FEDERAL SENTENCING GUIDELINES MANUAL

Volume 3

2013 EDITION

UNITED STATES SENTENCING COMMISSION

Including

**Amendments to Sentencing Guidelines Manual
Sentencing Worksheets
Related Federal Criminal Rules of Procedure
Tables**

THOMSON REUTERS™

For Customer Assistance Call 1-800-328-4880

Copyright © 1989 through 1995 West Publishing Co., 1997 through 2002 West Group, 2004 West, a Thomson business, 2005 Thomson/West

© 2013 Thomson Reuters
ISBN: 978-0-314-61588-6

Copyright is not claimed as to any part of the original work prepared by a United States Government officer or employee as part of the person's official duties.

This publication was created to provide you with accurate and authoritative information concerning the subject matter covered; however, this publication was not necessarily prepared by persons licensed to practice law in a particular jurisdiction. The publisher is not engaged in rendering legal or other professional advice and this publication is not a substitute for the advice of an attorney. If you require legal or other expert advice, you should seek the services of a competent attorney or other professional.

PUBLISHER'S PREFACE

This 2013 Edition contains the current text of the Sentencing Guidelines, Commentary, and Policy Statements of the United States Sentencing Commission, as most-recently amended.

Features in Volume 1 of this 2013 Edition include:

- Highlights of the 2013 Amendments, and Supreme Court decisions affecting the federal sentencing guidelines, by Thomas W. Hutchison.

- Statutory index. See Appendix A.

- Quick-reference "Sentencing Table" on the inside of the front cover.

Features in Volume 2 of this 2013 Edition include:

- Selected federal statutes relating to sentencing. See Appendix B.

Features in Volume 3 of this 2013 Edition include:

- Amendments to the Guidelines Manual. See Appendix C.

- Sentencing worksheets. See Appendix D.

- Federal Rules of Criminal Procedure relating to sentencing. See Appendix E.

- Fine and Revocation Tables. See Appendix G.

- Quick-reference "Sentencing Table." See Appendix G and the inside of the front cover.

For further coverage of the federal sentencing guidelines and related sentencing issues, refer to Thomas W. Hutchison, et al., *Federal Sentencing Law and Practice*. This comprehensive publication fully explains and annotates each Guideline and Policy Statement and provides related reference materials not readily available elsewhere.

Retention of Prior Editions

The 2012 Edition of the *Federal Sentencing Guidelines Manual*—along with prior editions—should be retained in the event there is a need to refer to the text of a specific Guidelines, Commentary, or Policy Statement at a particular point in time.

THE PUBLISHER

November, 2013

RELATED PRODUCTS

Courtroom Handbook on Federal Evidence
Steven Goode and Olin Guy Wellborn III

Modern Scientific Evidence
David L. Faigman, David H. Kaye, Michael J. Saks and Joseph Sanders

Federal Jury Practice and Instruction
Kevin F. O'Malley, Jay E. Grenig and William C. Lee
[Instructions available in CD-ROM]

Federal Trial Objections
Charles B. Gibbons

Federal Practice and Procedure
Charles Alan Wright, Arthur R. Miller, Mary Kay Kane, Edward H. Cooper, Richard L. Marcus, Kenneth W. Graham, Victor James Gold, Richard D. Freer, Vikram David Amar, Joan E. Steinman, Nancy J. King, Susan R. Klein, Andrew D. Leipold, Peter J. Henning, Sarah N. Welling, Charles H. Koch, Jr., Catherine T. Struve and Michael H. Graham
[Also available in CD-ROM]

Multidistrict Litigation Manual
David F. Herr

Legal Ethics: The Lawyer's Deskbook on Professional Responsibility
Ronald D. Rotunda and John S. Dzienkowski
[In joint venture with the American Bar Association]

West's Federal Administrative Practice
Federal Practice Experts

West's Federal Forms
Federal Practice Experts
[Also available in CD-ROM]

Federal Court of Appeals Manual
David G. Knibb

Federal Practice Deskbook
Charles Alan Wright and Mary Kay Kane

Handbook of Federal Evidence
Michael H. Graham

Treatise on Constitutional Law
Ronald D. Rotunda and John E. Nowak

Handbook of Federal Civil Discovery and Disclosure
Jay E. Grenig and Jeffrey S. Kinsler
[Includes Forms on Disk]

Annotated Manual for Complex Litigation
David F. Herr

Federal Sentencing Law and Practice
Thomas W. Hutchison, Peter B. Hoffman, Deborah Young, and Sigmund G. Popko

Federal Criminal Restitution
Catharine M. Goodwin, Jay E. Grenig, Nathan A. Fishbach

Administrative Law and Practice
Charles H. Koch, Jr.

Federal Case News

Federal Civil Judicial Procedure and Rules
Federal Sentencing Guidelines Manual
Manual for Complex Litigation
Reference Manual on Scientific Evidence
USCA

US Code Congressional and Administrative News

Westlaw®

West Books, CD-ROM Libraries, Disk Products and Westlaw
The Ultimate Research System

Thomson Reuters® thanks you for subscribing to this product. Should you have any questions regarding this product please contact Customer Service at 1-800-328-4880 or by fax at 1-800-340-9378. If you would like to inquire about related publications or place an order, please contact us at 1–800–344–5009.

THOMSON REUTERS

Thomson Reuters
610 Opperman Drive
Eagan, MN 55123

legalsolutions.thomsonreuters.com

Summary Table of Contents

	Page
Volume 1	
Highlights of the 2013 Amendments	ix
Supreme Court Decisions Affecting the Federal Sentencing Guidelines	xvii
Official Text of the United States Sentencing Commission Guidelines Manual	1
APPENDIX A - Statutory Index	533
INDEX TO GUIDELINES MANUAL	560
LIST OF DEPARTURE PROVISIONS	579
Volume 2	
APPENDIX B - Selected Sentencing Statutes	1
Volume 3	
APPENDIX C (Volume I) - Amendments to the Guidelines Manual (effective November 1, 1997, and earlier)	1
APPENDIX C (Volume II) - Amendments to the Guidelines Manual (effective November 1, 1998, through November 5, 2003)	499
APPENDIX C (Volume III) - Amendments to the Guidelines Manual (effective November 1, 1998, through November 5, 2003)	868
SUPPLEMENT to APPENDIX C - Amendments to the Guidelines Manual (effective November 1, 2013)	1248
APPENDIX D - Sentencing Worksheets	1298
Part A - Worksheets for Individuals	1299
Part B - Worksheets for Organizations	1308
APPENDIX E - Federal Rules of Criminal Procedure Relating to Sentencing	1317
APPENDIX F - Cases Applying Federal Sentencing Guidelines	1331
APPENDIX G - Tables	1332

APPENDIX C (VOLUME I) - AMENDMENTS TO THE GUIDELINES MANUAL

This Volume of Appendix C presents the amendments to the guidelines, policy statements, and official commentary promulgated effective January 15, 1988; June 15, 1988; October 15, 1988; November 1, 1989; November 1, 1990; November 1, 1991; November 27, 1991; November 1, 1992; November 1, 1993; September 23, 1994; November 1, 1994; November 1, 1995; November 1, 1996; May 1, 1997; November 1, 1997.*

For amendments effective after November 1, 1997, *see* Appendix C, Volume II.

The format under which the amendments are presented in this Appendix is designed to facilitate a comparison between previously existing and amended provisions, in the event it becomes necessary to reference the former guideline, policy statement, or commentary language.

AMENDMENTS

1. **Amendment:** Section 1B1.1(b) is amended by inserting "in the order listed" immediately following "Chapter Two".

    Section 1B1.1(d) is amended by deleting "one" and "three" and inserting in lieu thereof "(a)" and "(c)" respectively.

    The Commentary to § 1B1.1 captioned "Application Notes" is amended by inserting the following additional note:

    "4. The offense level adjustments from more than one specific offense characteristic within an offense guideline are cumulative (added together) unless the guideline specifies that only the greater (or greatest) is to be used. Within each specific offense characteristic subsection, however, the offense level adjustments are alternative; only the one that best describes the conduct is to be used. E.g., in § 2A2.2(b)(3), pertaining to degree of bodily injury, the subsection that best describes the level of bodily injury is used; the adjustments for different degrees of bodily injury (subsections (A), (B), and (C)) are not added together.".

    Reason for Amendment: The purposes of this amendment are to correct a clerical error and to clarify the operation of the guidelines by consolidating the former § 1B1.4 (Determining the Offense Level) with this section.

---

*In addition to the numbered amendments set forth in this Appendix, the following minor editorial revisions have been made to update the Manual to reflect that the guidelines system now constitutes current practice: the terms "current practice," "existing practice," and "present practice," where used to denote sentencing practice prior to guidelines, have been replaced by the term "pre-guidelines practice" and conforming tense changes have been made in § 2B3.1, comment. (backg'd); Chapter Two, Part C, intro. comment., § 2F1.1, comment. (backg'd); § 2J1.3, comment. (backg'd); § 2K2.1, comment. (backg'd); § 2R1.1, comment. (backg'd); § 2T1.1, comment. (backg'd); § 2T1.2, comment. (backg'd); § 2T1.8, comment. (backg'd); § 6A1.3, comment.; and Chapter Six, Part B, intro. comment. Also, an additional sentence ("For additional statutory provision(s), see Appendix A (Statutory Index).") has been inserted for clarity in the Commentary captioned "Statutory Provision[s]" of each Chapter Two offense guideline that has additional statutory provision(s) listed in Appendix A (Statutory Index).

Effective Date: The effective date of this amendment is November 1, 1990.

In addition, citations to court cases have been updated, as appropriate, in the Manual and this Appendix.

Amendment 1   APPENDIX C - VOLUME I   November 1, 2013

Effective Date: The effective date of this amendment is January 15, 1988.

2. **Amendment:** Section 1B1.2(a) is amended by deleting "guideline" the first time it appears and inserting in lieu thereof "offense guideline section".

    Section 1B1.2(a) is amended by inserting the following additional sentence at the end of the subsection: "Similarly, stipulations to additional offenses are treated as if the defendant had been convicted of separate counts charging those offenses.".

    Section 1B1.2(b) is amended by deleting:

    > "The court shall determine any applicable specific offense characteristic, victim-related adjustment, or departure from the guidelines attributable to offense conduct, according to the principles in § 1B1.3 (Relevant Conduct).",

    and inserting in lieu thereof:

    > "After determining the appropriate offense guideline section pursuant to subsection (a) of this section, determine the applicable guideline range in accordance with § 1B1.3 (Relevant Conduct).".

    The Commentary to § 1B1.2 captioned "Application Notes" is amended in Note 2 by deleting:

    > "any applicable victim-related adjustment from Chapter Three, Part A, and any guideline departures attributable to the offense conduct from Chapter Five, Part K, using a 'relevant conduct' standard, as that standard is defined in § 1B1.3.",

    and inserting in lieu thereof:

    > "and any other applicable sentencing factors pursuant to the relevant conduct definition in § 1B1.3.".

    The Commentary to § 1B1.2 captioned "Application Notes" is amended in Note 3 by deleting:

    > "In such instances, the court should consider all conduct, circumstances, and injury relevant to the offense (as well as all relevant offender characteristics). See § 1B1.3 (Relevant Conduct).",

    and inserting in lieu thereof:

    > "See §§ 1B1.3 (Relevant Conduct) and 1B1.4 (Information to be Used in Imposing Sentence).".

    Reason for Amendment: The purposes of this amendment are to correct a clerical error and to clarify the operation of the guidelines.

    Effective Date: The effective date of this amendment is January 15, 1988.

3. **Amendment:** Chapter One, Part B is amended by deleting § 1B1.3 in its entirety as follows:

    > "§ 1B1.3.   <u>Relevant Conduct</u>
    >
    > To determine the seriousness of the offense conduct, all conduct, circumstances, and injuries relevant to the offense of conviction shall be taken into account.

(a) Unless otherwise specified under the guidelines, conduct and circumstances relevant to the offense of conviction means:

acts or omissions committed or aided and abetted by the defendant, or by a person for whose conduct the defendant is legally accountable, that (1) are part of the same course of conduct, or a common scheme or plan, as the offense of conviction, or (2) are relevant to the defendant's state of mind or motive in committing the offense of conviction, or (3) indicate the defendant's degree of dependence upon criminal activity for a livelihood.

(b) Injury relevant to the offense of conviction means harm which is caused intentionally, recklessly or by criminal negligence in the course of conduct relevant to the offense of conviction.

Commentary

Application Note:

1. In sentencing, the court should consider all relevant offense and offender characteristics. For purposes of assessing offense conduct, the relevant conduct and circumstances of the offense of conviction are as follows:

   a. conduct directed toward preparation for or commission of the offense of conviction, and efforts to avoid detection and responsibility for the offense of conviction;

   b. conduct indicating that the offense of conviction was to some degree part of a broader purpose, scheme, or plan;

   c. conduct that is relevant to the state of mind or motive of the defendant in committing the crime;

   d. conduct that is relevant to the defendant's involvement in crime as a livelihood.

   The first three criteria are derived from two sources, Rule 8(a) of the Federal Rules of Criminal Procedure, governing joinder of similar or related offenses, and Rule 404(b) of the Federal Rules of Evidence, permitting admission of evidence of other crimes to establish motive, intent, plan, and common scheme. These rules provide standards that govern consideration at trial of crimes "of the same or similar character," and utilize concepts and terminology familiar to judges, prosecutors, and defenders. The governing standard should be liberally construed in favor of considering information generally appropriate to sentencing. When other crimes are inadmissible under the Rule 404(b) standard, such crimes may not be "relevant to the offense of conviction" under the criteria that determine this question for purposes of Chapter Two; such crimes would, however, be considered in determining the relevant offender characteristics to the extent authorized by Chapter Three (Adjustments), and Chapter Four (Criminal History and Criminal Livelihood) and Chapter Five, Part H (Specific Offender Characteristics). This construction is consistent with the existing rule that "[n]o limitation shall be placed on the information concerning the background, character, and conduct of a person convicted of an offense . . . for the purpose of imposing an appropriate sentence," 18 U.S.C. § 3577, so long as the information "has sufficient indicia of reliability to support its probable accuracy." United States v. Marshall, 519 F. Supp. 751 (D. Wis. 1981), aff'd, 719 F.2d 887 (7th Cir. 1983).

The last of these criteria is intended to ensure that a judge may consider at sentencing, information that, although not specifically within other criteria of relevance, indicates that the defendant engages in crime for a living. Inclusion of this information in sentencing considerations is consistent with 28 U.S.C. § 994(d)(11).".

A replacement guideline with accompanying commentary is inserted as § 1B1.3 (Relevant Conduct (Factors that Determine the Guideline Range)).

Reason for Amendment: The purpose of this amendment is to clarify the guideline. The amended language restates the intent of § 1B1.3 as originally promulgated.

Effective Date: The effective date of this amendment is January 15, 1988.

4. **Amendment:** Chapter One, Part B is amended by deleting § 1B1.4 in its entirety as follows:

"§ 1B1.4. Determining the Offense Level

In determining the offense level:

(a) determine the base offense level from Chapter Two;

(b) make any applicable adjustments for specific offense characteristics from Chapter Two in the order listed;

(c) make any applicable adjustments from Chapter Three;

(d) make any applicable adjustments from Chapter Four, Part B (Career Offenders and Criminal Livelihood).

Commentary

Application Notes:

1. A particular guideline (in the base offense level or in a specific offense characteristic) may expressly direct that a particular factor be applied only if the defendant was convicted of a particular statute. E.g., in § 2K2.3, a base offense level of 12 is used "if convicted under 26 U.S.C. § 5861." Unless such an express direction is included, conviction under the statute is not required. Thus, use of a statutory reference to describe a particular set of circumstances does not require a conviction under the referenced statute. Examples of this usage are found in § 2K1.3(b)(4) ("if the defendant was a person prohibited from receiving explosives under 18 U.S.C. § 842(i), or if the defendant knowingly distributed explosives to a person prohibited from receiving explosives under 18 U.S.C. § 842(i), increase by 10 levels"); and § 2A3.4(b)(2) ("if the abusive contact was accomplished as defined in 18 U.S.C. § 2242, increase by 4 levels"). In such cases, the particular circumstances described are to be evaluated under the "relevant conduct" standard of § 1B1.3.

2. Once the appropriate base offense level is determined, all specific offense characteristics are to be applied in the order listed.

3. The offense level adjustments from more than one specific offense characteristic within an offense guideline are cumulative (added together) unless the guideline specifies that only the greater (or greatest) is to be used. Within each specific offense characteristic subsection, however, the offense level adjustments are alternative; only the one that best describes the conduct is to be used. E.g., in § 2A2.2(b)(3), pertaining to degree of bodily injury, the subsection that best describes the level of bodily injury is used; the adjustments from different degrees of bodily injury (subsections (A), (B) and (C)) are not added together).

4. The adjustments in Chapter Three that may apply include Part A (Victim-Related Adjustments), Part B (Role in the Offense), Part C (Obstruction), Part D (Multiple Counts), and Part E (Acceptance of Responsibility).".

A replacement guideline with accompanying commentary is inserted as § 1B1.4 (Information to be Used in Imposing Sentence (Selecting a Point Within the Guideline Range or Departing from the Guidelines)).

Reason for Amendment: The purposes of this amendment are to remove material made redundant by the reorganization of this Part and to replace it with material that clarifies the operation of the guidelines. The material formerly in this section is now covered by § 1B1.1.

Effective Date: The effective date of this amendment is January 15, 1988.

5. **Amendment:** Chapter One, Part B, is amended by inserting an additional guideline with accompanying commentary as § 1B1.8 (Use of Certain Information).

Reason for Amendment: The purpose of this amendment is to facilitate cooperation agreements by ensuring that certain information revealed by a defendant, as part of an agreement to cooperate with the government by providing information concerning unlawful activities of others, will not be used to increase the guideline sentence.

Effective Date: The effective date of this amendment is June 15, 1988.

6. **Amendment:** Chapter One, Part B, is amended by inserting an additional guideline with accompanying commentary as § 1B1.9 (Petty Offenses).

Reason for Amendment: The purpose of this guideline is to delete coverage of petty offenses.

Effective Date: The effective date of this amendment is June 15, 1988.

7. **Amendment:** Section 2B1.1(b)(1) is amended by deleting "value of the property taken" and inserting in lieu thereof "loss".

The Commentary to § 2B1.1 captioned "Application Notes" is amended in Note 2 by deleting:

"Loss is to be based upon replacement cost to the victim or market value of the property, whichever is greater.",

and inserting in lieu thereof:

"'Loss' means the value of the property taken, damaged, or destroyed. Ordinarily, when property is taken or destroyed the loss is the fair market value of the particular property at issue. Where the market value is difficult to ascertain or inadequate to measure harm to the victim, the court may measure loss in some other way, such as reasonable replacement cost to the victim. When property is damaged the loss is the cost of repairs, not to exceed the loss had the property been destroyed. In cases of partially completed conduct, the loss is to be determined in accordance with the provisions of § 2X1.1 (Attempt, Solicitation, or Conspiracy Not Covered by a Specific Guideline). E.g., in the case of the theft of a government check or money order, loss refers to the loss that would have occurred if the check or money order had been cashed. Similarly, if a defendant is apprehended in the process of taking a vehicle, the loss refers to the value of the vehicle even if the vehicle is recovered immediately.".

Reason for Amendment: The purpose of this amendment is to clarify the guideline in respect to the determination of loss.

Effective Date: The effective date of this amendment is June 15, 1988.

8. **Amendment:** Section 2B1.2 is amended by transposing the texts of subsections (b)(2) and (3).

    The Commentary to § 2B1.2 captioned "Application Notes" is amended by deleting:

    "3. For consistency with § 2B1.1, it is the Commission's intent that specific offense characteristic (b)(3) be applied before (b)(2).",

    and by renumbering Note 4 as Note 3.

    Reason for Amendment: The purpose of this amendment is to correct a clerical error in the guideline. Correction of the error makes the deleted commentary unnecessary.

    Effective Date: The effective date of this amendment is January 15, 1988.

9. **Amendment:** Section 2B1.2(b)(1) is amended by deleting "taken", and inserting "stolen" immediately before "property".

    Reason for Amendment: The purpose of this amendment is to correct a clerical error.

    Effective Date: The effective date of this amendment is June 15, 1988.

10. **Amendment:** Section 2B1.3(b)(1) is amended by deleting "amount of the property damage or destruction, or the cost of restoration," and inserting in lieu thereof "loss".

    The Commentary to § 2B1.3 captioned "Application Notes" is amended in Note 2 by deleting "property" and inserting in lieu thereof "loss".

    Reason for Amendment: The purpose of this amendment is to clarify the guideline in respect to the determination of loss.

    Effective Date: The effective date of this amendment is June 15, 1988.

11. **Amendment:** The Commentary to § 2B2.1 captioned "Application Notes" is amended in Note 4 by inserting "or other dangerous weapon" immediately following "firearm".

    Reason for Amendment: The purpose of the amendment is to correct a clerical error.

    Effective Date: The effective date of this amendment is January 15, 1988.

12. **Amendment:** Section 2B2.1(b)(2) is amended by deleting "value of the property taken or destroyed" and inserting in lieu thereof "loss".

   The Commentary to § 2B2.1 captioned "Application Notes" is amended in Note 3 by deleting "property" and inserting in lieu thereof "loss".

   Reason for Amendment: The purpose of this amendment is to clarify the guideline in respect to the determination of loss.

   Effective Date: The effective date of this amendment is June 15, 1988.

13. **Amendment:** Section 2B2.2(b)(2) is amended by deleting "value of the property taken or destroyed" and inserting in lieu thereof "loss".

   The Commentary to § 2B2.2 captioned "Application Notes" is amended in Note 3 by deleting "property" and inserting in lieu thereof "loss".

   Reason for Amendment: The purpose of this amendment is to clarify the guideline in respect to the determination of loss.

   Effective Date: The effective date of this amendment is June 15, 1988.

14. **Amendment:** Section 2B3.1(b)(1) is amended by deleting "value of the property taken or destroyed" and inserting in lieu thereof "loss".

   The Commentary to § 2B3.1 captioned "Application Notes" is amended in Note 3 by deleting "property" and inserting in lieu thereof "loss".

   Reason for Amendment: The purpose of this amendment is to clarify the guideline in respect to the determination of loss.

   Effective Date: The effective date of this amendment is June 15, 1988.

15. **Amendment:** The Commentary to § 2B3.1 captioned "Application Notes" is amended in Note 2 by inserting "or attempted robbery" immediately following "robbery".

   Reason for Amendment: The purpose of this amendment is to clarify the guideline.

   Effective Date: The effective date of this amendment is June 15, 1988.

16. **Amendment:** The Commentary to § 2B5.1 captioned "Statutory Provisions" is amended by deleting "473" and inserting in lieu thereof "474", and by deleting "510," and ", 2314, 2315".

   Reason for Amendment: The purpose of this amendment is to correct a clerical error.

   Effective Date: The effective date of this amendment is January 15, 1988.

17. **Amendment:** The Commentary to § 2B5.2 is amended by deleting "Statutory Provision: 18 U.S.C. § 510" and inserting in lieu thereof "Statutory Provisions: 18 U.S.C. §§ 471-473, 500, 510, 1003, 2314, 2315".

   Reason for Amendment: The purpose of this amendment is to correct a clerical error.

   Effective Date: The effective date of this amendment is January 15, 1988.

18. **Amendment:** The Commentary to § 2C1.1 captioned "Application Notes" is amended in

Amendment 18 APPENDIX C - VOLUME I November 1, 2013

Note 3 by deleting "§ 3C1.1(c)(1)" and inserting in lieu thereof "§ 2C1.1(c)(1)".

Reason for Amendment: The purpose of this amendment is to correct a typographical error.

Effective Date: The effective date of this amendment is January 15, 1988.

19. **Amendment:** The Commentary to § 2D1.1 captioned "Application Notes" is amended in the Measurement Conversion Table in Note 10 by deleting "1 lb = .45 kg" and inserting in lieu thereof "1 lb = .4536 kg", by deleting "1 kg = 2.2 lbs", by deleting "1 gal = 3.8 liters" and inserting in lieu thereof "1 gal = 3.785 liters", and by deleting "1 qt = .95 liters" and inserting in lieu thereof "1 qt = .946 liters".

Reason for Amendment: The purpose of this amendment is to correct a clerical error.

Effective Date: The effective date of this amendment is January 15, 1988.

20. **Amendment:** The Commentary to § 2D1.1 captioned "Application Notes" is amended by deleting:

"11. If it is uncertain whether the quantity of drugs involved falls into one category in the table or an adjacent category, the court may use the intermediate level for sentencing purposes. For example, sale of 700-999 grams of heroin is at level 30, while sale of 400-699 grams is at level 28. If the exact quantity is uncertain, but near 700 grams, use of level 29 would be permissible.".

Reason for Amendment: The purpose of this amendment is to delete an erroneous reference to interpolation, which cannot apply as the guideline is written.

Effective Date: The effective date of this amendment is January 15, 1988.

21. **Amendment:** The Commentary to § 2D1.1 captioned "Application Notes" is amended by inserting the following additional note:

"11. Types and quantities of drugs not specified in the count of conviction may be considered in determining the offense level. See § 1B1.3(a)(2) (Relevant Conduct). If the amount seized does not reflect the scale of the offense, see Application Note 2 of the Commentary to § 2D1.4. If the offense involved negotiation to traffic in a controlled substance, see Application Note 1 of the Commentary to § 2D1.4.".

Reason for Amendment: The purpose of this amendment is to clarify the commentary.

Effective Date: The effective date of this amendment is January 15, 1988.

22. **Amendment:** Section 2D1.2(a)(1) is amended by deleting "less than fourteen years of age" and inserting in lieu thereof "fourteen years of age or less".

Section 2D1.2(a)(2) is amended by deleting "fourteen" and inserting in lieu thereof "fifteen".

The Commentary to § 2D1.2 captioned "Statutory Provision" is amended by deleting "21 U.S.C. § 845(b)" and inserting in lieu thereof "21 U.S.C. § 845b".

The Commentary to § 2D1.2 captioned "Background" is amended by deleting:

"(provided for by the minimum base offense level of 13) in addition to the punishment imposed for the applicable crime in which the defendant involved a juvenile. An increased penalty for the employment or use of persons under age fourteen is statutorily directed by 21 U.S.C. § 845b(d).",

and inserting in lieu thereof:

". An increased penalty for the employment or use of persons fourteen years of age or younger reflects the enhanced sentence authorized by 21 U.S.C. § 845b(d).".

Reason for Amendment: The purpose of this amendment is to correct clerical errors in the guideline and commentary.

Effective Date: The effective date of this amendment is January 15, 1988.

23. **Amendment:** The Commentary to § 2D1.3 captioned "Application Notes" is amended in Note 1 by deleting:

"If more than one enhancement provision is applicable in a particular case, the punishment imposed under the separate enhancement provisions should be added together in calculating the appropriate guideline sentence.",

and inserting in lieu thereof:

"If both subsections (a)(1) and (a)(2) apply to a single distribution (e.g., the distribution of 10 grams of a controlled substance to a pregnant woman under twenty-one years of age), the enhancements are applied cumulatively, i.e., by using four times rather than two times the amount distributed.".

Reason for Amendment: The purpose of this amendment is to clarify the commentary.

Effective Date: The effective date of this amendment is January 15, 1988.

24. **Amendment:** Section 2D2.1(a)(1) is amended by deleting "or LSD," immediately following "opiate".

Section 2D2.1(a)(2) is amended by inserting ", LSD," immediately following "cocaine".

Reason for Amendment: The purpose of this amendment is to correct a clerical error.

Effective Date: The effective date of this amendment is January 15, 1988.

25. **Amendment:** The Commentary to § 2D2.3 captioned "Statutory Provision" is amended by deleting "21 U.S.C. § 342" and inserting in lieu thereof "18 U.S.C. § 342".

Reason for Amendment: The purpose of this amendment is to correct a typographical error.

Effective Date: The effective date of this amendment is January 15, 1988.

26. **Amendment:** The Commentary to § 2E1.1 captioned "Application Notes" is amended in Note 1 by deleting:

"For purposes of subsection (a)(2), determine the offense level for each underlying offense. Use the provisions of Chapter Three, Part D (Multiple Counts), to determine the offense level, treating each underlying offense as if contained in a separate count of conviction.",

Amendment 26   APPENDIX C - VOLUME I   November 1, 2013

and inserting in lieu thereof:

"Where there is more than one underlying offense, treat each underlying offense as if contained in a separate count of conviction for the purposes of subsection (a)(2). To determine whether subsection (a)(1) or (a)(2) results in the greater offense level, apply Chapter Three, Parts A, B, C, and D to both (a)(1) and (a)(2). Use whichever subsection results in the greater offense level.".

Reason for Amendment: The purpose of this amendment is to clarify the guideline.

Effective Date: The effective date of this amendment is June 15, 1988.

27. **Amendment:** The Commentary to § 2E1.2 captioned "Application Notes" is amended in Note 1 by deleting:

"For purposes of subsection (a)(2), determine the offense level for each underlying offense. Use the provisions of Chapter Three, Part D (Multiple Counts), to determine the offense level, treating each underlying offense as if contained in a separate count of conviction.",

and inserting in lieu thereof:

"Where there is more than one underlying offense, treat each underlying offense as if contained in a separate count of conviction for the purposes of subsection (a)(2). To determine whether subsection (a)(1) or (a)(2) results in the greater offense level, apply Chapter Three, Parts A, B, C, and D to both (a)(1) and (a)(2). Use whichever subsection results in the greater offense level.".

Reason for Amendment: The purpose of this amendment is to clarify the guideline.

Effective Date: The effective date of this amendment is June 15, 1988.

28. **Amendment:** Section 2E5.2(b)(3) is amended by deleting "value of the property stolen" and inserting in lieu thereof "loss".

The Commentary to § 2E5.2 captioned "Application Notes" is amended in Note 1 by inserting immediately following the first sentence: "Valuation of loss is discussed in the Commentary to § 2B1.1 (Larceny, Embezzlement, and Other Forms of Theft).".

Reason for Amendment: The purpose of this amendment is to clarify the guideline in respect to the determination of loss.

Effective Date: The effective date of this amendment is June 15, 1988.

29. **Amendment:** Section 2E5.4(b)(3) is amended by deleting "value of the property stolen" and inserting in lieu thereof "loss".

The Commentary to § 2E5.4 captioned "Application Notes" is amended in Note 1 by inserting immediately following the first sentence: "Valuation of loss is discussed in the Commentary to § 2B1.1 (Larceny, Embezzlement, and Other Forms of Theft).".

Reason for Amendment: The purpose of this amendment is to clarify the guideline in respect to the determination of loss.

Effective Date: The effective date of this amendment is June 15, 1988.

30. **Amendment:** Section 2F1.1(b)(1) is amended by deleting "estimated, probable, or

intended" immediately before "loss".

The Commentary to § 2F1.1 captioned "Statutory Provisions" is amended by deleting "291" and inserting in lieu thereof "290".

The Commentary to § 2F1.1 captioned "Application Notes" is amended in Note 7 by inserting as the first sentence: "Valuation of loss is discussed in the Commentary to § 2B1.1 (Larceny, Embezzlement, and Other Forms of Theft).".

Reason for Amendment: The purposes of this amendment are to clarify the guideline in respect to the determination of loss and to delete an inadvertently included infraction.

Effective Date: The effective date of this amendment is June 15, 1988,

31. **Amendment:** Section 2G2.2(b)(1) is amended by inserting "a prepubescent minor or" immediately following "involved".

   Reason for Amendment: The purpose of this amendment is to provide an alternative measure to be used in determining whether the material involved an extremely young minor for cases in which the actual age of the minor is unknown.

   Effective Date: The effective date of this amendment is June 15, 1988.

32. **Amendment:** The Commentary to § 2J1.7 captioned "Application Notes" is amended by deleting:

    "1. By statute, a term of imprisonment imposed for this offense runs consecutively to any other term of imprisonment. 18 U.S.C. § 3147.

    2. This guideline assumes that the sentence imposed for the offense committed while on release, which may have been imposed by a state court, is reasonably consistent with that which the guidelines would provide for a similar federal offense. If this is not the case, a departure may be warranted. See Chapter Five, Part K (Departures).

    3. If the defendant was convicted in state court for the offense committed while on release, the term of imprisonment referred to in subdivision (b) is the maximum term of imprisonment authorized under state law.",

    and inserting in lieu thereof:

    "1. This guideline applies whenever a sentence pursuant to 18 U.S.C. § 3147 is imposed.

    2. By statute, a term of imprisonment imposed for a violation of 18 U.S.C. § 3147 runs consecutively to any other term of imprisonment. Consequently, a sentence for such a violation is exempt from grouping under the multiple count rules. See § 3D1.2.".

   The Commentary to § 2J1.7 captioned "Background" is amended by deleting "necessarily" and inserting in lieu thereof "generally".

   Reason for Amendment: The purposes of this amendment are to clarify the commentary and to delete erroneous references.

   Effective Date: The effective date of this amendment is January 15, 1988.

Amendment 33   APPENDIX C - VOLUME I   November 1, 2013

33. **Amendment:** Section 2J1.8(c) is amended by deleting "perjury" and inserting in lieu thereof "bribery of a witness".

    The Commentary to § 2J1.8 captioned "Application Notes" is amended by deleting:

    > "4. Subsection (c) refers to bribing a witness regarding his testimony in respect to a criminal offense.".

    Reason for Amendment: The purpose of this amendment is to correct a clerical error. Correction of this error makes the deleted commentary unnecessary.

    Effective Date: The effective date of this amendment is January 15, 1988.

34. **Amendment:** The Commentary to § 2K2.2 captioned "Application Note" is amended by deleting "<u>Application Note</u>" and inserting in lieu thereof "<u>Application Notes</u>", and by inserting the following additional note:

    > "2. Subsection (c)(1) refers to any situation in which the defendant possessed a firearm to facilitate another offense that he committed or attempted.".

    Reason for Amendment: The purpose of this amendment is to clarify the guideline.

    Effective Date: The effective date of this amendment is January 15, 1988.

35. **Amendment:** Section 2L1.1(a) is amended by deleting "6" and inserting in lieu thereof "9".

    Section 2L1.1(b)(1) is amended by deleting "for profit or with knowledge" and inserting in lieu thereof "other than for profit, and without knowledge", and by deleting "increase by 3 levels" and inserting in lieu thereof "decrease by 3 levels".

    The Commentary to § 2L1.1 captioned "Background" is amended by deleting:

    > "A specific offense characteristic provides an enhancement if the defendant committed the offense for profit or with knowledge that the alien was excludable as a subversive.",

    and inserting in lieu thereof:

    > "A specific offense characteristic provides a reduction if the defendant did not commit the offense for profit and did not know that the alien was excludable as a subversive.".

    Reason for Amendment: The purpose of this amendment is to make the guideline conform to the typical case.

    Effective Date: The effective date of this amendment is January 15, 1988.

36. **Amendment:** Section 2L1.1(b)(2) is amended by deleting "bringing illegal aliens into the United States" and inserting in lieu thereof "smuggling, transporting, or harboring an unlawful alien, or a related offense".

    The Commentary to § 2L1.1 captioned "Application Notes" is amended in Note 2 by deleting "bringing illegal aliens into the United States" and inserting in lieu thereof "smuggling, transporting, or harboring an unlawful alien, or a related offense".

    Reason for Amendment: The purpose of this amendment is to correct a clerical error in the guideline and conform the commentary to the corrected guideline.

Effective Date: The effective date of this amendment is January 15, 1988.

37. **Amendment:** The Commentary to § 2L1.1 captioned "Application Notes" is amended by inserting the following additional note:

    "8. The Commission has not considered offenses involving large numbers of aliens or dangerous or inhumane treatment. An upward departure should be considered in those circumstances.".

    Reason for Amendment: The purpose of this amendment is to clarify the factors considered by the Commission in promulgating the guideline.

    Effective Date: The effective date of this amendment is January 15, 1988.

38. **Amendment:** Section 2L1.2(a) is amended by deleting "6" and inserting in lieu thereof "8".

    Section 2L1.2(b) is amended by deleting:

    "(b) Specific Offense Characteristic

    (1) If the defendant previously has unlawfully entered or remained in the United States, increase by 2 levels.".

    The Commentary to § 2L1.2 captioned "Statutory Provisions" is amended by deleting "§§ 1325, 1326" and inserting in lieu thereof "§ 1325 (second or subsequent offense only), 8 U.S.C. § 1326".

    The Commentary to § 2L1.2 captioned "Application Notes" is amended in Note 1 by deleting:

    "The adjustment at § 2L1.2(b)(1) is to be applied where the previous entry resulted in deportation (voluntary or involuntary), with or without a criminal conviction. If the previous entry resulted in a conviction, this adjustment is to be applied in addition to any points added to the criminal history score for such conviction in Chapter Four, Part A (Criminal History).",

    and inserting in lieu thereof:

    "This guideline applies only to felonies. First offenses under 8 U.S.C. § 1325 are petty offenses for which no guideline has been promulgated.".

    Reason for Amendment: The purpose of this amendment is to delete coverage of a petty offense.

    Effective Date: The effective date of this amendment is January 15, 1988.

39. **Amendment:** The Commentary to § 2L2.2 captioned "Application Notes" is amended in Note 1 by deleting "an enhancement equivalent to that at § 2L1.2(b)(1)," and inserting in lieu thereof "a result equivalent to § 2L1.2.".

    Reason for Amendment: The purpose of this amendment is to make the commentary consistent with § 2L1.2, as amended.

    Effective Date: The effective date of this amendment is January 15, 1988.

Amendment 40   APPENDIX C - VOLUME I   November 1, 2013

40.   Amendment: The Commentary to § 2L2.4 captioned "Application Notes" is amended in Note 1 by deleting "an enhancement equivalent to that at § 2L1.2(b)(1)," and inserting in lieu thereof "a result equivalent to § 2L1.2.".

Reason for Amendment: The purpose of this amendment is to make the commentary consistent with § 2L1.2, as amended.

Effective Date: The effective date of this amendment is January 15, 1988.

41.   Amendment: The Commentary to § 2Q2.1 captioned "Statutory Provisions" is amended by deleting "707" and inserting in lieu thereof "707(b)".

Reason for Amendment: The purpose of this amendment is to correct a clerical error.

Effective Date: The effective date of this amendment is January 15, 1988.

42.   Amendment: The Commentary to § 2X1.1 captioned "Application Notes" is amended in Note 1 by deleting "§ 2A4.1" and inserting in lieu thereof "§ 2D1.4".

Reason for Amendment: The purpose of this amendment is to correct a typographical error.

Effective Date: The effective date of this amendment is January 15, 1988.

43.   Amendment: Chapter Two, Part X is amended by deleting § 2X5.1 in its entirety as follows:

"§ 2X5.1.   Other Offenses (Policy Statement)

For offenses for which no specific guideline has been promulgated:

(a)   If the offense is a felony or class A misdemeanor, the most analogous guideline should be applied. If no sufficiently analogous guideline exists, any sentence that is reasonable and consistent with the purposes of sentencing should be imposed. See 18 U.S.C. § 3553(b).

(b)   If the offense is a Class B or C misdemeanor or an infraction, any sentence that is reasonable and consistent with the purpose of sentencing should be imposed. See 18 U.S.C. § 3553(b).

Commentary

Background: This policy statement addresses cases in which a defendant has been convicted of an offense for which no specific guideline has been written. For a felony or a class A misdemeanor (see 18 U.S.C. §§ 3559(a) and 3581(b)), the court is directed to apply the most analogous guideline. If no sufficiently analogous guideline exists, the court is directed to sentence without reference to a specific guideline or guideline range, as provided in 18 U.S.C. § 3553(b).

For a class B or C misdemeanor or an infraction (see 18 U.S.C. §§ 3559(a) and 3581(b)) that is not covered by a specific guideline, the court is directed to sentence without reference to a specific guideline or guideline range, as provided in 18 U.S.C. § 3553(b). An inquiry as to whether there is a sufficiently analogous guideline that might be applied is not required. The Commission makes this distinction in treatment because for many lesser offenses (e.g., traffic infractions), gener-

November 1, 2013 APPENDIX C - VOLUME I **Amendment 45**

ally handled under assimilative offense provisions by magistrates, there will be no sufficiently analogous guideline, and a case-by-case determination in respect to this issue for the high volume of cases processed each year would be unduly burdensome and would not significantly reduce disparity.".

A replacement guideline with accompanying commentary is inserted as § 2X5.1 (Other Offenses).

Reason for Amendment: The purposes of this amendment are to make the section a binding guideline (as the Commission originally intended with respect to felonies and Class A misdemeanors) rather than a policy statement, to delete language relating to petty offenses, and to conform and clarify the commentary.

Effective Date: The effective date of this amendment is June 15, 1988.

44. **Amendment:** The Commentary to § 3A1.2 captioned "Application Notes" is amended in Note 1 by deleting:

" 'Victim' refers to an individual directly victimized by the offense. This term does not include an organization, agency, or the government itself.",

and inserting in lieu thereof:

"This guideline applies when specified individuals are victims of the offense. This guideline does not apply when the only victim is an organization, agency, or the government.".

Reason for Amendment: The purpose of this amendment is to clarify the commentary.

Effective Date: The effective date of this amendment is January 15, 1988.

45. **Amendment:** Section 3D1.2(d) is amended by deleting:

"(d) When counts involve the same general type of offense and the guidelines for that type of offense determine the offense level primarily on the basis of the total amount of harm or loss, the quantity of a substance involved, or some other measure of aggregate harm. Offenses of this kind are found in Chapter Two, Part B (except §§ 2B2.1-2B3.3), Part D (except §§ 2D1.6-2D3.4), Part E (except §§ 2E1.1-2E2.1), Part F, Part G (§§ 2G2.2-2G3.1), Part K (§ 2K2.3), Part N (§§ 2N2.1, 2N3.1), Part Q (§§ 2Q2.1, 2Q2.2), Part R, Part S, and Part T. This rule also applies where the guidelines deal with offenses that are continuing, e.g., §§ 2L1.3 and 2Q1.3(b)(1)(A).",

and inserting in lieu thereof:

"(d) Counts are grouped together if the offense level is determined largely on the basis of the total amount of harm or loss, the quantity of a substance involved, or some other measure of aggregate harm, or if the offense behavior is ongoing or continuous in nature and the offense guideline is written to cover such behavior.

Offenses covered by the following guidelines are specifically included under this subsection:

§§ 2B1.1, 2B1.2, 2B1.3, 2B4.1, 2B5.1, 2B5.2, 2B5.3, 2B5.4, 2B6.1;

– 15 –

§§ 2D1.1, 2D1.2, 2D1.3, 2D1.5;
§§ 2E4.1, 2E5.1, 2E5.2, 2E5.4, 2E5.6;
§§ 2F1.1, 2F1.2;
§ 2N3.1;
§ 2R1.1;
§§ 2S1.1, 2S1.2, 2S1.3;
§§ 2T1.1, 2T1.2, 2T1.3, 2T1.4, 2T1.6, 2T1.7, 2T1.9, 2T2.1, 2T3.1, 2T3.2.

Specifically excluded from the operation of this subsection are:

all offenses in Part A;
§§ 2B2.1, 2B2.2, 2B2.3, 2B3.1, 2B3.2, 2B3.3;
§§ 2C1.1, 2C1.5;
§§ 2D2.1, 2D2.2, 2D2.3;
§§ 2E1.3, 2E1.4, 2E1.5, 2E2.1;
§§ 2G1.1, 2G1.2, 2G2.1, 2G3.2;
§§ 2H1.1, 2H1.2, 2H1.3, 2H1.4, 2H2.1, 2H4.1;
§§ 2L1.1, 2L2.1, 2L2.2, 2L2.3, 2L2.4, 2L2.5;
§§ 2M2.1, 2M2.3, 2M3.1, 2M3.2, 2M3.3, 2M3.4, 2M3.5, 2M3.6, 2M3.7, 2M3.8, 2M3.9;
§§ 2P1.1, 2P1.2, 2P1.3, 2P1.4.

For multiple counts of offenses that are not listed, grouping under this subsection may or may not be appropriate; a case-by-case determination must be made based upon the facts of the case and the applicable guidelines (including specific offense characteristics and other adjustments) used to determine the offense level.

Exclusion of an offense from grouping under this subsection does not necessarily preclude grouping under another subsection.".

Reason for Amendment: The purpose of this amendment is to clarify the guideline.

Effective Date: The effective date of this amendment is June 15, 1988.

46. **Amendment:** Section 3E1.1(a) is amended by deleting "the offense of conviction" and inserting in lieu thereof "his criminal conduct".

   Reason for Amendment: The purpose of this amendment is to clarify the guideline.

   Effective Date: The effective date of this amendment is January 15, 1988.

47. **Amendment:** Section 4B1.1 is amended by deleting "(2) the instant offense is a crime of violence or trafficking in a controlled substance" and inserting in lieu thereof "(2) the instant offense of conviction is a felony that is either a crime of violence or a controlled substance offense".

   Reason for Amendment: The purposes of this amendment are to correct a clerical error and to clarify the guideline.

Effective Date: The effective date of this amendment is January 15, 1988.

48. **Amendment:** Section 4B1.1 is amended by deleting:

	"Offense Statutory Maximum	Offense Level
(A)	Life	37
(B)	20 years or more	34
(C)	10 years or more, but less than 20 years	26
(D)	5 years or more, but less than 10 years	19
(E)	More than 1 year, but less than 5 years	12
(F)	1 year or less	4",

and inserting in lieu thereof:

	"Offense Statutory Maximum	Offense Level
(A)	Life	37
(B)	25 years or more	34
(C)	20 years or more, but less than 25 years	32
(D)	15 years or more, but less than 20 years	29
(E)	10 years or more, but less than 15 years	24
(F)	5 years or more, but less than 10 years	17
(G)	More than 1 year, but less than 5 years	12".

The Commentary to § 4B1.1 captioned "Background" is amended by deleting the last paragraph as follows:

"The guideline levels for career offenders were established by using the statutory maximum for the offense of conviction to determine the class of felony provided in 18 U.S.C. § 3559. Then the maximum authorized sentence of imprisonment for each class of felony was determined as provided by 18 U.S.C. § 3581. A guideline range for each class of felony was then chosen so that the maximum of the guideline range was at or near the maximum provided in 18 U.S.C. § 3581.".

Reason for Amendment: The purpose of this amendment is to correct the guideline so that the table relating offense statutory maxima to offense levels is consistent with the current authorized statutory maximum terms.

Effective Date: The effective date of this amendment is January 15, 1988.

49. **Amendment:** Section 4B1.2(2) is amended by inserting "845b, 856," immediately following "841," and by deleting "§§ 405B and 416 of the Controlled Substance Act as amended in 1986," immediately following "959;".

Amendment 49

Section 4B1.2(3) is amended by deleting:

"(1) the defendant committed the instant offense subsequent to sustaining at least two felony convictions for either a crime of violence or a controlled substance offense (i.e., two crimes of violence, two controlled substance offenses, or one crime of violence and one controlled substance offense), and (2)",

and inserting in lieu thereof:

"(A) the defendant committed the instant offense subsequent to sustaining at least two felony convictions of either a crime of violence or a controlled substance offense (i.e., two felony convictions of a crime of violence, two felony convictions of a controlled substance offense, or one felony conviction of a crime of violence and one felony conviction of a controlled substance offense), and (B)".

The Commentary to § 4B1.2 captioned "Application Notes" is amended in Note 2 by deleting "means any of the federal offenses identified in the statutes referenced in § 4B1.2, or substantially equivalent state offenses" and inserting in lieu thereof "includes any federal or state offense that is substantially similar to any of those listed in subsection (2) of the guideline", by inserting "importing," immediately following "manufacturing,", and by inserting "import," immediately following "manufacture,".

The Commentary to § 4B1.2 captioned "Application Notes" is amended in Note 3 by deleting "Felony" and inserting in lieu thereof "Prior felony".

Reason for Amendment: The purposes of this amendment are to correct a clerical error and to clarify the guideline.

Effective Date: The effective date of this amendment is January 15, 1988.

50. **Amendment:** Section 4B1.3 is amended by deleting:

". In no such case will the defendant be eligible for a sentence of probation."

and inserting in lieu thereof:

", unless § 3E1.1 (Acceptance of Responsibility) applies, in which event his offense level shall be not less than 11.".

The Commentary to § 4B1.3 captioned "Application Note" is amended by deleting "(e.g., an ongoing fraudulent scheme)" immediately following "course of conduct", "(e.g., a number of burglaries or robberies, or both)" immediately following "independent offenses", and "or petty" immediately following "to minor".

The Commentary to § 4B1.3 captioned "Background" is amended by deleting "that offense" and inserting in lieu thereof "an offense", and by deleting the last sentence as follows: "Under this provision, the offense level is raised to 13, if it is not already 13 or greater".

Reason for Amendment: The purpose of this amendment is to provide that the adjustment from § 3E1.1 (Acceptance of Responsibility) applies to cases under § 4B1.3 (Criminal Livelihood).

Effective Date: The effective date of this amendment is June 15, 1988.

51. **Amendment:** The Commentary to § 5C2.1 captioned "Application Notes" is amended in

Note 4 by deleting "at least six" and inserting in lieu thereof "more than six", by deleting "6-12" whenever it appears and inserting in lieu thereof in each instance "8-14", and by deleting "three" whenever it appears and inserting in lieu thereof in each instance "four".

Reason for Amendment: The purpose of this amendment is to correct a clerical error.

Effective Date: The effective date of this amendment is January 15, 1988.

52. **Amendment:** Section 5D3.2(b) is amended by deleting:

    "(1)   three years for a defendant convicted of a Class A or B felony;

    (2)   two years for a defendant convicted of a Class C or D felony;

    (3)   one year for a defendant convicted of a Class E felony or a misdemeanor.",

and inserting in lieu thereof:

    "(1)   at least three years but not more than five years for a defendant convicted of a Class A or B felony;

    (2)   at least two years but not more than three years for a defendant convicted of a Class C or D felony;

    (3)   one year for a defendant convicted of a Class E felony or a Class A misdemeanor.".

Reason for Amendment: The purpose of this amendment is to permit implementation of the longer terms of supervised release authorized by the Sentencing Act of 1987.

Effective Date: The effective date of this amendment is January 15, 1988.

53. **Amendment:** Section 5E4.1(a) is amended by inserting immediately before the period at the end of the subsection: ", and may be ordered as a condition of probation or supervised release in any other case".

Reason for Amendment: The purpose of this amendment is to clarify the guideline.

Effective Date: The effective date of this amendment is January 15, 1988.

54. **Amendment:** Section 5E4.2 is amended by deleting:

    "(b)   The generally applicable minimum and maximum fine for each offense level is shown in the Fine Table in subsection (c) below. Unless a statute expressly authorizes a greater amount, no fine may exceed $250,000 for a felony or a misdemeanor resulting in the loss of human life; $25,000 for any other misdemeanor; or $1,000 for an infraction. 18 U.S.C. § 3571(b)(1).

    (c)   (1)   The minimum fine range is the greater of:

                  (A)   the amount shown in column A of the table below; or

                  (B)   any monetary gain to the defendant, less any restitution made or ordered.

           (2)   Except as specified in (4) below, the maximum fine is the greater of:

– 19 –

(A) the amount shown in column B of the table below;

(B) twice the estimated loss caused by the offense; or

(C) three times the estimated gain to the defendant.",

and inserting in lieu thereof:

"(b) Except as provided in subsections (f) and (i) below, or otherwise required by statute, the fine imposed shall be within the range specified in subsection (c) below.

(c) (1) The minimum of the fine range is the greater of:

(A) the amount shown in column A of the table below; or

(B) the pecuniary gain to the defendant, less restitution made or ordered.

(2) Except as specified in (4) below, the maximum of the fine range is the greater of:

(A) the amount shown in column B of the table below;

(B) twice the gross pecuniary loss caused by the offense; or

(C) three times the gross pecuniary gain to all participants in the offense.".

The Commentary to § 5E4.2 captioned "Application Notes" is amended by deleting:

"2. The maximum fines generally authorized by statute are restated in subsection (b). These apply to each count of conviction. Ordinarily, the maximum fines on each count are independent and cumulative. However, if the offenses 'arise from a common scheme or plan' and 'do not cause separable or distinguishable kinds of harm or damage,' the aggregate fine may not exceed 'twice the amount imposable for the most serious offense.' 18 U.S.C. § 3572(b) (former 18 U.S.C. § 3623(c)(2)).

3. Alternative fine limits are provided in subsection (c)(2). The term 'estimated gain' is used to emphasize that the Commission does not intend precise or detailed calculation of the monetary gain (nor of the loss) in using the alternative fine limits. In many cases, circumstances will make it unnecessary to consider these standards other than in the most general terms.",

and inserting in lieu thereof:

"2. In general, the maximum fine permitted by law as to each count of conviction is $250,000 for a felony or for any misdemeanor resulting in death; $100,000 for a Class A misdemeanor; and $5,000 for any other offense. 18 U.S.C. § 3571(b)(3)-(7). However, higher or lower limits may apply when specified by statute. 18 U.S.C. § 3571(b)(1), (e). As an alternative maximum, the court may fine the defendant up to the greater of twice the gross gain or twice the gross loss. 18 U.S.C. § 3571(b)(2), (d).

3. Alternative fine limits are provided in subsection (c). The terms 'pecuniary

gain' and 'pecuniary loss' are taken from 18 U.S.C. § 3571(d). The Commission does not intend precise or detailed calculation of the gain or loss in using the alternative fine limits. In many cases, circumstances will make it unnecessary to consider these standards other than in the most general terms.".

The Commentary to § 5E4.2 captioned "Application Notes" is amended in Note 4 by deleting "Any restitution" and inserting in lieu thereof "Restitution".

The Commentary to § 5E4.2 captioned "Background" is amended by deleting:

"defendant. In addition, the Commission concluded that greater latitude with a gain-based fine was justified; when the court finds it necessary to rely on the gain, rather than the loss, to set the fine, ordering restitution usually will not be feasible because of the difficulty in computing the amount.",

and inserting in lieu thereof:

"participants. In addition, in many such cases restitution will not be feasible.".

Reason for Amendment: The purposes of this amendment are to make the guideline consistent with 18 U.S.C. § 3571, as amended, to clarify the commentary, and to correct clerical errors in the guideline and commentary.

Effective Date: The effective date of this amendment is January 15, 1988.

55. **Amendment:** Chapter 5, Part J is amended in the title of the Part by deleting "PERTAINING TO CERTAIN EMPLOYMENT" immediately following "DISABILITY".

    Reason for Amendment: The purpose of this amendment is to eliminate the possible inference that this part covers only employment for compensation.

    Effective Date: The effective date of this amendment is June 15, 1988.

56. **Amendment:** Chapter Five, Part J is amended by deleting § 5J1.1 in its entirety as follows:

    "§ 5J1.1. Relief From Disability Pertaining to Certain Employment (Policy Statement)

    With regard to labor racketeering offenses, a part of the punishment imposed by 29 U.S.C. §§ 504 and 511 is the prohibition of convicted persons from service in labor unions, employer associations, employee benefit plans, and as labor relations consultants. Violations of these provisions are felony offenses. Persons convicted after October 12, 1984, may petition the sentencing court to reduce the statutory disability (thirteen years after sentence or imprisonment, whichever is later) to a lesser period (not less than three years after entry of judgment in the trial court). After November 1, 1987, petitions for exemption from the disability that were formerly administered by the United States Parole Commission will be transferred to the courts. Relief shall not be given in such cases to aid rehabilitation, but may be granted only following a clear demonstration by the convicted person that he has been rehabilitated since commission of the crime.".

    A replacement policy statement is inserted as § 5J1.1 (Relief from Disability Pertaining to

Convicted Persons Prohibited from Holding Certain Positions (Policy Statement)).

Reason for Amendment: The purpose of this amendment is to clarify the policy statement and conform it to the pertinent provisions of the Sentencing Act of 1987.

Effective Date: The effective date of this amendment is June 15, 1988.

57. **Amendment:** Section 5K2.0 is amended by deleting "an aggravating or mitigating circumstance exists that was" and inserting in lieu thereof "there exists an aggravating or mitigating circumstance of a kind, or to a degree".

    Reason for Amendment: The purpose of this amendment is to conform the quotation in this section to the wording in the Sentencing Act of 1987.

    Effective Date: The effective date of this amendment is June 15, 1988.

58. **Amendment:** Section 6A1.1 is amended by deleting "(a)" immediately before "A probation officer", and by deleting:

    > "(b) The presentence report shall be disclosed to the defendant, counsel for the defendant and the attorney for the government, to the maximum extent permitted by Rule 32(c), Fed. R. Crim. P. Disclosure shall be made at least ten days prior to the date set for sentencing, unless this minimum period is waived by the defendant. 18 U.S.C. § 3552(d).".

    Reason for Amendment: The purpose of this amendment is to delete material more properly covered elsewhere. See § 6A1.2 (Disclosure of Presentence Report; Issues in Dispute (Policy Statement)).

    Effective Date: The effective date of this amendment is June 15, 1988.

59. **Amendment:** Section 6A1.2 is amended by deleting:

    "Position of Parties with Respect to Sentencing Factors

    (a) After receipt of the presentence report and within a reasonable time before sentencing, the attorney for the government and the attorney for the defendant, or the pro se defendant, shall each file with the court a written statement of the sentencing factors to be relied upon at sentencing. The parties are not precluded from asserting additional sentencing factors if notice of the intention to rely upon another factor is filed with the court within a reasonable time before sentencing.

    (b) Copies of all sentencing statements filed with the court shall be contemporaneously served upon all other parties and submitted to the probation officer assigned to the case.

    (c) In lieu of the written statement required by § 6A1.2(a), any party may file:

    (1) a written statement adopting the findings of the presentence report;

    (2) a written statement adopting such findings subject to certain exceptions or additions; or

    (3) a written stipulation in which the parties agree to adopt the findings

of the presentence report or to adopt such findings subject to certain exceptions or additions.

(d) A district court may, by local rule, identify categories of cases for which the parties are authorized to make oral statements at or before sentencing, in lieu of the written statement required by this section.

(e) Except to the extent that a party may be privileged not to disclose certain information, all statements filed with the court or made orally to the court pursuant to this section shall:

(1) set forth, directly or by reference to the presentence report, the relevant facts and circumstances of the actual offense conduct and offender characteristics; and

(2) not contain misleading facts.",

and inserting in lieu thereof:

"Disclosure of Presentence Report; Issues in Dispute (Policy Statement)

Courts should adopt procedures to provide for the timely disclosure of the presentence report; the narrowing and resolution, where feasible, of issues in dispute in advance of the sentencing hearing; and the identification for the court of issues remaining in dispute. See Model Local Rule for Guideline Sentencing prepared by the Probation Committee of the Judicial Conference (August 1987).".

Reason for Amendment: This amendment deletes this guideline and inserts in lieu thereof a general policy statement. The Commission has determined that this subject is more appropriately covered by the Model Local Rule for Guideline Sentencing prepared by the Probation Committee of the Judicial Conference.

Effective Date: The effective date of this amendment is June 15, 1988.

60. **Amendment:** Appendix A is amended by inserting the following statutes in the appropriate place according to statutory title and section number:

"7 U.S.C. § 2024(b)	2F1.1",
"7 U.S.C. § 2024(c)	2F1.1",
"18 U.S.C. § 874	2B3.2, 2B3.3",
"18 U.S.C. § 914	2F1.1",
"18 U.S.C. § 923	2K2.3",
"18 U.S.C. § 1030(a)(1)	2M3.2",
"18 U.S.C. § 1030(a)(2)	2F1.1",
"18 U.S.C. § 1030(a)(3)	2F1.1",
"18 U.S.C. § 1030(a)(4)	2F1.1",
"18 U.S.C. § 1030(a)(5)	2F1.1",
"18 U.S.C. § 1030(a)(6)	2F1.1",
"18 U.S.C. § 1030(b)	2X1.1",
"18 U.S.C. § 1501	2A2.2, 2A2.3",
"18 U.S.C. § 1720	2F1.1",
"18 U.S.C. § 4082(d)	2P1.1",

Amendment 60 APPENDIX C - VOLUME I November 1, 2013

> "19 U.S.C. § 1304   2T3.1",
> "20 U.S.C. § 1097(c)   2B4.1",
> "20 U.S.C. § 1097(d)   2F1.1",
> "38 U.S.C. § 3502   2F1.1",
> "42 U.S.C. § 1307(a)   2F1.1",
> "42 U.S.C. § 1395nn(c)   2F1.1",
> "45 U.S.C. § 359(a)   2F1.1".

Reason for Amendment: The purpose of this amendment is to make the statutory index more comprehensive.

Effective Date: The effective date of this amendment is January 15, 1988.

61. **Amendment:** Appendix A is amended by deleting:

> "16 U.S.C. § 703   2Q2.1",
> "16 U.S.C. § 707   2Q2.1",

and inserting in lieu thereof:

> "16 U.S.C. § 707(b)   2Q2.1";

by deleting:

> "18 U.S.C. § 112(a)   2A2.1, 2A2.2, 2A2.3",

and inserting in lieu thereof:

> "18 U.S.C. § 112(a)   2A2.2, 2A2.3";

by deleting:

> "18 U.S.C. § 510(a)   2B5.1",

and inserting in lieu thereof:

> "18 U.S.C. § 510   2B5.2";

by deleting:

> "18 U.S.C. § 1005   2F1.1, 2S1.3",

and inserting in lieu thereof:

> "18 U.S.C. § 1005   2F1.1";

by deleting:

> "18 U.S.C. § 1701   2B1.1, 2H3.3",

and inserting in lieu thereof:

"18 U.S.C. § 1700   2H3.3";

by deleting:

"18 U.S.C. § 2113(a)   2B1.1, 2B3.1",

and inserting in lieu thereof:

"18 U.S.C. § 2113(a)   2B1.1, 2B2.2, 2B3.1, 2B3.2";

by deleting "2B5.1," from the line beginning with "18 U.S.C. § 2314"; and

by deleting "2B5.1," from the line beginning with "18 U.S.C. § 2315".

Reason for Amendment: The purpose of this amendment is to correct clerical errors.

Effective Date: The effective date of this amendment is January 15, 1988.

62. **Amendment:** Appendix A is amended by inserting the following statutes in the appropriate place according to statutory title and section number:

"18 U.S.C. § 911   2F1.1, 2L2.2",
"18 U.S.C. § 922(n)   2K2.1",
"18 U.S.C. § 2071   2B1.1, 2B1.3",
"26 U.S.C. § 7212(a)   2A2.2, 2A2.3",
"42 U.S.C. § 2278(a)(c)   2B2.3",
"46 U.S.C. § 3718(b)   2K3.1",
"47 U.S.C. § 553(b)(2)   2B5.3",
"49 U.S.C. § 1472(h)(2)   2K3.1".

Reason for Amendment: The purpose of this amendment is to make the statutory index more comprehensive.

Effective Date: The effective date of this amendment is June 15, 1988.

63. **Amendment:** Appendix A is amended by deleting:

"7 U.S.C. § 166   2N2.1",
"7 U.S.C. § 213   2F1.1",
"7 U.S.C. § 473   2N2.1";

by deleting:

"7 U.S.C. § 511e   2N2.1",
"7 U.S.C. § 511k   2N2.1",

and inserting in lieu thereof:

"7 U.S.C. § 511d   2N2.1",
"7 U.S.C. § 511i   2N2.1";

Amendment 63 — APPENDIX C - VOLUME I — November 1, 2013

by deleting:

"7 U.S.C. § 586	2N2.1",
"7 U.S.C. § 596	2N2.1",
"7 U.S.C. § 608e-1	2N2.1";

by deleting:

| "16 U.S.C. § 117(c) | 2B1.1, 2B1.3", |

and inserting in lieu thereof:

| "16 U.S.C. § 117c | 2B1.1, 2B1.3"; |

by deleting:

"16 U.S.C. § 414	2B2.3",
"16 U.S.C. § 426i	2B1.1, 2B1.3",
"16 U.S.C. § 428i	2B1.1, 2B1.3",
"18 U.S.C. § 291	2C1.3, 2F1.1",
"26 U.S.C. § 7269	2T1.2",
"41 U.S.C. § 51	2B4.1",
"42 U.S.C. § 4012	2Q1.3",
"50 U.S.C. § 2410	2M5.1";

and by deleting the first time it appears:

| "50 U.S.C. App. § 462 | 2M4.1". |

Reason for Amendment: The purposes of this amendment are to correct clerical errors and delete inadvertently included statutes.

Effective Date: The effective date of this amendment is June 15, 1988.

64. **Amendment:** Chapter Two, Part A is amended by inserting an additional guideline with accompanying commentary as § 2A2.4 (Obstructing or Impeding Officers).

The Commentary to § 2A2.3 captioned "Statutory Provisions" is amended by deleting "111".

Appendix A is amended by deleting "2A2.3," from the line beginning with "18 U.S.C. § 111", and inserting in lieu thereof "2A2.4";

by deleting "2A2.3," from the line beginning with "18 U.S.C. § 1501", and inserting in lieu thereof "2A2.4";

by inserting the following statutes in the appropriate place according to statutory title and section number:

| "18 U.S.C. § 1502 | 2A2.4", |
| "18 U.S.C. § 3056(d) | 2A2.4". |

– 26 –

Reason for Amendment: The purpose of this amendment is to make the guidelines more comprehensive.

Effective Date: The effective date of this amendment is October 15, 1988.

65. **Amendment:** Chapter Two, Part A is amended by inserting an additional guideline with accompanying commentary as § 2A5.3 (Committing Certain Crimes Aboard Aircraft).

Appendix A is amended by inserting the following statute in the appropriate place according to statutory title and section number:

"49 U.S.C. § 1472(k)(1)   2A5.3".

Reason for Amendment: The purpose of this amendment is to make the guidelines more comprehensive.

Effective Date: The effective date of this amendment is October 15, 1988.

66. **Amendment:** Chapter Two, Part D is amended by deleting § 2D1.5 in its entirety as follows:

"§ 2D1.5.   Continuing Criminal Enterprise

    (a)   Base Offense Level:

            (1)   32, for the first conviction of engaging in a continuing criminal enterprise; or

            (2)   38, for the second or any subsequent conviction of engaging in a continuing criminal enterprise; or

            (3)   43, for engaging in a continuing criminal enterprise as the principal administrator, leader, or organizer, if either the amount of drugs involved was 30 times the minimum in the first paragraph (i.e., the text corresponding to Level 36) of the Drug Quantity Table or 300 times the minimum in the third paragraph (i.e., the text corresponding to Level 32), or the principal received $10 million in gross receipts for any twelve-month period.

Commentary

Statutory Provision: 21 U.S.C. § 848.

Application Note:

1.   Do not apply any adjustment from Chapter Three, Part B (Role in the Offense).

Background: The base offense levels for continuing criminal enterprises are mandatory minimum sentences provided by the statute that mandate imprisonment for leaders of large scale drug enterprises. A conviction establishes that the defendant controlled and exercised decision-making authority over one of the most serious forms of ongoing criminal activity. Therefore, an adjustment for role in the offense in Chapter Three, Part B, is not applicable.".

A replacement guideline with accompanying commentary is inserted as § 2D1.5 (Continuing Criminal Enterprise).

Reason for Amendment: The purpose of this amendment is to ensure that the guideline adequately reflects the seriousness of the criminal conduct. The previous guideline specified sentences that were lower than sentences typically imposed on defendants convicted of engaging in a continuing criminal enterprise, a result that the Commission did not intend. The guideline is also amended to delete, as unnecessary, provisions that referred to statutory minimum sentences.

Effective Date: The effective date of this amendment is October 15, 1988.

67. **Amendment:** Chapter One, Part A (4)(b) is amended in the first sentence by deleting ". . . that was" and inserting in lieu thereof "of a kind, or to a degree,".

    Chapter One, Part A, section 4(b) is amended in the second sentence of the last paragraph by deleting "Part H" and inserting in lieu thereof "Part K (Departures)", and in the third sentence of the last paragraph by deleting "Part H" and inserting in lieu thereof "Part K".

    Reason for Amendment: The purposes of this amendment are to conform the quotation to the statute, as amended by Section 3 of the Sentencing Act of 1987, and to correct a clerical error.

    Effective Date: The effective date of this amendment is November 1, 1989.

68. **Amendment:** Chapter One, Part A, section 4(b) is amended in the first sentence of the fourth paragraph by deleting "three" and inserting in lieu thereof "two"; in the fourth paragraph by deleting the second through eighth sentences as follows:

    > "The first kind, which will most frequently be used, is in effect an interpolation between two adjacent, numerically oriented guideline rules. A specific offense characteristic, for example, might require an increase of four levels for serious bodily injury but two levels for bodily injury. Rather than requiring a court to force middle instances into either the 'serious' or the 'simple' category, the guideline commentary suggests that the court may interpolate and select a midpoint increase of three levels. The Commission has decided to call such an interpolation a 'departure' in light of the legal views that a guideline providing for a range of increases in offense levels may violate the statute's 25 percent rule (though other have presented contrary legal arguments). Since interpolations are technically departures, the courts will have to provide reasons for their selection, and it will be subject to review for 'reasonableness' on appeal. The Commission believes, however, that a simple reference by the court to the 'mid-category' nature of the facts will typically provide sufficient reason. It does not foresee serious practical problems arising out of the application of the appeal provisions to this form of departure.";

    in the first sentence of the fifth paragraph by deleting "second" and inserting in lieu thereof "first"; and, in the first sentence of the sixth paragraph by deleting "third" and inserting in lieu thereof "second".

    Reason for Amendment: The purpose of this amendment is to eliminate references to interpolation as a special type of departure. The Commission has reviewed the discussion of interpolation in Chapter One, which has been read as describing "interpolation" as a departure from an offense level rather than from the guideline range established after the determination of an offense level. The Commission concluded that it is simpler to add intermediate offense level adjustments to the guidelines in the cases where interpolation is most likely to be considered (i.e., degree of bodily injury). This amendment is not intended to preclude interpolation in other cases; where appropriate, the court will be able to achieve the same result by use of the regular departure provisions.

Effective Date: The effective date of this amendment is November 1, 1989.

69. **Amendment:** Section 1B1.1(a) is amended by deleting "guideline section in Chapter Two most applicable to the statute of conviction" and inserting in lieu thereof "applicable offense guideline section from Chapter Two", and by deleting the last sentence as follows: "If more than one guideline is referenced for the particular statute, select the guideline most appropriate for the conduct of which the defendant was convicted.".

    Reason for Amendment: The purposes of this amendment are to clarify the guideline and conform the language to § 1B1.2.

    Effective Date: The effective date of this amendment is November 1, 1989.

70. **Amendment:** Section 1B1.1(e) is amended by deleting the last sentence as follows: "The resulting offense level is the total offense level.".

    Section 1B1.1(g) is amended by deleting "total", and by inserting "determined above" immediately following "category".

    Reason for Amendment: The purpose of this amendment is to clarify the guideline.

    Effective Date: The effective date of this amendment is November 1, 1989.

71. **Amendment:** The Commentary to § 1B1.1 captioned "Application Notes" is amended in Note 1(c) by deleting "firearm or other dangerous weapon" and inserting in lieu thereof "dangerous weapon (including a firearm)".

    The Commentary to § 1B1.1 captioned "Application Notes" is amended in Note 1(d) by inserting the following additional sentence at the end: "Where an object that appeared to be a dangerous weapon was brandished, displayed, or possessed, treat the object as a dangerous weapon.".

    The Commentary to § 1B1.1 captioned "Application Notes" is amended in Note 1(g) by deleting "firearm or other dangerous weapon" the first time it appears and inserting in lieu thereof "dangerous weapon (including a firearm)".

    The Commentary to § 1B1.1 captioned "Application Notes" is amended by inserting the following additional note:

    > "5. Where two or more guideline provisions appear equally applicable, but the guidelines authorize the application of only one such provision, use the provision that results in the greater offense level. E.g., in § 2A2.2(b)(2), if a firearm is both discharged and brandished, the provision applicable to the discharge of the firearm would be used.".

    Reason for Amendment: The purposes of this amendment are to clarify the definition of a dangerous weapon; and to clarify that when two or more guideline provisions appear equally applicable, but the guidelines authorize the application of only one such provision, the provision that results in the greater offense level is to be used.

    Effective Date: The effective date of this amendment is November 1, 1989.

72. **Amendment:** The Commentary to § 1B1.1 captioned "Application Notes" is amended by inserting the following additional note:

> "6. In the case of a defendant subject to a sentence enhancement under 18 U.S.C. § 3147 (Penalty for an Offense Committed While on Release), see § 2J1.7 (Commission of Offense While on Release).".

Reason for Amendment: The purpose of this amendment is to clarify the treatment of a specific enhancement provision.

Effective Date: The effective date of this amendment is November 1, 1989.

73. **Amendment:** Section 1B1.2(a) is amended in the first sentence by deleting "The court shall apply" and inserting in lieu thereof "Determine"; and in the second sentence by deleting "the court shall apply" and inserting in lieu thereof "determine", and by deleting "guideline in such chapter" and inserting in lieu thereof "offense guideline section in Chapter Two".

Reason for Amendment: The purposes of this amendment are to clarify the guideline and to make the phraseology of this subsection more consistent with that of §§ 1B1.1 and 1B1.2(b).

Effective Date: The effective date of this amendment is November 1, 1989.

74. **Amendment:** Section 1B1.2(a) is amended in the first sentence by inserting immediately before the period: "(i.e., the offense conduct charged in the count of the indictment or information of which the defendant was convicted)".

The Commentary to § 1B1.2 captioned "Application Notes" is amended in the first paragraph of Note 1 by deleting:

> "As a general rule, the court is to apply the guideline covering the offense conduct most applicable to the offense of conviction. Where a particular statute proscribes a variety of conduct which might constitute the subject of different guidelines, the court will decide which guideline applies based upon the nature of the offense conduct charged.",

and inserting in lieu thereof:

> "As a general rule, the court is to use the guideline section from Chapter Two most applicable to the offense of conviction. The Statutory Index (Appendix A) provides a listing to assist in this determination. When a particular statute proscribes only a single type of criminal conduct, the offense of conviction and the conduct proscribed by the statute will coincide, and there will be only one offense guideline referenced. When a particular statute proscribes a variety of conduct that might constitute the subject of different offense guidelines, the court will determine which guideline section applies based upon the nature of the offense conduct charged in the count of which the defendant was convicted.".

Reason for Amendment: The purpose of this amendment is to clarify the guideline and commentary.

Effective Date: The effective date of this amendment is November 1, 1989.

75. **Amendment:** Section 1B1.2(a) is amended by deleting the last sentence as follows:

> "Similarly, stipulations to additional offenses are treated as if the defendant had been convicted of separate counts charging those offenses.",

and by inserting the following additional subsections:

> "(c) A conviction by a plea of guilty or nolo contendere containing a stipulation that specifically establishes the commission of additional offense(s) shall be treated as if the defendant had been convicted of additional count(s) charging those offense(s).
>
> (d) A conviction on a count charging a conspiracy to commit more than one offense shall be treated as if the defendant had been convicted on a separate count of conspiracy for each offense that the defendant conspired to commit.".

The Commentary to § 1B1.2 captioned "Application Notes" is amended in the second paragraph of Note 1 by deleting:

> "Similarly, if the defendant pleads guilty to one robbery but admits the elements of two additional robberies as part of a plea agreement, the guideline applicable to three robberies is to be applied.",

and by inserting the following additional notes:

> "4. Subsections (c) and (d) address circumstances in which the provisions of Chapter Three, Part D (Multiple Counts) are to be applied although there may be only one count of conviction. Subsection (c) provides that in the case of a stipulation to the commission of additional offense(s), the guidelines are to be applied as if the defendant had been convicted of an additional count for each of the offenses stipulated. For example, if the defendant is convicted of one count of robbery but, as part of a plea agreement, admits to having committed two additional robberies, the guidelines are to be applied as if the defendant had been convicted of three counts of robbery. Subsection (d) provides that a conviction on a conspiracy count charging conspiracy to commit more than one offense is treated as if the defendant had been convicted of a separate conspiracy count for each offense that he conspired to commit. For example, where a conviction on a single count of conspiracy establishes that the defendant conspired to commit three robberies, the guidelines are to be applied as if the defendant had been convicted on one count of conspiracy to commit the first robbery, one count of conspiracy to commit the second robbery, and one count of conspiracy to commit the third robbery.
>
> 5. Particular care must be taken in applying subsection (d) because there are cases in which the jury's verdict does not establish which offense(s) was the object of the conspiracy. In such cases, subsection (d) should only be applied with respect to an object offense alleged in the conspiracy count if the court, were it sitting as a trier of fact, would convict the defendant of conspiring to commit that object offense. Note, however, if the object offenses specified in the conspiracy count would be grouped together under § 3D1.2(d) (e.g., a conspiracy to steal three government checks) it is not necessary to engage in the foregoing analysis, because § 1B1.3(a)(2) governs consideration of the defendant's conduct.".

Reason for Amendment: The purpose of this amendment is to add a guideline subsection (subsection (d)) expressly providing that a conviction of conspiracy to commit more than one offense is treated for guideline purposes as if the defendant had been convicted of a separate conspiracy count for each offense that the defendant conspired to commit. The current instruction in Application Note 9 of § 3D1.2 is inadequate. For consistency, material now contained at § 1B1.2(a) concerning stipulations to having committed additional offenses is moved to a new subsection (subsection (c)).

Additional commentary (Application Note 5) is provided to address cases in which the jury's verdict does not specify how many or which offenses were the object of the conspiracy of which the defendant was convicted. Compare United States v. Johnson, 713 F.2d 633, 645-46 (11th Cir. 1983) (conviction stands if there is sufficient proof with respect to any one of the objectives) cert. denied sub nom. Wilkins v. United States, 465 U.S. 1081 (1984) with United States v. Tarnopol, 561 F.2d 466 (3d Cir. 1977) (failure of proof with respect to any one of the objectives renders the conspiracy conviction invalid). In order to maintain consistency with other § 1B1.2(a) determinations, this decision should be governed by a reasonable doubt standard. A higher standard of proof should govern the creation of what is, in effect, a new count of conviction for the purposes of Chapter Three, Part D (Multiple Counts). Because the guidelines do not explicitly establish standards of proof, the proposed new application note calls upon the court to determine which offense(s) was the object of the conspiracy as if it were "sitting as a trier of fact." The foregoing determination is not required, however, in the case of offenses that are grouped together under § 3D1.2(d) (e.g., fraud and theft) because § 1B1.3(a)(2) governs consideration of the defendant's conduct.

Effective Date: The effective date of this amendment is November 1, 1989.

76. **Amendment:** Section 1B1.3 is amended in subsection (a)(3) by deleting "or risk of harm" immediately following "all harm", and by deleting "if the harm or risk was caused intentionally, recklessly or by criminal negligence, and all harm or risk" and inserting in lieu thereof "and all harm".

Section 1B1.3(a) is amended by deleting:

"(4) the defendant's state of mind, intent, motive and purpose in committing the offense; and",

by renumbering subsection (a)(5) as (a)(4), and by inserting "and" at the end of subsection (a)(3) immediately following the semicolon.

The Commentary to § 1B1.3 captioned "Background" is amended by deleting:

"   Subsection (a)(4) requires consideration of the defendant's 'state of mind, intent, motive or purpose in committing the offense.' The defendant's state of mind is an element of the offense that may constitute a specific offense characteristic. See, e.g., § 2A1.4 (Involuntary Manslaughter) (distinction made between recklessness and criminal negligence). The guidelines also incorporate broader notions of intent or purpose that are not elements of the offense, e.g., whether the offense was committed for profit, or for the purpose of facilitating a more serious offense. Accordingly, such factors must be considered in determining the applicable guideline range.",

and inserting in lieu thereof:

"   Subsection (a)(4) requires consideration of any other information specified in the applicable guideline. For example, § 2A1.4 (Involuntary Manslaughter) specifies consideration of the defendant's state of mind; § 2K1.4 (Arson; Property Damage By Use of Explosives) specifies consideration of the risk of harm created.".

Reason for Amendment: The purpose of this amendment is to delete language pertaining to "risk of harm" and "state of mind" as unnecessary. Cases in which the guidelines specifically address risk of harm or state of mind are covered in the amended guideline under subsection (a)(4) [formerly subsection (a)(5)]. In addition, the amendment deletes reference to harm committed "intentionally, recklessly, or by criminal negligence" as unnecessary and potentially confusing.

Effective Date: The effective date of this amendment is November 1, 1989.

77. **Amendment:** Section 1B1.3 is amended by deleting the introductory sentence as follows: "The conduct that is relevant to determining the applicable guideline range includes that set forth below.".

Section 1B1.3(b) is amended by deleting:

> "(b) Chapter Four (Criminal History and Criminal Livelihood). To determine the criminal history category and the applicability of the career offender and criminal livelihood guidelines, the court shall consider all conduct relevant to a determination of the factors enumerated in the respective guidelines in Chapter Four.",

and inserting in lieu thereof:

> "(b) Chapters Four (Criminal History and Criminal Livelihood) and Five (Determining the Sentence). Factors in Chapters Four and Five that establish the guideline range shall be determined on the basis of the conduct and information specified in the respective guidelines.".

The Commentary to § 1B1.3 captioned "Background" is amended in the second paragraph by deleting "Chapter Four" and inserting in lieu thereof "Chapters Four and Five", and by deleting "that Chapter" and inserting in lieu thereof "those Chapters".

Reason for Amendment: The purpose of this amendment is to clarify the guideline.

Effective Date: The effective date of this amendment is November 1, 1989.

78. **Amendment:** The Commentary to § 1B1.3 captioned "Application Notes" is amended in Note 1 by deleting:

> "If the conviction is for conspiracy, it includes conduct in furtherance of the conspiracy that was known to or was reasonably foreseeable by the defendant. If the conviction is for solicitation, misprision or accessory after the fact, it includes all conduct relevant to determining the offense level for the underlying offense that was known to or reasonably should have been known by the defendant. See generally §§ 2X1.1-2X4.1.",

and inserting in lieu thereof:

> "In the case of criminal activity undertaken in concert with others, whether or not charged as a conspiracy, the conduct for which the defendant 'would be otherwise accountable' also includes conduct of others in furtherance of the execution of the jointly-undertaken criminal activity that was reasonably foreseeable by the defendant. Because a count may be broadly worded and include the conduct of many participants over a substantial period of time, the scope of the jointly-undertaken criminal activity, and hence relevant conduct, is not necessarily the same for every participant. Where it is established that the conduct was neither

within the scope of the defendant's agreement, nor was reasonably foreseeable in connection with the criminal activity the defendant agreed to jointly undertake, such conduct is not included in establishing the defendant's offense level under this guideline.

In the case of solicitation, misprision, or accessory after the fact, the conduct for which the defendant 'would be otherwise accountable' includes all conduct relevant to determining the offense level for the underlying offense that was known, or reasonably should have been known, by the defendant.

Illustrations of Conduct for Which the Defendant is Accountable

a. Defendant A, one of ten off-loaders hired by Defendant B, was convicted of importation of marihuana, as a result of his assistance in off-loading a boat containing a one-ton shipment of marihuana. Regardless of the number of bales of marihuana that he actually unloaded, and notwithstanding any claim on his part that he was neither aware of, nor could reasonably foresee, that the boat contained this quantity of marihuana, Defendant A is held accountable for the entire one-ton quantity of marihuana on the boat because he aided and abetted the unloading, and hence the importation, of the entire shipment.

b. Defendant C, the getaway driver in an armed bank robbery in which $15,000 is taken and a teller is injured, is convicted of the substantive count of bank robbery. Defendant C is accountable for the money taken because he aided and abetted the taking of the money. He is accountable for the injury inflicted because he participated in concerted criminal conduct that he could reasonably foresee might result in the infliction of injury.

c. Defendant D pays Defendant E a small amount to forge an endorsement on an $800 stolen government check. Unknown to Defendant E, Defendant D then uses that check as a down payment in a scheme to fraudulently obtain $15,000 worth of merchandise. Defendant E is convicted of forging the $800 check. Defendant E is not accountable for the $15,000 because the fraudulent scheme to obtain $15,000 was beyond the scope of, and not reasonably foreseeable in connection with, the criminal activity he jointly undertook with Defendant D.

d. Defendants F and G, working together, design and execute a scheme to sell fraudulent stocks by telephone. Defendant F fraudulently obtains $20,000. Defendant G fraudulently obtains $35,000. Each is convicted of mail fraud. Each defendant is accountable for the entire amount ($55,000) because each aided and abetted the other in the fraudulent conduct. Alternatively, because Defendants F and G engaged in concerted criminal activity, each is accountable for the entire $55,000 loss because the conduct of each was in furtherance of the jointly undertaken criminal activity and was reasonably foreseeable.

e. Defendants H and I engaged in an ongoing marihuana importation conspiracy in which Defendant J was hired only to help off-load a single shipment. Defendants H, I, and J are included in a single count charging conspiracy to import marihuana. For the purposes of determining the offense level under this guideline, Defendant J is accountable for the entire single shipment of marihuana he conspired to help import and any acts or omissions in furtherance of the importation that were reasonably foreseeable. He is not accountable for prior or subsequent shipments of marihuana imported by Defendants H or I if those acts were beyond the scope of, and not reasonably foreseeable in connection with, the criminal activity he agreed to jointly undertake with Defendants H and I (i.e., the importation of the single shipment of marihuana).".

Reason for Amendment: The purpose of this amendment is to clarify the definition of conduct for which the defendant is "otherwise accountable."

Effective Date: The effective date of this amendment is November 1, 1989.

79. **Amendment:** Section 1B1.5 is amended by deleting "adjustments for" immediately following "all applicable", and by inserting "and cross references" immediately before the period at the end of the sentence.

    The Commentary to § 1B1.5 captioned "Application Note" is amended in Note 1 by inserting "and cross references" immediately before "as well as the base offense level".

    Reason for Amendment: The purpose of this amendment is to clarify the guideline and commentary.

    Effective Date: The effective date of this amendment is November 1, 1989.

80. **Amendment:** The Commentary to § 1B1.5 captioned "Application Note" is amended in Note 1 by deleting the last sentence as follows: "If the victim was vulnerable, the adjustment from § 3A1.1 (Vulnerable Victim) also would apply.".

    Reason for Amendment: The purpose of this amendment is to delete an unnecessary sentence. No substantive change is made.

    Effective Date: The effective date of this amendment is November 1, 1989.

81. **Amendment:** Section 1B1.9 is amended in the title by deleting "Petty Offenses" and inserting in lieu thereof "Class B or C Misdemeanors and Infractions".

    Section 1B1.9 is amended by deleting "(petty offense)" immediately following "infraction".

    The Commentary to § 1B1.9 captioned "Application Notes is amended in the first sentence of Note 1 by deleting "petty offense" and inserting in lieu thereof "Class B or C misdemeanor or an infraction", in the second sentence of Note 1 by deleting "A petty offense is any offense for which the maximum sentence that may be imposed does not exceed six months' imprisonment." and inserting in lieu thereof "A Class B misdemeanor is any offense for which the maximum authorized term of imprisonment is more than thirty days but not more than six months; a Class C misdemeanor is any offense for which the maximum authorized term of imprisonment is more than five days but not more than thirty days; an infraction is any offense for which the maximum authorized term of imprisonment is not more than five days.", in the first sentence of Note 2 by deleting "petty offenses" and inserting in lieu thereof "Class B or C misdemeanors or infractions", in the second sentence of Note 2 by deleting "petty" and inserting in lieu thereof "such", in the third sentence of Note 2 by deleting "petty offense" and inserting in lieu thereof "Class B or C misdemeanor or infraction" and, in Note 3 by deleting:

    > "3. All other provisions of the guidelines should be disregarded to the extent that they purport to cover petty offenses.".

    The Commentary to § 1B1.9 captioned "Background" is amended by deleting:

    > "voted to adopt a temporary amendment to exempt all petty offenses from the coverage of the guidelines. Consequently, to the extent that some published guidelines may appear to cover petty offenses, they should be disregarded even if they appear in the Statutory Index",

and inserting in lieu thereof:

> "exempted all Class B and C misdemeanors and infractions from the coverage of the guidelines".

Reason for Amendment: The purposes of this amendment are to conform the guideline to a revision in the statutory definition of a petty offense, and to convert the wording of the Commission's emergency amendment at § 1B1.9 (effective June 15, 1988) to that appropriate for a permanent amendment. Section 7089 of the Anti-Drug Abuse Act of 1988 revises the definition of a petty offense so that it no longer exactly corresponds with a Class B or C misdemeanor or infraction. Under the revised definition, a Class B or C misdemeanor or infraction that has an authorized fine of more than $5,000 for an individual (or more than $10,000 for an organization) will not be a petty offense. This legislative revision does not affect the maximum terms of imprisonment authorized. The maximum authorized term of imprisonment remains controlled by the grade of the offense (i.e., the maximum term of imprisonment remains five days for an infraction, thirty days for a Class C misdemeanor, and six months for a Class B misdemeanor). Because the statutory grade of the offense (i.e., a Class B or C misdemeanor or an infraction) is the more relevant definition for guideline purposes, this amendment deletes the references in § 1B1.9 to "petty offenses" and in lieu thereof inserts references to "Class B and C misdemeanors and infractions."

Effective Date: The effective date of this amendment is November 1, 1989.

82. **Amendment:** The Commentary to § 2A1.1 captioned "Statutory Provision" is amended by deleting "Provision" and inserting in lieu thereof "Provisions", and by inserting "; 21 U.S.C. § 848(e)" at the end immediately before the period.

The Commentary to § 2A1.1 captioned "Application Note" is amended in the caption by deleting "Note" and inserting in lieu thereof "Notes", and by inserting the following additional note:

> "2. If the defendant is convicted under 21 U.S.C. § 848(e), a sentence of death may be imposed under the specific provisions contained in that statute. This guideline applies when a sentence of death is not imposed.".

The Commentary to § 2A1.1 captioned "Background" is amended by deleting "statute" and inserting in lieu thereof "18 U.S.C. § 1111", and by inserting immediately after the first sentence:

> "Prior to the applicability of the Sentencing Reform Act of 1984, a defendant convicted under this statute and sentenced to life imprisonment could be paroled (see 18 U.S.C. § 4205(a)). Because of the abolition of parole by that Act, the language of 18 U.S.C. § 1111(b) (which was not amended by the Act) appears on its face to provide a mandatory minimum sentence of life imprisonment for this offense. Other provisions of the Act, however, classify this offense as a Class A felony (see 18 U.S.C. § 3559(a)(1)), for which a term of imprisonment of any period of time is authorized as an alternative to imprisonment for the duration of the defendant's life (see 18 U.S.C. §§ 3559(b), 3581(b)(1), as amended); hence, the relevance of the discussion in Application Note 1, supra, regarding circumstances in which a sentence less than life may be appropriate for a conviction under this statute."

The Commentary to § 2A1.1 captioned "Background" is amended by inserting the following additional paragraph at the end:

"   The maximum penalty authorized under 21 U.S.C. § 848(e) is death or life imprisonment. If a term of imprisonment is imposed, the statutorily required minimum term is twenty years.".

Reason for Amendment: The purpose of this amendment is to incorporate new first-degree murder offenses created by Section 7001 of the Anti-Drug Abuse Act of 1988 where the death penalty is not imposed. This amendment also clarifies the existing commentary to this guideline.

Effective Date: The effective date of this amendment is November 1, 1989.

83. **Amendment:** Section 2A2.1 is amended in subsection (b)(2)(B) by deleting "a firearm or a dangerous weapon" and inserting in lieu thereof "a dangerous weapon (including a firearm)", and in subsection (b)(2)(C) by deleting "a firearm or other dangerous weapon" and inserting in lieu thereof "a dangerous weapon (including a firearm)".

Reason for Amendment: The purposes of this amendment are to clarify that a firearm is a type of dangerous weapon and to remove the inconsistency in the language between specific offense characteristic subdivisions (b)(2)(B) and (b)(2)(C).

Effective Date: The effective date of this amendment is November 1, 1989.

84. **Amendment:** Section 2A2.1(b)(3) is amended by inserting the following additional subdivisions:

> "(D) If the degree of injury is between that specified in subdivisions (A) and (B), add 3 levels; or
>
> (E) If the degree of injury is between that specified in subdivisions (B) and (C), add 5 levels.".

The Commentary to § 2A2.1 captioned "Application Notes" is amended in the caption by deleting "Notes" and inserting in lieu thereof "Note", and by deleting:

> "2. If the degree of bodily injury falls between two injury categories, use of the intervening level (i.e., interpolation) is appropriate."

Reason for Amendment: The purpose of this amendment is to provide intermediate adjustment levels for the degree of bodily injury.

Effective Date: The effective date of this amendment is November 1, 1989.

85. **Amendment:** Section 2A2.2 is amended in subsection (b)(2)(B) by deleting "a firearm or a dangerous weapon" and inserting in lieu thereof "a dangerous weapon (including a firearm)", and in subsection (b)(2)(C) by deleting "a firearm or other dangerous weapon" and inserting in lieu thereof "a dangerous weapon (including a firearm)".

Reason for Amendment: The purposes of this amendment are to clarify that a firearm is a type of dangerous weapon and to remove the inconsistency in language between specific offense characteristic subdivisions (b)(2)(B) and (b)(2)(C).

Effective Date: The effective date of this amendment is November 1, 1989.

86. **Amendment:** Section 2A2.2(b)(3) is amended by inserting the following additional subdivisions:

"(D) If the degree of injury is between that specified in subdivisions (A) and (B), add 3 levels; or

(E) If the degree of injury is between that specified in subdivisions (B) and (C), add 5 levels.".

The Commentary to § 2A2.2 captioned "Application Notes" is amended by deleting:

"3. If the degree of bodily injury falls between two injury categories, use of the intervening level (i.e., interpolation) is appropriate.",

and by renumbering Note 4 as Note 3.

Reason for Amendment: The purpose of this amendment is to provide intermediate adjustment levels for the degree of bodily injury.

Effective Date: The effective date of this amendment is November 1, 1989.

87. **Amendment:** Section 2A2.3(a)(1) is amended by deleting "striking, beating, or wounding" and inserting in lieu thereof "physical contact, or if a dangerous weapon (including a firearm) was possessed and its use was threatened".

The Commentary to § 2A2.3 captioned "Application Notes" is amended by deleting:

"2. 'Striking, beating, or wounding' means conduct sufficient to violate 18 U.S.C. § 113(d).",

and inserting in lieu thereof:

"2. Definitions of 'firearm' and 'dangerous weapon' are found in the Commentary to § 1B1.1 (Application Instructions).".

The Commentary to § 2A2.3 captioned "Background" is amended by deleting the last sentence as follows: "The distinction for striking, beating, or wounding reflects the statutory distinction found in 18 U.S.C. § 113(d) and (e).".

Reason for Amendment: The purpose of this amendment is to provide a clearer standard by replacing the phrase "striking, wounding, or beating" (a statutory phrase dealing with a petty offense) with "physical contact." The amendment also provides an enhanced offense level for the case in which a weapon is possessed and its use is threatened.

Effective Date: The effective date of this amendment is November 1, 1989.

88. **Amendment:** The Commentary to § 2A2.3 captioned "Statutory Provisions" is amended by deleting "113(d), 113(e),".

Reason for Amendment: The purpose of this amendment is to delete references to petty offenses.

Effective Date: The effective date of this amendment is November 1, 1989.

89. **Amendment:** The Commentary to § 2A2.4 captioned "Application Notes" is amended in Note 1 by deleting the first sentence as follows:

"Do not apply § 3A1.2 (Official Victim).",

and by inserting the following additional sentence at the end:

"Therefore, do not apply § 3A1.2 (Official Victim) unless subsection (c) requires the offense level to be determined under § 2A2.2 (Aggravated Assault).".

Reason for Amendment: The purpose of this amendment is to clarify the commentary.

Effective Date: The effective date of this amendment is November 1, 1989.

90. **Amendment:** Section 2A2.4(b)(1) is amended by deleting "striking, beating, or wounding", and inserting in lieu thereof "physical contact, or if a dangerous weapon (including a firearm) was possessed and its use was threatened".

The Commentary to § 2A2.4 captioned "Application Notes" is amended by deleting:

"2. 'Striking, beating, or wounding' is discussed in the Commentary to § 2A2.3 (Minor Assault).",

and inserting in lieu thereof:

"2. Definitions of 'firearm' and 'dangerous weapon' are found in the Commentary to § 1B1.1 (Application Instructions).".

Reason for Amendment: The purpose of this amendment is to provide a clearer standard by replacing the phrase "striking, wounding, or beating" (a statutory phrase dealing with a petty

offense) with "physical contact." The amendment also provides an enhanced offense level for the case in which a weapon is possessed and its use is threatened.

Effective Date: The effective date of this amendment is November 1, 1989.

91. **Amendment:** Section 2A3.1(b)(1) is amended by deleting:

"criminal sexual abuse was accomplished as defined in 18 U.S.C. § 2241",

and inserting in lieu thereof:

"offense was committed by the means set forth in 18 U.S.C. § 2241(a) or (b)".

The Commentary to § 2A3.1 captioned "Application Notes" is amended in Note 2 by deleting:

"'Accomplished as defined in 18 U.S.C. § 2241' means accomplished by force, threat, or other means as defined in 18 U.S.C. § 2241(a) or (b) (i.e., by using force against that person; by threatening or placing that other person",

and inserting in lieu thereof:

"'The means set forth in 18 U.S.C. § 2241(a) or (b)' are: by using force against the victim; by threatening or placing the victim",

by deleting the parenthesis immediately before the period at the end of the Note, and by inserting the following additional sentence at the end of the Note:

"This provision would apply, for example, where any dangerous weapon was used, brandished, or displayed to intimidate the victim.".

Amendment 91

The Commentary to § 2A3.1 captioned "Background" is amended in the fifth sentence of the first paragraph by deleting the comma immediately following "force" and inserting in lieu thereof a semicolon, and by deleting "kidnapping," and inserting in lieu thereof "or kidnapping;", and in the last sentence of the last paragraph by deleting "serious physical" and inserting in lieu thereof "permanent, life-threatening, or serious bodily".

Reason for Amendment: The purpose of this amendment is to clarify the guideline and commentary.

Effective Date: The effective date of this amendment is November 1, 1989.

92. **Amendment:** Section 2A3.1(b)(4) is amended by inserting immediately before the period at the end of the sentence: "; or (C) if the degree of injury is between that specified in subdivisions (A) and (B), increase by 3 levels".

Reason for Amendment: The purpose of this amendment is to provide an intermediate adjustment level for degree of bodily injury.

Effective Date: The effective date of this amendment is November 1, 1989.

93. **Amendment:** The Commentary to § 2A3.2 captioned "Statutory Provision" and "Background" is amended by deleting "2243" wherever it appears and inserting in lieu thereof "2243(a)".

The Commentary to § 2A3.2 captioned "Background" is amended by deleting "statutory rape, i.e.," immediately following "applies to", and by deleting "victim's incapacity to give lawful consent" and inserting in lieu thereof "age of the victim".

Reason for Amendment: The purposes of this amendment are to clarify that the relevant factor is the age of the victim, and to provide a more specific reference to the underlying statute.

Effective Date: The effective date of this amendment is November 1, 1989.

94. **Amendment:** Section 2A3.3 is amended in the title by deleting "(Statutory Rape)" immediately following "a Ward".

The Commentary to § 2A3.3 captioned "Statutory Provision" is amended by deleting "§ 2243" and inserting in lieu thereof "§ 2243(b)".

Reason for Amendment: The purposes of this amendment are to delete inapt language from the title and to provide a more specific reference to the underlying statute.

Effective Date: The effective date of this amendment is November 1, 1989.

95. **Amendment:** Chapter Two, Part A is amended by deleting § 2A3.4 in entirety as follows:

"§ 2A3.4.   Abusive Sexual Contact or Attempt to Commit Abusive Sexual Contact

    (a)   Base Offense Level: 6

    (b)   Specific Offense Characteristics

        (1)   If the abusive sexual contact was accomplished as defined in 18 U.S.C. § 2241 (including, but not limited to, the use or display of any dangerous weapon), increase by 9 levels.

November 1, 2013   APPENDIX C - VOLUME I   **Amendment 97**

       (2)   If the abusive sexual contact was accomplished as defined in 18 U.S.C. § 2242, increase by 4 levels.

Commentary

Statutory Provisions: 18 U.S.C. §§ 2244, 2245.

Application Notes:

1.   'Accomplished as defined in 18 U.S.C. § 2241' means accomplished by force, threat, or other means as defined in 18 U.S.C. § 2241(a) or (b) (i.e., by using force against that person; by threatening or placing that other person in fear that any person will be subject to death, serious bodily injury, or kidnapping; by rendering the victim unconscious; or by administering by force or threat of force, or without the knowledge or permission of the victim, a drug, intoxicant, or other similar substance and thereby substantially impairing the ability of the victim to appraise or control conduct).

2.   'Accomplished as defined in 18 U.S.C. § 2242' means accomplished by threatening or placing the victim in fear (other than by threatening or placing the victim in fear that any person will be subjected to death, serious bodily injury, or kidnapping); or when the victim is incapable of appraising the nature of the conduct or physically incapable of declining participation in, or communicating unwillingness to engage in, that sexual act.

Background: This section covers abusive sexual contact not amounting to criminal sexual abuse (criminal sexual abuse is covered under § 2A3.1-3.3). Enhancements are provided for the use of force or threats. The maximum term of imprisonment authorized by statute for offenses covered in this section is five years (if accomplished as defined in 18 U.S.C. § 2241), three years (if accomplished as defined in 18 U.S.C. § 2242), and six months otherwise. The base offense level applies to conduct that is consensual.".

A replacement guideline with accompanying commentary is inserted as § 2A3.4 (Abusive Sexual Contact or Attempt to Commit Abusive Sexual Contact).

Reason for Amendment: The purposes of the amendment are to make the offense levels under this guideline consistent with the structure of related guidelines (§§ 2A3.1, 2A3.2, 2G1.2, 2G2.1, and 2G2.2) and to reflect the increased maximum sentences for certain conduct covered by this guideline. The amendment increases all offense levels, but in particular provides enhanced punishment for victimization of minors and children.

Effective Date: The effective date of this amendment is November 1, 1989.

96.   **Amendment:** Section 2A4.1(b)(2) is amended by inserting immediately before the period at the end of the sentence: "; or (C) if the degree of injury is between that specified in subdivisions (A) and (B), increase by 3 levels".

     Reason for Amendment: The purpose of this amendment is to provide an intermediate adjustment level for the degree of bodily injury.

     Effective Date: The effective date of this amendment is November 1, 1989.

97.   **Amendment:** The Commentary to § 2A5.2 captioned "Application Note" is amended by deleting:

"Application Note:

1. If an assault occurred, apply the most analogous guideline from Part A, Subpart 2 (Assault) if the offense level under that guideline is greater.".

Reason for Amendment: The purpose of this amendment is to simplify the guideline by deleting redundant material.

Effective Date: The effective date of this amendment is November 1, 1989.

98. **Amendment:** The Commentary to § 2A5.3 captioned "Application Notes" is amended in Note 1 by deleting "that the defendant is convicted of violating" and inserting in lieu thereof "of which the defendant is convicted".

Reason for Amendment: The purpose of this amendment is to clarify the commentary.

Effective Date: The effective date of this amendment is November 1, 1989.

99. **Amendment:** Section 2B1.1(b)(1) is amended by deleting:

	"Loss	Increase in Level
(A)	$100 or less	no increase
(B)	$101 - $1,000	add 1
(C)	$1,001 - $2,000	add 2
(D)	$2,001 - $5,000	add 3
(E)	$5,001 - $10,000	add 4
(F)	$10,001 - $20,000	add 5
(G)	$20,001 - $50,000	add 6
(H)	$50,001 - $100,000	add 7
(I)	$100,001 - $200,000	add 8
(J)	$200,001 - $500,000	add 9
(K)	$500,001 - $1,000,000	add 10
(L)	$1,000,001 - $2,000,000	add 11
(M)	$2,000,001 - $5,000,000	add 12
(N)	over $5,000,000	add 13",

and inserting in lieu thereof:

	"Loss (Apply the Greatest)	Increase in Level
(A)	$100 or less	no increase
(B)	More than $100	add 1
(C)	More than $1,000	add 2
(D)	More than $2,000	add 3
(E)	More than $5,000	add 4
(F)	More than $10,000	add 5
(G)	More than $20,000	add 6
(H)	More than $40,000	add 7

(I)	More than $70,000	add 8
(J)	More than $120,000	add 9
(K)	More than $200,000	add 10
(L)	More than $350,000	add 11
(M)	More than $500,000	add 12
(N)	More than $800,000	add 13
(O)	More than $1,500,000	add 14
(P)	More than $2,500,000	add 15
(Q)	More than $5,000,000	add 16
(R)	More than $10,000,000	add 17
(S)	More than $20,000,000	add 18
(T)	More than $40,000,000	add 19
(U)	More than $80,000,000	add 20.".

Reason for Amendment: The purposes of this amendment are to conform the theft and fraud loss tables to the tax evasion table in order to remove an unintended inconsistency between these tables in cases where the amount is greater than $40,000, to increase the offense levels for larger losses to provide additional deterrence and better reflect the seriousness of the conduct, and to eliminate minor gaps in the loss table.

Effective Date: The effective date of this amendment is November 1, 1989.

100. **Amendment:** Section 2B1.1(b)(6) is amended by deleting "organized criminal activity" and inserting in lieu thereof "an organized scheme to steal vehicles or vehicle parts".

The Commentary to § 2B1.1 captioned "Application Notes" is amended by deleting:

"8. 'Organized criminal activity' refers to operations such as car theft rings or 'chop shops,' where the scope of the activity is clearly significant.",

and inserting in lieu thereof:

"8. Subsection (b)(6), referring to an 'organized scheme to steal vehicles or vehicle parts,' provides an alternative minimum measure of loss in the case of an ongoing, sophisticated operation such as an auto theft ring or 'chop shop.' 'Vehicles' refers to all forms of vehicles, including aircraft and watercraft.".

The Commentary to § 2B1.1 captioned "Background" is amended in the last paragraph by deleting:

"A minimum offense level of 14 is provided for organized criminal activity, i.e., operations such as car theft rings or 'chop shops,' where the scope of the activity is clearly significant but difficult to estimate. The guideline is structured so that if reliable information enables the court to estimate a volume of property loss that would result in a higher offense level, the higher offense level would govern.",

and inserting in lieu thereof:

"A minimum offense level of 14 is provided for offenses involving an organized scheme to steal vehicles or vehicle parts. Typically, the scope of such activity is substantial (i.e., the value of the stolen property, combined with an enhancement for 'more than minimal planning' would itself result in an offense level of at least 14), but the value of the property is particularly difficult to ascertain in individual cases because the stolen property is rapidly resold or otherwise disposed of in the course of the offense. Therefore, the specific offense characteristic of 'organized scheme' is used as an alternative to 'loss' in setting the offense level.".

Reason for Amendment: The purpose of this amendment is to clarify the coverage of a specific offense characteristic.

Effective Date: The effective date of this amendment is November 1, 1989.

101. **Amendment:** The Commentary to § 2B1.1 captioned "Background" is amended in the first paragraph by deleting "§ 5A1.1" and inserting in lieu thereof "Chapter Five, Part A".

Reason for Amendment: The purpose of this amendment is to correct a clerical error.

Effective Date: The effective date of this amendment is November 1, 1989.

102. **Amendment:** Section 2B1.2 is amended in the title by inserting ", Transporting, Transferring, Transmitting, or Possessing" immediately after "Receiving".

Section 2B1.2(b)(3)(A) is amended by inserting "receiving and" immediately before "selling".

The Commentary to § 2B1.2 captioned "Application Notes" is amended by deleting:

"1. If the defendant is convicted of transporting stolen property, either § 2B1.1 or this guideline would apply, depending upon whether the defendant stole the property.",

and by renumbering Notes 2 and 3 as Notes 1 and 2 respectively.

Reason for Amendment: The purpose of this amendment is to clarify the nature of the cases to which this guideline applies.

Effective Date: The effective date of this amendment is November 1, 1989.

103. **Amendment:** Section 2B1.2 is amended by renumbering subsection (b)(4) as (b)(5), and by inserting the following new subsection (b)(4):

"(4) If the property included undelivered United States mail and the offense level as determined above is less than level 6, increase to level 6.".

The Commentary to § 2B1.2 captioned "Application Notes", as amended, is further amended by inserting the following additional note:

"3. 'Undelivered United States mail' means mail that has not actually been received by the addressee or his agent (e.g., it includes mail that is in the addressee's mail box).".

Reason for Amendment: The purpose of this amendment is to add a specific offense characteristic where stolen property involved "undelivered mail" to conform to § 2B1.1.

Effective Date: The effective date of this amendment is November 1, 1989.

104. **Amendment:** Section 2B1.2(b)(5)[formerly (b)(4)] is amended by deleting "organized criminal activity" and inserting in lieu thereof "an organized scheme to receive stolen

vehicles or vehicle parts".

The Commentary to § 2B1.2 captioned "Application Notes" is amended by inserting the following additional note:

"4. Subsection (b)(5), referring to an 'organized scheme to receive stolen vehicles or vehicle parts,' provides an alternative minimum measure of loss in the case of an ongoing, sophisticated operation such as an auto theft ring or 'chop shop.' 'Vehicles' refers to all forms of vehicles, including aircraft and watercraft. See Commentary to § 2B1.1 (Larceny, Embezzlement, and Other Forms of Theft).".

Reason for Amendment: The purpose of this amendment is to clarify the coverage of a specific offense characteristic.

Effective Date: The effective date of this amendment is November 1, 1989.

105. **Amendment:** Section 2B2.1(b)(2) is amended by deleting:

	"Loss	Increase in Level
(A)	$2,500 or less	no increase
(B)	$2,501 - $10,000	add 1
(C)	$10,001 - $50,000	add 2
(D)	$50,001 - $250,000	add 3
(E)	$250,001 - $1,000,000	add 4
(F)	$1,000,001 - $5,000,000	add 5
(G)	more than $5,000,000	add 6",

and inserting in lieu thereof:

	"Loss (Apply the Greatest)	Increase in Level
(A)	$2,500 or less	no increase
(B)	More than $2,500	add 1
(C)	More than $10,000	add 2
(D)	More than $50,000	add 3
(E)	More than $250,000	add 4
(F)	More than $800,000	add 5
(G)	More than $1,500,000	add 6
(H)	More than $2,500,000	add 7
(I)	More than $5,000,000	add 8.".

Reason for Amendment: The purposes of this amendment are to eliminate minor gaps in the loss table and to conform the offense levels for larger losses to the amended loss table at § 2B1.1.

Effective Date: The effective date of this amendment is November 1, 1989.

106. **Amendment:** Section 2B2.1(b)(4) is amended by deleting "a firearm or other dangerous weapon" and inserting in lieu thereof "a dangerous weapon (including a firearm)".

Amendment 106

The Commentary to § 2B2.1 captioned "Application Notes" is amended in Note 4 by deleting "with respect to a firearm or other dangerous weapon" and inserting in lieu thereof "to possession of a dangerous weapon (including a firearm) that was".

Reason for Amendment: The purpose of this amendment is to clarify the guideline and commentary.

Effective Date: The effective date of this amendment is November 1, 1989.

107. **Amendment:** Section 2B2.2(b)(4) is amended by deleting "a firearm or other dangerous weapon" and inserting in lieu thereof "a dangerous weapon (including a firearm)".

The Commentary to § 2B2.2 captioned "Application Notes" is amended in Note 4 by deleting "with respect to a firearm", and inserting in lieu thereof "to possession of a dangerous weapon (including a firearm) that was".

Reason for Amendment: The purpose of this amendment is to clarify the guideline and commentary.

Effective Date: The effective date of this amendment is November 1, 1989.

108. **Amendment:** Section 2B2.3(b)(2) is amended by deleting "a firearm or other dangerous weapon" and inserting in lieu thereof "a dangerous weapon (including a firearm)".

Reason for Amendment: The purpose of this amendment is to clarify the guideline.

Effective Date: The effective date of this amendment is November 1, 1989.

109. **Amendment:** Section 2B2.3(b) is amended by deleting "Characteristic" and inserting in lieu thereof "Characteristics".

The Commentary to § 2B2.3 captioned "Statutory Provisions" is amended by deleting "Provisions" and inserting in lieu thereof "Provision", and by deleting "18 U.S.C. §§ 1382, 1854" and inserting in lieu thereof "42 U.S.C. § 7270b".

Reason for Amendment: The purposes of this amendment are to correct a clerical error, to delete a reference to a petty offense and an incorrect statutory reference, and to insert an additional statutory reference.

Effective Date: The effective date of this amendment is November 1, 1989.

110. **Amendment:** Section 2B3.1(a) is amended by deleting "18" and inserting in lieu thereof "20".

Section 2B3.1(b) is amended by deleting subdivisions (1) and (2) as follows:

"(1) If the loss exceeded $2,500, increase the offense level as follows:

	Loss	Increase in Level
(A)	$2,500 or less	no increase
(B)	$2,501 - $10,000	add 1
(C)	$10,001 - $50,000	add 2
(D)	$50,001 - $250,000	add 3

– 46 –

(E)	$250,001 - $1,000,000	add 4
(F)	$1,000,001 - $5,000,000	add 5
(G)	more than $5,000,000	add 6

Treat the loss for a financial institution or post office as at least $5,000.

(2) (A) If a firearm was discharged increase by 5 levels; (B) if a firearm or a dangerous weapon was otherwise used, increase by 4 levels; (C) if a firearm or other dangerous weapon was brandished, displayed or possessed, increase by 3 levels.",

and inserting in lieu thereof:

"(1) If the offense involved robbery or attempted robbery of the property of a financial institution or post office, increase by 2 levels.

(2) (A) If a firearm was discharged, increase by 5 levels; (B) if a dangerous weapon (including a firearm) was otherwise used, increase by 4 levels; (C) if a dangerous weapon (including a firearm) was brandished, displayed, or possessed, increase by 3 levels; or (D) if an express threat of death was made, increase by 2 levels.",

and by inserting the following additional subdivision:

"(6) If the loss exceeded $10,000, increase the offense level as follows:

Loss (Apply the Greatest)		Increase in Level
(A)	$10,000 or less	no increase
(B)	More than $10,000	add 1
(C)	More than $50,000	add 2
(D)	More than $250,000	add 3
(E)	More than $800,000	add 4
(F)	More than $1,500,000	add 5
(G)	More than $2,500,000	add 6
(H)	More than $5,000,000	add 7.".

The Commentary to § 2B3.1 captioned "Application Notes" is amended by deleting:

"2. Pursuant to the last sentence of § 2B3.1(b)(1), robbery or attempted robbery of a bank or post office results in a minimum one-level enhancement. There is no special enhancement for banks and post offices if the loss exceeds $10,000, however.",

and inserting in lieu thereof:

"2. When an object that appeared to be a dangerous weapon was brandished, displayed, or possessed, treat the object as a dangerous weapon for the purposes of subsection (b)(2)(C).".

The Commentary to § 2B3.1 captioned "Application Notes" is amended by inserting the

Amendment 110

following additional note:

> "8. An 'express threat of death,' as used in subsection (b)(2)(D), may be in the form of an oral or written statement, act, gesture, or combination thereof. For example, an oral or written demand using words such as 'Give me the money or I will kill you', 'Give me the money or I will pull the pin on the grenade I have in my pocket', 'Give me the money or I will shoot you', 'Give me your money or else (where the defendant draws his hand across his throat in a slashing motion)', or 'Give me the money or you are dead' would constitute an express threat of death. The court should consider that the intent of the underlying provision is to provide an increased offense level for cases in which the offender(s) engaged in conduct that would instill in a reasonable person, who is a victim of the offense, significantly greater fear than that necessary to constitute an element of the offense of robbery.".

The Commentary to § 2B3.1 captioned "Background" is amended in the first paragraph by deleting the third sentence as follows:

> "Banks and post offices carry a minimum 1 level enhancement for property loss because such institutions generally have more cash readily available, and whether the defendant obtains more or less than $2,500 is largely fortuitous.".

Reason for Amendment: The purposes of this amendment are to increase the offense level for robbery to better reflect the seriousness of the offense and past practice, to provide an increased enhancement for the robbery of the property of a financial institution or post office, to provide an enhancement for an express threat of death, and to provide that an object that appeared to be a dangerous weapon is to be treated as a dangerous weapon for the purposes of subsection (b)(2)(C).

Effective Date: The effective date of this amendment is November 1, 1989.

111. **Amendment:** Section 2B3.1(b)(3) is amended by inserting the following additional subdivisions:

> "(D)   If the degree of injury is between that specified in subdivisions (A) and (B), add 3 levels; or
>
> (E)   If the degree of injury is between that specified in subdivisions (B) and (C), add 5 levels.".

The Commentary to § 2B3.1 captioned "Application Notes" is amended by deleting:

> "4.   If the degree of bodily injury falls between two injury categories, use of the intervening level (i.e., interpolation) is appropriate.", and by renumbering Notes 5-8 as 4-7, respectively.

Reason for Amendment: The purpose of this amendment is to provide intermediate adjustment levels for the degree of bodily injury.

Effective Date: The effective date of this amendment is November 1, 1989.

112. **Amendment:** Section 2B3.2 is amended in subsection (b)(2)(B) by deleting "a firearm or a dangerous weapon" and inserting in lieu thereof "a dangerous weapon (including a firearm)", and in subsection (b)(2)(C) by deleting "a firearm or other dangerous weapon" and inserting in lieu thereof "a dangerous weapon (including a firearm)".

Reason for Amendment: The purposes of this amendment are to clarify that a firearm is a type of dangerous weapon and to remove the inconsistency in language between specific offense characteristic subdivisions (b)(2)(B) and (b)(2)(C).

Effective Date: The effective date of this amendment is November 1, 1989.

113. **Amendment:** Section 2B3.2(b)(3) is amended by inserting the following additional subdivisions:

> "(D) If the degree of injury is between that specified in subdivisions (A) and (B), add 3 levels; or
>
> (E) If the degree of injury is between that specified in subdivisions (B) and (C), add 5 levels.".

The Commentary to § 2B3.2 captioned "Application Notes" is amended by deleting:

> "4. If the degree of bodily injury falls between two injury categories, use of the intervening level (i.e., interpolation) is appropriate.",

and by renumbering Notes 5 and 6 as 4 and 5, respectively.

Reason for Amendment: The purpose of this amendment is to provide intermediate adjustment levels for the degree of bodily injury.

Effective Date: The effective date of this amendment is November 1, 1989.

114. **Amendment:** Section 2B3.3(b) is amended by deleting "Characteristics" and inserting in lieu thereof "Characteristic".

Reason for Amendment: The purpose of this amendment is to correct a clerical error.

Effective Date: The effective date of this amendment is November 1, 1989.

115. **Amendment:** Section 2B5.1 is amended in the title by inserting "Bearer" immediately before "Obligations".

The Commentary to § 2B5.1 captioned "Application Notes" is amended by renumbering Note 2 as Note 3, and by inserting the following new note 2:

> "2. 'Counterfeit,' as used in this section, means an instrument that purports to be genuine but is not, because it has been falsely made or manufactured in its entirety. Offenses involving genuine instruments that have been altered are covered under § 2B5.2.".

The Commentary to § 2B5.1 captioned "Application Notes" is amended in the renumbered Note 3 by deleting ", paste corners of notes on notes of a different denomination," immediately before "or otherwise produce".

Reason for Amendment: The purpose of this amendment is to clarify the coverage and operation of this guideline. The amendment revises the title of § 2B5.1 to make the coverage of the guideline clear from the title, and adopts the definition of "counterfeit" used in 18 U.S.C. § 513. "Altered" obligations (e.g., the corner of a note of one denomination pasted on a note of a different denomination) are covered under § 2B5.2.

Effective Date: The effective date of this amendment is November 1, 1989.

116. Amendment: Section 2B5.2 is amended in the title by inserting "Altered or" immediately following "Involving" and by inserting "Counterfeit Bearer" immediately following "Other than".

Reason for Amendment: The purpose of this amendment is to clarify the coverage of this guideline.

Effective Date: The effective date of this amendment is November 1, 1989.

117. Amendment: Section 2B6.1(b) is amended by renumbering subsection (b)(2) as (b)(3) and inserting the following new subsection (b)(2):

> "(2) If the defendant was in the business of receiving and selling stolen property, increase by 2 levels.".

Reason for Amendment: The purpose of this amendment is to resolve an inconsistency between this section and § 2B1.2 created by the lack of an enhancement in this section for a person in the business of selling stolen property. This amendment eliminates this inconsistency by adding a 2-level increase if the defendant was in the business of selling stolen property. Two levels rather than four levels is the applicable increase to conform to § 2B1.2 because the base offense level of § 2B6.1 already incorporates the adjustment for more than minimal planning.

Effective Date: The effective date of this amendment is November 1, 1989.

118. Amendment: Section 2B6.1(b)(3)[formerly (b)(2)] is amended by deleting "organized criminal activity" and inserting in lieu thereof "an organized scheme to steal vehicles or vehicle parts, or to receive stolen vehicles or vehicle parts".

The Commentary to § 2B6.1 captioned "Application Note" is amended by deleting:

> "1. See Commentary to § 2B1.1 (Larceny, Embezzlement, and other Forms of Theft) regarding the adjustment in subsection (b)(2) for organized criminal activity, such as car theft rings and 'chop shop' operations.",

and inserting in lieu thereof:

> "1. Subsection (b)(3), referring to an 'organized scheme to steal vehicles or vehicle parts, or to receive stolen vehicles or vehicle parts,' provides an alternative minimum measure of loss in the case of an ongoing, sophisticated operation such as an auto theft ring or 'chop shop.' 'Vehicles' refers to all forms of vehicles, including aircraft and watercraft. See Commentary to § 2B1.1 (Larceny, Embezzlement, and Other Forms of Theft).".

Reason for Amendment: The purpose of this amendment is to clarify the coverage of a specific offense characteristic.

Effective Date: The effective date of this amendment is November 1, 1989.

119. Amendment: Section 2B6.1(b) is amended by deleting "Characteristic" and inserting in lieu thereof "Characteristics".

The Commentary to § 2B6.1 captioned "Statutory Provisions" and "Background" is amended by deleting "2320" wherever it appears and inserting in lieu thereof in each instance "2321".

Reason for Amendment: The purpose of this amendment is to correct clerical errors.

Effective Date: The effective date of this amendment is November 1, 1989.

120. **Amendment:** Section 2C1.1(b)(1) is amended by deleting "action received" and inserting in lieu thereof "benefit received, or to be received,".

The Commentary to § 2C1.1 captioned "Application Notes" is amended in Note 2 in the first sentence by deleting "action received" and inserting in lieu thereof "benefit received, or to be received,", and by deleting "action (i.e., benefit or favor)" and inserting in lieu thereof "benefit"; in the second sentence by deleting "action received in return" and inserting in lieu thereof "benefit received or to be received", and by deleting "such action" and inserting in lieu thereof "such benefit"; and in the third sentence by deleting "action" and inserting in lieu thereof "benefit".

Reason for Amendment: The purpose of this amendment is to clarify the guideline and commentary.

Effective Date: The effective date of this amendment is November 1, 1989.

121. **Amendment:** Section 2C1.1(b) is amended by deleting "(1)" and "(2)" and inserting in lieu thereof "(A)" and "(B)" respectively; and by deleting "Apply the greater" and inserting in lieu thereof:

> "(1) If the offense involved more than one bribe, increase by 2 levels.
>
> (2) (If more than one applies, use the greater):".

The Commentary to § 2C1.1 captioned "Application Notes" is amended by deleting the text of Note 6 as follows:

> "When multiple counts are involved, each bribe is to be treated as a separate, unrelated offense not subject to § 3D1.2(d) or § 3D1.3(b). Instead, apply § 3D1.4. However, if a defendant makes several payments as part of a single bribe, that is to be treated as a single bribery offense involving the total amount of the bribe.",

and inserting in lieu thereof:

> "Related payments that, in essence, constitute a single bribe (e.g., a number of installment payments for a single action) are to be treated as a single bribe, even if charged in separate counts.".

Section 2C1.2(b) is amended by deleting "(1)" and "(2)" and inserting in lieu thereof "(A)" and "(B)" respectively; and by deleting "Apply the greater" and inserting in lieu thereof:

> "(1) If the offense involved more than one gratuity, increase by 2 levels.
>
> (2) (If more than one applies, use the greater):".

The Commentary to § 2C1.2 captioned "Application Notes" is amended by deleting the text of Note 4 as follows:

> "When multiple counts of receiving a gratuity are involved, each count is to be treated as a separate, unrelated offense not subject to § 3D1.2(d) or § 3D1.3(b). Instead, apply § 3D1.4.",

and inserting in lieu thereof:

"Related payments that, in essence, constitute a single gratuity (e.g., separate payments for airfare and hotel for a single vacation trip) are to be treated as a single gratuity, even if charged in separate counts.".

Section 3D1.2(d) is amended in the listing of offense sections in the third paragraph by deleting "§ 2C1.1,", and in the listing of offense sections in the second paragraph by inserting in order by section number "§§ 2C1.1, 2C1.2;".

The Introductory Commentary to Chapter Three, Part D, is amended in the fifth paragraph by deleting ", robbery, and bribery" and inserting in lieu thereof "and robbery", and in the seventh paragraph by deleting ", robbery, or bribery" and inserting in lieu thereof "or robbery".

Under the current bribery guideline, there is no enhancement for repeated instances of bribery if the conduct involves the same course of conduct or common scheme or plan and the same victim (as frequently is the case where the government is the victim) because such cases are grouped under § 3D1.2(b). In contrast, the fraud and theft guidelines generally provide a 2-level increase in cases of repeated instances under the second prong of the "more than minimal planning" definition.

Unlike the theft and fraud guidelines, it is arguable that the value of any bribe that was part of the same course of conduct or a common scheme or plan as the offense of conviction, but not included in the count of conviction, is excluded from consideration. This is because § 1B1.3(a)(2), which authorizes consideration of conduct not expressly included in the offense of conviction but part of the same course of conduct or common scheme or plan, applies only to offenses grouped under § 3D1.2(d). Thus, if the defendant pleads to one count of a bribery offense involving one $10,000 bribe in satisfaction of a 15 count indictment involving an additional $80,000 in separate bribes that were part of the same course of conduct, the current bribery guideline, unlike the theft and fraud guidelines, would not take into account the additional $80,000, and there would be no increase for repeated instances.

The current guideline may also create various anomalies because the multiple count rule (which applies only where the offenses are not grouped under § 3D1.2(b)) increases the offense level differently than the monetary table. For example, an elected public official who takes three unrelated $200 bribes has an offense level of 21; the same defendant who took two unrelated $500,000 bribes would have an offense level of 20.

Reason for Amendment: The purpose of this amendment is to address the above noted issues. A specific offense characteristic is added to provide a 2-level increase where the offense involved more than one bribe or gratuity. In addition, such offenses will be grouped under § 3D1.2(d) which allows for aggregation of the amount of the bribes from the same course of conduct or common scheme or plan under § 1B1.3(a)(2) (as in theft and fraud offenses).

Effective Date: The effective date of this amendment is November 1, 1989.

122. **Amendment:** The Commentary to § 2C1.1 captioned "Background" is amended in the eighth paragraph by deleting "extortions, conspiracies, and attempts" and inserting in lieu thereof "extortion, or attempted extortion,".

Reason for Amendment: The purpose of this amendment is to correct a technical error. This section expressly covers extortion and attempted extortion; conspiracy is covered through the operation of § 2X1.1.

Effective Date: The effective date of this amendment is November 1, 1989.

123. Amendment: Section 2D1.1(a) is amended by deleting:

"(a) Base Offense Level:

(1) 43, for an offense that results in death or serious bodily injury with a prior conviction for a similar drug offense; or

(2) 38, for an offense that results in death or serious bodily injury and involved controlled substances (except Schedule III, IV, and V controlled substances and less than: (A) fifty kilograms of marihuana, (B) ten kilograms of hashish, and (C) one kilogram of hashish oil); or

(3) For any other offense, the base offense level is the level specified in the Drug Quantity Table below.",

and inserting in lieu thereof:

"(a) Base Offense Level (Apply the greatest):

(1) 43, if the defendant is convicted under 21 U.S.C. § 841(b)(1)(A), (b)(1)(B), or (b)(1)(C), or 21 U.S.C. § 960(b)(1), (b)(2), or (b)(3), and the offense of conviction establishes that death or serious bodily injury resulted from the use of the substance and that the defendant committed the offense after one or more prior convictions for a similar offense; or

(2) 38, if the defendant is convicted under 21 U.S.C. § 841(b)(1)(A), (b)(1)(B), or (b)(1)(C), or 21 U.S.C. § 960(b)(1), (b)(2), or (b)(3), and the offense of conviction establishes that death or serious bodily injury resulted from the use of the substance; or

(3) the offense level specified in the Drug Quantity Table set forth in subsection (c) below.".

The Commentary to § 2D1.1 captioned "Application Notes" is amended in Note 1 by deleting "'Similar drug offense' as used in § 2D1.1(a)(1) means a prior conviction as described in 21 U.S.C. §§ 841(b) or 962(b).", and inserting in lieu thereof "'Mixture or substance' as used in this guideline has the same meaning as in 21 U.S.C. § 841.".

Reason for Amendment: The purpose of this amendment is to provide that subsections (a)(1) and (a)(2) apply only in the case of a conviction under circumstances specified in the statutes cited. The amendment also clarifies that the term "mixture or substance" has the same meaning as it has in the statute.

Effective Date: The effective date of this amendment is November 1, 1989.

124. Amendment: Section 2D1.1(b) is amended by deleting "a firearm or other dangerous weapon" and inserting in lieu thereof "a dangerous weapon (including a firearm)".

Reason for Amendment: The purpose of the amendment is to clarify the guideline.

Effective Date: The effective date of this amendment is November 1, 1989.

125. Amendment: Section 2D1.1 is amended by deleting the "Drug Quantity Table" in its en-

Amendment 125 APPENDIX C - VOLUME I November 1, 2013

tirety, including the title and footnotes, as follows:

"DRUG QUANTITY TABLE

Controlled Substances and Quantity*	Base Offense Level
10 KG Heroin or equivalent Schedule I or II Opiates, 50 KG Cocaine or equivalent Schedule I or II Stimulants, 500 G Cocaine Base, 10 KG PCP or 1 KG Pure PCP, 100 G LSD or equivalent Schedule I or II Hallucinogens, 4 KG Fentanyl or 1 KG Fentanyl Analogue, 10,000 KG Marihuana, 100,000 Marihuana Plants, 2000 KG Hashish, 200 KG Hashish Oil (or more of any of the above)	Level 36
3-9.9 KG Heroin or equivalent Schedule I or II Opiates, 15-49.9 KG Cocaine or equivalent Schedule I or II Stimulants, 150-499 G Cocaine Base, 3-9.9 KG PCP or 300-999 G Pure PCP, 30-99 G LSD or equivalent Schedule I or II Hallucinogens, 1.2-3.9 KG Fentanyl or 300-999 G Fentanyl Analogue, 3000-9999 KG Marihuana, 30,000-99,999 Marihuana Plants, 600-1999 KG Hashish, 60-199 KG Hashish Oil	Level 34
1-2.9 KG Heroin or equivalent Schedule I or II Opiates, 5-14.9 KG Cocaine or equivalent Schedule I or II Stimulants, 50-149 G Cocaine Base, 1-2.9 KG PCP or 100-299 G Pure PCP, 10-29 G LSD or equivalent Schedule I or II Hallucinogens, .4-1.1 KG Fentanyl or 100-299 G Fentanyl Analogue, 1000-2999 KG Marihuana, 10,000-29,999 Marihuana Plants, 200-599 KG Hashish, 20-59.9 KG Hashish Oil	Level 32**
700-999 G Heroin or equivalent Schedule I or II Opiates, 3.5-4.9 KG Cocaine or equivalent Schedule I or II Stimulants, 35-49 G Cocaine Base, 700-999 G PCP or 70-99 G Pure PCP, 7-9.9 G LSD or equivalent Schedule I or II Hallucinogens, 280-399 G Fentanyl or 70-99 G Fentanyl Analogue, 700-999 KG Marihuana, 7000-9999 Marihuana Plants, 140-199 KG Hashish, 14-19.9 KG Hashish Oil	Level 30
400-699 G Heroin or equivalent Schedule I or II Opiates, 2-3.4 KG Cocaine or equivalent Schedule I or II Stimulants, 20-34.9 G Cocaine Base, 400-699 G PCP or 40-69 G Pure PCP, 4-6.9 G LSD or equivalent Schedule I or II Hallucinogens, 160-279 G Fentanyl or 40-69 G Fentanyl Analogue, 400-699 KG Marihuana, 4000-6999 Marihuana Plants, 80-139 KG Hashish, 8.0-13.9 KG Hashish Oil	Level 28
100-399 G Heroin or equivalent Schedule I or II Opiates, .5-1.9 KG Cocaine or equivalent Schedule I or II Stimulants, 5-19 G Cocaine Base, 100-399 G PCP or 10-39 G Pure PCP, 1-3.9 G LSD or equivalent Schedule I or II Hallucinogens, 40-159 G Fentanyl or 10-39 G Fentanyl Analogue, 100-399 KG Marihuana, 1000-3999 Marihuana Plants, 20-79 KG Hashish, 2.0-7.9 KG Hashish Oil	Level 26**
80-99 G Heroin or equivalent Schedule I or II Opiates, 400-499 G Cocaine or equivalent Schedule I or II Stimulants, 4-4.9 G Cocaine Base, 80-99 G PCP or 8-9.9 G Pure PCP, 800-999 MG LSD or equivalent Schedule I or II Hallucinogens, 32-39 G Fentanyl or 8-9.9 G Fentanyl Analogue, 80-99 KG Marihuana, 800-999 Marihuana Plants, 16-19.9 KG Hashish, 1.6-1.9 KG Hashish Oil	Level 24
60-79 G Heroin or equivalent Schedule I or II Opiates, 300-399 G Cocaine or equivalent Schedule I or II Stimulants, 3-3.9 G Cocaine Base, 60-79 G PCP or 6-7.9 G Pure PCP, 600-799 MG LSD or equivalent Schedule I or II Hallucinogens, 24-31.9 G Fentanyl or 6-7.9 G Fentanyl Analogue, 60-79 KG Marihuana, 600-799 Marihuana Plants, 12-15.9 KG Hashish, 1.2-1.5 KG Hashish Oil	Level 22
40-59 G Heroin or equivalent Schedule I or II Opiates, 200-299 G Cocaine or equivalent Schedule I or II Stimulants, 2-2.9 G Cocaine Base, 40-59 G PCP or 4-5.9 G Pure PCP, 400-599 MG LSD or equivalent Schedule I or II Hallucinogens, 16-23.9 G Fentanyl or 4-5.9 G Fentanyl Analogue, 40-59 KG Marihuana, 400-599 Marihuana Plants, 8-11.9 KG Hashish, .8-1.1 KG Hashish Oil, 20 KG+ Schedule III or other Schedule I or II controlled substances	Level 20

20-39 G Heroin or equivalent Schedule I or II Opiates, 100-199 G Cocaine or equivalent Schedule I or II Stimulants, 1-1.9 G Cocaine Base, 20-39 G PCP or 2-3.9 G Pure PCP, 200-399 MG LSD or equivalent Schedule I or II Hallucinogens, 8-15.9 G Fentanyl or 2-3.9 G Fentanyl Analogue, 20-39 KG Marihuana, 200-399 Marihuana Plants, 5-7.9 KG Hashish, 500-799 G Hashish Oil, 10-19 KG Schedule III or other Schedule I or II controlled substances	Level 18
10-19 G Heroin or equivalent Schedule I or II Opiates, 50-99 G Cocaine or equivalent Schedule I or II Stimulants, 500-999 MG Cocaine Base, 10-19.9 G PCP or 1-1.9 G Pure PCP, 100-199 MG LSD or equivalent Schedule I or II Hallucinogens, 4-7.9 G Fentanyl or 1-1.9 G Fentanyl Analogue, 10-19 KG Marihuana, 100-199 Marihuana Plants, 2-4.9 KG Hashish, 200-499 G Hashish Oil, 5-9.9 KG Schedule III or other Schedule I or II controlled substances	Level 16
5-9.9 G Heroin or equivalent Schedule I or II Opiates, 25-49 G Cocaine or equivalent Schedule I or II Stimulants, 250-499 MG Cocaine Base, 5-9.9 G PCP or 500-999 MG Pure PCP, 50-99 MG LSD or equivalent Schedule I or II Hallucinogens, 2-3.9 G Fentanyl or.5-.9 G Fentanyl Analogue, 5-9.9 KG Marihuana, 50-99 Marihuana Plants, 1-1.9 KG Hashish, 100-199 G Hashish Oil, 2.5-4.9 KG Schedule III or other Schedule I or II controlled substances	Level 14
Less than the following: 5 G Heroin or equivalent Schedule I or II Opiates, 25 G Cocaine or equivalent Schedule I or II Stimulants, 250 MG Cocaine Base, 5 G PCP or 500 MG Pure PCP, 50 MG LSD or equivalent Schedule I or II Hallucinogens, 2 G Fentanyl or 500 MG Fentanyl Analogue; 2.5-4.9 KG Marihuana, 25-49 Marihuana Plants, 500-999 G Hashish, 50-99 G Hashish Oil, 1.25-2.4 KG Schedule III or other Schedule I or II controlled substances, 20 KG+ Schedule IV	Level 12
1-2.4 KG Marihuana, 10-24 Marihuana Plants, 200-499 G Hashish, 20-49 G Hashish Oil, .50- 1.24 KG Schedule III or other Schedule I or II controlled substances, 8-19 KG Schedule IV	Level 10
250-999 G Marihuana, 3-9 Marihuana Plants, 50-199 G Hashish, 10-19 G Hashish Oil, 125- 449 G Schedule III or other Schedule I or II controlled substances, 2-7.9 KG Schedule IV, 20 KG+ Schedule V	Level 8
Less than the following: 250 G Marihuana, 3 Marihuana Plants, 50 G Hashish, 10 G Hashish Oil, 125 G Schedule III or other Schedule I or II controlled substances, 2 KG Schedule IV, 20 KG Schedule V	Level 6

*   The scale amounts for all controlled substances refer to the total weight of the controlled substance. Consistent with the provisions of the Anti-Drug Abuse Act, if any mixture of a compound contains any detectable amount of a controlled substance, the entire amount of the mixture or compound shall be considered in measuring the quantity. If a mixture or compound contains a detectable amount of more than one controlled substance, the most serious controlled substance shall determine the categorization of the entire quantity.

**   Statute specifies a mandatory minimum sentence.",

and inserting in lieu thereof:

Amendment 125   APPENDIX C - VOLUME I   November 1, 2013

"(c) DRUG QUANTITY TABLE

	Controlled Substances and Quantity*	Base Offense Level
(1)	300 KG or more of Heroin (or the equivalent amount of other Schedule I or II Opiates); 1500 KG or more of Cocaine (or the equivalent amount of other Schedule I or II Stimulants); 15 KG or more of Cocaine Base; 300 KG or more of PCP, or 30 KG or more of Pure PCP; 300 KG or more of Methamphetamine, or 30 KG or more of Pure Methamphetamine; 3 KG or more of LSD (or the equivalent amount of other Schedule I or II Hallucinogens); 120 KG or more of Fentanyl; 30 KG or more of a Fentanyl Analogue; 300,000 KG or more of Marihuana; 60,000 KG or more of Hashish; 6,000 KG or more of Hashish Oil.	Level 42
(2)	At least 100 KG but less than 300 KG of Heroin (or the equivalent amount of other Schedule I or II Opiates); At least 500 KG but less than 1500 KG of Cocaine (or the equivalent amount of other Schedule I or II Stimulants); At least 5 KG but less than 15 KG of Cocaine Base; At least 100 KG but less than 300 KG of PCP, or at least 10 KG but less than 30 KG of Pure PCP; At least 100 KG but less than 300 KG of Methamphetamine, or at least 10 KG but less than 30 KG of Pure Methamphetamine; At least 1 KG but less than 3 KG of LSD (or the equivalent amount of other Schedule I or II Hallucinogens); At least 40 KG but less than 120 KG of Fentanyl; At least 10 KG but less than 30 KG of a Fentanyl Analogue; At least 100,000 KG but less than 300,000 KG of Marihuana; At least 20,000 KG but less than 60,000 KG of Hashish; At least 2,000 KG but less than 6,000 KG of Hashish Oil.	Level 40
(3)	At least 30 KG but less than 100 KG of Heroin (or the equivalent amount of other Schedule I or II Opiates); At least 150 KG but less than 500 KG of Cocaine (or the equivalent amount of other Schedule I or II Stimulants); At least 1.5 KG but less than 5 KG of Cocaine Base; At least 30 KG but less than 100 KG of PCP, or at least 3 KG but less than 10 KG of Pure PCP; At least 30 KG but less than 100 KG of Methamphetamine, or at least 3 KG but less than 10 KG of Pure Methamphetamine; At least 300 G but less than 1 KG of LSD (or the equivalent amount of other Schedule I or II Hallucinogens); At least 12 KG but less than 40 KG of Fentanyl; At least 3 KG but less than 10 KG of a Fentanyl Analogue; At least 30,000 KG but less than 100,000 KG of Marihuana; At least 6,000 KG but less than 20,000 KG of Hashish; At least 600 KG but less than 2,000 KG of Hashish Oil.	Level 38
(4)	At least 10 KG but less than 30 KG of Heroin (or the equivalent amount of other Schedule I or II Opiates); At least 50 KG but less than 150 KG of Cocaine (or the equivalent amount of other Schedule I or II Stimulants); At least 500 G but less than 1.5 KG of Cocaine Base; At least 10 KG but less than 30 KG of PCP, or at least 1 KG but less than 3 KG of Pure PCP; At least 10 KG but less than 30 KG of Methamphetamine, or at least 1 KG but less than 3 KG of Pure Methamphetamine; At least 100 G but less than 300 G of LSD (or the equivalent amount of other Schedule I or II Hallucinogens); At least 4 KG but less than 12 KG of Fentanyl; At least 1 KG but less than 3 KG of a Fentanyl Analogue; At least 10,000 KG but less than 30,000 KG of Marihuana; At least 2,000 KG but less than 6,000 KG of Hashish; At least 200 KG but less than 600 KG of Hashish Oil.	Level 36

(5)	At least 3 KG but less than 10 KG of Heroin Level 34
	(or the equivalent amount of other Schedule I or II Opiates);
	At least 15 KG but less than 50 KG of Cocaine
	(or the equivalent amount of other Schedule I or II Stimulants);
	At least 150 G but less than 500 G of Cocaine Base;
	At least 3 KG but less than 10 KG of PCP, or at least 300 G but
	less than 1 KG of Pure PCP;
	At least 3 KG but less than 10 KG of Methamphetamine, or at least
	300 G but less than 1 KG of Pure Methamphetamine;
	At least 30 G but less than 100 G of LSD
	(or the equivalent amount of other Schedule I or II Hallucinogens);
	At least 1.2 KG but less than 4 KG of Fentanyl;
	At least 300 G but less than 1 KG of a Fentanyl Analogue;
	At least 3,000 KG but less than 10,000 KG of Marihuana;
	At least 600 KG but less than 2,000 KG of Hashish;
	At least 60 KG but less than 200 KG of Hashish Oil.

(6)	At least 1 KG but less than 3 KG of Heroin Level 32
	(or the equivalent amount of other Schedule I or II Opiates);
	At least 5 KG but less than 15 KG of Cocaine
	(or the equivalent amount of other Schedule I or II Stimulants);
	At least 50 G but less than 150 G of Cocaine Base;
	At least 1 KG but less than 3 KG of PCP, or at least 100 G but less
	than 300 G of Pure PCP;
	At least 1 KG but less than 3 KG of Methamphetamine, or at least
	100 G but less than 300 G of Pure Methamphetamine;
	At least 10 G but less than 30 G of LSD
	(or the equivalent amount of other Schedule I or II Hallucinogens);
	At least 400 G but less than 1.2 KG of Fentanyl;
	At least 100 G but less than 300 G of a Fentanyl Analogue;
	At least 1,000 KG but less than 3,000 KG of Marihuana;
	At least 200 KG but less than 600 KG of Hashish;
	At least 20 KG but less than 60 KG of Hashish Oil.

(7)	At least 700 G but less than 1 KG of Heroin Level 30
	(or the equivalent amount of other Schedule I or II Opiates);
	At least 3.5 KG but less than 5 KG of Cocaine
	(or the equivalent amount of other Schedule I or II Stimulants);
	At least 35 G but less than 50 G of Cocaine Base;
	At least 700 G but less than 1 KG of PCP, or at least 70 G but less
	than 100 G of Pure PCP;
	At least 700 G but less than 1 KG of Methamphetamine, or at least
	70 G but less than 100 G of Pure Methamphetamine;
	At least 7 G but less than 10 G of LSD
	(or the equivalent amount of other Schedule I or II Hallucinogens);
	At least 280 G but less than 400 G of Fentanyl;
	At least 70 G but less than 100 G of a Fentanyl Analogue;
	At least 700 KG but less than 1,000 KG of Marihuana;
	At least 140 KG but less than 200 KG of Hashish;
	At least 14 KG but less than 20 KG of Hashish Oil.

(8)	At least 400 G but less than 700 G of Heroin Level 28
	(or the equivalent amount of other Schedule I or II Opiates);
	At least 2 KG but less than 3.5 KG of Cocaine
	(or the equivalent amount of other Schedule I or II Stimulants);
	At least 20 G but less than 35 G of Cocaine Base;
	At least 400 G but less than 700 G of PCP, or at least 40 G but less
	than 70 G of Pure PCP;
	At least 400 G but less than 700 G of Methamphetamine, or at least
	40 G but less than 70 G of Pure Methamphetamine;
	At least 4 G but less than 7 G of LSD
	(or the equivalent amount of other Schedule I or II Hallucinogens);
	At least 160 G but less than 280 G of Fentanyl;
	At least 40 G but less than 70 G of a Fentanyl Analogue;
	At least 400 KG but less than 700 KG of Marihuana;
	At least 80 KG but less than 140 KG of Hashish;
	At least 8 KG but less than 14 KG of Hashish Oil.

(9)	At least 100 G but less than 400 G of Heroin (or the equivalent amount of other Schedule I or II Opiates); At least 500 G but less than 2 KG of Cocaine (or the equivalent amount of other Schedule I or II Stimulants); At least 5 G but less than 20 G of Cocaine Base; At least 100 G but less than 400 G of PCP, or at least 10 G but less than 40 G of Pure PCP; At least 100 G but less than 400 G of Methamphetamine, or at least 10 G but less than 40 G of Pure Methamphetamine; At least 1 G but less than 4 G of LSD (or the equivalent amount of other Schedule I or II Hallucinogens); At least 40 G but less than 160 G of Fentanyl; At least 10 G but less than 40 G of a Fentanyl Analogue; At least 100 KG but less than 400 KG of Marihuana; At least 20 KG but less than 80 KG of Hashish; At least 2 KG but less than 8 KG of Hashish Oil.	Level 26
(10)	At least 80 G but less than 100 G of Heroin (or the equivalent amount of other Schedule I or II Opiates); At least 400 G but less than 500 G of Cocaine (or the equivalent amount of other Schedule I or II Stimulants); At least 4 G but less than 5 G of Cocaine Base; At least 80 G but less than 100 G of PCP, or at least 8 G but less than 10 G of Pure PCP; At least 80 G but less than 100 G of Methamphetamine, or at least 8 G but less than 10 G of Pure Methamphetamine; At least 800 MG but less than 1 G of LSD (or the equivalent amount of other Schedule I or II Hallucinogens); At least 32 G but less than 40 G of Fentanyl; At least 8 G but less than 10 G of a Fentanyl Analogue; At least 80 KG but less than 100 KG of Marihuana; At least 16 KG but less than 20 KG of Hashish; At least 1.6 KG but less than 2 KG of Hashish Oil.	Level 24
(11)	At least 60 G but less than 80 G of Heroin (or the equivalent amount of other Schedule I or II Opiates); At least 300 G but less than 400 G of Cocaine (or the equivalent amount of other Schedule I or II Stimulants); At least 3 G but less than 4 G of Cocaine Base; At least 60 G but less than 80 G of PCP, or at least 6 G but less than 8 G of Pure PCP; At least 60 G but less than 80 G of Methamphetamine, or at least 6 G but less than 8 G of Pure Methamphetamine; At least 600 MG but less than 800 MG of LSD (or the equivalent amount of other Schedule I or II Hallucinogens); At least 24 G but less than 32 G of Fentanyl; At least 6 G but less than 8 G of a Fentanyl Analogue; At least 60 KG but less than 80 KG of Marihuana; At least 12 KG but less than 16 KG of Hashish; At least 1.2 KG but less than 1.6 KG of Hashish Oil.	Level 22
(12)	At least 40 G but less than 60 G of Heroin (or the equivalent amount of other Schedule I or II Opiates); At least 200 G but less than 300 G of Cocaine (or the equivalent amount of other Schedule I or II Stimulants); At least 2 G but less than 3 G of Cocaine Base; At least 40 G but less than 60 G of PCP, or at least 4 G but less than 6 G of Pure PCP; At least 40 G but less than 60 G of Methamphetamine, or at least 4 G but less than 6 G of Pure Methamphetamine; At least 400 MG but less than 600 MG of LSD (or the equivalent amount of other Schedule I or II Hallucinogens); At least 16 G but less than 24 G of Fentanyl; At least 4 G but less than 6 G of a Fentanyl Analogue; At least 40 KG but less than 60 KG of Marihuana; At least 8 KG but less than 12 KG of Hashish; At least 800 G but less than 1.2 KG of Hashish Oil; 20 KG or more of Schedule I or II Depressants or Schedule III substances.	Level 20

(13)　At least 20 G but less than 40 G of Heroin　　　　　　　　　　Level 18
　　　(or the equivalent amount of other Schedule I or II Opiates);
　　　At least 100 G but less than 200 G of Cocaine
　　　(or the equivalent amount of other Schedule I or II Stimulants);
　　　At least 1 G but less than 2 G of Cocaine Base;
　　　At least 20 G but less than 40 G of PCP, or at least 2 G but less
　　　than 4 G of Pure PCP;
　　　At least 20 G but less than 40 G of Methamphetamine, or at least 2
　　　G but less than
　　　4 G of Pure Methamphetamine;
　　　At least 200 MG but less than 400 MG of LSD
　　　(or the equivalent amount of other Schedule I or II Hallucinogens);
　　　At least 8 G but less than 16 G of Fentanyl;
　　　At least 2 G but less than 4 G of a Fentanyl Analogue;
　　　At least 20 KG but less than 40 KG of Marihuana;
　　　At least 5 KG but less than 8 KG of Hashish;
　　　At least 500 G but less than 800 G of Hashish Oil;
　　　At least 10 KG but less than 20 KG of Schedule I or II Depressants
　　　or Schedule III substances.

(14)　At least 10 G but less than 20 G of Heroin　　　　　　　　　　Level 16
　　　(or the equivalent amount of other Schedule I or II Opiates);
　　　At least 50 G but less than 100 G of Cocaine
　　　(or the equivalent amount of other Schedule I or II Stimulants);
　　　At least 500 MG but less than 1 G of Cocaine Base;
　　　At least 10 G but less than 20 G of PCP, or at least 1 G but less
　　　than 2 G of Pure PCP;
　　　At least 10 G but less than 20 G of Methamphetamine, or at least 1
　　　G but less than 2 G of Pure Methamphetamine;
　　　At least 100 MG but less than 200 MG of LSD
　　　(or the equivalent amount of other Schedule I or II Hallucinogens);
　　　At least 4 G but less than 8 G of Fentanyl;
　　　At least 1 G but less than 2 G of a Fentanyl Analogue;
　　　At least 10 KG but less than 20 KG of Marihuana;
　　　At least 2 KG but less than 5 KG of Hashish;
　　　At least 200 G but less than 500 G of Hashish Oil;
　　　At least 5 KG but less than 10 KG of Schedule I or II Depressants
　　　or Schedule III substances.

(15)　At least 5 G but less than 10 G of Heroin　　　　　　　　　　Level 14
　　　(or the equivalent amount of other Schedule I or II Opiates);
　　　At least 25 G but less than 50 G of Cocaine (or the equivalent
　　　amount of other Schedule I or II Stimulants);
　　　At least 250 MG but less than 500 MG of Cocaine Base;
　　　At least 5 G but less than 10 G of PCP, or at least 500 MG but less
　　　than 1 G of Pure PCP;
　　　At least 5 G but less than 10 G of Methamphetamine, or at least
　　　500 MG but less than 1 G of Pure Methamphetamine;
　　　At least 50 MG but less than 100 MG of LSD
　　　(or the equivalent amount of other Schedule I or II Hallucinogens);
　　　At least 2 G but less than 4 G of Fentanyl;
　　　At least 500 MG but less than 1 G of a Fentanyl Analogue;
　　　At least 5 KG but less than 10 KG of Marihuana;
　　　At least 1 KG but less than 2 KG of Hashish;
　　　At least 100 G but less than 200 G of Hashish Oil;
　　　At least 2.5 KG but less than 5 KG of Schedule I or II Depressants
　　　or Schedule III substances.

Amendment 125 APPENDIX C - VOLUME I November 1, 2013

(16)	Less than 5 G Heroin (or the equivalent amount of other Schedule I or II Opiates); Less than 25 G Cocaine (or the equivalent amount of other Schedule I or II Stimulants); Less than 250 MG of Cocaine Base; Less than 5 G of PCP, or less than 500 MG of Pure PCP; Less than 5 G of Methamphetamine, or less than 500 MG of Pure Methamphetamine; Less than 50 MG of LSD (or the equivalent amount of other Schedule I or II Hallucinogens); Less than 2 G of Fentanyl; Less than 500 MG of a Fentanyl Analogue; At least 2.5 KG but less than 5 KG of Marihuana; At least 500 G but less than 1 KG of Hashish; At least 50 G but less than 100 G of Hashish Oil; At least 1.25 KG but less than 2.5 KG of Schedule I or II Depressants or Schedule III substances; 20 KG or more of Schedule IV substances.	Level 12
(17)	At least 1 KG but less than 2.5 KG of Marihuana; At least 200 G but less than 500 G of Hashish; At least 20 G but less than 50 G of Hashish Oil; At least 500 G but less than 1.25 KG of Schedule I or II Depressants or Schedule III substances; At least 8 KG but less than 20 KG of Schedule IV substances.	Level 10
(18)	At least 250 G but less than 1 KG of Marihuana; At least 50 G but less than 200 G of Hashish; At least 5 G but less than 20 G of Hashish Oil; At least 125 G but less than 500 G of Schedule I or II Depressants or Schedule III substances; At least 2 KG but less than 8 KG of Schedule IV substances; 20 KG or more of Schedule V substances.	Level 8
(19)	Less than 250 G of Marihuana; Less than 50 G of Hashish; Less than 5 G of Hashish Oil; Less than 125 G of Schedule I or II Depressants or Schedule III substances; Less than 2 KG of Schedule IV substances; Less than 20 KG of Schedule V substances.	Level 6

*Unless otherwise specified, the weight of a controlled substance set forth in the table refers to the entire weight of any mixture or substance containing a detectable amount of the controlled substance. If a mixture or substance contains more than one controlled substance, the weight of the entire mixture or substance is assigned to the controlled substance that results in the greater offense level. In the case of a mixture or substance containing PCP or methamphetamine, use the offense level determined by the entire weight of the mixture or substance or the offense level determined by the weight of the pure PCP or methamphetamine, whichever is greater.

In the case of an offense involving marihuana plants, if the offense involved (A) 50 or more marihuana plants, treat each plant as equivalent to 1 KG of marihuana; (B) fewer than 50 marihuana plants, treat each plant as equivalent to 100 G of marihuana. Provided, however, that if the actual weight of the marihuana is greater, use the actual weight of the marihuana.".

The Commentary to § 2D1.1 captioned "Application Notes" is amended in Note 9 by inserting immediately before the period at the end of the first sentence of the first paragraph:

", except in the case of PCP or methamphetamine for which the guideline itself provides for the consideration of purity (see the footnote to the Drug Quantity Table)",

and by deleting the second paragraph as follows:

"Congress provided an exception to purity considerations in the case of phencycli-

November 1, 2013 APPENDIX C - VOLUME I **Amendment 125**

dine (PCP). 21 U.S.C. § 841(b)(1)(A). The legislation designates amounts of pure PCP and mixtures in establishing mandatory sentences. The first row of the table illustrates this distinction as one kilogram of PCP or 100 grams of pure PCP. Allowance for higher sentences based on purity is not appropriate for PCP.".

The Commentary to § 2D1.1 captioned "Application Notes" is amended in the first paragraph of Note 10 by inserting "methamphetamine, fentanyl," immediately following "i.e., heroin, cocaine, PCP," and by deleting:

"one gram of a substance containing methamphetamine, a Schedule I stimulant, is to be treated as the equivalent of two grams of a substance containing cocaine in applying the Drug Quantity Table.",

and inserting in lieu thereof:

"one gram of a substance containing oxymorphone, a Schedule I opiate, is to be treated as the equivalent of five grams of a substance containing heroin in applying the Drug Quantity Table.".

The Commentary to § 2D1.1 captioned "Application Notes" is amended in Note 10, in the subdivision of the "Drug Equivalency Tables" captioned "Cocaine and Other Schedule I & II Stimulants" by deleting "2.0 gm. of cocaine/0.4 gm of heroin" immediately following "1 gm of Methamphetamine =" and inserting in lieu thereof "5.0 gm of cocaine/1.0 gm of heroin", and by deleting:

"1 gm of Phenylacetone/P_2P
(amphetamine precursor) =   0.375 gm of cocaine/0.075 gm of heroin

1 gm of Phenylacebone/P_2P
(methamphetamine precursor) =   0.833 gm of cocaine/0.167 gm of heroin",

and inserting in lieu thereof:

"1 gm Phenylacetone/P_2P
(when possessed for the purpose of
manufacturing methamphetamine) = 2.08 gm of cocaine/0.418 gm of heroin

1 gm Phenylacetone/P_2P
(in any other case) =   0.375 gm of cocaine/0.075 gm of heroin".

The Commentary to § 2D1.1 captioned "Application Notes" is amended in Note 10, in the subdivision of the "Drug Equivalency Tables" captioned "Schedule I Marihuana" by deleting:

"1 Marihuana/Cannabis Plant =   0.1 gm of heroin/100 gm of marihuana".

The Commentary to § 2D1.1 captioned "Application Notes" is amended in Note 10 in the second paragraph by deleting "Other Schedule I or II Substances" and inserting in lieu thereof "Schedule I or II Depressants", and in the "Drug Equivalency Tables" by deleting "Other Schedule I or II Substances" and inserting in lieu thereof "Schedule I or II Depressants".

The Commentary to 2D1.1 captioned "Background" is amended in the third paragraph by deleting "with two asterisks represent mandatory minimum sentences established by the

Amendment 125 APPENDIX C - VOLUME I November 1, 2013

Anti-Drug Abuse Act of 1986. These levels reflect sentences" and inserting in lieu thereof "at levels 26 and 32 establish guideline ranges", and by deleting "requirement" and inserting in lieu thereof "minimum".

Reason for Amendment: The purposes of this amendment are to expand the Drug Quantity Table to reflect offenses involving extremely large quantities of controlled substances, to eliminate minor gaps in the Drug Quantity Table, to reflect the statutory change with respect to methamphetamine (Section 6470 of the Anti-Drug Abuse Act of 1988) by inserting specific references to the quantity of this substance for each offense level set forth in the table, to reflect the statutory change with respect to fifty or more marihuana plants (Section 6479 of the Anti-Drug Abuse Act of 1988), to correct anomaly in the relationship of hashish oil to hashish in levels 6 and 8 of the Drug Quantity Table, to delete an unnecessary footnote, and to clarify the operation of the guideline.

Effective Date: The effective date of this amendment is November 1, 1989.

126. **Amendment:** The Commentary to § 2D1.1 captioned "Application Notes" is amended in Note 10 in the subdivision of the "Drug Equivalency Tables" captioned "Schedule I or II Opiates" on the line beginning "piperidinyl] Propanamide) =" by deleting "31.25 gm" and inserting in lieu thereof "2.5 gm"; on the line beginning "1 gm of Alpha-Methylfentanyl" by deleting "100 gm" and inserting in lieu thereof "10 gm"; and on the line beginning "1 gm of 3-Methylfentanyl" by deleting "125 gm" and inserting in lieu thereof "10 gm".

Reason for Amendment: The purpose of this amendment is to conform the equivalency for fentanyl and fentanyl analogues to that set forth in the Drug Quantity Table and statute.

Effective Date: The effective date of this amendment is November 1, 1989.

127. **Amendment:** The Commentary to § 2D1.1 captioned "Application Notes" is amended in Note 10 in the subdivision of "Dosage Equivalency Table" captioned "Hallucinogens" by deleting "STP (DOM) Dimethoxyamphetamine" and inserting in lieu thereof "2, 5-Dimethoxy-4-methylamphetamine (STP, DOM)".

The Commentary to § 2D1.1 captioned "Application Notes" is amended in Note 10 in the subdivision of the "Dosage Equivalency Table" captioned "Stimulants" by deleting "Preludin 25 mg" and inserting in lieu thereof "Phenmetrazine (Preludin) 75 mg".

Reason for Amendment: The purposes of this amendment are to substitute generic names for two substances and to conform the dosage of Phenmetrazine to that currently being manufactured.

Effective Date: The effective date of this amendment is November 1, 1989.

128. **Amendment:** The Commentary to § 2D1.1 captioned "Application Notes" is amended in Note 10 in the "Drug Equivalency Tables" in the subdivision captioned "Schedule III Substances" by deleting:

"1 gm of Thiohexethal =   2 mg of heroin/2 gm of marihuana",

in the "Dosage Equivalency Table" in the subdivision captioned "Hallucinogens" by deleting:

"Anhalamine   300 mg",
"Anhalonide   300 mg",

"Anhalonine	300 mg",
"Lophophorine	300 mg",
"Pellotine	300 mg",

and in the "Dosage Equivalency Table" in the subdivision captioned "Depressants" by deleting:

"Brallobarbital	30 mg",
"Eldoral	100 mg",
"Eunarcon	100 mg",
"Hexethel	100 mg",
"Thiohexethal	60 mg".

Reason for Amendment: The purpose of this amendment is to delete substances that either are not controlled substances or are no longer manufactured.

Effective Date: The effective date of this amendment is November 1, 1989.

129. **Amendment:** The Commentary to § 2D1.1 captioned "Application Notes" is amended in Note 10 in the "Drug Equivalency Tables" in the subdivision captioned "Cocaine and Other Schedule I and II Stimulants" by inserting the following as the eighth and ninth entries:

"1 gm of 4-Methylaminorex ('Euphoria') = 0.5 gm of cocaine/0.1 gm of heroin",
"1 gm of Methylphenidate (Ritalin) = 0.5gm of cocaine/0.1 gm of heroin",

in the subdivision captioned "LSD, PCP, and Other Schedule I and II Hallucinogens" by inserting the following as the twentieth entry:

"1 gm of 3, 4-Methylenedioxy - N - ethylamphetamine/MDEA = 0.03 gm of heroin or PCP",

in the subdivision captioned "Schedule III Substances" by inserting the following as the fourth entry:

"1 gm of Benzphetamine = 4 mg of heroin/4 gm of marihuana",

and in the "Dosage Equivalency Table" in the subdivision captioned "Depressants" by inserting the following in the appropriate place in alphabetical order:

"Glutethimide (Doriden) 500 mg".

The Commentary to § 2D1.1 captioned "Application Notes" is amended in Note 10 in the "Dosage Equivalency Table" by inserting the following immediately after the subdivision captioned "Depressants":

<u>"Marihuana</u>

1 marihuana cigarette 0.5 gm".

Reason for Amendment: The purpose of this amendment is to make the Drug Equivalency

Amendment 129   APPENDIX C - VOLUME I   November 1, 2013

Tables and Dosage Equivalency Table more comprehensive.

Effective Date: The effective date of this amendment is November 1, 1989.

130. **Amendment:** The Commentary to § 2D1.1 captioned "Application Notes" is amended in Note 10 in the "Drug Equivalency Tables" in the subdivision captioned "Schedule III Substances" by deleting "2 mg of heroin/2 gm of marihuana" immediately following "1 gm of Glutethimide = " and inserting in lieu thereof "0.4 mg of heroin/0.4 gm of marihuana", and by deleting:

"1 gm of Paregoric =	2 mg of heroin/2 gm of marihuana
1 gm of Hydrocodone Cough Syrups =	2 mg of heroin/2 gm of marihuana",

and inserting in lieu thereof:

"1 ml of Paregoric =	0.25 mg of heroin/0.25 gm of marihuana
1 ml of Hydrocodone Cough Syrup =	1 mg of heroin/1 gm of marihuana".

The Commentary to § 2D1.1 captioned "Application Notes" is amended in Note 10 in the "Dosage Equivalency Table" in the subdivision captioned "Hallucinogens" by deleting ".1 mg" in the line beginning "LSD (Lysergic acid diethylamide)" and inserting in lieu thereof ".05 mg", by deleting "LSD tartrate.05 mg", by deleting "Peyote 12 mg", and by inserting the following in the appropriate place in alphabetical order:

"Peyote (dry)	12 gm",
"Peyote (wet)	120 gm",
"Psilocybe mushrooms (dry)	5 gm",
"Psilocybe mushrooms (wet)	50 gm".

The Commentary to § 2D1.1 captioned "Application Notes" is amended in Note 10 in the "Dosage Equivalency Table" in the subdivision captioned "Stimulants" by deleting "Ethylamphetamine HCL 12 mg" and "Ethylamphetamine SO_4 12 mg", by deleting "Amphetamines" and inserting in lieu thereof "Amphetamine", by deleting "Methamphetamines" and inserting in lieu thereof "Methamphetamine", and by deleting "Methamphetamine combinations 5 mg".

Reason for Amendment: The purposes of this amendment are to provide more accurate approximations of the equivalencies and dosages for certain controlled substances, and to eliminate unnecessary references.

Effective Date: The effective date of this amendment is November 1, 1989.

131. **Amendment:** The Commentary to § 2D1.1 captioned "Application Notes" is amended in Note 10 in the subdivision of the "Drug Equivalency Tables" captioned "LSD, PCP, and Other Schedule I and II Hallucinogens" by deleting:

"1 gm of Liquid phencyclidine =	0.1 gm of heroin or PCP".

Reason for Amendment: The purpose of this amendment is to delete an incorrect equivalency.

Effective Date: The effective date of this amendment is November 1, 1989.

132. **Amendment:** The Commentary to § 2D1.1 captioned "Application Notes" is amended in

November 1, 2013 APPENDIX C - VOLUME I **Amendment 134**

Note 10 in the "Drug Equivalency Tables" by inserting immediately following the captions "Cocaine and Other Schedule I and II Stimulants" and "LSD, PCP, and Other Hallucinogens" in each instance "(and their immediate precursors)".

Reason for Amendment: The purpose of this amendment is to clarify the commentary.

Effective Date: The effective date of this amendment is November 1, 1989.

133. **Amendment:** The Commentary to § 2D1.1 captioned "Application Notes" is amended in Note 10 by deleting:

> "The following dosage equivalents for certain common drugs are provided by the Drug Enforcement Administration to facilitate the application of § 2D1.1 of the guidelines in cases where the number of doses, but not the weight of the controlled substances are known. The dosage equivalents provided in these tables reflect the amount of the pure drug contained in an average dose.
>
> DOSAGE EQUIVALENCY TABLE",

and inserting in lieu thereof:

> "11. If the number of doses, pills, or capsules but not the weight of the controlled substance is known, multiply the number of doses, pills, or capsules by the typical weight per dose to estimate the total weight of the controlled substance (e.g., 100 doses of Bufotenine at 1 mg per dose = 100 mg of Bufotenine). The Typical Weight Per Unit Table, prepared from information provided by the Drug Enforcement Administration, displays the typical weight per dose, pill, or capsule for common controlled substances.
>
> TYPICAL WEIGHT PER UNIT (DOSE, PILL, OR CAPSULE) TABLE".

The Commentary to § 2D1.1 captioned "Application Notes" is amended by renumbering the current Note 11 as Note 12.

Reason for Amendment: The purpose of this amendment is to clarify the commentary.

Effective Date: The effective date of this amendment is November 1, 1989.

134. **Amendment:** Section 2D1.1(b) is amended by deleting "Characteristic" and inserting in lieu thereof "Characteristics", and by inserting the following additional specific offense characteristic:

> "(2) If the defendant is convicted of violating 21 U.S.C. § 960(a) under circumstances in which (A) an aircraft other than a regularly scheduled commercial air carrier was used to import the controlled substance, or (B) the defendant acted as a pilot, copilot, captain, navigator, flight officer, or any other operation officer aboard any craft or vessel carrying a controlled substance, increase by 2 levels. If the resulting offense level is less than level 26, increase to level 26.";

The Commentary to § 2D1.1 captioned "Application Notes" is amended by inserting the following additional note:

> "13. If subsection (b)(2)(B) applies, do not apply § 3B1.3 (Abuse of Position of Trust or Use of Special Skill).";

The Commentary to § 2D1.1 captioned "Background" is amended by inserting the follow-

Amendment 134   APPENDIX C - VOLUME I   November 1, 2013

ing additional paragraph between the third and fourth paragraphs:

"   Specific Offense Characteristic (b)(2) is mandated by Section 6453 of the Anti-Drug Abuse Act of 1988.".

Reason for Amendment: The purpose of this amendment is to implement the directive to the Commission in Section 6453 of the Anti-Drug Abuse Act of 1988.

Effective Date: The effective date of this amendment is November 1, 1989.

135. **Amendment:**   Chapter Two, Part D is amended by deleting §§ 2D1.2 and 2D1.3 in their entirety as follows:

"§ 2D1.2.   Involving Juveniles in the Trafficking of Controlled Substances

   (a)   Base Offense Level:

      (1)   Level from § 2D1.1, corresponding to triple the drug amount involved, but in no event less than level 13, for involving an individual fourteen years of age or less; or

      (2)   Level from § 2D1.1, corresponding to double the drug amount involved, for involving an individual at least fifteen years of age and less than eighteen years of age.

Commentary

Statutory Provision: 21 U.S.C. § 845b.

Application Notes:

1.   If multiple drugs or offenses occur and all or some of them involve juveniles, double or triple the drug amounts for those offenses involving juveniles before totalling the amounts. For example, if there are three drug offenses of conviction and only one involves juveniles in trafficking, add the amount from the first and second offense, double the amount for the offense involving juveniles, and total. Use that total to determine the base offense level.

2.   The reference to the level from § 2D1.1 includes the base offense level plus the specific offense characteristic dealing with a weapon. Under § 2D1.1(b)(1) there is a 2-level increase for possession of a firearm or other dangerous weapon during commission of the offense.

Background: The statute addressed by this section punishes any person eighteen years of age or older who knowingly employs or uses any person younger than eighteen to violate or to conceal any violation of any provision of Title 21. Section 845b provides a minimum mandatory period of imprisonment of one year. An increased penalty for the employment or use of persons fourteen years of age or younger reflects the enhanced sentence authorized by 21 U.S.C. § 845b(d).

§ 2D1.3.   Distributing Controlled Substances to Individuals Younger than Twenty-One Years, To Pregnant Women, or Within 1000 Feet of a School or College

   (a)   Base Offense Level:

(1) Level from § 2D1.1, corresponding to double the drug amount involved, but in no event less than level 13, for distributing a controlled substance to a pregnant woman;

(2) (A) Level from § 2D1.1, corresponding to double the drug amount involved, but in no event less than level 13, for distributing a controlled substance other than five grams or less of marihuana to an individual under the age of twenty-one years; or

(B) Level from § 2D1.1, corresponding to double the drug amount involved, but in no event less than level 13, for distributing or manufacturing a controlled substance other than five grams or less of marihuana within 1000 feet of a schoolyard.

Commentary

Statutory Provisions: 21 U.S.C. §§ 845, 845a.

Application Notes:

1. The provisions addressed by this section contain a mandatory minimum period of imprisonment of one year. The base offense level is determined as in § 2D1.2. If both subsections (a)(1) and (a)(2) apply to a single distribution (e.g., the distribution of 10 grams of a controlled substance to a pregnant woman under twenty-one years of age), the enhancements are applied cumulatively, i.e., by using four times rather than two times the amount distributed. However, only one of the enhancements in § 2D1.3(a)(2) shall apply in a given case.

2. If multiple drugs or offenses occur, determine the offense level as described in the Commentary to § 2D1.2.

3. The reference to the level from § 2D1.1 includes the base offense level plus the specific offense characteristic dealing with a weapon. Under § 2D1.1(b)(1) there is a 2-level increase for possession of a firearm, or other dangerous weapon during the commission of the offense.

Background: The guideline sentences for distribution of controlled substances to individuals under twenty-one years of age or within 1000 feet of a school or college treat the distribution of less than five grams of marihuana less harshly than other controlled substances. This distinction is based on the statutory provisions that specifically exempt convictions for the distribution of less than five grams of marihuana from the mandatory minimum one-year imprisonment requirement.".

A replacement guideline with accompanying commentary is inserted as § 2D1.2 (Drug Offenses Occurring Near Protected Locations or Involving Underage or Pregnant Individuals).

Reason for Amendment: The purposes of this amendment are to implement the directive in Section 6454 of the Anti-Drug Abuse Act of 1988, and to expand the coverage of the guideline to include the provision of Sections 6458 and 6459 of that Act. The amendment also covers the provisions of 21 U.S.C. § 845, 845a, and 845b not included in the statutory direction to the Commission.

Effective Date: The effective date of this amendment is November 1, 1989.

136. Amendment: The Commentary to § 2D1.4 captioned "Application Notes" is amended in Note 1 by deleting:

> "Where the defendant was not reasonably capable of producing the negotiated amount, the court may depart and impose a sentence lower than the sentence that would otherwise result.",

and inserting in lieu thereof:

> "However, where the court finds that the defendant did not intend to produce and was not reasonably capable of producing the negotiated amount, the court shall exclude from the guideline calculation the amount that it finds the defendant did not intend to produce and was not reasonably capable of producing.".

Reason for Amendment: Application Note 1 currently provides that the "weight under negotiation in an uncompleted distribution shall be used to calculate the applicable amount." The instruction then provides "Where the defendant was not reasonably capable of producing the negotiated amount the court may depart and impose a sentence lower than the sentence that would otherwise result." This provision may result in inflated offense levels in uncompleted offenses where a defendant is merely "puffing," even though the court is then authorized to address the situation by a downward departure. The purpose of this amendment is to provide a more direct procedure for calculating the offense level where the court finds that the defendant did not intend to produce and was not reasonably capable of producing the negotiated amount.

Effective Date: The effective date of this amendment is November 1, 1989.

137. Amendment: The Commentary to § 2D1.4 captioned "Application Notes" is amended in Note 1 by deleting "the sentence should be imposed only on the basis of the defendant's conduct or the conduct of co-conspirators in furtherance of the conspiracy that was known to the defendant or was reasonably foreseeable" and inserting in lieu thereof "see Application Note 1 to § 1B1.3 (Relevant Conduct)".

Reason for Amendment: The purpose of this amendment is to conform this commentary to the revision of § 1B1.3.

Effective Date: The effective date of this amendment is November 1, 1989.

138. Amendment: Section 2D1.4(a) is amended by deleting "participating in an incomplete" and inserting in lieu thereof "a".

Reason for Amendment: The purpose of this amendment is to clarify the guideline.

Effective Date: The effective date of this amendment is November 1, 1989.

139. Amendment: Section 2D1.5 is amended by deleting: "(a) Base Offense Level: 36" and inserting in lieu thereof:

> "(a) Base Offense Level (Apply the greater):
>
> (1) 4 plus the offense level from § 2D1.1 applicable to the underlying offense; or
>
> (2) 38.".

The Commentary to § 2D1.5 captioned "Application Notes" is amended in Note 2 by deleting "if the quantity of drugs substantially exceeds that required for level 36 in the drug quantity table," immediately before "or if", and by deleting "is extremely" and inserting in lieu thereof "was extremely".

The Commentary to § 2D1.5 captioned "Background" is amended in the first paragraph by deleting "base offense level of 36" and inserting in lieu thereof "minimum base offense level of 38", and in the second paragraph by deleting "for second convictions" and inserting in lieu thereof "for the first conviction, a 30-year minimum mandatory penalty for a second conviction,".

Reason for Amendment: The purpose of this amendment is to reflect the increased mandatory minimum penalty for this offense pursuant to Section 6481 of the Anti-Drug Abuse Act of 1988.

Effective Date: The effective date of this amendment is November 1, 1989.

140. **Amendment:** Chapter Two, Part D is amended by inserting an additional guideline with accompanying commentary as § 2D1.10 (Endangering Human Life While Illegally Manufacturing a Controlled Substance).

    Reason for Amendment: The purpose of this amendment is to create a guideline covering the new offense in Section 6301 of the Anti-Drug Abuse Act of 1988.

    Effective Date: The effective date of this amendment is November 1, 1989.

141. **Amendment:** Section 2D2.3 is amended by deleting: "(a) Base Offense Level: 8" and inserting in lieu thereof:

    "(a)   Base Offense Level (Apply the greatest):

        (1)   26, if death resulted; or

        (2)   21, if serious bodily injury resulted; or

        (3)   13, otherwise.

    (b)   Special Instruction:

        (1)   If the defendant is convicted of a single count involving the death or serious bodily injury of more than one person, apply Chapter Three, Part D (Multiple Counts) as if the defendant had been convicted of a separate count for each such victim.".

    The Commentary to § 2D2.3 is amended by inserting at the end:

    "Background: This section implements the direction to the Commission in Section 6482 of the Anti-Drug Abuse Act of 1988. Offenses covered by this guideline may vary widely with regard to harm and risk of harm. The offense levels assume that the offense involved the operation of a common carrier carrying a number of passengers, e.g., a bus. If no or only a few passengers were placed at risk, a downward departure may be warranted. If the offense resulted in the death or serious bodily injury of a large number of persons, such that the resulting offense level under subsection (b) would not adequately reflect the seriousness of the offense, an upward departure may be warranted.".

Amendment 141 APPENDIX C - VOLUME I November 1, 2013

Reason for Amendment: The purpose of this amendment is to implement the directive to the Commission in Section 6482 of the Anti-Drug Abuse Act of 1988. In addition, the base offense level under subsection (a)(3) is increased to reflect the seriousness of the offense.

Effective Date: The effective date of this amendment is November 1, 1989.

142. **Amendment:** The Commentary to § 2E1.1 captioned "Application Notes" is amended by inserting the following additional note:

> "4. Certain conduct may be charged in the count of conviction as part of a 'pattern of racketeering activity' even though the defendant has previously been sentenced for that conduct. Where such previously imposed sentence resulted from a conviction prior to the last overt act of the instant offense, treat as a prior sentence under § 4A1.2(a)(1) and not as part of the instant offense. This treatment is designed to produce a result consistent with the distinction between the instant offense and criminal history found throughout the guidelines. If this treatment produces an anomalous result in a particular case, a guideline departure may be warranted.".

Reason for Amendment: The purpose of this amendment is to clarify the treatment of certain conduct for which the defendant previously has been sentenced as either part of the instant offense or prior criminal record.

Effective Date: The effective date of this amendment is November 1, 1989.

143. **Amendment:** The Commentary to § 2E1.3 captioned "Statutory Provision" is amended by deleting "1952B" and inserting in lieu thereof "1959 (formerly 18 U.S.C. § 1952B)".

Reason for Amendment: The purpose of this amendment is to reflect the redesignation of this statute.

Effective Date: The effective date of this amendment is November 1, 1989.

144. **Amendment:** The Commentary to § 2E1.4 captioned "Statutory Provision" is amended by deleting "1952A" and inserting in lieu thereof "1958 (formerly 18 U.S.C. § 1952A)".

Reason for Amendment: The purpose of this amendment is to reflect the redesignation of this statute.

Effective Date: The effective date of this amendment is November 1, 1989.

145. **Amendment:** Section 2E1.5 is amended by deleting "the guideline provision for extortion or robbery" and inserting in lieu thereof "§ 2B3.1 (Robbery), § 2B3.2 (Extortion by Force or Threat of Injury or Serious Damage), § 2B3.3 (Blackmail and Similar Forms of Extortion), or § 2C1.1 (Offering, Giving, Soliciting, or Receiving a Bribe; Extortion Under Color of Official Right)".

The Commentary to § 2E1.5 captioned "Application Note" is amended by deleting:

> "Application Note:
>
> 1. Apply the guideline most applicable to the underlying conduct, which may include § 2B3.1(Robbery), § 2B3.2 (Extortion by Force or Threat of Injury or Serious Damage), § 2B3.3 (Blackmail and Similar Forms of Extortion), or § 2C1.1 (Offering, Giving, Soliciting, or Receiving a Bribe).".

Reason for Amendment: The purpose of this amendment is to move material from the commentary to the guideline where it more appropriately belongs.

Effective Date: The effective date of this amendment is November 1, 1989.

146. **Amendment:** Section 2E2.1 is amended in subsection (b)(1)(B) by deleting "a firearm or a dangerous weapon" and inserting in lieu thereof "a dangerous weapon (including a firearm)", and in subsection (b)(1)(C) by deleting "a firearm or other dangerous weapon" and inserting in lieu thereof "a dangerous weapon (including a firearm)".

    Reason for Amendment: The purposes of this amendment are to clarify that a firearm is a type of dangerous weapon and to remove the inconsistency in language between specific offense characteristic subdivisions (b)(1)(B) and (b)(1)(C).

    Effective Date: The effective date of this amendment is November 1, 1989.

147. **Amendment:** Section 2E2.1(b)(2) is amended by inserting the following additional subdivisions:

    "(D) If the degree of injury is between that specified in subdivisions (A) and (B), add 3 levels; or

    (E) If the degree of injury is between that specified in subdivisions (B) and (C), add 5 levels.".

    Reason for Amendment: The purpose of this amendment is to provide intermediate adjustment levels for the degree of bodily injury.

    Effective Date: The effective date of this amendment is November 1, 1989.

148. **Amendment:** Section 2E2.1(b)(3)(A) is amended by inserting "or" immediately following "4 levels;".

    Reason for Amendment: The purpose of this amendment is to correct a clerical error.

    Effective Date: The effective date of this amendment is November 1, 1989.

149. **Amendment:** Section 2E5.1 is amended in the title by deleting "Bribery or Gratuity" and inserting in lieu thereof "Offering, Accepting, or Soliciting a Bribe or Gratuity".

    Reason for Amendment: The purpose of amending the title of this section is to ensure that attempts and solicitations are expressly covered by this guideline.

    Effective Date: The effective date of this amendment is November 1, 1989.

150. **Amendment:** Section 2E5.2 is amended by deleting:

    "(a) Base Offense Level: 4

    (b) Specific Offense Characteristics

    (1) If the offense involved more than minimal planning, increase by 2 levels.

    (2) If the defendant had a fiduciary obligation under the Employee Retirement Income Security Act, increase by 2 levels.

Amendment 150 APPENDIX C - VOLUME I November 1, 2013

     (3)   Increase by corresponding number of levels from the table in § 2B1.1 (Larceny, Embezzlement, and Other Forms of Theft) according to the loss.",

and inserting in lieu thereof:

"Apply § 2B1.1 (Larceny, Embezzlement, and Other Forms of Theft).".

The Commentary to § 2E5.2 captioned "Application Notes" is amended by deleting:

    "1.   'More than minimal planning' is defined in the Commentary to § 1B1.1 (Application Instructions). Valuation of loss is discussed in the Commentary to § 2B1.1 (Larceny, Embezzlement, and Other Forms of Theft)." and

    "3.   If the adjustment for a fiduciary obligation at § 2E5.2(b)(2) is applied, do not apply the adjustment at § 3B1.3 (Abuse of a Position of Trust or Use of a Special Skill).",

and by inserting in lieu of Note 1:

    "1.   In the case of a defendant who had a fiduciary obligation under the Employee Retirement Income Security Act, an adjustment under § 3B1.3 (Abuse of Position of Trust or Use of Special Skill) would apply.".

The Commentary to § 2E5.2 captioned "Background" is amended by deleting the second and third sentences as follows:

"The base offense level corresponds to the base offense level for other forms of theft. Specific offense characteristics address whether a defendant has a fiduciary relationship to the benefit plan, the sophistication of the offense, and the scale of the offense.".

Reason for Amendment: The purpose of this amendment is to simplify application of the guidelines.

Effective Date: The effective date of this amendment is November 1, 1989.

151. Amendment: Section 2E5.3(a)(2) is amended by deleting "false records were used for criminal conversion of funds or a scheme" and inserting in lieu thereof "the offense was committed to facilitate or conceal a theft or embezzlement, or an offense".

The Commentary to § 2E5.3 captioned "Application Note" is amended by deleting:

    "<u>Application Note</u>:

    1.   'Criminal conversion' means embezzlement.".

Reason for Amendment: The purpose of this amendment is to ensure that subsection (a)(2) covers any conduct engaged in for the purpose of facilitating or concealing a theft or embezzlement, or an offense involving a bribe or gratuity.

Effective Date: The effective date of this amendment is November 1, 1989.

152. Amendment: Section 2E5.4 is amended by deleting:

    "(a)   Base Offense Level: 4

-72-

(b) Specific Offense Characteristics

　　(1)　If the offense involved more than minimal planning, increase by 2 levels.

　　(2)　If the defendant was a union officer or occupied a position of trust in the union, as set forth in 29 U.S.C. § 501(a), increase by 2 levels.

　　(3)　Increase by the number of levels from the table in § 2B1.1 (Larceny, Embezzlement, and Other Forms of Theft) corresponding to the loss.",

and inserting in lieu thereof:

"Apply § 2B1.1 (Larceny, Embezzlement, and Other Forms of Theft).".

The Commentary to § 2E5.4 captioned "Application Notes" is amended by deleting:

"1.　'More than minimal planning' is defined in the Commentary to § 1B1.1 (Applicable Instructions). Valuation of loss is discussed in the Commentary to § 2B1.1 (Larceny, Embezzlement, and Other Forms of Theft).

2.　If the adjustment for being a union officer or occupying a position of trust in a union at § 2E5.4(b)(2) is applied, do not apply the adjustment at § 3B1.3 (Abuse of a Position of Trust or Use of a Special Skill).",

and inserting in lieu thereof:

"1.　In the case of a defendant who was a union officer or occupied a position of trust in the union, as set forth in 29 U.S.C. § 501(a), an adjustment under § 3B1.3 (Abuse of Position of Trust or Use of Special Skill) would apply.",

and by deleting in the caption "Notes" and inserting in lieu thereof "Note".

The Commentary to § 2E5.4 captioned "Background" is amended by deleting the last sentence as follows:

"The seriousness of this offense is determined by the amount of money taken, the sophistication of the offense, and the nature of the defendant's position in the union.".

Reason for Amendment: The purpose of this amendment is to simplify application of the guidelines.

Effective Date: The effective date of this amendment is November 1, 1989.

153.　Amendment: Section 2E5.5(a)(2) is amended by deleting "false records were used for criminal conversion of funds or a scheme" and inserting in lieu thereof "the offense was committed to facilitate or conceal a theft or embezzlement, or an offense".

Reason for Amendment: The purpose of this amendment is to ensure that subsection (a)(2) covers any conduct engaged in for the purpose of facilitating or concealing a theft or embezzlement, or an offense involving a bribe or gratuity.

Effective Date: The effective date of this amendment is November 1, 1989.

Amendment 154 APPENDIX C - VOLUME I November 1, 2013

154. Amendment: Section 2F1.1(b)(1) is amended by deleting:

	"Loss	Increase in Level
(A)	$2,000 or less	no increase
(B)	$2,001 - $5,000	add 1
(C)	$5,001 - $10,000	add 2
(D)	$10,001 - $20,000	add 3
(E)	$20,001 - $50,00	add 4
(F)	$50,001 - $100,000	add 5
(G)	$100,001 - $200,000	add 6
(H)	$200,001 - $500,000	add 7
(I)	$500,001 - $1,000,000	add 8
(J)	$1,000,001 - $2,000,000	add 9
(K)	$2,000,001 - $5,000,000	add 10
(L)	over $5,000,000	add 11",

and inserting in lieu thereof:

	"Loss (Apply the Greatest)	Increase in Level
(A)	$2,000 or less	no increase
(B)	More than $2,000	add 1
(C)	More than $5,000	add 2
(D)	More than $10,000	add 3
(E)	More than $20,000	add 4
(F)	More than $40,000	add 5
(G)	More than $70,000	add 6
(H)	More than $120,000	add 7
(I)	More than $200,000	add 8
(J)	More than $350,000	add 9
(K)	More than $500,000	add 10
(L)	More than $800,000	add 11
(M)	More than $1,500,000	add 12
(N)	More than $2,500,000	add 13
(O)	More than $5,000,000	add 14
(P)	More than $10,000,000	add 15
(Q)	More than $20,000,000	add 16
(R)	More than $40,000,000	add 17
(S)	More than $80,000,000	add 18.".

Reason for Amendment: The purposes of this amendment are to conform the theft and fraud loss tables to the tax evasion table in order to remove an unintended inconsistency between these tables in cases where the amount is greater than $40,000, to increase the offense levels for offenses with larger losses to provide additional deterrence and better reflect the seriousness of the conduct, and to eliminate minor gaps in the loss table.

Effective Date: The effective date of this amendment is November 1, 1989.

155. **Amendment:** The Commentary to § 2F1.1 captioned "Application Notes" is amended beginning in Note 14 by deleting:

"In such instances, although § 2F1.1 applies, a departure may be warranted.

15. In certain other cases, the mail or wire fraud statutes, or other relatively broad statutes, are used primarily as jurisdictional bases for the prosecution of other offenses. For example, a state law arson where a fraudulent insurance claim was mailed might be prosecuted as mail fraud. In such cases the most analogous guideline (in the above case, § 2K1.4) is to be applied.",

and by inserting at the end of Note 14:

"In certain other cases, the mail or wire fraud statutes, or other relatively broad statutes, are used primarily as jurisdictional bases for the prosecution of other offenses. For example, a state arson offense where a fraudulent insurance claim was mailed might be prosecuted as mail fraud. Where the indictment or information setting forth the count of conviction (or a stipulation as described in § 1B1.2(a)) establishes an offense more aptly covered by another guideline, apply that guideline rather than § 2F1.1. Otherwise, in such cases, § 2F1.1 is to be applied, but a departure from the guidelines may be considered.".

The Commentary to § 2F1.1 captioned "Application Notes" is amended in the second sentence of Note 14 by deleting "in which" and inserting in lieu thereof "for which".

Reason for Amendment: The purposes of this amendment are to ensure that this guideline is interpreted in a manner consistent with § 1B1.2 and to correct a clerical error.

Effective Date: The effective date of this amendment is November 1, 1989.

156. **Amendment:** Section 2F1.1(b)(2) is amended by deleting "; (B)" and inserting in lieu thereof ", or (B)", and by deleting "; (C) a misrepresentation that the defendant was acting on behalf of a charitable, educational, religious or political organization, or a government agency; or (D) violation of any judicial or administrative order, injunction, decree or process; increase by 2 levels, but if the result is less than level 10, increase to level 10" and inserting in lieu thereof ", increase by 2 levels".

Section 2F1.1(b)(3) is renumbered as (b)(5), and the following are inserted as new subsections:

"(3) If the offense involved (A) a misrepresentation that the defendant was acting on behalf of a charitable, educational, religious or political organization, or a government agency, or (B) violation of any judicial or administrative order, injunction, decree or process, increase by 2 levels. If the resulting offense level is less than level 10, increase to level 10.

(4) If the offense involved the conscious or reckless risk of serious bodily injury, increase by 2 levels. If the resulting offense level is less than level 13, increase to level 13.".

The Commentary to § 2F1.1 captioned "Statutory Provisions" is amended by inserting "1031," immediately following "1029,".

The Commentary to § 2F1.1 captioned "Application Notes" is amended in Note 4 by

Amendment 156 APPENDIX C - VOLUME I November 1, 2013

deleting "(b)(2)(C)" and inserting in lieu thereof "(b)(3)(A)", in Note 5 by deleting "(b)(2)(D)" and inserting in lieu thereof "(b)(3)(B)", and in Note 9(c) by deleting "or risked" immediately following "caused".

The Commentary to § 2F1.1 captioned "Background" is amended in the third paragraph by deleting "not only" immediately following "Accordingly, the guideline", by deleting ", but also specifies that the minimum offense level in such cases shall be 10" immediately following "is present", and by deleting the last sentence as follows:

> "A number of special cases are specifically broken out under subdivision (b)(2) to ensure that defendants in such cases are adequately punished.".

The Commentary to § 2F1.1 captioned "Application Notes" is amended by deleting:

> "10. The adjustments for loss do not distinguish frauds involving losses greater than $5,000,000. Departure above the applicable guideline may be warranted if the loss substantially exceeds that amount.",

and by renumbering Notes 11-14 as 10-13 respectively.

The Commentary to § 2F1.1 captioned "Application Notes" is amended in Note 1 by deleting "(b)(2)" and inserting in lieu thereof "(b)(3)", by deleting "several" and inserting in lieu thereof "both", and by deleting "upward" and inserting in lieu thereof "an upward".

Reason for Amendment: The purpose of this amendment is to reflect the instruction to the Commission in Section 2(b) of the Major Fraud Act of 1988. The Commission has concluded that a 2-level enhancement with a minimum offense level of 13 should apply to all fraud cases involving a conscious or reckless risk of serious bodily injury. In addition, the amendment divides former subsection (b)(2) into two separate specific offenses characteristics to better reflect their separate nature.

Effective Date: The effective date of this amendment is November 1, 1989.

157. **Amendment:** Section 2G1.1(b)(1) is amended by deleting "defendant used" and inserting in lieu thereof "offense involved the use of", and by deleting "drugs or otherwise" and inserting in lieu thereof "threats or drugs or in any manner".

The Commentary to § 2G1.1 captioned "Application Notes" is amended in Note 2 by deleting "by drugs or otherwise" immediately following "coercion".

Reason for Amendment: The purpose of this amendment is to clarify the guideline and commentary.

Effective Date: The effective date of this amendment is November 1, 1989.

158. **Amendment:** Section 2G1.1 is amended by inserting the following additional subsection:

> "(c)   Special Instruction
>
> > (1)   If the offense involves the transportation of more than one person, Chapter Three, Part D (Multiple Counts) shall be applied as if the transportation of each person had been contained in a separate count of conviction.".

Reason for Amendment: The purpose of this amendment is to provide a special instruction for the application of the multiple count rule in cases involving the transportation of more than one person.

Effective Date: The effective date of this amendment is November 1, 1989.

159. **Amendment:** Section 2G1.2(b)(1) is amended by deleting "drugs or otherwise" and inserting in lieu thereof "threats or drugs or in any manner".

    Section 2G1.2(b)(2) and (3) is amended by deleting "conduct" whenever it appears and inserting in lieu thereof in each instance "offense".

    The Commentary to § 2G1.2 captioned "Application Notes" is amended in Note 2 by deleting "by drugs or otherwise" immediately following "coercion", and in the caption by deleting "Note" and inserting in lieu thereof "Notes".

    Reason for Amendment: The purpose of this amendment is to clarify the guideline and commentary.

    Effective Date: The effective date of this amendment is November 1, 1989.

160. **Amendment:** Section 2G1.2 is amended by inserting the following additional subsection:

    "(c)   Special Instruction

        (1)   If the offense involves the transportation of more than one person, Chapter Three, Part D (Multiple Counts) shall be applied as if the transportation of each person had been contained in a separate count of conviction.".

    Reason for Amendment: The purpose of this amendment is to provide a special instruction for the application of the multiple count rule in cases involving the transportation of more than one person.

    Effective Date: The effective date of this amendment is November 1, 1989.

161. **Amendment:** The Commentary to § 2G2.1 captioned "Application Note" is amended in Note 1 by deleting ", distinct offense, even if several are exploited simultaneously." and inserting in lieu thereof "victim. Consequently, multiple counts involving the exploitation of different minors are not to be grouped together under § 3D1.2 (Groups of Closely-Related Counts).".

    Reason for Amendment: The purpose of this amendment is to clarify that multiple counts involving different minors are not grouped under § 3D1.2.

    Effective Date: The effective date of this amendment is November 1, 1989.

162. **Amendment:** Chapter Two, Part G, is amended by inserting an additional guideline with accompanying commentary as § 2G2.3 (Selling or Buying of Children for Use in the Production of Pornography).

    Reason for Amendment: The purpose of this amendment is to create a guideline covering the new offense in Section 7512 of the Anti-Drug Abuse Act of 1988.

    Effective Date: The effective date of this amendment is November 1, 1989.

163. **Amendment:** The Commentary to § 2G3.1 captioned "Statutory Provisions" is amended

Amendment 163

by deleting "§§ 1461-1465" and inserting in lieu thereof "§§ 1460-1463, 1465-1466".

Reason for Amendment: The purposes of this amendment are to conform the Statutory Provisions to the revision of § 2G3.2 and to make them more comprehensive.

Effective Date: The effective date of this amendment is November 1, 1989.

164. **Amendment:** Chapter Two, Part G is amended by deleting § 2G3.2 in its entirety as follows:

"§ 2G3.2. Obscene or Indecent Telephone Communications

(a) Base Offense Level: 6

Commentary

Statutory Provision: 47 U.S.C. § 223.

Background: This offense is a misdemeanor for which the maximum term of imprisonment authorized by statute is six months.".

A replacement guideline with accompanying commentary is inserted as § 2G3.2 (Obscene Telephone Communications for a Commercial Purpose; Broadcasting Obscene Material).

Reason for Amendment: The purposes of this amendment are to delete a guideline covering a petty offense; and to insert a guideline covering felony offenses, including two offenses created by Sections 7523 and 7524 of the Anti-Drug Abuse Act of 1988.

Effective Date: The effective date of this amendment is November 1, 1989.

165. **Amendment:** The title to § 2H1.3 is amended by inserting at the end "; Damage to Religious Real Property".

The Commentary to § 2H1.3 captioned "Application Notes" is amended in Note 3 by deleting "the adjustment at" immediately before "§ 3B1.3".

The Commentary to § 2H1.3 captioned "Background" is amended in the third sentence by deleting "injury occurs, ten years if injury occurs," and inserting in lieu thereof "bodily injury results, ten years if bodily injury results".

The Commentary to § 2H1.3 captioned "Statutory Provisions" is amended by deleting "18 U.S.C. § 245" and inserting in lieu thereof "18 U.S.C. §§ 245, 247".

Reason for Amendment: The purposes of this amendment are to include a recently enacted offense (18 U.S.C. § 247) expressly in the title of this guideline and to make editorial improvements.

Effective Date: The effective date of this amendment is November 1, 1989.

166. **Amendment:** Section 2H1.4(a)(2) is amended by deleting "2 plus" and inserting in lieu thereof "6 plus".

The Commentary to § 2H1.4 captioned "Application Notes" is amended in Note 1 by deleting "2 plus" and inserting in lieu thereof "6 plus", and by deleting "is defined" and inserting in lieu thereof "means 6 levels above the offense level for any underlying criminal conduct. See the discussion".

The Commentary to § 2H1.4 captioned "Background" is amended in the first paragraph by deleting ", except where death results, in which case the maximum term of imprisonment authorized is life imprisonment" and inserting in lieu there of "if no bodily injury results, ten years if bodily injury results, and life imprisonment if death results", by deleting "Given this one-year statutory maximum, a" and inserting in lieu thereof "A", by inserting "one-year" immediately following "near the", and by inserting "or bodily injury" immediately following "resulting in death".

The Commentary to § 2H1.4 captioned "Background" is amended by inserting the following sentences at the end of the first paragraph:

> "The 6-level increase under subsection (a)(2) reflects the 2-level increase that is applied to other offenses covered in this Part plus a 4-level increase for the commission of the offense under actual or purported legal authority. This 4-level increase is inherent in the base offense level of 10 under subsection (a)(1).".

Reason for Amendment: The purpose of this amendment is to correct an anomaly between the offense level under this section and § 2H1.5 when the offense level is determined under subsection (a)(2). Section 2H1.4 is similar to § 2H1.5 in that it may or may not involve the use of force. Under § 2H1.4, however, the offense must involve the abuse of actual or purported legal authority. The base offense level of 10 used in 2H1.4(a)(1) has a built-in 4-level enhancement (which corresponds to the base offense level of 6 under § 2H1.5(a)(1) plus the 4-level increase for a public official). There is an anomaly, however, when the base offense level from (a)(2) is used. In such cases, § 2H1.4 results in an offense level that is 4 levels less than § 2H1.5 when the offense is committed by a public official. The Commentary to § 2H1.4 is also amended to reflect the increase in the maximum authorized sentence from one to ten years in cases involving bodily injury.

Effective Date: The effective date of this amendment is November 1, 1989.

167. **Amendment:** The Commentary to § 2H1.5 captioned "Application Notes" is amended in Note 1 by deleting "explained" and inserting in lieu thereof "defined".

The Commentary to § 2H1.5 captioned "Application Notes" is amended in Note 2 by deleting "§ 2H1.4(b)(1)" and inserting in lieu thereof "§ 2H1.5(b)(1)", and by deleting "the adjustment at" immediately before "§ 3B1.3".

Reason for Amendment: The purposes of this amendment are to correct a clerical error and to make editorial improvements.

Effective Date: The effective date of this amendment is November 1, 1989.

168. **Amendment:** Section 2H2.1(a)(1) is amended by deleting "persons" and inserting in lieu thereof "person(s)".

The Commentary to § 2H2.1 captioned "Background" is amended by deleting "Specific offense characteristics" and inserting in lieu thereof "Alternative base offense levels".

Reason for Amendment: The purpose of this amendment is to correct two clerical errors.

Effective Date: The effective date of this amendment is November 1, 1989.

169. **Amendment:** Section 2H3.1 is amended by deleting:

> "(a)   Base Offense Level (Apply the greater):

(1) 9; or

(2) If the purpose of the conduct was to facilitate another offense, apply the guideline applicable to an attempt to commit that offense.

(b) Specific Offense Characteristic

(1) If the purpose of the conduct was to obtain direct or indirect commercial advantage or economic gain not covered by § 2H3.1(a)(2) above, increase by 3 levels.",

and inserting in lieu thereof:

"(a) Base Offense Level: 9

(b) Specific Offense Characteristic

(1) If the purpose of the conduct was to obtain direct or indirect commercial advantage or economic gain, increase by 3 levels.

(c) Cross Reference

(1) If the purpose of the conduct was to facilitate another offense, apply the guideline applicable to an attempt to commit that offense, if the resulting offense level is greater than that determined above.".

Reason for Amendment: The purpose of this amendment is to correct an anomaly in § 2H3.1. Currently, specific offense characteristic (b)(1) applies only to base offense level (a)(1). Consequently, conduct facilitating an offense for economic gain of level 8 or 9 would result in a greater offense level (11 or 12) than conduct facilitating a more serious (level 10 or 11) offense.

Effective Date: The effective date of this amendment is November 1, 1989.

170. **Amendment:** Section 2J1.1 is amended by deleting:

"If the defendant was adjudged guilty of contempt, the court shall impose a sentence based on stated reasons and the purposes of sentencing set forth in 18 U.S.C. § 3553(a)(2).",

and inserting in lieu thereof:

"Apply § 2X5.1 (Other Offenses).".

The Commentary to § 2J1.1 captioned "Application Note" is amended in Note 1 by deleting "See, however, § 2X5.1 (Other Offenses)." and inserting in lieu thereof "In certain cases, the offense conduct will be sufficiently analogous to § 2J1.2 (Obstruction of Justice) for that guideline to apply.".

Reason for Amendment: This section is designated as a guideline, but it is not a guideline contemplated by the Sentencing Reform Act. The purpose of this amendment is to clarify the Commission's original intent by referencing this section to § 2X5.1 (Other Offenses).

Effective Date: The effective date of this amendment is November 1, 1989.

171. **Amendment:** The Commentary to § 2J1.1 captioned "Statutory Provisions" is amended by deleting "Provisions" and inserting in lieu thereof "Provision", and by deleting "§ " and

", 402".

Reason for Amendment: The purpose of this amendment is to delete a reference to a petty offense.

Effective Date: The effective date of this amendment is November 1, 1989.

172. **Amendment:** Section 2J1.2(b)(1) is amended by deleting "defendant obstructed or attempted to obstruct the administration of justice by" and inserting in lieu thereof "offense involved", and by deleting "or property," and inserting in lieu thereof ", or property damage, in order to obstruct the administration of justice".

    Section 2J1.2(b)(2) is amended by deleting "defendant substantially interfered" and inserting in lieu thereof "offense resulted in substantial interference".

    Section 2J1.2(c)(1) is amended by deleting "conduct was" and inserting in lieu thereof "offense involved", and by deleting "such" and inserting in lieu thereof "that".

    The Commentary to § 2J1.2 captioned "Application Notes" is amended in Note 1 by deleting "'Substantially interfered" and inserting in lieu thereof " 'Substantial interference", and by deleting "offense conduct resulting in" immediately before "a premature".

    Reason for Amendment: The purposes of this amendment are to clarify the guideline and to ensure that an attempted obstruction is not excluded from subsection (c) because of the non-parallel language between (b)(1) and (c)(1).

    Effective Date: The effective date of this amendment is November 1, 1989.

173. **Amendment:** The Commentary to § 2J1.2 captioned "Statutory Provisions" is amended by deleting "1503-" and inserting in lieu thereof "1503, 1505-".

    Reason for Amendment: The purpose of this amendment is to delete a reference to a petty offense.

    Effective Date: The effective date of this amendment is November 1, 1989.

174. **Amendment:** The Commentary to § 2J1.2 captioned "Statutory Provisions" is amended by inserting ", 1516" immediately following "1513".

    Reason for Amendment: The purpose of this amendment is to expand the coverage of an existing guideline to include a new offense (Obstruction of a Federal Audit) created by Section 7078 of the Anti-Drug Abuse Act of 1988.

    Effective Date: The effective date of this amendment is November 1, 1989.

175. **Amendment:** Section 2J1.3 is amended in the caption by inserting "or Subornation of Perjury" immediately following "Perjury".

    Section 2J1.3(b)(1) is amended by deleting "defendant suborned perjury by" and inserting in lieu thereof "offense involved", and by deleting "or property" and inserting in lieu thereof ", or property damage, in order to suborn perjury".

    Section 2J1.3(b)(2) is amended by deleting "defendant's" immediately following "If the", and by deleting "substantially interfered" and inserting in lieu thereof "resulted in substantial interference".

Amendment 175   APPENDIX C - VOLUME I   November 1, 2013

Section 2J1.3(c)(1) is amended by deleting "conduct was perjury" and inserting in lieu thereof "offense involved perjury or subornation of perjury", and by deleting "such" and inserting in lieu thereof "that".

The Commentary to § 2J1.3 captioned "Application Notes" is amended in Note 1 by deleting "'Substantially interfered" and inserting in lieu thereof "'Substantial interference", and by deleting "offense conduct resulting in" immediately before "a premature".

Reason for Amendment: The purposes of this amendment are to clarify the guideline and to ensure that subornation of perjury is not excluded from subsection (c) due to a lack of parallel wording in the subsections.

Effective Date: The effective date of this amendment is November 1, 1989.

176. **Amendment:** Section 2J1.4(b)(1) is amended by deleting:

> "If the defendant falsely represented himself as a federal officer, agent or employee to demand or obtain any money, paper, document, or other thing of value or to conduct an unlawful arrest or search, increase by 6 levels.",

and inserting in lieu thereof:

> "If the impersonation was committed for the purpose of conducting an unlawful arrest, detention, or search, increase by 6 levels.".

Section 2J1.4 is amended by inserting the following additional subsection:

> "(c)   Cross Reference
>
>> (1)   If the impersonation was to facilitate another offense, apply the guideline for an attempt to commit that offense, if the resulting offense level is greater than the offense level determined above.".

Reason for Amendment: The purpose of this amendment is to relate the offense levels more directly to the underlying offense where the impersonation is committed for the purpose of facilitating another offense.

Effective Date: The effective date of this amendment is November 1, 1989.

177. **Amendment:** Section 2J1.5(b)(1) is amended by deleting "substantially interfered" and inserting in lieu thereof "resulted in substantial interference".

The Commentary to § 2J1.5 captioned "Application Notes" is amended in Note 1 by deleting "'Substantially interfered" and inserting in lieu thereof "'Substantial interference", and by deleting "offense conduct resulting in" immediately before "a premature".

Reason for Amendment: The purpose of this amendment is to clarify the guideline.

Effective Date: The effective date of this amendment is November 1, 1989.

178. **Amendment:** Chapter Two, Part J is amended by deleting § 2J1.7 in its entirety as follows:

> "§ 2J1.7.   Commission of Offense While on Release
>
>> (a)   Base Offense Level: 6

(b) Specific Offense Characteristics

> (1) If the offense committed while on release is punishable by death or imprisonment for a term of fifteen years or more, increase by 6 levels.
>
> (2) If the offense committed while on release is punishable by a term of imprisonment of five or more years, but less than fifteen years, increase by 4 levels.
>
> (3) If the offense committed while on release is a felony punishable by a maximum term of less than five years, increase by 2 levels.

Commentary

Statutory Provision: 18 U.S.C. § 3147.

Application Notes:

1. This guideline applies whenever a sentence pursuant to 18 U.S.C. § 3147 is imposed.

2. By statute, a term of imprisonment imposed for a violation of 18 U.S.C. § 3147 runs consecutively to any other term of imprisonment. Consequently, a sentence for such a violation is exempt from grouping under the multiple count rules. See § 3D1.2.

Background: Because defendants convicted under this section will generally have a prior criminal history, the guideline sentences provided are greater than they otherwise might appear.".

A replacement guideline with accompanying commentary is inserted as § 2J1.7 (Commission of Offense While on Release).

Reason for Amendment: The purpose of this amendment is to reflect the fact that 18 U.S.C. § 3147 is an enhancement provision, not a distinct offense. Created in 1984 as part of the Comprehensive Crime Control Act, the statute contained interim provisions (mandatory consecutive sentences that were subject to the parole and good time provisions of prior law) that were to be in effect until the sentencing guidelines took effect. The Senate Report to S.1762 indicates that the mandatory nature of the interim provisions was to be eliminated when the sentencing guidelines took effect ("Section 213(h) [220(g) of the CCCA of 1984] amends the new provision in title I of this Act relating to consecutive enhanced penalties for committing an offense while on release (new 18 U.S.C. § 3147)) by eliminating the mandatory nature of the penalties in favor of utilizing sentencing guidelines" (Senate Report 98-225 at 186). The statute, as amended, however, did not actually eliminate all language referring to mandatory penalties. A mandatory consecutive term of imprisonment is required but, unlike other mandatory provisions, there is no minimum required.

The amendment converts this section into an offense level adjustment for the offense committed while on release, a treatment that is considerably more consistent with the treatment of other offense/offender characteristics.

Effective Date: The effective date of this amendment is November 1, 1989.

179. Amendment: Section 2J1.8(b)(1) is amended by deleting "substantially interfered" and

Amendment 179

inserting in lieu thereof "resulted in substantial interference".

Section 2J1.8(c)(1) is amended by deleting "conduct was" and inserting in lieu thereof "offense involved", and by deleting "such" and inserting in lieu thereof "that".

The Commentary to § 2J1.8 captioned "Application Notes" is amended in Note 1 by deleting "Substantially interfered" and inserting in lieu thereof "Substantial interference", and by deleting "offense conduct resulting in" immediately before "a premature".

The Commentary to § 2J1.8 captioned "Application Notes" is amended in Note 2 by deleting the first sentence as follows: "This section applies only in the case of a conviction under the above referenced (or equivalent) statute.".

Reason for Amendment: The purpose of this amendment is to clarify the guideline.

Effective Date: The effective date of this amendment is November 1, 1989.

180. **Amendment:** The Commentary to § 2J1.9 captioned "Application Notes" is amended in Note 2 by deleting the first sentence as follows: "This section applies only in the case of a conviction under the above referenced (or equivalent) statute.".

Reason for Amendment: The purpose of this amendment is to clarify the commentary.

Effective Date: The effective date of this amendment is November 1, 1989.

181. **Amendment:** Section 2J1.9(b)(1) is amended by deleting "for refusing to testify" and inserting in lieu thereof "made or offered for refusing to testify or for the witness absenting himself to avoid testifying".

The Commentary to § 2J1.9 captioned "Application Notes" is amended by deleting:

"1. 'Refusing to testify' includes absenting oneself for the purpose of avoiding testifying.",

and by renumbering Notes 2 and 3 as 1 and 2 respectively.

Reason for Amendment: The purpose of this amendment is to move material from the commentary to the guideline itself where it more properly belongs.

Effective Date: The effective date of this amendment is November 1, 1989.

182. **Amendment:** Sections 2K1.4(c) and 2K1.5(c) are amended by deleting "higher" whenever it appears and inserting in lieu thereof "greater".

Reason for Amendment: The purpose of this amendment is to correct a clerical error.

Effective Date: The effective date of this amendment is November 1, 1989.

183. **Amendment:** Section 2K1.3(b) is amended by deleting "any of the following" and inserting in lieu thereof "more than one".

Section 2K1.3(b)(5) is amended by deleting "firearm offense" and inserting in lieu thereof "offense involving explosives".

Reason for Amendment: The purpose of this amendment is to clarify the guideline.

Effective Date: The effective date of this amendment is November 1, 1989.

184. Amendment: Section 2K1.4(b) is amended by deleting "any of the following" and inserting in lieu thereof "more than one".

Reason for Amendment: The purpose of this amendment is to clarify the guideline.

Effective Date: The effective date of this amendment is November 1, 1989.

185. Amendment: Section 2K1.4 is amended by inserting the following additional subsection:

> "(d) Note
>
> > (1) The specific offense characteristic in subsection (b)(4) applies only in the case of an offense committed prior to November 18, 1988.".

The Commentary to § 2K1.4 captioned "Statutory Provisions" is amended by inserting "(only in the case of an offense committed prior to November 18, 1988)" immediately following "(h)".

The Commentary to § 2K1.4 captioned "Background", is amended by deleting "used fire or an explosive in the commission of a felony," immediately before "used a destructive device", and by inserting the following additional sentences at the end of the paragraph:

> "As amended by Section 6474(b) of the Anti-Drug Abuse Act of 1988 (effective November 18, 1988), 18 U.S.C. § 844(h) sets forth a mandatory sentencing enhancement of five years for the first offense and ten years for subsequent offenses if the defendant was convicted of using fire or an explosive to commit a felony or of carrying an explosive during the commission of a felony. See § 2K1.7.".

Reason for Amendment: The purpose of this amendment is to conform the guideline to a statutory revision to 18 U.S.C. § 844(h).

Effective Date: The effective date of this amendment is November 1, 1989.

186. Amendment: Section 2K1.5(b) is amended by deleting "any of the following" and inserting in lieu thereof "more than one".

Reason for Amendment: The purpose of this amendment is to clarify the guideline.

Effective Date: The effective date of this amendment is November 1, 1989.

187. Amendment: Section 2K1.5(b)(1) is amended by deleting "(i.e., the defendant is convicted under 49 U.S.C. § 1472(l)(2)" immediately following "human life", and by inserting "is convicted under 49 U.S.C. § 1472(l)(2) (i.e., the defendant" immediately before "acted".

Reason for Amendment: The purpose of this amendment is to clarify the guideline.

Effective Date: The effective date of this amendment is November 1, 1989.

188. Amendment: Chapter Two, Part K is amended by inserting an additional guideline with accompanying commentary as § 2K1.7 (Use of Fire or Explosives to Commit a Federal Felony).

Reason for Amendment: The purpose of this amendment is to conform the guideline to a statutory revision of 18 U.S.C. § 844(h).

Effective Date: The effective date of this amendment is November 1, 1989.

189. Amendment: Section 2K2.1 is amended by deleting the entire guideline and accompanying commentary, except for the commentary captioned "Background", as follows:

> "§ 2K2.1. Receipt, Possession, or Transportation of Firearms and Other Weapons by Prohibited Persons
>
> (a) Base Offense Level: 9
>
> (b) Specific Offense Characteristics
>
> > (1) If the firearm was stolen or had an altered or obliterated serial number, increase by 1 level.
> >
> > (2) If the defendant obtained or possessed the firearm solely for sport or recreation, decrease by 4 levels.
>
> (c) Cross Reference
>
> > (1) If the defendant used the firearm in committing or attempting another offense, apply the guideline in respect to such other offense, or § 2X1.1 (Attempt or Conspiracy) if the resulting offense level is higher than that determined above.
>
> Commentary
>
> Statutory Provisions: 18 U.S.C. §§ 922(a)(6), (g), (h).
>
> Application Note:
>
> 1. Under § 2K2.1(b)(2), intended lawful use, as determined by the surrounding circumstances, provides a decrease in offense level. Relevant circumstances include, among others, the number and type of firearms (sawed-off shotguns, for example, have few legitimate uses) and ammunition, the location and circumstances of possession, the nature of the defendant's criminal history (e.g., whether involving firearms), and the extent to which possession is restricted by local law.",

and inserting in lieu thereof:

> "§ 2K2.1. Unlawful Receipt, Possession, or Transportation of Firearms or Ammunition
>
> (a) Base Offense Level (Apply the greatest):
>
> > (1) 16, if the defendant is convicted under 18 U.S.C. § 922(o) or 26 U.S.C. § 5861; or
> >
> > (2) 12, if the defendant is convicted under 18 U.S.C. § 922(g), (h), or (n); or if the defendant, at the time of the offense, had been convicted in any court of an offense punishable by imprisonment for a term exceeding one year; or
> >
> > (3) 6, otherwise.
>
> (b) Specific Offense Characteristics
>
> > (1) If the defendant obtained or possessed the firearm or ammunition solely for lawful sporting purposes or collection, decrease the offense level determined above to level 6.

(2) If the firearm was stolen or had an altered or obliterated serial number, increase by 2 levels.

(c) Cross References

(1) If the offense involved the distribution of a firearm or possession with intent to distribute, apply § 2K2.2 (Unlawful Trafficking and Other Prohibited Transactions Involving Firearms) if the resulting offense level is greater than that determined above.

(2) If the defendant used or possessed the firearm in connection with commission or attempted commission of another offense, apply § 2X1.1 (Attempt, Solicitation, or Conspiracy) in respect to that other offense, if the resulting offense level is greater than that determined above.

Commentary

Statutory Provisions: 18 U.S.C. § 922(a)(1), (a)(3), (a)(4), (a)(6), (e), (f), (g), (h), (i), (j), (k), (l), (n), and (o); 26 U.S.C. § 5861(b), (c), (d), (h), (i), (j), and (k).

Application Notes:

1. The definition of 'firearm' used in this section is that set forth in 18 U.S.C. § 921(a)(3) (if the defendant is convicted under 18 U.S.C. § 922) and 26 U.S.C. § 5845(a) (if the defendant is convicted under 26 U.S.C. § 5861). These definitions are somewhat broader than that used in Application Note 1(e) of the Commentary to § 1B1.1 (Application Instructions). Under 18 U.S.C. § 921(a)(3), the term 'firearm' means (A) any weapon (including a starter gun) which will or is designed to or may readily be converted to expel a projectile by the action of an explosive; (B) the frame or receiver of any such weapon; (C) any firearm muffler or firearm silencer; or (D) any destructive device. Under 26 U.S.C. § 5845(a), the term 'firearm' includes a shotgun, or a weapon made from a shotgun, with a barrel or barrels of less than 18 inches in length; a weapon made from a shotgun or rifle with an overall length of less than 26 inches; a rifle, or weapon made from a rifle, with a barrel or barrels less than 16 inches in length; a machine gun; a muffler or silencer for a firearm; a destructive device; and certain other large bore weapons.

2. Under § 2K2.1(b)(1), intended lawful use, as determined by the surrounding circumstances, provides a decrease in the offense level. Relevant circumstances include, among others, the number and type of firearms (sawed-off shotguns, for example, have few legitimate uses) and ammunition, the location and circumstances of possession, the nature of the defendant's criminal history (e.g., whether involving firearms), and the extent to which possession was restricted by local law.".

The Commentary to § 2K2.1 captioned "Background" is amended in the last paragraph by deleting "§ 2K2.1(c)" and inserting in lieu thereof "§ 2K2.1(c)(2)".

Chapter Two, Part K, Subpart 2 is amended by deleting §§ 2K2.2 and 2K2.3 in their entirety as follows:

"§ 2K2.2. Receipt, Possession, or Transportation of Firearms and Other Weapons in Violation of National Firearms Act

(a) Base Offense Level: 12

(b) Specific Offense Characteristics

(1) If the firearm was stolen or had an altered or obliterated serial number, increase by 1 level.

(2) If the firearm was a silencer, increase by 4 levels.

(3) If the defendant obtained or possessed the firearm solely for sport, recreation or collection, decrease by 6 levels.

(c) Cross Reference

(1) If the defendant used the firearm in committing or attempting another offense, apply the guideline for such other offense or § 2X1.1 (Attempt or Conspiracy), if the resulting offense level is higher than that determined above.

Commentary

Statutory Provisions: 26 U.S.C. §§ 5861(b) through (l).

Application Notes:

1. Under § 2K2.2(b)(3), intended lawful use, as determined by the surrounding circumstances, provides a decrease in offense level. Relevant circumstances include, among others, the number and type of firearms (sawed-off shotguns, for example, have few legitimate uses) and ammunition, the location and circumstances of possession, the nature of the defendant's criminal history (e.g., whether involving firearms), and the extent to which possession is restricted by local law.

2. Subsection (c)(1) refers to any situation in which the defendant possessed a firearm to facilitate another offense that he committed or attempted.

Background: 26 U.S.C. § 5861 prohibits the unlicensed receipt, possession, transportation, or manufacture of certain firearms, such as machine guns, silencers, rifles and shotguns with shortened barrels, and destructive devices. As with § 2K2.1, there is considerable variation in the conduct included under this statutory provision and some violations may be relatively technical.

§ 2K2.3. Prohibited Transactions in or Shipment of Firearms and Other Weapons

(a) Base Offense Level:

(1) 12, if convicted under 26 U.S.C. § 5861; or

(2) 6, otherwise.

(b) Specific Offense Characteristics

(1) If the number of firearms unlawfully dealt in exceeded 5, increase as follows:

	Number of Firearms	Increase in Level
(A)	6 - 10	add 1
(B)	11 - 20	add 2
(C)	21 - 50	add 3
(D)	51 - 100	add 4
(E)	101 - 200	add 5
(F)	more than 200	add 6

    (2)   If any of the following applies, use the greatest:

        (A)   If the defendant knew or had reason to believe that a purchaser was a person prohibited by federal law from owning the firearm, increase by 2 levels.

        (B)   If the defendant knew or had reason to believe that a purchaser resided in another state in which he was prohibited from owning the firearm, increase by 1 level.

        (C)   If the defendant knew or had reason to believe that a firearm was stolen or had an altered or obliterated serial number, increase by 1 level.

(c)   Cross Reference

    (1)   If the defendant provided the firearm to another for the purpose of committing another offense, or knowing that he planned to use it in committing another offense, apply § 2X1.1 (Attempt or Conspiracy) in respect to such other offense, if the resulting offense level is higher.

Commentary

Statutory Provisions: 18 U.S.C. § 922 (a)(1), (a)(5), (b)(2), (b)(3), (d), (i), (j), (k), (l); 26 U.S.C. § 5861(a).

Background: This section applies to a variety of offenses involving prohibited transactions in or transportation of firearms and certain other weapons.".

A replacement guideline with accompanying commentary is inserted as § 2K2.2 (Unlawful Trafficking and Other Prohibited Transactions Involving Firearms).

Chapter Two, Part K, Subpart 2 is amended by inserting an additional guideline with accompanying commentary as § 2K2.3 (Receiving, Transporting, Shipping or Transferring a Firearm or Ammunition With Intent to Commit Another Offense, or With Knowledge that It Will Be Used in Committing Another Offense).

Reason for Amendment: This amendment addresses a number of diverse substantive and technical issues, as well as the creation of several new offenses, and increased statutory maximum penalties for certain other offenses. Because there exist a large number of overlapping statutory provisions, the three basic guidelines, § 2K2.1 (Possession by a prohibited person), § 2K2.2 (Possession of certain types of weapons), and § 2K2.3

Amendment 189 APPENDIX C - VOLUME I November 1, 2013

(Unlawful trafficking) are not closely tied to the actual conduct. The amendment addresses this issue by consolidating the current three guidelines into two guidelines: (1) unlawful possession, receipt, or transportation, and (2) unlawful trafficking; and by more carefully drawing the distinctions between the base offense levels provided. The third guideline in this amendment is a new guideline to address transfer of a weapon with intent or knowledge that it will be used to commit another offense (formerly covered in a cross reference) and a new offense added by the Anti-Drug Abuse Act of 1988 (Section 6211)(Interstate travel to acquire a firearm for a criminal purpose).

The base offense level for conduct covered by the current § 2K2.1 is increased in the amendment from 9 to 12. The statutorily authorized maximum sentence for the conduct covered under § 2K2.1 was increased from five to ten years by the Anti-Drug Abuse Act of 1988 (Section 6462). Note, however, that the most aggravated conduct under § 2K2.1 (possession of a weapon during commission of another offense) is handled by the cross-reference at subsection (c) and is based upon the offense level for an attempt to commit the underlying offense. See Background Commentary to current § 2K2.1. The offense level for unlawful possession of a machine gun, sawed off shotgun, or destructive device is increased from 12 to 16. In addition, the amendment raises the enhancement for stolen weapons or obliterated serial numbers from 1 to 2 levels to better reflect the seriousness of this conduct. The numbers currently used in the table for the distribution of multiple weapons in § 2K2.2 are amended to increase the offense level more rapidly for sale of multiple weapons.

Effective Date: The effective date of this amendment is November 1, 1989.

190. **Amendment:** Section 2K2.4 is amended by deleting "penalties are those" and inserting in lieu thereof "term of imprisonment is that".

The Commentary to § 2K2.4 captioned "Application Notes" is amended by inserting the following additional note:

"3. Imposition of a term of supervised release is governed by the provisions of § 5D1.1 (Imposition of a Term of Supervised Release).".

Section 2K2.4 is amended by inserting "(a)" immediately before "If", and by inserting the following additional subsection:

"(b) Special Instructions for Fines

(1) Where there is a federal conviction for the underlying offense, the fine guideline shall be the fine guideline that would have been applicable had there only been a conviction for the underlying offense. This guideline shall be used as a consolidated fine guideline for both the underlying offense and the conviction underlying this section.".

The Commentary to § 2K2.4 captioned "Application Notes" is amended by inserting the following additional note:

"4. Subsection (b) sets forth special provisions concerning the imposition of fines. Where there is also a conviction for the underlying offense, a consolidated fine guideline is determined by the offense level that would have applied to the underlying offense absent a conviction under 18 U.S.C. § 924(c) or 929(a). This is because the offense level for the underlying offense may be reduced when there is also a conviction under 18 U.S.C.

– 90 –

§ 924(c) or 929(a) in that any specific offense characteristic for possession, use, or discharge of a firearm is not applied (see Application Note 2). The Commission has not established a fine guideline range for the unusual case in which there is no conviction for the underlying offense.".

Reason for Amendment: The purpose of this amendment is to address the imposition of a fine or term of supervised release when this guideline applies.

Effective Date: The effective date of this amendment is November 1, 1989.

191. **Amendment:** Chapter Two, Part K is amended by inserting an additional guideline with accompanying commentary as § 2K2.5 (Possession of Firearms and Dangerous Weapons in Federal Facilities).

    Reason for Amendment: The purpose of this amendment is to reflect a new offense enacted by Section 6215 of the Anti-Drug Abuse Act of 1988. A base offense level of 6 is provided for the misdemeanor portion of this statute. The felony portion of this statute (possession with intent to commit another offense) is treated as if an attempt to commit that other offense.

    Effective Date: The effective date of this amendment is November 1, 1989.

192. **Amendment:** Section 2L1.1(b) is amended by inserting the following additional subsection:

    "(3) If the defendant is an unlawful alien who has been deported (voluntarily or involuntarily) on one or more occasions prior to the instant offense, and the offense level determined above is less than level 8, increase to level 8.".

    The Commentary to § 2L1.1 captioned "Application Notes" is amended in Note 6 by deleting "enhancement at § 2L1.1(b)(1) does not apply" and inserting in lieu thereof "reduction at § 2L1.1(b)(1) applies".

    Reason for Amendment: The purposes of this amendment are to provide an offense level that is no less than that provided under § 2L1.2 in the case of a defendant who is a previously deported alien, and to conform Application Note 6 of the Commentary to § 2L1.1 to the January 1988 revision of § 2L1.1.

    Effective Date: The effective date of this amendment is November 1, 1989.

193. **Amendment:** Section 2L1.2 is amended by inserting the following additional subsection:

    "(b) Specific Offense Characteristic

    (1) If the defendant previously was deported after sustaining a conviction for a felony, other than a felony involving violation of the immigration laws, increase by 4 levels.",

    The Commentary to § 2L1.2 captioned "Application Notes" is amended by inserting the following additional notes:

    "3. A 4-level increase is provided under subsection (b)(1) in the case of a defendant who was previously deported after sustaining a conviction for a felony, other than a felony involving a violation of the immigration laws. In the case of a defendant previously deported after sustaining a conviction for an aggravated felony as defined in 8 U.S.C. § 1101(a), or for any other violent felony, an upward departure may be warranted.

4. The adjustment under § 2L1.2(b)(1) is in addition to any criminal history points added for such conviction in Chapter 4, Part A (Criminal History).".

Reason for Amendment: The purpose of this amendment is to add a specific offense characteristic to provide an increase in the case of an alien previously deported after conviction of a felony other than an immigration law violation. This specific offense characteristic is in addition to, and not in lieu of, criminal history points added for the prior sentence. The amendment provides for consideration of an upward departure where the previous deportation was for an "aggravated felony" or for any other violent felony.

Effective Date: The effective date of this amendment is November 1, 1989.

194. **Amendment:** Chapter Two, Part L, Subpart 1 is amended by deleting § 2L1.3 in its entirety as follows:

"§ 2L1.3. Engaging in a Pattern of Unlawful Employment of Aliens

(a) Base Offense Level: 6

Commentary

Statutory Provision: 8 U.S.C. § 1324a(f)(1).

Background: The offense covered under this section is a misdemeanor for which the maximum term of imprisonment authorized by statute is six months.".

Reason for Amendment: The purpose of this amendment is to delete a guideline applying only to a petty offense. Petty offenses were deleted from coverage of the guidelines by the adoption of § 1B1.9 (effective June 15, 1988).

Effective Date: The effective date of this amendment is November 1, 1989.

195. **Amendment:** Section 2L2.1(a) is amended by deleting "6" and inserting in lieu thereof "9".

Section 2L2.1(b)(1) is amended by deleting "for profit, increase by 3 levels" and inserting in lieu thereof "other than for profit, decrease by 3 levels".

Reason for Amendment: The purpose of this amendment is to conform the structure of this guideline to that of § 2L1.1.

Effective Date: The effective date of this amendment is November 1, 1989.

196. **Amendment:** Section 2L2.2 is amended by inserting the following additional subsection:

"(b) Specific Offense Characteristic

(1) If the defendant is an unlawful alien who has been deported (voluntarily or involuntarily) on one or more occasions prior to the instant offense, increase by 2 levels.".

The Commentary to § 2L2.2 captioned "Application Notes" is amended by deleting:

"1. In the case of a defendant who is an unlawful alien and has been deported (voluntarily or involuntarily) on one or more occasions prior to the instant offense, the Commission recommends an upward departure of 2 levels in order to provide a result equivalent to § 2L1.2.",

by renumbering Note 2 as Note 1, and by deleting "Notes" and inserting in lieu thereof "Note".

Reason for Amendment: The purpose of this amendment it to convert a departure recommendation into a specific offense characteristic.

Effective Date: The effective date of this amendment is November 1, 1989.

197. **Amendment:** Section 2L2.3(a) is amended by deleting "6" and inserting in lieu thereof "9".

Section 2L2.3(b)(1) is amended by deleting "for profit, increase by 3 levels" and inserting in lieu thereof "other than for profit, decrease by 3 levels".

Reason for Amendment: The purpose of this amendment is to conform the structure of this guideline to that of § 2L1.1.

Effective Date: The effective date of this amendment is November 1, 1989.

198. **Amendment:** Section 2L2.4 is amended by inserting the following additional subsection:

   "(b) Specific Offense Characteristic

   (1) If the defendant is an unlawful alien who has been deported (voluntarily or involuntarily) on one or more occasions prior to the instant offense, increase by 2 levels.".

The Commentary to § 2L2.4 captioned "Application Notes" is amended by deleting:

   "1. In the case of a defendant who is an unlawful alien and has been deported (voluntarily or involuntarily) on one or more occasions prior to the instant offense, the Commission recommends an upward departure of 2 levels in order to provide a result equivalent to § 2L1.2.",

by renumbering Note 2 as Note 1, and by deleting "Notes" and inserting in lieu thereof "Note".

Reason for Amendment: The purpose of this amendment is to convert a departure recommendation into a specific offense characteristic.

Effective Date: The effective date of this amendment is November 1, 1989.

199. **Amendment:** Section 2N3.1 is amended by deleting:

   "(b) If more than one vehicle was involved, apply § 2F1.1 (Offenses Involving Fraud or Deceit).",

and inserting in lieu thereof:

   "(b) Cross Reference

   (1) If the offense involved more than one vehicle, apply § 2F1.1 (Fraud and Deceit).".

Reason for Amendment: The purposes of this amendment are to correct a clerical error and to conform the phraseology of this subsection to that used elsewhere in the guidelines.

Effective Date: The effective date of this amendment is November 1, 1989.

200. **Amendment:** Section 2P1.1(a) is amended by deleting:

    "(1) 13, if from lawful custody resulting from a conviction or as a result of a lawful arrest for a felony;

    (2) 8, if from lawful custody awaiting extradition, pursuant to designation as a recalcitrant witness or as a result of a lawful arrest for a misdemeanor.",

and inserting in lieu thereof:

    "(1) 13, if the custody or confinement is by virtue of an arrest on a charge of felony, or conviction of any offense;

    (2) 8, otherwise.".

Reason for Amendment: The purpose of this amendment is to clarify the language of the guideline by making it conform more closely to that used in 18 U.S.C. § 751, the statute from which it was derived.

Effective Date: The effective date of this amendment is November 1, 1989.

201. **Amendment:** Section 2P1.1(b)(3) is amended by deleting:

    "If the defendant committed the offense while a correctional officer or other employee of the Department of Justice, increase by 2 levels.",

and inserting in lieu thereof:

    "If the defendant was a law enforcement or correctional officer or employee, or an employee of the Department of Justice, at the time of the offense, increase by 2 levels.".

Reason for Amendment: The current specific offense characteristic (b)(3) applies only to correctional officers or Justice Department employees, and not to local or state law enforcement officers who might have custody of a federal prisoner, or even to federal law enforcement officers who are not employed by the Department of Justice (e.g., Secret Service agents are employed by the Treasury Department). It also does not appear to apply to law enforcement or correctional employees who are not sworn officers unless they are Justice Department employees. The purpose of this amendment is to correct this anomaly.

Effective Date: The effective date of this amendment is November 1, 1989.

202. **Amendment:** Section 2P1.2(b)(1) is amended by deleting:

    "If the defendant committed the offense while a correctional officer or other employee of the Department of Justice, increase by 2 levels.",

and inserting in lieu thereof:

    "If the defendant was a law enforcement or correctional officer or employee, or an employee of the Department of Justice, at the time of the offense, increase by 2 levels.".

Reason for Amendment: The current specific offense characteristic (b)(1) applies only to correctional officers or Justice Department employees, and not to local or state law enforcement officers who might have custody of a federal prisoner, or even to federal law enforcement officers who are not employed by the Department of Justice (e.g., Secret Service agents are employed by the Treasury Department). It also does not appear to apply to law enforcement or correctional employees who are not sworn officers unless they are Justice Department employees. The purpose of this amendment is to correct this anomaly.

Effective Date: The effective date of this amendment is November 1, 1989.

203. **Amendment:** Section 2P1.2 is amended by inserting the following additional subsection:

> "(c) Cross Reference
>
> (1) If the defendant is convicted under 18 U.S.C. § 1791(a)(1) and is punishable under 18 U.S.C. § 1791(b)(1), the offense level is 2 plus the offense level from § 2D1.1, but in no event less than level 26.".

The Commentary to § 2P1.2 captioned "Application Note" is amended by deleting "Note" and inserting in lieu thereof "Notes", and by inserting the following additional note:

> "2. Pursuant to 18 U.S.C. § 1791(c), as amended, a sentence imposed upon an inmate for a violation of 18 U.S.C. § 1791 shall be consecutive to the sentence being served at the time of the violation.".

Reason for Amendment: The purpose of this amendment is to implement the direction to the Commission in Section 6468 of the Anti-Drug Abuse Act of 1988.

Effective Date: The effective date of this amendment is November 1, 1989.

204. **Amendment:** Chapter Two, Part P is amended by deleting § 2P1.4 in its entirety as follows:

> "§ 2P1.4. Trespass on Bureau of Prisons Facilities
>
> (a) Base Offense Level: 6
>
> Commentary
>
> Statutory Provision: 18 U.S.C. § 1793.".

Reason for Amendment: The purpose of this amendment is to delete a guideline applying only to a petty offense. Petty offenses were deleted from coverage of the guidelines by the adoption of § 1B1.9 (effective June 15, 1988).

Effective Date: The effective date of this amendment is November 1, 1989.

205. **Amendment:** The Commentary to § 2Q1.3 captioned "Statutory Provisions" is amended by deleting "§ 4912,".

Reason for Amendment: The purpose of this amendment is to delete a reference to a petty offense.

Effective Date: The effective date of this amendment is November 1, 1989.

206. **Amendment:** Section 2Q1.4(b)(1) is amended by inserting "bodily" immediately pre-

Amendment 206

ceding "injury".

The Commentary to § 2Q1.4 captioned "Application Note" is amended by deleting:

"1. 'Serious injury' means serious bodily injury as defined in the Commentary to § 1B1.1 (Applicable Instructions).",

and inserting in lieu thereof:

"1. 'Serious bodily injury' is defined in the Commentary to § 1B1.1 (Application Instructions).".

Reason for Amendment: The purpose of this amendment is to correct a clerical error.

Effective Date: The effective date of this amendment is November 1, 1989.

207. **Amendment:** Section 2Q1.5(b) is amended by deleting:

"(2) If the purpose of the offense was to influence government action or to extort money, increase by 8 levels.",

and by inserting the following additional subsection:

"(c) Cross Reference

(1) If the purpose of the offense was to influence government action or to extort money, apply § 2B3.2 (Extortion by Force or Threat of Injury or Serious Damage).".

Section 2Q1.5(b) is amended by deleting "Characteristics" and inserting in lieu thereof "Characteristic".

Reason for Amendment: The purposes of this amendment are to convert a specific offense characteristic to a cross-reference and render the guidelines internally more consistent.

Effective Date: The effective date of this amendment is November 1, 1989.

208. **Amendment:** Chapter Two, Part Q, Subpart 1, is amended by inserting an additional guideline with accompanying commentary as § 2Q1.6 (Hazardous or Injurious Devices on Federal Lands).

Reason for Amendment: The purpose of this amendment is to reflect a new offense created by Section 6254(f) of the Anti-Drug Abuse Act of 1988.

Effective Date: The effective date of this amendment is November 1, 1989.

209. **Amendment:** Section 2Q2.1 is amended in the title by inserting at the end "; Smuggling and Otherwise Unlawfully Dealing in Fish, Wildlife, and Plants".

The Commentary to § 2Q2.1 captioned "Statutory Provisions" is amended by inserting immediately before the period at the end ", 3373(d); 18 U.S.C. § 545".

The Commentary to § 2Q2.1 captioned "Background" is amended by deleting "and the Fur Seal Act. These statutes provide special protection to particular species of fish, wildlife and plants." and inserting in lieu thereof "the Fur Seal Act, the Lacey Act, and to violations of 18 U.S.C. § 545 where the smuggling activity involved fish, wildlife, or plants.".

Chapter Two, Part Q, Subpart 2 is amended by deleting § 2Q2.2 in its entirety as follows:

"§ 2Q2.2. Lacey Act; Smuggling and Otherwise Unlawfully Dealing in Fish, Wildlife, and Plants

    (a)   Base Offense Level:

        (1)   6, if the defendant knowingly imported or exported fish, wildlife, or plants, or knowingly engaged in conduct involving the sale or purchase of fish, wildlife, or plants with a market value greater than $350; or

        (2)   4.

    (b)   Specific Offense Characteristics

        (1)   If the offense involved a commercial purpose, increase by 2 levels.

        (2)   If the offense involved fish, wildlife, or plants that were not quarantined as required by law, increase by 2 levels.

        (3)   Apply the greater:

            (A)   If the market value of the fish, wildlife, or plants exceeded $2,000, increase the offense level by the corresponding number of levels from the table in § 2F1.1 (Fraud and Deceit); or

            (B)   If the offense involved a quantity of fish, wildlife, or plants that was substantial in relation either to the overall population of the species or to a discrete subpopulation, increase by 4 levels.

Commentary

Statutory Provisions: 16 U.S.C. § 3773(d); 18 U.S.C. § 545.

Application Note:

1.   This section applies to violations of 18 U.S.C. § 545 where the smuggling activity involved fish, wildlife, or plants. In other cases, see §§ 2T3.1 and 2T3.2.

Background: This section applies to violations of the Lacey Act Amendments of 1981, 16 U.S.C. § 3373(d), and to violations of 18 U.S.C. § 545 where the smuggling activity involved fish, wildlife, or plants. These are the principal enforcement statutes utilized to combat interstate and foreign commerce in unlawfully taken fish, wildlife, and plants. The adjustments for specific offense characteristics are identical to those in § 2Q2.1.".

Reason for Amendment: The purpose of this amendment is to consolidate two guidelines that cover very similar offenses.

Effective Date: The effective date of this amendment is November 1, 1989.

Amendment 210 APPENDIX C - VOLUME I November 1, 2013

210. Amendment: Section 2Q2.1(b)(3) is amended by deleting "Apply the greater:" and inserting in lieu thereof "(If more than one applies, use the greater):".

Reason for Amendment: The purpose of this amendment is to conform the guideline to the style of other guidelines.

Effective Date: The effective date of this amendment is November 1, 1989.

211. Amendment: Section 2R1.1(b)(2) is amended in the first column of the table by deleting:

"Volume of Commerce

(A)	less than $1,000,000
(B)	$1,000,000 - $4,000,000
(C)	$4,000,001 - $15,000,000
(D)	$15,000,001 - $50,000,000
(E)	over $50,000,000",

and inserting in lieu thereof:

"Volume of Commerce (Apply the Greatest)

(A)	Less than $1,000,000
(B)	$1,000,000 - $4,000,000
(C)	More than $4,000,000
(D)	More than $15,000,000
(E)	More than $50,000,000".

Reason for Amendment: The purpose of this amendment is to eliminate minor gaps in the loss table.

Effective Date: The effective date of this amendment is November 1, 1989.

212. Amendment: Section 2S1.1(b)(2) is amended in the first column of the table by deleting:

"Value

(A)	$100,000 or less
(B)	$100,001 - $200,000
(C)	$200,001 - $350,000
(D)	$350,001 - $600,000
(E)	$600,001 - $1,000,000
(F)	$1,000,001 - $2,000,000
(G)	$2,000,001 - $3,500,000
(H)	$3,500,001 - $6,000,000
(I)	$6,000,001 - $10,000,000
(J)	$10,000,001 - $20,000,000
(K)	$20,000,001 - $35,000,000
(L)	$35,000,001 - $60,000,000

(M) $60,000,001 - $100,000,000
(N) more than $100,000,000",

and inserting in lieu thereof:

"Value (Apply the Greatest)

(A) $100,000 or less
(B) More than $100,000
(C) More than $200,000
(D) More than $350,000
(E) More than $600,000
(F) More than $1,000,000
(G) More than $2,000,000
(H) More than $3,500,000
(I) More than $6,000,000
(J) More than $10,000,000
(K) More than $20,000,000
(L) More than $35,000,000
(M) More than $60,000,000
(N) More than $100,000,000".

Reason for Amendment: The purpose of this amendment is to eliminate minor gaps in the value table.

Effective Date: The effective date of this amendment is November 1, 1989.

213. **Amendment:** The Commentary to § 2S1.1 captioned "Background" is amended in the third paragraph by inserting the following additional sentences at the end: "Effective November 18, 1988, 18 U.S.C. § 1956(a)(1)(A) contains two subdivisions. The base offense level of 23 applies to § 1956(a)(1)(A)(i) and (ii).".

Reason for Amendment: The purpose of this amendment is to reflect a statutory revision made by Section 6471 of the Anti-Drug Abuse Act of 1988.

Effective Date: The effective date of this amendment is November 1, 1989.

214. **Amendment:** The Commentary to § 2S1.1 captioned "Background" is amended in the fourth paragraph by deleting "scope of the criminal enterprise as well as the degree of the defendant's involvement" and inserting in lieu thereof "magnitude of the criminal enterprise, and the extent to which the defendant aided the enterprise".

Reason for Amendment: The purpose of this amendment is to clarify the commentary.

Effective Date: The effective date of this amendment is November 1, 1989.

215. **Amendment:** Section 2S1.2(b)(1)(A) is amended by inserting at the end "or".

The Commentary to § 2S1.2 captioned "Background" is amended in the third paragraph by deleting "(b)(1)" and inserting in lieu thereof "(b)(1)(B)".

Reason for Amendment: The purpose of this amendment is to correct clerical errors.

Effective Date: The effective date of this amendment is November 1, 1989.

216. **Amendment:** Section 2S1.3(a)(1)(C) is amended by deleting "the proceeds of criminal activity" and inserting in lieu thereof "criminally derived property", and in subsection (b)(1) by inserting "property" immediately following "criminally derived".

The Commentary to § 2S1.3 captioned "Application Note" is amended by deleting:

"1. As used in this guideline, funds or other property are the 'proceeds of criminal activity' or 'criminally derived' if they are 'criminally derived property,' within the meaning of 18 U.S.C. § 1957.",

and inserting in lieu thereof:

"1. 'Criminally derived property' means any property constituting, or derived from, proceeds obtained from a criminal offense. See 18 U.S.C. § 1957(f)(2).".

Reason for Amendment: The purpose of this amendment is to clarify the guideline.

Effective Date: The effective date of this amendment is November 1, 1989.

217. **Amendment:** The Commentary to § 2S1.3 captioned "Statutory Provisions" is amended by inserting "26 U.S.C. § 7203 (if a willful violation of 26 U.S.C. § 6050I);" immediately before "31 U.S.C.".

Reason for Amendment: The purpose of this amendment is to conform the guideline to a revision of the relevant statute.

Effective Date: The effective date of this amendment is November 1, 1989.

218. **Amendment:** Section 2S1.3(a)(1)(A) is amended by inserting "or" immediately following "requirements;".

Section 2S1.3(a)(1)(B) is amended by deleting "activity" and inserting in lieu thereof "evasion of reporting requirements".

The Commentary to § 2S1.3 captioned "Application Note" is amended in the caption by deleting "Note" and inserting in lieu thereof "Notes", and by inserting the following additional note:

"2. Subsection (a)(1)(C) applies where a reasonable person would have believed from the circumstances that the funds were criminally derived property. Subsection (b)(1) applies if the defendant knew or believed the funds were criminally derived property. Subsection (b)(1) applies in addition to, and not in lieu of, subsection (a)(1)(C). Where subsection (b)(1) applies, subsection (a)(1)(C) also will apply. It is possible that a defendant 'believed' or 'reasonably should have believed' that the funds were criminally derived property even if, in fact, the funds were not so derived (e.g., in a 'sting' operation where the defendant is told the funds were derived from the unlawful sale of controlled substances).".

The Commentary to § 2S1.3 captioned "Background" is amended in the second paragraph

by deleting:

> "The base offense level is set at 13 for the great majority of cases. However, the base offense level is set at 5 for those cases in which these offenses may be committed with innocent motives and the defendant reasonably believed that the funds were from legitimate sources. The higher base offense level applies in all other cases. The offense level is increased by 5 levels if the defendant knew that the funds were criminally derived.",

and inserting in lieu thereof:

> "A base offense level of 13 is provided for those offenses where the defendant either structured the transaction to evade reporting requirements, made false statements to conceal or disguise the activity, or reasonably should have believed that the funds were criminally derived property. A lower alternative base offense level of 5 is provided in all other cases. The Commission anticipates that such cases will involve simple recordkeeping or other more minor technical violations of the regulatory scheme governing certain monetary transactions committed by defendants who reasonably believe that the funds at issue emanated from legitimate sources.
>
> Where the defendant actually knew or believed that the funds were criminally derived property, subsection (b)(1) provides for a 5 level increase in the offense level.".

The Commentary to § 2S1.3 captioned "Background" is amended in the last paragraph by deleting "The dollar value of the the transactions not reported is an important sentencing factor, except in rare cases. It is an" and inserting in lieu thereof "Except in rare cases, the dollar value of the transactions not reported is an important".

The Commentary to § 2S1.3 captioned "Statutory Provisions" is amended by inserting "18 U.S.C. § 1005;" immediately following "Provisions".

Reason for Amendment: The purposes of this amendment are to clarify the guideline and commentary, to provide more complete statutory references, and to conform the format of the guideline to that used in other guidelines.

Effective Date: The effective date of this amendment is November 1, 1989.

219. **Amendment:** Section 2T1.1(a) is amended by deleting the last sentence as follows: "When more than one year is involved, the tax losses are to be added.".

The Commentary to § 2T1.1 captioned "Application Notes" is amended in Note 2 by deleting:

> "The court is to determine this amount as it would any other guideline factor.",

and inserting in lieu thereof:

> "Although the definition of tax loss corresponds to what is commonly called the 'criminal deficiency,' its amount is to be determined by the same rules applicable in determining any other sentencing factor.".

The Commentary to § 2T1.1 captioned "Application Notes" is amended in Note 3 by deleting:

> "Although the definition of tax loss corresponds to what is commonly called the

'criminal deficiency,' its amount is to be determined by the same rules applicable in determining any other sentencing factor. In accordance with the 'relevant conduct' approach adopted by the guidelines, tax losses resulting from more than one year are to be added whether or not the defendant is convicted of multiple counts.",

and inserting in lieu thereof:

"In determining the total tax loss attributable to the offense (see § 1B1.3(a)(2)), all conduct violating the tax laws should be considered as part of the same course of conduct or common scheme or plan unless the evidence demonstrates that the conduct is clearly unrelated. The following examples are illustrative of conduct that is part of the same course of conduct or common scheme or plan: (a) there is a continuing pattern of violations of the tax laws by the defendant; (b) the defendant uses a consistent method to evade or camouflage income, e.g., backdating documents or using off-shore accounts; (c) the violations involve the same or a related series of transactions; (d) the violation in each instance involves a false or inflated claim of a similar deduction or credit; and (e) the violation in each instance involves a failure to report or an understatement of a specific source of income, e.g., interest from savings accounts or income from a particular business activity. These examples are not intended to be exhaustive.".

Reason for Amendment: The purposes of this amendment are to clarify the determination of tax loss and to make this instruction consistent among §§ 2T1.1-2T1.3.

Effective Date: The effective date of this amendment is November 1, 1989.

220. **Amendment:** Section 2T1.1(a) is amended by deleting ", including interest to the date of filing an indictment or information" immediately following "attempted to evade".

The Commentary to § 2T1.1 captioned "Application Notes" is amended in Note 2 in the first sentence by deleting ", plus interest to the date of the filing of an indictment or information" immediately following "attempted to evade", and in the second sentence by inserting "interest or" immediately before "penalties.".

Reason for Amendment: The purpose of this amendment is to simplify the application of the guideline by deleting interest from the calculation of tax loss.

Effective Date: The effective date of this amendment is November 1, 1989.

221. **Amendment:** Section 2T1.1(b)(1) is amended by deleting "(A)" immediately before "the defendant failed", by deleting ", or (B) the offense concealed or furthered criminal activity from which the defendant derived a substantial portion of his income" immediately following "criminal activity", by inserting "or to correctly identify the source of" immediately after "report", and by deleting "per" and inserting in lieu thereof "in any".

Reason for Amendment: The purposes of this amendment are to provide a more objective test for application of this enhancement, and to make clear that this enhancement applies if the defendant fails to report or disguises income exceeding $10,000 from criminal activity in any year.

Effective Date: The effective date of this amendment is November 1, 1989.

222. **Amendment:** The Commentary to § 2T1.1 captioned "Application Notes" is amended in Note 6 by deleting:

"Whether 'sophisticated means' were employed (§ 2T1.1(b)(2)) requires a subjective determination similar to that in § 2F1.1(b)(2).",

and inserting in lieu thereof:

"'Sophisticated means,' as used in § 2T1.1(b)(2), includes conduct that is more complex or demonstrates greater intricacy or planning than a routine tax-evasion case.".

Reason for Amendment: The purpose of this amendment is to clarify the commentary.

Effective Date: The effective date of this amendment is November 1, 1989.

223. **Amendment:** The Commentary to § 2T1.1 captioned "Background" is amended in the second paragraph by deleting "Tax Table" wherever it appears and inserting in lieu thereof in each instance "Sentencing Table".

    Reason for Amendment: The purpose of this amendment is to correct a clerical error.

    Effective Date: The effective date of this amendment is November 1, 1989.

224. **Amendment:** Section 2T1.2(b)(1) is amended by deleting "(A)" immediately before "the defendant failed", by deleting ", or (B) the offense concealed or furthered criminal activity from which the defendant derived a substantial portion of his income" immediately following "criminal activity", by inserting "or to correctly identify the source of" immediately after "report", and by deleting "per" and inserting in lieu thereof "in any".

    Reason for Amendment: The purposes of this amendment are to provide a more objective test for application of this enhancement, and to make clear that this enhancement applies if the defendant fails to report or disguises income exceeding $10,000 from criminal activity in any year.

    Effective Date: The effective date of this amendment is November 1, 1989.

225. **Amendment:** Section 2T1.2 is amended by inserting the following additional subsection:

    "(c)   Cross Reference

        (1)   If the defendant is convicted of a willful violation of 26 U.S.C. § 6050I, apply § 2S1.3 (Failure to Report Monetary Transactions) in lieu of this guideline.".

    The Commentary to § 2T1.2 captioned "Statutory Provision" is amended by inserting immediately before the period at the end "(other than a willful violation of 26 U.S.C. § 6050I)".

    Reason for Amendment: The purpose of this amendment is to reflect a revision of 26 U.S.C. § 6050I made by Section 7601 of the Anti-Drug Abuse Act of 1988.

    Effective Date: The effective date of this amendment is November 1, 1989.

226. **Amendment:** The Commentary to § 2T1.2 captioned "Application Note" is amended in Note 2 by deleting:

    "Whether 'sophisticated means' were employed (§ 2T1.2(b)(2)) requires a determination similar to that in § 2F1.1(b)(2).",

    and inserting in lieu thereof:

    "'Sophisticated means,' as used in § 2T1.2(b)(2), includes conduct that is more complex or demonstrates greater intricacy or planning than a routine tax-evasion case.".

Reason for Amendment: The purpose of this amendment is to clarify the commentary.

Effective Date: The effective date of this amendment is November 1, 1989.

227. **Amendment:** The Commentary to § 2T1.2 captioned "Application Note" is amended in the caption by deleting "Note" and inserting in lieu thereof "Notes", and by inserting the following additional note:

> "3. In determining the total tax loss attributable to the offense (see § 1B1.3(a)(2)), all conduct violating the tax laws should be considered as part of the same course of conduct or common scheme or plan unless the evidence demonstrates that the conduct is clearly unrelated. See Application Note 3 of the Commentary to § 2T1.1.".

Reason for Amendment: The purpose of this amendment is to clarify the determination of tax loss.

Effective Date: The effective date of this amendment is November 1, 1989.

228. **Amendment:** Section 2T1.3(b)(1) is amended by deleting "(A)" immediately before "the defendant failed", by deleting ", or (B) the offense concealed or furthered criminal activity from which the defendant derived a substantial portion of his income" immediately following "criminal activity", by inserting "or to correctly identify the source of" immediately after "report", and by deleting "per" and inserting in lieu thereof "in any".

Reason for Amendment: The purposes of this amendment are to provide a more objective test for application of this enhancement, and to make clear that this enhancement applies if the defendant fails to report or disguises income exceeding $10,000 from criminal activity in any year.

Effective Date: The effective date of this amendment is November 1, 1989.

229. **Amendment:** The Commentary to § 2T1.3 captioned "Application Notes" is amended in Note 2 by deleting:

> "Whether 'sophisticated means' were employed (§ 2T1.3(b)(2)) requires a determination similar to that in § 2F1.1(b)(2).",

and inserting in lieu thereof:

> "'Sophisticated means,' as used in § 2T1.3(b)(2), includes conduct that is more complex or demonstrates greater intricacy or planning than a routine tax-evasion case.".

Reason for Amendment: The purpose of this amendment is to clarify the commentary.

Effective Date: The effective date of this amendment is November 1, 1989.

230. **Amendment:** The Commentary to § 2T1.3 captioned "Application Notes" is amended by inserting the following additional note:

> "3. In determining the total tax loss attributable to the offense (see § 1B1.3(a)(2)), all conduct violating the tax laws should be considered as part of the

same course of conduct or common scheme or plan unless the evidence demonstrates that the conduct is clearly unrelated. See Application Note 3 of the Commentary to § 2T1.1.".

Reason for Amendment: The purpose of this amendment is to clarify the determination of tax loss.

Effective Date: The effective date of this amendment is November 1, 1989.

231. **Amendment:** The Commentary to § 2T1.4 captioned "Application Notes" is amended in Note 2 by deleting:

"Whether 'sophisticated means' were employed (§ 2T1.1(b)(2)) requires a determination similar to that in § 2F1.1(b)(2).",

and inserting in lieu thereof:

"'Sophisticated means,' as used in § 2T1.4(b)(2), includes conduct that is more complex or demonstrates greater intricacy or planning than a routine tax-evasion case.".

Reason for Amendment: The purpose of this amendment is to clarify the commentary.

Effective Date: The effective date of this amendment is November 1, 1989.

232. **Amendment:** Section 2T1.6(a) is amended by deleting ", plus interest" immediately following "paid over".

Reason for Amendment: The purpose of this amendment is to simplify the application of the guideline by deleting interest from the calculation of tax loss.

Effective Date: The effective date of this amendment is November 1, 1989.

233. **Amendment:** Section 2T1.9(b) is amended by deleting "either of the following adjustments" and inserting in lieu thereof "more than one".

Reason for Amendment: The purpose of this amendment is to correct a clerical error.

Effective Date: The effective date of this amendment is November 1, 1989.

234. **Amendment:** The Commentary to section 2T1.9 captioned "Application Notes" is amended by deleting:

"2. The minimum base offense level is 10. If a tax loss from the conspiracy can be established under either § 2T1.1 or § 2T1.3 (whichever applies to the underlying conduct), and that tax loss corresponds to a higher offense level in the Tax Table (§ 2T4.1), use that higher base offense level.

3. The specific offense characteristics are in addition to those specified in § 2T1.1 and § 2T1.3.

4. Because the offense is a conspiracy, adjustments from Chapter Three, Part B (Role in the Offense) usually will apply.",

and inserting in lieu thereof:

"2. The base offense level is the offense level (base offense level plus any ap-

– 105 –

plicable specific offense characteristics) from § 2T1.1 or § 2T1.3 (whichever is applicable to the underlying conduct), if that offense level is greater than 10. Otherwise, the base offense level is 10.

3. Specific offense characteristics from § 2T1.9(b) are to be applied to the base offense level determined under § 2T1.9(a)(1) or (2).".

Reason for Amendment: The purpose of this amendment is to clarify Application Notes 2 and 3. Application Note 4 (the content of which does not appear in any of the other guidelines covering conspiracy) is deleted as unnecessary.

Effective Date: The effective date of this amendment is November 1, 1989.

235. **Amendment:** The Commentary to § 2T3.1 captioned "Application Notes" is amended in Note 2 by inserting "if the increase in market value due to importation is not readily ascertainable" immediately following "United States".

Reason for Amendment: The purpose of this amendment is to clarify the commentary.

Effective Date: The effective date of this amendment is November 1, 1989.

236. **Amendment:** The Commentary to § 2T3.2 is amended by inserting at the end:

"Application Note:

1. Particular attention should be given to those items for which entry is prohibited, limited, or restricted. Especially when such items are harmful or protective quotas are in effect, the duties evaded on such items may not adequately reflect the harm to society or protected industries resulting from their importation. In such instances, the court should impose a sentence above the guideline. A sentence based upon an alternative measure of the 'duty' evaded, such as the increase in market value due to importation, or 25 percent of the items' fair market value in the United States if the increase in market value due to importation is not readily ascertainable, might be considered.".

Reason for Amendment: The purpose of this amendment is to clarify the application of the guideline by adding the text from Application Note 2 of the Commentary to § 2T3.1, which applies equally to this guideline section.

Effective Date: The effective date of this amendment is November 1, 1989.

237. **Amendment:** Section 2T4.1 is amended by deleting:

	"Tax Loss	Offense Level
(A)	less than $2,000	6
(B)	$2,000 - $5,000	7
(C)	$5,001 - $10,000	8
(D)	$10,001 - $20,000	9
(E)	$20,001 - $40,000	10
(F)	$40,001 - $80,000	11
(G)	$80,001 - $150,000	12

(H)	$150,001 - $300,000	13
(I)	$300,001 - $500,000	14
(J)	$500,001 - $1,000,000	15
(K)	$1,000,001 - $2,000,000	16
(L)	$2,000,001 - $5,000,000	17
(M)	more than $5,000,000	18",

and inserting in lieu thereof:

	"Tax Loss (Apply the Greatest)	Offense Level
(A)	$2,000 or less	6
(B)	More than $2,000	7
(C)	More than $5,000	8
(D)	More than $10,000	9
(E)	More than $20,000	10
(F)	More than $40,000	11
(G)	More than $70,000	12
(H)	More than $120,000	13
(I)	More than $200,000	14
(J)	More than $350,000	15
(K)	More than $500,000	16
(L)	More than $800,000	17
(M)	More than $1,500,000	18
(N)	More than $2,500,000	19
(O)	More than $5,000,000	20
(P)	More than $10,000,000	21
(Q)	More than $20,000,000	22
(R)	More than $40,000,000	23
(S)	More than $80,000,000	24.".

Reason for Amendment: The purposes of this amendment are to increase the offense levels for offenses with larger losses in order to provide additional deterrence and better reflect the seriousness of the conduct, and to eliminate minor gaps in the table.

Effective Date: The effective date of this amendment is November 1, 1989.

238. **Amendment:** Section 2X1.1(b)(1) is amended by deleting "or solicitation" immediately following "If an attempt".

Section 2X1.1(b) is amended by deleting:

"(3) If a solicitation, and the statute treats solicitation identically with the object of the offense, do not apply § 2X1.1(b)(1); i.e., the offense level for solicitation is the same as that for the object offense.",

and inserting in lieu thereof:

Amendment 238 APPENDIX C - VOLUME I November 1, 2013

"(3) (A) If a solicitation, decrease by 3 levels unless the person solicited to commit or aid the offense completed all the acts he believed necessary for successful completion of the object offense or the circumstances demonstrate that the person was about to complete all such acts but for apprehension or interruption by some similar event beyond such person's control.

(B) If the statute treats solicitation of the offense identically with the object offense, do not apply subdivision (A) above; i.e., the offense level for solicitation is the same as that for the object offense.".

Reason for Amendment: The current subsection (b)(1) does not clearly address how a solicitation is to be treated where the person solicited to commit the offense completes all the acts necessary for the successful completion of the offense. The purpose of this amendment is to clarify the treatment of such cases in a manner consistent with the treatment of attempts and conspiracies.

Effective Date: The effective date of this amendment is November 1, 1989.

239. **Amendment:** Section 2X1.1 is amended in the title by deleting "Not Covered by a Specific Guideline" and inserting in lieu thereof "(Not Covered by a Specific Offense Guideline)".

Section 2X1.1 is amended by inserting the following additional subsection:

"(c) Cross Reference

(1) When an attempt, solicitation, or conspiracy is expressly covered by another offense guideline section, apply that guideline section.".

The Commentary to § 2X1.1 captioned "Application Notes" is amended by deleting:

"1. Certain attempts, conspiracies, and solicitations are covered by specific guidelines (e.g., § 2A2.1 includes attempt, conspiracy, or solicitation to commit murder; § 2A3.1 includes attempted criminal sexual abuse; and § 2D1.4 includes attempts and conspiracies to commit controlled substance offenses). Section 2X1.1 applies only in the absence of a more specific guideline.",

and inserting in lieu thereof:

"1. Certain attempts, conspiracies, and solicitations are expressly covered by other offense guidelines.

Offense guidelines that expressly cover attempts include: § 2A2.1 (Assault With Intent to Commit Murder; Conspiracy or Solicitation to Commit Murder; Attempted Murder); § 2A3.1 (Criminal Sexual Abuse; Attempt or Assault with the Intent to Commit Criminal Sexual Abuse); § 2A3.2 (Criminal Sexual Abuse of a Minor (Statutory Rape) or Attempt to Commit Such Acts); § 2A3.3 (Criminal Sexual Abuse of a Ward or Attempt to Commit Such Acts); § 2A3.4 (Abusive Sexual Contact or Attempt to Commit Abusive Sexual Contact); § 2A4.2 (Demanding or Receiving Ransom Money); § 2A5.1 (Aircraft Piracy or Attempted Aircraft Piracy); § 2C1.1 (Offering,

Giving, Soliciting, or Receiving a Bribe; Extortion Under Color of Official Right); § 2C1.2 (Offering, Giving, Soliciting, or Receiving a Gratuity); § 2D1.4 (Attempts and Conspiracies); § 2E5.1 (Offering, Accepting, or Soliciting a Bribe or Gratuity Affecting the Operation of an Employee Welfare or Pension Benefit Plan); § 2N1.1 (Tampering or Attempting to Tamper Involving Risk of Death or Serious Injury); § 2Q1.4 (Tampering or Attempted Tampering with Public Water System).

Offense guidelines that expressly cover conspiracies include: § 2A2.1 (Assault With Intent to Commit Murder; Conspiracy or Solicitation to Commit Murder; Attempted Murder); § 2D1.4 (Attempts and Conspiracies); § 2H1.2 (Conspiracy to Interfere with Civil Rights); § 2T1.9 (Conspiracy to Impair, Impede or Defeat Tax).

Offense guidelines that expressly cover solicitations include: § 2A2.1 (Assault with Intent to Commit Murder; Conspiracy or Solicitation to Commit Murder; Attempted Murder); § 2C1.1 (Offering, Giving, Soliciting, or Receiving a Bribe; Extortion Under Color of Official Right); § 2C1.2 (Offering, Giving, Soliciting, or Receiving a Gratuity); § 2E5.1 (Offering, Accepting, or Soliciting a Bribe or Gratuity Affecting the Operation of an Employee Welfare or Pension Benefit Plan).".

Reason for Amendment: The purpose of this amendment is to clarify the guideline.

Effective Date: The effective date of this amendment is November 1, 1989.

240. **Amendment:** The Commentary to § 2X1.1 captioned "Application Notes" is amended by deleting:

> "4. If the defendant was convicted of conspiracy or solicitation and also for the completed offense, the conviction for the conspiracy or solicitation shall be imposed to run concurrently with the sentence for the object offense, except in cases where it is otherwise specifically provided for by the guidelines or by law. 28 U.S.C. § 994(l)(2).".

Reason for Amendment: The purpose of this amendment is to delete an application note that does not apply to any determination under this section. The circumstances which this application note addresses are covered under Chapter Three, Part D and Chapter Five, Part G.

Effective Date: The effective date of this amendment is November 1, 1989.

241. **Amendment:** The Commentary to § 2X1.1 captioned "Application Notes" is amended by inserting the following additional note:

> "4. In certain cases, the participants may have completed (or have been about to complete but for apprehension or interruption) all of the acts necessary for the successful completion of part, but not all, of the intended offense. In such cases, the offense level for the count (or group of closely-related multiple counts) is whichever of the following is greater: the offense level for the intended offense minus 3 levels (under § 2X1.1(b)(1), (b)(2), or (b)(3)(A)), or the offense level for the part of the offense for which the necessary acts were completed (or about to be completed but for apprehension or interruption). For example, where the intended offense was the theft of

$800,000 but the participants completed (or were about to complete) only the acts necessary to steal $30,000, the offense level is the offense level for the theft of $800,000 minus 3 levels, or the offense level for the theft of $30,000, whichever is greater.

In the case of multiple counts that are not closely-related counts, whether the 3-level reduction under § 2X1.1(b)(1) or (2) applies is determined separately for each count.".

Reason for Amendment: The purpose of this amendment is to clarify how the guidelines are to be applied to partially completed offenses.

Effective Date: The effective date of this amendment is November 1, 1989.

242. **Amendment:** The Commentary to § 2X1.1 captioned "Application Notes" is amended in the last sentence of Note 2 by deleting "intended" and inserting in lieu thereof "attempted".

Reason for Amendment: The purpose of this amendment is to clarify the commentary.

Effective Date: The effective date of this amendment is November 1, 1989.

243. **Amendment:** The Commentary to § 2X3.1 captioned "Application Notes" is amended in Note 1 by deleting:

"'Underlying offense' means the offense as to which the defendant was an accessory.",

and inserting in lieu thereof:

"'Underlying offense' means the offense as to which the defendant is convicted of being an accessory. Apply the base offense level plus any applicable specific offense characteristics that were known, or reasonably should have been known, by the defendant; see Application Note 1 of the Commentary to § 1B1.3 (Relevant Conduct).".

Reason for Amendment: The purpose of this amendment is to clarify the commentary.

Effective Date: The effective date of this amendment is November 1, 1989.

244. **Amendment:** The Commentary to § 2X4.1 captioned "Application Notes" is amended in Note 1 by deleting:

"'Underlying offense' means the offense as to which the misprision was committed.",

and inserting in lieu thereof:

"'Underlying offense' means the offense as to which the defendant is convicted of committing the misprision. Apply the base offense level plus any applicable specific offense characteristics that were known, or reasonably should have been known, by the defendant; see Application Note 1 of the Commentary to § 1B1.3 (Relevant Conduct).".

Reason for Amendment: The purpose of this amendment is to clarify the commentary.

Effective Date: The effective date of this amendment is November 1, 1989.

245. **Amendment:** Section 3A1.1 is amended by deleting "the victim" wherever it appears

and inserting in lieu thereof in each instance "a victim", and by inserting "otherwise" immediately before "particularly".

The Commentary to § 3A1.1 captioned Application Notes is amended in Note 1 by deleting:

"any offense where the victim's vulnerability played any part in the defendant's decision to commit the offense",

and inserting in lieu thereof:

"offenses where an unusually vulnerable victim is made a target of criminal activity by the defendant",

and by deleting:

"sold fraudulent securities to the general public and one of the purchasers",

and inserting in lieu thereof:

"sold fraudulent securities by mail to the general public and one of the victims".

Reason for Amendment: The purpose of the amendment is to clarify the guideline and commentary.

Effective Date: The effective date of this amendment is November 1, 1989.

246. **Amendment:** Section 3A1.2 is amended by deleting:

"any law-enforcement or corrections officer, any other official as defined in 18 U.S.C. § 1114, or a member of the immediate family thereof, and",

and inserting in lieu thereof:

"a law enforcement or corrections officer; a former law enforcement or corrections officer; an officer or employee included in 18 U.S.C. § 1114; a former officer or employee included in 18 U.S.C. § 1114; or a member of the immediate family of any of the above, and".

Reason for Amendment: The purpose of this amendment is to expand the coverage of this provision to reflect a statutory revision effected by Section 6487 of the Anti-Drug Abuse Act of 1988.

Effective Date: The effective date of this amendment is November 1, 1989.

247. **Amendment:** Section 3A1.2 is amended by deleting "If the victim" and inserting in lieu thereof:

"If--

(a) the victim",

and by deleting "crime was motivated by such status, increase by 3 levels." and inserting in lieu thereof:

"offense of conviction was motivated by such status; or

(b) during the course of the offense or immediate flight therefrom, the defendant or a person for whose conduct the defendant is otherwise accountable, knowing or having reasonable cause to believe that a person was a law enforcement or corrections officer, assaulted such officer in a manner creating a substantial risk of serious bodily injury,

increase by 3 levels.".

The Commentary to § 3A1.2 captioned "Application Notes" is amended by inserting the following additional notes:

"4. 'Motivated by such status' in subdivision (a) means that the offense of conviction was motivated by the fact that the victim was a law enforcement or corrections officer or other person covered under 18 U.S.C. § 1114, or a member of the immediate family thereof. This adjustment would not apply, for example, where both the defendant and victim were employed by the same government agency and the offense was motivated by a personal dispute.

5. Subdivision (b) applies in circumstances tantamount to aggravated assault against a law enforcement or corrections officer, committed in the course of, or in immediate flight following, another offense, such as bank robbery. While this subdivision may apply in connection with a variety of offenses that are not by nature targeted against official victims, its applicability is limited to assaultive conduct against law enforcement or corrections officers that is sufficiently serious to create at least a 'substantial risk of serious bodily injury' and that is proximate in time to the commission of the offense.

6. The phrase 'substantial risk of serious bodily injury' in subdivision (b) is a threshold level of harm that includes any more serious injury that was risked, as well as actual serious bodily injury (or more serious harm) if it occurs.".

Reason for Amendment: The purpose of the amendment is to set forth more clearly the categories of cases to which this adjustment is intended to apply.

Effective Date: The effective date of this amendment is November 1, 1989.

248. **Amendment:** The Commentary to § 3A1.2 captioned "Application Notes" is amended in Note 3 by inserting the following additional sentences at the end:

"In most cases, the offenses to which subdivision (a) will apply will be from Chapter Two, Part A (Offenses Against the Person). The only offense guideline in Chapter Two, Part A that specifically incorporates this factor is § 2A2.4 (Obstructing or Impeding Officers).".

Reason for Amendment: The purpose of this amendment is to clarify the application of the guideline.

Effective Date: The effective date of this amendment is November 1, 1989.

249. **Amendment:** Section 3A1.3 is amended by deleting "the victim of a crime" and inserting in lieu thereof "a victim".

The Commentary to § 3A1.3 captioned "Application Notes" is amended in Note 2 by deleting "the victim" and inserting in lieu thereof "a victim".

Reason for Amendment: The purpose of this amendment is to clarify the guideline.

Effective Date: The effective date of this amendment is November 1, 1989.

250. **Amendment:** The Commentary to § 3A1.3 captioned "Application Notes" is amended by inserting the following additional note:

> "3. If the restraint was sufficiently egregious, an upward departure may be warranted. See § 5K2.4 (Abduction or Unlawful Restraint).".

Reason for Amendment: The purpose of this amendment is to clarify the relationship between § 3A1.3 and § 5K2.4.

Effective Date: The effective date of this amendment is November 1, 1989.

251. **Amendment:** Section 3C1.1 is amended by deleting "from Chapter Two" immediately following "the offense level".

Reason for Amendment: The purpose of this amendment is to delete an incorrect reference.

Effective Date: The effective date of this amendment is November 1, 1989.

252. **Amendment:** The Commentary to § 3C1.1 captioned "Application Notes" is amended in Note 4 by deleting:

> ", except in determining the combined offense level as specified in Chapter Three, Part D (Multiple Counts). Under § 3D1.2(e), a count for obstruction will be grouped with the count for the underlying offense. Ordinarily, the offense level for that Group of Closely Related Counts will be the offense level for the underlying offense, as increased by the 2-level adjustment specified by this section. In some instances, however, the offense level for the obstruction offense may be higher, in which case that will be the offense level for the Group. See § 3D1.3(a). In cases in which a significant further obstruction occurred during the investigation or prosecution of an obstruction offense itself (one of the above listed offenses), an upward departure may be warranted (e.g., where a witness to an obstruction offense is threatened during the course of the prosecution for the obstruction offense).",

and inserting in lieu thereof:

> "to the offense level for that offense except where a significant further obstruction occurred during the investigation or prosecution of the obstruction offense itself (e.g., where the defendant threatened a witness during the course of the prosecution for the obstruction offense). Where the defendant is convicted both of the obstruction offense and the underlying offense, the count for the obstruction offense will be grouped with the count for the underlying offense under subsection (c) of § 3D1.2 (Groups of Closely-Related Counts). The offense level for that Group of Closely-Related Counts will be the offense level for the underlying offense increased by the 2-level adjustment specified by this section, or the offense level for the obstruction offense, whichever is greater.".

Reason for Amendment: The purpose of this amendment is to resolve an inconsistency between the commentary in this section and the Commentaries in Chapter Two, Part J.

Effective Date: The effective date of this amendment is November 1, 1989.

253. **Amendment:** Section 3D1.2(b)(3) is amended by deleting "§ 994(u)" and inserting in lieu thereof "§ 994(v)".

Amendment 253 APPENDIX C - VOLUME I November 1, 2013

Section 3D1.2(d) is amended in the second paragraph by deleting ", 2D1.3", and in the third paragraph by deleting ", 2G3.2" and ", 2P1.4".

Reason for Amendment: The purposes of this amendment are to correct an erroneous reference, and to delete references to two guidelines covering petty offenses that have been deleted and to a guideline that has been deleted by consolidation with another guideline.

Effective Date: The effective date of this amendment is November 1, 1989.

254. **Amendment:** The Commentary to § 3D1.2 captioned "Application Notes" is amended in Note 3 by deleting "(6)", "(7)", and "(8)" and inserting in lieu thereof "(5)", "(6)", and "(7)" respectively.

Reason for Amendment: The purpose of this amendment is to correct a clerical error.

Effective Date: The effective date of this amendment is November 1, 1989.

255. **Amendment:** The Commentary to § 3D1.2 captioned "Application Notes" is amended in Note 9 by inserting immediately following the second sentence: "See § 1B1.2(d) and accompanying commentary.".

Reason for Amendment: The purpose of this amendment is to cross reference the newly created guideline subsection dealing with a multiple object conspiracy.

Effective Date: The effective date of this amendment is November 1, 1989.

256. **Amendment:** The Commentary to § 3D1.2 captioned "Background" is amended in the second paragraph by deleting:

> "In general, counts are grouped together only when they involve both the same victim (or societal harm in 'victimless' offenses) and the same or contemporaneous transactions, except as provided in § 3D1.2(c) or (d).",

and inserting in lieu thereof:

> "Counts involving different victims (or societal harms in the case of 'victimless' crimes) are grouped together only as provided in subsection (c) or (d).".

Reason for Amendment: The purpose of this amendment is to clarify the commentary.

Effective Date: The effective date of this amendment is November 1, 1989.

257. **Amendment:** Section 3D1.3(b) is amended in the second sentence by deleting "varying" immediately following "involve", and by inserting "of the same general type to which different guidelines apply (e.g., theft and fraud)" immediately following "offenses".

Reason for Amendment: The purpose of this amendment is to enhance the clarity of the guideline.

Effective Date: The effective date of this amendment is November 1, 1989.

258. **Amendment:** The Commentary to § 3E1.1 captioned "Application Notes" is amended by deleting:

> "4. An adjustment under this section is not warranted where a defendant perjures himself, suborns perjury, or otherwise obstructs the trial or the administration of justice (see § 3C1.1), regardless of other factors.",

and inserting in lieu thereof:

> "4. Conduct resulting in an enhancement under § 3C1.1 (Willfully Obstructing or Impeding Proceedings) ordinarily indicates that the defendant has not accepted responsibility for his criminal conduct. There may, however, be extraordinary cases in which adjustments under both §§ 3C1.1 and 3E1.1 may apply.".

Reason for Amendment: The purposes of this amendment are to provide for extraordinary cases in which adjustments under both § 3C1.1 and § 3E1.1 are appropriate, and to clarify the reference to obstructive conduct.

Effective Date: The effective date of this amendment is November 1, 1989.

259. **Amendment:** Section 4A1.1(e) is amended by inserting "or while in imprisonment or escape status on such a sentence" immediately before the period at the end of the first sentence.

The Commentary to § 4A1.1 captioned "Application Notes" is amended in the second sentence of Note 5 by deleting "still in confinement" and inserting in lieu thereof "in imprisonment or escape status".

Reason for Amendment: The purpose of this amendment is to clarify that subsection (e) applies to defendants who are still in confinement status at the time of the instant offense (e.g., a defendant who commits the instant offense while in prison or on escape status).

Effective Date: The effective date of this amendment is November 1, 1989.

260. **Amendment:** The Commentary to § 4A1.1 captioned "Application Notes" is amended in Note 4 by inserting the following additional sentence at the end: "For the purposes of this item, a 'criminal justice sentence' means a sentence countable under § 4A1.2 (Definitions and Instructions for Computing Criminal History).".

Reason for Amendment: The purpose of this amendment is to clarify the application of the guideline.

Effective Date: The effective date of this amendment is November 1, 1989.

261. **Amendment:** The Commentary to § 4A1.1 captioned "Background" is amended in the third paragraph by inserting "a" immediately before "criminal", and by deleting "control" and inserting in lieu thereof "sentence".

Reason for Amendment: The purpose of this amendment is to conform the commentary to the guideline.

Effective Date: The effective date of this amendment is November 1, 1989.

262. **Amendment:** Section 4A1.2(e)(1) is amended by inserting ", whenever imposed," immediately before "that resulted", and by deleting "defendant's incarceration" and inserting in lieu thereof "defendant being incarcerated".

Reason for Amendment: The purpose of this amendment is to clarify that "resulted in the defendant's incarceration" applies to any part of the defendant's imprisonment and not only to the commencement of the defendant's imprisonment.

Effective Date: The effective date of this amendment is November 1, 1989.

Amendment 263 APPENDIX C - VOLUME I November 1, 2013

263. Amendment: Section 4A1.2(e) is amended by inserting the following additional subdivision:

"(4) The applicable time period for certain sentences resulting from offenses committed prior to age eighteen is governed by § 4A1.2(d)(2).".

Reason for Amendment: The purpose of this amendment is to clarify the relationship between § 4A1.2(d)(2) and (e).

Effective Date: The effective date of this amendment is November 1, 1989.

264. Amendment: Section 4A1.2(f) is amended by inserting ", or a plea of nolo contendere," immediately following "admission of guilt".

Reason for Amendment: The purpose of this amendment is to clarify that a plea of nolo contendere is equivalent to a finding of guilt for the purpose of § 4A1.2(f).

Effective Date: The effective date of this amendment is November 1, 1989.

265. Amendment: The Commentary to § 4A1.2 captioned "Application Notes" is amended in Note 8 by deleting "4A1.2(e)" and inserting in lieu thereof "4A1.2(d)(2) and (e)", and by inserting immediately following the first sentence:

"As used in § 4A1.2(d)(2) and (e), the term 'commencement of the instant offense' includes any relevant conduct. See § 1B1.3 (Relevant Conduct).".

Reason for Amendment: The purposes of this amendment are to correct a clerical error by inserting a reference to § 4A1.2(d)(2), and to clarify that "commencement of the instant offense" includes any relevant conduct.

Effective Date: The effective date of this amendment is November 1, 1989.

266. Amendment: Section 4B1.1 is amended by deleting "Offense Level" and inserting in lieu thereof "Offense Level*", and by inserting at the end:

"*If an adjustment from § 3E1.1 (Acceptance of Responsibility) applies, decrease the offense level by 2 levels.".

Reason for Amendment: The purpose of this amendment is to authorize the application of § 3E1.1 (Acceptance of Responsibility) to the determination of the offense level under this section to provide an incentive for the acceptance of responsibility by defendants subject to the career offender provision.

Effective Date: The effective date of this amendment is November 1, 1989.

267. Amendment: The Commentary to § 4B1.1 captioned "Application Note" is amended in Note 1 by deleting "felony conviction" and inserting in lieu thereof "two prior felony convictions".

The Commentary to § 4B1.1 captioned "Application Note" is amended by inserting the following additional note:

"2. 'Offense Statutory Maximum' refers to the maximum term of imprisonment authorized for the offense of conviction that is a crime of violence or controlled substance offense. If more than one count of conviction is of a crime of violence or controlled substance offense, use the maximum authorized term of imprisonment for the count that authorizes the greatest maximum term of imprisonment.",

and in the caption by deleting "Note" and inserting in lieu thereof "Notes".

The Commentary to § 4B1.1 captioned "Background" is amended by deleting:

"128 Cong. Rec. 12792, 97th Cong., 2d Sess. (1982) ('Career Criminals' amendment No. 13 by Senator Kennedy), 12796 (explanation of amendment), and 12798 (remarks by Senator Kennedy)",

and inserting in lieu thereof:

"128 Cong. Rec. 26, 511-12 (1982) (text of 'Career Criminals' amendment by Senator Kennedy), 26, 515 (brief summary of amendment), 26, 517-18 (statement of Senator Kennedy)".

Reason for Amendment: The purposes of this amendment are to clarify the operation of the guideline and to provide a citation to the more readily available edition of the Congressional Record.

Effective Date: The effective date of this amendment is November 1, 1989.

268. **Amendment:** Section 4B1.2(1) is amended by deleting "as used in this provision is defined under 18 U.S.C. § 16" and inserting in lieu thereof:

"means any offense under federal or state law punishable by imprisonment for a term exceeding one year that --

(i) has as an element the use, attempted use, or threatened use of physical force against the person of another, or

(ii) is burglary of a dwelling, arson, or extortion, involves use of explosives, or otherwise involves conduct that presents a serious potential risk of physical injury to another".

Section 4B1.2(2) is amended by deleting "as used in this provision" immediately before "means", and by deleting "identified in 21 U.S.C. §§ 841, 845(b), 856, 952(a), 955, 955(a), 959; and similar offenses" and inserting in lieu thereof:

"under a federal or state law prohibiting the manufacture, import, export, or distribution of a controlled substance (or a counterfeit substance) or the possession of a controlled substance (or a counterfeit substance) with intent to manufacture, import, export, or distribute".

The Commentary to § 4B1.2 captioned "Application Notes" is amended by deleting:

"1.   'Crime of violence' is defined in 18 U.S.C. § 16 to mean an offense that has as an element the use, attempted use, or threatened use of physical force against the person or property of another, or any other offense that is a felony and that by its nature involves a substantial risk that physical force against the person or property of another may be used in committing the offense. The Commission interprets this as follows: murder, manslaughter, kidnapping, aggravated assault, extortionate extension of credit, forcible sex offenses, arson, or robbery are covered by this provision. Other offenses are

Amendment 268

covered only if the conduct for which the defendant was specifically convicted meets the above definition. For example, conviction for an escape accomplished by force or threat of injury would be covered; conviction for an escape by stealth would not be covered. Conviction for burglary of a dwelling would be covered; conviction for burglary of other structures would not be covered.

2. 'Controlled substance offense' includes any federal or state offense that is substantially similar to any of those listed in subsection (2) of the guideline. These offenses include manufacturing, importing, distributing, dispensing, or possessing with intent to manufacture, import, distribute, or dispense, a controlled substance (or a counterfeit substance). This definition also includes aiding and abetting, conspiring, or attempting to commit such offenses, and other offenses that are substantially equivalent to the offenses listed.",

and inserting in lieu thereof:

"1. The terms 'crime of violence' and 'controlled substance offense' include the offenses of aiding and abetting, conspiring, and attempting to commit such offenses.

2. 'Crime of violence' includes murder, manslaughter, kidnapping, aggravated assault, forcible sex offenses, robbery, arson, extortion, extortionate extension of credit, and burglary of a dwelling. Other offenses are included where (A) that offense has as an element the use attempted use, or threatened use, of physical force against the person of another, or (B) the conduct set forth in the count of which the defendant was convicted involved use of explosives or, by its nature, presented a serious potential risk of physical injury to another.".

The caption of § 4B1.2 is amended by deleting "Definitions" and inserting in lieu thereof "Definitions of Terms Used in Section 4B1.1".

The Commentary to § 4B1.2 captioned "Application Notes" is amended in Note 4 by deleting "§ 4A1.2(e) (Applicable Time Period), § 4A1.2(h) (Foreign Sentences), and § 4A1.2(j) (Expunged Convictions)" and inserting in lieu thereof "§ 4A1.2 (Definitions and Instructions for Computing Criminal History)", and by deleting the last sentence as follows: "Also applicable is the Commentary to § 4A1.2 pertaining to invalid convictions.".

Reason for Amendment: The purpose of this amendment is to clarify the definitions of crime of violence and controlled substance offense used in this guideline. The definition of crime of violence used in this amendment is derived from 18 U.S.C. § 924(e). In addition, the amendment clarifies that all pertinent definitions and instructions in § 4A1.2 apply to this section.

Effective Date: The effective date of this amendment is November 1, 1989.

269. **Amendment:** Section 4B1.3 is amended by deleting "from which he derived a substantial portion of his income" and inserting in lieu thereof "engaged in as a livelihood".

The Commentary to § 4B1.3 captioned "Application Note" is amended by deleting "Note" and inserting in lieu thereof "Notes", and by inserting the following additional note:

"2. 'Engaged in as a livelihood' means that (1) the defendant derived income from the pattern of criminal conduct that in any twelve-month period exceeded 2,000 times the then existing hourly minimum wage under federal law (currently 2,000 times the hourly minimum wage under federal law is $6,700); and (2) the totality of circumstances shows that such criminal conduct was the defendant's primary occupation in that twelve-month period (e.g., the defendant engaged in criminal conduct rather than regular, legitimate employment; or the defendant's legitimate employment was merely a front for his criminal conduct).".

The Commentary to § 4B1.3 captioned "Application Notes" is amended in Note 1 by deleting the last sentence as follows: "This guideline is not intended to apply to minor offenses.".

The Commentary to § 4B1.3 captioned "Background" is amended by deleting "proportion" and inserting in lieu thereof "portion".

Reason for Amendment: The purpose of this amendment is to provide a better definition of the intended scope of this enhancement. Compare, for example, United States v. Kerr, 686 F. Supp. 1174 (W.D. Penn. 1988) with United States v. Rivera, 694 F. Supp. 1105 (S.D.N.Y. 1988). The first prong of the definition in application Note 2 above is derived from former 18 U.S.C. § 3575, the provision from which the statutory instruction underlying this guideline (28 U.S.C. § 994 (i)(2)) was itself derived.

Effective Date: The effective date of this amendment is November 1, 1989.

270. **Amendment:** Chapter Five, Part A, is amended in the Sentencing Table by deleting "0-1, 0-2, 0-3, 0-4, and 0-5" wherever it appears, and inserting in each instance "0-6".

Chapter Five, Part A, is amended in the Sentencing Table by inserting "(in months of imprisonment)" immediately under the title "Sentencing Table", by inserting "(Criminal History Points)" immediately following the caption "Criminal History Category", and by enclosing in parentheses each of the six sets of criminal history points displayed under that caption.

Reason for Amendment: This amendment provides that the maximum of the guideline range is six months wherever the minimum of the guideline range is zero months. The court has discretion to impose a sentence of up to 6 months imprisonment for a Class B misdemeanor (Class B or C misdemeanors and infractions are not covered by the guidelines; see § 1B1.9). It appears anomalous that the Commission guidelines allow less discretion for certain felonies and Class A misdemeanors. In fact, in certain cases, a plea to a reduced charge of a Class B misdemeanor could result in a higher potential sentence because the sentence for the felony or Class A misdemeanor might be restricted to less than 6 months by the guidelines. This can happen when the Sentencing Table provides a guideline range of 0-1 month, 0-2 months, 0-3, 0-4, or 0-5 months. These very narrow ranges are not required by statute, which allows a 6 month guideline range in such cases. This anomaly is removed by amending the guideline table to provide that whenever the lower limit of the guideline range is 0 months, the upper limit of the guideline range is six months.

In addition, this amendment makes minor editorial improvements to the title and caption of the Sentencing Table.

Effective Date: The effective date of this amendment is November 1, 1989.

271. **Amendment:** Section 5B1.4(b)(20) is amended by inserting ", but only as a substitute

Amendment 271   APPENDIX C - VOLUME I   November 1, 2013

for imprisonment" immediately following "release".

Section 5C2.1(c)(2) is amended by deleting "or community confinement" and inserting in lieu thereof ", community confinement, or home detention".

Section 5C2.1(c)(3) is amended by inserting "or home detention" immediately following "community confinement".

Section 5C2.1(d)(2) is amended by inserting "or home detention" immediately following "community confinement".

Section 5C2.1(e) is amended by inserting the following additional subdivision:

"(3)   One day of home detention for one day of imprisonment.",

and by deleting the period at the end of subsection (e)(2) and inserting a semicolon in lieu thereof.

The Commentary to § 5C2.1 captioned "Application Notes" is amended in the first sentence of the second subparagraph of Note 3 by deleting "intermittent confinement or community confinement, or combination of intermittent and community confinement," and inserting in lieu thereof "intermittent confinement, community confinement, or home detention, or combination of intermittent confinement, community confinement, and home detention,".

The Commentary to § 5C2.1 captioned "Application Notes" is amended in the second sentence of the second subparagraph of Note 3 by deleting "intermittent or community confinement" and inserting in lieu thereof "intermittent confinement, community confinement, or home detention".

The Commentary to § 5C2.1 captioned "Application Notes" is amended in the third subparagraph of Note 3 by inserting "or home detention" immediately following "community confinement", wherever the latter appears.

The Commentary to § 5C2.1 captioned "Application Notes" is amended in the last paragraph of Note 3 by inserting "or home detention" immediately following "community confinement", wherever the latter appears.

The Commentary to § 5C2.1 captioned "Application Notes" is amended in Note 4 by inserting "or home detention" immediately following "community confinement", wherever the latter appears.

The Commentary to § 5C2.1 captioned "Application Notes" is amended in Note 5 by deleting the last sentence as follows: "Home detention may not be substituted for imprisonment.".

Section 5F5.2 is amended by inserting ", but only as a substitute for imprisonment" immediately following "release".

The Commentary to § 5F5.2 captioned "Application Notes" is amended in Note 1 by deleting:

"'Home detention' means a program of confinement and supervision that restricts the defendant to his place of residence continuously, or during specified hours, enforced by appropriate means of surveillance by the probation office. The judge may also impose other conditions of probation or supervised release appropriate to effectuate home detention. If the confinement is only during specified hours, the defendant shall engage exclusively in gainful employment, community service or treatment during the nonresidential hours.",

and inserting in lieu thereof:

"'Home detention' means a program of confinement and supervision that restricts the defendant to his place of residence continuously, except for authorized absences, enforced by appropriate means of surveillance by the probation office. When an order of home detention is imposed, the defendant is required to be in his place of residence at all times except for approved absences for gainful employment, community service, religious services, medical care, educational or training programs, and such other times as may be specifically authorized. Electronic monitoring is an appropriate means of surveillance and ordinarily should be used in connection with home detention. However, alternative means of surveillance may be used so long as they are as effective as electronic monitoring.".

The Commentary to § 5F5.2 captioned "Application Notes" is amended in Note 2 by deleting:

"Home detention generally should not be imposed for a period in excess of six months. However, a longer term may be appropriate for disabled, elderly or extremely ill defendants who would otherwise be imprisoned.",

and inserting in lieu thereof:

"The court may impose other conditions of probation or supervised release appropriate to effectuate home detention. If the court concludes that the amenities available in the residence of a defendant would cause home detention not to be sufficiently punitive, the court may limit the amenities available.".

The Commentary to § 5F5.2 captioned "Application Notes" is amended by inserting the following additional note:

"3. The defendant's place of residence, for purposes of home detention, need not be the place where the defendant previously resided. It may be any place of residence, so long as the owner of the residence (and any other person(s) from whom consent is necessary) agrees to any conditions that may be imposed by the court, e.g., conditions that a monitoring system be installed, that there will be no 'call forwarding' or 'call waiting' services, or that there will be no cordless telephones or answering machines.".

The Commentary to § 5F5.2 is amended by inserting at the end:

"Background: The Commission has concluded that the surveillance necessary for effective use of home detention ordinarily requires electronic monitoring. However, in some cases home detention may effectively be enforced without electronic monitoring, e.g., when the defendant is physically incapacitated, or where some other effective means of surveillance is available. Accordingly, the Commission has not required that electronic monitoring be a necessary condition for home detention. Nevertheless, before ordering home detention without electronic monitoring, the court should be confident that an alternative form of surveillance will be equally effective.

In the usual case, the Commission assumes that a condition requiring that the defendant seek and maintain gainful employment will be imposed when home detention is ordered.".

Amendment 271   APPENDIX C - VOLUME I   November 1, 2013

Section 5B1.1(a)(2) is amended by deleting "or community confinement" and inserting in lieu thereof ", community confinement, or home detention".

The Commentary to § 5B1.1 captioned "Application Notes" is amended in Note 1 by inserting ", home detention," immediately after "community confinement" wherever the latter appears.

Chapter One, Part A, section 4(d) is amended in the third sentence of the third paragraph by deleting "or intermittent confinement" and inserting in lieu thereof ", intermittent confinement, or home detention", and in the fourth sentence of the third paragraph by inserting "or home detention" immediately following "of community confinement".

Reason for Amendment: The purpose of this amendment is to conform the guidelines with Section 7305 of the Anti-Drug Abuse Act of 1988.

Effective Date: The effective date of this amendment is November 1, 1989.

272. **Amendment:** Section 5B1.4(b) is amended by inserting the following additional paragraph at the end:

> "(25) Curfew
>
> If the court concludes that restricting the defendant to his place of residence during evening and nighttime hours is necessary to provide just punishment for the offense, to protect the public from crimes that the defendant might commit during those hours, or to assist in the rehabilitation of the defendant, a condition of curfew is recommended. Electronic monitoring may be used as a means of surveillance to ensure compliance with a curfew order.".

Section 5B1.4 is amended by inserting the following commentary:

> "Commentary
>
> Application Note:
>
> 1. Home detention, as defined by § 5F5.2, may only be used as a substitute for imprisonment. See § 5C2.1 (Imposition of a Term of Imprisonment). Under home detention, the defendant, with specified exceptions, is restricted to his place of residence during all non-working hours. Curfew, which limits the defendant to his place of residence during evening and nighttime hours, is less restrictive than home detention and may be imposed as a condition of probation whether or not imprisonment could have been ordered.".

Reason for Amendment: The purposes of this amendment are to set forth the conditions under which curfew is a recommended condition of probation and clarify that electronic monitoring may be used as a means of surveillance in connection with an order of curfew.

Effective Date: The effective date of this amendment is November 1, 1989.

273. **Amendment:** Section 5B1.3(c) is amended by inserting immediately before the period at the end of the first sentence:

> ", unless the court finds on the record that extraordinary circumstances exist that would make such a condition plainly unreasonable, in which event the court shall impose one or more of the other conditions set forth under 18 U.S.C. § 3563(b)".

Reason for Amendment: The purpose of this amendment is to conform the guideline to a statutory revision.

Effective Date: The effective date of this amendment is November 1, 1989.

274. **Amendment:** Section 5B1.3(a) is amended by inserting at the end: "The court shall also impose a condition that the defendant not possess illegal controlled substances. 18 U.S.C. § 3563(a)(3).".

Section 5B1.3 is amended by inserting the following commentary:

"Commentary

A broader form of the condition required under 18 U.S.C. § 3563(a)(3) (pertaining to possession of controlled substances) is set forth as recommended condition (7) at § 5B1.4 (Recommended Conditions of Probation and Supervised Release).".

Reason for Amendment: The purpose of this amendment is to reference a mandatory condition of probation added by Section 7303 of the Anti-Drug Abuse Act of 1988.

Effective Date: The effective date of this amendment is November 1, 1989.

275. **Amendment:** Section 5C2.1(e) is amended by deleting "Thirty days" and inserting in lieu thereof "One day", by deleting "one month" wherever it appears and inserting in lieu thereof in each instance "one day", and by deleting "One month" and inserting in lieu thereof "One day".

Reason for Amendment: The purpose of this amendment is to enhance the internal consistency of the guidelines.

Effective Date: The effective date of this amendment is November 1, 1989.

276. **Amendment:** Section 5D3.3 is amended by deleting:

"(b) In order to fulfill any authorized purposes of sentencing, the court may impose other conditions reasonably related to (1) the nature and circumstances of the offense, and (2) the history and characteristics of the defendant. 18 U.S.C. § 3583(d).",

and inserting in lieu thereof:

"(b) The court may impose other conditions of supervised release, to the extent that such conditions are reasonably related to (1) the nature and circumstances of the offense and the history and characteristics of the defendant, and (2) the need for the sentence imposed to afford adequate deterrence to criminal conduct, to protect the public from further crimes of the defendant, and to provide the defendant with needed educational or vocational training, medical care, or other correctional treatment in the most effective manner. 18 U.S.C. §§ 3553(a)(2) and 3583(d).".

Reason for Amendment: The purposes of this amendment are to clarify the guideline and conform it to the statute as amended by Section 7108 of the Anti-Drug Abuse Act of 1988.

Effective Date: The effective date of this amendment is November 1, 1989.

277. **Amendment:** Section 5D3.3(a) is amended by inserting at the end: "The court shall also impose a condition that the defendant not possess illegal controlled substances. 18 U.S.C.

§ 3563(a)(3).".

The Commentary to § 5D3.3 captioned "Background" is amended by inserting the following additional sentence at the end:

"A broader form of the condition required under 18 U.S.C. § 3563(a)(3) (pertaining to possession of controlled substances) is set forth as recommended condition (7) at § 5B1.4 (Recommended Conditions of Probation and Supervised Release).".

Reason for Amendment: The purpose of this amendment is to reference a mandatory condition of supervised release added by Section 7303 of the Anti-Drug Abuse Act of 1988.

Effective Date: The effective date of this amendment is November 1, 1989.

278. **Amendment:** Section 5E4.1 is amended by inserting the following additional subsection:

"(c) With the consent of the victim of the offense, the court may order a defendant to perform services for the benefit of the victim in lieu of monetary restitution or in conjunction therewith. 18 U.S.C. § 3663(b)(4).".

Reason for Amendment: The purpose of this amendment is to insert language previously contained in § 5F5.3(b) where it had been erroneously placed.

Effective Date: The effective date of this amendment is November 1, 1989.

279. **Amendment:** The Commentary to § 5E4.1 captioned "Background" is amended in the first paragraph by deleting:

"See S. Rep. No. 225, 98th Cong., 1st Sess. 95-96.",

and inserting in lieu thereof:

"See 18 U.S.C. § 3563(b)(3) as amended by Section 7110 of Pub. L. No. 100-690 (1988).".

Reason for Amendment: This amendment replaces a reference to legislative history with a citation to a revised statute. Section 7110 of the Anti-Drug Abuse Act of 1988 confirms the authority of a sentencing court to impose restitution as a condition of probation. Previously, such authority was inferred from 18 U.S.C. § 3563(b)(20) (defendant may be ordered to "satisfy such other conditions as the court may impose") and from legislative history.

Effective Date: The effective date of this amendment is November 1, 1989.

280. **Amendment:** Section 5E4.2(a) is amended by deleting the second sentence as follows:

"If the guideline for the offense in Chapter Two prescribes a different rule for imposing fines, that rule takes precedence over this subsection.".

Section 5E4.2(b) is amended by inserting at the end:

"If, however, the guideline for the offense in Chapter Two provides a specific rule for imposing a fine, that rule takes precedence over subsection (c) of this section.".

Reason for Amendment: The purpose of this amendment is to clarify the guideline. The last sentence of current § 5E4.2(a) is in the wrong place. This amendment moves the content of this sentence to subsection (b) where it belongs.

Effective Date: The effective date of this amendment is November 1, 1989.

281. **Amendment:** Section 5E4.2(c)(3) is amended by deleting:

    | "1 | $ 25 | $ 250 |
    | 2-3 | $100 | $1,000 |
    | 4-5 | $250 | $2,500", |

    and inserting in lieu thereof:

    | "3 and below | $100 | $5,000 |
    | 4-5 | $250 | $5,000". |

    Reason for Amendment: The purpose of this amendment is to increase the maximum in the fine table for offense levels 5 and below to $5,000, an amount equal to the maximum fine authorized for a petty offense. Moreover, because the guidelines now cover only felonies and class A misdemeanors, the minimum fine guideline is increased to $100.

    Effective Date: The effective date of this amendment is November 1, 1989.

282. **Amendment:** The Commentary to Section 5E4.3 captioned "Background" is amended in the first paragraph by inserting at the end:

    "Under the Victims of Crime Act, as amended by Section 7085 of the Anti-Drug Abuse Act of 1988, the court is required to impose assessments in the following amounts with respect to offenses committed on or after November 18, 1988:

    Individuals:

    $5, if the defendant is an individual convicted of an infraction or a Class C misdemeanor;
    $10, if the defendant is an individual convicted of a Class B misdemeanor;
    $25, if the defendant is an individual convicted of a Class A misdemeanor; and
    $50, if the defendant is an individual convicted of a felony.

    Organizations:

    $50, if the defendant is an organization convicted of a Class B misdemeanor;
    $125, if the defendant is an organization convicted of a Class A misdemeanor; and
    $200, if the defendant is an organization convicted of a felony. 18 U.S.C. § 3013.",

    and in the second paragraph by deleting "The Act requires the court" and inserting in lieu thereof "With respect to offenses committed prior to November 18, 1988, the court is required".

    Reason for Amendment: The purpose of this amendment is to conform the commentary to the statute as amended by Section 7085 of the Anti-Drug Abuse Act of 1988.

    Effective Date: The effective date of this amendment is November 1, 1989.

Amendment 283

283. Amendment: Section 5F5.3(a) is amended by deleting "(a)", and by inserting "and sentenced to probation" immediately following "felony".

Section 5F5.3(b) is amended by deleting:

"(b) With the consent of the victim of the offense, the court may order a defendant to perform services for the benefit of the victim in lieu of monetary restitution. 18 U.S.C. § 3663(b)(4).".

Reason for Amendment: The purposes of this amendment are to correct an erroneous statement in § 5F5.3(a) and to delete § 5F5.3(b), which deals with restitution, and therefore should appear at § 5E4.1.

Effective Date: The effective date of this amendment is November 1, 1989.

284. Amendment: The Commentary to § 5F5.4 captioned "Background" is amended by deleting the third paragraph as follows:

"The legislative history indicates that, although the sanction was designed to provide actual notice to victims, a court might properly limit notice to only those victims who could be most readily identified, if to do otherwise would unduly prolong or complicate the sentencing process.".

Reason for Amendment: The purpose of this amendment is to delete an unnecessary statement that could be subject to misinterpretation.

Effective Date: The effective date of this amendment is November 1, 1989.

285. Amendment: Section 5F5.5(a) is amended by deleting:

"(2) there is a risk that, absent such restriction, the defendant will continue to engage in unlawful conduct similar to that for which the defendant was convicted; and

(3) imposition of such a restriction is reasonably necessary to protect the public.",

and inserting in lieu thereof:

"(2) imposition of such a restriction is reasonably necessary to protect the public because there is reason to believe that, absent such restriction, the defendant will continue to engage in unlawful conduct similar to that for which the defendant was convicted.",

and by inserting "and" at the end of subsection (a)(1).

Reason for Amendment: The purpose of this amendment is to clarify the guideline.

Effective Date: The effective date of this amendment is November 1, 1989.

286. Amendment: Chapter Five, Part G is amended by deleting § 5G1.1 in its entirety as follows:

"§ 5G1.1. Sentencing on a Single Count of Conviction

(a) If application of the guidelines results in a sentence above the maximum authorized by statute for the offense of conviction, the statutory maximum shall be the guideline sentence.

(b) If application of the guidelines results in a sentence below the minimum sentence required by statute, the statutory minimum shall be the guideline sentence.

(c) In any other case, the sentence imposed shall be the sentence as determined from application of the guidelines.

Commentary

If the statute requires imposition of a sentence other than that required by the guidelines, the statute shall control. The sentence imposed should be consistent with the statute but as close as possible to the guidelines.".

A replacement guideline with accompanying commentary is inserted as § 5G1.1 (Sentencing on a Single Count of Conviction).

Reason for Amendment: The purpose of this amendment is to clarify the guideline.

Effective Date: The effective date of this amendment is November 1, 1989.

287. **Amendment:** The Commentary to § 5G1.2 is amended in the second paragraph by deleting "any combination of concurrent and consecutive sentences that produces the total punishment may be imposed" and inserting in lieu thereof "consecutive sentences are to be imposed to the extent necessary to achieve the total punishment".

Reason for Amendment: The purpose of this amendment is to clarify the commentary.

Effective Date: The effective date of this amendment is November 1, 1989.

288. **Amendment:** The Commentary to § 5G1.2 is amended by inserting the following additional paragraph immediately after the first paragraph:

" This section applies to multiple counts of conviction (1) contained in the same indictment or information, or (2) contained in different indictments or informations for which sentences are to be imposed at the same time or in a consolidated proceeding.".

Reason for Amendment: The purpose of this amendment is to clarify that this guideline applies in the case of separate indictments that are consolidated for purposes of sentencing.

Effective Date: The effective date of this amendment is November 1, 1989.

289. **Amendment:** Chapter Five, Part G is amended by deleting § 5G1.3 in its entirety as follows:

"§ 5G1.3. Convictions on Counts Related to Unexpired Sentences

If at the time of sentencing, the defendant is already serving one or more unexpired sentences, then the sentences for the instant offense(s) shall run consecutively to such unexpired sentences, unless one or more of the instant offenses(s) arose out of the same transactions or occurrences as the unexpired sentences. In the latter case, such instant sentences and the unexpired sentences shall run concurrently, except to the extent otherwise required by law.

Commentary

This section reflects the statutory presumption that sentences imposed at different times ordinarily run consecutively. See 18 U.S.C. § 3584(a). This presumption does

Amendment 289   APPENDIX C - VOLUME I   November 1, 2013

not apply when the new counts arise out of the same transaction or occurrence as a prior conviction.

Departure would be warranted when independent prosecutions produce anomalous results that circumvent or defeat the intent of the guidelines.".

A replacement guideline with accompanying commentary is inserted as § 5G1.3 (Imposition of a Sentence on a Defendant Serving an Unexpired Term of Imprisonment).

Reason for Amendment: The purpose of this amendment is to specify the circumstances in which a consecutive sentence is required by the guidelines.

Effective Date: The effective date of this amendment is November 1, 1989.

290. **Amendment:** Section 5K1.1 is amended by deleting "made a good faith effort to provide" and inserting in lieu thereof "provided".

Section 5K1.1(a) is amended in the first sentence by deleting "conduct" immediately following "of the following".

Reason for Amendment: The purpose of this amendment is to clarify the Commission's intent that departures under this policy statement be based upon the provision of substantial assistance. The existing policy statement could be interpreted as requiring only a willingness to provide such assistance. The amendment also makes an editorial correction.

Effective Date: The effective date of this amendment is November 1, 1989.

291. **Amendment:** The Commentary to § 5K1.2 is deleted in its entirety as follows:

"Commentary

Background: The Commission considered and rejected the use of a defendant's refusal to assist authorities as an aggravating sentencing factor. Refusal to assist authorities based upon continued involvement in criminal activities and association with accomplices may be considered, however, in evaluating a defendant's sincerity in claiming acceptance of responsibility.".

Reason for Amendment: The purpose of this amendment is to delete unnecessary commentary containing an unclear example.

Effective Date: The effective date of this amendment is November 1, 1989.

292. **Amendment:** Chapter Five, Part K, Subpart 2, is amended by inserting an additional policy statement as § 5K2.15 (Terrorism (Policy Statement)).

Reason for Amendment: The purpose of this amendment is to add a specific policy statement concerning consideration of an upward departure when the offense is committed for a terroristic purpose. This amendment does not make a substantive change. Such conduct is currently included in the broader policy statement at § 5K2.9 (Criminal Purpose) and other policy statements. See United States v. Kikumura, 706 F. Supp. 331 (D. N.J. 1989).

Effective Date: The effective date of this amendment is November 1, 1989.

293. **Amendment:** Section 6A1.1 is amended in the title by inserting at the end "(Policy Statement)".

Reason for Amendment: The purpose of this amendment is to designate § 6A1.1 as a policy statement. Designation of this section as a policy statement is more consistent with the nature of the subject matter.

Effective Date: The effective date of this amendment is November 1, 1989.

294. **Amendment:** Section 6A1.3 is amended in the title by inserting at the end "(Policy Statement)".

    Reason for Amendment: The purpose of this amendment is to designate § 6A1.3 as a policy statement. Designation of this section as a policy statement is more consistent with the nature of the subject matter.

    Effective Date: The effective date of this amendment is November 1, 1989.

295. **Amendment:** The Commentary to § 6B1.2 is amended in the second paragraph by deleting "and does not undermine the basic purposes of sentencing.", and inserting in lieu thereof "(i.e., that such departure is authorized by 18 U.S.C. § 3553(b)). See generally Chapter 1, Part A (4)(b)(Departures).".

    Reason for Amendment: The purpose of this amendment is to clarify the commentary.

    Effective Date: The effective date of this amendment is November 1, 1989.

296. **Amendment:** Appendix A (Statutory Index) is amended in the second sentence of the "Introduction" by deleting "conduct" and inserting in lieu thereof "nature of the offense conduct charged in the count", and by deleting "select" and inserting in lieu thereof "use"; and in the third sentence of the "Introduction" by deleting "the court is to apply" and inserting in lieu thereof "use", by deleting "which is" immediately before "most applicable", and by deleting "conduct for" and inserting in lieu thereof "nature of the offense conduct charged in the count of".

    Reason for Amendment: The purpose of this amendment is to clarify the operation of the Statutory Index in relation to §§ 1B1.1 and 1B1.2(a).

    Effective Date: The effective date of this amendment is November 1, 1989.

297. **Amendment:** Appendix A is amended by inserting the following additional paragraph at the end of the Introduction:

    "   The guidelines do not apply to any count of conviction that is a Class B or C misdemeanor or an infraction. (See § 1B1.9.)".

    Appendix A is amended by deleting:

"7 U.S.C. § 52	2N2.1",
"7 U.S.C. § 60	2N2.1",
"10 U.S.C. § 847	2J1.1, 2J1.5",
"16 U.S.C. § 198c	2B1.1, 2B1.3, 2B2.3",
"16 U.S.C. § 204c	2B1.1, 2B1.3",
"16 U.S.C. § 604	2B1.3",
"16 U.S.C. § 606	2B1.1, 2B1.3",
"16 U.S.C. § 668dd	2Q2.1",
"16 U.S.C. § 670j(a)(1)	2B2.3",

Amendment 297   APPENDIX C - VOLUME I   November 1, 2013

"16 U.S.C. § 676	2B2.3",
"16 U.S.C. § 682	2B2.3",
"16 U.S.C. § 683	2B2.3",
"16 U.S.C. § 685	2B2.3",
"16 U.S.C. § 689b	2B2.3",
"16 U.S.C. § 692a	2B2.3",
"16 U.S.C. § 694a	2B2.3",
"18 U.S.C. § 113(d)	2A2.3",
"18 U.S.C. § 113(e)	2A2.3",
"18 U.S.C. § 290	2F1.1",
"18 U.S.C. § 402	2J1.1",
"18 U.S.C. § 437	2C1.3",
"18 U.S.C. § 1164	2B1.3",
"18 U.S.C. § 1165	2B2.3",
"18 U.S.C. § 1382	2B2.3",
"18 U.S.C. § 1504	2J1.2",
"18 U.S.C. § 1726	2F1.1",
"18 U.S.C. § 1752	2B2.3",
"18 U.S.C. § 1793	2P1.4",
"18 U.S.C. § 1856	2B1.3",
"18 U.S.C. § 1863	2B2.3",
"40 U.S.C. § 193e	2B1.1, 2B1.3",
"42 U.S.C. § 1995	2J1.1",
"42 U.S.C. § 2000h	2J1.1",
"42 U.S.C. § 4912	2Q1.3".

Reason for Amendment: The purposes of this amendment are to clarify that the guidelines do not apply to any count of conviction that is a Class B or C misdemeanor or an infraction, and to delete references to statutes that apply solely to such offenses.

Effective Date: The effective date of this amendment is November 1, 1989.

298. **Amendment:**   Appendix A is amended by deleting:

"18 U.S.C. § 1512   2J1.2",

and inserting in lieu thereof:

"18 U.S.C. § 1512(a)	2A1.1, 2A1.2, 2A2.1
18 U.S.C. § 1512(b)	2A2.2, 2J1.2
18 U.S.C. § 1512(c)	2J1.2",

and by deleting:

"21 U.S.C. § 848   2D1.5",

and inserting in lieu thereof:

"21 U.S.C. § 848(a)	2D1.5
21 U.S.C. § 848(b)	2D1.5
21 U.S.C. § 848(e)	2A1.1".

Appendix A is amended by inserting the following statutes in the appropriate place according to statutory title and section number:

"18 U.S.C. § 247	2H1.3",
"18 U.S.C. § 709	2F1.1",
"18 U.S.C. § 930	2K2.5",
"18 U.S.C. § 1460	2G3.1",
"18 U.S.C. § 1466	2G3.1",
"18 U.S.C. § 1516	2J1.2",
"18 U.S.C. § 1716C	2B5.2",
"18 U.S.C. § 1958	2A2.1, 2E1.4",
"18 U.S.C. § 1959	2E1.3",
"42 U.S.C. § 7270b	2B2.3",
"43 U.S.C. § 1733(a)	
(43 C.F.R. 4140.1(b)(1)(i))	2B2.3",
"49 U.S.C. § 1472(c)	2A5.2".

Appendix A is amended on the line beginning "18 U.S.C. § 371" by inserting "2A2.1, 2D1.4," immediately before "2T1.9".

Appendix A is amended in the line beginning "18 U.S.C. § 1005" by inserting ", 2S1.3" immediately following "2F1.1".

Appendix A is amended in the line beginning "18 U.S.C. § 1028" by inserting ", 2L1.2, 2L2.1, 2L2.3" immediately following "2F1.1".

Appendix A is amended in the line beginning "26 U.S.C. § 7203" by inserting "2S1.3," immediately before "2T1.2".

Reason for Amendment: The purpose of this amendment is to make the statutory index more comprehensive.

Effective Date: The effective date of this amendment is November 1, 1989.

299. **Amendment:** Appendix A is amended in the line beginning "18 U.S.C. § 113(a)" by deleting ", 2A3.1".

Appendix A is amended in the line beginning "18 U.S.C. § 1854" by deleting ", 2B2.3".

Appendix A is amended in the line beginning "42 U.S.C. § 2278(a)(c)" by deleting "42 U.S.C. § 2278(a)(c)" and inserting in lieu thereof "42 U.S.C. § 2278a(c)".

Reason for Amendment: The purposes of this amendment are to delete incorrect references and to insert a correct reference.

Effective Date: The effective date of this amendment is November 1, 1989.

300. **Amendment:** Appendix A is amended by inserting the following statutes in the ap-

Amendment 300 APPENDIX C - VOLUME I November 1, 2013

propriate place according to statutory title and section number:

"18 U.S.C. § 2251A   2G2.3",
"21 U.S.C. § 858   2D1.10".

Appendix A is amended on the line beginning "18 U.S.C. § 1464" by deleting "2G3.1" and inserting in lieu thereof "2G3.2", and by inserting the following statute in the appropriate place according to statutory title and section number:

"18 U.S.C. § 1468   2G3.2".

Appendix A is amended on the line beginning "21 U.S.C. § 845" by deleting "2D1.3" and inserting in lieu thereof "2D1.2", and on the line beginning "21 U.S.C. § 845a" by deleting "2D1.3" and inserting in lieu thereof "2D1.2".

Appendix A is amended in the line beginning "47 U.S.C. § 223" by deleting "47 U.S.C. § 223" and inserting in lieu thereof "47 U.S.C. § 223(b)(1)(A)".

Reason for Amendment: The purpose of this amendment is to reflect the creation of new offense guidelines.

Effective Date: The effective date of this amendment is November 1, 1989.

301. **Amendment:** Appendix A is amended on the line beginning "18 U.S.C. § 844(h)" by deleting ", 2K1.6" and inserting in lieu thereof "(offenses committed prior to November 18, 1988), 2K1.6, 2K1.7".

Reason for Amendment: The purpose of this amendment is to reflect a revision in the offense covered by 18 U.S.C. § 844(h).

Effective Date: The effective date of this amendment is November 1, 1989.

302. **Amendment:** Sections 5C2.1, 5D3.1, 5D3.2, 5D3.3, 5E4.1, 5E4.2, 5E4.3, 5E4.4, 5F5.1, 5F5.2, 5F5.3, 5F5.4, and 5F5.5, and references thereto, are amended by deleting the number designating the subpart (i.e., the digit immediately following the letter in the section designation) wherever it appears and inserting in lieu thereof "1" in each instance.

Reason for Amendment: The purpose of this amendment is to correct a clerical error.

Effective Date: The effective date of this amendment is November 1, 1989.

303. **Amendment:** The Commentary to § 1B1.1 captioned "Application Notes" is amended in the third sentence of Note 4 by deleting "subsection" and inserting in lieu thereof "subdivision" and by deleting "subsections (A), (B) and (C)" and inserting in lieu thereof "subdivisions (A) - (E)".

The Commentary to § 1B1.2 captioned "Application Notes" is amended in Note 3 by deleting "at Sentencing)" and inserting in lieu thereof "in Imposing Sentence)".

The Commentary to § 1B1.3 captioned "Application Notes" is amended in the first sentence of Note 1 by deleting "is" and inserting in lieu thereof "would be".

The Commentary to § 1B1.3 captioned "Application Notes" is amended in Note 4 by deleting "(Assault)" and inserting in lieu thereof "(Aggravated Assault)", and by deleting "(Fraud)" and inserting in lieu thereof "(Fraud and Deceit)".

November 1, 2013　　APPENDIX C - VOLUME I　　**Amendment 303**

The Commentary to § 1B1.3 captioned "Application Notes" is amended in Note 5 by deleting "§ 2K2.3" and inserting in lieu thereof "§ 2K2.2", by deleting "12" and inserting in lieu thereof "16", by deleting "convicted under" and inserting in lieu thereof "the defendant is convicted under 18 U.S.C. § 922(o) or", by deleting "§ 2A3.4(b)(2)" and inserting in lieu thereof "§ 2A3.4(a)(2)", and by deleting "abusive contact was accomplished as defined in 18 U.S.C. § 2242, increase by 4 levels" and inserting in lieu thereof "offense was committed by the means set forth in 18 U.S.C. § 2242".

The Commentary to § 1B1.3 captioned "Background" is amended in the fourth sentence of the third paragraph by deleting "are part" and inserting in lieu thereof "were part".

The Commentary to § 1B1.4 captioned "Background" is amended by deleting "3557" and inserting in lieu thereof "3577".

The Commentary to § 2B3.2 captioned "Application Notes" is amended in the third sentence of Note 3 by inserting "and Racketeering" immediately before the period at the end of the sentence.

The Commentary to § 2B3.2 captioned "Application Notes" is amended in Note 5 by deleting "items taken" and inserting in lieu thereof "loss".

The Commentary to § 2A5.2 captioned "Background" is amended by inserting "or Aboard" immediately following "Materials While Boarding".

The Introductory Commentary to Chapter 2, Part B is amended by deleting "Order and" immediately before "Safety".

The Commentary to § 2B1.1 captioned "Application Notes" is amended in Note 2 by deleting "(Attempt, Solicitation, or Conspiracy Not Covered by a Specific Guideline)" and inserting in lieu thereof "(Attempt, Solicitation, or Conspiracy)".

The Commentary to § 2D1.1 captioned "Application Notes" is amended in Note 3 by deleting "§§ 2D1.2-2D1.4" and inserting in lieu thereof "§§ 2D1.2, 2D1.4, 2D1.5".

The Commentary to § 2D1.1 captioned "Background" is amended in the fifth paragraph by deleting "§§ 5D1.1-5D1.3" and inserting in lieu thereof "Part D (Supervised Release)".

The Commentary to § 2F1.1 captioned "Application Notes" is amended in the third sentence of Note 11 by deleting "Part B" and inserting in lieu thereof "Part B of this Chapter".

The Commentary to § 2H1.1 captioned "Application Notes" is amended in the last sentence of Note 1 by deleting "for any" and inserting in lieu thereof "applicable to".

The Commentary to § 2H1.2 captioned "Application Notes" is amended in Note 1 by deleting "explained" and inserting in lieu thereof "defined".

The Commentary to § 2H1.2 captioned "Background" is amended in the second sentence by deleting ", except where death results, in which case" and inserting in lieu thereof "; except where death results,".

Section 2K1.5(c)(1) is amended by deleting "(Attempt or Conspiracy)" and inserting in lieu thereof "(Attempt, Solicitation, or Conspiracy)".

Section 2K1.6(b)(1) is amended by deleting "(Attempt or Conspiracy)" and inserting in lieu thereof "(Attempt, Solicitation, or Conspiracy)".

Amendment 303

The Commentary to § 2R1.1 captioned "Application Notes" is amended in Note 7 by inserting "Category" immediately following "Criminal History".

The Commentary to § 2T1.4 captioned "Application Notes" is amended in Note 3 by inserting "Use of" immediately before "Special Skill".

The Commentary to § 3B1.4 is amended by deleting "(Role in the Offense)" the first time it appears and inserting in lieu thereof "(Aggravating Role)", and by deleting "(Role in the Offense)" the second time it appears and inserting in lieu thereof "(Mitigating Role)".

The Commentary to § 3D1.2 captioned "Application Notes" is amended in Note 1 by deleting "25 (18 + 1 + 6) rather than 28" and inserting in lieu thereof "28 (18 + 4 + 6) rather than 31".

The Commentary to § 3D1.3 captioned "Application Notes" is amended in the last sentence of Note 4 by deleting "Loss or Damage" and inserting in lieu thereof "Damage or Loss".

The Commentary following § 3D1.5 captioned "Illustrations of the Operation of the Multiple-Count Rules" is amended in example 1 by deleting "19" and inserting in lieu thereof "22", by deleting "1-Level" and inserting in lieu thereof "4-Level", by deleting "25." and inserting in lieu thereof "28.", by deleting "(25)" and inserting in lieu thereof "(28)", and by deleting "28" and inserting in lieu thereof "31".

The Commentary following § 3D1.5 captioned "Illustrations of the Operation of the Multiple-Count Rules" is amended in the last 2 sentences of example 3 by deleting "10" wherever it appears and inserting in lieu thereof in each instance "8".

The Commentary following § 3D1.5 captioned "Illustrations of the Operation of the Multiple-Count Rules" is amended in example 5 by deleting "13" wherever it appears and inserting in lieu thereof "14".

The Commentary following § 3D1.5 captioned "Illustrations of the Operation of the Multiple-Count Rules" is amended by deleting:

"2. Defendant B, a federal housing inspector, was convicted on four counts of bribery. Counts one and two charged receiving payments of $3,000 and $2,000 from Landlord X in return for a single action with respect to a single property. Count three charged receipt of $1,500 from Landlord X for taking action with respect to another property, and count four charged receipt of $1,000 from Landlord Y for taking action with respect to a third property. Counts one and two, which arise out of the same transaction, are combined into a single Group involving a $5,000 bribe and hence an offense level of 11 (§ 2C1.1(a)(1), § 2F1.1). Each of the two remaining counts represents a distinct Group, at offense level 10. As there are three Count Units, the offense level for the most serious (11) is increased by 3 levels. The combined offense level is 14.",

by renumbering Illustrations 3, 4, and 5 as 2, 3, and 4, respectively, and by redesignating defendants "C", "D", and "E" as "B", "C", and "D", respectively.

Reason for Amendment: The purposes of this amendment are to conform cross-references and illustrations of the operation of the guidelines to the guidelines, as amended, and to make editorial improvements.

Effective Date: The effective date of this amendment is November 1, 1989.

304. Amendment: Section 2D2.1 is amended by inserting the following additional subsection:

"(b)   Cross Reference

(1)   If the defendant is convicted of possession of more than 5 grams of a mixture or substance containing cocaine base, apply § 2D1.1 (Unlawful Manufacturing, Importing, Exporting, or Trafficking) as if the defendant had been convicted of possession of that mixture or substance with intent to distribute.".

The Commentary to § 2D2.1 captioned "Background" is amended by deleting the entire text as follows:

"<u>Background</u>: Absent a prior drug related conviction, the maximum term of imprisonment authorized by statute is one year. With a single prior drug related conviction, a mandatory minimum term of imprisonment of fifteen days is required by statute and the maximum term of imprisonment authorized is increased to two years. With two or more prior drug related convictions, a mandatory minimum term of imprisonment of ninety days is required by statute and the maximum term of imprisonment authorized is increased to three years.",

and inserting in lieu thereof:

"<u>Background</u>: Mandatory minimum penalties for several categories of cases, ranging from fifteen days' to five years' imprisonment, are set forth in 21 U.S.C. § 844(a). When a mandatory minimum penalty exceeds the guideline range, the mandatory minimum becomes the guideline sentence. § 5G1.1(b).

Section 2D2.1(b)(1) provides a cross reference to § 2D1.1 for possession of more than five grams of a mixture or substance containing cocaine base, an offense subject to an enhanced penalty under Section 6371 of the Anti-Drug Abuse Act of 1988. Other cases for which enhanced penalties are provided under Section 6371 of the Anti-Drug Abuse Act of 1988 (<u>e.g.</u>, for a person with one prior conviction, possession of more than three grams of a mixture or substance containing cocaine base; for a person with two or more prior convictions, possession of more than one gram of a mixture or substance containing cocaine base) are to be sentenced in accordance with § 5G1.1(b).".

Reason for Amendment: The purpose of this amendment is to reflect revisions in 21 U.S.C. § 844(a) made by Section 6371 of the Anti-Drug Abuse Act of 1988.

Effective Date: The effective date of this amendment is November 1, 1989.

305. Amendment: Chapter Five, Part F, is amended by inserting an additional guideline with accompanying commentary as § 5F1.6 (Denial of Federal Benefits to Drug Traffickers and Possessors).

Reason for Amendment: The purpose of this amendment is to reflect the enactment of 21 U.S.C. § 853a by Section 5301 of the Anti-Drug Abuse Act of 1988.

Effective Date: The effective date of this amendment is November 1, 1989.

306. Amendment: Chapter One, Part B, is amended by inserting an additional policy statement with accompanying commentary as § 1B1.10 (Retroactivity of Amended Guideline Range (Policy Statement)).

Reason for Amendment: The purpose of this amendment is to implement the directive in

28 U.S.C. § 994(u).

Effective Date: The effective date of this amendment is November 1, 1989.

307. **Amendment:** Chapter One, Part A, is amended by deleting subparts 2-5 in their entirety as follows:

"2. The Statutory Mission

The Comprehensive Crime Control Act of 1984 foresees guidelines that will further the basic purposes of criminal punishment, i.e., deterring crime, incapacitating the offender, providing just punishment, and rehabilitating the offender. It delegates to the Commission broad authority to review and rationalize the federal sentencing process.

The statute contains many detailed instructions as to how this determination should be made, but the most important of them instructs the Commission to create categories of offense behavior and offender characteristics. An offense behavior category might consist, for example, of 'bank robbery/committed with a gun/$2500 taken.' An offender characteristic category might be 'offender with one prior conviction who was not sentenced to imprisonment.' The Commission is required to prescribe guideline ranges that specify an appropriate sentence for each class of convicted persons, to be determined by coordinating the offense behavior categories with the offender characteristic categories. The statute contemplates the guidelines will establish a range of sentences for every coordination of categories. Where the guidelines call for imprisonment, the range must be narrow: the maximum imprisonment cannot exceed the minimum by more than the greater of 25 percent or six months. 28 U.S.C. § 994(b)(2).

The sentencing judge must select a sentence from within the guideline range. If, however, a particular case presents atypical features, the Act allows the judge to depart from the guidelines and sentence outside the range. In that case, the judge must specify reasons for departure. 18 U.S.C. § 3553(b). If the court sentences within the guideline range, an appellate court may review the sentence to see if the guideline was correctly applied. If the judge departs from the guideline range, an appellate court may review the reasonableness of the departure. 18 U.S.C. § 3742. The Act requires the offender to serve virtually all of any prison sentence imposed, for it abolishes parole and substantially restructures good behavior adjustments.

The law requires the Commission to send its initial guidelines to Congress by April 13, 1987, and under the present statute they take effect automatically on November 1, 1987. Pub. L. No. 98-473, § 235, reprinted at 18 U.S.C. § 3551. The Commission may submit guideline amendments each year to Congress between the beginning of a regular session and May 1. The amendments will take effect automatically 180 days after submission unless a law is enacted to the contrary. 28 U.S.C. § 994(p).

The Commission, with the aid of its legal and research staff, considerable public testimony, and written commentary, has developed an initial set of guidelines which it now transmits to Congress. The Commission emphasizes, however, that it views the guideline-writing process as evolutionary. It expects, and the governing statute anticipates, that continuing research, experience, and analysis will result in modifications and revisions to the guidelines by submission of amendments to Congress. To this end, the Commission is established as a permanent agency to monitor sentencing practices in the federal courts throughout the nation.

3. The Basic Approach (Policy Statement)

To understand these guidelines and the rationale that underlies them, one must begin with the three objectives that Congress, in enacting the new sentencing law, sought to achieve. Its basic objective was to enhance the ability of the criminal justice system to reduce crime through an effective, fair sentencing system. To achieve this objective, Congress first sought honesty in sentencing. It sought to avoid the confusion and implicit deception that arises out of the present sentencing system which requires a judge to impose an indeterminate sentence that is automatically reduced in most cases by 'good time' credits. In addition, the parole commission is permitted to determine how much of the remainder of any prison sentence an offender actually will serve. This usually results in a substantial reduction in the effective length of the sentence imposed, with defendants often serving only about one-third of the sentence handed down by the court.

Second, Congress sought uniformity in sentencing by narrowing the wide disparity in sentences imposed by different federal courts for similar criminal conduct by similar offenders. Third, Congress sought proportionality in sentencing through a system that imposes appropriately different sentences for criminal conduct of different severity.

Honesty is easy to achieve: The abolition of parole makes the sentence imposed by the court the sentence the offender will serve. There is a tension, however, between the mandate of uniformity (treat similar cases alike) and the mandate of proportionality (treat different cases differently) which, like the historical tension between law and equity, makes it difficult to achieve both goals simultaneously. Perfect uniformity -- sentencing every offender to five years -- destroys proportionality. Having only a few simple categories of crimes would make the guidelines uniform and easy to administer, but might lump together offenses that are different in important respects. For example, a single category for robbery that lumps together armed and unarmed robberies, robberies with and without injuries, robberies of a few dollars and robberies of millions, is far too broad.

At the same time, a sentencing system tailored to fit every conceivable wrinkle of each case can become unworkable and seriously compromise the certainty of punishment and its deterrent effect. A bank robber with (or without) a gun, which the robber kept hidden (or brandished), might have frightened (or merely warned), injured seriously (or less seriously), tied up (or simply pushed) a guard, a teller or a customer, at night (or at noon), for a bad (or arguably less bad) motive, in an effort to obtain money for other crimes (or for other purposes), in the company of a few (or many) other robbers, for the first (or fourth) time that day, while sober (or under the influence of drugs or alcohol), and so forth.

The list of potentially relevant features of criminal behavior is long; the fact that they can occur in multiple combinations means that the list of possible permutations of factors is virtually endless. The appropriate relationships among these different factors are exceedingly difficult to establish, for they are often context specific. Sentencing courts do not treat the occurrence of a simple bruise identically in all cases, irrespective of whether that bruise occurred in the context of a bank robbery or in the context of a breach of peace. This is so, in part, because the risk that such a harm will occur differs depending on the underlying offense with which it is connected (and therefore may already be counted, to a different degree, in the punishment for the underlying offense); and also because, in part, the relationship between punishment and multiple harms is not simply additive. The relation varies, depending on how much other harm has occurred. (Thus, one cannot easily assign points for each kind of harm and simply add them up, irrespective of context and total amounts.)

The larger the number of subcategories, the greater the complexity that is created and the less workable the system. Moreover, the subcategories themselves, sometimes too broad and sometimes too narrow, will apply and interact in unforeseen ways to unforeseen situations, thus failing to cure the unfairness of a simple, broad category system. Finally, and perhaps most importantly, probation officers and courts, in applying a complex system of subcategories, would have to make a host of decisions about whether the underlying facts are sufficient to bring the case within a particular subcategory. The greater the number of decisions required and the greater their complexity, the greater the risk that different judges will apply the guidelines differently to situations that, in fact, are similar, thereby reintroducing the very disparity that the guidelines were designed to eliminate.

In view of the arguments, it is tempting to retreat to the simple, broad-category approach and to grant judges the discretion to select the proper point along a broad sentencing range. Obviously, however, granting such broad discretion risks correspondingly broad disparity in sentencing, for different courts may exercise their discretionary powers in different ways. That is to say, such an approach risks a return to the wide disparity that Congress established the Commission to limit.

In the end, there is no completely satisfying solution to this practical stalemate. The Commission has had to simply balance the comparative virtues and vices of broad, simple categorization and detailed, complex subcategorization, and within the constraints established by that balance, minimize the discretionary powers of the sentencing court. Any ultimate system will, to a degree, enjoy the benefits and suffer from the drawbacks of each approach.

A philosophical problem arose when the Commission attempted to reconcile the differing perceptions of the purposes of criminal punishment. Most observers of the criminal law agree that the ultimate aim of the law itself, and of punishment in particular, is the control of crime. Beyond this point, however, the consensus seems to break down. Some argue that appropriate punishment should be defined primarily on the basis of the moral principle of 'just deserts.' Under this principle, punishment should be scaled to the offender's culpability and the resulting harms. Thus, if a defendant is less culpable, the defendant deserves less punishment. Others argue that punishment should be imposed primarily on the basis of practical 'crime control' considerations. Defendants sentenced under this scheme should receive the punishment that most effectively lessens the likelihood of future crime, either by deterring others or incapacitating the defendant.

Adherents of these points of view have urged the Commission to choose between them, to accord one primacy over the other. Such a choice would be profoundly difficult. The relevant literature is vast, the arguments deep, and each point of view has much to be said in its favor. A clear-cut Commission decision in favor of one of these approaches would diminish the chance that the guidelines would find the widespread acceptance they need for effective implementation. As a practical matter, in most sentencing decisions both philosophies may prove consistent with the same result.

For now, the Commission has sought to solve both the practical and philosophical problems of developing a coherent sentencing system by taking an empirical approach that uses data estimating the existing sentencing system as a starting point. It has analyzed data drawn from 10,000 presentence investigations, crimes as distinguished in substantive criminal statutes, the United States Parole Commission's guidelines and resulting statistics, and data from other relevant sources, in order to determine which distinctions are important in present practice. After examination, the Commission has accepted, modified, or rationalized the more important of these distinctions.

This empirical approach has helped the Commission resolve its practical problem by defining a list of relevant distinctions that, although of considerable length, is short enough to create a manageable set of guidelines. Existing categories are relatively broad and omit many distinctions that some may believe important, yet they include most of the major distinctions that statutes and presentence data suggest make a significant difference in sentencing decisions. Important distinctions that are ignored in existing practice probably occur rarely. A sentencing judge may take this unusual case into account by departing from the guidelines.

The Commission's empirical approach has also helped resolve its philosophical dilemma. Those who adhere to a just deserts philosophy may concede that the lack of moral consensus might make it difficult to say exactly what punishment is deserved for a particular crime, specified in minute detail. Likewise, those who subscribe to a philosophy of crime control may acknowledge that the lack of sufficient, readily available data might make it difficult to say exactly what punishment will best prevent that crime. Both groups might therefore recognize the wisdom of looking to those distinctions that judges and legislators have, in fact, made over the course of time. These established distinctions are ones that the community believes, or has found over time, to be important from either a moral or crime-control perspective.

The Commission has not simply copied estimates of existing practice as revealed by the data (even though establishing offense values on this basis would help eliminate disparity, for the data represent averages). Rather, it has departed from the data at different points for various important reasons. Congressional statutes, for example, may suggest or require departure, as in the case of the new drug law that imposes increased and mandatory minimum sentences. In addition, the data may reveal inconsistencies in treatment, such as punishing economic crime less severely than other apparently equivalent behavior.

Despite these policy-oriented departures from present practice, the guidelines represent an approach that begins with, and builds upon, empirical data. The guidelines will not please those who wish the Commission to adopt a single philosophical theory and then work deductively to establish a simple and perfect set of categorizations and distinctions. The guidelines may prove acceptable, however, to those who seek more modest, incremental improvements in the status quo, who believe the best is often the enemy of the good, and who recognize that these initial guidelines are but the first step in an evolutionary process. After spending considerable time and resources exploring alternative approaches, the Commission has developed these guidelines as a practical effort toward the achievement of a more honest, uniform, equitable, and therefore effective, sentencing system.

4. The Guidelines' Resolution of Major Issues (Policy Statement)

The guideline-writing process has required the Commission to resolve a host of important policy questions, typically involving rather evenly balanced sets of competing considerations. As an aid to understanding the guidelines, this introduction will briefly discuss several of those issues. Commentary in the guidelines explains others.

(a) Real Offense vs. Charge Offense Sentencing.

One of the most important questions for the Commission to decide was whether to base sentences upon the actual conduct in which the defendant engaged regardless of the charges for which he was indicted or convicted ('real offense' sentencing), or upon the conduct that constitutes the elements of the offense with which the defendant was charged and of which he was convicted ('charge offense' sentencing). A bank robber, for example, might have used a gun, frightened bystanders, taken $50,000, injured a teller, refused to stop when ordered, and raced away damaging property during escape. A pure real offense system would sentence on the basis of all identifiable conduct. A pure charge offense system would overlook some of the harms that did not constitute statutory elements of the offenses of which the defendant was convicted.

The Commission initially sought to develop a real offense system. After all, the present sentencing system is, in a sense, a real offense system. The sentencing court (and the parole commission) take account of the conduct in which the defendant actually engaged, as determined in a presentence report, at the sentencing hearing, or before a parole commission hearing officer. The Commission's initial efforts in this direction, carried out in the spring and early summer of 1986, proved unproductive mostly for practical reasons. To make such a system work, even to formalize and rationalize the status quo, would have required the Commission to decide precisely which harms to take into account, how to add them up, and what kinds of procedures the courts should use to determine the presence or absence of disputed factual elements. The Commission found no practical way to combine and account for the large number of diverse harms arising in different circumstances; nor did it find a practical way to reconcile the need for a fair adjudicatory procedure with the need for a speedy sentencing process, given the potential existence of hosts of adjudicated 'real harm' facts in many typical cases. The effort proposed as a solution to these problems required the use of, for example, quadratic roots and other mathematical operations that the Commission considered too complex to be workable, and, in the Commission's view, risked return to wide disparity in practice.

The Commission therefore abandoned the effort to devise a 'pure' real offense system and instead experimented with a 'modified real offense system,' which it published for public comment in a September 1986 preliminary draft.

This version also foundered in several major respects on the rock of practicality. It was highly complex and its mechanical rules for adding harms (e.g., bodily injury added the same punishment irrespective of context) threatened to work considerable unfairness. Ultimately, the Commission decided that it could not find a practical or fair and efficient way to implement either a pure or modified real offense system of the sort it originally wanted, and it abandoned that approach.

The Commission, in its January 1987 Revised Draft and the present guidelines, has moved closer to a 'charge offense' system. The system is not, however, pure; it has a number of real elements. For one thing, the hundreds of overlapping and duplicative statutory provisions that make up the federal criminal law have forced the Commission to write guidelines that are descriptive of generic conduct rather than tracking purely statutory language. For another, the guidelines, both through specific offense characteristics and adjustments, take account of a number of important, commonly occurring real offense elements such as role in the offense, the presence of a gun, or the amount of money actually taken.

Finally, it is important not to overstate the difference in practice between a real and a charge offense system. The federal criminal system, in practice, deals mostly with drug offenses, bank robberies and white collar crimes (such as fraud, embezzlement, and bribery). For the most part, the conduct that an indictment charges approximates the real and relevant conduct in which the offender actually engaged.

The Commission recognizes its system will not completely cure the problems of a real offense system. It may still be necessary, for example, for a court to determine some particular real facts that will make a difference to the sentence. Yet, the Commission believes that the instances of controversial facts will be far fewer; indeed, there will be few enough so that the court system will be able to devise fair procedures for their determination. See <u>United States v. Fatico</u>, 579 F.2d 707 (2d Cir. 1978) (permitting introduction of hearsay evidence at sentencing hearing under certain conditions), <u>on remand</u>, 458 F. Supp. 388 (E.D.N.Y. 1978), <u>aff'd</u>, 603 F.2d 1053 (2d Cir. 1979) (holding that the government need not prove facts at sentencing hearing beyond a reasonable doubt), <u>cert. denied</u>, 444 U.S. 1073 (1980).

The Commission also recognizes that a charge offense system has drawbacks of its own. One of the most important is its potential to turn over to the prosecutor the power to determine the sentence by increasing or decreasing the number (or content) of the counts in an indictment. Of course, the defendant's actual conduct (that which the prosecutor can prove in court) imposes a natural limit upon the prosecutor's ability to increase a defendant's sentence. Moreover, the Commission has written its rules for the treatment of multicount convictions with an eye toward eliminating unfair treatment that might flow from count manipulation. For example, the guidelines treat a three-count indictment, each count of which charges sale of 100 grams of heroin, or theft of $10,000, the same as a single-count indictment charging sale of 300 grams of heroin or theft of $30,000. Further, a sentencing court may control any inappropriate manipulation of the indictment through use of its power to depart from the specific guideline sentence. Finally, the Commission will closely monitor problems arising out of count manipulation and will make appropriate adjustments should they become necessary.

(b)   <u>Departures</u>.

The new sentencing statute permits a court to depart from a guideline-specified sentence only when it finds 'an aggravating or mitigating circumstance of a kind, or to a degree, not adequately taken into consideration by the Sentencing Commission . . .'. 18 U.S.C. § 3553(b). Thus, in principle, the Commission, by specifying that it had adequately considered a particular factor, could prevent a court from using it as grounds for departure. In this initial set of guidelines, however, the Commission does not so limit the courts' departure powers. The Commission intends the sentencing courts to treat each guideline as carving out a 'heartland,' a set of typical cases embodying the conduct that each guideline describes. When a court finds an atypical case, one to which a particular guideline linguistically applies but where conduct significantly differs from the norm, the court may consider whether a departure is warranted. Section 5H1.10 (Race, Sex, National Origin, Creed, Religion, Socio-Economic Status), the third sentence of § 5H1.4, and the last sentence of § 5K2.12, list a few factors that the court cannot take into account as grounds for departure. With those specific exceptions, however, the Commission does not intend to limit the kinds of factors (whether or not mentioned anywhere else in the guidelines) that could constitute grounds for departure in an unusual case.

The Commission has adopted this departure policy for two basic reasons. First is the difficulty of foreseeing and capturing a single set of guidelines that encompasses the vast range of human conduct potentially relevant to a sentencing decision. The Commission also recognizes that in the initial set of guidelines it need not do so. The Commission is a permanent body, empowered by law to write and rewrite guidelines, with progressive changes, over many years. By monitoring when courts depart from the guidelines and by analyzing their stated reasons for doing so, the Commission, over time, will be able to create more accurate guidelines that specify precisely where departures should and should not be permitted.

Second, the Commission believes that despite the courts' legal freedom to depart from the guidelines, they will not do so very often. This is because the guidelines, offense by offense, seek to take account of those factors that the Commission's sentencing data indicate make a significant difference in sentencing at the present time. Thus, for example, where the presence of actual physical injury currently makes an important difference in final sentences, as in the case of robbery, assault, or arson, the guidelines specifically instruct the judge to use this factor to augment the sentence. Where the guidelines do not specify an augmentation or diminution, this is generally because the sentencing data do not permit the Commission, at this time, to conclude that the factor is empirically important in relation to the particular offense. Of course, a factor (say physical injury) may nonetheless sometimes occur in connection with a crime (such as fraud) where it does not often occur. If, however, as the data indicate, such occurrences are rare, they are precisely the type of events that the court's departure powers were designed to cover -- unusual cases outside the range of the more typical offenses for which the guidelines were designed. Of course, the Commission recognizes that even its collection and analysis of 10,000 presentence reports are an imperfect source of data sentencing estimates. Rather than rely heavily at this time upon impressionistic accounts, however, the Commission believes it wiser to wait and collect additional data from our continuing monitoring process that may demonstrate how the guidelines work in practice before further modification.

It is important to note that the guidelines refer to two different kinds of departure.

The first kind involves instances in which the guidelines provide specific guidance for departure, by analogy or by other numerical or non-numerical suggestions. For example, the commentary to § 2G1.1 (Transportation for Prostitution), recommends a downward adjustment of eight levels where commercial purpose was not involved. The Commission intends such suggestions as policy guidance for the courts. The Commission expects that most departures will reflect the suggestions, and that the courts of appeals may prove more likely to find departures 'unreasonable' where they fall outside suggested levels.

A second kind of departure will remain unguided. It may rest upon grounds referred to in Chapter 5, Part K (Departures), or on grounds not mentioned in the guidelines. While Chapter 5, Part K lists factors that the Commission believes may constitute grounds for departure, those suggested grounds are not exhaustive. The Commission recognizes that there may be other grounds for departure that are not mentioned; it also believes there may be cases in which a departure outside suggested levels is warranted. In its view, however, such cases will be highly unusual.

(c) <u>Plea Agreements</u>.

Nearly ninety percent of all federal criminal cases involve guilty pleas, and many of these cases involve some form of plea agreement. Some commentators on early Commission guideline drafts have urged the Commission not to attempt any major reforms of the agreement process, on the grounds that any set of guidelines that threatens to radically change present practice also threatens to make the federal system unmanageable. Others, starting with the same facts, have argued that guidelines which fail to control and limit plea agreements would leave untouched a 'loophole' large enough to undo the good that sentencing guidelines may bring. Still other commentators make both sets of arguments.

The Commission has decided that these initial guidelines will not, in general, make significant changes in current plea agreement practices. The court will accept or reject any such agreements primarily in accordance with the rules set forth in

Fed.R.Crim.P. 11(e). The Commission will collect data on the courts' plea practices and will analyze this information to determine when and why the courts accept or reject plea agreements. In light of this information and analysis, the Commission will seek to further regulate the plea agreement process as appropriate.

The Commission nonetheless expects the initial set of guidelines to have a positive, rationalizing impact upon plea agreements for two reasons. First, the guidelines create a clear, definite expectation in respect to the sentence that a court will impose if a trial takes place. Insofar as a prosecutor and defense attorney seek to agree about a likely sentence or range of sentences, they will no longer work in the dark. This fact alone should help to reduce irrationality in respect to actual sentencing outcomes. Second, the guidelines create a norm to which judges will likely refer when they decide whether, under Rule 11(e), to accept or to reject a plea agreement or recommendation. Since they will have before them the norm, the relevant factors (as disclosed in the plea agreement), and the reason for the agreement, they will find it easier than at present to determine whether there is sufficient reason to accept a plea agreement that departs from the norm.

(d) <u>Probation and Split Sentences</u>.

The statute provides that the guidelines are to 'reflect the general appropriateness of imposing a sentence other than imprisonment in cases in which the defendant is a first offender who has not been convicted of a crime of violence or an otherwise serious offense . . .' 28 U.S.C. § 994(j). Under present sentencing practice, courts sentence to probation an inappropriately high percentage of offenders guilty of certain economic crimes, such as theft, tax evasion, antitrust offenses, insider trading, fraud, and embezzlement, that in the Commission's view are 'serious.' If the guidelines were to permit courts to impose probation instead of prison in many or all such cases, the present sentences would continue to be ineffective.

The Commission's solution to this problem has been to write guidelines that classify as 'serious' (and therefore subject to mandatory prison sentences) many offenses for which probation is now frequently given. At the same time, the guidelines will permit the sentencing court to impose short prison terms in many such cases. The Commission's view is that the definite prospect of prison, though the term is short, will act as a significant deterrent to many of these crimes, particularly when compared with the status quo where probation, not prison, is the norm.

More specifically, the guidelines work as follows in respect to a first offender. For offense levels one through six, the sentencing court may elect to sentence the offender to probation (with or without confinement conditions) or to a prison term. For offense levels seven through ten, the court may substitute probation for a prison term, but the probation must include confinement conditions (community confinement, intermittent confinement, or home detention). For offense levels eleven and twelve, the court must impose at least one half the minimum confinement sentence in the form of prison confinement, the remainder to be served on supervised release with a condition of community confinement or home detention. The Commission, of course, has not dealt with the single acts of aberrant behavior that still may justify probation at higher offense levels through departures.

(e) <u>Multi-Count Convictions</u>.

The Commission, like other sentencing commissions, has found it particularly difficult to develop rules for sentencing defendants convicted of multiple violations of law, each of which makes up a separate count in an indictment. The reason it is difficult is that when a defendant engages in conduct that causes several harms, each additional harm, even if it increases the extent to which punishment is warranted, does not necessarily warrant a proportionate increase in punishment. A defendant who assaults others during a fight, for example, may warrant more punishment if he injures ten people than if he injures one, but his conduct does not necessarily warrant ten times the punishment. If it did, many of the simplest offenses, for reasons that are often fortuitous, would lead to life sentences of imprisonment--sentences that neither 'just deserts' nor 'crime control' theories of punishment would find justified.

Several individual guidelines provide special instructions for increasing punishment when the conduct that is the subject of that count involves multiple occurrences or has caused several harms. The guidelines also provide general rules for aggravating punishment in light of multiple harms charged separately in separate counts. These rules may produce occasional anomalies, but normally they will permit an appropriate degree of aggravation of punishment when multiple offenses that are the subjects of separate counts take place.

These rules are set out in Chapter Three, Part D. They essentially provide: (1) When the conduct involves fungible items, e.g., separate drug transactions or thefts of money, the amounts are added and the guidelines apply to the total amount. (2) When nonfungible harms are involved, the offense level for the most serious count is increased (according to a somewhat diminishing scale) to reflect the existence of other counts of conviction.

The rules have been written in order to minimize the possibility that an arbitrary casting of a single transaction into several counts will produce a longer sentence. In addition, the sentencing court will have adequate power to prevent such a result through departures where necessary to produce a mitigated sentence.

(f)   Regulatory Offenses.

Regulatory statutes, though primarily civil in nature, sometimes contain criminal provisions in respect to particularly harmful activity. Such criminal provisions often describe not only substantive offenses, but also more technical, administratively-related offenses such as failure to keep accurate records or to provide requested information. These criminal statutes pose two problems. First, which criminal regulatory provisions should the Commission initially consider, and second, how should it treat technical or administratively-related criminal violations?

In respect to the first problem, the Commission found that it cannot comprehensively treat all regulatory violations in the initial set of guidelines. There are hundreds of such provisions scattered throughout the United States Code. To find all potential violations would involve examination of each individual federal regulation. Because of this practical difficulty, the Commission has sought to determine, with the assistance of the Department of Justice and several regulatory agencies, which criminal regulatory offenses are particularly important in light of the need for enforcement of the general regulatory scheme. The Commission has sought to treat these offenses in these initial guidelines. It will address the less common regulatory offenses in the future.

In respect to the second problem, the Commission has developed a system for treating technical recordkeeping and reporting offenses, dividing them into four categories.

First, in the simplest of cases, the offender may have failed to fill out a form intentionally, but without knowledge or intent that substantive harm would likely follow. He might fail, for example, to keep an accurate record of toxic substance transport, but that failure may not lead, nor be likely to lead, to the release or improper treatment of any toxic substance. Second, the same failure may be accompanied by a significant likelihood that substantive harm will occur; it may make a release of a toxic substance more likely. Third, the same failure may have led to substantive harm. Fourth, the failure may represent an effort to conceal a substantive harm that has occurred.

The structure of a typical guideline for a regulatory offense is as follows:

(1) The guideline provides a low base offense level (6) aimed at the first type of recordkeeping or reporting offense. It gives the court the legal authority to impose a punishment ranging from probation up to six months of imprisonment.

(2) Specific offense characteristics designed to reflect substantive offenses that do occur (in respect to some regulatory offenses), or that are likely to occur, increase the offense level.

(3) A specific offense characteristic also provides that a recordkeeping or reporting offense that conceals a substantive offense will be treated like the substantive offense.

The Commission views this structure as an initial effort. It may revise its approach in light of further experience and analysis of regulatory crimes.

(g) <u>Sentencing Ranges</u>.

In determining the appropriate sentencing ranges for each offense, the Commission began by estimating the average sentences now being served within each category. It also examined the sentence specified in congressional statutes, in the parole guidelines, and in other relevant, analogous sources. The Commission's forthcoming detailed report will contain a comparison between estimates of existing sentencing practices and sentences under the guidelines.

While the Commission has not considered itself bound by existing sentencing practice, it has not tried to develop an entirely new system of sentencing on the basis of theory alone. Guideline sentences in many instances will approximate existing practice, but adherence to the guidelines will help to eliminate wide disparity. For example, where a high percentage of persons now receive probation, a guideline may include one or more specific offense characteristics in an effort to distinguish those types of defendants who now receive probation from those who receive more severe sentences. In some instances, short sentences of incarceration for all offenders in a category have been substituted for a current sentencing practice of very wide variability in which some defendants receive probation while others receive several years in prison for the same offense. Moreover, inasmuch as those who currently plead guilty often receive lesser sentences, the guidelines also permit the court to impose lesser sentences on those defendants who accept responsibility and those who cooperate with the government.

The Commission has also examined its sentencing ranges in light of their likely impact upon prison population. Specific legislation, such as the new drug law and the career offender provisions of the sentencing law, require the Commission to promulgate rules that will lead to substantial prison population increases. These increases will occur irrespective of any guidelines. The guidelines themselves, insofar as they reflect policy decisions made by the Commission (rather than legislated mandatory minimum, or career offender, sentences), will lead to an increase in prison population that computer models, produced by the Commission and the Bureau of Prisons, estimate at approximately 10 percent, over a period of ten years.

    (h)   The Sentencing Table.

The Commission has established a sentencing table. For technical and practical reasons it has 43 levels. Each row in the table contains levels that overlap with the levels in the preceding and succeeding rows. By overlapping the levels, the table should discourage unnecessary litigation. Both prosecutor and defendant will realize that the difference between one level and another will not necessarily make a difference in the sentence that the judge imposes. Thus, little purpose will be served in protracted litigation trying to determine, for example, whether $10,000 or $11,000 was obtained as a result of a fraud. At the same time, the rows work to increase a sentence proportionately. A change of 6 levels roughly doubles the sentence irrespective of the level at which one starts. The Commission, aware of the legal requirement that the maximum of any range cannot exceed the minimum by more than the greater of 25 percent or six months, also wishes to permit courts the greatest possible range for exercising discretion. The table overlaps offense levels meaningfully, works proportionately, and at the same time preserves the maximum degree of allowable discretion for the judge within each level.

Similarly, many of the individual guidelines refer to tables that correlate amounts of money with offense levels. These tables often have many, rather than a few levels. Again, the reason is to minimize the likelihood of unnecessary litigation. If a money table were to make only a few distinctions, each distinction would become more important and litigation as to which category an offender fell within would become more likely. Where a table has many smaller monetary distinctions, it minimizes the likelihood of litigation, for the importance of the precise amount of money involved is considerably less.

5.   A Concluding Note

The Commission emphasizes that its approach in this initial set of guidelines is one of caution. It has examined the many hundreds of criminal statutes in the United States Code. It has begun with those that are the basis for a significant number of prosecutions. It has sought to place them in a rational order. It has developed additional distinctions relevant to the application of these provisions, and it has applied sentencing ranges to each resulting category. In doing so, it has relied upon estimates of existing sentencing practices as revealed by its own statistical analyses, based on summary reports of some 40,000 convictions, a sample of 10,000 augmented presentence reports, the parole guidelines and policy judgments.

The Commission recognizes that some will criticize this approach as overly cautious, as representing too little a departure from existing practice. Yet, it will cure wide disparity. The Commission is a permanent body that can amend the guidelines each year. Although the data available to it, like all data, are imperfect, experience with these guidelines will lead to additional information and provide a firm empirical basis for revision.

Finally, the guidelines will apply to approximately 90 percent of all cases in the federal courts. Because of time constraints and the nonexistence of statistical information, some offenses that occur infrequently are not considered in this initial set of guidelines. They will, however, be addressed in the near future. Their exclusion from this initial submission does not reflect any judgment about their seriousness.

The Commission has also deferred promulgation of guidelines pertaining to fines, probation and other sanctions for organizational defendants, with the exception of antitrust violations. The Commission also expects to address this area in the near future.".

Replacement subparts are inserted as Subparts 2 (The Statutory Mission), 3 (The Basic Approach (Policy Statement)), 4 (The Guidelines' Resolution of Major Issues (Policy Statement)), and 5 (A Concluding Note).

Reason for Amendment: This amendment updates this part to reflect the implementation of guideline sentencing on November 1, 1987, and makes various clarifying and editorial changes to enhance the usefulness of this part both as a historical overview and as an introduction to the structure and operation of the guidelines. For example, in the discussion of departures in subpart 4(b), language concerning what the Commission, in principle, might have done is deleted as unnecessary, but no substantive change is made.

Effective Date: The effective date of this amendment is November 1, 1990.

308. Amendment: Section 1B1.8(a) is amended by inserting "as part of that cooperation agreement" immediately following "unlawful activities of others, and"; and by deleting "so provided" and inserting in lieu thereof "provided pursuant to the agreement".

Section 1B1.8(b)(3) is amended by inserting "by the defendant" immediately before the period at the end of the sentence.

Section 1B1.8(b) is amended by renumbering subdivisions (2) and (3) as (3) and (4) respectively; and by inserting the following as subdivision (2):

> "(2)   concerning the existence of prior convictions and sentences in determining § 4A1.1 (Criminal History Category) and § 4B1.1 (Career Offender);".

The Commentary to § 1B1.8 captioned "Application Notes" is amended in Note 2 by deleting:

> "The Commission does not intend this guideline to interfere with determining adjustments under Chapter Four, Part A (Criminal History) or § 4B1.1 (Career Offender) (e.g., information concerning the defendant's prior convictions).",

and inserting in lieu thereof:

> "Subsection (b)(2) prohibits any cooperation agreement from restricting the use of information as to the existence of prior convictions and sentences in determining adjustments under § 4A1.1 (Criminal History Category) and § 4B1.1 (Career Offender).".

The Commentary to § 1B1.8 captioned "Application Notes" is amended in Note 3 by deleting "408" and inserting in lieu thereof "410".

Reason for Amendment: This amendment clarifies the Commission's intention that the use of information concerning the defendant's prior criminal convictions and sentences not be restricted by a cooperation agreement, makes several additional clarifying changes, and corrects a clerical error.

Effective Date: The effective date of this amendment is November 1, 1990.

309. Amendment: The Commentary to § 1B1.3 captioned "Application Notes" is amended in

Amendment 309

Note 2 by deleting:

"This subsection applies to offenses of types for which convictions on multiple counts would be grouped together pursuant to § 3D1.2(d); multiple convictions are not required.",

and inserting in lieu thereof:

"'Offenses of a character for which § 3D1.2(d) would require grouping of multiple counts,' as used in subsection (a)(2), applies to offenses for which grouping of counts would be required under § 3D1.2(d) had the defendant been convicted of multiple counts. Application of this provision does not require the defendant, in fact, to have been convicted of multiple counts. For example, where the defendant engaged in three drug sales of 10, 15, and 20 grams of cocaine, as part of the same course of conduct or common scheme or plan, subsection (a)(2) provides that the total quantity of cocaine involved (45 grams) is to be used to determine the offense level even if the defendant is convicted of a single count charging only one of the sales. If the defendant is convicted of multiple counts for the above noted sales, the grouping rules of Chapter Three, Part D (Multiple Counts) provide that the counts are grouped together. Although Chapter Three, Part D (Multiple Counts) applies to multiple counts of conviction, it does not limit the scope of subsection (a)(2). Subsection (a)(2) merely incorporates by reference the types of offenses set forth in § 3D1.2(d); thus, as discussed above, multiple counts of conviction are not required for subsection (a)(2) to apply.".

The Commentary to § 3D1.2 captioned "Application Notes" is amended in Note 4 by renumbering example (4) as (5); and by inserting, immediately before "But:", the following:

"(4) The defendant is convicted of two counts of distributing a controlled substance, each count involving a separate sale of 10 grams of cocaine that is part of a common scheme or plan. In addition, a finding is made that there are two other sales, also part of the common scheme or plan, each involving 10 grams of cocaine. The total amount of all four sales (40 grams of cocaine) will be used to determine the offense level for each count under § 1B1.3(a)(2). The two counts will then be grouped together under either this subsection or subsection (d) to avoid double counting.".

Reason for Amendment: This amendment clarifies the intended scope of § 1B1.3(a)(2) in conjunction with Chapter Three, Part D (Multiple Counts) to ensure that the latter is not read to limit the former only to conduct of which the defendant was convicted.

Effective Date: The effective date of this amendment is November 1, 1990.

310. **Amendment:** The Commentary to § 2A1.1 captioned "Statutory Provisions" is amended by deleting "18 U.S.C. § 1111" and inserting in lieu thereof "18 U.S.C. §§ 1111, 2113(e), 2118(c)(2)".

The Commentary to § 2A1.1 is amended in the first paragraph of Application Note 1 by deleting "the 'willful, deliberate, malicious, and premeditated killing' to which 18 U.S.C. § 1111 applies" and inserting in lieu thereof: "premeditated killing"; and by deleting:

"However, the same statute applies when death results from certain enumerated felonies -- arson, escape, murder, kidnapping, treason, espionage, sabotage, rape, burglary, or robbery.",

and inserting in lieu thereof:

"However, this guideline also applies when death results from the commission of certain felonies.".

The Commentary to § 2A1.1 captioned "Background" is amended in the first paragraph by deleting:

"Prior to the applicability of the Sentencing Reform Act of 1984, a defendant convicted under this statute and sentenced to life imprisonment could be paroled (see 18 U.S.C. § 4205(a)). Because of the abolition of parole by that Act, the language of 18 U.S.C. § 1111(b) (which was not amended by the Act) appears on its face to provide a mandatory minimum sentence of life imprisonment for this offense. Other provisions of the Act, however, classify this offense as a Class A felony (see 18 U.S.C. § 3559(a)(1)), for which a term of imprisonment of any period of time is authorized as an alternative to imprisonment for the duration of the defendant's life (see 18 U.S.C. §§ 3559(b), 3581(b)(1), as amended); hence, the relevance of the discussion in Application Note 1, supra, regarding circumstances in which a sentence less than life may be appropriate for a conviction under this statute.",

and inserting in lieu thereof:

"Whether a mandatory minimum term of life imprisonment is applicable to every defendant convicted of first degree murder under 18 U.S.C. § 1111 is a matter of statutory interpretation for the courts. The discussion in Application Note 1, supra, regarding circumstances in which a downward departure may be warranted is relevant in the event the penalty provisions of 18 U.S.C. § 1111 are construed to permit a sentence less than life imprisonment, or in the event the defendant is convicted under a statute that expressly authorizes a sentence of less than life imprisonment (e.g., 18 U.S.C. §§ 2113(e), 2118(c)(2), 21 U.S.C. § 848(e)).".

Reason for Amendment: This amendment clarifies the commentary with respect to circumstances that may warrant a departure below the guideline range for offenses to which this guideline applies. This amendment also reserves for the courts the issue of whether life imprisonment is the mandatory minimum sentence for first degree murder under 18 U.S.C. § 1111.

Effective Date: The effective date of this amendment is November 1, 1990.

311. **Amendment:** Section 2A2.1 is amended in the title by deleting "Conspiracy or Solicitation to Commit Murder;" immediately before "Attempted Murder".

Section 2A2.1 is amended by deleting:

"(a)   Base Offense Level: 20

(b)   Specific Offense Characteristics

(1)   If an assault involved more than minimal planning, increase by 2 levels.

(2)   (A) If a firearm was discharged, increase by 5 levels; (B) if a dangerous weapon (including a firearm) was otherwise used, increase by 4 levels; (C) if a dangerous weapon (including a firearm) was brandished or its use was threatened, increase by 3 levels.

(3)   If the victim sustained bodily injury, increase the offense level according to the seriousness of the injury:

	Degree of Bodily Injury	Increase in Level
(A)	Bodily Injury	add 2
(B)	Serious Bodily Injury	add 4
(C)	Permanent or Life-Threatening Bodily Injury	add 6

    (D)   If the degree of injury is between that specified in subdivisions (A) and (B), add 3 levels; or

    (E)   If the degree of injury is between that specified in subdivisions (B) and (C), add 5 levels.

Provided, however, that the cumulative adjustments from (2) and (3) shall not exceed 9 levels.

(4)   If a conspiracy or assault was motivated by a payment or offer of money or other thing of value, increase by 2 levels.",

and inserting in lieu thereof:

"(a)   Base Offense Level:

    (1)   28, if the object of the offense would have constituted first degree murder; or

    (2)   22, otherwise.

(b)   Specific Offense Characteristics

    (1)   (A) If the victim sustained permanent or life-threatening bodily injury, increase by 4 levels; (B) if the victim sustained serious bodily injury, increase by 2 levels; or (C) if the degree of injury is between that specified in subdivisions (A) and (B), increase by 3 levels.

    (2)   If the offense involved the offer or the receipt of anything of pecuniary value for undertaking the murder, increase by 4 levels.".

The Commentary to § 2A2.1 captioned "Statutory Provisions" is amended by deleting "(d), 373, 1113, 1116(a), 1117, 1751(c), (d), 1952A(a)" and inserting in lieu thereof "1113, 1116(a), 1751(c)".

The Commentary to § 2A2.1 captioned "Application Note" is amended in Note 1 by deleting "'more than minimal planning,' 'firearm,' 'dangerous weapon,' 'brandished,' 'otherwise used,' 'bodily injury,' 'serious bodily injury,'" and inserting in lieu thereof "'serious bodily injury'".

The Commentary to § 2A2.1 captioned "Application Note" is amended by inserting the following additional note:

"2.   'First degree murder,' as used in subsection (a)(1), means conduct that, if committed within the special maritime and territorial jurisdiction of the United States, would constitute first degree murder under 18 U.S.C. § 1111.";

and in the caption by deleting "Note" and inserting in lieu thereof "Notes".

The Commentary to § 2A2.1 captioned "Background" is amended in the first paragraph by deleting ", conspiracy to commit murder, solicitation to commit murder," immediately before "and attempted murder"; and by inserting the following additional sentence at the end:

> "An attempted manslaughter, or assault with intent to commit manslaughter, is covered under § 2A2.2 (Aggravated Assault).".

The Commentary to § 2A2.1 captioned "Background" is amended by deleting the second and third paragraphs as follows:

> "   The maximum term of imprisonment authorized by statute for conspiracy to murder is life imprisonment (18 U.S.C. § 1117). The maximum term of imprisonment authorized by statute for solicitation to murder is twenty years (18 U.S.C. § 373). The statutes that prohibit attempted murder, or assaults with intent to commit murder, vary widely in the maximum term of imprisonment authorized. Assault with intent to commit murder (18 U.S.C. § 113(a)) carries a maximum authorized term of twenty years imprisonment. An attempted assassination of certain essential government officials (18 U.S.C. § 351(c)) carries a maximum authorized term of life imprisonment. An attempted murder of foreign officials (18 U.S.C. § 1116(a)) carries a maximum authorized term of twenty years imprisonment. An attempt to commit murder, other than an assault with intent to commit murder covered by 18 U.S.C. § 113(a), carries a maximum term of three years imprisonment (18 U.S.C. § 1113).

>   Enhancements are provided for planning, weapon use, injury, and commission of the crime for hire. All of the factors can apply in the case of an assault; only the last can apply in the case of a conspiracy that does not include an assault; and none can apply in the case of a mere solicitation.".

The Commentary to § 2A2.2 captioned "Application Notes" is amended in Note 3 by inserting the following additional sentence as the first sentence: "This guideline also covers attempted manslaughter and assault with intent to commit manslaughter.".

The Commentary to § 2A2.2 captioned "Background" is amended in the first sentence of the first paragraph by deleting "where there is no intent to kill" immediately following " assaults".

Chapter Two, Part A, Subpart 1, is amended by inserting an additional guideline with accompanying commentary as § 2A1.5 (Conspiracy or Solicitation to Commit Murder).

Section 2E1.4(a)(1) is amended by deleting "23" and inserting in lieu thereof "32".

The Commentary to § 2E1.4 captioned "Application Notes" is amended by deleting Note 2 as follows:

> "2.   If the offense level for the underlying conduct is less than the alternative minimum base offense level specified (i.e., 23), the alternative minimum base offense level is to be used.";

and in the caption by deleting "Notes" and inserting in lieu thereof "Note".

The Commentary to § 2X1.1 captioned "Application Notes" is amended in Note 1 in the paragraph beginning "Offense guidelines that expressly cover attempts" by deleting "Con-

Amendment 311

spiracy or Solicitation to Commit Murder;" immediately before "Attempted Murder"; in the paragraph beginning "Offense guidelines that expressly cover conspiracies" by deleting "§ 2A2.1 (Assault With Intent to Commit Murder; Conspiracy or Solicitation to Commit Murder; Attempted Murder)" and inserting in lieu thereof "§ 2A1.5 (Conspiracy or Solicitation to Commit Murder)"; and in the paragraph beginning "Offense guidelines that expressly cover solicitations" by deleting "§ 2A2.1 (Assault With Intent to Commit Murder; Conspiracy or Solicitation to Commit Murder; Attempted Murder)" and inserting in lieu thereof "§ 2A1.5 (Conspiracy or Solicitation to Commit Murder)".

Reason for Amendment: This amendment restructures § 2A2.1, and increases the offense level for attempted murder and assault with intent to commit murder where the intended offense, if successful, would have constituted first degree murder to better reflect the seriousness of this conduct. For the same reason, the enhancement for an offense involving the offer or receipt of anything of pecuniary value for undertaking the murder is increased. For greater clarity, an additional guideline (§ 2A1.5) is inserted to cover conspiracy or solicitation to commit murder. Section 2E1.4 is amended to conform the offense level to that of § 2A1.5.

Effective Date: The effective date of this amendment is November 1, 1990.

312. **Amendment:** Section 2B1.1(b) is amended by transposing subdivisions (4) and (5); and by renumbering the transposed subdivisions accordingly.

Section 2B1.2(b) is amended by transposing subdivisions (3) and (4); and by renumbering the transposed subdivisions accordingly.

Section 2B1.3(b) is amended by transposing subdivisions (2) and (3); and by renumbering the transposed subdivisions accordingly.

Reason for Amendment: This amendment reorders the specific offense characteristics in §§ 2B1.1, 2B1.2, and 2B1.3 that address offenses involving U.S. mail. In cases involving the theft or destruction of U.S. mail, the theft guideline (§ 2B1.1), stolen property guideline (§ 2B1.2), property destruction guideline (§ 2B1.3), and forgery guideline (§ 2B5.2) produce identical results if the amount involved more than $1,000, or if the offense did not involve more than minimal planning. However, because of the ordering of the specific offense characteristics, there is a 1 or 2-level difference between §§ 2B1.1, 2B1.2 and 2B1.3 on the one hand, and § 2B5.2 on the other, in cases of stolen or destroyed mail involving more than minimal planning and a loss of $1,000 or less. In these cases, §§ 2B1.1, 2B1.2 and 2B1.3 produce a result that is 1 or 2-levels lower than § 2B5.2. This amendment corrects this anomaly by conforming the offense levels in §§ 2B1.1, 2B1.2, and 2B1.3 to that of § 2B5.2 in such cases.

Effective Date: The effective date of this amendment is November 1, 1990.

313. **Amendment:** Section 2B1.3 is amended by inserting the following additional subsection:

"(c)   Cross Reference

(1)   If the offense involved arson, or property damage by use of explosives, apply § 2K1.4 (Arson; Property Damage by Use of Explosives).";

and in the title by deleting "(Other than by Arson or Explosives)" immediately following "or Destruction".

The Commentary to § 2B1.3 captioned "Statutory Provisions" is amended by deleting the last sentence as follows:

"Arson is treated separately in Part K, Offenses Involving Public Order and Safety.".

The Commentary to § 2H1.1 captioned "Application Notes" is amended in Note 1 by deleting "(Other than by Arson or Explosives)" immediately following "or Destruction".

Section 2H3.3(a)(3) is amended by deleting "(Other than by Arson or Explosives)" immediately following "or Destruction".

The Commentary to § 2H3.3 captioned "Background" is amended by deleting "(Other than by Arson or Explosives)" immediately following "or Destruction".

Section 2Q1.6(a)(2) is amended by deleting "(Other Than by Arson or Explosives)" immediately following "or Destruction".

Reason for Amendment: This amendment inserts a cross reference providing that offense conduct constituting arson or property destruction by explosives is to be treated under § 2K1.4 (Arson, Property Destruction by Explosives). Because arson or property damage by use of explosives is an aggravated form of property destruction, just as armed robbery is an aggravated form of robbery, the use of the same "relevant conduct" standard to determine the offense level is appropriate.

Effective Date: The effective date of this amendment is November 1, 1990.

314. **Amendment:** Section 2B3.1(b)(1) is amended by deleting "offense involved robbery or attempted robbery of the" immediately following "If the"; and by inserting "was taken, or if the taking of such property was an object of the offense" immediately before ", increase".

The Commentary to § 2B3.1 captioned "Application Notes" is amended in Note 6 by deleting "actually" immediately following "defendant", and by inserting "; Attempted Murder" immediately following "Assault With Intent to Commit Murder".

Reason for Amendment: This amendment clarifies the guideline and Commentary.

Effective Date: The effective date of this amendment is November 1, 1990.

315. **Amendment:** Section 2B2.1(b)(3) is amended by deleting "obtaining" immediately before "a firearm", and by deleting "an object" and inserting in lieu thereof "taken, or if the taking of such item was an object".

The Commentary to § 2B2.1 is amended by inserting between "Commentary" and "Application Notes" the following:

"Statutory Provision: 18 U.S.C. § 1153.".

The Commentary to § 2B2.1 captioned "Application Notes" is amended by deleting Note 2 as follows:

"2. Obtaining a weapon or controlled substance is to be presumed to be an object of the offense if such an item was in fact taken.";

and by renumbering Notes 3 and 4 as 2 and 3, respectively.

Section 2B2.2(b)(3) is amended by deleting "obtaining" immediately before "a firearm"; and by deleting "an object" and inserting in lieu thereof "taken, or if the taking of such

Amendment 315 APPENDIX C - VOLUME I November 1, 2013

item was an object".

The Commentary to § 2B2.2 captioned "Application Notes" is amended by deleting Note 2 as follows:

"2. Obtaining a weapon or controlled substance is to be presumed to be an object of the offense if such an item was in fact taken.";

and by renumbering Notes 3 and 4 as 2 and 3, respectively.

Section 2B3.1(b)(5) is amended by deleting "obtaining" immediately before "a firearm"; and by deleting "the object" and inserting in lieu thereof "taken, or if the taking of such item was an object".

The Commentary to § 2B3.1 captioned "Application Notes" is amended by deleting Note 5 as follows:

"5. Obtaining a weapon or controlled substance is to be presumed to be an object of the offense if such an item was in fact taken.";

and by renumbering Notes 6, 7, and 8 as 5, 6, and 7 respectively.

The Commentary to § 2B3.1 captioned "Background" is amended by deleting the second paragraph as follows:

" Obtaining drugs or other controlled substances is often the motive for robberies of a Veterans Administration Hospital, a pharmacy on a military base, or a similar facility. A specific offense characteristic is included for robberies where drugs or weapons were the object of the offense to take account of the dangers involved when such items are taken.".

Reason for Amendment: This amendment provides that the specific offense characteristic related to the taking of a firearm or controlled substance applies whenever such item is taken or is an object of the offense. Also, it inserts additional Commentary to § 2B2.1 referencing a statutory provision contained in Appendix A (Statutory Index) to conform the format of this guideline to that of other offense guidelines.

Effective Date: The effective date of this amendment is November 1, 1990.

316. **Amendment:** Section 2B3.2(b)(1) is amended by deleting "§ 2B3.1" and inserting in lieu thereof "§ 2B2.1(b)(2)".

Reason for Amendment: This amendment references the loss table to § 2B2.1(b)(2) rather than § 2B3.1. The amendment to the loss table in § 2B3.1, effective November 1, 1989, inadvertently reduced the offense level for certain cases under this guideline by one level.

Effective Date: The effective date of this amendment is November 1, 1990.

317. **Amendment:** Section 2B1.1(b) is amended by inserting the following additional subdivision:

"(7) If the offense substantially jeopardized the safety and soundness of a financial institution, increase by 4 levels. If the resulting offense level is less than level 24, increase to level 24.".

The Commentary to § 2B1.1 captioned "Application Notes" is amended by inserting the following additional notes:

"9. 'Financial institution,' as used in this guideline, is defined to include any institution described in 18 U.S.C. §§ 215, 656-657, 1005-1008, 1014, and 1344; any state or foreign bank, trust company, credit union, insurance company, investment company, mutual fund, savings (building and loan) association, union or employee pension fund; any health, medical or hospital insurance association; brokers and dealers registered, or required to be registered, with the Securities and Exchange Commission; futures commodity merchants and commodity pool operators registered, or required to be registered, with the Commodity Futures Trading Commission; and any similar entity, whether or not insured by the federal government. 'Union or employee pension fund' and 'any health, medical, or hospital insurance association,' as used above, primarily include large pension funds that serve many individuals (e.g., pension funds of large national and international organizations, unions, and corporations doing substantial interstate business), and associations that undertake to provide pension, disability, or other benefits (e.g., medical or hospitalization insurance) to large numbers of persons.

10. An offense shall be deemed to have 'substantially jeopardized the safety and soundness of a financial institution' if as a consequence of the offense the institution became insolvent, substantially reduced benefits to pensioners or insureds, was unable on demand to refund fully any deposit, payment or investment, or was so depleted of its assets as to be forced to merge with another institution in order to continue active operations.".

The Commentary to § 2B1.1 captioned "Background" is amended by inserting the following additional paragraph at the end:

" Subsection (b)(7) implements, in a broader form, the statutory directive to the Commission in Section 961(m) of Public Law 101-73.".

Section 2B4.1(b) is amended by deleting "Characteristic" and inserting in lieu thereof "Characteristics"; and by inserting the following additional subdivision:

"(2) If the offense substantially jeopardized the safety and soundness of a financial institution, increase by 4 levels. If the resulting offense level is less than level 24, increase to level 24.".

The Commentary to § 2B4.1 captioned "Statutory Provisions" is amended by deleting "§§ 1," and inserting in lieu thereof "§§ ".

The Commentary to § 2B4.1 captioned "Application Notes" is amended by inserting the following additional notes:

"3. 'Financial institution,' as used in this guideline, is defined to include any institution described in 18 U.S.C. §§ 215, 656-657, 1005-1008, 1014, and 1344; any state or foreign bank, trust company, credit union, insurance company, investment company, mutual fund, savings (building and loan) association, union or employee pension fund; any health, medical or hospital insurance association; brokers and dealers registered, or required to be registered, with the Securities and Exchange Commission; futures commodity merchants and commodity pool operators registered, or required to be registered, with the Commodity Futures Trading Commission; and any similar entity, whether or not insured by the federal government. 'Union or employee pension fund' and 'any health, medical, or hospital insurance association,' as used above, primarily include large pension funds that serve many individuals (e.g., pension funds of large national and international organizations, unions, and corporations doing substantial interstate business), and associations that undertake to provide pension, disability, or other benefits (e.g., medical or hospitalization insurance) to large numbers of persons.

4. An offense shall be deemed to have 'substantially jeopardized the safety and soundness of a financial institution' if as a consequence of the offense the institution became insolvent, substantially reduced benefits to pensioners or insureds, was unable on demand to refund fully any deposit, payment or investment, or was so depleted of its assets as to be forced to merge with another institution in order to continue active operations.".

The Commentary to § 2B4.1 captioned "Background" is amended by inserting the following additional paragraph at the end:

" Subsection (b)(2) implements, in a broader form, the statutory directive to the Commission in Section 961(m) of Public Law 101-73.".

Section 2F1.1(b) is amended by inserting the following additional subdivision:

"(6) If the offense substantially jeopardized the safety and soundness of a financial institution, increase by 4 levels. If the resulting offense level is less than level 24, increase to level 24.".

The Commentary to § 2F1.1 captioned "Statutory Provisions" is amended by deleting "290" and inserting in lieu thereof "289".

The Commentary to § 2F1.1 captioned "Application Notes" is amended by inserting the following additional notes:

"14. 'Financial institution,' as used in this guideline, is defined to include any institution described in 18 U.S.C. §§ 215, 656-657, 1005-1008, 1014, and 1344; any state or foreign bank, trust company, credit union, insurance company, investment company, mutual fund, savings (building and loan) association, union or employee pension fund; any health, medical or hospital insurance association; brokers and dealers registered, or required to be registered, with the Securities and Exchange Commission; futures commodity merchants and commodity pool operators registered, or required to be registered, with the Commodity Futures Trading Commission; and any similar entity, whether or not insured by the federal government. 'Union or employee pension fund' and 'any health, medical, or hospital insurance association,' as used above, primarily include large pension funds that serve many individuals (e.g., pension funds of large national and international organizations, unions, and corporations doing substantial interstate business), and associations that undertake to provide pension, disability, or other benefits (e.g., medical or hospitalization insurance) to large numbers of persons.

15. An offense shall be deemed to have 'substantially jeopardized the safety and soundness of a financial institution' if as a consequence of the offense the institution became insolvent, substantially reduced benefits to pensioners or

insureds, was unable on demand to refund fully any deposit, payment or investment, or was so depleted of its assets as to be forced to merge with another institution in order to continue active operations.".

The Commentary to § 2F1.1 captioned "Background" is amended by inserting the following additional paragraph at the end:

" Subsection (b)(6) implements, in a broader form, the statutory directive to the Commission in Section 961(m) of Public Law 101-73.".

Reason for Amendment: This amendment implements, in a broader form, the following statutory directive in Section 961(m) of Public Law 101-73: "Pursuant to section 994 of title 28, United States Code, and section 21 of the Sentencing Act of 1987, the United States Sentencing Commission shall promulgate guidelines, or amend existing guidelines, to provide for a substantial period of incarceration for a violation of, or a conspiracy to violate, section 215, 656, 657, 1005, 1006, 1007, 1014, 1341, 1343, or 1344 of title 18, United States Code, that substantially jeopardizes the safety and soundness of a federally insured financial institution." In addition, this amendment deletes an incorrect statutory provision in the Commentary to § 2B4.1, and deletes a reference to a petty offense in the Commentary to § 2F1.1 that was inadvertently retained when other references to petty offenses were deleted.

Effective Date: The effective date of this amendment is November 1, 1990.

318. **Amendment:** The Commentary to § 2D1.1 captioned "Application Notes" is amended in Note 10 in the subdivision of the "Drug Equivalency Tables" captioned "Cocaine and Other Schedule I and II Stimulants (and their immediate precursors)" by inserting the following additional entry as the seventh entry: "1 gm of Methamphetamine (Pure) = 50 gm of cocaine/10 gm of heroin".

The Commentary to § 2D1.1 captioned "Application Notes" is amended in Note 10 in the subdivision of the "Drug Equivalency Tables" captioned "Cocaine and Other Schedule I and II Stimulants (and their immediate precursors)" in the twelfth (fomerly eleventh) entry by deleting "0.418 gm" and inserting in lieu thereof "0.416 gm".

The Commentary to § 2D1.1 captioned "Application Notes" is amended in Note 10 in the subdivision of the "Drug Equivalency Tables" captioned "Schedule IV Substances" by deleting the sixth entry as follows:

"1 gm of Mephobarbital = 0.125 mg of heroin/0.125 gm of marihuana".

The Commentary to § 2D1.1 captioned "Application Notes" is amended in Note 11 by inserting "in the table below" immediately before "to estimate"; by deleting "Bufotenine at 1 mg per dose = 100 mg of Bufotenine" and inserting in lieu thereof "Mescaline at 500 mg per dose = 50 gms of mescaline"; and by deleting "common controlled substances" and inserting in lieu thereof "certain controlled substances. Do not use this table if any more reliable estimate of the total weight is available from case-specific information".

The Commentary to § 2D1.1 captioned "Application Notes" is amended in Note 11 by deleting the following from the table captioned "Typical Weight Per Unit (Dose, Pill, or Capsule) Table":

"Bufotenine	1 mg
Diethyltryptamine	60 mg

Amendment 318 APPENDIX C - VOLUME I November 1, 2013

> Dimethyltryptamine   50 mg",
>
> "Barbiturates   100 mg
> Glutethimide (Doriden)   500 mg",
>
> "Thiobarbital   50 mg";

by inserting an asterisk immediately after each of the following:

> "LSD (Lysergic acid diethylamide)", "MDA", "PCP", "Psilocin", "Psilocybin", "2,5-Dimethoxy-4-methylamphetamine (STP, DOM)", "Methaqualone", "Amphetamine", "Methamphetamine", "Phenmetrazine (Preludin)";

and by inserting the following at the end:

> "*For controlled substances marked with an asterisk, the weight per unit shown is the weight of the actual controlled substance, and not generally the weight of the mixture or substance containing the controlled substance. Therefore, use of this table provides a very conservative estimate of the total weight.".

Reason for Amendment: This amendment provides an additional equivalency to reflect the distinction between methamphetamine and pure methamphetamine in the Drug Quantity Table at § 2D1.1(c), corrects an error in the equivalency for Phenylacetone/P_2P, and deletes a duplicate listing for Mephobarbital.

In addition, this amendment clarifies that the "Typical Weight Per Unit Table" in Note 11 of the Commentary to § 2D1.1 is not to be used where a more reliable estimate of the weight of the mixture or substance containing the controlled substance is available from case-specific information. This amendment also clarifies that for certain controlled substances this table provides an estimate of the weight of the actual controlled substance, not necessarily the weight of the mixture or substance containing the controlled substance, and therefore use of this table in such cases will provide a very conservative estimate. Finally, this amendment deletes listings for several controlled substances that are generally legitimately manufactured and then unlawfully diverted; in such cases, more accurate weight estimates can be obtained from other sources (*e.g.*, from the Drug Enforcement Administration or the manufacturer).

Effective Date: The effective date of this amendment is November 1, 1990.

319. **Amendment:** Section 2D1.2(a)(1) is amended by inserting "applicable to the quantity of controlled substances directly involving a protected location or an underage or pregnant individual" immediately following "§ 2D1.1".

Section § 2D1.2(a) is amended by renumbering subdivisions (2) and (3) as (3) and (4), respectively; and by inserting the following as subdivision (2):

> "(2)   1 plus the offense level from § 2D1.1 applicable to the total quantity of controlled substances involved in the offense; or".

The Commentary to § 2D1.2 is amended by inserting, immediately before "Background", the following:

> "<u>Application Note</u>:

– 158 –

1. Where only part of the relevant offense conduct directly involved a protected location or an underage or pregnant individual, subsections (a)(1) and (a)(2) may result in different offense levels. For example, if the defendant, as part of the same course of conduct or common scheme or plan, sold 5 grams of heroin near a protected location and 10 grams of heroin elsewhere, the offense level from subsection (a)(1) would be level 16 (2 plus the offense level for the sale of 5 grams of heroin, the amount sold near the protected location); the offense level from subsection (a)(2) would be level 17 (1 plus the offense level for the sale of 15 grams of heroin, the total amount of heroin involved in the offense).".

Reason for Amendment: This amendment provides for the determination of the offense level in cases in which only part of the relevant offense conduct involves a protected location or an underage or pregnant individual.

Effective Date: The effective date of this amendment is November 1, 1990.

320. **Amendment:** Section 2D1.6 is amended by deleting "12" and inserting in lieu thereof: "the offense level applicable to the underlying offense.".

The Commentary to § 2D1.6 is amended by inserting, immediately before "Background", the following:

"<u>Application Note</u>:

1. Where the offense level for the underlying offense is to be determined by reference to § 2D1.1, <u>see</u> Application Note 12 of the Commentary to § 2D1.1, and Application Notes 1 and 2 of the Commentary to § 2D1.4, for guidance in determining the scale of the offense. Note that the Drug Quantity Table in § 2D1.1 provides a minimum offense level of 12 where the offense involves heroin (or other Schedule I or II Opiates), cocaine (or other Schedule I or II Stimulants), cocaine base, PCP, Methamphetamine, LSD (or other Schedule I or II Hallucinogens), Fentanyl, or Fentanyl Analogue (§ 2D1.1(c)(16)); and a minimum offense level of 6 otherwise (§ 2D1.1(c)(19)).".

Reason for Amendment: This amendment is designed to reduce unwarranted disparity by requiring consideration in the guideline of the amount of the controlled substance involved in the offense, thus conforming this guideline section to the structure of §§ 2D1.1, 2D1.2, 2D1.4, and 2D1.5. The statute to which this guideline applies (21 U.S.C. § 843(b)) prohibits the use of a communications facility to commit, cause, or facilitate a felony controlled substance offense. Frequently, a conviction under this statute is the result of a plea bargain because the statute has a low maximum (four years with no prior felony drug conviction; eight years with a prior felony drug conviction) and no mandatory minimum. The current guideline has a base offense level of 12 and no specific offense characteristics. Therefore, the scale of the underlying drug offense is not reflected in the guideline. This results in a departure from the guideline range frequently being warranted. Without guidance as to whether or how far to depart, the potential for unwarranted disparity is substantial. Under this amendment, the guideline itself will take into account the scale of the underlying offense.

Effective Date: The effective date of this amendment is November 1, 1990.

321. **Amendment:** Section 2D2.1(a)(1) is amended by deleting "or an analogue of these" and

inserting in lieu thereof "an analogue of these, or cocaine base".

Reason for Amendment: This amendment specifies the appropriate offense level for possession of cocaine base ("crack") in cases not covered by the enhanced penalties created by section 6371 of the Anti-Drug Abuse Act of 1988.

Effective Date: The effective date of this amendment is November 1, 1990.

322. **Amendment:** Section 2G1.1(c)(1) is amended by deleting "involves" and inserting in lieu thereof "involved".

The Commentary to § 2G1.1 captioned "Application Notes" is amended in Note 3 by inserting at the end:

> "This factor would apply, for example, where the ability of the person being transported to appraise or control conduct was substantially impaired by drugs or alcohol. In the case of transportation involving an adult, rather than a minor, this characteristic generally will not apply where the alcohol or drug was voluntarily taken.".

The Commentary to § 2G1.1 captioned "Application Notes" is amended in Note 5 by deleting ", distinct offense, even if several persons are transported in a single act" and inserting in lieu thereof:

> "victim. Consequently, multiple counts involving the transportation of different persons are not to be grouped together under § 3D1.2 (Groups of Closely-Related Counts). Special instruction (c)(1) directs that if the relevant conduct of an offense of conviction includes more than one person being transported, whether specifically cited in the count of conviction or not, each such person shall be treated as if contained in a separate count of conviction".

Reason for Amendment: This amendment clarifies the application of this guideline and corrects a clerical error.

Effective Date: The effective date of this amendment is November 1, 1990.

323. **Amendment:** Section 2G1.2(c)(1) is amended by deleting "involves" and inserting in lieu thereof "involved".

Section 2G1.2 is amended by inserting the following additional subsection:

> "(d)   Cross Reference
>
> > (1)   If the offense involved the defendant causing, transporting, permitting, or offering or seeking by notice or advertisement, a minor to engage in sexually explicit conduct for the purpose of producing a visual depiction of such conduct, apply § 2G2.1 (Sexually Exploiting a Minor by Production of Sexually Explicit Visual or Printed Material; Custodian Permitting Minor to Engage in Sexually Explicit Conduct; Advertisement for Minors to Engage in Production).".

The Commentary to § 2G1.2 captioned "Statutory Provisions" is amended by deleting "§ 2423" and inserting in lieu thereof "§§ 2421, 2422, 2423".

The Commentary to § 2G1.2 captioned "Application Notes" is amended in Note 1 by deleting ", distinct offense, even if several persons are transported in a single act" and inserting in lieu thereof:

> "victim. Consequently, multiple counts involving the transportation of different persons are not to be grouped together under § 3D1.2 (Groups of Closely-Related Counts). Special instruction (c)(1) directs that if the relevant conduct of an offense of conviction includes more than one person being transported, whether specifically cited in the count of conviction or not, each such person shall be treated as if contained in a separate count of conviction".

The Commentary to § 2G1.2 captioned "Application Notes" is amended in Note 3 by inserting the following at the end:

> "This factor would apply, for example, where the ability of the person being transported to appraise or control conduct was substantially impaired by drugs or alcohol.".

The Commentary to § 2G1.2 captioned "Application Notes" is amended by inserting the following additional notes:

> "4. 'Sexually explicit conduct,' as used in this guideline, has the meaning set forth in 18 U.S.C. § 2256.
>
> 5. The cross reference in (d)(1) is to be construed broadly to include all instances where the offense involved employing, using, persuading, inducing, enticing, coercing, transporting, permitting, or offering or seeking by notice or advertisement, a minor to engage in sexually explicit conduct for the purpose of producing any visual depiction of such conduct.".

Reason for Amendment: This amendment clarifies the application of this guideline and corrects a clerical error. In addition, a cross reference to § 2G2.1 is inserted where the offense involves conduct that is more appropriately covered by that guideline to provide an offense level that more appropriately reflects the seriousness of such conduct.

Effective Date: The effective date of this amendment is November 1, 1990.

324. **Amendment:** Section 2G2.1 is amended in the title by inserting "; Custodian Permitting Minor to Engage in Sexually Explicit Conduct; Advertisement for Minors to Engage in Production" immediately following "Printed Material".

    Section 2G2.1 is amended by deleting:

    > "(1)   If the minor was under the age of twelve years, increase by 2 levels.";

    and inserting in lieu thereof:

    > "(1)   If the offense involved a minor under the age of twelve years, increase by 4 levels; otherwise, if the offense involved a minor under the age of sixteen years, increase by 2 levels.
    >
    > (2)   If the defendant was a parent, relative, or legal guardian of the minor involved in the offense, or if the minor was otherwise in the custody, care, or supervisory control of the defendant, increase by 2 levels.
    >
    > (c)   Special Instruction

(1) If the offense involved the exploitation of more than one minor, Chapter Three, Part D (Multiple Counts) shall be applied as if the exploitation of each minor had been contained in a separate count of conviction.";

and by deleting "Characteristic" and inserting in lieu thereof "Characteristics".

The Commentary to § 2G2.1 captioned "Statutory Provisions" is amended by deleting "8 U.S.C. § 1328;"; and by inserting "(a), (b), (c)(1)(B)" immediately following "18 U.S.C. § 2251".

The Commentary to § 2G2.1 captioned "Application Notes" is amended in Note 1 by inserting at the end:

"Special instruction (c)(1) directs that if the relevant conduct of an offense of conviction includes more than one minor being exploited, whether specifically cited in the count of conviction or not, each such minor shall be treated as if contained in a separate count of conviction.".

The Commentary to § 2G2.1 captioned "Application Note" is amended by inserting the following additional notes:

"2. Specific offense characteristic (b)(2) is intended to have broad application and includes offenses involving a minor entrusted to the defendant, whether temporarily or permanently. For example, teachers, day care providers, babysitters, or other temporary caretakers are among those who would be subject to this enhancement. In determining whether to apply this adjustment, the court should look to the actual relationship that existed between the defendant and the child and not simply to the legal status of the defendant-child relationship.

3. If specific offense characteristic (b)(2) applies, no adjustment is to be made under § 3B1.3 (Abuse of Position of Trust or Use of Special Skill).";

and in the caption by deleting "Note" and inserting in lieu thereof "Notes".

The Commentary to § 2G2.1 captioned "Background" is deleted in its entirety as follows:

"Background: This offense commonly involves the production source of a child pornography enterprise. Because the offense directly involves the exploitation of minors, the base offense level is higher than for the distribution of the sexually explicit material after production. An enhancement is provided when the conduct involves the exploitation of a minor under age twelve to reflect the more serious nature of exploiting young children.".

Reason for Amendment: This amendment revises subsection (b)(1) to provide distinctions for the age of the victim consistent with § 2G1.2, and adds subsection (b)(2) to provide an increase for defendants who abuse a position of trust in exploiting minor children. A special instruction is added to conform the operation of the multiple count rule in this guideline with §§ 2G1.1 and 2G1.2. A revision to the statutory provisions removes 8 U.S.C. § 1328; such offenses are now brought under this guideline by the cross reference appearing in § 2G1.2. In addition, the reference in the statutory provisions to 18 U.S.C. § 2251 is made specific to the appropriate subsections.

Effective Date: The effective date of this amendment is November 1, 1990.

325. Amendment: Section 2G2.2 is amended by inserting the following at the end:

>"(3) If the offense involved material that portrays sadistic or masochistic conduct or other depictions of violence, increase by 4 levels.

>(c) Cross Reference

>(1) If the offense involved causing, transporting, permitting, or offering or seeking by notice or advertisement, a minor to engage in sexually explicit conduct for the purpose of producing a visual depiction of such conduct, apply § 2G2.1 (Sexually Exploiting a Minor by Production of Sexually Explicit Visual or Printed Material; Custodian Permitting Minor to Engage in Sexually Explicit Conduct; Advertisement for Minors to Engage in Production) if the resulting offense level is greater than that determined above.".

The Commentary to § 2G2.2 captioned "Statutory Provision" is amended by deleting "Provision" and inserting in lieu thereof "Provisions"; and by inserting "§ 1460, 2251(c)(1)(A)," immediately before "2252".

The Commentary to § 2G2.2 captioned "Application Note" is amended by inserting the following additional notes:

>"2. 'Sexually explicit conduct,' as used in this guideline, has the meaning set forth in 18 U.S.C. § 2256.

>3. The cross reference in (c)(1) is to be construed broadly to include all instances where the offense involved employing, using, persuading, inducing, enticing, coercing, transporting, permitting, or offering or seeking by notice or advertisement, a minor to engage in sexually explicit conduct for the purpose of producing any visual depiction of such conduct.

>4. If the defendant sexually abused a minor at any time, whether or not such sexual abuse occurred during the course of the offense, an upward departure is warranted. In determining the extent of such a departure, the court should take into consideration the offense levels provided in §§ 2A3.1, 2A3.2, and 2A3.4 most commensurate with the defendant's conduct.";

and in the caption by deleting "Note" and inserting in lieu thereof "Notes".

Reason for Amendment: This amendment provides a specific offense characteristic for materials involving depictions of sadistic or masochistic conduct or other violence, and a cross reference for offenses more appropriately treated under § 2G2.1. It also provides Commentary recommending consideration of an upward departure in cases in which the defendant has sexually abused a minor at any time, whether or not such sexual abuse occurred during the course of the instant offense. In addition, it inserts a statutory provision indicating the applicability of this guideline to violations of 18 U.S.C. § 2251(c)(1)(A).

Effective Date: The effective date of this amendment is November 1, 1990.

326. Amendment: Section 2G3.1(b)(2) is amended by deleting "sadomasochistic" and inserting in lieu thereof "sadistic or masochistic".

Section 2G3.1(c) is amended by deleting:

>"(1) If the offense involved a criminal enterprise, apply the appropriate guideline

from Chapter Two, Part E (Offenses Involving Criminal Enterprises and Racketeering) if the resulting offense level is greater than that determined above.",

and inserting in lieu thereof:

"(1) If the offense involved transporting, distributing, receiving, possessing, or advertising to receive material involving the sexual exploitation of a minor, apply § 2G2.2 (Transporting, Receiving, or Trafficking in Material Involving the Sexual Exploitation of a Minor).".

Reason for Amendment: This amendment inserts a cross reference to § 2G2.2 for offenses involving materials which, in fact, depict children to ensure that the penalties for such offenses adequately reflect their seriousness. The current cross reference at subsection (c)(1) is deleted. In addition, the amendment conforms the terminology of specific offense characteristic (b)(2) to that used in other offense guidelines.

Effective Date: The effective date of this amendment is November 1, 1990.

327. **Amendment:** Section 2H1.1 is amended in the title by inserting "Conspiracy to Interfere with Civil Rights;" immediately before "Going".

Chapter Two, Part H, Subpart 1 is amended by deleting § 2H1.2 in its entirety as follows:

"§ 2H1.2. Conspiracy to Interfere with Civil Rights

(a) Base Offense Level (Apply the greater):

(1) 13; or

(2) 2 plus the offense level applicable to any underlying offense.

(b) Specific Offense Characteristic

(1) If the defendant was a public official at the time of the offense, increase by 4 levels.

Commentary

Statutory Provision: 18 U.S.C. § 241.

Application Notes:

1. '2 plus the offense level applicable to any underlying offense' is defined in the Commentary to § 2H1.1.

2. Where the adjustment in § 2H1.2(b)(1) is applied, do not apply § 3B1.3 (Abuse of Position of Trust or Use of Special Skill).

Background: This section applies to conspiracies to interfere with civil rights. The maximum term of imprisonment authorized by statute is ten years; except where death results, the maximum term of imprisonment authorized by statute is life imprisonment. The base offense level for this guideline assumes threatening or otherwise serious conduct.".

The Commentary to § 2X1.1 captioned "Application Notes" is amended in Note 1 in the paragraph beginning "Offense guidelines that expressly cover conspiracies" by deleting "§ 2H1.2 (Conspiracy to Interfere with Civil Rights)" and inserting in lieu thereof "§ 2H1.1 (Conspiracy to Interfere With Civil Rights; Going in Disguise to Deprive of Rights)".

Reason for Amendment: This amendment consolidates two guidelines and raises the minimum base offense level from level 13 to level 15 for cases currently covered under § 2H1.2 to better reflect the seriousness of this offense.

Effective Date: The effective date of this amendment is November 1, 1990.

328. **Amendment:** The Commentary to § 2H1.5 captioned "Statutory Provisions" is amended by deleting "Provisions" and inserting in lieu thereof "Provision"; and by deleting "; 42 U.S.C. § 3631".

    The Commentary to § 2H1.5 captioned "Application Notes" is amended by deleting Note 3 as follows:

    > "3. In the case of a violation of 42 U.S.C. § 3631, apply this guideline where the offense did not involve the threat or use of force. If the offense involved the threat or use of force, apply § 2H1.3.".

    Reason for Amendment: This amendment deletes references to a statute to which this guideline does not apply.

    Effective Date: The effective date of this amendment is November 1, 1990.

329. **Amendment:** Section 2J1.6 is amended by deleting:

    "(a) Base Offense Level: 6

    (b) Specific Offense Characteristics

       (1) If the underlying offense is punishable by death or imprisonment for a term of fifteen years or more, increase by 9 levels.

       (2) If the underlying offense is punishable by a term of imprisonment of five or more years, but less than fifteen years, increase by 6 levels.

       (3) If the underlying offense is a felony punishable by a maximum term of less than five years, increase by 3 levels.",

    and inserting in lieu thereof:

    "(a) Base Offense Level:

       (1) 11, if the offense constituted a failure to report for service of sentence; or

       (2) 6, otherwise.

    (b) Specific Offense Characteristics

       (1) If the base offense level is determined under subsection (a)(1), and the defendant --

          (A) voluntarily surrendered within 96 hours of the time he was originally scheduled to report, decrease by 5 levels; or

Amendment 329 APPENDIX C - VOLUME I November 1, 2013

       (B)   was ordered to report to a community corrections center, community treatment center, 'halfway house,' or similar facility, and subdivision (A) above does not apply, decrease by 2 levels.

       Provided, however, that this reduction shall not apply if the defendant, while away from the facility, committed any federal, state, or local offense punishable by a term of imprisonment of one year or more.

  (2)   If the base offense level is determined under subsection (a)(2), and the underlying offense is --

       (A)   punishable by death or imprisonment for a term of fifteen years or more, increase by 9 levels; or

       (B)   punishable by a term of imprisonment of five years or more, but less than fifteen years, increase by 6 levels; or

       (C)   a felony punishable by a term of imprisonment of less than five years, increase by 3 levels.".

The Commentary to § 2J1.6 captioned "Background" is amended by deleting "The offense level for this offense" and inserting in lieu thereof "Where the base offense level is determined under subsection (a)(2), the offense level".

Reason for Amendment: This amendment provides greater differentiation in the guideline offense levels for the various types of conduct covered by this guideline.

Effective Date: The effective date of this amendment is November 1, 1990.

330. Amendment: Chapter Two, Part K, Subpart 1 is amended by deleting § 2K1.4 in its entirety as follows:

  "§ 2K1.4.   <u>Arson; Property Damage By Use of Explosives</u>

    (a)   Base Offense Level: 6

    (b)   Specific Offense Characteristics

    If more than one applies, use the greatest:

       (1)   If the defendant knowingly created a substantial risk of death or serious bodily injury, increase by 18 levels.

       (2)   If the defendant recklessly endangered the safety of another, increase by 14 levels.

       (3)   If the offense involved destruction or attempted destruction of a residence, increase by 12 levels.

       (4)   If the defendant used fire or an explosive to commit another offense that is a felony under federal law, or carried explosives during the commission of any offense that is a felony under federal law (<u>i.e.</u>, the defendant is convicted under 18 U.S.C. § 844(h)), increase by 7 levels.

(5) If the defendant endangered the safety of another person, increase by 4 levels.

(6) If a destructive device was used, increase by 2 levels.

(c) Cross References

(1) If the defendant caused death, or intended to cause bodily injury, apply the most analogous guideline from Chapter Two, Part A (Offenses Against the Person) if the resulting offense level is greater than that determined above.

(2) Apply § 2B1.3 (Property Damage or Destruction) if the resulting offense level is greater than that determined above.

(d) Note

(1) The specific offense characteristic in subsection (b)(4) applies only in the case of an offense committed prior to November 18, 1988.

Commentary

Statutory Provisions: 18 U.S.C. §§ 32, 33, 81, 844(f), (h) (only in the case of an offense committed prior to November 18, 1988), (i), 1153, 1855, 2275.

Application Notes:

1. 'Destructive device' means any article described in 18 U.S.C. § 921(a)(4) (for example, explosive, incendiary, or poison gas bombs, grenades, mines, and similar devices and certain rockets, missiles, and large bore weapons).

2. If bodily injury resulted, an upward departure may be warranted. See Chapter Five, Part K (Departures).

Background: Review of presentence reports indicates that many arson cases involve 'malicious mischief,' i.e., minor property damage under circumstances that do not present an appreciable danger. A low base offense level is provided for these cases. However, aggravating factors are provided for instances where a defendant knowingly or recklessly endangered others, destroyed or attempted to destroy a residence, used a destructive device, or otherwise endangered others. As amended by Section 6474(b) of the Anti-Drug Abuse Act of 1988 (effective November 18, 1988), 18 U.S.C. § 844(h) sets forth a mandatory sentencing enhancement of five years for the first offense and ten years for subsequent offenses if the defendant was convicted of using fire or an explosive to commit a felony or of carrying an explosive during the commission of a felony. See § 2K1.7.".

A replacement guideline with accompanying commentary is inserted as § 2K1.4 (Arson; Property Damage by Use of Explosives).

Reason for Amendment: This amendment restructures this guideline to provide more appropriate offense levels for the conduct covered. The Commission has determined that the offense levels provided in the current guideline do not adequately reflect the seriousness of the offenses that are covered under this section.

Effective Date: The effective date of this amendment is November 1, 1990.

331. Amendment: Section 2K1.6(a) is amended by deleting "greater" and inserting in lieu thereof "greatest"; and by inserting the following additional subdivision:

"(3) If death resulted, apply the most analogous guideline from Chapter Two, Part A, Subpart 1 (Homicide).".

Section 2K1.6(a)(2) is amended by deleting the period at the end and inserting in lieu thereof "; or".

Reason for Amendment: This amendment adds an additional alternative base offense level to cover the situation in which the commission of this offense results in death.

Effective Date: The effective date of this amendment is November 1, 1990.

332. Amendment: Section 2K1.7 is amended by inserting "(a)" immediately before "If"; and by inserting the following additional subsection:

"(b) Special Instruction for Fines

(1) Where there is a federal conviction for the underlying offense, the fine guideline shall be the fine guideline that would have been applicable had there only been a conviction for the underlying offense. This guideline shall be used as a consolidated fine guideline for both the underlying offense and the conviction underlying this section.".

The Commentary to § 2K1.7 captioned "Application Notes" is amended by inserting the following additional notes:

"3. Where a sentence under this section is imposed in conjunction with a sentence for an underlying offense, any specific offense characteristic for the use of fire or explosives is not to be applied in respect to the guideline for the underlying offense.

4. Subsection (b) sets forth special provisions concerning the imposition of fines. Where there is also a conviction for the underlying offense, a consolidated fine guideline is determined by the offense level that would have applied to the underlying offense absent a conviction under 18 U.S.C. § 844(h). This is required because the offense level for the underlying offense may be reduced in that any specific offense characteristic for use of fire or explosives would not be applied (see Application Note 3). The Commission has not established a fine guideline range for the unusual case in which there is no conviction for the underlying offense, although a fine is authorized under 18 U.S.C. § 3571.".

The Commentary to § 2K2.4 captioned "Application Notes" is amended in Note 4 in the third sentence by inserting "required" immediately before "because"; and by inserting ", although a fine is authorized under 18 U.S.C. § 3571" immediately before the period at the end of the last sentence.

Reason for Amendment: This amendment conforms § 2K1.7 to § 2K2.4, which includes specific instructions concerning treatment of fines and double counting. Both sections are based upon similarly written statutes that provide for a fixed mandatory, consecutive sentence of imprisonment. In addition, Application Note 4 of the Commentary to § 2K2.4 is revised and expanded for greater clarity.

Effective Date: The effective date of this amendment is November 1, 1990.

333. **Amendment:** Section 2K2.1(a)(1) is amended by deleting "16" and inserting in lieu thereof "18".

Section 2K2.1(b)(1) is amended by inserting ", other than a firearm covered in 26 U.S.C. § 5845(a)," immediately following "ammunition".

Section 2K2.2(a)(1) is amended by deleting "16" and inserting in lieu thereof "18".

Reason for Amendment: This amendment provides that the reduction in offense level under subsection (b)(1) for possession of a weapon for sporting purposes or collection may not be applied in the case of any weapon described in 26 U.S.C. § 5845(a). In addition, the amendment increases the base offense level in subsection (a)(1) of §§ 2K2.1 and 2K2.2 from 16 to 18 to better reflect the seriousness of the conduct covered.

Effective Date: The effective date of this amendment is November 1, 1990.

334. **Amendment:** Chapter Two, Part K, Subpart 3 is amended by inserting an additional guideline with accompanying commentary as § 2K3.2 (Feloniously Mailing Injurious Articles).

Reason for Amendment: This amendment adds an additional guideline covering the felony provisions of 18 U.S.C. § 1716.

Effective Date: The effective date of this amendment is November 1, 1990.

335. **Amendment:** Section 2L1.1(b)(1) is amended by deleting "and without knowledge that the alien was excludable under 8 U.S.C. §§ 1182(a)(27), (28), (29)," immediately before "decrease".

The Commentary to § 2L1.1 captioned "Application Notes" is amended by deleting:

> "7. 8 U.S.C. §§ 1182(a)(27), (a)(28), and (a)(29) concern certain aliens who are excludable because they are subversives.",

and inserting in lieu thereof:

> "7. Where the defendant smuggled, transported, or harbored an alien knowing that the alien intended to enter the United States to engage in subversive activity, an upward departure may be warranted.".

The Commentary to § 2L1.1 captioned "Background" is amended in the second sentence by deleting "and did not know the alien was excludable as a subversive" immediately following "profit".

Reason for Amendment: This amendment deletes a portion of specific offense characteristic (b)(1) that is unclear in application, and in any event rarely occurs, and replaces it with an application note indicating that an upward departure may be warranted in the circumstances specified.

Effective Date: The effective date of this amendment is November 1, 1990.

336. **Amendment:** Section 2M4.1(b)(1) is amended by deleting "while" and inserting in lieu thereof "at a time when"; and by deleting "into the armed services, other than in time of war or armed conflict" and inserting in lieu thereof "for compulsory military service".

The Commentary to § 2M4.1 captioned "Application Notes" is amended by deleting:

Amendment 336   APPENDIX C - VOLUME I   November 1, 2013

"1. 'While persons were being inducted into the armed services' means at a time of compulsory military service under the Selective Service laws.

2. The Commission has not considered the appropriate sanction for this offense when persons are being inducted during time of war or armed conflict.",

and inserting in lieu thereof:

"1. Subsection (b)(1) does not distinguish between whether the offense was committed in peacetime or during time of war or armed conflict. If the offense was committed when persons were being inducted for compulsory military service during time of war or armed conflict, an upward departure may be warranted.";

and in the caption by deleting "Notes" and inserting in lieu thereof "Note".

Reason for Amendment: This amendment clarifies this guideline and deletes language that produced the anomalous result of a lower offense level for failure to register and evasion of military service in time of war or armed conflict than during a peacetime draft. In addition, the amendment makes a technical correction to the language of the guideline that enables the elimination of current Application Note 1.

Effective Date: The effective date of this amendment is November 1, 1990.

337. **Amendment:** Section 2M5.2 is amended by deleting:

"(a) Base Offense Level (Apply the greater):

(1) 22, if sophisticated weaponry was involved; or

(2) 14.",

and inserting in lieu thereof:

"(a) Base Offense Level:

(1) 22, except as provided in subdivision (2) below;

(2) 14, if the offense involved only non-fully-automatic small arms (rifles, handguns, or shotguns), and the number of weapons did not exceed ten.".

The Commentary to § 2M5.2 captioned "Statutory Provision" is amended by deleting "Provision" and inserting in lieu thereof "Provisions", and by deleting "§ 2778" and inserting in lieu thereof "§§ 2778, 2780".

The Commentary to § 2M5.2 captioned "Application Notes" is amended in Note 1 by inserting, immediately before "In the case of a violation", the following:

"Under 22 U.S.C. § 2778, the President is authorized, through a licensing system administered by the Department of State, to control exports of defense articles and defense services that he deems critical to a security or foreign policy interest of the United States. The items subject to control constitute the United States Munitions List, which is set out in 22 C.F.R. Part 121.1. Included in this list are such things as military aircraft, helicopters, artillery, shells, missiles, rockets, bombs, vessels of war, explosives, military and space electronics, and certain firearms.

The base offense level assumes that the offense conduct was harmful or had the potential to be harmful to a security or foreign policy interest of the United States. In the unusual case where the offense conduct posed no such risk, a downward departure may be warranted.".

The Commentary to § 2M5.2 captioned "Application Notes" is amended in the first sentence of Note 2 by inserting "or foreign policy" immediately before "interest".

Reason for Amendment: This amendment revises this guideline to better distinguish the more and less serious forms of offense conduct covered.

Effective Date: The effective date of this amendment is November 1, 1990.

338. **Amendment:** Section 2N1.1 is amended by inserting the following additional subsection:

"(b) Cross Reference

(1) If the offense involved extortion, apply § 2B3.2 (Extortion by Force or Threat of Injury or Serious Damage) if the resulting offense level is greater than that determined above.".

Reason for Amendment: This amendment adds a cross reference to ensure that in the case of an offense involving extortion, the offense level will not be lower than that under § 2B3.2.

Effective Date: The effective date of this amendment is November 1, 1990.

339. **Amendment:** Section 2N1.2 is amended by deleting:

"(a) Base Offense Level (Apply the greater):

(1) 16;

(2) If the offense involved extortion, apply § 2B3.2.",

and inserting in lieu thereof:

"(a) Base Offense Level: 16

(b) Cross Reference

(1) If the offense involved extortion, apply § 2B3.2 (Extortion by Force or Threat of Injury or Serious Damage).".

The Commentary to § 2N1.2 captioned "Application Notes" is amended by deleting Note 1 as follows:

"1. If the offense involved extortion, apply the guideline from § 2B3.2 (Extortion by Force or Threat of Injury or Serious Damage) rather than the guideline from this section.";

by renumbering Note 2 as Note 1; and in the caption by deleting "Notes" and inserting in lieu thereof "Note".

Reason for Amendment: This amendment conforms the structure of this guideline to that used in other guidelines. No substantive change results.

Effective Date: The effective date of this amendment is November 1, 1990.

340. **Amendment:** The Commentary to § 2N2.1 captioned "Statutory Provisions" is amended by inserting "(a)(1), (a)(2), (b)" immediately after "333".

The Commentary to § 2N2.1 captioned "Application Notes" is amended by inserting the following additional note:

> "4. The Commission has not promulgated a guideline for violations of 21 U.S.C. § 333(e) (offenses involving anabolic steroids).".

Reason for Amendment: This amendment provides that § 2N2.1 does not apply to convictions under 21 U.S.C. § 333(e).

Effective Date: The effective date of this amendment is November 1, 1990.

341. **Amendment:** Section 2P1.1(b)(2) is amended by inserting the following at the end:

> "*Provided*, however, that this reduction shall not apply if the defendant, while away from the facility, committed any federal, state, or local offense punishable by a term of imprisonment of one year or more.".

Section 2P1.1(b) is amended by renumbering subdivision (3) as (4); and by inserting the following as subdivision (3):

> "(3) If the defendant escaped from the non-secure custody of a community corrections center, community treatment center, 'halfway house,' or similar facility, and subsection (b)(2) is not applicable, decrease the offense level under subsection (a)(1) by 4 levels or the offense level under subsection (a)(2) by 2 levels. *Provided*, however, that this reduction shall not apply if the defendant, while away from the facility, committed any federal, state, or local offense punishable by a term of imprisonment of one year or more.".

The Commentary to § 2P1.1 captioned "Application Notes" is amended in Note 3 by deleting "§ 2P1.1(b)(3)" and inserting in lieu thereof "subsection (b)(4)".

The Commentary to § 2P1.1 captioned "Application Notes" is amended by inserting the following additional note:

> "5. Criminal history points under Chapter Four, Part A (Criminal History) are to be determined independently of the application of this guideline. For example, in the case of a defendant serving a one-year sentence of imprisonment at the time of the escape, criminal history points from § 4A1.1(b) (for the sentence being served at the time of the escape), § 4A1.1(d) (custody status), and § 4A1.1(e) (recency) would be applicable.".

Reason for Amendment: This amendment provides greater differentiation in the guideline offense levels for the various types of conduct covered by this guideline. In addition, it clarifies that, where the instant offense is escape, criminal history points from § 4A1.1(d) or (e), or both, may be applicable and that the addition of such points does not constitute unintended double counting.

Effective Date: The effective date of this amendment is November 1, 1990.

342. Amendment: The Introductory Commentary to Chapter Two, Part S, is deleted in its entirety as follows:

"Introductory Commentary

Money laundering activities are essential to the operation of organized crime. Congress recently enacted new statutes prohibiting these activities and increased the maximum penalties.

The guidelines provide substantially increased punishments for these offenses. In fiscal year 1985, the time served by defendants convicted of felonies involving monetary transaction reporting under 31 U.S.C. §§ 5313, 5316, and 5322 averaged about ten months, and only a few defendants served as much as four to five years. However, courts have been imposing higher sentences as they come to appreciate the seriousness of this activity, and sentences as long as thirty-five years have been reported. Specifically, Congress made all reporting violations felonies in 1984, and enacted the Money Laundering Control Act of 1986 (18 U.S.C. §§ 1956, 1957), which creates new offenses and provides higher maximum sentences when knowledge, facilitation or concealment of serious criminal activity is proved.".

Reason for Amendment: This amendment deletes the introductory commentary to this part as outdated, inconsistent with the commentaries to other sections, and better covered in the individual commentaries to the offenses contained in the part.

Effective Date: The effective date of this amendment is November 1, 1990.

343. Amendment: The Commentary to § 2T1.1 captioned "Application Notes" is amended in Note 5 by deleting:

"'racketeering activity' as defined in 18 U.S.C. § 1961. If § 2T1.1(b)(1) applies, do not apply § 4B1.3 (Criminal Livelihood), which is substantially duplicative",

and inserting in lieu thereof:

"conduct constituting a criminal offense under federal, state, or local law".

The Commentary to § 2T1.2 captioned "Application Notes" is amended in Note 1 by deleting:

"'racketeering activity' as defined in 18 U.S.C. § 1961. If § 2T1.2(b)(1) applies, do not apply § 4B1.3 (Criminal Livelihood), which is substantially duplicative",

and inserting in lieu thereof:

"conduct constituting a criminal offense under federal, state, or local law".

The Commentary to § 2T1.3 captioned "Application Notes" is amended in Note 1 by deleting:

"'racketeering activity' as defined in 18 U.S.C. § 1961. If § 2T1.3(b)(1) applies, do not apply § 4B1.3 (Criminal Livelihood), which is substantially duplicative",

and inserting in lieu thereof:

"conduct constituting a criminal offense under federal, state, or local law".

The Commentary to § 2T1.4 captioned "Application Notes" is amended in Note 1 by

Amendment 343

deleting the last sentence as follows:

>"If this subsection applies, do not apply § 4B1.3 (Criminal Livelihood) which is substantially duplicative.".

Reason for Amendment: This amendment deletes the portion of these application notes concerning application of § 4B1.3 (Criminal Livelihood) because this commentary conflicts with the principle expressed in Application Note 5 of the Commentary to § 1B1.1 (when two guideline provisions are equally applicable, the one producing the greater offense level controls). In addition, this amendment broadens the definition of "criminal activity" to cover any criminal violation of federal, state, or local law.

Effective Date: The effective date of this amendment is November 1, 1990.

344. **Amendment:** The Introductory Commentary to Chapter Three, Part A is amended by deleting the second sentence as follows: "They are to be treated as specific offense characteristics.".

The Commentary to § 3A1.1 (Vulnerable Victim) captioned "Application Notes" is amended in Note 2 by inserting the following at the end:

>"For example, where the offense guideline provides an enhancement for the age of the victim, this guideline should not be applied unless the victim was unusually vulnerable for reasons unrelated to age.".

Reason for Amendment: This amendment clarifies the application of § 3A1.1, and eliminates an unnecessary and confusing sentence in the introductory commentary to this part.

Effective Date: The effective date of this amendment is November 1, 1990.

345. **Amendment:** The Introductory Commentary to Chapter Three, Part B, is amended by beginning a new paragraph with the second sentence; and by inserting, immediately after the first sentence, the following:

>"The determination of a defendant's role in the offense is to be made on the basis of all conduct within the scope of § 1B1.3 (Relevant Conduct), i.e., all conduct included under § 1B1.3(a)(1)-(4), and not solely on the basis of elements and acts cited in the count of conviction. However, where the defendant has received mitigation by virtue of being convicted of an offense significantly less serious than his actual criminal conduct, e.g., the defendant is convicted of unlawful possession of a controlled substance but his actual conduct involved drug trafficking, a further reduction in the offense level under § 3B1.2 (Mitigating Role) ordinarily is not warranted because the defendant is not substantially less culpable than a defendant whose only conduct involved the less serious offense.".

Reason for Amendment: This amendment clarifies the conduct that is relevant to the determination of Chapter Three, Part B, and clarifies the operation of § 3B1.2 in certain cases.

Effective Date: The effective date of this amendment is November 1, 1990.

346. **Amendment:** Section 3B1.3 is amended in the second sentence by deleting "in addition to that provided for in § 3B1.1, nor may it be employed" immediately following "may not be employed"; and by inserting the following additional sentence at the end:

>"If this adjustment is based upon an abuse of a position of trust, it may be employed

in addition to an adjustment under § 3B1.1 (Aggravating Role); if this adjustment is based solely on the use of a special skill, it may not be employed in addition to an adjustment under § 3B1.1 (Aggravating Role).".

Reason for Amendment: This amendment provides that the enhancement for abuse of a position of trust may apply in addition to an enhancement for an aggravating role under § 3B1.1.

Effective Date: The effective date of this amendment is November 1, 1990.

347. **Amendment:** Section 3C1.1 is amended in the title by deleting "Willfully Obstructing or Impeding Proceedings" and inserting in lieu thereof "Obstructing or Impeding the Administration of Justice".

Section 3C1.1 is amended by deleting "impeded or obstructed, or attempted to impede or obstruct" and inserting in lieu thereof "obstructed or impeded, or attempted to obstruct or impede,"; and by deleting "or prosecution" and inserting in lieu thereof ", prosecution, or sentencing".

The Commentary to § 3C1.1 is amended by deleting the introductory paragraph immediately before "Application Notes" as follows:

" This section provides a sentence enhancement for a defendant who engages in conduct calculated to mislead or deceive authorities or those involved in a judicial proceeding, or otherwise to willfully interfere with the disposition of criminal charges, in respect to the instant offense.".

The Commentary to § 3C1.1 captioned "Application Notes" is amended by deleting Notes 1-4 as follows:

"1. The following conduct, while not exclusive, may provide a basis for applying this adjustment:

    (a) destroying or concealing material evidence, or attempting to do so;

    (b) directing or procuring another person to destroy or conceal material evidence, or attempting to do so;

    (c) testifying untruthfully or suborning untruthful testimony concerning a material fact, or producing or attempting to produce an altered, forged, or counterfeit document or record during a preliminary or grand jury proceeding, trial, sentencing proceeding, or any other judicial proceeding;

    (d) threatening, intimidating, or otherwise unlawfully attempting to influence a co-defendant, witness, or juror, directly or indirectly;

    (e) furnishing material falsehoods to a probation officer in the course of a presentence or other investigation for the court.

2. In applying this provision, suspect testimony and statements should be evaluated in a light most favorable to the defendant.

3. This provision is not intended to punish a defendant for the exercise of a constitutional right. A defendant's denial of guilt is not a basis for application of this provision.

Amendment 347 APPENDIX C - VOLUME I November 1, 2013

4. Where the defendant is convicted for an offense covered by § 2J1.1 (Contempt), § 2J1.2 (Obstruction of Justice), § 2J1.3 (Perjury), § 2J1.8 (Bribery of Witness), or § 2J1.9 (Payment to Witness), this adjustment is not to be applied to the offense level for that offense except where a significant further obstruction occurred during the investigation or prosecution of the obstruction offense itself (e.g., where the defendant threatened a witness during the course of the prosecution for the obstruction offense). Where the defendant is convicted both of the obstruction offense and the underlying offense, the count for the obstruction offense will be grouped with the count for the underlying offense under subsection (c) of § 3D1.2 (Groups of Closely-Related Counts). The offense level for that Group of Closely-Related Counts will be the offense level for the underlying offense increased by the 2-level adjustment specified by this section, or the offense level for the obstruction offense, whichever is greater.",

and inserting in lieu thereof:

"1. This provision is not intended to punish a defendant for the exercise of a constitutional right. A defendant's denial of guilt (other than a denial of guilt under oath that constitutes perjury), refusal to admit guilt or provide information to a probation officer, or refusal to enter a plea of guilty is not a basis for application of this provision. In applying this provision, the defendant's testimony and statements should be evaluated in a light most favorable to the defendant.

2. Obstructive conduct can vary widely in nature, degree of planning, and seriousness. Application Note 3 sets forth examples of the types of conduct to which this enhancement is intended to apply. Application Note 4 sets forth examples of less serious forms of conduct to which this enhancement is not intended to apply, but that ordinarily can appropriately be sanctioned by the determination of the particular sentence within the otherwise applicable guideline range. Although the conduct to which this enhancement applies is not subject to precise definition, comparison of the examples set forth in Application Notes 3 and 4 should assist the court in determining whether application of this enhancement is warranted in a particular case.

3. The following is a non-exhaustive list of examples of the types of conduct to which this enhancement applies:

    (a) threatening, intimidating, or otherwise unlawfully influencing a co-defendant, witness, or juror, directly or indirectly, or attempting to do so;

    (b) committing, suborning, or attempting to suborn perjury;

    (c) producing or attempting to produce a false, altered, or counterfeit document or record during an official investigation or judicial proceeding;

    (d) destroying or concealing or directing or procuring another person to destroy or conceal evidence that is material to an official investigation or judicial proceeding (e.g., shredding a document or destroying ledgers upon learning that an official investigation has commenced or is about to commence), or attempting to do so; however, if such conduct occurred contemporaneously with arrest (e.g., attempting to swallow or throw away a controlled substance), it shall not, standing alone, be sufficient to warrant an adjustment for obstruction unless it resulted in a material hindrance to the official investigation or prosecution of the instant offense or the sentencing of the offender;

(e) escaping or attempting to escape from custody before trial or sentencing; or willfully failing to appear, as ordered, for a judicial proceeding;

(f) providing materially false information to a judge or magistrate;

(g) providing a materially false statement to a law enforcement officer that significantly obstructed or impeded the official investigation or prosecution of the instant offense;

(h) providing materially false information to a probation officer in respect to a presentence or other investigation for the court;

(i) conduct prohibited by 18 U.S.C. §§ 1501-1516.

This adjustment also applies to any other obstructive conduct in respect to the official investigation, prosecution, or sentencing of the instant offense where there is a separate count of conviction for such conduct.

4. The following is a non-exhaustive list of examples of the types of conduct that, absent a separate count of conviction for such conduct, do not warrant application of this enhancement, but ordinarily can appropriately be sanctioned by the determination of the particular sentence within the otherwise applicable guideline range:

(a) providing a false name or identification document at arrest, except where such conduct actually resulted in a significant hindrance to the investigation or prosecution of the instant offense;

(b) making false statements, not under oath, to law enforcement officers, unless Application Note 3(g) above applies;

(c) providing incomplete or misleading information, not amounting to a material falsehood, in respect to a presentence investigation;

(d) avoiding or fleeing from arrest (see, however, § 3C1.2 (Reckless Endangerment During Flight)).

5. 'Material' evidence, fact, statement, or information, as used in this section, means evidence, fact, statement, or information that, if believed, would tend to influence or affect the issue under determination.

6. Where the defendant is convicted for an offense covered by § 2J1.1 (Contempt), § 2J1.2 (Obstruction of Justice), § 2J1.3 (Perjury or Subornation of Perjury), § 2J1.5 (Failure to Appear by Material Witness), § 2J1.6 (Failure to Appear by Defendant), § 2J1.8 (Bribery of Witness), or § 2J1.9 (Payment to Witness), this adjustment is not to be applied to the offense level for that offense except where a significant further obstruction occurred during the investigation or prosecution of the obstruction offense itself (e.g.,

Amendment 347 APPENDIX C - VOLUME I November 1, 2013

> where the defendant threatened a witness during the course of the prosecution for the obstruction offense). Where the defendant is convicted both of the obstruction offense and the underlying offense, the count for the obstruction offense will be grouped with the count for the underlying offense under subsection (c) of § 3D1.2 (Groups of Closely-Related Counts). The offense level for that group of closely-related counts will be the offense level for the underlying offense increased by the 2-level adjustment specified by this section, or the offense level for the obstruction offense, whichever is greater.".

Chapter Three, Part C, is amended by inserting an additional guideline with accompanying commentary as § 3C1.2 (Reckless Endangerment During Flight).

Reason for Amendment: This amendment clarifies the operation of § 3C1.1 and inserts an additional guideline to address reckless endangerment during flight. The Commission believes that reckless endangerment during flight is sufficiently different from other forms of obstructive conduct to warrant a separate enhancement.

Effective Date: The effective date of this amendment is November 1, 1990.

348. **Amendment:** Section 3D1.1 is amended by inserting "(a)" immediately before "When"; by deleting "(a)", "(b)", and "(c)", and inserting in lieu thereof "(1)", "(2)", and "(3)" respectively; and by inserting the following additional subsection:

> "(b) Any count for which the statute mandates imposition of a consecutive sentence is excluded from the operation of §§ 3D1.2-3D1.5. Sentences for such counts are governed by the provisions of § 5G1.2(a).".

The Commentary to § 3D1.1 captioned "Application Notes" is amended in Note 1 by deleting:

> "Certain offenses, e.g., 18 U.S.C. § 924(c) (use of a deadly or dangerous weapon in relation to a crime of violence or drug trafficking) by law carry mandatory consecutive sentences. Such offenses are exempted from the operation of these rules. See § 3D1.2.",

and inserting in lieu thereof:

> "Counts for which a statute mandates imposition of a consecutive sentence are excepted from application of the multiple count rules. Convictions on such counts are not used in the determination of a combined offense level under this Part, but may affect the offense level for other counts. A conviction for 18 U.S.C. § 924(c) (use of firearm in commission of a crime of violence) provides a common example. In the case of a conviction under 18 U.S.C. § 924(c), the specific offense characteristic for weapon use in the primary offense is to be disregarded to avoid double counting. See Commentary to § 2K2.4. Example: The defendant is convicted of one count of bank robbery (18 U.S.C. § 2113), and one count of use of a firearm in the commission of a crime of violence (18 U.S.C. § 924(c)). The two counts are not grouped together, and the offense level for the bank robbery count is computed without application of an enhancement for weapon possession or use. The mandatory five-year sentence on the weapon-use count runs consecutively, as required by law. See § 5G1.2(a).".

Section 3D1.2 is amended by deleting the second sentence as follows:

> "A count for which the statute mandates imposition of a consecutive sentence is excluded from such Groups for purposes of §§ 3D1.2-3D1.5.".

The Commentary to § 3D1.2 captioned "Application Notes" is amended by deleting Note 1 as follows:

"1. Counts for which the statute mandates imposition of a consecutive sentence are excepted from application of the multiple count rules. Convictions under such counts are excluded from the determination of the combined offense level. Convictions for 18 U.S.C. § 924(c) (use of firearm in commission of a crime of violence) provide a common example. Note that such a conviction usually does affect the offense level for other counts, however, in that in the event of such a conviction the specific offense characteristic for weapon use in the primary offense is to be disregarded. See Commentary to § 2K2.4. Example: The defendant is convicted of one count of bank robbery in which he took $5,000 and discharged a weapon causing permanent bodily injury (18 U.S.C. § 2113), and one count of use of a firearm in the commission of a crime of violence (18 U.S.C. § 924(c)). The two counts are not grouped together, but the offense level for the bank robbery count is 28 (18 + 4 + 6) rather than 31. The mandatory five year sentence on the weapon-use count runs consecutively, as required by law.".

Reason for Amendment: This amendment consolidates the provisions dealing with statutorily required consecutive sentences in § 3D1.1 for greater clarity.

Effective Date: The effective date of this amendment is November 1, 1990.

349. **Amendment:** Section 3D1.2(b) is amended by deleting, immediately following "common scheme or plan", the following:

" , including, but not limited to:

(1) A count charging conspiracy or solicitation and a count charging any substantive offense that was the sole object of the conspiracy or solicitation. 28 U.S.C. § 994(l)(2).

(2) A count charging an attempt to commit an offense and a count charging the commission of the offense. 18 U.S.C. § 3584(a).

(3) A count charging an offense based on a general prohibition and a count charging violation of a specific prohibition encompassed in the general prohibition. 28 U.S.C. § 994(v)".

Section 3D1.2(d) is amended by deleting "Counts are grouped together if" and inserting in lieu thereof "When".

Section 3D1.2(d) is amended by deleting "specifically included" and inserting in lieu thereof "to be grouped".

Section 3D1.2(d) is amended in the second paragraph by inserting in the appropriate place: "§ 2K2.2;".

Section 3D1.2(d) is amended in the third paragraph by inserting "Chapter Two," immediately before "Part A".

The Commentary to § 3D1.2 captioned "Application Notes" is amended by inserting the following as Note 1:

"1. Subsections (a)-(d) set forth circumstances in which counts are to be grouped

Amendment 349   APPENDIX C - VOLUME I   November 1, 2013

together into a single Group. Counts are to be grouped together into a single Group if any one or more of the subsections provide for such grouping. Counts for which the statute mandates imposition of a consecutive sentence are excepted from application of the multiple count rules. See § 3D1.1(b).".

The Commentary to § 3D1.2 captioned "Application Notes" is amended in Note 3 by inserting the following as the second paragraph:

"When one count charges an attempt to commit an offense and the other charges the commission of that offense, or when one count charges an offense based on a general prohibition and the other charges violation of a specific prohibition encompassed in the general prohibition, the counts will be grouped together under subsection (a).".

The Commentary to § 3D1.2 captioned "Application Notes" is amended in Note 4 in the first sentence of the first paragraph by deleting "states the principle" and inserting in lieu thereof "provides".

The Commentary to § 3D1.2 captioned "Application Notes" is amended in Note 4 by inserting the following sentence as the second sentence of the first paragraph:

"This provision does not authorize the grouping of offenses that cannot be considered to represent essentially one composite harm (e.g., robbery of the same victim on different occasions involves multiple, separate instances of fear and risk of harm, not one composite harm).";

and by inserting the following as the second paragraph:

"When one count charges a conspiracy or solicitation and the other charges a substantive offense that was the sole object of the conspiracy or solicitation, the counts will be grouped together under subsection (b).".

The Commentary to § 3D1.2 captioned "Application Notes" is amended in Note 6 by deleting the third sentence of the first paragraph as follows:

"'The same general type of offense' is to be construed broadly, and would include, for example, larceny, embezzlement, forgery, and fraud.";

and by inserting the following as the second paragraph:

"Counts involving offenses to which different offense guidelines apply are grouped together under subsection (d) if the offenses are of the same general type and otherwise meet the criteria for grouping under this subsection. In such cases, the offense guideline that results in the highest offense level is used; see § 3D1.3(b). The 'same general type' of offense is to be construed broadly, and would include, for example, larceny, embezzlement, forgery, and fraud.".

Reason for Amendment: This amendment clarifies the operation of § 3D1.2(b), makes editorial improvements in § 3D1.2(d), makes the listing of offenses in § 3D1.2(d) more comprehensive, clarifies the interaction of §§ 3D1.2(d) and 3D1.3(b), and clarifies the Commentary of § 3D1.2 by making explicit that offenses such as multiple robberies do not fit within the parameters of § 3D1.2(b).

Effective Date: The effective date of this amendment is November 1, 1990.

350. **Amendment:** Section 3D1.4 is amended in the fourth line of the Unit table by inserting

– 180 –

"2 1/2-" immediately before "3" the first time "3" appears; and in the fifth line of the Unit table by deleting "4 or" and inserting in lieu thereof "3 1/2-".

Section 3D1.4 is amended by deleting:

"(d) Except when the total number of Units is 1 1/2, round up to the next large whole number.".

The Commentary to § 3D1.4 captioned "Background" is amended in the first paragraph by deleting the fifth sentence as follows:

"When this approach produces a fraction in the total Units, other than 1 1/2, it is rounded up to the nearest whole number.".

The "Illustrations of the Operation of the Multiple-Count Rules" following § 3D1.5 are amended in example 1 in the third sentence by deleting "18" and "4-" and inserting in lieu thereof "20" and "2-" respectively; and in the sixth sentence by deleting "(rounded up to 3)" immediately following "2 1/2 Units".

The "Illustrations of the Operation of the Multiple-Count Rules" following § 3D1.5 are amended in example 3 in the sixth sentence by deleting "Obstruction" and inserting in lieu thereof "Obstructing or Impeding the Administration of Justice".

Reason for Amendment: This amendment simplifies the operation of § 3D1.4. In addition, the amendment conforms the illustrations of the operation of the multiple-count rules.

Effective Date: The effective date of this amendment is November 1, 1990.

351. **Amendment:** The Commentary to § 3E1.1 captioned "Application Notes" is amended by deleting:

"2. Conviction by trial does not preclude a defendant from consideration under this section. A defendant may manifest sincere contrition even if he exercises his constitutional right to a trial. This may occur, for example, where a defendant goes to trial to assert and preserve issues that do not relate to factual guilt (e.g., to make a constitutional challenge to a statute or a challenge to the applicability of a statute to his conduct).

3. A guilty plea may provide some evidence of the defendant's acceptance of responsibility. However, it does not, by itself, entitle a defendant to a reduced sentence under this section.",

and inserting in lieu thereof:

"2. This adjustment is not intended to apply to a defendant who puts the government to its burden of proof at trial by denying the essential factual elements of guilt, is convicted, and only then admits guilt and expresses remorse. Conviction by trial, however, does not automatically preclude a defendant from consideration for such a reduction. In rare situations a defendant may clearly demonstrate an acceptance of responsibility for his criminal conduct even though he exercises his constitutional right to a trial. This may occur, for example, where a defendant goes to trial to assert and preserve issues that do not relate to factual guilt (e.g., to make a constitutional challenge to a statute or a challenge to the applicability of a statute to his conduct). In each such instance, however, a determination that a defendant has accepted responsibility will be based primarily upon pre-trial statements and conduct.

3. Entry of a plea of guilty prior to the commencement of trial combined with truthful admission of involvement in the offense and related conduct will constitute significant evidence of acceptance of responsibility for the purposes of this section. However, this evidence may be outweighed by conduct of the defendant that is inconsistent with such acceptance of responsibility.".

The Commentary to § 3E1.1 captioned "Application Notes" is amended in Note 4 in the first sentence by deleting "Willfully Obstructing or Impeding Proceedings" and inserting in lieu thereof "Obstructing or Impeding the Administration of Justice".

The Commentary to § 3E1.1 captioned "Application Notes" is amended in Note 5 in the second sentence by deleting "and should not be disturbed unless it is without foundation" immediately following "review".

The Commentary to § 3E1.1 captioned "Background" is amended in the first paragraph in the second sentence by inserting "and related conduct" immediately before "by taking"; and in the third sentence by deleting "lesser sentence" and inserting in lieu thereof "lower offense level", and by deleting "sincere remorse" and inserting in lieu thereof "acceptance of responsibility".

The Commentary to § 3E1.1 captioned "Background" is amended by deleting the second paragraph as follows:

" The availability of a reduction under § 3E1.1 is not controlled by whether the conviction was by trial or plea of guilty. Although a guilty plea may show some evidence of acceptance of responsibility, it does not automatically entitle the defendant to a sentencing adjustment.".

Reason for Amendment: This amendment clarifies the operation of this guideline and conforms the title of a reference to another guideline.

Effective Date: The effective date of this amendment is November 1, 1990.

352. **Amendment:** Section 4A1.2(a)(3) is amended by inserting "or execution" immediately following "imposition".

Section 4A1.2(c)(1) is amended by inserting in the appropriate place by alphabetical order:

"Careless or reckless driving",
"Insufficient funds check".

Section 4A1.2(c)(1) is amended by inserting "(excluding local ordinance violations that are also criminal offenses under state law)" immediately following "Local ordinance violations".

Section 4A1.2(c)(2) is amended by inserting "(e.g., speeding)" immediately following "minor traffic infractions".

The Commentary to § 4A1.2 captioned "Application Notes" is amended by inserting the following additional notes:

November 1, 2013　　APPENDIX C - VOLUME I　　**Amendment 353**

"12.　Local ordinance violations. A number of local jurisdictions have enacted ordinances covering certain offenses (e.g., larceny and assault misdemeanors) that are also violations of state criminal law. This enables a local court (e.g., a municipal court) to exercise jurisdiction over such offenses. Such offenses are excluded from the definition of local ordinance violations in § 4A1.2(c)(1) and, therefore, sentences for such offenses are to be treated as if the defendant had been convicted under state law.

13.　Insufficient funds check. 'Insufficient funds check,' as used in § 4A1.2(c)(1), does not include any conviction establishing that the defendant used a false name or non-existent account.".

Reason for Amendment: This amendment clarifies that, for the purpose of computing criminal history points, there is no difference between the suspension of the "imposition" and "execution" of a prior sentence. This amendment also makes the provisions of § 4A1.2(c)(1) more comprehensive in respect to certain vehicular offenses and clarifies the application of § 4A1.2(c)(1) in respect to certain offenses prosecuted in municipal courts. In addition, this amendment expands the coverage of § 4A1.2(c)(1) to include a misdemeanor or petty offense conviction for an insufficient funds check.

Effective Date: The effective date of this amendment is November 1, 1990.

353.　**Amendment:**　The Commentary to § 4A1.2 captioned "Application Notes" is amended in Note 6 by deleting:

"Any other sentence resulting in a valid conviction is to be counted in the criminal history score. Convictions which the defendant shows to have been constitutionally invalid may not be counted in the criminal history score. Also, if to count an uncounseled misdemeanor conviction would result in the imposition of a sentence of imprisonment under circumstances that would violate the United States Constitution, then such conviction shall not be counted in the criminal history score. Nonetheless, any conviction that is not counted in the criminal history score may be considered pursuant to § 4A1.3 if it provides reliable evidence of past criminal activity.",

and inserting in lieu thereof:

"Also, sentences resulting from convictions that a defendant shows to have been previously ruled constitutionally invalid are not to be counted. Nonetheless, the criminal conduct underlying any conviction that is not counted in the criminal history score may be considered pursuant to § 4A1.3 (Adequacy of Criminal History Category).".

The Commentary to § 4A1.2 captioned "Application Notes" is amended in the caption of Note 6 by deleting "Invalid" and inserting in lieu thereof "Reversed, Vacated, or Invalidated". The Commentary to § 4A1.2 is amended by inserting at the end:

"Background: Prior sentences, not otherwise excluded, are to be counted in the criminal history score, including uncounseled misdemeanor sentences where imprisonment was not imposed.

The Commission leaves for court determination the issue of whether a defendant may collaterally attack at sentencing a prior conviction.".

Reason for Amendment: This amendment clarifies the circumstances under which prior

Amendment 353 APPENDIX C - VOLUME I November 1, 2013

sentences are excluded from the criminal history score. In particular, the amendment clarifies the Commission's intent regarding the counting of uncounseled misdemeanor convictions for which counsel constitutionally is not required because the defendant was not imprisoned. Lack of clarity regarding whether these prior sentences are to be counted may result not only in considerable disparity in guideline application, but also in the criminal history score not adequately reflecting the defendant's failure to learn from the application of previous sanctions and his potential for recidivism. This amendment expressly states the Commission's position that such convictions are to be counted for the purposes of criminal history under Chapter Four, Part A.

Effective Date: The effective date of this amendment is November 1, 1990.

354. **Amendment:** The Commentary to § 4B1.3 captioned "Application Notes" is amended in Note 2 by deleting "(currently 2,000x the hourly minimum wage under federal law is $6,700)" immediately following "then existing hourly minimum wage under federal law".

Reason for Amendment: This amendment deletes a reference to the federal minimum wage that is now outdated.

Effective Date: The effective date of this amendment is November 1, 1990.

355. **Amendment:** Chapter Four, Part B, is amended by inserting an additional guideline with accompanying commentary as § 4B1.4 (Armed Career Criminal).

Reason for Amendment: This amendment adds a new section to address cases subject to a sentence enhancement under 18 U.S.C. § 924(e).

Effective Date: The effective date of this amendment is November 1, 1990.

356. **Amendment:** Section 5E1.2 is amended by deleting:

> "(a) Except as provided in subsection (f) below, the court shall impose a fine in all cases.",

and inserting in lieu thereof:

> "(a) The court shall impose a fine in all cases, except where the defendant establishes that he is unable to pay and is not likely to become able to pay any fine.".

Section 5E1.2(d)(2) is amended by deleting "the ability of the defendant" and inserting in lieu thereof "any evidence presented as to the defendant's ability".

The Commentary to § 5E1.2 captioned "Application Notes" is amended in Note 3 by deleting the fourth sentence as follows:

> "In many cases, circumstances will make it unnecessary to consider these standards other than in the most general terms.";

and by inserting the following additional paragraphs at the end:

> "Where it is readily ascertainable that the defendant cannot, and is not likely to become able to, pay a fine greater than the maximum fine set forth in Column B of the Fine Table in subsection (c)(3), calculation of the alternative maximum fines under subsections (c)(2)(B) (twice the gross pecuniary loss caused by the offense)

– 184 –

and (c)(2)(C) (three times the gross pecuniary gain to all participants in the offense) is unnecessary. In such cases, a statement that 'the alternative maximums of the fine table were not calculated because it is readily ascertainable that the defendant cannot, and is not likely to become able to, pay a fine greater than the maximum set forth in the fine table' is recommended in lieu of such calculations.

The determination of the fine guideline range may be dispensed with entirely upon a court determination of present and future inability to pay any fine. The inability of a defendant to post bail bond (having otherwise been determined eligible for release) and the fact that a defendant is represented by (or was determined eligible for) assigned counsel are significant indicators of present inability to pay any fine. In conjunction with other factors, they may also indicate that the defendant is not likely to become able to pay any fine.".

Reason for Amendment: This amendment clarifies the operation of this guideline.

Effective Date: The effective date of this amendment is November 1, 1990.

357. **Amendment:** The Introductory Commentary to Chapter Five, Part H is amended by inserting the following additional paragraph at the end:

> "   In addition, 28 U.S.C. § 994(e) requires the Commission to assure that its guidelines and policy statements reflect the general inappropriateness of considering the defendant's education, vocational skills, employment record, family ties and responsibilities, and community ties in determining whether a term of imprisonment should be imposed or the length of a term of imprisonment.".

Reason for Amendment: This amendment clarifies the relationship of 28 U.S.C. § 994(e) to certain of the policy statements contained in this part.

Effective Date: The effective date of this amendment is November 1, 1990.

358. **Amendment:** Chapter Five, Part K, Subpart 2, is amended in the title by deleting "GENERAL PROVISIONS:" and inserting in lieu thereof "OTHER GROUNDS FOR DEPARTURE".

Section 5K2.0 is amended in the first sentence of the first paragraph by inserting a comma immediately following "degree", and by inserting "that should result in a sentence different from that described" immediately following "the guidelines"; in the third sentence of the first paragraph by deleting "court at the time of sentencing" and inserting in lieu thereof "courts"; in the fourth sentence of the first paragraph by deleting "the present section" and inserting in lieu thereof "this subpart", by deleting "fully" immediately before "take", by inserting "fully" immediately following "account", and by deleting "precise" and inserting in lieu thereof "the"; in the sixth sentence of the first paragraph by deleting "judge" and inserting in lieu thereof "court"; and in the seventh sentence of the first paragraph by deleting "listed elsewhere in the guidelines (e.g., as an adjustment or specific offense characteristic)" and inserting in lieu thereof "taken into consideration in the guidelines (e.g., as a specific offense characteristic or other adjustment)".

Section 5K2.0 is amended in the first sentence of the second paragraph by inserting ", for example," immediately following "Where", by deleting "guidelines, specific offense characteristics," and inserting in lieu thereof "offense guideline", by deleting "part" and inserting in lieu thereof "subpart", by deleting "guideline" and inserting in lieu thereof "applicable guideline range", and by deleting "of conviction" immediately following "the offense"; in the second sentence of the second paragraph by deleting "offense of convic-

Amendment 358 APPENDIX C - VOLUME I November 1, 2013

tion" and inserting in lieu thereof "applicable offense guideline"; in the third sentence of the second paragraph by deleting "offense of conviction is theft" and inserting in lieu thereof "theft offense guideline is applicable", by deleting "when" immediately before "the theft", and by inserting "range" immediately before "more readily"; and in the fourth sentence of the second paragraph by deleting "offense of conviction is robbery" and inserting in lieu thereof "robbery offense guideline is applicable", and by deleting "sentence" immediately before "adjustment".

Section 5K2.0 is amended by deleting the fourth paragraph as follows:

"Harms identified as a possible basis for departure from the guidelines should be taken into account only when they are relevant to the offense of conviction, within the limitations set forth in § 1B1.3.".

Reason for Amendment: This amendment makes various editorial and clarifying changes. In addition, the last paragraph is deleted as unclear and overly restrictive.

Effective Date: The effective date of this amendment is November 1, 1990.

359. **Amendment:** Appendix A (Statutory Index) is amended by inserting the following in the appropriate place by title and section:

"7 U.S.C. § 1361	2Q1.2",
"18 U.S.C. § 34	2A1.1, 2A1.2, 2A1.3, 2A1.4",
"18 U.S.C. § 35(b)	2A6.1",
"18 U.S.C. § 219	2C1.3",
"18 U.S.C. § 281	2C1.3",
"18 U.S.C. § 332	2B1.1, 2F1.1",
"18 U.S.C. § 335	2F1.1",
"18 U.S.C. § 608	2H2.1",
"18 U.S.C. § 647	2B1.1",
"18 U.S.C. § 650	2B1.1",
"18 U.S.C. § 665(b)	2B3.3, 2C1.1",
"18 U.S.C. § 667	2B1.1, 2B1.2",
"18 U.S.C. § 712	2F1.1",
"18 U.S.C. § 753	2P1.1",
"18 U.S.C. § 915	2F1.1",
"18 U.S.C. § 917	2F1.1",
"18 U.S.C. § 970(a)	2B1.3, 2K1.4",
"18 U.S.C. § 1015	2F1.1, 2J1.3, 2L2.1, 2L2.2",
"18 U.S.C. § 1023	2B1.1, 2F1.1",
"18 U.S.C. § 1024	2B1.2",
"18 U.S.C. § 1031	2F1.1",
"18 U.S.C. § 1091	2H1.3",
"18 U.S.C. § 1115	2A1.4",
"18 U.S.C. § 1167	2B1.1",
"18 U.S.C. § 1168	2B1.1",
"18 U.S.C. § 1201(c), (d)	2X1.1",
"18 U.S.C. § 1364	2K1.4",

"18 U.S.C. § 1422	2C1.2, 2F1.1",
"18 U.S.C. § 1541	2L2.3",
"18 U.S.C. § 1716	2K3.2",
(felony provisions only)	
"18 U.S.C. § 1860	2R1.1",
"18 U.S.C. § 1861	2F1.1",
"18 U.S.C. § 1864	2Q1.6",
"18 U.S.C. § 1991	2A2.1, 2X1.1",
"18 U.S.C. § 1992	2A1.1, 2B1.3, 2K1.4, 2X1.1",
"18 U.S.C. § 2072	2F1.1",
"18 U.S.C. § 2118(d)	2X1.1",
"18 U.S.C. § 2197	2B5.2, 2F1.1",
"18 U.S.C. § 2232	2J1.2",
"18 U.S.C. § 2233	2B1.1, 2B3.1",
"18 U.S.C. § 2272	2F1.1",
"18 U.S.C. § 2276	2B1.3, 2B2.2",
"18 U.S.C. § 2331(a)	2A1.1, 2A1.2, 2A1.3, 2A1.4",
"18 U.S.C. § 2331(b)	2A2.1",
"18 U.S.C. § 2331(c)	2A2.2",
"22 U.S.C. § 2780	2M5.2",
"42 U.S.C. § 300i-1	2Q1.4, 2Q1.5",
"42 U.S.C. § 1973j(c)	2X1.1".

Appendix A is amended:

in the line beginning "8 U.S.C. § 1328" by deleting ", 2G2.1, 2G2.2";

in the line beginning "16 U.S.C. § 1029" by deleting ", 2Q2.2";

in the line beginning "16 U.S.C. § 1030" by deleting ", 2Q2.2";

in the line beginning "16 U.S.C. § 1857(2)" by deleting ", 2Q2.2" and inserting in lieu thereof "2Q2.1";

in the line beginning "16 U.S.C. § 1859" by deleting "2Q2.2" and inserting in lieu thereof "2Q2.1";

and in the line beginning "16 U.S.C. § 3373(d)" by deleting "2Q2.2" and inserting in lieu thereof "2Q2.1";

by deleting:

"18 U.S.C. § 32(a)(1)-(4)	2K1.4, 2B1.3
18 U.S.C. § 32(b)	2A1.1-2A2.3, 2A4.1, 2A5.1-2A5.2, 2K1.4, 2B1.3",

and inserting in lieu thereof:

"18 U.S.C. § 32(a),(b) 2A1.1-2A2.3, 2A4.1, 2A5.1, 2A5.2, 2B1.3, 2K1.4";

Amendment 359 APPENDIX C - VOLUME I November 1, 2013

in the line beginning "18 U.S.C. § 33" by inserting "2A2.1, 2A2.2," immediately before ""2B1.3";

in the line beginning "18 U.S.C. § 112(a)" by inserting "2A2.1," immediately before "2A2.2," and by inserting ", 2A4.1, 2B1.3, 2K1.4" immediately following "2A2.3";

in the line beginning "18 U.S.C. § 152" by deleting "2F1.1," and by inserting ", 2F1.1, 2J1.3" immediately following "2B4.1";

in the line beginning "18 U.S.C. § 201(b)(1)" by deleting ", 2J1.3, 2J1.8, 2J1.9";

in the line beginning "18 U.S.C. § 241" by deleting "2H1.2,";

in the line beginning "18 U.S.C. § 351(d)" by deleting ", 2A2.1" and inserting in lieu thereof "2A1.5";

in the line beginning "18 U.S.C. § 371" by deleting "2A2.1" and inserting in lieu thereof "2A1.5";

in the line beginning "18 U.S.C. § 373" by deleting "2A2.1" and inserting in lieu thereof "2A1.5";

in the line beginning "18 U.S.C. § 474" by inserting ", 2B5.2" immediately following "2B5.1";

in the line beginning "18 U.S.C. § 476" by inserting ", 2B5.2" immediately following "2B5.1";

in the line beginning "18 U.S.C. § 477" by inserting ", 2B5.2" immediately following "2B5.1";

in the line beginning "18 U.S.C. § 496" by deleting "2T3.1" and inserting in lieu thereof "2F1.1, 2T3.1";

in the line beginning "18 U.S.C. § 545" by deleting "2Q2.2" and inserting in lieu thereof "2Q2.1";

in the line beginning "18 U.S.C. § 549" by inserting "2B1.1," immediately before "2T3.1", and by inserting ", 2T3.2" immediately following "2T3.1";

in the line beginning "18 U.S.C. § 551" by inserting "2J1.2," immediately before "2T3.1";

in the line beginning "18 U.S.C. § 642" by inserting ", 2B5.2" immediately following ""2B5.1";

by deleting:

    "18 U.S.C. § 666(a)   2B1.1, 2C1.1, 2C1.2, 2F1.1",

and inserting in lieu thereof:

"18 U.S.C. § 666(a)(1)(A)	2B1.1, 2F1.1
18 U.S.C. § 666(a)(1)(B)	2C1.1, 2C1.2
18 U.S.C. § 666(a)(1)(C)	2C1.1, 2C1.2";

in the line beginning "18 U.S.C. § 755" by deleting ", 2X2.1";

November 1, 2013 · APPENDIX C - VOLUME I · Amendment 359

in the line beginning "18 U.S.C. § 756" by deleting ", 2X2.1";

in the line beginning "18 U.S.C. § 757" by deleting "2X2.1" and inserting in lieu thereof "2X3.1";

in the line beginning "18 U.S.C. § 793(d), (e)" by inserting "2M3.2," immediately before "2M3.3";

in the line beginning "18 U.S.C. § 842(a)" by deleting ",(h),(i)" by inserting in lieu thereof "- (i)";

in the line beginning "18 U.S.C. § 844(f)" by inserting ", 2X1.1" immediately following "2K1.4";

by deleting:

"18 U.S.C. § 922(a)(1)-(5)	2K2.3
18 U.S.C. § 922(a)(6)	2K2.1
18 U.S.C. § 922(b)(1)-(3)	2K2.3
18 U.S.C. § 922(d)	2K2.3
18 U.S.C. § 922(g)	2K2.1
18 U.S.C. § 922(h)	2K2.1
18 U.S.C. § 922(i)	2B1.2, 2K2.3
18 U.S.C. § 922(j)	2B1.2, 2K2.3
18 U.S.C. § 922(k)	2K2.3
18 U.S.C. § 922(l)	2K2.3
18 U.S.C. § 922(n)	2K2.1
18 U.S.C. § 923	2K2.3
18 U.S.C. § 924(c)	2K2.4",

and inserting in lieu thereof:

"18 U.S.C. § 922(a)(1)	2K2.1, 2K2.2
18 U.S.C. § 922(a)(2)	2K2.2
18 U.S.C. § 922(a)(3)	2K2.1
18 U.S.C. § 922(a)(4)	2K2.1
18 U.S.C. § 922(a)(5)	2K2.2
18 U.S.C. § 922(a)(6)	2K2.1
18 U.S.C. § 922(b)-(d)	2K2.2
18 U.S.C. § 922(e)	2K2.1, 2K2.2
18 U.S.C. § 922(f)	2K2.1, 2K2.2
18 U.S.C. § 922(g)	2K2.1
18 U.S.C. § 922(h)	2K2.1
18 U.S.C. § 922(i)-(l)	2K2.1, 2K2.2
18 U.S.C. § 922(m)	2K2.2
18 U.S.C. § 922(n)	2K2.1
18 U.S.C. § 922(o)	2K2.1, 2K2.2
18 U.S.C. § 923(a)	2K2.2
18 U.S.C. § 924(a)(1)(A)	2K2.2

18 U.S.C. § 924(a)(1)(C)	2K2.1, 2K2.2
18 U.S.C. § 924(a)(3)(A)	2K2.2
18 U.S.C. § 924(b)	2K2.3
18 U.S.C. § 924(c)	2K2.4
18 U.S.C. § 924(f)	2K2.3
18 U.S.C. § 924(g)	2K2.3";

in the line beginning "18 U.S.C. § 1012" by inserting "2C1.3," immediately before "2F1.1";

in the line beginning "18 U.S.C. § 1028" by inserting ", 2L2.4" immediately following "2L2.3";

in the line beginning "18 U.S.C. § 1113" by inserting ", 2A2.2" immediately following "2A2.1";

in the line beginning "18 U.S.C. § 1117" by deleting "2A2.1" and inserting in lieu thereof "2A1.5";

in the line beginning "18 U.S.C. § 1362" by inserting ", 2K1.4" immediately following "2B1.3";

in the line beginning "18 U.S.C. § "1363" by inserting ", 2K1.4" immediately following "2B1.3";

in the line beginning "18 U.S.C. § 1426" by inserting ", 2L2.2" immediately following "2L2.1";

in the line beginning "18 U.S.C. § 1460" by inserting "2G2.2," immediately before "2G3.1";

in the line beginning "18 U.S.C. § 1512(a)" by inserting "2A1.3," immediately following "2A1.2,";

in the line beginning "18 U.S.C. § 1512(b) by inserting "2A1.2," immediately before "2A2.2";

in the line beginning "18 U.S.C. § 1704" by inserting ", 2F1.1" immediately following "2B5.2";

in the line beginning "18 U.S.C. § 1751(c)" by inserting ", 2X1.1" immediately following "2A4.1";

in the line beginning "18 U.S.C. § 1751(d)" by deleting "2A2.1" and inserting in lieu thereof "2A1.5", and by inserting ", 2X1.1" immediately following "2A4.1";

in the line beginning "18 U.S.C. § 1909" by inserting "2C1.3," immediately before "2C1.4";

in the line beginning "18 U.S.C. § 1951" by deleting "2B3.1, 2B3.2, 2C1.1,";

in the line beginning "18 U.S.C. § 1952A" by deleting "2A2.1,";

in the line beginning "18 U.S.C. § 1958" by deleting "2A2.1,";

by deleting:

    "18 U.S.C. § 2251   2G2.1",

and inserting in lieu thereof:

"18 U.S.C. § 2251(a), (b)	2G2.1
18 U.S.C. § 2251(c)(1)(A)	2G2.2
18 U.S.C. § 2251(c)(1)(B)	2G2.1";

in the line beginning "18 U.S.C. § 2271" by deleting "2F1.1,";

in the line beginning "18 U.S.C. § 2421" by inserting ", 2G1.2" immediately following "2G1.1";

in the line beginning "18 U.S.C. § 2422" by inserting ", 2G1.2" immediately following "2G1.1";

by deleting "18 U.S.C. § 4082(d) 2P1.1";

by deleting:

    "21 U.S.C. § 333   2N2.1",

and inserting in lieu thereof:

"21 U.S.C. § 333(a)(1)	2N2.1
21 U.S.C. § 333(a)(2)	2F1.1, 2N2.1
21 U.S.C. § 333(b)	2N2.1";

by deleting:

| "26 U.S.C. § 5861(a) | 2K2.3 |
| 26 U.S.C. § 5861(b)-(l) | 2K2.2", |

and inserting in lieu thereof:

"26 U.S.C. § 5861(a)	2K2.2
26 U.S.C. § 5861(b)	2K2.1
26 U.S.C. § 5861(c)	2K2.1
26 U.S.C. § 5861(d)	2K2.1
26 U.S.C. § 5861(e)	2K2.2
26 U.S.C. § 5861(f)	2K2.2
26 U.S.C. § 5861(g)	2K2.2
26 U.S.C. § 5861(h)	2K2.1
26 U.S.C. § 5861(i)	2K2.1
26 U.S.C. § 5861(j)	2K2.1, 2K2.2
26 U.S.C. § 5861(k)	2K2.1
26 U.S.C. § 5861(l)	2K2.2";

in the line beginning "26 U.S.C. § 5871" by deleting "2K2.2, 2K2.3" and inserting in lieu

Amendment 359 APPENDIX C - VOLUME I November 1, 2013

thereof "2K2.1, 2K2.2";

by deleting:

"33 U.S.C. § 1319   2Q1.1, 2Q1.2, 2Q1.3",

and inserting in lieu thereof:

"33 U.S.C. § 1319(c)(1),
(c)(2), (c)(4)   2Q1.2, 2Q1.3
33 U.S.C. § 1319(c)(3)   2Q1.1";

and in the line beginning "42 U.S.C. § 3631" by deleting ", 2H1.5".

The Commentary to § 2D3.4 captioned "Statutory Provisions" is amended by deleting "Provision" and inserting in lieu thereof "Provisions"; and by deleting "§ 842" and inserting in lieu thereof "§§ 954, 961".

The Commentary to § 2M6.2 is amended by inserting between "Commentary" and "Background" the following:

"Statutory Provision: 42 U.S.C. § 2273".

The Commentary to § 2T2.2 captioned "Statutory Provisions" is amended by deleting "5601-5605, 5607, 5608" and inserting in lieu thereof "5601, 5603-5605"; and by deleting "5691," immediately before "5762".

The Commentary to § 2X2.1 captioned "Statutory Provisions" is amended by deleting "Provisions" and inserting in lieu thereof "Provision"; and by deleting "§§ 2, 755-757" and inserting in lieu thereof "§ 2".

Reason for Amendment: This amendment makes the statutory index more comprehensive, conforms it to amended guidelines, and corrects erroneous references. In addition, this amendment conforms the statutory provisions of §§ 2D3.4, 2T2.2, 2X2.1 to the statutory index, and inserts additional Commentary in § 2M6.2 referencing a statutory provision contained in Appendix A (Statutory Index) to conform the format of this guideline to the format of other offense guidelines.

Effective Date: The effective date of this amendment is November 1, 1990.

360. **Amendment:** Section 1B1.10(d) is amended by deleting "and 269" and inserting in lieu thereof "269, 329, and 341".

Reason for Amendment: This amendment implements the directive in 28 U.S.C. § 994(u) in respect to the guideline amendments effective November 1, 1990.

Effective Date: The effective date of this amendment is November 1, 1990.

361. **Amendment:** The Commentary to § 1B1.1 captioned "Application Notes" is amended in Note 1 by inserting the following additional subdivision at the end:

"(k) 'Destructive device' means any article described in 18 U.S.C. § 921(a)(4) (including an explosive, incendiary, or poison gas - (i) bomb, (ii) grenade, (iii) rocket having a propellant charge of more than four ounces, (iv) missile having an explosive or incendiary charge of more than one-quarter ounce,

(v) mine, or (vi) device similar to any of the devices described in the proceeding clauses).".

The Commentary to § 2B1.1 captioned "Application Notes" is amended in Note 1 by deleting "and 'firearm'" and inserting in lieu thereof ",'firearm,' and 'destructive device'", and by deleting the last sentence as follows: "'Destructive device' is defined in the Commentary to § 2K1.4 (Arson: Property Damage by Use of Explosives).".

The Commentary to § 2B1.2 captioned "Application Notes" is amended in Note 1 by deleting "and 'firearm'" and inserting in lieu thereof ",'firearm,' and 'destructive device'", and by deleting the last sentence as follows: "'Destructive device' is defined in the Commentary to § 2K1.4 (Arson: Property Damage by Use of Explosives).".

The Commentary to § 2B2.1 captioned "Application Notes" is amended in Note 1 by inserting "'destructive device,'" immediately before "and 'dangerous weapon'", and by deleting the last sentence as follows: "'Destructive device' is defined in the Commentary to § 2K1.4 (Arson: Property Damage by Use of Explosives).".

The Commentary to § 2B2.2 captioned "Application Notes" is amended in Note 1 by deleting "and 'firearm'" and inserting in lieu thereof ", 'firearm,' 'destructive device,' and 'dangerous weapon'", and by deleting the last sentence as follows: "'Destructive device' is defined in the Commentary to § 2K1.4 (Arson: Property Damage by Use of Explosives).".

The Commentary to § 2B3.1 captioned "Application Notes" is amended in Note 1 by inserting "'destructive device,'" immediately before "'dangerous weapon,'".

Reason for Amendment: This amendment inserts the definition of a destructive device, formerly in the Commentary to § 2K1.4, in the Commentary to § 1B1.1, with minor revisions to the examples of the articles prohibited by 18 U.S.C. § 921(a)(4) to better reflect the statutory provision. This amendment also conforms the commentary of various offense guidelines to reference the definitions set forth in Application Note 1 of the Commentary to § 1B1.1.

Effective Date: The effective date of this amendment is November 1, 1990.

362. **Amendment:** Chapter Seven is deleted in its entirety as follows:

"CHAPTER SEVEN - VIOLATIONS OF PROBATION AND
SUPERVISED RELEASE

§ 7A1.1. <u>Reporting of Violations of Probation and Supervised Release</u> (Policy Statement)

(a) The Probation Officer shall promptly report to the court any alleged violation of a condition of probation or supervised release that constitutes new criminal conduct, other than conduct that would constitute a petty offense.

(b) The Probation Officer shall promptly report to the court any other alleged violation of a condition of probation or supervised release, unless the officer determines: (1) that such violation is minor, not part of a continuing pattern of violation, and not indicative of a serious adjustment problem; and (2) that non-reporting will not present an undue risk to the public or be inconsistent with any directive of the court relative to the reporting of violations.

Commentary

This policy statement addresses the reporting of violations of probation and supervised release. It is the Commission's intent that significant violations be promptly reported to the court. At the same time, the Commission realizes that it would neither be practical nor desirable to require such reporting for every minor violation.

§ 7A1.2.　　Revocation of Probation (Policy Statement)

(a)　　Upon a finding of a violation of probation involving new criminal conduct, other than criminal conduct constituting a petty offense, the court shall revoke probation.

(b)　　Upon a finding of a violation of probation involving conduct other than conduct under subsection (a), the court may: (1) revoke probation; or (2) extend the term of probation and/or modify the conditions of probation.

Commentary

This policy statement expresses a presumption that probation is to be revoked in the case of new criminal conduct other than a petty offense. For lesser violations, the policy statements provide that the court may revoke probation, extend the term of supervision, or modify the conditions of supervision.

§ 7A1.3.　　Revocation of Supervised Release (Policy Statement)

(a)　　Upon a finding of a violation of supervised release involving new criminal conduct, other than criminal conduct constituting a petty offense, the court shall revoke supervised release.

(b)　　Upon a finding of a violation of supervised release involving conduct other than conduct under subsection (a), the court may: (1) revoke supervised release; or (2) extend the term of supervised release and/or modify the conditions of supervised release.

Commentary

This policy statement expresses a presumption that supervised release is to be revoked in the case of new criminal conduct other than a petty offense. For lesser violations, the policy statements provide that the court may revoke supervised release, extend the term of supervision, or modify the conditions of supervision.

§ 7A1.4.　　No Credit for Time Under Supervision (Policy Statement)

(a)　　Upon revocation of probation, no credit shall be given (toward any sentence of imprisonment imposed) for any portion of the term of probation served prior to revocation.

(b)　　Upon revocation of supervised release, no credit shall be given (toward any term of imprisonment ordered) for time previously served on post-release supervision.

Commentary

This policy statement provides that time served on probation or supervised release is not to be credited in the determination of any term of imprisonment imposed upon revocation.".

A replacement chapter containing policy statements with accompanying commentary is inserted as Chapter Seven (Violations of Probation and Supervised Release).

Reason for Amendment: This amendment replaces Chapter Seven with a set of more detailed policy statements applicable to violations of probation and supervised release. Under 28 U.S.C. § 994(a)(3), the Sentencing Commission is required to issue guidelines or policy statements applicable to the revocation of probation and supervised release. At this time, the Commission has chosen to promulgate policy statements only. These policy statements will provide guidance while allowing for the identification of any substantive or procedural issues that require further review. The Commission views these policy statements as evolutionary and will review relevant data and materials concerning revocation determinations under these policy statements. Revocation guidelines will be issued after federal judges, probation officers, practitioners, and others have the opportunity to evaluate and comment on these policy statements.

Effective Date: The effective date of this amendment is November 1, 1990.

363. **Amendment:** Section 2A4.1(b) is amended by deleting:

"(5) If the victim was kidnapped, abducted, or unlawfully restrained to facilitate the commission of another offense: (A) increase by 4 levels; or (B) if the result of applying this guideline is less than that resulting from application of the guideline for such other offense, apply the guideline for such other offense.",

and inserting in lieu thereof:

"(5) If the victim was sexually exploited, increase by 3 levels.

(6) If the victim is a minor and, in exchange for money or other consideration, was placed in the care or custody of another person who had no legal right to such care or custody of the victim, increase by 3 levels.

(7) If the victim was kidnapped, abducted, or unlawfully restrained during the commission of, or in connection with, another offense or escape therefrom; or if another offense was committed during the kidnapping, abduction, or unlawful restraint, increase to --

(A) the offense level from the Chapter Two offense guideline applicable to that other offense if such offense guideline includes an adjustment for kidnapping, abduction, or unlawful restraint, or otherwise takes such conduct into account; or

(B) 4 plus the offense level from the offense guideline applicable to that other offense, but in no event greater than level 43, in any other case,

if the resulting offense level is greater than that determined above.

(c) Cross Reference

(1) If the victim was killed under circumstances that would constitute murder under 18 U.S.C. § 1111 had such killing taken place within

Amendment 363   APPENDIX C - VOLUME I   November 1, 2013

the territorial or maritime jurisdiction of the United States, apply § 2A1.1 (First Degree Murder).".

The Commentary to § 2A4.1 captioned "Application Notes" is amended by inserting the following additional note:

> "4. 'Sexually exploited' includes offenses set forth in 18 U.S.C. §§ 2241-2244, 2251, and 2421-2423.".

The Commentary to § 2A4.1 captioned "Background" is amended by inserting the following additional paragraph at the end:

> " Section 401 of Public Law 101-647 amended 18 U.S.C. § 1201 to require that courts take into account certain specific offense characteristics in cases involving a victim under eighteen years of age and directed the Commission to include those specific offense characteristics within the guidelines. Where the guidelines did not already take into account the conduct identified by the Act, additional specific offense characteristics have been provided.".

Reason for Amendment: This amendment implements the instructions in Section 401 of the Crime Control Act of 1990 (Public Law 101-647), in some cases with a broader scope, by adding specific offense characteristics at subsections (b)(5) and (b)(6). With respect to the portion of the Congressional instruction pertaining to aiders or abettors, no amendment was required because § 1B1.3 (Relevant Conduct) provides an offense level greater than that required by the Congressional instruction. A separate amendment (amendment 388) clarifies that maltreatment to a life threatening degree constitutes life-threatening bodily injury. In addition, this amendment replaces the current subsection (b)(5) with a revised subsection (b)(7) that addresses other offenses connected with kidnapping, abduction, or unlawful restraint in a manner that more appropriately reflects the combined seriousness of such offenses, and inserts a cross reference to address the case in which the victim was murdered.

Effective Date: The effective date of this amendment is November 1, 1991.

364. Amendment: Section 2B1.1(b)(7) is amended by inserting "-- (A)" immediately before "substantially"; and by deleting the comma immediately following "institution" and inserting in lieu thereof "; or (B) affected a financial institution and the defendant derived more than $1,000,000 in gross receipts from the offense,".

The Commentary to § 2B1.1 captioned "Statutory Provisions" is amended by inserting "225," immediately before "641".

The Commentary to § 2B1.1 captioned "Application Notes" is amended in Note 9 by deleting "215" and inserting in lieu thereof "20"; and by deleting "1008, 1014, and 1344" and inserting in lieu thereof "1007, and 1014".

The Commentary to § 2B1.1 captioned "Application Notes" is amended in Note 10 by deleting:

> "as a consequence of the offense the institution became insolvent, substantially reduced benefits to pensioners or insureds, was unable on demand to refund fully any deposit, payment or investment, or was so depleted of its assets as to be forced to merge with another institution in order to continue active operations",

and inserting in lieu thereof:

", as a consequence of the offense, the institution became insolvent; substantially reduced benefits to pensioners or insureds; was unable on demand to refund fully any deposit, payment, or investment; was so depleted of its assets as to be forced to merge with another institution in order to continue active operations; or was placed in substantial jeopardy of any of the above".

The Commentary to § 2B1.1 captioned "Application Notes" is amended by inserting the following additional notes:

"11. 'The defendant derived more than $1,000,000 in gross receipts from the offense,' as used in subsection (b)(7)(B), generally means that the gross receipts to the defendant individually, rather than to all participants, exceeded $1,000,000. 'Gross receipts from the offense' includes all property, real or personal, tangible or intangible, which is obtained directly or indirectly as a result of such offense. See 18 U.S.C. § 982(a)(4).

12. If the defendant is convicted under 18 U.S.C. § 225 (relating to a continuing financial crimes enterprise), the offense level is that applicable to the underlying series of offenses comprising the 'continuing financial crimes enterprise.'

13. If subsection (b)(7)(A) or (B) applies, there shall be a rebuttable presumption that the offense involved 'more than minimal planning.'".

The Commentary to § 2B1.1 captioned "Background" is amended in the seventh paragraph by deleting "(b)(7)" and inserting in lieu thereof "(b)(7)(A)", and by deleting "statutory directive" and inserting in lieu thereof "instruction"; and by inserting the following additional paragraph at the end:

" Subsection (b)(7)(B) implements the instruction to the Commission in Section 2507 of Public Law 101-647.".

Section 2B4.1(b)(2) is amended by inserting "-- (A)" immediately before "substantially"; and by deleting the comma immediately following "institution" and inserting in lieu thereof "; or (B) affected a financial institution and the defendant derived more than $1,000,000 in gross receipts from the offense,".

The Commentary to § 2B4.1 captioned "Statutory Provisions" is amended by inserting ", 225" immediately following "224".

The Commentary to § 2B4.1 captioned "Application Notes" is amended in Note 2 by deleting "Bribery" and inserting in lieu thereof "Offering, Giving, Soliciting, or Receiving a Bribe; Extortion Under Color of Official Right".

The Commentary to § 2B4.1 captioned "Application Notes" is amended in Note 3 by deleting "215" and inserting in lieu thereof "20"; and by deleting "1008, 1014, and 1344" and inserting in lieu thereof "1007, and 1014".

The Commentary to § 2B4.1 captioned "Application Notes" is amended in Note 4 by deleting:

"as a consequence of the offense the institution became insolvent, substantially reduced benefits to pensioners or insureds, was unable on demand to refund fully any deposit, payment or investment, or was so depleted of its assets as to be forced to merge with another institution in order to continue active operations",

and inserting in lieu thereof:

", as a consequence of the offense, the institution became insolvent; substantially reduced benefits to pensioners or insureds; was unable on demand to refund fully any deposit, payment, or investment; was so depleted of its assets as to be forced to merge with another institution in order to continue active operations; or was placed in substantial jeopardy of any of the above".

The Commentary to § 2B4.1 captioned "Application Notes" is amended by inserting the following additional notes:

> "5. 'The defendant derived more than $1,000,000 in gross receipts from the offense,' as used in subsection (b)(2)(B), generally means that the gross receipts to the defendant individually, rather than to all participants, exceeded $1,000,000. 'Gross receipts from the offense' includes all property, real or personal, tangible or intangible, which is obtained directly or indirectly as a result of such offense. See 18 U.S.C. § 982(a)(4).
>
> 6. If the defendant is convicted under 18 U.S.C. § 225 (relating to a continuing financial crimes enterprise), the offense level is that applicable to the underlying series of offenses comprising the 'continuing financial crimes enterprise.'".

The Commentary to § 2B4.1 captioned "Background" is amended in the second paragraph by deleting the second sentence as follows:

> "As is the case for most other offenses covered by this guideline, the maximum term of imprisonment authorized is five years.";

in the seventh paragraph by deleting "(b)(2)" and inserting in lieu thereof "(b)(2)(A)", and by deleting "statutory directive" and inserting in lieu thereof "instruction"; and by inserting the following additional paragraph at the end:

> "   Subsection (b)(2)(B) implements the instruction to the Commission in Section 2507 of Public Law 101-647.".

Section 2F1.1(b)(6) is amended by inserting "-- (A)" immediately before "substantially"; and by deleting the comma immediately following "institution" and inserting in lieu thereof "; or (B) affected a financial institution and the defendant derived more than $1,000,000 in gross receipts from the offense,".

The Commentary to § 2F1.1 captioned "Statutory Provisions" is amended by inserting "225," immediately before "285".

The Commentary to § 2F1.1 captioned "Application Notes" is amended in Note 14 by deleting "215" and inserting in lieu thereof "20"; and by deleting "1008, 1014, and 1344" and inserting in lieu thereof "1007, and 1014".

The Commentary to § 2F1.1 captioned "Application Notes" is amended in Note 15 by deleting:

> "as a consequence of the offense the institution became insolvent, substantially reduced benefits to pensioners or insureds, was unable on demand to refund fully any deposit, payment or investment, or was so depleted of its assets as to be forced to merge with another institution in order to continue active operations",

and inserting in lieu thereof:

> ", as a consequence of the offense, the institution became insolvent; substantially

reduced benefits to pensioners or insureds; was unable on demand to refund fully any deposit, payment, or investment; was so depleted of its assets as to be forced to merge with another institution in order to continue active operations; or was placed in substantial jeopardy of any of the above".

The Commentary to § 2F1.1 captioned "Application Notes" is amended by inserting the following additional notes:

"16. 'The defendant derived more than $1,000,000 in gross receipts from the offense,' as used in subsection (b)(6)(B), generally means that the gross receipts to the defendant individually, rather than to all participants, exceeded $1,000,000. 'Gross receipts from the offense' includes all property, real or personal, tangible or intangible, which is obtained directly or indirectly as a result of such offense. See 18 U.S.C. § 982(a)(4).

17. If the defendant is convicted under 18 U.S.C. § 225 (relating to a continuing financial crimes enterprise), the offense level is that applicable to the underlying series of offenses comprising the 'continuing financial crimes enterprise.'

18. If subsection (b)(6)(A) or (B) applies, there shall be a rebuttable presumption that the offense involved 'more than minimal planning.'".

The Commentary to § 2F1.1 captioned "Background" is amended in the sixth paragraph by deleting "(b)(6)" and inserting in lieu thereof "(b)(6)(A)", and by deleting "statutory directive" and inserting in lieu thereof "instruction"; and by inserting the following additional paragraph at the end:

" Subsection (b)(6)(B) implements the instruction to the Commission in Section 2507 of Public Law 101-647.".

Reason for Amendment: This amendment implements the instruction to the Commission in Section 2507 of the Crime Control Act of 1990 (Public Law 101-647). It also reflects the new offense relating to a continuing financial crimes enterprise created by Section 2510 of the Crime Control Act of 1990. In addition, it revises the Commentary to §§ 2B1.1, 2B4.1, and 2F1.1 with respect to the definition of "substantially jeopardized the safety and soundness of a financial institution" so that the commentary is read to include cases in which the offense created a substantial risk of any of the harms described in addition to cases in which such harm actually occurred.

Effective Date: The effective date of this amendment is November 1, 1991.

365. **Amendment:** Section 2B3.1(b) is amended by deleting:

"(2) (A) If a firearm was discharged, increase by 5 levels; (B) if a dangerous weapon (including a firearm) was otherwise used, increase by 4 levels; (C) if a dangerous weapon (including a firearm) was brandished, displayed, or possessed, increase by 3 levels; or (D) if an express threat of death was made, increase by 2 levels.",

and inserting in lieu thereof:

"(2) (A) If a firearm was discharged, increase by 7 levels; (B) if a firearm was otherwise used, increase by 6 levels; (C) if a firearm was brandished, displayed, or possessed, increase by 5 levels; (D) if a dangerous weapon was otherwise used, increase by 4 levels; (E) if a dangerous weapon was brandished, displayed, or possessed, increase by 3 levels; or (F) if an express threat of death was made, increase by 2 levels.".

Section 2B3.1(b)(3) is amended by deleting "9" and inserting in lieu thereof "11".

The Commentary to § 2B3.1 captioned "Application Notes" is amended in Note 1 by inserting "'bodily injury,' 'serious bodily injury,' 'permanent or life-threatening bodily injury,'" immediately before "'abducted'".

The Commentary to § 2B3.1 captioned "Application Notes" is amended in Note 2 by deleting "(b)(2)(C)" and inserting in lieu thereof "(b)(2)(E)".

The Commentary to § 2B3.1 captioned "Application Notes" is amended in Note 4 by deleting "9" and inserting in lieu thereof "11".

The Commentary to § 2B3.1 captioned "Application Notes" is amended in Note 7 by deleting "(b)(2)(D)" and inserting in lieu thereof "(b)(2)(F)".

Reason for Amendment: This amendment increases the offense levels for use or possession of a firearm by 2 levels to better reflect the seriousness of such offenses and to reduce the disparity resulting from the exercise of prosecutorial discretion in the charging of an offense under 18 U.S.C. § 924(c) or § 929(a). In addition, this amendment revises the commentary to make the reference to the terms defined in § 1B1.1 more comprehensive.

Effective Date: The effective date of this amendment is November 1, 1991.

366. **Amendment:** Section 2B3.2(b) is amended by deleting subdivisions (1) and (2) as follows:

> "(1) If the greater of the amount obtained or demanded exceeded $2,500, increase by the corresponding number of levels from the table in § 2B2.1(b)(2).
>
> (2) (A) If a firearm was discharged, increase by 5 levels; (B) if a dangerous weapon (including a firearm) was otherwise used, increase by 4 levels; (C) if a dangerous weapon (including a firearm) was brandished, displayed, or possessed, increase by 3 levels.";

by renumbering subdivisions (3) and (4) as (4) and (5) respectively; by inserting the following as subdivisions (1)-(3):

> "(1) If the offense involved an express or implied threat of death, bodily injury, or kidnapping, increase by 2 levels.
>
> (2) If the greater of the amount demanded or the loss to the victim exceeded $10,000, increase by the corresponding number of levels from the table in § 2B3.1(b)(6).
>
> (3) (A)(i) If a firearm was discharged, increase by 7 levels; (ii) if a firearm was otherwise used, increase by 6 levels; (iii) if a firearm was brandished, displayed, or possessed, increase by 5 levels; (iv) if a dangerous weapon was otherwise used, increase by 4 levels; or (v) if a dangerous weapon was brandished, displayed, or possessed, increase by 3 levels; or
>
> (B) If the offense involved preparation to carry out a threat of (i) death, (ii) serious bodily injury, (iii) kidnapping, or (iv) product tampering; or if the

November 1, 2013　　APPENDIX C - VOLUME I　　**Amendment 366**

participant(s) otherwise demonstrated the ability to carry out such threat, increase by 3 levels.";

and in the last sentence of the renumbered subdivision (4) (formerly (3)) by deleting "(2)", "(3)" and "9", and inserting in lieu thereof "(3)", "(4)", and "11", respectively.

Section 2B3.2 is amended by inserting the following additional subsection:

"(c)　Cross Reference

(1)　If the offense was tantamount to attempted murder, apply § 2A2.1 (Assault With Intent to Commit Murder; Attempted Murder) if the resulting offense level is greater than that determined above.".

The Commentary to § 2B3.2 captioned "Application Notes" is amended in Note 1 by inserting "'bodily injury,' 'serious bodily injury,' 'permanent or life-threatening bodily injury,'" immediately before "abducted"; and in Note 4 by deleting "9" and inserting in lieu thereof "11".

The Commentary to § 2B3.2 captioned "Application Notes" is amended by deleting:

"5.　Valuation of loss is discussed in the Commentary to § 2B1.1 (Larceny, Embezzlement, and Other Forms of Theft).",

and inserting in lieu thereof:

"5.　'Loss to the victim,' as used in subsection (b)(2), means any demand paid plus any additional consequential loss from the offense (e.g., the cost of defensive measures taken in direct response to the offense).

6.　In certain cases, an extortionate demand may be accompanied by conduct that does not qualify as a display of a dangerous weapon under subsection (b)(3)(A)(v) but is nonetheless similar in seriousness, demonstrating the defendant's preparation or ability to carry out the threatened harm (e.g., an extortionate demand containing a threat to tamper with a consumer product accompanied by a workable plan showing how the product's tamper-resistant seals could be defeated, or a threat to kidnap a person accompanied by information showing study of that person's daily routine). Subsection (b)(3)(B) addresses such cases.

7.　If the offense involved the threat of death or serious bodily injury to numerous victims (e.g., in the case of a plan to derail a passenger train or poison consumer products), an upward departure may be warranted.

8.　If the offense involved organized criminal activity, or a threat to a family member of the victim, an upward departure may be warranted.".

The Commentary to § 2B3.2 captioned "Background" is amended in the last sentence by deleting "§ 877" and inserting in lieu thereof "18 U.S.C. § 877".

Reason for Amendment: This amendment provides a specific offense characteristic to distinguish the greater seriousness of offenses that involve an express or implied threat of death, bodily injury, or kidnapping; conforms the loss table to that used in the robbery guideline to reflect that the typical case under the amended guideline will have an offense level that is more closely comparable to robbery; increases the offense levels for offenses

Amendment 366 APPENDIX C - VOLUME I November 1, 2013

involving use or possession of a firearm to conform to an amendment being made to the robbery guideline; adds a subdivision to the specific offense characteristic dealing with use or possession of a dangerous weapon to address cases in which the conduct is tantamount in seriousness to the brandishing, display, or possession of a dangerous weapon, but does not qualify under the current specific offense characteristic for weapon enhancement; modifies subsection (b)(1) to provide that the greater of the amount demanded or the loss to the victim is used; adds a cross reference to § 2A2.1 to address cases in which the conduct was tantamount to attempted murder; and sets forth commentary describing certain aggravating factors that may warrant an upward departure.

Effective Date: The effective date of this amendment is November 1, 1991.

367. **Amendment:** Section 2C1.1(b)(1) is amended by inserting "or extortion" immediately following "bribe".

Section 2C1.1(b)(2)(A) is amended by deleting "bribe or the benefit received, or to be received, in return for the bribe" and inserting in lieu thereof "payment, the benefit received or to be received in return for the payment, or the loss to the government from the offense, whichever is greatest,".

Section 2C1.1(b)(2)(B) is amended by deleting "bribe" and inserting in lieu thereof "payment".

Section 2C1.1(c) is amended by deleting:

> "(1) If the bribe was for the purpose of concealing or facilitating another criminal offense, or for obstructing justice in respect to another criminal offense, apply § 2X3.1 (Accessory After the Fact) in respect to such other criminal offense if the resulting offense level is greater than that determined above.";

by renumbering subsection (c)(2) as (c)(3); and by inserting the following as subsections (c)(1) and (2):

> "(1) If the offense was committed for the purpose of facilitating the commission of another criminal offense, apply the offense guideline applicable to a conspiracy to commit that other offense if the resulting offense level is greater than that determined above.
>
> (2) If the offense was committed for the purpose of concealing, or obstructing justice in respect to, another criminal offense, apply § 2X3.1 (Accessory After the Fact) or § 2J1.2 (Obstruction of Justice), as appropriate, in respect to that other offense if the resulting offense level is greater than that determined above.".

The Commentary to § 2C1.1 captioned "Application Notes" is amended by deleting Note 2 as follows:

> "2. 'Value of the bribe or the benefit received, or to be received, in return for the bribe' means the greater of the value of the bribe or the value of the benefit received, or to be received, in return for the bribe. The 'value of the benefit received or to be received' means the net value of such benefit. For example, if a $150,000 contract on which $20,000 profit was made was awarded in return for a bribe, the value of the benefit received in return is $20,000.",

and inserting in lieu thereof:

"2. 'Loss' is discussed in the Commentary to § 2B1.1 (Larceny, Embezzlement, and Other Forms of Theft) and includes both actual and intended loss. The value of 'the benefit received or to be received' means the net value of such benefit. Examples: (1) A government employee, in return for a $500 bribe, reduces the price of a piece of surplus property offered for sale by the government from $10,000 to $2,000; the value of the benefit received is $8,000. (2) A $150,000 contract on which $20,000 profit was made was awarded in return for a bribe; the value of the benefit received is $20,000. Do not deduct the value of the bribe itself in computing the value of the benefit received or to be received. In the above examples, therefore, the value of the benefit received would be the same regardless of the value of the bribe.";

The Commentary to § 2C1.1 captioned "Application Notes" is amended in Note 3 by deleting "§ 2C1.1(c)(1) or (2)." and inserting in lieu thereof "§ 2C1.1(c)(1), (2), or (3). In such cases, an adjustment from § 3B1.3 (Abuse of Position of Trust or Use of Special Skill) may apply.".

The Commentary to § 2C1.1 captioned "Application Notes" is amended in Note 4 by deleting "bribe" and inserting in lieu thereof "unlawful payment"; and by deleting "and (2)" and inserting in lieu thereof ", (2), and (3)".

The Commentary to § 2C1.1 captioned "Application Notes" is amended in Note 6 by inserting the following as the first sentence:

"Subsection (b)(1) provides an adjustment for offenses involving more than one incident of either bribery or extortion.";

by deleting "bribe" the first time it occurs and inserting in lieu thereof "incident of bribery or extortion"; and by inserting "or extortion" immediately before ", even if charged".

The Commentary to § 2C1.1 captioned "Background" is amended by deleting the third paragraph as follows:

"   The amount of the bribe is used as a factor in the guideline not because it directly measures harm to society, but because it is improbable that a large bribe would be given for a favor of little consequence. Moreover, for deterrence purposes, the punishment should be commensurate with the gain.",

and inserting in lieu thereof:

"   In determining the net value of the benefit received or to be received, the value of the bribe is not deducted from the gross value of such benefit; the harm is the same regardless of value of the bribe paid to receive the benefit. Where the value of the bribe exceeds the value of the benefit or the value of the benefit cannot be determined, the value of the bribe is used because it is likely that the payer of such a bribe expected something in return that would be worth more than the value of the bribe. Moreover, for deterrence purposes, the punishment should be commensurate with the gain to the payer or the recipient of the bribe, whichever is higher.".

The Commentary to § 2C1.1 captioned "Background" is amended in the fourth paragraph by deleting "bribe is" and inserting in lieu thereof "payment was".

The Commentary to § 2C1.1 captioned "Background" is amended by deleting the fifth, sixth, and seventh paragraphs as follows:

> "Under § 2C1.1(c)(1), if the purpose of the bribe involved the facilitation of another criminal offense or the obstruction of justice in respect to another criminal offense, the guideline for § 2X3.1 (Accessory After the Fact) in respect to that criminal offense will be applied, if the result is greater than that determined above. For example, if a bribe was given for the purpose of facilitating or covering up the offense of espionage, the guideline for accessory after the fact to espionage would be applied.
>
> Under § 2C1.1(c)(2), if the offense involved forcible extortion, the guideline from § 2B3.2 (Extortion by Force or Threat of Injury or Serious Damage) will apply if the result is greater than that determined above.
>
> Note that, when applying 2C1.1(c)(1) or (2), an adjustment from Chapter Three, Part B (Role in the Offense) will also apply. This normally will result in an increase of at least 2 levels.",

and inserting in lieu thereof:

> "   Under § 2C1.1(c)(1), if the payment was to facilitate the commission of another criminal offense, the guideline applicable to a conspiracy to commit that other offense will apply if the result is greater than that determined above. For example, if a bribe was given to a law enforcement officer to allow the smuggling of a quantity of cocaine, the guideline for conspiracy to import cocaine would be applied if it resulted in a greater offense level.
>
> Under § 2C1.1(c)(2), if the payment was to conceal another criminal offense or obstruct justice in respect to another criminal offense, the guideline from § 2X3.1 (Accessory After the Fact) or § 2J1.2 (Obstruction of Justice), as appropriate, will apply if the result is greater than that determined above. For example, if a bribe was given for the purpose of concealing the offense of espionage, the guideline for accessory after the fact to espionage would be applied.
>
> Under § 2C1.1(c)(3), if the offense involved forcible extortion, the guideline from § 2B3.2 (Extortion by Force or Threat of Injury or Serious Damage) will apply if the result is greater than that determined above.
>
> When the offense level is determined under § 2C1.1(c)(1), (2), or (3), an adjustment from § 3B1.3 (Abuse of Position of Trust or Use of Special Skill) may apply.".

Reason for Amendment: This amendment adds an additional factor in subsection (b)(2)(A) to take into account loss to the government from the offense; expands subsection (c) to distinguish an offense committed for the purpose of facilitating the commission of another offense from an offense committed to cover up or obstruct justice in respect to another offense; clarifies the term "value of the benefit received"; and substitutes "payment" for "bribe" and adds "or extortion" where necessary to reflect that this guideline covers both bribery and extortion under color of official right.

Effective Date: The effective date of this amendment is November 1, 1991.

368. **Amendment:** Chapter Two, Part C, is amended by inserting an additional guideline with accompanying commentary as § 2C1.7 (Fraud Involving Deprivation of the Intangible Right to the Honest Services of Public Officials; Conspiracy to Defraud by Interference with Governmental Functions).

Reason for Amendment: This amendment provides an additional guideline to cover certain offenses that involve public corruption but do not fall within the guidelines of Chapter Two, Part C (Official Corruption) as currently written. In some cases, the statutes covered are used to prosecute offenses more appropriately covered under § 2C1.1 (Offering, Giving, Soliciting, or Receiving a Bribe; Extortion Under Color of Official Right), § 2C1.2 (Offering, Giving, Soliciting, or Receiving a Gratuity), or § 2C1.3 (Conflict of Interest). A cross reference is provided to address such cases.

Effective Date: The effective date of this amendment is November 1, 1991.

369. **Amendment:** Section 2D1.1(c)(12) is amended by deleting the period immediately after "Schedule III substances" and inserting in lieu thereof "(except anabolic steroids);", and by inserting the following additional subdivision at the end:

"40,000 or more units of anabolic steroids.".

Section 2D1.1(c)(13) is amended by deleting the period immediately after "Schedule III substances" and inserting in lieu thereof "(except anabolic steroids);", and by inserting the following additional subdivision at the end:

"At least 20,000 but less than 40,000 units of anabolic steroids.".

Section 2D1.1(c)(14) is amended by deleting the period immediately after "Schedule III substances" and inserting in lieu thereof "(except anabolic steroids);", and by inserting the following additional subdivision at the end:

"At least 10,000 but less than 20,000 units of anabolic steroids.".

Section 2D1.1(c)(15) is amended by deleting the period immediately after "Schedule III substances" and inserting in lieu thereof "(except anabolic steroids);", and by inserting the following additional subdivision at the end:

"At least 5,000 but less than 10,000 units of anabolic steroids.".

Section 2D1.1(c)(16) is amended by inserting "(except anabolic steroids)" immediately after "Schedule III substances", and by inserting the following additional subdivision after the next to last subdivision:

"At least 2,500 but less than 5,000 units of anabolic steroids;".

Section 2D1.1(c)(17) is amended by inserting "(except anabolic steroids)" immediately after "Schedule III substances", and by inserting the following additional subdivision after the next to last subdivision:

"At least 1,000 but less than 2,500 units of anabolic steroids;".

Section 2D1.1(c)(18) is amended by inserting "(except anabolic steroids)" immediately after "Schedule III substances", and by inserting the following additional subdivision after the fourth subdivision:

"At least 250 but less than 1,000 units of anabolic steroids;".

Section 2D1.1(c)(19) is amended by inserting "(except anabolic steroids)" immediately after "Schedule III substances", and by inserting the following additional subdivision after the fourth subdivision:

"Less than 250 units of anabolic steroids;".

Section 2D1.1(c) is amended in the note following subdivision (19) by inserting the following additional paragraph at the end:

> "In the case of anabolic steroids, one 'unit' means a 10 cc vial of an injectable steroid or fifty tablets. All vials of injectable steroids are to be converted on the basis of their volume to the equivalent number of 10 cc vials (e.g., one 50 cc vial is to be counted as five 10 cc vials).".

Reason for Amendment: This amendment adds offenses involving anabolic steroids to § 2D1.1 to reflect that Title XIX of the Crime Control Act of 1990 (Public Law 101-647) reclassified anabolic steroids as Schedule III controlled substances under 21 U.S.C. § 812(c). Because of the variety of substances involved, the Commission has determined that a measure based on quantity unit, rather than weight, provides the most appropriate measure of the scale of the offense.

Effective Date: The effective date of this amendment is November 1, 1991.

370. **Amendment:** Section 2D1.1(c) is amended in subdivision (1) by inserting ", or 30 KG or more of 'Ice'" immediately following "Pure Methamphetamine"; in subdivision (2) by inserting ", or at least 10 KG but less than 30 KG of 'Ice'" immediately following "Pure Methamphetamine"; in subdivision (3) by inserting ", or at least 3 KG but less than 10 KG of 'Ice'" immediately following "Pure Methamphetamine"; in subdivision (4) by inserting ", or at least 1 KG but less than 3 KG of 'Ice'" immediately following "Pure Methamphetamine"; in subdivision (5) by inserting ", or at least 300 G but less than 1 KG of 'Ice'" immediately following "Pure Methamphetamine"; in subdivision (6) by inserting ", or at least 100 G but less than 300 G of 'Ice'" immediately following "Pure Methamphetamine"; in subdivision (7) by inserting ", or at least 70 G but less than 100 G of 'Ice'" immediately following "Pure Methamphetamine"; in subdivision (8) by inserting ", or at least 40 G but less than 70 G of 'Ice'" immediately following "Pure Methamphetamine"; subdivision (9) by inserting ", or at least 10 G but less than 40 G of 'Ice'" immediately following "Pure Methamphetamine"; in subdivision (10) by inserting ", or at least 8 G but less than 10 G of 'Ice'" immediately following "Pure Methamphetamine"; in subdivision (11) by inserting ", or at least 6 G but less than 8 G of 'Ice'" immediately following "Pure Methamphetamine"; in subdivision (12) by inserting ", or at least 4 G but less than 6 G of 'Ice'" immediately following "Pure Methamphetamine"; in subdivision (13) by inserting ", or at least 2 G but less than 4 G of 'Ice'" immediately following "Pure Methamphetamine"; subdivision (14) by inserting ", or at least 1 G but less than 2 G of 'Ice'" immediately following "Pure Methamphetamine"; in subdivision (15) by inserting ", or at least 500 MG but less than 1 G of 'Ice'" immediately following "Pure Methamphetamine"; in subdivision (16) by inserting ", or less than 500 MG of 'Ice'" immediately following "Pure Methamphetamine"; and in the note following subdivision (19) by inserting the following as the second paragraph:

> "'Ice,' for the purposes of this guideline, means a mixture or substance containing d-methamphetamine hydrochloride of at least 80% purity.".

Reason for Amendment: This amendment implements the instruction to the Commission in Section 2701 of the Crime Control Act of 1990 (Public Law 101-647) in a form compatible with the structure of the guidelines.

Effective Date: The effective date of this amendment is November 1, 1991.

371. **Amendment:** Chapter Two, Part D, Subpart 1, is amended by inserting additional guidelines with accompanying commentary as § 2D1.11 (Unlawfully Distributing, Import-

ing, Exporting or Possessing a Listed Chemical), § 2D1.12 (Unlawful Possession, Manufacture, Distribution, or Importation of Prohibited Flask or Equipment), and § 2D1.13 (Structuring Chemical Transactions or Creating a Chemical Mixture to Evade Reporting or Recordkeeping Requirements; Presenting False or Fraudulent Identification to Obtain a Listed Chemical).

Chapter Two, Part D, Subpart 3 is amended by inserting an additional guideline with accompanying commentary as § 2D3.5 (Violation of Recordkeeping or Reporting Requirements for Listed Chemicals and Certain Machines).

The Commentary to § 2D1.1 captioned "Statutory Provisions" is amended by deleting "841, 960" and inserting in lieu thereof "841(a), (b)(1)-(3), 960(a), (b)".

The Commentary to § 2D1.1 captioned "Application Notes" is amended by inserting the following additional note:

> "14. D-lysergic acid, which is generally used to make LSD, is classified as a Schedule III controlled substance (to which § 2D1.1 applies) and as a listed precursor (to which § 2D1.11 applies). Where the defendant is convicted under 21 U.S.C. §§ 841(b)(1)(D) or 860(b)(4) of an offense involving d-lysergic acid, apply § 2D1.1 or § 2D1.11, whichever results in the greater offense level. See Application Note 5 in the Commentary to § 1B1.1 (Application Instructions). Where the defendant is accountable for an offense involving the manufacture of LSD, see Application Note 12 above pertaining to the determination of the scale of the offense.".

Reason for Amendment: This amendment makes Chapter Two, Part D more comprehensive by providing additional guidelines to address violations involving listed chemicals, flasks, and certain machines that are used in the manufacture of controlled substances. Conforming changes are made to the Commentary to § 2D1.1.

Effective Date: The effective date of this amendment is November 1, 1991.

372. **Amendment:** Chapter Two, Part G, Subpart 2 is amended by inserting additional guidelines with accompanying commentary as § 2G2.4 (Receipt or Possession of Materials Depicting a Minor Engaged in Sexually Explicit Conduct) and § 2G2.5 (Recordkeeping Offenses Involving the Production of Sexually Explicit Materials).

Section 2G2.2 is amended in the title by deleting "Transporting, Receiving, or"; and by inserting at the end "; Receiving, Transporting, Advertising, or Possessing Material Involving the Sexual Exploitation of a Minor with Intent to Traffic".

The Commentary to § 2G2.2 captioned "Statutory Provisions" is amended by deleting "1460,".

Section 2G3.1(c)(1) is amended by deleting "(Transporting, Receiving, or Trafficking in Material Involving the Sexual Exploitation of a Minor)" and inserting in lieu thereof "(Trafficking in Material Involving the Sexual Exploitation of a Minor; Receiving, Transporting, Advertising, or Possessing Material Involving the Sexual Exploitation of a Minor with Intent to Traffic) or § 2G2.4 (Receipt or Possession of Materials Depicting a Minor Engaged in Sexually Explicit Conduct), as appropriate".

Reason for Amendment: This amendment inserts an additional guideline at § 2G2.4 to address offenses involving receipt or possession of materials depicting a minor engaged in sexually explicit conduct, as distinguished from offenses involving trafficking in such material, which continue to be covered under § 2G2.2. Offenses involving receipt or transportation of such material for the purpose of trafficking are referenced to § 2G2.2 on the basis of the underlying conduct (subsection (c)(2)). Similarly, offenses in which the underlying conduct is more appropriately addressed as sexual exploitation of a minor are referenced to that guideline (subsection (c)(1)). Among the offenses covered by this guideline is a new offense created by Section 323 of the Crime Control Act of 1990 (Public Law 101-647). In addition, this amendment inserts an additional guideline at § 2G2.5 to address a recordkeeping offense created by Section 311 of the Crime Control Act of 1990 (Public Law 101-647).

Effective Date: The effective date of this amendment is November 1, 1991.

373. **Amendment:** Chapter Two, Part K, Subpart 1 is amended by deleting §§ 2K1.3 and 2K1.6 in their entirety as follows:

"§ 2K1.3. Unlawfully Trafficking In, Receiving, or Transporting Explosives

(a) Base Offense Level: 6

(b) Specific Offense Characteristics

If more than one applies, use the greatest:

(1) If the defendant"s conduct involved any written or oral false or fictitious statement, false record, or misrepresented identification, increase by 4 levels.

(2) If the offense involved explosives that the defendant knew or had reason to believe were stolen, increase by 6 levels.

(3) If the defendant knowingly distributed explosives to a person under twenty-one years of age, to a person prohibited by state law or ordinance from receiving such explosives at the place of distribution, or to a person the defendant had reason to believe intended to transport such materials into a state in violation of the law of that state, increase by 4 levels.

(4) If the defendant was a person prohibited from receiving explosives under 18 U.S.C. § 842(i), or if the defendant knowingly distributed explosives to a person prohibited from receiving explosives under 18 U.S.C. § 842(i), increase by 10 levels.

(5) If a recordkeeping offense reflected an effort to conceal a substantive offense involving explosives, apply the guideline for the substantive offense.

Commentary

Statutory Provisions: 18 U.S.C. §§ 842(a), (h), (i), 844(b). For additional statutory provision(s), see Appendix A (Statutory Index).

Application Note:

1. 'A person prohibited from receiving explosives under 18 U.S.C. § 842(i)' is

anyone who is under indictment for or has been convicted of a crime punishable by imprisonment for more than one year; who is a fugitive from justice; who is an unlawful user of or addicted to marihuana, any depressant or stimulant or narcotic drug; or who has been adjudicated as a mental defective or has been committed to a mental institution.

Background: This section applies to conduct ranging from violations of a regulatory nature pertaining to licensees or persons otherwise lawfully involved in explosives commerce to more serious violations that involve substantial danger to public safety.",

"§ 2K1.6. Shipping, Transporting, or Receiving Explosives with Felonious Intent or Knowledge; Using or Carrying Explosives in Certain Crimes

    (a)   Base Offense Level (Apply the greatest):

        (1)   18; or

        (2)   If the defendant committed the offense with intent to commit another offense against a person or property, apply § 2X1.1 (Attempt, Solicitation, or Conspiracy) in respect to such other offense; or

        (3)   If death resulted, apply the most analogous guideline from Chapter Two, Part A, Subpart 1 (Homicide).

Commentary

Statutory Provisions: 18 U.S.C. § 844(d); 26 U.S.C. § 5685. For additional statutory provision(s), see Appendix A (Statutory Index).".

A replacement guideline with accompanying commentary is inserted as § 2K1.3 (Unlawful Receipt, Possession, or Transportation of Explosive Materials; Prohibited Transactions Involving Explosive Materials).

Chapter Two, Part K, Subpart 1 is amended by inserting an additional guideline with accompanying commentary as § 2K1.6 (Licensee Recordkeeping Violations Involving Explosive Materials).

Reason for Amendment: This amendment consolidates two guidelines, and revises the offense levels and characteristics to more adequately reflect the seriousness of such offenses, including enhancements for defendants previously convicted of felony crimes of violence or controlled substance offenses. In addition, the amendment inserts an additional guideline to cover certain recordkeeping offenses.

Effective Date: The effective date of this amendment is November 1, 1991.

374. **Amendment:** Chapter Two, Part K, Subpart 2 is amended by deleting §§ 2K2.1, 2K2.2, and 2K2.3 in their entirety as follows:

"§ 2K2.1. Unlawful Receipt, Possession, or Transportation of Firearms or Ammunition

    (a)   Base Offense Level (Apply the greatest):

        (1)   18, if the defendant is convicted under 18 U.S.C. § 922(o) or 26 U.S.C. § 5861; or

(2) 12, if the defendant is convicted under 18 U.S.C. § 922(g), (h), or (n); or if the defendant, at the time of the offense, had been convicted in any court of an offense punishable by imprisonment for a term exceeding one year; or

(3) 6, otherwise.

(b) Specific Offense Characteristics

(1) If the defendant obtained or possessed the firearm or ammunition, other than a firearm covered in 26 U.S.C. § 5845(a), solely for lawful sporting purposes or collection, decrease the offense level determined above to level 6.

(2) If the firearm was stolen or had an altered or obliterated serial number, increase by 2 levels.

(c) Cross References

(1) If the offense involved the distribution of a firearm or possession with intent to distribute, apply § 2K2.2 (Unlawful Trafficking and Other Prohibited Transactions Involving Firearms) if the resulting offense level is greater than that determined above.

(2) If the defendant used or possessed the firearm in connection with commission or attempted commission of another offense, apply § 2X1.1 (Attempt, Solicitation, or Conspiracy) in respect to that other offense, if the resulting offense level is greater than that determined above.

Commentary

Statutory Provisions: 18 U.S.C. § 922(a)(1), (a)(3), (a)(4), (a)(6), (e), (f), (g), (h), (i), (j), (k), (l), (n), and (o); 26 U.S.C. § 5861(b), (c), (d), (h), (i), (j), and (k). For additional statutory provision(s), see Appendix A (Statutory Index).

Application Notes:

1. The definition of 'firearm' used in this section is that set forth in 18 U.S.C. § 921(a)(3) (if the defendant is convicted under 18 U.S.C. § 922) and 26 U.S.C. § 5845(a) (if the defendant is convicted under 26 U.S.C. § 5861). These definitions are somewhat broader than that used in Application Note 1(e) of the Commentary to § 1B1.1 (Application Instructions). Under 18 U.S.C. § 921(a)(3), the term 'firearm' means (A) any weapon (including a starter gun) which will or is designed to or may readily be converted to expel a projectile by the action of an explosive; (B) the frame or receiver of any such weapon; (C) any firearm muffler or firearm silencer; or (D) any destructive device. Under 26 U.S.C. § 5845(a), the term 'firearm' includes a shotgun, or a weapon made from a shotgun, with a barrel or barrels of less than 18 inches in length; a weapon made from a shotgun or rifle with an overall length of less than 26 inches; a rifle, or weapon made from a rifle, with a barrel or barrels less than 16 inches in length; a machine gun; a muffler or silencer for a firearm; a destructive device; and certain other large bore weapons.

2. Under § 2K2.1(b)(1), intended lawful use, as determined by the surrounding circumstances, provides a decrease in the offense level. Relevant circumstances include, among others, the number and type of firearms (sawed-off shotguns, for example, have few legitimate uses) and ammunition, the location and circumstances of possession, the nature of the defendant's criminal history (e.g., whether involving firearms), and the extent to which possession was restricted by local law.

Background: Under pre-guidelines practice, there was substantial sentencing variation for these crimes. From the Commission's investigations, it appeared that the variation was attributable primarily to the wide variety of circumstances under which these offenses occur. Apart from the nature of the defendant's criminal history, his actual or intended use of the firearm was probably the most important factor in determining the sentence.

Statistics showed that pre-guidelines sentences averaged two to three months lower if the firearm involved was a rifle or an unaltered shotgun. This may reflect the fact that these weapons tend to be more suitable than others for recreational activities. However, some rifles or shotguns may be possessed for criminal purposes, while some handguns may be suitable primarily for recreation. Therefore, the guideline is not based upon the type of firearm. Intended lawful use, as determined by the surrounding circumstances, is a mitigating factor.

Available pre-guidelines data were not sufficient to determine the effect a stolen firearm had on the average sentence. However, reviews of pre-guidelines cases suggested that this factor tended to result in more severe sentences. Independent studies show that stolen firearms are used disproportionately in the commission of crimes.

The firearm statutes often are used as a device to enable the federal court to exercise jurisdiction over offenses that otherwise could be prosecuted only under state law. For example, a convicted felon may be prosecuted for possessing a firearm if he used the firearm to rob a gasoline station. In pre-guidelines practice, such prosecutions resulted in high sentences because of the true nature of the underlying conduct. The cross reference at § 2K2.1(c)(2) deals with such cases.

§ 2K2.2. Unlawful Trafficking and Other Prohibited Transactions Involving Firearms

(a) Base Offense Level:

(1) 18, if the defendant is convicted under 18 U.S.C. § 922(o) or 26 U.S.C. § 5861;

(2) 6, otherwise.

(b) Specific Offense Characteristics

(1) If the offense involved distribution of a firearm, or possession with intent to distribute, and the number of firearms unlawfully distributed, or to be distributed, exceeded two, increase as follows:

Number of Firearms   Increase in Level

(A)	3 - 4	add 1
(B)	5 - 7	add 2
(C)	8 - 12	add 3
(D)	13 - 24	add 4
(E)	25 - 49	add 5
(F)	50 or more	add 6.

  (2) If any of the firearms was stolen or had an altered or obliterated serial number, increase by 2 levels.

  (3) If more than one of the following applies, use the greater:

    (A) If the defendant is convicted under 18 U.S.C. § 922(d), increase by 6 levels; or

    (B) If the defendant is convicted under 18 U.S.C. § 922(b)(1) or (b)(2), increase by 1 level.

(c) Cross Reference

  (1) If the defendant, at the time of the offense, had been convicted in any court of a crime punishable by imprisonment for a term exceeding one year, apply § 2K2.1 (Unlawful Receipt, Possession, or Transportation of Firearms or Ammunition) if the resulting offense level is greater than that determined above.

Commentary

Statutory Provisions: 18 U.S.C. § 922(a)(1), (a)(2), (a)(5), (b), (c), (d), (e), (f), (i), (j), (k), (l), (m), (o); 26 U.S.C. § 5861(a), (e), (f), (g), (j), and (l). For additional statutory provision(s), see Appendix A (Statutory Index).

Application Notes:

1. The definition of 'firearm' used in this section is that set forth in 18 U.S.C. § 921(a)(3) (if the defendant is convicted under 18 U.S.C. § 922) and 26 U.S.C. § 5845(a) (if the defendant is convicted under 26 U.S.C § 5861). These definitions are somewhat broader than that used in Application Note 1(e) of the Commentary to § 1B1.1 (Application Instructions). Under 18 U.S.C. § 921(a)(3), the term 'firearm' means (A) any weapon (including a starter gun) which will or is designed to or may readily be converted to expel a projectile by the action of an explosive; (B) the frame or receiver of any such weapon; (C) any firearm muffler or firearm silencer; or (D) any destructive device. Under 26 U.S.C. § 5845(a), the term 'firearm' includes a shotgun, or a weapon made from a shotgun, with a barrel or barrels of less than 18 inches in length; a weapon made from a shotgun or rifle with an overall length of less than 26 inches; a rifle, or weapon made from a rifle, with a barrel or barrels less than 16 inches in length; a machine gun; a muffler or silencer for a firearm; a destructive device; and certain other large bore weapons.

2. If the number of weapons involved exceeded fifty, an upward departure may

be warranted. An upward departure especially may be warranted in the case of large numbers of military type weapons (e.g., machine guns, automatic weapons, assault rifles).

Background: This guideline applies to a variety of offenses involving firearms, ranging from unlawful distribution of silencers, machine guns, sawed-off shotguns and destructive devices, to essentially technical violations.

§ 2K2.3. Receiving, Transporting, Shipping or Transferring a Firearm or Ammunition With Intent to Commit Another Offense, or With Knowledge that It Will Be Used in Committing Another Offense

(a) Base Offense Level (Apply the greatest):

(1) The offense level from § 2X1.1 (Attempt, Solicitation, or Conspiracy) in respect to the offense that the defendant intended or knew was to be committed with the firearm; or

(2) The offense level from § 2K2.1 (Unlawful Receipt, Possession, or Transportation of Firearms or Ammunition), or § 2K2.2 (Unlawful Trafficking and Other Prohibited Transactions Involving Firearms), as applicable; or

(3) 12.

Commentary

Statutory Provisions: 18 U.S.C. § 924(b), (f), (g).".

A replacement guideline with accompanying commentary is inserted as § 2K2.1 (Unlawful Receipt, Possession, or Transportation of Firearms or Ammunition; Prohibited Transactions Involving Firearms or Ammunition).

Chapter Two, Part K, Subpart 2 is amended by deleting § 2K2.5 in its entirety as follows:

"§ 2K2.5. Possession of Firearms and Dangerous Weapons in Federal Facilities

(a) Base Offense Level: 6

(b) Cross Reference

(1) If the defendant possessed the firearm or other dangerous weapon with intent to use it in the commission of another offense, apply § 2X1.1 (Attempt, Solicitation, or Conspiracy) in respect to that other offense if the resulting offense level is greater than that determined above.

Commentary

Statutory Provision: 18 U.S.C. § 930.".

A replacement guideline with accompanying commentary is inserted as § 2K2.5 (Possession of Firearm or Dangerous Weapon in Federal Facility; Possession or Discharge of Firearm in School Zone).

Reason for Amendment: This amendment consolidates three firearms guidelines and

Amendment 374 APPENDIX C - VOLUME I November 1, 2013

revises the adjustments and offense levels to more adequately reflect the seriousness of such conduct, including enhancements for defendants previously convicted of felony crimes of violence or controlled substance offenses. In addition, § 2K1.5 is amended to address offenses committed within a school zone or federal court facility.

Effective Date: The effective date of this amendment is November 1, 1991.

375. Amendment: Section 2L1.1(a) is amended by deleting "9" and inserting in lieu thereof:

"(1) 20, if the defendant was convicted under 8 U.S.C. § 1327 of a violation involving an alien who previously was deported after a conviction for an aggravated felony; or

(2) 9, otherwise.".

Section 2L1.1(b)(1) is amended by inserting "and the base offense level is determined under subsection (a)(2)," immediately before "decrease".

The Commentary to § 2L1.1 captioned "Application Notes" is amended by inserting the following additional note:

"9. 'Aggravated felony' is defined in the Commentary to § 2L1.2 (Unlawfully Entering or Remaining in the United States).".

Section 2L1.2(b) is amended by deleting "Specific Offense Characteristic" and inserting in lieu thereof:

"Specific Offense Characteristics

If more than one applies, use the greater:".

Section 2L1.2(b)(1) is amended by deleting "sustaining" immediately before "a conviction"; and by inserting the following additional subdivision:

"(2) If the defendant previously was deported after a conviction for an aggravated felony, increase by 16 levels.".

The Commentary to § 2L1.2 captioned "Statutory Provisions" is amended by deleting "1325" and inserting in lieu thereof "1325(a)".

The Commentary to § 2L1.2 captioned "Application Notes" is amended in Note 1 by deleting:

"First offenses under 8 U.S.C. § 1325 are petty offenses for which no guideline has been promulgated.",

and inserting in lieu thereof:

"A first offense under 8 U.S.C. § 1325(a) is a Class B misdemeanor for which no guideline has been promulgated. A prior sentence for such offense, however, is to be considered under the provisions of Chapter Four, Part A (Criminal History).".

The Commentary to § 2L1.2 captioned "Application Notes" is amended in Note 3 by deleting "sustaining" immediately before "a conviction"; and by deleting the last sentence as follows:

"In the case of a defendant previously deported after sustaining a conviction for an aggravated felony as defined in 8 U.S.C. § 1101(a), or for any other violent felony, an upward departure may be warranted.".

The Commentary to § 2L1.2 captioned "Application Notes" is amended by deleting:

"4. The adjustment under § 2L1.2(b)(1) is in addition to any criminal history points added for such conviction in Chapter 4, Part A (Criminal History).",

and inserting in lieu thereof:

"4. A 16-level increase is provided under subsection (b)(2) in the case of a defendant who was previously deported after a conviction for an aggravated felony.

5. An adjustment under subsection (b)(1) or (b)(2) for a prior felony conviction applies in addition to any criminal history points added for such conviction in Chapter Four, Part A (Criminal History).

6. 'Deported after a conviction,' as used in subsections (b)(1) and (b)(2), means that the deportation was subsequent to the conviction, whether or not the deportation was in response to such conviction.

7. 'Aggravated felony,' as used in subsection (b)(2), means murder; any illicit trafficking in any controlled substance (as defined in 21 U.S.C. § 802), including any drug trafficking crime as defined in 18 U.S.C. § 924(c)(2); any illicit trafficking in any firearms or destructive devices as defined in 18 U.S.C. § 921; any offense described in 18 U.S.C. § 1956 (relating to laundering of monetary instruments); any crime of violence (as defined in 18 U.S.C. § 16, not including a purely political offense) for which the term of imprisonment imposed (regardless of any suspension of such imprisonment) is at least five years; or any attempt or conspiracy to commit any such act. The term 'aggravated felony' applies to offenses described in the previous sentence whether in violation of federal or state law and also applies to offenses described in the previous sentence in violation of foreign law for which the term of imprisonment was completed within the previous 15 years. See 8 U.S.C. § 1101(a)(43).".

Reason for Amendment: This amendment adds a specific offense characteristic providing an increase of 16 levels above the base offense level under § 2L1.2 for defendants who reenter the United States after having been deported subsequent to a conviction for an aggravated felony. Previously, such cases were addressed by a recommendation for consideration of an upward departure. This amendment also modifies § 2L1.1 to provide a base offense level of 20 for a defendant who is convicted under 8 U.S.C. § 1327 for an offense involving the smuggling, transporting, or harboring of an alien who was deported after a conviction for an aggravated felony. The Commission has determined that these increased offense levels are appropriate to reflect the serious nature of these offenses. In addition, this amendment revises the Commentary to § 2L1.2 to make the statutory reference more precise, and to clarify the operation of the guidelines in respect to prior criminal history.

Effective Date: The effective date of this amendment is November 1, 1991.

376. **Amendment:** Section 2N1.1 is amended in the title by deleting "Serious" and inserting in lieu thereof "Bodily".

Amendment 376 APPENDIX C - VOLUME I November 1, 2013

Section 2N1.1 is amended by deleting:

"(b) Cross Reference

(1) If the offense involved extortion, apply § 2B3.2 (Extortion by Force or Threat of Injury or Serious Damage) if the resulting offense level is greater than that determined above.",

and inserting in lieu thereof:

"(b) Specific Offense Characteristic

(1) (A) If any victim sustained permanent or life-threatening bodily injury, increase by 4 levels; (B) if any victim sustained serious bodily injury, increase by 2 levels; or (C) if the degree of injury is between that specified in subdivisions (A) and (B), increase by 3 levels.

(c) Cross References

(1) If the offense resulted in death, apply § 2A1.1 (First Degree Murder) if the death was caused intentionally or knowingly, or § 2A1.2 (Second Degree Murder) in any other case.

(2) If the offense was tantamount to attempted murder, apply § 2A2.1 (Assault With Intent to Commit Murder; Attempted Murder) if the resulting offense level is greater than that determined above.

(3) If the offense involved extortion, apply § 2B3.2 (Extortion by Force or Threat of Injury or Serious Damage) if the resulting offense level is greater than that determined above.

(d) Special Instruction

(1) If the defendant is convicted of a single count involving (A) the death or permanent, life-threatening, or serious bodily injury of more than one victim, or (B) conduct tantamount to the attempted murder of more than one victim, Chapter Three, Part D (Multiple Counts) shall be applied as if the defendant had been convicted of a separate count for each such victim.".

The Commentary to § 2N1.1 captioned "Application Note" is amended by deleting:

"1. If death, bodily injury, extreme psychological injury, or substantial property damage or monetary loss resulted, an upward departure may be warranted. See Chapter Five, Part K (Departures).",

and inserting in lieu thereof:

"1. The base offense level reflects that this offense typically poses a risk of death or serious bodily injury to one or more victims; or causes, or is intended to cause, bodily injury. Where the offense posed a substantial risk of death or serious bodily injury to numerous victims, or caused extreme psychological injury or substantial property damage or monetary loss, an upward departure may be warranted. In the unusual case in which the offense did not cause a risk of death or serious bodily injury, and neither caused nor was intended to cause bodily injury, a downward departure may be warranted.

2. The special instruction in subsection (d)(1) applies whether the offense level is determined under subsection (b)(1) or by use of a cross reference in subsection (c).";

and in the caption by deleting "Note" and inserting in lieu thereof "Notes".

The Commentary to § 2N1.1 captioned "Background" is deleted in its entirety as follows:

"<u>Background</u>: The base offense level reflects the risk of death or serious injury posed to significant numbers of people by this type of product tampering.".

Reason for Amendment: This amendment adds a specific offense characteristic for permanent, life-threatening, or serious bodily injury, and adds cross references for cases in which the offense resulted in death or was tantamount to attempted murder. In addition, a special instruction is added to address certain conduct involving multiple victims. Finally, the title of this guideline is revised to reflect more accurately the coverage of the guideline, and the background commentary is revised to clarify the "heartland" conduct to which the guideline applies.

Effective Date: The effective date of this amendment is November 1, 1991.

377. **Amendment:** Section 2R1.1(a) is amended by deleting "9" and inserting in lieu thereof "10".

Section 2R1.1(b)(2) is amended by deleting "less than $1,000,000 or more than $4,000,000" and inserting in lieu thereof "more than $400,000"; and by deleting:

"(A)	Less than $1,000,000	subtract 1
(B)	$1,000,000 - $4,000,000	no adjustment
(C)	More than $4,000,000	add 1
(D)	More than $15,000,000	add 2
(E)	More than $50,000,000	add 3",

and inserting in lieu thereof:

"(A)	More than $400,000	add 1
(B)	More than $1,000,000	add 2
(C)	More than $2,500,000	add 3
(D)	More than $6,250,000	add 4
(E)	More than $15,000,000	add 5
(F)	More than $37,500,000	add 6
(G)	More than $100,000,000	add 7.".

Section 2R1.1 is amended by deleting:

"(c) Fines

A fine shall be imposed in addition to any term of imprisonment. The guideline fine range for an individual conspirator is from 4 to 10 percent of the volume of commerce, but not less than $20,000. The fine range for an organization is from 20 to 50 percent of the volume of commerce, but not less than $100,000.",

and inserting in lieu thereof:

"(c) Special Instruction for Fines

(1) For an individual, the guideline fine range shall be from one to five percent of the volume of commerce, but not less than $20,000.".

The Commentary to § 2R1.1 captioned "Application Notes" is amended by deleting:

"1. Because the guideline sentences depend on the volume of commerce done by each firm, role in the offense is implicitly taken into account. Accordingly, the provisions of § 3B1.1 (Aggravating Role) are to be applied only in unusual circumstances. An increase for role under § 3B1.1 might be appropriate only where a defendant actually coerced others into participating in a conspiracy -- an unusual circumstance. Conversely, a decrease for role under § 3B1.2 (Mitigating Role) would not be appropriate merely because an individual defendant or his firm did not profit substantially from the violation. An individual defendant should be considered for a downward adjustment for a mitigating role in the offense only if he was responsible in some minor way for his firm's participation in the conspiracy. A complementary bidder who did not win a bid would not for that reason qualify for a downward adjustment, but a low-level employee who participated in only one of several agreements constituting a conspiracy would.",

and inserting in lieu thereof:

"1. The provisions of § 3B1.1 (Aggravating Role) and § 3B1.2 (Mitigating Role) should be applied to an individual defendant as appropriate to reflect the individual's role in committing the offense. For example, if a sales manager organizes or leads the price-fixing activity of five or more participants, a 4-level increase is called for under § 3B1.1. An individual defendant should be considered for a downward adjustment under § 3B1.2 for a mitigating role in the offense only if he was responsible in some minor way for his firm's participation in the conspiracy.".

The Commentary to § 2R1.1 captioned "Background" is amended in the third paragraph by deleting "four" and inserting in lieu thereof "six".

The Commentary to § 2R1.1 captioned "Background" is amended by deleting the fourth paragraph as follows:

" The guideline imprisonment terms represent a substantial change from pre-guidelines practice. Under pre-guidelines practice, approximately 39 percent of all individuals convicted of antitrust violations were imprisoned. Considering all defendants sentenced, the average time served under pre-guidelines practice was only forty-five days. The guideline prison terms are, however, consistent with the parole guidelines. The fines specified in the guideline represent substantial increases over pre-guidelines practice. Under pre-guidelines practice, the average fine for individuals was only approximately $27,000; for corporations, it was approximately $160,000.".

Reason for Amendment: This amendment increases the offense levels for antitrust violations to make them more comparable to the offense levels for fraud with similar amounts of loss. The base offense level for antitrust violations starts higher than the base offense level for fraud violations to reflect the serious nature of and the difficulty of detecting such violations, but the offense levels for antitrust offenses based on volume of commerce increase less rapidly than the offense levels for fraud, in part, because, on the average, the level of mark-up from an antitrust violation may tend to decline with the volume of commerce involved. This amendment also reduces the minimum guideline fine level based on the volume of commerce to reflect a marginal shift from fines to imprisonment as the more effective means to deter antitrust offenses. The provision addressing fines for organizational defendants in the current guideline is deleted. Such fines are addressed by the provisions pertaining to the sentencing of organizational defendants that are added by a separate amendment (amendment 422).

Effective Date: The effective date of this amendment is November 1, 1991.

378. **Amendment:** Section 2S1.1(a)(1) is amended by deleting "or (a)(2)(A)" and inserting in lieu thereof ", (a)(2)(A), or (a)(3)(A)".

Section 2S1.1(b)(1) is amended by inserting "or believed" immediately following "knew".

The Commentary to § 2S1.1 captioned "Background" is amended in the third paragraph by deleting "or (a)(2)(A)" and inserting in lieu thereof ", (a)(2)(A), or (a)(3)(A)"; and by deleting "did not merely conceal a serious crime that had already taken place, but" immediately before "encouraged".

Reason for Amendment: This amendment revises this guideline to reflect the enactment of subsection (a)(3) of 18 U.S.C. § 1956 that authorizes undercover "sting" operations in money laundering cases. Such cases differ from those prosecuted under subsection (a)(1) in that the money being laundered is not actually criminal proceeds, but is government "sting" money that an undercover officer represents to be criminal proceeds. In all other respects, subsections (a)(1) and (a)(3) are the same.

Effective Date: The effective date of this amendment is November 1, 1991.

379. **Amendment:** Section 2S1.3(a)(1) is amended by deleting:

> "(B) made false statements to conceal or disguise the evasion of reporting requirements; or
>
> (C) reasonably should have believed that the funds were criminally derived property;",

and inserting in lieu thereof:

> "(B) knowingly filed, or caused another to file, a report containing materially false statements; or".

Section 2S1.3(b)(1) is amended by deleting "5 levels." and inserting in lieu thereof "4 levels. If the resulting offense level is less than level 13, increase to level 13.".

The Commentary to § 2S1.3 captioned "Statutory Provisions" is amended by deleting "18 U.S.C. § 1005;"; and by deleting "5316," immediately before "5322".

The Commentary to § 2S1.3 captioned "Application Notes" is amended by deleting:

> "2. Subsection (a)(1)(C) applies where a reasonable person would have believed

Amendment 379

from the circumstances that the funds were criminally derived property. Subsection (b)(1) applies if the defendant knew or believed the funds were criminally derived property. Subsection (b)(1) applies in addition to, and not in lieu of, subsection (a)(1)(C). Where subsection (b)(1) applies, subsection (a)(1)(C) also will apply. It is possible that a defendant 'believed' or 'reasonably should have believed' that the funds were criminally derived property even if, in fact, the funds were not so derived (e.g., in a 'sting' operation where the defendant is told the funds were derived from the unlawful sale of controlled substances).";

and in the caption by deleting "Notes" and inserting in lieu thereof "Note".

The Commentary to § 2S1.3 captioned "Background" is amended by deleting the second and third paragraphs as follows:

" A base offense level of 13 is provided for those offenses where the defendant either structured the transaction to evade reporting requirements, made false statements to conceal or disguise the activity, or reasonably should have believed that the funds were criminally derived property. A lower alternative base offense level of 5 is provided in all other cases. The Commission anticipates that such cases will involve simple recordkeeping or other more minor technical violations of the regulatory scheme governing certain monetary transactions committed by defendants who reasonably believe that the funds at issue emanated from legitimate sources.

Where the defendant actually knew or believed that the funds were criminally derived property, subsection (b)(1) provides for a 5 level increase in the offense level.",

and inserting in lieu thereof:

" A base offense level of 13 is provided for those offenses where the defendant either structured the transaction to evade reporting requirements or knowingly filed, or caused another to file, a report containing materially false statements. A lower alternative base offense level of 5 is provided in all other cases.

Where the defendant actually knew or believed that the funds were criminally derived property, subsection (b)(1) provides for the greater of a 4-level increase or an increase to level 13.".

Chapter Two, Part S is amended by inserting an additional guideline with accompanying commentary as § 2S1.4 (Failure to File Currency and Monetary Instrument Report).

Reason for Amendment: This amendment clarifies the scope of the specific offense characteristics in § 2S1.3 and modifies subsection (b)(1) so that it does not produce a result that exceeds the comparable offense level under § 2S1.2. In addition, this amendment creates an additional offense guideline (§ 2S1.4) for offenses involving Currency and Monetary Instrument Reports (CMIR). Currently, such offenses are covered by § 2S1.3, which deals with all currency transaction reporting requirements. CMIR violations are committed by individuals who, when entering or leaving the country, knowingly conceal $10,000 or more in cash or bearer instruments on their persons or in their personal effects and knowingly fail to file the report required by the U.S. Customs Service. Such criminal conduct is sufficiently different from the other offenses covered by § 2S1.3 to merit treatment in a separate guideline.

Effective Date: The effective date of this amendment is November 1, 1991.

380. **Amendment:** Section 2X3.1(a) is amended by inserting the following additional

sentence at the end:

"*Provided*, that where the conduct is limited to harboring a fugitive, the offense level shall not be more than level 20.".

Reason for Amendment: This amendment distinguishes harboring a fugitive from other forms of accessory after the fact by providing a lower maximum offense level for such cases reflective, in part, of the lower statutory maximum provided for such offenses.

Effective Date: The effective date of this amendment is November 1, 1991.

381. **Amendment:** The Commentary to § 4A1.1 captioned "Application Notes" is amended by inserting the following additional sentence as the second sentence of Note 4 and the third sentence of Note 5:

"Failure to report for service of a sentence of imprisonment is to be treated as an escape from such sentence. See § 4A1.2(n).".

The Commentary to § 4A1.1 captioned "Application Notes" is amended in the third (formerly second) sentence of Note 4 by inserting the following immediately before the period at the end of the sentence:

"having a custodial or supervisory component, although active supervision is not required for this item to apply. For example, a term of unsupervised probation would be included; but a sentence to pay a fine, by itself, would not be included. A defendant who commits the instant offense while a violation warrant from a prior sentence is outstanding (e.g., a probation, parole, or supervised release violation warrant) shall be deemed to be under a criminal justice sentence for the purposes of this provision if that sentence is otherwise countable, even if that sentence would have expired absent such warrant. See § 4A1.2(m)".

Section 4A1.2(a) is amended by inserting the following additional subdivision:

"(4) Where a defendant has been convicted of an offense, but not yet sentenced, such conviction shall be counted as if it constituted a prior sentence under § 4A1.1(c) if a sentence resulting from that conviction otherwise would be countable. In the case of a conviction for an offense set forth in § 4A1.2(c)(1), apply this provision only where the sentence for such offense would be countable regardless of type or length.

'Convicted of an offense,' for the purposes of this provision, means that the guilt of the defendant has been established, whether by guilty plea, trial, or plea of nolo contendere.".

Section 4A1.2(k)(2) is amended by deleting the last sentence as follows:

"It may also affect the time period under which certain sentences are counted as provided in § 4A1.2(e)(1).";

by inserting "(A)" immediately after "(2)"; and by inserting the following additional subdivision:

"(B) Revocation of probation, parole, supervised release, special parole, or mandatory release may affect the time period under which certain sentences are counted as provided in § 4A1.2(d)(2) and (e). For the purposes of determining the applicable time period, use the following: (i) in the case of an adult term of imprisonment totaling more than one year and one month, the date of last release from incarceration on such sentence (see § 4A1.2(e)(1)); (ii) in the case of any other confinement sentence for an offense committed prior to the defendant's eighteenth birthday, the date of the defendant's last release from confinement on such sentence (see § 4A1.2(d)(2)(A)); and (iii) in any other case, the date of the original sentence (see § 4A1.2(d)(2)(B) and (e)(2)).".

Section 4A1.2 is amended by inserting the following additional subsections:

"(l) Sentences on Appeal

Prior sentences under appeal are counted except as expressly provided below. In the case of a prior sentence, the execution of which has been stayed pending appeal, § 4A1.1(a), (b), (c), (d), and (f) shall apply as if the execution of such sentence had not been stayed; § 4A1.1(e) shall not apply.

(m) Effect of a Violation Warrant

For the purposes of § 4A1.1(d), a defendant who commits the instant offense while a violation warrant from a prior sentence is outstanding (e.g., a probation, parole, or supervised release violation warrant) shall be deemed to be under a criminal justice sentence if that sentence is otherwise countable, even if that sentence would have expired absent such warrant.

(n) Failure to Report for Service of Sentence of Imprisonment

For the purposes of § 4A1.1(d) and (e), failure to report for service of a sentence of imprisonment shall be treated as an escape from such sentence.

(o) Felony Offense

For the purposes of § 4A1.2(c), a 'felony offense' means any federal, state, or local offense punishable by death or a term of imprisonment exceeding one year, regardless of the actual sentence imposed.".

The Commentary to § 4A1.2 captioned "Application Notes" is amended in Note 1 by inserting the following additional paragraph:

"Under § 4A1.2(a)(4), a conviction for which the defendant has not yet been sentenced is treated as if it were a prior sentence under § 4A1.1(c) if a sentence resulting from such conviction otherwise would have been counted. In the case of an offense set forth in § 4A1.2(c)(1) (which lists certain misdemeanor and petty offenses), a conviction for which the defendant has not yet been sentenced is treated as if it were a prior sentence under § 4A1.2(a)(4) only where the offense is similar to the instant offense (because sentences for other offenses set forth in § 4A1.2(c)(1) are counted only if they are of a specified type and length).".

The Commentary to § 4A1.2 captioned "Application Notes" is amended in Note 2 by inserting, immediately after "stated maximum", the following:

"(e.g., in the case of a determinate sentence of five years, the stated maximum is five years; in the case of an indeterminate sentence of one to five years, the stated maximum is five years; in the case of an indeterminate sentence for a term not to exceed five years, the stated maximum is five years; in the case of an indeterminate sentence for a term not to exceed the defendant's twenty-first birthday, the stated maximum is the amount of time in pre-trial detention plus the amount of time between the date of sentence and the defendant's twenty-first birthday)".

The Commentary to § 4A1.2 is amended in Note 11 by inserting the following additional paragraph at the end:

"Where a revocation applies to multiple sentences, and such sentences are counted separately under § 4A1.2(a)(2), add the term of imprisonment imposed upon revocation to the sentence that will result in the greatest increase in criminal history points. Example: A defendant was serving two probationary sentences, each counted separately under § 4A1.2(a)(2); probation was revoked on both sentences as a result of the same violation conduct; and the defendant was sentenced to a total of 45 days of imprisonment. If one sentence had been a 'straight' probationary sentence and the other had been a probationary sentence that had required service of 15 days of imprisonment, the revocation term of imprisonment (45 days) would be added to the probationary sentence that had the 15-day term of imprisonment. This would result in a total of 2 criminal history points under § 4A1.1(b) (for the combined 60-day term of imprisonment) and 1 criminal history point under § 4A1.1(c) (for the other probationary sentence).".

Section 4A1.3(d) is amended by deleting ", sentencing, or appeal" and inserting in lieu thereof "or sentencing".

Reason for Amendment: This amendment clarifies the meaning of the term "under a criminal justice sentence" as used in § 4A1.1; inserts a new subdivision in § 4A1.2(a) to address the case in which the defendant has been convicted of a prior offense, but has not yet been sentenced for that offense; inserts an additional subdivision in § 4A1.2(k) to clarify the determination of the applicable time periods in revocation cases; inserts additional subsections in § 4A1.2 to address the counting of sentences stayed pending appeal, the effect of a violation warrant on the counting of points under § 4A1.1(d), the counting of a failure to report for service of sentence under § 4A1.1(d) and (e), and the definition of a felony offense as used in § 4A1.2(c); adds an example to Application Note 2 in the Commentary to § 4A1.2 to illustrate the meaning of "stated maximum" sentence; adds an additional application note in the Commentary to § 4A1.2 addressing the counting of points in complex revocation cases; and conforms the Commentary of § 4A1.3 to the addition of § 4A1.2(l).

Effective Date: The effective date of this amendment is November 1, 1991.

382. **Amendment:** Section 4A1.1 is amended by inserting the following additional subsection:

"(f) Add 1 point for each prior sentence resulting from a conviction of a crime of violence that did not receive any points under (a), (b), or (c) above because such sentence was considered related to another sentence resulting from a conviction of a crime of violence, up to a total of 3 points for this item. *Provided*, that this item does not apply where the sentences are considered related because the offenses occurred on the same occasion.".

Section 4A1.1 is amended in the first sentence by deleting "(e)" and inserting in lieu thereof "(f)".

Section 4A1.1(c) is amended by deleting "included" and inserting in lieu thereof "counted".

The Commentary to § 4A1.1 captioned "Application Notes" is amended by inserting the following additional note:

> "6. § 4A1.1(f). Where the defendant received two or more prior sentences as a result of convictions for crimes of violence that are treated as related cases but did not arise from the same occasion (i.e., offenses committed on different occasions that were part of a single common scheme or plan or were consolidated for trial or sentencing; see Application Note 3 of the Commentary to § 4A1.2), one point is added under § 4A1.1(f) for each such sentence that did not result in any additional points under § 4A1.1(a), (b), or (c). A total of up to 3 points may be added under § 4A1.1(f). 'Crime of violence' is defined in § 4B1.2(1); see § 4A1.2(p).
>
> For example, a defendant's criminal history includes two robbery convictions for offenses committed on different occasions that were consolidated for sentencing and therefore are treated as related. If the defendant received a five-year sentence of imprisonment for one robbery and a four-year sentence of imprisonment for the other robbery (consecutively or concurrently), a total of 3 points is added under § 4A1.1(a). An additional point is added under § 4A1.1(f) because the second sentence did not result in any additional point(s) (under § 4A1.1(a), (b), or (c)). In contrast, if the defendant received a one-year sentence of imprisonment for one robbery and a nine-month consecutive sentence of imprisonment for the other robbery, a total of 3 points also is added under § 4A1.1(a) (a one-year sentence of imprisonment and a consecutive nine-month sentence of imprisonment are treated as a combined one-year-nine-month sentence of imprisonment). But no additional point is added under § 4A1.1(f) because the sentence for the second robbery already resulted in an additional point under § 4A1.1(a). Without the second sentence, the defendant would only have received two points under § 4A1.1(b) for the one-year sentence of imprisonment).".

Section 4A1.2(a)(2) is amended by deleting "the criminal history" and inserting in lieu thereof "§ 4A1.1(a), (b), and (c)".

Section 4A1.2 is amended by inserting the following additional subsection:

> "(p)   Crime of Violence Defined
>
> For the purposes of § 4A1.1(f), the definition of 'crime of violence' is that set forth in § 4B1.2(1).".

The Commentary to § 4A1.2 captioned "Application Notes" is amended in Note 3 by deleting:

> "Cases are considered related if they (1) occurred on a single occasion,",

and inserting in lieu thereof:

> "Prior sentences are not considered related if they were for offenses that were separated by an intervening arrest (i.e., the defendant is arrested for the first offense prior to committing the second offense). Otherwise, prior sentences are considered related if they resulted from offenses that (1) occurred on the same occasion,";

and by deleting:

> "For example, if the defendant commits a number of offenses on independent occa-

sions separated by arrests, and the resulting criminal cases are consolidated and result in a combined sentence of eight years, counting merely three points for this factor will not adequately reflect either the seriousness of the defendant's criminal history or the frequency with which he commits crimes. In such circumstances, the court should consider whether departure is warranted. See § 4A1.3.",

and inserting in lieu thereof:

"For example, if a defendant was convicted of a number of serious non-violent offenses committed on different occasions, and the resulting sentences were treated as related because the cases were consolidated for sentencing, the assignment of a single set of points may not adequately reflect the seriousness of the defendant's criminal history or the frequency with which he has committed crimes. In such circumstances, an upward departure may be warranted. Note that the above example refers to serious non-violent offenses. Where prior related sentences result from convictions of crimes of violence, § 4A1.1(f) will apply.".

Reason for Amendment: This amendment provides for a specific enhancement under § 4A1.2(f) in certain cases having prior convictions of crimes of violence not arising from the same incident that otherwise would be treated as related under § 4A1.2. In addition, the definition of related cases in Application Note 3 in the Commentary to § 4A1.2 is amended to provide that cases separated by an intervening arrest for one of the offenses are not treated as related cases.

Effective Date: The effective date of this amendment is November 1, 1991.

383. **Amendment:** Section 5E1.1 is amended by redesignating subsections (b) and (c) as (c) and (d), respectively; and by deleting:

"(a) Restitution shall be ordered for convictions under Title 18 of the United States Code or under 49 U.S.C. § 1472(h), (i), (j) or (n) in accordance with 18 U.S.C. § 3663(d), and may be ordered as a condition of probation or supervised release in any other case.",

and inserting in lieu thereof:

"(a) The court shall --

(1) enter a restitution order if such order is authorized under 18 U.S.C. §§ 3663-3664; or

(2) if a restitution order would be authorized under 18 U.S.C. §§ 3663-3664, except for the fact that the offense of conviction is not an offense set forth in Title 18, United States Code, or 49 U.S.C. § 1472(h), (i), (j), or (n), impose a term of probation or supervised release with a condition requiring restitution.

(b) *Provided*, that the provisions of subsection (a) do not apply when full restitution has been made, or to the extent the court determines that the complication and prolongation of the sentencing process resulting from the fashioning of a restitution requirement outweighs the need to provide restitution to any victims through the criminal process.".

The Commentary to § 5E1.1 captioned "Background" is amended in the first paragraph by deleting the last sentence as follows:

Amendment 383

"An order of restitution may be appropriate in offenses not specifically referenced in 18 U.S.C. § 3663 where victims require relief more promptly than the civil justice system provides.".

The Commentary to § 5E1.1 captioned "Background" is amended in the second paragraph by deleting "5E1.1 requires the court to order restitution for offenses under Title 18, or 49 U.S.C. § 1472(h), (i), (j) or (n), unless" and inserting in lieu thereof "(a)(1) of this guideline requires the court to order restitution for offenses under Title 18, United States Code, or 49 U.S.C. § 1472(h), (i), (j) or (n), unless full restitution has already been made or".

The Commentary to § 5E1.1 captioned "Background" is amended in the sixth paragraph by deleting "how and to whom" and by inserting in lieu thereof "the manner in which, and the persons to whom,".

The Commentary to § 5E1.1. captioned "Background" is amended by inserting the following additional paragraph at the end:

"   Subsection (a)(2) provides for restitution as a condition of probation or supervised release for offenses not set forth in Title 18, United States Code, or 49 U.S.C. § 1472(h), (i), (j), or (n).".

Reason for Amendment: This amendment expands § 5E1.1 to require restitution as a condition of probation or supervised release for offenses not set forth in Title 18 and 49 U.S.C. § 1472(h), (i), (j), and (n). Currently, § 5E1.1 permits, but does not require, restitution to be ordered as a condition of probation or supervised release for offenses not set forth in Title 18, United States Code, or 49 U.S.C. § 1472(h) (i), (j), and (n).

Effective Date: The effective date of this amendment is November 1, 1991.

384. **Amendment:** Section 5E1.2(c) is amended by deleting:

"(1)   The minimum of the fine range is the greater of:

   (A)   the amount shown in column A of the table below; or

   (B)   the pecuniary gain to the defendant, less restitution made or ordered.

(2)   Except as specified in (4) below, the maximum of the fine range is the greater of:

   (A)   the amount shown in column B of the table below;

   (B)   twice the gross pecuniary loss caused by the offense; or

   (C)   three times the gross pecuniary gain to all participants in the offense.",

and inserting in lieu thereof:

"(1)   The minimum of the fine range is the amount shown in column A of the table below.

(2)   Except as specified in (4) below, the maximum of the fine range is the amount shown in column B of the table below.".

The Commentary to § 5E1.2 captioned "Application Notes" is amended in Note 3 by deleting the first two paragraphs as follows:

> "Alternative fine limits are provided in subsection (c). The terms 'pecuniary gain' and 'pecuniary loss' are taken from 18 U.S.C. § 3571(d). The Commission does not intend precise or detailed calculation of the gain or loss in using the alternative fine limits.
>
> Where it is readily ascertainable that the defendant cannot, and is not likely to become able to, pay a fine greater than the maximum fine set forth in Column B of the Fine Table in subsection (c)(3), calculation of the alternative maximum fines under subsections (c)(2)(B) (twice the gross pecuniary loss caused by the offense) and (c)(2)(C) (three times the gross pecuniary gain to all participants in the offense) is unnecessary. In such cases, a statement that 'the alternative maximums of the fine table were not calculated because it is readily ascertainable that the defendant cannot, and is not likely to become able to, pay a fine greater than the maximum set forth in the fine table' is recommended in lieu of such calculations.".

The Commentary to § 5E1.2 captioned "Application Notes" is amended by deleting:

> "4. 'Restitution made or ordered' refers to restitution for the instant offense made before or at the time of sentencing, as well as any restitution ordered at the time of sentencing for the instant offense.",

and inserting in lieu thereof:

> "4. The Commission envisions that for most defendants, the maximum of the guideline fine range from subsection (c) will be at least twice the amount of gain or loss resulting from the offense. Where, however, two times either the amount of gain to the defendant or the amount of loss caused by the offense exceeds the maximum of the fine guideline, an upward departure from the fine guideline may be warranted.
>
> Moreover, where a sentence within the applicable fine guideline range would not be sufficient to ensure both the disgorgement of any gain from the offense that otherwise would not be disgorged (<u>e.g.</u>, by restitution or forfeiture) and an adequate punitive fine, an upward departure from the fine guideline range may be warranted.".

The Commentary to § 5E1.2 captioned "Background" is deleted in its entirety as follows:

> "<u>Background</u>: These guidelines permit a relatively wide range of fines. The Commission may promulgate more detailed guidelines for the imposition of fines after analyzing practice under these initial guidelines.
>
> Recent legislation provides for substantial increases in fines. 18 U.S.C. § 3571(b). With few restrictions, 42 U.S.C. § 10601(b), and (c) authorize fine payments up to $100 million to be deposited in the Crime Victims Fund in the United States Treasury. With vigorous enforcement, higher fines should be effective punitive and deterrent sanctions.
>
> A larger multiple of the gain than of the loss is used in subsection (c)(2) because most offenses result in losses to society that exceed the gain to the participants. In addition, in many such cases restitution will not be feasible. These larger fines authorized under subsection (c)(2) are, of course, subject to the absolute limits on fines that are imposed by statute.
>
> The Commission has not attempted to define gain or loss precisely. It is

expected that the terms will be used flexibly and consistently with their use in the criminal code, including former 18 U.S.C. § 3623(c)(1).".

Reason for Amendment: This amendment is designed to simplify the operation of this guideline and conserve probation and court resources by eliminating the need for the determination of loss and gain under this section in most cases. Experience has shown that for the vast majority of defendants, the amount from the fine table in subsection (c)(3) or the amount from subsection (c)(4), as applicable, is more than twice the gain or loss from the offense. This amendment provides that the guideline fine range is to be determined from subsection (c)(3) or (c)(4), as applicable. In the unusual case in which twice the defendant's gain from the offense or twice the loss caused by the offense exceeds the maximum of the guideline range, an upward departure may be considered.

Effective Date: The effective date of this amendment is November 1, 1991.

385. **Amendment:** Chapter Five, Part G is amended by deleting § 5G1.3 in its entirety as follows:

> "§ 5G1.3. Imposition of a Sentence on a Defendant Serving an Unexpired Term of Imprisonment
>
> If the instant offense was committed while the defendant was serving a term of imprisonment (including work release, furlough, or escape status), the sentence for the instant offense shall be imposed to run consecutively to the unexpired term of imprisonment.
>
> Commentary
>
> Under this guideline, the court shall impose a consecutive sentence where the instant offense (or any part thereof) was committed while the defendant was serving an unexpired term of imprisonment.
>
> Where the defendant is serving an unexpired term of imprisonment, but did not commit the instant offense while serving that term of imprisonment, the sentence for the instant offense may be imposed to run consecutively or concurrently with the unexpired term of imprisonment. The court may consider imposing a sentence for the instant offense that results in a combined sentence that approximates the total punishment that would have been imposed under § 5G1.2 (Sentencing on Multiple Counts of Conviction) had all of the offenses been federal offenses for which sentences were being imposed at the same time. Where the defendant is serving a term of imprisonment for a state offense, the information available may permit only a rough estimate of the total punishment that would have been imposed under the guidelines. It is not intended that the above methodology be applied in a manner that unduly complicates or prolongs the sentencing process.".

A replacement guideline with accompanying commentary is inserted as § 5G1.3 (Imposition of a Sentence on a Defendant Subject to an Undischarged Term of Imprisonment).

Reason for Amendment: This amendment provides additional structure and guidance for the decision to impose a consecutive or concurrent sentence upon a defendant subject to an undischarged term of imprisonment to reduce the potential for unwarranted disparity in such determinations.

Effective Date: The effective date of this amendment is November 1, 1991.

386. **Amendment:** The Introductory Commentary to Chapter Five, Part H is amended by

deleting:

"   Congress has directed the Commission to consider whether certain specific offender characteristics 'have any relevance to the nature, extent, place of service, or other incidents of an appropriate sentence' and to take them into account only to the extent they are determined relevant by the Commission. 28 U.S.C. § 994(d).",

and inserting in lieu thereof:

"   The following policy statements address the relevance of certain offender characteristics to the determination of whether a sentence should be outside the applicable guideline range and, in certain cases, to the determination of a sentence within the applicable guideline range. Under 28 U.S.C. § 994(d), the Commission is directed to consider whether certain specific offender characteristics 'have any relevance to the nature, extent, place of service, or other incidents of an appropriate sentence' and to take them into account only to the extent they are determined to be relevant by the Commission.

The Commission has determined that certain factors are not ordinarily relevant to the determination of whether a sentence should be outside the applicable guideline range. Unless expressly stated, this does not mean that the Commission views such factors as necessarily inappropriate to the determination of the sentence within the applicable guideline range or to the determination of various other incidents of an appropriate sentence (e.g., the appropriate conditions of probation or supervised release).".

Section 5H1.1 is amended by deleting:

"Age is not ordinarily relevant in determining whether a sentence should be outside the guidelines. Neither is it ordinarily relevant in determining the type of sentence to be imposed when the guidelines provide sentencing options. Age may be a reason to go below the guidelines when the offender is elderly and infirm and where a form of punishment (e.g., home confinement) might be equally efficient as and less costly than incarceration. If, independent of the consideration of age, a defendant is sentenced to probation or supervised release, age may be relevant in the determination of the length and conditions of supervision.",

and inserting in lieu thereof:

"Age (including youth) is not ordinarily relevant in determining whether a sentence should be outside the applicable guideline range. Age may be a reason to impose a sentence below the applicable guideline range when the defendant is elderly and infirm and where a form of punishment such as home confinement might be equally efficient as and less costly than incarceration. Physical condition, which may be related to age, is addressed at § 5H1.4 (Physical Condition, Including Drug or Alcohol Dependence or Abuse).

The guidelines are not applicable to a person sentenced as a juvenile delinquent under the provisions of 18 U.S.C. § 5037.".

Section 5H1.2 is amended by deleting:

"Education and vocational skills are not ordinarily relevant in determining whether a sentence should be outside the guidelines, but the extent to which a defendant may have misused special training or education to facilitate criminal activity is an express guideline factor. See § 3B1.3 (Abuse of Position of Trust or Use of Special Skill). Neither are education and vocational skills relevant in determining the type of sentence to be imposed when the guidelines provide sentencing options. If, independent of consideration of education and vocational skills, a defendant is sentenced to probation or supervised release, these considerations may be relevant in the determination of the length and conditions of supervision for rehabilitative purposes, for public protection by restricting activities that allow for the utilization of a certain skill, or in determining the type or length of community service.",

and by inserting in lieu thereof:

"Education and vocational skills are not ordinarily relevant in determining whether a sentence should be outside the applicable guideline range, but the extent to which a defendant may have misused special training or education to facilitate criminal activity is an express guideline factor. See § 3B1.3 (Abuse of Position of Trust or Use of Special Skill).

Education and vocational skills may be relevant in determining the conditions of probation or supervised release for rehabilitative purposes, for public protection by restricting activities that allow for the utilization of a certain skill, or in determining the appropriate type of community service.".

Section 5H1.3 is amended by deleting:

"Mental and emotional conditions are not ordinarily relevant in determining whether a sentence should be outside the guidelines, except as provided in the general provisions in Chapter Five. Mental and emotional conditions, whether mitigating or aggravating, may be relevant in determining the length and conditions of probation or supervised release.",

and inserting in lieu thereof:

"Mental and emotional conditions are not ordinarily relevant in determining whether a sentence should be outside the applicable guideline range, except as provided in Chapter Five, Part K, Subpart 2 (Other Grounds for Departure).

Mental and emotional conditions may be relevant in determining the conditions of probation or supervised release; e.g., participation in a mental health program (see recommended condition (24) at § 5B1.4 (Recommended Conditions of Probation and Supervised Release)).".

Section 5H1.4 is amended by deleting:

"Physical Condition, Including Drug Dependence and Alcohol Abuse (Policy Statement)

Physical condition is not ordinarily relevant in determining whether a sentence should be outside the guidelines or where within the guidelines a sentence should fall. However, an extraordinary physical impairment may be a reason to impose a sentence other than imprisonment.

Drug dependence or alcohol abuse is not a reason for imposing a sentence below the guidelines. Substance abuse is highly correlated to an increased propensity to commit crime. Due to this increased risk, it is highly recommended that a defendant who is incarcerated also be sentenced to supervised release with a requirement that the defendant participate in an appropriate substance abuse program. If participation in a substance abuse program is required, the length of supervised release should take into account the length of time necessary for the supervisory body to judge the success of the program.

This provision would also apply in cases where the defendant received a sentence of probation. The substance abuse condition is strongly recommended and the length of probation should be adjusted accordingly. Failure to comply would normally result in revocation of probation.",

and inserting in lieu thereof:

"Physical Condition, Including Drug or Alcohol Dependence or Abuse (Policy Statement)

Physical condition or appearance, including physique, is not ordinarily relevant in determining whether a sentence should be outside the applicable guideline range. However, an extraordinary physical impairment may be a reason to impose a sentence below the applicable guideline range; e.g., in the case of a seriously infirm defendant, home detention may be as efficient as, and less costly than, imprisonment.

Drug or alcohol dependence or abuse is not a reason for imposing a sentence below the guidelines. Substance abuse is highly correlated to an increased propensity to commit crime. Due to this increased risk, it is highly recommended that a defendant who is incarcerated also be sentenced to supervised release with a requirement that the defendant participate in an appropriate substance abuse program (see recommended condition (23) at § 5B1.4 (Recommended Conditions of Probation and Supervised Release)). If participation in a substance abuse program is required, the length of supervised release should take into account the length of time necessary for the supervisory body to judge the success of the program.

Similarly, where a defendant who is a substance abuser is sentenced to probation, it is strongly recommended that the conditions of probation contain a requirement that the defendant participate in an appropriate substance abuse program (see recommended condition (23) at § 5B1.4 (Recommended Conditions of Probation and Supervised Release)).".

Section 5H1.5 is amended by deleting:

"Employment record is not ordinarily relevant in determining whether a sentence should be outside the guidelines or where within the guidelines a sentence should fall. Employment record may be relevant in determining the type of sentence to be imposed when the guidelines provide for sentencing options. If, independent of the consideration of employment record, a defendant is sentenced to probation or supervised release, considerations of employment record may be relevant in the determination of the length and conditions of supervision.",

and inserting in lieu thereof:

"Employment record is not ordinarily relevant in determining whether a sentence should be outside the applicable guideline range.

Employment record may be relevant in determining the conditions of probation or supervised release (e.g., the appropriate hours of home detention).".

Section 5H1.6 is amended by deleting:

"Family ties and responsibilities and community ties are not ordinarily relevant in determining whether a sentence should be outside the guidelines. Family responsibilities that are complied with are relevant in determining whether to impose restitution and fines. Where the guidelines provide probation as an option, these factors may be relevant in this determination. If a defendant is sentenced to probation or supervised release, family ties and responsibilities that are met may be relevant in the determination of the length and conditions of supervision.",

and inserting in lieu thereof:

"Family ties and responsibilities and community ties are not ordinarily relevant in determining whether a sentence should be outside the applicable guideline range.

Family responsibilities that are complied with may be relevant to the determination of the amount of restitution or fine.".

Chapter Five, Part H is amended by inserting an additional policy statement as § 5H1.11 (Military, Civic, Charitable, or Public Service; Employment-Related Contributions; Record of Prior Good Works (Policy Statement)).

Reason for Amendment: This amendment expresses the Commission's intent that the factors set forth in this part are not ordinarily relevant in determining whether a sentence should be outside the applicable guideline range; but that, unless expressly stated, these policy statements do not mean that the Commission views such factors as necessarily inappropriate to the determination of the sentence within the applicable guideline range. The language within these sections is revised for clarity and consistency. In addition, this amendment adds language that expressly states that the guidelines do not apply to defendants sentenced as juvenile delinquents; and sets forth the Commission's position that physical appearance, including physique, military, civic, charitable, or public service, employment-related contributions, and record of prior good works are not ordinarily relevant in determining whether a sentence should be outside the applicable guideline range.

Effective Date: The effective date of this amendment is November 1, 1991.

387. **Amendment:** The Commentary to § 6A1.3 is amended by inserting the following additional paragraph as the third paragraph:

"The Commission believes that use of a preponderance of the evidence standard is appropriate to meet due process requirements and policy concerns in resolving disputes regarding application of the guidelines to the facts of a case.".

Reason for Amendment: This amendment expresses the Commission's approval of the use of a preponderance of the evidence standard in resolving disputes regarding application of the guidelines to the facts of a case.

Effective Date: The effective date of this amendment is November 1, 1991.

388. **Amendment:** The Commentary to § 1B1.1 captioned "Application Notes" is amended in Note 1 in the first sentence by inserting immediately before the colon:

"and are of general applicability (except to the extent expressly modified in respect to a particular guideline or policy statement)".

The Commentary to § 1B1.1 captioned "Application Notes" is amended in Note 2 by deleting the first two sentences as follows:

"Definitions or explanations of terms may also appear within the commentary to specific guidelines. Such commentary is not of general applicability.",

and inserting in lieu thereof:

"Definitions of terms also may appear in other sections. Such definitions are not designed for general applicability; therefore, their applicability to sections other than those expressly referenced must be determined on a case by case basis.";

and by beginning a new paragraph with the third sentence.

The Commentary to § 1B1.1 captioned "Application Notes" is amended in Note 1(e) by deleting:

"'Firearm' means any weapon which is designed to or may readily be converted to expel any projectile by the action of an explosive.",

and inserting in lieu thereof:

"'Firearm' means (i) any weapon (including a starter gun) which will or is designed to or may readily be converted to expel a projectile by the action of an explosive; (ii) the frame or receiver of any such weapon; (iii) any firearm muffler or silencer; or (iv) any destructive device.";

and by inserting "a" immediately before "'BB' or pellet gun".

The Commentary to § 1B1.1 captioned "Application Notes" is amended in Note (1)(f) by inserting ", other than conduct to which § 3C1.1 (Obstructing or Impeding the Administration of Justice) applies." immediately following "conceal the offense".

The Commentary to § 1B1.1 captioned "Application Notes" is amended in Note 1(h) by inserting the following additional sentence at the end:

"In the case of a kidnapping, for example, maltreatment to a life-threatening degree (e.g., by denial of food or medical care) would constitute life-threatening bodily injury.".

The Commentary to § 1B1.1 captioned "Application Notes" is amended in Note 1(k) by deleting "18 U.S.C. § 921(a)(4)" and inserting in lieu thereof "26 U.S.C. § 5845(f)"; and by deleting "proceeding" and inserting in lieu thereof "preceding".

The Commentary to § 1B1.1 captioned "Application Notes" is amended in Note 1 by inserting the following additional subdivision:

"(l) 'Offense' means the offense of conviction and all relevant conduct under § 1B1.3 (Relevant Conduct) unless a different meaning is specified or is otherwise clear from the context.".

Reason for Amendment: This amendment revises the definition of firearm in Note 1(e) to track more closely the definition of firearm in 18 U.S.C. § 921; clarifies Note 1(f) to prevent inappropriate "double counting;" clarifies in Note 1(h) that maltreatment to a life-threatening degree constitutes life-threatening bodily injury; conforms the statutory reference in Note 1(k) to conform to that used in § 2K2.1; and inserts an additional subdivision in Note 1 (subdivision (l)) that describes how the term "offense" is used in the guidelines. In addition, this amendment correct clerical errors and makes editorial improvements.

Effective Date: The effective date of this amendment is November 1, 1991.

389. **Amendment:** The Commentary to § 1B1.3 captioned "Application Notes" is amended in Note 2 in the first sentence by inserting "that were part of the same course of conduct or common scheme or plan as the offense of conviction" immediately following "'Such acts and omissions"; and by inserting ", that were part of the same course of conduct or com-

Amendment 389   APPENDIX C - VOLUME I   November 1, 2013

mon scheme or plan as the offense of conviction" immediately following "otherwise accountable".

The Commentary to § 1B1.3 captioned "Application Notes" is amended in Note 2 by inserting the following additional paragraph at the end:

"As noted above, subsection (a)(2) applies to offenses of a character for which § 3D1.2(d) would require grouping of multiple counts, had the defendant been convicted of multiple counts. For example, the defendant sells 30 grams of cocaine (a violation of 21 U.S.C. § 841) on one occasion and, as part of the same course of conduct or common scheme or plan, attempts to sell an additional 15 grams of cocaine (a violation of 21 U.S.C. 846) on another occasion. The defendant is convicted of one count charging the completed sale of 30 grams of cocaine. The two offenses (sale of cocaine and attempted sale of cocaine), although covered by different statutory provisions, are of a character for which § 3D1.2(d) would require the grouping of counts, had the defendant been convicted of both counts. Therefore, subsection (a)(2) applies and the total amount of cocaine (45 grams) involved is used to determine the offense level.".

The Commentary to § 1B1.3 captioned "Application Notes" is amended in Note 4 by inserting "; Property Damage by Use of Explosives" immediately following "Arson".

The Commentary to § 1B1.3 captioned "Application Notes is amended in Note 5 by deleting:

"E.g., in § 2K2.2, a base offense level of 16 is used 'if the defendant is convicted under 18 U.S.C. § 922(o) or 26 U.S.C. § 5861.'",

and inserting in lieu thereof:

"For example, in § 2K1.5, subsection (b)(1) applies 'If the defendant is convicted under 49 U.S.C. § 1472(l)(2).'";

by deleting:

"Examples of this usage are found in § 2K1.3(b)(4) ('If the defendant was a person prohibited from receiving explosives under 18 U.S.C. § 842(i), or if the defendant knowingly distributed explosives to a person prohibited from receiving explosives under 18 U.S.C. § 842(i), increase by 10 levels'); and",

and inserting in lieu thereof "An example of this usage is found in"; and by inserting the following additional paragraph at the end:

"An express direction to apply a particular factor only if the defendant was convicted of a particular statute includes the determination of the offense level where the defendant was convicted of conspiracy, attempt, solicitation, aiding or abetting, accessory after the fact, or misprision of felony in respect to that particular statute. For example, § 2K1.5(b)(1) (which is applicable only if the defendant is convicted under 49 U.S.C. § 1472(l)(2)) would be applied in determining the offense level under § 2X3.1 (Accessory After the Fact) where the defendant was convicted of accessory after the fact to a violation of 49 U.S.C. § 1472(l)(2).".

The Commentary to § 1B1.3 captioned "Application Notes" is amended by inserting the following additional notes:

"6.   In the case of a partially completed offense (e.g., an offense involving an attempted theft of $800,000 and a completed theft of $30,000), the offense level is to be determined in accordance with § 2X1.1 (Attempt, Solicitation, or Conspiracy) whether the conviction is for the substantive offense, the inchoate offense (attempt, solicitation, or conspiracy), or both. See Application Note 4 in the Commentary to § 2X1.1. Note, however, that Application Note 4 is not applicable where the offense level is determined under § 2X1.1(c)(1).

7. For the purposes of subsection (a)(2), offense conduct associated with a sentence that was imposed prior to the acts or omissions constituting the instant federal offense (the offense of conviction) is not considered as part of the same course of conduct or common scheme or plan as the offense of conviction.

Examples: (1) The defendant was convicted for the sale of cocaine and sentenced to state prison. Immediately upon release from prison, he again sold cocaine to the same person, using the same accomplices and modus operandi. The instant federal offense (the offense of conviction) charges this latter sale. In this example, the offense conduct relevant to the state prison sentence is considered as prior criminal history, not as part of the same course of conduct or common scheme or plan as the offense of conviction. The prior state prison sentence is counted under Chapter Four (Criminal History and Criminal Livelihood). (2) The defendant engaged in two cocaine sales constituting part of the same course of conduct or common scheme or plan. Subsequently, he is arrested by state authorities for the first sale and by federal authorities for the second sale. He is convicted in state court for the first sale and sentenced to imprisonment; he is then convicted in federal court for the second sale. In this case, the cocaine sales are not separated by an intervening sentence. Therefore, under subsection (a)(2), the cocaine sale associated with the state conviction is considered as relevant conduct to the instant federal offense. The state prison sentence for that sale is not counted as a prior sentence; see § 4A1.2(a)(1).

Note, however, in certain cases, offense conduct associated with a previously imposed sentence may be expressly charged in the offense of conviction. Unless otherwise provided, such conduct will be considered relevant conduct under subsection (a)(1), not (a)(2).".

The Commentary to § 1B1.3 captioned "Background" is amended by deleting the last paragraph as follows:

"This guideline and § 1B1.4 clarify the intent underlying § 1B1.3 as originally promulgated.".

Reason for Amendment: This amendment makes editorial improvements in Application Notes 1 and 2; inserts an additional paragraph in Application Note 2 to clarify that "offenses of a character for which § 3D1.2(d) would require grouping of multiple counts" is not limited to offenses proscribed by the same statutory provision; conforms a reference in Application Note 4 to the correct title of the guideline; conforms examples in Application Note 5 to amended guidelines and clarifies how a direction to apply a particular factor only if the defendant is convicted of a particular statute applies to the offenses of conspiracy, attempt, solicitation, aiding or abetting, accessory after the fact, and misprision of felony; inserts an additional application note (Note 6) that highlights the provision in § 2X1.1 dealing with cases of partially completed conduct; inserts an additional application note (Note 7) that clarifies the treatment of conduct for which the defendant has previously been sentenced; and deletes a surplus sentence of Background Commentary more appropriately contained in Appendix C in the paragraph describing the reason for amendment 3.

Effective Date: The effective date of this amendment is November 1, 1991.

390. **Amendment:** The Commentary to § 1B1.8 captioned "Application Notes" is amended by inserting the following additional notes:

> "5. This guideline limits the use of certain incriminating information furnished by a defendant in the context of a defendant-government agreement for the defendant to provide information concerning the unlawful activities of other persons. The guideline operates as a limitation on the use of such incriminating information in determining the applicable guideline range, and not merely as a restriction of the government's presentation of such information (e.g., where the defendant, subsequent to having entered into a cooperation agreement, repeats such information to the probation officer preparing the presentence report, the use of such information remains protected by this section).
>
> 6. Unless the cooperation agreement relates to the provision of information concerning the unlawful activities of others, this guideline does not apply (i.e., an agreement by the defendant simply to detail the extent of his own unlawful activities, not involving an agreement to provide information concerning the unlawful activity of another person, is not covered by this guideline).".

Reason for Amendment: This amendment clarifies the operation of this guideline.

Effective Date: The effective date of this amendment is November 1, 1991.

391. **Amendment:** The Commentary to § 2A2.1 captioned "Application Notes" is amended by inserting the following additional note:

> "3. If the offense created a substantial risk of death or serious bodily injury to more than one person, an upward departure may be warranted.".

Reason for Amendment: This amendment adds commentary to address the case in which an attempted murder results in a substantial risk of death or serious bodily injury to more than one person.

Effective Date: The effective date of this amendment is November 1, 1991.

392. **Amendment:** The Commentary to § 2A3.1 captioned "Application Notes" is amended by inserting the following additional note:

> "3. If the adjustment in subsection (b)(3) applies, do not apply § 3B1.3 (Abuse of Position of Trust or Use of Special Skill).".

Section 2A3.2(b)(1) is amended by deleting "1 level" and inserting in lieu thereof "2 levels".

The Commentary to § 2A3.2 captioned "Application Note" is amended by inserting the following additional note:

"2.	If the adjustment in subsection (b)(1) applies, do not apply § 3B1.3 (Abuse of Position of Trust or Use of Special Skill).";

and in the caption by deleting "Note" and inserting in lieu thereof "Notes".

Section 2A3.4(b) is amended by inserting the following additional subdivision:

"(3)	If the victim was in the custody, care, or supervisory control of the defendant, increase by 2 levels.".

The Commentary to § 2A3.4 captioned "Application Notes" is amended by inserting the following additional note:

"3.	If the adjustment in subsection (b)(3) applies, do not apply § 3B1.3 (Abuse of Position of Trust or Use of Special Skill).".

Reason for Amendment: This amendment provides for consistency among §§ 2A3.1, 2A3.2, and 2A3.4 with respect to an adjustment for a victim in the custody, care, or supervisory control of the defendant. In addition, the amendment adds an application note clarifying that when this adjustment applies, an adjustment from § 3B1.3 will not apply.

Effective Date: The effective date of this amendment is November 1, 1991.

393.	**Amendment:** The Commentary to § 2B1.1 captioned "Application Notes" is amended in Note 2 by deleting:

"In cases of partially completed conduct, the loss is to be determined in accordance with the provisions of § 2X1.1 (Attempt, Solicitation, or Conspiracy). E.g., in the case of the theft of a government check or money order, loss refers to the loss level that would have occurred if the check or money order had been cashed. Similarly, if a defendant is apprehended in the process of taking a vehicle, the loss refers to the value of the vehicle even if the vehicle is recovered immediately.",

and inserting in lieu thereof:

"Examples: (1) In the case of a theft of a check or money order, the loss is the loss that would have occurred if the check or money order had been cashed. (2) In the case of a defendant apprehended taking a vehicle, the loss is the value of the vehicle even if the vehicle is recovered immediately.

In the case of a partially completed offense (e.g., an offense involving a completed theft that is part of a larger, attempted theft), the offense level is to be determined in accordance with the provisions of § 2X1.1 (Attempt, Solicitation, or Conspiracy) whether the conviction is for the substantive offense, the inchoate offense (attempt, solicitation, or conspiracy), or both; see Application Note 4 in the Commentary to § 2X1.1.".

The Commentary to § 2B1.1 captioned "Application Notes" is amended in Note 4 by deleting "Attempts" and inserting in lieu thereof "Attempt, Solicitation, or Conspiracy"; and by inserting "and Deceit" immediately following "Fraud".

The Commentary to § 2F1.1 is amended by deleting Notes 7 and 8 as follows:

"7.	Valuation of loss is discussed in the Commentary to § 2B1.1 (Larceny, Embezzlement, and Other Forms of Theft). In keeping with the Commission's policy on attempts, if a probable or intended loss that the defendant was attempting to inflict can be determined, that figure would be used if it was larger than the actual loss. For example, if the fraud consisted of attempting to sell $40,000 in worthless securities, or representing that a forged check for $40,000 was genuine, the 'loss' would be treated as $40,000 for purposes of this guideline.

8. The amount of loss need not be precise. The court is not expected to identify each victim and the loss he suffered to arrive at an exact figure. The court need only make a reasonable estimate of the range of loss, given the available information. The estimate may be based on the approximate number of victims and an estimate of the average loss to each victim, or on more general factors, such as the nature and duration of the fraud and the revenues generated by similar operations. Estimates based upon aggregate 'market loss' (e.g., the aggregate decline in market value of a stock resulting from disclosure of information that was wrongfully withheld or misrepresented) are especially appropriate for securities cases. The offender's gross gain from committing the fraud is an alternative estimate that ordinarily will understate the loss.";

by deleting Note 10 as follows:

"10. In a few instances, the total dollar loss that results from the offense may overstate its seriousness. Such situations typically occur when a misrepresentation is of limited materiality or is not the sole cause of the loss. Examples would include understating debts to a limited degree in order to obtain a substantial loan which the defendant genuinely expected to repay; attempting to negotiate an instrument that was so obviously fraudulent that no one would seriously consider honoring it; and making a misrepresentation in a securities offering that enabled the securities to be sold at inflated prices, but where the value of the securities subsequently declined in substantial part for other reasons. In such instances, a downward departure may be warranted.";

by renumbering Note 9 as Note 10; by inserting the following as Notes 7, 8 and 9:

"7. Valuation of loss is discussed in the Commentary to § 2B1.1 (Larceny, Embezzlement, and Other Forms of Theft). Consistent with the provisions of § 2X1.1 (Attempt, Solicitation or Conspiracy), if an intended loss that the defendant was attempting to inflict can be determined, this figure will be used if it is greater than the actual loss. Frequently, loss in a fraud case will be the same as in a theft case. For example, if the fraud consisted of selling or attempting to sell $40,000 in worthless securities, or representing that a forged check for $40,000 was genuine, the loss would be $40,000. There are, however, instances where additional factors are to be considered in determining the loss or intended loss:

(a) Fraud Involving Misrepresentation of the Value of an Item or Product Substitution

A fraud may involve the misrepresentation of the value of an item that does have some value (in contrast to an item that is worthless). Where, for example, a defendant fraudulently represents that stock is worth $40,000 and the stock is worth only $10,000, the loss is the amount by which the stock was overvalued (i.e., $30,000). In a case involving a misrepresentation concerning the quality of a consumer product, the loss is the difference between the amount paid by the victim for the product and the amount for which the victim could resell the product received.

(b) Fraudulent Loan Application and Contract Procurement Cases

In fraudulent loan application cases and contract procurement cases where the defendant's capabilities are fraudulently represented, the loss is the actual loss to the victim (or if the loss has not yet come about, the expected loss). For example, if a defendant fraudulently obtains a loan by misrepresenting the value of his assets, the loss is the amount of the loan not repaid at the time the offense is discovered, reduced by the amount the lending institution has recovered, or can expect to recover, from any assets pledged to secure the loan.

In some cases, the loss determined above may significantly understate or overstate the seriousness of the defendant's conduct. For example, where the defendant substantially understated his debts to obtain a loan, which he nevertheless repaid, the loss determined above (zero loss) will tend not to reflect adequately the risk of loss created by the defendant's conduct. Conversely, a defendant may understate his debts to a limited degree to obtain a loan (e.g., to expand a grain export business), which he genuinely expected to repay and for which he would have qualified at a higher interest rate had he made truthful disclosure, but he is unable to repay the loan because of some unforeseen event (e.g., an embargo imposed on grain exports) which would have caused a default in any event. In such a case, the loss determined above may overstate the seriousness of the defendant's conduct.

(c) Consequential Damages in Procurement Fraud and Product Substitution Cases

In contrast to other types of cases, loss in a procurement fraud or product substitution case includes not only direct damages, but also consequential damages that were reasonably foreseeable. For example, in a case involving a defense product substitution offense, the loss includes the government's reasonably foreseeable costs of making substitute transactions and handling or disposing of the product delivered or retrofitting the product so that it can be used for its intended purpose, plus the government's reasonably foreseeable cost of rectifying the actual or potential disruption to government operations caused by the product substitution. Similarly, in the case of fraud affecting a defense contract award, loss includes the reasonably foreseeable administrative cost to the government and other participants of repeating or correcting the procurement action affected, plus any increased cost to procure the product or service involved that was reasonably foreseeable. Inclusion of reasonably foreseeable consequential damages directly in the calculation of loss in procurement fraud and product substitution cases reflects that such damages frequently are substantial in such cases.

(d) Diversion of Government Program Benefits

In a case involving diversion of government program benefits, loss is the value of the benefits diverted from intended recipients or uses.

(e) Davis-Bacon Act Cases

In a case involving a Davis-Bacon Act violation (a violation of 40 U.S.C. § 276a, criminally prosecuted under 18 U.S.C. § 1001), the loss is the difference between the legally required and actual wages paid.

8. For the purposes of subsection (b)(1), the loss need not be determined with precision. The court need only make a reasonable estimate of the loss, given the available information. This estimate, for example, may be based on the approximate number of victims and an estimate of the average loss to each victim, or on more general factors, such as the nature and duration of the fraud and the revenues generated by similar operations. The offender's gain from committing the fraud is an alternative estimate that ordinarily will underestimate the loss.

9. In the case of a partially completed offense (e.g., an offense involving a completed fraud that is part of a larger, attempted fraud), the offense level is to be determined in accordance with the provisions of § 2X1.1 (Attempt, Solicitation, or Conspiracy) whether the conviction is for the substantive offense, the inchoate offense (attempt, solicitation, or conspiracy), or both; see Application Note 4 in the Commentary to § 2X1.1.";

and in the renumbered Note 10 (formerly Note 9) by deleting:

"Dollar loss often does not fully capture the harmfulness and seriousness of the conduct. In such instances, an upward departure may be warranted.",

and inserting in lieu thereof:

"In cases in which the loss determined under subsection (b)(1) does not fully capture the harmfulness and seriousness of the conduct, an upward departure may be warranted.";

by deleting subdivision (f) as follows:

"(f) completion of the offense was prevented, or the offense was interrupted before it caused serious harm.";

by deleting the semicolon at the end of subdivision (e) and inserting in lieu thereof a period; and by inserting the following additional paragraph at the end:

"In a few instances, the loss determined under subsection (b)(1) may overstate the seriousness of the offense. This may occur, for example, where a defendant attempted to negotiate an instrument that was so obviously fraudulent that no one would seriously consider honoring it.".

Reason for Amendment: This amendment provides a more precise reference in the commentary of these guidelines to the discussion in § 2X1.1 that applies in the case of a partially completed offense. In addition, the amendment reorders the material in these notes, and divides them into separate paragraphs for greater clarity. The amendment also conforms the wording of Application Note 7 of the Commentary to § 2F1.1 to Application

Note 2 of the Commentary to § 2B1.1 to make clear that the treatment of attempts in cases of fraud and theft is identical. Finally, this amendment provides additional guidance with respect to the determination of loss, and makes editorial improvements.

Effective Date: The effective date of this amendment is November 1, 1991.

394. **Amendment:** Section 2D1.1(b)(1) is amended by deleting "during commission of the offense" immediately after "possessed".

The Commentary to § 2D1.1 captioned "Application Notes" is amended in Note 3 by deleting ". The adjustment is to be applied even if several counts are involved and the weapon was present in any of them." and inserting in lieu thereof ", 2D1.6, 2D1.7(b)(1).".

Section 2D1.8(b)(1) is amended by deleting "during commission of the offense" immediately after "possessed".

Reason for Amendment: This amendment clarifies that the provisions of § 1B1.3(a)(2) apply to the adjustments in §§ 2D1.1(b)(1) and 2D1.8(b)(1), and updates the list of referenced offense guidelines in Application Note 3 of the Commentary to § 2D1.1.

Effective Date: The effective date of this amendment is November 1, 1991.

395. **Amendment:** Section 2D1.1(c) is amended in the Drug Quantity Table by deleting "Pure PCP" wherever it appears and inserting in lieu thereof "PCP (actual)"; and by deleting "Pure Methamphetamine" wherever it appears and inserting in lieu thereof "Methamphetamine (actual)".

Section 2D1.1(c) is amended in the note designated by a single asterisk by inserting the following additional sentences as the third and fourth sentences of the first paragraph:

> "The terms 'PCP (actual)' and 'Methamphetamine (actual)' refer to the weight of the controlled substance, itself, contained in the mixture or substance. For example, a mixture weighing 10 grams containing PCP at 50% purity contains 5 grams of PCP (actual).";

and in the last sentence of the first paragraph by deleting "pure PCP or methamphetamine" and inserting in lieu thereof "PCP (actual) or methamphetamine (actual)".

Section 2D1.1(c) is amended by deleting "Schedule I or II Depressants" wherever it appears and inserting in lieu thereof "Secobarbital (or the equivalent amount of other Schedule I or II Depressants)".

Reason for Amendment: This amendment clarifies the operation of the guideline in cases involving methamphetamine or PCP by replacing the terms "Pure PCP" and "pure methamphetamine" with "PCP (actual)" and "methamphetamine (actual)," and by providing an example of their application. This amendment also clarifies the interaction of the guideline and drug equivalency tables with respect to Schedule I and II Depressants by using Secobarbital as the referenced substance.

Effective Date: The effective date of this amendment is November 1, 1991.

396. **Amendment:** The Commentary to § 2D1.1 captioned "Application Notes" is amended in Note 10 in the first paragraph by deleting "grams of a substance containing heroin" and inserting in lieu thereof "kilograms of marihuana"; in the second paragraph by deleting:

> "If all the drugs are 'equivalents' of the same drug, e.g., stimulants that are grouped

Amendment 396 APPENDIX C - VOLUME I November 1, 2013

with cocaine, convert them to that drug. In other cases, convert each of the drugs to either the heroin or marihuana equivalents, add the quantities, and look up the total in the Drug Quantity Table to obtain the combined offense level. Use the marihuana equivalents when the only substances involved are 'Schedule I Marihuana,' 'Schedule III Substances,' 'Schedule IV Substances,' 'Schedule V Substances' or 'Schedule I or II Depressants.' Otherwise, use the heroin equivalents.",

and inserting in lieu thereof:

"In each case, convert each of the drugs to its marihuana equivalent, add the quantities, and look up the total in the Drug Quantity Table to obtain the combined offense level.";

in the first example by deleting:

"a. The defendant is convicted of selling seventy grams of a substance containing PCP (Level 22) and 250 milligrams of a substance containing LSD (Level 18). Both PCP and LSD are grouped together in the Drug Equivalency Tables under the heading 'LSD, PCP, and Other Schedule I and II Hallucinogens,' which provide PCP equivalencies. The 250 milligrams of LSD is equivalent to twenty-five grams of PCP. The total is therefore ninety-five grams of PCP, for which the Drug Quantity Table provides an offense level of 24.",

and inserting in lieu thereof:

"a. The defendant is convicted of selling 70 grams of a substance containing PCP (Level 22) and 250 milligrams of a substance containing LSD (Level 18). The PCP converts to 70 kilograms of marihuana; the LSD converts to 25 kilograms of marihuana. The total is therefore equivalent to 95 kilograms of marihuana, for which the Drug Quantity Table provides an offense level of 24.";

and in the third example by deleting:

"c. The defendant is convicted of selling eighty grams of cocaine (Level 16) and five kilograms of marihuana (Level 14). The cocaine is equivalent to sixteen grams of heroin; the marihuana, to five grams of heroin. The total equivalent is twenty-one grams of heroin, which has an offense level of 18 in the Drug Quantity Table.",

and inserting in lieu thereof:

"c. The defendant is convicted of selling 80 grams of cocaine (Level 16) and five kilograms of marihuana (Level 14). The cocaine is equivalent to 16 kilograms of marihuana. The total is therefore equivalent to 21 kilograms of marihuana, which has an offense level of 18 in the Drug Quantity Table.".

The Commentary to § 2D1.1 captioned "Application Notes" is amended in Note 10 by inserting the following additional paragraph as the third paragraph:

"For certain types of controlled substances, the marihuana equivalencies in the Drug Equivalency Tables are 'capped' at specified amounts (e.g., the combined equivalent weight of all Schedule V controlled substances shall not exceed 999 grams of marihuana). Where there are controlled substances from more than one schedule (e.g., a quantity of a Schedule IV substance and a quantity of a Schedule V substance), determine the marihuana equivalency for each schedule separately (subject to the cap, if any, applicable to that schedule). Then add the marihuana equivalencies to determine the combined marihuana equivalency (subject to the cap, if any, applicable to the combined amounts).".

The Commentary to § 2D1.1 captioned "Application Notes" is amended in Note 10 by inserting the following additional example immediately after example (c):

"d. The defendant is convicted of selling 28 kilograms of a Schedule III substance, 50 kilograms of a Schedule IV substance, and 100 kilograms of a Schedule V substance. The marihuana equivalency for the Schedule III substance is 56 kilograms of marihuana (below the cap of 59.99 kilograms of marihuana set forth as the maximum equivalent weight for Schedule III substances). The marihuana equivalency for the Schedule IV substance is subject to a cap of 4.99 kilograms of marihuana set forth as the maximum equivalent weight for Schedule IV substances (without the cap it would have been 6.25 kilograms). The marihuana equivalency for the Schedule V substance is subject to the cap of 999 grams of marihuana set forth as the maximum equivalent weight for Schedule V substances (without the cap it would have been 1.25 kilograms). The combined equivalent weight, determined by adding together the above amounts, is subject to the cap of 59.99 kilograms of marihuana set forth as the maximum combined equivalent weight for Schedule III, IV, and V substances. Without the cap, the combined equivalent weight would have been 61.99 (56 + 4.99 + .999) kilograms.".

The Commentary to § 2D1.1 captioned "Application Notes" is amended in Note 10 by deleting:

"DRUG EQUIVALENCY TABLES

Schedule I or II Opiates

1 gm of Alpha-Methylfentanyl =	10 gm of heroin
1 gm of Dextromoramide =	0.67 gm of heroin
1 gm of Dipipanone =	0.25 gm of heroin
1 gm of 3-Methylfentanyl =	10 gm of heroin
1 gm of 1-Methyl-4-phenyl-4-propionoxypiperidine/MPPP =	0.7 gm of heroin
1 gm of 1-(2-Phenylethyl)-4-phenyl-4-acetyloxypiperidine/PEPAP =	0.7 gm of heroin
1 gm of Alphaprodine =	0.1 gm of heroin
1 gm of Fentanyl (N-phenyl-N-[1-(2-phenylethyl)-4-piperidinyl] Propanamide) =	2.5 gm of heroin
1 gm of Hydromorphone/Dihydromorphinone =	2.5 gm of heroin
1 gm of Levorphanol =	2.5 gm of heroin
1 gm of Meperidine/Pethidine =	0.05 gm of heroin
1 gm of Methadone =	0.5 gm of heroin
1 gm of 6-Monoacetylmorphine =	1 gm of heroin
1 gm of Morphine =	0.5 gm of heroin
1 gm of Oxycodone =	0.5 gm of heroin
1 gm of Oxymorphone =	5 gm of heroin
1 gm of Racemorphan =	0.8 gm of heroin
1 gm of Codeine =	0.08 gm of heroin
1 gm of Dextropropoxyphene/Propoxyphene-Bulk =	0.05 gm of heroin
1 gm of Ethylmorphine =	0.165 gm of heroin
1 gm of Hydrocodone/Dihydrocodeinone =	0.5 gm of heroin
1 gm of Mixed Alkaloids of Opium/Papaveretum =	0.25 gm of heroin

Amendment 396 APPENDIX C - VOLUME I November 1, 2013

1 gm of Opium = 0.05 gm of heroin

Cocaine and Other Schedule I and II Stimulants (and their immediate precursors)

1 gm of Cocaine = 0.2 gm of heroin
1 gm of N-Ethylamphetamine = 0.4 gm of cocaine/0.08 gm of heroin
1 gm of Fenethylline = 0.2 gm of cocaine/0.04 gm of heroin
1 gm of Amphetamine = 1.0 gm of cocaine/0.2 gm of heroin
1 gm of Dextroamphetamine = 1.0 gm of cocaine/0.2 gm of heroin
1 gm of Methamphetamine = 5.0 gm of cocaine/1.0 gm of heroin
1 gm of Methamphetamine (Pure) = 50 gm of cocaine/10 gm of heroin
1 gm of L-Methamphetamine/Levo-methamphetamine/L-Desoxyephedrine= 0.2 gm of cocaine/0.04 gm of heroin
1 gm of 4-Methylaminorex ("Euphoria")= 0.5 gm of cocaine/0.1 gm of heroin
1 gm of Methylphenidate (Ritalin)= 0.5 gm of cocaine/0.1 gm of heroin
1 gm of Phenmetrazine = 0.4 gm of cocaine/0.08 gm of heroin
1 gm Phenylacetone/P_2P (when possessed for the purpose of manufacturing methamphetamine) = 2.08 gm of cocaine/0.416 gm of heroin
1 gm Phenylacetone/P_2P (in any other case) = 0.375 gm of cocaine/0.075 gm of heroin
1 gm of Cocaine Base ("Crack") = 100 gm of cocaine/20 gm of heroin

LSD, PCP, and Other Schedule I and II Hallucinogens (and their immediate precursors)

1 gm of Bufotenine = 0.07 gm of heroin or PCP
1 gm of D-Lysergic Acid Diethylamide/Lysergide/LSD = 100 gm of heroin or PCP
1 gm of Diethyltryptamine/DET = 0.08 gm of heroin or PCP
1 gm of Dimethyltryptamine/DMT = 0.1 gm of heroin or PCP
1 gm of Mescaline = 0.01 gm of heroin or PCP
1 gm of Mushrooms containing Psilocin and/or Psilocybin (Dry) = 0.001 gm of heroin or PCP
1 gm of Mushrooms containing Psilocin and/or Psilocybin (Wet) = 0.0001 gm of heroin or PCP
1 gm of Peyote (Dry) = 0.0005 gm of heroin or PCP
1 gm of Peyote (Wet) = 0.00005 gm of heroin or PCP
1 gm of Phencyclidine/PCP = 1 gm of heroin
1 gm of Phencyclidine (Pure PCP) = 10 gm of heroin or PCP
1 gm of Psilocin = 0.5 gm of heroin or PCP
1 gm of Psilocybin = 0.5 gm of heroin or PCP
1 gm of Pyrrolidine Analog of Phencyclidine/PHP = 1 gm of heroin or PCP
1 gm of Thiophene Analog of Phencyclidine/TCP = 1 gm of heroin or PCP
1 gm of 4-Bromo-2,5-Dimethoxyamphetamine/DOB = 2.5 gm of heroin or PCP
1 gm of 2,5-Dimethoxy-4-methylamphetamine/DOM = 1.67 gm of heroin or PCP
1 gm of 3,4-Methylenedioxyamphetamine/MDA = 0.05 gm of heroin or PCP
1 gm of 3,4-Methylenedioxymethamphetamine/MDMA = 0.035 gm of heroin or PCP
1 gm of 3,4-Methylenedioxy-N-ethylamphetamine/MDEA= 0.03 gm of heroin or PCP
1 gm of 1-Piperidinocyclohexanecarbonitrile/PCC = 0.68 gm of heroin or PCP

Schedule I Marihuana

1 gm of Marihuana/Cannabis = 1 mg of heroin
1 gm of Marihuana/Cannabis, granulated, powdered, etc. = 1 mg of heroin/1 gm of marihuana
1 gm of Hashish Oil = 0.05 gm of heroin/50 gm of marihuana
1 gm of Cannabis Resin or Hashish = 5 mg of heroin/5 gm of marihuana
1 gm of Tetrahydrocannabinol, Organic = 0.167 gm of heroin/167 gm of marihuana
1 gm of Tetrahydrocannabinol, Synthetic = 0.167 gm of heroin/167 gm of marihuana

Schedule I or II Depressants

1 gm of Methaqualone = 0.7 mg of heroin/700 mg of marihuana
1 gm of Amobarbital = 2 mg of heroin/2 gm of marihuana
1 gm of Pentobarbital = 2 mg of heroin/2 gm of marihuana

1 gm of Secobarbital =   2 mg of heroin/2 gm of marihuana

Schedule III Substances

1 gm of Allobarbital =	2 mg of heroin/2 gm of marihuana
1 gm of Aprobarbital =	2 mg of heroin/2 gm of marihuana
1 gm of Barbiturate =	2 mg of heroin/2 gm of marihuana
1 gm of Benzphetamine=	4 mg of heroin/4 gm of marihuana
1 gm of Butabarbital =	2 mg of heroin/2 gm of marihuana
1 gm of Butalbital =	2 mg of heroin/2 gm of marihuana
1 gm of Butobarbital/butethal =	2 mg of heroin/2 gm of marihuana
1 gm of Cyclobarbital =	2 mg of heroin/2 gm of marihuana
1 gm of Cyclopentobarbital =	2 mg of heroin/2 gm of marihuana
1 gm of Glutethimide =	0.4 mg of heroin/0.4 gm of marihuana
1 gm of Heptabarbital =	2 mg of heroin/2 gm of marihuana
1 gm of Hexethal =	2 mg of heroin/2 gm of marihuana
1 gm of Hexobarbital =	2 mg of heroin/2 gm of marihuana
1 gm of Metharbital =	2 mg of heroin/2 gm of marihuana
1 gm of Talbutal =	2 mg of heroin/2 gm of marihuana
1 gm of Thialbarbital =	2 mg of heroin/2 gm of marihuana
1 gm of Thiamylal =	2 mg of heroin/2 gm of marihuana
1 gm of Thiobarbital =	2 mg of heroin/2 gm of marihuana
1 gm of Thiopental =	2 mg of heroin/2 gm of marihuana
1 gm of Vinbarbital =	2 mg of heroin/2 gm of marihuana
1 gm of Vinylbital =	2 mg of heroin/2 gm of marihuana
1 gm of Phendimetrazine =	2 mg of heroin/2 gm of marihuana
1 ml of Paregoric=	0.25 mg of heroin/0.25 gm of marihuana
1 ml of Hydrocodone Cough Syrup=	1 mg of heroin/ 1 gm of marihuana

Schedule IV Substances

1 gm of Phentermine =	0.125 mg of heroin/0.125 gm of marihuana
1 gm of Pentazocine =	0.125 mg of heroin/0.125 gm of marihuana
1 gm of Barbital =	0.125 mg of heroin/0.125 gm of marihuana
1 gm of Diazepam =	0.125 mg of heroin/0.125 gm of marihuana
1 gm of Phenobarbital =	0.125 mg of heroin/0.125 gm of marihuana
1 gm of Methohexital =	0.125 mg of heroin/0.125 gm of marihuana
1 gm of Methylphenobarbital/Mephobarbital =	0.125 mg of heroin/0.125 gm of marihuana
1 gm of Nitrazepam =	0.125 mg of heroin/0.125 gm of marihuana

Schedule V Substances

1 gm of codeine cough syrup =   0.0125 mg of heroin/12.5 mg of marihuana.",

and inserting in lieu thereof:

"DRUG EQUIVALENCY TABLES

Schedule I or II Opiates

1 gm of Heroin =	1 kg of marihuana
1 gm of Alpha-Methylfentanyl =	10 kg of marihuana
1 gm of Dextromoramide =	670 gm of marihuana
1 gm of Dipipanone =	250 gm of marihuana
1 gm of 3-Methylfentanyl =	10 kg of marihuana
1 gm of 1-Methyl-4-phenyl-4-propionoxypiperidine/MPPP =	700 gm of marihuana
1 gm of 1-(2-Phenylethyl)-4-phenyl-4-acetyloxypiperidine/PEPAP =	700 gm of marihuana

1 gm of Alphaprodine =	100 gm of marihuana
1 gm of Fentanyl (N-phenyl-N-[1-(2-phenylethyl)-4-piperidinyl] Propanamide) =	2.5 kg of marihuana
1 gm of Hydromorphone/Dihydromorphinone =	2.5 kg of marihuana
1 gm of Levorphanol =	2.5 kg of marihuana
1 gm of Meperidine/Pethidine =	50 gm of marihuana
1 gm of Methadone =	500 gm of marihuana
1 gm of 6-Monoacetylmorphine =	1 kg of marihuana
1 gm of Morphine =	500 gm of marihuana
1 gm of Oxycodone =	500 gm of marihuana
1 gm of Oxymorphone =	5 kg of marihuana
1 gm of Racemorphan =	800 gm of marihuana
1 gm of Codeine =	80 gm of marihuana
1 gm of Dextropropoxyphene/Propoxyphene-Bulk =	50 gm of marihuana
1 gm of Ethylmorphine =	165 gm of marihuana
1 gm of Hydrocodone/Dihydrocodeinone =	500 gm of marihuana
1 gm of Mixed Alkaloids of Opium/Papaveretum =	250 gm of marihuana
1 gm of Opium =	50 gm of marihuana

Cocaine and Other Schedule I and II Stimulants (and their immediate precursors)

1 gm of Cocaine =	200 gm of marihuana
1 gm of N-Ethylamphetamine =	80 gm of marihuana
1 gm of Fenethylline =	40 gm of marihuana
1 gm of Amphetamine =	200 gm of marihuana
1 gm of Dextroamphetamine =	200 gm of marihuana
1 gm of Methamphetamine =	1 kg of marihuana
1 gm of Methamphetamine (Actual) =	10 kg of marihuana
1 gm of "Ice" =	10 kg of marihuana
1 gm of L-Methamphetamine/Levo-methamphetamine/L-Desoxyephedrine=	40 gm of marihuana
1 gm of 4-Methylaminorex ("Euphoria")=	100 gm of marihuana
1 gm of Methylphenidate (Ritalin)=	100 gm of marihuana
1 gm of Phenmetrazine =	80 gm of marihuana
1 gm Phenylacetone/P$_2$P (when possessed for the purpose of manufacturing methamphetamine) =	416 gm of marihuana
1 gm Phenylacetone/P$_2$P (in any other case) =	75 gm of marihuana
1 gm of Cocaine Base ("Crack") =	20 kg of marihuana

LSD, PCP, and Other Schedule I and II Hallucinogens (and their immediate precursors)

1 gm of Bufotenine =	70 gm of marihuana
1 gm of D-Lysergic Acid Diethylamide/Lysergide/LSD =	100 kg of marihuana
1 gm of Diethyltryptamine/DET =	80 gm of marihuana
1 gm of Dimethyltryptamine/DMT =	100 gm of marihuana
1 gm of Mescaline =	10 gm of marihuana
1 gm of Mushrooms containing Psilocin and/or Psilocybin (Dry) =	1 gm of marihuana
1 gm of Mushrooms containing Psilocin and/or Psilocybin (Wet) =	0.1 gm of marihuana
1 gm of Peyote (Dry) =	0.5 gm of marihuana
1 gm of Peyote (Wet) =	0.05 gm of marihuana
1 gm of Phencyclidine/PCP =	1 kg of marihuana
1 gm of Phencyclidine (actual) /PCP (actual) =	10 kg of marihuana
1 gm of Psilocin =	500 gm of marihuana
1 gm of Psilocybin =	500 gm of marihuana
1 gm of Pyrrolidine Analog of Phencyclidine/PHP =	1 kg of marihuana
1 gm of Thiophene Analog of Phencyclidine/TCP =	1 kg of marihuana
1 gm of 4-Bromo-2,5-Dimethoxyamphetamine/DOB =	2.5 kg of marihuana
1 gm of 2,5-Dimethoxy-4-methylamphetamine/DOM =	1.67 kg of marihuana
1 gm of 3,4-Methylenedioxyamphetamine/MDA =	50 gm of marihuana
1 gm of 3,4-Methylenedioxymethamphetamine/MDMA =	35 gm of marihuana
1 gm of 3,4-Methylenedioxy-N-ethylamphetamine/MDEA =	30 gm of marihuana

November 1, 2013　　APPENDIX C - VOLUME I　　**Amendment 396**

　　1 gm of 1-Piperidinocyclohexanecarbonitrile/PCC =　　　　680 gm of marihuana

　　Schedule I Marihuana

　　1 gm of Marihuana/Cannabis, granulated, powdered, etc. =　　1 gm of marihuana
　　1 gm of Hashish Oil =　　　　　　　　　　　　　　　　　　50 gm of marihuana
　　1 gm of Cannabis Resin or Hashish =　　　　　　　　　　　5 gm of marihuana
　　1 gm of Tetrahydrocannabinol, Organic =　　　　　　　　　167 gm of marihuana
　　1 gm of Tetrahydrocannabinol, Synthetic =　　　　　　　　167 gm of marihuana

　　Secobarbital and Other Schedule I or II Depressants*

　　1 gm of Amobarbital =　　　　　　　　2 gm of marihuana
　　1 gm of Glutethimide =　　　　　　　　0.4 gm of marihuana
　　1 gm of Methaqualone =　　　　　　　　0.7 gm of marihuana
　　1 gm of Pentobarbital =　　　　　　　　2 gm of marihuana
　　1 gm of Secobarbital =　　　　　　　　2 gm of marihuana

　　*Provided, that the combined equivalent weight of all Schedule I or II depressants, Schedule III substances, Schedule IV substances, and Schedule V substances shall not exceed 59.99 kilograms of marihuana.

　　Schedule III Substances**

　　1 gm of a Schedule III Substance (except anabolic steroids) =　　2 gm of marihuana
　　1 unit of anabolic steroids =　　　　　　　　　　　　　　　　　1 gm of marihuana

　　**Provided, that the combined equivalent weight of all Schedule III substances, Schedule I or II depressants, Schedule IV substances, and Schedule V substances shall not exceed 59.99 kilograms of marihuana.

　　Schedule IV Substances***

　　1 gm of a Schedule IV Substance =　　　　　　　　0.125 gm of marihuana

　　***Provided, that the combined equivalent weight of all Schedule IV and V substances shall not exceed 4.99 kilograms of marihuana.

　　Schedule V Substances****

　　1 gm of a Schedule V Substance =　　　　　　　　0.0125 gm of marihuana

　　****Provided, that the combined equivalent weight of Schedule V substances shall not exceed 999 grams of marihuana.".

The Commentary to § 2D1.1 captioned "Background" is amended by inserting the following additional paragraph as the fourth paragraph:

　　"　　In cases involving fifty or more marihuana plants, an equivalency of one plant to one kilogram of marihuana is derived from the statutory penalty provisions of 21 U.S.C. § 841(b)(1)(A), (B), and (D). In cases involving fewer than fifty plants, the statute is silent as to the equivalency. For cases involving fewer than fifty plants, the Commission has adopted an equivalency of 100 grams per plant, or the actual weight of the usable marihuana, whichever is greater. The decision to treat each plant as equal to 100 grams is premised on the fact that the average yield from a mature marihuana plant equals 100 grams of marihuana. In controlled substance offenses, an attempt is assigned the same offense level as the object of the attempt (see § 2D1.4). Consequently, the Commission adopted the policy that, in the case of fewer than fifty marihuana plants, each plant is to be treated as the equivalent of an attempt to produce 100 grams of marihuana, except where the actual weight of the usable marihuana is greater.".

– 247 –

Amendment 396 APPENDIX C - VOLUME I November 1, 2013

Reason for Amendment: This amendment substitutes a single conversion for Schedule III substances (1 gm of a Schedule III substance = 2 gms of marihuana) that will simplify application of the guidelines as well as address currently unlisted Schedule III substances. Because the equivalencies for Schedule III substances are not statutorily based, nor are the pharmacological equivalencies as clear as with Schedule I or II Substances, a generic listing was deemed appropriate. For the same reasons, the amendment provides a single conversion for Schedule IV substances (1 gm of a Schedule IV substance = 0.125 gm of marihuana) and Schedule V substances (1 gm of a Schedule V substance = 0.0125 gm of marihuana). The amendment also adds a conversion for anabolic steroids consistent with their treatment in the Drug Quantity Table. In addition, the amendment adds footnotes to the Drug Equivalency Tables for Schedule I or II depressants and Schedule III, IV, and V substances to remove an ambiguity in guideline application by expressly limiting the combined equivalent weight of such substances to the marihuana amount consistent with the highest offense level for such substances provided in the Drug Quantity Table. See United States v. Gurgliolo, 894 F.2d 56 (3d Cir. 1990). The amendment inserts an additional listing under "Secobarbital and Other Schedule I and II Depressants" to reflect that glutethimide has been changed from a Schedule III to a Schedule II controlled substance under 21 C.F.R. § 1308.12. In addition, the amendment simplifies the application of the Drug Equivalency Table by referencing the conversions to one substance (marihuana) rather than to four substances; the use of one referent rather than four makes no substantive change but will make the required computations easier and reduce the likelihood of computational error. Finally, the amendment sets forth the rationale for the Commission's treatment of fewer than fifty marihuana plants.

Effective Date: The effective date of this amendment is November 1, 1991.

397. **Amendment:** Section 2D1.7 is amended in the title by deleting "Interstate Sale and Transporting" and inserting in lieu thereof "Sale or Transportation".

Section 2D1.7 is amended by inserting the following additional subsection:

"(b) Cross Reference

(1) If the offense involved a controlled substance, apply § 2D1.1 (Unlawful Manufacturing, Importing, Exporting, or Trafficking) or § 2D2.1 (Unlawful Possession), as appropriate, if the resulting offense level is greater than that determined above.".

The Commentary to § 2D1.7 captioned "Statutory Provision" is amended by deleting "21 U.S.C. § 857" and inserting in lieu thereof "21 U.S.C. § 863 (formerly 21 U.S.C. § 857)".

The Commentary to § 2D1.7 is amended by inserting the following at the end:

"Application Note:

1. The typical case addressed by this guideline involves small-scale trafficking in drug paraphernalia (generally from a retail establishment that also sells items that are not unlawful). In a case involving a large-scale dealer, distributor, or manufacturer, an upward departure may be warranted. Conversely, where the offense was not committed for pecuniary gain (e.g., transportation for the defendant's personal use), a downward departure may be warranted.".

Reason for Amendment: This amendment revises the title of the guideline to address the expanded coverage of the underlying statute, as amended by Section 2401 of the Crime

Control Act of 1990 (Public Law 101-647), adds a cross reference to address cases in which the underlying conduct involves a controlled substance offense, and adds an application note to specify the "heartland" types of cases addressed by the offense level set forth in the guideline.

Effective Date: The effective date of this amendment is November 1, 1991.

398. **Amendment:** Section 2E2.1 is amended in the title by deleting ", Financing, or Collecting an Extortionate Extension of Credit" and inserting in lieu thereof "or Financing an Extortionate Extension of Credit; Collecting an Extension of Credit by Extortionate Means".

Section 2E2.1(b)(3)(A) is amended by deleting "the commission of the offense or an escape from the scene of the crime" and inserting in lieu thereof "commission of the offense or to facilitate escape".

Reason for Amendment: This amendment corrects an error in the title of this section, and conforms the wording in subsection (b)(3)(A) with the wording used in subsection (b)(3)(B) and other guidelines.

Effective Date: The effective date of this amendment is November 1, 1991.

399. **Amendment:** The Commentary to § 2E5.2 captioned "Application Notes" is amended in Note 1 by deleting "had a fiduciary obligation under the Employee Retirement Income Security Act" and inserting in lieu thereof "was a fiduciary of the benefit plan"; and by deleting "would" and inserting in lieu thereof "will".

The Commentary to § 2E5.2 captioned "Application Notes" is amended by deleting Note 2 as follows:

"2. 'Fiduciary of the benefit plan' is defined in 29 U.S.C. § 1002(21)(A) to mean a person who exercises any discretionary authority or control in respect to the management of such plan or exercises authority or control in respect to management or disposition of its assets, or who renders investment advice for a fee or other direct or indirect compensation with respect to any moneys or other property of such plan, or has any authority or responsibility to do so, or who has any discretionary authority or responsibility in the administration of such plan.";

by inserting the text of former Note 2 as the last sentence of Note 1; and, in the caption, by deleting "Notes" and inserting in lieu thereof "Note".

Reason for Amendment: This amendment makes an editorial improvement in the language of this commentary.

Effective Date: The effective date of this amendment is November 1, 1991.

400. **Amendment:** Section 2G1.2(b) is amended by inserting the following additional subdivision:

"(4) If the defendant was a parent, relative, or legal guardian of the minor involved in the offense, or if the minor was otherwise in the custody, care, or supervisory control of the defendant, increase by 2 levels.".

Sections 2G1.2(c) and (d) are transposed and redesignated accordingly.

– 249 –

Amendment 400

Section 2G1.2(c) (formerly § 2G1.2(d)) is amended in the caption by deleting "Reference" and inserting in lieu thereof "References"; and by inserting the following additional subsections:

> "(2) If the offense involved criminal sexual abuse, attempted criminal sexual abuse, or assault with intent to commit criminal sexual abuse, apply § 2A3.1 (Criminal Sexual Abuse; Attempt or Assault with the Intent to Commit Criminal Sexual Abuse).
>
> (3) If neither subsection (c)(1) nor (c)(2) is applicable, and the offense did not involve transportation for the purpose of prostitution, apply § 2A3.2 (Criminal Sexual Abuse of a Minor or Attempt to Commit Such Acts) or § 2A3.4 (Abusive Sexual Contact or Attempt to Commit Abusive Sexual Contact), as appropriate.".

Section 2G1.2(c)(1) (formerly § 2G1.2(d)(1)) is amended by deleting "the defendant" immediately before "causing".

The Commentary to § 2G1.2 captioned "Application Notes" is amended by renumbering Note 5 as Note 7, and by inserting the following additional notes:

> "5. Subsection (b)(4) is intended to have broad application and includes offenses involving a minor entrusted to the defendant, whether temporarily or permanently. For example, teachers, day care providers, baby-sitters, or other temporary caretakers are among those who would be subject to this enhancement. In determining whether to apply this adjustment, the court should look to the actual relationship that existed between the defendant and the child and not simply to the legal status of the defendant-child relationship.
>
> 6. If the adjustment in subsection (b)(4) applies, do not apply § 3B1.3 (Abuse of Position of Trust or Use of Special Skill).".

The commentary to § 2G1.2 captioned "Application Notes" is amended in Note 1 by deleting "(c)(1)" and inserting in lieu thereof "(d)(1)"; and in Note 7 (formerly Note 5) by deleting "(d)(1)" and inserting in lieu thereof "subsection (c)(1)".

The Commentary to § 2G2.1 captioned "Application Notes" is amended in Note 2 by deleting "Specific offense characteristic" and inserting in lieu thereof "Subsection".

The Commentary to § 2G2.1 captioned "Application Notes" is amended by deleting:

> "3. If specific offense characteristic (b)(2) applies, no adjustment is to be made under § 3B1.3 (Abuse of Position of Trust or Use of Special Skill).",

and inserting in lieu thereof:

> "3. If the adjustment in subsection (b)(2) applies, do not apply § 3B1.3 (Abuse of Position of Trust or Use of Special Skill).".

Reason for Amendment: This amendment adds a specific offense characteristic and commentary to provide consistent treatment for similar conduct among the guidelines in this part, conforms the language used in § 2G1.2(c)(1) (formerly § 2G1.2(d)(1)) with the language used elsewhere in the guidelines, and makes editorial changes to improve clarity. In addition, as statutes referenced to § 2G1.2 may be used as "jurisdictional" statutes in some cases to prosecute conduct that is more appropriately covered under other guidelines

(§§ 2A3.1, 2A3.2, and 2A3.4), this amendment inserts cross references as § 2G1.2(c)(2) and (3) to provide consistent offense levels in such cases.

Effective Date: The effective date of this amendment is November 1, 1991.

401. **Amendment:** The Commentary to § 2J1.2 captioned "Application Notes" is amended in Note 1 by deleting:

> ", an indictment or verdict based upon perjury, false testimony, or other false evidence,"

and inserting in lieu thereof:

> "; an indictment, verdict, or any judicial determination based upon perjury, false testimony, or other false evidence;".

The Commentary to § 2J1.2 captioned "Application Notes" is amended by inserting the following additional note:

> "5. The inclusion of 'property damage' under subsection (b)(1) is designed to address cases in which property damage is caused or threatened as a means of intimidation or retaliation (e.g., to intimidate a witness from, or retaliate against a witness for, testifying). Subsection (b)(1) is not intended to apply, for example, where the offense consisted of destroying a ledger containing an incriminating entry.".

The Commentary to § 2J1.2 captioned "Background" is amended in the second paragraph by deleting:

> "assist another person to escape punishment for a crime he has committed, an alternative reference to the guideline for accessory after the fact is made",

and inserting in lieu thereof:

> "avoid punishment for an offense that the defendant has committed or to assist another person to escape punishment for an offense, a cross reference to § 2X3.1 (Accessory After the Fact) is provided. Use of this cross reference will provide an enhanced offense level when the obstruction is in respect to a particularly serious offense, whether such offense was committed by the defendant or another person".

The Commentary to § 2J1.3 captioned "Application Notes" is amended in Note 1 by deleting:

> ", an indictment or verdict based upon perjury, false testimony, or other false evidence,"

and inserting in lieu thereof:

> "; an indictment, verdict, or any judicial determination based upon perjury, false testimony, or other false evidence;".

The Commentary to § 2J1.5 captioned "Application Notes" is amended in Note 1 by deleting:

> ", an indictment or verdict based upon perjury, false testimony, or other false evidence,"

and inserting in lieu thereof:

"; an indictment, verdict, or any judicial determination based upon perjury, false testimony, or other false evidence;".

The Commentary to § 2J1.8 captioned "Application Notes" is amended in Note 1 by deleting:

", an indictment or verdict based upon perjury, false testimony, or other false evidence,"

and inserting in lieu thereof:

"; an indictment, verdict, or any judicial determination based upon perjury, false testimony, or other false evidence;".

Reason for Amendment: This amendment clarifies the types of circumstances to which §§ 2J1.2(b)(1) and 2J1.2(c)(1) apply. This amendment also clarifies the scope of the enhancement for "substantial interference with the administration of justice" in §§ 2J1.2, 2J1.3, 2J1.5, and 2J1.8.

Effective Date: The effective date of this amendment is November 1, 1991.

402. **Amendment:** Section 2J1.3 is amended by inserting the following additional subsection:

"(d) Special Instruction

(1) In the case of counts of perjury or subornation of perjury arising from testimony given, or to be given, in separate proceedings, do not group the counts together under § 3D1.2 (Groups of Closely-Related Counts).".

The Commentary to § 2J1.3 captioned "Application Notes" is amended by inserting the following additional note:

"5. 'Separate proceedings,' as used in subsection (d)(1), includes different proceedings in the same case or matter (e.g., a grand jury proceeding and a trial, or a trial and retrial), and proceedings in separate cases or matters (e.g., separate trials of codefendants), but does not include multiple grand jury proceedings in the same case.".

Reason for Amendment: This amendment provides a special instruction addressing the appropriate treatment of multiple instances of perjury under Chapter Three, Part D (Multiple Counts).

Effective Date: The effective date of this amendment is November 1, 1991.

403. **Amendment:** The Commentary to § 2J1.6 captioned "Application Notes" is amended by deleting:

"2. By statute, a term of imprisonment imposed for this offense runs consecutively to any other term of imprisonment imposed. 18 U.S.C. § 3146(b)(1).";

by renumbering Note 3 as Note 2; and by inserting the following additional notes:

"3. In the case of a failure to appear for service of sentence, any term of imprisonment imposed on the failure to appear count is to be imposed consecutively to any term of imprisonment imposed for the underlying offense. See § 5G1.3(a). The guideline range for the failure to appear count is to be determined independently and the grouping rules of §§ 3D1.2-3D1.5 do not apply.

Otherwise, in the case of a conviction on both the underlying offense and the failure to appear, the failure to appear is treated under § 3C1.1 (Obstructing or Impeding the Administration of Justice) as an obstruction of the underlying offense; and the failure to appear count and the count(s) for the underlying offense are grouped together under § 3D1.2(c). Note that although 18 U.S.C. § 3146(b)(2) does not require a sentence of imprisonment on a failure to appear count, it does require that any sentence of imprisonment on a failure to appear count be imposed consecutively to any other sentence of imprisonment. Therefore, in such cases, the combined sentence must be constructed to provide a 'total punishment' that satisfies the requirements both of § 5G1.2 (Sentencing on Multiple Counts of Conviction) and 18 U.S.C. § 3146(b)(2). For example, where the combined applicable guideline range for both counts is 30-37 months and the court determines a 'total punishment' of 36 months is appropriate, a sentence of thirty months for the underlying offense plus a consecutive six months sentence for the failure to appear count would satisfy these requirements.

4. In some cases, the defendant may be sentenced on the underlying offense (the offense in respect to which the defendant failed to appear) before being sentenced on the failure to appear offense. In such cases, criminal history points for the sentence imposed on the underlying offense are to be counted in determining the guideline range on the failure to appear offense only where the offense level is determined under subsection (a)(1) (i.e., where the offense constituted a failure to report for service of sentence).".

Reason for Amendment: This amendment inserts an application note (Note 3) to clarify the interaction of §§ 2J1.6, 3C1.1, 5G1.2, and 5G1.3; and inserts an application note (Note 4) to clarify the interaction of §§ 2J1.6 and 4A1.1.

Effective Date: The effective date of this amendment is November 1, 1991.

404. **Amendment:** Section 2K1.1 is amended in the title by deleting "Explosives" and inserting in lieu thereof "Explosive Materials".

Section 2K1.2 is amended in the title by deleting "Explosives" and inserting in lieu thereof "Explosive Materials".

The Commentary to § 2K1.4 captioned "Application Notes" is amended by inserting the following additional note:

"3. 'Explosives,' as used in the title of this guideline, includes any explosive, explosive material, or destructive device.".

Section 2K1.5(c)(1) is amended by inserting "or possessed" immediately following "used"; and by inserting ", as appropriate," immediately before "if the".

Reason for Amendment: This amendment revises the titles of § 2K1.1 and § 2K1.2, and the Commentary to § 2K1.4 to clarify that the term explosives, as used in those guidelines, includes explosives materials. In addition, this amendment clarifies the application of the cross reference in § 2K1.5(c)(1).

Effective Date: The effective date of this amendment is November 1, 1991.

405. **Amendment:** The Commentary to § 2K2.4 captioned "Application Notes" is amended in Note 2 by deleting "§ 2B3.1(b)(2)" and inserting in lieu thereof "§ 2B3.1(b)(2)(A)-(F)"; and by inserting the following additional paragraphs at the end:

> "*Provided*, that where the maximum of the guideline range from Chapter Five, Part A (Sentencing Table) determined by an offense level adjusted under the procedure described in the preceding paragraph, plus the term of imprisonment required under 18 U.S.C. § 924(c) or § 929(a), is less than the maximum of the guideline range that would apply to the underlying offense absent such adjustment, the procedure described in the preceding paragraph does not apply. Instead, the guideline range applicable to the underlying offense absent such adjustment is to be used after subtracting the term of imprisonment imposed under 18 U.S.C. § 924(c) or § 929(a) from both the minimum and maximum of such range.
>
> Example: A defendant, is to be sentenced under the robbery guideline; his unadjusted offense level from § 2B3.1 is 30, including a 7-level enhancement for discharging a firearm; no Chapter Three adjustments are applicable; and his criminal history category is Category IV. His unadjusted guideline range from Chapter Five, Part A (Sentencing Table) is 135-168 months. This defendant has also been convicted under 18 U.S.C. § 924(c) arising from the possession of a weapon during the robbery, and therefore must be sentenced to an additional consecutive five-year term of imprisonment. The defendant's adjusted guideline range, which takes into account the conviction under 18 U.S.C. § 924(c) by eliminating the 7-level weapon enhancement, is 70-87 months. Because the maximum of the defendant's adjusted guideline range plus the five year consecutive sentence (87 months + 60 months = 147 months) is less than the maximum of the defendant's unadjusted guideline range (168 months), the defendant is to be sentenced using the unadjusted guideline range after subtracting the 60 month sentence to be imposed under 18 U.S.C. § 924(c) from both the minimum and maximum of the unadjusted range (e.g., 135 months - 60 months = 75 months; 168 months - 60 months = 108 months). A sentence imposed for the underlying offense using the guideline range determined in this manner (75-108 months) when combined with the consecutive sentence imposed under 18 U.S.C. § 924(c) or § 929(a), will produce the appropriate total term of imprisonment."

Reason for Amendment: This amendment provides an additional instruction for the determination of the offense level in cases in which the defendant is convicted under 18 U.S.C. § 924(c) or § 929(a) in addition to a count for the offense in respect to which the firearm was used or possessed. The amendment is designed to prevent the anomalous result of the total punishment being less when there are convictions on both such counts than if the defendant was convicted only of the offense in respect to which the weapon was used or possessed.

Effective Date: The effective date of this amendment is November 1, 1991.

406. **Amendment:** The Commentary to § 2P1.1 captioned "Application Notes" is amended by inserting the following additional note:

> "6. If the adjustment in subsection (b)(1) applies as a result of conduct that involves an official victim, do not apply § 3A1.2 (Official Victim).".

Reason for Amendment: This amendment addresses the issue raised in United States v.

Dugan, 912 F.2d 942 (8th Cir. 1990) concerning the interaction between § 2P1.1(b)(1) and § 3A1.2 by expressly providing that where an enhancement from subsection (b)(1) applies, § 3A1.2 does not apply.

Effective Date: The effective date of this amendment is November 1, 1991.

407. **Amendment:** Section 2Q2.1(b)(3)(A) is amended by deleting "specially protected" immediately before "fish".

    Reason for Amendment: This amendment removes language inadvertently retained when this guideline was consolidated with the former § 2Q2.2.

    Effective Date: The effective date of this amendment is November 1, 1991.

408. **Amendment:** The Commentary to § 2T1.2 captioned "Background" is amended in the third paragraph by deleting:

    "difficulty of computing the tax loss, which may become the subject of protracted civil litigation. It is expected that the measure used will generally understate the tax due, and will not call for a sentence approaching the maximum unless very large incomes are involved. Thus, the burden will remain on the prosecution to provide a more accurate estimate of the tax loss if it seeks enhanced punishment",

    and inserting in lieu thereof:

    "potential difficulty of determining the amount of tax the taxpayer owed. It is expected that this alternative measure generally will understate the amount of tax owed".

    Reason for Amendment: This amendment clarifies the meaning of the commentary and deletes surplus material.

    Effective Date: The effective date of this amendment is November 1, 1991.

409. **Amendment:** Section 2T1.6 is amended by inserting the following additional subsection:

    "(b)   Cross Reference

        (1)   Where the offense involved embezzlement by withholding tax from an employee's earnings and willfully failing to account to the employee for it, apply § 2B1.1 (Larceny, Embezzlement, and Other Forms of Theft) if the resulting offense level is greater than that determined above.".

    The Commentary to § 2T1.6 captioned "Application Note" is amended in Note 1 by deleting "In such instances, an upward departure may be warranted" and inserting in lieu thereof "Subsection (b)(1) addresses such cases".

    Reason for Amendment: This amendment replaces the recommendation in the commentary of this guideline concerning consideration of an upward departure where the court finds that the offense involved embezzlement of an employee's funds with a cross reference that provides for the application of § 2B1.1 (Larceny, Embezzlement, and Other Forms of Theft) in such cases where that guideline results in the greater offense level.

    Effective Date: The effective date of this amendment is November 1, 1991.

410. **Amendment:** Section 2T3.1(a) is amended by deleting "Level from § 2T4.1 (Tax Table)

Amendment 410

corresponding to the tax loss." and inserting in lieu thereof:

"(1) The level from § 2T4.1 (Tax Table) corresponding to the tax loss, if the tax loss exceeded $1,000; or

(2) 5, if the tax loss exceeded $100 but did not exceed $1,000; or

(3) 4, if the tax loss did not exceed $100.".

Section 2T3.1 is amended by inserting the following additional subsection:

"(b) Specific Offense Characteristic

(1) If sophisticated means were used to impede discovery of the nature or existence of the offense, increase by 2 levels.".

Section 2T3.2(a) is amended by deleting "Level from § 2T4.1 (Tax Table) corresponding to the tax loss." and inserting in lieu thereof:

"(1) The level from § 2T4.1 (Tax Table) corresponding to the tax loss, if the tax loss exceeded $1,000; or

(2) 5, if the tax loss exceeded $100 but did not exceed $1,000; or

(3) 4, if the tax loss did not exceed $100.".

Section 2T3.2 is amended by inserting the following additional subsection:

"(b) Specific Offense Characteristic

(1) If sophisticated means were used to impede discovery of the nature or existence of the offense, increase by 2 levels.".

Reason for Amendment: This amendment lowers the offense level for the least serious offenses (evasion of import duty of $1,000 or less without use of sophisticated means) to provide an offense level equal to the offense level for theft of the same amount without more than minimal planning. In addition, it adds an adjustment for "sophisticated means" to conform with other tax evasion guidelines (e.g., § 2T1.1).

Effective Date: The effective date of this amendment is November 1, 1991.

411. **Amendment:** Section 2X1.1(a) and (b)(3) are amended by deleting "object" wherever it appears and inserting in lieu thereof in each instance "substantive".

Section 2X1.1(b)(1) is amended by inserting "substantive" immediately before "offense".

Section 2X1.1(b)(2) is amended by inserting "substantive" immediately before "offense".

Section 2X1.1(b)(3) is amended by deleting "the offense" the first two times it appears and inserting in lieu thereof in each instance "the substantive offense".

The Commentary to § 2X1.1 captioned "Application Notes" is amended in Note 2 by deleting:

"Under § 2X1.1(a) the base offense level will be the same as that for the object offense which the defendant solicited, or conspired or attempted to commit.",

and inserting in lieu thereof:

>"'Substantive offense,' as used in this guideline, means the offense that the defendant was convicted of soliciting, attempting, or conspiring to commit. Under § 2X1.1(a), the base offense level will be the same as that for the substantive offense.".

The Commentary to § 2X1.1 is amended by deleting "object" wherever it appears and inserting in lieu thereof "substantive".

The Commentary to § 2X1.1 captioned "Application Notes" is amended in Note 4 in the second paragraph by deleting "or (2)" and inserting in lieu thereof ", (b)(2), or (b)(3)(A)".

The Commentary to § 2X1.1 captioned "Background" is amended by deleting "necessary acts of" and inserting in lieu thereof "acts necessary for".

Reason for Amendment: This amendment replaces the term "object offense" with the more commonly used term "substantive offense," and makes clarifying and editorial changes.

Effective Date: The effective date of this amendment is November 1, 1991.

412. **Amendment:** Section 2X5.1 is amended by inserting, immediately before the period at the end of the second sentence, the following:

>", except that any guidelines and policy statements that can be applied meaningfully in the absence of a Chapter Two offense guideline shall remain applicable".

The Commentary to § 2X5.1 is amended by inserting, immediately after "Commentary", the following:

>"Application Note:
>
>1. Guidelines and policy statements that can be applied meaningfully in the absence of a Chapter Two offense guideline include: § 5B1.3 (Conditions of Probation); § 5B1.4 (Recommended Conditions of Probation and Supervised Release); § 5D1.1 (Imposition of a Term of Supervised Release); § 5D1.2 (Term of Supervised Release); § 5D1.3 (Conditions of Supervised Release); § 5E1.1 (Restitution); § 5E1.3 (Special Assessments); § 5E1.4 (Forfeiture); Chapter Five, Part F (Sentencing Options); § 5G1.3 (Imposition of a Sentence on a Defendant Subject to an Undischarged Term of Imprisonment); Chapter Five, Part H (Specific Offender Characteristics); Chapter Five, Part J (Relief from Disability); Chapter Five, Part K (Departures); Chapter Six, Part A (Sentencing Procedures); Chapter Six, Part B (Plea Agreements).".

The Commentary to § 2X5.1 captioned "Background" is amended by inserting the following additional paragraph:

>"   The sentencing guidelines apply to convictions under 18 U.S.C. § 13 (Assimilative Crimes Act) and 18 U.S.C. § 1153 (Indian Major Crimes Act); see 18 U.S.C. § 3551(a), as amended by section 1602 of Public Law 101-647.".

Reason for Amendment: This amendment inserts an application note to clarify that, in the case of an offense for which there is no sufficiently analogous offense guideline, any guidelines and policy statements that can be meaningfully applied in the absence of a Chapter Two offense guideline remain applicable. This amendment also clarifies the applicability of the sentencing guidelines to convictions under 18 U.S.C. §§ 13 (Assimilative Crimes Act) and 1153 (Indian Major Crimes Act). Section 1602 of the Crime Control Act of 1990 (Public Law 101-647) resolved this issue by amending 18 U.S.C. § 3551(a) to provide expressly that Chapter 227 of Title 18, United States Code (including the sentencing guidelines) applies to convictions under these statutes.

Effective Date: The effective date of this amendment is November 1, 1991.

413. **Amendment:** The Commentary to § 3A1.3 captioned "Application Notes" is amended by deleting:

> "2. This adjustment applies to any offense in which a victim was physically restrained in the course of the offense, except where such restraint is an element of the offense, specifically incorporated into the base offense level, or listed as a specific offense characteristic.",

and inserting in lieu thereof:

> "2. Do not apply this adjustment where the offense guideline specifically incorporates this factor, or where the unlawful restraint of a victim is an element of the offense itself (e.g., this adjustment does not apply to offenses covered by § 2A4.1 (Kidnapping, Abduction, Unlawful Restraint)).".

Reason for Amendment: This amendment clarifies the application of this guideline.

Effective Date: The effective date of this amendment is November 1, 1991.

414. **Amendment:** The Commentary to § 3B1.1 captioned "Application Notes" is amended in Note 1 by inserting the following additional sentence at the end:

> "A person who is not criminally responsible for the commission of the offense (e.g., an undercover law enforcement officer) is not a participant.".

Reason for Amendment: This amendment clarifies the operation of this guideline in accord with the holding in United States v. Carroll, 893 F.2d 1502 (6th Cir. 1990).

Effective Date: The effective date of this amendment is November 1, 1991.

415. **Amendment:** The Commentary to § 3C1.1 captioned "Application Notes" is amended in Note 1 in the last sentence by deleting ", the defendant's testimony and" and inserting in lieu thereof "in respect to alleged false testimony or statements by the defendant, such testimony or".

Reason for Amendment: This amendment more precisely states the meaning of this commentary.

Effective Date: The effective date of this amendment is November 1, 1991.

416. **Amendment:** The Commentary to § 3C1.2 captioned "Application Notes" is amended by redesignating note 3 as note 4; and by inserting the following additional note:

> "3. 'During flight' is to be construed broadly and includes preparation for flight. Therefore, this adjustment also is applicable where the conduct occurs in the course of resisting arrest.".

Reason for Amendment: This amendment clarifies that reckless endangerment in the course of resisting arrest that does not receive a 3-level enhancement under § 3A1.2 (Official Victim) may be considered under this section.

Effective Date: The effective date of this amendment is November 1, 1991.

417. Amendment: Section 3D1.2(d) is amended in the second paragraph by inserting ", 2C1.7" immediately following "2C1.2"; by inserting ", 2D1.11, 2D1.13" immediately following "2D1.5"; and by deleting "2K2.2" and inserting in lieu thereof "2K2.1".

The Commentary to § 3D1.2 captioned "Application Notes" is amended in Note 2 by inserting the following immediately after the second sentence:

"For offenses in which there are no identifiable victims (e.g., drug or immigration offenses, where society at large is the victim), the 'victim' for purposes of subsections (a) and (b) is the societal interest that is harmed. In such cases, the counts are grouped together when the societal interests that are harmed are closely related. Where one count, for example, involves unlawfully entering the United States and the other involves possession of fraudulent evidence of citizenship, the counts are grouped together because the societal interests harmed (the interests protected by laws governing immigration) are closely related. In contrast, where one count involves the sale of controlled substances and the other involves an immigration law violation, the counts are not grouped together because different societal interests are harmed.";

and by deleting the last sentence as follows:

"Thus, for so-called 'victimless' crimes (crimes in which society at large is the victim), the grouping decision must be based primarily upon the nature of the interest invaded by each offense.".

The Commentary to § 3D1.2 captioned "Application Notes" is amended by deleting Note 8, inserting the text of deleted Note 8 as the second paragraph of Note 5, and by renumbering Note 9 as Note 8.

The Commentary to § 3D1.2 captioned "Application Notes" is amended in the third (formerly second) paragraph of Note 5 by deleting "accessory after the fact for" and inserting in lieu thereof "a conspiracy to commit".

The Commentary to § 3D1.2 captioned "Application Notes" is amended in Note 6 by inserting the following additional paragraph as the second paragraph:

"A conspiracy, attempt, or solicitation to commit an offense is covered under subsection (d) if the offense that is the object of the conspiracy, attempt, or solicitation is covered under subsection (d).".

The Commentary following § 3D1.5 captioned "Illustrations of the Operation of the Multiple-Count Rules" is amended in example 1 by deleting "gun was discharged" and inserting in lieu thereof "firearm was displayed".

The Commentary following § 3D1.5 captioned "Illustrations of the Operation of the Multiple-Count Rules" is amended in example 2 by deleting:

"The base offense level is 6, and there is an aggravator of 1 level for property value. However, because the conduct involved repeated acts with some planning, the offense level is raised to 8 (§ 2F1.1(b)(2)(B)). The combined offense level therefore is 8.",

and inserting in lieu thereof:

> "The base offense level is 6; 1 level is added because of the value of the property (§ 2F1.1(b)(1)); and 2 levels are added because the conduct involved repeated acts with some planning (§ 2F1.1(b)(2)(A)). The resulting offense level is 9.".

The Commentary following § 3D1.5 captioned "Illustrations of the Operation of the Multiple-Count Rules" is amended in example 4 by deleting "§ 2B4.1 (Commercial Bribery)" and inserting in lieu thereof "§ 2B4.1 (Bribery in Procurement of Bank Loan and Other Commercial Bribery)".

Reason for Amendment: This amendment revises § 3D1.2(d) to reflect amendments to the offense guidelines of Chapter Two; clarifies the commentary in Note 1 to expressly state that a conspiracy, attempt, or solicitation to commit an offense covered under subsection (d) is also covered under subsection (d); clarifies the commentary in Note 2 with respect to the meaning of the term "victim" where society at large is the victim; merges former Note 8 with Note 5 for greater clarity; conforms two illustrations of the operation of the guidelines to the guidelines, as amended; corrects an inaccurate illustration; and corrects a reference to the title of an offense guideline.

Effective Date: The effective date of this amendment is November 1, 1991.

418. **Amendment:** The Commentary to Chapter Five, Part A (Sentencing Table) captioned "Application Notes" is amended in Note 3 by inserting ", except as provided in §§ 4B1.1 (Career Offender) and 4B1.4 (Armed Career Criminal)" immediately before the period at the end of the first sentence.

Reason for Amendment: This amendment conforms the commentary of this section to the provisions concerning the determination of the criminal history category set forth in §§ 4B1.1 and 4B1.4. No substantive change results.

Effective Date: The effective date of this amendment is November 1, 1991.

419. **Amendment:** Section 5F1.3 is amended by deleting:

> "If the defendant was convicted of a felony and sentenced to probation, the court must order one or more of the following sanctions: a fine, restitution, or community service. 18 U.S.C. § 3563(a)(2).".

Reason for Amendment: This amendment deletes a sentence in this guideline that is unnecessary and no longer accurate because of a change in the statute. The correct reference is found at § 5B1.3(a).

Effective Date: The effective date of this amendment is November 1, 1991.

420. **Amendment:** Chapter Five, Part K, Subpart 2 is amended by inserting an additional policy statement as § 5K2.16 (Voluntary Disclosure of Offense (Policy Statement)).

Reason for Amendment: This amendment sets forth an additional policy statement regarding a mitigating factor that may warrant a downward departure.

Effective Date: The effective date of this amendment is November 1, 1991.

421. **Amendment:** Appendix A (Statutory Index) is amended by inserting, in the appropriate place by title and section, the following:

"8 U.S.C. § 1160(b)(7)(A)	2L2.1, 2L2.2";
"18 U.S.C. § 225	2B1.1, 2B4.1, 2F1.1";
"18 U.S.C. § 403	2J1.1";
"18 U.S.C. § 1032	2B4.1, 2F1.1";
"18 U.S.C. § 1346	2C1.7";
"18 U.S.C. § 1517	2J1.2";
"18 U.S.C. § 2257	2G2.5";
"21 U.S.C. § 841(g)(1)	2D1.11, 2D1.13";
"21 U.S.C. § 843(a)(4)(B)	2D1.13";
"21 U.S.C. § 843(a)(6), (7)	2D1.12";
"21 U.S.C. § 843(a)(8)	2D1.13";
"21 U.S.C. § 859	2D1.2";
"21 U.S.C. § 860	2D1.2";
"21 U.S.C. § 861	2D1.2";
"21 U.S.C. § 863	2D1.7";
"42 U.S.C. § 1320a-7b	2B1.1, 2B4.1, 2F1.1".

Appendix A (Statutory Index) is amended in the line beginning "18 U.S.C. § 371" by inserting "2C1.7," immediately before "2D1.4";

by deleting:

"18 U.S.C. § 842(a)-(i)	2K1.3",

and inserting in lieu thereof:

"18 U.S.C. § 842(a)-(e)	2K1.3
18 U.S.C. § 842(f)	2K1.6
18 U.S.C. § 842(g)	2K1.6
18 U.S.C. § 842(h), (i)	2K1.3";

by deleting:

"18 U.S.C. § 844(a)	2K1.3
18 U.S.C. § 844(b)	2K1.1, 2K1.2, 2K1.3";

in the line beginning "18 U.S.C. § 844(d)" by deleting "§ 2K1.6" and inserting in lieu thereof "§ 2K1.3";

by deleting:

"18 U.S.C. § 922(a)(1)	2K2.1, 2K2.2
18 U.S.C. § 922(a)(2)	2K2.2
18 U.S.C. § 922(a)(3)	2K2.1
18 U.S.C. § 922(a)(4)	2K2.1
18 U.S.C. § 922(a)(5)	2K2.2
18 U.S.C. § 922(a)(6)	2K2.1
18 U.S.C. § 922(b)-(d)	2K2.2

Amendment 421 APPENDIX C - VOLUME I November 1, 2013

18 U.S.C. § 922(e)	2K2.1, 2K2.2
18 U.S.C. § 922(f)	2K2.1, 2K2.2
18 U.S.C. § 922(g)	2K2.1
18 U.S.C. § 922(h)	2K2.1
18 U.S.C. § 922(i)-(l)	2K2.1, 2K2.2
18 U.S.C. § 922(m)	2K2.2
18 U.S.C. § 922(n)	2K2.1
18 U.S.C. § 922(o)	2K2.1, 2K2.2
18 U.S.C. § 923(a)	2K2.2
18 U.S.C. § 924(a)(1)(A)	2K2.2
18 U.S.C. § 924(a)(1)(C)	2K2.1, 2K2.2
18 U.S.C. § 924(a)(3)(A)	2K2.2
18 U.S.C. § 924(b)	2K2.3",

and inserting in lieu thereof:

"18 U.S.C. § 922(a)-(p)	2K2.1
18 U.S.C. § 922(q)	2K2.5
18 U.S.C. § 922(r)	2K2.1
18 U.S.C. § 923	2K2.1
18 U.S.C. § 924(a)	2K2.1
18 U.S.C. § 924(b)	2K2.1";

by deleting:

"18 U.S.C. § 924(f)	2K2.3
18 U.S.C. § 924(g)	2K2.3",

and inserting in lieu thereof:

"18 U.S.C. § 924(e)	2K2.1 (see also 4B1.4)
18 U.S.C. § 924(f)	2K2.1
18 U.S.C. § 924(g)	2K2.1";

in the line beginning "18 U.S.C. § 1005" by deleting ", 2S1.3";

in the line beginning "18 U.S.C. § 1341" by inserting "2C1.7," immediately before "2F1.1";

in the line beginning "18 U.S.C. § 1342" by inserting "2C1.7," immediately before "2F1.1";

in the line beginning "18 U.S.C. § 1343" by inserting "2C1.7," immediately before "2F1.1";

in the line beginning "18 U.S.C. § 1460" by deleting "2G2.2,";

in the line beginning "18 U.S.C. § 1543" by inserting "2L2.3," immediately before "2L2.4";

November 1, 2013 APPENDIX C - VOLUME I **Amendment 421**

in the line beginning "18 U.S.C. § 1716" by inserting "2K1.3," immediately before "2K3.2";

in the line beginning "18 U.S.C. § 2252" by inserting ", 2G2.4" immediately following "2G2.2";

by deleting:

    "21 U.S.C. § 841(d)   2D1.1",

and inserting in lieu thereof:

    "21 U.S.C. § 841(d)(1), (2)   2D1.11
    21 U.S.C. § 841(d)(3)   2D1.13";

by deleting:

    "21 U.S.C. § 842(a)   2D3.1, 2D3.2, 2D3.3",

and inserting in lieu thereof:

    "21 U.S.C. § 842(a)(1)   2D3.1
    21 U.S.C. § 842(a)(2)   2D3.3
    21 U.S.C. § 842(a)(9), (10)   2D3.5";

in the line beginning "21 U.S.C. § 843(a)(1), (2), (4)" by deleting ", (1), (2), (4)" and inserting in lieu thereof "(1), (2)";

by deleting:

    "21 U.S.C. § 960   2D1.1",

and inserting in lieu thereof:

    "21 U.S.C. § 960(a), (b)   2D1.1
    21 U.S.C. § 960(d)(1), (2)   2D1.11";

in the line beginning 26 U.S.C. § 5685 by deleting "2K1.6,", and by deleting "2K2.2" and inserting in lieu thereof "2K2.1";

by deleting:

    "26 U.S.C. § 5861(a)   2K2.2
    26 U.S.C. § 5861(b)   2K2.1
    26 U.S.C. § 5861(c)   2K2.1
    26 U.S.C. § 5861(d)   2K2.1
    26 U.S.C. § 5861(e)   2K2.2
    26 U.S.C. § 5861(f)   2K2.2
    26 U.S.C. § 5861(g)   2K2.2
    26 U.S.C. § 5861(h)   2K2.1
    26 U.S.C. § 5861(i)   2K2.1

Amendment 421   APPENDIX C - VOLUME I   November 1, 2013

26 U.S.C. § 5861(j)	2K2.1, 2K2.2
26 U.S.C. § 5861(k)	2K2.1
26 U.S.C. § 5861(l)	2K2.2
26 U.S.C. § 5871	2K2.1, 2K2.2",

and inserting in lieu thereof:

"26 U.S.C. § 5861(a)-(l)	2K2.1
26 U.S.C. § 5871	2K2.1";

by deleting:

"31 U.S.C. § 5316(a)	2S1.3",

and inserting in lieu thereof:

"31 U.S.C. § 5316	2S1.4";

by deleting:

"46 U.S.C. § App. 1903	2D1.1",

and inserting in lieu thereof:

"46 U.S.C. App. § 1903(a)	2D1.1
46 U.S.C. App. § 1903(g)	2D1.1
46 U.S.C. App. § 1903(j)	2D1.4"; and

in the line beginning "47 U.S.C. § 605" by inserting "2B5.3," immediately before "2H3.1".

The Commentary to § 2D1.2 captioned "Statutory Provisions" is amended by deleting "21 U.S.C. §§ 845, 845a, 845b" and inserting in lieu thereof "21 U.S.C. §§ 859 (formerly 21 U.S.C. § 845), 860 (formerly 21 U.S.C. § 845a), 861 (formerly 21 U.S.C. § 845b)".

The Commentary to § 2D3.1 captioned "Statutory Provision" is amended by deleting "843(a). For additional statutory provision(s), see Appendix A (Statutory Index)." and inserting in lieu thereof "842(a)(1), 843(a)(1), (2)."; and by deleting "Provision" and inserting in lieu thereof "Provisions".

The Commentary to § 2D3.2 captioned "Statutory Provision" is amended by deleting "842" and inserting in lieu thereof "842(b), 843(a)(3)"; and by deleting "Provision" and inserting in lieu thereof "Provisions".

The Commentary to § 2D3.3 captioned "Statutory Provision" is amended by deleting "842" and inserting in lieu thereof "842(a)(2)".

Reason for Amendment: This amendment makes the statutory index more comprehensive, and conforms it to the offense guidelines, as amended.

Effective Date: The effective date of this amendment is November 1, 1991.

422. **Amendment:** The Guidelines Manual is amended by inserting an additional chapter

containing guidelines, policy statements, and accompanying commentary as Chapter Eight (Sentencing of Organizations).

Section 2B4.1 is amended by inserting the following additional subsection:

"(c) Special Instruction for Fines - Organizations

(1) In lieu of the pecuniary loss under subsection (a)(3) of § 8C2.4 (Base Fine), use the greatest of: (A) the value of the unlawful payment; (B) the value of the benefit received or to be received in return for the unlawful payment; or (C) the consequential damages resulting from the unlawful payment.".

Section 2C1.1 is amended by inserting the following additional subsection:

"(d) Special Instruction for Fines - Organizations

(1) In lieu of the pecuniary loss under subsection (a)(3) of § 8C2.4 (Base Fine), use the greatest of: (A) the value of the unlawful payment; (B) the value of the benefit received or to be received in return for the unlawful payment; or (C) the consequential damages resulting from the unlawful payment.".

Section 2C1.2 is amended by inserting the following additional subsection:

"(c) Special Instruction for Fines - Organizations

(1) In lieu of the pecuniary loss under subsection (a)(3) of § 8C2.4 (Base Fine), use the value of the unlawful payment.".

Section 2E5.1 is amended by inserting the following additional subsection:

"(c) Special Instruction for Fines - Organizations

(1) In lieu of the pecuniary loss under subsection (a)(3) of § 8C2.4 (Base Fine), use the greatest of: (A) the value of the unlawful payment; (B) if a bribe, the value of the benefit received or to be received in return for the unlawful payment; or (C) if a bribe, the consequential damages resulting from the unlawful payment.".

Section 2E5.6 is amended by inserting the following additional subsection:

"(c) Special Instruction for Fines - Organizations

(1) In lieu of the pecuniary loss under subsection (a)(3) of § 8C2.4 (Base Fine), use the greatest of: (A) the value of the unlawful payment; (B) if a bribe, the value of the benefit received or to be received in return for the unlawful payment; or (C) if a bribe, the consequential damages resulting from the unlawful payment.".

Section 2R1.1 is amended by inserting the following additional subsection:

"(d) Special Instructions for Fines - Organizations

(1) In lieu of the pecuniary loss under subsection (a)(3) of § 8C2.4 (Base Fine), use 20 percent of the volume of affected commerce.

Amendment 422

(2) When applying § 8C2.6 (Minimum and Maximum Multipliers), neither the minimum nor maximum multiplier shall be less than 0.75.

(3) In a bid-rigging case in which the organization submitted one or more complementary bids, use as the organization's volume of commerce the greater of (A) the volume of commerce done by the organization in the goods or services that were affected by the violation, or (B) the largest contract on which the organization submitted a complementary bid in connection with the bid-rigging conspiracy.".

The Commentary to § 2R1.1 captioned "Application Notes" is amended by deleting:

"3. In setting the fine for an organization, the court should consider whether the organization encouraged or took steps to prevent the violation, whether high-level management was aware of the violation, and whether the organization previously engaged in antitrust violations.",

and inserting in lieu thereof:

"3. The fine for an organization is determined by applying Chapter Eight (Sentencing of Organizations). In selecting a fine for an organization within the guideline fine range, the court should consider both the gain to the organization from the offense and the loss caused by the organization. It is estimated that the average gain from price-fixing is 10 percent of the selling price. The loss from price-fixing exceeds the gain because, among other things, injury is inflicted upon consumers who are unable or for other reasons do not buy the product at the higher prices. Because the loss from price-fixing exceeds the gain, subsection (d)(1) provides that 20 percent of the volume of affected commerce is to be used in lieu of the pecuniary loss under § 8C2.4(a)(3). The purpose for specifying a percent of the volume of commerce is to avoid the time and expense that would be required for the court to determine the actual gain or loss. In cases in which the actual monopoly overcharge appears to be either substantially more or substantially less than 10 percent, this factor should be considered in setting the fine within the guideline fine range.".

The Commentary to § 2R1.1 captioned "Background" is amended by deleting the last paragraph as follows:

" Substantial fines are an essential part of the sanction. It is estimated that the average additional profit attributable to price fixing is 10 percent of the selling price. The Commission has specified that a fine from two to five times that amount be imposed on organizational defendants as a deterrent because of the difficulty in identifying violators. Additional monetary penalties can be provided through private treble damage actions. A lower fine is specified for individuals. The Commission believes that most antitrust defendants have the resources and earning capacity to pay these fines, at least over time. The statutory maximum fine is $250,000 for individuals and $1,000,000 for organizations, but is increased when there are convictions on multiple counts.",

and inserting in lieu thereof:

" Substantial fines are an essential part of the sentence. For an individual, the guideline fine range is from one to five percent of the volume of commerce, but not less than $20,000. For an organization, the guideline fine range is determined under

Chapter Eight (Sentencing of Organizations), but pursuant to subsection (d)(2), the minimum multiplier is at least 0.75. This multiplier, which requires a minimum fine of 15 percent of the volume of commerce for the least serious case, was selected to provide an effective deterrent to antitrust offenses. At the same time, this minimum multiplier maintains incentives for desired organizational behavior. Because the Department of Justice has a well-established amnesty program for organizations that self-report antitrust offenses, no lower minimum multiplier is needed as an incentive for self-reporting. A minimum multiplier of at least 0.75 ensures that fines imposed in antitrust cases will exceed the average monopoly overcharge.

The Commission believes that most antitrust defendants have the resources and earning capacity to pay the fines called for by this guideline, at least over time on an installment basis. The statutory maximum fine is $350,000 for individuals and $10,000,000 for organizations, but is increased when there are convictions on multiple counts.".

Section 2S1.1 is amended by inserting the following additional subsection:

"(c) Special Instruction for Fines - Organizations

(1) In lieu of the applicable amount from the table in subsection (d) of § 8C2.4 (Base Fine), use:

(A) the greater of $250,000 or 100 percent of the value of the funds if subsections (a)(1) and (b)(1) are used to determine the offense level; or

(B) the greater of $200,000 or 70 percent of the value of the funds if subsections (a)(2) and (b)(1) are used to determine the offense level; or

(C) the greater of $200,000 or 70 percent of the value of the funds if subsection (a)(1) but not (b)(1) is used to determine the offense level; or

(D) the greater of $150,000 or 50 percent of the value of the funds if subsection (a)(2) but not (b)(1) is used to determine the offense level.".

Section 2S1.2 is amended by inserting the following additional subsection:

"(c) Special Instruction for Fines - Organizations

(1) In lieu of the applicable amount from the table in subsection (d) of § 8C2.4 (Base Fine), use:

(A) the greater of $175,000 or 60 percent of the value of the funds if subsection (b)(1)(A) is used to determine the offense level; or

(B) the greater of $150,000 or 50 percent of the value of the funds if subsection (b)(1)(B) is used to determine the offense level.".

Section 2S1.3 is amended by inserting the following additional subsection:

"(c) Special Instruction for Fines - Organizations

 (1) In lieu of the applicable amount from the table in subsection (d) of § 8C2.4 (Base Fine), use:

  (A) the greater of $125,000 or 30 percent of the value of the funds if subsections (a)(1) and (b)(1) are used to determine the offense level; or

  (B) the greater of $50,000 or 20 percent of the value of the funds if subsection (a)(1) but not (b)(1) are used to determine the offense level.".

Section 2S1.4 is amended by inserting the following additional subsection:

"(c) Special Instruction for Fines - Organizations

 (1) In lieu of the applicable amount from the table in subsection (d) of § 8C2.4 (Base Fine), use:

  (A) the greater of $50,000 or 20 percent of the value of the funds if subsection (b)(1) or (b)(2) is used to determine the offense level; or

  (B) the greater of $15,000 or 10 percent of the value of the funds, otherwise.".

Reason for Amendment: This amendment adds guidelines and policy statements to address the sentencing of organizational defendants.

Effective Date: The effective date of this amendment is November 1, 1991.

423. **Amendment:** Section 1B1.10(c) is amended by deleting:

"(c) *Provided*, however, that a reduction in a defendant's term of imprisonment --

 (1) is not authorized unless the maximum of the guideline range applicable to the defendant (from Chapter Five, Part A) has been lowered by at least six months; and

 (2) may, in no event, exceed the number of months by which the maximum of the guideline range applicable to the defendant (from Chapter Five, Part A) has been lowered.",

and inserting in lieu thereof:

"(c) *Provided*, that a reduction in a defendant's term of imprisonment may, in no event, exceed the number of months by which the maximum of the guideline range applicable to the defendant (from Chapter Five, Part A) has been lowered.".

Section 1B1.10(d) is amended by deleting "and 341" and inserting in lieu thereof "341, 379, and 380".

The Commentary to § 1B1.10 captioned "Background" is amended in the fourth paragraph

by deleting:

> "The requirement in subsection (c)(1) that the maximum of the guideline range be lowered by at least six months for a reduction to be considered",

and inserting in lieu thereof:

> "The Commission has not included in this policy statement amendments that generally reduce the maximum of the guideline range by less than six months. This criterion".

Reason for Amendment: This amendment expands the listing in subsection (d) to implement the directive in 28 U.S.C. § 994(u) in respect to the guideline amendments effective November 1, 1991. In addition, the amendment modifies subsection (c) to simplify the operation of this policy statement, expand eligibility under the policy statement to a few additional cases, and remove the potential for an anomalous result.

Effective Date: The effective date of this amendment is November 1, 1991.

424. **Amendment:** Chapter Five, Part F, is amended by inserting an additional policy statement as § 5F1.7 (Shock Incarceration Program (Policy Statement)).

Reason for Amendment: This amendment adds a policy statement at § 5F1.7 to reflect the provisions and implementation of 18 U.S.C. § 4046.

Effective Date: The effective date of this amendment is November 1, 1991.

425. **Amendment:** The Commentary to § 6A1.2 is amended by inserting, immediately after "Commentary", the following:

> "Application Note:
>
> 1. Under Rule 32, Fed.R.Crim. P., if the court intends to consider a sentence outside the applicable guideline range on a ground not identified as a ground for departure either in the presentence report or a pre-hearing submission, it shall provide reasonable notice that it is contemplating such ruling, specifically identifying the ground for the departure. Burns v. United States, __ U.S. __, 111 S.Ct. 2182 (1991).";

and by inserting "Background:" immediately before "In order".

Reason for Amendment: This amendment adds an application note to reflect the recent Supreme Court decision in Burns v. United States, __ U.S. __, 111 S.Ct. 2182 (1991).

Effective Date: The effective date of this amendment is November 1, 1991.

426. **Amendment:** The Commentary to § 2T1.3 captioned "Application Notes" is amended by inserting the following additional note:

> "4. The amount by which the greater of gross income and taxable income was understated, plus 100 percent of the total amount of any false credits claimed against tax is calculated as follows: (1) determine the amount, if any, by which the gross income was understated; (2) determine the amount, if any, by which the taxable income was understated; and (3) determine the amount of any false credit(s) claimed (a tax 'credit' is an item that reduces the amount

Amendment 426 APPENDIX C - VOLUME I November 1, 2013

of tax directly; in contrast, a 'deduction' is an item that reduces the amount of taxable income). Use the amount determined under step (1) or (2), whichever is greater, plus any amount determined under step (3).".

Reason for Amendment: This amendment clarifies the operation of the guideline.

Effective Date: The effective date of this amendment is November 1, 1991.

427. **Amendment:** Section 7B1.3 is amended by redesignating subsection (c)(1)(1) as (c)(1)(A), (c)(1)(2) as (c)(1)(B), (c)(2)(1) as (c)(2)(A), and (c)(2)(2) as (c)(2)(B).

The Commentary to § 7B1.3 captioned "Application Notes" is amended in Note 2 by deleting "§ 7B1.3(f)(2)" and inserting in lieu thereof "§ 7B1.3(g)(2)".

The Commentary to § 7B1.3 captioned "Application Notes" is amended in Note 3 by deleting "No. 89-10529 (9th Cir. July 3, 1990)" and inserting in lieu thereof "907 F.2d 896 (9th Cir. 1990)".

The Commentary to § 7B1.3 captioned "Application Notes" is amended by inserting the following additional note:

"7. 'Maximum term of imprisonment imposable upon revocation,' as used in subsection (g)(2), refers to the maximum term of imprisonment authorized by statute for the violation of supervised release, not to the maximum of the guideline range.".

Reason for Amendment: This amendment clarifies the operation of this policy statement, makes editorial improvements, and corrects a clerical error.

Effective Date: The effective date of this amendment is November 1, 1991.

428. **Amendment:** The Commentary to § 5F1.5 captioned "Background" is amended by deleting the last paragraph as follows:

"   The Comprehensive Crime Control Act expressly authorizes promulgation of policy statements regarding the appropriate use of conditions of probation and supervised release. 28 U.S.C. § 994(a)(2)(B). The Act does not expressly grant the authority to issue guidelines on the subject. The appellate review provisions of the Act, however, authorize appeals of occupational restrictions that deviate from the minimum and maximum limitations 'established in the guideline' (emphasis added).".

Reason for Amendment: This amendment deletes an outdated paragraph. Section 7103(b)(3) of Public Law 100-690 amended 28 U.S.C. § 994 by adding subsection (a)(1)(E), which expressly authorizes the Commission to promulgate guidelines addressing occupational restrictions as a condition of probation or supervised release.

Effective Date: The effective date of this amendment is November 1, 1991.

429. **Amendment:** The Commentary to § 1B1.5 captioned "Application Note" is amended in Note 1 by deleting "2D1.2(a)(1), 2H1.2(a)(2)" and inserting in lieu thereof "2D1.2(a)(1), (2), and 2H1.1(a)(2)"; by deleting "§§ 2A4.1(b)(5)(B), 2Q1.2(b)(5)" and inserting in lieu thereof "§ 2A4.1(b)(7)"; and by inserting the following additional paragraph:

"A reference may also be to a specific subsection of another guideline; e.g., the reference in § 2D1.10(a)(1) to '3 plus the offense level from the Drug Quantity Table in § 2D1.1'. In such case, only the specific subsection of that other guideline is used.".

The Commentary to § 1B1.5 captioned "Application Note" is amended by inserting the following additional notes:

"2. A reference may require that the offense level be determined under another offense guideline. In such case, the adjustments in Chapter Three, Parts A (Victim-Related Adjustments), B (Role in the Offense), and E (Acceptance of Responsibility) are also to be determined in respect to that other offense guideline. For example, a defendant convicted of possession of a firearm by a felon, to which § 2K2.1 (Unlawful Receipt, Possession, or Transportation of Firearms or Ammunition; Prohibited Transactions Involving Firearms or Ammunition) applies, is found to have used that firearm in the commission of a robbery. The cross reference at § 2K2.1(c) directs that the robbery offense guideline be used. The adjustments in Chapter Three, Parts A, B and E are to be applied as if the offense of conviction had directly referenced the robbery guideline.

3. A reference to another guideline may direct that such reference is to be used only if it results in a greater offense level. In such cases, the greater offense level means the greater final offense level (i.e., the greater offense level taking into account both the Chapter Two offense level and any applicable Chapter Three adjustments). Although the offense guideline that results in the greater offense level under Chapter Two will most frequently result in the greater final offense level, this will not always be the case. If, for example, a role or abuse of trust adjustment applies to the cross-referenced offense guideline, but not to the guideline initially applied, the greater Chapter Two offense level may not necessarily result in a greater final offense level.

4. A reference may direct that, if the conduct involved another offense, the offense guideline for such other offense is to be applied. Where there is more than one such other offense, the most serious such offense (or group of closely-related offenses in the case of offenses that would be grouped together under § 3D1.2(d)) is to be used. For example, if a defendant convicted of possession of a firearm by a felon, to which § 2K2.1 (Unlawful Receipt, Possession, or Transportation of Firearms or Ammunition; Prohibited Transactions Involving Firearms or Ammunition) applies, is found to have possessed that firearm during commission of a series of offenses, the cross reference at § 2K2.1(c) is applied to the offense resulting in the greatest offense level.";

and in the caption by deleting "Note" and inserting in lieu thereof "Notes".

Reason for Amendment: This amendment clarifies the operation of this guideline.

Effective Date: The effective date of this amendment is November 1, 1991.

430. **Amendment:** The Commentary to § 2H1.1 captioned "Application Notes" is amended by inserting the following additional paragraph as the first paragraph of Note 1:

"'Underlying offense,' as used in this guideline, includes any offense under federal, state, or local law other than an offense that is itself covered under Chapter Two,

Amendment 430 APPENDIX C - VOLUME I November 1, 2013

>Part H, Subpart 1, 2, or 4. For example, in the case of a conspiracy to interfere with a person's civil rights (a violation of 18 U.S.C. § 241) that involved an aggravated assault (the use of force) to deny certain rights or benefits in furtherance of discrimination (a violation of 18 U.S.C. § 245), the underlying offense in respect to both the violation of 18 U.S.C. § 241 (to which § 2H1.1 applies) and the violation of 18 U.S.C. § 245 (to which § 2H1.3 applies) would be the aggravated assault.".

The Commentary to § 2H1.1 captioned "Application Notes" is amended in Note 1 by inserting the following additional paragraph at the end:

>"In certain cases, the count of which the defendant is convicted may set forth conduct that constitutes more than one underlying offense (e.g., two instances of assault, or one instance of assault and one instance of arson). In such cases, determine the offense level for the underlying offense by treating each underlying offense as if contained in a separate count of conviction. To determine which of the alternative base offense levels (e.g., § 2H1.1(a)(1) or (a)(2)) results in the greater offense level, apply Chapter Three, Parts A, B, C, and D to each alternative base offense level. Use whichever results in the greater offense level. Example: The defendant is convicted of one count of conspiracy to violate civil rights that included two level 12 underlying offenses (of a type not grouped together under Chapter Three, Part D). No adjustment from Chapter Three, Parts A, B, or C applies. The base offense level from § 2H1.1(a)(1) is 15. The offense level for each underlying offense from § 2H1.1(a)(2) is 14 (2 + 12). Under Chapter Three, Part D (Multiple Counts), the two level 14 underlying offenses result in a combined offense level of 16. This offense level is greater than the alternative base offense level of 15 under § 2H1.1(a)(1). Therefore, the case is treated as if there were two counts, one for each underlying offense, with a base offense level under § 2H1.1(a)(2) of 14 for each underlying offense.".

The Commentary to § 2H1.1 captioned "Application Notes" is amended in the first sentence of the second paragraph of Note 1 (formerly the first paragraph) by deleting "contained in the particular guideline in Chapter Two) for any underlying criminal conduct" and inserting in lieu thereof "and cross references) from the offense guideline in Chapter Two that most closely corresponds to the underlying offense"; in the last sentence of the second paragraph of Note 1 (formerly the first paragraph) by deleting "an offense" and "that offense" and inserting in lieu thereof "arson" in each instance.

Reason for Amendment: This amendment clarifies the operation of this guideline.

Effective Date: The effective date of this amendment is November 1, 1991.

431. **Amendment:** The Commentary to § 2J1.7 captioned "Background" is amended by deleting the first paragraph as follows:

>"An enhancement under 18 U.S.C. § 3147 may be imposed only upon application of the government; it cannot be imposed on the court's own motion. In this respect, it is similar to a separate count of conviction and, for this reason, is placed in Chapter Two of the guidelines.",

and inserting in lieu thereof:

>"An enhancement under 18 U.S.C. § 3147 may be imposed only after sufficient notice to the defendant by the government or the court, and applies only in the case of a conviction for a federal offense that is committed while on release on another federal charge.".

Reason for Amendment: This amendment corrects the description in the Background

Commentary of the operation of the statute to which this guideline applies.

Effective Date: The effective date of this amendment is November 1, 1991.

432. **Amendment:** The Commentary to § 2N2.1 captioned "Application Notes" is amended in Note 1 by inserting "or reckless" immediately before "conduct".

The Commentary to § 2N2.1 captioned "Application Notes" is amended in Note 4 by deleting "anabolic steroids" and inserting in lieu thereof "human growth hormones", and by inserting at the end:

"Offenses involving anabolic steroids are covered by Chapter Two, Part D (Offenses Involving Drugs). In the case of an offense involving a substance purported to be an anabolic steroid, but not containing any active ingredient, apply § 2F1.1 (Fraud and Deceit) with 'loss' measured by the amount paid, or to be paid, by the victim for such substance.".

Reason for Amendment: This amendment clarifies Application Note 1 with respect to reckless conduct, conforms Application Note 4 to reflect that offenses involving anabolic steroids will be covered under § 2D1.1 (Amendment 369), and clarifies the treatment of an offense involving a substance purported to be an anabolic steroid, but containing no active ingredient.

Effective Date: The effective date of this amendment is November 1, 1991.

433. **Amendment:** Section 4B1.2(2) is amended by deleting "or distribution" and inserting in lieu thereof "distribution, or dispensing"; and by deleting "or distribute" and inserting in lieu thereof "distribute, or dispense".

Section 4B1.2(3) is amended by deleting "Part A of this Chapter" and inserting in lieu thereof "§ 4A1.1(a), (b), or (c)".

The Commentary to § 4B1.2 captioned "Application Notes" is amended in Note 2 by inserting "(i.e., expressly charged)" immediately following "set forth"; by inserting the following at the end:

"Under this section, the conduct of which the defendant was convicted is the focus of inquiry.

The term 'crime of violence' does not include the offense of unlawful possession of a firearm by a felon. Where the instant offense is the unlawful possession of a firearm by a felon, the specific offense characteristics of § 2K2.1 (Unlawful Receipt, Possession, or Transportation of Firearms or Ammunition; Prohibited Transactions Involving Firearms or Ammunition) provide an increase in offense level if the defendant has one or more prior felony convictions for a crime of violence or controlled substance offense; and, if the defendant is sentenced under the provisions of 18 U.S.C. § 924(e), § 4B1.4 (Armed Career Criminal) will apply.".

The Commentary to § 4B1.2 captioned "Application Notes" is amended in Note 2 by inserting "(including any explosive material or destructive device)" immediately following "explosives".

The Commentary to § 4B1.2 captioned "Application Notes" is amended in Note 3 by inserting the following additional sentences at the end:

"A conviction for an offense committed at age eighteen or older is an adult

Amendment 433

conviction. A conviction for an offense committed prior to age eighteen is an adult conviction if it is classified as an adult conviction under the laws of the jurisdiction in which the defendant was convicted (e.g., a federal conviction for an offense committed prior to the defendant's eighteenth birthday is an adult conviction if the defendant was expressly proceeded against as an adult).".

Reason for Amendment: This amendment clarifies that the application of § 4B1.2 is determined by the offense of conviction (i.e., the conduct charged in the count of which the defendant was convicted); clarifies that the offense of unlawful possession of a weapon is not a crime of violence for the purposes of this section; clarifies the definition of a prior adult conviction; makes the definitions in § 4B1.2(2) more comprehensive; and clarifies the application of § 4B1.2(3) by specifying the particular provisions of Chapter Four, Part A to which this subsection refers.

Effective Date: The effective date of this amendment is November 1, 1991.

434. **Amendment:** The Commentary to § 1B1.2 captioned "Application Notes" is amended in Note 1 in the second sentence of the second paragraph by deleting "as part of a plea of guilty or nolo contendere" and inserting in lieu thereof "that is set forth in a written plea agreement or made between the parties on the record during a plea proceeding"; in the second sentence of the third paragraph by deleting "the plea" and inserting in lieu thereof "a plea agreement"; and in the third sentence of the third paragraph by inserting "agreement" immediately following "plea".

Reason for Amendment: This amendment clarifies the meaning of the term "stipulation" used in § 1B1.2(a) and (c).

Effective Date: The effective date of this amendment is November 1, 1991.

435. **Amendment:** Section 2G2.2 is amended in the title by deleting "Advertising, or" and inserting in lieu thereof "Shipping, or Advertising Material Involving the Sexual Exploitation of a Minor;".

Section 2G2.2(a) is amended by deleting "13" and inserting in lieu thereof "15".

Section 2G2.2(b) is amended by inserting the following additional subdivision:

"(4) If the defendant engaged in a pattern of activity involving the sexual abuse or exploitation of a minor, increase by 5 levels.".

Section 2G2.2(b)(2) is amended by inserting "by" immediately following "event".

The Commentary to § 2G2.2 captioned "Statutory Provisions" is amended by deleting "2252" and inserting in lieu thereof "2252(a)(1)-(3)".

The Commentary to § 2G2.2 captioned "Application Notes" is amended by redesignating Note 4 as Note 5; by inserting the following as Note 4:

"'Pattern of activity involving the sexual abuse or exploitation of a minor,' for the purposes of subsection (b)(4), means any combination of two or more separate instances of the sexual abuse or the sexual exploitation of a minor, whether involving the same or different victims.";

and in Note 5 (formerly Note 4) by inserting "exploited or" immediately before "abused"; by deleting "is warranted" and inserting in lieu thereof "may be warranted"; and by inserting ", as well as whether the defendant has received an enhancement under subsection (b)(4) on account of such conduct" immediately after "conduct".

Reason for Amendment: This amendment implements the instructions to the Commission in Section 632 of Public Law 102-141, the Treasury, Postal Service and General Government Appropriations Act of 1992.

Effective Date: The effective date of this amendment is November 27, 1991.

436. **Amendment:** Section 2G2.4 is amended in the title by deleting "Receipt or" immediately before "Possession".

Section 2G2.4(a) is amended by deleting "10" and inserting in lieu thereof "13".

Section 2G2.4(b) is amended by inserting the following additional subdivision:

> "(2) If the offense involved possessing ten or more books, magazines, periodicals, films, video tapes, or other items, containing a visual depiction involving the sexual exploitation of a minor, increase by 2 levels.";

and in the caption by deleting "Characteristic" and inserting in lieu thereof "Characteristics".

Section 2G2.4(c)(2) is amended by inserting "shipping," immediately before "advertising, or"; and by deleting "Advertising, or" and inserting in lieu thereof "Shipping, or Advertising Material Involving the Sexual Exploitation of a Minor;".

The Commentary to § 2G2.4 captioned "Statutory Provision" is amended by deleting "2252" and inserting in lieu thereof "2252(a)(4)".

The Commentary to § 2G2.4 captioned "Application Note" is deleted in its entirety as follows:

> "Application Note:
>
> 1. This guideline assumes that the offense involved a small number of prohibited items. If the defendant possessed 50 or more books, magazines, periodicals, films, video tapes, or other items containing a visual depiction involving the sexual exploitation of a minor, and subsection (c)(1) or (c)(2) does not apply, an upward departure may be warranted.".

Reason for Amendment: This amendment implements the instructions to the Commission in Section 632 of Public Law 102-141, the Treasury, Postal Service and General Government Appropriations Act of 1992.

Effective Date: The effective date of this amendment is November 27, 1991.

437. **Amendment:** Section 2G3.1(a) is amended by deleting "6" and inserting in lieu thereof "10".

Section 2G3.1(c) is amended by deleting "Advertising, or" and inserting in lieu thereof "Shipping, or Advertising Material Involving the Sexual Exploitation of a Minor;"; and by deleting "Receipt or" immediately before "Possession".

The Commentary to § 2G3.1 captioned "Background" is amended by deleting "11" and inserting in lieu thereof "15".

Reason for Amendment: This amendment implements the instructions to the Commis-

Amendment 437

sion in Section 632 of Public Law 102-141, the Treasury, Postal Service and General Government Appropriations Act of 1992.

Effective Date: The effective date of this amendment is November 27, 1991.

438. Amendment: Section 1B1.2(a) is amended by deleting "conviction by a plea of guilty or nolo contendere" and inserting in lieu thereof "a plea agreement (written or made orally on the record)".

Section 1B1.2(c) is amended by deleting "conviction by a plea of guilty or nolo contendere" and inserting in lieu thereof "plea agreement (written or made orally on the record)".

The Commentary to § 1B1.2 captioned "Application Notes" is amended in Note 5 by deleting "jury's verdict" and inserting in lieu thereof "verdict or plea".

Reason for Amendment: This amendment revises the language of this guideline to clarify the meaning of the term "stipulation," complementing an amendment to the commentary of this guideline effective November 1, 1991 (amendment 434). Both this amendment and amendment 434 were made in response to Braxton v. United States, 111 S.Ct. 1854 (1991). In addition, the term "jury's verdict" in the commentary of this section is deleted and replaced with the more appropriate term "verdict or plea".

Effective Date: The effective date of this amendment is November 1, 1992.

439. Amendment: Section 1B1.3(a) is amended by deleting:

"(1) all acts and omissions committed or aided and abetted by the defendant, or for which the defendant would be otherwise accountable, that occurred during the commission of the offense of conviction, in preparation for that offense, or in the course of attempting to avoid detection or responsibility for that offense, or that otherwise were in furtherance of that offense;

(2) solely with respect to offenses of a character for which § 3D1.2(d) would require grouping of multiple counts, all such acts and omissions that were part of the same course of conduct or common scheme or plan as the offense of conviction;

(3) all harm that resulted from the acts or omissions specified in subsections (a)(1) and (a)(2) above, and all harm that was the object of such acts or omissions; and",

and inserting in lieu thereof:

"(1) (A) all acts and omissions committed, aided, abetted, counseled, commanded, induced, procured, or willfully caused by the defendant; and

(B) in the case of a jointly undertaken criminal activity (a criminal plan, scheme, endeavor, or enterprise undertaken by the defendant in concert with others, whether or not charged as a conspiracy), all reasonably foreseeable acts and omissions of others in furtherance of the jointly undertaken criminal activity,

that occurred during the commission of the offense of conviction, in preparation for that offense, or in the course of attempting to avoid detection or responsibility for that offense;

(2) solely with respect to offenses of a character for which § 3D1.2(d) would require grouping of multiple counts, all acts and omissions described in subdivisions (1)(A) and (1)(B) above that were part of the same course of conduct or common scheme or plan as the offense of conviction;

(3) all harm that resulted from the acts and omissions specified in subsections (a)(1) and (a)(2) above, and all harm that was the object of such acts and omissions; and".

The Commentary to § 1B1.3 captioned "Application Notes" is amended by renumbering Notes 2-7 as Notes 3-8, respectively; and by deleting Note 1 as follows:

"1. Conduct 'for which the defendant would be otherwise accountable,' as used in subsection (a)(1), includes conduct that the defendant counseled, commanded, induced, procured, or willfully caused. (Cf. 18 U.S.C. § 2.) In the case of criminal activity undertaken in concert with others, whether or not charged as a conspiracy, the conduct for which the defendant 'would be otherwise accountable' also includes conduct of others in furtherance of the execution of the jointly-undertaken criminal activity that was reasonably foreseeable by the defendant. Because a count may be broadly worded and include the conduct of many participants over a substantial period of time, the scope of the jointly-undertaken criminal activity, and hence relevant conduct, is not necessarily the same for every participant. Where it is established that the conduct was neither within the scope of the defendant's agreement, nor was reasonably foreseeable in connection with the criminal activity the defendant agreed to jointly undertake, such conduct is not included in establishing the defendant's offense level under this guideline.

In the case of solicitation, misprision, or accessory after the fact, the conduct for which the defendant 'would be otherwise accountable' includes all conduct relevant to determining the offense level for the underlying offense that was known, or reasonably should have been known, by the defendant.

Illustrations of Conduct for Which the Defendant is Accountable

a. Defendant A, one of ten off-loaders hired by Defendant B, was convicted of importation of marihuana, as a result of his assistance in off-loading a boat containing a one-ton shipment of marihuana. Regardless of the number of bales of marihuana that he actually unloaded, and notwithstanding any claim on his part that he was neither aware of, nor could reasonably foresee, that the boat contained this quantity of marihuana, Defendant A is held accountable for the entire one-ton quantity of marihuana on the boat because he aided and abetted the unloading, and hence the importation, of the entire shipment.

b. Defendant C, the getaway driver in an armed bank robbery in which $15,000 is taken and a teller is injured, is convicted of the substantive count of bank robbery. Defendant C is accountable for the money taken because he aided and abetted the taking of the money. He is accountable for the injury inflicted because he participated in concerted criminal conduct that he could reasonably foresee might result in the infliction of injury.

c. Defendant D pays Defendant E a small amount to forge an endorsement on an $800 stolen government check. Unknown to Defendant E, Defendant D then uses that check as a down payment in a scheme to fraudulently obtain $15,000 worth of merchandise. Defendant E is convicted of forging the $800 check.

Amendment 439 APPENDIX C - VOLUME I November 1, 2013

Defendant E is not accountable for the $15,000 because the fraudulent scheme to obtain $15,000 was beyond the scope of, and not reasonably foreseeable in connection with, the criminal activity he jointly undertook with Defendant D.

d. Defendants F and G, working together, design and execute a scheme to sell fraudulent stocks by telephone. Defendant F fraudulently obtains $20,000. Defendant G fraudulently obtains $35,000. Each is convicted of mail fraud. Each defendant is accountable for the entire amount ($55,000) because each aided and abetted the other in the fraudulent conduct. Alternatively, because Defendants F and G engaged in concerted criminal activity, each is accountable for the entire $55,000 loss because the conduct of each was in furtherance of the jointly undertaken criminal activity and was reasonably foreseeable.

e. Defendants H and I engaged in an ongoing marihuana importation conspiracy in which Defendant J was hired only to help off-load a single shipment. Defendants H, I, and J are included in a single count charging conspiracy to import marihuana. For the purposes of determining the offense level under this guideline, Defendant J is accountable for the entire single shipment of marihuana he conspired to help import and any acts or omissions in furtherance of the importation that were reasonably foreseeable. He is not accountable for prior or subsequent shipments of marihuana imported by Defendants H or I if those acts were beyond the scope of, and not reasonably foreseeable in connection with, the criminal activity he agreed to jointly undertake with Defendants H and I (i.e., the importation of the single shipment of marihuana).",

and inserting in lieu thereof:

"1. The principles and limits of sentencing accountability under this guideline are not always the same as the principles and limits of criminal liability. Under subsections (a)(1) and (a)(2), the focus is on the specific acts and omissions for which the defendant is to be held accountable in determining the applicable guideline range, rather than on whether the defendant is criminally liable for an offense as a principal, accomplice, or conspirator.

2. A 'jointly undertaken criminal activity' is a criminal plan, scheme, endeavor, or enterprise undertaken by the defendant in concert with others, whether or not charged as a conspiracy.

In the case of a jointly undertaken criminal activity, subsection (a)(1)(B) provides that a defendant is accountable for the conduct (acts and omissions) of others that was both:

(i) in furtherance of the jointly undertaken criminal activity; and

(ii) reasonably foreseeable in connection with that criminal activity.

Because a count may be worded broadly and include the conduct of many participants over a period of time, the scope of the criminal activity jointly undertaken by the defendant (the 'jointly undertaken criminal activity') is not necessarily the same as the scope of the entire conspiracy, and hence relevant conduct is not necessarily the same for every participant. In order to determine the defendant's accountability for the conduct of others under subsection (a)(1)(B), the court must first determine the scope of the criminal activity the particular defendant agreed to jointly undertake (i.e., the scope of the specific conduct and objectives embraced by the defendant's agreement). The conduct of others that was both in furtherance of, and reasonably foreseeable in connection with, the criminal activity jointly undertaken by the defendant is relevant conduct under this provision. The conduct of others that was not in furtherance of the criminal activity jointly undertaken by the defendant, or was not reasonably foreseeable in connection with that criminal activity, is not relevant conduct under this provision.

In determining the scope of the criminal activity that the particular defendant agreed to jointly undertake (i.e., the scope of the specific conduct and objectives embraced by the defendant's agreement), the court may consider any explicit agreement or implicit agreement fairly inferred from the conduct of the defendant and others.

Note that the criminal activity that the defendant agreed to jointly undertake, and the reasonably foreseeable conduct of others in furtherance of that criminal activity, are not necessarily identical. For example, two defendants agree to commit a robbery and, during the course of that robbery, the first defendant assaults and injures a victim. The second defendant is accountable for the assault and injury to the victim (even if the second defendant had not agreed to the assault and had cautioned the first defendant to be careful not to hurt anyone) because the assaultive conduct was in furtherance of the jointly undertaken criminal activity (the robbery) and was reasonably foreseeable in connection with that criminal activity (given the nature of the offense).

With respect to offenses involving contraband (including controlled substances), the defendant is accountable for all quantities of contraband with which he was directly involved and, in the case of a jointly undertaken criminal activity, all reasonably foreseeable quantities of contraband that were within the scope of the criminal activity that he jointly undertook.

The requirement of reasonable foreseeability applies only in respect to the conduct (i.e., acts and omissions) of others under subsection (a)(1)(B). It does not apply to conduct that the defendant personally undertakes, aids, abets, counsels, commands, induces, procures, or willfully causes; such conduct is addressed under subsection (a)(1)(A).

<u>Illustrations of Conduct for Which the Defendant is Accountable</u>

(a) <u>Acts and omissions aided or abetted by the defendant</u>

(1) Defendant A is one of ten persons hired by Defendant B to off-load a ship containing marihuana. The off-loading of the ship is interrupted by law enforcement officers and one ton of marihuana is seized (the amount on the ship as well as the amount off-loaded). Defendant A and the other off-loaders are arrested and convicted of importation of marihuana. Regardless of the number of bales he personally unloaded, Defendant A is accountable for the entire one-ton quantity of marihuana. Defendant A aided and abetted the off-loading of the entire shipment of marihuana by directly participating in the off-loading of that shipment (i.e., the specific objective of the criminal activity he joined was the off-loading of the entire shipment). Therefore, he is accountable for the entire shipment under subsection (a)(1)(A)

without regard to the issue of reasonable foreseeability. This is conceptually similar to the case of a defendant who transports a suitcase knowing that it contains a controlled substance and, therefore, is accountable for the controlled substance in the suitcase regardless of his knowledge or lack of knowledge of the actual type or amount of that controlled substance.

In certain cases, a defendant may be accountable for particular conduct under more than one subsection of this guideline. As noted in the preceding paragraph, Defendant A is accountable for the entire one-ton shipment of marihuana under subsection (a)(1)(A). Defendant A also is accountable for the entire one-ton shipment of marihuana on the basis of subsection (a)(1)(B)(applying to a jointly undertaken criminal activity). Defendant A engaged in a jointly undertaken criminal activity (the scope of which was the importation of the shipment of marihuana). A finding that the one-ton quantity of marihuana was reasonably foreseeable is warranted from the nature of the undertaking itself (the importation of marihuana by ship typically involves very large quantities of marihuana). The specific circumstances of the case (the defendant was one of ten persons off-loading the marihuana in bales) also support this finding. In an actual case, of course, if a defendant's accountability for particular conduct is established under one provision of this guideline, it is not necessary to review alternative provisions under which such accountability might be established.

(b) <u>Acts and omissions aided or abetted by the defendant; requirement that the conduct of others be in furtherance of the jointly undertaken criminal activity and reasonably foreseeable</u>

(1) Defendant C is the getaway driver in an armed bank robbery in which $15,000 is taken and a teller is assaulted and injured. Defendant C is accountable for the money taken under subsection (a)(1)(A) because he aided and abetted the act of taking the money (the taking of money was the specific objective of the offense he joined). Defendant C is accountable for the injury to the teller under subsection (a)(1)(B) because the assault on the teller was in furtherance of the jointly undertaken criminal activity (the robbery) and was reasonably foreseeable in connection with that criminal activity (given the nature of the offense).

As noted earlier, a defendant may be accountable for particular conduct under more than one subsection. In this example, Defendant C also is accountable for the money taken on the basis of subsection (a)(1)(B) because the taking of money was in furtherance of the jointly undertaken criminal activity (the robbery) and was reasonably foreseeable (as noted, the taking of money was the specific objective of the jointly undertaken criminal activity).

(c) <u>Requirement that the conduct of others be in furtherance of the jointly undertaken criminal activity and reasonably foreseeable; scope of the criminal activity</u>

(1) Defendant D pays Defendant E a small amount to forge an endorsement on an $800 stolen government check. Unknown to Defendant E, Defendant D then uses that check as a down payment in a scheme to fraudulently obtain $15,000 worth of merchandise. Defendant E is convicted of forging the $800 check and is accountable for the forgery of this check under subsection (a)(1)(A). Defendant E is not accountable for the $15,000 because the fraudulent scheme to obtain $15,000 was not in furtherance of the criminal activity he jointly undertook with Defendant D (i.e., the forgery of the $800 check).

(2) Defendants F and G, working together, design and execute a scheme to sell fraudulent stocks by telephone. Defendant F fraudulently obtains $20,000. Defendant G fraudulently obtains $35,000. Each is convicted of mail fraud. Defendants F and G each are accountable for the entire amount ($55,000). Each defendant is accountable for the amount he personally obtained under subsection (a)(1)(A). Each defendant is accountable for the amount obtained by his accomplice under subsection (a)(1)(B) because the conduct of each was in furtherance of the jointly undertaken criminal activity and was reasonably foreseeable in connection with that criminal activity.

(3) Defendants H and I engaged in an ongoing marihuana importation conspiracy in which Defendant J was hired only to help off-load a single shipment. Defendants H, I, and J are included in a single count charging conspiracy to import marihuana. Defendant J is accountable for the entire single shipment of marihuana he helped import under subsection (a)(1)(A) and any acts and omissions in furtherance of the importation of that shipment that were reasonably foreseeable (see the discussion in example (a)(1) above). He is not accountable for prior or subsequent shipments of marihuana imported by Defendants H or I because those acts were not in furtherance of his jointly undertaken criminal activity (the importation of the single shipment of marihuana).

(4) Defendant K is a wholesale distributor of child pornography. Defendant L is a retail-level dealer who purchases child pornography from Defendant K and resells it, but otherwise operates independently of Defendant K. Similarly, Defendant M is a retail-level dealer who purchases child pornography from Defendant K and resells it, but otherwise operates independently of Defendant K. Defendants L and M are aware of each other's criminal activity but operate independently. Defendant N is Defendant K's assistant who recruits customers for Defendant K and frequently supervises the deliveries to Defendant K's customers. Each

defendant is convicted of a count charging conspiracy to distribute child pornography. Defendant K is accountable under subsection (a)(1)(A) for the entire quantity of child pornography sold to Defendants L and M. Defendant N also is accountable for the entire quantity sold to those defendants under subsection (a)(1)(B) because the entire quantity was within the scope of his jointly undertaken criminal activity and reasonably foreseeable. Defendant L is accountable under subsection (a)(1)(A) only for the quantity of child pornography that he purchased from Defendant K because the scope of his jointly undertaken criminal activity is limited to that amount. For the same reason, Defendant M is accountable under subsection (a)(1)(A) only for the quantity of child pornography that he purchased from Defendant K.

(5) Defendant O knows about her boyfriend's ongoing drug-trafficking activity, but agrees to participate on only one occasion by making a delivery for him at his request when he was ill. Defendant O is accountable under subsection (a)(1)(A) for the drug quantity involved on that one occasion. Defendant O is not accountable for the other drug sales made by her boyfriend because those sales were not in furtherance of her jointly undertaken criminal activity (i.e., the one delivery).

(6) Defendant P is a street-level drug dealer who knows of other street-level drug dealers in the same geographic area who sell the same type of drug as he sells. Defendant P and the other dealers share a common source of supply, but otherwise operate independently. Defendant P is not accountable for the quantities of drugs sold by the other street-level drug dealers because he is not engaged in a jointly undertaken criminal activity with them. In contrast, Defendant Q, another street-level drug dealer, pools his resources and profits with four other street-level drug dealers. Defendant Q is engaged in a jointly undertaken criminal activity and, therefore, he is accountable under subsection (a)(1)(B) for the quantities of drugs sold by the four other dealers during the course of his joint undertaking with them because those sales were in furtherance of the jointly undertaken criminal activity and reasonably foreseeable in connection with that criminal activity.

(7) Defendant R recruits Defendant S to distribute 500 grams of cocaine. Defendant S knows that Defendant R is the prime figure in a conspiracy involved in importing much larger quantities of cocaine. As long as Defendant S's agreement and conduct is limited to the distribution of the 500 grams, Defendant S is accountable only for that 500 gram amount (under subsection (a)(1)(A)), rather than the much larger quantity imported by Defendant R.

(8) Defendants T, U, V, and W are hired by a supplier to backpack a quantity of marihuana across the border from

Mexico into the United States. Defendants T, U, V, and W receive their individual shipments from the supplier at the same time and coordinate their importation efforts by walking across the border together for mutual assistance and protection. Each defendant is accountable for the aggregate quantity of marihuana transported by the four defendants. The four defendants engaged in a jointly undertaken criminal activity, the object of which was the importation of the four backpacks containing marihuana (subsection (a)(1)(B)), and aided and abetted each other's actions (subsection (a)(1)(A)) in carrying out the jointly undertaken criminal activity. In contrast, if Defendants T, U, V, and W were hired individually, transported their individual shipments at different times, and otherwise operated independently, each defendant would be accountable only for the quantity of marihuana he personally transported (subsection (a)(1)(A)). As this example illustrates, in cases involving contraband (including controlled substances), the scope of the jointly undertaken criminal activity (and thus the accountability of the defendant for the contraband that was the object of that jointly undertaken activity) may depend upon whether, in the particular circumstances, the nature of the offense is more appropriately viewed as one jointly undertaken criminal activity or as a number of separate criminal activities.".

The Commentary to § 1B1.3 captioned "Application Notes" is amended in Note 3 (formerly Note 2) by deleting the first sentence as follows:

"'Such acts and omissions that were part of the same course of conduct or common scheme or plan as the offense of conviction,' as used in subsection (a)(2), refers to acts and omissions committed or aided and abetted by the defendant, or for which the defendant would be otherwise accountable, that were part of the same course of conduct or common scheme or plan as the offense of conviction.".

The Commentary to § 1B1.3 captioned "Application Notes" is amended in Note 6 (formerly Note 5) in the first paragraph by deleting:

"For example, in § 2K1.5, subsection (b)(1) applies 'If the defendant is convicted under 49 U.S.C. § 1472(l)(2).'",

and inserting in lieu thereof:

"For example, in § 2S1.1, subsection (a)(1) applies if the defendant 'is convicted under 18 U.S.C. § 1956(a)(1)(A), (a)(2)(A), or (a)(3)(A).'";

and in the second paragraph by deleting:

"For example, § 2K1.5(b)(1) (which is applicable only if the defendant is convicted under 49 U.S.C. § 1472(l)(2)) would be applied in determining the offense level under § 2X3.1 (Accessory After the Fact) where the defendant was convicted of accessory after the fact to a violation of 49 U.S.C. § 1472(l)(2).",

and inserting in lieu thereof:

"For example, § 2S1.1(a)(1) (which is applicable only if the defendant is convicted under 18 U.S.C. § 1956(a)(1)(A), (a)(2)(A), or (a)(3)(A)) would be applied in determining the offense level under § 2X3.1 (Accessory After the Fact) where the defendant was convicted of accessory after the fact to a violation of 18 U.S.C. § 1956(a)(1)(A),(a)(2)(A), or (a)(3)(A).".

The Commentary to § 1B1.3 captioned "Application Notes" is amended by inserting the following additional notes:

"9. 'Common scheme or plan' and 'same course of conduct' are two closely-related concepts.

(A) Common scheme or plan. For two or more offenses to constitute part of a common scheme or plan, they must be substantially connected to each other by at least one common factor, such as common victims, common accomplices, common purpose, or similar modus operandi. For example, the conduct of five defendants who together defrauded a group of investors by computer manipulations that unlawfully transferred funds over an eighteen-month period would qualify as a common scheme or plan on the basis of any of the above listed factors; i.e., the commonality of victims (the same investors were defrauded on an ongoing basis), commonality of offenders (the conduct constituted an ongoing conspiracy), commonality of purpose (to defraud the group of investors), or similarity of modus operandi (the same or similar computer manipulations were used to execute the scheme).

(B) Same course of conduct. Offenses that do not qualify as part of a common scheme or plan may nonetheless qualify as part of the same course of conduct if they are sufficiently connected or related to each other as to warrant the conclusion that they are part of a single episode, spree, or ongoing series of offenses. Factors that are appropriate to the determination of whether offenses are sufficiently connected or related to each other to be considered as part of the same course of conduct include the degree of similarity of the offenses and the time interval between the offenses. The nature of the offenses may also be a relevant consideration (e.g., a defendant's failure to file tax returns in three consecutive years appropriately would be considered as part of the same course of conduct because such returns are only required at yearly intervals).

10. In the case of solicitation, misprision, or accessory after the fact, the conduct for which the defendant is accountable includes all conduct relevant to determining the offense level for the underlying offense that was known, or reasonably should have been known, by the defendant.".

Reason for Amendment: This amendment clarifies and more fully illustrates the operation of this guideline. Material is moved from the commentary to the guideline itself and rephrased for greater clarity, the discussion of the application of this provision in the commentary is expanded, and additional examples are inserted. In addition, this amendment provides definitions of the terms "same course of conduct" and "common scheme or plan." Finally, this amendment conforms an example in Application Note 6 of the Commentary to a revision of a Chapter Two offense guideline.

Effective Date: The effective date of this amendment is November 1, 1992.

440. Amendment: Section 1B1.5 is amended by deleting:

"Unless otherwise expressly indicated, a reference to another guideline, or an instruction to apply another guideline, refers to the entire guideline, i.e., the base offense level plus all applicable specific offense characteristics and cross references.",

and inserting in lieu thereof:

"(a) A cross reference (an instruction to apply another offense guideline) refers to the entire offense guideline (i.e., the base offense level, specific offense characteristics, cross references, and special instructions).

(b) (1) An instruction to use the offense level from another offense guideline refers to the offense level from the entire offense guideline (i.e., the base offense level, specific offense characteristics, cross references, and special instructions), except as provided in subdivision (2) below.

(2) An instruction to use a particular subsection or table from another offense guideline refers only to the particular subsection or table referenced, and not to the entire offense guideline.

(c) If the offense level is determined by a reference to another guideline under subsection (a) or (b)(1) above, the adjustments in Chapter Three (Adjustments) also are determined in respect to the referenced offense guideline, except as otherwise expressly provided.

(d) A reference to another guideline under subsection (a) or (b)(1) above may direct that it be applied only if it results in the greater offense level. In such case, the greater offense level means the greater final offense level (i.e., the greater offense level taking into account both the Chapter Two offense level and any applicable Chapter Three adjustments).".

The Commentary to § 1B1.5 captioned "Application Notes" is amended in Note 1 by deleting:

"are to be construed to incorporate the specific offense characteristics and cross references",

and inserting in lieu thereof:

"incorporate the specific offense characteristics, cross references, and special instructions".

The Commentary to § 1B1.5 captioned "Application Notes" is amended by deleting Note 2 as follows:

"2. A reference may require that the offense level be determined under another offense guideline. In such case, the adjustments in Chapter Three, Parts A (Victim-Related Adjustments), B (Role in the Offense), and E (Acceptance of Responsibility) are also to be determined in respect to that other offense guideline. For example, a defendant convicted of possession of a firearm by a felon, to which § 2K2.1 (Unlawful Receipt, Possession, or Transportation of Firearms or Ammunition; Prohibited Transactions Involving Firearms or Ammunition) applies, is found to have used that firearm in the commission of a robbery. The cross reference at § 2K2.1(c) directs that the robbery offense guideline be used. The adjustments in Chapter Three, Parts A, B and E are to be applied as if the offense of conviction had directly referenced the robbery guideline.";

and by renumbering Notes 3 and 4 as Notes 2 and 3, respectively.

Reason for Amendment: This amendment clarifies the operation of this guideline and moves an instruction currently contained in the commentary into the guideline itself.

Effective Date: The effective date of this amendment is November 1, 1992.

441. **Amendment:** Section 1B1.8(b) is amended in subdivision (3) by deleting "or" immediately following the semicolon; in subdivision (4) by deleting the period at the end and inserting in lieu thereof "; or"; and by inserting the following additional subdivision:

> "(5) in determining whether, or to what extent, a downward departure from the guidelines is warranted pursuant to a government motion under § 5K1.1 (Substantial Assistance to Authorities).".

The Commentary to § 1B1.8 captioned "Application Notes" is amended in Note 1 by deleting the third sentence as follows:

> "Although this guideline, consistent with the general structure of these guidelines, affects only the determination of the guideline range, the policy of the Commission is that where a defendant as a result of a cooperation agreement with the government to assist in the investigation or prosecution of other offenders reveals information that implicates him in unlawful conduct not already known to the government, such defendant should not be subject to an increased sentence by virtue of that cooperation where the government agreed that the information revealed would not be used for such purpose.",

and inserting in lieu thereof:

> "Although the guideline itself affects only the determination of the guideline range, the policy of the Commission, as a corollary, is that information prohibited from being used to determine the applicable guideline range shall not be used to increase the defendant's sentence above the applicable guideline range by upward departure. In contrast, subsection (b)(5) provides that consideration of such information is appropriate in determining whether, and to what extent, a downward departure is warranted pursuant to a government motion under § 5K1.1 (Substantial Assistance to Authorities); e.g., a court may refuse to depart below the applicable guideline range on the basis of such information.".

The Commentary to § 1B1.8 captioned "Application Notes" is amended in Note 3 in the second sentence by deleting:

> "is governed by the provisions of Rule 11 of the Federal Rules of Criminal Procedure and Rule 410",

and inserting in lieu thereof:

> "in a sentencing proceeding is restricted by Rule 11(e)(6) (Inadmissibility of Pleas, Plea Discussions, and Related Statements) of the Federal Rules of Criminal Procedure and Rule 410 (Inadmissibility of Pleas, Plea Discussions, and Related Statements)".

The Commentary to § 1B1.8 captioned "Application Notes" is amended in Note 5 in the second sentence by deleting "repeats" and inserting in lieu thereof "provides".

Reason for Amendment: This amendment clarifies the operation of this guideline. Information protected by this guideline may not be used to determine the applicable guideline range. An upward departure on the basis of such information would be contrary to the Commission's policy (and, consequently, would be appealable under 18 U.S.C. § 3742(a)(2) and (3). See Williams v. United States, 112 S.Ct. 1112 (1992)). In contrast, the use of information covered by this guideline is appropriate in considering whether, and to what extent, a downward departure under § 5K1.1 (Substantial Assistance to Authorities) is appropriate. In addition, this amendment makes minor editorial improvements.

Effective Date: The effective date of this amendment is November 1, 1992.

442. **Amendment:** Chapter One, Part B, is amended by inserting an additional policy statement with accompanying commentary as § 1B1.11 (Use of Guidelines Manual in Effect on Date of Sentencing (Policy Statement)).

Reason for Amendment: This amendment inserts a policy statement addressing the use of the Guidelines Manual when the Guidelines Manual has been amended between the date the offense was committed and the date of sentencing.

Effective Date: The effective date of this amendment is November 1, 1992.

443. **Amendment:** Section 2A2.4(c)(1) is amended by deleting "defendant is convicted under 18 U.S.C. § 111 and the" immediately before "conduct".

Section 2K1.5(b)(1) is amended by deleting:

"defendant is convicted under 49 U.S.C. § 1472(l)(2) (i.e., the defendant acted willfully and without regard for the safety of human life, or with reckless disregard for the safety of human life)",

and inserting in lieu thereof:

"offense was committed willfully and without regard for the safety of human life, or with reckless disregard for the safety of human life".

Reason for Amendment: This amendment deletes the requirement of a conviction under a specific statute for these specific offense characteristics to apply and, consistent with the overall structure of the guidelines, provides for their application on the basis of the underlying conduct.

Effective Date: The effective date of this amendment is November 1, 1992.

444. **Amendment:** Section 2A3.1 is amended in the title by deleting "or Assault with the Intent" immediately following "Attempt".

Section 2A3.1(b)(3) is amended by deleting:

"in the custody, care, or supervisory control of the defendant, was a corrections employee, or",

and by inserting in lieu thereof:

"(A) in the custody, care, or supervisory control of the defendant; or (B)".

Section 2A3.1 is amended by inserting the following additional subsection:

"(c) Special Instruction

Amendment 444   APPENDIX C - VOLUME I   November 1, 2013

  (1) If the offense occurred in a correctional facility and the victim was a corrections employee, the offense shall be deemed to have an official victim for purposes of subsection (a) of § 3A1.2 (Official Victim).".

The Commentary to § 2A3.1 captioned "Application Notes" is amended by renumbering Note 3 as Note 4; and by inserting the following additional note:

  "3. Subsection (b)(3), as it pertains to a victim in the custody, care, or supervisory control of the defendant, is intended to have broad application and is to be applied whenever the victim is entrusted to the defendant, whether temporarily or permanently. For example, teachers, day care providers, baby-sitters, or other temporary caretakers are among those who would be subject to this enhancement. In determining whether to apply this enhancement, the court should look to the actual relationship that existed between the defendant and the victim and not simply to the legal status of the defendant-victim relationship.".

Section 2A3.2 is amended by inserting the following additional subsection:

  "(c) Cross Reference

    (1) If the offense involved criminal sexual abuse or attempt to commit criminal sexual abuse (as defined in 18 U.S.C. § 2241 or § 2242), apply § 2A3.1 (Criminal Sexual Abuse; Attempt to Commit Criminal Sexual Abuse).".

The Commentary to § 2A3.2 captioned "Application Notes" is amended by renumbering Note 2 as Note 3; and by inserting the following as Note 2:

  "2. Subsection (b)(1) is intended to have broad application and is to be applied whenever the victim is entrusted to the defendant, whether temporarily or permanently. For example, teachers, day care providers, baby-sitters, or other temporary caretakers are among those who would be subject to this enhancement. In determining whether to apply this enhancement, the court should look to the actual relationship that existed between the defendant and the victim and not simply to the legal status of the defendant-victim relationship.".

Section 2A3.4 is amended by inserting the following additional subsection:

  "(c) Cross References

    (1) If the offense involved criminal sexual abuse or attempt to commit criminal sexual abuse (as defined in 18 U.S.C. § 2241 or § 2242), apply § 2A3.1 (Criminal Sexual Abuse; Attempt to Commit Criminal Sexual Abuse).

    (2) If the offense involved criminal sexual abuse of a minor or attempt to commit criminal sexual abuse of a minor (as defined in 18 U.S.C. § 2243(a)), apply § 2A3.2 (Criminal Sexual Abuse of a Minor or Attempt to Commit Such Acts), if the resulting offense level is greater than that determined above.".

The Commentary to § 2A3.4 captioned "Application Notes" is amended by renumbering Note 3 as Note 4; and by inserting the following as Note 3:

"3. Subsection (b)(3) is intended to have broad application and is to be applied whenever the victim is entrusted to the defendant, whether temporarily or permanently. For example, teachers, day care providers, baby-sitters, or other temporary caretakers are among those who would be subject to this enhancement. In determining whether to apply this enhancement, the court should look to the actual relationship that existed between the defendant and the victim and not simply to the legal status of the defendant-victim relationship.".

Section 2G1.2(c)(2) is amended by deleting "or Assault with the Intent" immediately before "to Commit Criminal Sexual Abuse".

The Commentary to § 2X1.1 captioned "Application Notes" is amended in Note 1 in the second paragraph by deleting "or Assault with the Intent" immediately before "to Commit Criminal Sexual Abuse".

Reason for Amendment: This amendment cross references § 2A3.2 to § 2A3.1, and § 2A3.4 to §§ 2A3.1 and 2A3.2. A review of cases sentenced under these guidelines indicated that a significant proportion of cases sentenced under § 2A3.2 and § 2A3.4 clearly involved conduct that would more appropriately be covered under an offense guideline applicable to more serious sexual abuse cases. The addition of these cross references is designed to address this issue. In addition, this amendment removes an anomaly between § 2A3.1(b)(3) and § 3A1.2(a), and adds application notes to clarify the scope of §§ 2A3.1(b)(3), 2A3.2(b)(1), and 2A3.4(b)(3), using language derived from application notes pertaining to similar specific offense characteristics in Chapter Two, Part G.

Effective Date: The effective date of this amendment is November 1, 1992.

445. **Amendment:** The Commentary to § 2A4.1 captioned "Application Notes" is amended by inserting the following additional note:

"5. In the case of a conspiracy, attempt, or solicitation to kidnap, § 2X1.1 (Attempt, Solicitation, or Conspiracy) requires that the court apply any adjustment that can be determined with reasonable certainty. Therefore, for example, if an offense involved conspiracy to kidnap for the purpose of committing murder, subsection (b)(7) would reference first degree murder (resulting in an offense level of 43, subject to a possible 3-level reduction under § 2X1.1(b)). Similarly, for example, if an offense involved a kidnapping during which a participant attempted to murder the victim under circumstances that would have constituted first degree murder had death occurred, the offense referenced under subsection (b)(7) would be the offense of first degree murder.".

Reason for Amendment: This amendment clarifies the operation of this guideline.

Effective Date: The effective date of this amendment is November 1, 1992.

446. **Amendment:** Section 2D1.1(b)(2) is amended by deleting "is convicted of violating 21 U.S.C. § 960(a)" and inserting in lieu thereof "unlawfully imported or exported a controlled substance"; and by inserting "or export" immediately following "to import".

The Commentary to § 2D1.1 captioned "Application Notes" is amended in Note 10 in the "Drug Equivalency Tables" in the subdivision captioned "Cocaine and Other Schedule I

Amendment 446 APPENDIX C - VOLUME I November 1, 2013

and II Stimulants" by inserting the following additional entries at the end:

> "1 gm of Aminorex = 100 gm of marihuana
> 1 gm of Methcathinone = 380 gm of marihuana
> 1 gm of N-N-Dimethylamphetamine = 40 gm of marihuana";

and in the subdivision captioned "LSD, PCP, and Other Schedule I and II Hallucinogens" by inserting the following additional entry as the last entry:

> "1 gm of Phenylcyclohexamine (PCE) = 5.79 kg of marihuana".

The Commentary to § 2D1.1 captioned "Application Notes" is amended in Note 10 in the "Drug Equivalency Tables" by inserting an asterisk immediately following each of the following subdivision captions: "Schedule I or II Opiates", "Cocaine and Other Schedule I or II Stimulants (and their immediate precursors)", and "LSD, PCP, and Other Schedule I and II Hallucinogens (and their immediate precursors)"; and by inserting the following additional sentence at the end of each of the above noted subdivisions:

> "*Provided*, that the minimum offense level from the Drug Quantity Table for any of these controlled substances individually, or in combination with another controlled substance, is level 12.".

The Commentary to § 2D1.1 captioned "Application Notes" is amended by inserting the following additional note:

> "15. Certain pharmaceutical preparations are classified as Schedule III, IV, or V controlled substances by the Drug Enforcement Administration under 21 C.F.R. § 1308.13-15 even though they contain a small amount of a Schedule I or II controlled substance. For example, Tylenol 3 is classified as a Schedule III controlled substance even though it contains a small amount of codeine, a Schedule II opiate. For the purposes of the guidelines, the classification of the controlled substance under 21 C.F.R. § 1308.13-15 is the appropriate classification.".

The Commentary to § 2D1.1 captioned "Background" is amended in the fifth paragraph by deleting "mandated by" and inserting in lieu thereof "derived from".

Reason for Amendment: This amendment deletes the requirement of a conviction under a specific statute for the specific offense characteristic in subsection (b)(2) to apply and, consistent with the overall structure of the guidelines, provides for the application of this specific offense characteristic on the basis of the underlying conduct. In addition, this amendment adds equivalencies for four controlled substances to make the Drug Equivalency Tables more comprehensive, adds notes to the Drug Equivalency Tables to make clear the interaction between the minimum offense level for certain types of controlled substances in the Drug Quantity Table and the instructions for determining a combined offense level in a case with multiple controlled substances, and clarifies the treatment of certain pharmaceutical preparations that are classified as Schedule III, IV, or V substances under 21 C.F.R. § 1308.13-15.

Effective Date: The effective date of this amendment is November 1, 1992.

447. **Amendment:** Sections 2D1.1, 2D1.2, 2D1.5, 2D1.6, 2D1.7, 2D1.8, 2D1.9, 2D1.10, 2D1.11, 2D1.12, 2D1.13, 2D2.1, 2D2.2, 2D3.1, 2D3.2, 2D3.3, 2D3.4, and 2D3.5 are amended in their titles by inserting at the end thereof in each instance "; Attempt or

Conspiracy".

Section 2D1.4, including accompanying commentary, is deleted as follows:

"§ 2D1.4. Attempts and Conspiracies

(a) Base Offense Level: If a defendant is convicted of a conspiracy or an attempt to commit any offense involving a controlled substance, the offense level shall be the same as if the object of the conspiracy or attempt had been completed.

Commentary

Statutory Provisions: 21 U.S.C. §§ 846, 963. For additional statutory provision(s), see Appendix A (Statutory Index).

Application Notes:

1. If the defendant is convicted of a conspiracy that includes transactions in controlled substances in addition to those that are the subject of substantive counts of conviction, each conspiracy transaction shall be included with those of the substantive counts of conviction to determine scale. If the defendant is convicted of an offense involving negotiation to traffic in a controlled substance, the weight under negotiation in an uncompleted distribution shall be used to calculate the applicable amount. However, where the court finds that the defendant did not intend to produce and was not reasonably capable of producing the negotiated amount, the court shall exclude from the guideline calculation the amount that it finds the defendant did not intend to produce and was not reasonably capable of producing. If the defendant is convicted of conspiracy, see Application Note 1 to § 1B1.3 (Relevant Conduct).

2. Where there is no drug seizure or the amount seized does not reflect the scale of the offense, the sentencing judge shall approximate the quantity of the controlled substance. In making this determination, the judge may consider, for example, the price generally obtained for the controlled substance, financial or other records, similar transactions in controlled substances by the defendant, and the size or capability of any laboratory involved.

3. See Commentary to § 2D1.1 regarding weapon possession.".

The Commentary to § 2D1.1 captioned "Application Notes" is amended in Note 3 by deleting "reference § 2D1.1, i.e., §§ 2D1.2, 2D1.4, 2D1.5, 2D1.6, 2D1.7(b)(1)" and inserting in lieu thereof "are referenced to § 2D1.1; see §§ 2D1.2(a)(1) and (2), 2D1.5(a)(1), 2D1.6, 2D1.7(b)(1), 2D1.8, 2D1.11(c)(1), 2D1.12(b)(1), and 2D2.1(b)(1)".

The Commentary to § 2D1.1 captioned "Application Notes" is amended in Note 12 by deleting:

"If the amount seized does not reflect the scale of the offense, see Application Note 2 of the Commentary to § 2D1.4. If the offense involved negotiation to traffic in a controlled substance, see Application Note 1 of the Commentary to § 2D1.4.",

and inserting in lieu thereof:

"Where there is no drug seizure or the amount seized does not reflect the scale of the offense, the court shall approximate the quantity of the controlled substance. In making this determination, the court may consider, for example, the price generally obtained for the controlled substance, financial or other records, similar transactions in controlled substances by the defendant, and the size or capability of any laboratory involved.

If the offense involved both a substantive drug offense and an attempt or conspiracy (e.g., sale of five grams of heroin and an attempt to sell an additional ten grams of heroin), the total quantity involved shall be aggregated to determine the scale of the offense.

In an offense involving negotiation to traffic in a controlled substance, the weight under negotiation in an uncompleted distribution shall be used to calculate the applicable amount. However, where the court finds that the defendant did not intend to produce and was not reasonably capable of producing the negotiated amount, the court shall exclude from the guideline calculation the amount that it finds the defendant did not intend to produce and was not reasonably capable of producing.".

The Commentary to § 2D1.1 captioned "Background" is amended in the fifth sentence of the fourth paragraph by deleting "(see § 2D1.4)" immediately following "object of the attempt".

The Commentary to § 2D1.6 captioned "Application Note" is amended in the first sentence of Note 1 by deleting "Commentary to § 2D1.1, and Application Notes 1 and 2 of the Commentary to § 2D1.4," and inserting in lieu thereof "Commentary to § 2D1.1".

Section 2D1.11(c) is amended by deleting ", or § 2D1.4 (Attempts and Conspiracies), as appropriate," immediately before "if the resulting".

Section 2D1.12(b) is amended by deleting ", or § 2D1.4 (Attempts and Conspiracies), as appropriate," immediately before "if the resulting".

The Commentary to § 2X1.1 captioned "Application Notes" is amended in Note 1 by deleting "§ 2D1.4 (Attempts and Conspiracies)" wherever it appears and inserting in lieu thereof in each instance:

"§ 2D1.1 (Unlawful Manufacturing, Importing, Exporting, or Trafficking, Including Possession with Intent to Commit These Offenses; Attempt or Conspiracy); § 2D1.2 (Drug Offenses Occurring Near Protected Locations or Involving Underage or Pregnant Individuals; Attempt or Conspiracy); § 2D1.5 (Continuing Criminal Enterprise; Attempt or Conspiracy); § 2D1.6 (Use of Communication Facility in Committing Drug Offense; Attempt or Conspiracy); § 2D1.7 (Unlawful Sale or Transportation of Drug Paraphernalia; Attempt or Conspiracy); § 2D1.8 (Renting or Managing a Drug Establishment; Attempt or Conspiracy); § 2D1.9 (Placing or Maintaining Dangerous Devices on Federal Property to Protect the Unlawful Production of Controlled Substances; Attempt or Conspiracy); § 2D1.10 (Endangering Human Life While Illegally Manufacturing a Controlled Substance; Attempt or Conspiracy); § 2D1.11 (Unlawfully Distributing, Importing, Exporting or Possessing a Listed Chemical; Attempt or Conspiracy); § 2D1.12 (Unlawful Possession, Manufacture, Distribution, or Importation of Prohibited Flask or Equipment; Attempt or Conspiracy); § 2D1.13 (Structuring Chemical Transactions or Creating a Chemical Mixture to Evade Reporting or Recordkeeping Requirements; Presenting False or Fraudulent Identification to Obtain a Listed Chemical; Attempt or Conspiracy); § 2D2.1 (Unlawful Possession; Attempt or Conspiracy); § 2D2.2 (Acquiring a Controlled Substance by Forgery, Fraud, Deception, or Subterfuge; Attempt or Conspiracy); § 2D3.1 (Illegal Use of Registration Number to Manufacture, Distribute, Acquire, or Dispense a Controlled Substance; Attempt or Conspiracy); § 2D3.2

(Manufacture of Controlled Substance in Excess of or Unauthorized by Registration Quota; Attempt or Conspiracy); § 2D3.3 (Illegal Use of Registration Number to Distribute or Dispense a Controlled Substance to Another Registrant or Authorized Person; Attempt or Conspiracy); § 2D3.4 (Illegal Transfer or Transshipment of a Controlled Substance; Attempt or Conspiracy); and § 2D3.5 (Violation of Recordkeeping or Reporting Requirements for Listed Chemicals and Certain Machines; Attempt or Conspiracy)".

Reason for Amendment: This amendment clarifies and simplifies the guideline provisions dealing with attempts and conspiracies in drug cases and conforms the structure of these provisions to that of other offense guidelines that specifically address attempts and conspiracies (i.e., offense guidelines referenced by § 2X1.1(c)).

Effective Date: The effective date of this amendment is November 1, 1992.

448. **Amendment:** Section 2D1.8 is amended by deleting subsections (a) and (b) as follows:

"(a) Base Offense Level: 16

(b) Specific Offense Characteristic

(1) If a firearm or other dangerous weapon was possessed, increase by 2 levels.",

and inserting in lieu thereof:

"(a) Base Offense Level:

(1) The offense level from § 2D1.1 applicable to the underlying controlled substance offense, except as provided below.

(2) If the defendant had no participation in the underlying controlled substance offense other than allowing use of the premises, the offense level shall be 4 levels less than the offense level from § 2D1.1 applicable to the underlying controlled substance offense, but not greater than level 16.

(b) Special Instruction

(1) If the offense level is determined under subsection (a)(2), do not apply an adjustment under § 3B1.2 (Mitigating Role).".

The Commentary to § 2D1.8 captioned "Application Note" is amended by deleting Note 1 as follows:

"1. Definitions of 'firearm' and 'dangerous weapon' are found in the Commentary to § 1B1.1 (Application Instructions).",

and inserting in lieu thereof:

"1. Subsection (a)(2) does not apply unless the defendant had no participation in the underlying controlled substance offense other than allowing use of the premises. For example, subsection (a)(2) would not apply to a defendant who possessed a dangerous weapon in connection with the offense, a defendant who guarded the cache of controlled substances, a defendant who

– 293 –

Amendment 448 APPENDIX C - VOLUME I November 1, 2013

arranged for the use of the premises for the purpose of facilitating a drug transaction, a defendant who allowed the use of more than one premises, a defendant who made telephone calls to facilitate the underlying controlled substance offense, or a defendant who otherwise assisted in the commission of the underlying controlled substance offense. Furthermore, subsection (a)(2) does not apply unless the defendant initially leased, rented, purchased, or otherwise acquired a possessory interest in the premises for a legitimate purpose. Finally, subsection (a)(2) does not apply if the defendant had previously allowed any premises to be used as a drug establishment without regard to whether such prior misconduct resulted in a conviction.".

Reason for Amendment: This amendment is designed to reduce unwarranted disparity by requiring consideration in the guideline of the scale of the underlying controlled substance offense. The amendment parallels an amendment to § 2D1.6 made in 1990 (amendment 320).

Effective Date: The effective date of this amendment is November 1, 1992.

449. **Amendment:** The Commentary to § 2E1.4 captioned "Background" is amended by deleting:

"The statute does not require that a murder covered by this section has been committed. The maximum term of imprisonment authorized by statute ranges from five years to life imprisonment.",

and inserting in lieu thereof:

"This guideline and the statute to which it applies do not require that a murder actually have been committed.".

Reason for Amendment: This amendment makes editorial improvements, and deletes a reference to the length of the maximum term of imprisonment authorized by statute for the offense covered by this section that is no longer accurate.

Effective Date: The effective date of this amendment is November 1, 1992.

450. **Amendment:** Section 2L1.1(b)(2) is amended by deleting:

"If the defendant previously has been convicted of smuggling, transporting, or harboring an unlawful alien, or a related offense, increase by 2 levels.",

and inserting in lieu thereof:

"If the offense involved the smuggling, transporting, or harboring of six or more unlawful aliens, increase as follows:

	Number of Unlawful Aliens Smuggled, Transported, or Harbored	Increase in Level
(A)	6-24	add 2
(B)	25-99	add 4
(C)	100 or more	add 6.".

The Commentary to § 2L1.1 captioned "Application Notes" is amended in Note 1 by inserting the following additional sentence at the end:

> "The 'number of unlawful aliens smuggled, transported, or harbored' does not include the defendant.".

The Commentary to § 2L1.1 captioned "Application Notes" is amended by deleting Notes 2, 3, and 4 as follows:

> "2. 'Convicted of smuggling, transporting, or harboring an unlawful alien, or a related offense' includes any conviction for smuggling, transporting, or harboring an unlawful alien, and any conviction for aiding and abetting, conspiring or attempting to commit such offense.
>
> 3. If the defendant was convicted under 8 U.S.C. § 1328, apply the applicable guideline from Part G (see Statutory Index) rather than this guideline.
>
> 4. The adjustment under § 2L1.1(b)(2) for a previous conviction is in addition to any points added to the criminal history score for such conviction in Chapter Four, Part A (Criminal History). This adjustment is to be applied only if the previous conviction occurred prior to the last overt act of the instant offense.";

and by renumbering Notes 5, 6, 7, 8 and 9, as Notes 2, 3, 4, 5, and 6, respectively.

The Commentary to § 2L1.1 captioned "Application Notes" is amended in Note 4 (formerly Note 7) by inserting "drug trafficking, or other serious criminal behavior," immediately following "subversive activity,".

The Commentary to § 2L1.1 captioned "Application Notes" is amended by deleting the text of Note 5 (formerly Note 8) as follows:

> "The Commission has not considered offenses involving large numbers of aliens or dangerous or inhumane treatment. An upward departure should be considered in those circumstances.",

and inserting in lieu thereof:

> "If the offense involved dangerous or inhumane treatment, death or bodily injury, possession of a dangerous weapon, or substantially more than 100 aliens, an upward departure may be warranted.".

The Commentary to § 2L1.1 captioned "Background" is amended by deleting:

> "A second specific offense characteristic provides an enhancement if the defendant was previously convicted of a similar offense.",

and inserting in lieu thereof:

> "The offense level increases with the number of unlawful aliens smuggled, transported, or harbored. In large scale cases, an additional adjustment from § 3B1.1 (Aggravating Role) typically will apply to the most culpable defendants.".

The title of § 2L2.1 is amended by deleting "Evidence of Citizenship or Documents Authorizing Entry" and inserting in lieu thereof "Documents Relating to Naturalization, Citizenship, or Legal Resident Status; False Statement in Respect to the Citizenship or Immigration Status of Another; Fraudulent Marriage to Assist Alien to Evade Immigration

Amendment 450

Law".

Section 2L2.1(b) is amended by deleting "Characteristic" and inserting in lieu thereof "Characteristics"; and by inserting the following additional specific offense characteristic:

"(2) If the offense involved six or more sets of documents, increase as follows:

	Number of Sets of Documents	Increase in Level
(A)	6-24	add 2
(B)	25-99	add 4
(C)	100 or more	add 6.".

The Commentary to § 2L2.1 captioned "Statutory Provisions" is amended by deleting "18 U.S.C. §§ 1425-1427, 1546. For additional statutory provision(s), see Appendix A (Statutory Index)" and inserting in lieu thereof "8 U.S.C. §§ 1160(b)(7)(A), 1185(a)(3), (4), 1325(b), (c); 18 U.S.C. §§ 1015, 1028, 1425-1427, 1546".

The Commentary to § 2L2.1 captioned "Application Note" is amended by deleting "Note" and inserting in lieu thereof "Notes"; and by inserting the following additional note:

"2. Where it is established that multiple documents are part of a set intended for use by a single person, treat the set as one document.".

The title of § 2L2.2 is amended by deleting "Evidence of Citizenship or Documents Authorizing Entry for Own Use" and inserting in lieu thereof "Documents Relating to Naturalization, Citizenship, or Legal Resident Status for Own Use; False Personation or Fraudulent Marriage by Alien to Evade Immigration Law".

The Commentary to § 2L2.2 captioned "Statutory Provisions" is amended by deleting "18 U.S.C. §§ 1423, 1425, 1546. For additional statutory provision(s), see Appendix A (Statutory Index)" and inserting in lieu thereof "8 U.S.C. §§ 1160(b)(7)(A), 1185(a)(3), (5), 1325(b), (c); 18 U.S.C. §§ 911, 1015, 1028, 1423-1426, 1546".

Section 2L2.3(b) is amended by deleting "Characteristic" and inserting in lieu thereof "Characteristics"; and by inserting the following additional specific offense characteristic:

"(2) If the offense involved six or more passports, increase as follows:

	Number of Passports	Increase in Level
(A)	6-24	add 2
(B)	25-99	add 4
(C)	100 or more	add 6.".

Reason for Amendment: Prior to this amendment, § 2L1.1 provided the same offense level for a defendant who smuggles, transports, or harbors 1, 5, 25, 50, or any number of unlawful aliens. The inclusion of specific offense characteristic (b)(2) in § 2L1.1 in the guidelines as initially promulgated in April 1987 was intended to conform the guidelines to the offense level indicated by past practices data for "ongoing criminal conduct." However, further study has convinced the Commission that the specific offense characteristic "prior conviction for the same or similar offense" is not a good proxy for such conduct. Moreover, the inclusion of a prior criminal record variable in the offense guideline is inconsistent with the general treatment of prior record as a separate dimension in the guidelines.

This amendment addresses these issues by providing an enhancement in the guideline for the number of aliens smuggled, transported, or harbored as a more direct measure of the scope of the offense. Consistent with the Commission's general approach throughout the guidelines, the offense level increases gradually with the number of aliens. It should be noted that § 3B1.1 (Aggravating Role) generally provides an additional increase of 2, 3, or 4 levels for organizers, managers, and supervisors in large-scale cases. The enhancement in this amendment pertaining to the number of aliens is designed to work in conjunction with the operation of the role enhancements from § 3B1.1. Sections 2L2.1 and 2L2.3 are amended to follow the same structure.

In addition, this amendment expands the titles of §§ 2L2.1 and 2L2.2, and the statutory provisions to these sections, to include additional statutes appropriately covered by these guidelines.

Effective Date: The effective date of this amendment is November 1, 1992.

451. Amendment: Section 2N2.1 is amended by inserting the following additional subsection:

"(b) Cross References

(1) If the offense involved fraud, apply § 2F1.1 (Fraud and Deceit).

(2) If the offense was committed in furtherance of, or to conceal, an offense covered by another offense guideline, apply that other offense guideline if the resulting offense level is greater than that determined above.".

The Commentary to § 2N2.1 captioned "Application Notes" is amended by deleting Note 2 as follows:

"2. If the offense involved theft, fraud, bribery, revealing trade secrets, or destruction of property, apply the guideline applicable to the underlying conduct, rather than this guideline.",

and inserting in lieu thereof:

"2. The cross reference at subsection (b)(1) addresses cases in which the offense involved fraud. The cross reference at subsection (b)(2) addresses cases in which the offense was committed in furtherance of, or to conceal, an offense covered by another offense guideline (e.g., theft, bribery, revealing trade secrets, or destruction of property).".

Reason for Amendment: This amendment inserts cross references to cover cases more appropriately addressed by other offense guidelines. Previously, a similar instruction addressing such cases was contained in the commentary to this section.

Effective Date: The effective date of this amendment is November 1, 1992.

452. Amendment: Section 2Q2.1(b)(1) is amended by deleting "involved a commercial purpose" and inserting in lieu thereof "(A) was committed for pecuniary gain or otherwise involved a commercial purpose; or (B) involved a pattern of similar violations".

Section 2Q2.1(b)(2) is amended by deleting:

"involved fish, wildlife, or plants that were not quarantined as required by law",

and inserting in lieu thereof:

"(A) involved fish, wildlife, or plants that were not quarantined as required by law; or (B) otherwise created a significant risk of infestation or disease transmission potentially harmful to humans, fish, wildlife, or plants".

Section 2Q2.1(b)(3)(B) is amended by deleting:

"a quantity of fish, wildlife, or plants that was substantial in relation either to the overall population of the species or to a discrete subpopulation",

and inserting in lieu thereof:

"(i) marine mammals that are listed as depleted under the Marine Mammal Protection Act (as set forth in 50 C.F.R. § 216.15); (ii) fish, wildlife, or plants that are listed as endangered or threatened by the Endangered Species Act (as set forth in 50 C.F.R. Part 17); or (iii) fish, wildlife, or plants that are listed in Appendix I to the Convention on International Trade in Endangered Species of Wild Fauna or Flora (as set forth in 50 C.F.R. Part 23)".

The Commentary to § 2Q2.1 is amended by inserting, immediately before "Background", the following:

"Application Notes:

1. 'For pecuniary gain' means for receipt of, or in anticipation of receipt of, anything of value, whether monetary or in goods or services. Thus, offenses committed for pecuniary gain include both monetary and barter transactions. Similarly, activities designed to increase gross revenue are considered to be committed for pecuniary gain.

2. The acquisition of fish, wildlife, or plants for display to the public, whether for a fee or donation and whether by an individual or an organization, including a governmental entity, a private non-profit organization, or a private for-profit organization, shall be considered to involve a 'commercial purpose.'

3. For purposes of subsection (b)(2), the quarantine requirements include those set forth in 9 C.F.R. Part 92, and 7 C.F.R. Chapter III. State quarantine laws are included as well.

4. When information is reasonably available, 'market value' under subsection (b)(3)(A) shall be based on the fair-market retail price. Where the fair-market retail price is difficult to ascertain, the court may make a reasonable estimate using any reliable information, such as the reasonable replacement or restitution cost or the acquisition and preservation (e.g., taxidermy) cost. Market value, however, shall not be based on measurement of aesthetic loss (so called 'contingent valuation' methods).

5. If the offense involved the destruction of a substantial quantity of fish, wildlife, or plants, and the seriousness of the offense is not adequately measured by the market value, an upward departure may be warranted.".

The Commentary to § 2Q2.1 captioned "Background" is amended by deleting the last two sentences as follows:

"Enhancements are provided where the offense involved a commercial purpose, and where the fish, wildlife, or plants were not quarantined as required by law. An additional enhancement is provided where the market value of the species exceeded $2,000 or the offense involved a quantity of fish, wildlife, or plants that was substantial in relation either to the population of the species or to a discrete subpopulation of the species.".

Reason for Amendment: This amendment is designed to strengthen the deterrent effect of the sanctions for violations covered by this guideline. The amendment expands the specific offense characteristic in subsection (b)(1) to cover categories of offenses that appear to be equally serious to those committed for a commercial purpose. In addition, the amendment expands the specific offense characteristic in subsection (b)(2) to cover other comparable types of risk of harm. Furthermore, the amendment modifies the specific offense characteristic in subsection (b)(3) to better encompass the types of cases that the Commission intended to cover.

Effective Date: The effective date of this amendment is November 1, 1992.

453. **Amendment:** The Introductory Commentary to Chapter Two, Part T, Subpart 3, is amended by deleting "This part" and inserting in lieu thereof "This Subpart"; by deleting:

". These guidelines are primarily aimed at revenue collection or trade regulation. They are",

and inserting in lieu thereof:

", and is designed to address violations involving revenue collection or trade regulation. It is";

by deleting "legislation generally applies" and inserting in lieu thereof "criminal statutes apply"; and by deleting:

"or for imposing a sentence above that specified in these guidelines",

and inserting in lieu thereof:

"if applicable, or for imposing a sentence above that specified in the guideline in this Subpart".

Section 2T3.1 is amended in the title by inserting at the end "; Receiving or Trafficking in Smuggled Property".

Section 2T3.1 is amended by inserting the following additional subsection:

"(c)   Cross Reference

(1)   If the offense involves a contraband item covered by another offense guideline, apply that offense guideline if the resulting offense level is greater than that determined above.".

The Commentary to § 2T3.1 captioned "Application Notes" is amended in the third sentence of Note 2 by deleting "the court should impose a sentence above the guideline" and inserting in lieu thereof "an upward departure may be warranted".

Amendment 453

Section 2T3.2, including accompanying commentary, is deleted as follows:

"§ 2T3.2. Receiving or Trafficking in Smuggled Property

(a) Base Offense Level:

(1) The level from § 2T4.1 (Tax Table) corresponding to the tax loss, if the tax loss exceeded $1,000; or

(2) 5, if the tax loss exceeded $100 but did not exceed $1,000; or

(3) 4, if the tax loss did not exceed $100.

For purposes of this guideline, the 'tax loss' is the amount of the duty.

(b) Specific Offense Characteristic

(1) If sophisticated means were used to impede discovery of the nature or existence of the offense, increase by 2 levels.

Commentary

Statutory Provision: 18 U.S.C. § 545. For additional statutory provision(s), see Appendix A (Statutory Index).

Application Note:

1. Particular attention should be given to those items for which entry is prohibited, limited, or restricted. Especially when such items are harmful or protective quotas are in effect, the duties evaded on such items may not adequately reflect the harm to society or protected industries resulting from their importation. In such instances, the court should impose a sentence above the guideline. A sentence based upon an alternative measure of the 'duty' evaded, such as the increase in market value due to importation, or 25 percent of the items' fair market value in the United States if the increase in market value due to importation is not readily ascertainable, might be considered.".

Section 8C2.1(a) is amended by deleting ", 2T3.2" immediately following "2T3.1".

Reason for Amendment: This amendment inserts a cross reference in § 2T3.1 to cover cases more appropriately addressed by other offense guidelines. Previously, a similar instruction was set forth in the Introductory Commentary to this part. In addition, this amendment consolidates §§ 2T3.1 and 2T3.2 into one guideline as each contains the same offense levels and adjustments.

Effective Date: The effective date of this amendment is November 1, 1992.

454. **Amendment:** The Commentary to § 3A1.1 captioned "Application Notes" is amended in Note 1 by inserting the following additional sentence at the end:

"Similarly, for example, a bank teller is not an unusually vulnerable victim solely by virtue of the teller's position in a bank.".

Reason for Amendment: This amendment clarifies the circumstances in which the vulnerable victim adjustment is intended to be applied.

Effective Date: The effective date of this amendment is November 1, 1992.

455. **Amendment:** Section 3A1.2(a) is amended by deleting:

"a law enforcement or corrections officer; a former law enforcement or corrections officer; an officer or employee included in 18 U.S.C. § 1114; a former officer or employee included in 18 U.S.C. § 1114",

and inserting in lieu thereof:

"a government officer or employee; a former government officer or employee".

The Commentary to § 3A1.2 captioned "Application Notes" is amended in Note 2 by deleting:

"are not expressly covered by this section. The court should make an upward departure of at least three levels in those unusual cases in which such persons are victims",

and inserting in lieu thereof:

"although covered by this section, do not represent the heartland of the conduct covered. An upward departure to reflect the potential disruption of the governmental function in such cases typically would be warranted".

The Commentary to § 3A1.2 captioned "Application Notes" is amended in Note 4 by deleting "law enforcement or corrections officer or other person covered under 18 U.S.C. § 1114" and inserting in lieu thereof "government officer or employee"; and by inserting the following additional sentence at the end:

"This adjustment also would not apply in the case of a robbery of a postal employee because the offense guideline for robbery contains an enhancement (§ 2B3.1(a)) that takes such conduct into account.".

Reason for Amendment: This amendment expands the coverage of this guideline to apply in the case of any government officer or employee, former government officer or employee, or a member of the immediate family of any of the above, who is targeted because of the official conduct or position of that officer or employee.

Effective Date: The effective date of this amendment is November 1, 1992.

456. **Amendment:** The Introductory Commentary to Chapter Three, Part B is amended by deleting the third sentence of the first paragraph as follows:

"However, where the defendant has received mitigation by virtue of being convicted of an offense significantly less serious than his actual criminal conduct, _e.g._, the defendant is convicted of unlawful possession of a controlled substance but his actual conduct involved drug trafficking, a further reduction in the offense level under § 3B1.2 (Mitigating Role) ordinarily is not warranted because the defendant is not substantially less culpable than a defendant whose only conduct involved the less serious offense.".

The Commentary to § 3B1.2 captioned "Application Notes" is amended by inserting the following additional note:

"4. If a defendant has received a lower offense level by virtue of being convicted of an offense significantly less serious than warranted by his actual criminal conduct, a reduction for a mitigating role under this section ordinarily is not warranted because such defendant is not substantially less culpable than a defendant whose only conduct involved the less serious offense. For example, if a defendant whose actual conduct involved a minimal role in the distribution of 25 grams of cocaine (an offense having a Chapter Two offense level of 14 under § 2D1.1) is convicted of simple possession of cocaine (an offense having a Chapter Two offense level of 6 under § 2D2.1), no reduction for a mitigating role is warranted because the defendant is not substantially less culpable than a defendant whose only conduct involved the simple possession of cocaine.".

Reason for Amendment: This amendment clarifies a situation in which a defendant is not ordinarily eligible for a reduction under § 3B1.2 (Mitigating Role) and moves the discussion of this issue from the Introductory Commentary of Chapter Three, Part B, to the Commentary of § 3B1.2, where it more appropriately belongs.

Effective Date: The effective date of this amendment is November 1, 1992.

457. Amendment: The Commentary to § 3C1.1 captioned "Application Notes" is amended by inserting the following additional note:

"7. Under this section, the defendant is accountable for his own conduct and for conduct that he aided or abetted, counseled, commanded, induced, procured, or willfully caused.".

The Commentary to § 3C1.2 captioned "Application Notes" is amended by inserting the following additional notes:

"5. Under this section, the defendant is accountable for his own conduct and for conduct that he aided or abetted, counseled, commanded, induced, procured, or willfully caused.

6. If death or bodily injury results or the conduct posed a substantial risk of death or bodily injury to more than one person, an upward departure may be warranted. See Chapter Five, Part K (Departures).".

Reason for Amendment: This amendment clarifies the scope of the conduct for which the defendant is accountable under §§ 3C1.1 and 3C1.2. In addition, this amendment adds an application note to the Commentary of § 3C1.2 that describes circumstances in which an upward departure may be warranted.

Effective Date: The effective date of this amendment is November 1, 1992.

458. Amendment: Section 3D1.2(d) is amended in the second paragraph by inserting "§§ 2L1.1, 2L2.1, 2L2.3;" in the appropriate place by section; by inserting "§ 2Q2.1" in the appropriate place by section; and by deleting ", 2T3.2" immediately following "2T3.1".

Section 3D1.2(d) is amended in the third paragraph by deleting "§§ 2L1.1, 2L2.1, 2L2.2, 2L2.3" and inserting in lieu thereof "2L2.2".

The Commentary to § 3D1.2 captioned "Application Notes" is amended in Note 3 by

deleting example 7 as follows:

> "(7) The defendant is convicted of two counts, each for unlawfully bringing one alien into the United States, but on different occasions. The counts are not to be grouped together.".

Reason for Amendment: This amendment revises § 3D1.2(d) to reflect amendments to §§ 2L1.1, 2L2.1, and 2L2.3 (amendment 450); to clarify that offenses under § 2Q2.1 are to be grouped under this subsection; and to delete the reference to § 2T3.2 made obsolete by the deletion of that guideline (amendment 453).

Effective Date: The effective date of this amendment is November 1, 1992.

459. **Amendment:** Section 3E1.1 is amended by deleting:

> "(a) If the defendant clearly demonstrates a recognition and affirmative acceptance of personal responsibility for his criminal conduct, reduce the offense level by 2 levels.
>
> (b) A defendant may be given consideration under this section without regard to whether his conviction is based upon a guilty plea or a finding of guilt by the court or jury or the practical certainty of conviction at trial.
>
> (c) A defendant who enters a guilty plea is not entitled to a sentencing reduction under this section as a matter of right.",

and inserting in lieu thereof:

> "(a) If the defendant clearly demonstrates acceptance of responsibility for his offense, decrease the offense level by 2 levels.
>
> (b) If the defendant qualifies for a decrease under subsection (a), the offense level determined prior to the operation of subsection (a) is level 16 or greater, and the defendant has assisted authorities in the investigation or prosecution of his own misconduct by taking one or more of the following steps:
>
> > (1) timely providing complete information to the government concerning his own involvement in the offense; or
> >
> > (2) timely notifying authorities of his intention to enter a plea of guilty, thereby permitting the government to avoid preparing for trial and permitting the court to allocate its resources efficiently,
>
> decrease the offense level by 1 additional level.".

The Commentary to § 3E1.1 captioned "Application Notes" is amended in Note 1 by deleting "for this provision" and inserting in lieu thereof "under subsection (a)"; by deleting subdivision (c) as follows:

> "(c) voluntary and truthful admission to authorities of involvement in the offense and related conduct;";

by redesignating subdivisions (a) and (b) as subdivisions (b) and (c), respectively; by inserting the following as subdivision (a):

> "(a) truthfully admitting the conduct comprising the offense(s) of conviction, and truthfully admitting or not falsely denying any additional relevant conduct

for which the defendant is accountable under § 1B1.3 (Relevant Conduct). Note that a defendant is not required to volunteer, or affirmatively admit, relevant conduct beyond the offense of conviction in order to obtain a reduction under subsection (a). A defendant may remain silent in respect to relevant conduct beyond the offense of conviction without affecting his ability to obtain a reduction under this subsection. However, a defendant who falsely denies, or frivolously contests, relevant conduct that the court determines to be true has acted in a manner inconsistent with acceptance of responsibility;";

in subdivision (f) by deleting "and" immediately following "offense;";

by redesignating subdivision (g) as subdivision (h); and by inserting the following as subdivision (g):

"(g)　post-offense rehabilitative efforts (e.g., counseling or drug treatment); and".

The Commentary to § 3E1.1 captioned "Application Notes" is amended by deleting Note 3 as follows:

"3.　Entry of a plea of guilty prior to the commencement of trial combined with truthful admission of involvement in the offense and related conduct will constitute significant evidence of acceptance of responsibility for the purposes of this section. However, this evidence may be outweighed by conduct of the defendant that is inconsistent with such acceptance of responsibility.",

and by inserting in lieu thereof:

"3.　Entry of a plea of guilty prior to the commencement of trial combined with truthfully admitting the conduct comprising the offense of conviction, and truthfully admitting or not falsely denying any additional relevant conduct for which he is accountable under § 1B1.3 (Relevant Conduct) (see Application Note 1(a)), will constitute significant evidence of acceptance of responsibility for the purposes of subsection (a). However, this evidence may be outweighed by conduct of the defendant that is inconsistent with such acceptance of responsibility. A defendant who enters a guilty plea is not entitled to an adjustment under this section as a matter of right.".

The Commentary to § 3E1.1 captioned "Application Notes" is amended by inserting the following additional note:

"6.　Subsection (a) provides a 2-level decrease in offense level. Subsection (b) provides an additional 1-level decrease in offense level for a defendant at offense level 16 or greater prior to the operation of subsection (a) who both qualifies for a decrease under subsection (a) and who has assisted authorities in the investigation or prosecution of his own misconduct by taking one or both of the steps set forth in subsection (b). The timeliness of the defendant's acceptance of responsibility is a consideration under both subsections, and is context specific. In general, the conduct qualifying for a decrease in offense level under subsection (b)(1) or (2) will occur particularly early in the case. For example, to qualify under subsection (b)(2), the defendant must have notified authorities of his intention to enter a plea of guilty at a sufficiently early point in the process so that the government may avoid preparing for trial and the court may schedule its calendar efficiently.".

The Commentary to § 3E1.1 captioned "Background" is amended by deleting "a recognition and affirmative acceptance of personal responsibility for the offense and related conduct" and inserting in lieu thereof "acceptance of responsibility for his offense"; and by inserting the following additional paragraph at the end:

"   Subsection (a) provides a 2-level decrease in offense level. Subsection (b)provides an additional 1-level decrease for a defendant at offense level 16 or greater prior to operation of subsection (a) who both qualifies for a decrease under subsection (a) and has assisted authorities in the investigation or prosecution of his own misconduct by taking one or more of the steps specified in subsection (b). Such a defendant has accepted responsibility in a way that ensures the certainty of his just punishment in a timely manner, thereby appropriately meriting an additional reduction. Subsection (b) does not apply, however, to a defendant whose offense level is level 15 or lower prior to application of subsection (a). At offense level 15 or lower, the reduction in the guideline range provided by a 2-level decrease in offense level under subsection (a) (which is a greater proportional reduction in the guideline range than at higher offense levels due to the structure of the Sentencing Table) is adequate for the court to take into account the factors set forth in subsection (b) within the applicable guideline range.".

Section 4B1.1 is amended in the last sentence by deleting "2-levels" and inserting in lieu thereof "the number of levels corresponding to that adjustment".

Section 4B1.4(b) is amended by deleting the last sentence as follows:

"*If § 3E1.1 (Acceptance of Responsibility) applies, reduce by 2 levels.",

and inserting in lieu thereof:

"*If an adjustment from § 3E1.1 (Acceptance of Responsibility) applies, decrease the offense level by the number of levels corresponding to that adjustment.".

Reason for Amendment: This amendment provides an additional reduction of one level for certain defendants whose acceptance of responsibility includes assistance to the government in the investigation or prosecution of their own misconduct. In addition, it replaces the term "offense and related conduct" with the term "offense" and provides guidance as to the meaning of this term in the context of this guideline.

Effective Date: The effective date of this amendment is November 1, 1992.

460. **Amendment:** Section 4A1.3 is amended in the fourth paragraph by deleting "a Category IV criminal history" wherever it appears and inserting in lieu thereof in each instance "Criminal History Category IV"; and by deleting:

"The Commission contemplates that there may, on occasion, be a case of an egregious, serious criminal record in which even the guideline range for a Category VI criminal history is not adequate to reflect the seriousness of the defendant's criminal history. In such a case, a decision above the guideline range for a defendant with a Category VI criminal history may be warranted. However, this provision is not symmetrical. The lower limit of the range for a Category I criminal history is set for a first offender with the lowest risk of recidivism. Therefore, a departure below the lower limit of the guideline range for a Category I criminal history on the basis of the adequacy of criminal history cannot be appropriate.",

and inserting in lieu thereof:

"The Commission contemplates that there may, on occasion, be a case of an egregious, serious criminal record in which even the guideline range for Criminal History Category VI is not adequate to reflect the seriousness of the defendant's criminal history. In such a case, a departure above the guideline range for a defendant with Criminal History Category VI may be warranted. In determining whether an upward departure from Criminal History Category VI is warranted, the court should consider that the nature of the prior offenses rather than simply their number is often more indicative of the seriousness of the defendant's criminal record. For example, a defendant with five prior sentences for very large-scale fraud offenses may have 15 criminal history points, within the range of points typical for Criminal History Category VI, yet have a substantially more serious criminal history overall because of the nature of the prior offenses. On the other hand, a defendant with nine prior 60-day jail sentences for offenses such as petty larceny, prostitution, or possession of gambling slips has a higher number of criminal history points (18 points) than the typical Criminal History Category VI defendant, but not necessarily a more serious criminal history overall. Where the court determines that the extent and nature of the defendant's criminal history, taken together, are sufficient to warrant an upward departure from Criminal History Category VI, the court should structure the departure by moving incrementally down the sentencing table to the next higher offense level in Criminal History Category VI until it finds a guideline range appropriate to the case.

However, this provision is not symmetrical. The lower limit of the range for Criminal History Category I is set for a first offender with the lowest risk of recidivism. Therefore, a departure below the lower limit of the guideline range for Criminal History Category I on the basis of the adequacy of criminal history cannot be appropriate.".

Reason for Amendment: This amendment provides additional guidance concerning upward departure from Criminal History Category VI on the basis of adequacy of criminal history category, and makes minor editorial changes.

Effective Date: The effective date of this amendment is November 1, 1992.

461. **Amendment:** Section 4B1.2(3) is amended by deleting the last sentence as follows:

"The date that a defendant sustained a conviction shall be the date the judgment of conviction was entered.",

and inserting in lieu thereof:

"The date that a defendant sustained a conviction shall be the date that the guilt of the defendant has been established, whether by guilty plea, trial, or plea of nolo contendere.".

The Commentary to § 4B1.2 captioned "Application Notes" is amended by deleting the text of Note 2 as follows:

"'Crime of violence' includes murder, manslaughter, kidnapping, aggravated assault, forcible sex offenses, robbery, arson, extortion, extortionate extension of credit, and burglary of a dwelling. Other offenses are included where (A) that offense has as an element the use, attempted use, or threatened use of physical force against the person of another, or (B) the conduct set forth (i.e., expressly charged) in the count of which the defendant was convicted involved use of explosives (including any explosive material or destructive device) or, by its nature, presented a serious potential risk of physical injury to another. Under this section, the conduct of which the defendant was convicted is the focus of inquiry.

The term 'crime of violence' does not include the offense of unlawful possession of a firearm by a felon. Where the instant offense is the unlawful possession of a firearm by a felon, the specific offense characteristics of § 2K2.1 (Unlawful Receipt, Possession, or Transportation of Firearms or Ammunition; Prohibited Transactions Involving Firearms or Ammunition) provide an increase in offense level if the defendant has one or more prior felony convictions for a crime of violence or controlled substance offense; and, if the defendant is sentenced under the provisions of 18 U.S.C. § 924(e), § 4B1.4 (Armed Career Criminal) will apply.",

and inserting in lieu thereof:

"'Crime of violence' includes murder, manslaughter, kidnapping, aggravated assault, forcible sex offenses, robbery, arson, extortion, extortionate extension of credit, and burglary of a dwelling. Other offenses are included where (A) that offense has as an element the use, attempted use, or threatened use of physical force against the person of another, or (B) the conduct set forth (i.e., expressly charged) in the count of which the defendant was convicted involved use of explosives (including any explosive material or destructive device) or, by its nature, presented a serious potential risk of physical injury to another. Under this section, the conduct of which the defendant was convicted is the focus of inquiry.

The term 'crime of violence' does not include the offense of unlawful possession of a firearm by a felon. Where the instant offense is the unlawful possession of a firearm by a felon, § 2K2.1 (Unlawful Receipt, Possession, or Transportation of Firearms or Ammunition; Prohibited Transactions Involving Firearms or Ammunition) provides an increase in offense level if the defendant has one or more prior felony convictions for a crime of violence or controlled substance offense; and, if the defendant is sentenced under the provisions of 18 U.S.C. § 924(e), § 4B1.4 (Armed Career Criminal) will apply.".

Reason for Amendment: This amendment conforms the definition of "sustaining a conviction" in § 4B1.2 to the definition of "convicted of an offense" in § 4A1.2. In addition, this amendment ratifies a previous amendment to the commentary to § 4B1.2 (amendment 433, effective November 1, 1991) and corrects a clerical error in a reference in that commentary to § 2K2.1. The previous amendment to the text of Application Note 2 clarified that application of § 4B1.2 is governed by the offense of conviction, and that the offense of being a felon in possession of a firearm is not a crime of violence within the meaning of this guideline. As a clarifying and conforming change, the previous commentary amendment reflected Commission intent that the term "crime of violence," as that term is used in §§ 4B1.1 and 4B1.2, be interpreted consistently with that term as used in other provisions of the Guidelines Manual. For example, § 4B1.4, as promulgated by amendment 355, effective November 1, 1990, provides an increased offense level for a "felon-in-possession" defendant who is subject to an enhanced sentence under 18 U.S.C. § 924(e) and who used or possessed the firearm in connection with a crime of violence (§ 4B1.4(b)(3)(A)). This action to ratify a previous commentary amendment was taken because of concerns raised by United States v. Stinson, 957 F.2d 813 (11th Cir. 1992), in which the court stated it would not follow amendment 433 because the commentary amendment was not submitted to Congress.

Effective Date: The effective date of this amendment is November 1, 1992.

462. Amendment: Chapter Five, Part A, is amended in the Sentencing Table at Offense Level 7, Criminal History Category I, by deleting "1-7" and inserting in lieu thereof "0-6"; and at Offense Level 8, Criminal History Category I, by deleting "2-8" and inserting in lieu thereof "0-6".

Amendment 462 APPENDIX C - VOLUME I November 1, 2013

Chapter Five, Part A is amended in the Sentencing Table by designating four zones as follows: Zone A (containing all guideline ranges having a minimum of zero months); Zone B (containing all guideline ranges having a minimum of at least one but not more than six months); Zone C (containing all guideline ranges having a minimum of eight, nine, or ten months); and Zone D (containing all guideline ranges having a minimum of twelve months or more).

Section 5B1.1 is amended by deleting:

"(a) Subject to the statutory restrictions in subsection (b) below, sentence of probation is authorized:

 (1) if the minimum term of imprisonment in the range specified by the Sentencing Table in Part A, is zero months;

 (2) if the minimum term of imprisonment specified by the Sentencing Table is at least one but not more than six months, provided that the court imposes a condition or combination of conditions requiring intermittent confinement, community confinement, or home detention as provided in § 5C1.1(c)(2) (Imposition of a Term of Imprisonment).",

and inserting in lieu thereof:

"(a) Subject to the statutory restrictions in subsection (b) below, a sentence of probation is authorized if:

 (1) the applicable guideline range is in Zone A of the Sentencing Table; or

 (2) the applicable guideline range is in Zone B of the Sentencing Table and the court imposes a condition or combination of conditions requiring intermittent confinement, community confinement, or home detention as provided in subsection (c)(3) of § 5C1.1 (Imposition of a Term of Imprisonment).".

The Commentary to § 5B1.1 captioned "Application Notes" is amended in Note 1 by deleting:

"(a) Where the minimum term of imprisonment specified in the guideline range from the Sentencing Table is zero months. In such case, a condition requiring a period of community confinement, home detention, or intermittent confinement may be imposed but is not required.

(b) Where the minimum term of imprisonment specified in the guideline range from the Sentencing Table is at least one but not more than six months.",

and inserting in lieu thereof:

"(a) Where the applicable guideline range is in Zone A of the Sentencing Table (i.e., the minimum term of imprisonment specified in the applicable guideline range is zero months). In such cases, a condition requiring a period of community confinement, home detention, or intermittent confinement may be imposed but is not required.

(b) Where the applicable guideline range is in Zone B of the Sentencing Table (i.e., the minimum term of imprisonment specified in the applicable guideline rangeis at least one but not more than six months).";

and by deleting "Offense Level is 8 and the Criminal History Category is I" and inserting in lieu thereof "offense level is 7 and the criminal history category is II".

The Commentary to § 5B1.1 captioned "Application Notes" is amended in Note 2 by deleting:

"Where the minimum term of imprisonment specified in the guideline range from the Sentencing Table is more than six months",

and inserting in lieu thereof:

"Where the applicable guideline range is in Zone C or D of the Sentencing Table (i. e., the minimum term of imprisonment specified in the applicable guideline range is eight months or more)".

The Commentary to § 5B1.1 captioned "Background" is amended by deleting "1st Sess. 89). Subsection" and inserting in lieu thereof "1st Sess. 89 (1983)). Section".

Section 5C1.1(a) is amended by inserting "applicable" immediately before "guideline range".

Section 5C1.1(b) is amended by deleting "minimum term of imprisonment in the applicable guideline range in the Sentencing Table is zero months" and inserting in lieu thereof "applicable guideline range is in Zone A of the Sentencing Table".

Sections 5C1.1 is amended by deleting:

"(c) If the minimum term of imprisonment in the applicable guideline range in the Sentencing Table is at least one but not more than six months, the minimum term may be satisfied by (1) a sentence of imprisonment; (2) a sentence of probation that includes a condition or combination of conditions that substitute intermittent confinement, community confinement, or home detention for imprisonment according to the schedule in § 5C1.1(e); or (3) a sentence of imprisonment that includes a term of supervised release with a condition that substitutes community confinement or home detention according to the schedule in § 5C1.1(e), provided that at least one-half of the minimum term, but in no event less than one month, is satisfied by imprisonment.

(d) If the minimum term of imprisonment in the applicable guideline range in the Sentencing Table is more than six months but not more than ten months, the minimum term may be satisfied by (1) a sentence of imprisonment; or (2) a sentence of imprisonment that includes a term of supervised release with a condition that substitutes community confinement or home detention according to the schedule in § 5C1.1(e), provided that at least one-half of the minimum term is satisfied by imprisonment.",

and inserting in lieu thereof:

"(c) If the applicable guideline range is in Zone B of the Sentencing Table, the minimum term may be satisfied by --

(1) a sentence of imprisonment; or

Amendment 462 APPENDIX C - VOLUME I November 1, 2013

(2) a sentence of imprisonment that includes a term of supervised release with a condition that substitutes community confinement or home detention according to the schedule in subsection (e), provided that at least one month is satisfied by imprisonment; or

(3) a sentence of probation that includes a condition or combination of conditions that substitute intermittent confinement, community confinement, or home detention for imprisonment according to the schedule in subsection (e).

(d) If the applicable guideline range is in Zone C of the Sentencing Table, the minimum term may be satisfied by --

(1) a sentence of imprisonment; or

(2) a sentence of imprisonment that includes a term of supervised release with a condition that substitutes community confinement or home detention according to the schedule in subsection (e), provided that at least one-half of the minimum term is satisfied by imprisonment.".

Section 5C1.1 is amended by deleting:

"(f) If the minimum term of imprisonment in the applicable guideline range in the Sentencing Table is more than ten months, the guidelines require that the minimum term be satisfied by a sentence of imprisonment.",

and inserting in lieu thereof:

"(f) If the applicable guideline range is in Zone D of the Sentencing Table, the minimum term shall be satisfied by a sentence of imprisonment.".

The Commentary to § 5C1.1 captioned "Application Notes" is amended in Note 1 by deleting the first sentence as follows:

"Subsection 5C1.1(a) provides that a sentence conforms with the guidelines for imprisonment if it is within the minimum and maximum terms of the guideline range specified in the Sentencing Table.",

and inserting in lieu thereof:

"Subsection (a) provides that a sentence conforms with the guidelines for imprisonment if it is within the minimum and maximum terms of the applicable guideline range specified in the Sentencing Table in Part A of this Chapter.".

The Commentary to § 5C1.1 captioned "Application Notes" is amended in Note 2 by deleting: "Subsection 5C1.1(b) provides that where the minimum term of imprisonment specified in the guideline range from the Sentencing Table is zero months",

and inserting in lieu thereof:

"Subsection (b) provides that where the applicable guideline range is in Zone A of the Sentencing Table (i.e., the minimum term of imprisonment specified in the applicable guideline range is zero months)";

and by deleting "may, for example," and inserting in lieu thereof ", for example, may".

The Commentary to § 5C1.1 captioned "Application Notes" is amended in Note 3 by deleting:

"Subsection 5C1.1(c) provides that where the minimum term of imprisonment specified in the guideline range from the Sentencing Table is at least one but not more than six months",

and inserting in lieu thereof:

"Subsection (c) provides that where the applicable guideline range is in Zone B of the Sentencing Table (i.e., the minimum term of imprisonment specified in the applicable guideline range is at least one but not more than six months)";

by deleting:

"For example, where the guideline range is 3-9 months, a sentence of probation with a condition requiring at least three",

and inserting in lieu thereof:

"For example, where the guideline range is 4-10 months, a sentence of probation with a condition requiring at least four";

by deleting "one-half of the minimum term specified in the guideline range from the Sentencing Table, but in no event less than one month," and inserting in lieu thereof "one month"; by deleting "two months followed by a term of supervised release with a condition requiring two" and inserting in lieu thereof "one month followed by a term of supervised release with a condition requiring three"; and by deleting:

"For example, where the guideline range is 3-9 months, both a sentence of probation with a condition requiring six months of community confinement or home detention (under § 5C1.1(c)(2)) and a sentence of two months imprisonment followed by a term of supervised release with a condition requiring four months of community confinement or home detention (under § 5C1.1(c)(3)",

and inserting in lieu thereof:

"For example, where the guideline range is 4-10 months, both a sentence of probation with a condition requiring six months of community confinement or home detention (under subsection (c)(3)) and a sentence of two months imprisonment followed by a term of supervised release with a condition requiring four months of community confinement or home detention (under subsection (c)(2)".

The Commentary to § 5C1.1 captioned "Application Notes" is amended in Note 4 by deleting:

"Subsection 5C1.1(d) provides that where the minimum term specified in the guideline range from the Sentencing Table is more than six but not more than ten months",

and inserting in lieu thereof:

"Subsection (d) provides that where the applicable guideline range is in Zone C of the Sentencing Table (i.e., the minimum term specified in the applicable guideline range is eight, nine, or ten months)";

and by deleting "under § 5C1.1(d)" wherever it appears and inserting in lieu thereof in

Amendment 462

each instance "under subsection (d)".

The Commentary to § 5C1.1 captioned "Application Notes" is amended in Note 5 by deleting "Subsection 5C1.1(e)" and inserting in lieu thereof "Subsection (e)".

The Commentary to § 5C1.1 captioned "Application Notes" is amended in Note 7 by deleting "§ 5C1.1(c)" and inserting in lieu thereof "subsections (c)".

The Commentary to § 5C1.1 captioned "Application Notes" is amended by deleting Note 8 as follows:

> "8. Subsection 5C1.1(f) provides that, if the minimum term of imprisonment set forth in the Sentencing Table is more than ten months, the minimum term must be satisfied by a sentence of imprisonment without the use of any of the incarceration alternatives in § 5C1.1(e).",

and inserting in lieu thereof:

> "8. Subsection (f) provides that, where the applicable guideline range is in Zone D of the Sentencing Table (i.e., the minimum term of imprisonment specified in the applicable guideline range is twelve months or more), the minimum term must be satisfied by a sentence of imprisonment without the use of any of the imprisonment substitutes in subsection (e).".

Reason for Amendment: This amendment expands the number of categories in the Sentencing Table in Criminal History Category I in which the court has discretion to impose a sentence without imprisonment or confinement conditions. In addition, it removes the requirement that a "split sentence" include a term of imprisonment of at least one-half of the minimum of the guideline range for less serious categories of offenses and offenders and substitutes a requirement that such term of imprisonment be at least one month. Finally, this amendment reformats these sections to make their operation clearer.

Effective Date: The effective date of this amendment is November 1, 1992.

463. **Amendment:** Chapter Five, Part E, is amended by inserting an additional policy statement as § 5E1.5 (Costs of Prosecution (Policy Statement)).

Reason for Amendment: This amendment makes the Guidelines Manual more comprehensive by adding a section to provide notice of certain statutory requirements pertaining to the imposition of the costs of prosecution.

Effective Date: The effective date of this amendment is November 1, 1992.

464. **Amendment:** Section 5F1.6 is amended by deleting "21 U.S.C. § 853a" and inserting in lieu thereof "21 U.S.C. § 862".

The Commentary to § 5F1.6 captioned "Application Notes" is amended in Note 1 by deleting "21 U.S.C. § 853a(d)" and inserting in lieu thereof "21 U.S.C. § 862(d)".

The Commentary to § 5F1.6 captioned "Background" is amended by deleting "21 U.S.C. § 853a" wherever it appears and inserting in lieu thereof in each instance "21 U.S.C. § 862"; by deleting "21 U.S.C. § 853a(a)(1)" and inserting in lieu thereof "21 U.S.C. § 862(a)(1)"; by deleting "(a)(2)" and inserting in lieu thereof "(b)(1)"; by deleting "21 U.S.C. § 853a(a)(1)(C)" and inserting in lieu thereof "21 U.S.C. § 862(a)(1)(C)"; and by deleting "21 U.S.C. § 853a(c)" and inserting in lieu thereof "21 U.S.C. § 862(c)".

Reason for Amendment: This amendment conforms the references to the statutory provisions underlying this guideline as such provisions were renumbered by the Comprehensive Crime Control Act of 1990.

Effective Date: The effective date of this amendment is November 1, 1992.

465. **Amendment:** Section 5G1.3 is amended by deleting subsection (b) as follows:

> "(b) If subsection (a) does not apply, and the undischarged term of imprisonment resulted from offense(s) that constituted part of the same course of conduct as the instant offense and have been fully taken into account in the determination of the offense level for the instant offense, or if the prior undischarged term of imprisonment resulted from a federal offense and was imposed pursuant to the Sentencing Reform Act, the sentence for the instant offense shall be imposed to result in a combined sentence equal to the total punishment that would have been imposed under § 5G1.2 (Sentencing on Multiple Counts of Conviction) had all the sentences been imposed at the same time.",

and inserting in lieu thereof:

> "(b) If subsection (a) does not apply, and the undischarged term of imprisonment resulted from offense(s) that have been fully taken into account in the determination of the offense level for the instant offense, the sentence for the instant offense shall be imposed to run concurrently to the undischarged term of imprisonment.".

Section 5G1.3(c) is amended by inserting "(Policy Statement)" immediately before "In"; and by deleting "unexpired" and inserting in lieu thereof "undischarged".

The Commentary to § 5G1.3 captioned "Application Notes" is amended by deleting Notes 2-4 as follows:

> "2. Subsection (b) (which applies only if subsection (a) does not apply), applies in two situations. First, it applies if the sentence resulting in the undischarged term of imprisonment was a federal sentence imposed pursuant to the Sentencing Reform Act. In such cases, the court shall fashion a sentence equal to the total punishment that would have been imposed had both sentences been imposed at the same time. Second, it applies if the conduct resulting in the undischarged term of imprisonment was part of the same course of conduct as the instant offense and has been fully taken into account in determining the offense level for the instant offense (e.g., where a defendant is prosecuted in both federal and state court for the same criminal conduct; or where a defendant is prosecuted in federal and state court for different criminal transactions that are part of the same course of conduct, such as two drug sales, but the conduct underlying both transactions is fully taken into account under § 1B1.3 (Relevant Conduct) in determining the offense level for the instant offense).
>
> 3. When a sentence is imposed pursuant to subsection (b), the court should adjust for any term of imprisonment already served as a result of the conduct taken into account in determining the instant sentence (e.g., if the appropriate total punishment determined under this subsection for all offenses is 30 months and the defendant has already served 10 months of the prior undischarged term of imprisonment, the court should impose a sentence of 20 months concurrent with the prior undischarged term).

4. Where the defendant is serving an unexpired term of imprisonment in circumstances other than those set forth in subsections (a) or (b), the court shall impose a consecutive sentence to the extent necessary to fashion a sentence resulting in incremental punishment for the multiple offenses. To the extent practicable, the court shall impose a sentence for the instant offense that results in a combined sentence that approximates the total punishment that would have been imposed under § 5G1.2 (Sentencing on Multiple Counts of Conviction) had all of the offenses been federal offenses for which sentences were being imposed at the same time. Where the defendant is serving a term of imprisonment for a state offense, the information available may permit only a rough estimate of the total punishment that would have been imposed under the guidelines. It is not intended that the above methodology be applied in a manner that unduly complicates or prolongs the sentencing process. In fashioning an appropriate incremental punishment, the court should consider whether the offense was committed while the defendant was on bail or other release status from another offense. In such cases, a reasonable incremental penalty appropriately would include an additional enhancement equivalent to that provided in § 2J1.7 (Commission of Offense While on Release).",

and inserting in lieu thereof:

"2. Subsection (b) (which may apply only if subsection (a) does not apply), addresses cases in which the conduct resulting in the undischarged term of imprisonment has been fully taken into account under § 1B1.3 (Relevant Conduct) in determining the offense level for the instant offense. This can occur, for example, where a defendant is prosecuted in both federal and state court, or in two or more federal jurisdictions, for the same criminal conduct or for different criminal transactions that were part of the same course of conduct.

When a sentence is imposed pursuant to subsection (b), the court should adjust for any term of imprisonment already served as a result of the conduct taken into account in determining the sentence for the instant offense. Example: The defendant has been convicted of a federal offense charging the sale of 40 grams of cocaine. Under § 1B1.3 (Relevant Conduct), the defendant is held accountable for the sale of an additional 15 grams of cocaine that is part of the same course of conduct for which the defendant has been convicted and sentenced in state court (the defendant received a nine-month sentence of imprisonment, of which he has served six months at the time of sentencing on the instant federal offense). The guideline range applicable to the defendant is 10-16 months (Chapter Two offense level of 14 for sale of 55 grams of cocaine; 2-level reduction for acceptance of responsibility; final offense level of 12; Criminal History Category I). The court determines that a sentence of 13 months provides the appropriate total punishment. Because the defendant has already served six months on the related state charge, a sentence of seven months, imposed to run concurrently with the remainder of the defendant's state sentence, achieves this result. For clarity, the court should note on the Judgment in a Criminal Case Order that the sentence imposed is not a departure from the guidelines because the defendant has been credited for guideline purposes under § 5G1.3(b) with six months served in state custody.

3. Where the defendant is subject to an undischarged term of imprisonment

in circumstances other than those set forth in subsections (a) or (b), subsection (c) applies and the court shall impose a consecutive sentence to the extent necessary to fashion a sentence resulting in a reasonable incremental punishment for the multiple offenses. In some circumstances, such incremental punishment can be achieved by the imposition of a sentence that is concurrent with the remainder of the unexpired term of imprisonment. In such cases, a consecutive sentence is not required. To the extent practicable, the court should consider a reasonable incremental penalty to be a sentence for the instant offense that results in a combined sentence of imprisonment that approximates the total punishment that would have been imposed under § 5G1.2 (Sentencing on Multiple Counts of Conviction) had all of the offenses been federal offenses for which sentences were being imposed at the same time. It is recognized that this determination frequently will require an approximation. Where the defendant is serving a term of imprisonment for a state offense, the information available may permit only a rough estimate of the total punishment that would have been imposed under the guidelines. Where the offense resulting in the undischarged term of imprisonment is a federal offense for which a guideline determination has previously been made, the task will be somewhat more straightforward, although even in such cases a precise determination may not be possible.

It is not intended that the above methodology be applied in a manner that unduly complicates or prolongs the sentencing process. Additionally, this methodology does not, itself, require the court to depart from the guideline range established for the instant federal offense. Rather, this methodology is meant to assist the court in determining the appropriate sentence (e.g., the appropriate point within the applicable guideline range, whether to order the sentence to run concurrently or consecutively to the undischarged term of imprisonment, or whether a departure is warranted). Generally, the court may achieve an appropriate sentence through its determination of an appropriate point within the applicable guideline range for the instant federal offense, combined with its determination of whether that sentence will run concurrently or consecutively to the undischarged term of imprisonment.

Illustrations of the Application of Subsection (c):

(A) The guideline range applicable to the instant federal offense is 24-30 months. The court determines that a total punishment of 36 months' imprisonment would appropriately reflect the instant federal offense and the offense resulting in the undischarged term of imprisonment. The undischarged term of imprisonment is an indeterminate sentence of imprisonment with a 60-month maximum. At the time of sentencing on the instant federal offense, the defendant has served ten months on the undischarged term of imprisonment. In this case, a sentence of 26 months' imprisonment to be served concurrently with the remainder of the undischarged term of imprisonment would (1) be within the guideline range for the instant federal offense, and (2) achieve an appropriate total punishment (36 months).

(B) The applicable guideline range for the instant federal offense is 24-30 months. The court determines that a total punishment of 36 months' imprisonment would appropriately reflect the instant federal offense and the offense resulting in the undischarged term of imprisonment. The undischarged term of imprisonment is a six-

	month determinate sentence. At the time of sentencing on the instant federal offense, the defendant has served three months on the undischarged term of imprisonment. In this case, a sentence of 30 months' imprisonment to be served consecutively to the undischarged term of imprisonment would (1) be within the guideline range for the instant federal offense, and (2) achieve an appropriate total punishment (36 months).
(C)	The applicable guideline range for the instant federal offense is 24-30 months. The court determines that a total punishment of 60 months' imprisonment would appropriately reflect the instant federal offense and the offense resulting in the undischarged term of imprisonment. The undischarged term of imprisonment is a 12-month determinate sentence. In this case, a sentence of 30 months' imprisonment to be served consecutively to the undischarged term of imprisonment would be the greatest sentence imposable without departure for the instant federal offense.
(D)	The applicable guideline range for the instant federal offense is 24-30 months. The court determines that a total punishment of 36 months' imprisonment would appropriately reflect the instant federal offense and the offense resulting in the undischarged term of imprisonment. The undischarged term of imprisonment is an indeterminate sentence with a 60-month maximum. At the time of sentencing on the instant federal offense, the defendant has served 22 months on the undischarged term of imprisonment. In this case, a sentence of 24 months to be served concurrently with the remainder of the undischarged term of imprisonment would be the lowest sentence imposable without departure for the instant federal offense.".

Reason for Amendment: This amendment deletes the prong of § 5G1.3(b) pertaining to the sentencing of a defendant subject to an undischarged term of imprisonment previously imposed pursuant to the Sentencing Reform Act because the Commission found a number of problems in implementation. Cases previously addressed by this prong henceforth will be addressed by subsection (c), which is designed to produce a similar result but requires less precise calculations. Consistent with the structure of the Guidelines Manual, subsection (c) is expressly designated a policy statement. In addition, this amendment provides additional commentary explaining, and providing examples of, the operation of this section.

Effective Date: The effective date of this amendment is November 1, 1992.

466. Amendment: Chapter 5, Part H is amended by inserting an additional policy statement as § 5H1.12 (Lack of Guidance as a Youth and Similar Circumstances (Policy Statement)).

Chapter 1, Part A, Subpart 4(b) is amended in the first paragraph by inserting "§ 5H1.12 (Lack of Guidance as a Youth and Similar Circumstances)," immediately following "§ 5H1.10 (Race, Sex, National Origin, Creed, Religion, and Socio-Economic Status),".

Reason for Amendment: This amendment provides that the factors specified are not appropriate grounds for departure.

Effective Date: The effective date of this amendment is November 1, 1992.

467. Amendment: Section 6B1.2(a) is amended by inserting "or the sentencing guidelines" immediately following "statutory purposes of sentencing".

Section 6B1.2(a) is amended by inserting the following additional paragraph at the end:

"*Provided*, that a plea agreement that includes the dismissal of a charge or a plea agreement not to pursue a potential charge shall not preclude the conduct underlying such charge from being considered under the provisions of § 1B1.3 (Relevant Conduct) in connection with the count(s) of which the defendant is convicted.".

The Commentary to § 6B1.2 is amended in the first paragraph by deleting:

"This section makes clear that a court may accept a plea agreement provided that the judge complies with the obligations imposed by Rule 11(e), Fed. R. Crim. P. A judge",

and inserting in lieu thereof "The court".

The Commentary to § 6B1.2 is amended in the second paragraph by deleting:

"will accept a recommended sentence or a plea agreement requiring imposition of a specific sentence only if the court is satisfied either that the contemplated sentence is within the guidelines or, if not, that the recommended sentence or agreement",

and inserting in lieu thereof:

"should accept a recommended sentence or a plea agreement requiring imposition of a specific sentence only if the court is satisfied either that such sentence is an appropriate sentence within the applicable guideline range or, if not, that the sentence".

The Commentary to § 6B1.2 is amended by inserting the following additional paragraphs at the end:

"   A defendant who enters a plea of guilty in a timely manner will enhance the likelihood of his receiving a reduction in offense level under § 3E1.1 (Acceptance of Responsibility). Further reduction in offense level (or sentence) due to a plea agreement will tend to undermine the sentencing guidelines.

    The second paragraph of subsection (a) provides that a plea agreement that includes the dismissal of a charge, or a plea agreement not to pursue a potential charge, shall not prevent the conduct underlying that charge from being considered under the provisions of § 1B1.3 (Relevant Conduct) in connection with the count(s) of which the defendant is convicted. This paragraph prevents a plea agreement from restricting consideration of conduct that is within the scope of § 1B1.3 (Relevant Conduct) in respect to the count(s) of which the defendant is convicted; it does not in any way expand or modify the scope of § 1B1.3 (Relevant Conduct).".

Reason for Amendment: This amendment clarifies that a plea agreement to dismiss a charge or not to pursue a potential charge does not insulate the conduct underlying such charge from the operation of § 1B1.3 (Relevant Conduct) in respect to the count(s) of which the defendant is convicted. In addition, this amendment makes clearer the Commission's policy that plea agreements should not undermine the sentencing guidelines.

Effective Date: The effective date of this amendment is November 1, 1992.

Amendment 468

468. Amendment: Appendix A (Statutory Index) is amended by deleting:

"8 U.S.C. § 1325 2L1.2",

and inserting in lieu thereof:

"8 U.S.C. § 1325(a) 2L1.2
8 U.S.C. § 1325(b) 2L2.1, 2L2.2
8 U.S.C. § 1325(c) 2L2.1, 2L2.2";

in the line beginning "18 U.S.C. § 245(b)" by inserting ", 2J1.2" immediately following "2H2.1";

in the line beginning "18 U.S.C. § 371" by deleting "2D1.4," immediately following "2C1.7,";

in the line beginning "18 U.S.C. § 545" by deleting ", 2T3.2";

in the line beginning "18 U.S.C. § 547" by deleting ", 2T3.2";

in the line beginning "18 U.S.C. § 549" by deleting ", 2T3.2";

in the line beginning "18 U.S.C. § 656" by inserting ", 2F1.1" immediately following "2B1.1";

in the line beginning "18 U.S.C. § 657" by inserting ", 2F1.1" immediately following "2B1.1";

in the line beginning "18 U.S.C. § 1028" by deleting "2L1.2, 2L2.1" and inserting in lieu thereof "2L2.1, 2L2.2";

by deleting:

"18 U.S.C. § 1346 2C1.7";

in the line beginning "18 U.S.C. § 2331(a)" by deleting "18 U.S.C. § 2331(a)" and inserting in lieu thereof "18 U.S.C. § 2332(a)";

by deleting:

"18 U.S.C. § 2331(b) 2A2.1",

and inserting in lieu thereof:

"18 U.S.C. § 2332(b)(1) 2A2.1
18 U.S.C. § 2332(b)(2) 2A1.5";

in the line beginning "18 U.S.C. § 2331(c)" by deleting "18 U.S.C. § 2331(c)" and inserting in lieu thereof "18 U.S.C. § 2332(c)";

in the line beginning "19 U.S.C. § 1464" by deleting ", 2T3.2";

in the line beginning "21 U.S.C. § 846" by deleting "2D1.4" and inserting in lieu thereof "2D1.1, 2D1.2, 2D1.5, 2D1.6, 2D1.7, 2D1.8, 2D1.9, 2D1.10, 2D1.11, 2D1.12, 2D1.13, 2D2.1, 2D2.2, 2D3.1, 2D3.2, 2D3.3, 2D3.4, 2D3.5";

in the line beginning "21 U.S.C. § 963" by deleting "2D1.4" and inserting in lieu thereof "2D1.1, 2D1.2, 2D1.5, 2D1.6, 2D1.7, 2D1.8, 2D1.9, 2D1.10, 2D1.11, 2D1.12, 2D1.13, 2D2.1, 2D2.2, 2D3.1, 2D3.2, 2D3.3, 2D3.4, 2D3.5";

in the line beginning "31 U.S.C. § 5322" by inserting ", 2S1.4" immediately following "2S1.3";

and in the line beginning "46 U.S.C. App. § 1903(j)" by deleting "2D1.4" and inserting in lieu thereof "2D1.1".

The Commentary to § 2B4.1 captioned "Background" is amended in the sixth paragraph by deleting "§§ 77d-1 and 77d-2" and inserting in lieu thereof "78dd-1 and 78dd-2".

The Commentary to § 2C1.7 captioned "Statutory Provisions" is amended by deleting ", 1346".

The Commentary to § 2C1.7 captioned "Application Notes" is amended in Note 1 by inserting "(A)" immediately following "involve"; and by deleting ", 1346), or" and inserting in lieu thereof "), or (B)".

The Commentary to § 2C1.7 captioned "Background" is amended by deleting ", 1341-1343, and 1346" and inserting in lieu thereof "and 1341-1343".

The Commentary to § 2T1.1 captioned "Background" is amended in the fifth paragraph by deleting "28 U.S.C. § 994(n)" and inserting in lieu thereof "28 U.S.C. § 994(i)(2)".

Reason for Amendment: This amendment makes the statutory index more comprehensive, and conforms it to the amendments of the Chapter Two offense guidelines. In addition, it corrects clerical errors and makes an editorial improvement.

Effective Date: The effective date of this amendment is November 1, 1992.

469. **Amendment:** Section 1B1.10(d) is amended by deleting "and 380" and inserting in lieu thereof "380, 433, and 461".

Reason for Amendment: This amendment expands the listing in subsection (d) to implement the directive in 28 U.S.C. § 994(u) in respect to guideline amendments that may be considered for retroactive application.

Effective Date: The effective date of this amendment is November 1, 1992.

470. **Amendment:** The Commentary to § 2F1.1 captioned "Application Notes" is amended in Note 7 in the first paragraph by inserting the following additional sentence as the second sentence:

> "As in theft cases, loss is the value of the money, property, or services unlawfully taken; it does not, for example, include interest the victim could have earned on such funds had the offense not occurred.".

The Commentary to § 2F1.1 captioned "Application Notes" is amended in Note 7(b) by deleting:

> "In fraudulent loan application cases and contract procurement cases where the defendant's capabilities are fraudulently represented, the loss is the actual loss to the victim (or if the loss has not yet come about, the expected loss). For example, if a defendant fraudulently obtains a loan by misrepresenting the value of his assets,

Amendment 470 APPENDIX C - VOLUME I November 1, 2013

the loss is the amount of the loan not repaid at the time the offense is discovered, reduced by the amount the lending institution has recovered, or can expect to recover, from any assets pledged to secure the loan.",

and inserting in lieu thereof:

"In fraudulent loan application cases and contract procurement cases, the loss is the actual loss to the victim (or if the loss has not yet come about, the expected loss). For example, if a defendant fraudulently obtains a loan by misrepresenting the value of his assets, the loss is the amount of the loan not repaid at the time the offense is discovered, reduced by the amount the lending institution has recovered (or can expect to recover) from any assets pledged to secure the loan. However, where the intended loss is greater than the actual loss, the intended loss is to be used.".

Reason for Amendment: This amendment clarifies that interest is not included in the determination of loss. In, addition, it clarifies that in fraudulent loan application cases, as in other types of fraud, if the intended loss is greater than the actual loss, the intended loss is used. Finally, it makes an editorial improvement in this commentary by deleting an unnecessary phrase.

Effective Date: The effective date of this amendment is November 1, 1992.

471. **Amendment:** The Commentary to § 2K1.3 captioned "Application Notes" is amended by inserting the following additional note:

"11. As used in subsections (b)(3) and (c)(1), 'another felony offense' and 'another offense' refer to offenses other than explosives or firearms possession or trafficking offenses. However, where the defendant used or possessed a firearm or explosive to facilitate another firearms or explosives offense (e.g., the defendant used or possessed a firearm to protect the delivery of an unlawful shipment of explosives), an upward departure under § 5K2.6 (Weapons and Dangerous Instrumentalities) may be warranted.".

The Commentary to § 2K2.1 captioned "Application Notes" is amended in Note 15 by deleting "or (a)(5)" and inserting in lieu thereof "(a)(4)(B), or (a)(6)".

The Commentary to § 2K2.1 captioned "Application Notes" is amended by inserting the following additional note:

"18. As used in subsections (b)(5) and (c)(1), 'another felony offense' and 'another offense' refer to offenses other than explosives or firearms possession or trafficking offenses. However, where the defendant used or possessed a firearm or explosive to facilitate another firearms or explosives offense (e.g., the defendant used or possessed a firearm to protect the delivery of an unlawful shipment of explosives), an upward departure under § 5K2.6 (Weapons and Dangerous Instrumentalities) may be warranted.".

Reason for Amendment: This amendment clarifies the meaning of the terms "another felony offense' and "another offense," and corrects a clerical error.

Effective Date: The effective date of this amendment is November 1, 1992.

472. **Amendment:** The Commentary to § 4A1.2 captioned "Application Notes" is amended in Note 8 by deleting the last sentence as follows:

"If the government is able to show that a sentence imposed outside this time period is evidence of similar misconduct or the defendant's receipt of a substantial portion of income from criminal livelihood, the court may consider this information in determining whether to depart and sentence above the applicable guideline range.",

and by inserting in lieu thereof:

"If the court finds that a sentence imposed outside this time period is evidence of similar, or serious dissimilar, criminal conduct, the court may consider this information in determining whether an upward departure is warranted under § 4A1.3 (Adequacy of Criminal History Category).".

Reason for Amendment: This amendment clarifies that dissimilar, serious prior offenses outside the applicable time period may be considered in determining whether an upward departure is warranted under § 4A1.3. The amendment provides additional Commission guidance on an issue that has produced conflicting decisions among the courts of appeals. Compare, e.g., United States v. Leake, 908 F.2d 550, 554 (9th Cir. 1990) (upward departure impermissible for remote prior convictions dissimilar to instant offense) and United States v. Samuels, 938 F.2d 210, 215 (D.C. Cir. 1991) (suggesting the same) with United States v. Williams, 910 F.2d 1574, 1579 (7th Cir. 1990) (although older prior crimes dissimilar to instant offense, upward departure permissible if convictions are reliable information of increased recidivism risk), rev'd on other grounds, 112 S. Ct. 1112 (1992) and United States v. Russell, 905 F.2d 1439, 1444 (10th Cir. 1990) (same).

Effective Date: The effective date of this amendment is November 1, 1992.

473. **Amendment:** The Commentary to § 7B1.1 captioned "Application Notes" is amended by deleting Notes 2 and 3 as follows:

> "2. 'Crime of violence' has the same meaning as set forth in § 4B1.2(1), and includes any offense under federal or state law punishable by imprisonment for a term exceeding one year that --
>
>> (i) has as an element the use, attempted use, or threatened use of physical force against the person of another; or
>>
>> (ii) is burglary of a dwelling, arson, or extortion, involves use of explosives, or otherwise involves conduct that presents a serious potential risk of physical injury to another.
>
> A crime of violence includes murder, manslaughter, kidnapping, aggravated assault, forcible sex offenses, robbery, arson, extortion, extortionate extension of credit, and burglary of a dwelling. Other offenses are included where (A) that offense has as an element the use, attempted use, or threatened use of physical force against the person of another, or (B) the conduct set forth in the violation charged involved use of explosives or, by its nature, presented a serious potential risk of physical injury to another. A crime of violence also includes the offenses of aiding and abetting, conspiring, and attempting to commit such offenses.
>
> 3. 'Controlled substance offense' includes any offense under a federal or state law prohibiting the manufacture, import, export, distribution, or dispensing of a controlled substance (or a counterfeit substance) or the possession of a controlled substance (or a counterfeit substance) with the intent to manufacture, import, export, distribute, or dispense. A controlled substance offense also includes the offenses of aiding and abetting, conspiring, and attempting to commit such offenses.",

Amendment 473

and by inserting in lieu thereof:

"2. 'Crime of violence' is defined in § 4B1.2 (Definitions of Terms Used in Section 4B1.1). See § 4B1.2(1) and Application Notes 1 and 2 of the Commentary to § 4B1.2.

3. 'Controlled substance offense' is defined in § 4B1.2 (Definitions of Terms Used in Section 4B1.1). See § 4B1.2(2) and Application Note 1 of the Commentary to § 4B1.2.".

Reason for Amendment: This amendment clarifies the Commission's intent that the terms "crime of violence" and "controlled substance offense" in § 7B1.1 have the same meaning as these terms have in § 4B1.2.

Effective Date: The effective date of this amendment is November 1, 1992.

474. **Amendment:** Section 1B1.11(b) is amended by inserting the following additional subdivision:

"(3) If the defendant is convicted of two offenses, the first committed before, and the second after, a revised edition of the Guidelines Manual became effective, the revised edition of the Guidelines Manual is to be applied to both offenses.".

The Commentary to § 1B1.11 captioned "Application Note" is amended by inserting the following additional note:

"2. Under subsection (b)(1), the last date of the offense of conviction is the controlling date for ex post facto purposes. For example, if the offense of conviction (i.e., the conduct charged in the count of the indictment or information of which the defendant was convicted) was determined by the court to have been committed between October 15, 1991 and October 28, 1991, the date of October 28, 1991 is the controlling date for ex post facto purposes. This is true even if the defendant's conduct relevant to the determination of the guideline range under § 1B1.3 (Relevant Conduct) included an act that occurred on November 2, 1991 (after a revised Guideline Manual took effect).";

and in the caption by deleting "Note" and inserting in lieu thereof "Notes".

The Commentary to § 1B1.11 captioned "Background" is amended by inserting the following additional sentence as the first sentence of the first paragraph:

"Subsections (a) and (b)(1) provide that the court should apply the Guidelines Manual in effect on the date the defendant is sentenced unless the court determines that doing so would violate the ex post facto clause in Article I, § 9 of the United States Constitution.";

and by inserting the following additional paragraphs at the end:

" Subsection (b)(2) provides that the Guidelines Manual in effect on a particular date shall be applied in its entirety.

Subsection (b)(3) provides that where the defendant is convicted of two offenses, the first committed before, and the second after, a revised edition of the Guidelines Manual became effective, the revised edition of the Guidelines Manual is to be applied to both offenses, even if the revised edition results in an increased penalty for the first offense. Because the defendant completed the second offense after the amendment to the guidelines took effect, the ex post facto clause does not prevent determining the sentence for that count based on the amended guidelines. For example, if a defendant pleads guilty to a single count of embezzlement that occurred after the most recent edition of the Guidelines Manual became effective, the guideline range applicable in sentencing will encompass any relevant conduct (e.g., related embezzlement offenses that may have occurred prior to the effective date of the guideline amendments) for the offense of conviction. The same would be true for a defendant convicted of two counts of embezzlement, one committed before the amendments were enacted, and the second after. In this example, the ex post facto clause would not bar application of the amended guideline to the first conviction; a contrary conclusion would mean that such defendant was subject to a lower guideline range than if convicted only of the second offense. Decisions from several appellate courts addressing the analogous situation of the constitutionality of counting pre-guidelines criminal activity as relevant conduct for a guidelines sentence support this approach. See United States v. Ykema, 887 F.2d 697 (6th Cir. 1989) (upholding inclusion of pre-November 1, 1987, drug quantities as relevant conduct for the count of conviction, noting that habitual offender statutes routinely augment punishment for an offense of conviction based on acts committed before a law is passed), cert. denied, 493 U.S. 1062 (1990); United States v. Allen, 886 F.2d 143 (8th Cir. 1989) (similar); see also United States v. Cusack, 901 F.2d 29 (4th Cir. 1990) (similar).

Moreover, the approach set forth in subsection (b)(3) should be followed regardless of whether the offenses of conviction are the type in which the conduct is grouped under § 3D1.2(d). The ex post facto clause does not distinguish between groupable and nongroupable offenses, and unless that clause would be violated, Congress' directive to apply the sentencing guidelines in effect at the time of sentencing must be followed. Under the guideline sentencing system, a single sentencing range is determined based on the defendant's overall conduct, even if there are multiple counts of conviction (see §§ 3D1.1-3D1.5, 5G1.2). Thus, if a defendant is sentenced in January 1992 for a bank robbery committed in October 1988 and one committed in November 1991, the November 1991 Guidelines Manual should be used to determine a combined guideline range for both counts. See generally United States v. Stephenson, 921 F.2d 438 (2d Cir. 1990) (holding that the Sentencing Commission and Congress intended that the applicable version of the guidelines be applied as a 'cohesive and integrated whole' rather than in a piecemeal fashion).

Consequently, even in a complex case involving multiple counts that occurred under several different versions of the Guidelines Manual, it will not be necessary to compare more than two manuals to determine the applicable guideline range -- the manual in effect at the time the last offense of conviction was completed and the manual in effect at the time of sentencing.".

Reason for Amendment: This amendment expands § 1B1.11 to address what has become a frequently asked hotline question and troublesome application issue -- the application of amended guidelines to multiple count cases in which the effective date of guideline revision(s) occurs between the offenses of conviction. The issue has also produced litigation before several appellate courts. See United States v. Castro, 972 F.2d 1107 (9th Cir. 1992), cert. denied, 113 S. Ct. 1350 (1993); United States v. Seligsohn, 981 F.2d 1418 (3d Cir. 1992); United States v. Hartzog, 983 F.2d 604 (4th Cir. 1993). This amendment extends the Commission's "one book" rule to multiple count cases and sets forth the rationale for this policy.

Effective Date: The effective date of this amendment is November 1, 1993.

Amendment 475

475. Amendment: Chapter One, Part B, is amended by inserting an additional policy statement as § 1B1.12 (Persons Sentenced Under the Federal Juvenile Delinquency Act (Policy Statement)).

Section 5H1.1 is amended by deleting the last paragraph as follows:

"The guidelines are not applicable to a person sentenced as a juvenile delinquent under the provisions of 18 U.S.C. § 5037.".

Reason for Amendment: This amendment adds a policy statement as § 1B1.12 to address the determination of the maximum imposable sentence in the case of a juvenile delinquent. The Supreme Court's decision in United States v. R.L.C., 112 S. Ct. 1329 (1992), requires calculation of the guideline range in order to determine the maximum sentence imposable on a juvenile delinquent.

Effective Date: The effective date of this amendment is November 1, 1993.

476. Amendment: The Commentary to § 2A1.1 captioned "Background" is deleted as follows:

"Background: The maximum penalty authorized by 18 U.S.C. § 1111 for first degree murder is death or life imprisonment. Whether a mandatory minimum term of life imprisonment is applicable to every defendant convicted of first degree murder under 18 U.S.C. § 1111 is a matter of statutory interpretation for the courts. The discussion in Application Note 1, supra, regarding circumstances in which a downward departure may be warranted is relevant in the event the penalty provisions of 18 U.S.C. § 1111 are construed to permit a sentence less than life imprisonment, or in the event the defendant is convicted under a statute that expressly authorizes a sentence of less than life imprisonment (e.g., 18 U.S.C. §§ 2113(e), 2118(c)(2), 21 U.S.C. § 848(e)).

The maximum penalty authorized under 21 U.S.C. § 848(e) is death or life imprisonment. If a term of imprisonment is imposed, the statutorily required minimum term is twenty years.".

Reason for Amendment: This amendment deletes commentary that highlighted the question of whether 18 U.S.C. § 1111 provides a mandatory minimum term of life imprisonment. Since this commentary was written, appellate courts uniformly have held that 18 U.S.C. § 1111 does provide a mandatory minimum term of life imprisonment. See United States v. Sands, 968 F.2d 1058 (10th Cir. 1992), cert. denied, 113 S. Ct. 987 (1993); United States v. LaFleur, 952 F.2d 1537 (9th Cir), modfied and reh'g denied, 971 F.2d 200 (9th Cir. 1991); United States v. Gonzalez, 922 F.2d 1044 (2d Cir.), cert. denied, 112 S. Ct. 660 (1991); United States v. Donley, 878 F.2d 735 (3d Cir. 1989), cert. denied, 494 U.S. 1058 (1990). In addition, this amendment deletes, as unnecessary, several sentences of commentary that merely recite statutory penalties.

Effective Date: The effective date of this amendment is November 1, 1993.

477. Amendment: Section 2A3.1 is amended by redesignating subsection (c) as subsection (d); and by inserting the following additional subsection:

"(c) Cross Reference

(1) If a victim was killed under circumstances that would constitute murder under 18 U.S.C. § 1111 had such killing taken place within

the territorial or maritime jurisdiction of the United States, apply § 2A1.1 (First Degree Murder).".

Section 2A3.1(b)(2) is amended by deleting "otherwise, (B) if the victim was under the age of sixteen" and inserting in lieu thereof "or (B) if the victim had attained the age of twelve years but had not attained the age of sixteen years".

The Commentary to § 2A3.1 captioned "Application Notes" is amended by inserting the following additional note:

> "5. If the defendant was convicted (A) of more than one act of criminal sexual abuse and the counts are grouped under § 3D1.2 (Groups of Closely Related Counts), or (B) of only one such act but the court determines that the offense involved multiple acts of criminal sexual abuse of the same victim or different victims, an upward departure would be warranted.".

Reason for Amendment: This amendment adds a cross reference to § 2A3.1 to address the circumstance in which a victim is murdered during the offense. In addition, an editorial change in § 2A3.1(b)(2) is made to conform the phraseology used in this subsection to that used elsewhere in the guidelines. This amendment also authorizes an upward departure where the offense involved multiple acts of criminal sexual abuse that do not result in an increase in offense level under the multiple count rules in Chapter Three, Part D.

Effective Date: The effective date of this amendment is November 1, 1993.

478. **Amendment:** The Commentary to § 2A4.1 captioned "Background" is amended in the third paragraph by deleting:

> "or to facilitate the commission of another offense. Should the application of this guideline result in a penalty less than the result achieved by applying the guideline for the underlying offense, apply the guideline for the underlying offense (e.g., § 2A3.1, Criminal Sexual Abuse).",

and inserting in lieu thereof:

> "(subsection (b)(1)) or involves another federal, state, or local offense that results in a greater offense level (subsections (b)(7) and (c)(1)).".

The Commentary to § 2K1.3 captioned "Application Notes" is amended in Note 4 by inserting "(federal, state, or local)" immediately following "any offense".

The Commentary to § 2K1.3 captioned "Application Notes" is amended in Note 8 by inserting "(which may be a federal, state, or local offense)" immediately before "is".

The Commentary to § 2K2.1 captioned "Application Notes" is amended in Note 7 by inserting "(federal, state, or local)" immediately following "any offense".

The Commentary to § 2K2.1 captioned "Application Notes" is amended in Note 14 by inserting "(which may be a federal, state, or local offense)" immediately before "is".

The Commentary to § 2K2.1 captioned "Application Notes" is amended by inserting the following additional note:

> "19. The enhancement under subsection (b)(4) for a stolen firearm or a firearm with an altered or obliterated serial number applies whether or not the defendant knew or had reason to believe that the firearm was stolen or had an altered or obliterated serial number.".

Reason for Amendment: This amendment clarifies that the terms "another offense" and "other offense" in § 2A4.1(b)(7), and "felony offense," "another felony offense," "another offense," and "other offense" in §§ 2K1.3 and 2K2.1, refer to federal, state, or local offenses. In addition, this amendment clarifies that the enhancement in § 2K2.1(b)(4) applies whether or not the defendant knew or had reason to believe the firearm was stolen or had an altered or obliterated serial number.

Effective Date: The effective date of this amendment is November 1, 1993.

479. **Amendment:** Section 2A4.2 is amended by inserting the following additional subsection:

"(b)   Cross Reference

(1)   If the defendant was a participant in the kidnapping offense, apply § 2A4.1 (Kidnapping; Abduction; Unlawful Restraint).".

The Commentary to § 2A4.2 is amended by inserting the following immediately before "Background".

"Application Note:

1.   A 'participant' is a person who is criminally responsible for the commission of the offense, but need not have been convicted.".

Section 2B3.2(c) is amended by deleting "Reference" and inserting in lieu thereof "References"; by renumbering subdivision (1) as subdivision (2); and by inserting the following additional subdivision:

"(1)   If a victim was killed under circumstances that would constitute murder under 18 U.S.C. § 1111 had such killing taken place within the territorial or maritime jurisdiction of the United States, apply § 2A1.1 (First Degree Murder).".

Section 2B3.3 is amended by inserting the following additional subsection:

"(c)   Cross References

(1)   If the offense involved extortion under color of official right, apply § 2C1.1 (Offering, Giving, Soliciting, or Receiving a Bribe; Extortion Under Color of Official Right).

(2)   If the offense involved extortion by force or threat of injury or serious damage, apply § 2B3.2 (Extortion by Force or Threat of Injury or Serious Damage).".

Section 2D1.1 is amended by inserting the following additional subsection:

"(d)   Cross Reference

(1)   If a victim was killed under circumstances that would constitute murder under 18 U.S.C. § 1111 had such killing taken place within the territorial or maritime jurisdiction of the United States, apply § 2A1.1 (First Degree Murder).".

Section 2E2.1 is amended by inserting the following additional subsection:

"(c) Cross Reference

(1) If a victim was killed under circumstances that would constitute murder under 18 U.S.C. § 1111 had such killing taken place within the territorial or maritime jurisdiction of the United States, apply § 2A1.1 (First Degree Murder).".

Reason for Amendment: This amendment adds a cross reference to § 2A4.2 to address the circumstance in which the defendant was a participant in the underlying kidnapping offense. This amendment also adds cross references to §§ 2B3.2, 2D1.1, and 2E2.1 to address the circumstance in which a victim is murdered during the offense. Finally, this amendment adds cross references to § 2B3.3 to ensure the selection of the appropriate guideline.

Effective Date: The effective date of this amendment is November 1, 1993.

480. **Amendment:** Section 2A5.2(a)(1) is amended by deleting "defendant intentionally endangered" and inserting in lieu thereof "offense involved intentionally endangering".

Section 2A5.2(a)(2) is amended by deleting "defendant recklessly endangered" and inserting in lieu thereof "offense involved recklessly endangering".

Section 2A6.1(b)(1) is amended by deleting "defendant engaged in" and inserting in lieu thereof "offense involved".

Section 2A6.1(b)(2) is amended by deleting "the defendant's conduct" and inserting in lieu thereof "the offense".

Reason for Amendment: This amendment deletes language that could be construed as a limitation on the scope of conduct for which a defendant is accountable under § 1B1.3 (Relevant Conduct) and replaces it with language consistent with that used in other offense guidelines.

Effective Date: The effective date of this amendment is November 1, 1993.

481. **Amendment:** Section 2B1.1 is amended in the title by inserting "; Receiving, Transporting, Transferring, Transmitting, or Possessing Stolen Property" at the end thereof.

Section 2B1.1(b)(2) is amended by inserting "(A)" immediately following "If"; and by inserting "or the taking of such item was an object of the offense; or (B) the stolen property received, transported, transferred, transmitted, or possessed was a firearm, destructive device, or controlled substance," immediately following "taken,".

Section 2B1.1(b)(4) is amended by inserting "(A)" immediately following "If"; and by inserting "or the taking of such item was an object of the offense; or (B) the stolen property received, transported, transferred, transmitted, or possessed was undelivered United States mail," immediately following "taken,".

Section 2B1.1(b)(5) is amended by inserting "(A)" immediately before "If"; and by inserting "; or (B) If the offense involved receiving stolen property, and the defendant was a person in the business of receiving and selling stolen property, increase by 4 levels." immediately following "levels".

The Commentary to § 2B1.1 captioned "Statutory Provisions" is amended by inserting

Amendment 481 APPENDIX C - VOLUME I November 1, 2013

"553(a)(1)," immediately following "225,"; by inserting "662, 664," immediately before "1702"; and by deleting ", 2317" and inserting in lieu thereof "-2317; 29 U.S.C. § 501(c)".

The Commentary to § 2B1.1 captioned "Application Notes" is amended in Note 2 by inserting the following additional paragraph as the next to the last paragraph:

"In stolen property offenses (receiving, transporting, transferring, transmitting, or possessing stolen property), the loss is the value of the stolen property determined as in a theft offense.".

The Commentary to § 2B1.1 captioned "Application Notes" is amended by inserting the following additional note:

"14. If the offense involved theft or embezzlement from an employee pension or welfare benefit plan (a violation of 18 U.S.C. § 664) and the defendant was a fiduciary of the benefit plan, an adjustment under § 3B1.3 (Abuse of Position of Trust or Use of Special Skill) will apply. 'Fiduciary of the benefit plan' is defined in 29 U.S.C. § 1002(21)(A) to mean a person who exercises any discretionary authority or control in respect to the management of such plan or exercises authority or control in respect to management or disposition of its assets, or who renders investment advice for a fee or other direct or indirect compensation with respect to any moneys or other property of such plan, or has any authority or responsibility to do so, or who has any discretionary authority or responsibility in the administration of such plan.

If the offense involved theft or embezzlement from a labor union (a violation of 29 U.S.C. § 501(c)) and the defendant was a union officer or occupied a position of trust in the union as set forth in 29 U.S.C. § 501(a), an adjustment under § 3B1.3 (Abuse of Position of Trust or Use of Special Skill) will apply.".

The Commentary to § 2B1.1 captioned "Background" is amended in the first paragraph by deleting "property taken" and inserting in lieu thereof "the property stolen"; by deleting "theft offenses," and inserting in lieu thereof "theft and other offenses involving stolen property"; and by deleting "loss from the theft" and inserting in lieu thereof "loss".

Section 2B1.2 is deleted in its entirety as follows:

"§ 2B1.2. Receiving, Transporting, Transferring, Transmitting, or Possessing Stolen Property

(a) Base Offense Level: 4

(b) Specific Offense Characteristics

(1) If the value of the stolen property exceeded $100, increase by the corresponding number of levels from the table in § 2B1.1.

(2) If the property included a firearm, destructive device, or controlled substance, increase by 1 level; but if the resulting offense level is less than 7, increase to 7.

(3) If the property included undelivered United States mail and the offense level as determined above is less than level 6, increase to level 6.

(4) (A) If the offense was committed by a person in the business of receiving and selling stolen property, increase by 4 levels; or

(B) If the offense involved more than minimal planning, increase by 2 levels

(5) If the offense involved an organized scheme to receive stolen vehicles or vehicle parts, and the offense level as determined above is less than level 14, increase to level 14.

Commentary

Statutory Provisions: 18 U.S.C. §§ 553(a)(1), 659, 662, 1708, 2312-2317. For additional statutory provision(s), see Appendix A (Statutory Index).

Application Notes:

1. 'More than minimal planning,' 'firearm,' and 'destructive device' are defined in the Commentary to § 1B1.1 (Application Instructions).

2. Valuation of property is discussed in the Commentary to § 2B1.1.

3. 'Undelivered United States mail' means mail that has not actually been received by the addressee or his agent (e.g., it includes mail that is in the addressee's mail box).

4. Subsection (b)(5), referring to an 'organized scheme to receive stolen vehicles or vehicle parts,' provides an alternative minimum measure of loss in the case of an ongoing, sophisticated operation such as an auto theft ring or 'chop shop.' 'Vehicles' refers to all forms of vehicles, including aircraft and watercraft. See Commentary to § 2B1.1 (Larceny, Embezzlement, and Other Forms of Theft).

Background: The treatment accorded receiving stolen property parallels that given theft. Persons who receive stolen property for resale receive a sentence enhancement because the amount of property is likely to underrepresent the scope of their criminality and the extent to which they encourage or facilitate other crimes.".

Section 2B2.1 is amended in the title by inserting "or a Structure Other than a Residence" at the end thereof.

Section 2B2.1(a) is amended by deleting "Base Offense Level: 17" and inserting in lieu thereof:

"Base Offense Level:

(1) 17, if a residence; or

(2) 12, if a structure other than a residence.".

The Commentary to § 2B2.1 captioned "Statutory Provision" is amended by deleting "Provision: 18 U.S.C. § 1153" and inserting in lieu thereof "Provisions: 18 U.S.C. §§ 1153, 2113(a), 2115, 2117, 2118(b). For additional statutory provision(s), see Appendix A (Statutory Index)".

Section 2B2.2 is deleted in its entirety as follows:

"§ 2B2.2. Burglary of Other Structures

(a) Base Offense Level: 12

(b) Specific Offense Characteristics

(1) If the offense involved more than minimal planning, increase by 2 levels.

(2) If the loss exceeded $2,500, increase by the corresponding number of levels from the table in § 2B2.1.

(3) If a firearm, destructive device, or controlled substance was taken, or if the taking of such item was an object of the offense, increase by 1 level.

(4) If a dangerous weapon (including a firearm) was possessed, increase by 2 levels.

Commentary

Statutory Provisions: 18 U.S.C. §§ 2113(a), 2115, 2117, 2118(b). For additional statutory provision(s), see Appendix A (Statutory Index).

Application Notes:

1. 'More than minimal planning,' 'firearm,' 'destructive device,' and 'dangerous weapon' are defined in the Commentary to § 1B1.1 (Application Instructions).

2. Valuation of loss is discussed in the Commentary to § 2B1.1 (Larceny, Embezzlement, and Other Forms of Theft).

3. Subsection (b)(4) does not apply to possession of a dangerous weapon (including a firearm) that was stolen during the course of the offense.

Background: The offense level for burglary is significantly higher than that for theft for low losses, but is approximately the same for very high losses. Weapon possession, but not use, is a specific offense characteristic because use of a weapon (including to threaten) ordinarily would make the offense robbery. Weapon use would be a ground for upward departure.".

Chapter Two, Part B, Subpart 5 is amended in the title by deleting ", FORGERY," immediately before "AND".

Section 2B5.2 is deleted in its entirety as follows:

"§ 2B5.2. Forgery; Offenses Involving Altered or Counterfeit Instruments Other than Counterfeit Bearer Obligations of the United States

Apply § 2F1.1 (Fraud and Deceit).

Commentary

Statutory Provisions: 18 U.S.C. §§ 471-473, 500, 510, 1003, 2314, 2315. For additional statutory provision(s), see Appendix A (Statutory Index).".

November 1, 2013 APPENDIX C - VOLUME I **Amendment 481**

Section 2B5.3 is amended in the title by inserting "or Trademark" at the end thereof.

The Commentary to § 2B5.3 captioned "Statutory Provisions" is amended by deleting "2319" and inserting in lieu thereof "2318-2320".

The Commentary to § 2B5.3 captioned "Background" is amended in the first paragraph by inserting "and trademark" immediately following "copyright".

Section 2B5.4 is deleted in its entirety as follows:

"§ 2B5.4. Criminal Infringement of Trademark

(a) Base Offense Level: 6

(b) Specific Offense Characteristic

(1) If the retail value of the infringing items exceeded $2,000, increase by the corresponding number of levels from the table in § 2F1.1 (Fraud and Deceit).

Commentary

Statutory Provisions: 18 U.S.C. §§ 2318, 2320.

Background: The Commission concluded that trademark infringement is roughly comparable to copyright infringement.".

Section 2D3.2 is amended in the title by deleting "Manufacture of Controlled Substance in Excess of or Unauthorized by Registration Quota; Attempt or Conspiracy" and inserting in lieu thereof "Regulatory Offenses Involving Controlled Substances; Attempt or Conspiracy".

The Commentary to § 2D3.2 captioned "Statutory Provisions" is amended by deleting "842(b), 843(a)(3)" and inserting in lieu thereof "842(a)(2), (9), (10), (b), 954, 961".

The Commentary to § 2D3.2 captioned "Background" is amended by deleting "This offense is a misdemeanor" and inserting in lieu thereof "These offenses are misdemeanors".

Sections 2D3.3, 2D3.4, and 2D3.5 are deleted in their entirety as follows:

"§ 2D3.3. Illegal Use of Registration Number to Distribute or Dispense a Controlled Substance to Another Registrant or Authorized Person; Attempt or Conspiracy

(a) Base Offense Level: 4

Commentary

Statutory Provision: 21 U.S.C. § 842(a)(2).

Background: This offense is a misdemeanor. The maximum term of imprisonment authorized by statute is one year.

§ 2D3.4. Illegal Transfer or Transshipment of a Controlled Substance; Attempt or Conspiracy

(a) Base Offense Level: 4

– 331 –

Commentary

Statutory Provisions: 21 U.S.C. §§ 954, 961.

Background: This offense is a misdemeanor. The maximum term of imprisonment authorized by statute is one year.

§ 2D3.5.   Violation of Recordkeeping or Reporting Requirements for Listed Chemicals and Certain Machines; Attempt or Conspiracy

(a)   Base Offense Level: 4

Commentary

Statutory Provisions: 21 U.S.C. § 842(a)(9), (10).".

Section 2E1.5 is deleted in its entirety as follows:

"§ 2E1.5.   Hobbs Act Extortion or Robbery

Apply § 2B3.1 (Robbery), § 2B3.2 (Extortion by Force or Threat of Injury or Serious Damage), § 2B3.3 (Blackmail and Similar Forms of Extortion), or § 2C1.1 (Offering, Giving, Soliciting, or Receiving a Bribe; Extortion Under Color of Official Right), as applicable.

Commentary

Statutory Provision: 18 U.S.C. § 1951.".

Section 2E3.1 is amended in the title by deleting "Engaging in a Gambling Business" and inserting in lieu thereof "Gambling Offenses".

Section 2E3.1(a) is amended by deleting "12" and inserting in lieu thereof:

"(1)   12, if the offense was (A) engaging in a gambling business; (B) transmission of wagering information; or (C) committed as part of, or to facilitate, a commercial gambling operation; or

(2)   6, otherwise.".

The Commentary to § 2E3.1 captioned "Statutory Provision" is amended by deleting "Provision: 18 U.S.C. § 1955" and inserting in lieu thereof "Provisions: 15 U.S.C. §§ 1172-1175; 18 U.S.C. §§ 1082, 1301-1304, 1306, 1511, 1953, 1955. For additional statutory provision(s), see Appendix A (Statutory Index)".

Sections 2E3.2 and 2E3.3 are deleted in their entirety as follows:

"§ 2E3.2.   Transmission of Wagering Information

(a)   Base Offense Level: 12

Commentary

Statutory Provision: 18 U.S.C. § 1084.

§ 2E3.3.   Other Gambling Offenses

(a)   Base Offense Level: 6

(b) Specific Offense Characteristic

(1) If the offense is committed as part of, or to facilitate, a commercial gambling operation, increase by 6 levels.

Commentary

Statutory Provisions: 15 U.S.C. §§ 1172-1175; 18 U.S.C. §§ 1082, 1301-1304, 1306, 1511, 1953. For additional statutory provision(s), see Appendix A (Statutory Index).

Background: This section includes a wide variety of conduct. A specific offense characteristic has been included to distinguish commercial from other gambling offenses.".

Section 2E5.1 is amended in the title by inserting "; Prohibited Payments or Lending of Money by Employer or Agent to Employees, Representatives, or Labor Organizations" at the end thereof.

Section 2E5.1(b)(1) is amended by inserting "or labor organization" immediately following "plan".

The Commentary to § 2E5.1 captioned "Statutory Provision" is amended by deleting "Provision: 18 U.S.C. § 1954" and inserting in lieu thereof "Provisions: 18 U.S.C. § 1954; 29 U.S.C. § 186".

The Commentary to § 2E5.1 captioned "Background" is amended by inserting ", or labor organizations" immediately following "plans"; and by deleting the last sentence as follows:

"A more severe penalty is warranted in a bribery where the payment is the primary motivation for an action to be taken, as opposed to graft, where the prohibited payment is given because of a person's actions, duties, or decisions without a prior understanding that the recipient's performance will be directly influenced by the gift.".

Section 2E5.2 is deleted in its entirety as follows:

"§ 2E5.2. Theft or Embezzlement from Employee Pension and Welfare Benefit Plans

Apply § 2B1.1 (Larceny, Embezzlement, and Other Forms of Theft).

Commentary

Statutory Provision: 18 U.S.C. § 664.

Application Note:

1. In the case of a defendant who was a fiduciary of the benefit plan, an adjustment under § 3B1.3 (Abuse of Position of Trust or Use of Special Skill) will apply. 'Fiduciary of the benefit plan' is defined in 29 U.S.C. § 1002(21)(A) to mean a person who exercises any discretionary authority or control in respect to the management of such plan or exercises authority or control in respect to management or disposition of its assets, or who renders investment advice for a fee or other direct or indirect compensation with respect to any moneys or other property of such plan, or has any authority or responsibility to do so, or who has any discretionary authority or responsibility in the administration of such plan.

Amendment 481 APPENDIX C - VOLUME I November 1, 2013

Background: This section covers theft or conversion from employee benefit plans by fiduciaries, or by any person, including borrowers to whom loans are disbursed based upon materially defective loan applications, service providers who are paid on inflated billings, and beneficiaries paid as the result of fraudulent claims.".

Section 2E5.3 is amended in the title by inserting "; Failure to Maintain and Falsification of Records Required by the Labor Management Reporting and Disclosure Act" at the end thereof.

Section 2E5.3(a)(2) is amended by deleting "relating to the operation of an employee benefit plan, apply § 2E5.2" and inserting in lieu thereof ", apply § 2B1.1".

The Commentary to § 2E5.3 captioned "Statutory Provision" is amended by deleting "Provision: 18 U.S.C. § 1027" and inserting in lieu thereof "Provisions: 18 U.S.C. § 1027; 29 U.S.C. §§ 439, 461, 1131. For additional statutory provision(s), see Appendix A (Statutory Index)".

The Commentary to § 2E5.3 captioned "Background" is amended by inserting the following additional sentence as the second sentence:

"It also covers failure to maintain proper documents required by the LMRDA or falsification of such documents.".

Sections 2E5.4, 2E5.5, and 2E5.6 are deleted in their entirety as follows:

"§ 2E5.4. Embezzlement or Theft from Labor Unions in the Private Sector

Apply § 2B1.1 (Larceny, Embezzlement, and Other Forms of Theft).

Commentary

Statutory Provision: 29 U.S.C. § 501(c).

Application Note:

1. In the case of a defendant who was a union officer or occupied a position of trust in the union, as set forth in 29 U.S.C. § 501(a), an adjustment under § 3B1.3 (Abuse of Position of Trust or Use of Special Skill) would apply.

Background: This section includes embezzlement or theft from a labor organization. It is directed at union officers and persons employed by a union.

§ 2E5.5. Failure to Maintain and Falsification of Records Required by the Labor Management Reporting and Disclosure Act

(a) Base Offense Level (Apply the greater):

(1) 6; or

(2) If the offense was committed to facilitate or conceal a theft or embezzlement, or an offense involving a bribe or gratuity, apply § 2E5.4 or § 2E5.6, as applicable.

Commentary

Statutory Provisions: 29 U.S.C. §§ 439, 461. For additional statutory provision(s), see Appendix A (Statutory Index).

Background: This section covers failure to maintain proper documents required by the LMRDA or falsification of such documents. This offense is a misdemeanor.

§ 2E5.6. Prohibited Payments or Lending of Money by Employer or Agent to Employees, Representatives, or Labor Organizations

(a) Base Offense Level:

(1) 10, if a bribe; or

(2) 6, if a gratuity.

(b) Specific Offense Characteristic

(1) Increase by the number of levels from the table in § 2F1.1 (Fraud and Deceit) corresponding to the value of the prohibited payment or the value of the improper benefit to the payer, whichever is greater.

(c) Special Instruction for Fines - Organizations

(1) In lieu of the pecuniary loss under subsection (a)(3) of § 8C2.4 (Base Fine), use the greatest of: (A) the value of the unlawful payment; (B) if a bribe, the value of the benefit received or to be received in return for the unlawful payment; or (C) if a bribe, the consequential damages resulting from the unlawful payment.

Commentary

Statutory Provision: 29 U.S.C. § 186.

Application Notes:

1. 'Bribe' refers to the offer or acceptance of an unlawful payment with the specific understanding that it will corruptly affect an official action of the recipient.

2. 'Gratuity' refers to the offer or acceptance of an unlawful payment other than a bribe.

3. 'Value of the improper benefit to the payer' is explained in the Commentary to § 2C1.1 (Offering, Giving, Soliciting, or Receiving a Bribe; Extortion Under Color of Official Right).".

Section 2F1.1 is amended in the title by inserting "; Forgery; Offenses Involving Altered or Counterfeit Instruments Other than Counterfeit Bearer Obligations of the United States" at the end thereof.

The Commentary to § 2F1.1 captioned "Statutory Provisions" is amended by inserting "471-473, 500, 510," immediately following "289,"; and by inserting ", 2314, 2315" immediately following "1344".

Section 2J1.3 is amended in the title by inserting "; Bribery of Witness" at the end thereof.

Section 2J1.3(b)(2) is amended by deleting "perjury or subornation of perjury" and insert-

Amendment 481   APPENDIX C - VOLUME I   November 1, 2013

ing in lieu thereof "perjury, subornation of perjury, or witness bribery".

Section 2J1.3(c)(1) is amended by deleting "perjury or subornation of perjury" and inserting in lieu thereof "perjury, subornation of perjury, or witness bribery".

The Commentary to § 2J1.3 captioned "Statutory Provisions" is amended by inserting "201(b)(3), (4)," immediately before "1621".

The Commentary to § 2J1.3 captioned "Application Notes" is amended in Note 3 by inserting ", subornation of perjury, or witness bribery" immediately following "perjury".

The Commentary to § 2J1.3 captioned "Background" is amended by deleting "perjury and subornation of perjury" and inserting in lieu thereof "perjury, subornation of perjury, and witness bribery".

Section 2J1.8 is deleted in its entirety as follows:

"§ 2J1.8.   Bribery of Witness

     (a)   Base Offense Level: 12

     (b)   Specific Offense Characteristic

           (1)   If the offense resulted in substantial interference with the administration of justice, increase by 3 levels.

     (c)   Cross Reference

           (1)   If the offense involved bribery of a witness in respect to a criminal offense, apply § 2X3.1 (Accessory After the Fact) in respect to that criminal offense, if the resulting offense level is greater than that determined above.

Commentary

Statutory Provisions: 18 U.S.C. § 201(b)(3), (4).

Application Notes:

1.   'Substantial interference with the administration of justice' includes a premature or improper termination of a felony investigation; an indictment, verdict, or any judicial determination based upon perjury, false testimony, or other false evidence; or the unnecessary expenditure of substantial governmental or court resources.

2.   For offenses covered under this section, Chapter Three, Part C (Obstruction) does not apply, unless the defendant obstructed the investigation or trial of the witness bribery count.

3.   In the event that the defendant is convicted under this section as well as for the underlying offense (i.e., the offense with respect to which the bribery occurred), see the Commentary to Chapter Three, Part C (Obstruction), and to § 3D1.2(c) (Groups of Closely Related Counts).

Background: This section applies to witness bribery. The offense levels correspond to those for perjury (§ 2J1.3).".

Section 2K1.1 is amended in the title by inserting "; Improper Storage of Explosive Materials" at the end thereof.

The Commentary to § 2K1.1 captioned "Statutory Provisions" is amended by deleting "842(k), 844(b)" and inserting in lieu thereof "842(j), (k), 844(b). For additional statutory provision(s), see Appendix A (Statutory Index)".

Section 2K1.2 is deleted in its entirety as follows:

"§ 2K1.2. Improper Storage of Explosive Materials

    (a)   Base Offense Level: 6

Commentary

Statutory Provision: 18 U.S.C. § 842(j). For additional statutory provision(s), see Appendix A (Statutory Index).

Background: The above-referenced provision is a misdemeanor. The maximum term of imprisonment authorized by statute is one year.".

Section 2K1.7 is deleted in its entirety as follows:

"§ 2K1.7. Use of Fire or Explosives to Commit a Federal Felony

    (a)   If the defendant, whether or not convicted of another crime, was convicted under 18 U.S.C. § 844(h), the term of imprisonment is that required by statute.

    (b)   Special Instruction for Fines

        (1)   Where there is a federal conviction for the underlying offense, the fine guideline shall be the fine guideline that would have been applicable had there only been a conviction for the underlying offense. This guideline shall be used as a consolidated fine guideline for both the underlying offense and the conviction underlying this section.

Commentary

Statutory Provision: 18 U.S.C. § 844(h).

Application Notes:

1.   The statute requires a term of imprisonment imposed under this section to run consecutively to any other term of imprisonment.

2.   Imposition of a term of supervised release is governed by the provisions of § 5D1.1 (Imposition of a Term of Supervised Release).

3.   Where a sentence under this section is imposed in conjunction with a sentence for an underlying offense, any specific offense characteristic for the use of fire or explosives is not to be applied in respect to the guideline for the underlying offense.

4.   Subsection (b) sets forth special provisions concerning the imposition of

fines. Where there is also a conviction for the underlying offense, a consolidated fine guideline is determined by the offense level that would have applied to the underlying offense absent a conviction under 18 U.S.C. § 844(h). This is required because the offense level for the underlying offense may be reduced in that any specific offense characteristic for use of fire or explosives would not be applied (see Application Note 3). The Commission has not established a fine guideline range for the unusual case in which there is no conviction for the underlying offense, although a fine is authorized under 18 U.S.C. § 3571.".

Section 2K2.4 is amended in the title by deleting "Firearms or Armor-Piercing Ammunition" and inserting in lieu thereof "Firearm, Armor-Piercing Ammunition, or Explosive".

Section 2K2.4(a) is amended by deleting "§ 924(c)" and inserting in lieu thereof "§ 844(h), § 924(c),".

The Commentary to § 2K2.4 captioned "Statutory Provisions" is amended by inserting "844(h)," immediately before "924(c)".

The Commentary to § 2K2.4 captioned "Application Notes" is amended in Note 2 in the first paragraph by deleting "a firearm" and inserting in lieu thereof "an explosive or firearm"; and by deleting the comma immediately following "(Robbery))".

The Commentary to § 2K2.4 captioned "Application Notes" is amended in Note 4 by deleting "§ 924(c)" wherever it occurs and inserting in lieu thereof in each instance "§ 844(h), § 924(c),".

The Commentary to § 2K2.4 captioned "Background" is amended by deleting "924(c)" and inserting in lieu thereof "844(h), 924(c),"; and by inserting "explosive or" immediately before "firearm".

Chapter Two, Part K, Subpart 3 is amended in the title by deleting "TRANSPORTATION OF HAZARDOUS MATERIALS" and inserting in lieu thereof "MAILING INJURIOUS ARTICLES".

Section 2K3.1 is deleted in its entirety as follows:

"§ 2K3.1. Unlawfully Transporting Hazardous Materials in Commerce

Apply the guideline provision for § 2Q1.2 (Mishandling of Hazardous or Toxic Substances or Pesticides; Recordkeeping, Tampering, and Falsification).

Commentary

Statutory Provision: 49 U.S.C. § 1809(b). For additional statutory provision(s), see Appendix A (Statutory Index).

Background: This conduct involves the same risks as the conduct covered under § 2Q1.2 (Mishandling of Hazardous or Toxic Substances or Pesticides; Recordkeeping, Tampering, and Falsification). Accordingly, that guideline applies.".

Section 2L2.1 is amended in the title by deleting "Documents" and inserting in lieu thereof "a Document"; and by inserting ", or a United States Passport" immediately following "Status".

Section 2L2.1(b)(2) is amended by inserting "or passports" immediately following "documents"; and by inserting "/Passports" immediately following "Documents".

The Commentary to § 2L2.1 captioned "Statutory Provisions" is amended by inserting "1542, 1544," immediately following "1427,".

The Commentary to § 2L2.1 captioned "Application Notes" is amended in Note 2 by deleting "set as one document" and inserting in lieu thereof "documents as one set".

Section 2L2.2 is amended in the title by inserting "; Fraudulently Acquiring or Improperly Using a United States Passport" at the end thereof.

The Commentary to § 2L2.2 captioned "Statutory Provisions" is amended by inserting "1542-1544," immediately before "1546.".

Sections 2L2.3 and 2L2.4 are deleted in their entirety as follows:

"§ 2L2.3.   Trafficking in a United States Passport

(a) Base Offense Level: 9

(b) Specific Offense Characteristics

(1) If the defendant committed the offense other than for profit, decrease by 3 levels.

(2) If the offense involved six or more passports, increase as follows:

	Number of Passports	Increase in Level
(A)	6-24	add 2
(B)	25-99	add 4
(C)	100 or more	add 6.

Commentary

Statutory Provisions: 18 U.S.C. §§ 1542, 1544. For additional statutory provision(s), see Appendix A (Statutory Index).

Application Note:

1. 'For profit' means for financial gain or commercial advantage.

§ 2L2.4.   Fraudulently Acquiring or Improperly Using a United States Passport

(a) Base Offense Level: 6

(b) Specific Offense Characteristic

(1) If the defendant is an unlawful alien who has been deported (voluntarily or involuntarily) on one or more occasions prior to the instant offense, increase by 2 levels.

Commentary

Statutory Provisions: 18 U.S.C. §§ 1543, 1544. For additional statutory provision(s), see Appendix A (Statutory Index).

Amendment 481 APPENDIX C - VOLUME I November 1, 2013

Application Note:

1. For the purposes of Chapter Three, Part D (Multiple Counts), a conviction for unlawfully entering or remaining in the United States (§ 2L1.2) arising from the same course of conduct is treated as a closely related count, and is therefore grouped with an offense covered by this guideline.".

Section 2M2.1 is amended in the title by inserting ", or Production of Defective," immediately following "Destruction of".

The Commentary to § 2M2.1 captioned "Statutory Provisions" is amended by inserting ", 2154" immediately following "2153".

Section 2M2.2 is deleted in its entirety as follows:

"§ 2M2.2. Production of Defective War Material, Premises, or Utilities

(a) Base Offense Level: 32

Commentary

Statutory Provision: 18 U.S.C. § 2154.".

Section 2M2.3 is amended in the title by inserting ", or Production of Defective," immediately following "Destruction of".

The Commentary to § 2M2.3 captioned "Statutory Provisions" is amended by inserting ", 2156" immediately following "2155".

Section 2M2.4 is deleted in its entirety as follows:

"§ 2M2.4. Production of Defective National Defense Material, Premises, or Utilities

(a) Base Offense Level: 26

Commentary

Statutory Provision: 18 U.S.C. § 2156.".

Section 2M3.3 is amended in the title by inserting "; Disclosure of Classified Cryptographic Information; Unauthorized Disclosure to a Foreign Government or a Communist Organization of Classified Information by Government Employee; Unauthorized Receipt of Classified Information" at the end thereof.

Section 2M3.3(a)(1) is amended by deleting "was transmitted" immediately following "information".

The Commentary to § 2M3.3 captioned "Statutory Provisions" is amended by deleting ". For additional statutory provision(s), see Appendix A (Statutory Index)" and inserting in lieu thereof ", 798; 50 U.S.C. § 783(b), (c)".

The Commentary to § 2M3.3 captioned "Background" is amended by inserting the following additional paragraph at the end:

" This section also covers statutes that proscribe the disclosure of classified information concerning cryptographic or communication intelligence to the detriment of the United States or for the benefit of a foreign government, the unauthorized disclosure to a foreign government or a communist organization of classified information by a government employee, and the unauthorized receipt of classified information.".

Sections 2M3.6, 2M3.7, and 2M3.8 are deleted in their entirety as follows:

"§ 2M3.6. Disclosure of Classified Cryptographic Information

    (a)   Base Offense Level:

        (1)   29, if top secret information was disclosed; or

        (2)   24, otherwise.

Commentary

Statutory Provision: 18 U.S.C. § 798.

Application Note:

1.   See Commentary to § 2M3.1.

Background: The statute covered in this section proscribes the disclosure of classified information concerning cryptographic or communication intelligence to the detriment of the United States or for the benefit of a foreign government.

§ 2M3.7. Unauthorized Disclosure to Foreign Government or a Communist Organization of Classified Information by Government Employee

    (a)   Base Offense Level:

        (1)   29, if top secret information was disclosed; or

        (2)   24, otherwise.

Commentary

Statutory Provision: 50 U.S.C. § 783(b).

Application Note:

1.   See Commentary to § 2M3.1.

§ 2M3.8. Receipt of Classified Information

    (a)   Base Offense Level:

        (1)   29, if top secret information was received; or

        (2)   24, otherwise.

Commentary

Statutory Provision: 50 U.S.C. § 783(c).

Application Note:

Amendment 481

1. See Commentary to § 2M3.1.".

Section 2Q1.2 is amended in the title by inserting "; Unlawfully Transporting Hazardous Materials in Commerce" at the end thereof.

The Commentary to § 2Q1.2 captioned "Statutory Provisions" is amended by inserting "; 49 U.S.C. § 1809(b)" immediately following "1822(b)".

Reason for Amendment: This amendment deletes 25 offense guidelines by consolidating them with other offense guidelines that cover similar offense conduct and have identical or very similar base offense levels and adjustments. Consolidation of offense guidelines in this manner has a number of practical advantages: it shortens and simplifies the Guidelines Manual and reduces the likelihood of inconsistency in phraseology and definitions from section to section; it will reduce possible confusion and litigation as to which guideline applies to particular conduct; it will reduce the number of conforming amendments required whenever similar sections are amended; and it will aid the development of case law because cases involving similar or identical concepts and definitions can be referenced under one guideline rather than different guidelines.

Effective Date: The effective date of this amendment is November 1, 1993.

482. **Amendment:** The Commentary to § 2B1.1 captioned "Application Notes" is amended in Note 2 by inserting the following additional sentence as the fourth sentence of the first paragraph:

> "Loss does not include the interest that could have been earned had the funds not been stolen.";

and by inserting the following additional paragraphs as the second and third paragraphs:

> "Where the offense involved making a fraudulent loan or credit card application, or other unlawful conduct involving a loan or credit card, the loss is to be determined under the principles set forth in the Commentary to § 2F1.1 (Fraud and Deceit).
>
> In certain cases, an offense may involve a series of transactions without a corresponding increase in loss. For example, a defendant may embezzle $5,000 from a bank and conceal this embezzlement by shifting this amount from one account to another in a series of nine transactions over a six-month period. In this example, the loss is $5,000 (the amount taken), not $45,000 (the sum of the nine transactions), because the additional transactions did not increase the actual or potential loss.".

The Commentary to § 2B1.1 captioned "Application Notes" is amended by deleting Note 3 as follows:

> "3. The loss need not be determined with precision, and may be inferred from any reasonably reliable information available, including the scope of the operation.",

and inserting in lieu thereof:

> "3. For the purposes of subsection (b)(1), the loss need not be determined with precision. The court need only make a reasonable estimate of the loss, given the available information. This estimate, for example, may be based upon the approximate number of victims and the average loss to each victim, or on more general factors such as the scope and duration of the offense.".

The Commentary to § 2B5.3 is amended by inserting the following immediately before "Background":

"Application Note:

1. 'Infringing items' means the items that violate the copyright or trademark laws (not the legitimate items that are infringed upon).".

The Commentary to § 2B6.1 captioned "Application Note" is amended in the caption by deleting "Note" and inserting in lieu thereof "Notes"; and by inserting the following additional Note:

"2. The 'corresponding number of levels from the table in § 2F1.1 (Fraud and Deceit),' as used in subsection (b)(1), refers to the number of levels corresponding to the retail value of the motor vehicles or parts involved.".

Section 2F1.1(b)(3) is amended by deleting "or process" and by inserting in lieu thereof ", or process not addressed elsewhere in the guidelines".

The Commentary to § 2F1.1 captioned "Application Notes" is amended in Note 5 in the first sentence by inserting a comma immediately following "decree"; and by inserting the following additional sentence at the end:

"This subsection does not apply to conduct addressed elsewhere in the guidelines; e.g., a violation of a condition of release (addressed in § 2J1.7 (Offense Committed While on Release)) or a violation of probation (addressed in § 4A1.1 (Criminal History Category)).".

The Commentary to § 2F1.1 captioned "Application Notes" is amended in Note 7(b) in the second paragraph by inserting the following additional sentence at the end:

"Where the loss determined above significantly understates or overstates the seriousness of the defendant's conduct, an upward or downward departure may be warranted.".

The Commentary to § 2F1.1 captioned "Application Notes" is amended in Note 10 by deleting "the primary" and inserting in lieu thereof "a primary"; by inserting "; or the fraud caused or risked reasonably foreseeable, substantial non-monetary harm" immediately following "was non-monetary"; by deleting "physical or psychological harm" and inserting in lieu thereof "reasonably foreseeable, physical or psychological harm or severe emotional trauma"; by deleting the period immediately following "institution" and inserting in lieu thereof a semicolon; by inserting a new subdivision, immediately following subdivision (e), as follows:

"(f) the offense involved the knowing endangerment of the solvency of one or more victims.";

and by inserting the following additional sentence at the end of the last paragraph:

"In such cases, a downward departure may be warranted.".

The Commentary to § 2F1.1 captioned "Application Notes" is amended in Note 11 by deleting the last two sentences as follows:

"The statutes provide for increased maximum terms of imprisonment for the use or possession of device-making equipment and the production or transfer of more than

Amendment 482 APPENDIX C - VOLUME I November 1, 2013

five identification documents or fifteen access devices. The court may find it appropriate to enhance the sentence for violations of these statutes in a manner similar to the treatment of analogous counterfeiting offenses under Part B of this Chapter.",

and inserting in lieu thereof:

"Where the primary purpose of the offense involved the unlawful production, transfer, possession, or use of identification documents for the purpose of violating, or assisting another to violate, the laws relating to naturalization, citizenship, or legal resident status, apply § 2L2.1 or § 2L2.2, as appropriate, rather than § 2F1.1. In the case of an offense involving false identification documents or access devices, an upward departure may be warranted where the actual loss does not adequately reflect the seriousness of the conduct.".

Reason for Amendment: This amendment makes the definitions of loss in §§ 2B1.1 (Larceny, Embezzlement, and Other Forms of Theft) and 2F1.1 (Fraud and Deceit) more consistent. Although the term "reasonably reliable information" is deleted from § 2B1.1 (there is no corresponding term in § 2F1.1), no substantive change results because the reliability of the information considered in respect to all cases is already addressed in § 6A1.3 (Resolution of Disputed Factors). In addition, this amendment provides additional guidance for the determination of loss in cases that are referenced to § 2B1.1, but have loss characteristics closely resembling offenses referenced to § 2F1.1, and in cases in which simply adding the amounts from a series of transactions does not reflect the amount taken or put at risk. This amendment also clarifies the meaning of the term "infringing items" in § 2B5.3, and expressly provides that the reference in § 2B6.1 to the table in § 2F1.1 is to be applied using the retail value of the stolen parts. In addition, this amendment clarifies the operation of § 2F1.1(b)(3) to avoid inappropriate double counting. Finally, this amendment revises the Commentary to § 2F1.1 by expanding Application Note 10 to provide guidance in cases in which the monetary loss does not adequately reflect the seriousness of the offense, and by clarifying Application Note 11 and conforming the phraseology in this application note to that used elsewhere in the guidelines.

Effective Date: The effective date of this amendment is November 1, 1993.

483. **Amendment:** Section 2B3.1(b)(1) is amended by inserting "(A)" immediately following "If"; and by inserting "or (B) the offense involved carjacking," immediately before "increase".

Section 2B3.1 is amended by inserting the following additional subsection:

"(c) Cross Reference

(1) If a victim was killed under circumstances that would constitute murder under 18 U.S.C. § 1111 had such killing taken place within the territorial or maritime jurisdiction of the United States, apply § 2A1.1 (First Degree Murder).".

The Commentary to § 2B3.1 captioned "Statutory Provisions" is amended by inserting ", 2119" immediately following "2118(a)".

The Commentary to § 2B3.1 captioned "Application Notes" is amended in Note 1 by inserting the following additional paragraph at the end:

"'Carjacking' means the taking or attempted taking of a motor vehicle from the person or presence of another by force and violence or by intimidation.".

The Commentary to § 2B3.1 captioned "Application Notes" is amended by deleting Note 6 as follows:

> "6. If the defendant was convicted under 18 U.S.C. § 2113(e) and in committing the offense or attempting to flee or escape, a participant killed any person, apply § 2A1.1 (First Degree Murder). Otherwise, if death results, see Chapter Five, Part K (Departures).";

and by renumbering Note 7 as Note 6.

Reason for Amendment: This amendment adds a specific offense characteristic for carjacking to § 2B3.1, references 18 U.S.C. § 2119 (carjacking offenses) to this guideline, and adds a cross reference to this guideline to address the circumstance in which a victim is murdered during the offense.

Effective Date: The effective date of this amendment is November 1, 1993.

484. **Amendment:** The Commentary to § 2D1.1 captioned "Application Notes" is amended in Note 1 by deleting "21 U.S.C. § 841." and inserting in lieu thereof:

> "21 U.S.C. § 841, except as expressly provided. Mixture or substance does not include materials that must be separated from the controlled substance before the controlled substance can be used. Examples of such materials include the fiberglass in a cocaine/fiberglass bonded suitcase, beeswax in a cocaine/beeswax statue, and waste water from an illicit laboratory used to manufacture a controlled substance. If such material cannot readily be separated from the mixture or substance that appropriately is counted in the Drug Quantity Table, the court may use any reasonable method to approximate the weight of the mixture or substance to be counted.
>
> An upward departure nonetheless may be warranted when the mixture or substance counted in the Drug Quantity Table is combined with other, non-countable material in an unusually sophisticated manner in order to avoid detection.".

Reason for Amendment: This amendment addresses an inter-circuit conflict regarding the meaning of the term "mixture or substance," as used in § 2D1.1 by expressly providing that this term does not include portions of a drug mixture that have to be separated from the controlled substance before the controlled substance can be used. This issue has arisen, subsequent to the United States Supreme Court decision in Chapman v. United States, 111 S. Ct. 1919 (1991), in two types of cases. The first type of case involves a controlled substance bonded to, or suspended in, another substance (e.g., cocaine mixed with beeswax); however, the controlled substance is not usable until it is separated from the other substance. See, e.g., United States v. Mahecha-Onofre, 936 F.2d 623 (1st Cir.), cert. denied, 112 S. Ct. 648 (1991); United States v. Restrepo-Contreras, 942 F.2d 96 (1st Cir. 1991), cert. denied, 112 S. Ct. 955 (1992). The second type of case involves the waste produced from an illicit laboratory used to manufacture a controlled substance or chemicals confiscated before the chemical processing of the controlled substance is completed. The waste product is typically water or chemicals used to either remove impurities or form a precipitate (the precipitate, in some cases, being the controlled substance). Typically, a small amount of controlled substance remains in the waste water; often this amount is too small to quantify and is listed as a trace amount (no weight given) in DEA reports. In these types of cases, the waste product is not consumable. The chemicals seized before the end of processing are also not usable in that form because further processing must take place before they can be used. See, e.g., United States v. Sherrod, 964 F.2d 1501 (5th Cir.), cert. denied sub nom. Cooper v. United States, 113 S. Ct. 832 (1992) (White and Blackmun, JJ., dissenting from denial of cert.), and cert. denied sub nom. United States v. Sewell, 113 S. Ct. 1367 (1993) (White and Blackmun, JJ., opinion dissenting from denial of cert.).

Effective Date: The effective date of this amendment is November 1, 1993.

485. **Amendment:** The Commentary to § 2D1.1 captioned "Application Notes" is amended by inserting the following additional note:

> "16. Where (A) the amount of the controlled substance for which the defendant is accountable under § 1B1.3 (Relevant Conduct) results in a base offense level greater than 36, (B) the court finds that this offense level overrepresents the defendant's culpability in the criminal activity, and (C) the defendant qualifies for a mitigating role adjustment under § 3B1.2 (Mitigating Role), a downward departure may be warranted. The court may depart to a sentence no lower than the guideline range that would have resulted if the defendant's Chapter Two offense level had been offense level 36. Provided, that a defendant is not eligible for a downward departure under this provision if the defendant:
>
> (a) has one or more prior felony convictions for a crime of violence or a controlled substance offense as defined in § 4B1.2 (Definitions of Terms Used in Section 4B1.1);
>
> (b) qualifies for an adjustment under § 3B1.3 (Abuse of Position of Trust or Use of Special Skill);
>
> (c) possessed or induced another participant to use or possess a firearm in the offense;
>
> (d) had decision-making authority;
>
> (e) owned the controlled substance or financed any part of the offense; or
>
> (f) sold the controlled substance or played a substantial part in negotiating the terms of the sale.
>
> Example: A defendant, who the court finds meets the criteria for a downward departure under this provision, has a Chapter Two offense level of 40, a 2-level reduction for a minor role from § 3B1.2, and a 3-level reduction for acceptance of responsibility from § 3E1.1. His final offense level is 35. If the defendant's Chapter Two offense level had been 36, the 2-level reduction for a minor role and 3-level reduction for acceptance of responsibility would have resulted in a final offense level of 31. Therefore, under this provision, a downward departure not to exceed 4 levels (from level 35 to level 31) would be authorized.".

Reason for Amendment: Where a defendant's base offense level is greater than level 36 and the defendant had a minimal or minor role in the offense (and meets certain other qualifications), the quantity of the controlled substance for which the defendant is held accountable under § 1B1.3 (Relevant Conduct) may overrepresent the defendant's culpability in the criminal activity. To address this issue, this amendment adds an application note to § 2D1.1 that authorizes a downward departure in the specific circumstances described and sets forth the extent of a departure authorized on this basis.

Effective Date: The effective date of this amendment is November 1, 1993.

November 1, 2013   APPENDIX C - VOLUME I   **Amendment 488**

486. Amendment: The Commentary to § 2D1.1 captioned "Application Notes" is amended by inserting the following additional note:

> "17. If, in a reverse sting (an operation in which a government agent sells or negotiates to sell a controlled substance to a defendant), the court finds that the government agent set a price for the controlled substance that was substantially below the market value of the controlled substance, thereby leading to the defendant's purchase of a significantly greater quantity of the controlled substance than his available resources would have allowed him to purchase except for the artificially low price set by the government agent, a downward departure may be warranted.".

Reason for Amendment: This amendment adds an application note to § 2D1.1 authorizing a downward departure if, in a reverse sting operation, the court finds that the government agent set a price for the controlled substance that was substantially below market value and thereby significantly inflated the quantity of controlled substance purchased by the defendant beyond the amount the defendant otherwise could have afforded.

Effective Date: The effective date of this amendment is November 1, 1993.

487. Amendment: Section 2D1.1(c) is amended in the notes following the Drug Quantity Table by inserting the following additional paragraph as the third paragraph:

> "'Cocaine base,' for the purposes of this guideline, means 'crack.' 'Crack' is the street name for a form of cocaine base, usually prepared by processing cocaine hydrochloride and sodium bicarbonate, and usually appearing in a lumpy, rocklike form.".

Reason for Amendment: This amendment provides that, for purposes of the guidelines, "cocaine base" means "crack." The amendment addresses an inter-circuit conflict. Compare, e.g., United States v. Shaw, 936 F.2d 412 (9th Cir. 1991) (cocaine base means crack) with United States v. Jackson, 968 F.2d 158 (2d Cir) (cocaine base has a scientific, chemical definition that is more inclusive than crack), cert. denied, 113 S. Ct. 664 (1992). Under this amendment, forms of cocaine base other than crack (e.g., coca paste, an intermediate step in the processing of coca leaves into cocaine hydrochloride, scientifically is a base form of cocaine, but it is not crack) will be treated as cocaine.

Effective Date: The effective date of this amendment is November 1, 1993.

488. Amendment: Section 2D1.1(c) is amended in the notes following the Drug Quantity Table by inserting the following additional paragraph at the end:

> "In the case of LSD on a carrier medium (e.g., a sheet of blotter paper), do not use the weight of the LSD/carrier medium. Instead, treat each dose of LSD on the carrier medium as equal to 0.4 mg of LSD for the purposes of the Drug Quantity Table.".

The Commentary to § 2D1.1 captioned "Application Notes" is amended in note 11 by deleting the first entry in the "Typical Weight Per Unit Table" as follows:

> "LSD (Lysergic acid diethylamide) 0.05 mg".

The Commentary to § 2D1.1 captioned "Application Notes" is amended by inserting the following additional note:

> "18. LSD on a blotter paper carrier medium typically is marked so that the number

of doses ('hits') per sheet readily can be determined. When this is not the case, it is to be presumed that each 1/4 inch by 1/4 inch section of the blotter paper is equal to one dose.

In the case of liquid LSD (LSD that has not been placed onto a carrier medium), using the weight of the LSD alone to calculate the offense level may not adequately reflect the seriousness of the offense. In such a case, an upward departure may be warranted.".

The Commentary to § 2D1.1 captioned "Background" is amended by inserting the following paragraphs at the end:

"Because the weights of LSD carrier media vary widely and typically far exceed the weight of the controlled substance itself, the Commission has determined that basing offense levels on the entire weight of the LSD and carrier medium would produce unwarranted disparity among offenses involving the same quantity of actual LSD (but different carrier weights), as well as sentences disproportionate to those for other, more dangerous controlled substances, such as PCP. Consequently, in cases involving LSD contained in a carrier medium, the Commission has established a weight per dose of 0.4 milligram for purposes of determining the base offense level.

The dosage weight of LSD selected exceeds the Drug Enforcement Administration's standard dosage unit for LSD of 0.05 milligram (i.e., the quantity of actual LSD per dose) in order to assign some weight to the carrier medium. Because LSD typically is marketed and consumed orally on a carrier medium, the inclusion of some weight attributable to the carrier medium recognizes (A) that offense levels for most other controlled substances are based upon the weight of the mixture containing the controlled substance without regard to purity, and (B) the decision in Chapman v. United States, 111 S. Ct. 1919 (1991) (holding that the term 'mixture or substance' in 21 U.S.C. § 841(b)(1) includes the carrier medium in which LSD is absorbed). At the same time, the weight per dose selected is less than the weight per dose that would equate the offense level for LSD on a carrier medium with that for the same number of doses of PCP, a controlled substance that comparative assessments indicate is more likely to induce violent acts and ancillary crime than is LSD. (Treating LSD on a carrier medium as weighing 0.5 milligram per dose would produce offense levels equivalent to those for PCP.) Thus, the approach decided upon by the Commission will harmonize offense levels for LSD offenses with those for other controlled substances and avoid an undue influence of varied carrier weight on the applicable offense level. Nonetheless, this approach does not override the applicability of 'mixture or substance' for the purpose of applying any mandatory minimum sentence (see Chapman; § 5G1.1(b)).".

Reason for Amendment: The Commission has found that the weights of LSD carrier media vary widely and typically far exceed the weight of the controlled substance itself (e. g., LSD is typically placed on blotter paper which generally weighs from 5 to 10 milligrams per dose; the weight of the LSD itself per dose is generally from 0.02 to 0.08 milligram; the Drug Enforcement Administration describes a standard dose of LSD as containing 0.05 milligram of LSD). As a result, basing the offense level on the entire weight of the LSD and carrier medium produces unwarranted disparity among offenses involving the same quantity of actual LSD but different carrier weights, as well as sentences that are disproportionate to those for other, more dangerous controlled substances, such as PCP, heroin, and cocaine. Under the guidelines prior to the amendment, for example, 100 grams of heroin or 500 grams of cocaine (weights that correspond to several thousand doses, the number depending upon the purity) result in the same offense level as

125 doses of LSD on blotter paper (which has an average weight of 8 milligrams per dose) or 1 dose of LSD on a sugar cube (2000 milligrams per dose).

Consequently, in cases involving LSD contained in a carrier medium, this amendment establishes a weight per dose of 0.4 milligram to be used for purposes of determining the base offense level. The dosage weight of LSD selected by the Commission exceeds the Drug Enforcement Administration's standard dosage unit for LSD of 0.05 milligram (i.e., the quantity of actual LSD per dose) in order to assign some weight to the carrier medium. Because LSD typically is marketed and consumed orally on a carrier medium, the inclusion of some weight attributable to the carrier medium recognizes (A) that offense levels for most other controlled substances are based upon the weight of the mixture containing the controlled substance without regard to purity, and (B) the decision in Chapman v. United States, 111 S. Ct. 1919 (1991) (holding that the term "mixture or substance" in 21 U.S.C. § 841(b)(1) includes the carrier medium in which LSD is absorbed). At the same time, the weight per dose selected is less than the weight per dose that would equate the offense level for LSD on a carrier medium with that for the same number of doses of PCP, a controlled substance that comparative assessments indicate is more likely to induce violent acts and ancillary crime than is LSD. Treating LSD on a carrier medium as weighing 0.5 milligram per dose would produce offense levels equivalent to those for PCP (for example, 2000 doses of LSD at 0.5 milligram per dose equals 1 gram of LSD -- corresponding to the lower limit of offense level 26; similarly, 2000 doses of PCP at 5 milligrams per dose, the standard amount of actual PCP in a dose, equals 10 grams of actual PCP -- corresponding to the lower limit of offense level 26). Thus, the approach decided upon by the Commission will harmonize offense levels for LSD offenses with those for other controlled substances and avoid an undue influence of varied carrier weight on the applicable offense level. Nonetheless, this approach does not override the definition of mixture or substance for purposes of applying any mandatory minimum sentence (see Chapman; § 5G1.1(b)).

Effective Date: The effective date of this amendment is November 1, 1993.

489. **Amendment:** The Commentary to § 2K2.4 captioned "Application Notes" is amended in Note 2 by deleting:

> "Provided, that where the maximum of the guideline range from Chapter Five, Part A (Sentencing Table) determined by an offense level adjusted under the procedure described in the preceding paragraph, plus the term of imprisonment required under 18 U.S.C. § 924(c) or § 929(a), is less than the maximum of the guideline range that would apply to the underlying offense absent such adjustment, the procedure described in the preceding paragraph does not apply. Instead, the guideline range applicable to the underlying offense absent such adjustment is to be used after subtracting the term of imprisonment imposed under 18 U.S.C. § 924(c) or § 929(a) from both the minimum and maximum of such range.
>
> Example: A defendant, is to be sentenced under the robbery guideline; his unadjusted offense level from § 2B3.1 is 30, including a 7-level enhancement for discharging a firearm; no Chapter Three adjustments are applicable; and his criminal history category is Category IV. His unadjusted guideline range from Chapter Five, Part A (Sentencing Table) is 135-168 months. This defendant has also been convicted under 18 U.S.C. § 924(c) arising from the possession of a weapon during the robbery, and therefore must be sentenced to an additional consecutive five-year term of imprisonment. The defendant's adjusted guideline range, which takes into account the conviction under 18 U.S.C. § 924(c) by eliminating the 7-level weapon enhancement, is 70-87 months. Because the maximum of the defendant's adjusted guideline range plus the five year consecutive sentence (87 months + 60 months =

Amendment 489 APPENDIX C - VOLUME I November 1, 2013

147 months) is less than the maximum of the defendant's unadjusted guideline range (168 months), the defendant is to be sentenced using the unadjusted guideline range after subtracting the 60 month sentence to be imposed under 18 U.S.C. § 924(c) from both the minimum and maximum of the unadjusted range (e.g., 135 months - 60 months = 75 months; 168 months - 60 months = 108 months). A sentence imposed for the underlying offense using the guideline range determined in this manner (75-108 months) when combined with the consecutive sentence imposed under 18 U.S.C. § 924(c) or § 929(a), will produce the appropriate total term of imprisonment.",

and inserting in lieu thereof:

"In a few cases, the offense level for the underlying offense determined under the preceding paragraph may result in a guideline range that, when combined with the mandatory consecutive sentence under 18 U.S.C. § 844(h), § 924(c), or § 929(a), produces a total maximum penalty that is less than the maximum of the guideline range that would have resulted had there not been a count of conviction under 18 U.S.C. § 844(h), § 924(c), or § 929(a) (i.e., the guideline range that would have resulted if the enhancements for possession, use, or discharge of a firearm had been applied). In such a case, an upward departure may be warranted so that the conviction under 18 U.S.C. § 844(h), § 924(c), or § 929(a) does not result in a decrease in the total punishment. An upward departure under this paragraph shall not exceed the maximum of the guideline range that would have resulted had there not been a count of conviction under 18 U.S.C. § 844(h), § 924(c), or § 929(a).".

Reason for Amendment: This amendment simplifies the operation of § 2K2.4 in order to reduce erroneous application by deleting the proviso in Application Note 2 and, in lieu thereof, authorizing an upward departure in the unusual case in which the combined sentence for an underlying offense and a firearms or explosives offense (under 18 U.S.C. § 844(h), § 924(c), or § 929(a)) is less than the maximum of the guideline range that would have resulted if there had been no additional conviction for the firearms or explosives offense.

Effective Date: The effective date of this amendment is November 1, 1993.

490. **Amendment:** Sections 2S1.3 and 2S1.4 are deleted in their entirety as follows:

"§ 2S1.3. Failure to Report Monetary Transactions; Structuring Transactions to Evade Reporting Requirements

(a) Base Offense Level:

(1) 13, if the defendant:

(A) structured transactions to evade reporting requirements; or

(B) knowingly filed, or caused another to file, a report containing materially false statements; or

(2) 5, otherwise.

(b) Specific Offense Characteristics

(1) If the defendant knew or believed that the funds were criminally derived property, increase by 4 levels. If the

resulting offense level is less than level 13, increase to level 13.

(2) If the base offense level is from (a)(1) above and the value of the funds exceeded $100,000, increase the offense level as specified in § 2S1.1(b)(2).

(c) Special Instruction for Fines - Organizations

(1) In lieu of the applicable amount from the table in subsection (d) of § 8C2.4 (Base Fine), use:

(A) the greater of $125,000 or 30 percent of the value of the funds if subsections (a)(1) and (b)(1) are used to determine the offense level; or

(B) the greater of $50,000 or 20 percent of the value of the funds if subsection (a)(1) but not (b)(1) are used to determine the offense level.

Commentary

Statutory Provisions: 26 U.S.C. § 7203 (if a willful violation of 26 U.S.C. § 6050I); 31 U.S.C. §§ 5313, 5314, 5322, 5324. For additional statutory provision(s), see Appendix A (Statutory Index).

Application Note:

1. 'Criminally derived property' means any property constituting, or derived from, proceeds obtained from a criminal offense. See 18 U.S.C. § 1957(f)(2).

Background: The offenses covered by this guideline relate to records and reports of certain transactions involving currency and monetary instruments. The maximum prison sentence for these offenses is ten years if there is any pattern of unlawful activity, and five years otherwise.

A base offense level of 13 is provided for those offenses where the defendant either structured the transaction to evade reporting requirements or knowingly filed, or caused another to file, a report containing materially false statements. A lower alternative base offense level of 5 is provided in all other cases.

Where the defendant actually knew or believed that the funds were criminally derived property, subsection (b)(1) provides for the greater of a 4-level increase or an increase to level 13.

Except in rare cases, the dollar value of the transactions not reported is an important indicator of several factors that are pertinent to the sentence, including the size of the criminal enterprise, and the extent to which the defendant aided the enterprise.

§ 2S1.4. Failure to File Currency and Monetary Instrument Report

(a) Base Offense Level: 9

(b) Specific Offense Characteristics

(1) If the defendant knew or believed that the funds were criminally derived property, increase by 4 levels.

Amendment 490   APPENDIX C - VOLUME I   November 1, 2013

   (2) If the defendant knew or believed that the funds were intended to be used to promote criminal activity, increase by 4 levels.

   (3) If the value of the funds exceeded $100,000, increase the offense level as specified in § 2S1.1(b)(2).

  (c) Special Instruction for Fines - Organizations

   (1) In lieu of the applicable amount from the table in subsection (d) of § 8C2.4 (Base Fine), use:

    (A) the greater of $50,000 or 20 percent of the value of the funds if subsection (b)(1) or (b)(2) is used to determine the offense level; or

    (B) the greater of $15,000 or 10 percent of the value of the funds, otherwise.

<u>Commentary</u>

<u>Statutory Provision</u>: 31 U.S.C. § 5316. For additional statutory provision(s), <u>see</u> Appendix A (Statutory Index).

<u>Application Note</u>:

1. 'Criminally derived property' means any property constituting, or derived from, proceeds obtained from a criminal offense. <u>See</u> 18 U.S.C. § 1957(f)(2).".

A replacement guideline with accompanying commentary is inserted as "§ 2S1.3 (Structuring Transactions to Evade Reporting Requirements; Failure to Report Cash or Monetary Transactions; Failure to File Currency and Monetary Instrument Report; Knowingly Filing False Reports)".

Reason for Amendment: This amendment consolidates existing §§ 2S1.3 and 2S1.4 and modifies these guidelines to assure greater consistency of punishment for similar offenses and greater sensitivity to indicia of offense seriousness.

Effective Date: The effective date of this amendment is November 1, 1993.

491. **Amendment:** Chapter Two, Part T, Subpart 1 is amended in the title by inserting ", EMPLOYMENT TAXES, ESTATE TAXES, GIFT TAXES, AND EXCISE TAXES (OTHER THAN ALCOHOL, TOBACCO, AND CUSTOMS TAXES)" at the end thereof.

Section 2T1.1 is amended in the title by inserting "; Willful Failure to File Return, Supply Information, or Pay Tax; Fraudulent or False Returns, Statements, or Other Documents" at the end thereof.

Section 2T1.1(a) is amended by deleting:

 "Base Offense Level: Level from § 2T4.1 (Tax Table) corresponding to the tax loss.

 For purposes of this guideline, the 'tax loss' is the greater of: (A) the total amount of tax that the taxpayer evaded or attempted to evade; and (B) the 'tax loss' defined in § 2T1.3.",

and inserting in lieu thereof:

    "(a)   Base Offense Level:

        (1)   Level from § 2T4.1 (Tax Table) corresponding to the tax loss; or

        (2)   6, if there is no tax loss.".

Section 2T1.1(b)(2) is amended by deleting "nature" and inserting in lieu thereof "existence".

Section 2T1.1 is amended by inserting the following additional subsection:

    "(c)   Special Instructions

        For the purposes of this guideline --

        (1)   If the offense involved tax evasion or a fraudulent or false return, statement, or other document, the tax loss is the total amount of loss that was the object of the offense (i.e., the loss that would have resulted had the offense been successfully completed).

        Notes:

        (A) If the offense involved filing a tax return in which gross income was underreported, the tax loss shall be treated as equal to 28% of the unreported gross income (34% if the taxpayer is a corporation) plus 100% of any false credits claimed against tax, unless a more accurate determination of the tax loss can be made.

        (B) If the offense involved improperly claiming a deduction or an exemption, the tax loss shall be treated as equal to 28% of the amount of the improperly claimed deduction or exemption (34% if the taxpayer is a corporation) plus 100% of any false credits claimed against tax, unless a more accurate determination of the tax loss can be made.

        (C) If the offense involved improperly claiming a deduction to provide a basis for tax evasion in the future, the tax loss shall be treated as equal to 28% of the amount of the improperly claimed deduction (34% if the taxpayer is a corporation) plus 100% of any false credits claimed against tax, unless a more accurate determination of the tax loss can be made.

        (2)   If the offense involved failure to file a tax return, the tax loss is the amount of tax that the taxpayer owed and did not pay.

        Note: If the offense involved failure to file a tax return, the tax loss shall be treated as equal to 20% of the gross income (25% if the taxpayer is a corporation) less any tax withheld or otherwise paid, unless a more accurate determination of the tax loss can be made.

        (3)   If the offense involved willful failure to pay tax, the tax loss is the amount of tax that the taxpayer owed and did not pay.

        (4)   If the offense involved improperly claiming a refund to which the

claimant was not entitled, the tax loss is the amount of the claimed refund to which the claimant was not entitled.

    (5)   The tax loss is not reduced by any payment of the tax subsequent to the commission of the offense.".

The Commentary to § 2T1.1 captioned "Statutory Provision" is amended by deleting "Provision: 26 U.S.C. § 7201" and inserting in lieu thereof "Provisions: 26 U.S.C. §§ 7201, 7203 (other than a violation based upon 26 U.S.C. § 6050I), 7206 (other than a violation based upon 26 U.S.C. § 6050I or § 7206(2)), and 7207".

The Commentary to § 2T1.1 captioned "Application Notes" is amended by deleting Notes 1 and 4 as follows:

"1.   False statements in furtherance of the evasion (see §§ 2T1.3, 2T1.5, and 2T1.8) are considered part of the offense for purposes of this guideline.",

"4.   The guideline refers to § 2T1.3 to provide an alternative minimum standard for the tax loss, which is based on a percentage of the dollar amounts of certain misstatements made in returns filed by the taxpayer. This alternative standard may be easier to determine, and should make irrelevant the issue of whether the taxpayer was entitled to offsetting adjustments that he failed to claim.";

and by renumbering the remaining notes accordingly.

The Commentary to § 2T1.1 captioned "Application Notes" is amended in Note 1 (formerly Note 2) by deleting "For purposes of the guideline, the tax loss is the amount of tax that the taxpayer evaded or attempted to evade" and inserting in lieu thereof "'Tax loss' is defined in subsection (c)"; by deleting "deficiency" and inserting in lieu thereof "figures"; and by inserting the following additional paragraphs at the end:

"Notes under subsections (c)(1) and (c)(2) address certain situations in income tax cases in which the tax loss may not be reasonably ascertainable. In these situations, the 'presumptions' set forth are to be used unless the government or defense provides sufficient information for a more accurate assessment of the tax loss. In cases involving other types of taxes, the presumptions in the notes under subsections (c)(1) and (c)(2) do not apply.

Example 1: A defendant files a tax return reporting income of $40,000 when his income was actually $90,000. Under Note (A) to subsection (c)(1), the tax loss is treated as $14,000 ($90,000 of actual gross income minus $40,000 of reported gross income = $50,000 x 28%) unless sufficient information is available to make a more accurate assessment of the tax loss.

Example 2: A defendant files a tax return reporting income of $60,000 when his income was actually $130,000. In addition, the defendant claims $10,000 in false tax credits. Under Note (A) to subsection (c)(1), the tax loss is treated as $29,600 ($130,000 of actual gross income minus $60,000 of reported gross income = $70,000 x 28% = $19,600, plus $10,000 of false tax credits) unless sufficient information is available to make a more accurate assessment of the tax loss.

Example 3: A defendant fails to file a tax return for a year in which his salary was $24,000, and $2,600 in income tax was withheld by his employer. Under the note to subsection (c)(2), the tax loss is treated as $2,200 ($24,000 of gross income x 20%

= $4,800, minus $2,600 of tax withheld) unless sufficient information is available to make a more accurate assessment of the tax loss.

In determining the tax loss attributable to the offense, the court should use as many methods set forth in subsection (c) and this commentary as are necessary given the circumstances of the particular case. If none of the methods of determining the tax loss set forth fit the circumstances of the particular case, the court should use any method of determining the tax loss that appears appropriate to reasonably calculate the loss that would have resulted had the offense been successfully completed.".

The Commentary to § 2T1.1 captioned "Application Notes" is amended in Note 3 (formerly Note 5) by deleting "or local" and inserting in lieu thereof "local, or foreign".

The Commentary to § 2T1.1 captioned "Application Notes" is amended in Note 4 (formerly Note 6) by deleting "§ 2T1.1(b)(2)" and inserting in lieu thereof "subsection (b)(2)"; by inserting a comma immediately following "applied"; and by inserting "or fictitious entities" immediately following "shells".

The Commentary to § 2T1.1 captioned "Application Notes" is amended by inserting the following additional notes:

"5. A 'credit claimed against tax' is an item that reduces the amount of tax directly. In contrast, a 'deduction' is an item that reduces the amount of taxable income.

6. 'Gross income,' for the purposes of this section, has the same meaning as it has in 26 U.S.C. § 61 and 26 C.F.R. § 1.61.

7. If the offense involves both individual and corporate tax returns, the tax loss is the aggregate tax loss from the offenses taken together.".

The Commentary to § 2T1.1 captioned "Background" is amended by deleting:

" This guideline relies most heavily on the amount of tax evaded because the chief interest protected by the statute is the collection of taxes. A greater evasion is obviously more harmful to the treasury, and more serious than a smaller one with otherwise similar characteristics. Furthermore, as the potential benefit from tax evasion increases, the sanction necessary to deter also increases.

The overlapping imprisonment ranges in the Sentencing Table are intended to minimize the significance of disputes. The consequence of an inexact estimate of the tax loss is never severe, even when the tax loss is near the boundary of a range. For example, although the difference between $39,999 and $40,001 results in a change from level 10 to level 11, any sentence of eight to twelve months would be within the guidelines regardless of the offense level determination made by the court. Indeed, any sentence between ten and twelve months would be within the guidelines for a tax loss ranging from $20,000 to $150,000. As a consequence, for all dollar amounts, the Sentencing Table affords the court considerable latitude in evaluating other factors, even when the amount of the tax loss is uncertain.

Under pre-guidelines practice, roughly half of all tax evaders were sentenced to probation without imprisonment, while the other half received sentences that required them to serve an average prison term of twelve months. This guideline is intended to reduce disparity in sentencing for tax evasion and to somewhat increase average sentence length. As a result, the number of purely probationary sentences will be reduced. The Commission believes that any additional costs of imprisonment that may be incurred as a result of the increase in the average term of imprisonment for tax evasion are inconsequential in relation to the potential increase in revenue. According to estimates current at the time this guideline was originally developed (1987), income taxes are underpaid by approximately $90 billion annually.

Although under pre-guidelines practice some large-scale evaders served as much as five years in prison, the average sentence length for defendants sentenced to a term of imprisonment did not increase rapidly with the amount of tax evaded. Thus, the average time served by those sentenced to a term of imprisonment for evading less than $10,000 in taxes was about nine months, while the corresponding figure for those evading over $100,000 in taxes was about sixteen months. Guideline sentences should result in small increases in the average length of imprisonment for most tax cases that involve less than $100,000 in tax evaded. The increase is expected to be somewhat larger for cases involving more taxes.

Failure to report criminally derived income is included as a factor for deterrence purposes. Criminally derived income is generally difficult to establish, so that the tax loss in such cases will tend to be substantially understated. An enhancement for offenders who violate the tax laws as part of a pattern of criminal activity from which they derive a substantial portion of their income also serves to implement the mandate of 28 U.S.C. § 994(i)(2). Estimates from pre-guidelines practice were that, on average, the presence of this factor increased time served by the equivalent of 2 levels.

Although tax evasion always involves some planning, unusually sophisticated efforts to conceal the evasion decrease the likelihood of detection and therefore warrant an additional sanction for deterrence purposes. Analyses of pre-guidelines data for other frauds and property crimes showed that careful planning or sophistication generally resulted in an average increase of at least 2 levels.",

and inserting in lieu thereof:

"   This guideline relies most heavily on the amount of loss that was the object of the offense. Tax offenses, in and of themselves, are serious offenses; however, a greater tax loss is obviously more harmful to the treasury and more serious than a smaller one with otherwise similar characteristics. Furthermore, as the potential benefit from the offense increases, the sanction necessary to deter also increases.

Under pre-guidelines practice, roughly half of all tax evaders were sentenced to probation without imprisonment, while the other half received sentences that required them to serve an average prison term of twelve months. This guideline is intended to reduce disparity in sentencing for tax offenses and to somewhat increase average sentence length. As a result, the number of purely probationary sentences will be reduced. The Commission believes that any additional costs of imprisonment that may be incurred as a result of the increase in the average term of imprisonment for tax offenses are inconsequential in relation to the potential increase in revenue. According to estimates current at the time this guideline was originally developed (1987), income taxes are underpaid by approximately $90 billion annually. Guideline sentences should result in small increases in the average length of imprisonment for most tax cases that involve less than $100,000 in tax loss. The increase is expected to be somewhat larger for cases involving more taxes.

Failure to report criminally derived income is included as a factor for deterrence purposes. Criminally derived income is generally difficult to establish, so that the tax loss in such cases will tend to be substantially understated. An enhancement for offenders who violate the tax laws as part of a pattern of criminal activity from which they derive a substantial portion of their income also serves to implement the mandate of 28 U.S.C. § 994(i)(2).

Although tax offenses always involve some planning, unusually sophisticated efforts to conceal the offense decrease the likelihood of detection and therefore warrant an additional sanction for deterrence purposes.".

Sections 2T1.2 and 2T1.3 are deleted in their entirety as follows:

"§ 2T1.2.   Willful Failure To File Return, Supply Information, or Pay Tax

    (a)   Base Offense Level:

        (1)   1 level less than the level from § 2T4.1 (Tax Table) corresponding to the tax loss; or

        (2)   5, if there is no tax loss.

For purposes of this guideline, 'tax loss' means the total amount of tax that the taxpayer owed and did not pay, but, in the event of a failure to file in any year, not less than 10 percent of the amount by which the taxpayer's gross income for that year exceeded $20,000.

    (b)   Specific Offense Characteristics

        (1)   If the defendant failed to report or to correctly identify the source of income exceeding $10,000 in any year from criminal activity, increase by 2 levels. If the resulting offense level is less than level 12, increase to level 12.

        (2)   If sophisticated means were used to impede discovery of the nature or extent of the offense, increase by 2 levels.

    (c)   Cross Reference

        (1)   If the defendant is convicted of a willful violation of 26 U.S.C. § 6050I, apply § 2S1.3 (Failure to Report Monetary Transactions) in lieu of this guideline.

Commentary

Statutory Provision: 26 U.S.C. § 7203 (other than a willful violation of 26 U.S.C. § 6050I).

Application Notes:

1.   'Criminal activity' means any conduct constituting a criminal offense under federal, state, or local law.

2.   'Sophisticated means,' as used in § 2T1.2(b)(2), includes conduct that is more complex or demonstrates greater intricacy or planning than a routine tax-evasion case. An enhancement would be applied, for example, where the defendant used offshore bank accounts or transactions through corporate shells.

3.   In determining the total tax loss attributable to the offense (see § 1B1.3(a)(2)), all conduct violating the tax laws should be considered as part of the

same course of conduct or common scheme or plan unless the evidence demonstrates that the conduct is clearly unrelated. See Application Note 3 of the Commentary to § 2T1.1.

Background: Violations of 26 U.S.C. § 7203 are usually serious misdemeanors that are similar to tax evasion, except that there need be no affirmative act in support of the offense. They are rarely prosecuted unless the defendant also owed taxes that he failed to pay.

Because the conduct generally is tantamount to tax evasion, the guideline is similar to § 2T1.1. Because the offense is a misdemeanor, the offense level has been set at one below the level corresponding to evasion of the same amount of taxes.

An alternative measure of the tax loss, 10 percent of gross income in excess of $20,000, has been provided because of the potential difficulty of determining the amount of tax the taxpayer owed. It is expected that this alternative measure generally will understate the amount of tax owed.

The intended impact of this guideline is to increase the average time served for this offense, and to increase significantly the number of violators who receive a term of imprisonment. Under pre-guidelines practice, the average time served for this offense was approximately 2.5 months, including those who were not sentenced to prison. Considering only those who did serve a term of imprisonment, the average term was about six to seven months.

§ 2T1.3. Fraud and False Statements Under Penalty of Perjury

    (a)   Base Offense Level:

        (1)   Level from § 2T4.1 (Tax Table) corresponding to the tax loss, if the offense was committed in order to facilitate evasion of a tax; or

        (2)   6, otherwise.

For purposes of this guideline, the 'tax loss' is 28 percent of the amount by which the greater of gross income and taxable income was understated, plus 100 percent of the total amount of any false credits claimed against tax. If the taxpayer is a corporation, use 34 percent in lieu of 28 percent.

    (b)   Specific Offense Characteristics

        (1)   If the defendant failed to report or to correctly identify the source of income exceeding $10,000 in any year from criminal activity, increase by 2 levels. If the resulting offense level is less than level 12, increase to level 12.

        (2)   If sophisticated means were used to impede discovery of the nature or extent of the offense, increase by 2 levels.

Commentary

Statutory Provision: 26 U.S.C. § 7206, except § 7206(2). For additional statutory provision(s), see Appendix A (Statutory Index).

Application Notes:

1. 'Criminal activity' means any conduct constituting a criminal offense under federal, state, or local law.

2. 'Sophisticated means,' as used in § 2T1.3(b)(2), includes conduct that is more complex or demonstrates greater intricacy or planning than a routine tax-evasion case. An enhancement would be applied, for example, where the defendant used offshore bank accounts or transactions through corporate shells.

3. In determining the total tax loss attributable to the offense (see § 1B1.3(a)(2)), all conduct violating the tax laws should be considered as part of the same course of conduct or common scheme or plan unless the evidence demonstrates that the conduct is clearly unrelated. See Application Note 3 of the Commentary to § 2T1.1.

4. The amount by which the greater of gross income and taxable income was understated, plus 100 percent of the total amount of any false credits claimed against tax is calculated as follows: (1) determine the amount, if any, by which the gross income was understated; (2) determine the amount, if any, by which the taxable income was understated; and (3) determine the amount of any false credit(s) claimed (a tax 'credit' is an item that reduces the amount of tax directly; in contrast, a 'deduction' is an item that reduces the amount of taxable income). Use the amount determined under step (1) or (2), whichever is greater, plus any amount determined under step (3).

Background: This guideline covers conduct that usually is analogous to tax evasion, although the elements differ. Accordingly, the offense is treated much like tax evasion.

Existence of a tax loss is not an element of these offenses. Furthermore, in instances where the defendant is setting the groundwork for evasion of a tax that is expected to become due in the future, he may make false statements that under-report income that as of the time of conviction may not yet have resulted in a tax loss. In order to gauge the seriousness of these offenses, the guidelines establish a rule for determining a 'tax loss' based on the nature and magnitude of the false statements made. Use of this approach also avoids complex problems of proof and invasion of privacy when returns of persons other than the defendant and co-defendants are involved.".

Section 2T1.4(a)(1) is amended by deleting "resulting tax loss, if any" and inserting in lieu thereof "tax loss".

Section 2T1.4(a)(2) is amended by deleting "otherwise" and inserting in lieu thereof "if there is no tax loss".

Section 2T1.4(a) is amended by deleting "§ 2T1.3" and inserting in lieu thereof "§ 2T1.1".

Section 2T1.4(b)(1) is amended by inserting "(A)" immediately following "If"; and by inserting "; or (B) the defendant was in the business of preparing or assisting in the preparation of tax returns" immediately before ", increase".

Section 2T1.4(b)(2) is amended by deleting "nature" and inserting in lieu thereof "existence".

Amendment 491

Section 2T1.4(b) is amended by deleting:

> "(3) If the defendant was in the business of preparing or assisting in the preparation of tax returns, increase by 2 levels.".

The Commentary to § 2T1.4 captioned "Statutory Provision" is amended by inserting "(other than a violation based upon 26 U.S.C. § 6050I)" immediately following "§ 7206(2)".

The Commentary to § 2T1.4 captioned "Application Notes" is amended by deleting Notes 1, 3, and 4 as follows:

> "1. Subsection (b)(1) applies to persons who derive a substantial portion of their income through the promotion of tax fraud or tax evasion, e.g., through promoting fraudulent tax shelters.",
>
> "3. Subsection (b)(3) applies to persons who regularly act as tax preparers or advisers for profit. Do not employ § 3B1.3 (Abuse of Position of Trust or Use of Special Skill) if this adjustment applies. Subsection (b)(1) may also apply to such persons.
>
> 4. In certain instances, such as promotion of a tax shelter scheme, the defendant may advise other persons to violate their tax obligations through filing returns that find no support in the tax laws. If this type of conduct can be shown to have resulted in the filing of false returns (regardless of whether the principals were aware of their falsity), the misstatements in all such returns will contribute to one aggregate 'tax loss.'";

by renumbering Note 2 as Note 3; and by inserting the following as Notes 1 and 2:

> "1. For the general principles underlying the determination of tax loss, see § 2T1.1(c) and Application Note 1 of the Commentary to § 2T1.1 (Tax Evasion; Willful Failure to File Return, Supply Information, or Pay Tax; Fraudulent or False Returns, Statements, or Other Documents). In certain instances, such as promotion of a tax shelter scheme, the defendant may advise other persons to violate their tax obligations through filing returns that find no support in the tax laws. If this type of conduct can be shown to have resulted in the filing of false returns (regardless of whether the principals were aware of their falsity), the misstatements in all such returns will contribute to one aggregate 'tax loss.'
>
> 2. Subsection (b)(1) has two prongs. The first prong applies to persons who derive a substantial portion of their income through the promotion of tax schemes, e.g., through promoting fraudulent tax shelters. The second prong applies to persons who regularly prepare or assist in the preparation of tax returns for profit. If an enhancement from this subsection applies, do not apply § 3B1.3 (Abuse of Position of Trust or Use of Special Skill).".

The Commentary to § 2T1.4 captioned "Application Notes" is amended in Note 3 (formerly Note 2) by inserting "or fictitious entities" immediately following "corporate shells".

The Commentary to § 2T1.4 captioned "Background" is amended by deleting "tax preparers and advisers" and inserting in lieu thereof "those in the business of preparing or assisting in the preparation of tax returns and those who make a business of promoting tax fraud"; and by deleting "§ 2T1.3" and inserting in lieu thereof "§ 2T1.1".

Section 2T1.5 is deleted in its entirety as follows:

"§ 2T1.5. Fraudulent Returns, Statements, or Other Documents

(a) Base Offense Level: 6

Commentary

Statutory Provision: 26 U.S.C. § 7207.

Background: The offense is a misdemeanor. It is to be distinguished from 26 U.S.C. § 7206(1) (§ 2T1.3), which is a felony involving a false statement under penalty of perjury. The offense level has been set at 6 in order to give the sentencing judge considerable latitude because the conduct could be similar to tax evasion.".

Section 2T1.9 is amended in the title by deleting "Impair, Impede" and inserting in lieu thereof "Impede, Impair, Obstruct,".

Section 2T1.9(a)(1) is amended by deleting "§ 2T1.3, as applicable" and inserting in lieu thereof "§ 2T1.4, as appropriate".

Section 2T1.9(b)(1) is amended by inserting "to impede, impair, obstruct, or defeat the ascertainment, computation, assessment, or collection of revenue" immediately following "violence".

Section 2T1.9(b)(2) is amended by deleting "impede or impair the Internal Revenue Service in the assessment and" and inserting in lieu thereof "impede, impair, obstruct, or defeat the ascertainment, computation, assessment, or"; and by inserting the following additional sentence at the end:

"Do not, however, apply this adjustment if an adjustment from § 2T1.4(b)(1) is applied.".

The Commentary to § 2T1.9 captioned "Application Notes" is amended in Note 2 by deleting "§ 2T1.3 (whichever is applicable to the underlying conduct)" and inserting in lieu thereof "§ 2T1.4 (whichever guideline most closely addresses the harm that would have resulted had the conspirators succeeded in impeding, impairing, obstructing, or defeating the Internal Revenue Service)".

The Commentary to § 2T1.9 captioned "Application Notes" is amended by inserting the following additional note:

"4. Subsection (b)(2) provides an enhancement where the conduct was intended to encourage persons, other than the participants directly involved in the offense, to violate the tax laws (e.g., an offense involving a 'tax protest' group that encourages persons to violate the tax laws, or an offense involving the marketing of fraudulent tax shelters or schemes).".

Section 2T4.1 is amended by deleting:

"Tax Loss (Apply the Greatest)   Offense Level

(A)	$2,000 or less	6
(B)	More than $2,000	7
(C)	More than $5,000	8
(D)	More than $10,000	9
(E)	More than $20,000	10
(F)	More than $40,000	11
(G)	More than $70,000	12
(H)	More than $120,000	13
(I)	More than $200,000	14
(J)	More than $350,000	15
(K)	More than $500,000	16
(L)	More than $800,000	17
(M)	More than $1,500,000	18
(N)	More than $2,500,000	19
(O)	More than $5,000,000	20
(P)	More than $10,000,000	21
(Q)	More than $20,000,000	22
(R)	More than $40,000,000	23
(S)	More than $80,000,000	24.",

and inserting in lieu thereof:

"Tax Loss (Apply the Greatest)   Offense Level

(A)	$1,700 or less	6
(B)	More than $1,700	7
(C)	More than $3,000	8
(D)	More than $5,000	9
(E)	More than $8,000	10
(F)	More than $13,500	11
(G)	More than $23,500	12
(H)	More than $40,000	13
(I)	More than $70,000	14
(J)	More than $120,000	15
(K)	More than $200,000	16
(L)	More than $325,000	17
(M)	More than $550,000	18
(N)	More than $950,000	19
(O)	More than $1,500,000	20
(P)	More than $2,500,000	21
(Q)	More than $5,000,000	22
(R)	More than $10,000,000	23
(S)	More than $20,000,000	24
(T)	More than $40,000,000	25

(U) More than $80,000,000   26.".

Reason for Amendment: This amendment consolidates §§ 2T1.1, 2T1.2, 2T1.3, and 2T1.5, thereby eliminating the confusion that has arisen in some cases regarding which guideline applies. In addition, by adopting a uniform definition of tax loss, this amendment eliminates the anomaly of using actual tax loss in some cases and an amount that differs from actual tax loss in others. Furthermore, this amendment consolidates § 2T1.4(b)(1) and (b)(3) to reflect the substantial overlap between these subsections. Finally, this amendment adopts a revised "tax loss" table to provide increased deterrence for tax offenses.

Effective Date: The effective date of this amendment is November 1, 1993.

492. **Amendment:** The Commentary to § 3B1.3 captioned "Application Notes" is amended by deleting Note 1 as follows:

"1. The position of trust must have contributed in some substantial way to facilitating the crime and not merely have provided an opportunity that could as easily have been afforded to other persons. This adjustment, for example, would not apply to an embezzlement by an ordinary bank teller.",

and inserting in lieu thereof:

"1. 'Public or private trust' refers to a position of public or private trust characterized by professional or managerial discretion (i.e., substantial discretionary judgment that is ordinarily given considerable deference). Persons holding such positions ordinarily are subject to significantly less supervision than employees whose responsibilities are primarily nondiscretionary in nature. For this enhancement to apply, the position of trust must have contributed in some significant way to facilitating the commission or concealment of the offense (e.g., by making the detection of the offense or the defendant's responsibility for the offense more difficult). This adjustment, for example, would apply in the case of an embezzlement of a client's funds by an attorney serving as a guardian, a bank executive's fraudulent loan scheme, or the criminal sexual abuse of a patient by a physician under the guise of an examination. This adjustment would not apply in the case of an embezzlement or theft by an ordinary bank teller or hotel clerk because such positions are not characterized by the above-described factors.

Notwithstanding the preceding paragraph, because of the special nature of the United States mail an adjustment for an abuse of a position of trust will apply to any employee of the U.S. Postal Service who engages in the theft or destruction of undelivered United States mail.".

Reason for Amendment: This amendment reformulates the definition of an abuse of position of trust to better distinguish cases warranting this enhancement.

Effective Date: The effective date of this amendment is November 1, 1993.

493. **Amendment:** The Commentary to § 4A1.2 captioned "Application Notes" is amended in Note 1 by inserting the following additional sentence at the end of the first paragraph:

"Conduct that is part of the instant offense means conduct that is relevant conduct to the instant offense under the provisions of § 1B1.3 (Relevant Conduct).".

Amendment 493 APPENDIX C - VOLUME I November 1, 2013

The Commentary to § 4A1.2 captioned "Application Notes" is amended in Note 6 in the first sentence of the first paragraph by inserting "(A)" immediately before "have been reversed"; by deleting the comma following "law"; and by inserting "or (B) have been ruled constitutionally invalid in a prior case" immediately before "are not to be counted";

The Commentary to § 4A1.2 captioned "Application Notes" is amended in Note 6 by deleting the second sentence as follows:

"Also, sentences resulting from convictions that a defendant shows to have been previously ruled constitutionally invalid are not to be counted.",

and inserting in lieu thereof:

"With respect to the current sentencing proceeding, this guideline and commentary do not confer upon the defendant any right to attack collaterally a prior conviction or sentence beyond any such rights otherwise recognized in law (e.g., 21 U.S.C. § 851 expressly provides that a defendant may collaterally attack certain prior convictions).";

and by beginning a new paragraph with the third sentence.

The Commentary to § 4A1.2 captioned "Background" is amended by deleting the second paragraph as follows:

"The Commission leaves for court determination the issue of whether a defendant may collaterally attack at sentencing a prior conviction.".

Reason for Amendment: This amendment expressly provides that the term "part of the instant offense" in § 4A1.2(a)(1) means relevant conduct as defined in § 1B1.3 (Relevant Conduct) to avoid double counting and ensure consistency with other guideline provisions.

This amendment also clarifies the Commission's intent with respect to whether § 4A1.2 confers on defendants a right to attack prior convictions collaterally at sentencing, an issue on which the appellate courts have differed. Compare, e.g., United States v. Canales, 960 F.2d 1311, 1316 (5th Cir. 1992) (Section 4A1.2 commentary indicates Commission intended to grant sentencing courts discretion to entertain initial defendant challenges to prior convictions); United States v. Jacobetz, 955 F.2d 786, 805 (2d Cir.) (similar), cert. denied, 113 S. Ct. 104 (1992); United States v. Cornog, 945 F.2d 1504, 1511 (11th Cir. 1991) (similar) with United States v. Hewitt, 942 F.2d 1270, 1276 (8th Cir. 1991) (commentary indicates defendants may only challenge use of prior convictions at sentencing by showing such conviction previously ruled invalid). This amendment addresses this intercircuit conflict in interpreting the commentary by stating more clearly that the Commission does not intend to enlarge a defendant's right to attack collaterally a prior conviction at the current sentencing proceeding beyond any right otherwise recognized in law.

Effective Date: The effective date of this amendment is November 1, 1993.

494. Amendment: The Commentary to § 5G1.3 captioned "Application Notes" is amended in the second paragraph of Note 2 by deleting "40" and inserting in lieu thereof "30", and by deleting "55" and inserting in lieu thereof "45".

The Commentary to § 5G1.3 captioned "Application Notes" is amended by inserting the following additional note:

"4.   If the defendant was on federal or state probation, parole, or supervised release at the time of the instant offense, and has had such probation, parole, or supervised release revoked, the sentence for the instant offense should be imposed to be served consecutively to the term imposed for the violation of probation, parole, or supervised release in order to provide an incremental penalty for the violation of probation, parole, or supervised release (in accord with the policy expressed in §§ 7B1.3 and 7B1.4).".

Reason for Amendment: This amendment adds an application note to § 5G1.3 to provide guidance in the case of a defendant who was on federal or state probation, parole, or supervised release at the time of the instant federal offense and has had such term of supervision revoked prior to sentencing on the instant federal offense. In addition, this amendment corrects a mathematical error in an example.

Effective Date: The effective date of this amendment is November 1, 1993.

495. **Amendment:** The Commentary to § 6B1.2 is amended by inserting the following additional paragraph at the end:

> "   The Commission encourages the prosecuting attorney prior to the entry of a plea of guilty or nolo contendere under Rule 11 of the Federal Rules of Criminal Procedure to disclose to the defendant the facts and circumstances of the offense and offender characteristics, then known to the prosecuting attorney, that are relevant to the application of the sentencing guidelines. This recommendation, however, shall not be construed to confer upon the defendant any right not otherwise recognized in law.".

Reason for Amendment: This amendment adds commentary to § 6B1.2 recommending that the prosecuting attorney disclose to the defendant the facts and circumstances of the offense and offender characteristics then known to the prosecuting attorney that are relevant to the application of the guidelines in order to encourage plea negotiations that realistically reflect probable outcomes.

Effective Date: The effective date of this amendment is November 1, 1993.

496. **Amendment:** Appendix A (Statutory Index) is amended in the second paragraph of the introduction by deleting "or an attempt" and inserting in lieu thereof ", attempt, or solicitation".

Appendix A (Statutory Index) is amended by inserting the following at the appropriate place by title and section:

"16 U.S.C. § 742j-1(a)	2Q2.1",
"16 U.S.C. § 773e(a)(2), (3),(4),(6)	2A2.4",
"16 U.S.C. § 773g	2A2.4",
"16 U.S.C. § 916c	2Q2.1",
"16 U.S.C. § 916f	2Q2.1",
"16 U.S.C. § 973c(a)(8), (10),(11),(12)	2A2.4",
"16 U.S.C. § 973e	2A2.4",
"16 U.S.C. § 1417(a)(5),(6), (b)(2)	2A2.4",
"16 U.S.C. § 3606	2A2.4",

"16 U.S.C. § 3637(a)(2),(3),(4),(6),(c)	2A2.4",
"16 U.S.C. § 4223	2Q2.1",
"16 U.S.C. § 4224	2Q2.1",
"16 U.S.C. § 4910(a)	2Q2.1",
"16 U.S.C. § 4912(a)(2)(A)	2Q2.1",
"16 U.S.C. § 5009(5),(6),(7),(8)	2A2.4",
"16 U.S.C. § 5010(b)	2A2.4",
"18 U.S.C. § 43	2B1.3",
"18 U.S.C. § 228	2J1.1",
"18 U.S.C. § 924(h)	2K2.1",
"18 U.S.C. § 2119	2B3.1",
"18 U.S.C. § 2322	2B6.1",
"22 U.S.C. § 2197(n)	2F1.1",
"26 U.S.C. § 7208	2F1.1",
"26 U.S.C. § 7212(a) (omnibus clause)	2J1.2, 2T1.1",
"26 U.S.C. § 7232	2F1.1",
"29 U.S.C. § 530	2B3.2",
"29 U.S.C. § 1131	2E5.3",
"30 U.S.C. § 1461(a)(3),(4),(5),(7)	2A2.4",
"30 U.S.C. § 1463	2A2.4",
"42 U.S.C. § 1973gg-10	2H2.1",
"42 U.S.C. § 9151(2),(3),(4),(5),	2A2.4",
"42 U.S.C. § 9152(d)	2A2.4",
"46 U.S.C. App. § 1707a (f)(2)	2B1.1",
"49 U.S.C. App. § 1687(g)	2B1.3".

Appendix A (Statutory Index) is amended by deleting:

"7 U.S.C. § 13(a)	2B1.1
7 U.S.C. § 13(b)	2F1.1
7 U.S.C. § 13(c)	2F1.1
7 U.S.C. § 13(e)	2F1.2",

and inserting in lieu thereof:

"7 U.S.C. § 13(a)(1)	2B1.1
7 U.S.C. § 13(a)(2)	2F1.1
7 U.S.C. § 13(a)(3)	2F1.1
7 U.S.C. § 13(a)(4)	2F1.1
7 U.S.C. § 13(c)	2C1.3

7 U.S.C. § 13(d)	2F1.2
7 U.S.C. § 13(f)	2F1.2";

in the lines referenced to 15 U.S.C. §§ 1172, 1173, 1174, 1175, and 1176 by deleting "2E3.3" and inserting in lieu thereof "2E3.1";

in the lines referenced to 16 U.S.C. §§ 1029 and 1030 by deleting "2A2.2, 2A2.3, 2Q2.1" and inserting in lieu thereof "2A2.4";

in the line referenced to 16 U.S.C. § 1857(1)(D) by deleting "2A2.3" and inserting in lieu thereof "2A2.4";

in the line referenced to 16 U.S.C. § 1857(1)(E) by deleting "2A2.2, 2A2.3" and inserting in lieu thereof "2A2.4";

in the line referenced to 16 U.S.C. § 1857(1)(F) by deleting "2A2.3" and inserting in lieu thereof "2A2.4";

in the line referenced to 16 U.S.C. § 1857(1)(H) by deleting "2A2.2, 2A2.3" and inserting in lieu thereof "2A2.4";

by deleting:

"16 U.S.C. § 1857(2)   2Q2.1";

in the line referenced to 16 U.S.C. § 1859 by deleting "2A2.2, 2A2.3, 2Q2.1" and inserting in lieu thereof "2A2.4";

in the line referenced to 16 U.S.C. § 2435(4) by deleting "2A2.3" and inserting in lieu thereof "2A2.4";

in the lines referenced to 16 U.S.C. §§ 2435(5), 2435(6), 2435(7), and 2438 by deleting "2A2.2, 2A2.3" and inserting in lieu thereof "2A2.4";

in the line referenced to 18 U.S.C. § 32(a),(b) by deleting "2A1.1-2A2.3" and inserting in lieu thereof "2A1.1, 2A1.2, 2A1.3, 2A1.4, 2A2.1, 2A2.2, 2A2.3".

in the lines referenced to 18 U.S.C. §§ 201(b)(3) and 201(b)(4) by deleting "2J1.8" and inserting in lieu thereof "2J1.3";

in the lines referenced to 18 U.S.C. §§ 471, 472, 473, 474, 476, 477, 478, 479, 480, 481, 482, 483, 484, 485, 486, 488, 493, 494, 497, 498, 499, 500, 502, 503, 505, 506, 507, 508, 509, 510, and 513 by deleting "2B5.2" and inserting in lieu thereof "2F1.1";

in the lines referenced to 18 U.S.C. §§ 553(a)(1) and 553(a)(2) by deleting "2B1.2" and inserting in lieu thereof "2B1.1";

in the line referenced to 18 U.S.C. § 641 by deleting ", 2B1.2";

in the line referenced to 18 U.S.C. § 642 by deleting "2B5.2" and inserting in lieu thereof "2F1.1";

in the line referenced to 18 U.S.C. § 659 by deleting ", 2B1.2";

in the line referenced to 18 U.S.C. § 662 by deleting "2B1.2" and inserting in lieu thereof

Amendment 496

"2B1.1";

in the line referenced to 18 U.S.C. § 664 by deleting "2E5.2" and inserting in lieu thereof "2B1.1";

in the line referenced to 18 U.S.C. § 666(a)(1)(C) by deleting "18 U.S.C. § 666(a)(1)(C)"and inserting in lieu thereof "18 U.S.C. § 666(a)(2)";

in the line referenced to 18 U.S.C. § 667 by deleting ", 2B1.2";

in the line referenced to 18 U.S.C. § 798 by deleting ", 2M3.6";

in the line referenced to 18 U.S.C. § 842(j) by deleting "2K1.2" and inserting in lieu thereof "2K1.1";

in the line referenced to 18 U.S.C. § 844(h) by deleting "2K1.4 (offenses committed prior to November 18, 1988), 2K1.6, 2K1.7" and inserting in lieu thereof "2K2.4 (2K1.4 for offenses committed prior to November 18, 1988)";

in the lines referenced to 18 U.S.C. §§ 1003 and 1010 by deleting "2B5.2,";

in the line referenced to 18 U.S.C. § 1024 by deleting "2B1.2" and inserting in lieu thereof "2B1.1";

in the line referenced to 18 U.S.C. § 1028 by deleting ", 2L2.3, 2L2.4";

in the line referenced to 18 U.S.C. § 1082 by deleting "2E3.3" and inserting in lieu thereof "2E3.1";

in the line referenced to 18 U.S.C. § 1084 by deleting "2E3.2" and inserting in lieu thereof "2E3.1";

in the line referenced to 18 U.S.C. § 1153 by deleting "2B2.2,";

in the line referenced to 18 U.S.C. § 1163 by deleting ", 2B1.2";

in the lines referenced to 18 U.S.C. §§ 1301, 1302, 1303, 1304, 1306, and 1511 by deleting "2E3.3" and inserting in lieu thereof "2E3.1";

in the line referenced to 18 U.S.C. § 1541 by deleting "2L2.3" and inserting in lieu thereof "2L2.1";

in the lines referenced to 18 U.S.C. §§ 1542, 1543, and 1544 by deleting "2L2.3, 2L2.4" and inserting in lieu thereof "2L2.1, 2L2.2";

in the line referenced to 18 U.S.C. § 1704 by deleting "2B5.2,";

in the line referenced to 18 U.S.C. § 1708 by deleting "2B1.2,";

in the line referenced to 18 U.S.C. § 1716C by deleting "2B5.2" and inserting in lieu thereof "2F1.1";

in the lines referenced to 18 U.S.C. §§ 1852 and 1854 by deleting "2B1.2,";

in the line referenced to 18 U.S.C. § 1951 by deleting "2E1.5" and inserting in lieu thereof "2B3.1, 2B3.2, 2B3.3, 2C1.1";

in the line referenced to 18 U.S.C. § 1953 by deleting "2E3.3" and inserting in lieu thereof

"2E3.1";

in the line referenced to 18 U.S.C. § 2113(a) by deleting "2B2.2" and inserting in lieu thereof "2B2.1";

in the line referenced to 18 U.S.C. § 2113(c) by deleting ", 2B1.2";

in the lines referenced to 18 U.S.C. §§ 2115, 2116, 2117, and 2118(b) by deleting "2B2.2" and inserting in lieu thereof "2B2.1";

in the line referenced to 18 U.S.C. § 2154 by deleting "2M2.2" and inserting in lieu thereof "2M2.1";

in the line referenced to 18 U.S.C. § 2156 by deleting "2M2.4" and inserting in lieu thereof "2M2.3";

in the line referenced to 18 U.S.C. § 2197 by deleting "2B5.2,";

in the line referenced to 18 U.S.C. § 2276 by deleting "2B2.2" and inserting in lieu thereof "2B2.1";

in the lines referenced to 18 U.S.C. §§ 2312 and 2313 by deleting ", 2B1.2";

in the lines referenced to 18 U.S.C. §§ 2314 and 2315 by deleting "2B1.2, 2B5.2,";

in the lines referenced to 18 U.S.C. §§ 2316 and 2317 by deleting ", 2B1.2";

in the lines referenced to 18 U.S.C. §§ 2318 and 2320 by deleting "2B5.4" and inserting in lieu thereof "2B5.3";

in the line referenced to 20 U.S.C. § 1097(a) by deleting "2B5.2,"; by deleting:

> "21 U.S.C. § 842(a)(2)   2D3.3
> 21 U.S.C. § 842(a)(9),(10)   2D3.5",

and inserting in lieu thereof:

> "21 U.S.C. § 842(a)(2),(9),(10)   2D3.2";

in the line referenced to 21 U.S.C. § 846 by deleting ", 2D3.3, 2D3.4, 2D3.5";

in the lines referenced to 21 U.S.C. §§ 954 and 961 by deleting "2D3.4" and inserting in lieu thereof "2D3.2";

in the line referenced to 21 U.S.C. § 963 by deleting ", 2D3.3, 2D3.4, 2D3.5";

in the line referenced to 22 U.S.C. § 4221 by deleting "2B5.2" and inserting in lieu thereof "2F1.1";

in the line referenced to 26 U.S.C. § 7203 by deleting "2T1.2" and inserting in lieu thereof "2T1.1";

in the line referenced to 26 U.S.C. § 7206(1),(3),(4),(5) by deleting "2T1.3" and inserting in lieu thereof "2S1.3, 2T1.1";

in the line referenced to 26 U.S.C. § 7206(2) by inserting "2S1.3," immediately before

Amendment 496   APPENDIX C - VOLUME I   November 1, 2013

"2T1.4";

in the line referenced to 26 U.S.C. § 7207 by deleting "2T1.5" and inserting in lieu thereof "2T1.1";

in the line referenced to 26 U.S.C. § 7211 by deleting "2T1.3" and inserting in lieu thereof "2T1.1";

in the line referenced to 26 U.S.C. § 7212(a) by deleting "2A2.2, 2A2.3" and inserting in lieu thereof "2A2.4";

in the line referenced to 29 U.S.C. § 186 by deleting "2E5.6" and inserting in lieu thereof "2E5.1";

in the lines referenced to 29 U.S.C. §§ 431, 432, 433, 439, and 461 by deleting "2E5.5" and inserting in lieu thereof "2E5.3";

in the line referenced to 29 U.S.C. § 501(c) by deleting "2E5.4" and inserting in lieu thereof "2B1.1";

in the line referenced to 31 U.S.C. § 5316 by deleting "2S1.4" and inserting in lieu thereof "2S1.3";

in the line referenced to 31 U.S.C. § 5322 by deleting ", 2S1.4";

in the line referenced to 33 U.S.C. § 1232(b)(2) by deleting "2A2.2, 2A2.3" and inserting in lieu thereof "2A2.4";

in the line referenced to 33 U.S.C. § 1415(b) by inserting "§ 2Q1.2," immediately before "2Q1.3";

in the line referenced to 46 U.S.C. § 3718(b) by deleting "2K3.1" and inserting in lieu thereof "2Q1.2";

in the lines referenced to 49 U.S.C. §§ 1472(h)(2) and 1809(b) by deleting "2K3.1" and inserting in lieu thereof "2Q1.2";

in the line referenced to 50 U.S.C. § 783(b) by deleting "2M3.7" and inserting in lieu thereof "2M3.3"; and

in the line referenced to 50 U.S.C. § 783(c) by deleting "2M3.8" and inserting in lieu thereof "2M3.3".

The Commentary to § 2J1.1 captioned "Statutory Provision" is amended by deleting "Provision: 18 U.S.C. § 401" and inserting lieu thereof "Provisions: 18 U.S.C. §§ 401, 228".

The Commentary to § 2J1.1 captioned "Application Note" is amended in the caption by deleting "Note" and inserting lieu thereof "Notes"; and by inserting the following additional note:

    "2.   For offenses involving the willful failure to pay court-ordered child support (violations of 18 U.S.C. § 228), the most analogous guideline is § 2B1.1 (Larceny, Embezzlement, and Other Forms of Theft). The amount of the loss is the amount of child support that the defendant willfully failed to pay. Note: This guideline applies to second and subsequent offenses under 18

November 1, 2013 APPENDIX C - VOLUME I **Amendment 496**

U.S.C. § 228. A first offense under 18 U.S.C. § 228 is not covered by this guideline because it is a Class B misdemeanor.".

The Commentary to § 2X1.1 captioned "Application Notes" is amended in Note 1 by deleting:

"Offense guidelines that expressly cover attempts include: § 2A2.1 (Assault With Intent to Commit Murder; Attempted Murder); § 2A3.1 (Criminal Sexual Abuse; Attempt to Commit Criminal Sexual Abuse); § 2A3.2 (Criminal Sexual Abuse of a Minor (Statutory Rape) or Attempt to Commit Such Acts); § 2A3.3 (Criminal Sexual Abuse of a Ward or Attempt to Commit Such Acts); § 2A3.4 (Abusive Sexual Contact or Attempt to Commit Abusive Sexual Contact); § 2A4.2 (Demanding or Receiving Ransom Money); § 2A5.1 (Aircraft Piracy or Attempted Aircraft Piracy); § 2C1.1 (Offering, Giving, Soliciting, or Receiving a Bribe; Extortion Under Color of Official Right); § 2C1.2 (Offering, Giving, Soliciting, or Receiving a Gratuity); § 2D1.1 (Unlawful Manufacturing, Importing, Exporting, or Trafficking, Including Possession with Intent to Commit These Offenses; Attempt or Conspiracy); § 2D1.2 (Drug Offenses Occurring Near Protected Locations or Involving Underage or Pregnant Individuals; Attempt or Conspiracy); § 2D1.5 (Continuing Criminal Enterprise; Attempt or Conspiracy); § 2D1.6 (Use of Communication Facility in Committing Drug Offense; Attempt or Conspiracy); § 2D1.7 (Unlawful Sale or Transportation of Drug Paraphernalia; Attempt or Conspiracy); § 2D1.8 (Renting or Managing a Drug Establishment; Attempt or Conspiracy); § 2D1.9 (Placing or Maintaining Dangerous Devices on Federal Property to Protect the Unlawful Production of Controlled Substances; Attempt or Conspiracy); § 2D1.10 (Endangering Human Life While Illegally Manufacturing a Controlled Substance; Attempt or Conspiracy); § 2D1.11 (Unlawfully Distributing, Importing, Exporting or Possessing a Listed Chemical; Attempt or Conspiracy); § 2D1.12 (Unlawful Possession, Manufacture, Distribution, or Importation of Prohibited Flask or Equipment; Attempt or Conspiracy); § 2D1.13 (Structuring Chemical Transactions or Creating a Chemical Mixture to Evade Reporting or Recordkeeping Requirements; Presenting False or Fraudulent Identification to Obtain a Listed Chemical; Attempt or Conspiracy); § 2D2.1 (Unlawful Possession; Attempt or Conspiracy); § 2D2.2 (Acquiring a Controlled Substance by Forgery, Fraud, Deception, or Subterfuge; Attempt or Conspiracy); § 2D3.1 (Illegal Use of Registration Number to Manufacture, Distribute, Acquire, or Dispense a Controlled Substance; Attempt or Conspiracy); § 2D3.2 (Manufacture of Controlled Substance in Excess of or Unauthorized by Registration Quota; Attempt or Conspiracy); § 2D3.3 (Illegal Use of Registration Number to Distribute or Dispense a Controlled Substance to Another Registrant or Authorized Person; Attempt or Conspiracy); § 2D3.4 (Illegal Transfer or Transshipment of a Controlled Substance; Attempt or Conspiracy); and § 2D3.5 (Violation of Recordkeeping or Reporting Requirements for Listed Chemicals and Certain Machines; Attempt or Conspiracy); § 2E5.1 (Offering, Accepting, or Soliciting a Bribe or Gratuity Affecting the Operation of an Employee Welfare or Pension Benefit Plan); § 2N1.1 (Tampering or Attempting to Tamper Involving Risk of Death or Serious Injury); § 2Q1.4 (Tampering or Attempted Tampering with Public Water System).

Offense guidelines that expressly cover conspiracies include: § 2A1.5 (Conspiracy or Solicitation to Commit Murder); § 2D1.1 (Unlawful Manufacturing, Importing, Exporting, or Trafficking, Including Possession with Intent to Commit These Offenses; Attempt or Conspiracy); § 2D1.2 (Drug Offenses Occurring Near Protected Locations or Involving Underage or Pregnant Individuals; Attempt or Conspiracy); § 2D1.5 (Continuing Criminal Enterprise; Attempt or Conspiracy); § 2D1.6 (Use of Communication Facility in Committing Drug Offense; Attempt or Conspiracy); § 2D1.7 (Unlawful Sale or Transportation of Drug Paraphernalia; Attempt or Con-

Amendment 496 APPENDIX C - VOLUME I November 1, 2013

spiracy); § 2D1.8 (Renting or Managing a Drug Establishment; Attempt or Conspiracy); § 2D1.9 (Placing or Maintaining Dangerous Devices on Federal Property to Protect the Unlawful Production of Controlled Substances; Attempt or Conspiracy); § 2D1.10 (Endangering Human Life While Illegally Manufacturing a Controlled Substance; Attempt or Conspiracy); § 2D1.11 (Unlawfully Distributing, Importing, Exporting or Possessing a Listed Chemical; Attempt or Conspiracy); § 2D1.12 (Unlawful Possession, Manufacture, Distribution, or Importation of Prohibited Flask or Equipment; Attempt or Conspiracy); § 2D1.13 (Structuring Chemical Transactions or Creating a Chemical Mixture to Evade Reporting or Recordkeeping Requirements; Presenting False or Fraudulent Identification to Obtain a Listed Chemical; Attempt or Conspiracy); § 2D2.1 (Unlawful Possession; Attempt or Conspiracy); § 2D2.2 (Acquiring a Controlled Substance by Forgery, Fraud, Deception, or Subterfuge; Attempt or Conspiracy); § 2D3.1 (Illegal Use of Registration Number to Manufacture, Distribute, Acquire, or Dispense a Controlled Substance; Attempt or Conspiracy); § 2D3.2 (Manufacture of Controlled Substance in Excess of or Unauthorized by Registration Quota; Attempt or Conspiracy); § 2D3.3 (Illegal Use of Registration Number to Distribute or Dispense a Controlled Substance to Another Registrant or Authorized Person; Attempt or Conspiracy); § 2D3.4 (Illegal Transfer or Transshipment of a Controlled Substance; Attempt or Conspiracy); and § 2D3.5 (Violation of Recordkeeping or Reporting Requirements for Listed Chemicals and Certain Machines; Attempt or Conspiracy); § 2H1.1 (Conspiracy to Interfere with Civil Rights; Going in Disguise to Deprive of Rights); § 2T1.9 (Conspiracy to Impair, Impede or Defeat Tax).

Offense guidelines that expressly cover solicitations include: § 2A1.5 (Conspiracy or Solicitation to Commit Murder); § 2C1.1 (Offering, Giving, Soliciting, or Receiving a Bribe; Extortion Under Color of Official Right); § 2C1.2 (Offering, Giving, Soliciting, or Receiving a Gratuity); § 2E5.1 (Offering, Accepting, or Soliciting a Bribe or Gratuity Affecting the Operation of an Employee Welfare or Pension Benefit Plan).",

and inserting in lieu thereof:

"Offense guidelines that expressly cover attempts include:

§§ 2A2.1, 2A3.1, 2A3.2, 2A3.3, 2A3.4, 2A4.2, 2A5.1;
§§ 2C1.1, 2C1.2;
§§ 2D1.1, 2D1.2, 2D1.5, 2D1.6, 2D1.7, 2D1.8, 2D1.9, 2D1.10, 2D1.11, 2D1.12, 2D1.13, 2D2.1, 2D2.2, 2D3.1, 2D3.2;
§ 2E5.1;
§ 2N1.1;
§ 2Q1.4.

Offense guidelines that expressly cover conspiracies include:

§ 2A1.5;
§§ 2D1.1, 2D1.2, 2D1.5, 2D1.6, 2D1.7, 2D1.8, 2D1.9, 2D1.10, 2D1.11, 2D1.12, 2D1.13, 2D2.1, 2D2.2, 2D3.1, 2D3.2;
§ 2H1.1;
§ 2T1.9.

Offense guidelines that expressly cover solicitations include:

§ 2A1.5;

§§ 2C1.1, 2C1.2;
§ 2E5.1.".

The Commentary to § 2X3.1 captioned "Application Notes" is amended in Note 1 in the second sentence by deleting "Note 1" and inserting in lieu thereof "Note 10".

The Commentary to § 2X4.1 captioned "Application Notes" is amended in Note 1 in the second sentence by deleting "Note 1" and inserting in lieu thereof "Note 10".

The Commentary to § 3C1.1 captioned "Application Notes" is amended in Note 6 by inserting "; Bribery of Witness" immediately following "of Perjury"; by deleting "§ 2J1.8 (Bribery of Witness, or § 2J1.9 (Payment to Witness)" and inserting in lieu thereof "§ 2J1.9 (Payment to Witness), § 2X3.1 (Accessory After the Fact), or § 2X4.1 (Misprision of Felony)"; and by deleting "or prosecution" and inserting in lieu thereof ", prosecution, or sentencing".

Section 3D1.2(d) is amended in the second paragraph by deleting "2B1.2,", "2B5.2,", "2B5.4,", "2E5.2, 2E5.4, 2E5.6", ", 2L2.3,", and "2T1.2, 2T1.3,"; and in the third paragraph by deleting "2B2.2,", "2E1.5,", "2L2.4,", and "2M3.6, 2M3.7, 2M3.8,".

Section 8C2.1(a) is amended by deleting "2B1.2,", "2B5.4,", ", 2D3.4,", "2E3.2, 2E3.3,", "2E5.2,", ", 2E5.4, 2E5.5, 2E5.6", "2K1.2,", ", 2S1.4", "2T1.2, 2T1.3," and "2T1.5,".

The Commentary to § 8C2.4 captioned "Application Notes" is amended in Note 5 by inserting "; Prohibited Payments or Lending of Money by Employer or Agent to Employees, Representatives, or Labor Organizations" immediately following "Plan"; and by deleting "§ 2S1.3 (Failure to Report Monetary Transactions; Structuring Transactions to Evade Reporting Requirements); and § 2S1.4 (Failure to File Currency and Monetary Instrument Report)" and inserting in lieu thereof "and § 2S1.3 (Structuring Transactions to Evade Reporting Requirements; Failure to Report Cash or Monetary Transactions; Failure to File Currency and Monetary Instrument Report; Knowingly Filing False Reports)".

Reason for Amendment: This amendment makes Appendix A more comprehensive, conforms it to the consolidation of offense guidelines under amendments 481, 490, and 491, and deletes references to several Class B and C misdemeanor offenses to which the guidelines do not apply. In addition, this amendment conforms § 3D1.2(d), § 8C2.1, and the Commentary to §§ 2X1.1, 3C1.1, and 8C2.4 to the consolidation of offense guidelines under amendments 481, 490, and 491. In addition, this amendment reformats the Commentary to 2X1.1 for ease in application; corrects an omission in the second paragraph of the Introduction to Appendix A; revises Application Note 6 of the Commentary to § 3C1.1 to make the listing of offense guidelines more comprehensive and correct the omission of a reference to the sentencing of the instant offense; and revises a reference in the Commentary to §§ 2X3.1 and 2X4.1 to conform to a previous revision in the referenced provision.

Effective Date: The effective date of this amendment is November 1, 1993.

497. Amendment: The Commentary to § 1B1.1 captioned "Application Notes" is amended in Note 4 by inserting the following additional paragraph as the second paragraph:

"Absent an instruction to the contrary, the adjustments from different guideline sections are applied cumulatively (added together). For example, the adjustments from § 2F1.1(b)(2) (more than minimal planning) and § 3B1.1 (aggravating role) are applied cumulatively.".

Reason for Amendment: This amendment clarifies the Commission's intent that, absent an instruction to the contrary, adjustments from different guideline sections are to be applied cumulatively.

Effective Date: The effective date of this amendment is November 1, 1993.

498. **Amendment:** The Commentary to § 1B1.7 is amended by deleting the second paragraph as follows:

> " In stating that failure to follow certain commentary 'could constitute an incorrect application of the guidelines,' the Commission simply means that in seeking to understand the meaning of the guidelines courts likely will look to the commentary for guidance as an indication of the intent of those who wrote them. In such instances, the courts will treat the commentary much like legislative history or other legal material that helps determine the intent of a drafter.",

and inserting in lieu thereof:

> " '[C]ommentary in the Guidelines Manual that interprets or explains a guideline is authoritative unless it violates the Constitution or a federal statute, or is inconsistent with, or a plainly erroneous reading of, that guideline.' Stinson v. United States, 113 S. Ct. 1913, 1915 (1993).".

Reason for Amendment: This amendment revises the commentary to this section to reflect the decision of the Supreme Court in Stinson v. United States, 113 S. Ct. 1913, 1915 (1993).

Effective Date: The effective date of this amendment is November 1, 1993.

499. **Amendment:** The Commentary to § 2D1.1 captioned "Application Notes" is amended in Note 10 in the "Drug Equivalency Tables" in the subdivision captioned "LSD, PCP, and other Schedule I and II Hallucinogens" by deleting:

> "Phenylcyclohexamine (PCE) = 5.79 kg of marihuana"

and inserting in lieu thereof:

> "N-ethyl-1-phenylcyclohexylamine (PCE)= 1 kg of marihuana".

Reason for Amendment: This amendment revises the equivalency for PCE to reflect a reassessment of the potency of this controlled substance by the Drug Enforcement Administration. In addition, this amendment corrects an error in the scientific name for this controlled substance.

Effective Date: The effective date of this amendment is November 1, 1993.

500. **Amendment:** The Commentary to § 3B1.1 captioned "Application Notes" is amended by renumbering Notes 2 and 3 as 3 and 4, respectively; and by inserting the following additional note:

> "2. To qualify for an adjustment under this section, the defendant must have been the organizer, leader, manager, or supervisor of one or more other participants. An upward departure may be warranted, however, in the case of a defendant who did not organize, lead, manage, or supervise another participant, but who nevertheless exercised management responsibility over the property, assets, or activities of a criminal organization.".

Reason for Amendment: This amendment clarifies the operation of this section to resolve a split among the courts of appeal. Compare United States v. Carroll, 893 F.2d 1502 (6th Cir. 1990) (requiring degree of control over other persons for § 3B1.1 to apply); United States v. Fuller, 897 F.2d 1217 (1st Cir. 1990) (same); United States v. Mares-Molina, 913 F.2d 770 (9th Cir. 1990) (same) and United States v. Fuentes, 954 F.2d 151 (3d Cir.) (same), cert. denied, 112 S.Ct. 2950 (1992) with United States v. Chambers, 985 F.2d 1263 (4th Cir.) (defendant may be a "manager" even though he did not directly supervise other persons), petition for cert. filed, No. 92-8737 (U.S. May 17, 1993).

Effective Date: The effective date of this amendment is November 1, 1993.

501. **Amendment:** The Commentary to § 5E1.1 captioned "Background" is amended in the second paragraph by inserting the following additional sentence as the first sentence:

> "A court's authority to decline to order restitution is limited.";

by inserting, immediately after "18 U.S.C. § 3663(d).", the following:

> "The legislative history of 18 U.S.C. § 3579, the precursor of 18 U.S.C. § 3663, states that even '[i]n those unusual cases where the precise amount owed is difficult to determine, the section authorizes the court to reach an expeditious, reasonable determination of appropriate restitution by resolving uncertainties with a view toward achieving fairness to the victim.' S. Rep. No. 532, 97th Cong., 2d Sess. 31, reprinted in 1982 U.S. Code Cong. & Ad. News 2515, 2537.";

and by inserting the following additional sentence as the last sentence:

> "Subsection (a)(2) provides for restitution as a condition of probation or supervised release for offenses not set forth in Title 18, United States Code, or 49 U.S.C. § 1472(h), (i), (j), or (n).".

The Commentary to § 5E1.1 captioned "Background" is amended by deleting the fifth paragraph as follows:

> "   A court's authority to deny restitution is limited. Even 'in those unusual cases where the precise amount owed is difficult to determine, section 3579(d) authorizes the court to reach an expeditious, reasonable determination of appropriate restitution by resolving uncertainties with a view toward achieving fairness to the victim.' S. Rep. No. 532, 97th Cong., 2d Sess. 31, reprinted in 1982 U.S. Code Cong. & Ad. News 2515, 2537.";

and by deleting the seventh paragraph as follows:

> "   Subsection (a)(2) provides for restitution as a condition of probation or supervised release for offenses not set forth in Title 18, United States Code, or 49 U.S.C. § 1472(h), (i), (j), or (n).".

Reason for Amendment: This amendment updates the background commentary of § 5E1.1 to reflect the redesignation of 18 U.S.C. § 3579 as 18 U.S.C. § 3663. In addition, it moves material from the fifth and seventh paragraphs to the second paragraph to enhance clarity.

Effective Date: The effective date of this amendment is November 1, 1993.

502. **Amendment:** Section 1B1.10(d) is amended by deleting "and 461" and inserting in lieu thereof "454, 461, 484, 488, 490, and 499".

Reason for Amendment: This amendment expands the listing in § 1B1.10(d) to imple-

Amendment 502

ment the directive in 28 U.S.C. § 994(u) in respect to guideline amendments that may be considered for retroactive application.

Effective Date: The effective date of this amendment is November 1, 1993.

503. **Amendment:** The Commentary to § 1B1.3 captioned "Application Notes" is amended in Note 2 by inserting the following additional paragraph as the eighth paragraph:

> "A defendant's relevant conduct does not include the conduct of members of a conspiracy prior to the defendant joining the conspiracy, even if the defendant knows of that conduct (e.g., in the case of a defendant who joins an ongoing drug distribution conspiracy knowing that it had been selling two kilograms of cocaine per week, the cocaine sold prior to the defendant joining the conspiracy is not included as relevant conduct in determining the defendant's offense level). The Commission does not foreclose the possibility that there may be some unusual set of circumstances in which the exclusion of such conduct may not adequately reflect the defendant's culpability; in such a case, an upward departure may be warranted.".

The Commentary to § 1B1.3 captioned "Application Notes" is amended in Note 9(B) by deleting "and the time interval between the offenses" and inserting in lieu thereof:

> ", the regularity (repetitions) of the offenses, and the time interval between the offenses. When one of the above factors is absent, a stronger presence of at least one of the other factors is required. For example, where the conduct alleged to be relevant is relatively remote to the offense of conviction, a stronger showing of similarity or regularity is necessary to compensate for the absence of temporal proximity".

Reason for Amendment: This amendment clarifies the operation of § 1B1.3 with respect to the defendant's accountability for the actions of other conspirators prior to the defendant joining the conspiracy. The amendment is in accord with the rule stated in recent caselaw. See, e.g., United States v. Carreon, 11 F.3d 1225 (5th Cir. 1994); United States v. Petty, 982 F.2d 1374, 1377 (9th Cir. 1993); United States v. O'Campo, 973 F.2d 1015, 1026 (1st Cir. 1992). Cf. United States v. Miranda-Ortiz, 926 F.2d 172, 178 (2d Cir. 1991); United States v. Edwards, 945 F.2d 1387, 1393 (7th Cir. 1991)) (applying earlier versions of § 1B1.3). In addition, this amendment adds a well-phrased formulation, developed by the Ninth Circuit in United States v. Hahn, 960 F.2d 903 (9th Cir. 1992), addressing the circumstances in which multiple acts constitute the "same course of conduct."

Effective Date: The effective date of this amendment is November 1, 1994.

504. **Amendment:** Section 1B1.10(a) is amended by deleting "guidelines" and inserting in lieu thereof "Guidelines Manual"; by deleting "may be considered" and inserting in lieu thereof "is authorized"; by inserting "and thus is not authorized" immediately following "policy statement"; and by deleting "subsection (d)" wherever it appears and inserting in lieu thereof in each instance "subsection (c)".

Section 1B1.10(b) is amended by inserting ", and to what extent," immediately before "a reduction"; and by deleting:

> "originally imposed had the guidelines, as amended, been in effect at that time",

and inserting in lieu thereof:

> "imposed had the amendment(s) to the guidelines listed in subsection (c) been in effect at the time the defendant was sentenced".

Section 1B1.10 is amended by deleting:

"(c) *Provided*, that a reduction in a defendant's term of imprisonment may, in no event, exceed the number of months by which the maximum of the guideline range applicable to the defendant (from Chapter Five, Part A) has been lowered.";

and by redesignating subsection (d) as subsection (c).

Section 1B1.10(c)(formerly subsection (d)) is amended by inserting "371," immediately before "379"; and by deleting "and 499" and inserting in lieu thereof "499, and 506".

The Commentary to § 1B1.10 captioned "Application Note" is amended by deleting "Note" and inserting in lieu thereof "Notes"; and by deleting:

"1. Although eligibility for consideration under 18 U.S.C. § 3582(c)(2) is triggered only by an amendment listed in subsection (d) of this section, the amended guideline range referred to in subsections (b) and (c) of this section is to be determined by applying all amendments to the guidelines (i.e., as if the defendant was being sentenced under the guidelines currently in effect).",

and inserting in lieu thereof:

"1. Eligibility for consideration under 18 U.S.C. § 3582(c)(2) is triggered only by an amendment listed in subsection (c) that lowers the applicable guideline range.

2. In determining the amended guideline range under subsection (b), the court shall substitute only the amendments listed in subsection (c) for the corresponding guideline provisions that were applied when the defendant was sentenced. All other guideline application decisions remain unaffected.".

The Commentary to § 1B1.10 captioned "Background" is amended in the third paragraph by deleting "subsection (d)" and inserting in lieu thereof "subsection (c)".

Reason for Amendment: This amendment simplifies the operation of § 1B1.10 by providing that, in determining an amended guideline range, the court will use only those amendments expressly designated as retroactive. In addition, this amendment deletes § 1B1.10(c), a rather complex subsection, as an unnecessary restriction on the court's consideration of a revised sentence, redesignates § 1B1.10(d) as § 1B1.10(c), and makes a number of minor clarifying revisions. This amendment also expands the listing in § 1B1.10(c) (formerly § 1B1.10(d)) to implement the directive in 28 U.S.C. § 994(u) with respect to guideline amendments that may be considered for retroactive application.

Effective Date: The effective date of this amendment is November 1, 1994.

Amendment 505   APPENDIX C - VOLUME I   November 1, 2013

505. Amendment: Section 2D1.1(c) is amended by deleting:

    "(1) 300 KG or more of Heroin (or the equivalent amount of other   Level 42
        Schedule I or II Opiates);
        1500 KG or more of Cocaine (or the equivalent amount of other
        Schedule I or II Stimulants);
        15 KG or more of Cocaine Base;
        300 KG or more of PCP, or 30 KG or more of PCP (actual);
        300 KG or more of Methamphetamine, or 30 KG or more of
        Methamphetamine (actual), or 30 KG or more of "Ice";
        3 KG or more of LSD (or the equivalent amount of other
        Schedule I or II Hallucinogens);
        120 KG or more of Fentanyl;
        30 KG or more of a Fentanyl Analogue;
        300,000 KG or more of Marihuana;
        60,000 KG or more of Hashish;
        6,000 KG or more of Hashish Oil.

    (2) At least 100 KG but less than 300 KG of Heroin (or the   Level 40
        equivalent amount of other Schedule I or II Opiates);
        At least 500 KG but less than 1500 KG of Cocaine (or the
        equivalent amount of other Schedule I or II Stimulants);
        At least 5 KG but less than 15 KG of Cocaine Base;
        At least 100 KG but less than 300 KG of PCP, or at least
        10 KG but less than 30 KG of PCP (actual);
        At least 100 KG but less than 300 KG of Methamphetamine,
        or at least 10 KG but less than 30 KG of Methamphetamine
        (actual), or at least 10 KG but less than 30 KG of "Ice";
        At least 1 KG but less than 3 KG of LSD (or the equivalent
        amount of other Schedule I or II Hallucinogens);
        At least 40 KG but less than 120 KG of Fentanyl;
        At least 10 KG but less than 30 KG of a Fentanyl Analogue;
        At least 100,000 KG but less than 300,000 KG of Marihuana;
        At least 20,000 KG but less than 60,000 KG of Hashish;
        At least 2,000 KG but less than 6,000 KG of Hashish Oil.

    (3) At least 30 KG but less than 100 KG of Heroin (or the   Level 38
        equivalent amount of other Schedule I or II Opiates);
        At least 150 KG but less than 500 KG of Cocaine (or the
        equivalent amount of other Schedule I or II Stimulants);
        At least 1.5 KG but less than 5 KG of Cocaine Base;
        At least 30 KG but less than 100 KG of PCP, or at least 3 KG
        but less than 10 KG of PCP (actual);
        At least 30 KG but less than 100 KG of Methamphetamine, or
        at least 3 KG but less than 10 KG of Methamphetamine (actual),
        or at least 3 KG but less than 10 KG of "Ice";
        At least 300 G but less than 1 KG of LSD (or the equivalent
        amount of other Schedule I or II Hallucinogens);
        At least 12 KG but less than 40 KG of Fentanyl;
        At least 3 KG but less than 10 KG of a Fentanyl Analogue;
        At least 30,000 KG but less than 100,000 KG of Marihuana;
        At least 6,000 KG but less than 20,000 KG of Hashish;
        At least 600 KG but less than 2,000 KG of Hashish Oil.",

   and inserting in lieu thereof: ˆ

"(1) 30 KG or more of Heroin (or the equivalent amount of other Schedule I or II Opiates); 150 KG or more of Cocaine (or the equivalent amount of other Schedule I or II Stimulants); 1.5 KG or more of Cocaine Base; 30 KG or more of PCP, or 3 KG or more of PCP (actual); 30 KG or more of Methamphetamine, or 3 KG or more of Methamphetamine (actual), or 3 KG or more of 'Ice'; 300 G or more of LSD (or the equivalent amount of other Schedule I or II Hallucinogens); 12 KG or more of Fentanyl; 3 KG or more of a Fentanyl Analogue; 30,000 KG or more of Marihuana; 6,000 KG or more of Hashish; 600 KG or more of Hashish Oil.";	Level 38

and by renumbering subdivisions 4-19 as 2-17, respectively.

The Commentary to § 2D1.1 captioned "Application Notes" is amended in Note 14 by deleting "860(b)(4)" and inserting in lieu thereof "960(b)(4)".

The Commentary to § 2D1.1 captioned "Application Notes" is amended in Note 16 by deleting "40" and inserting in lieu thereof "38"; by deleting "35" wherever it appears and inserting in lieu thereof in each instance "33"; and by deleting "4 levels" and inserting in lieu thereof "2 levels".

The Commentary to § 2D1.1 captioned "Application Notes" is amended by inserting the following additional note:

"19. In an extraordinary case, an upward departure above offense level 38 on the basis of drug quantity may be warranted. For example, an upward departure may be warranted where the quantity is at least ten times the minimum quantity required for level 38.".

The Commentary to § 2D1.6 captioned "Application Note" is amended in Note 1 by deleting "(§ 2D1.1(c)(16))" and inserting in lieu thereof "(§ 2D1.1(c)(14))"; and by deleting "(§ 2D1.1(c)(19))" and inserting in lieu thereof "(§ 2D1.1(c)(17))".

Reason for Amendment: This amendment sets the upper limit of the Drug Quantity Table in § 2D1.1 at level 38. The Commission has determined that the extension of the Drug Quantity Table above level 38 for quantity itself is not required to ensure adequate punishment given that organizers, leaders, managers, and supervisors of such offenses will receive a 4-, 3-, or 2-level enhancement for their role in the offense, and any participant will receive an additional 2-level enhancement if a dangerous weapon is possessed in the offense. The Commission, however, has not foreclosed the possibility of an upward departure above offense level 38 on the basis of drug quantity in an extraordinary case. In addition, this amendment corrects a typographical error in a statutory reference.

Effective Date: The effective date of this amendment is November 1, 1994.

506. **Amendment:** The Commentary to § 4B1.1 captioned "Application Notes" is amended in Note 2 by deleting:

Amendment 506 APPENDIX C - VOLUME I November 1, 2013

> "'Offense Statutory Maximum' refers to the maximum term of imprisonment authorized for the offense of conviction that is a crime of violence or controlled substance offense.",

and inserting in lieu thereof:

> "'Offense Statutory Maximum,' for the purposes of this guideline, refers to the maximum term of imprisonment authorized for the offense of conviction that is a crime of violence or controlled substance offense, not including any increase in that maximum term under a sentencing enhancement provision that applies because of the defendant's prior criminal record (such sentencing enhancement provisions are contained, for example, in 21 U.S.C. § 841(b)(1)(A), (b)(1)(B), (b)(1)(C), and (b)(1)(D)). For example, where the statutory maximum term of imprisonment under 21 U.S.C. § 841(b)(1)(C) is increased from twenty years to thirty years because the defendant has one or more qualifying prior drug convictions, the 'Offense Statutory Maximum' for the purposes of this guideline is twenty years and not thirty years.".

Reason for Amendment: This amendment defines the term "offense statutory maximum" in § 4B1.1 to mean the statutory maximum prior to any enhancement based on prior criminal record (i.e., an enhancement of the statutory maximum sentence that itself was based upon the defendant's prior criminal record will not be used in determining the alternative offense level under this guideline). This rule avoids unwarranted double counting as well as unwarranted disparity associated with variations in the exercise of prosecutorial discretion in seeking enhanced penalties based on prior convictions. It is noted that when the instruction to the Commission that underlies § 4B1.1 (28 U.S.C. § 994(h)) was enacted by the Congress in 1984, the enhanced maximum sentences provided for recidivist drug offenders (e.g., under 21 U.S.C. § 841) did not exist.

Effective Date: The effective date of this amendment is November 1, 1994.

507. **Amendment:** The Commentary to § 5G1.2 is amended in the fourth paragraph by deleting "3D1.2" and inserting in lieu thereof "3D1.1"; and by inserting the following additional sentences at the end:

> "Note, however, that even in the case of a consecutive term of imprisonment imposed under subsection (a), any term of supervised release imposed is to run concurrently with any other term of supervised release imposed. See 18 U.S.C. § 3624(e).".

Reason for Amendment: This amendment revises the Commentary to § 5G1.2 to clarify that the Commission's interpretation is that 18 U.S.C. § 3624(e) requires multiple terms of supervised release to run concurrently in all cases. This interpretation is in accord with the view stated in United States v. Gullickson, 982 F.2d 1231, 1236 (8th Cir. 1993). In contrast, two courts of appeals have cited the current commentary as supporting the view that, notwithstanding the language in 18 U.S.C. § 3624(e) stating that terms of supervised release run concurrently, a court may order that supervised release terms run consecutively under certain circumstances. See United States v. Shorthouse, 7 F.3d 149 (9th Cir. 1993); United States v. Maxwell, 966 F.2d 545, 551 (10th Cir. 1992).

Effective Date: The effective date of this amendment is November 1, 1994.

508. **Amendment:** The Introductory Commentary to Chapter Five, Part H, is amended in the second paragraph by inserting the following additional sentences at the end:

> "Furthermore, although these factors are not ordinarily relevant to the determination

of whether a sentence should be outside the applicable guideline range, they may be relevant to this determination in exceptional cases. See § 5K2.0 (Grounds for Departure).".

Section 5K2.0 is amended by inserting the following additional paragraph as the fourth paragraph:

"An offender characteristic or other circumstance that is not ordinarily relevant in determining whether a sentence should be outside the applicable guideline range may be relevant to this determination if such characteristic or circumstance is present to an unusual degree and distinguishes the case from the 'heartland' cases covered by the guidelines in a way that is important to the statutory purposes of sentencing.".

Section 5K2.0 is amended by inserting the following commentary at the end:

"Commentary

The last paragraph of this policy statement sets forth the conditions under which an offender characteristic or other circumstance that is not ordinarily relevant to a departure from the applicable guideline range may be relevant to this determination. The Commission does not foreclose the possibility of an extraordinary case that, because of a combination of such characteristics or circumstances, differs significantly from the 'heartland' cases covered by the guidelines in a way that is important to the statutory purposes of sentencing, even though none of the characteristics or circumstances individually distinguishes the case. However, the Commission believes that such cases will be extremely rare.

In the absence of a characteristic or circumstance that distinguishes a case as sufficiently atypical to warrant a sentence different from that called for under the guidelines, a sentence outside the guideline range is not authorized. See 18 U.S.C. § 3553(b). For example, dissatisfaction with the available sentencing range or a preference for a different sentence than that authorized by the guidelines is not an appropriate basis for a sentence outside the applicable guideline range.".

Reason for Amendment: This amendment revises § 5K2.0 and the Introductory Commentary to Chapter Five, Part H to provide guidance as to when an offender characteristic or other circumstance (or combination of such characteristics or circumstances) that is not ordinarily relevant to a determination of whether a sentence should be outside the applicable guideline range may be relevant to this determination.

Effective Date: The effective date of this amendment is November 1, 1994.

509. **Amendment:** The Commentary to § 2D1.1 captioned "Application Notes" is amended in Note 7 by inserting the following additional sentences at the end:

"In addition, 18 U.S.C. § 3553(f) provides an exception to the applicability of mandatory minimum sentences in certain cases. See § 5C1.2 (Limitation on Applicability of Statutory Minimum Sentences in Certain Cases).".

The Commentary to § 2D2.1 captioned "Background" is amended in the first paragraph by inserting "(statutory)" immediately following "Mandatory"; and by deleting "§ 5G1.1(b)" and inserting in lieu thereof:

"See § 5G1.1(b). Note, however, that 18 U.S.C. § 3553(f) provides an exception to the applicability of mandatory minimum sentences in certain cases. See § 5C1.2 (Limitation on Applicability of Statutory Minimum Sentences in Certain Cases).".

Amendment 509 APPENDIX C - VOLUME I November 1, 2013

Chapter Five, Part C, is amended by inserting an additional guideline with accompanying commentary as § 5C1.2 (Limitation on Applicability of Statutory Minimum Sentences in Certain Cases).

Reason for Amendment: This amendment adds a new guideline as § 5C1.2, and revises the commentary in §§ 2D1.1 and 2D1.2, to reflect the addition of 18 U.S.C. § 3553(f) by section 80001 of the Violent Crime Control and Law Enforcement Act of 1994.

Effective Date: The effective date of this amendment is September 23, 1994.

510. **Amendment:** Section 2A2.3 is amended by inserting the following additional subsection:

"(b) Specific Offense Characteristic

(1) If the offense resulted in substantial bodily injury to an individual under the age of sixteen years, increase by 4 levels.".

The Commentary to § 2A2.3 captioned "Application Notes" is amended by inserting the following additional note:

"3. 'Substantial bodily injury' means 'bodily injury which involves - (A) a temporary but substantial disfigurement; or (B) a temporary but substantial loss or impairment of the function of any bodily member, organ, or mental faculty.' 18 U.S.C. § 113(b)(1).".

Reason for Amendment: This amendment addresses the enactment of 18 U.S.C. § 113(a)(7) (pertaining to certain assaults against minors) by section 170201 of the Violent Crime Control and Law Enforcement Act of 1994.

Effective Date: The effective date of this amendment is November 1, 1995.

511. **Amendment:** The Commentary to § 2A3.1 captioned "Application Notes" is amended by inserting the following additional notes:

"6. If a victim was sexually abused by more than one participant, an upward departure may be warranted. See § 5K2.8 (Extreme Conduct).

7. If the defendant's criminal history includes a prior sentence for conduct that is similar to the instant offense, an upward departure may be warranted.".

The Commentary to § 2A3.2 captioned "Application Notes" is amended by inserting the following additional note:

"4. If the defendant's criminal history includes a prior sentence for conduct that is similar to the instant offense, an upward departure may be warranted.".

The Commentary to § 2A3.3 captioned "Application Note" is amended by deleting "Note" and inserting in lieu thereof "Notes"; and by inserting the following additional note:

"2. If the defendant's criminal history includes a prior sentence for conduct that is similar to the instant offense, an upward departure may be warranted.".

The Commentary to § 2A3.4 captioned "Application Notes" is amended by inserting the following additional note:

"5. If the defendant's criminal history includes a prior sentence for conduct that is similar to the instant offense, an upward departure may be warranted.".

November 1, 2013 APPENDIX C - VOLUME I **Amendment 512**

Reason for Amendment: Section 40111 of the Violent Crime Control and Law Enforcement Act of 1994 doubles the authorized maximum term of imprisonment for defendants convicted of sexual abuse offenses who have been convicted previously of aggravated sexual abuse, sexual abuse, or aggravated sexual contact (18 U.S.C. § 2247) and directs the Sentencing Commission to implement this provision by promulgating amendments, if appropriate, to the applicable sentencing guidelines. Although the Chapter Two sexual abuse guidelines do not provide for enhancement for repeat sex offenses, Chapter Four (Criminal History and Criminal Livelihood) does include a determination of the seriousness of the defendant's criminal record based upon prior convictions (§ 4A1.1). Section 4B1.1 (Career Offender) also provides substantially enhanced penalties for offenders who engage in a crime of violence (including forcible sexual offenses) or controlled substance trafficking offense, having been sentenced previously on two or more occasions for offenses of either type. Moreover, § 4A1.3 (Adequacy of Criminal History category) provides that an upward departure may be considered "[i]f reliable information indicates that the criminal history category does not reflect the seriousness of the defendant's past criminal conduct or the likelihood that the defendant will commit other crimes." This amendment strengthens the sexual offense guidelines by expressly listing as a basis for upward departure the fact that the defendant has a prior sentence for conduct similar to the instant sexual offense.

Section 40112 of the Violent Crime Control and Law Enforcement Act of 1994 directs the Commission to conduct a study and consider the adequacy of the guidelines for sexual offenses with respect to a number of factors. The provision also requires the preparation of a report to Congress analyzing federal rape sentences and obtaining comment from independent experts. See Report to Congress: Analysis of Penalties for Federal Rape Cases (March 13, 1995). The Commission found that, in general, the current guidelines provide appropriate penalties for these offenses. This amendment strengthens § 2A3.1 (Criminal Sexual Abuse; Attempt to Commit Criminal Sexual Abuse) in one respect by expressly listing as a basis for an upward departure the fact that a victim was sexually abused by more than one participant.

Effective Date: The effective date of this amendment is November 1, 1995.

512. Amendment: Section 2B1.1(b) is amended by deleting:

"(2) If (A) a firearm, destructive device, or controlled substance was taken, or the taking of such item was an object of the offense; or (B) the stolen property received, transported, transferred, transmitted, or possessed was a firearm, destructive device, or controlled substance, increase by **1** level; but if the resulting offense level is less than **7**, increase to level **7**.";

and by renumbering the remaining subdivisions accordingly.

Section 2B1.1 is amended by inserting the following additional subsection:

"(c) Cross Reference

(1) If (A) a firearm, destructive device, explosive material, or controlled substance was taken, or the taking of such item was an object of the offense, or (B) the stolen property received, transported, transferred, transmitted, or possessed was a firearm, destructive device, explosive material, or controlled substance, apply § 2D1.1 (Unlawful Manufacturing, Importing, Exporting, or Trafficking; Attempt or Conspiracy), § 2D2.1 (Unlawful Possession; Attempt or Conspir-

- 383 -

acy), § 2K1.3 (Unlawful Receipt, Possession, or Transportation of Explosive Materials; Prohibited Transactions Involving Explosive Materials), or § 2K2.1 (Unlawful Receipt, Possession, or Transportation of Firearms or Ammunition; Prohibited Transactions Involving Firearms or Ammunition), as appropriate, if the resulting offense level is greater than that determined above.".

The Commentary to § 2B1.1 captioned "Application Notes" is amended in Note 8 by deleting "(b)(6)" and inserting in lieu thereof "(b)(5)".

The Commentary to § 2B1.1 captioned "Application Notes" is amended in Note 11 by deleting "(b)(7)(B)" and inserting in lieu thereof "(b)(6)(B)".

The Commentary to § 2B1.1 captioned "Application Notes" is amended in Note 13 by deleting "(b)(7)(A)" and inserting in lieu thereof "(b)(6)(A)".

The Commentary to § 2B1.1 captioned "Background" is amended by deleting the fourth paragraph as follows:

"   Studies show that stolen firearms are used disproportionately in the commission of crimes. The guidelines provide an enhancement for theft of a firearm to ensure that some amount of imprisonment is required. An enhancement is also provided when controlled substances are taken. Such thefts may involve a greater risk of violence, as well as a likelihood that the substance will be abused.".

The Commentary to § 2B1.1 captioned "Background" is amended in the sixth (formerly the seventh) paragraph by deleting "(b)(7)(A)" and inserting in lieu thereof "(b)(6)(A)"; and in the seventh (formerly the eighth) paragraph by deleting "(b)(7)(B)" and inserting in lieu thereof "(b)(6)(B)".

Reason for Amendment: This amendment addresses an inconsistency in guideline penalties between theft offenses involving the taking of firearms or controlled substances that are sentenced under § 2B1.1 (Larceny, Embezzlement, and Other Forms of Theft; Receiving, Transporting, Transferring, Transmitting, or Possessing Stolen Property) and similar offenses sentenced under § 2D1.1 (Unlawful Manufacturing, Importing, Exporting, or Trafficking; Attempt or Conspiracy), § 2D2.1 (Unlawful Possession; Attempt or Conspiracy), § 2K1.3 (Unlawful Receipt, Possession, or Transportation of Explosive Materials; Prohibited Transactions Involving Explosive Materials), or § 2K2.1 (Unlawful Receipt, Possession, or Transportation of Firearms or Ammunition; Prohibited Transactions Involving Firearms or Ammunition) by deleting the specific offense characteristic in § 2B1.1 applicable in such instances and inserting in lieu thereof a cross reference directing the application of § 2D1.1, § 2D2.1, § 2K1.3, or § 2K2.1, as appropriate, if the resulting offense level is greater.

Effective Date: The effective date of this amendment is November 1, 1995.

513. **Amendment:** Section 2B5.1(b) is amended by inserting the following additional subdivision:

"(3)   If a dangerous weapon (including a firearm) was possessed in connection with the offense, increase by 2 levels. If the resulting offense level is less than level 13, increase to level 13.".

The Commentary to § 2B5.1 captioned "Application Notes" is amended in Note 2 by deleting "2B5.2" and inserting in lieu thereof "2F1.1".

The Commentary to § 2B5.1 captioned "Background" is amended by inserting the following additional paragraph as the second paragraph:

> "   Subsection (b)(3) implements, in a broader form, the instruction to the Commission in section 110512 of Public Law 103-322.".

Section 2F1.1(b)(4) is amended by inserting "(A)" immediately following "involved"; and by inserting "or (B) possession of a dangerous weapon (including a firearm) in connection with the offense," immediately following "injury,".

The Commentary to § 2F1.1 captioned "Statutory Provisions" is amended by deleting "78d," immediately following "77x,".

The Commentary to § 2F1.1 captioned "Application Notes" is amended in Note 12 by inserting "Hate Crime Motivation or" immediately before "Vulnerable Victim".

The Commentary to § 2F1.1 captioned "Background" is amended by inserting the following additional paragraph as the sixth paragraph:

> "   Subsection (b)(4)(B) implements, in a broader form, the instruction to the Commission in section 110512 of Public Law 103-322.".

Reason for Amendment: Section 110512 of the Violent Crime Control and Law Enforcement Act of 1994 directs the Commission to amend its sentencing guidelines to provide an appropriate enhancement for a defendant convicted of a felony under Chapter 25 (Counterfeiting and Forgery) of title 18, United States Code, if the defendant used or carried a firearm during and in relation to the offense. This amendment implements this directive in a somewhat broader form.

In addition, this amendment corrects an outdated reference in the Commentary to § 2B5.1 (Offenses Involving Counterfeit Bearer Obligations of the United States) and conforms the Commentary to § 2F1.1 (Fraud and Deceit; Forgery; Offenses Involving Altered or Counterfeit Instruments Other than Counterfeit Bearer Obligations of the United States) with respect to the amended title of § 3A1.1 (Hate Crime Motivation or Vulnerable Victim).

Effective Date: The effective date of this amendment is November 1, 1995.

514. **Amendment:** Section 2D1.1(b) is amended by inserting the following additional subdivision:

> "(3)   If the object of the offense was the distribution of a controlled substance in a prison, correctional facility, or detention facility, increase by 2 levels.".

Section 2D2.1(b) is amended by deleting "Reference" and inserting in lieu thereof "References"; and by inserting the following new subdivision:

> "(2)   If the offense involved possession of a controlled substance in a prison, correctional facility, or detention facility, apply § 2P1.2 (Providing or Possessing Contraband in Prison).".

Reason for Amendment: Section 90103 of the Violent Crime Control and Law Enforcement Act of 1994 directs the Commission to amend the guidelines to provide an adequate enhancement for an offense under 21 U.S.C. § 841 that involves distributing a controlled substance in a federal prison or detention facility. This amendment addresses this directive by adding a two-level enhancement to § 2D1.1 (Unlawful Manufacturing, Importing, Exporting, or Trafficking; Attempt or Conspiracy) for an offense involving a prison or detention facility, similar to the enhancement provided for drug distribution in other protected locations at § 2D1.2 (Drug Offenses Occurring Near Protected Locations or Involving Underage or Pregnant Individuals; Attempt or Conspiracy).

Section 90103 also directs the Commission to amend the guidelines to provide an appropriate enhancement for an offense of simple possession of a controlled substance under 21 U.S.C. § 844 that occurs in a federal prison or detention facility. This amendment addresses this directive by providing a cross reference in § 2D2.1 (Unlawful Possession; Attempt or Conspiracy) that references § 2P1.2 (Providing or Possessing Contraband in Prison) in such cases.

Effective Date: The effective date of this amendment is November 1, 1995.

515. **Amendment:** Section 2D1.1(b) is amended by inserting the following additional subdivision:

> "(4) If the defendant meets the criteria set forth in subdivisions (1)-(5) of § 5C1.2 (Limitation on Applicability of Statutory Minimum Sentences in Certain Cases) and the offense level determined above is level 26 or greater, decrease by 2 levels.".

Section 5C1.2, effective September 23, 1994, is repromulgated with the editorial changes set forth below.

The Commentary to § 5C1.2 captioned "Application Notes" is amended in Note 6 by deleting "leader, organizer" and inserting in lieu thereof "organizer, leader".

The Commentary to § 5C1.2 captioned "Application Notes" is amended in Note 8 by deleting "Rule 32(a)(1), Fed. R. Crim. P." and inserting in lieu thereof "Fed. R. Crim. P. 32(c)(1), (3).".

The Commentary to § 5C1.2 captioned "Background" is amended by deleting "103-" immediately before "460".

Reason for Amendment: Section 80001(b) of the Violent Crime Control and Law Enforcement Act of 1994 directs the Commission to promulgate guidelines and policy statements to implement section 80001(a) (providing an exception to otherwise applicable statutory minimum sentences for certain defendants convicted of specified drug offenses). Pursuant to this provision, the Commission promulgated § 5C1.2 (Limitation on Applicability of Statutory Minimum Sentences in Certain Cases) as an emergency amendment, effective September 23, 1994. Under the terms of the congressionally-granted authority, this amendment is temporary unless repromulgated in the next amendment cycle under regularly applicable amendment procedures. See Pub. L. No. 100-182, § 21, set forth as an editorial note under 28 U.S.C. § 994. This amendment repromulgates § 5C1.2, as set forth in the 1994 edition of the Guidelines Manual, with minor editorial changes.

In addition, this amendment adds a new subsection to § 2D1.1 to implement this provision by providing a two-level decrease in offense level for cases meeting the criteria set forth in § 5C1.2(1)-(5).

Effective Date: The effective date of this amendment is November 1, 1995.

516. **Amendment:** Section 2D1.1(c) is amended in the fifth note immediately following the

Drug Quantity Table by deleting the first sentence as follows:

> "In the case of an offense involving marihuana plants, if the offense involved (A) 50 or more marihuana plants, treat each plant as equivalent to 1 KG of marihuana; (B) fewer than 50 marihuana plants, treat each plant as equivalent to 100 G of marihuana.",

and by inserting in lieu thereof:

> "In the case of an offense involving marihuana plants, treat each plant, regardless of sex, as equivalent to 100 G of marihuana.".

The Commentary to § 2D1.1 captioned "Background" is amended in the fourth paragraph by deleting the first three sentences as follows:

> "In cases involving fifty or more marihuana plants, an equivalency of one plant to one kilogram of marihuana is derived from the statutory penalty provisions of 21 U.S.C. § 841(b)(1)(A), (B), and (D). In cases involving fewer than fifty plants, the statute is silent as to the equivalency. For cases involving fewer than fifty plants, the Commission has adopted an equivalency of 100 grams per plant, or the actual weight of the usable marihuana, whichever is greater.",

and by inserting in lieu thereof:

> " For marihuana plants, the Commission has adopted an equivalency of 100 grams per plant, or the actual weight of the usable marihuana, whichever is greater.".

Reason for Amendment: For offenses involving 50 or more marihuana plants, the existing § 2D1.1 (Unlawful Manufacturing, Importing, Exporting, or Trafficking; Attempt or Conspiracy) uses an equivalency of one plant = one kilogram of marihuana, reflecting the quantities associated with the five- and ten-year mandatory minimum penalties in 21 U.S.C. § 841. For offenses involving fewer than 50 marihuana plants, the guidelines use an equivalency of one plant = 100 grams of marihuana, unless the weight of the actual marihuana is greater. In actuality, a marihuana plant does not produce a yield of one kilogram of marihuana. The one plant = 100 grams of marihuana equivalency used by the Commission for offenses involving fewer than 50 marihuana plants was selected as a reasonable approximation of the actual average yield of marihuana plants taking into account (1) studies reporting the actual yield of marihuana plants (37.5 to 412 grams depending on growing conditions); (2) that all plants regardless of size are counted for guideline purposes while, in actuality, not all plants will produce useable marihuana (*e.g.*, some plants may die of disease before maturity, and when plants are grown outdoors some plants may be consumed by animals); and (3) that male plants, which are counted for guideline purposes, are frequently culled because they do not produce the same quality of marihuana as do female plants. To enhance fairness and consistency, this amendment adopts the equivalency of 100 grams per marihuana plant for all guideline determinations.

Effective Date: The effective date of this amendment is November 1, 1995.

517. **Amendment:** Section 2D1.1(c)(10) is amended by deleting:

> "20 KG or more of Secobarbital (or the equivalent amount of other Schedule I or II Depressants) or Schedule III substances (except Anabolic Steroids);
> 40,000 or more units of Anabolic Steroids.",

and by inserting in lieu thereof:

Amendment 517   APPENDIX C - VOLUME I   November 1, 2013

"40,000 or more units of Schedule I or II Depressants or Schedule III substances.".

Section 2D1.1(c)(11) is amended by deleting:

"At least 10 KG but less than 20 KG of Secobarbital (or the equivalent amount of other Schedule I or II Depressants) or Schedule III substances (except Anabolic Steroids);
At least 20,000 but less than 40,000 units of Anabolic Steroids.",

and by inserting in lieu thereof:

"At least 20,000 but less than 40,000 units of Schedule I or II Depressants or Schedule III substances.".

Section 2D1.1(c)(12) is amended by deleting:

"At least 5 KG but less than 10 KG of Secobarbital (or the equivalent amount of other Schedule I or II Depressants) or Schedule III substances (except Anabolic Steroids);
At least 10,000 but less than 20,000 units of Anabolic Steroids."

and by inserting in lieu thereof:

"At least 10,000 but less than 20,000 units of Schedule I or II Depressants or Schedule III substances.".

Section 2D1.1(c)(13) is amended by deleting:

"At least 2.5 KG but less than 5 KG of Secobarbital (or the equivalent amount of other Schedule I or II Depressants) or Schedule III substances (except Anabolic Steroids);
At least 5,000 but less than 10,000 units of Anabolic Steroids.",

and by inserting in lieu thereof:

"At least 5,000 but less than 10,000 units of Schedule I or II Depressants or Schedule III substances.".

Section 2D1.1(c)(14) is amended by deleting:

"At least 1.25 KG but less than 2.5 KG of Secobarbital (or the equivalent amount of other Schedule I or II Depressants) or Schedule III substances (except Anabolic Steroids);
At least 2,500 but less than 5,000 units of Anabolic Steroids;
20 KG or more of Schedule IV substances.",

and inserting in lieu thereof:

"At least 2,500 but less than 5,000 units of Schedule I or II Depressants or Schedule III substances;
40,000 or more units of Schedule IV substances.".

Section 2D1.1(c)(15) is amended by deleting:

"At least 500 G but less than 1.25 KG of Secobarbital (or the equivalent amount of other Schedule I or II Depressants) or Schedule III substances (except Anabolic Steroids);
At least 1,000 but less than 2,500 units of Anabolic Steroids;
At least 8 KG but less than 20 KG of Schedule IV substances.",

and inserting in lieu thereof:

"At least 1,000 but less than 2,500 units of Schedule I or II Depressants or Schedule III substances
At least 16,000 but less than 40,000 units of Schedule IV substances.".

Section 2D1.1(c)(16) is amended by deleting:

"At least 125 G but less than 500 G of Secobarbital (or the equivalent amount of other Schedule I or II Depressants) or Schedule III substances (except Anabolic Steroids);
At least 250 but less than 1,000 units of Anabolic Steroids;
At least 2 KG but less than 8 KG of Schedule IV substances;
20 KG or more of Schedule V substances.",

and inserting in lieu thereof:

"At least 250 but less than 1,000 units of Schedule I or II Depressants or Schedule III substances;
At least 4,000 but less than 16,000 units of Schedule IV substances;
40,000 or more units of Schedule V substances.".

Section 2D1.1(c)(17) is amended by deleting:

"Less than 125 G of Secobarbital (or the equivalent amount of other Schedule I or II Depressants) or Schedule III substances (except Anabolic Steroids);
Less than 250 units of Anabolic Steroids;
Less than 2 KG of Schedule IV substances;
Less than 20 KG of Schedule V substances.",

and inserting in lieu thereof:

"Less than 250 units of Schedule I or II Depressants or Schedule III substances;
Less than 4,000 units of Schedule IV substances;
Less than 40,000 units of Schedule V substances.".

Section 2D1.1(c) is amended in the notes following the Drug Quantity Table by inserting the following additional note as the sixth note:

"In the case of Schedule I or II Depressants, Schedule III substances (except anabolic steroids), Schedule IV substances, and Schedule V substances, one 'unit' means one pill, capsule, or tablet. If the substance is in liquid form, one 'unit' means 0.5 gms.".

The Commentary to § 2D1.1 captioned "Application Notes" is amended in Note 10,

Amendment 517   APPENDIX C - VOLUME I   November 1, 2013

Example d, by deleting "28 kilograms" and inserting in lieu thereof "56,000 units"; by deleting "50 kilograms" and inserting in lieu thereof "100,000 units"; and by deleting "100 kilograms" and inserting in lieu thereof "200,000 units".

The Commentary to § 2D1.1 captioned "Application Notes" is amended in Note 10 in the Drug Equivalency Tables in the subsection captioned "Secobarbital and Other Schedule I or II Depressants" by deleting " Secobarbital and Other"; and by deleting:

"1 gm of Amobarbital = 2 gm of marihuana
1 gm of Glutethimide = 0.4 gm of marihuana
1 gm of Methaqualone = 0.7 gm of marihuana
1 gm of Pentobarbital = 2 gm of marihuana
1 gm of Secobarbital = 2 gm of marihuana",

and inserting in lieu thereof:

"1 unit of a Schedule I or II Depressant = 1 gm of marihuana".

The Commentary to § 2D1.1 captioned "Application Notes" is amended in Note 10 in the Drug Equivalency Tables in the subsection captioned "Schedule III Substances" by deleting:

"1 gm of a Schedule III Substance
(except anabolic steroids) = 2 gm of marihuana
1 unit of anabolic steroids = 1 gm of marihuana",

and inserting in lieu thereof:

"1 unit of a Schedule III Substance = 1 gm of marihuana".

The Commentary to § 2D1.1 captioned "Application Notes" is amended in Note 10 in the Drug Equivalency Tables in the subsection captioned "Schedule IV Substances" by deleting:

"1 gm of a Schedule IV Substance = 0.125 gm of marihuana",

and inserting in lieu thereof:

"1 unit of a Schedule IV Substance = 0.0625 gm of marihuana".

The Commentary to § 2D1.1 captioned "Application Notes" is amended in Note 10 in the Drug Equivalency Tables in the subsection captioned "Schedule V Substances" by deleting:

"1 gm of a Schedule V Substance = 0.0125 gm of marihuana",

and inserting in lieu thereof:

"1 unit of a Schedule V Substance = 0.00625 gm of marihuana".

The Commentary to § 2D1.1 captioned "Application Notes" is amended in Note 11 in the "Typical Weight Per Unit Table" by deleting the caption "Depressants"; and by deleting "Methaqualone* 300 mg".

Reason for Amendment: This amendment modifies § 2D1.1 (Unlawful Manufacturing,

Importing, Exporting, or Trafficking; Attempt or Conspiracy) with respect to the determination of the offense levels for Schedule I and II Depressants and Schedule III, IV, and V controlled substances by applying the Drug Quantity Table according to the number of pills, capsules, or tablets rather than by the gross weight of the pills, capsules, or tablets. Schedule I and II Depressants and Schedule III, IV, and V substances are almost always in pill, capsule, or tablet form. The current guidelines use the total weight of the pill, capsule, or tablet containing the controlled substance. This method leads to anomalies because the weight of most pills is determined primarily by the filler rather than the controlled substance. Thus, heavy pills lead to higher offense levels even though there is little or no relationship between gross weight and the potency of the pill. Applying the Drug Quantity Table according to the number of pills will both simplify guideline application and more fairly assess the scale and seriousness of the offense.

Effective Date: The effective date of this amendment is November 1, 1995.

518. Amendment: Section 2D1.1(c) is amended in the notes following the Drug Quantity Table by inserting the following additional notes at the end:

> "Hashish, for the purposes of this guideline, means a resinous substance of cannabis that includes (i) one or more of the tetrahydrocannabinols (as listed in 21 C.F.R. § 1308.11(d)(25)), (ii) at least two of the following: cannabinol, cannabidiol, or cannabichromene, and (iii) fragments of plant material (such as cystolith fibers).
>
> Hashish oil, for the purposes of this guideline, means a preparation of the soluble cannabinoids derived from cannabis that includes (i) one or more of the tetrahydrocannabinols (as listed in 21 C.F.R. § 1308.11(d)(25)), (ii) at least two of the following: cannabinol, cannabidiol, or cannabichromene, and (iii) is essentially free of plant material (e.g., plant fragments). Typically, hashish oil is a viscous, dark colored oil, but it can vary from a dry resin to a colorless liquid.".

Section 2D1.1(c) is amended by inserting "Notes to Drug Quantity Table:" immediately following the asterisk at the beginning of the notes to the Drug Quantity Table; and by inserting a letter designation immediately before each note in alphabetical order beginning with "(A)".

The Commentary to § 2D1.1 captioned "Application Notes" is amended in Note 1 by inserting the following additional paragraph at the end:

> "Similarly, in the case of marihuana having a moisture content that renders the marihuana unsuitable for consumption without drying (this might occur, for example, with a bale of rain-soaked marihuana or freshly harvested marihuana that had not been dried), an approximation of the weight of the marihuana without such excess moisture content is to be used.".

The Commentary to § 2D1.1 captioned "Application Notes" is amended in Note 8 by inserting the following additional paragraph at the end:

> "Note, however, that if an adjustment from subsection (b)(2)(B) applies, do not apply § 3B1.3 (Abuse of Position of Trust or Use of Special Skill).".

The Commentary to § 2D1.1 captioned "Application Notes" is amended in Note 10 in the Drug Equivalency Table in the subdivision captioned "Schedule I or II Opiates" by inserting at the end:

> "1 gm of Levo-alpha-acetylmethadol (LAAM)= 3 kg of marihuana".

Amendment 518 APPENDIX C - VOLUME I November 1, 2013

The Commentary to § 2D1.1 captioned "Application Notes" is amended in Note 10 in the Drug Equivalency Tables in the subdivision captioned "Cocaine and Other Schedule I and II Stimulants" by deleting:

"1 gm of L-Methamphetamine/Levo-methamphetamine/L-Desoxyephedrine = 40 gm of marihuana",

and inserting in lieu thereof:

"1 gm of Khat = .01 gm of marihuana".

The Commentary to § 2D1.1 captioned "Application Notes" is amended in Note 12 by deleting:

"In an offense involving negotiation to traffic in a controlled substance, the weight under negotiation in an uncompleted distribution shall be used to calculate the applicable amount. However, where the court finds that the defendant did not intend to produce and was not reasonably capable of producing the negotiated amount, the court shall exclude from the guideline calculation the amount that it finds the defendant did not intend to produce and was not reasonably capable of producing.",

and inserting in lieu thereof:

"In an offense involving an agreement to sell a controlled substance, the agreed-upon quantity of the controlled substance shall be used to determine the offense level unless the sale is completed and the amount delivered more accurately reflects the scale of the offense. For example, a defendant agrees to sell 500 grams of cocaine, the transaction is completed by the delivery of the controlled substance - actually 480 grams of cocaine, and no further delivery is scheduled. In this example, the amount delivered more accurately reflects the scale of the offense. In contrast, in a reverse sting, the agreed-upon quantity of the controlled substance would more accurately reflect the scale of the offense because the amount actually delivered is controlled by the government, not by the defendant. If, however, the defendant establishes that he or she did not intend to provide, or was not reasonably capable of providing, the agreed-upon quantity of the controlled substance, the court shall exclude from the offense level determination the amount of controlled substance that the defendant establishes that he or she did not intend to provide or was not reasonably capable of providing.".

The Commentary to § 2D1.1 captioned "Application Notes" is amended by deleting Note 13 as follows:

"13. If subsection (b)(2)(B) applies, do not apply § 3B1.3 (Abuse of Position of Trust or Use of Special Skill).".

The Commentary to § 2D1.1 captioned "Application Notes" is amended by deleting Note 14 as follows:

"14. D-lysergic acid, which is generally used to make LSD, is classified as a Schedule III controlled substance (to which § 2D1.1 applies) and as a listed precursor (to which § 2D1.11 applies). Where the defendant is convicted under 21 U.S.C. §§ 841(b)(1)(D) or 960(b)(4) of an offense involving d-lysergic acid, apply § 2D1.1 or § 2D1.11, whichever results in the greater offense level. See Application Note 5 in the Commentary to § 1B1.1 (Application Instructions). Where the defendant is accountable for an offense involving the manufacture of LSD, see Application Note 12 above pertaining to the determination of the scale of the offense.",

and by renumbering the remaining notes accordingly.

The Commentary to § 2D1.1 captioned "Application Notes" is amended by inserting the following additional note:

"18. For purposes of the guidelines, a 'plant' is an organism having leaves and a readily observable root formation (e.g., a marihuana cutting having roots, a rootball, or root hairs is a marihuana plant).".

Reason for Amendment: This is an eight-part amendment. First, this amendment adds definitions of hashish and hashish oil to § 2D1.1 (Unlawful Manufacturing, Importing, Exporting, or Trafficking; Attempt or Conspiracy) in the notes following the Drug Quantity Table. These terms are not defined by statute or in the existing guidelines, leading to litigation as to which substances are to be classified as hashish or hashish oil, as opposed to marihuana. See United States v. Gravelle, 819 F. Supp. 1076 (S.D. Fla. 1993); United States v. Schultz, 810 F. Supp. 230 (S.D. Ohio 1992).

Second, this amendment clarifies the treatment of marihuana that has a moisture content sufficient to render it unusable without drying (e.g., a bale of marihuana left in the rain or recently harvested marihuana that has not had time to dry). In such cases, using the weight of the wet marihuana can increase the offense level for a factor that bears no relationship to the scale of the offense or the marketable form of the marihuana. Prior to the effective date of the 1993 amendments, two circuits had approved weighing wet marihuana despite the fact that the marihuana was not in a usable form. United States v. Pinedo-Montoya, 966 F.2d 591 (10th Cir. 1992); United States v. Garcia, 925 F.2d 170 (7th Cir. 1991). Although Application Note 1 in the Commentary to § 2D1.1, effective November 1, 1993 (pertaining to unusable parts of a mixture or substance) should produce the appropriate result because marihuana must be dried before being used, this type of case is sufficiently distinct to warrant a specific reference in this application note to ensure correct application of the guideline.

Third, this amendment simplifies the Commentary to § 2D1.1 by consolidating application notes 8 and 13.

Fourth, this amendment deletes an outdated application note in the Commentary to § 2D1.1 pertaining to the classification of d-lysergic acid as a listed precursor chemical.

Fifth, this amendment addresses the issue of what constitutes a marihuana plant. Several circuits have confronted the issue of when a cutting from a marihuana plant becomes a "plant." The appellate courts generally have held that the term "plant" should be defined by "its plain and ordinary dictionary meaning. . .. [A] marihuana 'plant' includes those cuttings accompanied by root balls." United States v. Edge, 989 F.2d 871, 878 (6th Cir. 1993) (quoting United States v. Eves, 932 F.2d 856, 860 (10th Cir. 1991), appeal after remand, 30 F.3d 134 (6th Cir. 1994)). See also United States v. Malbrough, 922 F.2d 458, 465 (8th Cir. 1990) (acquiescing in the district court's apparent determination that certain marihuana cuttings that did not have their own "root system" should not be counted as plants), cert. denied, 501 S. Ct. 1258 (1991); United States v. Carlisle, 907 F.2d 94, 96 (9th Cir. 1990) (finding that cuttings were plants where each cutting had previous degrees of root formation not clearly erroneous); United States v. Angell, 794 F. Supp. 874, 875 (D. Minn. 1990) (refusing to count as plants marihuana cuttings that have no visible root structure), aff'd in part and rev'd in part, 11 F.3d 806 (8th Cir.), cert. denied, 114 S. Ct.

Amendment 518 APPENDIX C - VOLUME I November 1, 2013

3747 (1994); United States v. Fitol, 733 F. Supp. 1312, 1316 (D. Minn. 1990) ("individual cuttings, planted with the intent of growing full size plants, and which had grown roots, are 'plants' both within common parlance and within Section 841(b)"); United States v. Speltz, 733 F. Supp. 1311, 1312 (D. Minn. 1990) (small marihuana plants, e.g., cuttings with roots, are nonetheless still marihuana plants), aff'd, 938 F.2d 188 (8th Cir. 1991). Because this issue arises frequently, this amendment adds an application note to the Commentary of § 2D1.1 setting forth the definition of a plant for guidelines purposes.

Sixth, this amendment provides equivalencies for two additional controlled substances: (1) khat, and (2) levo-alpha-acetylmethadol (LAAM) in the Drug Equivalency Tables in the Commentary to § 2D1.1.

Seventh, this amendment deletes the distinction between d- and l-methamphetamine in the Drug Equivalency Tables in the Commentary to § 2D1.1. L-methamphetamine, which is a rather weak form of methamphetamine, is rarely seen and is not made intentionally, but rather results from a botched attempt to produce d-methamphetamine. Under this amendment, l-methamphetamine would be treated the same as d-methamphetamine (i.e., as if an attempt to manufacture or distribute d-methamphetamine). Currently, unless the methamphetamine is specifically tested to determine its form, litigation can result over whether the methamphetamine is l- methamphetamine or d-methamphetamine. In addition, there is another form of methamphetamine (dl-methamphetamine) that is not listed in the Drug Equivalency Table. The listing of l-methamphetamine as a separate form of methamphetamine has led to litigation as to how dl-methamphetamine should be treated. In United States v. Carroll, 6 F.3d 735 (11th Cir. 1993), cert. denied, 114 S. Ct. 1234 (1994), a case in which the Eleventh Circuit held that dl-methamphetamine should be treated as d-methamphetamine, the majority and dissenting opinions both point out the complexity engendered by the current distinction between d- and l- methamphetamine. Under this amendment, all forms of methamphetamine are treated alike, thereby simplifying guideline application.

Eighth, this amendment revises the Commentary to § 2D1.1 to provide that in a case involving negotiation for a quantity of a controlled substance, the negotiated quantity is used to determine the offense level unless the completed transaction establishes a different quantity, or the defendant establishes that he or she was not reasonably capable of producing the negotiated amount or otherwise did not intend to produce that amount. Disputes over the interpretation of this application note have produced much litigation. See, e.g., United States v. Tillman, 8 F.3d 17 (11th Cir. 1993); United States v. Smiley, 997 F.2d 475 (8th Cir. 1993); United States v. Barnes, 993 F.2d 680 (9th Cir. 1993), cert. denied, 115 S. Ct. 96 (1994); United States v. Rodriguez, 975 F.2d 999 (3d Cir. 1992); United States v. Christian, 942 F.2d 363 (6th Cir. 1991), cert. denied, 502 U.S. 1045 (1992); United States v. Richardson, 939 F.2d 135 (4th Cir.), 502 U.S. 987 (1991); United States v. Ruiz, 932 F.2d 1174 (7th Cir.), cert. denied, 502 U.S. 849 (1991); United States v. Bradley, 917 F.2d 601 (1st Cir. 1990).

Effective Date: The effective date of this amendment is November 1, 1995.

519. **Amendment:** Section 2D1.11(d) is amended in the Chemical Quantity Table by deleting "Listed Precursor" wherever it occurs and inserting in lieu thereof "List I"; and by deleting "Listed Essential" wherever it appears and inserting in lieu thereof "List II".

Section 2D1.11(d) is amended in subdivisions (1)-(9) by deleting the line referencing "D-Lysergic Acid" from each subdivision as set forth below:

(1) "200 G or more of D-Lysergic Acid;",

November 1, 2013　　APPENDIX C - VOLUME I　　**Amendment 519**

 (2) "At least 60 G but less than 200 G of D-Lysergic Acid;",

 (3) "At least 20 G but less than 60 G of D-Lysergic Acid;",

 (4) "At least 14 G but less than 20 G of D-Lysergic Acid;",

 (5) "At least 8 G but less than 14 G of D-Lysergic Acid;",

 (6) "At least 2 G but less than 8 G of D-Lysergic Acid;",

 (7) "At least 1.6 G but less than 2 G of D-Lysergic Acid;",

 (8) "At least 1.2 G but less than 1.6 G of D-Lysergic Acid;",

 (9) "Less than 1.2 G of D-Lysergic Acid;".

Section 2D1.11(d) is amended in subdivisions (1)-(9) by inserting the following list I chemicals (formerly Listed Precursor Chemicals) in the appropriate place in alphabetical order by subdivision as follows:

 (1) "17.8 KG or more of Benzaldehyde;",
    "12.6 KG or more of Nitroethane;",

 (2) "At least 5.3 KG but less than 17.8 KG of Benzaldehyde;",
    "At least 3.8 KG but less than 12.6 KG of Nitroethane;",

 (3) "At least 1.8 KG but less than 5.3 KG of Benzaldehyde;",
    "At least 1.3 KG but less than 3.8 KG of Nitroethane;",

 (4) "At least 1.2 KG but less than 1.8 KG of Benzaldehyde;",
    "At least 879 G but less than 1.3 KG of Nitroethane;",

 (5) "At least 712 G but less than 1.2 KG of Benzaldehyde;",
    "At least 503 G but less than 879 G of Nitroethane;",

 (6) "At least 178 G but less than 712 G of Benzaldehyde;",
    "At least 126 G but less than 503 G of Nitroethane;",

 (7) "At least 142 G but less than 178 G of Benzaldehyde;",
    "At least 100 G but less than 126 G of Nitroethane;",

 (8) "At least 107 G but less than 142 G of Benzaldehyde;",
    "At least 75 G but less than 100 G of Nitroethane;",

 (9) "Less than 107 G of Benzaldehyde;",
    "Less than 75 G of Nitroethane;".

Section 2D1.11 is amended in the List 1 Chemical Equivalency Table by inserting the following chemicals, in the appropriate place in alphabetical order:

 "1 gm of Benzaldehyde** = 1.124 gm of Ephedrine",
 "1 gm of Nitroethane** = 1.592 gm of Ephedrine";

and by deleting "1 gm of D-lysergic acid = 1 gm of Ephedrine".

Section 2D1.11(d) is amended in the notes following the Chemical Quantity Table by deleting Note (A) as follows:

Amendment 519 APPENDIX C - VOLUME I   November 1, 2013

> "(A) If more than one listed precursor chemical is involved, use the Precursor Chemical Equivalency Table to determine the offense level.",

and inserting in lieu thereof:

> "(A) The List I Chemical Equivalency Table provides a method for combining different precursor chemicals to obtain a single offense level. In a case involving two or more list I chemicals used to manufacture different controlled substances or to manufacture one controlled substance by different manufacturing processes, convert each to its ephedrine equivalency from the table below, add the quantities, and use the Chemical Quantity Table to determine the base offense level. In a case involving two or more list I chemicals used together to manufacture a controlled substance in the same manufacturing process, use the quantity of the single list I chemical that results in the greatest base offense level.";

in Notes (B) and (C) by deleting "listed essential" wherever it appears and inserting in lieu thereof in each instance "list II"; in Note (C) by deleting "listed precursor" and inserting in lieu thereof "list I"; by deleting Note (D) as follows:

> "(D) The Precursor Chemical Equivalency Table provides a means for combining different listed precursor chemicals to obtain a single offense level. In cases involving multiple precursor chemicals, convert each to its ephedrine equivalency from the table below, add the quantities, and apply the Chemical Quantity Table to obtain the applicable offense level.",

and inserting in lieu thereof:

> "(D) In a case involving ephedrine tablets, use the weight of the ephedrine contained in the tablets, not the weight of the entire tablets, in calculating the base offense level.";

and by deleting "PRECURSOR" and inserting in lieu thereof "(E) LIST I".

Section 2D1.11(d) is amended in the List I Chemical Equivalency Table (formerly the Precursor Chemical Equivalency Table) by inserting "**" immediately after each of the following substances: "Ethylamine", "N-Methylephedrine", "N-Methylpseudoephedrine", "Norpseudoephedrine", "Phenylpropanolamine", "Pseudoephedrine", and "3,4-Methylenedioxyphenyl-2-propanone".

Section 2D1.11(d) is amended in the note following the List I Chemical Equivalency Table (formerly the Precursor Chemical Equivalency Table) designated by two asterisks by deleting "both hydriodic acid and ephedrine" and inserting in lieu thereof:

> "(A) hydriodic acid and one of the following: ephedrine, N-methylephedrine, N-methylpseudoephedrine, norpseudoephedrine, phenylpropanolamine, or pseudoephedrine; or (B) ethylamine and 3,4-methylenedioxyphenyl-2-propanone; or (C) benzaldehyde and nitroethane".

The Commentary to § 2D1.11 captioned "Application Notes" is amended in Note 3 by deleting "3, 4 methylenedioxphenyl-2-propanone" wherever it appears and inserting in lieu thereof in each instance "methylamine"; and by deleting "LSD, PCP, and other Schedule I and II Hallucinogens" and inserting in lieu thereof "Cocaine and Other Schedule I and II Stimulants".

The Commentary to § 2D1.11 captioned "Application Notes" is amended by deleting:

"4. Where there are multiple listed precursor chemicals, the quantities of all listed precursors are added together for purposes of determining the base offense level, except as expressly noted (see Note A to the Chemical Quantity Table). This reflects that only one listed precursor typically is used in a given manufacturing process. For example, in the case of an offense involving 300 grams of piperidine and 800 grams of benzyl cyanide, the piperidine is converted to 600 grams of ephedrine and the benzyl cyanide is converted to 800 grams of ephedrine, using the Precursor Chemical Equivalency Table, for a total of 1400 grams of ephedrine. Applying the Chemical Quantity Table to 1400 grams (1.4 kilograms) of ephedrine results in a base offense level of 22.",

and inserting in lieu thereof:

"4. When two or more list I chemicals are used together in the same manufacturing process, calculate the offense level for each separately and use the quantity that results in the greatest base offense level. In any other case, the quantities should be added together (using the List I Chemical Equivalency Table) for the purpose of calculating the base offense level.

Examples:

(a) The defendant was in possession of five kilograms of ephedrine and three kilograms of hydriodic acid. Ephedrine and hydriodic acid typically are used together in the same manufacturing process to manufacture methamphetamine. Therefore, the base offense level for each listed chemical is calculated separately and the list I chemical with the higher base offense level is used. Five kilograms of ephedrine result in a base offense level of 24; 300 grams of hydriodic acid result in a base offense level of 14. In this case, the base offense level would be 24.

(b) The defendant was in possession of five kilograms of ephedrine and two kilograms of phenylacetic acid. Although both of these chemicals are used to manufacture methamphetamine, they are not used together in the same manufacturing process. Therefore, the quantity of phenylacetic acid should be converted to an ephedrine equivalency using the List I Chemical Equivalency Table and then added to the quantity of ephedrine. In this case, the two kilograms of phenylacetic acid convert to two kilograms of ephedrine (see List I Chemical Equivalency Table), resulting in a total equivalency of seven kilograms of ephedrine.".

The Commentary to § 2D1.11 is amended by deleting "listed precursor" wherever it appears and inserting in lieu thereof "list I"; and by deleting "listed essential" and inserting in lieu thereof in each instance "list II".

The Commentary to § 2D1.11 captioned "Background" is amended in the second sentence by deleting "Listed precursor chemicals are critical to the formation of a controlled substance and" and inserting in lieu thereof "List I chemicals are important to the manufacture of a controlled substance and usually".

The Commentary to § 2D1.11 captioned "Background" is amended by deleting the last

Amendment 519 APPENDIX C - VOLUME I November 1, 2013

sentence as follows:

> "Listed essential chemicals are generally solvents, catalysts, and reagents, and do not become part of the finished product.",

and inserting in lieu thereof:

> "List II chemicals are generally used as solvents, catalysts, and reagents.".

Reason for Amendment: The Domestic Chemical Diversion Act of 1993, Pub. L. 103-200, 107 Stat. 2333, changed the designations of the listed chemicals from "listed precursor chemicals" and "listed essential chemicals" to "list I chemicals" and "list II chemicals," respectively. This amendment conforms § 2D1.11 (Unlawfully Distributing, Importing, Exporting or Possessing a Listed Chemical; Attempt or Conspiracy) to these statutory changes.

The Act also adds pills containing ephedrine as a list I chemical. Ephedrine itself is a list I chemical under 21 U.S.C. § 802(34). Pills containing ephedrine previously were not covered by the statute and, thus, legally could be purchased "over the counter." Purchases of these pills were sometimes made in large quantities and the pills crushed and processed to extract the ephedrine (which can be used to make methamphetamine). Unlike ephedrine, which is purchased from a chemical company and is virtually 100 percent pure, these tablets contain a substantially lower percentage of ephedrine (about 25 percent). To avoid unwarranted disparity, this amendment adds a note to § 2D1.11 providing that the amount of actual ephedrine contained in a pill is to be used in determining the offense level.

In addition, the Act removes three chemicals from, and adds two others to, the listed chemicals controlled under the Controlled Substances Act. Two of the chemicals removed from the list are not currently listed in § 2D1.11 because the Commission was aware that they are not used in the manufacture of any controlled substance. The third chemical removed from the list, d-lysergic acid, was listed both as a listed chemical in § 2D1.11 and as a controlled substance in § 2D1.1 (Unlawful Manufacturing, Importing, Exporting, or Trafficking; Attempt or Conspiracy). This amendment conforms § 2D1.11 by deleting all references to d-lysergic acid. The two chemicals added as listed chemicals are benzaldehyde and nitroethane. Both of these chemicals are used to make methamphetamine. The base offense levels for listed chemicals in § 2D1.11 are determined by reference to the most common controlled substance the chemical is used to manufacture; consequently, this amendment adds these chemicals to the Chemical Quantity Table based on information provided by the Drug Enforcement Administration regarding their use in the production of methamphetamine.

A number of the chemicals in the Chemical Quantity Table in § 2D1.11 are used in the same process to make a controlled substance. A note at the end of the existing Precursor Chemical Equivalency Table addresses this situation for hydriodic acid and ephedrine. This amendment expands this note to cover other chemicals that similarly are used together.

In addition, this amendment corrects Application Note 3 of the Commentary to § 2D1.11 with respect to an example of a listed chemical that is used with P_2P to manufacture methamphetamine and a reference to a subdivision of the Drug Equivalency Tables in the Commentary to § 2D1.1.

Effective Date: The effective date of this amendment is November 1, 1995.

520. Amendment: Section 2D1.12(a) is amended by inserting "(Apply the greater)" immediately after "Base Offense Level"; and by deleting "12" and inserting in lieu thereof:

"(1) 12, if the defendant intended to manufacture a controlled substance or knew or believed the prohibited equipment was to be used to manufacture a controlled substance; or

(2) 9, if the defendant had reasonable cause to believe the prohibited equipment was to be used to manufacture a controlled substance.".

Reason for Amendment: The Domestic Chemical Diversion Act of 1993, Pub. L. 103-200, 107 Stat. 2333, broadens the prohibition in 21 U.S.C. § 843(a) to cover possessing, manufacturing, distributing, exporting, or importing three-neck, round-bottom flasks, tableting machines, encapsulating machines, or gelatin capsules having reasonable cause to believe they will be used to manufacture a controlled substance. Section 2D1.12 (Unlawful Possession, Manufacture, Distribution, or Importation of Prohibited Flask or Equipment; Attempt or Conspiracy) applies to this conduct. Consistent with the treatment of similar conduct under §§ 2D1.11(b)(2) and 2D1.13(b)(2), this amendment provides an alternative base offense level in § 2D1.12 to address the case in which the defendant had reasonable cause to believe, but not actual knowledge or belief, that the equipment was to be used to manufacture a controlled substance.

Effective Date: The effective date of this amendment is November 1, 1995.

521. **Amendment:** Chapter Two, Part H, Subpart 1 is amended by deleting:

"Introductory Commentary

This subpart covers violations of civil rights statutes that typically penalize conduct involving death or bodily injury more severely than discriminatory or intimidating conduct not involving such injury.

The addition of two levels to the offense level applicable to the underlying offense in this subpart reflects the fact that the harm involved both the underlying conduct and activity intended to deprive a person of his civil rights. An added penalty is imposed on an offender who was a public official at the time of the offense to reflect the likely damage to public confidence in the integrity and fairness of government, and the added likely force of the threat because of the official's involvement.".

Sections 2H1.1, 2H1.3, 2H1.4, and 2H1.5 are deleted in their entirety as follows:

"§ 2H1.1. Conspiracy to Interfere with Civil Rights; Going in Disguise to Deprive of Rights

    (a) Base Offense Level (Apply the greater):

        (1) 15; or

        (2) 2 plus the offense level applicable to any underlying offense.

    (b) Specific Offense Characteristic

        (1) If the defendant was a public official at the time of the offense, increase by 4 levels.

Commentary

Statutory Provision: 18 U.S.C. § 241.

Application Notes:

1. 'Underlying offense,' as used in this guideline, includes any offense under federal, state, or local law other than an offense that is itself covered under Chapter Two, Part H, Subpart 1, 2, or 4. For example, in the case of a conspiracy to interfere with a person's civil rights (a violation of 18 U.S.C. § 241) that involved an aggravated assault (the use of force) to deny certain rights or benefits in furtherance of discrimination (a violation of 18 U.S.C. § 245), the underlying offense in respect to both the violation of 18 U.S.C. § 241 (to which § 2H1.1 applies) and the violation of 18 U.S.C. § 245 (to which § 2H1.3 applies) would be the aggravated assault.

   '2 plus the offense level applicable to any underlying offense' means 2 levels above the offense level (base offense level plus any applicable specific offense characteristics and cross references) from the offense guideline in Chapter Two that most closely corresponds to the underlying offense. For example, if the underlying offense was second degree murder, which under § 2A1.2 has an offense level of 33, '2 plus the offense level applicable to any underlying offense' would be 33 + 2 = 35. If the underlying offense was assault, criminal sexual conduct, kidnapping, abduction or unlawful restraint, the offense level from the guideline for the most comparable offense in §§ 2A2.1-2A4.2 (Assault, Criminal Sexual Abuse, and Kidnapping, Abduction, or Unlawful Restraint) would first be determined, and 2 levels then would be added. If the underlying offense was damage to property by means of arson or an explosive device, the offense level from § 2K1.4 (Arson; Property Damage By Use of Explosives) would first be determined and 2 levels would be added. If the offense was property damage by other means, the offense level from § 2B1.3 (Property Damage or Destruction) would first be determined and 2 levels would be added. If the offense was a conspiracy or attempt to commit arson, '2 plus the offense level applicable to any underlying offense' would be the offense level from the guideline applicable to a conspiracy or attempt to commit arson plus 2 levels.

   In certain cases, the count of which the defendant is convicted may set forth conduct that constitutes more than one underlying offense (e.g., two instances of assault, or one instance of assault and one instance of arson). In such cases, determine the offense level for the underlying offense by treating each underlying offense as if contained in a separate count of conviction. To determine which of the alternative base offense levels (e.g., § 2H1.1(a)(1) or (a)(2)) results in the greater offense level, apply Chapter Three, Parts A, B, C, and D to each alternative base offense level. Use whichever results in the greater offense level. Example: The defendant is convicted of one count of conspiracy to violate civil rights that included two level 12 underlying offenses (of a type not grouped together under Chapter Three, Part D). No adjustment from Chapter Three, Parts A, B, or C applies. The base offense level from § 2H1.1(a)(1) is 15. The offense level for each underlying offense from § 2H1.1(a)(2) is 14 (2 + 12). Under Chapter Three, Part D (Multiple Counts), the two level 14 underlying offenses result in a combined offense level of 16. This offense level is greater than the alternative base offense level of 15 under § 2H1.1(a)(1). Therefore, the case is treated as if there were two counts, one for each underlying offense, with a base offense level under § 2H1.1(a)(2) of 14 for each underlying offense.

2. Where the adjustment in § 2H1.1(b)(1) is applied, do not apply § 3B1.3 (Abuse of Position of Trust or Use of Special Skill).

Background: This section applies to intimidating activity by various groups, including formally and informally organized groups as well as hate groups. The maximum term of imprisonment authorized by statute is ten years; except where death results, the maximum term of imprisonment authorized by statute is life imprisonment. The base offense level for this guideline assumes threatening or otherwise serious conduct.

§ 2H1.3. Use of Force or Threat of Force to Deny Benefits or Rights in Furtherance of Discrimination; Damage to Religious Real Property

    (a)   Base Offense Level (Apply the greatest):

        (1)   10, if no injury occurred; or

        (2)   15, if injury occurred; or

        (3)   2 plus the offense level applicable to any underlying offense.

    (b)   Specific Offense Characteristic

        (1)   If the defendant was a public official at the time of the offense, increase by 4 levels.

Commentary

Statutory Provisions: 18 U.S.C. §§ 245, 247; 42 U.S.C. § 3631. For additional statutory provision(s), see Appendix A (Statutory Index).

Application Notes:

1. '2 plus the offense level applicable to any underlying offense' is defined in the Commentary to § 2H1.1.

2. 'Injury' means 'bodily injury,' 'serious bodily injury,' or 'permanent or life-threatening bodily injury' as defined in the Commentary to § 1B1.1 (Application Instructions).

3. Where the adjustment in § 2H1.3(b)(1) is applied, do not apply § 3B1.3 (Abuse of Position of Trust or Use of Special Skill).

4. In the case of a violation of 42 U.S.C. § 3631, apply this guideline where the offense involved the threat or use of force. Otherwise, apply § 2H1.5.

Background: The statutes covered by this guideline provide federal protection for the exercise of civil rights in a variety of contexts (e.g., voting, employment, public accommodations, etc.). The base offense level in § 2H1.3(a) reflects that the threat or use of force is inherent in the offense. The maximum term of imprisonment authorized by statute is one year if no bodily injury results, ten years if bodily injury results, and life imprisonment if death results.

§ 2H1.4. Interference with Civil Rights Under Color of Law

    (a)   Base Offense Level (Apply the greater):

        (1)   10; or

        (2)   6 plus the offense level applicable to any underlying offense.

Amendment 521

APPENDIX C - VOLUME I

November 1, 2013

Commentary

Statutory Provision: 18 U.S.C. § 242.

Application Notes:

1. '6 plus the offense level applicable to any underlying offense' means 6 levels above the offense level for any underlying criminal conduct. See the discussion in the Commentary to § 2H1.1.

2. Do not apply the adjustment from § 3B1.3 (Abuse of Position of Trust or Use of Special Skill).

Background: This maximum term of imprisonment authorized by 18 U.S.C. § 242 is one year if no bodily injury results, ten years if bodily injury results, and life imprisonment if death results. A base offense level of 10 is prescribed at § 2H1.4(a)(1) providing a guideline sentence near the one-year statutory maximum for cases not resulting in death or bodily injury because of the compelling public interest in deterring and adequately punishing those who violate civil rights under color of law. The Commission intends to recommend that this one-year statutory maximum penalty be increased. An alternative base offense level is provided at § 2H1.4(a)(2). The 6-level increase under subsection (a)(2) reflects the 2-level increase that is applied to other offenses covered in this Part plus a 4-level increase for the commission of the offense under actual or purported legal authority. This 4-level increase is inherent in the base offense level of 10 under subsection (a)(1).

Enhancement under § 3B1.3 (Abuse of Position of Trust or Use of Special Skill) is inappropriate because the base offense level in § 2H1.4(a) reflects that the abuse of actual or purported legal authority is inherent in the offense.

§ 2H1.5. Other Deprivations of Rights or Benefits in Furtherance of Discrimination

    (a) Base Offense Level (Apply the greater):

        (1) 6; or

        (2) 2 plus the offense level applicable to any underlying offense.

    (b) Specific Offense Characteristic

        (1) If the defendant was a public official at the time of the offense, increase by 4 levels.

Commentary

Statutory Provision: 18 U.S.C. § 246.

Application Notes:

1. '2 plus the offense level applicable to any underlying offense' is defined in the Commentary to § 2H1.1.

2. Where the adjustment in § 2H1.5(b)(1) is applied, do not apply § 3B1.3 (Abuse of Position of Trust or Use of Special Skill).

Background: Violations of the statutes covered by this provision do not necessarily involve the use of force or threatening conduct or violations by public officials. Accordingly, the minimum base offense level (level 6) provided is lower than that of the other guidelines in this subpart.".

A replacement guideline with accompanying commentary is inserted as § 2H1.1 (Offenses Involving Individual Rights).

Section 3A1.1 (Vulnerable Victim) is deleted in its entirety as follows:

"§ 3A1.1. Vulnerable Victim

> If the defendant knew or should have known that a victim of the offense was unusually vulnerable due to age, physical or mental condition, or that a victim was otherwise particularly susceptible to the criminal conduct, increase by 2 levels.

> Commentary

Application Notes:

1. This adjustment applies to offenses where an unusually vulnerable victim is made a target of criminal activity by the defendant. The adjustment would apply, for example, in a fraud case where the defendant marketed an ineffective cancer cure or in a robbery where the defendant selected a handicapped victim. But it would not apply in a case where the defendant sold fraudulent securities by mail to the general public and one of the victims happened to be senile. Similarly, for example, a bank teller is not an unusually vulnerable victim solely by virtue of the teller's position in a bank.

2. Do not apply this adjustment if the offense guideline specifically incorporates this factor. For example, where the offense guideline provides an enhancement for the age of the victim, this guideline should not be applied unless the victim was unusually vulnerable for reasons unrelated to age.".

A replacement guideline with accompanying commentary is inserted as § 3A1.1 (Hate Crime Motivation or Vulnerable Victim).

The Commentary to § 2H4.1 captioned "Application Note" is amended in Note 1 by deleting "2 plus the offense" and inserting in lieu thereof "Offense".

Reason for Amendment: This is a five-part amendment. First, the amendment adds an additional subsection to § 3A1.1 (Vulnerable Victim) to implement the directive contained in Section 280003 of the Violent Crime Control and Law Enforcement Act of 1994 by providing a three-level increase in the offense level for offenses that are "hate crimes." Second, the amendment consolidates §§ 2H1.1 (Offenses Involving Individual Rights), 2H1.3 (Use of Force or Threat of Force to Deny Benefits or Rights in Furtherance of Discrimination; Damage to Religious Real Property), 2H1.4 (Interference with Civil Rights Under Color of Law), and 2H1.5 (Other Deprivations of Rights Benefits in Furtherance of Discrimination) into a revised § 2H1.1 (Offenses Involving Individual Rights). This revised guideline provides greater consistency in offense levels for similar conduct, reflects the additional enhancement now contained in § 3A1.1, and better reflects the seriousness of the underlying conduct. Third, the amendment references violations of 18 U.S.C. § 248 (the Freedom of Access to Clinic Entrances Act of 1994, Pub. L. 103-259, 108 Stat. 694) to the consolidated § 2H1.1. Fourth, the amendment clarifies the operation of § 3A1.1 with respect to a vulnerable victim. Fifth, the amendment addresses the directive to the Commission in section 240002 of the Violent Crime Control and Law Enforcement Act of 1994 (pertaining to elderly victims of crimes of violence).

Section 280003 of the Violent Crime Control and Law Enforcement Act of 1994 directs the Commission to provide a minimum enhancement of three levels for offenses that the finder of fact at trial determines are hate crimes. This directive also instructs the Commission to ensure that there is reasonable consistency with other guidelines and that duplicative punishments for the same offense are avoided. The congressional directive in section 280003 requires that the three-level hate crimes enhancement apply where "the finder of fact at trial determines beyond a reasonable doubt" that the offense of conviction was a hate crime. This amendment makes the enhancement applicable if either the finder of fact at trial or, in the case of a guilty or nolo contendere plea, the court at sentencing determines that the offense was a hate crime. By broadening the applicability of the congressionally mandated enhancement, this amendment will avoid unwarranted sentencing disparity based on the mode of conviction. The Commission's general guideline promulgation authority, see 28 U.S.C. § 994, permits such a broadening of the enhancement.

The addition of a generally applicable Chapter Three hate crimes enhancement requires amendment of the civil rights offense guidelines to avoid duplicative punishments. In addition, to further the Commission's goal of simplifying the operation of the guidelines, the proposed amendment consolidates the four current civil rights offense guidelines into one guideline and adjusts these guidelines to take into account the new enhancement under § 3A1.1(a).

The Freedom of Access to Clinic Entrances Act of 1994 makes it a crime to interfere with access to reproductive services or to interfere with certain religious activities. This Act criminalizes a broad array of conduct, from non-violent obstruction of the entrance to a clinic to murder. The amendment treats these violations in the same way as other offenses involving individual rights.

Section 240002 of the Violent Crime Control and Law Enforcement Act of 1994 directs the Commission to ensure that the guidelines provide sufficiently stringent penalties for crimes of violence against elderly victims. Upon review of the guidelines, the Commission determined that the penalties currently provided generally appear appropriate; however, this amendment strengthens the Commentary to § 3A1.1 in one area by expressly providing a basis for an upward departure if both the current offense and a prior offense involved a vulnerable victim (including an elderly victim), regardless of the type of offense.

Finally, Section 250003 of the Violent Control and Law Enforcement Act of 1994 directs the Commission to review, and if necessary, amend the sentencing guidelines to ensure that victim-related adjustments for fraud offenses against older victims are adequate. Section 250003 also directs the Commission to study and report to the Congress on this issue. See Report to Congress: Adequacy of Penalties for Fraud Offenses Involving Elderly Victims (March 13, 1995). Although the Commission found that the current guidelines generally provided adequate penalties in these cases, it noted some inconsistency in the application of § 3A1.1 regarding whether this adjustment required proof that the defendant had "targeted the victim on account of the victim's vulnerability." This amendment revises the Commentary of § 3A1.1 to clarify application with respect to this issue.

Effective Date: The effective date of this amendment is November 1, 1995.

522. Amendment: Section § 2K2.1(a)(1) is amended by deleting:

"defendant had at least two prior felony convictions of either a crime of violence or a controlled substance offense, and the instant offense involved a firearm listed in 26 U.S.C. § 5845(a)",

and inserting in lieu thereof:

"offense involved a firearm described in 26 U.S.C. § 5845(a) or 18 U.S.C. § 921(a)(30), and the defendant had at least two prior felony convictions of either a crime of violence or a controlled substance offense".

Section § 2K2.1(a)(3) is amended by deleting:

"defendant had one prior felony conviction of either a crime of violence or a controlled substance offense, and the instant offense involved a firearm listed in 26 U.S.C. § 5845(a)",

and inserting in lieu thereof:

"offense involved a firearm described in 26 U.S.C. § 5845(a) or 18 U.S.C. § 921(a)(30), and the defendant had one prior conviction of either a crime of violence or controlled substance offense".

Section § 2K2.1(a)(4)(B) is amended by deleting "listed in 26 U.S.C. § 5845(a)" and inserting in lieu thereof "described in 26 U.S.C. § 5845(a) or 18 U.S.C. § 921(a)(30)".

Section 2K2.1(a)(5) is amended by deleting "listed in 26 U.S.C. § 5845(a)" and inserting in lieu thereof "described in 26 U.S.C. § 5845(a) or 18 U.S.C. § 921(a)(30)".

Section 2K2.1(a)(8) is amended by deleting "or (m)" and by inserting in lieu thereof "(m), (s), (t), or (x)(1)".

The Commentary to § 2K2.1 captioned "Statutory Provisions" is amended by deleting "(r)" and inserting in lieu thereof "(r)-(w), (x)(1)"; and by deleting "(g)" and inserting in lieu thereof "(g), (h), (j)-(n)".

The Commentary to § 2K2.1 captioned "Application Notes" is amended by deleting:

"3. 'Firearm listed in 26 U.S.C. § 5845(a)' includes: (i) any short-barreled rifle or shotgun or any weapon made therefrom; (ii) a machinegun; (iii) a silencer; (iv) a destructive device; or (v) any 'other weapon,' as that term is defined by 26 U.S.C. § 5845(e). A firearm listed in 26 U.S.C. § 5845(a) does not include unaltered handguns or regulation-length rifles or shotguns. For a more detailed definition, refer to 26 U.S.C. § 5845.",

and inserting in lieu thereof:

"3. A 'firearm described in 26 U.S.C. § 5845(a)' includes: (i) a shotgun having a barrel or barrels of less than 18 inches in length; a weapon made from a shotgun if such weapon as modified has an overall length of less than 26 inches or a barrel or barrels of less than 18 inches in length; a rifle having a barrel or barrels of less than 16 inches in length; or a weapon made from a rifle if such weapon as modified has an overall length of less than 26 inches or a barrel or barrels of less than 16 inches in length; (ii) a machinegun; (iii) a silencer; (iv) a destructive device; and (v) certain unusual weapons defined in 26 U.S.C. § 5845(e) (that are not conventional, unaltered handguns, rifles, or shotguns). For a more detailed definition, refer to 26 U.S.C. § 5845.

A 'firearm described in 18 U.S.C. § 921(a)(30)' (pertaining to semiautomatic

Amendment 522 APPENDIX C - VOLUME I   November 1, 2013

>assault weapons) does not include a weapon exempted under the provisions of 18 U.S.C. § 922(v)(3).".

The Commentary to § 2K2.1 captioned "Application Notes" is amended in Note 6 by deleting:

>"or (v) being an alien, is illegally or unlawfully in the United States",

and inserting in lieu thereof:

>"(v) being an alien, is illegally or unlawfully in the United States; or (vi) is subject to a court order that restrains such person from harassing, stalking, or threatening an intimate partner of such person or child of such intimate partner or person, or engaging in other conduct that would place an intimate partner in reasonable fear of bodily injury to the partner or child as defined in 18 U.S.C. § 922(d)(8)".

The Commentary to § 2K2.1 captioned "Application Notes" is amended by deleting:

>"12. If the defendant is convicted under 18 U.S.C. § 922(i), (j), or (k), or 26 U.S.C. § 5861(g) or (h) (offenses involving stolen firearms or ammunition), and is convicted of no other offense subject to this guideline, do not apply the adjustment in subsection (b)(4) because the base offense level itself takes such conduct into account.".

and inserting in lieu thereof:

>"12. If the only offense to which § 2K2.1 applies is 18 U.S.C. § 922 (i), (j), or (u), 18 U.S.C. § 924(j) or (k), or 26 U.S.C. § 5861(g) or (h) (offenses involving a stolen firearm or stolen ammunition) and the base offense level is determined under subsection (a)(7), do not apply the adjustment in subsection (b)(4) unless the offense involved a firearm with an altered or obliterated serial number. This is because the base offense level takes into account that the firearm or ammunition was stolen.
>
>Similarly, if the only offense to which § 2K2.1 applies is 18 U.S.C. § 922(k) (offenses involving an altered or obliterated serial number) and the base offense level is determined under subsection (a)(7), do not apply the adjustment in subsection (b)(4) unless the offense involved a stolen firearm or stolen ammunition. This is because the base offense level takes into account that the firearm had an altered or obliterated serial number.".

Reason for Amendment: This is a five-part amendment. First, the amendment revises § 2K2.1 (Unlawful Receipt, Possession, or Transportation of Firearms or Ammunition; Prohibited Transactions Involving Firearms or Ammunition) to provide increased offense levels for possession of a semiautomatic assault weapon that correspond to the offense levels currently provided for possession of machineguns and other firearms described in 26 U.S.C. § 5845(a). Second, the amendment addresses section 110201 of the Violent Crime Control Law Enforcement Act of 1994 by providing an offense level of six for the misdemeanor portion of 18 U.S.C. § 922(x)(1) (involving sale or transfer of a handgun or ammunition to a juvenile). For an offense under the felony portion of 18 U.S.C. § 922(x)(1) (involving the sale or transfer of a handgun or handgun ammunition to a juvenile knowing or having reasonable cause to believe that the handgun or ammunition was intended to be used in a crime), the enhancement in subsection (b)(5) will provide a minimum offense level of 18. Third, the amendment addresses section 110401 of the Violent Crime Control and Law Enforcement Act of 1994 by adding to the definition of a "prohibited person" in

§ 2K2.1 a person under the court order described in that section of the Act. Fourth, the amendment provides an offense level of six for the misdemeanors set forth in 18 U.S.C. § 922 (s) and (t) (involving violations of the Brady Act). Fifth, the amendment clarifies that Application Note 12 in § 2K2.1 applies only to cases in which the base offense level is determined under § 2K2.1(a)(7).

Effective Date: The effective date of this amendment is November 1, 1995.

523. **Amendment:** The Commentary to § 2L1.2 captioned "Application Notes" is amended in Note 2 by deleting:

> "a sentence at or near the maximum of the applicable guideline range may be warranted",

and inserting in lieu thereof:

> "an upward departure may be warranted. See § 4A1.3 (Adequacy of Criminal History Category)".

Reason for Amendment: This amendment revises § 2L1.2 (Unlawfully Entering or Remaining in the United States) to authorize the court to consider an upward departure in the case of a defendant with repeated prior instances of deportation not resulting in a criminal conviction.

Effective Date: The effective date of this amendment is November 1, 1995.

524. **Amendment:** Section 2L2.1(b)(2) is amended by deleting "sets of documents" and inserting in lieu thereof "documents"; and by deleting "Sets of Documents" and inserting in lieu thereof "Documents".

Section 2L2.1(b) is amended by inserting the following additional subdivision:

> "(3) If the defendant knew, believed, or had reason to believe that a passport or visa was to be used to facilitate the commission of a felony offense, other than an offense involving violation of the immigration laws, increase by 4 levels.".

The Commentary to § 2L2.1 captioned "Application Notes" is amended in Note 2 by inserting "of documents" immediately before "intended"; and by deleting "documents as one set" and inserting in lieu thereof "set as one document".

The Commentary to § 2L2.1 captioned "Application Notes" is amended by inserting the following additional note:

> "3. Subsection (b)(3) provides an enhancement if the defendant knew, believed, or had reason to believe that a passport or visa was to be used to facilitate the commission of a felony offense, other than an offense involving violation of the immigration laws. If the defendant knew, believed, or had reason to believe that the felony offense to be committed was of an especially serious type, an upward departure may be warranted.".

Section 2L2.2 is amended by inserting the following additional subsection:

> "(c) Cross Reference
>
> (1) If the defendant used a passport or visa in the commission or at-

tempted commission of a felony offense, other than an offense involving violation of the immigration laws, apply --

(A) § 2X1.1 (Attempt, Solicitation, or Conspiracy) in respect to that felony offense, if the resulting offense level is greater than that determined above; or

(B) if death resulted, the most analogous offense guideline from Chapter Two, Part A, Subpart 1 (Homicide), if the resulting offense level is greater than that determined above.".

Reason for Amendment: This is a three-part amendment. First, this amendment provides an enhancement in § 2L2.1 (Trafficking in a Document Relating to Naturalization, Citizenship, or Legal Resident Status, or a United States Passport; False Statement in Respect to the Citizenship or Immigration Status of Another; Fraudulent Marriage to Assist Alien to Evade Immigration Law) if the defendant trafficked in a passport or visa knowing, believing, or having reason to believe that the passport or visa was to be used to facilitate the commission of a felony offense, other than an offense involving violation of the immigration laws. Second, this amendment corrects a technical error in § 2L2.1(b)(2). Third, this amendment adds a cross reference to § 2L2.2 (Fraudulently Acquiring Documents Relating to Naturalization, Citizenship, or Legal Resident Status for Own Use; False Personation or Fraudulent Marriage by Alien to Evade Immigration Law; Fraudulently Acquiring or Improperly Using a United States Passport) that addresses the case of a defendant who uses a passport or visa in the commission or attempted commission of a felony offense, other than an offense involving violation of the immigration laws.

Effective Date: The effective date of this amendment is November 1, 1995.

525. **Amendment:** Section 2P1.2(a)(2) is amended by inserting "methamphetamine," immediately following "PCP,".

Section 2P1.2(a)(3) is amended by inserting "methamphetamine," immediately following "PCP,".

Section 2P1.2 is amended by deleting subsection (c)(1) as follows:

"(1) If the defendant is convicted under 18 U.S.C. § 1791(a)(1) and is punishable under 18 U.S.C. § 1791(b)(1), the offense level is 2 plus the offense level from § 2D1.1, but in no event less than level 26.",

and inserting in lieu thereof:

"(1) If the object of the offense was the distribution of a controlled substance, apply the offense level from § 2D1.1 (Unlawful Manufacturing, Importing, Exporting, or Trafficking; Attempt or Conspiracy). *Provided*, that if the defendant is convicted under 18 U.S.C. § 1791(a)(1) and is punishable under 18 U.S.C. § 1791(b)(1), and the resulting offense level is less than level 26, increase to level 26.".

Reason for Amendment: This amendment conforms the offense level for methamphetamine offenses in a correctional or detention facility to that of other controlled substance offenses committed in a correctional or detention facility that have the same statutory maximum penalty. This change reflects the increase in the maximum penalty for methamphetamine offenses in section 90101 of the Violent Crime Control and Law Enforcement Act of 1994. In addition, the amendment expands the cross reference in

§ 2P1.2(c)(1) to cover distribution of all controlled substances in a correctional or detention facility.

Effective Date: The effective date of this amendment is November 1, 1995.

526. **Amendment:** Chapter Three, Part A, is amended by inserting an additional section as § 3A1.4 (International Terrorism).

Section 5K2.15 (Terrorism) is deleted in its entirety as follows:

"§ 5K2.15. Terrorism (Policy Statement)

If the defendant committed the offense in furtherance of a terroristic action, the court may increase the sentence above the authorized guideline range.".

Reason for Amendment: Section 120004 of the Violent Crime Control and Law Enforcement Act of 1994 directs the Commission to provide an appropriate enhancement for any felony that involves or is intended to promote international terrorism. The amendment addresses this directive by adding a Chapter Three enhancement at § 3A1.4 (International Terrorism) in place of the upward departure provision at § 5K2.15 (Terrorism).

Effective Date: The effective date of this amendment is November 1, 1995.

527. **Amendment:** Section 3B1.4 is deleted in its entirety as follows:

"§ 3B1.4. In any other case, no adjustment is made for role in the offense.

Commentary

Many offenses are committed by a single individual or by individuals of roughly equal culpability so that none of them will receive an adjustment under this Part. In addition, some participants in a criminal organization may receive increases under § 3B1.1 (Aggravating Role) while others receive decreases under § 3B1.2 (Mitigating Role) and still other participants receive no adjustment.".

A new § 3B1.4 (Using a Minor To Commit a Crime) is inserted in lieu thereof.

Reason for Amendment: This amendment implements the directive in Section 140008 of the Violent Crime Control and Law Enforcement Act of 1994 (pertaining to the use of a minor in the commission of an offense) in a slightly broader form by adding a new § 3B1.4 (Using a Minor to Commit a Crime). The existing § 3B1.4 (untitled) is deleted as unnecessary.

Effective Date: The effective date of this amendment is November 1, 1995.

528. **Amendment:** The Commentary to § 4B1.1 captioned "Background" is amended by deleting:

"28 U.S.C. § 994(h) mandates that the Commission assure that certain 'career' offenders, as defined in the statute, receive a sentence of imprisonment 'at or near the maximum term authorized.' Section 4B1.1 implements this mandate. The legislative history of this provision suggests that the phrase 'maximum term authorized' should be construed as the maximum term authorized by statute. See S. Rep. 98-225, 98th Cong., 1st Sess. 175 (1983), 128 Cong. Rec. 26, 511-12 (1982) (text of 'Career Criminals' amendment by Senator Kennedy), 26, 515 (brief summary of amendment), 26, 517-18 (statement of Senator Kennedy).",

and inserting in lieu thereof:

> "Section 994(h) of Title 28, United States Code, mandates that the Commission assure that certain 'career' offenders receive a sentence of imprisonment 'at or near the maximum term authorized.' Section 4B1.1 implements this directive, with the definition of a career offender tracking in large part the criteria set forth in 28 U.S.C. § 994(h). However, in accord with its general guideline promulgation authority under 28 U.S.C. § 994(a)-(f), and its amendment authority under 28 U.S.C. § 994(o) and (p), the Commission has modified this definition in several respects to focus more precisely on the class of recidivist offenders for whom a lengthy term of imprisonment is appropriate and to avoid 'unwarranted sentencing disparities among defendants with similar records who have been found guilty of similar criminal conduct . . . .' 28 U.S.C. § 991(b)(1)(B). The Commission's refinement of this definition over time is consistent with Congress's choice of a directive to the Commission rather than a mandatory minimum sentencing statute ('The [Senate Judiciary] Committee believes that such a directive to the Commission will be more effective; the guidelines development process can assure consistent and rational implementation for the Committee's view that substantial prison terms should be imposed on repeat violent offenders and repeat drug traffickers.' S. Rep. No. 225, 98th Cong., 1st Sess. 175 (1983)).
>
> The legislative history of this provision suggests that the phrase 'maximum term authorized' should be construed as the maximum term authorized by statute. See S. Rep. No. 225, 98th Cong., 1st Sess. 175 (1983); 128 Cong. Rec. 26,511-12 (1982) (text of 'Career Criminals' amendment by Senator Kennedy); id. at 26,515 (brief summary of amendment); id. at 26,517-18 (statement of Senator Kennedy).".

Application Note 1 of the Commentary to § 4B1.2 is repromulgated without change.

Reason for Amendment: This amendment repromulgates Application Note 1 of the Commentary to § 4B1.2 (Definition of Terms Used in Section 4B1.1) and inserts additional background commentary in § 4B1.1 (Career Offender) explaining the Commission's rationale and authority for its implementation of this guideline. The amendment responds to a decision by the United States Court of Appeals for the District of Columbia Circuit in United States v. Price, 990 F.2d 1367 (D.C. Cir. 1993). In Price, the court invalidated application of the career offender guideline to a defendant convicted of a drug conspiracy because 28 U.S.C. § 994(h), which the Commission cites as the mandating authority for the career offender guideline, does not expressly refer to inchoate offenses. The court indicated that it did not foreclose Commission authority to include conspiracy offenses under the career offender guideline by drawing upon its broader guideline promulgation authority in 28 U.S.C. § 994(a). See also United States v. Mendoza-Figueroa, 28 F.3d 766 (8th Cir. 1994), vacated (Sept. 2, 1994); United States v. Bellazerius, 24 F.3d 698 (5th Cir.), cert. denied, 115 S. Ct. 375 (1994). Other circuits have rejected the Price analysis and upheld the Commission's definition of "controlled substance offense." For example, the Ninth Circuit considered the legislative history to 994(h) and determined that the Senate Report clearly indicated that 994(h) was not the sole enabling statute for the career offender guidelines. United States v. Heim, 15 F.3d 830 (9th Cir.), cert. denied, 115 S. Ct. 55 (1994). See also United States v. Hightower, 25 F.3d 182 (3d Cir.), cert. denied, 115 S. Ct. 370 (1994); United States v. Damerville, 27 F.3d 254 (7th Cir.), cert. denied, 115 S. Ct. 445 (1994); United States v. Allen, 24 F.3d 1180 (10th Cir.), cert. denied, 115 S. Ct. 493 (1994); United States v. Baker, 16 F.3d 854 (8th Cir. 1994); United States v. Linnear, 40 F.3d 215 (7th Cir. 1994); United States v. Kennedy, 32 F.3d 876 (4th Cir. 1994), cert. denied, 115 S. Ct. 939 (1995); United States v. Piper, 35 F.3d 611 (1st Cir. 1994), cert. denied, 115 S. Ct. 1118 (1995).

Effective Date: The effective date of this amendment is November 1, 1995.

529. Amendment: The Commentary to § 5D1.1 captioned "Application Notes" is amended by deleting Note 1 as follows:

> "Subsection 5D1.1(a) requires imposition of supervised release following any sentence of imprisonment for a term of more than one year or if required by a specific statute. While there may be cases within this category that do not require post release supervision, these cases are the exception and may be handled by a departure from this guideline.",

and inserting in lieu thereof:

> "Under subsection (a), the court is required to impose a term of supervised release to follow imprisonment if a sentence of imprisonment of more than one year is imposed or if a term of supervised release is required by a specific statute. The court may depart from this guideline and not impose a term of supervised release if it determines that supervised release is neither required by statute nor required for any of the following reasons: (1) to protect the public welfare; (2) to enforce a financial condition; (3) to provide drug or alcohol treatment or testing; (4) to assist the reintegration of the defendant into the community; or (5) to accomplish any other sentencing purpose authorized by statute.".

The Commentary to § 5D1.1 captioned "Application Notes" is amended by deleting Note 2 as follows:

> "2. Under § 5D1.1(b), the court may impose a term of supervised release in cases involving imprisonment for a term of one year or less. The court may consider the need for a term of supervised release to facilitate the reintegration of the defendant into the community; to enforce a fine, restitution order, or other condition; or to fulfill any other purpose authorized by statute.",

and inserting in lieu thereof:

> "2. Under subsection (b), the court may impose a term of supervised release to follow a term of imprisonment of one year or less for any of the reasons set forth in Application Note 1.".

Section 5D1.2 is amended by deleting:

> "(a) If a defendant is convicted under a statute that requires a term of supervised release, the term shall be at least three years but not more than five years, or the minimum period required by statute, whichever is greater.",

and by redesignating subsection (b) as subsection (a).

Section 5D1.2(a) (formerly § 5D1.2(b)) is amended by deleting "Otherwise, when" and inserting in lieu thereof "If".

Section 5D1.2 is amended by inserting the following additional subsection:

> "(b) *Provided*, that the term of supervised release imposed shall in no event be less than any statutorily required term of supervised release.".

The Commentary to § 5D1.2 captioned "Background" is amended in the second sentence by deleting "(a)" and inserting in lieu thereof "(b)"; and by deleting the third sentence as follows:

> "Subsection (b) applies to all other statutes.".

Amendment 529

Reason for Amendment: This amendment sets forth with greater specificity the circumstances under which the court may depart from the requirements of § 5D1.1 (Imposition of a Term of Supervised Release) and impose no term of supervised release. In addition, the amendment deletes, as unnecessary, the requirement in § 5D1.2 (Term of Supervised Release) of a term of supervised release of three to five years whenever a statute requires any term of supervised release. Instead, the amendment provides that, in the case of a statute requiring a term of supervised release, the length of the term of supervised release shall be determined by the class of felony of which the defendant was convicted, but shall not be less than any minimum term of supervised release required by statute.

Effective Date: The effective date of this amendment is November 1, 1995.

530. **Amendment:** Section 5E1.1(a)(2) is amended by deleting "49 U.S.C. § 1472(h), (i), (j), or (n)" and inserting in lieu thereof "49 U.S.C. § 46312, § 46502, or § 46504".

The Commentary to § 5E1.1 captioned "Background" is amended in the first paragraph by deleting "and of designated subdivisions of 49 U.S.C. § 1472" and inserting in lieu thereof "or 49 U.S.C. § 46312, § 46502, or § 46504".

The Commentary to § 5E1.1 captioned "Background" is amended in the second paragraph by deleting "§ 1472(h), (i), (j), or (n)" wherever it appears and inserting in lieu there of in each instance "§ 46312, § 46502, or § 46504".

The Commentary to § 5E1.1 captioned "Background" is amended in the fourth paragraph by deleting "Rule 32(c)(2)(D)" and inserting in lieu thereof "Rule 32(b)(4)(D)".

The Commentary to § 5E1.1 is amended by inserting the following immediately before "Background":

"Application Note:

1. In the case of a conviction under certain statutes, additional requirements regarding restitution apply. See 18 U.S.C. §§ 2248 and 2259 (applying to convictions under 18 U.S.C. §§ 2241-2258 for sexual-abuse offenses and sexual exploitation of minors); 18 U.S.C. § 2327 (applying to convictions under 18 U.S.C. §§ 1028-1029, 1341-1344 for telemarketing-fraud offenses); 18 U.S.C. § 2264 (applying to convictions under 18 U.S.C. §§ 2261-2262 for domestic-violence offenses). To the extent that any of the above-noted statutory provisions conflict with the provisions of this guideline, the applicable statutory provision shall control.".

Reason for Amendment: Section 40113 of the Violent Crime Control and Law Enforcement Act of 1994 requires "mandatory" restitution for offenses involving sexual abuse and sexual exploitation of children under 18 U.S.C. §§ 2241-2258. Sections 40221 and 250002 add similar "mandatory" restitution provisions for offenses involving domestic violence (18 U.S.C. § 2264) and telemarketing fraud (18 U.S.C. § 2327). These provisions also require that compliance with a restitution order be a condition of probation or supervised release, have broader definitions of loss than 18 U.S.C. § 3663, and apply "notwithstanding section 3663, and in addition to any civil or criminal penalty authorized by law." This amendment adds commentary to § 5E1.1 (Restitution) to alert courts to these statutory provisions.

In addition, this amendment conforms § 5E1.1 to the redesignation of 49 U.S.C. § 1472(h), (i), (j), and (n) as 49 U.S.C. §§ 46312, 46502(a), (b), and 46504, and the redesignation of Rule 32(c)(2)(D) as Rule 32(b)(4)(D).

Effective Date: The effective date of this amendment is November 1, 1995.

531. **Amendment:** Chapter Five, Part K, Subpart Two is amended by inserting an additional policy statement as § 5K2.17 (High-Capacity, Semiautomatic Firearms).

    Reason for Amendment: This amendment addresses the directive in section 110501 of the Violent Crime Control and Law Enforcement Act of 1994 to provide an appropriate enhancement for a crime of violence or drug trafficking crime if a semiautomatic firearm is involved.

    According to data reviewed by the Commission, semiautomatic firearms are used in 50-70 percent of offenses involving a firearm. Thus, offenses involving a semiautomatic firearm represent the typical or "heartland" case under the guidelines. Consequently, the firearms enhancements in the guidelines for crimes of violence and drug trafficking can be considered to take into account the fact that firearms involved in these offenses typically are semiautomatic. Moreover, the "firepower" or "dangerousness" of semiautomatic firearms, compared to other types of firearms, varies substantially with caliber and magazine capacity. For example, a.25 caliber, six-shot semiautomatic pistol is not considered as having as much firepower as a.38 caliber, six-shot revolver or a.357 magnum, six-shot revolver. A nine-millimeter semiautomatic pistol fires a somewhat more powerful cartridge than a.38 caliber revolver and a somewhat less powerful cartridge than a.357 magnum revolver. But some nine-millimeter semiautomatic pistols hold from 14-18 cartridges, compared to six cartridges for a revolver. A high magazine capacity, nine-millimeter semiautomatic pistol can be said to have significantly more firepower than a revolver because it can fire a significantly larger number of shots without reloading.

    If harm actually results (e.g., death or bodily injury), the guidelines generally take that harm into account directly. Consequently, in considering any distinction between semiautomatic firearms and other firearms, the issue is whether there is any significant difference in the risk of harm. The difference in the risk of harm also varies widely with the circumstances of the offense. For example, in a robbery at very close range, the difference in the likelihood of death or bodily injury between a revolver and semiautomatic pistol would seem to be small. In contrast, in a drive-by shooting the greater firepower of a semiautomatic weapon likely would have a more significant effect on the likelihood of death or injury.

    After considering the above factors, the Commission determined that the most appropriate approach at this time was to provide a specific basis for an upward departure when a high-capacity semiautomatic firearm is possessed in connection with a crime of violence or drug trafficking offense, thereby allowing the courts the flexibility to take this factor into account as appropriate in the circumstances of the particular case.

    Effective Date: The effective date of this amendment is November 1, 1995.

532. **Amendment:** Chapter Five, Part K, Subpart Two is amended by inserting an additional policy statement as § 5K1.18 (Violent Street Gangs).

    Reason for Amendment: This amendment expressly provides a basis for an upward departure in the case of a defendant subject to a statutorily enhanced maximum penalty under 18 U.S.C. § 521 (pertaining to criminal street gangs), as enacted by section 150000 of the Violent Crime and Law Enforcement Act of 1994.

    Effective Date: The effective date of this amendment is November 1, 1995.

533. **Amendment:** Section 7B1.3(g)(2) is amended by deleting "the defendant may, to the

extent permitted by law, be ordered to recommence supervised release upon release from imprisonment" and inserting in lieu thereof:

> "the court may include a requirement that the defendant be placed on a term of supervised release upon release from imprisonment. The length of such a term of supervised release shall not exceed the term of supervised release authorized by statute for the offense that resulted in the original term of supervised release, less any term of imprisonment that was imposed upon revocation of supervised release. 18 U.S.C. § 3583(h)".

The Commentary to § 7B1.3 captioned "Application Notes" is amended in Note 2 by deleting:

> ". This statute, however, neither expressly authorizes nor precludes a court from ordering that a term of supervised release recommence after revocation. Under § 7B1.3(g)(2), the court may order, to the extent permitted by law, the recommencement of a supervised release term following revocation",

and inserting in lieu thereof:

> ", (g)-(i). Under 18 U.S.C. § 3583(h) (effective September 13, 1994), the court, in the case of revocation of supervised release and imposition of less than the maximum imposable term of imprisonment, may order an additional period of supervised release to follow imprisonment".

The Commentary to § 7B1.3 captioned "Application Notes is amended by deleting:

> "3. Subsection (c) provides for the use of certain alternatives to imprisonment upon revocation. It is to be noted, however, that a court may decide that not every alternative is authorized by statute in every circumstance. For example, in United States v. Behnezhad, 907 F.2d 896 (9th Cir. 1990), the Ninth Circuit held that where a term of supervised release was revoked there was no statutory authority to impose a further term of supervised release. Under this decision, in the case of a revocation of a term of supervised release, an alternative that is contingent upon imposition of a further term of supervised release (e.g., a period of imprisonment followed by a period of community confinement or detention as a condition of supervised release) cannot be implemented. The Commission has transmitted to the Congress a proposal for a statutory amendment to address this issue.";

and by renumbering the remaining notes accordingly.

The Commentary to § 7B1.4 captioned "Application Notes" is amended by deleting:

> "5. Under 18 U.S.C. § 3565(a), upon a finding that a defendant violated a condition of probation by being in possession of a controlled substance, the court is required 'to revoke the sentence of probation and sentence the defendant to not less than one-third of the original sentence.' Under 18 U.S.C. § 3583(g), upon a finding that a defendant violated a condition of supervised release by being in possession of a controlled substance, the court is required 'to terminate supervised release and sentence the defendant to serve in prison not less than one-third of the term of supervised release.' The Commission leaves to the court the determination of whether evidence of drug usage established solely by laboratory analysis constitutes 'possession of a controlled substance' as set forth in 18 U.S.C. §§ 3565(a) and 3583(g).
>
> 6. Under 18 U.S.C. § 3565(b), upon a finding that a defendant violated a condi-

tion of probation by the actual possession of a firearm, the court is required 'to revoke the sentence of probation and impose any other sentence that was available . . . at the time of initial sentencing.'",

and inserting in lieu thereof:

"5. Upon a finding that a defendant violated a condition of probation or supervised release by being in possession of a controlled substance or firearm or by refusing to comply with a condition requiring drug testing, the court is required to revoke probation or supervised release and impose a sentence that includes a term of imprisonment. 18 U.S.C. §§ 3565(b), 3583(g).

6. In the case of a defendant who fails a drug test, the court shall consider whether the availability of appropriate substance abuse programs, or a defendant's current or past participation in such programs, warrants an exception from the requirement of mandatory revocation and imprisonment under 18 U.S.C. §§ 3565(b) and 3583(g). 18 U.S.C. §§ 3563(a), 3583(d).".

Reason for Amendment: Section 110505 of the Violent Crime Control and Law Enforcement Act of 1994 amends 18 U.S.C. § 3583(e)(3) by specifying that a defendant whose supervised release term is revoked may not be required to serve more than five years in prison if the offense that resulted in the term of supervised release is a Class A felony. The provision also amends section 3583(g) by eliminating the mandatory re-imprisonment period of at least one-third of the term of supervised release if the defendant possesses a controlled substance. Additionally, the provision requires the courts to revoke probation or supervised release and impose a sentence that includes a term of imprisonment if the defendant is found to be in possession of a firearm, or refuses to participate in drug testing. Finally, the provision expressly authorizes the court to order an additional, limited period of supervision following revocation of supervised release and re-imprisonment.

Section 20414 of the Violent Crime Control and Law Enforcement Act of 1994 makes mandatory a condition of probation requiring that the defendant refrain from any unlawful use of a controlled substance. 18 U.S.C. § 3563(a)(4). The section also establishes a condition that the defendant, with certain exceptions, submit to periodic drug tests. The existing mandatory condition of probation requiring the defendant not to possess a controlled substance remains unchanged. 18 U.S.C. § 3563(a)(3). Similar requirements are made with respect to conditions of supervised release. 18 U.S.C. § 3583(d).

Section 110506 of the Violent Crime Control and Law Enforcement Act of 1994 mandates revocation of probation and imposition of a term of imprisonment if the defendant violates probation by possessing a controlled substance or a firearm, or by refusing to comply with drug testing. 18 U.S.C. § 3565(b). It does not require revocation in the case of use of a controlled substance (although use presumptively may establish possession). No minimum term of imprisonment is required other than a sentence that includes a "term of imprisonment" consistent with the sentencing guidelines and revocation policy statements. Similar requirements are set forth in 18 U.S.C. § 3583(g) with respect to conditions of supervised release.

Section 20414 permits "an exception in accordance with United States Sentencing Commission guidelines" from the mandatory revocation provisions of section 3565(b), "when considering any action against a defendant who fails a drug test administered in accordance with [section 3563(a)(4)]." The exception from the mandatory revocation provisions appears limited to a defendant who fails the test and does not appear to apply to a defendant who refuses to take the test.

This amendment conforms §§ 7B1.3 (Revocation of Probation or Supervised Release) and 7B1.4 (Term of Imprisonment) to these revised statutory provisions.

Effective Date: The effective date of this amendment is November 1, 1995.

534. **Amendment:** Appendix A (Statutory Index) is amended by inserting the following at the appropriate place by title and section:

"7 U.S.C. § 2018(c)	2N2.1",
"7 U.S.C. § 6810	2N2.1",
"18 U.S.C. § 36	2D1.1",
"18 U.S.C. § 37	2A1.1, 2A1.2, 2A1.3, 2A1.4, 2A2.1, 2A2.2, 2A2.3, 2A3.1, 2A3.4, 2A4.1, 2A5.1, 2A5.2, 2B1.3, 2B3.1, 2K1.4",
"18 U.S.C. § 113(a)(1)	2A2.1",
"18 U.S.C. § 113(a)(2)	2A2.2",
"18 U.S.C. § 113(a)(3)	2A2.2",
"18 U.S.C. § 113(a)(5) (Class A misdemeanor provisions only)	2A2.3",
"18 U.S.C. § 113(a)(6)	2A2.2",
"18 U.S.C. § 113(a)(7)	2A2.3",
"18 U.S.C. § 470	2B5.1, 2F1.1",
"18 U.S.C. § 668	2B1.1",
"18 U.S.C. § 844(m)	2K1.3",
"18 U.S.C. § 880	2B1.1",
"18 U.S.C. § 922(x)(1)	2K2.1",
"18 U.S.C. § 924(i)	2A1.1, 2A1.2",
"18 U.S.C. § 924(j)-(n)	2K2.1",
"18 U.S.C. § 1033	2B1.1, 2F1.1, 2J1.2",
"18 U.S.C. § 1118	2A1.1, 2A1.2",
"18 U.S.C. § 1119	2A1.1, 2A1.2, 2A1.3, 2A1.4, 2A2.1",
"18 U.S.C. § 1120	2A1.1, 2A1.2, 2A1.3, 2A1.4",
"18 U.S.C. § 1121	2A1.1, 2A1.2",
"18 U.S.C. § 1204	2J1.2",
"18 U.S.C. § 1716D	2Q2.1",
"18 U.S.C. § 2258(a),(b)	2G2.1, 2G2.2",
"18 U.S.C. § 2261	2A1.1, 2A1.2, 2A2.1, 2A2.2, 2A2.3, 2A3.1, 2A3.4, 2A4.1, 2B3.1, 2B3.2, 2K1.4",
"18 U.S.C. § 2262	2A1.1, 2A1.2, 2A2.1,

	2A2.2, 2A2.3, 2A3.1, 2A3.4, 2A4.1, 2B3.1, 2B3.2, 2K1.4",
"18 U.S.C. § 2280	2A1.1, 2A1.2, 2A1.3, 2A1.4, 2A2.1, 2A2.2, 2A2.3, 2A4.1, 2B1.3 2B3.1, 2B3.2, 2K1.4",
"18 U.S.C. § 2281	2A1.1, 2A1.2, 2A1.3, 2A1.4, 2A2.1, 2A2.2, 2A2.3, 2A4.1, 2B1.3, 2B3.1, 2B3.2, 2K1.4",
"18 U.S.C. § 2332a	2A1.1, 2A1.2, 2A1.3, 2A1.4, 2A1.5, 2A2.1, 2A2.2, 2B1.3, 2K1.4",
"18 U.S.C. § 2423(b)	2A3.1, 2A3.2, 2A3.3",
"21 U.S.C. § 843(a)(9)	2D3.1",
"21 U.S.C. § 843(c)	2D3.1",
"21 U.S.C. § 849	2D1.2",
"21 U.S.C. § 854	2S1.2",
"21 U.S.C. § 960(d)(3), (4)	2D1.11",
"21 U.S.C. § 960(d)(5)	2D1.13",
"21 U.S.C. § 960(d)(6)	2D3.1",
"42 U.S.C. § 1307(b)	2F1.1",
"49 U.S.C. § 46308	2A5.2",
"49 U.S.C. § 46312	2Q1.2",
"49 U.S.C. § 46502(a),(b)	2A5.1",
"49 U.S.C. § 46504	2A5.2",
"49 U.S.C. § 46505	2K1.5",
"49 U.S.C. § 46506	2A5.3".

Appendix A (Statutory Index) is amended in the line referenced to 18 U.S.C. § 113(a) by inserting "(for offenses committed prior to September 13, 1994)" immediately following "2A2.1";

in the line referenced to 18 U.S.C. § 113(b) by inserting "(for offenses committed prior to September 13, 1994)" immediately following "2A2.2";

in the line referenced to 18 U.S.C. § 113(c) by inserting "(for offenses committed prior to September 13, 1994)" immediately following "2A2.2";

in the line referenced to 18 U.S.C. § 113(f) by inserting "(for offenses committed prior to September 13, 1994)" immediately following "2A2.2";

in the line referenced to 18 U.S.C. § 242 by deleting "2H1.4" and inserting in lieu thereof "2H1.1";

in the line referenced to 18 U.S.C. § 245(b) by deleting "2H1.3" and inserting in lieu thereof "2H1.1";

Amendment 534

in the line referenced to 18 U.S.C. § 246 by deleting "2H1.5" and inserting in lieu thereof "2H1.1";

in the line referenced to 18 U.S.C. § 247 by deleting "2H1.3" and inserting in lieu thereof "2H1.1";

in the line referenced to 18 U.S.C. § 371 by inserting "2K2.1 (if a conspiracy to violate 18 U.S.C. § 924(c))," immediately before "2X1.1";

in the line referenced to 18 U.S.C. § 922(r) by deleting "(r)" and inserting in lieu thereof "(r)-(w)";

in the line referenced to 18 U.S.C. § 1153 by inserting "2A2.3," immediately before "2A3.1";

in the line referenced to 18 U.S.C. § 2114 by deleting "2114" and inserting in lieu thereof "2114(a)";

in the line referenced to 18 U.S.C. § 2423 by deleting "2423" and by inserting in lieu thereof "2423(a)"; and

in the line referenced to 42 U.S.C. § 3631 by deleting "2H1.3" and inserting in lieu thereof "2H1.1".

Appendix A (Statutory Index) is amended by deleting:

"49 U.S.C. § 1472(c)	2A5.2
49 U.S.C. § 1472(h)(2)	2Q1.2
49 U.S.C. § 1472(i)(1)	2A5.1
49 U.S.C. § 1472(j)	2A5.2
49 U.S.C. § 1472(k)(1)	2A5.3
49 U.S.C. § 1472(l)	2K1.5
49 U.S.C. § 1472(n)(1)	2A5.1".

Chapter 1, Part A, Subpart 4(d) is amended in the second sentence of the third paragraph by deleting "six" and inserting in lieu thereof "eight"; and in the third sentence of the third paragraph by deleting "seven through" and inserting in lieu thereof "nine and".

The Commentary to § 1B1.5 captioned "Application Notes" is amended in Note 1 by deleting "2H1.1(a)(2)" and inserting in lieu thereof "2H1.1(a)(1)".

The Commentary to § 2A2.1 captioned "Statutory Provisions" is amended by deleting "113(a)" and inserting in lieu thereof "113(a)(1)".

The Commentary to § 2A2.2 captioned "Statutory Provisions" is amended by deleting "113(b), (c), (f)" and inserting in lieu thereof "113(a)(2), (3), (6)".

The Commentary to § 2A5.1 captioned "Statutory Provisions" is amended by deleting "49 U.S.C. § 1472 (i), (n)" and inserting in lieu thereof "49 U.S.C. § 46502 (a), (b) (formerly 49 U.S.C. § 1472 (i), (n))".

The Commentary to § 2A5.1 captioned "Background" is amended by deleting "49 U.S.C. § 1472(i)" and inserting in lieu thereof "49 U.S.C. § 46502(a)", and by deleting "49 U.S.C. § 1472(n)" and inserting in lieu thereof "49 U.S.C. § 46502(b)".

The Commentary to § 2A5.2 captioned "Statutory Provisions" is amended by deleting "49 U.S.C. § 1472(c), (j)" and inserting in lieu thereof "49 U.S.C. §§ 46308, 46504 (formerly 49 U.S.C. § 1472(c), (j))".

The Commentary to § 2A5.2 captioned "Background" is amended by deleting "49 U.S.C. § 1472(l) and inserting in lieu thereof "49 U.S.C. § 46505".

The Commentary to § 2A5.3 captioned "Statutory Provision" is amended by deleting "49 U.S.C. § 1472(k)(1)" and inserting in lieu thereof "49 U.S.C. § 46506 (formerly 49 U.S.C. § 1472(k)(1))".

The Commentary to § 2A5.3 captioned "Application Notes" is amended in Note 1 by deleting "49 U.S.C. § 1472(k)(1)" and inserting in lieu thereof "49 U.S.C. § 46506".

The Commentary to 2C1.2 captioned "Background" is amended by deleting the third sentence as follows:

"The maximum term of imprisonment authorized by statute for these offenses is two years.".

The Commentary to 2C1.3 captioned "Background" is amended by deleting the second sentence as follows:

"The maximum term of imprisonment authorized by statute is two years.".

Section 2D3.1 is amended in the title by deleting "Illegal Use of Registration Number to Manufacture, Distribute, Acquire, or Dispense a Controlled Substance" and inserting in lieu thereof "Regulatory Offenses Involving Registration Numbers; Unlawful Advertising Relating to Schedule I Substances".

The Commentary to § 2D3.1 captioned "Background" is amended by deleting:

"Background: The maximum term of imprisonment authorized by statute is four years, except in a case with a prior drug-related felony where the maximum term of imprisonment authorized by statute is eight years.".

Section 2D3.2 is amended in the title by inserting "or Listed Chemicals" immediately after "Controlled Substances".

The Commentary to § 2D3.2 captioned "Background" is amended by deleting:

"Background: These offenses are misdemeanors. The maximum term of imprisonment authorized by statute is one year.".

The Commentary to § 2H2.1 captioned "Statutory Provisions" is amended by deleting "1973j" and inserting in lieu thereof "1973j(a), (b)".

The Commentary to § 2K1.3 captioned "Statutory Provisions" is amended by deleting "5865" and inserting in lieu thereof "5685".

Section 2K1.5(b)(3) is amended by deleting "49 U.S.C. § 1472(l)" and inserting in lieu thereof "49 U.S.C. § 46505".

The Commentary to § 2K1.5 captioned "Statutory Provision" is amended by deleting "49 U.S.C. § 1472(l)" and inserting in lieu thereof "49 U.S.C. § 46505 (formerly 49 U.S.C. § 1472(l))".

Amendment 534 APPENDIX C - VOLUME I November 1, 2013

The Commentary to § 2K1.5 captioned "Background" is amended by deleting "49 U.S.C. § 1472(l)(2)" and inserting in lieu thereof "49 U.S.C. § 46505(c)".

Section 2Q2.1 is amended in the title by deleting "Specially Protected Fish, Wildlife, and Plants; Smuggling and Otherwise Unlawfully Dealing in Fish, Wildlife, and Plants", and inserting in lieu thereof "Offenses Involving Fish, Wildlife, and Plants".

Section 3D1.2(d) is amended in the third paragraph by deleting the semicolon immediately following "2B2.3" and inserting in lieu thereof a comma; and by deleting "2H1.2, 2H1.3, 2H1.4,".

The Commentary following § 3D1.5 captioned "Illustrations of the Operation of the Multiple-Count Rules" is amended in Illustration 3 by deleting "seventy-five" and inserting in lieu thereof "75"; by deleting "heroin equivalents" and inserting in lieu thereof "marihuana equivalents (using the Drug Equivalency Tables in the Commentary to § 2D1.1)"; by deleting "forty-six grams of heroin" and inserting in lieu thereof "46 kilograms of marihuana"; by deleting "thirty grams of heroin" and inserting in lieu thereof "30 kilograms of marihuana; and the third count translates into 75 kilograms of marihuana"; and by deleting "151 grams of heroin" and inserting in lieu thereof "151 kilograms of marihuana".

The Commentary to § 8C2.4 captioned "Application Notes" is amended by deleting:

> "5. Special instructions regarding the determination of the base fine are contained in: § 2B4.1 (Bribery in Procurement of Bank Loan and Other Commercial Bribery); § 2C1.1 (Offering, Giving, Soliciting, or Receiving a Bribe; Extortion Under Color of Official Right); § 2C1.2 (Offering, Giving, Soliciting, or Receiving a Gratuity); § 2E5.1 (Offering, Accepting, or Soliciting a Bribe or Gratuity Affecting the Operation of an Employee Welfare or Pension Benefit Plan; Prohibited Payments or Lending of Money by Employer or Agent to Employees, Representatives, or Labor Organizations); § 2R1.1 (Bid-Rigging, Price-Fixing or Market-Allocation Agreements Among Competitors); § 2S1.1 (Laundering of Monetary Instruments); § 2S1.2 (Engaging in Monetary Transactions in Property Derived from Specified Unlawful Activity); and § 2S1.3 (Structuring Transactions to Evade Reporting Requirements; Failure to Report Cash or Monetary Transactions; Failure to File Currency and Monetary Instrument Report; Knowingly Filing False Reports).",

and inserting in lieu thereof:

> "5. Special instructions regarding the determination of the base fine are contained in §§ 2B4.1 (Bribery in Procurement of Bank Loan and Other Commercial Bribery); 2C1.1 (Offering, Giving, Soliciting, or Receiving a Bribe; Extortion Under Color of Official Right); 2C1.2 (Offering, Giving, Soliciting, or Receiving a Gratuity); 2E5.1 (Offering, Accepting, or Soliciting a Bribe or Gratuity Affecting the Operation of an Employee Welfare or Pension Benefit Plan; Prohibited Payments or Lending of Money by Employer or Agent to Employees, Representatives, or Labor Organizations); 2R1.1 (Bid-Rigging, Price-Fixing or Market-Allocation Agreements Among Competitors); 2S1.1 (Laundering of Monetary Instruments); and 2S1.2 (Engaging in Monetary Transactions in Property Derived from Specified Unlawful Activity).".

Reason for Amendment: This amendment makes Appendix A (Statutory Index) more comprehensive. References are added for new offenses enacted by the Violent Crime Control and Law Enforcement Act of 1994, Pub. L. 103-322, 108 Stat. 1796; the Fresh Cut Flowers and Fresh Cut Greens Promotion and Information Act of 1993, Pub. L. 103-190, 107 Stat. 2266; the Food Stamp Program Improvements Act of 1994, Pub. L. 103-225, 108 Stat. 106; the Social Security Independence and Program Improvements Act of 1994, Pub. L. 103-296 108 Stat. 1464; the Domestic Chemical Diversion Act of 1993, Pub. L. 103-200, 107 Stat. 2333; and the International Parental Kidnapping Crime Act of 1993, Pub. L. 103-173, 107 Stat. 1998. In addition, the amendment conforms Appendix A to other statutory revisions; revises the titles of §§ 2D3.1 (Regulatory Offenses Involving Registration Numbers; Unlawful Advertising Relating to Schedule I Substances; Attempt or Conspiracy), 2D3.2 (Regulatory Offenses Involving Controlled Substances or Listed Chemicals; Attempt or Conspiracy), and 2Q2.1 (Offenses Involving Fish, Wildlife, and Plants) to better reflect their scope; conforms Chapter One, Part A, Subpart (4)(d), §§ 1B1.5 (Interpretation of References to Other Offense Guidelines), 2A5.1 (Aircraft Piracy or Attempted Aircraft Piracy), 2A5.2 (Interference with Flight Crew Member or Flight Attendant), 2A5.3 (Committing Certain Crimes Aboard Aircraft), 2H2.1 (Obstructing an Election or Registration), 2K1.3 (Unlawful Receipt, Possession, or Transportation of Explosive Materials; Prohibited Transactions Involving Explosive Materials), 2K1.5 (Possessing Dangerous Weapons or Materials While Boarding or Aboard an Aircraft), 3D1.2 (Groups of Closely Related Counts), the Illustrations of the Operation of the Multiple-Count Rules following § 3D1.5 (Determining the Total Punishment), and § 8C2.4 (Base Fine) to revisions made by guideline or statutory amendments; and deletes obsolete background commentary in §§ 2C1.2 (Offering, Giving, Soliciting, or Receiving a Gratuity), 2C1.3 (Conflict of Interest), 2D3.1, and 2D3.2.

Effective Date: The effective date of this amendment is November 1, 1995.

535. Amendment: Section 5G1.3 is amended by deleting:

"(c) (Policy Statement) In any other case, the sentence for the instant offense shall be imposed to run consecutively to the prior undischarged term of imprisonment to the extent necessary to achieve a reasonable incremental punishment for the instant offense.",

and inserting in lieu thereof:

"(c) (Policy Statement) In any other case, the sentence for the instant offense may be imposed to run concurrently, partially concurrently, or consecutively to the prior undischarged term of imprisonment to achieve a reasonable punishment for the instant offense.".

The Commentary to § 5G1.3 captioned "Application Notes" is amended in Note 1 by inserting "Consecutive sentence - subsection (a) cases." immediately before "Under"; and by deleting "where the instant offense (or any part thereof)" and inserting in lieu thereof "when the instant offense".

The Commentary to § 5G1.3 captioned "Application Notes" is amended by deleting:

"2. Subsection (b) (which may apply only if subsection (a) does not apply), addresses cases in which the conduct resulting in the undischarged term of imprisonment has been fully taken into account under § 1B1.3 (Relevant Conduct) in determining the offense level for the instant offense. This can occur, for example, where a defendant is prosecuted in both federal and state court, or in two or more federal jurisdictions, for the same criminal conduct or for different criminal transactions that were part of the same course of conduct.

When a sentence is imposed pursuant to subsection (b), the court should adjust for any term of imprisonment already served as a result of the conduct taken into account in determining the sentence for the instant offense. Example: The defendant has been convicted of a federal offense charging the sale of 30 grams of cocaine. Under § 1B1.3 (Relevant Conduct), the defendant is held accountable for the sale of an additional 15 grams of cocaine that is part of the same course of conduct for which the defendant has been convicted and sentenced in state court (the defendant received a nine-month sentence of imprisonment, of which he has served six months at the time of sentencing on the instant federal offense). The guideline range applicable to the defendant is 10-16 months (Chapter Two offense level of 14 for sale of 45 grams of cocaine; 2-level reduction for acceptance of responsibility; final offense level of 12; Criminal History Category I). The court determines that a sentence of 13 months provides the appropriate total punishment. Because the defendant has already served six months on the related state charge, a sentence of seven months, imposed to run concurrently with the remainder of the defendant's state sentence, achieves this result. For clarity, the court should note on the Judgment in a Criminal Case Order that the sentence imposed is not a departure from the guidelines because the defendant has been credited for guideline purposes under § 5G1.3(b) with six months served in state custody.

3. Where the defendant is subject to an undischarged term of imprisonment in circumstances other than those set forth in subsections (a) or (b), subsection (c) applies and the court shall impose a consecutive sentence to the extent necessary to fashion a sentence resulting in a reasonable incremental punishment for the multiple offenses. In some circumstances, such incremental punishment can be achieved by the imposition of a sentence that is concurrent with the remainder of the unexpired term of imprisonment. In such cases, a consecutive sentence is not required. To the extent practicable, the court should consider a reasonable incremental penalty to be a sentence for the instant offense that results in a combined sentence of imprisonment that approximates the total punishment that would have been imposed under § 5G1.2 (Sentencing on Multiple Counts of Conviction) had all of the offenses been federal offenses for which sentences were being imposed at the same time. It is recognized that this determination frequently will require an approximation. Where the defendant is serving a term of imprisonment for a state offense, the information available may permit only a rough estimate of the total punishment that would have been imposed under the guidelines. Where the offense resulting in the undischarged term of imprisonment is a federal offense for which a guideline determination has previously been made, the task will be somewhat more straightforward, although even in such cases a precise determination may not be possible.

It is not intended that the above methodology be applied in a manner that unduly complicates or prolongs the sentencing process. Additionally, this methodology does not, itself, require the court to depart from the guideline range established for the instant federal offense. Rather, this methodology is meant to assist the court in determining the appropriate sentence (e.g., the appropriate point within the applicable guideline range, whether to order the sentence to run concurrently or consecutively to the undischarged term of imprisonment, or whether a departure is warranted). Generally, the court may achieve an appropriate sentence through its determination of an appropriate point within the applicable guideline range for the instant federal offense, combined with its determination of whether that sentence will run concurrently or consecutively to the undischarged term of imprisonment.

Illustrations of the Application of Subsection (c):

(A) The guideline range applicable to the instant federal offense is 24-30 months. The court determines that a total punishment of 36 months' imprisonment would appropriately reflect the instant federal offense and the offense resulting in the undischarged term of imprisonment. The undischarged term of imprisonment is an indeterminate sentence of imprisonment with a 60-month maximum. At the time of sentencing on the instant federal offense, the defendant has served ten months on the undischarged term of imprisonment. In this case, a sentence of 26 months' imprisonment to be served concurrently with the remainder of the undischarged term of imprisonment would (1) be within the guideline range for the instant federal offense, and (2) achieve an appropriate total punishment (36 months).

(B) The applicable guideline range for the instant federal offense is 24-30 months. The court determines that a total punishment of 36 months' imprisonment would appropriately reflect the instant federal offense and the offense resulting in the undischarged term of imprisonment. The undischarged term of imprisonment is a six-month determinate sentence. At the time of sentencing on the instant federal offense, the defendant has served three months on the undischarged term of imprisonment. In this case, a sentence of 30 months' imprisonment to be served consecutively to the undischarged term of imprisonment would (1) be within the guideline range for the instant federal offense, and (2) achieve an appropriate total punishment (36 months).

(C) The applicable guideline range for the instant federal offense is 24-30 months. The court determines that a total punishment of 60 months' imprisonment would appropriately reflect the instant federal offense and the offense resulting in the undischarged term of imprisonment. The undischarged term of imprisonment is a 12-month determinate sentence. In this case, a sentence of 30 months' imprisonment to be served consecutively to the undischarged term of imprisonment would be the greatest sentence imposable without departure for the instant federal offense.

(D) The applicable guideline range for the instant federal offense is 24-30 months. The court determines that a total punishment of 36 months' imprisonment would appropriately reflect the instant federal offense and the offense resulting in the undischarged term of imprisonment. The undischarged term of imprisonment is an indeterminate sentence with a 60-month maximum. At the time of sentencing on the instant federal offense, the defendant has served 22 months on the undischarged term of imprisonment. In this case, a sentence of 24 months to be served concurrently with the remainder of the undischarged term of imprisonment would be the lowest sentence imposable without departure for the instant federal offense.

Amendment 535 APPENDIX C - VOLUME I November 1, 2013

    4.   If the defendant was on federal or state probation, parole, or supervised release at the time of the instant offense, and has had such probation, parole, or supervised release revoked, the sentence for the instant offense should be imposed to be served consecutively to the term imposed for the violation of probation, parole, or supervised release in order to provide an incremental penalty for the violation of probation, parole, or supervised release (in accord with the policy expressed in §§ 7B1.3 and 7B1.4)",

and inserting in lieu thereof:

"2.   <u>Adjusted concurrent sentence - subsection (b) cases</u>. When a sentence is imposed pursuant to subsection (b), the court should adjust the sentence for any period of imprisonment already served as a result of the conduct taken into account in determining the guideline range for the instant offense if the court determines that period of imprisonment will not be credited to the federal sentence by the Bureau of Prisons. <u>Example</u>: The defendant is convicted of a federal offense charging the sale of 30 grams of cocaine. Under § 1B1.3 (Relevant Conduct), the defendant is held accountable for the sale of an additional 15 grams of cocaine, an offense for which the defendant has been convicted and sentenced in state court. The defendant received a nine-month sentence of imprisonment for the state offense and has served six months on that sentence at the time of sentencing on the instant federal offense. The guideline range applicable to the defendant is 10-16 months (Chapter Two offense level of 14 for sale of 45 grams of cocaine; 2-level reduction for acceptance of responsibility; final offense level of 12; Criminal History Category I). The court determines that a sentence of 13 months provides the appropriate total punishment. Because the defendant has already served six months on the related state charge as of the date of sentencing on the instant federal offense, a sentence of seven months, imposed to run concurrently with the three months remaining on the defendant's state sentence, achieves this result. For clarity, the court should note on the Judgment in a Criminal Case Order that the sentence imposed is not a departure from the guideline range because the defendant has been credited for guideline purposes under § 5G1.3(b) with six months served in state custody that will not be credited to the federal sentence under 18 U.S.C. § 3585(b).

3.   <u>Concurrent or consecutive sentence - subsection (c) cases</u>. In circumstances not covered under subsection (a) or (b), subsection (c) applies. Under this subsection, the court may impose a sentence concurrently, partially concurrently, or consecutively. To achieve a reasonable punishment and avoid unwarranted disparity, the court should consider the factors set forth in 18 U.S.C. § 3584 (referencing 18 U.S.C. § 3553(a)) and be cognizant of:

(a)   the type (<u>e.g.</u>, determinate, indeterminate/parolable) and length of the prior undischarged sentence;

(b)   the time served on the undischarged sentence and the time likely to be served before release;

(c)   the fact that the prior undischarged sentence may have been imposed in state court rather than federal court, or at a different time before the same or different federal court; and

(d)   any other circumstance relevant to the determination of an appropriate sentence for the instant offense.

4. Partially concurrent sentence. In some cases under subsection (c), a partially concurrent sentence may achieve most appropriately the desired result. To impose a partially concurrent sentence, the court may provide in the Judgment in a Criminal Case Order that the sentence for the instant offense shall commence (A) when the defendant is released from the prior undischarged sentence, or (B) on a specified date, whichever is earlier. This order provides for a fully consecutive sentence if the defendant is released on the undischarged term of imprisonment on or before the date specified in the order, and a partially concurrent sentence if the defendant is not released on the undischarged term of imprisonment by that date.

5. Complex situations. Occasionally, the court may be faced with a complex case in which a defendant may be subject to multiple undischarged terms of imprisonment that seemingly call for the application of different rules. In such a case, the court may exercise its discretion in accordance with subsection (c) to fashion a sentence of appropriate length and structure it to run in any appropriate manner to achieve a reasonable punishment for the instant offense.

6. Revocations. If the defendant was on federal or state probation, parole, or supervised release at the time of the instant offense, and has had such probation, parole, or supervised release revoked, the sentence for the instant offense should be imposed to run consecutively to the term imposed for the violation of probation, parole, or supervised release in order to provide an incremental penalty for the violation of probation, parole, or supervised release. See § 7B1.3 (Revocation of Probation or Supervised Release) (setting forth a policy that any imprisonment penalty imposed for violating probation or supervised release should be consecutive to any sentence of imprisonment being served or subsequently imposed).".

The Commentary to § 5G1.3 captioned "Background" is amended by deleting:

"This guideline provides direction to the court when a term of imprisonment is imposed on a defendant who is already subject to an undischarged term of imprisonment. See 18 U.S.C. § 3584. Except in the cases in which subsection (a) applies, this guideline is intended to result in an appropriate incremental punishment for the instant offense that most nearly approximates the sentence that would have been imposed had all the sentences been imposed at the same time.",

and inserting in lieu thereof:

"In a case in which a defendant is subject to an undischarged sentence of imprisonment, the court generally has authority to impose an imprisonment sentence on the current offense to run concurrently with or consecutively to the prior undischarged term. 18 U.S.C. § 3584(a). Exercise of that authority, however, is predicated on the court's consideration of the factors listed in 18 U.S.C. § 3553(a), including any applicable guidelines or policy statements issued by the Sentencing Commission.".

Reason for Amendment: This is a two-part amendment. First, this amendment clarifies the application of subsections (a) and (b) of this guideline. Second, in circumstances covered by the policy statement in subsection (c), this amendment affords the sentencing court additional flexibility to impose, as appropriate, a consecutive, concurrent, or partially concurrent sentence in order to achieve a reasonable punishment for the instant offense.

Authority to impose a partially concurrent sentence is found in the Sentencing Reform Act

Amendment 535   APPENDIX C - VOLUME I   November 1, 2013

of 1984 (SRA). In enacting 28 U.S.C. § 994(l)(1), Congress contemplated that 18 U.S.C. § 3584 would allow imposition of partially concurrent sentences, in addition to fully concurrent or consecutive sentences. ("It is the Committee's intent that, to the extent feasible, the sentences for each of the multiple offenses be determined separately and the degree to which they should overlap be specified.") S. Rep. No. 225, 98th Cong., 1st Sess. 177 (1983). Without the ability to fashion such a sentence, the instruction to the Commission in 28 U.S.C. § 994(l)(1) to provide a reasonable incremental penalty for additional offenses could not be implemented successfully in certain situations, particularly when the defendant's release date on an undischarged term of imprisonment cannot be determined readily in advance (e.g., in the case of an indeterminate sentence subject to parole release).

Prior to the SRA, only the Bureau of Prisons had the authority to commence a federal sentence prior to the defendant's release from imprisonment on a state sentence. See, e.g., United States v. Segal, 549 F.2d 1293, 1301 (9th Cir. 1977). SRA legislative history pertaining to 18 U.S.C. § 3584 indicates that this new section was intended to authorize imposition of a federal prison sentence to run concurrently or consecutively to a state prison sentence. "This . . . [section 3584] changes the law that now applies to a person sentenced for a Federal offense who is already serving a term of imprisonment for a state offense." S. Rep. No. 225, supra at 127. "Thus, it is intended that this provision be construed contrary to the holding in United States v. Segal. . ." Id. (at 127 n.314). See United States v. Hardesty, 958 F.2d 910, 914 (stating that, under section 3584, "Congress has expressly granted federal judges the discretion to impose a sentence concurrent to a state prison term"), aff'd en banc, 977 F.2d 1347 (9th Cir. 1992).

Effective Date: The effective date of this amendment is November 1, 1995.

536. **Amendment:** Section 1B1.10(c) is amended by deleting "and 506" and inserting in lieu thereof "505, 506, and 516".

The Commentary to § 1B1.10 captioned "Background" is amended in the fourth paragraph by inserting an asterisk immediately following "old guidelines"; and by inserting, as a note, following the Background Commentary:

"*So in original. Probably should be 'to fall above the amended guidelines'.".

Reason for Amendment: This amendment expands the listing in § 1B1.10(d) to implement the directive in 28 U.S.C. § 994(u) in respect to guideline amendments that may be considered for retroactive application. The amendment also makes an editorial addition to the Commentary to § 1B1.10 (Retroactivity of Amended Guideline Range).

Effective Date: The effective date of this amendment is November 1, 1995.

537. **Amendment:** Section 2G2.1(a) is amended by deleting "25" and inserting in lieu thereof "27".

Section 2G2.1(b) is amended by deleting:

"(1) If the offense involved a minor under the age of twelve years, increase by 4 levels; otherwise, if the offense involved a minor under the age of sixteen years, increase by 2 levels.",

and inserting in lieu thereof:

"(1) If the offense involved a victim who had (A) not attained the age of twelve years, increase by 4 levels; or (B) attained the age of twelve years but not attained the age of sixteen years, increase by 2 levels.".

Section 2G2.1(b) is amended by inserting after subdivision (2) the following additional subdivision:

> "(3) If a computer was used to solicit participation by or with a minor in sexually explicit conduct for the purpose of producing sexually explicit material, increase by 2 levels.".

The Commentary to § 2G2.1 captioned "Statutory Provisions" is amended by deleting "§ 2251(a), (b), (c)(1)(B)" and inserting in lieu thereof "§§ 2251(a), (b), (c)(1)(B), 2258(a), (b)".

Section 2G2.2(a) is amended by deleting "15" and inserting in lieu thereof "17".

Section 2G2.2(b) is amended by inserting after subdivision (4) the following additional subdivision:

> "(5) If a computer was used for the transmission of the material or a notice or advertisement of the material, increase by 2 levels.".

The Commentary to § 2G2.2 captioned "Statutory Provisions" is amended by inserting ", 2258(a), (b)" immediately before the period.

The Commentary to § 2G2.2 captioned "Application Notes" is amended by deleting:

> "1. 'Distribution,' as used in this guideline, includes any act related to distribution for pecuniary gain, including production, transportation, and possession with intent to distribute.
>
> 2. 'Sexually explicit conduct,' as used in this guideline, has the meaning set forth in 18 U.S.C. § 2256.",

and inserting in lieu thereof:

> "1. For purposes of this guideline—
>
> 'Distribution' includes any act related to distribution for pecuniary gain, including production, transportation, and possession with intent to distribute.
>
> 'Pattern of activity involving the sexual abuse or exploitation of a minor' means any combination of two or more separate instances of the sexual abuse or sexual exploitation of a minor by the defendant, whether or not the abuse or exploitation (A) occurred during the course of the offense, (B) involved the same or different victims, or (C) resulted in a conviction for such conduct.
>
> 'Sexual abuse or exploitation' means conduct constituting criminal sexual abuse of a minor, sexual exploitation of a minor, abusive sexual contact of a minor, any similar offense under state law, or an attempt or conspiracy to commit any of the above offenses. 'Sexual abuse or exploitation' does not include trafficking in material relating to the sexual abuse or exploitation of a minor.
>
> 'Sexually explicit conduct' has the meaning set forth in 18 U.S.C. § 2256.
>
> 2. If the defendant engaged in the sexual abuse or exploitation of a minor at any time (whether or not such abuse or exploitation occurred during the

Amendment 537 APPENDIX C - VOLUME I November 1, 2013

course of the offense or resulted in a conviction for such conduct) and subsection (b)(4) does not apply, an upward departure may be warranted. In addition, an upward departure may be warranted if the defendant received an enhancement under subsection (b)(4) but that enhancement does not adequately reflect the seriousness of the sexual abuse or exploitation involved.

Prior convictions taken into account under subsection (b)(4) are also counted for purposes of determining criminal history points pursuant to Chapter Four, Part A (Criminal History).".

The Commentary to § 2G2.2 captioned "Application Notes" is amended in Note 3 by deleting "(c)(1)" and inserting in lieu thereof "subsection (c)(1)".

The Commentary to § 2G2.2 captioned "Application Notes" is amended by deleting Notes 4 and 5 as follows:

"4. 'Pattern of activity involving the sexual abuse or exploitation of a minor,' for the purposes of subsection (b)(4), means any combination of two or more separate instances of the sexual abuse or the sexual exploitation of a minor, whether involving the same or different victims.

5. If the defendant sexually exploited or abused a minor at any time, whether or not such sexual abuse occurred during the course of the offense, an upward departure may be warranted. In determining the extent of such a departure, the court should take into consideration the offense levels provided in §§ 2A3.1, 2A3.2, and 2A3.4 most commensurate with the defendant's conduct, as well as whether the defendant has received an enhancement under subsection (b)(4) on account of such conduct.".

Section 2G2.4(a) is amended by deleting "13" and inserting in lieu thereof "15".

Section 2G2.4(b) is amended by inserting after subdivision (2) the following additional subdivision:

"(3) If the defendant's possession of the material resulted from the defendant's use of a computer, increase by 2 levels.".

Reason for Amendment: This is a four-part amendment. First, the amendment implements the congressional directives in section 2 of the Sex Crimes Against Children Prevention Act of 1995, Pub. L. 104-71, 109 Stat. 774, by providing a two-level enhancement above the currently prescribed offense level for offenses involving the sexual exploitation of minors. The two-level enhancement is provided in the base offense levels under §§ 2G2.1, 2G2.2, and 2G2.4.

Second, the amendment implements the congressional directive in section 3 of the above-noted Act by providing a two-level enhancement for offenses involving the sexual exploitation of a minor if a computer was used to transmit certain notices or advertisements of material involving minors engaged in sexually explicit conduct or to transport or ship that material. The enhancement in § 2G2.2(b)(5) applies to the transmission of the material or of the notice or advertisement of the material. The enhancement in § 2G2.4(b)(3) applies only if the defendant's possession of the material resulted from the defendant's use of a computer. In addition to these congressionally directed enhancements, the amendment adds a two-level enhancement under § 2G2.1(b)(3) if a computer was used to solicit participation in sexually explicit conduct by or with a minor for the purpose of producing sexually explicit material.

Third, the amendment revises the Commentary to § 2G2.2 to consolidate the definitions applicable to this guideline in the first application note and address several additional issues. The amendment revises the definition of "pattern of activity involving the sexual abuse or exploitation of a minor" to clarify that "sexual abuse or exploitation," for purposes of § 2G2.2(b)(4), requires that the defendant personally had participated in such conduct. The amendment defines "sexual abuse or exploitation" to mean conduct constituting criminal sexual abuse, sexual exploitation, or abusive sexual contact and to exclude trafficking in child pornography. These revisions are consistent with United States v. Chapman, 60 F.3d 894 (1st Cir. 1995) and United States v. Ketcham, 80 F.3d 789 (3d Cir. 1996), both of which held that the defendant's transportation or distribution of child pornography is not sexual exploitation within the meaning of the "pattern of activity" enhancement in § 2G2.2(b)(4). In addition, the amendment clarifies that the "pattern of activity" may include acts of sexual abuse or exploitation that were not committed during the course of the offense or that did not result in a conviction. This revision responds in part to the holding in Chapman, 60 F.3d at 901, that the "pattern of activity" enhancement is inapplicable to past sexual abuse or exploitation unrelated to the offense of conviction. The amended language expressly provides that such conduct may be considered. Accordingly, the conduct considered for purposes of the "pattern of activity" enhancement is broader than the scope of relevant conduct typically considered under § 1B1.3 (Relevant Conduct). In addition, the amendment provides that an upward departure may be warranted if the defendant (1) did not engage in a "pattern of activity" but nevertheless abused a minor at any time, or (2) engaged in a "pattern of activity" but the enhancement does not adequately reflect the seriousness of the sexual abuse or exploitation. In addition, the amendment clarifies that prior convictions counted as part of the "pattern of activity" also may be counted as part of the defendant's criminal history under Chapter Four, if those convictions meet the criteria set forth in the relevant guidelines of that chapter.

Fourth, the amendment makes the "Statutory Provisions" in the Commentary to §§ 2G2.1 and 2G2.2 more comprehensive by adding 18 U.S.C. § 2258(a) and (b) to the list of statutory provisions covered by those guidelines.

Effective Date: The effective date of this amendment is November 1, 1996.

538. **Amendment:** Sections 2G1.1 and 2G1.2 are deleted in their entirety as follows:

"§ 2G1.1. Transportation for the Purpose of Prostitution or Prohibited Sexual Conduct

(a) Base Offense Level: 14

(b) Specific Offense Characteristic

(1) If the offense involved the use of physical force, or coercion by threats or drugs or in any manner, increase by 4 levels.

(c) Special Instruction

(1) If the offense involved the transportation of more than one person, Chapter Three, Part D (Multiple Counts) shall be applied as if the transportation of each person had been contained in a separate count of conviction.

Commentary

Statutory Provisions: 8 U.S.C. § 1328; 18 U.S.C. §§ 2421, 2422.

Application Notes:

1. The base offense level assumes that the offense was committed for profit. In the infrequent case where the defendant did not commit the offense for profit and the offense did not involve physical force or coercion, the Commission recommends a downward departure of 8 levels.

2. The enhancement for physical force, or coercion, anticipates no bodily injury. If bodily injury results, an upward departure may be warranted. See Chapter Five, Part K (Departures).

3. 'Coercion,' as used in this guideline, includes any form of conduct that negates the voluntariness of the behavior of the person transported. This factor would apply, for example, where the ability of the person being transported to appraise or control conduct was substantially impaired by drugs or alcohol. In the case of transportation involving an adult, rather than a minor, this characteristic generally will not apply where the alcohol or drug was voluntarily taken.

4. For the purposes of § 3B1.1 (Aggravating Role), the persons transported are considered participants only if they assisted in the unlawful transportation of others.

5. For the purposes of Chapter Three, Part D (Multiple Counts), each person transported is to be treated as a separate victim. Consequently, multiple counts involving the transportation of different persons are not to be grouped together under § 3D1.2 (Groups of Closely Related Counts). Special instruction (c)(1) directs that if the relevant conduct of an offense of conviction includes more than one person being transported, whether specifically cited in the count of conviction or not, each such person shall be treated as if contained in a separate count of conviction.

§ 2G1.2. Transportation of a Minor for the Purpose of Prostitution or Prohibited Sexual Conduct

    (a) Base Offense Level: 16

    (b) Specific Offense Characteristics

        (1) If the offense involved the use of physical force, or coercion by threats or drugs or in any manner, increase by 4 levels.

        (2) If the offense involved the transportation of a minor under the age of twelve years, increase by 4 levels.

        (3) If the offense involved the transportation of a minor at least twelve years of age but under the age of sixteen years, increase by 2 levels.

        (4) If the defendant was a parent, relative, or legal guardian of the minor involved in the offense, or if the minor was

otherwise in the custody, care, or supervisory control of the defendant, increase by 2 levels.

(c) Cross References

(1) If the offense involved causing, transporting, permitting, or offering or seeking by notice or advertisement, a minor to engage in sexually explicit conduct for the purpose of producing a visual depiction of such conduct, apply § 2G2.1 (Sexually Exploiting a Minor by Production of Sexually Explicit Visual or Printed Material; Custodian Permitting Minor to Engage in Sexually Explicit Conduct; Advertisement for Minors to Engage in Production).

(2) If the offense involved criminal sexual abuse, attempted criminal sexual abuse, or assault with intent to commit criminal sexual abuse, apply § 2A3.1 (Criminal Sexual Abuse; Attempt to Commit Criminal Sexual Abuse).

(3) If neither subsection (c)(1) nor (c)(2) is applicable, and the offense did not involve transportation for the purpose of prostitution, apply § 2A3.2 (Criminal Sexual Abuse of a Minor or Attempt to Commit Such Acts) or § 2A3.4 (Abusive Sexual Contact or Attempt to Commit Abusive Sexual Contact), as appropriate.

(d) Special Instruction

(1) If the offense involved the transportation of more than one person, Chapter Three, Part D (Multiple Counts) shall be applied as if the transportation of each person had been contained in a separate count of conviction.

Commentary

Statutory Provisions: 8 U.S.C. § 1328; 18 U.S.C. §§ 2421, 2422, 2423.

Application Notes:

1. For the purposes of Chapter Three, Part D (Multiple Counts), each person transported is to be treated as a separate victim. Consequently, multiple counts involving the transportation of different persons are not to be grouped together under § 3D1.2 (Groups of Closely Related Counts). Special instruction (d)(1) directs that if the relevant conduct of an offense of conviction includes more than one person being transported, whether specifically cited in the count of conviction or not, each such person shall be treated as if contained in a separate count of conviction.

2. The enhancement for physical force, or coercion, anticipates no bodily injury. If bodily injury results, an upward departure may be warranted. See Chapter Five, Part K (Departures).

3. 'Coercion,' as used in this guideline, includes any form of conduct that negates the voluntariness of the behavior of the person transported. This factor would apply, for example, where the ability of the person being

Amendment 538 APPENDIX C - VOLUME I November 1, 2013

>   transported to appraise or control conduct was substantially impaired by drugs or alcohol.

> 4. 'Sexually explicit conduct,' as used in this guideline, has the meaning set forth in 18 U.S.C. § 2256.

> 5. Subsection (b)(4) is intended to have broad application and includes offenses involving a minor entrusted to the defendant, whether temporarily or permanently. For example, teachers, day care providers, baby-sitters, or other temporary caretakers are among those who would be subject to this enhancement. In determining whether to apply this adjustment, the court should look to the actual relationship that existed between the defendant and the child and not simply to the legal status of the defendant-child relationship.

> 6. If the adjustment in subsection (b)(4) applies, do not apply § 3B1.3 (Abuse of Position of Trust or Use of Special Skill).

> 7. The cross reference in subsection (c)(1) is to be construed broadly to include all instances where the offense involved employing, using, persuading, inducing, enticing, coercing, transporting, permitting, or offering or seeking by notice or advertisement, a minor to engage in sexually explicit conduct for the purpose of producing any visual depiction of such conduct.".

A replacement guideline with accompanying commentary is inserted as § 2G1.1 (Promoting Prostitution or Prohibited Sexual Conduct).

Chapter 1, Part A, Subpart 4(b) is amended in the fourth paragraph by deleting:

> "For example, the Commentary to § 2G1.1 (Transportation for the Purpose of Prostitution or Prohibited Sexual Conduct) recommends a downward departure of eight levels where a commercial purpose was not involved.".

Section 3D1.2(d) is amended in the third paragraph by deleting "2G1.2,".

Reason for Amendment: This is a three-part amendment. First, this amendment consolidates §§ 2G1.1 (Transportation for the Purpose of Prostitution or Prohibited Sexual Conduct) and 2G1.2 (Transportation of a Minor for the Purpose of Prostitution or Prohibited Sexual Conduct) in furtherance of the Commission's goal of simplifying the operation of the guidelines. The enhancement pertaining to the age of the victim in subsection (b)(2) is increased by two levels to reflect the two-level higher base offense level of former § 2G1.2. The consolidated offense guideline incorporates the cross references of § 2G1.2, provides a definition of the term "victim," and clarifies that the guideline covers offenses under 18 U.S.C. § 2423(a), but not 18 U.S.C. § 2423(b) (a statutory provision referenced in Appendix A to §§ 2A3.1, 2A3.2, and 2A3.3).

Second, this amendment implements the congressional directive in section 4 of the Sex Crimes Against Children Prevention Act of 1995, Pub. L. 104-71, 109 Stat. 774, by providing a three-level increase in the enhancement for offenses involving the transportation of minors with intent to engage in prostitution or other prohibited sexual conduct. This three-level increase is provided in the specific offense characteristic pertaining to the age of the victim in subsection (b)(2) and is in addition to the two-level increase in this enhancement described in the first part of this amendment.

Third, this amendment addresses 18 U.S.C. § 2422(b), a new offense created by section 508 of the Telecommunications Act of 1996, Pub. L. 104-104, 110 Stat. 56. That offense makes it unlawful, in interstate or foreign commerce, including through the mail, or within the special maritime or territorial jurisdiction of the United States, to knowingly persuade, induce, entice, or coerce an individual under the age of 18 years to engage in prostitution or other prohibited sexual conduct. The amendment brings this new offense within the scope of the consolidated guideline. As revised, the guideline is broadly applicable to offenses that involve "promoting prostitution or prohibited sexual conduct." That term is defined to encompass conduct covered by the new Telecommunications Act offense as well as conduct previously covered by the guideline; i.e., transporting a person, or inducing a person to travel, for the purpose of prostitution or other prohibited sexual conduct.

Effective Date: The effective date of this amendment is November 1, 1996.

539. **Amendment:** Section 3A1.4 is amended in the title by deleting "International".

Section 3A1.4(a) is amended by deleting "international" and inserting in lieu thereof "a federal crime of".

The Commentary to § 3A1.4 captioned "Application Notes" is amended in Note 1 in the first sentence by deleting "international" and inserting in lieu thereof "a federal crime of"; and in the second sentence by deleting "International" and inserting in lieu thereof "Federal crime of", and by deleting "2331" and inserting in lieu thereof "2332b(g)".

Reason for Amendment: This amendment implements section 730 of the Antiterrorism and Effective Death Penalty Act of 1996, Pub. L. 104-132, 110 Stat. 1303. That section requires the Commission to amend the sentencing guidelines so that the adjustment in § 3A1.4 (relating to international terrorism) applies more broadly to a "Federal crime of terrorism," as defined in 18 U.S.C. § 2332b(g), and provides that the Commission shall have the authority to promulgate this amendment as an emergency amendment under procedures set forth in section 21(a) of the Sentencing Act of 1987.

Effective Date: The effective date of this amendment is November 1, 1996.

540. **Amendment:** Appendix A (Statutory Index) is amended by inserting at the appropriate place by title and section:

"8 U.S.C. § 1255a(c)(6)	2L2.1, 2L2.2",
"16 U.S.C. § 1372	2Q2.1",
"16 U.S.C. § 1387	2Q2.1",
"18 U.S.C. § 474A	2B5.1, 2F1.1",
"18 U.S.C. § 842(l)-(o)	2K1.3",
"18 U.S.C. § 844(b)	2K1.1",
"18 U.S.C. § 844(g)	2K1.3",
"18 U.S.C. § 844(n)	2X1.1",
"18 U.S.C. § 844(o)	2K2.4",
"18 U.S.C. § 956	2A1.5, 2X1.1",
"18 U.S.C. § 1073	2J1.5, 2J1.6",
"18 U.S.C. § 2319A	2B5.3",
"21 U.S.C. § 843(a)(4)(A)	2D1.13",
"26 U.S.C. § 7212(b)	2B1.1, 2B2.1, 2B3.1",
"41 U.S.C. § 423(e)	2C1.1, 2C1.7, 2F1.1",
"49 U.S.C. § 11902	2B4.1",

"49 U.S.C. § 11903	2F1.1",
"49 U.S.C. § 14904	2B4.1",
"49 U.S.C. § 14103(b)	2B1.1",
"49 U.S.C. § 14905(b)	2B1.1",
"49 U.S.C. § 14909	2J1.1",
"49 U.S.C. § 14912	2F1.1",
"49 U.S.C. § 16102	2F1.1",
"49 U.S.C. § 16104	2J1.1".

Appendix A (Statutory Index) is amended in the line referenced to 8 U.S.C. § 1328, by deleting ", 2G1.2";

in the line referenced to 18 U.S.C. § 32(a),(b) by inserting ", 2X1.1" immediately following "2K1.4";

in the line referenced to 18 U.S.C. § 37 by inserting ", 2X1.1" immediately following "2K1.4";

in the line referenced to 18 U.S.C. § 115(a) by inserting ", 2X1.1" immediately following "2A6.1";

in the line referenced to 18 U.S.C. § 115(b)(2) by inserting ", 2X1.1" immediately following "2A4.1";

in the line referenced to 18 U.S.C. § 115 (b)(3) by inserting ", 2X1.1" immediately following "2A2.1";

in the line referenced to 18 U.S.C. § 491 by inserting "2B5.1," immediately before "2F1.1";

in the line referenced to 18 U.S.C. § 752 by inserting ", 2X3.1" immediately following "2P1.1";

in the line referenced to 18 U.S.C. § 1203 by inserting ", 2X1.1" immediately following "2A4.1";

in the line referenced to 18 U.S.C. § 2280 by inserting ", 2X1.1" immediately following "2K1.4";

in the line referenced to 18 U.S.C. § 2281 by inserting ", 2X1.1" immediately following "2K1.4";

in the line referenced to 18 U.S.C. § 2421, by deleting ", 2G1.2";

in the line referenced to 18 U.S.C. § 2422, by deleting ", 2G1.2";

in the line referenced to 18 U.S.C. § 2423(a), by deleting "2G1.2" and inserting in lieu thereof "2G1.1";

by deleting:

"42 U.S.C. § 7413   2Q1.2, 2Q1.3",

and inserting in lieu thereof:

"42 U.S.C. § 7413(c)(1)-(4)	2Q1.2, 2Q1.3
42 U.S.C. § 7413(c)(5)	2Q1.1";

in the line referenced to 49 U.S.C. § 11904 by deleting "2B4.1" and inserting in lieu thereof "2F1.1 (2B4.1 for offenses committed prior to January 1, 1996)";

in the line referenced to 49 U.S.C. § 11907(a) by inserting "(for offenses committed prior to January 1, 1996)" immediately following "2B4.1";

in the line referenced to 49 U.S.C. § 11907(b) by inserting "(for offenses committed prior to January 1, 1996)" immediately following "2B4.1"; and

in the line referenced to 49 U.S.C. § 46502(a),(b) by inserting ", 2X1.1" immediately following "2A5.1".

The Commentary to § 3B1.4 captioned "Application Notes" is amended in Note 1 by deleting "processing" and inserting in lieu thereof "procuring".

The Commentary to § 5C1.2 captioned "Application Notes" is amended in Note 6 in the second sentence by deleting "a 'organizer," and inserting in lieu thereof "an 'organizer,".

Reason for Amendment: This amendment makes Appendix A (Statutory Index) more comprehensive. References are added for additional offenses, including offenses enacted by the Marine Mammal Protection Act Amendments of 1994, Pub. L. 103-238, 108 Stat. 532; the ICC Termination Act of 1995, Pub. L. 104-88, 109 Stat. 803; the National Defense Authorization Act for Fiscal Year 1996, Pub. L. 104-106, 110 Stat. 186; and the Antiterrorism and Effective Death Penalty Act of 1996, Pub. L. 104-132, 110 Stat. 1214. In addition, this amendment revises Appendix A to conform to the revision of existing statutes and reflect the consolidation of §§ 2G1.1 and 2G1.2. Finally, this amendment corrects clerical errors in §§ 3B1.4 and 5C1.2.

Effective Date: The effective date of this amendment is November 1, 1996.

541. **Amendment:** Section 2D1.11(d) is amended by deleting:

"(1)　List I Chemicals　　　　　　　　　　　　　　　　　　　　　　　　　　Level 28
17.8 KG or more of Benzaldehyde;
20 KG or more of Benzyl Cyanide;
20 KG or more of Ephedrine;
200 G or more of Ergonovine;
400 G or more of Ergotamine;
20 KG or more of Ethylamine;
44 KG or more of Hydriodic Acid;
320 KG or more of Isoafrole;
4 KG or more of Methylamine;
500 KG or more of N-Methylephedrine;
500 KG or more of N-Methylpseudoephedrine;
12.6 KG or more of Nitroethane;
200 KG or more of Norpseudoephedrine;
20 KG or more of Phenylacetic Acid;
200 KG or more of Phenylpropanolamine;
10 KG or more of Piperidine;
320 KG or more of Piperonal;
1.6 KG or more of Propionic Anhydride;

Amendment 541   APPENDIX C - VOLUME I   November 1, 2013

20 KG or more of Pseudoephedrine;
320 KG or more of Safrole;
400 KG or more of 3, 4-Methylenedioxyphenyl-2-propanone;

List II Chemicals
11 KG or more of Acetic Anhydride;
1175 KG or more of Acetone;
20 KG or more of Benzyl Chloride;
1075 KG or more of Ethyl Ether;
1200 KG or more of Methyl Ethyl Ketone;
10 KG or more of Potassium Permanganate;
1300 KG or more of Toluene.

(2) List I Chemicals   Level 26
At least 5.3 KG but less than 17.8 KG of Benzaldehyde;
At least 6 KG but less than 20 KG of Benzyl Cyanide;
At least 6 KG but less than 20 KG of Ephedrine;
At least 60 G but less than 200 G of Ergonovine;
At least 120 G but less than 400 G of Ergotamine;
At least 6 KG but less than 20 KG of Ethylamine;
At least 13.2 KG but less than 44 KG of Hydriodic Acid;
At least 96 KG but less than 320 KG of Isoafrole;
At least 1.2 KG but less than 4 KG of Methylamine;
At least 150 KG but less than 500 KG of N-Methylephedrine;
At least 150 KG but less than 500 KG of
N-Methylpseudoephedrine;
At least 3.8 KG but less than 12.6 KG of Nitroethane;
At least 60 KG but less than 200 KG of Norpseudoephedrine;
At least 6 KG but less than 20 KG of Phenylacetic Acid;
At least 60 KG but less than 200 KG of Phenylpropanolamine;
At least 3 KG but less than 10 KG of Piperidine;
At least 96 KG but less than 320 KG of Piperonal;
At least 480 G but less than 1.6 KG of Propionic Anhydride;
At least 6 KG but less than 20 KG of Pseudoephedrine;
At least 96 KG but less than 320 KG of Safrole;
At least 120 KG but less than 400 KG of 3,
4-Methylenedioxyphenyl-2-propanone;

List II Chemicals
At least 3.3 KG but less than 11 KG of Acetic Anhydride;
At least 352.5 KG but less than 1175 KG of Acetone;
At least 6 KG but less than 20 KG of Benzyl Chloride;
At least 322.5 KG but less than 1075 KG of Ethyl Ether;
At least 360 KG but less than 1200 KG of Methyl Ethyl Ketone;
At least 3 KG but less than 10 KG of Potassium Permanganate;
At least 390 KG but less than 1300 KG of Toluene.

(3) List I Chemicals   Level 24
At least 1.8 KG but less than 5.3 KG of Benzaldehyde;
At least 2 KG but less than 6 KG of Benzyl Cyanide;
At least 2 KG but less than 6 KG of Ephedrine;
At least 20 G but less than 60 G of Ergonovine;
At least 40 G but less than 120 G of Ergotamine;

At least 2 KG but less than 6 KG of Ethylamine;
At least 4.4 KG but less than 13.2 KG of Hydriodic Acid;
At least 32 KG but less than 96 KG of Isoafrole;
At least 400 G but less than 1.2 KG of Methylamine;
At least 50 KG but less than 150 KG of N-Methylephedrine;
At least 50 KG but less than 150 KG of
N-Methylpseudoephedrine;
At least 1.3 KG but less than 3.8 KG of Nitroethane;
At least 20 KG but less than 60 KG of Norpseudoephedrine;
At least 2 KG but less than 6 KG of Phenylacetic Acid;
At least 20 KG but less than 60 KG of Phenylpropanolamine;
At least 1 KG but less than 3 KG of Piperidine;
At least 32 KG but less than 96 KG of Piperonal;
At least 160 G but less than 480 G of Propionic Anhydride;
At least 2 KG but less than 6 KG of Pseudoephedrine;
At least 32 KG but less than 96 KG of Safrole;
At least 40 KG but less than 120 KG of 3,
4-Methylenedioxyphenyl-2-propanone;

List II Chemicals
At least 1.1 KG but less than 3.3 KG of Acetic Anhydride;
At least 117.5 KG but less than 352.5 KG of Acetone;
At least 2 KG but less than 6 KG of Benzyl Chloride;
At least 107.5 KG but less than 322.5 KG of Ethyl Ether;
At least 120 KG but less than 360 KG of Methyl Ethyl Ketone;
At least 1 KG but less than 3 KG of Potassium Permanganate;
At least 130 KG but less than 390 KG of Toluene.

(4) List I Chemicals   Level 22
At least 1.2 KG but less than 1.8 KG of Benzaldehyde;
At least 1.4 KG but less than 2 KG of Benzyl Cyanide;
At least 1.4 KG but less than 2 KG of Ephedrine;
At least 14 G but less than 20 G of Ergonovine;
At least 28 G but less than 40 G of Ergotamine;
At least 1.4 KG but less than 2 KG of Ethylamine;
At least 3.08 KG but less than 4.4 KG of Hydriodic Acid;
At least 22.4 KG but less than 32 KG of Isoafrole;
At least 280 G but less than 400 G of Methylamine;
At least 35 KG but less than 50 KG of N-Methylephedrine;
At least 35 KG but less than 50 KG of
N-Methylpseudoephedrine;
At least 879 G but less than 1.3 KG of Nitroethane;
At least 14 KG but less than 20 KG of Norpseudoephedrine;
At least 1.4 KG but less than 2 KG of Phenylacetic Acid;
At least 14 KG but less than 20 KG of Phenylpropanolamine;
At least 700 G but less than 1 KG of Piperidine;
At least 22.4 KG but less than 32 KG of Piperonal;
At least 112 G but less than 160 G of Propionic Anhydride;
At least 1.4 KG but less than 2 KG of Pseudoephedrine;
At least 22.4 KG but less than 32 KG of Safrole;
At least 28 KG but less than 40 KG of 3,
4-Methylenedioxyphenyl-2-propanone;

Amendment 541 APPENDIX C - VOLUME I November 1, 2013

List II Chemicals
At least 726 G but less than 1.1 KG of Acetic Anhydride;
At least 82.25 KG but less than 117.5 KG of Acetone;
At least 1.4 KG but less than 2 KG of Benzyl Chloride;
At least 75.25 KG but less than 107.5 KG of Ethyl Ether;
At least 84 KG but less than 120 KG of Methyl Ethyl Ketone;
At least 700 G but less than 1 KG of Potassium Permanganate;
At least 91 KG but less than 130 KG of Toluene.

(5) List I Chemicals Level 20
At least 712 G but less than 1.2 KG of Benzaldehyde;
At least 800 G but less than 1.4 KG of Benzyl Cyanide;
At least 800 G but less than 1.4 KG of Ephedrine;
At least 8 G but less than 14 G of Ergonovine;
At least 16 G but less than 28 G of Ergotamine;
At least 800 G but less than 1.4 KG of Ethylamine;
At least 1.76 KG but less than 3.08 KG of Hydriodic Acid;
At least 12.8 KG but less than 22.4 KG of Isoafrole;
At least 160 G but less than 280 G of Methylamine;
At least 20 KG but less than 35 KG of N-Methylephedrine;
At least 20 KG but less than 35 KG of
N-Methylpseudoephedrine;
At least 503 G but less than 879 G of Nitroethane;
At least 8 KG but less than 14 KG of Norpseudoephedrine;
At least 800 G but less than 1.4 KG of Phenylacetic Acid;
At least 8 KG but less than 14 KG of Phenylpropanolamine;
At least 400 G but less than 700 G of Piperidine;
At least 12.8 KG but less than 22.4 KG of Piperonal;
At least 64 G but less than 112 G of Propionic Anhydride;
At least 800 G but less than 1.4 KG of Pseudoephedrine;
At least 12.8 KG but less than 22.4 KG of Safrole;
At least 16 KG but less than 28 KG of 3,
4-Methylenedioxyphenyl-2-propanone;

List II Chemicals

At least 440 G but less than 726 G of Acetic Anhydride;
At least 47 KG but less than 82.25 KG of Acetone;
At least 800 G but less than 1.4 KG of Benzyl Chloride;
At least 43 KG but less than 75.25 KG of Ethyl Ether;
At least 48 KG but less than 84 KG of Methyl Ethyl Ketone;
At least 400 G but less than 700 G of Potassium Permanganate;
At least 52 KG but less than 91 KG of Toluene.

(6) List I Chemicals Level 18
At least 178 G but less than 712 G of Benzaldehyde;
At least 200 G but less than 800 G of Benzyl Cyanide;
At least 200 G but less than 800 G of Ephedrine;
At least 2 G but less than 8 G of Ergonovine;
At least 4 G but less than 16 G of Ergotamine;
At least 200 G but less than 800 G of Ethylamine;
At least 440 G but less than 1.76 KG of Hydriodic Acid;
At least 3.2 KG but less than 12.8 KG of Isoafrole;
At least 40 G but less than 160 G of Methylamine;
At least 5 KG but less than 20 KG of N-Methylephedrine;

November 1, 2013   APPENDIX C - VOLUME I   **Amendment 541**

At least 5 KG but less than 20 KG of N-Methylpseudoephedrine;
At least 126 G but less than 503 G of Nitroethane;
At least 2 KG but less than 8 KG of Norpseudoephedrine;
At least 200 G but less than 800 G of Phenylacetic Acid;
At least 2 KG but less than 8 KG of Phenylpropanolamine;
At least 100 G but less than 400 G of Piperidine;
At least 3.2 KG but less than 12.8 KG of Piperonal;
At least 16 G but less than 64 G of Propionic Anhydride;
At least 200 G but less than 800 G of Pseudoephedrine;
At least 3.2 KG but less than 12.8 KG of Safrole;
At least 4 KG but less than 16 KG of 3, 4-Methylenedioxyphenyl-2-propanone;

List II Chemicals

At least 110 G but less than 440 G of Acetic Anhydride;
At least 11.75 KG but less than 47 KG of Acetone;
At least 200 G but less than 800 G of Benzyl Chloride;
At least 10.75 KG but less than 43 KG of Ethyl Ether;
At least 12 KG but less than 48 KG of Methyl Ethyl Ketone;
At least 100 G but less than 400 G of Potassium Permanganate;
At least 13 KG but less than 52 KG of Toluene.

(7)   List I Chemicals   Level 16
At least 142 G but less than 178 G of Benzaldehyde;
At least 160 G but less than 200 G of Benzyl Cyanide;
At least 160 G but less than 200 G of Ephedrine;
At least 1.6 G but less than 2 G of Ergonovine;
At least 3.2 G but less than 4 G of Ergotamine;
At least 160 G but less than 200 G of Ethylamine;
At least 352 G but less than 440 G of Hydriodic Acid;
At least 2.56 KG but less than 3.2 KG of Isoafrole;
At least 32 G but less than 40 G of Methylamine;
At least 4 KG but less than 5 KG of N-Methylephedrine;
At least 4 KG but less than 5 KG of N-Methylpseudoephedrine;
At least 100 G but less than 126 G of Nitroethane;
At least 1.6 KG but less than 2 KG of Norpseudoephedrine;
At least 160 G but less than 200 G of Phenylacetic Acid;
At least 1.6 KG but less than 2 KG of Phenylpropanolamine;
At least 80 G but less than 100 G of Piperidine;
At least 2.56 KG but less than 3.2 KG of Piperonal;
At least 12.8 G but less than 16 G of Propionic Anhydride;
At least 160 G but less than 200 G of Pseudoephedrine;
At least 2.56 KG but less than 3.2 KG of Safrole;
At least 3.2 KG but less than 4 KG of 3, 4-Methylenedioxyphenyl-2-propanone;

List II Chemicals

At least 88 G but less than 110 G of Acetic Anhydride;
At least 9.4 KG but less than 11.75 KG of Acetone;
At least 160 G but less than 200 G of Benzyl Chloride;
At least 8.6 KG but less than 10.75 KG of Ethyl Ether;
At least 9.6 KG but less than 12 KG of Methyl Ethyl Ketone;
At least 80 G but less than 100 G of Potassium Permanganate;
At least 10.4 KG but less than 13 KG of Toluene.

Amendment 541　　APPENDIX C - VOLUME I　　November 1, 2013

(8)　List I Chemicals　　　　　　　　　　　　　　　　　　　　　　　　Level 14
　　3.6 KG or more of Anthranilic Acid;
　　At least 107 G but less than 142 G of Benzaldehyde;
　　At least 120 G but less than 160 G of Benzyl Cyanide;
　　At least 120 G but less than 160 G of Ephedrine;
　　At least 1.2 G but less than 1.6 G of Ergonovine;
　　At least 2.4 G but less than 3.2 G of Ergotamine;
　　At least 120 G but less than 160 G of Ethylamine;
　　At least 264 G but less than 352 G of Hydriodic Acid;
　　At least 1.92 KG but less than 2.56 KG of Isoafrole;
　　At least 24 G but less than 32 G of Methylamine;
　　4.8 KG or more of N-Acetylanthranilic Acid;
　　At least 3 KG but less than 4 KG of N-Methylephedrine;
　　At least 3 KG but less than 4 KG of N-Methylpseudoephedrine;
　　At least 75 G but less than 100 G of Nitroethane;
　　At least 1.2 KG but less than 1.6 KG of Norpseudoephedrine;
　　At least 120 G but less than 160 G of Phenylacetic Acid;
　　At least 1.2 KG but less than 1.6 KG of Phenylpropanolamine;
　　At least 60 G but less than 80 G of Piperidine;
　　At least 1.92 KG but less than 2.56 KG of Piperonal;
　　At least 9.6 G but less than 12.8 G of Propionic Anhydride;
　　At least 120 G but less than 160 G of Pseudoephedrine;
　　At least 1.92 KG but less than 2.56 KG of Safrole;
　　At least 2.4 KG but less than 3.2 KG of 3,
　　4-Methylenedioxyphenyl-2-propanone;

　　List II Chemicals
　　At least 66 G but less than 88 G of Acetic Anhydride;
　　At least 7.05 KG but less than 9.4 KG of Acetone;
　　At least 120 G but less than 160 G of Benzyl Chloride;
　　At least 6.45 KG but less than 8.6 KG of Ethyl Ether;
　　At least 7.2 KG but less than 9.6 KG of Methyl Ethyl Ketone;
　　At least 60 G but less than 80 G of Potassium Permanganate;
　　At least 7.8 KG but less than 10.4 KG of Toluene.

(9)　List I Chemicals　　　　　　　　　　　　　　　　　　　　　　　　Level 12
　　Less than 3.6 KG of Anthranilic Acid;
　　Less than 107 G of Benzaldehyde;
　　Less than 120 G of Benzyl Cyanide;
　　Less than 120 G of Ephedrine;
　　Less than 1.2 G of Ergonovine;
　　Less than 2.4 G of Ergotamine;
　　Less than 120 G of Ethylamine;
　　Less than 264 G of Hydriodic Acid;
　　Less than 1.92 KG of Isoafrole;
　　Less than 24 G of Methylamine;
　　Less than 4.8 KG of N-Acetylanthranilic Acid;
　　Less than 3 KG of N-Methylephedrine;
　　Less than 3 KG of N-Methylpseudoephedrine;
　　Less than 75 G of Nitroethane;
　　Less than 1.2 KG of Norpseudoephedrine;
　　Less than 120 G of Phenylacetic Acid;
　　Less than 1.2 KG of Phenylpropanolamine;

November 1, 2013   APPENDIX C - VOLUME I   **Amendment 541**

        Less than 60 G of Piperidine;
        Less than 1.92 KG of Piperonal;
        Less than 9.6 G of Propionic Anhydride;
        Less than 120 G of Pseudoephedrine;
        Less than 1.92 KG of Safrole;
        Less than 2.4 KG of 3, 4-Methylenedioxyphenyl-2-propanone;

        List II Chemicals
        Less than 66 G of Acetic Anhydride;
        Less than 7.05 KG of Acetone;
        Less than 120 G of Benzyl Chloride;
        Less than 6.45 KG of Ethyl Ether;
        Less than 7.2 KG of Methyl Ethyl Ketone;
        Less than 60 G of Potassium Permanganate;
        Less than 7.8 KG of Toluene.",

and inserting in lieu thereof:

   "(1)   List I Chemicals   Level 30
              17.8 KG or more of Benzaldehyde;
              20 KG or more of Benzyl Cyanide;
              20 KG or more of Ephedrine;
              200 G or more of Ergonovine;
              400 G or more of Ergotamine;
              20 KG or more of Ethylamine;
              44 KG or more of Hydriodic Acid;
              320 KG or more of Isosafrole;
              4 KG or more of Methylamine;
              500 KG or more of N-Methylephedrine;
              500 KG or more of N-Methylpseudoephedrine;
              12.6 KG or more of Nitroethane;
              200 KG or more of Norpseudoephedrine;
              20 KG or more of Phenylacetic Acid;
              200 KG or more of Phenylpropanolamine;
              10 KG or more of Piperidine;
              320 KG or more of Piperonal;
              1.6 KG or more of Propionic Anhydride;
              20 KG or more of Pseudoephedrine;
              320 KG or more of Safrole;
              400 KG or more of 3, 4-Methylenedioxyphenyl-2-propanone;

   (2)   List I Chemicals   Level 28
              At least 5.3 KG but less than 17.8 KG of Benzaldehyde;
              At least 6 KG but less than 20 KG of Benzyl Cyanide;
              At least 6 KG but less than 20 KG of Ephedrine;
              At least 60 G but less than 200 G of Ergonovine;
              At least 120 G but less than 400 G of Ergotamine;
              At least 6 KG but less than 20 KG of Ethylamine;
              At least 13.2 KG but less than 44 KG of Hydriodic Acid;
              At least 96 KG but less than 320 KG of Isosafrole;
              At least 1.2 KG but less than 4 KG of Methylamine;
              At least 150 KG but less than 500 KG of N-Methylephedrine;
              At least 150 KG but less than 500 KG of
              N-Methylpseudoephedrine;

At least 3.8 KG but less than 12.6 KG of Nitroethane;
At least 60 KG but less than 200 KG of Norpseudoephedrine;
At least 6 KG but less than 20 KG of Phenylacetic Acid;
At least 60 KG but less than 200 KG of Phenylpropanolamine;
At least 3 KG but less than 10 KG of Piperidine;
At least 96 KG but less than 320 KG of Piperonal;
At least 480 G but less than 1.6 KG of Propionic Anhydride;
At least 6 KG but less than 20 KG of Pseudoephedrine;
At least 96 KG but less than 320 KG of Safrole;
At least 120 KG but less than 400 KG of 3,
4-Methylenedioxyphenyl-2-propanone;

List II Chemicals
11 KG or more of Acetic Anhydride;
1175 KG or more of Acetone;
20 KG or more of Benzyl Chloride;
1075 KG or more of Ethyl Ether;
1200 KG or more of Methyl Ethyl Ketone;
10 KG or more of Potassium Permanganate;
1300 KG or more of Toluene.

(3)   List I Chemicals   Level 26
At least 1.8 KG but less than 5.3 KG of Benzaldehyde;
At least 2 KG but less than 6 KG of Benzyl Cyanide;
At least 2 KG but less than 6 KG of Ephedrine;
At least 20 G but less than 60 G of Ergonovine;
At least 40 G but less than 120 G of Ergotamine;
At least 2 KG but less than 6 KG of Ethylamine;
At least 4.4 KG but less than 13.2 KG of Hydriodic Acid;
At least 32 KG but less than 96 KG of Isosafrole;
At least 400 G but less than 1.2 KG of Methylamine;
At least 50 KG but less than 150 KG of N-Methylephedrine;
At least 50 KG but less than 150 KG of
N-Methylpseudoephedrine;
At least 1.3 KG but less than 3.8 KG of Nitroethane;
At least 20 KG but less than 60 KG of Norpseudoephedrine;
At least 2 KG but less than 6 KG of Phenylacetic Acid;
At least 20 KG but less than 60 KG of Phenylpropanolamine;
At least 1 KG but less than 3 KG of Piperidine;
At least 32 KG but less than 96 KG of Piperonal;
At least 160 G but less than 480 G of Propionic Anhydride;
At least 2 KG but less than 6 KG of Pseudoephedrine;
At least 32 KG but less than 96 KG of Safrole;
At least 40 KG but less than 120 KG of 3,
4-Methylenedioxyphenyl-2-propanone;

List II Chemicals
At least 3.3 KG but less than 11 KG of Acetic Anhydride;
At least 352.5 KG but less than 1175 KG of Acetone;
At least 6 KG but less than 20 KG of Benzyl Chloride;
At least 322.5 KG but less than 1075 KG of Ethyl Ether;
At least 360 KG but less than 1200 KG of Methyl Ethyl Ketone;
At least 3 KG but less than 10 KG of Potassium Permanganate;
At least 390 KG but less than 1300 KG of Toluene.

(4) List I Chemicals   Level 24
At least 1.2 KG but less than 1.8 KG of Benzaldehyde;
At least 1.4 KG but less than 2 KG of Benzyl Cyanide;
At least 1.4 KG but less than 2 KG of Ephedrine;
At least 14 G but less than 20 G of Ergonovine;
At least 28 G but less than 40 G of Ergotamine;
At least 1.4 KG but less than 2 KG of Ethylamine;
At least 3.08 KG but less than 4.4 KG of Hydriodic Acid;
At least 22.4 KG but less than 32 KG of Isosafrole;
At least 280 G but less than 400 G of Methylamine;
At least 35 KG but less than 50 KG of N-Methylephedrine;
At least 35 KG but less than 50 KG of N-Methylpseudoephedrine;
At least 879 G but less than 1.3 KG of Nitroethane;
At least 14 KG but less than 20 KG of Norpseudoephedrine;
At least 1.4 KG but less than 2 KG of Phenylacetic Acid;
At least 14 KG but less than 20 KG of Phenylpropanolamine;
At least 700 G but less than 1 KG of Piperidine;
At least 22.4 KG but less than 32 KG of Piperonal;
At least 112 G but less than 160 G of Propionic Anhydride;
At least 1.4 KG but less than 2 KG of Pseudoephedrine;
At least 22.4 KG but less than 32 KG of Safrole;
At least 28 KG but less than 40 KG of 3, 4-Methylenedioxyphenyl-2-propanone;

List II Chemicals
At least 1.1 KG but less than 3.3 KG of Acetic Anhydride;
At least 117.5 KG but less than 352.5 KG of Acetone;
At least 2 KG but less than 6 KG of Benzyl Chloride;
At least 107.5 KG but less than 322.5 KG of Ethyl Ether;
At least 120 KG but less than 360 KG of Methyl Ethyl Ketone;
At least 1 KG but less than 3 KG of Potassium Permanganate;
At least 130 KG but less than 390 KG of Toluene.

(5) List I Chemicals   Level 22
At least 712 G but less than 1.2 KG of Benzaldehyde;
At least 800 G but less than 1.4 KG of Benzyl Cyanide;
At least 800 G but less than 1.4 KG of Ephedrine;
At least 8 G but less than 14 G of Ergonovine;
At least 16 G but less than 28 G of Ergotamine;
At least 800 G but less than 1.4 KG of Ethylamine;
At least 1.76 KG but less than 3.08 KG of Hydriodic Acid;
At least 12.8 KG but less than 22.4 KG of Isosafrole;
At least 160 G but less than 280 G of Methylamine;
At least 20 KG but less than 35 KG of N-Methylephedrine;
At least 20 KG but less than 35 KG of N-Methylpseudoephedrine;
At least 503 G but less than 879 G of Nitroethane;
At least 8 KG but less than 14 KG of Norpseudoephedrine;
At least 800 G but less than 1.4 KG of Phenylacetic Acid;
At least 8 KG but less than 14 KG of Phenylpropanolamine;
At least 400 G but less than 700 G of Piperidine;
At least 12.8 KG but less than 22.4 KG of Piperonal;

Amendment 541   APPENDIX C - VOLUME I   November 1, 2013

At least 64 G but less than 112 G of Propionic Anhydride;
At least 800 G but less than 1.4 KG of Pseudoephedrine;
At least 12.8 KG but less than 22.4 KG of Safrole;
At least 16 KG but less than 28 KG of 3, 4-Methylenedioxyphenyl-2-propanone;

List II Chemicals
At least 726 G but less than 1.1 KG of Acetic Anhydride;
At least 82.25 KG but less than 117.5 KG of Acetone;
At least 1.4 KG but less than 2 KG of Benzyl Chloride;
At least 75.25 KG but less than 107.5 KG of Ethyl Ether;
At least 84 KG but less than 120 KG of Methyl Ethyl Ketone;
At least 700 G but less than 1 KG of Potassium Permanganate;
At least 91 KG but less than 130 KG of Toluene.

(6) List I Chemicals   Level 20
At least 178 G but less than 712 G of Benzaldehyde;
At least 200 G but less than 800 G of Benzyl Cyanide;
At least 200 G but less than 800 G of Ephedrine;
At least 2 G but less than 8 G of Ergonovine;
At least 4 G but less than 16 G of Ergotamine;
At least 200 G but less than 800 G of Ethylamine;
At least 440 G but less than 1.76 KG of Hydriodic Acid;
At least 3.2 KG but less than 12.8 KG of Isosafrole;
At least 40 G but less than 160 G of Methylamine;
At least 5 KG but less than 20 KG of N-Methylephedrine;
At least 5 KG but less than 20 KG of N-Methylpseudoephedrine;
At least 126 G but less than 503 G of Nitroethane;
At least 2 KG but less than 8 KG of Norpseudoephedrine;
At least 200 G but less than 800 G of Phenylacetic Acid;
At least 2 KG but less than 8 KG of Phenylpropanolamine;
At least 100 G but less than 400 G of Piperidine;
At least 3.2 KG but less than 12.8 KG of Piperonal;
At least 16 G but less than 64 G of Propionic Anhydride;
At least 200 G but less than 800 G of Pseudoephedrine;
At least 3.2 KG but less than 12.8 KG of Safrole;
At least 4 KG but less than 16 KG of 3, 4-Methylenedioxyphenyl-2-propanone;

List II Chemicals
At least 440 G but less than 726 G of Acetic Anhydride;
At least 47 KG but less than 82.25 KG of Acetone;
At least 800 G but less than 1.4 KG of Benzyl Chloride;
At least 43 KG but less than 75.25 KG of Ethyl Ether;
At least 48 KG but less than 84 KG of Methyl Ethyl Ketone;
At least 400 G but less than 700 G of Potassium Permanganate;
At least 52 KG but less than 91 KG of Toluene.

(7) List I Chemicals   Level 18
At least 142 G but less than 178 G of Benzaldehyde;
At least 160 G but less than 200 G of Benzyl Cyanide;
At least 160 G but less than 200 G of Ephedrine;
At least 1.6 G but less than 2 G of Ergonovine;

November 1, 2013 APPENDIX C - VOLUME I **Amendment 541**

At least 3.2 G but less than 4 G of Ergotamine;
At least 160 G but less than 200 G of Ethylamine;
At least 352 G but less than 440 G of Hydriodic Acid;
At least 2.56 KG but less than 3.2 KG of Isosafrole;
At least 32 G but less than 40 G of Methylamine;
At least 4 KG but less than 5 KG of N-Methylephedrine;
At least 4 KG but less than 5 KG of N-Methylpseudoephedrine;
At least 100 G but less than 126 G of Nitroethane;
At least 1.6 KG but less than 2 KG of Norpseudoephedrine;
At least 160 G but less than 200 G of Phenylacetic Acid;
At least 1.6 KG but less than 2 KG of Phenylpropanolamine;
At least 80 G but less than 100 G of Piperidine;
At least 2.56 KG but less than 3.2 KG of Piperonal;
At least 12.8 G but less than 16 G of Propionic Anhydride;
At least 160 G but less than 200 G of Pseudoephedrine;
At least 2.56 KG but less than 3.2 KG of Safrole;
At least 3.2 KG but less than 4 KG of 3,
4-Methylenedioxyphenyl-2-propanone;

List II Chemicals
At least 110 G but less than 440 G of Acetic Anhydride;
At least 11.75 KG but less than 47 KG of Acetone;
At least 200 G but less than 800 G of Benzyl Chloride;
At least 10.75 KG but less than 43 KG of Ethyl Ether;
At least 12 KG but less than 48 KG of Methyl Ethyl Ketone;
At least 100 G but less than 400 G of Potassium Permanganate;
At least 13 KG but less than 52 KG of Toluene.

(8) List I Chemicals   Level 16
3.6 KG or more of Anthranilic Acid;
At least 107 G but less than 142 G of Benzaldehyde;
At least 120 G but less than 160 G of Benzyl Cyanide;
At least 120 G but less than 160 G of Ephedrine;
At least 1.2 G but less than 1.6 G of Ergonovine;
At least 2.4 G but less than 3.2 G of Ergotamine;
At least 120 G but less than 160 G of Ethylamine;
At least 264 G but less than 352 G of Hydriodic Acid;
At least 1.92 KG but less than 2.56 KG of Isosafrole;
At least 24 G but less than 32 G of Methylamine;
4.8 KG or more of N-Acetylanthranilic Acid;
At least 3 KG but less than 4 KG of N-Methylephedrine;
At least 3 KG but less than 4 KG of N-Methylpseudoephedrine;
At least 75 G but less than 100 G of Nitroethane;
At least 1.2 KG but less than 1.6 KG of Norpseudoephedrine;
At least 120 G but less than 160 G of Phenylacetic Acid;
At least 1.2 KG but less than 1.6 KG of Phenylpropanolamine;
At least 60 G but less than 80 G of Piperidine;
At least 1.92 KG but less than 2.56 KG of Piperonal;
At least 9.6 G but less than 12.8 G of Propionic Anhydride;
At least 120 G but less than 160 G of Pseudoephedrine;
At least 1.92 KG but less than 2.56 KG of Safrole;
At least 2.4 KG but less than 3.2 KG of 3,
4-Methylenedioxyphenyl-2-propanone;

– 445 –

Amendment 541 APPENDIX C - VOLUME I   November 1, 2013

List II Chemicals
At least 88 G but less than 110 G of Acetic Anhydride;
At least 9.4 KG but less than 11.75 KG of Acetone;
At least 160 G but less than 200 G of Benzyl Chloride;
At least 8.6 KG but less than 10.75 KG of Ethyl Ether;
At least 9.6 KG but less than 12 KG of Methyl Ethyl Ketone;
At least 80 G but less than 100 G of Potassium Permanganate;
At least 10.4 KG but less than 13 KG of Toluene.

(9) List I Chemicals   Level 14
At least 2.7 KG but less than 3.6 KG of Anthranilic Acid;
At least 71.2 G but less than 107 G of Benzaldehyde;
At least 80 G but less than 120 G of Benzyl Cyanide;
At least 80 G but less than 120 G of Ephedrine;
At least 800 MG but less than 1.2 G of Ergonovine;
At least 1.6 G but less than 2.4 G of Ergotamine;
At least 80 G but less than 120 G of Ethylamine;
At least 176 G but less than 264 G of Hydriodic Acid;
At least 1.44 G but less than 1.92 KG of Isosafrole;
At least 16 G but less than 24 G of Methylamine;
At least 3.6 KG but less than 4.8 KG of N-Acetylanthranilic Acid;
At least 2.25 KG but less than 3 KG of N-Methylephedrine;
At least 2.25 KG but less than 3 KG of
N-Methylpseudoephedrine;
At least 56.25 G but less than 75 G of Nitroethane;
At least 800 G but less than 1.2 KG of Norpseudoephedrine;
At least 80 G but less than 120 G of Phenylacetic Acid;
At least 800 G but less than 1.2 KG of Phenylpropanolamine;
At least 40 G but less than 60 G of Piperidine;
At least 1.44 KG but less than 1.92 KG of Piperonal;
At least 7.2 G but less than 9.6 G of Propionic Anhydride;
At least 80 G but less than 120 G of Pseudoephedrine;
At least 1.44 KG but less than 1.92 KG of Safrole;
At least 1.8 KG but less than 2.4 KG of 3,
4-Methylenedioxyphenyl-2-propanone;

List II Chemicals
At least 66 G but less than 88 G of Acetic Anhydride;
At least 7.05 KG but less than 9.4 KG of Acetone;
At least 120 G but less than 160 G of Benzyl Chloride;
At least 6.45 KG but less than 8.6 KG of Ethyl Ether;
At least 7.2 KG but less than 9.6 KG of Methyl Ethyl Ketone;
At least 60 G but less than 80 G of Potassium Permanganate;
At least 7.8 KG but less than 10.4 KG of Toluene.

(10) List I Chemicals   Level 12
Less than 2.7 KG of Anthranilic Acid;
Less than 71.2 G of Benzaldehyde;
Less than 80 G of Benzyl Cyanide;
Less than 80 G of Ephedrine;
Less than 800 MG of Ergonovine;
Less than 1.6 G of Ergotamine;
Less than 80 G of Ethylamine;
Less than 176 G of Hydriodic Acid;

Less than 1.44 G of Isosafrole;
Less than 16 G of Methylamine;
Less than 3.6 KG of N-Acetylanthranilic Acid;
Less than 2.25 KG of N-Methylephedrine;
Less than 2.25 KG of N-Methylpseudoephedrine;
Less than 56.25 G of Nitroethane;
Less than 800 G of Norpseudoephedrine;
Less than 80 G of Phenylacetic Acid;
Less than 800 G of Phenylpropanolamine;
Less than 40 G of Piperidine;
Less than 1.44 KG of Piperonal;
Less than 7.2 G of Propionic Anhydride;
Less than 80 G of Pseudoephedrine;
Less than 1.44 G of Safrole;
Less than 1.8 KG of 3, 4-Methylenedioxyphenyl-2-propanone;

List II Chemicals
Less than 66 G of Acetic Anhydride;
Less than 7.05 KG of Acetone;
Less than 120 G of Benzyl Chloride;
Less than 6.45 KG of Ethyl Ether;
Less than 7.2 KG of Methyl Ethyl Ketone;
Less than 60 G of Potassium Permanganate;
Less than 7.8 KG of Toluene.".

Section 2D1.11(d) is amended in Note E (List I Chemical Equivalency Table) by deleting "Isoafrole" and inserting in lieu thereof "Isosafrole".

The Commentary to § 2D1.11 captioned "Application Notes" is amended in Note 4(a) in the first sentence by deleting "three kilograms" and inserting in lieu thereof "300 grams"; in the fourth sentence by deleting "24" and inserting in lieu thereof "26" and by deleting "14" and inserting in lieu thereof "16"; and in the fifth sentence by deleting "24" and inserting in lieu thereof "26".

Reason for Amendment: This amendment implements section 302 of the Comprehensive Methamphetamine Control Act of 1996, Pub. L. 104-237, 110 Stat. 3099, which directs the Commission to increase by at least two levels the offense levels for offenses involving list I chemicals under 21 U.S.C. §§ 841(d)(1) and (2) and 960(d)(1) and (3).

Effective Date: The effective date of this amendment is May 1, 1997.

542. **Amendment:** Section 2H4.1(a) is amended by deleting "(Apply the greater):" and inserting in lieu thereof ": 22"; and by deleting subdivisions (1) and (2) as follows:

"(1)   15; or

(2)   2 plus the offense level applicable to any underlying offense.".

Section 2H4.1 is amended by inserting after subsection (a) the following additional subsection:

"(b)   Specific Offense Characteristics

(1)   (A) If any victim sustained permanent or life-threatening bodily injury, increase by 4 levels; or (B) if any victim sustained serious bodily injury, increase by 2 levels.

Amendment 542 APPENDIX C - VOLUME I November 1, 2013

> (2) If a dangerous weapon was used, increase by 2 levels.
>
> (3) If any victim was held in a condition of peonage or involuntary servitude for (A) more than one year, increase by 3 levels; (B) between 180 days and one year, increase by 2 levels; or (C) more than 30 days but less than 180 days, increase by 1 level.
>
> (4) If any other felony offense was committed during the commission of, or in connection with, the peonage or involuntary servitude offense, increase to the greater of:
>
> > (A) 2 plus the offense level as determined above, or
> >
> > (B) 2 plus the offense level from the offense guideline applicable to that other offense, but in no event greater than level 43.".

The Commentary to § 2H4.1 captioned "Statutory Provisions" is amended by inserting "241," before "1581".

The Commentary to § 2H4.1 captioned "Application Note" is amended by deleting "Note" and inserting in lieu thereof "Notes"; by deleting:

> "1. 'Offense level applicable to the underlying offense' is explained in the Commentary to § 2H1.1.",

and inserting in lieu thereof:

> "1. For purposes of this guideline—
>
> 'A dangerous weapon was used' means that a firearm was discharged, or that a firearm or dangerous weapon was otherwise used.
>
> Definitions of 'firearm,' 'dangerous weapon,' 'otherwise used,' 'serious bodily injury,' and 'permanent or life-threatening bodily injury' are found in the Commentary to § 1B1.1 (Application Instructions).";

and by inserting after Note 1 the following additional notes:

> "2. Under subsection (b)(4), 'any other felony offense' means any conduct that constitutes a felony offense under federal, state, or local law (other than an offense that is itself covered by this subpart). When there is more than one such other offense, the most serious such offense (or group of closely related offenses in the case of offenses that would be grouped together under § 3D1.2(d)) is to be used. See Application Note 3 of § 1B1.5 (Interpretation of References to other Offense Guidelines).
>
> 3. If the offense involved the holding of more than ten victims in a condition of peonage or involuntary servitude, an upward departure may be warranted.".

The Commentary to § 2H4.1 captioned "Background" is deleted as follows:

> "Background: This section covers statutes that prohibit peonage, involuntary servitude, and slave trade. For purposes of deterrence and just punishment, the minimum base offense level is 15. However, these offenses frequently involve other

serious offenses. In such cases, the offense level will be increased under § 2H4.1(a)(2).".

Reason for Amendment: This amendment implements section 218 of the Illegal Immigration Reform and Immigrant Responsibility Act of 1996, Pub. L. 104-208, 110 Stat. 3009-573, which directs the Commission to review the guideline for peonage, involuntary servitude and slave trade offenses and amend the guideline pursuant to that review.

Effective Date: The effective date of this amendment is May 1, 1997.

543. **Amendment:** Section 2L1.1(a)(1) is amended by deleting "20" and inserting in lieu thereof "23".

Section 2L1.1(a)(2) is amended by deleting "9" and inserting in lieu thereof "12".

Section 2L1.1(b) is amended by deleting:

"(1) If the defendant committed the offense other than for profit, and the base offense level is determined under subsection (a)(2), decrease by 3 levels.",

and inserting in lieu thereof:

"(1) If (A) the defendant committed the offense other than for profit, or the offense involved the smuggling, transporting, or harboring only of the defendant's spouse or child (or both the defendant's spouse and child), and (B) the base offense level is determined under subsection (a)(2), decrease by 3 levels.".

Section 2L1.1(b)(2) is amended in the column captioned "Increase in Level" by deleting "2" in subdivision (A), and inserting in lieu thereof "3"; by deleting "4" in subdivision (B) and inserting in lieu thereof "6"; and by deleting in "6" subdivision (C) and inserting in lieu thereof "9".

Section 2L1.1(b) is amended by deleting:

"(3) If the defendant is an unlawful alien who has been deported (voluntarily or involuntarily) on one or more occasions prior to the instant offense, and the offense level determined above is less than level 8, increase to level 8.",

and by inserting in lieu thereof:

"(3) If the defendant committed any part of the instant offense after sustaining (A) a conviction for a felony immigration and naturalization offense, increase by 2 levels; or (B) two (or more) convictions for felony immigration and naturalization offenses, each such conviction arising out of a separate prosecution, increase by 4 levels.".

Section 2L1.1(b) is amended by inserting after subdivision (3) the following additional subdivisions:

"(4) (Apply the greatest):

(A) If a firearm was discharged, increase by 6 levels, but if the resulting offense level is less than level 22, increase to level 22.

(B) If a dangerous weapon (including a firearm) was brandished or

Amendment 543 APPENDIX C - VOLUME I November 1, 2013

>>otherwise used, increase by 4 levels, but if the resulting offense level is less than level 20, increase to level 20.
>
>>(C) If a dangerous weapon (including a firearm) was possessed, increase by 2 levels, but if the resulting offense level is less than level 18, increase to level 18.
>
>(5) If the offense involved intentionally or recklessly creating a substantial risk of death or serious bodily injury to another person, increase by 2 levels, but if the resulting offense level is less than level 18, increase to level 18.
>
>(6) If any person died or sustained bodily injury, increase the offense level according to the seriousness of the injury:

Death or Degree of Injury		Increase in Level
(1)	Bodily Injury	add 2 levels
(2)	Serious Bodily Injury	add 4 levels
(3)	Permanent or Life-Threatening Bodily Injury	add 6 levels
(4)	Death	add 8 levels.".

Section 2L1.1 is amended by inserting after subsection (b) the following additional subsection:

>"(c) Cross Reference
>
>>If any person was killed under circumstances that would constitute murder under 18 U.S.C. § 1111 had such killing taken place within the special maritime and territorial jurisdiction of the United States, apply the appropriate murder guideline from Chapter Two, Part A, Subpart 1.".

The Commentary to § 2L1.1 captioned "Application Notes" is amended in Note 1 by inserting at the beginning "For purposes of this guideline—";

by deleting:

>"'For profit' means for financial gain or commercial advantage, but this definition does not include a defendant who commits the offense solely in return for his own entry or transportation.",

and inserting in lieu thereof:

>"'The defendant committed the offense other than for profit' means that there was no payment or expectation of payment for the smuggling, transporting, or harboring of any of the unlawful aliens."; and

by inserting at the end the following paragraphs:

>"'Aggravated felony' is defined in the Commentary to § 2L1.2 (Unlawfully Entering or Remaining in the United States).
>
>'Child' has the meaning set forth in section 101(b)(1) of the Immigration and Nationality Act (8 U.S.C. § 1101(b)(1)).
>
>'Spouse' has the meaning set forth in 101(a)(35) of the Immigration and Nationality Act (8 U.S.C. § 1101(a)(35)).

'Immigration and naturalization offense' means any offense covered by Chapter Two, Part L.".

The Commentary to § 2L1.1 captioned "Application Notes" is amended by deleting:

"3. For the purposes of § 3B1.2 (Mitigating Role), a defendant who commits the offense solely in return for his own entry or transportation is not entitled to a reduction for a minor or minimal role. This is because the reduction at § 2L1.1(b)(1) applies to such a defendant.";

and by redesignating Note 4 as Note 3.

The Commentary to § 2L1.1 captioned "Application Notes" is amended in Note 5 by deleting "dangerous or inhumane treatment, death or bodily injury, possession of a dangerous weapon, or" following "involved"; and by redesignating Note 5 as Note 4.

The Commentary to § 2L1.1 captioned "Application Notes" is amended by deleting:

"6. 'Aggravated felony' is defined in the Commentary to § 2L1.2 (Unlawfully Entering or Remaining in the United States).".

The Commentary to § 2L1.1 captioned "Application Notes" is amended by inserting after Note 4, as redesignated, the following additional notes:

"5. Prior felony conviction(s) resulting in an adjustment under subsection (b)(3) are also counted for purposes of determining criminal history points pursuant to Chapter Four, Part A (Criminal History).

6. Reckless conduct to which the adjustment from subsection (b)(5) applies includes a wide variety of conduct (e.g., transporting persons in the trunk or engine compartment of a motor vehicle, carrying substantially more passengers than the rated capacity of a motor vehicle or vessel, or harboring persons in a crowded, dangerous, or inhumane condition). If subsection (b)(5) applies solely on the basis of conduct related to fleeing from a law enforcement officer, do not apply an adjustment from § 3C1.2 (Reckless Endangerment During Flight). Additionally, do not apply the adjustment in subsection (b)(5) if the only reckless conduct that created a substantial risk of death or serious bodily injury is conduct for which the defendant received an enhancement under subsection (b)(4).".

The Commentary to § 2L1.1 captioned "Background" is amended by deleting:

"A specific offense characteristic provides a reduction if the defendant did not commit the offense for profit. The offense level increases with the number of unlawful aliens smuggled, transported, or harbored.".

The Commentary to § 2L1.1 captioned "Background" is amended in the last sentence by inserting "smuggling, transporting, or harboring" immediately following "scale".

Reason for Amendment: This amendment implements section 203 of the Illegal Immigration Reform and Immigrant Responsibility Act of 1996, Pub. L. 104-208, 110 Stat. 3009-566, which directs the Commission to amend the guidelines for offenses related to smuggling, transporting, or harboring illegal aliens.

Effective Date: The effective date of this amendment is May 1, 1997.

Amendment 544   APPENDIX C - VOLUME I   November 1, 2013

544. Amendment: Section 2L2.1(a) is amended by deleting "9" and inserting in lieu thereof "11".

Section 2L2.1(b) is amended by deleting:

"(1)   If the defendant committed the offense other than for profit, decrease by 3 levels.",

and inserting in lieu thereof:

"(1)   If the defendant committed the offense other than for profit, or the offense involved the smuggling, transporting, or harboring only of the defendant's spouse or child (or both the defendant's spouse and child), decrease by 3 levels.".

Section 2L2.1(b)(2) is amended in the column captioned "Increase in Level" by deleting "2" in subdivision (A) and inserting in lieu thereof "3"; by deleting "4" in subdivision (B) and inserting in lieu thereof "6"; and by deleting "6" subdivision (C) and inserting in lieu thereof "9".

Section 2L2.1(b) is amended by inserting after subdivision (3) the following additional subdivision:

"(4)   If the defendant committed any part of the instant offense after sustaining (A) a conviction for a felony immigration and naturalization offense, increase by 2 levels; or (B) two (or more) convictions for felony immigration and naturalization offenses, each such conviction arising out of a separate prosecution, increase by 4 levels.".

The Commentary to § 2L2.1 captioned "Application Notes" is amended by deleting Note 1 as follows:

"1.   'For profit' means for financial gain or commercial advantage.",

and inserting in lieu thereof:

"1.   For purposes of this guideline—

'The defendant committed the offense other than for profit' means that there was no payment or expectation of payment for the smuggling, transporting, or harboring of any of the unlawful aliens.

'Immigration and naturalization offense' means any offense covered by Chapter Two, Part L.

'Child' has the meaning set forth in section 101(b)(1) of the Immigration and Nationality Act (8 U.S.C. § 1101(b)(1)).

'Spouse' has the meaning set forth in section 101(a)(35) of the Immigration and Nationality Act (8 U.S.C. § 1101(a)(35)).".

The Commentary to § 2L2.1 captioned "Application Notes" is amended by inserting after Note 3 the following additional notes:

"4.   Prior felony conviction(s) resulting in an adjustment under subsection (b)(4) are also counted for purposes of determining criminal history points pursuant to Chapter Four, Part A (Criminal History).

5. If the offense involved substantially more than 100 documents, an upward departure may be warranted.".

Section 2L2.2(a) is amended by deleting "6" and inserting in lieu thereof "8".

Section 2L2.2(b) is amended by deleting "Characteristic" and inserting in lieu thereof "Characteristics"; and by inserting after subdivision (1) the following additional subdivision:

"(2) If the defendant committed any part of the instant offense after sustaining (A) a conviction for a felony immigration and naturalization offense, increase by 2 levels; or (B) two (or more) convictions for felony immigration and naturalization offenses, each such conviction arising out of a separate prosecution, increase by 4 levels.".

The Commentary to § 2L2.2 captioned "Application Note" is amended by deleting "Note" and inserting in lieu thereof "Notes"; by redesignating Note 1 as Note 2; and by inserting the following as the new Note 1:

"1. For purposes of this guideline—

'Immigration and naturalization offense' means any offense covered by Chapter Two, Part L.".

The Commentary to § 2L2.2 captioned "Application Notes" is amended by inserting after Note 2, as redesignated, the following additional note:

"3. Prior felony conviction(s) resulting in an adjustment under subsection (b)(2) are also counted for purposes of determining criminal history points pursuant to Chapter Four, Part A (Criminal History).".

Reason for Amendment: This amendment implements section 211 of the Illegal Immigration Reform and Immigrant Responsibility Act of 1996, Pub. L. 104-208, 110 Stat. 3009-569, which directs the Commission to amend the guidelines for offenses related to the fraudulent use of government-issued documents.

Effective Date: The effective date of this amendment is May 1, 1997.

545. **Amendment:** The Commentary to § 1B1.1 captioned "Application Notes" is amended in Note 1(b) by deleting:

"As used in the guidelines, the definition of this term is somewhat different than that used in various statutes.".

The Commentary to § 1B1.1 captioned "Application Notes" is amended in Note 1(j) by inserting "protracted" before "impairment"; and by deleting "As used in the guidelines, the definition of this term is somewhat different than that used in various statutes." and inserting in lieu thereof "In addition, 'serious bodily injury' is deemed to have occurred if the offense involved conduct constituting criminal sexual abuse under 18 U.S.C. § 2241 or § 2242 or any similar offense under state law.".

The Commentary to § 2A3.1 captioned "Application Notes" is amended in Note 1 by

Amendment 545

inserting "For purposes of this guideline—" before "'Permanent"; and by inserting at the end the following:

> "However, for purposes of this guideline, 'serious bodily injury' means conduct other than criminal sexual abuse, which already is taken into account in the base offense level under subsection (a).
>
> 'The means set forth in 18 U.S.C. § 2241(a) or (b)' are: by using force against the victim; by threatening or placing the victim in fear that any person will be subject to death, serious bodily injury, or kidnaping; by rendering the victim unconscious; or by administering by force or threat of force, or without the knowledge or permission of the victim, a drug, intoxicant, or other similar substance and thereby substantially impairing the ability of the victim to appraise or control conduct. This provision would apply, for example, where any dangerous weapon was used, brandished, or displayed to intimidate the victim.".

The Commentary to § 2A3.1 captioned "Application Notes" is amended by deleting:

> "2. 'The means set forth in 18 U.S.C. § 2241(a) or (b)' are: by using force against the victim; by threatening or placing the victim in fear that any person will be subject to death, serious bodily injury, or kidnapping; by rendering the victim unconscious; or by administering by force or threat of force, or without the knowledge or permission of the victim, a drug, intoxicant, or other similar substance and thereby substantially impairing the ability of the victim to appraise or control conduct. This provision would apply, for example, where any dangerous weapon was used, brandished, or displayed to intimidate the victim.";

and by redesignating Notes 3, 4, 5, 6, and 7, as Notes 2, 3, 4, 5, and 6, respectively.

The Commentary to § 2A4.1 captioned "Application Notes" is amended in Note 1 by inserting "For purposes of this guideline—" before "Definitions"; and by inserting at the end the following:

> "However, for purposes of this guideline, 'serious bodily injury' means conduct other than criminal sexual abuse, which is taken into account in the specific offense characteristic under subsection (b)(5).".

Section 2B3.1(b)(1) is amended by deleting "(A)" following "If"; and by deleting "or (B) the offense involved carjacking," before "increase".

Section 2B3.1(b) is amended by redesignating subdivisions (5) and (6) as subdivisions (6) and (7), respectively; and by inserting after subdivision (4) the following new subdivision (5):

> "(5) If the offense involved carjacking, increase by 2 levels.".

Reason for Amendment: This amendment implements, in a broader form, section 2 of the Carjacking Correction Act of 1996, Pub.L. 104-217, 110 Stat. 3020. The Act amended 18 U.S.C. § 2119(2) to include aggravated sexual abuse under 18 U.S.C. § 2241 and sexual abuse under 18 U.S.C. § 2242 within the meaning of "serious bodily injury." In implementing this legislation, the Commission has elected to broaden the term "serious bodily injury," as used in a number of offense conduct guidelines, so that such injury will be deemed to have occurred in the case of a sexual assault. The amendment also makes a number of conforming changes in other guidelines. In addition, this amendment amends

§ 2B3.1(b)(1) to provide cumulative enhancements if the offense involved both bank robbery and carjacking.

Effective Date: The effective date of this amendment is November 1, 1997.

546. Amendment: Section 1B1.1(b) is amended by inserting ", cross references, and special instructions" after "characteristics".

The Commentary to § 1B1.1 captioned "Application Notes" is amended in Note 1(l) by inserting at the end the following:

> "The term 'instant' is used in connection with 'offense,' 'federal offense,' or 'offense of conviction,' as the case may be, to distinguish the violation for which the defendant is being sentenced from a prior or subsequent offense, or from an offense before another court (e.g., an offense before a state court involving the same underlying conduct).".

Section 4B1.1 is amended by deleting "of the instant offense" and inserting in lieu thereof "the defendant committed the instant offense of conviction".

Section 4B1.2(3) is amended by inserting "of conviction" before "subsequent".

The Commentary to § 4B1.2 captioned "Application Notes" is amended in Note 2 in the second paragraph by inserting "of conviction" after "instant offense".

The Commentary to § 8A1.2 captioned "Application Notes" is amended in Note 3(a) by inserting at the end the following:

> "The term 'instant' is used in connection with 'offense,' 'federal offense,' or 'offense of conviction,' as the case may be, to distinguish the violation for which the defendant is being sentenced from a prior or subsequent offense, or from an offense before another court (e.g., an offense before a state court involving the same underlying conduct).".

Reason for Amendment: This amendment has two primary purposes. First, it corrects a technical error in § 1B1.1(b). Second, it explains the purpose of the term "instant" as that term is employed throughout the Guidelines Manual, as a modifier of the term "offense," "federal offense," or "offense of conviction." It also clarifies the usage of the term "instant offense of conviction" at several places in the Guidelines Manual.

Effective Date: The effective date of this amendment is November 1, 1997.

547. Amendment: Section § 1B1.5(d) is amended by deleting "final offense level (i.e., the greater offense level taking into account both the Chapter Two offense level and any applicable Chapter Three adjustments)" and inserting in lieu thereof "Chapter Two offense level, except as otherwise expressly provided".

The Commentary to § 1B1.5 captioned "Application Notes" is amended in Note 1 by deleting "§ " before "2D1.2(a)(1)"; and by deleting ", (2), and 2H1.1(a)(1)" and inserting in lieu thereof "and (2))".

The Commentary to § 1B1.5 captioned "Application Notes" is amended in Note 2 in the second sentence by deleting "greater final"; by deleting "(i.e., the greater offense level"; and by deleting "both" and inserting in lieu thereof "only".

The Commentary to § 1B1.5 captioned "Application Notes" is amended in Note 2 by

Amendment 547 APPENDIX C - VOLUME I November 1, 2013

deleting:

"and any applicable Chapter Three adjustments). Although the offense guideline that results in the greater offense level under Chapter Two will most frequently result in the greater final offense level, this will not always be the case. If, for example, a role or abuse of trust adjustment applies to the cross-referenced offense guideline, but not to the guideline initially applied, the greater Chapter Two offense level may not necessarily result in a greater final offense level.",

and inserting in lieu thereof:

", unless the offense guideline expressly provides for consideration of both the Chapter Two offense level and applicable Chapter Three adjustments. For situations in which a comparison involving both Chapters Two and Three is necessary, see the Commentary to §§ 2C1.1 (Offering, Giving, Soliciting, or Receiving a Bribe); 2C1.7 (Fraud Involving Deprivation of the Intangible Right to the Honest Services of Public Officials); 2E1.1 (Unlawful Conduct Relating to Racketeer Influenced and Corrupt Organizations); and 2E1.2 (Interstate or Foreign Travel or Transportation in Aid of a Racketeering Enterprise).".

The Commentary to § 2C1.1 captioned "Application Notes" is amended by inserting after Note 6 the following additional note:

"7. For the purposes of determining whether to apply the cross references in this section, the 'resulting offense level' means the greater final offense level (i.e., the offense level determined by taking into account both the Chapter Two offense level and any applicable adjustments from Chapter Three, Parts A-D).".

The Commentary to § 2C1.7 captioned "Application Notes" is amended by inserting after Note 5 the following additional note:

"6. For the purposes of determining whether to apply the cross references in this section, the 'resulting offense level' means the greater final offense level (i.e., the offense level determined by taking into account both the Chapter Two offense level and any applicable adjustments from Chapter Three, Parts A-D).".

Reason for Amendment: This amendment simplifies the guidelines by restricting the cross-reference comparison to the Chapter Two offense levels, unless a different procedure is expressly specified. With respect to §§ 2C1.1, 2C1.7, 2E1.1, and 2E1.2, the amendment, and an express provision in each of these guidelines, provide a different procedure because these guidelines are the only four offense guidelines in which the inclusion of Chapter Three adjustments in the comparison is likely to make a difference.

Effective Date: The effective date of this amendment is November 1, 1997.

548. **Amendment:** Section 1B1.10 is amended in the title by deleting "Retroactivity" and inserting in lieu thereof "Reduction in Term of Imprisonment as a Result".

Section 1B1.10(b) is amended by deleting "sentence" in both instances and inserting in lieu thereof "the term of imprisonment"; and by inserting ", except that in no event may the reduced term of imprisonment be less than the term of imprisonment the defendant has already served" after "sentenced".

The Commentary to § 1B1.10 captioned "Application Notes" is amended by inserting after Note 2 the following additional notes:

> "3. Under subsection (b), the amended guideline range and the term of imprisonment already served by the defendant limit the extent to which an eligible defendant's sentence may be reduced under 18 U.S.C. § 3582(c)(2). When the original sentence represented a downward departure, a comparable reduction below the amended guideline range may be appropriate; however, in no case shall the term of imprisonment be reduced below time served. Subject to these limitations, the sentencing court has the discretion to determine whether, and to what extent, to reduce a term of imprisonment under this section.
>
> 4. Only a term of imprisonment imposed as part of the original sentence is authorized to be reduced under this section. This section does not authorize a reduction in the term of imprisonment imposed upon revocation of supervised release.
>
> 5. If the limitation in subsection (b) relating to time already served precludes a reduction in the term of imprisonment to the extent the court determines otherwise would have been appropriate as a result of the amended guideline range, the court may consider any such reduction that it was unable to grant in connection with any motion for early termination of a term of supervised release under 18 U.S.C. § 3583(e)(1). However, the fact that a defendant may have served a longer term of imprisonment than the court determines would have been appropriate in view of the amended guideline range shall not, without more, provide a basis for early termination of supervised release. Rather, the court should take into account the totality of circumstances relevant to a decision to terminate supervised release, including the term of supervised release that would have been appropriate in connection with a sentence under the amended guideline range.".

The Commentary to § 1B1.10 captioned "Background" is amended in the third paragraph by inserting "to determine an amended guideline range under subsection (b)" after "retroactively"; and by inserting before the fourth paragraph the following additional paragraph:

> "The listing of an amendment in subsection (c) reflects policy determinations by the Commission that a reduced guideline range is sufficient to achieve the purposes of sentencing and that, in the sound discretion of the court, a reduction in the term of imprisonment may be appropriate for previously sentenced, qualified defendants. The authorization of such a discretionary reduction does not otherwise affect the lawfulness of a previously imposed sentence, does not authorize a reduction in any other component of the sentence, and does not entitle a defendant to a reduced term of imprisonment as a matter of right.".

Reason for Amendment: This amendment makes a number of substantive and clarifying changes in the policy statement relating to retroactive application of an amendment that reduces a guideline range. The amendment provides that, in exercising discretion to reduce the term of imprisonment of an incarcerated defendant, a court may not reduce the term of imprisonment below time served (or, put differently, grant a greater reduction in imprisonment than the imprisonment time remaining to be served). In those cases in which the combination of time already served and this limitation preclude a defendant from receiving the full reduction the court would be inclined to grant as a result of an amended guideline range, the amended commentary instructs that the court may weigh the equities

Amendment 548 APPENDIX C - VOLUME I November 1, 2013

of such a situation in connection with a separate motion for early termination of supervised release under 18 U.S.C. § 3583(e)(1). The amendment also makes clear that, contrary to the holding in United States v. Etherton, 101 F.3d 80 (9th Cir. 1996), a reduction in the term of imprisonment imposed upon revocation of supervised release is not authorized by the policy statement. Finally, the amendment makes a number of changes in the title and text of the policy statement to improve the precision of the language, adds commentary emphasizing court discretion in applying amendments that the Commission has listed for possible retroactive application, and adds background commentary more fully describing the legal consequences flowing from a Commission decision to list an amendment for possible retroactive application.

Effective Date: The effective date of this amendment is November 1, 1997.

549. **Amendment:** Section 2A2.2(b) is amended by inserting after subdivision (4) the following additional subdivision:

> "(5) If the offense involved the violation of a court protection order, increase by 2 levels.".

Chapter Two, Part A, Subpart 6 is amended in the title by inserting "or Harassing" after "Threatening"; and by inserting ", Stalking, and Domestic Violence" after "Communications".

Section 2A6.1 is amended in the title by inserting "or Harassing" after "Threatening".

Section 2A6.1 is amended by deleting subsection (a) as follows:

> "(a) Base Offense Level: 12",

and inserting in lieu thereof:

> "(a) Base Offense Level:
>
> (1) 12; or
>
> (2) 6, if the defendant is convicted of an offense under 47 U.S.C. § 223(a)(1)(C), (D), or (E) that did not involve a threat to injure a person or property.".

Section 2A6.1(b) is amended by redesignating subdivision (2) as subdivision (4); and by inserting after subdivision (1) the following new subdivisions:

> "(2) If the offense involved more than two threats, increase by 2 levels.
>
> (3) If the offense involved the violation of a court protection order, increase by 2 levels.".

Section 2A6.1(b)(4), as redesignated, is amended by deleting "If specific offense characteristic § 2A6.1(b)(1) does not apply, and" and inserting in lieu thereof "If (A) subsection (a)(2) and subdivisions (1), (2), and (3) do not apply, and (B)".

The Commentary to § 2A6.1 captioned "Statutory Provisions" is amended by inserting "; 47 U.S.C. § 223(a)(1)(C)-(E)" after "879".

The Commentary to § 2A6.1 captioned "Application Note" is amended by deleting "Note" and inserting in lieu thereof "Notes"; and by inserting after Note 1 the following additional note:

"2. In determining whether subsections (b)(1), (b)(2), and (b)(3) apply, the court shall consider both conduct that occurred prior to the offense and conduct that occurred during the offense; however, conduct that occurred prior to the offense must be substantially and directly connected to the offense, under the facts of the case taken as a whole. For example, if the defendant engaged in several acts of mailing threatening letters to the same victim over a period of years (including acts that occurred prior to the offense), then for purposes of determining whether subsections (b)(1), (b)(2), and (b)(3) apply, the court shall consider only those prior acts of threatening the victim that have a substantial and direct connection to the offense.

For purposes of Chapter Three, Part D (Multiple Counts), multiple counts involving making a threatening or harassing communication to the same victim are grouped together under § 3D1.2 (Groups of Closely Related Counts). Multiple counts involving different victims are not to be grouped under § 3D1.2.

If the conduct involved substantially more than two threatening communications to the same victim or a prolonged period of making harassing communications to the same victim, an upward departure may be warranted.".

Chapter Two, Part A, Subpart 6 is amended by adding after § 2A6.1 the following new guideline:

"§ 2A6.2. <u>Stalking or Domestic Violence</u>

    (a)   Base Offense Level: 14

    (b)   Specific Offense Characteristic

        (1)   If the offense involved one of the following aggravating factors: (A) the violation of a court protection order; (B) bodily injury; (C) possession, or threatened use, of a dangerous weapon; or (D) a pattern of activity involving stalking, threatening, harassing, or assaulting the same victim, increase by 2 levels. If the offense involved more than one of these aggravating factors, increase by 4 levels.

    (c)   Cross Reference

        (1)   If the offense involved conduct covered by another offense guideline from Chapter Two, Part A (Offenses Against the Person), apply that offense guideline, if the resulting offense level is greater than that determined above.

Commentary

<u>Statutory Provisions</u>: 18 U.S.C. §§ 2261-2262.

<u>Application Notes</u>:

1. For purposes of this guideline—

'Bodily injury' and 'dangerous weapon' are defined in the Commentary to § 1B1.1 (Application Instructions).

'Pattern of activity involving stalking, threatening, harassing, or assaulting the same victim' means any combination of two or more separate instances of stalking, threatening, harassing, or assaulting the same victim, whether or not such conduct resulted in a conviction. For example, a single instance of stalking accompanied by a separate instance of threatening, harassing, or assaulting the same victim constitutes a pattern of activity for purposes of this guideline.

'Stalking' means traveling with the intent to injure or harass another person and, in the course of, or as a result of, such travel, placing the person in reasonable fear of death or serious bodily injury to the person or the person's immediate family. See 18 U.S.C. § 2261A. 'Immediate family' has the meaning set forth in 18 U.S.C. § 115(c)(2).

2. Subsection (b)(1) provides for a two-level or four-level enhancement based on the degree to which the offense involved aggravating factors listed in that subsection. If the offense involved aggravating factors more serious than the factors listed in subsection (b)(1), the cross reference in subsection (c) most likely will apply, if the resulting offense level is greater, because the more serious conduct will be covered by another offense guideline from Chapter Two, Part A. For example, § 2A2.2 (Aggravated Assault) most likely would apply pursuant to subsection (c) if the offense involved assaultive conduct in which injury more serious than bodily injury occurred or if a dangerous weapon was used rather than merely possessed.

3. In determining whether subsection (b)(1)(D) applies, the court shall consider, under the totality of the circumstances, any conduct that occurred prior to or during the offense; however, conduct that occurred prior to the offense must be substantially and directly connected to the offense. For example, if a defendant engaged in several acts of stalking the same victim over a period of years (including acts that occurred prior to the offense), then for purposes of determining whether subsection (b)(1)(D) applies, the court shall look to the totality of the circumstances, considering only those prior acts of stalking the victim that have a substantial and direct connection to the offense.

Prior convictions taken into account under subsection (b)(1)(D) are also counted for purposes of determining criminal history points pursuant to Chapter Four, Part A (Criminal History).

4. For purposes of Chapter Three, Part D (Multiple Counts), multiple counts involving stalking, threatening, or harassing the same victim are grouped together (and with counts of other offenses involving the same victim that are covered by this guideline) under § 3D1.2 (Groups of Closely Related Counts). For example, if the defendant is convicted of two counts of stalking the defendant's ex-spouse under 18 U.S.C. § 2261A and one count of interstate domestic violence involving an assault of the ex-spouse under 18 U.S.C. § 2261, the stalking counts would be grouped together with the interstate domestic violence count. This grouping procedure avoids unwarranted 'double counting' with the enhancement in subsection (b)(1)(D) (for multiple acts of stalking, threatening, harassing, or assaulting the same victim) and recognizes that the stalking and interstate domestic violence counts are sufficiently related to warrant grouping.

Multiple counts that are cross referenced to another offense guideline pursuant to subsection (c) are to be grouped together if § 3D1.2 would require grouping of those counts under that offense guideline. Similarly, multiple counts cross referenced pursuant to subsection (c) are not to be grouped together if § 3D1.2 would preclude grouping of the counts under that offense guideline. For example, if the defendant is convicted of multiple counts of threatening an ex-spouse in violation of a court protection order under 18 U.S.C. § 2262 and the counts are cross referenced to § 2A6.1 (Threatening or Harassing Communications), the counts would group together because Application Note 2 of § 2A6.1 specifically requires grouping. In contrast, if the defendant is convicted of multiple counts of assaulting the ex-spouse in violation of a court protection order under 18 U.S.C. § 2262 and the counts are cross referenced to § 2A2.2 (Aggravated Assault), the counts probably would not group together inasmuch as § 3D1.2(d) specifically precludes grouping of counts covered by § 2A2.2 and no other provision of § 3D1.2 would likely apply to require grouping.

Multiple counts involving different victims are not to be grouped under § 3D1.2.

5. If the defendant received an enhancement under subsection (b)(1) but that enhancement does not adequately reflect the extent or seriousness of the conduct involved, an upward departure may be warranted. For example, an upward departure may be warranted if the defendant stalked the victim on many occasions over a prolonged period of time.".

Reason for Amendment: This is a five-part amendment. First, this amendment addresses the new offense of interstate stalking, 18 U.S.C. § 2261A, which was enacted as section 1069 of the National Defense Authorization Act for Fiscal Year 1997, Pub. L. 104–201, 110 Stat. 2422. That offense makes it unlawful to travel across a state line or within federal jurisdiction with the intent to injure or harass another person and, in the course of, or as a result of, such travel, to place that person in reasonable fear of death or serious bodily injury to that person or that person's immediate family.

The amendment adds a new guideline, § 2A6.2 (Stalking or Domestic Violence), to cover the stalking offense. The new guideline provides for a base offense level of 14 and an enhancement for the presence of one or more aggravating factors that are often part of a stalking offense, including the violation of a court protection order and the presence of a pattern of stalking, harassing, threatening, or assaultive conduct. The new guideline also provides for a cross reference to other Chapter Two guidelines if the offense involved more serious conduct, such as aggravated assault or kidnapping, that would produce a greater offense level. In addition, the new guideline permits the consideration of prior stalking, harassing, threatening, or assaultive conduct if that conduct is directly and substantially related to the offense.

The new guideline also incorporates the definitions of "bodily injury" and "dangerous weapon" found in § 1B1.1 (Application Instructions). The definition of bodily injury found in the guidelines differs from the definition of bodily injury in 18 U.S.C. § 2266 that is applicable to interstate stalking and interstate domestic violence offenses. The definition of "bodily injury" in 18 U.S.C. § 2266 explicitly includes sexual abuse, but the guideline definition of "bodily injury" does not. However, the Commission is fully aware that criminal sexual abuse often is part of a domestic violence offense under 18 U.S.C. §§ 2261 and 2262 and may be part of a stalking offense under 18 U.S.C. § 2261A. It is the view of the Commission that the new guideline provides an adequate mechanism for taking into ac-

Amendment 549 APPENDIX C - VOLUME I November 1, 2013

count the occurrence of criminal sexual abuse in any of these offenses. This is because the guideline definition of "serious bodily injury" in § 1B1.1 deems serious bodily injury -- a more serious gradient of bodily injury -- to have occurred if the offense involved conduct constituting criminal sexual abuse under 18 U.S.C. § 2241 or § 2242 or any similar offense under state law. Under the new guideline, any offense that involved criminal sexual abuse almost certainly will be subject to the cross reference to another offense guideline and to the rule deeming such conduct to be serious bodily injury (for purposes of applying a serious bodily injury enhancement in that other guideline to the offense). Therefore, in all likelihood, the sentence will be enhanced for the occurrence of criminal sexual abuse because the case will be cross referenced to another guideline that enhances for serious bodily injury.

Second, the amendment changes the manner in which the offenses of interstate domestic violence, 18 U.S.C. § 2261, and interstate violation of a protection order, 18 U.S.C. § 2262, are treated under the guidelines. Instead of being referenced to the guidelines that may cover underlying conduct, the amendment brings those offenses under the ambit of the new guideline, § 2A6.2. This change recognizes that the aggravating factors accounted for in the new guideline often are present in these offenses as well.

Third, the amendment adds an enhancement to § 2A2.2 (Aggravated Assault), if the offense involved the violation of a court protection order, to ensure an appropriately severe offense level for stalking, domestic violence, and other cases that are sentenced under the aggravated assault guideline and involve this factor.

Fourth, the amendment addresses several new harassing telecommunications offenses, 47 U.S.C. § 223(a)(1)(C)-(E), which were enacted in section 502 of the Telecommunications Act of 1996, Pub. L. 104–104, 110 Stat. 56. Those offenses make it unlawful to make a telephone call or utilize a telecommunications device, whether or not conversation or communication ensues, without disclosing one's identity and with the intent to annoy, abuse, threaten, or harass any person at the called number or who receives the communication; make or cause the telephone of another to repeatedly or continuously ring, with the intent to harass any person at the called number; or make repeated telephone calls or repeatedly initiate conversation with a telecommunications device, during which conversation or communication ensues, solely to harass any person at the called number or who receives the communication.

The amendment incorporates these new offenses into § 2A6.1 (Threatening Communications). Recognizing that these offenses carry only a two-year maximum term of imprisonment, the amendment provides an alternative offense level of 6 (as compared to 12), if the defendant is convicted of any of these offenses and there was no threat to injure a person or property. The amendment also adds enhancements if the offense involved more than two threats or the violation of a court protection order.

Fifth, this amendment addresses a circuit conflict regarding the enhancement in § 2A6.1 that provides a 6-level increase if the offense involved any conduct evidencing an intent to carry out a threat. Specifically, the conflict is whether or not conduct which occurred prior to the making of the threat can evidence an intent to carry out the threat. Compare United States v. Hornick, 942 F.2d 105 (2d Cir. 1991) ("a person cannot take action that will constitute proof of his intent to carry out a threat until after the threat has been made") cert. denied, 502 U.S. 1061 (1992) with United States v. Taylor, 88 F.3d 938 (11th Cir. 1996) ("the essential inquiry for § 2A6.1(b)(1) is whether the facts of the case, taken as a whole, establish a sufficiently direct connection between the defendant's pre-threat conduct and his threat"); United States v. Sullivan, 75 F.3d 297 (7th Cir. 1996)(same); United States v. Gary, 18 F.3d 1123 (4th Cir.) (same), cert. denied 513 U.S. 844 (1994); United States v.

– 462 –

Hines, 26 F.3d 1469 (9th Cir. 1994)(same).

The amendment essentially adopts the Eleventh Circuit's view by adding an application note to both §§ 2A6.1 and 2A6.2 to provide that conduct which occurred prior to the offense shall be considered in determining specified enhancements in those guidelines if the prior conduct is substantially and directly connected to the offense.

Effective Date: The effective date of this amendment is November 1, 1997.

550. Amendment: The Commentary to § 2A2.4 captioned "Application Notes" is amended in Note 1 by inserting the following after "(Aggravated Assault).":

> "Conversely, the base offense level does not reflect the possibility that the defendant may create a substantial risk of death or serious bodily injury to another person in the course of fleeing from a law enforcement official (although an offense under 18 U.S.C. § 758 for fleeing or evading a law enforcement checkpoint at high speed will often, but not always, involve the creation of that risk). If the defendant creates that risk and no higher guideline adjustment is applicable for the conduct creating the risk, apply § 3C1.2 (Reckless Endangerment During Flight).".

Reason for Amendment: This amendment clarifies the interaction of this guideline with the enhancement under § 3C1.2 (Reckless Endangerment During Flight), particularly when the defendant is convicted under 18 U.S.C. § 758 of fleeing an immigration checkpoint at high speed.

Effective Date: The effective date of this amendment is November 1, 1997.

551. Amendment: Section 2B1.1(b) is amended by inserting after subdivision (6) the following additional subdivision:

> "(7) If the offense involved misappropriation of a trade secret and the defendant knew or intended that the offense would benefit any foreign government, foreign instrumentality, or foreign agent, increase by 2 levels.".

The Commentary to § 2B1.1 captioned "Statutory Provisions" is amended by inserting "1831, 1832," before "2113(b)".

The Commentary to § 2B1.1 captioned "Application Notes" is amended in Note 1 by inserting after the first paragraph the following additional paragraphs:

> "'Trade secret' is defined in 18 U.S.C. § 1839(3).
>
> 'Foreign instrumentality' and 'foreign agent' are defined in 18 U.S.C. § 1839(1) and (2), respectively.".

The Commentary to § 2B1.1 captioned "Application Notes" is amended in Note 2 by inserting after the fourth paragraph the following additional paragraph:

> "In an offense involving unlawfully accessing, or exceeding authorized access to, a 'protected computer' as defined in 18 U.S.C. § 1030(e)(2)(A) or (B), 'loss' includes the reasonable cost to the victim of conducting a damage assessment, restoring the system and data to their condition prior to the offense, and any lost revenue due to interruption of service.".

The Commentary to § 2B1.1 captioned "Application Notes" is amended by inserting after Note 14 the following additional notes:

"15. In cases where the loss determined under subsection (b)(1) does not fully capture the harmfulness of the conduct, an upward departure may be warranted. For example, the theft of personal information or writings (e.g., medical records, educational records, a diary) may involve a substantial invasion of a privacy interest that would not be addressed by the monetary loss provisions of subsection (b)(1).

16. In cases involving theft of information from a 'protected computer', as defined in 18 U.S.C. § 1030(e)(2)(A) or (B), an upward departure may be warranted where the defendant sought the stolen information to further a broader criminal purpose.".

Section 2B1.3 is amended by inserting after subsection (c) the following additional subsection:

"(d) Special Instruction

(1) If the defendant is convicted under 18 U.S.C. § 1030(a)(5), the minimum guideline sentence, notwithstanding any other adjustment, shall be six months' imprisonment.".

The Commentary to § 2B1.3 captioned "Statutory Provisions" is amended by inserting "1030(a)(5)," before "1361,".

The Commentary to § 2B1.3 captioned "Application Notes" is amended in Note 4 by inserting "or interference with a telecommunications network" after "line"; by inserting ", with attendant life-threatening delay in the delivery of emergency medical treatment or disruption of other important governmental or private services" after "hours"; by deleting "instances" and inserting in lieu thereof "cases"; by deleting "would" and inserting in lieu thereof "may"; and by inserting at the end the following:

"See §§ 5K2.2 (Physical Injury), 5K2.7 (Disruption of Governmental Function), and 5K2.14 (Public Welfare).".

The Commentary to § 2B1.3 is amended by adding at the end the following:

"Background: Subsection (d) implements the instruction to the Commission in section 805(c) of Public Law 104-132.".

Section 2B2.3(b) is amended by inserting after subdivision (2) the following additional subdivision:

"(3) If the offense involved invasion of a protected computer resulting in a loss exceeding $2000, increase the offense level by the number of levels from the table in § 2F1.1 corresponding to the loss.".

The Commentary to § 2B2.3 captioned "Statutory Provision" is amended by deleting "Provision" and inserting in lieu thereof "Provisions"; and by inserting "18 U.S.C. § 1030(a)(3);" before "42 U.S.C.".

The Commentary to § 2B2.3 captioned "Application Note" is amended in Note 1 by inserting "For purposes of this guideline—" before "'Firearm'"; and by inserting after the first paragraph the following additional paragraph:

"'Protected computer' means a computer described in 18 U.S.C. § 1030(e)(2)(A) or (B).".

The Commentary to § 2B2.3 captioned "Application Note" is amended by deleting "Note" and inserting "Notes" and by inserting after Note 1 the following additional note:

"2. Valuation of loss is discussed in the Commentary to § 2B1.1 (Larceny, Embezzlement, and Other Forms of Theft).".

The Commentary to § 2B3.2 captioned "Statutory Provisions" is amended by inserting "1030(a)(7)," following "877,".

The Commentary to § 2B3.2 captioned "Background" is amended by inserting at the end:

"This guideline also applies to offenses under 18 U.S.C. § 1030(a)(7) involving a threat to impair the operation of a 'protected computer.'".

Section 2F1.1 is amended by inserting after subsection (b) the following additional subsection:

"(c) Special Instruction

(1) If the defendant is convicted under 18 U.S.C. § 1030(a)(4), the minimum guideline sentence, notwithstanding any other adjustment, shall be six months' imprisonment.".

The Commentary to § 2F1.1 captioned "Statutory Provisions" is amended by inserting "1030(a)(4)," before "1031,".

The Commentary to § 2F1.1 captioned "Background" is amended by inserting at the end the following additional paragraph:

" Subsection (c) implements the instruction to the Commission in section 805(c) of Public Law 104-132.".

Reason for Amendment: This amendment makes a number of changes in the theft, property destruction, trespass, extortion, and fraud guidelines to more effectively punish computer-related offenses. The amendment also addresses new offenses under 18 U.S.C. § 1030(a)(7), prohibiting extortion by threats of damage to a non-public government computer or a computer of a financial institution; 18 U.S.C. § 1831, prohibiting "economic espionage"; and 18 U.S.C. § 1832, prohibiting theft of "trade secrets," as broadly defined at 18 U.S.C. § 1839. Offenses under 18 U.S.C. § 1030(a)(7) are referenced to § 2B3.2 (Extortion by Force or Threat of Injury or Serious Damage); offenses under 18 U.S.C. §§ 1031 and 1832 are referenced to § 2B1.1 (Larceny, Embezzlement, and Other Forms of Theft).

Special instructions have been added to §§ 2B1.3 and 2F1.1 to provide that the minimum guideline sentence for those convicted under 18 U.S.C. § 1030(a)(4) and (5) is six months' imprisonment. These provisions implement a directive to the Commission in section 805(c) of the Antiterrorism and Effective Death Penalty Act of 1996, Pub. L. 104–132, 110 Stat. 1305.

Effective Date: The effective date of this amendment is November 1, 1997.

552. Amendment: Section 2B3.1(b)(2)(F) is amended by deleting "an express" and inserting in lieu thereof "a".

The Commentary to § 2B3.1 captioned "Application Notes" is amended in Note 6 by

Amendment 552

deleting "An 'express" and inserting in lieu thereof "'A"; by inserting after the first sentence the following additional sentence:

"Accordingly, the defendant does not have to state expressly his intent to kill the victim in order for the enhancement to apply.";

by deleting "an express" after "constitute" and inserting in lieu thereof "a"; by deleting "the underlying" and inserting in lieu thereof "this"; and by deleting "significantly greater fear than that necessary to constitute an element of the offense of robbery" and inserting in lieu thereof "a fear of death".

Reason for Amendment: This amendment addresses a circuit court conflict regarding the application of the "express threat of death" enhancement in § 2B3.1 (Robbery). The amendment adopts the majority appellate view which holds that the enhancement applies when the combination of the defendant's actions and words would instill in a reasonable person in the position of the immediate victim (e.g., a bank teller) a greater amount of fear than necessary to commit the robbery. See, e.g., United States v. Robinson, 86 F.3d 1197, 1202 (D.C. Cir. 1996) (enhancement applies if (1) a reasonable person in the position of the immediate victim would very likely believe the defendant made a threat and the threat was to kill, and (2) the victim likely thought his life was in peril); United States v. Murray, 65 F.3d 1161, 1167 (4th Cir. 1995) ("any combination of statements, gestures, or actions that would put an ordinary victim in reasonable fear for his or her life is an express threat of death").

Effective Date: The effective date of this amendment is November 1, 1997.

553. **Amendment:** The Commentary to § 2B4.1 captioned "Statutory Provisions" is amended by deleting "§§ 11907(a), (b)" and inserting in lieu thereof "§ 11902".

The Commentary to § 2N3.1 captioned "Statutory Provisions" is amended by deleting "15 U.S.C. §§ 1983-1988, 1990c" and inserting in lieu thereof "49 U.S.C. §§ 32703-32705, 32709(b).".

The Commentary to § 2Q1.2 captioned "Statutory Provisions" is amended by deleting "§ 1809(b)" and inserting in lieu thereof "§ 60123(d)".

Reason for Amendment: This amendment makes technical corrections to § 2B4.1 (Bribery in Procurement of Bank Loan and Other Commercial Bribery), § 2N3.1(Odometer Laws and Regulations), § 2Q1.2 (Mishandling of Hazardous or Toxic Substances or Pesticides; Recordkeeping, Tampering, and Falsification; Unlawfully Transporting Hazardous Materials in Commerce), to reflect changes made to statutory references when Congress codified Title 49 (Transportation), United States Code. Pub. L. 103-272, § 1(e), July 5, 1994, 108 Stat. 1356; Pub. L. 104-88, Title I, § 102(a), December 29, 1995, 109 Stat. 850.

Effective Date: The effective date of this amendment is November 1, 1997.

554. **Amendment:** Section 2B5.1(b) is amended by inserting after subdivision (3) the following additional subdivision:

"(4) If any part of the offense was committed outside the United States, increase by 2 levels.".

The Commentary to § 2B5.1 captioned "Statutory Provisions" is amended by deleting "471" and inserting in lieu thereof "470".

The Commentary to § 2B5.1 captioned "Application Notes" is amended by redesignating Notes 1 through 3 as Notes 2 through 4; and by inserting as the new Note 1:

> "1. For purposes of this guideline, 'United States' means each of the fifty states, the District of Columbia, the Commonwealth of Puerto Rico, the Virgin Islands, Guam, the Northern Mariana Islands, and American Samoa.".

Reason for Amendment: This amendment addresses section 807(h) of the Antiterrorism and Effective Death Penalty Act of 1996, Pub. L. 104-132, 110 Stat. 1308, which requires the Commission to amend the sentencing guidelines to provide an appropriate enhancement for a defendant convicted of an international counterfeiting offense under 18 U.S.C. § 470. The amendment adds a specific offense characteristic in § 2B5.1 (Offenses Involving Counterfeit Bearer Obligations of the United States) to provide a two-level enhancement if the offense occurred outside the United States.

Effective Date: The effective date of this amendment is November 1, 1997.

555. Amendment: Section 2D1.1(b) is amended by redesignating subdivision (4) as subdivision (6) and inserting after subdivision (3) the following additional subdivisions:

> "(4) If (A) the offense involved the importation of methamphetamine or the manufacture of methamphetamine from listed chemicals that the defendant knew were imported unlawfully, and (B) the defendant is not subject to an adjustment under § 3B1.2 (Mitigating Role), increase by 2 levels.
>
> (5) If the offense involved (A) an unlawful discharge, emission, or release into the environment of a hazardous or toxic substance, or (B) the unlawful transportation, treatment, storage, or disposal of a hazardous waste, increase by 2 levels.".

Section 2D1.1(c) is amended in subdivision (1) by deleting "30 KG" before "or more of Methamphetamine" and inserting in lieu thereof "15 KG".

Section 2D1.1(c) is amended in subdivision (2) by deleting "10 KG but less than 30 KG" before "of Methamphetamine" and inserting in lieu thereof "5 KG but less than 15 KG".

Section 2D1.1(c) is amended in subdivision (3) by deleting "3 KG but less than 10 KG" before "of Methamphetamine" and inserting in lieu thereof "1.5 G but less than 5 KG".

Section 2D1.1(c) is amended in subdivision (4) by deleting "1 KG but less than 3 KG" before "of Methamphetamine" and inserting in lieu thereof "500 G but less than 1.5 KG".

Section 2D1.1(c) is amended in subdivision (5) by deleting "700 G but less than 1 KG" before "of Methamphetamine" and inserting in lieu thereof "350 G but less than 500 G".

Section 2D1.1(c) is amended in subdivision (6) by deleting "400 G but less than 700 G" before "of Methamphetamine" and inserting in lieu thereof "200 G but less than 350 G".

Section 2D1.1(c) is amended in subdivision (7) by deleting "100 G but less than 400 G" before "of Methamphetamine" and inserting in lieu thereof "50 G but less than 200 G".

Section 2D1.1(c) is amended in subdivision (8) by deleting "80 G but less than 100 G" before "of Methamphetamine" and inserting in lieu thereof "40 G but less than 50 G".

Section 2D1.1(c) is amended in subdivision (9) by deleting "60 G but less than 80 G"

Amendment 555 APPENDIX C - VOLUME I November 1, 2013

before "of Methamphetamine" and inserting in lieu thereof "30 G but less than 40 G".

Section 2D1.1(c) is amended in subdivision (10) by deleting "40 G but less than 60 G" before "of Methamphetamine" and inserting in lieu thereof "20 G but less than 30 G".

Section 2D1.1(c) is amended in subdivision (11) by deleting "20 G but less than 40 G" before "of Methamphetamine" and inserting in lieu thereof "10 G but less than 20 G".

Section 2D1.1(c) is amended in subdivision (12) by deleting "10 G but less than 20 G" before "of Methamphetamine" and inserting in lieu thereof "5 G but less than 10 G".

Section 2D1.1(c) is amended in subdivision (13) by deleting "5 G but less than 10 G" before "of Methamphetamine" and inserting in lieu thereof "2.5 G but less than 5 G".

Section 2D1.1(c) is amended in subdivision (14) by deleting "5 G" before "of Methamphetamine" and inserting in lieu thereof "2.5 G".

The Commentary to § 2D1.1 captioned "Application Notes" is amended in Note 10 in the "Drug Equivalency Tables" in the subdivision captioned "Cocaine and Other Schedule I and II Stimulants" in the entry beginning "1 gm of Methamphetamine =" by deleting "1 kg" before "of marihuana" and inserting in lieu thereof "2 kg".

The Commentary to § 2D1.1 captioned "Application Notes" is amended by inserting after Note 18 the following additional notes:

"19. If the offense involved importation of methamphetamine, and an adjustment from subsection (b)(2) applies, do not apply subsection (b)(4).

20. Under subsection (b)(5), the enhancement applies if the conduct for which the defendant is accountable under § 1B1.3 (Relevant Conduct) involved any discharge, emission, release, transportation, treatment, storage, or disposal violation covered by the Resource Conservation and Recovery Act, 42 U.S.C. § 6928(d), the Federal Water Pollution Control Act, 33 U.S.C. § 1319(c), or the Comprehensive Environmental Response, Compensation, and Liability Act, 42 U.S.C. §§ 5124, 9603(b). In some cases, the enhancement under this subsection may not adequately account for the seriousness of the environmental harm or other threat to public health or safety (including the health or safety of law enforcement and cleanup personnel). In such cases, an upward departure may be warranted. Additionally, any costs of environmental cleanup and harm to persons or property should be considered by the court in determining the amount of restitution under § 5E1.1 (Restitution) and in fashioning appropriate conditions of supervision under § 5B1.3 (Conditions of Probation) and § 5D1.3 (Conditions of Supervised Release).".

The Commentary to § 2D1.1 captioned "Background" is amended in the second paragraph by inserting as the last sentence "Where necessary, this scheme has been modified in response to specific congressional directives to the Commission.".

Reason for Amendment: This multi-part amendment responds to the Comprehensive Methamphetamine Control Act of 1996, Pub. L. 104-237, 110 Stat. 3099, including the directives to the Commission in sections 301 and 303 of that Act. First, as directed by section 301 of the Act, the amendment increases penalties for methamphetamine trafficking offenses. This penalty increase is accomplished by reducing by one-half the quantity of a mixture or substance containing methamphetamine corresponding to each offense level in the Drug Quantity Table. This part of the amendment makes no change, however, in the

November 1, 2013 APPENDIX C - VOLUME I **Amendment 556**

quantities of methamphetamine (actual) (i.e., "pure" methamphetamine) and "Ice" methamphetamine that correspond to the various offense levels. The Commission has arrived at these particular changes after careful analysis of recent sentencing data, including its own intensive study of methamphetamine offenses, information provided by the Strategic Intelligence Section of the Drug Enforcement Administration concerning recent methamphetamine trafficking levels, dosage unit size, price, and drug quantity, and a variety of other information.

Second, in response to the directive in section 303 of the Act, this amendment provides an enhancement of two levels, with an invited upward departure in more extreme cases, for environmental violations occurring in association with an illicit manufacturing or other drug trafficking offense.

Third, in response to evidence of a recent, substantial increase in the importation of methamphetamine and precursor chemicals used to manufacture methamphetamine, the amendment provides an enhancement of two levels directed at such activity. An exception to this enhancement is provided for defendants who have a mitigating role in the offense under § 3B1.2 (Mitigating Role).

Effective Date: The effective date of this amendment is November 1, 1997.

556. **Amendment:** Section 2D1.1(d) is amended by deleting "Reference" and inserting in lieu thereof "References";

and by inserting after subdivision (1) the following additional subdivision:

"(2) If the defendant was convicted under 21 U.S.C. § 841(b)(7) (of distributing a controlled substance with intent to commit a crime of violence), apply § 2X1.1 (Attempt, Solicitation, or Conspiracy) in respect to the crime of violence that the defendant committed, or attempted or intended to commit, if the resulting offense level is greater than that determined above.".

Section 2D1.1(c)(10) is amended by deleting the period after "Schedule III substances" and inserting in lieu thereof a semicolon; and by inserting at the end the following additional subdivision:

"2,500 or more units of Flunitrazepam.".

Section 2D1.1(c)(11) is amended by deleting the period after "Schedule III substances" and inserting in lieu thereof a semicolon; and by inserting at the end the following additional subdivision:

"At least 1,250 but less than 2,500 units of Flunitrazepam.".

Section 2D1.1(c)(12) is amended by deleting the period after "Schedule III substances" and inserting in lieu thereof a semicolon; and by inserting at the end the following additional subdivision:

"At least 625 but less than 1,250 units of Flunitrazepam.".

Section 2D1.1(c)(13) is amended by deleting the period after "Schedule III substances" and inserting in lieu thereof a semicolon; and by inserting at the end the following additional subdivision:

"At least 312 but less than 625 units of Flunitrazepam.".

Amendment 556

Section 2D1.1(c)(14) is amended by inserting after "Schedule III substances;" the following additional subdivision:

"At least 156 but less than 312 units of Flunitrazepam;";

and by inserting "(except Flunitrazepam)" after "Schedule IV substances".

Section 2D1.1(c)(15) is amended by inserting after "Schedule III substances;" the following additional subdivision:

"At least 62 but less than 156 units of Flunitrazepam;";

and by inserting "(except Flunitrazepam)" after "Schedule IV substances".

Section 2D1.1(c)(16) is amended by inserting after "Schedule III substances;" the following additional subdivision:

"Less than 62 units of Flunitrazepam;";

and by inserting "(except Flunitrazepam)" after "Schedule IV substances".

Section 2D1.1(c)(17) is amended by inserting "(except Flunitrazepam)" after "Schedule IV substances".

The Commentary to § 2D1.1 captioned "Statutory Provisions" is amended by inserting "(7)," after "(3),".

The Commentary to § 2D1.1 captioned "Application Notes" is amended in Note 10 in the "Drug Equivalency Tables" by inserting before the subdivision captioned "Schedule I or II Depressants**" the following additional subdivision:

"Flunitrazepam **

1 unit of Flunitrazepam =   16 gm of marihuana

** Provided, that the combined equivalent weight of flunitrazepam, all Schedule I or II depressants, Schedule III substances, Schedule IV substances, and Schedule V substances shall not exceed 99.99 kilograms of marihuana.

The minimum offense level from the Drug Quantity Table for flunitrazepam individually, or in combination with any Schedule I or II depressants, Schedule III substances, Schedule IV substances, and Schedule V substances is level 8.".

The Commentary to § 2D1.1 captioned "Application Notes" is amended in Note 10 in the "Drug Equivalency Tables" in the subdivision captioned "Schedule I or II Depressants" by inserting an additional asterisk after "**" in both instances; and by inserting "(except flunitrazepam)" after "Schedule IV substances".

The Commentary to § 2D1.1 captioned "Application Notes" is amended in Note 10 in the "Drug Equivalency Tables" in the subdivision captioned "Schedule III Substances" by inserting an additional asterisk after "***" in both instances; and by inserting "(except flunitrazepam)" after "Schedule IV substances".

The Commentary to § 2D1.1 captioned "Application Notes" is amended in Note 10 in the "Drug Equivalency Tables" in the subdivision captioned "Schedule IV Substances" is amended by inserting "(except Flunitrazepam)" after "Substances"; by inserting an additional asterisk after "****" in both instances; by inserting "(except flunitrazepam)" after "Substance"; and by inserting "(except flunitrazepam)" before "and V".

The Commentary to § 2D1.1 captioned "Application Notes" is amended in Note 10 in the Drug Equivalency Tables in the subdivision captioned "Schedule V Substances" by inserting an additional asterisk after "*****" in both instances.

The Commentary to § 2D1.1 captioned "Application Notes" is amended in Note 17 by adding at the end:

> "Similarly, in the case of a controlled substance for which the maximum offense level is less than level 38 (e.g., the maximum offense level in the Drug Quantity Table for flunitrazepam is level 20), an upward departure may be warranted if the drug quantity substantially exceeds the quantity for the highest offense level established for that particular controlled substance.".

Section 2D2.1(a)(2) is amended by inserting "flunitrazepam," after "cocaine,".

The Commentary to § 2D2.1 is amended by inserting before "Background:":

> "Application Note:
>
> 1. The typical case addressed by this guideline involves possession of a controlled substance by the defendant for the defendant's own consumption. Where the circumstances establish intended consumption by a person other than the defendant, an upward departure may be warranted.".

Reason for Amendment: This amendment implements the directive to the Commission in the Drug-Induced Rape Prevention and Punishment Act of 1996, Pub. L. 104-305, 110 Stat. 3807. Section 2 of the Act directs the Commission to amend the guidelines to reflect the serious nature of offenses involving flunitrazepam. This amendment reflects the increases in statutory maximum penalties for offenses involving trafficking and simple possession, respectively, of flunitrazepam. In addition, the amendment contains a cross reference to cover the new offense created under this Act involving the distribution of a controlled substance to an individual in order to commit a crime of violence against that individual.

Effective Date: The effective date of this amendment is November 1, 1997.

557. **Amendment:** Section 2D1.11(d)(1)-(10), Note "E" (List Chemical Equivalency Table) of § 2D1.11(d), and Note 4(a) of the Commentary to § 2D1.11 captioned "Application Notes" are repromulgated without change.

Reason for Amendment: Section 302 of the Comprehensive Methamphetamine Control Act of 1996, Pub. L. 104-237, 110 Stat. 3099, directs the Commission to increase by at least two levels the offense levels for offenses involving list I chemicals under 21 U.S.C. §§ 841(d)(1) and (2) and 960(d)(1) and (3). Pursuant to this provision, the Commission promulgated an emergency amendment to § 2D1.11, effective May 1, 1997. Under the terms of the congressionally-granted authority, the emergency amendment is temporary unless repromulgated in the next amendment cycle under regularly applicable amendment procedures. See Pub.L. 100-182, § 21 set forth as an editorial note under 28 U.S.C. § 994. This amendment repromulgates § 2D1.11(d)(1)-(10), Note "E" (List Chemical Equivalency Table) of § 2D1.11(d), and Note 4(a) of the Commentary to § 2D1.11 captioned "Application Notes", as set forth in the May 1, 1997 Revised Supplement to the 1995 edition of the Guidelines Manual.

Effective Date: The effective date of this amendment is November 1, 1997.

558. Amendment: Section 2D1.12 is amended by redesignating subsection (b) as subsection (c); and by inserting the following new subsection (b):

> "(b) Specific Offense Characteristic
>
> (1) If the defendant (A) intended to manufacture methamphetamine, or (B) knew, believed, or had reasonable cause to believe that prohibited equipment was to be used to manufacture methamphetamine, increase by 2 levels.".

The Commentary to § 2D1.12 captioned "Application Notes" is amended in Note 2 by deleting "(b)(1)" and inserting in lieu thereof "(c)(1)".

Section 2D2.1(a)(3) is amended by inserting "or a list I chemical" after "controlled substance".

Reason for Amendment: This amendment implements the directive to the Commission in section 203 of the Comprehensive Methamphetamine Control Act of 1996, Pub. L. 104-237, 110 Stat. 3099, to ensure that possession of equipment used to make methamphetamine is treated as a significant violation. Additionally, the amendment includes list I chemicals under § 2D2.1 (Unlawful Possession; Attempt or Conspiracy), in response to section 201 of the Act, which amends 21 U.S.C. § 844 to include list I chemicals.

Effective Date: The effective date of this amendment is November 1, 1997.

559. Amendment: Section 2H4.1 is repromulgated without change.

Reason for Amendment: This amendment implements section 218 of the Illegal Immigration Reform and Immigrant Responsibility Act of 1996, Pub. L. 104-208, 110 Stat. 3009, which directs the Commission to review the guideline for peonage, involuntary servitude, and slave trade offenses and amend the guideline pursuant to that review. Pursuant to the emergency amendment authority of that Act, this amendment previously was promulgated as a temporary measure effective May 1, 1997.

Effective Date: The effective date of this amendment is November 1, 1997.

560. Amendment: The Commentary to § 2K1.5 captioned "Background" is amended by deleting:

> "Except under the circumstances specified in 49 U.S.C. § 46505(c), the offense covered by this section is a misdemeanor for which the maximum term of imprisonment authorized by statute is one year.";

by deleting "An" and inserting in lieu thereof "This guideline provides an"; and by deleting "is provided" immediately after "enhancement".

Reason for Amendment: This amendment strikes background commentary in guideline § 2K1.5 that is no longer correct because of a recent change in statutory penalties. Specifically, the Antiterrorism Act of 1996 increased the statutory maximum penalty for violations of 49 U.S.C. § 46505(b) from not more than one year to not more than 10 years. This increase changes the classification of an offense under subsection (b) from a class A misdemeanor to a class D felony.

Effective Date: The effective date of this amendment is November 1, 1997.

561. Amendment: Section 2L1.1 is repromulgated with the following changes:

Section 2L1.1(b)(1)(A) is amended by deleting "the defendant committed the offense" and inserting in lieu thereof "the offense was committed".

The Commentary to § 2L1.1 captioned "Application Notes" is amended in Note 1 by deleting:

> "'The defendant committed the offense other than for profit' means that there was no payment or expectation of payment for the smuggling, transporting, or harboring of any of the unlawful aliens. The 'number of unlawful aliens smuggled, transported, or harbored' does not include the defendant.",

and inserting in lieu thereof:

> "'The offense was committed other than for profit' means that there was no payment or expectation of payment for the smuggling, transporting, or harboring of any of the unlawful aliens.
>
> 'Number of unlawful aliens smuggled, transported, or harbored' does not include the defendant.".

Section 5K2.0 is amended in the third paragraph by deleting "immigration violations" and inserting in lieu thereof "other guidelines"; and by deleting "for an immigration violation" and inserting in lieu thereof "under one of these other guidelines".

Reason for Amendment: This amendment implements section 203 of the Illegal Immigration Reform and Immigrant Responsibility Act of 1996, Pub. L. 104-208, 110 Stat. 3009, which directs the Commission to amend the guidelines for offenses related to smuggling, transporting, or harboring illegal aliens. Pursuant to the emergency amendment authority of that Act, this amendment previously was promulgated as a temporary measure effective May 1, 1997. This version of the amendment changes § 2L1.1(b)(1)(A) (pertaining to a reduction for non-profit offenses) to narrow somewhat the class of cases that would qualify for the reduced offense level under that provision. This amendment also makes a conforming change to § 5K2.0.

Effective Date: The effective date of this amendment is November 1, 1997.

562. Amendment: Section 2L1.2 is amended by deleting subsection (b) as follows:

> "(b) Specific Offense Characteristics
>
> If more than one applies, use the greater:
>
> (1) If the defendant previously was deported after a conviction for a felony, other than a felony involving violation of the immigration laws, increase by 4 levels.
>
> (2) If the defendant previously was deported after a conviction for an aggravated felony, increase by 16 levels.",

and inserting in lieu thereof:

> "(b) Specific Offense Characteristic
>
> (1) If the defendant previously was deported after a criminal conviction, or if the defendant unlawfully remained in the United States follow-

ing a removal order issued after a criminal conviction, increase as follows (if more than one applies, use the greater):

(A) If the conviction was for an aggravated felony, increase by 16 levels.

(B) If the conviction was for (i) any other felony, or (ii) three or more misdemeanor crimes of violence or misdemeanor controlled substance offenses, increase by 4 levels.".

The Commentary to § 2L1.2 captioned "Application Notes" is amended by deleting Notes 3 and 4 as follows:

"3. A 4-level increase is provided under subsection (b)(1) in the case of a defendant who was previously deported after a conviction for a felony, other than a felony involving a violation of the immigration laws.

4. A 16-level increase is provided under subsection (b)(2) in the case of a defendant who was previously deported after a conviction for an aggravated felony.";

by redesignating Notes 1 and 2 as Notes 2 and 3, respectively; by deleting in Note 3, as redesignated, "without criminal conviction" after "deportation"; and by inserting the following as the new Note 1:

"1. For purposes of this guideline—

'Deported after a conviction,' means that the deportation was subsequent to the conviction, whether or not the deportation was in response to such conviction. An alien has previously been 'deported' if he or she has been removed or has departed the United States while an order of exclusion, deportation, or removal was outstanding.

'Remained in the United States following a removal order issued after a conviction,' means that the removal order was subsequent to the conviction, whether or not the removal order was in response to such conviction.

'Aggravated felony,' is defined at 8 U.S.C. § 1101(a)(43) without regard to the date of conviction of the aggravated felony.

'Crime of violence' and 'controlled substance offense' are defined in § 4B1.2. For purposes of subsection (b)(1)(B), 'crime of violence' includes offenses punishable by imprisonment for a term of one year or less.

'Firearms offense' means any offense covered by Chapter Two, Part K, Subpart 2, or any similar offense under state or local law.

'Felony offense' means any federal, state, or local offense punishable by imprisonment for a term exceeding one year.".

The Commentary to § 2L1.2 captioned "Application Notes" is amended by redesignating Note 5 as Note 4; in Note 4, as redesignated, by deleting "(b)(1) or (b)(2)" and inserting in lieu thereof "(b)"; and by inserting after Note 4, as redesignated, the following new note:

"5. Aggravated felonies that trigger the adjustment from subsection (b)(1)(A) vary widely. If subsection (b)(1)(A) applies, and (A) the defendant has previously been convicted of only one felony offense; (B) such offense was not a crime of violence or firearms offense; and (C) the term of imprisonment imposed for such offense did not exceed one year, a downward departure may be warranted based on the seriousness of the aggravated felony.".

The Commentary to § 2L1.2 captioned "Application Notes" is amended by deleting Notes 6 and 7 as follows:

"6. 'Deported after a conviction,' as used in subsections (b)(1) and (b)(2), means that the deportation was subsequent to the conviction, whether or not the deportation was in response to such conviction.

7. 'Aggravated felony,' as used in subsection (b)(2), means murder; any illicit trafficking in any controlled substance (as defined in 21 U.S.C. § 802), including any drug trafficking crime as defined in 18 U.S.C. § 924(c)(2); any illicit trafficking in any firearms or destructive devices as defined in 18 U.S.C. § 921; any offense described in 18 U.S.C. § 1956 (relating to laundering of monetary instruments); any crime of violence (as defined in 18 U.S.C. § 16, not including a purely political offense) for which the term of imprisonment imposed (regardless of any suspension of such imprisonment) is at least five years; or any attempt or conspiracy to commit any such act. The term 'aggravated felony' applies to offenses described in the previous sentence whether in violation of federal or state law and also applies to offenses described in the previous sentence in violation of foreign law for which the term of imprisonment was completed within the previous 15 years. See 8 U.S.C. § 1101(a)(43).".

Reason for Amendment: This amendment implements sections 321 and 334 of the Illegal Immigration and Immigrant Responsibility Act of 1996, Pub. L. 104-208, 110 Stat. 3009. Section 321 of the Act adds to the definition of "aggravated felony" crimes of rape and sexual abuse of a minor, as well as any crime of violence for which the term of imprisonment is at least one year. This amendment conforms the definition of "aggravated felony" in the guidelines with the amended definition in the Immigration and Nationality Act.

Section 334 directs the Sentencing Commission to promulgate amendments to the guidelines for the crimes of unlawfully remaining and illegally entering the United States corresponding to changes made in statutory penalties for these offenses in the Violent Crime Control and Law Enforcement Act of 1994, Pub. L. 103-322, 108 Stat. 1796. This amendment enhances penalties for those who unlawfully enter or remain in the United States following conviction for an aggravated felony, any other felony, or three misdemeanor crimes of violence or controlled substance offenses. The amendment also makes clarifying changes to the commentary.

Effective Date: The effective date of this amendment is November 1, 1997.

563. **Amendment:** Section 2L2.1 is repromulgated with the following changes:

Section 2L2.1(b) is amended by deleting:

"(1) If the defendant committed the offense other than for profit, or the offense involved the smuggling, transporting, or harboring only of the defendant's spouse or child (or both the defendant's spouse and child), decrease by 3 levels.",

and inserting in lieu thereof:

> "(1) If the offense was committed other than for profit, or the offense involved the smuggling, transporting, or harboring only of the defendant's spouse or child (or both the defendant's spouse and child), decrease by 3 levels.".

The Commentary to § 2L2.1 captioned "Application Notes" is amended in Note 1 by deleting:

> "'The defendant committed the offense other than for profit' means that there was no payment or expectation of payment for the smuggling, transporting, or harboring of any of the unlawful aliens.",

and inserting in lieu thereof:

> "'The offense was committed other than for profit' means that there was no payment or expectation of payment for the smuggling, transporting, or harboring of any of the unlawful aliens.".

Section 2L2.2 is repromulgated without change.

Reason for Amendment: This amendment implements section 211 of the Illegal Immigration Reform and Immigrant Responsibility Act of 1996, Pub. L. 104-208, 110 Stat. 3009, which directs the Commission to amend the guidelines for offenses related to the fraudulent use of government-issued documents. Pursuant to the emergency amendment authority of that Act, this amendment previously was promulgated as a temporary measure effective May 1, 1997. This version of the amendment changes § 2L2.1(b)(1)(pertaining to a reduction for non-profit offenses) to narrow somewhat the class of cases that would qualify for the reduced offense level under that provision.

Effective Date: The effective date of this amendment is November 1, 1997.

564. **Amendment:** Section 3A1.1(a) is amended by inserting "of conviction" after "the offense".

The Commentary to § 3A1.1 captioned "Application Notes" is amended in Note 2 by inserting at the beginning the following new paragraph:

> "For purposes of subsection (b), 'victim' includes any person who is a victim of the offense of conviction and any conduct for which the defendant is accountable under § 1B1.3 (Relevant Conduct).".

Reason for Amendment: This amendment addresses a circuit court conflict regarding whether "victim of the offense" in § 3A1.1 (Hate Crime Motivation or Vulnerable Victim) refers only to a victim of the defendant's offense of conviction or, more broadly, to a victim of any relevant conduct. The amendment adopts the majority appellate view, which holds that a sentencing court should consider the defendant's relevant conduct when determining whether the vulnerable victim enhancement applies. See, e.g., United States v. Haggard, 41 F.3d 1320, 1326 (9th Cir. 1994) (proper to consider harm caused to victims beyond the defendant's offense of conviction); United States v. Yount, 960 F.2d 955 (11th Cir. 1992).

This amendment also clarifies a possible ambiguity regarding the scope of conduct to be considered when applying the hate crime motivation enhancement in § 3A1.1(a). Consistent with Congress's intent to punish a defendant whose primary objective in committing the hate crime was to harm a member of a particular class of individuals, this amendment clarifies that the enhancement in subsection (a) is limited to victims of the defendant's offense of conviction.

Effective Date: The effective date of this amendment is November 1, 1997.

565. **Amendment:** Section 3A1.4 is repromulgated without change.

Reason for Amendment: Section 730 of the Antiterrorism and Effective Death Penalty Act of 1996, Pub. L. 104-132, 110 Stat. 1303, requires the Commission to amend the sentencing guidelines so that the adjustment in § 3A1.4 (relating to international terrorism) applies more broadly to "Federal crimes of terrorism," as defined in 18 U.S.C. § 2332b(g). Pursuant to this provision, the Commission promulgated § 3A1.4 (Terrorism) as an emergency amendment, effective November 1, 1996. Under the terms of the congressionally granted authority, this amendment is temporary unless repromulgated in the next amendment cycle under regularly applicable amendment procedures. See Pub. L. No. 100-182, § 21, set forth as an editorial note under 28 U.S.C. § 994. This amendment repromulgates § 3A1.4, as set forth in the May 1, 1997 Revised Supplement to the 1995 Guidelines Manual.

Effective Date: The effective date of this amendment is November 1, 1997.

566. **Amendment:** The Commentary to § 3C1.1 captioned "Application Notes" is amended in Note 1 by deleting in the third sentence "such testimony or statements should be evaluated in a light most favorable to the defendant." and inserting in lieu thereof:

> "the court should be cognizant that inaccurate testimony or statements sometimes may result from confusion, mistake, or faulty memory and, thus, not all inaccurate testimony or statements necessarily reflect a willful attempt to obstruct justice.".

The Commentary to § 3C1.1 captioned "Application Notes" is amended in Note 3(i) by deleting "conduct prohibited by 18 U.S.C. §§ 1501-1516." and inserting in lieu thereof "other conduct prohibited by obstruction of justice provisions under Title 18, United States Code (e.g., 18 U.S.C. §§ 1510, 1511).".

The Commentary to § 3C1.1 captioned "Application Notes" is amended in Note 4 by deleting "The following is a non-exhaustive list of examples of the" and inserting in lieu thereof "Some"; by deleting "that, absent a separate count of conviction for such conduct," and inserting in lieu thereof "ordinarily"; by deleting ", but ordinarily can appropriately be sanctioned by the determination of the particular" and inserting in lieu thereof "but may warrant a greater"; and by inserting the following after "guideline range":

> ". However, if the defendant is convicted of a separate count for such conduct, this enhancement will apply and increase the offense level for the underlying offense (i. e., the offense with respect to which the obstructive conduct occurred). See Application Note 7, below.
>
> The following is a non-exhaustive list of examples of the types of conduct to which this application note applies".

The Commentary to § 3C1.1 captioned "Application Notes" is amended in Note 6 by deleting:

> "Where the defendant is convicted both of the obstruction offense and the underlying offense, the count for the obstruction offense will be grouped with the count for

Amendment 566

the underlying offense under subsection (c) of § 3D1.2 (Groups of Closely Related Counts). The offense level for that group of closely related counts will be the offense level for the underlying offense increased by the 2-level adjustment specified by this section, or the offense level for the obstruction offense, whichever is greater.".

The Commentary to § 3C1.1 captioned "Application Notes" is amended by redesignating Note 7 as Note 8; and by inserting the following as new Note 7:

> "7. Where the defendant is convicted both of the obstruction offense and the underlying offense (the offense with respect to which the obstructive conduct occurred), the count for the obstruction offense will be grouped with the count for the underlying offense under subsection (c) of § 3D1.2 (Groups of Closely Related Counts). The offense level for that group of closely related counts will be the offense level for the underlying offense increased by the 2-level adjustment specified by this section, or the offense level for the obstruction offense, whichever is greater.".

Reason for Amendment: This amendment addresses a circuit court conflict regarding the meaning of the last sentence of Application Note 1 in § 3C1.1. The issue is whether that sentence requires the use of a heightened standard of proof when the court applies an enhancement for perjury. Compare United States v. Montague, 40 F.3d 1251 (D.C. Cir. 1994) (applying the clear and convincing standard) with United States v. Zajac, 62 F.3d 145 (6th Cir.) (applying the preponderance of the evidence standard), cert. denied 116 S. Ct. 681 (1995). The amendment changes the last sentence of Application Note 1 so that it no longer suggests the use of a heightened standard of proof. Instead, it clarifies that the court should be mindful that not all inaccurate testimony or statements reflect a willful attempt to obstruct justice.

The amendment also (A) modifies subdivision (i) of Application Note 3 in § 3C1.1 to make the language more precise; (B) in response to concerns expressed in a Seventh Circuit opinion, clarifies the meaning of the phrase "absent a separate count of conviction" by adding an additional sentence at the end of Application Note 4, see United States v. Giacometti, 28 F.3d 698 (7th Cir. 1994); and (C) clarifies that the guidance in the last two sentences of Application Note 6 applies to a broader set of cases than the cases described in the first two sentences of Application Note 6.

Effective Date: The effective date of this amendment is November 1, 1997.

567. **Amendment:** The Commentary to § 4B1.1 captioned "Application Notes" is amended in Note 2 by deleting "not" after "offense," in the first sentence; by deleting "(b)(1)(B), (b)(1)(C), and (b)(1)(D)" and inserting in lieu thereof "(B), (C), and (D)"; by deleting "where" and inserting in lieu thereof "in a case in which"; by inserting "for that defendant" after "Maximum'"; by deleting "twenty years and not thirty years" and inserting in lieu thereof "thirty years and not twenty years"; by deleting "authorizes" and inserting in lieu thereof "has"; and by deleting "maximum term of imprisonment" and inserting in lieu thereof "offense statutory maximum".

The Commentary to § 4B1.1 captioned "Background" is amended by deleting:

> "The legislative history of this provision suggests that the phrase 'maximum term authorized' should be construed as the maximum term authorized by statute. See S. Rep. No. 225, 98th Cong., 1st Sess. 175 (1983); 128 Cong. Rec. 26,511-12 (1982) (text of 'Career Criminals' amendment by Senator Kennedy); id. at 26,515 (brief summary of amendment); id. at 26,517-18 (statement of Senator Kennedy).".

Reason for Amendment: This amendment responds to United States v. LaBonte, 520 U.S. 751. In LaBonte, the Supreme Court held that the way in which the Commission defined "maximum term authorized", for purposes of fulfilling the requirement under 28 U.S.C. § 994(h) to specify sentences for certain categories of career offenders at or near the maximum term authorized for those offenders, is inconsistent with § 994(h)'s plain and unambiguous language and is therefore invalid. The Commission defined "maximum term authorized" to mean the maximum term authorized for the offense of conviction not including any sentencing enhancement provisions that apply because of the defendant's prior criminal record. The Supreme Court held that under § 994's plain and unambiguous language, "maximum term authorized" must be read to include all applicable statutory sentencing enhancements. The proposed amendment makes a straightforward change to the commentary to § 4B1.1, the career offender guideline, to reflect the LaBonte decision. Specifically, the definition of "maximum term authorized" is proposed to be changed to reflect that the "maximum term authorized" includes all sentencing enhancements that apply because of the defendant's prior criminal record.

Effective Date: The effective date of this amendment is November 1, 1997.

568. Amendment: Section § 4B1.2(1) is amended by deleting "(1)" and inserting in lieu thereof "(a)"; by inserting a comma after "law" and after "one year"; by deleting "(i)" and inserting in lieu thereof "(1)"; and by deleting "(ii)" and inserting in lieu thereof "(2)".

Section § 4B1.2(2) is amended by deleting "(2)" and inserting in lieu thereof "(b)"; by deleting "a" after "under"; and by deleting "prohibiting" and inserting in lieu thereof ", punishable by imprisonment for a term exceeding one year, that prohibits".

Section § 4B1.2(3) is amended by deleting "(3)" and inserting in lieu thereof "(c)"; by deleting "(A)" and inserting in lieu thereof "(1)"; and by deleting "(B)" and inserting in lieu thereof "(2)".

The Commentary to § 4B1.2 captioned "Application Notes" is amended in Note 1 by inserting at the beginning "For purposes of this guideline—"; by deleting "The terms 'crime" and inserting in lieu thereof "'Crime";

and by inserting at the end the following new paragraphs:

> "'Crime of violence' includes murder, manslaughter, kidnapping, aggravated assault, forcible sex offenses, robbery, arson, extortion, extortionate extension of credit, and burglary of a dwelling. Other offenses are included as 'crimes of violence' if (A) that offense has as an element the use, attempted use, or threatened use of physical force against the person of another, or (B) the conduct set forth (i.e., expressly charged) in the count of which the defendant was convicted involved use of explosives (including any explosive material or destructive device) or, by its nature, presented a serious potential risk of physical injury to another.

> 'Crime of violence' does not include the offense of unlawful possession of a firearm by a felon. Where the instant offense of conviction is the unlawful possession of a firearm by a felon, § 2K2.1 (Unlawful Receipt, Possession, or Transportation of Firearms or Ammunition; Prohibited Transactions Involving Firearms or Ammunition) provides an increase in offense level if the defendant had one or more prior felony convictions for a crime of violence or controlled substance offense; and, if the defendant is sentenced under the provisions of 18 U.S.C. § 924(e), § 4B1.4 (Armed Career Criminal) will apply.

> Unlawfully possessing a listed chemical with intent to manufacture a controlled substance (21 U.S.C. § 841(d)(1)) is a 'controlled substance offense.'

Amendment 568 APPENDIX C - VOLUME I November 1, 2013

Unlawfully possessing a prohibited flask or equipment with intent to manufacture a controlled substance (21 U.S.C. § 843(a)(6)) is a 'controlled substance offense.'

Maintaining any place for the purpose of facilitating a drug offense (21 U.S.C. § 856) is a 'controlled substance offense' if the offense of conviction established that the underlying offense (the offense facilitated) was a 'controlled substance offense.'

Using a communications facility in committing, causing, or facilitating a drug offense (21 U.S.C. § 843(b)) is a 'controlled substance offense' if the offense of conviction established that the underlying offense (the offense committed, caused, or facilitated) was a 'controlled substance offense.'

Possessing a firearm during and in relation to a crime of violence or drug offense (18 U.S.C. § 924(c)) is a 'crime of violence' or 'controlled substance offense' if the offense of conviction established that the underlying offense (the offense during and in relation to which the firearm was carried or possessed) was a 'crime of violence' or 'controlled substance offense.' (Note that if the defendant also was convicted of the underlying offense, the two convictions will be treated as related cases under § 4A1.2 (Definitions and Instruction for Computing Criminal History)).

'Prior felony conviction' means a prior adult federal or state conviction for an offense punishable by death or imprisonment for a term exceeding one year, regardless of whether such offense is specifically designated as a felony and regardless of the actual sentence imposed. A conviction for an offense committed at age eighteen or older is an adult conviction. A conviction for an offense committed prior to age eighteen is an adult conviction if it is classified as an adult conviction under the laws of the jurisdiction in which the defendant was convicted (e.g., a federal conviction for an offense committed prior to the defendant's eighteenth birthday is an adult conviction if the defendant was expressly proceeded against as an adult).".

The Commentary to § 4B1.2 captioned "Application Notes" is amended by deleting Notes 2 and 3 as follows:

"2. 'Crime of violence' includes murder, manslaughter, kidnapping, aggravated assault, forcible sex offenses, robbery, arson, extortion, extortionate extension of credit, and burglary of a dwelling. Other offenses are included where (A) that offense has as an element the use, attempted use, or threatened use of physical force against the person of another, or (B) the conduct set forth (i.e., expressly charged) in the count of which the defendant was convicted involved use of explosives (including any explosive material or destructive device) or, by its nature, presented a serious potential risk of physical injury to another. Under this section, the conduct of which the defendant was convicted is the focus of inquiry.

The term 'crime of violence' does not include the offense of unlawful possession of a firearm by a felon. Where the instant offense of conviction is the unlawful possession of a firearm by a felon, § 2K2.1 (Unlawful Receipt, Possession, or Transportation of Firearms or Ammunition; Prohibited Transactions Involving Firearms or Ammunition) provides an increase in offense level if the defendant has one or more prior felony convictions for a crime of violence or controlled substance offense; and, if the defendant is sentenced under the provisions of 18 U.S.C. § 924(e), § 4B1.4 (Armed Career Criminal) will apply.

3. 'Prior felony conviction' means a prior adult federal or state conviction for

an offense punishable by death or imprisonment for a term exceeding one year, regardless of whether such offense is specifically designated as a felony and regardless of the actual sentence imposed. A conviction for an offense committed at age eighteen or older is an adult conviction. A conviction for an offense committed prior to age eighteen is an adult conviction if it is classified as an adult conviction under the laws of the jurisdiction in which the defendant was convicted (e.g., a federal conviction for an offense committed prior to the defendant's eighteenth birthday is an adult conviction if the defendant was expressly proceeded against as an adult).";

and by inserting after Note 1 the following new Note 2:

"2. Section 4B1.1 (Career Offender) expressly provides that the instant and prior offenses must be crimes of violence or controlled substance offenses of which the defendant was convicted. Therefore, in determining whether an offense is a crime of violence or controlled substance for the purposes of § 4B1.1 (Career Offender), the offense of conviction (i.e., the conduct of which the defendant was convicted) is the focus of inquiry.".

The Commentary to § 4B1.2 captioned "Application Notes" is amended by redesignating Note 4 as Note 3.

The Commentary to § 2K1.3 captioned "Application Notes" is amended in Note 2 by deleting "Note 3" and inserting in lieu thereof "Note 1".

The Commentary to § 2K2.1 captioned "Application Notes" is amended in Note 5 by deleting "Note 3" and inserting in lieu thereof "Note 1".

The Commentary to § 7B1.1 captioned "Application Notes" is amended in Note 2 by deleting "§ 4B1.2(1)" and inserting in lieu thereof "§ 4B1.2(a)"; and by deleting "Notes 1 and 2" and inserting in lieu thereof "Note 1".

The Commentary to § 7B1.1 captioned "Application Notes" is amended in Note 3 by deleting "§ 4B1.2(2)" and inserting in lieu thereof "§ 4B1.2(b)".

Reason for Amendment: This amendment addresses a circuit court conflict regarding whether the offenses of possessing a listed chemical with intent to manufacture a controlled substance or possessing a prohibited flask or equipment with intent to manufacture a controlled substance are "controlled substance offenses" under the career offender guideline. Compare United States v. Calverley, 11 F.3d 505 (5th Cir. 1993) (possession of a listed chemical with intent to manufacture a controlled substance is a controlled substance offense under § 4B1.2) with United States v. Wagner, 994 F.2d 1467, 1475 (10th Cir. 1993) (possession of a listed chemical with intent to manufacture a controlled substance is not a controlled substance offense). This amendment makes each of these offenses a "controlled substance offense" under the career offender guideline. This decision is based on the Commission's view that there is such a close connection between possession of a listed chemical or prohibited flask or equipment with intent to manufacture a controlled substance and actually manufacturing a controlled substance that the former offenses are fairly considered as controlled substance trafficking offenses.

The amendment also clarifies that certain other offenses are "crimes of violence" or "controlled substance offenses" if the offense of conviction established that the underlying offense was a "crime of violence" or "controlled substance offense." See United States v. Baker, 16 F.3d 854 (8th Cir. 1994); United States v. Vea-Gonzalez, 999 F.2d 1326 (9th Cir. 1993), effectively overruled on other grounds by Custis v. United States, 114 S.Ct.

Amendment 568 APPENDIX C - VOLUME I November 1, 2013

1732 (1994). Additionally, the amendment makes the following nonsubstantive changes to § 4B1.2 to improve the internal consistency of the guidelines: (A) adding the phrase "punishable by a term of imprisonment of more than one year, that prohibits" in subsection (2) to make it consistent with subsection (1); and (B) conforming the second paragraph of Application Note 2 of § 4B1.2 to the language of §§ 2K1.3 and 2K2.1.

Effective Date: The effective date of this amendment is November 1, 1997.

569. Amendment: Chapter Five, Part B, Subpart 1 is amended by deleting §§ 5B1.3 and 5B1.4 in their entirety as follows:

"§ 5B1.3. Conditions of Probation

(a) If a term of probation is imposed, the court shall impose a condition that the defendant shall not commit another federal, state, or local crime during the term of probation. 18 U.S.C. § 3563(a)(1). The court shall also impose a condition that the defendant not possess illegal controlled substances. 18 U.S.C. § 3563(a)(3).

(b) The court may impose other conditions that (1) are reasonably related to the nature and circumstances of the offense, the history and characteristics of the defendant, and the purposes of sentencing and (2) involve only such deprivations of liberty or property as are reasonably necessary to effect the purposes of sentencing. 18 U.S.C. § 3563(b). Recommended conditions are set forth in § 5B1.4.

(c) If a term of probation is imposed for a felony, the court shall impose at least one of the following as a condition of probation: a fine, an order of restitution, or community service, unless the court finds on the record that extraordinary circumstances exist that would make such a condition plainly unreasonable, in which event the court shall impose one or more of the other conditions set forth under 18 U.S.C. § 3563(b). 18 U.S.C. § 3563(a)(2).

(d) Intermittent confinement (custody for intervals of time) may be ordered as a condition of probation during the first year of probation. 18 U.S.C. § 3563(b)(11). Intermittent confinement shall be credited toward the guideline term of imprisonment at § 5C1.1 as provided in the schedule at § 5C1.1(e).

Commentary

A broader form of the condition required under 18 U.S.C. § 3563(a)(3) (pertaining to possession of controlled substances) is set forth as recommended condition (7) at § 5B1.4 (Recommended Conditions of Probation and Supervised Release).

§ 5B1.4. Recommended Conditions of Probation and Supervised Release (Policy Statement)

(a) The following 'standard' conditions (1-13) are generally recommended for both probation and supervised release:

(1) the defendant shall not leave the judicial district or other specified geographic area without the permission of the court or probation officer;

(2) the defendant shall report to the probation officer as directed by the court or probation officer and shall submit a truthful and complete written report within the first five days of each month;

(3) the defendant shall answer truthfully all inquiries by the probation officer and follow the instructions of the probation officer;

(4) the defendant shall support his dependents and meet other family responsibilities;

(5) the defendant shall work regularly at a lawful occupation unless excused by the probation officer for schooling, training, or other acceptable reasons;

(6) the defendant shall notify the probation officer within seventy-two hours of any change in residence or employment;

(7) the defendant shall refrain from excessive use of alcohol and shall not purchase, possess, use, distribute, or administer any narcotic or other controlled substance, or any paraphernalia related to such substances, except as prescribed by a physician;

(8) the defendant shall not frequent places where controlled substances are illegally sold, used, distributed, or administered, or other places specified by the court;

(9) the defendant shall not associate with any persons engaged in criminal activity, and shall not associate with any person convicted of a felony unless granted permission to do so by the probation officer;

(10) the defendant shall permit a probation officer to visit him at any time at home or elsewhere and shall permit confiscation of any contraband observed in plain view by the probation officer;

(11) the defendant shall notify the probation officer within seventy-two hours of being arrested or questioned by a law enforcement officer;

(12) the defendant shall not enter into any agreement to act as an informer or a special agent of a law enforcement agency without the permission of the court;

(13) as directed by the probation officer, the defendant shall notify third parties of risks that may be occasioned by the defendant's criminal record or personal history or characteristics, and shall permit the probation officer to make such notifications and to confirm the defendant's compliance with such notification requirement.

(b) The following 'special' conditions of probation and supervised release (14-24) are either recommended or required by law under the circumstances described, or may be appropriate in a particular case:

- (14) Possession of Weapons

    If the instant conviction is for a felony, or if the defendant was previously convicted of a felony or used a firearm or other dangerous weapon in the course of the instant offense, it is recommended that the court impose a condition prohibiting the defendant from possessing a firearm or other dangerous weapon.

- (15) Restitution

    If the court imposes an order of restitution, it is recommended that the court impose a condition requiring the defendant to make payment of restitution or adhere to a court ordered installment schedule for payment of restitution. See § 5E1.1 (Restitution).

- (16) Fines

    If the court imposes a fine, it is recommended that the court impose a condition requiring the defendant to pay the fine or adhere to a court ordered installment schedule for payment of the fine.

- (17) Debt Obligations

    If an installment schedule of payment of restitution or fines is imposed, it is recommended that the court impose a condition prohibiting the defendant from incurring new credit charges or opening additional lines of credit without approval of the probation officer unless the defendant is in compliance with the payment schedule.

- (18) Access to Financial Information

    If the court imposes an order of restitution, forfeiture, or notice to victims, or orders the defendant to pay a fine, it is recommended that the court impose a condition requiring the defendant to provide the probation officer access to any requested financial information.

- (19) Community Confinement

    Residence in a community treatment center, halfway house or similar facility may be imposed as a condition of probation or supervised release. See § 5F1.1 (Community Confinement).

- (20) Home Detention

    Home detention may be imposed as a condition of probation or supervised release, but only as a substitute for imprisonment. See § 5F1.2 (Home Detention).

(21) Community Service

Community service may be imposed as a condition of probation or supervised release. See § 5F1.3 (Community Service).

(22) Occupational Restrictions

Occupational restrictions may be imposed as a condition of probation or supervised release. See § 5F1.5 (Occupational Restrictions).

(23) Substance Abuse Program Participation

If the court has reason to believe that the defendant is an abuser of narcotics, other controlled substances or alcohol, it is recommended that the court impose a condition requiring the defendant to participate in a program approved by the United States Probation Office for substance abuse, which program may include testing to determine whether the defendant has reverted to the use of drugs or alcohol.

(24) Mental Health Program Participation

If the court has reason to believe that the defendant is in need of psychological or psychiatric treatment, it is recommended that the court impose a condition requiring that the defendant participate in a mental health program approved by the United States Probation Office.

(25) Curfew

If the court concludes that restricting the defendant to his place of residence during evening and nighttime hours is necessary to provide just punishment for the offense, to protect the public from crimes that the defendant might commit during those hours, or to assist in the rehabilitation of the defendant, a condition of curfew is recommended. Electronic monitoring may be used as a means of surveillance to ensure compliance with a curfew order.

Commentary

Application Note:

1. Home detention, as defined by § 5F1.2, may only be used as a substitute for imprisonment. See § 5C1.1 (Imposition of a Term of Imprisonment). Under home detention, the defendant, with specified exceptions, is restricted to his place of residence during all non-working hours. Curfew, which limits the defendant to his place of residence during evening and nighttime hours, is less restrictive than home detention and may be imposed as a condition of probation whether or not imprisonment could have been ordered.".

A replacement guideline with accompanying commentary is inserted as § 5B1.3 (Condi-

Amendment 569   APPENDIX C - VOLUME I   November 1, 2013

tions of Probation).

Chapter Five, Part D, Subpart 1 is amended by deleting § 5D1.3 in its entirety as follows:

"§ 5D1.3.   Conditions of Supervised Release

     (a)   If a term of supervised release is imposed, the court shall impose a condition that the defendant not commit another federal, state, or local crime. 18 U.S.C. § 3583(d). The court shall also impose a condition that the defendant not possess illegal controlled substances. 18 U.S.C. § 3563(a)(3).

     (b)   The court may impose other conditions of supervised release, to the extent that such conditions are reasonably related to (1) the nature and circumstances of the offense and the history and characteristics of the defendant, and (2) the need for the sentence imposed to afford adequate deterrence to criminal conduct, to protect the public from further crimes of the defendant, and to provide the defendant with needed educational or vocational training, medical care, or other correctional treatment in the most effective manner. 18 U.S.C. §§ 3553(a)(2) and 3583(d).

     (c)   Recommended conditions of supervised release are set forth in § 5B1.4.

Commentary

Background: This section applies to conditions of supervised release. The conditions generally recommended for supervised release are those recommended for probation. See § 5B1.4. A broader form of the condition required under 18 U.S.C. § 3563(a)(3) (pertaining to possession of controlled substances) is set forth as recommended condition (7) at § 5B1.4 (Recommended Conditions of Probation and Supervised Release).".

A replacement guideline with accompanying commentary is inserted as § 5D1.3 (Conditions of Supervised Release).

The Commentary to § 2X5.1 captioned "Application Note" is amended in Note 1 by deleting: "§ 5B1.4 (Recommended Conditions of Probation and Supervised Release);".

Section 5H1.3 is amended by deleting "recommended condition (24) at § 5B1.4 (Recommended Conditions of Probation and Supervised Release)" and inserting in lieu thereof "§§ 5B1.3(d)(5) and 5D1.3(d)(5)".

Section 5H1.4 is amended in the second paragraph by deleting "recommended condition (23) at § 5B1.4 (Recommended Conditions of Probation and Supervised Release)" and inserting in lieu thereof "§ 5D1.3(d)(4)"; and in the third paragraph by deleting "recommended condition (23) at § 5B1.4 (Recommended Conditions of Probation and Supervised Release)" and inserting in lieu thereof "§ 5B1.3(d)(4)".

Section 8D1.3(a) is amended by deleting "shall" immediately after "organization".

Section 8D1.3(b) is amended by deleting "a fine, restitution, or community service," and inserting in lieu thereof "(1) restitution, (2) notice to victims of the offense pursuant to 18 U.S.C. § 3555, or (3) an order requiring the organization to reside, or refrain from residing, in a specified place or area,";

and by adding at the end:

> "Note: Section 3563(a)(2) of Title 18, United States Code, provides that, absent unusual circumstances, a defendant convicted of a felony shall abide by at least one of the conditions set forth in 18 U.S.C. § 3563(b)(2), (b)(3), and (b)(13). Before the enactment of the Antiterrorism and Effective Death Penalty Act of 1996, those conditions were a fine ((b)(2)), an order of restitution ((b)(3)), and community service ((b)(13)). Whether or not the change was intended, the Act deleted the fine condition and renumbered the restitution and community service conditions in 18 U.S.C. § 3563(b), but failed to make a corresponding change in the referenced paragraphs under 18 U.S.C. § 3563(a)(2). Accordingly, the conditions now referenced are restitution ((b)(2)), notice to victims pursuant to 18 U.S.C. § 3555 ((b)(3)), and an order that the defendant reside, or refrain from residing, in a specified place or area ((b)(13)).".

Reason for Amendment: The purposes of this amendment are twofold. First, the amendment revises the pertinent guidelines to reflect statutorily required conditions of probation and supervised release added by Section 203 of the Antiterrorism and Effective Death Penalty Act of 1996, Pub. L. 104-132, 110 Stat. 1227, and other laws. Second, the amendment revises §§ 5B1.3 (Conditions of Probation), 5B1.4 (Recommended Conditions of Probation and Supervised Release), and 5D1.3 (Conditions of Supervised Release) so as to better distinguish among the statutorily required, standard, and special conditions of probation and supervised release. Section 5B1.4 has been eliminated. Provisions of § 5B1.4 relating to recommended conditions of probation have been incorporated into § 5B1.3, and provisions of § 5B1.4 relating to recommended conditions of supervised release have been incorporated into § 5D1.3.

Effective Date: The effective date of this amendment is November 1, 1997.

570. **Amendment:** Section 5D1.2(a) is amended by deleting "If" and inserting in lieu thereof "Subject to subsection (b), if".

Section 5D1.2(b) is amended by deleting "Provided, that" and inserting in lieu thereof "Except as otherwise provided,"; and by deleting "in no event" and inserting in lieu thereof "not".

The Commentary to § 5D1.2 is amended by inserting the following before "Background":

> "Application Notes:
>
> 1. A defendant who qualifies under § 5C1.2 (Applicability of Statutory Minimum Sentence in Certain Cases) is not subject to any statutory minimum sentence of supervised release. See 18 U.S.C. § 3553(f). In such a case, the term of supervised release shall be determined under subsection (a).
>
> 2. Upon motion of the Government, a defendant who has provided substantial assistance in the investigation or prosecution of another person who has committed an offense may be sentenced to a term of supervised release that is less than any minimum required by statute or the guidelines. See 18 U.S.C. § 3553(e), § 5K1.1 (Substantial Assistance to Authorities).".

The Commentary to § 5C1.2 captioned "Application Notes" is amended by inserting after Note 8 the following additional note:

> "9. A defendant who meets the criteria under this section is exempt from any

Amendment 570   APPENDIX C - VOLUME I   November 1, 2013

otherwise applicable statutory minimum sentence of imprisonment and statutory minimum term of supervised release.".

Reason for Amendment: This amendment amends § 5D1.2 (Term of Supervised Release) to make clear that a defendant who qualifies under the "safety valve" (§ 5C1.2, 18 U.S.C. § 3553(f)), or who is the beneficiary of a Government substantial assistance motion under 18 U.S.C. § 3553(e), is not subject to any statutory minimum term of supervised release. This issue has arisen in a number of hotline calls. This amendment also clarifies that the requirement in subsection (a), with respect to the length of a term of supervised release, is subject to the requirement in subsection (b) that the term be not less than any statutorily required term of supervised release.

Effective Date: The effective date of this amendment is November 1, 1997.

571. **Amendment:** Chapter Five, Part E, Subpart 1 is amended by deleting § 5E1.1 in its entirety as follows:

"§ 5E1.1. Restitution

(a) The court shall --

(1) enter a restitution order if such order is authorized under 18 U.S.C. §§ 3663-3664; or

(2) if a restitution order would be authorized under 18 U.S.C. §§ 3663-3664, except for the fact that the offense of conviction is not an offense set forth in Title 18, United States Code, or 49 U.S.C. § 46312, § 46502, or § 46504, impose a term of probation or supervised release with a condition requiring restitution.

(b) *Provided*, that the provisions of subsection (a) do not apply when full restitution has been made, or to the extent the court determines that the complication and prolongation of the sentencing process resulting from the fashioning of a restitution requirement outweighs the need to provide restitution to any victims through the criminal process.

(c) If a defendant is ordered to make restitution and to pay a fine, the court shall order that any money paid by the defendant shall first be applied to satisfy the order of restitution.

(d) With the consent of the victim of the offense, the court may order a defendant to perform services for the benefit of the victim in lieu of monetary restitution or in conjunction therewith. 18 U.S.C. § 3663(b)(4).

Commentary

Application Note:

1. In the case of a conviction under certain statutes, additional requirements regarding restitution apply. See 18 U.S.C. §§ 2248 and 2259 (applying to convictions under 18 U.S.C. §§ 2241-2258 for sexual-abuse offenses and sexual exploitation of minors); 18 U.S.C. § 2327 (applying to convictions

under 18 U.S.C. §§ 1028-1029, 1341-1344 for telemarketing-fraud offenses); 18 U.S.C. § 2264 (applying to convictions under 18 U.S.C. §§ 2261-2262 for domestic-violence offenses). To the extent that any of the above-noted statutory provisions conflict with the provisions of this guideline, the applicable statutory provision shall control.

Background: Section 3553(a)(7) of Title 18 requires the court, 'in determining the particular sentence to be imposed,' to consider 'the need to provide restitution to any victims of the offense.' Section 3556 of Title 18 authorizes the court to impose restitution in accordance with 18 U.S.C. §§ 3663 and 3664, which authorize restitution for violations of Title 18 or 49 U.S.C. § 46312, § 46502, or § 46504. For other offenses, restitution may be imposed as a condition of probation or supervised release. See 18 U.S.C. § 3563(b)(3) as amended by Section 7110 of Pub. L. No. 100-690 (1988).

A court's authority to decline to order restitution is limited. Subsection (a)(1) of this guideline requires the court to order restitution for offenses under Title 18, United States Code, or 49 U.S.C. § 46312, § 46502, or § 46504, unless full restitution has already been made or 'the court determines that the complication and prolongation of the sentencing process resulting from the fashioning of an order of restitution . . . outweighs the need to provide restitution to any victims.' 18 U.S.C. § 3663(d). The legislative history of 18 U.S.C. § 3579, the precursor of 18 U.S.C. § 3663, states that even '[i]n those unusual cases where the precise amount owed is difficult to determine, the section authorizes the court to reach an expeditious, reasonable determination of appropriate restitution by resolving uncertainties with a view toward achieving fairness to the victim.' S. Rep. No. 532, 97th Cong., 2d Sess. 31, reprinted in 1982 U.S. Code Cong. & Ad. News 2515, 2537. If the court does not order restitution, or orders only partial restitution, it must state its reasons for doing so. 18 U.S.C. § 3553(c). Subsection (a)(2) provides for restitution as a condition of probation or supervised release for offenses not set forth in Title 18, United States Code, or 49 U.S.C. § 46312, § 46502, or § 46504.

In determining whether to impose an order of restitution, and the amount of restitution, the court shall consider the amount of loss the victim suffered as a result of the offense, the financial resources of the defendant, the financial needs of the defendant and his dependents, and other factors the court deems appropriate. 18 U.S.C. § 3664(a).

Pursuant to Rule 32(b)(4)(D), Federal Rules of Criminal Procedure, the probation officer's presentence investigation report must contain a victim impact statement. That report must contain information about the financial impact on the victim and the defendant's financial condition. The sentencing judge may base findings on the presentence report or other testimony or evidence supported by a preponderance of the evidence. 18 U.S.C. § 3664(d).

Unless the court orders otherwise, restitution must be made immediately. 18 U.S.C. § 3663(f)(3). The court may permit the defendant to make restitution within a specified period or in specified installments, provided that the last installment is paid not later than the expiration of probation, five years after the end of the defendant's term of imprisonment, or in any other case five years after the date of sentencing. 18 U.S.C. § 3663(f)(1) and (2). The restitution order should specify the manner in which, and the persons to whom, payment is to be made.".

A replacement guideline with accompanying commentary is inserted as § 5E1.1 (Restitution).

Chapter Eight, Part B, Subpart 1 is amended by deleting § 8B1.1 in its entirety as follows:

Amendment 571   APPENDIX C - VOLUME I   November 1, 2013

"§ 8B1.1. Restitution - Organizations

   (a)   The court shall --

        (1)   enter a restitution order if such order is authorized under 18 U.S.C. §§ 3663-3664; or

        (2)   if a restitution order would be authorized under 18 U.S.C. §§ 3663-3664, except for the fact that the offense of conviction is not an offense set forth in Title 18, United States Code, or 49 U.S.C. § 1472(h), (i), (j), or (n), sentence the organization to probation with a condition requiring restitution.

   (b)   *Provided*, that the provisions of subsection (a) do not apply when the organization has made full restitution, or to the extent the court determines that the complication and prolongation of the sentencing process resulting from the fashioning of a restitution requirement outweighs the need to provide restitution to any victims through the criminal process.

Commentary

Background: This guideline provides for restitution either as a sentence under 18 U.S.C. §§ 3663-3664 or as a condition of probation.".

A replacement guideline with accompanying commentary is inserted as § 8B1.1 (Restitution - Organizations).

Reason for Amendment: This amendment conforms the provisions of §§ 5E1.1 and 8B1.1 to section 204 of the Antiterrorism and Effective Death Penalty Act of 1996, Pub. L. 104-132, 110 Stat. 1227, which includes procedures for payment of full restitution to a victim of the offense. The amendment also implements the directive to the Commission in section 205 of the Act to issue guidelines to assist courts in determining an appropriate amount of "community restitution" when the defendant is convicted of certain drug offenses and there is no identifiable victim of the offense. As a starting point, the Commission has elected to issue a guideline that permits broad court discretion to determine an amount of community restitution not exceeding the fine imposed. Over time, the Commission intends to evaluate and refine this guideline in light of sentencing experience.

Effective Date: The effective date of this amendment is November 1, 1997.

572. **Amendment:** Section § 5E1.2(b) is amended by deleting "Except as provided in subsections (f) and (i) below, or otherwise required by statute, the fine imposed shall be within the range" and inserting in lieu thereof "The applicable fine guideline range is that".

Section 5E1.2(c)(1) is amended by inserting "guideline" after "fine".

Section 5E1.2(c)(2) is amended by inserting "guideline" after "fine".

Section 5E1.2(d) is amended in subdivision (6) by deleting "and"; by redesignating subdivision (7) as subdivision (8); and by inserting after subdivision (6) the following new subdivision (7):

November 1, 2013 APPENDIX C - VOLUME I **Amendment 573**

> "(7) the expected costs to the government of any term of probation, or term of imprisonment and term of supervised release imposed; and".

Section 5E1.2 is amended by deleting "(e)"; by redesignating subsections (f), (g), and (h) as subsections (e), (f), and (g) respectively; and by deleting:

> "(i) Notwithstanding of the provisions of subsection (c) of this section, but subject to the provisions of subsection (f) herein, the court shall impose an additional fine amount that is at least sufficient to pay the costs to the government of any imprisonment, probation, or supervised release ordered.".

The Commentary to § 5E1.2 captioned "Application Notes" is amended in Note 6 by deleting "§ 5E1.2" and inserting in lieu thereof "this section".

The Commentary to § 5E1.2 captioned "Application Notes" is amended in Note 7 by deleting:

> "Subsection (i) provides for an additional fine sufficient to pay the costs of any imprisonment, probation, or supervised release ordered, subject to the defendant's ability to pay as prescribed in subsection (f). In making a determination as to the amount of any fine to be imposed under this provision,"

and inserting in lieu thereof "In considering subsection (d)(7),".

Reason for Amendment: This amendment indirectly addresses a circuit court conflict regarding whether a court may impose a fine for costs of imprisonment and/or supervision when it has not imposed any punitive fine. Compare, United States v. Labat, 915 F.2d 603 (10th Cir. 1990)(requiring imposition of punitive fine before costs of imprisonment fine can be imposed) with United States v. Sellers, 42 F.3d 116 (2d Cir. 1994)(not requiring imposition of punitive fine before ordering costs of imprisonment fine), cert. denied, 116 S.Ct. 93 (1995).

Recognizing that a fine for costs of imprisonment and/or supervision is not statutorily required and rarely is imposed, the Commission has elected to dispense with the requirement that courts determine a separate, additional fine for such costs. Instead, the amendment provides that the court shall take such costs into consideration in determining the appropriate amount of a punitive fine.

Because, under the amended procedure, it no longer will be necessary to determine a separate fine increment for costs associated with implementing the sentence, the issue on which the circuit courts have differed should not arise. This procedure also should substantially simplify fine calculations, thereby allowing court and probation officer resources to be used more efficiently and productively.

Effective Date: The effective date of this amendment is November 1, 1997.

573. Amendment: The Commentary to § 5E1.3 captioned "Background" is amended by deleting the entire text as follows:

> "Background: The Victims of Crime Act of 1984, Pub. L. No. 98-473, Title II, Chap. XIV, requires the courts to impose special assessments on convicted defendants for the purpose of funding the Crime Victims Fund established by the same legislation. Monies deposited in the fund are awarded to the states by the Attorney General for victim assistance and compensation programs. Under the Victims of Crime Act, as amended by Section 7085 of the Anti-Drug Abuse Act of 1988, the

Amendment 573   APPENDIX C - VOLUME I   November 1, 2013

court is required to impose assessments in the following amounts with respect to offenses committed on or after November 18, 1988:

Individuals:

$5, if the defendant is an individual convicted of an infraction or a Class C misdemeanor;
$10, if the defendant is an individual convicted of a Class B misdemeanor;
$25, if the defendant is an individual convicted of a Class A misdemeanor; and
$50, if the defendant is an individual convicted of a felony.

Organizations:

$50, if the defendant is an organization convicted of a Class B misdemeanor;
$125, if the defendant is an organization convicted of a Class A misdemeanor; and
$200, if the defendant is an organization convicted of a felony. 18 U.S.C. § 3013.

With respect to offenses committed prior to November 18, 1988, the court is required to impose assessments in the following amounts:

$25, if the defendant is an individual convicted of a misdemeanor;
$50, if the defendant is an individual convicted of a felony;
$100, if the defendant is an organization convicted of a misdemeanor; and
$200, if the defendant is an organization convicted of a felony. 18 U.S.C. § 3013.

The Act does not authorize the court to waive imposition of the assessment.",

and inserting in lieu thereof:

"Application Notes:

1. This guideline applies only if the defendant is an individual. See § 8E1.1 for special assessments applicable to organizations.

2. The following special assessments are provided by statute (18 U.S.C. § 3013):

   For Offenses Committed By Individuals On Or After April 24, 1996:

   (A) $100, if convicted of a felony;
   (B) $25, if convicted of a Class A misdemeanor;
   (C) $10, if convicted of a Class B misdemeanor;
   (D) $5, if convicted of a Class C misdemeanor or an infraction.

   For Offenses Committed By Individuals On Or After November 18, 1988 But Prior To April 24, 1996:

   (E) $50, if convicted of a felony;

(F) $25, if convicted of a Class A misdemeanor;
(G) $10, if convicted of a Class B misdemeanor;
(H) $5, if convicted of a Class C misdemeanor or an infraction.

For Offenses Committed By Individuals Prior To November 18, 1988:

(I) $50, if convicted of a felony;
(J) $25, if convicted of a misdemeanor.

3. A special assessment is required by statute for each count of conviction.

Background: Section 3013 of Title 18, United States Code, added by The Victims of Crimes Act of 1984, Pub. L. No. 98-473, Title II, Chap. XIV, requires courts to impose special assessments on convicted defendants for the purpose of funding the Crime Victims Fund established by the same legislation.".

The Commentary to § 8E1.1 captioned "Background" is amended by deleting the entire text as follows:

"Background: Pursuant to 18 U.S.C. § 3013(a), the court is required to impose assessments in the following amounts:

$50,   if the organization is convicted of a Class B misdemeanor;
$125, if the organization is convicted of a Class A misdemeanor; and
$200, if the organization is convicted of a felony. 18 U.S.C. § 3013.

The Act does not authorize the court to waive imposition of the assessment.",

and inserting in lieu thereof the following:

"Application Notes:

1. This guideline applies if the defendant is an organization. It does not apply if the defendant is an individual. See § 5E1.3 for special assessments applicable to individuals.

2. The following special assessments are provided by statute (see 18 U.S.C. § 3013):

For Offenses Committed By Organizations On Or After April 24, 1996:

(A) $400, if convicted of a felony;
(B) $125, if convicted of a Class A misdemeanor;
(C) $50, if convicted of a Class B misdemeanor; or
(D) $25, if convicted of a Class C misdemeanor or an infraction.

For Offenses Committed By Organizations On Or After November 18, 1988 But Prior To April 24, 1996:

(E) $200, if convicted of a felony;

(F) $125, if convicted of a Class A misdemeanor;
(G) $50, if convicted of a Class B misdemeanor; or
(H) $25, if convicted of a Class C misdemeanor or an infraction.

For Offenses Committed By Organizations Prior To November 18, 1988:

(I) $200, if convicted of a felony;
(J) $100, if convicted of a misdemeanor.

3. A special assessment is required by statute for each count of conviction.

Background: Section 3013 of Title 18, United States Code, added by The Victims of Crimes Act of 1984, Pub. L. No. 98-473, Title II, Chap. XIV, requires courts to impose special assessments on convicted defendants for the purpose of funding the Crime Victims Fund established by the same legislation.".

Reason for Amendment: This amendment conforms §§ 5E1.3 (Special Assessments) and 8E1.1 (Special Assessments - Organizations) to changes made by section 210 of the Antiterrorism and Effective Death Penalty Act, Pub. L. 104-132, 110 Stat. 1240, and section 601(r)(4) of Pub. L. 104-294, 110 Stat. 3502. As amended, the felony assessments for offenses committed after April 24, 1996, are raised to $100 for individuals and $400 for organizations.

Effective Date: The effective date of this amendment is November 1, 1997.

574. Amendment: Section 6A1.1 is amended by deleting "(c)(1)" and inserting in lieu thereof "(b)(1)".

The Commentary to 6A1.1 is amended by deleting "(c)(1)" and inserting in lieu thereof "(b)(1)".

Section 6A1.2 is amended by deleting "See Model Local Rule for Guideline Sentencing prepared by the Probation Committee of the Judicial Conference (August 1987)." and insert in lieu thereof "Rule 32(b)(6), Fed. R. Crim. P.".

The Commentary to § 6A1.2 captioned "Application Note" is amended in Note 1 by deleting "111 S. Ct. 2182" and inserting in lieu thereof "501 U.S. 129, 135-39".

The Commentary to § 6A1.2 captioned "Background" is amended by inserting "in writing" after "respond"; and by deleting:

"The potential complexity of factors important to the sentencing determination normally requires that the position of the parties be presented in writing. However, because courts differ greatly with respect to their reliance on written plea agreements and with respect to the feasibility of written statements under guidelines, district courts are encouraged to consider the approach that is most appropriate under local conditions. The Commission intends to reexamine this issue in light of experience under the guidelines.",

and inserting in lieu thereof "Rule 32(b)(6)(B), Fed. R. Crim. P.".

Section 6A1.3(a) is amended in the second sentence by deleting "reasonable" before "dispute".

Section 6A1.3(b) is amended by inserting "at a sentencing hearing" after "factors"; by deleting "(a)(1)" and inserting in lieu thereof "(c)(1)"; and by deleting "(effective Nov. 1, 1987), notify the parties of its tentative findings and provide a reasonable opportunity for the submission of oral written objections before imposition of sentence.".

The Commentary to § 6A1.3 is amended in the first paragraph by deleting "will no longer exist" and inserting in lieu thereof "no longer exists"; by deleting "will usually have" and inserting in lieu thereof "usually has";

and by deleting:

> "Although lengthy sentencing hearings should seldom be necessary, disputes about sentencing factors must be resolved with care. When a reasonable dispute exists about any factor important to the sentencing determination, the court must ensure that the parties have an adequate opportunity to present relevant information. Written statements of counsel or affidavits of witnesses may be adequate under many circumstances. An evidentiary hearing may sometimes be the only reliable way to resolve disputed issues. See United States v. Fatico, 603 F.2d 1053, 1057 n.9 (2d Cir. 1979) cert. denied, 444 U.S. 1073 (1980). The sentencing court must determine the appropriate procedure in light of the nature of the dispute, its relevance to the sentencing determination, and applicable case law.",

and inserting in lieu thereof:

> "   Although lengthy sentencing hearings seldom should be necessary, disputes about sentencing factors must be resolved with care. When a dispute exists about any factor important to the sentencing determination, the court must ensure that the parties have an adequate opportunity to present relevant information. Written statements of counsel or affidavits of witnesses may be adequate under many circumstances. See, e.g., United States v. Ibanez, 924 F.2d 427 (2d Cir. 1991). An evidentiary hearing may sometimes be the only reliable way to resolve disputed issues. See, e.g., United States v. Jimenez Martinez, 83 F.3d 488, 494-95 (1st Cir. 1996) (finding error in district court's denial of defendant's motion for evidentiary hearing given questionable reliability of affidavit on which the district court relied at sentencing); United States v. Roberts, 14 F.3d 502, 521(10th Cir. 1993) (remanding because district court did not hold evidentiary hearing to address defendants' objections to drug quantity determination or make requisite findings of fact regarding drug quantity); see also, United States v. Fatico, 603 F.2d 1053, 1057 n.9 (2d Cir. 1979), cert. denied, 444 U.S. 1073 (1980). The sentencing court must determine the appropriate procedure in light of the nature of the dispute, its relevance to the sentencing determination, and applicable case law.".

The Commentary to § 6A1.3 is amended by deleting:

> "   In determining the relevant facts, sentencing judges are not restricted to information that would be admissible at trial. 18 U.S.C. § 3661. Any information may be considered, so long as it has 'sufficient indicia of reliability to support its probable accuracy.' United States v. Marshall, 519 F. Supp. 751 (E.D. Wis. 1981), aff'd, 719 F.2d 887 (7th Cir. 1983); United States v. Fatico, 579 F.2d 707 (2d Cir. 1978) cert. denied, 444 U.S. 1073 (1980). Reliable hearsay evidence may be considered. Out-of-court declarations by an unidentified informant may be considered 'where there is good cause for the nondisclosure of his identity and there is sufficient corroboration by other means.' United States v. Fatico, 579 F.2d at 713. Unreliable allegations shall not be considered. United States v. Weston, 448 F.2d 626 (9th Cir. 1971) cert. denied, 404 U.S. 1061 (1972).",

and inserting in lieu thereof:

Amendment 574 APPENDIX C - VOLUME I November 1, 2013

> "   In determining the relevant facts, sentencing judges are not restricted to information that would be admissible at trial. See 18 U.S.C. § 3661; see also United States v. Watts, 117 U.S. 633, 635 (1997) (holding that lower evidentiary standard at sentencing permits sentencing court's consideration of acquitted conduct); Witte v. United States, 515 U.S. 389, 399-401 (1995) (noting that sentencing courts have traditionally considered wide range of information without the procedural protections of a criminal trial, including information concerning criminal conduct that may be the subject of a subsequent prosecution); Nichols v. United States, 511 U.S. 738, 747-48 (1994) (noting that district courts have traditionally considered defendant's prior criminal conduct even when the conduct did not result in a conviction). Any information may be considered, so long as it has sufficient indicia of reliability to support its probable accuracy. Watts, 117 U.S. at 637; Nichols, 511 U.S. at 748; United States v. Zuleta-Alvarez, 922 F.2d 33 (1st Cir. 1990), cert. denied, 500 U.S. 927 (1991); United States v. Beaulieu, 893 F.2d 1177 (10th Cir.), cert. denied, 497 U.S. 1038 (1990). Reliable hearsay evidence may be considered. United States v. Petty, 982 F.2d 1365 (9th Cir. 1993), cert. denied, 510 U.S. 1040 (1994); United States v. Sciarrino, 884 F.2d 95 (3d Cir.), cert. denied, 493 U.S. 997 (1989). Out-of-court declarations by an unidentified informant may be considered where there is good cause for the nondisclosure of the informant's identity and there is sufficient corroboration by other means. United States v. Rogers, 1 F.3d 341 (5th Cir. 1993); see also United States v. Young, 981 F.2d 180 (5th Cir.), cert. denied, 508 U.S. 980 (1993); United States v. Fatico, 579 F.2d 707, 713 (2d Cir. 1978), cert. denied, 444 U.S. 1073 (1980). Unreliable allegations shall not be considered. United States v. Ortiz, 993 F.2d 204 (10th Cir. 1993).".

The Commentary to § 6A1.3 is amended by deleting:

> "   If sentencing factors are the subject of reasonable dispute, the court should, where appropriate, notify the parties of its tentative findings and afford an opportunity for correction of oversight or error before sentence is imposed.".

Reason for Amendment: This amendment makes a number of technical and conforming changes to the policy statements in Chapter Six, Part A (Sentencing Procedures) to reflect changes in Rule 32, Fed. R. Crim. P. and updates the case law references in the commentary to § 6A1.3 to include references to sentencing guideline cases.

Effective Date: The effective date of this amendment is November 1, 1997.

575. **Amendment:** Appendix A (Statutory Index) is amended by inserting, in the appropriate place by title and section:

"18 U.S.C. § 514	2F1.1";
"18 U.S.C. § 611	2H2.1";
"18 U.S.C. § 669	2B1.1";
"18 U.S.C. § 758	2A2.4";
"18 U.S.C. § 1030(a)(7)	2B3.2";
"18 U.S.C. § 1035	2F1.1";
"18 U.S.C. § 1347	2F1.1";
"18 U.S.C. § 1518	2J1.2";
"18 U.S.C. § 1831	2B1.1";
"18 U.S.C. § 1832	2B1.1";
"18 U.S.C. § 2261A	2A6.2";
"21 U.S.C. § 841(b)(7)	2D1.1";

"21 U.S.C. § 960(d)(7)	2D1.11";
"47 U.S.C. § 223(a)(1)(C)	2A6.1";
"47 U.S.C. § 223(a)(1)(D)	2A6.1";
"47 U.S.C. § 223(a)(1)(E)	2A6.1";
"49 U.S.C. § 5124	2Q1.2";
"49 U.S.C. § 32703	2N3.1";
"49 U.S.C. § 32704	2N3.1";
"49 U.S.C. § 32705	2N3.1";
"49 U.S.C. § 32709(b)	2N3.1";
"49 U.S.C. § 60123(d)	2B1.3";
"49 U.S.C. § 80116	2F1.1";
"49 U.S.C. § 80501	2B1.3";

in the line referenced to "15 U.S.C. § 1281" by inserting "(for offenses committed prior to July 5, 1994)" immediately after "2B1.3";

in the line referenced to "15 U.S.C. § 1983" by inserting "(for offenses committed prior to July 5, 1994)" immediately after "2N3.1";

in the line referenced to "15 U.S.C. § 1984" by inserting "(for offenses committed prior to July 5, 1994)" immediately after "2N3.1";

in the line referenced to "15 U.S.C. § 1985" by inserting "(for offenses committed prior to July 5, 1994)" immediately after "2N3.1";

in the line referenced to "15 U.S.C. § 1986" by inserting "(for offenses committed prior to July 5, 1994)" immediately after "2N3.1";

in the line referenced to "15 U.S.C. § 1987" by inserting "(for offenses committed prior to July 5, 1994)" immediately after "2N3.1";

in the line referenced to "15 U.S.C. § 1988" by inserting "(for offenses committed prior to July 5, 1994)" immediately after "2N3.1";

in the line referenced to "15 U.S.C. § 1990c" by inserting "(for offenses committed prior to July 5, 1994)" immediately after "2N3.1";

by deleting "18 U.S.C. § 1008   2F1.1, 2S1.3";

in the line referenced to "18 U.S.C. § 1030(a)(2)" by deleting "2F1.1" and inserting in lieu thereof "2B1.1";

in the line referenced to "18 U.S.C. § 1030(a)(3)" by deleting "2F1.1" and inserting in lieu thereof "2B2.3";

in the line referenced to "18 U.S.C. § 1030(a)(5)" by deleting "2F1.1" and inserting in lieu thereof "2B1.3";

by deleting:

"18 U.S.C. § 2258(a), (b)   2G2.1, 2G2.2",

and inserting in lieu thereof:

Amendment 575

"18 U.S.C. § 2260   2G2.1, 2G2.2";

in the line referenced to "18 U.S.C. § 2261" by deleting "2A1.1, 2A1.2, 2A2.1, 2A2.2, 2A2.3, 2A3.1, 2A3.4, 2A4.1, 2B3.1, 2B3.2, 2K1.4" and inserting in lieu thereof "2A6.2";

in the line referenced to "18 U.S.C. § 2262" by deleting "2A1.1, 2A1.2, 2A2.1, 2A2.2, 2A2.3, 2A3.1, 2A3.4, 2A4.1, 2B3.1, 2B3.2, 2K1.4" and inserting in lieu thereof "2A6.2";

in the line referenced to "21 U.S.C. § 959" by inserting ", 2D1.11" immediately after "2D1.1".

in the line referenced to "49 U.S.C. § 121" by inserting "(for offenses committed prior to July 5, 1994)" immediately after "2F1.1";

in the line referenced to "49 U.S.C. § 1809(b)" by inserting "(for offenses committed prior to July 5, 1994)" immediately after "2Q1.2";

in the line referenced to "49 U.S.C. App. § 1687(g)" by inserting "(for offenses committed prior to July 5, 1994)" immediately after "2B1.3"; and

by deleting "49 U.S.C. § 14904   2B4.1".

The Commentary to § 2G2.1 captioned "Statutory Provisions" is amended by deleting "2258(a), (b)" and inserting in lieu thereof "2260".

The Commentary to § 2G2.2 captioned "Statutory Provisions" is amended by deleting "2258(a), (b)" and inserting in lieu thereof "2260".

Section 2K2.1(a)(3) is amended by inserting "felony" before "prior".

Reason for Amendment: This amendment makes Appendix A (Statutory Index) more comprehensive. This amendment adds references for additional offenses, including offenses created by recently enacted legislation. In addition, this amendment revises Appendix A to conform to the revision of existing statutes and to reflect the codification of Title 49, United States Code. This amendment also corrects clerical errors in §§ 2G2.1 and 2G2.2.

Finally, this amendment corrects a clerical error in § 2K2.1(a)(3), as amended by amendment 522, effective November 1, 1995. During the execution of that amendment, which equalized offense levels for semiautomatic assault weapon possession with machinegun possession, the word "felony" was inadvertently omitted from the phrase "prior conviction" in subsection (a)(3).

Effective Date: The effective date of this amendment is November 1, 1997.

APPENDIX C (VOLUME II) - AMENDMENTS TO THE GUIDELINES MANUAL

This volume of Appendix C presents the amendments to the guidelines, policy statements, and official commentary effective November 1, 1998; May 1, 2000; November 1, 2000; December 16, 2000; May 1, 2001; November 1, 2001; November 1, 2002; January 25, 2003; April 30, 2003; October 27, 2003; November 1, 2003; and November 5, 2003.

For amendments to the guidelines, policy statements, and official commentary effective November 1, 1997, and earlier, *see* Appendix C, Volume I.

The format under which the amendments are presented in Appendix C, including this supplement, is designed to facilitate a comparison between previously existing and amended provisions, in the event it becomes necessary to reference the former guideline, policy statement, or commentary language.

AMENDMENTS

576. Amendment: Section 2B1.1(b) is amended by adding at the end the following new subdivision:

"(8) If the offense involved theft of property from a national cemetery, increase by 2 levels.".

The Commentary to § 2B1.1 captioned "Application Notes" is amended in Note 1 by adding at the end the following new paragraph:

"'National cemetery' means a cemetery (A) established under section 2400 of title 38, United States Code; or (B) under the jurisdiction of the Secretary of the Army, the Secretary of the Navy, the Secretary of the Air Force, or the Secretary of the Interior.".

The Commentary to § 2B1.1 captioned "Background" is amended by adding at the end the following new paragraph:

" Subsection (b)(8) implements the instruction to the Commission in section 2 of Public Law 105–101.".

Section 2B1.3(b) is amended by adding at the end the following new subdivision:

"(4) If property of a national cemetery was damaged or destroyed, increase by 2 levels.".

The Commentary to § 2B1.3 captioned "Application Notes" is amended in Note 1 by adding at the end the following new paragraph:

"'National cemetery' means a cemetery (A) established under section 2400 of title 38, United States Code; or (B) under the jurisdiction of the Secretary of the Army, the Secretary of the Navy, the Secretary of the Air Force, or the Secretary of the Interior.".

The Commentary to § 2B1.3 captioned "Background" is amended by inserting before the first paragraph the following:

" Subsection (b)(4) implements the instruction to the Commission in section 2 of Public Law 105–101.".

Section 2K1.4(b) is amended by striking "Characteristic" and inserting "Characteristics"; and by adding at the end the following new subdivision:

> "(2) If the base offense level is not determined under (a)(4), and the offense occurred on a national cemetery, increase by 2 levels.".

The Commentary to § 2K1.4 is amended by adding at the end the following new application note and background commentary:

> "4. 'National cemetery' means a cemetery (A) established under section 2400 of title 38, United States Code; or (B) under the jurisdiction of the Secretary of the Army, the Secretary of the Navy, the Secretary of the Air Force, or the Secretary of the Interior.
>
> Background: Subsection (b)(2) implements the directive to the Commission in section 2 of Public Law 105–101.".

Reason for Amendment: The purpose of this amendment is to provide an increase for property offenses committed against national cemeteries. This amendment implements the directive to the Commission in the Veterans' Cemetery Protection Act of 1997, Pub. L. 105–101, § 2, 111 Stat. 2202, 2202 (1997). This Act directs the Commission to provide a sentence enhancement of not less than two levels for any offense against the property of a national cemetery. In response to the legislation, this amendment adds a two-level enhancement to §§ 2B1.1 (Theft), 2B1.3 (Property Destruction), and 2K1.4 (Arson). "National cemetery" is defined in the same way as that term is defined in the statute.

Effective Date: The effective date of this amendment is November 1, 1998.

577. **Amendment:** Section 2F1.1(b) is amended by striking subdivision (5) in its entirety as follows:

> "(5) If the offense involved the use of foreign bank accounts or transactions to conceal the true nature or extent of the fraudulent conduct, and the offense level as determined above is less than level 12, increase to level 12.",

and inserting:

> "(5) (A) If the defendant relocated, or participated in relocating, a fraudulent scheme to another jurisdiction to evade law enforcement or regulatory officials; (B) if a substantial part of a fraudulent scheme was committed from outside the United States; or (C) if the offense otherwise involved sophisticated concealment, increase by 2 levels. If the resulting offense level is less than level 12, increase to level 12.".

Section 2F1.1(b) is amended by adding at the end the following new subdivision:

> "(7) If the offense was committed through mass-marketing, increase by 2 levels.".

The Commentary to § 2F1.1 captioned "Application Notes" is amended by redesignating Notes 14 through 18, as Notes 15 through 19, respectively; and by inserting after Note 13 the following new Note 14:

> "14. For purposes of subsection (b)(5)(B), 'United States' means each of the 50 states, the District of Columbia, the Commonwealth of Puerto Rico, the United States Virgin Islands, Guam, the Northern Mariana Islands, and American Samoa.

For purposes of subsection (b)(5)(C), 'sophisticated concealment' means especially complex or especially intricate offense conduct in which deliberate steps are taken to make the offense, or its extent, difficult to detect. Conduct such as hiding assets or transactions, or both, through the use of fictitious entities, corporate shells, or offshore bank accounts ordinarily indicates sophisticated concealment.".

The Commentary to § 2F1.1 captioned "Application Notes" is amended by adding at the end the following new note:

"20. 'Mass-marketing,' as used in subsection (b)(7), means a plan, program, promotion, or campaign that is conducted through solicitation by telephone, mail, the Internet, or other means to induce a large number of persons to (A) purchase goods or services; (B) participate in a contest or sweepstakes; or (C) invest for financial profit. The enhancement would apply, for example, if the defendant conducted or participated in a telemarketing campaign that solicited a large number of individuals to purchase fraudulent life insurance policies.".

Section 2T1.1(b) is amended by striking subdivision (2) in its entirety as follows:

"(2) If sophisticated means were used to impede discovery of the existence or extent of the offense, increase by 2 levels.",

and inserting the following:

"(2) If the offense involved sophisticated concealment, increase by 2 levels.".

The Commentary to § 2T1.1 captioned "Application Notes" is amended by striking Note 4 in its entirety as follows:

"4. 'Sophisticated means,' as used in subsection (b)(2), includes conduct that is more complex or demonstrates greater intricacy or planning than a routine tax-evasion case. An enhancement would be applied, for example, where the defendant used offshore bank accounts, or transactions through corporate shells or fictitious entities.",

and inserting the following:

"4. For purposes of subsection (b)(2), 'sophisticated concealment' means especially complex or especially intricate offense conduct in which deliberate steps are taken to make the offense, or its extent, difficult to detect. Conduct such as hiding assets or transactions, or both, through the use of fictitious entities, corporate shells, or offshore bank accounts ordinarily indicates sophisticated concealment.".

Section 2T1.4(b) is amended by striking subdivision (2) in its entirety as follows:

"(2) If sophisticated means were used to impede discovery of the existence or extent of the offense, increase by 2 levels.",

and inserting the following:

"(2) If the offense involved sophisticated concealment, increase by 2 levels.".

The Commentary to § 2T1.4 captioned "Application Notes" is amended by striking Note 3

Amendment 577

in its entirety as follows:

"3. 'Sophisticated means,' as used in § 2T1.4(b)(2), includes conduct that is more complex or demonstrates greater intricacy or planning than a routine tax-evasion case. An enhancement would be applied, for example, where the defendant used offshore bank accounts or transactions through corporate shells or fictitious entities.",

and inserting the following:

"3. For purposes of subsection (b)(2), 'sophisticated concealment' means especially complex or especially intricate offense conduct in which deliberate steps are taken to make the offense, or its extent, difficult to detect. Conduct such as hiding assets or transactions, or both, through the use of fictitious entities, corporate shells, or offshore bank accounts ordinarily indicates sophisticated concealment.".

Section 2T3.1(b) is amended by striking subdivision (1) in its entirety as follows:

"(1) If sophisticated means were used to impede discovery of the nature or existence of the offense, increase by 2 levels.",

and inserting the following:

"(1) If the offense involved sophisticated concealment, increase by 2 levels.".

The Commentary to § 2T3.1 captioned "Application Notes" is amended by adding at the end the following new note:

"3. For purposes of subsection (b)(1), 'sophisticated concealment' means especially complex or especially intricate offense conduct in which deliberate steps are taken to make the offense, or its extent, difficult to detect. Conduct such as hiding assets or transactions, or both, through the use of fictitious entities, corporate shells, or offshore bank accounts ordinarily indicates sophisticated concealment.".

Reason for Amendment: This amendment has three purposes: (1) to provide an increase for fraud offenses that use mass-marketing to carry out the fraud; (2) to provide an increase for fraud offenses that involve conduct, such as sophisticated concealment, that makes it difficult for law enforcement authorities to discover the offense or apprehend the offender; and (3) to clarify and conform an existing enhancement that provides an increase for tax offenses that similarly involve sophisticated concealment.

First, this amendment adds a two-level enhancement in the fraud guideline for offenses that are committed through mass-marketing. The Commission identified mass-marketing as a central component of telemarketing fraud and also determined that there were other fraudulent schemes that relied on mass-marketing to perpetrate the offense (for example, Internet fraud). Accordingly, rather than provide a limited enhancement for telemarketing fraud only, the Commission determined that a generally applicable specific offense characteristic in the fraud guideline would better provide consistent and proportionate sentencing increases for similar types of fraud, while also ensuring increased sentences for persons who engage in mass-marketed telemarketing fraud.

Second, this amendment provides an increase for fraud offenses that involve conduct, such as sophisticated concealment, that makes it difficult for law enforcement authorities to discover the offense or apprehend the offenders. The new enhancement provides a two-level increase and a "floor" offense level of level 12 in the fraud guideline and replaces the current enhancement for "the use of foreign bank accounts or transactions to conceal the true nature or extent of fraudulent conduct." There are three alternative provisions to the enhancement. The first two prongs address conduct that the Commission has been informed often relates to telemarketing fraud, although the conduct also may occur in connection with fraudulent schemes perpetrated by other means. Specifically, the Commission has been informed that fraudulent telemarketers increasingly are conducting their operations from Canada and other locations outside the United States. Additionally, testimony offered at a Commission hearing on telemarketing fraud indicated that telemarketers often relocate their schemes to other jurisdictions once they know or suspect that enforcement authorities have discovered the scheme. Both types of conduct are specifically covered by the new enhancement. The third prong provides an increase if any offense covered by the fraud guideline otherwise involves sophisticated concealment. This prong addresses cases in which deliberate steps are taken to make the offense, or its extent, difficult to detect.

Third, this amendment provides a two-level enhancement for conduct related to sophisticated concealment of a tax offense. The primary purpose of this amendment is to conform the language of the current enhancement for "sophisticated means" in the tax guidelines to the essentially equivalent language of the new sophisticated concealment enhancement provided in the fraud guideline. Additionally, the amendment resolves a circuit conflict regarding whether the enhancement applies based on the personal conduct of the defendant or the overall offense conduct for which the defendant is accountable. Consistent with the usual relevant conduct rules, application of this new enhancement for sophisticated concealment accordingly is based on the overall offense conduct for which the defendant is accountable.

Effective Date: The effective date of this amendment is November 1, 1998.

578. Amendment: Section 2K2.1(a) is amended in subdivision (4) by striking "the defendant" after "20, if"; in subdivision (4)(A) by inserting "the defendant" before "had one"; in subdivision (4)(B) by striking "is a prohibited person, and"; and in subdivision (4)(B) by inserting "; and the defendant (i) is a prohibited person; or (ii) is convicted under 18 U.S.C. § 922(d)" after "§ 921(a)(30)".

Section 2K2.1(a)(6) is amended by inserting "(A)" after "defendant"; and by inserting "; or (B) is convicted under 18 U.S.C. § 922(d)" after "person".

The Commentary to § 2K2.1 captioned "Application Notes" is amended in Note 6 by striking "or" before "(vi)"; and by inserting "; or (vii) has been convicted in any court of a misdemeanor crime of domestic violence as defined in 18 U.S.C. § 921(a)(33)" after "§ 922(d)(8)".

The Commentary to § 2K2.1 captioned "Application Notes" is amended in Note 12 in the first paragraph by striking "924(j) or (k), or 26 U.S.C. § 5861(g) or (h)" and inserting "924 (l) or (m)"; and in the second paragraph by striking "only" after "if the"; and by inserting "or 26 U.S.C. § 5861(g) or (h)" after "922(k)".

Reason for Amendment: This amendment has three purposes: (1) to change the definition of "prohibited person" in the firearms guideline so that it includes a person convicted of a misdemeanor crime of domestic violence; (2) to provide the same base offense levels for both a prohibited person and a person who is convicted under 18 U.S.C. § 922(d) of transferring a firearm to a prohibited person; and (3) to make several technical and

Amendment 578   APPENDIX C - VOLUME II   November 1, 2013

conforming changes to the firearms guideline.

The first part of the amendment amends Application Note 6 of § 2K2.1 (Unlawful Receipt, Possession, or Transportation of Firearms or Ammunition; Prohibited Transactions Involving Firearms or Ammunition) to include a person convicted of a misdemeanor crime of domestic violence within the scope of "prohibited person" for purposes of that guideline. It also defines "misdemeanor crime of domestic violence" by reference to the new statutory definition of that term in 18 U.S.C. § 921(a).

This part of the amendment addresses section 658 of the Treasury, Postal Service, and General Government Appropriations Act, Pub. L. 104–208, 110 Stat. 3009 (1996) (contained in the Omnibus Consolidated Appropriations Act for Fiscal Year 1997). Section 658 amended 18 U.S.C. § 922(d) to prohibit the sale of a firearm or ammunition to a person who has been convicted in any court of a misdemeanor crime of domestic violence. It also amended 18 U.S.C. § 922(g) to prohibit a person who has been convicted in any court of a misdemeanor crime of domestic violence from transporting or receiving a firearm or ammunition. Section 922(s)(3)(B)(i), which lists the information a person not licensed under 18 U.S.C. § 923 must include in a statement to the handgun importer, manufacturer, or dealer, was amended to require certification that the person to whom the gun is transferred was not convicted in any court of a misdemeanor crime of domestic violence. Section 658 also amended 18 U.S.C. § 921(a) to define "misdemeanor crime of domestic violence".

Violations of 18 U.S.C. § 922(d) and (g) are covered by § 2K2.1. The new provisions at § 922(d) (sale of a firearm to a "prohibited person") and § 922(g) (transporting, possession, and receipt of a firearm by a "prohibited person") affect Application Note 6 of § 2K2.1, which defines "prohibited person". This part of the amendment conforms Application Note 6 of § 2K2.1 to the new statutory provisions.

The second part of this amendment increases the base offense level for a defendant who is convicted under 18 U.S.C. § 922(d), which prohibits the transfer of a firearm to a prohibited person. Specifically, this part amends the two alternative base offense levels that pertain to prohibited persons in the firearms guideline in order to make those offense levels applicable to the person who transfers the firearm to the prohibited person. A person who is convicted under 18 U.S.C. § 922(d) has been shown beyond a reasonable doubt either to have known, or to have had reasonable cause to believe, that the transferee was a prohibited person.

The third part of this amendment makes two technical and conforming changes in Application Note 12 of § 2K2.1. First, the amendment corrects statutory references to 18 U.S.C. § 924(j) and (k), which were added as a result of the Violent Crime Control and Law Enforcement Act of 1994, Pub. L. 103–322, 108 Stat. 1796 (1994). In the Economic Espionage Act of 1996, Pub. L. 104–294, 110 Stat. 3488 (1996), Congress again amended 18 U.S.C. § 924 and redesignated the provisions as subsections (l) and (m). The amendment conforms Application Note 12 to that redesignation. Second, the amendment corrects the misplacement of the reference to 26 U.S.C. § 5861(g) and (h).

Effective Date: The effective date of this amendment is November 1, 1998.

579. **Amendment:** The Commentary to § 2J1.6 captioned "Application Notes" is amended in Note 3 in the first paragraph by striking "3D1.2" and inserting "3D1.1"; and by striking the second paragraph in its entirety as follows:

"Otherwise, in the case of a conviction on both the underlying offense and the fail-

November 1, 2013 APPENDIX C - VOLUME II **Amendment 579**

ure to appear, the failure to appear is treated under § 3C1.1 (Obstructing or Impeding the Administration of Justice) as an obstruction of the underlying offense; and the failure to appear count and the count(s) for the underlying offense are grouped together under § 3D1.2(c). Note that although 18 U.S.C. § 3146(b)(2) does not require a sentence of imprisonment on a failure to appear count, it does require that any sentence of imprisonment on a failure to appear count be imposed consecutively to any other sentence of imprisonment. Therefore, in such cases, the combined sentence must be constructed to provide a 'total punishment' that satisfies the requirements both of § 5G1.2 (Sentencing on Multiple Counts of Conviction) and 18 U.S.C. § 3146(b)(2). For example, where the combined applicable guideline range for both counts is 30-37 months and the court determines a 'total punishment' of 36 months is appropriate, a sentence of thirty months for the underlying offense plus a consecutive six months sentence for the failure to appear count would satisfy these requirements.",

and inserting the following as the new second paragraph:

"In the case of a conviction on both the underlying offense and the failure to appear, the failure to appear is treated under § 3C1.1 (Obstructing or Impeding the Administration of Justice) as an obstruction of the underlying offense, and the failure to appear count and the count or counts for the underlying offense are grouped together under § 3D1.2(c). (Note that 18 U.S.C. § 3146(b)(2) does not require a sentence of imprisonment on a failure to appear count, although if a sentence of imprisonment on the failure to appear count is imposed, the statute requires that the sentence be imposed to run consecutively to any other sentence of imprisonment. Therefore, unlike a count in which the statute mandates both a minimum and a consecutive sentence of imprisonment, the grouping rules of §§ 3D1.1-3D1.5 apply. See § 3D1.1(b), comment. (n.1), and § 3D1.2, comment. (n.1).) The combined sentence will then be constructed to provide a 'total punishment' that satisfies the requirements both of § 5G1.2 (Sentencing on Multiple Counts of Conviction) and 18 U.S.C. § 3146(b)(2). For example, if the combined applicable guideline range for both counts is 30-37 months and the court determines that a 'total punishment' of 36 months is appropriate, a sentence of 30 months for the underlying offense plus a consecutive six months' sentence for the failure to appear count would satisfy these requirements. (Note that the combination of this instruction and increasing the offense level for the obstructive, failure to appear conduct has the effect of ensuring an incremental, consecutive punishment for the failure to appear count, as required by 18 U.S.C. § 3146(b)(2).)".

The Commentary to § 2J1.6 captioned "Application Notes" is amended by redesignating Note 4 as Note 5; and by inserting the following as new Note 4:

"4. If a defendant is convicted of both the underlying offense and the failure to appear count, and the defendant committed additional acts of obstructive behavior (e.g., perjury) during the investigation, prosecution, or sentencing of the instant offense, an upward departure may be warranted. The upward departure will ensure an enhanced sentence for obstructive conduct for which no adjustment under § 3C1.1 (Obstruction of Justice) is made because of the operation of the rules set out in Application Note 3.".

The Commentary to § 2P1.2 captioned "Application Notes" is amended in Note 2 by striking "as amended," after "18 U.S.C. § 1791(c),"; and by inserting "by the inmate" after "served".

The Commentary to § 2P1.2 captioned "Application Notes" is amended in Note 2 by inserting before the first paragraph the following:

-505-

Amendment 579 APPENDIX C - VOLUME II November 1, 2013

> "In a case in which the defendant is convicted of the underlying offense and an offense involving providing or possessing a controlled substance in prison, group the offenses together under § 3D1.2(c). (Note that 18 U.S.C. § 1791(b) does not require a sentence of imprisonment, although if a sentence of imprisonment is imposed on a count involving providing or possessing a controlled substance in prison, section 1791(c) requires that the sentence be imposed to run consecutively to any other sentence of imprisonment for the controlled substance. Therefore, unlike a count in which the statute mandates both a minimum and a consecutive sentence of imprisonment, the grouping rules of §§ 3D1.1-3D1.5 apply. See § 3D1.1(b), comment. (n.1), and § 3D1.2, comment. (n.1).) The combined sentence will then be constructed to provide a 'total punishment' that satisfies the requirements both of § 5G1.2 (Sentencing on Multiple Counts of Conviction) and 18 U.S.C. § 1791(c). For example, if the combined applicable guideline range for both counts is 30-37 months and the court determines a 'total punishment' of 36 months is appropriate, a sentence of 30 months for the underlying offense plus a consecutive six months' sentence for the providing or possessing a controlled substance in prison count would satisfy these requirements.".

The Commentary to § 3C1.1 captioned "Application Notes" is amended in Note 6 by striking "Where" and inserting "If"; and by striking "where" both places it appears and inserting "if".

The Commentary to § 3C1.1 captioned "Application Notes" is amended in Note 7 in the first sentence by striking "Where" and inserting "If"; by striking "both of the" and inserting "both of an"; by inserting "(e.g., 18 U.S.C. § 3146 (Penalty for failure to appear); 18 U.S.C. § 1621 (Perjury generally))" after "obstruction offense" the first place it appears; and by striking "the underlying" the first place it appears and inserting "an underlying".

Section 3D1.1(b) is amended by striking the first sentence in its entirety as follows:

> "Any count for which the statute mandates imposition of a consecutive sentence is excluded from the operation of §§ 3D1.2-3D1.5.",

and inserting the following:

> "Exclude from the application of §§ 3D1.2-3D1.5 any count for which the statute (1) specifies a term of imprisonment to be imposed; and (2) requires that such term of imprisonment be imposed to run consecutively to any other term of imprisonment.".

The Commentary to § 3D1.1 captioned "Application Note" is amended by striking Note 1 in its entirety as follows:

> "1. Counts for which a statute mandates imposition of a consecutive sentence are excepted from application of the multiple count rules. Convictions on such counts are not used in the determination of a combined offense level under this Part, but may affect the offense level for other counts. A conviction for 18 U.S.C. § 924(c) (use of firearm in commission of a crime of violence) provides a common example. In the case of a conviction under 18 U.S.C. § 924(c), the specific offense characteristic for weapon use in the primary offense is to be disregarded to avoid double counting. See Commentary to § 2K2.4 (Use of Firearm, Armor-Piercing Ammunition, or Explosive During or in Relation to Certain Crimes). Example: The defendant is convicted of one count of bank robbery (18 U.S.C. § 2113), and one count of use of a firearm in the commission of a crime of violence (18 U.S.C. § 924(c)). The

two counts are not grouped together, and the offense level for the bank robbery count is computed without application of an enhancement for weapon possession or use. The mandatory five-year sentence on the weapon-use count runs consecutively, as required by law. See § 5G1.2(a).",

and inserting the following:

"1. Subsection (b) applies if a statute (A) specifies a term of imprisonment to be imposed; and (B) requires that such term of imprisonment be imposed to run consecutively to any other term of imprisonment. See, e.g., 18 U.S.C. § 924(c) (requiring mandatory term of five years to run consecutively). The multiple count rules set out under this Part do not apply to a count of conviction covered by subsection (b). However, a count covered by subsection (b) may affect the offense level determination for other counts. For example, a defendant is convicted of one count of bank robbery (18 U.S.C. § 2113), and one count of use of a firearm in the commission of a crime of violence (18 U.S.C. § 924(c)). The two counts are not grouped together pursuant to this guideline, and, to avoid unwarranted double counting, the offense level for the bank robbery count under § 2B3.1 (Robbery) is computed without application of the enhancement for weapon possession or use as otherwise required by subsection (b)(2) of that guideline. Pursuant to 18 U.S.C. § 924(c), the mandatory five-year sentence on the weapon-use count runs consecutively to the guideline sentence imposed on the bank robbery count. See § 5G1.2(a).

Unless specifically instructed, subsection (b) does not apply when imposing a sentence under a statute that requires the imposition of a consecutive term of imprisonment only if a term of imprisonment is imposed (i.e., the statute does not otherwise require a term of imprisonment to be imposed). See, e.g., 18 U.S.C. § 3146 (Penalty for failure to appear); 18 U.S.C. § 924(a)(4) (regarding penalty for 18 U.S.C. § 922(q) (possession or discharge of a firearm in a school zone)); 18 U.S.C. § 1791(c) (penalty for providing or possessing a controlled substance in prison). Accordingly, the multiple count rules set out under this Part do apply to a count of conviction under this type of statute.".

The Commentary to § 3D1.2 captioned "Application Notes" is amended in Note 1 in the third sentence by striking "mandates imposition of a consecutive sentence" and inserting "(A) specifies a term of imprisonment to be imposed; and (B) requires that such term of imprisonment be imposed to run consecutively to any other term of imprisonment"; and by inserting "; id., comment. (n.1)" after "§ 3D1.1(b)".

Section 5G1.2(a) is amended by striking "mandates a consecutive sentence" and inserting "(1) specifies a term of imprisonment to be imposed; and (2) requires that such term of imprisonment be imposed to run consecutively to any other term of imprisonment"; and by inserting "by that statute" after "determined".

The Commentary to § 5G1.2 is amended in the last paragraph by striking the first three sentences as follows:

"Counts for which a statute mandates a consecutive sentence, such as counts charging the use of a firearm in a violent crime (18 U.S.C. § 924(c)) are treated separately. The sentence imposed on such a count is the sentence indicated for the particular offense of conviction. That sentence then runs consecutively to the sentences imposed on the other counts.",

Amendment 579 APPENDIX C - VOLUME II November 1, 2013

and inserting the following:

> "Subsection (a) applies if a statute (1) specifies a term of imprisonment to be imposed; and (2) requires that such term of imprisonment be imposed to run consecutively to any other term of imprisonment. See, e.g., 18 U.S.C. § 924(c) (requiring mandatory term of five years to run consecutively to any other term of imprisonment). The term of years to be imposed consecutively is determined by the statute of conviction, and is independent of a guideline sentence on any other count.".

The Commentary to § 5G1.2 is amended in the last paragraph in the fourth sentence by inserting ", e.g.," after "See"; and by adding at the end the following new sentence:

> "Subsection (a) also applies in certain other instances in which an independently determined and consecutive sentence is required. See, e.g., Application Note 3 of the Commentary to § 2J1.6 (Failure to Appear by Defendant), relating to failure to appear for service of sentence.".

Reason for Amendment: The purpose of this amendment is to clarify how several guideline provisions, including those on grouping multiple counts of conviction, work together to ensure an incremental, consecutive penalty for a failure to appear count. This amendment addresses a circuit conflict regarding whether the guideline procedure of grouping the failure to appear count of conviction with the count of conviction for the underlying offense violates the statutory mandate of imposing a consecutive sentence. Compare United States v. Agoro, 996 F.2d 1288 (1st Cir. 1993) (grouping rules apply), and United States v. Flores, No. 93-3771, 1994 WL 163766 (6th Cir. May 2, 1994) (unpublished) (same), with United States v. Packer, 70 F.3d 357 (5th Cir. 1995) (grouping rules defeat statutory purposes of 18 U.S.C. § 3146), cert. denied, 117 S. Ct. 75 (1996). The amendment maintains the current grouping rules for failure to appear and obstruction of justice, but addresses internal inconsistencies among different guidelines and explains how the guideline provisions work together to ensure an incremental, consecutive penalty for the failure to appear count. Specifically, the amendment (1) more clearly distinguishes between statutes that require imposition of a consecutive term of imprisonment only if imprisonment is imposed (e.g., 18 U.S.C. § 3146 (Penalty for failure to appear); 18 U.S.C. § 1791(b), (c) (Penalty for providing or possessing contraband in prison)), and statutes that require both a minimum term of imprisonment and a consecutive sentence (e.g., 18 U.S.C. § 924(c) (Use of a firearm in relation to crime of violence or drug trafficking offense)); (2) states that the method outlined for determining a sentence for failure to appear and similar statutes ensures an incremental, consecutive punishment; (3) adds an upward departure provision if offense conduct involves multiple obstructive acts; (4) makes conforming changes in § 2P1.2 (Providing or Possessing Contraband in Prison) because the relevant statute, 18 U.S.C. § 1791, is similar to 18 U.S.C. § 3146; and (5) makes conforming changes in §§ 3C1.1, 3D1.1, 3D1.2, and 5G1.2.

Effective Date: The effective date of this amendment is November 1, 1998.

580. Amendment: The Commentary to § 3B1.3 captioned "Application Notes" is amended in the first paragraph of Note 1 in the third sentence by striking "enhancement" and inserting "adjustment"; by inserting "public or private" after "position of"; in the fourth sentence by striking "would apply" and inserting "applies"; and in the last sentence by striking "would" and inserting "does.".

The Commentary to § 3B1.3 captioned "Application Notes" is amended by redesignating Note 2 as Note 3; and by inserting the following as new Note 2:

"2. This adjustment also applies in a case in which the defendant provides sufficient indicia to the victim that the defendant legitimately holds a position of private or public trust when, in fact, the defendant does not. For example, the adjustment applies in the case of a defendant who (A) perpetrates a financial fraud by leading an investor to believe the defendant is a legitimate investment broker; or (B) perpetrates a fraud by representing falsely to a patient or employer that the defendant is a licensed physician. In making the misrepresentation, the defendant assumes a position of trust, relative to the victim, that provides the defendant with the same opportunity to commit a difficult-to-detect crime that the defendant would have had if the position were held legitimately.".

The Commentary to § 3B1.3 captioned "Background" is amended by inserting after the first sentence the following:

"The adjustment also applies to persons who provide sufficient indicia to the victim that they legitimately hold a position of public or private trust when, in fact, they do not.".

Reason for Amendment: The purpose of this amendment is to establish that the two-level increase for abuse of a position of trust applies to a defendant who is an imposter, as well as to a person who legitimately holds and abuses a position of trust. This amendment resolves a circuit conflict on that issue. Compare United States v. Gill, 99 F.3d 484 (1st Cir. 1996) (adjustment applied to defendant who posed as licensed psychologist), and United States v. Queen, 4 F.3d 925 (10th Cir. 1993) (adjustment applied to defendant who posed as financial broker), cert. denied, 510 U.S. 1182 (1994), with United States v. Echevarria, 33 F.3d 175 (2d Cir. 1994) (defendant who poses as physician does not occupy a position of trust). The amendment adopts the majority appellate view and provides that the abuse of position of trust adjustment applies to an imposter who pretends to hold a position of trust when in fact he does not. The Commission has determined that, particularly from the perspective of the crime victim, an imposter who falsely assumes and takes advantage of a position of trust is as culpable and deserving of increased punishment as is a defendant who abuses an actual position of trust.

Effective Date: The effective date of this amendment is November 1, 1998

581. Amendment: Section 3C1.1 is amended by inserting "(A)" after "If"; by inserting "the course of" after "during"; and by inserting "of conviction, and (B) the obstructive conduct related to (i) the defendant's offense of conviction and any relevant conduct; or (ii) a closely related offense" after "instant offense".

The Commentary to § 3C1.1 captioned "Application Notes" is amended in Note 2 by striking "enhancement" each place it appears, and inserting "adjustment"; in the second sentence by striking "Note 3" and inserting "Note 4"; in the third sentence by striking "Note 4" and inserting "Note 5"; and in the fourth sentence by striking "Notes 3 and 4" and inserting "Notes 4 and 5".

The Commentary to § 3C1.1 captioned "Application Notes" is amended in Note 4 in the first paragraph by striking "Note 7" and inserting "Note 8".

The Commentary to § 3C1.1 captioned "Application Notes" is amended by redesignating Notes 1 through 8, as Notes 2 through 9, respectively; and by inserting the following as new Note 1:

"1. This adjustment applies if the defendant's obstructive conduct (A) occurred

Amendment 581 APPENDIX C - VOLUME II November 1, 2013

during the course of the investigation, prosecution, or sentencing of the defendant's instant offense of conviction, and (B) related to (i) the defendant's offense of conviction and any relevant conduct; or (ii) an otherwise closely related case, such as that of a co-defendant.".

Reason for Amendment: The purpose of this amendment is to clarify what the term "instant offense" means in the obstruction of justice guideline, § 3C1.1. This amendment resolves a circuit conflict on the issue of whether the adjustment applies to obstructions that occur in cases closely related to the defendant's case or only those specifically related to the offense of which the defendant convicted. Compare United States v. Powell, 113 F.3d 464 (3d Cir.) (adjustment applies if defendant attempts to impede the prosecution of a codefendant who is charged with the same offense for which defendant was convicted), cert. denied, 118 S. Ct. 454 (1997), United States v. Walker, 119 F.3d 403 (6th Cir.) (same), cert. denied, 118 S. Ct. 643 (1997), United States v. Acuna, 9 F.3d 1442 (9th Cir. 1993) (adjustment applies if defendant attempts to obstruct justice in a case closely related to his own), and United States v. Bernaugh, 969 F.2d 858 (10th Cir. 1992) (adjustment applies when defendant testifies falsely at his own hearing about co-defendants' roles in the offense), with United States v. Perdomo, 927 F.2d 111 (2d Cir. 1991) (cannot apply adjustment based on obstructive conduct outside the scope of charged offense), and United States v. Partee, 31 F.3d 529 (7th Cir. 1994) (same). The amendment, which adopts the majority view, instructs that the obstruction must relate either to the defendant's offense of conviction (including any relevant conduct) or to a closely related case. The amendment also clarifies the temporal element of the obstruction guideline (i.e., that the obstructive conduct must occur during the investigation, prosecution, or sentencing of the defendant's offense of conviction).

Effective Date: The effective date of this amendment is November 1, 1998.

582. **Amendment:** The Commentary to § 3C1.1 captioned "Application Notes" is amended in Note 4 (redesignated as Note 5 by Amendment 581, see supra) in the first sentence of the first paragraph by striking "enhancement" and inserting "adjustment"; and by inserting "or affect the determination of whether other guideline adjustments apply (e.g., § 3E1.1 (Acceptance of Responsibility))" after "guideline range"; in the second sentence by striking "enhancement" and inserting "adjustment"; in subdivision (d) by striking the period at the end and inserting a semicolon; and by adding at the end the following new subdivision:

> "(e) lying to a probation or pretrial services officer about defendant's drug use while on pre-trial release, although such conduct may be a factor in determining whether to reduce the defendant's sentence under § 3E1.1 (Acceptance of Responsibility).".

Reason for Amendment: The purpose of this amendment is to establish that lying to a probation officer about drug use while released on bail does not warrant an obstruction of justice adjustment under § 3C1.1. This amendment resolves a circuit conflict on that issue. Compare United States v. Belletiere, 971 F.2d 961 (3d Cir. 1992) (lying about drug use is not obstructive conduct that impedes government's investigation of instant offense), and United States v. Thompson, 944 F.2d 1331 (7th Cir. 1991) (same), cert. denied, 502 U.S. 1097 (1992), with United States v. Garcia, 20 F.3d 670 (6th Cir. 1994) (falsely denying drug use, while not outcome-determinative, is relevant), cert. denied, 513 U.S. 1159 (1995). The amendment, which adopts the majority view, excludes from application of § 3C1.1 a defendant's denial of drug use while on pre-trial release, although the amendment provides that such conduct may be relevant in determining the application of other guidelines, such as § 3E1.1 (Acceptance of Responsibility).

Effective Date: The effective date of this amendment is November 1, 1998.

583. Amendment: Section 5K2.13 is amended by striking the text in its entirety as follows:

"If the defendant committed a non-violent offense while suffering from significantly reduced mental capacity not resulting from voluntary use of drugs or other intoxicants, a lower sentence may be warranted to reflect the extent to which reduced mental capacity contributed to the commission of the offense, provided that the defendant's criminal history does not indicate a need for incarceration to protect the public.",

and inserting:

"A sentence below the applicable guideline range may be warranted if the defendant committed the offense while suffering from a significantly reduced mental capacity. However, the court may not depart below the applicable guideline range if (1) the significantly reduced mental capacity was caused by the voluntary use of drugs or other intoxicants; (2) the facts and circumstances of the defendant's offense indicate a need to protect the public because the offense involved actual violence or a serious threat of violence; or (3) the defendant's criminal history indicates a need to incarcerate the defendant to protect the public. If a departure is warranted, the extent of the departure should reflect the extent to which the reduced mental capacity contributed to the commission of the offense.

Commentary

Application Note:

1. For purposes of this policy statement—

    'Significantly reduced mental capacity' means the defendant, although convicted, has a significantly impaired ability to (A) understand the wrongfulness of the behavior comprising the offense or to exercise the power of reason; or (B) control behavior that the defendant knows is wrongful.".

Reason for Amendment: The purpose of this amendment is to allow (except under certain circumstances) a diminished capacity departure if there is sufficient evidence that the defendant committed the offense while suffering from a significantly reduced mental capacity. This amendment addresses a circuit conflict regarding whether the diminished capacity departure is precluded if the defendant committed a "crime of violence" as that term is defined in the career offender guideline. Compare United States v. Poff, 926 F.2d 588 (7th Cir.) (en banc) (definition of "non-violent offense" necessarily excludes a crime of violence), cert. denied, 502 U.S. 827 (1991), United States v. Maddalena, 893 F.2d 815 (6th Cir. 1989) (same), United States v. Mayotte, 76 F.3d 887 (8th Cir. 1996) (same), United States v. Borrayo, 898 F.2d 91 (9th Cir. 1989) (same), and United States v. Dailey, 24 F.3d 1323 (11th Cir. 1994) (same), with United States v. Chatman, 986 F.2d 1446 (D.C. Cir. 1993) (court must consider all the facts and circumstances to determine whether offense was non-violent; terms are not mutually exclusive), United States v. Weddle, 30 F.3d 532 (4th Cir. 1994) (same), and United States v. Askari, 140 F. 3d 536 (3d Cir. 1998) (en banc) ("non-violent offenses" are those that do not involve a reasonable perception that force against persons may be used in committing the offense), abrogating United States v. Rosen, 896 F.2d 789 (3d Cir. 1990) (non-violent offense means the opposite of crime of violence). The amendment replaces the current policy statement with a new provision that essentially represents a compromise approach to the circuit conflict. The new policy statement allows a diminished capacity departure if there is sufficient evidence that the defendant committed the offense while suffering from a significantly reduced mental capacity, except under the following three circumstances: (1) the significantly reduced mental

Amendment 583   APPENDIX C - VOLUME II   November 1, 2013

capacity was caused by the voluntary use of drugs or other intoxicants; (2) the facts and circumstances of the defendant's offense indicate a need to protect the public because the offense involved actual violence or a serious threat of violence; or (3) the defendant's criminal history indicates a need to incarcerate the defendant to protect the public. The amendment also adds an application note that defines "significantly reduced mental capacity" in accord with the decision in United States v. McBroom, 124 F.3d 533 (3d Cir. 1997). The McBroom court concluded that "significantly reduced mental capacity" included both cognitive impairments (i.e., an inability to understand the wrongfulness of the conduct or to exercise the power of reason) and volitional impairments (i.e., an inability to control behavior that the person knows is wrongful). The application note specifically includes both types of impairments in the definition of "significantly reduced mental capacity".

Effective Date: The effective date of this amendment is November 1, 1998.

584. **Amendment:** Section 5B1.3(d) is amended by adding at the end the following new subdivision:

> "(6)   Deportation
>
> > If (A) the defendant and the United States entered into a stipulation of deportation pursuant to section 238(c)(5) of the Immigration and Nationality Act (8 U.S.C. § 1228(c)(5)); or (B) in the absence of a stipulation of deportation, if, after notice and hearing pursuant to such section, the Attorney General demonstrates by clear and convincing evidence that the alien is deportable -- a condition ordering deportation by a United States district court or a United States magistrate judge.".

Section 5D1.3(d) is amended by adding at the end the following new subdivision:

> "(6)   Deportation
>
> > If (A) the defendant and the United States entered into a stipulation of deportation pursuant to section 238(c)(5) of the Immigration and Nationality Act (8 U.S.C. § 1228(c)(5)); or (B) in the absence of a stipulation of deportation, if, after notice and hearing pursuant to such section, the Attorney General demonstrates by clear and convincing evidence that the alien is deportable -- a condition ordering deportation by a United States district court or a United States magistrate judge.".

Section 5D1.3(e)(5) is amended by striking "to provide just punishment for the offense,".

Section 5B1.3(c) is amended by inserting "(Policy Statement)" before "The following".

Section 5B1.3(d) is amended by inserting "(Policy Statement)" before "The following".

Section 5B1.3(e) is amended in the title by adding "(Policy Statement)" at the end.

Section 5D1.3(c) is amended by inserting "(Policy Statement)" before "The following".

Section 5D1.3(d) is amended by inserting "(Policy Statement)" before "The following".

Section 5D1.3(e) is amended in the title by adding "(Policy Statement)" at the end.

Reason for Amendment: The purpose of this amendment is to make several technical and conforming changes to the guidelines relating to conditions of probation and supervised release. The amendment has three parts. First, the amendment adds to §§ 5B1.3 and 5D1.3 a condition of probation and supervised release regarding deportation, in response to section 374 of the Illegal Immigration Reform and Immigrant Responsibility Act of 1996, Pub. L 104–208, 110 Stat. 3009 (1996). That section amended 18 U.S.C. § 3563(b) to add a new discretionary condition of probation with respect to deportation. Second, this amendment deletes the reference in the supervised release guideline to "just punishment" as a reason for the imposition of curfew as a condition of supervised release. The need to provide "just punishment" is not included in 18 U.S.C. § 3583(c) as a permissible factor to be considered in imposing a term of supervised release. Third, this amendment amends the guidelines pertaining to conditions of probation and supervised release to indicate that discretionary (as opposed to mandatory) conditions are advisory policy statements of the Commission, not binding guidelines.

Effective Date: The effective date of this amendment is November 1, 1998.

585. **Amendment:** Section 5K2.0 is amended in the first paragraph in the first sentence by inserting a comma after "3553(b)"; by striking "guideline" and inserting "guidelines"; in the second sentence by striking "guidelines" and inserting "guideline range"; in the third sentence by striking "controlling" after "The"; by striking "can only be made by the courts" and inserting "rests with the sentencing court on a case-specific basis"; in the last sentence by inserting "determining" after "consideration in"; by striking "guidelines" the second place it appears and inserting "guideline range"; by striking "guideline level" and inserting "weight"; by inserting "under the guidelines" after "factor"; and by inserting before the period at the end "or excessive".

Section 5K2.0 is amended in the last paragraph by striking "An" and inserting "Finally, an"; by striking "not ordinarily relevant" and inserting ", in the Commission's view, 'not ordinarily relevant'"; and by striking "in a way that is important to the statutory purposes of sentencing".

The Commentary to § 5K2.0 is amended by inserting before the first paragraph the following:

> "   The United States Supreme Court has determined that, in reviewing a district court's decision to depart from the guidelines, appellate courts are to apply an abuse of discretion standard, because the decision to depart embodies the traditional exercise of discretion by the sentencing court. Koon v. United States, 116 S. Ct. 2035 (1996). Furthermore, '[b]efore a departure is permitted, certain aspects of the case must be found unusual enough for it to fall outside the heartland of cases in the Guideline. To resolve this question, the district court must make a refined assessment of the many facts bearing on the outcome, informed by its vantage point and day-to-day experience in criminal sentencing. Whether a given factor is present to a degree not adequately considered by the Commission, or whether a discouraged factor nonetheless justifies departure because it is present in some unusual or exceptional way, are matters determined in large part by comparison with the facts of other Guidelines cases. District Courts have an institutional advantage over appellate courts in making these sorts of determinations, especially as they see so many more Guidelines cases than appellate courts do.' Id. at 2046-47.".

Reason for Amendment: The purpose of this amendment is to reference specifically in the general departure policy statement the United States Supreme Court's decision in United States v. Koon, 116 S. Ct. 2035 (1996). This amendment (1) incorporates the principal holding and key analytical points from the Koon decision into the general departure policy statement, § 5K2.0; (2) deletes language inconsistent with the holding of

Amendment 585 APPENDIX C - VOLUME II November 1, 2013

Koon; and (3) makes minor, non-substantive changes that improve the precision of the language of § 5K2.0.

Effective Date: The effective date of this amendment is November 1, 1998.

586. Amendment: Section 2B3.2(b) is amended in subdivision (2) by striking "(b)(6)" and inserting "(b)(7)".

The Commentary to § 2K1.3 captioned "Application Note" is amended in Note 2 by striking " subsections (1) and (2)" and inserting "subsection (a), subsection (b)".

The Commentary to § 2K2.1 captioned "Application Notes" is amended in Note 5 in the first sentence by striking "subsections (1) and (2)" and inserting "subsection (a), subsection (b)".

The Commentary to § 6A1.3 is amended in the third paragraph by striking "117 U.S." after "Watts," both places it appears and inserting "117 S. Ct.".

Reason for Amendment: This amendment corrects technical errors in §§ 2B3.1, 2K2.1, and 6A1.3.

Effective Date: The effective date of this amendment is November 1, 1998.

587. Amendment: Section 2F1.1(b), as amended by Amendment 577, is further amended by striking subdivision (3) and all that follows through the end of the subsection as follows:

> "(3) If the offense involved (A) a misrepresentation that the defendant was acting on behalf of a charitable, educational, religious or political organization, or a government agency, or (B) violation of any judicial or administrative order, injunction, decree, or process not addressed elsewhere in the guidelines, increase by 2 levels. If the resulting offense level is less than level 10, increase to level 10.
>
> (4) If the offense involved (A) the conscious or reckless risk of serious bodily injury, or (B) possession of a dangerous weapon (including a firearm) in connection with the offense, increase by 2 levels. If the resulting offense level is less than level 13, increase to level 13.
>
> (5) (A) If the defendant relocated, or participated in relocating, a fraudulent scheme to another jurisdiction to evade law enforcement or regulatory officials; (B) if a substantial part of a fraudulent scheme was committed from outside the United States; or (C) if the offense otherwise involved sophisticated concealment, increase by 2 levels. If the resulting offense level is less than level 12, increase to level 12.
>
> (6) If the offense --
>
> > (A) substantially jeopardized the safety and soundness of a financial institution; or
> >
> > (B) affected a financial institution and the defendant derived more than $1,000,000 in gross receipts from the offense,
>
> increase by 4 levels. If the resulting offense level is less than level 24, increase to level 24.

(7) If the offense was committed through mass-marketing, increase by 2 levels.";

and inserting the following:

"(3) If the offense was committed through mass-marketing, increase by 2 levels.

(4) If the offense involved (A) a misrepresentation that the defendant was acting on behalf of a charitable, educational, religious or political organization, or a government agency; or (B) violation of any judicial or administrative order, injunction, decree, or process not addressed elsewhere in the guidelines, increase by 2 levels. If the resulting offense level is less than level 10, increase to level 10.

(5) If (A) the defendant relocated, or participated in relocating, a fraudulent scheme to another jurisdiction to evade law enforcement or regulatory officials; (B) a substantial part of a fraudulent scheme was committed from outside the United States; or (C) the offense otherwise involved sophisticated means, increase by 2 levels. If the resulting offense level is less than level 12, increase to level 12.

(6) If the offense involved (A) the conscious or reckless risk of serious bodily injury; or (B) possession of a dangerous weapon (including a firearm) in connection with the offense, increase by 2 levels. If the resulting offense level is less than level 13, increase to level 13.

(7) If the offense --

  (A) substantially jeopardized the safety and soundness of a financial institution; or

  (B) affected a financial institution and the defendant derived more than $1,000,000 in gross receipts from the offense,

  increase by 4 levels. If the resulting offense level is less than level 24, increase to level 24.".

The Commentary to § 2F1.1 captioned "Application Notes", as amended by Amendment 577, is further amended by striking Application Note 14 and all that follows through the end of the Application Notes as follows:

"14. For purposes of subsection (b)(5)(B), 'United States' means each of the 50 states, the District of Columbia, the Commonwealth of Puerto Rico, the United States Virgin Islands, Guam, the Northern Mariana Islands, and American Samoa.

For purposes of subsection (b)(5)(C), 'sophisticated concealment' means especially complex or especially intricate offense conduct in which deliberate steps are taken to make the offense, or its extent, difficult to detect. Conduct such as hiding assets or transactions, or both, through the use of fictitious entities, corporate shells, or offshore bank accounts ordinarily indicates sophisticated concealment.

15. 'Financial institution,' as used in this guideline, is defined to include any institution described in 18 U.S.C. §§ 20, 656, 657, 1005-1007, and 1014; any state or foreign bank, trust company, credit union, insurance company,

investment company, mutual fund, savings (building and loan) association, union or employee pension fund; any health, medical or hospital insurance association; brokers and dealers registered, or required to be registered, with the Securities and Exchange Commission; futures commodity merchants and commodity pool operators registered, or required to be registered, with the Commodity Futures Trading Commission; and any similar entity, whether or not insured by the federal government. 'Union or employee pension fund' and 'any health, medical, or hospital insurance association,' as used above, primarily include large pension funds that serve many individuals (e.g., pension funds of large national and international organizations, unions, and corporations doing substantial interstate business), and associations that undertake to provide pension, disability, or other benefits (e.g., medical or hospitalization insurance) to large numbers of persons.

16. An offense shall be deemed to have 'substantially jeopardized the safety and soundness of a financial institution' if, as a consequence of the offense, the institution became insolvent; substantially reduced benefits to pensioners or insureds; was unable on demand to refund fully any deposit, payment, or investment; was so depleted of its assets as to be forced to merge with another institution in order to continue active operations; or was placed in substantial jeopardy of any of the above.

17. 'The defendant derived more than $1,000,000 in gross receipts from the offense,' as used in subsection (b)(7)(B), generally means that the gross receipts to the defendant individually, rather than to all participants, exceeded $1,000,000. 'Gross receipts from the offense' includes all property, real or personal, tangible or intangible, which is obtained directly or indirectly as a result of such offense. See 18 U.S.C. § 982(a)(4).

18. If the defendant is convicted under 18 U.S.C. § 225 (relating to a continuing financial crimes enterprise), the offense level is that applicable to the underlying series of offenses comprising the 'continuing financial crimes enterprise.'

19. If subsection (b)(7)(A) or (B) applies, there shall be a rebuttable presumption that the offense involved 'more than minimal planning.'

20. 'Mass-marketing,' as used in subsection (b)(7), means a plan, program, promotion, or campaign that is conducted through solicitation by telephone, mail, the Internet, or other means to induce a large number of persons to (A) purchase goods or services; (B) participate in a contest or sweepstakes; or (C) invest for financial profit. The enhancement would apply, for example, if the defendant conducted or participated in a telemarketing campaign that solicited a large number of individuals to purchase fraudulent life insurance policies.",

and inserting the following:

"15. For purposes of subsection (b)(5)(B), 'United States' means each of the 50 states, the District of Columbia, the Commonwealth of Puerto Rico, the United States Virgin Islands, Guam, the Northern Mariana Islands, and American Samoa.

For purposes of subsection (b)(5)(C), 'sophisticated means' means especially complex or especially intricate offense conduct pertaining to the execution or concealment of an offense. For example, in a telemarketing scheme, locating the main office of the scheme in one jurisdiction but locating soliciting operations in another jurisdiction would ordinarily indicate sophisticated means. Conduct such as hiding assets or transactions, or both, through the use of fictitious entities, corporate shells, or offshore bank accounts also ordinarily would indicate sophisticated means.

The enhancement for sophisticated means under subsection (b)(5)(C) requires conduct that is significantly more complex or intricate than the conduct that may form the basis for an enhancement for more than minimal planning under subsection (b)(2)(A).

If the conduct that forms the basis for an enhancement under subsection (b)(5) is the only conduct that forms the basis for an adjustment under § 3C1.1 (Obstruction of Justice), do not apply an adjustment under § 3C1.1.

16. 'Financial institution,' as used in this guideline, is defined to include any institution described in 18 U.S.C. §§ 20, 656, 657, 1005-1007, and 1014; any state or foreign bank, trust company, credit union, insurance company, investment company, mutual fund, savings (building and loan) association, union or employee pension fund; any health, medical or hospital insurance association; brokers and dealers registered, or required to be registered, with the Securities and Exchange Commission; futures commodity merchants and commodity pool operators registered, or required to be registered, with the Commodity Futures Trading Commission; and any similar entity, whether or not insured by the federal government. 'Union or employee pension fund' and 'any health, medical, or hospital insurance association,' as used above, primarily include large pension funds that serve many individuals (e.g., pension funds of large national and international organizations, unions, and corporations doing substantial interstate business), and associations that undertake to provide pension, disability, or other benefits (e.g., medical or hospitalization insurance) to large numbers of persons.

17. An offense shall be deemed to have 'substantially jeopardized the safety and soundness of a financial institution' if, as a consequence of the offense, the institution became insolvent; substantially reduced benefits to pensioners or insureds; was unable on demand to refund fully any deposit, payment, or investment; was so depleted of its assets as to be forced to merge with another institution in order to continue active operations; or was placed in substantial jeopardy of any of the above.

18. 'The defendant derived more than $1,000,000 in gross receipts from the offense,' as used in subsection (b)(7)(B), generally means that the gross receipts to the defendant individually, rather than to all participants, exceeded $1,000,000. 'Gross receipts from the offense' includes all property, real or personal, tangible or intangible, which is obtained directly or indirectly as a result of such offense. See 18 U.S.C. § 982(a)(4).

19. If the defendant is convicted under 18 U.S.C. § 225 (relating to a continuing financial crimes enterprise), the offense level is that applicable to the underlying series of offenses comprising the 'continuing financial crimes enterprise.'

20. If subsection (b)(7)(A) or (B) applies, there shall be a rebuttable presumption that the offense involved 'more than minimal planning.'".

Amendment 587 APPENDIX C - VOLUME II November 1, 2013

The Commentary to § 2F1.1 captioned "Application Notes ", as amended by Amendment 577, is further amended by redesignating Notes 3 through 13 as Notes 4 through 14, respectively; and by inserting after Note 2 the following new Note 3:

> "3. 'Mass-marketing,' as used in subsection (b)(3), means a plan, program, promotion, or campaign that is conducted through solicitation by telephone, mail, the Internet, or other means to induce a large number of persons to (A) purchase goods or services; (B) participate in a contest or sweepstakes; or (C) invest for financial profit. The enhancement would apply, for example, if the defendant conducted or participated in a telemarketing campaign that solicited a large number of individuals to purchase fraudulent life insurance policies.".

The Commentary to § 2F1.1 captioned "Application Notes" is amended in Note 1 by striking "§ 2F1.1(b)(3)" and inserting "§ 2F1.1(b)(4)"; in redesignated Note 5 (formerly Note 4), by striking "(b)(3)(A)" and inserting "(b)(4)(A)"; and in redesignated Note 6 (formerly Note 5), by striking "(b)(3)(B)" and inserting "(b)(4)(B)".

The Commentary to § 2F1.1 captioned "Background" is amended by inserting after the fifth paragraph the following new paragraph:

> "   Subsection (b)(5) implements, in a broader form, the instruction to the Commission in section 6(c)(2) of Public Law 105-184.".

Section 3A1.1 is amended by striking subsection (b) in its entirety as follows:

> "(b) If the defendant knew or should have known that a victim of the offense was unusually vulnerable due to age, physical or mental condition, or that a victim was otherwise particularly susceptible to the criminal conduct, increase by 2 levels.",

and inserting:

> "(b) (1) If the defendant knew or should have known that a victim of the offense was a vulnerable victim, increase by 2 levels.
>
>   (2) If (A) subdivision (1) applies; and (B) the offense involved a large number of vulnerable victims, increase the offense level determined under subdivision (1) by 2 additional levels.".

The Commentary to § 3A1.1 captioned "Application Notes" is amended in Note 2 in the first paragraph by striking "'victim' includes any person" before "who is" and inserting "'vulnerable victim' means a person (A)"; and by inserting after "(Relevant Conduct)" the following:

> "; and (B) who is unusually vulnerable due to age, physical or mental condition, or who is otherwise particularly susceptible to the criminal conduct".

The Commentary to § 3A1.1 captioned "Application Notes" is amended in Note 2 in the second paragraph by striking "where" each place it appears and inserting "in which".

The Commentary to § 3A1.1 captioned "Application Notes" is amended in Note 2 in the third paragraph by striking "offense guideline specifically incorporates this factor" and inserting "factor that makes the person a vulnerable victim is incorporated in the offense guideline".

The Commentary to § 3A1.1 captioned "Background" is amended by adding at the end the following additional paragraph:

"   Subsection (b)(2) implements, in a broader form, the instruction to the Commission in section 6(c)(3) of Public Law 105-184.".

The Commentary to § 2B5.1 captioned "Application Notes" is amended in Note 1 by inserting "United States" before "Virgin Islands".

Reason for Amendment: This amendment implements, in a broader form, the directives to the Commission in section 6 of the Telemarketing Fraud Prevention Act of 1998, Pub. L. 105–184 ("the Act").

The Act directs the Commission to provide for "substantially increased penalties" for telemarketing frauds. It also more specifically requires that the guidelines provide "an additional appropriate sentencing enhancement, if the offense involved sophisticated means, including but not limited to sophisticated concealment efforts, such as perpetrating the offense from outside the United States," and "an additional appropriate sentencing enhancement for cases in which a large number of vulnerable victims, including but not limited to [telemarketing fraud victims over age 55], are affected by a fraudulent scheme or schemes."

This amendment responds to the directives by building upon the amendments to the fraud guideline, § 2F1.1, that were submitted to Congress on May 1, 1998. (See amendment 577, supra.) Those amendments added a specific offense characteristic for "mass-marketing," which is defined to include telemarketing, and a specific offense characteristic for sophisticated concealment.

This amendment broadens the "sophisticated concealment" enhancement to cover "sophisticated means" of executing or concealing a fraud offense. In addition, the amendment increases the enhancement under the vulnerable victim guideline, § 3A1.1, for offenses that impact a large number of vulnerable victims.

This amendment also makes a conforming amendment to § 2B5.1 in the definition of "United States".

In designing enhancements that may apply more broadly than the Act's above-stated directives minimally require, the Commission acts consistently with other directives in the Act (e.g., section 6(c)(4) (requiring the Commission to ensure that its implementing amendments are reasonably consistent with other relevant directives to the Commission and other parts of the sentencing guidelines)) and with its basic mandate in sections 991 and 994 of title 28, United States Code (e.g., 28 U.S.C. § 991(b)(1)(B)) (requiring sentencing policies that avoid unwarranted disparities among similarly situated defendants)).

Effective Date: The effective date of this amendment is November 1, 1998.

588. **Amendment:** The Commentary to § 2C1.4 captioned "Background" is amended by striking the last sentence as follows:

"Both offenses are misdemeanors for which the maximum term of imprisonment authorized by statute is one year.".

The Commentary to § 2J1.1 captioned "Application Notes" is amended in Note 2 in the third sentence by inserting "(a)(1) and to any offense under 18 U.S.C. § 228(a)(2) and (3)" after "228"; and in the fourth sentence by inserting "(a)(1)" after "228".

Reason for Amendment: This is a two-part amendment. First, this amendment amends

Amendment 588

the commentary in the contempt guideline, § 2J1.1, pertaining to offenses under 18 U.S.C. § 228 involving the willful failure to pay court-ordered child support. The commentary notes that the contempt guideline applies to second and subsequent offenses under 18 U.S.C. § 228 because a first offense is a Class B misdemeanor not covered by the guidelines.

However, in the Deadbeat Parents Punishment Act of 1998, Pub. L. 105-187, Congress amended 18 U.S.C. § 228 to add two new violations of that section (found at 18 U.S.C. § 228(a)(2) and (3)) and to make even the first offense under those new violations a felony that would be subject to the guidelines. Accordingly, the commentary in the contempt guideline is amended to reflect that it is only the first offense under a violation of 18 U.S.C. § 228(a)(1) that is not covered by the guideline.

Second, this amendment updates and corrects the background commentary of § 2C1.4, the guideline that covers offenses involving unlawful compensation for federal employees and bank officials. Currently the background commentary states that 18 U.S.C. § 209 (involving the unlawful supplementation of the salary of various federal employees) and 18 U.S.C. § 1909 (prohibiting bank examiners from performing any service for compensation for banks or bank officials) both are misdemeanors for which the maximum term of imprisonment is one year. In fact, however, as a result of enacted legislation, the maximum term of imprisonment for violations of 18 U.S.C. § 209 is now five years if the conduct is willful.

The amendment deletes the sentence of the commentary that describes the maximum term of imprisonment for these offenses.

Effective Date: The effective date of this amendment is November 1, 1998.

589. **Amendment:** Appendix A (Statutory Index) is amended in the line referenced to "18 U.S.C. § 924(i)" by striking "2A1.1, 2A1.2" and inserting "2K2.1";

by striking:

"18 U.S.C. § 924(j)-(n)   2K2.1",

and inserting:

"18 U.S.C. § 924(j)(1)   2A1.1, 2A1.2",
"18 U.S.C. § 924(j)(2)   2A1.3, 2A1.4",
"18 U.S.C. § 924(k)-(o)   2K2.1";

and by inserting, after the line referenced to "18 U.S.C. § 2252" the following new line:

"18 U.S.C. § 2252A   2G2.2, 2G2.4".

Reason for Amendment: This amendment updates the Statutory Index by adding a reference to a recently created offense (pertaining to the use of a computer to commit certain child pornography offenses) and by correcting the references to a number of firearms offenses in response to congressional redesignations of those offenses.

Specifically, Congress recently enacted 18 U.S.C. § 2252A, which makes it unlawful to traffic in, receive, or possess child pornography, including by computer. The amendment references this offense to § 2G2.2 (trafficking in child pornography) and § 2G2.4 (possession of child pornography).

In addition, in the Violent Crime Control and Law Enforcement Act of 1994, Pub. L. 103–322, and the Economic Espionage Act of 1996, Pub. L. 104-294, Congress redesignated a number of firearms provisions in 18 U.S.C. § 924. The amendment changes the references in the Statutory Index to a number of these offenses in response to the congressional redesignations.

Effective Date: The effective date of this amendment is November 1, 1998.

590. Amendment: Chapter Two, Part B, Subpart 5 is amended by striking § 2B5.3 in its entirety as follows:

> "§ 2B5.3. <u>Criminal Infringement of Copyright or Trademark</u>
>
> (a) Base Offense Level: 6
>
> (b) Specific Offense Characteristic
>
> (1) If the retail value of the infringing items exceeded $2,000, increase by the corresponding number of levels from the table in § 2F1.1 (Fraud and Deceit).
>
> Commentary
>
> <u>Statutory Provisions</u>: 17 U.S.C. § 506(a); 18 U.S.C. §§ 2318-2320, 2511. For additional statutory provision(s), <u>see</u> Appendix A (Statutory Index).
>
> <u>Application Note</u>:
>
> 1. 'Infringing items' means the items that violate the copyright or trademark laws (not the legitimate items that are infringed upon).
>
> <u>Background</u>: This guideline treats copyright and trademark violations much like fraud. Note that the enhancement is based on the value of the infringing items, which will generally exceed the loss or gain due to the offense.
>
> The Electronic Communications Act of 1986 prohibits the interception of satellite transmission for purposes of direct or indirect commercial advantage or private financial gain. Such violations are similar to copyright offenses and are therefore covered by this guideline.".

A replacement guideline with accompanying commentary is inserted as § 2B5.3 (Criminal Infringement of Copyright or Trademark).

Reason for Amendment: This amendment is in response to section 2(g) of the No Electronic Theft (NET) Act of 1997, Pub. L. 105–147 ("the Act"). The Act directs the Commission to ensure that the applicable guideline range for intellectual property offenses (including offenses set forth at section 506(a) of title 17, United States Code, and sections 2319, 2319A, and 2320 of title 18, United States Code) is "sufficiently stringent to deter such a crime." It also more specifically requires that the guidelines "provide for consideration of the retail value and quantity of the items with respect to which the intellectual property offense was committed."

The amendment responds to the directives, first, by making changes to the monetary calculation found in the copyright and trademark infringement guideline, § 2B5.3. In addition, the amendment makes a number of other modifications to the infringement guideline, including the addition of several mitigating and aggravating factors, as further means of providing just and proportionate punishment while also seeking to achieve sufficient deterrence.

The monetary calculation in § 2B5.3(b)(1), similar to the loss enhancement in the theft and fraud guidelines, serves as an approximation of the pecuniary harm caused by the offense and is a principal factor in determining the offense level for intellectual property offenses. Prior to this amendment, the monetary calculation for all intellectual property crimes was based on the retail value of the infringing item multiplied by the quantity of infringing items. In response to the directive, the Commission refashioned this enhancement so as to use the retail value of the infringed item, multiplied by the number of infringing items, as a means of approximating the pecuniary harm for cases in which that calculation is believed most likely to provide a reasonable estimate of the resulting harm. Use of that calculation is believed to provide a reasonable approximation for those classes of infringement cases in which it is highly likely that the sale of an infringing item results in a displaced sale of the legitimate, infringed item. The amendment also requires that the retail value of the infringed item, multiplied by the number of infringing items, be used in certain other cases for reasons of practicality.

However, based upon a review of cases sentenced under the former § 2B5.3 over two years, the Commission further determined that using the above formula likely would overstate substantially the pecuniary harm caused to copyright and trademark owners in some cases currently sentenced under the guideline. For those cases, a one-to-one correlation between the sale of infringing items and the displaced sale of legitimate, infringed items is unlikely because the inferior quality of the infringing item and/or the greatly discounted price at which it is sold suggests that many purchasers of infringing items would not, or could not, have purchased the infringed item in the absence of the availability of the infringing item. The Commission therefore determined that, for these latter classes of cases (referred to in Application Note 2(B)), the retail value of the infringing item, multiplied by the number of those items, provides a more reasonable approximation of lost revenues to the copyright or trademark owner, and hence, of the pecuniary harm resulting from the offense.

This amendment also increases the base offense level from level 6 to level 8. The two-level increase in the base offense level brings the infringement guideline more in line with offense levels that would pertain under the fraud guideline, § 2F1.1, assuming applicability under that guideline of the two-level enhancement for more than minimal planning. Based on a review of cases sentenced under the infringement guideline, if a more than minimal planning enhancement did exist in that guideline, it would apply in the vast majority of such cases because they involve this kind of aggravating conduct. Rather than provide a separate enhancement within the revised guideline for "more than minimal planning" conduct, the Commission determined that the infringement guideline should incorporate this type of conduct into the base offense level.

This amendment also provides an enhancement of two levels, and a minimum offense level of level 12, if the offense involved the manufacture, importation, or uploading of infringing items. The Commission determined that defendants who engage in such conduct are more culpable than other intellectual property offenders because they place infringing items into the stream of commerce, thereby enabling others to infringe the copyright or trademark. A review of cases sentenced under the guideline indicated applicability of this enhancement to approximately two-thirds of the cases.

This amendment also provides a two-level downward adjustment (but not less than offense level 8) if the offense was not committed for commercial advantage or private financial gain. This adjustment reflects the fact that the Act establishes lower statutory penalties for offenses that were not committed for commercial advantage or private financial gain.

This amendment also provides an enhancement of two levels, and a minimum offense level of level 13, if the offense involved the conscious or reckless risk of serious bodily injury or possession of a dangerous weapon in connection with the offense. Testimony received by the Commission indicated that the conscious or reckless risk of serious bodily injury may occur in some cases involving counterfeit consumer products. The Commission determined that this kind of aggravating conduct in connection with infringement cases should be treated under the guidelines in the same way it is treated in connection with fraud cases; therefore, this enhancement is consistent with an identical provision in the fraud guideline.

The amendment also contains an application note expressly providing that the adjustment in § 3B1.3 (Abuse of Position of Trust or Use of Special Skill) will apply if the defendant de-encrypted or otherwise circumvented a technological security measure to gain initial access to an infringed item. As stated in the background commentary to § 3B1.3, persons who use such a special skill to facilitate or commit a crime generally are viewed as more culpable.

Finally, this amendment contains two encouraged upward departure provisions. The Commission received public comment that indicated that infringement may cause substantial harm to the reputation of the copyright or trademark owner that is not accounted for in the monetary calculation. Public comment also indicated that some copyright and trademark offenses are committed in connection with, or in furtherance of, the criminal activities of certain organized crime enterprises. The amendment invites the court to consider an appropriate upward departure if either of these aggravating circumstances are present.

Effective Date: The effective date of this amendment is May 1, 2000.

591. **Amendment:** Section 1B1.1 is amended by striking subsection (a) in its entirety and inserting:

> "(a) Determine, pursuant to § 1B1.2 (Applicable Guidelines), the offense guideline section from Chapter Two (Offense Conduct) applicable to the offense of conviction. See § 1B1.2.".

Section 1B1.2(a) is amended by striking "most" each place it appears; by striking "Provided, however" and inserting "However"; and by adding at the end the following:

> "Refer to the Statutory Index (Appendix A) to determine the Chapter Two offense guideline, referenced in the Statutory Index for the offense of conviction. If the offense involved a conspiracy, attempt, or solicitation, refer to § 2X1.1 (Attempt, Solicitation, or Conspiracy) as well as the guideline referenced in the Statutory Index for the substantive offense. For statutory provisions not listed in the Statutory Index, use the most analogous guideline. See § 2X5.1 (Other Offenses). The guidelines do not apply to any count of conviction that is a Class B or C misdemeanor or an infraction. See § 1B1.9 (Class B or C Misdemeanors and Infractions).".

The Commentary to § 1B1.2 captioned "Application Notes" is amended by striking the first paragraph of Note 1 and inserting the following:

> "This section provides the basic rules for determining the guidelines applicable to the offense conduct under Chapter Two (Offense Conduct). The court is to use the Chapter Two guideline section referenced in the Statutory Index (Appendix A) for the offense of conviction. However, (A) in the case of a plea agreement containing a

Amendment 591

stipulation that specifically establishes a more serious offense than the offense of conviction, the Chapter Two offense guideline section applicable to the stipulated offense is to be used; and (B) for statutory provisions not listed in the Statutory Index, the most analogous guideline, determined pursuant to § 2X5.1 (Other Offenses), is to be used.

In the case of a particular statute that proscribes only a single type of criminal conduct, the offense of conviction and the conduct proscribed by the statute will coincide, and the Statutory Index will specify only one offense guideline for that offense of conviction. In the case of a particular statute that proscribes a variety of conduct that might constitute the subject of different offense guidelines, the Statutory Index may specify more than one offense guideline for that particular statute, and the court will determine which of the referenced guideline sections is most appropriate for the offense conduct charged in the count of which the defendant was convicted. If the offense involved a conspiracy, attempt, or solicitation, refer to § 2X1.1 (Attempt, Solicitation, or Conspiracy) as well as the guideline referenced in the Statutory Index for the substantive offense. For statutory provisions not listed in the Statutory Index, the most analogous guideline is to be used. See § 2X5.1 (Other Offenses).".

The Commentary to § 1B1.2 captioned "Application Notes" is amended by striking Note 3 in its entirety; and by redesignating Notes 4 and 5 as Notes 3 and 4, respectively.

The Commentary to § 2D1.2 captioned "Application Note" is amended in Note 1 by striking "Where" and inserting the following:

"This guideline applies only in a case in which the defendant is convicted of a statutory violation of drug trafficking in a protected location or involving an underage or pregnant individual (including an attempt or conspiracy to commit such a violation) or in a case in which the defendant stipulated to such a statutory violation. See § 1B1.2(a). In a case involving such a conviction but in which".

Appendix A (Statutory Index) is amended by striking the entire text of the "Introduction" and inserting the following:

"This index specifies the offense guideline section(s) in Chapter Two (Offense Conduct) applicable to the statute of conviction. If more than one guideline section is referenced for the particular statute, use the guideline most appropriate for the offense conduct charged in the count of which the defendant was convicted. For the rules governing the determination of the offense guideline section(s) from Chapter Two, and for any exceptions to those rules, see § 1B1.2 (Applicable Guidelines).".

The Commentary to § 2H1.1 captioned "Application Notes" is amended in Note 1 in the second paragraph by striking "Application Note 5" and inserting "Application Note 4".

Reason for Amendment: This amendment addresses a circuit conflict regarding whether the enhanced penalties in § 2D1.2 (Drug Offenses Occurring Near Protected Locations or Involving Underage or Pregnant Individuals) apply only in a case in which the defendant was convicted of an offense referenced to that guideline or, alternatively, in any case in which the defendant's relevant conduct included drug sales in a protected location or involving a protected individual. Compare United States v. Chandler, 125 F.3d 892, 897-98 (5th Cir. 1997) ("First, utilizing the Statutory Index located in Appendix A, the court determines the offense guideline section 'most applicable to the offense of conviction.'" Once the appropriate guideline is identified, a court can take relevant conduct into account only as it relates to factors set forth in that guideline); United States v. Locklear, 24 F.3d 641 (4th Cir. 1994) (finding that § 2D1.2 does not apply to convictions under 21 U.S.C. § 841 based on the fact that the commentary to § 2D1.2 lists as the "Statutory Provisions" to which it is applicable 21 U.S.C. §§ 859, 860, and 861, but not § 841. "[S]ection 2D1.2 is intended not to identify a specific offense characteristic which would, where applicable, increase the offense level over the base level assigned by § 2D1.1, but rather to define the base offense level for violations of 21 U.S.C. §§ 859, 860 and 861."); United States v. Saavedra, 148 F.3d 1311 (11th Cir. 1998) (defendant's uncharged but relevant conduct is actually irrelevant to determining the sentencing guideline applicable to the defendant's offense; such conduct is properly considered only after the applicable guideline has been selected when the court is analyzing the various sentencing considerations within the guideline chosen, such as the base offense level, specific offense characteristics, and any cross references), with United States v. Clay, 117 F.3d 317 (6th Cir.), cert. denied, 118 S. Ct. 395 (1997) (applying § 2D1.2 to defendant convicted only of possession with intent to distribute under 21 U.S.C. § 841 but not convicted of any statute referenced to § 2D1.2 based on underlying facts indicating defendant involved a juvenile in drug sales); United States v. Oppedahl, 998 F.2d 584 (8th Cir. 1993) (applying § 2D1.2 to defendant convicted of conspiracy to distribute and possess with intent to distribute based on fact that defendant's relevant conduct involved distribution within 1,000 feet of a school); United States v. Robles, 814 F. Supp. 1249 (E.D. Pa), aff'd (unpub.), 8 F.3d 814 (3d Cir. 1993) (looking to relevant conduct to determine appropriate guideline).

In promulgating this amendment, the Commission also was aware of case law that raises a similar issue regarding selection of a Chapter Two (Offense Conduct) guideline, different from that referenced in the Statutory Index (Appendix A), based on factors other than the conduct charged in the offense of conviction. See United States v. Smith, 186 F.3d 290 (3d Cir. 1999) (determining that § 2F1.1 (Fraud and Deceit) was most appropriate guideline rather than the listed guideline of § 2S1.1 (Laundering of Monetary Instruments)); United States v. Brunson, 882 F. 2d 151, 157 (5th Cir. 1989) ("It is not completely clear to us under what circumstances the Commission contemplated deviation from the suggested guidelines for an 'atypical' case.").

The amendment modifies §§ 1B1.1(a), 1B1.2(a), and the Statutory Index's introductory commentary to clarify the inter-relationship among these provisions. The clarification is intended to emphasize that the sentencing court must apply the offense guideline referenced in the Statutory Index for the statute of conviction unless the case falls within the limited "stipulation" exception set forth in § 1B1.2(a). Therefore, in order for the enhanced penalties in § 2D1.2 to apply, the defendant must be convicted of an offense referenced to § 2D1.2, rather than simply have engaged in conduct described by that guideline. Furthermore, the amendment deletes Application Note 3 of § 1B1.2 (Applicable Guidelines), which provided that in many instances it would be appropriate for the court to consider the actual conduct of the offender, even if such conduct did not constitute an element of the offense. This application note describes a consideration that is more appropriate when applying § 1B1.3 (Relevant Conduct), and its current placement in § 1B1.2 apparently has caused confusion in applying that guideline's principles to determine the offense conduct guideline in Chapter Two most appropriate for the offense of conviction. In particular, the note has been used by some courts to permit a court to decline to use the offense guideline referenced in the Statutory Index in cases that were allegedly "atypical" or "outside the heartland." See United States v. Smith, supra.

Effective Date: The effective date of this amendment is November 1, 2000.

592. Amendment: Section 2A3.1(b) is amended by adding at the end the following:

"(6) If, to persuade, induce, entice, or coerce a minor to engage in prohibited sexual conduct, or if, to facilitate transportation or travel, by a minor or a

Amendment 592

participant, to engage in prohibited sexual conduct, the offense involved (A) the knowing misrepresentation of a participant's identity; or (B) the use of a computer or an Internet-access device, increase by 2 levels.".

The Commentary to § 2A3.1 captioned "Application Notes" is amended in Note 1 by inserting after "For purposes of this guideline —" the following:

"'Minor' means an individual who had not attained the age of 18 years.

'Participant' has the meaning given that term in Application Note 1 of the Commentary to § 3B1.1 (Aggravating Role).".

The Commentary to § 2A3.1 captioned "Application Notes" is amended in Note 1 by inserting after "the base offense level under subsection (a)." the following paragraph:

"'Prohibited sexual conduct' (A) means any sexual activity for which a person can be charged with a criminal offense; (B) includes the production of child pornography; and (C) does not include trafficking in, or possession of, child pornography. 'Child pornography' has the meaning given that term in 18 U.S.C. § 2256(8).".

The Commentary to § 2A3.1 captioned "Application Notes" is amended by redesignating Notes 4 through 6 as Notes 5 through 7, respectively; and by inserting after Note 3 the following:

"4. The enhancement in subsection (b)(6)(A) applies in cases involving the misrepresentation of a participant's identity to (A) persuade, induce, entice, or coerce a minor to engage in prohibited sexual conduct; or (B) facilitate transportation or travel, by a minor or a participant, to engage in prohibited sexual conduct. Subsection (b)(6)(A) is intended to apply only to misrepresentations made directly to a minor or to a person who exercises custody, care, or supervisory control of the minor. Accordingly, the enhancement in subsection (b)(6)(A) would not apply to a misrepresentation made by a participant to an airline representative in the course of making travel arrangements for the minor.

The misrepresentation to which the enhancement in subsection (b)(6)(A) may apply includes misrepresentation of a participant's name, age, occupation, gender, or status, as long as the misrepresentation was made with the intent to (A) persuade, induce, entice, or coerce a minor to engage in prohibited sexual conduct; or (B) facilitate transportation or travel, by a minor or a participant, to engage in prohibited sexual conduct. Accordingly, use of a computer screen name, without such intent, would not be a sufficient basis for application of the enhancement.

Subsection (b)(6)(B) provides an enhancement if a computer or an Internet-access device was used to (A) persuade, induce, entice, or coerce a minor to engage in prohibited sexual conduct; or (B) facilitate transportation or travel, by a minor or a participant, to engage in prohibited sexual conduct. Subsection (b)(6)(B) is intended to apply only to the use of a computer or an Internet-access device to communicate directly with a minor or with a person who exercises custody, care, or supervisory control of the minor. Accordingly, the enhancement would not apply to the use of a computer or an Internet-access device to obtain airline tickets for the minor from an airline's Internet site.".

Chapter Two, Part A, Subpart 3 is amended by striking § 2A3.2 in its entirety and inserting the following:

"§ 2A3.2.   Criminal Sexual Abuse of a Minor Under the Age of Sixteen Years (Statutory Rape) or Attempt to Commit Such Acts

    (a)   Base Offense Level:

        (1)   18, if the offense involved a violation of chapter 117 of title 18, United States Code; or

        (2)   15, otherwise.

    (b)   Specific Offense Characteristics

        (1)   If the victim was in the custody, care, or supervisory control of the defendant, increase by 2 levels.

        (2)   If subsection (b)(1) does not apply; and—

            (A)   the offense involved the knowing misrepresentation of a participant's identity to (i) persuade, induce, entice, or coerce the victim to engage in prohibited sexual conduct; or (ii) facilitate transportation or travel, by the victim or a participant, to engage in prohibited sexual conduct; or

            (B)   a participant otherwise unduly influenced the victim to engage in prohibited sexual conduct,

        increase by 2 levels.

        (3)   If a computer or an Internet-access device was used to (A) persuade, induce, entice, or coerce the victim to engage in prohibited sexual conduct; or (B) facilitate transportation or travel, by the victim or a participant, to engage in prohibited sexual conduct, increase by 2 levels.

        (4)   If (A) subsection (a)(1) applies; and (B) none of subsections (b)(1) through (b)(3) applies, decrease by 3 levels.

    (c)   Cross Reference

        (1)   If the offense involved criminal sexual abuse or attempt to commit criminal sexual abuse (as defined in 18 U.S.C. § 2241 or § 2242), apply § 2A3.1 (Criminal Sexual Abuse; Attempt to Commit Criminal Sexual Abuse). If the victim had not attained the age of 12 years, § 2A3.1 shall apply, regardless of the 'consent' of the victim.

Commentary

Statutory Provision: 18 U.S.C. § 2243(a). For additional statutory provision(s), see Appendix A (Statutory Index).

Application Notes:

1.   For purposes of this guideline—

'Participant' has the meaning given that term in Application Note 1 of § 3B1.1 (Aggravating Role).

'Prohibited sexual conduct' has the meaning given that term in Application Note 1 of § 2A3.1 (Criminal Sexual Abuse; Attempt to Commit Criminal Sexual Abuse).

'Victim' means (A) an individual who, except as provided in subdivision (B), had not attained the age of 16 years; or (B) an undercover law enforcement officer who represented to a participant that the officer had not attained the age of 16 years.

2. If the defendant committed the criminal sexual act in furtherance of a commercial scheme such as pandering, transporting persons for the purpose of prostitution, or the production of pornography, an upward departure may be warranted. See Chapter Five, Part K (Departures).

3. Subsection (b)(1) is intended to have broad application and is to be applied whenever the victim is entrusted to the defendant, whether temporarily or permanently. For example, teachers, day care providers, baby-sitters, or other temporary caretakers are among those who would be subject to this enhancement. In determining whether to apply this enhancement, the court should look to the actual relationship that existed between the defendant and the victim and not simply to the legal status of the defendant-victim relationship.

4. If the enhancement in subsection (b)(1) applies, do not apply subsection (b)(2) or § 3B1.3 (Abuse of Position of Trust or Use of Special Skill).

5. The enhancement in subsection (b)(2)(A) applies in cases involving the misrepresentation of a participant's identity to (A) persuade, induce, entice, or coerce the victim to engage in prohibited sexual conduct; or (B) facilitate transportation or travel, by the victim or a participant, to engage in prohibited sexual conduct. Subsection (b)(2)(A) is intended to apply only to misrepresentations made directly to the victim or to a person who exercises custody, care, or supervisory control of the victim. Accordingly, the enhancement in subsection (b)(2)(A) would not apply to a misrepresentation made by a participant to an airline representative in the course of making travel arrangements for the victim.

The misrepresentation to which the enhancement in subsection (b)(2)(A) may apply includes misrepresentation of a participant's name, age, occupation, gender, or status, as long as the misrepresentation was made with the intent to (A) persuade, induce, entice, or coerce the victim to engage in prohibited sexual conduct; or (B) facilitate transportation or travel, by the victim or a participant, to engage in prohibited sexual conduct. Accordingly, use of a computer screen name, without such intent, would not be a sufficient basis for application of the enhancement.

In determining whether subsection (b)(2)(B) applies, the court should closely consider the facts of the case to determine whether a participant's influence over the victim compromised the voluntariness of the victim's behavior.

In a case in which a participant is at least 10 years older than the victim, there shall be a rebuttable presumption, for purposes of subsection (b)(2)(B), that such participant unduly influenced the victim to engage in prohibited sexual conduct. In such a case, some degree of undue influence can be presumed because of the substantial difference in age between the participant and the victim.

If the victim was threatened or placed in fear, the cross reference in subsection (c)(1) will apply.

6. Subsection (b)(3) provides an enhancement if a computer or an Internet-access device was used to (A) persuade, induce, entice, coerce the victim to engage in prohibited sexual conduct; or (B) facilitate transportation or travel, by the victim or a participant, to engage in prohibited sexual conduct. Subsection (b)(3) is intended to apply only to the use of a computer or an Internet-access device to communicate directly with the victim or with a person who exercises custody, care, or supervisory control of the victim. Accordingly, the enhancement would not apply to the use of a computer or an Internet-access device to obtain airline tickets for the victim from an airline's Internet site.

7. Subsection (c)(1) provides a cross reference to § 2A3.1 (Criminal Sexual Abuse; Attempt to Commit Criminal Sexual Abuse) if the offense involved criminal sexual abuse or attempt to commit criminal sexual abuse, as defined in 18 U.S.C. § 2241 or § 2242. For example, the cross reference to § 2A3.1 shall apply if (A) the victim had not attained the age of 12 years (see 18 U.S.C. § 2241(c)); (B) the victim had attained the age of 12 years but not attained the age of 16 years, and was placed in fear of death, serious bodily injury, or kidnaping (see 18 U.S.C. § 2241(a),(c)); or (C) the victim was threatened or placed in fear other than fear of death, serious bodily injury, or kidnaping (see 18 U.S.C. § 2242(1)).

8. If the defendant's criminal history includes a prior sentence for conduct that is similar to the instant offense, an upward departure may be warranted.

Background: This section applies to offenses involving the criminal sexual abuse of an individual who had not attained the age of 16 years. While this section applies to consensual sexual acts prosecuted under 18 U.S.C. § 2243(a) that would be lawful but for the age of the victim, it also applies to cases, prosecuted under 18 U.S.C. § 2243(a) or chapter 117 of title 18, United States Code, in which a participant took active measure(s) to unduly influence the victim to engage in prohibited sexual conduct and, thus, the voluntariness of the victim's behavior was compromised. A two-level enhancement is provided in subsection (b)(2) for such cases. It is assumed that at least a four-year age difference exists between the victim and the defendant, as specified in 18 U.S.C. § 2243(a). A two-level enhancement is provided in subsection (b)(1) for a defendant who victimizes a minor under his supervision or care. However, if the victim had not attained the age of 12 years, § 2A3.1 (Criminal Sexual Abuse; Attempt to Commit Criminal Sexual Abuse) will apply, regardless of the 'consent' of the victim.".

Section 2A3.3 is amended by inserting after subsection (a) the following:

"(b) Specific Offense Characteristics

(1) If the offense involved the knowing misrepresentation of a participant's identity to (A) persuade, induce, entice, or coerce a minor to engage in prohibited sexual conduct; or (B) facilitate transportation

Amendment 592 APPENDIX C - VOLUME II November 1, 2013

or travel, by a minor or a participant, to engage in prohibited sexual conduct, increase by 2 levels.

(2) If a computer or an Internet-access device was used to (A) persuade, induce, entice, or coerce a minor to engage in prohibited sexual conduct; or (B) facilitate transportation or travel, by a minor or a participant, to engage in prohibited sexual conduct, increase by 2 levels.".

The Commentary to § 2A3.3 captioned "Application Notes" is amended by striking Note 1 in its entirety and inserting the following:

"1. For purposes of this guideline—

'Minor' means an individual who had not attained the age of 18 years.

'Participant' has the meaning given that term in Application Note 1 of the Commentary to § 3B1.1 (Aggravating Role).

'Prohibited sexual conduct' has the meaning given that term in Application Note 1 of the Commentary to § 2A3.1 (Criminal Sexual Abuse; Attempt to Commit Criminal Sexual Abuse).

'Ward' means a person in official detention under the custodial, supervisory, or disciplinary authority of the defendant.";

by redesignating Note 2 as Note 4; and by inserting after Note 1 the following:

"2. The enhancement in subsection (b)(1) applies in cases involving the misrepresentation of a participant's identity to (A) persuade, induce, entice, or coerce a minor to engage in prohibited sexual conduct; or (B) facilitate transportation or travel, by a minor or a participant, to engage in prohibited sexual conduct. Subsection (b)(1) is intended to apply only to misrepresentations made directly to a minor or to a person who exercises custody, care, or supervisory control of the minor. Accordingly, the enhancement in subsection (b)(1) would not apply to a misrepresentation made by a participant to an airline representative in the course of making travel arrangements for the minor.

The misrepresentation to which the enhancement in subsection (b)(1) may apply includes misrepresentation of a participant's name, age, occupation, gender, or status, as long as the misrepresentation was made with the intent to (A) persuade, induce, entice, or coerce a minor to engage in prohibited sexual conduct; or (B) facilitate transportation or travel, by a minor or a participant, to engage in prohibited sexual conduct. Accordingly, use of a computer screen name, without such intent, would not be a sufficient basis for application of the enhancement.

3. Subsection (b)(2) provides an enhancement if a computer or an Internet-access device was used to (A) persuade, induce, entice, or coerce a minor to engage in prohibited sexual conduct; or (B) facilitate transportation or travel, by a minor or a participant, to engage in prohibited sexual conduct. Subsection (b)(2) is intended to apply only to the use of a computer or an Internet-access device to communicate directly with a minor or with a person who exercises custody, care, or supervisory control of the minor. Accordingly,

the enhancement would not apply to the use of a computer or an Internet-access device to obtain airline tickets for the minor from an airline's Internet site.".

Section 2A3.4(b) is amended by adding at the end the following:

"(4) If the offense involved the knowing misrepresentation of a participant's identity to (A) persuade, induce, entice, or coerce a minor to engage in prohibited sexual conduct; or (B) facilitate transportation or travel, by a minor or a participant, to engage in prohibited sexual conduct, increase by 2 levels.

(5) If a computer or an Internet-access device was used to (A) persuade, induce, entice, or coerce a minor to engage in prohibited sexual conduct; or (B) facilitate transportation or travel, by a minor or a participant, to engage in prohibited sexual conduct, increase by 2 levels.".

Section 2A3.4(c)(2) is amended by inserting "Under the Age of Sixteen Years" before "(Statutory Rape)".

The Commentary to § 2A3.4 captioned "Application Notes" is amended by redesignating Note 5 as Note 8; by redesignating Notes 1 through 4 as Notes 2 through 5, respectively; by inserting before redesignated Note 2 (formerly Note 1) the following:

"1. For purposes of this guideline— 'Minor' means an individual who had not attained the age of 18 years.

'Participant' has the meaning given that term in Application Note 1 of the Commentary to § 3B1.1 (Aggravating Role).

'Prohibited sexual conduct' has the meaning given that term in Application Note 1 of the Commentary to § 2A3.1 (Criminal Sexual Abuse; Attempt to Commit Criminal Sexual Abuse).";

and by adding after redesignated Note 5 (formerly Note 4), the following:

"6. The enhancement in subsection (b)(4) applies in cases involving the misrepresentation of a participant's identity to (A) persuade, induce, entice, or coerce a minor to engage in prohibited sexual conduct; or (B) facilitate transportation or travel, by a minor or a participant, to engage in prohibited sexual conduct. Subsection (b)(4) is intended to apply only to misrepresentations made directly to a minor or to a person who exercises custody, care, or supervisory control of the minor. Accordingly, the enhancement in subsection (b)(4) would not apply to a misrepresentation made by a participant to an airline representative in the course of making travel arrangements for the minor.

The misrepresentation to which the enhancement in subsection (b)(4) may apply includes misrepresentation of a participant's name, age, occupation, gender, or status, as long as the misrepresentation was made with the intent to (A) persuade, induce, entice, or coerce a minor to engage in prohibited sexual conduct; or (B) facilitate transportation or travel, by a minor or a participant, to engage in prohibited sexual conduct. Accordingly, use of a computer screen name, without such intent, would not be a sufficient basis for application of the enhancement.

Amendment 592 APPENDIX C - VOLUME II November 1, 2013

> 7. Subsection (b)(5) provides an enhancement if a computer or an Internet-access device was used to (A) persuade, induce, entice, or coerce a minor to engage in prohibited sexual conduct; or (B) facilitate transportation or travel, by a minor or a participant, to engage in prohibited sexual conduct. Subsection (b)(5) is intended to apply only to the use of a computer or an Internet-access device to communicate directly with a minor or with a person who exercises custody, care, or supervisory control of the minor. Accordingly, the enhancement would not apply to the use of a computer or an Internet-access device to obtain airline tickets for the minor from an airline's Internet site.".

Chapter Two, Part G, Subpart One is amended by striking the text of the title to Subpart One in its entirety and inserting the following:

"PROMOTING PROSTITUTION OR PROHIBITED SEXUAL CONDUCT";

and by striking § 2G1.1 in its entirety and inserting the following:

"§ 2G1.1. Promoting Prostitution or Prohibited Sexual Conduct

    (a)   Base Offense Level:

        (1)   19, if the offense involved a minor; or

        (2)   14, otherwise.

    (b)   Specific Offense Characteristics

        (1)   If the offense involved (A) prostitution; and (B) the use of physical force, or coercion by threats or drugs or in any manner, increase by 4 levels.

        (2)   If the offense involved a victim who had (A) not attained the age of 12 years, increase by 4 levels; or (B) attained the age of 12 years but not attained the age of 16 years, increase by 2 levels.

        (3)   If subsection (b)(2) applies; and—

            (A)   the defendant was a parent, relative, or legal guardian of the victim; or

            (B)   the victim was otherwise in the custody, care, or supervisory control of the defendant,

        increase by 2 levels.

        (4)   If subsection (b)(3) does not apply; and—

            (A)   the offense involved the knowing misrepresentation of a participant's identity to persuade, induce, entice, coerce, or facilitate the travel of, a minor to engage in prostitution; or

            (B)   a participant otherwise unduly influenced a minor to engage in prostitution, increase by 2 levels.

November 1, 2013   APPENDIX C - VOLUME II   **Amendment 592**

> (5) If a computer or an Internet-access device was used to (A) persuade, induce, entice, coerce, or facilitate the travel of, a minor to engage in prostitution; or (B) entice, encourage, offer, or solicit a person to engage in prohibited sexual conduct with a minor, increase by 2 levels.
>
> (c) Cross References
>
> > (1) If the offense involved causing, transporting, permitting, or offering or seeking by notice or advertisement, a person less than 18 years of age to engage in sexually explicit conduct for the purpose of producing a visual depiction of such conduct, apply § 2G2.1 (Sexually Exploiting a Minor by Production of Sexually Explicit Visual or Printed Material; Custodian Permitting Minor to Engage in Sexually Explicit Conduct; Advertisement for Minors to Engage in Production).
> >
> > (2) If the offense involved criminal sexual abuse, attempted criminal sexual abuse, or assault with intent to commit criminal sexual abuse, apply § 2A3.1 (Criminal Sexual Abuse; Attempt to Commit Criminal Sexual Abuse). If the offense involved criminal sexual abuse of a minor who had not attained the age of 12 years, § 2A3.1 shall apply, regardless of the 'consent' of the victim.
> >
> > (3) If the offense did not involve promoting prostitution, and neither subsection (c)(1) nor (c)(2) is applicable, apply § 2A3.2 (Criminal Sexual Abuse of a Minor Under the Age of Sixteen Years (Statutory Rape) or Attempt to Commit Such Acts) or § 2A3.4 (Abusive Sexual Contact or Attempt to Commit Abusive Sexual Contact), as appropriate.
>
> (d) Special Instruction
>
> > (1) If the offense involved more than one victim, Chapter Three, Part D (Multiple Counts) shall be applied as if the promoting of prostitution or prohibited sexual conduct in respect to each victim had been contained in a separate count of conviction.

Commentary

<u>Statutory Provisions</u>: 8 U.S.C. § 1328; 18 U.S.C. §§ 2421, 2422, 2423(a), 2425.

<u>Application Notes</u>:

1. For purposes of this guideline—

    'Minor' means an individual who had not attained the age of 18 years.

    'Participant' has the meaning given that term in Application Note 1 of § 3B1.1 (Aggravating Role).

    'Prohibited sexual conduct' has the meaning given that term in Application

-533-

Amendment 592 APPENDIX C - VOLUME II November 1, 2013

Note 1 of § 2A3.1 (Criminal Sexual Abuse; Attempt to Commit Criminal Sexual Abuse).

'Promoting prostitution' means persuading, inducing, enticing, or coercing a person to engage in prostitution, or to travel to engage in, prostitution.

'Victim' means a person transported, persuaded, induced, enticed, or coerced to engage in, or travel for the purpose of engaging in, prostitution or prohibited sexual conduct, whether or not the person consented to the prostitution or prohibited sexual conduct. Accordingly, 'victim' may include an undercover law enforcement officer.

2. Subsection (b)(1) provides an enhancement for physical force, or coercion, that occurs as part of a prostitution offense and anticipates no bodily injury. If bodily injury results, an upward departure may be warranted. See Chapter Five, Part K (Departures). For purposes of subsection (b)(1), 'coercion' includes any form of conduct that negates the voluntariness of the behavior of the victim. This enhancement would apply, for example, in a case in which the ability of the victim to appraise or control conduct was substantially impaired by drugs or alcohol. In the case of an adult victim, rather than a victim less than 18 years of age, this characteristic generally will not apply if the drug or alcohol was voluntarily taken.

3. For the purposes of § 3B1.1 (Aggravating Role), a victim, as defined in this guideline, is considered a participant only if that victim assisted in the promoting of prostitution or prohibited sexual conduct in respect to another victim.

4. For the purposes of Chapter Three, Part D (Multiple Counts), each person transported, persuaded, induced, enticed, or coerced to engage in, or travel to engage in, prostitution or prohibited sexual conduct is to be treated as a separate victim. Consequently, multiple counts involving more than one victim are not to be grouped together under § 3D1.2 (Groups of Closely-Related Counts). In addition, subsection (d)(1) directs that if the relevant conduct of an offense of conviction includes the promoting of prostitution or prohibited sexual conduct in respect to more than one victim, whether specifically cited in the count of conviction, each such victim shall be treated as if contained in a separate count of conviction.

5. Subsection (b)(3) is intended to have broad application and includes offenses involving a victim less than 18 years of age entrusted to the defendant, whether temporarily or permanently. For example, teachers, day care providers, baby-sitters, or other temporary caretakers are among those who would be subject to this enhancement. In determining whether to apply this enhancement, the court should look to the actual relationship that existed between the defendant and the victim and not simply to the legal status of the defendant-victim relationship.

6. If the enhancement in subsection (b)(3) applies, do not apply subsection (b)(4) or § 3B1.3 (Abuse of Position of Trust or Use of Special Skill).

7. The enhancement in subsection (b)(4)(A) applies in cases involving the misrepresentation of a participant's identity to persuade, induce, entice, coerce, or facilitate the travel of, a minor to engage in prostitution. Subsec-

tion (b)(4)(A) is intended to apply only to misrepresentations made directly to a minor or to a person who exercises custody, care, or supervisory control of the minor. Accordingly, the enhancement in subsection (b)(4)(A) would not apply to a misrepresentation made by a participant to an airline representative in the course of making travel arrangements for the minor.

The misrepresentation to which the enhancement in subsection (b)(4)(A) may apply includes misrepresentation of a participant's name, age, occupation, gender, or status, as long as the misrepresentation was made with the intent to persuade, induce, entice, coerce, or facilitate the travel of, a minor to engage in prostitution. Accordingly, use of a computer screen name, without such intent, would not be a sufficient basis for application of the enhancement.

In determining whether subsection (b)(4)(B) applies, the court should closely consider the facts of the case to determine whether a participant's influence over the minor compromised the voluntariness of the minor's behavior.

In a case in which a participant is at least 10 years older than the minor, there shall be a rebuttable presumption, for purposes of subsection (b)(4)(B), that such participant unduly influenced the minor to engage in prostitution. In such a case, some degree of undue influence can be presumed because of the substantial difference in age between the participant and the minor.

8. Subsection (b)(5) provides an enhancement if a computer or an Internet-access device was used to (A) persuade, induce, entice, coerce, or facilitate the travel of, a minor to engage in prostitution; or (B) entice, encourage, offer, or solicit a person to engage in prohibited sexual conduct with a minor. Subsection (b)(5)(A) is intended to apply only to the use of a computer or an Internet-access device to communicate directly with a minor or with a person who exercises custody, care, or supervisory control of the minor. Accordingly, the enhancement in subsection (b)(5)(A) would not apply to the use of a computer or an Internet-access device to obtain airline tickets for the minor from an airline's Internet site.

9. The cross reference in subsection (c)(1) is to be construed broadly to include all instances in which the offense involved employing, using, persuading, inducing, enticing, coercing, transporting, permitting, or offering or seeking by notice or advertisement, a person less than 18 years of age to engage in sexually explicit conduct for the purpose of producing any visual depiction of such conduct. For purposes of subsection (c)(1), 'sexually explicit conduct' has the meaning given that term in 18 U.S.C. § 2256.

10. Subsection (c)(2) provides a cross reference to § 2A3.1 (Criminal Sexual Abuse; Attempt to Commit Criminal Sexual Abuse) if the offense involved criminal sexual abuse or attempt to commit criminal sexual abuse, as defined in 18 U.S.C. § 2241 or § 2242. For example, the cross reference to § 2A3.1 shall apply if the offense involved criminal sexual abuse; and (A) the victim had not attained the age of 12 years (see 18 U.S.C. § 2241(c)); (B) the victim had attained the age of 12 years but had not attained the age of 16 years, and was placed in fear of death, serious bodily injury, or kidnaping (see 18 U.S.C. § 2241(a),(c)); or (C) the victim was threatened

Amendment 592 APPENDIX C - VOLUME II November 1, 2013

or placed in fear other than fear of death, serious bodily injury, or kidnaping (see 18 U.S.C. § 2242(1)).

11. The cross reference in subsection (c)(3) addresses the case in which the offense did not involve promoting prostitution, neither subsection (c)(1) nor (c)(2) is applicable, and the offense involved prohibited sexual conduct other than the conduct covered by subsection (c)(1) or (c)(2). In such case, the guideline for the underlying prohibited sexual conduct is to be used; i.e., § 2A3.2 (Criminal Sexual Abuse of a Minor Under the Age of Sixteen Years (Statutory Rape) or Attempt to Commit Such Acts) or § 2A3.4 (Abusive Sexual Contact or Attempt to Commit Abusive Sexual Contact).

Background: This guideline covers offenses under chapter 117 of title 18, United States Code. Those offenses involve promoting prostitution or prohibited sexual conduct through a variety of means. Offenses that involve promoting prostitution under chapter 117 of such title are sentenced under this guideline, unless other prohibited sexual conduct occurs as part of the prostitution offense, in which case one of the cross references would apply. Offenses under chapter 117 of such title that do not involve promoting prostitution are to be sentenced under § 2G2.1 (Sexually Exploiting a Minor by Production of Sexually Explicit Visual or Printed Material; Custodian Permitting Minor to Engage in Sexually Explicit Conduct; Advertisement for Minors to Engage in Production), § 2A3.1 (Criminal Sexual Abuse; Attempt to Commit Criminal Sexual Abuse), § 2A3.2 (Criminal Sexual Abuse of a Minor Under the Age of Sixteen Years (Statutory Rape) or Attempt to Commit Such Acts) or § 2A3.4 (Abusive Sexual Contact or Attempt to Commit Abusive Sexual Contact), as appropriate, pursuant to the cross references provided in subsection (c).".

Section 2G2.1(b) is amended by striking subdivision (3) in its entirety and inserting the following:

"(3) If, for the purpose of producing sexually explicit material, the offense involved (A) the knowing misrepresentation of a participant's identity to persuade, induce, entice, coerce, or facilitate the travel of, a minor to engage sexually explicit conduct; or (B) the use of a computer or an Internet-access device to (i) persuade, induce, entice, coerce, or facilitate the travel of, a minor to engage in sexually explicit conduct, or to otherwise solicit participation by a minor in such conduct; or (ii) solicit participation with a minor in sexually explicit conduct, increase by 2 levels.".

The Commentary to § 2G2.1 captioned "Application Notes" is amended by redesignating Notes 1 through 3 as Notes 2 through 4, respectively; by inserting before redesignated Note 2 (formerly Note 1) the following:

"1. For purposes of this guideline, 'minor' means an individual who had not attained the age of 18 years.";

and by adding at the end the following:

"5. The enhancement in subsection (b)(3)(A) applies in cases involving the misrepresentation of a participant's identity to persuade, induce, entice, coerce, or facilitate the travel of, a minor to engage in sexually explicit conduct for the purpose of producing sexually explicit material. Subsection (b)(3)(A) is intended to apply only to misrepresentations made directly to a minor or to a person who exercises custody, care, or supervisory control of the minor. Accordingly, the enhancement in subsection (b)(3)(A) would not apply to a misrepresentation made by a participant to an airline representative in the course of making travel arrangements for the minor.

The misrepresentation to which the enhancement in subsection (b)(3)(A) may apply includes misrepresentation of a participant's name, age, occupation, gender, or status, as long as the misrepresentation was made with the intent to persuade, induce, entice, coerce, or facilitate the travel of, a minor to engage in sexually explicit conduct for the purpose of producing sexually explicit material. Accordingly, use of a computer screen name, without such intent, would not be a sufficient basis for application of the enhancement.

Subsection (b)(3)(B)(i) provides an enhancement if a computer or an Internet-access device was used to persuade, induce, entice, coerce, or facilitate the travel of, a minor to engage in sexually explicit conduct for the purpose of producing sexually explicit material or otherwise to solicit participation by a minor in such conduct for such purpose. Subsection (b)(3)(B)(i) is intended to apply only to the use of a computer or an Internet-access device to communicate directly with a minor or with a person who exercises custody, care, or supervisory control of the minor. Accordingly, the enhancement would not apply to the use of a computer or an Internet-access device to obtain airline tickets for the minor from an airline's Internet site.".

Section 2G2.2(b) is amended by striking subdivision (2) in its entirety and inserting the following:

"(2)   (Apply the Greatest) If the offense involved:

   (A)   Distribution for pecuniary gain, increase by the number of levels from the table in § 2F1.1 (Fraud and Deceit) corresponding to the retail value of the material, but by not less than 5 levels.

   (B)   Distribution for the receipt, or expectation of receipt, of a thing of value, but not for pecuniary gain, increase by 5 levels.

   (C)   Distribution to a minor, increase by 5 levels.

   (D)   Distribution to a minor that was intended to persuade, induce, entice, coerce, or facilitate the travel of, the minor to engage in prohibited sexual conduct, increase by 7 levels.

   (E)   Distribution other than distribution described in subdivisions (A) through (D), increase by 2 levels.".

The Commentary to § 2G2.2 captioned "Application Notes" is amended by striking Note 1 in its entirety and inserting the following:

"1.   For purposes of this guideline—

   'Distribution' means any act, including production, transportation, and possession with intent to distribute, related to the transfer of material involving the sexual exploitation of a minor.

   'Distribution for pecuniary gain' means distribution for profit.

'Distribution for the receipt, or expectation of receipt, of a thing of value, but not for pecuniary gain' means any transaction, including bartering or other in-kind transaction, that is conducted for a thing of value, but not for profit. 'Thing of value' means anything of valuable consideration. For example, in a case involving the bartering of child pornographic material, the 'thing of value' is the child pornographic material received in exchange for other child pornographic material bartered in consideration for the material received.

'Distribution to a minor' means the knowing distribution to an individual who is a minor at the time of the offense, knowing or believing the individual is a minor at that time.

'Minor' means an individual who had not attained the age of 18 years.

'Pattern of activity involving the sexual abuse or exploitation of a minor' means any combination of two or more separate instances of the sexual abuse or sexual exploitation of a minor by the defendant, whether or not the abuse or exploitation (A) occurred during the course of the offense; (B) involved the same or different victims; or (C) resulted in a conviction for such conduct.

'Prohibited sexual conduct' has the meaning given that term in Application Note 1 of the Commentary to § 2A3.1 (Criminal Sexual Abuse; Attempt to Commit Criminal Sexual Abuse).

'Sexual abuse or exploitation' means conduct constituting criminal sexual abuse of a minor, sexual exploitation of a minor, abusive sexual contact of a minor, any similar offense under state law, or an attempt or conspiracy to commit any of the above offenses. 'Sexual abuse or exploitation' does not include trafficking in material relating to the sexual abuse or exploitation of a minor.

'Sexually explicit conduct' has the meaning given that term in 18 U.S.C. § 2256.".

The Commentary to § 2G2.4 is amended by adding at the end the following:

"Application Notes:

1. For purposes of this guideline—

    'Minor' means an individual who had not attained the age of 18 years.

    'Visual depiction' means any visual depiction described in 18 U.S.C. § 2256(5) and (8).

2. For purposes of subsection (b)(2), a file that (A) contains a visual depiction; and (B) is stored on a magnetic, optical, digital, other electronic, or other storage medium or device, shall be considered to be one item.

    If the offense involved a large number of visual depictions, an upward departure may be warranted, regardless of whether subsection (b)(2) applies.".

Section 2G3.1 is amended in the title by adding at the end "; Transferring Obscene Matter to a Minor".

Section 2G3.1(b) is amended by striking subdivision (1) in its entirety and inserting the following:

"(1) (Apply the Greatest) If the offense involved:

(A) Distribution for pecuniary gain, increase by the number of levels from the table in § 2F1.1 (Fraud and Deceit) corresponding to the retail value of the material, but by not less than 5 levels.

(B) Distribution for the receipt, or expectation of receipt, of a thing of value, but not for pecuniary gain, increase by 5 levels.

(C) Distribution to a minor, increase by 5 levels.

(D) Distribution to a minor that was intended to persuade, induce, entice, coerce, or facilitate the travel of, the minor to engage in prohibited sexual conduct, increase by 7 levels.

(E) Distribution other than distribution described in subdivisions (A) through (D), increase by 2 levels.".

The Commentary to § 2G3.1 captioned "Statutory Provisions" is amended by inserting ", 1470" after "1466".

The Commentary to § 2G3.1 captioned "Application Note" is amended by striking Note 1 in its entirety and inserting the following:

"1. For purposes of this guideline—

'Distribution' means any act, including production, transportation, and possession with intent to distribute, related to the transfer of obscene matter.

'Distribution for pecuniary gain' means distribution for profit.

'Distribution for the receipt, or expectation of receipt, of a thing of value, but not for pecuniary gain' means any transaction, including bartering or other in-kind transaction, that is conducted for a thing of value, but not for profit. 'Thing of value' means anything of valuable consideration.

'Distribution to a minor' means the knowing distribution to an individual who is a minor at the time of the offense, knowing or believing the individual is a minor at that time.

'Minor' means an individual who had not attained the age of 16 years.

'Prohibited sexual conduct' has the meaning given that term in Application Note 1 of the Commentary to § 2A3.1 (Criminal Sexual Abuse; Attempt to Commit Criminal Sexual Abuse).".

The Commentary to § 2G3.2 captioned "Background" is amended by inserting "; Transferring Obscene Matter to a Minor" after "Transporting Obscene Matter".

Appendix A (Statutory Index) is amended by inserting after the line referenced to "18 U.S.C. § 1468" the following new line:

"18 U.S.C. § 1470   2G3.1";

and by inserting after the line referenced to "18 U.S.C. § 2423(b)" the following new line:

"18 U.S.C. § 2425   2G1.1".

Reason for Amendment: This is a six-part amendment. The amendment is promulgated primarily in response to the Protection of Children from Sexual Predators Act of 1998, Pub. L. 105–314 (the "Act"), which contained several directives to the Commission.

First, the amendment addresses the Act's directives to provide enhancements to the guidelines covering aggravated sexual abuse, sexual abuse, and sexual abuse of a minor if (1) the defendant used a computer with the intent to persuade, induce, entice, coerce, or facilitate the transport of a minor to engage in any prohibited sexual activity; and (2) the defendant knowingly misrepresented the defendant's actual identity with the intent to persuade, induce, entice, coerce, or facilitate the transport of a minor to engage in any prohibited sexual conduct. The legislative history of the Act indicates congressional intent to ensure that persons who misrepresent themselves to a minor, or use computers or Internet-access devices to locate and gain access to a minor, are severely punished.

In response to these directives, the amendment provides separate, cumulative two-level enhancements in the sexual abuse guidelines, §§ 2A3.2 (Criminal Sexual Abuse of a Minor Under the Age of Sixteen Years (Statutory Rape) or Attempt to Commit Such Acts), 2A3.3 (Criminal Sexual Abuse of a Ward), and 2A3.4 (Abusive Sexual Contact), and in § 2G1.1 (Promoting Prostitution or Prohibited Sexual Conduct) for (1) the use of a computer or Internet-access device with the intent to persuade, induce, entice, coerce, or facilitate the transport of a minor to engage in any prohibited sexual conduct; and (2) misrepresentation of a criminally responsible person's identity with such an intent. The Commission has determined that, for offenses sentenced under these guidelines, the use of a computer or Internet-access device and the misrepresentation of identity represent separate, additional harms and increase the culpability of a defendant or criminal participant who engages, or attempts to engage, in such conduct. With respect to §§ 2A3.1 (Criminal Sexual Abuse; Attempt to Commit Criminal Sexual Abuse) and 2G2.1 (Sexually Exploiting a Minor by Production of Sexually Explicit Visual or Printed Material), the amendment treats these two types of aggravating conduct as alternative triggers for one enhancement. In these guidelines, the substantially higher base offense levels and other specific offense characteristics provide alternative guideline mechanisms to account, at least in part, for these harms and the defendant's increased culpability. Accordingly, the Commission determined that, in these guidelines, a single, two-level increase for the use of a computer or misrepresentation adequately addresses the increased seriousness of these offenses.

Second, this amendment responds to the directive in the Act to provide a sentencing enhancement for offenses under chapter 117 of title 18, United States Code (relating to the transportation of minors for illegal sexual activity), while ensuring that the sentences, guidelines, and policy statements for offenders convicted of such offenses are appropriately severe and reasonably consistent with the other relevant directives and the relevant existing guidelines. In furtherance of this directive, the Commission initiated a comprehensive examination of §§ 2A3.2 and 2G1.1, the guidelines under which most cases prosecuted under such chapter are sentenced. The Commission intends to continue its comprehensive review of these guidelines and other guidelines that cover chapter 117 offenses in the next amendment cycle.

The amendment implements the directive to provide an enhancement for chapter 117 offenses, in part, through the enhancements provided in §§ 2A3.2 and 2G1.1 for misrepresentation of identity and use of a computer to facilitate such offenses. In addition, the amendment provides an alternative basis for a sentencing enhancement if a participant otherwise unduly influenced the victim to engage in prohibited sexual conduct. Despite the fact that § 2A3.2 nominally applies to consensual sexual acts with a person who had not attained the age of 16 years, Commission data indicated that many of the cases sentenced under § 2A3.2, directly or via a cross reference from § 2G1.1, involve some aspect of undue influence over the victim on the part of the defendant or other criminally responsible person. Analysis of these cases revealed conduct such as coercion, enticement, or other forms of undue influence by the defendant that compromised the voluntariness of the victim's behavior and, accordingly, increased the defendant's culpability for the crime. This prong of the new enhancement is designed to allow courts to consider closely the facts of the individual case. Furthermore, a rebuttable presumption is created that the offense involved undue influence if a participant was at least 10 years older than the victim. Data reviewed by the Commission suggested that such a presumption is appropriate because persons who are much older than a minor are frequently in a position to manipulate the minor due to increased knowledge, influence, and resources.

As a result of the Commission's comprehensive assessment of §§ 2A3.2 and 2G1.1, the amendment also makes several other modifications to these guidelines. The amendment provides, in § 2A3.2, an alternative base offense level of level 18 if the offense involved a violation of chapter 117 of title 18, United States Code. This alternative base offense level more fully implements a directive in the Sex Crimes Against Children Prevention Act of 1995, Pub. L. 104–71, to provide at least a three-level increase for offenses under 18 U.S.C. § 2423(a) involving the transportation of minors for prostitution or other prohibited sexual conduct. However, the amendment also provides for a three-level decrease if a defendant receives the higher alternative base offense level of level 18 and none of certain listed aggravating specific offense characteristics apply. This reduction recognizes that not all defendants convicted under chapter 117 have necessarily engaged in a more aggravated form of statutory rape conduct. The amendment also adds several definitions to § 2A3.2, including clarifying that "victim" includes an undercover police officer who represents to the perpetrator of the offense that the officer was under the age of 16 years. This change was made to ensure that offenders who are apprehended in an undercover operation are appropriately punished. In § 2G1.1, the amendment reallocates, without substantive change, five offense levels from subsection (b)(2) to the base offense level, for offenses involving a minor. Section 2G1.1(b)(1) also is amended to clarify that the offense must have involved prostitution in order for the enhancement for coercion, threats, or drugs to apply. The amendment also clarifies that, in §§ 2A3.2(c)(1) and 2G1.1(c)(2), the cross reference to § 2A3.1 shall apply if the offense involved criminal sexual abuse of a minor under the age of 12 years, regardless of the "consent" of the victim. Review of Commission data indicated that the cross reference to § 2A3.1 currently is not being applied in many cases in which the offense conduct suggests it should. In both §§ 2A3.2 and 2G1.1, the amendment also precludes application of the new enhancement for misrepresentation of identity and/or undue influence if the victim is in the custody, care, or supervisory control of the defendant.

Third, the amendment addresses the directive in the Act to clarify that the term "distribution of pornography" applies to the distribution of pornography for both monetary remuneration and a non-pecuniary interest. In response to the directive, the amendment modifies the enhancement in § 2G2.2 (Trafficking in Material Involving the Sexual Exploitation of a Minor), relating to the distribution of child pornographic material, as well as a similar enhancement in § 2G3.1 (Importing, Mailing, or Transporting Obscene Matter; Transferring Obscene Matter to a Minor), relating to the distribution of obscene material. For each of these enhancements, the amendment (1) modifies the definition of "distribution" to mean any act, including production, transportation, and possession with intent to distribute, related to the transfer of the material, regardless of whether it was for pecuniary gain; and (2) provides for varying levels of enhancement depending upon the purpose and audience of the distribution. These varying levels are intended to respond to increased congressional concerns, as indicated in the legislative history of the Act, that pedophiles, including those who use the Internet, are using child pornographic and obscene material to desensitize children to sexual activity, to convince children that sexual activity involving children is normal, and to entice children to engage in sexual activity.

Fourth, the amendment clarifies the meaning of the term "item" in subsection (b)(2) of § 2G2.4 (Possession of Materials Depicting a Minor Engaged in Sexually Explicit Conduct). That subsection provides a two-level enhancement if the offense involved possession of ten or more items of child pornography. The amendment adopts the holding of all circuits that have addressed the matter that a computer file qualifies as an item for purposes of the enhancement. The amendment also provides for an invited upward departure if the offense involves a large number of visual depictions of child pornography, regardless of the number of "items" involved. This provision invites courts to depart upward in cases in which a particular item, such as a book or a computer file, contains an unusually large number of pornographic images involving children.

Fifth, the amendment addresses the new offense of transferring obscene matter to a minor, codified at 18 U.S.C. § 1470, by referencing the offense in the Statutory Index (Appendix A) to § 2G3.1.

Sixth, the amendment addresses the new offense of prohibiting the knowing transmittal of identifying information about minors for criminal sexual purposes, codified at 18 U.S.C. § 2425, by referencing the new offense in the Statutory Index to § 2G1.1.

Effective Date: The effective date of this amendment is November 1, 2000.

593. **Amendment:** Section 2B5.3, effective May 1, 2000 (see Amendment 590, supra), is repromulgated, with minor editorial changes, as follows:

"§ 2B5.3. Criminal Infringement of Copyright or Trademark

(a) Base Offense Level: 8

(b) Specific Offense Characteristics

(1) If the infringement amount exceeded $2,000, increase by the number of levels from the table in § 2F1.1 (Fraud and Deceit) corresponding to that amount.

(2) If the offense involved the manufacture, importation, or uploading of infringing items, increase by 2 levels. If the resulting offense level is less than level 12, increase to level 12.

(3) If the offense was not committed for commercial advantage or private financial gain, decrease by 2 levels, but the resulting offense level shall be not less than level 8.

(4) If the offense involved (A) the conscious or reckless risk of serious bodily injury; or (B) possession of a dangerous

weapon (including a firearm) in connection with the offense, increase by 2 levels. If the resulting offense level is less than level 13, increase to level 13.

Commentary

Statutory Provisions: 17 U.S.C. § 506(a); 18 U.S.C. §§ 2318-2320, 2511. For additional statutory provision(s), see Appendix A (Statutory Index).

Application Notes:

1. Definitions.—For purposes of this guideline:

'Commercial advantage or private financial gain' means the receipt, or expectation of receipt, of anything of value, including other protected works.

'Infringed item' means the copyrighted or trademarked item with respect to which the crime against intellectual property was committed.

'Infringing item' means the item that violates the copyright or trademark laws.

'Uploading' means making an infringing item available on the Internet or a similar electronic bulletin board with the intent to enable other persons to download or otherwise copy, or have access to, the infringing item.

2. Determination of Infringement Amount.—This note applies to the determination of the infringement amount for purposes of subsection (b)(1).

   (A) Use of Retail Value of Infringed Item.—The infringement amount is the retail value of the infringed item, multiplied by the number of infringing items, in a case involving any of the following:

      (i) The infringing item (I) is, or appears to a reasonably informed purchaser to be, identical or substantially equivalent to the infringed item; or (II) is a digital or electronic reproduction of the infringed item.

      (ii) The retail price of the infringing item is not less than 75% of the retail price of the infringed item.

      (iii) The retail value of the infringing item is difficult or impossible to determine without unduly complicating or prolonging the sentencing proceeding.

      (iv) The offense involves the illegal interception of a satellite cable transmission in violation of 18 U.S.C. § 2511. (In a case involving such an offense, the 'retail value of the infringed item' is the price the user of the transmission would have paid to lawfully receive that transmission, and the 'infringed item' is the satellite transmission rather than the intercepting device.)

      (v) The retail value of the infringed item provides a more accurate assessment of the pecuniary harm to the copyright or trademark owner than does the retail value of the infringing item.

(B) Use of Retail Value of Infringing Item.—The infringement amount is the retail value of the infringing item, multiplied by the number of infringing items, in any case not covered by subdivision (A) of this Application Note, including a case involving the unlawful recording of a musical performance in violation of 18 U.S.C. § 2319A.

(C) Retail Value Defined.—For purposes of this Application Note, the 'retail value' of an infringed item or an infringing item is the retail price of that item in the market in which it is sold.

(D) Determination of Infringement Amount in Cases Involving a Variety of Infringing Items.—In a case involving a variety of infringing items, the infringement amount is the sum of all calculations made for those items under subdivisions (A) and (B) of this Application Note. For example, if the defendant sold both counterfeit videotapes that are identical in quality to the infringed videotapes and obviously inferior counterfeit handbags, the infringement amount, for purposes of subsection (b)(1), is the sum of the infringement amount calculated with respect to the counterfeit videotapes under subdivision (A)(i) (i.e., the quantity of the infringing videotapes multiplied by the retail value of the infringed videotapes) and the infringement amount calculated with respect to the counterfeit handbags under subdivision (B) (i.e., the quantity of the infringing handbags multiplied by the retail value of the infringing handbags).

3. Uploading.—With respect to uploading, subsection (b)(2) applies only to uploading with the intent to enable other persons to download or otherwise copy, or have access to, the infringing item. For example, this subsection applies in the case of illegally uploading copyrighted software to an Internet site, but it does not apply in the case of downloading or installing that software on a hard drive on the defendant's personal computer.

4. Application of § 3B1.3.—If the defendant de-encrypted or otherwise circumvented a technological security measure to gain initial access to an infringed item, an adjustment under § 3B1.3 (Abuse of Position of Trust or Use of Special Skill) shall apply.

5. Upward Departure Considerations.—If the offense level determined under this guideline substantially understates the seriousness of the offense, an upward departure may be warranted. The following is a non-exhaustive list of factors that the court may consider in determining whether an upward departure may be warranted:

(A) The offense involved substantial harm to the reputation of the copyright or trademark owner.

(B) The offense was committed in connection with, or in furtherance of, the criminal activities of a national, or international, organized criminal enterprise.

Background: This guideline treats copyright and trademark violations much like theft and fraud. Similar to the sentences for theft and fraud offenses, the sentences for defendants convicted of intellectual property offenses should reflect the nature and magnitude of the pecuniary harm caused by their crimes. Accordingly, similar to the loss enhancement in the theft and fraud guidelines, the infringement amount in subsection (b)(1) serves as a principal factor in determining the offense level for intellectual property offenses.

Subsection (b)(1) implements section 2(g) of the No Electronic Theft (NET) Act of 1997, Pub. L. 105–147, by using the retail value of the infringed item, multiplied by the number of infringing items, to determine the pecuniary harm for cases in which use of the retail value of the infringed item is a reasonable estimate of that harm. For cases referred to in Application Note 2(B), the Commission determined that use of the retail value of the infringed item would overstate the pecuniary harm or otherwise be inappropriate. In these types of cases, use of the retail value of the infringing item, multiplied by the number of those items, is a more reasonable estimate of the resulting pecuniary harm.

Section 2511 of title 18, United States Code, as amended by the Electronic Communications Act of 1986, prohibits the interception of satellite transmission for purposes of direct or indirect commercial advantage or private financial gain. Such violations are similar to copyright offenses and are therefore covered by this guideline.".

Reason for Amendment: This amendment is in response to section 2(g) of the No Electronic Theft (NET) Act of 1997, Pub. L. 105–147 ("the Act"). The Act directs the Commission to ensure that the applicable guideline range for intellectual property offenses (including offenses set forth at section 506(a) of title 17, United States Code, and sections 2319, 2319A, and 2320 of title 18, United States Code) is "sufficiently stringent to deter such a crime." It also more specifically requires that the guidelines "provide for consideration of the retail value and quantity of the items with respect to which the intellectual property offense was committed."

The amendment responds to the directives by making changes to the monetary calculation found in § 2B5.3 (Criminal Infringement of Copyright or Trademark). In addition, the amendment makes a number of other modifications to the infringement guideline, including the addition of several mitigating and aggravating factors, as further means of providing just and proportionate punishment while also seeking to achieve sufficient deterrence.

The monetary calculation in § 2B5.3(b)(1), similar to the loss enhancement in the theft and fraud guidelines, serves as an approximation of the pecuniary harm caused by the offense and is a principal factor in determining the offense level for intellectual property offenses. Prior to this amendment, the monetary calculation for all intellectual property crimes was based on the retail value of the infringing item multiplied by the quantity of infringing items. In response to the directive, the Commission refashioned this enhancement so as to use the retail value of the infringed item, multiplied by the number of infringing items, as a means of approximating the pecuniary harm for cases in which that calculation is believed most likely to provide a reasonable estimate of the resulting harm. Use of that calculation is believed to provide a reasonable approximation for those classes of infringement cases in which it is highly likely that the sale of an infringing item results in a displaced sale of the legitimate, infringed item. The amendment also requires that the retail value of the infringed item, multiplied by the number of infringing items, be used in certain other cases for reasons of practicality.

However, based upon a review of cases sentenced under the former § 2B5.3 over two years, the Commission further determined that using the above formula likely would overstate substantially the pecuniary harm caused to copyright and trademark owners in some cases currently sentenced under the guideline. For those cases, a one-to-one correlation between the sale of infringing items and the displaced sale of legitimate, infringed items is unlikely because the inferior quality of the infringing item and/or the greatly discounted price at which it is sold suggests that many purchasers of infringing items would not, or could not, have purchased the infringed item in the absence of the availability of the infringing item. The Commission therefore determined that, for these latter classes of cases (referred to in Application Note 2(B)), the retail value of the infringing item, multiplied by the number of those items, provides a more reasonable approximation of lost revenues to the copyright or trademark owner, and hence, of the pecuniary harm resulting from the offense.

This amendment also increases the base offense level from level 6 to level 8. The two-level increase in the base offense level brings the infringement guideline more in line with offense levels that would pertain under § 2F1.1 (Fraud and Deceit), assuming applicability under that guideline of the two-level enhancement for more than minimal planning. Based on a review of cases sentenced under the infringement guideline, if a more than minimal planning enhancement did exist in that guideline, it would apply in the vast majority of such cases because they involve this kind of aggravating conduct. Rather than provide a separate enhancement within the revised guideline for "more than minimal planning" conduct, the Commission determined that the infringement guideline should incorporate this type of conduct into the base offense level.

This amendment also provides an enhancement of two levels, and a minimum offense level of level 12, if the offense involved the manufacture, importation, or uploading of infringing items. The Commission determined that defendants who engage in such conduct are more culpable than other intellectual property offenders because they place infringing items into the stream of commerce, thereby enabling others to infringe the copyright or trademark. A review of cases sentenced under the guideline indicated applicability of this enhancement to approximately two-thirds of the cases.

This amendment also provides a two-level downward adjustment (but to a resulting offense level that is not less than offense level 8) if the offense was not committed for commercial advantage or private financial gain. This adjustment reflects the fact that the Act establishes lower statutory penalties for offenses that were not committed for commercial advantage or private financial gain.

This amendment also provides an enhancement of two levels, and a minimum offense level of level 13, if the offense involved the conscious or reckless risk of serious bodily injury or possession of a dangerous weapon in connection with the offense. Testimony received by the Commission indicated that the conscious or reckless risk of serious bodily injury may occur in some cases involving counterfeit consumer products. The Commission determined that this kind of aggravating conduct in connection with infringement cases should be treated under the guidelines in the same way it is treated in connection with fraud cases; therefore, this enhancement is consistent with an identical provision in the fraud guideline.

The amendment also contains an application note expressly providing that the adjustment in § 3B1.3 (Abuse of Position of Trust or Use of Special Skill) shall apply if the defendant de-encrypted or otherwise circumvented a technological security measure to gain initial access to an infringed item. As stated in the background commentary to § 3B1.3, persons who use such a special skill to facilitate or commit a crime generally are viewed as more culpable.

Finally, this amendment contains two encouraged upward departure provisions. The Commission received public comment that indicated that infringement may cause substantial harm to the reputation of the copyright or trademark owner that is not accounted for in the monetary calculation. Public comment also indicated that some copyright and trademark offenses are committed in connection with, or in furtherance of, the criminal activities of certain organized crime enterprises. The amendment invites the court to consider an appropriate upward departure if either of these aggravating circumstances are present.

Pursuant to the emergency amendment authority of the Act, this amendment previously was promulgated as a temporary measure effective May 1, 2000. (See Amendment 590, supra).

Effective Date: The effective date of this amendment is November 1, 2000.

594. **Amendment:** Section 2D1.1(c)(1) is amended by striking "3 KG or more" before "of Methamphetamine (actual)" and inserting "1.5 KG or more"; and by striking "3 KG or more" before "of 'Ice'" and inserting "1.5 KG or more".

Section 2D1.1(c)(2) is amended by striking "at least 1 KG but less than 3 KG" before "of Methamphetamine (actual)" and inserting "at least 500 G but less than 1.5 KG"; and by striking "at least 1 KG but less than 3 KG" before "of 'Ice'" and inserting "at least 500 G but less than 1.5 KG".

Section 2D1.1(c)(3) is amended by striking "at least 300 G but less than 1 KG" before "of Methamphetamine (actual)" and inserting "at least 150 G but less than 500 G"; and by striking "at least 300 G but less than 1 KG" before "of 'Ice'" and inserting "at least 150 G but less than 500 G".

Section 2D1.1(c)(4) is amended by striking "at least 100 G but less than 300 G" before "of Methamphetamine (actual)" and inserting "at least 50 G but less than 150 G"; and by striking "at least 100 G but less than 300 G" before "of 'Ice'" and inserting "at least 50 G but less than 150 G".

Section 2D1.1(c)(5) is amended by striking "at least 70 G but less than 100 G" before "of Methamphetamine (actual)" and inserting "at least 35 G but less than 50 G"; and by striking "at least 70 G but less than 100 G" before "of 'Ice'" and inserting "at least 35 G but less than 50 G".

Section 2D1.1(c)(6) is amended by striking "at least 40 G but less than 70 G" before "of Methamphetamine (actual)" and inserting "at least 20 G but less than 35 G"; and by striking "at least 40 G but less than 70 G" before "of 'Ice'" and inserting "at least 20 G but less than 35 G".

Section 2D1.1(c)(7) is amended by striking "at least 10 G but less than 40 G" before "of Methamphetamine (actual)" and inserting "at least 5 G but less than 20 G"; and by striking "at least 10 G but less than 40 G" before "of 'Ice'" and inserting "at least 5 G but less than 20 G".

Section 2D1.1(c)(8) is amended by striking "at least 8 G but less than 10 G" before "of Methamphetamine (actual)" and inserting "at least 4 G but less than 5 G"; and by striking "at least 8 G but less than 10 G" before "of 'Ice'" and inserting "at least 4 G but less than 5 G".

Section 2D1.1(c)(9) is amended by striking "at least 6 G but less than 8 G" before "of Methamphetamine (actual)" and inserting "at least 3 G but less than 4 G"; and by striking "at least 6 G but less than 8 G" before "of 'Ice'" and inserting "at least 3 G but less than 4 G".

Section 2D1.1(c)(10) is amended by striking "at least 4 G but less than 6 G" before "of

Methamphetamine (actual)" and inserting "at least 2 G but less than 3 G"; and by striking "at least 4 G but less than 6 G" before "of 'Ice'" and inserting "at least 2 G but less than 3 G".

Section 2D1.1(c)(11) is amended by striking "at least 2 G but less than 4 G" before "of Methamphetamine (actual)" and inserting "at least 1 G but less than 2 G"; and by striking "at least 2 G but less than 4 G" before "of 'Ice'" and inserting "at least 1 G but less than 2 G".

Section 2D1.1(c)(12) is amended by striking "at least 1 G but less than 2 G" before "of Methamphetamine (actual)" and inserting "at least 500 MG but less than 1 G"; and by striking "at least 1 G but less than 2 G" before "of 'Ice'" and inserting "at least 500 MG but less than 1 G".

Section 2D1.1(c)(13) is amended by striking "at least 500 MG but less than 1 G" before "of Methamphetamine (actual)" and inserting "at least 250 MG but less than 500 MG"; and by striking "at least 500 MG but less than 1 G" before "of 'Ice'" and inserting "at least 250 MG but less than 500 MG".

Section 2D1.1(c)(14) is amended by striking "less than 500 MG" before "of Methamphetamine (actual)" and inserting "less than 250 MG"; and by striking "less than 500 MG" before "of 'Ice'" and inserting "less than 250 MG".

The Commentary to § 2D1.1 captioned "Application Notes" is amended in Note 10 in the subdivision of the "Drug Equivalency Tables" captioned "Cocaine and Other Schedule I and II Stimulants (and their immediate precursors)" in the line referenced to "Methamphetamine (Actual)" by striking "10 kg" and inserting "20 kg"; and in the line referenced to "Ice" by striking "10 kg" and inserting "20 kg".

Reason for Amendment: This amendment responds to statutory changes to the quantity of methamphetamine substance triggering mandatory minimum penalties, as prescribed in the Methamphetamine Trafficking Penalty Enhancement Act of 1998, Pub. L. 105–277 (the "Act"). This amendment conforms methamphetamine (actual) penalties, as specified in the Drug Quantity Table in § 2D1.1 (Unlawful Manufacturing, Importing, Exporting, or Trafficking), to the more stringent mandatory minimums established by the Act. In taking this action, the Commission follows the approach set forth in the original guidelines for the other principal controlled substances for which mandatory minimum penalties have been established by Congress. No change was made in the guideline penalties for methamphetamine mixture offenses because those penalties already corresponded to the mandatory minimum penalties as amended by the Act. See USSC Guidelines Manual Appendix C, Amendment 555, effective November 1, 1997.

Effective Date: The effective date of this amendment is November 1, 2000.

595. **Amendment:** Sections 2B5.1, 2F1.1, and 3A1.1, effective November 1, 1998 (see Amendment 587, supra), are repromulgated without change.

Reason for Amendment: This amendment implements, in a broader form, the directives to the Commission in section 6 of the Telemarketing Fraud Prevention Act of 1998, Pub. L. 105–184 ("the Act").

The Act directs the Commission to provide for "substantially increased penalties" for telemarketing frauds. It also more specifically requires that the guidelines provide "an additional appropriate sentencing enhancement, if the offense involved sophisticated means, including but not limited to sophisticated concealment efforts, such as perpetrating the of-

November 1, 2013 APPENDIX C - VOLUME II **Amendment 596**

fense from outside the United States," and "an additional appropriate sentencing enhancement for cases in which a large number of vulnerable victims, including but not limited to [telemarketing fraud victims over age 55], are affected by a fraudulent scheme or schemes."

This amendment responds to the directives by building upon the amendments to the fraud guideline, § 2F1.1 (Fraud and Deceit), that were submitted to Congress on May 1, 1998. (See Amendment 577, supra). Those amendments added a specific offense characteristic for "mass-marketing," which is defined to include telemarketing, and a specific offense characteristic for sophisticated concealment.

This amendment broadens the "sophisticated concealment" enhancement to cover "sophisticated means" of executing or concealing a fraud offense. In addition, the amendment increases the enhancement under § 3A1.1 (Hate Crime Motivation or Vulnerable Victim), for offenses that impact a large number of vulnerable victims.

This amendment also makes a conforming amendment to § 2B5.1 in the definition of "United States".

In designing enhancements that may apply more broadly than the Act's above-stated directives minimally require, the Commission acts consistently with other directives in the Act (e.g., section 6(c)(4) (requiring the Commission to ensure that its implementing amendments are reasonably consistent with other relevant directives to the Commission and other parts of the sentencing guidelines)) and with its basic mandate in sections 991 and 994 of title 28, United States Code (e.g., 28 U.S.C. § 991(b)(1)(B)) (requiring sentencing policies that avoid unwarranted disparities among similarly situated defendants)).

Pursuant to the emergency amendment authority of the Act, this amendment previously was promulgated as a temporary measure effective November 1, 1998. (See Amendment 587, supra).

Effective Date: The effective date of this amendment is November 1, 2000.

596. **Amendment:** The Commentary to § 2B1.1 captioned "Application Notes" is amended by striking Note 4 in its entirety; by redesignating Notes 5 through 16 as Notes 4 through 15, respectively; and in Note 2 by striking the second paragraph in its entirety and inserting the following:

> "If the offense involved making a fraudulent loan or credit card application, or other unlawful conduct involving a loan, a counterfeit access device, or an unauthorized access device, the loss is to be determined in accordance with the Commentary to § 2F1.1 (Fraud and Deceit). For example, in accordance with Application Note 17 of the Commentary to § 2F1.1, in a case involving an unauthorized access device (such as a stolen credit card), loss includes any unauthorized charge(s) made with the access device. In such a case, the loss shall be not less than $500 per unauthorized access device. For purposes of this application note, 'counterfeit access device' and 'unauthorized access device' have the meaning given those terms in 18 U.S.C. § 1029(e)(2) and (e)(3), respectively.".

Section 2F1.1, as amended by Amendment 595 (see supra), is further amended by redesignating subsections (b)(5) through (b)(7) as subsections (b)(6) through (b)(8), respectively; and by inserting after subsection (b)(4) the following:

> "(5) If the offense involved—
>
> (A) the possession or use of any device-making equipment;

Amendment 596

> (B) the production or trafficking of any unauthorized access device or counterfeit access device; or
>
> (C) (i) the unauthorized transfer or use of any means of identification unlawfully to produce or obtain any other means of identification; or (ii) the possession of 5 or more means of identification that unlawfully were produced from another means of identification or obtained by the use of another means of identification,
>
> increase by 2 levels. If the resulting offense level is less than level 12, increase to level 12.".

The Commentary to § 2F1.1 captioned "Application Notes", as amended by Amendment 595 (see supra), is further amended in Note 12 in the first sentence by striking "fraudulent identification documents and"; by striking the second sentence in its entirety; in the third sentence, by striking "the case of an offense involving false identification documents or access devices," and inserting "such a case,"; and by adding at the end the following paragraph:

> "Offenses involving identification documents, false identification documents, and means of identification, in violation of 18 U.S.C. § 1028, also are covered by this guideline. If the primary purpose of the offense was to violate, or assist another to violate, the law pertaining to naturalization, citizenship, or legal resident status, apply § 2L2.1 (Trafficking in a Document Relating to Naturalization) or § 2L2.2 (Fraudulently Acquiring Documents Relating to Naturalization), as appropriate, rather than § 2F1.1.".

The Commentary to § 2F1.1 captioned "Application Notes", as amended by Amendment 595 (see supra), is further amended by redesignating Notes 15 through 20 as Notes 18 through 23, respectively; and by inserting after Note 14 the following:

> "15. For purposes of subsection (b)(5)—
>
> 'Counterfeit access device' (A) has the meaning given that term in 18 U.S.C. § 1029(e)(2); and (B) also includes a telecommunications instrument that has been modified or altered to obtain unauthorized use of telecommunications service. 'Telecommunications service' has the meaning given that term in 18 U.S.C. § 1029(e)(9).
>
> 'Device-making equipment' (A) has the meaning given that term in 18 U.S.C. § 1029(e)(6); and (B) also includes (i) any hardware or software that has been configured as described in 18 U.S.C. § 1029(a)(9); and (ii) a scanning receiver referred to in 18 U.S.C. § 1029(a)(8). 'Scanning receiver' has the meaning given that term in 18 U.S.C. § 1029(e)(8).
>
> 'Means of identification' has the meaning given that term in 18 U.S.C. § 1028(d)(3), except that such means of identification shall be of an actual (i. e., not fictitious) individual other than the defendant or a person for whose conduct the defendant is accountable under § 1B1.3 (Relevant Conduct).
>
> 'Produce' includes manufacture, design, alter, authenticate, duplicate, or assemble. 'Production' includes manufacture, design, alteration, authentication, duplication, or assembly.
>
> 'Unauthorized access device' has the meaning given that term in 18 U.S.C. § 1029(e)(3).

16. Subsection (b)(5)(C)(i) applies in a case in which a means of identification of an individual other than the defendant (or a person for whose conduct the defendant is accountable under § 1B1.3 (Relevant Conduct)) is used without that individual's authorization unlawfully to produce or obtain another means of identification.

   Examples of conduct to which this subsection should apply are as follows:

   (A) A defendant obtains an individual's name and social security number from a source (e.g., from a piece of mail taken from the individual's mailbox) and obtains a bank loan in that individual's name. In this example, the account number of the bank loan is the other means of identification that has been obtained unlawfully.

   (B) A defendant obtains an individual's name and address from a source (e.g., from a driver's license in a stolen wallet) and applies for, obtains, and subsequently uses a credit card in that individual's name. In this example, the credit card is the other means of identification that has been obtained unlawfully.

   Examples of conduct to which subsection (b)(5)(C)(i) should not apply are as follows:

   (A) A defendant uses a credit card from a stolen wallet only to make a purchase. In such a case, the defendant has not used the stolen credit card to obtain another means of identification.

   (B) A defendant forges another individual's signature to cash a stolen check. Forging another individual's signature is not producing another means of identification.

   Subsection (b)(5)(C)(ii) applies in any case in which the offense involved the possession of 5 or more means of identification that unlawfully were produced or obtained, regardless of the number of individuals in whose name (or other identifying information) the means of identification were so produced or so obtained.

   In a case involving unlawfully produced or unlawfully obtained means of identification, an upward departure may be warranted if the offense level does not adequately address the seriousness of the offense. Examples may include the following:

   (A) The offense caused substantial harm to the victim's reputation or credit record, or the victim suffered a substantial inconvenience related to repairing the victim's reputation or a damaged credit record.

   (B) An individual whose means of identification the defendant used to obtain unlawful means of identification is erroneously arrested or denied a job because an arrest record has been made in the individual's name.

   (C) The defendant produced or obtained numerous means of identification with respect to one individual and essentially assumed that individual's identity.

17. In a case involving any counterfeit access device or unauthorized access de-

vice, loss includes any unauthorized charges made with the counterfeit access device or unauthorized access device. In any such case, loss shall be not less than $500 per access device. However, if the unauthorized access device is a means of telecommunications access that identifies a specific telecommunications instrument or telecommunications account (including an electronic serial number/mobile identification number (ESN/MIN) pair), and that means was only possessed, and not used, during the commission of the offense, loss shall be not less than $100 per unused means. For purposes of this application note, 'counterfeit access device' and 'unauthorized access device' have the meaning given those terms in Application Note 15.".

The Commentary to § 2F1.1 captioned "Application Notes", as amended by Amendment 595 (see supra), is further amended in redesignated Note 18 (formerly Note 15) by striking "(b)(5)" each place it appears and inserting "(b)(6)".

The Commentary to § 2F1.1 captioned "Application Notes", as amended by Amendment 595 (see supra), is further amended in redesignated Note 21 (formerly Note 18), by striking "(b)(7)" and inserting "(b)(8)".

The Commentary to § 2F1.1 captioned "Application Notes", as amended by Amendment 595 (see supra), is further amended by striking redesignated Note 23 (formerly Note 20), in its entirety and inserting the following:

"23. If subsection (b)(5), subsection (b)(8)(A), or subsection (b)(8)(B) applies, there shall be a rebuttable presumption that the offense also involved more than minimal planning for purposes of subsection (b)(2).

If the conduct that forms the basis for an enhancement under subsection (b)(5) is the only conduct that forms the basis of an enhancement under subsection (b)(6), do not apply an enhancement under subsection (b)(6).".

The Commentary to § 2F1.1 captioned "Background", as amended by Amendment 595 (see supra), is further amended by striking the sixth paragraph and all that follows through the end of the "Background" and inserting the following:

" Subsections (b)(5)(A) and (B) implement the instruction to the Commission in section 4 of the Wireless Telephone Protection Act, Public Law 105–172.

Subsection (b)(5)(C) implements the directive to the Commission in section 4 of the Identity Theft and Assumption Deterrence Act of 1998, Public Law 105–318. This subsection focuses principally on an aggravated form of identity theft known as 'affirmative identity theft' or 'breeding,' in which a defendant uses another individual's name, social security number, or some other form of identification (the 'means of identification') to 'breed' (i.e., produce or obtain) new or additional forms of identification. Because 18 U.S.C. § 1028(d) broadly defines 'means of identification,' the new or additional forms of identification can include items such as a driver's license, a credit card, or a bank loan. This subsection provides a minimum offense level of level 12, in part, because of the seriousness of the offense. The minimum offense level accounts for the fact that the means of identification that were 'bred' (i.e., produced or obtained) often are within the defendant's exclusive control, making it difficult for the individual victim to detect that the victim's identity has been 'stolen.' Generally, the victim does not become aware of the offense until certain harms have already occurred (e.g., a damaged credit rating or inability to obtain a loan). The minimum offense level also accounts for the non-monetary harm associated with these types of offenses, much of which may be difficult or impossible to quantify (e.g., harm to the individual's reputation or credit rating, inconvenience, and other difficulties resulting from the offense). The legislative history of the Identity Theft and Assumption Deterrence Act of 1998 indicates that Congress was especially concerned with providing increased punishment for this type of harm.

Subsection (b)(6) implements, in a broader form, the instruction to the Commission in section 6(c)(2) of Public Law 105–184.

Subsection (b)(7)(B) implements, in a broader form, the instruction to the Commission in section 110512 of Public Law 103–322.

Subsection (b)(8)(A) implements, in a broader form, the instruction to the Commission in section 961(m) of Public Law 101–73.

Subsection (b)(8)(B) implements the instruction to the Commission in section 2507 of Public Law 101–647.

Subsection (c) implements the instruction to the Commission in section 805(c) of Public Law 104–132.".

Reason for Amendment: This is a five-part amendment. First, this amendment provides a two-level increase and a minimum offense level of level 12 for offenses involving (1) the possession or use of equipment that is used to manufacture access devices; (2) the production of, or trafficking in, unauthorized and counterfeit access devices, such as stolen credit cards and cloned wireless telephones; or (3) affirmative identity theft (i.e., unlawfully producing from any means of identification any other means of identification). Affirmative identity theft, referred to in the research and analysis conducted by the Commission as the "breeding" of identification means, will result in an enhanced penalty in any case in which there is a transfer or use of another person's means of identification unlawfully to produce or "breed" additional means of identification, or in which there is the possession of five or more means of identification that were unlawfully produced.

Second, this amendment provides a rebuttable presumption that the offense involved more than minimal planning, and it contains a rule to avoid "double counting" between the existing enhancement for "sophisticated means" based on the same conduct.

Third, the amendment provides a revised minimum loss rule for offenses involving counterfeit or unauthorized access devices. Specifically, this rule requires that a minimum loss amount of $500 per access device be used when calculating the loss involved in the offense. However, for offenses that involve only the possession, and not the use, of a means of telecommunications access that identifies a specific telecommunications instrument or telecommunications account (e.g., an ESN/MIN pair used to obtain telecommunications service in a wireless telephone), the rule provides a minimum loss amount of $100 per unused means.

Fourth, this amendment provides an encouraged upward departure if the offense level does not adequately reflect the seriousness of the offense conduct. Examples of cases in which a departure may be warranted include those in which (1) an identity theft caused substantial harm to the victim's reputation or credit record; (2) an individual is arrested, or is denied a job, because of a misidentification that results from an identity theft; or (3) a defendant essentially assumed the victim's identity.

Fifth, this amendment incorporates the statutory definitions of 18 U.S.C. §§ 1028 and 1029, although it also broadens the definitions of "counterfeit access device" and "device-making equipment" for guideline purposes.

This amendment responds to the directives to the Commission contained in section 4 of the Identity Theft and Assumption Deterrence Act of 1998, Pub. L. 105–318(b)(1) ("ITADA") and section 2 of the Wireless Telephone Protection Act, Pub. L. 105–172 ("WTPA"). For the reasons discussed below and because of the overlap in some of the statutory definitions in the ITADA and the WTPA (particularly "access device," "telecommunication identifying information," and "means of identification"), enhancements have been consolidated into a single guideline amendment.

The ITADA and the WTPA directed the Commission to "review and amend the Federal sentencing guidelines and the policy statements of the Commission" to provide appropriate punishment for identity theft offenses under 18 U.S.C. § 1028 and for offenses under 18 U.S.C. § 1029 related to the cloning of wireless telephones.

The WTPA directed the Commission to review, among other factors, "the range of conduct covered by" cloning offenses. Although cloned telephones may be possessed and used in connection with a variety of offenses, the Commission determined that the possession or use of a cloned phone does not necessarily increase the seriousness of the underlying offense. However, the Commission decided that offenders who manufacture or distribute cloned telephones are more culpable than offenders who only possess them. Accordingly, the new enhancements at § 2F1.1(b)(5)(A) and (B) recognize that such offenders warrant greater punishment. However, to ensure that the guidelines apply consistently to similarly serious conduct regardless of the technology employed, this amendment provides for a broader enhancement that applies to the manufacture or distribution of any access device, including a cloned telephone.

The ITADA directed the Commission to assess certain specific factors in its consideration of appropriate penalties for identity theft, including: the number of victims; the harm to a victim's reputation and inconvenience caused by the offense; the number of means of identification, identification documents, or false identification documents involved in the offense; the range of offense conduct; and, the adequacy of the value of loss to an individual victim as a measure for establishing penalties.

In conducting research pursuant to the ITADA, the Commission learned that identity theft, as defined broadly under the new statutory provisions at 18 U.S.C. §§ 1028(a)(7) and 1028(d)(3), occurs along a continuum of offense conduct. The most basic type of identity theft occurs when a thief steals a wallet and uses a stolen credit card to make a purchase or forges a signature to cash a stolen check. However, after analyzing the legislative history of the ITADA and Commission data, the Commission determined that the more aggravated and sophisticated forms of identity theft, about which Congress seemed particularly concerned, should be the focus of enhanced punishment under the guidelines. Such offense conduct, which generally occurs within the context of financial and credit account takeovers, involves affirmative activity to generate or "breed" another level of identification means without the knowledge of the individual victim whose identification means are misused, purloined, or "taken over". This activity is considered more sophisticated because of the additional steps the perpetrator takes to "breed" additional means of identification in order to conceal and continue the fraudulent conduct. Such sophisticated conduct makes detection by both the individual and institutional victims much more difficult. It also has the potential to increase harm, both monetary and non-monetary, to the individual victims (about whom Congress was particularly concerned in enacting the ITADA), and can result in substantial disruption of record-keeping by governmental agencies and private financial institutions upon which the stream of commerce depends. Thus, the Commission determined that this aggravated offense conduct, in contrast to the most basic forms of identity theft, merits enhanced punishment.

Accordingly, amended section § 2F1.1(b)(5)(C) recognizes that the conduct of generating or "breeding" identification means warrants substantial additional penalties. The minimum offense level of level 12 accounts for the fact that the defendant in an identity theft case typically has exclusive control over the "bred" means of identification, making it difficult for the individual victim to detect that the victim's identity has been stolen until substantial harms (e.g., a damaged credit rating) have occurred. The minimum offense level also accounts for the non-monetary harms associated with identity theft (e.g., harm to reputation or credit rating), which typically are difficult to quantify. However, for cases in which the nature and scope of the harm to an individual victim is so egregious that the two-level enhancement and minimum offense level provide insufficient punishment, the amendment invites an upward departure.

The WTPA directed the Commission to review "the extent to which the value of the loss caused by the offenses. . . is an adequate measure for establishing penalties. . . ." The amendment provides a minimum loss rule in § 2F1.1 that extends to all access devices, not just to cloned wireless telephones. In so doing, similar fraud cases will be treated similarly regardless of the technology or type of access device used in the offense. Additionally, the Commission's research and data supported increasing the minimum loss amount, previously provided only in § 2B1.1 (Larceny, Embezzlement, and Other Forms of Theft), from $100 to $500 per access device. However, the data were insufficient to support using this increased amount in cases that involve only the possession, and not the use, of means of telecommunications access that identify a specific telecommunications instrument or account (e.g., ESN/MIN pairs of wireless telephones). (An example of such a case is a defendant who possesses a list of ESN/MIN pairs but has not used any of those pairs to clone wireless telephones.) For such cases, the Commission decided that the minimum loss amount should be $100 per unused means.

Effective Date: The effective date of this amendment is November 1, 2000.

597. Amendment: Section 2F1.1(b), as amended by Amendment 595 (see supra), is further amended in subdivision (4) by striking "; or" after "agency" and inserting a semicolon; by inserting "a misrepresentation or other fraudulent action during the course of a bankruptcy proceeding; or (C) a" after "(B)"; and by inserting "prior, specific" before "judicial".

The Commentary to § 2F1.1 captioned "Application Notes", as amended by Amendment 595 (see supra), is further amended by striking Note 6 in its entirety and inserting the following:

"6. Subsection (b)(4)(C) provides an enhancement if the defendant commits a fraud in contravention of a prior, official judicial or administrative warning, in the form of an order, injunction, decree, or process, to take or not to take a specified action. A defendant who does not comply with such a prior, official judicial or administrative warning demonstrates aggravated criminal intent and deserves additional punishment. If it is established that an entity the defendant controlled was a party to the prior proceeding that resulted in the official judicial or administrative action, and the defendant had knowledge of that prior decree or order, this enhancement applies even if the defendant was not a specifically named party in that prior case. For example, a defendant whose business previously was enjoined from selling a dangerous product, but who nonetheless engaged in fraudulent conduct to sell the product, is subject to this enhancement. This enhancement does not apply if the same conduct resulted in an enhancement pursuant to a provision found

Amendment 597 APPENDIX C - VOLUME II November 1, 2013

elsewhere in the guidelines (e.g., a violation of a condition of release addressed in § 2J1.7 (Commission of Offense While on Release) or a violation of probation addressed in § 4A1.1 (Criminal History Category)).

If the conduct that forms the basis for an enhancement under (b)(4)(B) or (C) is the only conduct that forms the basis for an adjustment under § 3C1.1 (Obstruction of Justice), do not apply an adjustment under § 3C1.1.".

The Commentary to § 2F1.1 captioned "Background", as amended by Amendment 595 (see supra), is further amended by striking the fourth sentence of the fourth paragraph and inserting the following:

"The commission of a fraud in the course of a bankruptcy proceeding subjects the defendant to an enhanced sentence because that fraudulent conduct undermines the bankruptcy process as well as harms others with an interest in the bankruptcy estate.".

Reason for Amendment: The amendment was prompted by the circuit conflict regarding whether the enhancement in § 2F1.1 (Fraud and Deceit) for "violation of any judicial or administrative order, injunction, decree, or process" applies to false statements made during bankruptcy proceedings. Compare United States v. Saacks, 131 F.3d 540 (5th Cir. 1997) (bankruptcy fraud implicates the violation of a judicial or administrative order or process within the meaning of the enhancement; United States v. Michalek, 54 F.3d 325 (7th Cir. 1995) (bankruptcy fraud is a "special procedure"; it is a violation of a specific adjudicatory process); United States v. Lloyd, 947 F.2d 339 (8th Cir. 1991) (knowing concealment of assets in bankruptcy fraud violates "judicial process"); United States v. Welch, 103 F.3d 906 (9th Cir. 1996) (same); United States v. Messner, 107 F.3d 1448 (10th Cir. 1997) (same); United States v. Bellew, 35 F.3d 518 (11th Cir. 1994) (knowing concealment of assets during bankruptcy proceedings qualifies as a violation of a "judicial order"), with United States v. Shadduck, 112 F.3d 523 (1st Cir. 1997) (falsely filling out bankruptcy forms does not violate judicial process since the debtor is not accorded a position of trust). See also United States v. Carrozella, 105 F. 3d 796 (2d Cir. 1997) (district court erred in enhancing the sentence for violation of judicial process in the case of a defendant who filed false accounts in probate court).

The majority of circuits have held that the current enhancement applies to a defendant who conceals assets in a bankruptcy case because the conduct violates a judicial order or violates judicial process. Commission data indicate that, in fiscal year 1998, 41 defendants received an increase for either "violation of a judicial order . . . or misrepresentation of a charitable organization." The data did not distinguish between the two parts of the enhancement.

This amendment creates a separate and distinct basis for a two-level enhancement under the fraud guideline for a misrepresentation or false statement made in the course of a bankruptcy proceeding. Additionally, the existing enhancement and its accompanying commentary are modified to make clear that, in order for the enhancement to apply in a fraud case not involving a bankruptcy proceeding, there must be a false statement in violation of a specific, prior order. Therefore, any case involving a bankruptcy fraud will result in a two-level enhancement, but in the case of a non-bankruptcy fraud, the enhancement will apply only if a defendant was given prior notice of a particular action. The Commission has decided to treat bankruptcy fraud more severely because of its adverse impact on the bankruptcy judicial process and because of the additional harm and seriousness involved in such conduct. See United States v. Saacks, 131 F.3d 540, 543 (5th Cir. 1997) (noting that bankruptcy fraud is more serious than "the most pedestrian federal fraud offense").

Effective Date: The effective date of this amendment is November 1, 2000.

598. Amendment: Section 2K2.4 is amended by striking subsection (a) in its entirety and inserting the following:

"(a) If the defendant, whether or not convicted of another crime, was convicted of violating:

(1) Section 844(h) of title 18, United States Code, the guideline sentence is the term of imprisonment required by statute.

(2) Section 924(c) or section 929(a) of title 18, United States Code, the guideline sentence is the minimum term of imprisonment required by statute.".

The Commentary to § 2K2.4 captioned "Application Notes" is amended by striking Note 1 in its entirety and inserting the following:

"1. Section 844(h) of title 18, United State Code, provides a mandatory term of imprisonment of 10 years (or 20 years for the second or subsequent offense). Sections 924(c) and 929(a) of title 18, United States Code, provide mandatory minimum terms of imprisonment (e.g., not less than five years). Subsection (a) reflects this distinction. Accordingly, the guideline sentence for a defendant convicted under 18 U.S.C. § 844(h) is the term required by the statute, and the guideline sentence for a defendant convicted under 18 U.S.C. § 924(c) or § 929(a) is the minimum term required by the relevant statute. Each of 18 U.S.C. §§ 844(h), 924(c), and 929(a) requires a term of imprisonment imposed under this section to run consecutively to any other term of imprisonment.

A sentence above the minimum term required by 18 U.S.C. § 924(c) or § 929(a) is an upward departure from the guideline sentence. A departure may be warranted, for example, to reflect the seriousness of the defendant's criminal history, particularly in a case in which the defendant is convicted of an 18 U.S.C. § 924(c) or § 929(a) offense and has at least two prior felony convictions for a crime of violence or a controlled substance offense that would have resulted in application of § 4B1.1 (Career Offender) if that guideline applied to these offenses. See Application Note 3.".

The Commentary to § 2K2.4 captioned "Background" is amended by striking the first sentence in its entirety and inserting the following:

"Section 844(h) of title 18, United States Code, provides a mandatory term of imprisonment. Sections 924(c) and 929(a) of title 18, United States Code, provide mandatory minimum terms of imprisonment. A sentence imposed pursuant to any of these statutes must be imposed to run consecutively to any other term of imprisonment.".

The Commentary to § 3D1.1 captioned "Application Note" is amended in Note 1 in the second sentence by striking "mandatory term of five years" and inserting "mandatory minimum terms of imprisonment, based on the conduct involved,"; and in the seventh sentence by inserting "minimum" after "mandatory".

The Commentary to § 5G1.2 is amended in the second sentence of the last paragraph by

Amendment 598

striking "mandatory term of five years" and inserting "mandatory minimum terms of imprisonment, based on the conduct involved,".

Reason for Amendment: This amendment revises § 2K2.4 (Use of Firearm, Armor-Piercing Ammunition, or Explosive During or in Relation to Certain Crimes) to (1) clarify how the minimum, consecutive terms of imprisonment mandated by the statutes indexed to this guideline should be treated for purposes of guideline application; and (2) specify guideline sentences, for all statutes indexed to § 2K2.4, that comply with the Commission's mandate in 28 U.S.C. § 994(b)(2) (requiring guideline sentencing ranges in which the maximum shall not exceed the minimum by more than the greater of 25 percent or six months). The Act to Throttle the Criminal Use of Guns, Pub. L. 105–386, changed the penalty provisions in 18 U.S.C. § 924(c) from fixed terms of years to ranges of "not less than" various terms of years. This effectively establishes mandatory minimum terms of imprisonment with implicit maximum terms of life. Section 929(a) of title 18, United States Code, contains similar provisions. Section 2K2.4 continues to provide that, in both cases, the term of imprisonment imposed under the statute should be determined independently of the usual guideline application rules and the sentence imposed should run consecutively to any other term of imprisonment. See § 5G1.2(a). However, § 2K2.4 previously stated that the term of imprisonment was that "required by statute." Because two of the statutes indexed to the guideline now provide for terms of a range of years, questions arose as to whether any sentence within the statutorily authorized range complied with the guidelines.

The amendment clarifies that the guideline sentence is the minimum term required by the statute of conviction, that a term greater than this minimum is an upward departure and should be imposed using the normal standards and procedures that apply to departures from the guideline range, and that such upward departures are invited under certain circumstances. See 18 U.S.C. § 3553(b). For example, career offenders who are convicted both of an offense under 18 U.S.C. § 924(c) and of an underlying crime of violence or drug trafficking typically will receive lengthy guideline sentences. This amendment modifies Application Note 1 of § 2K2.4 to encourage an upward departure in the unusual circumstance in which an offender is convicted only of 18 U.S.C. § 924(c) and would have qualified as a career offender if that guideline applied to such convictions, or in other unusual circumstances in which the sentence in a particular case does not adequately reflect the seriousness of the defendant's criminal history. Because 18 U.S.C. § 844(h) still provides for fixed terms of imprisonment, the amendment differentiates it from the two statutes that provide for terms of a range of years.

The amendment also contains technical and conforming changes: §§ 3D1.1 (Procedure for Determining Offense Level on Multiple Counts) and 5G1.2 (Sentencing on Multiple Counts of Conviction) are revised to reflect a change to the penalty provision of 18 U.S.C. § 924(c).

Effective Date: The effective date of this amendment is November 1, 2000.

599. **Amendment:** The Commentary to § 2K2.4 captioned "Application Notes" is amended in Note 2 in the second paragraph by striking "paragraph" after "preceding" and inserting "paragraphs"; and by striking the first paragraph in its entirety and inserting the following:

"If a sentence under this guideline is imposed in conjunction with a sentence for an underlying offense, do not apply any specific offense characteristic for possession, brandishing, use, or discharge of an explosive or firearm when determining the sentence for the underlying offense. A sentence under this guideline accounts for any explosive or weapon enhancement for the underlying offense of conviction, including any such enhancement that would apply based on conduct for which the defendant is accountable under § 1B1.3 (Relevant Conduct). Do not apply any weapon enhancement in the guideline for the underlying offense, for example, if (A) a co-defendant, as part of the jointly undertaken criminal activity, possessed a firearm different from the one for which the defendant was convicted under 18 U.S.C. § 924(c); or (B) in an ongoing drug trafficking offense, the defendant possessed a firearm other than the one for which the defendant was convicted under 18 U.S.C. § 924(c). However, if a defendant is convicted of two armed bank robberies, but is convicted under 18 U.S.C. § 924(c) in connection with only one of the robberies, a weapon enhancement would apply to the bank robbery which was not the basis for the 18 U.S.C. § 924(c) conviction.

If the explosive or weapon that was possessed, brandished, used, or discharged in the course of the underlying offense also results in a conviction that would subject the defendant to an enhancement under § 2K1.3(b)(3) (pertaining to possession of explosive material in connection with another felony offense) or § 2K2.1(b)(5) (pertaining to possession of any firearm or ammunition in connection with another felony offense), do not apply that enhancement. A sentence under this guideline accounts for the conduct covered by these enhancements because of the relatedness of that conduct to the conduct that forms the basis for the conviction under 18 U.S.C. § 844(h), § 924(c) or § 929(a). For example, if in addition to a conviction for an underlying offense of armed bank robbery, the defendant was convicted of being a felon in possession under 18 U.S.C. § 922(g), the enhancement under § 2K2.1(b)(5) would not apply.".

The Commentary to § 2K2.4 captioned "Application Notes", as amended by Amendment 600 (see supra), is further amended in Note 5 (formerly Note 4) in the third sentence by inserting "brandishing," after "possession,".

The Commentary to § 2K2.4 captioned "Background" is amended in the second sentence by inserting "brandishing," after "use,".

Reason for Amendment: This amendment expands the commentary in Application Note 2 of § 2K2.4 (Use of Firearm, Armor-Piercing Ammunition, or Explosive During or in Relation to Certain Crimes) to clarify under what circumstances defendants sentenced for violations of 18 U.S.C. § 924(c) in conjunction with convictions for other offenses may receive weapon enhancements contained in the guidelines for those other offenses. The amendment directs that no guideline weapon enhancement should be applied when determining the sentence for the crime of violence or drug trafficking offense underlying the 18 U.S.C. § 924(c) conviction, nor for any conduct with respect to that offense for which the defendant is accountable under § 1B1.3 (Relevant Conduct). Guideline weapon enhancements may be applied, however, when determining the sentence for counts of conviction outside the scope of relevant conduct for the underlying offense (e.g., a conviction for a second armed bank robbery for which no 18 U.S.C. § 924(c) conviction was obtained).

For similar reasons, this amendment also expands the application note to clarify that offenders who receive a sentence under § 2K2.4 should not receive enhancements under § 2K1.3(b)(3) (pertaining to explosive material connected with another offense), or § 2K2.1(b)(5) (pertaining to firearms or ammunition possessed, used, or transferred in connection with another offense) with respect to any weapon, ammunition, or explosive connected to the offense underlying the count of conviction sentenced under § 2K2.4.

The purposes of this amendment are to (1) avoid unwarranted disparity and duplicative punishment; and (2) conform application of guideline weapon enhancements with general guideline principles. The relevant application note to § 2K2.4 previously stated that if a sentence was imposed under § 2K2.4 in conjunction with a sentence for "an underlying offense," no weapon enhancement should be applied with respect to the guideline for the underlying offense. Some courts interpreted "underlying offense" narrowly to mean only the "crime of violence" or "drug trafficking offense" that forms the basis for the 18 U.S.C. § 924(c) conviction. See, e.g., United States v. Flennory, 145 F.3d 1264, 1268-69 (11th Cir. 1998), cert. denied, 119 S.Ct. 1130 (1999). But see United States v. Smith, 196 F.3d 676, 679-82 (6th Cir. 1999) (a conviction under 18 U.S.C. § 922(g) qualifies as an "underlying offense," and thus, application of the enhancement in § 2K2.1(b)(5) was impermissible double-counting). In other cases, offenders have received both the mandated statutory penalty and a guideline weapon enhancement in circumstances in which the guidelines generally would require a single weapon enhancement. See United States v. Gonzalez, 183 F.3d 1315, 1325-26 (11th Cir.), cert. denied, 120 S.Ct. 996 (2000) (both statutory and guideline increases may be imposed if defendant and accomplice used different weapons as part of a joint undertaking); United States v. Willett, 90 F.3d 404, 407-08 (9th Cir. 1996) (not double counting to apply both increases for separate weapons possessed by defendant). But see United States v. Knobloch, 131 F.3d 366, 372 (3d Cir. 1996) (error to apply guideline enhancement in addition to statutory penalty "even if the section 924(c)(1) sentence is for a different weapon than the weapon upon which the enhancement is predicated.").

The amendment clarifies application of the commentary, consistent with the definition of "offense" found in § 1B1.1 (Application Note 1(*l*)) and with general guideline principles. It addresses disparate application arising from conflicting interpretations of the current guideline in different courts, and is intended to avoid the duplicative punishment that results when sentences are increased under both the statutes and the guidelines for substantially the same harm.

Finally, Application Notes 2 and 4 and the Background Commentary of § 2K2.4 are revised to reflect changes to 18 U.S.C. § 924(c), made by the Act to Throttle the Criminal Use of Guns, Pub. L. 105–386, with respect to "brandishing" a firearm.

Effective Date: The effective date of this amendment is November 1, 2000.

600. **Amendment:** The Commentary to § 2K2.4 captioned "Application Notes" is amended by redesignating Notes 3 and 4 as Notes 4 and 5, respectively; and by inserting after Note 2 the following:

> "3. Do not apply Chapter Three (Adjustments) and Chapter Four (Criminal History and Criminal Livelihood) to any offense sentenced under this guideline. Such offenses are excluded from application of these chapters because the guideline sentence for each offense is determined only by the relevant statute. See §§ 3D1.1 (Procedure for Determining Offense Level on Multiple Counts) and 5G1.2 (Sentencing on Multiple Counts of Conviction).".

The Commentary to § 4B1.2 captioned "Application Notes" is amended in Note 1 by striking "Possessing a firearm during and in relation to a crime of violence" and all that follows through the end of the first sentence and inserting the following:

> "A prior conviction for violating 18 U.S.C. § 924(c) or § 929(a) is a 'prior felony conviction' for purposes of applying § 4B1.1 (Career Offender) if the prior offense of conviction established that the underlying offense was a 'crime of violence' or 'controlled substance offense.'".

The Commentary to § 4B1.2 captioned "Application Notes" is amended by redesignating

November 1, 2013 APPENDIX C - VOLUME II **Amendment 601**

Notes 2 and 3 as Notes 3 and 4, respectively; and by inserting after Note 1 the following:

"2. The guideline sentence for a conviction under 18 U.S.C. § 924(c) or § 929(a) is determined only by the statute and is imposed independently of any other sentence. See §§ 2K2.4 (Use of Firearm, Armor-Piercing Ammunition, or Explosive During or in Relation to Certain Crimes), 3D1.1 (Procedure for Determining Offense Level on Multiple Counts), and subsection (a) of § 5G1.2 (Sentencing on Multiple Counts of Conviction). Accordingly, do not apply this guideline if the only offense of conviction is for violating 18 U.S.C. § 924(c) or § 929(a). For provisions pertaining to an upward departure from the guideline sentence for a conviction under 18 U.S.C. § 924(c) or § 929(a), see Application Note 1 of § 2K2.4.".

Reason for Amendment: This amendment revises §§ 2K2.4 (Use of Firearm, Armor-Piercing Ammunition, or Explosive During or in Relation to Certain Crimes) and 4B1.2 (Definitions of Terms Used in Section 4B1.1) to clarify guideline application for offenders convicted under 18 U.S.C. §§ 924(c) and 929(a) who might also qualify as career offenders under the rules and definitions provided in §§ 4B1.1 (Career Offender) and 4B1.2. This amendment preserves the status quo as it existed prior to the statutory changes to 18 U.S.C. § 924(c), made by the Act to Throttle the Criminal Use of Guns, Pub. L. 105–386, that established a statutory maximum of life for all violations of the statute.

This amendment adds a new Application Note 3 to § 2K2.4 directing courts not to apply Chapter Three (Adjustments) or Chapter Four (Criminal History and Criminal Livelihood) to any offense sentenced under § 2K2.4. This effectively prohibits the use of 18 U.S.C. § 924(c) convictions either to trigger application of the career offender guideline, § 4B1.1, or to determine the appropriate offense level under that guideline. Application Note 1 of § 4B1.2 also is amended to clarify, however, that prior convictions for violating 18 U.S.C. § 924(c) will continue to qualify as "prior felony convictions" under the career offender guideline in most circumstances.

Effective Date: The effective date of this amendment is November 1, 2000.

601. Amendment: The Commentary to § 1B1.1 captioned "Application Notes" is amended in Note 1(c) by striking "that the weapon was pointed or waved about, or displayed in a threatening manner." and inserting the following:

"that all or part of the weapon was displayed, or the presence of the weapon was otherwise made known to another person, in order to intimidate that person, regardless of whether the weapon was directly visible to that person. Accordingly, although the dangerous weapon does not have to be directly visible, the weapon must be present.".

The Commentary to § 1B1.1 captioned "Application Notes" is amended in Note 1 by striking subdivision (d) in its entirety and inserting the following:

"(d) 'Dangerous weapon' means (i) an instrument capable of inflicting death or serious bodily injury; or (ii) an object that is not an instrument capable of inflicting death or serious bodily injury but (I) closely resembles such an instrument; or (II) the defendant used the object in a manner that created the impression that the object was such an instrument (e.g. a defendant wrapped a hand in a towel during a bank robbery to create the appearance of a gun).".

Section 2A3.1(b)(1) is amended by striking "(including, but not limited to, the use or

Amendment 601 APPENDIX C - VOLUME II November 1, 2013

display of any dangerous weapon)".

The Commentary to § 2A3.1 captioned "Application Notes" is amended in Note 1 by striking "where any dangerous weapon was used," and inserting "if any dangerous weapon was used or"; and by striking ", or displayed to intimidate the victim".

Section 2B3.1(b)(2) is amended by striking "displayed," each place it appears.

The Commentary to § 2B3.1 captioned "Application Notes" is amended by striking Note 2 in its entirety and inserting the following:

> "2. Consistent with Application Note 1(d)(ii) of § 1B1.1 (Application Instructions), an object shall be considered to be a dangerous weapon for purposes of subsection (b)(2)(E) if (A) the object closely resembles an instrument capable of inflicting death or serious bodily injury; or (B) the defendant used the object in a manner that created the impression that the object was an instrument capable of inflicting death or serious bodily injury (e.g., a defendant wrapped a hand in a towel during a bank robbery to create the appearance of a gun).".

Section 2B3.2(b)(3) is amended by striking "displayed," each place it appears.

Section 2E2.1(b)(1)(C) is amended by striking ", displayed".

Reason for Amendment: This amendment conforms the guideline definition of "brandish" found at Application Note 1(c) of § 1B1.1 (Application Instructions) to a statutory definition, which was added by the Act to Throttle the Criminal Use of Guns, Pub. L. 105–386, and is codified at 18 U.S.C. § 924(c)(4). The purposes of this amendment are to (1) avoid confusion that can be caused by different guideline and statutory definitions of identical terms; and (2) increase punishment in some circumstances for persons who "make the presence of the weapon known to another person, in order to intimidate that person," regardless of whether the weapon is visible. As was the case prior to this amendment, the guideline definition of "brandish" applies to all dangerous weapons and not only to firearms.

The definition of "dangerous weapon" in Application Note 1(d) of § 1B1.1 also is amended to clarify under what circumstances an object that is not an actual, dangerous weapon should be treated as one for purposes of guideline application. The amendment is in accord with the decisions in United States v. Shores, 966 F.2d 1383 (11th Cir. 1992) (toy gun carried but never used by a defendant qualifies as a dangerous weapon because of its potential, if it were used, to arouse fear in victims and dangerous reactions by police or security personnel) and United States v. Dixon, 982 F.2d 116 (3rd Cir. 1992) (hand wrapped in a towel qualifies as a dangerous weapon if the defendant's actions created the impression that the defendant possessed a dangerous weapon).

The amendment also deletes the term "displayed" wherever it appears in the Guidelines Manual in an enhancement with "brandished." Because "brandished" applies in any case in which "all or part of the weapon was displayed," the Commission determined the inclusion of "displayed" in these enhancements is redundant. This part of the amendment is not intended to make a substantive change in the guidelines.

Effective Date: The effective date of this amendment is November 1, 2000.

602. **Amendment:** Chapter One, Part A, Subpart 4(b) is amended in the fifth sentence of the first paragraph by striking "and" before "the last"; and by inserting ", and § 5K2.19 (Post-

Sentencing Rehabilitative Efforts)" after "(Coercion and Duress)".

Chapter Five, Part K, Subpart 2, is amended by inserting at the end the following:

"§ 5K2.19. <u>Post-Sentencing Rehabilitative Efforts</u> (Policy Statement)

Post-sentencing rehabilitative efforts, even if exceptional, undertaken by a defendant after imposition of a term of imprisonment for the instant offense are not an appropriate basis for a downward departure when resentencing the defendant for that offense. (Such efforts may provide a basis for early termination of supervised release under 18 U.S.C. § 3583(e)(1).)

Commentary

<u>Background</u>: The Commission has determined that post-sentencing rehabilitative measures should not provide a basis for downward departure when resentencing a defendant initially sentenced to a term of imprisonment because such a departure would (1) be inconsistent with the policies established by Congress under 18 U.S.C. § 3624(b) and other statutory provisions for reducing the time to be served by an imprisoned person; and (2) inequitably benefit only those who gain the opportunity to be resentenced <u>de novo</u>.".

Reason for Amendment: This amendment was prompted by the circuit conflict regarding whether sentencing courts may consider an offender's post-offense rehabilitative efforts while in prison or on probation as a basis for downward departure at resentencing following an appeal. <u>Compare</u> <u>United States v. Rhodes</u>, 145 F.3d 1375, 1379 (D.C. Cir. 1998) (post-conviction rehabilitation is not a prohibited factor and, therefore, sentencing courts may consider it as a possible ground for downward departure at resentencing); <u>United States v. Bradstreet</u>, 207 F.3d 76 (1st Cir. 2000); <u>United States v. Core</u>, 125 F.3d 74, 75 (2d Cir. 1997) ("We find nothing in the pertinent statutes or the Sentencing Guidelines that prevents a sentencing judge from considering post-conviction rehabilitation in prison as a basis for departure if resentencing becomes necessary.") <u>cert. denied</u>, 118 S. Ct. 735 (1998); <u>United States v. Sally</u>, 116 F.3d 76, 80 (3d Cir. 1997) (holding that "post-offense rehabilitations efforts, including those which occur post-conviction, may constitute a sufficient factor warranting a downward departure"); <u>United States v. Rudolph</u>, 190 F.3d 720, 723 (6th Cir. 1999); <u>United States v. Green</u>, 152 F.3d 1202, 1207 (9th Cir. 1998) (<u>same</u>), <u>with</u> <u>United States v. Sims</u>, 174 F.3d 911 (8th Cir. 1999) (district court lacks authority at resentencing following an appeal to depart on ground of post-conviction rehabilitation which occurred after the original sentencing; refuses to extend holding regarding departures for post-offense rehabilitation to conduct that occurs in prison; departure based on post-conviction conduct infringes on statutory authority of the Bureau of Prisons to grant good-time credits). In <u>Sims</u>, the Eighth Circuit concluded that a rule allowing a departure at resentencing based on post-sentencing rehabilitation would result in unwarranted disparity because resentencing would be a fortuitous event benefitting only some defendants; would reinstate a parole-like system; and would interfere with the authority of the Bureau of Prisons to award good-time credits. <u>See</u> <u>Sims</u>, 174 F.3d at 912-13; <u>Rhodes</u>, 145 F.3d at 1384 (Silberman, J., dissenting).

The Commission determined that post-sentencing rehabilitative efforts should not provide a basis for a downward departure when resentencing a defendant initially sentenced to a term of imprisonment because such a departure would (1) be inconsistent with policies established by Congress under the Sentencing Reform Act, including the provisions of 18 U.S.C. § 3624(b) for reducing the time to be served by an imprisoned person; and (2) inequitably benefit only those few who gain the opportunity to be resentenced <u>de novo</u>, while others, whose rehabilitative efforts may have been more substantial, could not bene-

Amendment 602

fit simply because they chose not to appeal or appealed unsuccessfully. Additionally, prohibition on downward departure for post-sentencing rehabilitative efforts is consistent with Commission policies expressed in § 1B1.10 (Reduction in Term of Imprisonment as a Result of Amended Guideline Range). This amendment does not restrict departures based on extraordinary post-offense rehabilitative efforts prior to sentencing. Such departures have been allowed by every circuit that has ruled on the matter post-Koon. See e.g., United States v. Brock, 108 F.3d 31 (4th Cir. 1997).

Effective Date: The effective date of this amendment is November 1, 2000.

603. **Amendment:** Chapter One, Part A, Subpart 4(d) is amended by adding an asterisk at the end of the last paragraph after the period; and by adding at the end the following footnote:

> "*Note: Although the Commission had not addressed 'single acts of aberrant behavior' at the time the Introduction to the Guidelines Manual originally was written, it subsequently addressed the issue in Amendment 603, effective November 1, 2000. (See Supplement to Appendix C, Amendment 603.)".

Chapter Five, Part K, Subpart 2, as amended by Amendment 602 (see supra), is further amended by adding at the end the following:

> "§ 5K2.20. Aberrant Behavior (Policy Statement)
>
> > A sentence below the applicable guideline range may be warranted in an extraordinary case if the defendant's criminal conduct constituted aberrant behavior. However, the court may not depart below the guideline range on this basis if (1) the offense involved serious bodily injury or death; (2) the defendant discharged a firearm or otherwise used a firearm or a dangerous weapon; (3) the instant offense of conviction is a serious drug trafficking offense; (4) the defendant has more than one criminal history point, as determined under Chapter Four (Criminal History and Criminal Livelihood); or (5) the defendant has a prior federal, or state, felony conviction, regardless of whether the conviction is countable under Chapter Four.
>
> > Commentary
>
> Application Notes:
>
> 1. For purposes of this policy statement—
>
> > 'Aberrant behavior' means a single criminal occurrence or single criminal transaction that (A) was committed without significant planning; (B) was of limited duration; and (C) represents a marked deviation by the defendant from an otherwise law-abiding life.
>
> > 'Dangerous weapon,' 'firearm,' 'otherwise used,' and 'serious bodily injury' have the meaning given those terms in the Commentary to § 1B1.1 (Application Instructions).
>
> > 'Serious drug trafficking offense' means any controlled substance offense under title 21, United States Code, other than simple possession under 21 U.S.C. § 844, that, because the defendant does not meet the criteria under § 5C1.2 (Limitation on Applicability of Statutory Mandatory Minimum Sentences in Certain Cases), results in the imposition of a mandatory minimum term of imprisonment upon the defendant.

2. In determining whether the court should depart on the basis of aberrant behavior, the court may consider the defendant's (A) mental and emotional conditions; (B) employment record; (C) record of prior good works; (D) motivation for committing the offense; and (E) efforts to mitigate the effects of the offense.".

Reason for Amendment: This amendment responds to a circuit conflict regarding whether, for purposes of downward departure from the guideline range, a "single act of aberrant behavior" (Chapter One, Part A, Subpart 4(d)) includes multiple acts occurring over a period of time. Compare United States v. Grandmaison, 77 F.3d 555 (1st Cir. 1996) (Sentencing Commission intended the word "single" to refer to the crime committed; therefore, "single acts of aberrant behavior" include multiple acts leading up to the commission of the crime; the district court should review the totality of circumstances); Zecevic v. United States Parole Commission, 163 F.3d 731 (2d Cir. 1998) (aberrant behavior is conduct which constitutes a short-lived departure from an otherwise law-abiding life, and the best test is the totality of the circumstances); United States v. Takai, 941 F.2d 738 (9th Cir. 1991) ("single act" refers to the particular action that is criminal, even though a whole series of acts lead up to the commission of the crime); United States v. Pena, 930 F.2d 1486 (10th Cir. 1991) (aberrational nature of the defendant's conduct and other circumstances justified departure), with United States v. Marcello, 13 F.3d 752 (3d Cir. 1994) (single act of aberrant behavior requires a spontaneous, thoughtless, single act involving lack of planning); United States v. Glick, 946 F.2d 335 (4th Cir. 1991) (conduct over a ten-week period involving a number of actions and extensive planning was not "single act of aberrant behavior"); United States v. Williams, 974 F.2d 25 (5th Cir. 1992) (a single act of aberrant behavior is generally spontaneous or thoughtless); United States v. Carey, 895 F.2d 318 (7th Cir. 1990) (single act of aberrant behavior contemplates a spontaneous and seemingly thoughtless act rather than one which was the result of substantial planning); United States v. Garlich, 951 F.2d 161 (8th Cir. 1991) (fraud spanning one year and several transactions was not a "single act of aberrant behavior"); United States v. Withrow, 85 F.3d 527 (11th Cir. 1996) (a single act of aberrant behavior is not established unless the defendant is a first-time offender and the crime was a thoughtless act rather than one that was the result of substantial planning); United States v. Dyce, 78 F.3d 610 (D.C. Cir.), amd. on reh. 91 F.3d 1462 (D.C. Cir. 1996) (same).

This amendment addresses the circuit conflict but does not adopt in toto either the majority or minority circuit view on this issue. As a threshold matter, this amendment provides that the departure is available only in an extraordinary case. However, the amendment defines and describes "aberrant behavior" more flexibly than the interpretation of existing guideline language followed by the majority of circuits that have allowed a departure for aberrant behavior only in a case involving a single act that was spontaneous and seemingly thoughtless. The Commission concluded that this application of the current language in Chapter One is overly restrictive and may preclude departures for aberrant behavior in circumstances in which such a departure might be warranted. For this reason, the Commission attempted to slightly relax the "single act" rule in some respects, and provide guidance and limitations regarding what can be considered aberrant behavior. At the same time, the Commission also chose not to adopt the "totality of circumstances" approach endorsed by the minority of circuits, concluding that the latter approach is overly broad and vague. The Commission anticipates that this compromise amendment will not broadly expand departures for aberrant behavior.

The amendment creates a new policy statement and accompanying commentary in Chapter Five, Part K (Departures) that sets forth the parameters of conduct and criminal history that the Commission believes appropriately may warrant departure as "aberrant behavior."

The policy statement provides, in pertinent part, that "'aberrant behavior' means a single criminal occurrence or single criminal transaction." The Commission intends that the phrases "single criminal occurrence" and "single criminal transaction" will be somewhat broader than "single act", but will be limited in potential applicability to offenses (1) committed without significant planning; (2) of limited duration; and (3) that represent a marked deviation by the defendant from an otherwise law-abiding life. For offense conduct to be considered for departure as aberrant behavior, the offense conduct must, at a minimum, have these characteristics. The Commission chose these characteristics after reviewing case law and public comment that indicated some support for the appropriateness of these factors.

The policy statement places significant restrictions on the type of offense and the criminal history of the offender that can be considered for this departure. The restrictions on the type of offense that can qualify reflect a Commission concern that certain offense conduct is so serious that a departure premised on a finding of aberrant behavior should not be available to those offenders who engage in such conduct. Similarly, the restrictions on criminal history reflect a Commission view that defendants with significant prior criminal records should not qualify for a departure premised on the aberrant nature of their current conduct.

The Commission recognizes that a number of other factors may have some relevance in evaluating the appropriateness of a departure based on aberrant behavior. Some of the relevant factors identified in the case law and public comment are listed in an application note.

Effective Date: The effective date of this amendment is November 1, 2000.

604. Amendment: The Commentary to § 1B1.4 captioned "Background" is amended by striking:

> ". For example, if the defendant committed two robberies, but as part of a plea negotiation entered a guilty plea to only one, the robbery that was not taken into account by the guidelines would provide a reason for sentencing at the top of the guideline range. In addition, information that does not enter into the determination of the applicable guideline sentencing range may be considered in determining whether and to what extent to depart from the guidelines.",

and inserting:

> "in determining a sentence within the guideline range or from considering that information in determining whether and to what extent to depart from the guidelines. For example, if the defendant committed two robberies, but as part of a plea negotiation entered a guilty plea to only one, the robbery that was not taken into account by the guidelines would provide a reason for sentencing at the top of the guideline range and may provide a reason for sentencing above the guideline range.".

Chapter Five, Part K, Subpart 2, as amended by Amendment 603 (see supra), is further amended by adding at the end the following:

> "§ 5K2.21. Dismissed and Uncharged Conduct (Policy Statement)
>
> The court may increase the sentence above the guideline range to reflect the actual seriousness of the offense based on conduct (1) underlying a charge dismissed as part of a plea agreement in the case, or underlying a potential charge not pursued in the case as part of a plea agreement or for any other

reason; and (2) that did not enter into the determination of the applicable guideline range.".

Section 6B1.2(a) is amended in the second paragraph by striking "Provided, that" and inserting "However,".

The Commentary to § 6B1.2 is amended in the fourth paragraph by adding at the end the following:

> "Section 5K2.21 (Dismissed and Uncharged Conduct) addresses the use, as a basis for upward departure, of conduct underlying a charge dismissed as part of a plea agreement in the case, or underlying a potential charge not pursued in the case as part of a plea agreement.".

Reason for Amendment: This amendment addresses the circuit conflict regarding whether a court can base an upward departure on conduct that was dismissed or not charged as part of a plea agreement in the case. According to the majority of circuits, the sentencing court, in determining the sentence to impose within the guideline range, or whether a departure from the guidelines is warranted, may consider without limitation any information concerning the background, character and conduct of the defendant, unless otherwise prohibited by law. See § 1B1.4 (Information to be Used in Imposing Sentence) and 18 U.S.C. § 3661. These courts hold that § 6B1.2 (Standards for Acceptance of Plea Agreements) does not prohibit a court from considering conduct underlying counts dismissed pursuant to a plea agreement. The minority circuit view holds that a departure based on conduct uncharged or dismissed in the context of a plea agreement is inappropriate. Courts holding the minority view emphasize the need to protect the expectations of the parties to the plea agreement. Compare United States v. Figaro, 935 F.2d 4 (1st Cir. 1991) (allowing upward departure based on uncharged conduct); United States v. Kim, 896 F.2d 678 (2d Cir. 1990) (allowing upward departure based on related conduct that formed the basis of dismissed counts and based on prior similar misconduct not resulting in conviction); United States v. Baird, 109 F.3d 856 (3d Cir.), cert. denied, 118 S. Ct. 243 (1997) (allowing upward departure based on dismissed counts if the conduct underlying the dismissed counts is related to the offense of conviction conduct) (citing United States v. Watts, 519 U.S. 148 (1997)); United States v. Barber, 119 F.2d 276, 283-84 (4th Cir. 1997) (en banc); United States v. Cross, 121 F.3d 234 (6th Cir. 1997) (allowing upward departure based on dismissed conduct) (citing Watts); United States v. Ashburn, 38 F.3d 803 (5th Cir. 1994) (allowing upward departure based on dismissed conduct); United States v. Big Medicine, 73 F.3d 994 (10th Cir. 1995) (allowing departure based on uncharged conduct), with United States v. Ruffin, 997 F.2d 343 (7th Cir. 1993) (error to depart based on counts dismissed as part of plea agreement); United States v. Harris, 70 F.3d 1001 (8th Cir. 1995) (same); United States v. Lawton, 193 F.3d 1087 (9th Cir. 1999) (court may not accept plea bargain and later consider dismissed charges for upward departure in sentencing).

This amendment allows courts to consider for upward departure purposes aggravating conduct that is dismissed or not charged in connection with a plea agreement. This approach is consistent with the principles that underlie § 1B1.4 and 18 U.S.C. § 3661 and preserves flexibility for the sentencing judge to impose an appropriate sentence within the context of a charge-reduction plea agreement.

Effective Date: The effective date of this amendment is November 1, 2000.

605. **Amendment:** Section 2B5.1(b)(2) is amended by inserting "level" after "increase to".

The Commentary to § 2D1.1 captioned "Application Notes" is amended in Note 20 by

striking "Under subsection (b)(5), the enhancement" and inserting "Subsection (b)(5)"; by striking "under this subsection" and inserting "under subsection (b)(5)"; by striking "§ 5B1.3" and inserting "§§ 5B1.3"; and by striking "§ " before "5D1.3".

Section 2D1.11(b) is amended by adding at the end the following:

"(3) If the offense involved (A) an unlawful discharge, emission, or release into the environment of a hazardous or toxic substance; or (B) the unlawful transportation, treatment, storage, or disposal of a hazardous waste, increase by 2 levels.".

The Commentary to § 2D1.11 captioned "Application Notes" is amended by adding at the end the following:

"8. Subsection (b)(3) applies if the conduct for which the defendant is accountable under § 1B1.3 (Relevant Conduct) involved any discharge, emission, release, transportation, treatment, storage, or disposal violation covered by the Resource Conservation and Recovery Act, 42 U.S.C. § 6928(d), the Federal Water Pollution Control Act, 33 U.S.C. § 1319(c), or the Comprehensive Environmental Response, Compensation, and Liability Act, 42 U.S.C. §§ 5124, 9603(b). In some cases, the enhancement under subsection (b)(3) may not adequately account for the seriousness of the environmental harm or other threat to public health or safety (including the health or safety of law enforcement and cleanup personnel). In such cases, an upward departure may be warranted. Additionally, any costs of environmental cleanup and harm to persons or property should be considered by the court in determining the amount of restitution under § 5E1.1 (Restitution) and in fashioning appropriate conditions of supervision under §§ 5B1.3 (Conditions of Probation) and 5D1.3 (Conditions of Supervised Release).".

Section 2D1.12(b) is amended by striking "Characteristic" and inserting "Characteristics"; and by adding at the end the following:

"(2) If the offense involved (A) an unlawful discharge, emission, or release into the environment of a hazardous or toxic substance; or (B) the unlawful transportation, treatment, storage, or disposal of a hazardous waste, increase by 2 levels.".

The Commentary to 2D1.12 captioned "Application Notes" is amended by adding at the end the following:

"3. Subsection (b)(2) applies if the conduct for which the defendant is accountable under § 1B1.3 (Relevant Conduct) involved any discharge, emission, release, transportation, treatment, storage, or disposal violation covered by the Resource Conservation and Recovery Act, 42 U.S.C. § 6928(d), the Federal Water Pollution Control Act, 33 U.S.C. § 1319(c), or the Comprehensive Environmental Response, Compensation, and Liability Act, 42 U.S.C. §§ 5124, 9603(b). In some cases, the enhancement under subsection (b)(2) may not adequately account for the seriousness of the environmental harm or other threat to public health or safety (including the health or safety of law enforcement and cleanup personnel). In such cases, an upward departure may be warranted. Additionally, any costs of environmental cleanup and harm to persons or property should be considered by the court in determining the amount of restitution under § 5E1.1 (Restitution) and in fashioning appropriate conditions of supervision under §§ 5B1.3 (Conditions of Probation) and 5D1.3 (Conditions of Supervised Release).".

The Commentary to § 2K2.1 captioned "Statutory Provisions" is amended by striking "(e), (f), (g), (h), (j)-(n)" and inserting "(e)-(i), (k)-(o)".

Section 5B1.3(a) is amended by striking the asterisk after "Conditions"; in subdivision (8) by striking the period after "§ 3563(a))" and inserting a semi-colon; and by adding at the end the following:

"(9) a defendant convicted of a sexual offense as described in 18 U.S.C. § 4042(c)(4) shall report the address where the defendant will reside and any subsequent change of residence to the probation officer responsible for supervision, and shall register as a sex offender in any State where the person resides, is employed, carries on a vocation, or is a student.";

Section 5B1.3 is amended by striking the footnote at the end in its entirety as follows:

"*Note: Effective one year after November 26, 1997, section 3563(a) of Title 18, United States Code, was amended (by section 115 of Pub. L. 105–119) to add the following new mandatory condition of probation:

(9) a defendant convicted of a sexual offense as described in 18 U.S.C. § 4042(c)(4) (as amended by section 115 of Pub. L. 105–119) shall report the address where the defendant will reside and any subsequent change of residence to the probation officer responsible for supervision, and shall register as a sex offender in any State where the person resides, is employed, carries on a vocation, or is a student.".

Section 5D1.3(a) is amended by striking the asterisk after "Conditions"; in subdivision (6) by striking the period after "§ 3013" and inserting a semi-colon; and by adding at the end the following:

"(7) a defendant convicted of a sexual offense as described in 18 U.S.C. § 4042(c)(4) shall report the address where the defendant will reside and any subsequent change of residence to the probation officer responsible for supervision, and shall register as a sex offender in any State where the person resides, is employed, carries on a vocation, or is a student.";

Section 5D1.3 is amended by striking the footnote at the end in its entirety as follows:

"*Note: Effective one year after November 26, 1997, section 3583(a) of Title 18, United States Code, was amended (by section 115 of Pub. L. 105–119) to add the following new mandatory condition of supervised release:

(7) a defendant convicted of a sexual offense as described in 18 U.S.C. § 4042(c)(4) (as amended by section 115 of Pub. L. 105–119) shall report the address where the defendant will reside and any subsequent change of residence to the probation officer responsible for supervision, and shall register as a sex offender in any State where the person resides, is employed, carries on a vocation, or is a student.".

Reason for Amendment: This four-part amendment makes various technical and conforming changes.

First, the amendment corrects a typographical error in § 2B5.1 (Offenses Involving

Amendment 605

Counterfeit Bearer Obligations of the United States) by inserting a missing word in subsection (b)(2).

Second, the amendment corrects an omission that was made during prior, final deliberations by the Commission on amendments to implement the Comprehensive Methamphetamine Control Act of 1996 (the "Act"), Pub. L. 104-237. Specifically, the amendment amends §§ 2D1.11 and 2D1.12 (Unlawful Possession, Manufacture, Distribution, or Importation of Prohibited Flask or Equipment) to add an enhancement for environmental damage associated with methamphetamine offenses. The Commission previously had intended to amend these guidelines in this manner, but due to a technical oversight, the final amendment did not implement that intent.

The Act directed the Commission to determine whether the guidelines adequately punish environmental violations occurring in connection with precursor chemical offenses under 21 U.S.C. § 841(d) and (g) (sentenced under § 2D1.11), and manufacturing equipment offenses under 21 U.S.C. § 843(a)(6) and (7) (sentenced under § 2D1.12). On February 25, 1997, the Commission published two options to provide an increase for environmental damage associated with the manufacture of methamphetamine, the first by a specific offense characteristic, the second by an invited upward departure. See 62 Fed. Reg. 8487 (proposed Feb. 25, 1997). Both options proposed to make amendments to §§ 2D1.11, 2D1.12, and 2D1.13. Additionally, although the directive did not address manufacturing offenses under 21 U.S.C. § 841(a), the Commission elected to use its broader guideline promulgation authority under 28 U.S.C. § 994(a) to ensure that environmental violations occurring in connection with this more frequently occurring offense were treated similarly. Accordingly, the published options also included amendments to § 2D1.1 (Unlawful Manufacturing, Importing, Exporting, or Trafficking).

The published options were revised prior to final action by the Commission. However, in the revision that was presented to the Commission for promulgation in late April 1997, amendments to §§ 2D1.11 and 2D1.12 mistakenly were omitted from the option to provide a specific offense characteristic, although that revision did refer to §§ 2D1.11 and 2D1.12 in the synopsis and included amendments to these guidelines in the upward departure option. (The revision did not include any amendments to guideline § 2D1.13, covering record-keeping offenses, because, upon further examination, it seemed unlikely that offenses sentenced under this guideline would involve environmental damage.) Accordingly, when the Commission voted to adopt the option providing the specific offense characteristic for §§ 2D1.1, 2D1.11, and 2D1.12, the vote effectively was limited to what was before the Commission, i.e., an environmental damage enhancement for § 2D1.1 only. This amendment corrects that error and makes minor, conforming changes to the relevant application note in § 2D1.1.

Third, the amendment updates the Statutory Provisions of § 2K2.1 (Unlawful Receipt, Possession, or Transportation of Firearms or Ammunition) to conform to statutory redesignations made to 18 U.S.C. § 924 (and already conformed in Appendix A (Statutory Index)).

Finally, the amendment updates §§ 5B1.3 (Conditions of Probation) and 5D1.3 (Conditions of Supervised Release). Effective November 26, 1998, 18 U.S.C. §§ 3563(a) and 3583(a) were amended to add a new mandatory condition of probation and supervised release requiring a person convicted of a sexual offense described in 18 U.S.C. § 4042(c)(4) (enumerating several sex offenses) to report to the probation officer the person's address and any subsequent change of address, and to register as a sex offender in the state in which the person resides. See section 115 of Departments of Commerce, Justice, and State, the Judiciary, and Related Agencies Appropriations Act, 1998 (Pub. L. 105-119).

Because the effective date of this change was later than the effective date of the last issued Guidelines Manual (November 1, 1998), the Commission did not amend §§ 5B1.3 and 5D1.3 to reflect the new condition. However, the Commission did provide a footnote in each guideline setting forth the new condition and alerting the user as to the date on which the condition became effective. This amendment includes the sex offender condition as a specific mandatory condition of probation and supervised release in both guidelines rather than in a footnote.

Effective Date: The effective date of this amendment is November 1, 2000.

606. **Amendment:** Section 2D1.11(d) is amended in subdivision (9) by striking "At least 1.44 G but less than 1.92 KG of Isosafrole;" and inserting "At least 1.44 KG but less than 1.92 KG of Isosafrole;"; and by striking "At least 1.44 G but less than 1.92 KG of Safrole;" and inserting "At least 1.44 KG but less than 1.92 KG of Safrole;".

Section 2D1.11(d) is amended in subdivision (10) by striking "Less than 1.44 G" before "of Isosafrole;" and inserting "Less than 1.44 KG"; and by striking "Less than 1.44 G" before "of Safrole;" and inserting "Less than 1.44 KG".

Reason for Amendment: The amendment corrects a typographical error in the Chemical Quantity Table in § 2D1.11 (Unlawfully Distributing, Importing, Exporting, or Possessing a Listed Chemical) regarding certain quantities of Isosafrole and Safrole by changing those quantities from grams to kilograms.

Effective Date: The effective date of this amendment is November 1, 2000.

607. **Amendment:** Section 1B1.10(c) is amended by striking "and 516." and inserting "516, 591, 599, and 606.".

Reason for Amendment: This amendment expands the listing in § 1B1.10(c) to implement the directive in 28 U.S.C. § 994(u) with respect to guideline amendments that may be considered for retroactive application.

Effective Date: The effective date of this amendment is November 1, 2000.

608. **Amendment:** Section 2D1.1(b)(5) is amended by striking the comma after "substance" and inserting a semicolon.

Section 2D1.1(b) is amended by redesignating subdivision (6) as subdivision (7); and by inserting after subdivision (5) the following:

"(6)   (Apply the greater):

    (A)   If the offense (i) involved the manufacture of amphetamine or methamphetamine; and (ii) created a substantial risk of harm to (I) human life other than a life described in subsection (b)(6)(B); or (II) the environment, increase by 3 levels. If the resulting offense level is less than level 27, increase to level 27.

    (B)   If the offense (i) involved the manufacture of amphetamine or methamphetamine; and (ii) created a substantial risk of harm to the life of a minor or an incompetent, increase by 6 levels. If the resulting offense level is less than level 30, increase to level 30.".

The Commentary to § 2D1.1 captioned "Application Notes" is amended in Note 20 by inserting "Hazardous or Toxic Substances.—" before "Subsection (b)(5)".

Amendment 608 APPENDIX C - VOLUME II November 1, 2013

The Commentary to § 2D1.1 captioned "Application Notes" is amended by adding at the end the following:

"21. <u>Substantial Risk of Harm Associated with the Manufacture of Amphetamine and Methamphetamine.</u>—

(A) <u>Factors to Consider.</u>—In determining, for purposes of subsection (b)(6), whether the offense created a substantial risk of harm to human life or the environment, the court may consider factors such as the following:

(i) The quantity of any chemicals or hazardous or toxic substances found at the laboratory, or the manner in which the chemicals or substances were stored.

(ii) The manner in which hazardous or toxic substances were disposed, or the likelihood of release into the environment of hazardous or toxic substances.

(iii) The duration of the offense, or the extent of the manufacturing operation.

(iv) The location of the amphetamine or methamphetamine laboratory (<u>e.g.</u>, in a residential neighborhood or a remote area), and the number of human lives placed at substantial risk of harm.

(B) <u>Definitions.</u>—For purposes of subsection (b)(6)(B):

'Incompetent' means an individual who is incapable of taking care of the individual's self or property because of a mental or physical illness or disability, mental retardation, or senility.

'Minor' has the meaning given that term in Application Note 1 of the Commentary to § 2A3.1 (Criminal Sexual Abuse).".

The Commentary to § 2D1.1 captioned "Background" is amended by adding at the end the following:

" Subsection (b)(5) implements the instruction to the Commission in section 303 of Public Law 103–237.

Subsection (b)(6) implements the instruction to the Commission in section 102 of Public Law 106–878.".

Section 2D1.10 is amended by inserting after subsection (a) the following:

"(b) Specific Offense Characteristic

(1) (Apply the greater):

(A) If the offense involved the manufacture of amphetamine or methamphetamine, increase by 3 levels. If the resulting offense level is less than level 27, increase to level 27.

(B) If the offense (i) involved the manufacture of amphetamine or methamphetamine; and (ii) created a substantial risk of harm to the life of a minor or an incompetent, increase by 6 levels. If the resulting offense level is less than level 30, increase to level 30.".

The Commentary to § 2D1.10 is amended by adding at the end the following:

"Application Note:

1. Substantial Risk of Harm Associated with the Manufacture of Amphetamine and Methamphetamine.—

    (A) Factors to Consider.— In determining, for purposes of subsection (b)(1)(B), whether the offense created a substantial risk of harm to the life of a minor or an incompetent, the court may consider factors such as the following:

        (i) The quantity of any chemicals or hazardous or toxic substances found at the laboratory, or the manner in which the chemicals or substances were stored.

        (ii) The manner in which hazardous or toxic substances were disposed, or the likelihood of release into the environment of hazardous or toxic substances.

        (iii) The duration of the offense, or the extent of the manufacturing operation.

        (iv) The location of the amphetamine or methamphetamine laboratory (e.g., in a residential neighborhood or a remote area), and the number of human lives placed at substantial risk of harm.

    (B) Definitions.—For purposes of subsection (b)(1)(B):

        'Incompetent' means an individual who is incapable of taking care of the individual's self or property because of a mental or physical illness or disability, mental retardation, or senility.

        'Minor' has the meaning given that term in Application Note 1 of the Commentary to § 2A3.1 (Criminal Sexual Abuse).

Background: Subsection (b)(1) implements the instruction to the Commission in section 102 of Public Law 106–878.".

Reason for Amendment: This amendment addresses the directive in section 102 (the "substantial risk directive") of the Methamphetamine and Club Drug Anti-Proliferation Act of 2000 (the "Act"), Pub. L. 106–878.

The Act requires the Commission to promulgate amendments under emergency amendment authority. Although the Act generally provides that the Commission shall promulgate various amendments "as soon as practicable," the substantial risk directive specifically requires that the amendment implementing the directive shall apply "to any offense occurring on or after the date that is 60 days after the date of the enactment" of the Act.

The directive instructs the Commission to amend the federal sentencing guidelines with

Amendment 608 APPENDIX C - VOLUME II November 1, 2013

respect to any offense relating to the manufacture, attempt to manufacture, or conspiracy to manufacture amphetamine or methamphetamine in (1) the Controlled Substances Act (21 U.S.C. § 801 et seq.); (2) the Controlled Substances Import and Export Act (21 U.S.C. § 951 et seq.); or (3) the Maritime Drug Law Enforcement Act (46 U.S.C. App. § 1901 et seq.).

The Act requires the Commission, in carrying out the substantial risk directive, to provide the following enhancements—

(A) if the offense created a substantial risk of harm to human life (other than a life described in subparagraph (B)) or the environment, increase the base offense level for the offense—

(i) by not less than 3 offense levels above the applicable level in effect on the date of the enactment of this Act; or

(ii) if the resulting base offense level after an increase under clause (i) would be less than level 27, to not less than level 27; or

(B) if the offense created a substantial risk of harm to the life of a minor or incompetent, increase the base offense level for the offense—

(i) by not less than 6 offense levels above the applicable level in effect on the date of the enactment of this Act; or

(ii) if the resulting base offense level after an increase under clause (i) would be less than level 30, to not less than level 30.

The pertinent aspects of this amendment are as follows:

(1) <u>Guidelines Amended</u>.—The amendment provides new enhancements in §§ 2D1.1 (Unlawful Manufacturing, Importing, Exporting, or Trafficking) and 2D1.10 (Endangering Human Life While Illegally Manufacturing a Controlled Substance) that also apply in the case of an attempt or a conspiracy to manufacture amphetamine or methamphetamine. The amendment does not amend § 2D1.11 (Unlawfully Distributing, Importing, Exporting or Possessing a Listed Chemical) or § 2D1.12 (Unlawful Possession, Manufacture, Distribution, or Importation or Prohibited Flask or Equipment). Although offenses that involve the manufacture of amphetamine or methamphetamine also are referenced in Appendix (A) (Statutory Index) to §§ 2D1.11 and 2D1.12, the cross reference in these guidelines, which applies if the offense involved the manufacture of a controlled substance, will result in application of § 2D1.1 and accordingly, the new enhancements.

(2) <u>Structure</u>.—The basic structure of the amendment to §§ 2D1.1 and 2D1.10 tracks the structure of the directive. Accordingly, in § 2D1.1, the amendment provides a three-level increase and a minimum offense level of level 27 if the offense (A) involved the manufacture of amphetamine or methamphetamine; and (B) created a substantial risk of either harm to human life or the environment. For offenses that created a substantial risk of harm to the life of a minor or an incompetent, the amendment provides a six-level increase and a minimum offense level of 30.

However, the structure of the amendment in § 2D1.10 differs from that in § 2D1.1 with respect to the first prong of the enhancement (regarding substantial risk of harm to human life or to the environment). Specifically, the amendment provides a three-level increase and a minimum offense level of level 27 if the offense involved the manufacture of amphetamine or methamphetamine without making application of the enhancement dependent upon whether the offense also involved a substantial risk of either harm to human life or the environment. Consideration of whether the offense involved a substantial risk of harm to human life is unnecessary because § 2D1.10 applies only to convictions under 21 U.S.C. § 858, and the creation of a substantial risk of harm to human life is an element of a § 858 offense. Therefore, the base offense level already takes into account the substantial risk of harm to human life. Consideration of whether the offense involved a substantial risk of harm to the environment is unnecessary because the directive predicated application of the enhancement on substantial risk of harm either to human life or to the environment, and the creation of a substantial risk of harm to human life is necessarily present because it is an element of the offense.

(3) <u>Determining "Substantial Risk of Harm"</u>.—Neither the directive nor any statutory provision defines "substantial risk of harm". Based on an analysis of relevant case law that interpreted "substantial risk of harm", the amendment provides commentary setting forth factors that may be relevant in determining whether a particular offense created a substantial risk of harm.

(4) <u>Definitions</u>.—The definition of "incompetent" is modeled after several state statutes, which proved useful for purposes of this amendment.

The definition of "minor" has the meaning given that term in Application Note 1 of the Commentary to § 2A3.1 (Criminal Sexual Abuse).

Effective Date: The effective date of this amendment is December 16, 2000.

609. **Amendment:** The Commentary to § 2D1.1 captioned "Application Notes" is amended in Note 10 in the Drug Equivalency Tables in the subdivision captioned "LSD, PCP, and Other Schedule I and II Hallucinogens (and their immediate precursors)*" in the line referenced to "MDA" by striking "50 gm" and inserting "500 gm"; in the line referenced to "MDMA" by striking "35 gm" and inserting "500 gm"; in the line referenced "MDEA" by striking "30 gm" and inserting "500 gm"; and by inserting "1 gm of Paramethoxymethamphetamine/PMA = 500 gm of marihuana" after the line referenced to "MDEA".

Reason for Amendment: This amendment addresses the directive in the Ecstasy Anti-Proliferation Act of 2000 (the "Act"), section 3664 of Pub. L. 106–310, which instructs the Commission to provide, under emergency amendment authority, increased penalties for the manufacture, importation, exportation, or trafficking of Ecstasy. The directive specifically requires the Commission to increase the base offense level for 3,4-Methylenedioxymethamphetamine (MDMA), 3,4-Methylenedioxyamphetamine (MDA), 3,4-Methylenedioxy-N-ethylamphetamine (MDEA), Paramethoxymethamphetamine (PMA), and any other controlled substance that is marketed as Ecstasy and that has either a chemical structure similar to MDMA or an effect on the central nervous system substantially similar to or greater than MDMA.

The amendment addresses the directive by amending the Drug Equivalency Table in § 2D1.1, Application Note 10, to increase substantially the marihuana equivalencies for the specified controlled substances, which has the effect of substantially increasing the penalties for offenses involving Ecstasy. The new penalties for Ecstasy trafficking provide penalties which, gram for gram, are more severe than those for powder cocaine. Currently under the Drug Equivalency Table, one gram of powder cocaine has a marihuana equivalency of 200 grams. This amendment sets the marihuana equivalency for one gram of Ecstasy at 500 grams.

There are a combination of reasons why the Commission has substantially increased the

Amendment 609   APPENDIX C - VOLUME II   November 1, 2013

penalties in response to the congressional directive. Much evidence received by the Commission indicated that Ecstasy: (1) has powerful pharmacological effects; (2) has the capacity to cause lasting physical harms, including brain damage; and (3) is being abused by rapidly increasing numbers of teenagers and young adults. Indeed, the market for Ecstasy is overwhelmingly comprised of people under the age of 25 years.

Before voting to promulgate this amendment, the Commission considered whether the penalty levels for Ecstasy should be set at the same levels as for heroin (i.e., one gram of heroin has a marihuana equivalency of 1000 grams) and decided that somewhat lesser penalties were appropriate for Ecstasy for a number of reasons: (1) the potential for addiction is greater with heroin; (2) heroin distribution often involves violence while, at this time, violence is not reported in Ecstasy markets; (3) because it is a narcotic and is often injected, the risk of death from overdose is much greater from heroin; and (4) because heroin is often injected, there are more secondary health consequences, such as infections and the transmission of the human immunodeficiency virus (HIV) and hepatitis.

Finally, based on information regarding Ecstasy trafficking patterns, the penalty levels chosen are appropriate and sufficient to target serious and high-level traffickers and to provide appropriate punishment, deterrence, and incentives for cooperation. The penalty levels chosen for Ecstasy offenses provide five year sentences for serious traffickers (those whose relevant conduct involved at least 800 pills) and ten year sentences for high-level traffickers (those whose relevant conduct involved at least 8,000 pills).

Effective Date: The effective date of this amendment is May 1, 2001.

610. **Amendment:** Section 2D1.1(c)(1) is amended by inserting after the fifth entry the following:

"15 KG or more of Amphetamine, or 1.5 KG or more of Amphetamine (actual);".

Section 2D1.1(c)(2) is amended by inserting after the fifth entry the following:

"At least 5 KG but less than 15 KG of Amphetamine, or at least 500 G but less than 1.5 KG of Amphetamine (actual);".

Section 2D1.1(c)(3) is amended by inserting after the fifth entry the following:

"At least 1.5 KG but less than 5 KG of Amphetamine, or at least 150 G but less than 500 G of Amphetamine (actual);".

Section 2D1.1(c)(4) is amended by inserting after the fifth entry the following:

"At least 500 G but less than 1.5 KG of Amphetamine, or at least 50 G but less than 150 G of Amphetamine (actual);".

Section 2D1.1(c)(5) is amended by inserting after the fifth entry the following:

"At least 350 G but less than 500 G of Amphetamine, or at least 35 G but less than 50 G of Amphetamine (actual);".

Section 2D1.1(c)(6) is amended by inserting after the fifth entry the following:

"At least 200 G but less than 350 G of Amphetamine, or at least 20 G but less than 35 G of Amphetamine (actual);".

Section 2D1.1(c)(7) is amended by inserting after the fifth entry the following:

"At least 50 G but less than 200 G of Amphetamine, or at least 5 G but less than 20 G of Amphetamine (actual);".

Section 2D1.1(c)(8) is amended by inserting after the fifth entry the following:

"At least 40 G but less than 50 G of Amphetamine, or at least 4 G but less than 5 G of Amphetamine (actual);".

Section 2D1.1(c)(9) is amended by inserting after the fifth entry the following:

"At least 30 G but less than 40 G of Amphetamine, or at least 3 G but less than 4 G of Amphetamine (actual);".

Section 2D1.1(c)(10) is amended by inserting after the fifth entry the following:

"At least 20 G but less than 30 G of Amphetamine, or at least 2 G but less than 3 G of Amphetamine (actual);".

Section 2D1.1(c)(11) is amended by inserting after the fifth entry the following:

"At least 10 G but less than 20 G of Amphetamine, or at least 1 G but less than 2 G of Amphetamine (actual);".

Section 2D1.1(c)(12) is amended by inserting after the fifth entry the following:

"At least 5 G but less than 10 G of Amphetamine, or at least 500 MG but less than 1 G of Amphetamine (actual);".

Section 2D1.1(c)(13) is amended by inserting after the fifth entry the following:

"At least 2.5 G but less than 5 G of Amphetamine, or at least 250 MG but less than 500 MG of Amphetamine (actual);".

Section 2D1.1(c)(14) is amended by inserting after the fifth entry the following:

"Less than 2.5 G of Amphetamine, or less than 250 MG of Amphetamine (actual);".

Section 2D1.1(c) is amended in Note (B) of the "Notes to Drug Quantity Table" by inserting ", 'Amphetamine (actual)'," after "terms 'PCP (actual)'"; by inserting ", amphetamine," after "substance containing PCP"; and by inserting ", amphetamine (actual)," after "weight of the PCP (actual)".

The Commentary to § 2D1.1 captioned "Application Notes" is amended in Note 9 by inserting ", amphetamine," after "PCP".

The Commentary to § 2D1.1 captioned "Application Notes" is amended in Note 10 in the Drug Equivalency Tables in the subdivision captioned "Cocaine and Other Schedule I and II Stimulants (and their immediate precursors)*" by striking "200 gm" after "1 gm of Amphetamine =" and inserting "2 kg"; and by inserting "1 gm of Amphetamine (Actual) = 20 kg of marihuana" after the line referenced to "Amphetamine".

Reason for Amendment: This emergency amendment implements the directive in the Methamphetamine Anti-Proliferation Act of 2000, section 3611 of Pub. L. 106–310 (the "Act"), which directs the Commission to provide, under emergency amendment authority, increased guideline penalties for amphetamine such that those penalties are comparable to the base offense level for methamphetamine.

This amendment revises § 2D1.1 to include amphetamine in the Drug Quantity Table.

Amendment 610 APPENDIX C - VOLUME II November 1, 2013

This amendment also treats amphetamine and methamphetamine identically, at a 1:1 ratio (i.e., the same quantities of amphetamine and methamphetamine would result in the same base offense level) because of the similarities of the two substances. Specifically, amphetamine and methamphetamine (1) chemically are similar; (2) are produced by a similar method and are trafficked in a similar manner; (3) share similar methods of use; (4) affect the same parts of the brain; and (5) have similar intoxicating effects. The amendment also distinguishes between pure amphetamine (i.e., amphetamine (actual)) and amphetamine mixture in the same manner, and at the same quantities, as pure methamphetamine (i.e., methamphetamine (actual)) and methamphetamine mixture, respectively. The amendment reflects the view that the 1:1 ratio is appropriate given the seriousness of these two controlled substances.

Effective Date: The effective date of this amendment is May 1, 2001.

611. **Amendment:** Section 2D1.11 is amended by striking subsection (d), captioned "Chemical Quantity Table*" and by striking the Notes that follow subsection (d), captioned "*Notes" as follows:

"   (d) CHEMICAL QUANTITY TABLE*

Listed Chemicals and Quantity   Base Offense Level

(1)   List I Chemicals   Level 30
         17.8 KG or more of Benzaldehyde;
         20 KG or more of Benzyl Cyanide;
         20 KG or more of Ephedrine;
         200 G or more of Ergonovine;
         400 G or more of Ergotamine;
         20 KG or more of Ethylamine;
         44 KG or more of Hydriodic Acid;
         320 KG or more of Isosafrole;
         4 KG or more of Methylamine;
         500 KG or more of N-Methylephedrine;
         500 KG or more of N-Methylpseudoephedrine;
         12.6 KG or more of Nitroethane;
         200 KG or more of Norpseudoephedrine;
         20 KG or more of Phenylacetic Acid;
         200 KG or more of Phenylpropanolamine;
         10 KG or more of Piperidine;
         320 KG or more of Piperonal;
         1.6 KG or more of Propionic Anhydride;
         20 KG or more of Pseudoephedrine;
         320 KG or more of Safrole;
         400 KG or more of 3, 4-Methylenedioxyphenyl-2-propanone;

(2)   List I Chemicals   Level 28
         At least 5.3 KG but less than 17.8 KG of Benzaldehyde;
         At least 6 KG but less than 20 KG of Benzyl Cyanide;

At least 6 KG but less than 20 KG of Ephedrine;
At least 60 G but less than 200 G of Ergonovine;
At least 120 G but less than 400 G of Ergotamine;
At least 6 KG but less than 20 KG of Ethylamine;
At least 13.2 KG but less than 44 KG of Hydriodic Acid;
At least 96 KG but less than 320 KG of Isosafrole;
At least 1.2 KG but less than 4 KG of Methylamine;
At least 150 KG but less than 500 KG of N-Methylephedrine;
At least 150 KG but less than 500 KG of N-Methylpseudoephedrine;
At least 3.8 KG but less than 12.6 KG of Nitroethane;
At least 60 KG but less than 200 KG of Norpseudoephedrine;
At least 6 KG but less than 20 KG of Phenylacetic Acid;
At least 60 KG but less than 200 KG of Phenylpropanolamine;
At least 3 KG but less than 10 KG of Piperidine;
At least 96 KG but less than 320 KG of Piperonal;
At least 480 G but less than 1.6 KG of Propionic Anhydride;
At least 6 KG but less than 20 KG of Pseudoephedrine;
At least 96 KG but less than 320 KG of Safrole;
At least 120 KG but less than 400 KG of 3, 4-Methylenedioxyphenyl-2-propanone;

List II Chemicals
11 KG or more of Acetic Anhydride;
1175 KG or more of Acetone;
20 KG or more of Benzyl Chloride;
1075 KG or more of Ethyl Ether;
1200 KG or more of Methyl Ethyl Ketone;
10 KG or more of Potassium Permanganate;
1300 KG or more of Toluene.

(3) List I Chemicals   Level 26
At least 1.8 KG but less than 5.3 KG of Benzaldehyde;
At least 2 KG but less than 6 KG of Benzyl Cyanide;
At least 2 KG but less than 6 KG of Ephedrine;
At least 20 G but less than 60 G of Ergonovine;
At least 40 G but less than 120 G of Ergotamine;
At least 2 KG but less than 6 KG of Ethylamine;
At least 4.4 KG but less than 13.2 KG of Hydriodic Acid;
At least 32 KG but less than 96 KG of Isosafrole;
At least 400 G but less than 1.2 KG of Methylamine;
At least 50 KG but less than 150 KG of N-Methylephedrine;
At least 50 KG but less than 150 KG of N-Methylpseudoephedrine;
At least 1.3 KG but less than 3.8 KG of Nitroethane;
At least 20 KG but less than 60 KG of Norpseudoephedrine;

Amendment 611 APPENDIX C - VOLUME II November 1, 2013

At least 2 KG but less than 6 KG of Phenylacetic Acid;
At least 20 KG but less than 60 KG of Phenylpropanolamine;
At least 1 KG but less than 3 KG of Piperidine;
At least 32 KG but less than 96 KG of Piperonal;
At least 160 G but less than 480 G of Propionic Anhydride;
At least 2 KG but less than 6 KG of Pseudoephedrine;
At least 32 KG but less than 96 KG of Safrole;
At least 40 KG but less than 120 KG of 3, 4-Methylenedioxyphenyl-2-propanone;

List II Chemicals
At least 3.3 KG but less than 11 KG of Acetic Anhydride;
At least 352.5 KG but less than 1175 KG of Acetone;
At least 6 KG but less than 20 KG of Benzyl Chloride;
At least 322.5 KG but less than 1075 KG of Ethyl Ether;
At least 360 KG but less than 1200 KG of Methyl Ethyl Ketone;
At least 3 KG but less than 10 KG of Potassium Permanganate;
At least 390 KG but less than 1300 KG of Toluene.

(4) List I Chemicals Level 24
At least 1.2 KG but less than 1.8 KG of Benzaldehyde;
At least 1.4 KG but less than 2 KG of Benzyl Cyanide;
At least 1.4 KG but less than 2 KG of Ephedrine;
At least 14 G but less than 20 G of Ergonovine;
At least 28 G but less than 40 G of Ergotamine;
At least 1.4 KG but less than 2 KG of Ethylamine;
At least 3.08 KG but less than 4.4 KG of Hydriodic Acid;
At least 22.4 KG but less than 32 KG of Isosafrole;
At least 280 G but less than 400 G of Methylamine;
At least 35 KG but less than 50 KG of N-Methylephedrine;
At least 35 KG but less than 50 KG of N-Methylpseudoephedrine;
At least 879 G but less than 1.3 KG of Nitroethane;
At least 14 KG but less than 20 KG of Norpseudoephedrine;
At least 1.4 KG but less than 2 KG of Phenylacetic Acid;
At least 14 KG but less than 20 KG of Phenylpropanolamine;
At least 700 G but less than 1 KG of Piperidine;
At least 22.4 KG but less than 32 KG of Piperonal;
At least 112 G but less than 160 G of Propionic Anhydride;
At least 1.4 KG but less than 2 KG of Pseudoephedrine;
At least 22.4 KG but less than 32 KG of Safrole;
At least 28 KG but less than 40 KG of 3, 4-Methylenedioxyphenyl-2-propanone;

November 1, 2013   APPENDIX C - VOLUME II   **Amendment 611**

List II Chemicals
At least 1.1 KG but less than 3.3 KG of Acetic Anhydride;
At least 117.5 KG but less than 352.5 KG of Acetone;
At least 2 KG but less than 6 KG of Benzyl Chloride;
At least 107.5 KG but less than 322.5 KG of Ethyl Ether;
At least 120 KG but less than 360 KG of Methyl Ethyl Ketone;
At least 1 KG but less than 3 KG of Potassium Permanganate;
At least 130 KG but less than 390 KG of Toluene.

(5)   List I Chemicals   Level 22
At least 712 G but less than 1.2 KG of Benzaldehyde;
At least 800 G but less than 1.4 KG of Benzyl Cyanide;
At least 800 G but less than 1.4 KG of Ephedrine;
At least 8 G but less than 14 G of Ergonovine;
At least 16 G but less than 28 G of Ergotamine;
At least 800 G but less than 1.4 KG of Ethylamine;
At least 1.76 KG but less than 3.08 KG of Hydriodic Acid;
At least 12.8 KG but less than 22.4 KG of Isosafrole;
At least 160 G but less than 280 G of Methylamine;
At least 20 KG but less than 35 KG of N-Methylephedrine;
At least 20 KG but less than 35 KG of N-Methylpseudoephedrine;
At least 503 G but less than 879 G of Nitroethane;
At least 8 KG but less than 14 KG of Norpseudoephedrine;
At least 800 G but less than 1.4 KG of Phenylacetic Acid;
At least 8 KG but less than 14 KG of Phenylpropanolamine;
At least 400 G but less than 700 G of Piperidine;
At least 12.8 KG but less than 22.4 KG of Piperonal;
At least 64 G but less than 112 G of Propionic Anhydride;
At least 800 G but less than 1.4 KG of Pseudoephedrine;
At least 12.8 KG but less than 22.4 KG of Safrole;
At least 16 KG but less than 28 KG of 3, 4-Methylenedioxyphenyl-2-propanone;

List II Chemicals
At least 726 G but less than 1.1 KG of Acetic Anhydride;
At least 82.25 KG but less than 117.5 KG of Acetone;
At least 1.4 KG but less than 2 KG of Benzyl Chloride;
At least 75.25 KG but less than 107.5 KG of Ethyl Ether;
At least 84 KG but less than 120 KG of Methyl Ethyl Ketone;
At least 700 G but less than 1 KG of Potassium Permanganate;
At least 91 KG but less than 130 KG of Toluene.

(6)   List I Chemicals   Level 20
At least 178 G but less than 712 G of Benzaldehyde;

– 581 –

At least 200 G but less than 800 G of Benzyl Cyanide;
At least 200 G but less than 800 G of Ephedrine;
At least 2 G but less than 8 G of Ergonovine;
At least 4 G but less than 16 G of Ergotamine;
At least 200 G but less than 800 G of Ethylamine;
At least 440 G but less than 1.76 KG of Hydriodic Acid;
At least 3.2 KG but less than 12.8 KG of Isosafrole;
At least 40 G but less than 160 G of Methylamine;
At least 5 KG but less than 20 KG of N-Methylephedrine;
At least 5 KG but less than 20 KG of N-Methylpseudoephedrine;
At least 126 G but less than 503 G of Nitroethane;
At least 2 KG but less than 8 KG of Norpseudoephedrine;
At least 200 G but less than 800 G of Phenylacetic Acid;
At least 2 KG but less than 8 KG of Phenylpropanolamine;
At least 100 G but less than 400 G of Piperidine;
At least 3.2 KG but less than 12.8 KG of Piperonal;
At least 16 G but less than 64 G of Propionic Anhydride;
At least 200 G but less than 800 G of Pseudoephedrine;
At least 3.2 KG but less than 12.8 KG of Safrole;
At least 4 KG but less than 16 KG of 3, 4-Methylenedioxyphenyl-2-propanone;

List II Chemicals
At least 440 G but less than 726 G of Acetic Anhydride;
At least 47 KG but less than 82.25 KG of Acetone;
At least 800 G but less than 1.4 KG of Benzyl Chloride;
At least 43 KG but less than 75.25 KG of Ethyl Ether;
At least 48 KG but less than 84 KG of Methyl Ethyl Ketone;
At least 400 G but less than 700 G of Potassium Permanganate;
At least 52 KG but less than 91 KG of Toluene.

(7) List I Chemicals   Level 18
At least 142 G but less than 178 G of Benzaldehyde;
At least 160 G but less than 200 G of Benzyl Cyanide;
At least 160 G but less than 200 G of Ephedrine;
At least 1.6 G but less than 2 G of Ergonovine;
At least 3.2 G but less than 4 G of Ergotamine;
At least 160 G but less than 200 G of Ethylamine;
At least 352 G but less than 440 G of Hydriodic Acid;
At least 2.56 KG but less than 3.2 KG of Isosafrole;
At least 32 G but less than 40 G of Methylamine;
At least 4 KG but less than 5 KG of N-Methylephedrine;
At least 4 KG but less than 5 KG of N-Methylpseudoephedrine;
At least 100 G but less than 126 G of Nitroethane;

At least 1.6 KG but less than 2 KG of Norpseudoephedrine;
At least 160 G but less than 200 G of Phenylacetic Acid;
At least 1.6 KG but less than 2 KG of Phenylpropanolamine;
At least 80 G but less than 100 G of Piperidine;
At least 2.56 KG but less than 3.2 KG of Piperonal;
At least 12.8 G but less than 16 G of Propionic Anhydride;
At least 160 G but less than 200 G of Pseudoephedrine;
At least 2.56 KG but less than 3.2 KG of Safrole;
At least 3.2 KG but less than 4 KG of 3, 4-Methylenedioxyphenyl-2-propanone;

List II Chemicals
At least 110 G but less than 440 G of Acetic Anhydride;
At least 11.75 KG but less than 47 KG of Acetone;
At least 200 G but less than 800 G of Benzyl Chloride;
At least 10.75 KG but less than 43 KG of Ethyl Ether;
At least 12 KG but less than 48 KG of Methyl Ethyl Ketone;
At least 100 G but less than 400 G of Potassium Permanganate;
At least 13 KG but less than 52 KG of Toluene.

(8) List I Chemicals   Level 16
3.6 KG or more of Anthranilic Acid;
At least 107 G but less than 142 G of Benzaldehyde;
At least 120 G but less than 160 G of Benzyl Cyanide;
At least 120 G but less than 160 G of Ephedrine;
At least 1.2 G but less than 1.6 G of Ergonovine;
At least 2.4 G but less than 3.2 G of Ergotamine;
At least 120 G but less than 160 G of Ethylamine;
At least 264 G but less than 352 G of Hydriodic Acid;
At least 1.92 KG but less than 2.56 KG of Isosafrole;
At least 24 G but less than 32 G of Methylamine;
4.8 KG or more of N-Acetylanthranilic Acid;
At least 3 KG but less than 4 KG of N-Methylephedrine;
At least 3 KG but less than 4 KG of N-Methylpseudoephedrine;
At least 75 G but less than 100 G of Nitroethane;
At least 1.2 KG but less than 1.6 KG of Norpseudoephedrine;
At least 120 G but less than 160 G of Phenylacetic Acid;
At least 1.2 KG but less than 1.6 KG of Phenylpropanolamine;
At least 60 G but less than 80 G of Piperidine;
At least 1.92 KG but less than 2.56 KG of Piperonal;
At least 9.6 G but less than 12.8 G of Propionic Anhydride;
At least 120 G but less than 160 G of Pseudoephedrine;
At least 1.92 KG but less than 2.56 KG of Safrole;
At least 2.4 KG but less than 3.2 KG of 3, 4-Methylenedioxyphenyl-2-

Amendment 611 APPENDIX C - VOLUME II November 1, 2013

propanone;

List II Chemicals
At least 88 G but less than 110 G of Acetic Anhydride;
At least 9.4 KG but less than 11.75 KG of Acetone;
At least 160 G but less than 200 G of Benzyl Chloride;
At least 8.6 KG but less than 10.75 KG of Ethyl Ether;
At least 9.6 KG but less than 12 KG of Methyl Ethyl Ketone;
At least 80 G but less than 100 G of Potassium Permanganate;
At least 10.4 KG but less than 13 KG of Toluene.

(9) List I Chemicals   Level 14
At least 2.7 KG but less than 3.6 KG of Anthranilic Acid;
At least 71.2 G but less than 107 G of Benzaldehyde;
At least 80 G but less than 120 G of Benzyl Cyanide;
At least 80 G but less than 120 G of Ephedrine;
At least 800 MG but less than 1.2 G of Ergonovine;
At least 1.6 G but less than 2.4 G of Ergotamine;
At least 80 G but less than 120 G of Ethylamine;
At least 176 G but less than 264 G of Hydriodic Acid;
At least 1.44 KG but less than 1.92 KG of Isosafrole;
At least 16 G but less than 24 G of Methylamine;
At least 3.6 KG but less than 4.8 KG of N-Acetylanthranilic Acid;
At least 2.25 KG but less than 3 KG of N-Methylephedrine;
At least 2.25 KG but less than 3 KG of N-Methylpseudoephedrine;
At least 56.25 G but less than 75 G of Nitroethane;
At least 800 G but less than 1.2 KG of Norpseudoephedrine;
At least 80 G but less than 120 G of Phenylacetic Acid;
At least 800 G but less than 1.2 KG of Phenylpropanolamine;
At least 40 G but less than 60 G of Piperidine;
At least 1.44 KG but less than 1.92 KG of Piperonal;
At least 7.2 G but less than 9.6 G of Propionic Anhydride;
At least 80 G but less than 120 G of Pseudoephedrine;
At least 1.44 KG but less than 1.92 KG of Safrole;
At least 1.8 KG but less than 2.4 KG of 3, 4-Methylenedioxyphenyl-2-propanone;

List II Chemicals
At least 66 G but less than 88 G of Acetic Anhydride;
At least 7.05 KG but less than 9.4 KG of Acetone;
At least 120 G but less than 160 G of Benzyl Chloride;
At least 6.45 KG but less than 8.6 KG of Ethyl Ether;
At least 7.2 KG but less than 9.6 KG of Methyl Ethyl Ketone;
At least 60 G but less than 80 G of Potassium Permanganate;

November 1, 2013   APPENDIX C - VOLUME II   **Amendment 611**

        At least 7.8 KG but less than 10.4 KG of Toluene.

(10)   <u>List I Chemicals</u>   Level 12
        Less than 2.7 KG of Anthranilic Acid;
        Less than 71.2 G of Benzaldehyde;
        Less than 80 G of Benzyl Cyanide;
        Less than 80 G of Ephedrine;
        Less than 800 MG of Ergonovine;
        Less than 1.6 G of Ergotamine;
        Less than 80 G of Ethylamine;
        Less than 176 G of Hydriodic Acid;
        Less than 1.44 KG of Isosafrole;
        Less than 16 G of Methylamine;
        Less than 3.6 KG of N-Acetylanthranilic Acid;
        Less than 2.25 KG of N-Methylephedrine;
        Less than 2.25 KG of N-Methylpseudoephedrine;
        Less than 56.25 G of Nitroethane;
        Less than 800 G of Norpseudoephedrine;
        Less than 80 G of Phenylacetic Acid;
        Less than 800 G of Phenylpropanolamine;
        Less than 40 G of Piperidine;
        Less than 1.44 KG of Piperonal;
        Less than 7.2 G of Propionic Anhydride;
        Less than 80 G of Pseudoephedrine;
        Less than 1.44 KG of Safrole;
        Less than 1.8 KG of 3, 4-Methylenedioxyphenyl-2-propanone;

        <u>List II Chemicals</u>
        Less than 66 G of Acetic Anhydride;
        Less than 7.05 KG of Acetone;
        Less than 120 G of Benzyl Chloride;
        Less than 6.45 KG of Ethyl Ether;
        Less than 7.2 KG of Methyl Ethyl Ketone;
        Less than 60 G of Potassium Permanganate;
        Less than 7.8 KG of Toluene.

---

*<u>Notes</u>:

(A)   The List I Chemical Equivalency Table provides a method for combining different precursor chemicals to obtain a single offense level. In a case involving two or more list I chemicals used to manufacture different controlled substances or to manufacture one controlled substance by different manufacturing processes, convert each to its ephedrine equivalency from the table below, add the quantities, and use the Chemical Quantity Table to determine the base offense level. In a case involving two or more list I

-585-

Amendment 611 APPENDIX C - VOLUME II November 1, 2013

(continued)

chemicals used together to manufacture a controlled substance in the same manufacturing process, use the quantity of the single list I chemical that results in the greatest base offense level.

(B) If more than one list II chemical is involved, use the single list II chemical resulting in the greatest offense level.

(C) If both list I and list II chemicals are involved, use the offense level determined under (A) or (B) above, whichever is greater.

(D) In a case involving ephedrine tablets, use the weight of the ephedrine contained in the tablets, not the weight of the entire tablets, in calculating the base offense level.

(E) LIST I CHEMICAL EQUIVALENCY TABLE

1 gm of Anthranilic Acid* =	0.033 gm of Ephedrine
1 gm of Benzaldehyde** =	1.124 gm of Ephedrine
1 gm of Benzyl Cyanide =	1 gm of Ephedrine
1 gm of Ergonovine =	100 gm of Ephedrine
1 gm of Ergotamine =	50 gm of Ephedrine
1 gm of Ethylamine** =	1 gm of Ephedrine
1 gm of Hydriodic Acid** =	0.4545 gm of Ephedrine
1 gm of Isosafrole =	0.0625 gm of Ephedrine
1 gm of Methylamine =	5 gm of Ephedrine
1 gm of N-Acetylanthranilic Acid* =	0.025 gm of Ephedrine
1 gm of N-Methylephedrine** =	0.04 gm of Ephedrine
1 gm of N-Methylpseudoephedrine** =	0.04 gm of Ephedrine
1 gm of Nitroethane** =	1.592 gm of Ephedrine
1 gm of Norpseudoephedrine** =	0.1 gm of Ephedrine
1 gm of Phenylacetic Acid =	1 gm of Ephedrine
1 gm of Phenylpropanolamine** =	0.1 gm of Ephedrine
1 gm of Piperidine =	2 gm of Ephedrine
1 gm of Piperonal =	0.0625 gm of Ephedrine
1 gm of Propionic Anhydride =	12.5 gm of Ephedrine
1 gm of Pseudoephedrine** =	1 gm of Ephedrine
1 gm of Safrole =	0.0625 gm of Ephedrine
1 gm of 3,4-Methylenedioxyphenyl-2-propanone** =	0.05 gm of Ephedrine

* The ephedrine equivalency for anthranilic acid or N-acetylanthranilic acid, or both, shall not exceed 159.99 grams of ephedrine.

** In cases involving (A) hydriodic acid and one of the following: ephedrine, N-methylephedrine, N-methylpseudoephedrine, norpseudoephedrine, phenylpropanolamine, or pseudoephedrine; or (B) ethylamine and 3,4-methylenedioxyphenyl-2-propanone; or (C) benzaldehyde and nitroethane, calculate the offense level for each separately and use the quantity that results in the greater offense level.".

and inserting the following:

"(d)(1) EPHEDRINE, PSEUDOEPHEDRINE, AND PHENYLPROPANOLAMINE QUANTITY TABLE*
(Methamphetamine and Amphetamine Precursor Chemicals)

	Quantity	Base Offense Level
(1)	3 KG or more of Ephedrine; 3 KG or more of Phenylpropanolamine; 3 KG or More of Pseudoephedrine.	Level 38
(2)	At least 1 KG but less than 3 KG of Ephedrine; At least 1 KG but less than 3 KG of Phenylpropanolamine; At least 1 KG but less than 3 KG of Pseudoephedrine.	Level 36
(3)	At least 300 G but less than 1 KG of Ephedrine; At least 300 G but less than 1 KG of Phenylpropanolamine; At least 300 G but less than 1 KG of Pseudoephedrine.	Level 34
(4)	At least 100 G but less than 300 G of Ephedrine; At least 100 G but less than 300 G of Phenylpropanolamine; At least 100 G but less than 300 G of Pseudoephedrine.	Level 32
(5)	At least 70 G but less than 100 G of Ephedrine; At least 70 G but less than 100 G of Phenylpropanolamine; At least 70 G but less than 100 G of Pseuodoephedrine.	Level 30
(6)	At least 40 G but less than 70 G of Ephedrine; At least 40 G but less than 70 G of Phenylpropanolamine; At least 40 G but less than 70 G of Pseudoephedrine.	Level 28
(7)	At least 10 G but less than 40 G of Ephedrine; At least 10 G but less than 40 G of Phenylpropanolamine; At least 10 G but less than 40 G of Pseudoephedrine.	Level 26
(8)	At least 8 G but less than 10 G of Ephedrine; At least 8 G but less than 10 G of Phenylpropanolamine; At least 8 G but less than 10 G of Pseudoephedrine.	Level 24
(9)	At least 6 G but less than 8 G of Ephedrine; At least 6 G but less than 8 G of Phenylpropanolamine;	Level 22

	At least 6 G but less than 8 G of Pseudoephedrine.	
(10)	At least 4 G but less than 6 G of Ephedrine; At least 4 G but less than 6 G of Phenylpropanolamine; At least 4 G but less than 6 G of Pseudoephedrine.	Level 20
(11)	At least 2 G but less than 4 G of Ephedrine; At least 2 G but less than 4 G of Phenylpropanolamine; At least 2 G but less than 4 G of Pseudoephedrine.	Level 18
(12)	At least 1 G but less than 2 G of Ephedrine; At least 1 G but less than 2 G of Phenylpropanolamine; At least 1 G but less than 2 G of Pseudoephedrine.	Level 16
(13)	At least 500 MG but less than 1 G of Ephedrine; At least 500 MG but less than 1 G of Phenylpropanolamine; At least 500 MG but less than 1 G of Pseudoephedrine.	Level 14
(14)	Less than 500 MG of Ephedrine; Less than 500 MG of Phenylpropanolamine; Less than 500 MG of Pseudoephedrine.	Level 12

(d)(2) CHEMICAL QUANTITY TABLE*
(All Other Precursor Chemicals)

Listed Chemicals and Quantity		Base Offense Level
(1)	<u>List I Chemicals</u> 890 G or more of Benzaldehyde; 20 KG or more of Benzyl Cyanide; 200 G or more of Ergonovine; 400 G or more of Ergotamine; 20 KG or more of Ethylamine; 2.2 KG or more of Hydriodic Acid; 320 KG or more of Isosafrole; 200 G or more of Methylamine; 500 KG or more of N-Methylephedrine; 500 KG or more of N-Methylpseudoephedrine; 625 G or more of Nitroethane; 10 KG or more of Norpseudoephedrine; 20 KG or more of Phenylacetic Acid; 10 KG or more of Piperidine; 320 KG or more of Piperonal; 1.6 KG or more of Propionic Anhydride;	Level 30

320 KG or more of Safrole;
400 KG or more of 3, 4-Methylenedioxyphenyl-2-propanone.

(2) List I Chemicals Level 28
At least 267 G but less than 890 G of Benzaldehyde;
At least 6 KG but less than 20 KG of Benzyl Cyanide;
At least 60 G but less than 200 G of Ergonovine;
At least 120 G but less than 400 G of Ergotamine;
At least 6 KG but less than 20 KG of Ethylamine;
At least 660 G but less than 2.2 KG of Hydriodic Acid;
At least 96 KG but less than 320 KG of Isosafrole;
At least 60 G but less than 200 G of Methylamine;
At least 150 KG but less than 500 KG of N-Methylephedrine;
At least 150 KG but less than 500 KG of N-Methylpseudoephedrine;
At least 187.5 G but less than 625 G of Nitroethane;
At least 3 KG but less than 10 KG of Norpseudoephedrine;
At least 6 KG but less than 20 KG of Phenylacetic Acid;
At least 3 KG but less than 10 KG of Piperidine;
At least 96 KG but less than 320 KG of Piperonal;
At least 480 G but less than 1.6 KG of Propionic Anhydride;
At least 96 KG but less than 320 KG of Safrole;
At least 120 KG but less than 400 KG of 3, 4-Methylenedioxyphenyl-2-propanone;

List II Chemicals
11 KG or more of Acetic Anhydride;
1175 KG or more of Acetone;
20 KG or more of Benzyl Chloride;
1075 KG or more of Ethyl Ether;
1200 KG or more of Methyl Ethyl Ketone;
10 KG or more of Potassium Permanganate;
1300 KG or more of Toluene.

(3) List I Chemicals Level 26
At least 89 G but less than 267 G of Benzaldehyde;
At least 2 KG but less than 6 KG of Benzyl Cyanide;
At least 20 G but less than 60 G of Ergonovine;
At least 40 G but less than 120 G of Ergotamine;
At least 2 KG but less than 6 KG of Ethylamine;
At least 220 G but less than 660 G of Hydriodic Acid;
At least 32 KG but less than 96 KG of Isosafrole;
At least 20 G but less than 60 G of Methylamine;
At least 50 KG but less than 150 KG of N-Methylephedrine;
At least 50 KG but less than 150 KG of N-Methylpseudoephedrine;

Amendment 611 APPENDIX C - VOLUME II November 1, 2013

At least 62.5 G but less than 187.5 G of Nitroethane;
At least 1 KG but less than 3 KG of Norpseudoephedrine;
At least 2 KG but less than 6 KG of Phenylacetic Acid;
At least 1 KG but less than 3 KG of Piperidine;
At least 32 KG but less than 96 KG of Piperonal;
At least 160 G but less than 480 G of Propionic Anhydride;
At least 32 KG but less than 96 KG of Safrole; At least 40 KG but less than 120 KG of 3, 4-Methylenedioxyphenyl-2-propanone;

List II Chemicals
At least 3.3 KG but less than 11 KG of Acetic Anhydride;
At least 352.5 KG but less than 1175 KG of Acetone;
At least 6 KG but less than 20 KG of Benzyl Chloride;
At least 322.5 KG but less than 1075 KG of Ethyl Ether;
At least 360 KG but less than 1200 KG of Methyl Ethyl Ketone;
At least 3 KG but less than 10 KG of Potassium Permanganate;
At least 390 KG but less than 1300 KG of Toluene.

(4)   List I Chemicals   Level 24
At least 62.3 G but less than 89 G of Benzaldehyde;
At least 1.4 KG but less than 2 KG of Benzyl Cyanide;
At least 14 G but less than 20 G of Ergonovine;
At least 28 G but less than 40 G of Ergotamine;
At least 1.4 KG but less than 2 KG of Ethylamine;
At least 154 G but less than 220 G of Hydriodic Acid;
At least 22.4 KG but less than 32 KG of Isosafrole;
At least 14 G but less than 20 G of Methylamine;
At least 35 KG but less than 50 KG of N-Methylephedrine;
At least 35 KG but less than 50 KG of N-Methylpseudoephedrine;
At least 43.8 G but less than 62.5 G of Nitroethane;
At least 700 G but less than 1 KG of Norpseudoephedrine;
At least 1.4 KG but less than 2 KG of Phenylacetic Acid;
At least 700 G but less than 1 KG of Piperidine;
At least 22.4 KG but less than 32 KG of Piperonal;
At least 112 G but less than 160 G of Propionic Anhydride;
At least 22.4 KG but less than 32 KG of Safrole;
At least 28 KG but less than 40 KG of 3, 4-Methylenedioxyphenyl-2-propanone;

List II Chemicals
At least 1.1 KG but less than 3.3 KG of Acetic Anhydride;
At least 117.5 KG but less than 352.5 KG of Acetone;
At least 2 KG but less than 6 KG of Benzyl Chloride;
At least 107.5 KG but less than 322.5 KG of Ethyl Ether;

November 1, 2013　　APPENDIX C - VOLUME II　　**Amendment 611**

At least 120 KG but less than 360 KG of Methyl Ethyl Ketone;
At least 1 KG but less than 3 KG of Potassium Permanganate;
At least 130 KG but less than 390 KG of Toluene.

(5)　List I Chemicals　　　　　　　　　　　　　　　　　　　Level 22
At least 35.6 G but less than 62.3 G of Benzaldehyde;
At least 800 G but less than 1.4 KG of Benzyl Cyanide;
At least 8 G but less than 14 G of Ergonovine;
At least 16 G but less than 28 G of Ergotamine;
At least 800 G but less than 1.4 KG of Ethylamine;
At least 88 G but less than 154 G of Hydriodic Acid;
At least 12.8 KG but less than 22.4 KG of Isosafrole;
At least 8 G but less than 14 G of Methylamine;
At least 20 KG but less than 35 KG of N-Methylephedrine;
At least 20 KG but less than 35 KG of N-Methylpseudoephedrine;
At least 25 G but less than 43.8 G of Nitroethane;
At least 400 G but less than 700 G of Norpseudoephedrine;
At least 800 G but less than 1.4 KG of Phenylacetic Acid;
At least 400 G but less than 700 G of Piperidine;
At least 12.8 KG but less than 22.4 KG of Piperonal;
At least 64 G but less than 112 G of Propionic Anhydride;
At least 12.8 KG but less than 22.4 KG of Safrole;
At least 16 KG but less than 28 KG of 3, 4-Methylenedioxyphenyl-2-propanone;

List II Chemicals
At least 726 G but less than 1.1 KG of Acetic Anhydride;
At least 82.25 KG but less than 117.5 KG of Acetone;
At least 1.4 KG but less than 2 KG of Benzyl Chloride;
At least 75.25 KG but less than 107.5 KG of Ethyl Ether;
At least 84 KG but less than 120 KG of Methyl Ethyl Ketone;
At least 700 G but less than 1 KG of Potassium Permanganate;
At least 91 KG but less than 130 KG of Toluene.

(6)　List I Chemicals　　　　　　　　　　　　　　　　　　　Level 20
At least 8.9 G but less than 35.6 G of Benzaldehyde;
At least 200 G but less than 800 G of Benzyl Cyanide;
At least 2 G but less than 8 G of Ergonovine;
At least 4 G but less than 16 G of Ergotamine;
At least 200 G but less than 800 G of Ethylamine;
At least 22 G but less than 88 G of Hydriodic Acid;
At least 3.2 KG but less than 12.8 KG of Isosafrole;
At least 2 G but less than 8 G of Methylamine;
At least 5 KG but less than 20 KG of N-Methylephedrine;

– 591 –

Amendment 611   APPENDIX C - VOLUME II   November 1, 2013

At least 5 KG but less than 20 KG of N-Methylpseudoephedrine;
At least 6.3 G but less than 25 G of Nitroethane;
At least 100 G but less than 400 of Norpseudoephedrine;
At least 200 G but less than 800 G of Phenylacetic Acid;
At least 100 G but less than 400 G of Piperidine;
At least 3.2 KG but less than 12.8 KG of Piperonal;
At least 16 G but less than 64 G of Propionic Anhydride;
At least 3.2 KG but less than 12.8 KG of Safrole;
At least 4 KG but less than 16 KG of 3, 4-Methylenedioxyphenyl-2-propanone;

List II Chemicals
At least 440 G but less than 726 G of Acetic Anhydride;
At least 47 KG but less than 82.25 KG of Acetone;
At least 800 G but less than 1.4 KG of Benzyl Chloride;
At least 43 KG but less than 75.25 KG of Ethyl Ether;
At least 48 KG but less than 84 KG of Methyl Ethyl Ketone;
At least 400 G but less than 700 G of Potassium Permanganate;
At least 52 KG but less than 91 KG of Toluene.

(7)   List I Chemicals   Level 18
At least 7.1 G but less than 8.9 G of Benzaldehyde;
At least 160 G but less than 200 G of Benzyl Cyanide;
At least 1.6 G but less than 2 G of Ergonovine;
At least 3.2 G but less than 4 G of Ergotamine;
At least 160 G but less than 200 G of Ethylamine;
At least 17.6 G but less than 22 G of Hydriodic Acid;
At least 2.56 KG but less than 3.2 KG of Isosafrole;
At least 1.6 G but less than 2 G of Methylamine;
At least 4 KG but less than 5 KG of N-Methylephedrine;
At least 4 KG but less than 5 KG of N-Methylpseudoephedrine;
At least 5 G but less than 6.3 G of Nitroethane;
At least 80 G but less than 100 G of Norpseudoephedrine;
At least 160 G but less than 200 G of Phenylacetic Acid;
At least 80 G but less than 100 G of Piperidine;
At least 2.56 KG but less than 3.2 KG of Piperonal;
At least 12.8 G but less than 16 G of Propionic Anhydride;
At least 2.56 KG but less than 3.2 KG of Safrole;
At least 3.2 KG but less than 4 KG of 3, 4-Methylenedioxyphenyl-2-propanone;

List II Chemicals
At least 110 G but less than 440 G of Acetic Anhydride;
At least 11.75 KG but less than 47 KG of Acetone;

- 592 -

At least 200 G but less than 800 G of Benzyl Chloride;
At least 10.75 KG but less than 43 KG of Ethyl Ether;
At least 12 KG but less than 48 KG of Methyl Ethyl Ketone;
At least 100 G but less than 400 G of Potassium Permanganate;
At least 13 KG but less than 52 KG of Toluene.

(8) List I Chemicals Level 16
3.6 KG or more of Anthranilic Acid;
At least 5.3 G but less than 7.1 G of Benzaldehyde;
At least 120 G but less than 160 G of Benzyl Cyanide;
At least 1.2 G but less than 1.6 G of Ergonovine;
At least 2.4 G but less than 3.2 G of Ergotamine;
At least 120 G but less than 160 G of Ethylamine;
At least 13.2 G but less than 17.6 G of Hydriodic Acid;
At least 1.92 KG but less than 2.56 KG of Isosafrole;
At least 1.2 G but less than 1.6 G of Methylamine;
4.8 KG or more of N-Acetylanthranilic Acid;
At least 3 KG but less than 4 KG of N-Methylephedrine;
At least 3 KG but less than 4 KG of N-Methylpseudoephedrine;
At least 3.8 G but less than 5 G of Nitroethane;
At least 60 G but less than 80 G of Norpseudoephedrine;
At least 120 G but less than 160 G of Phenylacetic Acid;
At least 60 G but less than 80 G of Piperidine;
At least 1.92 KG but less than 2.56 KG of Piperonal;
At least 9.6 G but less than 12.8 G of Propionic Anhydride;
At least 1.92 KG but less than 2.56 KG of Safrole;
At least 2.4 KG but less than 3.2 KG of 3, 4-Methylenedioxyphenyl-2-propanone;

List II Chemicals
At least 88 G but less than 110 G of Acetic Anhydride;
At least 9.4 KG but less than 11.75 KG of Acetone;
At least 160 G but less than 200 G of Benzyl Chloride;
At least 8.6 KG but less than 10.75 KG of Ethyl Ether;
At least 9.6 KG but less than 12 KG of Methyl Ethyl Ketone;
At least 80 G but less than 100 G of Potassium Permanganate;
At least 10.4 KG but less than 13 KG of Toluene.

(9) List I Chemicals Level 14
At least 2.7 KG but less than 3.6 KG of Anthranilic Acid;
At least 3.6 G but less than 5.3 G of Benzaldehyde;
At least 80 G but less than 120 G of Benzyl Cyanide;
At least 800 MG but less than 1.2 G of Ergonovine;
At least 1.6 G but less than 2.4 G of Ergotamine;

At least 80 G but less than 120 G of Ethylamine;
At least 8.8 G but less than 13.2 G of Hydriodic Acid;
At least 1.44 KG but less than 1.92 KG of Isosafrole;
At least 800 MG but less than 1.2 G of Methylamine;
At least 3.6 KG but less than 4.8 KG of N-Acetylanthranilic Acid;
At least 2.25 KG but less than 3 KG of N-Methylephedrine;
At least 2.25 KG but less than 3 KG of N-Methylpseudoephedrine;
At least 2.5 G but less than 3.8 G of Nitroethane;
At least 40 G but less than 60 G of Norpseudoephedrine;
At least 80 G but less than 120 G of Phenylacetic Acid;
At least 40 G but less than 60 G of Piperidine;
At least 1.44 KG but less than 1.92 KG of Piperonal;
At least 7.2 G but less than 9.6 G of Propionic Anhydride;
At least 1.44 KG but less than 1.92 KG of Safrole;
At least 1.8 KG but less than 2.4 KG of 3, 4-Methylenedioxyphenyl-2-propanone;

List II Chemicals
At least 66 G but less than 88 G of Acetic Anhydride;
At least 7.05 KG but less than 9.4 KG of Acetone;
At least 120 G but less than 160 G of Benzyl Chloride;
At least 6.45 KG but less than 8.6 KG of Ethyl Ether;
At least 7.2 KG but less than 9.6 KG of Methyl Ethyl Ketone;
At least 60 G but less than 80 G of Potassium Permanganate;
At least 7.8 KG but less than 10.4 KG of Toluene.

(10) List I Chemicals Level 12
Less than 2.7 KG of Anthranilic Acid;
Less than 3.6 G of Benzaldehyde;
Less than 80 G of Benzyl Cyanide;
Less than 800 MG of Ergonovine;
Less than 1.6 G of Ergotamine;
Less than 80 G of Ethylamine;
Less than 8.8 G of Hydriodic Acid;
Less than 1.44 KG of Isosafrole;
Less than 800 MG of Methylamine;
Less than 3.6 KG of N-Acetylanthranilic Acid;
Less than 2.25 KG of N-Methylephedrine;
Less than 2.25 KG of N-Methylpseudoephedrine;
Less than 2.5 G of Nitroethane;
Less than 40 G of Norpseudoephedrine;
Less than 80 G of Phenylacetic Acid;
Less than 40 G of Piperidine;
Less than 1.44 KG of Piperonal;

Less than 7.2 G of Propionic Anhydride;
Less than 1.44 KG of Safrole;
Less than 1.8 KG of 3, 4-Methylenedioxyphenyl-2-propanone;

<u>List II Chemicals</u>
Less than 66 G of Acetic Anhydride;
Less than 7.05 KG of Acetone;
Less than 120 G of Benzyl Chloride;
Less than 6.45 KG of Ethyl Ether;
Less than 7.2 KG of Methyl Ethyl Ketone;
Less than 60 G of Potassium Permanganate;
Less than 7.8 KG of Toluene.

*Notes:

(A) Except as provided in Note (B), to calculate the base offense level in an offense that involves two or more chemicals, use the quantity of the single chemical that results in the greatest offense level, regardless of whether the chemicals are set forth in different tables or in different categories (i.e., list I or list II) under subsection (d) of this guideline.

(B) To calculate the base offense level in an offense that involves two or more chemicals each of which is set forth in the Ephedrine, Pseudoephedrine, and Phenylpropanolamine Quantity Table, (i) aggregate the quantities of all such chemicals, and (ii) determine the base offense level corresponding to the aggregate quantity.

(C) In a case involving ephedrine, pseudoephedrine, or phenylpropanolamine tablets, use the weight of the ephedrine, pseudoephedrine, or phenylpropanolamine contained in the tablets, not the weight of the entire tablets, in calculating the base offense level.".

The Commentary to § 2D1.11 captioned "Application Notes" is amended by striking Note 4 in its entirety as follows:

"4. When two or more list I chemicals are used together in the same manufacturing process, calculate the offense level for each separately and use the quantity that results in the greatest base offense level. In any other case, the quantities should be added together (using the List I Chemical Equivalency Table) for the purpose of calculating the base offense level.

<u>Examples</u>:

(a) The defendant was in possession of five kilograms of ephedrine and 300 grams of hydriodic acid. Ephedrine and hydriodic acid typically are used together in the same manufacturing process to manufacture methamphetamine. Therefore, the base offense level for each listed chemical is calculated separately and the list I chemical with the higher base offense level is used. Five kilograms of ephedrine result in a base offense level of 26; 300 grams of hydriodic acid result in a

Amendment 611 APPENDIX C - VOLUME II November 1, 2013

> base offense level of 16. In this case, the base offense level would be 26.
>
> (b) The defendant was in possession of five kilograms of ephedrine and two kilograms of phenylacetic acid. Although both of these chemicals are used to manufacture methamphetamine, they are not used together in the same manufacturing process. Therefore, the quantity of phenylacetic acid should be converted to an ephedrine equivalency using the List I Chemical Equivalency Table and then added to the quantity of ephedrine. In this case, the two kilograms of phenylacetic acid convert to two kilograms of ephedrine (see List I Chemical Equivalency Table), resulting in a total equivalency of seven kilograms of ephedrine.",

and inserting the following:

> "4. Cases Involving Multiple Chemicals.—
>
> (A) Determining the Base Offense Level for Two or More Chemicals.—Except as provided in subdivision (B), if the offense involves two or more chemicals, use the quantity of the single chemical that results in the greatest offense level, regardless of whether the chemicals are set forth in different tables or in different categories (i.e., list I or list II) under subsections (d) and (e) of this guideline.
>
> Example: The defendant was in possession of five kilograms of ephedrine and 300 grams of hydriodic acid. Ephedrine and hydriodic acid typically are used together in the same manufacturing process to manufacture methamphetamine. The base offense level for each chemical is calculated separately and the chemical with the higher base offense level is used. Five kilograms of ephedrine result in a base offense level of level 38; 300 grams of hydriodic acid result in a base offense level of level 26. In this case, the base offense level would be level 38.
>
> (B) Determining the Base Offense Level for Offenses involving Ephedrine, Pseudoephedrine, or Phenylpropanolamine.—If the offense involves two or more chemicals each of which is set forth in the Ephedrine, Pseudoephedrine, and Phenylpropanolamine Quantity Table, (i) aggregate the quantities of all such chemicals, and (ii) determine the base offense level corresponding to the aggregate quantity.
>
> Example: The defendant was in possession of 80 grams of ephedrine and 50 grams of phenylpropanolamine, an aggregate quantity of 130 grams of such chemicals. The base offense level corresponding to that aggregate quantity is level 32.
>
> (C) Upward Departure.—In a case involving two or more chemicals used to manufacture different controlled substances, or to manufacture one controlled substance by different manufacturing processes, an upward departure may be warranted if the offense level does not adequately address the seriousness of the offense.".

The Commentary to § 2D1.11 captioned "Application Notes" is amended by striking

Notes 5 and 6 in their entirety as follows:

> "5. Where there are multiple list II chemicals, all quantities of the same list II chemical are added together for purposes of determining the base offense level. However, quantities of different list II chemicals are not aggregated (see Note B to the Chemical Quantity Table). Thus, where multiple list II chemicals are involved in the offense, the base offense level is determined by using the base offense level for the single list II chemical resulting in the greatest base offense level. For example, in the case of an offense involving seven kilograms of methyl ethyl ketone and eight kilograms of acetone, the base offense level for the methyl ethyl ketone is 12 and the base offense level for the acetone is 14; therefore, the base offense level is 14.
>
> 6. Where both list I chemicals and list II chemicals are involved, use the greater of the base offense level for the list I chemicals or the list II chemicals (see Note C to the Chemical Quantity Table).";

and by redesignating Notes 7 and 8 as Notes 5 and 6, respectively.

The Commentary to § 2D1.11 captioned "Background" is amended in the first sentence by inserting "(including ephedrine, pseudoephedrine, and phenylpropanolamine)" after "list I chemicals".

The Commentary to 2D1.1 captioned "Application Notes" is amended in Note 10 in the "Drug Equivalency Tables" by inserting after the subdivision captioned "Schedule V Substances******" the following new subdivision:

> "List I Chemicals (relating to the manufacture of amphetamine or methamphetamine)*******
>
> | | |
> |---|---|
> | 1 gm of Ephedrine = | 10 kg of marihuana |
> | 1 gm of Phenylpropanolamine = | 10 kg of marihuana |
> | 1 gm of Pseudoephedrine = | 10 kg of marihuana |
>
> *******Provided, that in a case involving ephedrine, pseudoephedrine, or phenylpropanolamine tablets, use the weight of the ephedrine, pseudoephedrine, or phenylpropanolamine contained in the tablets, not the weight of the entire tablets, in calculating the base offense level.".

Reason for Amendment: This amendment is in response to the three-part directive in section 3651 of the Methamphetamine Anti-Proliferation Act of 2000, Pub. L. 106–310 (the "Act"), regarding enhanced punishment for trafficking in List I chemicals. That section requires the Commission to promulgate an amendment implementing the directive under emergency amendment authority.

First, this amendment provides a new chemical quantity table specifically for ephedrine, pseudoephedrine, and phenylpropanolamine (PPA). The table ties the base offense levels for these chemicals to the base offense levels for methamphetamine (actual) set forth in § 2D1.1, assuming a 50 percent actual yield of the controlled substance from the chemicals. (Methamphetamine (actual) is used rather than methamphetamine mixture because ephedrine, pseudoephedrine, and PPA produce methamphetamine (actual)). This yield is based on information provided by the Drug Enforcement Administration (DEA) that the typical yield of these substances for clandestine laboratories is 50 to 75 percent.

This new chemical quantity table has a maximum base offense level of level 38 (as opposed to a maximum base offense level of level 30 for all other precursor chemicals). Providing a maximum base offense level of level 38 complies with the directive to establish penalties for these precursors that "correspond to the quantity of controlled substance that could have reasonably been manufactured using the quantity of ephedrine, phenylpropanolamine, or pseudoephedrine possessed or distributed." Additionally, this adjustment will have an impact on the relationship between §§ 2D1.1 and 2D1.11 by eliminating the six-level distinction that currently exists between offenses that involve intent to manufacture methamphetamine and offenses that involve an attempt to manufacture methamphetamine, at least for offenses involving ephedrine, pseudoephedrine, and PPA.

This amendment eliminates the Ephedrine Equivalency Table in § 2D1.11 and, in its place, provides an instruction for the court to determine the base offense level in cases involving multiple precursors (other than ephedrine, pseudoephedrine, or PPA) by using the quantity of the single chemical resulting in the greatest offense level. An upward departure is provided for cases in which the offense level does not adequately address the seriousness of the offense.

However, this amendment provides an exception to the rule for offenses that involve a combination of ephedrine, pseudoephedrine, or PPA because these chemicals often are used in the same manufacturing process. In a case that involves two or more of these chemicals, the base offense level will be determined using the total quantity of these chemicals involved. The purpose of this exception is twofold: (1) any of the three primary precursors in the same table can be combined without difficulty; and (2) studies conducted by the DEA indicate that because the manufacturing process for amphetamine and methamphetamine is identical, there are cases in which the different precursors are included in the same batch of drugs. If the chemical is PPA, amphetamine results; and if the chemical is ephedrine, methamphetamine results.

Second, the amendment adds to the Drug Equivalency Tables in § 2D1.1 a conversion table for these precursor chemicals, providing for a 50 percent conversion ratio. This is based on data from the DEA that the actual yield from ephedrine, pseudoephedrine, or PPA typically is in the range of 50 to 75 percent. The purpose of this part of the amendment is to achieve the same punishment level (as is achieved by the first part of this amendment) for an offense involving any of these precursor chemicals when such offense involved the manufacture of methamphetamine and, as a result, is sentenced under § 2D1.1 pursuant to the cross reference in § 2D1.11.

Third, this amendment increases the base offense level for Benzaldehyde, Hydriodic Acid, Methylamine, Nitroethane, and Norpseudoephedrine by re-calibrating these levels to the appropriate quantity of methamphetamine (actual) that could be produced assuming a 50 percent yield of chemical to drug and retaining a cap at level 30. Previously, these chemicals had been linked to methamphetamine (mixture) penalty levels. Based on a study conducted by the DEA, ephedrine and pseudoepehdrine are the primary precursors used to make methamphetamine in the United States. Phenylproponolamine is the primary precursor used to make amphetamine. Unlike the five additional List I chemicals, the chemical structures of ephedrine, pseudoephedrine, and PPA are so similar to the resulting drug (i.e., methamphetamine or amphetamine) that the manufacture of methamphetamine or amphetamine from ephedrine, pseudoephedrine, or PPA is a very simple one-step synthesis which anyone can perform using a variety of chemical reagents. The manufacture of methamphetamine or amphetamine from the five additional List I chemicals is a more complex process which requires a heightened level of expertise.

Effective Date: The effective date of this amendment is May 1, 2001.

612. Amendment: The Commentary to § 2G1.1 captioned "Statutory Provisions" is amended by inserting "1591," before "2421".

The Commentary to § 2G1.1 captioned "Application Notes" is amended in Note 2 in the fourth sentence by adding "(B)" after "purposes of subsection (b)(1)".

The Commentary to § 2G1.1 captioned "Application Notes" is amended by adding at the end the following:

"12. <u>Upward Departure Provisions</u>.—An upward departure may be warranted in either of the following circumstances:

(A) The defendant was convicted under 18 U.S.C. § 1591 and the offense involved a victim who had not attained the age of 14 years.

(B) The offense involved more than 10 victims.".

The Commentary to § 2G1.1 captioned "Background" is amended by adding at the end the following paragraph:

"This guideline also covers offenses under section 1591 of title 18, United States Code. These offenses involve recruiting or transporting a person in interstate commerce knowing either that (1) force, fraud, or coercion will be used to cause the person to engage in a commercial sex act; or (2) the person (A) had not attained the age of 18 years; and (B) will be caused to engage in a commercial sex act.".

The Commentary to § 2G2.1 captioned "Statutory Provisions" is amended by inserting "1591," before "2251(a)".

The Commentary to § 2G2.1 captioned "Application Notes" is amended by adding at the end the following:

"6. <u>Upward Departure Provisions</u>.—An upward departure may be warranted in either of the following circumstances:

(A) The defendant was convicted under 18 U.S.C. § 1591 and the offense involved a victim who had not attained the age of 14 years.

(B) The offense involved more than 10 victims.".

Section 2H4.1 is amended by striking subsection (a) in its entirety as follows:

"(a) Base Offense Level: 22",

and inserting the following:

"(a) Base Offense Level (Apply the greater):

(1) 22; or

(2) 18, if the defendant was convicted of an offense under 18 U.S.C. § 1592.".

Section 2H4.1(b) is amended by striking subdivision (2) in its entirety as follows:

"(2) If a dangerous weapon was used, increase by 2 levels.",

Amendment 612

and inserting the following:

> "(2) If (A) a dangerous weapon was used, increase by 4 levels; or (B) a dangerous weapon was brandished, or the use of a dangerous weapon was threatened, increase by 2 levels.".

The Commentary to § 2H4.1 captioned "Statutory Provisions" is amended by striking "1588" and inserting "1590, 1592".

The Commentary to § 2H4.1 captioned "Application Notes" is amended in Note 1 in the second paragraph by inserting "other" after "that a firearm or"; and by adding after "otherwise used." the following:

> "'The use of a dangerous weapon was threatened' means that the use of a dangerous weapon was threatened regardless of whether a dangerous weapon was present.".

Chapter Two, Part H, is amended in Subpart 4 by adding at the end the following:

> "§ 2H4.2.   Willful Violations of the Migrant and Seasonal Agricultural Worker Protection Act
>
> (a)   Base Offense Level: 6
>
> (b)   Specific Offense Characteristics
>
> > (1)   If the offense involved (i) serious bodily injury, increase by 4 levels; or (ii) bodily injury, increase by 2 levels.
> >
> > (2)   If the defendant committed any part of the instant offense subsequent to sustaining a civil or administrative adjudication for similar misconduct, increase by 2 levels.
>
> Commentary
>
> Statutory Provision: 29 U.S.C. § 1851.
>
> Application Notes:
>
> 1.   Definitions.—For purposes of subsection (b)(1), 'bodily injury' and 'serious bodily injury' have the meaning given those terms in Application Note 1 of the Commentary to § 1B1.1 (Application Instructions).
>
> 2.   Application of Subsection (b)(2).—Section 1851 of title 29, United States Code, covers a wide range of conduct. Accordingly, the enhancement in subsection (b)(2) applies only if the instant offense is similar to previous misconduct that resulted in a civil or administrative adjudication under the provisions of the Migrant and Seasonal Agricultural Worker Protection Act (29 U.S.C. § 1801 et. seq.).".

Section 5E1.1(a)(1) is amended by inserting "§ 1593," after "18 U.S.C.".

The Commentary to § 5E1.1 captioned "Background" is amended in the first paragraph by inserting "1593," after "18 U.S.C. §§ ".

Appendix A (Statutory Index) is amended in the line referenced to "18 U.S.C. § 241" by inserting ", 2H4.1" after "2H2.1".

Appendix A (Statutory Index) is amended by inserting after the line referenced to "18 U.S.C. § 1588" the following new lines:

"18 U.S.C. § 1589   2H4.1
18 U.S.C. § 1590   2H4.1
18 U.S.C. § 1591   2G1.1, 2G2.1
18 U.S.C. § 1592   2H4.1".

Appendix A (Statutory Index) is amended by inserting after the line referenced to "29 U.S.C. § 1141" the following:

"29 U.S.C. § 1851   2H4.2".

Reason for Amendment: In promulgating this amendment, the Commission is cognizant of the extraordinarily serious nature of offenses that involve trafficking in human lives. This amendment is in response to the directive found at section 112(b) of the Victims of Trafficking and Violence Protection Act of 2000 (the "Act"), Pub. L. 106–386. The Commission expects to consider further revisions and additions to the specific offense characteristics and punishment levels for these offenses, such as the possibility of providing an alternative base offense level in § 2G1.1 (Promoting Prostitution or Prohibited Sexual Conduct) for convictions under 18 U.S.C. § 1591 involving victims under the age of 14 years.

The directive confers emergency authority on the Commission to amend the federal sentencing guidelines to reflect changes to 18 U.S.C. §§ 1581(a) (Peonage), 1583 (Enticement into Slavery), and 1584 (Sale into Involuntary Servitude). The Commission also is directed to consider how to address four new statutes: 18 U.S.C. §§ 1589 (Forced Labor); 1590 (Trafficking with Respect to Peonage, Involuntary Servitude or Forced Labor); 1591 (Sex Trafficking of Children by Force, Fraud or Coercion); and 1592 (Unlawful Conduct with Respect to Documents in Furtherance of Peonage, Involuntary Servitude or Forced Labor).

Specifically, the Commission is directed to "review and, if appropriate, amend the sentencing guidelines applicable to . . . the trafficking of persons including . . . peonage, involuntary servitude, slave trade offenses, and possession, transfer or sale of false immigration documents in furtherance of trafficking, and the Fair Labor Standards Act and the Migrant and Seasonal Agricultural Worker Protection Act."

The Commission further is directed to "take all appropriate measures to ensure that these sentencing guidelines . . . are sufficiently stringent to deter and adequately reflect the heinous nature of these offenses." The Commission also is directed to "consider providing sentencing enhancements" in cases which involve: (1) a large number of victims; (2) a pattern of continued and flagrant violations; (3) the use or threatened use of a dangerous weapon; or (4) the death or bodily injury of any person.

To address this multi-faceted directive, this amendment makes changes to several existing guidelines and creates a new guideline for criminal violations of the Migrant and Seasonal Agricultural Worker Protection Act. Although the directive instructs the Commission to amend the guidelines applicable to the Fair Labor Standards Act (29 U.S.C. § 201 et. seq.), a criminal violation of the Fair Labor Standards Act is only a Class B misdemeanor. See 29 U.S.C. § 216. Thus, the guidelines are not applicable to those offenses.

The amendment references the new offense at 18 U.S.C. § 1591 to § 2G1.1. Section 1591 punishes a defendant who participates in the transporting or harboring of a person, or who benefits from participating in such a venture, with the knowledge that force, fraud, or coercion will be used to cause that person to engage in a commercial sex act or with knowledge that the person is not 18 years old and will be forced to engage in a commercial sex act. Despite the statute's inclusion in a chapter of title 18 devoted mainly to peonage offenses, section 1591 offenses are more analogous to the offenses referenced to the prostitution guideline.

Section 1591 cases alternatively have been referred in Appendix A to § 2G2.1 (Sexually Exploiting a Minor by Production of Sexually Explicit Visual or Printed Material; Custodian Permitting Minor to Engage in Sexually Explicit Conduct; Advertisement for Minors to Engage in Production). This has been done in anticipation that some portion of section 1591 cases will involve children being forced or coerced to engage in commercial sex acts for the purpose of producing pornography. Such offenses, as recognized by the higher base offense level at § 2G2.1, are more serious because they both involve specific harm to an individual victim and further an additional criminal purpose, namely, commercial pornography.

The amendment maintains the view that § 2H4.1 (Peonage, Involuntary Servitude, and Slave Trade) continues to be an appropriate tool for determining sentences for violations of 18 U.S.C. §§ 1581, 1583, and 1584. Section 2H4.1 also is designed to cover offenses under three new statutes, 18 U.S.C. §§ 1589, 1590, and 1592. Section 1589 punishes defendants who provide or obtain the labor or services of another by the use of threats of serious harm or physical restraint against a person, or by a scheme or plan intended to make the person believe that if he or she did not perform the labor or services, he or she would suffer physical restraint or serious harm. This statute also applies to defendants who provide or obtain labor or services of another by abusing or threatening abuse of the law or the legal process. See 18 U.S.C. § 1589.

Section 1590 punishes defendants who harbor, transport, or are otherwise involved in obtaining, a person for labor or services. Section 1592 punishes a defendant who knowingly possesses, destroys, or removes an actual passport, other immigration document, or government identification document of another person in the course of a violation of § 1581 (peonage), § 1583 (enticement into slavery), § 1584 (sale into involuntary servitude), § 1589 (forced labor), § 1590 (trafficking with respect to these offenses), § 1591 (sex trafficking of children by force, fraud or coercion), or § 1594(a) (attempts to violate these offenses). Section 1592 also punishes a defendant who, with intent to violate § 1581, § 1583, § 1584, § 1589, § 1590, or § 1591, knowingly possesses, destroys, or removes an actual passport, other immigration document, or government identification document of another person. These statutes prohibit the types of behaviors that have been traditionally sentenced under § 2H4.1.

The amendment provides an alternative, less punitive base offense level of level 18 for those who violate 18 U.S.C. § 1592, an offense which limits participation in peonage cases to the destruction or wrongful confiscation of a passport or other immigration document. This alternative, lower base level reflects the lower statutory maximum sentence for § 1592 offenses (i.e., 5 years).

Section 2H4.1(b)(2) has been expanded to provide a 4-level increase if a dangerous weapon was used and a 2-level increase if a dangerous weapon was brandished or its use was threatened. Currently, only actual use of a dangerous weapon is covered. This change reflects the directive to consider an enhancement for the "use or threatened use of a dangerous weapon." The commentary to § 2H4.1 is amended to clarify that the threatened use of a dangerous weapon applies regardless of whether a dangerous weapon was actually present.

The amendment also creates a new guideline, § 2H4.2 (Willful Violations of the Migrant and Seasonal Agricultural Worker Protection Act), in response to the directive to amend the guidelines applicable to such offenses. These offenses, which have a statutory maximum sentence of one year imprisonment for first offenses and three years' imprisonment for subsequent offenses, currently are not referred to any specific guideline. The amendment provides a base offense level of level 6 in recognition of the low statutory maximum sentences set for these cases by Congress. Further, these offenses typically involve violations of regulatory provisions. Setting the base offense level at level 6 provides consistency with guidelines for other regulatory offenses. See, e.g., §§ 2N2.1 (Violations of Statutes and Regulations Dealing With Any Food, Drug, Biological Product, Device, Cosmetic, or Agricultural Product) and 2N3.1 (Odometer Laws and Regulations). Subsections (b)(1), an enhancement for bodily injury, and (b)(2), an enhancement applicable to defendants who commit the instant offense after previously sustaining a civil penalty for similar misconduct, have been established to respond to the directive that the Commission consider sentencing enhancement for these offense characteristics. This section addresses the Department of Justice's and the Department of Labor's concern regarding prior administrative and civil adjudications.

This amendment also addresses that portion of section 112 of the Act that amends chapter 77 of title 18, United States Code, to provide mandatory restitution for peonage and involuntary servitude offenses. The amendment amends § 5E1.1 (Restitution) to include a reference to 18 U.S.C. § 1593 in the guideline provision regarding mandatory restitution.

By enactment of various sentencing enhancements and encouraged upward departures for areas of concern identified by Congress, the Commission has provided for more severe sentences for perpetrators of human trafficking offenses in keeping with the conclusion that the offenses covered by this amendment are both heinous in nature and being committed with rapidly increasing frequency.

Effective Date: The effective date of this amendment is May 1, 2001.

613. **Amendment:** The Commentary to § 1B1.2 captioned "Application Notes" is amended in Note 1 in the third sentence of the first paragraph by inserting "(written or made orally on the record)" after "agreement".

The Commentary to § 1B1.2 captioned "Application Notes" is amended in Note 1 by striking the first two sentences of the third paragraph as follows:

> "However, there is a limited exception to this general rule. Where a stipulation that is set forth in a written plea agreement or made between the parties on the record during a plea proceeding specifically establishes facts that prove a more serious offense or offenses than the offense or offenses of conviction, the court is to apply the guideline most applicable to the more serious offense or offenses established.",

and inserting:

> "As set forth in the first paragraph of this note, an exception to this general rule is that if a plea agreement (written or made orally on the record) contains a stipulation that establishes a more serious offense than the offense of conviction, the guideline section applicable to the stipulated offense is to be used. A factual statement or a stipulation contained in a plea agreement (written or made orally on the record) is a stipulation for purposes of subsection (a) only if both the defendant and the government explicitly agree that the factual statement or stipulation is a stipulation for such purposes. However, a factual statement or stipulation made after the plea agreement has been entered, or after any modification to the plea agreement has been made, is not a stipulation for purposes of subsection (a).".

Amendment 613

The Commentary to § 1B1.2 captioned "Application Notes" is amended in Note 1 in the third paragraph by striking "may be imposed" and inserting "shall be imposed".

The Commentary to § 1B1.2 captioned "Application Notes" is amended in Note 1 in the second sentence of the fourth paragraph by striking "cases where" and inserting "a case in which".

Reason for Amendment: This amendment addresses the circuit conflict regarding whether admissions made by a defendant during a guilty plea hearing, without more, can be considered stipulations for purposes of subsection (a) of § 1B1.2 (Application Instructions). Compare, e.g., United States v. Nathan, 188 F.3d 190, 201 (3d Cir. 1999) (statements made by defendants during the factual-basis hearing for a plea agreement do not constitute stipulations for the purpose of this enhancement; a statement is a stipulation only if it is part of a defendant's written plea agreement or if both the government and the defendant explicitly agree at a factual-basis hearing that the facts being placed on the record are stipulations that might subject the defendant to § 1B1.2(a)); United States v. Saaverda, 148 F.3d 1311 (11th Cir. 1998) (same); United States v. McCall, 915 F.2d 811 (2d Cir. 1990) (same); United States v. Gardner, 940 F.2d 587 (10th Cir. 1991) (requiring a "knowing agreement by the defendant, as part of a plea bargain, that facts supporting a more serious offense occurred and could be presented to the court"); and United States v. Rutter, 897 F.2d 1558, 1561 (10th Cir. 1990) (once the government agrees to a plea bargain without extracting an admission, facts admitted by the defendant can be considered only as relevant conduct in determining appropriate guideline range, not as stipulations under § 1B1.2(a)), with United States v. Loos, 165 F.3d 504, 508 (7th Cir. 1998) (the objective behind § 1B1.2(a) is best answered by interpreting "stipulations" to mean any acknowledgment by the defendant that the defendant committed the acts that justify use of the more serious guideline, not in the formal agreement); and United States v. Domino, 62 F.3d 716 (5th Cir. 1995) (same).

This amendment represents a narrow approach to the majority view that a factual statement made by the defendant during the plea colloquy must be made as part of the plea agreement in order to be considered a stipulation for purposes of § 1B1.2(a). This approach lessens the possibility that the plea agreement will be modified during the course of the plea proceeding without providing the parties, especially the defendant, with notice of the defendant's potential sentencing range.

Effective Date: The effective date of this amendment is November 1, 2001.

614. **Amendment:** The Commentary to § 2A2.2 captioned "Application Notes" is amended by striking Notes 1 through 3 as follows:

> "1. 'Aggravated assault' means a felonious assault that involved (A) a dangerous weapon with intent to do bodily harm (i.e., not merely to frighten), or (B) serious bodily injury, or (C) an intent to commit another felony.
>
> 2. Definitions of 'more than minimal planning,' 'firearm,' 'dangerous weapon,' 'brandished,' 'otherwise used,' 'bodily injury,' 'serious bodily injury," and 'permanent or life-threatening bodily injury,' are found in the Commentary to § 1B1.1 (Application Instructions).
>
> 3. This guideline also covers attempted manslaughter and assault with intent to commit manslaughter. Assault with intent to commit murder is covered by § 2A2.1 (Assault With Intent to Commit Murder). Assault with intent to commit rape is covered by § 2A3.1 (Criminal Sexual Abuse).",

and inserting the following:

> "1. Definitions.—For purposes of this guideline:
>
>   'Aggravated assault' means a felonious assault that involved (A) a dangerous weapon with intent to cause bodily injury (i.e., not merely to frighten) with that weapon; (B) serious bodily injury; or (C) an intent to commit another felony.
>
>   'Brandished,' 'bodily injury,' 'firearm,' 'otherwise used,' 'permanent or life-threatening bodily injury,' and 'serious bodily injury,' have the meaning given those terms in § 1B1.1 (Application Instructions), Application Note 1.
>
>   'Dangerous weapon' has the meaning given that term in § 1B1.1, Application Note 1, and includes any instrument that is not ordinarily used as a weapon (e.g., a car, a chair, or an ice pick) if such an instrument is involved in the offense with the intent to commit bodily injury.
>
> 2. Application of Subsection (b)(2).—In a case involving a dangerous weapon with intent to cause bodily injury, the court shall apply both the base offense level and subsection (b)(2).
>
> 3. More than Minimal Planning.—For purposes of subsection (b)(1), 'more than minimal planning' means more planning than is typical for commission of the offense in a simple form. 'More than minimal planning' also exists if significant affirmative steps were taken to conceal the offense, other than conduct to which § 3C1.1 (Obstructing or Impeding the Administration of Justice) applies. For example, waiting to commit the offense when no witnesses were present would not alone constitute more than minimal planning. By contrast, luring the victim to a specific location or wearing a ski mask to prevent identification would constitute more than minimal planning.".

The Commentary to § 2A2.2 captioned "Background" is amended by striking the text of the background as follows:

> "   This section applies to serious (aggravated) assaults. Such offenses occasionally may involve planning or be committed for hire. Consequently, the structure follows § 2A2.1.
>
>   There are a number of federal provisions that address varying degrees of assault and battery. The punishments under these statutes differ considerably, even among provisions directed to substantially similar conduct. For example, if the assault is upon certain federal officers 'while engaged in or on account of . . . official duties,' the maximum term of imprisonment under 18 U.S.C. § 111 is three years. If a dangerous weapon is used in the assault on a federal officer, the maximum term of imprisonment is ten years. However, if the same weapon is used to assault a person not otherwise specifically protected, the maximum term of imprisonment under 18 U.S.C. § 113(c) is five years. If the assault results in serious bodily injury, the maximum term of imprisonment under 18 U.S.C. § 113(f) is ten years, unless the injury constitutes maiming by scalding, corrosive, or caustic substances under 18 U.S.C. § 114, in which case the maximum term of imprisonment is twenty years.",

and inserting the following:

> "   This guideline covers felonious assaults that are more serious than minor as-

saults because of the presence of an aggravating factor, i.e., serious bodily injury, the involvement of a dangerous weapon with intent to cause bodily injury, or the intent to commit another felony. Such offenses occasionally may involve planning or be committed for hire. Consequently, the structure follows § 2A2.1 (Assault with Intent to Commit Murder; Attempted Murder). This guideline also covers attempted manslaughter and assault with intent to commit manslaughter. Assault with intent to commit murder is covered by § 2A2.1. Assault with intent to commit rape is covered by § 2A3.1 (Criminal Sexual Abuse; Attempt to Commit Criminal Sexual Abuse).

An assault that involves the presence of a dangerous weapon is aggravated in form when the presence of the dangerous weapon is coupled with the intent to cause bodily injury. In such a case, the base offense level and the weapon enhancement in subsection (b)(2) take into account different aspects of the offense, even if application of the base offense level and the weapon enhancement is based on the same conduct.".

Reason for Amendment: This amendment responds to a circuit conflict regarding whether the four-level enhancement in subsection (b)(2)(B) of § 2A2.2 (Aggravated Assault) for use of a dangerous weapon during an aggravated assault is impermissible double counting. Compare United States v. Williams, 954 F.2d 204, 205-08 (4th Cir. 1992) (applying the dangerous weapon enhancement under § 2A2.2(b)(2)(B) for defendant's use of his chair as a dangerous weapon did not constitute impermissible double counting even though that conduct increased the defendant's offense level twice: first, by triggering the application of the aggravated assault guideline, and second, as the basis for the four-level enhancement for use of a dangerous weapon), with United States v. Hudson, 972 F.2d 504, 506-07 (2d Cir. 1992) (in a case in which the use of an automobile caused the crime to be classified as an aggravated assault, the court may not enhance the base offense level under § 2A2.2(b) for use of the same, non-inherently dangerous weapon).

This amendment addresses the circuit conflict by providing in the aggravated assault guideline that (1) both the base offense level of level 15 and the weapon use enhancement in subsection (b)(2) shall apply to aggravated assaults that involve a dangerous weapon with intent to cause bodily harm; and (2) an instrument, such as a car or chair, that ordinarily is not used as a weapon may qualify as a dangerous weapon for purposes of the use of the aggravated assault guideline and the application of subsection (b)(2) when the defendant involves it in the offense with the intent to cause bodily harm.

Effective Date: The effective date of this amendment is November 1, 2001.

615. **Amendment:** The Commentary to § 2A3.1 captioned "Application Notes" is amended by striking Note 5 as follows:

"5. If the defendant was convicted (A) of more than one act of criminal sexual abuse and the counts are grouped under § 3D1.2 (Groups of Closely Related Counts), or (B) of only one such act but the court determines that the offense involved multiple acts of criminal sexual abuse of the same victim or different victims, an upward departure would be warranted.";

by striking Note 7 as follows:

"7. If the defendant's criminal history includes a prior sentence for conduct that is similar to the instant offense, an upward departure may be warranted.";

and by redesignating Note 6 as Note 5.

Section 2A3.2(a) is amended by striking subdivisions (1) and (2) as follows:

"(1) 18, if the offense involved a violation of chapter 117 of title 18, United States Code; or

(2) 15, otherwise.",

and inserting the following:

"(1) 24, if the offense involved (A) a violation of chapter 117 of title 18, United States Code; and (B)(i) the commission of a sexual act; or (ii) sexual contact;

(2) 21, if the offense (A) involved a violation of chapter 117 of title 18, United States Code; but (B) did not involve (i) the commission of a sexual act; or (ii) sexual contact; or

(3) 18, otherwise.".

Section 2A3.2(b) is amended by striking subdivision (4) as follows:

"(4) If (A) subsection (a)(1) applies; and (B) none of subsections (b)(1) through (b)(3) applies, decrease by 3 levels.",

and inserting the following:

"(4) If (A) subsection (a)(1) applies; and (B) none of subsections (b)(1) through (b)(3) applies, decrease by 6 levels.".

The Commentary to § 2A3.2 captioned "Application Notes" is amended in Note 1 by striking "For purposes of this guideline—" and inserting "Definitions.—For purposes of this guideline:"; and by inserting before "'Victim' means" the following new paragraphs:

"'Sexual act' has the meaning given that term in 18 U.S.C. § 2246(2).

'Sexual contact' has the meaning given that term in 18 U.S.C. § 2246(3).".

The Commentary to § 2A3.2 captioned "Application Notes" is amended by striking Note 2 as follows:

"2. If the defendant committed the criminal sexual act in furtherance of a commercial scheme such as pandering, transporting persons for the purpose of prostitution, or the production of pornography, an upward departure may be warranted. See Chapter Five, Part K (Departures).";

by striking Note 8 as follows:

"8. If the defendant's criminal history includes a prior sentence for conduct that is similar to the instant offense, an upward departure may be warranted.";

by redesignating Notes 3 through 7 as Notes 2 through 6, respectively; and by inserting after Note 6, as redesignated by this amendment, the following:

"7. Upward Departure Consideration.—There may be cases in which the offense level determined under this guideline substantially understates the seriousness of the offense. In such cases, an upward departure may be warranted. For example, an upward departure may be warranted if the defendant committed the criminal sexual act in furtherance of a commercial scheme such as pandering, transporting persons for the purpose of prostitution, or the production of pornography.".

The Commentary to § 2A3.2 captioned "Application Notes" is amended in Note 2, as redesignated by this amendment, by inserting "Custody, Care, and Supervisory Control Enhancement.—" before "Subsection".

The Commentary to § 2A3.2 captioned "Application Notes" is amended in Note 3, as redesignated by this amendment, by inserting "Abuse of Position of Trust.—" before "If the".

The Commentary to § 2A3.2 captioned "Application Notes" is amended in Note 4, as redesignated by this amendment, by inserting "Misrepresentation of Identity.—" before "The enhancement".

The Commentary to § 2A3.2 captioned "Application Notes" is amended in Note 5, as redesignated by this amendment, by inserting "Use of Computer or Internet-Access Device.—" before "Subsection (b)(3) provides".

The Commentary to § 2A3.2 captioned "Application Notes" is amended in Note 6, as redesignated by this amendment, by inserting "Cross Reference.—" before "Subsection (c)(1)".

The Commentary to § 2A3.3 captioned "Application Notes" is amended by striking Note 4 as follows:

> "4. If the defendant's criminal history includes a prior sentence for conduct that is similar to the instant offense, an upward departure may be warranted.".

Section 2A3.4(b) is amended by adding at the end the following:

> "(6) If the offense involved a violation of chapter 117 of title 18, United States Code, increase by 3 levels.".

The Commentary to § 2A3.4 captioned "Application Notes" is amended by striking Note 8 as follows:

> "8. If the defendant's criminal history includes a prior sentence for conduct that is similar to the instant offense, an upward departure may be warranted.".

Section 3D1.2(d) is amended in the second paragraph by inserting after "§§ 2E4.1, 2E5.1;" the following new line:

> "§§ 2G2.2, 2G2.4;".

Chapter Four, Part B is amended by adding at the end the following:

> "§ 4B1.5. Repeat and Dangerous Sex Offender Against Minors
>
> > (a) In any case in which the defendant's instant offense of conviction is a covered sex crime, § 4B1.1 (Career Offender) does not apply, and the defendant committed the instant offense of conviction subsequent to sustaining at least one sex offense conviction:
> >
> > > (1) The offense level shall be the greater of:

(A) the offense level determined under Chapters Two and Three; or

(B) the offense level from the table below decreased by the number of levels corresponding to any applicable adjustment from § 3E1.1 (Acceptance of Responsibility):

	Offense Statutory Maximum	Offense Level
(i)	Life	37
(ii)	25 years or more	34
(iii)	20 years or more, but less than 25 years	32
(iv)	15 years or more, but less than 20 years	29
(v)	10 years or more, but less than 15 years	24
(vi)	5 years or more, but less than 10 years	17
(vii)	More than 1 year, but less than 5 years	12.

(2) The criminal history category shall be the greater of:(A) the criminal history category determined under Chapter Four, Part A (Criminal History); or (B) criminal history Category V.

(b) In any case in which the defendant's instant offense of conviction is a covered sex crime, neither § 4B1.1 nor subsection (a) of this guideline applies, and the defendant engaged in a pattern of activity involving prohibited sexual conduct:

(1) The offense level shall be 5 plus the offense level determined under Chapters Two and Three. However, if the resulting offense level is less than level 22, the offense level shall be level 22, decreased by the number of levels corresponding to any applicable adjustment from § 3E1.1.

(2) The criminal history category shall be the criminal history category determined under Chapter Four, Part A.

Commentary

Application Notes:

1. Definitions.—For purposes of this guideline:

'Minor' means an individual who had not attained the age of 18 years.

'Minor victim' includes (A) an undercover law enforcement officer who represented to the defendant that the officer was a minor; or (B) any minor the officer represented to the defendant would be involved in the prohibited sexual conduct.

2. Covered Sex Crime as Instant Offense of Conviction.—For purposes of this guideline, the instant offense of conviction must be a covered sex crime, i.e.: (A) an offense, perpetrated against a minor, under (i) chapter 109A of title 18, United States Code; (ii) chapter 110 of such title, not including traffick-

Amendment 615 APPENDIX C - VOLUME II November 1, 2013

ing in, receipt of, or possession of, child pornography, or a recordkeeping offense; (iii) chapter 117 of such title, not including transmitting information about a minor or filing a factual statement about an alien individual; or (B) an attempt or a conspiracy to commit any offense described in subdivisions (A)(i) through (iii) of this note.

3. Application of Subsection (a).—

   (A) Definitions.—For purposes of subsection (a):

   (i) 'Offense statutory maximum' means the maximum term of imprisonment authorized for the instant offense of conviction that is a covered sex crime, including any increase in that maximum term under a sentencing enhancement provision (such as a sentencing enhancement provision contained in 18 U.S.C. § 2247(a) or § 2426(a)) that applies to that covered sex crime because of the defendant's prior criminal record.

   (ii) 'Sex offense conviction' (I) means any offense described in 18 U.S.C. § 2426(b)(1)(A) or (B), if the offense was perpetrated against a minor; and (II) does not include trafficking in, receipt of, or possession of, child pornography. 'Child pornography' has the meaning given that term in 18 U.S.C. § 2256(8).

   (B) Determination of Offense Statutory Maximum in the Case of Multiple Counts of Conviction.—In a case in which more than one count of the instant offense of conviction is a felony that is a covered sex crime, the court shall use the maximum authorized term of imprisonment for the count that has the greatest offense statutory maximum, for purposes of determining the offense statutory maximum under subsection (a).

4. Application of Subsection (b).—

   (A) Definition.—For purposes of subsection (b), 'prohibited sexual conduct' (i) means any offense described in 18 U.S.C. § 2426(b)(1)(A) or (B); (ii) includes the production of child pornography; (iii) includes trafficking in child pornography only if, prior to the commission of the instant offense of conviction, the defendant sustained a felony conviction for that trafficking in child pornography; and (iv) does not include receipt or possession of child pornography. 'Child pornography' has the meaning given that term in 18 U.S.C. § 2256(8).

   (B) Determination of Pattern of Activity.—

   (i) In General.—For purposes of subsection (b), the defendant engaged in a pattern of activity involving prohibited sexual conduct if—

   (I) on at least two separate occasions, the defendant engaged in prohibited sexual conduct with a minor; and

(II) there were at least two minor victims of the prohibited sexual conduct.

For example, the defendant engaged in a pattern of activity involving prohibited sexual conduct if there were two separate occasions of prohibited sexual conduct and each such occasion involved a different minor, or if there were two separate occasions of prohibited sexual conduct involving the same two minors.

(ii) Occasion of Prohibited Sexual Conduct.—An occasion of prohibited sexual conduct may be considered for purposes of subsection (b) without regard to whether the occasion (I) occurred during the course of the instant offense; or (II) resulted in a conviction for the conduct that occurred on that occasion.

5. Treatment and Monitoring.—

(A) Recommended Maximum Term of Supervised Release.—The statutory maximum term of supervised release is recommended for offenders sentenced under this guideline.

(B) Recommended Conditions of Probation and Supervised Release.—Treatment and monitoring are important tools for supervising offenders and should be considered as special conditions of any term of probation or supervised release that is imposed.

Background: This guideline is intended to provide lengthy incarceration for offenders who commit sex offenses against minors and who present a continuing danger to the public. It applies to offenders whose instant offense of conviction is a sex offense committed against a minor victim. The relevant criminal provisions provide for increased statutory maximum penalties for repeat sex offenders and make those increased statutory maximum penalties available if the defendant previously was convicted of any of several federal and state sex offenses (see 18 U.S.C. §§ 2247, 2426). In addition, section 632 of Pub. L. 102–141 and section 505 of Pub. L. 105–314 directed the Commission to ensure lengthy incarceration for offenders who engage in a pattern of activity involving the sexual abuse or exploitation of minors.".

Section 5B1.3(d) is amended by adding at the end the following:

"(7) Sex Offenses

If the instant offense of conviction is a sex offense, as defined in § 5D1.2 (Term of Supervised Release) -- a condition requiring the defendant to participate in a program approved by the United States Probation Office for the treatment and monitoring of sex offenders.".

Section 5D1.2 is amended by adding after subsection (b) the following:

"(c) If the instant offense of conviction is a sex offense, the statutory maximum term of supervised release is recommended.".

The Commentary to § 5D1.2 captioned "Application Notes" is amended by redesignating Notes 1 and 2 as Notes 2 and 3, respectively; by inserting before Note 2, as redesignated

Amendment 615

by this amendment, the following:

"1. Definition.—For purposes of this guideline, 'sex offense' means (A) an offense, perpetrated against a minor, under (i) chapter 109A of title 18, United States Code; (ii) chapter 110 of such title, not including a recordkeeping offense; or (iii) chapter 117 of such title, not including transmitting information about a minor or filing a factual statement about an alien individual; or (B) an attempt or a conspiracy to commit any offense described in subdivisions (A)(i) through (iii) of this note.";

in Note 2, as redesignated by this amendment, by inserting "Safety Valve Cases.—" before "A defendant"; and in Note 3, as redesignated by this amendment, by inserting "Substantial Assistance Cases.—" before "Upon motion".

Section 5D1.3(d) is amended by inserting at the end the following:

"(7) Sex Offenses

If the instant offense of conviction is a sex offense, as defined in § 5D1.2 (Term of Supervised Release) -- a condition requiring the defendant to participate in a program approved by the United States Probation Office for the treatment and monitoring of sex offenders.".

Reason for Amendment: This is a three-part amendment promulgated primarily in response to the Protection of Children from Sexual Predators Act of 1998, Pub. L. 105–314 (the "Act"), which contains several directives to the Commission. In furtherance of the directives, the Commission initiated a comprehensive examination of the guidelines under which most sex crimes are sentenced. Amendment 592, effective November 1, 2000, addressed a number of these directives. (See Amendment 592.)

The first part of the amendment addresses the Act's directive to increase penalties in any case in which the defendant engaged in a pattern of activity of sexual abuse or sexual exploitation of a minor. In response to this directive, the amendment provides a new Chapter Four (Criminal History and Criminal Livelihood) guideline, § 4B1.5 (Repeat and Dangerous Sex Offender Against Minors), that focuses on repeat child sex offenders. This new guideline works in a coordinated manner with § 4B1.1 (Career Offender) and creates a tiered approach to punishing repeat child sex offenders.

The first tier, in § 4B1.5(a), aims to incapacitate repeat child sex offenders who have an instant offense of conviction of sexual abuse of a minor and a prior felony conviction for sexual abuse of a minor (but to whom § 4B1.1 does not apply). This provision subjects a defendant to the greater of the offense level determined under Chapters Two and Three or the offense level obtained from a table that, like the table in § 4B1.1, bases the applicable offense level on the statutory maximum for the offense. In addition, the defendant is subject to an enhanced criminal history category of not less than Category V, similar to § 4B1.1 (which provides for Category VI). By statute, defendants convicted of a federal sex offense are subject to twice the statutory maximum penalty for a subsequent sex offense conviction. This guideline provision effectuates the Commission's and Congress's intent to punish repeat child sex offenders severely.

The second tier, in § 4B1.5(b), provides a five-level increase in the offense level and a minimum offense level of level 22 for defendants who are not subject to either § 4B1.1 or to § 4B1.5(a) and who have engaged in a pattern of activity involving prohibited sexual conduct with minors. This part of the guideline does not rely on prior convictions to increase the penalty for those who have a pattern of activity of sexual abuse or exploitation of a minor. The pattern of activity enhancement requires that the defendant engaged in prohibited sexual conduct on at least two separate occasions and that at least two minors were victims of the sexual conduct. This provision is similar to the existing five-level pattern of activity enhancement in subsection (b)(4) of § 2G2.2 (Trafficking in Material Involving the Sexual Exploitation of a Minor; Receiving, Transporting, Shipping, or Advertising Material Involving the Sexual Exploitation of a Minor; Possessing Material Involving the Sexual Exploitation of a Minor with Intent to Traffic) and effectuates the Commission's and Congress's intent to punish severely offenders who engage in a pattern of activity involving the sexual abuse or exploitation of minors.

Conforming amendments are made to the criminal sexual abuse guidelines in Chapter Two, Part A, Subpart 3 to delete the upward departure provisions for prior sentences for similar conduct; that factor is now taken into account in the new guideline.

In addition to creating a new guideline, this part of the amendment also modifies § 5D1.2 (Term of Supervised Release) to provide that the recommended term of supervised release for a defendant convicted of a sex crime is the maximum term authorized by statute. Amendments to §§ 5B1.3 (Conditions of Probation) and 5D1.3 (Conditions of Supervised Release) effectuate the Commission's intent that offenders who commit sex crimes receive appropriate treatment and monitoring.

The second part of the amendment addresses a circuit conflict regarding whether multiple counts of possession, receipt, or transportation of images containing child pornography should be grouped together pursuant to subsection (a) or (b) of § 3D1.2 (Groups of Closely Related Counts). Resolution of the conflict depends, in part, on determining who is the victim of the offense: the child depicted in the pornography images or society as a whole. Six circuits have held that the child depicted is the victim, and, therefore, that the counts are not grouped. See United States v. Norris, 159 F.3d 926 (5th Cir. 1998); United States v. Hibbler, 159 F.3d 233 (6th Cir. 1998); United States v. Ketcham, 80 F.3d 789 (3d Cir. 1996); United States v. Rugh, 968 F.2d 750 (8th Cir. 1992); United States v. Boos, 127 F.3d 1207 (9th Cir. 1997), cert. denied, 522 U.S. 1066 (1998); and United States v. Tillmon, 195 F.3d 640 (11th Cir. 1999). In contrast, one circuit has held that society as a whole is the victim of these types of offenses, and, therefore, that one count of interstate transportation of child pornography does not group with a count of interstate transportation of a minor with intent to engage in illegal sexual activity in a case in which the child portrayed in the pornography was the same child transported. See United States v. Toler, 901 F.2d 399 (4th Cir. 1990).

In addressing the circuit conflict, the Commission adopted a position that provides for grouping of multiple counts of child pornography distribution, receipt, and possession pursuant to § 3D1.2(d). Grouping multiple counts of these offenses pursuant to § 3D1.2(d) is appropriate because these offenses typically are continuous and ongoing enterprises. This grouping provision does not require the determination of whether counts involve the same victim in order to calculate a combined adjusted offense level for multiple counts of conviction which, particularly in these kinds of cases, could be complex and time consuming. Consistent with the provisions of subsection (a)(2) of § 1B1.3 (Relevant Conduct), this approach provides that additional images of child pornography (often involved in the case, but outside of the offense of conviction) shall be considered by the court in determining the appropriate sentence for the defendant if the conduct related to those images is part of the same course of conduct or common scheme or plan.

The third part of the amendment makes several modifications to § 2A3.2 (Criminal Sexual Abuse of a Minor Under the Age of Sixteen Years (Statutory Rape) or Attempt to Commit

Amendment 615 APPENDIX C - VOLUME II November 1, 2013

Such Acts). The amendment responds to the directive in the Act to provide an enhancement for offenses under chapter 117 of title 18, United States Code, involving the transportation of minors for prostitution or prohibited sexual conduct. The amendment increases the offense levels in § 2A3.2 and in § 2A3.4 (Abusive Sexual Contact or Attempt to Commit Abusive Sexual Contact). The Act focuses on those individuals who travel to meet or transport minors for illegal sexual activity by providing increased statutory maximum penalties for those individuals. In response, the increase in penalties in these guidelines were geared toward those individuals. Specifically, the amendment distinguishes between chapter 117 offenses that involve the commission of a sexual act or sexual contact and those offenses (e.g., sting cases) that do not, by providing an alternative base offense level in § 2A3.2 for chapter 117 offenses that also involve the commission of a sexual act or sexual contact that is three levels greater (i.e., level 24) than the base offense level applicable to chapter 117 offenses that do not involve a sexual act or sexual contact.

The amendment provides a three-level increase in the base offense level for offenses sentenced under § 2A3.2, such that the base offense level (1) for statutory rape unaccompanied by aggravating conduct is increased from level 15 to level 18; (2) for a chapter 117 offense (unaccompanied by a sexual act or sexual contact) is increased from level 18 to level 21; and (3) for a chapter 117 offense (accompanied by a sexual act or sexual contact) results in a base offense level of level 24. The amendment reflects the seriousness accorded criminal sexual abuse offenses by Congress, which provided for statutory maximum penalties of 15 years' imprisonment (or 30 years' imprisonment with a prior conviction for a sex crime). A defendant who transmits child pornography to a minor as a means of enticing the minor to engage in illegal sexual activity will receive a sentence increase when that defendant subsequently travels across state lines to engage in illegal sexual activity with that minor. Therefore, this increase also maintains the proportionality between §§ 2A3.2 and 2G2.2.

The third part of the amendment also makes conforming changes to § 2A3.2 to ensure that some chapter 117 offenses that do not include aggravating conduct receive the offense level applicable to statutory rape in its basic form. Technical changes made by the amendment (such as the addition of headings and the reordering of applications notes) are not intended to have substantive effect.

Effective Date: The effective date of this amendment is November 1, 2001.

616. **Amendment:** Section 2A6.2(a) is amended by striking "14" and inserting "18".

Section 2A6.2(c) is amended by striking subdivision (1) as follows:

"(1) If the offense involved conduct covered by another offense guideline from Chapter Two, Part A (Offenses Against the Person), apply that offense guideline, if the resulting offense level is greater than that determined above.",

and inserting the following:

"(1) If the offense involved the commission of another criminal offense, apply the offense guideline from Chapter Two, Part A (Offenses Against the Person) most applicable to that other criminal offense, if the resulting offense level is greater than that determined above.".

The Commentary to § 2A6.2 captioned "Application Notes" is amended in Note 1 by striking the 1-em dash and inserting a colon; and by striking the last paragraph as follows:

"'Stalking' means traveling with the intent to injure or harass another person and, in the course of, or as a result of, such travel, placing the person in reasonable fear of death or serious bodily injury to the person or the person's immediate family. See 18 U.S.C. § 2261A. 'Immediate family' has the meaning set forth in 18 U.S.C. § 115(c)(2).",

and inserting the following:

"'Stalking' means (A) traveling with the intent to kill, injure, harass, or intimidate another person and, in the course of, or as a result of, such travel, placing the person in reasonable fear of death or serious bodily injury to that person or an immediate family member of that person; or (B) using the mail or any facility of interstate or foreign commerce to engage in a course of conduct that places that person in reasonable fear of the death of, or serious bodily injury to, that person or an immediate family member of that person. See 18 U.S.C. § 2261A. 'Immediate family member' (A) has the meaning given that term in 18 U.S.C. § 115(c)(2); and (B) includes a spouse or intimate partner. 'Course of conduct' and 'spouse or intimate partner' have the meaning given those terms in 18 U.S.C. § 2266(2) and (7), respectively.".

The Commentary to § 1B1.5 captioned "Application Notes" is amended in Note 3 by inserting after the first sentence the following:

"Consistent with the provisions of § 1B1.3 (Relevant Conduct), such other offense includes conduct that may be a state or local offense and conduct that occurred under circumstances that would constitute a federal offense had the conduct taken place within the territorial or maritime jurisdiction of the United States.".

Reason for Amendment: This amendment addresses section 1107 of the Victims of Trafficking and Violence Protection Act of 2000, Pub. L 106–386 (the "Act"). That section amends 18 U.S.C. §§ 2261, 2261A, and 2262 to broaden the reach of those statutes to include international travel to stalk, commit domestic violence, or violate a protective order. Section 2261A also is amended to broaden the category of persons protected by this statute to include intimate partners of the person stalked. The Act also creates a new offense at section 2261A(2) that prohibits the use of the mail or any facility of interstate or foreign commerce to commit a stalking offense. Several technical changes were also made to these statutes.

The Act includes a directive to the Commission to amend the federal sentencing guidelines to reflect the changes made to 18 U.S.C. § 2261, with specific consideration to be given to the following factors: (1) whether the guidelines relating to stalking offenses should be modified in light of the amendment made by this subsection; and (2) whether any changes the Commission may make to the guidelines pursuant to clause (1) should also be made with respect to offenses under chapter 110A of title 18, United States Code (stalking and domestic violence offenses).

For several reasons, the amendment refers the new stalking by mail offense, like other stalking offenses, to § 2A6.2 (Stalking or Domestic Violence). First, the statutory penalties for stalking by mail are the same as the statutory penalties for other stalking offenses. Second, although there was some consideration to refer this new offense to § 2A6.1 (Threatening or Harassing Communications), stalking by mail offenses differ significantly from threatening communications in that the former require the defendant's intent to kill, or injure a person, or place a person in reasonable fear of death or serious bodily injury. Third, referencing stalking by mail offenses to § 2A6.1 could result in these offenses receiving higher penalties than other stalking offenses. For example, a defendant who writes a threatening letter, violates a protective order, and engages in some conduct evidencing an intent to carry out such threat, would receive an offense level of level 20 under § 2A6.1. A defendant who engages in stalking by mail, violates a protective order, and actually commits bodily injury on the person who is the subject of the protection order would have received, prior to this amendment, an offense level of level 18 under § 2A6.2. This amendment reflects the policy judgment that the second defendant should receive punishment equal to, or perhaps greater than, that received by the first defendant. Accordingly, because of concern for proportionality in sentencing stalking and domestic violence offenses relative to other crimes, such as threatening or harassing communications, this amendment increases the base offense level in § 2A6.2 from level 14 to level 18. Setting the base offense level at level 18 for stalking and domestic violence crimes ensures that these offenses are sentenced at or above the offense levels for offenses involving threatening and harassing communications.

The amendment also conforms the definition of "stalking" in Application Note 1 of § 2A6.2 to the statutory changes made by the Act. Additionally, the amendment modifies the language of subsection (c) in § 2A6.2 to clarify application of the cross reference. This change is consistent with the amendment to Application Note 3 of § 1B1.5 (Interpretation of References to Other Offense Guidelines), which also clarifies the operation of cross references generally.

These revisions are designed to clarify that, unless otherwise specified, cross references in Chapter Two (Offense Conduct) are to be determined consistently with the provisions of § 1B1.3 (Relevant Conduct). Therefore, in a case in which the guideline includes a reference to use another guideline if the conduct involved another offense, the other offense includes conduct that may be a state or local offense and conduct that occurred under circumstances that would constitute a federal offense had the conduct taken place within the territorial or maritime jurisdiction of the United States.

Effective Date: The effective date of this amendment is November 1, 2001.

617. **Amendment:** Chapter Two is amended by striking the heading to Part B, the heading to Subpart 1 of Part B, and the Introductory Commentary to such subpart as follows:

"   PART B - OFFENSES INVOLVING PROPERTY

1.   THEFT, EMBEZZLEMENT, RECEIPT OF STOLEN PROPERTY, AND PROPERTY DESTRUCTION

Introductory Commentary

These sections address the most basic forms of property offenses: theft, embezzlement, transactions in stolen goods, and simple property damage or destruction. (Arson is dealt with separately in Part K, Offenses Involving Public Safety.) These guidelines apply to offenses prosecuted under a wide variety of federal statutes, as well as offenses that arise under the Assimilative Crimes Act.",

and inserting the following:

"   PART B - BASIC ECONOMIC OFFENSES

1.   THEFT, EMBEZZLEMENT, RECEIPT OF STOLEN PROPERTY, PROPERTY DESTRUCTION, AND OFFENSES INVOLVING FRAUD OR DECEIT

November 1, 2013 — APPENDIX C - VOLUME II — **Amendment 617**

Introductory Commentary

These sections address basic forms of property offenses: theft, embezzlement, fraud, forgery, counterfeiting (other than offenses involving altered or counterfeit bearer obligations of the United States), insider trading, transactions in stolen goods, and simple property damage or destruction. (Arson is dealt with separately in Chapter Two, Part K (Offenses Involving Public Safety)). These guidelines apply to offenses prosecuted under a wide variety of federal statutes, as well as offenses that arise under the Assimilative Crimes Act.".

Chapter Two, Part B is amended by striking § 2B1.1, and its accompanying commentary, as follows:

"§ 2B1.1. Larceny, Embezzlement, and Other Forms of Theft; Receiving, Transporting, Transferring, Transmitting, or Possessing Stolen Property

    (a)   Base Offense Level: 4

    (b)   Specific Offense Characteristics

        (1)   If the loss exceeded $100, increase the offense level as follows:

	Loss (Apply the Greatest)	Increase in Level
(A)	$100 or less	no increase
(B)	More than $100	add 1
(C)	More than $1,000	add 2
(D)	More than $2,000	add 3
(E)	More than $5,000	add 4
(F)	More than $10,000	add 5
(G)	More than $20,000	add 6
(H)	More than $40,000	add 7
(I)	More than $70,000	add 8
(J)	More than $120,000	add 9
(K)	More than $200,000	add 10
(L)	More than $350,000	add 11
(M)	More than $500,000	add 12
(N)	More than $800,000	add 13
(O)	More than $1,500,000	add 14
(P)	More than $2,500,000	add 15
(Q)	More than $5,000,000	add 16
(R)	More than $10,000,000	add 17
(S)	More than $20,000,000	add 18
(T)	More than $40,000,000	add 19
(U)	More than $80,000,000	add 20.

        (2)   If the theft was from the person of another, increase by 2 levels.

        (3)   If (A) undelivered United States mail was taken, or the tak-

ing of such item was an object of the offense; or (B) the stolen property received, transported, transferred, transmitted, or possessed was undelivered United States mail, and the offense level as determined above is less than level 6, increase to level 6.

(4) (A) If the offense involved more than minimal planning, increase by 2 levels; or

(B) If the offense involved receiving stolen property, and the defendant was a person in the business of receiving and selling stolen property, increase by 4 levels.

(5) If the offense involved an organized scheme to steal vehicles or vehicle parts, and the offense level as determined above is less than level 14, increase to level 14.

(6) If the offense --

(A) substantially jeopardized the safety and soundness of a financial institution; or

(B) affected a financial institution and the defendant derived more than $1,000,000 in gross receipts from the offense,

increase by 4 levels. If the resulting offense level is less than level 24, increase to level 24.

(7) If the offense involved misappropriation of a trade secret and the defendant knew or intended that the offense would benefit any foreign government, foreign instrumentality, or foreign agent, increase by 2 levels.

(8) If the offense involved theft of property from a national cemetery, increase by 2 levels.

(c) Cross Reference

(1) If (A) a firearm, destructive device, explosive material, or controlled substance was taken, or the taking of such item was an object of the offense, or (B) the stolen property received, transported, transferred, transmitted, or possessed was a firearm, destructive device, explosive material, or controlled substance, apply § 2D1.1 (Unlawful Manufacturing, Importing, Exporting, or Trafficking; Attempt or Conspiracy), § 2D2.1 (Unlawful Possession; Attempt or Conspiracy), § 2K1.3 (Unlawful Receipt, Possession, or Transportation of Explosive Materials; Prohibited Transactions Involving Explosive Materials), or § 2K2.1 (Unlawful Receipt, Possession, or Transportation of Firearms or Ammunition; Prohibited Transactions Involving Firearms or Ammunition), as appropriate, if the resulting offense level is greater than that determined above.

Commentary

Statutory Provisions: 18 U.S.C. §§ 225, 553(a)(1), 641, 656, 657, 659, 662, 664, 1702, 1708, 1831, 1832, 2113(b), 2312-2317; 29 U.S.C. § 501(c). For additional statutory provision(s), see Appendix A (Statutory Index).

Application Notes:

1. 'More than minimal planning,' 'firearm,' and 'destructive device' are defined in the Commentary to § 1B1.1 (Application Instructions).

   'Trade secret' is defined in 18 U.S.C. § 1839(3).

   'Foreign instrumentality' and 'foreign agent' are defined in 18 U.S.C. § 1839(1) and (2), respectively.

   'National cemetery' means a cemetery (A) established under section 2400 of title 38, United States Code; or (B) under the jurisdiction of the Secretary of the Army, the Secretary of the Navy, the Secretary of the Air Force, or the Secretary of the Interior.

2. 'Loss' means the value of the property taken, damaged, or destroyed. Ordinarily, when property is taken or destroyed the loss is the fair market value of the particular property at issue. Where the market value is difficult to ascertain or inadequate to measure harm to the victim, the court may measure loss in some other way, such as reasonable replacement cost to the victim. Loss does not include the interest that could have been earned had the funds not been stolen. When property is damaged, the loss is the cost of repairs, not to exceed the loss had the property been destroyed. Examples: (1) In the case of a theft of a check or money order, the loss is the loss that would have occurred if the check or money order had been cashed. (2) In the case of a defendant apprehended taking a vehicle, the loss is the value of the vehicle even if the vehicle is recovered immediately.

   If the offense involved making a fraudulent loan or credit card application, or other unlawful conduct involving a loan, a counterfeit access device, or an unauthorized access device, the loss is to be determined in accordance with the Commentary to § 2F1.1 (Fraud and Deceit). For example, in accordance with Application Note 17 of the Commentary to § 2F1.1, in a case involving an unauthorized access device (such as a stolen credit card), loss includes any unauthorized charge(s) made with the access device. In such a case, the loss shall be not less than $500 per unauthorized access device. For purposes of this application note, 'counterfeit access device' and 'unauthorized access device' have the meaning given those terms in 18 U.S.C. § 1029(e)(2) and (e)(3), respectively.

   In certain cases, an offense may involve a series of transactions without a corresponding increase in loss. For example, a defendant may embezzle $5,000 from a bank and conceal this embezzlement by shifting this amount from one account to another in a series of nine transactions over a six-month period. In this example, the loss is $5,000 (the amount taken), not $45,000 (the sum of the nine transactions), because the additional transactions did not increase the actual or potential loss.

   In stolen property offenses (receiving, transporting, transferring, transmit-

Amendment 617 APPENDIX C - VOLUME II November 1, 2013

ting, or possessing stolen property), the loss is the value of the stolen property determined as in a theft offense.

In an offense involving unlawfully accessing, or exceeding authorized access to, a 'protected computer' as defined in 18 U.S.C. § 1030(e)(2)(A) or (B), 'loss' includes the reasonable cost to the victim of conducting a damage assessment, restoring the system and data to their condition prior to the offense, and any lost revenue due to interruption of service.

In the case of a partially completed offense (e.g., an offense involving a completed theft that is part of a larger, attempted theft), the offense level is to be determined in accordance with the provisions of § 2X1.1 (Attempt, Solicitation, or Conspiracy) whether the conviction is for the substantive offense, the inchoate offense (attempt, solicitation, or conspiracy), or both; see Application Note 4 in the Commentary to § 2X1.1.

3. For the purposes of subsection (b)(1), the loss need not be determined with precision. The court need only make a reasonable estimate of the loss, given the available information. This estimate, for example, may be based upon the approximate number of victims and the average loss to each victim, or on more general factors such as the scope and duration of the offense.

4. Controlled substances should be valued at their estimated street value.

5. 'Undelivered United States mail' means mail that has not actually been received by the addressee or his agent (e.g., it includes mail that is in the addressee's mail box).

6. 'From the person of another' refers to property, taken without the use of force, that was being held by another person or was within arms' reach. Examples include pick-pocketing or non-forcible purse-snatching, such as the theft of a purse from a shopping cart.

7. Subsection (b)(5), referring to an 'organized scheme to steal vehicles or vehicle parts,' provides an alternative minimum measure of loss in the case of an ongoing, sophisticated operation such as an auto theft ring or 'chop shop.' 'Vehicles' refers to all forms of vehicles, including aircraft and watercraft.

8. 'Financial institution,' as used in this guideline, is defined to include any institution described in 18 U.S.C. §§ 20, 656, 657, 1005-1007, and 1014; any state or foreign bank, trust company, credit union, insurance company, investment company, mutual fund, savings (building and loan) association, union or employee pension fund; any health, medical or hospital insurance association; brokers and dealers registered, or required to be registered, with the Securities and Exchange Commission; futures commodity merchants and commodity pool operators registered, or required to be registered, with the Commodity Futures Trading Commission; and any similar entity, whether or not insured by the federal government. 'Union or employee pension fund' and 'any health, medical, or hospital insurance association,' as used above, primarily include large pension funds that serve many individuals (e.g., pension funds of large national and international organizations, unions, and corporations doing substantial interstate busi-

ness), and associations that undertake to provide pension, disability, or other benefits (e.g., medical or hospitalization insurance) to large numbers of persons.

9. An offense shall be deemed to have 'substantially jeopardized the safety and soundness of a financial institution' if, as a consequence of the offense, the institution became insolvent; substantially reduced benefits to pensioners or insureds; was unable on demand to refund fully any deposit, payment, or investment; was so depleted of its assets as to be forced to merge with another institution in order to continue active operations; or was placed in substantial jeopardy of any of the above.

10. 'The defendant derived more than $1,000,000 in gross receipts from the offense,' as used in subsection (b)(6)(B), generally means that the gross receipts to the defendant individually, rather than to all participants, exceeded $1,000,000. 'Gross receipts from the offense' includes all property, real or personal, tangible or intangible, which is obtained directly or indirectly as a result of such offense. See 18 U.S.C. § 982(a)(4).

11. If the defendant is convicted under 18 U.S.C. § 225 (relating to a continuing financial crimes enterprise), the offense level is that applicable to the underlying series of offenses comprising the 'continuing financial crimes enterprise.'

12. If subsection (b)(6)(A) or (B) applies, there shall be a rebuttable presumption that the offense involved 'more than minimal planning.'

13. If the offense involved theft or embezzlement from an employee pension or welfare benefit plan (a violation of 18 U.S.C. § 664) and the defendant was a fiduciary of the benefit plan, an adjustment under § 3B1.3 (Abuse of Position of Trust or Use of Special Skill) will apply. 'Fiduciary of the benefit plan' is defined in 29 U.S.C. § 1002(21)(A) to mean a person who exercises any discretionary authority or control in respect to the management of such plan or exercises authority or control in respect to management or disposition of its assets, or who renders investment advice for a fee or other direct or indirect compensation with respect to any moneys or other property of such plan, or has any authority or responsibility to do so, or who has any discretionary authority or responsibility in the administration of such plan.

If the offense involved theft or embezzlement from a labor union (a violation of 29 U.S.C. § 501(c)) and the defendant was a union officer or occupied a position of trust in the union as set forth in 29 U.S.C. § 501(a), an adjustment under § 3B1.3 (Abuse of Position of Trust or Use of Special Skill) will apply.

14. In cases where the loss determined under subsection (b)(1) does not fully capture the harmfulness of the conduct, an upward departure may be warranted. For example, the theft of personal information or writings (e.g., medical records, educational records, a diary) may involve a substantial invasion of a privacy interest that would not be addressed by the monetary loss provisions of subsection (b)(1).

15. In cases involving theft of information from a 'protected computer', as defined in 18 U.S.C. § 1030(e)(2)(A) or (B), an upward departure may be

warranted where the defendant sought the stolen information to further a broader criminal purpose.

Background: The value of the property stolen plays an important role in determining sentences for theft and other offenses involving stolen property because it is an indicator of both the harm to the victim and the gain to the defendant. Because of the structure of the Sentencing Table (Chapter 5, Part A), subsection (b)(1) results in an overlapping range of enhancements based on the loss.

The guidelines provide an enhancement for more than minimal planning, which includes most offense behavior involving affirmative acts on multiple occasions. Planning and repeated acts are indicative of an intention and potential to do considerable harm. Also, planning is often related to increased difficulties of detection and proof.

Consistent with statutory distinctions, an increased minimum offense level is provided for the theft of undelivered mail. Theft of undelivered mail interferes with a governmental function, and the scope of the theft may be difficult to ascertain.

Theft from the person of another, such as pickpocketing or non-forcible purse-snatching, receives an enhanced sentence because of the increased risk of physical injury. This guideline does not include an enhancement for thefts from the person by means of force or fear; such crimes are robberies.

A minimum offense level of 14 is provided for offenses involving an organized scheme to steal vehicles or vehicle parts. Typically, the scope of such activity is substantial (i.e., the value of the stolen property, combined with an enhancement for 'more than minimal planning' would itself result in an offense level of at least 14), but the value of the property is particularly difficult to ascertain in individual cases because the stolen property is rapidly resold or otherwise disposed of in the course of the offense. Therefore, the specific offense characteristic of 'organized scheme' is used as an alternative to 'loss' in setting the offense level.

Subsection (b)(6)(A) implements, in a broader form, the instruction to the Commission in section 961(m) of Public Law 101-73.

Subsection (b)(6)(B) implements the instruction to the Commission in section 2507 of Public Law 101-647.

Subsection (b)(8) implements the instruction to the Commission in section 2 of Public Law 105–101.".

A replacement guideline with accompanying commentary is inserted as § 2B1.1 (Larceny, Embezzlement, and Other Forms of Theft; Offenses Involving Stolen Property; Property Damage or Destruction; Fraud and Deceit; Forgery; Offenses Involving Altered or Counterfeit Instruments Other than Counterfeit Bearer Obligations of the United States).

Chapter Two, Part B is amended by striking § 2B1.3 and its accompanying commentary as follows:

"§ 2B1.3.   Property Damage or Destruction

    (a)   Base Offense Level: 4

    (b)   Specific Offense Characteristics

        (1)   If the loss exceeded $100, increase by the corresponding number of levels from the table in § 2B1.1.

(2) If undelivered United States mail was destroyed, and the offense level as determined above is less than level 6, increase to level 6.

(3) If the offense involved more than minimal planning, increase by 2 levels.

(4) If property of a national cemetery was damaged or destroyed, increase by 2 levels.

(c) Cross Reference

(1) If the offense involved arson, or property damage by use of explosives, apply § 2K1.4 (Arson; Property Damage by Use of Explosives).

(d) Special Instruction

(1) If the defendant is convicted under 18 U.S.C. § 1030(a)(5), the minimum guideline sentence, notwithstanding any other adjustment, shall be six months' imprisonment.

Commentary

Statutory Provisions: 18 U.S.C. §§ 1030(a)(5), 1361, 1363, 1702, 1703 (if vandalism or malicious mischief, including destruction of mail is involved). For additional statutory provision(s), see Appendix A (Statutory Index).

Application Notes:

1. 'More than minimal planning' is defined in the Commentary to § 1B1.1 (Application Instructions).

   'National cemetery' means a cemetery (A) established under section 2400 of title 38, United States Code; or (B) under the jurisdiction of the Secretary of the Army, the Secretary of the Navy, the Secretary of the Air Force, or the Secretary of the Interior.

2. Valuation of loss is discussed in the Commentary to § 2B1.1 (Larceny, Embezzlement, and Other Forms of Theft).

3. 'Undelivered United States mail' means mail that has not been received by the addressee or his agent (e.g., it includes mail that is in the addressee's mailbox).

4. In some cases, the monetary value of the property damaged or destroyed may not adequately reflect the extent of the harm caused. For example, the destruction of a $500 telephone line or interference with a telecommunications network may cause an interruption in service to thousands of people for several hours, with attendant life-threatening delay in the delivery of emergency medical treatment or disruption of other important governmental or private services. In such cases, an upward departure may be warranted. See §§ 5K2.2 (Physical Injury), 5K2.7 (Disruption of Governmental Function), and 5K2.14 (Public Welfare).

Background: Subsection (b)(4) implements the instruction to the Commission in section 2 of Public Law 105–101.

Amendment 617   APPENDIX C - VOLUME II   November 1, 2013

    Subsection (d) implements the instruction to the Commission in section 805(c) of Public Law 104-132.".

Chapter Two is amended by striking Part F in its entirety as follows:

"PART F - OFFENSES INVOLVING FRAUD OR DECEIT

§ 2F1.1.   Fraud and Deceit; Forgery; Offenses Involving Altered or Counterfeit Instruments Other than Counterfeit Bearer Obligations of the United States

    (a)   Base Offense Level: 6

    (b)   Specific Offense Characteristics

        (1)   If the loss exceeded $2,000, increase the offense level as follows:

	Loss (Apply the Greatest)	Increase in Level
(A)	$2,000 or less	no increase
(B)	More than $2,000	add 1
(C)	More than $5,000	add 2
(D)	More than $10,000	add 3
(E)	More than $20,000	add 4
(F)	More than $40,000	add 5
(G)	More than $70,000	add 6
(H)	More than $120,000	add 7
(I)	More than $200,000	add 8
(J)	More than $350,000	add 9
(K)	More than $500,000	add 10
(L)	More than $800,000	add 11
(M)	More than $1,500,000	add 12
(N)	More than $2,500,000	add 13
(O)	More than $5,000,000	add 14
(P)	More than $10,000,000	add 15
(Q)	More than $20,000,000	add 16
(R)	More than $40,000,000	add 17
(S)	More than $80,000,000	add 18.

        (2)   If the offense involved (A) more than minimal planning, or (B) a scheme to defraud more than one victim, increase by 2 levels.

        (3)   If the offense was committed through mass-marketing, increase by 2 levels.

        (4)   If the offense involved (A) a misrepresentation that the defendant was acting on behalf of a charitable, educational, religious or political organization, or a government agency; (B) a misrepresentation or other fraudulent action during the course of a bankruptcy proceeding; or (C) a violation of

any prior, specific judicial or administrative order, injunction, decree, or process not addressed elsewhere in the guidelines, increase by 2 levels. If the resulting offense level is less than level 10, increase to level 10.

(5) If the offense involved—

    (A) the possession or use of any device-making equipment;

    (B) the production or trafficking of any unauthorized access device or counterfeit access device; or

    (C) (i) the unauthorized transfer or use of any means of identification unlawfully to produce or obtain any other means of identification; or (ii) the possession of 5 or more means of identification that unlawfully were produced from another means of identification or obtained by the use of another means of identification,

increase by 2 levels. If the resulting offense level is less than level 12, increase to level 12.

(6) If (A) the defendant relocated, or participated in relocating, a fraudulent scheme to another jurisdiction to evade law enforcement or regulatory officials; (B) a substantial part of a fraudulent scheme was committed from outside the United States; or (C) the offense otherwise involved sophisticated means, increase by 2 levels. If the resulting offense level is less than level 12, increase to level 12.

(7) If the offense involved (A) the conscious or reckless risk of serious bodily injury; or (B) possession of a dangerous weapon (including a firearm) in connection with the offense, increase by 2 levels. If the resulting offense level is less than level 13, increase to level 13.

(8) If the offense -

    (A) substantially jeopardized the safety and soundness of a financial institution; or

    (B) affected a financial institution and the defendant derived more than $1,000,000 in gross receipts from the offense,

increase by 4 levels. If the resulting offense level is less than level 24, increase to level 24.

(c) Special Instruction

(1) If the defendant is convicted under 18 U.S.C. § 1030(a)(4), the minimum guideline sentence, notwithstanding any other adjustment, shall be six months' imprisonment.

Amendment 617 APPENDIX C - VOLUME II November 1, 2013

Commentary

Statutory Provisions: 7 U.S.C. §§ 6, 6b, 6c, 6h, 6o, 13, 23; 15 U.S.C. §§ 50, 77e, 77q, 77x, 78j, 78ff, 80b-6, 1644; 18 U.S.C. §§ 225, 285-289, 471-473, 500, 510, 659, 1001-1008, 1010-1014, 1016-1022, 1025, 1026, 1028, 1029, 1030(a)(4), 1031, 1341-1344, 2314, 2315. For additional statutory provision(s), see Appendix A (Statutory Index).

Application Notes:

1. The adjustments in § 2F1.1(b)(4) are alternative rather than cumulative. If in a particular case, however, both of the enumerated factors applied, an upward departure might be warranted.

2. 'More than minimal planning' (subsection (b)(2)(A)) is defined in the Commentary to § 1B1.1 (Application Instructions).

3. 'Mass-marketing,' as used in subsection (b)(3), means a plan, program, promotion, or campaign that is conducted through solicitation by telephone, mail, the Internet, or other means to induce a large number of persons to (A) purchase goods or services; (B) participate in a contest or sweepstakes; or (C) invest for financial profit. The enhancement would apply, for example, if the defendant conducted or participated in a telemarketing campaign that solicited a large number of individuals to purchase fraudulent life insurance policies.

4. 'Scheme to defraud more than one victim,' as used in subsection (b)(2)(B), refers to a design or plan to obtain something of value from more than one person. In this context, "victim" refers to the person or entity from which the funds are to come directly. Thus, a wire fraud in which a single telephone call was made to three distinct individuals to get each of them to invest in a pyramid scheme would involve a scheme to defraud more than one victim, but passing a fraudulently endorsed check would not, even though the maker, payee and/or payor all might be considered victims for other purposes, such as restitution.

5. Subsection (b)(4)(A) provides an adjustment for a misrepresentation that the defendant was acting on behalf of a charitable, educational, religious or political organization, or a government agency. Examples of conduct to which this factor applies would include a group of defendants who solicit contributions to a non-existent famine relief organization by mail, a defendant who diverts donations for a religiously affiliated school by telephone solicitations to church members in which the defendant falsely claims to be a fund-raiser for the school, or a defendant who poses as a federal collection agent in order to collect a delinquent student loan.

6. Subsection (b)(4)(C) provides an enhancement if the defendant commits a fraud in contravention of a prior, official judicial or administrative warning, in the form of an order, injunction, decree, or process, to take or not to take a specified action. A defendant who does not comply with such a prior, official judicial or administrative warning demonstrates aggravated criminal intent and deserves additional punishment. If it is established that an entity the defendant controlled was a party to the prior proceeding that resulted in the official judicial or administrative action, and the defendant had knowl-

edge of that prior decree or order, this enhancement applies even if the defendant was not a specifically named party in that prior case. For example, a defendant whose business previously was enjoined from selling a dangerous product, but who nonetheless engaged in fraudulent conduct to sell the product, is subject to this enhancement. This enhancement does not apply if the same conduct resulted in an enhancement pursuant to a provision found elsewhere in the guidelines (e.g., a violation of a condition of release addressed in § 2J1.7 (Commission of Offense While on Release) or a violation of probation addressed in § 4A1.1 (Criminal History Category)).

If the conduct that forms the basis for an enhancement under (b)(4)(B) or (C) is the only conduct that forms the basis for an adjustment under § 3C1.1 (Obstruction of Justice), do not apply an adjustment under § 3C1.1.

7. Some fraudulent schemes may result in multiple-count indictments, depending on the technical elements of the offense. The cumulative loss produced by a common scheme or course of conduct should be used in determining the offense level, regardless of the number of counts of conviction. See Chapter Three, Part D (Multiple Counts).

8. Valuation of loss is discussed in the Commentary to § 2B1.1 (Larceny, Embezzlement, and Other Forms of Theft). As in theft cases, loss is the value of the money, property, or services unlawfully taken; it does not, for example, include interest the victim could have earned on such funds had the offense not occurred. Consistent with the provisions of § 2X1.1 (Attempt, Solicitation, or Conspiracy), if an intended loss that the defendant was attempting to inflict can be determined, this figure will be used if it is greater than the actual loss. Frequently, loss in a fraud case will be the same as in a theft case. For example, if the fraud consisted of selling or attempting to sell $40,000 in worthless securities, or representing that a forged check for $40,000 was genuine, the loss would be $40,000.

There are, however, instances where additional factors are to be considered in determining the loss or intended loss:

(a) Fraud Involving Misrepresentation of the Value of an Item or Product Substitution

A fraud may involve the misrepresentation of the value of an item that does have some value (in contrast to an item that is worthless). Where, for example, a defendant fraudulently represents that stock is worth $40,000 and the stock is worth only $10,000, the loss is the amount by which the stock was overvalued (i.e., $30,000). In a case involving a misrepresentation concerning the quality of a consumer product, the loss is the difference between the amount paid by the victim for the product and the amount for which the victim could resell the product received.

(b) Fraudulent Loan Application and Contract Procurement Cases

In fraudulent loan application cases and contract procurement cases, the loss is the actual loss to the victim (or if the loss has not yet come about, the expected loss). For example, if a defendant fraudulently obtains a loan by misrepresenting the value of his assets, the loss is the amount of the loan not repaid at the time the offense is discovered, reduced by the amount the lending institution has recovered (or can expect to recover) from any assets pledged to secure the loan. However, where the intended loss is greater than the actual loss, the intended loss is to be used.

In some cases, the loss determined above may significantly understate or overstate the seriousness of the defendant's conduct. For example, where the defendant substantially understated his debts to obtain a loan, which he nevertheless repaid, the loss determined above (zero loss) will tend not to reflect adequately the risk of loss created by the defendant's conduct. Conversely, a defendant may understate his debts to a limited degree to obtain a loan (e.g., to expand a grain export business), which he genuinely expected to repay and for which he would have qualified at a higher interest rate had he made truthful disclosure, but he is unable to repay the loan because of some unforeseen event (e.g., an embargo imposed on grain exports) which would have caused a default in any event. In such a case, the loss determined above may overstate the seriousness of the defendant's conduct. Where the loss determined above significantly understates or overstates the seriousness of the defendant's conduct, an upward or downward departure may be warranted.

(c) Consequential Damages in Procurement Fraud and Product Substitution Cases

In contrast to other types of cases, loss in a procurement fraud or product substitution case includes not only direct damages, but also consequential damages that were reasonably foreseeable. For example, in a case involving a defense product substitution offense, the loss includes the government's reasonably foreseeable costs of making substitute transactions and handling or disposing of the product delivered or retrofitting the product so that it can be used for its intended purpose, plus the government's reasonably foreseeable cost of rectifying the actual or potential disruption to government operations caused by the product substitution. Similarly, in the case of fraud affecting a defense contract award, loss includes the reasonably foreseeable administrative cost to the government and other participants of repeating or correcting the procurement action affected, plus any increased cost to procure the product or service involved that was reasonably foreseeable. Inclusion of reasonably foreseeable consequential damages directly in the calculation of loss in procurement fraud and product substitution cases reflects that such damages frequently are substantial in such cases.

(d) Diversion of Government Program Benefits

In a case involving diversion of government program benefits, loss is the value of the benefits diverted from intended recipients or uses.

(e) Davis-Bacon Act Cases

In a case involving a Davis-Bacon Act violation (a violation of 40 U.S.C. § 276a, criminally prosecuted under 18 U.S.C. § 1001), the loss is the difference between the legally required and actual wages paid.

9. For the purposes of subsection (b)(1), the loss need not be determined with precision. The court need only make a reasonable estimate of the loss, given the available information. This estimate, for example, may be based on the approximate number of victims and an estimate of the average loss to each victim, or on more general factors, such as the nature and duration of the fraud and the revenues generated by similar operations. The offender's gain from committing the fraud is an alternative estimate that ordinarily will underestimate the loss.

10. In the case of a partially completed offense (e.g., an offense involving a completed fraud that is part of a larger, attempted fraud), the offense level is to be determined in accordance with the provisions of § 2X1.1 (Attempt, Solicitation, or Conspiracy) whether the conviction is for the substantive offense, the inchoate offense (attempt, solicitation, or conspiracy), or both; see Application Note 4 in the Commentary to § 2X1.1.

11. In cases in which the loss determined under subsection (b)(1) does not fully capture the harmfulness and seriousness of the conduct, an upward departure may be warranted. Examples may include the following:

    (a) a primary objective of the fraud was non-monetary; or the fraud caused or risked reasonably foreseeable, substantial non-monetary harm;

    (b) false statements were made for the purpose of facilitating some other crime;

    (c) the offense caused reasonably foreseeable, physical or psychological harm or severe emotional trauma;

    (d) the offense endangered national security or military readiness;

    (e) the offense caused a loss of confidence in an important institution;

    (f) the offense involved the knowing endangerment of the solvency of one or more victims.

    In a few instances, the loss determined under subsection (b)(1) may overstate the seriousness of the offense. This may occur, for example, where a defendant attempted to negotiate an instrument that was so obviously fraudulent that no one would seriously consider honoring it. In such cases, a downward departure may be warranted.

12. Offenses involving access devices, in violation of 18 U.S.C. §§ 1028 and 1029, are also covered by this guideline. In such a case, an upward departure may be warranted where the actual loss does not adequately reflect the seriousness of the conduct.

    Offenses involving identification documents, false identification documents, and means of identification, in violation of 18 U.S.C. § 1028, also are

Amendment 617 APPENDIX C - VOLUME II November 1, 2013

covered by this guideline. If the primary purpose of the offense was to violate, or assist another to violate, the law pertaining to naturalization, citizenship, or legal resident status, apply § 2L2.1 (Trafficking in a Document Relating to Naturalization) or § 2L2.2 (Fraudulently Acquiring Documents Relating to Naturalization), as appropriate, rather than § 2F1.1.

13. If the fraud exploited vulnerable victims, an enhancement will apply. See § 3A1.1 (Hate Crime Motivation or Vulnerable Victim).

14. Sometimes, offenses involving fraudulent statements are prosecuted under 18 U.S.C. § 1001, or a similarly general statute, although the offense is also covered by a more specific statute. Examples include false entries regarding currency transactions, for which § 2S1.3 would be more apt, and false statements to a customs officer, for which § 2T3.1 likely would be more apt. In certain other cases, the mail or wire fraud statutes, or other relatively broad statutes, are used primarily as jurisdictional bases for the prosecution of other offenses. For example, a state arson offense where a fraudulent insurance claim was mailed might be prosecuted as mail fraud. Where the indictment or information setting forth the count of conviction (or a stipulation as described in § 1B1.2(a)) establishes an offense more aptly covered by another guideline, apply that guideline rather than § 2F1.1. Otherwise, in such cases, § 2F1.1 is to be applied, but a departure from the guidelines may be considered.

15. For purposes of subsection (b)(5)—

    'Counterfeit access device' (A) has the meaning given that term in 18 U.S.C. § 1029(e)(2); and (B) also includes a telecommunications instrument that has been modified or altered to obtain unauthorized use of telecommunications service. 'Telecommunications service' has the meaning given that term in 18 U.S.C. § 1029(e)(9).

    'Device-making equipment' (A) has the meaning given that term in 18 U.S.C. § 1029(e)(6); and (B) also includes (i) any hardware or software that has been configured as described in 18 U.S.C. § 1029(a)(9); and (ii) a scanning receiver referred to in 18 U.S.C. § 1029(a)(8). 'Scanning receiver' has the meaning given that term in 18 U.S.C. § 1029(e)(8).

    'Means of identification' has the meaning given that term in 18 U.S.C. § 1028(d)(3), except that such means of identification shall be of an actual (i.e., not fictitious) individual other than the defendant or a person for whose conduct the defendant is accountable under § 1B1.3 (Relevant Conduct).

    'Produce' includes manufacture, design, alter, authenticate, duplicate, or assemble. 'Production' includes manufacture, design, alteration, authentication, duplication, or assembly.

    'Unauthorized access device' has the meaning given that term in 18 U.S.C. § 1029(e)(3).

16. Subsection (b)(5)(C)(i) applies in a case in which a means of identification of an individual other than the defendant (or a person for whose conduct the defendant is accountable under § 1B1.3 (Relevant Conduct)) is used without that individual's authorization unlawfully to produce or obtain another means of identification.

Examples of conduct to which this subsection should apply are as follows:

(A) A defendant obtains an individual's name and social security number from a source (e.g., from a piece of mail taken from the individual's mailbox) and obtains a bank loan in that individual's name. In this example, the account number of the bank loan is the other means of identification that has been obtained unlawfully.

(B) A defendant obtains an individual's name and address from a source (e.g., from a driver's license in a stolen wallet) and applies for, obtains, and subsequently uses a credit card in that individual's name. In this example, the credit card is the other means of identification that has been obtained unlawfully.

Examples of conduct to which subsection (b)(5)(C)(i) should not apply are as follows:

(A) A defendant uses a credit card from a stolen wallet only to make a purchase. In such a case, the defendant has not used the stolen credit card to obtain another means of identification.

(B) A defendant forges another individual's signature to cash a stolen check. Forging another individual's signature is not producing another means of identification.

Subsection (b)(5)(C)(ii) applies in any case in which the offense involved the possession of 5 or more means of identification that unlawfully were produced or obtained, regardless of the number of individuals in whose name (or other identifying information) the means of identification were so produced or so obtained.

In a case involving unlawfully produced or unlawfully obtained means of identification, an upward departure may be warranted if the offense level does not adequately address the seriousness of the offense. Examples may include the following:

(A) The offense caused substantial harm to the victim's reputation or credit record, or the victim suffered a substantial inconvenience related to repairing the victim's reputation or a damaged credit record.

(B) An individual whose means of identification the defendant used to obtain unlawful means of identification is erroneously arrested or denied a job because an arrest record has been made in the individual's name.

(C) The defendant produced or obtained numerous means of identification with respect to one individual and essentially assumed that individual's identity.

17. In a case involving any counterfeit access device or unauthorized access device, loss includes any unauthorized charges made with the counterfeit access device or unauthorized access device. In any such case, loss shall be not less than $500 per access device. However, if the unauthorized access device is a means of telecommunications access that identifies a specific

telecommunications instrument or telecommunications account (including an electronic serial number/mobile identification number (ESN/MIN) pair), and that means was only possessed, and not used, during the commission of the offense, loss shall be not less than $100 per unused means. For purposes of this application note, 'counterfeit access device' and 'unauthorized access device' have the meaning given those terms in Application Note 15.

18. For purposes of subsection (b)(6)(B), 'United States' means each of the 50 states, the District of Columbia, the Commonwealth of Puerto Rico, the United States Virgin Islands, Guam, the Northern Mariana Islands, and American Samoa.

For purposes of subsection (b)(6)(C), 'sophisticated means' means especially complex or especially intricate offense conduct pertaining to the execution or concealment of an offense. For example, in a telemarketing scheme, locating the main office of the scheme in one jurisdiction but locating soliciting operations in another jurisdiction would ordinarily indicate sophisticated means. Conduct such as hiding assets or transactions, or both, through the use of fictitious entities, corporate shells, or offshore bank accounts also ordinarily would indicate sophisticated means.

The enhancement for sophisticated means under subsection (b)(6)(C) requires conduct that is significantly more complex or intricate than the conduct that may form the basis for an enhancement for more than minimal planning under subsection (b)(2)(A).

If the conduct that forms the basis for an enhancement under subsection (b)(6) is the only conduct that forms the basis for an adjustment under § 3C1.1 (Obstruction of Justice), do not apply an adjustment under § 3C1.1.

19. 'Financial institution,' as used in this guideline, is defined to include any institution described in 18 U.S.C. §§ 20, 656, 657, 1005-1007, and 1014; any state or foreign bank, trust company, credit union, insurance company, investment company, mutual fund, savings (building and loan) association, union or employee pension fund; any health, medical or hospital insurance association; brokers and dealers registered, or required to be registered, with the Securities and Exchange Commission; futures commodity merchants and commodity pool operators registered, or required to be registered, with the Commodity Futures Trading Commission; and any similar entity, whether or not insured by the federal government. 'Union or employee pension fund' and 'any health, medical, or hospital insurance association,' as used above, primarily include large pension funds that serve many individuals (e.g., pension funds of large national and international organizations, unions, and corporations doing substantial interstate business), and associations that undertake to provide pension, disability, or other benefits (e.g., medical or hospitalization insurance) to large numbers of persons.

20. An offense shall be deemed to have 'substantially jeopardized the safety and soundness of a financial institution' if, as a consequence of the offense, the institution became insolvent; substantially reduced benefits to pensioners or insureds; was unable on demand to refund fully any deposit, payment, or investment; was so depleted of its assets as to be forced to merge with another institution in order to continue active operations; or was placed in substantial jeopardy of any of the above.

21. 'The defendant derived more than $1,000,000 in gross receipts from the offense,' as used in subsection (b)(8)(B), generally means that the gross receipts to the defendant individually, rather than to all participants, exceeded $1,000,000. 'Gross receipts from the offense' includes all property, real or personal, tangible or intangible, which is obtained directly or indirectly as a result of such offense. See 18 U.S.C. § 982(a)(4).

22. If the defendant is convicted under 18 U.S.C. § 225 (relating to a continuing financial crimes enterprise), the offense level is that applicable to the underlying series of offenses comprising the 'continuing financial crimes enterprise.'

23. If subsection (b)(5), subsection (b)(8)(A), or subsection (b)(8)(B) applies, there shall be a rebuttable presumption that the offense also involved more than minimal planning for purposes of subsection (b)(2).

    If the conduct that forms the basis for an enhancement under subsection (b)(5) is the only conduct that forms the basis of an enhancement under subsection (b)(6), do not apply an enhancement under subsection (b)(6).

Background: This guideline is designed to apply to a wide variety of fraud cases. The statutory maximum term of imprisonment for most such offenses is five years. The guideline does not link offense characteristics to specific code sections. Because federal fraud statutes are so broadly written, a single pattern of offense conduct usually can be prosecuted under several code sections, as a result of which the offense of conviction may be somewhat arbitrary. Furthermore, most fraud statutes cover a broad range of conduct with extreme variation in severity.

Empirical analyses of pre-guidelines practice showed that the most important factors that determined sentence length were the amount of loss and whether the offense was an isolated crime of opportunity or was sophisticated or repeated. Accordingly, although they are imperfect, these are the primary factors upon which the guideline has been based.

The extent to which an offense is planned or sophisticated is important in assessing its potential harmfulness and the dangerousness of the offender, independent of the actual harm. A complex scheme or repeated incidents of fraud are indicative of an intention and potential to do considerable harm. In pre-guidelines practice, this factor had a significant impact, especially in frauds involving small losses. Accordingly, the guideline specifies a 2-level enhancement when this factor is present.

Use of false pretenses involving charitable causes and government agencies enhances the sentences of defendants who take advantage of victims' trust in government or law enforcement agencies or their generosity and charitable motives. Taking advantage of a victim's self-interest does not mitigate the seriousness of fraudulent conduct. However, defendants who exploit victims' charitable impulses or trust in government create particular social harm. The commission of a fraud in the course of a bankruptcy proceeding subjects the defendant to an enhanced sentence because that fraudulent conduct undermines the bankruptcy process as well as harms others with an interest in the bankruptcy estate.

Offenses that involve the use of transactions or accounts outside the United States in an effort to conceal illicit profits and criminal conduct involve a particularly high level of sophistication and complexity. These offenses are difficult to detect and require costly investigations and prosecutions. Diplomatic processes often must be used to secure testimony and evidence beyond the jurisdiction of United States courts. Consequently, a minimum level of 12 is provided for these offenses.

Amendment 617 APPENDIX C - VOLUME II November 1, 2013

Subsections (b)(5)(A) and(B) implement the instruction to the Commission in section 4 of the Wireless Telephone Protection Act, Public Law 105–172.

Subsection (b)(5)(C) implements the directive to the Commission in section 4 of the Identity Theft and Assumption Deterrence Act of 1998, Public Law 105–318. This subsection focuses principally on an aggravated form of identity theft known as 'affirmative identity theft' or 'breeding,' in which a defendant uses another individual's name, social security number, or some other form of identification (the 'means of identification') to 'breed' (i.e., produce or obtain) new or additional forms of identification. Because 18 U.S.C. § 1028(d) broadly defines 'means of identification,' the new or additional forms of identification can include items such as a driver's license, a credit card, or a bank loan. This subsection provides a minimum offense level of level 12, in part, because of the seriousness of the offense. The minimum offense level accounts for the fact that the means of identification that were 'bred' (i.e., produced or obtained) often are within the defendant's exclusive control, making it difficult for the individual victim to detect that the victim's identity has been 'stolen.' Generally, the victim does not become aware of the offense until certain harms have already occurred (e.g., a damaged credit rating or inability to obtain a loan). The minimum offense level also accounts for the non-monetary harm associated with these types of offenses, much of which may be difficult or impossible to quantify (e.g., harm to the individual's reputation or credit rating, inconvenience, and other difficulties resulting from the offense). The legislative history of the Identity Theft and Assumption Deterrence Act of 1998 indicates that Congress was especially concerned with providing increased punishment for this type of harm.

Subsection (b)(6) implements, in a broader form, the instruction to the Commission in section 6(c)(2) of Public Law 105–184.

Subsection (b)(7)(B) implements, in a broader form, the instruction to the Commission in section 110512 of Public Law 103–322.

Subsection (b)(8)(A) implements, in a broader form, the instruction to the Commission in section 961(m) of Public Law 101–73.

Subsection (b)(8)(B) implements the instruction to the Commission in section 2507 of Public Law 101–647.

Subsection (c) implements the instruction to the Commission in section 805(c) of Public Law 104–132.

§ 2F1.2.   Insider Trading

(a) Base Offense Level: 8

(b) Specific Offense Characteristic

(1) Increase by the number of levels from the table in § 2F1.1 corresponding to the gain resulting from the offense.

Commentary

Statutory Provisions: 15 U.S.C. § 78j and 17 C.F.R. § 240.10b-5. For additional statutory provision(s), see Appendix A (Statutory Index).

Application Note:

1. Section 3B1.3 (Abuse of Position of Trust or Use of Special Skill) should be applied only if the defendant occupied and abused a position of special trust.

Examples might include a corporate president or an attorney who misused information regarding a planned but unannounced takeover attempt. It typically would not apply to an ordinary 'tippee.'

Background: This guideline applies to certain violations of Rule 10b-5 that are commonly referred to as 'insider trading.' Insider trading is treated essentially as a sophisticated fraud. Because the victims and their losses are difficult if not impossible to identify, the gain, i.e., the total increase in value realized through trading in securities by the defendant and persons acting in concert with him or to whom he provided inside information, is employed instead of the victims' losses.

Certain other offenses, e.g., 7 U.S.C. § 13(e), that involve misuse of inside information for personal gain also may appropriately be covered by this guideline.".

Chapter Two, Part B, Subpart 1, is amended by adding at the end the following:

"§ 2B1.4.   Insider Trading

(a)   Base Offense Level: 8

(b)   Specific Offense Characteristic

(1)   If the gain resulting from the offense exceeded $5,000, increase by the number of levels from the table in § 2B1.1 (Theft, Property Destruction, and Fraud) corresponding to that amount.

Commentary

Statutory Provisions: 15 U.S.C. § 78j and 17 C.F.R. § 240.10b-5. For additional statutory provision(s), see Appendix A (Statutory Index).

Application Note:

1.   Application of Subsection of § 3B1.3.—Section 3B1.3 (Abuse of Position of Trust or Use of Special Skill) should be applied only if the defendant occupied and abused a position of special trust. Examples might include a corporate president or an attorney who misused information regarding a planned but unannounced takeover attempt. It typically would not apply to an ordinary 'tippee'.

Background: This guideline applies to certain violations of Rule 10b-5 that are commonly referred to as 'insider trading'. Insider trading is treated essentially as a sophisticated fraud. Because the victims and their losses are difficult if not impossible to identify, the gain, i.e., the total increase in value realized through trading in securities by the defendant and persons acting in concert with the defendant or to whom the defendant provided inside information, is employed instead of the victims' losses.

Certain other offenses, e.g., 7 U.S.C. § 13(e), that involve misuse of inside information for personal gain also appropriately may be covered by this guideline.".

The Commentary to § 1B1.1 captioned "Application Notes" is amended in Note 1 by striking subdivision (f) as follows:

"(f)   'More than minimal planning' means more planning than is typical for commission of the offense in a simple form. 'More than minimal planning' also exists if significant affirmative steps were taken to conceal the offense, other than conduct to which § 3C1.1 (Obstructing or Impeding the Administration of Justice) applies.

'More than minimal planning' is deemed present in any case involving repeated acts over a period of time, unless it is clear that each instance was purely opportune. Consequently, this adjustment will apply especially frequently in property offenses.

In an assault, for example, waiting to commit the offense when no witnesses were present would not alone constitute more than minimal planning. By contrast, luring the victim to a specific location, or wearing a ski mask to prevent identification, would constitute more than minimal planning.

In a commercial burglary, for example, checking the area to make sure no witnesses were present would not alone constitute more than minimal planning. By contrast, obtaining building plans to plot a particular course of entry, or disabling an alarm system, would constitute more than minimal planning.

In a theft, going to a secluded area of a store to conceal the stolen item in one's pocket would not alone constitute more than minimal planning. However, repeated instances of such thefts on several occasions would constitute more than minimal planning. Similarly, fashioning a special device to conceal the property, or obtaining information on delivery dates so that an especially valuable item could be obtained, would constitute more than minimal planning.

In an embezzlement, a single taking accomplished by a false book entry would constitute only minimal planning. On the other hand, creating purchase orders to, and invoices from, a dummy corporation for merchandise that was never delivered would constitute more than minimal planning, as would several instances of taking money, each accompanied by false entries.";

and by redesignating subdivisions (g) through (l) as subdivisions (f) through (k), respectively.

The Commentary to § 1B1.1 captioned "Application Notes" is amended in Note 4 in the second paragraph by striking the last sentence as follows:

"For example, the adjustments from § 2F1.1(b)(2) (more than minimal planning) and § 3B1.1 (Aggravating Role) are applied cumulatively.".

The Commentary to § 1B1.2 captioned "Application Notes" is amended in Note 1 in the fourth paragraph by striking "§ 2B1.1 (Larceny, Embezzlement, and Other Forms of Theft)" and inserting "§ 2B1.1 (Theft, Property Destruction, and Fraud)".

The Commentary to § 1B1.3 captioned "Application Notes" is amended in Note 5 by striking "§ 2F1.1 (Fraud and Deceit)" and inserting "§ 2B1.1 (Theft, Property Destruction, and Fraud)".

The Commentary to § 2B2.1 captioned "Application Notes" is amended in Note 1 by striking "'More than minimal planning,' 'firearm,'" and inserting "'Firearm,'".

The Commentary to § 2B2.1 captioned "Application Notes" is amended by striking the text of Note 2 as follows:

"Valuation of loss is discussed in the Commentary to § 2B1.1 (Larceny, Embezzlement, and Other Forms of Theft).",

and inserting the following:

"'Loss' means the value of the property taken, damaged, or destroyed.".

The Commentary to § 2B2.1 captioned "Application Notes" is amended by adding at the end the following:

"4. <u>More than Minimal Planning</u>.—'More than minimal planning' means more planning than is typical for commission of the offense in a simple form. 'More than minimal planning' also exists if significant affirmative steps were taken to conceal the offense, other than conduct to which § 3C1.1 (Obstructing or Impeding the Administration of Justice) applies. 'More than minimal planning' shall be considered to be present in any case involving repeated acts over a period of time, unless it is clear that each instance was purely opportune. For example, checking the area to make sure no witnesses were present would not alone constitute more than minimal planning. By contrast, obtaining building plans to plot a particular course of entry, or disabling an alarm system, would constitute more than minimal planning.".

Section 2B2.3(b) is amended by striking subdivision (3) as follows:

"(3) If the offense involved invasion of a protected computer resulting in a loss exceeding $2000, increase the offense level by the number of levels from the table in § 2F1.1 corresponding to the loss.",

and inserting the following:

"(3) If (A) the offense involved invasion of a protected computer; and (B) the loss resulting from the invasion (i) exceeded $2,000 but did not exceed $5,000, increase by 1 level; or (ii) exceeded $5,000, increase by the number of levels from the table in § 2B1.1 (Theft, Property Destruction, and Fraud) corresponding to that amount.".

The Commentary to § 2B2.3 captioned "Application Notes" is amended in Note 2 by striking "§ 2B1.1 (Larceny, Embezzlement, and Other Forms of Theft)" and inserting "§ 2B1.1 (Theft, Property Destruction, and Fraud)".

The Commentary to § 2B3.1 captioned "Application Notes" is amended by striking the text of Note 3 as follows:

"Valuation of loss is discussed in the Commentary to § 2B1.1 (Larceny, Embezzlement, and Other Forms of Theft).",

and inserting:

"'Loss' means the value of the property taken, damaged, or destroyed.".

Section 2B3.3(b) is amended by striking subdivision (1) as follows:

"(1) If the greater of the amount obtained or demanded exceeded $2,000, increase by the corresponding number of levels from the table in § 2F1.1.",

Amendment 617 APPENDIX C - VOLUME II November 1, 2013

and inserting the following:

"(1) If the greater of the amount obtained or demanded (A) exceeded $2,000 but did not exceed $5,000, increase by 1 level; or (B) exceeded $5,000, increase by the number of levels from the table in § 2B1.1 (Theft, Property Destruction, and Fraud) corresponding to that amount.".

Section 2B4.1(b) is amended by striking subdivision (1) as follows:

"(1) If the greater of the value of the bribe or the improper benefit to be conferred exceeded $2,000, increase the offense level by the corresponding number of levels from the table in § 2F1.1.",

and inserting the following:

"(1) If the greater of the value of the bribe or the improper benefit to be conferred (A) exceeded $2,000 but did not exceed $5,000, increase by 1 level; or (B) exceeded $5,000, increase by the number of levels from the table in § 2B1.1 (Theft, Property Destruction, and Fraud) corresponding to that amount.".

Section 2B5.1(b) is amended by striking subdivision (1) as follows:

"(1) If the face value of the counterfeit items exceeded $2,000, increase by the corresponding number of levels from the table at § 2F1.1 (Fraud and Deceit).",

and inserting the following:

"(1) If the face value of the counterfeit items (A) exceeded $2,000 but did not exceed $5,000, increase by 1 level; or (B) exceeded $5,000, increase by the number of levels from the table in § 2B1.1 (Theft, Property Destruction, and Fraud) corresponding to that amount.".

The Commentary to § 2B5.1 captioned "Application Notes" is amended in Note 3 by striking "§ 2F1.1 (Fraud and Deceit)" and inserting "§ 2B1.1 (Theft, Property Destruction, and Fraud)".

Section 2B5.3(b) is amended by striking subdivision (1) as follows:

"(1) If the infringement amount exceeded $2,000, increase by the number of levels from the table in § 2F1.1 (Fraud and Deceit) corresponding to that amount.",

and inserting the following:

"(1) If the infringement amount (A) exceeded $2,000 but did not exceed $5,000, increase by 1 level; or (B) exceeded $5,000, increase by the number of levels from the table in § 2B1.1 (Theft, Property Destruction, and Fraud) corresponding to that amount.".

The Commentary to § 2B5.3 captioned "Background" is amended in the first paragraph by striking "guidelines" and inserting "guideline".

Section 2B6.1(b) is amended by striking subdivision (1) as follows:

"(1) If the retail value of the motor vehicles or parts involved exceeded $2,000, increase the offense level by the corresponding number of levels from the table in § 2F1.1 (Fraud and Deceit).",

and inserting the following:

"(1) If the retail value of the motor vehicles or parts (A) exceeded $2,000 but did not exceed $5,000, increase by 1 level; or (B) exceeded $5,000, increase by the number of levels from the table in § 2B1.1 (Theft, Property Destruction, and Fraud) corresponding to that amount.".

The Commentary to § 2B6.1 captioned "Application Notes" is amended in Note 1 by striking "§ 2B1.1 (Larceny, Embezzlement, and Other Forms of Theft)" and inserting "§ 2B1.1 (Theft, Property Destruction, and Fraud)".

The Commentary to § 2B6.1 captioned "Application Notes" is amended in Note 2 by striking "'corresponding" before "number" and inserting "term 'increase by the"; and by striking "§ 2F1.1 (Fraud and Deceit)" and inserting "§ 2B1.1 (Theft, Property Destruction, and Fraud) corresponding to that amount".

Section 2C1.1(b) is amended by striking subdivision (2)(A) as follows:

"(A) If the value of the payment, the benefit received or to be received in return for the payment, or the loss to the government from the offense, whichever is greatest, exceeded $2,000, increase by the corresponding number of levels from the table in § 2F1.1 (Fraud and Deceit).",

and inserting the following:

"(A) If the value of the payment, the benefit received or to be received in return for the payment, or the loss to the government from the offense, whichever is greatest (i) exceeded $2,000 but did not exceed $5,000, increase by 1 level; or (ii) exceeded $5,000, increase by the number of levels from the table in § 2B1.1 (Theft, Property Destruction, and Fraud) corresponding to that amount.".

The Commentary to § 2C1.1 captioned "Application Notes" is amended in Note 2 by striking "'Loss' is discussed in the Commentary to § 2B1.1 (Larceny, Embezzlement, and Other Forms of Theft) and includes both actual and intended loss" and inserting "'Loss', for purposes of subsection (b)(2)(A), shall be determined in accordance with Application Note 2 of the Commentary to § 2B1.1 (Theft, Property Destruction, and Fraud)".

Section 2C1.2(b) is amended by striking subdivision (2)(A) as follows:

"(A) If the value of the gratuity exceeded $2,000, increase by the corresponding number of levels from the table in § 2F1.1 (Fraud and Deceit).",

and inserting the following:

"(A) If the value of the gratuity (i) exceeded $2,000 but did not exceed $5,000, increase by 1 level; or (ii) exceeded $5,000, increase by the number of levels from the table in § 2B1.1 (Theft, Property Destruction, and Fraud) corresponding to that amount.".

Section 2C1.6(b) is amended by striking subdivision (1) as follows:

"(1) If the value of the gratuity exceeded $2,000, increase by the corresponding number of levels from the table in § 2F1.1 (Fraud and Deceit).",

Amendment 617　　APPENDIX C - VOLUME II　　November 1, 2013

and inserting the following:

"(1)　If the value of the gratuity (i) exceeded $2,000 but did not exceed $5,000, increase by 1 level; or (ii) exceeded $5,000, increase by the number of levels from the table in § 2B1.1 (Theft, Property Destruction, and Fraud) corresponding to that amount.".

Section 2C1.7(b) is amended by striking subdivision (1)(A) as follows:

"(A)　If the loss to the government, or the value of anything obtained or to be obtained by a public official or others acting with a public official, whichever is greater, exceeded $2,000, increase by the corresponding number of levels from the table in § 2F1.1 (Fraud and Deceit); or"

and inserting the following:

"(A)　If the loss to the government, or the value of anything obtained or to be obtained by a public official or others acting with a public official, whichever is greater (i) exceeded $2,000 but did not exceed $5,000, increase by 1 level; or (ii) exceeded $5,000, increase by the number of levels from the table in § 2B1.1 (Theft, Property Destruction, and Fraud) corresponding to that amount.".

The Commentary to § 2C1.7 captioned "Application Notes" is amended by striking the text of Note 3 as follows:

"'Loss' is discussed in the Commentary to § 2B1.1 (Larceny, Embezzlement, and Other Forms of Theft) and includes both actual and intended loss.",

and inserting the following:

"'Loss', for purposes of subsection (b)(1)(A), shall be determined in accordance with Application Note 2 of the Commentary to § 2B1.1 (Theft, Property Destruction, and Fraud).".

Section 2E5.1(b) is amended by striking subdivision (2) as follows:

"(2)　Increase by the number of levels from the table in § 2F1.1 (Fraud and Deceit) corresponding to the value of the prohibited payment or the value of the improper benefit to the payer, whichever is greater.",

and inserting the following:

"(2)　If the value of the prohibited payment or the value of the improper benefit to the payer, whichever is greater (A) exceeded $2,000 but did not exceed $5,000, increase by 1 level; or (B) exceeded $5,000, increase by the number of levels from the table in § 2B1.1 (Theft, Property Destruction, and Fraud) corresponding to that amount.".

Section 2G2.2(b)(2)(A) is amended by striking "§ 2F1.1 (Fraud and Deceit)" and inserting "§ 2B1.1 (Theft, Property Destruction, and Fraud)".

Section 2G3.1(b)(1)(A) is amended by striking "§ 2F1.1 (Fraud and Deceit)" and inserting "§ 2B1.1 (Theft, Property Destruction, and Fraud)".

Section 2G3.2(b)(2) is amended by striking "at § 2F1.1(b)(1)" and inserting "in § 2B1.1

– 640 –

(Theft, Property Destruction, and Fraud)".

Section 2H3.3(a) is amended by striking the text of subdivision (2) as follows:

"if the conduct was theft of mail, apply § 2B1.1 (Larceny, Embezzlement, and Other Forms of Theft);",

and inserting the following:

"if the conduct was theft or destruction of mail, apply § 2B1.1 (Theft, Property Destruction, and Fraud).";

and by striking subdivision (3) as follows:

"(3) if the conduct was destruction of mail, apply § 2B1.3 (Property Damage or Destruction).".

The Commentary to § 2H3.3 captioned "Background" is amended by striking "§ 2B1.1 (Larceny, Embezzlement, and Other Forms of Theft) or § 2B1.3 (Property Damage or Destruction)" and inserting "§ 2B1.1 (Theft, Property Destruction, and Fraud)".

The Commentary to § 2J1.1 captioned "Application Notes" is amended in Note 2 by striking "(Larceny, Embezzlement, and Other Forms of Theft)" and inserting "(Theft, Property Destruction, and Fraud)".

Section 2K1.4(a) subdivision (2) is amended by inserting "or" after "or a structure other than a dwelling;"; by striking the text of subdivision (3) as follows:

"2 plus the offense level from § 2F1.1 (Fraud and Deceit) if the offense was committed in connection with a scheme to defraud; or",

and inserting the following:

"2 plus the offense level from § 2B1.1 (Theft, Property Destruction, and Fraud).";

and by striking subdivision (4) as follows:

"(4) 2 plus the offense level from § 2B1.3 (Property Damage or Destruction).".

Section 2K1.4(b)(2) is amended by striking "(4)" and inserting "(3)".

Section 2N2.1(b)(1) is amended by striking "§ 2F1.1 (Fraud and Deceit)" and inserting "§ 2B1.1 (Theft, Property Destruction, and Fraud)".

The Commentary to § 2N2.1 captioned "Statutory Provisions" is amended by inserting ", 6810, 7734" after "150gg".

The Commentary to § 2N2.1 captioned "Application Notes" is amended in Note 2 by inserting "theft, property destruction, or" after "involved"; and by striking "theft, bribery, revealing trade secrets, or destruction of property" and inserting "bribery".

The Commentary to § 2N2.1 captioned "Application Notes" is amended in Note 4 by striking "§ 2F1.1 (Fraud and Deceit)" and inserting "§ 2B1.1 (Theft, Property Destruction, and Fraud)".

Section 2N3.1(b)(1) is amended by striking "§ 2F1.1 (Fraud and Deceit)" and inserting "§ 2B1.1 (Theft, Property Destruction, and Fraud)".

Amendment 617 APPENDIX C - VOLUME II November 1, 2013

The Commentary to § 2N3.1 captioned "Background" is amended by striking "the guideline for fraud and deception, § 2F1.1," and inserting "§ 2B1.1 (Theft, Property Destruction, and Fraud)".

Section 2Q1.6(a)(2) is amended by striking "§ 2B1.3 (Property Damage or Destruction)" and inserting "§ 2B1.1 (Theft, Property Destruction, and Fraud)".

Section 2Q2.1(b) is amended by striking subdivision (3)(A) as follows:

"(A) If the market value of the fish, wildlife, or plants exceeded $2,000, increase the offense level by the corresponding number of levels from the table in § 2F1.1 (Fraud and Deceit); or",

and inserting the following:

"(A) If the market value of the fish, wildlife, or plants (i) exceeded $2,000 but did not exceed $5,000, increase by 1 level; or (ii) exceeded $5,000, increase by the number of levels from the table in § 2B1.1 (Theft, Property Destruction, and Fraud) corresponding to that amount; or".

Section 2S1.3(a) is amended by striking "§ 2F1.1 (Fraud and Deceit)" and inserting "§ 2B1.1 (Theft, Property Destruction, and Fraud)".

Section 2T1.1(b)(2) is amended by striking "concealment" and inserting "means"; and by inserting after "levels." the following:

"If the resulting offense level is less than level 12, increase to level 12.".

Section 2T1.1(c)(1) is amended by adding at the end the following:

"(D) If the offense involved (i) conduct described in subdivisions (A), (B), or (C) of these Notes; and (ii) both individual and corporate tax returns, the tax loss is the aggregate tax loss from the offenses added together.".

Section 2T1.1(c)(2) is amended in the second paragraph by striking "Note" and inserting "Notes"; by inserting "(A)" before "If"; and by adding at the end the following:

"(B) If the offense involved (i) conduct described in subdivision (A) of these Notes; and (ii) both individual and corporate tax returns, the tax loss is the aggregate tax loss from the offenses added together.".

The Commentary to § 2T1.1 captioned "Application Notes" is amended in Note 1 in the first paragraph by inserting ", except in willful evasion of payment cases under 26 U.S.C. § 7201 and willful failure to pay cases under 26 U.S.C. § 7203" after "penalties".

The Commentary to § 2T1.1 captioned "Application Notes" is amended by striking the text of Note 4 as follows:

"For purposes of subsection (b)(2), 'sophisticated concealment' means especially complex or especially intricate offense conduct in which deliberate steps are taken to make the offense, or its extent, difficult to detect. Conduct such as hiding assets or transactions, or both, through the use of fictitious entities, corporate shells, or offshore bank accounts ordinarily indicates sophisticated concealment.",

and inserting the following:

"Sophisticated Means Enhancement.—For purposes of subsection (b)(2), 'sophisticated means' means especially complex or especially intricate offense conduct pertaining to the execution or concealment of an offense. Conduct such as hiding assets or transactions, or both, through the use of fictitious entities, corporate shells, or offshore financial accounts ordinarily indicates sophisticated means.".

The Commentary to § 2T1.1 captioned "Application Notes" is amended by striking the text of Note 7 as follows:

"If the offense involves both individual and corporate tax returns, the tax loss is the aggregate tax loss from the offenses taken together.",

and inserting the following:

"If the offense involved both individual and corporate tax returns, the tax loss is the aggregate tax loss from the individual tax offense and the corporate tax offense added together. Accordingly, in a case in which a defendant fails to report income derived from a corporation on both the defendant's individual tax return and the defendant's corporate tax return, the tax loss is the sum of (A) the unreported or diverted amount multiplied by (i) 28%; or (ii) the tax rate for the individual tax offense, if sufficient information is available to make a more accurate assessment of that tax rate; and (B) the unreported or diverted amount multiplied by (i) 34%; or (ii) the tax rate for the corporate tax offense, if sufficient information is available to make a more accurate assessment of that tax rate. For example, the defendant, the sole owner of a Subchapter C corporation, fraudulently understates the corporation's income in the amount of $100,000 on the corporation's tax return, diverts the funds to the defendant's own use, and does not report these funds on the defendant's individual tax return. For purposes of this example, assume the use of 34% with respect to the corporate tax loss and the use of 28% with respect to the individual tax loss. The tax loss attributable to the defendant's corporate tax return is $34,000 ($100,000 multiplied by 34%). The tax loss attributable to the defendant's individual tax return is $28,000 ($100,000 multiplied by 28%). The tax loss for the offenses are added together to equal $62,000 ($34,000 + $28,000).".

Section 2T1.4(b)(2) is amended by striking "concealment" and inserting "means"; and by inserting after "levels." the following:

"If the resulting offense level is less than level 12, increase to level 12.".

The Commentary to § 2T1.4 captioned "Application Notes" is amended by striking the text of Note 3 as follows:

"For purposes of subsection (b)(2), 'sophisticated concealment' means especially complex or especially intricate offense conduct in which deliberate steps are taken to make the offense, or its extent, difficult to detect. Conduct such as hiding assets or transactions, or both, through the use of fictitious entities, corporate shells, or offshore bank accounts ordinarily indicates sophisticated concealment.",

and inserting the following:

"<u>Sophisticated Means</u>.—For purposes of subsection (b)(2), 'sophisticated means' means especially complex or especially intricate offense conduct pertaining to the execution or concealment of an offense. Conduct such as hiding assets or transactions, or both, through the use of fictitious entities, corporate shells, or offshore financial accounts ordinarily indicates sophisticated means.".

Section 2T1.6(b)(1) is amended by striking "(Larceny, Embezzlement, and Other Forms of Theft)" and inserting "(Theft, Property Destruction, and Fraud)".

Amendment 617   APPENDIX C - VOLUME II   November 1, 2013

Section 2T3.1(b)(1) is amended by striking "concealment" and inserting "means"; and by inserting after "levels." the following:

"If the resulting offense level is less than level 12, increase to level 12.".

The Commentary to § 2T3.1 captioned "Application Notes" is amended by striking the text of Note 3 as follows:

"For purposes of subsection (b)(1), 'sophisticated concealment' means especially complex or especially intricate offense conduct in which deliberate steps are taken to make the offense, or its extent, difficult to detect. Conduct such as hiding assets or transactions, or both, through the use of fictitious entities, corporate shells, or offshore bank accounts ordinarily indicates sophisticated concealment.",

and inserting the following:

"Sophisticated Means.—For purposes of subsection (b)(1), 'sophisticated means' means especially complex or especially intricate offense conduct pertaining to the execution or concealment of an offense. Conduct such as hiding assets or transactions, or both, through the use of fictitious entities, corporate shells, or offshore financial accounts ordinarily indicates sophisticated means.".

Section 2T4.1 is amended by striking the text as follows:

"Tax Loss (Apply the Greatest)		Offense Level
(A)	$1,700 or less	6
(B)	More than $1,700	7
(C)	More than $3,000	8
(D)	More than $5,000	9
(E)	More than $8,000	10
(F)	More than $13,500	11
(G)	More than $23,500	12
(H)	More than $40,000	13
(I)	More than $70,000	14
(J)	More than $120,000	15
(K)	More than $200,000	16
(L)	More than $325,000	17
(M)	More than $550,000	18
(N)	More than $950,000	19
(O)	More than $1,500,000	20
(P)	More than $2,500,000	21
(Q)	More than $5,000,000	22
(R)	More than $10,000,000	23
(S)	More than $20,000,000	24
(T)	More than $40,000,000	25
(U)	More than $80,000,000	26.",

and inserting the following:

"Tax Loss (Apply the Greatest)		Offense Level
(A)	$2,000 or less	6
(B)	More than $2,000	8
(C)	More than $5,000	10
(D)	More than $12,500	12
(E)	More than $30,000	14
(F)	More than $80,000	16
(G)	More than $200,000	18
(H)	More than $400,000	20
(I)	More than $1,000,000	22
(J)	More than $2,500,000	24
(K)	More than $7,000,000	26
(L)	More than $20,000,000	28
(M)	More than $50,000,000	30
(N)	More than $100,000,000	32.".

The Commentary to § 3B1.3 captioned "Application Notes" is amended by adding after Note 3 the following:

"4. The following additional illustrations of an abuse of a position of trust pertain to theft or embezzlement from employee pension or welfare benefit plans or labor unions:

(A) If the offense involved theft or embezzlement from an employee pension or welfare benefit plan and the defendant was a fiduciary of the benefit plan, an adjustment under this section for abuse of a position of trust will apply. 'Fiduciary of the benefit plan' is defined in 29 U.S.C. § 1002(21)(A) to mean a person who exercises any discretionary authority or control in respect to the management of such plan or exercises authority or control in respect to management or disposition of its assets, or who renders investment advice for a fee or other direct or indirect compensation with respect to any moneys or other property of such plan, or has any authority or responsibility to do so, or who has any discretionary authority or responsibility in the administration of such plan.

(B) If the offense involved theft or embezzlement from a labor union and the defendant was a union officer or occupied a position of trust in the union (as set forth in 29 U.S.C. § 501(a)), an adjustment under this section for an abuse of a position of trust will apply.".

Section 3D1.2(d) is amended in the second paragraph by striking "2B1.3" and inserting "2B1.4"; and by striking "§§ 2F1.1, 2F1.2;".

The Commentary to § 3D1.2 captioned "Application Notes" is amended in Note 6 in the third paragraph by striking ", and would include, for example, larceny, embezzlement, forgery, and fraud".

Section 3D1.3(b) is amended by striking "(e.g., theft and fraud)".

The Commentary to § 3D1.3 captioned "Application Notes" is amended in Note 3 by

Amendment 617

striking "(e.g., theft and fraud)"; and by striking the last sentence as follows:

> "In addition, the adjustment for 'more than minimal planning' frequently will apply to multiple count convictions for property offenses.".

The Commentary following § 3D1.5 captioned "Illustrations of the Operation of the Multiple-Count Rules" is amended by striking Illustration 2 as follows:

> "2. Defendant B was convicted on the following seven counts: (1) theft of a $2,000 check; (2) uttering the same $2,000 check; (3) possession of a stolen $1,200 check; (4) forgery of a $600 check; (5) possession of a stolen $1,000 check; (6) forgery of the same $1,000 check; (7) uttering the same $1,000 check. Counts 1, 3 and 5 involve offenses under Part B (Offenses Involving Property), while Counts 2, 4, 6 and 7 involve offenses under Part F (Offenses Involving Fraud and Deceit). For purposes of § 3D1.2(d), fraud and theft are treated as offenses of the same kind, and therefore all counts are grouped into a single Group, for which the offense level depends on the aggregate harm. The total value of the checks is $4,800. The fraud guideline is applied, because it produces an offense level that is as high as or higher than the theft guideline. The base offense level is 6; 1 level is added because of the value of the property (§ 2F1.1(b)(1)); and 2 levels are added because the conduct involved repeated acts with some planning (§ 2F1.1(b)(2)(A)). The resulting offense level is 9.";

and by redesignating Illustrations 3 and 4 as Illustrations 2 and 3, respectively.

The Commentary following § 3D1.5 captioned "Illustrations of the Operation of the Multiple-Count Rules" is amended in Illustration 3, as redesignated by this amendment, by striking "§ 2F1.1 (Fraud and Deceit)" and inserting "§ 2B1.1 (Theft, Property Destruction, and Fraud)"; by striking "14" each place it appears and inserting "16"; and by striking "§ 2B4.1 or § 2F1.1" and inserting "§ 2B1.1 (assuming the application of the 'sophisticated means' enhancement in § 2B1.1(b)(8)) or § 2B4.1".

The Commentary to § 8A1.2 captioned "Application Notes" is amended in Note 3(i) by striking "§§ 2B1.1 (Larceny, Embezzlement, and Other Forms of Theft), 2F1.1 (Fraud and Deceit)" and inserting "§ 2B1.1 (Theft, Property Destruction, and Fraud)".

Section 8C2.1(a) is amended by striking "2B1.3" and inserting "2B1.4"; and by striking "§§ 2F1.1, 2F1.2;".

The Commentary to § 8C2.1 captioned "Application Notes" is amended in Note 2 by striking "§ 2F1.1 (Fraud and Deceit)" each place it appears and inserting "§ 2B1.1 (Theft, Property Destruction, and Fraud)".

Appendix A (Statutory Index) is amended in the line referenced to 7 U.S.C. § 6 by striking "2F1.1" and inserting "2B1.1";

in the line referenced to 7 U.S.C. § 6b(A) by striking "2F1.1" and inserting "2B1.1";

in the line referenced to 7 U.S.C. § 6b(B) by striking "2F1.1" and inserting "2B1.1";

in the line referenced to 7 U.S.C. § 6b(C) by striking "2F1.1" and inserting "2B1.1";

in the line referenced to 7 U.S.C. § 6c by striking "2F1.1" and inserting "2B1.1";

in the line referenced to 7 U.S.C. § 6h by striking "2F1.1" and inserting "2B1.1";

in the line referenced to 7 U.S.C. § 6o by striking "2F1.1" and inserting "2B1.1";

in the line referenced to 7 U.S.C. § 13(a)(2) by striking "2F1.1" and inserting "2B1.1";

in the line referenced to 7 U.S.C. § 13(a)(3) by striking "2F1.1" and inserting "2B1.1";

in the line referenced to 7 U.S.C. § 13(a)(4) by striking "2F1.1" and inserting "2B1.1";

in the line referenced to 7 U.S.C. § 13(d) by striking "2F1.2" and inserting "2B1.4";

in the line referenced to 7 U.S.C. § 13(f) by striking "2F1.2" and inserting "2B1.4";

in the line referenced to 7 U.S.C. § 23 by striking "2F1.1" and inserting "2B1.1";

in the line referenced to 7 U.S.C. § 270 by striking "2F1.1" and inserting "2B1.1";

in the line referenced to 7 U.S.C. § 2024(b) by striking "2F1.1" and inserting "2B1.1";

in the line referenced to 7 U.S.C. § 2024(c) by striking "2F1.1" and inserting "2B1.1";

by inserting after the line referenced to 7 U.S.C. § 6810 the following new line:

"7 U.S.C. § 7734   2N2.1";

in the line referenced to 12 U.S.C. § 631 by striking "2F1.1" and inserting "2B1.1";

in the line referenced to 15 U.S.C. § 50 by striking "2F1.1" and inserting "2B1.1";

in the line referenced to 15 U.S.C. § 77e by striking "2F1.1" and inserting "2B1.1";

in the line referenced to 15 U.S.C. § 77q by striking "2F1.1" and inserting "2B1.1";

in the line referenced to 15 U.S.C. § 77x by striking "2F1.1" and inserting "2B1.1";

in the line referenced to 15 U.S.C. § 78j by striking "2F1.1" and inserting "2B1.1"; and by striking "2F1.2" and inserting "2B1.4";

in the line referenced to 15 U.S.C. § 78ff by striking "2B4.1, 2F1.1" and inserting "2B1.1, 2B4.1";

in the line referenced to 15 U.S.C. § 80b-6 by striking "2F1.1" and inserting "2B1.1";

in the line referenced to 15 U.S.C. § 158 by striking "2F1.1" and inserting "2B1.1";

in the line referenced to 15 U.S.C. § 645(a) by striking "2F1.1" and inserting "2B1.1";

in the line referenced to 15 U.S.C. § 645(b) by striking ", 2F1.1";

in the line referenced to 15 U.S.C. § 645(c) by striking ", 2F1.1";

in the line referenced to 15 U.S.C. § 714m(a) by striking "2F1.1" and inserting "2B1.1";

in the line referenced to 15 U.S.C. § 714m(b) by striking ", 2F1.1";

in the line referenced to 15 U.S.C. § 1281 by striking "2B1.3" and inserting "2B1.1";

in the line referenced to 15 U.S.C. § 1644 by striking "2F1.1" and inserting "2B1.1";

in the line referenced to 15 U.S.C. § 1681q by striking "2F1.1" and inserting "2B1.1";

in the line referenced to 15 U.S.C. § 1693n(a) by striking "2F1.1" and inserting "2B1.1";

by inserting after the line referenced to 15 U.S.C. § 2615 the following new line:

"15 U.S.C. § 6821   2B1.1";

in the line referenced to 16 U.S.C. § 114 by striking ", 2B1.3";

in the line referenced to 16 U.S.C. § 117c by striking ", 2B1.3";

in the line referenced to 16 U.S.C. § 123 by striking "2B1.3,";

in the line referenced to 16 U.S.C. § 146 by striking "2B1.3,";

in the line referenced to 16 U.S.C. § 413 by striking ", 2B1.3";

in the line referenced to 16 U.S.C. § 433 by striking ", 2B1.3";

in the line referenced to 16 U.S.C. § 831t(b) by striking "2F1.1" and inserting "2B1.1";

in the line referenced to 16 U.S.C. § 831t(c) by striking "2F1.1" and inserting "2B1.1";

in the line referenced to 18 U.S.C. § 32(a),(b) by striking "2B1.3" and inserting "2B1.1";

in the line referenced to 18 U.S.C. § 33 by striking "2B1.3"and inserting "2B1.1";

in the line referenced to 18 U.S.C. § 37 by striking "2B1.3" and inserting "2B1.1";

by inserting after the line referenced to 18 U.S.C. § 37 the following new line:

"18 U.S.C. § 38   2B1.1";

in the line referenced to 18 U.S.C. § 43 by striking "2B1.3" and inserting "2B1.1";

in the line referenced to 18 U.S.C. § 112(a) by striking "2B1.3" and inserting "2B1.1";

in the line referenced to 18 U.S.C. § 152 by striking "2B4.1, 2F1.1" and inserting "2B1.1, 2B4.1";

in the line referenced to 18 U.S.C. § 153 by striking ", 2F1.1";

in the line referenced to 18 U.S.C. § 155 by striking "2F1.1" and inserting "2B1.1";

in the line referenced to 18 U.S.C. § 225 by striking ", 2F1.1";

in the line referenced to 18 U.S.C. § 285 by striking ", 2F1.1";

in the line referenced to 18 U.S.C. § 286 by striking "2F1.1" and inserting "2B1.1";

in the line referenced to 18 U.S.C. § 287 by striking "2F1.1" and inserting "2B1.1";

in the line referenced to 18 U.S.C. § 288 by striking "2F1.1" and inserting "2B1.1";

in the line referenced to 18 U.S.C. § 289 by striking "2F1.1" and inserting "2B1.1";

in the line referenced to 18 U.S.C. § 332 by striking ", 2F1.1";

in the line referenced to 18 U.S.C. § 335 by striking "2F1.1" and inserting "2B1.1";

in the line referenced to 18 U.S.C. § 470 by inserting "2B1.1," before "2B5.1"; and by striking ", 2F1.1";

in the line referenced to 18 U.S.C. § 471 by inserting "2B1.1," before "2B5.1"; and by striking ", 2F1.1";

in the line referenced to 18 U.S.C. § 472 by inserting "2B1.1," before "2B5.1"; and by striking ", 2F1.1";

in the line referenced to 18 U.S.C. § 473 by inserting "2B1.1," before "2B5.1"; and by striking ", 2F1.1";

in the line referenced to 18 U.S.C. § 474 by inserting "2B1.1," before "2B5.1"; and by striking ", 2F1.1";

in the line referenced to 18 U.S.C. § 474A by inserting "2B1.1," before "2B5.1"; and by striking ", 2F1.1";

in the line referenced to 18 U.S.C. § 476 by inserting "2B1.1," before "2B5.1"; and by striking ", 2F1.1";

in the line referenced to 18 U.S.C. § 477 by inserting "2B1.1," before "2B5.1"; and by striking ", 2F1.1";

in the line referenced to 18 U.S.C. § 478 by striking "2F1.1" and inserting "2B1.1";

in the line referenced to 18 U.S.C. § 479 by striking "2F1.1" and inserting "2B1.1";

in the line referenced to 18 U.S.C. § 480 by striking "2F1.1" and inserting "2B1.1";

in the line referenced to 18 U.S.C. § 481 by striking "2F1.1" and inserting "2B1.1";

in the line referenced to 18 U.S.C. § 482 by striking "2F1.1" and inserting "2B1.1";

in the line referenced to 18 U.S.C. § 483 by striking "2F1.1" and inserting "2B1.1";

in the line referenced to 18 U.S.C. § 484 by inserting "2B1.1," before "2B5.1"; and by striking ", 2F1.1";

in the line referenced to 18 U.S.C. § 485 by inserting "2B1.1," before "2B5.1"; and by striking ", 2F1.1";

in the line referenced to 18 U.S.C. § 486 by inserting "2B1.1," before "2B5.1"; and by striking ", 2F1.1";

in the line referenced to 18 U.S.C. § 488 by striking "2F1.1" and inserting "2B1.1";

in the line referenced to 18 U.S.C. § 491 by inserting "2B1.1," before "2B5.1"; and by striking ", 2F1.1";

in the line referenced to 18 U.S.C. § 493 by inserting "2B1.1," before "2B5.1"; and by striking ", 2F1.1";

in the line referenced to 18 U.S.C. § 494 by striking "2F1.1" and inserting "2B1.1";

in the line referenced to 18 U.S.C. § 495 by striking "2F1.1" and inserting "2B1.1";

Amendment 617   APPENDIX C - VOLUME II   November 1, 2013

in the line referenced to 18 U.S.C. § 496 by striking "2F1.1" and inserting "2B1.1";

in the line referenced to 18 U.S.C. § 497 by striking "2F1.1" and inserting "2B1.1";

in the line referenced to 18 U.S.C. § 498 by striking "2F1.1" and inserting "2B1.1";

in the line referenced to 18 U.S.C. § 499 by striking "2F1.1" and inserting "2B1.1";

in the line referenced to 18 U.S.C. § 500 by striking ", 2F1.1";

in the line referenced to 18 U.S.C. § 501 by inserting "2B1.1," before "2B5.1"; and by striking ", 2F1.1";

in the line referenced to 18 U.S.C. § 502 by striking "2F1.1" and inserting "2B1.1";

in the line referenced to 18 U.S.C. § 503 by striking "2F1.1" and inserting "2B1.1";

in the line referenced to 18 U.S.C. § 505 by striking "2F1.1" and inserting "2B1.1";

in the line referenced to 18 U.S.C. § 506 by striking "2F1.1" and inserting "2B1.1";

in the line referenced to 18 U.S.C. § 507 by striking "2F1.1" and inserting "2B1.1";

in the line referenced to 18 U.S.C. § 508 by striking "2F1.1" and inserting "2B1.1";

in the line referenced to 18 U.S.C. § 509 by striking "2F1.1" and inserting "2B1.1";

in the line referenced to 18 U.S.C. § 510 by striking "2F1.1" and inserting "2B1.1";

in the line referenced to 18 U.S.C. § 513 by striking "2F1.1" and inserting "2B1.1";

in the line referenced to 18 U.S.C. § 514 by striking "2F1.1" and inserting "2B1.1";

in the line referenced to 18 U.S.C. § 642 by inserting "2B1.1," before "2B5.1" and striking ", 2F1.1";

in the line referenced to 18 U.S.C. § 656 by striking ", 2F1.1";

in the line referenced to 18 U.S.C. § 657 by striking ", 2F1.1";

in the line referenced to 18 U.S.C. § 659 by striking ", 2F1.1";

in the line referenced to 18 U.S.C. § 663 by striking ", 2F1.1";

in the line referenced to 18 U.S.C. § 665(a) by striking ", 2F1.1";

in the line referenced to 18 U.S.C. § 666(a)(1)(A) by striking ", 2F1.1";

in the line referenced to 18 U.S.C. § 709 by striking "2F1.1" and inserting "2B1.1";

in the line referenced to 18 U.S.C. § 712 by striking "2F1.1" and inserting "2B1.1";

in the line referenced to 18 U.S.C. § 911 by striking "2F1.1" and inserting "2B1.1";

in the line referenced to 18 U.S.C. § 914 by striking "2F1.1" and inserting "2B1.1";

in the line referenced to 18 U.S.C. § 915 by striking "2F1.1" and inserting "2B1.1";

in the line referenced to 18 U.S.C. § 917 by striking "2F1.1" and inserting "2B1.1";

November 1, 2013   APPENDIX C - VOLUME II   **Amendment 617**

in the line referenced to 18 U.S.C. § 970(a) by striking "2B1.3" and inserting "2B1.1";

in the line referenced to 18 U.S.C. § 1001 by striking "2F1.1" and inserting "2B1.1";

in the line referenced to 18 U.S.C. § 1002 by striking "2F1.1" and inserting "2B1.1";

in the line referenced to 18 U.S.C. § 1003 by inserting "2B1.1," before "2B5.1" and striking ", 2F1.1";

in the line referenced to 18 U.S.C. § 1004 by striking "2F1.1" and inserting "2B1.1";

in the line referenced to 18 U.S.C. § 1005 by striking "2F1.1" and inserting "2B1.1";

in the line referenced to 18 U.S.C. § 1006 by striking "2F1.1" and inserting "2B1.1";

in the line referenced to 18 U.S.C. § 1007 by striking "2F1.1" and inserting "2B1.1";

in the line referenced to 18 U.S.C. § 1010 by striking "2F1.1" and inserting "2B1.1";

in the line referenced to 18 U.S.C. § 1011 by striking "2F1.1" and inserting "2B1.1";

in the line referenced to 18 U.S.C. § 1012 by inserting "2B1.1," before "2C1.3"; and by striking ", 2F1.1";

in the line referenced to 18 U.S.C. § 1013 by striking "2F1.1" and inserting "2B1.1";

in the line referenced to 18 U.S.C. § 1014 by striking "2F1.1" and inserting "2B1.1";

in the line referenced to 18 U.S.C. § 1015 by striking "2F1.1" and inserting "2B1.1";

in the line referenced to 18 U.S.C. § 1016 by striking "2F1.1" and inserting "2B1.1";

in the line referenced to 18 U.S.C. § 1017 by striking "2F1.1" and inserting "2B1.1";

in the line referenced to 18 U.S.C. § 1018 by striking "2F1.1" and inserting "2B1.1";

in the line referenced to 18 U.S.C. § 1019 by striking "2F1.1" and inserting "2B1.1";

in the line referenced to 18 U.S.C. § 1020 by striking "2F1.1" and inserting "2B1.1";

in the line referenced to 18 U.S.C. § 1021 by striking "2F1.1" and inserting "2B1.1";

in the line referenced to 18 U.S.C. § 1022 by striking "2F1.1" and inserting "2B1.1";

in the line referenced to 18 U.S.C. § 1023 by striking ", 2F1.1";

in the line referenced to 18 U.S.C. § 1025 by striking "2F1.1" and inserting "2B1.1";

in the line referenced to 18 U.S.C. § 1026 by striking "2F1.1" and inserting "2B1.1";

in the line referenced to 18 U.S.C. § 1028 by striking "2F1.1" and inserting "2B1.1";

in the line referenced to 18 U.S.C. § 1029 by striking "2F1.1" and inserting "2B1.1";

in the line referenced to 18 U.S.C. § 1030(a)(4) by striking "2F1.1" and inserting "2B1.1";

in the line referenced to 18 U.S.C. § 1030(a)(5) by striking "2B1.3" and inserting "2B1.1";

in the line referenced to 18 U.S.C. § 1030(a)(6) by striking "2F1.1" and inserting "2B1.1";

Amendment 617

in the line referenced to 18 U.S.C. § 1031 by striking "2F1.1" and inserting "2B1.1";

in the line referenced to 18 U.S.C. § 1032 by inserting "2B1.1," before "2B4.1"; and by striking ", 2F1.1";

in the line referenced to 18 U.S.C. § 1033 by striking "2F1.1,";

in the line referenced to 18 U.S.C. § 1035 by striking "2F1.1" and inserting "2B1.1";

in the line referenced to 18 U.S.C. § 1341 by inserting "2B1.1," before "2C1.7"; and by striking ", 2F1.1";

in the line referenced to 18 U.S.C. § 1342 by inserting "2B1.1," before "2C1.7"; and by striking ", 2F1.1";

in the line referenced to 18 U.S.C. § 1343 by inserting "2B1.1," before "2C1.7"; and by striking ", 2F1.1";

in the line referenced to 18 U.S.C. § 1344 by striking "2F1.1" and inserting "2B1.1";

in the line referenced to 18 U.S.C. § 1347 by striking "2F1.1" and inserting "2B1.1";

in the line referenced to 18 U.S.C. § 1361 by striking "2B1.3" and inserting "2B1.1";

in the line referenced to 18 U.S.C. § 1362 by striking "2B1.3" and inserting "2B1.1";

in the line referenced to 18 U.S.C. § 1363 by striking "2B1.3" and inserting "2B1.1";

in the line referenced to 18 U.S.C. § 1366 by striking "2B1.3" and inserting "2B1.1";

in the line referenced to 18 U.S.C. § 1422 by inserting "2B1.1," before "2C1.2"; and by striking ", 2F1.1";

in the line referenced to 18 U.S.C. § 1702 by striking "2B1.3,";

in the line referenced to 18 U.S.C. § 1703 by striking "2B1.3,";

in the line referenced to 18 U.S.C. § 1704 by striking ", 2F1.1";

in the line referenced to 18 U.S.C. § 1705 by striking "2B1.3" and inserting "2B1.1";

in the line referenced to 18 U.S.C. § 1706 by striking "2B1.3" and inserting "2B1.1";

in the line referenced to 18 U.S.C. § 1708 by striking ", 2F1.1";

in the line referenced to 18 U.S.C. § 1712 by striking "2F1.1" and inserting "2B1.1";

in the line referenced to 18 U.S.C. § 1716C by striking "2F1.1" and inserting "2B1.1";

in the line referenced to 18 U.S.C. § 1720 by striking "2F1.1" and inserting "2B1.1";

in the line referenced to 18 U.S.C. § 1728 by striking "2F1.1" and inserting "2B1.1";

in the line referenced to 18 U.S.C. § 1852 by striking ", 2B1.3";

in the line referenced to 18 U.S.C. § 1853 by striking ", 2B1.3";

in the line referenced to 18 U.S.C. § 1854 by striking ", 2B1.3";

in the line referenced to 18 U.S.C. § 1857 by striking "2B1.3," and inserting "2B1.1,";

in the line referenced to 18 U.S.C. § 1861 by striking "2F1.1" and inserting "2B1.1";

in the line referenced to 18 U.S.C. § 1902 by striking "2F1.2" and inserting "2B1.4";

in the line referenced to 18 U.S.C. § 1919 by striking "2F1.1" and inserting "2B1.1";

in the line referenced to 18 U.S.C. § 1920 by striking "2F1.1" and inserting "2B1.1";

in the line referenced to 18 U.S.C. § 1923 by striking "2F1.1" and inserting "2B1.1";

in the line referenced to 18 U.S.C. § 1992 by striking "2B1.3" and inserting "2B1.1";

in the line referenced to 18 U.S.C. § 2071 by striking ", 2B1.3";

in the line referenced to 18 U.S.C. § 2072 by striking "2F1.1" and inserting "2B1.1";

in the line referenced to 18 U.S.C. § 2073 by striking "2F1.1" and inserting "2B1.1";

in the line referenced to 18 U.S.C. § 2197 by striking "2F1.1" and inserting "2B1.1";

in the line referenced to 18 U.S.C. § 2272 by striking "2F1.1" and inserting "2B1.1";

in the line referenced to 18 U.S.C. § 2275 by striking "2B1.3" and inserting "2B1.1";

in the line referenced to 18 U.S.C. § 2276 by striking "2B1.3" and inserting "2B1.1";

in the line referenced to 18 U.S.C. § 2280 by striking "2B1.3" and inserting "2B1.1";

in the line referenced to 18 U.S.C. § 2281 by striking "2B1.3" and inserting "2B1.1";

in the line referenced to 18 U.S.C. § 2314 by striking ", 2F1.1";

in the line referenced to 18 U.S.C. § 2315 by striking ", 2F1.1";

in the line referenced to 19 U.S.C. § 1434 by striking "2F1.1" and inserting "2B1.1";

in the line referenced to 19 U.S.C. § 1435 by striking "2F1.1" and inserting "2B1.1";

in the line referenced to 19 U.S.C. § 1436 by striking "2F1.1" and inserting "2B1.1";

in the line referenced to 19 U.S.C. § 1919 by striking "2F1.1" and inserting "2B1.1";

in the line referenced to 19 U.S.C. § 2316 by striking "2F1.1" and inserting "2B1.1";

in the line referenced to 20 U.S.C. § 1097(a) by striking ", 2F1.1";

in the line referenced to 20 U.S.C. § 1097(b) by striking "2F1.1" and inserting "2B1.1";

in the line referenced to 20 U.S.C. § 1097(d) by striking "2F1.1" and inserting "2B1.1";

in the line referenced to 21 U.S.C. § 333(a)(2) by striking "2F1.1" and inserting "2B1.1";

in the line referenced to 22 U.S.C. § 1980(g) by striking "2F1.1" and inserting "2B1.1";

in the line referenced to 22 U.S.C. § 2197(n) by striking "2F1.1" and inserting "2B1.1";

in the line referenced to 22 U.S.C. § 4221 by striking "2F1.1" and inserting "2B1.1";

Amendment 617 — APPENDIX C - VOLUME II — November 1, 2013

in the line referenced to 25 U.S.C. § 450d by striking ", 2F1.1";

in the line referenced to 26 U.S.C. § 7208 by striking "2F1.1" and inserting "2B1.1";

in the line referenced to 26 U.S.C. § 7214 by inserting "2B1.1," before "2C1.1"; and by striking ", 2F1.1";

in the line referenced to 26 U.S.C. § 7232 by striking "2F1.1" and inserting "2B1.1";

in the line referenced to 29 U.S.C. § 1141 by inserting "2B1.1," before "2B3.2"; and by striking ", 2F1.1";

in the line referenced to 38 U.S.C. § 787 by striking "2F1.1" and inserting "2B1.1";

in the line referenced to 38 U.S.C. § 3502 by striking "2F1.1" and inserting "2B1.1";

in the line referenced to 41 U.S.C. § 423(e) by inserting "2B1.1," before "2C1.1"; and by striking ", 2F1.1";

in the line referenced to 42 U.S.C. § 408 by striking "2F1.1" and inserting "2B1.1";

by inserting after the line referenced to 42 U.S.C. § 408 the following new line:

"42 U.S.C. § 1011   2B1.1";

in the line referenced to 42 U.S.C. § 1307(a) by striking "2F1.1" and inserting "2B1.1";

in the line referenced to 42 U.S.C. § 1307(b) by striking "2F1.1" and inserting "2B1.1";

in the line referenced to 42 U.S.C. § 1307a-7b by striking ", 2F1.1";

in the line referenced to 42 U.S.C. § 1383(d)(2) by striking "2F1.1" and inserting "2B1.1";

in the line referenced to 42 U.S.C. § 1383a(a) by striking "2F1.1" and inserting "2B1.1";

in the line referenced to 42 U.S.C. § 1383a(b) by striking "2F1.1" and inserting "2B1.1";

in the line referenced to 42 U.S.C. § 1395nn(a) by striking "2F1.1" and inserting "2B1.1";

in the line referenced to 42 U.S.C. § 1395nn(c) by striking "2F1.1" and inserting "2B1.1";

in the line referenced to 42 U.S.C. § 1396h(a) by striking "2F1.1" and inserting "2B1.1";

in the line referenced to 42 U.S.C. § 1713 by striking "2F1.1" and inserting "2B1.1";

in the line referenced to 42 U.S.C. § 1760(g) by striking ", 2F1.1";

in the line referenced to 42 U.S.C. § 1761(o)(1) by striking "2F1.1" and inserting "2B1.1";

in the line referenced to 42 U.S.C. § 1761(o)(2) by striking ", 2F1.1";

in the line referenced to 42 U.S.C. § 3220(a) by striking "2F1.1" and inserting "2B1.1";

in the line referenced to 42 U.S.C. § 3220(b) by striking ", 2F1.1";

in the line referenced to 42 U.S.C. § 3426 by striking "2F1.1" and inserting "2B1.1";

in the line referenced to 42 U.S.C. § 3791 by striking ", 2F1.1";

November 1, 2013　APPENDIX C - VOLUME II　**Amendment 617**

in the line referenced to 42 U.S.C. § 3792 by striking "2F1.1" and inserting "2B1.1";

in the line referenced to 42 U.S.C. § 3795 by striking ", 2F1.1";

in the line referenced to 42 U.S.C. § 5157(a) by striking "2F1.1" and inserting "2B1.1";

in the line referenced to 45 U.S.C. § 359(a) by striking "2F1.1" and inserting "2B1.1";

in the line referenced to 46 U.S.C. § 1276 by striking "2F1.1" and inserting "2B1.1";

in the line referenced to 49 U.S.C. § 121 by striking "2F1.1" and inserting "2B1.1";

in the line referenced to 49 U.S.C. § 11903 by striking "2F1.1" and inserting "2B1.1";

in the line referenced to 49 U.S.C. § 11904 by striking "2F1.1" and inserting "2B1.1";

in the line referenced to 49 U.S.C. § 14912 by striking "2F1.1" and inserting "2B1.1";

in the line referenced to 49 U.S.C. § 16102 by striking "2F1.1" and inserting "2B1.1";

by inserting after the line referenced to 49 U.S.C. § 16104 the following new line:

"49 U.S.C. § 30170　　　　2B1.1";

by inserting after the line referenced to 49 U.S.C. § 46312 the following new line:

"49 U.S.C. § 46317(a)　　　2B1.1";

in the line referenced to 49 U.S.C. § 60123(d) by striking "2B1.3" and inserting "2B1.1";

in the line referenced to 49 U.S.C. § 80116 by striking "2F1.1" and inserting "2B1.1";

in the line referenced to 49 U.S.C. § 80501 by striking "2B1.3" and inserting "2B1.1"; and

in the line referenced to 49 U.S.C. App. § 1687(g) by striking "2B1.3" and inserting "2B1.1".

Reason for Amendment: This "Economic Crime Package" is a six-part amendment that is the result of Commission study of economic crime issues over a number of years. The major parts of the amendment are: (1) consolidation of the theft, property destruction, and fraud guidelines; (2) a revised, common loss table for the consolidated guideline, and a similar table for tax offenses; (3) a revised, common definition of loss for the consolidated guideline; (4) revisions to guidelines that refer to the loss table in the consolidated guideline; (5) technical and conforming amendments; and (6) amendments regarding tax loss.

Consolidation of Theft, Property Destruction, and Fraud; Miscellaneous Revisions

The first part of this amendment consolidates the guidelines for theft, § 2B1.1 (Larceny, Embezzlement, and Other Forms of Theft; Receiving, Transporting, Transferring, Transmitting, or Possessing Stolen Property), property destruction, § 2B1.3 (Property Damage or Destruction), and fraud, § 2F1.1 (Fraud and Deceit; Forgery; Offenses Involving Altered or Counterfeit Instruments Other than Counterfeit Bearer Obligations of the United States) into one guideline, § 2B1.1 (Theft, Property Destruction, and Fraud). Consolidation will provide similar treatment for similar offenses for which pecuniary harm is a major factor in determining the offense level and, therefore, decrease unwarranted sentencing disparity that may be caused by undue complexity in the guidelines. Consolidation addresses concerns raised over several years by probation officers, judges, and practitioners about the difficulties of determining for particular cases, whether to apply § 2B1.1 or § 2F1.1 and the disparate sentencing outcomes that can result depending on that decision. Commentators have noted that inasmuch as theft and fraud offenses are conceptually similar, there is no strong reason to sentence them differently.

The base offense level for the consolidated guideline is level 6. This maintains the base offense level for fraud offenses, but represents a two-level increase for theft and property destruction offenses, which prior to this amendment was level 4. The increase of two levels in the base offense levels for theft and property destruction offenses will have minimal impact for low-level theft offenses involving offenders in criminal history Category I or Category II. Commission analysis indicates that only a few defendants will move from Zone A (where probation without conditions of confinement is possible) to Zone B or Zone C, and those that are moved into a zone at higher offense levels in the Sentencing Table generally will have criminal history categories above Category I. As a result, the Commission decided against promulgating a two-level reduction for offenses involving loss amounts less than $2,000.

The amendment deletes the two-level enhancement for more than minimal planning previously at §§ 2B1.1(b)(4)(A) and 2F1.1(b)(2)(A). The two-fold reason for this change was to obviate the need for judicial fact-finding about this frequently occurring enhancement and to avoid the potential overlap between the more than minimal planning enhancement and the sophisticated means enhancement previously at § 2F1.1(b)(6) and now, by this amendment, at § 2B1.1(b)(8).

The amendment also eliminates the alternative prong of the more than minimal planning enhancement, at § 2F1.1(b)(2)(B) prior to this amendment, which provided a two-level increase if the offense involved more than one victim. The amendment replaces this enhancement with a specific offense characteristic for offenses that involved large numbers of victims. This change addresses three concerns. First, as a result of the consolidation, the more-than-one-victim enhancement, if retained, would apply in cases that, prior to this amendment, were not subject to such an enhancement. Second, a two-level increase in every case involving more than one victim is arguably inconsistent with the approach in subsection (b)(2) of § 3A1.1 (Hate Crime Motivation or Vulnerable Victim), which provides a two-level increase if the offense involved a large number of vulnerable victims. Third, in practice, the more than minimal planning enhancement was so closely linked with this enhancement that the decision to eliminate the former argues strongly for also eliminating the latter.

The amendment provides a two-level enhancement for offenses involving ten or more, but fewer than 50, victims, and a four-level increase for offenses involving 50 or more victims. This provision is designed to provide a measured increment that results in increased punishment for offenses involving larger numbers of victims. Its applicability to those cases in which victims, both individuals and organizations, sustain an actual loss under subsection (b)(1) or sustain bodily injury.

A special rule is provided for application of the victim enhancement for offenses involving United States mail because of (i) the unique proof problems often attendant to such offenses, (ii) the frequently significant, but difficult to quantify, non-monetary losses in such offenses, and (iii) the importance of maintaining the integrity of the United States mail.

In addition, the amendment moves the mass-marketing enhancement into the new victim-related specific offense characteristic, as an alternative to the two-level adjustment for more than ten, but fewer than 50, victims. The provision is retained to remain responsive to the congressional directive that led to its original promulgation and reflects the Commission's expectation that most telemarketing cases, or similar mass-marketing cases, will have at least ten victims and, receive this enhancement. The mass-marketing alternative enhancement also will continue to apply in cases in which mass-marketing has been used to target a large number of persons, regardless of the number of persons who have sustained an actual loss or injury.

In addition, the amendment provides that if a victim enhancement applies, the enhancement under § 3A1.1(b)(2) for "a large number of vulnerable victims" does not also apply because the more serious conduct already would have resulted in a higher penalty level.

In response to issues raised in a circuit conflict, the amendment revises the commentary related to subsection (b)(4)(B) of § 2B1.1 to clarify the meaning of "person in the business of receiving and selling stolen property." The amendment addresses an issue that has arisen in case law regarding what conduct receives a defendant for the 4-level enhancement.

In determining the meaning of "in the business of", some circuits apply what has been termed the "fence test", under which the court must consider (1) if the stolen property was bought and sold, and (2) to what extent the stolen property transactions encouraged others to commit property crimes. Other circuits have adopted the "totality of the circumstances test" that focuses on the regularity and sophistication of the defendant's operation. Compare United States v. Esquivel, 919 F.2d 957 (5th Cir. 1990), with United States v. St. Cyr, 997 F.2d 698 (1st Cir. 1992). Under either test, courts consider the sophistication and regularity of the business as well as the control, volume, turnover, relationship with thieves, and connections with buyers. Although the factors considered by all of these circuits are similar, the approaches are different.

After consideration, the Commission adopted the totality of circumstances approach because it is more objective and more properly targets the conduct of the individual who is actually in the business of fencing. See United States v. St. Cyr, supra.

In addition, this amendment resolves a circuit conflict regarding the scope of the enhancement in the consolidated guideline for a misrepresentation that the defendant was acting on behalf of a charitable, educational, religious, or political organization, or a government agency. (Prior to this amendment, the enhancement was at subsection (b)(4)(A) of § 2F1.1). The conflict concerns whether the misrepresentation enhancement applies only in cases in which the defendant does not have any authority to act on behalf of the covered organization or government agency or if it applies more broadly to cases in which the defendant has a legitimate connection to the covered organization or government agency, but misrepresents that the defendant is acting solely on behalf of that organization or agency. Compare, e.g., United States v. Marcum, 16 F.3d 599 (4th Cir. 1994) (enhancement appropriate even though defendant did not misrepresent his authority to act on behalf of the organization but rather only misrepresented that he was conducting an activity wholly on behalf of the organization), with United States v. Frazier, 53 F.3d 1105 (10th Cir. 1995) (application of the enhancement is limited to cases in which the defendant exploits the victim by claiming to have authority which in fact does not exist).

The amendment follows the broader view of the Fourth Circuit. It provides for application of the enhancement, now, by this amendment, at § 2B1.1(b)(7)(A), if the defendant falsely represented that the defendant was acting to obtain a benefit for a covered organization or agency when, in fact, the defendant intended to divert all or part of that benefit (for example, for the defendant's personal gain), regardless of whether the defendant actually was associated with the organization or government agency. The Commission determined that the enhancement was appropriate in such cases because the representation that the defendant was acting to obtain a benefit for the organization enables the defendant to commit the offense. In the case of an employee who also holds a position of trust, the amendment provides an application note instructing the court not to apply § 3B1.3 (Abuse of Position of Trust or Use of Special Skill) if the same conduct forms the basis both for the enhancement and the adjustment in § 3B1.3.

The amendment implements the directive in section 3 of the College Scholarship Fraud Prevention Act of 2000, Public Law 106-420, by providing an additional alternative enhancement that applies if the offense involves a misrepresentation to a consumer in connection with obtaining, providing, or furnishing financial assistance for an institution of higher education. The enhancement targets the provider of the financial assistance or scholarship services, not the individual applicant for such assistance or scholarship, consistent with the intent of the legislation.

This amendment makes two minor substantive changes to the enhancement for conscious or reckless risk of serious bodily injury, now, by this amendment, at subsection (b)(11)(A). First, it increases the minimum offense level from level 13 to level 14 to promote proportionality within this guideline. For example, within the theft and fraud guidelines prior to this amendment, there were other specific offense characteristics that had a higher floor offense level than the risk of bodily injury enhancement: (1) "chop shops" (level 14); (2) jeopardizing the solvency of a financial institution (level 24); and (3) personally receiving more than $1,000,000 from a financial institution (level 24). Second, it inserts "death" before the term "or serious bodily injury" to clarify that the risk of the greater harm also is covered. Including risk of death also provides consistency with similar provisions in other parts of the Guidelines Manual, where risk of death is always included with risk of serious bodily injury.

The amendment modifies the four-level increase and minimum offense level of level 24 for a defendant who personally derives more than $1,000,000 in gross receipts from an offense that affected a financial institution, now, by this amendment, at subsection (b)(12)(A). The amendment retains the minimum offense level but reduces the four-level enhancement to two levels because of the increased offense levels that will result from the loss table for the consolidated guideline. The two-level increase was retained because elimination of the enhancement entirely would not provide an appropriate punishment for those offenders involved with losses that are in the $1,000,000 to $2,500,000 range of loss.

The enhancement also was modified to address issues about what it means to "affect" a financial institution and how to apply the enhancement to a case in which there are more than one financial institution involved. Accordingly, the revised provision focuses on whether the defendant derived more than $1,000,000 in gross receipts from one or more financial institutions as a result of the offense.

The amendment includes a new cross reference (subsection (c)(3)) that is more generally applicable and intended to apply whenever a broadly applicable fraud statute is used to reach conduct that is addressed more specifically in another Chapter Two guideline. Prior to this amendment, the fraud guideline contained an application note that instructed the user to move to another, more appropriate Chapter Two guideline, under specified circumstances. Although this note was not a cross reference, but rather a reminder of the principles enunciated in § 1B1.2, it operated like a cross reference in the sense that it required use of a different guideline.

This amendment also makes a minor revision (adding "in a broader form") to the background commentary regarding the implementation of the directive in section 2507 of Public Law 101–647, nullifying the effect of United States v. Tomasino, 206 F. 3d 739 (7th Cir. 2000).

Loss Tables

The amendment provides revised loss tables for this consolidated guideline and for the tax offense guidelines. A principle feature of the new tables is that they expand the previously existing one-level increments into two-level increments, thus increasing the range of losses that correspond to an individual increment, compressing the table, and reducing fact-finding. The new loss tables also provide substantial increases in penalties for moderate and higher loss amounts, even, for fraud and theft offenses, notwithstanding the elimination of the two-level enhancement for more than minimal planning. These higher penalty levels respond to comments received from the Department of Justice, the Criminal Law Committee of the Judicial Conference, and others, that the offenses sentenced under the guidelines consolidated by this amendment under-punish individuals involved with moderate and high loss amounts, relative to penalty levels for offenses of similar seriousness sentenced under other guidelines.

Some offenders accountable for relatively low dollar losses will receive slightly lower offense levels under the new loss table for the consolidated guideline because of (1) the elimination of the enhancement for more than minimal planning; (2) the change from one-level to two-level increments for increasing loss amounts; (3) the selection of the breakpoints for the loss increments (including $5,000 as the first loss amount that results in an increase); and (4) the slope chosen for the relationship between increases in loss amount and increases in offense level at the lower loss amounts. This amendment reflects a decision by the Commission that this effect on penalty levels at lower loss amounts is appropriate for several reasons: (1) the lower offense levels provide appropriate deterrence and punishment, generally, (2) at lower offense levels more defendants will be subject to the court's ability to fashion sentencing alternatives as appropriate (see, e.g., § 5C1.1 (Imposition of a Term of Imprisonment)); and (3) these penalty levels may facilitate the payment of restitution.

The loss table for the consolidated guideline provides the first of incremental increases for cases in which loss exceeds $5,000, rather than $2,000 provided previously in § 2F1.1, or $100 provided previously in § 2B1.1. The Commission believes this will reduce the fact-finding burden on courts for less serious offenses that are generally subject to greater sentencing flexibility because of the availability of alternatives to incarceration.

The amendment also provides a revised loss table in § 2T4.1 (Tax Table) for tax offenses that ensures significantly higher penalty levels for offenses involving moderate and high tax loss in a similar manner and degree as the loss table for the consolidated guideline. The new table is designed to reflect more appropriately the seriousness of tax offenses and to maintain proportionality with the offenses sentenced under the consolidated guideline.

The tax loss table is similar to the loss table for the consolidated guideline, except it does not reduce generally any sentences for offenders involved with lower loss amounts. The tax table provides its first increment for loss at $2,000, rather than the $5,000 threshold under the consolidated guideline (and the $1,700 threshold under the tax loss table prior to this amendment). These differences are intended to avoid unintended decreases that would occur otherwise. The increases in the new tax loss table for offenders involved with lower loss amounts are intended to maintain the long-standing treatment of tax offenses relative to theft and fraud offenses.

Definition of Loss

Amendment 617

This amendment provides a new definition of loss applicable to offenses previously sentenced under §§ 2B1.1, 2B1.3, and 2F1.1. The revised definition makes clarifying and substantive revisions to the definitions of loss previously in the commentary to §§ 2B1.1 and 2F1.1, resolves a number of circuit conflicts, addresses a variety of application issues, and promotes consistency in application.

Significantly, the new definition of loss retains the core rule that loss is the greater of actual and intended loss. The Commission concluded that, for cases in which intended loss is greater than actual loss, the intended loss is a more appropriate initial measure of the culpability of the offender. Conversely, in cases which the actual loss is greater, that amount is a more appropriate measure of the seriousness of the offense.

A definition is provided for intended loss that is consistent with the rule regarding the interaction of actual and intended loss.

The amendment includes a resolution of the circuit conflict relating to the meaning and application of intended loss.

The amendment resolves the conflict to provide that intended loss includes unlikely or impossible losses that are intended, because their inclusion better reflects the culpability of the offender. Compare United States v. Geevers, 226 F.3d 186 (3d Cir. 2000) (agreeing with the majority of circuits holding that impossibility is not in and of itself a limit on the intended loss for purposes of calculating sentences under the guidelines . . . impossibility does not require a sentencing court to lower its calculations of intended loss); and United States v. Coffman, 94 F.3d 330 (7th Cir. 1996) (rejecting the argument that a loss that cannot possibly occur cannot be intended); United States v. Koenig, 952 F.2d 267 (9th Cir. 1991) (holding that § 2F1.1 only requires a calculation of intended loss and does not require a finding that the intentions were realistic); United States v. Klisser, 190 F. 3d 34, 36 (2d Cir. 1999) (same); United States v. Blitz, 151 F. 3d 1002, 1010 (9th Cir. 1998) (same); United States v. Studevent, 116 F. 3d 1559, 1563 (D.C. Cir. 1997) (same); United States v. Wai-Keung, 115 F. 3d 874, 877 (11th Cir. 1997) (same), with United States v. Galbraith, 20 F. 3d 1054, 1059 (10th Cir. 1993) (because intended loss only includes losses that are possible, in an undercover sting operation the intended loss is zero); and United States v. Watkins, 994 F.2d 1192, 1196 (6th Cir. 1993) (holding that a limitation on the broad reach of the intended loss rule is that the intended loss must have been possible to be considered relevant).

Accordingly, concepts such as "economic reality" or "amounts put at risk" will no longer be considerations in the determination of intended loss. See United States v. Bonanno, 146 F.3d 502 (7th Cir. 1998) (holding that the relevant inquiry is how much the scheme put at risk); and United States v. Wells, 127 F. 3d 739 (8th Cir. 1997) (citing United States v. Morris, 18 F.3d 562 (8th Cir. 1994)) (holding that intended loss properly was measured by the possible loss the defendant intended, and did not hinge on actual or net loss).

This amendment also resolves differing circuit interpretations of the standard of causation applicable for actual loss, an issue that was not addressed expressly in the prior definition of actual loss. Various circuits recognized three arguably inconsistent standards for loss causation. First, § 1B1.3 (Relevant Conduct) provides that a defendant is responsible for all losses – foreseen or unforeseen – that result from the defendant's actions or that result from the foreseeable actions of co-participants. See United States v. Sarno, 73 F.3d 1470 (9th Cir. 1995) (holding that "[a] sentence calculated pursuant to the loss tables . . . is properly based on actual loss notwithstanding the fact that this loss may be greater than the intended, expected or foreseeable loss"), cert. denied, 518 U.S. 1020 (1996); and United States v. Lopreato, 83 F.3d 571 (2d Cir. 1996) (holding that in a bribery case, the defendant is responsible for all losses, foreseeable or not). A second view is premised on the fact that prior to this amendment commentary in § 2F1.1 limited the loss amount to the value of the money, property, or services unlawfully taken. See United States v. Marlatt, 24 F.3d 1005 (7th Cir. 1994) (refusing to count foreseeable losses in loss figure because they did not represent the actual thing taken). A third view is that the commentary's explicit inclusion of consequential damages in the loss determination for contract procurement and product substitution cases implies that only non-consequential or direct damages are included in other cases. See United States v. Thomas, 62 F.3d 1332 (11th Cir. 1995), cert. denied, 516 U.S. 1166 (1996) (only non-consequential or direct damages are included in loss). See also United States v. Daddona, 34 F.3d 163 (3d Cir.), cert. denied, 513 U.S. 1002 (1994) (holding that merely incidental or consequential damages may not be counted in computing loss); and United States v. Newman, 6 F.3d 623 (9th Cir. 1993) (holding that loss caused by the defendant arsonist was only the value of the property destroyed by the fire, not costs of putting out the fire).

The amendment defines "actual loss" as the "reasonably foreseeable pecuniary harm" that resulted from the offense. The amendment incorporates this causation standard that, at a minimum, requires factual causation (often called "but for" causation) and provides a rule for legal causation (i.e., guidance to courts regarding how to draw the line as to what losses should be included and excluded from the loss determination). Significantly, the application of this causation standard in the great variety of factual contexts in which it is expected to occur appropriately is entrusted to sentencing judges.

"Pecuniary harm" is defined in a manner that excludes emotional distress, harm to reputation, and other non-economic harm, in order to foreclose the laborious effort sometimes necessary to quantify non-economic harms (as in some tort proceedings, for example).

"Reasonably foreseeable pecuniary harm" is defined to include pecuniary harms that the defendant knew or, under the circumstances, reasonably should have known, was a potential result of the offense. The Commission determined that this standard better ensures the inclusion in loss of those harms that reflect the seriousness of the offense and the culpability of the offender.

The definition deletes the previous rule that, by negative implication, excludes consequential damages (except in specified cases), thus resolving a circuit conflict. Compare United States v. Izydore, 167 F.3d 213 (5th Cir. 1999) (the fact that the Commission prescribed consequential losses in only specific fraud cases, and not others, is strong evidence that consequential damages were omitted from the general loss definition by design rather than mistake), with United States v. Gottfried, 58 F.3d 648 (D.C. Cir. 1995) (holding that merely incidental or consequential damages may not be counted in computing loss). The Commission decided, however, not to use the term "consequential damages," or any similar civil law distinction between direct and indirect harms. Rather, the Commission determined that the reasonable foreseeability standard provides sufficient guidance to courts as to what type of harms are included in loss.

In addition, this amendment preserves the special provisions addressing loss in protected computer offenses and the inclusion of consequential damages in product substitution and contract procurement offenses; however, these special cases are re-characterized as rules of construction to avoid any negative implications regarding other types of offenses.

The amendment reflects a decision by the Commission that interest and similar costs shall be excluded from loss. However, the amendment provides that a departure may be warranted in the rare case in which exclusion of interest will under-punish the offender. Thus, the rule resolves the circuit split regarding whether "bargained for" interest may be included in loss. Compare United States v. Henderson, 19 F.3d 917 (5th Cir.), cert. denied, 513 U.S. 877 (1994) (holding that interest should be included if the victim had a reasonable expectation of receiving interest from the transaction); United States v. Gilberg, 75 F.3d 15 (1st Cir. 1996) (including in loss interest on fraudulently procured mortgage loan); and United States v. Sharma, 190 F.3d 220 (3d Cir. 1999) (holding that Application Note 8 of § 2F1.1 requires the exclusion of "opportunity cost" interest, but did not intend to exclude bargained-for interest), with United States v. Hoyle, 33 F.3d 415 (4th Cir. 1994), cert. denied, 513 U.S. 1133 (1995) (excluding interest from the determination of loss for sentencing purposes); and United States v. Guthrie, 144 F.3d 1006 (6th Cir. 1998) (holding that when the defendant concealed assets in a bankruptcy proceeding, the lower court's determination that loss to creditors included interest was erroneous). This rule is consistent with the general purpose of the loss determination to serve as a rough measurement of the seriousness of the offense and culpability of the offender and avoids unnecessary litigation regarding the amount of interest to be included.

The loss definition also excludes from loss certain costs incurred by the government and victims in connection with criminal investigation and prosecution of the offense. Such losses are likely to occur in a broad range of cases, would present a fact-finding burden in those cases, and would not contribute to the ability of loss to perform its essential function.

The loss definition also provides for the exclusion from loss of certain economic benefits transferred to victims, to be measured at the time of detection. This provision codifies the "net loss" approach that has developed in the case law, with some modifications made for policy reasons. This crediting approach is adopted because the seriousness of the offense and the culpability of a defendant is better determined by using a net approach. This approach recognizes that the offender who transfers something of value to the victim(s) generally is committing a less serious offense than an offender who does not.

The amendment adopts "time of detection" as the most appropriate and least burdensome time for measuring the value of the transferred benefits. The Commission determined that valuing such benefits at the time of transfer would be especially problematic in cases in which the offender misrepresented the value of an item that is difficult to value. Although the time of detection standard will allow some fluctuation in value which may inure to the defendant's benefit or detriment, the Commission determined that, because the time of detection is closer in time to the sentencing and occurs at a point when the authorities are aware of the criminality, its use generally would make it easier to determine a more accurate value of the benefit.

The definition of "time of detection" was adopted because there may be situations in which it is difficult to prove that the defendant knew the offense was detected even if it was already discovered. In addition, the words "about to be detected" are included to cover those situations in which the offense is not yet detected, but the defendant knows it is about to be detected. In such a case, it would be inappropriate to credit the defendant with benefits transferred to the victim after that defendant's awareness.

The definition of "loss" also provides special rules for certain schemes. One rule includes in loss (and excludes from crediting) the benefits received by victims of persons fraudulently providing professional services. This rule reverses case law that has allowed crediting (or exclusion from loss) in cases in which services were provided by persons posing as attorneys and medical personnel. See United States v. Maurello, 76 F.3d 1304 (3d Cir. 1996) (calculating loss by subtracting the value of satisfactory legal services from amount of fees paid to a person posing as a lawyer); and United States v. Reddeck, 22 F.3d 1504 (10th Cir. 1994) (reducing loss by the value of education received from a sham university). The Commission determined that the seriousness of these offenses and the culpability of these offenders is best reflected by a loss determination that does not credit the value of the unlicensed benefits provided. In addition, this provision eliminates the additional burden that would be imposed on courts if required to determine the value of these benefits.

Similarly, the definition of loss provides a special rule that includes in loss (and excludes from crediting) the value of items that were falsely represented as approved by a regulatory agency, for which regulatory approval was obtained by fraud, or for which regulatory approval was required but not obtained. The Commission determined that the seriousness of these offenses and the culpability of these offenders is best reflected by a loss determination that does not credit the value of these items. This decision reflects the importance of the regulatory approval process to public health, safety, and confidence.

Regarding investment schemes, the amendment resolves a circuit conflict regarding whether and how to credit payments made to victims. Compare United States v. Mucciante, 21 F.3d 1228 (2nd Cir. 1994) (under the Guidelines, loss includes the value of all property taken, even though all or part of it was returned.); United States v. Deavours, 219 F.3d 400 (5th Cir. 2000) (intended loss is not reduced by any sums returned to investors); and United States v. Loayza, 107 F.3d 257 (4th Cir. 1997) (declining to follow the approach of net loss and holding defendants responsible for the value of all property taken, even though all or a part is returned), with United States v. Holiusa, 13 F.3d 1043 (7th Cir. 1994) (holding that only the net loss should be included in loss, thus allowing a credit for returned interest), and United States v. Orton, 73 F.3d 331 (11th Cir. 1996) (only payments made to losing investors should be credited, not payments to investors who made a profit).

This amendment adopts the approach of the Eleventh Circuit that excludes the gain to any individual investor in the scheme from being used to offset the loss to other individual investors because any gain realized by an individual investor is designed to lure others into the fraudulent scheme. See United States v. Orton, supra.

The definition retains the rule providing for the use of gain when loss cannot reasonably be determined. It clarifies that there must be a loss for gain to be considered. In doing so, the Commission resolved another circuit conflict. Compare United States v. Robie, 166 F.3d 444 (2d Cir. 1999) (holding that use of defendant's gain for purposes of subsection (b)(1) is improper if there is no economic loss to the victim), with United States v. Haas, 171 F.3d 259 (5th Cir. 1999) (stating that "if the loss is either incalculable or zero, the district court must determine the § 2F1.1 sentence enhancement by estimating the gain to the defendant as a result of his fraud"). The Commission decided not to expand the use of gain to situations in which loss can be determined but the gain is greater than the loss because such instances should occur infrequently, the efficiency of the criminal operation as reflected in the amount of gain ordinarily should not determine the penalty level, and the traditional use of loss is generally adequate.

The amendment revises the special rule on determining loss in cases involving diversion of government program benefits to resolve another circuit conflict. The revision is intended to clarify that loss in such cases only includes amounts that were diverted from intended recipients or uses, not benefits received or used by authorized persons. In other words, even if such benefits flowed through an unauthorized intermediary, as long as they went to intended recipients for intended uses, the amount of those benefits should not be included in loss. Compare United States v. Henry, 164 F.3d 1304 (10th Cir. 1999) (holding that loss includes the value of gross benefits paid, rather than the value of benefits improperly received or diverted in determining the loss), with United States v. Peters, 59 F.3d 732 (8th Cir. 1995) (determining that loss is the value of benefits diverted from intended

Amendment 617 APPENDIX C - VOLUME II November 1, 2013

recipients); and United States v. Barnes, 117 F.3d 328 (7th Cir. 1997) (holding that the sentence is calculated only on the value of the government benefits diverted from intended recipients or users). This net loss approach is more consistent with general rules for determining loss.

Referring Guidelines for Theft and Fraud

The amendment includes revisions to the guidelines that, prior to this amendment, referred to the loss tables in § 2B1.1 or § 2F1.1. Pursuant to this amendment, these guidelines will refer to the loss tables in the consolidated guideline. Prior to this amendment, the referring guidelines used the tables in §§ 2B1.1 and 2F1.1, which provided the first loss increment for losses in excess of $2,000. Because the consolidated loss table provides the first loss increment for losses in excess of $5,000, the referring guidelines are amended to provide a one-level increase in a case in which the loss is more than $2,000, but did not exceed $5,000. This increase is provided to avoid a one-level decrease that would otherwise occur for an offense involving losses of more than $2,000 but not more than $5,000.

Two referring guidelines (§§ 2B2.1 (Burglary of a Residence or a Structure Other than a Residence) and 2B3.1 (Robbery)) that use the definition of loss previously in § 2B1.1 will retain that definition of loss rather than the new loss definition in the consolidated guideline. The existing definition has not proven problematic for cases sentenced under these guidelines.

Technical and Conforming Amendments

The amendment includes a number of technical and conforming amendments, most of which are necessitated by the consolidation and the deletion of the more than minimal planning enhancement.

Computing Tax Loss

This amendment addresses several issues related to tax loss. It addresses a circuit conflict regarding how tax loss under § 2T1.1 (Tax Evasion) is computed for cases that involve a defendant's under-reporting of income on both individual and corporate tax returns. Such a case often arises when (1) the defendant fails to report, and pay corporate income taxes on, income earned by the corporation; (2) the defendant diverts that unreported corporate income for the defendant's personal use; and (3) the defendant fails to report, and to pay personal income taxes on, that diverted income. The amendment provides that the amount of the federal tax loss is the sum of the federal income tax due from the corporation and the amount of federal income tax due from the individual.

The amendment thereby resolves a circuit conflict as to the methodology used to calculate tax loss in cases involving a corporate diversion. Two circuits use a sequential method to aggregate the tax loss. Under this method, the court determines the corporate federal income tax that would have been due, subtracts that amount from the amount diverted to the defendant personally, then determines the personal federal income tax that would have been due on the reduced diverted amount. See United States v. Harvey, 996 F.2d 919 (7th Cir. 1993); and United States v. Martinez-Rios, 143 F.3d 662 (2d Cir. 1998). The Commission adopted the alternative method used in United States v. Cseplo, 42 F.3d 360 (6th Cir. 1994), in which the court determines the corporate federal income tax due on the diverted amount, and adds that amount to the personal federal income tax due on the total amount diverted. This clarifies the prior rule in Application Note 7 of § 2T1.1 that "if the offense involves both individual and corporate tax returns, the tax loss is the aggregate tax loss from the offenses taken together" and reflects the Commission's conclusion that, in cases of corporate diversions, the method for computing total tax loss adopted by the Sixth

Circuit in Cseplo more accurately reflects the seriousness of the total harm caused by these offenses than would be reflected by the alternative method.

In evasion-of-payment tax cases, the Commission amended the definition of "tax loss" to include interest and penalties because, in contrast to evasion-of-assessment tax cases, such amounts appropriately are included in tax loss for such cases. This amendment limits the inclusion of interest or penalties to willful evasion of payment cases under 26 U.S.C. § 7201 and willful failure to pay cases under 26 U.S.C. § 7203. The nature of these cases is such that the interest and penalties often greatly exceed the assessed tax amount constituting the bulk of the harm associated with these offenses.

This amendment also revises the sophisticated concealment enhancement in subsection (b)(2) of §§ 2T1.1 (Tax Evasion) and 2T1.4 (Aiding, Assisting, Procuring, Counseling, or Advising Tax Fraud) to conform to the sophisticated means enhancement in the consolidated guideline, including imposition of a minimum offense level of level 12. This revision is appropriate inasmuch as certain tax offenses can be committed using sophisticated means in addition to being concealed in a sophisticated manner. Indeed, tax offenses committed in a sophisticated manner are more serious offenses, and reflect a greater culpability on the part of the offender (just as a tax offense concealed in a sophisticated manner reflects greater culpability). Consequently, this revision will allow the enhancement to apply to a somewhat greater range of tax offenses than the previously existing sophisticated concealment enhancement.

In addition, the amendment revises "offshore bank accounts" by substituting "financial" for "bank", to ensure that the enhancement applies to conduct involving similar kinds of accounts, consistent with language in § 2S1.1 (Laundering of Monetary Instruments; Engaging in Monetary Transactions in Property Derived from Unlawful Activity). A similar revision is made in § 2B1.1.

Effective Date: The effective date of this amendment is November 1, 2001.

618. **Amendment:** Section 2B5.1(b)(2) is amended by inserting "(A)" after "defendant"; and by striking ", and the offense level as determined above is less than 15, increase to level 15." and inserting "; or (B) controlled or possessed (i) counterfeiting paper similar to a distinctive paper; or (ii) a feature or device essentially identical to a distinctive counterfeit deterrent, increase by 2 levels.".

Section 2B5.1(b) is amended by redesignating subdivisions (3) and (4) as subdivisions (4) and (5), respectively; and by inserting after subdivision (2) the following:

> "(3) If subsection (b)(2)(A) applies, and the offense level determined under that subsection is less than level 15, increase to level 15.".

The Commentary to § 2B5.1 captioned "Statutory Provisions" is amended by inserting "A" after "474".

The Commentary to § 2B5.1 captioned "Application Notes" is amended by striking Note 1 as follows:

> "1. For purposes of this guideline, 'United States' means each of the fifty states, the District of Columbia, the Commonwealth of Puerto Rico, the United States Virgin Islands, Guam, the Northern Mariana Islands, and American Samoa.",

and inserting the following:

"1. Definitions.—For purposes of this guideline:

'Distinctive counterfeit deterrent' and 'distinctive paper' have the meaning given those terms in 18 U.S.C. § 474A(c)(2) and (1), respectively.

'United States' means each of the fifty states, the District of Columbia, the Commonwealth of Puerto Rico, the United States Virgin Islands, Guam, the Northern Mariana Islands, and American Samoa.".

The Commentary to § 2B5.1 captioned "Application Notes" is amended in Note 2 by inserting "Applicability to Counterfeit Bearer Obligations of the United States.—" before "This guideline".

The Commentary to § 2B5.1 captioned "Application Notes" is amended in Note 3 by inserting "Inapplicability to Genuine but Fraudulently Altered Instruments.—" before "'Counterfeit,".

The Commentary to § 2B5.1 captioned "Application Notes" is amended by striking Note 4 as follows:

"4. Subsection (b)(2) does not apply to persons who merely photocopy notes or otherwise produce items that are so obviously counterfeit that they are unlikely to be accepted even if subjected to only minimal scrutiny.",

and inserting the following:

"4. Inapplicability to Certain Obviously Counterfeit Items.—Subsection (b)(2)(A) does not apply to persons who produce items that are so obviously counterfeit that they are unlikely to be accepted even if subjected to only minimal scrutiny.".

The Commentary to § 2B5.1 captioned "Background" is amended by striking "(b)(3)" and inserting "(b)(4)".

Reason for Amendment: The frequency of counterfeiting offenses has increased significantly since 1995 due to the increasing affordability and availability of personal computers and digital printers. This amendment addresses concerns raised by the Department of the Treasury and the United States Secret Service regarding both the operation of, and the penalties provided by, § 2B5.1 (Offenses Involving Counterfeit Bearer Obligations of the United States). The amendment increases penalties for counterfeiting activity in two ways.

First, the amendment adds a two-level enhancement for manufacturing, in addition to the minimum offense level of level 15 for manufacturing. This change will ensure some degree of additional punishment for all offenders who engage in manufacturing activity.

Second, the amendment adds a two-level enhancement (which would apply alternatively to the manufacturing enhancement) if the offense involved possessing or controlling (1) paper that is similar to a distinctive paper used by the United States for its currency, obligations, or securities; or (2) a feature or device that is essentially identical to a distinctive counterfeit deterrent used by the United States for its currency, obligations, or securities. This enhancement is justified because of the higher statutory maximum penalties under 18 U.S.C. § 474A (i.e., a term of imprisonment of up to 25 years compared to

10, 15, and 20 years for other counterfeiting offenses). In addition, use of paper similar to "distinctive paper" and use of features and devices essentially identical to "distinctive counterfeit deterrents" (both of which are defined in § 2B5.1 consistently with the statute) make the counterfeit item more passable and the offense more sophisticated.

In addition, the amendment deletes the language in the commentary of § 2B5.1 that suggests that the manufacturing adjustment does not apply if the defendant "merely photocopies". That commentary was intended to make the manufacturing minimum offense level of level 15 inapplicable to notes that are so obviously counterfeit that they are unlikely to be accepted. Particularly with the advent of digital technology, it cannot be said that photocopying necessarily produces a note so obviously counterfeit as to be impassible.

Effective Date: The effective date of this amendment is November 1, 2001.

619. **Amendment:** Section 2C1.3 is amended in the title by adding "; Payment or Receipt of Unauthorized Compensation" after "Interest".

Section 2C1.3 is amended by adding after subsection (b) the following:

"(c) Cross Reference

(1) If the offense involved a bribe or gratuity, apply § 2C1.1 (Offering, Giving, Soliciting, or Receiving a Bribe; Extortion Under Color of Official Right) or § 2C1.2 (Offering, Giving, Soliciting, or Receiving a Gratuity), as appropriate, if the resulting offense level is greater than the offense level determined above.".

The Commentary to § 2C1.3 captioned "Statutory Provisions" is amended by inserting ", 209, 1909" after "208".

The Commentary to § 2C1.3 captioned "Application Note" is amended in Note 1 by inserting "Abuse of Position of Trust.—" before "Do not".

The Commentary to § 2C1.3 is amended by striking the background as follows:

"Background: This section applies to financial and non-financial conflicts of interest by present and former federal officers and employees.".

Chapter Two, Part C is amended by striking § 2C1.4 and its accompanying commentary as follows:

"§ 2C1.4. Payment or Receipt of Unauthorized Compensation

(a) Base Offense Level: 6

Commentary

Statutory Provisions: 18 U.S.C. §§ 209, 1909.

Application Note:

1. Do not apply the adjustment in § 3B1.3 (Abuse of Position of Trust or Use of Special Skill).

Background: Violations of 18 U.S.C. § 209 involve the unlawful supplementation

Amendment 619

of salary of various federal employees. 18 U.S.C. § 1909 prohibits bank examiners from performing any service for compensation for banks or bank officials.".

Section 8C2.1(a) is amended by striking "2C1.4,".

Reason for Amendment: The amendment (1) consolidates §§ 2C1.3 (Conflict of Interest) and 2C1.4 (Payment or Receipt of Unauthorized Compensation) covering payments to obtain public office, to promote ease of application; and (2) adds a cross reference in § 2C1.3 (Conflict of Interest; Payment or Receipt of Unauthorized Compensation) to § 2C1.1 (Offering, Giving, Soliciting, or Receiving a Bribe; Extortion Under Color of Official Right) and § 2C1.2 (Offering, Giving, Soliciting, or Receiving a Gratuity) to account for aggravating conduct often occurring in offenses involving the unlawful supplementation of the salary of various federal officials and employees committed in violation of 18 U.S.C. § 209.

The amendment simplifies guideline operation by consolidating §§ 2C1.3 and 2C1.4. Consolidation is appropriate because the gravamen of the offenses covered by §§ 2C1.3 and 2C1.4 is similar: unauthorized receipt of a payment in respect to an official act. The cross reference to § 2C1.1 or § 2C1.2 was added by this amendment because the cases to which these guidelines apply usually involve a conflict of interest offense that is associated with a bribe or gratuity.

Effective Date: The effective date of this amendment is November 1, 2001.

620. **Amendment:** Section 2D1.1(b)(5) through (7), Notes 20 and 21 of the Commentary to § 2D1.1 captioned "Application Notes", the ninth and tenth paragraphs of the Commentary to § 2D1.1 captioned "Background", and § 2D1.10, effective December 16, 2000 (see Amendment 608), are repromulgated with the following changes:

Section 2D1.1(b) is amended by striking subdivision (5) as follows:

"(5) If the offense involved (A) an unlawful discharge, emission, or release into the environment of a hazardous or toxic substance; or (B) the unlawful transportation, treatment, storage, or disposal of a hazardous waste, increase by 2 levels.";

by redesignating subdivisions (6) and (7) as subdivisions (5) and (6), respectively; by redesignating subdivisions (5)(A) and (5)(B), as redesignated by this amendment, as subdivisions (5)(B) and (5)(C), respectively; and by inserting before subdivision (5)(B), as redesignated by this amendment, the following:

"(A) If the offense involved (i) an unlawful discharge, emission, or release into the environment of a hazardous or toxic substance; or (ii) the unlawful transportation, treatment, storage, or disposal of a hazardous waste, increase by 2 levels.".

Section 2D1.1(b)(5)(B), as redesignated by this amendment, is amended by striking "subsection (b)(6)(B)" and inserting "subdivision (C)".

The Commentary to § 2D1.1 captioned "Application Notes" is amended by striking Note 20 (redesignated as Note 19 by amendment 624) as follows:

"20. Hazardous or Toxic Substances.—Subsection (b)(5) applies if the conduct for which the defendant is accountable under § 1B1.3 (Relevant Conduct) involved any discharge, emission, release, transportation, treatment, storage, or disposal violation covered by the Resource Conservation and Recovery Act, 42 U.S.C. § 6928(d), the Federal Water Pollution Control Act, 33 U.S.C. § 1319(c), or the Comprehensive Environmental Response, Compensation, and Liability Act, 42 U.S.C. §§ 5124, 9603(b). In some cases, the enhancement under subsection (b)(5) may not adequately account for the seriousness of the environmental harm or other threat to public health or safety (including the health or safety of law enforcement and cleanup personnel). In such cases, an upward departure may be warranted. Additionally, any costs of environmental cleanup and harm to persons or property should be considered by the court in determining the amount of restitution under § 5E1.1 (Restitution) and in fashioning appropriate conditions of supervision under §§ 5B1.3 (Conditions of Probation) and 5D1.3 (Conditions of Supervised Release).",

and inserting the following:

"20.   Hazardous or Toxic Substances.—Subsection (b)(5)(A) applies if the conduct for which the defendant is accountable under § 1B1.3 (Relevant Conduct) involved any discharge, emission, release, transportation, treatment, storage, or disposal violation covered by the Resource Conservation and Recovery Act, 42 U.S.C. § 6928(d); the Federal Water Pollution Control Act, 33 U.S.C. § 1319(c); the Comprehensive Environmental Response, Compensation, and Liability Act, 42 U.S.C. § 9603(b); or 49 U.S.C. § 5124 (relating to violations of laws and regulations enforced by the Department of Transportation with respect to the transportation of hazardous material). In some cases, the enhancement under subsection (b)(5)(A) may not account adequately for the seriousness of the environmental harm or other threat to public health or safety (including the health or safety of law enforcement and cleanup personnel). In such cases, an upward departure may be warranted. Additionally, in determining the amount of restitution under § 5E1.1 (Restitution) and in fashioning appropriate conditions of probation and supervision under §§ 5B1.3 (Conditions of Probation) and 5D1.3 (Conditions of Supervised Release), respectively, any costs of environmental cleanup and harm to individuals or property shall be considered by the court in cases involving the manufacture of amphetamine or methamphetamine and should be considered by the court in cases involving the manufacture of a controlled substance other than amphetamine or methamphetamine. See 21 U.S.C. § 853(q) (mandatory restitution for cleanup costs relating to the manufacture of amphetamine and methamphetamine).".

The Commentary to § 2D1.1 captioned "Application Notes" is amended in Note 21(A) (redesignated as Note 20(A) by amendment 624) by striking "(b)(6)" and inserting "(b)(5)(B) or (C)"; by striking "may consider factors such as the following" and inserting "shall include consideration of the following factors"; by striking "or" after "at the laboratory," and inserting "and"; by striking "or" after "disposed," and inserting "and"; by striking "or" after "the offense" and inserting "and"; by striking "amphetamine or methamphetamine"; and by inserting "whether the laboratory is located" after "e.g.,".

The Commentary to § 2D1.1 captioned "Application Notes" is amended in Note 21(B) (redesignated as Note 20(B) by amendment 624) by striking "(b)(6)(B)" and inserting "(b)(5)(C)".

The Commentary to § 2D1.1 captioned "Background" is amended in the ninth paragraph by inserting "(A)" after "(b)(5)"; and in the tenth paragraph by striking "Subsection (b)(6) implements" and inserting "Subsections (b)(5)(B) and (C) implement, in a broader form,";

Amendment 620 APPENDIX C - VOLUME II November 1, 2013

and by striking "878" and inserting "310".

The Commentary to § 2D1.10 captioned "Application Note" is amended in Note 1 by striking "may consider factors such as the following" and inserting "shall include consideration of the following factors"; by striking "or" after "at the laboratory," and inserting "and"; by striking "or" after "disposed," and inserting "and"; by striking "or" after "the offense" and inserting "and"; by striking "amphetamine or methamphetamine"; and by inserting "whether the laboratory is located" after "e.g.,".

The Commentary to § 2D1.10 captioned "Background" is amended by striking "878" and inserting "310".

Reason for Amendment: The Commission promulgated an emergency amendment addressing the directive in section 102 (the "substantial risk directive") of the Methamphetamine Anti-Proliferation Act of 2000, Pub. L. 106–310 (the "Act"), with an effective date of December 16, 2000. (See Amendment 608.) This amendment repromulgates the emergency amendment, with modifications, as a permanent amendment.

The substantial risk directive instructs the Commission to amend the federal sentencing guidelines with respect to any offense relating to the manufacture, attempt to manufacture, or conspiracy to manufacture amphetamine or methamphetamine in (1) the Controlled Substances Act, 21 U.S.C. §§ 801-90; (2) the Controlled Substances Import and Export Act, 21 U.S.C. §§ 951-71; or (3) the Maritime Drug Law Enforcement Act, 46 U.S.C. App. §§ 1901-04.

The Act requires the Commission, in carrying out the substantial risk directive, to provide the following enhancements—

> (A) if the offense created a substantial risk of harm to human life (other than a life described in subparagraph (B)) or the environment, increase the base offense level for the offense—
>
>> (i) by not less than 3 offense levels above the applicable level in effect on the date of the enactment of this Act; or
>>
>> (ii) if the resulting base offense level after an increase under clause (i) would be less than level 27, to not less than level 27; or
>
> (B) if the offense created a substantial risk of harm to the life of a minor or incompetent, increase the base offense level for the offense—
>
>> (i) by not less than 6 offense levels above the applicable level in effect on the date of the enactment of this Act; or
>>
>> (ii) if the resulting base offense level after an increase under clause (i) would be less than level 30, to not less than level 30.

The emergency amendment provided enhancements in §§ 2D1.1 (Unlawful Manufacturing, Importing, Exporting, or Trafficking (Including Possession with Intent to Commit These Offenses); Attempt or Conspiracy) and 2D1.10 (Endangering Human Life While Illegally Manufacturing a Controlled Substance) that also apply in the case of an attempt or a conspiracy to manufacture amphetamine or methamphetamine. The amendment did not amend § 2D1.11 (Unlawfully Distributing, Importing, Exporting or Possessing a Listed Chemical; Attempt or Conspiracy) or § 2D1.12 (Unlawful Possession, Manufacture, Distribution, or Importation of Prohibited Flask or Equipment). Although offenses that involve the manufacture of amphetamine or methamphetamine also are referenced in Appendix A

(Statutory Index) to §§ 2D1.11 and 2D1.12, the cross references in these guidelines, which apply if the offense involved the manufacture of a controlled substance, will result in application of § 2D1.1 and accordingly, the enhancements.

The basic structure of the emergency amendment to §§ 2D1.1 and 2D1.10 tracked the structure of the substantial risk directive. Accordingly, in § 2D1.1, the amendment provided a three-level increase and a minimum offense level of level 27 if the offense (1) involved the manufacture of amphetamine or methamphetamine; and (2) created a substantial risk of harm either to human life or the environment. For offenses that created a substantial risk of harm to the life of a minor or an incompetent, the amendment provided a six-level increase and a minimum offense level of level 30.

However, the structure of the emergency amendment to § 2D1.10 differed from the structure of the emergency amendment to § 2D1.1 with respect to the first prong of the enhancement (regarding substantial risk of harm to human life or to the environment). Specifically, the emergency amendment provided a three-level increase and a minimum offense level of level 27 if the offense involved the manufacture of amphetamine or methamphetamine without making application of the enhancement dependent upon whether the offense also involved a substantial risk of either harm to human life or the environment. Consideration of whether the offense involves a substantial risk of harm to human life also is unnecessary because § 2D1.10 applies only to convictions under 21 U.S.C. § 858, and the creation of a substantial risk of harm to human life is an element of an offense under 21 U.S.C. § 858. Therefore, the base offense level already takes into account the substantial risk of harm to human life. Consideration of whether the offense involved a substantial risk of harm to the environment was unnecessary because the directive predicated application of the enhancement on substantial risk of harm either to human life or to the environment, and the creation of a substantial risk of harm to human life necessarily is taken into account as an element of the offense.

Neither the substantial risk directive nor any statutory provision defines "substantial risk of harm." Based on an analysis of relevant case law that interpreted "substantial risk of harm," the emergency amendment provided commentary setting forth factors that may be relevant in determining whether a particular offense created a substantial risk of harm. The definition of "incompetent" was modeled after several state statutes.

This permanent amendment re-promulgates, with modifications, the emergency amendment regarding the substantial risk directive. This amendment differs from the emergency amendment in several respects:

First, in § 2D1.1, this amendment treats the existing specific offense characteristic in § 2D1.1(b)(5), relating to a two-level enhancement for environmental violations occurring in the course of a drug trafficking offense, as an alternative to the three-level enhancement for substantial risk of harm to human life or the environment. This portion of the amendment is in response to an issue related to the substantial risk directive regarding how to implement it in a manner consistent with the earlier environmental hazard directive in section 303 of the Comprehensive Methamphetamine Control Act, Pub. L. 104–237. The emergency amendment made the enhancements cumulative. However, this permanent amendment makes the new guideline provision alternative with the pre-existing enhancement for environmental hazards in § 2D1.1.

Second, in § 2D1.1, this amendment lists four factors that the court "shall", as opposed to "may", consider to determine whether subsection (b)(6)(A) or (B) applies. Similarly, in § 2D1.10, this amendment lists four factors the court "shall" consider to determine whether subsection (b)(1)(B) applies. The list of four factors was identified by the Commission to

Amendment 620

assist the courts in defining the meaning of "substantial risk of harm" for offenses related to the production and trafficking of precursor chemicals and the manufacture of amphetamine and methamphetamine.

Third, in § 2D1.1, this amendment provides that the court (1) shall consider any costs of environmental cleanup and harm to individuals and property in cases involving the manufacture of amphetamine or methamphetamine in determining the amount of restitution under § 5E1.1 (Restitution) and in fashioning appropriate conditions of probation and supervision under §§ 5B1.3 (Conditions of Probation) and 5D1.3 (Conditions of Supervised Release), and (2) should consider such costs and harms in cases involving the manufacture of a controlled substance other than amphetamine or methamphetamine.

The amendment also makes a minor technical change in the background commentary.

Effective Date: The effective date of this amendment is November 1, 2001.

621. **Amendment:** The subdivision captioned "LSD, PCP, and Other Schedule I and II Hallucinogens (and their immediate precursors)*" of the Drug Equivalency Tables of Note 10 of the Commentary to § 2D1.1 captioned "Application Notes", effective May 1, 2001 (see Amendment 609), is repromulgated without change.

Reason for Amendment: This amendment repromulgates (as a permanent amendment) without change the emergency amendment previously promulgated that addressed the directive in section 3664 of the Ecstasy Anti-Proliferation Act of 2000, Pub. L. 106–310 (the "Act"). (See Amendment 609). That directive instructs the Commission to provide increased penalties for the manufacture, importation, exportation, or trafficking of "Ecstasy". The directive specifically requires the Commission to increase the base offense level for 3,4-Methylenedioxymethamphetamine (MDMA), 3,4-Methylenedioxyamphetamine (MDA), 3,4-Methylenedioxy-N-ethylamphetamine (MDEA), Paramethoxymethamphetamine (PMA), and any other controlled substance that is marketed as "Ecstasy" and that has either a chemical structure similar to MDMA or an effect on the central nervous system substantially similar to or greater than MDMA.

The amendment addresses the directive by amending the Drug Equivalency Tables in § 2D1.1, Application Note 10, to increase substantially the marihuana equivalencies for the specified controlled substances, which has the effect of substantially increasing the penalties for offenses involving "Ecstasy". The new penalties for "Ecstasy" trafficking provide penalties which, gram for gram, are more severe than those for powder cocaine. Under the Drug Equivalency Tables, one gram of powder cocaine has a marihuana equivalency of 200 grams. This amendment sets the marihuana equivalency for one gram of "Ecstasy" at 500 grams.

There is a combination of reasons why the Commission has substantially increased the penalties in response to the congressional directive. Much evidence received by the Commission indicated that "Ecstasy" (1) has powerful pharmacological effects; (2) has the capacity to cause lasting physical harms, including brain damage; and (3) is being abused by rapidly increasing numbers of teenagers and young adults. Indeed, the market for "Ecstasy" is overwhelmingly comprised of persons under the age of 25 years.

The Commission considered whether the penalty levels for "Ecstasy" should be set at the same levels as for heroin (one gram of heroin has a marihuana equivalency of 1000 grams) and decided that somewhat lesser penalties were appropriate for "Ecstasy" for a number of reasons: (1) the potential for addiction is greater with heroin; (2) heroin distribution often involves violence while, at this time, violence is not reported in "Ecstasy" markets; (3)

because heroin it is a narcotic and is often injected, the risk of death from overdose is much greater than for "Ecstasy"; and (4) because heroin is often injected, there are more secondary health consequences, such as infections and the transmission of the human immunodeficiency virus (HIV) and hepatitis than for "Ecstasy".

Finally, based on information regarding "Ecstasy" trafficking patterns, the penalty levels chosen are appropriate and sufficient to target serious and high-level traffickers and to provide appropriate punishment, deterrence, and incentives for cooperation. The penalty levels chosen for "Ecstasy" offenses provide five year sentences for serious traffickers (those whose relevant conduct involved approximately 800 pills) and ten year sentences for high-level traffickers (those whose relevant conduct involved approximately 8,000 pills).

Effective Date: The effective date of this amendment is November 1, 2001.

622. **Amendment:** Section 2D1.1(b)(4) is amended by inserting "amphetamine or" before "methamphetamine" each place it appears.

The Commentary to § 2D1.1 captioned "Statutory Provisions" is amended by inserting "; 49 U.S.C. § 46317(b)" after "960(a), (b)".

The Commentary to § 2D1.1 captioned "Application Notes" is amended in Note 19 by inserting "amphetamine or" before "methamphetamine".

Appendix A (Statutory Index), as amended by amendment 617, is further amended by inserting after the line referenced to 49 U.S.C. § 46317(a) the following new line:

"49 U.S.C. § 46317(b)   2D1.1".

The sixth entry, relating to Amphetamine and Amphetamine (actual), in each of subdivisions (1) through (14) of section 2D1.1(c), Note (B) of the "*Notes to Drug Quantity Table" in § 2D1.1(c), Note 9 of the Commentary to § 2D1.1 captioned "Application Notes", and the subdivision captioned "Cocaine and Other Schedule I and II Stimulants (and their immediate precursors)*" of the Drug Equivalency Tables in Note 10 of the Commentary to § 2D1.1 captioned "Application Notes", effective May 1, 2001 (see Amendment 610), are repromulgated with the following change:

The Commentary to § 2D1.1 captioned "Application Notes" is amended in Note 10 in the Drug Equivalency Tables in the subdivision captioned "Cocaine and Other Schedule I and II Stimulants (and their immediate precursors)*" by striking "1 gm of Dextroamphetamine = 200 gm of marihuana".

Reason for Amendment: This amendment repromulgates as a permanent amendment the emergency amendment previously promulgated to implement the directive in section 3611 of the Methamphetamine Anti-Proliferation Act of 2000, Pub. L. 106-310 (the "Act"), which directs the Commission to provide increased guideline penalties for amphetamine offenses such that those penalties are comparable to the base offense level for methamphetamine offenses. The directive provided the Commission emergency amendment authority. (See Amendment 610.)

This amendment revises § 2D1.1 to include amphetamine in the Drug Quantity Table in § 2D1.1 (Unlawful Manufacturing, Importing, Exporting, or Trafficking (Including Possession with Intent to Commit These Offenses); Attempt or Conspiracy). This amendment also treats amphetamine and methamphetamine identically, at a 1:1 ratio (i.e., the same quantities of amphetamine and methamphetamine will result in the same base offense level) because of the similarities of the two substances. Specifically, amphetamine and methamphetamine (1) are chemically similar; (2) are produced by a similar method and are trafficked in a similar manner; (3) share similar methods of use; (4) affect the same parts of the brain; and (5) have similar intoxicating effects. The amendment also distinguishes between pure amphetamine (i.e., amphetamine (actual)) and amphetamine mixture in the same manner, and at the same quantities, as pure methamphetamine (i.e., methamphetamine (actual)) and methamphetamine mixture, respectively. The Commission determined that the 1:1 ratio is appropriate given the similarity of these two controlled substances.

This amendment differs from the emergency amendment in that it also (1) amends § 2D1.1(b)(4) to make the enhancement for the importation of methamphetamine applicable to amphetamine offenses as well, and makes a conforming change in the commentary to § 2D1.1 in Application Note 19; (2) deletes as unnecessary the marihuana equivalency for dextroamphetamine in the Drug Equivalency Tables in § 2D1.1; and (3) amends Appendix A (Statutory Index) to refer a new offense at 49 U.S.C. § 46317(b), (prohibiting transportation of controlled substances by aircraft) to § 2D1.1.

Effective Date: The effective date of this amendment is November 1, 2001.

623. Amendment: Section 2D1.1(c)(1) is amended by striking the period after "Hashish Oil" and inserting a semi-colon; and by adding at the end the following:

> "30,000,000 units or more of Schedule I or II Depressants;
> 1,875,000 units or more of Flunitrazepam.".

Section 2D1.1(c)(2) is amended by striking the period after "Hashish Oil" and inserting a semi-colon; and by adding at the end the following:

> "At least 10,000,000 but less than 30,000,000 units of Schedule I or II Depressants;
> At least 625,000 but less than 1,875,000 units of Flunitrazepam.".

Section 2D1.1(c)(3) is amended by striking the period after "Hashish Oil" and inserting a semi-colon; and by adding at the end the following:

> "At least 3,000,000 but less than 10,000,000 units of Schedule I or II Depressants;
> At least 187,500 but less than 625,000 units of Flunitrazepam.".

Section 2D1.1(c)(4) is amended by striking the period after "Hashish Oil" and inserting a semi-colon; and by adding at the end the following:

> "At least 1,000,000 but less than 3,000,000 units of Schedule I or II Depressants;
> At least 62,500 but less than 187,500 units of Flunitrazepam.".

Section 2D1.1(c)(5) is amended by striking the period after "Hashish Oil" and inserting a semi-colon; and by adding at the end the following:

> "At least 700,000 but less than 1,000,000 units of Schedule I or II Depressants;
> At least 43,750 but less than 62,500 units of Flunitrazepam.".

Section 2D1.1(c)(6) is amended by striking the period after "Hashish Oil" and inserting a semi-colon; and by adding at the end the following:

"At least 400,000 but less than 700,000 units of Schedule I or II Depressants;
At least 25,000 but less than 43,750 units of Flunitrazepam.".

Section 2D1.1(c)(7) is amended by striking the period after "Hashish Oil" and inserting a semi-colon; and by adding at the end the following:

"At least 100,000 but less than 400,000 units of Schedule I or II Depressants;
At least 6,250 but less than 25,000 units of Flunitrazepam.".

Section 2D1.1(c)(8) is amended by striking the period after "Hashish Oil" and inserting a semi-colon; and by adding at the end the following:

"At least 80,000 but less than 100,000 units of Schedule I or II Depressants;
At least 5,000 but less than 6,250 units of Flunitrazepam.".

Section 2D1.1(c)(9) is amended by striking the period after "Hashish Oil" and inserting a semi-colon; and by adding at the end the following:

"At least 60,000 but less than 80,000 units of Schedule I or II Depressants;
At least 3,750 but less than 5,000 units of Flunitrazepam.".

Section 2D1.1(c)(10) is amended in the line referenced to Schedule I or II Depressants by striking "40,000 or more" and inserting "At least 40,000 but less than 60,000"; and in the line referenced to Flunitrazepam, by striking "2,500 or more" and inserting "At least 2,500 but less than 3,750".

The Commentary to § 2D1.1 captioned "Application Notes" is amended in Note 10 in the Drug Equivalency Tables in the subdivision captioned "Flunitrazepam**" by striking the following:

"** Provided, that the combined equivalent weight of flunitrazepam, all Schedule I or II depressants, Schedule III substances, Schedule IV substances, and Schedule V substances shall not exceed 99.99 kilograms of marihuana.

The minimum offense level from the Drug Quantity Table for flunitrazepam individually, or in combination with any Schedule I or II depressants, Schedule III substances, Schedule IV substances, and Schedule V substances is level 8.",

and inserting the following:

"**Provided, that the minimum offense level from the Drug Quantity Table for flunitrazepam individually, or in combination with any Schedule I or II depressants, Schedule III substances, Schedule IV substances, and Schedule V substances is level 8.".

The Commentary to § 2D1.1 captioned "Application Notes" is amended in Note 10 in the Drug Equivalency Tables in the subdivision captioned "Schedule I or II Depressants***" in the heading by striking "***" after "Schedule I or II Depressants"; and by striking the following:

"***Provided, that the combined equivalent weight of all Schedule I or II depressants, Schedule III substances, Schedule IV substances (except flunitrazepam), and Schedule V substances shall not exceed 59.99 kilograms of marihuana.".

Amendment 623 APPENDIX C - VOLUME II November 1, 2013

The Commentary to § 2D1.1 captioned "Application Notes" is amended in Note 10 in the Drug Equivalency Tables in the subdivision captioned "Schedule III Substances****" in the heading by striking "****" and inserting "***"; by striking "****Provided," and inserting "***Provided,"; and by striking "Schedule I or II depressants," after "Schedule III substances,".

The Commentary to § 2D1.1 captioned "Application Notes" is amended in Note 10 in the Drug Equivalency Tables in the subdivision captioned "Schedule IV Substances (except flunitrazepam)*****" in the heading by striking "*****" and inserting "****"; and by striking "*****Provided," and inserting "****Provided,".

The Commentary to § 2D1.1 captioned "Application Notes" is amended in Note 10 in the Drug Equivalency Tables in the subdivision captioned "Schedule V Substances******" in the heading by striking "******" and inserting "*****"; and by striking "******Provided," and inserting "*****Provided,".

The Commentary to § 2D1.1 captioned "Application Notes" is amended in Note 17 by striking "(e.g., the maximum offense level in the Drug Quantity Table for flunitrazepam is level 20)".

Reason for Amendment: This amendment implements the Hillory J. Farias and Samantha Reid Date-Rape Drug Prohibition Act of 2000, Pub. L. 106–172 (the "Act"), which provides the emergency scheduling of gamma hydroxybutyric acid ("GHB") as a Schedule I controlled substance under the Controlled Substances Act when the drug is used illicitly. The Act also amended section 401(b)(1)(C) of the Controlled Substances Act, 21 U.S.C. § 841(b)(1)(C), and section 1010(b)(3) of the Controlled Substances Import and Export Act, 21 U.S.C. § 960(b)(3), to provide penalties of not more than 20 years' imprisonment for an offense that involves GHB.

This amendment eliminates the maximum base offense level of level 20 in the Drug Quantity Table of § 2D1.1 (Unlawful Manufacturing, Importing, Exporting, or Trafficking (Including Possession with Intent to Commit These Offenses); Attempt or Conspiracy) for Schedule I and II depressants (including GHB). The same change is made with respect to flunitrazepam, which, for sentencing purposes, is tied to Schedule I and II depressants. The Commission determined that increased penalties for the more serious offenses involving Schedule I and II depressants are appropriate.

Corresponding changes to the Drug Equivalency Tables in § 2D1.1 were made for both Flunitrazepam and Schedule I or II depressants by eliminating the maximum marihuana equivalency when offenses involving these controlled substances also involve offenses for controlled substances in Schedules III, IV, or V.

Effective Date: The effective date of this amendment is November 1, 2001.

624. **Amendment:** Section 2D1.1(b)(6), as redesignated by amendment 620, is amended by inserting "subsection (a) of" after "(1)-(5) of"; and by striking "and the offense level determined above is level 26 or greater".

The Commentary to § 2D1.1 captioned "Application Notes", as amended by amendments 620, 621, 622, and 623, is further amended by striking Note 14 as follows:

"14. Where (A) the amount of the controlled substance for which the defendant is accountable under § 1B1.3 (Relevant Conduct) results in a base offense level greater than 36, (B) the court finds that this offense level overrepresents the defendant's culpability in the criminal activity, and (C) the defendant qualifies for a mitigating role adjustment under § 3B1.2 (Mitigating Role), a downward departure may be warranted. The court may depart to a sentence no lower than the guideline range that would have resulted if the defendant's Chapter Two offense level had been offense level 36. Provided, that a defendant is not eligible for a downward departure under this provision if the defendant:

(a) has one or more prior felony convictions for a crime of violence or a controlled substance offense as defined in § 4B1.2 (Definitions of Terms Used in Section 4B1.1);

(b) qualifies for an adjustment under § 3B1.3 (Abuse of Position of Trust or Use of Special Skill);

(c) possessed or induced another participant to use or possess a firearm in the offense;

(d) had decision-making authority;

(e) owned the controlled substance or financed any part of the offense; or

(f) sold the controlled substance or played a substantial part in negotiating the terms of the sale.

Example: A defendant, who the court finds meets the criteria for a downward departure under this provision, has a Chapter Two offense level of 38, a 2-level reduction for a minor role from § 3B1.2, and a 3-level reduction for acceptance of responsibility from § 3E1.1. His final offense level is 33. If the defendant's Chapter Two offense level had been 36, the 2-level reduction for a minor role and 3-level reduction for acceptance of responsibility would have resulted in a final offense level of 31. Therefore, under this provision, a downward departure not to exceed 2 levels (from level 33 to level 31) would be authorized.";

and by redesignating Notes 15 through 21 as Notes 14 through 20, respectively.

Section 5C1.2 is amended in the first paragraph by striking "In" and inserting "(a) Except as provided in subsection (b), in".

Section 5C1.2 is amended by inserting after subsection (a), as so designated by this amendment, the following:

"(b) In the case of a defendant (1) who meets the criteria set forth in subsection (a); and (2) for whom the statutorily required minimum sentence is at least five years, the offense level applicable from Chapters Two (Offense Conduct) and Three (Adjustments) shall be not less than level 17.".

The Commentary to § 5C1.2 captioned "Application Notes" is amended in Notes 1 and 2 by striking "subdivision" each place it appears and inserting "subsection (a)".

The Commentary to § 5C1.2 captioned "Application Notes" is amended in Note 3 by striking "subdivisions" and inserting "subsection (a)"; and striking "subdivision" and inserting "subsection (a)".

The Commentary to § 5C1.2 captioned "Application Notes" is amended in Notes 4 through

Amendment 624 APPENDIX C - VOLUME II November 1, 2013

7 by striking "subdivision" each place it appears and inserting "subsection (a)".

Reason for Amendment: This amendment expands the eligibility for the two-level reduction in subsection (b)(6) of § 2D1.1 (Unlawful Manufacturing, Importing, Exporting, or Trafficking (Including Possession with Intent to Commit These Offenses); Attempt or Conspiracy) for persons who meet the criteria set forth in § 5C1.2 (Limitation on Applicability of Statutory Minimum Sentences in Certain Cases) to include defendants with an offense level less than level 26. The Commission determined that limiting the applicability of this reduction to defendants with an offense level of level 26 or greater is inconsistent with the general principles underlying this two-level reduction (and the related safety valve provision, see 18 U.S.C. § 3553(f)) to provide lesser punishment for first time, nonviolent offenders.

This amendment also establishes in § 5C1.2 a minimum offense level of level 17 for a defendant who meets the requirements set forth in § 5C1.2, and for whom the statutorily required minimum sentence is at least five years, in order to comply more strictly with the directive to the Commission at section 80001(b) of the Violent Crime Control and Law Enforcement Act of 1994, Pub. L. 103–322.

Effective Date: The effective date of this amendment is November 1, 2001.

625. **Amendment:** The subdivision captioned "List I Chemicals (relating to the manufacture of amphetamine or methamphetamine)*******" in the Drug Equivalency Tables in Note 10 of the Commentary to § 2D1.1 captioned "Application Notes" and § 2D1.11, effective May 1, 2001 (see Amendment 611), are repromulgated with the following changes:

Section 2D1.11 is amended in the heading to subsection (d)(1) by striking "(d)(1)" before "Ephedrine," and inserting "(d)".

Section 2D1.11 is amended in the heading to subsection (d)(2) by striking "(d)(2)" before "Chemical" and inserting "(e)".

Section 2D1.11(e)(1), as redesignated by this amendment, is amended by striking the period after "3, 4-Methylenedioxyphenyl-2-propanone" and inserting a semicolon; and by adding at the end the following:

"10,000 KG or more of Gamma-butyrolactone.".

Section 2D1.11(e)(2), as redesignated by this amendment, is amended in the subdivision captioned "List I Chemicals" by adding at the end the following:

"At least 3,000 KG but less than 10,000 KG of Gamma-butyrolactone;";

and in the subdivision captioned "List II Chemicals" by striking the period after "Toluene" and inserting a semi-colon; and by adding at the end the following:

"376.2 G or more of Iodine.".

Section 2D1.11(e)(3), as redesignated by this amendment, is amended in the subdivision captioned "List I Chemicals" by adding at the end the following:

"At least 1,000 KG but less than 3,000 KG of Gamma-butyrolactone;";

and in the subdivision captioned "List II Chemicals" by striking the period after "Toluene" and inserting a semi-colon; and by adding at the end the following:

"At least 125.4 G but less than 376.2 G of Iodine.".

November 1, 2013 APPENDIX C - VOLUME II **Amendment 625**

Section 2D1.11(e)(4), as redesignated by this amendment, is amended in the subdivision captioned "List I Chemicals" by adding at the end the following:

"At least 700 KG but less than 1,000 KG of Gamma-butyrolactone;";

and in the subdivision captioned "List II Chemicals" by striking the period after "Toluene" and inserting a semi-colon; and by adding at the end the following:

"At least 87.8 G but less than 125.4 G of Iodine.".

Section 2D1.11(e)(5), as redesignated by this amendment, is amended in the subdivision captioned "List I Chemicals" by adding at the end the following:

"At least 400 KG but less than 700 KG of Gamma-butyrolactone;";

and in the subdivision captioned "List II Chemicals" by striking the period after "Toluene" and inserting a semi-colon; and by adding at the end the following:

"At least 50.2 G but less than 87.8 G of Iodine.".

Section 2D1.11(e)(6), as redesignated by this amendment, is amended in the subdivision captioned "List I Chemicals" by adding at the end the following:

"At least 100 KG but less than 400 KG of Gamma-butyrolactone;";

and in the subdivision captioned "List II Chemicals" by striking the period after "Toluene" and inserting a semi-colon; and by adding at the end the following:

"At least 12.5 G but less than 50.2 G of Iodine.".

Section 2D1.11(e)(7), as redesignated by this amendment, is amended in the subdivision captioned "List I Chemicals" by adding at the end the following:

"At least 80 KG but less than 100 KG of Gamma-butyrolactone;";

and in the subdivision captioned "List II Chemicals" by striking the period after "Toluene" and inserting a semi-colon; and by adding at the end the following:

"At least 10 G but less than 12.5 G of Iodine.".

Section 2D1.11(e)(8), as redesignated by this amendment, is amended in the subdivision captioned "List I Chemicals" by adding at the end the following:

"At least 60 KG but less than 80 KG of Gamma-butyrolactone;";

and in the subdivision captioned "List II Chemicals" by striking the period after "Toluene" and inserting a semi-colon; and by adding at the end the following:

"At least 7.5 G but less than 10 G of Iodine.".

Section 2D1.11(e)(9), as redesignated by this amendment, is amended in the subdivision captioned "List I Chemicals" by adding at the end the following:

"At least 40 KG but less than 60 KG of Gamma-butyrolactone;";

and in the subdivision captioned "List II Chemicals" by striking the period after "Toluene" and inserting a semi-colon; and by adding at the end the following:

"At least 5 G but less than 7.5 G of Iodine.".

Section 2D1.11(e)(10), as redesignated by this amendment, is amended in the subdivision captioned "List I Chemicals" by adding at the end the following:

"Less than 40 KG of Gamma-butyrolactone;";

and in the subdivision captioned "List II Chemicals" by striking the period after "Toluene" and inserting a semi-colon; and by adding at the end the following:

"Less than 5 G of Iodine.".

The Commentary to § 2D1.11 captioned "Application Notes" is amended in the first paragraph of Note 4(A) by striking "subsection (d) of".

The Commentary to § 2D1.1 captioned "Application Notes" is amended in Note 10 in the Drug Equivalency Tables in the subdivision captioned "List I Chemicals (relating to the manufacture of amphetamine or methamphetamine)*******" in the heading by striking "*******" and inserting "******"; and by striking "*******Provided," and inserting "******Provided,".

Reason for Amendment: This amendment repromulgates, with additional changes, the emergency amendment previously promulgated in response to the three-part directive in section 3651 of the Methamphetamine Anti-Proliferation Act of 2000, Pub. L. 106–310 (the "Act"), regarding enhanced punishment for trafficking in List I chemicals. (See Amendment 611). That section provided the Commission emergency amendment authority to implement the directive.

This amendment provides a new chemical quantity table in § 2D1.11 (Unlawfully Distributing, Importing, Exporting or Possessing a Listed Chemical; Attempt or Conspiracy) specifically for ephedrine, pseudoephedrine, and phenylpropanolamine (PPA). The table ties the base offense levels for these chemicals to the base offense levels for methamphetamine (actual) set forth in § 2D1.1 (Unlawful Manufacturing, Importing, Exporting, or Trafficking (Including Possession with Intent to Commit These Offenses); Attempt or Conspiracy), assuming a 50 percent actual yield of the controlled substance from the chemicals. (Methamphetamine (actual) is used rather than methamphetamine mixture because ephedrine and pseudoephedrine produce methamphetamine (actual), and PPA produces amphetamine (actual)). This yield is based on information provided by the Drug Enforcement Administration (DEA) that the typical yield of these substances for clandestine laboratories is 50 to 75 percent.

This new chemical quantity table has a maximum base offense level of level 38 (as opposed to a maximum base offense level of level 30 for all other precursor chemicals). Providing a maximum base offense level of level 38 complies with the directive to establish penalties for these precursors that "correspond to the quantity of controlled substance that reasonably could have been manufactured using the quantity of ephedrine, phenylpropanolamine, or pseudoephedrine possessed or distributed." Additionally, this eliminates the six-level distinction that currently exists between precursor chemical offenses that involve intent to manufacture amphetamine or methamphetamine and such offenses that also involve an actual attempt to manufacture amphetamine or methamphetamine.

This amendment eliminates the Ephedrine Equivalency Table in § 2D1.11 and, in its place, provides a general rule for the court to determine the base offense level in cases involving multiple precursors (other than ephedrine, pseudoephedrine, or PPA) by using the quantity of the single chemical resulting in the greatest offense level. An upward departure is provided for cases in which the offense level does not adequately address the seriousness of the offense.

However, this amendment provides an exception to that general rule for offenses that involve a combination of ephedrine, pseudoephedrine, or PPA because these chemicals often are used in the same manufacturing process. In a case that involves two or more of these chemicals, the base offense level will be determined using the total quantity of these chemicals involved. The purpose of this exception is twofold: (1) any of the three primary precursors in the same table can be combined without difficulty; and (2) studies conducted by the DEA indicate that because the manufacturing process for amphetamine is essentially identical to the manufacturing process for methamphetamine, there are cases in which the different precursors are included in the same batch of drugs. If the chemical is PPA, amphetamine results; if the chemical is ephedrine or pseudoephedrine, methamphetamine results.

The amendment also adds to the Drug Equivalency Tables in § 2D1.1 a conversion table for these precursor chemicals, providing for a 50 percent conversion ratio. This is based on data from the DEA that the actual yield from ephedrine, pseudoephedrine, or PPA typically is in the range of 50 to 75 percent. The purpose of this part of the amendment is to achieve the same punishment level (as is achieved by the first part of this amendment) for an offense involving any of these precursor chemicals when such offense involved the manufacture of amphetamine or methamphetamine and, as a result, is sentenced under § 2D1.1 pursuant to the cross reference in § 2D1.11.

This amendment also increases the base offense level for Benzaldehyde, Hydriodic Acid, Methylamine, Nitroethane, and Norpseudoephedrine by re-calibrating these levels to the appropriate quantity of methamphetamine (actual) that could be produced assuming a 50 percent yield of chemical to drug and retaining a cap at level 30. Previously, these chemicals had been linked to methamphetamine (mixture) penalty levels. Based on a study conducted by the DEA, ephedrine and pseudoepehdrine are the primary precursors used to make methamphetamine in the United States. Phenylproponolamine is the primary precursor used to make amphetamine. Unlike the five additional List I chemicals, the chemical structures of ephedrine, pseudoephedrine, and PPA are so similar to the resulting drug (i.e., methamphetamine or amphetamine) that the manufacture of methamphetamine or amphetamine from ephedrine, pseudoephedrine, or PPA is a very simple one-step synthesis which anyone can perform using a variety of chemical reagents. The manufacture of methamphetamine or amphetamine from the five additional List I chemicals is a more complex process which requires a heightened level of expertise.

This amendment adds to the emergency amendment in two ways. First, it amends the Chemical Quantity Table in § 2D1.11 to include gamma-butyrolactone (GBL), a precursor for gamma hydroxybutyric acid (GHB), as a List I chemical. This change is in response to the Hillory J. Farias and Samantha Reid Date Rape Prohibition Act of 2000, Pub. L. 106–172, which added GBL to the list of List 1 chemicals in section 401 (b)(1)(C) of the Controlled Substances Act, 21 U.S.C. § 841(b)(1)(C). Offense levels for GBL were established in the same manner as other List I chemicals. The offense level for a specific quantity of GHB that can be produced from a given quantity of GBL, assuming a 50 percent yield, was determined using the Drug Quantity Table in § 2D1.1. From this offense level, six levels were subtracted to reflect the fact that an attempt to manufacture is not a required element of these offenses and, therefore, they are less serious offenses than offenses covered by § 2D1.1.

Second, the amendment adds iodine to the Chemical Quantity Table in § 2D1.11(e) in response to a recent classification of iodine as a List II chemical. Iodine is used to produce

Amendment 625   APPENDIX C - VOLUME II   November 1, 2013

hydrogen iodide which, in the presence of water, becomes hydriodic acid, a List I chemical that is a reagent used in the production of amphetamine and methamphetamine. The penalties for iodine were established based upon its conversion to hydriodic acid.

Effective Date: The effective date of this amendment is November 1, 2001.

626. Amendment: Section 2D1.12 is amended in the title by inserting "Transportation, Exportation," after "Distribution,"; and by striking "or Equipment" and inserting ", Equipment, Chemical, Product, or Material".

Section 2D1.12(a)(1), (a)(2), and (b)(1) are amended by inserting "flask," after "prohibited" each place it appears; and by inserting ", chemical, product, or material" after "equipment" each place it appears.

The Commentary to § 2D1.12 captioned "Statutory Provisions" is amended by inserting "§ " before "843"; and by inserting ", 864" after "(7)".

The Commentary to § 2D1.12 captioned "Application Notes" is amended by striking the text of Note 1 as follows:

"If the offense involved the large-scale manufacture, distribution, or importation of prohibited flasks or equipment, an upward departure may be warranted.",

and inserting the following:

"If the offense involved the large-scale manufacture, distribution, transportation, exportation, or importation of prohibited flasks, equipment, chemicals, products, or material, an upward departure may be warranted.".

Appendix A (Statutory Index) is amended by inserting after the line referenced to 21 U.S.C. § 863 the following:

"21 U.S.C. § 864   2D1.12".

Reason for Amendment: This amendment addresses the new offense, in section 423 of the Controlled Substances Act, 21 U.S.C. § 864, of stealing or transporting across state lines anhydrous ammonia knowing, intending, or having reasonable cause to believe that such anhydrous ammonia will be used to manufacture a controlled substance. This new offense, created by section 3653 of the Methamphetamine Anti-Proliferation Act of 2000, Pub. L. 106–310, carries the statutory penalties contained in section 403(d) of the Controlled Substances Act, 21 U.S.C. § 843, i.e., not more than four years' imprisonment (or not more than eight years' imprisonment in the case of certain prior convictions), or not more than ten years' imprisonment (or not more than 20 years' imprisonment in the case of certain prior convictions) if the offense involved the manufacture of methamphetamine.

The amendment references the new offense to § 2D1.12 (Unlawful Possession, Manufacture, Distribution, or Importation of Prohibited Flask or Equipment; Attempt or Conspiracy). Reference to this guideline is appropriate because the new offense is similar to other offenses that already are referenced to the guideline and have the same penalty structure, such as 21 U.S.C. § 843(a)(6), which among other things, makes it unlawful to possess any chemical, product, or material that may be used to manufacture a controlled substance. In addition, this amendment expands the coverage of Application Note 1 to also apply to cases involving the transportation and exportation of prohibited chemicals, products, or material. Finally, the amendment makes minor, non-substantive changes to the guideline in order to fully incorporate the new and existing offenses.

November 1, 2013 APPENDIX C - VOLUME II **Amendment 627**

Effective Date: The effective date of this amendment is November 1, 2001.

627. **Amendment:** Sections 2G1.1, 2G2.1, 2H4.1, 2H4.2, and 5E1.1, and each line in Appendix A (Statutory Index) referenced to 18 U.S.C. § 241, § 1589, § 1590, § 1591, or § 1592, or to 29 U.S.C. § 1851, effective May 1, 2001 (see Amendment 612), are repromulgated with the following changes:

Section 5E1.1(a)(1) is amended by inserting ", or 21 U.S.C. § 853(q)" after "3663A".

The Commentary to § 5E1.1 captioned "Background" is amended in the first paragraph by inserting ", and 21 U.S.C. § 853(q)" after "3663A".

Reason for Amendment: This amendment repromulgates as a permanent amendment the previously promulgated emergency amendment on human trafficking. (See Amendment 612.) The amendment implements the congressional directive in section 112(b) of the Victims of Trafficking and Violence Protection Act of 2000, Pub. L. 106–386 (the "Act").

The directive requires the Commission to amend, if appropriate, the guidelines applicable to human trafficking (i.e., peonage, involuntary servitude, and forced labor) offenses. It also requires the Commission to ensure that the guidelines "are sufficiently stringent to deter and adequately reflect the heinous nature of these offenses." In compliance with the directive, the amendment (1) creates a new guideline, § 2H4.2 (Willful Violations of the Migrant and Seasonal Agricultural Worker Protection Act); (2) refers violations of four new statutes, 18 U.S.C. §§ 1589 (Forced Labor), 1590 (Trafficking with Respect to Peonage, Involuntary Servitude or Forced Labor), 1591 (Sex Trafficking of Children by Force, Fraud or Coercion), and 1592 (Unlawful Conduct with Respect to Documents in Furtherance of Peonage, Involuntary Servitude, or Forced Labor) to the appropriate guidelines; and (3) makes changes, consistent with the directive, which both enhance sentences and reflect changes to three existing statutes: 18 U.S.C. §§ 1581(a) (Peonage), 1583 (Enticement into Slavery) and 1584 (Sale into Involuntary Servitude).

To address this multi-faceted directive, the amendment makes changes to several existing guidelines and creates a new guideline for criminal violations of the Migrant and Seasonal Agricultural Worker Protection Act. Although the directive instructs the Commission to amend the guidelines applicable to the Fair Labor Standards Act (29 U.S.C. § 201 et. seq.), a criminal violation of the Fair Labor Standards Act is only a Class B misdemeanor. See 29 U.S.C. § 216. Thus, the guidelines are not applicable to those offenses.

The amendment references the new offense at 18 U.S.C. § 1591 to § 2G1.1 (Promoting Prostitution or Prohibited Sexual Conduct). Section 1591 provides criminal penalties for a defendant who participates in the transporting or harboring of a person, or who benefits from participating in such a venture, with the knowledge that force, fraud, or coercion will be used to cause that person to engage in a commercial sex act or with knowledge that the person is not 18 years old and will be forced to engage in a commercial sex act. Despite the statute's inclusion in a chapter of title 18 devoted mainly to peonage offenses, section 1591 offenses are more analogous to the offenses referenced to the prostitution guideline.

Section 1591 cases alternatively have been referred in Appendix A (Statutory Index) to § 2G2.1 (Sexually Exploiting a Minor by Production of Sexually Explicit Visual or Printed Material; Custodian Permitting Minor to Engage in Sexually Explicit Conduct; Advertisement for Minors to Engage in Production). This has been done in anticipation that some portion of section 1591 cases will involve forcing or coercing children to engage in commercial sex acts for the purpose of producing pornography. Such offenses, as recognized by the higher base offense level at § 2G2.1, are more serious because they both involve

Amendment 627

specific harm to an individual victim and further an additional criminal purpose, namely, commercial pornography.

The amendment maintains the view that § 2H4.1 (Peonage, Involuntary Servitude, and Slave Trade) continues to be an appropriate tool for determining sentences for violations of 18 U.S.C. §§ 1581, 1583, and 1584. Section 2H4.1 also is designed to cover offenses under three new statutes: 18 U.S.C. §§ 1589, 1590, and 1592. Section 1589 provides criminal penalties for a defendant who provides or obtains the labor or services of another by the use of threats of serious harm or physical restraint against a person, or by a scheme or plan intended to make the person believe that physical restraint or serious harm would result from not performing the labor or services. This statute also applies to defendants who provide or obtain labor or services of another by abusing or threatening abuse of the law or the legal process. See 18 U.S.C. § 1589.

Section 1590 provides criminal penalties for a defendant who harbors, transports, or is otherwise involved in obtaining, a person for labor or services. Section 1592 provides criminal penalties for a defendant who knowingly possesses, destroys, or removes an actual passport, other immigration document, or government identification document of another person in the course of a violation of § 1581 (peonage), § 1583 (enticement into slavery), § 1584 (sale into involuntary servitude), § 1589 (forced labor), § 1590 (trafficking with respect to these offenses), § 1591 (sex trafficking of children by force, fraud, or coercion), or § 1594(a) (attempts to violate these offenses). Section 1592 also provides criminal penalties for a defendant who, with intent to violate § 1581, § 1583, § 1584, § 1589, § 1590, or § 1591, knowingly possesses, destroys, or removes an actual passport, other immigration document, or government identification document of another person. These statutes prohibit the types of behaviors that traditionally have been sentenced under § 2H4.1.

The amendment provides an alternative, less punitive base offense level of level 18 for those who violate 18 U.S.C. § 1592, an offense which limits participation in peonage cases to the destruction or wrongful confiscation of a passport or other immigration document. This alternative, lower base level reflects the lower statutory maximum sentence for section 1592 offenses (i.e., 5 years' imprisonment).

Section 2H4.1(b)(2) has been expanded to provide a four-level increase if a dangerous weapon was used and a two-level increase if a dangerous weapon was brandished or its use was threatened. Prior to this amendment, only actual use of a dangerous weapon was covered. This change reflects the directive to consider an enhancement for the use or threatened use of a dangerous weapon. The commentary to § 2H4.1 is amended to clarify that the threatened use of a dangerous weapon applies regardless of whether a dangerous weapon was actually present.

The amendment also creates a new guideline, § 2H4.2 (Willful Violations of the Migrant and Seasonal Agricultural Worker Protection Act), in response to the directive to amend the guidelines applicable to such offenses. These offenses, which have a statutory maximum sentence of one year imprisonment for first offenses and three years' imprisonment for subsequent offenses, were not, prior to this amendment, referred to any specific guideline. The amendment provides a base offense level of level 6 in recognition of the low statutory maximum sentences set for these cases by Congress. Further, these offenses typically involve violations of regulatory provisions. Setting the base offense level at level 6 provides consistency with guidelines for other regulatory offenses. See, e.g., §§ 2N2.1 (Violations of Statutes and Regulations Dealing With Any Food, Drug, Biological Product, Device, Cosmetic, or Agricultural Product) and 2N3.1 (Odometer Laws and Regulations). Subsections (b)(1), an enhancement for bodily injury, and (b)(2), an enhancement applicable to defendants who commit the instant offense after previously sustaining a civil penalty for similar misconduct, have been established to respond to the directive that the Commission consider sentencing enhancement for this aggravated conduct. This provision addresses the Department of Justice's and the Department of Labor's concern regarding the need for enhanced penalties in cases involving prior administrative and civil adjudications.

This amendment also addresses that portion of section 112 of the Act that amends chapter 77 of title 18, United States Code, to provide mandatory restitution for peonage and involuntary servitude offenses. The amendment amends § 5E1.1 (Restitution) to include a reference to 18 U.S.C. § 1593 in the guideline provision regarding mandatory restitution.

By enactment of various sentencing enhancements and encouraged upward departures for areas of concern identified by Congress, the Commission has provided for more severe sentences for perpetrators of human trafficking offenses in keeping with the conclusion that the offenses covered by this amendment are both heinous in nature and being committed with increasing frequency.

In addition, to repromulgating the emergency amendment, this amendment responds to section 3613 of the Methamphetamine Anti-Proliferation Act of 2000, Pub. L. 106–310, that amends 21 U.S.C. § 853(q) to provide mandatory restitution for offenses involving the manufacture of methamphetamine. Accordingly, the amendment amends § 5E1.1 (Restitution) to include a reference to 21 U.S.C. § 853(q) in the guideline provision regarding mandatory restitution.

Effective Date: The effective date of this amendment is November 1, 2001.

628. **Amendment:** Section 2H3.1 is amended in the title by striking "or" and inserting a semicolon; and by inserting "; Disclosure of Tax Return Information" after "Eavesdropping".

Section 2H3.1 is amended by striking subsection (a) as follows:

"(a) Base Offense Level: 9",

and inserting the following:

"(a) Base Offense Level (Apply the greater):

(1) 9; or

(2) 6, if the defendant was convicted of 26 U.S.C. § 7213A or 26 U.S.C. § 7216.".

Section 2H3.1(b)(1) is amended by striking "conduct" and inserting "offense".

Section 2H3.1(c)(1) is amended by striking "conduct" and inserting "offense"; and by striking "that offense" and inserting "that other offense".

The Commentary to § 2H3.1 captioned "Statutory Provisions" is amended by inserting "26 U.S.C. §§ 7213(a)(1)-(3), (a)(5), (d), 7213A, 7216;" after "2511;".

The Commentary to § 2H3.1 captioned "Application Note" is amended by striking "Note" and inserting "Notes"; by redesignating Note 1 as Note 2; and by inserting before Note 2, as redesignated by this amendment, the following:

"1. Definitions.—For purposes of this guideline, 'tax return' and 'tax return information' have the meaning given the terms 'return' and 'return information' in 26 U.S.C. § 6103(b)(1) and (2), respectively.".

The Commentary to § 2H3.1 captioned "Application Notes" as re-captioned by this amendment, is amended in Note 2, as redesignated by this amendment, by inserting "Satellite Cable Transmissions.—" before "If the".

The Commentary to § 2H3.1 captioned "Background" is amended by adding at the end the following additional paragraph:

" This section also refers to conduct relating to the disclosure and inspection of tax returns and tax return information, which is proscribed by 26 U.S.C. §§ 7213(a)(1)-(3), (5), (d), 7213A, and 7216. These statutes provide for a maximum term of imprisonment of five years for most types of disclosure of tax return information, but provide a maximum term of imprisonment of one year for violations of 26 U.S.C. §§ 7213A and 7216.".

Appendix A (Statutory Index) is amended by inserting after the line referenced to 26 U.S.C. § 7212(b) the following new lines:

"26 U.S.C. § 7213(a)(1)	2H3.1
26 U.S.C. § 7213(a)(2)	2H3.1
26 U.S.C. § 7213(a)(3)	2H3.1
26 U.S.C. § 7213(a)(5)	2H3.1
26 U.S.C. § 7213(d)	2H3.1
26 U.S.C. § 7213A	2H3.1";

and by inserting after the line referenced to 26 U.S.C. § 7215 the following new line:

"26 U.S.C. § 7216   2H3.1".

Reason for Amendment: This amendment responds to the Internal Revenue Service Restructuring and Reform Act of 1998, Public Law 105–206 ("the Act"). The Act created new tax offenses pertaining to the unlawful disclosure of tax-related information contained on computer software and to unlawful requests for tax audits. In addition, the Taxpayer Browsing Protection Act of 1997, Public Law 105–35, created another tax offense pertaining to the unlawful inspection of tax information.

Specifically, Public Law 105–35 expanded 26 U.S.C. § 7213 to prohibit federal and state employees and certain other persons from disclosing tax-related computer software. Public Law 105–35 also created an offense at 26 U.S.C. § 7213A making it unlawful for federal and state employees and certain other persons to inspect tax return information in any way other than that authorized under the Internal Revenue Code.

This is a two-part amendment. First, this amendment updates Appendix A (Statutory Index) by referring most of these offenses to § 2H3.1 (Interception of Communications and Eavesdropping). Prior to this amendment, no guideline provision or statutory reference was expressly promulgated to address tax offenses that implicated privacy interests. Under subsection (a) of § 1B1.2 (Applicable Guidelines) and under § 2X5.1 (Other Offenses), courts are required to use the most analogous offense guideline from Chapter Two (Offense Conduct) in each pending case brought under a statute having no reference in the guidelines' statutory index.

In general, the guideline most analogous for these offenses is § 2H3.1. Section 2H3.1 concerns offenses against privacy and, in large measure, these tax-related offenses are devoted to protecting taxpayer privacy interests. Section 2H3.1 also contains a cross reference to "another offense" if a greater offense level will result.

Second, this amendment adds a three-level decrease in the base offense level under § 2H3.1 for the least serious types of offense behavior, in which there was no intent to harm or obtain pecuniary gain. The base offense level for § 2H3.1 is level 9 with a range of 4 to 10 months (in criminal history Category I). The Commission determined that a base offense level of level 9 is too severe for the misdemeanor offenses contained in 26 U.S.C. §§ 7213A (Unauthorized Inspection) and 7216 (Unauthorized Disclosure), and the three-level decrease addresses this concern.

Effective Date: The effective date of this amendment is November 1, 2001.

629. **Amendment:** Section 2K1.3(a) is amended by striking the text of subdivision (3) as follows:

> "16, if the defendant is a prohibited person; or knowingly distributed explosive materials to a prohibited person; or",

and inserting the following:

> "16, if the defendant (A) was a prohibited person at the time the defendant committed the instant offense; or (B) knowingly distributed explosive materials to a prohibited person; or".

The Commentary to § 2K1.3 captioned "Statutory Provisions" is amended by inserting "(l)-(o), (p)(2)," after "(i),".

The Commentary to § 2K1.3 captioned "Application Notes" is amended by striking the text of Note 3 as follows:

> "'Prohibited person,' as used in subsection (a)(3), means anyone who: (i) is under indictment for, or has been convicted of, a 'crime punishable by imprisonment for a term exceeding one year,' as defined at 18 U.S.C. § 841(l); (ii) is a fugitive from justice; (iii) is an unlawful user of, or is addicted to, any controlled substance; or (iv) has been adjudicated as a mental defective or involuntarily committed to a mental institution.",

and inserting the following:

> "For purposes of subsection (a)(3), 'prohibited person' means any person described in 18 U.S.C. § 842(i).".

Section 2K2.1(a)(4)(B) is amended by striking "is" after "(i)" and inserting "was"; and by inserting "at the time the defendant committed the instant offense" after "prohibited person".

Section 2K2.1(a)(6) is amended by striking "is" after "(A)" and inserting "was"; and by inserting "at the time the defendant committed the instant offense" after "prohibited person".

The Commentary to § 2K2.1 captioned "Application Notes" is amended by striking the

Amendment 629   APPENDIX C - VOLUME II   November 1, 2013

text of Note 6 as follows:

> 'Prohibited person,' as used in subsections (a)(4)(B) and (a)(6), means anyone who: (i) is under indictment for, or has been convicted of, a 'crime punishable by imprisonment for more than one year,' as defined by 18 U.S.C. § 921(a)(20); (ii) is a fugitive from justice; (iii) is an unlawful user of, or is addicted to, any controlled substance; (iv) has been adjudicated as a mental defective or involuntarily committed to a mental institution; (v) being an alien, is illegally or unlawfully in the United States; (vi) is subject to a court order that restrains such person from harassing, stalking, or threatening an intimate partner of such person or child of such intimate partner or person, or engaging in other conduct that would place an intimate partner in reasonable fear of bodily injury to the partner or child as defined in 18 U.S.C. § 922(d)(8); or (vii) has been convicted in any court of a misdemeanor crime of domestic violence as defined in 18 U.S.C. § 921(a)(33).",

and inserting the following:

> "For purposes of subsections (a)(4)(B) and (a)(6), 'prohibited person' means any person described in 18 U.S.C. § 922(g) or § 922(n).".

Reason for Amendment: This amendment makes two revisions regarding the definition of "prohibited person" in subsection (a)(3) of § 2K1.3 (Unlawful Receipt, Possession, or Transportation of Explosive Materials; Prohibited Transactions Involving Explosive Materials) and subsections (a)(4)(B) and (a)(6) of § 2K2.1 (Unlawful Receipt, Possession, or Transportation of Firearms or Ammunition; Prohibited Transactions Involving Firearms or Ammunition). First, the amendment adopts the definitions of prohibited person found in specific statutes for explosive and firearm offenses. (There is no uniform statutory definition of prohibited person.) The relevant statutory provision for § 2K1.3 is 18 U.S.C. § 842(i), and the relevant statutory provisions for § 2K2.1 are 18 U.S.C. § 922(g) and (n).

Second, the amendment clarifies that the pertinent alternative base offense level applies only when the offender attains the requisite status prior to committing the instant offense. This clarification is consistent with the amendment on prior felonies, which provides for increased punishment only when the offender sustains certain felony convictions prior to committing the instant offense.

Effective Date: The effective date of this amendment is November 1, 2001.

630. **Amendment:** Section 2K1.3(a)(1) is amended by striking "had at least two prior felony convictions of either a crime of violence or a controlled substance offense; or" and inserting "committed any part of the instant offense subsequent to sustaining at least two felony convictions of either a crime of violence or a controlled substance offense;";

Section 2K1.3(a)(2) is amended by striking "had one prior felony conviction of either a crime of violence or a controlled substance offense; or" and inserting "committed any part of the instant offense subsequent to sustaining one felony conviction of either a crime of violence or a controlled substance offense;".

The Commentary to § 2K1.3 captioned "Application Notes" is amended by striking the text of Note 2 as follows:

> 'Crime of violence,' 'controlled substance offense,' and 'prior felony conviction(s),' as used in subsections (a)(1) and (a)(2), are defined at § 4B1.2 (Definitions of Terms Used in Section 4B1.1), subsection (a), subsection (b), and Application Note 1 of the Commentary, respectively. For purposes of determining the number of such

convictions under subsections (a)(1) and (a)(2), count any such prior conviction that receives any points under § 4A1.1 (Criminal History Category).",

and inserting the following:

"For purposes of this guideline:

'Controlled substance offense' has the meaning given that term in § 4B1.2(b) and Application Note 1 of the Commentary to § 4B1.2 (Definitions of Terms Used in Section 4B1.1).

'Crime of violence' has the meaning given that term in § 4B1.2(a) and Application Note 1 of the Commentary to § 4B1.2.

'Felony conviction' means a prior adult federal or state conviction for an offense punishable by death or imprisonment for a term exceeding one year, regardless of whether such offense is specifically designated as a felony and regardless of the actual sentence imposed. A conviction for an offense committed at age eighteen years or older is an adult conviction. A conviction for an offense committed prior to age eighteen years is an adult conviction if it is classified as an adult conviction under the laws of the jurisdiction in which the defendant was convicted (e.g., a federal conviction for an offense committed prior to the defendant's eighteenth birthday is an adult conviction if the defendant was expressly proceeded against as an adult).".

The Commentary to § 2K1.3 captioned "Application Notes" is amended in Note 9 by inserting before the first paragraph the following:

"For purposes of applying subsection (a)(1) or (2), use only those felony convictions that receive criminal history points under § 4A1.1(a), (b), or (c). In addition, for purposes of applying subsection (a)(1), use only those felony convictions that are counted separately under § 4A1.1(a), (b), or (c). See § 4A1.2(a)(2); § 4A1.2, comment. (n.3).".

Section 2K2.1(a)(1) is amended by striking "had at least two prior felony convictions of either a crime of violence or a controlled substance offense; or" and inserting "committed any part of the instant offense subsequent to sustaining at least two felony convictions of either a crime of violence or a controlled substance offense;".

Section 2K2.1(a)(2) is amended by striking "had at least two prior felony convictions of either a crime of violence or a controlled substance offense; or" and inserting "committed any part of the instant offense subsequent to sustaining at least two felony convictions of either a crime of violence or a controlled substance offense;".

Section 2K2.1(a)(3) is amended by striking "had one prior felony conviction of either a crime of violence or controlled substance offense; or" and inserting "committed any part of the instant offense subsequent to sustaining one felony conviction of either a crime of violence or a controlled substance offense;".

Section 2K2.1(a)(4)(A) is amended by striking "had one prior felony conviction of either a crime of violence or controlled substance offense; or" and inserting "committed any part of the instant offense subsequent to sustaining one felony conviction of either a crime of violence or a controlled substance offense; or".

Section 2K2.1(a) is amended in subdivision (4)(B) by striking "; or" after "922(d)" and inserting a semi-colon; in subdivision (5), by striking "; or" after "921(a)(30)" and insert-

Amendment 630

ing a semi-colon; and in subdivision (6) by striking "; or" after "§ 922(d)" and inserting a semicolon.

The Commentary to § 2K2.1 captioned "Application Notes" is amended by striking Note 5 as follows:

> "5. 'Crime of violence,' 'controlled substance offense,' and 'prior felony conviction(s),' are defined in § 4B1.2 (Definitions of Terms Used in Section 4B1.1), subsection (a), subsection (b), and Application Note 1 of the Commentary, respectively. For purposes of determining the number of such convictions under subsections (a)(1), (a)(2), (a)(3), and (a)(4)(A), count any such prior conviction that receives any points under § 4A1.1 (Criminal History Category).

and inserting the following:

> "5. For purposes of this guideline:
>
> 'Controlled substance offense' has the meaning given that term in § 4B1.2(b) and Application Note 1 of the Commentary to § 4B1.2 (Definitions of Terms Used in Section 4B1.1).
>
> 'Crime of violence' has the meaning given that term in § 4B1.2(a) and Application Note 1 of the Commentary to § 4B1.2.
>
> 'Felony conviction' means a prior adult federal or state conviction for an offense punishable by death or imprisonment for a term exceeding one year, regardless of whether such offense is specifically designated as a felony and regardless of the actual sentence imposed. A conviction for an offense committed at age eighteen years or older is an adult conviction. A conviction for an offense committed prior to age eighteen years is an adult conviction if it is classified as an adult conviction under the laws of the jurisdiction in which the defendant was convicted (e.g., a federal conviction for an offense committed prior to the defendant's eighteenth birthday is an adult conviction if the defendant was expressly proceeded against as an adult).".

The Commentary to § 2K2.1 captioned "Application Notes" is amended in Note 15 by inserting before the first paragraph the following:

> "For purposes of applying subsection (a)(1), (2), (3), or (4)(A), use only those felony convictions that receive criminal history points under § 4A1.1(a), (b), or (c). In addition, for purposes of applying subsection (a)(1) and (a)(2), use only those felony convictions that are counted separately under § 4A1.1(a), (b), or (c). See § 4A1.2(a)(2); § 4A1.2, comment. (n.3).".

Reason for Amendment: This amendment modifies subsections (a)(1) and (a)(2) of § 2K1.3 (Unlawful Receipt, Possession, or Transportation of Explosive Materials; Prohibited Transactions Involving Explosive Materials) and subsections (a)(1), (a)(2), (a)(3) and (a)(4)(A) of § 2K2.1 (Unlawful Receipt, Possession or Transportation of Firearms or Ammunition) to resolve a circuit conflict regarding whether a crime committed after the commission of the instant offense and before sentencing for the instant offense is counted as a prior felony conviction for purposes of determining the defendant's base offense level. Compare United States v. Pugh, 158 F.3d 1308, 1311 (D.C. Cir. 1998) (finding the guideline language ambiguous but the commentary language clear, thereby counting prior felony conviction that was sentenced prior to sentencing for the instant federal offense, even if the defendant committed the prior felony offense after the instant federal offense); United States v. McCary, 14 F.3d 1502, 1506 (10th Cir. 1994) (the defendant's base offense level is to be determined on the basis of the defendant's status as of the date the district court imposed sentence, not the date of the offense for which he had previously been convicted); and United States v. Laihben, 167 F.3d 1364 (11th Cir. 1999) (district court properly considered defendant's conviction, which occurred after commission of, but before sentencing, on the federal firearms offense, in determining offense level), with United States v. Barton, 100 F.3d 43, 46 (6th Cir. 1996) (defendant's state drug crime, which was committed after federal offense of being a felon in possession of firearm, could not have been counted as prior felony conviction under § 2K2.1(a), even though defendant was convicted and sentenced on state offense prior to sentencing on federal charge; only those convictions that occur prior to the commission of the firearm offense may be counted against the defendant in determining the base offense level)) and United States v. Oetken, 241 F.3d 1057 (8th Cir. 2001) (only convictions that occur prior to the commission of the offense qualify as "prior convictions").

The amendment adopts the minority view that an offense committed after the commission of any part of the offense cannot be counted as a prior felony conviction. The amendment clarifies, in § 2K1.3(a)(1) and (a)(2) and in § 2K2.1(a)(1), (a)(2), (a)(3) and (a)(4)(A), that the instant offense must have been committed subsequent to sustaining the prior felony conviction. In so doing, this amendment adopts a rule that is consistent with the requirements concerning the use of prior convictions under §§ 4B1.1 (Career Offender) and 4B1.2 (Definitions of Terms Used in Section 4B1.1).

This amendment also clarifies that in cases in which more than one prior felony conviction is required for application of the base offense level in § 2K1.3 or § 2K2.1, the prior felony convictions must be counted separately under Chapter Four (Criminal History and Criminal Livelihood).

The amendment makes nonsubstantive clarifying changes in the definitions of "controlled substance offense", "crime of violence", and "felony conviction" for purposes of §§ 2K1.3 and 2K2.1.

Effective Date: The effective date of this amendment is November 1, 2001.

631. Amendment: Section 2K2.1(b)(1) is amended in the table by striking subdivisions (A) through (F) as follows:

"(A)	3-4	add 1
(B)	5-7	add 2
(C)	8-12	add 3
(D)	13-24	add 4
(E)	25-49	add 5
(F)	50 or more	add 6.",

and inserting the following:

"(A)	3-7	add 2
(B)	8-24	add 4
(C)	25-99	add 6
(D)	100-199	add 8
(E)	200 or more	add 10.".

Amendment 631   APPENDIX C - VOLUME II   November 1, 2013

The Commentary to § 2K2.1 captioned "Application Notes" is amended in Note 16 by striking "significantly" and inserting "substantially"; and by striking "fifty" and inserting "200".

Reason for Amendment: This amendment responds to a recommendation from the Bureau of Alcohol, Tobacco and Firearms (ATF) to increase the penalties in § 2K2.1 (Unlawful Receipt, Possession or Transportation of Firearms or Ammunition) for offenses involving more than 100 firearms.

The amendment modifies the firearms table at § 2K2.1(b)(1), to provide enhancements in two-level increments. Prior to this amendment, the table provided enhancements in one-level increments. This change has the effect of compressing the table by providing a wider range in each subdivision of the table for the number of firearms involved in the offense. Compressing the table in this manner diminishes some of the fact-finding required to determine how many firearms were involved in the offense and provides some increase in penalties. The amendment provides additional two-level increases for offenses that involve either 100-199 firearms, or 200 or more firearms. These increases are provided to ensure adequate and proportionate punishment in cases that involve large numbers of firearms.

The amendment also makes a conforming change to Application Note 16 of § 2K2.1 regarding upward departures.

Effective Date: The effective date of this amendment is November 1, 2001.

632. **Amendment:** Chapter Two, Part L, Subpart 1 is amended by striking § 2L1.2 and its accompanying commentary as follows:

"§ 2L1.2. Unlawfully Entering or Remaining in the United States

  (a) Base Offense Level: 8

  (b) Specific Offense Characteristic

   (1) If the defendant previously was deported after a criminal conviction, or if the defendant unlawfully remained in the United States following a removal order issued after a criminal conviction, increase as follows (if more than one applies, use the greater):

    (A) If the conviction was for an aggravated felony, increase by 16 levels.

    (B) If the conviction was for (i) any other felony, or (ii) three or more misdemeanor crimes of violence or misdemeanor controlled substance offenses, increase by 4 levels.

Commentary

Statutory Provisions: 8 U.S.C. § 1325(a) (second or subsequent offense only), 8 U.S.C. § 1326. For additional statutory provision(s), see Appendix A (Statutory Index).

Application Notes:

1. For purposes of this guideline—

'Deported after a conviction,' means that the deportation was subsequent to the conviction, whether or not the deportation was in response to such conviction. An alien has previously been 'deported' if he or she has been removed or has departed the United States while an order of exclusion, deportation, or removal was outstanding.

'Remained in the United States following a removal order issued after a conviction,' means that the removal order was subsequent to the conviction, whether or not the removal order was in response to such conviction.

'Aggravated felony,' is defined at 8 U.S.C. § 1101(a)(43) without regard to the date of conviction of the aggravated felony.

'Crime of violence' and 'controlled substance offense' are defined in § 4B1.2. For purposes of subsection (b)(1)(B), "crime of violence" includes offenses punishable by imprisonment for a term of one year or less.

'Firearms offense' means any offense covered by Chapter Two, Part K, Subpart 2, or any similar offense under state or local law.

'Felony offense' means any federal, state, or local offense punishable by imprisonment for a term exceeding one year.

2. This guideline applies only to felonies. A first offense under 8 U.S.C. § 1325(a) is a Class B misdemeanor for which no guideline has been promulgated. A prior sentence for such offense, however, is to be considered under the provisions of Chapter Four, Part A (Criminal History).

3. In the case of a defendant with repeated prior instances of deportation, an upward departure may be warranted. See § 4A1.3 (Adequacy of Criminal History Category).

4. An adjustment under subsection (b) for a prior felony conviction applies in addition to any criminal history points added for such conviction in Chapter Four, Part A (Criminal History).

5. Aggravated felonies that trigger the adjustment from subsection (b)(1)(A) vary widely. If subsection (b)(1)(A) applies, and (A) the defendant has previously been convicted of only one felony offense; (B) such offense was not a crime of violence or firearms offense; and (C) the term of imprisonment imposed for such offense did not exceed one year, a downward departure may be warranted based on the seriousness of the aggravated felony.".

A replacement guideline is inserted as § 2L1.2 (Unlawfully Entering or Remaining in the United States).

Reason for Amendment: This amendment responds to concerns raised by a number of judges, probation officers, and defense attorneys, particularly in districts along the southwest border between the United States and Mexico, that § 2L1.2 (Unlawfully Entering or Remaining in the United States) sometimes results in disproportionate penalties because of the 16-level enhancement provided in the guideline for a prior conviction for an aggravated felony. The disproportionate penalties result because the breadth of the definition of "aggravated felony" provided in 8 U.S.C. § 1101(a)(43), which is incorporated into the guideline by reference, means that a defendant who previously was convicted of murder, for example, receives the same 16-level enhancement as a defendant previously convicted of simple assault. The Commission also observed that the criminal justice system has been addressing this inequity on an ad hoc basis in such cases by increased use of departures.

This amendment responds to these concerns by providing a more graduated sentencing enhancement of between 8 levels and 16 levels, depending on the seriousness of the prior aggravated felony and the dangerousness of the defendant. In doing so, the Commission determined that the 16-level enhancement is warranted if the defendant previously was deported, or unlawfully remained in the United States, after a conviction for certain serious offenses, specifically, a drug trafficking offense for which the sentence imposed exceeded 13 months, a felony that is a crime of violence, a felony that is a firearms offense, a felony that is a national security or terrorism offense, a felony that is a human trafficking offense, and a felony that is an alien smuggling offense committed for profit. Other felony drug trafficking offenses will receive a 12-level enhancement. All other aggravated felony offenses will receive an 8-level enhancement.

This amendment also deletes an application note providing that a downward departure may be warranted based on the seriousness of the offense if the 16-level enhancement applied and (1) the defendant has previously been convicted of only one felony offense; (2) such offense was not a crime of violence or firearms offense; and (3) the term of imprisonment for such offenses did not exceed one year. The Commission determined that the graduation of the 16-level enhancement based on the seriousness of the prior conviction negated the need for this departure provision. As a result, this amendment may have the indirect result of reducing the departure rate for cases sentenced under § 2L1.2. In addition, this amendment renders moot a circuit conflict regarding whether the three criteria set forth in the application note are the exclusive basis for a downward departure from the 16-level enhancement. Compare United States v. Sanchez-Rodriguez, 161 F.3d 556 (9th Cir. 1998) (holding that Application Note 5 to § 2L1.2 does not limit the circumstances under which a downward departure from the 16-level enhancement is warranted); and United States v. Alfaro-Zayas, 196 F.3d 1338 (11th Cir. 1999) (same), with United States v. Tappin, 205 F.3d 536 (2d Cir. 2000) (holding that a defendant must satisfy all three criteria set forth in Application Note 5 in § 2L1.2 to receive a downward departure from the 16-level enhancement).

This amendment also makes a number of other minor changes to § 2L1.2, to provide guidance regarding the application of the enhancement for the commission of three or more prior misdemeanors and to provide definitions for terms used in the guideline.

Effective Date: The effective date of this amendment is November 1, 2001.

633. **Amendment:** The heading to Chapter Two, Part M is amended by adding at the end "And Weapons of Mass Destruction".

Section 2M5.1 is amended by striking subsection (a) as follows:

"(a) Base Offense Level (Apply the greater):

(1) 22, if national security or nuclear proliferation controls were evaded; or

(2) 14.",

and inserting the following:

"(a) Base Offense Level (Apply the greater):

    (1) 26, if national security controls or controls relating to the proliferation of nuclear, biological, or chemical weapons or materials were evaded; or

    (2) 14, otherwise.".

Section 2M5.2(a)(1) is amended by striking "22" and inserting "26".

The heading to Chapter Two, Part M, Subpart 6 is amended by striking "Atomic Energy" and inserting "Nuclear, Biological, And Chemical Weapons And Materials, And Other Weapons of Mass Destruction".

Chapter Two, Part M is amended by striking § 2M6.1 as follows:

"§ 2M6.1. Unlawful Acquisition, Alteration, Use, Transfer, or Possession of Nuclear Material, Weapons, or Facilities

    (a) Base Offense Level: 30

    (b) Specific Offense Characteristic

        (1) If the offense was committed with intent to injure the United States or to aid a foreign nation, increase by 12 levels.

Commentary

Statutory Provisions: 42 U.S.C. §§ 2077(b), 2122, 2131. Also, 18 U.S.C. § 831 (only where the conduct is similar to that proscribed by the aforementioned statutory provisions). For additional statutory provision(s), see Appendix A (Statutory Index).".

A replacement guideline is inserted as § 2M6.1 (Unlawful Production, Development, Acquisition, Stockpiling, Alteration, Use, Transfer, or Possession of Nuclear Material, Weapons, or Facilities, Biological Agents, Toxins, or Delivery Systems, Chemical Weapons, or Other Weapons of Mass Destruction; Attempt or Conspiracy).

The Commentary to § 2X1.1 captioned "Application Notes" is amended in Note 1 by inserting after the line referenced to "§ 2E5.1;" the following:

"§ 2M6.1;".

The Commentary to § 2X1.1 captioned "Application Notes" is amended in Note 1 by inserting after the line referenced to "§ 2H1.1" the following:

"§ 2M6.1;".

Appendix A (Statutory Index) is amended by inserting after the line referenced to 18 U.S.C. § 155 the following new line:

"18 U.S.C. § 175   2M6.1";

by inserting after the line referenced to 18 U.S.C. § 228 the following new line:

Amendment 633   APPENDIX C - VOLUME II   November 1, 2013

"18 U.S.C. § 229   2M6.1";

by inserting after the line referenced to 18 U.S.C. § 842(l)-(o) the following new line:

"18 U.S.C. § 842(p)(2)   2K1.3, 2M6.1";

in the line referenced to 18 U.S.C. § 2332a by striking "2A1.1, 2A1.2, 2A1.3, 2A1.4, 2A1.5, 2A2.1, 2A2.2, 2B1.3," and by inserting ", 2M6.1" after "2K1.4"; and

by inserting after the line referenced to 50 U.S.C. App. § 462 the following new line:

"50 U.S.C. App. § 1701   2M5.1, 2M5.2".

Reason for Amendment: This amendment responds to a statutory provision expressing a sense of Congress and addresses two offenses relating to biological and chemical weapons. Specifically, the amendment responds to section 1423(a) of the National Defense Authorization Act for Fiscal Year 1997, Public Law 104–201, that expressed a sense of Congress that guideline penalties are inadequate for certain offenses involving the importation and exportation of nuclear, chemical, and biological weapons, materials, or technologies by providing a four-level increase for those offenses in subsection (a)(1) of both §§ 2M5.1 (Evasion of Export Controls) and 2M5.2 (Exportation of Arms, Munitions, or Military Equipment or Services Without a Required Validated Export License). This increase serves to make the penalty structure for those offenses proportional to other national security guidelines in Chapter Two, Part M. In addition, Appendix A (Statutory Index) is amended to refer one of the offenses, 50 U.S.C. § 1701 (which prior to this amendment was not referenced in the Statutory Index), to both §§ 2M5.1 and 2M5.2.

The amendment also substantially revises § 2M6.1 to incorporate offenses at 18 U.S.C. § 175, relating to biological weapons, and 18 U.S.C. § 229, relating to chemical weapons. Specifically, the amendment modifies § 2M6.1 as follows:

First, the amendment provides three alternative base offense levels. The first alternative base offense level of level 42 applies if the offense was committed with the intent to injure the United States or to aid a foreign government or foreign terrorist organization and incorporates the 12-level enhancement previously at subsection (b)(1). Therefore, this change does not affect the overall offense level for these offenses. "Foreign terrorist organizations" are added because such groups are investing in the acquisition of unconventional weapons such as nuclear, biological, and chemical agents. This first alternative base offense level is expected to apply to cases previously covered by the guideline (i.e., the acquisition of nuclear material from nuclear facilities in order to assist foreign governments, thereby creating a threat to the national security), as well as to cases that implicate the national security and involve biological and chemical weapons and other weapons of mass destruction.

The amendment provides that, if the base offense level of level 42 applies, none of the adjustments in subsection (b) shall apply. However, if death results, the cross reference allows for the possibility of a greater offense level through application of the first degree murder guideline.

The second alternative base offense level of level 28 applies to those cases that do not threaten the national security of the United States, and is expected to apply in most cases.

The third alternative base offense level of level 20 applies to cases which involve a threat to use a nuclear, biological, or chemical weapon or material, or other weapon of mass destruction, but do not involve any conduct evidencing an intent or ability to carry out the threat and, accordingly, are less serious offenses.

Second, the amendment provides a two-level enhancement in subsection (b)(1) if the offense or threat involved particularly dangerous types of nuclear, chemical, and biological weapons and materials that are defined in the guideline commentary by reference to the applicable statutory and regulatory provisions. This enhancement reflects the distinctions already made in international treaties, provisions of title 18, United States Code, relevant regulatory schemes, and the fact that certain types of weapons and materials are inherently more lethal and pose a greater threat to the public safety.

Third, the amendment provides a four-level enhancement in subsection (b)(2) if any victim died or sustained permanent or life-threatening bodily injury, and a two-level enhancement if any victim sustained serious bodily injury. If the degree of injury is between permanent or life-threatening bodily injury and serious bodily injury, a three-level enhancement is provided. This enhancement is modeled after the enhancement found in § 2N1.1 (Tampering or Attempting to Tamper Involving Risk of Death or Bodily Injury).

Fourth, the amendment provides a four-level enhancement for cases involving a substantial disruption of public, governmental, or business functions or services, or the substantial expenditure of funds to clean up, decontaminate, or otherwise respond to the offense.

Fifth, the amendment provides two cross references, applicable if the resulting offense level is greater and either death resulted (in which case the first or second degree murder guideline would apply), or if the offense was tantamount to attempted murder (in which case the attempted murder guideline would apply). These cross references are also modeled after the cross reference found in § 2N1.1.

Sixth, the amendment provides a special instruction that if the defendant is convicted of one count involving the death of, serious bodily injury to, or attempted murder of, more than one victim, the grouping rules will be applied as if the defendant had been convicted of separate counts for each such victim.

Seventh, the amendment amends Appendix A to refer violations of 18 U.S.C. §§ 175 and 229 to § 2M6.1 and to delete a number of guideline references for violations of 18 U.S.C. § 2332a and instead provide a reference for that offense to §§ 2K1.4 (Arson; Property Damage by Use of Explosives) and 2M6.1 (in the case of other weapons of mass destruction).

Finally, the amendment amends the title of § 2M6.1 to include attempts and conspiracies, and adds § 2M6.1 under the sections addressing attempts and conspiracies in Application Note 1 of § 2X1.1 (Attempt, Solicitation, or Conspiracy) to indicate that attempts and conspiracies are covered expressly by the § 2M6.1 offense guideline.

Effective Date: The effective date of this amendment is November 1, 2001.

634. **Amendment:** Chapter Two, Part S is amended by striking § 2S1.1 as follows:

"§ 2S1.1. Laundering of Monetary Instruments

(a) Base Offense Level:

(1) 23, if convicted under 18 U.S.C. § 1956(a)(1)(A), (a)(2)(A), or (a)(3)(A);

Amendment 634 APPENDIX C - VOLUME II November 1, 2013

    (2) 20, otherwise.

 (b) Specific Offense Characteristics

    (1) If the defendant knew or believed that the funds were the proceeds of an unlawful activity involving the manufacture, importation, or distribution of narcotics or other controlled substances, increase by 3 levels.

    (2) If the value of the funds exceeded $100,000, increase the offense level as follows:

Value (Apply the Greatest)		Increase in Level
(A)	$100,000 or less	no increase
(B)	More than $100,000	add 1
(C)	More than $200,000	add 2
(D)	More than $350,000	add 3
(E)	More than $600,000	add 4
(F)	More than $1,000,000	add 5
(G)	More than $2,000,000	add 6
(H)	More than $3,500,000	add 7
(I)	More than $6,000,000	add 8
(J)	More than $10,000,000	add 9
(K)	More than $20,000,000	add 10
(L)	More than $35,000,000	add 11
(M)	More than $60,000,000	add 12
(N)	More than $100,000,000	add 13.

 (c) Special Instruction for Fines - Organizations

    (1) In lieu of the applicable amount from the table in subsection (d) of § 8C2.4 (Base Fine), use:

      (A) the greater of $250,000 or 100 percent of the value of the funds if subsections (a)(1) and (b)(1) are used to determine the offense level; or

      (B) the greater of $200,000 or 70 percent of the value of the funds if subsections (a)(2) and (b)(1) are used to determine the offense level; or

      (C) the greater of $200,000 or 70 percent of the value of the funds if subsection (a)(1) but not (b)(1) is used to determine the offense level; or

      (D) the greater of $150,000 or 50 percent of the value of the funds if subsection (a)(2) but not (b)(1) is used to determine the offense level.

<u>Commentary</u>

<u>Statutory Provision</u>: 18 U.S.C. § 1956.

Background: The statute covered by this guideline is a part of the Anti-Drug Abuse Act of 1986, and prohibits financial transactions involving funds that are the proceeds of 'specified unlawful activity,' if such transactions are intended to facilitate that activity, or conceal the nature of the proceeds or avoid a transaction reporting requirement. The maximum term of imprisonment authorized is twenty years.

In keeping with the clear intent of the legislation, this guideline provides for substantial punishment. The punishment is higher than that specified in § 2S1.2 and § 2S1.3 because of the higher statutory maximum, and the added elements as to source of funds, knowledge, and intent.

A higher base offense level is specified if the defendant is convicted under 18 U.S.C. § 1956(a)(1)(A), (a)(2)(A), or (a)(3)(A) because those subsections apply to defendants who encouraged or facilitated the commission of further crimes. Effective November 18, 1988, 18 U.S.C. § 1956(a)(1)(A) contains two subdivisions. The base offense level of 23 applies to § 1956(a)(1)(A)(i) and (ii).

The amount of money involved is included as a factor because it is an indicator of the magnitude of the criminal enterprise, and the extent to which the defendant aided the enterprise. Narcotics trafficking is included as a factor because of the clearly expressed Congressional intent to adequately punish persons involved in that activity.".

A replacement guideline with accompanying commentary is inserted as § 2S1.1 (Laundering of Monetary Instruments; Engaging in Monetary Transactions in Property Derived from Unlawful Activity).

Chapter Two, Part S is amended by striking § 2S1.2 as follows:

"§ 2S1.2.   Engaging in Monetary Transactions in Property Derived from Specified Unlawful Activity

(a)   Base Offense Level: 17

(b)   Specific Offense Characteristics

(1)   If the defendant knew that the funds were the proceeds of:

(A)   an unlawful activity involving the manufacture, importation, or distribution of narcotics or other controlled substances, increase by 5 levels; or

(B)   any other specified unlawful activity (see 18 U.S.C. § 1956(c)(7)), increase by 2 levels.

(2)   If the value of the funds exceeded $100,000, increase the offense level as specified in § 2S1.1(b)(2).

(c)   Special Instruction for Fines - Organizations

(1)   In lieu of the applicable amount from the table in subsection (d) of § 8C2.4 (Base Fine), use:

(A)   the greater of $175,000 or 60 percent of the value of the funds if subsection (b)(1)(A) is used to determine the offense level; or

(B) the greater of $150,000 or 50 percent of the value of the funds if subsection (b)(1)(B) is used to determine the offense level.

Commentary

Statutory Provisions: 18 U.S.C. § 1957. For additional statutory provision(s), see Appendix A (Statutory Index).

Application Note:

1. 'Specified unlawful activity' is defined in 18 U.S.C. § 1956(c)(7) to include racketeering offenses (18 U.S.C. § 1961(1)), drug offenses, and most other serious federal crimes but does not include other money-laundering offenses.

Background: The statute covered by this guideline is a part of the Anti-Drug Abuse Act of 1986, and prohibits monetary transactions that exceed $10,000 and involve the proceeds of 'specified unlawful activity' (as defined in 18 U.S.C. § 1956), if the defendant knows that the funds are criminally derived property. (Knowledge that the property is from a specified unlawful activity is not an element of the offense.) The maximum term of imprisonment specified is ten years.

The statute is similar to 18 U.S.C. § 1956, but does not require that the recipient exchange or 'launder' the funds, that he have knowledge that the funds were proceeds of a specified unlawful activity, nor that he have any intent to further or conceal such an activity. In keeping with the intent of the legislation, this guideline provides for substantial punishment. The offense levels are higher than in § 2S1.3 because of the higher statutory maximum and the added element of knowing that the funds were criminally derived property.

The 2-level increase in subsection (b)(1)(B) applies if the defendant knew that the funds were not merely criminally derived, but were in fact the proceeds of a specified unlawful activity. Such a distinction is not made in § 2S1.1, because the level of intent required in that section effectively precludes an inference that the defendant was unaware of the nature of the activity.".

The Commentary to § 2S1.3 captioned "Statutory Provisions" is amended by inserting "18 U.S.C. § 1960;" before "26 U.S.C. § 7203"; and by inserting ", 5326" after "5324".

Appendix A (Statutory Index) is amended in the line referenced to 18 U.S.C. § 1957 and the line referenced to 21 U.S.C. § 854 by striking "2S1.2" and inserting "2S1.1";

by inserting after the line referenced to 18 U.S.C. § 1959 the following new line:

"18 U.S.C. § 1960   2S1.3";

and by inserting after the line referenced to 31 U.S.C. § 5324 the following new line:

"31 U.S.C. § 5326   2S1.3, 2T2.2".

The Commentary to § 1B1.3 captioned "Application Notes" is amended in Note 6 in the first paragraph by striking the second sentence as follows:

"For example, in § 2S1.1 (Laundering of Monetary Instruments), subsection (a)(1) applies if the defendant 'is convicted under 18 U.S.C. § 1956(a)(1)(A), (a)(2)(A), or (a)(3)(A).'",

and inserting the following:

> "For example, in § 2S1.1 (Laundering of Monetary Instruments; Engaging in Monetary Transactions in Property Derived from Unlawful Activity), subsection (b)(2)(B) applies if the defendant 'is convicted under 18 U.S.C. § 1956'.".

The Commentary to § 1B1.3 captioned "Application Notes" is amended in Note 6 in the second paragraph by striking "An express" and inserting "Unless otherwise specified, an express"; and by striking the last sentence as follows:

> "For example, § 2S1.1(a)(1) (which is applicable only if the defendant is convicted under 18 U.S.C. § 1956(a)(1)(A), (a)(2)(A), or (a)(3)(A)) would be applied in determining the offense level under § 2X3.1 (Accessory After the Fact) where the defendant was convicted of accessory after the fact to a violation of 18 U.S.C. § 1956(a)(1)(A), (a)(2)(A), or (a)(3)(A).",

and inserting the following:

> "For example, § 2S1.1(b)(2)(B) (which is applicable only if the defendant is convicted under 18 U.S.C. § 1956) would be applied in determining the offense level under § 2X3.1 (Accessory After the Fact) in a case in which the defendant was convicted of accessory after the fact to a violation of 18 U.S.C. § 1956 but would not be applied in a case in which the defendant is convicted of a conspiracy under 18 U.S.C. § 1956(h) and the sole object of that conspiracy was to commit an offense set forth in 18 U.S.C. § 1957. See Application Note 3(C) of § 2S1.1.".

Section 3D1.2(d) is amended in the second paragraph by striking "2S1.2,".

Section 8C2.1(a) is amended by striking "2S1.2,".

The Commentary to § 8C2.4 captioned "Application Notes" is amended in Note 5 by striking "; 2S1.1 (Laundering of Monetary Instruments); and 2S1.2 (Engaging in Monetary Transactions in Property Derived from Specified Unlawful Activity)"; and by inserting "and" before "2R1.1".

The Commentary to § 8C2.4 captioned "Background" is amended in the seventh sentence by striking "and money laundering".

Reason for Amendment: This amendment consolidates the money laundering guidelines, §§ 2S1.1 (Laundering of Monetary Instruments) and 2S1.2 (Engaging in Monetary Transactions in Property Derived from Specified Unlawful Activity), into one guideline that applies to convictions under 18 U.S.C. § 1956 or § 1957, or 21 U.S.C. § 854. The amendment responds in several ways to concerns that the penalty structure existing prior to this amendment for such offenses did not reflect adequately the culpability of the defendant or the seriousness of the money laundering conduct because the offense level for money laundering was determined without sufficient consideration of the defendant's involvement in, or the relative seriousness of, the underlying offense. This amendment is designed to promote proportionality by providing increased penalties for defendants who launder funds derived from more serious underlying criminal conduct, such as drug trafficking, crimes of violence, and fraud offenses that generate relatively high loss amounts, and decreased penalties for defendants who launder funds derived from less serious underlying criminal conduct, such as basic fraud offenses that generate relatively low loss amounts.

First, this amendment ties offense levels for money laundering more closely to the underlying conduct that was the source of the criminally derived funds by separating money laundering offenders into two categories for purposes of determining the base offense level. For direct money launderers (offenders who commit or would be accountable under § 1B1.3(a)(1)(A) (Relevant Conduct) for the underlying offense which generated the criminal proceeds), subsection (a)(1) sets the base offense level at the offense level in Chapter Two (Offense Conduct) for the underlying offense (i.e., the base offense level, specific offense characteristics, cross references, and special instructions for the underlying offense). For third party money launderers (offenders who launder the proceeds generated from underlying offenses that the defendant did not commit or would not be accountable for under § 1B1.3(a)(1)(A)), subsection (a)(2) sets the base offense level at level 8, plus an increase based on the value of the laundered funds from the table in subsection (b)(1) of § 2B1.1 (Theft, Fraud, Property Destruction).

Second, in addition to the base offense level calculation, this amendment provides an enhancement designed to reflect the differing seriousness of the underlying conduct that was the source of the criminally derived funds. Subsection (b)(1) provides a six-level enhancement for third party money launderers who knew or believed that any of the laundered funds were the proceeds of, or were intended to promote, certain types of more serious underlying criminal conduct; specifically, drug trafficking, crimes of violence, offenses involving firearms, explosives, national security, terrorism, and the sexual exploitation of a minor. The Commission determined that defendants who knowingly launder the proceeds of these more serious underlying offenses are substantially more culpable than third party launderers of criminally derived proceeds of less serious underlying offenses.

Third, this amendment provides three alternative enhancements, with the greatest applicable enhancement to be applied. These enhancements are designed to (1) ensure that all direct money launderers receive additional punishment for committing both the money laundering offense and the underlying offense, and (2) reflect the differing seriousness of money laundering conduct depending on the nature and sophistication of the offense. Specifically, subsection (b)(2)(A) provides a one-level increase if the defendant was convicted under 18 U.S.C. § 1957, and subsection (b)(2)(B) provides a two-level increase if the defendant was convicted under 18 U.S.C. § 1956. The one-level difference between these two enhancements reflects the fact that 18 U.S.C. § 1956 has a statutory maximum penalty (20 years' imprisonment) that is twice as long as the statutory maximum penalty for violations of 18 U.S.C. § 1957 (10 years' imprisonment). In addition, subsection (b)(3) provides an additional two-level increase if subsection (b)(2)(B) applies and the offense involved sophisticated laundering such as the use of fictitious entities, shell corporations, two or more levels of transactions, or offshore financial accounts. The Commission determined that, similar to fraud and tax offenses that involve sophisticated means, see subsection (b)(8) of § 2B1.1 (Theft, Property Destruction, and Fraud), subsection (b)(2) of § 2T1.1 (Tax Evasion; Willful Failure to File Return, Supply Information, or Pay Tax; Fraudulent or False Returns, Statements, or Other Documents), violations of 18 U.S.C. § 1956 that involve sophisticated laundering warrant additional punishment because such offenses are more difficult and time consuming for law enforcement to detect than less sophisticated laundering. As a result of the enhancements provided by subsections (b)(2)(A), (b)(2)(B), and (b)(3), all direct money launderers will receive an offense level that is one to four levels greater than the Chapter Two offense level for the underlying offense, depending on the statute of conviction and sophistication of the money laundering offense conduct.

With respect to third party money launderers, subsection (b)(2)(C) provides a four-level enhancement if the defendant is "in the business" of laundering funds. The Commission determined that, similar to a professional "fence", see § 2B1.1(b)(4)(B), defendants who routinely engage in laundering funds on behalf of others, and who gain financially from engaging in such transactions, warrant substantial additional punishment because they encourage the commission of additional criminal conduct.

Fourth, this amendment contains an application note expressly providing instructions regarding the grouping of money laundering counts with a count of conviction for the underlying offense. In a case in which the defendant is to be sentenced on a count of conviction for money laundering and a count of conviction for the underlying offense that generated the laundered funds, this application note instructs that such counts shall be grouped pursuant to subsection (c) of § 3D1.2 (Groups of Closely-Related Counts), thereby resolving a circuit conflict on this issue. Compare United States v. Cusumano, 943 F.2d 305 (3d Cir. 1991), cert. denied, 502 U.S. 1036 (1992) (affirming decision to group under § 3D1.2(b) money laundering count with other offenses that "were all part of one scheme to obtain money" from an employee benefit fund); United States v. Leonard, 61 F.3d 1181 (5th Cir. 1995) (affirming decision to group fraud and money laundering offenses under § 3D1.2(d) because defendant's money laundering activity and fraudulent telemarketing scheme constituted the same common plan and had the same victims); and United States v. Wilson, 98 F.3d 281 (7th Cir. 1996) (district court erred in not grouping money laundering and mail fraud convictions under § 3D1.2(d)), with United States v. Kneeland, 148 F.3d 6 (1st Cir. 1998) (affirming district court decision not to group fraud and money laundering counts under § 3D1.2(d) because the offense level for fraud, unlike money laundering, is determined "largely on the basis of total amount of harm or loss"); United States v. Napoli, 179 F.3d 1 (2d Cir. 1999), cert. denied, 528 U.S. 1162 (2000) (affirming decision not to group wire fraud and money laundering counts under § 3D1.2(b) or (d) because the offenses have different victims and the offense level for money laundering, unlike fraud, is not based primarily on the amount of money involved); United States v. Hildebrand, 152 F.3d 756 (8th Cir.), cert. denied, 525 U.S. 1033 (1998) (finding that money laundering and fraud counts should not be grouped because the fraud and money laundering guidelines do not measure the same types of harm); United States v. Hanley, 190 F.3d 1017 (9th Cir. 1999) (affirming decision not to group money laundering and wire fraud counts under § 3D1.2(d) because the guidelines for such offenses measure harm differently); and United States v. Johnson, 971 F.2d 562 (10th Cir. 1992) (district court erred in grouping money laundering and fraud counts under § 3D1.2(d) because the measurement of harm for fraud is not the same as that for money laundering).

Finally, this amendment provides that convictions under 18 U.S.C. § 1960 are referenced to § 2S1.3 (Structuring Transactions to Evade Reporting Requirements). Operation of money transmitting businesses without an appropriate license is proscribed by 18 U.S.C. § 1960, as are failures to comply with certain reporting requirements issued under 31 U.S.C. § 5330. The Commission determined that offenses involving these regulatory requirements serve many of the same purposes as Currency Transaction Reports, Currency and Monetary Instrument Reports, Reports of Foreign Bank and Financial Accounts, and Reports of Cash Payments over $10,000 Received in a Trade or Business, violations regarding which currently are referenced to § 2S1.3, and that, therefore, violations of 18 U.S.C. § 1960 also should be referenced to § 2S1.3.

Effective Date: The effective date of this amendment is November 1, 2001.

635. **Amendment:** The Commentary to § 3B1.2 is amended by striking Notes 1 through 4 and the background as follows:

> "1. Subsection (a) applies to a defendant who plays a minimal role in concerted activity. It is intended to cover defendants who are plainly among the least culpable of those involved in the conduct of a group. Under this provision, the defendant's lack of knowledge or understanding of the scope and structure of the enterprise and of the activities of others is indicative of a role as minimal participant.

Amendment 635　　APPENDIX C - VOLUME II　　November 1, 2013

2. It is intended that the downward adjustment for a minimal participant will be used infrequently. It would be appropriate, for example, for someone who played no other role in a very large drug smuggling operation than to offload part of a single marihuana shipment, or in a case where an individual was recruited as a courier for a single smuggling transaction involving a small amount of drugs.

3. For purposes of § 3B1.2(b), a minor participant means any participant who is less culpable than most other participants, but whose role could not be described as minimal.

4. If a defendant has received a lower offense level by virtue of being convicted of an offense significantly less serious than warranted by his actual criminal conduct, a reduction for a mitigating role under this section ordinarily is not warranted because such defendant is not substantially less culpable than a defendant whose only conduct involved the less serious offense. For example, if a defendant whose actual conduct involved a minimal role in the distribution of 25 grams of cocaine (an offense having a Chapter Two offense level of 14 under § 2D1.1) is convicted of simple possession of cocaine (an offense having a Chapter Two offense level of 6 under § 2D2.1), no reduction for a mitigating role is warranted because the defendant is not substantially less culpable than a defendant whose only conduct involved the simple possession of cocaine.

Background: This section provides a range of adjustments for a defendant who plays a part in committing the offense that makes him substantially less culpable than the average participant. The determination whether to apply subsection (a) or subsection (b), or an intermediate adjustment, involves a determination that is heavily dependent upon the facts of the particular case.",

and inserting the following:

"1. Definition.—For purposes of this guideline, 'participant' has the meaning given that term in Application Note 1 of § 3B1.1 (Aggravating Role).

2. Requirement of Multiple Participants.—This guideline is not applicable unless more than one participant was involved in the offense. See the Introductory Commentary to this Part (Role in the Offense). Accordingly, an adjustment under this guideline may not apply to a defendant who is the only defendant convicted of an offense unless that offense involved other participants in addition to the defendant and the defendant otherwise qualifies for such an adjustment.

3. Applicability of Adjustment.—

    (A) Substantially Less Culpable than Average Participant.—This section provides a range of adjustments for a defendant who plays a part in committing the offense that makes him substantially less culpable than the average participant.

    A defendant who is accountable under § 1B1.3 (Relevant Conduct) only for the conduct in which the defendant personally was involved and who performs a limited function in concerted criminal activity is not precluded from consideration for an adjustment under this guideline. For example, a defendant who is convicted of a drug trafficking offense, whose role in that offense was limited to transporting or storing drugs and who is accountable under § 1B1.3 only for the quantity of drugs the defendant personally transported or stored is not precluded from consideration for an adjustment under this guideline.

(B) <u>Conviction of Significantly Less Serious Offense</u>.—If a defendant has received a lower offense level by virtue of being convicted of an offense significantly less serious than warranted by his actual criminal conduct, a reduction for a mitigating role under this section ordinarily is not warranted because such defendant is not substantially less culpable than a defendant whose only conduct involved the less serious offense. For example, if a defendant whose actual conduct involved a minimal role in the distribution of 25 grams of cocaine (an offense having a Chapter Two offense level of level 14 under § 2D1.1 (Unlawful Manufacturing, Importing, Exporting, or Trafficking (Including Possession with Intent to Commit These Offenses); Attempt or Conspiracy)) is convicted of simple possession of cocaine (an offense having a Chapter Two offense level of level 6 under § 2D2.1 (Unlawful Possession; Attempt or Conspiracy)), no reduction for a mitigating role is warranted because the defendant is not substantially less culpable than a defendant whose only conduct involved the simple possession of cocaine.

(C) <u>Fact-Based Determination</u>.—The determination whether to apply subsection (a) or subsection (b), or an intermediate adjustment, involves a determination that is heavily dependent upon the facts of the particular case. As with any other factual issue, the court, in weighing the totality of the circumstances, is not required to find, based solely on the defendant's bare assertion, that such a role adjustment is warranted.

4. <u>Minimal Participant</u>.—Subsection (a) applies to a defendant described in Application Note 3(A) who plays a minimal role in concerted activity. It is intended to cover defendants who are plainly among the least culpable of those involved in the conduct of a group. Under this provision, the defendant's lack of knowledge or understanding of the scope and structure of the enterprise and of the activities of others is indicative of a role as minimal participant. It is intended that the downward adjustment for a minimal participant will be used infrequently.

5. <u>Minor Participant</u>.— Subsection (b) applies to a defendant described in Application Note 3(A) who is less culpable than most other participants, but whose role could not be described as minimal.".

Reason for Amendment: This amendment resolves a circuit conflict regarding whether a defendant who is accountable under § 1B1.3 (Relevant Conduct) only for conduct in which the defendant personally was involved, and who performs a limited function in concerted criminal activity, is precluded from consideration for an adjustment under § 3B1.2 (Mitigating Role). Compare <u>United States v. Burnett</u>, 66 F.3d 137 (7th Cir. 1995) ("where a defendant is sentenced only for the amount of drugs he handled, he is not entitled to a § 3B1.2 reduction"), <u>with</u> <u>United States v. Rodriguez De Varon</u>, 175 F.3d 930 (11th Cir. 1999) (a defendant is not automatically precluded from consideration for a mitigating role adjustment in a case in which the defendant is held accountable solely for the amount

Amendment 635 APPENDIX C - VOLUME II November 1, 2013

of drugs he personally handled). Although this circuit conflict arose in the context of a drug offense, the amendment resolves it in a manner that makes the rule applicable to all types of offenses.

The amendment adopts the approach articulated by the Eleventh Circuit in <u>United States v. Rodriguez De Varon</u>, supra, that § 3B1.2 does not automatically preclude a defendant from being considered for a mitigating role adjustment in a case in which the defendant is held accountable under § 1B1.3 solely for the amount of drugs the defendant personally handled. In considering a § 3B1.2 adjustment, a court must measure the defendant's role against the relevant conduct for which the defendant is held accountable at sentencing, whether or not other defendants are charged.

In contrast to the holding in <u>United States v. Burnett</u>, supra, this amendment allows the court to apply traditional analysis on the applicability of a reduction pursuant to § 3B1.2, even in a case in which a defendant is held liable under § 1B1.3 only for conduct (such as drug quantities) in which the defendant was involved personally.

The substantive impact of this amendment in resolving the circuit conflict is to provide, in the context of a drug courier, for example, that the court is not precluded from considering a § 3B1.2 adjustment simply because the defendant's role in the offense was limited to transporting or storing drugs, and the defendant was accountable under § 1B1.3 only for the quantity of drugs the defendant personally transported or stored. The amendment does not require that such a defendant receive a reduction under § 3B1.2, or suggest that such a defendant can receive a reduction based only on those facts; rather, the amendment provides only that such a defendant is not precluded from consideration for such a reduction if the defendant otherwise qualifies for the reduction pursuant to the terms of § 3B1.2.

In addition to resolving the circuit conflict, the amendment makes the following non-substantive revisions to § 3B1.2 to clarify guideline application: (1) incorporating commentary from the Introduction to Chapter Three, Part B (Role in the Offense) that there must be more than one participant before application of a mitigating role adjustment may be considered; (2) incorporating into this guideline the definition of "participant" from § 3B1.1 (Aggravating Role); (3) moving into an application note significant background commentary that has been cited frequently in appellate decisions; (4) adding a section on fact-based determinations to Application Note 3 that emphasizes the significant judicial role in decision-making on the applicability of § 3B1.2; (5) maintaining commentary language that the minimal role adjustment is intended to be used infrequently; and (6) making technical amendments to the Commentary to clarify applicable rules (such as the addition of headings for, and the reordering of, application notes in the commentary) that are intended to have no substantive impact.

The language regarding "average participant" is moved from the Background into Application Note 3(A) to provide guidance as to the applicability of § 3B1.2. For a reduction to apply, the court, at a minimum, must make a factual determination that the defendant's role was significantly less culpable than the average participant.

Effective Date: The effective date of this amendment is November 1, 2001.

636. **Amendment:** The Commentary to § 2J1.6 captioned "Application Notes" is amended in Note 3 in the first sentence of the second paragraph by striking "In" and inserting "However, in"; and by inserting "other than a case of failure to appear for service of sentence," after "offense and the failure to appear,".

The Commentary to § 2M3.9 captioned "Application Notes" is amended by inserting after

November 1, 2013 APPENDIX C - VOLUME II **Amendment 637**

Note 2 the following:

"3. A term of imprisonment imposed for a conviction under 50 U.S.C. § 421 shall be imposed consecutively to any other term of imprisonment.".

Reason for Amendment: This amendment makes two minor technical changes. First, the amendment makes an editorial change in the commentary to § 2J1.6 (Failure to Appear by Defendant) to improve the transition between the first and second paragraphs of Application Note 3. Second, the amendment adds an application note to § 2M3.9 (Disclosure of Information Identifying a Covert Agent) that implements the consecutive sentencing requirement of 50 U.S.C. § 421, relating to the disclosure of information identifying a covert agent.

Effective Date: The effective date of this amendment is November 1, 2001.

637. **Amendment:** The Commentary to § 2A1.1 captioned "Statutory Provisions" is amended by inserting ", 2332b(a)(1), 2340A" after "2118(c)(2)".

The Commentary to § 2A1.2 captioned "Statutory Provision" is amended by striking "Provision" and inserting "Provisions"; by inserting "§ " before "1111"; and by inserting ", 2332b(a)(1), 2340A" after "1111".

The Commentary to § 2A1.3 captioned "Statutory Provision" is amended by striking "Provision" and inserting "Provisions"; by inserting "§ " before "1112"; and by inserting ", 2332b(a)(1)" after "1112".

The Commentary to § 2A1.4 captioned "Statutory Provision" is amended by striking "Provision" and inserting "Provisions"; by inserting "§ " before "1112"; and by inserting ", 2332b(a)(1)" after "1112".

The Commentary to § 2A2.1 captioned "Statutory Provisions" is amended by inserting ", 1993(a)(6)" after "1751(c)".

The Commentary to § 2A2.2 captioned "Statutory Provisions" is amended by inserting ", 1993(a)(6), 2332b(a)(1), 2340A" after "1751(e)".

The Commentary to § 2A4.1 captioned "Statutory Provisions" is amended by inserting ", 2340A" after "1751(b)".

Chapter Two, Part A is amended in the heading of Subpart 5 by adding at the end "AND OFFENSES AGAINST MASS TRANSPORTATION SYSTEMS".

Section 2A5.2 is amended in the heading by adding at the end "; Interference with Dispatch, Operation, or Maintenance of Mass Transportation Vehicle or Ferry".

Section 2A5.2(a)(1) is amended by striking "the aircraft and passengers; or" and inserting ": (A) an airport or an aircraft; or (B) a mass transportation facility, a mass transportation vehicle, or a ferry;".

Section 2A5.2(a)(2) is amended by striking "the aircraft and passengers; or" and inserting ": (A) an airport or an aircraft; or (B) a mass transportation facility, a mass transportation vehicle, or a ferry;".

Section 2A5.2 is amended by inserting after subsection (a) the following:

"(b) Specific Offense Characteristic

Amendment 637

(1) If (A) subsection (a)(1) or (a)(2) applies; and (B)(i) a firearm was discharged, increase by 5 levels; (ii) a dangerous weapon was otherwise used, increase by 4 levels; or (iii) a dangerous weapon was brandished or its use was threatened, increase by 3 levels. If the resulting offense level is less than level 24, increase to level 24.

(c) Cross References

(1) If death resulted, apply the most analogous guideline from Chapter Two, Part A, Subpart 1 (Homicide), if the resulting offense level is greater than that determined above.

(2) If the offense involved possession of, or a threat to use (A) a nuclear weapon, nuclear material, or nuclear byproduct material; (B) a chemical weapon; (C) a biological agent, toxin, or delivery system; or (D) a weapon of mass destruction, apply § 2M6.1 (Nuclear, Biological, and Chemical Weapons, and Other Weapons of Mass Destruction), if the resulting offense level is greater than that determined above.".

The Commentary to § 2A5.2 captioned "Statutory Provisions" is amended by inserting "18 U.S.C. § 1993(a)(4), (5), (6), (b);" before "49 U.S.C. §§ "; and by inserting "46503," after "46308,".

Section 2A5.2 is amended by striking the Commentary captioned "Background" as follows:

"Background: An adjustment is provided where the defendant intentionally or recklessly endangered the safety of the aircraft and passengers. The offense of carrying a weapon aboard an aircraft, which is proscribed by 49 U.S.C. § 46505, is covered in § 2K1.5 (Possessing Dangerous Weapons or Materials While Boarding or Aboard an Aircraft).",

and inserting the following:

"Application Note:

1. Definitions.—For purposes of this guideline:

'Biological agent', 'chemical weapon', 'nuclear byproduct material', 'nuclear material', 'toxin', and 'weapon of mass destruction' have the meaning given those terms in Application Note 1 of the Commentary to § 2M6.1 (Nuclear, Biological, and Chemical Weapons, and Other Weapons of Mass Destruction).

'Brandished', 'dangerous weapon', 'firearm', and 'otherwise used' have the meaning given those terms in Application Note 1 of the Commentary to § 1B1.1 (Application Instructions).

'Mass transportation' has the meaning given that term in 18 U.S.C. § 1993(c)(5).".

Section 2A6.1 is amended by redesignating subsection (b)(4) as subsection (b)(5); by striking "and (3)" in subsection (b)(5), as redesignated by this amendment, and inserting "(3), and (4)"; and by inserting after subsection (b)(3) the following:

"(4) If the offense resulted in (A) substantial disruption of public, governmental, or business functions or services; or (B) a substantial expenditure of funds to clean up, decontaminate, or otherwise respond to the offense, increase by 4 levels.".

The Commentary to § 2A6.1 captioned "Statutory Provisions" is amended by inserting "32(c), 35(b)," before "871"; by inserting ", 1993(a)(7), (8), 2332b(a)(2)" after "879"; and by inserting "; 49 U.S.C. § 46507" after "(C)-(E)".

The Commentary to § 2A6.1 captioned "Application Notes" is amended by striking Note 1 as follows:

"1. The Commission recognizes that this offense includes a particularly wide range of conduct and that it is not possible to include all of the potentially relevant circumstances in the offense level. Factors not incorporated in the guideline may be considered by the court in determining whether a departure from the guidelines is warranted. See Chapter Five, Part K (Departures).";

and by redesignating Note 2 as Note 1.

The Commentary to § 2A6.1 captioned "Application Notes" is amended in Note 1, as redesignated by this amendment, by inserting "Scope of Conduct to Be Considered.—" before "In determining"; and by striking the last two paragraphs as follows:

"For purposes of Chapter Three, Part D (Multiple Counts), multiple counts involving making a threatening or harassing communication to the same victim are grouped together under § 3D1.2 (Groups of Closely Related Counts). Multiple counts involving different victims are not to be grouped under § 3D1.2.

If the conduct involved substantially more than two threatening communications to the same victim or a prolonged period of making harassing communications to the same victim, an upward departure may be warranted.".

The Commentary to § 2A6.1 captioned "Application Notes" is amended by adding at the end the following:

"2. Grouping.—For purposes of Chapter Three, Part D (Multiple Counts), multiple counts involving making a threatening or harassing communication to the same victim are grouped together under § 3D1.2 (Groups of Closely Related Counts). Multiple counts involving different victims are not to be grouped under § 3D1.2.

3. Departure Provisions.—

   (A) In General.—The Commission recognizes that offenses covered by this guideline may include a particularly wide range of conduct and that it is not possible to include all of the potentially relevant circumstances in the offense level. Factors not incorporated in the guideline may be considered by the court in determining whether a departure from the guidelines is warranted. See Chapter Five, Part K (Departures).

   (B) Multiple Threats or Victims.—If the offense involved substantially more than two threatening communications to the same victim or a prolonged period of making harassing communications to the same victim, or if the offense involved multiple victims, an upward departure may be warranted.".

Section 2B1.1 is amended by striking subsection (d) as follows:

"(d) Special Instruction

(1) If the defendant is convicted under 18 U.S.C. § 1030(a)(4) or (5), the minimum guideline sentence, notwithstanding any other adjustment, shall be six months' imprisonment.".

The Commentary to § 2B1.1 captioned "Statutory Provisions" is amended by inserting "1992, 1993(a)(1), (a)(4)," after "1832,"; by inserting ", 2332b(a)(1)" after "2317"; and by inserting ", 60123(b)" after "46317(a)".

The Commentary to § 2B1.1 captioned "Background" is amended by striking the last paragraph as follows:

" Subsection (d) implements the instruction to the Commission in section 805(c) of Public Law 104–132.".

Section 2B2.3(b)(1) is amended by inserting "(A)" after "occurred"; by striking the comma after "government facility" and inserting "; (B) at"; and by striking ", or" after "energy facility" and inserting "; (C) on a vessel or aircraft of the United States; (D) in a secured area of an airport; or (E) at".

Section 2B2.3 is amended by inserting after subsection (b) the following:

"(c) Cross Reference

(1) If the offense was committed with the intent to commit a felony offense, apply § 2X1.1 (Attempt, Solicitation, or Conspiracy) in respect to that felony offense, if the resulting offense level is greater than that determined above.".

The Commentary to § 2B2.3 captioned "Statutory Provisions" is amended by inserting "§ " before "1030"; and by inserting ", 1036" after "(a)(3)".

The Commentary to § 2B2.3 captioned "Application Notes" is amended in Note 1 by striking "For purposes of this guideline—" and inserting the following:

"Definitions.—For purposes of this guideline:

'Airport' has the meaning given that term in section 47102 of title 49, United States Code.

'Felony offense' means any offense (federal, state, or local) punishable by imprisonment for a term exceeding one year, whether or not a criminal charge was brought or a conviction was obtained.".

Section 2K1.4(a)(1)(B) is amended by inserting ", an airport, an aircraft, a mass transportation facility, a mass transportation vehicle, or a ferry" after "dwelling".

Section 2K1.4(a)(2) is amended by striking "a dwelling; or (C) endangered a dwelling, or a structure other than a dwelling" and inserting "(i) a dwelling, or (ii) an airport, an aircraft, a mass transportation facility, a mass transportation vehicle, or a ferry; or (C) endangered

(i) a dwelling, (ii) a structure other than a dwelling, or (iii) an aircraft, a mass transportation vehicle, or a ferry".

The Commentary to § 2K1.4 captioned "Statutory Provisions" is amended by inserting "1992, 1993(a)(1), (a)(2), (a)(3), (b)," after "1855,"; and by inserting ", 2332a; 49 U.S.C. § 60123(b)" after "2275".

The Commentary to § 2K1.4 captioned "Application Notes" is amended by striking Note 1 as follows:

"1. If bodily injury resulted, an upward departure may be warranted. See Chapter Five, Part K (Departures).",

and inserting the following:

"1. Definitions.—For purposes of this guideline:

'Explosives' includes any explosive, explosive material, or destructive device.

'National cemetery' means a cemetery (A) established under section 2400 of title 38, United States Code; or (B) under the jurisdiction of the Secretary of the Army, the Secretary of the Navy, the Secretary of the Air Force, or the Secretary of the Interior.

'Mass transportation' has the meaning given that term in 18 U.S.C. § 1993(c)(5).".

The Commentary to § 2K1.4 captioned "Application Notes" is amended in Note 2 by inserting "Risk of Death or Serious Bodily Injury.—" before "Creating".

The Commentary to § 2K1.4 captioned "Application Notes" is amended by striking Notes 3 and 4 as follows:

"3. 'Explosives,' as used in the title of this guideline, includes any explosive, explosive material, or destructive device.

4. 'National cemetery' means a cemetery (A) established under section 2400 of title 38, United States Code; or (B) under the jurisdiction of the Secretary of the Army, the Secretary of the Navy, the Secretary of the Air Force, or the Secretary of the Interior.",

and inserting the following:

"3. Upward Departure Provision.—If bodily injury resulted, an upward departure may be warranted. See Chapter Five, Part K (Departures).".

The Commentary to § 2L1.2 captioned "Application Notes" is amended by inserting at the end of subdivision (B) of Note 1 the following:

"(vi) 'Terrorism offense' means any offense involving, or intending to promote, a 'federal crime of terrorism', as that term is defined in 18 U.S.C. § 2332b(g)(5).".

The Commentary to § 2M2.1 captioned "Statutory Provisions" is amended by inserting ";

49 U.S.C. § 60123(b)" after "2284".

The Commentary to § 2M2.3 captioned "Statutory Provisions" is amended by inserting "; 49 U.S.C. § 60123(b)" after "2284".

Chapter Two, Part M is amended in the heading of Subpart 5 by adding at the end ", AND PROVIDING MATERIAL SUPPORT TO DESIGNATED FOREIGN TERRORIST ORGANIZATIONS".

Section 2M5.1 is amended in the heading by adding at the end "; Financial Transactions with Countries Supporting International Terrorism".

Section 2M5.1(a)(1) is amended by inserting "(A)" after "26, if"; and by inserting "; or (B) the offense involved a financial transaction with a country supporting international terrorism" after "evaded".

The Commentary to § 2M5.1 captioned "Statutory Provisions" is amended by inserting "18 U.S.C. § 2332d;" before "50 U.S.C.".

The Commentary to § 2M5.1 captioned "Application Notes" is amended by adding at the end the following:

>"4. For purposes of subsection (a)(1)(B), 'a country supporting international terrorism' means a country designated under section 6(j) of the Export Administration Act (50 U.S.C. App. 2405).".

Chapter Two, Part M, Subpart 5 is amended by adding at the end the following:

>"§ 2M5.3. Providing Material Support or Resources to Designated Foreign Terrorist Organizations
>
>(a) Base Offense Level: 26
>
>(b) Specific Offense Characteristic
>
>   (1) If the offense involved the provision of (A) dangerous weapons; (B) firearms; (C) explosives; or (D) funds with knowledge or reason to believe such funds would be used to purchase any of the items described in subdivisions (A) through (C), increase by 2 levels.
>
>(c) Cross References
>
>   (1) If the offense resulted in death, apply § 2A1.1 (First Degree Murder) if the death was caused intentionally or knowingly, or § 2A1.2 (Second Degree Murder) otherwise, if the resulting offense level is greater than that determined above.
>
>   (2) If the offense was tantamount to attempted murder, apply § 2A2.1 (Assault with Intent to Commit Murder; Attempted Murder), if the resulting offense level is greater than that determined above.
>
>   (3) If the offense involved the provision of (A) a nuclear weapon, nuclear material, or nuclear byproduct material;

(B) a chemical weapon; (C) a biological agent, toxin, or delivery system; or (D) a weapon of mass destruction, apply § 2M6.1 (Nuclear, Biological, and Chemical Weapons, and Other Weapons of Mass Destruction), if the resulting offense level is greater than that determined above.

Commentary

Statutory Provision: 18 U.S.C. § 2339B.

Application Notes:

1. Definitions.—For purposes of this guideline:

   'Biological agent', 'chemical weapon', 'nuclear byproduct material', 'nuclear material', 'toxin', and 'weapon of mass destruction' have the meaning given those terms in Application Note 1 of the Commentary to § 2M6.1 (Nuclear, Biological, and Chemical Weapons, and Other Weapons of Mass Destruction).

   'Dangerous weapon', 'firearm', and 'destructive device' have the meaning given those terms in Application Note 1 of the Commentary to § 1B1.1 (Application Instructions).

   'Explosives' has the meaning given that term in Application Note 1 of the Commentary to § 2K1.4 (Arson; Property Damage by Use of Explosives).

   'Foreign terrorist organization' has the meaning given the term "terrorist organization" in 18 U.S.C. § 2339B(g)(6).

   'Material support or resources' has the meaning given that term in 18 U.S.C. § 2339B(g)(4).

2. Departure Provisions.—

   (A) In General.—In determining the sentence within the applicable guideline range, the court may consider the degree to which the violation threatened a security interest of the United States, the volume of the material support or resources involved, the extent of planning or sophistication, and whether there were multiple occurrences. In a case in which such factors are present in an extreme form, a departure from the guidelines may be warranted. See Chapter Five, Part K (Departures).

   (B) War or Armed Conflict.—In the case of a violation during time of war or armed conflict, an upward departure may be warranted.".

Section 2M6.1(a)(2) is amended by striking "and" and inserting a comma; by inserting ", (a)(4), and (a)(5)" after "(a)(3)"; and by striking "or".

Section 2M6.1(a) is amended by redesignating subdivision (3) as subdivision (5); by inserting after subdivision (2) the following:

"(3) 22, if the defendant is convicted under 18 U.S.C. § 175b;

(4) 20, if the defendant is convicted under 18 U.S.C. § 175(b); or";

and by striking "by-product" in subdivision (5), as redesignated by this amendment, and inserting "byproduct".

Section 2M6.1(b)(1) is amended by striking "or (a)(3)" and inserting ", (a)(4), or (a)(5)".

Section 2M6.1(b)(2) is amended by inserting ", (a)(3), or (a)(4)" after "(a)(2)".

Section 2M6.1(b)(3) is amended by striking "or" after "(a)(2)" and inserting a comma; and by inserting ", (a)(4), or (a)(5)" after "(a)(3)".

The Commentary to § 2M6.1 captioned "Statutory Provisions" is amended by inserting "175b," after "175,"; and by inserting "1993(a)(2), (3), (b)," after "842(p)(2),".

The Commentary to § 2M6.1 captioned "Application Notes" is amended in Note 1 by inserting after "18 U.S.C. § 831(f)(1)." the following paragraph:

> "'Restricted person' has the meaning given that term in 18 U.S.C. § 175b(b)(2).".

Section 2S1.3 is amended in the heading by adding at the end "; Bulk Cash Smuggling; Establishing or Maintaining Prohibited Accounts".

Section 2S1.3 is amended by striking subsection (a) as follows:

> "(a)   Base Offense Level: 6 plus the number of offense levels from the table in § 2B1.1 (Theft, Property Destruction, and Fraud) corresponding to the value of the funds.",

and inserting the following:

> "(a)   Base Offense Level:
>
> > (1)   8, if the defendant was convicted under 31 U.S.C. § 5318 or § 5318A; or
> >
> > (2)   6 plus the number of offense levels from the table in § 2B1.1 (Theft, Property Destruction, and Fraud) corresponding to the value of the funds, if subsection (a)(1) does not apply.".

Section 2S1.3(b)(1) is amended by inserting "(A)" after "If"; and by inserting "; or (B) the offense involved bulk cash smuggling" after "promote unlawful activity".

Section 2S1.3(b) is amended by redesignating subdivision (2) as subdivision (3); and by inserting after subdivision (1) the following:

> "(2)   If the defendant (A) was convicted of an offense under subchapter II of chapter 53 of title 31, United States Code; and (B) committed the offense as part of a pattern of unlawful activity involving more than $100,000 in a 12-month period, increase by 2 levels.".

Section 2S1.3(b)(3), as redesignated by this amendment, is amended by striking "subsection (b)(1) does not apply" and inserting "subsection (a)(2) applies and subsections (b)(1) and (b)(2) do not apply".

The Commentary to § 2S1.3 captioned "Statutory Provisions" is amended by inserting "§ " before "7203"; by striking "§ " before "7206"; by inserting "5318, 5318A(b), 5322," after "5316,"; and by inserting ", 5331, 5332" after "5326".

November 1, 2013 — APPENDIX C - VOLUME II — **Amendment 637**

The Commentary to § 2S1.3 captioned "Application Note" is amended by striking "Note" and inserting "Notes"; by inserting "Definition of 'Value of the Funds'.—" before "For purposes of this guideline" in Note 1; and by adding after Note 1 the following:

"2. Bulk Cash Smuggling.—For purposes of subsection (b)(1)(B), 'bulk cash smuggling' means (A) knowingly concealing, with the intent to evade a currency reporting requirement under 31 U.S.C. § 5316, more than $10,000 in currency or other monetary instruments; and (B) transporting or transferring (or attempting to transport or transfer) such currency or monetary instruments into or outside of the United States. 'United States' has the meaning given that term in Application Note 1 of the Commentary to § 2B5.1 (Offenses Involving Counterfeit Bearer Obligations of the United States).

3. Enhancement for Pattern of Unlawful Activity.—For purposes of subsection (b)(2), 'pattern of unlawful activity' means at least two separate occasions of unlawful activity involving a total amount of more than $100,000 in a 12-month period, without regard to whether any such occasion occurred during the course of the offense or resulted in a conviction for the conduct that occurred on that occasion.".

The Commentary to § 2S1.3 captioned "Background" is amended by striking "The" and inserting "Some of the"; and by adding at the end the following:

"   This guideline also covers offenses under 31 U.S.C. §§ 5318 and 5318A, pertaining to records, reporting and identification requirements, prohibited accounts involving certain foreign jurisdictions, foreign institutions, and foreign banks, and other types of transactions and types of accounts.".

Section 2X1.1 is amended by adding after subsection (c) the following:

"(d) Special Instruction

(1) Subsection (b) shall not apply to any of the following offenses, if such offense involved, or was intended to promote, a federal crime of terrorism as defined in 18 U.S.C. § 2332b(g)(5):

18 U.S.C. § 81;
18 U.S.C. § 930(c);
18 U.S.C. § 1362;
18 U.S.C. § 1363;
18 U.S.C. § 1992;
18 U.S.C. § 2339A;
18 U.S.C. § 2340A;
49 U.S.C. § 46504;
49 U.S.C. § 46505; and
49 U.S.C. § 60123(b).".

The Commentary to § 2X2.1 captioned "Statutory Provision" is amended by striking the following:

"Statutory Provision: 18 U.S.C. § 2.",

and inserting:

Amendment 637 APPENDIX C - VOLUME II November 1, 2013

"Statutory Provisions: 18 U.S.C. §§ 2, 2339, 2339A.".

The Commentary to § 2X2.1 captioned "Application Note" is amended in Note 1 by striking "'Underlying" and inserting "Definition.—For purposes of this guideline, 'underlying"; and by inserting ", or in the case of a violation of 18 U.S.C. § 2339A, 'underlying offense' means the offense the defendant is convicted of having materially supported prior to or during its commission" after "abetting".

Section 2X3.1(a) is amended by striking "Provided, that where" and inserting "However, in a case in which"; and by striking "offense level shall" and inserting "base offense level under this subsection shall".

The Commentary to § 2X3.1 captioned "Statutory Provisions" is amended by inserting ", 2339, 2339A" after "1072".

The Commentary to § 2X3.1 captioned "Application Notes" is amended in Note 1 by striking "'Underlying" and inserting "Definition.—For purposes of this guideline, 'underlying"; and by inserting ", or in the case of a violation of 18 U.S.C. § 2339A, 'underlying offense' means the offense the defendant is convicted of having materially supported after its commission (i.e., in connection with the concealment of or an escape from that offense)" after "accessory".

The Commentary to § 2X3.1 captioned "Application Notes" is amended in Note 2 by inserting "Application of Mitigating Role Adjustment.—" before "The adjustment".

The Commentary to § 3A1.4 captioned "Application Notes" is amended by striking Note 1 as follows:

> "1. Subsection (a) increases the offense level if the offense involved, or was intended to promote, a federal crime of terrorism. 'Federal crime of terrorism' is defined at 18 U.S.C. § 2332b(g).",

and inserting the following:

> "1. 'Federal Crime of Terrorism' Defined.—For purposes of this guideline, 'federal crime of terrorism' has the meaning given that term in 18 U.S.C. § 2332b(g)(5).".

The Commentary to § 3A1.4 captioned "Application Notes" is amended by redesignating Note 2 as Note 3; and by inserting after Note 1 the following:

> "2. Harboring, Concealing, and Obstruction Offenses.—For purposes of this guideline, an offense that involved (A) harboring or concealing a terrorist who committed a federal crime of terrorism (such as an offense under 18 U.S.C. § 2339 or § 2339A); or (B) obstructing an investigation of a federal crime of terrorism, shall be considered to have involved, or to have been intended to promote, that federal crime of terrorism.".

The Commentary to § 3A1.4 captioned "Application Notes" is amended in Note 3, as redesignated by this amendment, by inserting "Computation of Criminal History Category.—" before "Under subsection (b)".

The Commentary to § 3A1.4 captioned "Application Notes" is amended by adding at the end the following:

> "4. Upward Departure Provision.—By the terms of the directive to the Commis-

sion in section 730 of the Antiterrorism and Effective Death Penalty Act of 1996, the adjustment provided by this guideline applies only to federal crimes of terrorism. However, there may be cases in which (A) the offense was calculated to influence or affect the conduct of government by intimidation or coercion, or to retaliate against government conduct but the offense involved, or was intended to promote, an offense other than one of the offenses specifically enumerated in 18 U.S.C. § 2332b(g)(5)(B); or (B) the offense involved, or was intended to promote, one of the offenses specifically enumerated in 18 U.S.C. § 2332b(g)(5)(B), but the terrorist motive was to intimidate or coerce a civilian population, rather than to influence or affect the conduct of government by intimidation or coercion, or to retaliate against government conduct. In such cases an upward departure would be warranted, except that the sentence resulting from such a departure may not exceed the top of the guideline range that would have resulted if the adjustment under this guideline had been applied.".

The Commentary to § 3C1.1 captioned "Application Notes" is amended in Note 4 by striking the period at the end of subdivision (i) and inserting a semicolon; and by inserting after subdivision (i) the following:

"(j) failing to comply with a restraining order or injunction issued pursuant to 21 U.S.C. § 853(e) or with an order to repatriate property issued pursuant to 21 U.S.C. § 853(p).".

Section 5D1.2(a) is amended by adding at the end the following:

"Notwithstanding subdivisions (1) through (3), the length of the term of supervised release for any offense listed in 18 U.S.C. § 2332b(g)(5)(B) the commission of which resulted in, or created a foreseeable risk of, death or serious bodily injury to another person (A) shall be not less than the minimum term of years specified for that class of offense under subdivisions (1) through (3); and (B) may be up to life.".

Appendix A (Statutory Index) is amended by inserting after the line referenced to 18 U.S.C. § 175 the following new line:

"18 U.S.C. § 175b   2M6.1";

by inserting after the line referenced to 18 U.S.C. § 1992 the following new lines:

"18 U.S.C. § 1993(a)(1)	2B1.1, 2K1.4
18 U.S.C. § 1993(a)(2)	2K1.4, 2M6.1
18 U.S.C. § 1993(a)(3)	2K1.4, 2M6.1
18 U.S.C. § 1993(a)(4)	2A5.2, 2B1.1
18 U.S.C. § 1993(a)(5)	2A5.2
18 U.S.C. § 1993(a)(6)	2A2.1, 2A2.2, 2A5.2
18 U.S.C. § 1993(a)(7)	2A6.1
18 U.S.C. § 1993(a)(8)	2A6.1
18 U.S.C. § 1993(b)	2A5.2, 2K1.4, 2M6.1";

by inserting after the line referenced to 18 U.S.C. § 2332a the following new lines:

"18 U.S.C. § 2332b(a)(1)   2A1.1, 2A1.2, 2A1.3, 2A1.4, 2A2.1, 2A2.2, 2A4.1, 2B1.1

Amendment 637

18 U.S.C. § 2332b(a)(2)	2A6.1
18 U.S.C. § 2332d	2M5.1
18 U.S.C. § 2339	2X2.1, 2X3.1
18 U.S.C. § 2339A	2X2.1, 2X3.1
18 U.S.C. § 2339B	2M5.3
18 U.S.C. § 2340A	2A1.1, 2A1.2, 2A2.1, 2A2.2, 2A4.1";

by inserting after the line referenced to 30 U.S.C. § 1463 the following new line:

"31 U.S.C. § 5311 note (section 329 of the USA PATRIOT Act of 2001)	2C1.1";

by inserting after the line referenced to 31 U.S.C. § 5316 the following new lines:

"31 U.S.C. § 5318	2S1.3
31 U.S.C. § 5318A(b)	2S1.3";

by inserting after the line referenced to 31 U.S.C. § 5326 the following new lines:

"31 U.S.C. § 5331	2S1.3
31 U.S.C. § 5332	2S1.3";

by inserting after the line referenced to 49 U.S.C. § 46502(a),(b) the following new line:

"49 U.S.C. § 46503	2A5.2"; and

by inserting after the line referenced to 49 U.S.C. § 46506 the following new lines:

"49 U.S.C. § 46507	2A6.1
49 U.S.C. § 60123(b)	2B1.1, 2K1.4, 2M2.1, 2M2.3".

Reason for Amendment: This amendment is a six-part amendment that responds to the Uniting and Strengthening America by Providing Appropriate Tools Required to Intercept and Obstruct Terrorism (USA PATRIOT Act) Act of 2001, Pub. L. 107–204 (the "Act").

Among its many provisions are appropriately severe penalties for offenses against mass transportation systems and interstate gas or hazardous liquid pipelines. The amendment also increases sentences for threats that substantially disrupt governmental or business operations or result in costly cleanup measures. It expands the guideline coverage of offenses involving bioterrorism, and it creates a new guideline for providing material support to foreign terrorist organizations. It punishes attempts and conspiracies to commit terrorism as if the offense had been carried out and adds an invited upward departure to the guidelines' terrorism enhancement for appropriate cases. Finally, it authorizes a term of supervised release up to life for a defendant convicted of a federal crime of terrorism that resulted in substantial risk of death or serious bodily injury to another person.

First, this amendment makes a number of changes to Appendix A (Statutory Index) and several guidelines in Chapter Two (Offense Conduct) in order to incorporate several new predicate offenses to federal crimes of terrorism. This amendment addresses section 801 of the Act, which added 18 U.S.C. § 1993, generally pertaining to offenses against mass transportation systems and facilities. The amendment also addresses 49 U.S.C. § 46507 pertaining to false information and threats, that heretofore was not listed in the Statutory Index, as well as the new offense at 49 U.S.C. § 46503, pertaining to interference with security screening personnel.

Specifically, the amendment makes a number of changes to § 2A5.2 (Interference with Flight Crew Member or Flight Attendant) and the guidelines in Chapter Two, Part A, Subpart 2 (Assault). First, this amendment references violations of 18 U.S.C. § 1993(a)(4), (a)(5), (a)(6), and (b) and 49 U.S.C. § 46503 to § 2A5.2 because that guideline presently covers other similar offenses and because the guideline's alternative base offense levels cover offenses that involve reckless or intentional endangerment, conduct which is an element of some of these new offenses.

In order to take into account aggravating conduct which may occur in such offenses, the amendment adds a specific offense characteristic for use of a weapon, borrowing language from § 2A2.2 (Aggravated Assault). The specific offense characteristic provides a graduated enhancement with a minimum offense level of level 24 at § 2A5.2(b)(1) for the involvement of a dangerous weapon in the offense. This enhancement addresses concerns that the current base offense level of level 18 (in § 2A5.2(a)(2)) for reckless endangerment may be inadequate in situations involving a dangerous weapon and reckless disregard for the safety of human life. The minimum offense level of level 24 mirrors the offense level that applies for conduct amounting to reckless endangerment under subsection (b)(1) of § 2K1.5 (Possessing Dangerous Weapons or Materials While Boarding or Aboard an Aircraft). A cross reference to the appropriate homicide guideline also is provided for offenses in which death results; death as an aggravating circumstance is included in 18 U.S.C. § 1993(b).

The amendment also amends § 2A6.1 (Threatening or Harassing Communications) to incorporate offenses against mass transportation systems under 18 U.S.C. § 1993(a)(7) and (a)(8) and 49 U.S.C. § 46507 and provides corresponding references in the Statutory Index. These three provisions require the same type of threatening conduct or conveyance of false information as two other offenses referenced to § 2A6.1, specifically 18 U.S.C. §§ 32(c) and 35(b), which cover aircraft, railroads, and shipping, rather than mass transportation systems. Additionally, a specific offense characteristic is added if the offense resulted in a substantial disruption of public, governmental, or business functions or services, or a substantial expenditure of funds to clean up, decontaminate, or otherwise respond to the offense. This enhancement recognizes that a terrorist threat usually will be directed at a large number of individuals, governmental buildings or operations, or infrastructure. Unless such a terrorist threat is immediately dismissed as not credible, the conduct may result in significant disruption and response costs. This specific offense characteristic is the same as that contained in subsection (b)(3) of § 2M6.1 (Nuclear, Biological, and Chemical Weapons, and Other Weapons of Mass Destruction). An invited upward departure provision is added for situations in which the offense involved multiple victims, a circumstance which might occur in the context of these new offenses.

This amendment also amends § 2K1.4 (Arson; Property Damage by Use of Explosives) and § 2B1.1 (Theft, Property Destruction, and Fraud) to cover violations of 18 U.S.C. § 1993(a)(1) and (b). Offenses under 18 U.S.C. § 1993(a)(1) are similar to another offense referenced to these guidelines, 18 U.S.C. § 32(a)(1), with respect to the intent standard required to commit the offense, offense conduct, and resulting harm. The amendment references violations of 18 U.S.C. § 1993(a)(2), (a)(3), and (b) to §§ 2K1.4 and 2M6.1. These offenses encompass a wide range of conduct. For example, a violation of 18 U.S.C. § 1993(a)(3) may occur if the defendant sets fire to a garage or places a biological agent or toxin for use as a destructive substance near an aircraft and this likely endangered the

Amendment 637   APPENDIX C - VOLUME II   November 1, 2013

safety of that aircraft.

The amendment expands § 2M6.1 to cover 18 U.S.C. §§ 175(b) and 175b, two new offenses created by section 817 of the Act, involving possession of biological agents, toxins, and delivery systems. Section 2M6.1 is the most appropriate guideline for these offenses because they involve the knowing possession of certain biological substances. A base offense level of level 20 is provided for 18 U.S.C. § 175(b) offenses, the same base offense level as is currently provided for threat cases under that guideline. The current two level increase for particularly dangerous biological agents would be available for the most serious substances.

A base offense level of level 22 is provided for offenses under 18 U.S.C. § 175b, which forbids certain restricted persons (defined in the statute) to ship or transport in interstate or foreign commerce, or possess in or affecting commerce, any biological agent or toxin, or to receive any biological agent or toxin that has been shipped or transported in interstate or foreign commerce, if the biological agent or toxin is listed as a select agent (e.g., ebola, anthrax). Because this offense already takes into account the serious nature of a select agent, the amendment treats these offenses separately from offenses under 18 U.S.C. § 175(b), with a higher base offense level and an instruction that the enhancement for select biological agents does not apply.

The amendment also amends the Statutory Index to reference 18 U.S.C. § 2339 to §§ 2X2.1 (Aiding and Abetting) and 2X3.1 (Accessory After the Fact). This offense prohibits harboring or concealing any person who the defendant knows, or has reasonable grounds to believe, has committed or is about to commit, one of several enumerated offenses.

Second, this amendment provides Statutory Index references, as well as modifications to various Chapter Two guidelines, for a number of offenses that, prior to enactment of the Act, were enumerated in 18 U.S.C. § 2332b(g)(5) as predicate offenses for federal crimes of terrorism but were not explicitly incorporated in the guidelines.

Specifically, the amendment references 18 U.S.C. § 2332b(a)(1) offenses to §§ 2A1.1 (First Degree Murder), 2A1.2 (Second Degree Murder), 2A1.3 (Voluntary Manslaughter), 2A1.4 (Involuntary Manslaughter), 2A2.1 (Assault with Intent to Commit Murder; Attempted Murder), 2A2.2 (Aggravated Assault), and 2A4.1 (Kidnapping, Abduction, Unlawful Restraint), inasmuch as 18 U.S.C. § 2332b offenses are analogous to offenses currently referenced to those guidelines.

The amendment also provides a Statutory Index reference to § 2A6.1 (Threatening or Harassing Communications) for cases under 18 U.S.C. § 2332b(a)(2), which prohibits threats, attempts and conspiracies to commit an offense under 18 U.S.C. § 2332b(a)(1).

This amendment also creates a new guideline, at § 2M5.3 (Providing Material Support or Resources to Designated Foreign Terrorist Organizations), for offenses under 18 U.S.C. § 2339B, which prohibits the provision of material support or resources to a foreign terrorist organization. The amendment references offenses under 18 U.S.C. § 2339A to §§ 2X2.1 and 2X3.1. Section 2339A offenses concern providing material support to terrorists that the defendant knows or intends will be used in preparation for, or in carrying out, certain specified predicate offenses. Thus, the essence of 18 U.S.C. § 2339A offenses is akin to aiding and abetting or accessory after the fact offenses, which warrants reference to §§ 2X2.1 and 2X3.1. In contrast, 18 U.S.C. § 2339B offenses are referenced to a new guideline, § 2M5.3, primarily because they are not statutorily linked to the commission of any specified predicate offenses. To account for the variety of ways in which such offenses may be committed, the new guideline provides two specific offense characteristics that enhance the sentence for cases in which the material support involved dangerous weapons and in which the material support involved nuclear, biological, or chemical weapons.

The amendment references torture offenses under 18 U.S.C. § 2340A to §§ 2A1.1, 2A1.2, 2A2.1, 2A2.2, and 2A4.1. The amendment also references 49 U.S.C. § 60123(b), pertaining to damaging or destroying an interstate gas or hazardous liquid pipeline facility, to §§ 2B1.1, 2K1.4, 2M2.1 (Destruction of, or Production of Defective, War Material, Premises, or Utilities), and 2M2.3 (Destruction of, or Production of Defective, National Defense Material, Premises, or Utilities).

Third, the amendment responds to section 811 of the Act, which amended a number of offenses to ensure that attempts and conspiracies to commit any of those offenses subject the offender to the same penalties prescribed for the object offense. This amendment provides a special instruction in § 2X1.1 (Attempt, Solicitation, or Conspiracy) that the three level reduction in § 2X1.1(b) does not apply to these offenses when committed for a terrorist objective.

Fourth, the amendment adds an encouraged, structured upward departure in § 3A1.4 (Terrorism) for offenses that involve terrorism but do not otherwise qualify as offenses that involved or were intended to promote "federal crimes of terrorism" for purposes of the terrorism adjustment in § 3A1.4. The amendment provides an upward departure, rather than a specified guideline adjustment, because of the expected infrequency of these terrorism offenses and to provide the court with a viable tool to account for the harm involved during the commission of these offenses on a case-by-case basis. In addition, the structured upward departure provision makes it possible to impose punishment equal in severity to that which would be imposed if the § 3A1.4 adjustment actually applied.

The amendment adds an application note to § 3A1.4 regarding harboring and concealing offenses to clarify that § 3A1.4 may apply in the case of offenses that occurred after the commission of the federal crime of terrorism (e.g., a case in which the defendant, in violation of 18 U.S.C. § 2339A, concealed an individual who had committed a federal crime of terrorism).

Fifth, the amendment amends § 2S1.3 (Structuring Transactions to Evade Reporting Requirements; Failure to Report Cash or Monetary Transactions; Failure to File Currency and Monetary Instrument Report; Knowingly Filing False Reports) to incorporate new money laundering provisions created by the Act.

Specifically, the amendment provides an alternative base offense level of level 8 in § 2S1.3(a) in order to incorporate offenses under 31 U.S.C. §§ 5318 and 5318A. The base offense level of level 8 recognizes the heightened due diligence requirements placed on financial institutions with respect to payable-through accounts, correspondent accounts, and shell banks.

The amendment also amends § 2S1.3(b)(1), relating to the promotion of unlawful activity, to provide an alternative prong if the offense involved bulk cash smuggling. This amendment addresses 31 U.S.C. § 5332, added by section 371 of the Act, which prohibits concealing, with intent to evade a currency reporting requirement under 31 U.S.C. § 5316, more than $10,000 in currency or other monetary instruments and transporting or transferring such currency or monetary instruments into or outside of the United States. Findings set forth in that section of the Act indicate that bulk cash smuggling typically involves the promotion of unlawful activity.

The amendment also provides an enhancement in § 2S1.3(b) to give effect to the enhanced penalty provisions under 31 U.S.C. § 5322(b) for offenses under subchapter II of chapter

Amendment 637

53 of title 31, United Stated Code, if such offenses were committed as part of a pattern of unlawful activity involving more than $100,000 in a 12-month period.

Sixth, the amendment addresses a number of miscellaneous issues related to terrorism. Specifically, it provides a definition of terrorism for purposes of the prior conviction enhancement in § 2L1.2 (Unlawfully Entering or Remaining in the United States). For consistency, the definition is the same as that found in the current Chapter Three terrorism adjustment.

It also amends § 3C1.1 (Obstructing or Impeding the Administration of Justice), in response to section 319(d) of the Act, which amends the Controlled Substances Act at 21 U.S.C. § 853(e) to require a defendant to repatriate any property that may be seized and forfeited and to deposit that property in the registry of the court or with the United States Marshals Service or the Secretary of the Treasury. Section 319(d) of the Act also states that the failure to comply with a protective order and an order to repatriate property "may also result in an enhancement of the sentence of the defendant under the obstruction of justice provision of the Federal Sentencing Guidelines." Accordingly, the amendment adds Application Note 4(j) to § 3C1.1 to provide that failure to comply with an order issued pursuant to 21 U.S.C. § 835(e) is an example of the types of conduct to which the adjustment applies.

It also amends § 5D1.2 (Term of Supervised Release), in response to section 812 of the Act, which authorizes a term of supervised release of any term of years or life for a defendant convicted of a federal crime of terrorism the commission of which resulted in, or created a foreseeable risk of, death or serious bodily injury to another person.

It also amends § 2B1.1 to delete the special instruction pertaining to the imposition of not less than six months' imprisonment for a defendant convicted under 18 U.S.C. § 1030(a)(4) or (5). This amendment is in response to section 814(f) of the Act, which directed the Commission to amend the guidelines "to ensure that any individual convicted of a violation of section 1030 of title 18, United States Code, can be subjected to appropriate penalties, without regard to any mandatory minimum term of imprisonment."

It also adds a reference in the Statutory Index to § 2C1.1 (Offering, Giving, Soliciting, or Receiving a Bribe; Extortion Under Color of Official Right), for the new offense created by section 329 of the Act, which prohibits a federal official or employee, in connection with administration of the money laundering provisions of the Act, to corruptly demand, seek, receive, accept, or agree to receive or accept anything of value in return for being influenced in the performance of an official act, being influenced to commit or aid in committing any fraud on the United States, or being induced to do or omit to do any act in violation of official duties.

It also amends § 2M5.1 (Evasion of Export Controls) to incorporate 18 U.S.C. § 2332d, which prohibits a United States person, knowing or having reasonable cause to know that a country is designated under the Export Administration Act as a country supporting international terrorism, to engage in a financial transaction with the government of that country. The amendment provides a base offense level of level 26 for these offenses.

Finally, it amends § 2B2.3 (Trespass) to incorporate the offense under 18 U.S.C. § 1036. That offense, added by section 2 of the Enhanced Federal Security Act of 2000, Pub. L. 106–547, prohibits, by fraud or pretense, the entering or attempting to enter any real property, vessel, or aircraft of the United States, or secure area of an airport. The amendment amends the existing two level enhancement in § 2B2.3(b)(1) to provide an additional ground for application of the enhancement if the trespass involved a vessel, aircraft of the

United States, or secure area of an airport. It also adds a cross reference to § 2X1.1 if the offense involved the intent to commit another felony.

Effective Date: **The effective date of this amendment is November 1, 2002.**

638. **Amendment:** Section 2B1.1(c) is amended by adding at the end the following:

> "(4) If the offense involved a cultural heritage resource, apply § 2B1.5 (Theft of, Damage to, or Destruction of, Cultural Heritage Resources; Unlawful Sale, Purchase, Exchange, Transportation, or Receipt of Cultural Heritage Resources), if the resulting offense level is greater than that determined above.".

The Commentary to § 2B1.1 captioned "Application Notes" is amended in Note 1 by inserting after "For purposes of this guideline:" the following paragraph:

> "'Cultural heritage resource' has the meaning given that term in Application Note 1 of the Commentary to § 2B1.5 (Theft of, Damage to, or Destruction of, Cultural Heritage Resources; Unlawful Sale, Purchase, Exchange, Transportation, or Receipt of Cultural Heritage Resources).".

The Commentary to § 2B1.1 captioned "Application Notes" is amended in subdivision (F) of Note 2 by adding at the end the following:

> "(vii) <u>Value of Cultural Heritage Resources</u>.—In a case involving a cultural heritage resource, loss attributable to that cultural heritage resource shall be determined in accordance with the rules for determining the 'value of the cultural heritage resource' set forth in Application Note 2 of the Commentary to § 2B1.5.".

Chapter Two, Part B, Subpart 1 is amended by adding at the end the following new guideline and accompanying commentary:

> "§ 2B1.5. <u>Theft of, Damage to, or Destruction of, Cultural Heritage Resources; Unlawful Sale, Purchase, Exchange, Transportation, or Receipt of Cultural Heritage Resources</u>
>
> (a) Base Offense Level: 8
>
> (b) Specific Offense Characteristics
>
> > (1) If the value of the cultural heritage resource (A) exceeded $2,000 but did not exceed $5,000, increase by 1 level; or (B) exceeded $5,000, increase by the number of levels from the table in § 2B1.1 (Theft, Property Destruction, and Fraud) corresponding to that amount.
> >
> > (2) If the offense involved a cultural heritage resource from, or that, prior to the offense, was on, in, or in the custody of (A) the national park system; (B) a National Historic Landmark; (C) a national monument or national memorial; (D) a national marine sanctuary; (E) a national cemetery; (F) a museum; or (G) the World Heritage List, increase by 2 levels.
> >
> > (3) If the offense involved a cultural heritage resource constituting (A) human remains; (B) a funerary object; (C) cultural

patrimony; (D) a sacred object; (E) cultural property; (F) designated archaeological or ethnological material; or (G) a pre-Columbian monumental or architectural sculpture or mural, increase by 2 levels.

(4) If the offense was committed for pecuniary gain or otherwise involved a commercial purpose, increase by 2 levels.

(5) If the defendant engaged in a pattern of misconduct involving cultural heritage resources, increase by 2 levels.

(6) If a dangerous weapon was brandished or its use was threatened, increase by 2 levels. If the resulting offense level is less than level 14, increase to level 14.

(c) Cross Reference

(1) If the offense involved arson, or property damage by the use of any explosive, explosive material, or destructive device, apply § 2K1.4 (Arson; Property Damage by Use of Explosives), if the resulting offense level is greater than that determined above.

Commentary

Statutory Provisions: 16 U.S.C. §§ 470ee, 668(a), 707(b); 18 U.S.C. §§ 541-546, 641, 661-662, 666, 668, 1152-1153, 1163, 1168, 1170, 1361, 2232, 2314-2315.

Application Notes:

1. 'Cultural Heritage Resource' Defined.—For purposes of this guideline, 'cultural heritage resource' means any of the following:

    (A) A historic property, as defined in 16 U.S.C. § 470w(5) (see also section 16(l) of 36 C.F.R. pt. 800).

    (B) A historic resource, as defined in 16 U.S.C. § 470w(5).

    (C) An archaeological resource, as defined in 16 U.S.C. § 470bb(1) (see also section 3(a) of 43 C.F.R. pt. 7; 36 C.F.R. pt. 296; 32 C.F.R. pt. 299; 18 C.F.R. pt. 1312).

    (D) A cultural item, as defined in section 2(3) of the Native American Graves Protection and Repatriation Act, 25 U.S.C. § 3001(3) (see also 43 C.F.R. § 10.2(d)).

    (E) A commemorative work. 'Commemorative work' (A) has the meaning given that term in section 2(c) of Public Law 99–652 (40 U.S.C. § 1002(c)); and (B) includes any national monument or national memorial.

    (F) An object of cultural heritage, as defined in 18 U.S.C. § 668(a)(2).

    (G) Designated ethnological material, as described in 19 U.S.C. §§ 2601(2)(ii), 2601(7), and 2604.

2. Value of the Cultural Heritage Resource Under Subsection (b)(1).—This application note applies to the determination of the value of the cultural heritage resource under subsection (b)(1).

(A) General Rule.—For purposes of subsection (b)(1), the value of the cultural heritage resource shall include, as applicable to the particular resource involved, the following:

    (i) The archaeological value. (Archaeological value shall be included in the case of any cultural heritage resource that is an archaeological resource.)

    (ii) The commercial value.

    (iii) The cost of restoration and repair.

(B) Estimation of Value.—For purposes of subsection (b)(1), the court need only make a reasonable estimate of the value of the cultural heritage resource based on available information.

(C) Definitions.—For purposes of this application note:

    (i) 'Archaeological value' of a cultural heritage resource means the cost of the retrieval of the scientific information which would have been obtainable prior to the offense, including the cost of preparing a research design, conducting field work, conducting laboratory analysis, and preparing reports, as would be necessary to realize the information potential. (See 43 C.F.R. § 7.14(a); 36 C.F.R. § 296.14(a); 32 C.F.R. § 229.14(a); 18 C.F.R. § 1312.14(a).)

    (ii) 'Commercial value' of a cultural heritage resource means the fair market value of the cultural heritage resource at the time of the offense. (See 43 C.F.R. § 7.14(b); 36 C.F.R. § 296.14(b); 32 C.F.R. § 229.14(b); 18 C.F.R. § 1312.14(b).)

    (iii) 'Cost of restoration and repair' includes all actual and projected costs of curation, disposition, and appropriate reburial of, and consultation with respect to, the cultural heritage resource; and any other actual and projected costs to complete restoration and repair of the cultural heritage resource, including (I) its reconstruction and stabilization; (II) reconstruction and stabilization of ground contour and surface; (III) research necessary to conduct reconstruction and stabilization; (IV) the construction of physical barriers and other protective devices; (V) examination and analysis of the cultural heritage resource as part of efforts to salvage remaining information about the resource; and (VI) preparation of reports. (See 43 C.F.R. § 7.14(c); 36 C.F.R. § 296.14(c); 32 C.F.R. § 229.14(c); 18 C.F.R. § 1312.14(c).)

(D) Determination of Value in Cases Involving a Variety of Cultural Heritage Resources.—In a case involving a variety of cultural heritage resources, the value of the cultural heritage resources is the sum of all calculations made for those resources under this application note.

3. Enhancement in Subsection (b)(2).—For purposes of subsection (b)(2):

(A) 'Museum' has the meaning given that term in 18 U.S.C. § 668(a)(1) except that the museum may be situated outside the United States.

(B) 'National cemetery' has the meaning given that term in Application Note 1 of the Commentary to § 2B1.1 (Theft, Property Destruction, and Fraud).

(C) 'National Historic Landmark' means a property designated as such pursuant to 16 U.S.C. § 470a(a)(1)(B).

(D) 'National marine sanctuary' means a national marine sanctuary designated as such by the Secretary of Commerce pursuant to 16 U.S.C. § 1433.

(E) 'National monument or national memorial' means any national monument or national memorial established as such by Act of Congress or by proclamation pursuant to the Antiquities Act of 1906 (16 U.S.C. § 431).

(F) 'National park system' has the meaning given that term in 16 U.S.C. § 1c(a).

(G) 'World Heritage List' means the World Heritage List maintained by the World Heritage Committee of the United Nations Educational, Scientific, and Cultural Organization in accordance with the Convention Concerning the Protection of the World Cultural and Natural Heritage.

4. Enhancement in Subsection (b)(3).—For purposes of subsection (b)(3):

(A) 'Cultural patrimony' has the meaning given that term in 25 U.S.C. § 3001(3)(D) (see also 43 C.F.R. 10.2(d)(4)).

(B) 'Cultural property' has the meaning given that term in 19 U.S.C. § 2601(6).

(C) 'Designated archaeological or ethnological material' means archaeological or ethnological material described in 19 U.S.C. § 2601(7) (see also 19 U.S.C. §§ 2601(2) and 2604).

(D) 'Funerary object' means an object that, as a part of the death rite or ceremony of a culture, was placed intentionally, at the time of death or later, with or near human remains.

(E) 'Human remains' (i) means the physical remains of the body of a human; and (ii) does not include remains that reasonably may be determined to have been freely disposed of or naturally shed by the human from whose body the remains were obtained, such as hair made into ropes or nets.

(F) 'Pre-Columbian monumental or architectural sculpture or mural' has the meaning given that term in 19 U.S.C. § 2095(3).

(G) 'Sacred object' has the meaning given that term in 25 U.S.C. § 3001(3)(C) (see also 43 C.F.R. § 10.2(d)(3)).

5. Pecuniary Gain and Commercial Purpose Enhancement Under Subsection (b)(4).—

   (A) 'For Pecuniary Gain'.—For purposes of subsection (b)(4), 'for pecuniary gain' means for receipt of, or in anticipation of receipt of, anything of value, whether monetary or in goods or services. Therefore, offenses committed for pecuniary gain include both monetary and barter transactions, as well as activities designed to increase gross revenue.

   (B) Commercial Purpose.—The acquisition of cultural heritage resources for display to the public, whether for a fee or donation and whether by an individual or an organization, including a governmental entity, a private non-profit organization, or a private for-profit organization, shall be considered to involve a 'commercial purpose' for purposes of subsection (b)(4).

6. Pattern of Misconduct Enhancement Under Subsection (b)(5).—

   (A) Definition.—For purposes of subsection (b)(5), 'pattern of misconduct involving cultural heritage resources' means two or more separate instances of offense conduct involving a cultural heritage resource that did not occur during the course of the offense (i.e., that did not occur during the course of the instant offense of conviction and all relevant conduct under § 1B1.3 (Relevant Conduct)). Offense conduct involving a cultural heritage resource may be considered for purposes of subsection (b)(5) regardless of whether the defendant was convicted of that conduct.

   (B) Computation of Criminal History Points.—A conviction taken into account under subsection (b)(5) is not excluded from consideration of whether that conviction receives criminal history points pursuant to Chapter Four, Part A (Criminal History).

7. Dangerous Weapons Enhancement Under Subsection (b)(6).—For purposes of subsection (b)(6), 'brandished' and 'dangerous weapon' have the meaning given those terms in Application Note 1 of the Commentary to § 1B1.1 (Application Instructions).

8. Multiple Counts.—For purposes of Chapter Three, Part D (Multiple Counts), multiple counts involving cultural heritage offenses covered by this guideline are grouped together under subsection (d) of § 3D1.2 (Groups of Closely Related Counts). Multiple counts involving cultural heritage offenses covered by this guideline and offenses covered by other guidelines are not to be grouped under § 3D1.2(d).

9. Upward Departure Provision.—There may be cases in which the offense level determined under this guideline substantially understates the seriousness of the offense. In such cases, an upward departure may be warranted. For example, an upward departure may be warranted if (A) in addition to cultural heritage resources, the offense involved theft of, damage to, or destruction of, items that are not cultural heritage resources (such as an offense involving the theft from a national cemetery of lawnmowers and other administrative property in addition to historic gravemarkers or other cultural

Amendment 638 APPENDIX C - VOLUME II November 1, 2013

heritage resources); or (B) the offense involved a cultural heritage resource that has profound significance to cultural identity (e.g., the Statue of Liberty or the Liberty Bell).".

Section 2Q2.1 is amended by adding after subsection (b) the following:

"(c) Cross Reference

    (1) If the offense involved a cultural heritage resource, apply § 2B1.5 (Theft of, Damage to, or Destruction of, Cultural Heritage Resources; Unlawful Sale, Purchase, Exchange, Transportation, or Receipt of Cultural Heritage Resources), if the resulting offense level is greater than that determined above.".

The Commentary to § 2Q2.1 captioned "Application Notes" is amended by adding at the end the following:

"6. For purposes of subsection (c)(1), 'cultural heritage resource' has the meaning given that term in Application Note 1 of the Commentary to § 2B1.5 (Theft of, Damage to, or Destruction of, Cultural Heritage Resources; Unlawful Sale, Purchase, Exchange, Transportation, or Receipt of Cultural Heritage Resources).".

Section 3D1.2(d) is amended by inserting "2B1.5," after "2B1.4,".

Appendix A (Statutory Index) is amended by striking the line referenced to 16 U.S.C. § 433;

by inserting before the line referenced to 16 U.S.C. § 668(a) the following new line:

"16 U.S.C. § 470ee   2B1.5";

in the line referenced to 16 U.S.C. § 668(a) by inserting "2B1.5," before "2Q2.1";

in the line referenced to 16 U.S.C. § 707(b) by inserting "2B1.5," before "2Q2.1";

in the line referenced to 18 U.S.C. § 541 by inserting "2B1.5," before "2T3.1";

in the line referenced to 18 U.S.C. § 542 by inserting "2B1.5," before "2T3.1";

in the line referenced to 18 U.S.C. § 543 by inserting "2B1.5," before "2T3.1";

in the line referenced to 18 U.S.C. § 544 by inserting "2B1.5," before "2T3.1";

in the line referenced to 18 U.S.C. § 545 by inserting "2B1.5," before "2Q2.1";

by inserting after the line referenced to 18 U.S.C. § 545 the following new line:

"18 U.S.C. § 546   2B1.5";

in the line referenced to 18 U.S.C. § 641 by inserting ", 2B1.5" after "2B1.1";

in the line referenced to 18 U.S.C. § 661 by inserting ", 2B1.5" after "2B1.1";

in the line referenced to 18 U.S.C. § 662 by inserting ", 2B1.5" after "2B1.1";

in the line referenced to 18 U.S.C. § 666(a)(1)(A) by inserting ", 2B1.5" after "2B1.1";

in the line referenced to 18 U.S.C. § 668 by striking "2B1.1" and inserting "2B1.5";

by inserting after the line referenced to 18 U.S.C. § 1121 the following new line:

"18 U.S.C. § 1152   2B1.5";

in the line referenced to 18 U.S.C. § 1153 by inserting "2B1.5," after "2B1.1,";

in the line referenced to 18 U.S.C. § 1163 by inserting ", 2B1.5" after "2B1.1";

by inserting after the line referenced to 18 U.S.C. § 1168 the following new line:

"18 U.S.C. § 1170   2B1.5";

in the line referenced to 18 U.S.C. § 1361 by inserting ", 2B1.5" after "2B1.1";

in the line referenced to 18 U.S.C. § 2232 by inserting "2B1.5," before "2J1.2";

in the line referenced to 18 U.S.C. § 2314 by inserting ", 2B1.5" after "2B1.1"; and

in the line referenced to 18 U.S.C. § 2315 by inserting ", 2B1.5" after "2B1.1".

Reason for Amendment: This amendment provides a new guideline at § 2B1.5 (Theft of, Damage to, Destruction of, Cultural Heritage Resources; Unlawful Sale, Purchase, Exchange, Transportation, or Receipt of Cultural Heritage Resources) for offenses involving cultural heritage resources. This amendment reflects the Commission's conclusion that the existing sentencing guidelines for economic and property destruction crimes are inadequate to punish in an appropriate and proportional way the variety of federal crimes involving the theft of, damage to, destruction of, or illicit trafficking in, cultural heritage resources. The Commission has determined that a separate guideline, which specifically recognizes both the federal government's long-standing obligation and role in preserving such resources, and the harm caused to both the nation and its inhabitants when its history is degraded through the destruction of cultural heritage resources, is needed.

Cultural heritage resources include national memorials, landmarks, parks, archaeological and other historic and cultural resources, specifically designated by Congress and the President for the preservation of the cultural heritage of this nation and its ancestors. The federal government acts either as a trustee for the public generally, or as a fiduciary on behalf of American Indians, Alaska Natives and Native Hawaiian Organizations, to protect these cultural heritage resources. Because individuals, communities, and nations identify themselves through intellectual, emotional, and spiritual connections to places and objects, the effects of cultural heritage resource crimes transcend mere monetary considerations. Accordingly, this new guideline takes into account the transcendent and irreplaceable value of cultural heritage resources and punishes in a proportionate way the aggravating conduct associated with cultural heritage resource crimes.

This guideline incorporates into the definition of "cultural heritage resource" a broad range of existing federal statutory definitions for various historical, cultural, and archaeological items. If a defendant is convicted of an offense that charges illegal conduct involving a cultural heritage resource, this guideline will apply, irrespective of whether the conviction is obtained under general property theft or damage statutes, such as laws concerning the theft and destruction of government property, 18 U.S.C. § 641, interstate sale or receipt of stolen property, 18 U.S.C. §§ 2314-15, and smuggling, 18 U.S.C. §§ 541 et seq., or under specific cultural heritage statutes, such as the Archaeological Resources Protection Act of 1979, 16 U.S.C. § 470ee (ARPA), the criminal provisions of the Native American Graves

Protection and Repatriation Act (NAGPRA) at 18 U.S.C. § 1170, and 18 U.S.C. § 668, which concerns theft from museums. In addition, if a more general offense is charged that is referenced in Appendix A to § 2B1.1 (Theft, Property Destruction, and Fraud), this guideline will apply by cross reference if the offense conduct involves a cultural heritage resource and results in a higher offense level.

This new guideline has a base offense level of level 8, which is two levels higher than the base offense level for general economic and property destruction crimes. The higher base offense level represents the Commission's determination that offenses involving cultural heritage resources are more serious because they involve essentially irreplaceable resources and cause intangible harm to society.

The new guideline also provides that the monetary value of the cultural heritage resource is an important, although not the sole, factor in determining the appropriate punishment. The Commission has elected not to use the concept of "loss," which is an integral part of the theft, fraud, and property destruction guideline at § 2B1.1, because cultural heritage offenses do not involve the same fungible and compensatory values embodied in "loss." Instead, under this new guideline, value is to be based on commercial value, archaeological value, and the cost of restoration and repair. These methods of valuation are derived from existing federal law. See 16 U.S.C. § 470ee(d); 43 C.F.R. § 7.14.

The Commission has recognized that archaeological value shall be used in calculating the value of archaeological resources but has provided flexibility for the sentencing court to determine whether either commercial value or the cost of restoration and repair, or both, should be added to archaeological value in determining the appropriate value of archaeological resources. For all other types of cultural heritage resources covered by this guideline, the Commission has provided flexibility for the sentencing court regarding whether and when to use all or some of the methods of valuation, as appropriate, for calculating the total value associated with the harm to the particular resource caused by the defendant's offense conduct. The value of the cultural heritage resource is then referenced to the monetary table provided at § 2B1.1(b)(1) in order to determine appropriate and proportionate offense levels in a manner consistent with the overall guidelines structure.

The new guideline provides five additional specific offense characteristics to provide proportionate enhancements for aggravating conduct that may occur in connection with cultural heritage resource offenses. In providing enhancements for these non-pecuniary aggravating factors, the Commission seeks to ensure that the nonquantifiable harm caused by the offense to affected cultural groups, and society as a whole, is adequately reflected in the penalty structure.

The first two of these enhancements, at subsections (b)(2) and (b)(3), relate to whether the offense involves a place or resource that Congress has designated for special protection. A two level enhancement attaches if the offense involves a resource from one of eight locations specifically designated by Congress for historic commemoration, resource preservation, or public education. These are the national park system, national historic landmarks, national monuments, national memorials, national marine sanctuaries, national cemeteries, sites contained on the World Heritage List, and museums.

Consistent with the definition in 18 U.S.C. § 668(a)(1), museums are defined broadly to include all organized and permanent institutions, with an essentially educational or aesthetic purpose, which exhibit tangible objects to the public on a regular schedule. Adoption of this definition reflects the Commission's recognition that cultural heritage resource crimes affecting institutions dedicated to the preservation of resources and associated knowledge, irrespective of the institution's size, ownership, or funding, deprive the public and future generations of the opportunity to learn and appreciate the richness of the nation's heritage. Similarly, this enhancement reflects the Commission's assessment that damage to the other listed places degrades not only the resource itself but also the historical and cultural aspects which the resource commemorates.

An additional two level enhancement attaches to offense conduct that involves any of a number of specified resources, including human remains and other resources that have been designated by Congress for special treatment and heightened protection under federal law. Funerary objects, items of cultural patrimony, and sacred objects are included because they are domestic cultural heritage resources protected under NAGPRA. See 25 U.S.C. § 3001. Cultural property, designated archaeological and ethnological material, and pre-Columbian monumental and architectural sculpture and murals are included in the enhancement because these are cultural heritage resources of foreign provenance for which Congress has chosen, in the implementation of international treaties and bilateral agreements, to impose import restrictions. See 19 U.S.C. §§ 2092, 2606, and 2607.

This guideline also provides a two level enhancement at subsection (b)(4) if the offense was committed for pecuniary gain or otherwise involved a commercial purpose. This increase is based on a determination that offenders who are motivated by financial gain or other commercial incentive are more culpable than offenders who are motivated solely by their personal interest in possessing cultural heritage resources. Those motivated by financial gain contribute to illicit trafficking and support dealers and brokers who earn a livelihood from illegal activities. Mindful of INTERPOL's findings, as reported by the Department of Justice, that the annual dollar value of art and cultural property theft is exceeded only by trafficking in illicit narcotics, money laundering, and arms trafficking, the Commission seeks to ensure that the penalty structure adequately accounts for these increased harms.

This guideline also provides a two level enhancement at subsection (b)(5) if the offense involves a pattern of misconduct, and provides a definition of "pattern of misconduct" that is designed to interact with other requirements of the guidelines regarding relevant conduct and criminal history. "Pattern of misconduct" is defined as "two or more separate instances of offense conduct involving cultural heritage resources that did not occur during the course of the instant offense (i.e., that did not occur during the offense of conviction and all relevant conduct under § 1B1.3 (Relevant Conduct))". Accordingly, under this guideline, separate instances of offense conduct need not result in a criminal conviction or legal adjudication in order for this enhancement to apply. Separate instances of offense conduct involving cultural heritage resources that are included in the defendant's criminal history may also form the factual basis for the application of this enhancement. The Commission considers such increased punishment to be appropriate for offenders who repeatedly disregard cultural heritage resource laws and regulations and the social values underlying them. These repeat offenders cause serious harm, not only to the resources themselves, but to the nation and the individuals who treasure them.

This guideline also provides at subsection (b)(6) a two level enhancement and a minimum offense level of level 14 if a dangerous weapon, including a firearm, is brandished or its use threatened. This enhancement reflects the increased culpability of offenders who pose a threat to law enforcement officers and innocent passersby. Recognizing that there are legitimate uses in remote expanses of tribal and federal land for certain tools and firearms that may otherwise qualify as "dangerous weapons" under the guideline definitions, the Commission has limited the scope of this enhancement by requiring that the dangerous weapon or firearm be brandished or its use threatened, in order for increased punishment to attach under this provision.

Amendment 638

In light of the increased potential for the symbols of our nation's heritage and culture to be targets of violent individuals, including terrorists, the Commission also has provided for increased punishment through a cross reference to § 2K1.4 (Arson; Property Damage by Use of Explosives), if the offense involved arson or property damage by the use of any explosive, explosive material, or destructive devices, when the resulting offense level is greater under § 2K1.4 than the offense level under this guideline.

This guideline also includes a special rule in the Commentary to address multiple counts of cultural heritage resource offenses, as well as multiple counts of conviction involving offenses under this and other guidelines. Consistent with the principles underlying the rules for grouping multiple counts of conviction in § 3D1.2 (Groups of Closely Related Counts) and the unique concerns sought to be addressed by this amendment, the new guideline provides that multiple counts of cultural heritage resource offenses are to be grouped under § 3D1.2(d). However, because the monetary harm is measured differently, a count of conviction for an offense sentenced under § 2B1.5 may not be grouped under this provision with a conviction for an offense sentenced under a different guideline.

This guideline also invites an upward departure if the determined offense level substantially understates the seriousness of the cultural heritage resource offense. Two illustrations of such situations are given. Finally, this amendment provides a cross reference within § 2B1.1. Theft, fraud, and property destruction offenses which also involve cultural heritage resources are cross referenced to the new guideline at § 2B1.5 if the resulting offense level under it would be greater than under § 2B1.1. When a case involving a cultural heritage resource is sentenced under § 2B1.1, loss attributable to that cultural heritage resource is to be determined using the definition of "value of the cultural heritage resource" from § 2B1.5.

The Commission recognizes that the full implementation of this new guideline for the most serious offenders often will be limited in its application because of the extremely low statutory maxima of some of the potentially applicable statutes, such as the criminal provisions of ARPA, NAGPRA, and 18 U.S.C. § 1163 (covering the theft of tribal property). Currently ARPA has either a one year or two year statutory maximum term of imprisonment for the first offense, depending on whether the value exceeds $500, and NAGPRA has a statutory maximum term of imprisonment of one year for the first offense irrespective of value. These statutes all have five year statutory maximum terms of imprisonment for second and subsequent offenses. Consequently, the statutory ceiling may limit the full range of proportionate guideline sentencing, but the Commission has promulgated this new guideline to cover the wide variety of potential offense conduct that can occur in connection with cultural heritage resources. The Commission has recommended to Congress that the statutory maximum terms of imprisonment for these offenses be raised appropriately.

Effective Date: The effective date of this amendment is November 1, 2002.

639. Amendment: The Commentary to § 2B4.1 captioned "Statutory Provisions" is amended by striking "15 U.S.C. §§ 78dd-1, 78dd-2;".

The Commentary to § 2B4.1 captioned "Application Notes" is amended in Note 1 by inserting ", foreign governments, or public international organizations" after "local government"; and by striking "governmental" and inserting "any such".

The Commentary to § 2B4.1 captioned "Background" is amended in the sixth paragraph by striking "to violations of the Foreign Corrupt Practices Act, 15 U.S.C. §§ 78dd-1 and 78dd-2, and".

The Commentary to § 2C1.1 captioned "Statutory Provisions" is amended by inserting "15 U.S.C. §§ 78dd-1, 78dd-2, 78dd-3;" before "18 U.S.C.".

The Commentary to § 2C1.1 captioned "Background" is amended by inserting after the ninth paragraph the following:

"   Section 2C1.1 also applies to offenses under 15 U.S.C. §§ 78dd-1, 78dd-2, and 78dd-3. Such offenses generally involve a payment to a foreign public official, candidate for public office, or agent or intermediary, with the intent to influence an official act or decision of a foreign government or political party. Typically, a case prosecuted under these provisions will involve an intent to influence governmental action.".

Appendix A (Statutory Index) is amended in the line referenced to 15 U.S.C. § 78dd-1 by striking "2B4.1" and inserting "2C1.1";

in the line referenced to 15 U.S.C. § 78dd-2 by striking "2B4.1" and inserting "2C1.1";

by inserting after the line referenced to 15 U.S.C. § 78dd-2 following new line:

"15 U.S.C. § 78dd-3   2C1.1";

and n the line referenced to 15 U.S.C. § 78ff by striking "2B4.1" and inserting "2C1.1".

Reason for Amendment: This amendment changes the Statutory Index reference for violations of section 30A of the Securities Exchange Act of 1934 (15 U.S.C. § 78dd-1) and sections 104 and 104A of the Foreign Corrupt Practices Act of 1977 (15 U.S.C. §§ 78dd-2 and 78dd-3), from § 2B4.1 (Bribery in Procurement of Bank Loan and Other Commercial Bribery) to § 2C1.1 (Offering, Giving, Soliciting, or Receiving a Bribe; Extortion Under Color of Official Right).

This change is made because violations of 15 U.S.C. §§ 78dd-1 through 78dd-3 involve public corruption of foreign officials and are, therefore, more akin to public corruption cases than commercial bribery cases. Violations of the 15 U.S.C. §§ 78dd-1 through 78dd-3 typically involve payments to foreign officials for the purposes of influencing their official acts or decisions, inducing them to do or omit an act in violation of their lawful duty, inducing them to influence a foreign government, or securing any improper advantage. These cases also involve payments to foreign political parties or officials, candidates for foreign political office, or persons who act as conduits to these individuals. Most cases prosecuted under 15 U.S.C. §§ 78dd-1 through 78dd-3 involve an intent to influence governmental action.

Conversely, commercial bribery cases sentenced under § 2B4.1 often involve kickback and gratuity payments made to bank officials or others who accept payments in return for influence or some type of exchange from the other person. These cases typically do not involve bribery of public or governmental officials and indeed, the Commentary to the guideline makes this clear in Application Note 1.

This change also is made to comply with the mandate of a mulitlateral treaty entered into by the United States, the Convention on Combating Bribery of Foreign Public Officials in International Business Transactions. In part, this Convention requires signatory countries to impose comparable sentences in both domestic and foreign bribery cases. Domestic public bribery cases are referenced to § 2C1.1. To comply with the treaty, offenses committed in violation of 15 U.S.C. §§ 78dd-1 through 78dd-3 are now similarly referenced to § 2C1.1.

Effective Date: The effective date of this amendment is November 1, 2002.

640. Amendment: Section 2D1.1(a)(3) is amended by striking "below." and inserting ", except that if the defendant receives an adjustment under § 3B1.2 (Mitigating Role), the base offense level under this subsection shall be not more than level 30.".

The Commentary to § 2D1.1 captioned "Application Notes" is amended in Note 11 in the "TYPICAL WEIGHT PER UNIT (DOSE, PILL, OR CAPSULE) TABLE" by striking "MDA* 100 mg" and inserting the following:

"MDA   250 mg
MDMA   250 mg".

The Commentary to § 2D1.1 captioned "Application Notes" is amended by adding at the end the following:

"21. Applicability of Subsection (b)(6).—The applicability of subsection (b)(6) shall be determined without regard to whether the defendant was convicted of an offense that subjects the defendant to a mandatory minimum term of imprisonment. Section § 5C1.2(b), which provides a minimum offense level of level 17, is not pertinent to the determination of whether subsection (b)(6) applies.".

Section 2D1.8(a)(2) is amended by striking "16" and inserting "26".

The Commentary to § 3B1.2 captioned "Application Notes" is amended by adding at the end the following:

"6. Application of Role Adjustment in Certain Drug Cases.—In a case in which the court applied § 2D1.1 and the defendant's base offense level under that guideline was reduced by operation of the maximum base offense level in § 2D1.1(a)(3), the court also shall apply the appropriate adjustment under this guideline.".

Reason for Amendment: This amendment responds to concerns that the guidelines pertaining to drug offenses do not satisfactorily reflect the culpability of certain offenders. The amendment also clarifies the operation of certain provisions in § 2D1.1 (Unlawful Manufacturing, Importing, Exporting, or Trafficking (Including Possession with Intent to Commit These Offenses); Attempt or Conspiracy).

First, the amendment increases the maximum base offense level under subsection (a)(2) of § 2D1.8 (Renting or Managing a Drug Establishment; Attempt or Conspiracy) from level 16 to level 26. This part of the amendment responds to concerns that § 2D1.8 did not adequately punish defendants convicted under 21 U.S.C. § 856, pertaining to the establishment of manufacturing operations. That statute originally was enacted to target defendants who maintain, manage, or control so-called "crack houses" and more recently has been applied to defendants who facilitate drug use at commercial dance clubs, frequently called "raves".

Prior to this amendment, § 2D1.8(a)(2) provided a maximum base offense level of level 16 for defendants convicted under 21 U.S.C. § 856 who had no participation in the underlying controlled substance offense other than allowing use of their premises. The Commission determined that the maximum base offense level of level 16 did not adequately reflect the culpability of offenders who permit distribution of drugs in quantities that under § 2D1.1

result in offense levels higher than level 16. Such offenders knowingly and intentionally facilitate and profit, at least indirectly, from the trafficking of illegal drugs, even though they may not participate directly in the underlying controlled substance offense.

Second, the amendment modifies § 2D1.1(a)(3) to provide a maximum base offense level of level 30 if the defendant receives an adjustment under § 3B1.2 (Mitigating Role). The maximum base offense level somewhat limits the sentencing impact of drug quantity for offenders who perform relatively low level trafficking functions, have little authority in the drug trafficking organization, and have a lower degree of individual culpability (e.g., "mules" or "couriers" whose most serious trafficking function is transporting drugs and who qualify for a mitigating role adjustment).

This part of the amendment responds to concerns that base offense levels derived from the Drug Quantity Table in § 2D1.1 overstate the culpability of certain drug offenders who meet the criteria for a mitigating role adjustment under § 3B1.2. The Commission determined that, ordinarily, a maximum base offense level of level 30 adequately reflects the culpability of a defendant who qualifies for a mitigating role adjustment. Other aggravating adjustments in the trafficking guideline (e.g., the weapon enhancement at § 2D1.1(b)(1)), or other general, aggravating adjustments in Chapter Three (Adjustments), may increase the offense level above level 30. The maximum base offense level is expected to apply narrowly, affecting approximately six percent of all drug trafficking offenders.

The amendment also adds an application note in § 3B1.2 that instructs the court to apply the appropriate adjustment under that guideline in a case in which the maximum base offense level in § 2D1.1(a)(3) operates to reduce the defendant's base offense level under § 2D1.1.

Third, the amendment modifies the Typical Weight Per Unit (Dose, Pill, or Capsule) Table in the commentary to § 2D1.1 to reflect more accurately the type and weight of ecstasy pills typically trafficked and consumed. Specifically, the amendment adds a reference for MDMA (3,4-methylenedioxymethamphetamine) in the Typical Weight Per Unit Table and lists the typical weight as 250 milligrams per pill. The amendment also revises the typical weight for MDA to 250 milligrams of the mixture or substance containing the controlled substance. Prior to this amendment, the Table listed the typical weight of MDA as 100 milligrams of the actual controlled substance.

Information provided by the Drug Enforcement Administration indicates that ecstasy usually is trafficked and used as MDMA in pills weighing approximately 250 to 350 milligrams.

The absence of MDMA from the Typical Weight Per Unit (Dose, Pill, or Capsule) Table and the listing for MDA of an estimate of the actual weight of the controlled substance created the potential for misapplying the MDA estimate in a case in which MDMA is involved, which could result in underpunishment in some ecstasy cases. This part of the amendment thus promotes uniform application of § 2D1.1 for offenses involving ecstasy by adding a reference for MDMA and revising the estimated weight for MDA.

Fourth, the amendment addresses two application concerns regarding the two level reduction under § 2D1.1(b)(6) for defendants who meet the criteria set forth in § 5C1.2 (Limitation on Applicability of Statutory Minimum Sentences in Certain Cases). The amendment provides an application note that clarifies that the two level reduction under § 2D1.1(b)(6) does not depend on whether the defendant is convicted under a statute that carries a mandatory minimum term of imprisonment. The application note also clarifies that § 5C1.2(b), which provides a minimum offense level of level 17 for certain offenders, is not applicable

Amendment 640

to § 2D1.1(b)(6).

Effective Date: The effective date of this amendment is November 1, 2002.

641. Amendment: Chapter Two is amended in the heading of Part G by striking "PROSTITUTION" and inserting "COMMERCIAL SEX ACTS".

Chapter Two, Part G is amended in the heading of Subpart 1 by striking "PROSTITUTION" and inserting "A COMMERCIAL SEX ACT".

Section 2G1.1 is amended in the heading by striking "Prostitution" and inserting "A Commercial Sex Act".

Section 2G1.1(b)(1) is amended by striking "prostitution" and inserting "a commercial sex act"; by inserting "fraud," after "force,"; and by striking "by threats or drugs or in any manner".

Section 2G1.1(b)(4) is amended by striking "prostitution" each place it appears and inserting "a commercial sex act".

Section 2G1.1(b)(5) is amended by striking "prostitution" and inserting "a commercial sex act".

Section 2G1.1(c)(3) is amended by striking "prostitution" and inserting "a commercial sex act".

Section 2G1.1(d)(1) is amended by striking "prostitution" and inserting "a commercial sex act".

The Commentary to § 2G1.1 captioned "Application Notes" is amended in Note 1 by inserting after "For purposes of this guideline—" the following paragraph:

"'Commercial sex act' has the meaning given that term in 18 U.S.C. § 1591(c)(1).";

and by striking the last two paragraphs as follows:

"'Promoting prostitution' means persuading, inducing, enticing, or coercing a person to engage in prostitution, or to travel to engage in, prostitution.

'Victim' means a person transported, persuaded, induced, enticed, or coerced to engage in, or travel for the purpose of engaging in, prostitution or prohibited sexual conduct, whether or not the person consented to the prostitution or prohibited sexual conduct. Accordingly, 'victim' may include an undercover law enforcement officer.",

and inserting the following:

"'Promoting a commercial sex act' means persuading, inducing, enticing, or coercing a person to engage in a commercial sex act, or to travel to engage in, a commercial sex act.

'Victim' means a person transported, persuaded, induced, enticed, or coerced to engage in, or travel for the purpose of engaging in, a commercial sex act or prohibited sexual conduct, whether or not the person consented to the commercial sex act or prohibited sexual conduct. Accordingly, 'victim' may include an undercover law enforcement officer.".

The Commentary to § 2G1.1 captioned "Application Notes" is amended in Note 2 by inserting "fraud," after "force,"; and by striking "prostitution" and inserting "commercial sex act".

The Commentary to § 2G1.1 captioned "Application Notes" is amended in Notes 3, 4, 7, 8, and 11 by striking "prostitution" each place it appears and inserting "a commercial sex act".

The Commentary to § 2G1.1 captioned "Application Notes" is amended in Note 10 by striking "kidnaping" each place it appears and inserting "kidnapping".

The Commentary to § 2G1.1 captioned "Application Notes" is amended by striking Note 12 as follows:

"12. Upward Departure Provisions.—An upward departure may be warranted in either of the following circumstances:

(A) The defendant was convicted under 18 U.S.C. § 1591 and the offense involved a victim who had not attained the age of 14 years.

(B) The offense involved more than 10 victims.",

and inserting the following:

"12. Upward Departure Provision.—An upward departure may be warranted if the offense involved more than 10 victims.".

Reason for Amendment: This amendment ensures that appropriately severe sentences for sex trafficking crimes apply to commercial sex acts such as production of child pornography, in addition to prostitution, and also targets offenders who use fraud to entrap victims. It makes several changes to § 2G1.1 (Promoting Prostitution or Prohibited Sexual Conduct) to address more adequately the portion of section 112(b) of the Victims of Trafficking and Violence Protection Act of 2000 (the "Act"), Pub. L. 106–386, pertaining to the new offense at 18 U.S.C. § 1591, which prohibits knowingly transporting or harboring any person, or benefitting from such transporting or harboring, knowing either that force, fraud, or coercion will be used to cause that person to engage in a commercial sex act, or that the person has not attained the age of 18 years and will be forced to engage in a commercial sex act.

In response to the Act, the Commission in 2001 promulgated an amendment that referenced 18 U.S.C. § 1591 to §§ 2G1.1 and 2G2.1 (Sexually Exploiting a Minor by Production of Sexually Explicit Visual or Printed Material) and provided an encouraged upward departure in those guidelines to address cases in which (1) the defendant was convicted under 18 U.S.C. § 1591 and the offense involved a victim who had not attained the age of 14 years; or (2) the offense involved more than 10 victims. (See Supplement to Appendix C, Amendment 612, effective May 1, 2001, and Amendment 627, effective November 1, 2001).

This amendment makes three substantive changes to § 2G1.1. First, this amendment broadens the conduct covered by the guideline beyond prostitution to encompass all commercial sex acts, consistent with the scope of the Act. Second, this amendment expands the "force or coercion" prong of § 2G1.1(b)(1) to also cover offenses involving fraud. This change addresses the increased punishment provided by 18 U.S.C. § 1591 for offenses effected by force, fraud, or coercion. Third, the amendment deletes the portion of the encouraged upward departure provision in § 2G1.1 pertaining to the age of the victim because such conduct already is taken into account by that guideline.

Effective Date: The effective date of this amendment is November 1, 2002.

642. Amendment: Section 2K2.4 is amended by redesignating subsection (b) as subsection (d); and by striking subsection (a) as follows:

> "(a) If the defendant, whether or not convicted of another crime, was convicted of violating:
>
> > (1) Section 844(h) of title 18, United States Code, the guideline sentence is the term of imprisonment required by statute.
> >
> > (2) Section 924(c) or section 929(a) of title 18, United States Code, the guideline sentence is the minimum term of imprisonment required by statute.",

and inserting the following:

> "(a) If the defendant, whether or not convicted of another crime, was convicted of violating section 844(h) of title 18, United States Code, the guideline sentence is the term of imprisonment required by statute. Chapters Three (Adjustments) and Four (Criminal History and Criminal Livelihood) shall not apply to that count of conviction.
>
> (b) Except as provided in subsection (c), if the defendant, whether or not convicted of another crime, was convicted of violating section 924(c) or section 929(a) of title 18, United States Code, the guideline sentence is the minimum term of imprisonment required by statute. Chapters Three and Four shall not apply to that count of conviction.
>
> (c) If the defendant (1) was convicted of violating section 924(c) or section 929(a) of title 18, United States Code; and (2) as a result of that conviction (alone or in addition to another offense of conviction), is determined to be a career offender under § 4B1.1 (Career Offender), the guideline sentence shall be determined under § 4B1.1(c). Except for §§ 3E1.1 (Acceptance of Responsibility), 4B1.1, and 4B1.2 (Definitions of Terms Used in Section 4B1.1), Chapters Three and Four shall not apply to that count of conviction.".

The Commentary to § 2K2.4 captioned "Application Notes" is amended by redesignating Notes 2 through 5 as Notes 4 through 7, respectively; and by striking Note 1 as follows:

> "1. Section 844(h) of title 18, United State Code, provides a mandatory term of imprisonment of 10 years (or 20 years for the second or subsequent offense). Sections 924(c) and 929(a) of title 18, United States Code, provide mandatory minimum terms of imprisonment (e.g., not less than five years). Subsection (a) reflects this distinction. Accordingly, the guideline sentence for a defendant convicted under 18 U.S.C. § 844(h) is the term required by the statute, and the guideline sentence for a defendant convicted under 18 U.S.C. § 924(c) or § 929(a) is the minimum term required by the relevant statute. Each of 18 U.S.C. §§ 844(h), 924(c), and 929(a) requires a term of imprisonment imposed under this section to run consecutively to any other term of imprisonment.
>
> A sentence above the minimum term required by 18 U.S.C. § 924(c) or

§ 929(a) is an upward departure from the guideline sentence. A departure may be warranted, for example, to reflect the seriousness of the defendant's criminal history, particularly in a case in which the defendant is convicted of an 18 U.S.C. § 924(c) or § 929(a) offense and has at least two prior felony convictions for a crime of violence or a controlled substance offense that would have resulted in application of § 4B1.1 (Career Offender) if that guideline applied to these offenses. See Application Note 3.",

and inserting the following:

"1. Application of Subsection (a).—Section 844(h) of title 18, United State Code, provides a mandatory term of imprisonment of 10 years (or 20 years for the second or subsequent offense). Accordingly, the guideline sentence for a defendant convicted under 18 U.S.C. § 844(h) is the term required by that statute. Section 844(h) of title 18, United State Code, also requires a term of imprisonment imposed under this section to run consecutively to any other term of imprisonment.

2. Application of Subsection (b).—

   (A) In General.—Sections 924(c) and 929(a) of title 18, United States Code, provide mandatory minimum terms of imprisonment (e.g., not less than five years). Except as provided in subsection (c), in a case in which the defendant is convicted under 18 U.S.C. § 924(c) or § 929(a), the guideline sentence is the minimum term required by the relevant statute. Each of 18 U.S.C. §§ 924(c) and 929(a) also requires that a term of imprisonment imposed under that section shall run consecutively to any other term of imprisonment.

   (B) Upward Departure Provision.—In a case in which the guideline sentence is determined under subsection (b), a sentence above the minimum term required by 18 U.S.C. § 924(c) or § 929(a) is an upward departure from the guideline sentence. A departure may be warranted, for example, to reflect the seriousness of the defendant's criminal history in a case in which the defendant is convicted of an 18 U.S.C. § 924(c) or § 929(a) offense but is not determined to be a career offender under § 4B1.1.

3. Application of Subsection (c).—In a case in which the defendant (A) was convicted of violating 18 U.S.C. § 924(c) or 18 U.S.C. § 929(a); and (B) as a result of that conviction (alone or in addition to another offense of conviction), is determined to be a career offender under § 4B1.1 (Career Offender), the guideline sentence shall be determined under § 4B1.1(c). In a case involving multiple counts, the sentence shall be imposed according to the rules in subsection (e) of § 5G1.2 (Sentencing on Multiple Counts of Conviction).".

The Commentary to § 2K2.4 captioned "Application Notes" is amended in Note 4, as redesignated by this amendment, by inserting "Weapon Enhancement.—" before "If a sentence under"; and by inserting in the last paragraph "in which the defendant is determined not to be a career offender" after "In a few cases".

The Commentary to § 2K2.4 captioned "Application Notes" is amended by striking Note 5, as redesignated by this amendment, as follows:

"5. Do not apply Chapter Three (Adjustments) and Chapter Four (Criminal History and Criminal Livelihood) to any offense sentenced under this guideline. Such offenses are excluded from application of these chapters because the guideline sentence for each offense is determined only by the relevant statute. See §§ 3D1.1 (Procedure for Determining Offense Level on Multiple Counts) and 5G1.2 (Sentencing on Multiple Counts of Conviction).",

and inserting the following:

"5. Chapters Three and Four.—Except for those cases covered by subsection (c), do not apply Chapter Three (Adjustments) and Chapter Four (Criminal History and Criminal Livelihood) to any offense sentenced under this guideline. Such offenses are excluded from application of those chapters because the guideline sentence for each offense is determined only by the relevant statute. See §§ 3D1.1 (Procedure for Determining Offense Level on Multiple Counts) and 5G1.2. In determining the guideline sentence for those cases covered by subsection (c): (A) the adjustment in § 3E1.1 (Acceptance of Responsibility) may apply, as provided in § 4B1.1(c); and (B) no other adjustments in Chapter Three and no provisions of Chapter Four, other than §§ 4B1.1 and 4B1.2, shall apply.".

The Commentary to § 2K2.4 captioned "Application Notes" is amended in Note 6, as redesignated by this amendment, by inserting "Terms of Supervised Release.—" before "Imposition of a term".

The Commentary to § 2K2.4 captioned "Application Notes" is amended in Note 7, as redesignated by this amendment, by inserting "Fines.—" before "Subsection"; by striking "(b)" and inserting "(d)"; and by striking "Note 2" and inserting "Note 4".

Section 4B1.1 is amended by striking the following:

"A defendant is a career offender if (1) the defendant was at least eighteen years old at the time the defendant committed the instant offense of conviction, (2) the instant offense of conviction is a felony that is either a crime of violence or a controlled substance offense, and (3) the defendant has at least two prior felony convictions of either a crime of violence or a controlled substance offense. If the offense level for a career criminal from the table below is greater than the offense level otherwise applicable, the offense level from the table below shall apply. A career offender's criminal history category in every case shall be Category VI.",

and inserting the following:

"(a) A defendant is a career offender if (1) the defendant was at least eighteen years old at the time the defendant committed the instant offense of conviction; (2) the instant offense of conviction is a felony that is either a crime of violence or a controlled substance offense; and (3) the defendant has at least two prior felony convictions of either a crime of violence or a controlled substance offense.

(b) Except as provided in subsection (c), if the offense level for a career offender from the table in this subsection is greater than the offense level otherwise applicable, the offense level from the table in this subsection shall apply. A career offender's criminal history category in every case under this subsection shall be Category VI.".

Section 4B1.1 is amended by adding after "corresponding to that adjustment." the following:

"(c) If the defendant is convicted of 18 U.S.C. § 924(c) or § 929(a), and the defendant is determined to be a career offender under subsection (a), the applicable guideline range shall be determined as follows:

(1) If the only count of conviction is 18 U.S.C. § 924(c) or § 929(a), the applicable guideline range shall be determined using the table in subsection (c)(3).

(2) In the case of multiple counts of conviction in which at least one of the counts is a conviction other than a conviction for 18 U.S.C. § 924(c) or § 929(a), the guideline range shall be the greater of—

(A) the guideline range that results by adding the mandatory minimum consecutive penalty required by the 18 U.S.C. § 924(c) or § 929(a) count(s) to the minimum and the maximum of the otherwise applicable guideline range determined for the count(s) of conviction other than the 18 U.S.C. § 924(c) or § 929(a) count(s); and

(B) the guideline range determined using the table in subsection (c)(3).

(3) Career Offender Table for 18 U.S.C. § 924(c) or § 929(a) Offenders

§ 3E1.1 Reduction	Guideline Range for the 18 U.S.C. § 924(c) or § 929(a) Count(s)
No reduction	360-life
2-level reduction	292-365
3-level reduction	262-327.".

The Commentary to § 4B1.1 captioned "Application Notes" is amended by adding at the end the following:

"3. Application of Subsection (c).—

(A) In General.—Subsection (c) applies in any case in which the defendant (i) was convicted of violating 18 U.S.C. § 924(c) or § 929(a); and (ii) as a result of that conviction (alone or in addition to another offense of conviction), is determined to be a career offender under § 4B1.1(a).

(B) Subsection (c)(2).—To determine the greater guideline range under subsection (c)(2), the court shall use the guideline range with the highest minimum term of imprisonment.

(C) 'Otherwise Applicable Guideline Range'.—For purposes of subsection (c)(2)(A), 'otherwise applicable guideline range' for the count(s) of conviction other than the 18 U.S.C. § 924(c) or 18 U.S.C. § 929(a) count(s) is determined as follows:

Amendment 642 APPENDIX C - VOLUME II November 1, 2013

(i) If the count(s) of conviction other than the 18 U.S.C. § 924(c) or 18 U.S.C. § 929(a) count(s) does not qualify the defendant as a career offender, the otherwise applicable guideline range for that count(s) is the guideline range determined using: (I) the Chapter Two and Three offense level for that count(s); and (II) the appropriate criminal history category determined under §§ 4A1.1 (Criminal History Category) and 4A1.2 (Definitions and Instructions for Computing Criminal History).

(ii) If the count(s) of conviction other than the 18 U.S.C. § 924(c) or 18 U.S.C. § 929(a) count(s) qualifies the defendant as a career offender, the otherwise applicable guideline range for that count(s) is the guideline range determined for that count(s) under § 4B1.1(a) and (b).

(D) Imposition of Consecutive Term of Imprisonment.—In a case involving multiple counts, the sentence shall be imposed according to the rules in subsection (e) of § 5G1.2 (Sentencing on Multiple Counts of Conviction).

(E) Example.—The following example illustrates the application of subsection (c)(2) in a multiple count situation:

The defendant is convicted of one count of violating 18 U.S.C. § 924(c) for possessing a firearm in furtherance of a drug trafficking offense (5 year mandatory minimum), and one count of violating 21 U.S.C. § 841(b)(1)(B) (5 year mandatory minimum, 40 year statutory maximum). Applying subsection (c)(2)(A), the court determines that the drug count (without regard to the 18 U.S.C. § 924(c) count) qualifies the defendant as a career offender under § 4B1.1(a). Under § 4B1.1(a), the otherwise applicable guideline range for the drug count is 188-235 months (using offense level 34 (because the statutory maximum for the drug count is 40 years), minus 3 levels for acceptance of responsibility, and criminal history category VI). The court adds 60 months (the minimum required by 18 U.S.C. § 924(c)) to the minimum and the maximum of that range, resulting in a guideline range of 248-295 months. Applying subsection (c)(2)(B), the court then determines the career offender guideline range from the table in subsection (c)(3) is 262-327 months. The range with the greatest minimum, 262-327 months, is used to impose the sentence in accordance with § 5G1.2(e).".

The Commentary to § 4B1.1 captioned "Background" is amended by adding at the end the following:

"   Subsection (c) provides rules for determining the sentence for career offenders who have been convicted of 18 U.S.C. § 924(c) or § 929(a). The Career Offender Table in subsection (c)(3) provides a sentence at or near the statutory maximum for these offenders by using guideline ranges that correspond to criminal history category VI and offense level 37 (assuming § 3E1.1 (Acceptance of Responsibility) does not apply), offense level 35 (assuming a 2-level reduction under § 3E1.1 applies), and offense level 34 (assuming a 3-level reduction under § 3E1.1 applies).".

The Commentary to § 4B1.2 captioned "Application Notes" is amended in Note 1 by striking the following:

"A prior conviction for violating 18 U.S.C. § 924(c) or § 929(a) is a 'prior felony conviction' for purposes of applying § 4B1.1 (Career Offender) if the prior offense of conviction established that the underlying offense was a 'crime of violence' or 'controlled substance offense.' (Note that if the defendant also was convicted of the underlying offense, the two convictions will be treated as related cases under § 4A1.2 (Definitions and Instruction for Computing Criminal History)).",

and inserting the following:

"A violation of 18 U.S.C. § 924(c) or § 929(a) is a 'crime of violence' or a 'controlled substance offense' if the offense of conviction established that the underlying offense was a 'crime of violence' or a 'controlled substance offense'. (Note that in the case of a prior 18 U.S.C. § 924(c) or § 929(a) conviction, if the defendant also was convicted of the underlying offense, the two prior convictions will be treated as related cases under § 4A1.2 (Definitions and Instructions for Computing Criminal History).)".

The Commentary to § 4B1.2 captioned "Application Notes" is amended by striking Note 2 as follows:

"2. The guideline sentence for a conviction under 18 U.S.C. § 924(c) or § 929(a) is determined only by the statute and is imposed independently of any other sentence. See §§ 2K2.4 (Use of Firearm, Armor-Piercing Ammunition, or Explosive During or in Relation to Certain Crimes), 3D1.1 (Procedure for Determining Offense Level on Multiple Counts), and subsection (a) of § 5G1.2 (Sentencing on Multiple Counts of Conviction). Accordingly, do not apply this guideline if the only offense of conviction is for violating 18 U.S.C. § 924(c) or § 929(a). For provisions pertaining to an upward departure from the guideline sentence for a conviction under 18 U.S.C. § 924(c) or § 929(a), see Application Note 1 of § 2K2.4.";

and by redesignating Notes 3 and 4 as Notes 2 and 3, respectively.

Section 5G1.2(a) is amended by striking "The" and inserting "Except as provided in subsection (e), the"; and by inserting a comma after "other term of imprisonment".

Section 5G1.2 is amended by adding after subsection (d) the following:

"(e) In a case in which subsection (c) of § 4B1.1 (Career Offender) applies, to the extent possible, the total punishment is to be apportioned among the counts of conviction, except that (1) the sentence to be imposed on a count requiring a minimum term of imprisonment shall be at least the minimum required by statute; and (2) the sentence to be imposed on the 18 U.S.C. § 924(c) or § 929(a) count shall be imposed to run consecutively to any other count.".

The Commentary to § 5G1.2 is amended by striking the first paragraph as follows:

"This section specifies the procedure for determining the specific sentence to be formally imposed on each count in a multiple-count case. The combined length of the sentences ("total punishment") is determined by the adjusted combined offense level. To the extent possible, the total punishment is to be imposed on each count. Sentences on all counts run concurrently, except as required to achieve the total sentence, or as required by law.",

Amendment 642

and inserting the following:

"Application Notes:

1. <u>In General</u>.—This section specifies the procedure for determining the specific sentence to be formally imposed on each count in a multiple-count case. The combined length of the sentences ('total punishment') is determined by the court after determining the adjusted combined offense level and the Criminal History Category. Except as otherwise required by subsection (e) or any other law, the total punishment is to be imposed on each count and the sentences on all counts are to be imposed to run concurrently to the extent allowed by the statutory maximum sentence of imprisonment for each count of conviction.";

by indenting the second and third paragraphs 2 ems from the left margin; and by striking the fourth paragraph as follows:

" Subsection (a) applies if a statute (1) specifies a term of imprisonment to be imposed; and (2) requires that such term of imprisonment be imposed to run consecutively to any other term of imprisonment. See, e.g., 18 U.S.C. § 924(c) (requiring mandatory minimum terms of imprisonment, based on the conduct involved, to run consecutively to any other term of imprisonment). The term of years to be imposed consecutively is determined by the statute of conviction, and is independent of a guideline sentence on any other count. See, e.g., Commentary to §§ 2K2.4 (Use of Firearm, Armor-Piercing Ammunition, or Explosive During or in Relation to Certain Crimes) and 3D1.1 (Procedure for Determining Offense Level on Multiple Counts) regarding determination of the offense levels for related counts when a conviction under 18 U.S.C. § 924(c) is involved. Note, however, that even in the case of a consecutive term of imprisonment imposed under subsection (a), any term of supervised release imposed is to run concurrently with any other term of supervised release imposed. See 18 U.S.C. § 3624(e). Subsection (a) also applies in certain other instances in which an independently determined and consecutive sentence is required. See, e.g., Application Note 3 of the Commentary to § 2J1.6 (Failure to Appear by Defendant), relating to failure to appear for service of sentence.",

and inserting the following:

"2. <u>Mandatory Minimum and Mandatory Consecutive Terms of Imprisonment (Not Covered by Subsection (e))</u>.—Subsection (a) applies if a statute (A) specifies a term of imprisonment to be imposed; and (B) requires that such term of imprisonment be imposed to run consecutively to any other term of imprisonment. See, e.g., 18 U.S.C. § 924(c) (requiring mandatory minimum terms of imprisonment, based on the conduct involved, and also requiring the sentence imposed to run consecutively to any other term of imprisonment). Except for certain career offender situations in which subsection (c) of § 4B1.1 (Career Offender) applies, the term of years to be imposed consecutively is the minimum required by the statute of conviction and is independent of the guideline sentence on any other count. See, e.g., the Commentary to §§ 2K2.4 (Use of Firearm, Armor-Piercing Ammunition, or Explosive During or in Relation to Certain Crimes) and 3D1.1 (Procedure for Determining Offense Level on Multiple Counts) regarding the determination of the offense levels for related counts when a conviction under 18 U.S.C. § 924(c) is involved. Note, however, that even in the case of a consecutive term of imprisonment imposed under subsection (a), any term of supervised release imposed is to run concurrently with any other term of supervised release imposed. See 18 U.S.C. § 3624(e). Subsection (a) also applies in certain other instances in which an independently determined and consecutive sentence is required. See, e.g., Application Note 3 of the Commentary to § 2J1.6 (Failure to Appear by Defendant), relating to failure to appear for service of sentence.

3. Career Offenders Covered under Subsection (e).—

(A) Imposing Sentence.—The sentence imposed for a conviction under 18 U.S.C. § 924(c) or § 929(a) shall, under that statute, consist of a minimum term of imprisonment imposed to run consecutively to the sentence on any other count. Subsection (e) requires that the total punishment determined under § 4B1.1(c) be apportioned among all the counts of conviction. In most cases this can be achieved by imposing the statutory minimum term of imprisonment on the 18 U.S.C. § 924(c) or § 929(a) count, subtracting that minimum term of imprisonment from the total punishment determined under § 4B1.1(c), and then imposing the balance of the total punishment on the other counts of conviction. In some cases covered by subsection (e), a consecutive term of imprisonment longer than the minimum required by 18 U.S.C. § 924(c) or § 929(a) will be necessary in order both to achieve the total punishment determined by the court and to comply with the applicable statutory requirements.

(B) Examples.—The following examples illustrate the application of subsection (e) in a multiple count situation:

(i) The defendant is convicted of one count of violating 18 U.S.C. § 924(c) for possessing a firearm in furtherance of a drug trafficking offense (5 year mandatory minimum), and one count of violating 21 U.S.C. § 841(b)(1)(C) (20 year statutory maximum). Applying § 4B1.1(c), the court determines that a sentence of 300 months is appropriate (applicable guideline range of 262-327). The court then imposes a sentence of 60 months on the 18 U.S.C. § 924(c) count, subtracts that 60 months from the total punishment of 300 months and imposes the remainder of 240 months on the 21 U.S.C. § 841 count. As required by statute, the sentence on the 18 U.S.C. § 924(c) count is imposed to run consecutively.

(ii) The defendant is convicted of one count of 18 U.S.C. § 924(c) (5 year mandatory minimum), and one count of violating 21 U.S.C. § 841(b)(1)(C) (20 year statutory maximum). Applying § 4B1.1(c), the court determines that a sentence of 327 months is appropriate (applicable guideline range of 262-327). The court then imposes a sentence of 240 months on the 21 U.S.C. § 841 count and a sentence of 87 months on the 18 U.S.C. § 924(c) count to run consecutively to the sentence on the 21 U.S.C. § 841 count.

(iii) The defendant is convicted of two counts of 18 U.S.C.

§ 924(c) (5 year mandatory minimum on first count, 25 year mandatory minimum on second count) and one count of violating 18 U.S.C. § 2113(a) (20 year statutory maximum). Applying § 4B1.1(c), the court determines that a sentence of 400 months is appropriate (applicable guideline range of 360-life). The court then imposes (I) a sentence of 60 months on the first 18 U.S.C. § 924(c) count; (II) a sentence of 300 months on the second 18 U.S.C. § 924(c) count; and (III) a sentence of 40 months on the 18 U.S.C. § 2113(a) count. The sentence on each count is imposed to run consecutively to the other counts.".

Reason for Amendment: This amendment is intended to comply with the statutory directive in 28 U.S.C. § 994(h) by providing a guideline sentence at or near the statutory maximum of life imprisonment for cases in which certain serious firearm offenses establish the defendant as a career offender.

This amendment provides special rules in §§ 4B1.1 (Career Offender) and 5G1.2 (Sentencing on Multiple Counts of Conviction) for determining and imposing a guideline sentence in a case in which the defendant is convicted of an offense under 18 U.S.C. § 924(c) or § 929(a) and, as a result of that conviction, is determined to be a career offender under §§ 4B1.1 and 4B1.2 (Definitions of Terms Used in Section 4B1.1). The amendment supplements Amendment 600 (effective November 1, 2000) in which the Commission first addressed implementation of the statutory changes in penalties for 18 U.S.C. §§ 924(c) and 929(a) offenses made by the Act to Throttle the Criminal Use of Guns, Pub. L. 105–386. At that time, the Commission deferred addressing the more complicated issues of whether convictions under 18 U.S.C. §§ 924(c) and 929(a) can qualify as instant offenses for purposes of § 4B1.1, and if they do so qualify, how the sentence would be imposed. Promulgation of this amendment reflects the Commission's decision that the amendment, while somewhat complex, is necessary to comply appropriately with 28 U.S.C. § 994(h).

Operationally, this amendment achieves two goals. First, it permits 18 U.S.C. § 924(c) or § 929(a) offenses, whether as the instant or prior offense of conviction, to qualify for career offender purposes. Second, it ensures that, in a case in which such an instant offense establishes the defendant as a career offender, the resulting guideline sentence is determined under § 4B1.1 using a count of conviction that has a statutory maximum of life imprisonment. The special rule necessarily is somewhat more complex because of the need to address certain anomalies that infrequently would occur in the absence of such a rule, i.e., that a very serious offender could receive a lower sentence by virtue of the application of § 4B1.1 than that which would otherwise be received by imposing the statutorily required minimum sentence consecutively to the otherwise applicable guideline range.

This amendment does not change the current guideline rules precluding application of guideline weapon enhancements in a case in which the defendant is convicted of a 18 U.S.C. § 924(c) or § 929(a) offense. Furthermore, under this amendment, in a case in which the defendant is convicted of a 18 U.S.C. § 924(c) or § 929(a) offense but that offense, together with any prior convictions, does not establish the defendant as a career offender, the current guideline rules for sentencing on that 18 U.S.C. § 924(c) or § 929(a) count continue to apply. Accordingly, under § 2K2.4 (Use of Firearm, Armor-Piercing Ammunition, or Explosive During or in Relation to Certain Crimes), the guideline sentence on that count is the statutory minimum, and that sentence is imposed independently and consecutively to the sentence on other counts. No adjustments in Chapter Three

(Adjustments) or Chapter Four (Criminal History and Criminal Livelihood) apply to adjust the guideline sentence for that 18 U.S.C. § 924(c) or § 929(a) count.

However, under this amendment, in a case in which the 18 U.S.C. § 924(c) or § 929(a) count establishes the defendant as a career offender, which the court will determine under §§ 4B1.1 and 4B1.2, new special rules and instructions will apply. To determine the guideline sentence on the 18 U.S.C. § 924(c) or § 929(a) count, the court moves directly from § 2K2.4 to § 4B1.1 and applies the new special instruction therein. New special instructions for imposing sentence in these cases also have been added to § 5G1.2.

Effective Date: The effective date of this amendment is November 1, 2002.

643. **Amendment:** Chapter Three, Part A, is amended by striking § 3A1.2 as follows:

"§ 3A1.2. Official Victim

If --

(a) the victim was a government officer or employee; a former government officer or employee; or a member of the immediate family of any of the above, and the offense of conviction was motivated by such status; or

(b) during the course of the offense or immediate flight therefrom, the defendant or a person for whose conduct the defendant is otherwise accountable, knowing or having reasonable cause to believe that a person was a law enforcement or corrections officer, assaulted such officer in a manner creating a substantial risk of serious bodily injury,

increase by 3 levels.",

and inserting the following:

"§ 3A1.2. Official Victim

(a) If (1) the victim was (A) a government officer or employee; (B) a former government officer or employee; or (C) a member of the immediate family of a person described in subdivision (A) or (B); and (2) the offense of conviction was motivated by such status, increase by 3 levels.

(b) If, in a manner creating a substantial risk of serious bodily injury, the defendant or a person for whose conduct the defendant is otherwise accountable—

(1) knowing or having reasonable cause to believe that a person was a law enforcement officer, assaulted such officer during the course of the offense or immediate flight therefrom; or

(2) knowing or having reasonable cause to believe that a person was a prison official, assaulted such official while the defendant (or a person for whose conduct the defendant is otherwise accountable) was in the custody or control of a prison or other correctional facility,

increase by 3 levels.".

Amendment 643

The Commentary to § 3A1.2 captioned "Application Notes" is amended in Note 1 by inserting "Applicability to Certain Victims.—" before "This guideline applies".

The Commentary to § 3A1.2 captioned "Application Notes" is amended by striking Note 2 as follows:

"2. Certain high-level officials, e.g., the President and Vice President, although covered by this section, do not represent the heartland of the conduct covered. An upward departure to reflect the potential disruption of the governmental function in such cases typically would be warranted.";

and by redesignating Notes 3 through 6 as Notes 2 through 5, respectively.

The Commentary to § 3A1.2 captioned "Application Notes" is amended in Note 2, as redesignated by this amendment, by inserting "Nonapplicability in Case of Incorporation of Factor in Chapter Two.—" before "Do not apply".

The Commentary to § 3A1.2 captioned "Application Notes" is amended in Note 3, as redesignated by this amendment, by inserting "Application of Subsection (a).—" before "'Motivated by such"; and by striking "subdivision" and inserting "subsection".

The Commentary to § 3A1.2 captioned "Application Notes" is amended by striking Note 4, as redesignated by this amendment, as follows:

"4. Subdivision (b) applies in circumstances tantamount to aggravated assault against a law enforcement or corrections officer, committed in the course of, or in immediate flight following, another offense, such as bank robbery. While this subdivision may apply in connection with a variety of offenses that are not by nature targeted against official victims, its applicability is limited to assaultive conduct against law enforcement or corrections officers that is sufficiently serious to create at least a 'substantial risk of serious bodily injury' and that is proximate in time to the commission of the offense.",

and inserting the following:

"4. Application of Subsection (b).—

(A) In General.—Subsection (b) applies in circumstances tantamount to aggravated assault (i) against a law enforcement officer, committed in the course of, or in immediate flight following, another offense; or (ii) against a prison official, while the defendant (or a person for whose conduct the defendant is otherwise accountable) was in the custody or control of a prison or other correctional facility. While subsection (b) may apply in connection with a variety of offenses that are not by nature targeted against official victims, its applicability is limited to assaultive conduct against such official victims that is sufficiently serious to create at least a 'substantial risk of serious bodily injury'.

(B) Definitions.—For purposes of subsection (b):

'Custody and control' includes 'non-secure custody', i.e., custody with no significant physical restraint. For example, a defendant is in the custody and control of a prison or other correctional facility if the defendant (i) is on a work detail outside the security perimeter of the prison or correctional facility; (ii) is physically away from the prison or correctional facility while on a pass or furlough; or (iii) is in custody at a community corrections center, community treatment center, 'halfway house', or similar facility. The defendant also shall be deemed to be in the custody and control of a prison or other correctional facility while the defendant is in the status of having escaped from that prison or correctional facility.

'Prison official' means any individual (including a director, officer, employee, independent contractor, or volunteer, but not including an inmate) authorized to act on behalf of a prison or correctional facility. For example, this enhancement would be applicable to any of the following: (i) an individual employed by a prison as a corrections officer; (ii) an individual employed by a prison as a work detail supervisor; and (iii) a nurse who, under contract, provides medical services to prisoners in a prison health facility.

'Substantial risk of serious bodily injury' includes any more serious injury that was risked, as well as actual serious bodily injury (or more serious injury) if it occurs.".

The Commentary to § 3A1.2 captioned "Application Notes" is amended by striking Note 5, as redesignated by this amendment, as follows:

"5. The phrase 'substantial risk of serious bodily injury' in subdivision (b) is a threshold level of harm that includes any more serious injury that was risked, as well as actual serious bodily injury (or more serious harm) if it occurs.",

and inserting the following:

"5. Upward Departure Provision.—Certain high level officials, e.g., the President and Vice President, although covered by this section, do not represent the heartland of the conduct covered. An upward departure to reflect the potential disruption of the governmental function in such cases typically would be warranted.".

Reason for Amendment: This amendment expands the category of persons who may be considered official victims for purposes of triggering the two level enhancement at § 3A1.2 (Official Victim). This amendment is promulgated in response to concerns expressed by the Bureau of Prisons regarding United States v. Walker, 202 F.3d 181 (3d Cir. 2000). Walker held that an individual employed by the prison to supervise food service functions who was attacked by an inmate subordinate was not a "corrections officer" within the scope of § 3A1.2. The Bureau of Prisons advised the Commission that the Bureau uses a variety of employees, contractors, and volunteers to supervise inmates and that maintenance of a safe and stable institutional environment is fostered by knowledge on the part of inmates that anyone in prison employment or performing an authorized role within a prison is afforded the protection of § 3A1.2. In accord with the Bureau's recommendation, the amendment includes a broad definition of "prison official" to include prison employees, as well as independent contractors and volunteers on prison premises with official authorization, but does not include inmates.

Effective Date: The effective date of this amendment is November 1, 2002.

644. **Amendment:** Section 5B1.3(a) is amended by striking the period at the end of subdivi-

sion (9) and inserting a semicolon; and by adding after subdivision (9) the following:

"(10) the defendant shall submit to the collection of a DNA sample from the defendant at the direction of the United States Probation Office if the collection of such a sample is authorized pursuant to section 3 of the DNA Analysis Backlog Elimination Act of 2000 (42 U.S.C. § 14135a).".

Section 5D1.3(a) is amended by striking the period at the end of subdivision (7) and inserting a semicolon; and by adding after subdivision (7) the following:

"(8) the defendant shall submit to the collection of a DNA sample from the defendant at the direction of the United States Probation Office if the collection of such a sample is authorized pursuant to section 3 of the DNA Analysis Backlog Elimination Act of 2000 (42 U.S.C. § 14135a).".

Reason for Amendment: This amendment adds a mandatory condition to §§ 5B1.3 (Conditions of Probation) and 5D1.3 (Conditions of Supervised Release) that the defendant provide a DNA sample if the defendant is required to do so by the DNA Analysis Backlog Elimination Act of 2000, Pub. L. 106–546. Pursuant to section 3 of the Act, a defendant is required to provide a DNA sample if the defendant is convicted of certain offenses (e.g., murder, kidnapping).

Effective Date: The effective date of this amendment is November 1, 2002.

645. **Amendment:** The Commentary to § 5G1.3 captioned "Application Notes" is amended by adding at the end the following:

"7. Downward Departure Provision.—In the case of a discharged term of imprisonment, a downward departure is not prohibited if subsection (b) would have applied to that term of imprisonment had the term been undischarged. Any such departure should be fashioned to achieve a reasonable punishment for the instant offense.".

Reason for Amendment: This amendment modifies § 5G1.3 (Imposition of a Sentence on a Defendant Subject to an Undischarged Term of Imprisonment) to include certain discharged terms of imprisonment. Specifically, the amendment adds commentary to § 5G1.3 to provide that courts are not prohibited from considering a downward departure in a case in which § 5G1.3(b) would have applied if the term of imprisonment had not been discharged. In the case of undischarged terms of imprisonment, § 5G1.3(b) currently authorizes a court to adjust the sentence if the conduct underlying the undischarged term of imprisonment has been fully taken into account in the offense level for the instant federal offense. See Application Note 2 of the Commentary to § 5G1.3. By adding the new commentary, the Commission makes clear that discharged terms of imprisonment may merit a downward departure for a similar reason. The amendment thereby addresses a circuit conflict regarding the propriety of a downward departure under such circumstances. Compare, e.g., United States v. O'Hagan, 139 F.3d 641, 657 (8th Cir. 1998) (holding that a sentencing court could downwardly depart to adjust for time served on a discharged state sentence); United States v. Blackwell, 49 F.3d 1232, 1241-42 (7th Cir. 1995) (same) with United States v. McHan, 101 F.3d 1027, 1040 (4th Cir. 1996) (holding that downward departure to allow an adjustment for a discharged term was based on an error of law and therefore an abuse of discretion), cert. denied, 520 U.S. 1281 (1997).

Effective Date: The effective date of this amendment is November 1, 2002.

646. **Amendment:** The Commentary to § 2B1.1 captioned "Application Notes" is amended in

subdivision (A) of Note 7 by striking "18 U.S.C. 1028(d)(3)" and inserting "18 U.S.C. 1028(d)(4)".

Section 2B4.1 is amended by striking subsection (b)(2) as follows:

"(2) If the offense --

(A) substantially jeopardized the safety and soundness of a financial institution; or

(B) affected a financial institution and the defendant derived more than $1,000,000 in gross receipts from the offense,

increase by 4 levels. If the resulting offense level is less than level 24, increase to level 24.",

and inserting the following:

"(2) (Apply the greater) If—

(A) the defendant derived more than $1,000,000 in gross receipts from one or more financial institutions as a result of the offense, increase by 2 levels; or

(B) the offense substantially jeopardized the safety and soundness of a financial institution, increase by 4 levels.

If the resulting offense level determined under subdivision (A) or (B) is less than level 24, increase to level 24.".

The Commentary to § 2B4.1 captioned "Application Notes" is amended by striking Notes 4 and 5 as follows:

"4. An offense shall be deemed to have 'substantially jeopardized the safety and soundness of a financial institution' if, as a consequence of the offense, the institution became insolvent; substantially reduced benefits to pensioners or insureds; was unable on demand to refund fully any deposit, payment, or investment; was so depleted of its assets as to be forced to merge with another institution in order to continue active operations; or was placed in substantial jeopardy of any of the above.

5. 'The defendant derived more than $1,000,000 in gross receipts from the offense,' as used in subsection (b)(2)(B), generally means that the gross receipts to the defendant individually, rather than to all participants, exceeded $1,000,000. 'Gross receipts from the offense' includes all property, real or personal, tangible or intangible, which is obtained directly or indirectly as a result of such offense. See 18 U.S.C. § 982(a)(4).",

and inserting the following:

"4. Gross Receipts Enhancement under Subsection (b)(2)(A).—

(A) In General.—For purposes of subsection (b)(2)(A), the defendant shall be considered to have derived more than $1,000,000 in gross receipts if the gross receipts to the defendant individually, rather than to all participants, exceeded $1,000,000.

(B) Definition.—'Gross receipts from the offense' includes all property, real or personal, tangible or intangible, which is obtained directly or indirectly as a result of such offense. See 18 U.S.C. § 982(a)(4).

5. Enhancement for Substantially Jeopardizing the Safety and Soundness of a Financial Institution under Subsection (b)(2)(B).—For purposes of subsection (b)(2)(B), an offense shall be considered to have substantially jeopardized the safety and soundness of a financial institution if, as a consequence of the offense, the institution (A) became insolvent; (B) substantially reduced benefits to pensioners or insureds; (C) was unable on demand to refund fully any deposit, payment, or investment; (D) was so depleted of its assets as to be forced to merge with another institution in order to continue active operations; or (E) was placed in substantial jeopardy of any of subdivisions (A) through (D) of this note.".

The Commentary to § 2D1.9 captioned "Statutory Provision" is amended by striking "(e)" and inserting "(d)".

Section 2D1.11(a) is amended by striking "below" and inserting "or (e), as appropriate".

Section 2D1.11(e) is amended in Note (A) of the Notes following the "CHEMICAL QUANTITY TABLE" by striking "of this guideline" and inserting "or (e) of this guideline, as appropriate".

The Commentary to § 2D1.11 captioned "Statutory Provisions" is amended by striking "841(d)(1)" and inserting "841(c)(1)"; and by striking "(g)(1)" and inserting "(f)(1)".

The Commentary to § 2D1.13 captioned "Statutory Provisions" is amended by striking "841(d)(3)" and inserting "841(c)(3)"; and by striking "(g)(1)" and inserting "(f)(1)".

The Commentary to § 2N2.1 captioned "Application Notes" is amended in Note 2 by striking "theft, property destruction, or".

Section 2Q1.6(a)(3) is amended by inserting "or" after "(Aggravated Assault);".

Section 2T1.1(c) is amended in Note (D) of subdivision (1) by striking "subdivisions" and inserting "subdivision".

Amendment 568 (effective November 1, 1997) is repromulgated with the following changes:

Section 4B1.4(b)(3)(A) is amended to read as follows:

"(3) (A) 34, if the defendant used or possessed the firearm or ammunition in connection with either a crime of violence, as defined in § 4B1.2(a), or a controlled substance offense, as defined in § 4B1.2(b), or if the firearm possessed by the defendant was of a type described in 26 U.S.C. § 5845(a)*; or";

and § 4B1.4(c)(2) is amended to read as follows:

"(2) Category VI, if the defendant used or possessed the firearm or ammunition in connection with either a crime of violence, as defined in § 4B1.2(a), or a controlled substance offense, as defined in § 4B1.2(b), or if the firearm possessed by the defendant was of a type described in 26 U.S.C. § 5845(a); or".

Section 5C1.1(c)(2) is amended by inserting an asterisk after "confinement".

Section 5C1.1(d)(2) is amended by inserting an asterisk after "confinement".

The Commentary to § 5C1.1 captioned "Application Notes" is amended in the first sentence of subdivision (C) of Note 3 by inserting an asterisk after "confinement".

The Commentary to § 5C1.1 captioned "Application Notes" is amended in the first sentence of subdivision (B) of Note 4 by inserting an asterisk after "confinement".

The Commentary to § 5C1.1 captioned "Application Notes" is amended in the first sentence of Note 6 by inserting an asterisk after "confinement".

The Commentary to § 5C1.1 captioned "Application Notes" is amended by inserting after Application Note 8 the following:

"*Note: Section 3583(d) of title 18, United States Code, provides that '[t]he court may order, as a further condition of supervised release. . .any condition set forth as a discretionary condition of probation in section 3563(b)(1) through (b)(10) and (b)(12) through (b)(20), and any other condition it considers to be appropriate.' Subsection (b)(11) of section 3563 of title 18, United States Code, is explicitly excluded as a condition of supervised release. Before the enactment of the Antiterrorism and Effective Death Penalty Act of 1996, the condition at 18 U.S.C. § 3563(b)(11) was intermittent confinement. The Act deleted 18 U.S.C. § 3563(b)(2), authorizing the payment of a fine as a condition of probation, and redesignated the remaining conditions of probation set forth in 18 U.S.C. § 3563(b); intermittent confinement is now set forth at subsection (b)(10), whereas subsection (b)(11) sets forth the condition of residency at a community corrections facility. It would appear that intermittent confinement now is authorized as a condition of supervised release and that community confinement now is not authorized as a condition of supervised release.

However, there is some question as to whether Congress intended this result. Although the Antiterrorism and Effective Death Penalty Act of 1996 redesignated the remaining paragraphs of section 3563(b), it failed to make the corresponding redesignations in 18 U.S.C. § 3583(d), regarding discretionary conditions of supervised release.".

Section 5D1.2(c) is amended by inserting "(Policy Statement)" before "If the".

Section 5D1.3 is amended by inserting an asterisk after "Confinement" in the heading of subsection (e)(1); and by inserting after subsection (e)(1) the following:

"*Note: Section 3583(d) of title 18, United States Code, provides that '[t]he court may order, as a further condition of supervised release. . .any condition set forth as a discretionary condition of probation in section 3563(b)(1) through (b)(10) and (b)(12) through (b)(20), and any other condition it considers to be appropriate.' Subsection (b)(11) of section 3563 of title 18, United States Code, is explicitly excluded as a condition of supervised release. Before the enactment of the Antiterrorism and Effective Death Penalty Act of 1996, the condition at 18 U.S.C. § 3563(b)(11) was intermittent confinement. The Act deleted 18 U.S.C. § 3563(b)(2), authorizing the payment of a fine as a condition of probation, and redesignated the remaining conditions of probation set forth in 18 U.S.C. § 3563(b); intermittent confinement is now set forth at subsection (b)(10), whereas subsection (b)(11) sets forth the condition of residency at a community corrections facility. It would appear that intermittent confinement now is authorized as a condition of supervised release and that community confinement now is not authorized as a condition of supervised release.

However, there is some question as to whether Congress intended this result. Although the Antiterrorism and Effective Death Penalty Act of 1996 redesignated the remaining paragraphs of section 3563(b), it failed to make the corresponding redesignations in 18 U.S.C. § 3583(d), regarding discretionary conditions of supervised release.".

The Commentary to § 5E1.2 captioned "Application Notes" is amended in Note 5 by inserting "and" before "42 U.S.C. § 6928(d)"; and by striking "; and 42 U.S.C. § 7413(c), which authorizes a fine of up to $25,000 per day for violations of the Clean Air Act".

Section 5F1.1 is amended by striking "release." and inserting the following:

"release.*

*Note: Section 3583(d) of title 18, United States Code, provides that '[t]he court may order, as a further condition of supervised release. . .any condition set forth as a discretionary condition of probation in section 3563(b)(1) through (b)(10) and (b)(12) through (b)(20), and any other condition it considers to be appropriate.' Subsection (b)(11) of section 3563 of title 18, United States Code, is explicitly excluded as a condition of supervised release. Before the enactment of the Antiterrorism and Effective Death Penalty Act of 1996, the condition at 18 U.S.C. § 3563(b)(11) was intermittent confinement. The Act deleted 18 U.S.C. § 3563(b)(2), authorizing the payment of a fine as a condition of probation, and redesignated the remaining conditions of probation set forth in 18 U.S.C. § 3563(b); intermittent confinement is now set forth at subsection (b)(10), whereas subsection (b)(11) sets forth the condition of residency at a community corrections facility. It would appear that intermittent confinement now is authorized as a condition of supervised release and that community confinement now is not authorized as a condition of supervised release.

However, there is some question as to whether Congress intended this result. Although the Antiterrorism and Effective Death Penalty Act of 1996 redesignated the remaining paragraphs of section 3563(b), it failed to make the corresponding redesignations in 18 U.S.C. § 3583(d), regarding discretionary conditions of supervised release.".

The Commentary to § 5F1.5 captioned "Background" is amended in the first paragraph by striking "(b)(6)" each place it appears and inserting "(b)(5)".

The Commentary to § 5F1.5 captioned "Background" is amended by striking the last paragraph as follows:

"   The appellate review provisions permit a defendant to challenge the imposition of a probation condition under 18 U.S.C. § 3563(b)(6) if 'the sentence includes . . . a more limiting condition of probation or supervised release under section 3563(b)(6) . . . than the maximum established in the guideline.' 18 U.S.C. § 3742(a)(3)(A). The government may appeal if the sentence includes a 'less limiting' condition of probation than the minimum established in the guideline. 18 U.S.C. § 3742(b)(3)(A).",

and inserting the following:

"   The appellate review provisions permit a defendant to challenge the imposition of a probation condition under 18 U.S.C. § 3563(b)(5) if the sentence includes a more limiting condition of probation or supervised release than the maximum established in the guideline. See 18 U.S.C. § 3742(a)(3). The government may appeal if the sentence includes a less limiting condition of probation than the minimum established in the guideline. See 18 U.S.C. § 3742(b)(3).".

The Commentary to § 5F1.7 is amended in the first paragraph by inserting "Background:" before "Section 4046"; and by striking "Title" and inserting "title".

Chapter Seven, Part A, Subpart 2 is amended in the second paragraph of subdivision (b) by striking "intermittent confinement," and inserting "residency in, or participation in the program of, a community corrections facility,*"; and by inserting after subdivision (b) the following:

> *Note: Section 3583(d) of title 18, United States Code, provides that '[t]he court may order, as a further condition of supervised release. . .any condition set forth as a discretionary condition of probation in section 3563(b)(1) through (b)(10) and (b)(12) through (b)(20), and any other condition it considers to be appropriate.' Subsection (b)(11) of section 3563 of title 18, United States Code, is explicitly excluded as a condition of supervised release. Before the enactment of the Antiterrorism and Effective Death Penalty Act of 1996, the condition at 18 U.S.C. § 3563(b)(11) was intermittent confinement. The Act deleted 18 U.S.C. § 3563(b)(2), authorizing the payment of a fine as a condition of probation, and redesignated the remaining conditions of probation set forth in 18 U.S.C. § 3563(b); intermittent confinement is now set forth at subsection (b)(10), whereas subsection (b)(11) sets forth the condition of residency at a community corrections facility. It would appear that intermittent confinement now is authorized as a condition of supervised release and that community confinement now is not authorized as a condition of supervised release.
>
> However, there is some question as to whether Congress intended this result. Although the Antiterrorism and Effective Death Penalty Act of 1996 redesignated the remaining paragraphs of section 3563(b), it failed to make the corresponding redesignations in 18 U.S.C. § 3583(d), regarding discretionary conditions of supervised release.".

The Commentary to § 7B1.3 captioned "Application Notes" is amended in Note 5 by striking "(11). Intermittent confinement is not authorized as a condition of supervised release. 18 U.S.C. § 3583(d)." and inserting the following:

> "(10).*
>
> *Note: Section 3583(d) of title 18, United States Code, provides that '[t]he court may order, as a further condition of supervised release. . .any condition set forth as a discretionary condition of probation in section 3563(b)(1) through (b)(10) and (b)(12) through (b)(20), and any other condition it considers to be appropriate.' Subsection (b)(11) of section 3563 of title 18, United States Code, is explicitly excluded as a condition of supervised release. Before the enactment of the Antiterrorism and Effective Death Penalty Act of 1996, the condition at 18 U.S.C. § 3563(b)(11) was intermittent confinement. The Act deleted 18 U.S.C. § 3563(b)(2), authorizing the payment of a fine as a condition of probation, and redesignated the remaining conditions of probation set forth in 18 U.S.C. § 3563(b); intermittent confinement is now set forth at subsection (b)(10), whereas subsection (b)(11) sets forth the condition of residency at a community corrections facility. It would appear that intermittent confinement now is authorized as a condition of supervised release and that community confinement now is not authorized as a condition of supervised release.
>
> However, there is some question as to whether Congress intended this result. Al-

though the Antiterrorism and Effective Death Penalty Act of 1996 redesignated the remaining paragraphs of section 3563(b), it failed to make the corresponding redesignations in 18 U.S.C. § 3583(d), regarding discretionary conditions of supervised release.".

Appendix A (Statutory Index) is amended by inserting after the line referenced to 16 U.S.C. § 1417(a)(5),(6),(b)(2) the following new line:

"16 U.S.C. § 1437(c)   2A2.4";

by inserting after the line referenced to 18 U.S.C. § 2244 the following new line:

"18 U.S.C. § 2245   2A1.1";

in the line referenced to 21 U.S.C. § 841(d)(1),(2) by striking "(d)" and inserting "(c)";

in the line referenced to 21 U.S.C. § 841(d)(3) by striking "(d)" and inserting "(c)";

in the line referenced to 21 U.S.C. § 841(e) by striking "(e)" and inserting "(d)";

in the line referenced to 21 U.S.C. § 841(g)(1) by striking "(g)" and inserting "(f)";

by inserting after the line referenced to 42 U.S.C. § 5157(a) the following new line:

"42 U.S.C. § 5409   2N2.1"; and

by inserting after the line referenced to 42 U.S.C. § 9603(d) the following new line:

"42 U.S.C. § 14905   2B1.1".

Reason for Amendment: This thirteen-part amendment makes several technical and conforming changes to various guideline provisions.

First, the amendment conforms the language concerning offenses that "affected a financial institution" in subsection (b)(2) of § 2B4.1 (Bribery in Procurement of Bank Loan and Other Commercial Bribery) with subsection (b)(12) of § 2B1.1 (Theft, Property Destruction, and Fraud).

Second, the amendment: (1) updates statutory references in §§ 2D1.9 (Placing or Maintaining Dangerous Devices on Federal Property to Protect the Unlawful Production of Controlled Substances; Attempt or Conspiracy), 2D1.11 (Unlawfully Distributing, Importing, Exporting or Possessing a Listed Chemical; Attempt or Conspiracy), and 2D1.13 (Structuring Chemical Transactions or Creating a Chemical Mixture to Evade Reporting or Recordkeeping Requirements; Presenting False or Fraudulent Identification to Obtain a Listed Chemical; Attempt or Conspiracy) and Appendix A (Statutory Index) to correspond to statutory redesignations made by the Hillory J. Farias and Samantha Reid Date-Rape Drug Prohibition Act of 2000, Pub. L. 106–172; and (2) corrects references to the new chemical quantity tables in § 2D1.11.

Third, the amendment corrects a change to the commentary of § 2N2.1 (Violations of Statutes and Regulations Dealing With Any Food, Drug, Biological Product, Device, Cosmetic, or Agricultural Product) that was inadvertently made as part of the conforming package of amendments in the Economic Crime Package (see Supplement to Appendix C, Amendment 617, effective November 1, 2001).

Fourth, the amendment inserts a missing "or" in subsection (a)(3) of § 2Q1.6 (Hazardous or Injurious Devices on Federal Lands).

Fifth, the amendment corrects a grammatical error in Note (D) of subsection (c)(1) of § 2T1.1 (Tax Evasion; Willful Failure to File Return, Supply Information, or Pay Tax; Fraudulent or False Returns, Statements, or Other Documents) by replacing "subdivisions (A), (B), or (C)" with "subdivision (A), (B), or (C)".

Sixth, the amendment repromulgates amendment 568, effective November 1, 1997, to correct an inadvertent omission of a conforming amendment to § 4B1.4 (Armed Career Criminal) from amendment 568.

Seventh, the amendment conforms §§ 5C1.1 (Imposition of a Term of Imprisonment), 5D1.3 (Conditions of Supervised Release), and 5F1.1 (Community Confinement), Part A of Chapter Seven (Violations of Probation and Supervised Release), and § 7B1.3 (Revocation of Probation or Supervised Release) to current statutory provisions at 18 U.S.C. §§ 3563 and 3583 and provides an explanatory note concerning the status of intermittent confinement and community confinement as conditions of supervised release.

Eighth, the amendment clarifies that language in subsection (c) of § 5D1.2 (Term of Supervised Release) is a policy statement (because it recommends the maximum term of supervised release for sex offenders rather than requires it).

Ninth, the amendment deletes from Application Note 5 of § 5E1.2 (Fines for Individual Defendants) an incorrect statement concerning the Clean Air Act.

Tenth, the amendment updates statutory references in § 5F1.5 (Occupational Restrictions).

Eleventh, the amendment inserts a missing "Background" heading in § 5F1.7 (Shock Incarceration Program).

Twelfth, the amendment references 18 U.S.C. § 2245, which covers sexual abuse resulting in death, to § 2A1.1 (First Degree Murder) in Appendix A (Statutory Index) because the offense requires the death of a person.

Finally, the amendment responds to new legislation as follows:

(1) It updates, in § 2B1.1, a statutory reference in the definition of "means of identification" to correspond to a redesignation made by the Internet False Identification Prevention Act of 2000, Pub. L. 106–578.

(2) It provides guideline references in Appendix A for two new offenses created by the American Homeownership and Economic Opportunity Act of 2000, Pub. L. 106–569 ("the Act"). First, section 608 of the Act amends section 610(a) of the National Manufactured Housing Construction and Safety Standards Act of 1974 (42 U.S.C. § 5409(a)) which makes it unlawful to fail to comply with a state's installation program. Under section 611 of the National Housing Construction and Safety Standard Act of 1974 (42 U.S.C. § 5410(b)), knowing and willful violations of subsection 610(a) are punishable by imprisonment of not more than one year. The amendment references this provision to § 2N2.1. Second, section 708 of the Act created section 543 in Title V of the Housing Act of 1949 (42 U.S.C. § 1490(s)(a)), which provides a criminal penalty of not more than five years' imprisonment for equity skimming. The amendment references this provision to § 2B1.1.

(3) It references offenses under section 307(c) of the National Marine Sanctuar-

ies Act (16 U.S.C. § 1437(c)) to § 2A2.4 (Obstructing or Impeding Officers). Section 307(c) of the National Marine Sanctuaries Act, as amended by the National Marine Sanctuaries Amendments Act of 2000, Pub. L. 106–513, prohibits the interference with the enforcement of conservation activities authorized in title 16, United States Code, including refusing to permit any officer authorized to enforce such title to board a vessel for purposes of conducting a search or inspection in connection with the enforcement of such title.

Effective Date: The effective date of this amendment is November 1, 2002.

647. Amendment: Section 2B1.1(b)(1) is amended by striking the period; and by adding at the end the following:

"(O)   More than $200,000,000   add 28
(P)   More than $400,000,000   add 30.".

Section 2B1.1 is amended by striking subsection (b)(2) as follows:

"(2)   (Apply the greater) If the offense—

(A)   (i) involved more than 10, but less than 50, victims; or (ii) was committed through mass-marketing, increase by 2 levels; or

(B)   involved 50 or more victims, increase by 4 levels.",

and inserting the following:

"(2)   (Apply the greatest) If the offense—

(A)   (i) involved 10 or more victims; or (ii) was committed through mass-marketing, increase by 2 levels;

(B)   involved 50 or more victims, increase by 4 levels; or

(C)   involved 250 or more victims, increase by 6 levels.".

Section 2B1.1 is amended by striking subsection (b)(12)(B) as follows:

"(B)   the offense substantially jeopardized the safety and soundness of a financial institution, increase by 4 levels.",

and inserting the following:

"(B)   the offense (i) substantially jeopardized the safety and soundness of a financial institution; (ii) substantially endangered the solvency or financial security of an organization that, at any time during the offense, (I) was a publicly traded company; or (II) had 1,000 or more employees; or (iii) substantially endangered the solvency or financial security of 100 or more victims, increase by 4 levels.".

Section 2B1.1(b) is amended by adding at the end the following:

"(13)   If the offense involved a violation of securities law and, at the time of the offense, the defendant was an officer or a director of a publicly traded company, increase by 4 levels.".

The Commentary to § 2B1.1 captioned "Statutory Provisions" is amended by inserting "1348, 1350," after "1341-1344,".

The Commentary to § 2B1.1 captioned "Application Notes" is amended in Note 1 by adding after "Resources)." the following new paragraph:

"'Equity securities' has the meaning given that term in section 3(a)(11) of the Securities Exchange Act of 1934 (15 U.S.C. § 78c(a)(11)).";

by inserting after "Secretary of the Interior." the following new paragraph:

"'Publicly traded company' means an issuer (A) with a class of securities registered under section 12 of the Securities Exchange Act of 1934 (15 U.S.C. § 78l); or (B) that is required to file reports under section 15(d) of the Securities Exchange Act of 1934 (15 U.S.C. § 78o(d)). 'Issuer' has the meaning given that term in section 3 of the Securities Exchange Act of 1934 (15 U.S.C. § 78c).";

and by adding at the end the following:

"'Victim' means (A) any person who sustained any part of the actual loss determined under subsection (b)(1); or (B) any individual who sustained bodily injury as a result of the offense. 'Person' includes individuals, corporations, companies, associations, firms, partnerships, societies, and joint stock companies.".

The Commentary to § 2B1.1 captioned "Application Notes" is amended in Note 2(C) by redesignating subdivision (iv) as (v); and by adding after subdivision (iii) the following new subdivision:

"(iv) The reduction that resulted from the offense in the value of equity securities or other corporate assets.".

The Commentary to § 2B1.1 captioned "Application Notes" is amended in Note 3 by striking "Victim and Mass-Marketing Enhancement under" in the heading and inserting "Application of"; by striking subdivision (A) as follows:

"(A) Definitions.— For purposes of subsection (b)(2):

(i) 'Mass-marketing' means a plan, program, promotion, or campaign that is conducted through solicitation by telephone, mail, the Internet, or other means to induce a large number of persons to (I) purchase goods or services; (II) participate in a contest or sweepstakes; or (III) invest for financial profit. 'Mass-marketing' includes, for example, a telemarketing campaign that solicits a large number of individuals to purchase fraudulent life insurance policies.

(ii) 'Victim' means (I) any person who sustained any part of the actual loss determined under subsection (b)(1); or (II) any individual who sustained bodily injury as a result of the offense. 'Person' includes individuals, corporations, companies, associations, firms, partnerships, societies, and joint stock companies.",

and inserting the following:

"(A) Definition.— For purposes of subsection (b)(2), 'mass-marketing' means a plan, program, promotion, or campaign that is conducted through solicitation by telephone, mail, the Internet, or other means to induce a large number of persons to (i) purchase goods or services; (ii) participate in a contest or sweepstakes; or (iii) invest for financial profit. 'Mass-marketing' includes, for example, a telemarketing campaign that solicits a large number of individuals to purchase fraudulent life insurance policies.";

in subdivision (B)(i)(I) by striking "described in subdivision (A)(ii) of this note;" and inserting "any victim as defined in Application Note 1;";

in subdivision (B)(ii)(IV) by inserting "at least" after "to have involved"; and in subdivision (C) by inserting "or (C)" after "(B)".

The Commentary to § 2B1.1 captioned "Application Notes" is amended by redesignating Notes 11 through 15 as Notes 12 through 16, respectively.

The Commentary to § 2B1.1 captioned "Application Notes" is amended by striking Note 10 as follows:

"10. Enhancement for Substantially Jeopardizing the Safety and Soundness of a Financial Institution under Subsection (b)(12)(B).—For purposes of subsection (b)(12)(B), an offense shall be considered to have substantially jeopardized the safety and soundness of a financial institution if, as a consequence of the offense, the institution (A) became insolvent; (B) substantially reduced benefits to pensioners or insureds; (C) was unable on demand to refund fully any deposit, payment, or investment; (D) was so depleted of its assets as to be forced to merge with another institution in order to continue active operations; or (E) was placed in substantial jeopardy of any of subdivisions (A) through (D) of this note.",

and inserting the following:

"10. Application of Subsection (b)(12)(B).—

(A) Application of Subsection (b)(12)(B)(i).—The following is a non-exhaustive list of factors that the court shall consider in determining whether, as a result of the offense, the safety and soundness of a financial institution was substantially jeopardized:

(i) The financial institution became insolvent.

(ii) The financial institution substantially reduced benefits to pensioners or insureds.

(iii) The financial institution was unable on demand to refund fully any deposit, payment, or investment.

(iv) The financial institution was so depleted of its assets as to be forced to merge with another institution in order to continue active operations.

(B) Application of Subsection (b)(12)(B)(ii).—

(i) Definition.—For purposes of this subsection, 'organization' has the meaning given that term in Application Note 1 of § 8A1.1 (Applicability of Chapter Eight).

(ii) In General.—The following is a non-exhaustive list of factors that the court shall consider in determining whether, as a result of the offense, the solvency or financial security of an organization that was a publicly traded company or that had more than 1000 employees was substantially endangered:

(I) The organization became insolvent or suffered a substantial reduction in the value of its assets.

(II) The organization filed for bankruptcy under Chapters 7, 11, or 13 of the Bankruptcy Code (title 11, United States Code).

(III) The organization suffered a substantial reduction in the value of its equity securities or the value of its employee retirement accounts.

(IV) The organization substantially reduced its workforce.

(V) The organization substantially reduced its employee pension benefits.

(VI) The liquidity of the equity securities of a publicly traded company was substantially endangered. For example, the company was delisted from its primary listing exchange, or trading of the company's securities was halted for more than one full trading day.

11. Application of Subsection (b)(13).—

(A) Definition.—For purposes of this subsection, 'securities law' (i) means 18 U.S.C. §§ 1348, 1350, and the provisions of law referred to in section 3(a)(47) of the Securities Exchange Act of 1934 (15 U.S.C. § 78c(a)(47)); and (ii) includes the rules, regulations, and orders issued by the Securities and Exchange Commission pursuant to the provisions of law referred to in such section.

(B) In General.—A conviction under a securities law is not required in order for subsection (b)(13) to apply. This subsection would apply in the case of a defendant convicted under a general fraud statute if the defendant's conduct violated a securities law. For example, this subsection would apply if an officer of a publicly traded company violated regulations issued by the Securities and Exchange Commission by fraudulently influencing an independent audit of the company's financial statements for the purposes of rendering such financial statements materially misleading, even if the officer is convicted only of wire fraud.

(C) Nonapplicability of § 3B1.3 (Abuse of Position of Trust or Use of Special Skill).—If subsection (b)(13) applies, do not apply § 3B1.3.".

The Commentary to § 2B1.1 captioned "Application Notes" is amended in Note 16, as redesignated by this amendment, by striking subdivision (v) as follows:

Amendment 647

"(v) The offense endangered the solvency or financial security of one or more victims.";

and by redesignating subdivisions (vi) and (vii) as subdivisions (v) and (vi), respectively.

The Commentary to § 2B1.1 captioned "Background" is amended in the last paragraph by inserting "(i)" after "(B)".

Section 2E5.3 is amended in the heading by adding at the end "; Destruction and Failure to Maintain Corporate Audit Records".

Section 2E5.3 is amended by striking subsection (a)(2) as follows:

"(2) If the offense was committed to facilitate or conceal a theft or embezzlement, or an offense involving a bribe or a gratuity, apply § 2B1.1 or § 2E5.1, as applicable.",

and inserting the following:

"(2) If the offense was committed to facilitate or conceal (A) an offense involving a theft, a fraud, or an embezzlement; (B) an offense involving a bribe or a gratuity; or (C) an obstruction of justice offense, apply § 2B1.1 (Theft, Property Destruction, and Fraud), § 2E5.1 (Offering, Accepting, or Soliciting a Bribe or Gratuity Affecting the Operation of an Employee Welfare or Pension Benefit Plan; Prohibited Payments or Lending of Money by Employer or Agent to Employees, Representatives, or Labor Organizations), or § 2J1.2 (Obstruction of Justice), as applicable.".

The Commentary to § 2E5.3 captioned "Statutory Provisions" is amended by inserting "§ " before "1027"; and by inserting ", 1520" after "1027".

Section 2J1.2(a) is amended by striking "12" and inserting "14".

Section 2J1.2(b) is amended by adding at the end the following:

"(3) If the offense (A) involved the destruction, alteration, or fabrication of a substantial number of records, documents, or tangible objects; (B) involved the selection of any essential or especially probative record, document, or tangible object, to destroy or alter; or (C) was otherwise extensive in scope, planning, or preparation, increase by 2 levels.".

The Commentary to § 2J1.2 captioned "Statutory Provisions" is amended by inserting ", 1519" after "1516".

Section 2T4.1 is amended in the table by striking the period; and by adding at the end the following:

"(O) More than $200,000,000   34
 (P) More than $400,000,000   36.".

Appendix A (Statutory Index) is amended by inserting after the line referenced to 18 U.S.C. § 1347 the following new lines:

```
"18 U.S.C. § 1348     2B1.1
 18 U.S.C. § 1349     2X1.1
 18 U.S.C. § 1350     2B1.1".
```

Appendix A (Statutory Index) is amended in the line referenced to 18 U.S.C. § 1512(c) by striking "(c)" and inserting "(d)".

Appendix A (Statutory Index) is amended by inserting after the line referenced to 18 U.S.C. § 1512(b) the following new line:

```
"18 U.S.C. § 1512(c)    2J1.2".
```

Appendix A (Statutory Index) is amended by inserting after the line referenced to 18 U.S.C. § 1518 the following new lines:

```
"18 U.S.C. § 1519     2J1.2
 18 U.S.C. § 1520     2E5.3".
```

Reason for Amendment: This amendment implements directives to the Commission contained in sections 805, 905, and 1104 of the Sarbanes-Oxley Act of 2002, Pub. L. 107–56 (the "Act"), by making several modifications to § 2B1.1 (Larceny, Embezzlement, and Other Forms of Theft; Offenses Involving Stolen Property; Property Damage or Destruction; Fraud and Deceit; Forgery; Offenses Involving Altered or Counterfeit Instruments Other than Counterfeit Bearer Obligations of the United States) and § 2J1.2 (Obstruction of Justice). The directives pertain to serious fraud and related offenses and obstruction of justice offenses. The directives require the Commission under emergency amendment authority to promulgate amendments addressing, among other things, officers and directors of publicly traded companies who commit fraud and related offenses, fraud offenses that endanger the solvency or financial security of a substantial number of victims, fraud offenses that involve significantly greater than 50 victims, and obstruction of justice offenses that involve the destruction of evidence.

First, the amendment addresses the directive contained in section 1104(b)(5) of the Act to "ensure that the guideline offense levels and enhancements under United States Sentencing Guideline § 2B1.1 (as in effect on the date of enactment of this Act) are sufficient for a fraud offense when the number of victims adversely involved is significantly greater than 50." The amendment implements this directive by expanding the existing enhancement at § 2B1.1(b)(2) based on the number of victims involved in the offense. Prior to the amendment, subsection (b)(2) provided a two level enhancement if the offense involved more than 10, but less than 50, victims (or was committed through mass-marketing), and a four level enhancement if the offense involved 50 or more victims. The amendment provides an additional two level increase, for a total of six levels, if the offense involved 250 or more victims. The Commission determined that an enhancement of this magnitude appropriately responds to the pertinent directive and reflects the extensive nature of, and the large scale victimization caused by, such offenses.

Second, the amendment addresses directives contained in sections 805 and 1104 of the Act pertaining to securities and accounting fraud offenses and fraud offenses that endanger the solvency or financial security of a substantial number of victims. Specifically, section 805(a)(4) directs the Commission to ensure that "a specific offense characteristic enhancing sentencing is provided under United States Sentencing Guideline 2B1.1 (as in effect on the date of enactment of this Act) for a fraud offense that endangers the solvency or financial security of a substantial number of victims." In addition, section 1104(b)(1) directs the Commission to "ensure that the sentencing guidelines and policy statements reflect the serious nature of securities, pension, and accounting fraud and the need for aggressive and appropriate law enforcement action to prevent such offenses." The amendment implements these directives by expanding the scope of the existing enhancement at § 2B1.1(b)(12)(B).

Prior to the amendment, § 2B1.1(b)(12)(B) provided a four level enhancement and a minimum offense level of 24 if the offense substantially jeopardized the safety and soundness of a financial institution. The amendment expands the scope of this enhancement by providing two additional prongs. The first prong applies to offenses that substantially endanger the solvency or financial security of an organization that, at any time during the offense, was a publicly traded company or had 1,000 or more employees. The addition of this prong reflects the Commission's determination that such an offense undermines the public's confidence in the securities and investment market much in the same manner as an offense that jeopardizes the safety and soundness of a financial institution undermines the public's confidence in the banking system. This prong also reflects the likelihood that an offense that endangers the solvency or financial security of an employer of this size will similarly affect a substantial number of individual victims, without requiring the court to determine whether the solvency or financial security of each individual victim was substantially endangered.

A corresponding application note for § 2B1.1(b)(12)(B) sets forth a non-exhaustive list of factors that the court shall consider in determining whether the offense endangered the solvency or financial security of a publicly traded company or an organization with 1,000 or more employees. The list of factors includes references to insolvency, filing for bankruptcy, substantially reducing the value of the company's stock, and substantially reducing the company's workforce among the list of factors that the court shall consider when applying the new enhancement, and other factors not enumerated in the application note could be considered by the court as appropriate.

The amendment also modifies the application note of the previously existing prong of § 2B1.1(b)(12)(B), the financial institutions enhancement, to be consistent structurally with the new prongs of the enhancement. Prior to the amendment, the presence of any one of the factors enumerated in the application note would trigger the financial institutions enhancement under § 2B1.1(b)(12)(B). Under the amendment, the application note to the financial institutions enhancement sets forth a non-exhaustive list of factors that the court shall consider in determining whether the offense substantially jeopardized the safety and soundness of a financial institution. The list of factors that the court shall consider when applying this enhancement includes references to insolvency, substantially reducing benefits to pensioners and insureds, and an inability to refund fully any deposit, payment, or investment on demand.

The second prong added to § 2B1.1(b)(12)(B) by the amendment applies to offenses that substantially endangered the solvency or financial security of 100 or more victims, regardless of whether a publicly traded company or other organization was affected by the offense. The Commission concluded that the specificity of the directive in section 805(a)(4) required an enhancement focused specifically on conduct that endangers the financial security of individual victims. Thus, use of this prong of the enhancement will be appropriate in cases in which there is sufficient evidence for the court to determine that the amount of loss suffered by individual victims of the offense substantially endangered the solvency or financial security of those victims. The Commission also determined that the enhancement provided in § 2B1.1(b)(12)(B) shall apply cumulatively with the enhancement at § 2B1.1(b)(2), which is based solely on the number of victims involved in the offense, to reflect the particularly acute harm suffered by victims of offenses for which the new prongs of subsection (b)(12)(B) apply.

Third, the amendment addresses the directive contained at section 1104(a)(2) of the Act to "consider the promulgation of new sentencing guidelines or amendments to existing sentencing guidelines to provide an enhancement for officers or directors of publicly traded corporations who commit fraud and related offenses." The amendment implements this directive by providing a new, four level enhancement at § 2B1.1(b)(13) that applies if the offense involved a violation of securities law and, at the time of the offense, the defendant was an officer or director of a publicly traded company. The Commission concluded that a four level enhancement appropriately reflects that an officer or director of a publicly traded company who commits such an offense violates certain heightened fiduciary duties imposed by securities law upon such individuals. Accordingly, the court is not required to determine specifically whether the defendant abused a position of trust in order for the enhancement to apply, and a corresponding application note provides that, in cases in which the new, four level enhancement applies, the existing two level enhancement for abuse of position of trust at § 3B1.3 (Abuse of Position of Trust or Use of Special Skill) shall not apply.

The corresponding application note also expressly provides that the enhancement would apply regardless of whether the defendant was convicted under a specific securities fraud statute (e.g., 18 U.S.C. § 1348, a new offense created by the Act specifically prohibiting securities fraud) or under a general fraud statute (e.g., 18 U.S.C. § 1341, prohibiting mail fraud), provided that the offense involved a violation of "securities law" as defined in the application note.

Fourth, the amendment expands the loss table at § 2B1.1(b)(1) to punish adequately offenses that cause catastrophic losses of magnitudes previously unforeseen, such as the serious corporate scandals that gave rise to several portions of the Act. Prior to the amendment, the loss table at § 2B1.1(b)(1) provided sentencing enhancements in two level increments up to a maximum of 26 levels for offenses in which the loss exceeded $100,000,000. The amendment adds two additional loss amount categories to the table; an increase of 28 levels for offenses in which the loss exceeded $200,000,000, and an increase of 30 levels for offenses in which the loss exceeded $400,000,000. These additions to the loss table address congressional concern regarding particularly extensive and serious fraud offenses, and more fully effectuate increases in statutory maximum penalties provided by the Act (e.g., the increase in the statutory maximum penalties for wire fraud and mail fraud offenses from five to 20 years set forth in section 903 of the Act). The amendment also modifies the tax table in § 2T4.1 in a similar manner to maintain the longstanding proportional relationship between the loss table in § 2B1.1 and the tax table.

The amendment also adds a new factor to the general, enumerated factors that the court may consider in determining the amount of loss under § 2B1.1(b)(1). Specifically, the amendment adds the reduction in the value of equity securities or other corporate assets that resulted from the offense to the list of general factors set forth in Application Note 2(C) of § 2B1.1. This factor was added to provide courts additional guidance in determining loss in certain cases, particularly in complex white collar cases.

Fifth, the amendment modifies § 2J1.2 to address the directives pertaining to obstruction of justice offenses contained in sections 805 and 1104 of the Act. Specifically, section 805(a) of the Act directs the Commission to ensure that the base offense level and existing enhancements in § 2J1.2 are sufficient to deter and punish obstruction of justice offenses generally, and specifically are adequate in cases involving the destruction, alteration, or fabrication of a large amount of evidence, a large number of participants, the selection of

Amendment 647

evidence that is particularly probative or essential to the investigation, more than minimal planning, or abuse of a special skill or a position of trust. Section 1104(b) of the Act further directs the Commission to ensure that the "guideline offense levels and enhancements for an obstruction of justice offense are adequate in cases where documents or other physical evidence are actually destroyed or fabricated."

The amendment implements these directives by making two modifications to § 2J1.2. First, the amendment increases the base offense level in § 2J1.2 from level 12 to level 14. Second, the amendment adds a new two level enhancement to § 2J1.2. This enhancement applies if the offense (i) involved the destruction, alteration, or fabrication of a substantial number of records, documents or tangible objects; (ii) involved the selection of any essential or especially probative record, document, or tangible object to destroy or alter; or (iii) was otherwise extensive in scope, planning, or preparation. The Commission determined that existing adjustments in Chapter Three for aggravating role, § 3B1.1, and abuse of position of trust or use of special skill, § 3B1.3, adequately account for those particular factors described in section 805(a) of the Act.

Sixth, the amendment addresses new offenses created by the Act. Section 1520 of title 18, United States Code, relating to destruction of corporate audit records, is referenced to § 2E5.3 (False Statements and Concealment of Facts in Relation to Documents Required by the Employee Retirement Income Security Act; Failure to Maintain and Falsification of Records Required by the Labor Management Reporting and Disclosure Act; Destruction and Failure to Maintain Corporate Audit Records). Section 1520 provides a statutory maximum penalty of ten years' imprisonment for knowing and willful violations of document maintenance requirements as set forth in that section or in rules or regulations to be promulgated by the Securities and Exchange Commission pursuant to that section. The amendment also expands the existing cross reference in § 2E5.3(a)(2) specifically to cover fraud and obstruction of justice offenses. Accordingly, if a defendant who is convicted under 18 U.S.C. § 1520 committed the offense in order to obstruct justice, the amendment to the cross reference provision requires the court to apply § 2J1.2 instead of § 2E5.3. Other new offenses are listed in Appendix A (Statutory Index), as well as in the statutory provisions of the relevant guidelines.

Effective Date: The effective date of this amendment is January 25, 2003.

648. Amendment: Chapter Two, Part C is amended in the heading by adding at the end "AND VIOLATIONS OF FEDERAL ELECTION CAMPAIGN LAWS".

Chapter Two, Part C is amended by striking the introductory commentary as follows:

> "   Introductory Commentary
>
> The Commission believes that pre-guidelines sentencing practice did not adequately reflect the seriousness of public corruption offenses. Therefore, these guidelines provide for sentences that are considerably higher than average pre-guidelines practice.".

Chapter Two, Part C is amended by adding at the end the following new guideline and accompanying commentary:

> "§ 2C1.8. Making, Receiving, or Failing to Report a Contribution, Donation, or Expenditure in Violation of the Federal Election Campaign Act; Fraudulently Misrepresenting Campaign Authority; Soliciting or Receiving a Donation in Connection with an Election While on Certain Federal Property

(a) Base Offense Level: 8

(b) Specific Offense Characteristics

    (1) If the value of the illegal transactions exceeded $5,000, increase by the number of levels from the table in § 2B1.1 (Theft, Property Destruction, and Fraud) corresponding to that amount.

    (2) (Apply the greater) If the offense involved, directly or indirectly, an illegal transaction made by or received from—

        (A) a foreign national, increase by 2 levels; or

        (B) a government of a foreign country, increase by 4 levels.

    (3) If (A) the offense involved the contribution, donation, solicitation, expenditure, disbursement, or receipt of governmental funds; or (B) the defendant committed the offense for the purpose of obtaining a specific, identifiable non-monetary Federal benefit, increase by 2 levels.

    (4) If the defendant engaged in 30 or more illegal transactions, increase by 2 levels.

    (5) If the offense involved a contribution, donation, solicitation, or expenditure made or obtained through intimidation, threat of pecuniary or other harm, or coercion, increase by 4 levels.

(c) Cross Reference

    (1) If the offense involved a bribe or gratuity, apply § 2C1.1 (Offering, Giving, Soliciting, or Receiving a Bribe; Extortion Under Color of Official Right) or § 2C1.2 (Offering, Giving, Soliciting, or Receiving a Gratuity), as appropriate, if the resulting offense level is greater than the offense level determined above.

<u>Commentary</u>

<u>Statutory Provisions</u>: 2 U.S.C. §§ 437g(d)(1), 439a, 441a, 441a-1, 441b, 441c, 441d, 441e, 441f, 441g, 441h(a), 441i, 441k; 18 U.S.C. § 607. For additional provision(s), <u>see</u> Statutory Index (Appendix A).

<u>Application Notes</u>:

1. <u>Definitions</u>.—For purposes of this guideline:

'Foreign national' has the meaning given that term in section 319(b) of the Federal Election Campaign Act of 1971, 2 U.S.C. § 441e(b).

'Government of a foreign country' has the meaning given that term in section 1(e) of the Foreign Agents Registration Act of 1938 (22 U.S.C. § 611(e)).

'Governmental funds' means money, assets, or property, of the United States government, of a State government, or of a local government, including any branch, subdivision, department, agency, or other component of any such government. 'State' means any of the fifty States, the District of Columbia, the Commonwealth of Puerto Rico, the United States Virgin Islands, Guam, the Northern Mariana Islands, or American Samoa. 'Local government' means the government of a political subdivision of a State.

'Illegal transaction' means (A) any contribution, donation, solicitation, or expenditure of money or anything of value, or any other conduct, prohibited by the Federal Election Campaign Act of 1971, 2 U.S.C. § 431 et seq; (B) any contribution, donation, solicitation, or expenditure of money or anything of value made in excess of the amount of such contribution, donation, solicitation, or expenditure that may be made under such Act; and (C) in the case of a violation of 18 U.S.C. § 607, any solicitation or receipt of money or anything of value under that section. The terms 'contribution' and 'expenditure' have the meaning given those terms in section 301(8) and (9) of the Federal Election Campaign Act of 1971 (2 U.S.C. § 431(8) and (9)), respectively.

2. Application of Subsection (b)(3)(B).—Subsection (b)(3)(B) provides an enhancement for a defendant who commits the offense for the purpose of achieving a specific, identifiable non-monetary Federal benefit that does not rise to the level of a bribe or a gratuity. Subsection (b)(3)(B) is not intended to apply to offenses under this guideline in which the defendant's only motivation for commission of the offense is generally to achieve increased visibility with, or heightened access to, public officials. Rather, subsection (b)(3)(B) is intended to apply to defendants who commit the offense to obtain a specific, identifiable non-monetary Federal benefit, such as a Presidential pardon or information proprietary to the government.

3. Application of Subsection (b)(4).—Subsection (b)(4) shall apply if the defendant engaged in any combination of 30 or more illegal transactions during the course of the offense, whether or not the illegal transactions resulted in a conviction for such conduct.

4. Departure Provision.—In a case in which the defendant's conduct was part of a systematic or pervasive corruption of a governmental function, process, or office that may cause loss of public confidence in government, an upward departure may be warranted.".

Section 3D1.2(d) is amended by inserting ", 2C1.8" after "2C1.7".

The Commentary to § 5E1.2 captioned "Application Notes" is amended in the second sentence of Note 5 by striking "and" after "Control Act;" and by inserting before the period at the end the following:

"; and 2 U.S.C. § 437g(d)(1)(D), which authorizes, for violations of the Federal Election Campaign Act under 2 U.S.C. § 441f, a fine up to the greater of $50,000 or 1,000 percent of the amount of the violation, and which requires, in the case of such a violation, a minimum fine of not less than 300 percent of the amount of the violation.

There may be cases in which the defendant has entered into a conciliation agreement with the Federal Election Commission under section 309 of the Federal Election Campaign Act of 1971 in order to correct or prevent a violation of such Act by the defendant. The existence of a conciliation agreement between the defendant and Federal Election Commission, and the extent of compliance with that conciliation agreement, may be appropriate factors in determining at what point within the applicable fine guideline range to sentence the defendant, unless the defendant began negotiations toward a conciliation agreement after becoming aware of a criminal investigation".

Appendix A (Statutory Index) is amended by inserting before the line referenced to 7 U.S.C. § 6 the following new lines:

"2 U.S.C. § 437g(d)	2C1.8
2 U.S.C. § 439a	2C1.8
2 U.S.C. § 441a	2C1.8
2 U.S.C. § 441a-1	2C1.8
2 U.S.C. § 441b	2C1.8
2 U.S.C. § 441c	2C1.8
2 U.S.C. § 441d	2C1.8
2 U.S.C. § 441e	2C1.8
2 U.S.C. § 441f	2C1.8
2 U.S.C. § 441g	2C1.8
2 U.S.C. § 441h(a)	2C1.8
2 U.S.C. § 441i	2C1.8
2 U.S.C. § 441k	2C1.8".

Appendix A (Statutory Index) is amended by inserting after the line referenced to 18 U.S.C. § 597 the following new line:

"18 U.S.C. § 607   2C1.8".

Reason for Amendment: This amendment implements the directive from Congress contained in the Bipartisan Campaign Reform Act of 2002, Pub. L. 107–155, (the "BCRA") to the effect that the Commission "promulgate a guideline, or amend an existing guideline . . ., for penalties for violations of the Federal Election Campaign Act of 1971 (the "FECA") and related election laws . . . .". The BCRA significantly increased statutory penalties for campaign finance crimes, formerly misdemeanors under the FECA. The new statutory maximum term of imprisonment for even the least serious of these offenses is now two years and for more serious offenses, the maximum term of imprisonment is five years.

To effectively punish these offenses, the Commission chose to create a new guideline at § 2C1.8 (Making, Receiving, or Failing to Report a Contribution, Donation, or Expenditure in Violation of the Federal Election Campaign Act; Fraudulently Misrepresenting Campaign Authority; Soliciting or Receiving a Donation in Connection with an Election While on Certain Federal Property). The Commission opted against simply amending an existing guideline because it determined after review that the characteristics of election-violation cases did not bear sufficient similarity to cases sentenced under any existing guideline. The offenses which will be sentenced under § 2C1.8 include: violations of the statutory prohibitions against "soft money" (2 U.S.C. § 441i); restrictions on "hard money" contributions (2 U.S.C. § 441a); contributions by foreign nationals (2 U.S.C. § 441e); restrictions on "electioneering communications" as defined at 2 U.S.C. § 434(f)(3)(C)); certain fraudulent misrepresentations (2 U.S.C. § 441h); and "conduit contributions" (2

U.S.C. § 441f).

The new guideline has a base offense level of level 8, which reflects the fact that these offenses, while they are somewhat similar to fraud offenses (sentenced under § 2B1.1 (Theft, Property Destruction, and Fraud) at a base offense level of level 6), generally are more serious due to the additional harm, or the potential harm, of corrupting the elective process.

The new guideline provides five specific offense characteristics to ensure appropriate penalty enhancements for aggravating conduct which may occur during the commission of certain campaign finance offenses. First, the new guideline provides a specific offense characteristic, at § 2C1.8(b)(1), that uses the fraud loss table in § 2B1.1 to incrementally increase the offense level in proportion to the monetary amounts involved in the illegal transactions. This both assures proportionality with penalties for fraud offenses and responds to Congress' directive to provide an enhancement for "a large aggregate amount of illegal contributions."

Second, the new guideline provides alternative enhancements, at § 2C1.8(b)(2), if the offense involved a foreign national (two levels) or a foreign government (four levels). These enhancements respond to another specific directive in the BCRA and reflect the seriousness of foreign entities attempting to tamper with the United States' election processes.

Third, the new guideline provides alternative two level enhancements, at § 2C1.8(b)(3), when the offense involves either "governmental funds," defined broadly to include Federal, State, or local funds, or an intent to derive "a specific, identifiable non-monetary Federal benefit" (e.g., a presidential pardon). Each of these enhancements responds to specific directives of the BCRA.

Fourth, the new guideline provides a two level enhancement, at subsection (b)(4), when the offender engages in "30 or more illegal transactions." After a review of all campaign finance cases in the Commission's datafile, the Commission chose 30 transactions as the number best illustrative of a "large number" in that context. This enhancement also responds to a specific directive in the BCRA to the effect that the Commission provide enhanced sentencing for cases involving "a large number of illegal transactions."

Fifth, the new guideline provides a 4 level enhancement, at § 2C1.8(b)(5), if the offense involves the use of "intimidation, threat of pecuniary or other harm, or coercion." This enhancement responds to information received from the Federal Election Commission and the Public Integrity Section of the Department of Justice which characterizes offenses of this type as some of the most aggravated offenses committed under the FECA.

The new guideline also provides a cross reference, at subsection (c), which directs the sentencing court to apply either § 2C1.1 or § 2C1.2, as appropriate, if the offense involved a bribe or a gratuity and the resulting offense level would be greater than that determined under § 2C1.8.

Section 3D1.2 (Groups of Closely Related Counts) has been amended, consistent with the principles underlying the rules for grouping multiple counts of conviction, to include § 2C1.8 offenses among those in which the offense level is determined largely on the basis of the total amount of harm or loss or some other measure of aggregate harm. (See § 3D1.2(d)).

Finally, § 5E1.2 (Fines for Individual Defendants) has been amended to specifically reflect fine provisions unique to the FECA. This part of the amendment also provides that the defendant's participation in a conciliation agreement with the Federal Election Commission may be an appropriate factor for use in determining the specific fine within the applicable fine guideline range unless the defendant began negotiations with the Federal Election Commission after the defendant became aware that he or it was the subject of a criminal investigation.

Effective Date: The effective date of this amendment is January 25, 2003.

649. **Amendment:** Section 2G2.2(b) is amended by adding at the end the following:

> "(6) If the offense involved—
>
>> (A) at least 10 images, but fewer than 150, increase by 2 levels;
>>
>> (B) at least 150 images, but fewer than 300, increase by 3 levels;
>>
>> (C) at least 300 images, but fewer than 600, increase by 4 levels; and
>>
>> (D) 600 or more images, increase by 5 levels.".

The Commentary to § 2G2.2 is amended by adding at the end the following:

> "<u>Background</u>: Section 401(i)(1)(C) of Public Law 108–121 directly amended subsection (b) to add subdivision (6), effective April 30, 2003.".

Section 2G2.4(b) is amended by adding at the end the following:

> "(4) If the offense involved material that portrays sadistic or masochistic conduct or other depictions of violence, increase by 4 levels.
>
> (5) If the offense involved—
>
>> (A) at least 10 images, but fewer than 150, increase by 2 levels;
>>
>> (B) at least 150 images, but fewer than 300, increase by 3 levels;
>>
>> (C) at least 300 images, but fewer than 600, increase by 4 levels; and
>>
>> (D) 600 or more images, increase by 5 levels.".

The Commentary to § 2G2.4 is amended by adding at the end the following:

> "<u>Background</u>: Section 401(i)(1)(B) of Public Law 108–21 directly amended subsection (b) to add subdivisions (4) and (5), effective April 30, 2003.".

Section 3E1.1(b) is amended by inserting "upon motion of the government stating that" before "the defendant has assisted authorities"; and by striking the following:

> "taking one or more of the following steps:
>
> (1) timely providing complete information to the government concerning his own involvement in the offense; or
>
> (2) timely notifying authorities of his intention to enter a plea of guilty, thereby permitting the government to avoid preparing for trial and permitting the court to allocate its resources efficiently,

decrease the offense level by 1 additional level",

and inserting "timely notifying authorities of his intention to enter a plea of guilty, thereby permitting the government to avoid preparing for trial and permitting the government and the court to allocate their resources efficiently, decrease the offense level by 1 additional level".

The Commentary to § 3E1.1 captioned "Application Notes" is amended in Note 6 by striking "one or both of"; by striking "(1) or (2)"; by striking "(b)(2)" and inserting "(b)"; and by adding at the end the following new paragraph:

> "Because the Government is in the best position to determine whether the defendant has assisted authorities in a manner that avoids preparing for trial, an adjustment under subsection (b) may only be granted upon a formal motion by the Government at the time of sentencing. See section 401(g)(2)(B) of Pub. L. 108–21.".

The Commentary to § 3E1.1 captioned "Background" is amended by striking "one or more of" both places it appears; and by adding at the end the following:

> "   Section 401(g) of Public Law 108–21 directly amended subsection (b), Application Note 6 (including adding the last paragraph of that application note), and the Background Commentary, effective April 30, 2003.".

The Commentary to § 4B1.5 captioned "Application Notes" is amended in Note 4(B) by striking subdivision (i) as follows:

> "(i)   In General.—For purposes of subsection (b), the defendant engaged in a pattern of activity involving prohibited sexual conduct if—
>
> > (I)   on at least two separate occasions, the defendant engaged in prohibited sexual conduct with a minor; and
> >
> > (II)   there were at least two minor victims of the prohibited sexual conduct.
>
> For example, the defendant engaged in a pattern of activity involving prohibited sexual conduct if there were two separate occasions of prohibited sexual conduct and each such occasion involved a different minor, or if there were two separate occasions of prohibited sexual conduct involving the same two minors.";

and inserting:

> "(i)   In General.—For purposes of subsection (b), the defendant engaged in a pattern of activity involving prohibited sexual conduct if on at least two separate occasions, the defendant engaged in prohibited sexual conduct with a minor.".

The Commentary to § 4B1.5 captioned "Background" is amended by striking "section 632 of Pub. L. 102–141 and section 505 of Pub. L. 105–314" and inserting "section 632 of Public Law 102–141 and section 505 of Public Law 105–314"; and by adding at the end the following:

> "   Section 401(i)(1)(A) of Public Law 108–21 directly amended Application Note 4(b)(i), effective April 30, 2003.".

Section 5H1.6 is amended by striking "Family ties" and inserting "In sentencing a defendant convicted of an offense other than an offense described in the following paragraph, family ties";

and by inserting after the first sentence the following new paragraph:

"In sentencing a defendant convicted of an offense involving a minor victim under section 1201, an offense under section 1591, or an offense under chapter 71, 109A, 110, or 117, of title 18, United States Code, family ties and responsibilities and community ties are not relevant in determining whether a sentence should be below the applicable guideline range.".

Section 5H1.6 is amended by adding at the end the following:

"Commentary

Background: Section 401(b)(4) of Public Law 108–21 directly amended this policy statement to add the second paragraph, effective April 30, 2003.".

Section 5K2.0 is amended by striking "Under" and inserting the following:

"(a) DOWNWARD DEPARTURES IN CRIMINAL CASES OTHER THAN CHILD CRIMES AND SEXUAL OFFENSES.—Under";

and by adding at the end the following:

(b) DOWNWARD DEPARTURES IN CHILD CRIMES AND SEXUAL OFFENSES.—Under 18 U.S.C. § 3553(b)(2), the sentencing court may impose a sentence below the range established by the applicable guidelines only if the court finds that there exists a mitigating circumstance of a kind, or to a degree, that—

(1) has been affirmatively and specifically identified as a permissible ground of downward departure in the sentencing guidelines or policy statements issued under section 994(a) of title 28, United States Code, taking account of any amendments to such sentencing guidelines or policy statements by act of Congress;

(2) has not adequately been taken into consideration by the Sentencing Commission in formulating the guidelines; and

(3) should result in a sentence different from that described.

The grounds enumerated in this Part K of chapter 5 are the sole grounds that have been affirmatively and specifically identified as a permissible ground of downward departure in these sentencing guidelines and policy statements. Thus, notwithstanding any other reference to authority to depart downward elsewhere in this Sentencing Manual, a ground of downward departure has not been affirmatively and specifically identified as a permissible ground of downward departure within the meaning of section 3553(b)(2) unless it is expressly enumerated in this Part K as a ground upon which a downward departure may be granted.".

The Commentary to § 5K2.0 is amended by inserting an asterisk after "Commentary" and by inserting the following new paragraph before "The United":

"[*Section 401(m)(2)(C) of Public Law 108–21 directs the Commission to revise § 5K2.0, within 180 days after the date of the enactment of that Public Law, or

October 27, 2003, to conform § 5K2.0 to changes made by that Public Law, including changes to the appellate standard of review for decisions to depart from the guidelines. That directive has not been implemented yet in the following commentary.]".

The Commentary to § 5K2.0 is amended by striking "of this policy statement" and inserting "of subsection (a)".

The Commentary to § 5K2.0 is amended by adding at the end the following:

" Section 401(b)(1) of Public Law 108–21 directly amended this policy statement to add subsection (b), effective April 30, 2003.".

Section 5K2.13 is amended by striking "or" before "(3)"; and by striking "public." and inserting "public; or (4) the defendant has been convicted of an offense under chapter 71, 109A, 110, or 117, of title 18, United States Code.".

The Commentary to § 5K2.13 is amended by adding at the end the following:

"Background: Section 401(b)(5) of Public Law 108–21 directly amended this policy statement to add subdivision (4), effective April 30, 2003.".

Section 5K2.20 is amended by striking "A sentence" and inserting "Except where a defendant is convicted of an offense involving a minor victim under section 1201, an offense under section 1591, or an offense under chapter 71, 109A, 110, or 117, of title 18, United States Code, a sentence".

The Commentary to § 5K2.20 is amended by adding at the end the following:

"Background: Section 401(b)(3) of Public Law 108–21 directly amended this policy statement, effective April 30, 2003.".

Chapter Five, Part K, is amended by adding at the end the following:

"§ 5K2.22. Specific Offender Characteristics as Grounds for Downward Departure in Child Crimes and Sexual Offenses (Policy Statement)

In sentencing a defendant convicted of an offense involving a minor victim under section 1201, an offense under section 1591, or an offense under chapter 71, 109A, 110, or 117, of title 18, United States Code:

(1) Age may be a reason to impose a sentence below the applicable guideline range only if and to the extent permitted by § 5H1.1.

(2) An extraordinary physical impairment may be a reason to impose a sentence below the applicable guideline range only if and to the extent permitted by § 5H1.4.

(3) Drug, alcohol, or gambling dependence or abuse is not a reason for imposing a sentence below the guidelines.

Commentary

Background: Section 401(b)(2) of Public Law 108–21 directly amended Chapter Five, Part K, to add this policy statement, effective April 30, 2003.".

Reason for Amendment: This amendment implements amendments to the guidelines made directly by the PROTECT Act, Pub. L. 108–21. In addition to amendments made directly by the PROTECT Act, this amendment makes technical and conforming amendments to those direct congressional amendments, pursuant to the Commission's authority to promulgate such technical and conforming amendments under section 401(m) of the PROTECT Act and 28 U.S.C. § 994.

Effective Date: The effective date of this amendment is April 30, 2003.

650. **Amendment:** Section 2A4.1 is amended in subsection (a) by striking "24" and inserting the following:

    "(1)   24 (effective before, but not on or after, May 30, 2003).

    (1)   32 (effective on and after May 30, 2003).";

in subsection (b)(4)(C), by inserting "(effective before, but not on or after, May 30, 2003)" after "level";

and by striking subsection (b)(5) as follows:

    "(5)   If the victim was sexually exploited, increase by 3 levels."

and inserting the following:

    "(5)   If the victim was sexually exploited:

        (A)   increase by 3 levels (effective before, but not on or after, May 30, 2003).

        (A)   increase by 6 levels (effective on and after May 30, 2003).".

The Commentary to § 2A4.1 captioned "Application Notes" is amended in Note 3 by inserting "(effective before, but not on or after, May 30, 2003)" after "resistance".

The Commentary to § 2A4.1 captioned "Background" is amended by adding at the end the following:

    "   Subsections (a) and (b)(5), and the deletion of subsection (b)(4)(C), effective May 30, 2003, implement the directive to the Commission in section 104 of Public Law 108–21.".

Reason for Amendment: This amendment implements the directive to the Commission in section 104 of the PROTECT Act, Pub. L. 108–21.

Effective Date: The effective date of this amendment is May 30, 2003.

651. **Amendment:** Chapter One is amended by striking the heading as follows:

    "   CHAPTER ONE - INTRODUCTION
                AND GENERAL APPLICATION PRINCIPLES";

and by inserting:

Amendment 651

"   CHAPTER ONE - AUTHORITY
AND GENERAL APPLICATION PRINCIPLES".

Chapter One is amended by striking Part A as follows:

"   PART A - INTRODUCTION

1. Authority

The United States Sentencing Commission ('Commission') is an independent agency in the judicial branch composed of seven voting and two nonvoting, ex officio members. Its principal purpose is to establish sentencing policies and practices for the federal criminal justice system that will assure the ends of justice by promulgating detailed guidelines prescribing the appropriate sentences for offenders convicted of federal crimes.

The guidelines and policy statements promulgated by the Commission are issued pursuant to Section 994(a) of Title 28, United States Code.

2. The Statutory Mission

The Sentencing Reform Act of 1984 (Title II of the Comprehensive Crime Control Act of 1984) provides for the development of guidelines that will further the basic purposes of criminal punishment: deterrence, incapacitation, just punishment, and rehabilitation. The Act delegates broad authority to the Commission to review and rationalize the federal sentencing process.

The Act contains detailed instructions as to how this determination should be made, the most important of which directs the Commission to create categories of offense behavior and offender characteristics. An offense behavior category might consist, for example, of 'bank robbery/committed with a gun/$2500 taken.' An offender characteristic category might be 'offender with one prior conviction not resulting in imprisonment.' The Commission is required to prescribe guideline ranges that specify an appropriate sentence for each class of convicted persons determined by coordinating the offense behavior categories with the offender characteristic categories. Where the guidelines call for imprisonment, the range must be narrow: the maximum of the range cannot exceed the minimum by more than the greater of 25 percent or six months. 28 U.S.C. § 994(b)(2).

Pursuant to the Act, the sentencing court must select a sentence from within the guideline range. If, however, a particular case presents atypical features, the Act allows the court to depart from the guidelines and sentence outside the prescribed range. In that case, the court must specify reasons for departure. 18 U.S.C. § 3553(b). If the court sentences within the guideline range, an appellate court may review the sentence to determine whether the guidelines were correctly applied. If the court departs from the guideline range, an appellate court may review the reasonableness of the departure. 18 U.S.C. § 3742. The Act also abolishes parole, and substantially reduces and restructures good behavior adjustments.

The Commission's initial guidelines were submitted to Congress on April 13, 1987. After the prescribed period of Congressional review, the guidelines took effect on November 1, 1987, and apply to all offenses committed on or after that date. The Commission has the authority to submit guideline amendments each year to Congress between the beginning of a regular Congressional session and May 1. Such amendments automatically take effect 180 days after submission unless a law is enacted to the contrary. 28 U.S.C. § 994(p).

The initial sentencing guidelines and policy statements were developed after extensive hearings, deliberation, and consideration of substantial public comment. The Commission emphasizes, however, that it views the guideline-writing process as evolutionary. It expects, and the governing statute anticipates, that continuing research, experience, and analysis will result in modifications and revisions to the guidelines through submission of amendments to Congress. To this end, the Commission is established as a permanent agency to monitor sentencing practices in the federal courts.

3. The Basic Approach (Policy Statement)

To understand the guidelines and their underlying rationale, it is important to focus on the three objectives that Congress sought to achieve in enacting the Sentencing Reform Act of 1984. The Act's basic objective was to enhance the ability of the criminal justice system to combat crime through an effective, fair sentencing system. To achieve this end, Congress first sought honesty in sentencing. It sought to avoid the confusion and implicit deception that arose out of the pre-guidelines sentencing system which required the court to impose an indeterminate sentence of imprisonment and empowered the parole commission to determine how much of the sentence an offender actually would serve in prison. This practice usually resulted in a substantial reduction in the effective length of the sentence imposed, with defendants often serving only about one-third of the sentence imposed by the court.

Second, Congress sought reasonable uniformity in sentencing by narrowing the wide disparity in sentences imposed for similar criminal offenses committed by similar offenders. Third, Congress sought proportionality in sentencing through a system that imposes appropriately different sentences for criminal conduct of differing severity.

Honesty is easy to achieve: the abolition of parole makes the sentence imposed by the court the sentence the offender will serve, less approximately fifteen percent for good behavior. There is a tension, however, between the mandate of uniformity and the mandate of proportionality. Simple uniformity -- sentencing every offender to five years -- destroys proportionality. Having only a few simple categories of crimes would make the guidelines uniform and easy to administer, but might lump together offenses that are different in important respects. For example, a single category for robbery that included armed and unarmed robberies, robberies with and without injuries, robberies of a few dollars and robberies of millions, would be far too broad.

A sentencing system tailored to fit every conceivable wrinkle of each case would quickly become unworkable and seriously compromise the certainty of punishment and its deterrent effect. For example: a bank robber with (or without) a gun, which the robber kept hidden (or brandished), might have frightened (or merely warned), injured seriously (or less seriously), tied up (or simply pushed) a guard, teller, or customer, at night (or at noon), in an effort to obtain money for other crimes (or for other purposes), in the company of a few (or many) other robbers, for the first (or fourth) time.

The list of potentially relevant features of criminal behavior is long; the fact that they can occur in multiple combinations means that the list of possible permutations of factors is virtually endless. The appropriate relationships among these different factors are exceedingly difficult to establish, for they are often context specific. Sentencing courts do not treat the occurrence of a simple bruise identically in all cases, irrespective of whether that bruise occurred in the context of a bank robbery or in the context of a breach of peace. This is so, in part, because the risk that such a harm will occur differs depending on the underlying offense with which it is connected; and also because, in part, the relationship between punishment and multiple harms is not simply additive. The relation varies depending on how much other harm has occurred. Thus, it would not be proper to assign points for each kind of harm and simply add them up, irrespective of context and total amounts.

The larger the number of subcategories of offense and offender characteristics included in the guidelines, the greater the complexity and the less workable the system. Moreover, complex combinations of offense and offender characteristics would apply and interact in unforeseen ways to unforeseen situations, thus failing to cure the unfairness of a simple, broad category system. Finally, and perhaps most importantly, probation officers and courts, in applying a complex system having numerous subcategories, would be required to make a host of decisions regarding whether the underlying facts were sufficient to bring the case within a particular subcategory. The greater the number of decisions required and the greater their complexity, the greater the risk that different courts would apply the guidelines differently to situations that, in fact, are similar, thereby reintroducing the very disparity that the guidelines were designed to reduce.

In view of the arguments, it would have been tempting to retreat to the simple, broad category approach and to grant courts the discretion to select the proper point along a broad sentencing range. Granting such broad discretion, however, would have risked correspondingly broad disparity in sentencing, for different courts may exercise their discretionary powers in different ways. Such an approach would have risked a return to the wide disparity that Congress established the Commission to reduce and would have been contrary to the Commission's mandate set forth in the Sentencing Reform Act of 1984.

In the end, there was no completely satisfying solution to this problem. The Commission had to balance the comparative virtues and vices of broad, simple categorization and detailed, complex subcategorization, and within the constraints established by that balance, minimize the discretionary powers of the sentencing court. Any system will, to a degree, enjoy the benefits and suffer from the drawbacks of each approach.

A philosophical problem arose when the Commission attempted to reconcile the differing perceptions of the purposes of criminal punishment. Most observers of the criminal law agree that the ultimate aim of the law itself, and of punishment in particular, is the control of crime. Beyond this point, however, the consensus seems to break down. Some argue that appropriate punishment should be defined primarily on the basis of the principle of 'just deserts.' Under this principle, punishment should be scaled to the offender's culpability and the resulting harms. Others argue that punishment should be imposed primarily on the basis of practical 'crime control' considerations. This theory calls for sentences that most effectively lessen the likelihood of future crime, either by deterring others or incapacitating the defendant.

Adherents of each of these points of view urged the Commission to choose between them and accord one primacy over the other. As a practical matter, however, this choice was unnecessary because in most sentencing decisions the application of either philosophy will produce the same or similar results.

In its initial set of guidelines, the Commission sought to solve both the practical and philosophical problems of developing a coherent sentencing system by taking an empirical approach that used as a starting point data estimating pre-guidelines sentencing practice. It analyzed data drawn from 10,000 presentence investigations, the differing elements of various crimes as distinguished in substantive criminal statutes, the United States Parole Commission's guidelines and statistics, and data from other relevant sources in order to determine which distinctions were important in pre-guidelines practice. After consideration, the Commission accepted, modified, or rationalized these distinctions.

This empirical approach helped the Commission resolve its practical problem by defining a list of relevant distinctions that, although of considerable length, was short enough to create a manageable set of guidelines. Existing categories are relatively broad and omit distinctions that some may believe important, yet they include most of the major distinctions that statutes and data suggest made a significant difference in sentencing decisions. Relevant distinctions not reflected in the guidelines probably will occur rarely and sentencing courts may take such unusual cases into account by departing from the guidelines.

The Commission's empirical approach also helped resolve its philosophical dilemma. Those who adhere to a just deserts philosophy may concede that the lack of consensus might make it difficult to say exactly what punishment is deserved for a particular crime. Likewise, those who subscribe to a philosophy of crime control may acknowledge that the lack of sufficient data might make it difficult to determine exactly the punishment that will best prevent that crime. Both groups might therefore recognize the wisdom of looking to those distinctions that judges and legislators have, in fact, made over the course of time. These established distinctions are ones that the community believes, or has found over time, to be important from either a just deserts or crime control perspective.

The Commission did not simply copy estimates of pre-guidelines practice as revealed by the data, even though establishing offense values on this basis would help eliminate disparity because the data represent averages. Rather, it departed from the data at different points for various important reasons. Congressional statutes, for example, suggested or required departure, as in the case of the Anti-Drug Abuse Act of 1986 that imposed increased and mandatory minimum sentences. In addition, the data revealed inconsistencies in treatment, such as punishing economic crime less severely than other apparently equivalent behavior.

Despite these policy-oriented departures from pre-guidelines practice, the guidelines represent an approach that begins with, and builds upon, empirical data. The guidelines will not please those who wish the Commission to adopt a single philosophical theory and then work deductively to establish a simple and perfect set of categorizations and distinctions. The guidelines may prove acceptable, however, to those who seek more modest, incremental improvements in the status quo, who believe the best is often the enemy of the good, and who recognize that these guidelines are, as the Act contemplates, but the first step in an evolutionary process. After spending considerable time and resources exploring alternative approaches, the Commission developed these guidelines as a practical effort toward the achievement of a more honest, uniform, equitable, proportional, and therefore effective sentencing system.

4. The Guidelines' Resolution of Major Issues (Policy Statement)

The guideline-drafting process required the Commission to resolve a host of important policy questions typically involving rather evenly balanced sets of competing considerations. As an aid to understanding the guidelines, this introduction briefly discusses several of those issues; commentary in the guidelines explains others.

(a) <u>Real Offense vs. Charge Offense Sentencing</u>.

One of the most important questions for the Commission to decide was whether to base sentences upon the actual conduct in which the defendant engaged regardless of the charges for which he was indicted or convicted ('real offense' sentencing), or upon the conduct that constitutes the elements of the offense for which the defendant was charged and of which he was convicted ('charge offense' sentencing). A bank robber, for example, might have used a gun, frightened bystanders, taken $50,000, injured a teller, refused to stop when ordered, and raced away damaging property during his escape. A pure real offense system would sentence on the basis of all identifiable conduct. A pure charge offense system would overlook some of the harms that did not constitute statutory elements of the offenses of which the defendant was convicted.

The Commission initially sought to develop a pure real offense system. After all, the pre-guidelines sentencing system was, in a sense, this type of system. The sentencing court and the parole commission took account of the conduct in which the defendant actually engaged, as determined in a presentence report, at the sentencing hearing, or before a parole commission hearing officer. The Commission's initial efforts in this direction, carried out in the spring and early summer of 1986, proved unproductive, mostly for practical reasons. To make such a system work, even to formalize and rationalize the status quo, would have required the Commission to decide precisely which harms to take into account, how to add them up, and what kinds of procedures the courts should use to determine the presence or absence of disputed factual elements. The Commission found no practical way to combine and account for the large number of diverse harms arising in different circumstances; nor did it find a practical way to reconcile the need for a fair adjudicatory procedure with the need for a speedy sentencing process given the potential existence of hosts of adjudicated 'real harm' facts in many typical cases. The effort proposed as a solution to these problems required the use of, for example, quadratic roots and other mathematical operations that the Commission considered too complex to be workable. In the Commission's view, such a system risked return to wide disparity in sentencing practice.

In its initial set of guidelines submitted to Congress in April 1987, the Commission moved closer to a charge offense system. This system, however, does contain a significant number of real offense elements. For one thing, the hundreds of overlapping and duplicative statutory provisions that make up the federal criminal law forced the Commission to write guidelines that are descriptive of generic conduct rather than guidelines that track purely statutory language. For another, the guidelines take account of a number of important, commonly occurring real offense elements such as role in the offense, the presence of a gun, or the amount of money actually taken, through alternative base offense levels, specific offense characteristics, cross references, and adjustments.

The Commission recognized that a charge offense system has drawbacks of its own. One of the most important is the potential it affords prosecutors to influence sentences by increasing or decreasing the number of counts in an indictment. Of course, the defendant's actual conduct (that which the prosecutor can prove in court) imposes a natural limit upon the prosecutor's ability to increase a defendant's sentence. Moreover, the Commission has written its rules for the treatment of multicount convictions with an eye toward eliminating unfair treatment that might flow from count manipulation. For example, the guidelines treat a three-count indictment, each count of which charges sale of 100 grams of heroin or theft of $10,000, the same as a single-count indictment charging sale of 300 grams of heroin or theft of $30,000. Furthermore, a sentencing court may control any inappropriate manipulation of the indictment through use of its departure power. Finally, the Commission will closely monitor charging and plea agreement practices and will make appropriate adjustments should they become necessary.

(b) Departures.

The sentencing statute permits a court to depart from a guideline-specified sentence only when it finds 'an aggravating or mitigating circumstance of a kind, or to a degree, not adequately taken into consideration by the Sentencing Commission in formulating the guidelines that should result in a sentence different from that described.' 18 U.S.C. § 3553(b). The Commission intends the sentencing courts to treat each guideline as carving out a 'heartland,' a set of typical cases embodying the conduct that each guideline describes. When a court finds an atypical case, one to which a particular guideline linguistically applies but where conduct significantly differs from the norm, the court may consider whether a departure is warranted. Section 5H1.10 (Race, Sex, National Origin, Creed, Religion, and Socio-Economic Status), § 5H1.12 (Lack of Guidance as a Youth and Similar Circumstances), the third sentence of § 5H1.4 (Physical Condition, Including Drug or Alcohol Dependence or Abuse), the last sentence of § 5K2.12 (Coercion and Duress), and § 5K2.19 (Post-Sentencing Rehabilitative Efforts) list several factors that the court cannot take into account as grounds for departure. With those specific exceptions, however, the Commission does not intend to limit the kinds of factors, whether or not mentioned anywhere else in the guidelines, that could constitute grounds for departure in an unusual case.

The Commission has adopted this departure policy for two reasons. First, it is difficult to prescribe a single set of guidelines that encompasses the vast range of human conduct potentially relevant to a sentencing decision. The Commission also recognizes that the initial set of guidelines need not do so. The Commission is a permanent body, empowered by law to write and rewrite guidelines, with progressive changes, over many years. By monitoring when courts depart from the guidelines and by analyzing their stated reasons for doing so and court decisions with references thereto, the Commission, over time, will be able to refine the guidelines to specify more precisely when departures should and should not be permitted.

Second, the Commission believes that despite the courts' legal freedom to depart from the guidelines, they will not do so very often. This is because the guidelines, offense by offense, seek to take account of those factors that the Commission's data indicate made a significant difference in pre-guidelines sentencing practice. Thus, for example, where the presence of physical injury made an important difference in pre-guidelines sentencing practice (as in the case of robbery or assault), the guidelines specifically include this factor to enhance the sentence. Where the guidelines do not specify an augmentation or diminution, this is generally because the sentencing data did not permit the Commission to conclude that the factor was empirically important in relation to the particular offense. Of course, an important factor (e.g., physical injury) may infrequently occur in connection with a particular crime (e.g., fraud). Such rare occurrences are precisely the type of events that the courts' departure powers were designed to cover -- unusual cases outside the range of the more typical offenses for which the guidelines were designed.

It is important to note that the guidelines refer to two different kinds of departure. The first involves instances in which the guidelines provide specific guidance for departure by analogy or by other numerical or non-numerical suggestions. The Commission intends such suggestions as policy guidance for the courts. The Commission expects that most departures will reflect the suggestions and that the courts of appeals may prove more likely to find departures 'unreasonable' where they fall outside suggested levels.

A second type of departure will remain unguided. It may rest upon grounds referred to in Chapter Five, Part K (Departures) or on grounds not mentioned in the guidelines. While Chapter Five, Part K lists factors that the Commission believes may constitute grounds for departure, the list is not exhaustive. The Commission recognizes that there may be other grounds for departure that are not mentioned; it also believes there may be cases in which a departure outside suggested levels is warranted. In its view, however, such cases will be highly infrequent.

(c) Plea Agreements.

Nearly ninety percent of all federal criminal cases involve guilty pleas and many of these cases involve some form of plea agreement. Some commentators on early Commission guideline drafts urged the Commission not to attempt any major reforms of the plea agreement process on the grounds that any set of guidelines that threatened to change pre-guidelines practice radically also threatened to make the federal system unmanageable. Others argued that guidelines that failed to control and limit plea agreements would leave untouched a 'loophole' large enough to undo the good that sentencing guidelines would bring.

The Commission decided not to make major changes in plea agreement practices in the initial guidelines, but rather to provide guidance by issuing general policy statements concerning the acceptance of plea agreements in Chapter Six, Part B (Plea Agreements). The rules set forth in Fed. R. Crim. P. 11(e) govern the acceptance or rejection of such agreements. The Commission will collect data on the courts' plea practices and will analyze this information to determine when and why the courts accept or reject plea agreements and whether plea agreement practices are undermining the intent of the Sentencing Reform Act. In light of this information and analysis, the Commission will seek to further regulate the plea agreement process as appropriate. Importantly, if the policy statements relating to plea agreements are followed, circumvention of the Sentencing Reform Act and the guidelines should not occur.

The Commission expects the guidelines to have a positive, rationalizing impact upon plea agreements for two reasons. First, the guidelines create a clear, definite expectation in respect to the sentence that a court will impose if a trial takes place. In the event a prosecutor and defense attorney explore the possibility of a negotiated plea, they will no longer work in the dark. This fact alone should help to reduce irrationality in respect to actual sentencing outcomes. Second, the guidelines create a norm to which courts will likely refer when they decide whether, under Rule 11(e), to accept or to reject a plea agreement or recommendation.

(d) Probation and Split Sentences.

The statute provides that the guidelines are to 'reflect the general appropriateness of imposing a sentence other than imprisonment in cases in which the defendant is a first offender who has not been convicted of a crime of violence or an otherwise serious offense . . . .' 28 U.S.C. § 994(j). Under pre-guidelines sentencing practice, courts sentenced to probation an inappropriately high percentage of offenders guilty of certain economic crimes, such as theft, tax evasion, antitrust offenses, insider trading, fraud, and embezzlement, that in the Commission's view are 'serious.'

The Commission's solution to this problem has been to write guidelines that classify as serious many offenses for which probation previously was frequently given and provide for at least a short period of imprisonment in such cases. The Commission concluded that the definite prospect of prison, even though the term may be short, will serve as a significant deterrent, particularly when compared with pre-guidelines practice where probation, not prison, was the norm.

More specifically, the guidelines work as follows in respect to a first offender. For offense levels one through eight, the sentencing court may elect to sentence the offender to probation (with or without confinement conditions) or to a prison term. For offense levels nine and ten, the court may substitute probation for a prison term, but the probation must include confinement conditions (community confinement, intermittent confinement, or home detention). For offense levels eleven and twelve, the court must impose at least one-half the minimum confinement sentence in the form of prison confinement, the remainder to be served on supervised release with a condition of community confinement or home detention. The Commission, of course, has not dealt with the single acts of aberrant behavior that still may justify probation at higher offense levels through departures.*

*Note: Although the Commission had not addressed 'single acts of aberrant behavior' at the time the Introduction to the Guidelines Manual originally was written, it subsequently addressed the issue in Amendment 603, effective November 1, 2000. (See Supplement to Appendix C, amendment 603.)

(e) Multi-Count Convictions.

The Commission, like several state sentencing commissions, has found it particularly difficult to develop guidelines for sentencing defendants convicted of multiple violations of law, each of which makes up a separate count in an indictment. The difficulty is that when a defendant engages in conduct that causes several harms, each additional harm, even if it increases the extent to which punishment is warranted, does not necessarily warrant a proportionate increase in punishment. A defendant who assaults others during a fight, for example, may warrant more punishment if he injures ten people than if he injures one, but his conduct does not necessarily warrant ten times the punishment. If it did, many of the simplest offenses, for reasons that are often fortuitous, would lead to sentences of life imprisonment -- sentences that neither just deserts nor crime control theories of punishment would justify.

Several individual guidelines provide special instructions for increasing punishment when the conduct that is the subject of that count involves multiple occurrences or has caused several harms. The guidelines also provide general rules for aggravating punishment in light of multiple harms charged separately in separate counts. These rules may produce occasional anomalies, but normally they will permit an appropriate degree of aggravation of punishment for multiple offenses that are the subjects of separate counts.

These rules are set out in Chapter Three, Part D (Multiple Counts). They essentially provide: (1) when the conduct involves fungible items (e.g., separate drug transactions or thefts of money), the amounts are added and the guidelines apply to the total amount; (2) when nonfungible harms are involved, the offense level for the most serious count is increased (according to a diminishing scale) to reflect the existence of other counts of conviction. The guidelines have been written in order to minimize the possibility that an arbitrary casting of a single transaction into several counts will produce a longer sentence. In addition, the sentencing court will have adequate power to prevent such a result through departures.

(f) Regulatory Offenses.

Regulatory statutes, though primarily civil in nature, sometimes contain criminal provisions in respect to particularly harmful activity. Such criminal provisions often describe not only substantive offenses, but also more technical, administratively-related offenses such as failure to keep accurate records or to provide requested information. These statutes pose two problems: first, which criminal regulatory provisions should the Commission initially consider, and second, how should it treat technical or administratively-related criminal violations?

In respect to the first problem, the Commission found that it could not comprehensively treat all regulatory violations in the initial set of guidelines. There are hundreds of such provisions scattered throughout the United States Code. To find all potential violations would involve examination of each individual federal regulation. Because of this practical difficulty, the Commission sought to determine, with the assistance of the Department of Justice and several regulatory agencies, which criminal regulatory offenses were particularly important in light of the need for enforcement of the general regulatory scheme. The Commission addressed these offenses in the initial guidelines.

In respect to the second problem, the Commission has developed a system for treating technical recordkeeping and reporting offenses that divides them into four categories. First, in the simplest of cases, the offender may have failed to fill out a form intentionally, but without knowledge or intent that substantive harm would likely follow. He might fail, for example, to keep an accurate record of toxic substance transport, but that failure may not lead, nor be likely to lead, to the release or improper handling of any toxic substance. Second, the same failure may be accompanied by a significant likelihood that substantive harm will occur; it may make a release of a toxic substance more likely. Third, the same failure may have led to substantive harm. Fourth, the failure may represent an effort to conceal a substantive harm that has occurred.

The structure of a typical guideline for a regulatory offense provides a low base offense level (e.g., 6) aimed at the first type of recordkeeping or reporting offense. Specific offense characteristics designed to reflect substantive harms that do occur in respect to some regulatory offenses, or that are likely to occur, increase the offense level. A specific offense characteristic also provides that a recordkeeping or reporting offense that conceals a substantive offense will have the same offense level as the substantive offense.

(g) Sentencing Ranges.

In determining the appropriate sentencing ranges for each offense, the Commission estimated the average sentences served within each category under the pre-guidelines sentencing system. It also examined the sentences specified in federal statutes, in the parole guidelines, and in other relevant, analogous sources. The Commission's Supplementary Report on the Initial Sentencing Guidelines (1987) contains a comparison between estimates of pre-guidelines sentencing practice and sentences under the guidelines.

While the Commission has not considered itself bound by pre-guidelines sentencing practice, it has not attempted to develop an entirely new system of sentencing on the basis of theory alone. Guideline sentences, in many instances, will approximate average pre-guidelines practice and adherence to the guidelines will help to eliminate wide disparity. For example, where a high percentage of persons received probation under pre-guidelines practice, a guideline may include one or more specific offense characteristics in an effort to distinguish those types of defendants who received probation from those who received more severe sentences. In some instances, short sentences of incarceration for all offenders in a category have been substituted for a pre-guidelines sentencing practice of very wide variability in which some defendants received probation while others received several years in prison for the same offense. Moreover, inasmuch as those who pleaded guilty under pre-guidelines practice often received lesser sentences, the guidelines permit the court to impose lesser sentences on those defendants who accept responsibility for their misconduct. For defendants who provide substantial assistance to the government in the investigation or prosecution of others, a downward departure may be warranted.

The Commission has also examined its sentencing ranges in light of their likely impact upon prison population. Specific legislation, such as the Anti-Drug Abuse Act of 1986 and the career offender provisions of the Sentencing Reform Act of 1984 (28 U.S.C. § 994(h)), required the Commission to promulgate guidelines that will lead to substantial prison population increases. These increases will occur irrespective of the guidelines. The guidelines themselves, insofar as they reflect policy decisions made by the Commission (rather than legislated mandatory minimum or career offender sentences), are projected to lead to an increase in prison population that computer models, produced by the Commission and the Bureau of Prisons in 1987, estimated at approximately 10 percent over a period of ten years.

(h) The Sentencing Table.

The Commission has established a sentencing table that for technical and practical reasons contains 43 levels. Each level in the table prescribes ranges that overlap with the ranges in the preceding and succeeding levels. By overlapping the ranges, the table should discourage unnecessary litigation. Both prosecution and defense will realize that the difference between one level and another will not necessarily make a difference in the sentence that the court imposes. Thus, little purpose will be served in protracted litigation trying to determine, for example, whether $10,000 or $11,000 was obtained as a result of a fraud. At the same time, the levels work to increase a sentence proportionately. A change of six levels roughly doubles the sentence irrespective of the level at which one starts. The guidelines, in keeping with the statutory requirement that the maximum of any range cannot exceed the minimum by more than the greater of 25 percent or six months (28 U.S.C. § 994(b)(2)), permit courts to exercise the greatest permissible range of sentencing discretion. The table overlaps offense levels meaningfully, works proportionately, and at the same time preserves the maximum degree of allowable discretion for the court within each level.

Similarly, many of the individual guidelines refer to tables that correlate amounts of money with offense levels. These tables often have many rather than a few levels. Again, the reason is to minimize the likelihood of unnecessary litigation. If a money table were to make only a few distinctions, each distinction would become more important and litigation over which category an offender fell within would become more likely. Where a table has many small monetary distinctions, it minimizes the likelihood of litigation because the precise amount of money involved is of considerably less importance.

5. A Concluding Note

The Commission emphasizes that it drafted the initial guidelines with considerable caution. It examined the many hundreds of criminal statutes in the United States Code. It began with those that were the basis for a significant number of prosecutions and sought to place them in a rational order. It developed additional distinctions relevant to the application of these provisions and it applied sentencing ranges to each resulting category. In doing so, it relied upon pre-guidelines sentencing practice as revealed by its own statistical analyses based on summary reports of some 40,000 convictions, a sample of 10,000 augmented presentence reports, the parole guidelines, and policy judgments.

The Commission recognizes that some will criticize this approach as overly cautious, as representing too little a departure from pre-guidelines sentencing practice. Yet, it will cure wide disparity. The Commission is a permanent body that can amend the guidelines each year. Although the data available to it, like all data, are imperfect, experience with the guidelines will lead to additional information and provide a firm empirical basis for consideration of revisions.

Finally, the guidelines will apply to more than 90 percent of all felony and Class A misdemeanor cases in the federal courts. Because of time constraints and the nonexistence of statistical information, some offenses that occur infrequently are not considered in the guidelines. Their exclusion does not reflect any judgment regarding their seriousness and they will be addressed as the Commission refines the guidelines over time.";

and inserting:

" PART A - AUTHORITY

§ 1A1.1. Authority

The guidelines, policy statements, and commentary set forth in this Guidelines Manual, including amendments thereto, are promulgated by the United States Sentencing Commission pursuant to: (1) section 994(a) of title 28, United States Code; and (2) with respect to guidelines, policy statements, and commentary promulgated or amended pursuant to specific congressional directive, pursuant to the authority contained in that directive in addition to the authority under section 994(a) of title 28, United States Code.

Commentary

Application Note:

1. Historical Review of Original Introduction.—Part A of Chapter One originally was an introduction to the Guidelines Manual that explained a number of policy decisions made by the Commission when it promulgated the initial set of guidelines. This introduction was amended occasionally between 1987 and 2003. In 2003, as part of the Commission's implementation of the Prosecutorial Remedies and Other Tools to end the Exploitation of Children Today Act of 2003 (the 'PROTECT Act', Public Law 108–21), the original introduction was transferred to the Editorial Note at the end of this guideline. The Commission encourages the review of this material for context and historical purposes.

Background: The Sentencing Reform Act of 1984 changed the course of federal sentencing. Among other things, the Act created the United States Sentencing Commission as an independent agency in the Judicial Branch, and directed it to develop guidelines and policy statements for sentencing courts to use when sentencing offenders convicted of federal crimes. Moreover, it empowered the Commission with ongoing responsibilities to monitor the guidelines, submit to Congress appropriate modifications of the guidelines and recommended changes in criminal statutes, and establish education and research programs. The mandate rested on Congressional awareness that sentencing was a dynamic field that requires continuing review by an expert body to revise sentencing policies, in light of application experience, as new criminal statutes are enacted, and as more is learned about what motivates and controls criminal behavior.";

and adding an editorial note following the guideline.

The Commentary to § 1B1.1 captioned "Application Notes" is amended by striking Note 1 as follows:

"1. The following are definitions of terms that are used frequently in the guidelines and are of general applicability (except to the extent expressly modified in respect to a particular guideline or policy statement):

(a) 'Abducted' means that a victim was forced to accompany an offender to a different location. For example, a bank robber's forcing a bank teller from the bank into a getaway car would constitute an abduction.

(b) 'Bodily injury' means any significant injury; e.g., an injury that is painful and obvious, or is of a type for which medical attention ordinarily would be sought.

(c) 'Brandished' with reference to a dangerous weapon (including a firearm) means that all or part of the weapon was displayed, or the presence of the weapon was otherwise made known to another person, in order to intimidate that person, regardless of whether the weapon was directly visible to that person. Accordingly, although the dangerous weapon does not have to be directly visible, the weapon must be present.

(d) 'Dangerous weapon' means (i) an instrument capable of inflicting death or serious bodily injury; or (ii) an object that is not an instrument capable of inflicting death or serious bodily injury but (I) closely resembles such an instrument; or (II) the defendant used the object in a manner that created the impression that the object was such an instrument (e.g. a defendant wrapped a hand in a towel during a bank robbery to create the appearance of a gun).

(e) 'Firearm' means (i) any weapon (including a starter gun) which will or is designed to or may readily be converted to expel a projectile by the action of an explosive; (ii) the frame or receiver of any such weapon; (iii) any firearm muffler or silencer; or (iv) any destructive device. A weapon, commonly known as a 'BB' or pellet gun, that uses air or carbon dioxide pressure to expel a projectile is a dangerous weapon but not a firearm.

(f) 'Otherwise used' with reference to a dangerous weapon (including a firearm) means that the conduct did not amount to the discharge of a firearm but was more than brandishing, displaying, or possessing a firearm or other dangerous weapon.

(g) 'Permanent or life-threatening bodily injury' means injury involving a substantial risk of death; loss or substantial impairment of the function of a bodily member, organ, or mental faculty that is likely to be permanent; or an obvious disfigurement that is likely to be permanent. In the case of a kidnapping, for example, maltreatment to a life-threatening degree (e.g., by denial of food or medical care) would constitute life-threatening bodily injury.

(h) 'Physically restrained' means the forcible restraint of the victim such as by being tied, bound, or locked up.

Amendment 651 APPENDIX C - VOLUME II November 1, 2013

(i) 'Serious bodily injury' means injury involving extreme physical pain or the protracted impairment of a function of a bodily member, organ, or mental faculty; or requiring medical intervention such as surgery, hospitalization, or physical rehabilitation. In addition, 'serious bodily injury' is deemed to have occurred if the offense involved conduct constituting criminal sexual abuse under 18 U.S.C. § 2241 or § 2242 or any similar offense under state law.

(j) 'Destructive device' means any article described in 26 U.S.C. § 5845(f) (including an explosive, incendiary, or poison gas - (i) bomb, (ii) grenade, (iii) rocket having a propellant charge of more than four ounces, (iv) missile having an explosive or incendiary charge of more than one-quarter ounce, (v) mine, or (vi) device similar to any of the devices described in the preceding clauses).

(k) 'Offense' means the offense of conviction and all relevant conduct under § 1B1.3 (Relevant Conduct) unless a different meaning is specified or is otherwise clear from the context. The term 'instant' is used in connection with 'offense,' 'federal offense,' or 'offense of conviction,' as the case may be, to distinguish the violation for which the defendant is being sentenced from a prior or subsequent offense, or from an offense before another court (e.g., an offense before a state court involving the same underlying conduct).",

and inserting the following:

"1. The following are definitions of terms that are used frequently in the guidelines and are of general applicability (except to the extent expressly modified in respect to a particular guideline or policy statement):

(A) 'Abducted' means that a victim was forced to accompany an offender to a different location. For example, a bank robber's forcing a bank teller from the bank into a getaway car would constitute an abduction.

(B) 'Bodily injury' means any significant injury; e.g., an injury that is painful and obvious, or is of a type for which medical attention ordinarily would be sought.

(C) 'Brandished' with reference to a dangerous weapon (including a firearm) means that all or part of the weapon was displayed, or the presence of the weapon was otherwise made known to another person, in order to intimidate that person, regardless of whether the weapon was directly visible to that person. Accordingly, although the dangerous weapon does not have to be directly visible, the weapon must be present.

(D) 'Dangerous weapon' means (i) an instrument capable of inflicting death or serious bodily injury; or (ii) an object that is not an instrument capable of inflicting death or serious bodily injury but (I) closely resembles such an instrument; or (II) the defendant used the object in a manner that created the impression that the object was such an instrument (e.g. a defendant wrapped a hand in a towel during a bank robbery to create the appearance of a gun).

(E) 'Departure' means (i) for purposes other than those specified in subdivision (ii), imposition of a sentence outside the applicable guideline range or of a sentence that is otherwise different from the guideline sentence; and (ii) for purposes of § 4A1.3 (Departures Based on Inadequacy of Criminal History Category), assignment of a criminal history category other than the otherwise applicable criminal history category, in order to effect a sentence outside the applicable guideline range. 'Depart' means grant a departure.

'Downward departure' means departure that effects a sentence less than a sentence that could be imposed under the applicable guideline range or a sentence that is otherwise less than the guideline sentence. 'Depart downward' means grant a downward departure.

'Upward departure' means departure that effects a sentence greater than a sentence that could be imposed under the applicable guideline range or a sentence that is otherwise greater than the guideline sentence. 'Depart upward' means grant an upward departure.

(F) 'Destructive device' means any article described in 26 U.S.C. § 5845(f) (including an explosive, incendiary, or poison gas - (i) bomb, (ii) grenade, (iii) rocket having a propellant charge of more than four ounces, (iv) missile having an explosive or incendiary charge of more than one-quarter ounce, (v) mine, or (vi) device similar to any of the devices described in the preceding clauses).

(G) 'Firearm' means (i) any weapon (including a starter gun) which will or is designed to or may readily be converted to expel a projectile by the action of an explosive; (ii) the frame or receiver of any such weapon; (iii) any firearm muffler or silencer; or (iv) any destructive device. A weapon, commonly known as a 'BB' or pellet gun, that uses air or carbon dioxide pressure to expel a projectile is a dangerous weapon but not a firearm.

(H) 'Offense' means the offense of conviction and all relevant conduct under § 1B1.3 (Relevant Conduct) unless a different meaning is specified or is otherwise clear from the context. The term 'instant' is used in connection with 'offense,' 'federal offense,' or 'offense of conviction,' as the case may be, to distinguish the violation for which the defendant is being sentenced from a prior or subsequent offense, or from an offense before another court (e.g., an offense before a state court involving the same underlying conduct).

(I) 'Otherwise used' with reference to a dangerous weapon (including a firearm) means that the conduct did not amount to the discharge of a firearm but was more than brandishing, displaying, or possessing a firearm or other dangerous weapon.

(J) 'Permanent or life-threatening bodily injury' means injury involving a substantial risk of death; loss or substantial impairment of the function of a bodily member, organ, or mental faculty that is likely to be permanent; or an obvious disfigurement that is likely to be permanent. In the case of a kidnapping, for example, maltreatment to a life-threatening degree (e.g., by denial of food or medical care) would constitute life-threatening bodily injury.

(K) 'Physically restrained' means the forcible restraint of the victim such as by being tied, bound, or locked up.

(L) 'Serious bodily injury' means injury involving extreme physical pain or the protracted impairment of a function of a bodily member, organ, or mental faculty; or requiring medical intervention such as surgery, hospitalization, or physical rehabilitation. In addition, 'serious bodily injury' is deemed to have occurred if the offense involved conduct constituting criminal sexual abuse under 18 U.S.C. § 2241 or § 2242 or any similar offense under state law.".

Section 2A4.1 is amended by striking:

"(a) Base Offense Level:

(1) 24 (effective before, but not on or after, May 30, 2003).

(1) 32 (effective on and after May 30, 2003).",

and inserting:

"(a) Base Offense Level: 32".

Section 2A4.1(b)(4) is amended by striking:

"(C) If the victim was released before twenty-four hours had elapsed, decrease by 1 level (effective before, but not on or after, May 30, 2003).".

Section 2A4.1(b) is amended by striking:

"(5) If the victim was sexually exploited:

(A) increase by 3 levels (effective before, but not on or after, May 30, 2003).

(A) increase by 6 levels (effective on and after May 30, 2003).";

and inserting:

"(5) If the victim was sexually exploited, increase by 6 levels.".

The Commentary to § 2A4.1 captioned "Application Notes" is amended by striking Note 3 as follows:

"3. For the purpose of subsection (b)(4)(C), 'released' includes allowing the victim to escape or turning him over to law enforcement authorities without resistance (effective before, but not on or after, May 30, 2003).";

and by redesignating Notes 4 and 5 and Notes 3 and 4, respectively.

The Commentary to § 4A1.1 captioned "Background" is amended by striking "permits information about the significance or similarity of past conduct underlying prior convictions to be used as a basis for imposing a sentence outside the applicable guideline range." and inserting "authorizes the court to depart from the otherwise applicable criminal history category in certain circumstances.".

Chapter Four, Part A, Subpart One is amended by striking the following guideline and accompanying commentary:

"§ 4A1.3.   Adequacy of Criminal History Category (Policy Statement)

If reliable information indicates that the criminal history category does not adequately reflect the seriousness of the defendant's past criminal conduct or the likelihood that the defendant will commit other crimes, the court may consider imposing a sentence departing from the otherwise applicable guideline range. Such information may include, but is not limited to, information concerning:

(a)   prior sentence(s) not used in computing the criminal history category (e.g., sentences for foreign and tribal offenses);

(b)   prior sentence(s) of substantially more than one year imposed as a result of independent crimes committed on different occasions;

(c)   prior similar misconduct established by a civil adjudication or by a failure to comply with an administrative order;

(d)   whether the defendant was pending trial or sentencing on another charge at the time of the instant offense;

(e)   prior similar adult criminal conduct not resulting in a criminal conviction.

A departure under this provision is warranted when the criminal history category significantly under-represents the seriousness of the defendant's criminal history or the likelihood that the defendant will commit further crimes. Examples might include the case of a defendant who (1) had several previous foreign sentences for serious offenses, (2) had received a prior consolidated sentence of ten years for a series of serious assaults, (3) had a similar instance of large scale fraudulent misconduct established by an adjudication in a Securities and Exchange Commission enforcement proceeding, (4) committed the instant offense while on bail or pretrial release for another serious offense, or (5) for appropriate reasons, such as cooperation in the prosecution of other defendants, had previously received an extremely lenient sentence for a serious offense. The court may, after a review of all the relevant information, conclude that the defendant's criminal history was significantly more serious than that of most defendants in the same criminal history category, and therefore consider an upward departure from the guidelines. However, a prior arrest record itself shall not be considered under § 4A1.3.

There may be cases where the court concludes that a defendant's criminal history category significantly over-represents the seriousness of a defendant's criminal history or the likelihood that the defendant will commit further crimes. An example might include the case of a defendant with two minor misdemeanor convictions close to ten years prior to the instant offense and no other evidence of prior criminal behavior in the intervening period. The court may conclude that the defendant's criminal history was significantly less serious than that of most defendants in the same criminal history category (Category II), and therefore consider a downward departure from the guidelines.

In considering a departure under this provision, the Commission intends that

Amendment 651 APPENDIX C - VOLUME II November 1, 2013

the court use, as a reference, the guideline range for a defendant with a higher or lower criminal history category, as applicable. For example, if the court concludes that the defendant's criminal history category of III significantly under-represents the seriousness of the defendant's criminal history, and that the seriousness of the defendant's criminal history most closely resembles that of most defendants with Criminal History Category IV, the court should look to the guideline range specified for a defendant with Criminal History Category IV to guide its departure. The Commission contemplates that there may, on occasion, be a case of an egregious, serious criminal record in which even the guideline range for Criminal History Category VI is not adequate to reflect the seriousness of the defendant's criminal history. In such a case, a departure above the guideline range for a defendant with Criminal History Category VI may be warranted. In determining whether an upward departure from Criminal History Category VI is warranted, the court should consider that the nature of the prior offenses rather than simply their number is often more indicative of the seriousness of the defendant's criminal record. For example, a defendant with five prior sentences for very large-scale fraud offenses may have 15 criminal history points, within the range of points typical for Criminal History Category VI, yet have a substantially more serious criminal history overall because of the nature of the prior offenses. On the other hand, a defendant with nine prior 60-day jail sentences for offenses such as petty larceny, prostitution, or possession of gambling slips has a higher number of criminal history points (18 points) than the typical Criminal History Category VI defendant, but not necessarily a more serious criminal history overall. Where the court determines that the extent and nature of the defendant's criminal history, taken together, are sufficient to warrant an upward departure from Criminal History Category VI, the court should structure the departure by moving incrementally down the sentencing table to the next higher offense level in Criminal History Category VI until it finds a guideline range appropriate to the case.

However, this provision is not symmetrical. The lower limit of the range for Criminal History Category I is set for a first offender with the lowest risk of recidivism. Therefore, a departure below the lower limit of the guideline range for Criminal History Category I on the basis of the adequacy of criminal history cannot be appropriate.

Commentary

Background: This policy statement recognizes that the criminal history score is unlikely to take into account all the variations in the seriousness of criminal history that may occur. For example, a defendant with an extensive record of serious, assaultive conduct who had received what might now be considered extremely lenient treatment in the past might have the same criminal history category as a defendant who had a record of less serious conduct. Yet, the first defendant's criminal history clearly may be more serious. This may be particularly true in the case of younger defendants (e.g., defendants in their early twenties or younger) who are more likely to have received repeated lenient treatment, yet who may actually pose a greater risk of serious recidivism than older defendants. This policy statement authorizes the consideration of a departure from the guidelines in the limited circumstances where reliable information indicates that the criminal history category does not adequately reflect the seriousness of the defendant's criminal history or likelihood of recidivism, and provides guidance for the consideration of such departures.",

and inserting:

"§ 4A1.3. Departures Based on Inadequacy of Criminal History Category (Policy Statement)

(a) UPWARD DEPARTURES.—

    (1) STANDARD FOR UPWARD DEPARTURE.—If reliable information indicates that the defendant's criminal history category substantially under-represents the seriousness of the defendant's criminal history or the likelihood that the defendant will commit other crimes, an upward departure may be warranted.

    (2) TYPES OF INFORMATION FORMING THE BASIS FOR UPWARD DEPARTURE.—The information described in subsection (a) may include information concerning the following:

        (A) Prior sentence(s) not used in computing the criminal history category (e.g., sentences for foreign and tribal offenses).

        (B) Prior sentence(s) of substantially more than one year imposed as a result of independent crimes committed on different occasions.

        (C) Prior similar misconduct established by a civil adjudication or by a failure to comply with an administrative order.

        (D) Whether the defendant was pending trial or sentencing on another charge at the time of the instant offense.

        (E) Prior similar adult criminal conduct not resulting in a criminal conviction.

    (3) PROHIBITION.—A prior arrest record itself shall not be considered for purposes of an upward departure under this policy statement.

    (4) DETERMINATION OF EXTENT OF UPWARD DEPARTURE.—

        (A) IN GENERAL.—Except as provided in subdivision (B), the court shall determine the extent of a departure under this subsection by using, as a reference, the criminal history category applicable to defendants whose criminal history or likelihood to recidivate most closely resembles that of the defendant's.

        (B) UPWARD DEPARTURES FROM CATEGORY VI.—In a case in which the court determines that the extent and nature of the defendant's criminal history, taken together, are sufficient to warrant an upward departure from Criminal History Category VI, the court should structure the departure by moving incrementally down the sentencing table to the next higher offense level in Criminal History Category VI until it finds a guideline range appropriate to the case.

(b) DOWNWARD DEPARTURES.—

    (1) STANDARD FOR DOWNWARD DEPARTURE.—If reliable information indicates that the defendant's criminal history category substantially over-represents the seriousness of the defendant's criminal history or the likelihood that the defendant will commit other crimes, a downward departure may be warranted.

    (2) PROHIBITIONS.—

        (A) CRIMINAL HISTORY CATEGORY I.—A departure below the lower limit of the applicable guideline range for Criminal History Category I is prohibited.

        (B) ARMED CAREER CRIMINAL AND REPEAT AND DANGEROUS SEX OFFENDER.—A downward departure under this subsection is prohibited for (i) an armed career criminal within the meaning of § 4B1.4 (Armed Career Criminal); and (ii) a repeat and dangerous sex offender against minors within the meaning of § 4B1.5 (Repeat and Dangerous Sex Offender Against Minors).

    (3) LIMITATIONS.—

        (A) LIMITATION ON EXTENT OF DOWNWARD DEPARTURE FOR CAREER OFFENDER.—The extent of a downward departure under this subsection for a career offender within the meaning of § 4B1.1 (Career Offender) may not exceed one criminal history category.

        (B) LIMITATION ON APPLICABILITY OF § 5C1.2 IN EVENT OF DOWNWARD DEPARTURE TO CATEGORY I.—A defendant whose criminal history category is Category I after receipt of a downward departure under this subsection does not meet the criterion of subsection (a)(1) of § 5C1.2 (Limitation on Applicability of Statutory Maximum Sentences in Certain Cases) if, before receipt of the downward departure, the defendant had more than one criminal history point under § 4A1.1 (Criminal History Category).

(c) WRITTEN SPECIFICATION OF BASIS FOR DEPARTURE.—In departing from the otherwise applicable criminal history category under this policy statement, the court shall specify in writing the following:

(1) In the case of an upward departure, the specific reasons why the applicable criminal history category substantially under-represents the seriousness of the defendant's criminal history or the likelihood that the defendant will commit other crimes.

(2) In the case of a downward departure, the specific reasons why the applicable criminal history category substantially over-represents the seriousness of the defendant's criminal history or the likelihood that the defendant will commit other crimes.

Commentary

Application Notes:

1. Definitions.—For purposes of this policy statement, the terms 'depart', 'departure', 'downward departure', and 'upward departure' have the meaning given those terms in Application Note 1 of the Commentary to § 1B1.1 (Application Instructions).

2. Upward Departures.—

(A) Examples.—An upward departure from the defendant's criminal history category may be warranted based on any of the following circumstances:

(i) A previous foreign sentence for a serious offense.

(ii) Receipt of a prior consolidated sentence of ten years for a series of serious assaults.

(iii) A similar instance of large scale fraudulent misconduct established by an adjudication in a Securities and Exchange Commission enforcement proceeding.

(iv) Commission of the instant offense while on bail or pretrial release for another serious offense.

(B) Upward Departures from Criminal History Category VI.—In the case of an egregious, serious criminal record in which even the guideline range for Criminal History Category VI is not adequate to reflect the seriousness of the defendant's criminal history, a departure above the guideline range for a defendant with Criminal History Category VI may be warranted. In determining whether an upward departure from Criminal History Category VI is warranted, the court should consider that the nature of the prior offenses rather than simply their number is often more indicative of the seriousness of the defendant's criminal record. For example, a defendant with five prior sentences for very large-scale fraud offenses may have 15 criminal history points, within the range of points typical for Criminal History Category VI, yet have a substantially more serious criminal history overall because of the nature of the prior offenses.

3. Downward Departures.—A downward departure from the defendant's criminal history category may be warranted if, for example, the defendant had two minor misdemeanor convictions close to ten years prior to the instant offense and no other evidence of prior criminal behavior in the intervening period. A departure below the lower limit of the applicable guideline range for Criminal History Category I is prohibited under subsection (b)(2)(B), due to the fact that the lower limit of the guideline range for Criminal History Category I is set for a first offender with the lowest risk of recidivism.

Background: This policy statement recognizes that the criminal history score is unlikely to take into account all the variations in the seriousness of criminal history that may occur. For example, a defendant with an extensive record of serious, assaultive conduct who had received what might now be considered extremely lenient treatment in the past might have the same criminal history category as a defendant who had a record of less serious conduct. Yet, the first defendant's criminal history clearly may be more serious. This may be particularly true in the case of younger defendants (e.g., defendants in their early twenties or younger) who are more likely to have received repeated lenient treatment, yet who may actually pose a greater risk of serious recidivism than older defendants. This policy statement authorizes the consideration of a departure from the guidelines in the limited circumstances where reliable information indicates that the criminal history category does not adequately reflect the seriousness of the defendant's criminal history or likelihood of recidivism, and provides guidance for the consideration of such departures.".

Section 5C1.2 is amended in subsection (a)(1) by inserting "before application of subsection (b) of § 4A1.3 (Departures Based on Inadequacy of Criminal History Category)" after "guidelines".

The Commentary to § 5C1.2 captioned "Application Notes" is amended in Note 1 by inserting "before application of subsection (b) of § 4A1.3 (Departures Based on Inadequacy of Criminal History Category)" after "Category)".

Chapter Five, Part H is amended by striking the Introductory Commentary as follows:

"   Introductory Commentary

The following policy statements address the relevance of certain offender characteristics to the determination of whether a sentence should be outside the applicable guideline range and, in certain cases, to the determination of a sentence within the applicable guideline range. Under 28 U.S.C. § 994(d), the Commission is directed to consider whether certain specific offender characteristics "have any relevance to the nature, extent, place of service, or other incidents of an appropriate sentence" and to take them into account only to the extent they are determined to be relevant by the Commission.

The Commission has determined that certain factors are not ordinarily relevant to the determination of whether a sentence should be outside the applicable guideline range. Unless expressly stated, this does not mean that the Commission views such factors as necessarily inappropriate to the determination of the sentence within the applicable guideline range or to the determination of various other incidents of an appropriate sentence (e.g., the appropriate conditions of probation or supervised release). Furthermore, although these factors are not ordinarily relevant to the determination of whether a sentence should be outside the applicable guideline range, they may be relevant to this determination in exceptional cases. See § 5K2.0 (Grounds for Departure).

In addition, 28 U.S.C. § 994(e) requires the Commission to assure that its guidelines and policy statements reflect the general inappropriateness of considering the defendant's education, vocational skills, employment record, family ties and responsibilities, and community ties in determining whether a term of imprisonment should be imposed or the length of a term of imprisonment.",

and inserting:

"   Introductory Commentary

The following policy statements address the relevance of certain offender characteristics to the determination of whether a sentence should be outside the applicable guideline range and, in certain cases, to the determination of a sentence within the applicable guideline range. Under 28 U.S.C. § 994(d), the Commission is directed to consider whether certain specific offender characteristics 'have any relevance to the nature, extent, place of service, or other incidents of an appropriate sentence' and to take them into account only to the extent they are determined to be relevant by the Commission.

The Commission has determined that certain circumstances are not ordinarily relevant to the determination of whether a sentence should be outside the applicable guideline range. Unless expressly stated, this does not mean that the Commission views such circumstances as necessarily inappropriate to the determination of the sentence within the applicable guideline range or to the determination of various other incidents of an appropriate sentence (e.g., the appropriate conditions of probation or supervised release). Furthermore, although these circumstances are not ordinarily relevant to the determination of whether a sentence should be outside the applicable guideline range, they may be relevant to this determination in exceptional cases. They also may be relevant if a combination of such circumstances makes the case an exceptional one, but only if each such circumstance is identified as an affirmative ground for departure and is present in the case to a substantial degree. See § 5K2.0 (Grounds for Departure).

In addition, 28 U.S.C. § 994(e) requires the Commission to assure that its guidelines and policy statements reflect the general inappropriateness of considering the defendant's education, vocational skills, employment record, and family ties and responsibilities in determining whether a term of imprisonment should be imposed or the length of a term of imprisonment.";

by striking:

"§ 5H1.4.   Physical Condition, Including Drug or Alcohol Dependence or Abuse
             (Policy Statement)

Physical condition or appearance, including physique, is not ordinarily relevant in determining whether a sentence should be outside the applicable guideline range. However, an extraordinary physical impairment may be a reason to impose a sentence below the applicable guideline range; e.g., in the case of a seriously infirm defendant, home detention may be as efficient as, and less costly than, imprisonment.

Drug or alcohol dependence or abuse is not a reason for imposing a sentence below the guidelines. Substance abuse is highly correlated to an increased propensity to commit crime. Due to this increased risk, it is highly recommended that a defendant who is incarcerated also be sentenced to supervised release with a requirement that the defendant participate in an appropriate substance abuse program (see § 5D1.3(d)(4)). If participation in a substance abuse program is required, the length of supervised release should take into account the length of time necessary for the supervisory body to judge the success of the program.

Similarly, where a defendant who is a substance abuser is sentenced to probation, it is strongly recommended that the conditions of probation contain a requirement that the defendant participate in an appropriate substance abuse program (see § 5B1.3(d)(4)).",

and inserting:

"§ 5H1.4. Physical Condition, Including Drug or Alcohol Dependence or Abuse; Gambling Addiction (Policy Statement)

Physical condition or appearance, including physique, is not ordinarily relevant in determining whether a departure may be warranted. However, an extraordinary physical impairment may be a reason to depart downward; e.g., in the case of a seriously infirm defendant, home detention may be as efficient as, and less costly than, imprisonment.

Drug or alcohol dependence or abuse is not a reason for a downward departure. Substance abuse is highly correlated to an increased propensity to commit crime. Due to this increased risk, it is highly recommended that a defendant who is incarcerated also be sentenced to supervised release with a requirement that the defendant participate in an appropriate substance abuse program (see § 5D1.3(d)(4)). If participation in a substance abuse program is required, the length of supervised release should take into account the length of time necessary for the supervisory body to judge the success of the program.

Similarly, where a defendant who is a substance abuser is sentenced to probation, it is strongly recommended that the conditions of probation contain a requirement that the defendant participate in an appropriate substance abuse program (see § 5B1.3(d)(4)).

Addiction to gambling is not a reason for a downward departure.";

by striking:

"§ 5H1.6. Family Ties and Responsibilities, and Community Ties (Policy Statement)

In sentencing a defendant convicted of an offense other than an offense described in the following paragraph, family ties and responsibilities and community ties are not ordinarily relevant in determining whether a sentence should be outside the applicable guideline range.

In sentencing a defendant convicted of an offense involving a minor victim under section 1201, an offense under section 1591, or an offense under chapter 71, 109A, 110, or 117, of title 18, United States Code, family ties and responsibilities and community ties are not relevant in determining whether a sentence should be below the applicable guideline range.

Family responsibilities that are complied with may be relevant to the determination of the amount of restitution or fine.

Commentary

Background: Section 401(b)(4) of Public Law 108–21 directly amended this policy statement to add the second paragraph, effective April 30, 2003.",

and inserting:

"§ 5H1.6.   Family Ties and Responsibilities (Policy Statement)

Family ties and responsibilities are not ordinarily relevant in determining whether a departure may be warranted.

Family responsibilities that are complied with may be relevant to the determination of the amount of restitution or fine.

Commentary

Application Note:

1. Circumstances to Consider.—

    (A) In General.—In determining whether a departure is warranted under this policy statement, the court shall consider the following non-exhaustive list of circumstances:

        (i) The seriousness of the offense.

        (ii) The involvement in the offense, if any, of members of the defendant's family.

        (iii) The danger, if any, to members of the defendant's family as a result of the offense.

    (B) Departures Based on Loss of Caretaking or Financial Support.—A departure under this policy statement based on the loss of caretaking or financial support of the defendant's family requires, in addition to the court's consideration of the non-exhaustive list of circumstances in subdivision (A), the presence of the following circumstances:

        (i) The defendant's service of a sentence within the applicable guideline range will cause a substantial, direct, and specific loss of essential caretaking, or essential financial support, to the defendant's family.

        (ii) The loss of caretaking or financial support substantially exceeds the harm ordinarily incident to incarceration for a similarly situated defendant. For example, the fact that the defendant's family might incur some degree of financial hardship or suffer to some extent from the absence of a parent through incarceration is not in itself sufficient as a basis for departure because such hardship or suffering is of a sort ordinarily incident to incarceration.

(iii) The loss of caretaking or financial support is one for which no effective remedial or ameliorative programs reasonably are available, making the defendant's caretaking or financial support irreplaceable to the defendant's family.

(iv) The departure effectively will address the loss of caretaking or financial support.",

by striking:

"§ 5H1.7. Role in the Offense (Policy Statement)

A defendant's role in the offense is relevant in determining the appropriate sentence. See Chapter Three, Part B (Role in the Offense).",

and inserting:

"§ 5H1.7. Role in the Offense (Policy Statement)

A defendant's role in the offense is relevant in determining the applicable guideline range (see Chapter Three, Part B (Role in the Offense)) but is not a basis for departing from that range (see subsection (d) of § 5K2.0 (Grounds for Departures)).";

and by striking:

"§ 5H1.8. Criminal History (Policy Statement)

A defendant's criminal history is relevant in determining the appropriate sentence. See Chapter Four (Criminal History and Criminal Livelihood).",

and inserting:

"§ 5H1.8. Criminal History (Policy Statement)

A defendant's criminal history is relevant in determining the applicable criminal history category. See Chapter Four (Criminal History and Criminal Livelihood). For grounds of departure based on the defendant's criminal history, see § 4A1.3 (Departures Based on Inadequacy of Criminal History Category).".

Chapter Five Part K, Subpart Two is amended by striking the following guideline and accompanying commentary in its entirety:

"§ 5K2.0. Grounds for Departure (Policy Statement)

(a) DOWNWARD DEPARTURES IN CRIMINAL CASES OTHER THAN CHILD CRIMES AND SEXUAL OFFENSES.—Under 18 U.S.C. § 3553(b), the sentencing court may impose a sentence outside the range established by the applicable guidelines, if the court finds 'that there exists an aggravating or mitigating circumstance of a kind, or to a degree, not adequately taken into consideration by the Sentencing Commission in formulating the guidelines that should result in a sentence different from that described.' Circumstances that may warrant departure from the guideline range pursuant to this provision cannot, by their very nature, be comprehensively listed and analyzed in advance. The decision as to whether and to what extent departure is warranted rests with the sentencing court on a case-specific basis. Nonetheless, this subpart seeks to aid the court by identifying some of the factors that the Commission has not been able to take into account fully in formulating the guidelines. Any case may involve factors in addition to those identified that have not been given adequate consideration by the Commission. Presence of any such factor may warrant departure from the guidelines, under some circumstances, in the discretion of the sentencing court. Similarly, the court may depart from the guidelines, even though the reason for departure is taken into consideration in determining the guideline range (e.g., as a specific offense characteristic or other adjustment), if the court determines that, in light of unusual circumstances, the weight attached to that factor under the guidelines is inadequate or excessive.

Where, for example, the applicable offense guideline and adjustments do take into consideration a factor listed in this subpart, departure from the applicable guideline range is warranted only if the factor is present to a degree substantially in excess of that which ordinarily is involved in the offense. Thus, disruption of a governmental function, § 5K2.7, would have to be quite serious to warrant departure from the guidelines when the applicable offense guideline is bribery or obstruction of justice. When the theft offense guideline is applicable, however, and the theft caused disruption of a governmental function, departure from the applicable guideline range more readily would be appropriate. Similarly, physical injury would not warrant departure from the guidelines when the robbery offense guideline is applicable because the robbery guideline includes a specific adjustment based on the extent of any injury. However, because the robbery guideline does not deal with injury to more than one victim, departure would be warranted if several persons were injured.

Also, a factor may be listed as a specific offense characteristic under one guideline but not under all guidelines. Simply because it was not listed does not mean that there may not be circumstances when that factor would be relevant to sentencing. For example, the use of a weapon has been listed as a specific offense characteristic under many guidelines, but not under other guidelines. Therefore, if a weapon is a relevant factor to sentencing under one of these other guidelines, the court may depart for this reason.

Finally, an offender characteristic or other circumstance that is, in the Commission's view, 'not ordinarily relevant' in determining whether a sentence should be outside the applicable guideline range may be relevant to this determination if such characteristic or circumstance is present to an unusual degree and distinguishes the case from the 'heartland' cases covered by the guidelines.

(b) DOWNWARD DEPARTURES IN CHILD CRIMES AND SEXUAL OFFENSES.—Under 18 U.S.C. § 3553(b)(2), the sentencing court may impose a sentence below the range established by the applicable guidelines only if the court finds that there exists a mitigating circumstance of a kind, or to a degree, that—

(1) has been affirmatively and specifically identified as a permissible ground of downward departure in the sentencing guidelines or policy statements issued under section 994(a) of title 28, United States Code, taking account of any amendments to such sentencing guidelines or policy statements by act of Congress;

(2) has not adequately been taken into consideration by the Sentencing Commission in formulating the guidelines; and

(3) should result in a sentence different from that described.

The grounds enumerated in this Part K of Chapter Five are the sole grounds that have been affirmatively and specifically identified as a permissible ground of downward departure in these sentencing guidelines and policy statements. Thus, notwithstanding any other reference to authority to depart downward elsewhere in this Sentencing Manual, a ground of downward departure has not been affirmatively and specifically identified as a permissible ground of downward departure within the meaning of section 3553(b)(2) unless it is expressly enumerated in this Part K as a ground upon which a downward departure may be granted.

Commentary*

[*Section 401(m)(2)(C) of Public Law 108–21 directs the Commission to revise § 5K2.0, within 180 days after the date of the enactment of that Public Law, or October 27, 2003, to conform § 5K2.0 to changes made by that Public Law, including changes to the appellate standard of review for decisions to depart from the guidelines. That directive has not been implemented yet in the following commentary.]

The United States Supreme Court has determined that, in reviewing a district court's decision to depart from the guidelines, appellate courts are to apply an abuse of discretion standard, because the decision to depart embodies the traditional exercise of discretion by the sentencing court. Koon v. United States, 518 U.S. 81 (1996). Furthermore, '[b]efore a departure is permitted, certain aspects of the case must be found unusual enough for it to fall outside the heartland of cases in the Guideline. To resolve this question, the district court must make a refined assessment of the many facts bearing on the outcome, informed by its vantage point and day-to-day experience in criminal sentencing. Whether a given factor is present to a degree not adequately considered by the Commission, or whether a discouraged factor nonetheless justifies departure because it is present in some unusual or exceptional way, are matters determined in large part by comparison with the facts of other Guidelines cases. District Courts have an institutional advantage over appellate courts in making these sorts of determinations, especially as they see so many more Guidelines cases than appellate courts do.' Id. at 98.

The last paragraph of subsection (a) sets forth the conditions under which an offender characteristic or other circumstance that is not ordinarily relevant to a departure from the applicable guideline range may be relevant to this determination. The Commission does not foreclose the possibility of an extraordinary case that, because of a combination of such characteristics or circumstances, differs significantly from the "heartland" cases covered by the guidelines in a way that is important to the statutory purposes of sentencing, even though none of the characteristics or circumstances individually distinguishes the case. However, the Commission believes that such cases will be extremely rare.

In the absence of a characteristic or circumstance that distinguishes a case as sufficiently atypical to warrant a sentence different from that called for under the guidelines, a sentence outside the guideline range is not authorized. See 18 U.S.C. § 3553(b). For example, dissatisfaction with the available sentencing range or a preference for a different sentence than that authorized by the guidelines is not an appropriate basis for a sentence outside the applicable guideline range.

Section 401(b)(1) of Public Law 108–21 directly amended this policy statement to add subsection (b), effective April 30, 2003.",

and inserting:

"§ 5K2.0.   Grounds for Departure (Policy Statement)

    (a)   UPWARD DEPARTURES IN GENERAL AND DOWNWARD DEPARTURES IN CRIMINAL CASES OTHER THAN CHILD CRIMES AND SEXUAL OFFENSES.—

        (1)   IN GENERAL.—The sentencing court may depart from the applicable guideline range if—

            (A)   in the case of offenses other than child crimes and sexual offenses, the court finds, pursuant to 18 U.S.C. § 3553(b)(1), that there exists an aggravating or mitigating circumstance; or

            (B)   in the case of child crimes and sexual offenses, the court finds, pursuant to 18 U.S.C. § 3553(b)(2)(A)(i), that there exists an aggravating circumstance, of a kind, or to a degree, not adequately taken into consideration by the Sentencing Commission in formulating the guidelines that, in order to advance the objectives set forth in 18 U.S.C. § 3553(a)(2), should result in a sentence different from that described.

        (2)   DEPARTURES BASED ON CIRCUMSTANCES OF A KIND NOT ADEQUATELY TAKEN INTO CONSIDERATION.—

            (A)   IDENTIFIED CIRCUMSTANCES.—This subpart (Chapter Five, Part K, Subpart 2 (Other Grounds for Departure)) identifies some of the circumstances that the Commission may have not adequately taken into consideration in determining the applicable guideline range (e.g., as a specific offense characteristic or other adjustment). If any such circumstance is present in the case and has not adequately been taken into consideration in determining the applicable guideline range, a departure consistent with 18 U.S.C. § 3553(b) and the provisions of this subpart may be warranted.

  (B) UNIDENTIFIED CIRCUMSTANCES.—A departure may be warranted in the exceptional case in which there is present a circumstance that the Commission has not identified in the guidelines but that nevertheless is relevant to determining the appropriate sentence.

(3) DEPARTURES BASED ON CIRCUMSTANCES PRESENT TO A DEGREE NOT ADEQUATELY TAKEN INTO CONSIDERATION.—A departure may be warranted in an exceptional case, even though the circumstance that forms the basis for the departure is taken into consideration in determining the guideline range, if the court determines that such circumstance is present in the offense to a degree substantially in excess of, or substantially below, that which ordinarily is involved in that kind of offense.

(4) DEPARTURES BASED ON NOT ORDINARILY RELEVANT OFFENDER CHARACTERISTICS AND OTHER CIRCUMSTANCES.—An offender characteristic or other circumstance identified in Chapter Five, Part H (Offender Characteristics) or elsewhere in the guidelines as not ordinarily relevant in determining whether a departure is warranted may be relevant to this determination only if such offender characteristic or other circumstance is present to an exceptional degree.

(b) DOWNWARD DEPARTURES IN CHILD CRIMES AND SEXUAL OFFENSES.—Under 18 U.S.C. § 3553(b)(2)(A)(ii), the sentencing court may impose a sentence below the range established by the applicable guidelines only if the court finds that there exists a mitigating circumstance of a kind, or to a degree, that—

(1) has been affirmatively and specifically identified as a permissible ground of downward departure in the sentencing guidelines or policy statements issued under section 994(a) of title 28, United States Code, taking account of any amendments to such sentencing guidelines or policy statements by act of Congress;

(2) has not adequately been taken into consideration by the Sentencing Commission in formulating the guidelines; and

(3) should result in a sentence different from that described.

The grounds enumerated in this Part K of Chapter Five are the sole grounds that have been affirmatively and specifically identified as a permissible ground of downward departure in these sentencing guidelines and policy statements. Thus, notwithstanding any other reference to authority to depart downward elsewhere in this Sentencing Manual, a ground of downward departure has not been affirmatively and specifically identified as a permissible ground of downward departure within the meaning of section 3553(b)(2) unless it is expressly enumerated in this Part K as a ground upon which a downward departure may be granted.

(c) LIMITATION ON DEPARTURES BASED ON MULTIPLE CIRCUMSTANCES.—The court may depart from the applicable guideline range based on a combination of two or more offender characteristics or other circumstances, none of which independently is sufficient to provide a basis for departure, only if—

   (1) such offender characteristics or other circumstances, taken together, make the case an exceptional one; and

   (2) each such offender characteristic or other circumstance is—

      (A) present to a substantial degree; and

      (B) identified in the guidelines as a permissible ground for departure, even if such offender characteristic or other circumstance is not ordinarily relevant to a determination of whether a departure is warranted.

(d) PROHIBITED DEPARTURES.—Notwithstanding subsections (a) and (b) of this policy statement, or any other provision in the guidelines, the court may not depart from the applicable guideline range based on any of the following circumstances:

   (1) Any circumstance specifically prohibited as a ground for departure in §§ 5H1.10 (Race, Sex, National Origin, Creed, Religion, and Socio-Economic Status), 5H1.12 (Lack of Guidance as a Youth and Similar Circumstances), the third and last sentences of 5H1.4 (Physical Condition, Including Drug or Alcohol Dependence or Abuse; Gambling Addiction), the last sentence of 5K2.12 (Coercion and Duress), and 5K2.19 (Post-Sentencing Rehabilitative Efforts).

   (2) The defendant's acceptance of responsibility for the offense, which may be taken into account only under § 3E1.1 (Acceptance of Responsibility).

   (3) The defendant's aggravating or mitigating role in the offense, which may be taken into account only under § 3B1.1 (Aggravating Role) or § 3B1.2 (Mitigating Role), respectively.

   (4) The defendant's decision, in and of itself, to plead guilty to the offense or to enter a plea agreement with respect to the offense (i.e., a departure may not be based merely on the fact that the defendant decided to plead guilty or to enter into a plea agreement, but a departure may be based on justifiable, non-prohibited reasons as part of a sentence that is recommended, or agreed to, in the plea agreement and ac-

cepted by the court. See § 6B1.2 (Standards for Acceptance of Plea Agreement).

(5) The defendant's fulfillment of restitution obligations only to the extent required by law including the guidelines (i.e., a departure may not be based on unexceptional efforts to remedy the harm caused by the offense).

(6) Any other circumstance specifically prohibited as a ground for departure in the guidelines.

(e) REQUIREMENT OF SPECIFIC WRITTEN REASONS FOR DEPARTURE.—If the court departs from the applicable guideline range, it shall state, pursuant to 18 U.S.C. § 3553(c), its specific reasons for departure in open court at the time of sentencing and, with limited exception in the case of statements received in camera, shall state those reasons with specificity in the written judgment and commitment order.

Commentary

Application Notes:

1. Definitions.—For purposes of this policy statement:

'Circumstance' includes, as appropriate, an offender characteristic or any other offense factor.

'Depart', 'departure', 'downward departure', and 'upward departure' have the meaning given those terms in Application Note 1 of the Commentary to § 1B1.1 (Application Instructions).

2. Scope of this Policy Statement.—

(A) Departures Covered by this Policy Statement.—This policy statement covers departures from the applicable guideline range based on offense characteristics or offender characteristics of a kind, or to a degree, not adequately taken into consideration in determining that range. See 18 U.S.C. § 3553(b).

Subsection (a) of this policy statement applies to upward departures in all cases covered by the guidelines and to downward departures in all such cases except for downward departures in child crimes and sexual offenses.

Subsection (b) of this policy statement applies only to downward departures in child crimes and sexual offenses.

(B) Departures Covered by Other Guidelines.—This policy statement does not cover the following departures, which are addressed elsewhere in the guidelines: (i) departures based on the defendant's criminal history (see Chapter Four (Criminal History and Criminal Livelihood), particularly § 4A1.3 (Departures Based on Inadequacy of Criminal History Category)); (ii) departures based on the defendant's substantial assistance to the authorities (see § 5K1.1

(Substantial Assistance to Authorities)); and (iii) departures based on early disposition programs (see § 5K3.1 (Early Disposition Programs)).

3. Kinds and Expected Frequency of Departures under Subsection (a).—As set forth in subsection (a), there generally are two kinds of departures from the guidelines based on offense characteristics and/or offender characteristics: (A) departures based on circumstances of a kind not adequately taken into consideration in the guidelines; and (B) departures based on circumstances that are present to a degree not adequately taken into consideration in the guidelines.

(A) Departures Based on Circumstances of a Kind Not Adequately Taken into Account in Guidelines.—Subsection (a)(2) authorizes the court to depart if there exists an aggravating or a mitigating circumstance in a case under 18 U.S.C. § 3553(b)(1), or an aggravating circumstance in a case under 18 U.S.C. § 3553(b)(2)(A)(i), of a kind not adequately taken into consideration in the guidelines.

(i) Identified Circumstances.—This subpart (Chapter Five, Part K, Subpart 2) identifies several circumstances that the Commission may have not adequately taken into consideration in setting the offense level for certain cases. Offense guidelines in Chapter Two (Offense Conduct) and adjustments in Chapter Three (Adjustments) sometimes identify circumstances the Commission may have not adequately taken into consideration in setting the offense level for offenses covered by those guidelines. If the offense guideline in Chapter Two or an adjustment in Chapter Three does not adequately take that circumstance into consideration in setting the offense level for the offense, and only to the extent not adequately taken into consideration, a departure based on that circumstance may be warranted.

(ii) Unidentified Circumstances.—A case may involve circumstances, in addition to those identified by the guidelines, that have not adequately been taken into consideration by the Commission, and the presence of any such circumstance may warrant departure from the guidelines in that case. However, inasmuch as the Commission has continued to monitor and refine the guidelines since their inception to take into consideration relevant circumstances in sentencing, it is expected that departures based on such unidentified circumstances will occur rarely and only in exceptional cases.

(B) Departures Based on Circumstances Present to a Degree Not Adequately Taken into Consideration in Guidelines.—

(i) In General.—Subsection (a)(3) authorizes the court to depart if there exists an aggravating or a mitigating circumstance in a case under 18 U.S.C. § 3553(b)(1), or an aggravating circumstance in a case under 18 U.S.C.

§ 3553(b)(2)(A)(i), to a degree not adequately taken into consideration in the guidelines. However, inasmuch as the Commission has continued to monitor and refine the guidelines since their inception to determine the most appropriate weight to be accorded the mitigating and aggravating circumstances specified in the guidelines, it is expected that departures based on the weight accorded to any such circumstance will occur rarely and only in exceptional cases.

(ii) Examples.—As set forth in subsection (a)(3), if the applicable offense guideline and adjustments take into consideration a circumstance identified in this subpart, departure is warranted only if the circumstance is present to a degree substantially in excess of that which ordinarily is involved in the offense. Accordingly, a departure pursuant to § 5K2.7 for the disruption of a governmental function would have to be substantial to warrant departure from the guidelines when the applicable offense guideline is bribery or obstruction of justice. When the guideline covering the mailing of injurious articles is applicable, however, and the offense caused disruption of a governmental function, departure from the applicable guideline range more readily would be appropriate. Similarly, physical injury would not warrant departure from the guidelines when the robbery offense guideline is applicable because the robbery guideline includes a specific adjustment based on the extent of any injury. However, because the robbery guideline does not deal with injury to more than one victim, departure may be warranted if several persons were injured.

(C) Departures Based on Circumstances Identified as Not Ordinarily Relevant.—Because certain circumstances are specified in the guidelines as not ordinarily relevant to sentencing (see, e.g., Chapter Five, Part H (Specific Offender Characteristics)), a departure based on any one of such circumstances should occur only in exceptional cases, and only if the circumstance is present in the case to an exceptional degree. If two or more of such circumstances each is present in the case to a substantial degree, however, and taken together make the case an exceptional one, the court may consider whether a departure would be warranted pursuant to subsection (c). Departures based on a combination of not ordinarily relevant circumstances that are present to a substantial degree should occur extremely rarely and only in exceptional cases.

In addition, as required by subsection (e), each circumstance forming the basis for a departure described in this subdivision shall be stated with specificity in the written judgment and commitment order.

4. Downward Departures in Child Crimes and Sexual Offenses.—

(A) Definition.—For purposes of this policy statement, the term 'child crimes and sexual offenses' means offenses under any of the following: 18 U.S.C. § 1201 (involving a minor victim), 18 U.S.C. § 1591, or chapter 71, 109A, 110, or 117 of title 18, United States Code.

    (B)   <u>Standard for Departure</u>.—

        (i)   <u>Requirement of Affirmative and Specific Identification of Departure Ground</u>.—The standard for a downward departure in child crimes and sexual offenses differs from the standard for other departures under this policy statement in that it includes a requirement, set forth in 18 U.S.C. § 3553(b)(2)(A)(ii)(I) and subsection (b)(1) of this guideline, that any mitigating circumstance that forms the basis for such a downward departure be affirmatively and specifically identified as a ground for downward departure in this part (i.e., Chapter Five, Part K).

        (ii)   <u>Application of Subsection (b)(2)</u>.—The commentary in Application Note 3 of this policy statement, except for the commentary in Application Note 3(A)(ii) relating to unidentified circumstances, shall apply to the court's determination of whether a case meets the requirement, set forth in subsection 18 U.S.C. § 3553(b)(2)(A)(ii)(II) and subsection (b)(2) of this policy statement, that the mitigating circumstance forming the basis for a downward departure in child crimes and sexual offenses be of kind, or to a degree, not adequately taken into consideration by the Commission.

5.   <u>Departures Based on Plea Agreements</u>.—Subsection (d)(4) prohibits a downward departure based only on the defendant's decision, in and of itself, to plead guilty to the offense or to enter a plea agreement with respect to the offense. Even though a departure may not be based merely on the fact that the defendant agreed to plead guilty or enter a plea agreement, a departure may be based on justifiable, non-prohibited reasons for departure as part of a sentence that is recommended, or agreed to, in the plea agreement and accepted by the court. <u>See</u> § 6B1.2 (Standards for Acceptance of Plea Agreements). In cases in which the court departs based on such reasons as set forth in the plea agreement, the court must state the reasons for departure with specificity in the written judgment and commitment order, as required by subsection (e).

<u>Background</u>: This policy statement sets forth the standards for departing from the applicable guideline range based on offense and offender characteristics of a kind, or to a degree, not adequately considered by the Commission. Circumstances the Commission has determined are not ordinarily relevant to determining whether a departure is warranted or are prohibited as bases for departure are addressed in Chapter Five, Part H (Offender Characteristics) and in this policy statement. Other departures, such as those based on the defendant's criminal history, the defendant's substantial assistance to authorities, and early disposition programs, are addressed elsewhere in the guidelines.

As acknowledged by Congress in the Sentencing Reform Act and by the

Commission when the first set of guidelines was promulgated, 'it is difficult to prescribe a single set of guidelines that encompasses the vast range of human conduct potentially relevant to a sentencing decision.' (See Historical Note to § 1A1.1 (Authority)). Departures, therefore, perform an integral function in the sentencing guideline system. Departures permit courts to impose an appropriate sentence in the exceptional case in which mechanical application of the guidelines would fail to achieve the statutory purposes and goals of sentencing. Departures also help maintain 'sufficient flexibility to permit individualized sentences when warranted by mitigating or aggravating factors not taken into account in the establishment of general sentencing practices.' 28 U.S.C. § 991(b)(1)(B). By monitoring when courts depart from the guidelines and by analyzing their stated reasons for doing so, along with appellate cases reviewing these departures, the Commission can further refine the guidelines to specify more precisely when departures should and should not be permitted.

As reaffirmed in the Prosecutorial Remedies and Other Tools to end the Exploitation of Children Today Act of 2003 (the 'PROTECT Act', Public Law 108–21), circumstances warranting departure should be rare. Departures were never intended to permit sentencing courts to substitute their policy judgments for those of Congress and the Sentencing Commission. Departure in such circumstances would produce unwarranted sentencing disparity, which the Sentencing Reform Act was designed to avoid.

In order for appellate courts to fulfill their statutory duties under 18 U.S.C. § 3742 and for the Commission to fulfill its ongoing responsibility to refine the guidelines in light of information it receives on departures, it is essential that sentencing courts state with specificity the reasons for departure, as required by the PROTECT Act.

This policy statement, including its commentary, was substantially revised, effective October 27, 2003, in response to directives contained in the PROTECT Act, particularly the directive in section 401(m) of that Act to—

'(1) review the grounds of downward departure that are authorized by the sentencing guidelines, policy statements, and official commentary of the Sentencing Commission; and

(2) promulgate, pursuant to section 994 of title 28, United States Code—

(A) appropriate amendments to the sentencing guidelines, policy statements, and official commentary to ensure that the incidence of downward departures is substantially reduced;

(B) a policy statement authorizing a departure pursuant to an early disposition program; and

(C) any other conforming amendments to the sentencing guidelines, policy statements, and official commentary of the Sentencing Commission necessitated by the Act, including a revision of . . .section 5K2.0'.

The substantial revision of this policy statement in response to the PROTECT Act was intended to refine the standards applicable to departures while giving due regard for concepts, such as the 'heartland', that have evolved in departure jurisprudence over time.

Section 401(b)(1) of the PROTECT Act directly amended this policy statement to add subsection (b), effective April 30, 2003.";

by striking:

"§ 5K2.10. Victim's Conduct (Policy Statement)

If the victim's wrongful conduct contributed significantly to provoking the offense behavior, the court may reduce the sentence below the guideline range to reflect the nature and circumstances of the offense. In deciding the extent of a sentence reduction, the court should consider:

(a) the size and strength of the victim, or other relevant physical characteristics, in comparison with those of the defendant;

(b) the persistence of the victim's conduct and any efforts by the defendant to prevent confrontation;

(c) the danger reasonably perceived by the defendant, including the victim's reputation for violence;

(d) the danger actually presented to the defendant by the victim; and

(e) any other relevant conduct by the victim that substantially contributed to the danger presented.

Victim misconduct ordinarily would not be sufficient to warrant application of this provision in the context of offenses under Chapter Two, Part A.3 (Criminal Sexual Abuse). In addition, this provision usually would not be relevant in the context of nonviolent offenses. There may, however, be unusual circumstances in which substantial victim misconduct would warrant a reduced penalty in the case of a non-violent offense. For example, an extended course of provocation and harassment might lead a defendant to steal or destroy property in retaliation.",

and inserting:

"§ 5K2.10. Victim's Conduct (Policy Statement)

If the victim's wrongful conduct contributed significantly to provoking the offense behavior, the court may reduce the sentence below the guideline range to reflect the nature and circumstances of the offense. In deciding whether a sentence reduction is warranted, and the extent of such reduction, the court should consider the following:

(1) The size and strength of the victim, or other relevant physical characteristics, in comparison with those of the defendant.

(2) The persistence of the victim's conduct and any efforts by the defendant to prevent confrontation.

(3) The danger reasonably perceived by the defendant, including the victim's reputation for violence.

(4) The danger actually presented to the defendant by the victim.

(5) Any other relevant conduct by the victim that substantially contributed to the danger presented.

(6) The proportionality and reasonableness of the defendant's response to the victim's provocation.

Victim misconduct ordinarily would not be sufficient to warrant application of this provision in the context of offenses under Chapter Two, Part A, Subpart 3 (Criminal Sexual Abuse). In addition, this provision usually would not be relevant in the context of non-violent offenses. There may, however, be unusual circumstances in which substantial victim misconduct would warrant a reduced penalty in the case of a non-violent offense. For example, an extended course of provocation and harassment might lead a defendant to steal or destroy property in retaliation.";

by striking:

"§ 5K2.12. Coercion and Duress (Policy Statement)

If the defendant committed the offense because of serious coercion, blackmail or duress, under circumstances not amounting to a complete defense, the court may decrease the sentence below the applicable guideline range. The extent of the decrease ordinarily should depend on the reasonableness of the defendant's actions and on the extent to which the conduct would have been less harmful under the circumstances as the defendant believed them to be. Ordinarily coercion will be sufficiently serious to warrant departure only when it involves a threat of physical injury, substantial damage to property or similar injury resulting from the unlawful action of a third party or from a natural emergency. The Commission considered the relevance of economic hardship and determined that personal financial difficulties and economic pressures upon a trade or business do not warrant a decrease in sentence.",

and inserting:

"§ 5K2.12. Coercion and Duress (Policy Statement)

If the defendant committed the offense because of serious coercion, blackmail or duress, under circumstances not amounting to a complete defense, the court may decrease the sentence below the applicable guideline range. The extent of the decrease ordinarily should depend on the reasonableness of the defendant's actions, on the proportionality of the defendant's actions to the seriousness of coercion, blackmail, or duress involved, and on the extent to which the conduct would have been less harmful under the circumstances as the defendant believed them to be. Ordinarily coercion will be sufficiently serious to warrant departure only when it involves a threat of physical injury, substantial damage to property or similar injury resulting from the unlawful action of a third party or from a natural emergency. Notwithstanding this policy statement, personal financial difficulties and economic pressures upon a trade or business do not warrant a downward departure.";

by striking:

"§ 5K2.13. Diminished Capacity (Policy Statement)

A sentence below the applicable guideline range may be warranted if the defendant committed the offense while suffering from a significantly reduced mental capacity. However, the court may not depart below the applicable guideline range if (1) the significantly reduced mental capacity was caused by the voluntary use of drugs or other intoxicants; (2) the facts and circumstances of the defendant's offense indicate a need to protect the public because the offense involved actual violence or a serious threat of violence; (3) the defendant's criminal history indicates a need to incarcerate the defendant to protect the public; or (4) the defendant has been convicted of an offense under chapter 71, 109A, 110, or 117, of title 18, United States Code. If a departure is warranted, the extent of the departure should reflect the extent to which the reduced mental capacity contributed to the commission of the offense.

Commentary

Application Note:

1. For purposes of this policy statement—

"Significantly reduced mental capacity" means the defendant, although convicted, has a significantly impaired ability to (A) understand the wrongfulness of the behavior comprising the offense or to exercise the power of reason; or (B) control behavior that the defendant knows is wrongful.

Background: Section 401(b)(5) of Public Law 108–21 directly amended this policy statement to add subdivision (4), effective April 30, 2003.",

and inserting:

"§ 5K2.13. Diminished Capacity (Policy Statement)

A sentence below the applicable guideline range may be warranted if (1) the defendant committed the offense while suffering from a significantly reduced mental capacity; and (2) the significantly reduced mental capacity contributed substantially to the commission of the offense. Similarly, if a departure is warranted under this policy statement, the extent of the departure should reflect the extent to which the reduced mental capacity contributed to the commission of the offense.

However, the court may not depart below the applicable guideline range if (1) the significantly reduced mental capacity was caused by the voluntary use of drugs or other intoxicants; (2) the facts and circumstances of the defendant's offense indicate a need to protect the public because the offense involved actual violence or a serious threat of violence; (3) the defendant's criminal history indicates a need to incarcerate the defendant to protect the public; or (4) the defendant has been convicted of an offense under chapter 71, 109A, 110, or 117, of title 18, United States Code.

Commentary

Application Note:

1. For purposes of this policy statement—

'Significantly reduced mental capacity' means the defendant, although convicted, has a significantly impaired ability to (A) understand the wrongfulness of the behavior comprising the offense or to exercise the power of reason; or (B) control behavior that the defendant knows is wrongful.

Background: Section 401(b)(5) of Public Law 108–21 directly amended this policy statement to add subdivision (4), effective April 30, 2003.";

and by striking:

"§ 5K2.20. Aberrant Behavior (Policy Statement)

Except where a defendant is convicted of an offense involving a minor victim under section 1201, an offense under section 1591, or an offense under chapter 71, 109A, 110, or 117, of title 18, United States Code, a sentence below the applicable guideline range may be warranted in an extraordinary case if the defendant's criminal conduct constituted aberrant behavior. However, the court may not depart below the guideline range on this basis if (1) the offense involved serious bodily injury or death; (2) the defendant discharged a firearm or otherwise used a firearm or a dangerous weapon; (3) the instant offense of conviction is a serious drug trafficking offense; (4) the defendant has more than one criminal history point, as determined under Chapter Four (Criminal History and Criminal Livelihood); or (5) the defendant has a prior federal, or state, felony conviction, regardless of whether the conviction is countable under Chapter Four.

Commentary

Application Notes:

1. For purposes of this policy statement—

    'Aberrant behavior' means a single criminal occurrence or single criminal transaction that (A) was committed without significant planning; (B) was of limited duration; and (C) represents a marked deviation by the defendant from an otherwise law-abiding life.

    'Dangerous weapon,' 'firearm,' 'otherwise used,' and 'serious bodily injury' have the meaning given those terms in the Commentary to § 1B1.1 (Application Instructions).

    'Serious drug trafficking offense' means any controlled substance offense under title 21, United States Code, other than simple possession under 21 U.S.C. § 844, that, because the defendant does not meet the criteria under § 5C1.2 (Limitation on Applicability of Statutory Mandatory Minimum Sentences in Certain Cases), results in the imposition of a mandatory minimum term of imprisonment upon the defendant.

2. In determining whether the court should depart on the basis of aberrant behavior, the court may consider the defendant's (A) mental and emotional conditions; (B) employment record; (C) record of prior good works; (D) motivation for committing the offense; and (E) efforts to mitigate the effects of the offense.

Background: Section 401(b)(3) of Public Law 108–21 directly amended this policy statement, effective April 30, 2003.",

and inserting:

"§ 5K2.20. Aberrant Behavior (Policy Statement)

(a) IN GENERAL.—Except where a defendant is convicted of an offense involving a minor victim under section 1201, an offense under section 1591, or an offense under chapter 71, 109A, 110, or 117, of title 18, United States Code, a downward departure may be warranted in an exceptional case if (1) the defendant's criminal conduct meets the requirements of subsection (b); and (2) the departure is not prohibited under subsection (c).

(b) REQUIREMENTS.—The court may depart downward under this policy statement only if the defendant committed a single criminal occurrence or single criminal transaction that (1) was committed without significant planning; (2) was of limited duration; and (3) represents a marked deviation by the defendant from an otherwise law-abiding life.

(c) PROHIBITIONS BASED ON THE PRESENCE OF CERTAIN CIRCUMSTANCES.—The court may not depart downward pursuant to this policy statement if any of the following circumstances are present:

(1) The offense involved serious bodily injury or death.

(2) The defendant discharged a firearm or otherwise used a firearm or a dangerous weapon.

(3) The instant offense of conviction is a serious drug trafficking offense.

(4) The defendant has either of the following: (A) more than one criminal history point, as determined under Chapter Four (Criminal History and Criminal Livelihood) before application of subsection (b) of § 4A1.3 (Departures Based on Inadequacy of Criminal History Category); or (B) a prior federal or state felony conviction, or any other significant prior criminal behavior, regardless of whether the conviction or significant prior criminal behavior is countable under Chapter Four.

Commentary

Application Notes:

1. Definitions.—For purposes of this policy statement:

'Dangerous weapon,' 'firearm,' 'otherwise used,' and 'serious bodily injury' have the meaning given those terms in the Commentary to § 1B1.1 (Application Instructions).

'Serious drug trafficking offense' means any controlled substance offense under title 21, United States Code, other than simple possession under 21 U.S.C. § 844, that provides for a mandatory minimum term of imprisonment of five years or greater, regardless of whether the defendant meets the criteria of § 5C1.2 (Limitation on Applicability of Statutory Mandatory Minimum Sentences in Certain Cases).

2. Repetitious or Significant, Planned Behavior.—Repetitious or significant,

planned behavior does not meet the requirements of subsection (b). For example, a fraud scheme generally would not meet such requirements because such a scheme usually involves repetitive acts, rather than a single occurrence or single criminal transaction, and significant planning.

3. Other Circumstances to Consider.—In determining whether the court should depart under this policy statement, the court may consider the defendant's (A) mental and emotional conditions; (B) employment record; (C) record of prior good works; (D) motivation for committing the offense; and (E) efforts to mitigate the effects of the offense.

Background: Section 401(b)(3) of Public Law 108–21 directly amended subsection (a) of this policy statement, effective April 30, 2003.".

Chapter 5, Part K, is amended by adding at the end the following:

"3. EARLY DISPOSITION PROGRAMS

§ 5K3.1. Early Disposition Programs (Policy Statement)

Upon motion of the Government, the court may depart downward not more than 4 levels pursuant to an early disposition program authorized by the Attorney General of the United States and the United States Attorney for the district in which the court resides.

Commentary

Background: This policy statement implements the directive to the Commission in section 401(m)(2)(B) of the Prosecutorial Remedies and Other Tools to end the Exploitation of Children Today Act of 2003 (the 'PROTECT Act', Public Law 108–21).".

Section 6B1.2 is amended in subsection (a) by striking "[Rule 11(e)(1)(A)]" and inserting "(Rule 11(c)(1)(A))".

Section 6B1.2 is amended in subsection (b) by striking "[Rule 11(e)(1)(B)]" and inserting "(Rule 11(c)(1)(B))"; and by striking subdivision (2) as follows:

"(2) the recommended sentence departs from the applicable guideline range for justifiable reasons.",

and inserting the following:

"(2) (A) the recommended sentence departs from the applicable guideline range for justifiable reasons; and (B) those reasons are specifically set forth in writing in the statement of reasons or judgment and commitment order.".

Section 6B1.2 is amended in subsection (c) by striking "[Rule 11(e)(1)(C)]" and inserting "(Rule 11(c)(1)(C))"; and by striking subdivision (2) as follows:

"(2) the agreed sentence departs from the applicable guideline range for justifiable reasons.",

and inserting the following:

"(2) (A) the agreed sentence departs from the applicable guideline range for justi-

November 1, 2013 APPENDIX C - VOLUME II **Amendment 651**

fiable reasons; and (B) those reasons are specifically set forth in writing in the statement of reasons or judgment and commitment order.".

The Commentary to § 6B1.2 is amended in the second paragraph by striking ". See generally Chapter 1, Part A, Subpart 4(b)(Departures)." and inserting "and those reasons are specifically set forth in writing in the statement of reasons or the judgment and commitment order. As set forth in subsection (d) of § 5K2.0 (Grounds for Departure), however, the court may not depart below the applicable guideline range merely because of the defendant's decision to plead guilty to the offense or to enter a plea agreement with respect to the offense.".

Reason for Amendment: This emergency amendment continues the Commission's work in the area of departures and implements the directive in section 401(m) of the "Prosecutorial Remedies and Other Tools to end the Exploitation of Children Today Act of 2003" or "PROTECT Act," Pub. L. 108–21. The PROTECT Act was enacted on April 30, 2003, and directs the Commission, not later than 180 days after the enactment of the Act, to promulgate: (1) appropriate amendments to the sentencing guidelines, policy statements, and official commentary to ensure that the incidence of downward departures is substantially reduced; (2) a policy statement authorizing a downward departure of not more than 4 levels if the Government files a motion for such departure pursuant to an early disposition program authorized by the Attorney General and the United States Attorney for the district in which the court resides; (3) any other necessary conforming amendments, including a revision of paragraph 4(b) of Part A of Chapter One and a revision of § 5K2.0 (Grounds for Departure). The analysis underlying this amendment will be set forth more fully in a forthcoming report to Congress.

The Commission anticipates that this amendment will substantially reduce the incidence of downward departures by prohibiting several factors as grounds for departure, restricting the availability of certain departures, clarifying when certain departures are appropriate, and limiting the extent of departure permissible for certain offenders. The amendment also reduces the incidence of downward departures generally by restructuring departure provisions throughout the Guidelines Manual to track more closely both the statutory criteria for imposing a sentence outside the guideline sentencing range and the newly enacted statutory requirement that reasons for departure be stated with specificity in the written order of judgment and commitment. See 18 U.S.C. §§ 3553 (Imposition of a sentence), 3742(e) (Review of a sentence). The Commission determined that requiring sentencing courts to document reasons for departure with greater specificity complements the findings required of sentencing courts by the PROTECT Act, increases the accountability of sentencing courts for departures by facilitating appellate review, and improves the Commission's ability to monitor departure decisions and refine the guidelines as necessary.

The eight-part amendment makes modifications to §§ 5K2.0 (Grounds for Departure), 5H1.4 (Physical Condition, Including Drug or Alcohol Dependence or Abuse; Gambling Addiction), 5H1.6 (Family Ties and Responsibilities), 5H1.7 (Role in the Offense), 5H1.8 (Criminal History), 5K2.10 (Victim's Conduct), 5K2.12 (Coercion and Duress), 5K2.13 (Diminished Capacity), 5K2.20 (Aberrant Behavior), 4A1.3 (Departures Based on Inadequacy of Criminal History Category), and 6B1.2 (Standards for Acceptance of Plea Agreements). The amendment also creates one new policy statement, § 5K3.1 (Early Disposition Programs), and one new guideline, § 1A1.1 (Authority), among other changes.

First, this amendment makes several significant modifications to § 5K2.0 (Grounds for Departure) to limit, and in certain circumstances, to prohibit downward departures. The amendment generally restructures § 5K2.0 to set forth more clearly the standards governing departures in order to facilitate and emphasize the analysis required of the court. The amendment does so by: (1) integrating throughout the policy statement the statutory language of 18 U.S.C. §§ 3553(b) and 3742(e), as amended by the PROTECT Act, which provide the statutory criteria for sentencing outside the guideline range; (2) adopting, when provided in the policy statement, a uniform qualitative description of the type of case in which a departure may be warranted, the "exceptional case"; (3) restating in the application notes and background commentary to § 5K2.0 longstanding commentary in the Guidelines Manual, which was reaffirmed by the PROTECT Act, that the frequency of departures under § 5K2.0 generally should be rare, and that certain types of departures under § 5K2.0 should be extremely rare; and (4) deleting certain language in the commentary taken from Koon v. United States, 518 U.S. 81 (1996) that effectively was overruled by the PROTECT Act.

Accordingly, § 5K2.0(a) sets forth the general governing principle that, in cases other than child crimes and sexual offenses, the sentencing court may depart if the court finds pursuant to 18 U.S.C. § 3553(b)(1) that there exists an aggravating or mitigating circumstance of a kind, or to a degree, not adequately taken into consideration by the Sentencing Commission that, in order to advance the objectives set forth in 18 U.S.C. § 3553(a)(2), should result in a sentence different from a sentence within the applicable guideline range.

The amendment also prohibits several grounds for departure, in addition to the departure prohibitions in § 5K2.0 for child crimes and sexual offenses enacted by the PROTECT Act, and other prohibitions elsewhere in the Guidelines Manual. The amendment creates a new subsection, § 5K2.0(d), that clearly lists the forbidden departure grounds. These include several longstanding prohibitions, as well as a number of new prohibitions added by the amendment, specifically: (1) the defendant's acceptance of responsibility; (2) the defendant's aggravating or mitigating role in the offense; (3) the defendant's decision, in itself, to plead guilty to the offense or to enter into a plea agreement with respect to the offense; and (4) the defendant's fulfillment of restitution only to the extent required by law, including the guidelines. The Commission determined that these circumstances are never appropriate grounds for departure.

The amendment also revises § 5K2.0 to restrict the availability of departures based on multiple circumstances, often referred to as a "combination of factors." The Commission determined that heightened criteria are appropriate for cases in which no single offender characteristic or other circumstance independently is sufficient to provide a basis for departure. Under § 5K2.0(c) a departure based on multiple circumstances can be based only on offender characteristics or other circumstances that are identified in the guidelines as permissible grounds for departure. Circumstances unmentioned in the guidelines, therefore, can no longer be used for a departure based on multiple circumstances pursuant to § 5K2.0(c). In addition, in order to support a departure based on a combination of circumstances, each offender characteristic or other circumstance must be present individually to a substantial degree and must make the case exceptional when considered together. Emphasizing the Commission's expectation as to the infrequency of such departures, the accompanying application note retains previously existing guidance and states that departures under § 5K2.0(c) based on a combination of not ordinarily relevant circumstances should occur extremely rarely.

In addition, the amendment clarifies when a departure may be based on a circumstance present to a degree not adequately taken into consideration. Section 5K2.0(a)(3) provides that a departure may be warranted in an exceptional case, even though the circumstance that forms the basis for the departure is taken into consideration, only if the court determines that such circumstance is present to a degree substantially different from that ordinarily involved in that kind of offense.

The amendment also modifies § 5K2.0 in two additional ways to underscore the need for courts to state with specificity their reasons for departure. First, § 5K2.0(e) provides that if the court departs, it shall state, pursuant to 18 U.S.C. § 3553(c), as amended by the PROTECT Act, its specific reasons for departure in open court at the time of sentencing and, with limited exception in the case of statements received in camera, shall state those factors with specificity in the written judgment and commitment order. Second, Application Note 5 provides that in cases in which the court departs based on reasons set forth in a plea agreement, the court must state the reasons for departure with specificity in the written judgment and commitment order.

Second, the amendment limits several departure provisions in Chapter Five, Part H (Specific Offender Characteristics). First, the amendment adds a prohibition to § 5H1.4 (Physical Condition, Including Drug or Alcohol Dependence or Abuse; Gambling Addiction) against departures based on addiction to gambling and renames the policy statement accordingly. The Commission determined that addiction to gambling is never a relevant ground for departure.

The amendment limits the availability of departures pursuant to § 5H1.6 (Family Ties and Responsibilities) by requiring the court to conduct certain more rigorous analyses. In determining whether a departure is warranted under this policy statement, a new application note instructs the court to consider the seriousness of the offense; the involvement in the offense, if any, of members of the defendant's family; and the danger, if any to members of the defendant's immediate family as a result of the offense.

In addition to considering those factors, the amendment further restricts family ties departures by adding an application note that establishes heightened criteria for departures based on loss of caretaking or financial support. In such cases, the court must find all of the following four circumstances: (1) that a sentence within the applicable guideline range will cause a substantial, direct, and specific loss of essential caretaking or essential financial support to the defendant's family; (2) that such loss exceeds the harm ordinarily incident to incarceration; (3) that there are no effective remedial or ameliorative programs reasonably available, making the defendant's caretaking or financial support irreplaceable to the defendant's family; and (4) that the departure effectively will address the loss of caretaking or financial support. The Commission determined that these heightened criteria are appropriate and necessary in order to distinguish hardship or suffering that is ordinarily incident to incarceration from that which is exceptional.

The amendment also eliminates community ties as a separate ground for departure and renames § 5H1.6 accordingly.

The amendment makes conforming modifications to § 5H1.7 (Role in the Offense), reiterating that a defendant's role in the offense is not a basis for departure, and to § 5H1.8 (Criminal History), providing that the only grounds for departure based on the defendant's criminal history are set forth in § 4A1.3 (Departures Based on Inadequacy of Criminal History Category).

Third, the amendment limits several departure provisions in Chapter Five, Part K (Departures). The amendment adds a factor to § 5K2.10 (Victim's Conduct) that the court should consider when determining whether a departure is warranted based on victim's conduct. The amendment provides that, in addition to five previously existing factors, the court should consider the proportionality and reasonableness of the defendant's response to the victim's provocation.

The amendment adds a similar factor to § 5K2.12 (Coercion and Duress). The amendment provides that the extent of a departure based on coercion and duress ordinarily should depend on several considerations, including the proportionality of the defendant's actions to the seriousness of the coercion, blackmail, or duress involved.

The amendment limits the availability of departures pursuant to § 5K2.13 (Diminished Capacity) by adding a causation element. The amendment provides that in order to receive a departure for diminished capacity, the significantly reduced mental capacity must have contributed substantially to the commission of the offense. The amendment similarly limits the extent of departure by stating that the extent of the departure should reflect the extent to which the reduced mental capacity contributed to the commission of the offense.

The amendment significantly restructures § 5K2.20 (Aberrant Behavior) and further restricts the availability of departures based on aberrant behavior. The Commission promulgated § 5K2.20 effective November 1, 2000, in order to resolve a longstanding circuit conflict and more properly define when a departure based on aberrant behavior may be warranted. See Appendix C, amendment 603. A departure based on aberrant behavior may be warranted only if the defendant committed a single criminal occurrence or single criminal transaction that (1) was without significant planning; (2) was of limited duration; and (3) represents a marked deviation by the defendant from an otherwise law-abiding life.

The amendment provides greater emphasis to these strict requirements by moving them from an application note to the body of the policy statement. The amendment also gives the court greater guidance in applying these requirements with a new application note that clarifies that repetitious or significant, planned behavior does not meet the requirements for receiving a departure under § 5K2.20. A fraud scheme, for example, generally would be prohibited from receiving a departure pursuant to § 5K2.20 because such a scheme usually involves repetitive acts, rather than a single occurrence or single criminal transaction, as well as significant planning.

The amendment also further restricts the availability of departures based on aberrant behavior by adding several strict prohibitions to the list that has existed in § 5K2.20 since its initial promulgation. Prior to this amendment, § 5K2.20 prohibited the court from departing based on aberrant behavior if (1) the offense involved serious bodily injury or death; (2) the defendant discharged a firearm or otherwise used a firearm or a dangerous weapon; (3) the instant offense of conviction is a serious drug trafficking offense; (4) the defendant has more than one criminal history point, as determined under Chapter Four (Criminal History and Criminal Livelihood); or (5) the defendant has a prior federal, or state, felony conviction, regardless of whether the conviction is countable under Chapter Four.

The amendment gives greater prominence to those previously existing prohibitions and expands them in significant ways. The amendment eliminates defendants who have any significant prior criminal behavior from consideration for a departure pursuant to § 5K2.20, regardless of whether such behavior is countable under Chapter Four, and even if such behavior is not a state or federal felony. In addition, the amendment expands the class of drug trafficking defendants prohibited from consideration for a departure pursuant to § 5K2.20 by expanding the definition of "serious drug trafficking offense." Specifically, the amendment expands the definition of "serious drug trafficking offense" in the accompanying application note to include any controlled substance offense under title 21, United States Code, other than simple possession under 21 U.S.C. § 844, that provides a mandatory minimum term of imprisonment of five years or greater, regardless of whether the defendant meets the criteria of § 5C1.2 (Limitation on Applicability of Statutory Mandatory Minimum Sentences in Certain Cases). Prior to this amendment, only drug trafficking defendants who were subject to such mandatory minimum penalties and who did not meet the criteria set forth in § 5C1.2 were precluded categorically from consideration for a departure under § 5K2.20.

Fourth, the amendment substantially restructures § 4A1.3 (Departures Based on Inadequacy of Criminal History Category) to set forth more clearly the standards governing departures based on criminal history, to prohibit and limit the extent of departures based on criminal history for certain offenders with significant criminal history, and to require written specification of the basis for a criminal history departure.

Section 4A1.3(a) provides that an upward departure may be warranted if reliable information indicates that the defendant's criminal history category substantially under-represents the seriousness of the defendant's criminal history or the likelihood that the defendant will commit other crimes. Section 4A1.3(a) also more clearly sets forth previously existing guidance regarding determination of the extent of an upward departure based on criminal history. Similarly, § 4A1.3(b) provides that a downward departure may be warranted if reliable information indicates that the defendant's criminal history category substantially over-represents the seriousness of the defendant's criminal history or the likelihood that the defendant will commit other crimes.

The amendment, however, adds several prohibitions and limitations to the availability of downward departures based on criminal history. It prohibits a downward departure based on § 4A1.3(b) if the defendant is an armed career criminal within the meaning of § 4B1.3 (Armed Career Criminal) or a repeat and dangerous sex offender against minors within the meaning of § 4B1.5 (Repeat and Dangerous Sex Offender Against Minors). The Commission determined that such offenders should never receive a criminal history-based downward departure.

Section 4A1.3(b) reiterates the longstanding prohibition against a departure below the lower limit of the applicable guideline range for Criminal History Category I.

Section 4A1.3(b) also contains certain limitations on the extent of departure available under this provision. Specifically, a downward departure pursuant to this section for a career offender within the meaning of § 4B1.1 (Career Offender) may not exceed one criminal history category.

In addition, the amendment provides that a defendant whose criminal history category is Category I after receipt of a downward departure under § 4A1.3(b) does not meet the criterion of subsection (a)(1) of § 5C1.2 if, before receipt of the departure, the defendant had more than one criminal history point under § 4A1.1 (Criminal History Category). Thus, a departure to Category I cannot qualify an otherwise ineligible defendant for relief from an applicable mandatory minimum sentence under § 5C1.2, which is consistent with case law.

The amendment adds a new subsection, § 4A1.3(c), that requires the court, in departing based on criminal history, to set forth in writing the specific reasons why the applicable criminal history category under-represents or over-represents the seriousness of the defendant's criminal history or the likelihood that the defendant will commit other crimes. This specificity requirement is consistent with the PROTECT Act and is intended to facilitate both the necessary statutory and guideline departure analysis, as well as to improve the Commission's ability to refine the criminal history guidelines in light of criminal history departure decisions.

The amendment also makes conforming modifications to § 4A1.1 and § 5C1.2.

The amendment implements the directive at section 401(m)(2)(B) of the PROTECT Act

Amendment 651

by adding a new policy statement at § 5K3.1 entitled Early Disposition Programs. The provision restates the language contained in the directive and provides that, upon motion of the Government, the court may depart downward not more than 4 levels pursuant to an early disposition program authorized by the Attorney General of the United States and the United States Attorney for the district in which the court resides. The Commission determined that implementing the directive in this manner is appropriate at this time, pending further study and monitoring of the implementation of early disposition programs.

The amendment revises subsections (b) and (c) of § 6B1.2 (Standards for Acceptance of Plea Agreements) to require greater specificity in the sentencing documentation in a case involving a departure either recommended or agreed to in a Rule 11(c)(1)(B) or Rule 11(c)(1)(C) plea agreement. Specifically, if the court accepts such a plea agreement, and the recommended or agreed to sentence departs from the applicable guideline range for justifiable reasons, the amendment requires the court to set forth specifically those reasons in writing in the statement of reasons or judgment and commitment order. This specificity requirement is consistent with the PROTECT Act and is intended to facilitate the necessary statutory and guideline departure analysis, as well as to improve the Commission's ability to understand the underlying reasons for departures in cases involving plea agreements.

The amendment creates a new guideline, § 1A1.1 (Authority), that clearly sets forth the Commission's authority to promulgate guidelines, policy statements, and commentary and implements the Protect Act directive requiring conforming amendments to paragraph 4(b) of Part A of Chapter One. In addition, the amendment moves in toto Part A of Chapter One, as in effect on November 1, 1987, to the commentary as a historical note. Part A of Chapter One was an introduction to the Guidelines Manual that explained a number of policy decisions made by the Commission when it promulgated the initial set of guidelines. This introduction was amended occasionally between 1987 and 2003. The Commission determined that in order to preserve its historical significance and context, the introduction should be returned to its original form and placed in a historical note. The Commission encourages review of this material. The amendment also incorporates relevant portions of paragraph 4(b) of Part A of the former introduction regarding departures in the background commentary to § 5K2.0.

The amendment amends § 1B1.1 (Application Instructions) to provide uniform definitions of departure, upward departure, and downward departure.

The amendment also makes technical amendments to § 2A4.1 (Kidnapping, Abduction, Unlawful Restraint).

This amendment complements other significant policy initiatives affecting sentencing, including the statutory changes in sentencing law and guideline changes directly made by the PROTECT Act, and recent policies implemented by the Department of Justice. The Commission believes that these general policy changes, working together, will substantially reduce the incidence of downward departures. In addition to the significant modifications made by this amendment, the Commission has identified several aspects of the guidelines affecting departures that it intends to continue studying during the current amendment cycle and beyond, including aberrant behavior, criminal history, immigration, early disposition, or "fast track," programs, and collateral consequences, among others.

Effective Date: The effective date of this amendment is October 27, 2003.

652. Amendment: Section 2A1.4(a)(1) is amended by striking "10" and inserting "12".

Section 2A1.4(a)(2) is amended by striking "14" and inserting "18".

Reason for Amendment: This amendment responds to a concern that the federal sentencing guidelines do not adequately reflect the seriousness of involuntary manslaughter offenses. Specifically, the Department of Justice, some members of Congress, and an ad hoc advisory group formed by the Commission to address Native American sentencing guideline issues expressed concern that most federal involuntary manslaughter cases involve vehicular homicides, which analysis of Commission data confirmed. These commentators also indicated that these offenses appear to be underpunished, particularly when compared to comparable cases arising under state law. This disparity with state punishments has been confirmed by studies undertaken by the Commission. In addition, Congress increased the maximum statutory penalty for involuntary manslaughter from three to six years' imprisonment in 1994.

In response to these concerns and the Commission's analysis, this amendment increases the base offense level in § 2A1.4(a)(2) for reckless involuntary manslaughter offenses from level 14 to level 18. This four level increase corresponds to an approximate 50 percent increase in sentence length for these offenses. This amendment also increases the base offense level in § 2A4.1(a)(1) for criminally negligent involuntary manslaughter offenses from level 10 to level 12. The two level increase represents an approximate 25 percent increase in the sentence length for these offenses.

Effective Date: The effective date of this amendment is November 1, 2003.

653. **Amendment:** Sections 2B1.1, 2E5.3, 2J1.2, and 2T4.1, effective January 25, 2003 (see USSC Guidelines Manual Appendix C (Volume II), Amendment 647), are repromulgated with the following changes:

Section 2B1.1 is amended by striking subsection (a) as follows:

"(a) Base Offense Level: 6",

and inserting the following:

"(a) Base Offense Level:

(1) 7, if (A) the defendant was convicted of an offense referenced to this guideline; and (B) that offense of conviction has a statutory maximum term of imprisonment of 20 years or more; or

(2) 6, otherwise.".

Section 2B1.1(b)(12) is amended by striking "If the resulting offense level determined under subdivision (A) or (B) is less than level 24, increase to level 24.";

and inserting after subdivision (B) the following:

"(C) The cumulative adjustments from application of both subsections (b)(2) and (b)(12)(B) shall not exceed 8 levels, except as provided in subdivision (D).

(D) If the resulting offense level determined under subdivision (A) or (B) is less than level 24, increase to level 24.".

Section 2B1.1(b) is amended by striking the following:

"(13) If the offense involved a violation of securities law and, at the time of the offense, the defendant was an officer or a director of a publicly traded company, increase by 4 levels.",

Amendment 653

and inserting the following:

"(14) If the offense involved—

(A) a violation of securities law and, at the time of the offense, the defendant was (i) an officer or a director of a publicly traded company; (ii) a registered broker or dealer, or a person associated with a broker or dealer; or (iii) an investment adviser, or a person associated with an investment adviser; or

(B) a violation of commodities law and, at the time of the offense, the defendant was (i) an officer or a director of a futures commission merchant or an introducing broker; (ii) a commodities trading advisor; or (iii) a commodity pool operator,

increase by 4 levels.".

The Commentary to § 2B1.1 captioned "Application Notes" is amended by redesignating Notes 2 through 9 as Notes 3 through 10, respectively; by redesignating Notes 11 through 16 as Notes 13 through 18, respectively; by inserting after Note 1 the following:

"2. Application of Subsection (a)(1).—

(A) 'Referenced to This Guideline'.—For purposes of subsection (a)(1), an offense is 'referenced to this guideline' if (i) this guideline is the applicable Chapter Two guideline determined under the provisions of § 1B1.2 (Applicable Guidelines) for the offense of conviction; or (ii) in the case of a conviction for conspiracy, solicitation, or attempt to which § 2X1.1 (Attempt, Solicitation, or Conspiracy) applies, this guideline is the appropriate guideline for the offense the defendant was convicted of conspiring, soliciting, or attempting to commit.

(B) Definition of 'Statutory Maximum Term of Imprisonment'.—For purposes of this guideline, 'statutory maximum term of imprisonment' means the maximum term of imprisonment authorized for the offense of conviction, including any increase in that maximum term under a statutory enhancement provision.

(C) Base Offense Level Determination for Cases Involving Multiple Counts.—In a case involving multiple counts sentenced under this guideline, the applicable base offense level is determined by the count of conviction that provides the highest statutory maximum term of imprisonment.";

and by striking "10. Application of Subsection (b)(12)(B).—" and inserting "11. Application of Subsection (b)(12)(B).—".

The Commentary to § 2B1.1 captioned "Application Notes" is amended in Note 4, as redesignated by this amendment, in subdivision (B), by striking subdivision (i) as follows:

"(i) In General.—In a case in which undelivered United States mail was taken, or the taking of such item was an object of the offense, or in a case in which the stolen property received, transported, transferred, transmitted, or possessed was undelivered United States mail, 'victim' means any person (I) any victim

November 1, 2013   APPENDIX C - VOLUME II   **Amendment 653**

as defined in Application Note 1; or (II) any person who was the intended recipient, or addressee, of the undelivered United States mail.",

and inserting the following:

"(i)   In General.—In a case in which undelivered United States mail was taken, or the taking of such item was an object of the offense, or in a case in which the stolen property received, transported, transferred, transmitted, or possessed was undelivered United States mail, 'victim' means (I) any victim as defined in Application Note 1; or (II) any person who was the intended recipient, or addressee, of the undelivered United States mail.";

and in subdivision (ii)(IV) by striking "or more".

The Commentary to § 2B1.1 captioned "Application Notes" is amended in Note 13, as redesignated by this amendment, by striking "(b)(13)" each place it appears and inserting "(b)(14)"; by striking subdivision (A) as follows:

"(A)   Definition.—For purposes of this subsection, 'securities law' (i) means 18 U.S.C. §§ 1348, 1350, and the provisions of law referred to in section 3(a)(47) of the Securities Exchange Act of 1934 (15 U.S.C. § 78c(a)(47)); and (ii) includes the rules, regulations, and orders issued by the Securities and Exchange Commission pursuant to the provisions of law referred to in such section.",

and inserting the following:

"(A)   Definitions.—For purposes of this subsection:

'Commodities law' means (i) the Commodities Exchange Act (7 U.S.C. § 1 et seq.); and (ii) includes the rules, regulations, and orders issued by the Commodities Futures Trading Commission.

'Commodity pool operator' has the meaning given that term in section 1a(4) of the Commodities Exchange Act (7 U.S.C. § 1a(4)).

'Commodity trading advisor' has the meaning given that term in section 1a(5) of the Commodities Exchange Act (7 U.S.C. § 1a(5)).

'Futures commission merchant' has the meaning given that term in section 1a(20) of the Commodities Exchange Act (7 U.S.C. § 1a(20)).

'Introducing broker' has the meaning given that term in section 1a(23) of the Commodities Exchange Act (7 U.S.C. § 1a(23)).

'Investment adviser' has the meaning given that term in section 202 of the Investment Advisers Act of 1940 (15 U.S.C. § 80b-2(a)(11)).

'Person associated with a broker or dealer' has the meaning given that term in section 3(a)(48) of the Securities Exchange Act of 1934 (15 U.S.C. § 78c(a)(18)).

'Person associated with an investment adviser' has the meaning given that term in section 202 of the Investment Advisers Act of 1940 (15 U.S.C. § 80b-2(a)(17)).

'Registered broker or dealer' has the meaning given that term in section 3(a)(48) of the Securities Exchange Act of 1934 (15 U.S.C. § 78c(a)(48)).

'Securities law' (i) means 18 U.S.C. §§ 1348, 1350, and the provisions of law referred to in section 3(a)(47) of the Securities Exchange Act of 1934 (15 U.S.C. § 78c(a)(47)); and (ii) includes the rules, regulations, and orders issued by the Securities and Exchange Commission pursuant to the provisions of law referred to in such section.";

and in subdivision (B) by inserting "or commodities law" after "securities law" each place it appears.

The Commentary to § 2B1.1 captioned "Background" is amended in the first paragraph by striking the last sentence as follows:

"It also covers offenses involving altering or removing motor vehicle identification numbers, trafficking in automobiles or automobile parts with altered or obliterated identification numbers, odometer laws and regulations, obstructing correspondence, the falsification of documents or records relating to a benefit plan covered by the Employment Retirement Income Security Act, and the failure to maintain, or falsification of, documents required by the Labor Management Reporting and Disclosure Act.".

The Commentary to § 2C1.1 captioned "Application Notes" is amended in Note 2 by striking "Note 2" and inserting "Note 3".

The Commentary to § 2C1.7 captioned "Application Notes" is amended in Note 3 by striking "Note 2" and inserting "Note 3".

The Commentary to § 2J1.1 captioned "Application Notes" is amended in Note 1 by inserting "In General.—" before "Because".

The Commentary to § 2J1.1 captioned "Application Notes" is amended in Note 2 by inserting "Willful Failure to Pay Court-Ordered Child Support.—" before "For offenses".

The Commentary to § 2J1.1 captioned "Application Notes" is amended by adding at the end the following:

"3. Violation of Judicial Order Enjoining Fraudulent Behavior.—In a case involving a violation of a judicial order enjoining fraudulent behavior, the most analogous guideline is § 2B1.1. In such a case, § 2B1.1(b)(7)(C) (pertaining to a violation of a prior, specific judicial order) ordinarily would apply.".

The Commentary to § 2J1.2 captioned "Application Notes" is amended in Note 1 by inserting before the paragraph that begins "'Substantial interference" the following:

"Definitions.—For purposes of this guideline:

'Records, documents, or tangible objects' includes (A) records, documents, or tangible objects that are stored on, or that are, magnetic, optical, digital, other electronic, or other storage mediums or devices; and (B) wire or electronic communications.".

The Commentary to § 2J1.2 captioned "Application Notes" is amended in Note 2 by inserting "Nonapplicability of Chapter Three, Part C.—" before "For offenses"; by inserting ", prosecution," after "investigation"; and by striking "trial" and inserting "sentencing".

The Commentary to § 2J1.2 captioned "Application Notes" is amended in Note 3 by inserting "Convictions for the Underlying Offense.—" before "In the event"; and by inserting "of an offense sentenced" after "convicted".

The Commentary to § 2J1.2 captioned "Application Notes" is amended in Note 4 by inserting "Upward Departure Considerations.—" before "If a weapon"; by striking "a departure" and inserting "an upward departure"; and by inserting at the end the following:

> "In a case involving an act of extreme violence (for example, retaliating against a government witness by throwing acid in the witness's face), an upward departure would be warranted.".

The Commentary to § 2J1.2 captioned "Application Notes" is amended in Note 5 by inserting "Subsection (b)(1).—" before "The inclusion".

Section 2J1.3(a) is amended by striking "12" and inserting "14".

Appendix A (Statutory Index), effective January 25, 2003 (see USSC Guidelines Manual Appendix C (Volume II), Amendments 647 and 648; see also this document, Amendment 656), is repromulgated without change.

Reason for Amendment: With this amendment the Commission continues its work to deter and punish economic and white collar crimes, building on its Economic Crime Package of 2001 and subsequent formation in early 2002 of an Ad Hoc Advisory Group on the Organizational Guidelines for sentencing corporations and other organizations. This 2003 amendment also implements directives in sections 805, 905, and 1104 of the Sarbanes-Oxley Act of 2002, Pub. L. 107-204 (the "Act"), by making several modifications to §§ 2B1.1 (Larceny, Embezzlement, and Other Forms of Theft; Offenses Involving Stolen Property; Property Damage or Destruction; Fraud and Deceit; Forgery; Offenses Involving Altered or Counterfeit Instruments Other than Counterfeit Bearer Obligations of the United States), 2J1.2 (Obstruction of Justice), and 2E5.3 (False Statements and Concealment of Facts in Relation to Documents Required by the Employee Retirement Income Security Act; Failure to Maintain and Falsification of Records Required by the Labor Management Reporting and Disclosure Act; Destruction and Failure to Maintain Corporate Audit Records), as well as conforming changes to §§ 2J1.1 (Contempt), 2J1.3 (Perjury or Subornation of Perjury; Bribery of Witness), and 2T4.1 (Tax Table). The amendment also responds to increased statutory penalties for existing crimes and several severely punished new crimes created by the Act.

The directives in the Act generally pertain to serious fraud and related offenses and obstruction of justice offenses. Congress gave the Commission emergency amendment authority to promulgate amendments addressing, among other things, officers and directors of publicly traded companies who commit fraud and related offenses, fraud offenses that endanger the solvency or financial security of a substantial number of victims, fraud offenses that involve significantly greater than 50 victims, and obstruction of justice offenses that involve the destruction of evidence. This amendment expands upon the temporary emergency amendment effective January 25, 2003, and repromulgates it as a permanent amendment.

First, the amendment modifies the base offense level in § 2B1.1 to implement more fully the directive contained in section 905(b)(2) of the Act to consider whether the guidelines "for violations of the sections amended by this Act are sufficient to deter and punish such offenses, and specifically, are adequate in view of the statutory increases in penalties contained in this Act." Section 903 of the Act, for example, quadrupled the statutory maximum penalties for wire fraud and mail fraud from five to 20 years' imprisonment, while section 902 made attempts and conspiracies subject to these same heightened penalties. Specifically, the amendment provides a new higher alternative base offense level of level 7 if the defendant was convicted of an offense referenced to § 2B1.1 and the offense carries a statutory maximum term of imprisonment of 20 years or more. The alternative base offense levels are intended to calibrate better the base guideline penalty to the seriousness of the wide variety of offenses referenced to that guideline, as reflected by statutory maximum penalties established by Congress.

For those offenses to which the higher alternative base offense will apply (including wire fraud and mail fraud), the effect of the amendment is to limit the availability of a probation only sentence in Zone A of the sentencing table to offenses involving loss amounts of $10,000 or less, assuming a two level reduction for acceptance of responsibility. Prior to the amendment, a Zone A sentence was available for all offenses sentenced under § 2B1.1 involving loss amounts of $30,000 or less. Similarly, for those offenses for which the higher alternative base offense level will apply, the effect of the amendment is to require an imprisonment sentence in Zone D for offenses involving loss amounts of more than $70,000. Prior to the amendment, a Zone D sentence was required for all offenses sentenced under § 2B1.1 involving loss amounts of more than $120,000.

Second, the amendment expands the loss table at § 2B1.1(b)(1) to punish adequately offenses that cause catastrophic losses of magnitudes previously unforeseen, such as the serious corporate scandals that gave rise to several portions of the Act. Prior to the emergency amendment, the loss table at § 2B1.1(b)(1) provided sentencing enhancements in two level increments up to a maximum of 26 levels for offenses in which the loss exceeded $100,000,000. The amendment adds two additional loss amount categories to the table; an increase of 28 levels for offenses in which the loss exceeded $200,000,000, and an increase of 30 levels for offenses in which the loss exceeded $400,000,000. These additions to the loss table address congressional concern regarding particularly extensive and serious fraud offenses and also more fully effectuate increases in statutory maximum penalties provided by the Act. The amendment also modifies the tax table in § 2T4.1 in a similar manner to maintain the longstanding proportional relationship between the loss table in § 2B1.1 and the tax table.

The amendment also adds a new factor to the general, enumerated factors that the court may consider in determining the amount of loss under § 2B1.1(b)(1). Specifically, the amendment adds the reduction in the value of equity securities or other corporate assets that resulted from the offense to the list of general factors set forth in Application Note 3(C) of § 2B1.1. This factor was added to provide courts additional guidance in determining loss in certain cases, particularly in complex white collar cases.

Third, the amendment addresses the directive contained in section 1104(b)(5) of the Act to "ensure that the guideline offense levels and enhancements under United States Sentencing Guideline 2B1.1 (as in effect on the date of enactment of this Act) are sufficient for a fraud offense when the number of victims adversely involved is significantly greater than 50." The amendment implements this directive by expanding the existing enhancement at § 2B1.1(b)(2) based on the number of victims involved in the offense. Prior to the emergency amendment, subsection (b)(2) provided a two level enhancement if the offense involved more than 10, but less than 50, victims (or was committed through mass-marketing), and a four level enhancement if the offense involved 50 or more victims. The amendment provides an additional two level increase, for a total of six levels, if the offense involved 250 or more victims. The Commission determined that an enhancement of this magnitude appropriately responds to the pertinent directive and accounts for the extensive nature of, and the large scale victimization caused by, such offenses.

Fourth, the amendment addresses directives contained in sections 805 and 1104 of the Act pertaining to securities and accounting fraud offenses and fraud offenses that endanger the solvency or financial security of a substantial number of victims. Specifically, section 805(a)(4) directs the Commission to ensure that "a specific offense characteristic enhancing sentencing is provided under United States Sentencing Guideline 2B1.1 (as in effect on the date of enactment of this Act) for a fraud offense that endangers the solvency or financial security of a substantial number of victims." In addition, section 1104(b)(1) directs the Commission to "ensure that the sentencing guidelines and policy statements reflect the serious nature of securities, pension, and accounting fraud and the need for aggressive and appropriate law enforcement action to prevent such offenses." The amendment implements these directives by expanding the scope of the existing enhancement at § 2B1.1(b)(12)(B).

Prior to the emergency amendment, § 2B1.1(b)(12)(B) provided a four level enhancement and a minimum offense level of level 24 if the offense substantially jeopardized the safety and soundness of a financial institution. The amendment expands the scope of this enhancement by providing two additional parts. The first part applies to offenses that substantially endanger the solvency or financial security of an organization that, at any time during the offense, was a publicly traded company or had 1,000 or more employees. The addition of this part reflects the Commission's determination that such an offense undermines the public's confidence in the securities and investment market much in the same manner as an offense that jeopardizes the safety and soundness of a financial institution undermines the public's confidence in the banking system. This part also reflects the likelihood that an offense that endangers the solvency or financial security of an employer of this size will similarly affect a substantial number of individual victims, without requiring the court to determine whether the solvency or financial security of each individual victim was substantially endangered.

A corresponding application note for § 2B1.1(b)(12)(B) sets forth a non-exhaustive list of factors that the court shall consider in determining whether the offense endangered the solvency or financial security of a publicly traded company or an organization with 1,000 or more employees. The list of factors that the court shall consider when applying the new enhancement includes references to insolvency, filing for bankruptcy, substantially reducing the value of the company's stock, and substantially reducing the company's workforce. As appropriate, the court may consider other factors not enumerated in the application note.

The amendment also modifies the application note to previously existing § 2B1.1(b)(12)(B), the financial institutions enhancement, to be consistent structurally with the new part of the enhancement. Prior to the emergency amendment, the presence of any one of the factors enumerated in the application note would trigger the financial institutions enhancement under § 2B1.1(b)(12)(B). Under the amendment, the application note to the financial institutions enhancement sets forth a non-exhaustive list of factors that the court shall consider in determining whether the offense substantially jeopardized the safety and soundness of a financial institution. The list of factors that the court shall consider when applying this enhancement includes references to insolvency, substantially reducing benefits to pensioners and insureds, and an inability to refund fully any deposit, payment, or investment on demand.

The second part added to § 2B1.1(b)(12)(B) by the amendment applies to offenses that substantially endangered the solvency or financial security of 100 or more victims, regardless of whether a publicly traded company or other organization was affected by the

Amendment 653

offense. The Commission concluded that the specificity of the directive in section 805(a)(4) required an enhancement focused specifically on conduct that endangers the financial security of individual victims. Thus, use of this part of the enhancement will be appropriate in cases in which there is sufficient evidence for the court to determine that the amount of loss suffered by individual victims of the offense substantially endangered the solvency or financial security of those victims. The Commission also determined that the enhancement provided in § 2B1.1(b)(12)(B) shall apply cumulatively with the enhancement at § 2B1.1(b)(2), which is based solely on the number of victims involved in the offense, to reflect the particularly acute harm suffered by victims of offenses to which the new parts of subsection (b)(12)(B) apply. To account for the overlapping nature of such conduct in some cases, however, the Commission added a provision at subsection (b)(12)(C) that limits the cumulative impact of subsections (b)(2) and (b)(12)(B) to eight levels, except for application of the minimum offense level of level 24.

Fifth, the amendment addresses the directive contained at section 1104(a)(2) of the Act to "consider the promulgation of new sentencing guidelines or amendments to existing sentencing guidelines to provide an enhancement for officers or directors of publicly traded corporations who commit fraud and related offenses." The emergency amendment implemented this directive by providing a new, four level enhancement that applies if the offense involved a violation of securities law and, at the time of the offense, the defendant was an officer or director of a publicly traded company.

The amendment expands the scope of this enhancement to cover registered brokers and dealers, associated persons of a broker or dealer, investment advisers, and associated persons of an investment adviser. The amendment also expands the scope of this enhancement to apply if the offense involves a violation of commodities law and, at the time of the offense, the defendant was an officer or director of a futures commission merchant or introducing broker, a commodities trading advisor, or a commodity pool operator. The Commission concluded that a four level enhancement appropriately reflects the culpability of offenders who occupy such positions and who are subject to heightened fiduciary duties imposed by securities law or commodities law similar to duties imposed on officers and directors of publicly traded corporations. Accordingly, the court is not required to determine specifically whether the defendant abused a position of trust in order for the enhancement to apply, and a corresponding application note provides that, in cases in which the new, four level enhancement applies, the existing two level enhancement for abuse of position of trust at § 3B1.3 (Abuse of Position of Trust or Use of Special Skill) shall not apply.

The corresponding application note also expressly provides that the enhancement would apply regardless of whether the defendant was convicted under a specific securities fraud or commodities fraud statute (e.g., 18 U.S.C. § 1348, a new offense created by the Act specifically prohibiting securities fraud) or under a general fraud statute (e.g., 18 U.S.C. § 1341, prohibiting mail fraud), provided that the offense involved a violation of "securities law" or "commodities law" as defined in the application note.

Sixth, the amendment modifies § 2J1.2 to address the directives pertaining to obstruction of justice offenses contained in sections 805 and 1104 of the Act. Specifically, section 805(a) of the Act directs the Commission to ensure that the base offense level and existing enhancements in § 2J1.2 are sufficient to deter and punish obstruction of justice offenses generally, and specifically are adequate in cases involving the destruction, alteration, or fabrication of a large amount of evidence, a large number of participants, the selection of evidence that is particularly probative or essential to the investigation, more than minimal planning, or abuse of a special skill or a position of trust. Section 1104(b) of the Act further directs the Commission to ensure that the "guideline offense levels and enhancements for an obstruction of justice offense are adequate in cases where documents or other physical evidence are actually destroyed or fabricated."

The amendment implements these directives by making two modifications to § 2J1.2. First, the amendment increases the base offense level in § 2J1.2 from level 12 to level 14. Second, the amendment adds a new two level enhancement to § 2J1.2. This enhancement applies if the offense (1) involved the destruction, alteration, or fabrication of a substantial number of records, documents or tangible objects; (2) involved the selection of any essential or especially probative record, document, or tangible object to destroy or alter; or (3) was otherwise extensive in scope, planning, or preparation. The amendment also adds an upward departure provision for offenses sentenced under § 2J1.2 that involve extreme acts of violence, for example, retaliating against a government witness by throwing acid in the witness's face. The Commission determined that existing adjustments in Chapter Three for aggravating role, § 3B1.1, and abuse of position of trust or use of special skill, § 3B1.3, adequately account for those particular factors described in section 805(a) of the Act.

Seventh, the amendment also increases the base offense level in the perjury guideline, § 2J1.3, from level 12 to level 14 in order to maintain the longstanding proportional relationship between the offense levels provided in the guidelines for perjury and obstruction of justice.

Eighth, the amendment addresses new offenses created by the Act. Section 1520 of title 18, United States Code, relating to destruction of corporate audit records, is referenced to § 2E5.3. Section 1520 provides a statutory maximum penalty of ten years' imprisonment for knowing and willful violations of document maintenance requirements as set forth in that section or in rules or regulations to be promulgated by the Securities and Exchange Commission pursuant to that section. The amendment also expands the existing cross reference in § 2E5.3(a)(2) specifically to cover fraud and obstruction of justice offenses. Accordingly, if a defendant violated 18 U.S.C. § 1520 in order to obstruct justice, the cross reference provision in § 2E5.3 requires the court to apply § 2J1.2 instead of § 2E5.3. Other new offenses are listed in Appendix A (Statutory Index), as well as in the statutory provisions of the relevant guidelines.

Finally, the amendment amends the contempt guideline, § 2J1.1, by adding an application note clarifying that (1) § 2B1.1 is the most analogous guideline in a case involving a violation of a judicial order enjoining fraudulent behavior; and (2) the enhancement at § 2B1.1(b)(7)(C) (pertaining to a violation of a prior, specific judicial order) ordinarily would apply in such a case.

Effective Date: The effective date of this amendment is November 1, 2003.

654. **Amendment:** Section 2B1.1(b) is amended by inserting after subsection (b)(12) the following:

"(13) (A) (Apply the greatest) If the defendant was convicted of an offense under:

(i) 18 U.S.C. § 1030, and the offense involved (I) a computer system used to maintain or operate a critical infrastructure, or used by or for a government entity in furtherance of the administration of justice, national defense, or national security; or (II) an intent to obtain personal information, increase by 2 levels.

Amendment 654   APPENDIX C - VOLUME II   November 1, 2013

> (ii) 18 U.S.C. § 1030(a)(5)(A)(i), increase by 4 levels.
>
> (iii) 18 U.S.C. § 1030, and the offense caused a substantial disruption of a critical infrastructure, increase by 6 levels.
>
> (B) If subdivision (A)(iii) applies, and the offense level is less than level 24, increase to level 24.".

The Commentary to § 2B1.1 captioned "Statutory Provisions" is amended by inserting ", 2701" after "2332b(a)(1)".

The Commentary to § 2B1.1 captioned "Application Notes" is amended in Note 3(A)(v), as redesignated by Amendment 653, by striking subdivision (III) as follows:

> "(III) Protected Computer Cases.—In the case of an offense involving unlawfully accessing, or exceeding authorized access to, a "protected computer" as defined in 18 U.S.C. § 1030(e)(2), actual loss includes the following pecuniary harm, regardless of whether such pecuniary harm was reasonably foreseeable: reasonable costs to the victim of conducting a damage assessment, and restoring the system and data to their condition prior to the offense, and any lost revenue due to interruption of service.",

and inserting the following:

> "(III) Offenses Under 18 U.S.C. § 1030.—In the case of an offense under 18 U.S.C. § 1030, actual loss includes the following pecuniary harm, regardless of whether such pecuniary harm was reasonably foreseeable: any reasonable cost to any victim, including the cost of responding to an offense, conducting a damage assessment, and restoring the data, program, system, or information to its condition prior to the offense, and any revenue lost, cost incurred, or other damages incurred because of interruption of service.".

The Commentary to § 2B1.1 captioned "Application Notes" is amended by inserting before Note 13, as redesignated by Amendment 653, the following:

> "12. Application of Subsection (b)(13).—
>
> (A) Definitions.—For purposes of subsection (b)(13):
>
> 'Critical infrastructure' means systems and assets vital to national defense, national security, economic security, public health or safety, or any combination of those matters. A critical infrastructure may be publicly or privately owned. Examples of critical infrastructures include gas and oil production, storage, and delivery systems, water supply systems, telecommunications networks, electrical power delivery systems, financing and banking systems, emergency services (including medical, police, fire, and rescue services), transportation systems and services (including highways, mass transit, airlines, and airports), and government operations that provide essential services to the public.
>
> 'Government entity' has the meaning given that term in 18 U.S.C. § 1030(e)(9).
>
> 'Personal information' means sensitive or private information

(including such information in the possession of a third party), including (i) medical records; (ii) wills; (iii) diaries; (iv) private correspondence, including e-mail; (v) financial records; (vi) photographs of a sensitive or private nature; or (vii) similar information.

    (B)   Subsection (b)(13)(iii).—If the same conduct that forms the basis for an enhancement under subsection (b)(13)(iii) is the only conduct that forms the basis for an enhancement under subsection (b)(12)(B), do not apply the enhancement under subsection (b)(12)(B).".

The Commentary to § 2B1.1 captioned "Application Notes" is amended in Note 18, as redesignated by Amendment 653, by adding at the end of subdivision (A)(ii) the following:

"An upward departure would be warranted, for example, in an 18 U.S.C. § 1030 offense involving damage to a protected computer, if, as a result of that offense, death resulted.";

by redesignating subdivision (B) as subdivision (C); and by inserting after subdivision (A) the following:

"(B)   Upward Departure for Debilitating Impact on a Critical Infrastructure.—An upward departure would be warranted in a case in which subsection (b)(13)(iii) applies and the disruption to the critical infrastructure(s) is so substantial as to have a debilitating impact on national security, national economic security, national public health or safety, or any combination of those matters.".

The Commentary to § 2B1.1 captioned "Background" is amended by adding at the end the following paragraph:

"   Subsection (b)(13) implements the directive in section 225(b) of Public Law 107–296. The minimum offense level of level 24 provided in subsection (b)(13)(B) for an offense that resulted in a substantial disruption of a critical infrastructure reflects the serious impact such an offense could have on national security, national economic security, national public health or safety, or a combination of any of these matters.".

Section 2B2.3(b)(1) is amended by striking "or" after "airport;" and by inserting after "residence" the following:

"; or (F) on a computer system used (i) to maintain or operate a critical infrastructure; or (ii) by or for a government entity in furtherance of the administration of justice, national defense, or national security".

The Commentary to § 2B2.3 captioned "Application Notes" is amended in Note 1 by inserting after "United States Code." the following paragraph:

"'Critical infrastructure' means systems and assets vital to national defense, national security, economic security, public health or safety, or any combination of those matters. A critical infrastructure may be publicly or privately owned. Examples of critical infrastructures include gas and oil production, storage, and delivery systems, water supply systems, telecommunications networks, electrical power delivery systems, financing and banking systems, emergency services (including medical, police, fire, and rescue services), transportation systems and services (including highways, mass transit, airlines, and airports), and government operations that provide essential services to the public.";

and by inserting after "Instructions)." the following paragraph:

"'Government entity' has the meaning given that term in 18 U.S.C. § 1030(e)(9).".

Section 2B3.2(b)(3) is amended by striking subdivision (B) as follows:

"(B) If the offense involved preparation to carry out a threat of (i) death, (ii) serious bodily injury, (iii) kidnapping, or (iv) product tampering; or if the participant(s) otherwise demonstrated the ability to carry out such threat, increase by 3 levels.",

and inserting the following:

"(B) If (i) the offense involved preparation to carry out a threat of (I) death; (II) serious bodily injury; (III) kidnapping; (IV) product tampering; or (V) damage to a computer system used to maintain or operate a critical infrastructure, or by or for a government entity in furtherance of the administration of justice, national defense, or national security; or (ii) the participant(s) otherwise demonstrated the ability to carry out a threat described in any of subdivisions (i)(I) through (i)(V), increase by 3 levels.".

The Commentary to § 2B3.2 captioned "Application Notes" is amended by striking Note 1 as follows:

"1. 'Firearm,' 'dangerous weapon,' 'otherwise used,' 'brandished,' 'bodily injury,' 'serious bodily injury,' 'permanent or life-threatening bodily injury,' 'abducted,' and 'physically restrained' are defined in the Commentary to § 1B1.1 (Application Instructions).",

and inserting the following:

"1. Definitions.—For purposes of this guideline:

'Abducted,' 'bodily injury,' 'brandished,' 'dangerous weapon,' 'firearm,' 'otherwise used,' 'permanent or life-threatening bodily injury,' 'physically restrained,' and 'serious bodily injury' have the meaning given those terms in Application Note 1 of the Commentary to § 1B1.1 (Application Instructions).

'Critical infrastructure' means systems and assets vital to national defense, national security, economic security, public health or safety, or any combination of those matters. A critical infrastructure may be publicly or privately owned. Examples of critical infrastructures include gas and oil production, storage, and delivery systems, water supply systems, telecommunications networks, electrical power delivery systems, financing and banking systems, emergency services (including medical, police, fire, and rescue services), transportation systems and services (including highways, mass transit, airlines, and airports), and government operations that provide essential services to the public.

'Government entity' has the meaning given that term in 18 U.S.C. § 1030(e)(9).".

The Commentary to § 2M3.2 captioned "Statutory Provisions" is amended by inserting

"§ " before "793(a)"; and by inserting ", 1030(a)(1)" after "(g)".

Appendix A (Statutory Index) is amended by inserting after the line referenced to 18 U.S.C. § 2512 the following:

"18 U.S.C. § 2701   2B1.1".

Reason for Amendment: This amendment addresses the serious harm and invasion of privacy that can result from offenses involving the misuse of, or damage to, computers. It implements the directive in section 225(b) of the Homeland Security Act of 2002, Pub. L. 107–296, which required the Commission to review, and if appropriate amend, the guidelines and policy statements applicable to persons convicted of offenses under 18 U.S.C. § 1030 (fraud and related activity in connection with computers) to ensure that the guidelines and policy statements reflect the serious nature and growing incidence of such offenses and the need for an effective deterrent and appropriate punishment. The directive further requires the Commission to consider the extent to which eight specific factors were or were not accounted for by the guidelines. The amendment responds to the directive by making several changes to §§ 2B1.1 (Larceny, Embezzlement, and Other Forms of Theft; Offenses Involving Stolen Property; Property Damage or Destruction; Fraud and Deceit; Forgery; Offenses Involving Altered or Counterfeit Instruments Other than Counterfeit Bearer Obligations of the United States), 2B2.3 (Trespass), and 2B3.2 (Extortion by Force or Threat of Injury or Serious Damage). These changes are designed to supplement existing guidelines and policy statements and thereby ensure that offenses under 18 U.S.C. § 1030 are adequately addressed and punished.

First, the amendment adds a new specific offense characteristic at § 2B1.1(b)(13) with three alternative enhancements of two, four, and six levels. The first enhancement provides a two level increase for convictions under 18 U.S.C. § 1030 that involve either (1) a computer system used to maintain or operate a critical infrastructure or used in furtherance of the administration of justice, national defense, or national security; or (2) an intent to obtain private personal information. The second enhancement provides a four level increase for a conviction under 18 U.S.C. § 1030(a)(5)(A)(i), which requires a heightened showing of intent to cause damage. The third enhancement provides a six level increase, with a minimum offense level of level 24, for a conviction under 18 U.S.C. § 1030 that resulted in a substantial disruption of a critical infrastructure. The graduated levels ensure incremental punishment for increasingly serious conduct, and were chosen in recognition of the fact that conduct supporting application of a more serious enhancement frequently will encompass behavior relevant to a lesser enhancement as well. Accordingly, the most serious applicable enhancement will apply in any particular case.

The minimum offense level of level 24 applicable to the third such enhancement was chosen to maintain parity with the minimum offense level that applies to an offense that substantially jeopardized the safety and soundness of a financial institution, substantially endangered the solvency or financial security of a publicly traded company or an organization of at least 1,000 employees, or substantially endangered the solvency or financial security of 100 or more victims. See § 2B1.1(b)(12)(B). Because of the potential overlap in certain cases, the commentary provides that the enhancement at § 2B1.1(b)(12)(B) will not apply in a case in which the conduct supporting the six level critical infrastructure enhancement is the only conduct that forms the basis for the § 2B1.1(b)(12)(B) enhancement.

The minimum offense level of level 24 applicable to the third enhancement also reflects the fact that some offenders to whom the enhancement may apply will be subject to a statutory maximum penalty of five years' imprisonment, i.e., those convicted of an offense under 18 U.S.C. § 1030(a)(5)(A)(ii). To ensure that the most egregious cases involving critical infrastructure are adequately addressed, the amendment also provides an encouraged upward departure for cases in which the disruption of the critical infrastructure has a debilitating impact on national security, national economic security, national public health or safety, or any combination of these matters.

A definition of critical infrastructure is provided in the commentary. This definition is derived in part from the definition of critical infrastructure in the USA PATRIOT Act (see Pub. L. 107–56, section 1016; 42 U.S.C. § 5195c(e)) but was modified to ensure that the enhancement will apply to substantial disruptions of critical infrastructure that are regional, rather than national, in scope. Examples of critical infrastructures are provided.

Second, the amendment modifies the rule of construction relating to the calculation of loss in protected computer cases. This change was made to incorporate more fully the statutory definition of loss at 18 U.S.C. § 1030(e)(11), added as part of the USA PATRIOT Act, and to clarify its application to all 18 U.S.C. § 1030 offenses sentenced under § 2B1.1.

Third, the amendment expands the upward departure note in § 2B1.1. That note provides that an upward departure may be warranted if an offense caused or risked substantial nonmonetary harm, including physical harm. The amendment adds a provision that expressly states that an upward departure would be warranted for an offense under 18 U.S.C. § 1030 involving damage to a protected computer that results in death.

Fourth, the amendment modifies § 2B2.3, to which 18 U.S.C. § 1030(a)(3) (misdemeanor trespass on a government computer) offenses are referenced, and § 2B3.2, to which 18 U.S.C. § 1030(a)(7) (extortionate demand to damage protected computer) offenses are referenced, to provide enhancements relating to computer systems used to maintain or operate a critical infrastructure, or by or for a government entity in furtherance of the administration of justice, national defense, or national security. The amendment expands the scope of existing enhancements to ensure that trespasses and extortions involving these types of important computer systems are addressed.

Finally, the amendment references offenses under 18 U.S.C. § 2701 (unlawful access to stored communications) to § 2B1.1. Prior to the Act, a first offense under section 2701 was classified as a misdemeanor offense, and the guidelines did not reference the statute in Appendix A (Statutory Index). Given that the Act increased the penalties available for 18 U.S.C. § 2701 offenses, the amendment references the statute in Appendix A. Section 2701 offenses are referenced to § 2B1.1 because such offenses involve the obtaining, altering, or denial of authorized access to stored wire or electronic communications, conduct that is related to fraud, theft, and property damage, which are covered by § 2B1.1.

Effective Date: The effective date of this amendment is November 1, 2003.

655. **Amendment:** The Commentary to § 2B1.1 captioned "Application Notes", as amended by Amendment 654, is further amended in subdivision (A)(ii) of Note 18, as redesignated by Amendment 653, by adding at the end the following:

> "An upward departure also would be warranted, for example, in a case involving animal enterprise terrorism under 18 U.S.C. § 43, if, in the course of the offense, serious bodily injury or death resulted, or substantial scientific research or information were destroyed.".

Section 2K1.3(a) is amended by redesignating subdivisions (3) and (4) as subdivisions (4) and (5), respectively; and by inserting after subdivision (2) the following:

> "(3)   18, if the defendant was convicted under 18 U.S.C. § 842(p)(2);".

Section 2K1.3(b)(3) is amended by inserting "(A) was convicted under 18 U.S.C. § 842(p)(2); or (B)" after "defendant".

Section 2K1.3(c)(1) is amended by inserting "(A) was convicted under 18 U.S.C. § 842(p)(2); or (B)" after "defendant".

The Commentary to § 2K1.3 captioned "Application Notes" is amended in Note 3 by striking "(3)" and inserting "(4)".

The Commentary to § 2K1.3 captioned "Application Notes" is amended in the second paragraph of Note 9 by striking "(3)" and inserting "(4)".

The Commentary to § 2K1.3 captioned "Application Notes" is amended in Note 11 by adding at the end the following new paragraph:

> "In addition, for purposes of subsection (c)(1)(A), 'that other offense' means, with respect to an offense under 18 U.S.C. § 842(p)(2), the underlying Federal crime of violence.".

Section 2K1.4(a)(1)(B) is amended by striking "or a ferry" and inserting "a ferry, a public transportation system, a state or government facility, an infrastructure facility, or a place of public use".

Section 2K1.4(a) is amended by striking subdivision (2) as follows:

> "(2)   20, if the offense (A) created a substantial risk of death or serious bodily injury to any person other than a participant in the offense; (B) involved the destruction or attempted destruction of a structure other than (i) a dwelling, or (ii) an airport, an aircraft, a mass transportation facility, a mass transportation vehicle, or a ferry; or (C) endangered (i) a dwelling, (ii) a structure other than a dwelling, or (iii) an aircraft, a mass transportation vehicle, or a ferry; or",

and inserting the following:

> "(2)   20, if the offense (A) created a substantial risk of death or serious bodily injury to any person other than a participant in the offense; (B) involved the destruction or attempted destruction of a structure other than (i) a dwelling, or (ii) an airport, an aircraft, a mass transportation facility, a mass transportation vehicle, a ferry, a public transportation system, a state or government facility, an infrastructure facility, or a place of public use; or (C) endangered (i) a dwelling, (ii) a structure other than a dwelling, or (iii) an airport, an aircraft, a mass transportation facility, a mass transportation vehicle, a ferry, a public transportation system, a state or government facility, an infrastructure facility, or a place of public use; or".

The Commentary to § 2K1.4 captioned "Statutory Provisions" is amended by inserting ", 2332f" after "2332a".

The Commentary to § 2K1.4 captioned "Application Notes" is amended in Note 1 by adding at the end the following new paragraph:

> "'State or government facility', 'infrastructure facility', 'place of public use', and 'public transportation system' have the meaning given those terms in 18 U.S.C. § 2332f(e)(3), (5), (6), and (7), respectively.".

Amendment 655

Section 2M5.3 is amended in the heading by adding "or For a Terrorist Purpose" after "Organizations".

Section 2M5.3(b)(1) is amended in subdivision (C) by striking "or" after "explosives;"; in subdivision (D) by inserting "the intent," after "with" and by inserting a comma after "knowledge"; and by inserting "; or (E) funds or other material support or resources with the intent, knowledge, or reason to believe they are to be used to commit or assist in the commission of a violent act" after "(A) through (C)".

The Commentary to § 2M5.3 captioned "Statutory Provision" is amended by striking "Provision" and inserting "Provisions"; by inserting "§ " before "2339B"; and by inserting ", 2339C(a)(1)(B), (c)(2)(B) (but only with respect to funds known or intended to have been provided or collected in violation of 18 U.S.C. § 2339C(a)(1)(B))" after "2339B".

The Commentary to § 2M5.3 captioned "Application Notes" is amended in Note 2(A) by inserting "funds or other" after "volume of the".

Section 2M6.1(a)(2) is amended by inserting "and" after "(a)(3),"; and by striking ", and (a)(5)".

Section 2M6.1(a)(3) is amended by inserting "or" after the semicolon.

Section 2M6.1(a)(4) is amended by inserting "(A)" after "if"; and by inserting "(B) the offense (i) involved a threat to use a nuclear weapon, nuclear material, or nuclear byproduct material, a chemical weapon, a biological agent, toxin, or delivery system, or a weapon of mass destruction; but (ii) did not involve any conduct evidencing an intent or ability to carry out the threat." after "or".

Section § 2M6.1(a) is amended by striking subdivision (5) as follows:

"(5)   20, if the offense (A) involved a threat to use a nuclear weapon, nuclear material, or nuclear byproduct material, a chemical weapon, a biological agent, toxin, or delivery system, or a weapon of mass destruction; but (B) did not involve any conduct evidencing an intent or ability to carry out the threat.".

Section 2M6.1(b)(1) is amended by striking the comma after "(a)(2)" and inserting "or"; and by striking ", or (a)(5)".

Section 2M6.1(b)(2) is amended by inserting "(A)" after "(a)(4)".

Section 2M6.1(b)(3) is amended by inserting "or" after "(a)(3),"; and by striking ", or (a)(5)".

The Commentary to § 2M6.1 captioned "Statutory Provisions" is amended by inserting "(only with respect to weapons of mass destruction as defined in 18 U.S.C. § 2332a(c)(2)(B), (C), and (D))," after "842(p)(2)"; and by striking ", but including any biological agent, toxin, or vector".

The Commentary to § 2M6.1 captioned "Application Notes" is amended in Note 1 in the paragraph that begins "'Select biological agent'" by inserting "(A)" after "identified"; by inserting "and maintained" after "established"; and by striking "511(d) of the Antiterrorism and Effective Death Penalty Act, Pub. L. 104–132. See 42 C.F.R. part 72." and inserting "351A of the Public Health Service Act (42 U.S.C. § 262a); or (B) by the Secretary of Agriculture on the list established and maintained pursuant to section 212 of the Agricultural Bioterrorism Protection Act of 2002 (7 U.S.C. § 8401).".

The Commentary to § 2M6.1 captioned "Application Notes" is amended in Note 2 by striking "(a)(3)" each place it appears and inserting "(a)(4)(B)".

Chapter Two, Part Q, is amended by striking § 2Q1.4 in its entirety as follows:

"§ 2Q1.4. Tampering or Attempted Tampering with Public Water System

(a) Base Offense Level: 18

(b) Specific Offense Characteristics

(1) If a risk of death or serious bodily injury was created, increase by 6 levels.

(2) If the offense resulted in disruption of a public water system or evacuation of a community, or if cleanup required a substantial expenditure, increase by 4 levels.

(3) If the offense resulted in an ongoing, continuous, or repetitive release of a contaminant into a public water system or lasted for a substantial period of time, increase by 2 levels.

(4) If the purpose of the offense was to influence government action or to extort money, increase by 6 levels.

Commentary

Statutory Provision: 42 U.S.C. § 300i-1.

Application Note:

1. 'Serious bodily injury' is defined in the Commentary to § 1B1.1 (Application Instructions).",

and inserting the following new guideline:

"§ 2Q1.4. Tampering or Attempted Tampering with a Public Water System; Threatening to Tamper with a Public Water System

(a) Base Offense Level (Apply the greatest):

(1) 26;

(2) 22, if the offense involved (A) a threat to tamper with a public water system; and (B) any conduct evidencing an intent to carry out the threat; or

(3) 16, if the offense involved a threat to tamper with a public water system but did not involve any conduct evidencing an intent to carry out the threat.

(b) Specific Offense Characteristics

(1) If (A) any victim sustained permanent or life-threatening bodily injury, increase by 4 levels; (B) any victim sustained serious bodily injury, increase by 2 levels; or (C) the degree

of injury is between that specified in subdivisions (A) and (B), increase by 3 levels.

  (2) If the offense resulted in (A) a substantial disruption of public, governmental, or business functions or services; or (B) a substantial expenditure of funds to clean up, decontaminate, or otherwise respond to the offense, increase by 4 levels.

  (3) If the offense resulted in an ongoing, continuous, or repetitive release of a contaminant into a public water system or lasted for a substantial period of time, increase by 2 levels.

(c) Cross References

  (1) If the offense resulted in death, apply § 2A1.1 (First Degree Murder) if the death was caused intentionally or knowingly, or § 2A1.2 (Second Degree Murder) in any other case, if the resulting offense level is greater than that determined above.

  (2) If the offense was tantamount to attempted murder, apply § 2A2.1 (Assault with Intent to Commit Murder; Attempted Murder) if the resulting offense level is greater than that determined above.

  (3) If the offense involved extortion, apply § 2B3.2 (Extortion by Force or Threat of Injury or Serious Damage) if the resulting offense level is greater than that determined above.

(d) Special Instruction

  (1) If the defendant is convicted of a single count involving (A) the death or permanent, life-threatening, or serious bodily injury of more than one victim; or (B) conduct tantamount to the attempted murder of more than one victim, Chapter Three, Part D (Multiple Counts) shall be applied as if the defendant had been convicted of a separate count for each such victim.

Commentary

Statutory Provision: 42 U.S.C. § 300i-1.

Application Notes:

1. Definitions.—For purposes of this guideline, 'permanent or life-threatening bodily injury' and 'serious bodily injury' have the meaning given those terms in Note 1 of the Commentary to § 1B1.1 (Application Instructions).

2. Application of Special Instruction.—Subsection (d) applies in any case in which the defendant is convicted of a single count involving (A) the death or permanent, life-threatening, or serious bodily injury of more than one victim; or (B) conduct tantamount to the attempted murder of more than one victim, regardless of whether the offense level is determined under this guideline or

under another guideline in Chapter Two (Offense Conduct) by use of a cross reference under subsection (c).

3. Departure Provisions.—

(A) Downward Departure Provision.—The base offense level in subsection (a)(1) reflects that offenses covered by that subsection typically pose a risk of death or serious bodily injury to one or more victims, or cause, or are intended to cause, bodily injury. In the unusual case in which such an offense did not cause a risk of death or serious bodily injury, and neither caused nor was intended to cause bodily injury, a downward departure may be warranted.

(B) Upward Departure Provisions.—If the offense caused extreme psychological injury, or caused substantial property damage or monetary loss, an upward departure may be warranted.

If the offense was calculated to influence or affect the conduct of government by intimidation or coercion, or to retaliate against government conduct, an upward departure would be warranted. See Application Note 4 of § 3A1.4 (Terrorism).".

Chapter Two, Part Q, is amended by striking § 2Q1.5 in its entirety as follows:

"§ 2Q1.5. Threatened Tampering with Public Water System

(a) Base Offense Level: 10

(b) Specific Offense Characteristic

(1) If the threat or attempt resulted in disruption of a public water system or evacuation of a community or a substantial public expenditure, increase by 4 levels.

(c) Cross Reference

(1) If the purpose of the offense was to influence government action or to extort money, apply § 2B3.2 (Extortion by Force or Threat of Injury or Serious Damage).

Commentary

Statutory Provision: 42 U.S.C. § 300i-1.".

Section § 2S1.1(b)(1)(B)(iii) is amended by striking "terrorism,".

The Commentary to § 2S1.1 captioned "Statutory Provisions" is amended by inserting ", 1960 (but only with respect to unlicensed money transmitting businesses as defined in 18 U.S.C. § 1960(b)(1)(C))" after "1957".

The Commentary to § 2S1.3 captioned "Statutory Provisions" is amended by inserting "(but only with respect to unlicensed money transmitting businesses as defined in 18 U.S.C. § 1960(b)(1)(A) and (B))" after "1960".

The Commentary to § 2X2.1 captioned "Statutory Provisions" is amended by inserting ", 2339C(a)(1)(A)" after "2339A".

The Commentary to § 2X2.1 captioned "Application Notes" is amended in Note 1 by inserting "or § 2339C(a)(1)(A)" after "2339A"; and by inserting ", or provided or collected funds for, "after "supported".

Section 2X3.1 is amended by striking the following:

"(a) Base Offense Level: 6 levels lower than the offense level for the underlying offense, but in no event less than 4, or more than 30. However, in a case in which the conduct is limited to harboring a fugitive, the base offense level under this subsection shall not be more than level 20.",

and inserting the following:

"(a) Base Offense Level:

(1) 6 levels lower than the offense level for the underlying offense, except as provided in subdivisions (2) and (3).

(2) The base offense level under this guideline shall be not less than level 4.

(3) (A) The base offense level under this guideline shall be not more than level 30, except as provided in subdivision (B).

(B) In any case in which the conduct is limited to harboring a fugitive, other than a case described in subdivision (C), the base offense level under this guideline shall be not more than level 20.

(C) The limitation in subdivision (B) shall not apply in any case in which (i) the defendant is convicted under 18 U.S.C. § 2339 or § 2339A; or (ii) the conduct involved harboring a person who committed any offense listed in 18 U.S.C. § 2339 or § 2339A or who committed any offense involving or intending to promote a federal crime of terrorism, as defined in 18 U.S.C. § 2332b(g)(5). In such a case, the base offense level under this guideline shall be not more than level 30, as provided in subdivision (A).".

The Commentary to § 2X3.1 captioned "Statutory Provisions" is amended by inserting ", 2339C(c)(2)(A), (c)(2)(B) (but only with respect to funds known or intended to have been provided or collected in violation of 18 U.S.C. § 2339C (a)(1)(A))" after "2339A".

The Commentary to § 2X3.1 captioned "Application Notes" is amended in Note 1 by inserting ", or in the case of a violation of 18 U.S.C. § 2339C(c)(2)(A), 'underlying offense' means the violation of 18 U.S.C. § 2339B with respect to which the material support or resources were concealed or disguised" after "that offense)".

Appendix A (Statutory Index) is amended in the line referenced to 18 U.S.C. § 1960 by inserting "2S1.1," before "2S1.3";

by inserting after the line referenced to 18 U.S.C. § 2332d the following new line:

"18 U.S.C. § 2332f   2K1.4, 2M6.1";

by inserting after the line referenced to 18 U.S.C. § 2339B the following new lines:

"18 U.S.C. § 2339C(a)(1)(A)	2X2.1
18 U.S.C. § 2339C(a)(1)(B)	2M5.3
18 U.S.C. § 2339C(c)(2)(A)	2X3.1
18 U.S.C. § 2339C(c)(2)(B)	2M5.3, 2X3.1";

and in the line referenced to 42 U.S.C. § 300i-1 by striking ", 2Q1.5".

Reason for Amendment: This amendment is a three part amendment that (1) further responds to the Uniting and Strengthening America by Providing Appropriate Tools Required to Intercept and Obstruct Terrorism (USA PATRIOT Act) Act of 2001, Pub. L. 107–56; (2) responds to the Public Health Security and Bioterrorism Preparedness and Response Act of 2002, Pub. L. 107–188; and (3) responds to the Terrorist Bombings Preparedness and Response Act of 2002, Pub. L. 107–197.

First, this amendment makes changes to the money laundering and transactions structuring guidelines to complete work begun in 2002 to address the provisions of the USA PATRIOT Act. The amendment eliminates the six level enhancement for terrorism in § 2S1.1 (Laundering of Monetary Instruments; Engaging in Monetary Transactions in Property Derived from Unlawful Activity) because such conduct is adequately accounted for by the terrorism adjustment at § 3A1.4 (Terrorism). The terrorism adjustment at § 3A1.4 applies if the offense is a felony that involved, or was intended to promote, a federal crime of terrorism as defined in 18 U.S.C. § 2332b(g)(5). Therefore, if the defendant knew or believed that any of the laundered funds were the proceeds of, or were intended to promote, an offense involving terrorism, as defined in § 3A1.4, that adjustment will apply. This amendment also provides for the treatment of certain offenses under 18 U.S.C. § 1960. The amendment changes Appendix A (Statutory Index) to refer violations of 18 U.S.C. § 1960 to both §§ 2S1.1 and 2S1.3 (Structuring Transactions to Evade Reporting Requirements; Failure to Report Case or Monetary Transactions; Failure to File Currency and Monetary Instrument Report; Knowingly Filing False Reports; Bulk Cash Smuggling; Establishing or Maintaining Prohibited Accounts). Referring violations of 18 U.S.C. § 1960(b)(1)(C) to § 2S1.1 is appropriate because the essence of this offense is money laundering, rather than structuring transactions to evade reporting requirements.

The amendment also raises the maximum offense level in § 2X3.1 (Accessory After the Fact) from level 20 to level 30 for offenses in which the conduct involves harboring or concealing a fugitive involved in a terrorism offense. The Commission determined that the heightened maximum offense level of level 30 is appropriate for offenses involving the harboring of terrorists because of the relative seriousness of those offenses. Specifically, the heightened maximum offense level applies in any case in which the defendant is convicted under 18 U.S.C. § 2339 or § 2339A or in which the conduct involved harboring a person who committed any offense listed under those statutes, or who committed any offense involving or intending to promote a federal crime of terrorism as defined in 18 U.S.C. § 2332b(g)(5).

Second, the amendment responds to the Public Health Security and Bioterrorism Preparedness and Response Act of 2002. The amendment refers certain new offenses involving biological agents and toxins to the guideline covering nuclear, biological, and chemical weapons and materials, § 2M6.1 (Unlawful Production, Development, Acquisition, Stockpiling, Alteration, Use, Transfer, or Possession of Nuclear Material, Weapons, or Facilities, Biological Agents, Toxins, or Delivery Systems, Chemical Weapons, or Other Weapons of Mass Destruction; Attempt or Conspiracy).

The amendment also responds to amendments made to the Safe Drinking Water Act (42

Amendment 655 APPENDIX C - VOLUME II November 1, 2013

U.S.C. § 300i-1(a)) made by section 403 of the Public Health Security and Bioterrorism Preparedness and Response Act of 2002. Section 1432(a) of the Safe Drinking Water Act prohibits any person from tampering with a public water system. The statutory maximum penalty was increased from five years' imprisonment to 20 years' imprisonment. Section 1432(b) of the Act prohibits anyone from attempting or threatening to tamper with a public water system. The statutory maximum penalty was increased from three years' imprisonment to ten years' imprisonment.

The amendment consolidates §§ 2Q1.5 (Threatened Tampering with Public Water System) and 2Q1.4 (Tampering or Attempted Tampering with Public Water System). This consolidation reflects the similar manner in which threats to carry out a nuclear, biological, or chemical weapons offense are treated under § 2M6.1. Three alternative base offense levels are provided for the substantive offense and for a threat to carry out the substantive offense, either accompanied or unaccompanied by other conduct evidencing an intent to carry out the threat.

The amendment also increases the base offense level for offenses involving tampering and threatened tampering with a public water system. The amendment increases the base offense level for tampering with a public water system from level 18 to level 26. The six level enhancement for the risk of death or serious bodily injury (in the predecessor guideline) is incorporated into the base offense level, as are two levels for bodily injury (similar to the treatment of this aggravated conduct in the consumer product tampering guideline). A graduated enhancement for serious or life-threatening bodily injury, modeled after the nuclear, biological, and chemical guideline and the consumer product tampering guideline, is added. Likewise, the base offense level for threatening to tamper with a public water system, without conduct evidencing an intent to carry out the threat, is increased from level 10 to level 16. A base offense level of level 22 is provided if there is conduct evidencing an intent to carry out the threat. For point of comparison, the existing base offense levels for threatening communications under § 2A6.1 (Threatening or Harassing Communications) is level 12, and for threatened use of nuclear, biological, and chemical weapons under § 2M6.1 is level 20. These substantial increases in the base offense levels for threatened tampering of a public water system are provided to ensure proportionality with similar offenses and to respond to the increased statutory maximum penalties made by section 403 of the Public Health Security and Bioterrorism Preparedness and Response Act of 2002. Additionally, the enhancement in subsection (b)(2) regarding the disruption of the public water system has been expanded slightly to make it consistent with similar enhancements in other related guidelines, such as the nuclear, biological, and chemical guideline, § 2M6.1.

This amendment adds an invited upward departure provision in § 2B1.1 (Larceny, Embezzlement, and Other Forms of Theft; Offenses Involving Stolen Property; Property Damage or Destruction; Fraud and Deceit; Forgery; Offenses Involving Altered or Counterfeit Instruments Other than Counterfeit Bearer Obligations of the United States), to account for aggravating conduct that may occur in connection with an animal enterprise offense under 18 U.S.C. § 43. While reference only to that guideline generally continues to be appropriate for violations under 18 U.S.C. § 43, that guideline fails to account for aggravated situations in which serious bodily injury or death results. Although the property damage guideline contains an enhancement for the risk of serious bodily injury or death, there is no enhancement or cross reference in that guideline that would provide a higher offense level if actual serious bodily injury or death resulted. Given the highly unusual occurrence of death or serious bodily injury in property damage cases generally and the infrequency of these specific offenses, the amendment adds an invited upward departure provision in the commentary of § 2B1.1 if death or serious bodily injury occurs in an offense under 18 U.S.C. § 43, or if substantial or significant scientific information or research is lost as part of such an offense.

Third, the amendment amends Appendix A (and the Statutory Provisions of the pertinent Chapter Two guidelines) to add three new offenses created by the Terrorist Bombings Convention Implementation Act of 2002, and provides conforming amendments within a number of Chapter Two guidelines to incorporate more fully the new offenses into the offense guidelines. Section 102 of the Act created a new offense at 18 U.S.C. § 2332f, which provides in subsection (a) that "whoever unlawfully delivers, places, discharges, or detonates an explosive or other lethal device in, into, or against a place of public use, a state or government facility, a public transportation system, or an infrastructure facility (1) with the intent to cause death or serious bodily injury, or (2) with the intent to cause extensive destruction of such a place, facility, or system, where such destruction results in or is likely to result in major economic loss" and in subsection (b) that "whoever attempts or conspires to commit [such] an offense" shall be punished as provided under 18 U.S.C. § 2332a(a). Section 2332a offenses currently are referenced to §§ 2K1.4 (Arson; Property Damage by Use of Explosives) and 2M6.1. The amendment refers this new offense to those guidelines as well. In addition, the amendment amends the alternative base offense levels in § 2K1.4(a)(1) so that the base offense level of level 24 applies to targets of 18 U.S.C. § 2332f offenses, namely, state or government facilities, infrastructure facilities, public transportation systems and "places of public use".

Section 202 of the Act created a new offense at 18 U.S.C. § 2339C. The amendment refers the new offense at 18 U.S.C. § 2339C(1)(A) to § 2X2.1 (Aiding and Abetting). The new offense involves providing or collecting funds knowing or intending that the funds would be used to carry out any of a number of specified offenses. Accordingly, the amendment treats these offenses in the same manner as 18 U.S.C. § 2339A offenses, which aid and abet a predicate offense listed in the statute. An amendment is also made in § 2X2.1 to provide a definition for the "underlying offense" that is aided and abetted.

The amendment also refers the new offense at 18 U.S.C. § 2339C(a)(1)(B) to § 2M5.3 (Providing Material Support or Resources to Designated Foreign Terrorist Organizations). Reference to § 2M5.3 is appropriate because this offense involves generally providing or collecting funds knowing or intending that the funds would be used to carry out an act which by its nature is a terrorist act (because it is meant to intimidate a civilian population or to compel a government or international organization to do something or to refrain from doing something). Therefore, the essence of the offense is the provision of material support to terrorists, which appropriately is referenced to § 2M5.3. The amendment expands § 2M5.3 to include not only designated foreign terrorist organizations but other terrorists as well.

Additionally, 18 U.S.C. § 2339C(c)(2) makes it unlawful in the United States, or outside the United States by a national of the United States or an entity organized under the laws of the United States, to knowingly conceal or disguise the nature, location, source, ownership, or control of any material support, resources, or funds knowing or intending that they were (1) provided in violation of 18 U.S.C. § 2339B, or (2) provided or collected in violation of 18 U.S.C. § 2339C(a)(1) or (2). The maximum term of imprisonment for a violation of subsection 18 U.S.C. § 2339C(c) is 10 years. The amendment references offenses under 18 U.S.C. § 2339C(c)(2)(A) to § 2X3.1 (Accessory After the Fact), because the essence of such an offense is the concealment of resources that were known or intended to have been provided in violation of another substantive offense, namely, 18 U.S.C. § 2339B. An amendment is made in § 2X3.1 to provide a definition of the "underlying offense" to which the defendant is an accessory.

The amendment references offenses under 18 U.S.C. § 2339C(c)(2)(B) to §§ 2M5.3 and

2X3.1. To the extent the offense involved knowingly concealing or disguising the nature, location, source, ownership, or control of any funds knowing or intending that they were provided or collected in violation of 18 U.S.C. § 2339C(a)(1)(A), the offense should be sentenced under § 2X3.1. This is because the concealment occurs with respect to funds the defendant knows are to be used, in full or in part, in order to carry out an act which constitutes any number of specified offenses. To the extent the offense involved knowingly concealing or disguising the nature, location, source, ownership, or control of any funds knowing or intending that they were provided or collected in violation of 18 U.S.C. § 2339C(a)(1)(B), the offense should be sentenced under § 2M5.3. This is because the concealment occurs with respect to material support the defendant knows is to be used, in full or in part, in order to carry out an act which by its nature is a terrorist act (because it is meant to intimidate a civilian population or to compel a government or international organization to do something or to refrain from doing something). A conforming amendment is added to the Statutory Provisions of §§ 2M5.3 and 2X3.1.

Finally, an amendment is made to § 2K1.3 (Unlawful Receipt, Possession, or Transportation of Explosive Materials; Prohibited Transaction Involving Explosive Materials) to add an additional base offense level of level 18 for certain offenses committed under 18 U.S.C. § 842(p)(2) involving explosives, destructive devices, or weapons of mass destruction. The statute is referenced in Appendix A to §§ 2K1.3 and 2M6.1. The applicable offense levels at § 2M6.1 are levels 42 and 28. The applicable base offense level at § 2K1.3 is level 12. The base offense level of level 12 appears to be disproportionately low compared with other 20 year offenses and compared with the treatment of 18 U.S.C. § 842(p)(2) offenses under § 2M6.1. This is especially true in light of the definition of destructive device, defined at 18 U.S.C. § 921(a)(4) to include any explosive, incendiary, or poison gas (1) bomb; (2) grenade; (3) rocket having a propellant charge of more than four ounces; (4) missile having an explosive or incendiary charge of more than one-quarter ounce; (5) mine; or (6) device similar to any of the devices described in the preceding clauses.

The amendment makes the enhancement at § 2K1.3(b)(3) and the cross reference at § 2K1.3(c)(1) applicable to 18 U.S.C. § 842(p)(2) offenses. In cases in which the defendant used or possessed any explosive material in connection with another felony offense or possessed or transferred any explosive material with knowledge, intent, or reason to believe that it would be used or possessed in connection with another felony offense, subsection (b)(3) provides a four level enhancement and a minimum offense level of level 18. Alternatively, the cross reference at subsection (c)(1) references such cases either to § 2X1.1 (Attempt, Solicitation, or Conspiracy (Not Covered by a Specific Guideline)), or to the most analogous homicide guideline if death resulted, if the resulting offense level is greater. Application of both subsection (b)(3) and subsection (c)(1) to 18 U.S.C. § 842(p)(2) offenses is appropriate because of the defendant's knowledge and/or intent that the defendant's teaching would be used to carry out another felony.

Effective Date: The effective date of this amendment is November 1, 2003.

656. **Amendment:** The heading of Part C of Chapter Two, amendments to the Introductory Commentary of Part C of Chapter Two, §§ 2C1.8, 3D1.2 and 5E1.2, effective January 25, 2003 (see USSC Guidelines Manual Appendix C (Volume II), Amendment 648), are repromulgated without change. Appendix A, effective January 25, 2003 (see USSC Guidelines Manual Appendix C (Volume II), Amendments 647 and 648; see also this document, Amendment 653), is repromulgated without change.

Reason for Amendment: The Commission promulgated an emergency amendment addressing the directive from Congress contained in the Bipartisan Campaign Reform Act of 2002, Pub. L. 107–155, (the "BCRA"), with an effective date of January 25, 2003. (See

Amendment 648.) This amendment repromulgates without change the emergency amendment as a permanent amendment.

This amendment implements the directive from Congress contained in the BCRA to the effect that the Commission "promulgate a guideline, or amend an existing guideline . . ., for penalties for violations of the Federal Election Campaign Act of 1971 [the "FECA"] and related election laws . . . ." The BCRA significantly increased statutory penalties for campaign finance crimes, formerly misdemeanors under the FECA. The new statutory maximum term of imprisonment for even the least serious of these offenses is now two years, and for more serious offenses, the maximum term of imprisonment is five years.

To punish these offenses effectively, the Commission chose to create a new guideline at § 2C1.8 (Making, Receiving, or Failing to Report a Contribution, Donation, or Expenditure in Violation of the Federal Election Campaign Act; Fraudulently Misrepresenting Campaign Authority; Soliciting or Receiving a Donation in Connection with an Election While on Certain Federal Property). The Commission opted against simply amending an existing guideline because it determined after review that the characteristics of election violation cases did not bear sufficient similarity to cases sentenced under any existing guideline. The offenses that will be sentenced under § 2C1.8 include: violations of the statutory prohibitions against "soft money" (2 U.S.C. § 441i); restrictions on "hard money" contributions (2 U.S.C. § 441a); contributions by foreign nationals (2 U.S.C. § 441e); restrictions on "electioneering communications" (as defined in 2 U.S.C. § 434(f)(3)(C)); certain fraudulent misrepresentations (2 U.S.C. § 441h); and "conduit contributions" (2 U.S.C. § 441f).

The new guideline has a base offense level of level 8, which reflects the fact that these offenses, while they are somewhat similar to fraud offenses (sentenced under § 2B1.1 (Larceny, Embezzlement, and Other Forms of Theft; Offenses Involving Stolen Property; Property Damage or Destruction; Fraud and Deceit; Forgery; Offenses Involving Altered or Counterfeit Instruments Other than Counterfeit Bearer Obligations of the United States) at a base offense level of level 6), nevertheless are more serious due to the additional harm, or the potential harm, of corrupting the elective process.

The new guideline provides five specific offense characteristics to ensure appropriate penalty enhancements for aggravating conduct that may occur during the commission of certain campaign finance offenses. First, the new guideline provides a specific offense characteristic, at § 2C1.8(b)(1), that uses the fraud loss table in § 2B1.1 incrementally to increase the offense level in proportion to the monetary amounts involved in the illegal transactions. This both assures proportionality with penalties for fraud offenses and responds to Congress' directive to provide an enhancement for "a large aggregate amount of illegal contributions."

Second, the new guideline provides alternative enhancements, at § 2C1.8(b)(2), if the offense involved a foreign national (two levels) or a foreign government (four levels). These enhancements respond to another specific directive in the BCRA and reflect the seriousness of attempts by foreign entities to tamper with the United States' election processes.

Third, the new guideline provides alternative enhancements of two levels each, at § 2C1.8(b)(3), when the offense involves either "governmental funds," defined broadly to include federal, state, or local funds, or an intent to derive "a specific, identifiable nonmonetary Federal benefit" (e.g., a presidential pardon). Each of these enhancements responds to specific directives of the BCRA.

Fourth, the new guideline provides a two level enhancement, at subsection (b)(4), when

Amendment 656

the offender engages in "30 or more illegal transactions." After a review of all campaign finance cases in the Commission's datafile, the Commission chose 30 transactions as the number best illustrative of a "large number" in that context. This enhancement also responds to a specific directive in the BCRA to the effect that the Commission provide enhanced sentencing for cases involving "a large number of illegal transactions."

Fifth, the new guideline provides a four level enhancement, at § 2C1.8(b)(5), if the offense involves the use of "intimidation, threat of pecuniary or other harm, or coercion." This enhancement responds to information, received from the Federal Election Commission and the Public Integrity Section of the Department of Justice, which characterizes offenses of this type as some of the most aggravated offenses committed under the FECA.

The new guideline also provides a cross reference, at subsection (c), which directs the sentencing court to apply either § 2C1.1 (Offering, Giving, Soliciting, or Receiving a Bribe; Extortion Under Color of Official Right) or § 2C1.2 (Offering, Giving, Soliciting, or Receiving a Gratuity), as appropriate, if the offense involved a bribe or a gratuity and the resulting offense level would be greater than that determined under § 2C1.8.

Section 3D1.2 (Groups of Closely Related Counts) has been amended, consistent with the principles underlying the rules for grouping multiple counts of conviction, to include § 2C1.8 offenses among those in which the offense level is determined largely on the basis of the total amount of harm or loss or some other measure of aggregate harm. (See § 3D1.2(d)).

Finally, § 5E1.2 (Fines for Individual Defendants) has been amended specifically to reflect fine provisions unique to the FECA. This part of the amendment also provides that the defendant's participation in a conciliation agreement with the Federal Election Commission may be an appropriate factor for use in determining the specific fine within the applicable fine guideline range unless the defendant began negotiations with the Federal Election Commission only after the defendant became aware that the defendant was the subject of a criminal investigation.

Effective Date: The effective date of this amendment is November 1, 2003.

657. Amendment: Section 2D1.1(c) is amended in Note (B) of the "*Notes to Drug Quantity Table" by adding at the end the following new paragraph:

> "The term 'Oxycodone (actual)' refers to the weight of the controlled substance, itself, contained in the pill, capsule, or mixture.".

The Commentary to § 2D1.1 captioned "Application Notes" is amended in Note 9 by striking "or" after "amphetamine,"; and by inserting ", or oxycodone" after "methamphetamine".

The Commentary to § 2D1.1 captioned "Application Notes" is amended in Note 10, in the Drug Equivalency Tables, in the subdivision captioned "Schedule I or II Opiates*" by striking "1 gm of Oxycodone = 500 gm of marihuana" and inserting "1 gm of Oxycodone (actual) = 6700 gm of marihuana".

Reason for Amendment: This amendment responds to proportionality issues in the sentencing of oxycodone trafficking offenses. Oxycodone is an opium alkaloid found in certain prescription pain relievers such as Percocet and OxyContin. This prescription drug generally is sold in pill form and, prior to this amendment, the sentencing guidelines established penalties for oxycodone trafficking based on the entire weight of the pill. The proportionality issues arise (1) because of the formulations of the different medicines; and

(2) because different amounts of oxycodone are found in pills of identical weight.

As an example of the first issue, the drug Percocet contains, in addition to oxycodone, the non-prescription pain reliever acetaminophen. The weight of the oxycodone component accounts for a very small proportion of the total weight of the pill. In contrast, the weight of the oxycodone accounts for a substantially greater proportion of the weight of an OxyContin pill. To illustrate this difference, a Percocet pill containing five milligrams (mg) of oxycodone weighs approximately 550 mg with oxycodone accounting for 0.9 percent of the total weight of the pill. By comparison, the weight of an OxyContin pill containing 10 mg of oxycodone is approximately 135 mg with oxycodone accounting for 7.4 percent of the total weight. Consequently, prior to this amendment, trafficking 364 Percocet pills or 1,481 OxyContin pills resulted in the same five year sentence of imprisonment. Additionally, the total amount of the narcotic oxycodone involved in this example is vastly different depending on the drug. The 364 Percocets produce 1.8 grams of actual oxycodone while the 1,481 OxyContin pills produce 14.8 grams of oxycodone.

The second issue results from differences in the formulation of OxyContin. Three different amounts of oxycodone (10, 20, and 40 mg) are contained in pills of identical weight (135 mg). As a result, prior to this amendment, an individual trafficking in a particular number of OxyContin pills would receive the same sentence regardless of the amount of oxycodone contained in the pills.

To remedy these proportionality issues, the amendment changes the Drug Equivalency Tables in § 2D1.1 (Unlawful Manufacturing, Importing, Exporting, or Trafficking (Including Possession with Intent to Commit These Offenses); Attempt or Conspiracy) to provide sentences for oxycodone offenses using the weight of the actual oxycodone instead of calculating the weight of the entire pill. The amendment equates 1 gram of actual oxycodone to 6,700 grams of marihuana. This equivalency keeps penalties for offenses involving 10 mg OxyContin pills identical to levels that existed prior to the amendment, substantially increases penalties for all other doses of OxyContin, and decreases somewhat the penalties for offenses involving Percocet.

Effective Date: The effective date of this amendment is November 1, 2003.

658. Amendment: Section 2L1.2(b)(1)(A)(vii) is amended by striking "committed for profit".

The Commentary to § 2L1.2 captioned "Application Notes" is amended in Note 1 by striking subdivision (A)(iv) as follows:

> "(iv)   If all or any part of a sentence of imprisonment was probated, suspended, deferred, or stayed, "sentence imposed" refers only to the portion that was not probated, suspended, deferred, or stayed.",

and inserting the following:

> "(iv)   Subsection (b)(1) does not apply to a conviction for an offense committed before the defendant was eighteen years of age unless such conviction is classified as an adult conviction under the laws of the jurisdiction in which the defendant was convicted.".

The Commentary to § 2L1.2 captioned "Application Notes" is amended in Note 1 by striking subdivision (B) as follows:

> "(B)   <u>Definitions</u>.—For purposes of subsection (b)(1):
>
> > (i)   'Committed for profit' means committed for payment or expectation of payment.

Amendment 658

(ii) 'Crime of violence'—

    (I) means an offense under federal, state, or local law that has as an element the use, attempted use, or threatened use of physical force against the person of another; and

    (II) includes murder, manslaughter, kidnapping, aggravated assault, forcible sex offenses (including sexual abuse of a minor), robbery, arson, extortion, extortionate extension of credit, and burglary of a dwelling.

(iii) 'Drug trafficking offense' means an offense under federal, state, or local law that prohibits the manufacture, import, export, distribution, or dispensing of a controlled substance (or a counterfeit substance) or the possession of a controlled substance (or a counterfeit substance) with intent to manufacture, import, export, distribute, or dispense.

(iv) 'Felony' means any federal, state, or local offense punishable by imprisonment for a term exceeding one year.

(v) 'Firearms offense' means any of the following:

    (I) An offense under federal, state, or local law that prohibits the importation, distribution, transportation, or trafficking of a firearm described in 18 U.S.C. § 921, or of an explosive material as defined in 18 U.S.C. § 841(c).

    (II) An offense under federal, state, or local law that prohibits the possession of a firearm described in 26 U.S.C. § 5845(a), or of an explosive material as defined in 18 U.S.C. § 841(c).

    (III) A violation of 18 U.S.C. § 844(h).

    (IV) A violation of 18 U.S.C. § 924(c).

    (V) A violation of 18 U.S.C. § 929(a).

(vi) 'Terrorism offense' means any offense involving, or intending to promote, a 'federal crime of terrorism', as that term is defined in 18 U.S.C. § 2332b(g)(5),

and inserting the following:

"(B) Definitions.—For purposes of subsection (b)(1):

(i) 'Alien smuggling offense' has the meaning given that term in section 101(a)(43)(N) of the Immigration and Nationality Act (8 U.S.C. § 1101(a)(43)(N)).

(ii) 'Child pornography offense' means (I) an offense described in 18 U.S.C. § 2251, § 2251A, § 2252, § 2252A, or § 2260; or (II) an offense under state or local law consisting of conduct that would have been an offense under any such section if the offense had occurred within the special maritime and territorial jurisdiction of the United States.

(iii) 'Crime of violence' means any of the following: murder, manslaughter, kidnapping, aggravated assault, forcible sex offenses, statutory rape, sexual abuse of a minor, robbery, arson, extortion, extortionate extension of credit, burglary of a dwelling, or any offense under federal, state, or local law that has as an element the use, attempted use, or threatened use of physical force against the person of another.

(iv) 'Drug trafficking offense' means an offense under federal, state, or local law that prohibits the manufacture, import, export, distribution, or dispensing of a controlled substance (or a counterfeit substance) or the possession of a controlled substance (or a counterfeit substance) with intent to manufacture, import, export, distribute, or dispense.

(v) 'Firearms offense' means any of the following:

(I) An offense under federal, state, or local law that prohibits the importation, distribution, transportation, or trafficking of a firearm described in 18 U.S.C. § 921, or of an explosive material as defined in 18 U.S.C. § 841(c).

(II) An offense under federal, state, or local law that prohibits the possession of a firearm described in 26 U.S.C. § 5845(a), or of an explosive material as defined in 18 U.S.C. § 841(c).

(III) A violation of 18 U.S.C. § 844(h).

(IV) A violation of 18 U.S.C. § 924(c).

(V) A violation of 18 U.S.C. § 929(a).

(VI) An offense under state or local law consisting of conduct that would have been an offense under subdivision (III), (IV), or (V) if the offense had occurred within the special maritime and territorial jurisdiction of the United States.

(vi) 'Human trafficking offense' means (I) any offense described in 18 U.S.C. § 1581, § 1582, § 1583, § 1584, § 1585, § 1588, § 1589, § 1590, or § 1591; or (II) an offense under state or local law consisting of conduct that would have been an offense under any such section if the offense had occurred within the special maritime and territorial jurisdiction of the United States.

(vii) 'Sentence imposed' has the meaning given the term 'sentence of imprisonment' in Application Note 2 and subsection (b) of § 4A1.2 (Definitions and Instructions for Computing Criminal History), without regard to the date of the conviction. The length of the sentence imposed includes any term of imprisonment given upon revocation of probation, parole, or supervised release.

(viii) 'Terrorism offense' means any offense involving, or intending to promote, a 'Federal crime of terrorism', as that term is defined in 18 U.S.C. § 2332b(g)(5).".

Section 2L1.2 captioned "Application Notes" is amended by striking Note 2 as follows:

"2. Application of Subsection (b)(1)(C).—For purposes of subsection (b)(1)(C), 'aggravated felony' has the meaning given that term in section 101(a)(43) of the Immigration and Nationality Act (8 U.S.C. § 1101(a)(43)), without regard to the date of conviction of the aggravated felony.",

and inserting the following:

"2. Definition of 'Felony'.—For purposes of subsection (b)(1)(A), (B), and (D), 'felony' means any federal, state, or local offense punishable by imprisonment for a term exceeding one year.".

Section 2L1.2 captioned "Application Notes" is amended by redesignating Notes 4 and 5 as Notes 5 and 6, respectively; and

by redesignating Note 3 as Note 4; and by inserting after Note 2 the following:

"3. Application of Subsection (b)(1)(C).—

(A) Definitions.—For purposes of subsection (b)(1)(C), 'aggravated felony' has the meaning given that term in section 101(a)(43) of the Immigration and Nationality Act (8 U.S.C. § 1101(a)(43)), without regard to the date of conviction for the aggravated felony.

(B) In General.—The offense level shall be increased under subsection (b)(1)(C) for any aggravated felony (as defined in subdivision (A)), with respect to which the offense level is not increased under subsections (b)(1)(A) or (B).".

Section 2L1.2 captioned "Application Notes" is amended in Note 4, as redesignated by this amendment, by striking subdivision (B) as follows:

"(B) 'Three or more convictions' means at least three convictions for offenses that (i) were separated by an intervening arrest; (ii) did not occur on the same occasion; (iii) were not part of a single common scheme or plan; or (iv) were not consolidated for trial or sentencing.",

and inserting the following:

"(B) 'Three or more convictions' means at least three convictions for offenses that are not considered 'related cases', as that term is defined in Application Note 3 of § 4A1.2 (Definitions and Instructions for Computing Criminal History).".

Appendix A (Statutory Index) is amended by striking the following:

"8 U.S.C. § 1252(e)   2L1.2",

and inserting the following:

"8 U.S.C. § 1253   2L1.2".

Reason for Amendment: In 2001 the Commission comprehensively revised § 2L1.2 (Unlawfully Entering or Remaining in the United States) to provide more graduated enhancements at subsection (b)(1) for illegal re-entrants previously deported after criminal convictions. In response to application issues raised by a number of judges, probation officers, defense attorneys, and prosecutors, particularly along the southwest border between the United States and Mexico, this amendment builds upon the 2001 amendment by clarifying the meaning of some of the terms used in § 2L1.2(b)(1).

First, the amendment adds commentary to define the following offenses: "alien smuggling", "child pornography", and "human trafficking." Prior to the amendment, these offenses received a 16 level increase but were not defined. The lack of definitions led to litigation regarding the meaning and scope of some of these terms. The Commission has determined that these offenses warrant application of the 16 level enhancement even though some of these offenses, as defined by the amendment, may not meet the statutory definition of an aggravated felony in 8 U.S.C. § 1101(a)(43).

The amendment provides a definition of "alien smuggling offense" in a manner consistent with the "aggravated felony" definition in 8 U.S.C. § 1101(a)(43)(N). This statutory definition excludes "a first offense for which the alien has affirmatively shown that the alien committed the offense for the purpose of assisting, abetting, or aiding only the alien's spouse, child, or parent (and no other person)". This definition generally is consistent with the guideline's previous terminology of "alien smuggling offense committed for profit," and results in a 16 level increase only for the most serious of such offenses. The new definition also responds to concerns about whether an alien smuggling offense includes the offenses of harboring or transporting aliens. By explicitly incorporating the statutory definition of alien smuggling within the guideline definition, the amendment, in effect, adopts the Fifth Circuit's interpretation of "alien smuggling". See United States v. Solis-Campozano, 312 F.3d 164 (5th Cir. 2002) (holding that "alien smuggling offense" was not limited to the "offense of alien smuggling" but includes transporting aliens brought into the country as well).

Second, the amendment adds commentary that clarifies the meaning of the term "crime of violence" by providing that the term "means any of the following: murder, manslaughter, kidnapping, aggravated assault, forcible sex offenses, statutory rape, sexual abuse of a minor, robbery, arson, extortion, extortionate extension of credit, burglary of a dwelling, or any offense under federal, state, or local law that has as an element the use, attempted use, or threatened use of physical force against the person of another." The previous definition often led to confusion over whether the specified offenses listed in that definition, particularly sexual abuse of a minor and residential burglary, also had to include as an element of the offense "the use, attempted use, or threatened use of physical force against the person of another." The amended definition makes clear that the enumerated offenses are always classified as "crimes of violence," regardless of whether the prior offense expressly has as an element the use, attempted use, or threatened use of physical force against the person of another.

Third, the amendment adds commentary at Application Note 1(B)(vii) explaining that the term "sentence imposed" has the meaning given the term "sentence of imprisonment" in Application Note 2 and subsection (b) of § 4A1.2 (Definitions and Instructions for Computing Criminal History), without regard to the date of the conviction. The length of the sentence of imprisonment includes any term of imprisonment given upon revocation of probation, parole, or supervised release. The Commission's approach in clarifying this definition is consistent with the case law interpreting the term and the use of the term in Chapter Four of the guidelines. See, e.g., United States v. Moreno-Cisneros, 319 F.3d 456 (9th Cir. 2003) (holding that the length of the sentence of imprisonment includes any term of imprisonment given upon revocation of probation, parole, or supervised release); United States v. Compian-Torres, 320 F.3d 514 (5th Cir. 2003) (same). Compare United States v. Hidalgo-Macias, 300 F.3d 281 (2d Cir. 2002) (holding that the imposition of a sentence of imprisonment following revocation of probation is a modification of the original sentence and must be considered part of the sentence imposed for the original offense), with United States v. Rodriguez-Arreola, 313 F.3d 1064 (8th Cir. 2002) (holding that the term "sentence imposed" when applied to an indeterminate sentence is the maximum term that a defendant may serve).

Fourth, the amendment adds commentary providing that the enhancements in subsection (b)(1) do not apply to a conviction for an offense committed before the defendant was eighteen years of age, unless such conviction is classified as an adult conviction under the laws of the jurisdiction in which the defendant was convicted. This provision is consistent with the approach in Chapter Four of the guidelines.

The amendment also makes other minor technical and clarifying changes.

Effective Date: The effective date of this amendment is November 1, 2003.

659. **Amendment:** Chapter Three, Part B, is amended by adding at the end the following new guideline:

"§ 3B1.5. Use of Body Armor in Drug Trafficking Crimes and Crimes of Violence

If—

(1) the defendant was convicted of a drug trafficking crime or a crime of violence; and

(2) (apply the greater)—

(A) the offense involved the use of body armor, increase by 2 levels; or

(B) the defendant used body armor during the commission of the offense, in preparation for the offense, or in an attempt to avoid apprehension for the offense, increase by 4 levels.

Commentary

Application Notes:

1. Definitions.—For purposes of this guideline:

'Body armor' means any product sold or offered for sale, in interstate or foreign commerce, as personal protective body covering intended to protect against gunfire, regardless of whether the product is to be worn alone or is sold as a complement to another product or garment. See 18 U.S.C. § 921(a)(35).

'Crime of violence' has the meaning given that term in 18 U.S.C. § 16.

'Drug trafficking crime' has the meaning given that term in 18 U.S.C. § 924(c)(2).

'Offense' has the meaning given that term in Application Note 1 of the Commentary to § 1B1.1 (Application Instructions).

'Use' means (A) active employment in a manner to protect the person from gunfire; or (B) use as a means of bartering. 'Use' does not mean mere possession (e.g., 'use' does not mean that the body armor was found in the trunk of the car but not used actively as protection). 'Used' means put into 'use' as defined in this paragraph.

2. Application of Subdivision (2)(B).—Consistent with § 1B1.3 (Relevant Conduct), the term 'defendant', for purposes of subdivision (2)(B), limits the accountability of the defendant to the defendant's own conduct and conduct that the defendant aided or abetted, counseled, commanded, induced, procured, or willfully caused.

Background: This guideline implements the directive in the James Guelff and Chris McCurley Body Armor Act of 2002 (section 11009(d) of the 21st Century Department of Justice Appropriations Authorization Act, Pub. L. 107–273).".

Reason for Amendment: This amendment responds to the directive in section 11009 of the 21st Century Department of Justice Appropriations Authorization Act (the "Act"), Pub. L. 107–273. The directive requires the Sentencing Commission to review and amend the guidelines, as appropriate, to provide an appropriate sentencing enhancement for any crime of violence (as defined in 18 U.S.C. § 16) or drug trafficking crime (as defined in 18 U.S.C. § 924(c)) (including a crime of violence or drug trafficking crime that provides for an enhanced punishment if committed by the use of a deadly or dangerous weapon or device) in which the defendant used body armor. The Act included a sense of Congress that any such enhancement should be at least two levels.

In response to the directive, the amendment creates a new Chapter Three adjustment at § 3B1.5 (Use of Body Armor in Drug Trafficking Crimes and Crimes of Violence). The new adjustment provides for the greater of a two level adjustment if the defendant was convicted of a crime of violence or a drug trafficking crime and the offense involved the use of body armor, or a four level adjustment if the defendant used body armor in preparation for, during the commission of, or in an attempt to avoid apprehension for, the offense.

An application note defines "drug trafficking crime" (as defined in 18 U.S.C. § 924(e)(2)). This definition includes any felony punishable under the Controlled Substances Act. The application note also defines "crime of violence" (as defined in 18 U.S.C. § 16). This definition includes offenses that involve the use or attempted use of physical force against property as well as persons. Both of these definitions are somewhat broader than the definitions of "crime of violence" and "drug trafficking offense" used in a number of other guidelines. The definition of "body armor" is the same as the statutory definition provided in 18 U.S.C. § 921(a)(35).

An application note makes clear that in order for § 3B1.5 to apply, the body armor must be used, i.e., actively employed either in a manner to protect the person from gunfire or as a means of bartering. Mere possession is insufficient to trigger the adjustment.

Another application note explains that in order for the heightened, four level adjustment to apply, the defendant must have used the body armor or aided, abetted, counseled, commanded, induced, procured, or willfully caused someone else to use the body armor.

Effective Date: The effective date of this amendment is November 1, 2003.

660. **Amendment:** Section 5G1.3 is amended by striking subsection (b) as follows:

"(b) If subsection (a) does not apply, and the undischarged term of imprisonment

Amendment 660

resulted from offense(s) that have been fully taken into account in the determination of the offense level for the instant offense, the sentence for the instant offense shall be imposed to run concurrently to the undischarged term of imprisonment.",

and inserting the following:

"(b) If subsection (a) does not apply, and a term of imprisonment resulted from another offense that is relevant conduct to the instant offense of conviction under the provisions of subsections (a)(1), (a)(2), or (a)(3) of § 1B1.3 (Relevant Conduct) and that was the basis for an increase in the offense level for the instant offense under Chapter Two (Offense Conduct) or Chapter Three (Adjustments), the sentence for the instant offense shall be imposed as follows:

   (1) the court shall adjust the sentence for any period of imprisonment already served on the undischarged term of imprisonment if the court determines that such period of imprisonment will not be credited to the federal sentence by the Bureau of Prisons; and

   (2) the sentence for the instant offense shall be imposed to run concurrently to the remainder of the undischarged term of imprisonment.".

Section 5G1.3(c) is amended by inserting "involving an undischarged term of imprisonment" after "case".

The Commentary to § 5G1.3 captioned "Application Notes" is amended by striking Notes 2 through 7 as follows:

"2. *Adjusted concurrent sentence - subsection (b) cases*. When a sentence is imposed pursuant to subsection (b), the court should adjust the sentence for any period of imprisonment already served as a result of the conduct taken into account in determining the guideline range for the instant offense if the court determines that period of imprisonment will not be credited to the federal sentence by the Bureau of Prisons. Example: The defendant is convicted of a federal offense charging the sale of 30 grams of cocaine. Under § 1B1.3 (Relevant Conduct), the defendant is held accountable for the sale of an additional 15 grams of cocaine, an offense for which the defendant has been convicted and sentenced in state court. The defendant received a nine-month sentence of imprisonment for the state offense and has served six months on that sentence at the time of sentencing on the instant federal offense. The guideline range applicable to the defendant is 10-16 months (Chapter Two offense level of 14 for sale of 45 grams of cocaine; 2-level reduction for acceptance of responsibility; final offense level of 12; Criminal History Category I). The court determines that a sentence of 13 months provides the appropriate total punishment. Because the defendant has already served six months on the related state charge as of the date of sentencing on the instant federal offense, a sentence of seven months, imposed to run concurrently with the three months remaining on the defendant's state sentence, achieves this result. For clarity, the court should note on the Judgment in a Criminal Case Order that the sentence imposed is not a departure from the guideline range because the defendant has been credited for guideline purposes under § 5G1.3(b) with six months served in state custody that will not be credited to the federal sentence under 18 U.S.C. § 3585(b).

3. Concurrent or consecutive sentence - subsection (c) cases. In circumstances not covered under subsection (a) or (b), subsection (c) applies. Under this subsection, the court may impose a sentence concurrently, partially concurrently, or consecutively. To achieve a reasonable punishment and avoid unwarranted disparity, the court should consider the factors set forth in 18 U.S.C. § 3584 (referencing 18 U.S.C. § 3553(a)) and be cognizant of:

    (a) the type (e.g., determinate, indeterminate/parolable) and length of the prior undischarged sentence;

    (b) the time served on the undischarged sentence and the time likely to be served before release;

    (c) the fact that the prior undischarged sentence may have been imposed in state court rather than federal court, or at a different time before the same or different federal court; and

    (d) any other circumstance relevant to the determination of an appropriate sentence for the instant offense.

4. Partially concurrent sentence. In some cases under subsection (c), a partially concurrent sentence may achieve most appropriately the desired result. To impose a partially concurrent sentence, the court may provide in the Judgment in a Criminal Case Order that the sentence for the instant offense shall commence (A) when the defendant is released from the prior undischarged sentence, or (B) on a specified date, whichever is earlier. This order provides for a fully consecutive sentence if the defendant is released on the undischarged term of imprisonment on or before the date specified in the order, and a partially concurrent sentence if the defendant is not released on the undischarged term of imprisonment by that date.

5. Complex situations. Occasionally, the court may be faced with a complex case in which a defendant may be subject to multiple undischarged terms of imprisonment that seemingly call for the application of different rules. In such a case, the court may exercise its discretion in accordance with subsection (c) to fashion a sentence of appropriate length and structure it to run in any appropriate manner to achieve a reasonable punishment for the instant offense.

6. Revocations. If the defendant was on federal or state probation, parole, or supervised release at the time of the instant offense, and has had such probation, parole, or supervised release revoked, the sentence for the instant offense should be imposed to run consecutively to the term imposed for the violation of probation, parole, or supervised release in order to provide an incremental penalty for the violation of probation, parole, or supervised release. See § 7B1.3 (Revocation of Probation or Supervised Release) (setting forth a policy that any imprisonment penalty imposed for violating probation or supervised release should be consecutive to any sentence of imprisonment being served or subsequently imposed).

7. Downward Departure Provision.—In the case of a discharged term of imprisonment, a downward departure is not prohibited if subsection (b) would have applied to that term of imprisonment had the term been undischarged. Any such departure should be fashioned to achieve a reasonable punishment for the instant offense.",

and inserting the following:

"2. Application of Subsection (b).—

(A) In General.—Subsection (b) applies in cases in which all of the prior offense (i) is relevant conduct to the instant offense under the provisions of subsection (a)(1), (a)(2), or (a)(3) of § 1B1.3 (Relevant Conduct); and (ii) has resulted in an increase in the Chapter Two or Three offense level for the instant offense. Cases in which only part of the prior offense is relevant conduct to the instant offense are covered under subsection (c).

(B) Inapplicability of Subsection (b).—Subsection (b) does not apply in cases in which the prior offense increased the Chapter Two or Three offense level for the instant offense but was not relevant conduct to the instant offense under § 1B1.3(a)(1), (a)(2), or (a)(3) (e.g., the prior offense is an aggravated felony for which the defendant received an increase under § 2L1.2 (Unlawfully Entering or Remaining in the United States), or the prior offense was a crime of violence for which the defendant received an increased base offense level under § 2K2.1 (Unlawful Receipt, Possession, or Transportation of Firearms or Ammunition; Prohibited Transactions Involving Firearms or Ammunition)).

(C) Imposition of Sentence.—If subsection (b) applies, and the court adjusts the sentence for a period of time already served, the court should note on the Judgement in a Criminal Case Order (i) the applicable subsection (e.g., § 5G1.3(b)); (ii) the amount of time by which the sentence is being adjusted; (iii) the undischarged term of imprisonment for which the adjustment is being given; and (iv) that the sentence imposed is a sentence reduction pursuant to § 5G1.3(b) for a period of imprisonment that will not be credited by the Bureau of Prisons.

(D) Example.—The following is an example in which subsection (b) applies and an adjustment to the sentence is appropriate:

The defendant is convicted of a federal offense charging the sale of 40 grams of cocaine. Under § 1B1.3, the defendant is held accountable for the sale of an additional 15 grams of cocaine, an offense for which the defendant has been convicted and sentenced in state court. The defendant received a nine-month sentence of imprisonment for the state offense and has served six months on that sentence at the time of sentencing on the instant federal offense. The guideline range applicable to the defendant is 12-18 months (Chapter Two offense level of level 16 for sale of 55 grams of cocaine; 3 level reduction for acceptance of responsibility; final offense level of level 13; Criminal History Category I). The court determines that a sentence of 13 months provides the appropriate total punishment. Because the defendant has already served six months on the related state charge as of the date of sentencing on the instant federal offense, a sentence of seven months, imposed to run concurrently with the three months remaining on the defendant's state sentence, achieves this result.

3. Application of Subsection (c).—

   (A) In General.—Under subsection (c), the court may impose a sentence concurrently, partially concurrently, or consecutively to the undischarged term of imprisonment. In order to achieve a reasonable incremental punishment for the instant offense and avoid unwarranted disparity, the court should consider the following:

   (i) the factors set forth in 18 U.S.C. § 3584 (referencing 18 U.S.C. § 3553(a));

   (ii) the type (e.g., determinate, indeterminate/parolable) and length of the prior undischarged sentence;

   (iii) the time served on the undischarged sentence and the time likely to be served before release;

   (iv) the fact that the prior undischarged sentence may have been imposed in state court rather than federal court, or at a different time before the same or different federal court; and

   (v) any other circumstance relevant to the determination of an appropriate sentence for the instant offense.

   (B) Partially Concurrent Sentence.—In some cases under subsection (c), a partially concurrent sentence may achieve most appropriately the desired result. To impose a partially concurrent sentence, the court may provide in the Judgment in a Criminal Case Order that the sentence for the instant offense shall commence on the earlier of (i) when the defendant is released from the prior undischarged sentence; or (ii) on a specified date. This order provides for a fully consecutive sentence if the defendant is released on the undischarged term of imprisonment on or before the date specified in the order, and a partially concurrent sentence if the defendant is not released on the undischarged term of imprisonment by that date.

   (C) Undischarged Terms of Imprisonment Resulting from Revocations of Probation, Parole or Supervised Release.—Subsection (c) applies in cases in which the defendant was on federal or state probation, parole, or supervised release at the time of the instant offense and has had such probation, parole, or supervised release revoked. Consistent with the policy set forth in Application Note 4 and subsection (f) of § 7B1.3 (Revocation of Probation or Supervised Release), the Commission recommends that the sentence for the instant offense be imposed consecutively to the sentence imposed for the revocation.

   (D) Complex Situations.—Occasionally, the court may be faced with a complex case in which a defendant may be subject to multiple undischarged terms of imprisonment that seemingly call for the application of different rules. In such a case, the court may exercise its discretion in accordance with subsection (c) to fashion a sentence of appropriate length and structure it to run in any appropriate manner to achieve a reasonable punishment for the instant offense.

(E) Downward Departure.—Unlike subsection (b), subsection (c) does not authorize an adjustment of the sentence for the instant offense for a period of imprisonment already served on the undischarged term of imprisonment. However, in an extraordinary case involving an undischarged term of imprisonment under subsection (c), it may be appropriate for the court to downwardly depart. This may occur, for example, in a case in which the defendant has served a very substantial period of imprisonment on an undischarged term of imprisonment that resulted from conduct only partially within the relevant conduct for the instant offense. In such a case, a downward departure may be warranted to ensure that the combined punishment is not increased unduly by the fortuity and timing of separate prosecutions and sentencings. Nevertheless, it is intended that a departure pursuant to this application note result in a sentence that ensures a reasonable incremental punishment for the instant offense of conviction.

To avoid confusion with the Bureau of Prisons' exclusive authority provided under 18 U.S.C. § 3585(b) to grant credit for time served under certain circumstances, the Commission recommends that any downward departure under this application note be clearly stated on the Judgment in a Criminal Case Order as a downward departure pursuant to § 5G1.3(c), rather than as a credit for time served.

4. Downward Departure Provision.—In the case of a discharged term of imprisonment, a downward departure is not prohibited if the defendant (A) has completed serving a term of imprisonment; and (B) subsection (b) would have provided an adjustment had that completed term of imprisonment been undischarged at the time of sentencing for the instant offense. See § 5K2.23 (Discharged Terms of Imprisonment).".

Chapter Five, Part K, is amended by adding at the end the following new policy statement:

"§ 5K2.23. Discharged Terms of Imprisonment (Policy Statement)

A sentence below the applicable guideline range may be appropriate if the defendant (1) has completed serving a term of imprisonment; and (2) subsection (b) of § 5G1.3 (Imposition of a Sentence on a Defendant Subject to Undischarged Term of Imprisonment) would have provided an adjustment had that completed term of imprisonment been undischarged at the time of sentencing for the instant offense. Any such departure should be fashioned to achieve a reasonable punishment for the instant offense.".

Reason for Amendment: This amendment addresses a number of issues in § 5G1.3 (Imposition of a Sentence on a Defendant Subject to an Undischarged Term of Imprisonment).

First, this amendment clarifies the rule for application of subsection (b) (mandating a concurrent term of imprisonment) with respect to a prior term of imprisonment by stating that subsection (b) shall apply only to prior offenses that are relevant conduct to the instant offense of conviction and that resulted in an increase in the offense level for the instant offense. By clarifying the application of subsection (b), this amendment addresses conflicting litigation regarding the meaning of "fully taken into account." Compare, e.g., United States v. Garcia-Hernandez, 237 F.3d 105, 109 (2d Cir. 2000) (determining that a prior offense is "fully taken into account" if and only if the guidelines provide for sentencing as if both the offense of conviction and the separate offense had been prosecuted in a single proceeding), with United States v. Fuentes, 107 F.3d 1515, 1524 (11th Cir. 1997) (finding that a prior offense has been "fully taken into account" when the prior offense is part of the same course of conduct, common scheme, or plan).

Second, this amendment addresses how this guideline applies in cases in which an instant offense is committed while the defendant is on federal or state probation, parole, or supervised release, and has had such probation, parole, or supervised release revoked. Under this amendment, the sentence for the instant offense may be imposed concurrently, partially concurrently, or consecutively to the undischarged term of imprisonment; however, the Commission recommends a consecutive sentence in this situation. This amendment also resolves a circuit conflict concerning whether the imposition of such sentence is required to be consecutive. The amendment follows holdings of the Second, Third, and Tenth Circuits stating that imposition of sentence for the instant offense is not required to be consecutive to the sentence imposed upon revocation of probation, parole, or supervised release. See United States v. Maria, 186 F.3d 65, 70-73 (2d Cir. 1999); United States v. Swan, 275 F.3d 272, 279-83 (3d Cir. 2002); United States v. Tisdale, 248 F.3d 964, 977-79 (10th Cir. 2001).

Third, this amendment provides a new downward departure provision in § 5K2.23 (Discharged Terms of Imprisonment) regarding the effect of discharged terms of imprisonment. This provision replaces the departure provision previously set forth in Application Note 7 of § 5G1.3. By placing the departure provision in Chapter Five, Part K, this amendment brings structural clarity to § 5G1.3 because the guideline applies to undischarged, rather than discharged, terms of imprisonment. For ease of application, the new commentary in § 5G1.3 provides a reference to § 5K2.23.

Finally, this amendment addresses a circuit conflict regarding whether the sentencing court may grant "credit" or adjust the instant sentence for time served on a prior undischarged term covered under subsection (c). Compare Ruggiano v. Reish, 307 F.3d 121 (3d Cir. 2002) (federal sentencing court may grant such credit), with United States v. Fermin, 252 F.3d 102 (2d Cir. 2001) (court may not grant such credit). The amendment makes clear that the court may not adjust or give "credit" for time served on an undischarged term of imprisonment covered under subsection (c). However, the amendment adds commentary to § 5G1.3 to provide that courts may consider a downward departure in an extraordinary case, in order to achieve a reasonable punishment for the instant offense.

Effective Date: The effective date of this amendment is November 1, 2003.

661. **Amendment:** Section 1B1.1 is amended by inserting before subsection (a) the following new paragraph:

> "Except as specifically directed, the provisions of this manual are to be applied in the following order:".

The Commentary to § 1B1.1 captioned "Application Notes" is amended by striking Note 4 as follows:

> "4. The offense level adjustments from more than one specific offense characteristic within an offense guideline are cumulative (added together) unless the guideline specifies that only the greater (or greatest) is to be used. Within each specific offense characteristic subsection, however, the offense level

adjustments are alternative; only the one that best describes the conduct is to be used. E.g., in § 2A2.2(b)(3), pertaining to degree of bodily injury, the subdivision that best describes the level of bodily injury is used; the adjustments for different degrees of bodily injury (subdivisions (A)-(E)) are not added together.

Absent an instruction to the contrary, the adjustments from different guideline sections are applied cumulatively (added together).",

and inserting the following:

"4. (A) Cumulative Application of Multiple Adjustments within One Guideline.—The offense level adjustments from more than one specific offense characteristic within an offense guideline are applied cumulatively (added together) unless the guideline specifies that only the greater (or greatest) is to be used. Within each specific offense characteristic subsection, however, the offense level adjustments are alternative; only the one that best describes the conduct is to be used. For example, in § 2A2.2(b)(3), pertaining to degree of bodily injury, the subdivision that best describes the level of bodily injury is used; the adjustments for different degrees of bodily injury (subdivisions (A)-(E)) are not added together.

(B) Cumulative Application of Multiple Adjustments from Multiple Guidelines.—Absent an instruction to the contrary, enhancements under Chapter Two, adjustments under Chapter Three, and determinations under Chapter Four are to be applied cumulatively. In some cases, such enhancements, adjustments, and determinations may be triggered by the same conduct. For example, shooting a police officer during the commission of a robbery may warrant an injury enhancement under § 2B3.1(b)(3) and an official victim adjustment under § 3A1.2, even though the enhancement and the adjustment both are triggered by the shooting of the officer.".

The Commentary to § 1B1.1 captioned "Application Notes" is amended by adding at the end the following:

"(7) Use of Abbreviated Guideline Titles.—Whenever a guideline makes reference to another guideline, a parenthetical restatement of that other guideline's heading accompanies the initial reference to that other guideline. This parenthetical is provided only for the convenience of the reader and is not intended to have substantive effect. In the case of lengthy guideline headings, such a parenthetical restatement of the guideline heading may be abbreviated for ease of reference. For example, references to § 2B1.1 (Larceny, Embezzlement, and Other Forms of Theft; Offenses Involving Stolen Property; Property Damage or Destruction; Fraud and Deceit; Forgery; Offenses Involving Altered or Counterfeit Instruments Other than Counterfeit Bearer Obligations of the United States) may be abbreviated as follows: § 2B1.1 (Theft, Property Destruction, and Fraud).".

The Commentary to § 2A3.1 captioned "Application Notes" is amended in Note 1 in the paragraph beginning "'Prohibited sexual conduct'" by striking the following:

"'Prohibited sexual conduct' (A) means any sexual activity for which a person can be charged with a criminal offense; (B) includes the production of child pornography; and (C) does not include trafficking in, or possession of, child pornography.",

and inserting:

> "'Prohibited sexual conduct' means any sexual activity for which a person can be charged with a criminal offense. 'Prohibited sexual conduct' includes the production of child pornography, but does not include trafficking in, or possession of, child pornography.".

The Commentary to § 2B1.1 captioned "Statutory Provisions" is amended by inserting "19 U.S.C. § 2401f;" before "29 U.S.C.".

The Commentary to § 2C1.3 captioned "Statutory Provisions" is amended by inserting "; 40 U.S.C. § 14309(a), (b)" after "1909".

Section § 2D1.11(e)(1) is amended in the subdivision captioned "List I Chemicals" by striking the period after "Gamma-butyrolactone" and inserting a semi-colon; and by adding at the end the following:

> "714 G or more of Red Phosphorus.".

Section § 2D1.11(e)(2) is amended in the subdivision captioned "List I Chemicals" by adding at the end the following:

> "At least 214 G but less than 714 G of Red Phosphorus;".

Section § 2D1.11(e)(3) is amended in the subdivision captioned "List I Chemicals" by adding at the end the following:

> "At least 71 G but less than 214 G of Red Phosphorus;".

Section § 2D1.11(e)(4) is amended in the subdivision captioned "List I Chemicals" by adding at the end the following:

> "At least 50 G but less than 71 G of Red Phosphorus;".

Section § 2D1.11(e)(5) is amended in the subdivision captioned "List I Chemicals" by adding at the end the following:

> "At least 29 G but less than 50 G of Red Phosphorus;".

Section § 2D1.11(e)(6) is amended in the subdivision captioned "List I Chemicals" by adding at the end the following:

> "At least 7 G but less than 29 G of Red Phosphorus;".

Section § 2D1.11(e)(7) is amended in the subdivision captioned "List I Chemicals" by adding at the end the following:

> "At least 6 G but less than 7 G of Red Phosphorus;".

Section § 2D1.11(e)(8) is amended in the subdivision captioned "List I Chemicals" by adding at the end the following:

> "At least 4 G but less than 6 G of Red Phosphorus;".

Section § 2D1.11(e)(9) is amended in the subdivision captioned "List I Chemicals" by adding at the end the following:

> "At least 3 G but less than 4 G of Red Phosphorus;".

Section § 2D1.11(e)(10) is amended in the subdivision captioned "List I Chemicals" by adding at the end the following:

"Less than 3 G of Red Phosphorus;".

The Commentary to § 2G2.1 captioned "Application Notes" is amended by striking Note 6 as follows:

> "6. Upward Departure Provisions.—An upward departure may be warranted in either of the following circumstances:
>
>   (A) The defendant was convicted under 18 U.S.C. § 1591 and the offense involved a victim who had not attained the age of 14 years.
>
>   (B) The offense involved more than 10 victims.",

and inserting the following:

> "6. Upward Departure Provision.—An upward departure may be warranted if the offense involved more than 10 victims.".

Section 2G2.2(b)(5) is amended by inserting ", receipt, or distribution" after "transmission".

The Commentary to § 2H2.1 captioned "Statutory Provisions" is amended by inserting ", 1015(f)" after "597".

The Commentary to § 2K2.5 captioned "Statutory Provisions" is amended by inserting "; 40 U.S.C. § 5104(e)(1)" after "930".

The Commentary to § 2N2.1 captioned "Statutory Provisions" is amended by inserting ", 8313" after "7734".

The Commentary to § 2R1.1 captioned "Statutory Provision" is amended by striking "Provision" and inserting "Provisions"; and by striking " § 1" and inserting "§§ 1, 3(b)".

The Commentary to § 4B1.5 captioned "Application Notes" is amended Note 4(A) by striking "(i) means" and inserting "means any of the following: (i)"; by striking "includes" each place it appears; by inserting "or" before "(iii)"; and by striking "; and (iv)" and inserting ". It".

Appendix A (Statutory Index) is amended by inserting after the line referenced to 7 U.S.C. § 7734 the following new line:

> "7 U.S.C. § 8313   2N2.1";

by inserting after the line referenced to 15 U.S.C. § 1 the following new line:

> "15 U.S.C. § 3(b)   2R1.1";

in the line referenced to 18 U.S.C. § 1015 by inserting "(a)-(e)" after "1015";

by inserting after the line referenced to 18 U.S.C. § 1015(a)-(e), as amended by this amendment, the following new line:

> "18 U.S.C. § 1015(f)   2H2.1";

by inserting after the line referenced to 19 U.S.C. § 2316 the following new line:

    "19 U.S.C. § 2401f   2B1.1"; and

by inserting after the line referenced to 38 U.S.C. § 3502 the following new lines:

    "40 U.S.C. § 5104(e)(1)   2K2.5
    40 U.S.C. § 14309(a), (b)   2C1.3".

Reason for Amendment: This six-part amendment makes several technical and conforming changes to various guideline provisions.

First, this amendment makes changes to § 1B1.1 (Application Instructions) to (1) provide an instruction making clear that the application instructions are to be applied in the order presented in the guideline; (2) provide an application note making clear that, absent an instruction to the contrary, Chapter Two enhancements, Chapter Three adjustments, and determinations under Chapter Four triggered by the same conduct are to be applied cumulatively; and (3) provide an application note concerning the use of abbreviated guideline titles to ease reference to guidelines that have exceptionally long titles.

Second, this amendment adds red phosphorus to the Chemical Quantity Table in § 2D1.11 (Unlawfully Distributing, Importing, Exporting or Possessing a Listed Chemical) in response to a recent classification of red phosphorus as a List I chemical.

Third, this amendment conforms the departure provision in Application Note 6 of § 2G2.1 (Sexually Exploiting a Minor by Production of Sexually Explicit Visual or Printed Material; Custodian Permitting Minor to Engage in Sexually Explicit Conduct; Advertisement for Minors to Engage in Production) to Application Note 12 of § 2G1.1 (Promoting A Commercial Sex Act or Prohibited Sexual Conduct).

Fourth, this amendment amends subsection (b)(5) of § 2G2.2 (Trafficking in Material Involving the Sexual Exploitation of a Minor; Receiving, Transporting, Shipping, or Advertising Material Involving the Sexual Exploitation of a Minor; Possessing Material Involving the Sexual Exploitation of a Minor with Intent to Traffic) to include receipt and distribution in the enhancement for use of a computer.

Fifth, this amendment restructures the definitions of "prohibited sexual conduct" in §§ 2A3.1 (Criminal Sexual Abuse; Attempt to Commit Criminal Sexual Abuse) and 4B1.5 (Repeat and Dangerous Sex Offender Against Minors) to eliminate possible ambiguity regarding the interaction of "means" and "includes".

Finally, this amendment responds to new legislation and makes other technical amendments as follows:

    (1)   Amends Appendix A (Statutory Index) and § 2N2.1 (Violations of Statutes and Regulations Dealing with any Food, Drug, Biological Product, Device, Cosmetic, or Agricultural Product) in response to new offenses created by the Farm Security and Rural Investment Act of 2002 (the "Act"), Pub. L. 107–171. The first new offense provides a statutory maximum of one year of imprisonment for violating the Animal Health Protection Act (Subtitle E of the Act), or for counterfeiting or destroying certain documents specified in the Animal Health Protection Act. The second new offense provides a statutory maximum term of imprisonment of five years for importing, entering, exporting, or moving any animal or article for distribution or sale. The

Amendment 661 APPENDIX C - VOLUME II November 1, 2013

Act also provides a statutory maximum of ten years' imprisonment for a subsequent violation of either offense.

(2) Amends Appendix A and § 2B1.1 (Larceny, Embezzlement, and Other Forms of Theft; Offenses Involving Stolen Property; Property Damage or Destruction; Fraud and Deceit; Forgery; Offenses Involving Altered or Counterfeit Instruments Other than Counterfeit Bearer Obligations of the United States) in response to a new offense (19 U.S.C. § 2401f) created by the Trade Act of 2002, Pub. L. 107–210. The new offense provides a statutory maximum term of imprisonment of one year for knowingly making a false statement of material fact for the purpose of obtaining or increasing a payment of federal adjustment assistance to qualifying agricultural commodity producers.

(3) Amends Appendix A, §§ 2C1.3 (Conflict of Interest; Payment or Receipt of Unauthorized Compensation) and 2K2.5 (Possession of Firearm or Dangerous Weapon in Federal Facility; Possession or Discharge of Firearm in School Zone) in response to the codification of title 40, United States Code, by Pub. L. 107–217. Section 5104(e)(1) of title 40, United States Code, prohibits anyone (except as authorized by the Capitol Police Board) from carrying or having readily accessible a firearm, dangerous weapon, explosive, or incendiary device on the Capitol Grounds or in any of the Capitol Buildings. The statutory maximum term of imprisonment is five years. The amendment references 40 U.S.C. § 5104(e)(1) to § 2K2.5. Section 14309(a) of title 40, United States Code, prohibits certain conflicts of interests of members of the Appalachian Regional Commission and provides a statutory maximum term of imprisonment of two years. Section 14309(b) prohibits certain additional sources of salary and provides a statutory maximum term of imprisonment of one year. The amendment references 40 U.S.C. § 14309(a) and (b) to § 2C1.3.

(4) Amends Appendix A and § 2H2.1 (Obstructing an Election or Registration) to provide a guideline reference for offenses under 18 U.S.C. § 1015(f). Prior to this amendment, 18 U.S.C. § 1015 was referenced to §§ 2B1.1, 2J1.3 (Perjury or Subornation of Perjury; Bribery of Witness), 2L2.1 (Trafficking in a Document Relating to Naturalization, Citizenship, or Legal Resident Status, or a United States Passport; False Statement in Respect to the Citizenship or Immigration Status of Another; Fraudulent Marriage to Assist Alien to Evade Immigration Law), and 2L2.2 (Fraudulently Acquiring Documents Relating to Naturalization, Citizenship, or Legal Resident Status for Own Use; False Personation or Fraudulent Marriage by Alien to Evade Immigration Law; Fraudulently Acquiring or Improperly Using a United States Passport). However, 18 U.S.C. § 1015(f) specifically relates to knowingly making false statements in order to register to vote, or to vote, in a Federal, State, or local election. Accordingly, the amendment references 18 U.S.C. § 1015(f) to § 2H2.1 (Obstructing an Election or Registration).

(5) Amends Appendix A and § 2R1.1 (Bid-Rigging, Price-Fixing or Market-Allocation Agreements Among Competitors) in response to a new offense (15 U.S.C. § 3) created by section 14102 (the Antitrust Technical Corrections Act of 2002) of the 21st Century Department of Justice Appropriations Authorization Act, Pub. L. 107–273. The new offense provides a statutory maximum term of imprisonment of three years, and a maximum fine of

$10,000,000 for a corporation, or $350,000 for an individual, for monopolizing, or attempting or conspiring to monopolize, any part of the trade or commerce in or between any states, or territories of the United States, or between any such states, or territories of the United States and any foreign nations.

Effective Date: The effective date of this amendment is November 1, 2003.

662. **Amendment:** Section 1B1.10(c) is amended by striking "and 606" and inserting "606, and 657".

Reason for Amendment: This amendment expands the listing in § 1B1.10(c) to implement the directive in 28 U.S.C. § 994(u) with respect to guideline amendments that may be considered for retroactive application.

Effective Date: The effective date of this amendment is November 5, 2003.

APPENDIX C (VOLUME III) - AMENDMENTS TO THE GUIDELINES MANUAL

This volume of Appendix C presents amendments to the guidelines, policy statements, and official commentary effective November 1, 2004; October 24, 2005; November 1, 2005; March 27, 2006; September 12, 2006; November 1, 2006; May 1, 2007; November 1, 2007; February 6, 2008; March 3, 2008; May 1, 2008; November 1, 2008; November 1, 2009; November 1, 2010; and November 1, 2011.

For amendments to the guidelines, policy statements, and official commentary effective November 1, 1998; May 1, 2000; November 1, 2000; December 16, 2000; May 1, 2001; November 1, 2001; November 1, 2002; January 25, 2003; April 30, 2003; October 27, 2003; November 1, 2003; and November 5, 2003, see Appendix C, Volume II. For amendments effective November 1, 1997, and earlier, see Appendix C, Volume I.

The format under which the amendments are presented in Appendix C, including this volume, is designed to facilitate a comparison between previously existing and amended provisions, in the event it becomes necessary to reference the former guideline, policy statement, or commentary language.

AMENDMENTS

663. Amendment: The Commentary to § 2A1.1 captioned "Application Notes" is amended by striking Notes 1 and 2 as follows:

> "1. The Commission has concluded that in the absence of capital punishment life imprisonment is the appropriate punishment for premeditated killing. However, this guideline also applies when death results from the commission of certain felonies. Life imprisonment is not necessarily appropriate in all such situations. For example, if in robbing a bank, the defendant merely passed a note to the teller, as a result of which she had a heart attack and died, a sentence of life imprisonment clearly would not be appropriate.
>
> If the defendant did not cause the death intentionally or knowingly, a downward departure may be warranted. The extent of the departure should be based upon the defendant's state of mind (e.g., recklessness or negligence), the degree of risk inherent in the conduct, and the nature of the underlying offense conduct. However, the Commission does not envision that departure below that specified in § 2A1.2 (Second Degree Murder) is likely to be appropriate. Also, because death obviously is an aggravating factor, it necessarily would be inappropriate to impose a sentence at a level below that which the guideline for the underlying offense requires in the absence of death.
>
> 2. If the defendant is convicted under 21 U.S.C. § 848(e), a sentence of death may be imposed under the specific provisions contained in that statute. This guideline applies when a sentence of death is not imposed.",

and inserting the following:

> "1. Applicability of Guideline.—This guideline applies in cases of premeditated killing. This guideline also applies when death results from the commission of certain felonies. For example, this guideline may be applied as a result of a cross reference (e.g., a kidnapping in which death occurs), or in cases in

which the offense level of a guideline is calculated using the underlying crime (e.g., murder in aid of racketeering).

2. Imposition of Life Sentence.—

   (A) Offenses Involving Premeditated Killing.—In the case of premeditated killing, life imprisonment is the appropriate sentence if a sentence of death is not imposed. A downward departure would not be appropriate in such a case. A downward departure from a mandatory statutory term of life imprisonment is permissible only in cases in which the government files a motion for a downward departure for the defendant's substantial assistance, as provided in 18 U.S.C. § 3553(e).

   (B) Felony Murder.—If the defendant did not cause the death intentionally or knowingly, a downward departure may be warranted. For example, a downward departure may be warranted if in robbing a bank, the defendant merely passed a note to the teller, as a result of which the teller had a heart attack and died. The extent of the departure should be based upon the defendant's state of mind (e.g., recklessness or negligence), the degree of risk inherent in the conduct, and the nature of the underlying offense conduct. However, departure below the minimum guideline sentence provided for second degree murder in § 2A1.2 (Second Degree Murder) is not likely to be appropriate. Also, because death obviously is an aggravating factor, it necessarily would be inappropriate to impose a sentence at a level below that which the guideline for the underlying offense requires in the absence of death.

3. Applicability of Guideline When Death Sentence Not Imposed.—If the defendant is sentenced pursuant to 18 U.S.C. § 3591 et seq. or 21 U.S.C. § 848(e), a sentence of death may be imposed under the specific provisions contained in that statute. This guideline applies when a sentence of death is not imposed under those specific provisions.".

Section 2A1.2(a) is amended by striking "33" and inserting "38".

Section 2A1.2 is amended by striking the commentary captioned "Background" as follows:

"Background: The maximum term of imprisonment authorized by statute for second degree murder is life.",

and inserting the following:

"Application Note:

1. Upward Departure Provision.—If the defendant's conduct was exceptionally heinous, cruel, brutal, or degrading to the victim, an upward departure may be warranted. See § 5K2.8 (Extreme Conduct).".

Section 2A1.3(a) is amended by striking "25" and inserting "29".

Section 2A1.3 is amended by striking the commentary captioned "Background" as follows:

"Background: The maximum term of imprisonment authorized by statute for voluntary manslaughter is ten years.".

Section 2A1.4(a) is amended in subdivision (1) by striking "conduct was criminally negligent" and inserting "offense involved criminally negligent conduct"; and by striking subdivision (2) as follows:

"(2)   18, if the conduct was reckless.",

and inserting the following:

"(2)   (Apply the greater):

(A)   18, if the offense involved reckless conduct; or

(B)   22, if the offense involved the reckless operation of a means of transportation.".

Section 2A1.4 is amended by adding at the end the following:

"(b)   Special Instruction

(1)   If the offense involved the involuntary manslaughter of more than one person, Chapter Three, Part D (Multiple Counts) shall be applied as if the involuntary manslaughter of each person had been contained in a separate count of conviction.".

The Commentary to § 2A1.4 captioned "Application Notes" is amended in the heading by striking "Notes" and inserting "Note"; and by striking Notes 1 and 2 as follows:

"1.   'Reckless' refers to a situation in which the defendant was aware of the risk created by his conduct and the risk was of such a nature and degree that to disregard that risk constituted a gross deviation from the standard of care that a reasonable person would exercise in such a situation. The term thus includes all, or nearly all, convictions for involuntary manslaughter under 18 U.S.C. § 1112. A homicide resulting from driving, or similarly dangerous actions, while under the influence of alcohol or drugs ordinarily should be treated as reckless.

2.   'Criminally negligent' refers to conduct that involves a gross deviation from the standard of care that a reasonable person would exercise under the circumstances, but which is not reckless. Offenses with this characteristic usually will be encountered as assimilative crimes.".

and inserting the following:

"1.   Definitions.—For purposes of this guideline:

'Criminally negligent' means conduct that involves a gross deviation from the standard of care that a reasonable person would exercise under the circumstances, but which is not reckless. Offenses with this characteristic usually will be encountered as assimilative crimes.

'Means of transportation' includes a motor vehicle (including an automobile or a boat) and a mass transportation vehicle. 'Mass transportation' has the meaning given that term in 18 U.S.C. § 1993(c)(5).

'Reckless' means a situation in which the defendant was aware of the risk created by his conduct and the risk was of such a nature and degree that to disregard that risk constituted a gross deviation from the standard of care that a reasonable person would exercise in such a situation. 'Reckless' includes all, or nearly all, convictions for involuntary manslaughter under 18 U.S.C. § 1112. A homicide resulting from driving a means of transportation, or similarly dangerous actions, while under the influence of alcohol or drugs ordinarily should be treated as reckless.".

Section 2A1.5(a) is amended by striking "28" and inserting "33".

Section 2A2.1(a) is amended in subdivision (1) by striking "28" and inserting "33"; and in subdivision (2) by striking "22" and inserting "27".

Section 2A2.1(b)(1) is amended by striking "(A) If" and inserting "If (A)"; and by striking "if" each place it appears.

The Commentary to § 2A2.1 captioned "Application Notes" is amended by striking Notes 1 through 3 as follows:

"1. Definitions of 'serious bodily injury' and 'permanent or life-threatening bodily injury' are found in the Commentary to § 1B1.1 (Application Instructions).

2. 'First degree murder,' as used in subsection (a)(1), means conduct that, if committed within the special maritime and territorial jurisdiction of the United States, would constitute first degree murder under 18 U.S.C. § 1111.

3. If the offense created a substantial risk of death or serious bodily injury to more than one person, an upward departure may be warranted.",

and inserting the following:

"1. Definitions.—For purposes of this guideline:

'First degree murder' means conduct that, if committed within the special maritime and territorial jurisdiction of the United States, would constitute first degree murder under 18 U.S.C. § 1111.

'Permanent or life-threatening bodily injury' and 'serious bodily injury' have the meaning given those terms in Application Note 1 of the Commentary to § 1B1.1 (Application Instructions).

2. Upward Departure Provision.—If the offense created a substantial risk of death or serious bodily injury to more than one person, an upward departure may be warranted.".

Section 2A2.2(a) is amended by striking "15" and inserting "14".

Section 2A2.2(b)(2) is amended by striking "(A) If" and inserting "If (A)"; and by striking "if" each place it appears.

Section 2A2.2(b)(3) is amended in subdivision (A) by striking "2" and inserting "3"; in subdivision (B) by striking "4" and inserting "5"; in subdivision (C) by striking "6" and inserting "7"; in subdivision (D) by striking "3" and inserting "4"; and in subdivision (E) by striking "5" and inserting "6".

Amendment 663 APPENDIX C - VOLUME III November 1, 2013

Section 2A2.2(b)(3) is amended by striking "Provided, however, that the cumulative adjustments from (2) and (3) shall not exceed 9 levels.", and inserting "However, the cumulative adjustments from application of subdivisions (2) and (3) shall not exceed 10 levels.".

Section 2A2.2(b) is amended by adding at the end the following:

"(6) If the defendant was convicted under 18 U.S.C. § 111(b) or § 115, increase by 2 levels.".

The Commentary to § 2A2.2 captioned "Application Notes" is amended by striking Note 2 as follows:

"2. Application of Subsection (b)(2).—In a case involving a dangerous weapon with intent to cause bodily injury, the court shall apply both the base offense level and subsection (b)(2).".

The Commentary to § 2A2.2 captioned "Application Notes" is amended in Note 3 by striking:

"3. More than Minimal Planning.—For purposes of subsection (b)(1),",

and inserting the following:

"2. Application of Subsection (b)(1).—For purposes of subsection (b)(1),".

The Commentary to § 2A2.2 captioned "Application Notes" is amended by adding at the end the following:

"3. Application of Subsection (b)(2).—In a case involving a dangerous weapon with intent to cause bodily injury, the court shall apply both the base offense level and subsection (b)(2).

4. Application of Official Victim Adjustment.—If subsection (b)(6) applies, § 3A1.2 (Official Victim) also shall apply.".

The Commentary to § 2A2.2 captioned "Background" is amended by adding at the end the following:

" Subsection (b)(6) implements the directive to the Commission in subsection 11008(e) of the 21st Century Department of Justice Appropriations Act (the 'Act'), Public Law 107–273. The enhancement in subsection (b)(6) is cumulative to the adjustment in § 3A1.2 (Official Victim) in order to address adequately the directive in section 11008(e)(2)(D) of the Act, which provides that the Commission shall consider 'the extent to which sentencing enhancements within the Federal guidelines and the authority of the court to impose a sentence in excess of the applicable guideline range are adequate to ensure punishment at or near the maximum penalty for the most egregious conduct covered by' 18 U.S.C. §§ 111 and 115.".

Section 2A2.3(a) is amended in subdivision (1) by striking "6" and inserting "7", and by striking "conduct" and inserting "offense"; and in subdivision (2) by striking "3" and inserting "4".

Section 2A2.3(b)(1) is amended by inserting "(A) the victim sustained bodily injury, increase by 2 levels; or (B)" after "If".

– 872 –

Section 2A2.3 is amended by adding at the end the following:

"(c) Cross Reference

(1) If the conduct constituted aggravated assault, apply § 2A2.2 (Aggravated Assault).".

The Commentary to § 2A2.3 captioned "Application Notes" is amended by striking Notes 1 through 3 as follows:

"1. 'Minor assault' means a misdemeanor assault, or a felonious assault not covered by § 2A2.2.

2. Definitions of 'firearm' and 'dangerous weapon' are found in the Commentary to § 1B1.1 (Application Instructions).

3. 'Substantial bodily injury' means 'bodily injury which involves - (A) a temporary but substantial disfigurement; or (B) a temporary but substantial loss or impairment of the function of any bodily member, organ, or mental faculty.' 18 U.S.C. § 113(b)(1).",

and inserting the following:

"1. Definitions.—For purposes of this guideline:

'Bodily injury', 'dangerous weapon', and 'firearm' have the meaning given those terms in Application Note 1 of the Commentary to § 1B1.1 (Application Instructions).

'Minor assault' means a misdemeanor assault, or a felonious assault not covered by § 2A2.2 (Aggravated Assault).

'Substantial bodily injury' means 'bodily injury which involves (A) a temporary but substantial disfigurement; or (B) a temporary but substantial loss or impairment of the function of any bodily member, organ, or mental faculty.' See 18 U.S.C. § 113(b)(1).

2. Application of Subsection (b)(1).—Conduct that forms the basis for application of subsection (a)(1) also may form the basis for application of the enhancement in subsection (b)(1)(A) or (B).".

Section 2A2.4(a) is amended by striking "6" and inserting "10".

Section 2A2.4(b) is amended by striking "Characteristic" and inserting "Characteristics"; by striking in subdivision (1) "If the conduct involved physical contact, or if" and inserting "If (A) the offense involved physical contact; or (B)"; and by adding at the end the following:

"(2) If the victim sustained bodily injury, increase by 2 levels.".

The Commentary to § 2A2.4 captioned "Application Notes" is amended by striking Notes 1 and 2 as follows:

"1. The base offense level reflects the fact that the victim was a governmental officer performing official duties. Therefore, do not apply § 3A1.2 (Official

– 873 –

Victim) unless subsection (c) requires the offense level to be determined under § 2A2.2 (Aggravated Assault). Conversely, the base offense level does not reflect the possibility that the defendant may create a substantial risk of death or serious bodily injury to another person in the course of fleeing from a law enforcement official (although an offense under 18 U.S.C. § 758 for fleeing or evading a law enforcement checkpoint at high speed will often, but not always, involve the creation of that risk). If the defendant creates that risk and no higher guideline adjustment is applicable for the conduct creating the risk, apply § 3C1.2 (Reckless Endangerment During Flight).

2. Definitions of 'firearm' and 'dangerous weapon' are found in the Commentary to § 1B1.1 (Application Instructions).",

and inserting the following:

"1. Definitions.—For purposes of this guideline, 'bodily injury', 'dangerous weapon', and 'firearm' have the meaning given those terms in Application Note 1 of the Commentary to § 1B1.1 (Application Instructions).

2. Application of Certain Chapter Three Adjustments.—The base offense level incorporates the fact that the victim was a governmental officer performing official duties. Therefore, do not apply § 3A1.2 (Official Victim) unless, pursuant to subsection (c), the offense level is determined under § 2A2.2 (Aggravated Assault). Conversely, the base offense level does not incorporate the possibility that the defendant may create a substantial risk of death or serious bodily injury to another person in the course of fleeing from a law enforcement official (although an offense under 18 U.S.C. § 758 for fleeing or evading a law enforcement checkpoint at high speed will often, but not always, involve the creation of that risk). If the defendant creates that risk and no higher guideline adjustment is applicable for the conduct creating the risk, apply § 3C1.2 (Reckless Endangerment During Flight).".

The Commentary to § 2A2.4 captioned "Application Notes" is amended in Note 3 by inserting "Upward Departure Provision.—" before "The base".

The Commentary to § 2A2.4 captioned "Background" is amended by striking the last sentence as follows:

"The guideline has been drafted to provide offense levels that are identical to those otherwise provided for assaults involving an official victim; when no assault is involved, the offense level is 6.".

Section 3A1.2 is amended by striking:

"§ 3A1.2. Official Victim

(a) If (1) the victim was (A) a government officer or employee; (B) a former government officer or employee; or (C) a member of the immediate family of a person described in subdivision (A) or (B); and (2) the offense of conviction was motivated by such status, increase by 3 levels.

(b) If, in a manner creating a substantial risk of serious bodily injury, the defendant or a person for whose conduct the defendant is otherwise accountable—

(1) knowing or having reasonable cause to believe that a person was a law enforcement officer, assaulted such officer during the course of the offense or immediate flight therefrom; or

(2) knowing or having reasonable cause to believe that a person was a prison official, assaulted such official while the defendant (or a person for whose conduct the defendant is otherwise accountable) was in the custody or control of a prison or other correctional facility,

increase by 3 levels.",

and inserting:

"§ 3A1.2.   Official Victim

(Apply the greatest):

(a) If (1) the victim was (A) a government officer or employee; (B) a former government officer or employee; or (C) a member of the immediate family of a person described in subdivision (A) or (B); and (2) the offense of conviction was motivated by such status, increase by 3 levels.

(b) If subsection (a)(1) and (2) apply, and the applicable Chapter Two guideline is from Chapter Two, Part A (Offenses Against the Person), increase by 6 levels.

(c) If, in a manner creating a substantial risk of serious bodily injury, the defendant or a person for whose conduct the defendant is otherwise accountable—

(1) knowing or having reasonable cause to believe that a person was a law enforcement officer, assaulted such officer during the course of the offense or immediate flight therefrom; or

(2) knowing or having reasonable cause to believe that a person was a prison official, assaulted such official while the defendant (or a person for whose conduct the defendant is otherwise accountable) was in the custody or control of a prison or other correctional facility,

increase by 6 levels.".

The Commentary to § 3A1.2 captioned "Application Notes" is amended in Note 2 by striking the second sentence as follows: "In most cases, the offenses to which subdivision (a) will apply will be from Chapter Two, Part A (Offenses Against the Person)."; and by striking in the third sentence ", Part A,".

The Commentary to § 3A1.2 captioned "Application Notes" is amended in Note 3 by striking "Subsection (a)" and inserting "Subsections (a) and (b)"; and by striking "in subsection (a)" and inserting ", for purposes of subsections (a) and (b),".

The Commentary to § 3A1.2 captioned "Application Notes" is amended in Note 4 by striking "Subsection (b)" each place it appears and inserting "Subsection (c)"; by striking "subsection (b)" each place it appears and inserting "subsection (c)"; and by striking "and control" each place it appears and inserting "or control".

The Commentary to § 3A1.2 captioned "Application Notes" is amended by striking Note 5 as follows:

> "5. Upward Departure Provision.—Certain high level officials, e.g., the President and Vice President, although covered by this section, do not represent the heartland of the conduct covered. An upward departure to reflect the potential disruption of the governmental function in such cases typically would be warranted.",

and inserting the following:

> "5. Upward Departure Provision.—If the official victim is an exceptionally high-level official, such as the President or the Vice President of the United States, an upward departure may be warranted due to the potential disruption of the governmental function.".

Reason for Amendment: This amendment increases the base offense levels for the homicide and manslaughter guidelines to address longstanding proportionality concerns and new proportionality issues prompted by changes to other Chapter Two guidelines pursuant to the Prosecutorial Remedies and Other Tools to end the Exploitation of Children Today Act of 2003, Pub. L. 108–21 (the "PROTECT Act"). It also amends the assault guidelines and the adjustment at § 3A1.2 (Official Victim) to implement the directive in section 11008(e) of the 21st Century Department of Justice Appropriations Authorization Act, Pub. L. 107–273 (the "Act").

First, this amendment makes a number of changes to the homicide guidelines. The amendment revises the commentary in guideline § 2A1.1 (First Degree Murder) and deletes outdated language. One effect of this revision is to clarify that a downward departure from a mandatory statutory sentence of life imprisonment is permissible only in cases in which the government files a motion for a downward departure for the defendant's substantial assistance, as provided in 18 U.S.C. § 3553(e).

In addition, the Commission received public comment that the guideline penalties for all homicides, other than for first degree murder, were inadequate and in need of review. An examination of the homicide and manslaughter guidelines also was prompted by section 104 of the PROTECT Act, which directed the Commission to increase the base offense level for § 2A4.1 (Kidnapping, Abduction, Unlawful Restraint). The Commission increased the base offense level for kidnapping by eight levels, from base offense level 24 to base offense level 32, effective May 30, 2003. This increase brought kidnapping without injury to within one level of the base offense of level 33 for second degree murder. The Commission examined data on second degree murder offenses and found that in 2002, courts departed upward from the guideline range in 34.3% of the cases. The Commission also received public comment expressing concern that an individual convicted of second degree murder who accepted responsibility might serve as little as eight years' imprisonment. By increasing the base offense level in § 2A1.2 (Second Degree Murder) to level 38, the Commission has established an approximate 20-year sentence of imprisonment for second degree murder.

Data also showed a high level of upward departure sentences for some other homicide offenses, such as voluntary manslaughter, which had a 28.6% upward departure rate in 2002. Based upon such indications that the sentences may be inadequate for these offenses, the Commission increased the base offense levels of many of the homicide guidelines to punish them more appropriately and with an eye toward restoring the proportionality found in the original guidelines. For example, the original base offense level of 28 for attempted first degree murder, § 2A2.1 (Assault with Intent to Commit Murder; Attempted Murder) is five levels lower than the original base offense level of level 33 for second degree murder. In this amendment, the five-level increase from a base offense level of level 28 to level 33 for attempted first degree murder mirrors the five-level increase for second degree murder from offense level of level 33 to level 38 and maintains the five-level difference that exists between the two. The amendment increases the base offense levels in the guidelines for §§ 2A1.2, 2A1.3 (Voluntary Manslaughter), 2A1.5 (Conspiracy or Solicitation to Commit Murder), and 2A2.1.

Additionally, the amendment adds a third alternative base offense level in § 2A1.4 (Involuntary Manslaughter) of level 22 for reckless involuntary manslaughter offenses that involved the reckless operation of a means of transportation. This new offense level completes work undertaken in the previous amendment cycle to address disparities between federal and state sentences for vehicular manslaughter and to account for the 1994 increase in the statutory maximum term of imprisonment from three to six years. The new alternative offense level focusing on the reckless operation of a means of transportation addresses concerns raised by some members of Congress and comports with a recommendation from the Commission's Native American Advisory Group that vehicular manslaughter involving alcohol or drugs should be sentenced at offense level 22. The amendment also adds a special instruction to apply § 3D1.2 (Groups of Closely Related Counts) as if there had been a separate count of conviction for each victim in cases in which more than one victim died. The purpose of the instruction is to ensure an incremental increase in punishment for single count offenses involving multiple victims.

Second, this amendment makes a number of changes to the assault guidelines and the Chapter Three adjustment relating to official victims, to implement the congressional directive and the changes in statutory maximum terms of imprisonment in the 21st Century Department of Justice Appropriations Authorization Act. The Act increased the statutory maximum term of imprisonment for a number of offenses against current or former officers or employees of the United States, including Federal judges and magistrate judges, their families, or persons assisting in the performance of those official duties, or offenses committed on account of those duties. In response to the directive, the Commission added a new specific offense characteristic in § 2A2.2 (Aggravated Assault) to provide a two-level increase if the defendant was convicted under 18 U.S.C. § 111(b) or § 115. The Commission also amended the guideline to decrease the base offense level from level 15 to level 14, based upon information received from the Native American Advisory Group and studies indicating that federal aggravated assault sentences generally are more severe than many state aggravated assault sentences. To ensure that individuals who cause bodily injury to victims do not benefit from this decrease in the base offense level, the specific offense characteristics addressing degrees of bodily injury each were increased by one level. To maintain proportionality, reflect increased statutory penalties, and comply with the directive, the two non-aggravated assault guidelines also were amended. For § 2A2.3 (Minor Assault), the alternative base offense levels each were increased by one level, a specific offense characteristic was added to provide a two-level enhancement if the victim sustained bodily injury, and a cross-reference to § 2A2.2 was added. Similarly, § 2A2.4 (Obstructing or Impeding Officers) was amended by increasing the base offense level to level 10, and by adding a specific offense characteristic providing a two-level increase if the victim sustained bodily injury.

The amendment restructures § 3A1.2 (Official Victim) and provides a two-tiered adjustment. The amendment maintains the three-level adjustment for offenses motivated by the status of the official victim, but increases the adjustment to six levels if that defendant's offense guideline was from Chapter Two, Part A (Offenses Against the Person). For example, a threat against a federal judge sentenced pursuant to § 2A6.1 (Threatening or Harassing Communications) that is calculated at base offense level 12 could have received, before this amendment, a three-level enhancement under § 3A1.2, which would have resulted in an adjusted offense level of level 15 and a guideline range of 18 to 24 months. Under this amendment, the defendant could receive a six-level adjustment, resulting in an enhanced offense level of level 18 and a guideline range of 27 to 33 months. The six level enhancement also applies to assaultive conduct against law enforcement officers or prison officials if the defendant committed the assault in a manner creating a substantial risk of serious bodily injury. This increase comports with the directive in the Act to "ensure punishment at or near the maximum penalty for the most egregious conduct covered by the offense" for offenses against federal officers, officials and employees.

Effective Date: The effective date of this amendment is November 1, 2004.

664. Amendment: Section 2A3.1(a) is amended by striking "27" and inserting "30".

Section 2A3.1(b)(1) is amended by striking "was committed by the means set forth" and inserting "involved conduct described".

Section 2A3.1(b)(6) is amended by striking "Internet-access device" and inserting "interactive computer service".

Section 2A3.1(c) is amended in the heading by striking "Cross Reference" and inserting "Cross References".

Section 2A3.1(c)(1) is amended by inserting ", if the resulting offense level is greater than that determined above" after "Murder)".

Section 2A3.1(c) is amended by adding at the end the following:

> "(2) If the offense involved causing, transporting, permitting, or offering or seeking by notice or advertisement, a minor to engage in sexually explicit conduct for the purpose of producing a visual depiction of such conduct, apply § 2G2.1 (Sexually Exploiting a Minor by Production of Sexually Explicit Visual or Printed Material; Custodian Permitting Minor to Engage in Sexually Explicit Conduct; Advertisement for Minors to Engage in Production), if the resulting offense level is greater than that determined above.".

Section 2A3.1(d)(1) is amended by striking "a correctional facility and the victim was a corrections employee" and inserting "the custody or control of a prison or other correctional facility and the victim was a prison official"; and by striking "(a)" and inserting "(c)(2)".

The Commentary to § 2A3.1 captioned "Application Notes" is amended by striking Notes 1 through 3 as follows:

> "1. For purposes of this guideline—
>
> > 'Minor' means an individual who had not attained the age of 18 years.
> >
> > 'Participant' has the meaning given that term in Application Note 1 of the Commentary to § 3B1.1 (Aggravating Role).
> >
> > 'Permanent or life-threatening bodily injury,' 'serious bodily injury,' and

'abducted' are defined in the Commentary to § 1B1.1 (Application Instructions). However, for purposes of this guideline, 'serious bodily injury' means conduct other than criminal sexual abuse, which already is taken into account in the base offense level under subsection (a).

'Prohibited sexual conduct' means any sexual activity for which a person can be charged with a criminal offense. 'Prohibited sexual conduct' includes the production of child pornography, but does not include trafficking in, or possession of, child pornography. 'Child pornography' has the meaning given that term in 18 U.S.C. § 2256(8).

'The means set forth in 18 U.S.C. § 2241(a) or (b)' are: by using force against the victim; by threatening or placing the victim in fear that any person will be subject to death, serious bodily injury, or kidnaping; by rendering the victim unconscious; or by administering by force or threat of force, or without the knowledge or permission of the victim, a drug, intoxicant, or other similar substance and thereby substantially impairing the ability of the victim to appraise or control conduct. This provision would apply, for example, if any dangerous weapon was used or brandished.

2. Subsection (b)(3), as it pertains to a victim in the custody, care, or supervisory control of the defendant, is intended to have broad application and is to be applied whenever the victim is entrusted to the defendant, whether temporarily or permanently. For example, teachers, day care providers, baby-sitters, or other temporary caretakers are among those who would be subject to this enhancement. In determining whether to apply this enhancement, the court should look to the actual relationship that existed between the defendant and the victim and not simply to the legal status of the defendant-victim relationship.

3. If the adjustment in subsection (b)(3) applies, do not apply § 3B1.3 (Abuse of Position of Trust or Use of Special Skill).",

and inserting the following:

"1. Definitions.—For purposes of this guideline:

'Abducted', 'permanent or life-threatening bodily injury', and 'serious bodily injury' have the meaning given those terms in Application Note 1 of the Commentary to § 1B1.1 (Application Instructions). However, for purposes of this guideline, 'serious bodily injury' means conduct other than criminal sexual abuse, which already is taken into account in the base offense level under subsection (a).

'Custody or control' and 'prison official' have the meaning given those terms in Application Note 4 of the Commentary to § 3A1.2 (Official Victim).

'Child pornography' has the meaning given that term in 18 U.S.C. § 2256(8).

'Computer' has the meaning given that term in 18 U.S.C. § 1030(e)(1).

'Distribution' means any act, including possession with intent to distribute, production, transportation, and advertisement, related to the transfer of material involving the sexual exploitation of a minor. Accordingly, distribution includes posting material involving the sexual exploitation of a minor on a website for public viewing, but does not include the mere solicitation of such material by a defendant.

'Interactive computer service' has the meaning given that term in section 230(e)(2) of the Communications Act of 1934 (47 U.S.C. § 230(f)(2)).

'Minor' means (A) an individual who had not attained the age of 18 years; (B) an individual, whether fictitious or not, who a law enforcement officer represented to a participant (i) had not attained the age of 18 years, and (ii) could be provided for the purposes of engaging in sexually explicit conduct; or (C) an undercover law enforcement officer who represented to a participant that the officer had not attained the age of 18 years.

'Participant' has the meaning given that term in Application Note 1 of the Commentary to § 3B1.1 (Aggravating Role).

'Prohibited sexual conduct' (A) means any sexual activity for which a person can be charged with a criminal offense; (B) includes the production of child pornography; and (C) does not include trafficking in, or possession of, child pornography.

'Victim' includes an undercover law enforcement officer.

2. Application of Subsection (b)(1).—For purposes of subsection (b)(1), 'conduct described in 18 U.S.C. § 2241(a) or (b)' is engaging in, or causing another person to engage in, a sexual act with another person by: (A) using force against the victim; (B) threatening or placing the victim in fear that any person will be subject to death, serious bodily injury, or kidnapping; (C) rendering the victim unconscious; or (D) administering by force or threat of force, or without the knowledge or permission of the victim, a drug, intoxicant, or other similar substance and thereby substantially impairing the ability of the victim to appraise or control conduct. This provision would apply, for example, if any dangerous weapon was used or brandished, or in a case in which the ability of the victim to appraise or control conduct was substantially impaired by drugs or alcohol.

3. Application of Subsection (b)(3).—

   (A) Care, Custody, or Supervisory Control.—Subsection (b)(3) is to be construed broadly and includes offenses involving a victim less than 18 years of age entrusted to the defendant, whether temporarily or permanently. For example, teachers, day care providers, babysitters, or other temporary caretakers are among those who would be subject to this enhancement. In determining whether to apply this enhancement, the court should look to the actual relationship that existed between the defendant and the minor and not simply to the legal status of the defendant-minor relationship.

   (B) Inapplicability of Chapter Three Adjustment.—If the enhancement in subsection (b)(3) applies, do not apply § 3B1.3 (Abuse of Position of Trust or Use of Special Skill).".

The Commentary to § 2A3.1 captioned "Application Notes" is amended in Note 4 by inserting before "The enhancement" the following:

"Application of Subsection (b)(6).—

(A) Misrepresentation of Participant's Identity.—";

and by striking the last paragraph as follows:

"Subsection (b)(6)(B) provides an enhancement if a computer or an Internet-access device was used to (A) persuade, induce, entice, or coerce a minor to engage in prohibited sexual conduct; or (B) facilitate transportation or travel, by a minor or a participant, to engage in prohibited sexual conduct. Subsection (b)(6)(B) is intended to apply only to the use of a computer or an Internet-access device to communicate directly with a minor or with a person who exercises custody, care, or supervisory control of the minor. Accordingly, the enhancement would not apply to the use of a computer or an Internet-access device to obtain airline tickets for the minor from an airline's Internet site.",

and inserting the following:

"(B) Use of a Computer or Interactive Computer Service.— Subsection (b)(6)(B) provides an enhancement if a computer or an interactive computer service was used to (i) persuade, induce, entice, or coerce a minor to engage in prohibited sexual conduct; or (ii) facilitate transportation or travel, by a minor or a participant, to engage in prohibited sexual conduct. Subsection (b)(6)(B) is intended to apply only to the use of a computer or an interactive computer service to communicate directly with a minor or with a person who exercises custody, care, or supervisory control of the minor. Accordingly, the enhancement would not apply to the use of a computer or an interactive computer service to obtain airline tickets for the minor from an airline's Internet site.".

The Commentary to § 2A3.1 captioned "Application Notes" is amended by redesignating Note 5 as Note 6; and by inserting after Note 4 the following:

"5. Application of Subsection (c)(1).—

(A) In General.—The cross reference in subsection (c)(1) is to be construed broadly and includes all instances where the offense involved employing, using, persuading, inducing, enticing, coercing, transporting, permitting, or offering or seeking by notice or advertisement, a minor to engage in sexually explicit conduct for the purpose of producing any visual depiction of such conduct.

(B) Definition.—For purposes of subsection (c)(1), 'sexually explicit conduct' has the meaning given that term in 18 U.S.C. § 2256(2).".

The Commentary to § 2A3.1 captioned "Application Notes" is amended in Note 6, as redesignated by this amendment, by inserting "Upward Departure Provision.—" before "If a victim".

Section 2A3.2 is amended by striking subsection (a) as follows:

"(a) Base Offense Level:

(1) 24, if the offense involved (A) a violation of chapter 117 of title 18, United States Code; and (B)(i) the commission of a sexual act; or (ii) sexual contact;

(2) 21, if the offense (A) involved a violation of chapter 117 of title 18, United States Code; but (B) did not involve (i) the commission of a sexual act; or (ii) sexual contact; or

(3) 18, otherwise.",

and inserting the following:

"(a) Base Offense Level: 18".

Section 2A3.2(b)(1) is amended by striking "victim" and inserting "minor"; and by striking "2 levels" and inserting "4 levels".

Section 2A3.2(b) is amended by striking subdivisions (2) through (4) as follows:

"(2) If subsection (b)(1) does not apply; and—

(A) the offense involved the knowing misrepresentation of a participant's identity to (i) persuade, induce, entice, or coerce the victim to engage in prohibited sexual conduct; or (ii) facilitate transportation or travel, by the victim or a participant, to engage in prohibited sexual conduct; or

(B) a participant otherwise unduly influenced the victim to engage in prohibited sexual conduct, increase by 2 levels.

(3) If a computer or an Internet-access device was used to (A) persuade, induce, entice, or coerce the victim to engage in prohibited sexual conduct; or (B) facilitate transportation or travel, by the victim or a participant, to engage in prohibited sexual conduct, increase by 2 levels.

(4) If (A) subsection (a)(1) applies; and (B) none of subsections (b)(1) through (b)(3) applies, decrease by 6 levels.",

and inserting the following:

"(2) If (A) subsection (b)(1) does not apply; and (B)(i) the offense involved the knowing misrepresentation of a participant's identity to persuade, induce, entice, or coerce the minor to engage in prohibited sexual conduct; or (ii) a participant otherwise unduly influenced the minor to engage in prohibited sexual conduct, increase by 4 levels.

(3) If a computer or an interactive computer service was used to persuade, induce, entice, or coerce the minor to engage in prohibited sexual conduct, increase by 2 levels.".

The Commentary to § 2A3.2 captioned "Application Notes" is amended in Note 1 by inserting after "Definitions.—For purposes of this guideline:" the following:

"'Computer' has the meaning given that term in 18 U.S.C. § 1030(e)(1).

'Interactive computer service' has the meaning given that term in section 230(e)(2) of the Communications Act of 1934 (47 U.S.C. § 230(f)(2)).

'Minor' means (A) an individual who had not attained the age of 16 years; (B) an individual, whether fictitious or not, who a law enforcement officer represented to a participant (i) had not attained the age of 16 years, and (ii) could be provided for the purposes of engaging in sexually explicit conduct; or (C) an undercover law enforcement officer who represented to a participant that the officer had not attained the age of 16 years.";

and by striking the following:

"'Sexual act' has the meaning given that term in 18 U.S.C. § 2246(2).

'Sexual contact' has the meaning given that term in 18 U.S.C. § 2246(3).

'Victim' means (A) an individual who, except as provided in subdivision (B), had not attained the age of 16 years; or (B) an undercover law enforcement officer who represented to a participant that the officer had not attained the age of 16 years.".

The Commentary to § 2A3.2 captioned "Application Notes" is amended in Note 2 by striking "Custody, Care, and Supervisory Control Enhancement.— Subsection (b)(1)" and inserting the following:

"Custody, Care, or Supervisory Control Enhancement.—

(A)   In General.—Subsection (b)(1)";

by striking "victim" each place it appears and inserting "minor"; and by adding at the end the following:

"(B)   Inapplicability of Chapter Three Adjustment.—If the enhancement in subsection (b)(1) applies, do not apply subsection (b)(2) or § 3B1.3 (Abuse of Position of Trust or Use of Special Skill).".

The Commentary to § 2A3.2 captioned "Application Notes" is amended by striking Notes 3 through 5 as follows:

"3.   Abuse of Position of Trust.— If the enhancement in subsection (b)(1) applies, do not apply subsection (b)(2) or § 3B1.3 (Abuse of Position of Trust or Use of Special Skill).

4.   Misrepresentation of Identity.—The enhancement in subsection (b)(2)(A) applies in cases involving the misrepresentation of a participant's identity to (A) persuade, induce, entice, or coerce the victim to engage in prohibited sexual conduct; or (B) facilitate transportation or travel, by the victim or a participant, to engage in prohibited sexual conduct. Subsection (b)(2)(A) is intended to apply only to misrepresentations made directly to the victim or to a person who exercises custody, care, or supervisory control of the victim. Accordingly, the enhancement in subsection (b)(2)(A) would not apply to a misrepresentation made by a participant to an airline representative in the course of making travel arrangements for the victim.

The misrepresentation to which the enhancement in subsection (b)(2)(A) may apply includes misrepresentation of a participant's name, age, occupation, gender, or status, as long as the misrepresentation was made with the intent to (A) persuade, induce, entice, or coerce the victim to engage in prohibited sexual conduct; or (B) facilitate transportation or travel, by the victim or a participant, to engage in prohibited sexual conduct. Accordingly, use of a computer screen name, without such intent, would not be a sufficient basis for application of the enhancement.

Amendment 664   APPENDIX C - VOLUME III   November 1, 2013

In determining whether subsection (b)(2)(B) applies, the court should closely consider the facts of the case to determine whether a participant's influence over the victim compromised the voluntariness of the victim's behavior.

In a case in which a participant is at least 10 years older than the victim, there shall be a rebuttable presumption, for purposes of subsection (b)(2)(B), that such participant unduly influenced the victim to engage in prohibited sexual conduct. In such a case, some degree of undue influence can be presumed because of the substantial difference in age between the participant and the victim.

If the victim was threatened or placed in fear, the cross reference in subsection (c)(1) will apply.

5. Use of Computer or Internet-Access Device.—Subsection (b)(3) provides an enhancement if a computer or an Internet-access device was used to (A) persuade, induce, entice, coerce the victim to engage in prohibited sexual conduct; or (B) facilitate transportation or travel, by the victim or a participant, to engage in prohibited sexual conduct. Subsection (b)(3) is intended to apply only to the use of a computer or an Internet-access device to communicate directly with the victim or with a person who exercises custody, care, or supervisory control of the victim. Accordingly, the enhancement would not apply to the use of a computer or an Internet-access device to obtain airline tickets for the victim from an airline's Internet site.",

and inserting the following:

"3. Application of Subsection (b)(2).—

(A) Misrepresentation of Identity.—The enhancement in subsection (b)(2)(B)(i) applies in cases involving the misrepresentation of a participant's identity to persuade, induce, entice, or coerce the minor to engage in prohibited sexual conduct. Subsection (b)(2)(B)(i) is intended to apply only to misrepresentations made directly to the minor or to a person who exercises custody, care, or supervisory control of the minor. Accordingly, the enhancement in subsection (b)(2)(B)(i) would not apply to a misrepresentation made by a participant to an airline representative in the course of making travel arrangements for the minor.

The misrepresentation to which the enhancement in subsection (b)(2)(B)(i) may apply includes misrepresentation of a participant's name, age, occupation, gender, or status, as long as the misrepresentation was made with the intent to persuade, induce, entice, or coerce the minor to engage in prohibited sexual conduct. Accordingly, use of a computer screen name, without such intent, would not be a sufficient basis for application of the enhancement.

(B) Undue Influence.—In determining whether subsection (b)(2)(B)(ii) applies, the court should closely consider the facts of the case to determine whether a participant's influence over the minor compromised the voluntariness of the minor's behavior.

In a case in which a participant is at least 10 years older than the minor, there shall be a rebuttable presumption, for purposes of subsection (b)(2)(B)(ii), that such participant unduly influenced the minor to engage in prohibited sexual conduct. In such a case, some degree of undue influence can be presumed because of the substantial difference in age between the participant and the minor.

4. Application of Subsection (b)(3).—Subsection (b)(3) provides an enhancement if a computer or an interactive computer service was used to persuade, induce, entice, or coerce the minor to engage in prohibited sexual conduct. Subsection (b)(3) is intended to apply only to the use of a computer or an interactive computer service to communicate directly with the minor or with a person who exercises custody, care, or supervisory control of the minor.".

The Commentary to § 2A3.2 captioned "Application Notes" is amended by redesignating Notes 6 and 7 as Notes 5 and 6, respectively.

The Commentary to § 2A3.2 captioned "Background" is amended by striking "or chapter 117 of title 18, United States Code"; by striking "victim" each place it appears and inserting "minor"; and by striking "victim's" and inserting "minor's".

Section 2A3.3(a) is amended by striking "9" and inserting "12".

Section 2A3.3(b)(1) is amended by striking "(A)"; and by striking "; or (B) facilitate transportation or travel, by a minor or a participant, to engage in prohibited sexual conduct".

Section 2A3.3(b)(2) is amended by striking "(A)"; by striking "; or (B) facilitate transportation or travel, by a minor or a participant, to engage in prohibited sexual conduct"; and by striking "Internet-access device" and inserting "interactive computer service".

The Commentary to § 2A3.3 captioned "Application Notes" is amended in Note 1 by striking "For purposes of this guideline—" and inserting the following:

"Definitions.—For purposes of this guideline:

'Computer' has the meaning given that term in 18 U.S.C. § 1030(e)(1).

'Interactive computer service' has the meaning given that term in section 230(e)(2) of the Communications Act of 1934 (47 U.S.C. § 230(f)(2)).".

The Commentary to § 2A3.3 captioned "Application Notes" is amended by striking Notes 2 and 3 as follows:

"2. The enhancement in subsection (b)(1) applies in cases involving the misrepresentation of a participant's identity to (A) persuade, induce, entice, or coerce a minor to engage in prohibited sexual conduct; or (B) facilitate transportation or travel, by a minor or a participant, to engage in prohibited sexual conduct. Subsection (b)(1) is intended to apply only to misrepresentations made directly to a minor or to a person who exercises custody, care, or supervisory control of the minor. Accordingly, the enhancement in subsection (b)(1) would not apply to a misrepresentation made by a participant to an airline representative in the course of making travel arrangements for the minor.

The misrepresentation to which the enhancement in subsection (b)(1) may apply includes misrepresentation of a participant's name, age, occupation, gender, or status, as long as the misrepresentation was made with the intent to (A) persuade, induce, entice, or coerce a minor to engage in prohibited sexual conduct; or (B) facilitate transportation or travel, by a minor or a participant, to engage in prohibited sexual conduct. Accordingly, use of a computer screen name, without such intent, would not be a sufficient basis for application of the enhancement.

3. Subsection (b)(2) provides an enhancement if a computer or an Internet-access device was used to (A) persuade, induce, entice, or coerce a minor to engage in prohibited sexual conduct; or (B) facilitate transportation or travel, by a minor or a participant, to engage in prohibited sexual conduct. Subsection (b)(2) is intended to apply only to the use of a computer or an Internet-access device to communicate directly with a minor or with a person who exercises custody, care, or supervisory control of the minor. Accordingly, the enhancement would not apply to the use of a computer or an Internet-access device to obtain airline tickets for the minor from an airline's Internet site.",

and inserting the following:

"2. Application of Subsection (b)(1).—The enhancement in subsection (b)(1) applies in cases involving the misrepresentation of a participant's identity to persuade, induce, entice, or coerce a minor to engage in prohibited sexual conduct. Subsection (b)(1) is intended to apply only to misrepresentations made directly to a minor or to a person who exercises custody, care, or supervisory control of the minor.

The misrepresentation to which the enhancement in subsection (b)(1) may apply includes misrepresentation of a participant's name, age, occupation, gender, or status, as long as the misrepresentation was made with the intent to persuade, induce, entice, or coerce a minor to engage in prohibited sexual conduct. Accordingly, use of a computer screen name, without such intent, would not be a sufficient basis for application of the enhancement.

3. Application of Subsection (b)(2).—Subsection (b)(2) provides an enhancement if a computer or an interactive computer service was used to persuade, induce, entice, or coerce a minor to engage in prohibited sexual conduct. Subsection (b)(2) is intended to apply only to the use of a computer or an interactive computer service to communicate directly with a minor or with a person who exercises custody, care, or supervisory control of the minor.".

Section 2A3.4(a) is amended by striking subdivisions (1) through (3) as follows:

"(1) 16, if the offense was committed by the means set forth in 18 U.S.C. § 2241(a) or (b);

(2) 12, if the offense was committed by the means set forth in 18 U.S.C. § 2242;

(3) 10, otherwise.",

and inserting the following:

"(1) 20, if the offense involved conduct described in 18 U.S.C. § 2241(a) or (b);

(2) 16, if the offense involved conduct described in 18 U.S.C. § 2242; or

(3) 12, otherwise.".

Section 2A3.4(b)(1) is amended by striking "16" each place it appears and inserting "20".

Section 2A3.4(b) is amended by striking subdivisions (4) through (6) as follows:

"(4) If the offense involved the knowing misrepresentation of a participant's identity to (A) persuade, induce, entice, or coerce a minor to engage in prohibited sexual conduct; or (B) facilitate transportation or travel, by a minor or a participant, to engage in prohibited sexual conduct, increase by 2 levels.

(5) If a computer or an Internet-access device was used to (A) persuade, induce, entice, or coerce a minor to engage in prohibited sexual conduct; or (B) facilitate transportation or travel, by a minor or a participant, to engage in prohibited sexual conduct, increase by 2 levels.

(6) If the offense involved a violation of chapter 117 of title 18, United States Code, increase by 3 levels.",

and inserting the following:

"(4) If the offense involved the knowing misrepresentation of a participant's identity to persuade, induce, entice, or coerce a minor to engage in prohibited sexual conduct, increase by 2 levels.

(5) If a computer or an interactive computer service was used to persuade, induce, entice, or coerce a minor to engage in prohibited sexual conduct, increase by 2 levels.".

The Commentary to § 2A3.4 captioned "Application Notes" is amended in Note 1 by striking the following:

"For purposes of this guideline—

'Minor' means an individual who had not attained the age of 18 years.",

and inserting the following:

"1. Definitions.—For purposes of this guideline:

'Computer' has the meaning given that term in 18 U.S.C. § 1030(e)(1).

'Interactive computer service' has the meaning given that term in section 230(e)(2) of the Communications Act of 1934 (47 U.S.C. § 230(f)(2)).

'Minor' means (A) an individual who had not attained the age of 18 years; (B) an individual, whether fictitious or not, who a law enforcement officer represented to a participant (i) had not attained the age of 18 years, and (ii) could be provided for the purposes of engaging in sexually explicit conduct; or (C) an undercover law enforcement officer who represented to a participant that the officer had not attained the age of 18 years.".

The Commentary to § 2A3.4 captioned "Application Notes" is amended by striking Notes 2 and 3 as follows:

"2.   'The means set forth in 18 U.S.C. § 2241(a) or (b)' are: by using force against the victim; by threatening or placing the victim in fear that any person will be subjected to death, serious bodily injury, or kidnapping; by rendering the victim unconscious; or by administering by force or threat of force, or without the knowledge or permission of the victim, a drug, intoxicant, or other similar substance and thereby substantially impairing the ability of the victim to appraise or control conduct.

3.   'The means set forth in 18 U.S.C. § 2242' are: by threatening or placing the victim in fear (other than by threatening or placing the victim in fear that any person will be subjected to death, serious bodily injury, or kidnapping); or by victimizing an individual who is incapable of appraising the nature of the conduct or physically incapable of declining participation in, or communicating unwillingness to engage in, that sexual act.",

and inserting the following:

"2.   Application of Subsection (a)(1).—For purposes of subsection (a)(1), 'conduct described in 18 U.S.C. § 2241(a) or (b)' is engaging in, or causing sexual contact with, or by another person by: (A) using force against the victim; (B) threatening or placing the victim in fear that any person will be subjected to death, serious bodily injury, or kidnapping; (C) rendering the victim unconscious; or (D) administering by force or threat of force, or without the knowledge or permission of the victim, a drug, intoxicant, or other similar substance and thereby substantially impairing the ability of the victim to appraise or control conduct.

3.   Application of Subsection (a)(2).—For purposes of subsection (a)(2), 'conduct described in 18 U.S.C. § 2242' is: (A) engaging in, or causing sexual contact with, or by another person by threatening or placing the victim in fear (other than by threatening or placing the victim in fear that any person will be subjected to death, serious bodily injury, or kidnapping); or (B) engaging in, or causing sexual contact with, or by another person who is incapable of appraising the nature of the conduct or physically incapable of declining participation in, or communicating unwillingness to engage in, the sexual act.".

The Commentary to § 2A3.4 captioned "Application Notes" is amended in Note 4 by inserting before "Subsection (b)(3)" the following:

"Application of Subsection (b)(3).—

(A)   Custody, Care, or Supervisory Control.—";

and by adding at the end the following:

"(B)   Inapplicability of Chapter Three Adjustment.—If the enhancement in subsection (b)(3) applies, do not apply § 3B1.3 (Abuse of Position of Trust or Use of Special Skill).".

The Commentary to § 2A3.4 captioned "Application Notes" is amended by striking Note 5 as follows:

"5.   If the adjustment in subsection (b)(3) applies, do not apply § 3B1.3 (Abuse of Position of Trust or Use of Special Skill).";

and by redesignating Notes 6 and 7 as Notes 5 and 6, respectively.

The Commentary to § 2A3.4 captioned "Application Notes" is amended in Note 5, as redesignated by this amendment, by inserting "Misrepresentation of a Participant's Identity.—" before "The enhancement"; by striking "(A)" each place it appears; and by striking "; or (B) facilitate transportation or travel, by a minor or a participant, to engage in prohibited sexual conduct" each place it appears.

The Commentary to § 2A3.4 captioned "Application Notes" is amended in Note 6, as redesignated by this amendment, by striking the text as follows:

> "Subsection (b)(5) provides an enhancement if a computer or an Internet-access device was used to (A) persuade, induce, entice, or coerce a minor to engage in prohibited sexual conduct; or (B) facilitate transportation or travel, by a minor or a participant, to engage in prohibited sexual conduct. Subsection (b)(5) is intended to apply only to the use of a computer or an Internet-access device to communicate directly with a minor or with a person who exercises custody, care, or supervisory control of the minor. Accordingly, the enhancement would not apply to the use of a computer or an Internet-access device to obtain airline tickets for the minor from an airline's Internet site.",

and inserting the following:

> "Application of Subsection (b)(5).—Subsection (b)(5) provides an enhancement if a computer or an interactive computer service was used to persuade, induce, entice, or coerce a minor to engage in prohibited sexual conduct. Subsection (b)(5) is intended to apply only to the use of a computer or an interactive computer service to communicate directly with a minor or with a person who exercises custody, care, or supervisory control of the minor.".

The Commentary to § 2A3.4 captioned "Background" is amended by striking the following:

> "For cases involving consensual sexual contact involving victims that have achieved the age of 12 but are under age 16, the offense level assumes a substantial difference in sexual experience between the defendant and the victim. If the defendant and the victim are similar in sexual experience, a downward departure may be warranted. For such cases, the Commission recommends a downward departure to the equivalent of an offense level of level 6.".

Chapter Two, Part G, Subpart 1 is amended by striking § 2G1.1 and its accompanying commentary as follows:

"§ 2G1.1.   Promoting A Commercial Sex Act or Prohibited Sexual Conduct

    (a)   Base Offense Level:

        (1)   19, if the offense involved a minor; or

        (2)   14, otherwise.

    (b)   Specific Offense Characteristics

        (1)   If the offense involved (A) a commercial sex act; and (B) the use of physical force, fraud, or coercion, increase by 4 levels.

Amendment 664 APPENDIX C - VOLUME III November 1, 2013

   (2) If the offense involved a victim who had (A) not attained the age of 12 years, increase by 4 levels; or (B) attained the age of 12 years but not attained the age of 16 years, increase by 2 levels.

   (3) If subsection (b)(2) applies; and—

     (A) the defendant was a parent, relative, or legal guardian of the victim; or

     (B) the victim was otherwise in the custody, care, or supervisory control of the defendant,

   increase by 2 levels.

   (4) If subsection (b)(3) does not apply; and—

     (A) the offense involved the knowing misrepresentation of a participant's identity to persuade, induce, entice, coerce, or facilitate the travel of, a minor to engage in a commercial sex act; or

     (B) a participant otherwise unduly influenced a minor to engage in a commercial sex act,

   increase by 2 levels.

   (5) If a computer or an Internet-access device was used to (A) persuade, induce, entice, coerce, or facilitate the travel of, a minor to engage in a commercial sex act; or (B) entice, encourage, offer, or solicit a person to engage in prohibited sexual conduct with a minor, increase by 2 levels.

(c) Cross References

   (1) If the offense involved causing, transporting, permitting, or offering or seeking by notice or advertisement, a person less than 18 years of age to engage in sexually explicit conduct for the purpose of producing a visual depiction of such conduct, apply § 2G2.1 (Sexually Exploiting a Minor by Production of Sexually Explicit Visual or Printed Material; Custodian Permitting Minor to Engage in Sexually Explicit Conduct; Advertisement for Minors to Engage in Production).

   (2) If the offense involved criminal sexual abuse, attempted criminal sexual abuse, or assault with intent to commit criminal sexual abuse, apply § 2A3.1 (Criminal Sexual Abuse; Attempt to Commit Criminal Sexual Abuse). If the offense involved criminal sexual abuse of a minor who had not attained the age of 12 years, § 2A3.1 shall apply, regardless of the 'consent' of the victim.

   (3) If the offense did not involve promoting a commercial sex act, and neither subsection (c)(1) nor (c)(2) is applicable,

apply § 2A3.2 (Criminal Sexual Abuse of a Minor Under the Age of Sixteen Years (Statutory Rape) or Attempt to Commit Such Acts) or § 2A3.4 (Abusive Sexual Contact or Attempt to Commit Abusive Sexual Contact), as appropriate.

    (d)   Special Instruction

        (1)   If the offense involved more than one victim, Chapter Three, Part D (Multiple Counts) shall be applied as if the promoting of a commercial sex act or prohibited sexual conduct in respect to each victim had been contained in a separate count of conviction.

Commentary

<u>Statutory Provisions</u>: 8 U.S.C. § 1328; 18 U.S.C. §§ 1591, 2421, 2422, 2423(a), 2425.

<u>Application Notes</u>:

1.   For purposes of this guideline—

'Commercial sex act' has the meaning given that term in 18 U.S.C. § 1591(c)(1).

'Minor' means an individual who had not attained the age of 18 years.

'Participant' has the meaning given that term in Application Note 1 of § 3B1.1 (Aggravating Role).

'Prohibited sexual conduct' has the meaning given that term in Application Note 1 of § 2A3.1 (Criminal Sexual Abuse; Attempt to Commit Criminal Sexual Abuse).

'Promoting a commercial sex act' means persuading, inducing, enticing, or coercing a person to engage in a commercial sex act, or to travel to engage in, a commercial sex act.

'Victim' means a person transported, persuaded, induced, enticed, or coerced to engage in, or travel for the purpose of engaging in, a commercial sex act or prohibited sexual conduct, whether or not the person consented to the commercial sex act or prohibited sexual conduct. Accordingly, 'victim' may include an undercover law enforcement officer.

2.   Subsection (b)(1) provides an enhancement for physical force, fraud, or coercion, that occurs as part of a commercial sex act offense and anticipates no bodily injury. If bodily injury results, an upward departure may be warranted. <u>See</u> Chapter Five, Part K (Departures). For purposes of subsection (b)(1)(B), 'coercion' includes any form of conduct that negates the voluntariness of the behavior of the victim. This enhancement would apply, for example, in a case in which the ability of the victim to appraise or control conduct was substantially impaired by drugs or alcohol. In the case of an adult victim, rather than a victim less than 18 years of age, this characteristic generally will not apply if the drug or alcohol was voluntarily taken.

Amendment 664 APPENDIX C - VOLUME III November 1, 2013

3. For the purposes of § 3B1.1 (Aggravating Role), a victim, as defined in this guideline, is considered a participant only if that victim assisted in the promoting of a commercial sex act or prohibited sexual conduct in respect to another victim.

4. For the purposes of Chapter Three, Part D (Multiple Counts), each person transported, persuaded, induced, enticed, or coerced to engage in, or travel to engage in, a commercial sex act or prohibited sexual conduct is to be treated as a separate victim. Consequently, multiple counts involving more than one victim are not to be grouped together under § 3D1.2 (Groups of Closely-Related Counts). In addition, subsection (d)(1) directs that if the relevant conduct of an offense of conviction includes the promoting of a commercial sex act or prohibited sexual conduct in respect to more than one victim, whether specifically cited in the count of conviction, each such victim shall be treated as if contained in a separate count of conviction.

5. Subsection (b)(3) is intended to have broad application and includes offenses involving a victim less than 18 years of age entrusted to the defendant, whether temporarily or permanently. For example, teachers, day care providers, baby-sitters, or other temporary caretakers are among those who would be subject to this enhancement. In determining whether to apply this enhancement, the court should look to the actual relationship that existed between the defendant and the victim and not simply to the legal status of the defendant-victim relationship.

6. If the enhancement in subsection (b)(3) applies, do not apply subsection (b)(4) or § 3B1.3 (Abuse of Position of Trust or Use of Special Skill).

7. The enhancement in subsection (b)(4)(A) applies in cases involving the misrepresentation of a participant's identity to persuade, induce, entice, coerce, or facilitate the travel of, a minor to engage in a commercial sex act. Subsection (b)(4)(A) is intended to apply only to misrepresentations made directly to a minor or to a person who exercises custody, care, or supervisory control of the minor. Accordingly, the enhancement in subsection (b)(4)(A) would not apply to a misrepresentation made by a participant to an airline representative in the course of making travel arrangements for the minor.

The misrepresentation to which the enhancement in subsection (b)(4)(A) may apply includes misrepresentation of a participant's name, age, occupation, gender, or status, as long as the misrepresentation was made with the intent to persuade, induce, entice, coerce, or facilitate the travel of, a minor to engage in a commercial sex act. Accordingly, use of a computer screen name, without such intent, would not be a sufficient basis for application of the enhancement.

In determining whether subsection (b)(4)(B) applies, the court should closely consider the facts of the case to determine whether a participant's influence over the minor compromised the voluntariness of the minor's behavior.

In a case in which a participant is at least 10 years older than the minor, there shall be a rebuttable presumption, for purposes of subsection (b)(4)(B), that such participant unduly influenced the minor to engage in a commercial sex act. In such a case, some degree of undue influence can be presumed because of the substantial difference in age between the participant and the minor.

8. Subsection (b)(5) provides an enhancement if a computer or an Internet-access device was used to (A) persuade, induce, entice, coerce, or facilitate the travel of, a minor to engage in a commercial sex act; or (B) entice, encourage, offer, or solicit a person to engage in prohibited sexual conduct with a minor. Subsection (b)(5)(A) is intended to apply only to the use of a computer or an Internet-access device to communicate directly with a minor or with a person who exercises custody, care, or supervisory control of the minor. Accordingly, the enhancement in subsection (b)(5)(A) would not apply to the use of a computer or an Internet-access device to obtain airline tickets for the minor from an airline's Internet site.

9. The cross reference in subsection (c)(1) is to be construed broadly to include all instances in which the offense involved employing, using, persuading, inducing, enticing, coercing, transporting, permitting, or offering or seeking by notice or advertisement, a person less than 18 years of age to engage in sexually explicit conduct for the purpose of producing any visual depiction of such conduct. For purposes of subsection (c)(1), 'sexually explicit conduct' has the meaning given that term in 18 U.S.C. § 2256.

10. Subsection (c)(2) provides a cross reference to § 2A3.1 (Criminal Sexual Abuse; Attempt to Commit Criminal Sexual Abuse) if the offense involved criminal sexual abuse or attempt to commit criminal sexual abuse, as defined in 18 U.S.C. § 2241 or § 2242. For example, the cross reference to § 2A3.1 shall apply if the offense involved criminal sexual abuse; and (A) the victim had not attained the age of 12 years (see 18 U.S.C. § 2241(c)); (B) the victim had attained the age of 12 years but had not attained the age of 16 years, and was placed in fear of death, serious bodily injury, or kidnapping (see 18 U.S.C. § 2241(a),(c)); or (C) the victim was threatened or placed in fear other than fear of death, serious bodily injury, or kidnapping (see 18 U.S.C. § 2242(1)).

11. The cross reference in subsection (c)(3) addresses the case in which the offense did not involve promoting a commercial sex act, neither subsection (c)(1) nor (c)(2) is applicable, and the offense involved prohibited sexual conduct other than the conduct covered by subsection (c)(1) or (c)(2). In such case, the guideline for the underlying prohibited sexual conduct is to be used; i.e., § 2A3.2 (Criminal Sexual Abuse of a Minor Under the Age of Sixteen Years (Statutory Rape) or Attempt to Commit Such Acts) or § 2A3.4 (Abusive Sexual Contact or Attempt to Commit Abusive Sexual Contact).

12. Upward Departure Provision.—An upward departure may be warranted if the offense involved more than 10 victims.

Background: This guideline covers offenses under chapter 117 of title 18, United States Code. Those offenses involve promoting prostitution or prohibited sexual conduct through a variety of means. Offenses that involve promoting prostitution under chapter 117 of such title are sentenced under this guideline, unless other prohibited sexual conduct occurs as part of the prostitution offense, in which case one of the cross references would apply. Offenses under chapter 117 of such title that do not involve promoting prostitution are to be sentenced under § 2G2.1 (Sexually Exploiting a Minor by Production of Sexually Explicit Visual or Printed Material; Custodian Permitting Minor to Engage in Sexually Explicit Conduct; Advertisement for Minors to Engage in Production), § 2A3.1 (Criminal Sexual Abuse; Attempt to Commit Criminal Sexual Abuse), § 2A3.2 (Criminal Sexual Abuse of a Minor Under the Age of Sixteen Years (Statutory Rape) or Attempt to Commit Such Acts) or § 2A3.4 (Abusive Sexual Contact or Attempt to Commit Abusive Sexual Contact), as appropriate, pursuant to the cross references provided in subsection (c).

This guideline also covers offenses under section 1591 of title 18, United States Code. These offenses involve recruiting or transporting a person in interstate commerce knowing either that (1) force, fraud, or coercion will be used to cause the person to engage in a commercial sex act; or (2) the person (A) had not attained the age of 18 years; and (B) will be caused to engage in a commercial sex act.",

and inserting the following:

"§ 2G1.1. Promoting a Commercial Sex Act or Prohibited Sexual Conduct with an Individual Other than a Minor

    (a)   Base Offense Level: 14

    (b)   Specific Offense Characteristic

            (1)   If the offense involved fraud or coercion, increase by 4 levels.

    (c)   Cross Reference

            (1)   If the offense involved conduct described in 18 U.S.C. § 2241(a) or (b) or 18 U.S.C. § 2242, apply § 2A3.1 (Criminal Sexual Abuse; Attempt to Commit Criminal Sexual Abuse).

    (d)   Special Instruction

            (1)   If the offense involved more than one victim, Chapter Three, Part D (Multiple Counts) shall be applied as if the promoting of a commercial sex act or prohibited sexual conduct in respect to each victim had been contained in a separate count of conviction.

Commentary

Statutory Provisions: 8 U.S.C. § 1328 (only if the offense involved a victim other than a minor); 18 U.S.C. §§ 1591 (only if the offense involved a victim other than a minor), 2421 (only if the offense involved a victim other than a minor), 2422(a) (only if the offense involved a victim other than a minor).

Application Notes:

1.   Definitions.—For purposes of this guideline:

    'Commercial sex act' has the meaning given that term in 18 U.S.C. § 1591(c)(1).

    'Prohibited sexual conduct' has the meaning given that term in Application

Note 1 of § 2A3.1 (Criminal Sexual Abuse; Attempt to Commit Criminal Sexual Abuse).

'Promoting a commercial sex act' means persuading, inducing, enticing, or coercing a person to engage in a commercial sex act, or to travel to engage in, a commercial sex act.

'Victim' means a person transported, persuaded, induced, enticed, or coerced to engage in, or travel for the purpose of engaging in, a commercial sex act or prohibited sexual conduct, whether or not the person consented to the commercial sex act or prohibited sexual conduct. Accordingly, 'victim' may include an undercover law enforcement officer.

2. Application of Subsection (b)(1).—Subsection (b)(1) provides an enhancement for fraud or coercion that occurs as part of the offense and anticipates no bodily injury. If bodily injury results, an upward departure may be warranted. See Chapter Five, Part K (Departures). For purposes of subsection (b)(1), 'coercion' includes any form of conduct that negates the voluntariness of the victim. This enhancement would apply, for example, in a case in which the ability of the victim to appraise or control conduct was substantially impaired by drugs or alcohol. This characteristic generally will not apply if the drug or alcohol was voluntarily taken.

3. Application of Chapter Three Adjustment.—For the purposes of § 3B1.1 (Aggravating Role), a victim, as defined in this guideline, is considered a participant only if that victim assisted in the promoting of a commercial sex act or prohibited sexual conduct in respect to another victim.

4. Application of Subsection (c)(1).—

    (A) Conduct Described in 18 U.S.C. § 2241(a) or (b).—For purposes of subsection (c)(1), conduct described in 18 U.S.C. § 2241(a) or (b) is engaging in, or causing another person to engage in, a sexual act with another person by: (i) using force against the victim; (ii) threatening or placing the victim in fear that any person will be subject to death, serious bodily injury, or kidnapping; (iii) rendering the victim unconscious; or (iv) administering by force or threat of force, or without the knowledge or permission of the victim, a drug, intoxicant, or other similar substance and thereby substantially impairing the ability of the victim to appraise or control conduct. This provision would apply, for example, if any dangerous weapon was used or brandished, or in a case in which the ability of the victim to appraise or control conduct was substantially impaired by drugs or alcohol.

    (B) Conduct Described in 18 U.S.C. § 2242.—For purposes of subsection (c)(1), conduct described in 18 U.S.C. § 2242 is: (i) engaging in, or causing another person to engage in, a sexual act with another person by threatening or placing the victim in fear (other than by threatening or placing the victim in fear that any person will be subject to death, serious bodily injury, or kidnapping); or (ii) engaging in, or causing another person to engage in, a sexual act with a victim who is incapable of appraising the nature of the conduct or who is physically incapable of declining participation in, or communicating unwillingness to engage in, the sexual act.

Amendment 664 APPENDIX C - VOLUME III November 1, 2013

5. <u>Special Instruction at Subsection (d)(1)</u>.—For the purposes of Chapter Three, Part D (Multiple Counts), each person transported, persuaded, induced, enticed, or coerced to engage in, or travel to engage in, a commercial sex act or prohibited sexual conduct is to be treated as a separate victim. Consequently, multiple counts involving more than one victim are not to be grouped together under § 3D1.2 (Groups of Closely Related Counts). In addition, subsection (d)(1) directs that if the relevant conduct of an offense of conviction includes the promoting of a commercial sex act or prohibited sexual conduct in respect to more than one victim, whether specifically cited in the count of conviction, each such victim shall be treated as if contained in a separate count of conviction.

6. <u>Upward Departure Provision</u>.—If the offense involved more than ten victims, an upward departure may be warranted.

<u>Background</u>: This guideline covers offenses that involve promoting prostitution or prohibited sexual conduct with an adult through a variety of means. Offenses that involve promoting prostitution or prohibited sexual conduct with an adult are sentenced under this guideline, unless criminal sexual abuse occurs as part of the offense, in which case the cross reference would apply.

This guideline also covers offenses under section 1591 of title 18, United States Code, that involve recruiting or transporting a person, other than a minor, in interstate commerce knowing that force, fraud, or coercion will be used to cause the person to engage in a commercial sex act.

Offenses of promoting prostitution or prohibited sexual conduct in which a minor victim is involved are to be sentenced under § 2G1.3 (Promoting a Commercial Sex Act or Prohibited Sexual Conduct with a Minor; Transportation of Minors to Engage in a Commercial Sex Act or Prohibited Sexual Conduct; Travel to Engage in Commercial Sex Act or Prohibited Sexual Conduct with a Minor; Sex Trafficking of Children; Use of Interstate Facilities to Transport Information about a Minor).".

Chapter Two, Part G, Subpart 1, is amended by adding at the end the following new guideline and accompanying commentary:

"§ 2G1.3. <u>Promoting a Commercial Sex Act or Prohibited Sexual Conduct with a Minor; Transportation of Minors to Engage in a Commercial Sex Act or Prohibited Sexual Conduct; Travel to Engage in Commercial Sex Act or Prohibited Sexual Conduct with a Minor; Sex Trafficking of Children; Use of Interstate Facilities to Transport Information about a Minor</u>

(a) Base Offense Level: 24

(b) Specific Offense Characteristics

(1) If (A) the defendant was a parent, relative, or legal guardian of the minor; or (B) the minor was otherwise in the custody, care, or supervisory control of the defendant, increase by 2 levels.

(2) If (A) the offense involved the knowing misrepresentation of a participant's identity to persuade, induce, entice, coerce, or facilitate the travel of, a minor to engage in

prohibited sexual conduct; or (B) a participant otherwise unduly influenced a minor to engage in prohibited sexual conduct, increase by 2 levels.

(3) If the offense involved the use of a computer or an interactive computer service to (A) persuade, induce, entice, coerce, or facilitate the travel of, the minor to engage in prohibited sexual conduct; or (B) entice, encourage, offer, or solicit a person to engage in prohibited sexual conduct with the minor, increase by 2 levels.

(4) If the offense involved (A) the commission of a sex act or sexual contact; or (B) a commercial sex act, increase by 2 levels.

(5) If the offense involved a minor who had not attained the age of 12 years, increase by 8 levels.

(c) Cross References

(1) If the offense involved causing, transporting, permitting, or offering or seeking by notice or advertisement, a minor to engage in sexually explicit conduct for the purpose of producing a visual depiction of such conduct, apply § 2G2.1 (Sexually Exploiting a Minor by Production of Sexually Explicit Visual or Printed Material; Custodian Permitting Minor to Engage in Sexually Explicit Conduct; Advertisement for Minors to Engage in Production), if the resulting offense level is greater than that determined above.

(2) If a minor was killed under circumstances that would constitute murder under 18 U.S.C. § 1111 had such killing taken place within the territorial or maritime jurisdiction of the United States, apply § 2A1.1 (First Degree Murder), if the resulting offense level is greater than that determined above.

(3) If the offense involved conduct described in 18 U.S.C. § 2241 or § 2242, apply § 2A3.1 (Criminal Sexual Abuse; Attempt to Commit Criminal Sexual Abuse), if the resulting offense level is greater than that determined above. If the offense involved interstate travel with intent to engage in a sexual act with a minor who had not attained the age of 12 years, or knowingly engaging in a sexual act with a minor who had not attained the age of 12 years, § 2A3.1 shall apply, regardless of the 'consent' of the minor.

(d) Special Instruction

(1) If the offense involved more than one minor, Chapter Three, Part D (Multiple Counts) shall be applied as if the persuasion, enticement, coercion, travel, or transportation to engage in a commercial sex act or prohibited sexual conduct of each victim had been contained in a separate count of conviction.

Amendment 664

Commentary

Statutory Provisions: 8 U.S.C. § 1328 (only if the offense involved a minor); 18 U.S.C. §§ 1591 (only if the offense involved a minor), 2421 (only if the offense involved a minor), 2422 (only if the offense involved a minor), 2422(b), 2423, 2425.

Application Notes:

1. Definitions.—For purposes of this guideline:

    'Commercial sex act' has the meaning given that term in 18 U.S.C. § 1591(c)(1).

    'Computer' has the meaning given that term in 18 U.S.C. § 1030(e)(1).

    'Illicit sexual conduct' has the meaning given that term in 18 U.S.C. § 2423(f).

    'Interactive computer service' has the meaning given that term in section 230(e)(2) of the Communications Act of 1934 (47 U.S.C. § 230(f)(2)).

    'Minor' means (A) an individual who had not attained the age of 18 years; (B) an individual, whether fictitious or not, who a law enforcement officer represented to a participant (i) had not attained the age of 18 years, and (ii) could be provided for the purposes of engaging in sexually explicit conduct; or (C) an undercover law enforcement officer who represented to a participant that the officer had not attained the age of 18 years.

    'Participant' has the meaning given that term in Application Note 1 of the Commentary to § 3B1.1 (Aggravating Role).

    'Prohibited sexual conduct' has the meaning given that term in Application Note 1 of the Commentary to § 2A3.1 (Criminal Sexual Abuse; Attempt to Commit Criminal Sexual Abuse).

    'Sexual act' has the meaning given that term in 18 U.S.C. § 2246(2).

    'Sexual contact' has the meaning given that term in 18 U.S.C. § 2246(3).

2. Application of Subsection (b)(1).—

    (A) Custody, Care, or Supervisory Control.—Subsection (b)(1) is intended to have broad application and includes offenses involving a victim less than 18 years of age entrusted to the defendant, whether temporarily or permanently. For example, teachers, day care providers, baby-sitters, or other temporary caretakers are among those who would be subject to this enhancement. In determining whether to apply this enhancement, the court should look to the actual relationship that existed between the defendant and the minor and not simply to the legal status of the defendant-minor relationship.

    (B) Inapplicability of Chapter Three Adjustment.—If the enhancement under subsection (b)(1) applies, do not apply § 3B1.3 (Abuse of Position of Trust or Use of Special Skill).

3. Application of Subsection (b)(2).—

   (A) Misrepresentation of Participant's Identity.—The enhancement in subsection (b)(2)(A) applies in cases involving the misrepresentation of a participant's identity to persuade, induce, entice, coerce, or facilitate the travel of, a minor to engage in prohibited sexual conduct. Subsection (b)(2)(A) is intended to apply only to misrepresentations made directly to a minor or to a person who exercises custody, care, or supervisory control of the minor. Accordingly, the enhancement in subsection (b)(2)(A) would not apply to a misrepresentation made by a participant to an airline representative in the course of making travel arrangements for the minor.

   The misrepresentation to which the enhancement in subsection (b)(2)(A) may apply includes misrepresentation of a participant's name, age, occupation, gender, or status, as long as the misrepresentation was made with the intent to persuade, induce, entice, coerce, or facilitate the travel of, a minor to engage in prohibited sexual conduct. Accordingly, use of a computer screen name, without such intent, would not be a sufficient basis for application of the enhancement.

   (B) Undue Influence.—In determining whether subsection (b)(2)(B) applies, the court should closely consider the facts of the case to determine whether a participant's influence over the minor compromised the voluntariness of the minor's behavior.

   In a case in which a participant is at least 10 years older than the minor, there shall be a rebuttable presumption, for purposes of subsection (b)(2)(B), that such participant unduly influenced the minor to engage in prohibited sexual conduct. In such a case, some degree of undue influence can be presumed because of the substantial difference in age between the participant and the minor.

4. Application of Subsection (b)(3).—Subsection (b)(3) is intended to apply only to the use of a computer or an interactive computer service to communicate directly with a minor or with a person who exercises custody, care, or supervisory control of the minor. Accordingly, the enhancement in subsection (b)(3) would not apply to the use of a computer or an interactive computer service to obtain airline tickets for the minor from an airline's Internet site.

5. Application of Subsection (c).—

   (A) Application of Subsection (c)(1).—The cross reference in subsection (c)(1) is to be construed broadly and includes all instances in which the offense involved employing, using, persuading, inducing, enticing, coercing, transporting, permitting, or offering or seeking by notice, advertisement or other method, a minor to engage in sexually explicit conduct for the purpose of producing any visual depiction of such conduct. For purposes of subsection (c)(1), 'sexually explicit conduct' has the meaning given that term in 18 U.S.C. § 2256(2).

   (B) Application of Subsection (c)(3).—For purposes of subsection (c)(3), conduct described in 18 U.S.C. § 2241 means conduct described in 18 U.S.C. § 2241(a), (b), or (c). Accordingly, for purposes of subsection (c)(3):

(i) Conduct described in 18 U.S.C. § 2241(a) or (b) is engaging in, or causing another person to engage in, a sexual act with another person: (I) using force against the minor; (II) threatening or placing the minor in fear that any person will be subject to death, serious bodily injury, or kidnapping; (III) rendering the minor unconscious; or (IV) administering by force or threat of force, or without the knowledge or permission of the minor, a drug, intoxicant, or other similar substance and thereby substantially impairing the ability of the minor to appraise or control conduct. This provision would apply, for example, if any dangerous weapon was used or brandished, or in a case in which the ability of the minor to appraise or control conduct was substantially impaired by drugs or alcohol.

(ii) Conduct described in 18 U.S.C. § 2241(c) is: (I) interstate travel with intent to engage in a sexual act with a minor who has not attained the age of 12 years; (II) knowingly engaging in a sexual act with a minor who has not attained the age of 12 years; or (III) knowingly engaging in a sexual act under the circumstances described in 18 U.S.C. § 2241(a) and (b) with a minor who has attained the age of 12 years but has not attained the age of 16 years (and is at least 4 years younger than the person so engaging).

(iii) Conduct described in 18 U.S.C. § 2242 is: (I) engaging in, or causing another person to engage in, a sexual act with another person by threatening or placing the minor in fear (other than by threatening or placing the minor in fear that any person will be subject to death, serious bodily injury, or kidnapping); or (II) engaging in, or causing another person to engage in, a sexual act with a minor who is incapable of appraising the nature of the conduct or who is physically incapable of declining participation in, or communicating unwillingness to engage in, the sexual act.

6. Application of Subsection (d)(1).—For the purposes of Chapter Three, Part D (Multiple Counts), each minor transported, persuaded, induced, enticed, or coerced to engage in, or travel to engage in, a commercial sex act or prohibited sexual conduct is to be treated as a separate minor. Consequently, multiple counts involving more than one minor are not to be grouped together under § 3D1.2 (Groups of Closely Related Counts). In addition, subsection (d)(1) directs that if the relevant conduct of an offense of conviction includes travel or transportation to engage in a commercial sex act or prohibited sexual conduct in respect to more than one minor, whether specifically cited in the count of conviction, each such minor shall be treated as if contained in a separate count of conviction.

7. Upward Departure Provision.—If the offense involved more than ten minors, an upward departure may be warranted.

Background: This guideline covers offenses under chapter 117 of title 18, United States Code, involving transportation of a minor for illegal sexual activity through a variety of means. This guideline also covers offenses involving a minor under section 1591 of title 18, United States Code. Offenses involving an individual who had attained the age of 18 years are covered under § 2G1.1 (Promoting A Commercial Sex Act or Prohibited Sexual Conduct with an Individual Other than a Minor).".

Section 2G2.1(a) is amended by striking "27" and inserting "32".

Section 2G2.1(b) is amended in subdivision (1) by striking "victim" and inserting "minor"; by redesignating subdivisions (2) and (3) as subdivisions (5) and (6), respectively; and by inserting after subdivision (1) the following:

"(2) (Apply the greater) If the offense involved—

    (A) the commission of a sexual act or sexual contact, increase by 2 levels; or

    (B) (i) the commission of a sexual act; and (ii) conduct described in 18 U.S.C. § 2241(a) or (b), increase by 4 levels.

(3) If the offense involved distribution, increase by 2 levels.

(4) If the offense involved material that portrays sadistic or masochistic conduct or other depictions of violence, increase by 4 levels.".

Section 2G2.1(b)(6), as redesignated by this amendment, is amended by striking "Internet-access device" and inserting "interactive computer service".

Section 2G2.1 is amended by redesignating subsection (c) as subsection (d); and by inserting after subsection (b) the following:

"(c) Cross Reference

    (1) If the victim was killed in circumstances that would constitute murder under 18 U.S.C. § 1111 had such killing taken place within the territorial or maritime jurisdiction of the United States, apply § 2A1.1 (First Degree Murder), if the resulting offense level is greater than that determined above.".

The Commentary to § 2G2.1 captioned "Statutory Provisions" is amended by striking "(a), (b), (c)(1)(B), 2260" and inserting ", 2260(b)".

The Commentary to § 2G2.1 captioned "Application Notes" is amended by striking Notes 1 through 5 as follows:

"1. For purposes of this guideline, 'minor' means an individual who had not attained the age of 18 years.

2. For the purposes of Chapter Three, Part D (Multiple Counts), each minor exploited is to be treated as a separate victim. Consequently, multiple counts involving the exploitation of different minors are not to be grouped together under § 3D1.2 (Groups of Closely Related Counts). Special instruction (c)(1)

Amendment 664 APPENDIX C - VOLUME III November 1, 2013

directs that if the relevant conduct of an offense of conviction includes more than one minor being exploited, whether specifically cited in the count of conviction or not, each such minor shall be treated as if contained in a separate count of conviction.

3. Subsection (b)(2) is intended to have broad application and includes offenses involving a minor entrusted to the defendant, whether temporarily or permanently. For example, teachers, day care providers, baby-sitters, or other temporary caretakers are among those who would be subject to this enhancement. In determining whether to apply this adjustment, the court should look to the actual relationship that existed between the defendant and the child and not simply to the legal status of the defendant-child relationship.

4. If the adjustment in subsection (b)(2) applies, do not apply § 3B1.3 (Abuse of Position of Trust or Use of Special Skill).

5. The enhancement in subsection (b)(3)(A) applies in cases involving the misrepresentation of a participant's identity to persuade, induce, entice, coerce, or facilitate the travel of, a minor to engage in sexually explicit conduct for the purpose of producing sexually explicit material. Subsection (b)(3)(A) is intended to apply only to misrepresentations made directly to a minor or to a person who exercises custody, care, or supervisory control of the minor. Accordingly, the enhancement in subsection (b)(3)(A) would not apply to a misrepresentation made by a participant to an airline representative in the course of making travel arrangements for the minor.

The misrepresentation to which the enhancement in subsection (b)(3)(A) may apply includes misrepresentation of a participant's name, age, occupation, gender, or status, as long as the misrepresentation was made with the intent to persuade, induce, entice, coerce, or facilitate the travel of, a minor to engage in sexually explicit conduct for the purpose of producing sexually explicit material. Accordingly, use of a computer screen name, without such intent, would not be a sufficient basis for application of the enhancement.

Subsection (b)(3)(B)(i) provides an enhancement if a computer or an Internet-access device was used to persuade, induce, entice, coerce, or facilitate the travel of, a minor to engage in sexually explicit conduct for the purpose of producing sexually explicit material or otherwise to solicit participation by a minor in such conduct for such purpose. Subsection (b)(3)(B)(i) is intended to apply only to the use of a computer or an Internet-access device to communicate directly with a minor or with a person who exercises custody, care, or supervisory control of the minor. Accordingly, the enhancement would not apply to the use of a computer or an Internet-access device to obtain airline tickets for the minor from an airline's Internet site.",

and inserting the following:

"1. Definitions.—For purposes of this guideline:

'Computer' has the meaning given that term in 18 U.S.C. § 1030(e)(1).

'Distribution' means any act, including possession with intent to distribute, production, advertisement, and transportation, related to the transfer of material involving the sexual exploitation of a minor. Accordingly, distribution includes posting material involving the sexual exploitation of a minor on a website for public viewing but does not include the mere solicitation of such material by a defendant.

'Interactive computer service' has the meaning given that term in section 230(e)(2) of the Communications Act of 1934 (47 U.S.C. § 230(f)(2)).

'Minor' means (A) an individual who had not attained the age of 18 years; (B) an individual, whether fictitious or not, who a law enforcement officer represented to a participant (i) had not attained the age of 18 years, and (ii) could be provided for the purposes of engaging in sexually explicit conduct; or (C) an undercover law enforcement officer who represented to a participant that the officer had not attained the age of 18 years.

'Sexually explicit conduct' has the meaning given that term in 18 U.S.C. § 2256(2).

2. Application of Subsection (b)(2).—For purposes of subsection (b)(2):

'Conduct described in 18 U.S.C. § 2241(a) or (b)' is: (i) using force against the minor; (ii) threatening or placing the minor in fear that any person will be subject to death, serious bodily injury, or kidnapping; (iii) rendering the minor unconscious; or (iv) administering by force or threat of force, or without the knowledge or permission of the minor, a drug, intoxicant, or other similar substance and thereby substantially impairing the ability of the minor to appraise or control conduct. This provision would apply, for example, if any dangerous weapon was used or brandished, or in a case in which the ability of the minor to appraise or control conduct was substantially impaired by drugs or alcohol.

'Sexual act' has the meaning given that term in 18 U.S.C. § 2246(2).

'Sexual contact' has the meaning given that term in 18 U.S.C. § 2246(3).

3. Application of Subsection (b)(5).—

  (A) In General.—Subsection (b)(5) is intended to have broad application and includes offenses involving a minor entrusted to the defendant, whether temporarily or permanently. For example, teachers, day care providers, baby-sitters, or other temporary caretakers are among those who would be subject to this enhancement. In determining whether to apply this adjustment, the court should look to the actual relationship that existed between the defendant and the minor and not simply to the legal status of the defendant-minor relationship.

  (B) Inapplicability of Chapter Three Adjustment.—If the enhancement in subsection (b)(5) applies, do not apply § 3B1.3 (Abuse of Position of Trust or Use of Special Skill).

4. Application of Subsection (b)(6).—

  (A) Misrepresentation of Participant's Identity.—The enhancement in subsection (b)(6)(A) applies in cases involving the misrepresentation of a participant's identity to persuade, induce, entice, coerce, or facilitate the travel of, a minor to engage in sexually explicit conduct for the purpose of producing sexually explicit material. Subsection (b)(6)(A) is intended to apply only to misrepresentations made directly to a minor or to a person who exercises custody, care, or supervisory control of the minor. Accordingly, the enhancement in subsection (b)(6)(A) would not apply to a misrepresentation made by a participant to an airline representative in the course of making travel arrangements for the minor.

The misrepresentation to which the enhancement in subsection (b)(6)(A) may apply includes misrepresentation of a participant's name, age, occupation, gender, or status, as long as the misrepresentation was made with the intent to persuade, induce, entice, coerce, or facilitate the travel of, a minor to engage in sexually explicit conduct for the purpose of producing sexually explicit material. Accordingly, use of a computer screen name, without such intent, would not be a sufficient basis for application of the enhancement.

(B) Use of a Computer or an Interactive Computer Service.—Subsection (b)(6)(B) provides an enhancement if the offense involved the use of a computer or an interactive computer service to persuade, induce, entice, coerce, or facilitate the travel of, a minor to engage in sexually explicit conduct for the purpose of producing sexually explicit material or otherwise to solicit participation by a minor in such conduct for such purpose. Subsection (b)(6)(B) is intended to apply only to the use of a computer or an interactive computer service to communicate directly with a minor or with a person who exercises custody, care, or supervisory control of the minor. Accordingly, the enhancement would not apply to the use of a computer or an interactive computer service to obtain airline tickets for the minor from an airline's Internet site.

5. Application of Subsection (d)(1).—For the purposes of Chapter Three, Part D (Multiple Counts), each minor exploited is to be treated as a separate minor. Consequently, multiple counts involving the exploitation of different minors are not to be grouped together under § 3D1.2 (Groups of Closely Related Counts). Subsection (d)(1) directs that if the relevant conduct of an offense of conviction includes more than one minor being exploited, whether specifically cited in the count of conviction or not, each such minor shall be treated as if contained in a separate count of conviction.".

The Commentary to § 2G2.1 captioned "Application Notes" is amended in Note 6 by striking "victims" and inserting "minors".

Chapter Two, Part G, Subpart 2, is amended by striking § 2G2.2 and its accompanying commentary as follows:

"§ 2G2.2. Trafficking in Material Involving the Sexual Exploitation of a Minor; Receiving, Transporting, Shipping, or Advertising Material Involving the Sexual Exploitation of a Minor; Possessing Material Involving the Sexual Exploitation of a Minor with Intent to Traffic

(a) Base Offense Level: 17

(b) Specific Offense Characteristics

    (1) If the material involved a prepubescent minor or a minor under the age of twelve years, increase by 2 levels.

    (2) (Apply the Greatest) If the offense involved:

        (A) Distribution for pecuniary gain, increase by the number of levels from the table in § 2B1.1 (Theft, Property Destruction, and Fraud) corresponding to the retail value of the material, but by not less than 5 levels.

        (B) Distribution for the receipt, or expectation of receipt, of a thing of value, but not for pecuniary gain, increase by 5 levels.

        (C) Distribution to a minor, increase by 5 levels.

        (D) Distribution to a minor that was intended to persuade, induce, entice, coerce, or facilitate the travel of, the minor to engage in prohibited sexual conduct, increase by **7** levels.

        (E) Distribution other than distribution described in subdivisions (A) through (D), increase by 2 levels.

    (3) If the offense involved material that portrays sadistic or masochistic conduct or other depictions of violence, increase by 4 levels.

    (4) If the defendant engaged in a pattern of activity involving the sexual abuse or exploitation of a minor, increase by 5 levels.

    (5) If a computer was used for the transmission, receipt, or distribution of the material or a notice or advertisement of the material, increase by 2 levels.

    (6) If the offense involved—

        (A) at least 10 images, but fewer than 150, increase by 2 levels;

        (B) at least 150 images, but fewer than 300, increase by 3 levels;

        (C) at least 300 images, but fewer than 600, increase by 4 levels; and

        (D) 600 or more images, increase by 5 levels.

(c) Cross Reference

    (1) If the offense involved causing, transporting, permitting, or

offering or seeking by notice or advertisement, a minor to engage in sexually explicit conduct for the purpose of producing a visual depiction of such conduct, apply § 2G2.1 (Sexually Exploiting a Minor by Production of Sexually Explicit Visual or Printed Material; Custodian Permitting Minor to Engage in Sexually Explicit Conduct; Advertisement for Minors to Engage in Production) if the resulting offense level is greater than that determined above.

Commentary

Statutory Provisions: 18 U.S.C. §§ 2251(c)(1)(A), 2252(a)(1)-(3), 2260.

Application Notes:

1. For purposes of this guideline—

   'Distribution' means any act, including production, transportation, and possession with intent to distribute, related to the transfer of material involving the sexual exploitation of a minor.

   'Distribution for pecuniary gain' means distribution for profit.

   'Distribution for the receipt, or expectation of receipt, of a thing of value, but not for pecuniary gain' means any transaction, including bartering or other in-kind transaction, that is conducted for a thing of value, but not for profit. 'Thing of value' means anything of valuable consideration. For example, in a case involving the bartering of child pornographic material, the 'thing of value' is the child pornographic material received in exchange for other child pornographic material bartered in consideration for the material received.

   'Distribution to a minor' means the knowing distribution to an individual who is a minor at the time of the offense, knowing or believing the individual is a minor at that time.

   'Minor' means an individual who had not attained the age of 18 years.

   'Pattern of activity involving the sexual abuse or exploitation of a minor' means any combination of two or more separate instances of the sexual abuse or sexual exploitation of a minor by the defendant, whether or not the abuse or exploitation (A) occurred during the course of the offense; (B) involved the same or different victims; or (C) resulted in a conviction for such conduct.

   'Prohibited sexual conduct' has the meaning given that term in Application Note 1 of the Commentary to § 2A3.1 (Criminal Sexual Abuse; Attempt to Commit Criminal Sexual Abuse).

   'Sexual abuse or exploitation' means conduct constituting criminal sexual abuse of a minor, sexual exploitation of a minor, abusive sexual contact of a minor, any similar offense under state law, or an attempt or conspiracy to commit any of the above offenses. 'Sexual abuse or exploitation' does not include trafficking in material relating to the sexual abuse or exploitation of a minor.

   'Sexually explicit conduct' has the meaning given that term in 18 U.S.C. § 2256.

2. If the defendant engaged in the sexual abuse or exploitation of a minor at any time (whether or not such abuse or exploitation occurred during the course of the offense or resulted in a conviction for such conduct) and subsection (b)(4) does not apply, an upward departure may be warranted. In addition, an upward departure may be warranted if the defendant received an enhancement under subsection (b)(4) but that enhancement does not adequately reflect the seriousness of the sexual abuse or exploitation involved.

Prior convictions taken into account under subsection (b)(4) are also counted for purposes of determining criminal history points pursuant to Chapter Four, Part A (Criminal History).

3. The cross reference in subsection (c)(1) is to be construed broadly to include all instances where the offense involved employing, using, persuading, inducing, enticing, coercing, transporting, permitting, or offering or seeking by notice or advertisement, a minor to engage in sexually explicit conduct for the purpose of producing any visual depiction of such conduct.

Background: Section 401(i)(1)(C) of Public Law 108–21 directly amended subsection (b) to add subdivision (6), effective April 30, 2003.",

and inserting the following:

"§ 2G2.2. Trafficking in Material Involving the Sexual Exploitation of a Minor; Receiving, Transporting, Shipping, Soliciting, or Advertising Material Involving the Sexual Exploitation of a Minor; Possessing Material Involving the Sexual Exploitation of a Minor with Intent to Traffic; Possessing Material Involving the Sexual Exploitation of a Minor

(a) Base Offense Level:

(1) 18, if the defendant is convicted of 18 U.S.C. § 1466A(b), § 2252(a)(4), or § 2252A(a)(5).

(2) 22, otherwise.

(b) Specific Offense Characteristics

(1) If (A) subsection (a)(2) applies; (B) the defendant's conduct was limited to the receipt or solicitation of material involving the sexual exploitation of a minor; and (C) the defendant did not intend to traffic in, or distribute, such material, decrease by 2 levels.

(2) If the material involved a prepubescent minor or a minor who had not attained the age of 12 years, increase by 2 levels.

(3) (Apply the greatest) If the offense involved:

(A) Distribution for pecuniary gain, increase by the number of levels from the table in § 2B1.1 (Theft, Property Destruction, and Fraud) corresponding to the retail value of the material, but by not less than 5 levels.

(B) Distribution for the receipt, or expectation of receipt, of a thing of value, but not for pecuniary gain, increase by 5 levels.

(C) Distribution to a minor, increase by 5 levels.

(D) Distribution to a minor that was intended to persuade, induce, entice, or coerce the minor to engage in any illegal activity, other than illegal activity covered under subdivision (E), increase by 6 levels.

(E) Distribution to a minor that was intended to persuade, induce, entice, coerce, or facilitate the travel of, the minor to engage in prohibited sexual conduct, increase by 7 levels.

(F) Distribution other than distribution described in subdivisions (A) through (E), increase by 2 levels.

(4) If the offense involved material that portrays sadistic or masochistic conduct or other depictions of violence, increase by 4 levels.

(5) If the defendant engaged in a pattern of activity involving the sexual abuse or exploitation of a minor, increase by 5 levels.

(6) If the offense involved the use of a computer or an interactive computer service for the possession, transmission, receipt, or distribution of the material, increase by 2 levels.

(7) If the offense involved—

(A) at least 10 images, but fewer than 150, increase by 2 levels;

(B) at least 150 images, but fewer than 300, increase by 3 levels;

(C) at least 300 images, but fewer than 600, increase by 4 levels; and

(D) 600 or more images, increase by 5 levels.

(c) Cross Reference

(1) If the offense involved causing, transporting, permitting, or offering or seeking by notice or advertisement, a minor to engage in sexually explicit conduct for the purpose of producing a visual depiction of such conduct, apply § 2G2.1 (Sexually Exploiting a Minor by Production of Sexually Explicit Visual or Printed Material; Custodian Permitting Minor to Engage in Sexually Explicit Conduct; Advertisement for Minors to Engage in Production), if the resulting offense level is greater than that determined above.

Commentary

Statutory Provisions: 18 U.S.C. §§ 1466A, 2252, 2252A, 2260(b).

Application Notes:

1. Definitions.—For purposes of this guideline:

'Computer' has the meaning given that term in 18 U.S.C. § 1030(e)(1).

'Distribution' means any act, including possession with intent to distribute, production, advertisement, and transportation, related to the transfer of material involving the sexual exploitation of a minor. Accordingly, distribution includes posting material involving the sexual exploitation of a minor on a website for public viewing but does not include the mere solicitation of such material by a defendant.

'Distribution for pecuniary gain' means distribution for profit.

'Distribution for the receipt, or expectation of receipt, of a thing of value, but not for pecuniary gain' means any transaction, including bartering or other in-kind transaction, that is conducted for a thing of value, but not for profit. 'Thing of value' means anything of valuable consideration. For example, in a case involving the bartering of child pornographic material, the 'thing of value' is the child pornographic material received in exchange for other child pornographic material bartered in consideration for the material received.

'Distribution to a minor' means the knowing distribution to an individual who is a minor at the time of the offense.

'Interactive computer service' has the meaning given that term in section 230(e)(2) of the Communications Act of 1934 (47 U.S.C. § 230(f)(2)).

'Minor' means (A) an individual who had not attained the age of 18 years; (B) an individual, whether fictitious or not, who a law enforcement officer represented to a participant (i) had not attained the age of 18 years, and (ii) could be provided for the purposes of engaging in sexually explicit conduct; or (C) an undercover law enforcement officer who represented to a participant that the officer had not attained the age of 18 years.

'Pattern of activity involving the sexual abuse or exploitation of a minor' means any combination of two or more separate instances of the sexual abuse or sexual exploitation of a minor by the defendant, whether or not the abuse or exploitation (A) occurred during the course of the offense; (B) involved the same minor; or (C) resulted in a conviction for such conduct.

'Prohibited sexual conduct' has the meaning given that term in Application Note 1 of the Commentary to § 2A3.1 (Criminal Sexual Abuse; Attempt to Commit Criminal Sexual Abuse).

'Sexual abuse or exploitation' means any of the following: (A) conduct described in 18 U.S.C. § 2241, § 2242, § 2243, § 2251, § 2251A, § 2260(b), § 2421, § 2422, or § 2423; (B) an offense under state law, that would have been an offense under any such section if the offense had occurred within the special maritime or territorial jurisdiction of the United States; or (C) an attempt or conspiracy to commit any of the offenses under subdivisions (A) or (B). 'Sexual abuse or exploitation' does not include possession, receipt, or trafficking in material relating to the sexual abuse or exploitation of a minor.

2. Application of Subsection (b)(4).—Subsection (b)(4) applies if the offense involved material that portrays sadistic or masochistic conduct or other depictions of violence, regardless of whether the defendant specifically intended to possess, receive, or distribute such materials.

3. Application of Subsection (b)(5).—A conviction taken into account under subsection (b)(5) is not excluded from consideration of whether that conviction receives criminal history points pursuant to Chapter Four, Part A (Criminal History).

4. Application of Subsection (b)(7).—

   (A) Definition of 'Images'.—'Images' means any visual depiction, as defined in 18 U.S.C. § 2256(5), that constitutes child pornography, as defined in 18 U.S.C. § 2256(8).

   (B) Determining the Number of Images.—For purposes of determining the number of images under subsection (b)(7):

      (i) Each photograph, picture, computer or computer-generated image, or any similar visual depiction shall be considered to be one image. If the number of images substantially underrepresents the number of minors depicted, an upward departure may be warranted.

      (ii) Each video, video-clip, movie, or similar recording shall be considered to have 75 images. If the length of the recording is substantially more than 5 minutes, an upward departure may be warranted.

5. Application of Subsection (c)(1).—

   (A) In General.—The cross reference in subsection (c)(1) is to be construed broadly and includes all instances where the offense involved employing, using, persuading, inducing, enticing, coercing, transporting, permitting, or offering or seeking by notice or advertisement, a minor to engage in sexually explicit conduct for the purpose of producing any visual depiction of such conduct.

   (B) Definition.—'Sexually explicit conduct' has the meaning given that term in 18 U.S.C. § 2256(2).

6. Upward Departure Provision.—If the defendant engaged in the sexual abuse or exploitation of a minor at any time (whether or not such abuse or exploitation occurred during the course of the offense or resulted in a conviction for such conduct) and subsection (b)(5) does not apply, an upward departure may be warranted. In addition, an upward departure may be warranted if the defendant received an enhancement under subsection (b)(5) but that enhancement does not adequately reflect the seriousness of the sexual abuse or exploitation involved.

Background: Section 401(i)(1)(C) of Public Law 108–21 directly amended subsection (b) to add subdivision (7), effective April 30, 2003.".

Chapter Two, Part G, Subpart 2, is amended by striking § 2G2.4 and its accompanying commentary as follows:

"§ 2G2.4. Possession of Materials Depicting a Minor Engaged in Sexually Explicit Conduct

    (a)   Base Offense Level: 15

    (b)   Specific Offense Characteristics

        (1)   If the material involved a prepubescent minor or a minor under the age of twelve years, increase by 2 levels.

        (2)   If the offense involved possessing ten or more books, magazines, periodicals, films, video tapes, or other items, containing a visual depiction involving the sexual exploitation of a minor, increase by 2 levels.

        (3)   If the defendant's possession of the material resulted from the defendant's use of a computer, increase by 2 levels.

        (4)   If the offense involved material that portrays sadistic or masochistic conduct or other depictions of violence, increase by 4 levels.

        (5)   If the offense involved—

            (A)   at least 10 images, but fewer than 150, increase by 2 levels;

            (B)   at least 150 images, but fewer than 300, increase by 3 levels;

            (C)   at least 300 images, but fewer than 600, increase by 4 levels; and

            (D)   600 or more images, increase by 5 levels.

    (c)   Cross References

        (1)   If the offense involved causing, transporting, permitting, or offering or seeking by notice or advertisement, a minor to engage in sexually explicit conduct for the purpose of producing a visual depiction of such conduct, apply § 2G2.1 (Sexually Exploiting a Minor by Production of Sexually Explicit Visual or Printed Material; Custodian Permitting Minor to Engage in Sexually Explicit Conduct; Advertisement for Minors to Engage in Production).

        (2)   If the offense involved trafficking in material involving the sexual exploitation of a minor (including receiving, transporting, shipping, advertising, or possessing material

Amendment 664   APPENDIX C - VOLUME III   November 1, 2013

involving the sexual exploitation of a minor with intent to traffic), apply § 2G2.2 (Trafficking in Material Involving the Sexual Exploitation of a Minor; Receiving, Transporting, Shipping, or Advertising Material Involving the Sexual Exploitation of a Minor; Possessing Material Involving the Sexual Exploitation of a Minor with Intent to Traffic).

Commentary

Statutory Provision: 18 U.S.C. § 2252(a)(4).

Application Notes:

1. For purposes of this guideline—

    'Minor' means an individual who had not attained the age of 18 years.

    'Visual depiction' means any visual depiction described in 18 U.S.C. § 2256(5) and (8).

2. For purposes of subsection (b)(2), a file that (A) contains a visual depiction; and (B) is stored on a magnetic, optical, digital, other electronic, or other storage medium or device, shall be considered to be one item.

    If the offense involved a large number of visual depictions, an upward departure may be warranted, regardless of whether subsection (b)(2) applies.

Background: Section 401(i)(1)(B) of Public Law 108–21 directly amended subsection (b) to add subdivisions (4) and (5), effective April 30, 2003.".

Section 2G3.1 is amended in the heading by adding at the end "; Misleading Domain Names".

Section 2G3.1(b)(1) is amended by redesignating subdivisions (D) and (E) as subdivisions (E) and (F), respectively; and by inserting after subdivision (C) the following:

"(D) Distribution to a minor that was intended to persuade, induce, entice, or coerce the minor to engage in any illegal activity, other than illegal activity covered under subdivision (E), increase by 6 levels.";

and in subdivision (F), as redesignated by this amendment, by striking "(D)" and inserting "(E)".

Section 2G3.1(b) is amended by redesignating subdivision (2) as subdivision (4); and by inserting after subdivision (1) the following:

"(2) If the offense involved the use of a misleading domain name on the Internet with the intent to deceive a minor into viewing material on the Internet that is harmful to minors, increase by 2 levels.

(3) If the offense involved the use of a computer or an interactive computer service, increase by 2 levels.".

The Commentary to § 2G3.1 captioned "Statutory Provisions" is amended by inserting ", 2252B" after "1470".

The Commentary to § 2G3.1 captioned "Application Note" is amended by striking "Note" in the heading and inserting "Notes"; and by striking Application Note 1 as follows:

"1. For purposes of this guideline—

'Distribution' means any act, including production, transportation, and possession with intent to distribute, related to the transfer of obscene matter.

'Distribution for pecuniary gain' means distribution for profit.

'Distribution for the receipt, or expectation of receipt, of a thing of value, but not for pecuniary gain' means any transaction, including bartering or other in-kind transaction, that is conducted for a thing of value, but not for profit. 'Thing of value' means anything of valuable consideration.

'Distribution to a minor' means the knowing distribution to an individual who is a minor at the time of the offense, knowing or believing the individual is a minor at that time.

'Minor' means an individual who had not attained the age of 16 years.

'Prohibited sexual conduct' has the meaning given that term in Application Note 1 of the Commentary to § 2A3.1 (Criminal Sexual Abuse; Attempt to Commit Criminal Sexual Abuse).",

and inserting the following:

"1. Definitions.—For purposes of this guideline:

'Computer' has the meaning given that term in 18 U.S.C. § 1030(e)(1).

'Distribution' means any act, including possession with intent to distribute, production, advertisement, and transportation, related to the transfer of obscene matter. Accordingly, distribution includes posting material involving the sexual exploitation of a minor on a website for public viewing but does not include the mere solicitation of such material by a defendant.

'Distribution for pecuniary gain' means distribution for profit.

'Distribution for the receipt, or expectation of receipt, of a thing of value, but not for pecuniary gain' means any transaction, including bartering or other in-kind transaction, that is conducted for a thing of value, but not for profit. 'Thing of value' means anything of valuable consideration.

'Distribution to a minor' means the knowing distribution to an individual who is a minor at the time of the offense.

'Interactive computer service' has the meaning given that term in section 230(e)(2) of the Communications Act of 1934 (47 U.S.C. § 230(f)(2)).

'Material that is harmful to minors' has the meaning given that term in 18 U.S.C. § 2252B(d).

'Minor' means (A) an individual who had not attained the age of 18 years; (B) an individual, whether fictitious or not, who a law enforcement officer represented to a participant (i) had not attained the age of 18 years, and (ii) could be provided for the purposes of engaging in sexually explicit conduct;

or (C) an undercover law enforcement officer who represented to a participant that the officer had not attained the age of 18 years.

'Prohibited sexual conduct' has the meaning given that term in Application Note 1 of the Commentary to § 2A3.1 (Criminal Sexual Abuse; Attempt to Commit Criminal Sexual Abuse).

'Sexually explicit conduct' has the meaning given that term in 18 U.S.C. § 2256(2).

2. Inapplicability of Subsection (b)(3).—If the defendant is convicted of 18 U.S.C. § 2252B, subsection (b)(3) shall not apply.

3. Application of Subsection (b)(4).—Subsection (b)(4) applies if the offense involved material that portrays sadistic or masochistic conduct or other depictions of violence, regardless of whether the defendant specifically intended to possess, receive, or distribute such materials.".

Section 3D1.2(d) is amended by striking "2G2.4" and inserting "2G3.1".

Section 5B1.3(d)(7) is amended by striking:

"If the instant offense of conviction is a sex offense, as defined in § 5D1.2 (Term of Supervised Release) -- a condition requiring the defendant to participate in a program approved by the United States Probation Office for the treatment and monitoring of sex offenders.",

and inserting the following:

"If the instant offense of conviction is a sex offense, as defined in Application Note 1 of the Commentary to § 5D1.2 (Term of Supervised Release) --

(A) A condition requiring the defendant to participate in a program approved by the United States Probation Office for the treatment and monitoring of sex offenders.

(B) A condition limiting the use of a computer or an interactive computer service in cases in which the defendant used such items.".

Section 5D1.2 is amended by striking subsections (a) through (c) as follows:

"(a) Subject to subsection (b), if a term of supervised release is ordered, the length of the term shall be:

(1) at least three years but not more than five years for a defendant convicted of a Class A or B felony;

(2) at least two years but not more than three years for a defendant convicted of a Class C or D felony;

(3) one year for a defendant convicted of a Class E felony or a Class A misdemeanor.

Notwithstanding subdivisions (1) through (3), the length of the term of supervised release for any offense listed in 18 U.S.C. § 2332b(g)(5)(B) the commission of which resulted in, or created a foreseeable risk of, death or serious bodily injury to another person (A) shall be not less than the minimum term of years specified for that class of offense under subdivisions (1) through (3); and (B) may be up to life.

(b) Except as otherwise provided, the term of supervised release imposed shall not be less than any statutorily required term of supervised release.

(c) (Policy Statement) If the instant offense of conviction is a sex offense, the statutory maximum term of supervised release is recommended.",

and inserting following:

"(a) Except as provided in subsections (b) and (c), if a term of supervised release is ordered, the length of the term shall be:

(1) At least three years but not more than five years for a defendant convicted of a Class A or B felony.

(2) At least two years but not more than three years for a defendant convicted of a Class C or D felony.

(3) One year for a defendant convicted of a Class E felony or a Class A misdemeanor.

(b) Notwithstanding subdivisions (a)(1) through (3), the length of the term of supervised release shall be not less than the minimum term of years specified for the offense under subdivisions (a)(1) through (3) and may be up to life, if the offense is—

(1) any offense listed in 18 U.S.C. § 2332b(g)(5)(B), the commission of which resulted in, or created a foreseeable risk of, death or serious bodily injury to another person; or

(2) a sex offense.

(Policy Statement) If the instant offense of conviction is a sex offense, however, the statutory maximum term of supervised release is recommended.

(c) The term of supervised release imposed shall be not less than any statutorily required term of supervised release.".

Section 5D1.3(d)(7) is amended by striking:

"If the instant offense of conviction is a sex offense, as defined in § 5D1.2 (Term of Supervised Release) -- a condition requiring the defendant to participate in a program approved by the United States Probation Office for the treatment and monitoring of sex offenders.",

and inserting the following:

"If the instant offense of conviction is a sex offense, as defined in Application Note 1 of the Commentary to § 5D1.2 (Term of Supervised Release) --

(A) A condition requiring the defendant to participate in a program approved by the United States Probation Office for the treatment and monitoring of sex offenders.

(B) A condition limiting the use of a computer or an interactive computer service in cases in which the defendant used such items.".

Section 7B1.3(g) is amended by striking "Where" each place it appears and inserting "If"; and in subdivision (2) by striking "and the term of imprisonment imposed is less than the maximum term of imprisonment imposable upon revocation".

The Commentary to § 7B1.3 captioned "Application Notes" is amended in Note 2 by striking "and imposition of less than the maximum imposable term of imprisonment"; and by striking Note 6 as follows:

"6. 'Maximum term of imprisonment imposable upon revocation,' as used in subsection (g)(2), refers to the maximum term of imprisonment authorized by statute for the violation of supervised release, not to the maximum of the guideline range.".

Appendix A (Statutory Index) is amended in the line referenced to 8 U.S.C. § 1328 by inserting ", 2G1.3" after "2G1.1";

by inserting after the line referenced to 18 U.S.C. § 1466 the following:

"18 U.S.C. § 1466A   2G2.2";

in the line referenced to 18 U.S.C. § 1591 by inserting ", 2G1.3" after "2G1.1";

in the line referenced to 18 U.S.C. § 2252 by striking ", 2G2.4";

in the line referenced to 18 U.S.C. § 2252A by striking ", 2G2.4";

by inserting before the line referenced to 18 U.S.C. § 2257 the following new line:

"18 U.S.C. § 2252B   2G3.1";

by striking the following:

"18 U.S.C. § 2260   2G2.1, 2G2.2",

and inserting the following:

"18 U.S.C. § 2260(a)   2G2.1
18 U.S.C. § 2260(b)   2G2.2";

in the line referenced to 18 U.S.C. § 2421 by inserting ", 2G1.3" after "2G1.1";

in the line referenced to 18 U.S.C. § 2422 by inserting ", 2G1.3" after "2G1.1";

in the line referenced to 18 U.S.C. § 2423(a) by striking "2G1.1" and inserting "2G1.3";

in the line referenced to 18 U.S.C. § 2423(b) by striking "2A3.1, 2A3.2, 2A3.3" and inserting "2G1.3"; and

in the line referenced to 18 U.S.C. § 2425 by striking "2G1.1" and inserting "2G1.3".

Reason for Amendment: This amendment implements the directives to the Commission regarding child pornography and sexual abuse offenses in the Prosecutorial Remedies and

Other Tools to end the Exploitation of Children Today Act of 2003, (the "PROTECT Act"), Pub. L. 108–21. This amendment makes changes to Chapter Two, Part A (Criminal Sexual Abuse), Chapter Two, Part G (Offenses Involving Commercial Sex Acts, Sexual Exploitation of Minors, and Obscenity), §§ 3D1.2 (Groups of Closely Related Counts), 5B1.3 (Conditions of Probation), 5D1.2 (Term of Supervised Release), and 5D1.3 (Conditions of Supervised Release), and Appendix A (Statutory Index).

First, the amendment consolidates §§ 2G2.2 (Trafficking in Material Involving the Sexual Exploitation of a Minor; Receiving, Transporting, Shipping, or Advertising Material Involving the Sexual Exploitation of a Minor; Possessing Material Involving the Sexual Exploitation of a Minor with Intent to Traffic), and 2G2.4 (Possession of Materials Depicting a Minor Engaged in Sexually Explicit Conduct), into one guideline, § 2G2.2 (Trafficking in Material Involving the Sexual Exploitation of a Minor; Receiving, Transporting, Shipping, or Advertising Material Involving the Sexual Exploitation of a Minor; Possessing Material Involving the Sexual Exploitation of a Minor with Intent to Traffic; Possession of Materials Depicting a Minor Engaged in Sexually Explicit Conduct). Consolidation addresses concerns raised by judges, probation officers, prosecutors, and defense attorneys regarding difficulties in determining the appropriate guideline (§ 2G2.2 or § 2G2.4) for cases involving convictions of 18 U.S.C. § 2252 or § 2252A. Furthermore, as a result of amendments directed by the PROTECT Act, these guidelines have a number of similar specific offense characteristics.

Section 103 of the PROTECT Act established five-year mandatory minimum terms of imprisonment for offenses related to trafficking and receipt of child pornography under 18 U.S.C. §§ 2252(a)(1)-(3) and 2252A(a)(1), (2), (3), (4) and (6). This section also increased the statutory maximum terms of imprisonment for these offenses from 15 years to 20 years. Furthermore, the PROTECT Act increased the statutory maximum penalty for possession offenses from five to ten years. As a result of these new mandatory minimum penalties and the increases in the statutory maxima for these offenses, the Commission increased the base offense level for these offenses.

The amendment provides two alternative base offense levels depending upon the statute of conviction. The base offense level is set at level 18 for a defendant convicted of the possession of child pornography under 18 U.S.C. § 2252(a)(4), 18 U.S.C. § 2252A(a)(5), or 18 U.S.C. § 1466A(b), and at level 22 for a defendant convicted of any other offense referenced to this guideline, primarily trafficking and receipt of child pornography. The Commission determined that a base offense level of level 22 is appropriate for trafficking offenses because, when combined with several specific offense characteristics which are expected to apply in almost every case (e.g., use of a computer, material involving children under 12 years of age, number of images), the mandatory minimum of 60 months' imprisonment will be reached or exceeded in almost every case by the Chapter Two calculations. The Commission increased the base offense level for possession offenses from level 15 to level 18 because of the increase in the statutory maximum term of imprisonment from 5 to 10 years, and to maintain proportionality with receipt and trafficking offenses. The amendment also provides a two-level decrease at § 2G2.2(b)(1) for a defendant whose base offense level is level 22, whose conduct was limited to the receipt or solicitation of material involving the sexual exploitation of a minor, and whose conduct did not involve an intent to traffic in or distribute the material. Thus, individuals convicted of receipt of child pornography with no intent to traffic or distribute the material essentially will have an adjusted offense level of level 20, as opposed to an offense level of level 22, for receipt with intent to traffic, prior to application of any other specific offense characteristics. The Commission's review of these cases indicated the conduct involved in such "simple receipt" cases in most instances was indistinguishable from "simple possession" cases. The statutory penalties for "simple receipt" cases, however, are the same as the statutory penalties for trafficking cases. Reconciling these competing concerns, the Commission determined that a two-level reduction from the base offense level of level 22 is warranted, if the defendant establishes that there was no intent to distribute the material.

The amendment also provides a new, six-level enhancement at § 2G2.2(b)(3)(D) for offenses that involve distribution to a minor with intent to persuade, induce, entice, or coerce the minor to engage in any illegal activity, other than sexual activity.

The amendment also makes a number of changes to the commentary at § 2G2.2, as follows. The amendment adds several definitions, including definitions of "computer," "image," and "interactive computer service," to provide greater guidance for these terms and uniformity in application of the guideline. The amendment also broadens the "use of a computer" enhancement at § 2G2.2(b)(5) in two ways. First, the amendment expands the enhancement to include an "interactive computer service" (e.g., Internet access devices), as defined in 47 U.S.C. § 230(f)(2). The Commission concluded that the term "computer" did not capture all types of Internet devices. Thus, the amendment expands the definition of "computer" to include other devices that involve interactive computer services (e.g., Web-Tv). In addition, the amendment broadens the enhancement by explicitly providing that the enhancement applies to offenses in which the computer or interactive computer service was used to obtain possession of child pornographic material. Prior to this amendment, the enhancement only applied if the computer was used for the transmission, receipt or distribution of the material.

The PROTECT Act directly amended §§ 2G2.2 and 2G2.4 to create a specific offense characteristic related to the number of child pornography images. That specific offense characteristic provides a graduated enhancement of two to five levels, depending on the number of images. However, the congressional amendment did not provide a definition of "image," which raised questions regarding how to apply the specific offense characteristic. This amendment defines the term "image" and provides an instruction regarding how to apply the specific offense characteristic to videotapes. Application Note 4 states that an "image" means any visual depiction described in 18 U.S.C. § 2256(5) and (8) and instructs that each photograph, picture, computer or computer-generated image, or any similar visual depiction shall be considered one image. Furthermore, the application note provides that each video, video-clip, movie, or similar recording shall be considered to have 75 images for purposes of the specific offense characteristic. Application Note 4 also provides two possible grounds for an upward departure (if the number of images substantially underrepresents the number of minors or if the length of the videotape or recording is substantially more than five minutes). Because the image specific offense characteristic created directly by Congress in the PROTECT Act essentially supercedes an earlier directive regarding a specific offense characteristic relating to the number of items (see Pub. L. 102–141 and Amendment 436), the Commission deleted the specific offense characteristic for possessing ten or more child pornographic items (formerly § 2G2.4(b)(3)). This deletion avoids potential litigation regarding issues of "double counting" if both specific offense characteristics were retained in the guideline.

In response to the increase in the use of undercover officers in child pornography investigations, the amendment expands the definition of "minor." "Minor" is defined as (1) an individual who had not attained the age of 18 years; (2) an individual, whether fictitious or not, who a law enforcement officer represented to a participant (A) had not attained the age of 18 years, and (B) could be provided to a participant for the purposes of engaging in sexually explicit conduct; or (3) an undercover law enforcement officer who represented to a participant that the officer had not attained the age of 18 years.

The amendment also makes clear that distribution includes advertising and posting material involving the sexual exploitation of a minor on a website for public viewing but does not include soliciting such material. In response to a circuit conflict, the amendment adds an application note to make clear that the specific offense characteristic for material portraying sadistic or masochistic conduct applies regardless of whether the defendant specifically intended to possess, receive, or distribute such material. The circuit courts have disagreed regarding whether a defendant must have specifically intended to receive the sadistic or masochistic images. Some circuit courts have required that the defendant must have intended to receive these images. See United States v. Kimbrough, 69 F.3d 723 (5th Cir. 1995); United States v. Tucker, 136 F.3d 763 (11th Cir. 1998). The Seventh Circuit has held that this specific offense characteristic is applied based on a strict liability standard, and that no proof of intent is necessary. See United States v. Richardson, 238 F.3d 837 (7th Cir. 2001). The Commission followed the Seventh Circuit's holding that the enhancement applies regardless of whether the defendant specifically intended to possess, receive, or distribute such material.

Second, section 103 of the PROTECT Act increased the mandatory minimum term of imprisonment from 10 to 15 years for offenses related to the production of child pornography under 18 U.S.C. § 2251. In response, the amendment increases the base offense level at § 2G2.1 (Sexually Exploiting a Minor by Production of Sexually Explicit Visual or Printed Material; Custodian Permitting Minor to Engage in Sexually Explicit Conduct; Advertisement for Minors to Engage in Production) from level 27 to level 32. A base offense level of level 32 is appropriate for production offenses because, combined with the application of several specific offense characteristics that are expected to apply in almost all production cases (e.g., age of the victim), this base offense level will ensure that the 15 year mandatory minimum (180 months) will be met in by the Chapter Two calculations almost every case.

The amendment adds three new specific offense characteristics that are associated with the production of child pornography. The amendment provides, at § 2G2.1(b)(2), a two-level increase if the offense involved the commission of a sex act or sexual contact, or a four-level increase if the offense involved a sex act and conduct described in 18 U.S.C. § 2241(a) or (b) (i.e., the use of force was involved). The Commission concluded that this type of conduct is more serious than the production of a picture without a sex act or the use of force, and therefore, a two- or four-level increase is appropriate. The amendment also adds a two-level increase if the production offense also involved distribution. The Commission concluded that because traffickers sentenced at § 2G2.2 receive an increase for distributing images of child pornography, an individual who produces and distributes the image(s) also should be punished for distributing the item. Lastly, the amendment adds a new, four-level increase if the offense involved material portraying sadistic or masochistic conduct. Similar to the distribution specific offense characteristic, the Commission concluded that, because § 2G2.2 contains a four-level increase for possessing, receiving or trafficking these images, the producers of such images also should receive comparable additional punishment.

Third, this amendment creates a new guideline, § 2G1.3 (Promoting a Commercial Sex Act or Prohibited Sexual Conduct with a Minor; Transportation of Minors to Engage in a Commercial Sex Act or Prohibited Sexual Conduct; Travel to Engage in Commercial Sex Act or Prohibited Sexual Conduct with a Minor; Sex Trafficking of Children; Use of Interstate Facilities to Transport Information about a Minor), to specifically address offenses under chapter 117 of title 18, United States Code (Transportation for Illegal Sexual Activity and Related Crimes). Prior to the amendment, chapter 117 offenses, primarily 18 U.S.C. §§ 2422 (Coercion and Enticement) and 2423 (Transportation of Minors), were referenced by Appendix A (Statutory Index) to either § 2G1.1 or § 2A3.2. Offenses under 18 U.S.C. §§ 2422 and 2423(a) (Transportation with Intent to Engage in Criminal Sexual Activity) are referenced to § 2G1.1 (Promoting A Commercial Sex Act or Prohibited Sexual Conduct), but are then cross referenced from § 2G1.1 to § 2A3.2 (Criminal Sexual Abuse of a Minor Under the Age of Sixteen Years (Statutory Rape) or Attempt to Commit Such Acts) in order to account for certain underlying behavior. Application of this cross reference has led to confusion among courts and practitioners. Offenses under 18 U.S.C. § 2423(b) (Travel with Intent to Engage in Sexual Act with a Juvenile) are referenced to § 2A3.1, § 2A3.2, or § 2A3.3, but most are sentenced at § 2A3.2. Until recently, the majority of cases sentenced under § 2A3.2 were statutory rape cases that occurred on federal property (e.g., military bases) or Native American lands. In fiscal years 2001 and 2002, the majority of cases sentenced under the statutory rape guideline were coercion, travel, and transportation offenses. The creation of a new guideline for these cases is intended to address more appropriately the issues specific to these offenses. In addition, the removal of these cases from § 2A3.2 will permit the Commission to more appropriately tailor that guideline to actual statutory rape cases. Furthermore, travel and transportation cases have a different statutory penalty structure than § 2243(a) statutory rape cases.

Prior to the amendment, § 2A3.2 provided alternative base offense levels of (1) level 24 for a chapter 117 violation with a sexual act; (2) level 21 for a chapter 117 violation with no sexual act (e.g., a sting case); or (3) level 18 for statutory rape with no travel. The PROTECT Act created a five year mandatory minimum term of imprisonment for 18 U.S.C. §§ 2422(a) and 2423(a) and increased the statutory maximum term of imprisonment for these offenses from 15 to 30 years. The PROTECT Act, however, did not increase the statutory maximum penalty, nor did the Act add a mandatory minimum, for 18 U.S.C. § 2243(a) offenses.

This new guideline has a base offense level of level 24 to account for the new mandatory minimum terms of imprisonment established by the PROTECT Act. The new guideline provides six specific offense characteristics to provide proportionate enhancements for aggravating conduct that may occur in connection with these cases. The guideline contains enhancements for commission of a sex act or commercial sex act, use of a computer, misrepresentations of identity, undue influence, custody issues, and involvement of a minor under the age of 12 years. The amendment also provides three cross references to account for certain more serious sexual abuse conduct, including a cross reference if the offense involved conduct described in 18 U.S.C. § 2241 or § 2242. Furthermore, the amendment makes conforming changes to § 2G1.1 (Promoting a Commercial Sex Act or Prohibited Sexual Conduct) as a result of the creation of the new travel guideline. Section 2G1.1 is expected to apply primarily to adult prostitution cases because of the creation of § 2G1.3.

Fourth, section 521 of the PROTECT Act created a new offense at 18 U.S.C. § 2252B (Misleading Domain Names on the Internet). Section 2252B(a) prohibits the knowing use of a misleading domain name on the Internet with the intent to deceive a person into viewing material constituting obscenity. Offenses under this subsection are punishable by a maximum term of imprisonment of two years. Section 2252B(b) prohibits the knowing use of a misleading domain name with the intent to deceive a minor into viewing material that is harmful to minors, with a maximum term of imprisonment of four years. The amendment refers the new offense to § 2G3.1 (Importing, Mailing, or Transporting Obscene Matter; Transferring Obscene Matter to a Minor), modifies the title of the guideline to include "Misleading Domain Names", and provides a two-level enhancement at § 2G3.1(b)(2), if "the offense involved the use of a misleading domain name on the Internet with the intent to deceive a minor into viewing material on the Internet that is harmful to minors." In addition, the amendment also provides enhancements for the following conduct: (1) distribution to a minor that was intended to persuade, induce, entice, or coerce a minor to engage in any illegal activity; and (2) use of a computer or interactive computer service. Finally, the amendment adds § 2G3.1 to the list of guidelines at subsection (d) of § 3D1.2 (Groups of Closely Related Counts). Grouping multiple counts of these offenses pursuant to § 3D1.2(d) is appropriate because typically these offenses, as well as other pornography distribution offenses, are ongoing or continuous in nature. The amendment makes other minor technical changes to the commentary to make this guideline consistent with other Chapter Two, Part G guidelines.

Fifth, in response to a circuit conflict, this amendment adds a condition to §§ 5B1.3 (Conditions of Probation) and 5D1.3 (Conditions of Supervised Release) permitting the court to limit the use of a computer or an interactive computer service for sex offenses in which the defendant used such items. The circuit courts have disagreed over imposition of restrictive computer use and Internet-access conditions. Some circuit courts have refused to allow complete prohibitions on computer use and Internet access (see United States v. Sofsky, 287 F.3d 122 (2nd Cir. 2002) (invalidating restrictions on computer use and Internet use); United States v. Freeman, 316 F.3d 386 (3d Cir. 2003) (same)), but other circuit courts have upheld restrictions on computer use and Internet access with probation officer permission (see United States v. Fields, 324 F.3d 1025 (8th Cir. 2003) (upholding condition prohibiting defendant from having Internet service in his home and allowing possessing of a computer only if granted permission by his probation officer); United States v. Walser, 275 F.3d 981 (10th Cir. 2001) (prohibiting Internet use but allowing Internet use with probation officer's permission); United States v. Zinn, 321 F.3d 1084 (11th Cir. 2003) (same)). Other courts have permitted a complete ban on a convicted sex offender's Internet use while on supervised release. See United States v. Paul, 274 F.3d 155 (5th Cir. 2001) (upholding complete ban on Internet use).

In addition, this amendment makes § 5D1.2 (Term of Supervised Release) consistent with changes made by the PROTECT Act regarding the applicable terms of supervised release under 18 U.S.C. § 3583 for sex offenders.

Sixth, section 401(i)(2) of the PROTECT Act directs the Commission to "amend the Sentencing Guidelines to ensure that the Guidelines adequately reflect the seriousness of the offenses" under sections 2243(b) (Sexual Abuse of a Ward), 2244(a)(4) (Abusive Sexual Contact), and 2244(b) (Sexual Contact with a Person without that Person's Permission) of title 18, United States Code. This amendment makes several amendments to the guidelines in Chapter Two, Part A (Criminal Sexual Abuse) to address this directive and to account for proportionality issues created by the increases in the Chapter Two, Part G guidelines. In addition, the amendment makes changes to the commentary to make the definitions in these guidelines consistent with definitions in the pornography guidelines.

Seventh, the amendment increases the base offense level at § 2A3.1 (Criminal Sexual Abuse; Attempt to Commit Criminal Sexual Abuse) from level 27 to level 30 to maintain proportionality between this guideline and § 2G2.1, the production of child pornography guideline, the base offense level of which was raised to level 32 by this amendment. Furthermore, the amendment adds the term "interactive computer service" to the computer enhancement in § 2A3.1.

Eighth, the amendment increases the offense levels for two specific offense characteristics at § 2A3.2. The amendment increases the custody, care, or supervisory control enhancement from two to four levels at § 2A3.2(b)(1), and changes § 2A3.2(b)(3), which involves the misrepresentation or undue influence by the defendant, from a two- to a four-level increase. The Commission concluded that an increase in the magnitude of these enhancements is appropriate because of the seriousness of such conduct. The amendment also deletes the alternative base offense level of level 21 or level 24 because these cases will be referenced to the new travel guideline at § 2G1.3.

Ninth, in response to section 401 of the PROTECT Act, the amendment increases the base offense level at § 2A3.3 (Criminal Sexual Abuse of a Ward) from level 9 to a level 12. Although 18 U.S.C. § 2243(b) offenses have only a one-year statutory maximum term of imprisonment, the Commission determined that these offenses were serious in nature and deserved punishment near that statutory maximum.

Finally, the amendment increases the alternative base offense levels in § 2A3.4 (Abusive Sexual Contact or Attempt to Commit Abusive Sexual Contact) to level 20, 16, or 12, depending on the conduct involved in the offense. Prior to the amendment, these base offenses levels were level 16, 12, or 10. Base offense level 20 applies if the offense involved conduct described in 18 U.S.C. § 2241(a) or (b). Base offense level 16 applies if the offense involved conduct described in 18 U.S.C. § 2242, and base offense level 12 applies for all other cases sentenced at this guideline. The Commission concluded that these increases were appropriate to account for the serious conduct committed by the defendant and to maintain proportionality with other Chapter Two, Part A guidelines.

Effective Date: The effective date of this amendment is November 1, 2004.

665. Amendment: Section 2B1.1(b) is amended by redesignating subdivisions (7) through (14) as subdivisions (8) through (15), respectively; and by inserting after subdivision (6) the following:

> "(7)   If (A) the defendant was convicted of an offense under 18 U.S.C. § 1037; and (B) the offense involved obtaining electronic mail addresses through improper means, increase by 2 levels.".

The Commentary to § 2B1.1 captioned "Statutory Provisions" is amended by inserting "1037," after "1031,".

The Commentary to § 2B1.1 captioned "Application Notes" is amended in Note 4 by redesignating subdivisions (B) and (C) as subdivisions (C) and (D), respectively; and by inserting after subdivision (A) the following:

> "(B)   Applicability to Transmission of Multiple Commercial Electronic Mail Messages.—For purposes of subsection (b)(2), an offense under 18 U.S.C. § 1037, or any other offense involving conduct described in 18 U.S.C. § 1037, shall be considered to have been committed through mass-marketing. Accordingly, the defendant shall receive at least a two-level enhancement under subsection (b)(2) and may, depending on the facts of the case, receive a greater enhancement under such subsection, if the defendant was convicted under, or the offense involved conduct described in, 18 U.S.C. § 1037.".

The Commentary to § 2B1.1 captioned "Application Notes" is amended by redesignating Notes 6 through 18 as Notes 7 through 19, respectively; and by inserting after Note 5 the following:

> "6.   Application of Subsection (b)(7).—For purposes of subsection (b)(7), 'improper means' includes the unauthorized harvesting of electronic mail addresses of users of a website, proprietary service, or other online public forum.".

Appendix A (Statutory Index) is amended by inserting after the line referenced to 18 U.S.C. § 1035 the following new line:

"18 U.S.C. § 1037   2B1.1".

Reason for Amendment: This amendment responds to the directive in section 4(b) of the Controlling the Assault of Non-Solicited Pornography and Marketing Act (CAN-SPAM Act) of 2003, Pub. L. 108–187. The Act creates five new felony offenses codified at 18 U.S.C. § 1037 and directs the Commission to review and as appropriate amend the sentencing guidelines and policy statements to establish appropriate penalties for violations of 18 U.S.C. § 1037 and other offenses that may be facilitated by sending large volumes of unsolicited electronic mail, including fraud, identity theft, obscenity, child pornography and sexual exploitation of children. The Act also requires that the Commission consider providing sentencing enhancements for several factors, including defendants convicted under 18 U.S.C. § 1037 who obtained electronic mail addresses through improper means.

The amendment refers violations of subsections of 18 U.S.C. § 1037 to § 2B1.1 (Larceny, Embezzlement, and Other Forms of Theft; Offenses Involving Stolen Property; Property Damage or Destruction; Fraud and Deceit; Forgery; Offenses involving Altered or Counterfeit Instruments Other than Counterfeit Bearer Obligations of the United States). The Commission determined that reference to § 2B1.1 is appropriate because subsection 18 U.S.C. § 1037(a)(1) involves misappropriation of another's computer, and 18 U.S.C. § 1037(a)(2) through (a)(5) involve deceit. Because each offense under 18 U.S.C. § 1037 contains as an element the transmission of multiple commercial electronic messages (where "multiple" is defined in the statute as "more than 100 electronic mail messages during a 24-hour period, more than 1,000 electronic mail messages during a 30-day period, or more than 10,000 electronic mail messages during a 1-year period"), the amendment provides in Application Note 4 that the mass-marketing enhancement in § 2B1.1(b)(2)(A)(ii) shall apply automatically to any defendant who is convicted of 18 U.S.C. § 1037, or who committed an offense involving conduct described in 18 U.S.C. § 1037. Broadening application of the mass marketing enhancement to all defendants sentenced under § 2B1.1 whose offense involves conduct described in 18 U.S.C. § 1037, whether or not the defendant is convicted under 18 U.S.C. § 1037, responds specifically to that part of the directive concerning offenses that are facilitated by sending large volumes of electronic mail.

Additionally, in response to the directive, a new specific offense characteristic in § 2B1.1(b)(7) provides for a two-level increase if the defendant is convicted under 18 U.S.C. § 1037 and the offense involved obtaining electronic mail addressed through improper means. A corresponding application note provides a definition of "improper means." Finally, the Commission also responded to the directive concerning other offenses by making several modifications to other guidelines, as set forth in Amendment 2 of this document. For example, an amendment to the obscenity guideline, § 2G3.1 (Importing, Mailing, or Transporting Obscene Matter; Transferring Obscene Matter to a Minor), added a two-level enhancement if the offense involved the use of a computer or interactive computer service.

Effective Date: The effective date of this amendment is November 1, 2004.

666. **Amendment:** The Commentary to § 1B1.5 captioned "Application Notes" is amended in Note 2 by striking "(Offering, Giving, Soliciting, or Receiving a Bribe); 2C1.7 (Fraud Involving Deprivation of the Intangible Right to the Honest Services of Public Officials)" and inserting "(Offering, Giving, Soliciting, or Receiving a Bribe; Extortion Under Color of Official Right; Fraud Involving the Deprivation of the Intangible Right to Honest Services of Public Officials; Conspiracy to Defraud by Interference with Governmental Functions)".

Amendment 666

The Commentary to § 2B1.1 captioned "Application Notes" is amended in Note 15, as redesignated by Amendment 665, by adding at the end the following:

"For example, a state employee who improperly influenced the award of a contract and used the mails to commit the offense may be prosecuted under 18 U.S.C. § 1341 for fraud involving the deprivation of the intangible right of honest services. Such a case would be more aptly sentenced pursuant to § 2C1.1 (Offering, Giving, Soliciting, or Receiving a Bribe; Extortion Under Color of Official Right; Fraud involving the Deprivation of the Intangible Right to Honest Services of Public Officials; Conspiracy to Defraud by Interference with Governmental Functions).".

The Commentary to § 2B4.1 captioned "Application Notes" is amended in Note 2 by inserting "; Fraud Involving the Deprivation of the Intangible Right to Honest Services of Public Officials; Conspiracy to Defraud by Interference with Governmental Functions" after "Official Right".

Chapter Two, Part C is amended by striking §§ 2C1.1 and 2C1.2 and their accompanying commentary as follows:

"§ 2C1.1. Offering, Giving, Soliciting, or Receiving a Bribe; Extortion Under Color of Official Right

(a) Base Offense Level: 10

(b) Specific Offense Characteristics

(1) If the offense involved more than one bribe or extortion, increase by 2 levels.

(2) (If more than one applies, use the greater):

(A) If the value of the payment, the benefit received or to be received in return for the payment, or the loss to the government from the offense, whichever is greatest (i) exceeded $2,000 but did not exceed $5,000, increase by 1 level; or (ii) exceeded $5,000, increase by the number of levels from the table in § 2B1.1 (Theft, Property Destruction, and Fraud) corresponding to that amount.

(B) If the offense involved a payment for the purpose of influencing an elected official or any official holding a high-level decision-making or sensitive position, increase by 8 levels.

(c) Cross References

(1) If the offense was committed for the purpose of facilitating the commission of another criminal offense, apply the offense guideline applicable to a conspiracy to commit that other offense if the resulting offense level is greater than that determined above.

(2) If the offense was committed for the purpose of concealing, or obstructing justice in respect to, another criminal offense,

apply § 2X3.1 (Accessory After the Fact) or § 2J1.2 (Obstruction of Justice), as appropriate, in respect to that other offense if the resulting offense level is greater than that determined above.

 (3) If the offense involved a threat of physical injury or property destruction, apply § 2B3.2 (Extortion by Force or Threat of Injury or Serious Damage) if the resulting offense level is greater than that determined above.

(d) Special Instruction for Fines - Organizations

 (1) In lieu of the pecuniary loss under subsection (a)(3) of § 8C2.4 (Base Fine), use the greatest of: (A) the value of the unlawful payment; (B) the value of the benefit received or to be received in return for the unlawful payment; or (C) the consequential damages resulting from the unlawful payment.

Commentary

Statutory Provisions: 15 U.S.C. §§ 78dd-1, 78dd-2, 78dd-3; 18 U.S.C. §§ 201(b)(1), (2), 872, 1951. For additional statutory provision(s), see Appendix A (Statutory Index).

Application Notes:

1. 'Official holding a high-level decision-making or sensitive position' includes, for example, prosecuting attorneys, judges, agency administrators, supervisory law enforcement officers, and other governmental officials with similar levels of responsibility.

2. 'Loss', for purposes of subsection (b)(2)(A), shall be determined in accordance with Application Note 3 of the Commentary to § 2B1.1 (Theft, Property Destruction, and Fraud). The value of 'the benefit received or to be received' means the net value of such benefit. Examples: (1) A government employee, in return for a $500 bribe, reduces the price of a piece of surplus property offered for sale by the government from $10,000 to $2,000; the value of the benefit received is $8,000. (2) A $150,000 contract on which $20,000 profit was made was awarded in return for a bribe; the value of the benefit received is $20,000. Do not deduct the value of the bribe itself in computing the value of the benefit received or to be received. In the above examples, therefore, the value of the benefit received would be the same regardless of the value of the bribe.

3. Do not apply § 3B1.3 (Abuse of Position of Trust or Use of Special Skill) except where the offense level is determined under § 2C1.1(c)(1), (2), or (3). In such cases, an adjustment from § 3B1.3 (Abuse of Position of Trust or Use of Special Skill) may apply.

4. In some cases the monetary value of the unlawful payment may not be known or may not adequately reflect the seriousness of the offense. For example, a small payment may be made in exchange for the falsification of inspection records for a shipment of defective parachutes or the destruction of evidence in a major narcotics case. In part, this issue is addressed by the adjustments

in § 2C1.1(b)(2), and § 2C1.1(c)(1), (2), and (3). However, in cases in which the seriousness of the offense is still not adequately reflected, an upward departure is warranted. See Chapter Five, Part K (Departures).

5. Where the court finds that the defendant's conduct was part of a systematic or pervasive corruption of a governmental function, process, or office that may cause loss of public confidence in government, an upward departure may be warranted. See Chapter Five, Part K (Departures).

6. Subsection (b)(1) provides an adjustment for offenses involving more than one incident of either bribery or extortion. Related payments that, in essence, constitute a single incident of bribery or extortion (e.g., a number of installment payments for a single action) are to be treated as a single bribe or extortion, even if charged in separate counts.

7. For the purposes of determining whether to apply the cross references in this section, the 'resulting offense level' means the greater final offense level (i.e., the offense level determined by taking into account both the Chapter Two offense level and any applicable adjustments from Chapter Three, Parts A-D).

Background: This section applies to a person who offers or gives a bribe for a corrupt purpose, such as inducing a public official to participate in a fraud or to influence his official actions, or to a public official who solicits or accepts such a bribe. The maximum term of imprisonment authorized by statute for these offenses is fifteen years under 18 U.S.C. § 201(b) and (c), twenty years under 18 U.S.C. § 1951, and three years under 18 U.S.C. § 872.

The object and nature of a bribe may vary widely from case to case. In some cases, the object may be commercial advantage (e.g., preferential treatment in the award of a government contract). In others, the object may be issuance of a license to which the recipient is not entitled. In still others, the object may be the obstruction of justice. Consequently, a guideline for the offense must be designed to cover diverse situations.

In determining the net value of the benefit received or to be received, the value of the bribe is not deducted from the gross value of such benefit; the harm is the same regardless of value of the bribe paid to receive the benefit. Where the value of the bribe exceeds the value of the benefit or the value of the benefit cannot be determined, the value of the bribe is used because it is likely that the payer of such a bribe expected something in return that would be worth more than the value of the bribe. Moreover, for deterrence purposes, the punishment should be commensurate with the gain to the payer or the recipient of the bribe, whichever is higher.

Under § 2C1.1(b)(2)(B), if the payment was for the purpose of influencing an official act by certain officials, the offense level is increased by 8 levels if this increase is greater than that provided under § 2C1.1(b)(2)(A).

Under § 2C1.1(c)(1), if the payment was to facilitate the commission of another criminal offense, the guideline applicable to a conspiracy to commit that other offense will apply if the result is greater than that determined above. For example, if a bribe was given to a law enforcement officer to allow the smuggling of a quantity of cocaine, the guideline for conspiracy to import cocaine would be applied if it resulted in a greater offense level.

Under § 2C1.1(c)(2), if the payment was to conceal another criminal offense or obstruct justice in respect to another criminal offense, the guideline from § 2X3.1 (Accessory After the Fact) or § 2J1.2 (Obstruction of Justice), as appropriate, will apply if the result is greater than that determined above. For example, if a bribe was given for the purpose of concealing the offense of espionage, the guideline for accessory after the fact to espionage would be applied.

Under § 2C1.1(c)(3), if the offense involved forcible extortion, the guideline from § 2B3.2 (Extortion by Force or Threat of Injury or Serious Damage) will apply if the result is greater than that determined above.

When the offense level is determined under § 2C1.1(c)(1), (2), or (3), an adjustment from § 3B1.3 (Abuse of Position of Trust or Use of Special Skill) may apply.

Section 2C1.1 also applies to extortion by officers or employees of the United States in violation of 18 U.S.C. § 872, and Hobbs Act extortion, or attempted extortion, under color of official right in violation of 18 U.S.C. § 1951. The Hobbs Act, 18 U.S.C. § 1951(b)(2), applies in part to any person who acts 'under color of official right.' This statute applies to extortionate conduct by, among others, officials and employees of state and local governments. The panoply of conduct that may be prosecuted under the Hobbs Act varies from a city building inspector who demands a small amount of money from the owner of an apartment building to ignore code violations to a state court judge who extracts substantial interest-free loans from attorneys who have cases pending in his court.

Section 2C1.1 also applies to offenses under 15 U.S.C. §§ 78dd-1, 78dd-2, and 78dd-3. Such offenses generally involve a payment to a foreign public official, candidate for public office, or agent or intermediary, with the intent to influence an official act or decision of a foreign government or political party. Typically, a case prosecuted under these provisions will involve an intent to influence governmental action.

Offenses involving attempted bribery are frequently not completed because the victim reports the offense to authorities or is acting in an undercover capacity. Failure to complete the offense does not lessen the defendant's culpability in attempting to use public position for personal gain. Therefore, solicitations and attempts are treated as equivalent to the underlying offense.

§ 2C1.2. Offering, Giving, Soliciting, or Receiving a Gratuity

(a) Base Offense Level: 7

(b) Specific Offense Characteristics

(1) If the offense involved more than one gratuity, increase by 2 levels.

(2) (If more than one applies, use the greater):

(A) If the value of the gratuity (i) exceeded $2,000 but did not exceed $5,000, increase by 1 level; or (ii) exceeded $5,000, increase by the number of levels from the table in § 2B1.1 (Theft, Property Destruction, and Fraud) corresponding to that amount.

(B) If the gratuity was given, or to be given, to an

elected official or any official holding a high-level decision-making or sensitive position, increase by 8 levels.

    (c)   Special Instruction for Fines - Organizations

        (1)   In lieu of the pecuniary loss under subsection (a)(3) of § 8C2.4 (Base Fine), use the value of the unlawful payment.

Commentary

Statutory Provision: 18 U.S.C. § 201(c)(1). For additional statutory provision(s), see Appendix A (Statutory Index).

Application Notes:

1. 'Official holding a high-level decision-making or sensitive position' includes, for example, prosecuting attorneys, judges, agency administrators, supervisory law enforcement officers, and other governmental officials with similar levels of responsibility.

2. Do not apply the adjustment in § 3B1.3 (Abuse of Position or Trust or Use of Special Skill).

3. In some cases, the public official is the instigator of the offense. In others, a private citizen who is attempting to ingratiate himself or his business with the public official may be the initiator. This factor may appropriately be considered in determining the placement of the sentence within the applicable guideline range.

4. Related payments that, in essence, constitute a single gratuity (e.g., separate payments for airfare and hotel for a single vacation trip) are to be treated as a single gratuity, even if charged in separate counts.

Background: This section applies to the offering, giving, soliciting, or receiving of a gratuity to a public official in respect to an official act. A corrupt purpose is not an element of this offense. An adjustment is provided where the value of the gratuity exceeded $2,000, or where the public official was an elected official or held a high-level decision-making or sensitive position.",

and inserting the following:

"§ 2C1.1.   Offering, Giving, Soliciting, or Receiving a Bribe; Extortion Under Color of Official Right; Fraud Involving the Deprivation of the Intangible Right to Honest Services of Public Officials; Conspiracy to Defraud by Interference with Governmental Functions

    (a)   Base Offense Level:

        (1)   14, if the defendant was a public official; or

        (2)   12, otherwise.

    (b)   Specific Offense Characteristics

        (1)   If the offense involved more than one bribe or extortion, increase by 2 levels.

(2) If the value of the payment, the benefit received or to be received in return for the payment, the value of anything obtained or to be obtained by a public official or others acting with a public official, or the loss to the government from the offense, whichever is greatest, exceeded $5,000, increase by the number of levels from the table in § 2B1.1 (Theft, Property Destruction, and Fraud) corresponding to that amount.

(3) If the offense involved an elected public official or any public official in a high-level decision-making or sensitive position, increase by 4 levels. If the resulting offense level is less than level 18, increase to level 18.

(4) If the defendant was a public official who facilitated (A) entry into the United States for a person, a vehicle, or cargo; (B) the obtaining of a passport or a document relating to naturalization, citizenship, legal entry, or legal resident status; or (C) the obtaining of a government identification document, increase by 2 levels.

(c) Cross References

(1) If the offense was committed for the purpose of facilitating the commission of another criminal offense, apply the offense guideline applicable to a conspiracy to commit that other offense, if the resulting offense level is greater than that determined above.

(2) If the offense was committed for the purpose of concealing, or obstructing justice in respect to, another criminal offense, apply § 2X3.1 (Accessory After the Fact) or § 2J1.2 (Obstruction of Justice), as appropriate, in respect to that other offense, if the resulting offense level is greater than that determined above.

(3) If the offense involved a threat of physical injury or property destruction, apply § 2B3.2 (Extortion by Force or Threat of Injury or Serious Damage), if the resulting offense level is greater than that determined above.

(d) Special Instruction for Fines - Organizations

(1) In lieu of the pecuniary loss under subsection (a)(3) of § 8C2.4 (Base Fine), use the greatest of: (A) the value of the unlawful payment; (B) the value of the benefit received or to be received in return for the unlawful payment; or (C) the consequential damages resulting from the unlawful payment.

Commentary

Statutory Provisions: 15 U.S.C. §§ 78dd-1, 78dd-2, 78dd-3; 18 U.S.C. §§ 201(b)(1), (2), 371 (if conspiracy to defraud by interference with governmental functions), 872, 1341 (if the scheme or artifice to defraud was to deprive another of the intangible right of honest services of a public official), 1342 (if the scheme or artifice to defraud was to deprive another of the intangible right of honest services of a public official), 1343 (if the scheme or artifice to defraud was to deprive another of the intangible right of honest services of a public official), 1951. For additional statutory provision(s), see Appendix A (Statutory Index).

Application Notes:

1. Definitions.—For purposes of this guideline:

    'Government identification document' means a document made or issued by or under the authority of the United States Government, a State, or a political subdivision of a State, which, when completed with information concerning a particular individual, is of a type intended or commonly accepted for the purpose of identification of individuals.

    'Payment' means anything of value. A payment need not be monetary.

    'Public official' shall be construed broadly and includes the following:

    (A) 'Public official' as defined in 18 U.S.C. § 201(a)(1).

    (B) A member of a state or local legislature. 'State' means a State of the United States, and any commonwealth, territory, or possession of the United States.

    (C) An officer or employee or person acting for or on behalf of a state or local government, or any department, agency, or branch of government thereof, in any official function, under or by authority of such department, agency, or branch of government, or a juror in a state or local trial.

    (D) Any person who has been selected to be a person described in subdivisions (A), (B), or (C), either before or after such person has qualified.

    (E) An individual who, although not otherwise covered by subdivisions (A) through (D): (i) is in a position of public trust with official responsibility for carrying out a government program or policy; (ii) acts under color of law or official right; or (iii) participates so substantially in government operations as to possess de facto authority to make governmental decisions (e.g., which may include a leader of a state or local political party who acts in the manner described in this subdivision).

2. More than One Bribe or Extortion.—Subsection (b)(1) provides an adjustment for offenses involving more than one incident of either bribery or extortion. Related payments that, in essence, constitute a single incident of bribery or extortion (e.g., a number of installment payments for a single action) are to be treated as a single bribe or extortion, even if charged in separate counts.

    In a case involving more than one incident of bribery or extortion, the applicable amounts under subsection (b)(2) (i.e., the greatest of the value of the payment, the benefit received or to be received, the value of anything obtained or to be obtained by a public official or others acting with a public official, or the loss to the government) are determined separately for each incident and then added together.

3. Application of Subsection (b)(2).—'Loss', for purposes of subsection (b)(2)(A), shall be determined in accordance with Application Note 3 of the Commentary to § 2B1.1 (Theft, Property Destruction, and Fraud). The value of 'the benefit received or to be received' means the net value of such benefit. Examples: (A) A government employee, in return for a $500 bribe, reduces the price of a piece of surplus property offered for sale by the government from $10,000 to $2,000; the value of the benefit received is $8,000. (B) A $150,000 contract on which $20,000 profit was made was awarded in return for a bribe; the value of the benefit received is $20,000. Do not deduct the value of the bribe itself in computing the value of the benefit received or to be received. In the preceding examples, therefore, the value of the benefit received would be the same regardless of the value of the bribe.

4. Application of Subsection (b)(3).—

   (A) Definition.—'High-level decision-making or sensitive position' means a position characterized by a direct authority to make decisions for, or on behalf of, a government department, agency, or other government entity, or by a substantial influence over the decision-making process.

   (B) Examples.—Examples of a public official in a high-level decision-making position include a prosecuting attorney, a judge, an agency administrator, and any other public official with a similar level of authority. Examples of a public official who holds a sensitive position include a juror, a law enforcement officer, an election official, and any other similarly situated individual.

5. Application of Subsection (c).—For the purposes of determining whether to apply the cross references in this section, the 'resulting offense level' means the final offense level (i.e., the offense level determined by taking into account both the Chapter Two offense level and any applicable adjustments from Chapter Three, Parts A-D). See § 1B1.5(d); Application Note 2 of the Commentary to § 1B1.5 (Interpretation of References to Other Offense Guidelines).

6. Inapplicability of § 3B1.3.—Do not apply § 3B1.3 (Abuse of Position of Trust or Use of Special Skill).

7. Upward Departure Provisions.—In some cases the monetary value of the unlawful payment may not be known or may not adequately reflect the seriousness of the offense. For example, a small payment may be made in exchange for the falsification of inspection records for a shipment of defective parachutes or the destruction of evidence in a major narcotics case. In part, this issue is addressed by the enhancements in § 2C1.1(b)(2) and (c)(1), (2), and (3). However, in cases in which the seriousness of the offense is still not adequately reflected, an upward departure is warranted. See Chapter Five, Part K (Departures).

In a case in which the court finds that the defendant's conduct was part of a systematic or pervasive corruption of a governmental function, process, or office that may cause loss of public confidence in government, an upward departure may be warranted. See § 5K2.7 (Disruption of Governmental Function).

Background: This section applies to a person who offers or gives a bribe for a corrupt purpose, such as inducing a public official to participate in a fraud or to influence such individual's official actions, or to a public official who solicits or accepts such a bribe.

The object and nature of a bribe may vary widely from case to case. In some cases, the object may be commercial advantage (e.g., preferential treatment in the award of a government contract). In others, the object may be issuance of a license to which the recipient is not entitled. In still others, the object may be the obstruction of justice. Consequently, a guideline for the offense must be designed to cover diverse situations.

In determining the net value of the benefit received or to be received, the value of the bribe is not deducted from the gross value of such benefit; the harm is the same regardless of value of the bribe paid to receive the benefit. In a case in which the value of the bribe exceeds the value of the benefit, or in which the value of the benefit cannot be determined, the value of the bribe is used because it is likely that the payer of such a bribe expected something in return that would be worth more than the value of the bribe. Moreover, for deterrence purposes, the punishment should be commensurate with the gain to the payer or the recipient of the bribe, whichever is greater.

Under § 2C1.1(b)(3), if the payment was for the purpose of influencing an official act by certain officials, the offense level is increased by 4 levels.

Under § 2C1.1(c)(1), if the payment was to facilitate the commission of another criminal offense, the guideline applicable to a conspiracy to commit that other offense will apply if the result is greater than that determined above. For example, if a bribe was given to a law enforcement officer to allow the smuggling of a quantity of cocaine, the guideline for conspiracy to import cocaine would be applied if it resulted in a greater offense level.

Under § 2C1.1(c)(2), if the payment was to conceal another criminal offense or obstruct justice in respect to another criminal offense, the guideline from § 2X3.1 (Accessory After the Fact) or § 2J1.2 (Obstruction of Justice), as appropriate, will apply if the result is greater than that determined above. For example, if a bribe was given for the purpose of concealing the offense of espionage, the guideline for accessory after the fact to espionage would be applied.

Under § 2C1.1(c)(3), if the offense involved forcible extortion, the guideline from § 2B3.2 (Extortion by Force or Threat of Injury or Serious Damage) will apply if the result is greater than that determined above.

Section 2C1.1 also applies to offenses under 15 U.S.C. §§ 78dd-1, 78dd-2, and 78dd-3. Such offenses generally involve a payment to a foreign public official, candidate for public office, or agent or intermediary, with the intent to influence an official act or decision of a foreign government or political party. Typically, a case prosecuted under these provisions will involve an intent to influence governmental action.

Section 2C1.1 also applies to fraud involving the deprivation of the intangible right to honest services of government officials under 18 U.S.C. §§ 1341-1343 and conspiracy to defraud by interference with governmental functions under 18 U.S.C. § 371. Such fraud offenses typically involve an improper use of government influence that harms the operation of government in a manner similar to bribery offenses.

Offenses involving attempted bribery are frequently not completed because the offense is reported to authorities or an individual involved in the offense is acting in an undercover capacity. Failure to complete the offense does not lessen the defendant's culpability in attempting to use public position for personal gain. Therefore, solicitations and attempts are treated as equivalent to the underlying offense.

§ 2C1.2. Offering, Giving, Soliciting, or Receiving a Gratuity

(a) Base Offense Level:

(1) 11, if the defendant was a public official; or

(2) 9, otherwise.

(b) Specific Offense Characteristics

(1) If the offense involved more than one gratuity, increase by 2 levels.

(2) If the value of the gratuity exceeded $5,000, increase by the number of levels from the table in § 2B1.1 (Theft, Property Destruction, and Fraud) corresponding to that amount.

(3) If the offense involved an elected public official or any public official in a high-level decision-making or sensitive position, increase by 4 levels. If the resulting offense level is less than level 15, increase to level 15.

(4) If the defendant was a public official who facilitated (A) entry into the United States for a person, a vehicle, or cargo; (B) the obtaining of a passport or a document relating to naturalization, citizenship, legal entry, or legal resident status; or (C) the obtaining of a government identification document, increase by 2 levels.

(c) Special Instruction for Fines - Organizations

(1) In lieu of the pecuniary loss under subsection (a)(3) of § 8C2.4 (Base Fine), use the value of the unlawful payment.

Commentary

Statutory Provisions: 18 U.S.C. §§ 201(c)(1), 212-214, 217. For additional statutory provision(s), see Appendix A (Statutory Index).

Application Notes:

1. Definitions.—For purposes of this guideline:

'Government identification document' means a document made or issued by or under the authority of the United States Government, a State, or a political subdivision of a State, which, when completed with information concerning a particular individual, is of a type intended or commonly accepted for the purpose of identification of individuals.

'Public official' shall be construed broadly and includes the following:

(A) 'Public official' as defined in 18 U.S.C. § 201(a)(1).

(B) A member of a state or local legislature. 'State' means a State of the United States, and any commonwealth, territory, or possession of the United States.

(C) An officer or employee or person acting for or on behalf of a state or local government, or any department, agency, or branch of government thereof, in any official function, under or by authority of such department, agency, or branch of government, or a juror.

(D) Any person who has been selected to be a person described in subdivisions (A), (B), or (C), either before or after such person has qualified.

(E) An individual who, although not otherwise covered by subdivisions (A) through (D): (i) is in a position of public trust with official responsibility for carrying out a government program or policy; (ii) acts under color of law or official right; or (iii) participates so substantially in government operations as to possess de facto authority to make governmental decisions (e.g., which may include a leader of a state or local political party who acts in the manner described in this subdivision).

2. Application of Subsection (b)(1).—Related payments that, in essence, constitute a single gratuity (e.g., separate payments for airfare and hotel for a single vacation trip) are to be treated as a single gratuity, even if charged in separate counts.

3. Application of Subsection (b)(3).—

(A) Definition.—'High-level decision-making or sensitive position' means a position characterized by a direct authority to make decisions for, or on behalf of, a government department, agency, or other government entity, or by a substantial influence over the decision-making process.

(B) Examples.—Examples of a public official in a high-level decision-making position include a prosecuting attorney, a judge, an agency administrator, a law enforcement officer, and any other public official with a similar level of authority. Examples of a public official who holds a sensitive position include a juror, a law enforcement officer, an election official, and any other similarly situated individual.

4. Inapplicability of § 3B1.3.—Do not apply the adjustment in § 3B1.3 (Abuse of Position or Trust or Use of Special Skill).

Background: This section applies to the offering, giving, soliciting, or receiving of a gratuity to a public official in respect to an official act. It also applies in cases involving (1) the offer to, or acceptance by, a bank examiner of a loan or gratuity; (2) the offer or receipt of anything of value for procuring a loan or discount of commercial bank paper from a Federal Reserve Bank; and (3) the acceptance of a fee or other consideration by a federal employee for adjusting or cancelling a farm debt.".

Chapter Two, Part C, Subpart 1, is amended by striking §§ 2C1.6 and 2C1.7 and their accompanying commentary as follows:

"§ 2C1.6. Loan or Gratuity to Bank Examiner, or Gratuity for Adjustment of Farm Indebtedness, or Procuring Bank Loan, or Discount of Commercial Paper

(a) Base Offense Level: 7

(b) Specific Offense Characteristic

(1) If the value of the gratuity (i) exceeded $2,000 but did not exceed $5,000, increase by 1 level; or (ii) exceeded $5,000, increase by the number of levels from the table in § 2B1.1 (Theft, Property Destruction, and Fraud) corresponding to that amount.

Commentary

Statutory Provisions: 18 U.S.C. §§ 212-214, 217.

Application Note:

1. Do not apply the adjustment in § 3B1.3 (Abuse of Position of Trust or Use of Special Skill).

Background: Violations of 18 U.S.C. §§ 212 and 213 involve the offer to, or acceptance by, a bank examiner of a loan or gratuity. Violations of 18 U.S.C. § 214 involve the offer or receipt of anything of value for procuring a loan or discount of commercial paper from a Federal Reserve bank. Violations of 18 U.S.C. § 217 involve the acceptance of a fee or other consideration by a federal employee for adjusting or cancelling a farm debt. These offenses are misdemeanors for which the maximum term of imprisonment authorized by statute is one year.

§ 2C1.7. Fraud Involving Deprivation of the Intangible Right to the Honest Services of Public Officials; Conspiracy to Defraud by Interference with Governmental Functions

(a) Base Offense Level: 10

(b) Specific Offense Characteristic

(1) (If more than one applies, use the greater):

(A) If the loss to the government, or the value of anything obtained or to be obtained by a public official or others acting with a public official, whichever is greater (i) exceeded $2,000 but did not exceed $5,000, increase by 1 level; or (ii) exceeded $5,000, increase by the number of levels from the table in § 2B1.1 (Theft, Property Destruction, and Fraud) corresponding to that amount.

(B) If the offense involved an elected official or any official holding a high-level decision-making or sensitive position, increase by 8 levels.

(c) Cross References

(1) If the offense was committed for the purpose of facilitating the commission of another criminal offense, apply the offense guideline applicable to a conspiracy to commit that other offense if the resulting offense level is greater than that determined above.

(2) If the offense was committed for the purpose of concealing, or obstructing justice in respect to, another criminal offense, apply § 2X3.1 (Accessory After the Fact) or § 2J1.2 (Obstruction of Justice), as appropriate, in respect to that other offense if the resulting offense level is greater than that determined above.

(3) If the offense involved a threat of physical injury or property destruction, apply § 2B3.2 (Extortion by Force or Threat of Injury or Serious Damage) if the resulting offense level is greater than that determined above.

(4) If the offense is covered more specifically under § 2C1.1 (Offering, Giving, Soliciting, or Receiving a Bribe; Extortion Under Color of Official Right), § 2C1.2 (Offering, Giving, Soliciting, or Receiving a Gratuity), or § 2C1.3 (Conflict of Interest), apply the offense guideline that most specifically covers the offense.

Commentary

Statutory Provisions: 18 U.S.C. §§ 371, 1341-1343.

Application Notes:

1. This guideline applies only to offenses committed by public officials or others acting with them that involve (A) depriving others of the intangible right to honest services (such offenses may be prosecuted under 18 U.S.C. §§ 1341-1343), or (B) conspiracy to defraud the United States by interfering with governmental functions (such offenses may be prosecuted under 18 U.S.C. § 371). 'Public official,' as used in this guideline, includes officers and employees of federal, state, or local government.

2. 'Official holding a high-level decision-making or sensitive position' includes, for example, prosecuting attorneys, judges, agency administrators, supervisory law enforcement officers, and other governmental officials with similar levels of responsibility.

3. 'Loss', for purposes of subsection (b)(1)(A), shall be determined in accordance with Application Note 3 of the Commentary to § 2B1.1 (Theft, Property Destruction, and Fraud).

4. Do not apply § 3B1.3 (Abuse of Position of Trust or Use of Special Skill)

except where the offense level is determined under § 2C1.7(c)(1), (2), or (3). In such cases, an adjustment from § 3B1.3 (Abuse of Position of Trust or Use of Special Skill) may apply.

5. Where the court finds that the defendant's conduct was part of a systematic or pervasive corruption of a governmental function, process, or office that may cause loss of public confidence in government, an upward departure may be warranted. See Chapter Five, Part K (Departures).

6. For the purposes of determining whether to apply the cross references in this section, the 'resulting offense level' means the greater final offense level (i. e., the offense level determined by taking into account both the Chapter Two offense level and any applicable adjustments from Chapter Three, Parts A-D).

Background: The maximum term of imprisonment authorized by statute under 18 U.S.C. §§ 371 and 1341-1343 is five years.".

The Commentary to § 2E5.1 captioned "Application Notes" is amended in Note 4 by inserting "; Fraud Involving the Deprivation of the Intangible Right to Honest Services of Public Officials; Conspiracy to Defraud by Interference with Governmental Functions" after "Official Right".

The Commentary to § 8C2.4 captioned "Application Notes" is amended in Note 5 by inserting "; Fraud Involving the Deprivation of the Intangible Right to Honest Services of Public Officials; Conspiracy to Defraud by Interference with Governmental Functions" after "Official Right".

Appendix A (Statutory Index) is amended in the line referenced to 18 U.S.C. § 209 by striking "2C1.4" and inserting "2C1.3";

in the line referenced to 18 U.S.C. § 212 by striking "2C1.6" and inserting "2C1.2";

in the line referenced to 18 U.S.C. § 213 by striking "2C1.6" and inserting "2C1.2";

in the line referenced to 18 U.S.C. § 214 by striking "2C1.6" and inserting "2C1.2";

in the line referenced to 18 U.S.C. § 217 by striking "2C1.6" and inserting "2C1.2";

in the line referenced to 18 U.S.C. § 371 by striking "2C1.7" and inserting "2C1.1 (if conspiracy to defraud by interference with governmental functions)"; and by striking "924(c)" and inserting "924(c))";

in the line referenced to 18 U.S.C. § 1341 by striking "2C1.7" and inserting "2C1.1";

in the line referenced to 18 U.S.C. § 1342 by striking "2C1.7" and inserting "2C1.1";

in the line referenced to 18 U.S.C. § 1343 by striking "2C1.7" and inserting "2C1.1";

in the line referenced to 18 U.S.C. § 1909 by striking ", 2C1.4"; and

in the line referenced to 41 U.S.C. § 423(e) by striking ", 2C1.7".

Reason for Amendment: This amendment increases punishment for bribery, gratuity, and "honest services" cases while providing additional enhancements to address previously unrecognized aggravating factors inherent in some of these offenses. This amendment reflects the Commission's conclusion that, in general, public corruption offenses previously did not receive punishment commensurate with the gravity of such offenses. The amendment also ensures that punishment levels for public corruption offenses remain proportionate to those for closely analogous offenses sentenced under § 2B1.1 (Larceny, Embezzlement, and Other Forms of Theft; Offenses Involving Stolen Property; Property Damage or Destruction; Fraud and Deceit; Forgery; Offenses Involving Altered or Counterfeit Instruments Other than Counterfeit Bearer Obligations of the United States) and § 2J1.2 (Obstruction of Justice). To simplify guideline application, this amendment also consolidates § 2C1.1 (Offering, Giving, Soliciting, or Receiving a Bribe; Extortion Under Color of Official Right) with § 2C1.7 (Fraud Involving Deprivation of the Intangible Right to the Honest Services of Public Officials; Conspiracy to Defraud by Interference with Governmental Functions) and consolidates § 2C1.2 (Offering, Giving, Soliciting, or Receiving a Gratuity) with § 2C1.6 (Loan or Gratuity to Bank Examiner, or Gratuity for Adjustment of Farm Indebtedness, or Procuring Bank Loan, or Discount of Commercial Paper).

Sections 2C1.1 and 2C1.2 each are amended to include alternative base offense levels, with an increase of two levels for public official defendants who violate their offices or responsibilities by accepting bribes, gratuities, or anything else of value. The higher alternative base offense levels for public officials reflect the Commission's view that offenders who abuse their positions of public trust are inherently more culpable than those who seek to corrupt them, and their offenses present a somewhat greater threat to the integrity of governmental processes.

A specific offense characteristic in the former §§ 2C1.1, 2C1.2, and 2C1.7 that raised offense levels incrementally with the financial magnitude of the offense or, if greater, by eight levels for the defendant's status as a "high-level decision-maker" is replaced by two separate specific offense characteristics in the amended guidelines. These new specific offense characteristics for "loss" and "status" are to be applied cumulatively when they both co-exist in the case. Their operation in tandem ensures that the offense level will always rise commensurate with the financial magnitude of the offense, and that all offenses involving "an elected public official or any public official in a high-level decision-making or sensitive position" will receive four additional offense levels and, when applicable, a minimum offense level of level 18 (in § 2C1.1) or level 15 (in § 2C1.2). The minimum offense level ensures that an offender sentenced under the amended guidelines will not receive a less severe sentence than a similarly situated offender under the former guidelines. Application notes and illustrative examples have been added to the amended guidelines to clarify the meaning of "high-level decision-making or sensitive position."

A new specific offense characteristic has been added to §§ 2C1.1 and 2C1.2 that provides two additional offense levels when the offender is a public official whose position involves the security of the borders of the United States or the integrity of the process for generating documents related to naturalization, legal entry, legal residence, or other government identification documents. This specific offense characteristic recognizes the extreme sensitivity of these positions in light of heightened threats from international terrorism.

Effective Date: The effective date of this amendment is November 1, 2004.

667. Amendment: Section 2D1.1(b) is amended by redesignating subdivisions (5) and (6) as subdivisions (6) and (7), respectively; and by inserting after subdivision (4) the following:

"(5) If the defendant, or a person for whose conduct the defendant is accountable under § 1B1.3 (Relevant Conduct), distributed a controlled substance through mass-marketing by means of an interactive computer service, increase by 2 levels.".

Section 2D1.1 is amended by adding after subsection (d) the following:

"(e) Special Instruction

(1) If (A) subsection (d)(2) does not apply; and (B) the defendant committed, or attempted to commit, a sexual offense against another individual by distributing, with or without that individual's knowledge, a controlled substance to that individual, an adjustment under § 3A1.1(b)(1) shall apply.".

Section 2D1.1(c) is amended in subdivision (10) by striking "or Schedule III substances" in the thirteenth entry; and by inserting after the thirteenth entry the following:

"40,000 or more units of Schedule III substances;";

in subdivision (11) by striking "or Schedule III substances" in the thirteenth entry; and by inserting after the thirteenth entry the following:

"At least 20,000 but less than 40,000 units of Schedule III substances;";

in subdivision (12) by striking "or Schedule III substances" in the thirteenth entry; and by inserting after the thirteenth entry the following:

"At least 10,000 but less than 20,000 units of Schedule III substances;";

in subdivision (13) by striking "or Schedule III substances" in the thirteenth entry; and by inserting after the thirteenth entry the following:

"At least 5,000 but less than 10,000 units of Schedule III substances;";

in subdivision (14) by striking "or Schedule III substances" in the thirteenth entry; and by inserting after the thirteenth entry the following:

"At least 2,500 but less than 5,000 units of Schedule III substances;";

in subdivision (15) by striking "or Schedule III substances" in the fourth entry; and by inserting after the fourth entry the following:

"At least 1,000 but less than 2,500 units of Schedule III substances;";

in subdivision (16) by striking "or Schedule III substances" in the fourth entry; and by inserting after the fourth entry the following:

"At least 250 but less than 1,000 units of Schedule III substances;"; and

in subdivision (17) by striking "or Schedule III substances" in the fourth entry; and by inserting after the fourth entry the following:

"Less than 250 units of Schedule III substances;".

Section 2D1.1 is amended in the subdivision captioned "*Notes to Drug Quantity Table" in Note (F) in the first sentence by inserting "(except gamma-hydroxybutyric acid)" after "Depressants"; and in the second sentence by inserting "(except gamma-hydroxybutyric acid)" after "substance", and by striking "gm" and inserting "ml".

The Commentary to § 2D1.1 captioned "Application Notes" is amended by striking Note 5 as follows:

| **Amendment 667** | APPENDIX C - VOLUME III | November 1, 2013 |

"5. Any reference to a particular controlled substance in these guidelines includes all salts, isomers, and all salts of isomers. Any reference to cocaine includes ecgonine and coca leaves, except extracts of coca leaves from which cocaine and ecgonine have been removed.",

and inserting the following:

"5. <u>Analogues and Controlled Substances Not Referenced in this Guideline.</u>— Any reference to a particular controlled substance in these guidelines includes all salts, isomers, all salts of isomers, and, except as otherwise provided, any analogue of that controlled substance. Any reference to cocaine includes ecgonine and coca leaves, except extracts of coca leaves from which cocaine and ecgonine have been removed. For purposes of this guideline 'analogue' has the meaning given the term 'controlled substance analogue' in 21 U.S.C. § 802(32). In determining the appropriate sentence, the court also may consider whether a greater quantity of the analogue is needed to produce a substantially similar effect on the central nervous system as the controlled substance for which it is an analogue.

In the case of a controlled substance that is not specifically referenced in this guideline, determine the base offense level using the marihuana equivalency of the most closely related controlled substance referenced in this guideline. In determining the most closely related controlled substance, the court shall, to the extent practicable, consider the following:

(A) Whether the controlled substance not referenced in this guideline has a chemical structure that is substantially similar to a controlled substance referenced in this guideline.

(B) Whether the controlled substance not referenced in this guideline has a stimulant, depressant, or hallucinogenic effect on the central nervous system that is substantially similar to the stimulant, depressant, or hallucinogenic effect on the central nervous system of a controlled substance referenced in this guideline.

(C) Whether a lesser or greater quantity of the controlled substance not referenced in this guideline is needed to produce a substantially similar effect on the central nervous system as a controlled substance referenced in this guideline.".

The Commentary to § 2D1.1 captioned "Application Notes" is amended in Note 10 in the Drug Equivalency Tables by striking the subdivision captioned "Schedule I or II Depressants" as follows:

"<u>Schedule I or II Depressants</u>

1 unit of a Schedule I or II Depressant = 1 gm of marihuana",

and inserting the following new subdivisions:

"<u>Schedule I or II Depressants (except gamma-hydroxybutyric acid)</u>

1 unit of a Schedule I or II Depressant

– 940 –

(except gamma-hydroxybutyric acid) =   1 gm of marihuana

Gamma-hydroxybutyric Acid

1 ml of gamma-hydroxybutyric acid =   8.8 gm of marihuana".

The Commentary to § 2D1.1 captioned "Application Notes" is amended in Note 12 by striking the last sentence of the third paragraph as follows:

"If, however, the defendant establishes that he or she did not intend to provide, or was not reasonably capable of providing, the agreed-upon quantity of the controlled substance, the court shall exclude from the offense level determination the amount of controlled substance that the defendant establishes that he or she did not intend to provide or was not reasonably capable of providing.",

and inserting the following:

"If, however, the defendant establishes that the defendant did not intend to provide or purchase, or was not reasonably capable of providing or purchasing, the agreed-upon quantity of the controlled substance, the court shall exclude from the offense level determination the amount of controlled substance that the defendant establishes that the defendant did not intend to provide or purchase or was not reasonably capable of providing or purchasing.".

The Commentary to § 2D1.1 captioned "Application Notes" is amended by adding at the end the following:

"22. Application of Subsection (b)(5).—For purposes of subsection (b)(5), 'mass-marketing by means of an interactive computer service' means the solicitation, by means of an interactive computer service, of a large number of persons to induce those persons to purchase a controlled substance. For example, subsection (b)(5) would apply to a defendant who operated a web site to promote the sale of Gamma-hydroxybutyric Acid (GHB) but would not apply to coconspirators who use an interactive computer service only to communicate with one another in furtherance of the offense. 'Interactive computer service', for purposes of subsection (b)(5) and this note, has the meaning given that term in section 230(e)(2) of the Communications Act of 1934 (47 U.S.C. § 230(f)(2)).

23. Application of Subsection (e)(1).—

   (A)   Definition.—For purposes of this guideline, 'sexual offense' means a 'sexual act' or 'sexual contact' as those terms are defined in 18 U.S.C. § 2246(2) and (3), respectively.

   (B)   Upward Departure Provision.—If the defendant committed a sexual offense against more than one individual, an upward departure would be warranted.".

Section 2D1.11(b)(2) is amended by striking "21 U.S.C. §§ 841(d)(2), (g)(1), or 960(d)(2)," and inserting "21 U.S.C. § 841(c)(2) or (f)(1), or § 960(d)(2), (d)(3), or (d)(4),".

Section 2D1.11(b) is amended by adding at the end the following:

Amendment 667   APPENDIX C - VOLUME III   November 1, 2013

"(4) If the defendant, or a person for whose conduct the defendant is accountable under § 1B1.3 (Relevant Conduct), distributed a listed chemical through mass-marketing by means of an interactive computer service, increase by 2 levels.".

Section 2D1.11(e) is amended in subdivision (1) by striking "10,000 KG or more of Gamma-butyrolactone;" and inserting "2271 L or more of Gamma-butyrolactone;"; and by inserting ", White Phosphorus, or Hypophosphorous Acid" after "Red Phosphorus";

in subdivision (2) by striking "At least 3,000 KG but less than 10,000 KG of Gamma-butyrolactone;" and inserting "At least 681.3 L but less than 2271 L of Gamma-butyrolactone;"; and by inserting ", White Phosphorus, or Hypophosphorous Acid" after "Red Phosphorus";

in subdivision (3) by striking "At least 1,000 KG but less than 3,000 KG of Gamma-butyrolactone;" and inserting "At least 227.1 L but less than 681.3 L of Gamma-butyrolactone;"; and by inserting ", White Phosphorus, or Hypophosphorous Acid" after "Red Phosphorus";

in subdivision (4) by striking "At least 700 KG but less than 1,000 KG of Gamma-butyrolactone;" and inserting "At least 159 L but less than 227.1 L of Gamma-butyrolactone;"; and by inserting ", White Phosphorus, or Hypophosphorous Acid" after "Red Phosphorus";

in subdivision (5) by striking "At least 400 KG but less than 700 KG of Gamma-butyrolactone;" and inserting "At least 90.8 L but less than 159 L of Gamma-butyrolactone;"; and by inserting ", White Phosphorus, or Hypophosphorous Acid" after "Red Phosphorus";

in subdivision (6) by striking "At least 100 KG but less than 400 KG of Gamma-butyrolactone;" and inserting "At least 22.7 L but less than 90.8 L of Gamma-butyrolactone;"; and by inserting ", White Phosphorus, or Hypophosphorous Acid" after "Red Phosphorus";

in subdivision (7) by striking "At least 80 KG but less than 100 KG of Gamma-butyrolactone;" and inserting "At least 18.2 L but less than 22.7 L of Gamma-butyrolactone;"; and by inserting ", White Phosphorus, or Hypophosphorous Acid" after "Red Phosphorus";

in subdivision (8) by striking "At least 60 KG but less than 80 KG of Gamma-butyrolactone;" and inserting "At least 13.6 L but less than 18.2 L of Gamma-butyrolactone;"; and by inserting ", White Phosphorus, or Hypophosphorous Acid" after "Red Phosphorus";

in subdivision (9) by striking "At least 40 KG but less than 60 KG of Gamma-butyrolactone;" and inserting "At least 9.1 L but less than 13.6 L of Gamma-butyrolactone;"; and by inserting ", White Phosphorus, or Hypophosphorous Acid" after "Red Phosphorus";

in subdivision (10) by striking "Less than 40 KG of Gamma-butyrolactone;" and inserting "Less than 9.1 L of Gamma-butyrolactone;"; and by inserting ", White Phosphorus, or Hypophosphorous Acid" after "Red Phosphorus".

The Commentary to § 2D1.11 captioned "Statutory Provisions" is amended by inserting ", (3), (4)" after "(d)(1), (2)".

The Commentary to § 2D1.11 captioned "Application Notes" is amended in Note 5 by striking "21 U.S.C. §§ 841(d)(2), (g)(1), and 960(d)(2)" and inserting "21 U.S.C. §§ 841(c)(2) and (f)(1), and 960(d)(2), (d)(3), and (d)(4)"; and by striking "Where" and inserting "In a case in which".

The Commentary to § 2D1.11 captioned "Application Notes" is amended by adding at the end the following:

"7. Application of Subsection (b)(4).—For purposes of subsection (b)(4), 'mass-marketing by means of an interactive computer service' means the solicitation, by means of an interactive computer service, of a large number of persons to induce those persons to purchase a controlled substance. For example, subsection (b)(4) would apply to a defendant who operated a web site to promote the sale of Gamma-butyrolactone (GBL) but would not apply to coconspirators who use an interactive computer service only to communicate with one another in furtherance of the offense. 'Interactive computer service', for purposes of subsection (b)(4) and this note, has the meaning given that term in section 230(e)(2) of the Communications Act of 1934 (47 U.S.C. § 230(f)(2)).".

Section 2D1.12(b) is amended by adding at the end the following:

"(3) If the defendant, or a person for whose conduct the defendant is accountable under § 1B1.3 (Relevant Conduct), distributed any prohibited flask, equipment, chemical, product, or material through mass-marketing by means of an interactive computer service, increase by 2 levels.

(4) If the offense involved stealing anhydrous ammonia or transporting stolen anhydrous ammonia, increase by 6 levels.".

The Commentary to § 2D1.12 captioned "Application Notes" is amended by adding at the end the following:

"4. Application of Subsection (b)(3).—For purposes of subsection (b)(3), 'mass-marketing by means of an interactive computer service' means the solicitation, by means of an interactive computer service, of a large number of persons to induce those persons to purchase a controlled substance. For example, subsection (b)(3) would apply to a defendant who operated a web site to promote the sale of prohibited flasks but would not apply to coconspirators who use an interactive computer service only to communicate with one another in furtherance of the offense. 'Interactive computer service', for purposes of subsection (b)(3) and this note, has the meaning given that term in section 230(e)(2) of the Communications Act of 1934 (47 U.S.C. § 230(f)(2)).".

Appendix A (Statutory Index) is amended by striking the following:

"21 U.S.C. § 957   2D1.1".

Reason for Amendment: This amendment makes several modifications to the guidelines in Chapter Two, Part D (Offenses Involving Drugs). First, this amendment implements section 608 of the Prosecutorial Remedies and Other Tools to end the Exploitation of Children Today Act of 2003, (the "PROTECT Act"), Pub. L. 108–21, which directs the Commission to review and consider amending the guidelines with respect to gamma-hydroxybutyric acid (GHB) to provide increased penalties that reflect the seriousness of offenses involving GHB and the need to deter them. The Commission identified several harms associated with GHB offenses and separately increased penalties for Internet trafficking and drug facilitated sexual assault, two harms associated with trafficking and use of this and other controlled substances. Specifically, the amendment modifies § 2D1.1 (Unlawful Manufacturing, Importing, Exporting, or Trafficking (Including Possession with Intent to Commit These Offenses); Attempt or Conspiracy) to provide an approximate five-year term of imprisonment (equivalent to base offense level 26, Criminal History Category I) for distribution of three gallons of GHB. The Commission determined, based on information provided by the Drug Enforcement Administration, that this quantity typically reflects a mid-level distributor. The trigger for the ten-year penalty (base offense level 32) is set at 30 gallons, reflecting quantities associated with a high-level distributor. This amendment also increases the penalties under § 2D1.11 (Unlawfully Distributing, Importing, Exporting or Possessing a Listed Chemical; Attempt or Conspiracy) for offenses involving gamma-butyrolactone (GBL), a precursor for GHB. The quantities in § 2D1.11 track the quantities used in § 2D1.1.

Second, this amendment adds a two-level enhancement in §§ 2D1.1, 2D1.11, and 2D1.12 (Unlawful Possession, Manufacture, Distribution, Transportation, Exportation, or Importation of Prohibited Flask, Equipment, Chemical, Product, or Material; Attempt or Conspiracy) for mass marketing of a controlled substance, listed chemical, or prohibited equipment, respectively, through the use of an interactive computer service. The Commission identified use of an interactive computer service as a tool providing easier access to illegal products. Use of an interactive computer service enables drug traffickers to market their illegal products more efficiently and anonymously to a wider audience than through traditional drug trafficking means, while making it more difficult for law enforcement authorities to discover the offense and apprehend the offenders.

Third, this amendment provides a special instruction in § 2D1.1(e) that requires application of the vulnerable victim adjustment in § 3A1.1(b)(1) (Hate Crime Motivation or Vulnerable Victim) if the defendant commits a sexual offense by distributing a controlled substance to another individual, with or without that individual's knowledge. The amendment addresses cases in which the cross reference in § 2D1.1(d)(2) does not apply. The cross reference in § 2D1.1(d)(2) is limited to cases involving a conviction under 21 U.S.C. § 841(b)(7), which prescribes a 20-year statutory maximum penalty for the distribution of a controlled substance to another individual, without that individual's knowledge, with the intent to commit a crime of violence (including rape). Because the statute requires that the distribution occur without knowledge, the cross reference does not apply to drug facilitated sexual assaults when the victim of the sexual assault knowingly ingests the controlled substance. This amendment reflects the Commission's view that a defendant who commits a drug-facilitated sexual assault should receive increased punishment whether or not the victim knowingly ingested the controlled substance distributed by the defendant.

Fourth, this amendment modifies the existing rule at Application Note 5 of § 2D1.1 to provide a uniform mechanism for determining sentences in cases involving analogues of controlled substances or controlled substances not specifically referenced in this guideline. The genesis of this amendment was the Commission's investigation of GHB, during which the Commission learned that analogues of GHB, specifically GBL and 1,4 Butanediol (BD), among others, often are used in its stead and cause the same effects as GHB. The Commission was concerned that analogues of other drugs might be similarly used. Additionally, the Commission became aware that courts employ a variety of means to determine the applicable guideline range for defendants charged with offenses involving controlled substances not specifically referenced in § 2D1.1, resulting in disparate sentences. The purpose of the amendment is to provide a more uniform mechanism for determining sentences in cases involving analogues or controlled substances not specifically referenced in this guideline.

Fifth, this amendment corrects a technical error in the Drug Quantity Table at § 2D1.1(c) with respect to Schedule III substances. Specifically, the maximum base offense level for Schedule III substances is level 20, but prior to the amendment there was no corresponding language in the Drug Quantity Table to so indicate.

Sixth, this amendment addresses a circuit conflict regarding the interpretation of the last sentence in Application Note 12 of § 2D1.1. See United States v. Smack, 347 F.3d 533 (3rd Cir. 2003) (criticizing language of note); compare United States v. Gomez, 103 F.3d 249, 252-53 (2d Cir. 1997) (holding that the last sentence of the note is intended to apply only to sellers); United States v. Perez de Dios, 237 F.3d 1192 (10th Cir. 2001) (same); United States v. Brassard, 212 F.3d 54, 58 (1st Cir. 2000) (same), with United States v. Minore, 40 Fed. Appx. 536, 537 (9th Cir. 2002) (mem.op.) (applying the final sentence of the new Note 12 to a buyer in reverse sting operation); United States v. Estrada, 256 F.3d 466, 476 (7th Cir. 2001) (same). Application Note 12 covers offenses involving an agreement to sell a specific quantity of a controlled substance. This amendment makes clear that the court shall exclude from the offense level determination the amount of the controlled substance, if any, that the defendant establishes that he or she did not intend to provide or purchase, or was not reasonably capable of providing or purchasing, regardless of whether the defendant agreed to be the seller or the buyer of the controlled substance.

Seventh, this amendment updates the statutory references in § 2D1.11(b)(2) and accompanying commentary to conform to statutory redesignations of certain offenses, and also expands application of § 2D1.11(b)(2) to include 21 U.S.C. § 960(d)(3) and (d)(4) among the statutes of conviction for which the three-level reduction at subsection (b)(2) is available. The reduction formerly applied in cases in which the defendant, convicted under 21 U.S.C. § 841(c)(2), (f)(1), or § 960(d)(2), as properly redesignated, did not have knowledge or actual belief that the listed chemical would be used to manufacture a controlled substance. Section 841(c)(2) of title 21, United States Code, requires a finding of either knowledge or a reasonable cause to believe that the listed chemical would be used to manufacture a controlled substance. Sections 960(d)(3) and (d)(4) of title 21, United States Code, similarly require a finding that a person who imports, exports, or serves as a broker for, a listed chemical knows or has a reasonable cause to believe, that the listed chemical will be used to manufacture a controlled substance. Given that the reduction applies in 21 U.S.C. § 841(c)(2) cases in which the defendant had a reasonable cause to believe, but not knowledge or actual belief, that the listed chemical would be used to manufacture a controlled substance, and the mens rea in 21 U.S.C. § 841(c)(2) is the same as in 21 U.S.C. § 960(d)(3) and (d)(4), the amendment adds 21 U.S.C. § 960(d)(3) and (d)(4) to § 2D1.11(b)(2).

Eighth, this amendment adds white phosphorus and hypophosphorous acid to the Chemical Quantity Table in § 2D1.11(e). Both substances are List I chemicals that can be substituted for red phosphorus in the manufacture of methamphetamine. Red phosphorus was added to the Chemical Quantity Table effective November 1, 2003 (see Amendment 661), but notice and comment requirements prevented white phosphorus and hypophosphorous acid from being added contemporaneously.

Ninth, this amendment provides an enhancement of six levels at § 2D1.12 if the offense involved stealing anhydrous ammonia or transporting stolen anhydrous ammonia. A widely used source of nitrogen fertilizer for crops, anhydrous ammonia also is used in the manufacture of methamphetamine. Anhydrous ammonia must be stored and handled under high pressure, which requires specially designed and well-maintained equipment. The improper handling and storage of anhydrous ammonia can result in permanent injury (such as cell destruction and severe chemical burns) and explosions. Methamphetamine manufacturers often obtain anhydrous ammonia by siphoning large-volume tanks at fertilizer plants and farms, and rarely have the knowledge or equipment required to properly handle it. This enhancement accounts for the inherent dangers created by such conduct, as well as the likely intended unlawful use.

Finally, this amendment modifies Appendix A (Statutory Index) by deleting the reference to 21 U.S.C. § 957, which is not a substantive criminal offense, but rather a registration provision for which violations are prosecuted under 21 U.S.C. § 960(a) or (b) (for controlled substances) or § 960(d)(6) (for listed chemicals).

Effective Date: The effective date of this amendment is November 1, 2004.

668. Amendment: Section 2D1.1(a) is amended by striking subdivision (3) as follows:

"(3) the offense level specified in the Drug Quantity Table set forth in subsection (c), except that if the defendant receives an adjustment under § 3B1.2 (Mitigating Role), the base offense level under this subsection shall be not more than level 30.",

and inserting the following:

"(3) the offense level specified in the Drug Quantity Table set forth in subsection (c), except that if (A) the defendant receives an adjustment under § 3B1.2 (Mitigating Role); and (B) the base offense level under subsection (c) is (i) level 32, decrease by 2 levels; (ii) level 34 or level 36, decrease by 3 levels; or (iii) level 38, decrease by 4 levels.".

Section 2D1.11 is amended by striking subsection (a) as follows:

"(a) Base Offense Level: The offense level from the Chemical Quantity Table set forth in subsection (d) or (e), as appropriate.",

and inserting the following:

"(a) Base Offense Level: The offense level from the Chemical Quantity Table set forth in subsection (d) or (e), as appropriate, except that if (A) the defendant receives an adjustment under § 3B1.2 (Mitigating Role); and (B) the base offense level under subsection (e) is (i) level 32, decrease by 2 levels; (ii) level 34 or level 36, decrease by 3 levels; or (iii) level 38, decrease by 4 levels.".

Reason for Amendment: The amendment modifies the maximum base offense level for certain offenders provided at § 2D1.1(a)(3) (Unlawful Manufacturing, Importing, Exporting, or Trafficking (Including Possession with Intent to Commit These Offenses); Attempt or Conspiracy). Prior to the amendment, subsection (a)(3) limited the maximum base offense level to level 30 for all offenders sentenced under § 2D1.1 who also received an adjustment under § 3B1.2 (Mitigating Role). In order to address proportionality concerns arising from the "mitigating role cap," the amendment modifies § 2D1.1(a)(3) to provide a graduated reduction for offenders whose quantity level under § 2D1.1(c) results in a base offense level greater than level 30 and who qualify for a mitigating role adjustment under § 3B1.2. Specifically, the amendment provides a two-level reduction if the defendant receives an adjustment under § 3B1.2 and the base offense level determined at the Drug Quantity Table in § 2D1.1 is level 32. If the base offense level determined at § 2D1.1(c) is level 34 or 36, and the defendant receives an adjustment under § 3B1.2, a three-level reduction is provided. A four-level reduction is provided if the defendant receives an adjustment under § 3B1.2 and the base offense level under § 2D1.1(c) is level 38. This amendment also provides an identical reduction in § 2D1.11 (Unlawfully Distributing, Importing, Exporting or Possessing a Listed Chemical; Attempt or Conspiracy).

Effective Date: The effective date of this amendment is November 1, 2004.

669. Amendment: Section 2K2.1(b) is amended by striking subdivision (3) as follows:

"(3) If the offense involved a destructive device, increase by 2 levels.",

and inserting the following:

"(3) If the offense involved—

(A) a destructive device that is a portable rocket, a missile, or a device for use in launching a portable rocket or a missile, increase by 15 levels; or

(B) a destructive device other than a destructive device referred to in subdivision (A), increase by 2 levels.".

Section 2K2.1(b) is amended by striking:

"Provided, that the cumulative offense level determined above shall not exceed level 29.",

and inserting the following:

"The cumulative offense level determined from the application of subsections (b)(1) through (b)(4) may not exceed level 29, except if subsection (b)(3)(A) applies.".

The Commentary to § 2K2.1 captioned "Application Notes" is amended by striking Notes 1 through 4 as follows:

"1. 'Firearm' includes (i) any weapon (including a starter gun) which will, or is designed to, or may readily be converted to, expel a projectile by the action of an explosive; (ii) the frame or receiver of any such weapon; (iii) any firearm muffler or silencer; or (iv) any destructive device. See 18 U.S.C. § 921(a)(3).

2. 'Ammunition' includes ammunition or cartridge cases, primer, bullets, or propellent powder designed for use in any firearm. See 18 U.S.C. § 921(a)(17)(A).

3. A 'firearm described in 26 U.S.C. § 5845(a)' includes: (i) a shotgun having a barrel or barrels of less than 18 inches in length; a weapon made from a shotgun if such weapon as modified has an overall length of less than 26 inches or a barrel or barrels of less than 18 inches in length; a rifle having a barrel or barrels of less than 16 inches in length; or a weapon made from a rifle if such weapon as modified has an overall length of less than 26 inches or a barrel or barrels of less than 16 inches in length; (ii) a machinegun; (iii) a silencer; (iv) a destructive device; and (v) certain unusual weapons defined in 26 U.S.C. § 5845(e) (that are not conventional, unaltered handguns, rifles, or shotguns). For a more detailed definition, refer to 26 U.S.C. § 5845.

A 'firearm described in 18 U.S.C. § 921(a)(30)' (pertaining to semiautomatic assault weapons) does not include a weapon exempted under the provisions of 18 U.S.C. § 922(v)(3).

4. 'Destructive device' is a type of firearm listed in 26 U.S.C. § 5845(a), and includes any explosive, incendiary, or poison gas -- (i) bomb, (ii) grenade, (iii) rocket having a propellant charge of more than four ounces, (iv) missile having an explosive or incendiary charge of more than one-quarter ounce, (v) mine, or (vi) device similar to any of the devices described in the preceding clauses; any type of weapon which will, or which may be readily converted to, expel a projectile by the action of an explosive or other propellant, and which has any barrel with a bore of more than one-half inch in diameter; or any combination of parts either designed or intended for use in converting any device into any destructive device listed above. For a more detailed definition, refer to 26 U.S.C. § 5845(f).",

and by redesignating Note 5 as Note 1.

The Commentary to § 2K2.1 captioned "Application Notes" is amended in Note 1, as redesignated by this amendment, by inserting "Definitions.—" before "For purposes of this guideline:"; by inserting before "'Controlled substance offense'" the following paragraph:

"'Ammunition' has the meaning given that term in 18 U.S.C. § 921(a)(17)(A).";

by inserting after the paragraph that begins "'Crime of violence'" the following paragraph:

"'Destructive device' has the meaning given that term in 26 U.S.C. § 5845(f).";

and by adding at the end the following paragraph:

"'Firearm' has the meaning given that term in 18 U.S.C. § 921(a)(3).".

The Commentary to § 2K2.1 captioned "Application Notes" is amended by inserting after Note 1, as redesignated by this amendment, the following:

"2. Firearm Described in 18 U.S.C. § 921(a)(30).—For purposes of subsection (a), a 'firearm described in 18 U.S.C. § 921(a)(30)' (pertaining to semiautomatic assault weapons) does not include a weapon exempted under the provisions of 18 U.S.C. § 922(v)(3).".

The Commentary to § 2K2.1 captioned "Application Notes" is amended by redesignating Notes 6 through 19 as Notes 3 through 16, respectively.

The Commentary to § 2K2.1 captioned "Application Notes" is amended in Note 8, as redesignated by this amendment, by striking "a two-level" and inserting "the applicable"; and by adding at the end the following paragraph:

"Offenses involving such devices cover a wide range of offense conduct and involve different degrees of risk to the public welfare depending on the type of destructive device involved and the location or manner in which that destructive device was possessed or transported. For example, a pipe bomb in a populated train station creates a substantially greater risk to the public welfare, and a substantially greater risk of death or serious bodily injury, than an incendiary device in an isolated area. In a case in which the cumulative result of the increased base offense level and the enhancement under subsection (b)(3) does not adequately capture the seriousness of

November 1, 2013 APPENDIX C - VOLUME III **Amendment 669**

the offense because of the type of destructive device involved, the risk to the public welfare, or the risk of death or serious bodily injury that the destructive device created, an upward departure may be warranted. See also §§ 5K2.1 (Death), 5K2.2 (Physical Injury), and 5K2.14 (Public Welfare).".

The Commentary to § 2K2.1 captioned "Application Notes" is amended in Note 13, as redesignated by this amendment, by inserting "(see Application Note 8)" after "multiple individuals".

Section 2X1.1 is amended by striking subsection (d) as follows:

"(d) Special Instruction

(1) Subsection (b) shall not apply to any of the following offenses, if such offense involved, or was intended to promote, a federal crime of terrorism as defined in 18 U.S.C. § 2332b(g)(5):

18 U.S.C. § 81;
18 U.S.C. § 930(c);
18 U.S.C. § 1362;
18 U.S.C. § 1363;
18 U.S.C. § 1992;
18 U.S.C. § 2339A;
18 U.S.C. § 2340A;
49 U.S.C. § 46504;
49 U.S.C. § 46505; and
49 U.S.C. § 60123(b).",

and inserting the following:

"(d) Special Instruction

(1) Subsection (b) shall not apply to:

(A) Any of the following offenses, if such offense involved, or was intended to promote, a federal crime of terrorism as defined in 18 U.S.C. § 2332b(g)(5):

18 U.S.C. § 81;
18 U.S.C. § 930(c);
18 U.S.C. § 1362;
18 U.S.C. § 1363;
18 U.S.C. § 1992;
18 U.S.C. § 2339A;
18 U.S.C. § 2340A;
49 U.S.C. § 46504;
49 U.S.C. § 46505; and
49 U.S.C. § 60123(b).

(B) Any of the following offenses:

18 U.S.C. § 32;

18 U.S.C. § 1993; and
18 U.S.C. § 2332a.".

Appendix A (Statutory Index) is amended in the line referenced to 18 U.S.C. § 1993(a)(8) by inserting "2A5.2 (if attempt or conspiracy to commit 18 U.S.C. § 1993(a)(4), (a)(5), or (a)(6))," before "2A6.1".

Reason for Amendment: Before promulgation of this amendment, subsection (b)(3) of § 2K2.1 (Unlawful Receipt, Possession, or Transportation of Firearms or Ammunition; Prohibited Transactions Involving Firearms or Ammunition) generally provided a two-level enhancement if the offense involved a destructive device, without regard to the type of destructive device involved. This amendment increases that enhancement to 15 levels if the destructive device was a man-portable air defense system (MANPADS), portable rocket, missile, or device used for launching a portable rocket or missile. It maintains the two-level enhancement for all other destructive devices. MANPADS and similar weapons are highly regulated under chapter 53 of title 26, United States Code, and chapter 44 of title 18, United States Code, and are classified as "destructive devices" under 26 U.S.C. § 5845(f).

This amendment responds to concerns that these types of weapons, which have been used overseas, have the ability to inflict death or injury on large numbers of persons if fired at an aircraft, train, building, or similar target. Because of the inherent risks of such weapons and the fact that there is no legitimate reason to possess them, the Commission determined that the statutory maximum penalty for possession of such devices should apply in all such offenses, even after possible application of acceptance of responsibility. The amendment also re-designates Application Note 11 as Application Note 8, and adds an invited upward departure for non-MANPADS destructive devices in a case in which the two-level enhancement for such devices does not adequately capture the seriousness of the offense because of the type of destructive device involved, the risk to public welfare, and the risk of death or serious bodily injury that the destructive device created. Furthermore, in response to concerns that it is unclear whether certain types of firearms qualify as "destructive devices" using the guideline definition of "destructive device," the amendment adopts the statutory definition provided in 26 U.S.C. § 5845(f). For consistency, similar statutory definitions are substituted for the definitions of "ammunition" and "firearm."

The amendment also increases guideline penalties for attempts and conspiracies to commit certain offenses if those offenses involved the use of a MANPADS or similar destructive device. Affected offenses include 18 U.S.C. § 32 (Destruction of aircraft or aircraft facilities), 18 U.S.C. § 1993 (Terrorist attacks and other acts of violence against mass transportation systems), and 18 U.S.C. § 2332a (Use of certain weapons of mass destruction). The Commission amended the special instruction in subsection (d) of § 2X1.1 (Attempt, Solicitation, or Conspiracy (Not Covered by a Specific Offense Guideline)) to prohibit application of the three-level reduction for attempts and conspiracies for these offenses generally, and not just in the context of the use of a MANPADS or similar destructive device.

Finally, the amendment modifies the Statutory Index (Appendix A) reference for convictions under 18 U.S.C. § 1993(a)(8), relating to attempts, threats, or conspiracies to commit any of the substantive terrorist offenses in 18 U.S.C. § 1993(a). Under this amendment, these offenses will be referred to § 2A5.2 (Interference with Flight Crew Member or Flight Attendant; Interference with Dispatch, Operation, or Maintenance of Mass Transportation Vehicle or Ferry) rather than § 2A6.1 (Threatening or Harassing Communications).

Effective Date: The effective date of this amendment is November 1, 2004.

670. Amendment: Chapter Two, Part K, Subpart 2, is amended by adding at the end the following new guideline and accompanying commentary:

"§ 2K2.6. Possessing, Purchasing, or Owning Body Armor by Violent Felons

    (a)   Base Offense Level: 10

    (b)   Specific Offense Characteristic

        (1)   If the defendant used the body armor in connection with another felony offense, increase by 4 levels.

Commentary

Statutory Provision: 18 U.S.C. § 931.

Application Notes:

1. Application of Subsection (b)(1).—

    (A) Meaning of 'Defendant'.—Consistent with § 1B1.3 (Relevant Conduct), the term 'defendant', for purposes of subsection (b)(1), limits the accountability of the defendant to the defendant's own conduct and conduct that the defendant aided or abetted, counseled, commanded, induced, procured, or willfully caused.

    (B) Meaning of 'Felony Offense'.—For purposes of subsection (b)(1), 'felony offense' means any offense (federal, state, or local) punishable by imprisonment for a term exceeding one year, regardless of whether a criminal charge was brought, or a conviction obtained.

    (C) Meaning of 'Used'.—For purposes of subsection (b)(1), 'used' means the body armor was (i) actively employed in a manner to protect the person from gunfire; or (ii) used as a means of bartering. Subsection (b)(1) does not apply if the body armor was merely possessed. For example, subsection (b)(1) would not apply if the body armor was found in the trunk of a car but was not being actively used as protection.

2. Inapplicability of § 3B1.5.—If subsection (b)(1) applies, do not apply the adjustment in § 3B1.5 (Use of Body Armor in Drug Trafficking Crimes and Crimes of Violence).

3. Grouping of Multiple Counts.—If subsection (b)(1) applies (because the defendant used the body armor in connection with another felony offense) and the instant offense of conviction includes a count of conviction for that other felony offense, the counts of conviction for the 18 U.S.C. § 931 offense and that other felony offense shall be grouped pursuant to subsection (c) of § 3D1.2 (Groups of Closely Related Counts).".

The Commentary to § 3B1.5 captioned "Application Notes" is amended by adding at the end the following:

"3. Interaction with § 2K2.6 and Other Counts of Conviction.—If the defendant is convicted only of 18 U.S.C. § 931 and receives an enhancement under subsection (b)(1) of § 2K2.6 (Possessing, Purchasing, or Owning Body Armor by Violent Felons), do not apply an adjustment under this guideline. However, if, in addition to the count of conviction under 18 U.S.C. § 931, the defendant (A) is convicted of an offense that is a drug trafficking crime or a crime of violence; and (B) used the body armor with respect to that offense, an adjustment under this guideline shall apply with respect to that offense.".

Reason for Amendment: This amendment addresses the new offense at 18 U.S.C. § 931, which was created by section 11009 of the 21st Century Department of Justice Appropriations Authorization Act, Pub. L. 107–273. Section 931 of title 18, United States Code, prohibits the purchase, ownership, or possession of body armor by individuals who have been convicted of either a federal or state felony that is a crime of violence. The statutory maximum term of imprisonment for 18 U.S.C. § 931 is three years.

This amendment creates a new guideline at § 2K2.6 (Possessing, Purchasing, or Owning Body Armor by Violent Felons) because there is no guideline that covers conduct sufficiently analogous to the conduct constituting a violation of 18 U.S.C. § 931.

The new guideline provides a base offense level of 10 because 18 U.S.C. § 931 offenses have lesser statutory maximum punishments than offenses involving weapon possession and trafficking. Those offenses, which are sentenced at § 2K2.1 (Unlawful Receipt, Possession, or Transportation of Firearms or Ammunition; Prohibited Transactions Involving Firearms or Ammunition), have a base offense level of 12 if there is no aggravating circumstance present in the case.

The new guideline provides a four-level increase at § 2K2.6(b)(1) "[i]f the defendant used the body armor in connection with another felony offense" because violations in which the body armor was used in connection with another felony offense are more serious than those involving only possession, purchase, or ownership of body armor. "Felony offense" is defined as "any offense (federal, state, or local) punishable by imprisonment for a term exceeding one year" and does not require that a charge be brought or a conviction sustained.

The commentary also provides guidance for the scope of the terms "defendant" and "used" for purposes of § 2K2.6(b)(1). Use of the term "defendant" limits the accountability of the defendant to the defendant's own conduct and conduct that the defendant aided or abetted, counseled, commanded, induced, procured, or willfully caused. The term "used" requires that the body armor be actively used in order to protect from gunfire or be used as a means of bartering. Finally, the commentary provides that when subsection (b)(1) applies and the defendant also is convicted of the underlying offense (the offense with respect to which the body armor was used), the counts shall be grouped pursuant to subsection (c) of § 3D1.2 (Groups of Closely Related Counts).

Section 3B1.5 (Use of Body Armor in Drug Trafficking Crimes and Crimes of Violence) has been amended so that the adjustment in that guideline does not apply with respect to the 18 U.S.C. § 931 offense. However, if the defendant is convicted of the offense with respect to which the body armor was used, § 3B1.5 will apply to that offense.

Effective Date: The effective date of this amendment is November 1, 2004.

671. **Amendment:** Section 2L2.2(b) is amended by adding at the end the following:

> "(3) If the defendant fraudulently obtained or used a United States passport, increase by 4 levels.".

The Commentary to § 2L2.2 captioned "Application Notes" is amended by striking Note 1 as follows:

> "1. For purposes of this guideline—
>
> 'Immigration and naturalization offense' means any offense covered by Chapter Two, Part L.",

and inserting the following:

> "1. Definition.—For purposes of this guideline, 'immigration and naturalization offense' means any offense covered by Chapter Two, Part L.";

by striking Note 2 as follows:

> "2. For the purposes of Chapter Three, Part D (Multiple Counts), a conviction for unlawfully entering or remaining in the United States (§ 2L1.2) arising from the same course of conduct is treated as a closely related count, and is therefore grouped with an offense covered by this guideline.";

and redesignating Note 3 as Note 2; and in Note 2, as redesignated by this amendment, by inserting "Application of Subsection (b)(2).—" before "Prior".

The Commentary to § 2L2.2 captioned "Application Notes" is amended by adding at the end the following:

> "3. Application of Subsection (b)(3).—The term 'used' is to be construed broadly and includes the attempted renewal of previously-issued passports.
>
> 4. Multiple Counts.—For the purposes of Chapter Three, Part D (Multiple Counts), a count of conviction for unlawfully entering or remaining in the United States covered by § 2L1.2 (Unlawfully Entering or Remaining in the United States) arising from the same course of conduct as the count of conviction covered by this guideline shall be considered a closely related count to the count of conviction covered by this guideline, and therefore is to be grouped with the count of conviction covered by this guideline.
>
> 5. Upward Departure Provision.—If the defendant fraudulently obtained or used a United States passport for the purpose of entering the United States to engage in terrorist activity, an upward departure may be warranted. See Application Note 4 of the Commentary to § 3A1.4 (Terrorism).".

Reason for Amendment: The purpose of this amendment is to provide increased punishment for defendants who fraudulently use or obtain United States passports. The amendment adds a new specific offense characteristic at subsection (b)(3) of § 2L2.2 (Smuggling, Transporting, or Harboring an Unlawful Alien) that provides an increase of four levels if the defendant fraudulently obtained or used a United States passport. Application Note 3 clarifies that "use" is to be construed broadly and includes the attempted renewal of a previously issued United States passport. Application Note 5 invites an upward departure if the defendant fraudulently obtained or used a United States passport with the intent to engage in terrorist activity.

This amendment responds to comments received from the Departments of State and Justice to the effect that maintaining the integrity of United States passports is at the core of United States border and security efforts. Accordingly, this amendment ensures increased

Amendment 671

punishment for those defendants who threaten the security of the United States by their fraudulent abuse of United States passports.

Effective Date: The effective date of this amendment is November 1, 2004.

672. **Amendment:** Section 2Q1.2(b) is amended by adding at the end the following:

> "(7) If the defendant was convicted under 49 U.S.C. § 5124 or § 46312, increase by 2 levels.".

The Commentary to § 2Q1.2 captioned "Statutory Provisions" is amended by striking "; 49 U.S.C. § 60123(d)" and inserting "; 49 U.S.C. §§ 5124, 46312".

The Commentary to § 2Q1.2 captioned "Application Notes" is amended by striking Note 9 as follows:

> "9. Where a defendant has previously engaged in similar misconduct established by a civil adjudication or has failed to comply with an administrative order, an upward departure may be warranted. See § 4A1.3 (Adequacy of Criminal History Category).",

and inserting the following:

> "9. Other Upward Departure Provisions.—
>
> (A) Civil Adjudications and Failure to Comply with Administrative Order.—In a case in which the defendant has previously engaged in similar misconduct established by a civil adjudication or has failed to comply with an administrative order, an upward departure may be warranted. See § 4A1.3 (Departures Based on Inadequacy of Criminal History Category).
>
> (B) Extreme Psychological Injury.—If the offense caused extreme psychological injury, an upward departure may be warranted. See § 5K2.3 (Extreme Psychological Injury).
>
> (C) Terrorism.—If the offense was calculated to influence or affect the conduct of government by intimidation or coercion, or to retaliate against government conduct, an upward departure would be warranted. See Application Note 4 of the Commentary to § 3A1.4 (Terrorism).".

Reason for Amendment: This amendment adds a two-level enhancement in § 2Q1.2 (Mishandling of Hazardous or Toxic Substances or Pesticides; Recordkeeping, Tampering, and Falsification; Unlawfully Transporting Hazardous Materials in Commerce) for offenders convicted under 49 U.S.C. § 5124 or § 46312. These offenses pose an inherent risk to large populations in a manner not typically associated with other pollution offenses sentenced under the same guideline.

In addition, this amendment adds an application note inviting an upward departure if the offense was calculated to influence or affect the conduct of the government by intimidation or coercion, or to retaliate against government conduct. The Commission added this departure provision to address concerns that terrorists may commit hazardous material transportation offenses because of their potential to cause a one-time, catastrophic event. The upward departure provision would apply in cases in which a defendant who has a terrorist motive is not also convicted of a "federal crime of terrorism" that would trigger application of § 3A1.4 (Terrorism).

This amendment also adds an upward departure provision that could apply if the offense resulted in extreme psychological injury. This provision conforms to the upward departure provision found at § 2Q1.4 (Tampering or Attempted Tampering with a Public Water System; Threatening to Tamper with a Public Water System).

Effective Date: The effective date of this amendment is November 1, 2004.

673. **Amendment:** Chapter Eight is amended by striking the "Introductory Commentary" as follows:

"   Introductory Commentary

The guidelines and policy statements in this chapter apply when the convicted defendant is an organization. Organizations can act only through agents and, under federal criminal law, generally are vicariously liable for offenses committed by their agents. At the same time, individual agents are responsible for their own criminal conduct. Federal prosecutions of organizations therefore frequently involve individual and organizational co-defendants. Convicted individual agents of organizations are sentenced in accordance with the guidelines and policy statements in the preceding chapters. This chapter is designed so that the sanctions imposed upon organizations and their agents, taken together, will provide just punishment, adequate deterrence, and incentives for organizations to maintain internal mechanisms for preventing, detecting, and reporting criminal conduct.

This chapter reflects the following general principles: First, the court must, whenever practicable, order the organization to remedy any harm caused by the offense. The resources expended to remedy the harm should not be viewed as punishment, but rather as a means of making victims whole for the harm caused. Second, if the organization operated primarily for a criminal purpose or primarily by criminal means, the fine should be set sufficiently high to divest the organization of all its assets. Third, the fine range for any other organization should be based on the seriousness of the offense and the culpability of the organization. The seriousness of the offense generally will be reflected by the highest of the pecuniary gain, the pecuniary loss, or the amount in a guideline offense level fine table. Culpability generally will be determined by the steps taken by the organization prior to the offense to prevent and detect criminal conduct, the level and extent of involvement in or tolerance of the offense by certain personnel, and the organization's actions after an offense has been committed. Fourth, probation is an appropriate sentence for an organizational defendant when needed to ensure that another sanction will be fully implemented, or to ensure that steps will be taken within the organization to reduce the likelihood of future criminal conduct.",

and inserting the following:

"   Introductory Commentary

The guidelines and policy statements in this chapter apply when the convicted defendant is an organization. Organizations can act only through agents and, under federal criminal law, generally are vicariously liable for offenses committed by their agents. At the same time, individual agents are responsible for their own criminal conduct. Federal prosecutions of organizations therefore frequently involve individual and organizational co-defendants. Convicted individual agents of organizations are sentenced in accordance with the guidelines and policy statements in the pre-

Amendment 673

ceding chapters. This chapter is designed so that the sanctions imposed upon organizations and their agents, taken together, will provide just punishment, adequate deterrence, and incentives for organizations to maintain internal mechanisms for preventing, detecting, and reporting criminal conduct.

This chapter reflects the following general principles:

First, the court must, whenever practicable, order the organization to remedy any harm caused by the offense. The resources expended to remedy the harm should not be viewed as punishment, but rather as a means of making victims whole for the harm caused.

Second, if the organization operated primarily for a criminal purpose or primarily by criminal means, the fine should be set sufficiently high to divest the organization of all its assets.

Third, the fine range for any other organization should be based on the seriousness of the offense and the culpability of the organization. The seriousness of the offense generally will be reflected by the greatest of the pecuniary gain, the pecuniary loss, or the amount in a guideline offense level fine table. Culpability generally will be determined by six factors that the sentencing court must consider. The four factors that increase the ultimate punishment of an organization are: (i) the involvement in or tolerance of criminal activity; (ii) the prior history of the organization; (iii) the violation of an order; and (iv) the obstruction of justice. The two factors that mitigate the ultimate punishment of an organization are: (i) the existence of an effective compliance and ethics program; and (ii) self-reporting, cooperation, or acceptance of responsibility.

Fourth, probation is an appropriate sentence for an organizational defendant when needed to ensure that another sanction will be fully implemented, or to ensure that steps will be taken within the organization to reduce the likelihood of future criminal conduct.

These guidelines offer incentives to organizations to reduce and ultimately eliminate criminal conduct by providing a structural foundation from which an organization may self-police its own conduct through an effective compliance and ethics program. The prevention and detection of criminal conduct, as facilitated by an effective compliance and ethics program, will assist an organization in encouraging ethical conduct and in complying fully with all applicable laws.".

Section 8A1.2(a) is amended by inserting ", Subpart 1" after "Part B".

Section 8A1.2(b)(2)(D) is amended by adding at the end the following:

"To determine whether the organization had an effective compliance and ethics program for purposes of § 8C2.5(f), apply § 8B2.1 (Effective Compliance and Ethics Program).".

The Commentary to § 8A1.2 captioned "Application Notes" is amended in Note 3(c) in the second sentence by inserting "of the organization" after "high-level personnel".

The Commentary to § 8A1.2 captioned "Application Notes" is amended by striking Note 3(k) as follows:

"(k) An 'effective program to prevent and detect violations of law' means a program that has been reasonably designed, implemented, and enforced so that it generally will be effective in preventing and detecting criminal conduct. Failure to prevent or detect the instant offense, by itself, does not mean that the program was not effective. The hallmark of an effective program to prevent and detect violations of law is that the organization exercised due diligence in seeking to prevent and detect criminal conduct by its employees and other agents. Due diligence requires at a minimum that the organization must have taken the following types of steps:

(1) The organization must have established compliance standards and procedures to be followed by its employees and other agents that are reasonably capable of reducing the prospect of criminal conduct.

(2) Specific individual(s) within high-level personnel of the organization must have been assigned overall responsibility to oversee compliance with such standards and procedures.

(3) The organization must have used due care not to delegate substantial discretionary authority to individuals whom the organization knew, or should have known through the exercise of due diligence, had a propensity to engage in illegal activities.

(4) The organization must have taken steps to communicate effectively its standards and procedures to all employees and other agents, e.g., by requiring participation in training programs or by disseminating publications that explain in a practical manner what is required.

(5) The organization must have taken reasonable steps to achieve compliance with its standards, e.g., by utilizing monitoring and auditing systems reasonably designed to detect criminal conduct by its employees and other agents and by having in place and publicizing a reporting system whereby employees and other agents could report criminal conduct by others within the organization without fear of retribution.

(6) The standards must have been consistently enforced through appropriate disciplinary mechanisms, including, as appropriate, discipline of individuals responsible for the failure to detect an offense. Adequate discipline of individuals responsible for an offense is a necessary component of enforcement; however, the form of discipline that will be appropriate will be case specific.

(7) After an offense has been detected, the organization must have taken all reasonable steps to respond appropriately to the offense and to prevent further similar offenses -- including any necessary modifications to its program to prevent and detect violations of law.

The precise actions necessary for an effective program to prevent and detect violations of law will depend upon a number of factors. Among the relevant factors are:

(i) Size of the organization -- The requisite degree of formality of a program to prevent and detect violations of law will vary with the size of the organization: the larger the organization, the more formal the program typically should be. A larger organization

Amendment 673 APPENDIX C - VOLUME III November 1, 2013

                    generally should have established written policies defining the standards and procedures to be followed by its employees and other agents.

(ii)   Likelihood that certain offenses may occur because of the nature of its business-- If because of the nature of an organization's business there is a substantial risk that certain types of offenses may occur, management must have taken steps to prevent and detect those types of offenses. For example, if an organization handles toxic substances, it must have established standards and procedures designed to ensure that those substances are properly handled at all times. If an organization employs sales personnel who have flexibility in setting prices, it must have established standards and procedures designed to prevent and detect price-fixing. If an organization employs sales personnel who have flexibility to represent the material characteristics of a product, it must have established standards and procedures designed to prevent fraud.

(iii)   Prior history of the organization -- An organization's prior history may indicate types of offenses that it should have taken actions to prevent. Recurrence of misconduct similar to that which an organization has previously committed casts doubt on whether it took all reasonable steps to prevent such misconduct. An organization's failure to incorporate and follow applicable industry practice or the standards called for by any applicable governmental regulation weighs against a finding of an effective program to prevent and detect violations of law.".

Chapter Eight, Part B is amended by striking the heading as follows:

"PART B - REMEDYING HARM FROM CRIMINAL CONDUCT",

and inserting the following:

"PART B - REMEDYING HARM FROM CRIMINAL CONDUCT, AND EFFECTIVE COMPLIANCE AND ETHICS PROGRAM

1.   REMEDYING HARM FROM CRIMINAL CONDUCT";

and by adding at the end the following new subpart:

"2.   EFFECTIVE COMPLIANCE AND ETHICS PROGRAM

§ 8B2.1.   <u>Effective Compliance and Ethics Program</u>

(a)   To have an effective compliance and ethics program, for purposes of subsection (f) of § 8C2.5 (Culpability Score) and subsection (c)(1) of § 8D1.4 (Recommended Conditions of Probation - Organizations), an organization shall—

(1)   exercise due diligence to prevent and detect criminal conduct; and

(2)   otherwise promote an organizational culture that encour-

ages ethical conduct and a commitment to compliance with the law.

Such compliance and ethics program shall be reasonably designed, implemented, and enforced so that the program is generally effective in preventing and detecting criminal conduct. The failure to prevent or detect the instant offense does not necessarily mean that the program is not generally effective in preventing and detecting criminal conduct.

(b) Due diligence and the promotion of an organizational culture that encourages ethical conduct and a commitment to compliance with the law within the meaning of subsection (a) minimally require the following:

(1) The organization shall establish standards and procedures to prevent and detect criminal conduct.

(2) (A) The organization's governing authority shall be knowledgeable about the content and operation of the compliance and ethics program and shall exercise reasonable oversight with respect to the implementation and effectiveness of the compliance and ethics program.

(B) High-level personnel of the organization shall ensure that the organization has an effective compliance and ethics program, as described in this guideline. Specific individual(s) within high-level personnel shall be assigned overall responsibility for the compliance and ethics program.

(C) Specific individual(s) within the organization shall be delegated day-today operational responsibility for the compliance and ethics program. Individual(s) with operational responsibility shall report periodically to high-level personnel and, as appropriate, to the governing authority, or an appropriate subgroup of the governing authority, on the effectiveness of the compliance and ethics program. To carry out such operational responsibility, such individual(s) shall be given adequate resources, appropriate authority, and direct access to the governing authority or an appropriate subgroup of the governing authority.

(3) The organization shall use reasonable efforts not to include within the substantial authority personnel of the organization any individual whom the organization knew, or should have known through the exercise of due diligence, has engaged in illegal activities or other conduct inconsistent with an effective compliance and ethics program.

(4) (A) The organization shall take reasonable steps to communicate periodically and in a practical manner its standards and procedures, and other aspects of the compliance and ethics program, to the indi-

viduals referred to in subdivision (B) by conducting effective training programs and otherwise disseminating information appropriate to such individuals' respective roles and responsibilities.

  (B) The individuals referred to in subdivision (A) are the members of the governing authority, high-level personnel, substantial authority personnel, the organization's employees, and, as appropriate, the organization's agents.

 (5) The organization shall take reasonable steps—

  (A) to ensure that the organization's compliance and ethics program is followed, including monitoring and auditing to detect criminal conduct;

  (B) to evaluate periodically the effectiveness of the organization's compliance and ethics program; and

  (C) to have and publicize a system, which may include mechanisms that allow for anonymity or confidentiality, whereby the organization's employees and agents may report or seek guidance regarding potential or actual criminal conduct without fear of retaliation.

 (6) The organization's compliance and ethics program shall be promoted and enforced consistently throughout the organization through (A) appropriate incentives to perform in accordance with the compliance and ethics program; and (B) appropriate disciplinary measures for engaging in criminal conduct and for failing to take reasonable steps to prevent or detect criminal conduct.

 (7) After criminal conduct has been detected, the organization shall take reasonable steps to respond appropriately to the criminal conduct and to prevent further similar criminal conduct, including making any necessary modifications to the organization's compliance and ethics program.

(c) In implementing subsection (b), the organization shall periodically assess the risk of criminal conduct and shall take appropriate steps to design, implement, or modify each requirement set forth in subsection (b) to reduce the risk of criminal conduct identified through this process.

Commentary

Application Notes:

1. <u>Definitions</u>.—For purposes of this guideline:

 'Compliance and ethics program' means a program designed to prevent and detect criminal conduct.

'Governing authority' means the (A) the Board of Directors; or (B) if the organization does not have a Board of Directors, the highest-level governing body of the organization.

'High-level personnel of the organization' and 'substantial authority personnel' have the meaning given those terms in the Commentary to § 8A1.2 (Application Instructions - Organizations).

'Standards and procedures' means standards of conduct and internal controls that are reasonably capable of reducing the likelihood of criminal conduct.

2. <u>Factors to Consider in Meeting Requirements of this Guideline.</u>—

    (A)   <u>In General</u>.—Each of the requirements set forth in this guideline shall be met by an organization; however, in determining what specific actions are necessary to meet those requirements, factors that shall be considered include: (i) applicable industry practice or the standards called for by any applicable governmental regulation; (ii) the size of the organization; and (iii) similar misconduct.

    (B)   <u>Applicable Governmental Regulation and Industry Practice</u>.—An organization's failure to incorporate and follow applicable industry practice or the standards called for by any applicable governmental regulation weighs against a finding of an effective compliance and ethics program.

    (C)   <u>The Size of the Organization</u>.—

        (i)   <u>In General</u>.—The formality and scope of actions that an organization shall take to meet the requirements of this guideline, including the necessary features of the organization's standards and procedures, depend on the size of the organization.

        (ii)   <u>Large Organizations</u>.—A large organization generally shall devote more formal operations and greater resources in meeting the requirements of this guideline than shall a small organization. As appropriate, a large organization should encourage small organizations (especially those that have, or seek to have, a business relationship with the large organization) to implement effective compliance and ethics programs.

        (iii)   <u>Small Organizations</u>.—In meeting the requirements of this guideline, small organizations shall demonstrate the same degree of commitment to ethical conduct and compliance with the law as large organizations. However, a small organization may meet the requirements of this guideline with less formality and fewer resources than would be expected of large organizations. In appropriate circumstances, reliance on existing resources and simple systems can demonstrate a degree of commitment that, for a large organization, would only be demonstrated through more formally planned and implemented systems.

Examples of the informality and use of fewer resources with which a small organization may meet the requirements of this guideline include the following: (I) the governing authority's discharge of its responsibility for oversight of the compliance and ethics program by directly managing the organization's compliance and ethics efforts; (II) training employees through informal staff meetings, and monitoring through regular 'walk-arounds' or continuous observation while managing the organization; (III) using available personnel, rather than employing separate staff, to carry out the compliance and ethics program; and (IV) modeling its own compliance and ethics program on existing, well-regarded compliance and ethics programs and best practices of other similar organizations.

(D) Recurrence of Similar Misconduct.—Recurrence of similar misconduct creates doubt regarding whether the organization took reasonable steps to meet the requirements of this guideline. For purposes of this subdivision, 'similar misconduct' has the meaning given that term in the Commentary to § 8A1.2 (Application Instructions - Organizations).

3. Application of Subsection (b)(2).—High-level personnel and substantial authority personnel of the organization shall be knowledgeable about the content and operation of the compliance and ethics program, shall perform their assigned duties consistent with the exercise of due diligence, and shall promote an organizational culture that encourages ethical conduct and a commitment to compliance with the law.

If the specific individual(s) assigned overall responsibility for the compliance and ethics program does not have day-to-day operational responsibility for the program, then the individual(s) with day-to-day operational responsibility for the program typically should, no less than annually, give the governing authority or an appropriate subgroup thereof information on the implementation and effectiveness of the compliance and ethics program.

4. Application of Subsection (b)(3).—

(A) Consistency with Other Law.—Nothing in subsection (b)(3) is intended to require conduct inconsistent with any Federal, State, or local law, including any law governing employment or hiring practices.

(B) Implementation.—In implementing subsection (b)(3), the organization shall hire and promote individuals so as to ensure that all individuals within the high-level personnel and substantial authority personnel of the organization will perform their assigned duties in a manner consistent with the exercise of due diligence and the promotion of an organizational culture that encourages ethical conduct and a commitment to compliance with the law under subsection (a). With respect to the hiring or promotion of such individuals, an organization shall consider the relatedness of the individual's illegal activities and other misconduct (i.e., other conduct inconsistent with an effective compliance and ethics program) to the specific responsibilities the individual is anticipated to be assigned and other factors such as: (i) the recency of the individual's illegal activities and other misconduct; and (ii) whether the individual has engaged in other such illegal activities and other such misconduct.

5. Application of Subsection (b)(6).—Adequate discipline of individuals responsible for an offense is a necessary component of enforcement; however, the form of discipline that will be appropriate will be case specific.

6. Application of Subsection (c).—To meet the requirements of subsection (c), an organization shall:

   (A) Assess periodically the risk that criminal conduct will occur, including assessing the following:

      (i) The nature and seriousness of such criminal conduct.

      (ii) The likelihood that certain criminal conduct may occur because of the nature of the organization's business. If, because of the nature of an organization's business, there is a substantial risk that certain types of criminal conduct may occur, the organization shall take reasonable steps to prevent and detect that type of criminal conduct. For example, an organization that, due to the nature of its business, employs sales personnel who have flexibility to set prices shall establish standards and procedures designed to prevent and detect price-fixing. An organization that, due to the nature of its business, employs sales personnel who have flexibility to represent the material characteristics of a product shall establish standards and procedures designed to prevent and detect fraud.

      (iii) The prior history of the organization. The prior history of an organization may indicate types of criminal conduct that it shall take actions to prevent and detect.

   (B) Prioritize periodically, as appropriate, the actions taken pursuant to any requirement set forth in subsection (b), in order to focus on preventing and detecting the criminal conduct identified under subdivision (A) of this note as most serious, and most likely, to occur.

   (C) Modify, as appropriate, the actions taken pursuant to any requirement set forth in subsection (b) to reduce the risk of criminal conduct identified under subdivision (A) of this note as most serious, and most likely, to occur.

Background: This section sets forth the requirements for an effective compliance and ethics program. This section responds to section 805(a)(2)(5) of the Sarbanes-Oxley Act of 2002, Public Law 107–204, which directed the Commission to review and amend, as appropriate, the guidelines and related policy statements to ensure that the guidelines that apply to organizations in this chapter 'are sufficient to deter and punish organizational criminal misconduct.'

Amendment 673

The requirements set forth in this guideline are intended to achieve reasonable prevention and detection of criminal conduct for which the organization would be vicariously liable. The prior diligence of an organization in seeking to prevent and detect criminal conduct has a direct bearing on the appropriate penalties and probation terms for the organization if it is convicted and sentenced for a criminal offense.".

The Commentary to § 8C2.4 captioned "Application Notes" is amended in Note 2 by striking "(Larceny, Embezzlement, and Other Forms of Theft)" and inserting "(Theft, Property Destruction, and Fraud)".

Section 8C2.5 is amended by striking subsection (f) as follows:

"(f) Effective Program to Prevent and Detect Violations of Law

If the offense occurred despite an effective program to prevent and detect violations of law, subtract 3 points.

Provided, that this subsection does not apply if an individual within high-level personnel of the organization, a person within high-level personnel of the unit of the organization within which the offense was committed where the unit had 200 or more employees, or an individual responsible for the administration or enforcement of a program to prevent and detect violations of law participated in, condoned, or was willfully ignorant of the offense. Participation of an individual within substantial authority personnel in an offense results in a rebuttable presumption that the organization did not have an effective program to prevent and detect violations of law.

Provided, further, that this subsection does not apply if, after becoming aware of an offense, the organization unreasonably delayed reporting the offense to appropriate governmental authorities.",

and inserting the following:

"(f) Effective Compliance and Ethics Program

(1) If the offense occurred even though the organization had in place at the time of the offense an effective compliance and ethics program, as provided in § 8B2.1 (Effective Compliance and Ethics Program), subtract 3 points.

(2) Subsection (f)(1) shall not apply if, after becoming aware of an offense, the organization unreasonably delayed reporting the offense to appropriate governmental authorities.

(3) (A) Except as provided in subdivision (B), subsection (f)(1) shall not apply if an individual within high-level personnel of the organization, a person within high-level personnel of the unit of the organization within which the offense was committed where the unit had 200 or more employees, or an individual described in § 8B2.1(b)(2)(B) or (C), participated in, condoned, or was willfully ignorant of the offense.

(B) There is a rebuttable presumption, for purposes of subsection (f)(1), that the organization did not have an effective compliance and ethics program if an individual—

> (i) within high-level personnel of a small organization; or
>
> (ii) within substantial authority personnel, but not within high-level personnel, of any organization,
>
> participated in, condoned, or was willfully ignorant of, the offense.".

The Commentary to § 8C2.5 captioned "Application Notes" is amended by striking Note 1 as follows:

> "1. 'Substantial authority personnel,' 'condoned,' 'willfully ignorant of the offense,' 'similar misconduct,' 'prior criminal adjudication,' and 'effective program to prevent and detect violations of law,' are defined in the Commentary to § 8A1.2 (Application Instructions - Organizations).",

and inserting the following:

> "1. Definitions.—For purposes of this guideline, 'condoned', 'prior criminal adjudication', 'similar misconduct', 'substantial authority personnel', and 'willfully ignorant of the offense' have the meaning given those terms in Application Note 3 of the Commentary to § 8A1.2 (Application Instructions - Organizations).
>
> 'Small Organization', for purposes of subsection (f)(3), means an organization that, at the time of the instant offense, had fewer than 200 employees.".

The Commentary to § 8C2.5 captioned "Application Notes" is amended in Note 3 in the last sentence by striking "entire organization" and inserting "organization in its entirety".

The Commentary to § 8C2.5 captioned "Application Notes" is amended in Note 10 by striking "The second proviso in subsection (f)" and inserting "Subsection (f)(2)"; and by striking "this proviso" and inserting "subsection (f)(2)".

The Commentary to § 8C2.5 captioned "Application Notes" is amended in Note 12 by adding at the end the following:

> "Waiver of attorney-client privilege and of work product protections is not a prerequisite to a reduction in culpability score under subdivisions (1) and (2) of subsection (g) unless such waiver is necessary in order to provide timely and thorough disclosure of all pertinent information known to the organization.".

Section 8C2.8(a) is amended in subdivision (9) by striking "and"; in subdivision (10) by striking the period at the end of the subdivision and inserting "; and"; and by adding at the end the following:

> "(11) whether the organization failed to have, at the time of the instant offense, an effective compliance and ethics program within the meaning of § 8B2.1 (Effective Compliance and Ethics Program).".

The Commentary to § 8C2.8 captioned "Application Notes" is amended in Note 4 in the first sentence by inserting "within high-level personnel of" after "organization or".

Amendment 673 APPENDIX C - VOLUME III November 1, 2013

Section 8C4.10 is amended by striking "(Effective Program to Prevent and Detect Violations of Law)" and inserting "(Effective Compliance and Ethics Program)"; and by adding at the end the following paragraph:

"Similarly, if, at the time of the instant offense, the organization was required by law to have an effective compliance and ethics program, but the organization did not have such a program, an upward departure may be warranted.".

Chapter Eight, Part D, is amended in the "Introductory Commentary" by striking "8D1.5" and inserting "8D1.4, and § 8F1.1,".

Section 8D1.1(a) is amended by striking subdivision (3) as follows:

"(3) if, at the time of sentencing, an organization having 50 or more employees does not have an effective program to prevent and detect violations of law;",

and inserting the following:

"(3) if, at the time of sentencing, (A) the organization (i) has 50 or more employees, or (ii) was otherwise required under law to have an effective compliance and ethics program; and (B) the organization does not have such a program;".

Section 8D1.4(b)(4) is amended by striking "(1)" and inserting "(A)"; by striking "(2)" and inserting "(B)"; and by striking "(3)" and inserting "(C)".

Section 8D1.4(c) is amended by striking subdivision (1) as follows:

"(1) The organization shall develop and submit to the court a program to prevent and detect violations of law, including a schedule for implementation.",

and inserting the following:

"(1) The organization shall develop and submit to the court an effective compliance and ethics program consistent with § 8B2.1 (Effective Compliance and Ethics Program). The organization shall include in its submission a schedule for implementation of the compliance and ethics program.";

and in subdivisions (2), (3), and (4) by striking "to prevent and detect violations of law" each place it appears and inserting "referred to in subdivision (1)".

The Commentary to § 8D1.4 captioned "Application Notes" is amended by striking "Notes" in the heading and inserting "Note"; and in Note 1 by striking "a program to prevent and detect violations of law" and inserting "a compliance and ethics program"; and by striking the last sentence of the first paragraph as follows:

"The court should approve any program that appears reasonably calculated to prevent and detect violations of law, provided it is consistent with any applicable statutory or regulatory requirement.",

and inserting the following:

"The court should approve any program that appears reasonably calculated to prevent and detect criminal conduct, as long as it is consistent with § 8B2.1 (Effective Compliance and Ethics Program), and any applicable statutory and regulatory requirements.".

Chapter Eight, Part D is amended by striking § 8D1.5 and its accompanying commentary as follows:

> "§ 8D1.5. <u>Violations of Conditions of Probation - Organizations</u> (Policy Statement)
>
> Upon a finding of a violation of a condition of probation, the court may extend the term of probation, impose more restrictive conditions of probation, or revoke probation and resentence the organization.
>
> Commentary
>
> Application Note:
>
> 1. In the event of repeated, serious violations of conditions of probation, the appointment of a master or trustee may be appropriate to ensure compliance with court orders.".

Chapter Eight is amended by adding at the end the following Part:

> "PART F - VIOLATIONS OF PROBATION - ORGANIZATIONS
>
> § 8F1.1. <u>Violations of Conditions of Probation - Organizations</u> (Policy Statement)
>
> Upon a finding of a violation of a condition of probation, the court may extend the term of probation, impose more restrictive conditions of probation, or revoke probation and resentence the organization.
>
> Commentary
>
> Application Notes:
>
> 1. <u>Appointment of Master or Trustee</u>.—In the event of repeated violations of conditions of probation, the appointment of a master or trustee may be appropriate to ensure compliance with court orders.
>
> 2. <u>Conditions of Probation</u>.—Mandatory and recommended conditions of probation are specified in §§ 8D1.3 (Conditions of Probation - Organizations) and 8D1.4 (Recommended Conditions of Probation - Organizations).".

Reason for Amendment: This amendment modifies existing provisions of Chapter Eight and provides a new guideline at § 8B2.1 (Effective Compliance and Ethics Program). Most notably, § 8B2.1 strengthens the existing criteria an organization must follow in order to establish and maintain an effective program to prevent and detect criminal conduct for purposes of mitigating its sentencing culpability for an offense. This amendment is the culmination of a multi-year review of the organizational guidelines, implements several recommendations issued on October 7, 2003, by the Commission's Ad Hoc Advisory Group on the Organizational Sentencing Guidelines (Advisory Group), and responds to the Sarbanes-Oxley Act ("the Act"), Pub. L. 107–204, which in section 805 directed the Commission to review and amend the organizational guidelines and related policy statements to ensure that they are sufficient to deter and punish organizational misconduct.

Consistent with the Act's focus on deterring criminal misconduct, this amendment revises the introductory commentary to Chapter Eight to highlight the importance of structural safeguards designed to prevent and detect criminal conduct. First and foremost among these safeguards is a regime of internal crime prevention and self-policing ("an effective

Amendment 673   APPENDIX C - VOLUME III   November 1, 2013

compliance and ethics program"). While Chapter Eight derives its authority and content from the federal criminal law, an effective compliance and ethics program not only will prevent and detect criminal conduct, but also should facilitate compliance with all applicable laws.

Under § 8C2.5(g) (Culpability Score), an effective compliance and ethics program is one of the mitigating factors that can reduce an organization's fine punishment under Chapter Eight. The absence of an effective program may be a reason for the court to place an organization on probation, and the implementation of an effective program may be a condition of probation for organizations under § 8D1.4(c) (Recommended Conditions of Probation-Organizations).

In order to emphasize the importance of compliance and ethics programs and to provide more prominent guidance on the requirements for an effective program, the amendment elevates the criteria for an effective compliance program previously set forth in the Commentary to § 8A1.2 (Application Instructions - Organizations) into a separate guideline. Furthermore, the amendment elaborates upon these criteria, introducing additional rigor generally and imposing significantly greater responsibilities on the organization's governing authority and executive leadership.

Section 8B2.1(a)(1) sets forth the existing requirement that an organization exercise due diligence to prevent and detect criminal conduct, but adds the requirement that an organization "otherwise promote an organizational culture that encourages ethical conduct and a commitment to compliance with the law." This addition is intended to reflect the emphasis on ethical conduct and values incorporated into recent legislative and regulatory reforms, such as those provided by the Act.

Section 8B2.1(b) provides that due diligence and the promotion of desired organizational culture are indicated by the fulfilment of seven minimum requirements, which are the hallmarks of an effective program that encourages compliance with the law and ethical conduct. While the framework of requirements is derived from the existing criteria for an effective compliance program at Application Note 3(k) to § 8A1.2, significant additional guidance is provided.

First, § 8B2.1(b)(1) provides that organizations must establish "standards and procedures to prevent and detect criminal conduct." Application Note 1 establishes that "standards and procedures" encompass "standards of conduct and internal controls that are reasonably capable of reducing the likelihood of criminal conduct."

Second, the new guideline replaces the requirement in Application Note 3(k)(2) to § 8A1.2 that "specific individual(s) within high-level personnel of the organization must have been assigned overall responsibility to oversee compliance" with more specific and exacting requirements. Section 8B2.1(b)(2) defines the specific roles and reporting relationships of particular categories of personnel with respect to compliance and ethics program responsibilities. Specifically, the Commission has determined that the organization's governing authority must "be knowledgeable about the content and operation of the compliance and ethics program and shall exercise reasonable oversight with respect to the implementation and effectiveness of the compliance and ethics program." Application Note 1 defines "governing authority" as the "(A) Board of Directors, or (B) if the organization does not have a Board of Directors, the highest-level governing body of the organization."

Section 8B2.1(b)(2) provides that it is the organizational leadership, defined in the guidelines as "high-level personnel," who must ensure that the organization's program is effective. The accompanying commentary at Application Note 1 retains existing definitions for the terms "high-level personnel" and "substantial authority personnel" of the organization. Section 8B2.1(b)(2)(B) provides that the organization must assign someone in high-level personnel "overall responsibility" for the program. This prescription makes explicit that, while another individual or individuals may be assigned operational responsibility for the program, someone within high-level personnel must be assigned the ultimate responsibility for the program's effectiveness.

Section 8B2.1(b)(2)(C) requires that certain individual(s) have day-to-day responsibility for the compliance and ethics program and adequate resources to carry out the associated tasks. Specifically, § 8B2.1 requires that the individual assigned day-to-day operational responsibility for the program, whether it be a high-level person or an employee to whom this task is assigned, report to organizational leadership and the governing authority on the program. If authority is delegated, the governing authority must receive reports from such individuals at least annually, according to the commentary in Application Note 3. In order to carry out such responsibility, the new guideline mandates that such individual or individuals, no matter the level, must "be given adequate resources, appropriate authority, and direct access to the governing authority or an appropriate subgroup of the governing authority."

Third, § 8B2.1(b)(3) replaces the previous requirement that substantial authority personnel be screened for their "propensity to engage in violations of law" with the requirement that the organization "use reasonable efforts not to include within the substantial authority personnel of the organization any individual whom the organization knew, or should have known through the exercise of due diligence, has engaged in illegal activities or other conduct inconsistent with an effective compliance and ethics program." Application Note 4(A) makes explicit that this provision does not require any "conduct inconsistent with any Federal, State, or local law, including any law governing employment or hiring practices." Application Note 4(B) provides that the organization shall hire and promote individuals so as to ensure that all individuals within the organizational leadership will perform their assigned duties in a manner consistent with the exercise of due diligence and the promotion of an organizational culture that encourages a commitment to compliance with ethics and the law. If an individual has engaged in illegal activities, the organization has an obligation to consider the relatedness of the individual's illegal activities and other misconduct to the specific responsibilities such individual is expected to be assigned. The recency of the individual's illegal activities and other misconduct also should be considered.

Fourth, § 8B2.1(b)(4) makes compliance and ethics training a requirement, and specifically extends the training requirement to the upper levels of an organization, including the governing authority and high-level personnel, in addition to all of the organization's employees and agents, as appropriate. Furthermore, subsection (b)(4) establishes that this communication and training obligation is ongoing, requiring "periodic" updates.

Fifth, § 8B2.1(b)(5) expands the existing requirement regarding reasonable steps to achieve compliance. Specifically, the amendment mandates that organizations use auditing and monitoring systems designed to detect criminal conduct. It also adds the specific requirement that the organization periodically evaluate the effectiveness of its compliance and ethics program. Significantly, the new guideline expands the focus of internal reporting from simply reporting "the criminal conduct . . . of others" to using internal systems to either "report or seek guidance regarding potential or actual criminal conduct." The addition of "seeking guidance" is consistent with the increased focus of this guideline on the prevention and deterrence of wrongdoing within organizations. This section also replaces the existing reference to "reporting systems without fear of retribution" with the more specific requirement that the organization must have "a system, which may include mechanisms that allow for anonymity or confidentiality, whereby the organization's employees and agents may report or seek guidance regarding potential or actual criminal conduct without fear of retaliation."

The Commission is aware that both anonymous and confidential mechanisms have inherent value and limitations. For example, anonymous mechanisms may hinder an organization from engaging in an effective dialogue with the potential whistleblower to discover additional information that might lead to a more efficient detection of the wrongdoing. Confidential mechanisms may permit the dialogue and development of maximum information, but the ability of organizations to ensure total confidentiality may be limited by legal obligations relating to self-disclosure, law enforcement subpoenas, and civil discovery requests. The Commission intends for an organization to have maximum flexibility in implementing a system that is best suited to its culture and conforms to applicable law. A responsible organization is expected, as appropriate, to communicate to its employees any applicable limitations of its internal reporting mechanisms.

Sixth, § 8B2.1(b)(6) broadens the existing criterion that the compliance standards be enforced through disciplinary measures by adding that such standards also be encouraged through "appropriate incentives to perform in accordance with the compliance and ethics program." This addition articulates both a duty to promote proper conduct in whatever manner an organization deems appropriate, as well as a duty to sanction improper conduct.

Finally, § 8B2.1(b)(7) retains the requirement that an organization take reasonable steps to respond to and prevent further similar criminal conduct. This dual duty underscores the organization's obligation to address both specific instances of misconduct and systemic shortcomings that compromise the deterrent effect of its compliance and ethics program.

In addition to the seven requirements for a compliance and ethics program, § 8B2.1(c) expressly provides, as an essential component of the design, implementation, and modification of an effective program, that an organization must periodically assess the risk of the occurrence of criminal conduct. The new guideline includes at Application Note 6 various factors that should be addressed when assessing relevant risks. Specifically, organizations should evaluate the nature and seriousness of potential criminal conduct, the likelihood that certain criminal conduct may occur because of the nature of the organization's business, and the prior history of the organization. To be effective, this process must be ongoing. Organizations must periodically prioritize their compliance and ethics resources to target those potential criminal activities that pose the greatest threat in light of the risks identified.

The amendment also provides additional guidance with respect to the implementation of compliance and ethics programs by small organizations by including frequent references to small organizations throughout the commentary of § 8B2.1 and providing illustrations (see e.g., Application Note 2(C)(ii)). It also encourages larger organizations to promote the adoption of compliance and ethics programs by smaller organizations, including those with which they conduct or seek to conduct business.

This amendment also changes the automatic preclusion for compliance program credit provided in § 8C2.5(f) (Culpability Score) for "small organizations." A "small organization" is defined, for this subsection only, as an organization having fewer than 200 employees. This modification is intended to assist smaller organizations that previously may have been automatically precluded, because of their size, from arguing for a culpability score reduction based upon an effective compliance and ethics program that fulfills all of the guideline requirements. Rather than precluding absolutely these small organizations from obtaining the reduction if certain categories of high-level personnel are involved in the offense of conviction, § 8C2.5(f)(3) establishes that an offense by an individual within high-level personnel of the organization results in a rebuttable presumption for a small organization that it did not have an effective program. The small organization, however, can rebut that presumption by demonstrating that it had an effective program, despite the involvement in the offense of a person high in the organization's structure.

This amendment also addresses concerns about the relationship between obtaining credit under § 8C2.5(g) and waiver of the attorney-client privilege and the work product protection doctrine. Pursuant to § 8C2.5(g)(1) and (2), an organization's culpability score will be reduced if it "fully cooperated in the investigation" of its wrongdoing, among other factors. The Commission's Ad Hoc Advisory Group on the Organizational Sentencing Guidelines studied the relationship between waivers and § 8C2.5(g) by obtaining testimony and conducting its own research, including a survey of United States Attorneys' Offices (all of which are described at Part V of the Advisory Group Report of October 7, 2003). The Commission addresses some of these concerns by providing at Application Note 12 that waiver of the attorney-client privilege and of work product protections "is not a prerequisite to a reduction in culpability score under subdivisions (1) and (2) of subsection (g) unless such waiver is necessary in order to provide timely and thorough disclosure of all pertinent information known to the organization." The Commission expects that such waivers will be required on a limited basis. See "United States Attorneys' Bulletin", November 2003, Volume 51, Number 6, pp. 1, 8.

Effective Date: The effective date of this amendment is November 1, 2004.

674. **Amendment:** The Commentary to § 1B1.3 captioned "Application Notes" is amended in Note 5 by striking the fifth sentence as follows:

> "When not adequately taken into account by the applicable offense guideline, creation of a risk may provide a ground for imposing a sentence above the applicable guideline range.",

and inserting the following:

> "In a case in which creation of risk is not adequately taken into account by the applicable offense guideline, an upward departure may be warranted.".

The Commentary to § 1B1.4 captioned "Background" is amended in the fifth sentence by striking "sentencing above the guideline range" and inserting "an upward departure".

The Commentary to § 1B1.8 captioned "Application Notes" is amended in Note 1 in the third sentence by striking "increase the defendant's sentence above the applicable guideline range by upward departure" and inserting "depart upward"; and in the last sentence by striking "below the applicable guideline range" and inserting "downward".

Section 2B1.1(b)(10), as redesignated by Amendment 665, is amended in subdivision (A) by striking "device-making equipment" and inserting "(i) device-making equipment, or (ii) authentication feature"; in subdivision (B) by inserting "(i)" before "unauthorized access"; and by inserting ", or (ii) authentication feature" after "counterfeit access device"; and in subdivision (C)(i) by striking the semi-colon and inserting a comma.

The Commentary to § 2B1.1 captioned "Application Notes" is amended in Note 4 by striking subdivision (C)(ii), as redesignated by Amendment 665, as follows:

> "(ii) Special Rule.—A case described in subdivision (B)(i) of this note that

Amendment 674   APPENDIX C - VOLUME III   November 1, 2013

involved a Postal Service (I) relay box; (II) collection box; (III) delivery vehicle; or (IV) satchel or cart, shall be considered to have involved at least 50 victims.",

and inserting the following:

"(ii) Special Rule.—A case described in subdivision (C)(i) of this note that involved—

(I) a United States Postal Service relay box, collection box, delivery vehicle, satchel, or cart, shall be considered to have involved at least 50 victims.

(II) a housing unit cluster box or any similar receptacle that contains multiple mailboxes, whether such receptacle is owned by the United States Postal Service or otherwise owned, shall, unless proven otherwise, be presumed to have involved the number of victims corresponding to the number of mailboxes in each cluster box or similar receptacle.".

The Commentary to § 2B1.1 captioned "Application Notes" is amended in Note 7, as redesignated by Amendment 665, by striking "(b)(7)" each place it appears and inserting "(b)(8)"; and in Note 8, as redesignated by Amendment 665, by striking "(b)(8)" each place it appears and inserting "(b)(9)".

The Commentary to § 2B1.1 captioned "Application Notes" is amended in Note 9, as redesignated by Amendment 665, by striking "(b)(9)" each place it appears and inserting "(b)(10)"; in subdivision (A) by inserting before the paragraph that begins "'Counterfeit access device'" the following paragraph:

"'Authentication feature' has the meaning given that term in 18 U.S.C. § 1028(d)(1).";

in the paragraph that begins "'Means of identification'" by striking "(d)(4)" and inserting "(d)(7)"; and in subdivision (B) by inserting "Authentication Features and" before "Identification Documents."; and by inserting "authentication features," after "involving".

The Commentary § 2B1.1 captioned "Application Notes" is amended in Note 10, as redesignated by Amendment 665, by striking "(b)(10)" each place it appears and inserting "(b)(11)"; in Note 11, as redesignated by Amendment 665, by striking "(b)(12)" each place it appears and inserting "(b)(13)"; in Note 12, as redesignated by Amendment 665, by striking "(b)(12)" each place it appears and inserting "(b)(13)"; in Note 13, as redesignated by Amendment 665, by striking "(b)(13)" each place it appears and inserting "(b)(14)"; and by striking "(b)(12)(B)" each place it appears and inserting "(b)(13)(B)"; in Note 14, as redesignated by Amendment 665, by striking "(b)(14)" each place it appears and inserting "(b)(15)"; and in Note 19(B), as redesignated by Amendment 665, by striking "(b)(13)(iii)" and inserting "(b)(14)(iii)".

The Commentary to § 2B1.1 captioned "Background" is amended in the ninth paragraph by striking "Subsection (b)(7)(D)" and inserting "Subsection (b)(8)(D)"; in the tenth paragraph by striking "Subsection (b)(8)" and inserting "Subsection (b)(9)"; in the eleventh paragraph by striking "Subsections (b)(9)(A) and (B)" and inserting "Subsections (b)(10)(A)(i) and (B)(i)"; in the twelfth paragraph by striking "Subsection (b)(9)(C)" and inserting "Subsection (b)(10)(C)"; in the thirteenth paragraph by striking "Subsection (b)(11)(B)" and inserting "Subsection (b)(12)(B)"; in the fourteenth paragraph by striking

"Subsection (b)(12)(A)" and inserting "Subsection (b)(13)(A)"; in the fifteenth paragraph by striking "Subsection (b)(12)(B)" and inserting "Subsection (b)(13)(B)"; in the sixteenth paragraph by striking "Subsection (b)(13) implements" and inserting "Subsection (b)(14) implements"; and by striking "subsection (b)(13)(B)" and inserting "subsection (b)(14)(B)".

The Commentary to § 2D1.1 captioned "Application Notes" is amended in Note 7 by striking "sentence below the applicable guideline range" and inserting "downward departure".

The Commentary to § 2R1.1 captioned "Application Notes" is amended in Note 7 by striking ", or even above,"; and by inserting ", or an upward departure," after "guideline range".

The Commentary to § 2T1.8 captioned "Application Note" is amended in Note 1 by striking "a sentence above the guidelines" and inserting "an upward departure".

Chapter Two, Part T, Subpart 3, is amended in the "Introductory Commentary" by striking "imposing a sentence above that specified in the guideline in this Subpart" and inserting "departing upward".

Chapter Two, Part X is amended by adding at the end the following new Subpart:

"6. OFFENSES INVOLVING USE OF A MINOR IN A CRIME OF VIOLENCE

§ 2X6.1.   Use of a Minor in a Crime of Violence

(a)   Base Offense Level: 4 plus the offense level from the guideline applicable to the underlying crime of violence.

Commentary

Statutory Provision: 18 U.S.C. § 25.

Application Notes:

1. Definition.—For purposes of this guideline, 'underlying crime of violence' means the crime of violence as to which the defendant is convicted of using a minor.

2. Inapplicability of § 3B1.4.—Do not apply the adjustment under § 3B1.4 (Using a Minor to Commit a Crime).

3. Multiple Counts.—

    (A)   In a case in which the defendant is convicted under both 18 U.S.C. § 25 and the underlying crime of violence, the counts shall be grouped pursuant to subsection (a) of § 3D1.2 (Groups of Closely Related Counts).

    (B)   Multiple counts involving the use of a minor in a crime of violence shall not be grouped under § 3D1.2.".

The Commentary to § 3C1.1 captioned "Application Notes" is amended in Note 5(b) by striking "3(g)" and inserting "4(g)".

Amendment 674   APPENDIX C - VOLUME III   November 1, 2013

Section 3D1.2(d) is amended by striking the period after "2P1.3" and inserting a semi-colon; and by inserting after the line that begins "§§ 2P1.1," the following new line:

"§ 2X6.1.".

The Commentary to § 3D1.3 captioned "Application Notes" is amended in Note 4 by striking "a sentence above the guideline range" and inserting "an upward departure".

The Commentary to § 4B1.2 captioned "Application Notes" is amended in Note 1 in the first sentence of the paragraph that begins "'Crime of violence' does not include" by inserting ", unless the possession was of a firearm described in 26 U.S.C. § 5845(a)" before the period.

The Commentary to § 4B1.2 captioned "Application Notes" is amended in Note 1 by inserting before the paragraph that begins "Unlawfully possessing a prohibited flask" the following paragraph:

"Unlawfully possessing a firearm described in 26 U.S.C. § 5845(a) (e.g., a sawed-off shotgun or sawed-off rifle, silencer, bomb, or machine gun) is a 'crime of violence'.".

The Commentary to § 4B1.4 captioned "Application Note" is amended by striking "Note" in the heading and inserting "Notes"; and by adding at the end the following:

"2. Application of § 4B1.4 in Cases Involving Convictions Under 18 U.S.C. § 844(h), § 924(c), or § 929(a).—If a sentence under this guideline is imposed in conjunction with a sentence for a conviction under 18 U.S.C. § 844(h), § 924(c), or § 929(a), do not apply either subsection (b)(3)(A) or (c)(2). A sentence under 18 U.S.C. § 844(h), § 924(c), or § 929(a) accounts for the conduct covered by subsections (b)(3)(A) and (c)(2) because of the relatedness of the conduct covered by these subsections to the conduct that forms the basis for the conviction under 18 U.S.C. § 844(h), § 924(c), or § 929(a).

In a few cases, the rule provided in the preceding paragraph may result in a guideline range that, when combined with the mandatory consecutive sentence under 18 U.S.C. § 844(h), § 924(c), or § 929(a), produces a total maximum penalty that is less than the maximum of the guideline range that would have resulted had there not been a count of conviction under 18 U.S.C. § 844(h), § 924(c), or § 929(a) (i.e., the guideline range that would have resulted if subsections (b)(3)(A) and (c)(2) had been applied). In such a case, an upward departure may be warranted so that the conviction under 18 U.S.C. § 844(h), § 924(c), or § 929(a) does not result in a decrease in the total punishment. An upward departure under this paragraph shall not exceed the maximum of the guideline range that would have resulted had there not been a count of conviction under 18 U.S.C. § 844(h), § 924(c), or § 929(a).".

Section 5C1.2(a) is amended by striking "verbatim".

The Commentary to § 5G1.2 captioned "Application Notes" is amended in Note 3(B)(iii) in the first sentence by striking "2113(a) (20 year" and inserting "113(a)(3) (10 year"; in the second sentence by striking "400" and inserting "460", and by striking "360-life" and inserting "460-485 months"; and in the third sentence by striking "40" and inserting "100", and by striking "2113(a)" and inserting "113(a)(3)".

Section 5H1.1 is amended by striking "sentence should be outside the applicable guideline range" and inserting "departure is warranted"; by striking "impose a sentence below the applicable guideline range when" and inserting "depart downward in a case in which"; and by inserting "; Gambling Addiction" after "Abuse".

Section 5H1.2 is amended by striking "sentence should be outside the applicable guideline range" and inserting "departure is warranted".

Section 5H1.3 is amended by striking "sentence should be outside the applicable guideline range" and inserting "departure is warranted".

Section 5H1.5 is amended by striking "sentence should be outside the applicable guideline range" and inserting "departure is warranted".

Chapter Five, Part H is amended by striking § 5H1.6 as follows:

"§ 5H1.6. Family Ties and Responsibilities (Policy Statement)

Family ties and responsibilities are not ordinarily relevant in determining whether a departure may be warranted.

In sentencing a defendant convicted of an offense involving a minor victim under section 1201, an offense under section 1591, or an offense under chapter 71, 109A, 110, or 117, of title 18, United States Code, family ties and responsibilities and community ties are not relevant in determining whether a sentence should be below the applicable guideline range.*

Family responsibilities that are complied with may be relevant to the determination of the amount of restitution or fine.

*Note: Section 401(b)(4) of Public Law 108-21 (the "Protect Act") directly amended § 5H1.6 to add the second paragraph, effective April 30, 2003. The Commission incorporated this direct amendment in the Supplement to the 2002 Guidelines Manual but inadvertently omitted the second paragraph in the Federal Register notice of amendments dated October 21, 2003. The policy statement should be read as containing the second paragraph, pursuant to the direct amendment made by Public Law 108–21.",

and inserting the following:

"§ 5H1.6. Family Ties and Responsibilities (Policy Statement)

In sentencing a defendant convicted of an offense other than an offense described in the following paragraph, family ties and responsibilities are not ordinarily relevant in determining whether a departure may be warranted.

In sentencing a defendant convicted of an offense involving a minor victim under section 1201, an offense under section 1591, or an offense under chapter 71, 109A, 110, or 117, of title 18, United States Code, family ties and responsibilities and community ties are not relevant in determining whether a sentence should be below the applicable guideline range.

Family responsibilities that are complied with may be relevant to the determination of the amount of restitution or fine.".

The Commentary to § 5H1.6 is amended by adding at the end the following:

"Background: Section 401(b)(4) of Public Law 108–21 directly amended this policy statement to add the second paragraph, effective April 30, 2003.".

Amendment 674

Section 5H1.11 is amended by striking "sentence should be outside the applicable guideline range" and inserting "departure is warranted".

Section 5H1.12 is amended by striking "grounds for imposing a sentence outside the applicable guideline range" and inserting "in determining whether a departure is warranted".

Section 5K2.12 is amended by striking "decrease the sentence below the applicable guideline range" and inserting "depart downward".

Section 5K2.13 is amended by striking "sentence below the applicable guideline range" and inserting "downward departure".

Section 5K2.14 is amended by striking "increase the sentence above the guideline range" and inserting "depart upward".

Section 5K2.16 is amended by striking "departure below the applicable guideline range for that offense" and inserting "downward departure".

Section 5K2.21 is amended by striking "increase the sentence above the guideline range" and inserting "depart upward".

Section 5K2.22 is amended by striking "impose a sentence below the applicable guideline range" each place it appears and inserting "depart downward"; and by striking "for imposing a sentence below the guidelines" and inserting "to depart downward".

Section 5K2.23 is amended by striking "sentence below the applicable guideline range" and inserting "downward departure".

Section 6A1.1 is amended by striking the following:

> "A probation officer shall conduct a presentence investigation and report to the court before the imposition of sentence unless the court finds that there is information in the record sufficient to enable the meaningful exercise of sentencing authority pursuant to 18 U.S.C. § 3553, and the court explains this finding on the record. Rule 32(b)(1), Fed. R. Crim. P. The defendant may not waive preparation of the presentence report.",

and inserting the following:

> "(a) The probation officer must conduct a presentence investigation and submit a report to the court before it imposes sentence unless—
>
>   (1) 18 U.S.C. § 3593(c) or another statute requires otherwise; or
>
>   (2) the court finds that the information in the record enables it to meaningfully exercise its sentencing authority under 18 U.S.C. § 3553, and the court explains its finding on the record.
>
>   Rule 32(c)(1)(A), Fed. R. Crim. P.
>
> (b) The defendant may not waive preparation of the presentence report.".

The Commentary to § 6A1.1 is amended by striking:

> "   A thorough presentence investigation is essential in determining the facts relevant to sentencing. In order to ensure that the sentencing judge will have informa-

tion sufficient to determine the appropriate sentence, Congress deleted provisions of Rule 32(c), Fed. R. Crim. P., which previously permitted the defendant to waive the presentence report. Rule 32(b)(1) permits the judge to dispense with a presentence report, but only after explaining, on the record, why sufficient information is already available.",

and inserting the following:

" A thorough presentence investigation ordinarily is essential in determining the facts relevant to sentencing. Rule 32(c)(1)(A) permits the judge to dispense with a presentence report in certain limited circumstances, as when a specific statute requires or when the court finds sufficient information in the record to enable it to exercise its statutory sentencing authority meaningfully and explains its finding on the record.".

Chapter Six, Part A is amended by striking § 6A1.2 and its accompanying commentary as follows:

"§ 6A1.2. Disclosure of Presentence Report; Issues in Dispute (Policy Statement)

Courts should adopt procedures to provide for the timely disclosure of the presentence report; the narrowing and resolution, where feasible, of issues in dispute in advance of the sentencing hearing; and the identification for the court of issues remaining in dispute. Rule 32(b)(6), Fed. R. Crim. P.

Commentary

Application Note:

1. Under Rule 32, Fed. R. Crim. P., if the court intends to consider a sentence outside the applicable guideline range on a ground not identified as a ground for departure either in the presentence report or a pre-hearing submission, it shall provide reasonable notice that it is contemplating such ruling, specifically identifying the grounds for the departure. Burns v. United States, 501 U.S. 129, 135-39 (1991).

Background: In order to focus the issues prior to sentencing, the parties are required to respond in writing to the presentence report and to identify any issues in dispute. Rule 32(b)(6)(B), Fed. R. Crim. P.",

and inserting the following:

"§ 6A1.2. Disclosure of Presentence Report; Issues in Dispute (Policy Statement)

(a) The probation officer must give the presentence report to the defendant, the defendant's attorney, and an attorney for the government at least 35 days before sentencing unless the defendant waives this minimum period. Rule 32(e)(2), Fed. R. Crim. P.

(b) Within 14 days after receiving the presentence report, the parties must state in writing any objections, including objections to material information, sentencing guideline ranges, and policy statements contained in or omitted from the report. An objecting party must provide a copy of its objections to the opposing party and to the probation officer. After receiving objections, the probation officer may meet with the parties to discuss the objections. The probation

>> officer may then investigate further and revise the presentence report accordingly. Rule 32(f), Fed. R. Crim. P.

> (c) At least 7 days before sentencing, the probation officer must submit to the court and to the parties the presentence report and an addendum containing any unresolved objections, the grounds for those objections, and the probation officer's comments on them. Rule 32(g), Fed. R. Crim. P.

> Background: In order to focus the issues prior to sentencing, the parties are required to respond in writing to the presentence report and to identify any issues in dispute. See Rule 32(f), Fed. R. Crim. P.".

Section 6A1.3(b) is amended by striking "Rule 32(c)(1)" and inserting "Rule 32(i)".

The Commentary to § 6A1.3 is amended by striking the first paragraph as follows:

> "   In pre-guidelines practice, factors relevant to sentencing were often determined in an informal fashion. The informality was to some extent explained by the fact that particular offense and offender characteristics rarely had a highly specific or required sentencing consequence. This situation no longer exists under sentencing guidelines. The court's resolution of disputed sentencing factors usually has a measurable effect on the applicable punishment. More formality is therefore unavoidable if the sentencing process is to be accurate and fair.";

by striking "117 S. Ct. 633, 635" and inserting "519 U.S. 148, 154"; and by striking "117 S. Ct. at 637" and inserting "519 U.S. at 157".

Chapter Six, Part A is amended by adding at the end the following:

> "§ 6A1.4.   Notice of Possible Departure (Policy Statement)

>> Before the court may depart from the applicable sentencing guideline range on a ground not identified for departure either in the presentence report or in a party's prehearing submission, the court must give the parties reasonable notice that it is contemplating such a departure. The notice must specify any ground on which the court is contemplating a departure. Rule 32(h), Fed. R. Crim. P.

>> Commentary

> Background: The Federal Rules of Criminal Procedure were amended, effective December 1, 2002, to incorporate into Rule 32(h) the holding in Burns v. United States, 501 U.S. 129, 138-39 (1991). This policy statement parallels Rule 32(h), Fed. R. Crim. P.".

Chapter Six, Part B is amended by striking the Introductory Commentary as follows:

> "   Introductory Commentary

>> Policy statements governing the acceptance of plea agreements under Rule 11(e)(1), Fed. R. Crim. P., are intended to ensure that plea negotiation practices:

> (1)   promote the statutory purposes of sentencing prescribed in 18 U.S.C. § 3553(a); and

> (2)   do not perpetuate unwarranted sentencing disparity.

These policy statements are a first step toward implementing 28 U.S.C. § 994(a)(2)(E). Congress indicated that it expects judges 'to examine plea agreements to make certain that prosecutors have not used plea bargaining to undermine the sentencing guidelines.' S. Rep. 98-225, 98th Cong., 1st Sess. 63, 167 (1983). In pursuit of this goal, the Commission shall study plea agreement practice under the guidelines and ultimately develop standards for judges to use in determining whether to accept plea agreements. Because of the difficulty in anticipating problems in this area, and because the sentencing guidelines are themselves to some degree experimental, substantive restrictions on judicial discretion would be premature at this stage of the Commission's work.

The present policy statements move in the desired direction in two ways. First, the policy statements make clear that sentencing is a judicial function and that the appropriate sentence in a guilty plea case is to be determined by the judge. This is a reaffirmation of pre-guidelines practice. Second, the policy statements ensure that the basis for any judicial decision to depart from the guidelines will be explained on the record. Explanations will be carefully analyzed by the Commission and will pave the way for more detailed policy statements presenting substantive criteria to achieve consistency in this aspect of the sentencing process.",

and inserting the following:

"   Introductory Commentary

Policy statements governing the acceptance of plea agreements under Rule 11(c), Fed. R. Crim. P., are intended to ensure that plea negotiation practices: (1) promote the statutory purposes of sentencing prescribed in 18 U.S.C. § 3553(a); and (2) do not perpetuate unwarranted sentencing disparity.

These policy statements make clear that sentencing is a judicial function and that the appropriate sentence in a guilty plea case is to be determined by the judge. The policy statements also ensure that the basis for any judicial decision to depart from the guidelines will be explained on the record.".

Section 6B1.1 is amended by striking subsections (a), (b), and (c) as follows:

"(a)   If the parties have reached a plea agreement, the court shall, on the record, require disclosure of the agreement in open court or, on a showing of good cause, in camera. Rule 11(e)(2), Fed. R. Crim. P.

(b)   If the plea agreement includes a nonbinding recommendation pursuant to Rule 11(e)(1)(B), the court shall advise the defendant that the court is not bound by the sentencing recommendation, and that the defendant has no right to withdraw the defendant's guilty plea if the court decides not to accept the sentencing recommendation set forth in the plea agreement.

(c)   The court shall defer its decision to accept or reject any nonbinding recommendation pursuant to Rule 11(e)(1)(B), and the court's decision to accept or reject any plea agreement pursuant to Rules 11(e)(1)(A) and 11(e)(1)(C) until there has been an opportunity to consider the presentence report, unless a report is not required under § 6A1.1.",

and inserting the following:

"(a)   The parties must disclose the plea agreement in open court when the plea is offered, unless the court for good cause allows the parties to disclose the plea agreement in camera. Rule 11(c)(2), Fed. R. Crim. P.

(b) To the extent the plea agreement is of the type specified in Rule 11(c)(1)(B), the court must advise the defendant that the defendant has no right to withdraw the plea if the court does not follow the recommendation or request. Rule 11(c)(3)(B), Fed. R. Crim. P.

(c) To the extent the plea agreement is of the type specified in Rule 11(c)(1)(A) or (C), the court may accept the agreement, reject it, or defer a decision until the court has reviewed the presentence report. Rule 11(c)(3)(A), Fed. R. Crim. P.".

The Commentary to § 6B1.1 is amended in the first paragraph by striking "Rule 11(e)" and inserting "Rule 11(c)";

and by striking the second paragraph as follows:

" Section 6B1.1(c) deals with the timing of the court's decision whether to accept the plea agreement. Rule 11(e)(2) gives the court discretion to accept the plea agreement immediately or defer acceptance pending consideration of the presentence report. Prior to the guidelines, an immediate decision was permissible because, under Rule 32(c), Fed. R. Crim. P., the defendant could waive preparation of the presentence report. Section 6B1.1(c) reflects the changes in practice required by § 6A1.1 (Presentence Report) and amended Rule 32(c)(1). Since a presentence report normally will be prepared, the court must defer acceptance of the plea agreement until the court has had an opportunity to consider the presentence report.",

and inserting the following:

" Section 6B1.1(c) deals with the timing of the court's decision regarding whether to accept or reject the plea agreement. Rule 11(c)(3)(A) gives the court discretion to accept or reject the plea agreement immediately or defer a decision pending consideration of the presentence report. Given that a presentence report normally will be prepared, the Commission recommends that the court defer acceptance of the plea agreement until the court has reviewed the presentence report.".

Section 6B1.3 is amended by striking:

"If a plea agreement pursuant to Rule 11(e)(1)(A) or Rule 11(e)(1)(C) is rejected, the court shall afford the defendant an opportunity to withdraw the defendant's guilty plea. Rule 11(e)(4), Fed. R. Crim. P.",

and inserting the following:

"If the court rejects a plea agreement containing provisions of the type specified in Rule 11(c)(1)(A) or (C), the court must do the following on the record and in open court (or, for good cause, in camera)—

(a) inform the parties that the court rejects the plea agreement;

(b) advise the defendant personally that the court is not required to follow the plea agreement and give the defendant an opportunity to withdraw the plea; and

(c) advise the defendant personally that if the plea is not withdrawn, the court may dispose of the case less favorably toward the defendant than the plea agreement contemplated.

Rule 11(c)(5), Fed. R. Crim. P.".

The Commentary to § 6B1.3 is amended by striking "Rule 11(e)(4)" and inserting "Rule 11(c)(5)"; and by striking "that would require dismissal of charges or imposition of a specific sentence." and inserting a period.

Appendix A is amended by inserting after the line referenced to 18 U.S.C. § 4 the following new line:

"18 U.S.C. § 25   2X6.1".

Reason for Amendment: This nine-part amendment consists of four technical and conforming amendments and five amendments of a more substantive nature, some of which are in response to new legislation.

First, this amendment corrects a typographical error in Application Note 4 to § 3C1.1 (Obstructing or Impeding the Administration of Justice) by changing a reference to Application Note 3(g) to 4(g).

Second, this amendment makes a number of conforming changes to various guideline provisions and commentary as a result of departure amendments previously made in furtherance of the Prosecutorial Remedies and Other Tools to end the Exploitation of Children Today Act of 2003, Pub. L. 108–21 (the "PROTECT Act").

Third, this amendment corrects an error in an example provided in Application Note 3(B)(iii) of § 5G1.2 (Sentencing on Multiple Counts of Conviction).

Fourth, this amendment generally updates Chapter Six (Sentencing Procedures and Plea Agreements) in response to a number of amendments that were made to the Federal Rules of Criminal Procedure effective December 1, 2002. While some of these changes to the Rules were substantive, the bulk of the changes to Rules 11 and 32 of the Federal Rules of Criminal Procedure were organizational and stylistic. These guideline amendments conform to those changes made to the Federal Rules of Criminal Procedure with respect to such issues as deadlines for disputed issues and requirements for disclosure of presentence reports, as well as procedures the court must follow in rejecting certain plea agreements. Certain outdated commentary also has been deleted.

Fifth, this amendment broadens the special multiple victim rule in Application Note 4(C)(ii) of § 2B1.1 (Larceny, Embezzlement, and Other Forms of Theft; Offenses Involving Stolen Property; Property Damage or Destruction; Fraud and Deceit; Forgery; Offenses Involving Altered or Counterfeit Instruments Other than Counterfeit Bearer Obligations of the United States), as redesignated by Amendment 3 of this document, for offenses involving stolen United States mail. The rule is expanded to include theft of mail from housing unit cluster boxes, whether owned by the United States Postal Service or otherwise. The amendment provides a presumption that a theft from such a cluster box involves the number of victims corresponding to the number of mailboxes contained in the cluster box. The same rationale for the original special rule applies to this expansion: (i) unique proof problems in that once entry is gained to such a cluster box and mail is removed, it is difficult to determine the number of persons from whom mail was stolen; (ii) the frequently significant, but difficult to quantify, non-monetary losses; and (iii) the importance of maintaining the integrity of the United States mail service. See USSG App. C (Vol. II) (Amendment 617). These reasons are equally valid whether the mail receptacle is owned by the United States Postal Service or is privately owned.

Sixth, this amendment modifies § 2B1.1(b)(10), as redesignated by Amendment 3 of this document, which provides a two-level enhancement and a minimum offense level of 12, in response to the Secure Authentication Feature and Enhanced Identification Defense Act of

2003 (the "SAFE ID Act") (section 607 of the PROTECT Act, Pub. L. 108–21). That Act created a new offense at 18 U.S.C. § 1028(a)(8), prohibiting the trafficking of authentication features (e.g., a hologram or symbol used by a government agency to determine whether a document is counterfeit, altered, or otherwise falsified), and amended 18 U.S.C. § 1028 to prohibit the transfer or possession of authentication features. This amendment makes § 2B1.1(b)(10) applicable to offenses involving authentication features.

Seventh, this amendment creates a new guideline at § 2X6.1 (Use of a Minor to Commit a Crime of Violence). This new guideline is in response to a new offense provided at 18 U.S.C. § 25 (Use of Minors in Crimes of Violence), which was created by section 601 of the PROTECT Act. The new offense prohibits any person 18 years of age or older from intentionally using a minor to commit a crime of violence or to assist in avoiding detection or apprehension for such offense. For a first conviction, the penalty is twice the maximum term of imprisonment that would otherwise be authorized for the offense, and for each subsequent conviction, three times the maximum term of imprisonment that would otherwise be authorized for the offense.

While consideration was given to expanding the existing two-level adjustment at § 3B1.4 (Using a Minor to Commit a Crime), the Commission determined it was more appropriate and consistent with guideline construction to create a new guideline for the new substantive offense created by Congress in the PROTECT Act. This new guideline at § 2X6.1 directs the court to increase by 4 levels the offense level from the guideline applicable to the underlying crime of violence. Application notes are included to provide that the adjustment under § 3B1.4 is inapplicable if § 2X6.1 is used and to provide rules for the grouping of multiple counts.

Eighth, this amendment expands the definition of "crime of violence" in Application Note 1 to § 4B1.2 (Definitions of Terms Used in Section 4B1.1) to include unlawful possession of any firearm described in 26 U.S.C. § 5845(a). The amendment also excepts possession of those firearms described in 26 U.S.C. § 5845(a) from the rule that excludes felon in possession offenses from the definition of "crime of violence." Congress has determined that those firearms described in 26 U.S.C. § 5845(a) are inherently dangerous and when possessed unlawfully, serve only violent purposes. In the National Firearms Act, Pub. L. 90–618, Congress required that these firearms be registered with the National Firearms Registration and Transfer Record. A number of courts have held that possession of certain of these firearms, such as a sawed-off shotgun, is a "crime of violence" due to the serious potential risk of physical injury to another person. The amendment's categorical rule incorporating 26 U.S.C. § 5845(a) firearms includes short-barreled rifles and shotguns, machine guns, silencers, and destructive devices. It will affect determinations both of career offender status under Chapter Four, Part B and also of appropriate base offense levels in § 2K2.1 (Unlawful Receipt, Possession, or Transportation of Firearms or Ammunition; Prohibited Transactions Involving Firearms or Ammunition).

Ninth, this amendment provides an application note in § 4B1.4 (Armed Career Criminal) to address an apparent "double counting" issue that appears to be present when a defendant is convicted both of 18 U.S.C. § 922(g) (Felon in Possession) and also of an offense such as 18 U.S.C. § 924(c) (Use of a Firearm in Relation to Any Crime of Violence or Drug Trafficking Crime) or a similar offense carrying a mandatory minimum consecutive penalty, such as 18 U.S.C. § 844(h) relating to use of explosives, or 18 U.S.C. § 929(a) relating to use of restricted ammunition.

The basis for the mandatory minimum, consecutive penalties in these offenses is the same as the basis for the enhanced guideline offense level 34 at § 4B1.4(b)(3)(A) and the enhanced Criminal History Category VI at § 4B1.4(c)(2); i.e., the use or possession of the firearm in connection with a crime of violence or controlled substance offense. The Commission determined that the mandatory minimum, consecutive sentences in these statutes are sufficient to take into account the aggravated conduct referenced in § 4B1.4.

An upward departure is provided for those cases that result in a total maximum penalty that is less than the maximum of the guideline range that would have resulted if the enhanced offense level under § 4B1.4(b)(3)(A) and the criminal history enhancement under § 4B1.4(c)(2) had been applied. However, the extent of the upward departure shall not exceed the maximum of the guideline range that would have resulted had there not been a conviction under 18 U.S.C. § 924(c), § 844(h), or § 929(a).

Effective Date: The effective date of this amendment is November 1, 2004.

675. **Amendment:** Section 2B5.3(b) is amended by redesignating subsections (b)(2) through (b)(4) as subsections (b)(3) through (b)(5), respectively; and by inserting after subsection (b)(1) the following:

> "(2) If the offense involved the display, performance, publication, reproduction, or distribution of a work being prepared for commercial distribution, increase by 2 levels.".

The Commentary to § 2B5.3 captioned "Application Notes" is amended in Note 1 by striking the last paragraph as follows:

> "'Uploading' means making an infringing item available on the Internet or a similar electronic bulletin board with the intent to enable other persons to download or otherwise copy, or have access to, the infringing item.",

and inserting the following:

> "'Uploading' means making an infringing item available on the Internet or a similar electronic bulletin board with the intent to enable other persons to (A) download or otherwise copy the infringing item; or (B) have access to the infringing item, including by storing the infringing item in an openly shared file. 'Uploading' does not include merely downloading or installing an infringing item on a hard drive on a defendant's personal computer unless the infringing item is placed in an openly shared file.
>
> 'Work being prepared for commercial distribution' has the meaning given that term in 17 U.S.C. § 506(a)(3).".

The Commentary to § 2B5.3 captioned "Application Notes" is amended in Note 2 in subdivision (A) by inserting after subdivision (v) the following:

> "(vi) The offense involves the display, performance, publication, reproduction, or distribution of a work being prepared for commercial distribution. In a case involving such an offense, the 'retail value of the infringed item' is the value of that item upon its initial commercial distribution.";

and by inserting after subdivision (D) the following:

> "(E) <u>Indeterminate Number of Infringing Items</u>.—In a case in which the court cannot determine the number of infringing items, the court need only make a reasonable estimate of the infringement amount using any relevant information, including financial records.".

The Commentary to § 2B5.3 captioned "Application Notes" is amended by striking Note 3 as follows:

"3. Uploading.—With respect to uploading, subsection (b)(2) applies only to uploading with the intent to enable other persons to download or otherwise copy, or have access to, the infringing item. For example, this subsection applies in the case of illegally uploading copyrighted software to an Internet site, but it does not apply in the case of downloading or installing that software on a hard drive on the defendant's personal computer.";

and by redesignating Notes 4 and 5 as Notes 3 and 4, respectively.

Appendix A (Statutory Index) is amended by inserting after the line reference to "18 U.S.C. § 2319A" the following:

"18 U.S.C. § 2319B   2B5.3".

Reason for Amendment: This amendment implements the directive in section 105 of the Family Entertainment and Copyright Act of 2005, Pub. L. 109–9. The directive, which requires the Commission to promulgate an amendment under emergency amendment authority by October 24, 2005, instructs the Commission to "review and, if appropriate, amend the Federal sentencing guidelines and policy statements applicable to persons convicted of intellectual property rights crimes. . ."

"In carrying out [the directive], the Commission shall—

(1) take all appropriate measures to ensure that the Federal sentencing guidelines and policy statements. . .are sufficiently stringent to deter, and adequately reflect the nature of, intellectual property rights crimes;

(2) determine whether to provide a sentencing enhancement for those convicted of the offenses [involving intellectual property rights], if the conduct involves the display, performance, publication, reproduction, or distribution of a copyrighted work before it has been authorized by the copyright owner, whether in the media format used by the infringing party or in any other media format;

(3) determine whether the scope of 'uploading' set forth in application note 3 of section 2B5.3 of the Federal sentencing guidelines is adequate to address the loss attributable to people who, without authorization, broadly distribute copyrighted works over the Internet; and

(4) determine whether the sentencing guideline and policy statements applicable to the offenses [involving intellectual property rights] adequately reflect any harm to victims from copyright infringement if law enforcement authorities cannot determine how many times copyrighted material has been reproduced or distributed."

Pre-Release Works

The amendment provides a separate two-level enhancement if the offense involved a pre-release work. The enhancement and the corresponding definition use language directly from 17 U.S.C. § 506(a) (criminal infringement). The amendment adds language to Application Note 2 that explains that in cases involving pre-release works, the infringement amount should be determined by using the retail value of the infringed item, rather than any premium price attributed to the infringing item because of its pre-release status. The amendment addresses concerns that distribution of an item before it is legally available to the consumer is more serious conduct than distribution of other infringing items and involves a harm not addressed by the current guideline.

Uploading

The concern underlying the uploading directive pertains to offenses in which the copyrighted work is transferred through file sharing. The amendment builds on the current definition of "uploading" to include making an infringing item available on the Internet by storing an infringing item in an openly shared file. The amendment also clarifies that uploading does not include merely downloading or installing infringing items on a hard drive of the defendant's computer unless the infringing item is in an openly shared file. By clarifying the definition of uploading in this manner, Application Note 3, which is a restatement of the uploading definition, is no longer necessary and the amendment deletes the application note from the guideline.

Indeterminate Number

The amendment addresses the final directive by amending Application Note 2, which sets forth the rules for determining the infringement amount. The note provides that the court may make a reasonable estimate of the infringement amount using any relevant information including financial records in cases in which the court cannot determine the number of infringing items.

New Offense

Finally, the amendment provides a reference in Appendix A (Statutory Index) for the new offense at 18 U.S.C. § 2319B. This offense is to be referenced to § 2B5.3.

Effective Date: The effective date of this amendment is October 24, 2005.

676. **Amendment:** Section 2J1.2(b) is amended by striking subdivision (1) as follows:

> "(1) If the offense involved causing or threatening to cause physical injury to a person, or property damage, in order to obstruct the administration of justice, increase by 8 levels.",

and inserting the following:

> "(1) (Apply the greater):
>
> (A) If the offense involved causing or threatening to cause physical injury to a person, or property damage, in order to obstruct the administration of justice, increase by 8 levels.
>
> (B) If (i) defendant was convicted under 18 U.S.C. § 1001 or § 1505; and (ii) the statutory maximum term of imprisonment relating to international terrorism or domestic terrorism is applicable, increase by 12 levels.".

The Commentary to § 2J1.2 captioned "Statutory Provisions" is amended by striking "18 U.S.C. §§ 1503" and inserting the following:

> "18 U.S.C. §§ 1001 when the statutory maximum term of imprisonment relating to international terrorism or domestic terrorism is applicable, 1503".

The Commentary to § 2J1.2 captioned "Application Notes" is amended in Note 1 by insert-

Amendment 676

ing after "<u>Definitions</u>.—For purposes of this guideline:" the following:

"'Domestic terrorism' has the meaning given that term in 18 U.S.C. § 2331(5).

'International terrorism' has the meaning given that term in 18 U.S.C. § 2331(1).".

The Commentary to § 2J1.2 captioned "Application Notes" is amended by striking Note 2 as follows:

"2. <u>Nonapplicability of Chapter Three, Part C</u>.—For offenses covered under this section, Chapter Three, Part C (Obstruction) does not apply, unless the defendant obstructed the investigation, prosecution, or sentencing of the obstruction of justice count.",

and inserting the following:

"2. <u>Chapter Three Adjustments</u>.—

(A) <u>Inapplicability of Chapter Three, Part C</u>.—For offenses covered under this section, Chapter Three, Part C (Obstruction) does not apply, unless the defendant obstructed the investigation, prosecution, or sentencing of the obstruction of justice count.

(B) <u>Interaction with Terrorism Adjustment</u>.—If § 3A1.4 (Terrorism) applies, do not apply subsection (b)(1)(B).".

Appendix A (Statutory Index) is amended in the line referenced to "18 U.S.C. § 1001" by inserting ", 2J1.2 when the statutory maximum term of imprisonment relating to international terrorism or domestic terrorism is applicable" after 2B1.1".

Reason for Amendment: This amendment implements section 6703 of the Intelligence Reform and Terrorism Prevention Act of 2004 (the "Act"), Pub. L. 108–458. Section 6703(a) provides an enhanced penalty of not more than 8 years of imprisonment for offenses under sections 1001(a) and 1505 of title 18, United States Code, "if the offense involves international or domestic terrorism (as defined in section 2331)." Section 6703(b) requires the Sentencing Commission to amend the sentencing guidelines to provide for "an increased offense level for an offense under sections 1001(a) and 1505 of title 18, United States Code, if the offense involves international or domestic terrorism, as defined in section 2331 of such title." The Commission is directed under section 3 of the United States Parole Commission Extension and Sentencing Commission Authority Act of 2005, Pub. L. 109–76, to promulgate this amendment as an emergency amendment.

First, the amendment references convictions under 18 U.S.C. § 1001 to § 2J1.2 (Obstruction of Justice) "when the statutory maximum term of imprisonment relating to international or domestic terrorism is applicable." It also adds a new specific offense characteristic at § 2J1.2(b)(1)(B) providing for a 12 level increase for a defendant convicted under 18 U.S.C. §§ 1001 and 1505 "when the statutory maximum term of imprisonment relating to international or domestic terrorism is applicable." This 12 level increase is applied in lieu of the current 8 level increase for injury or threats to persons or property. The increase of 12 levels is intended to provide parity with the treatment of federal crimes of terrorism within the limits of the 8 year statutory maximum penalty. It is also provided to ensure a 5 year sentence of imprisonment for offenses that involve international or domestic terrorism.

Second, the amendment adds to Application Note 1 definitions for "domestic terrorism" and "international terrorism," using the meanings given the terms at 18 U.S.C. § 2331(5) and (1), respectively.

Third, the amendment adds to Application Note 2 an instruction that if § 3A1.4 (Terrorism) applies, do not apply § 2J1.2(b)(1)(B).

Effective Date: The effective date of this amendment is October 24, 2005.

677. **Amendment:** Chapter Two, Part B, Subpart 1 is amended by adding at the end the following new guideline and accompanying commentary:

"§ 2B1.6.   Aggravated Identity Theft

(a) If the defendant was convicted of violating 18 U.S.C. § 1028A, the guideline sentence is the term of imprisonment required by statute. Chapters Three (Adjustments) and Four (Criminal History and Criminal Livelihood) shall not apply to that count of conviction.

Commentary

Statutory Provision: 18 U.S.C. § 1028A. For additional statutory provision(s), see Appendix A (Statutory Index).

Application Notes:

1. Imposition of Sentence.—

    (A) In General.—Section 1028A of title 18, United State Code, provides a mandatory term of imprisonment. Accordingly, the guideline sentence for a defendant convicted under 18 U.S.C. § 1028A is the term required by that statute. Except as provided in subdivision (B), 18 U.S.C. § 1028A also requires a term of imprisonment imposed under this section to run consecutively to any other term of imprisonment.

    (B) Multiple Convictions Under Section 1028A.—Section 1028A(b)(4) of title 18, United State Code, provides that in the case of multiple convictions under 18 U.S.C. § 1028A, the terms of imprisonment imposed on such counts may, in the discretion of the court, run concurrently, in whole or in part, with each other. See the Commentary to § 5G1.2 (Sentencing on Multiple Counts of Conviction) for guidance regarding imposition of sentence on multiple counts of 18 U.S.C. § 1028A.

2. Inapplicability of Chapter Two Enhancement.—If a sentence under this guideline is imposed in conjunction with a sentence for an underlying offense, do not apply any specific offense characteristic for the transfer, possession, or use of a means of identification when determining the sentence for the underlying offense. A sentence under this guideline accounts for this factor for the underlying offense of conviction, including any such enhancement that would apply based on conduct for which the defendant is accountable under § 1B1.3 (Relevant Conduct). 'Means of identification' has the meaning given that term in 18 U.S.C. § 1028(d)(7).

3. Inapplicability of Chapters Three and Four.—Do not apply Chapters Three

Amendment 677   APPENDIX C - VOLUME III   November 1, 2013

(Adjustments) and Four (Criminal History and Criminal Livelihood) to any offense sentenced under this guideline. Such offenses are excluded from application of those chapters because the guideline sentence for each offense is determined only by the relevant statute. See §§ 3D1.1 (Procedure for Determining Offense Level on Multiple Counts) and 5G1.2.".

The Commentary to § 3B1.3 captioned "Application Notes" is amended in Note 1 by inserting "Definition of 'Public or Private Trust'.—" before "'Public or private trust' refers to", and by striking the second paragraph as follows:

"Notwithstanding the preceding paragraph, because of the special nature of the United States mail an adjustment for an abuse of a position of trust will apply to any employee of the U.S. Postal Service who engages in the theft or destruction of undelivered United States mail.";

by redesignating Notes 2 through 4 as Notes 3 through 5, respectively; and by inserting after Note 1 the following:

"2.   Application of Adjustment in Certain Circumstances.—Notwithstanding Application Note 1, or any other provision of this guideline, an adjustment under this guideline shall apply to the following:

(A)   An employee of the United States Postal Service who engages in the theft or destruction of undelivered United States mail.

(B)   A defendant who exceeds or abuses the authority of his or her position in order to obtain unlawfully, or use without authority, any means of identification. 'Means of identification' has the meaning given that term in 18 U.S.C. § 1028(d)(7). The following are examples to which this subdivision would apply: (i) an employee of a state motor vehicle department who exceeds or abuses the authority of his or her position by knowingly issuing a driver's license based on false, incomplete, or misleading information; (ii) a hospital orderly who exceeds or abuses the authority of his or her position by obtaining or misusing patient identification information from a patient chart; and (iii) a volunteer at a charitable organization who exceeds or abuses the authority of his or her position by obtaining or misusing identification information from a donor's file.".

Section 3D1.1 is amended by striking subsection (b) as follows:

"(b)   Exclude from the application of §§ 3D1.2-3D1.5 any count for which the statute (1) specifies a term of imprisonment to be imposed; and (2) requires that such term of imprisonment be imposed to run consecutively to any other term of imprisonment. Sentences for such counts are governed by the provisions of § 5G1.2(a).",

and inserting the following:

"(b)   Exclude from the application of §§ 3D1.2-3D1.5 the following:

(1)   Any count for which the statute (A) specifies a term of imprisonment to be imposed; and (B) requires that such term of imprisonment be imposed to run consecutively to any other term of imprisonment. Sentences for such counts are governed by the provisions of § 5G1.2(a).

(2) Any count of conviction under 18 U.S.C. § 1028A. See Application Note 2(B) of the Commentary to § 5G1.2 (Sentencing on Multiple Counts of Conviction) for guidance on how sentences for multiple counts of conviction under 18 U.S.C. § 1028A should be imposed.".

The Commentary to § 5G1.2 captioned "Application Notes" is amended in Note 2 by inserting "(A) In General.—" before "Subsection (a) applies"; by inserting "and 18 U.S.C. § 1028A (requiring a mandatory term of imprisonment of either two or five years, based on the conduct involved, and also requiring, except in the circumstances described in subdivision (B), the sentence imposed to run consecutively to any other term of imprisonment)" after "imprisonment)"; by striking the following:

"Note, however, that even in the case of a consecutive term of imprisonment imposed under subsection (a), any term of supervised release imposed is to run concurrently with any other term of supervised release imposed. See 18 U.S.C. § 3624(e).";

and by adding at the end the following:

"(B) Multiple Convictions Under 18 U.S.C. § 1028A.—Section 1028A of title 18, United States Code, generally requires that the mandatory term of imprisonment for a violation of such section be imposed consecutively to any other term of imprisonment. However, 18 U.S.C. § 1028A(b)(4) permits the court, in its discretion, to impose the mandatory term of imprisonment on a defendant for a violation of such section 'concurrently, in whole or in part, only with another term of imprisonment that is imposed by the court at the same time on that person for an additional violation of this section, provided that such discretion shall be exercised in accordance with any applicable guidelines and policy statements issued by the Sentencing Commission. . . .'.

In determining whether multiple counts of 18 U.S.C. § 1028A should run concurrently with, or consecutively to, each other, the court should consider the following non-exhaustive list of factors:

(i) The nature and seriousness of the underlying offenses. For example, the court should consider the appropriateness of imposing consecutive, or partially consecutive, terms of imprisonment for multiple counts of 18 U.S.C. § 1028A in a case in which an underlying offense for one of the 18 U.S.C. § 1028A offenses is a crime of violence or an offense enumerated in 18 U.S.C. § 2332b(g)(5)(B).

(ii) Whether the underlying offenses are groupable under § 3D1.2 (Multiple Counts). Generally, multiple counts of 18 U.S.C. § 1028A should run concurrently with one another in cases in which the underlying offenses are groupable under § 3D1.2.

(iii) Whether the purposes of sentencing set forth in 18 U.S.C. § 3553(a)(2) are better achieved by imposing a concurrent or a consecutive sentence for multiple counts of 18 U.S.C. § 1028A.

(C) Imposition of Supervised Release.—In the case of a consecutive term of imprisonment imposed under subsection (a), any term of supervised release imposed is to run concurrently with any other term of supervised release imposed. See 18 U.S.C. § 3624(e).".

Amendment 677

Appendix A (Statutory Index) is amended by inserting after the line referenced to 18 U.S.C. § 1028 the following:

"18 U.S.C. § 1028A   2B1.6".

Reason for Amendment: This amendment implements sections 2 and 5 of the Identity Theft Penalty Enhancement Act, Pub. L. 108–275, 118 Stat. 831 ("the Act"), which create two new criminal offenses at 18 U.S.C. § 1028A and direct the Sentencing Commission to expand the upward adjustment at § 3B1.3 (Abuse of Position of Trust or Use of Special Skill). This amendment also provides guidance to the courts on imposing sentences for multiple violations of section 1028A.

The Act creates a new offense at 18 U.S.C. § 1028A(a)(1) that prohibits the unauthorized transfer, use, or possession of a means of identification of another person during, or in relation to, specific enumerated felonies. These felonies consist of various types of fraud, including mail and wire fraud in connection with passports, visas and other immigration, nationality, and citizenship laws, programs under the Social Security Act, and the acquisition of firearms. A conviction under section 1028A(a)(1) carries a two-year mandatory term of imprisonment that must run consecutively to any other term of imprisonment, including the sentence for the underlying felony conviction. The Act also creates a new offense at 18 U.S.C. § 1028A(b)(1) that prohibits the unauthorized transfer, use, or possession of a means of identification of another person during, or in relation to, specific felonies enumerated in 18 U.S.C. § 2332b(g)(5)(B) ("federal crimes of terrorism"). Section 1028A(b)(1) provides a five-year mandatory term of imprisonment that must run consecutively to any other term of imprisonment, including the sentence for the underlying felony conviction. As described below, section 1028A(b)(4) creates an exception to the requirement for consecutive terms of imprisonment in cases involving multiple violations of the statute sentenced at the same time.

First, in response to the creation of these new criminal offenses, the amendment creates a new guideline at § 2B1.6 (Aggravated Identity Theft). This guideline is patterned after § 2K2.4 (Use of Firearm, Armor-Piercing Ammunition, or Explosive During or in Relation to Certain Crimes). Because the new offenses carry a fixed, mandatory consecutive term of imprisonment, the new guideline, as does § 2K2.4, provides that the guideline sentence is the term of imprisonment required by statute. To avoid unwarranted double-counting, the amendment contains an application note that prohibits the application of any specific offense characteristic for the transfer, possession, or use of a means of identification when determining the sentence for the underlying offense in cases in which a sentence under § 2B1.6 is imposed in conjunction with a sentence for an underlying offense. Also, consistent with § 2K2.4, the new guideline at § 2B1.6 contains an application note that provides that adjustments under Chapters Three and Four are inapplicable to sentences under this guideline.

Second, in response to the directive in section 5 to amend § 3B1.3 (Abuse of Position of Trust or Use of Special Skill) to include a "defendant [who] exceeds or abuses the authority of his or her position in order to obtain unlawfully or use without authority any means of identification," the Commission created Application Note 2 to § 3B1.3 to include such defendants within the scope of the guideline. The application note contains several examples to illustrate the types of conduct intended to be within the scope of the new provision.

Third, the amendment adds a number of provisions at appropriate guidelines in order to provide guidance to courts in accordance with section 2 of the Act (18 U.S.C. § 1028A(b)(4)). That section states that "a term of imprisonment imposed on a person for violation of this section may, in the discretion of the court, run concurrently, in whole or in part, only with another term of imprisonment that is imposed by the court at the same time on that person for an additional violation of this section, provided that such discretion shall be exercised in accordance with any applicable guidelines and policy statements issued by the Sentencing Commission. . . ." The amendment states a general rule, at § 5G1.2 (Sentencing on Multiple Counts of Conviction), Application Note 2(B), providing that the court has discretion to impose concurrent or consecutive, or partially concurrent and partially consecutive, terms of imprisonment for multiple violations of 18 U.S.C. § 1028A. A non-exhaustive list of factors for courts to consider in making this determination is provided, including the nature and seriousness of the underlying offenses and whether the offenses would be groupable under § 3D1.2 (Group of Closely Related Counts).

Finally, the amendment modifies § 3D1.1 (Procedure for Determining Offense Level on Multiple Counts) to make clear that section 1028A offenses are excluded from the general grouping rules in §§ 3D1.2 - 3D1.5 and makes conforming additions and changes to the new guideline at § 2B1.6 (Aggravated Identity Theft) in Application Note 1 and § 3D1.1(b)(1) and (2).

Effective Date: The effective date of this amendment is November 1, 2005.

678. Amendment: Section 2R1.1(a) is amended by striking "10" and inserting "12".

Section 2R1.1(b) is amended by striking subdivision (2) as follows:

"(2) If the volume of commerce attributable to the defendant was more than $400,000, adjust the offense level as follows:

Volume of Commerce (Apply the Greatest)		Adjustment to Offense Level
(A)	More than $400,000	add 1
(B)	More than $1,000,000	add 2
(C)	More than $2,500,000	add 3
(D)	More than $6,250,000	add 4
(E)	More than $15,000,000	add 5
(F)	More than $37,500,000	add 6
(G)	More than $100,000,000	add 7.

For purposes of this guideline, the volume of commerce attributable to an individual participant in a conspiracy is the volume of commerce done by him or his principal in goods or services that were affected by the violation. When multiple counts or conspiracies are involved, the volume of commerce should be treated cumulatively to determine a single, combined offense level.",

and inserting the following:

"(2) If the volume of commerce attributable to the defendant was more than $1,000,000, adjust the offense level as follows:

Volume of
Commerce (Apply the Greatest)   Adjustment to
                                  Offense Level

(A)	More than $1,000,000	add 2
(B)	More than $10,000,000	add 4
(C)	More than $40,000,000	add 6
(D)	More than $100,000,000	add 8
(E)	More than $250,000,000	add 10
(F)	More than $500,000,000	add 12
(G)	More than $1,000,000,000	add 14
(H)	More than $1,500,000,000	add 16.

> For purposes of this guideline, the volume of commerce attributable to an individual participant in a conspiracy is the volume of commerce done by him or his principal in goods or services that were affected by the violation. When multiple counts or conspiracies are involved, the volume of commerce should be treated cumulatively to determine a single, combined offense level.".

The Commentary to § 2R1.1 captioned "Application Notes" is amended by striking Note 1 as follows:

> "1. The provisions of § 3B1.1 (Aggravating Role) and § 3B1.2 (Mitigating Role) should be applied to an individual defendant as appropriate to reflect the individual's role in committing the offense. For example, if a sales manager organizes or leads the price-fixing activity of five or more participants, a 4-level increase is called for under § 3B1.1. An individual defendant should be considered for a downward adjustment under § 3B1.2 for a mitigating role in the offense only if he was responsible in some minor way for his firm's participation in the conspiracy.",

and inserting the following:

> "1. Application of Chapter Three (Adjustments).—Sections 3B1.1 (Aggravating Role), 3B1.2 (Mitigating Role), 3B1.3 (Abuse of Position of Trust or Use of Special Skill), and 3C1.1 (Obstructing or Impeding the Administration of Justice) may be relevant in determining the seriousness of the defendant's offense. For example, if a sales manager organizes or leads the price-fixing activity of five or more participants, the 4-level increase at § 3B1.1(a) should be applied to reflect the defendant's aggravated role in the offense. For purposes of applying § 3B1.2, an individual defendant should be considered for a mitigating role adjustment only if he were responsible in some minor way for his firm's participation in the conspiracy.".

The Commentary to § 2R1.1 captioned "Application Notes" is amended in Note 2 by striking the first sentence as follows:

> "In setting the fine for individuals, the court should consider the extent of the defendant's participation in the offense, his role, and the degree to which he personally profited from the offense (including salary, bonuses, and career enhancement).",

and inserting the following:

> "Considerations in Setting Fine for Individuals.—In setting the fine for individuals, the court should consider the extent of the defendant's participation in the offense, the defendant's role, and the degree to which the defendant personally profited from the offense (including salary, bonuses, and career enhancement).".

The Commentary to § 2R1.1 captioned "Background" is amended in the second paragraph by striking the following:

> "The Commission believes that the most effective method to deter individuals from committing this crime is through imposing short prison sentences coupled with large fines. The controlling consideration underlying this guideline is general deterrence.";

in the third paragraph by striking "confinement of six months or longer" and inserting "some period of confinement"; and in the last paragraph by striking the last sentence as follows:

> "The statutory maximum fine is $350,000 for individuals and $10,000,000 for organizations, but is increased when there are convictions on multiple counts.".

Reason for Amendment: This amendment responds to the Antitrust Criminal Penalty Enhancement and Reform Act of 2004, Pub. L. 108–237 (the "Act"). The Act increased the statutory maximum term of imprisonment for antitrust offenses under 15 U.S.C. §§ 1 and 3(b) from three to ten years. The amendment responds to congressional concern about the seriousness of antitrust offenses and provides for antitrust penalties that are more proportionate to those for sophisticated frauds sentenced under § 2B1.1 (Larceny, Embezzlement, and Other Forms of Theft; Offenses Involving Stolen Property; Property Damage or Destruction; Fraud and Deceit; Forgery; Offenses Involving Altered or Counterfeit Instruments Other than Counterfeit Bearer Obligations of the United States). The Commission has long recognized the similarity of antitrust offenses to sophisticated frauds.

The amendment increases the base offense level for antitrust offenses in § 2R1.1 (Bid-Rigging, Price-Fixing or Market-Allocation Agreements Among Competitors) to level 12. The higher base offense level ensures that penalties for antitrust offenses will be coextensive with those for sophisticated frauds sentenced under § 2B1.1 and recognizes congressional concern about the inherent seriousness of antitrust offenses. The penalties for sophisticated fraud have been increased incrementally due to a series of amendments to § 2B1.1, while no commensurate increases for antitrust offenses had occurred. Raising the base offense level of § 2R1.1 helps restore the historic proportionality in the treatment of antitrust offenses and sophisticated frauds.

The "volume of commerce" table at § 2R1.1(b)(2) is amended to provide up to 16 additional offense levels for the defendant whose offense involves more than $1,500,000,000, while the new table's first threshold is raised from $400,000 to $1,000,000. The new volume of commerce table: (1) recognizes the depreciation in the value of the dollar since the table was last revised in 1991; (2) responds to data indicating that the financial magnitude of antitrust offenses has increased significantly; and (3) provides greater deterrence of large scale price-fixing crimes.

Application Note 1 to § 2R1.1 is amended to emphasize the potential relevance of such Chapter Three enhancements as § 3B1.1 (Aggravating Role), § 3B1.3 (Abuse of Position of Trust or Use of Special Skill), and § 3C1.1 (Obstructing or Impeding the Administration of Justice) in determining the appropriate sentence for an antitrust offender. Application Note 2 also is amended to highlight the potential relevance of the defendant's role in the offense in determining the amount of fine to be imposed. Finally, the amendment strikes outdated background commentary.

Effective Date: The effective date of this amendment is November 1, 2005.

679. Amendment: Section 2A2.4 is amended by striking the Commentary captioned

Amendment 679 APPENDIX C - VOLUME III November 1, 2013

"Background" as follows:

"Background: Violations of 18 U.S.C. §§ 1501, 1502, and 3056(d) are misdemeanors; violation of 18 U.S.C. § 111 is a felony.".

The Commentary to § 2B1.1 captioned "Application Notes" is amended in Note 15 in the first sentence by inserting "involving fraudulent conduct that is" after "establishes an offense"; and in the second sentence by inserting "involves fraudulent conduct that" after "the offense".

Section 2B3.3(c)(1) is amended by inserting "; Fraud Involving the Deprivation of the Intangible Right to Honest Services of Public Officials; Conspiracy to Defraud by Interference with Governmental Functions" after "Official Right".

Section 2C1.3(c)(1) is amended by inserting "; Fraud Involving the Deprivation of the Intangible Right to Honest Services of Public Officials; Conspiracy to Defraud by Interference with Governmental Functions" after "Official Right".

Section 2C1.8(c)(1) is amended by inserting "; Fraud Involving the Deprivation of the Intangible Right to Honest Services of Public Officials; Conspiracy to Defraud by Interference with Governmental Functions" after "Official Right".

The Commentary to § 2D1.1 captioned "Application Notes" is amended in Note 5 in the first paragraph by striking "whether a greater quantity of the analogue is needed to produce a substantially similar effect on the central nervous system as" and inserting "whether the same quantity of analogue produces a greater effect on the central nervous system than".

The Commentary to § 2D1.1 captioned "Application Notes" is amended in Note 19 by striking "(b)(5)(A)" each place it appears and inserting "(b)(6)(A)"; in Note 20 by striking "(b)(5)(B) or (C)" and inserting "(b)(6)(B) or (C)"; and by striking "(b)(5)(C)" and inserting "(b)(6)(C)"; and in Note 21 by striking "(b)(6)" each place it appears and inserting "(b)(7)".

The Commentary to § 2D1.1 captioned "Background" is amended in the ninth paragraph by striking "(b)(5)(A)" and inserting "(b)(6)(A)"; and in the last paragraph by striking "(b)(5)(B) and (C)" and inserting "(b)(6)(B) and (C)".

Section 2D1.11(e) is amended in subdivision (1) by striking "2271 L or more of Gamma-butyrolactone;" and inserting "1135.5 L or more of Gamma-butyrolactone;";

in subdivision (2) by striking "At least 681.3 L but less than 2271 L of Gamma-butyrolactone;" and inserting "At least 340.7 L but less than 1135.5 L of Gamma-butyrolactone;";

in subdivision (3) by striking "At least 227.1 L but less than 681.3 L of Gamma-butyrolactone;" and inserting "At least 113.6 L but less than 340.7 L of Gamma-butyrolactone;";

in subdivision (4) by striking "At least 159 L but less than 227.1 L of Gamma-butyrolactone;" and inserting "At least 79.5 L but less than 113.6 L of Gamma-butyrolactone;";

in subdivision (5) by striking "At least 90.8 L but less than 159 L of Gamma-butyrolactone;" and inserting "At least 45.4 L but less than 79.5 L of Gamma-butyrolactone;";

in subdivision (6) by striking "At least 22.7 L but less than 90.8 L of Gamma-butyrolactone;" and inserting "At least 11.4 L but less than 45.4 L of Gamma-butyrolactone;";

in subdivision (7) by striking "At least 18.2 L but less than 22.7 L of Gamma-butyrolactone;" and inserting "At least 9.1 L but less than 11.4 L of Gamma-butyrolactone;";

in subdivision (8) by striking "At least 13.6 L but less than 18.2 L of Gamma-butyrolactone;" and inserting "At least 6.8 L but less than 9.1 L of Gamma-butyrolactone;";

in subdivision (9) by striking "At least 9.1 L but less than 13.6 L of Gamma-butyrolactone;" and inserting "At least 4.5 L but less than 6.8 L of Gamma-butyrolactone;"; and

in subdivision (10) by striking "Less than 9.1 L of Gamma-butyrolactone;" and inserting "Less than 4.5 L of Gamma-butyrolactone;".

The Commentary to § 2K2.1 captioned "Statutory Provisions" is amended by striking "(e)-(i), (k)-(o)" and inserting "(e)-(h), (j)-(n)".

Section 2M6.1 is amended by striking "(a)(4)*" in subsection (b)(1)(A) and inserting "(a)(4)(A)"; and by striking "*Note: The reference to '(a)(4)' should be to '(a)(4)(A)'.".

Section 3D1.2(d) is amended by striking "2C1.7,".

The Commentary to § 5D1.2 captioned "Application Notes" is amended in Note 2 by inserting "Limitation on" before "Applicability of Statutory".

Section 8C2.1(a) is amended by striking ", 2C1.7".

Appendix A (Statutory Index) is amended by striking the following:

"18 U.S.C. § 924(i) 2K2.1
18 U.S.C. § 924(j)(1) 2A1.1, 2A1.2
18 U.S.C. § 924(j)(2) 2A1.3, 2A1.4
18 U.S.C. § 924(k)-(o) 2K2.1",

and inserting the following:

"18 U.S.C. § 924(i)(1) 2A1.1, 2A1.2
18 U.S.C. § 924(i)(2) 2A1.3, 2A1.4
18 U.S.C. § 924(j)-(n) 2K2.1".

Reason for Amendment: This ten-part amendment consists of technical and conforming amendments to various guidelines.

First, this amendment deletes unnecessary background commentary in § 2A2.4 (Obstructing or Impeding Officers).

Second, this amendment makes minor clarifying amendments to Application Note 15 in the fraud guideline, § 2B1.1, to make clear that, in order for the cross reference at § 2B1.1(c)(3) to apply, the conduct set forth in the count of conviction must establish a fraud or false statement-type offense.

Third, this amendment makes technical amendments to several guidelines to conform to

Amendment 679 APPENDIX C - VOLUME III November 1, 2013

changes made in the public corruption guidelines in the 2004 amendment cycle (see Appendix C to the Guidelines Manual, Amendment 666). Specifically, the amendment corrects title references to § 2C1.1 in §§ 2B3.3(c)(1), 2C1.3(c)(1), and 2C1.8(c)(1) and strikes references to § 2C1.7 in §§ 3D1.2(d) and 8C2.1.

Fourth, this amendment clarifies Application Note 5 in the drug guideline, § 2D1.1, regarding drug analogues. The current note suggests that drug analogues are less potent than the drug for which it is an analogue. However, by statute, analogues can only be the same or more potent.

Fifth, this amendment redesignates incorrect references in a number of Application Notes in the drug guideline, § 2D1.1.

Sixth, this amendment conforms § 2D1.11 (Unlawfully Distributing, Importing, Exporting or Possessing a Listed Chemical; Attempt or Conspiracy) to changes made in the drug guideline, § 2D1.1, in the 2004 amendment cycle (see Appendix C to the Guidelines Manual, Amendment 667). Specifically, the amendment amends the Chemical Quantity Table in § 2D1.11(e) so that the amount of gamma-butyrolactone (GBL), at any particular offense level, is the amount that provides a 100 percent yield of gamma-hydroxybutyric acid (GHB).

Seventh, this amendment updates the statutory provisions in § 2K2.1 (Unlawful Receipt, Possession, or Transportation of Firearms or Ammunition; Prohibited Transactions Involving Firearms or Ammunition) to account for redesignations of 18 U.S.C. § 924 offenses.

Eighth, this amendment corrects a typographical error in § 2M6.1 (Unlawful Production, Development, Acquisition, Stockpiling, Alteration, Use, Transfer, or Possession of Nuclear Material, Weapons, or Facilities, Biological Agents, Toxins, or Delivery Systems, Chemical Weapons, or Other Weapons of Mass Destruction; Attempt or Conspiracy).

Ninth, this amendment corrects the title to § 5C1.2 (Limitation on Applicability of Statutory Minimum Sentences in Certain Cases) in Application Note 2 of § 5D1.2 (Term of Supervised Release.).

Tenth, this amendment corrects Appendix A (Statutory Index) to account for redesignations of 18 U.S.C. § 924 offenses.

Effective Date: The effective date of this amendment is November 1, 2005.

680. Amendment: The Commentary to § 2J1.6 captioned "Application Notes" is amended in Note 3 in the second paragraph in the fourth sentence by striking "See § 3D1.1(b)" and inserting "See § 3D1.1(b)(1)".

The Commentary to § 2K2.1 captioned "Statutory Provisions", as amended by Amendment 679, is amended by striking "(e)-(h), (j)-(n)" and inserting "(e)-(i), (k)-(o)".

The Commentary to § 2P1.2 captioned "Application Notes" is amended in Note 2 in the first paragraph in the fourth sentence by striking "See § 3D1.1(b)" and inserting "See § 3D1.1(b)(1)".

The Commentary to § 3D1.1 captioned "Application Notes" is amended in Note 1 in the first paragraph by striking "Subsection (b)" and inserting "Subsection (b)(1)"; in the fourth sentence by striking "subsection (b)" and inserting "subsection (b)(1)"; and in the second paragraph by striking "subsection (b)" and inserting "subsection (b)(1)".

The Commentary to § 3D1.2 captioned "Application Notes" is amended in Note 1 by

striking "See § 3D1.1(b)" and inserting "See § 3D1.1(b)(1)".

The Commentary to § 5G1.2 captioned "Application Notes", as amended by Amendment 677, is amended in Note 2 in subdivision (A) by striking "(A) specifies" and inserting "(i) specifies" and by striking "(B) requires" and inserting "(ii) requires"; and in subdivision (B)(ii) by striking "(Multiple Counts)" and inserting "(Groups of Closely Related Counts)".

Appendix A (Statutory Index), as amended by Amendment 679, is amended by striking the following:

"18 U.S.C. § 924(i)(1)	2A1.1, 2A1.2
18 U.S.C. § 924(i)(2)	2A1.3, 2A1.4
18 U.S.C. § 924(j)-(n)	2K2.1".

and inserting the following:

"18 U.S.C. § 924(i)	2K2.1
18 U.S.C. § 924(j)(1)	2A1.1, 2A1.2
18 U.S.C. § 924(j)(2)	2A1.3, 2A1.4
18 U.S.C. § 924(k)-(o)	2K2.1".

Reason for Amendment: This amendment makes various technical and conforming changes in order to more fully implement amendments submitted to Congress on April 29, 2005 (see Amendments 677 and 679).

Effective Date: The effective date of this amendment is November 1, 2005.

681. **Amendment:** Section 2D1.1 is amended by redesignating subsections (b)(6) and (b)(7) as subsections (b)(8) and (b)(9), respectively; and by inserting the following after subsection (b)(5):

"(6) If the offense involved the distribution of an anabolic steroid and a masking agent, increase by 2 levels.

(7) If the defendant distributed an anabolic steroid to an athlete, increase by 2 levels.".

Section 2D1.1(c) is amended in the "*Notes to Drug Quantity Table" in subdivision (F) by striking "(except anabolic steroids)"; and by adding at the end the following:

"For an anabolic steroid that is not in a pill, capsule, tablet, or liquid form (e.g., patch, topical cream, aerosol), the court shall determine the base offense level using a reasonable estimate of the quantity of anabolic steroid involved in the offense. In making a reasonable estimate, the court shall consider that each 25 mg of an anabolic steroid is one 'unit'.".

Section 2D1.1(c) is amended in the "*Notes to Drug Quantity Table" by striking subdivision (G) as follows:

"(G) In the case of anabolic steroids, one 'unit' means a 10 cc vial of an injectable steroid or fifty tablets. All vials of injectable steroids are to be converted on the basis of their volume to the equivalent number of 10 cc vials (e.g., one 50 cc vial is to be counted as five 10 cc vials).";

and by redesignating subdivisions (H) through (J) as subdivisions (G) through (I), respectively.

The Commentary to § 2D1.1 captioned "Application Notes" is amended in the first paragraph of Note 8 by inserting "Interaction with § 3B1.3.—" before "A defendant who"; by striking "enhancement" and inserting "adjustment"; and by adding at the end the following:

> "Additionally, an enhancement under § 3B1.3 ordinarily would apply in a case in which the defendant used his or her position as a coach to influence an athlete to use an anabolic steroid.".

The Commentary to § 2D1.1 captioned "Application Notes" is amended in Notes 19 and 20 by striking "(b)(6)" each place it appears and inserting "(b)(8)"; and in Note 21 by striking "(b)(7)" each place it appears and inserting "(b)(9)".

The Commentary to § 2D1.1 captioned "Application Notes" is amended by adding at the end the following:

> "24. Application of Subsection (b)(6).—For purposes of subsection (b)(6), 'masking agent' means a substance that, when taken before, after, or in conjunction with an anabolic steroid, prevents the detection of the anabolic steroid in an individual's body.
>
> 25. Application of Subsection (b)(7).—For purposes of subsection (b)(7), 'athlete' means an individual who participates in an athletic activity conducted by (i) an intercollegiate athletic association or interscholastic athletic association; (ii) a professional athletic association; or (iii) an amateur athletic organization.".

The Commentary to § 2D1.1 captioned "Background" is amended in the ninth paragraph by striking "(b)(6)(A)" and inserting "(b)(8)(A)"; and in the last paragraph by striking "(b)(6)(B) and (C)" and inserting "(b)(8)(B) and (C)".

Reason for Amendment: This amendment implements the directive in the United States Parole Commission Extension and Sentencing Commission Authority Act of 2005, Pub. L. 109–76, which required the Commission, under emergency amendment authority, to implement section 3 of the Anabolic Steroid Control Act of 2004, Pub. L. 108–358 (the "ASC Act"). The ASC Act directed the Commission to "review the Federal sentencing guidelines with respect to offenses involving anabolic steroids" and "consider amending the. . .guidelines to provide for increased penalties with respect to offenses involving anabolic steroids in a manner that reflects the seriousness of such offenses and the need to deter anabolic steroid trafficking and use. . .."

The amendment implements the directives by increasing the penalties for offenses involving anabolic steroids. It does so by changing the manner in which anabolic steroids are treated under § 2D1.1 (Unlawful Manufacturing, Importing, Exporting, or Trafficking (Including Possession with Intent to Commit These Offenses); Attempt or Conspiracy). The amendment eliminates the sentencing distinction between anabolic steroids and other Schedule III substances when the steroid is in a pill, capsule, tablet, or liquid form. For anabolic steroids in other forms (e.g., patch, topical cream, aerosol), the amendment instructs the court that it shall make a reasonable estimate of the quantity of anabolic steroid involved in the offense, and in making such estimate, the court shall consider that each 25 mg of anabolic steroid is one "unit".

In addition, the amendment addresses two harms often associated with anabolic steroid offenses by providing new enhancements in § 2D1.1(b)(6) and (b)(7). Subsection (b)(6) provides a two-level enhancement if the offense involved the distribution of an anabolic steroid and a masking agent. Subsection (b)(7) provides a two-level enhancement if the defendant distributed an anabolic steroid to an athlete. Both enhancements address congressional concern with distribution of anabolic steroids to athletes, particularly the impact that steroids distribution and steroids use has on the integrity of sport, either because of the unfair advantage gained by the use of steroids or because of the concealment of such use.

The amendment also amends Application Note 8 of § 2D1.1 to provide that an adjustment under § 3B1.3 (Abuse of Position of Trust or Use of Special Skill) ordinarily would apply in the case of a defendant who used his or her position as a coach to influence an athlete to use an anabolic steroid.

Effective Date: The effective date of this amendment is March 27, 2006.

682. **Amendment:** The Commentary to § 2B5.3 captioned "Application Notes" is amended in Note 2(A) by adding at the end the following:

> "(vii) A case under 18 U.S.C. § 2318 or § 2320 that involves a counterfeit label, patch, sticker, wrapper, badge, emblem, medallion, charm, box, container, can, case, hangtag, documentation, or packaging of any type or nature (I) that has not been affixed to, or does not enclose or accompany a good or service; and (II) which, had it been so used, would appear to a reasonably informed purchaser to be affixed to, enclosing or accompanying an identifiable, genuine good or service. In such a case, the 'infringed item' is the identifiable, genuine good or service.".

Reason for Amendment: This amendment implements the emergency directive in section 1(c) of the Stop Counterfeiting in Manufactured Goods Act, Pub. L. 109–181. The directive, which requires the Commission to promulgate an amendment under emergency amendment authority by September 12, 2006, instructs the Commission to "review, and if appropriate, amend the Federal sentencing guidelines and policy statements applicable to persons convicted of any offense under section 2318 or 2320 of title 18, United States Code . . .." The directive further provides that the Commission shall:

> determine whether the definition of "infringement amount" set forth in application note 2 of section 2B5.3 of the Federal sentencing guidelines is adequate to address situations in which the defendant has been convicted of one of the offenses [under section 2318 or 2320 of title 18, United States Code,] and the item in which the defendant trafficked was not an infringing item but rather was intended to facilitate infringement, such as an anti-circumvention device, or the item in which the defendant trafficked was infringing and also was intended to facilitate infringement in another good or service, such as a counterfeit label, documentation, or packaging, taking into account cases such as U.S. v. Sung, 87 F.3d 194 (7th Cir. 1996).

The emergency amendment adds subdivision (vii) to Application Note 2(A) of § 2B5.3 (Criminal Infringement of Copyright or Trademark) to provide that the infringement amount is based on the retail value of the infringed item in a case under 18 U.S.C. § 2318 or § 2320 that involves a counterfeit label, patch, sticker, wrapper, badge, emblem, medallion, charm, box, container, can, case, hangtag, documentation, or packaging of any type or nature (I) that has not been affixed to, or does not enclose or accompany a good or service; and (II) which, had it been so used, would appear to a reasonably informed purchaser to be affixed to, enclosing or accompanying an identifiable, genuine good or service. In

Amendment 682

such a case, the "infringed item" is the identifiable, genuine good or service.

Effective Date: The effective date of this amendment is September 12, 2006.

683. **Amendment:** Chapter One, Part B is amended by adding at the end the following:

"§ 1B1.13. Reduction in Term of Imprisonment as a Result of Motion by Director of Bureau of Prisons (Policy Statement)

Upon motion of the Director of the Bureau of Prisons under 18 U.S.C. § 3582(c)(1)(A), the court may reduce a term of imprisonment (and may impose a term of supervised release with or without conditions that does not exceed the unserved portion of the original term of imprisonment) if, after considering the factors set forth in 18 U.S.C. § 3553(a), to the extent that they are applicable, the court determines that—

(1)   (A)   extraordinary and compelling reasons warrant the reduction; or

       (B)   the defendant (i) is at least 70 years old; and (ii) has served at least 30 years in prison pursuant to a sentence imposed under 18 U.S.C. § 3559(c) for the offense or offenses for which the defendant is imprisoned;

(2)   the defendant is not a danger to the safety of any other person or to the community, as provided in 18 U.S.C. § 3142(g); and

(3)   the reduction is consistent with this policy statement.

Commentary

Application Notes:

1. Application of Subsection (1)(A).—

     (A)   Extraordinary and Compelling Reasons.—A determination made by the Director of the Bureau of Prisons that a particular case warrants a reduction for extraordinary and compelling reasons shall be considered as such for purposes of subdivision (1)(A).

     (B)   Rehabilitation of the Defendant.—Pursuant to 28 U.S.C. § 994(t), rehabilitation of the defendant is not, by itself, an extraordinary and compelling reason for purposes of subdivision (1)(A).

2. Application of Subdivision (3).—Any reduction made pursuant to a motion by the Director of the Bureau of Prisons for the reasons set forth in subdivisions (1) and (2) is consistent with this policy statement.

Background: This policy statement is an initial step toward implementing 28 U.S.C. § 994(t). The Commission intends to develop further criteria to be applied and a list of specific examples of extraordinary and compelling reasons for sentence reduction pursuant to such statute.".

Reason for Amendment: This amendment creates a new policy statement at § 1B1.13 (Reduction in Term of Imprisonment as a Result of Motion by Director of Bureau of Prisons) as a first step toward implementing the directive in 28 U.S.C. § 994(t) that the Commission "in promulgating general policy statements regarding the sentence modification provisions in section 3582(c)(1)(A) of title 18, shall describe what should be considered extraordinary and compelling reasons for sentence reduction, including the criteria to be applied and a list of specific examples." The policy statement restates the statutory bases for a reduction in sentence under 18 U.S.C. § 3582(c)(1)(A). In addition, the policy statement provides that in all cases there must be a determination made by the court that the defendant is not a danger to the safety of any other person or to the community. The amendment also provides background commentary that states the Commission's intent to develop criteria to be applied and a list of specific examples pursuant to 28 U.S.C. § 994(t).

Effective Date: The effective date of this amendment is November 1, 2006.

684. **Amendment:** The Commentary to § 1B1.1 captioned "Application Notes" is amended by striking Note 6 as follows:

> "6. In the case of a defendant subject to a sentence enhancement under 18 U.S.C. § 3147 (Penalty for an Offense Committed While on Release), see § 2J1.7 (Commission of Offense While on Release).";

and by redesignating Note 7 as Note 6.

Section 2D1.1(c) is amended by striking "(or the equivalent amount of other Schedule I or II Opiates)" each place it appears; by striking "(or the equivalent amount of other Schedule I or II Stimulants)" each place it appears; and by striking "(or the equivalent amount of other Schedule I or II Hallucinogens)" each place it appears.

Section 2D1.1(d)(1) is amended by inserting "or § 2A1.2 (Second Degree Murder), as appropriate, if the resulting offense level is greater than that determined under this guideline" after "Murder)".

The Commentary to § 2D1.1 captioned "Application Notes" is amended in Note 10 in the first paragraph by striking the third and fourth sentences as follows:

> "The Drug Equivalency Tables set forth below provide conversion factors for other substances, which the Drug Quantity Table refers to as 'equivalents' of these drugs. For example, one gram of a substance containing oxymorphone, a Schedule I opiate, is to be treated as the equivalent of five kilograms of marihuana in applying the Drug Quantity Table.",

and inserting the following:

> "In the case of a controlled substance that is not specifically referenced in the Drug Quantity Table, determine the base offense level as follows:
>
> (A) Use the Drug Equivalency Tables to convert the quantity of the controlled substance involved in the offense to its equivalent quantity of marihuana.
>
> (B) Find the equivalent quantity of marihuana in the Drug Quantity Table.
>
> (C) Use the offense level that corresponds to the equivalent quantity of marihuana as the base offense level for the controlled substance involved in the offense.
>
> (See also Application Note 5.) For example, in the Drug Equivalency Tables set forth in this Note, 1 gm of a substance containing oxymorphone, a Schedule I opi-

Amendment 684

ate, converts to an equivalent quantity of 5 kg of marihuana. In a case involving 100 gm of oxymorphone, the equivalent quantity of marihuana would be 500 kg, which corresponds to a base offense level of 28 in the Drug Quantity Table.".

Chapter Two, Part J is amended by striking § 2J1.7 and its accompanying commentary as follows:

"§ 2J1.7.   Commission of Offense While on Release

If an enhancement under 18 U.S.C. § 3147 applies, add 3 levels to the offense level for the offense committed while on release as if this section were a specific offense characteristic contained in the offense guideline for the offense committed while on release.

Commentary

Statutory Provision: 18 U.S.C. § 3147.

Application Notes:

1. Because 18 U.S.C. § 3147 is an enhancement provision, rather than an offense, this section provides a specific offense characteristic to increase the offense level for the offense committed while on release.

2. Under 18 U.S.C. § 3147, a sentence of imprisonment must be imposed in addition to the sentence for the underlying offense, and the sentence of imprisonment imposed under 18 U.S.C. § 3147 must run consecutively to any other sentence of imprisonment. Therefore, the court, in order to comply with the statute, should divide the sentence on the judgment form between the sentence attributable to the underlying offense and the sentence attributable to the enhancement. The court will have to ensure that the 'total punishment' (i.e., the sentence for the offense committed while on release plus the sentence enhancement under 18 U.S.C. § 3147) is in accord with the guideline range for the offense committed while on release, as adjusted by the enhancement in this section. For example, if the applicable adjusted guideline range is 30-37 months and the court determines 'total punishment' of 36 months is appropriate, a sentence of 30 months for the underlying offense plus 6 months under 18 U.S.C. § 3147 would satisfy this requirement.

Background: An enhancement under 18 U.S.C. § 3147 may be imposed only after sufficient notice to the defendant by the government or the court, and applies only in the case of a conviction for a federal offense that is committed while on release on another federal charge.

Legislative history indicates that the mandatory nature of the penalties required by 18 U.S.C. § 3147 was to be eliminated upon the implementation of the sentencing guidelines. 'Section 213(h) [renumbered as § 200(g) in the Crime Control Act of 1984] amends the new provision in title I of this Act relating to consecutive enhanced penalties for committing an offense on release (new 18 U.S.C. § 3147) by eliminating the mandatory nature of the penalties in favor of utilizing sentencing guidelines.' (Senate Report 98-225 at 186). Not all of the phraseology relating to the requirement of a mandatory sentence, however, was actually deleted from the statute. Consequently, it appears that the court is required to impose a consecutive sentence of imprisonment under this provision, but there is no requirement as to any minimum term. This guideline is drafted to enable the court to determine and implement a combined 'total punishment' consistent with the overall structure of the guidelines, while at the same time complying with the statutory requirement. Guideline provisions that prohibit the grouping of counts of conviction requiring consecutive sentences (e.g., the introductory paragraph of § 3D1.2; § 5G1.2(a)) do not apply to this section because 18 U.S.C. § 3147 is an enhancement, not a count of conviction.".

Chapter 3, Part C is amended in the heading by adding at the end "AND RELATED ADJUSTMENTS".

Chapter Three, Part C is amended by adding at the end the following:

"§ 3C1.3. Commission of Offense While on Release

If a statutory sentencing enhancement under 18 U.S.C. § 3147 applies, increase the offense level by 3 levels.

Commentary

Application Note:

1. Under 18 U.S.C. § 3147, a sentence of imprisonment must be imposed in addition to the sentence for the underlying offense, and the sentence of imprisonment imposed under 18 U.S.C. § 3147 must run consecutively to any other sentence of imprisonment. Therefore, the court, in order to comply with the statute, should divide the sentence on the judgment form between the sentence attributable to the underlying offense and the sentence attributable to the enhancement. The court will have to ensure that the 'total punishment' (i.e., the sentence for the offense committed while on release plus the statutory sentencing enhancement under 18 U.S.C. § 3147) is in accord with the guideline range for the offense committed while on release, as adjusted by the enhancement in this section. For example, if the applicable adjusted guideline range is 30-37 months and the court determines a 'total punishment' of 36 months is appropriate, a sentence of 30 months for the underlying offense plus 6 months under 18 U.S.C. § 3147 would satisfy this requirement.

Background: An enhancement under 18 U.S.C. § 3147 applies, after appropriate sentencing notice, when a defendant is sentenced for an offense committed while released in connection with another federal offense.

This guideline enables the court to determine and implement a combined 'total punishment' consistent with the overall structure of the guidelines, while at the same time complying with the statutory requirement.".

Reason for Amendment: This amendment addresses several problematic areas of guideline application. First, the amendment adds language to the cross reference at subsection (d) of § 2D1.1 (Unlawful Manufacturing, Importing, Exporting, or Trafficking (Including Possession with Intent to Commit These Offenses); Attempt or Conspiracy) to allow the application of § 2A1.2 (Second Degree Murder) in cases in which the conduct involved is second degree murder, if the resulting offense level is greater than the offense level determined under § 2D1.1.

Second, the amendment creates a new guideline at § 3C1.3 (Commission of Offense While on Release), which provides a three-level adjustment in cases in which the statutory sentencing enhancement at 18 U.S.C. § 3147 (Penalty for an offense committed while on release) applies. The amendment also deletes § 2J1.7 (Commission of Offense While on

Release), the Chapter Two guideline to which the statutory enhancement at 18 U.S.C. § 3147 had been referenced prior to the amendment. Despite its reference in Appendix A (Statutory Index), 18 U.S.C. § 3147 is not an offense of conviction and thus does not require reference in Appendix A. Creating a Chapter Three adjustment for 18 U.S.C. § 3147 cases ensures the enhancement is not overlooked and is consistent with other adjustments in Chapter Three, all of which apply to a broad range of offenses.

Third, the amendment deletes from the Drug Quantity Table in § 2D1.1(c) language that indicates the court should apply "the equivalent amount of other Schedule I or II Opiates" (in the line referenced to Heroin), "the equivalent amount of other Schedule I or II Stimulants" (in the line referenced to Cocaine), and "the equivalent amount of other Schedule I or II Hallucinogens" (in the line referenced to LSD). This language caused some guideline users to erroneously calculate the base offense level without converting the controlled substance to its marihuana equivalency, even though Application Note 10 of § 2D1.1 sets forth the marihuana equivalencies for substances not specifically referenced in the Drug Quantity Table. For example, instead of converting 10 KG of morphine (an opiate) to 5000 KG of marihuana and determining the base offense level on that marihuana equivalency (resulting in a base offense level of 34), some guideline users determined the base offense level on the 10 KG of morphine by using the equivalent amount of heroin (resulting in a base offense level of 36). This amendment deletes the problematic language and also clarifies in Application Note 10 that, for cases involving a substance not specifically referenced in the Drug Quantity Table, the court is to determine the base offense level using the marihuana equivalency for that controlled substance.

Effective Date: The effective date of this amendment is November 1, 2006.

685. Amendment: The Commentary to § 2A1.1 captioned "Statutory Provisions" is amended by inserting "1841(a)(2)(C)," after "1111,".

The Commentary to § 2A1.2 captioned "Statutory Provisions" is amended by inserting "1841(a)(2)(C)," after "1111,".

The Commentary to § 2A1.3 captioned "Statutory Provisions" is amended by inserting "1841(a)(2)(C)," after "1112,".

The Commentary to § 2A1.4 captioned "Statutory Provisions" is amended by inserting "1841(a)(2)(C)," after "1112,".

The Commentary to § 2A2.1 captioned "Statutory Provisions" is amended by inserting "1841(a)(2)(C)," after "1751(c),".

The Commentary to § 2A2.2 captioned "Statutory Provisions" is amended by inserting "1841(a)(2)(C)," after "1751(e),".

Section 2B1.1(b)(6) is amended by inserting "or veterans' memorial" after "national cemetery".

The Commentary to § 2B1.1 captioned "Statutory Provisions" is amended by inserting "1369," after "1363,".

The Commentary to § 2B1.1 captioned "Application Notes" is amended in Note 1 by inserting after the paragraph that begins "'Trade secret'" the following paragraph:

"'Veterans' memorial' means any structure, plaque, statue, or other monument described in 18 U.S.C. § 1369(a).".

Section 2B1.5(b)(2)(E) is amended by inserting "or veterans' memorial" after "cemetery".

The Commentary to § 2B1.5 captioned "Statutory Provisions" is amended by inserting "1369," after "1361,".

The Commentary to § 2B1.5 captioned "Application Notes" is amended in Note 3 in subdivision (B) by striking "has the meaning given that term" and inserting "and 'veterans' memorial' have the meaning given those terms".

The Commentary to § 2N2.1 captioned "Application Notes" is amended by striking Note 3 as follows:

> "3. If death or bodily injury, extreme psychological injury, property damage or monetary loss resulted, an upward departure may be warranted. See Chapter Five, Part K (Departures).",

and inserting the following:

> "3. <u>Upward Departure Provisions</u>.—The following are circumstances in which an upward departure may be warranted:
>
> (A) Death or bodily injury, extreme psychological injury, property damage, or monetary loss resulted. <u>See</u> Chapter Five, Part K (Departures).
>
> (B) The defendant was convicted under 7 U.S.C. § 7734.".

Chapter Two, Part T, Subpart 3 is amended in the "Introductory Commentary" in the first sentence by inserting "and 3907," after "1708(b),"; in the second sentence by striking "It is not intended to deal with the importation of contraband," and inserting "It is intended to deal with some types of contraband, such as certain uncertified diamonds, but is not intended to deal with the importation of other types of contraband,"; in the last sentence by inserting "not specifically covered by this Subpart" after "stolen goods"; and by inserting "if there is not another more specific applicable guideline" after "upward".

The Commentary to § 2T3.1 captioned "Statutory Provisions" is amended by inserting ", 3907" after "1708(b)".

Chapter Two, Part X, Subpart 5 is amended in the heading by inserting "FELONY" after "OTHER"; and by adding at the end "AND CLASS A MISDEMEANORS".

Section 2X5.1 is amended in the heading by inserting "Felony" after "Other".

Section 2X5.1 is amended by striking "or Class A misdemeanor"; by striking "(b)" after "18 U.S.C. § 3553"; and by adding at the end the following paragraph:

> "If the defendant is convicted under 18 U.S.C. § 1841(a)(1), apply the guideline that covers the conduct the defendant is convicted of having engaged in, as that conduct is described in 18 U.S.C. § 1841(a)(1) and listed in 18 U.S.C. § 1841(b).".

The Commentary the § 2X5.1 is amended by inserting before "<u>Application Note</u>:" the following:

> "<u>Statutory Provision</u>: 18 U.S.C. § 1841(a)(1).".

The Commentary the § 2X5.1 captioned "Application Note" is amended by striking "Note" and inserting "Notes"; in Note 1 by inserting "In General.—" before "Guidelines"; and by adding at the end the following:

"2. Convictions under 18 U.S.C. § 1841(a)(1).—

(A) In General.—If the defendant is convicted under 18 U.S.C. § 1841(a)(1), the Chapter Two offense guideline that applies is the guideline that covers the conduct the defendant is convicted of having engaged in, i.e., the conduct of which the defendant is convicted that violates a specific provision listed in 18 U.S.C. § 1841(b) and that results in the death of, or bodily injury to, a child in utero at the time of the offense of conviction. For example, if the defendant committed aggravated sexual abuse against the unborn child's mother and it caused the death of the child in utero, the applicable Chapter Two guideline would be § 2A3.1 (Criminal Sexual Abuse; Attempt to Commit Criminal Sexual Abuse).

(B) Upward Departure Provision.—For offenses under 18 U.S.C. § 1841(a)(1), an upward departure may be warranted if the offense level under the applicable guideline does not adequately account for the death of, or serious bodily injury to, the child in utero.

3. Application of § 2X5.2.—This guideline applies only to felony offenses not referenced in Appendix A (Statutory Index). For Class A misdemeanor offenses that have not been referenced in Appendix A, apply § 2X5.2 (Class A Misdemeanors (Not Covered by Another Specific Offense Guideline)).".

The Commentary to § 2X5.1 captioned "Background" is amended in the first paragraph by striking the following:

"Where there is no sufficiently analogous guideline, the provisions of 18 U.S.C. § 3553(b) control. That statute provides in relevant part as follows: 'In the absence of an applicable sentencing guideline, the court shall impose an appropriate sentence, having due regard for the purposes set forth in [18 U.S.C. § 3553] subsection (a)(2). In the absence of an applicable sentencing guideline in the case of an offense other than a petty offense, the court shall also have due regard for the relationship of the sentence imposed to sentences prescribed by guidelines applicable to similar offenses and offenders, and to the applicable policy statements of the Sentencing Commission.'",

and inserting the following:

"In a case in which there is no sufficiently analogous guideline, the provisions of 18 U.S.C. § 3553 control.".

Chapter Two, Part X, Subpart 5 is amended by adding at the end the following:

"§ 2X5.2. Class A Misdemeanors (Not Covered by Another Specific Offense Guideline)

(a) Base Offense Level: 6

Commentary

Statutory Provisions: 7 U.S.C. § 2156; 18 U.S.C. §§ 1365(f), 1801; 42 U.S.C. §§ 1129(a), 14133.

Application Note:

1. Ｉｎ General.—This guideline applies to Class A misdemeanor offenses that are specifically referenced in Appendix A (Statutory Index) to this guideline. This guideline also applies to Class A misdemeanor offenses that have not been referenced in Appendix A. Do not apply this guideline to a Class A misdemeanor that has been specifically referenced in Appendix A to another Chapter Two guideline.".

Appendix A (Statutory Index) is amended by inserting after the line referenced to 7 U.S.C. § 2024(c) the following:

"7 U.S.C. § 2156   2X5.2";

by inserting after the line referenced to 18 U.S.C. § 1121 the following:

"18 U.S.C. § 1129(a)   2X5.2";

by inserting after the line referenced to 18 U.S.C. § 1365(e) the following:

"18 U.S.C. § 1365(f)   2X5.2";

by inserting after the line referenced to 18 U.S.C. § 1366 the following:

"18 U.S.C. § 1369   2B1.1, 2B1.5";

by inserting after the line referenced to 18 U.S.C. § 1792 the following:

"18 U.S.C. § 1801   2X5.2";

by inserting after the line referenced to 18 U.S.C. § 1832 the following:

"18 U.S.C. § 1841(a)(1)   2X5.1
18 U.S.C. § 1841(a)(2)(C) 2A1.1, 2A1.2, 2A1.3,
                           2A1.4, 2A2.1, 2A2.2";

by inserting after the line referenced to 19 U.S.C. § 2401f the following:

"19 U.S.C. § 3907   2T3.1"; and

by inserting after the line referenced to 42 U.S.C. § 9603(d) the following:

"42 U.S.C. § 14133   2X5.2".

Reason for Amendment: This five-part amendment makes several additions to various guideline provisions in response to recently-enacted legislation, and creates a new guideline at § 2X5.2 to cover certain Class A misdemeanors.

First, this amendment responds to section 2 of the Veterans' Memorial Preservation and Recognition Act of 2003, Pub. L. 108–29. This Act created a new offense at 18 U.S.C. § 1369 that prohibits the destruction of veterans' memorials and imposes a ten-year statutory maximum term of imprisonment. This amendment refers this new offense to both §§ 2B1.1 (Theft, Property Destruction, and Fraud) and 2B1.5 (Theft of, Damage to, or Destruction of, Cultural Heritage Resources), and broadens the application of the two-level enhancement under both §§ 2B1.1(b)(6) and 2B1.5(b)(2) to include veterans' memorials. The two-level enhancement at § 2B1.1(b)(6), combined with the cross reference at § 2B1.1(c)(4), ensures that the penalty for the destruction of veterans' memorials will reflect the status of a veterans' memorial as a specially protected cultural heritage resource.

Second, this amendment addresses the Plant Protection Act of 2002, Pub. L. 107–171, which created a new offense under 7 U.S.C. § 7734 for knowingly importing or exporting plants, plant products, biological control organisms, and like products for distribution or sale. The statutory maximum term of imprisonment for the first offense is five years, and for subsequent offenses the statutory maximum term of imprisonment is ten years. This amendment modifies Application Note 3 of § 2N2.1 (Violations of Statutes and Regulations Dealing with Any Food, Drug, Biological Product, Device, Cosmetic, or Agricultural Product) to provide that an upward departure may be warranted if a defendant is convicted under 7 U.S.C. § 7734.

Third, this amendment addresses the Clean Diamond Trade Act of 2003, Pub. L. 108–19, and accompanying Executive Order 13312, which prohibits (1) "the importation into, or exportation from, the United States . . . of any rough diamond, from whatever source, unless the rough diamond has been controlled through the [Kimberley Process Certification Scheme]; and (2) any transaction by a United States person anywhere, or any transaction that occurs in whole or in part within the United States, that evades or avoids, or has the purpose of evading or avoiding, or attempts to violate, any of the prohibitions set forth in this section," and conspiracies to commit such acts. This amendment references the new offense at 19 U.S.C. § 3907 to § 2T3.1 (Evading Import Duties or Restrictions (Smuggling); Receiving or Trafficking in Smuggled Property) because the offense involves importing into the United States "conflict" diamonds (so-called because the profits from their sale are frequently used to fund rebel and military activities) without proper certification or payment of duty fees according to the Kimberley Process Certification Scheme, a process that legitimizes the quality and original source of the diamond. Because the essence of this new statutory offense is to avoid proper certification and evade duty fees, penalties for its violation are appropriately covered by § 2T3.1. This amendment also adds language referencing "contraband diamonds" to the introductory commentary of Chapter Two, Part T, Subpart Three to indicate that uncertified diamonds are contraband covered by § 2T3.1 even if other types of contraband are covered by other, more specific guidelines.

Fourth, this amendment implements the Unborn Victims of Violence Act of 2004, Pub. L. 108–212, which created a new offense at 18 U.S.C. § 1841 for causing death or serious bodily injury to a child in utero while engaging in conduct violative of any of over 60 offenses enumerated at 18 U.S.C. § 1841(b). Under 18 U.S.C. § 1841(a)(1) and (a)(2)(A), the statutory maximum term of imprisonment for the conduct that "caused the death of, or bodily injury to a child in utero shall be the penalty provided under Federal law for that conduct had that injury or death occurred to the unborn child's mother." Otherwise, under 18 U.S.C. § 1841(a)(2)(C), if the person "engaging in the conduct . . . intentionally kills or attempts to kill the unborn child, that person shall be punished . . . under sections 1111, 1112, and 1113 for intentionally killing or attempting to kill a human being." The amendment references 18 U.S.C. § 1841(a)(2)(C) to the guidelines designated in Appendix A for 18 U.S.C. §§ 1111, 1112, and 1113, which are §§ 2A1.1 (First Degree Murder), 2A1.2 (Second Degree Murder), 2A1.3 (Voluntary Manslaughter), and 2A1.4 (Involuntary Manslaughter). This amendment also refers the provisions under 18 U.S.C. § 1841(a)(1) and (a)(2)(A) to 2X5.1 (Other Offenses) and adds a special instruction that the most analogous guideline for these offenses is the guideline that covers the underlying offenses. Fifth, this amendment creates a new guideline at § 2X5.2 (Class A Misdemeanors) that covers all Class A misdemeanors not otherwise referenced to a more specific

Chapter Two guideline. The amendment assigns a base offense level of 6 for such offenses, consistent with the guidelines' treatment of many Class A misdemeanor and regulatory offenses. The amendment also references several new Class A Misdemeanors to this guideline. With the promulgation of this new guideline, the Commission will reference new Class A Misdemeanor offenses either to this guideline or to another, more specific Chapter Two guideline, as appropriate.

Effective Date: The effective date of this amendment is November 1, 2006.

686. Amendment: Chapter Two, Part A, Subpart 6 is amended in the heading by inserting "HOAXES," after "COMMUNICATIONS,".

Section 2A6.1 is amended in the heading by adding at the end "; Hoaxes".

Section 2A6.1 is amended by adding at the end the following:

"(c) Cross Reference

(1) If the offense involved any conduct evidencing an intent to carry out a threat to use a weapon of mass destruction, as defined in 18 U.S.C. § 2332a(c)(2)(B), (C), and (D), apply § 2M6.1 (Weapons of Mass Destruction), if the resulting offense level is greater than that determined under this guideline.".

The Commentary to § 2A6.1 captioned "Statutory Provisions" is amended by inserting "1038," after "879,".

The Commentary to § 2K2.1 captioned "Statutory Provisions" is amended by inserting ", 2332g" after "(k)-(o)".

Section 2L1.1(b), as amended by Amendment 692, is further amended by adding at the end the following:

"(9) If the defendant was convicted under 8 U.S.C. § 1324(a)(4), increase by 2 levels.".

The Commentary to § 2M6.1 captioned "Statutory Provisions" is amended by inserting "175c," after "175b,"; by inserting "832," after "831,"; and by inserting ", 2332h" before "; 42 U.S.C.".

Appendix A (Statutory Index) is amended by inserting after the line referenced to 18 U.S.C. § 175b the following:

"18 U.S.C. § 175c   2M6.1";

by inserting after the line referenced to 18 U.S.C. § 831 the following:

"18 U.S.C. § 832   2M6.1";

by inserting after the line referenced to 18 U.S.C. § 1037 the following:

"18 U.S.C. § 1038   2A6.1"; and

by inserting after the line referenced to 18 U.S.C. § 2332f the following:

Amendment 686 APPENDIX C - VOLUME III November 1, 2013

    "18 U.S.C. § 2332g   2K2.1
    18 U.S.C. § 2332h   2M6.1".

Reason for Amendment: This amendment implements various provisions of the Intelligence Reform and Terrorism Prevention Act of 2004 (the "Act"), Pub. L. 108-458. Section 5401 of the Act adds a new subsection (a)(4) to 8 U.S.C. § 1324 that increases the otherwise applicable penalties by up to ten years' imprisonment for bringing aliens into the United States if (A) the conduct is part of an ongoing commercial organization or enterprise; (B) aliens were transported in groups of 10 or more; and (C)(i) aliens were transported in a manner that endangered their lives; or (ii) the aliens presented a life-threatening health risk to people in the United States. Offenses under 18 U.S.C. § 1324 are referenced to § 2L1.1 (Smuggling, Transporting, or Harboring an Unlawful Alien). In response to the new offense, the amendment adds a two-level specific offense characteristic at § 2L1.1(b)(7) applicable to offenses of conviction under 8 U.S.C. § 1324(a)(4), to account for the increased statutory maximum penalty for such offenses.

Section 6702 of the Act creates a new offense at 18 U.S.C. § 1038 (False Information and Hoaxes). The amendment references the new offense to § 2A6.1 (Threatening or Harassing Communications) and adds a cross reference to § 2M6.1 (Unlawful Production, Development, Acquisition, Stockpiling, Alteration, Use, Transfer, or Possession of Nuclear Material, Weapons, or Facilities, Biological Agents, Toxins, or Delivery Systems, Chemical Weapons, or Other Weapons of Mass Destruction; Attempt or Conspiracy) if the conduct supports a threat to use a weapon of mass destruction. The Commission referenced the new offense to these guidelines because the conduct criminalized by the new statute is analogous to conduct already covered by other statutes referenced to these two guidelines.

Section 6803 of the Act creates a new offense at 18 U.S.C. § 832 (Participation in Nuclear and Weapons of Mass Destruction Threats in the United States), relating to participation in nuclear, and weapons of mass destruction, threats to the United States. Section 6803 also adds this new offense to the list of predicate offenses at 18 U.S.C. § 2332b(g)(5)(B)(i) and amends sections 57(b) and 92 of the Atomic Energy Act of 1954 (42 U.S.C. § 2077(b)) to cover the participation of an individual in the development of special nuclear material. The amendment references 18 U.S.C. § 832 to § 2M6.1 because this offense is similar to other offenses referenced to this guideline.

Section 6903 of the Act creates a new offense at 18 U.S.C. § 2332g (Missile Systems Designed to Destroy Aircraft) prohibiting the production or transfer of missile systems designed to destroy aircraft. The amendment references 18 U.S.C. § 2332g to § 2K2.1 (Unlawful Receipt, Possession, or Transportation of Firearms or Ammunition; Prohibited Transactions Involving Firearms or Ammunition) because the types of weapons described in the offense would be covered as destructive devices under 26 U.S.C. § 5845(a).

Section 6905 of the Act creates a new offense at 18 U.S.C. § 2332h (Radiological Dispersal Devices) prohibiting the production, transfer, receipt, possession, or threat to use, any radiological dispersal device. The amendment references 18 U.S.C. § 2332h to § 2M6.1 because of the nature of the offense. Section 2M6.1 covers conduct dealing with the production of certain types of nuclear, biological, or chemical weapons or other weapons of mass destruction, including weapons of mass destruction that, as defined in 18 U.S.C. § 2332a, are designed to release radiation or radioactivity at levels dangerous to human life.

Section 6906 of the Act creates a new offense at 18 U.S.C. § 175c (Variola Virus) that prohibits the production, acquisition, transfer, or possession of, or the threat to use, the variola virus. The amendment references the new offense to § 2M6.1 because the variola virus may be used as a biological agent or toxin and, therefore, it is appropriate to reference this new offense to this guideline.

Effective Date: The effective date of this amendment is November 1, 2006.

687. **Amendment:** Section 2B5.3 and Appendix A (Statutory Index), effective October 24, 2005 (see USSC Guidelines Manual, Supplement to Appendix C, Amendment 675), are repromulgated with the following changes:

The Commentary to § 2B5.3 captioned "Application Notes" is amended in Note 1, in the paragraph that begins 'Uploading' by striking "item in an openly shared file" and inserting "item as an openly shared file"; and by striking "placed in".

Reason for Amendment: This amendment re-promulgates as a permanent amendment the temporary, emergency amendment to § 2B5.3 (Criminal Infringement of Copyright or Trademark), and Appendix A (Statutory Index), which became effective on October 24, 2005. The amendment implements the directive in section 105 of the Family Entertainment and Copyright Act of 2005, Pub. L. 109–9, which instructs the Commission, under emergency authority, to "review and, if appropriate, amend the Federal sentencing guidelines and policy statements applicable to persons convicted of intellectual property rights crimes. . ."

"In carrying out [the directive], the Commission shall—

(1) take all appropriate measures to ensure that the Federal sentencing guidelines and policy statements. . .are sufficiently stringent to deter, and adequately reflect the nature of, intellectual property rights crimes;

(2) determine whether to provide a sentencing enhancement for those convicted of the offenses [involving intellectual property rights], if the conduct involves the display, performance, publication, reproduction, or distribution of a copyrighted work before it has been authorized by the copyright owner, whether in the media format used by the infringing party or in any other media format;

(3) determine whether the scope of 'uploading' set forth in application note 3 of section 2B5.3 of the Federal sentencing guidelines is adequate to address the loss attributable to people who, without authorization, broadly distribute copyrighted works over the Internet; and

(4) determine whether the sentencing guideline and policy statements applicable to the offenses [involving intellectual property rights] adequately reflect any harm to victims from copyright infringement if law enforcement authorities cannot determine how many times copyrighted material has been reproduced or distributed."

Pre-Release Works

The amendment provides a separate two-level enhancement if the offense involved a pre-release work. The enhancement and the corresponding definition use language directly from 17 U.S.C. § 506(a) (criminal infringement). The amendment adds language to Application Note 2 that explains that in cases involving pre-release works, the infringement amount should be determined by using the retail value of the infringed item, rather than any premium price attributed to the infringing item because of its pre-release status. The amendment addresses concerns that distribution of an item before it is legally available to the consumer is more serious conduct than distribution of other infringing items and involves a harm not addressed by the current guideline.

Uploading

The concern underlying the uploading directive pertains to offenses in which the copyrighted work is transferred through file sharing. The amendment builds on the current definition of "uploading" to include making an infringing item available on the Internet by storing an infringing item as an openly shared file. The amendment also clarifies that uploading does not include merely downloading or installing infringing items on a hard drive of the defendant's computer unless the infringing item is in an openly shared file. By clarifying the definition of uploading in this manner, Application Note 3, which is a restatement of the uploading definition, is no longer necessary and the amendment deletes the application note from the guideline.

Indeterminate Number

The amendment addresses the final directive by amending Application Note 2, which sets forth the rules for determining the infringement amount. The note provides that the court may make a reasonable estimate of the infringement amount using any relevant information including financial records in cases in which the court cannot determine the number of infringing items.

New Offense

Finally, the amendment provides a reference in Appendix A (Statutory Index) for the new offense at 18 U.S.C. § 2319B. This offense is to be referenced to § 2B5.3.

Effective Date: The effective date of this amendment is November 1, 2006.

688. **Amendment:** Section 2D1.1, effective March 27, 2006 (USSC Guidelines Manual, Supplement to the 2005 Supplement to Appendix C, Amendment 681), is repromulgated without change.

Reason for Amendment: This amendment re-promulgates as a permanent amendment the temporary, emergency amendment that implemented the directive in the United States Parole Commission Extension and Sentencing Commission Authority Act of 2005, Pub. L. 109–76. That Act requires the Commission, under emergency amendment authority, to implement section 3 of the Anabolic Steroid Control Act of 2004, Pub. L. 108–358 (the "ASC Act"), which directs the Commission to "review the Federal sentencing guidelines with respect to offenses involving anabolic steroids" and "consider amending the. . . guidelines to provide for increased penalties with respect to offenses involving anabolic steroids in a manner that reflects the seriousness of such offenses and the need to deter anabolic steroid trafficking and use . . .." The emergency amendment became effective on March 27, 2006 (See Supplement to Appendix C, Amendment 681).

The amendment implements the directives by increasing the penalties for offenses involving anabolic steroids. It does so by changing the manner in which anabolic steroids are treated under § 2D1.1 (Unlawful Manufacturing, Importing, Exporting, or Trafficking (Including Possession with Intent to Commit These Offenses); Attempt or Conspiracy). The amendment eliminates the sentencing distinction between anabolic steroids and other Schedule III substances when the steroid is in a pill, capsule, tablet, or liquid form. For anabolic steroids in other forms (e.g., patch, topical cream, aerosol), the amendment instructs the court that it shall make a reasonable estimate of the quantity of anabolic steroid involved in the offense, and in making such estimate, the court shall consider that

November 1, 2013 APPENDIX C - VOLUME III **Amendment 689**

each 25 mg of anabolic steroid is one "unit".

In addition, the amendment addresses two harms often associated with anabolic steroid offenses by providing new enhancements in § 2D1.1(b)(6) and (b)(7). Subsection (b)(6) provides a two-level enhancement if the offense involved the distribution of an anabolic steroid and a masking agent. Subsection (b)(7) provides a two-level enhancement if the defendant distributed an anabolic steroid to an athlete. Both enhancements address congressional concern with distribution of anabolic steroids to athletes, particularly the impact that steroids distribution and steroids use has on the integrity of sport, either because of the unfair advantage gained by the use of steroids or because of the concealment of such use.

The amendment also amends Application Note 8 of § 2D1.1 to provide that an adjustment under § 3B1.3 (Abuse of Position of Trust or Use of Special Skill) ordinarily would apply in the case of a defendant who used his or her position as a coach to influence an athlete to use an anabolic steroid.

Effective Date: The effective date of this amendment is November 1, 2006.

689. **Amendment:** Section 2G2.5 is amended in the heading by adding at the end "; Failure to Provide Required Marks in Commercial Electronic Email".

The Commentary to § 2G2.5 captioned "Statutory Provision" is amended by striking "Provision:" and inserting "Provisions: 15 U.S.C. § 7704(d);".

Chapter Three, Part C, as amended by Amendment 684 of this document, is further amended by adding at the end the following:

"§ 3C1.4. False Registration of Domain Name

If a statutory enhancement under 18 U.S.C. § 3559(f)(1) applies, increase by 2 levels.

Commentary

Background: This adjustment implements the directive to the Commission in section 204(b) of Pub. L. 108–482.".

Appendix A (Statutory Index) is amended by inserting after the line referenced to 15 U.S.C. § 6821 the following:

"15 U.S.C. § 7704(d) 2G2.5".

Reason for Amendment: This amendment (A) implements the directive to the Commission in section 204(b) of the Intellectual Property Protection and Courts Administration Act of 2004, Pub. L 109–9; and (B) addresses the new offense in section 5(d) of the Controlling the Assault of Non-Solicited Pornography and Marketing Act of 2003, Pub L. 108–187 ("CAN-SPAM Act")(15 U.S.C. § 7704(d)).

Section 204(b) of the Intellectual Property Protection and Courts Administration Act of 2004 directed the Commission to ensure that the applicable guideline range for a defendant convicted of any felony offense carried out online that may be facilitated through the use of a domain name registered with materially false contact information is sufficiently stringent to deter commission of such acts. The amendment implements this directive by creating a new guideline, at § 3C1.4 (False Registration of Domain Names), which

Amendment 689

provides a two-level adjustment for cases in which a statutory enhancement under 18 U.S.C. § 3559(f)(1) applies. Section 3559(f)(1), created by section 204(a) of the Intellectual Property Protection and Courts Administration Act of 2004, doubles the statutory maximum term of imprisonment, or increases the maximum sentence by seven years, whichever is less, if a defendant who is convicted of a felony offense knowingly falsely registered a domain name and used that domain name in the course of the offense. Basing the adjustment in the new guideline on application of the statutory enhancement in 18 U.S.C. § 3559(f)(1) satisfies the directive in a straightforward and uncomplicated manner.

Section 5(d)(1) of the CAN-SPAM Act prohibits the transmission of commercial electronic messages that contain "sexually oriented material" unless such messages include certain marks, notices, and information. The amendment references the new offense, found at 15 U.S.C. § 7704(d), to § 2G2.5 (Recordkeeping Offenses Involving the Production of Sexually Explicit Materials). Prior to this amendment, § 2G2.5 applied to violations of 18 U.S.C. § 2257, which requires producers of sexually explicit materials to maintain detailed records regarding their production activities and to make such records available for inspection by the Attorney General in accordance with applicable regulations. Although offenses under 15 U.S.C. § 7704(d) do not involve the same recording and reporting functions, section 7704(d) offenses essentially are regulatory in nature and in this manner are similar to other offenses sentenced under § 2G2.5. In addition to the statutory reference changes, the amendment also expands the heading of § 2G2.5 specifically to cover offenses under 15 U.S.C. § 7704(d).

Effective Date: The effective date of this amendment is November 1, 2006.

690. **Amendment:** Section 2J1.2 and Appendix A (Statutory Index), effective October 24, 2005 (see USSC Guidelines Manual, Supplement to Appendix C, Amendment 676), are repromulgated without change.

Reason for Amendment: This amendment repromulgates as a permanent amendment the temporary, emergency amendment to § 2J1.2 and Appendix A (Statutory Index), which became effective on October 24, 2005 (see Supplement to Appendix C, Amendment 676). The amendment implements section 6703 of the Intelligence Reform and Terrorism Prevention Act of 2004 (the "Act"), Pub. L. 108–458, which provides an enhanced penalty of not more than 8 years of imprisonment for offenses under sections 1001(a) and 1505 of title 18, United States Code, "if the offense involves international or domestic terrorism (as defined in section 2331)." Section 6703(b) requires the Sentencing Commission to amend the sentencing guidelines to provide for "an increased offense level for an offense under sections 1001(a) and 1505 of title 18, United States Code, if the offense involves international or domestic terrorism, as defined in section 2331 of such title." Section 3 of the United States Parole Commission Extension and Sentencing Commission Authority Act of 2005, Pub. L. 109–76, directed the Commission, under emergency authority, to promulgate an amendment implementing section 6703(b).

First, the amendment references convictions under 18 U.S.C. § 1001 to § 2J1.2 (Obstruction of Justice) "when the statutory maximum term of imprisonment relating to international or domestic terrorism is applicable." It also adds a new specific offense characteristic at § 2J1.2(b)(1)(B) providing for a 12 level increase for a defendant convicted under 18 U.S.C. §§ 1001 and 1505 "when the statutory maximum term of imprisonment relating to international or domestic terrorism is applicable." This 12 level increase is applied in lieu of the current 8 level increase for injury or threats to persons or property. The increase of 12 levels is intended to provide parity with the treatment of federal crimes of terrorism within the limits of the 8 year statutory maximum penalty. It is also provided to ensure a 5 year sentence of imprisonment for offenses that involve international or domestic terrorism.

Second, the amendment adds to Application Note 1 definitions for "domestic terrorism" and "international terrorism," using the meanings given the terms at 18 U.S.C. § 2331(5) and (1), respectively.

Third, the amendment adds to Application Note 2 an instruction that if § 3A1.4 (Terrorism) applies, do not apply § 2J1.2(b)(1)(B).

Effective Date: The effective date of this amendment is November 1, 2006.

691. **Amendment:** Section 2K2.1(a) is amended by striking subdivision (1) as follows:

> "(1) 26, if the offense involved a firearm described in 26 U.S.C. § 5845(a) or 18 U.S.C. § 921(a)(30), and the defendant committed any part of the instant offense subsequent to sustaining at least two felony convictions of either a crime of violence or a controlled substance offense;",

and inserting the following:

> "(1) 26, if (A) the offense involved a (i) semiautomatic firearm that is capable of accepting a large capacity magazine; or (ii) firearm that is described in 26 U.S.C. § 5845(a); and (B) the defendant committed any part of the instant offense subsequent to sustaining at least two felony convictions of either a crime of violence or a controlled substance offense;";

by striking subdivision (3) as follows:

> "(3) 22, if the offense involved a firearm described in 26 U.S.C. § 5845(a) or 18 U.S.C. § 921(a)(30), and the defendant committed any part of the instant offense subsequent to sustaining one felony conviction of either a crime of violence or a controlled substance offense;",

and inserting the following:

> "(3) 22, if (A) the offense involved a (i) semiautomatic firearm that is capable of accepting a large capacity magazine; or (ii) firearm that is described in 26 U.S.C. § 5845(a); and (B) the defendant committed any part of the instant offense subsequent to sustaining one felony conviction of either a crime of violence or a controlled substance offense;";

by striking subdivision (4)(B) as follows:

> "(B) the offense involved a firearm described in 26 U.S.C. § 5845(a) or 18 U.S.C. § 921(a)(30); and the defendant (i) was a prohibited person at the time the defendant committed the instant offense; or (ii) is convicted under 18 U.S.C. § 922(d);",

and inserting the following:

> "(B) the (i) offense involved a (I) semiautomatic firearm that is capable of accepting a large capacity magazine; or (II) firearm that is described in 26 U.S.C. § 5845(a); and (ii) defendant (I) was a prohibited person at the time the defendant committed the instant offense; or (II) is convicted under 18 U.S.C. § 922(d);";

Amendment 691

APPENDIX C - VOLUME III

November 1, 2013

and in subdivision (5) by striking "or 18 U.S.C. § 921(a)(30)".

Section 2K2.1(b) is amended by striking subdivision (4) as follows:

"(4) If any firearm was stolen, or had an altered or obliterated serial number, increase by 2 levels.",

and inserting the following:

"(4) If any firearm (A) was stolen, increase by 2 levels; or (B) had an altered or obliterated serial number, increase by 4 levels.".

Section 2K2.1(b) is amended by redesignating subdivisions (5) and (6) as subdivisions (6) and (7), respectively; and by inserting after "except if subsection (b)(3)(A) applies." the following subdivision:

"(5) If the defendant engaged in the trafficking of firearms, increase by 4 levels.".

The Commentary to § 2K2.1 captioned "Application Notes" is amended by striking Note 2 as follows:

"2. Firearm Described in 18 U.S.C. § 921(a)(30).—For purposes of subsection (a), a 'firearm described in 18 U.S.C. § 921(a)(30)' (pertaining to semiautomatic assault weapons) does not include a weapon exempted under the provisions of 18 U.S.C. § 922(v)(3).",

and inserting the following:

"2. Semiautomatic Firearm Capable of Accepting a Large Capacity Magazine.— For purposes of subsections (a)(1), (a)(3), and (a)(4), a 'semiautomatic firearm capable of accepting a large capacity magazine' means a semiautomatic firearm that has the ability to fire many rounds without reloading because at the time of the offense (A) the firearm had attached to it a magazine or similar device that could accept more than 15 rounds of ammunition; or (B) a magazine or similar device that could accept more than 15 rounds of ammunition was in close proximity to the firearm. This definition does not include a semiautomatic firearm with an attached tubular device capable of operating only with .22 caliber rim fire ammunition.".

The Commentary to § 2K2.1 captioned "Application Notes" is amended by striking Note 4 as follows:

"4. 'Felony offense,' as used in subsection (b)(5), means any offense (federal, state, or local) punishable by imprisonment for a term exceeding one year, whether or not a criminal charge was brought, or conviction obtained.";

by redesignating Notes 5 through 10 as Notes 4 through 9, respectively; by striking Note 11 as follows:

"11. Under subsection (c)(1), the offense level for the underlying offense (which may be a federal, state, or local offense) is to be determined under § 2X1.1 (Attempt, Solicitation, or Conspiracy) or, if death results, under the most analogous guideline from Chapter Two, Part A, Subpart 1 (Homicide).";

by redesignating Notes 12 through 14 as Notes 10 through 12, respectively; and by striking Notes 15 and 16 as follows:

"15. As used in subsections (b)(5) and (c)(1), 'another felony offense' and 'another offense' refer to offenses other than explosives or firearms possession or trafficking offenses. However, where the defendant used or possessed a firearm or explosive to facilitate another firearms or explosives offense (e.g., the defendant used or possessed a firearm to protect the delivery of an unlawful shipment of explosives), an upward departure under § 5K2.6 (Weapons and Dangerous Instrumentalities) may be warranted.

16. The enhancement under subsection (b)(4) for a stolen firearm or a firearm with an altered or obliterated serial number applies whether or not the defendant knew or had reason to believe that the firearm was stolen or had an altered or obliterated serial number.".

The Commentary to § 2K2.1 captioned "Application Notes" is amended by striking Note 8, as redesignated by this amendment, and inserting the following:

"8. Application of Subsection (b)(4).—

(A) Interaction with Subsection (a)(7).—If the only offense to which § 2K2.1 applies is 18 U.S.C. § 922(i), (j), or (u), or 18 U.S.C. § 924(l) or (m) (offenses involving a stolen firearm or stolen ammunition) and the base offense level is determined under subsection (a)(7), do not apply the enhancement in subsection (b)(4)(A). This is because the base offense level takes into account that the firearm or ammunition was stolen. However, if the offense involved a firearm with an altered or obliterated serial number, apply subsection (b)(4)(B).

Similarly, if the offense to which § 2K2.1 applies is 18 U.S.C. § 922(k) or 26 U.S.C. § 5861(g) or (h) (offenses involving an altered or obliterated serial number) and the base offense level is determined under subsection (a)(7), do not apply the enhancement in subsection (b)(4)(B). This is because the base offense level takes into account that the firearm had an altered or obliterated serial number. However, it the offense involved a stolen firearm or stolen ammunition, apply subsection (b)(4)(A).

(B) Knowledge or Reason to Believe.—Subsection (b)(4) applies regardless of whether the defendant knew or had reason to believe that the firearm was stolen or had an altered or obliterated serial number.".

The Commentary to § 2K2.1 captioned "Application Notes" is amended in Note 4, as redesignated by this amendment, by inserting "Application of Subsection (a)(7).—" before "Subsection (a)(7)"; in Note 5, as redesignated by this amendment, by inserting "Application of Subsection (b)(1).—" before "For purposes of calculating"; in Note 6, as redesignated by this amendment, by inserting "Application of Subsection (b)(2).—" before "Under subsection (b)(2)"; in Note 7, as redesignated by this amendment, by inserting "Destructive Devices.—" before "A defendant"; in Note 9, as redesignated by this amendment, by inserting "Application of Subsection (b)(7).—" before "Under"; and by striking "(b)(6), if" and inserting "(b)(7), if"; in Note 10, as redesignated by this amendment, by inserting "Prior Felony Convictions.—" before "For purposes of"; in Note 11, as redesignated by this amendment, by inserting "Upward Departure Provisions.—" before "An upward departure"; in Note 12, as redesignated by this amendment, by inserting "Armed Career Criminal.—" before "A defendant who"; and by inserting at the end the following:

"13. Application of Subsection (b)(5).—

    (A) In General.—Subsection (b)(5) applies, regardless of whether anything of value was exchanged, if the defendant—

        (i) transported, transferred, or otherwise disposed of two or more firearms to another individual, or received two or more firearms with the intent to transport, transfer, or otherwise dispose of firearms to another individual; and

        (ii) knew or had reason to believe that such conduct would result in the transport, transfer, or disposal of a firearm to an individual—

            (I) whose possession or receipt of the firearm would be unlawful; or

            (II) who intended to use or dispose of the firearm unlawfully.

    (B) Definitions.—For purposes of this subsection:

'Individual whose possession or receipt of the firearm would be unlawful' means an individual who (i) has a prior conviction for a crime of violence, a controlled substance offense, or a misdemeanor crime of domestic violence; or (ii) at the time of the offense was under a criminal justice sentence, including probation, parole, supervised release, imprisonment, work release, or escape status. 'Crime of violence' and 'controlled substance offense' have the meaning given those terms in § 4B1.2 (Definitions of Terms Used in Section 4B1.1). 'Misdemeanor crime of domestic violence' has the meaning given that term in 18 U.S.C. § 921(a)(33)(A).

The term 'defendant', consistent with § 1B1.3 (Relevant Conduct), limits the accountability of the defendant to the defendant's own conduct and conduct that the defendant aided or abetted, counseled, commanded, induced, procured, or willfully caused.

    (C) Upward Departure Provision.—If the defendant trafficked substantially more than 25 firearms, an upward departure may be warranted.

    (D) Interaction with Other Subsections.—In a case in which three or more firearms were both possessed and trafficked, apply both subsections (b)(1) and (b)(5). If the defendant used or transferred one of such firearms in connection with another felony offense (i.e., an offense other than a firearms possession or trafficking offense) an enhancement under subsection (b)(6) also would apply.

14. 'In Connection With'.—

    (A) In General.—Subsections (b)(6) and (c)(1) apply if the firearm or ammunition facilitated, or had the potential of facilitating, another felony offense or another offense, respectively.

(B) <u>Application When Other Offense is Burglary or Drug Offense</u>.—Subsections (b)(6) and (c)(1) apply (i) in a case in which a defendant who, during the course of a burglary, finds and takes a firearm, even if the defendant did not engage in any other conduct with that firearm during the course of the burglary; and (ii) in the case of a drug trafficking offense in which a firearm is found in close proximity to drugs, drug-manufacturing materials, or drug paraphernalia. In these cases, application of subsections (b)(1) and (c)(1) is warranted because the presence of the firearm has the potential of facilitating another felony offense or another offense, respectively.

(C) <u>Definitions</u>.—

'Another felony offense', for purposes of subsection (b)(6), means any federal, state, or local offense, other than the explosive or firearms possession or trafficking offense, punishable by imprisonment for a term exceeding one year, regardless of whether a criminal charge was brought, or a conviction obtained.

'Another offense', for purposes of subsection (c)(1), means any federal, state, or local offense, other than the explosive or firearms possession or trafficking offense, regardless of whether a criminal charge was brought, or a conviction obtained.

(D) <u>Upward Departure Provision</u>.—In a case in which the defendant used or possessed a firearm or explosive to facilitate another firearms or explosives offense (<u>e.g.</u>, the defendant used or possessed a firearm to protect the delivery of an unlawful shipment of explosives), an upward departure under § 5K2.6 (Weapons and Dangerous Instrumentalities) may be warranted.".

Chapter Five, Part K is amended by striking § 5K2.17 as follows:

"§ 5K2.17. <u>High-Capacity, Semiautomatic Firearms</u> (Policy Statement)

If the defendant possessed a high-capacity, semiautomatic firearm in connection with a crime of violence or controlled substance offense, an upward departure may be warranted. A 'high-capacity, semiautomatic firearm' means a semiautomatic firearm that has a magazine capacity of more than ten cartridges. The extent of any increase should depend upon the degree to which the nature of the weapon increased the likelihood of death or injury in the circumstances of the particular case.",

and inserting:

"§ 5K2.17. <u>Semiautomatic Firearms Capable of Accepting Large Capacity Magazine</u> (Policy Statement)

If the defendant possessed a semiautomatic firearm capable of accepting a large capacity magazine in connection with a crime of violence or controlled substance offense, an upward departure may be warranted. A 'semiautomatic firearm capable of accepting a large capacity magazine' means a semiautomatic firearm that has the ability to fire many rounds without reloading because at the time of the offense (A) the firearm had attached to it a magazine or similar device that could accept more than 15 rounds of ammunition; or (B) a magazine or similar device that could accept more than 15 rounds of ammunition was in close proximity to the firearm. The extent of any increase should depend upon the degree to which the nature of the weapon increased the likelihood of death or injury in the circumstances of the particular case.".

Reason for Amendment: This four part amendment addresses various issues pertaining to the primary firearms guideline, § 2K2.1 (Unlawful Receipt, Possession, or Transportation of Firearms or Ammunition; Prohibited Transactions Involving Firearms or Ammunition). First, the amendment modifies four base offense levels that provide enhanced penalties for offenses involving a firearm described in 18 U.S.C. § 921(a)(30), the semiautomatic assault weapon ban that expired on September 13, 2004. The Commission received information regarding inconsistent application as to whether the enhanced base offense levels apply to these types of firearms in light of the ban's expiration. The amendment deletes the reference to 18 U.S.C. § 921(a)(30) at § 2K2.1(a)(1), (a)(3), and (a)(4) and replaces the reference with the term, "a semiautomatic firearm capable of accepting a large capacity magazine," which is defined in Application Note 2.

While the amendment deletes the reference to 18 U.S.C. § 921(a)(30) at § 2K2.1(a)(5), it does not include the phrase "a semiautomatic firearm that is capable of accepting a large capacity magazine" in this subsection because a defendant sentenced under subsection (a)(5) does not have the same "prohibited person" status as a defendant sentenced under subsections (a)(1), (a)(3), or (a)(4).

The amendment also amends § 5K2.17 (High-Capacity, Semiautomatic Firearms) in a manner consistent with § 2K2.1, as amended, except that it excludes the language pertaining to .22 caliber rim fire ammunition in order to remain in conformity with a prior congressional directive. As amended, § 5K2.17 (Semiautomatic Firearms Capable of Accepting Large Capacity Magazine) provides that an upward departure may be warranted if a defendant possesses a semiautomatic firearm capable of accepting a large capacity magazine in connection with a crime of violence or controlled substance offense.

Second, the amendment provides a 4-level enhancement at § 2K2.1(b)(5) if the defendant engaged in the trafficking of firearms. The definition of trafficking encompasses transporting, transferring, or otherwise disposing of two or more firearms, or receipt of two or more firearms with the intent to transport, transfer, or otherwise dispose of firearms to another individual. The definition also requires that the defendant know or have reason to believe that such conduct would result in the transport, transfer, or disposal of a firearm to an individual whose possession or receipt would be unlawful or who intended to use or dispose of the firearm unlawfully. With respect to an individual whose possession would be unlawful, the amendment includes individuals who previously have been convicted of a crime of violence, a controlled substance offense, or a misdemeanor crime of domestic violence, or who at the time of the offense were under a criminal justice sentence, including probation, parole, supervised release, imprisonment, work release, or escape status. Additionally, the definition provides that the enhancement applies regardless of whether anything of value was exchanged.

Third, the amendment modifies § 2K2.1(b)(4) to increase penalties for offenses involving altered or obliterated serial numbers. Prior to this amendment, § 2K2.1(b)(4) provided a 2-level enhancement if the offense involved either a stolen firearm or a firearm with an altered or obliterated serial number. The amendment provides a 4-level enhancement for offenses involving altered or obliterated serial numbers. This increase reflects both the difficulty in tracing firearms with altered or obliterated serial numbers, and the increased market for these types of weapons.

Fourth, the amendment addresses a circuit conflict pertaining to the application of current § 2K2.1(b)(5) (re-designated by this amendment as § 2K2.1(b)(6)) and (c)(1)), specifically with respect to the use of a firearm "in connection with" burglary and drug offenses. The amendment, adopting the language from <u>Smith v. United States</u>, 508 U.S. 223 (1993), provides at Application Note 14 that the provisions apply if the firearm facilitated, or had the potential of facilitating, another felony offense or another offense, respectively. Furthermore, the amendment provides that in burglary offenses, these provisions apply to a defendant who takes a firearm during the course of the burglary, even if the defendant did not engage in any other conduct with that firearm during the course of the burglary. In addition, the provisions apply in the case of a drug trafficking offense in which a firearm is found in close proximity to drugs, drug manufacturing materials, or drug paraphernalia. The Commission determined that application of these provisions is warranted in these cases because of the potential that the presence of the firearm has for facilitating another felony offense or another offense.

Effective Date: The effective date of this amendment is November 1, 2006.

692. Amendment: Section 2L1.1 is amended by redesignating subsections (a)(1) and (a)(2) as subsections (a)(2) and (a)(3), respectively; and by inserting after "Base Offense Level:" the following:

"(1)   25, if the defendant was convicted under 8 U.S.C. § 1327 of a violation involving an alien who was inadmissible under 8 U.S.C. § 1182(a)(3);".

Section 2L1.1 is amended by redesignating subsections (b)(4) through (b)(6) as subsections (b)(5) through (b)(7), respectively; and by inserting after subsection (b)(3) the following:

"(4)   If the defendant smuggled, transported, or harbored a minor who was unaccompanied by the minor's parent or grandparent, increase by 2 levels.".

Subsection (b)(7), as redesignated by this amendment, is amended by striking "8 levels" and inserting "10 levels"; and by redesignating subdivisions (1) through (4) as subdivisions (A) through (D), respectively.

Section 2L1.1(b) is amended by adding at the end the following:

"(8)   If an alien was involuntarily detained through coercion or threat, or in connection with a demand for payment, (A) after the alien was smuggled into the United States; or (B) while the alien was transported or harbored in the United States, increase by 2 levels. If the resulting offense level is less than level 18, increase to level 18.".

Section 2L1.1(c) is amended by striking "If any person" through the end of "Subpart 1." and inserting the following:

"(1)   If death resulted, apply the appropriate homicide guideline from Chapter Two, Part A, Subpart 1, if the resulting offense level is greater than that determined under this guideline.".

The Commentary to § 2L1.1 captioned "Application Notes" is amended in Note 1 by striking "For purposes of this guideline—" and inserting "<u>Definitions</u>.—For purposes of this guideline:"; and by adding at the end the following:

"'Minor' means an individual who had not attained the age of 16 years.

'Parent' means (A) a natural mother or father; (B) a stepmother or stepfather; or (C) an adoptive mother or father.".

The Commentary to § 2L1.1 captioned "Application Notes" is amended in Note 2 by inserting "Interaction with § 3B1.1.—" before "For"; and by adding at the end the following:

"In large scale smuggling, transporting, or harboring cases, an additional adjustment from § 3B1.1 typically will apply.".

The Commentary to § 2L1.1 captioned "Application Notes" is amended by striking Notes 3 and 4 as follows:

"3. Where the defendant smuggled, transported, or harbored an alien knowing that the alien intended to enter the United States to engage in subversive activity, drug trafficking, or other serious criminal behavior, an upward departure may be warranted.

4. If the offense involved substantially more than 100 aliens, an upward departure may be warranted.",

and inserting the following:

"3. Upward Departure Provisions.—An upward departure may be warranted in any of the following cases:

(A) The defendant smuggled, transported, or harbored an alien knowing that the alien intended to enter the United States to engage in subversive activity, drug trafficking, or other serious criminal behavior.

(B) The defendant smuggled, transported, or harbored an alien the defendant knew was inadmissible for reasons of security and related grounds, as set forth under 8 U.S.C. § 1182(a)(3).

(C) The offense involved substantially more than 100 aliens.";

by redesignating Notes 5 and 6 as Notes 4 and 5, respectively; in Note 4, as redesignated by this amendment, by inserting "Prior Convictions Under Subsection (b)(3).—" before "Prior felony"; and in Note 5, as redesignated by this amendment, by inserting "Application of Subsection (b)(6).—" before "Reckless"; by striking "(b)(5)" each place it appears and inserting "(b)(6)"; and by striking "(b)(4)" and inserting "(b)(5)".

The Commentary to § 2L1.1 captioned "Application Notes" is amended by adding at the end the following:

"6. Inapplicability of § 3A1.3.—If an enhancement under subsection (b)(8) applies, do not apply § 3A1.3 (Restraint of Victim).".

The Commentary to § 2L1.1 captioned "Background" is amended by striking the last sentence as follows:

"In large scale smuggling, transporting, or harboring cases, an additional adjustment from § 3B1.1 (Aggravating Role) typically will apply to the most culpable defendants.".

Section 2L2.1(b) is amended by adding at the end the following:

"(5) If the defendant fraudulently obtained or used (A) a United States passport, increase by 4 levels; or (B) a foreign passport, increase by 2 levels.".

Section 2L2.2(b)(3) is amended by inserting "(A)" after "used" and by inserting "; or (B) a foreign passport, increase by 2 levels" after "4 levels".

Reason for Amendment: This two-part amendment addresses various issues pertaining to §§ 2L1.1 (Smuggling, Transporting, or Harboring an Unlawful Alien), 2L2.1 (Trafficking in a Document Relating to Naturalization, Citizenship, or Legal Resident Status, or a United States Passport; False Statement in Respect to the Citizenship or Immigration Status of Another; Fraudulent Marriage to Assist Alien to Evade Immigration Law), and 2L2.2 (Fraudulently Acquiring Documents Relating to Naturalization, Citizenship, or Legal Resident Status for Own Use; False Personation or Fraudulent Marriage by Alien to Evade Immigration Law; Fraudulently Acquiring or Improperly Using a United States Passport).

The first part of this amendment modifies § 2L1.1. First, this amendment addresses national security concerns pertaining to the smuggling of illegal aliens. Specifically, a new base offense level of 25 at § 2L1.1(a)(1) provides increased punishment for defendants convicted of 8 U.S.C. § 1327 involving an alien who is inadmissible because of "security or related grounds," as defined in 8 U.S.C. 1182(a)(3). To further address concerns related to national security, an application note provides that an upward departure may be warranted if the defendant had specific knowledge that the alien the defendant smuggled, transported, or harbored was inadmissible for reasons of security and related grounds, as set forth in 8 U.S.C. § 1182(a)(3). This upward departure note applies regardless of whether the defendant is convicted of 8 U.S.C. § 1327.

Second, the amendment provides a two-level enhancement for a case in which the defendant smuggled, transported, or harbored a minor unaccompanied by the minor's parent or grandparent. This enhancement addresses concerns regarding the increased risk involved when unaccompanied minors are smuggled into, or harbored or transported within, the United States. Application Note 1 defines "minor" as "an individual who had not attained the age of 16 years" and defines "parent" as "(A) a natural mother or father; (B) a stepmother or stepfather; or (C) an adoptive mother or father."

Third, the amendment makes two changes with respect to offenses involving death. First, the amendment increases the enhancement from 8 levels to 10 levels if any person died as a result of the offense. Additionally, the cross reference at § 2L1.1(c)(1) is expanded to cover homicides other than murder. This amendment ensures that any offense involving the death of an alien will be sentenced under the guideline appropriate for the particular type of homicide involved if the resulting offense level is greater than the offense level determined under § 2L1.1.

Fourth, the amendment adds a two-level enhancement and a minimum offense level of 18 in a case in which an alien was involuntarily detained through coercion or threat, or in connection with a demand for payment, after the alien was smuggled into the United States, or while the alien was transported or harbored in the United States. This conduct may not be covered by § 3A1.3 (Restraint of Victim) because an illegal alien, as a participant in the offense, may not be considered a "victim" for purposes of that adjustment. Additionally, application of § 3A1.3 requires "physical restraint," as that term is defined in

§ 1B1.1, and the involuntary detainment involved in offenses sentenced under § 2L1.1 may not involve physical restraint. Finally, the amendment provides an application note, as a corollary to Application Note 2 in § 3A1.3, that instructs the court not to apply § 3A1.3 if the involuntary detainment enhancement applies

The second part of the amendment modifies §§ 2L2.1 and 2L2.2. First, this part of the amendment adds a new specific offense characteristic at § 2L2.1(b)(5)(A) that provides a four-level enhancement in a case in which the defendant fraudulently used or obtained a United States passport. The same specific offense characteristic was added to § 2L2.2, effective November 1, 2004 (see USSC Guidelines Manual Supplement to Appendix C, Amendment 671). The addition of this specific offense characteristic to § 2L2.1 promotes proportionality between the document fraud guidelines, §§ 2L2.1 and 2L2.2.

Second, the amendment provides, at § 2L2.1(b)(5)(B) and § 2L2.2(b)(3)(B), a two-level enhancement if the defendant fraudulently obtained or used a foreign passport. This modification addresses concern regarding the threat to the security of the United States in document fraud offenses involving foreign passports.

Effective Date: The effective date of this amendment is November 1, 2006.

693. **Amendment:** Section 3C1.1 is amended by striking "during the course of" and inserting "with respect to".

The Commentary to § 3C1.1 captioned "Application Notes" is amended in Note 1 by inserting "In General.—" before "This adjustment"; by striking "during the course of" and inserting "with respect to"; and by inserting at the end the following:

"Obstructive conduct that occurred prior to the start of the investigation of the instant offense of conviction may be covered by this guideline if the conduct was purposefully calculated, and likely, to thwart the investigation or prosecution of the offense of conviction.".

The Commentary to § 3C1.1 captioned "Application Notes" is amended in Note 2 by inserting "Limitations on Applicability of Adjustment.—" before "This provision"; in Note 3 by inserting "Covered Conduct Generally.—" before "Obstructive"; in Note 5 by inserting "Examples of Conduct Ordinarily Not Covered.—" before "Some types"; in Note 6 by inserting "'Material' Evidence Defined.—" before "'Material' evidence"; in Note 7 by inserting "Inapplicability of Adjustment in Certain Circumstances.—" before "If the defendant"; in Note 8 by inserting "Grouping Under § 3D1.2(c).—" before "If the defendant"; and in Note 9 by inserting "Accountability for § 1B1.3(a)(1)(A) Conduct.—" before "Under this section".

The Commentary to § 3C1.1 captioned "Application Notes" is amended in Note 4 by inserting "Examples of Covered Conduct.—" before "The following"; in subdivision (b) by inserting ", including during the course of a civil proceeding if such perjury pertains to conduct that forms the basis of the offense of conviction" after "suborn perjury"; by striking the period at the end of subdivision (j) and inserting a semi-colon; and by adding at the end the following subdivision:

"(k) threatening the victim of the offense in an attempt to prevent the victim from reporting the conduct constituting the offense of conviction.".

Reason for Amendment: This amendment addresses a circuit conflict regarding the issue of whether pre-investigative conduct can form the basis of an adjustment under § 3C1.1 (Obstructing or Impeding the Administration of Justice). The First, Second, Seventh,

Tenth, and District of Columbia Circuits have held that pre-investigation conduct can be used to support an obstruction adjustment under § 3C1.1. Compare United States v. McGovern, 329 F.3d 247, 252 (1st Cir. 2003)(holding that the submission of false run sheets to Medicare and Medicaid representatives qualified for the enhancement even though "the fact that there was no pending federal criminal investigation at the time of the obstruction did not disqualify a defendant from an enhancement when there was a 'close connection' between the obstructive conduct and the offense of conviction.'"(quoting United States v. Emery, 991 F.2d 907, 911(1st Cir. 1992))); United States v. Fiore, 381 F.3d 89, 94 (2nd Cir. 2004)(defendant's perjury in an SEC civil investigation into defendant's securities fraud constituted obstruction of justice of the criminal investigation of the same "precise conduct" for which defendant was criminally convicted, even though the perjury occurred before the criminal investigation commenced); United States v. Snyder, 189 F.3d 640, 649 (7th Cir. 1999)(holding the adjustment appropriate in case in which defendant made pre-investigation threat to victim and did not withdraw his threat after the investigation began, thus obstructing justice during the course of the investigation); United States v. Mills, 194 F.3d 1108, 1115 (10th Cir. 1999)(holding that destruction of tape that occurred before an investigation began warranted application of the enhancement because the defendant knew an investigation would be conducted and understood the importance of the tape to that investigation); and United States v. Barry, 938 F.2d 1327, 1333-34 (D.C. Cir. 1991)("Given the commentary and the case law interpreting § 3C1.1, we conclude that the enhancement applies if the defendant attempted to obstruct justice in respect to the investigation or prosecution of the offense of conviction, even if the obstruction occurred before the police or prosecutors began investigating or prosecuting the specific offense of conviction."), with United States v. Baggett, 342 F.3d 536, 542 (6th Cir. 2003)(holding that the obstruction of justice enhancement could not be justified on the basis of the threats that the defendant made to the victim prior to the investigation, prosecution, or sentencing of the offense); United States v. Stolba, 357 F.3d 850, 852-53 (8th Cir. 2004)(holding that an obstruction adjustment is not available when destruction of documents occurred before an official investigation had commenced); United States v. DeGeorge, 380 F.3d 1203, 1222 (9th Cir. 2004)(perjury during a civil trial as part of a scheme to defraud was not an obstruction of justice of a criminal investigation of the fraudulent scheme because the criminal investigation had not yet begun at the time the defendant perjured himself); see also United States v. Clayton, 172 F.3d 347, 355 (5th Cir. 1999)(holding that defendant's threats to witnesses warrant the enhancement under § 3C1.1, but stating in dicta that the guideline "specifically limits applicable conduct to that which occurs during an investigation. . . .").

The amendment, which adopts the majority view, permits application of the guideline to obstructive conduct that occurs prior to the start of the investigation of the instant offense of conviction by allowing the court to consider such conduct if it was purposefully calculated, and likely, to thwart the investigation or prosecution of the offense of conviction. The amendment also adds, as examples of covered conduct in Application Note 4, (A) perjury that occurs during the course of a civil proceeding if such perjury pertains to the conduct that forms the basis of the offense of conviction; and (B) conduct involving threats to the victim of the offense if those threats were intended to prevent the victim from reporting the conduct constituting the offense of conviction. Finally, the amendment changes language in § 3C1.1(A) from "during the course of" to "with respect to."

Effective Date: The effective date of this amendment is November 1, 2006.

694. **Amendment:** Chapter Six is amended in the heading by striking "AND" and inserting a comma; and by adding at the end ", AND CRIME VICTIMS' RIGHTS".

Chapter Six, Part A is amended by adding at the end the following:

"§ 6A1.5. Crime Victims' Rights (Policy Statement)

> In any case involving the sentencing of a defendant for an offense against a crime victim, the court shall ensure that the crime victim is afforded the rights described in 18 U.S.C. § 3771 and in any other provision of Federal law pertaining to the treatment of crime victims.

Commentary

Application Note:

1. Definition.—For purposes of this policy statement, 'crime victim' has the meaning given that term in 18 U.S.C. § 3771(e).".

Reason for Amendment: This amendment creates a new policy statement at § 6A1.5 (Crime Victims' Rights) in response to the Justice for All Act of 2004, Pub. L. 108-405, which sets forth at 18 U.S.C. § 3771 various rights for crime victims during the criminal justice process, including at subsection (a)(4) the right to be "reasonably heard at any public proceeding . . . involving release, plea, sentencing, or any parole proceeding." The amendment also changes the title of Chapter Six to reflect the addition of the policy statement.

Effective Date: The effective date of this amendment is November 1, 2006.

695. Amendment: The Commentary to § 8C2.5 captioned "Application Notes" is amended in Note 12 by striking the last sentence as follows:

> "Waiver of attorney-client privilege and of work product protections is not a prerequisite to a reduction in culpability score under subdivisions (1) and (2) of subsection (g) unless such waiver is necessary in order to provide timely and thorough disclosure of all pertinent information known to the organization.".

Reason for Amendment: This amendment deletes the last sentence of Application Note 12 to § 8C2.5 (Culpability Score), which stated that "[w]aiver of attorney-client privilege and of work product protections is not a prerequisite to a reduction in culpability score . . . unless such waiver is necessary in order to provide timely and thorough disclosure of all pertinent information known to the organization." The Commission added this sentence to address some concerns regarding the relationship between waivers and § 8C2.5(g), and at the time stated that "[t]he Commission expects that such waivers will be required on a limited basis." See Supplement to Appendix C (Amendment 673, effective November 1, 2004). Subsequently, the Commission received public comment and heard testimony at public hearings on November 15, 2005, and March 15, 2006, that the sentence at issue could be misinterpreted to encourage waivers.

Effective Date: The effective date of this amendment is November 1, 2006.

696. Amendment: The Commentary to § 2B1.1 captioned "Application Notes" is amended in Note 7(C) by striking "§ 2J1.7" and inserting "§ 3C1.3".

The Commentary to § 2K2.1 captioned "Application Notes", as amended by Amendment 691, is further amended in Note 3 by inserting "Definition of 'Prohibited Person'.—" before "For purposes"; and in Note 11, as redesignated by Amendment 691, by striking "Note 8" and inserting "Note 7".

The Commentary to § 2K2.4 captioned "Application Notes" is amended in Note 4 by striking "(b)(5)" each place it appears and inserting "(b)(6)".

Reason for Amendment: This amendment makes various technical and conforming amendments in order to execute properly amendments submitted to the Congress on May 1, 2006, and that will become effective on November 1, 2006. Specifically, the amendment conforms guideline references in the commentary of §§ 2B1.1 (Theft, Property Destruction, and Fraud), 2K2.1 (Unlawful Receipt, Possession, or Transportation of Firearms or Ammunition), and 2K2.4 (Use of Firearm, Armor-Piercing Ammunition, or Explosive During or in Relation to Certain Crimes) to redesignated guideline provisions and adds a heading to Application Note 3 in § 2K2.1.

Effective Date: The effective date of this amendment is November 1, 2006.

697. **Amendment:** Section 2H3.1 is amended in the heading by striking "Tax Return Information" and inserting "Certain Private or Protected Information".

Section 2H3.1(b)(1) is amended by inserting "(A) the defendant is convicted under 18 U.S.C. § 1039(d) or (e); or (B)" after "If".

The Commentary to § 2H3.1 captioned "Statutory Provisions" is amended by inserting "§ 1039," after "18 U.S.C. § ".

The Commentary to § 2H3.1 captioned "Application Notes" is amended by striking Note 1 as follows:

"1. Definitions.—For purposes of this guideline, 'tax return' and 'tax return information' have the meaning given the terms 'return' and 'return information' in 26 U.S.C. § 6103(b)(1) and (2), respectively.";

by redesignating Note 2 as Note 1; and by inserting after Note 1, as redesignated by this amendment, the following:

"2. Imposition of Sentence for 18 U.S.C. § 1039(d) and (e).—Subsections 1039(d) and (e) of title 18, United States Code, require a term of imprisonment of not more than 5 years to be imposed in addition to any sentence imposed for a conviction under 18 U.S.C. § 1039(a), (b), or (c). In order to comply with the statute, the court should determine the appropriate 'total punishment' and divide the sentence on the judgment form between the sentence attributable to the conviction under 18 U.S.C. § 1039(d) or (e) and the sentence attributable to the conviction under 18 U.S.C. § 1039(a), (b), or (c), specifying the number of months to be served for the conviction under 18 U.S.C. § 1039(d) or (e). For example, if the applicable adjusted guideline range is 15-21 months and the court determines a 'total punishment' of 21 months is appropriate, a sentence of 9 months for conduct under 18 U.S.C. § 1039(a) plus 12 months for 18 U.S.C. § 1039(d) conduct would achieve the 'total punishment' in a manner that satisfies the statutory requirement.

3. Upward Departure.—There may be cases in which the offense level determined under this guideline substantially understates the seriousness of the offense. In such a case, an upward departure may be warranted. The following are examples of cases in which an upward departure may be warranted:

(i) The offense involved confidential phone records information of a substantial number of individuals.

(ii) The offense caused or risked substantial non-monetary harm (e.g. physical harm, psychological harm, or severe emotional trauma, or resulted in a substantial invasion of privacy interest) to individuals whose private or protected information was obtained.".

Section 2H3.1 is amended by striking the Commentary captioned "Background" as follows:

"Background: This section refers to conduct proscribed by 47 U.S.C. § 605 and the Electronic Communications Privacy Act of 1986, which amends 18 U.S.C. § 2511 and other sections of Title 18 dealing with unlawful interception and disclosure of communications. These statutes proscribe the interception and divulging of wire, oral, radio, and electronic communications. The Electronic Communications Privacy Act of 1986 provides for a maximum term of imprisonment of five years for violations involving most types of communication.

This section also refers to conduct relating to the disclosure and inspection of tax returns and tax return information, 26 U.S.C. §§ 7213(a)(1)-(3), (5), (d), 7213A, and 7216. These statutes provide for a maximum term of imprisonment of five years for most types of disclosure of tax return information, but provide a maximum term of imprisonment of one year for violations of 26 U.S.C. §§ 7213A and 7216.".

Appendix A (Statutory Index) is amended by inserting after the line referenced to 18 U.S.C. § 1038 the following new line:

"18 U.S.C. § 1039   2H3.1".

Reason for Amendment: This amendment implements the emergency directive in section 4 of the Telephone Records and Privacy Protection Act of 2006, Pub. L. 109-476. The directive, which requires the Commission to promulgate an amendment under emergency amendment authority by July 11, 2007, instructs the Commission to "review and, if appropriate, amend the Federal sentencing guidelines and policy statements applicable to persons convicted of any offense under section 1039 of title 18, United States Code." Section 1039 criminalizes the fraudulent acquisition or disclosure of confidential phone records. The penalties for violating the statute include fines and imprisonment for a term not to exceed 10 years. The statute also includes enhanced penalties for certain forms of aggravated conduct, providing for up to a five year term of imprisonment, in addition to the penalties for a violation of section 1039(a), (b), or (c). See 18 U.S.C. § 1039 (d), (e).

The amendment refers the new offense at 18 U.S.C. § 1039 to § 2H3.1 (Interception of Communications; Eavesdropping; Disclosure of Tax Return Information). The Commission concluded that disclosure of telephone records is similar to the types of privacy offenses referenced to this guideline. In addition, this guideline includes a cross reference, instructing that if the purpose of the offense was to facilitate another offense, that the guideline applicable to an attempt to commit the other offenses should be applied, if the resulting offense level is higher. The Commission concluded that operation of the cross reference would capture the harms associated with the aggravated forms of this offense referenced at 18 U.S.C. § 1039(d) or (e). Finally, the amendment expands the scope of the existing three-level enhancement in the guideline to include cases in which the defendant is convicted under 18 U.S.C. § 1039(d) or (e). Thus, in cases where the cross reference does not apply, application of the enhancement will capture the increased harms associated with the aggravated offenses.

Effective Date: The effective date of this amendment is May 1, 2007.

698. Amendment: The Commentary to § 1B1.13 captioned "Application Notes" is amended in Note 1 by striking subdivision (A) as follows:

"(A) <u>Extraordinary and Compelling Reasons</u>.—A determination made by the Director of the Bureau of Prisons that a particular case warrants a reduction for extraordinary and compelling reasons shall be considered as such for purposes of subdivision (1)(A).",

and inserting the following:

"(A) <u>Extraordinary and Compelling Reasons</u>.—Provided the defendant meets the requirements of subdivision (2), extraordinary and compelling reasons exist under any of the following circumstances:

(i) The defendant is suffering from a terminal illness.

(ii) The defendant is suffering from a permanent physical or medical condition, or is experiencing deteriorating physical or mental health because of the aging process, that substantially diminishes the ability of the defendant to provide self-care within the environment of a correctional facility and for which conventional treatment promises no substantial improvement.

(iii) The death or incapacitation of the defendant's only family member capable of caring for the defendant's minor child or minor children.

(iv) As determined by the Director of the Bureau of Prisons, there exists in the defendant's case an extraordinary and compelling reason other than, or in combination with, the reasons described in subdivisions (i), (ii), and (iii).".

The Commentary to § 1B1.13 is amended by striking the commentary captioned "Background" as follows:

"<u>Background</u>: This policy statement is an initial step toward implementing 28 U.S.C. § 994(t). The Commission intends to develop further criteria to be applied and a list of specific examples of extraordinary and compelling reasons for sentence reduction pursuant to such statute.",

and inserting the following:

"<u>Background</u>: This policy statement implements 28 U.S.C. § 994(t).".

Reason for Amendment: This amendment modifies the policy statement at § 1B1.13 (Reduction in Term of Imprisonment as a Result of Motion by Director of Bureau of Prisons) to further effectuate the directive in 28 U.S.C. § 994(t). Section 994(t) provides that the Commission "in promulgating general policy statements regarding the sentence modification provisions in section 3582(c)(1)(A) of title 18, shall describe what should be considered extraordinary and compelling reasons for sentence reduction, including the criteria to be applied and a list of specific examples." The amendment revises Application Note 1(A) of § 1B1.13 to provide four examples of circumstances that, provided the defendant is not a danger to the safety of any other person or to the community, would constitute "extraordinary and compelling reasons" for purposes of 18 U.S.C. § 3582(c)(1)(A).

Effective Date: The effective date of this amendment is November 1, 2007.

Amendment 699

699. Amendment: The Commentary to § 2A1.1 captioned "Statutory Provisions" is amended by inserting "1992(a)(7)," after "1841(a)(2)(C),"; and by inserting "2199, 2291," after "2118(c)(2),".

The Commentary to § 2A1.2 captioned "Statutory Provisions" is amended by inserting "2199, 2291," after "1841(a)(2)(C),".

The Commentary to § 2A1.3 captioned "Statutory Provisions" is amended by inserting "2199, 2291," after "1841(a)(2)(C),".

The Commentary to § 2A1.4 captioned "Statutory Provisions" is amended by inserting "2199, 2291," after "1841(a)(2)(C),".

The Commentary to § 2A1.4 captioned "Application Note" is amended in Note 1 by striking "18 U.S.C. § 1993(c)(5)" and inserting "18 U.S.C. § 1992(d)(7)".

The Commentary to § 2A2.1 captioned "Statutory Provisions" is amended by striking "1993(a)(6)" and inserting "1992(a)(7), 2199, 2291".

The Commentary to § 2A2.2 captioned "Statutory Provisions" is amended by striking "1993(a)(6)," and inserting "1992(a)(7), 2199, 2291,".

The Commentary to § 2A2.3 captioned "Statutory Provisions" is amended by inserting ", 2199, 2291" after "1751(e)".

The Commentary to § 2A2.4 captioned "Statutory Provisions" is amended by inserting "2237(a)(1), (a)(2)(A)," after "1502,".

Section 2A5.2 is amended in the heading by inserting "Navigation," after "Dispatch,"; and by striking "or Ferry".

Sections 2A5.2(a)(1) and (a)(2) are amended by striking the comma after "facility" each place it appears and inserting "or"; and by striking ", or a ferry" each place it appears.

The Commentary to § 2A5.2 captioned "Statutory Provisions" is amended by striking "1993(a)(4), (5), (6), (b);" and inserting "1992(a)(1), (a)(4), (a)(5), (a)(6);".

The Commentary to § 2A5.2 captioned "Application Note" is amended in Note 1 in the last paragraph by striking "18 U.S.C. § 1993(c)(5)" and inserting "18 U.S.C. § 1992(d)(7)".

The Commentary to § 2A6.1 captioned "Statutory Provisions" is amended by striking "1993(a)(7), (8)," and inserting "1992(a)(9), (a)(10), 2291(a)(8), 2291(e), 2292,".

Section 2B1.1(b) is amended by striking subdivision (11) as follows:

"(11) If the offense involved an organized scheme to steal vehicles or vehicle parts, and the offense level is less than level 14, increase to level 14.",

and inserting the following:

"(11) If the offense involved an organized scheme to steal or to receive stolen (A) vehicles or vehicle parts; or (B) goods or chattels that are part of a cargo shipment, increase by 2 levels. If the offense level is less than level 14, increase to level 14.".

The Commentary to § 2B1.1 captioned "Statutory Provisions" is amended by inserting "(a)(1), (a)(5)" after "1992"; by striking "1993(a)(1), (a)(4),"; by inserting "2291," after "2113(b),"; and by inserting "14915," after "49 U.S.C. §§ ".

The Commentary to § 2B1.1 captioned "Application Notes" is amended by striking Note 10 as follows:

> "10. Chop Shop Enhancement under Subsection (b)(11).—Subsection (b)(11) provides a minimum offense level in the case of an ongoing, sophisticated operation (such as an auto theft ring or 'chop shop') to steal vehicles or vehicle parts, or to receive stolen vehicles or vehicle parts. 'Vehicles' refers to all forms of vehicles, including aircraft and watercraft.",

and inserting the following:

> "10. Application of Subsection (b)(11).—Subsection (b)(11) provides a minimum offense level in the case of an ongoing, sophisticated operation (e.g., an auto theft ring or 'chop shop') to steal or to receive stolen (A) vehicles or vehicle parts; or (B) goods or chattels that are part of a cargo shipment. For purposes of this subsection, 'vehicle' means motor vehicle, vessel, or aircraft. A 'cargo shipment' includes cargo transported on a railroad car, bus, steamboat, vessel, or airplane.".

Section 2B2.3(b)(1) is amended by striking "secured" each place it appears and inserting "secure"; and by inserting "or a seaport" after "airport".

The Commentary to § 2B2.3 captioned "Statutory Provisions" is amended by inserting ", 2199" after "1036".

The Commentary to § 2B2.3 captioned "Application Notes" is amended in Note 1 by adding at the end the following:

> "'Seaport' has the meaning given that term in 18 U.S.C. § 26.".

The Commentary to § 2B2.3 captioned "Background" is amended by striking "secured" before "government" and inserting "secure"; and by striking ", such as nuclear facilities," and inserting "(such as nuclear facilities) and other locations (such as airports and seaports)".

The Commentary to § 2C1.1 captioned "Statutory Provisions" is amended by inserting "226," after "§§ 201(b)(1), (2),".

The Commentary to § 2K1.4 captioned "Statutory Provisions" is amended by inserting "(a)(1), (a)(2), (a)(4)" after "1992"; by striking "1993(a)(1), (a)(2), (a)(3), (b),"; and by inserting "2291," after "2275,".

The Commentary to § 2K1.4 captioned "Application Notes" is amended in Note 1 by striking "18 U.S.C. § 1993(c)(5)" and inserting "18 U.S.C. § 1992(d)(7)".

The Commentary to § 2M6.1 captioned "Statutory Provisions" is amended by striking "1993(a)(2), (3), (b), 2332a (only with respect to weapons of mass destruction as defined in 18 U.S.C. § 2332a(c)(2)(B), (C), and (D))," and inserting "1992(a)(2), (a)(3), (a)(4), (b)(2), 2291,".

The Commentary to § 2Q1.1 captioned "Statutory Provisions" is amended by inserting "18 U.S.C. § 1992(b)(3);" before "33 U.S.C. § 1319(c)(3);".

Amendment 699 APPENDIX C - VOLUME III November 1, 2013

Section 2X1.1 is amended in subsection (d)(1)(A) by inserting "(a)(1)-(a)(7), (a)(9), (a)(10)" after "1992"; and in subsection (d)(1)(B) by inserting "and" after "§ 32;"; and by striking "18 U.S.C. § 1993; and".

The Commentary to § 2X5.2 captioned "Statutory Provisions" is amended by inserting "; 49 U.S.C. § 31310" after "14133".

Appendix A (Statutory Index) is amended by inserting after the line referenced to 18 U.S.C. § 225 the following:

"18 U.S.C. § 226   2C1.1";

by inserting after the line referenced to 18 U.S.C. § 1035 the following:

"18 U.S.C. § 1036   2B2.3";

by striking the following:

"18 U.S.C. § 1992	2A1.1, 2B1.1, 2K1.4, 2X1.1
18 U.S.C. § 1993(a)(1)	2B1.1, 2K1.4
18 U.S.C. § 1993(a)(2)	2K1.4, 2M6.1
18 U.S.C. § 1993(a)(3)	2K1.4, 2M6.1
18 U.S.C. § 1993(a)(4)	2A5.2, 2B1.1
18 U.S.C. § 1993(a)(5)	2A5.2
18 U.S.C. § 1993(a)(6)	2A2.1, 2A2.2, 2A5.2
18 U.S.C. § 1993(a)(7)	2A6.1
18 U.S.C. § 1993(a)(8)	2A5.2 (if attempt or conspiracy to commit 18 U.S.C. § 1993(a)(4), (a)(5), or (a)(6)), 2A6.1
18 U.S.C. § 1993(b)	2A5.2, 2K1.4, 2M6.1",

and inserting the following:

"18 U.S.C. § 1992(a)(1)	2A5.2, 2B1.1, 2K1.4, 2X1.1
18 U.S.C. § 1992(a)(2)	2K1.4, 2M6.1, 2X1.1
18 U.S.C. § 1992(a)(3)	2M6.1, 2X1.1
18 U.S.C. § 1992(a)(4)	2A5.2, 2K1.4, 2M6.1, 2X1.1
18 U.S.C. § 1992(a)(5)	2A5.2, 2B1.1, 2X1.1
18 U.S.C. § 1992(a)(6)	2A5.2, 2X1.1
18 U.S.C. § 1992(a)(7)	2A1.1, 2A2.1, 2A2.2, 2X1.1
18 U.S.C. § 1992(a)(8)	2X1.1
18 U.S.C. § 1992(a)(9)	2A6.1, 2X1.1
18 U.S.C. § 1992(a)(10)	2A6.1, 2X1.1";

in the line referenced to 18 U.S.C. § 2199 by inserting "2A1.1, 2A1.2, 2A1.3, 2A1.4, 2A2.1, 2A2.2, 2A2.3," before "2B1.1";

by inserting after the line referenced to 18 U.S.C. § 2233 the following:

"18 U.S.C. § 2237(a)(1), (a)(2)(A)	2A2.4
18 U.S.C. § 2237(a)(2)(B)	2B1.1";

by inserting after the line referenced to 18 U.S.C. § 2281 the following:

"18 U.S.C. § 2291   2A1.1, 2A1.2, 2A1.3, 2A1.4, 2A2.1, 2A2.2, 2A2.3,
                    2A6.1, 2B1.1, 2K1.4, 2M6.1
18 U.S.C. § 2292   2A6.1";

by inserting after the line referenced to 49 U.S.C. § 14912 the following:

"49 U.S.C. § 14915   2B1.1"; and

by inserting after the line referenced to 49 U.S.C. § 30170 the following:

"49 U.S.C. § 31310   2X5.2".

Reason for Amendment: This amendment implements various provisions of the USA PATRIOT Improvement and Reauthorization Act of 2005, Pub. L. 109–177 (the "PATRIOT Reauthorization Act") and the Safe, Accountable, Flexible, Efficient Transportation Equity Act: A Legacy for Users, Pub. L. 109–59 ("SAFETEA-LU").

The PATRIOT Reauthorization Act created several new offenses and increased the scope of or penalty for several existing offenses. SAFETEA-LU also created two new offenses. This amendment references both the new statutes and those with increased scope and penalties to existing guidelines. The amendment also provides a corresponding amendment to Appendix A (Statutory Index). The Commission concluded that referencing the new offenses to existing guidelines was appropriate because the type of conduct criminalized by the new statutes was adequately addressed and penalized by the guidelines.

Section 307(c) of the PATRIOT Reauthorization Act directed the Commission to review the guidelines to determine whether a sentencing enhancement is appropriate for any offense under sections 659 or 2311 of title 18, United States Code. This amendment responds to the directive by revising the enhancement at subsection (b)(11) of § 2B1.1 (Larceny, Embezzlement, and Other Forms of Theft; Offenses Involving Stolen Property; Property Damage or Destruction; Fraud and Deceit; Forgery; Offenses Involving Altered or Counterfeit Instruments Other than Counterfeit Bearer Obligations of the United States). The amendment expands the scope of this enhancement to cover cargo theft and adds a reference to the receipt of stolen vehicles or goods to ensure application of the enhancement is consistent with the scope of 18 U.S.C. §§ 659 and 2313. The Commission determined that the two-level increase, and the minimum offense level of 14, appropriately responds to concerns regarding the increased instances of organized cargo theft operations.

Effective Date: The effective date of this amendment is November 1, 2007.

700. **Amendment:** The Commentary to § 2A1.1 captioned "Statutory Provisions", as amended by Amendment 699, is further amended by inserting "2282A," after "2199,".

The Commentary to § 2A1.2 captioned "Statutory Provisions", as amended by Amendment 699, is further amended by inserting "2282A," after "2199,".

The Commentary to § 2B1.1 captioned "Statutory Provisions", as amended by Amendment 699, is further amended by inserting "2282A, 2282B," after "2113(b),".

The Commentary to § 2B1.5 captioned "Statutory Provisions" is amended by inserting "554," before "641,".

Chapter Two, Part D, Subpart One, is amended by adding at the end the following new guideline and accompanying commentary:

"§ 2D1.14. Narco-Terrorism

    (a)   Base Offense Level:

        (1)   The offense level from § 2D1.1 (Unlawful Manufacturing, Importing, Exporting, or Trafficking (Including Possession with Intent to Commit These Offenses); Attempt or Conspiracy) applicable to the underlying offense, except that § 2D1.1(a)(3)(A), (a)(3)(B), and (b)(11) shall not apply.

    (b)   Specific Offense Characteristic

        (1)   If § 3A1.4 (Terrorism) does not apply, increase by 6 levels.

Commentary

Statutory Provision: 21 U.S.C. § 960a.".

Chapter Two, Part E, Subpart Four, is amended in the heading by adding at the end "AND SMOKELESS TOBACCO".

Section 2E4.1 is amended in the heading by adding at the end "and Smokeless Tobacco".

The Commentary to § 2E4.1 captioned "Background" is amended by striking "60,000" and inserting "10,000".

The Commentary to § 2K1.3 captioned "Statutory Provisions" is amended by inserting ", 2283" after "1716".

Section 2K1.4 is amended in subsections (a)(1) and (a)(2) by striking "a ferry," each place it appears and inserting "a maritime facility, a vessel, or a vessel's cargo,"; in subsection (a)(2) by striking "or" the last place it appears; by redesignating subsection (a)(3) as subsection (a)(4); and by inserting the following after subsection (a)(2):

    "(3)   16, if the offense involved the destruction of or tampering with aids to maritime navigation; or".

Section 2K1.4(b)(2) is amended by striking "(a)(3)" and inserting "(a)(4)".

The Commentary to § 2K1.4 captioned "Statutory Provisions", as amended by Amendment 699, is further amended by inserting "2282A, 2282B," after "2275,".

The Commentary to § 2K1.4 captioned "Application Notes" is amended in Note 1 by inserting after "For purposes of this guideline:" the following paragraph:

"'Aids to maritime navigation' means any device external to a vessel intended to assist the navigator to determine position or save course, or to warn of dangers or obstructions to navigation.";

by inserting after "destructive device." the following paragraph:

"'Maritime facility' means any structure or facility of any kind located in, on, under, or adjacent to any waters subject to the jurisdiction of the United States and used, operated, or maintained by a public or private entity, including any contiguous or adjoining property under common ownership or operation.";

by striking "1993(c)(5)" and inserting "1992(d)(7)"; and by adding at the end the following:

> "'Vessel' includes every description of watercraft or other artificial contrivance used, or capable of being used, as a means of transportation on water.".

The Commentary to § 2M5.2 captioned "Statutory Provisions" is amended by inserting "18 U.S.C. § 554;" before "22 U.S.C. §§ 2778, 2780.".

Section 2M5.3 is amended in the heading by inserting "Specially Designated Global Terrorists, or" after "Organizations or"

The Commentary to § 2M5.3 captioned "Statutory Provisions" is amended by inserting "2283, 2284," after "18 U.S.C. §§ "; and by striking the period at the end and inserting "; 50 U.S.C. §§ 1701, 1705.".

The Commentary to § 2M5.3 captioned "Application Notes" is amended in Note 1 by adding at the end the following paragraph:

> "'Specially designated global terrorist' has the meaning given that term in 31 C.F.R. § 594.513.".

Section 2M6.1 is amended in the heading by striking "Production, Development, Acquisition, Stockpiling, Alteration, Use, Transfer, or Possession of" and inserting "Activity Involving".

The Commentary to § 2M6.1 captioned "Statutory Provisions", as amended by Amendment 699, is further amended by inserting "2283," before "2291,".

The Commentary to § 2Q2.1 captioned "Statutory Provisions" is amended by inserting "§ " before "545" and by inserting ", 554" after "545".

The Commentary to § 2Q2.1 captioned "Background" is amended by striking "§ 545 where" and inserting "§§ 545 and 554 if".

The Commentary to § 2X1.1 captioned "Statutory Provisions" is amended by inserting ", 2282A, 2282B" after "2271".

The Commentary to § 2X2.1 captioned "Statutory Provisions" is amended by inserting "2284," after "2,".

The Commentary to § 2X3.1 captioned "Statutory Provisions" is amended by inserting "2284," after "1072,".

Chapter Two, Part X is amended by adding at the end the following new subpart, guideline, and accompanying commentary:

> "7. OFFENSES INVOLVING BORDER TUNNELS
>
> § 2X7.1. Border Tunnels and Subterranean Passages
>
> (a) Base Offense Level:
>
> (1) If the defendant was convicted under 18 U.S.C. § 554(c), 4 plus the offense level applicable to the underlying smuggling offense. If the resulting offense level is less than level 16, increase to level 16.

(2) 16, if the defendant was convicted under 18 U.S.C. § 554(a); or

(3) 8, if the defendant was convicted under 18 U.S.C. § 554(b).

Commentary

Statutory Provision: 18 U.S.C. § 554.

Application Note:

1. Definition.—For purposes of this guideline, 'underlying smuggling offense' means the smuggling offense the defendant committed through the use of the tunnel or subterranean passage.".

Chapter Five, Part K is amended by adding at the end the following new policy statement and accompanying commentary:

"§ 5K2.24. Commission of Offense While Wearing or Displaying Unauthorized or Counterfeit Insignia or Uniform (Policy Statement)

If, during the commission of the offense, the defendant wore or displayed an official, or counterfeit official, insignia or uniform received in violation of 18 U.S.C. § 716, an upward departure may be warranted.

Commentary

Application Note:

1. Definition.—For purposes of this policy statement, 'official insignia or uniform' has the meaning given that term in 18 U.S.C. § 716(c)(3).".

Appendix A (Statutory Index) is amended by inserting after the line referenced to 18 U.S.C. § 553(a)(2) the following:

"18 U.S.C. § 554
(Border tunnels and passages)   2X7.1
18 U.S.C. § 554
(Smuggling goods from
the United States)   2B1.5, 2M5.2, 2Q2.1".

Appendix A (Statutory Index), as amended by Amendment 699, is further amended by inserting after the line referenced to 18 U.S.C. § 2281 the following:

"18 U.S.C. § 2282A   2A1.1, 2A1.2, 2B1.1,
                     2K1.4, 2X1.1
18 U.S.C. § 2282B   2B1.1, 2K1.4, 2X1.1
18 U.S.C. § 2283   2K1.3, 2M5.3, 2M6.1
18 U.S.C. § 2284   2M5.3, 2X2.1, 2X3.1".

Appendix A (Statutory Index) is amended in the line referenced to 18 U.S.C. § 2339 by inserting "2M5.3," before "2X2.1";

by inserting after the line referenced to 21 U.S.C. § 960(d)(7) the following:

"21 U.S.C. § 960a   2D1.14".

by inserting after the line referenced to 50 U.S.C. § 783(c) the following:

"50 U.S.C. § 1701   2M5.1, 2M5.2, 2M5.3
50 U.S.C. § 1705   2M5.3"; and

by striking the following:

"50 U.S.C. App. § 1701   2M5.1, 2M5.2".

Reason for Amendment: This amendment implements the USA PATRIOT Improvement and Reauthorization Act of 2005 (the "PATRIOT Reauthorization Act"), Pub. L. 109–177, and the Department of Homeland Security Appropriations Act, 2007 (the "Homeland Security Act"), Pub. L. 109–295.

First, the amendment addresses section 122 of the PATRIOT Reauthorization Act, which created a new offense at 21 U.S.C. § 960a covering narco-terrorism. This new offense prohibits engaging in conduct that would be covered under 21 U.S.C. § 841(a) if committed under the jurisdiction of the United States, knowing or intending to provide, directly or indirectly, anything of pecuniary value to any person or organization that has engaged or engages in terrorist activity (as defined in section 212(a)(3)(B) of the Immigration and Nationality Act) or terrorism (as defined in section 140(d)(2) of the Foreign Relations Authorization Act, Fiscal Years 1988 and 1989 (This act is made up of separate parts divided by fiscal year)). The penalty is not less than twice the statutory minimum punishment under 21 U.S.C. § 841(b)(1) and not more than life. Section 960a also provides a mandatory term of supervised release of at least five years.

The amendment creates a new guideline at § 2D1.14 (Narco-Terrorism) because an offense under 21 U.S.C. § 960a differs from basic drug offenses because it involves trafficking that benefits terrorist activity. The guideline also provides that the base offense level is the offense level determined under § 2D1.1 (Unlawful Manufacturing, Importing, Exporting, or Trafficking (Including Possession with Intent to Commit These Offenses); Attempt or Conspiracy) for the underlying offense, except that the "mitigating role cap" in § 2D1.1(a)(3)(A) and (B) and the two-level reduction for meeting the criteria set forth in subdivisions (1)-(5) of subsection (a) of § 5C1.2 (Limitation on Applicability of Statutory Minimum Sentences in Certain Cases) shall not apply. The Commission determined that these exclusions are appropriate to reflect that this is not a typical drug offense, in that an individual convicted under this provision must have had knowledge that the person or organization receiving the funds or support generated by the drug trafficking "has engaged or engages in terrorist activity . . . or terrorism . . . ." The guideline also contains a specific offense characteristic that provides a six-level increase if the adjustment in § 3A1.4 (Terrorism) does not apply. This six-level increase fully effectuates the statute's doubling of the minimum punishment for the underlying drug offense, while avoiding potential double counting with the 12-level adjustment at § 3A1.4. The amendment also provides a corresponding reference for the new offense to § 2D1.14 in Appendix A (Statutory Index).

Second, the amendment responds to the directive in section 551 of the Homeland Security Act, which created a new offense in 18 U.S.C. § 554 regarding the construction of border tunnels and subterranean passages that cross the international boundary between the United States and another country. Section 551(c) of the Homeland Security Act directed the Commission to promulgate or amend the guidelines to provide for increased penalties for persons convicted of offenses under 18 U.S.C. § 554 and required the Commission to consider a number of factors. Section 554(a) prohibits the construction or financing of such tunnels and passages and provides a statutory maximum term of imprisonment of 20 years. Section 554(b) prohibits the knowing or reckless disregard of the construction on land the person owns or controls and provides a statutory maximum term of imprisonment of 10 years. Section 554(c) prohibits the use of the tunnels to smuggle an alien, goods (in violation of 18 U.S.C. § 545), controlled substances, weapons of mass destruction (including biological weapons), or a member of a terrorist organization (defined in 18 U.S.C. § 2339B(g)(6)) and provides a penalty of twice the maximum term of imprisonment that otherwise would have been applicable had the unlawful activity not made use of the tunnel or passage.

The amendment creates a new guideline at § 2X7.1 (Border Tunnels and Subterranean Passages) for convictions under 18 U.S.C. § 554. The new guideline provides that a conviction under 18 U.S.C. § 554(a) receives a base offense level 16, which is commensurate with certain other offenses with statutory maximum terms of imprisonment of 20 years and ensures a sentence of imprisonment. A conviction under 18 U.S.C. § 554(c) will receive a four-level increase over the offense level applicable to the underlying smuggling offense, which ensures that the seriousness of the underlying offense is the primary measure of offense severity. The four-level increase also satisfies the directive's instruction to account for the aggravating nature of the use of a tunnel or subterranean passage to breach the border to accomplish the smuggling offense and effectuates the statute's doubling of the statutory maximum penalty. A conviction under 18 U.S.C. § 554(b) receives a base offense level of 8, which reflects the less aggravated nature of this offense.

Third, the amendment addresses other new offenses created by the PATRIOT Reauthorization Act. Based on an assessment of similar offenses already covered by the relevant guidelines, the amendment provides as follows:

(A) The new offense in 18 U.S.C. § 554, pertaining to smuggling of goods from the United States, is referenced to §§ 2B1.5 (Theft of, Damage to, or Destruction of, Cultural Heritage Resources; Unlawful Sale, Purchase, Exchange, Transportation, or Receipt of Cultural Heritage Resources), 2M5.2 (Exportation of Arms, Munitions, or Military Equipment or Services Without Required Validated Export License), and 2Q2.1 (Offenses Involving Fish, Wildlife, and Plants).

(B) The new offense in 18 U.S.C. § 2282A, pertaining to mining of United States navigable waters, is referenced to §§ 2A1.1 (First Degree Murder), 2A1.2 (Second Degree Murder), 2B1.1 (Larceny, Embezzlement, and Other Forms of Theft; Offenses Involving Stolen Property; Property Damage or Destruction; Fraud and Deceit; Forgery; Offenses Involving Altered or Counterfeit Instruments Other than Counterfeit Bearer Obligations of the United States), 2K1.4 (Arson; Property Damage by Use of Explosives), and 2X1.1 (Attempt, Solicitation, or Conspiracy (Not Covered by a Specific Offense Guideline)). The amendment also adds vessel, maritime facility, and a vessel's cargo to § 2K1.4(a)(1) and (a)(2) to cover conduct described in 18 U.S.C. § 2282A. The definitions provided for "vessel," "maritime facility," and "aids to maritime navigation" come from title 33 of the Code of Federal Regulations pertaining to the United States Coast Guard, specifically Navigation and Navigable Waters.

Section 2282B, pertaining to violence against maritime navigational aids, is referenced to §§ 2B1.1, 2K1.4, and 2X1.1. Section 2K1.4(a) is amended to provide a new base offense level of 16 if the offense involved the destruction of or tampering with aids to maritime navigation.

November 1, 2013 APPENDIX C - VOLUME III **Amendment 701**

(C) The new offense in 18 U.S.C. § 2283 pertaining to transporting biological and chemical weapons is referenced to §§ 2K1.3 (Unlawful Receipt, Possession, or Transportation of Explosive Materials; Prohibited Transactions Involving Explosive Materials), 2M5.3 (Providing Material Support or Resources to Designated Foreign Terrorism Organizations or For a Terrorist Purpose), and 2M6.1 (Unlawful Production, Development, Acquisition, Stockpiling, Alteration, Use, Transfer, or Possession of Nuclear Material, Weapons, or Facilities, Biological Agents, Toxins, or Delivery Systems, Chemical Weapons, or Other Weapons of Mass Destruction; Attempt or Conspiracy). The new offense in 18 U.S.C. § 2284 pertaining to transporting terrorists is referenced to §§ 2M5.3 (Providing Material Support or Resources to Designated Foreign Terrorist Organizations or For a Terrorist Purpose), 2X2.1 (Aiding and Abetting), and 2X3.1 (Accessory After the Fact).

(D) Section 2341 of title 18, United States Code, which provides definitions for offenses involving contraband cigarettes and smokeless tobacco, was amended to reduce the number of contraband cigarettes necessary to violate the substantive offenses set forth in 18 U.S.C. §§ 2342 and 2344 from 60,000 to 10,000. The amendment makes conforming changes to the background commentary of § 2E4.1 (Unlawful Conduct Relating to Contraband Cigarettes) and expands the headings of Chapter Two, Part E, Subpart 4 and § 2E4.1 to include smokeless tobacco.

(E) The Patriot Reauthorization Act increased the statutory maximum term of imprisonment for offenses covered by the International Emergency Economic Powers Act (50 U.S.C. § 1705) from 10 years to 20 years' imprisonment. The amendment references 50 U.S.C. § 1705 to § 2M5.3 and modifies the heading of the guideline to include "specially designated global terrorist".

Fourth, the amendment sets forth the statutory references in Appendix A (Statutory Index) for the new offenses. Appendix A is amended to provide a parenthetical description for the two statutory references to 18 U.S.C. § 554.

Fifth, the amendment implements a directive in section 1191(c) of the Violence Against Women and Department of Justice Reauthorization Act of 2005, Pub. L. 109–162. The Act directed the Commission to amend the guidelines "to assure that the sentence imposed on a defendant who is convicted of a Federal offense while wearing or displaying insignia and uniform received in violation of section 716 of title 18, United States Code, reflects the gravity of this aggravating factor." Section 716 of title 18, United States Code, is a Class B misdemeanor which is not covered by the guidelines, see § 1B1.9 (Class B or C Misdemeanors and Infractions); however, the amendment creates a new policy statement at § 5K2.24 (Commission of Offense While Wearing or Displaying Unauthorized or Counterfeit Insignia or Uniform) providing that an upward departure may be warranted if, during the commission of the offense, the defendant wore or displayed an official, or counterfeit official, insignia or uniform received in violation of 18 U.S.C. § 716.

Effective Date: The effective date of this amendment is November 1, 2007.

701. Amendment: Chapter Two, Part A, Subpart Three, is amended in the heading by adding at the end "AND OFFENSES RELATED TO REGISTRATION AS A SEX OFFENDER".

Section 2A3.1(a) is amended by striking "30" and inserting the following:

"(1) 38, if the defendant was convicted under 18 U.S.C. § 2241(c); or

(2) 30, otherwise.".

Section 2A3.1(b)(2) is amended by striking "(A) If" and inserting "If subsection (a)(2) applies and (A)"; and by striking "if" after "(B)".

The Commentary to § 2A3.1 captioned "Application Notes" is amended in Note 2 by inserting "(A) <u>Definitions</u>.—" before "For purposes of"; and by adding at the end the following subdivision:

"(B) <u>Application in Cases Involving a Conviction under 18 U.S.C. § 2241(c)</u>.—If the conduct that forms the basis for a conviction under 18 U.S.C. § 2241(c) is that the defendant engaged in conduct described in 18 U.S.C. § 2241(a) or (b), do not apply subsection (b)(1).".

Section 2A3.1 is amended by striking the Commentary captioned "Background" as follows:

"<u>Background</u>: Sexual offenses addressed in this section are crimes of violence. Because of their dangerousness, attempts are treated the same as completed acts of criminal sexual abuse. The maximum term of imprisonment authorized by statute is life imprisonment. The base offense level represents sexual abuse as set forth in 18 U.S.C. § 2242. An enhancement is provided for use of force; threat of death, serious bodily injury, or kidnapping; or certain other means as defined in 18 U.S.C. § 2241. This includes any use or threatened use of a dangerous weapon.

An enhancement is provided when the victim is less than sixteen years of age. An additional enhancement is provided where the victim is less than twelve years of age. Any criminal sexual abuse with a child less than twelve years of age, regardless of 'consent,' is governed by § 2A3.1 (Criminal Sexual Abuse).

An enhancement for a custodial relationship between defendant and victim is also provided. Whether the custodial relationship is temporary or permanent, the defendant in such a case is a person the victim trusts or to whom the victim is entrusted. This represents the potential for greater and prolonged psychological damage. Also, an enhancement is provided where the victim was an inmate of, or a person employed in, a correctional facility. Finally, enhancements are provided for permanent, life-threatening, or serious bodily injury and abduction.".

Section 2A3.3(a) is amended by striking "12" and inserting "14".

The Commentary to § 2A3.3 captioned "Application Notes" is amended in Note 1 by striking "'Minor' means an individual who had not attained the age of 18 years." and inserting the following:

"'Minor' means (A) an individual who had not attained the age of 18; (B) an individual, whether fictitious or not, who a law enforcement officer represented to a participant (i) had not attained the age of 18 years; and (ii) could be provided for the purposes of engaging in sexually explicit conduct; or (C) an undercover law enforcement officer who represented to a participant that the officer had not attained the age of 18 years.".

The Commentary to § 2A3.3 captioned "Application Notes" is amended by adding at the end the following:

> "4. Inapplicability of § 3B1.3.—Do not apply § 3B1.3 (Abuse of Position of Trust or Use of Special Skill).".

Section 2A3.3 is amended by striking the Commentary captioned "Background" as follows:

> "Background: The offense covered by this section is a misdemeanor. The maximum term of imprisonment authorized by statute is one year.".

Section 2A3.4(b)(1) is amended by striking "20" each place it appears and inserting "22".

The Commentary to § 2A3.4 captioned "Statutory Provisions" is amended by striking "(a)(1), (2), (3)" after "§ 2244".

The Commentary to § 2A3.4 captioned "Background" is amended by striking the following:

> "Enhancements are provided for victimizing children or minors. The enhancement under subsection (b)(2) does not apply, however, where the base offense level is determined under subsection (a)(3) because an element of the offense to which that offense level applies is that the victim had attained the age of twelve years but had not attained the age of sixteen years.".

Chapter Two, Part A, Subpart Three, is amended by adding at the end the following new guidelines and accompanying commentaries:

> "§ 2A3.5. Failure to Register as a Sex Offender
>
> (a) Base Offense Level (Apply the greatest):
>
> (1) 16, if the defendant was required to register as a Tier III offender;
>
> (2) 14, if the defendant was required to register as a Tier II offender; or
>
> (3) 12, if the defendant was required to register as a Tier I offender.
>
> (b) Specific Offense Characteristics
>
> (1) (Apply the greatest):
>
> If, while in a failure to register status, the defendant committed—
>
> (A) a sex offense against someone other than a minor increase by 6 levels;
>
> (B) a felony offense against a minor not otherwise covered by subdivision (C), increase by 6 levels; or
>
> (C) a sex offense against a minor, increase by 8 levels.

(2) If the defendant voluntarily (A) corrected the failure to register; or (B) attempted to register but was prevented from registering by uncontrollable circumstances and the defendant did not contribute to the creation of those circumstances, decrease by 3 levels.

Commentary

Statutory Provision: 18 U.S.C. § 2250(a).

Application Notes:

1. Definitions.—For purposes of this guideline:

    'Minor' means (A) an individual who had not attained the age of 18 years; (B) an individual, whether fictitious or not, who a law enforcement officer represented to a participant (i) had not attained the age of 18 years; and (ii) could be provided for the purposes of engaging in sexually explicit conduct; or (C) an undercover law enforcement officer who represented to a participant that the officer had not attained the age of 18 years.

    'Sex offense' has the meaning given that term in 42 U.S.C. § 16911(5).

    'Tier I offender', 'Tier II offender', and 'Tier III offender' have the meaning given those terms in 42 U.S.C. § 16911(2), (3) and (4), respectively.

2. Application of Subsection (b)(2).—

    (A) In General.—In order for subsection (b)(2) to apply, the defendant's voluntary attempt to register or to correct the failure to register must have occurred prior to the time the defendant knew or reasonably should have known a jurisdiction had detected the failure to register.

    (B) Interaction with Subsection (b)(1).—Do not apply subsection (b)(2) if subsection (b)(1) also applies.

§ 2A3.6. Aggravated Offenses Relating to Registration as a Sex Offender

If the defendant was convicted under—

(a) 18 U.S.C. § 2250(c), the guideline sentence is the minimum term of imprisonment required by statute; or

(b) 18 U.S.C. § 2260A, the guideline sentence is the term of imprisonment required by statute.

Chapters Three (Adjustments) and Four (Criminal History and Criminal Livelihood) shall not apply to any count of conviction covered by this guideline.

Commentary

Statutory Provisions: 18 U.S.C. §§ 2250(c), 2260A.

Application Notes:

1. In General.—Section 2250(c) of title 18, United States Code, provides a mandatory minimum term of five years' imprisonment and a statutory

maximum term of 30 years' imprisonment. The statute also requires a sentence to be imposed consecutively to any sentence imposed for a conviction under 18 U.S.C. § 2250(a). Section 2260A of title 18, United States Code, provides a term of imprisonment of 10 years that is required to be imposed consecutively to any sentence imposed for an offense enumerated under that section.

2. Inapplicability of Chapters Three and Four.—Do not apply Chapters Three (Adjustments) and Four (Criminal History and Criminal Livelihood) to any offense sentenced under this guideline. Such offenses are excluded from application of those chapters because the guideline sentence for each offense is determined only by the relevant statute. See §§ 3D1.1 (Procedure for Determining Offense Level on Multiple Counts) and 5G1.2 (Sentencing on Multiple Counts of Conviction).

3. Inapplicability of Chapter Two Enhancement.—If a sentence under this guideline is imposed in conjunction with a sentence for an underlying offense, do not apply any specific offense characteristic that is based on the same conduct as the conduct comprising the conviction under 18 U.S.C. § 2250(c) or § 2260A.

4. Upward Departure.—In a case in which the guideline sentence is determined under subsection (a), a sentence above the minimum term required by 18 U.S.C. § 2250(c) is an upward departure from the guideline sentence. A departure may be warranted, for example, in a case involving a sex offense committed against a minor or if the offense resulted in serious bodily injury to a minor.".

Section 2G1.1(a) is amended by striking "14" and inserting the following:

"(1) 34, if the offense of conviction is 18 U.S.C. § 1591(b)(1); or

(2) 14, otherwise.".

Section 2G1.1(b)(1) is amended by inserting "(A) subsection (a)(2) applies; and (B)" after "If".

Section 2G1.1 is amended by striking the Commentary captioned "Background" as follows:

"Background: This guideline covers offenses that involve promoting prostitution or prohibited sexual conduct with an adult through a variety of means. Offenses that involve promoting prostitution or prohibited sexual conduct with an adult are sentenced under this guideline, unless criminal sexual abuse occurs as part of the offense, in which case the cross reference would apply.

This guideline also covers offenses under section 1591 of title 18, United States Code, that involve recruiting or transporting a person, other than a minor, in interstate commerce knowing that force, fraud, or coercion will be used to cause the person to engage in a commercial sex act.

Offenses of promoting prostitution or prohibited sexual conduct in which a minor victim is involved are to be sentenced under § 2G1.3 (Promoting a Commercial Sex Act or Prohibited Sexual Conduct with a Minor; Transportation of Minors to Engage in a Commercial Sex Act or Prohibited Sexual Conduct; Travel

Amendment 701

to Engage in Commercial Sex Act or Prohibited Sexual Conduct with a Minor; Sex Trafficking of Children; Use of Interstate Facilities to Transport Information about a Minor).".

Section 2G1.3(a) is amended by striking "24" and inserting the following:

"(1) 34, if the defendant was convicted under 18 U.S.C. § 1591(b)(1);

(2) 30, if the defendant was convicted under 18 U.S.C. § 1591(b)(2);

(3) 28, if the defendant was convicted under 18 U.S.C. § 2422(b) or § 2423(a); or

(4) 24, otherwise.".

Section 2G1.3(b) is amended by striking subdivision (4) as follows:

"(4) If the offense involved (A) the commission of a sex act or sexual contact; or (B) a commercial sex act, increase by 2 levels.".

and inserting the following:

"(4) If (A) the offense involved the commission of a sex act or sexual contact; or (B) subsection (a)(3) or (a)(4) applies and the offense involved a commercial sex act, increase by 2 levels.".

Section 2G1.3(b)(5) is amended by inserting "(A) subsection (a)(3) or (a)(4) applies; and (B)" after "If".

The Commentary to § 2G1.3 captioned "Statutory Provisions" is amended by striking "2422(b),".

Section 2G1.3 is amended by striking the Commentary captioned "Background" as follows:

"Background: This guideline covers offenses under chapter 117 of title 18, United States Code, involving transportation of a minor for illegal sexual activity through a variety of means. This guideline also covers offenses involving a minor under section 1591 of title 18, United States Code. Offenses involving an individual who had attained the age of 18 years are covered under § 2G1.1 (Promoting A Commercial Sex Act or Prohibited Sexual Conduct with an Individual Other than a Minor).".

The Commentary to § 2G2.5 captioned "Statutory Provisions" is amended by inserting "§ " after "18 U.S. C. § "; and by inserting ", 2257A" after "2257".

Chapter Two, Part G, Subpart Two, is amended by adding at the end the following new guideline and accompanying commentary:

"§ 2G2.6. Child Exploitation Enterprises

(a) Base Offense Level: 35

(b) Specific Offense Characteristics

(1) If a victim (A) had not attained the age of 12 years, increase by 4 levels; or (B) had attained the age of 12 years but had not attained the age of 16 years, increase by 2 levels.

(2) If (A) the defendant was a parent, relative, or legal guardian of a minor victim; or (B) a minor victim was otherwise in the custody, care, or supervisory control of the defendant, increase by 2 levels.

(3) If the offense involved conduct described in 18 U.S.C. § 2241(a) or (b), increase by 2 levels.

(4) If a computer or an interactive computer service was used in furtherance of the offense, increase by 2 levels.

Commentary

Statutory Provision: 18 U.S.C. § 2252A(g).

Application Notes:

1. Definitions.—For purposes of this guideline:

'Computer' has the meaning given that term in 18 U.S.C. § 1030(e)(1).

'Interactive computer service' has the meaning given that term in section 230(e)(2) of the Communications Act of 1934 (47 U.S.C. § 230(f)(2)).

'Minor' means (A) an individual who had not attained the age of 18 years; (B) an individual, whether fictitious or not, who a law enforcement officer represented to a participant (i) had not attained the age of 18 years; and (ii) could be provided for the purposes of engaging in sexually explicit conduct; or (C) an undercover law enforcement officer who represented to a participant that the officer had not attained the age of 18 years.

2. Application of Subsection (b)(2).—

   (A) Custody, Care, or Supervisory Control.—Subsection (b)(2) is intended to have broad application and includes offenses involving a victim less than 18 years of age entrusted to the defendant, whether temporarily or permanently. For example, teachers, day care providers, baby-sitters, or other temporary caretakers are among those who would be subject to this enhancement. In determining whether to apply this enhancement, the court should look to the actual relationship that existed between the defendant and the minor and not simply to the legal status of the defendant-minor relationship.

   (B) Inapplicability of Chapter Three Adjustment.—If the enhancement under subsection (b)(2) applies, do not apply § 3B1.3 (Abuse of Position of Trust or Use of Special Skill).

3. Application of Subsection (b)(3).—For purposes of subsection (b)(3), 'conduct described in 18 U.S.C. § 2241(a) or (b)' is: (i) using force against the minor; (ii) threatening or placing the minor in fear that any person will be subject to death, serious bodily injury, or kidnapping; (iii) rendering the minor unconscious; or (iv) administering by force or threat of force, or without the knowledge or permission of the minor, a drug, intoxicant, or other similar substance and thereby substantially impairing the ability of the

Amendment 701 APPENDIX C - VOLUME III November 1, 2013

minor to appraise or control conduct. This provision would apply, for example, if any dangerous weapon was used or brandished, or in a case in which the ability of the minor to appraise or control conduct was substantially impaired by drugs or alcohol.".

Section 2G3.1(b) is amended by striking subdivision (2) as follows:

"(2) If the offense involved the use of a misleading domain name on the Internet with the intent to deceive a minor into viewing material on the Internet that is harmful to minors, increase by 2 levels.",

and inserting the following:

"(2) If, with the intent to deceive a minor into viewing material that is harmful to minors, the offense involved the use of (A) a misleading domain name on the Internet; or (B) embedded words or digital images in the source code of a website, increase by 2 levels.".

The Commentary to § 2G3.1 captioned "Statutory Provisions" is amended by inserting ", 2252C" after "2252B".

The Commentary to § 2G3.1 captioned "Application Notes" is amended in Note 2 by inserting "or § 2252C" after "2252B".

Section 2J1.2(b) is amended in subdivision (1) by striking "greater" and inserting "greatest"; by redesignating subdivisions (A) and (B) as subdivisions (B) and (C), respectively; by inserting before subdivision (B), as redesignated by this amendment, the following:

"(A) If the (i) defendant was convicted under 18 U.S.C. § 1001; and (ii) statutory maximum term of eight years' imprisonment applies because the matter relates to sex offenses under 18 U.S.C. § 1591 or chapters 109A, 109B, 110, or 117 of title 18, United States Code, increase by 4 levels.";

and by striking subdivision (C), as redesignated by this amendment, as follows:

"(C) If (i) defendant was convicted under 18 U.S.C. § 1001 or § 1505; and (ii) the statutory maximum term of imprisonment relating to international terrorism or domestic terrorism is applicable, increase by 12 levels.",

and inserting the following:

"(C) If the (i) defendant was convicted under 18 U.S.C. § 1001 or § 1505; and (ii) statutory maximum term of eight years' imprisonment applies because the matter relates to international terrorism or domestic terrorism, increase by 12 levels.".

The Commentary to § 2J1.2 captioned "Statutory Provisions" is amended by striking "when the statutory maximum term of imprisonment relating to international terrorism or domestic terrorism is applicable," and inserting the following:

"(when the statutory maximum term of eight years' imprisonment applies because the matter relates to international terrorism or domestic terrorism, or to sex offenses under 18 U.S.C. § 1591 or chapters 109A, 109B, 110, or 117 of title 18, United States Code),".

The Commentary to § 2J1.2 captioned "Application Notes" is amended in Note 2(B) by striking "(b)(1)(B)" and inserting "(b)(1)(C)".

The Commentary to § 2J1.2 captioned "Application Notes" is amended in Note 4 by inserting "or a particularly serious sex offense" after "face)".

The Commentary to § 2J1.2 captioned "Application Notes" is amended in Note 5 by inserting "(B)" after "Subsection (b)(1)" each place it appears; and by inserting "(B)" after "under subsection (b)(1)".

Section 3D1.2(d) is amended by inserting as a new line "§ 2A3.5;" before the line that begins "§§ 2B1.1"; and by inserting "(except § 2A3.5)" after "Chapter Two, Part A".

The Commentary to § 4B1.5 captioned "Application Notes" is amended by striking Note 1 as follows:

> "1. Definitions.—For purposes of this guideline:
>
> 'Minor' means an individual who had not attained the age of 18 years.
>
> 'Minor victim' includes (A) an undercover law enforcement officer who represented to the defendant that the officer was a minor; or (B) any minor the officer represented to the defendant would be involved in the prohibited sexual conduct.",

and inserting the following:

> "1. Definition.—For purposes of this guideline, 'minor' means (A) an individual who had not attained the age of 18 years; (B) an individual, whether fictitious or not, who a law enforcement officer represented to a participant (i) had not attained the age of 18 years; and (ii) could be provided for the purposes of engaging in sexually explicit conduct; or (C) an undercover law enforcement officer who represented to a participant that the officer had not attained the age of 18 years.".

The Commentary to § 4B1.5 captioned "Application Notes" is amended in Note 2 by inserting "or (iv) 18 U.S.C. § 1591;" after "individual;"; and by striking "(iii)" after "through" and inserting "(iv)".

The Commentary to § 4B1.5 captioned "Background" is amended by striking the following:

> "This guideline is intended to provide lengthy incarceration for offenders who commit sex offenses against minors and who present a continuing danger to the public. It applies to offenders whose instant offense of conviction is a sex offense committed against a minor victim.".

and inserting:

> "This guideline applies to offenders whose instant offense of conviction is a sex offense committed against a minor and who present a continuing danger to the public.".

Section 5B1.3(a)(9) is amended by inserting "(A) in a state in which the requirements of the Sex Offender Registration and Notification Act (see 42 U.S.C. §§ 16911 and 16913) do not apply," before "a defendant convicted"; by inserting "(Pub. L. 105–119, § 115(a)(8), Nov. 26, 1997)" after "4042(c)(4)"; by inserting "or" after "student;" and by adding at the

Amendment 701

end the following:

"(B) in a state in which the requirements of Sex Offender Registration and Notification Act apply, a sex offender shall (i) register, and keep such registration current, where the offender resides, where the offender is an employee, and where the offender is a student, and for the initial registration, a sex offender also shall register in the jurisdiction in which convicted if such jurisdiction is different from the jurisdiction of residence; (ii) provide information required by 42 U.S.C. § 16914; and (iii) keep such registration current for the full registration period as set forth in 42 U.S.C. § 16915;".

Section 5B1.3(d)(7) is amended by adding at the end the following:

"(C) A condition requiring the defendant to submit to a search, at any time, with or without a warrant, and by any law enforcement or probation officer, of the defendant's person and any property, house, residence, vehicle, papers, computer, other electronic communication or data storage devices or media, and effects, upon reasonable suspicion concerning a violation of a condition of probation or unlawful conduct by the defendant, or by any probation officer in the lawful discharge of the officer's supervision functions.".

Section 5B1.3 is amended by adding at the end the following:

"   Commentary

Application Note:

1. Application of Subsection (b)(9)(A) and (B).—Some jurisdictions continue to register sex offenders pursuant to the sex offender registry in place prior to July 27, 2006, the date of enactment of the Adam Walsh Act, which contained the Sex Offender Registration and Notification Act. In such a jurisdiction, subsection (b)(9)(A) will apply. In a jurisdiction that has implemented the requirements of the Sex Offender Registration and Notification Act, subsection (b)(9)(B) will apply. (See 42 U.S.C. §§ 16911 and 16913.)".

The Commentary to § 5D1.2 captioned "Application Notes" is amended by striking Note 1 as follows:

"1. Definition.—For purposes of this guideline, "sex offense" means (A) an offense, perpetrated against a minor, under (i) chapter 109A of title 18, United States Code; (ii) chapter 110 of such title, not including a recordkeeping offense; or (iii) chapter 117 of such title, not including transmitting information about a minor or filing a factual statement about an alien individual; or (B) an attempt or a conspiracy to commit any offense described in subdivisions (A)(i) through (iii) of this note.",

and inserting:

"1. Definitions.—For purposes of this guideline:

'Sex offense' means (A) an offense, perpetrated against a minor, under (i) chapter 109A of title 18, United States Code; (ii) chapter 109B of such title; (iii) chapter 110 of such title, not including a recordkeeping offense; (iv) chapter 117 of such title, not including transmitting information about a minor or filing a factual statement about an alien individual; (v) an offense under 18 U.S.C. § 1201; or (vi) an offense under 18 U.S.C. § 1591; or (B) an attempt or a conspiracy to commit any offense described in subdivisions (A)(i) through (vi) of this note.

'Minor' means (A) an individual who had not attained the age of 18 years; (B) an individual, whether fictitious or not, who a law enforcement officer represented to a participant (i) had not attained the age of 18 years; and (ii) could be provided for the purposes of engaging in sexually explicit conduct; or (C) an undercover law enforcement officer who represented to a participant that the officer had not attained the age of 18 years.".

Section 5D1.3(a)(7) is amended by inserting "(A) in a state in which the requirements of the Sex Offender Registration and Notification Act (see 42 U.S.C. §§ 16911 and 16913) do not apply," before "a defendant"; by inserting "(Pub. L. 105–119, § 115(a)(8), Nov. 26, 1997)" after "4042(c)(4)"; by inserting "or" after "student;" and by adding at the end the following:

"(B) in a state in which the requirements of Sex Offender Registration and Notification Act apply, a sex offender shall (i) register, and keep such registration current, where the offender resides, where the offender is an employee, and where the offender is a student, and for the initial registration, a sex offender also shall register in the jurisdiction in which convicted if such jurisdiction is different from the jurisdiction of residence; (ii) provide information required by 42 U.S.C. § 16914; and (iii) keep such registration current for the full registration period as set forth in 42 U.S.C. § 16915;".

Section 5D1.3(d)(7) is amended by adding at the end the following:

"(C) A condition requiring the defendant to submit to a search, at any time, with or without a warrant, and by any law enforcement or probation officer, of the defendant's person and any property, house, residence, vehicle, papers, computer, other electronic communication or data storage devices or media, and effects upon reasonable suspicion concerning a violation of a condition of supervised release or unlawful conduct by the defendant, or by any probation officer in the lawful discharge of the officer's supervision functions.".

Section 5D1.3 is amended by adding at the end the following:

"   Commentary

Application Note:

1. Application of Subsection (b)(7)(A) and (B).—Some jurisdictions continue to register sex offenders pursuant to the sex offender registry in place prior to July 27, 2006, the date of enactment of the Adam Walsh Act, which contained the Sex Offender Registration and Notification Act. In such a jurisdiction, subsection (b)(7)(A) will apply. In a jurisdiction that has implemented the requirements of the Sex Offender Registration and Notification Act, subsection (b)(7)(B) will apply. (See 42 U.S.C. §§ 16911 and 16913.)".

Appendix A (Statutory Index) is amended in the line referenced to 18 U.S.C. § 1001 by striking the following:

"when the statutory maximum term of imprisonment relating to international terrorism or domestic terrorism is applicable",

and inserting the following:

> "(when the statutory maximum term of eight years' imprisonment applies because the matter relates to international terrorism or domestic terrorism, or to sex offenses under 18 U.S.C. § 1591 or chapters 109A, 109B, 110, or 117 of title 18, United States Code)".

Appendix A (Statutory Index) is amended by inserting after the line referenced to 18 U.S.C. § 2245 the following:

> "18 U.S.C. § 2250(a)   2A3.5
> 18 U.S.C. § 2250(c)   2A3.6";

by inserting after the line referenced to 18 U.S.C. § 2252B the following:

> "18 U.S.C. § 2252C   2G3.1";

by inserting after the line referenced to 18 U.S.C. § 2257 the following:

> "18 U.S.C. § 2257A   2G2.5"; and

by inserting after the line referenced to 18 U.S.C. § 2260(b) the following:

> "18 U.S.C. § 2260A   2A3.6".

Reason for Amendment: This amendment responds to the Adam Walsh Child Protection and Safety Act of 2006 (the "Adam Walsh Act"), Pub. L. 109–248, which contained a directive to the Commission, created new sexual offenses, and enhanced penalties for existing sexual offenses. The amendment implements the directive by creating two new guidelines, §§ 2A3.5 (Failure to Register as a Sex Offender) and 2A3.6 (Aggravated Offenses Relating to Registration as a Sex Offender). It further addresses relevant provisions in the Adam Walsh Act by making changes to Chapter Two, Part A, Subpart 3 (Criminal Sexual Abuse) and Part G (Offenses Involving Commercial Sex Acts, Sexual Exploitation of Minors, and Obscenity), § 2J1.2 (Obstruction of Justice), § 3D1.2 (Groups of Closely Related Counts), § 4B1.5 (Repeat and Dangerous Sex Offender Against Minors), § 5B1.3 (Conditions of Probation), § 5D1.2 (Term of Supervised Release), § 5D1.3 (Conditions of Supervised Release) and Appendix A (Statutory Index).

First, section 206 of the Adam Walsh Act amended 18 U.S.C. § 2241(c) to add a new mandatory minimum term of imprisonment of 30 years for offenses related to the aggravated sexual abuse of a child under 12 years old, or of a child between 12 and 16 years old if force, threat, or other means was used. In response to the new mandatory minimum for these offenses, the amendment increases the base offense level at § 2A3.1 (Criminal Sexual Abuse; Attempt to Commit Criminal Sexual Abuse) from level 30 to level 38. The base offense level of 30 has been retained for all other offenses. At least one specific offense characteristic applied to every conviction under 18 U.S.C. § 2241(c) sentenced under § 2A3.1 in fiscal year 2006. Accordingly, the mandatory minimum 360 months' imprisonment is expected to be reached or exceeded in every case with a base offense level of 38.

The amendment provides a new application note that precludes application of the specific offense characteristic at § 2A3.1(b)(1) regarding conduct described in 18 U.S.C. § 2241(a) or (b) if the conduct that forms the basis for a conviction under 18 U.S.C. § 2241(c) is that the defendant engaged in conduct described in 18 U.S.C. § 2241(a) or (b) (force, threat, or other means). The amendment also precludes application of the specific offense characteristic for the age of a victim at § 2A3.1(b)(2) if the defendant was convicted under section 2241(c). The heightened base offense level of 38 takes into account the age of the victim. These instructions, therefore, avoid unwarranted double counting.

Second, section 207 of the Adam Walsh Act increased the statutory maximum term of imprisonment under 18 U.S.C. § 2243(b) from 5 years to 15 years for the sexual abuse of a person in official detention or under custodial authority. In response to increased penalty, the amendment increases the base offense level from 12 to 14 in § 2A3.3 (Criminal Sexual Abuse of a Ward or Attempt to Commit Such Acts). The amendment also adds a new definition of "minor" consistent with how this term is defined elsewhere in the guidelines manual. In addition, the amendment includes an application note precluding application of § 3B1.3 (Abuse of Position of Trust or Use of Special Skill) for these offenses because an abuse of position of trust is assumed in all such cases and, therefore, is built into the base offense level.

Third, section 206 of the Adam Walsh Act created a new subsection at 18 U.S.C. § 2244. Section 2244(a)(5) provides a penalty of any term of years if the sexual conduct would have violated 18 U.S.C. § 2241(c) had the contact been a sexual act. Section 2241(c) conduct involves the aggravated sexual abuse of a child under 12 years old or of a child between 12 and 16 years old if force, threat, or other means was used, as defined in 18 U.S.C. § 2241(a) and (b). Prior to the Adam Walsh Act, the penalty for offenses involving children under 12 years old was "twice that otherwise provided," and the penalty for sexual contact involving behavior described in 18 U.S.C. § 2241 was a statutory maximum term of imprisonment of 10 years.

The amendment addresses this new offense by increasing the minimum offense level in the age enhancement in subsection (b)(1) of § 2A3.4 (Abusive Sexual Contact or Attempt to Commit Abusive Sexual Contact) from level 20 to level 22.

Fourth, section 141 of the Adam Walsh Act created a new offense under 18 U.S.C. § 2250(a) for the failure to register as a sex offender. The basic offense carries a statutory maximum term of imprisonment of 10 years. Section 141 also included a directive to the Commission that when promulgating guidelines for the offense, to consider, among other factors, the seriousness of the sex offender's conviction that gave rise to the requirement to register; relevant further offense conduct during the period for which the defendant failed to register; and the offender's criminal history.

The amendment creates a new guideline, § 2A3.5 (Failure to Register as a Sex Offender), to address the directive. The new guideline provides three alternative base offense levels based on the tiered category of the sex offender: level 16 if the defendant was required to register as a Tier III offender; level 14 if the defendant was required to register as a Tier II offender; and level 12 if the defendant was required to register as a Tier I offender.

The amendment also provides two specific offense characteristics. First, subsection (b)(1) provides a tiered enhancement to address criminal conduct committed while the defendant is in a failure to register status. Specifically, § 2A3.5(b)(1) provides a six-level increase if, while in a failure to register status, the defendant committed a sex offense against an adult, a six-level increase if the defendant committed a felony offense against a minor, and an eight-level increase if the defendant committed a sex offense against a minor. Second, § 2A3.5(b)(2) provides a three-level decrease if the defendant voluntarily corrected the failure to register or voluntarily attempted to register but was prevented from registering by uncontrollable circumstances, and the defendant did not contribute to the creation of those circumstances. The reduction covers cases in which (1) the defendant either does not

Amendment 701   APPENDIX C - VOLUME III   November 1, 2013

attempt to register until after the relevant registration period has expired but subsequently successfully registers, thereby correcting the failure to register status, or (2) the defendant, either before or after the registration period has expired, attempted to register but circumstances beyond the defendant's control prevented the defendant from successfully registering. An application note specifies that the voluntary attempt to register or to correct the failure to register must have occurred prior to the time the defendant knew or reasonably should have known a jurisdiction had detected the failure to register. The application note also provides that the reduction does not apply if the enhancement for committing one of the enumerated offenses in § 2A3.5(b)(1) applies.

Additionally, the amendment adds § 2A3.5 to the list of offenses that are considered groupable under § 3D1.2(d) because the failure to register offense is an ongoing and continuous offense.

Fifth, section 141 of the Adam Walsh Act created two new aggravated offenses relating to the registration as a sex offender. Section 141 of the Act created 18 U.S.C. § 2250(c), which carries a mandatory minimum term of imprisonment of 5 years and a statutory maximum term of imprisonment of 30 years if a defendant commits a crime of violence while in a failure to register status, with the sentence to be consecutive to the punishment provided for the failure to register. Section 702 of the Adam Walsh Act created a new offense at 18 U.S.C. § 2260A that prohibits the commission of various enumerated offenses while in a failure to register status. The penalty for this offense is a mandatory term of imprisonment of 10 years to be imposed consecutively to the underlying offense.

The amendment creates a new guideline at § 2A3.6 (Aggravated Offenses Relating to Registration as a Sex Offender) to address these new offenses. The new guideline provides that for offenses under section 2250(c), the guideline sentence is the minimum term of imprisonment required by statute, and for offenses under section 2260A, the guideline sentence is the term of imprisonment required by statute. Chapters Three and Four are not to apply. This is consistent with how the guidelines treat other offenses that carry both a specified term of imprisonment and a requirement that such term be imposed consecutively. See §§ 3D1.1 (Procedure for Determining Offense Level on Multiple Counts) and 5G1.2 (Sentencing on Multiple Counts of Conviction).

The guideline includes an application note that provides an upward departure stating that a sentence above the minimum term required by section 2250(c) is an upward departure from the guideline sentence. An upward departure may be warranted, for example, in a case involving a sex offense committed against a minor or if the offense resulted in serious bodily injury to a minor.

Sixth, section 208 of the Adam Walsh Act added a new mandatory minimum term of imprisonment of 15 years under 18 U.S.C. § 1591(b)(1) for sex trafficking of an adult by force, fraud, or coercion. In response, the amendment provides a new base offense level of 34 in § 2G1.1 (Promoting a Commercial Sex Act or Prohibited Sexual Conduct with an Individual Other than a Minor) if the offense of conviction is 18 U.S.C. § 1591(b)(1), but retains a base offense level of 14 for all other offenses. In addition, the amendment limits application of the specific offense characteristic at § 2G1.1(b)(1) that applies if the offense involved fraud or coercion only to those offenses receiving a base offense level of 14. Offenses under 18 U.S.C. § 1591(b)(1) necessarily involve fraud and coercion and, therefore, such conduct is built into the heightened base offense level of 34. This limitation thus avoids unwarranted double counting.

Seventh, section 208 of the Adam Walsh Act added a new mandatory minimum term of imprisonment of 15 years under 18 U.S.C. § 1591(b)(1) for sex trafficking of children under 14 years of age and added a new mandatory minimum term of imprisonment of 10 years and increased the statutory maximum term of imprisonment from 40 years to life under 18 U.S.C. § 1591(b)(2) for sex trafficking of children who had attained the age of 14 years but had not attained the age of 18 years. Further, the Adam Walsh Act increased the mandatory minimum term of imprisonment from 5 years to 10 years and increased the statutory maximum term of imprisonment from 30 years to life under both 18 U.S.C. § 2422(b), for persuading or enticing any person who has not attained the age of 18 years to engage in prostitution or any sexual activity for which any person can be charged with a criminal offense, and 18 U.S.C. § 2423(a), for transporting a person who has not attained the age of 18 years in interstate or foreign commerce, with the intent that the person engage in prostitution, or in any sexual activity for which any person can be charged with a criminal offense.

In response, the amendment provides alternative base offense levels in § 2G1.3 (Promoting a Commercial Sex Act or Prohibited Sexual Conduct with a Minor; Transportation of Minors to Engage in a Commercial Sex Act or Prohibited Sexual Conduct; Travel to Engage in Commercial Sex Act or Prohibited Sexual Conduct with a Minor; Sex Trafficking of Children; Use of Interstate Facilities to Transport Information about a Minor) based on the statute of conviction and the conduct described in that conviction. For convictions under 18 U.S.C. § 1591(b)(1), the base offense level is 34. For convictions under 18 U.S.C. § 1591(b)(2), the base offense level is 30.

The amendment further provides a base offense level of 28 for convictions under 18 U.S.C. §§ 2422(b) and 2423(a). The two-level enhancement for the use of a computer at § 2G1.3(b)(3) applied to 95 percent of offenders convicted under 18 U.S.C. § 2422(b) and sentenced under § 2G1.3 in fiscal year 2006. In addition, the two-level enhancement for the offense involving a sexual act or sexual contact at § 2G1.3(b)(4) applied to 95 percent of offenders convicted under 18 U.S.C. § 2423(a) and sentenced under this guideline in fiscal year 2006. With application of either enhancement, the mandatory minimum term of imprisonment of 120 months will be reached in the majority of convictions under 18 U.S.C. §§ 2422(b) and 2423(a), before application of other guidelines adjustments.

Further, the amendment addresses the interaction of two specific offense characteristics with the alternative base offense levels. First, every conviction under 18 U.S.C. § 1591 necessarily involves a commercial sex act. With the base offense levels being determined based on the statute of conviction, the amendment clarifies that § 2G1.3(b)(4)(B), which provides a two-level enhancement if the offense involved a commercial sex act, does not apply if the defendant is convicted under 18 U.S.C. § 1591. Second, the amendment precludes application of the age enhancement in § 2G1.3(b)(5) if the base offense level is determined under subsection (a)(1) of § 2G1.3 for a conviction under 18 U.S.C. § 1591(b)(1). The base offense level provided by subsection (a)(1) of § 2G1.3 takes into account the age of the victim and, therefore, limitations on application of subsections (b)(4)(B) and (b)(5) of § 2G1.3 avoid unwarranted double counting.

Eighth, section 503 of the Adam Walsh Act created a new section, 18 U.S.C. § 2257A, adopting new recordkeeping obligations for the production of any book, magazine, periodical, film, videotape, or digital image that contains a visual depiction of simulated sexually explicit conduct. Section 2257A has a statutory maximum of one year imprisonment for the failure to comply with the recordkeeping requirements and a statutory maximum term of imprisonment of five years if the violation was to conceal a substantive offense that involves either causing a minor to engage in sexually explicit conduct for the purpose of producing a visual depiction or trafficking in material involving the sexual exploitation of a minor. The new offense is similar to 18 U.S.C. § 2257, which is referenced to § 2G2.5 (Recordkeeping Offenses Involving the Production of Sexually Explicit Materials; Failure to Provide Required Marks in Commercial Electronic Mail). Accordingly, the amendment refers the new offense to § 2G2.5.

Ninth, section 701 of the Adam Walsh Act created a new offense in 18 U.S.C. § 2252A(g) that prohibits engaging in child exploitation enterprises, defined as violating 18 U.S.C. §§ 1591, 1201 (if the victim is a minor), chapter 109A (involving a minor victim), chapter 110 (except for 18 U.S.C. §§ 2257 and 2257A), or chapter 117 (involving a minor victim), as part of a series of felony violations constituting three or more separate incidents and involving more than one victim, and committing those offenses in concert with three or more other people. The statute provides a mandatory minimum term of imprisonment of 20 years. The amendment creates a new guideline at § 2G2.6 (Child Exploitation Enterprises) to cover this new offense. The guideline provides a base offense level of 35 and four specific offense characteristics. The Commission anticipates these offenses typically will involve conduct encompassing at least one of the specific offense characteristics, resulting in an offense level of at least level 37. Thus, the mandatory minimum term of imprisonment of 240 months typically is expected to be reached or exceeded, before application of other guideline adjustments.

Tenth, section 206 of the Adam Walsh Act increased the statutory maximum term of imprisonment from 4 years to 10 years under 18 U.S.C. § 2252B(b) for knowingly using a misleading domain name with the intent to deceive a minor into viewing material harmful to minors on the Internet. In addition, section 703 of the Act created a new section, 18 U.S.C. § 2252C, that carries a statutory maximum term of imprisonment of 10 years for knowingly embedding words or digital images into the source code of a website with the intent to deceive a person into viewing material constituting obscenity. Section 2252C(b) carries a statutory maximum term of imprisonment of 20 years for knowingly embedding words or digital images into the source code of a website with the intent to deceive a minor into viewing material harmful to minors on the Internet.

In response to the new offense, the amendment expands the scope of subsection (b)(2) of § 2G3.1 (Importing, Mailing, or Transporting Obscene Matter; Transferring Obscene Matter to a Minor; Misleading Domain Names) by adding to this enhancement "embedded words or digital images into the source code on a website."

Eleventh, section 141 of the Adam Walsh Act added a new provision in 18 U.S.C. § 1001 that carries a statutory maximum term of imprisonment of 8 years for falsifying or covering up by any scheme or making materially false or fraudulent statements or making or using any false writings or documents that relate to offenses under chapters 109A, 109B, 110, and 117, and under section 1591 of chapter 77. The amendment adds a new specific offense characteristic at subsection (b)(1)(A) of § 2J1.2 (Obstruction of Justice) enhancing the offense level by four levels if the defendant was convicted under 18 U.S.C. § 1001 and the statutory maximum term of 8 years' imprisonment applies because the matter relates to sex offenses. The amendment also added language to Application Note 4 stating an upward departure may be warranted under the guideline in a case involving a particularly serious sex offense.

Twelfth, section 206 of the Adam Walsh Act added 18 U.S.C. § 1591 to the list of offenses for which a defendant is to be sentenced to life under 18 U.S.C. § 3559(e)(2)(A). The amendment adds 18 U.S.C. § 1591 to the list of instant offenses of convictions that are covered sex crimes under § 4B1.5.

Thirteenth, section 141 of the Adam Walsh Act amended 18 U.S.C. §§ 3563 and 3583. The amendment adds a new subdivision to (a)(9) of § 5B1.3 and to (d)(7) of § 5D1.3 to require a defendant to comply with the new registration requirements provided by the

Adam Walsh Act. The amendment also modifies the language in §§ 5B1.3(a)(9) and 5D1.3(d)(7) relating to defendants convicted of a sexual offense described in 18 U.S.C. § 4042(c)(4). Not all states have implemented the new requirements, continuing to register sex offenders pursuant to the sex offender registry in place prior to July 27, 2006, the date of enactment of the Adam Walsh Act. Thus, it is necessary to maintain the language in the guidelines providing for conditions of probation and supervised release for those offenders.

Fourteenth, section 141 of the Act amended 18 U.S.C. § 3583(k), which provides that the authorized term of supervised release for any offense under enumerated sex offenses is any term of years or life. In response, the amendment adds offenses under chapter 109B and sections 1201 and 1591 of title 18 United States Code or 18 U.S.C. §§ 1201 and 1591 to the definition of sex offense under § 5D1.2(b)(2) for which the length of the term of supervised release shall be not less than the minimum term of years specified for the offense and may be up to life.

Finally, the amendment provides a definition of "minor" in relevant guidelines that is consistent with how this term is defined elsewhere in the guidelines. Outdated background commentary also is deleted by this amendment.

Effective Date: The effective date of this amendment is November 1, 2007.

702. **Amendment:** Section 2B1.1(b)(13)(C) is amended by striking "(b)(12)(B)" and inserting "(b)(13)(B)".

Section 2L1.1(b)(1) is amended by striking "(a)(2)" and inserting "(a)(3)".

Reason for Amendment: This amendment corrects typographical errors in subsection (b)(13)(C) of § 2B1.1 (Larceny, Embezzlement, and Other Forms of Theft; Offenses Involving Stolen Property; Property Damage or Destruction; Fraud and Deceit; Forgery; Offenses Involving Altered or Counterfeit Instruments Other than Counterfeit Bearer Obligations of the United States) and subsection (b)(1) of § 2L1.1 (Smuggling, Transporting, or Harboring an Unlawful Alien).

The typographical error to § 2B1.1(b)(13)(C) stems from redesignations made to § 2B1.1 in 2004 when the Commission added a new subsection (b)(7) in response to the Controlling the Assault of Non-Solicited Pornography and Marketing Act of 2003 ("CAN-SPAM Act"), Pub. L. 108–187. (USSG App. C Amendment 665) (November 1, 2004).

The typographical error in § 2L1.1(b)(1) stems from redesignations made to § 2L1.1 in 2006 when the Commission added a new subsection (a)(1) for aliens who are inadmissible for national security related reasons. (USSG App. C Amendment 692) (November 1, 2006).

The Commission has determined that this amendment should be applied retroactively because (A) the purpose of the amendment is to correct typographical errors; (B) the number of cases involved is minimal even given the potential change in guideline ranges (i.e., ensuring application of the maximum increase of 8 levels in § 2B1.1(b)(13)(C) and providing correct application of the three-level reduction in § 2L1.1(b)(1)); and (C) the amendment would not be difficult to apply retroactively. These factors, combined, meet the standards set forth in the relevant background commentary to § 1B1.10 (Reduction in Term of Imprisonment as a Result of Amended Guideline Range).

Effective Date: The effective date of this amendment is November 1, 2007.

703. **Amendment:** Section 2B2.3(b)(1) is amended by redesignating subdivision (F) as

Amendment 703

subdivision (G); and by inserting "(F) at Arlington National Cemetery or a cemetery under the control of the National Cemetery Administration;" after "residence;".

The Commentary to § 2B2.3 captioned "Statutory Provisions", as amended by Amendment 699, is further amended by inserting "38 U.S.C. § 2413;" after "2199;".

The Commentary to § 2E3.1 captioned "Statutory Provisions" is amended by inserting "; 31 U.S.C. § 5363" after "1955".

Appendix A (Statutory Index) is amended by inserting after the line referenced to 31 U.S.C. § 5332 the following:

"31 U.S.C. § 5363   2E3.1"; and

by inserting after the line referenced to 38 U.S.C. § 787 the following:

"38 U.S.C. § 2413   2B2.3".

Reason for Amendment: This amendment addresses two new offenses, 38 U.S.C. § 2413, which was created by the Respect for America's Fallen Heroes Act, Pub. L. 109–228, and 31 U.S.C. § 5363, which was created by the Security and Accountability for Every Port Act of 2006, Pub. L. 109–347.

The new offense at 38 U.S.C. § 2413 prohibits certain demonstrations at Arlington National Cemetery and at cemeteries controlled by the National Cemetery Administration and provides a statutory maximum penalty of imprisonment of not more than one year, a fine, or both. The amendment references convictions under 38 U.S.C. § 2413 to § 2B2.3 (Trespass) and expands the scope of the two-level enhancement at § 2B2.3(b)(1) for trespass offenses that occur in certain locations to include trespass at Arlington National Cemetery or a cemetery under the control of the National Cemetery Administration. The Commission determined that the need to protect the final resting places of the nation's war dead and the need to discourage violent confrontations at the funerals of veterans who are killed in action justifies expanding the scope of the enhancement to cover such conduct.

The new offense at 31 U.S.C. § 5363 prohibits acceptance of any financial instrument for unlawful Internet gambling and provides a statutory maximum term of imprisonment of five years. The amendment references convictions under 31 U.S.C. § 5363 to § 2E3.1 (Gambling Offenses).

Effective Date: The effective date of this amendment is November 1, 2007.

704. **Amendment:** The amendment to § 2B5.3, effective September 12, 2006 (see Appendix C amendment 682), is repromulgated with the following changes:

Section 2B5.3(b)(3) is amended by inserting "(A)" before "offense involved" and by inserting "; or (B) defendant was convicted under 17 U.S.C. §§ 1201 and 1204 for trafficking in circumvention devices" after "items".

The Commentary to § 2B5.3 captioned "Statutory Provisions" is amended by inserting "§ " after "17 U.S.C. § "; and by inserting ", 1201, 1204" after "506(a)".

The Commentary to § 2B5.3 captioned "Application Notes" is amended in Note 1 by inserting after "Definitions.—For purposes of this guideline:" the following paragraph:

"'Circumvention devices' are devices used to perform the activity described in 17 U.S.C. §§ 1201(a)(3)(A) and 1201(b)(2)(A).".

The Commentary to § 2B5.3 captioned "Application Notes" is amended in Note 2(A) by adding at the end the following:

"(vii) A case under 18 U.S.C. § 2318 or § 2320 that involves a counterfeit label, patch, sticker, wrapper, badge, emblem, medallion, charm, box, container, can, case, hangtag, documentation, or packaging of any type or nature (I) that has not been affixed to, or does not enclose or accompany a good or service; and (II) which, had it been so used, would appear to a reasonably informed purchaser to be affixed to, enclosing or accompanying an identifiable, genuine good or service. In such a case, the 'infringed item' is the identifiable, genuine good or service.

(viii) A case under 17 U.S.C. §§ 1201 and 1204 in which the defendant used a circumvention device. In such an offense, the 'retail value of the infringed item' is the price the user would have paid to access lawfully the copyrighted work, and the 'infringed item' is the accessed work.".

The Commentary to § 2B5.3 captioned "Application Notes" is amended in Note 3 by striking "shall" and inserting "may".

The Commentary to § 2B5.3 captioned "Application Notes" is amended in Note 4 by striking "Upward" before "Departure"; by inserting "or overstates" after "understates"; and by striking "an upward" each place it appears and inserting "a"; and by adding at the end the following:

"(C) The method used to calculate the infringement amount is based upon a formula or extrapolation that results in an estimated amount that may substantially exceed the actual pecuniary harm to the copyright or trademark owner.".

Appendix A (Statutory Index) is amended by inserting after the line referenced to 17 U.S.C. § 506(a) the following new lines:

"17 U.S.C. § 1201   2B5.3
17 U.S.C. § 1204   2B5.3".

Reason for Amendment: This amendment re-promulgates as permanent the temporary, emergency amendment (effective Sept. 12, 2006) that implemented the emergency directive in section 1(c) of the Stop Counterfeiting in Manufactured Goods Act, Pub. L. 109–181 (2006). The directive, which required the Commission to promulgate an amendment under emergency amendment authority by September 12, 2006, instructs the Commission to "review, and if appropriate, amend the Federal sentencing guidelines and policy statements applicable to persons convicted of any offense under section 2318 or 2320 of title 18, United States Code."

In carrying out [the directive], the United States Sentencing Commission shall determine whether the definition of "infringement amount" set forth in application note 2 of section 2B5.3 of the Federal sentencing guidelines is adequate to address situations in which the defendant has been convicted of one of the offenses [under section 2318 or 2320 of title 18, United States Code,] and the item in which the defendant trafficked was not an infringing item but rather was intended to facilitate infringement, such as an anti-circumvention device, or the item in which the defendant trafficked was infringing and also was intended to facilitate infringement in another good or service, such as a counterfeit label, documentation, or packaging, taking into account cases such as *U.S. v. Sung*, 87 F.3d 194 (7th Cir. 1996).

The amendment adds subdivision (vii) to Application Note 2(A) of § 2B5.3 (Criminal Infringement of Copyright or Trademark) to provide that the infringement amount is based on the retail value of the infringed item in a case under 18 U.S.C. § 2318 or § 2320 that involves a counterfeit label, patch, sticker, wrapper, badge, emblem, medallion, charm, box, container, can, case, hangtag, documentation, or packaging of any type or nature (i) that has not been affixed to, or does not enclose or accompany a good or service; and (ii) which, had it been so used, would appear to a reasonably informed purchaser to be affixed to, enclosing or accompanying an identifiable, genuine good or service. In such a case, the "infringed item" is the identifiable, genuine good or service.

In addition to re-promulgating the emergency amendment, the amendment responds to the directive by addressing violations of 17 U.S.C. §§ 1201 and 1204 involving circumvention devices. The amendment addresses circumvention devices in two ways. First, the amendment adds an application note regarding the determination of the infringement amount in cases under 17 U.S.C. §§ 1201 and 1204 in which the defendant used a circumvention device and thus obtained unauthorized access to a copyrighted work. Such an offense would involve an identifiable copyrighted work. Accordingly, consistent with the existing rules in § 2B5.3, the "retail value of the infringed item" would be used for purposes of determining the infringement amount. The amendment adds subsection (viii) to Application Note 2(A), and explains that the "retail value of the infringed item" is the price the user would have paid to access lawfully the copyrighted work, and the "infringed item" is the accessed work. If the defendant violated 17 U.S.C. §§ 1201 and 1204 by conduct that did not include use of a circumvention device, Application Note 2(B) would apply by default. Thus, as it does in any case not otherwise covered by Application Note 2(A), the infringement amount would be determined by reference to the value of the infringing item, which in these cases would be the circumvention device.

Second, the amendment expands the sentencing enhancement in § 2B5.3(b)(3) to include convictions under 17 U.S.C. §§ 1201 and 1204 for trafficking in circumvention devices. Prior to the amendment, § 2B5.3(b)(3) provided a two-level enhancement and a minimum offense level of 12 for cases involving the manufacture, importation, or uploading of infringing items. The purpose of the enhancement in § 2B5.3(b)(3) is to provide greater punishment for defendants who put infringing items into the stream of commerce in a manner that enables others to infringe the copyright or trademark. The Commission determined that trafficking in circumvention devices similarly enables others to infringe a copyright and warrants greater punishment.

The amendment also strikes language in Application Note 3 mandating an adjustment under § 3B1.3 (Abuse of Position of Trust or Use of Special Skill) in every case in which the defendant de-encrypted or otherwise circumvented a technological security measure to gain initial access to an infringed item. Instead, the note indicates that application of the adjustment may be appropriate in such a case because the Commission determined that not every case involving de-encryption or circumvention requires the level of skill contemplated by the special skill adjustment.

Finally, the amendment modifies Application Note 4 to address downward departures. The addition of this language recognizes that in some instances the method for calculating the infringement amount may be based on a formula or extrapolation that overstates the actual pecuniary harm to the copyright or trademark owner. This language is analogous to departure language in § 2B1.1 (Larceny, Embezzlement, and Other Forms of Theft; Offenses Involving Stolen Property; Property Damage or Destruction; Fraud and Deceit; Forgery; Offenses Involving Altered or Counterfeit Instruments Other than Counterfeit Bearer Obligations of the United States) and thus promotes consistency between these two economic crime guidelines.

Effective Date: The effective date of this amendment is November 1, 2007.

705. Amendment: Section 2D1.1(b) is amended by redesingating subdivisions (8) and (9), as subdivisions (10) and (11), respectively; by redesignating subdivisions (5) through (7) as subdivisions (6) through (8), respectively; by inserting after subdivision (4) the following:

> "(5) If the defendant is convicted under 21 U.S.C. § 865, increase by 2 levels.";

and by inserting after subdivision (8), as redesignated by this amendment, the following:

> "(9) If the defendant was convicted under 21 U.S.C. § 841(g)(1)(A), increase by 2 levels.".

Section 2D1.1(b) is amended in subdivision (10), as redesignated by this amendment, by striking "greater" and inserting "greatest"; by redesignating subdivision (C) as subdivision (D); and by striking subdivision (B) as follows:

> "(B) If the offense (i) involved the manufacture of amphetamine or methamphetamine; and (ii) created a substantial risk of harm to (I) human life other than a life described in subdivision (C); or (II) the environment, increase by 3 levels. If the resulting offense level is less than level 27, increase to level 27.".

and inserting the following:

> "(B) If the defendant was convicted under 21 U.S.C. § 860a of distributing, or possessing with intent to distribute, methamphetamine on premises where a minor is present or resides, increase by 2 levels. If the resulting offense level is less than level 14, increase to level 14.
>
> (C) If—
>
>> (i) the defendant was convicted under 21 U.S.C. § 860a of manufacturing, or possessing with intent to manufacture, methamphetamine on premises where a minor is present or resides; or
>>
>> (ii) the offense involved the manufacture of amphetamine or methamphetamine and the offense created a substantial risk of harm to (I) human life other than a life described in subdivision (D); or (II) the environment,
>
> increase by 3 levels. If the resulting offense level is less than level 27, increase to level 27.".

Section 2D1.1(c)(1) is amended by inserting "30,000,000 units or more of Ketamine;" after the line referenced to "Hashish Oil".

Section 2D1.1(c)(2) is amended by inserting "At least 10,000,000 but less than 30,000,000 units of Ketamine;" after the line referenced to "Hashish Oil".

Section 2D1.1(c)(3) is amended by inserting "At least 3,000,000 but less than 10,000,000 units of Ketamine;" after the line referenced to "Hashish Oil".

Section 2D1.1(c)(4) is amended by inserting "At least 1,000,000 but less than 3,000,000 units of Ketamine;" after the line referenced to "Hashish Oil".

Amendment 705

Section 2D1.1(c)(5) is amended by inserting "At least 700,000 but less than 1,000,000 units of Ketamine;" after the line referenced to "Hashish Oil".

Section 2D1.1(c)(6) is amended by inserting "At least 400,000 but less than 700,000 units of Ketamine;" after the line referenced to "Hashish Oil".

Section 2D1.1(c)(7) is amended by inserting "At least 100,000 but less than 400,000 units of Ketamine;" after the line referenced to "Hashish Oil".

Section 2D1.1(c)(8) is amended by inserting "At least 80,000 but less than 100,000 units of Ketamine;" after the line referenced to "Hashish Oil".

Section 2D1.1(c)(9) is amended by inserting "At least 60,000 but less than 80,000 units of Ketamine;" after the line referenced to "Hashish Oil".

Section 2D1.1(c)(10) is amended by inserting "At least 40,000 but less than 60,000 units of Ketamine;" after the line referenced to "Hashish Oil"; and by inserting "(except Ketamine)" after "Schedule III substances".

Section 2D1.1(c)(11) is amended by inserting "At least 20,000 but less than 40,000 units of Ketamine;" after the line referenced to "Hashish Oil"; and by inserting "(except Ketamine)" after "Schedule III substances".

Section 2D1.1(c)(12) is amended by inserting "At least 10,000 but less than 20,000 units of Ketamine;" after the line referenced to "Hashish Oil"; and by inserting "(except Ketamine)" after "Schedule III substances".

Section 2D1.1(c)(13) is amended by inserting "At least 5,000 but less than 10,000 units of Ketamine;" after the line referenced to "Hashish Oil"; and by inserting "(except Ketamine)" after "Schedule III substances".

Section 2D1.1(c)(14) is amended by inserting "At least 2,500 but less than 5,000 units of Ketamine;" after the line referenced to "Hashish Oil"; and by inserting "(except Ketamine)" after "Schedule III substances".

Section 2D1.1(c)(15) is amended by inserting "At least 1,000 but less than 2,500 units of Ketamine;" after the line referenced to "Hashish Oil"; and by inserting "(except Ketamine)" after "Schedule III substances".

Section 2D1.1(c)(16) is amended by inserting "At least 250 but less than 1,000 units of Ketamine;" after the line referenced to "Hashish Oil"; and by inserting "(except Ketamine)" after "Schedule III substances".

Section 2D1.1(c)(17) is amended by inserting "Less than 250 units of Ketamine;" after the line referenced to "Hashish Oil"; and by inserting "(except Ketamine)" after "Schedule III substances".

The Commentary to § 2D1.1 captioned "Statutory Provisions" is amended by inserting "(g), 860a, 865," after "(3), (7),".

The Commentary to § 2D1.1 captioned "Application Notes" is amended in Note 10 in the section captioned "Drug Equivalency Tables" in the subdivision captioned "Schedule III Substances" by inserting in the heading "(except ketamine)" after "Substances";

by adding after the subdivision captioned "Schedule III Substances" the following new subdivision:

"Ketamine

1 unit of ketamine =   1 gm of marihuana";

and by adding after the subdivision captioned "List I Chemicals (relating to the manufacture of amphetamine or methamphetamine)" the following new subdivision:

"Date Rape Drugs (except flunitrazipam, GHB, or ketamine)

1 ml of 1,4-butanediol =   8.8 gm marihuana
1 ml of gamma butyrolactone =   8.8 gm marihuana".

The Commentary to § 2D1.1 captioned "Application Notes" is amended in Note 19 by striking "(b)(8)" each place it appears and inserting "(b)(10)".

The Commentary to § 2D1.1 captioned "Application Notes" is amended in Note 20 in subdivision (A) by striking "(b)(8)(B) or (C)" and inserting "(b)(10)(C)(ii) or (D)"; and in subdivision (B) by striking "(b)(8)(C)" and inserting (b)(10)(D)".

The Commentary to § 2D1.1 captioned "Application Notes" is amended in Note 21 by striking "(9)" each place it appears and inserting "(11)".

The Commentary to § 2D1.1 captioned "Application Notes" is amended by redesignating Notes 22 through 25 as Notes 23 through 26, respectively; and by inserting after Note 21 the following:

"22. Imposition of Consecutive Sentence for 21 U.S.C. § 860a or § 865.—Sections 860a and 865 of title 21, United States Code, require the imposition of a mandatory consecutive term of imprisonment of not more than 20 years and 15 years, respectively. In order to comply with the relevant statute, the court should determine the appropriate 'total punishment' and divide the sentence on the judgment form between the sentence attributable to the underlying drug offense and the sentence attributable to 21 U.S.C. § 860a or § 865, specifying the number of months to be served consecutively for the conviction under 21 U.S.C. § 860a or § 865. For example, if the applicable adjusted guideline range is 151-188 months and the court determines a 'total punishment' of 151 months is appropriate, a sentence of 130 months for the underlying offense plus 21 months for the conduct covered by 21 U.S.C. § 860a or § 865 would achieve the 'total punishment' in a manner that satisfies the statutory requirement of a consecutive sentence.".

The Commentary to § 2D1.1 captioned "Application Notes" is amended in Note 23, as redesignated by this amendment, by striking "(5)" each place it appears and inserting "(6)".

The Commentary to § 2D1.1 captioned "Application Notes" is amended in Note 25, as redesignated by this amendment, by striking "(6)" each place it appears and inserting "(7)".

The Commentary to § 2D1.1 captioned "Application Notes" is amended in Note 26, as redesignated by this amendment, by striking "(7)" each place it appears and inserting "(8)".

The Commentary to § 2D1.1 captioned "Background" is amended in the ninth paragraph by striking "(b)(8)" and inserting "(b)(10)"; and in the last paragraph by striking "(b)(8)(B)

Amendment 705

and (C)" and inserting "(b)(10)(C)(ii) and (D)".

Section 2D1.11(b) is amended by adding at the end the following subdivision:

"(5) If the defendant is convicted under 21 U.S.C. § 865, increase by 2 levels.".

The Commentary to § 2D1.11 captioned "Statutory Provisions" is amended by inserting "865," after "(f)(1),".

The Commentary to § 2D1.11 captioned "Application Notes" is amended by adding at the end the following:

"8. Imposition of Consecutive Sentence for 21 U.S.C. § 865.—Section 865 of title 21, United States Code, requires the imposition of a mandatory consecutive term of imprisonment of not more than 15 years. In order to comply with the relevant statute, the court should determine the appropriate 'total punishment' and, on the judgment form, divide the sentence between the sentence attributable to the underlying drug offense and the sentence attributable to 21 U.S.C. § 865, specifying the number of months to be served consecutively for the conviction under 21 U.S.C. § 865. For example, if the applicable adjusted guideline range is 151-188 months and the court determines a 'total punishment' of 151 months is appropriate, a sentence of 130 months for the underlying offense plus 21 months for the conduct covered by 21 U.S.C. § 865 would achieve the 'total punishment' in a manner that satisfies the statutory requirement of a consecutive sentence.".

Appendix A (Statutory Index) is amended by inserting after the line referenced to 21 U.S.C. § 841(f)(1) the following:

"21 U.S.C. § 841(g)   2D1.1";

by inserting after the line referenced to 21 U.S.C. § 860 the following:

"21 U.S.C. § 860a   2D1.1";

and by inserting after the line referenced to 21 U.S.C. § 864 the following:

"21 U.S.C. § 865   2D1.1, 2D1.11".

Reason for Amendment: This amendment responds to the new offenses created by the USA PATRIOT Improvement and Reauthorization Act of 2005 (the "PATRIOT Reauthorization Act"), Pub. L. 109–177, and the Adam Walsh Child Protection and Safety Act of 2006 (the "Adam Walsh Act"), Pub. L. 109–248.

First, the amendment addresses section 731 of the PATRIOT Reauthorization Act, which created a new offense at 21 U.S.C. § 865. The new offense provides a mandatory consecutive sentence of 15 years' imprisonment for smuggling of methamphetamine or its precursor chemicals into the United States by a person enrolled in, or acting on behalf of someone or some entity enrolled in, any dedicated commuter lane, alternative or accelerated inspection system, or other facilitated entry program administered by the federal government for use in entering the United States. The amendment refers the new offense to both §§ 2D1.1 (Unlawful Manufacturing, Importing, Exporting, or Trafficking (Including Possession with Intent to Commit These Offenses); Attempt or Conspiracy) and 2D1.11 (Unlawfully Distributing, Importing, Exporting or Possessing a Listed Chemical; Attempt or Conspiracy), and provides a new two-level enhancement in §§ 2D1.1(b)(5) and 2D1.11(b)(5) if the defendant is convicted under 21 U.S.C. § 865. The Commission determined that a two-level enhancement is appropriate because such conduct is analogous to abusing a position of trust, which receives a two-level adjustment under § 3B1.3 (Abuse of Position of Trust or Use of Special Skill).

Second, the amendment modifies § 2D1.1 to address the new offense in 21 U.S.C. § 841(g) (Internet Sales of Date Rape Drugs) created by the Adam Walsh Act. This offense, which is punishable up to statutory maximum term of imprisonment of 20 years, prohibits the use of the Internet to distribute a date rape drug to any person, "knowing or with reasonable cause to believe that — (A) the drug would be used in the commission of criminal sexual conduct; or (B) the person is not an authorized purchaser." The statute defines "date rape drug" as "(i) gamma hydroxybutyric acid (GHB) or any controlled substance analogue of GHB, including gamma butyrolactone (GBL) or 1,4-butanediol; (ii) ketamine; (iii) flunitrazipam; or (iv) any substance which the Attorney General designates . . . to be used in committing rape or sexual assault." The amendment provides a new two-level enhancement in § 2D1.1(b)(9) that is tailored to focus on the more serious conduct covered by the new statute, specifically conviction under 21 U.S.C. § 841(g)(1)(A), which covers individuals who know or have reasonable cause to believe the drug would be used in the commission of criminal sexual conduct.

Third, the amendment eliminates the maximum base offense level of level 20 for ketamine offenses. Ketamine is a Schedule III controlled substance. The Drug Quantity Table at § 2D1.1(c) provides a maximum offense level of 20 for most Schedule III substances because such substances are subject to a statutory maximum term of imprisonment of 5 years. If a defendant is convicted under 21 U.S.C. § 841(g) for distributing ketamine, however, the defendant is subject to a statutory maximum term of imprisonment of 20 years. Accordingly, the amendment modifies the Drug Quantity Table in order to allow for appropriate sentencing of 21 U.S.C. § 841(g) offenses involving larger quantities of ketamine that correspond to offense levels greater than level 20. This approach is consistent with how other drug offenses with a statutory maximum term of imprisonment of 20 years are penalized and with how other date rape drugs are penalized. The amendment also provides a marihuana equivalency in Application Note 10 for ketamine (1 unit of ketamine = 1 gram of marihuana).

Fourth, the amendment adds to § 2D1.1, Application Note 10, a new drug equivalency for 1,4-butanediol (BD) and gamma butyrolactone (GBL), both of which are included in the definition of date rape drugs under 21 U.S.C. § 841(g). Neither is a controlled substance. The drug equivalency is 1 ml of BD or GBL equals 8.8 grams of marihuana. The Commission has received testimony that both substances are at least equipotent as GHB, which is punished at the same marihuana equivalency.

Fifth, the amendment addresses the new offense in 21 U.S.C. § 860a (Consecutive sentence for manufacturing or distributing, or possessing with intent to manufacture or distribute, methamphetamine on premises where children are present or reside), created by the PATRIOT Reauthorization Act. The new offense provides that a term of not more than 20 years' imprisonment is to be imposed, in addition to any other sentence imposed, for manufacturing, distributing, or possessing with the intent to manufacture or distribute, methamphetamine on a premises where a minor is present or resides. The amendment modifies § 2D1.1(b)(8)(C) to provide a two-level increase (with a minimum offense level of 14) if the defendant is convicted under 21 U.S.C. § 860a involving the distribution or possession with intent to distribute methamphetamine and a three-level increase (with a minimum offense level of 27) if the defendant is convicted under 21 U.S.C. § 860a involving the manufacture or possession with intent to manufacture methamphetamine.

Amendment 705   APPENDIX C - VOLUME III   November 1, 2013

To account for the spectrum of harms created by methamphetamine offenses, and to address the specific harms created by 21 U.S.C. § 860a, the amendment builds on the "substantial risk enhancement." This multi-tiered enhancement was added to § 2D1.1 in 2000 in response to the Methamphetamine Anti-Proliferation Act of 2000, Pub. L. 106-310, Title XXXVI. See USSG App. C (Amendments 608 and 620 (effective Dec. 12, 2000, and Nov. 1, 2001, respectively)). Prior to this amendment, the first tier provided a two-level increase for basic environmental harms, such as discharging hazardous substances into the environment. The second tier provided a three-level increase, and a minimum offense level of 27, for the substantial risk of harm to the life of someone other than a minor or an incompetent. The final tier provided a six-level increase and a minimum offense level of 30 for the substantial risk of harm to the life of a minor or incompetent or the environment.

The Commission determined that distributing, or possessing with the intent to distribute, methamphetamine on a premises where a minor is present or resides presents a greater harm than discharging a hazardous substance into the environment, but is a lesser harm than the substantial risk of harm to adults or to the environment created by the manufacture of methamphetamine. Therefore, the amendment adds a new tier to the enhancement in the new subdivision (b)(10)(B) in order to account for this conduct. A defendant convicted under 21 U.S.C. § 860a for distributing, or possessing with the intent to distribute, methamphetamine on a premises where a minor is present or resides will receive a two-level enhancement, with a minimum offense level of 14.

To address the overlap of conduct covered by the enhancement for the substantial risk of harm to the life of a minor and the new offense of manufacturing, or possessing with the intent to manufacture, methamphetamine on a premises where a minor is present or resides, a three-level enhancement and a minimum offense level of level 27 will apply in a case in which a minor is present, but in which the offense did not create a substantial risk of harm to the life of a minor. In any methamphetamine manufacturing offense which creates a substantial risk of harm to the life of a minor, a six-level enhancement and a minimum offense level of level 30 will apply.

Sixth, the amendment updates Appendix A (Statutory Index) to include references to the new offenses created by the PATRIOT Reauthorization and Adam Walsh Acts.

Effective Date: The effective date of this amendment is November 1, 2007.

706. Amendment: Section 2D1.1(c)(1) is amended by striking "1.5 KG or more of Cocaine Base" and inserting "4.5 KG or more of Cocaine Base".

Section 2D1.1(c)(2) is amended by striking "At least 500 G but less than 1.5 KG of Cocaine Base" and inserting "At least 1.5 KG but less than 4.5 KG of Cocaine Base".

Section 2D1.1(c)(3) is amended by striking "At least 150 G but less than 500 G of Cocaine Base" and inserting "At least 500 G but less than 1.5 KG of Cocaine Base".

Section 2D1.1(c)(4) is amended by striking "At least 50 G but less than 150 G of Cocaine Base" and inserting "At least 150 G but less than 500 G of Cocaine Base".

Section 2D1.1(c)(5) is amended by striking "At least 35 G but less than 50 G of Cocaine Base" and inserting "At least 50 G but less than 150 G of Cocaine Base".

Section 2D1.1(c)(6) is amended by striking "At least 20 G but less than 35 G of Cocaine Base" and inserting "At least 35 G but less than 50 G of Cocaine Base".

Section 2D1.1(c)(7) is amended by striking "At least 5 G but less than 20 G of Cocaine

Base" and inserting "At least 20 G but less than 35 G of Cocaine Base".

Section 2D1.1(c)(8) is amended by striking "At least 4 G but less than 5 G of Cocaine Base" and inserting "At least 5 G but less than 20 G of Cocaine Base".

Section 2D1.1(c)(9) is amended by striking "At least 3 G but less than 4 G of Cocaine Base" and inserting "At least 4 G but less than 5 G of Cocaine Base".

Section 2D1.1(c)(10) is amended by striking "At least 2 G but less than 3 G of Cocaine Base" and inserting "At least 3 G but less than 4 G of Cocaine Base".

Section 2D1.1(c)(11) is amended by striking "At least 1 G but less than 2 G of Cocaine Base" and inserting "At least 2 G but less than 3 G of Cocaine Base".

Section 2D1.1(c)(12) is amended by striking "At least 500 MG but less than 1 G of Cocaine Base" and inserting "At least 1 G but less than 2 G of Cocaine Base".

Section 2D1.1(c)(13) is amended by striking "At least 250 MG but less than 500 MG of Cocaine Base" and inserting "At least 500 MG but less than 1 G of Cocaine Base".

Section 2D1.1(c)(14) is amended by striking "Less than 250 MG of Cocaine Base" and inserting "Less than 500 MG of Cocaine Base".

The Commentary to § 2D1.1 captioned "Application Notes" is amended in Note 10 in the first paragraph by inserting before "The Commission has used the sentences" the following:

> "Use of Drug Equivalency Tables.—
>
> (A)   Controlled Substances Not Referenced in Drug Quantity Table.—";

by striking "(A)" before "Use" and inserting "(i)"; by striking "(B)" before "Find" and inserting "(ii)"; and by striking "(C)" before "Use" and inserting "(iii)";

in the second paragraph by striking "The Drug Equivalency Tables also provide" and inserting the following:

> "(B)   Combining Differing Controlled Substances (Except Cocaine Base).—The Drug Equivalency Tables also provide";

and by adding at the end the following:

> "To determine a single offense level in a case involving cocaine base and other controlled substances, see subdivision (D) of this note.".

The Commentary to § 2D1.1 captioned "Application Notes" is amended in Note 10 in the subdivision captioned "Examples:" by striking "Examples:" and inserting the following:

> "(C)   Examples for Combining Differing Controlled Substances (Except Cocaine Base).—";

and by redesignating examples "a." through "d." as examples (i) through (iv), respectively.

The Commentary to § 2D1.1 captioned "Application Notes" is amended in Note 10 by inserting after example (iv), as redesignated by this amendment, the following:

> "(D)   Determining Base Offense Level in Offenses Involving Cocaine Base and Other Controlled Substances.—

(i) <u>In General</u>.—If the offense involves cocaine base ('crack') and one or more other controlled substance, determine the base offense level as follows:

    (I) Determine the combined base offense level for the other controlled substance or controlled substances as provided in subdivision (B) of this note.

    (II) Use the combined base offense level determined under subdivision (B) of this note to obtain the appropriate marihuana equivalency for the cocaine base involved in the offense using the following table:

Base Offense Level	Marihuana Equivalency
38	6.7 kg of marihuana
36	6.7 kg of marihuana
34	6 kg of marihuana
32	6.7 kg of marihuana
30	14 kg of marihuana
28	11.4 kg of marihuana
26	5 kg of marihuana
24	16 kg of marihuana
22	15 kg of marihuana
20	13.3 kg of marihuana
18	10 kg of marihuana
16	10 kg of marihuana
14	10 kg of marihuana
12	10 kg of marihuana.

    (III) Using the marihuana equivalency obtained from the table in subdivision (II), convert the quantity of cocaine base involved in the offense to its equivalent quantity of marihuana.

    (IV) Add the quantity of marihuana determined under subdivisions (I) and (III), and look up the total in the Drug Quantity Table to obtain the combined base offense level for all the controlled substances involved in the offense.

(ii) <u>Example</u>.—The case involves 1.5 kg of cocaine, 10 kg of marihuana, and 20 g of cocaine base. Pursuant to subdivision (B), the equivalent quantity of marihuana for the cocaine and the marihuana is 310 kg. (The cocaine converts to an equivalent of 300 kg of marihuana (1.5 kg x 200 g = 300 kg), which when added to the quantity of marihuana involved in the offense, results in an equivalent quantity of 310 kg of marihuana.) This corresponds to a base offense level 26. Pursuant to the table in subdivision (II), the base offense level of 26 results in a marihuana equivalency of 5 kg for the cocaine base. Using this marihuana equivalency for the cocaine base results in a marihuana equivalency of 100 kg (20 g x 5 kg =

– 1066 –

100 kg). Adding the quantities of marihuana of all three controlled substances results in a combined quantity of 410 kg of marihuana, which corresponds to a combined base offense level of 28 in the Drug Quantity Table.".

The Commentary to § 2D1.1 captioned "Application Notes" is amended in Note 10 by striking "DRUG EQUIVALENCY TABLES" and inserting the following:

"(E)   Drug Equivalency Tables.—";

and in the subdivision captioned "Cocaine and Other Schedule I and II Stimulants (and their immediate precursors)" by striking "1 gm of Cocaine Base ('Crack') = 20 kg of marihuana".

Reason for Amendment: The Commission identified as a policy priority for the amendment cycle ending May 1, 2007, "continuation of its work with the congressional, executive, and judicial branches of the government and other interested parties on cocaine sentencing policy," including reevaluating the Commission's 2002 report to Congress, Cocaine and Federal Sentencing Policy. As a result of the Anti-Drug Abuse Act of 1986, Pub. L. 99–570, 21 U.S.C. § 841(b)(1) requires a five-year mandatory minimum penalty for a first-time trafficking offense involving 5 grams or more of crack cocaine, or 500 grams of powder cocaine, and a ten-year mandatory minimum penalty for a first-time trafficking offense involving 50 grams or more of crack cocaine, or 5,000 grams or more of powder cocaine. Because 100 times more powder cocaine than crack cocaine is required to trigger the same mandatory minimum penalty, this penalty structure is commonly referred to as the "100-to-1 drug quantity ratio."

To assist the Commission in its consideration of Federal cocaine sentencing policy, the Commission received statements and heard expert testimony from the Executive Branch, the Federal judiciary, defense practitioners, state and local law enforcement representatives, medical and treatment experts, academicians, social scientists, and interested community representatives at hearings on November 14, 2006, and March 20, 2007. The Commission also received substantial written public comment on Federal cocaine sentencing policy throughout the amendment cycle.

During the amendment cycle, the Commission updated its analysis of key sentencing data about cocaine offenses and offenders; reviewed recent scientific literature regarding cocaine use, effects, dependency, prenatal effects, and prevalence; researched trends in cocaine trafficking patterns, price, and use; surveyed the state laws regarding cocaine penalties; and monitored case law developments.

Current data and information continue to support the Commission's consistently held position that the 100-to-1 drug quantity ratio significantly undermines various congressional objectives set forth in the Sentencing Reform Act and elsewhere. These findings will be more thoroughly explained in a forthcoming report that will present to Congress, on or before May 15, 2007, a number of recommendations for modifications to the statutory penalties for crack cocaine offenses. It is the Commission's firm desire that this report will facilitate prompt congressional action addressing the 100-to-1 drug quantity ratio.

The Commission's recommendation and strong desire for prompt legislative action notwithstanding, the problems associated with the 100-to-1 drug quantity ratio are so urgent and compelling that this amendment is promulgated as an interim measure to alleviate some of those problems. The Commission has concluded that the manner in which the Drug Quantity Table in § 2D1.1 (Unlawful Manufacturing, Importing, Exporting, or

Amendment 706

Trafficking (Including Possession with Intent to Commit These Offenses); Attempt or Conspiracy)) was constructed to incorporate the statutory mandatory minimum penalties for crack cocaine offenses is an area in which the Federal sentencing guidelines contribute to the problems associated with the 100-to-1 drug quantity ratio.

When Congress passed the 1986 Act, the Commission responded by generally incorporating the statutory mandatory minimum sentences into the guidelines and extrapolating upward and downward to set guideline sentencing ranges for all drug quantities. The drug quantity thresholds in the Drug Quantity Table are set so as to provide base offense levels corresponding to guideline ranges that are above the statutory mandatory minimum penalties. Accordingly, offenses involving 5 grams or more of crack cocaine were assigned a base offense level (level 26) corresponding to a sentencing guideline range of 63 to 78 months for a defendant in Criminal History Category I (a guideline range that exceeds the five-year statutory minimum for such offenses by at least three months). Similarly, offenses involving 50 grams or more of crack cocaine were assigned a base offense level (level 32) corresponding to a sentencing guideline range of 121 to 151 months for a defendant in Criminal History Category I (a guideline range that exceeds the ten-year statutory minimum for such offenses by at least one month). Crack cocaine offenses for quantities above and below the mandatory minimum threshold quantities were set accordingly using the 100-to-1 drug quantity ratio.

This amendment modifies the drug quantity thresholds in the Drug Quantity Table so as to assign, for crack cocaine offenses, base offense levels corresponding to guideline ranges that include the statutory mandatory minimum penalties. Accordingly, pursuant to the amendment, 5 grams of cocaine base are assigned a base offense level of 24 (51 to 63 months at Criminal History Category I, which includes the five-year (60 month) statutory minimum for such offenses), and 50 grams of cocaine base are assigned a base offense level of 30 (97 to 121 months at Criminal History Category I, which includes the ten-year (120 month) statutory minimum for such offenses). Crack cocaine offenses for quantities above and below the mandatory minimum threshold quantities similarly are adjusted downward by two levels. The amendment also includes a mechanism to determine a combined base offense level in an offense involving crack cocaine and other controlled substances.

The Commission's prison impact model predicts that, assuming no change in the existing statutory mandatory minimum penalties, this modification to the Drug Quantity Table will affect 69.7 percent of crack cocaine offenses sentenced under § 2D1.1 and will result in a reduction in the estimated average sentence of all crack cocaine offenses from 121 months to 106 months, based on an analysis of cases sentenced in fiscal year 2006 under § 2D1.1 involving crack cocaine.

Having concluded once again that the 100-to-1 drug quantity ratio should be modified, the Commission recognizes that establishing federal cocaine sentencing policy ultimately is Congress's prerogative. Accordingly, the Commission tailored the amendment to fit within the existing statutory penalty scheme by assigning base offense levels that provide guideline ranges that include the statutory mandatory minimum penalties for crack cocaine offenses. The Commission, however, views the amendment only as an interim solution to some of the problems associated with the 100-to-1 drug quantity ratio. It is neither a permanent nor a complete solution to those problems. Any comprehensive solution to the 100-to-1 drug quantity ratio requires appropriate legislative action by Congress.

Effective Date: The effective date of this amendment is November 1, 2007.

707. Amendment: Section 2D1.11(a) is amended by striking "(e)" after "under subsection" and inserting "(d)".

The Commentary to § 2K2.1 captioned "Application Notes" is amended in Note 14 in subdivision (B) by striking "(b)(1)" and inserting "(b)(6)".

Appendix A (Statutory Index) is amended by inserting after the line referenced to 18 U.S.C. § 930 the following:

"18 U.S.C. § 931   2K2.6";

and by striking the following:

"18 U.S.C. § 3147   2J1.7".

Chapter Three, Part D is amended in the Introductory Commentary in the first paragraph by inserting after the first sentence the following:

"These rules apply to multiple counts of conviction (A) contained in the same indictment or information; or (B) contained in different indictments or informations for which sentences are to be imposed at the same time or in a consolidated proceeding.".

The Commentary to § 3D1.1 captioned "Application Note" is amended by striking "Note" and inserting "Notes"; by redesignating Note 1 as Note 2; and by inserting the following as new Note 1:

"1.   In General.—For purposes of sentencing multiple counts of conviction, counts can be (A) contained in the same indictment or information; or (B) contained in different indictments or informations for which sentences are to be imposed at the same time or in a consolidated proceeding.".

Reason for Amendment: This amendment makes various technical and conforming changes to the guidelines.

First, the amendment corrects typographical errors in subsection (a) of § 2D1.11 (Unlawfully Distributing, Importing, Exporting or Possessing a Listed Chemical; Attempt or Conspiracy) and Application Note 14 of § 2K2.1 (Unlawful Receipt, Possession, or Transportation of Firearms or Ammunition; Prohibited Transactions Involving Firearms or Ammunition). Second, the amendment addresses application of the grouping rules when a defendant is sentenced on multiple counts contained in different indictments as, for example, when a case is transferred to another district for purposes of sentencing, pursuant to Fed. R. Crim. P. 20(a).

The amendment adopts the reasoning of recent case law and clarifies that the grouping rules apply not only to multiple counts in the same indictment, but also to multiple counts contained in different indictments when a defendant is sentenced on the indictments simultaneously. The amendment provides clarifying language in the Introductory Commentary of Chapter Three, Part D, as well as in § 3D1.1 (Procedure for Determining Offense Level on Multiple Counts). The language is the same as that provided in § 5G1.2 (Sentencing on Multiple Counts of Conviction).

Effective Date: The effective date of this amendment is November 1, 2007.

708. **Amendment:** The amendments to § 2H3.1 and Appendix A, effective May 1, 2007 (see Appendix C, Amendment 697), are repromulgated with the following changes:

Section 2H3.1 is amended in the heading by striking "Tax Return Information" and inserting "Certain Private or Protected Information".

Section 2H3.1(a) is amended by striking subdivision (2) as follows:

"(2) 6, if the defendant was convicted of 26 U.S.C. § 7213A or 26 U.S.C. § 7216.",

and inserting the following:

"(2) 6, if the offense of conviction has a statutory maximum term of imprisonment of one year or less but more than six months.".

Section 2H3.1(b)(1) is amended by inserting "(A) the defendant is convicted under 18 U.S.C. § 1039(d) or (e); or (B)" after "If".

The Commentary to § 2H3.1 captioned "Statutory Provisions" is amended by inserting "8 U.S.C. § 1375a(d)(3)(C), (d)(5)(B);" before "18 U.S.C."; by inserting "§ 1039, 1905," after "18 U.S.C. § "; and by inserting "42 U.S.C. §§ 16962, 16984;" after "7216;".

The Commentary to § 2H3.1 captioned "Application Notes" is amended by striking Note 1 as follows:

"1. Definitions.—For purposes of this guideline, 'tax return' and 'tax return information' have the meaning given the terms 'return' and 'return information' in 26 U.S.C. § 6103(b)(1) and (2), respectively.";

by redesignating Note 2 as Note 1; and by adding at the end the following:

"2. Imposition of Sentence for 18 U.S.C. § 1039(d) and (e).—Subsections 1039(d) and (e) of title 18, United States Code, require a term of imprisonment of not more than 5 years to be imposed in addition to any sentence imposed for a conviction under 18 U.S.C. § 1039(a), (b), or (c).

In order to comply with the statute, the court should determine the appropriate 'total punishment' and divide the sentence on the judgment form between the sentence attributable to the conviction under 18 U.S.C. § 1039(d) or (e) and the sentence attributable to the conviction under 18 U.S.C. § 1039(a), (b), or (c), specifying the number of months to be served for the conviction under 18 U.S.C. § 1039(d) or (e). For example, if the applicable adjusted guideline range is 15-21 months and the court determines a 'total punishment' of 21 months is appropriate, a sentence of 9 months for conduct under 18 U.S.C. § 1039(a) plus 12 months for 18 U.S.C. § 1039(d) conduct would achieve the 'total punishment' in a manner that satisfies the statutory requirement.

3. Upward Departure.—There may be cases in which the offense level determined under this guideline substantially understates the seriousness of the offense. In such a case, an upward departure may be warranted. The following are examples of cases in which an upward departure may be warranted:

(i) The offense involved confidential phone records information or tax return information of a substantial number of individuals.

(ii) The offense caused or risked substantial non-monetary harm (e.g.

physical harm, psychological harm, or severe emotional trauma, or resulted in a substantial invasion of privacy interest) to individuals whose private or protected information was obtained.".

Section 2H3.1 is amended by striking the Commentary captioned "Background" as follows:

"Background: This section refers to conduct proscribed by 47 U.S.C. § 605 and the Electronic Communications Privacy Act of 1986, which amends 18 U.S.C. § 2511 and other sections of Title 18 dealing with unlawful interception and disclosure of communications. These statutes proscribe the interception and divulging of wire, oral, radio, and electronic communications. The Electronic Communications Privacy Act of 1986 provides for a maximum term of imprisonment of five years for violations involving most types of communication.

This section also refers to conduct relating to the disclosure and inspection of tax returns and tax return information, which is proscribed by 26 U.S.C. §§ 7213(a)(1)-(3), (5), (d), 7213A, and 7216. These statutes provide for a maximum term of imprisonment of five years for most types of disclosure of tax return information, but provide a maximum term of imprisonment of one year for violations of 26 U.S.C. §§ 7213A and 7216.".

Appendix A (Statutory Index) is amended by inserting after the line referenced to 8 U.S.C. § 1328 the following:

"8 U.S.C. § 1375a(d)(3)(C), (d)(5)(B)   2H3.1";

by inserting after the line referenced to 18 U.S.C. § 1038 the following:

"18 U.S.C. § 1039   2H3.1"; and

by inserting after the line referenced to 42 U.S.C. § 14905 the following:

"42 U.S.C. § 16962   2H3.1
42 U.S.C. § 16984   2H3.1".

Reason for Amendment: This amendment addresses several offenses that pertain to unauthorized access or disclosure of private or protected information. Specifically, this amendment pertains to (A) the re-promulgation of the emergency amendment that implemented the directive in section 4 of the Telephone Records and Privacy Protection Act of 2006, Pub. L. 109–476 (the "Telephone Records Act"); (B) offenses involving improper use of a child's fingerprints under 42 U.S.C. §§ 16984 and 16962; and (C) various other offenses related to private or protected information.

This amendment re-promulgates as permanent the temporary emergency amendment (effective May 1, 2007) that implemented the directive in section 4 of the Telephone Records Act. The amendment refers the new offense at 18 U.S.C. § 1039 to § 2H3.1 (Interception of Communications; Eavesdropping; Disclosure of Tax Information). The Commission concluded that disclosure of telephone records is similar to the types of privacy offenses referenced to this guideline. In addition, this guideline includes a cross reference, instructing that if the purpose of the 18 U.S.C. § 1039 offense was to facilitate another offense, the guideline applicable to an attempt to commit the other offense should be applied, if the resulting offense level is higher. The Commission concluded that operation of the cross reference would capture the harms associated with the aggravated forms of this offense referenced at 18 U.S.C. § 1039(d) or (e). The amendment also expands the scope of the existing three-level enhancement in the guideline to include cases in which the defendant is convicted under 18 U.S.C. § 1039(d) or (e). Thus, in a case in which the cross reference does not apply, application of the enhancement will capture the increased harms associated with the aggravated offenses. Finally, the amendment expands the upward departure note to include tax return information of a substantial number of individuals.

Section 153 of the Adam Walsh Child Protection and Safety Act of 2006, Pub. L. 109–248 (the "Adam Walsh Act"), added a new offense at 42 U.S.C. § 16962, which provides a statutory maximum term of imprisonment of 10 years for the improper release of information obtained in fingerprint-based checks for the background check of either foster or adoptive parents or of individuals employed by, or considering employment with, a private or public educational agency. Additionally, section 627 of the Adam Walsh Act added a new Class A Misdemeanor offense at 42 U.S.C. § 16984 prohibiting the use of a child's fingerprints for any purpose other than providing those fingerprints to the child's parent or legal guardian. This amendment references both offenses to § 2H3.1, providing a base offense level of 9 under § 2H3.1(a)(1) if the defendant was convicted of violating 42 U.S.C. § 16962, and a base offense level of 6 if the defendant was convicted of violating 42 U.S.C. § 16984.

Finally, this amendment implements the Violence Against Women and Department of Justice Reauthorization Act of 2005, Pub. L. 109–162 ("VAWA"). VAWA included the International Marriage Broker Regulation Act of 2005 ("IMBRA"), which requires marriage brokers to keep private information gathered in the course of their business confidential.

New offenses at 8 U.S.C. §§ 1375a(d)(3)(C) and 1375a(d)(5)(B) involve invasions of protected privacy interests and, as such, are referenced to § 2H3.1.

The Commission concluded that referencing these new offenses to § 2H3.1 was appropriate because each of the new offenses is similar to the types of privacy offenses referenced to this guideline.

Effective Date: The effective date of this amendment is November 1, 2007.

709. Amendment: Section 4A1.1(f) is amended by striking "was considered related to another sentence resulting from a conviction of a crime of violence" and inserting "was counted as a single sentence"; and by striking the last sentence as follows:

> "Provided, that this item does not apply where the sentences are considered related because the offenses occurred on the same occasion.".

The Commentary to § 4A1.1 captioned "Application Notes" is amended in Note 6 by striking the first paragraph as follows:

> "§ 4A1.1(f). Where the defendant received two or more prior sentences as a result of convictions for crimes of violence that are treated as related cases but did not arise from the same occasion (i.e., offenses committed on different occasions that were part of a single common scheme or plan or were consolidated for trial or sentencing; see Application Note 3 of the Commentary to § 4A1.2), one point is added under § 4A1.1(f) for each such sentence that did not result in any additional points under § 4A1.1(a), (b), or (c). A total of up to 3 points may be added under § 4A1.1(f). "Crime of violence" is defined in § 4B1.2(a); see § 4A1.2(p).",

and inserting the following:

"§ 4A1.1(f). In a case in which the defendant received two or more prior sentences as a result of convictions for crimes of violence that are counted as a single sentence (see § 4A1.2(a)(2)), one point is added under § 4A1.1(f) for each such sentence that did not result in any additional points under § 4A1.1(a), (b), or (c). A total of up to 3 points may be added under § 4A1.1(f). For purposes of this guideline, 'crime of violence' has the meaning given that term in § 4B1.2(a). See § 4A1.2(p).";

and in the second paragraph by striking "that were consolidated for sentencing and therefore are treated as related." and inserting ". The sentences for these offenses were imposed on the same day and are counted as a single prior sentence. See § 4A1.2(a)(2).".

Section 4A1.2(a) is amended in the heading by striking "Defined"; and by striking subdivision (2) as follows:

"(2) Prior sentences imposed in unrelated cases are to be counted separately. Prior sentences imposed in related cases are to be treated as one sentence for purposes of § 4A1.1(a), (b), and (c). Use the longest sentence of imprisonment if concurrent sentences were imposed and the aggregate sentence of imprisonment imposed in the case of consecutive sentences.",

and inserting the following:

"(2) If the defendant has multiple prior sentences, determine whether those sentences are counted separately or as a single sentence. Prior sentences always are counted separately if the sentences were imposed for offenses that were separated by an intervening arrest (i.e., the defendant is arrested for the first offense prior to committing the second offense). If there is no intervening arrest, prior sentences are counted separately unless (A) the sentences resulted from offenses contained in the same charging instrument; or (B) the sentences were imposed on the same day. Count any prior sentence covered by (A) or (B) as a single sentence. See also § 4A1.1(f).

For purposes of applying § 4A1.1(a), (b), and (c), if prior sentences are counted as a single sentence, use the longest sentence of imprisonment if concurrent sentences were imposed. If consecutive sentences were imposed, use the aggregate sentence of imprisonment.".

Section 4A1.2(c)(1) is amended by striking "at least one" and inserting "more than one"; by striking "Fish and game violations"; and by striking "Local ordinance violations (excluding local ordinance violations that are also criminal offenses under state law)".

Section 4A1.2(c)(2) is amended by inserting "Fish and game violations" as a new line before the line referenced to "Hitchhiking"; and by inserting "Local ordinance violations (except those violations that are also violations under state criminal law)" as a new line before the line referenced to "Loitering".

The Commentary to § 4A1.2 captioned "Application Notes" is amended by striking Note 3 as follows:

"3. Related Cases. Prior sentences are not considered related if they were for offenses that were separated by an intervening arrest (i.e., the defendant is arrested for the first offense prior to committing the second offense). Otherwise, prior sentences are considered related if they resulted from offenses that (A) occurred on the same occasion, (B) were part of a single common scheme or plan, or (C) were consolidated for trial or sentencing. The court should be

Amendment 709

aware that there may be instances in which this definition is overly broad and will result in a criminal history score that underrepresents the seriousness of the defendant's criminal history and the danger that he presents to the public. For example, if a defendant was convicted of a number of serious non-violent offenses committed on different occasions, and the resulting sentences were treated as related because the cases were consolidated for sentencing, the assignment of a single set of points may not adequately reflect the seriousness of the defendant's criminal history or the frequency with which he has committed crimes. In such circumstances, an upward departure may be warranted. Note that the above example refers to serious non-violent offenses. Where prior related sentences result from convictions of crimes of violence, § 4A1.1(f) will apply.",

and inserting the following:

"3. Upward Departure Provision.—Counting multiple prior sentences as a single sentence may result in a criminal history score that underrepresents the seriousness of the defendant's criminal history and the danger that the defendant presents to the public. In such a case, an upward departure may be warranted. For example, if a defendant was convicted of a number of serious non-violent offenses committed on different occasions, and the resulting sentences were counted as a single sentence because either the sentences resulted from offenses contained in the same charging instrument or the defendant was sentenced for these offenses on the same day, the assignment of a single set of points may not adequately reflect the seriousness of the defendant's criminal history or the frequency with which the defendant has committed crimes.".

The Commentary to § 4A1.2 captioned "Application Notes" is amended in Note 12 by striking "Local Ordinance Violations." and inserting the following:

"Application of Subsection (c).—

(A) In General.—In determining whether an unlisted offense is similar to an offense listed in subdivision (c)(1) or (c)(2), the court should use a common sense approach that includes consideration of relevant factors such as (i) a comparison of punishments imposed for the listed and unlisted offenses; (ii) the perceived seriousness of the offense as indicated by the level of punishment; (iii) the elements of the offense; (iv) the level of culpability involved; and (v) the degree to which the commission of the offense indicates a likelihood of recurring criminal conduct.

(B) Local Ordinance Violations.—";

by striking "§ 4A1.2(c)(1)" after "violations in" and inserting "§ 4A1.2(c)(2)"; and by inserting at the end the following:

"(C) Insufficient Funds Check.—'Insufficient funds check,' as used in § 4A1.2(c)(1), does not include any conviction establishing that the defendant used a false name or non-existent account.".

The Commentary to § 4A1.2 captioned "Application Notes" is amended by striking Note 13 as follows:

"13. Insufficient Funds Check. 'Insufficient funds check,' as used in § 4A1.2(c)

(1), does not include any conviction establishing that the defendant used a false name or non-existent account.".

The Commentary to § 4B1.2 captioned "Application Notes" is amended in Note 1 in the paragraph that begins "A violation of 18 U.S.C. § 924(c)" by inserting "sentences for the" before "two prior"; and by striking "treated as related cases" and inserting "counted as a single sentence".

The Commentary to § 2L1.2 captioned "Application Notes" is amended in Note 4(B) by striking "considered 'related cases', as that term is defined in Application Note 3" and inserting "counted as a single sentence pursuant to subsection (a)(2)".

Reason for Amendment: This amendment addresses two areas of the Chapter Four criminal history rules: the counting of multiple prior sentences and the use of misdemeanor and petty offenses in determining a defendant's criminal history score. In November 2006 the Commission hosted round-table discussions to receive input on criminal history issues from federal judges, prosecutors, defense attorneys, probation officers, and members of academia. In addition, the Commission gathered information through its training programs, the public comment process, and comments received during a public hearing of the Commission in March 2007. This amendment addresses two issues that were raised during this process.

First, the amendment addresses the counting of multiple prior sentences. The Commission has heard from a number of practitioners throughout the criminal justice system that the "related cases" rules at subsection (a)(2) of § 4A1.2 (Definitions and Instructions for Computing Criminal History) and Application Note 3 of § 4A1.2 are too complex and lead to confusion. Moreover, a significant amount of litigation has arisen concerning application of the rules, and circuit conflicts have developed over the meaning of terms in the commentary that define when prior sentences may be considered "related." For example, the commentary provides that prior sentences for offenses not separated by an intervening arrest are to be considered related if the sentences resulted from offenses that were consolidated for sentencing. In determining whether offenses were consolidated for sentencing, some courts have required that the record reflect a formal order of consolidation, while others have not. Compare, e.g., United States v. Correa, 114 F.3d 314, 317 (1st Cir. 1997) (order required) with United States v. Huskey, 137 F.3d 283, 288 (5th Cir. 1998) (order not required).

The amendment simplifies the rules for counting multiple prior sentences and promotes consistency in the application of the guideline. The amendment eliminates use of the term "related cases" at § 4A1.2(a)(2) and instead uses the terms "single" and "separate" sentences. This change in terminology was made because some have misunderstood the term "related cases" to suggest a relationship between the prior sentences and the instant offense. Prior sentences for conduct that is part of the instant offense are separately addressed at § 4A1.2(a)(1) and Application Note 1 of that guideline.

Under the amendment, the initial inquiry will be whether the prior sentences were for offenses that were separated by an intervening arrest (i.e., the defendant was arrested for the first offense prior to committing the second offense). If so, they are to be considered separate sentences, counted separately, and no further inquiry is required.

If the prior sentences were for offenses that were not separated by an intervening arrest, the sentences are to be counted as separate sentences unless the sentences (1) were for offenses that were named in the same charging document, or (2) were imposed on the same day. In either of these situations they are treated as a single sentence.

Amendment 709

The amendment further provides that in the case of a single sentence that comprises multiple concurrent sentences of varying lengths, the longest sentence is to be used for purposes of applying subsection (a), (b) and (c) of § 4A1.1 (Criminal History Category). In the case of a single sentence that comprises multiple sentences that include one or more consecutive sentences, the aggregate sentence is to be used for purposes of applying § 4A1.1(a), (b), and (c).

Instances may arise in which a single sentence comprises multiple prior sentences for crimes of violence. In such a case, § 4A1.1(f) will apply. Consistent with § 4A1.1(f) and Application Note 6 to § 4A1.1, additional criminal history points will be awarded for certain sentences that otherwise do not receive points because they have been determined to be part of a single sentence. For example, if a defendant's criminal history contains two robbery convictions for which the defendant received concurrent five-year sentences of imprisonment and the sentences are considered a single sentence because the offenses were not separated by an intervening arrest and were imposed on the same day, a total of 3 points would be added under § 4A1.1(a). An additional point would be added under § 4A1.1(f) because the second sentence was for a crime of violence that did not receive any points under § 4A1.1(a), (b), or (c).

The amendment also provides for an upward departure at Application Note 12(A) to § 4A1.1 if counting multiple prior sentences as a single sentence would underrepresent the seriousness of the defendant's criminal history and the danger that the defendant presents to the public.

Second, the amendment addresses the use of misdemeanor and petty offenses in determining a defendant's criminal history score. Sections 4A1.2(c)(1) and (2) govern whether and when certain misdemeanor and petty offenses are counted. Section 4A1.2(c)(1) lists offenses that are counted only when the prior sentence was a term of probation of at least one year or a term of imprisonment of at least 30 days. Section 4A1.2(c)(2) lists offenses that are never counted toward the defendant's criminal history score. The amendment responds to concerns that (1) some misdemeanor and petty offenses counted under the guidelines involve conduct that is not serious enough to warrant increased punishment upon sentencing for a subsequent offense; (2) the presence of a prior misdemeanor or petty offense in a rare case can affect the sentence in the instant offense in a way that is greatly disproportionate to the seriousness of the prior offense (such as when such a prior offense alone disqualifies a defendant from safety valve eligibility); and (3) jurisdictional differences in defining misdemeanor and petty offenses can result in inconsistent application of criminal history points for substantially similar conduct.

To evaluate these concerns, the Commission conducted a study of misdemeanor and petty offenses and the criminal history rules that govern them, particularly § 4A1.2(c)(1). The Commission examined a sample of 11,300 offenders sentenced in fiscal year 2006 to determine the type of misdemeanor and petty offenses counted in the criminal history score, the frequency with which they occurred, and the particular guideline provisions that caused them to be counted. In addition, the Commission examined a sample of offenders sentenced in 1992 who were subsequently released from imprisonment and monitored for two years for evidence of recidivism. (See U.S. Sentencing Commission *Measuring Recidivism: The Criminal History Computation of the Federal Sentencing Guidelines* (2004) for additional information concerning this sample.) Furthermore, the Commission examined how state guidelines treat minor offenses.

The results of these analyses led the Commission to make three modifications to § 4A1.2(c)(1) and (2). First, the amendment moves from § 4A1.2(c)(1) to § 4A1.2(c)(2) two classes of offenses: fish and game violations and local ordinance violations (except those violations that are also violations under state criminal law). Second, the amendment changes the probation criterion at § 4A1.2(c)(1) from a term of "at least" one year to a term of "more than" one year. Finally, the amendment resolves a circuit conflict over the manner in which a non-listed offense is determined to be "similar to" an offense listed at § 4A1.2(c)(1) and (2).

Fish and game violations were moved from § 4A1.2(c)(1) to § 4A1.2(c)(2) so that they will not be counted in a defendant's criminal history score. Fish and game violations generally do not involve criminal conduct that is more serious than the offense of conviction, and the relatively minor sentences received by fish and game offenders in the fiscal year 2006 study suggest that these offenses are not considered to be among the more serious offenses listed at § 4A1.2(c)(1).

In addition, local ordinance violations (except those that are also violations of state law) were moved from § 4A1.2(c)(1) to § 4A1.2(c)(2) so that they also will not be counted in a defendant's criminal history score. Similar to fish and game violations, local ordinance violations generally do not represent conduct criminalized under state law. Moreover, these offenses also frequently received minor sentences. The exception in this amendment for violations that are also criminal violations under state law will ensure that only the more serious prior criminal conduct will continue to be included in the criminal history score.

Section 4A1.2(c)(1)(A) is amended to provide that the offenses listed at § 4A1.2(c)(1) will be counted "only if (A) the sentence was a term of probation of more than one year or a term of imprisonment of at least thirty days, or (B) the prior offense was similar to the instant offense" (emphasis added). The Commission received comment that some sentences of a one-year term of probation constitute a default punishment summarily imposed by the state sentencing authority, particularly in those instances in which the probation imposed lacked a supervision component or was imposed in lieu of a fine or to enable the payment of a fine. The Commission determined that prior misdemeanor and petty offenses that receive such a relatively minor default sentence should not be counted for criminal history purposes.

The amendment resolves a circuit conflict over the manner in which a court should determine whether a non-listed offense is "similar to" an offense listed at § 4A1.2(c)(1) or (2). Some courts have adopted a "common sense approach," first articulated by the Fifth Circuit in United States v. Hardeman, 933 F.2d 278, 281 (5th Cir. 1991). This common sense approach includes consideration of all relevant factors of similarity such as "punishments imposed for the listed and unlisted offenses, the perceived seriousness of the offense as indicated by the level of punishment, the elements of the offense, the level of culpability involved, and the degree to which the commission of the offense indicates a likelihood of recurring criminal conduct." Id. See also United States v. Martinez-Santos, 184 F.3d 196, 205-06 (2d Cir. 1999) (adopting Hardeman approach); United States v. Booker, 71 F.3d 685, 689 (7th Cir. 1995) (same). Other courts have adopted a strict "elements" test, which involves solely a comparison between the elements of the two offenses to determine whether or not the offenses are similar. See United States v. Elmore, 108 F.3d 23, 27 (3d Cir. 1997); United States v. Tigney, 367 F.3d 200, 201-02 (4th Cir. 2004); United States v. Borer, 412 F.3d 987, 992 (8th Cir. 2005). This amendment, at Application Note 12(A), adopts the Hardeman "common sense approach" as a means of ensuring that courts are guided by a number of relevant factors that may help them determine whether a non-listed offense is similar to a listed one.

Effective Date: The effective date of this amendment is November 1, 2007.

710. **Amendment:** Section 1B1.10(c) is amended by striking "and" and by inserting ", and

Amendment 710   APPENDIX C - VOLUME III   November 1, 2013

702" before the period.

Reason for Amendment: Amendment 702 corrects typographical errors in subsection (b)(13)(C) of § 2B1.1 (Larceny, Embezzlement, and Other Forms of Theft; Offenses Involving Stolen Property; Property Damage or Destruction; Fraud and Deceit; Forgery; Offenses Involving Altered or Counterfeit Instruments Other than Counterfeit Bearer Obligations of the United States) and subsection (b)(1) of § 2L1.1 (Smuggling, Transporting, or Harboring an Unlawful Alien). As stated in the reason for amendment accompanying Amendment 702, this amendment adds Amendment 702 to § 1B1.10 (Reduction in Term of Imprisonment as a Result of Amended Guideline Range) as an amendment that the court may consider for retroactive application.

Effective Date: The effective date of this amendment is November 1, 2007.

711. **Amendment:** The Commentary to § 2A3.4 captioned "Statutory Provisions" is amended by striking "Provisions" and inserting "Provision".

Section 2A3.5(b)(1)(A), as added by Amendment 701, is amended by inserting a comma after "minor".

Chapter Two, Part D is amended in the heading by inserting "AND NARCO-TERRORISM" after "DRUGS".

The Commentary to § 2D1.1 captioned "Application Notes", as amended by Amendment 706, is further amended by striking subdivision (D) as follows:

"(D) Determining Base Offense Level in Offenses Involving Cocaine Base and Other Controlled Substances.—

(i) In General.—If the offense involves cocaine base ('crack') and one or more other controlled substance, determine the base offense level as follows:

(I) Determine the combined base offense level for the other controlled substance or controlled substances as provided in subdivision (B) of this note.

(II) Use the combined base offense level determined under subdivision (B) of this note to obtain the appropriate marihuana equivalency for the cocaine base involved in the offense using the following table:

Base Offense Level	Marihuana Equivalency
38	6.7 kg of marihuana
36	6.7 kg of marihuana
34	6 kg of marihuana
32	6.7 kg of marihuana
30	14 kg of marihuana
28	11.4 kg of marihuana
26	5 kg of marihuana
24	16 kg of marihuana
22	15 kg of marihuana

20	13.3 kg of marihuana
18	10 kg of marihuana
16	10 kg of marihuana
14	10 kg of marihuana
12	10 kg of marihuana.

        (III)   Using the marihuana equivalency obtained from the table in subdivision (II), convert the quantity of cocaine base involved in the offense to its equivalent quantity of marihuana.

        (IV)   Add the quantity of marihuana determined under subdivisions (I) and (III), and look up the total in the Drug Quantity Table to obtain the combined base offense level for all the controlled substances involved in the offense.

    (ii)   Example.—The case involves 1.5 kg of cocaine, 10 kg of marihuana, and 20 g of cocaine base. Pursuant to subdivision (B), the equivalent quantity of marihuana for the cocaine and the marihuana is 310 kg. (The cocaine converts to an equivalent of 300 kg of marihuana (1.5 kg x 200 g = 300 kg), which when added to the quantity of marihuana involved in the offense, results in an equivalent quantity of 310 kg of marihuana.) This corresponds to a base offense level 26. Pursuant to the table in subdivision (II), the base offense level of 26 results in a marihuana equivalency of 5 kg for the cocaine base. Using this marihuana equivalency for the cocaine base results in a marihuana equivalency of 100 kg (20 g x 5 kg = 100 kg). Adding the quantities of marihuana of all three controlled substances results in a combined quantity of 410 kg of marihuana, which corresponds to a combined base offense level of 28 in the Drug Quantity Table.".

and inserting the following:

  "(D)   <u>Determining Base Offense Level in Offenses Involving Cocaine Base and Other Controlled Substances</u>.—

    (i)   <u>In General</u>.—If the offense involves cocaine base ('crack') and one or more other controlled substance, determine the base offense level as follows:

        (I)   Determine the base offense level for the quantity of cocaine base involved in the offense.

        (II)   Using the marihuana equivalency obtained from the table in this subdivision, convert the quantity of cocaine base involved in the offense to its equivalent quantity of marihuana.

<u>Base Offense Level</u>	<u>Marihuana Equivalency</u>
38	6.7 kg of marihuana per g of cocaine base

Amendment 711 APPENDIX C - VOLUME III November 1, 2013

36	6.7 kg of marihuana per g of cocaine base
34	6 kg of marihuana per g of cocaine base
32	6.7 kg of marihuana per g of cocaine base
30	14 kg of marihuana per g of cocaine base
28	11.4 kg of marihuana per g of cocaine base
26	5 kg of marihuana per g of cocaine base
24	16 kg of marihuana per g of cocaine base
22	15 kg of marihuana per g of cocaine base
20	13.3 kg of marihuana per g of cocaine base
18	10 kg of marihuana per g of cocaine base
16	10 kg of marihuana per g of cocaine base
14	10 kg of marihuana per g of cocaine base
12	10 kg of marihuana per g of cocaine base

       (III)   Determine the combined marihuana equivalency for the other controlled substance or controlled substances involved in the offense as provided in subdivision (B) of this note.

       (IV)   Add the quantity of marihuana determined under subdivisions (II) and (III), and look up the total in the Drug Quantity Table to obtain the combined base offense level for all the controlled substances involved in the offense.

  (ii)   Example.—The case involves 1.5 kg of cocaine, 10 kg of marihuana, and 20 g of cocaine base. Under the Drug Quantity Table, 20 g of cocaine base corresponds to a base offense level of 26. Pursuant to the table in subdivision (II), the base offense level of 26 corresponds to a marihuana equivalency of 5 kg per gram of cocaine base. Therefore, the equivalent quantity of marihuana for the cocaine base is 100 kg (20 g x 5 kg = 100 kg). Pursuant to subdivision (B), the equivalent quantity of marihuana for the cocaine and marihuana is 310 kg. (The cocaine converts to an equivalent of 300 kg of marihuana (1.5 kg x 200 g = 300 kg), which, when added to the 10 kg of marihuana, results in an equivalent quantity of 310 kg of marihuana.) Adding the equivalent quantities of marihuana of all three drug types results in a combined quantity of 410 kg of marihuana (100 kg + 310 kg = 410 kg), which corresponds to a combined base offense level of 28 in the Drug Quantity Table.".

The Commentary to § 2N2.1 captioned "Application Notes" is amended in Note 4 by inserting "and Narco-Terrorism" after "Drugs".

The Commentary to § 5B1.3 captioned "Application Note", as added by Amendment 701, is amended by striking "(b)" each place it appears and inserting "(a)".

The Commentary to § 5D1.3 captioned "Application Note", as added by Amendment 701, is amended by striking "(b)" each place it appears and inserting "(a)".

Appendix A (Statutory Index) is amended by striking the lines referenced to "50 U.S.C. § 421" and "50 U.S.C. § 783(b)" the first place they appear.

November 1, 2013   APPENDIX C - VOLUME III   **Amendment 712**

Reason for Amendment: This amendment makes various technical and conforming amendments in order to execute properly amendments submitted to Congress on May 1, 2007, and that will become effective on November 1, 2007. Specifically, the amendment corrects grammatical errors in the commentary to § 2A3.4 (Abusive Sexual Contact or Attempt to Commit Abusive Sexual Contact); amends the commentary to § 2D1.1 (Unlawful Manufacturing, Importing, Exporting, or Trafficking (Including Possession with Intent to Commit These Offenses); Attempt or Conspiracy); changes the heading in Chapter Two, Part D and makes the conforming change to § 2N2.1 (Violations of Statutes and Regulations Dealing With Any Food, Drug, Biological Product, Device, Cosmetic, or Agricultural Product); corrects typographical errors in §§ 5B1.3 (Conditions of Probation) and 5D1.3 (Conditions of Supervised Release); and amends Appendix A to remove duplicate listings.

Effective Date: The effective date of this amendment is November 1, 2007.

712. **Amendment:** Chapter One, Part B, Subpart One, is amended by striking § 1B1.10 and its accompanying commentary as follows:

> "§ 1B1.10. <u>Reduction in Term of Imprisonment as a Result of Amended Guideline Range</u> (Policy Statement)
>
> (a) Where a defendant is serving a term of imprisonment, and the guideline range applicable to that defendant has subsequently been lowered as a result of an amendment to the Guidelines Manual listed in subsection (c) below, a reduction in the defendant's term of imprisonment is authorized under 18 U.S.C. § 3582(c)(2). If none of the amendments listed in subsection (c) is applicable, a reduction in the defendant's term of imprisonment under 18 U.S.C. § 3582(c)(2) is not consistent with this policy statement and thus is not authorized.
>
> (b) In determining whether, and to what extent, a reduction in the term of imprisonment is warranted for a defendant eligible for consideration under 18 U.S.C. § 3582(c)(2), the court should consider the term of imprisonment that it would have imposed had the amendment(s) to the guidelines listed in subsection (c) been in effect at the time the defendant was sentenced, except that in no event may the reduced term of imprisonment be less than the term of imprisonment the defendant has already served.
>
> (c) Amendments covered by this policy statement are listed in Appendix C as follows: 126, 130, 156, 176, 269, 329, 341, 371, 379, 380, 433, 454, 461, 484, 488, 490, 499, 505, 506, 516, 591, 599, 606, 657, and 702.
>
> <u>Commentary</u>
>
> <u>Application Notes</u>:
>
> 1. Eligibility for consideration under 18 U.S.C. § 3582(c)(2) is triggered only by an amendment listed in subsection (c) that lowers the applicable guideline range.
>
> 2. In determining the amended guideline range under subsection (b), the court shall substitute only the amendments listed in subsection (c) for the corresponding guideline provisions that were applied when the defendant was sentenced. All other guideline application decisions remain unaffected.

– 1081 –

3. Under subsection (b), the amended guideline range and the term of imprisonment already served by the defendant limit the extent to which an eligible defendant's sentence may be reduced under 18 U.S.C. § 3582(c)(2). When the original sentence represented a downward departure, a comparable reduction below the amended guideline range may be appropriate; however, in no case shall the term of imprisonment be reduced below time served. Subject to these limitations, the sentencing court has the discretion to determine whether, and to what extent, to reduce a term of imprisonment under this section.

4. Only a term of imprisonment imposed as part of the original sentence is authorized to be reduced under this section. This section does not authorize a reduction in the term of imprisonment imposed upon revocation of supervised release.

5. If the limitation in subsection (b) relating to time already served precludes a reduction in the term of imprisonment to the extent the court determines otherwise would have been appropriate as a result of the amended guideline range, the court may consider any such reduction that it was unable to grant in connection with any motion for early termination of a term of supervised release under 18 U.S.C. § 3583(e)(1). However, the fact that a defendant may have served a longer term of imprisonment than the court determines would have been appropriate in view of the amended guideline range shall not, without more, provide a basis for early termination of supervised release. Rather, the court should take into account the totality of circumstances relevant to a decision to terminate supervised release, including the term of supervised release that would have been appropriate in connection with a sentence under the amended guideline range.

Background: Section 3582(c)(2) of Title 18, United States Code, provides: '[I]n the case of a defendant who has been sentenced to a term of imprisonment based on a sentencing range that has subsequently been lowered by the Sentencing Commission pursuant to 28 U.S.C. § 994(o), upon motion of the defendant or the Director of the Bureau of Prisons, or on its own motion, the court may reduce the term of imprisonment, after considering the factors set forth in section 3553(a) to the extent that they are applicable, if such a reduction is consistent with applicable policy statements issued by the Sentencing Commission.'

This policy statement provides guidance for a court when considering a motion under 18 U.S.C. § 3582(c)(2) and implements 28 U.S.C. § 994(u), which provides: 'If the Commission reduces the term of imprisonment recommended in the guidelines applicable to a particular offense or category of offenses, it shall specify in what circumstances and by what amount the sentences of prisoners serving terms of imprisonment for the offense may be reduced.'

Among the factors considered by the Commission in selecting the amendments included in subsection (c) were the purpose of the amendment, the magnitude of the change in the guideline range made by the amendment, and the difficulty of applying the amendment retroactively to determine an amended guideline range under subsection (b).

The listing of an amendment in subsection (c) reflects policy determinations by the Commission that a reduced guideline range is sufficient to achieve the purposes of sentencing and that, in the sound discretion of the court, a reduction in the term of imprisonment may be appropriate for previously sentenced, qualified defendants. The authorization of such a discretionary reduction does not otherwise affect the lawfulness of a previously imposed sentence, does not authorize a reduction in any other component of the sentence, and does not entitle a defendant to a reduced term of imprisonment as a matter of right.

The Commission has not included in this policy statement amendments that generally reduce the maximum of the guideline range by less than six months. This criterion is in accord with the legislative history of 28 U.S.C. § 994(u) (formerly § 994(t)), which states: 'It should be noted that the Committee does not expect that the Commission will recommend adjusting existing sentences under the provision when guidelines are simply refined in a way that might cause isolated instances of existing sentences falling above the old guidelines* or when there is only a minor downward adjustment in the guidelines. The Committee does not believe the courts should be burdened with adjustments in these cases.' S. Rep. 225, 98th Cong., 1st Sess. 180 (1983).

* So in original. Probably should be 'to fall above the amended guidelines'.",

and inserting the following:

"§ 1B1.10. Reduction in Term of Imprisonment as a Result of Amended Guideline Range (Policy Statement)

(a) Authority.—

(1) In General.—In a case in which a defendant is serving a term of imprisonment, and the guideline range applicable to that defendant has subsequently been lowered as a result of an amendment to the Guidelines Manual listed in subsection (c) below, the court may reduce the defendant's term of imprisonment as provided by 18 U.S.C. § 3582(c)(2). As required by 18 U.S.C. § 3582(c)(2), any such reduction in the defendant's term of imprisonment shall be consistent with this policy statement.

(2) Exclusions.—A reduction in the defendant's term of imprisonment is not consistent with this policy statement and therefore is not authorized under 18 U.S.C. § 3582(c)(2) if—

(A) none of the amendments listed in subsection (c) is applicable to the defendant; or

(B) an amendment listed in subsection (c) does not have the effect of lowering the defendant's applicable guideline range.

(3) Limitation.—Consistent with subsection (b), proceedings under 18 U.S.C. § 3582(c)(2) and this policy statement do not constitute a full resentencing of the defendant.

(b) Determination of Reduction in Term of Imprisonment.—

(1) In General.—In determining whether, and to what extent, a reduction in the defendant's term of imprisonment under 18

U.S.C. § 3582(c)(2) and this policy statement is warranted, the court shall determine the amended guideline range that would have been applicable to the defendant if the amendment(s) to the guidelines listed in subsection (c) had been in effect at the time the defendant was sentenced. In making such determination, the court shall substitute only the amendments listed in subsection (c) for the corresponding guideline provisions that were applied when the defendant was sentenced and shall leave all other guideline application decisions unaffected.

(2) Limitations and Prohibition on Extent of Reduction.—

(A) In General.—Except as provided in subdivision (B), the court shall not reduce the defendant's term of imprisonment under 18 U.S.C. § 3582(c)(2) and this policy statement to a term that is less than the minimum of the amended guideline range determined under subdivision (1) of this subsection.

(B) Exception.—If the original term of imprisonment imposed was less than the term of imprisonment provided by the guideline range applicable to the defendant at the time of sentencing, a reduction comparably less than the amended guideline range determined under subdivision (1) of this subsection may be appropriate. However, if the original term of imprisonment constituted a non-guideline sentence determined pursuant to 18 U.S.C. § 3553(a) and United States v. Booker, 543 U.S. 220 (2005), a further reduction generally would not be appropriate.

(C) Prohibition.—In no event may the reduced term of imprisonment be less than the term of imprisonment the defendant has already served.

(c) Amendments covered by this policy statement are listed in Appendix C as follows: 126, 130, 156, 176, 269, 329, 341, 371, 379, 380, 433, 454, 461, 484, 488, 490, 499, 505, 506, 516, 591, 599, 606, 657, and 702.

Commentary

Application Notes:

1. Application of Subsection (a).—

(A) Eligibility.—Eligibility for consideration under 18 U.S.C. § 3582(c)(2) is triggered only by an amendment listed in subsection (c) that lowers the applicable guideline range. Accordingly, a reduction in the defendant's term of imprisonment is not authorized under 18 U.S.C. § 3582(c)(2) and is not consistent with this policy statement if: (i) none of the amendments listed in subsection (c) is applicable to the defendant; or (ii) an amendment listed in subsection

(c) is applicable to the defendant but the amendment does not have the effect of lowering the defendant's applicable guideline range because of the operation of another guideline or statutory provision (e.g., a statutory mandatory minimum term of imprisonment).

(B) Factors for Consideration.—

(i) In General.—Consistent with 18 U.S.C. § 3582(c)(2), the court shall consider the factors set forth in 18 U.S.C. § 3553(a) in determining: (I) whether a reduction in the defendant's term of imprisonment is warranted; and (II) the extent of such reduction, but only within the limits described in subsection (b).

(ii) Public Safety Consideration.—The court shall consider the nature and seriousness of the danger to any person or the community that may be posed by a reduction in the defendant's term of imprisonment in determining: (I) whether such a reduction is warranted; and (II) the extent of such reduction, but only within the limits described in subsection (b).

(iii) Post-Sentencing Conduct.—The court may consider post-sentencing conduct of the defendant that occurred after imposition of the original term of imprisonment in determining: (I) whether a reduction in the defendant's term of imprisonment is warranted; and (II) the extent of such reduction, but only within the limits described in subsection (b).

2. Application of Subsection (b)(1).—In determining the amended guideline range under subsection (b)(1), the court shall substitute only the amendments listed in subsection (c) for the corresponding guideline provisions that were applied when the defendant was sentenced. All other guideline application decisions remain unaffected.

3. Application of Subsection (b)(2).—Under subsection (b)(2), the amended guideline range determined under subsection (b)(1) and the term of imprisonment already served by the defendant limit the extent to which the court may reduce the defendant's term of imprisonment under 18 U.S.C. § 3582(c)(2) and this policy statement. Specifically, if the original term of imprisonment imposed was within the guideline range applicable to the defendant at the time of sentencing, the court shall not reduce the defendant's term of imprisonment to a term that is less than the minimum term of imprisonment provided by the amended guideline range determined under subsection (b)(1). For example, in a case in which: (A) the guideline range applicable to the defendant at the time of sentencing was 41 to 51 months; (B) the original term of imprisonment imposed was 41 months; and (C) the amended guideline range determined under subsection (b)(1) is 30 to 37 months, the court shall not reduce the defendant's term of imprisonment to a term less than 30 months.

If the original term of imprisonment imposed was less than the term of imprisonment provided by the guideline range applicable to the defendant at

Amendment 712 APPENDIX C - VOLUME III November 1, 2013

the time of sentencing, a reduction comparably less than the amended guideline range determined under subsection (b)(1) may be appropriate. For example, in a case in which: (A) the guideline range applicable to the defendant at the time of sentencing was 70 to 87 months; (B) the defendant's original term of imprisonment imposed was 56 months (representing a downward departure of 20 percent below the minimum term of imprisonment provided by the guideline range applicable to the defendant at the time of sentencing); and (C) the amended guideline range determined under subsection (b)(1) is 57 to 71 months, a reduction to a term of imprisonment of 46 months (representing a reduction of approximately 20 percent below the minimum term of imprisonment provided by the amended guideline range determined under subsection (b)(1)) would amount to a comparable reduction and may be appropriate. In no case, however, shall the term of imprisonment be reduced below time served. Subject to these limitations, the sentencing court has the discretion to determine whether, and to what extent, to reduce a term of imprisonment under this section.

4. Supervised Release.—

    (A) Exclusion Relating to Revocation.—Only a term of imprisonment imposed as part of the original sentence is authorized to be reduced under this section. This section does not authorize a reduction in the term of imprisonment imposed upon revocation of supervised release.

    (B) Modification Relating to Early Termination.—If the prohibition in subsection (b)(2)(C) relating to time already served precludes a reduction in the term of imprisonment to the extent the court determines otherwise would have been appropriate as a result of the amended guideline range determined under subsection (b)(1), the court may consider any such reduction that it was unable to grant in connection with any motion for early termination of a term of supervised release under 18 U.S.C. § 3583(e)(1). However, the fact that a defendant may have served a longer term of imprisonment than the court determines would have been appropriate in view of the amended guideline range determined under subsection (b)(1) shall not, without more, provide a basis for early termination of supervised release. Rather, the court should take into account the totality of circumstances relevant to a decision to terminate supervised release, including the term of supervised release that would have been appropriate in connection with a sentence under the amended guideline range determined under subsection (b)(1).

Background: Section 3582(c)(2) of Title 18, United States Code, provides: '[I]n the case of a defendant who has been sentenced to a term of imprisonment based on a sentencing range that has subsequently been lowered by the Sentencing Commission pursuant to 28 U.S.C. § 994(o), upon motion of the defendant or the Director of the Bureau of Prisons, or on its own motion, the court may reduce the term of imprisonment, after considering the factors set forth in section 3553(a) to the extent that they are applicable, if such a reduction is consistent with applicable policy statements issued by the Sentencing Commission.'

This policy statement provides guidance and limitations for a court when considering a motion under 18 U.S.C. § 3582(c)(2) and implements 28 U.S.C.

§ 994(u), which provides: 'If the Commission reduces the term of imprisonment recommended in the guidelines applicable to a particular offense or category of offenses, it shall specify in what circumstances and by what amount the sentences of prisoners serving terms of imprisonment for the offense may be reduced.'

Among the factors considered by the Commission in selecting the amendments included in subsection (c) were the purpose of the amendment, the magnitude of the change in the guideline range made by the amendment, and the difficulty of applying the amendment retroactively to determine an amended guideline range under subsection (b)(1).

The listing of an amendment in subsection (c) reflects policy determinations by the Commission that a reduced guideline range is sufficient to achieve the purposes of sentencing and that, in the sound discretion of the court, a reduction in the term of imprisonment may be appropriate for previously sentenced, qualified defendants. The authorization of such a discretionary reduction does not otherwise affect the lawfulness of a previously imposed sentence, does not authorize a reduction in any other component of the sentence, and does not entitle a defendant to a reduced term of imprisonment as a matter of right.

The Commission has not included in this policy statement amendments that generally reduce the maximum of the guideline range by less than six months. This criterion is in accord with the legislative history of 28 U.S.C. § 994(u) (formerly § 994(t)), which states: 'It should be noted that the Committee does not expect that the Commission will recommend adjusting existing sentences under the provision when guidelines are simply refined in a way that might cause isolated instances of existing sentences falling above the old guidelines* or when there is only a minor downward adjustment in the guidelines. The Committee does not believe the courts should be burdened with adjustments in these cases.' S. Rep. 225, 98th Cong., 1st Sess. 180 (1983).

* So in original. Probably should be 'to fall above the amended guidelines'.".

Reason for Amendment: This amendment makes a number of modifications to § 1B1.10 (Reduction in Term of Imprisonment as a Result of Amended Guideline Range) to clarify when, and to what extent, a reduction in the defendant's term of imprisonment is consistent with the policy statement and is therefore authorized under 18 U.S.C. § 3582(c)(2).

The amendment modifies subsection (a) to state the statutory requirement under 18 U.S.C. § 3582(c)(2) that a reduction in the defendant's term of imprisonment be consistent with the policy statement. The amendment also modifies subsection (a) to state that, consistent with subsection (b), proceedings under 18 U.S.C. § 3582(c)(2) do not constitute a full resentencing of the defendant.

In addition, the amendment amends subsection (a) to clarify circumstances in which a reduction in the defendant's term of imprisonment is not consistent with the policy statement and therefore is not authorized under 18 U.S.C. § 3582(c)(2). Specifically, the amendment provides that a reduction in the defendant's term of imprisonment is not consistent with § 1B1.10 and therefore is not authorized under 18 U.S.C. § 3582(c)(2) if (1) none of the amendments listed in subsection (c) is applicable to the defendant; or (2) an amendment listed in subsection (c) does not have the effect of lowering the defendant's applicable guideline range. Application Note 1 provides further explanation that an amendment may be listed in subsection (c) but not have the effect of lowering the defendant's applicable guideline range because of the operation of another guideline or statutory provision (e.g., a statutory mandatory minimum term of imprisonment). In such a case, a reduction in the defendant's term of imprisonment is not consistent with § 1B1.10 and therefore is not authorized under 18 U.S.C. § 3582(c)(2).

The amendment modifies subsection (b) to clarify the limitations on the extent to which a court may reduce the defendant's term of imprisonment under 18 U.S.C. § 3582(c)(2) and § 1B1.10. Specifically, in subsection (b)(1) the amendment provides that, in determining whether, and to what extent, a reduction in the defendant's term of imprisonment is warranted, the court shall determine the amended guideline range that would have been applicable to the defendant if the amendment(s) to the guidelines listed in subsection (c) had been in effect at the time the defendant was sentenced, substituting only the amendments listed in subsection (c) for the corresponding guideline provisions that were applied when the defendant was sentenced and leaving all other guideline application decisions unaffected.

In subsection (b)(2) the amendment provides further clarification that the court shall not reduce the defendant's term of imprisonment to a term that is less than the minimum of the amended guideline range, except if the original term of imprisonment imposed was less than the term of imprisonment provided by the guideline range applicable to the defendant at the time of sentencing, a reduction comparably less than the amended guideline range may be appropriate. However, if the original term of imprisonment constituted a non-guideline sentence determined pursuant to 18 U.S.C. § 3553(a) and United States v. Booker, 543 U.S. 220 (2005), a further reduction generally would not be appropriate. The amendment clarifies that in no event may the reduced term of imprisonment be less than the term of imprisonment the defendant has already served. The amendment adds in Application Note 3 examples illustrating the limitations on the extent to which a court may reduce a defendant's term of imprisonment under 18 U.S.C. § 3582(c)(2) and § 1B1.10.

The amendment also modifies Application Note 1 to delineate more clearly factors for consideration by the court in determining whether, and to what extent, a reduction in the defendant's term of imprisonment is warranted under 18 U.S.C. § 3582(c)(2). Specifically, the amendment provides that the court shall consider the factors set forth in 18 U.S.C. § 3553(a), as required by 18 U.S.C. § 3582(c)(2), and the nature and seriousness of the danger to any person or the community that may be posed by such a reduction, but only within the limits described in subsection (b). In addition, the amendment provides that the court may consider post-sentencing conduct of the defendant that occurred after imposition of the original term of imprisonment, but only within the limits described in subsection (b).

The amendment makes conforming changes and adds headings to the application notes, and makes conforming changes to the background commentary.

Effective Date: The effective date of this amendment is March 3, 2008.

713. **Amendment:** Section 1B1.10, as amended by Amendment 712, is further amended in subsection (c) by inserting "Covered Amendments.—" before "Amendments"; by striking "and 702"; and by inserting "702, and 706 as amended by 711" before the period.

Reason for Amendment: This amendment expands the listing in § 1B1.10(c) to implement the directive in 28 U.S.C. § 994(u) with respect to guideline amendments that may be considered for retroactive application. The Commission has determined that Amendment 706, as amended by Amendment 711, should be applied retroactively because the applicable standards set forth in the background commentary to § 1B1.10 (Reduction in Term of Imprisonment as a Result of Amended Guideline Range) appear to be met. Specifically: (1) as stated in the reason for amendment accompanying Amendment 706, the purpose of that amendment was to alleviate some of the urgent and compelling problems associated with the penalty structure for crack cocaine offenses; (2) the Commission's analysis of cases potentially eligible for retroactive application of Amendment 706 (available on the Commission's website at www.ussc.gov) indicates that the number of cases potentially involved is substantial, and the magnitude of the change in the guideline range, i.e., two levels, is not difficult to apply in individual cases; and (3) the Commission received persuasive written comment and testimony at its November 13, 2007 public hearing on retroactivity that the administrative burdens of applying Amendment 706 retroactively are manageable. In addition, public safety will be considered in every case because § 1B1.10, as amended by Amendment 712, requires the court, in determining whether and to what extent a reduction in the defendant's term of imprisonment is warranted, to consider the nature and seriousness of the danger to any person or the community that may be posed by such a reduction.

Effective Date: The effective date of this amendment is March 3, 2008.

714. **Amendment:** Section 2B1.1(b) is amended by adding at the end the following:

> "(16) If the offense involved fraud or theft involving any benefit authorized, transported, transmitted, transferred, disbursed, or paid in connection with a declaration of a major disaster or an emergency, increase by 2 levels.".

The Commentary to § 2B1.1 captioned "Application Notes" is amended in Note 3 by inserting after the paragraph that begins "(III) Offenses Under 18 U.S.C. § 1030.—" the following:

> "(IV) Disaster Fraud Cases.—In a case in which subsection (b)(16) applies, reasonably foreseeable pecuniary harm includes the administrative costs to any federal, state, or local government entity or any commercial or not-for-profit entity of recovering the benefit from any recipient thereof who obtained the benefit through fraud or was otherwise ineligible for the benefit that were reasonably foreseeable.".

The Commentary to § 2B1.1 captioned "Application Notes" is amended by redesignating Notes 15 through 19 as Notes 16 through 20, respectively; and by inserting after Note 14 the following:

> "15. Application of Subsection (b)(16).—
>
> Definitions.—For purposes of this subsection:
>
> 'Emergency' has the meaning given that term in 42 U.S.C. § 5122.
>
> 'Major disaster' has the meaning given that term in 42 U.S.C. § 5122.".

The Commentary to § 2B1.1 captioned "Background" is amended by adding at the end the following:

> "Subsection (b)(16) implements the directive in section 5 of Public Law 110–179.".

Appendix A (Statutory Index) is amended by inserting after the line reference to 18 U.S.C. § 1039 the following:

> "18 U.S.C. § 1040   2B1.1".

Amendment 714 APPENDIX C - VOLUME III November 1, 2013

Reason for Amendment: This amendment implements the emergency directive in section 5 of the Emergency and Disaster Assistance Fraud Penalty Enhancement Act of 2007, Pub. L. 110–179. The directive, which requires the Commission to promulgate an amendment under emergency amendment authority by February 6, 2008, directs that the Commission forthwith shall—

> promulgate sentencing guidelines or amend existing sentencing guidelines to provide for increased penalties for persons convicted of fraud or theft offenses in connection with a major disaster declaration under section 401 of the Robert T. Stafford Disaster Relief and Emergency Assistance Act (42 U.S.C. 5170) or an emergency declaration under section 501 of the Robert T. Stafford Disaster Relief and Emergency Assistance Act (42 U.S.C. 5191) . . ..

Section 5(b) of the Act further requires the Commission to—

> (1) ensure that the sentencing guidelines and policy statements reflect the serious nature of the offenses described in subsection (a) and the need for aggressive and appropriate law enforcement action to prevent such offenses;
>
> (2) assure reasonable consistency with other relevant directives and with other guidelines;
>
> (3) account for any aggravating or mitigating circumstances that might justify exceptions, including circumstances for which the sentencing guidelines currently provide sentencing enhancements;
>
> (4) make any necessary conforming changes to the sentencing guidelines; and
>
> (5) assure that the guidelines adequately meet the purposes of sentencing as set forth in section 3553(a)(2) of title 18, United States Code.

The amendment addresses the directive by creating a two-level enhancement that applies if the offense involved fraud or theft in connection with a declaration of a major disaster or emergency, as those terms are defined in 42 U.S.C. § 5122. In addition, the amendment modifies Application Note 3 to provide that for purposes of determining loss under subsection (b)(1), reasonably foreseeable pecuniary harm includes certain administrative costs in such cases.

Effective Date: The effective date of this amendment is February 6, 2008.

715. Amendment: The Commentary to § 2D1.1 captioned "Application Notes" is amended in Note 10 by striking subdivision (D) as follows:

> "(D) Determining Base Offense Level in Offenses Involving Cocaine Base and Other Controlled Substances.—
>
>> (i) In General.—If the offense involves cocaine base ("crack") and one or more other controlled substance, determine the base offense level as follows:
>>
>>> (I) Determine the base offense level for the quantity of cocaine base involved in the offense.
>>>
>>> (II) Using the marihuana equivalency obtained from the table

-1090-

in this subdivision, convert the quantity of cocaine base involved in the offense to its equivalent quantity of marihuana.

Base Offense Level	Marihuana Equivalency
38	6.7 kg of marihuana per g of cocaine base
36	6.7 kg of marihuana per g of cocaine base
34	6 kg of marihuana per g of cocaine base
32	6.7 kg of marihuana per g of cocaine base
30	14 kg of marihuana per g of cocaine base
28	11.4 kg of marihuana per g of cocaine base
26	5 kg of marihuana per g of cocaine base
24	16 kg of marihuana per g of cocaine base
22	15 kg of marihuana per g of cocaine base
20	13.3 kg of marihuana per g of cocaine base
18	10 kg of marihuana per g of cocaine base
16	10 kg of marihuana per g of cocaine base
14	10 kg of marihuana per g of cocaine base
12	10 kg of marihuana per g of cocaine base

(III) Determine the combined marihuana equivalency for the other controlled substance or controlled substances involved in the offense as provided in subdivision (B) of this note.

(IV) Add the quantity of marihuana determined under subdivisions (II) and (III), and look up the total in the Drug Quantity Table to obtain the combined base offense level for all the controlled substances involved in the offense.

(ii) Example.—The case involves 1.5 kg of cocaine, 10 kg of marihuana, and 20 g of cocaine base. Under the Drug Quantity Table, 20 g of cocaine base corresponds to a base offense level of 26. Pursuant to the table in subdivision (II), the base offense level of 26 corresponds to a marihuana equivalency of 5 kg per gram of cocaine base. Therefore, the equivalent quantity of marihuana for the cocaine base is 100 kg (20 g x 5 kg = 100 kg). Pursuant to subdivision (B), the equivalent quantity of marihuana for the cocaine and marihuana is 310 kg. (The cocaine converts to an equivalent of 300 kg of marihuana (1.5 kg x 200 g = 300 kg), which, when added to the 10 kg of marihuana, results in an equivalent quantity of 310 kg of marihuana.) Adding the equivalent quantities of marihuana of all three drug types results in a combined quantity of 410 kg of marihuana (100 kg + 310 kg = 410 kg), which corresponds to a combined base offense level of 28 in the Drug Quantity Table.",

and inserting the following:

"(D) Determining Base Offense Level in Offenses Involving Cocaine Base and Other Controlled Substances.—

(i) In General.—Except as provided in subdivision (ii), if the offense involves cocaine base ('crack') and one or more other controlled substance, determine the combined offense level as provided by subdivision (B) of this note, and reduce the combined offense level by 2 levels.

(ii) Exceptions to 2-level Reduction.—The 2-level reduction provided in subdivision (i) shall not apply in a case in which:

(I) the offense involved 4.5 kg or more, or less than 250 mg, of cocaine base; or

(II) the 2-level reduction results in a combined offense level that is less than the combined offense level that would apply under subdivision (B) of this note if the offense involved only the other controlled substance(s) (i.e., the controlled substance(s) other than cocaine base).

(iii) Examples.—

(I) The case involves 20 gm of cocaine base, 1.5 kg of cocaine, and 10 kg of marihuana. Under the Drug Equivalency Tables in subdivision (E) of this note, 20 gm of cocaine base converts to 400 kg of marihuana (20 gm x 20 kg = 400 kg), and 1.5 kg of cocaine converts to 300 kg of marihuana (1.5 kg x 200 gm = 300 kg), which, when added to the 10 kg of marihuana results in a combined equivalent quantity of 710 kg of marihuana. Under the Drug Quantity Table, 710 kg of marihuana corresponds to a combined offense level of 30, which is reduced by two levels to level 28. For the cocaine and marihuana, their combined equivalent quantity of 310 kg of marihuana corresponds to a combined offense level of 26 under the Drug Quantity Table. Because the combined offense level for all three drug types after the 2-level reduction is not less than the combined base offense level for the cocaine and marihuana, the combined offense level for all three drug types remains level 28.

(II) The case involves 5 gm of cocaine base and 6 kg of heroin. Under the Drug Equivalency Tables in subdivision (E) of this note, 5 gm of cocaine base converts to 100 kg of marihuana (5 gm x 20 kg = 100 kg), and 6 kg of heroin converts to 6,000 kg of marihuana (6,000 gm x 1 kg = 6,000 kg), which, when added together results in a combined equivalent quantity of 6,100 kg of marihuana. Under the Drug Quantity Table, 6,100 kg of marihuana corresponds to a combined offense level of 34, which is reduced by two levels to 32. For the heroin, the 6,000 kg of marihuana corresponds to an offense level 34 under the Drug Quantity Table. Because the combined offense level for the two drug types after the 2-level reduction is less than the offense level for the heroin, the reduction does not apply and the combined offense level for the two drugs remains level 34.".

The Commentary to § 2D1.1 captioned "Application Notes" is amended in Note 10, in subdivision (E), by inserting under the heading "Cocaine and Other Schedule I and II Stimulants (and their immediate precursors)*" the following as the fifteenth entry:

"1 gm Cocaine Base ('Crack') = 20 kg of marihuana".

Reason for Amendment: This amendment modifies the commentary to § 2D1.1 (Unlawful Manufacturing, Importing, Exporting, or Trafficking (Including Possession with Intent to Commit These Offenses); Attempt or Conspiracy) to revise the manner in which combined offense levels are determined in cases involving cocaine base ("crack cocaine") and one or more other controlled substance. Specifically, Application Note 10(D) has resulted in a certain sentencing anomaly in which some offenders have not received the benefit of the two-level reduction provided by Amendment 706 because of the conversion of cocaine base to its marihuana equivalent, and some offenders have received a reduction greater than intended (see Amendment 706).

In order to remedy this anomaly, this amendment modifies the Drug Equivalency Tables to provide that 1 gram of cocaine base equals 20 kilograms of marihuana, as it did prior to Amendment 706, and amends Application Note 10(D) to provide that the combined offense level for an offense involving cocaine base and one or more other controlled substance is determined initially in the same manner as for other polydrug cases under Application Note 10(B). In order to effectuate the two-level reduction intended by Amendment 706, this amendment further provides that the resulting combined offense level is reduced by two levels. However, the amendment provides three exclusions to application of the two-level reduction. First, the two-level reduction does not apply if the offense involved 4.5 kilograms or more of cocaine base because the offense levels for such offenses were unaffected by Amendment 706. Second, the two-level reduction does not apply if the offense involved less than 250 milligrams of cocaine base in order to ensure that the offense level does not reduce below level 12, the minimum offense level in the Drug Quantity Table for offenses involving cocaine base. Third, the two-level reduction does not apply if it would result in a combined offense level that is less than the combined offense level that would apply if the offense involved only the other controlled substance(s) (i.e., the controlled substance(s) other than cocaine base). This third exclusion ensures that offenses involving controlled substances other than cocaine base do not receive a lower offense level than they otherwise would receive merely because cocaine base also is involved in the offense.

Effective Date: The effective date of this amendment is May 1, 2008.

716. **Amendment:** Section 1B1.10 is amended in subsection (c) by striking "and"; and by inserting ", and 715" before the period.

Reason for Amendment: This amendment expands the listing in § 1B1.10(c) (Reduction in Term of Imprisonment as a Result of Amended Guideline Range (Policy Statement)) to include Amendment 715 as an amendment that may be applied retroactively pursuant to 28 U.S.C. § 994(u). The Commission determined for the same reasons accompanying Amendment 713 that Amendment 715 also should be applied retroactively (see Amendment 713).

Effective Date: The effective date of this amendment is May 1, 2008.

717. **Amendment:** Chapter One is amended in the heading by inserting "Introduction," before "Authority and General"; and by striking Part A, including the Editorial Note as follows:

"   PART A - AUTHORITY

§ 1A1.1. Authority

The guidelines, policy statements, and commentary set forth in this Guidelines Manual, including amendments thereto, are promulgated by the United States Sentencing Commission pursuant to: (1) section 994(a) of title 28, United States Code; and (2) with respect to guidelines, policy statements, and commentary promulgated or amended pursuant to specific congressional directive, pursuant to the authority contained in that directive in addition to the authority under section 994(a) of title 28, United States Code.

Commentary

Application Note:

1. Historical Review of Original Introduction.—Part A of Chapter One originally was an introduction to the Guidelines Manual that explained a number of policy decisions made by the Commission when it promulgated the initial set of guidelines. This introduction was amended occasionally between 1987 and 2003. In 2003, as part of the Commission's implementation of the Prosecutorial Remedies and Other Tools to end the Exploitation of Children Today Act of 2003 (the "PROTECT Act", Public Law 108–21), the original introduction was transferred to the Editorial Note at the end of this guideline. The Commission encourages the review of this material for context and historical purposes.

Background: The Sentencing Reform Act of 1984 changed the course of federal sentencing. Among other things, the Act created the United States Sentencing Commission as an independent agency in the Judicial Branch, and directed it to develop guidelines and policy statements for sentencing courts to use when sentencing offenders convicted of federal crimes. Moreover, it empowered the Commission with ongoing responsibilities to monitor the guidelines, submit to Congress appropriate modifications of the guidelines and recommended changes in criminal statutes, and establish education and research programs. The mandate rested on Congressional awareness that sentencing was a dynamic field that requires continuing review by an expert body to revise sentencing policies, in light of application experience, as new criminal statutes are enacted, and as more is learned about what motivates and controls criminal behavior.

Editorial Note: Chapter One, Part A, as in effect on November 1, 1987, read as follows:

"   CHAPTER ONE - INTRODUCTION
        AND GENERAL APPLICATION PRINCIPLES

                PART A - INTRODUCTION

1. Authority

The United States Sentencing Commission ('Commission') is an independent agency in the judicial branch composed of seven voting and two non-voting, ex officio members. Its principal purpose is to establish sentencing policies and practices for the federal criminal justice system that will assure the ends of justice by promulgating detailed guidelines prescribing the appropriate sentences for offenders convicted of federal crimes.

The guidelines and policy statements promulgated by the Commission are issued pursuant to Section 994(a) of Title 28, United States Code.

2. The Statutory Mission

The Comprehensive Crime Control Act of 1984 foresees guidelines that will further the basic purposes of criminal punishment, i.e., deterring crime, incapacitating the offender, providing just punishment, and rehabilitating the offender. It delegates to the Commission broad authority to review and rationalize the federal sentencing process.

The statute contains many detailed instructions as to how this determination should be made, but the most important of them instructs the Commission to create categories of offense behavior and offender characteristics. An offense behavior category might consist, for example, of 'bank robbery/committed with a gun/$2500 taken.' An offender characteristic category might be 'offender with one prior conviction who was not sentenced to imprisonment.' The Commission is required to prescribe guideline ranges that specify an appropriate sentence for each class of convicted persons, to be determined by coordinating the offense behavior categories with the offender characteristic categories. The statute contemplates the guidelines will establish a range of sentences for every coordination of categories. Where the guidelines call for imprisonment, the range must be narrow: the maximum imprisonment cannot exceed the minimum by more than the greater of 25 percent or six months. 28 U.S.C. § 994(b)(2).

The sentencing judge must select a sentence from within the guideline range. If, however, a particular case presents atypical features, the Act allows the judge to depart from the guidelines and sentence outside the range. In that case, the judge must specify reasons for departure. 18 U.S.C. § 3553(b). If the court sentences within the guideline range, an appellate court may review the sentence to see if the guideline was correctly applied. If the judge departs from the guideline range, an appellate court may review the reasonableness of the departure. 18 U.S.C. § 3742. The Act requires the offender to serve virtually all of any prison sentence imposed, for it abolishes parole and substantially restructures good behavior adjustments.

The law requires the Commission to send its initial guidelines to Congress by April 13, 1987, and under the present statute they take effect automatically on November 1, 1987. Pub. L. No. 98-473, § 235, reprinted at 18 U.S.C. § 3551. The Commission may submit guideline amendments each year to Congress between the beginning of a regular session and May 1. The amendments will take effect automatically 180 days after submission unless a law is enacted to the contrary. 28 U.S.C. § 994(p).

The Commission, with the aid of its legal and research staff, considerable public testimony, and written commentary, has developed an initial set of guidelines which it now transmits to Congress. The Commission emphasizes, however, that it views the guideline-writing process as evolutionary. It expects, and the governing statute anticipates, that continuing research, experience, and analysis will result in modifications and revisions to the guidelines by submission of amendments to Congress. To this end, the Commission is established as a permanent agency to monitor sentencing practices in the federal courts throughout the nation.

3. The Basic Approach (Policy Statement)

To understand these guidelines and the rationale that underlies them, one must begin with the three objectives that Congress, in enacting the new sentencing law, sought to achieve. Its basic objective was to enhance the ability of the criminal justice system to reduce crime through an effective, fair sentencing system. To achieve this objective, Congress first sought honesty in sentencing. It sought to avoid the confusion and implicit deception that arises out of the present sentencing system which requires a judge to impose an indeterminate sentence that is automatically reduced in most cases by 'good time' credits. In addition, the parole commission is permitted to determine how much of the remainder of any prison sentence an offender actually will serve. This usually results in a substantial reduction in the effective length of the sentence imposed, with defendants often serving only about one-third of the sentence handed down by the court.

Second, Congress sought <u>uniformity</u> in sentencing by narrowing the wide disparity in sentences imposed by different federal courts for similar criminal conduct by similar offenders. Third, Congress sought <u>proportionality</u> in sentencing through a system that imposes appropriately different sentences for criminal conduct of different severity.

Honesty is easy to achieve: The abolition of parole makes the sentence imposed by the court the sentence the offender will serve. There is a tension, however, between the mandate of uniformity (treat similar cases alike) and the mandate of proportionality (treat different cases differently) which, like the historical tension between law and equity, makes it difficult to achieve both goals simultaneously. Perfect uniformity -- sentencing every offender to five years -- destroys proportionality. Having only a few simple categories of crimes would make the guidelines uniform and easy to administer, but might lump together offenses that are different in important respects. For example, a single category for robbery that lumps together armed and unarmed robberies, robberies with and without injuries, robberies of a few dollars and robberies of millions, is far too broad.

At the same time, a sentencing system tailored to fit every conceivable wrinkle of each case can become unworkable and seriously compromise the certainty of punishment and its deterrent effect. A bank robber with (or without) a gun, which the robber kept hidden (or brandished), might have frightened (or merely warned), injured seriously (or less seriously), tied up (or simply pushed) a guard, a teller or a customer, at night (or at noon), for a bad (or arguably less bad) motive, in an effort to obtain money for other crimes (or for other purposes), in the company of a few (or many) other robbers, for the first (or fourth) time that day, while sober (or under the influence of drugs or alcohol), and so forth.

The list of potentially relevant features of criminal behavior is long; the fact that they can occur in multiple combinations means that the list of possible permutations of factors is virtually endless. The appropriate relationships among these different factors are exceedingly difficult to establish, for they are often context specific. Sentencing courts do not treat the occurrence of a simple bruise identically in all cases, irrespective of whether that bruise occurred in the context of a bank robbery or in the context of a breach of peace. This is so, in part, because the risk that such a harm will occur differs depending on the underlying offense with which it is connected (and therefore may already be counted, to a different degree, in the punishment for the underlying offense); and also because, in part, the relationship between punishment and multiple harms is not simply additive. The relation varies, depending on how much other harm has occurred. (Thus, one cannot easily assign points for each kind of harm and simply add them up, irrespective of context and total amounts.)

The larger the number of subcategories, the greater the complexity that is created and the less workable the system. Moreover, the subcategories themselves, sometimes too broad and sometimes too narrow, will apply and interact in unforeseen ways to unforeseen situations, thus failing to cure the unfairness of a simple, broad category system. Finally, and perhaps most importantly, probation officers and courts, in applying a complex system of subcategories, would have to make a host of decisions about whether the underlying facts are sufficient to bring the case within a particular subcategory. The greater the number of decisions required and the greater their complexity, the greater the risk that different judges will apply the guidelines differently to situations that, in fact, are similar, thereby reintroducing the very disparity that the guidelines were designed to eliminate.

In view of the arguments, it is tempting to retreat to the simple, broad-category approach and to grant judges the discretion to select the proper point along a broad sentencing range. Obviously, however, granting such broad discretion risks correspondingly broad disparity in sentencing, for different courts may exercise their discretionary powers in different ways. That is to say, such an approach risks a return to the wide disparity that Congress established the Commission to limit.

In the end, there is no completely satisfying solution to this practical stalemate. The Commission has had to simply balance the comparative virtues and vices of broad, simple categorization and detailed, complex subcategorization, and within the constraints established by that balance, minimize the discretionary powers of the sentencing court. Any ultimate system will, to a degree, enjoy the benefits and suffer from the drawbacks of each approach.

A philosophical problem arose when the Commission attempted to reconcile the differing perceptions of the purposes of criminal punishment. Most observers of the criminal law agree that the ultimate aim of the law itself, and of punishment in particular, is the control of crime. Beyond this point, however, the consensus seems to break down. Some argue that appropriate punishment should be defined primarily on the basis of the moral principle of 'just deserts.' Under this principle, punishment should be scaled to the offender's culpability and the resulting harms. Thus, if a defendant is less culpable, the defendant deserves less punishment. Others argue that punishment should be imposed primarily on the basis of practical 'crime control' considerations. Defendants sentenced under this scheme should receive the punishment that most effectively lessens the likelihood of future crime, either by deterring others or incapacitating the defendant.

Adherents of these points of view have urged the Commission to choose between them, to accord one primacy over the other. Such a choice would be profoundly difficult. The relevant literature is vast, the arguments deep, and each point of view has much to be said in its favor. A clear-cut Commission decision in favor of one of these approaches would diminish the chance that the guidelines would find the widespread acceptance they need for effective implementation. As a practical matter, in most sentencing decisions both philosophies may prove consistent with the same result.

For now, the Commission has sought to solve both the practical and philosophical problems of developing a coherent sentencing system by taking an empirical approach that uses data estimating the existing sentencing system as a starting point. It has analyzed data drawn from 10,000 presentence investigations, crimes as distinguished in substantive criminal statutes, the United States Parole Commission's guidelines and resulting statistics, and data from other relevant sources, in order to determine which distinctions are important in present practice. After examination, the Commission has accepted, modified, or rationalized the more important of these distinctions.

This empirical approach has helped the Commission resolve its practical problem by defining a list of relevant distinctions that, although of considerable length, is short enough to create a manageable set of guidelines. Existing categories are relatively broad and omit many distinctions that some may believe important, yet they include most of the major distinctions that statutes and presentence data suggest make a significant difference in sentencing decisions. Important distinctions that are ignored in existing practice probably occur rarely. A sentencing judge may take this unusual case into account by departing from the guidelines.

The Commission's empirical approach has also helped resolve its philosophical dilemma. Those who adhere to a just deserts philosophy may concede that the lack of moral consensus might make it difficult to say exactly what punishment is deserved for a particular crime, specified in minute detail. Likewise, those who subscribe to a philosophy of crime control may acknowledge that the lack of sufficient, readily available data might make it difficult to say exactly what punishment will best prevent that crime. Both groups might therefore recognize the wisdom of looking to those distinctions that judges and legislators have, in fact, made over the course of time. These established distinctions are ones that the community believes, or has found over time, to be important from either a moral or crime-control perspective.

The Commission has not simply copied estimates of existing practice as revealed by the data (even though establishing offense values on this basis would help eliminate disparity, for the data represent averages). Rather, it has departed from the data at different points for various important reasons. Congressional statutes, for example, may suggest or require departure, as in the case of the new drug law that imposes increased and mandatory minimum sentences. In addition, the data may reveal inconsistencies in treatment, such as punishing economic crime less severely than other apparently equivalent behavior.

Despite these policy-oriented departures from present practice, the guidelines represent an approach that begins with, and builds upon, empirical data. The guidelines will not please those who wish the Commission to adopt a single philosophical theory and then work deductively to establish a simple and perfect set of categorizations and distinctions. The guidelines may prove acceptable, however, to those who seek more modest, incremental improvements in the status quo, who believe the best is often the enemy of the good, and who recognize that these initial guidelines are but the first step in an evolutionary process. After spending considerable time and resources exploring alternative approaches, the Commission has developed these guidelines as a practical effort toward the achievement of a more honest, uniform, equitable, and therefore effective, sentencing system.

4. The Guidelines' Resolution of Major Issues (Policy Statement)

The guideline-writing process has required the Commission to resolve a host of important policy questions, typically involving rather evenly balanced sets of competing considerations. As an aid to understanding the guidelines, this introduction will briefly discuss several of those issues. Commentary in the guidelines explains others.

(a) Real Offense vs. Charge Offense Sentencing.

One of the most important questions for the Commission to decide was whether to base sentences upon the actual conduct in which the defendant engaged regardless of the charges for which he was indicted or convicted ('real offense' sentencing), or upon the conduct that constitutes the elements of the offense with which the defendant was charged and of which he was convicted ('charge offense' sentencing). A bank robber, for example, might have used a gun, frightened bystanders, taken $50,000, injured a teller, refused to stop when ordered, and raced away damaging property during escape. A pure real offense system would sentence on the basis of all identifiable conduct. A pure charge offense system would overlook some of the harms that did not constitute statutory elements of the offenses of which the defendant was convicted.

The Commission initially sought to develop a real offense system. After all, the present sentencing system is, in a sense, a real offense system. The sentencing court (and the parole commission) take account of the conduct in which the defendant actually engaged, as determined in a presentence report, at the sentencing hearing, or before a parole commission hearing officer. The Commission's initial efforts in this direction, carried out in the spring and early summer of 1986, proved unproductive mostly for practical reasons. To make such a system work, even to formalize and rationalize the status quo, would have required the Commission to decide precisely which harms to take into account, how to add them up, and what kinds of procedures the courts should use to determine the presence or absence of disputed factual elements. The Commission found no practical way to combine and account for the large number of diverse harms arising in different circumstances; nor did it find a practical way to reconcile the need for a fair adjudicatory procedure with the need for a speedy sentencing process, given the potential existence of hosts of adjudicated 'real harm' facts in many typical cases. The effort proposed as a solution to these problems required the use of, for example, quadratic roots and other mathematical operations that the Commission considered too complex to be workable, and, in the Commission's view, risked return to wide disparity in practice.

The Commission therefore abandoned the effort to devise a 'pure' real offense system and instead experimented with a 'modified real offense system,' which it published for public comment in a September 1986 preliminary draft.

This version also foundered in several major respects on the rock of practicality. It was highly complex and its mechanical rules for adding harms (e.g., bodily injury added the same punishment irrespective of context) threatened to work considerable unfairness. Ultimately, the Commission decided that it could not find a practical or fair and efficient way to implement either a pure or modified real offense system of the sort it originally wanted, and it abandoned that approach.

The Commission, in its January 1987 Revised Draft and the present guidelines, has moved closer to a 'charge offense' system. The system is not, however, pure; it has a number of real elements. For one thing, the hundreds of overlapping and duplicative statutory provisions that make up the federal criminal law have forced the Commission to write guidelines that are descriptive of generic conduct rather than tracking purely statutory language. For another, the guidelines, both through specific offense characteristics and adjustments, take account of a number of important, commonly occurring real offense elements such as role in the offense, the presence of a gun, or the amount of money actually taken.

Finally, it is important not to overstate the difference in practice between a real and a charge offense system. The federal criminal system, in practice, deals mostly with drug offenses, bank robberies and white collar crimes (such as fraud, embezzlement, and bribery). For the most part, the conduct that an indictment charges approximates the real and relevant conduct in which the offender actually engaged.

The Commission recognizes its system will not completely cure the problems of a real offense system. It may still be necessary, for example, for a court to determine some particular real facts that will make a difference to the sentence. Yet, the Commission believes that the instances of controversial facts will be far fewer; indeed, there will be few enough so that the court system will be able to devise fair procedures for their determination. See United States v. Fatico, 579 F.2d 707 (2d Cir. 1978) (permitting introduction of hearsay evidence at sentencing hearing under certain conditions), on remand, 458 F. Supp. 388 (E.D.N.Y. 1978), aff'd, 603 F.2d 1053 (2d Cir. 1979) (holding that the government need not prove facts at sentencing hearing beyond a reasonable doubt), cert. denied, 444 U.S. 1073 (1980).

The Commission also recognizes that a charge offense system has drawbacks of its own. One of the most important is its potential to turn over to the prosecutor the power to determine the sentence by increasing or decreasing the number (or content) of the counts in an indictment. Of course, the defendant's actual conduct (that which the prosecutor can prove in court) imposes a natural limit upon the prosecutor's ability to increase a defendant's sentence. Moreover, the Commission has written its rules for the treatment of multicount convictions with an eye toward eliminating unfair treatment that might flow from count manipulation. For example, the guidelines treat a three-count indictment, each count of which charges sale of 100 grams of heroin, or theft of $10,000, the same as a single-count indictment charging sale of 300 grams of heroin or theft of $30,000. Further, a sentencing court may control any inappropriate manipulation of the indictment through use of its power to depart from the specific guideline sentence. Finally, the Commission will closely monitor problems arising out of count manipulation and will make appropriate adjustments should they become necessary.

(b) Departures.

The new sentencing statute permits a court to depart from a guideline-specified sentence only when it finds 'an aggravating or mitigating circumstance . . .that was not adequately taken into consideration by the Sentencing Commission . . .'. 18 U.S.C. § 3553(b). Thus, in principle, the Commission, by specifying that it had adequately considered a particular factor, could prevent a court from using it as grounds for departure. In this initial set of guidelines, however, the Commission does not so limit the courts' departure powers. The Commission intends the sentencing courts to treat each guideline as carving out a 'heartland,' a set of typical cases embodying the conduct that each guideline describes. When a court finds an atypical case, one to which a particular guideline linguistically applies but where conduct significantly differs from the norm, the court may consider whether a departure is warranted. Section 5H1.10 (Race, Sex, National Origin, Creed, Religion, Socio-Economic Status), the third sentence of § 5H1.4, and the last sentence of § 5K2.12, list a few factors that the court cannot take into account as grounds for departure. With those specific exceptions, however, the Commission does not intend to limit the kinds of factors (whether or not mentioned anywhere else in the guidelines) that could constitute grounds for departure in an unusual case.

The Commission has adopted this departure policy for two basic reasons. First is the difficulty of foreseeing and capturing a single set of guidelines that encompasses the vast range of human conduct potentially relevant to a sentencing decision. The Commission also recognizes that in the initial set of guidelines it need not do so. The Commission is a permanent body, empowered by law to write and rewrite guidelines, with progressive changes, over many years. By monitoring when courts depart from the guidelines and by analyzing their stated reasons for doing so, the Commission, over time, will be able to create more accurate guidelines that specify precisely where departures should and should not be permitted.

Second, the Commission believes that despite the courts' legal freedom to depart from the guidelines, they will not do so very often. This is because the guidelines, offense by offense, seek to take account of those factors that the Commission's sentencing data indicate make a significant difference in sentencing at the present time. Thus, for example, where the presence of actual physical injury currently makes an important difference in final sentences, as in the case of robbery, assault, or arson, the guidelines specifically instruct the judge to use this factor to augment the sentence. Where the guidelines do not specify an augmentation or diminution, this is generally because the sentencing data do not permit the Commission, at this time, to conclude that the factor is empirically important in relation to the particular offense. Of course, a factor (say physical injury) may nonetheless sometimes occur in connection with a crime (such as fraud) where it does not often occur. If, however, as the data indicate, such occurrences are rare, they are precisely the type of events that the court's departure powers were designed to cover -- unusual cases outside the range of the more typical offenses for which the guidelines were designed. Of course, the Commission recognizes that even its collection and analysis of 10,000 presentence reports are an imperfect source of data sentencing estimates. Rather than rely heavily at this time upon impressionistic accounts, however, the Commission believes it wiser to wait and collect additional data from our continuing monitoring process that may demonstrate how the guidelines work in practice before further modification.

It is important to note that the guidelines refer to three different kinds of departure. The first kind, which will most frequently be used, is in effect an interpolation between two adjacent, numerically oriented guideline rules. A specific offense characteristic, for example, might require an increase of four levels for serious bodily injury but two levels for bodily injury. Rather than requiring a court to force middle instances into either the 'serious' or the 'simple' category, the guideline commentary suggests that the court may interpolate and select a midpoint increase of three levels. The Commission has decided to call such an interpolation a 'departure' in light of the legal views that a guideline providing for a range of increases in offense levels may violate the statute's 25 percent rule (though others have presented contrary legal arguments). Since interpolations are technically departures, the courts will have to provide reasons for their selection, and it will be subject to review for 'reasonableness' on appeal. The Commission believes, however, that a simple reference by the court to the 'mid-category' nature of the facts will typically provide sufficient reason. It does not foresee serious practical problems arising out of the application of the appeal provisions to this form of departure.

The second kind involves instances in which the guidelines provide specific guidance for departure, by analogy or by other numerical or non-numerical suggestions. For example, the commentary to § 2G1.1 (Transportation for Prostitution), recommends a downward adjustment of eight levels where commercial purpose was not involved. The Commission intends such suggestions as policy guidance for the courts. The Commission expects that most departures will reflect the suggestions, and that the courts of appeals may prove more likely to find departures 'unreasonable' where they fall outside suggested levels.

A third kind of departure will remain unguided. It may rest upon grounds referred to in Chapter 5, Part H, or on grounds not mentioned in the guidelines. While Chapter 5, Part H lists factors that the Commission believes may constitute grounds for departure, those suggested grounds are not exhaustive. The Commission recognizes that there may be other grounds for departure that are not mentioned; it also believes there may be cases in which a departure outside suggested levels is warranted. In its view, however, such cases will be highly unusual.

(c) <u>Plea Agreements</u>.

Nearly ninety percent of all federal criminal cases involve guilty pleas, and many of these cases involve some form of plea agreement. Some commentators on early Commission guideline drafts have urged the Commission not to attempt any major reforms of the agreement process, on the grounds that any set of guidelines that threatens to radically change present practice also threatens to make the federal system unmanageable. Others, starting with the same facts, have argued that guidelines which fail to control and limit plea agreements would leave untouched a 'loophole' large enough to undo the good that sentencing guidelines may bring. Still other commentators make both sets of arguments.

The Commission has decided that these initial guidelines will not, in general, make significant changes in current plea agreement practices. The court will accept or reject any such agreements primarily in accordance with the rules set forth in Fed.R.Crim.P. 11(e). The Commission will collect data on the courts' plea practices and will analyze this information to determine when and why the courts accept or reject plea agreements. In light of this information and analysis, the Commission will seek to further regulate the plea agreement process as appropriate.

The Commission nonetheless expects the initial set of guidelines to have a positive, rationalizing impact upon plea agreements for two reasons. First, the guidelines create a clear, definite expectation in respect to the sentence that a court will impose if a trial takes place. Insofar as a prosecutor and defense attorney seek to agree about a likely sentence or range of sentences, they will no longer work in the dark. This fact alone should help to reduce irrationality in respect to actual sentencing outcomes. Second, the guidelines create a norm to which judges will likely refer when they decide whether, under Rule 11(e), to accept or to reject a plea agreement or recommendation. Since they will have before them the norm, the relevant factors (as disclosed in the plea agreement), and the reason for the agreement, they will find it easier than at present to determine whether there is sufficient reason to accept a plea agreement that departs from the norm.

(d) Probation and Split Sentences.

The statute provides that the guidelines are to 'reflect the general appropriateness of imposing a sentence other than imprisonment in cases in which the defendant is a first offender who has not been convicted of a crime of violence or an otherwise serious offense . . .' 28 U.S.C. § 994(j). Under present sentencing practice, courts sentence to probation an inappropriately high percentage of offenders guilty of certain economic crimes, such as theft, tax evasion, antitrust offenses, insider trading, fraud, and embezzlement, that in the Commission's view are 'serious.' If the guidelines were to permit courts to impose probation instead of prison in many or all such cases, the present sentences would continue to be ineffective.

The Commission's solution to this problem has been to write guidelines that classify as 'serious' (and therefore subject to mandatory prison sentences) many offenses for which probation is now frequently given. At the same time, the guidelines will permit the sentencing court to impose short prison terms in many such cases. The Commission's view is that the definite prospect of prison, though the term is short, will act as a significant deterrent to many of these crimes, particularly when compared with the status quo where probation, not prison, is the norm.

More specifically, the guidelines work as follows in respect to a first offender. For offense levels one through six, the sentencing court may elect to sentence the offender to probation (with or without confinement conditions) or to a prison term. For offense levels seven through ten, the court may substitute probation for a prison term, but the probation must include confinement conditions (community confinement or intermittent confinement). For offense levels eleven and twelve, the court must impose at least one half the minimum confinement sentence in the form of prison confinement, the remainder to be served on supervised release with a condition of community confinement. The Commission, of course, has not dealt with the single acts of aberrant behavior that still may justify probation at higher offense levels through departures.

    (e)   <u>Multi-Count Convictions</u>.

The Commission, like other sentencing commissions, has found it particularly difficult to develop rules for sentencing defendants convicted of multiple violations of law, each of which makes up a separate count in an indictment. The reason it is difficult is that when a defendant engages in conduct that causes several harms, each additional harm, even if it increases the extent to which punishment is warranted, does not necessarily warrant a proportionate increase in punishment. A defendant who assaults others during a fight, for example, may warrant more punishment if he injures ten people than if he injures one, but his conduct does not necessarily warrant ten times the punishment. If it did, many of the simplest offenses, for reasons that are often fortuitous, would lead to life sentences of imprisonment -- sentences that neither 'just deserts' nor 'crime control' theories of punishment would find justified.

Several individual guidelines provide special instructions for increasing punishment when the conduct that is the subject of that count involves multiple occurrences or has caused several harms. The guidelines also provide general rules for aggravating punishment in light of multiple harms charged separately in separate counts. These rules may produce occasional anomalies, but normally they will permit an appropriate degree of aggravation of punishment when multiple offenses that are the subjects of separate counts take place.

These rules are set out in Chapter Three, Part D. They essentially provide: (1) When the conduct involves fungible items, <u>e.g.</u>, separate drug transactions or thefts of money, the amounts are added and the guidelines apply to the total amount. (2) When nonfungible harms are involved, the offense level for the most serious count is increased (according to a somewhat diminishing scale) to reflect the existence of other counts of conviction.

The rules have been written in order to minimize the possibility that an arbitrary casting of a single transaction into several counts will produce a longer sentence. In addition, the sentencing court will have adequate power to prevent such a result through departures where necessary to produce a mitigated sentence.

    (f)   <u>Regulatory Offenses</u>.

Regulatory statutes, though primarily civil in nature, sometimes contain criminal provisions in respect to particularly harmful activity. Such criminal provisions often describe not only substantive offenses, but also more technical, administratively-related offenses such as failure to keep accurate records or to provide requested information. These criminal statutes pose two problems. First, which criminal regulatory provisions should the Commission initially consider, and second, how should it treat technical or administratively-related criminal violations?

In respect to the first problem, the Commission found that it cannot comprehensively treat all regulatory violations in the initial set of guidelines. There are hundreds of such provisions scattered throughout the United States Code. To find all potential violations would involve examination of each individual federal regulation. Because of this practical difficulty, the Commission has sought to determine, with the assistance of the Department of Justice and several regulatory agencies, which criminal regulatory offenses are particularly important in light of the need for enforcement of the general regulatory scheme. The Commission has sought to treat these offenses in these initial guidelines. It will address the less common regulatory offenses in the future.

In respect to the second problem, the Commission has developed a system for treating technical recordkeeping and reporting offenses, dividing them into four categories.

First, in the simplest of cases, the offender may have failed to fill out a form intentionally, but without knowledge or intent that substantive harm would likely follow. He might fail, for example, to keep an accurate record of toxic substance transport, but that failure may not lead, nor be likely to lead, to the release or improper treatment of any toxic substance. Second, the same failure may be accompanied by a significant likelihood that substantive harm will occur; it may make a release of a toxic substance more likely. Third, the same failure may have led to substantive harm. Fourth, the failure may represent an effort to conceal a substantive harm that has occurred.

The structure of a typical guideline for a regulatory offense is as follows:

(1) The guideline provides a low base offense level (6) aimed at the first type of recordkeeping or reporting offense. It gives the court the legal authority to impose a punishment ranging from probation up to six months of imprisonment.

(2) Specific offense characteristics designed to reflect substantive offenses that do occur (in respect to some regulatory offenses), or that are likely to occur, increase the offense level.

(3) A specific offense characteristic also provides that a recordkeeping or reporting offense that conceals a substantive offense will be treated like the substantive offense.

The Commission views this structure as an initial effort. It may revise its approach in light of further experience and analysis of regulatory crimes.

(g) Sentencing Ranges.

In determining the appropriate sentencing ranges for each offense, the Commission began by estimating the average sentences now being served within each category. It also examined the sentence specified in congressional statutes, in the parole guidelines, and in other relevant, analogous sources. The Commission's forthcoming detailed report will contain a comparison between estimates of existing sentencing practices and sentences under the guidelines.

While the Commission has not considered itself bound by existing sentencing practice, it has not tried to develop an entirely new system of sentencing on the basis of theory alone. Guideline sentences in many instances will approximate existing practice, but adherence to the guidelines will help to eliminate wide disparity. For example, where a high percentage of persons now receive probation, a guideline may include one or more specific offense characteristics in an effort to distinguish those types of defendants who now receive probation from those who receive more severe sentences. In some instances, short sentences of incarceration for all offenders in a category have been substituted for a current sentencing practice of very wide variability in which some defendants receive probation while others receive several years in prison for the same offense. Moreover, inasmuch as those who currently plead guilty often receive lesser sentences, the guidelines also permit the court to impose lesser sentences on those defendants who accept responsibility and those who cooperate with the government.

The Commission has also examined its sentencing ranges in light of their likely impact upon prison population. Specific legislation, such as the new drug law and the career offender provisions of the sentencing law, require the Commission to promulgate rules that will lead to substantial prison population increases. These increases will occur irrespective of any guidelines. The guidelines themselves, insofar as they reflect policy decisions made by the Commission (rather than legislated mandatory minimum, or career offender, sentences), will lead to an increase in prison population that computer models, produced by the Commission and the Bureau of Prisons, estimate at approximately 10 percent, over a period of ten years.

(h) The Sentencing Table.

The Commission has established a sentencing table. For technical and practical reasons it has 43 levels. Each row in the table contains levels that overlap with the levels in the preceding and succeeding rows. By overlapping the levels, the table should discourage unnecessary litigation. Both prosecutor and defendant will realize that the difference between one level and another will not necessarily make a difference in the sentence that the judge imposes. Thus, little purpose will be served in protracted litigation trying to determine, for example, whether $10,000 or $11,000 was obtained as a result of a fraud. At the same time, the rows work to increase a sentence proportionately. A change of 6 levels roughly doubles the sentence irrespective of the level at which one starts. The Commission, aware of the legal requirement that the maximum of any range cannot exceed the minimum by more than the greater of 25 percent or six months, also wishes to permit courts the greatest possible range for exercising discretion. The table overlaps offense levels meaningfully, works proportionately, and at the same time preserves the maximum degree of allowable discretion for the judge within each level.

Similarly, many of the individual guidelines refer to tables that correlate amounts of money with offense levels. These tables often have many, rather than a few levels. Again, the reason is to minimize the likelihood of unnecessary litigation. If a money table were to make only a few distinctions, each distinction would become more important and litigation as to which category an offender fell within would become more likely. Where a table has many smaller monetary distinctions, it minimizes the likelihood of litigation, for the importance of the precise amount of money involved is considerably less.

5. A Concluding Note

The Commission emphasizes that its approach in this initial set of guidelines is one of caution. It has examined the many hundreds of criminal statutes in the United States Code. It has begun with those that are the basis for a significant number of prosecutions. It has sought to place them in a rational order. It has developed additional distinctions relevant to the application of these provisions, and it has applied sentencing ranges to each resulting category. In doing so, it has relied upon estimates of existing sentencing practices as revealed by its own statistical analyses, based on summary reports of some 40,000 convictions, a sample of 10,000 augmented presentence reports, the parole guidelines and policy judgments.

The Commission recognizes that some will criticize this approach as overly cautious, as representing too little a departure from existing practice. Yet, it will cure wide disparity. The Commission is a permanent body that can amend the guidelines each year. Although the data available to it, like all data, are imperfect, experience with these guidelines will lead to additional information and provide a firm empirical basis for revision.

Finally, the guidelines will apply to approximately 90 percent of all cases in the federal courts. Because of time constraints and the nonexistence of statistical information, some offenses that occur infrequently are not considered in this initial set of guidelines. They will, however, be addressed in the near future. Their exclusion from this initial submission does not reflect any judgment about their seriousness. The Commission has also deferred promulgation of guidelines pertaining to fines, probation and other sanctions for organizational defendants, with the exception of antitrust violations. The Commission also expects to address this area in the near future.".

Amendments

1989 Amendments

Amendment 67 amended Subpart 4(b) in the first sentence of the first paragraph by striking ". . .that was" and inserting "of a kind, or to a degree,"; in the second sentence of the last paragraph by striking "Part H" and inserting "Part K (Departures)"; and in the third sentence of the last paragraph by striking "Part H" and inserting "Part K".

Amendment 68 amended Subpart 4(b) in the first sentence of the fourth paragraph by striking "three" and inserting "two"; in the fourth paragraph by striking the second through eighth sentences as follows:

"The first kind, which will most frequently be used, is in effect an interpolation between two adjacent, numerically oriented guideline rules. A specific offense characteristic, for example, might require an increase of four levels for serious bodily injury but two levels for bodily injury. Rather than requiring a court to force middle instances into either the 'serious' or the 'simple' category, the guideline commentary suggests that the court may interpolate and select a midpoint increase of three levels. The Commission has decided to call such an interpolation a 'departure' in light of the legal views that a guideline providing for a range of increases in offense levels may violate the statute's 25 percent rule (though other have presented contrary legal arguments). Since interpolations are technically departures, the courts will have to provide reasons for their selection, and it will be subject to review for 'reasonableness' on appeal. The Commission believes, however, that a simple reference by the court to the 'mid-category' nature of the facts will typically provide sufficient reason. It does not foresee serious practical problems arising out of the application of the appeal provisions to this form of departure.";

in the first sentence of the fifth paragraph by striking "second" and inserting "first"; and in the first sentence of the sixth paragraph by striking "third" and inserting "second".

1990 Amendment

Amendment 307 amended Subparts 2 through 5 to read as follows:

"2.   The Statutory Mission

The Sentencing Reform Act of 1984 (Title II of the Comprehensive Crime

Control Act of 1984) provides for the development of guidelines that will further the basic purposes of criminal punishment: deterrence, incapacitation, just punishment, and rehabilitation. The Act delegates broad authority to the Commission to review and rationalize the federal sentencing process.

The Act contains detailed instructions as to how this determination should be made, the most important of which directs the Commission to create categories of offense behavior and offender characteristics. An offense behavior category might consist, for example, of 'bank robbery/committed with a gun/ $2500 taken.' An offender characteristic category might be 'offender with one prior conviction not resulting in imprisonment.' The Commission is required to prescribe guideline ranges that specify an appropriate sentence for each class of convicted persons determined by coordinating the offense behavior categories with the offender characteristic categories. Where the guidelines call for imprisonment, the range must be narrow: the maximum of the range cannot exceed the minimum by more than the greater of 25 percent or six months. 28 U.S.C. § 994(b)(2).

Pursuant to the Act, the sentencing court must select a sentence from within the guideline range. If, however, a particular case presents atypical features, the Act allows the court to depart from the guidelines and sentence outside the prescribed range. In that case, the court must specify reasons for departure. 18 U.S.C. § 3553(b). If the court sentences within the guideline range, an appellate court may review the sentence to determine whether the guidelines were correctly applied. If the court departs from the guideline range, an appellate court may review the reasonableness of the departure. 18 U.S.C. § 3742. The Act also abolishes parole, and substantially reduces and restructures good behavior adjustments.

The Commission's initial guidelines were submitted to Congress on April 13, 1987. After the prescribed period of Congressional review, the guidelines took effect on November 1, 1987, and apply to all offenses committed on or after that date. The Commission has the authority to submit guideline amendments each year to Congress between the beginning of a regular Congressional session and May 1. Such amendments automatically take effect 180 days after submission unless a law is enacted to the contrary. 28 U.S.C. § 994(p).

The initial sentencing guidelines and policy statements were developed after extensive hearings, deliberation, and consideration of substantial public comment. The Commission emphasizes, however, that it views the guideline-writing process as evolutionary. It expects, and the governing statute anticipates, that continuing research, experience, and analysis will result in modifications and revisions to the guidelines through submission of amendments to Congress. To this end, the Commission is established as a permanent agency to monitor sentencing practices in the federal courts.

3. <u>The Basic Approach</u> (Policy Statement)

To understand the guidelines and their underlying rationale, it is important to focus on the three objectives that Congress sought to achieve in enacting the Sentencing Reform Act of 1984. The Act's basic objective was to enhance the ability of the criminal justice system to combat crime through an effective, fair sentencing system. To achieve this end, Congress first sought honesty in sentencing. It sought to avoid the confusion and implicit deception that arose out of the pre-guidelines sentencing system which required the court to impose an indeterminate sentence of imprisonment and empowered the parole commission to determine how much of the sentence an offender actually would serve in prison. This practice usually resulted in a substantial reduction in the effective length of the sentence imposed, with defendants often serving only about one-third of the sentence imposed by the court.

Second, Congress sought reasonable uniformity in sentencing by narrowing the wide disparity in sentences imposed for similar criminal offenses committed by similar offenders. Third, Congress sought proportionality in sentencing through a system that imposes appropriately different sentences for criminal conduct of differing severity.

Honesty is easy to achieve: the abolition of parole makes the sentence imposed by the court the sentence the offender will serve, less approximately fifteen percent for good behavior. There is a tension, however, between the mandate of uniformity and the mandate of proportionality. Simple uniformity -- sentencing every offender to five years -- destroys proportionality.

Having only a few simple categories of crimes would make the guidelines uniform and easy to administer, but might lump together offenses that are different in important respects. For example, a single category for robbery that included armed and unarmed robberies, robberies with and without injuries, robberies of a few dollars and robberies of millions, would be far too broad.

A sentencing system tailored to fit every conceivable wrinkle of each case would quickly become unworkable and seriously compromise the certainty of punishment and its deterrent effect. For example: a bank robber with (or without) a gun, which the robber kept hidden (or brandished), might have frightened (or merely warned), injured seriously (or less seriously), tied up (or simply pushed) a guard, teller, or customer, at night (or at noon), in an effort to obtain money for other crimes (or for other purposes), in the company of a few (or many) other robbers, for the first (or fourth) time.

The list of potentially relevant features of criminal behavior is long; the fact that they can occur in multiple combinations means that the list of possible permutations of factors is virtually endless. The appropriate relationships among these different factors are exceedingly difficult to establish, for they are often context specific. Sentencing courts do not treat the occurrence of a simple bruise identically in all cases, irrespective of whether that bruise occurred in the context of a bank robbery or in the context of a breach of peace. This is so, in part, because the risk that such a harm will occur differs depending on the underlying offense with which it is connected; and also because, in part, the relationship between punishment and multiple harms is not simply additive. The relation varies depending on how much other harm has occurred. Thus, it would not be proper to assign points for each kind of harm and simply add them up, irrespective of context and total amounts.

The larger the number of subcategories of offense and offender characteristics included in the guidelines, the greater the complexity and the less workable the system. Moreover, complex combinations of offense and offender characteristics would apply and interact in unforeseen ways to unforeseen situations, thus failing to cure the unfairness of a simple, broad category system. Finally, and perhaps most importantly, probation officers and courts, in applying a complex system having numerous subcategories, would be required to make a host of decisions regarding whether the underlying facts were sufficient to bring the case within a particular subcategory. The greater the number of decisions required and the greater their complexity, the greater the risk that different courts would apply the guidelines differently to situations that, in fact, are similar, thereby reintroducing the very disparity that the guidelines were designed to reduce.

In view of the arguments, it would have been tempting to retreat to the simple, broad category approach and to grant courts the discretion to select the proper point along a broad sentencing range. Granting such broad discretion, however, would have risked correspondingly broad disparity in sentencing, for different courts may exercise their discretionary powers in different ways. Such an approach would have risked a return to the wide disparity that Congress established the Commission to reduce and would have been contrary to the Commission's mandate set forth in the Sentencing Reform Act of 1984.

In the end, there was no completely satisfying solution to this problem. The Commission had to balance the comparative virtues and vices of broad, simple categorization and detailed, complex subcategorization, and within the constraints established by that balance, minimize the discretionary powers of the sentencing court. Any system will, to a degree, enjoy the benefits and suffer from the drawbacks of each approach.

A philosophical problem arose when the Commission attempted to reconcile the differing perceptions of the purposes of criminal punishment. Most observers of the criminal law agree that the ultimate aim of the law itself, and of punishment in particular, is the control of crime. Beyond this point, however, the consensus seems to break down. Some argue that appropriate punishment should be defined primarily on the basis of the principle of 'just deserts.' Under this principle, punishment should be scaled to the offender's culpability and the resulting harms. Others argue that punishment should be imposed primarily on the basis of practical 'crime control' considerations. This theory calls for sentences that most effectively lessen the likelihood of future crime, either by deterring others or incapacitating the defendant.

Adherents of each of these points of view urged the Commission to choose between them and accord one primacy over the other. As a practical matter, however, this choice was unnecessary because in most sentencing decisions the application of either philosophy will produce the same or similar results.

In its initial set of guidelines, the Commission sought to solve both the practical and philosophical problems of developing a coherent sentencing system by taking an empirical approach that used as a starting point data estimating pre-guidelines sentencing practice. It analyzed data drawn from 10,000 presentence investigations, the differing elements of various crimes as distinguished in substantive criminal statutes, the United States Parole Commission's guidelines and statistics, and data from other relevant sources in order to determine which distinctions were important in pre-guidelines practice. After consideration, the Commission accepted, modified, or rationalized these distinctions.

This empirical approach helped the Commission resolve its practical problem by defining a list of relevant distinctions that, although of considerable length, was short enough to create a manageable set of guidelines. Existing categories are relatively broad and omit distinctions that some may believe important, yet they include most of the major distinctions that statutes and data suggest made a significant difference in sentencing decisions. Relevant distinctions not reflected in the guidelines probably will occur rarely and sentencing courts may take such unusual cases into account by departing from the guidelines.

The Commission's empirical approach also helped resolve its philosophical dilemma. Those who adhere to a just deserts philosophy may concede that the lack of consensus might make it difficult to say exactly what punishment is deserved for a particular crime. Likewise, those who subscribe to a philosophy of crime control may acknowledge that the lack of sufficient data might make it difficult to determine exactly the punishment that will best prevent that crime. Both groups might therefore recognize the wisdom of looking to those distinctions that judges and legislators have, in fact, made over the course of time. These established distinctions are ones that the community believes, or has found over time, to be important from either a just deserts or crime control perspective.

The Commission did not simply copy estimates of pre-guidelines practice as revealed by the data, even though establishing offense values on this basis would help eliminate disparity because the data represent averages. Rather, it departed from the data at different points for various important reasons. Congressional statutes, for example, suggested or required departure, as in the case of the Anti-Drug Abuse Act of 1986 that imposed increased and mandatory minimum sentences. In addition, the data revealed inconsistencies in treatment, such as punishing economic crime less severely than other apparently equivalent behavior.

Despite these policy-oriented departures from pre-guidelines practice, the guidelines represent an approach that begins with, and builds upon, empirical data. The guidelines will not please those who wish the Commission to adopt a single philosophical theory and then work deductively to establish a simple and perfect set of categorizations and distinctions. The guidelines may prove acceptable, however, to those who seek more modest, incremental improvements in the status quo, who believe the best is often the enemy of the good, and who recognize that these guidelines are, as the Act contemplates, but the first step in an evolutionary process. After spending considerable time and resources exploring alternative approaches, the Commission developed these guidelines as a practical effort toward the achievement of a more honest, uniform, equitable, proportional, and therefore effective sentencing system.

4. <u>The Guidelines' Resolution of Major Issues</u> (Policy Statement)

The guideline-drafting process required the Commission to resolve a host of important policy questions typically involving rather evenly balanced sets of competing considerations. As an aid to understanding the guidelines, this introduction briefly discusses several of those issues; commentary in the guidelines explains others.

(a) <u>Real Offense vs. Charge Offense Sentencing</u>.

One of the most important questions for the Commission to decide was whether to base sentences upon the actual conduct in which the defendant engaged regardless of the charges for which he was indicted or convicted ('real offense' sentencing), or upon the conduct that constitutes the elements of the offense for which the defendant was charged and of which he was convicted ('charge offense' sentencing). A bank robber, for example, might have used a gun, frightened bystanders, taken $50,000, injured a teller, refused to stop when ordered, and raced away damaging property during his escape. A pure real offense system would sentence on the basis of all identifiable conduct. A pure charge offense system would overlook some of the harms that did not constitute statutory elements of the offenses of which the defendant was convicted.

The Commission initially sought to develop a pure real offense system. After all, the pre-guidelines sentencing system was, in a sense, this type of system. The sentencing court and the parole commission took account of the conduct in which the defendant actually engaged, as determined in a presentence report, at the sentencing hearing, or before a parole commission hearing officer. The Commission's initial efforts in this direction, carried out in the spring and early summer of 1986, proved unproductive, mostly for practical reasons. To make such a system work, even to formalize and rationalize the status quo, would have required the Commission to decide precisely which harms to take into account, how to add them up, and what kinds of procedures the courts should use to determine the presence or absence of disputed factual elements. The Commission found no practical way to combine and account for the large number of diverse harms arising in different circumstances; nor did it find a practical way to reconcile the need for a fair adjudicatory procedure with the need for a speedy sentencing process given the potential existence of hosts of adjudicated 'real harm' facts in many typical cases. The effort proposed as a solution to these problems required the use of, for example, quadratic roots and other mathematical operations that the Commission considered too complex to be workable. In the Commission's view, such a system risked return to wide disparity in sentencing practice.

In its initial set of guidelines submitted to Congress in April 1987, the Commission moved closer to a charge offense system. This system, however, does contain a significant number of real offense elements. For one thing, the hundreds of overlapping and duplicative statutory provisions that make up the federal criminal law forced the Commission to write guidelines that are descriptive of generic conduct rather than guidelines that track purely statutory language. For another, the guidelines take account of a number of important, commonly occurring real offense elements such as role in the offense, the presence of a gun, or the amount of money actually taken, through alternative base offense levels, specific offense characteristics, cross references, and adjustments.

The Commission recognized that a charge offense system has drawbacks of its own. One of the most important is the potential it affords prosecutors to influence sentences by increasing or decreasing the number of counts in an indictment. Of course, the defendant's actual conduct (that which the prosecutor can prove in court) imposes a natural limit upon the prosecutor's ability to increase a defendant's sentence. Moreover, the Commission has written its rules for the treatment of multicount convictions with an eye toward eliminating unfair treatment that might flow from count manipulation. For example, the guidelines treat a three-count indictment, each count of which charges sale of 100 grams of heroin or theft of $10,000, the same as a single-count indictment charging sale of 300 grams of heroin or theft of $30,000. Furthermore, a sentencing court may control any inappropriate manipulation of the indictment through use of its departure power. Finally, the Commission will closely monitor charging and plea agreement practices and will make appropriate adjustments should they become necessary.

(b)   Departures.

The sentencing statute permits a court to depart from a guideline-specified sentence only when it finds 'an aggravating or mitigating circumstance of a kind, or to a degree, not adequately taken into consideration by the Sentencing Commission in formulating the guidelines that should result in a sentence different from that described.' 18 U.S.C. § 3553(b). The Commission intends the sentencing courts to treat each guideline as carving out a 'heartland,' a set of typical cases embodying the conduct that each guideline describes. When a court finds an atypical case, one to which a particular guideline linguistically applies but where conduct significantly differs from the norm, the court may consider whether a departure is warranted. Section 5H1.10 (Race, Sex, National Origin, Creed, Religion, and Socio-Economic Status), the third sentence of § 5H1.4 (Physical Condition, Including Drug or Alcohol Dependence or Abuse), and the last sentence of § 5K2.12 (Coercion and Duress) list several factors that the court cannot take into account as grounds for departure. With those specific exceptions, however, the Commission does not intend to limit the kinds of factors, whether or not mentioned anywhere else in the guidelines, that could constitute grounds for departure in an unusual case.

The Commission has adopted this departure policy for two reasons. First, it is difficult to prescribe a single set of guidelines that encompasses the vast range of human conduct potentially relevant to a sentencing decision. The Commission also recognizes that the initial set of guidelines need not do so. The Commission is a permanent body, empowered by law to write and rewrite guidelines, with progressive changes, over many years. By monitoring when courts depart from the guidelines and by analyzing their stated reasons for doing so and court decisions with references thereto, the Commission, over time, will be able to refine the guidelines to specify more precisely when departures should and should not be permitted.

Second, the Commission believes that despite the courts' legal freedom to depart from the guidelines, they will not do so very often. This is because the guidelines, offense by offense, seek to take account of those factors that the Commission's data indicate made a significant difference in pre-guidelines sentencing practice. Thus, for example, where the presence of physical injury made an important difference in pre-guidelines sentencing practice (as in the case of robbery or assault), the guidelines specifically include this factor to enhance the sentence. Where the guidelines do not specify an augmentation or diminution, this is generally because the sentencing data did not permit the Commission to conclude that the factor was empirically important in relation to the particular offense. Of course, an important factor (e.g., physical injury) may infrequently occur in connection with a particular crime (e.g., fraud). Such rare occurrences are precisely the type of events that the courts' departure powers were designed to cover -- unusual cases outside the range of the more typical offenses for which the guidelines were designed.

It is important to note that the guidelines refer to two different kinds of departure. The first involves instances in which the guidelines provide specific guidance for departure by analogy or by other numerical or non-numerical suggestions. For example, the Commentary to § 2G1.1 (Transportation for the Purpose of Prostitution or Prohibited Sexual Conduct) recommends a downward departure of eight levels where a commercial purpose was not involved. The Commission intends such suggestions as policy guidance for the courts. The Commission expects that most departures will reflect the suggestions and that the courts of appeals may prove more likely to find departures 'unreasonable' where they fall outside suggested levels.

A second type of departure will remain unguided. It may rest upon grounds referred to in Chapter Five, Part K (Departures) or on grounds not mentioned in the guidelines. While Chapter Five, Part K lists factors that the Commission believes may constitute grounds for departure, the list is not exhaustive. The Commission recognizes that there may be other grounds for departure that are not mentioned; it also believes there may be cases in which a departure outside suggested levels is warranted. In its view, however, such cases will be highly infrequent.

(c) Plea Agreements.

Nearly ninety percent of all federal criminal cases involve guilty pleas and many of these cases involve some form of plea agreement. Some commentators on early Commission guideline drafts urged the Commission not to attempt any major reforms of the plea agreement process on the grounds that any set of guidelines that threatened to change pre-guidelines practice radically also threatened to make the federal system unmanageable. Others argued that guidelines that failed to control and limit plea agreements would leave untouched a 'loophole' large enough to undo the good that sentencing guidelines would bring.

The Commission decided not to make major changes in plea agreement practices in the initial guidelines, but rather to provide guidance by issuing general policy statements concerning the acceptance of plea agreements in Chapter Six, Part B (Plea Agreements). The rules set forth in Fed. R. Crim. P. 11(e) govern the acceptance or rejection of such agreements. The Commission will collect data on the courts' plea practices and will analyze this information to determine when and why the courts accept or reject plea agreements and whether plea agreement practices are undermining the intent of the Sentencing Reform Act. In light of this information and analysis, the Commission will seek to further regulate the plea agreement process as appropriate. Importantly, if the policy statements relating to plea agreements are followed, circumvention of the Sentencing Reform Act and the guidelines should not occur.

The Commission expects the guidelines to have a positive, rationalizing impact upon plea agreements for two reasons. First, the guidelines create a clear, definite expectation in respect to the sentence that a court will impose if a trial takes place. In the event a prosecutor and defense attorney explore the possibility of a negotiated plea, they will no longer work in the dark. This fact alone should help to reduce irrationality in respect to actual sentencing outcomes. Second, the guidelines create a norm to which courts will likely refer when they decide whether, under Rule 11(e), to accept or to reject a plea agreement or recommendation.

(d) Probation and Split Sentences.

The statute provides that the guidelines are to 'reflect the general appropriateness of imposing a sentence other than imprisonment in cases in which the defendant is a first offender who has not been convicted of a crime of violence or an otherwise serious offense . . . .' 28 U.S.C. § 994(j). Under pre-guidelines sentencing practice, courts sentenced to probation an inappropriately high percentage of offenders guilty of certain economic crimes, such as theft, tax evasion, antitrust offenses, insider trading, fraud, and embezzlement, that in the Commission's view are 'serious.'

The Commission's solution to this problem has been to write guidelines that classify as serious many offenses for which probation previously was frequently given and provide for at least a short period of imprisonment in such cases. The Commission concluded that the definite prospect of prison, even though the term may be short, will serve as a significant deterrent, particularly when compared with pre-guidelines practice where probation, not prison, was the norm.

More specifically, the guidelines work as follows in respect to a first offender. For offense levels one through six, the sentencing court may elect to sentence the offender to probation (with or without confinement conditions) or to a prison term. For offense levels seven through ten, the court may substitute probation for a prison term, but the probation must include confinement conditions (community confinement, intermittent confinement, or home detention). For offense levels eleven and twelve, the court must impose at least one-half the minimum confinement sentence in the form of prison confinement, the remainder to be served on supervised release with a condition of community confinement or home detention. The Commission, of course, has not dealt with the single acts of aberrant behavior that still may justify probation at higher offense levels through departures.

(e) Multi-Count Convictions.

The Commission, like several state sentencing commissions, has found it particularly difficult to develop guidelines for sentencing defendants convicted of multiple violations of law, each of which makes up a separate count in an indictment. The difficulty is that when a defendant engages in conduct that causes several harms, each additional harm, even if it increases the extent to which punishment is warranted, does not necessarily warrant a proportionate increase in punishment. A defendant who assaults others during a fight, for example, may warrant more punishment if he injures ten people than if he injures one, but his conduct does not necessarily warrant ten times the punishment. If it did, many of the simplest offenses, for reasons that are often fortuitous, would lead to sentences of life imprisonment -- sentences that neither just deserts nor crime control theories of punishment would justify.

Several individual guidelines provide special instructions for increasing punishment when the conduct that is the subject of that count involves multiple occurrences or has caused several harms. The guidelines also provide general rules for aggravating punishment in light of multiple harms charged separately in separate counts. These rules may produce occasional anomalies, but normally they will permit an appropriate degree of aggravation of punishment for multiple offenses that are the subjects of separate counts.

These rules are set out in Chapter Three, Part D (Multiple Counts). They essentially provide: (1) when the conduct involves fungible items (e.g., separate drug transactions or thefts of money), the amounts are added and the guidelines apply to the total amount; (2) when nonfungible harms are involved, the offense level for the most serious count is increased (according to a diminishing scale) to reflect the existence of other counts of conviction. The guidelines have been written in order to minimize the possibility that an arbitrary casting of a single transaction into several counts will produce a longer sentence. In addition, the sentencing court will have adequate power to prevent such a result through departures.

(f) Regulatory Offenses.

Regulatory statutes, though primarily civil in nature, sometimes contain criminal provisions in respect to particularly harmful activity. Such criminal provisions often describe not only substantive offenses, but also more technical, administratively-related offenses such as failure to keep accurate records or to provide requested information. These statutes pose two problems: first, which criminal regulatory provisions should the Commission initially consider, and second, how should it treat technical or administratively-related criminal violations?

In respect to the first problem, the Commission found that it could not comprehensively treat all regulatory violations in the initial set of guidelines. There are hundreds of such provisions scattered throughout the United States Code. To find all potential violations would involve examination of each individual federal regulation. Because of this practical difficulty, the Commission sought to determine, with the assistance of the Department of Justice and several regulatory agencies, which criminal regulatory offenses were particularly important in light of the need for enforcement of the general regulatory scheme. The Commission addressed these offenses in the initial guidelines.

In respect to the second problem, the Commission has developed a system for treating technical recordkeeping and reporting offenses that divides them into four categories. First, in the simplest of cases, the offender may have failed to fill out a form intentionally, but without knowledge or intent that substantive harm would likely follow. He might fail, for example, to keep an accurate record of toxic substance transport, but that failure may not lead, nor be likely to lead, to the release or improper handling of any toxic substance. Second, the same failure may be accompanied by a significant likelihood that substantive harm will occur; it may make a release of a toxic substance more likely. Third, the same failure may have led to substantive harm. Fourth, the failure may represent an effort to conceal a substantive harm that has occurred.

The structure of a typical guideline for a regulatory offense provides a low base offense level (e.g., 6) aimed at the first type of recordkeeping or reporting offense. Specific offense characteristics designed to reflect substantive harms that do occur in respect to some regulatory offenses, or that are likely to occur, increase the offense level. A specific offense characteristic also provides that a recordkeeping or reporting offense that conceals a substantive offense will have the same offense level as the substantive offense.

(g) Sentencing Ranges.

In determining the appropriate sentencing ranges for each offense, the Commission estimated the average sentences served within each category under the pre-guidelines sentencing system. It also examined the sentences specified in federal statutes, in the parole guidelines, and in other relevant, analogous sources. The Commission's Supplementary Report on the Initial Sentencing Guidelines (1987) contains a comparison between estimates of pre-guidelines sentencing practice and sentences under the guidelines.

While the Commission has not considered itself bound by pre-guidelines sentencing practice, it has not attempted to develop an entirely new system of sentencing on the basis of theory alone. Guideline sentences, in many instances, will approximate average pre-guidelines practice and adherence to the guidelines will help to eliminate wide disparity. For example, where a high percentage of persons received probation under pre-guidelines practice, a guideline may include one or more specific offense characteristics in an effort to distinguish those types of defendants who received probation from those who received more severe sentences. In some instances, short sentences of incarceration for all offenders in a category have been substituted for a pre-guidelines sentencing practice of very wide variability in which some defendants received probation while others received several years in prison for the same offense. Moreover, inasmuch as those who pleaded guilty under pre-guidelines practice often received lesser sentences, the guidelines permit the court to impose lesser sentences on those defendants who accept responsibility for their misconduct. For defendants who provide substantial assistance to the government in the investigation or prosecution of others, a downward departure may be warranted.

The Commission has also examined its sentencing ranges in light of their likely impact upon prison population. Specific legislation, such as the Anti-Drug Abuse Act of 1986 and the career offender provisions of the Sentencing Reform Act of 1984 (28 U.S.C. § 994(h)), required the Commission to promulgate guidelines that will lead to substantial prison population increases. These increases will occur irrespective of the guidelines. The guidelines themselves, insofar as they reflect policy decisions made by the Commission (rather than legislated mandatory minimum or career offender sentences), are projected to lead to an increase in prison population that computer models, produced by the Commission and the Bureau of Prisons in 1987, estimated at approximately 10 percent over a period of ten years.

(h) The Sentencing Table.

The Commission has established a sentencing table that for technical and practical reasons contains 43 levels. Each level in the table prescribes ranges that overlap with the ranges in the preceding and succeeding levels. By overlapping the ranges, the table should discourage unnecessary litigation. Both prosecution and defense will realize that the difference between one level and another will not necessarily make a difference in the sentence that the court imposes. Thus, little purpose will be served in protracted litigation trying to determine, for example, whether $10,000 or $11,000 was obtained as a result of a fraud. At the same time, the levels work to increase a sentence proportionately. A change of six levels roughly doubles the sentence irrespective of the level at which one starts. The guidelines, in keeping with the statutory requirement that the maximum of any range cannot exceed the minimum by more than the greater of 25 percent or six months (28 U.S.C. § 994(b)(2)), permit courts to exercise the greatest permissible range of sentencing discretion. The table overlaps offense levels meaningfully, works proportionately, and at the same time preserves the maximum degree of allowable discretion for the court within each level.

Similarly, many of the individual guidelines refer to tables that correlate amounts of money with offense levels. These tables often have many rather than a few levels. Again, the reason is to minimize the likelihood of unnecessary litigation. If a money table were to make only a few distinctions, each distinction would become more important and litigation over which category an offender fell within would become more likely. Where a table has many small monetary distinctions, it minimizes the likelihood of litigation because the precise amount of money involved is of considerably less importance.

5. A Concluding Note

The Commission emphasizes that it drafted the initial guidelines with considerable caution. It examined the many hundreds of criminal statutes in the United States Code. It began with those that were the basis for a significant number of prosecutions and sought to place them in a rational order. It developed additional distinctions relevant to the application of these provisions and it applied sentencing ranges to each resulting category. In doing so, it relied upon pre-guidelines sentencing practice as revealed by its own statistical analyses based on summary reports of some 40,000 convictions, a sample of 10,000 augmented presentence reports, the parole guidelines, and policy judgments.

The Commission recognizes that some will criticize this approach as overly cautious, as representing too little a departure from pre-guidelines sentencing practice. Yet, it will cure wide disparity. The Commission is a permanent body that can amend the guidelines each year. Although the data available to it, like all data, are imperfect, experience with the guidelines will lead to additional information and provide a firm empirical basis for consideration of revisions.

Finally, the guidelines will apply to more than 90 percent of all felony and Class A misdemeanor cases in the federal courts. Because of time constraints and the nonexistence of statistical information, some offenses that occur infrequently are not considered in the guidelines. Their exclusion does not reflect any judgment regarding their seriousness and they will be addressed as the Commission refines the guidelines over time.".

1992 Amendment

Amendment 466 amended Subpart 4(b) in the first paragraph by inserting "§ 5H1.12 (Lack of Guidance as a Youth and Similar Circumstances)" after "§ 5H1.10 (Race, Sex, National Origin, Creed, Religion, and Socio-Economic Status)".

1995 Amendment

Amendment 534 amended Subpart 4(d) in the second sentence of the third paragraph by striking "six" and inserting "eight"; and in the third sentence of the third paragraph by striking "seven through" and inserting "nine and".

1996 Amendment

Amendment 538 amended Subpart 4(b) in the fourth paragraph by striking the third sentence as follows:

"For example, the Commentary to § 2G1.1 (Transportation for the Purpose of Prostitution or Prohibited Sexual Conduct) recommends a downward departure of eight levels where a commercial purpose was not involved.".

2000 Amendments

Amendment 602 amended Subpart 4(b) in the fifth sentence of the first paragraph by striking "and" before "the last"; and by inserting ", and § 5K2.19 (Post-Sentencing Rehabilitative Efforts)" after "(Coercion and Duress)".

Amendment 603 amended Subpart 4(d) by adding an asterisk at the end of the last paragraph after the period; and by adding at the end the following footnote:

"*Note: Although the Commission had not addressed 'single acts of aberrant behavior' at the time the Introduction to the Guidelines Manual originally was written, it subsequently addressed the issue in Amendment 603, effective November 1, 2000. (See Supplement to Appendix C, Amendment 603.)".",

and inserting:

" PART A - INTRODUCTION AND AUTHORITY

Introductory Commentary

Subparts 1 and 2 of this Part provide an introduction to the Guidelines Manual describing the historical development and evolution of the federal sentencing guidelines. Subpart 1 sets forth the original introduction to the Guidelines Manual as it first appeared in 1987, with the inclusion of amendments made occasionally thereto between 1987 and 2000. The original introduction, as so amended, explained a number of policy decisions made by the United States Sentencing Commission ('Commission') when it promulgated the initial set of guidelines and therefore provides a useful reference for contextual and historical purposes. Subpart 2 further describes the evolution of the federal sentencing guidelines after the initial guidelines were promulgated.

Subpart 3 of this Part states the authority of the Commission to promulgate federal sentencing guidelines, policy statements, and commentary.

1. ORIGINAL INTRODUCTION TO THE GUIDELINES MANUAL

The following provisions of this Subpart set forth the original introduction to this manual, effective November 1, 1987, and as amended through November 1, 2000:

1. Authority

The United States Sentencing Commission ('Commission') is an independent agency in the judicial branch composed of seven voting and two non-voting, ex officio members. Its principal purpose is to establish sentencing policies and practices for the federal criminal justice system that will assure the ends of justice by promulgating detailed guidelines prescribing the appropriate sentences for offenders convicted of federal crimes.

The guidelines and policy statements promulgated by the Commission are issued pursuant to Section 994(a) of Title 28, United States Code.

2. The Statutory Mission

The Sentencing Reform Act of 1984 (Title II of the Comprehensive Crime Control Act of 1984) provides for the development of guidelines that will further the basic purposes of criminal punishment: deterrence, incapacitation, just punishment, and rehabilitation. The Act delegates broad authority to the Commission to review and rationalize the federal sentencing process.

The Act contains detailed instructions as to how this determination should be made, the most important of which directs the Commission to create categories of offense behavior and offender characteristics. An offense behavior category might consist, for example, of 'bank robbery/committed with a gun/ $2500 taken.' An offender characteristic category might be 'offender with one prior conviction not resulting in imprisonment.' The Commission is required to prescribe guideline ranges that specify an appropriate sentence for each class of convicted persons determined by coordinating the offense behavior categories with the offender characteristic categories. Where the guidelines call for imprisonment, the range must be narrow: the maximum of the range cannot exceed the minimum by more than the greater of 25 percent or six months. 28 U.S.C. § 994(b)(2).

Pursuant to the Act, the sentencing court must select a sentence from within the guideline range. If, however, a particular case presents atypical features, the Act allows the court to depart from the guidelines and sentence outside the prescribed range. In that case, the court must specify reasons for departure. 18 U.S.C. § 3553(b). If the court sentences within the guideline range, an appellate court may review the sentence to determine whether the guidelines were correctly applied. If the court departs from the guideline range, an appellate court may review the reasonableness of the departure. 18 U.S.C. § 3742. The Act also abolishes parole, and substantially reduces and restructures good behavior adjustments.

The Commission's initial guidelines were submitted to Congress on April 13, 1987. After the prescribed period of Congressional review, the guidelines took effect on November 1, 1987, and apply to all offenses committed on or after that date. The Commission has the authority to submit guideline amendments each year to Congress between the beginning of a regular Congressional session and May 1. Such amendments automatically take effect 180 days after submission unless a law is enacted to the contrary. 28 U.S.C. § 994(p).

The initial sentencing guidelines and policy statements were developed after extensive hearings, deliberation, and consideration of substantial public comment. The Commission emphasizes, however, that it views the guideline-writing process as evolutionary. It expects, and the governing statute anticipates, that continuing research, experience, and analysis will result in modifications and revisions to the guidelines through submission of amendments to Congress. To this end, the Commission is established as a permanent agency to monitor sentencing practices in the federal courts.

3. The Basic Approach (Policy Statement)

To understand the guidelines and their underlying rationale, it is important to focus on the three objectives that Congress sought to achieve in enacting the Sentencing Reform Act of 1984. The Act's basic objective was to enhance the ability of the criminal justice system to combat crime through an effective, fair sentencing system. To achieve this end, Congress first sought honesty in sentencing. It sought to avoid the confusion and implicit deception that arose out of the pre-guidelines sentencing system which required the court to impose an indeterminate sentence of imprisonment and empowered the parole commission to determine how much of the sentence an offender actually would serve in prison. This practice usually resulted in a substantial reduction in the effective length of the sentence imposed, with defendants often serving only about one-third of the sentence imposed by the court.

Second, Congress sought reasonable uniformity in sentencing by narrowing the wide disparity in sentences imposed for similar criminal offenses committed by similar offenders. Third, Congress sought proportionality in sentencing through a system that imposes appropriately different sentences for criminal conduct of differing severity.

Honesty is easy to achieve: the abolition of parole makes the sentence imposed by the court the sentence the offender will serve, less approximately fifteen percent for good behavior. There is a tension, however, between the mandate of uniformity and the mandate of proportionality. Simple uniformity -- sentencing every offender to five years -- destroys proportionality. Having only a few simple categories of crimes would make the guidelines uniform and easy to administer, but might lump together offenses that are different in important respects. For example, a single category for robbery that included armed and unarmed robberies, robberies with and without injuries, robberies of a few dollars and robberies of millions, would be far too broad.

A sentencing system tailored to fit every conceivable wrinkle of each case would quickly become unworkable and seriously compromise the certainty of punishment and its deterrent effect. For example: a bank robber with (or without) a gun, which the robber kept hidden (or brandished), might have frightened (or merely warned), injured seriously (or less seriously), tied up (or simply pushed) a guard, teller, or customer, at night (or at noon), in an effort to obtain money for other crimes (or for other purposes), in the company of a few (or many) other robbers, for the first (or fourth) time.

The list of potentially relevant features of criminal behavior is long; the fact that they can occur in multiple combinations means that the list of possible permutations of factors is virtually endless. The appropriate relationships among these different factors are exceedingly difficult to establish, for they are often context specific. Sentencing courts do not treat the occurrence of a simple bruise identically in all cases, irrespective of whether that bruise occurred in the context of a bank robbery or in the context of a breach of peace. This is so, in part, because the risk that such a harm will occur differs depending on the underlying offense with which it is connected; and also because, in part, the relationship between punishment and multiple harms is not simply additive. The relation varies depending on how much other harm has occurred. Thus, it would not be proper to assign points for each kind of harm and simply add them up, irrespective of context and total amounts.

The larger the number of subcategories of offense and offender characteristics included in the guidelines, the greater the complexity and the less workable the system. Moreover, complex combinations of offense and offender characteristics would apply and interact in unforeseen ways to unforeseen situations, thus failing to cure the unfairness of a simple, broad category system. Finally, and perhaps most importantly, probation officers and courts, in applying a complex system having numerous subcategories, would be required to make a host of decisions regarding whether the underlying facts were sufficient to bring the case within a particular subcategory. The greater the number of decisions required and the greater their complexity, the greater the risk that different courts would apply the guidelines differently to situations that, in fact, are similar, thereby reintroducing the very disparity that the guidelines were designed to reduce.

In view of the arguments, it would have been tempting to retreat to the simple, broad category approach and to grant courts the discretion to select the proper point along a broad sentencing range. Granting such broad discretion, however, would have risked correspondingly broad disparity in sentencing, for different courts may exercise their discretionary powers in different ways. Such an approach would have risked a return to the wide disparity that Congress established the Commission to reduce and would have been contrary to the Commission's mandate set forth in the Sentencing Reform Act of 1984.

In the end, there was no completely satisfying solution to this problem. The Commission had to balance the comparative virtues and vices of broad, simple categorization and detailed, complex subcategorization, and within the constraints established by that balance, minimize the discretionary powers of the sentencing court. Any system will, to a degree, enjoy the benefits and suffer from the drawbacks of each approach.

A philosophical problem arose when the Commission attempted to reconcile the differing perceptions of the purposes of criminal punishment. Most observers of the criminal law agree that the ultimate aim of the law itself, and of punishment in particular, is the control of crime. Beyond this point, however, the consensus seems to break down. Some argue that appropriate punishment should be defined primarily on the basis of the principle of 'just deserts.' Under this principle, punishment should be scaled to the offender's culpability and the resulting harms. Others argue that punishment should be imposed primarily on the basis of practical 'crime control' considerations. This theory calls for sentences that most effectively lessen the likelihood of future crime, either by deterring others or incapacitating the defendant.

Adherents of each of these points of view urged the Commission to choose between them and accord one primacy over the other. As a practical matter, however, this choice was unnecessary because in most sentencing decisions the application of either philosophy will produce the same or similar results.

In its initial set of guidelines, the Commission sought to solve both the practical and philosophical problems of developing a coherent sentencing system by taking an empirical approach that used as a starting point data estimating pre-guidelines sentencing practice. It analyzed data drawn from 10,000 presentence investigations, the differing elements of various crimes as distinguished in substantive criminal statutes, the United States Parole Commission's guidelines and statistics, and data from other relevant sources in order to determine which distinctions were important in pre-guidelines practice. After consideration, the Commission accepted, modified, or rationalized these distinctions.

This empirical approach helped the Commission resolve its practical problem by defining a list of relevant distinctions that, although of considerable length, was short enough to create a manageable set of guidelines. Existing categories are relatively broad and omit distinctions that some may believe important, yet they include most of the major distinctions that statutes and data suggest made a significant difference in sentencing decisions. Relevant distinctions not reflected in the guidelines probably will occur rarely and sentencing courts may take such unusual cases into account by departing from the guidelines.

The Commission's empirical approach also helped resolve its philosophical dilemma. Those who adhere to a just deserts philosophy may concede that the lack of consensus might make it difficult to say exactly what punishment is deserved for a particular crime. Likewise, those who subscribe to a philosophy of crime control may acknowledge that the lack of sufficient data might make it difficult to determine exactly the punishment that will best prevent that crime. Both groups might therefore recognize the wisdom of looking to those distinctions that judges and legislators have, in fact, made over the course of time. These established distinctions are ones that the community believes, or has found over time, to be important from either a just deserts or crime control perspective.

The Commission did not simply copy estimates of pre-guidelines practice as revealed by the data, even though establishing offense values on this basis would help eliminate disparity because the data represent averages. Rather, it departed from the data at different points for various important reasons. Congressional statutes, for example, suggested or required departure, as in the case of the Anti-Drug Abuse Act of 1986 that imposed increased and mandatory minimum sentences. In addition, the data revealed inconsistencies in treatment, such as punishing economic crime less severely than other apparently equivalent behavior.

Despite these policy-oriented departures from pre-guidelines practice, the guidelines represent an approach that begins with, and builds upon, empirical data. The guidelines will not please those who wish the Commission to adopt a single philosophical theory and then work deductively to establish a simple and perfect set of categorizations and distinctions. The guidelines may prove acceptable, however, to those who seek more modest, incremental improvements in the status quo, who believe the best is often the enemy of the good, and who recognize that these guidelines are, as the Act contemplates, but the first step in an evolutionary process. After spending considerable time and resources exploring alternative approaches, the Commission developed these guidelines as a practical effort toward the achievement of a more honest, uniform, equitable, proportional, and therefore effective sentencing system.

4. The Guidelines' Resolution of Major Issues (Policy Statement)

The guideline-drafting process required the Commission to resolve a host of important policy questions typically involving rather evenly balanced sets of competing considerations. As an aid to understanding the guidelines, this introduction briefly discusses several of those issues; commentary in the guidelines explains others.

(a) Real Offense vs. Charge Offense Sentencing.

One of the most important questions for the Commission to decide was whether to base sentences upon the actual conduct in which the defendant engaged regardless of the charges for which he was indicted or convicted ('real offense' sentencing), or upon the conduct that constitutes the elements of the offense for which the defendant was charged and of which he was convicted ('charge offense' sentencing). A bank robber, for example, might have used a gun, frightened bystanders, taken $50,000, injured a teller, refused to stop when ordered, and raced away damaging property during his escape. A pure real offense system would sentence on the basis of all identifiable conduct. A pure charge offense system would overlook some of the harms that did not constitute statutory elements of the offenses of which the defendant was convicted.

The Commission initially sought to develop a pure real offense system. After all, the pre-guidelines sentencing system was, in a sense, this type of system. The sentencing court and the parole commission took account of the conduct in which the defendant actually engaged, as determined in a presentence report, at the sentencing hearing, or before a parole commission hearing officer. The Commission's initial efforts in this direction, carried out in the spring and early summer of 1986, proved unproductive, mostly for practical reasons. To make such a system work, even to formalize and rationalize the status quo, would have required the Commission to decide precisely which harms to take into account, how to add them up, and what kinds of procedures the courts should use to determine the presence or absence of disputed factual elements. The Commission found no practical way to combine and account for the large number of diverse harms arising in different circumstances; nor did it find a practical way to reconcile the need for a fair adjudicatory procedure with the need for a speedy sentencing process given the potential existence of hosts of adjudicated 'real harm' facts in many typical cases. The effort proposed as a solution to these problems required the use of, for example, quadratic roots and other mathematical operations that the Commission considered too complex to be workable. In the Commission's view, such a system risked return to wide disparity in sentencing practice.

In its initial set of guidelines submitted to Congress in April 1987, the Commission moved closer to a charge offense system. This system, however, does contain a significant number of real offense elements. For one thing, the hundreds of overlapping and duplicative statutory provisions that make up the federal criminal law forced the Commission to write guidelines that are descriptive of generic conduct rather than guidelines that track purely statutory language. For another, the guidelines take account of a number of important, commonly occurring real offense elements such as role in the offense, the presence of a gun, or the amount of money actually taken, through alternative base offense levels, specific offense characteristics, cross references, and adjustments.

The Commission recognized that a charge offense system has drawbacks of its own. One of the most important is the potential it affords prosecutors to influence sentences by increasing or decreasing the number of counts in an indictment. Of course, the defendant's actual conduct (that which the prosecutor can prove in court) imposes a natural limit upon the prosecutor's ability to increase a defendant's sentence. Moreover, the Commission has written its rules for the treatment of multicount convictions with an eye toward eliminating unfair treatment that might flow from count manipulation. For example, the guidelines treat a three-count indictment, each count of which charges sale of 100 grams of heroin or theft of $10,000, the same as a single-count indictment charging sale of 300 grams of heroin or theft of $30,000. Furthermore, a sentencing court may control any inappropriate manipulation of the indictment through use of its departure power. Finally, the Commission will closely monitor charging and plea agreement practices and will make appropriate adjustments should they become necessary.

(b)   Departures.

The sentencing statute permits a court to depart from a guideline-specified sentence only when it finds 'an aggravating or mitigating circumstance of a kind, or to a degree, not adequately taken into consideration by the Sentencing Commission in formulating the guidelines that should result in a sentence different from that described.' 18 U.S.C. § 3553(b). The Commission intends the sentencing courts to treat each guideline as carving out a 'heartland,' a set of typical cases embodying the conduct that each guideline describes. When a court finds an atypical case, one to which a particular guideline linguistically applies but where conduct significantly differs from the norm, the court may consider whether a departure is warranted. Section 5H1.10 (Race, Sex, National Origin, Creed, Religion, and Socio-Economic Status), § 5H1.12 (Lack of Guidance as a Youth and Similar Circumstances), the third sentence of § 5H1.4 (Physical Condition, Including Drug or Alcohol Dependence or Abuse), the last sentence of § 5K2.12 (Coercion and Duress), and § 5K2.19 (Post-Sentencing Rehabilitative Efforts) list several factors that the court cannot take into account as grounds for departure. With those specific exceptions, however, the Commission does not intend to limit the kinds of factors, whether or not mentioned anywhere else in the guidelines, that could constitute grounds for departure in an unusual case.

The Commission has adopted this departure policy for two reasons. First, it is difficult to prescribe a single set of guidelines that encompasses the vast range of human conduct potentially relevant to a sentencing decision. The Commission also recognizes that the initial set of guidelines need not do so. The Commission is a permanent body, empowered by law to write and rewrite guidelines, with progressive changes, over many years. By monitoring when courts depart from the guidelines and by analyzing their stated reasons for doing so and court decisions with references thereto, the Commission, over time, will be able to refine the guidelines to specify more precisely when departures should and should not be permitted.

Second, the Commission believes that despite the courts' legal freedom to depart from the guidelines, they will not do so very often. This is because the guidelines, offense by offense, seek to take account of those factors that the Commission's data indicate made a significant difference in pre-guidelines sentencing practice. Thus, for example, where the presence of physical injury made an important difference in pre-guidelines sentencing practice (as in the case of robbery or assault), the guidelines specifically include this factor to enhance the sentence. Where the guidelines do not specify an augmentation or diminution, this is generally because the sentencing data did not permit the Commission to conclude that the factor was empirically important in relation to the particular offense. Of course, an important factor (e.g., physical injury) may infrequently occur in connection with a particular crime (e.g., fraud). Such rare occurrences are precisely the type of events that the courts' departure powers were designed to cover -- unusual cases outside the range of the more typical offenses for which the guidelines were designed.

It is important to note that the guidelines refer to two different kinds of departure. The first involves instances in which the guidelines provide specific guidance for departure by analogy or by other numerical or non-numerical suggestions. The Commission intends such suggestions as policy guidance for the courts. The Commission expects that most departures will reflect the suggestions and that the courts of appeals may prove more likely to find departures 'unreasonable' where they fall outside suggested levels.

A second type of departure will remain unguided. It may rest upon grounds referred to in Chapter Five, Part K (Departures) or on grounds not mentioned in the guidelines. While Chapter Five, Part K lists factors that the Commission believes may constitute grounds for departure, the list is not exhaustive. The Commission recognizes that there may be other grounds for departure that are not mentioned; it also believes there may be cases in which a departure outside suggested levels is warranted. In its view, however, such cases will be highly infrequent.

(c) Plea Agreements.

Nearly ninety percent of all federal criminal cases involve guilty pleas and many of these cases involve some form of plea agreement. Some commentators on early Commission guideline drafts urged the Commission not to attempt any major reforms of the plea agreement process on the grounds that any set of guidelines that threatened to change pre-guidelines practice radically also threatened to make the federal system unmanageable. Others argued that guidelines that failed to control and limit plea agreements would leave untouched a 'loophole' large enough to undo the good that sentencing guidelines would bring.

The Commission decided not to make major changes in plea agreement practices in the initial guidelines, but rather to provide guidance by issuing general policy statements concerning the acceptance of plea agreements in Chapter Six, Part B (Plea Agreements). The rules set forth in Fed. R. Crim. P. 11(e) govern the acceptance or rejection of such agreements. The Commission will collect data on the courts' plea practices and will analyze this information to determine when and why the courts accept or reject plea agreements and whether plea agreement practices are undermining the intent of the Sentencing Reform Act. In light of this information and analysis, the Commission will seek to further regulate the plea agreement process as appropriate. Importantly, if the policy statements relating to plea agreements are followed, circumvention of the Sentencing Reform Act and the guidelines should not occur.

The Commission expects the guidelines to have a positive, rationalizing impact upon plea agreements for two reasons. First, the guidelines create a clear, definite expectation in respect to the sentence that a court will impose if a trial takes place. In the event a prosecutor and defense attorney explore the possibility of a negotiated plea, they will no longer work in the dark. This fact alone should help to reduce irrationality in respect to actual sentencing outcomes. Second, the guidelines create a norm to which courts will likely refer when they decide whether, under Rule 11(e), to accept or to reject a plea agreement or recommendation.

(d) Probation and Split Sentences.

The statute provides that the guidelines are to 'reflect the general appropriateness of imposing a sentence other than imprisonment in cases in which the defendant is a first offender who has not been convicted of a crime of violence or an otherwise serious offense . . . .' 28 U.S.C. § 994(j). Under pre-guidelines sentencing practice, courts sentenced to probation an inappropriately high percentage of offenders guilty of certain economic crimes, such as theft, tax evasion, antitrust offenses, insider trading, fraud, and embezzlement, that in the Commission's view are 'serious.'

The Commission's solution to this problem has been to write guidelines that classify as serious many offenses for which probation previously was frequently given and provide for at least a short period of imprisonment in such cases. The Commission concluded that the definite prospect of prison, even though the term may be short, will serve as a significant deterrent, particularly when compared with pre-guidelines practice where probation, not prison, was the norm.

More specifically, the guidelines work as follows in respect to a first offender. For offense levels one through eight, the sentencing court may elect to sentence the offender to probation (with or without confinement conditions) or to a prison term. For offense levels nine and ten, the court may substitute probation for a prison term, but the probation must include confinement conditions (community confinement, intermittent confinement, or home detention). For offense levels eleven and twelve, the court must impose at least one-half the minimum confinement sentence in the form of prison confinement, the remainder to be served on supervised release with a condition of community confinement or home detention. The Commission, of course, has not dealt with the single acts of aberrant behavior that still may justify probation at higher offense levels through departures.*

*Note: Although the Commission had not addressed 'single acts of aberrant behavior' at the time the Introduction to the Guidelines Manual originally was written, it subsequently addressed the issue in Amendment 603, effective November 1, 2000. (See Supplement to Appendix C, amendment 603.)

(e) Multi-Count Convictions.

The Commission, like several state sentencing commissions, has found it particularly difficult to develop guidelines for sentencing defendants convicted of multiple violations of law, each of which makes up a separate count in an indictment. The difficulty is that when a defendant engages in conduct that causes several harms, each additional harm, even if it increases the extent to which punishment is warranted, does not necessarily warrant a proportionate increase in punishment. A defendant who assaults others during a fight, for example, may warrant more punishment if he injures ten people than if he injures one, but his conduct does not necessarily warrant ten times the punishment. If it did, many of the simplest offenses, for reasons that are often fortuitous, would lead to sentences of life imprisonment -- sentences that neither just deserts nor crime control theories of punishment would justify.

Several individual guidelines provide special instructions for increasing punishment when the conduct that is the subject of that count involves multiple occurrences or has caused several harms. The guidelines also provide general rules for aggravating punishment in light of multiple harms charged separately in separate counts. These rules may produce occasional anomalies, but normally they will permit an appropriate degree of aggravation of punishment for multiple offenses that are the subjects of separate counts.

These rules are set out in Chapter Three, Part D (Multiple Counts). They essentially provide: (1) when the conduct involves fungible items (e.g., separate drug transactions or thefts of money), the amounts are added and the guidelines apply to the total amount; (2) when nonfungible harms are involved, the offense level for the most serious count is increased (according to a diminishing scale) to reflect the existence of other counts of conviction. The guidelines have been written in order to minimize the possibility that an arbitrary casting of a single transaction into several counts will produce a longer sentence. In addition, the sentencing court will have adequate power to prevent such a result through departures.

(f) Regulatory Offenses.

Regulatory statutes, though primarily civil in nature, sometimes contain criminal provisions in respect to particularly harmful activity. Such criminal provisions often describe not only substantive offenses, but also more technical, administratively-related offenses such as failure to keep accurate records or to provide requested information. These statutes pose two problems: first, which criminal regulatory provisions should the Commission initially consider, and second, how should it treat technical or administratively-related criminal violations?

In respect to the first problem, the Commission found that it could not comprehensively treat all regulatory violations in the initial set of guidelines. There are hundreds of such provisions scattered throughout the United States Code. To find all potential violations would involve examination of each individual federal regulation. Because of this practical difficulty, the Commission sought to determine, with the assistance of the Department of Justice and several regulatory agencies, which criminal regulatory offenses were particularly important in light of the need for enforcement of the general regulatory scheme. The Commission addressed these offenses in the initial guidelines.

In respect to the second problem, the Commission has developed a system for treating technical recordkeeping and reporting offenses that divides them into four categories. First, in the simplest of cases, the offender may have failed to fill out a form intentionally, but without knowledge or intent that substantive harm would likely follow. He might fail, for example, to keep an accurate record of toxic substance transport, but that failure may not lead, nor be likely to lead, to the release or improper handling of any toxic substance. Second, the same failure may be accompanied by a significant likelihood that substantive harm will occur; it may make a release of a toxic substance more likely. Third, the same failure may have led to substantive harm. Fourth, the failure may represent an effort to conceal a substantive harm that has occurred.

The structure of a typical guideline for a regulatory offense provides a low base offense level (e.g., 6) aimed at the first type of recordkeeping or reporting offense. Specific offense characteristics designed to reflect substantive harms that do occur in respect to some regulatory offenses, or that are likely to occur, increase the offense level. A specific offense characteristic also provides that a recordkeeping or reporting offense that conceals a substantive offense will have the same offense level as the substantive offense.

    (g)   <u>Sentencing Ranges</u>.

In determining the appropriate sentencing ranges for each offense, the Commission estimated the average sentences served within each category under the pre-guidelines sentencing system. It also examined the sentences specified in federal statutes, in the parole guidelines, and in other relevant, analogous sources. The Commission's Supplementary Report on the Initial Sentencing Guidelines (1987) contains a comparison between estimates of pre-guidelines sentencing practice and sentences under the guidelines.

While the Commission has not considered itself bound by pre-guidelines sentencing practice, it has not attempted to develop an entirely new system of sentencing on the basis of theory alone. Guideline sentences, in many instances, will approximate average pre-guidelines practice and adherence to the guidelines will help to eliminate wide disparity. For example, where a high percentage of persons received probation under pre-guidelines practice, a guideline may include one or more specific offense characteristics in an effort to distinguish those types of defendants who received probation from those who received more severe sentences. In some instances, short sentences of incarceration for all offenders in a category have been substituted for a pre-guidelines sentencing practice of very wide variability in which some defendants received probation while others received several years in prison for the same offense. Moreover, inasmuch as those who pleaded guilty under pre-guidelines practice often received lesser sentences, the guidelines permit the court to impose lesser sentences on those defendants who accept responsibility for their misconduct. For defendants who provide substantial assistance to the government in the investigation or prosecution of others, a downward departure may be warranted.

The Commission has also examined its sentencing ranges in light of their likely impact upon prison population. Specific legislation, such as the Anti-Drug Abuse Act of 1986 and the career offender provisions of the Sentencing Reform Act of 1984 (28 U.S.C. § 994(h)), required the Commission to promulgate guidelines that will lead to substantial prison population increases. These increases will occur irrespective of the guidelines. The guidelines themselves, insofar as they reflect policy decisions made by the Commission (rather than legislated mandatory minimum or career offender sentences), are projected to lead to an increase in prison population that computer models, produced by the Commission and the Bureau of Prisons in 1987, estimated at approximately 10 percent over a period of ten years.

(h) The Sentencing Table.

The Commission has established a sentencing table that for technical and practical reasons contains 43 levels. Each level in the table prescribes ranges that overlap with the ranges in the preceding and succeeding levels. By overlapping the ranges, the table should discourage unnecessary litigation. Both prosecution and defense will realize that the difference between one level and another will not necessarily make a difference in the sentence that the court imposes. Thus, little purpose will be served in protracted litigation trying to determine, for example, whether $10,000 or $11,000 was obtained as a result of a fraud. At the same time, the levels work to increase a sentence proportionately. A change of six levels roughly doubles the sentence irrespective of the level at which one starts. The guidelines, in keeping with the statutory requirement that the maximum of any range cannot exceed the minimum by more than the greater of 25 percent or six months (28 U.S.C. § 994(b)(2)), permit courts to exercise the greatest permissible range of sentencing discretion. The table overlaps offense levels meaningfully, works proportionately, and at the same time preserves the maximum degree of allowable discretion for the court within each level.

Similarly, many of the individual guidelines refer to tables that correlate amounts of money with offense levels. These tables often have many rather than a few levels. Again, the reason is to minimize the likelihood of unnecessary litigation. If a money table were to make only a few distinctions, each distinction would become more important and litigation over which category an offender fell within would become more likely. Where a table has many small monetary distinctions, it minimizes the likelihood of litigation because the precise amount of money involved is of considerably less importance.

5. A Concluding Note

The Commission emphasizes that it drafted the initial guidelines with considerable caution. It examined the many hundreds of criminal statutes in the United States Code. It began with those that were the basis for a significant number of prosecutions and sought to place them in a rational order. It developed additional distinctions relevant to the application of these provisions and it applied sentencing ranges to each resulting category. In doing so, it relied upon pre-guidelines sentencing practice as revealed by its own statistical analyses based on summary reports of some 40,000 convictions, a sample of 10,000 augmented presentence reports, the parole guidelines, and policy judgments.

The Commission recognizes that some will criticize this approach as overly cautious, as representing too little a departure from pre-guidelines sentencing practice. Yet, it will cure wide disparity. The Commission is a permanent body that can amend the guidelines each year. Although the data available to it, like all data, are imperfect, experience with the guidelines will lead to additional information and provide a firm empirical basis for consideration of revisions.

Finally, the guidelines will apply to more than 90 percent of all felony and Class A misdemeanor cases in the federal courts. Because of time constraints and the nonexistence of statistical information, some offenses that occur infrequently are not considered in the guidelines. Their exclusion does not reflect any judgment regarding their seriousness and they will be addressed as the Commission refines the guidelines over time.

2. CONTINUING EVOLUTION AND ROLE OF THE GUIDELINES

The Sentencing Reform Act of 1984 changed the course of federal sentencing. Among other things, the Act created the United States Sentencing Commission as an independent agency in the Judicial Branch, and directed it to develop guidelines and policy statements for sentencing courts to use when sentencing offenders convicted of federal crimes. Moreover, it empowered the Commission with ongoing responsibilities to monitor the guidelines, submit to Congress appropriate modifications of the guidelines and recommended changes in criminal statutes, and establish education and research programs. The mandate rested on congressional awareness that sentencing is a dynamic field that requires continuing review by an expert body to revise sentencing policies, in light of application experience, as new criminal statutes are enacted, and as more is learned about what motivates and controls criminal behavior.

This statement finds resonance in a line of Supreme Court cases that, taken together, echo two themes. The first theme is that the guidelines are the product of a deliberative process that seeks to embody the purposes of sentencing set forth in the Sentencing Reform Act, and as such they continue to play an important role in the sentencing court's determination of an appropriate sentence in a particular case. The Supreme Court alluded to this in Mistretta v. United States, 488 U.S. 361 (1989), which upheld the constitutionality of both the federal sentencing guidelines and the Commission against nondelegation and separation of powers challenges. Therein the Court stated:

> Developing proportionate penalties for hundreds of different crimes by a virtually limitless array of offenders is precisely the sort of intricate, labor-intensive task for which delegation to an expert body is especially appropriate. Although Congress has delegated significant discretion to the Commission to draw judgments from its analysis of existing sentencing practice and alternative sentencing models, . . . [w]e have no doubt that in the hands of the Commission 'the criteria which Congress has supplied are wholly adequate for carrying out the general policy and purpose' of the Act.

Id. at 379 (internal quotation marks and citations omitted).

The continuing importance of the guidelines in federal sentencing was further acknowledged by the Court in United States v. Booker, 543 U.S. 220 (2005), even as that case rendered the guidelines advisory in nature. In Booker, the Court held that the imposition of an enhanced sentence under the federal sentencing guidelines based on the sentencing judge's determination of a fact (other than a prior conviction) that was not found by the jury or admitted by the defendant violated the Sixth Amendment. The Court reasoned that an advisory guideline system, while lacking the mandatory features that Congress enacted, retains other features that help to further congressional objectives, including providing certainty and fairness in meeting the purposes of sentencing, avoiding unwarranted sentencing disparities, and maintaining sufficient flexibility to permit individualized sentences when warranted. The Court concluded that an advisory guideline system would 'continue to move sentencing in Congress' preferred direction, helping to avoid excessive sentencing disparities while maintaining flexibility sufficient to individualize sentences where necessary.' Id. at 264-65. An advisory guideline system continues to assure transparency by requiring that sentences be based on articulated reasons stated in open court that are subject to appellate review. An advisory guideline system also continues to promote certainty and predictability in sentencing, thereby enabling the parties to better anticipate the likely sentence based on the individualized facts of the case.

The continuing importance of the guidelines in the sentencing determination is predicated in large part on the Sentencing Reform Act's intent that, in promulgating guidelines, the Commission must take into account the purposes of sentencing as set forth in 18 U.S.C. § 3553(a). See 28 U.S.C. §§ 994(f), 991(b)(1). The Supreme Court reinforced this view in Rita v. United States, 127 S. Ct. 2456 (2007), which held that a court of appeals may apply a presumption of reasonableness to a sentence imposed by a district court within a properly calculated guideline range without violating the Sixth Amendment. In Rita, the Court relied heavily on the complementary roles of the Commission and the sentencing court in federal sentencing, stating:

> [T]he presumption reflects the nature of the Guidelines-writing task that Congress set for the Commission and the manner in which the Commission carried out that task. In instructing both the sentencing judge and the Commission what to do, Congress referred to the basic sentencing objectives that the statute sets forth in 18 U.S.C. § 3553(a) . . . . The provision also tells the sentencing judge to 'impose a sentence sufficient, but not greater than necessary, to comply with' the basic aims of sentencing as set out above. Congressional statutes then tell the Commission to write Guidelines that will carry out these same § 3553(a) objectives.

Id. at 2463 (emphasis in original). The Court concluded that '[t]he upshot is that the sentencing statutes envision both the sentencing judge and the Commission as carrying out the same basic § 3553(a) objectives, the one, at retail, the other at wholesale,' id., and that the Commission's process for promulgating guidelines results in 'a set of Guidelines that seek to embody the § 3553(a) considerations, both in principle and in practice.' Id. at 2464.

Consequently, district courts are required to properly calculate and consider the guidelines when sentencing, even in an advisory guideline system. See 18 U.S.C. § 3553(a)(4), (a)(5); Booker, 543 U.S. at 264 ('The district courts, while not bound to apply the Guidelines, must . . . take them into account when sentencing.'); Rita, 127 S. Ct. at 2465 (stating that a district court should begin all sentencing proceedings by correctly calculating the applicable Guidelines range); Gall v. United States, 128 S. Ct. 586, 596 (2007) ('As a matter of administration and to secure nationwide consistency, the Guidelines should be the starting point and the initial benchmark.'). The district court, in determining the appropriate sentence in a particular case, therefore, must consider the properly calculated guideline range, the grounds for departure provided in the policy statements, and then the factors under 18 U.S.C. § 3553(a). See Rita, 127 S. Ct. at 2465. The appellate court engages in a two-step process upon review. The appellate court 'first ensure[s] that the district court committed no significant procedural error, such as failing to calculate (or improperly calculating) the Guidelines range . . . [and] then consider[s] the substantive reasonableness of the sentence imposed under an abuse-of-discretion standard[,] . . . tak[ing] into account the totality of the circumstances, including the extent of any variance from the Guidelines range.' Gall, 128 S. Ct. at 597.

The second and related theme resonant in this line of Supreme Court cases is that, as contemplated by the Sentencing Reform Act, the guidelines are evolutionary in nature. They are the product of the Commission's fulfillment of its statutory duties to monitor federal sentencing law and practices, to seek public input on the operation of the guidelines, and to revise the guidelines accordingly. As the Court acknowledged in Rita:

> The Commission's work is ongoing. The statutes and the Guidelines themselves foresee continuous evolution helped by the sentencing courts and courts of appeals in that process. The sentencing courts, applying the Guidelines in individual cases may depart (either pursuant to the Guidelines or, since Booker, by imposing a non-Guidelines sentence). The judges will set forth their reasons. The Courts of Appeals will determine the reasonableness of the resulting sentence. The Commission will collect and examine the results. In doing so, it may obtain advice from prosecutors, defenders, law enforcement groups, civil liberties associations, experts in penology, and others. And it can revise the Guidelines accordingly.

Id. at 2464; see also Booker, 543 U.S. at 264 ('[T]he Sentencing Commission remains in place, writing Guidelines, collecting information about actual district court sentencing decisions, undertaking research, and revising the Guidelines accordingly.'); Gall, 128 S. Ct. at 594 ('[E]ven though the Guidelines are advisory rather than mandatory, they are, as we pointed out in Rita, the product of careful study based on extensive empirical evidence derived from the review of thousands of individual sentencing decisions.').

Provisions of the Sentencing Reform Act promote and facilitate this evolutionary process. For example, pursuant to 28 U.S.C. § 994(x), the Commission publishes guideline amendment proposals in the Federal Register and conducts hearings to solicit input on those proposals from experts and other members of the public. Pursuant to 28 U.S.C. § 994(o), the Commission periodically reviews and revises the guidelines in consideration of comments it receives from members of the federal criminal justice system, including the courts, probation officers, the Department of Justice, the Bureau of Prisons, defense attorneys and the federal public defenders, and in consideration of data it receives from sentencing courts and other sources. Statutory mechanisms such as these bolster the Commission's ability to take into account fully the purposes of sentencing set forth in 18 U.S.C. § 3553(a)(2) in its promulgation of the guidelines.

Congress retains authority to require certain sentencing practices and may exercise its authority through specific directives to the Commission with respect to the guidelines. As the Supreme Court noted in Kimbrough v. United States, 128 S. Ct. 558 (2007), 'Congress has shown that it knows how to direct sentencing practices in express terms. For example, Congress has specifically required the Sentencing Commission to set Guideline sentences for serious recidivist offenders 'at or near' the statutory maximum.' Id. at 571; 28 U.S.C. § 994(h).

As envisioned by Congress, implemented by the Commission, and reaffirmed by the Supreme Court, the guidelines are the product of a deliberative and dynamic process that seeks to embody within federal sentencing policy the purposes of sentencing set forth in the Sentencing Reform Act. As such, the guidelines continue to be a key component of federal sentencing and to play an important role in the sentencing court's determination of an appropriate sentence in any particular case.

3. AUTHORITY

§ 1A3.1.   Authority

The guidelines, policy statements, and commentary set forth in this Guidelines Manual, including amendments thereto, are promulgated by the United States Sentencing Commission pursuant to: (1) section 994(a) of title 28, United States Code; and (2) with respect to guidelines, policy statements, and commentary promulgated or amended pursuant to specific congressional directive, pursuant to the authority contained in that directive in addition to the authority under section 994(a) of title 28, United States Code.".

Reason for Amendment: This amendment sets forth the introduction to the Guidelines Manual as it first appeared in 1987, with the inclusion of amendments occasionally made thereto between 1987 and 2000, in Subpart 1 of Chapter One. In 2003, the introduction was moved to an editorial note. (See Appendix C to the Guidelines Manual, Amendment 651.) This amendment removes the introduction from the editorial note to Subpart 1 of Chapter One, representing the original introduction as it first appeared in 1987, as amended by Amendments 67, 68, 307, 466, 534, 538, 602, and 603.

The amendment also supplements the original introduction with an updated discussion of the role of the guidelines, their evolution, and Supreme Court case law, and redesignates § 1A1.1 (Authority) as § 1A3.1.

Effective Date: The effective date of this amendment is November 1, 2008.

718. **Amendment:** Section 2A6.1 is amended in the heading by adding at the end "; False Liens".

Section 2A6.1(b) is amended by striking subdivision (2) as follows:

"(2) If the offense involved more than two threats, increase by 2 levels.",

and inserting the following:

"(2) If (A) the offense involved more than two threats; or (B) the defendant is convicted under 18 U.S.C. § 1521 and the offense involved more than two false liens or encumbrances, increase by 2 levels.".

The Commentary to § 2A6.1 captioned "Statutory Provisions" is amended by inserting "1521," after "1038,".

The Commentary to § 2A6.1 captioned "Application Notes" is amended by redesignating Notes 2 and 3 as Notes 3 and 4, respectively; and by inserting after Note 1 the following:

"2. Applicability of Chapter Three Adjustments.—If the defendant is convicted under 18 U.S.C. § 1521, apply § 3A1.2 (Official Victim).".

The Commentary to § 2A6.1 captioned "Application Notes" is amended in Note 4, as redesignated by this amendment, by striking subdivision (B) as follows:

"(B) Multiple Threats or Victims.—If the offense involved substantially more than two threatening communications to the same victim or a prolonged period of making harassing communications to the same victim, or if the offense involved multiple victims, an upward departure may be warranted.",

and inserting the following:

"(B) Multiple Threats, False Liens or Encumbrances, or Victims; Pecuniary

Harm.—If the offense involved (i) substantially more than two threatening communications to the same victim, (ii) a prolonged period of making harassing communications to the same victim, (iii) substantially more than two false liens or encumbrances against the real or personal property of the same victim, (iv) multiple victims, or (v) substantial pecuniary harm to a victim, an upward departure may be warranted.".

Section 2H3.1(b) is amended by striking "Characteristic" and inserting "Characteristics"; and by adding at the end the following:

"(2) (Apply the greater) If—

(A) the defendant is convicted under 18 U.S.C. § 119, increase by 8 levels; or

(B) the defendant is convicted under 18 U.S.C. § 119, and the offense involved the use of a computer or an interactive computer service to make restricted personal information about a covered person publicly available, increase by 10 levels.".

The Commentary to § 2H3.1 captioned "Statutory Provisions" is amended by inserting "119," before "1039,".

The Commentary to § 2H3.1 captioned "Application Notes" is amended by redesignating Note 3 as Note 5 and inserting after Note 2 the following:

"3. Inapplicability of Chapter Three (Adjustments).—If the enhancement under subsection (b)(2) applies, do not apply § 3A1.2 (Official Victim).

4. Definitions.—For purposes of subsection (b)(2)(B):

'Computer' has the meaning given that term in 18 U.S.C. § 1030(e)(1).

'Covered person' has the meaning given that term in 18 U.S.C. § 119(b).

'Interactive computer service' has the meaning given that term in section 230(e)(2) of the Communications Act of 1934 (47 U.S.C. § 230(f)(2)).

'Restricted personal information' has the meaning given that term in 18 U.S.C. § 119(b).".

Appendix A (Statutory Index) is amended by inserting after the line reference to 18 U.S.C. § 115(b)(4) the following:

"18 U.S.C. § 119   2H3.1"; and

by inserting after the line reference to 18 U.S.C. § 1520 the following:

"18 U.S.C. § 1521   2A6.1".

Reason for Amendment: This amendment responds to two new offenses created by the Court Security Improvement Act of 2007 (the "Act"), Pub. L. 110–177.

First, the amendment addresses section 201 of the Act, which created a new offense at 18 U.S.C. § 1521 prohibiting the filing of, attempts, or conspiracies to file any false lien or encumbrance against the real or personal property of officers or employees of the United States Government, on account of that individual's performance of official duties. The offense is punishable by a statutory maximum term of imprisonment of ten years. The amendment references the new offense to § 2A6.1 (Threatening or Harassing Communications; Hoaxes), and expands the heading of § 2A6.1 accordingly. The Commission determined that referencing offenses under 18 U.S.C. § 1521 to § 2A6.1 is appropriate because the harassment and threatening of an official by the filing of fraudulent encumbrances is analogous to conduct covered by other statutes referenced to this guideline.

The amendment also makes a number of modifications to § 2A6.1 to address specific harms associated with violations of 18 U.S.C. § 1521. Specifically, the amendment expands the scope of the two-level enhancement at subsection (b)(2) to apply if the defendant is convicted under 18 U.S.C. § 1521 and the offense involved more than two false liens or encumbrances, and also provides an upward departure provision that may apply if the offense involved substantially more than two false liens or encumbrances against the real or personal property of the same victim. These modifications reflect the additional time and resources required to remove multiple false liens or encumbrances and provide proportionality between such offenses and other offenses referenced to this guideline that involve more than two threats.

The amendment also provides an upward departure provision that may apply if the offense involved substantial pecuniary harm to a victim. The upward departure provision reflects the increased seriousness of those offenses that result in substantial costs.

In addition, the amendment adds a new application note specifying that if the defendant is convicted under 18 U.S.C. § 1521, the adjustment under § 3A1.2 (Official Victim) shall apply. The addition of this note clarifies that the official status of the victim is not taken into account in the base offense level.

Second, the amendment addresses section 202 of the Act, which created a new offense at 18 U.S.C. § 119 prohibiting the public disclosure of restricted personal information about a federal officer or employee, witness, juror, or immediate family member of such a person, with the intent to threaten or facilitate a crime of violence against such a person. The offense is punishable by a statutory maximum term of imprisonment of five years. The amendment references the new offense to § 2H3.1 (Interception of Communications; Eavesdropping; Disclosure of Certain Private or Protected Information). The Commission determined that referencing offenses under 18 U.S.C. § 119 to § 2H3.1 is appropriate because the prohibited conduct is analogous to conduct covered by other statutes referenced to this guideline.

The amendment also creates a two-pronged enhancement at subsection (b)(2), the greater of which applies. The first prong, at subsection (b)(2)(A), is an eight-level enhancement applicable if the defendant is convicted under 18 U.S.C. § 119. A corresponding application note provides that § 3A1.2 shall not apply in such cases. Thus, the enhancement at subsection (b)(2)(A) accounts for the official victim adjustment under § 3A1.2 that would otherwise apply in many offenses under 18 U.S.C. § 119. Incorporating the official victim adjustment into subsection (b)(2)(A) was appropriate because the adjustment in § 3A1.2 does not apply to some individuals, such as witnesses and jurors, who are covered by 18 U.S.C. § 119. The enhancement at subsection (b)(2)(A) also reflects the intent to threaten or facilitate a crime of violence, which is an element of an offense under 18 U.S.C. § 119. The cross reference at subsection (c)(1) will apply, however, if the purpose of the offense was to facilitate another offense and the guideline applicable to an attempt to commit that other offense results in a greater offense level.

The second prong, at subsection (b)(2)(B), is a ten-level enhancement applicable if the defendant is convicted under 18 U.S.C. § 119 and the offense involved the use of a computer or an interactive computer service to make restricted personal information about a covered person publicly available. This greater enhancement accounts for the more substantial risk of harm posed by widely disseminating such protected information via the Internet.

Effective Date: The effective date of this amendment is November 1, 2008.

719. **Amendment:** Section 2B1.1, effective February 6, 2008 (see Amendment 714), is repromulgated with the following changes:

Section 2B1.1(b) is amended by striking subdivision (16) as follows:

> "(16) If the offense involved fraud or theft involving any benefit authorized, transported, transmitted, transferred, disbursed, or paid in connection with a declaration of a major disaster or an emergency, increase by 2 levels.";

by redesignating subdivisions (11) through (15) as subdivisions (12) through (16), respectively; by inserting after subdivision (10) the following:

> "(11) If the offense involved conduct described in 18 U.S.C. § 1040, increase by 2 levels. If the resulting offense level is less than level 12, increase to level 12.";

in subdivision (12), as redesignated by this amendment, by inserting "resulting" before "offense level"; and

in subdivision (14), as redesignated by this amendment, by striking "(b)(13)(B)" and inserting "(b)(14)(B)".

The Commentary to § 2B1.1 captioned "Statutory Provisions" is amended by inserting "1040," before "1341-1344,".

The Commentary to § 2B1.1 captioned "Application Notes" is amended in Note 3 by striking subdivision (A)(v)(IV) as follows:

> "(IV) Disaster Fraud Cases.—In a case in which subsection (b)(16) applies, reasonably foreseeable pecuniary harm includes the administrative costs to any federal, state, or local government entity or any commercial or not-for-profit entity of recovering the benefit from any recipient thereof who obtained the benefit through fraud or was otherwise ineligible for the benefit that were reasonably foreseeable.".

The Commentary to § 2B1.1 captioned "Application Notes" is amended in Note 10 by striking "(b)(11)" and inserting "(b)(12)" each place it appears.

The Commentary to § 2B1.1 captioned "Application Notes" is amended in Note 11 by striking "(b)(13)(A)" and inserting "(b)(14)(A)" each place it appears.

The Commentary to § 2B1.1 captioned "Application Notes" is amended in Note 12 by striking "(b)(13)(B)" and inserting "(b)(14)(B)"; by striking "(b)(13)(B)(i)" and inserting "(b)(14)(B)(i)"; and by striking "(b)(13)(B)(ii)" and inserting "(b)(14)(B)(ii)".

The Commentary to § 2B1.1 captioned "Application Notes" is amended in Note 13 by

Amendment 719 APPENDIX C - VOLUME III November 1, 2013

striking "(b)(14)" and inserting "(b)(15)" each place it appears; by striking "(b)(14)(iii)" and inserting "(b)(15)(iii)" each place it appears; and by striking "(b)(13)(B)" and inserting "(b)(14)(B)" each place it appears.

The Commentary to § 2B1.1 captioned "Application Notes" is amended in Note 14 by striking "(b)(15)" and inserting "(b)(16)" each place it appears.

The Commentary to § 2B1.1 captioned "Application Notes" is amended by striking Note 15 as follows:

"15. Application of Subsection (b)(16).—

Definitions.—For purposes of this subsection:

'Emergency' has the meaning given that term in 42 U.S.C. § 5122.

'Major disaster' has the meaning given that term in 42 U.S.C. § 5122.",

and by redesignating Notes 16 through 20 as Notes 15 through 19, respectively.

The Commentary to § 2B1.1 captioned "Application Notes" is amended in Note 19, as redesignated by this amendment, by striking "(b)(14)(iii)" and inserting "(b)(15)(iii)"; and by adding at the end the following:

"(D) Downward Departure for Major Disaster or Emergency Victims.—If (i) the minimum offense level of level 12 in subsection (b)(11) applies; (ii) the defendant sustained damage, loss, hardship, or suffering caused by a major disaster or an emergency as those terms are defined in 42 U.S.C. § 5122; and (iii) the benefits received illegally were only an extension or overpayment of benefits received legitimately, a downward departure may be warranted.".

The Commentary to § 2B1.1 captioned "Background" is amended by inserting after the paragraph that begins "Subsection (b)(10)(C)" the following:

"Subsection (b)(11) implements the directive in section 5 of Public Law 110–179.".

The Commentary to § 2B1.1 captioned "Background" is amended in the paragraph that begins "Subsection (b)(12)(B)" by striking "(b)(12)(B)" and inserting "(b)(13)(B)";

in the paragraph that begins "Subsection (b)(13)(A)" by striking "(b)(13)(A)" and inserting "(b)(14)(A)";

in the paragraph that begins "Subsection (b)(13)(B)(i)" by striking "(b)(13)(B)(i)" and inserting "(b)(14)(B)(i)";

in the paragraph that begins "Subsection (b)(14)" by striking "(b)(14)" and inserting "(b)(15)"; and by striking "(b)(14)(B)" and inserting "(b)(15)(B)"; and

by striking the paragraph that begins "Subsection (b)(16) implements" as follows:

"Subsection (b)(16) implements the directive in section 5 of Public Law 110–179.".

Reason for Amendment: This amendment re-promulgates as permanent the temporary, emergency amendment (effective Feb. 6, 2008) that implemented the emergency directive in section 5 of the "Emergency and Disaster Assistance Fraud Penalty Enhancement Act of 2007," Pub. L. 110–179 (the "Act"). The directive, which required the Commission to promulgate an amendment under emergency amendment authority by February 6, 2008, directed that the Commission forthwith shall –

> promulgate sentencing guidelines or amend existing sentencing guidelines to provide for increased penalties for persons convicted of fraud or theft offenses in connection with a major disaster declaration under section 401 of the Robert T. Stafford Disaster Relief and Emergency Assistance Act (42 U.S.C. 5170) or an emergency declaration under section 501 of the Robert T. Stafford Disaster Relief and Emergency Assistance Act (42 U.S.C. 5191) . . ..

Section 5(b) of the Act further required the Commission to –

> (1) ensure that the sentencing guidelines and policy statements reflect the serious nature of the offenses described in subsection (a) and the need for aggressive and appropriate law enforcement action to prevent such offenses;
>
> (2) assure reasonable consistency with other relevant directives and with other guidelines;
>
> (3) account for any aggravating or mitigating circumstances that might justify exceptions, including circumstances for which the sentencing guidelines currently provide sentencing enhancements;
>
> (4) make any necessary conforming changes to the sentencing guidelines; and
>
> (5) assure that the guidelines adequately meet the purposes of sentencing as set forth in section 3553(a)(2) of title 18, United States Code.

The emergency amendment addressed concerns that disaster fraud involves harms not adequately addressed by § 2B1.1 (Larceny, Embezzlement, and Other Forms of Theft; Offenses Involving Stolen Property; Property Damage or Destruction; Fraud and Deceit; Forgery; Offenses Involving Altered or Counterfeit Instruments Other than Counterfeit Bearer Obligations of the United States) by (1) adding a two-level enhancement if the offense involved fraud or theft involving any benefit authorized, transported, transmitted, transferred, disbursed, or paid in connection with a declaration of a major disaster or an emergency; (2) modifying the commentary to the guideline as it relates to the calculation of loss; and (3) providing a reference to § 2B1.1 in Appendix A (Statutory Index) for the offense at 18 U.S.C. § 1040 (Fraud in connection with major disaster or emergency benefits) created by the Act.

This amendment repromulgates the temporary, emergency amendment as permanent, with the following changes. First, the amendment expands the scope of the two-level enhancement to include all conduct described in 18 U.S.C. § 1040. Thus, the amendment expands the scope of the enhancement to include fraud or theft involving procurement of property or services as a contractor, subcontractor or supplier, rather than limiting it to the conduct described in the emergency directive. The limited emergency amendment authority did not permit the Commission to include such conduct in the enhancement promulgated in the emergency amendment. However, the directive in section 5 of the Act covers all "fraud or theft offenses in connection with a major disaster declaration" and, therefore, expansion of the scope of the enhancement to apply to all conduct described in 18 U.S.C. § 1040 is appropriate.

Second, the amendment modifies the enhancement to include a minimum offense level of 12. The Commission frequently adopts a minimum offense level in circumstances in which, as in these cases, loss as calculated by the guidelines is difficult to compute or does not adequately account for the harm caused by the offense. The Commission studied a sample of disaster fraud cases and compared those cases to other cases of defrauding government programs. This analysis supported claims made in testimony to the Commission that the majority of the disaster fraud cases resulted in probationary sentences because the amount of loss calculated under subsection (b)(1) of § 2B1.1 had little impact on the sentences. The Commission also received testimony and public comment identifying various harms unique to disaster fraud cases. For example, charitable institutions may have a more difficult time soliciting contributions because fraud in connection with disasters may erode public trust in these institutions. Moreover, the pool of funds available to aid legitimate disaster victims is adversely affected when fraud occurs. Further, the inherent tension between the imposition of fraud controls and the need to provide aid to disaster victims quickly makes it difficult for relief agencies and charitable institutions to prevent disaster fraud. All of these factors provide support for a minimum offense level.

Third, the amendment adds a downward departure provision that may apply in a case in which the minimum offense level applies, the defendant is a victim of a major disaster or emergency, and the benefits received illegally were only an extension or overpayment of benefits received legitimately. This provision recognizes that a defendant's legitimate status as a disaster victim may be a mitigating factor warranting a downward departure in certain cases involving relatively small amounts of loss.

Fourth, the amendment deletes certain commentary relating to the definition of loss that was promulgated in the emergency amendment. Specifically, the emergency amendment added subdivision (IV) to Application Note 3(A)(v) of § 2B1.1 providing that in disaster fraud cases, "reasonably foreseeable pecuniary harm includes the administrative costs to any federal, state, or local government entity or any commercial or not-for-profit entity of recovering the benefit from any recipient thereof who obtained the benefit through fraud or was otherwise ineligible for the benefit that were reasonably foreseeable." The amendment deletes this provision because of concerns that administrative costs might be difficult to determine or in some instances could over-represent the harm caused by the offense.

Finally, the amendment makes conforming changes to the guideline and the commentary.

Effective Date: The effective date of this amendment is November 1, 2008.

720. **Amendment:** The Commentary to § 2C1.1 captioned "Statutory Provisions" is amended by inserting "227," after "226,".

Appendix A (Statutory Index) is amended by inserting after the line reference to 18 U.S.C. § 226 the following:

"18 U.S.C. § 227   2C1.1".

Reason for Amendment: This amendment responds to the Honest Leadership and Open Government Act of 2007, Pub. L. 110–81 ("the Act"). The Act created a criminal offense at 18 U.S.C. § 227 prohibiting a member or employee of Congress from influencing or attempting to influence, on the basis of political affiliation, employment decisions or practices of a private entity. The offense is punishable by a 15-year statutory maximum term of imprisonment.

The amendment modifies Appendix A (Statutory Index) to reference offenses under 18 U.S.C. § 227 to § 2C1.1 (Offering, Giving, Soliciting, or Receiving a Bribe; Extortion Under Color of Official Right; Fraud Involving the Deprivation of the Intangible Right to Honest Services of Public Officials; Conspiracy to Defraud by Interference with

Governmental Functions) because this guideline covers similar offenses.

Effective Date: The effective date of this amendment is November 1, 2008.

721. Amendment: Section 2E3.1 is amended in the heading by adding at the end "; Animal Fighting Offenses".

Section 2E3.1(a) is amended by inserting "(Apply the greatest)" after "Level:"; by redesignating subdivision (2) as subdivision (3); and by inserting after subdivision (1) the following:

"(2) 10, if the offense involved an animal fighting venture; or".

The Commentary to § 2E3.1 captioned "Statutory Provisions" is amended by inserting "7 U.S.C. § 2156;" before "15 U.S.C. §§ ".

The Commentary to § 2E3.1 is amended by adding at the end the following:

"Application Notes:

1. Definition.—For purposes of this guideline: 'Animal fighting venture' has the meaning given that term in 7 U.S.C. § 2156(g).

2. Upward Departure Provision.—If the offense involved extraordinary cruelty to an animal that resulted in, for example, maiming or death to an animal, an upward departure may be warranted.".

The Commentary to § 2X5.2 captioned "Statutory Provisions" is amended by striking "7 U.S.C. § 2156;".

Appendix A (Statutory Index) is amended in the line reference to 7 U.S.C. § 2156 by striking "2X5.2" and inserting "2E3.1".

Reason for Amendment: This amendment implements the Animal Fighting Prohibition Enforcement Act of 2007, Pub. L. 110–22 (the "Act"). The Act amended the Animal Welfare Act, 7 U.S.C. § 2156, to increase penalties for existing offenses and to create a new offense. Specifically, the Act increased penalties for criminal violations of 7 U.S.C. § 2156 from a one-year statutory maximum term of imprisonment to a three-year statutory maximum term of imprisonment. The penalties are set forth in section 49 of title 18, United States Code. In addition, the Act created an offense at 7 U.S.C. § 2156(e) making it unlawful to "sell, buy, transport, or deliver in interstate or foreign commerce a knife, a gaff, or any other sharp instrument attached, or designed or intended to be attached, to the leg of a bird for use in an animal fighting venture." This new offense also carries a three-year statutory maximum term of imprisonment.

Because 7 U.S.C. § 2156 is now a felony offense, the amendment deletes the reference of 7 U.S.C. § 2156 to § 2X5.2 (Class A Misdemeanors) in Appendix A (Statutory Index), and deletes the listing of 7 U.S.C. § 2156 from the statutory provisions listed in the commentary to § 2X5.2. The amendment references offenses under 7 U.S.C. § 2156 to § 2E3.1 (Gambling Offenses) as the legislative history and public comment indicate that such offenses often involve gambling. Accordingly, the amendment expands the title of § 2E3.1 to include animal fighting offenses.

The amendment also creates a new alternative base offense level at § 2E3.1(a)(2) that provides a base offense level of level 10 if the offense involved an "animal fighting venture," which is defined in Application Note 1 as having the meaning given that term in 7 U.S.C. § 2156(g), i.e., "any event which involves a fight between at least two animals and is conducted for purposes of sport, wagering, or entertainment." The alternative base offense level reflects the increased harm, i.e., cruelty to animals, resulting from offenses under 7 U.S.C. § 2156(g) that is not associated with offenses that typically receive a base offense level of level 6 under the guideline. Additionally, the amendment adds an instruction to apply the greatest applicable base offense level at § 2E3.1(a) because an offense involving an animal fighting venture may also involve conduct covered by subsection (a)(1) and, therefore, should receive the higher base offense level provided by that subsection.

The amendment also provides an upward departure provision that may apply if an offense involves extraordinary cruelty to an animal that resulted in, for example, maiming or death to an animal.

Effective Date: The effective date of this amendment is November 1, 2008.

722. **Amendment:** The Commentary to § 2L1.2 captioned "Application Notes" is amended in Note 1 by striking subdivision (B)(iii) as follows:

"(iii) 'Crime of violence' means any of the following: murder, manslaughter, kidnapping, aggravated assault, forcible sex offenses, statutory rape, sexual abuse of a minor, robbery, arson, extortion, extortionate extension of credit, burglary of a dwelling, or any offense under federal, state, or local law that has as an element the use, attempted use, or threatened use of physical force against the person of another.",

and inserting the following:

"(iii) 'Crime of violence' means any of the following offenses under federal, state, or local law: murder, manslaughter, kidnapping, aggravated assault, forcible sex offenses (including where consent to the conduct is not given or is not legally valid, such as where consent to the conduct is involuntary, incompetent, or coerced), statutory rape, sexual abuse of a minor, robbery, arson, extortion, extortionate extension of credit, burglary of a dwelling, or any other offense under federal, state, or local law that has as an element the use, attempted use, or threatened use of physical force against the person of another.";

and in subdivision (B)(iv) by inserting ", or offer to sell" after "dispensing of".

The Commentary to § 2L1.2 captioned "Application Notes" is amended by adding at the end the following:

"7. Departure Consideration.—There may be cases in which the applicable offense level substantially overstates or understates the seriousness of a prior conviction. In such a case, a departure may be warranted. Examples: (A) In a case in which subsection (b)(1)(A) or (b)(1)(B) does not apply and the defendant has a prior conviction for possessing or transporting a quantity of a controlled substance that exceeds a quantity consistent with personal use, an upward departure may be warranted. (B) In a case in which subsection (b)(1)(A) applies, and the prior conviction does not meet the definition of aggravated felony at 8 U.S.C. § 1101(a)(43), a downward departure may be warranted.".

Reason for Amendment: This amendment addresses certain discrete issues that have arisen in the application of § 2L1.2 (Unlawfully Entering or Remaining in the United States). The amendment reflects input the Commission has received from federal judges, prosecutors, defense attorneys, and probation officers at several roundtable discussions and public hearings on the operation of § 2L1.2.

First, the amendment clarifies the scope of the term "forcible sex offense" as that term is used in the definition of "crime of violence" in § 2L1.2, Application Note 1(B)(iii). The amendment provides that the term "forcible sex offense" includes crimes "where consent to the conduct is not given or is not legally valid, such as where consent to the conduct is involuntary, incompetent, or coerced." The amendment makes clear that forcible sex offenses, like all offenses enumerated in Application Note 1(B)(iii), "are always classified as 'crimes of violence,' regardless of whether the prior offense expressly has as an element the use, attempted use, or threatened use of physical force against the person of another," USSC, Guideline Manual, Supplement to Appendix C, Amendment 658. Application of the amendment, therefore, would result in an outcome that is contrary to cases excluding crimes in which "there may be assent in fact but no legally valid consent" from the scope of "forcible sex offenses." See, e.g., United States v. Gomez-Gomez, 493 F.3d 562, 567 (5th Cir. 2007) (holding that a rape conviction was not a forcible sex offense because it could have been based on assent given in response to a threat "to reveal embarrassing secrets" or after "an employer threatened to fire a subordinate"); United States v. Luciano-Rodriguez, 442 F.3d 320, 322–23 (5th Cir. 2006) (holding that a conviction for a sexual assault was not a forcible sex offense because it could have been based on assent when "the actor knows that as a result of mental disease or defect the other person is at the time of the sexual assault incapable either of appraising the nature of the act or of resisting it," when "the actor is a public servant who coerces the other person to submit or participate," or when "the actor is a member of the clergy or is a mental health service provider who exploits the emotional dependency engendered by their position"); United States v. Sarmiento-Funes, 374 F.3d 336, 341 (5th Cir. 2004) (holding that a conviction for sexual assault was not a forcible sex offense because it could have been based on assent that is "the product of deception or a judgment impaired by intoxication").

Second, the amendment clarifies that an "offer to sell" a controlled substance is a "drug trafficking offense" for purposes of subsection (b)(1) of § 2L1.2 by adding "offer to sell" to the conduct listed in Application Note 1(B)(iv).

Finally, the amendment addresses the concern that in some cases the categorical enhancements in subsection (b) may not adequately reflect the seriousness of a prior offense. The amendment adds a departure provision that may apply in a case "in which the applicable offense level substantially overstates or understates the seriousness of a prior conviction." The amendment provides two examples of cases that may warrant such a departure. The first example suggests that an upward departure may be warranted in a case in which "subsection (b)(1)(A) or (b)(1)(B) does not apply and the defendant has a prior conviction for possessing or transporting a quantity of a controlled substance that exceeds a quantity consistent with personal use." The second example suggests that a downward departure may be warranted in a case in which "subsection (b)(1)(A) applies, and the prior conviction does not meet the definition of aggravated felony at 8 U.S.C. § 1101(a)(43)."

Effective Date: The effective date of this amendment is November 1, 2008.

723. **Amendment:** Section 2N2.1 is amended by redesignating subsection (b) as subsection (c) and inserting after subsection (a) the following:

"(b) Specific Offense Characteristic

(1) If the defendant was convicted under 21 U.S.C. § 331 after sustaining a prior conviction under 21 U.S.C. § 331, increase by 4 levels.".

The Commentary to § 2N2.1 captioned "Application Notes" is amended in Note 2 by striking "(b)(1)" and inserting "(c)(1)"; and by striking "(b)(2)" and inserting "(c)(2)".

The Commentary to § 2N2.1 captioned "Application Notes" is amended in Note 3 by striking "Death" and inserting "The offense created a substantial risk of bodily injury or death;"; by inserting "death," before "extreme"; and by inserting "from the offense" after "resulted".

Reason for Amendment: This amendment makes two changes to § 2N2.1 (Violations of Statutes and Regulations Dealing With Any Food, Drug, Biological Product, Device, Cosmetic, or Agricultural Product) to address offenses under the Federal Food, Drug, and Cosmetic Act, 21 U.S.C. §§ 301 et seq. (the "FDCA") and the Prescription Drug Marketing Act of 1987, Pub L. 100–293 (the "PDMA"). First, the amendment adds a specific offense characteristic at subsection (b)(1) of § 2N2.1 that provides a four-level enhancement for repeat violations of the FDCA. First time violations of the FDCA, absent fraud, carry a maximum term of imprisonment of one year. 21 U.S.C. § 333(a)(1). In contrast, second or subsequent violations of the FDCA carry a maximum term of imprisonment of three years. 21 U.S.C. § 333(a)(2). The Commission determined based on public comment and testimony that an enhancement is appropriate to account for the increased statutory maximum penalties provided for second or subsequent FDCA violations.

Second, the amendment expands the upward departure provision at Application Note 3(A) of § 2N2.1 to include an offense that created a substantial risk of bodily injury or death. Public comment and testimony indicated that § 2N2.1 may not adequately account for the substantial risk of bodily injury or death created by certain offenses. The PDMA, for example, includes certain offenses that may create such risks, such as the re-importation into the United States of any previously exported prescription drug, except by the drug's manufacturer; the sale or purchase of any prescription drug sample or coupon; and the wholesale distribution of prescription drugs without the necessary state or federal licenses. 21 U.S.C. § 353(c), (d), (e). Thus, the amendment expanded the scope of the upward departure provision to address such risks.

Effective Date: The effective date of this amendment is November 1, 2008.

724. **Amendment:** The Commentary to § 2E4.1 captioned "Application Note" is amended in Note 1 by inserting "and local" before "excise"; and by striking "tax" and inserting "taxes".

The Commentary to § 2E4.1 captioned "Background" is amended by inserting "and local" before "excise".

Section 2X7.1 is amended in subsection (a) by striking "554" and inserting "555" each place it appears.

The Commentary to § 2X7.1 captioned "Statutory Provision" is amended by striking "554" and inserting "555".

Section 3C1.4 is amended by striking "3559(f)(1)" and inserting "3559(g)(1)".

Appendix A (Statutory Index) is amended by striking both line references to 18 U.S.C. § 554 as follows:

"18 U.S.C. § 554   2X7.1

(Border tunnels and passages)
18 U.S.C. § 554
(Smuggling goods from the   2B1.5, 2M5.2, 2Q2.1",
United States)

and inserting the following:

"18 U.S.C. § 554   2B1.5, 2M5.2, 2Q2.1
18 U.S.C. § 555   2X7.1";

in the line reference to 18 U.S.C. § 1091 by striking "2H1.3" and inserting "2H1.1";

in the line reference to 18 U.S.C. § 1512(a) by inserting ", 2A2.2, 2A2.3, 2J1.2" after "2A2.1"; and

in the line reference to 18 U.S.C. § 1512(b) by striking "2A1.2, 2A2.2,".

Reason for Amendment: This amendment makes various technical and conforming changes to the guidelines.

First, the amendment addresses section 121 of the USA PATRIOT Improvement and Reauthorization Act of 2005, Pub. L. 109–177, which expanded the definition of "contraband cigarette" in subsection (2) of 18 U.S.C. § 2341 to include the failure to pay local cigarette taxes. The amendment reflects this statutory change by expanding the scope of Application Note 1 of § 2E4.1 (Unlawful Conduct Relating to Contraband Cigarettes and Smokeless Tobacco) to include local excise taxes within the meaning of "taxes evaded." The amendment also amends the background commentary to § 2E4.1 to include local excise taxes.

Second, the amendment implements technical corrections made by section 553 of Pub. L. 110–161 by changing the statutory references in § 2X7.1 (Border Tunnels and Subterranean Passages) from "18 U.S.C. § 554" to "18 U.S.C. § 555," and by amending Appendix A (Statutory Index) to refer violations of 18 U.S.C. § 555 to § 2X7.1.

Third, the amendment addresses a statutory redesignation made by section 202 of the Adam Walsh Child Protection and Safety Act of 2006, Pub. L. 109–248, by changing statutory references in § 3C1.4 (False Registration of Domain Name) from "18 U.S.C. § 3559(f)(1)" to "18 U.S.C. § 3559(g)(1)."

Fourth, the amendment addresses statutory changes to 18 U.S.C. § 1512 (Tampering with a witness, victim, or an informant) made by the 21st Century Department of Justice Appropriations Act, Pub. L. 107–273, by deleting in Appendix A the references to §§ 2A1.2 (Second Degree Murder) and 2A2.2 (Aggravated Assault) for violations of 18 U.S.C. § 1512(b), and adding those guidelines as references for violations of 18 U.S.C. § 1512(a). The amendment also adds a reference to § 2J1.2 (Obstruction of Justice) for a violation of 18 U.S.C. § 1512(a) to reflect the broad range of obstructive conduct, including the use of physical force against a witness, covered by that subsection.

Fifth, the amendment changes the reference in Appendix A for offenses under 18 U.S.C. § 1091 (Genocide) from § 2H1.3 (Use of Force or Threat of Force to Deny Benefits or Rights in Furtherance of Discrimination; Damage to Religious Real Property), which no longer exists as a result of a guideline consolidation (see Appendix C to the Guidelines Manual, Amendment 521), to § 2H1.1 (Offenses Involving Individual Rights).

Effective Date: The effective date of this amendment is November 1, 2008.

725. **Amendment:** Chapter One, as amended by Amendment 717, is amended in the heading by inserting a comma after "AUTHORITY".

The Commentary to § 2A3.1 captioned "Application Notes" is amended in Note 5 by striking "(c)(1)" each place it appears and inserting "(c)(2)".

The Commentary to § 2B1.1 captioned "Application Notes" is amended in Note 3(F)(i) by striking "7(A)" and inserting "9(A)".

The Commentary to § 5K2.0 captioned "Background" is amended in the second paragraph by striking "Historical Note to § 1A1.1 (Authority)" and inserting "Chapter One, Part A".

Appendix A (Statutory Index) is amended by inserting after the line reference to 18 U.S.C. § 1039 the following:

"18 U.S.C. § 1040   2B1.1".

Reason for Amendment: This amendment makes various technical and conforming changes. Specifically, the amendment makes a clerical change to the chapter heading of Chapter One; corrects inaccurate references in the Commentary to § 2A3.1 Criminal Sexual Abuse; Attempt to Commit Criminal Sexual Abuse), § 2B1.1 (Larceny, Embezzlement, and Other Forms of Theft; Offenses Involving Stolen Property; Property Damage or Destruction; Fraud and Deceit; Forgery; Offenses Involving Altered or Counterfeit Instruments Other than Counterfeit Bearer Obligations of the United States), and § 5K2.0 (Grounds for Departure), and amends Appendix A (Statutory Index) to repromulgate the line reference to 18 U.S.C. § 1040, which had been added by Amendment 714.

Effective Date: The effective date of this amendment is November 1, 2008.

726. **Amendment:** Section 2B1.1(b) is amended by redesignating subdivisions (15) and (16) as subdivisions (16) and (17); and by inserting after subdivision (14) the following:

"(15) If (A) the defendant was convicted of an offense under 18 U.S.C. § 1030, and the offense involved an intent to obtain personal information, or (B) the offense involved the unauthorized public dissemination of personal information, increase by 2 levels.".

Section 2B1.1(b) is amended in subdivision (16), as redesignated by this amendment, by striking "(I)" after "involved"; by striking "; or (II) an intent to obtain personal information" after "security"; and by striking "(i)" after "(5)(A)".

The Commentary to § 2B1.1 captioned "Application Notes" is amended in Note 1 by inserting after the paragraph that begins "'Foreign instrumentality'" the following:

"'Means of identification' has the meaning given that term in 18 U.S.C. § 1028(d)(7), except that such means of identification shall be of an actual (i.e., not fictitious) individual, other than the defendant or a person for whose conduct the defendant is accountable under § 1B1.3 (Relevant Conduct).";

and by inserting after the paragraph that begins "'National cemetery'" the following:

"'Personal information' means sensitive or private information involving an identifiable individual (including such information in the possession of a third party), including (i) medical records; (ii) wills; (iii) diaries; (iv) private correspondence, including e-mail; (v) financial records; (vi) photographs of a sensitive or private nature; or (vii) similar information.".

The Commentary to § 2B1.1 captioned "Application Notes" is amended in Note 3(C) in subdivision (i) by inserting ", copied," after "taken"; by redesignating subdivisions (ii) through (v) as subdivisions (iii) through (vi); and by inserting after subdivision (i) the following:

> "(ii) In the case of proprietary information (e.g., trade secrets), the cost of developing that information or the reduction in the value of that information that resulted from the offense.".

The Commentary to § 2B1.1 captioned "Application Notes" is amended in Note 4 by adding at the end the following:

> "(E) <u>Cases Involving Means of Identification</u>.—For purposes of subsection (b)(2), in a case involving means of identification 'victim' means (i) any victim as defined in Application Note 1; or (ii) any individual whose means of identification was used unlawfully or without authority.".

The Commentary to § 2B1.1 captioned "Application Notes" is amended in Note 9(A) by striking the paragraph that begins "'Means of identification'" as follows:

> "'Means of identification' has the meaning given that term in 18 U.S.C. § 1028(d)(7), except that such means of identification shall be of an actual (i.e., not fictitious) individual, other than the defendant or a person for whose conduct the defendant is accountable under § 1B1.3 (Relevant Conduct).".

The Commentary to § 2B1.1 captioned "Application Notes" is amended in Note 13 by striking "(15)" and inserting "(16)" each place it appears; by striking the paragraph that begins "'Personal information'" as follows:

> "'Personal information' means sensitive or private information (including such information in the possession of a third party), including (i) medical records; (ii) wills; (iii) diaries; (iv) private correspondence, including e-mail; (v) financial records; (vi) photographs of a sensitive or private nature; or (vii) similar information.";

and by inserting "(A)" before "(iii)" each place it appears.

The Commentary to § 2B1.1 captioned "Application Notes" is amended in Note 14 by striking "(b)(16)" and inserting "(b)(17)" each place it appears.

The Commentary to § 2B1.1 captioned "Application Notes" is amended in Note 19(B) by striking "(15)" and inserting "(16)(A)".

The Commentary to § 2B1.1 captioned "Background" is amended by inserting after the paragraph that begins "Subsection (b)(14)(B)(i)" the following:

> " Subsection (b)(15) implements the directive in section 209 of Public Law 110–326.";

and in the paragraph that begins "Subsection (b)(15)" by striking "(15)" and inserting "(16)" each place it appears.

The Commentary to § 2H3.1 captioned "Application Notes" is amended in Note 4 by striking "Definitions.—For purposes of subsection (b)(2)(B):" and inserting "Definitions.—For purposes of this guideline:"; and by inserting after the paragraph that begins "'Interactive computer service'" the following:

> "'Means of identification' has the meaning given that term in 18 U.S.C. § 1028(d)(7), except that such means of identification shall be of an actual (i.e., not fictitious) individual, other than the defendant or a person for whose conduct the defendant is accountable under § 1B1.3 (Relevant Conduct).
>
> 'Personal information' means sensitive or private information involving an identifiable individual (including such information in the possession of a third party), including (i) medical records; (ii) wills; (iii) diaries; (iv) private correspondence, including e-mail; (v) financial records; (vi) photographs of a sensitive or private nature; or (vii) similar information.".

The Commentary to § 2H3.1 captioned "Application Notes" is amended in Note 5(i) by inserting "personal information, means of identification," after "offense involved"; and by inserting a comma before "or tax".

The Commentary to § 3B1.3 captioned "Application Notes" is amended in Note 2(B) by inserting ", transfer, or issue" after "in order to obtain".

Reason for Amendment: This multi-part amendment responds to the directive in section 209 of the Identity Theft Enforcement and Restitution Act of 2008, Title II of Pub. L. 110–326 (the "Act"), and addresses other related issues arising from case law. Section 209(a) of the Act directed the Commission to—

> review its guidelines and policy statements applicable to persons convicted of offenses under sections 1028, 1028A, 1030, 2511, and 2701 of title 18, United States Code, and any other relevant provisions of law, in order to reflect the intent of Congress that such penalties be increased in comparison to those currently provided by such guidelines and policy statements.

The Act further required the Commission, in determining the appropriate sentence for the above referenced offenses, to consider the extent to which the guidelines and policy statements adequately account for 13 factors listed in section 209(b) of the Act.

In response to the congressional directive, the amendment increases penalties provided by the applicable guidelines and policy statements by adding a new enhancement and a new upward departure provision. In addition, the amendment expands both the definition of "victim" and the factors to be considered in the calculation of loss; each of these expansions may, in an appropriate case, increase penalties in comparison to those provided prior to the amendment.

First, the amendment adds a new two-level enhancement in § 2B1.1 (Larceny, Embezzlement, and Other Forms of Theft; Offenses Involving Stolen Property; Property Damage or Destruction; Fraud and Deceit; Forgery; Offenses Involving Altered or Counterfeit Instruments Other than Counterfeit Bearer Obligations of the United States). The new enhancement, which addresses offenses involving personal information, is at subsection (b)(15). An existing enhancement, which addresses offenses under 18 U.S.C. § 1030 (i.e., computer crimes), was at subsection (b)(15) but has been redesignated as subsection (b)(16).

The new enhancement for offenses involving personal information applies if (A) the defendant was convicted of an offense under 18 U.S.C. § 1030 and the offense involved an intent to obtain personal information, or (B) the offense involved the unauthorized public dissemination of personal information. The "(A)" prong of the new personal information enhancement had been a prong of the existing computer crime enhancement, but the tiered structure of that enhancement was such that if a computer crime involved both an intent to obtain personal information and another harm (such as an intrusion into a government computer, an intent to cause damage, or a disruption of a critical infrastructure), only the greatest applicable increase would apply. The amendment responds to concerns that a case involving those other harms is different in kind from a case involving an intent to obtain personal information. Moving the intent to obtain personal information prong out of the computer crime enhancement and into the new enhancement ensures that a defendant convicted under section 1030 receives an incremental increase in punishment if the offense involved both an intent to obtain personal information and another harm addressed by the computer crime enhancement. The "(B)" prong of the new personal information enhancement ensures that any defendant, regardless of the statute of conviction, receives an additional incremental increase in punishment if the offense involved the unauthorized public dissemination of personal information. This prong accounts for the greater harm to privacy caused by such an offense.

Second, the amendment amends the Commentary to § 2B1.1 to provide that, for purposes of the victims table in subsection (b)(2), an individual whose means of identification was used unlawfully or without authority is considered a "victim." The Commentary to § 2B1.1 in Application Note 1 defines "victim" in pertinent part to mean "any person who sustained any part of the actual loss determined under subsection (b)(1)". An identity theft case may involve an individual whose means of identification was taken and used but who was fully reimbursed by a third party (e.g., a bank or credit card company). Some courts have held that such an individual is not counted as a "victim" for purposes of the victims table at § 2B1.1(b)(2). See United States v. Kennedy, 554 F.3d 415 (3d Cir. 2009) (discussing various cases addressing this issue, including United States v. Armstead, 552 F.3d 769 (9th Cir. 2008); United States v. Abiodun, 536 F.3d 162 (2d Cir. 2008); United States v. Connor, 537 F.3d 480 (5th Cir. 2008); United States v. Icaza, 492 F.3d 967 (8th Cir. 2007); United States v. Lee, 427 F.3d 881 (11th Cir. 2005); and United States v. Yagar, 404 F.3d 967 (6th Cir. 2005)). The Commission determined that such an individual should be considered a "victim" for purposes of subsection (b)(2) because such an individual, even if fully reimbursed, must often spend significant time resolving credit problems and related issues, and such lost time may not be adequately accounted for in the loss calculations under the guidelines. The Commission received testimony that the incidence of data breach cases, in which large numbers of means of identification are compromised, is increasing. This new category of "victim" for purposes of subsection (b)(2) is appropriately limited, however, to cover only those individuals whose means of identification are actually used.

Third, the amendment makes two changes to Application Note 3(C) regarding the calculation of loss. The first change specifies that the estimate of loss may be based upon the fair market value of property that is copied. This change responds to concerns that the calculation of loss does not adequately account for a case in which an owner of proprietary information retains possession of such information, but the proprietary information is unlawfully copied. The amendment recognizes, for example, that a computer crime that does not deprive the owner of the information in the computer nonetheless may cause loss inasmuch as it reduces the value of the information. The amendment makes clear that in such a case the court may use the fair market value of the copied property to estimate loss. The second change adds a new provision to Application Note 3(C) specifying that, in a case involving proprietary information (e.g., trade secrets), the court may estimate loss using the cost of developing that information or the reduction in the value of that information that resulted from the offense. The new provision responds to concerns that the guidelines did not adequately explain how to estimate loss in a case involving proprietary information such as trade secrets.

Fourth, the amendment moves the definitions of "means of identification" and "personal information" to Application Note 1, and clarifies that for information to be considered "personal information," it must involve information of an identifiable individual.

Fifth, the amendment amends § 2H3.1 (Interception of Communications; Eavesdropping; Disclosure of Certain Private or Protected Information) to provide that an upward departure may be warranted in a case in which the offense involved personal information or means of identification of a substantial number of individuals. As a conforming change, in Application Note 4 the amendment adds definitions of "means of identification" and "personal information" that are identical to the definitions of those terms in § 2B1.1. The departure provision responds to concerns that the guideline may not adequately account for the rare wiretapping offense that involves a substantial number of victims.

Sixth, the amendment clarifies Application Note 2(B) of § 3B1.3 (Abuse of Position of Trust or Use of Special Skill). The first sentence of Application Note 2(B) specifies that an adjustment under § 3B1.3 shall apply to a defendant who exceeds or abuses his or her authority to "obtain" or "use" a means of identification. The second sentence then provides, as an example of such a defendant, an employee of a state motor vehicle department who exceeds or abuses his or her authority by "issuing" a means of identification. To make the two sentences consistent, the amendment clarifies the first sentence so that it expressly applies not only to obtaining or using a means of identification, but also to issuing or transferring a means of identification.

Finally, the amendment makes several technical changes. In particular, it corrects several places in the Guidelines Manual that erroneously refer to subsection "(b)(15)(iii)" of § 2B1.1; the reference should be to subsection (b)(15)(A)(iii) (redesignated by the amendment as (b)(16)(A)(iii)). Also, it conforms a statutory reference in § 2B1.1(b)(15)(A)(ii) (redesignated by the amendment as (b)(16)(A)(ii)), which refers to 18 U.S.C. § 1030(a)(5)(A)(i); the Act redesignated this statute as 18 U.S.C. § 1030(a)(5)(A).

The Commission determined that certain factors listed in the directive are adequately accounted for by existing provisions in the Guidelines Manual. See, e.g., §§ 2B1.1(b)(1), (b)(9)(C), (b)(13), (b)(16) (as redesignated by the amendment); 2B2.3(b)(1), (b)(3); 2B3.2(b)(3)(B); 2H3.1(b)(1)(B); and 3B1.4 (Using a Minor To Commit a Crime)).

Effective Date: The effective date of this amendment is November 1, 2009.

727. **Amendment:** Section 2D1.1(a) is amended by redesignating subdivision (3) as subdivision (5); and by inserting after subdivision (2) the following:

    "(3)   30, if the defendant is convicted under 21 U.S.C. § 841(b)(1)(E) or 21 U.S.C. § 960(b)(5), and the offense of conviction establishes that death or serious bodily injury resulted from the use of the substance and that the defendant committed the offense after one or more prior convictions for a similar offense; or

    (4)   26, if the defendant is convicted under 21 U.S.C. § 841(b)(1)(E) or 21 U.S.C. § 960(b)(5), and the offense of conviction establishes that death or serious bodily injury resulted from the use of the substance; or".

Section 2D1.1(c)(5) is amended by inserting "700,000 or more units of Schedule III Hydrocodone;" after the line referenced to "Schedule I or II Depressants".

Section 2D1.1(c)(6) is amended by inserting "At least 400,000 but less than 700,000 units of Schedule III Hydrocodone;" after the line referenced to "Schedule I or II Depressants".

Section 2D1.1(c)(7) is amended by inserting "At least 100,000 but less than 400,000 units of Schedule III Hydrocodone;" after the line referenced to "Schedule I or II Depressants".

Section 2D1.1(c)(8) is amended by inserting "At least 80,000 but less than 100,000 units of Schedule III Hydrocodone;" after the line referenced to "Schedule I or II Depressants".

Section 2D1.1(c)(9) is amended by inserting "At least 60,000 but less than 80,000 units of Schedule III Hydrocodone;" after the line referenced to "Schedule I or II Depressants".

Section 2D1.1(c)(10) is amended by inserting "At least 40,000 but less than 60,000 units of Schedule III Hydrocodone;" after the line referenced to "Schedule I or II Depressants"; and by inserting "or Hydrocodone" after "(except Ketamine".

Section 2D1.1(c)(11) is amended by inserting "At least 20,000 but less than 40,000 units of Schedule III Hydrocodone;" after the line referenced to "Schedule I or II Depressants"; and by inserting "or Hydrocodone" after "(except Ketamine".

Section 2D1.1(c)(12) is amended by inserting "At least 10,000 but less than 20,000 units of Schedule III Hydrocodone;" after the line referenced to "Schedule I or II Depressants"; and by inserting "or Hydrocodone" after "(except Ketamine".

Section 2D1.1(c)(13) is amended by inserting "At least 5,000 but less than 10,000 units of Schedule III Hydrocodone;" after the line referenced to "Schedule I or II Depressants"; and by inserting "or Hydrocodone" after "(except Ketamine".

Section 2D1.1(c)(14) is amended by inserting "At least 2,500 but less than 5,000 units of Schedule III Hydrocodone;" after the line referenced to "Schedule I or II Depressants"; and by inserting "or Hydrocodone" after "(except Ketamine".

Section 2D1.1(c)(15) is amended by inserting "At least 1,000 but less than 2,500 units of Schedule III Hydrocodone;" after the line referenced to "Schedule I or II Depressants"; and by inserting "or Hydrocodone" after "(except Ketamine".

Section 2D1.1(c)(16) is amended by inserting "At least 250 but less than 1,000 units of Schedule III Hydrocodone;" after the line referenced to "Schedule I or II Depressants"; and by inserting "or Hydrocodone" after "(except Ketamine".

Section 2D1.1(c)(17) is amended by inserting "Less than 250 units of Schedule III Hydrocodone;" after the line referenced to "Schedule I or II Depressants"; and by inserting "or Hydrocodone" after "(except Ketamine".

The Commentary to § 2D1.1 captioned "Application Notes" is amended in Note 10(E) in the subdivision captioned "Schedule III Substances (except ketamine)" by inserting in the heading "and hydrocodone" after "(except ketamine"; and in the sentence that begins "* * *Provided" by inserting "(except ketamine and hydrocodone)" after "Schedule III substances".

The Commentary to § 2D1.1 captioned "Application Notes" is amended in Note 10(E) by inserting after the subdivision captioned "Schedule III Substances (except ketamine)" the following subdivision:

"Schedule III Hydrocodone****

Amendment 727 APPENDIX C - VOLUME III November 1, 2013

1 unit of Schedule III hydrocodone =   1 gm of marihuana

****Provided, that the combined equivalent weight of all Schedule III substances (except ketamine), Schedule IV substances (except flunitrazepam), and Schedule V substances shall not exceed 999.99 kilograms of marihuana.".

The Commentary to § 2D1.1 captioned "Application Notes" is amended in Note 10(E) in the subdivision captioned "Schedule IV Substances (except flunitrazepam)" by inserting an additional asterisk after "****" each place it appears.

The Commentary to § 2D1.1 captioned "Application Notes" is amended in Note 10(E) in the subdivision captioned "Schedule V Substances" by inserting an additional asterisk after "*****" each place it appears.

The Commentary to § 2D1.1 captioned "Application Notes" is amended in Note 10(E) in the subdivision captioned "List I Chemicals (relating to the manufacture of amphetamine or methamphetamine)" by inserting an additional asterisk after "******" each place it appears.

Section 2D3.1 is amended in the heading by striking "Schedule I" and inserting "Scheduled".

Appendix A (Statutory Index) is amended by inserting after the line referenced to 21 U.S.C. § 841(g) the following:

"21 U.S.C. § 841(h)   2D1.1".

Reason for Amendment: This amendment responds to the Ryan Haight Online Pharmacy Consumer Protection Act of 2008, Pub. L. 110–425 (the "Act").

The Act amended the Controlled Substances Act (21 U.S.C. § 801 et seq.) to create two new offenses involving controlled substances, increased the statutory maximum terms of imprisonment for all Schedule III and IV controlled substance offenses and for second and subsequent Schedule V controlled substance offenses, and added a sentencing enhancement for Schedule III controlled substance offenses in a case in which "death or serious bodily injury results from the use of such substance". The Act also included a directive to the Commission that states:

> The United States Sentencing Commission, in determining whether to amend, or establish new, guidelines or policy statements, to conform the Federal sentencing guidelines and policy statements to this Act and the amendments made by this Act, should not construe any change in the maximum penalty for a violation involving a controlled substance in a particular schedule as being the sole reason to amend, or establish a new, guideline or policy statement.

First, the amendment addresses the sentencing enhancement added by the Act, which applies when the offense involved a Schedule III controlled substance and death or serious bodily injury resulted from the use of such substance. The statutory enhancement provides a maximum term of imprisonment of 15 years, or 30 years if the violation is committed after a prior conviction for a felony drug offense. See 21 U.S.C. §§ 841(b)(1)(E), 960(b)(5). The amendment addresses the statutory enhancement by amending § 2D1.1 (Unlawful Manufacturing, Importing, Exporting, or Trafficking (Including Possession with Intent to Commit These Offenses); Attempt or Conspiracy) to provide two new alternative base offense levels at subsections (a)(3) and (a)(4) for offenses involving Schedule III controlled substances in which death or injury results that are comparable to the alternative base offense levels at subsections (a)(1) and (a)(2) for offenses involving Schedule I and II controlled substances in which death or injury results. To reflect the harms involved in these offenses and the criminal histories of repeat drug offenders, the alternative base offense levels are set at level 30 if the defendant committed the offense after one or more prior convictions for a similar offense and level 26 otherwise.

Second, the amendment modifies the Drug Quantity Table in § 2D1.1 to increase the maximum base offense level for offenses involving Schedule III hydrocodone from level 20 to level 30, without modifying any other offense level. The amendment extends the Drug Quantity Table for Schedule III hydrocodone offenses to level 30 using the existing marihuana equivalency (i.e., 1 pill of Schedule III hydrocodone = 1 gram of marihuana). The Commission determined that a maximum base offense level of 30 is appropriate for Schedule III hydrocodone offenses because of data and testimony indicating a relatively high prevalence of misuse (when compared to other, non-marihuana drugs of abuse), an increasing number of emergency room visits involving this drug, and the very large volume of hydrocodone pills illicitly distributed, either over the Internet or in specialized pain clinics.

Finally, the amendment addresses the two new offenses created by the Act. The first new offense, at 21 U.S.C. § 841(h), prohibits the delivery, distribution, or dispensing of controlled substances over the Internet without a valid prescription. The applicable statutory maximum term of imprisonment depends on the controlled substance involved. The amendment amends Appendix A (Statutory Index) to reference 21 U.S.C. § 841(h) to § 2D1.1 because distribution of a controlled substance is an element of the offense. That guideline also is appropriate because it includes an enhancement at subsection (b)(6) that provides a two-level increase in a case in which "a person distributes a controlled substance through mass-marketing by means of an interactive computer service" (e.g., sale of a controlled substance by means of the Internet).

The second new offense, at 21 U.S.C. § 843(c)(2)(A), prohibits the use of the Internet to advertise for sale a controlled substance and has a statutory maximum term of imprisonment of four years. Offenses under 21 U.S.C. § 843(c) already are referenced in Appendix A (Statutory Index) to § 2D3.1 (Regulatory Offenses Involving Registration Numbers; Unlawful Advertising Relating to Schedule I Substances; Attempt or Conspiracy). The amendment modifies the title of that guideline to indicate that it covers any scheduled controlled substance.

Effective Date: The effective date of this amendment is November 1, 2009.

728. **Amendment:** Section 2D1.1(b)(2) is amended by striking "or" before "(B)"; and by inserting "a submersible vessel or semi-submersible vessel as described in 18 U.S.C. § 2285 was used, or (C)" after "(B)".

The Commentary to § 2D1.1 captioned "Application Notes" is amended in Note 8 in the paragraph that begins "Note, however" by striking "(B)" and inserting "(C)".

Chapter Two, Part X, Subpart 7 is amended in the heading by adding at the end "AND SUBMERSIBLE AND SEMI-SUBMERSIBLE VESSELS".

Chapter Two, Part X, Subpart 7 is amended by adding at the end the following guideline and accompanying commentary:

"§ 2X7.2.   Submersible and Semi-Submersible Vessels

(a) Base Offense Level: 26

(b) Specific Offense Characteristic

(1) (Apply the greatest) If the offense involved—

(A) a failure to heave to when directed by law enforcement officers, increase by 2 levels;

(B) an attempt to sink the vessel, increase by 4 levels; or

(C) the sinking of the vessel, increase by 8 levels.

Commentary

Statutory Provision: 18 U.S.C. § 2285.

Application Note:

1. Upward Departure Provisions.—An upward departure may be warranted in any of the following cases:

(A) The defendant engaged in a pattern of activity involving use of a submersible vessel or semi-submersible vessel described in 18 U.S.C. § 2285 to facilitate other felonies.

(B) The offense involved use of the vessel as part of an ongoing criminal organization or enterprise.

Background: This guideline implements the directive to the Commission in section 103 of Public Law 110-407.".

Appendix A (Statutory Index) is amended by inserting after the line referenced to 18 U.S.C. § 2284 the following:

"18 U.S.C. § 2285   2X7.2".

Reason for Amendment: This amendment responds to the Drug Trafficking Vessel Interdiction Act of 2008, Pub. L. 110-407 (the "Act"). The Act created a new offense at 18 U.S.C. § 2285 making it unlawful to operate, attempt or conspire to operate, or embark in an unflagged submersible or semi-submersible vessel in international waters with the intent to evade detection. Section 103 of the Act directed the Commission to amend the guidelines, or promulgate new guidelines, to provide adequate penalties for persons convicted of offenses under 18 U.S.C. § 2285 and included a list of circumstances for the Commission to consider.

First, the amendment amends § 2D1.1 (Unlawful Manufacturing, Importing, Exporting, or Trafficking (Including Possession with Intent to Commit These Offenses); Attempt or Conspiracy) by expanding the scope of the specific offense characteristic at subsection (b)(2) to apply if a submersible or semi-submersible vessel was used in a drug importation offense. The Commission determined that a drug importation offense involving the use of a submersible or semi-submersible vessel poses similar risks and harms as a drug importation offense involving an unscheduled aircraft (which subsection (b)(2) already covers). The amendment also makes a conforming change to a reference in Application Note 8.

Second, the amendment creates a new guideline at § 2X7.2 (Submersible and Semi-

Submersible Vessels) for the new offense at 18 U.S.C. § 2285. The new guideline provides a base offense level of 26 and includes a tiered specific offense characteristic and upward departure provisions to address certain aggravating circumstances listed in the directive. Public testimony indicates that submersible and semi-submersible vessels to date have been used for the purpose of transporting drugs. Such conduct receives a minimum offense level of 26 under § 2D1.1(b)(2), discussed above, regardless of the type or quantity of drug involved in the offense. The Commission determined that a base offense level of 26 in § 2X7.2 for an offense under section 2285 would be appropriate to promote proportionality.

The specific offense characteristic in § 2X7.2 provides a two-level enhancement for failing to heave to, a four-level enhancement for attempting to sink the vessel, and an eight-level enhancement for sinking the vessel; the greatest applicable enhancement applies. Offenses involving such conduct are more serious because they create greater risk of harm to the crew of the illegal vessel and the interdicting law enforcement personnel, particularly in a case in which the illegal vessel is sunk and its crew must be rescued. In addition, sinking the vessel destroys evidence of illegal activity. The upward departure provisions provide that an upward departure may be warranted if the defendant engaged in a pattern of activity involving the use of a submersible or semi-submersible vessel, or if the offense involved the use of the vessel as a part of an ongoing criminal organization or criminal enterprise.

Third, the amendment amends Appendix A (Statutory Index) to reference 18 U.S.C. § 2285 to § 2X7.2.

Effective Date: The effective date of this amendment is November 1, 2009.

729. **Amendment:** Section 2A6.1(b) is amended by redesignating subdivision (5) as subdivision (6); by inserting after subdivision (4) the following:

> "(5) If the defendant (A) is convicted under 18 U.S.C. § 115, (B) made a public threatening communication, and (C) knew or should have known that the public threatening communication created a substantial risk of inciting others to violate 18 U.S.C. § 115, increase by 2 levels.";

and in subdivision (6), as redesignated by this amendment, by striking "and (4)" and inserting "(4), and (5)".

The Commentary to § 2A6.1 captioned "Background" is amended by adding at the end the following:

> "   Subsection (b)(5) implements, in a broader form, the directive to the Commission in section 209 of the Court Security Improvement Act of 2007, Public Law 110–177.".

Appendix A (Statutory Index) is amended in the line referenced to 18 U.S.C. § 1513 by inserting "2A1.1, 2A1.2, 2A1.3, 2A2.1, 2A2.2, 2A2.3, 2B1.1," before "2J1.2".

Reason for Amendment: This amendment responds to the Court Security Improvement Act of 2007, Pub. L. 110–177 (the "Act"), and other related issues.

First, the amendment responds to the directive in section 209 of the Act, which required the Commission to review the guidelines applicable to threats punishable under 18 U.S.C. § 115 (Influencing, impeding, or retaliating against a Federal official by threatening or injuring a family member) that occur over the Internet, and determine "whether and by how much that circumstance should aggravate the punishment pursuant to section 994 of title 28, United States Code." The directive further required the Commission to consider the number of such threats made, the intended number of recipients of such threats, and whether the initial senders of such threats were acting in an individual capacity or as part of a larger group.

The amendment implements the directive by amending § 2A6.1 (Threatening or Harassing Communications; Hoaxes; False Liens) to provide a new two-level enhancement for a case in which the defendant is convicted under 18 U.S.C. § 115, made a public threatening communication, and knew or should have known that the public threatening communication created a substantial risk of inciting others to violate 18 U.S.C. § 115. The Commission determined that the policy concerns underlying the directive regarding threats occurring over the Internet apply equally to threats made public by other means (e.g., radio, television broadcast) and that the response to the directive therefore should be technology neutral. The threat guideline, § 2A6.1, adequately accounts for offenses involving multiple threats and multiple victims through the existing specific offense characteristic at subsection (b)(2) and the upward departure provision in Application Note 4.

Second, the amendment amends Appendix A (Statutory Index) to add references for 18 U.S.C. § 1513 (Retaliating against a witness, victim, or an informant) to §§ 2A1.1 (First Degree Murder), 2A1.2 (Second Degree Murder), 2A1.3 (Voluntary Manslaughter), 2A2.1 (Assault with Intent to Commit Murder; Attempted Murder), 2A2.2 (Aggravated Assault), 2A2.3 (Minor Assault), and 2B1.1 (Larceny, Embezzlement, and Other Forms of Theft; Offenses Involving Stolen Property; Property Damage or Destruction; Fraud and Deceit; Forgery; Offenses Involving Altered or Counterfeit Instruments Other than Counterfeit Bearer Obligations of the United States), in addition to § 2J1.2 (Obstruction of Justice). The additional references more adequately reflect the range of conduct covered by 18 U.S.C. § 1513, including killing or attempting to kill a witness, causing bodily injury to a witness, and damaging the tangible property of a witness. In addition, 18 U.S.C. § 1512 (Tampering with a witness, victim, or an informant), which covers a similar range of conduct, including killing or attempting to kill a witness and using physical force against a witness, is referenced to the same Chapter Two, Part A guidelines.

Effective Date: The effective date of this amendment is November 1, 2009.

730. **Amendment:** Section 2H4.1(a) is amended by striking "(Apply the greater)" after "Offense Level"; and by striking subdivision (2) as follows:

"(2)   18, if the defendant was convicted of an offense under 18 U.S.C. § 1592.",

and inserting the following:

"(2)   18, if (A) the defendant was convicted of an offense under 18 U.S.C. § 1592, or (B) the defendant was convicted of an offense under 18 U.S.C. § 1593A based on an act in violation of 18 U.S.C. § 1592.".

The Commentary to § 2H4.1 captioned "Statutory Provisions" is amended by inserting ", 1593A" after "1592".

The Commentary to § 2H4.1 captioned "Application Notes" is amended by adding at the end the following:

"4.   In a case in which the defendant was convicted under 18 U.S.C. §§ 1589(b) or 1593A, a downward departure may be warranted if the defendant benefitted from participating in a venture described in those sections without know-

– 1154 –

ing that (i.e., in reckless disregard of the fact that) the venture had engaged in the criminal activity described in those sections.".

Section 2L1.1(b) is amended by striking subdivision (8) as follows:

"(8) If an alien was involuntarily detained through coercion or threat, or in connection with a demand for payment, (A) after the alien was smuggled into the United States; or (B) while the alien was transported or harbored in the United States, increase by 2 levels. If the resulting offense level is less than level 18, increase to level 18.",

and inserting the following:

"(8) (Apply the greater):

(A) If an alien was involuntarily detained through coercion or threat, or in connection with a demand for payment, (i) after the alien was smuggled into the United States; or (ii) while the alien was transported or harbored in the United States, increase by 2 levels. If the resulting offense level is less than level 18, increase to level 18.

(B) If (i) the defendant was convicted of alien harboring, (ii) the alien harboring was for the purpose of prostitution, and (iii) the defendant receives an adjustment under § 3B1.1 (Aggravating Role), increase by 2 levels, but if the alien engaging in the prostitution had not attained the age of 18 years, increase by 6 levels.".

The Commentary to § 2L1.1 captioned "Application Notes" is amended in Note 6 by inserting "(A)" after "(b)(8)".

Appendix A (Statutory Index) is amended by inserting after the line referenced to 18 U.S.C. § 1350 the following:

"18 U.S.C. § 1351   2B1.1";

and by inserting after the line referenced to 18 U.S.C. § 1592 the following:

"18 U.S.C. § 1593A   2H4.1".

Reason for Amendment: This amendment responds to the William Wilberforce Trafficking Victims Protection Reauthorization Act of 2008, Pub. L. 110–457 (the "Act"), which included a directive to the Commission and created two new offenses.

First, the amendment responds to the directive in section 222(g) of the Act. It directed the Commission to—

review and, if appropriate, amend the sentencing guidelines and policy statements applicable to persons convicted of alien harboring to ensure conformity with the sentencing guidelines applicable to persons convicted of promoting a commercial sex act if–

(1) the harboring was committed in furtherance of prostitution; and

(2) the defendant to be sentenced is an organizer, leader, manager, or supervisor of the criminal activity.

Amendment 730

The amendment amends § 2L1.1 (Smuggling, Transporting, or Harboring an Unlawful Alien) to provide an alternative prong to the enhancement at subsection (b)(8), which covers cases in which an alien was involuntarily detained through coercion or threat, or in connection with a demand for payment. The new alternative prong, at subsection (b)(8)(B), applies in a case in which the defendant was convicted of alien harboring, the alien harboring was for the purpose of prostitution, and the defendant receives an adjustment under § 3B1.1 (Aggravating Role). In such a case, a two-level increase applies, but if the alien engaging in the prostitution had not attained the age of 18 years, a six-level increase applies. Because this is an alternative enhancement, it does not apply if the enhancement for coercion at § 2L1.1(b)(8)(A) is greater.

The amendment also amends Application Note 6 to provide that, while an adjustment under § 3A1.3 (Restraint of Victim) does not apply in a case that receives an enhancement under § 2L1.1(b)(8)(A), such an adjustment may apply in a case that receives an enhancement under § 2L1.1(b)(8)(B).

Second, the amendment responds to a new offense created by the Act, 18 U.S.C. § 1351 (Fraud in foreign labor contracting). The new offense has a statutory maximum term of imprisonment of five years. Because this new offense has fraud as an element, the amendment references this new offense in Appendix A (Statutory Index) to § 2B1.1 (Larceny, Embezzlement, and Other Forms of Theft; Offenses Involving Stolen Property; Property Damage or Destruction; Fraud and Deceit; Forgery; Offenses Involving Altered or Counterfeit Instruments Other than Counterfeit Bearer Obligations of the United States).

Third, the amendment responds to another new offense created by the Act, 18 U.S.C. § 1593A (Benefitting financially from peonage, slavery, and trafficking in persons). This new offense applies when a person has knowingly benefitted financially from participating in a venture that has engaged in a violation of 18 U.S.C. §§ 1581(a), 1592, or 1595(a), knowing or in reckless disregard of the fact that the venture has engaged in such violation. The amendment amends Appendix A (Statutory Index) to reference 18 U.S.C. § 1593A to § 2H4.1 (Peonage, Involuntary Servitude, and Slave Trade) because that guideline covers the relevant underlying statutes, 18 U.S.C. §§ 1581(a) and 1592. The amendment also amends § 2H4.1 to provide that a defendant convicted of 18 U.S.C. § 1593A receives the same base offense level as if the defendant were convicted of committing the underlying violation. Accordingly, if the defendant was convicted under section 1593A under circumstances in which the defendant benefitted from participation in a venture that engaged in a violation of 18 U.S.C. § 1592, the defendant would receive the same base offense level, 18, as if the defendant had been convicted of 18 U.S.C. § 1592. If the defendant was convicted under section 1593A under circumstances in which the defendant benefitted from participation in a venture that engaged in a violation of 18 U.S.C. § 1581(a), the defendant would receive the same base offense level, 22, as if the defendant had been convicted of 18 U.S.C. § 1581(a).

The amendment also amends the Commentary to § 2H4.1 to provide that a downward departure may be warranted in a case in which the defendant is convicted under 18 U.S.C. §§ 1589(b) or 1593A if the defendant benefitted from participating in a venture described in those sections in reckless disregard of the fact that the venture had engaged in the criminal activities described in those sections. This downward departure provision recognizes that a defendant who commits such an offense in reckless disregard of the fact that the venture engaged in such criminal activities may be less culpable than a defendant who acts with knowledge of that fact.

Finally, the amendment makes a technical change to § 2H4.1(a) by striking the phrase "(Apply the greater)".

November 1, 2013 APPENDIX C - VOLUME III **Amendment 731**

Effective Date: The effective date of this amendment is November 1, 2009.

731. **Amendment:** Section 2B5.1(b)(2)(B) is amended by inserting "(ii) genuine United States currency paper from which the ink or other distinctive counterfeit deterrent has been completely or partially removed;" after "paper;"; and by striking "or (ii)" and inserting "or (iii)".

The Commentary to § 2B5.1 captioned "Application Notes" is amended in Note 1 by inserting after the paragraph that begins "Definitions.—" the following:

> "'Counterfeit' refers to an instrument that has been falsely made, manufactured, or altered. For example, an instrument that has been falsely made or manufactured in its entirety is 'counterfeit', as is a genuine instrument that has been falsely altered (such as a genuine $5 bill that has been altered to appear to be a genuine $100 bill).".

The Commentary to § 2B5.1 captioned "Application Notes" is amended by striking Note 3 as follows:

> "3. Inapplicability to Genuine but Fraudulently Altered Instruments.— 'Counterfeit,' as used in this section, means an instrument that purports to be genuine but is not, because it has been falsely made or manufactured in its entirety. Offenses involving genuine instruments that have been altered are covered under § 2B1.1 (Theft, Property Destruction, and Fraud).";

and by redesignating Note 4 as Note 3.

Appendix A (Statutory Index) is amended in the line referenced to 18 U.S.C. § 474A by striking "2B1.1,"; and in the line referenced to 18 U.S.C. § 476 by striking "2B1.1,".

Reason for Amendment: This amendment amends § 2B5.1 (Offenses Involving Counterfeit Bearer Obligations of the United States) to clarify guideline application issues regarding the sentencing of counterfeiting offenses involving "bleached notes." A bleached note is genuine United States currency stripped of its original image through the use of solvents or other chemicals and then reprinted to appear to be a note of higher denomination. The amendment responds to concerns expressed by federal judges and members of Congress regarding which guideline should apply to offenses involving bleached notes.

Courts in different circuits have resolved differently the question of whether an offense involving bleached notes should be sentenced under § 2B5.1 or § 2B1.1 (Larceny, Embezzlement, and Other Forms of Theft; Offenses Involving Stolen Property; Property Damage or Destruction; Fraud and Deceit; Forgery; Offenses Involving Altered or Counterfeit Instruments Other than Counterfeit Bearer Obligations of the United States). Compare United States v. Schreckengost, 384 F.3d 922 (7th Cir. 2004) (holding that bleached notes should be sentenced under § 2B1.1), and United States v. Inclema, 363 F.3d 1177 (11th Cir. 2004) (same), with United States v. Dison, 2008 WL 351935 (W.D. La. Feb. 8, 2008) (applying § 2B5.1 in a case involving bleached notes), and United States v. Vice, 2008 WL 113970 (W.D. La. Jan. 3, 2008) (same).

The amendment resolves this issue by providing that an offense involving bleached notes is sentenced under § 2B5.1. The amendment does so by deleting Application Note 3 and revising the definition of "counterfeit" to more closely parallel relevant counterfeiting statutes, including 18 U.S.C. §§ 471 (Obligations or securities of the United States) and 472 (Uttering counterfeit obligations or securities). It establishes a new definition at Application Note 1 providing that counterfeit "refers to an instrument that has been falsely made, manufactured, or altered." Under the new definition, altered instruments are treated as counterfeit and sentenced under § 2B5.1. Technological advances in counterfeiting, such as bleaching notes, have rendered obsolete the previous distinction in the guidelines between an instrument falsely made or manufactured in its entirety and a genuine instrument that is altered.

The amendment also adds a prong to the enhancement at subsection (b)(2)(B) to cover a case in which the defendant controlled or possessed genuine United States currency paper from which the ink or other distinctive counterfeit deterrent has been completely or partially removed. Blank or partially blank bleached notes are similar to counterfeiting paper in how they are involved in counterfeiting offenses. Accordingly, this new prong ensures that an offender who controlled or possessed blank or partially blank bleached notes is subject to the same two-level enhancement as an offender who controlled or possessed "counterfeiting paper similar to a distinctive paper", as subsection (b)(2)(B)(i) already provides.

Finally, the amendment amends Appendix A (Statutory Index) by striking the reference to § 2B1.1 for two offenses that do not involve elements of fraud. Specifically, the amendment deletes the reference to § 2B1.1 for offenses under 18 U.S.C. §§ 474A (Deterrents to counterfeiting of obligations and securities) and 476 (Taking impressions of tools used for obligations or securities).

Effective Date: The effective date of this amendment is November 1, 2009.

732. **Amendment:** The Commentary to § 2A3.2 captioned "Application Notes" is amended in Note 3(B) in the paragraph that begins "<u>Undue Influence</u>" by adding at the end "The voluntariness of the minor's behavior may be compromised without prohibited sexual conduct occurring."; by inserting after the paragraph that begins "<u>Undue Influence</u>" the following:

> "However, subsection (b)(2)(B)(ii) does not apply in a case in which the only 'minor' (as defined in Application Note 1) involved in the offense is an undercover law enforcement officer.";

and in the paragraph that begins "In a case" by striking ", for purposes of subsection (b)(2)(B), that such participant unduly influenced the minor to engage in prohibited sexual conduct" and inserting "that subsection (b)(2)(B)(ii) applies".

The Commentary to § 2A3.2 captioned "Background" is amended by striking "two-level" and inserting "four-level" each place it appears.

The Commentary to § 2G1.3 captioned "Application Notes" is amended in Note 3(B) in the paragraph that begins "<u>Undue Influence</u>" by adding at the end "The voluntariness of the minor's behavior may be compromised without prohibited sexual conduct occurring."; by inserting after the paragraph that begins "<u>Undue Influence</u>" the following:

> "However, subsection (b)(2)(B) does not apply in a case in which the only 'minor' (as defined in Application Note 1) involved in the offense is an undercover law enforcement officer.";

and in the paragraph that begins "In a case" by striking ", for purposes of subsection (b)(2)(B), that such participant unduly influenced the minor to engage in prohibited sexual conduct" and inserting "that subsection (b)(2)(B) applies".

Reason for Amendment: This amendment addresses a circuit conflict regarding application of the undue influence enhancement at subsection (b)(2)(B)(ii) of § 2A3.2 (Criminal Sexual Abuse of a Minor Under the Age of Sixteen Years (Statutory Rape) or Attempt to Commit Such Acts) and at subsection (b)(2)(B) of § 2G1.3 (Promoting a Commercial Sex Act or Prohibited Sexual Conduct with a Minor; Transportation of Minors to Engage in a Commercial Sex Act or Prohibited Sexual Conduct; Travel to Engage in Commercial Sex Act or Prohibited Sexual Conduct with a Minor; Sex Trafficking of Children; Use of Interstate Facilities to Transport Information about a Minor). The undue influence enhancement applies if "a participant otherwise unduly influenced the minor to engage in prohibited sexual conduct." The Commentary to both guidelines states that in determining whether the undue influence enhancement applies, "the court should closely consider the facts of the case to determine whether a participant's influence over the minor compromised the voluntariness of the minor's behavior." The Commentary also provides for a rebuttable presumption of undue influence "[i]n a case in which a participant is at least 10 years older than the minor."

In both guidelines, the term "minor" is defined to include "an individual, whether fictitious or not, who a law enforcement officer represented to a participant . . . could be provided for the purposes of engaging in sexually explicit conduct" or "an undercover law enforcement officer who represented to a participant that the officer had not attained" the age of majority.

Three circuits have expressed different views on two issues: first, whether the undue influence enhancement can apply in a case involving attempted sexual conduct; and second, whether the undue influence enhancement can apply in a case in which the only minor involved is a law enforcement officer. Compare United States v. Root, 296 F.3d 1222, 1234 (11th Cir. 2002) (holding that the undue influence enhancement in § 2A3.2 can apply in instances of attempted sexual conduct, including a case in which the only "victim" involved in the case is an undercover law enforcement officer), and United States v. Vance, 494 F.3d 985, 996 (11th Cir. 2007) (holding that the undue influence enhancement in § 2G1.3 can apply in a case in which the minor is fictitious), with United States v. Mitchell, 353 F.3d 552, 554, 557 (7th Cir. 2003) (holding that the undue influence enhancement in § 2A3.2 "cannot apply in the case of an attempt where the victim is an undercover police officer", and suggesting that it cannot apply in any case in which "the offender and victim have not engaged in illicit sexual conduct"), and United States v. Chriswell, 401 F.3d 459, 469 (6th Cir. 2005) (holding that the undue influence enhancement in § 2A3.2 "is not applicable in cases where the victim is an undercover agent representing himself to be a child under the age of sixteen" but leaving open the possibility that it can apply in other instances of attempted sexual conduct).

The amendment resolves the first issue by providing that the undue influence enhancement can apply in a case involving attempted sexual conduct. Specifically, the amendment amends the Commentary in §§ 2A3.2 and 2G1.3 to provide that "[t]he voluntariness of the minor's behavior may be compromised without prohibited sexual conduct occurring."

The amendment resolves the second issue by providing in the Commentary to §§ 2A3.2 and 2G1.3 that the undue influence enhancement does not apply in a case in which the only "minor" involved in the offense is an undercover law enforcement officer. The Commission determined that the undue influence enhancement should not apply in a case involving only an undercover law enforcement officer because, unlike other enhancements in the sex offense guidelines, the undue influence enhancement is properly focused on the effect of the defendant's actions on the minor's behavior.

The amendment also makes a stylistic change to the language in the Commentary of both §§ 2A3.2 and 2G1.3, and makes a technical change to the Background of § 2A3.2.

Amendment 732

Effective Date: The effective date of this amendment is November 1, 2009.

733. Amendment: Section 2B1.1(b)(6) is amended by striking "or" after "damage to,"; and by inserting "or trafficking in," after "destruction of,".

The Commentary to § 2B1.1 captioned "Background" is amended in the paragraph that begins "Subsection (b)(6)" by inserting "and the directive to the Commission in section 3 of Public Law 110–384" after "105–101".

Section 2G2.1(b)(6) is amended by inserting "or for the purpose of transmitting such material live" after "explicit material".

The Commentary to § 2G2.1 captioned "Application Notes" is amended in Note 1 in the paragraph that begins "'Distribution' means" by inserting "transmission," after "production,"; and by inserting after the paragraph that begins "'Interactive computer service'" the following:

"'Material' includes a visual depiction, as defined in 18 U.S.C. § 2256.".

The Commentary to § 2G2.1 captioned "Application Notes" is amended in Note 4 by inserting "or for the purpose of transmitting such material live" after "explicit material" each place it appears; and in subdivision (B) by striking "purpose" after "for such" and inserting "purposes".

Section 2G2.2(a)(1) is amended by striking "or" after "2252(a)(4),"; and by inserting ", or § 2252A(a)(7)" after "2252A(a)(5)".

Section 2G2.2(b)(6) is amended by inserting "or for accessing with intent to view the material," after "material,".

Section 2G2.2(c)(1) is amended by inserting "or for the purpose of transmitting a live visual depiction of such conduct" after "such conduct".

The Commentary to § 2G2.2 captioned "Application Notes" is amended in Note 1 in the paragraph that begins "'Distribution' means" by inserting "transmission," after "production,"; by inserting after the paragraph that begins "'Interactive computer service'" the following:

"'Material' includes a visual depiction, as defined in 18 U.S.C. § 2256."; and

in the paragraph that begins "'Sexual abuse or exploitation'" by inserting "accessing with intent to view," after "possession,".

The Commentary to § 2G2.2 captioned "Application Notes" is amended in Note 2 by inserting "access with intent to view," after "possess,".

The Commentary to § 2G2.2 captioned "Application Notes" is amended in Note 4(B)(ii) by striking "recording" and inserting "visual depiction" each place it appears.

The Commentary to § 2G2.2 captioned "Application Notes" is amended in Note 5(A) by inserting "or for the purpose of transmitting live any visual depiction of such conduct" after "such conduct".

The Commentary to § 2G2.2 captioned "Application Notes" is amended by redesignating Note 6 as Note 7; and by inserting after Note 5 the following:

"6. Cases Involving Adapted or Modified Depictions.—If the offense involved material that is an adapted or modified depiction of an identifiable minor (e. g., a case in which the defendant is convicted under 18 U.S.C. § 2252A(a)(7)), the term 'material involving the sexual exploitation of a minor' includes such material.".

Chapter Two, Part H, Subpart 4 is amended in the heading by striking "AND" after "SERVITUDE,"; and by adding at the end ", AND CHILD SOLDIERS".

Section 2H4.1 is amended in the heading by striking "and" after "Servitude,"; and by adding at the end ", and Child Soldiers".

The Commentary to § 2H4.1 captioned "Statutory Provisions" is amended by inserting ", 2442" before the period at the end.

The Commentary to § 2H4.1 captioned "Application Notes" is amended in Note 1 by adding at the end the following:

"'Peonage or involuntary servitude' includes forced labor, slavery, and recruitment or use of a child soldier.".

Chapter Two, Part N is amended in the heading by inserting "CONSUMER PRODUCTS," after "PRODUCTS,".

Chapter Two, Part N, Subpart 2 is amended in the heading by striking "AND" after "DRUGS,"; and by adding at the end ", AND CONSUMER PRODUCTS".

Section 2N2.1 is amended in the heading by striking "or" after "Cosmetic,"; and by adding at the end ", or Consumer Product".

Section 5B1.3(a) is amended in subdivision (2) by striking "(B) give notice to victims of the offense pursuant to 18 U.S.C. § 3555, or (C) reside, or refrain from residing, in a specified place or area," and inserting "(B) work in community service, or (C) both, unless the court has imposed a fine, or"; and by striking the paragraph that begins "Note: Section 3563(a)(2)" as follows:

"Note: Section 3563(a)(2) of Title 18, United States Code, provides that, absent unusual circumstances, a defendant convicted of a felony shall abide by at least one of the conditions set forth in 18 U.S.C. § 3563(b)(2), (b)(3), and (b)(13). Before the enactment of the Antiterrorism and Effective Death Penalty Act of 1996, those conditions were a fine ((b)(2)), an order of restitution ((b)(3)), and community service ((b)(13)). Whether or not the change was intended, the Act deleted the fine condition and renumbered the restitution and community service conditions in 18 U.S.C. § 3563(b), but failed to make a corresponding change in the referenced paragraphs under 18 U.S.C. § 3563(a)(2). Accordingly, the conditions now referenced are restitution ((b)(2)), notice to victims pursuant to 18 U.S.C. § 3555 ((b)(3)), and an order that the defendant reside, or refrain from residing, in a specified place or area ((b)(13)).".

Section 5B1.3(e)(1) is amended by adding at the end "See § 5F1.1 (Community Confinement).".

Section 5B1.3(e)(6) is amended by adding at the end "See § 5F1.8 (Intermittent Confinement).".

Section 5C1.1(c)(2) is amended by striking the asterisk after "confinement".

Section 5C1.1(d)(2) is amended by striking the asterisk after "confinement".

Amendment 733 APPENDIX C - VOLUME III November 1, 2013

The Commentary to § 5C1.1 captioned "Application Notes" is amended in Note 3(C) in the first sentence by striking the asterisk after "confinement".

The Commentary to § 5C1.1 captioned "Application Notes" is amended in Note 4(B) in the first sentence by striking the asterisk after "confinement".

The Commentary to § 5C1.1 captioned "Application Notes" is amended in Note 6 by striking the asterisk after "confinement".

The Commentary to § 5C1.1 captioned "Application Notes" is amended by striking the paragraph that begins "*Note:" and the paragraph that begins "However," as follows:

> "*Note: Section 3583(d) of title 18, United States Code, provides that "[t]he court may order, as a further condition of supervised release. . .any condition set forth as a discretionary condition of probation in section 3563(b)(1) through (b)(10) and (b)(12) through (b)(20), and any other condition it considers to be appropriate." Subsection (b)(11) of section 3563 of title 18, United States Code, is explicitly excluded as a condition of supervised release. Before the enactment of the Antiterrorism and Effective Death Penalty Act of 1996, the condition at 18 U.S.C. § 3563(b)(11) was intermittent confinement. The Act deleted 18 U.S.C. § 3563(b)(2), authorizing the payment of a fine as a condition of probation, and redesignated the remaining conditions of probation set forth in 18 U.S.C. § 3563(b); intermittent confinement is now set forth at subsection (b)(10), whereas subsection (b)(11) sets forth the condition of residency at a community corrections facility. It would appear that intermittent confinement now is authorized as a condition of supervised release and that community confinement now is not authorized as a condition of supervised release.
>
> However, there is some question as to whether Congress intended this result. Although the Antiterrorism and Effective Death Penalty Act of 1996 redesignated the remaining paragraphs of section 3563(b), it failed to make the corresponding redesignations in 18 U.S.C. § 3583(d), regarding discretionary conditions of supervised release.".

Section 5D1.3(e)(1) is amended by striking the asterisk after "Confinement"; and by striking the paragraph that begins "*Note: Section 3583(d)" and the paragraph that begins "However," as follows:

> "*Note: Section 3583(d) of title 18, United States Code, provides that '[t]he court may order, as a further condition of supervised release. . .any condition set forth as a discretionary condition of probation in section 3563(b)(1) through (b)(10) and (b)(12) through (b)(20), and any other condition it considers to be appropriate.' Subsection (b)(11) of section 3563 of title 18, United States Code, is explicitly excluded as a condition of supervised release. Before the enactment of the Antiterrorism and Effective Death Penalty Act of 1996, the condition at 18 U.S.C. § 3563(b)(11) was intermittent confinement. The Act deleted 18 U.S.C. § 3563(b)(2), authorizing the payment of a fine as a condition of probation, and redesignated the remaining conditions of probation set forth in 18 U.S.C. § 3563(b); intermittent confinement is now set forth at subsection (b)(10), whereas subsection (b)(11) sets forth the condition of residency at a community corrections facility. It would appear that intermittent confinement now is authorized as a condition of supervised release and that community confinement now is not authorized as a condition of supervised release.
>
> However, there is some question as to whether Congress intended this result. Although the Antiterrorism and Effective Death Penalty Act of 1996 redesignated the

remaining paragraphs of section 3563(b), it failed to make the corresponding redesignations in 18 U.S.C. § 3583(d), regarding discretionary conditions of supervised release.".

Section 5D1.3(e) is amended by adding at the end the following:

"(6) Intermittent Confinement

Intermittent confinement (custody for intervals of time) may be ordered as a condition of supervised release during the first year of supervised release, but only for a violation of a condition of supervised release in accordance with 18 U.S.C. § 3583(e)(2) and only when facilities are available. See § 5F1.8 (Intermittent Confinement).".

Section 5F1.1 is amended by striking the asterisk after "release."; and by striking the paragraph that begins "*Note: Section 3583(d)" and the paragraph that begins "However," as follows:

"*Note: Section 3583(d) of title 18, United States Code, provides that "[t]he court may order, as a further condition of supervised release. . .any condition set forth as a discretionary condition of probation in section 3563(b)(1) through (b)(10) and (b)(12) through (b)(20), and any other condition it considers to be appropriate." Subsection (b)(11) of section 3563 of title 18, United States Code, is explicitly excluded as a condition of supervised release. Before the enactment of the Antiterrorism and Effective Death Penalty Act of 1996, the condition at 18 U.S.C. § 3563(b)(11) was intermittent confinement. The Act deleted 18 U.S.C. § 3563(b)(2), authorizing the payment of a fine as a condition of probation, and redesignated the remaining conditions of probation set forth in 18 U.S.C. § 3563(b); intermittent confinement is now set forth at subsection (b)(10), whereas subsection (b)(11) sets forth the condition of residency at a community corrections facility. It would appear that intermittent confinement now is authorized as a condition of supervised release and that community confinement now is not authorized as a condition of supervised release.

However, there is some question as to whether Congress intended this result. Although the Antiterrorism and Effective Death Penalty Act of 1996 redesignated the remaining paragraphs of section 3563(b), it failed to make the corresponding redesignations in 18 U.S.C. § 3583(d), regarding discretionary conditions of supervised release.".

Chapter Five, Part F is amended by adding at the end the following guideline and accompanying commentary:

"§ 5F1.8. Intermittent Confinement

Intermittent confinement may be imposed as a condition of probation during the first year of probation. See 18 U.S.C. § 3563(b)(10). It may be imposed as a condition of supervised release during the first year of supervised release, but only for a violation of a condition of supervised release in accordance with 18 U.S.C. § 3583(e)(2) and only when facilities are available. See 18 U.S.C. § 3583(d).

Commentary

Application Note:

1. 'Intermittent confinement' means remaining in the custody of the Bureau of

Prisons during nights, weekends, or other intervals of time, totaling no more than the lesser of one year or the term of imprisonment authorized for the offense, during the first year of the term of probation or supervised release. See 18 U.S.C. § 3563(b)(10).".

Chapter Seven, Part A, Subpart 2(b) is amended in the paragraph that begins "With the exception" by striking the first sentence as follows:

"With the exception of residency in, or participation in the program of, a community corrections facility,* which is available only for a sentence of probation, the conditions of supervised release authorized by statute are the same as those for a sentence of probation.",

and inserting the following:

"The conditions of supervised release authorized by statute are the same as those for a sentence of probation, except for intermittent confinement. (Intermittent confinement is available for a sentence of probation, but is available as a condition of supervised release only for a violation of a condition of supervised release.)";

and by striking the paragraph that begins "*Note: Section 3583(d)" and the paragraph that begins "However," as follows:

"*Note: Section 3583(d) of title 18, United States Code, provides that "[t]he court may order, as a further condition of supervised release. . .any condition set forth as a discretionary condition of probation in section 3563(b)(1) through (b)(10) and (b)(12) through (b)(20), and any other condition it considers to be appropriate." Subsection (b)(11) of section 3563 of title 18, United States Code, is explicitly excluded as a condition of supervised release. Before the enactment of the Antiterrorism and Effective Death Penalty Act of 1996, the condition at 18 U.S.C. § 3563(b)(11) was intermittent confinement. The Act deleted 18 U.S.C. § 3563(b)(2), authorizing the payment of a fine as a condition of probation, and redesignated the remaining conditions of probation set forth in 18 U.S.C. § 3563(b); intermittent confinement is now set forth at subsection (b)(10), whereas subsection (b)(11) sets forth the condition of residency at a community corrections facility. It would appear that intermittent confinement now is authorized as a condition of supervised release and that community confinement now is not authorized as a condition of supervised release.

However, there is some question as to whether Congress intended this result. Although the Antiterrorism and Effective Death Penalty Act of 1996 redesignated the remaining paragraphs of section 3563(b), it failed to make the corresponding redesignations in 18 U.S.C. § 3583(d), regarding discretionary conditions of supervised release.".

The Commentary to § 7B1.3 captioned "Application Notes" is amended by striking Note 5 as follows:

"5. Intermittent confinement is authorized only as a condition of probation during the first year of the term of probation. 18 U.S.C. § 3563(b)(10).*

*Note: Section 3583(d) of title 18, United States Code, provides that "[t]he court may order, as a further condition of supervised release. . .any condition set forth as a discretionary condition of probation in section 3563(b)(1) through (b)(10) and (b)(12) through (b)(20), and any other condition it considers to be appropriate." Subsection (b)(11) of section 3563 of title 18,

United States Code, is explicitly excluded as a condition of supervised release. Before the enactment of the Antiterrorism and Effective Death Penalty Act of 1996, the condition at 18 U.S.C. § 3563(b)(11) was intermittent confinement. The Act deleted 18 U.S.C. § 3563(b)(2), authorizing the payment of a fine as a condition of probation, and redesignated the remaining conditions of probation set forth in 18 U.S.C. § 3563(b); intermittent confinement is now set forth at subsection (b)(10), whereas subsection (b)(11) sets forth the condition of residency at a community corrections facility. It would appear that intermittent confinement now is authorized as a condition of supervised release and that community confinement now is not authorized as a condition of supervised release.

However, there is some question as to whether Congress intended this result. Although the Antiterrorism and Effective Death Penalty Act of 1996 redesignated the remaining paragraphs of section 3563(b), it failed to make the corresponding redesignations in 18 U.S.C. § 3583(d), regarding discretionary conditions of supervised release.",

and inserting the following:

"5. Intermittent confinement is authorized as a condition of probation during the first year of the term of probation. 18 U.S.C. § 3563(b)(10). Intermittent confinement is authorized as a condition of supervised release during the first year of supervised release, but only for a violation of a condition of supervised release in accordance with 18 U.S.C. § 3583(e)(2) and only when facilities are available. See § 5F1.8 (Intermittent Confinement).".

Section 8D1.3(b) is amended by striking ", (2) notice to victims of the offense pursuant to 18 U.S.C. § 3555, or (3) an order requiring the organization to reside, or refrain from residing, in a specified place or area," and inserting "or (2) community service, unless the court has imposed a fine, or";

and by striking the paragraph that begins "<u>Note</u>:" as follows:

"<u>Note</u>: Section 3563(a)(2) of Title 18, United States Code, provides that, absent unusual circumstances, a defendant convicted of a felony shall abide by at least one of the conditions set forth in 18 U.S.C. § 3563(b)(2), (b)(3), and (b)(13). Before the enactment of the Antiterrorism and Effective Death Penalty Act of 1996, those conditions were a fine ((b)(2)), an order of restitution ((b)(3)), and community service ((b)(13)). Whether or not the change was intended, the Act deleted the fine condition and renumbered the restitution and community service conditions in 18 U.S.C. § 3563(b), but failed to make a corresponding change in the referenced paragraphs under 18 U.S.C. § 3563(a)(2). Accordingly, the conditions now referenced are restitution ((b)(2)), notice to victims pursuant to 18 U.S.C. § 3555 ((b)(3)), and an order that the defendant reside, or refrain from residing, in a specified place or area ((b)(13)).".

Appendix A (Statutory Index) is amended by inserting before the line referenced to 2 U.S.C. § 437g(d) the following:

"2 U.S.C. § 192   2J1.1, 2J1.5
2 U.S.C. § 390   2J1.1, 2J1.5";

by inserting after the line referenced to 7 U.S.C. § 87b the following:

"7 U.S.C. § 87f(e)   2J1.1, 2J1.5";

by inserting after the line referenced to 8 U.S.C. § 1375a(d)(3)(C),(d)(5)(B) the following:

"10 U.S.C. § 987(f)   2X5.2";

by inserting after the line referenced to 12 U.S.C. § 631 the following:

"12 U.S.C. § 1818(j)   2B1.1
12 U.S.C. § 1844(f)   2J1.1, 2J1.5
12 U.S.C. § 2273   2J1.1, 2J1.5
12 U.S.C. § 3108(b)(6)   2J1.1, 2J1.5
12 U.S.C. § 4636b   2B1.1
12 U.S.C. § 4641   2J1.1, 2J1.5";

by inserting after the line referenced to 15 U.S.C. § 78ff the following:

"15 U.S.C. § 78u(c)   2J1.1, 2J1.5
15 U.S.C. § 80a-41(c)   2J1.1, 2J1.5";

by inserting after the line referenced to 15 U.S.C. § 80b-6 the following:

"15 U.S.C. § 80b-9(c)   2J1.1, 2J1.5";

by inserting after the line referenced to 15 U.S.C. § 714m(c) the following:

"15 U.S.C. § 717m(d)   2J1.1, 2J1.5";

by inserting after the line referenced to 15 U.S.C. § 1176 the following:

"15 U.S.C. § 1192   2N2.1
15 U.S.C. § 1197(b)   2N2.1
15 U.S.C. § 1202(c)   2N2.1
15 U.S.C. § 1263   2N2.1";

by inserting after the line referenced to 15 U.S.C. § 1990c the following:

"15 U.S.C. § 2068   2N2.1";

by inserting after the line referenced to 16 U.S.C. § 773g the following:

"16 U.S.C. § 825f(c)   2J1.1, 2J1.5";

by inserting after the line referenced to 18 U.S.C. § 115(b)(4) the following:

"18 U.S.C. § 117   2A6.2";

in the line referenced to 18 U.S.C. § 2280 by inserting "2A6.1," after "2A4.1,";

in the line referenced to 18 U.S.C. § 2332a by inserting "2A6.1," before "2K1.4";

by inserting after the line referenced to 18 U.S.C. § 2425 the following:

"18 U.S.C. § 2442   2H4.1";

in the line referenced to 26 U.S.C. § 7210 by inserting ", 2J1.5" after "2J1.1";

by striking the line referenced to 33 U.S.C. § 506 as follows:

"33 U.S.C. § 506   2J1.1";

in the line referenced to 33 U.S.C. § 1227(b) by inserting ", 2J1.5" after "2J1.1";

in the line referenced to 42 U.S.C. § 3611(f) by inserting ", 2J1.5" after "2J1.1";

by inserting after the line referenced to 47 U.S.C. § 223(b)(1)(A) the following:

"47 U.S.C. § 409(m)   2J1.1, 2J1.5";

in the line referenced to 49 U.S.C. § 14909 by inserting ", 2J1.5" after "2J1.1";

in the line referenced to 49 U.S.C. § 16104 by inserting ", 2J1.5" after "2J1.1";

and by inserting after the line referenced to 50 U.S.C. § 783(c) the following:

"50 U.S.C. App. § 527(e)   2X5.2".

Reason for Amendment: This multi-part amendment responds to miscellaneous issues arising from legislation recently enacted and other miscellaneous guideline application issues.

First, the amendment amends Appendix A (Statutory Index) to include offenses created by the Housing and Economic Recovery Act of 2008, Pub. L. 110–289, and other offenses similar to those offenses, as follows:

(1)   The new offense at 12 U.S.C. § 4636b is referenced to § 2B1.1 (Larceny, Embezzlement, and Other Forms of Theft; Offenses Involving Stolen Property; Property Damage or Destruction; Fraud and Deceit; Forgery; Offenses Involving Altered or Counterfeit Instruments Other than Counterfeit Bearer Obligations of the United States). The similar existing offense at 12 U.S.C. § 1818(j) is also referenced to § 2B1.1. These offenses are similar to economic crimes and are best accounted for by § 2B1.1.

(2)   The new offense at 12 U.S.C. § 4641 is referenced to § 2J1.1 (Contempt) and § 2J1.5 (Failure to Appear by Material Witness); similar existing offenses (2 U.S.C. §§ 192, 390; 7 U.S.C. § 87f(e); 12 U.S.C. §§ 1844(f), 2273, 3108(b)(6); 15 U.S.C. §§ 78u(c), 80a-41(c), 80b-9(c), 717m(d); 16 U.S.C. § 825f(c); 26 U.S.C. § 7210; 33 U.S.C. § 1227(b); 42 U.S.C. § 3611; 47 U.S.C. § 409(m); 49 U.S.C. §§ 14909, 16104) are also referenced to § 2J1.1 and § 2J1.5. Contempt offenses can involve a range of conduct. The Commission determined that referencing these offenses to both § 2J1.1 and § 2J1.5 will best account for the range of conduct involved. Another similar offense, 33 U.S.C. § 506, is deleted from Appendix A (Statutory Index) because it has been repealed.

Second, the amendment amends Appendix A (Statutory Index) to include offenses upgraded from misdemeanors to felonies by the Consumer Product Safety Improvement Act of 2008, Pub. L. 110–314. These offenses (15 U.S.C. §§ 1192, 1197(b), 1202(c), 1263, 2068) are referenced to § 2N2.1 (Violations of Statutes and Regulations Dealing With Any Food, Drug, Biological Product, Device, Cosmetic, or Agricultural Product). These offenses cover a range of conduct (from paperwork violations to making or selling a nonconforming product) and a range of mental states (from strict liability to knowing, willful, or intentional misconduct). The Commission determined that these offenses are similar to offenses referenced to § 2N2.1, which has provisions to account for aggravating and mitigating circumstances that may be involved in such offenses. Technical and conforming changes are also made to indicate that § 2N2.1 covers consumer product safety offenses.

Third, the amendment amends Appendix A (Statutory Index) to include an offense created by the Veterans' Benefits Improvement Act of 2008, Pub. L. 110–389. The new offense, 50 U.S.C. App. § 527(e), is a Class A misdemeanor and, accordingly, is referenced to § 2X5.2 (Class A Misdemeanors (Not Covered by Another Specific Offense Guideline)). The amendment also references 10 U.S.C. § 987(f), a similar Class A misdemeanor, to § 2X5.2.

Fourth, the amendment amends Appendix A (Statutory Index) to include an offense created by the Violence Against Women and Department of Justice Reauthorization Act of 2005, Pub. L. 109–162. The offense, 18 U.S.C. § 117, covers domestic assault by a person with two or more prior convictions for domestic assault offenses. It is similar to the offenses referenced to § 2A6.2 (Stalking or Domestic Violence) and, therefore, is referenced to that guideline.

Fifth, the amendment amends Appendix A (Statutory Index) to include an offense created by the Child Soldiers Accountability Act of 2008, Pub. L. 110–340. The offense, 18 U.S.C. § 2442, is referenced to § 2H4.1 (Peonage, Involuntary Servitude, and Slave Trade). The offenses currently indexed to § 2H4.1 include five offenses that relate to illegal use of an individual's labor and have the same statutory maximum term of imprisonment as the new child soldiers offense (20 years imprisonment or, if death results, life). Likewise, § 2H4.1 has provisions to account for aggravating and mitigating circumstances that may be involved in a child soldiers offense. Technical and conforming changes are also made to indicate that § 2H4.1 applies to the new offense.

Sixth, the amendment makes changes throughout the Guidelines Manual to reflect the amendments made by the Judicial Administration and Technical Amendments Act of 2008, Pub. L. 110–406, to the probation and supervised release statutes (18 U.S.C. §§ 3563, 3583). The changes include a new guideline for intermittent confinement at § 5F1.8 (Intermittent Confinement) that parallels the statutory language, as well as technical and conforming changes. These changes conform the Guidelines Manual to reflect what Congress has provided.

Seventh, the amendment responds to the Let Our Veterans Rest in Peace Act of 2008, Pub. L. 110–384, which directed the Commission to review and, if appropriate, amend the guidelines to "provide adequate sentencing enhancements" for any offense involving "desecration, theft, or trafficking" in a veteran's grave marker. There is a specific offense characteristic at subsection (b)(6) of § 2B1.1 for damage, destruction, or theft of a veteran's grave marker. The amendment amends this specific offense characteristic so that it also covers trafficking in a veteran's grave marker.

Eighth, the amendment makes changes in the child pornography guidelines, § 2G2.1 (Sexually Exploiting a Minor by Production of Sexually Explicit Visual or Printed Material; Custodian Permitting Minor to Engage in Sexually Explicit Conduct; Advertisement for Minors to Engage in Production) and § 2G2.2 (Trafficking in Material Involving the Sexual Exploitation of a Minor; Receiving, Transporting, Shipping, Soliciting, or Advertising Material Involving the Sexual Exploitation of a Minor; Possessing Material Involving the Sexual Exploitation of a Minor with Intent to Traffic; Possessing Material Involving the Sexual Exploitation of a Minor), so that they reflect the amendments made to the child pornography statutes (18 U.S.C. §§ 2251 et seq.) by the Effective Child Pornography Prosecution Act of 2007, Pub. L. 110–358, and the PROTECT Our Children Act of 2008, Pub. L. 110–401. The changes relate primarily to cases in which child pornography is transmitted over the Internet. Under the amendment, where the guidelines refer to the purpose of producing a visual depiction, they will also refer to the purpose of transmitting a live visual depiction; where the guidelines refer to possessing material, they will also refer to accessing with intent to view the material. The amendment also amends the child pornography guidelines so that the term "distribution" includes "transmission", and the term "material" includes any visual depiction, as now defined by 18 U.S.C. § 2256 (i.e., to include data which is capable of conversion into a visual image that has been transmitted by any means, whether or not stored in a permanent format). These changes conform the child pornography guidelines to reflect what Congress has provided.

Ninth, the amendment amends Appendix A (Statutory Index) so that the threat guideline, § 2A6.1 (Threatening or Harassing Communications; Hoaxes; False Liens), is included on the list of guidelines to which 18 U.S.C. § 2280 and § 2332a are referenced. A person may be charged and convicted of committing such an offense by threat. In such a case, § 2A6.1 may be the most appropriate guideline.

Tenth, the amendment addresses subsection (a)(7) of 18 U.S.C. § 2252A, a new child pornography offense created by the PROTECT Our Children Act of 2008, Pub. L. 110–401. The offense makes it unlawful to knowingly produce with intent to distribute, or to knowingly distribute, "child pornography that is an adapted or modified depiction of an identifiable minor." A violator is subject to a maximum term of imprisonment of 15 years. This offense is already referenced in Appendix A (Statutory Index) to the child pornography distribution guideline, § 2G2.2, by virtue of the fact that all offenses under section 2252A(a) are referenced to that guideline. The Commission determined that the distribution guideline is the appropriate guideline for this offense because distribution is a required element of this offense, in that the offender must either distribute the material or produce it with intent to distribute. The distribution guideline also has provisions to account for aggravating and mitigating circumstances that may be involved in these offenses. The amendment provides a base offense level of 18 for this offense, which is four levels lower than the base offense level for other child pornography distribution offenses referenced to § 2G2.2. The Commission determined that the lower base offense level was appropriate for this offense because, unlike for other child pornography distribution offenses, the process of creating the image does not involve the sexual exploitation of a child, and Congress provided a lower penalty structure for this offense (a maximum term of imprisonment of 15 years, and no mandatory minimum term of imprisonment) than for other child pornography distribution offenses (typically, a maximum term of imprisonment of 20 years and a mandatory minimum of 5 years). The lower base offense level also accounts for the fact that the enhancements at subsections (b)(3) (for distribution) and (b)(6) (for use of a computer) will likely apply in these cases. Finally, to ensure that § 2G2.2 treats material involving an adapted or modified image in the same manner as it treats material involving any other form of child pornography, the amendment provides a new Application Note to § 2G2.2 to clarify that, if the offense involved material that is an adapted or modified depiction of an identifiable minor, the term "material involving the sexual exploitation of a minor" includes such material.

Effective Date: The effective date of this amendment is November 1, 2009.

734. Amendment: The Commentary to § 3C1.3 captioned "Application Note" is amended in Note 1 by striking "as adjusted" and inserting "including, as in any other case in which a Chapter Three adjustment applies (see § 1B1.1 (Application Instructions)), the adjustment provided"; and by adding at the end "Similarly, if the applicable adjusted guideline range is 30-37 months and the court determines a 'total punishment' of 30 months is appropriate, a sentence of 24 months for the underlying offense plus 6 months under 18 U.S.C. § 3147 would satisfy this requirement.".

Reason for Amendment: This amendment clarifies Application Note 1 in § 3C1.3 (Commission of Offense While on Release). Section 3C1.3 (formerly § 2J1.7, see Appendix C to the Guidelines Manual, Amendment 684) provides a three-level adjustment if the defendant is subject to the statutory enhancement at 18 U.S.C. § 3147—that is, if the defendant has committed the underlying offense while on release. Application Note 1 to § 3C1.3 states that, in order to comply with the statute's requirement that a consecutive sentence be imposed, the sentencing court must "divide the sentence on the judgment form between the sentence attributable to the underlying offense and the sentence attributable to the enhancement."

The Second and Seventh Circuits have held that, according to the terms of Application Note 2 to § 2J1.7 (now Application Note 1 to § 3C1.3), a sentencing court cannot apportion to the underlying offense more than the maximum of the guideline range absent the three-level adjustment. See United States v. Confredo, 528 F.3d 143 (2d Cir. 2008); United States v. Stevens, 66 F.3d 431 (2d Cir. 1995); United States v. Wilson, 966 F.2d 243 (7th Cir. 1992).

The amendment clarifies that the court determines the applicable guideline range for a defendant who committed an offense while on release and is subject to the enhancement at 18 U.S.C. § 3147 as in any other case. Therefore, under ordinary guideline application principles, only one guideline range applies to such a defendant. See § 1B1.1 (Application Instructions) (instructing the sentencing court to, in this order: (1) determine the offense guideline applicable to the offense of conviction (the underlying offense); (2) determine the base offense level and specific offense characteristics, and follow other instructions in Chapter Two; (3) apply adjustments from Chapter Three; and, ultimately, (4) "[d]etermine the guideline range in Part A of Chapter Five that corresponds to the offense level and criminal history category determined above"). At that point, the court determines an appropriate "total punishment" using that applicable guideline range, and then divides the total sentence between the underlying offense and the section 3147 enhancement as the court considers appropriate.

Effective Date: The effective date of this amendment is November 1, 2009.

735. Amendment: Section 2B5.3(b)(5) is amended by inserting "death or" after "risk of"; and by striking "13" and inserting "14" each place it appears.

Reason for Amendment: This amendment responds to the Prioritizing Resources and Organization for Intellectual Property Act of 2008, Pub. L. 110–403, which added two sentencing enhancements to violations of 18 U.S.C. § 2320 (Trafficking in counterfeit goods or services). Under those sentencing enhancements, if the offender causes or attempts to cause serious bodily injury, the statutory maximum term of imprisonment is increased from 10 years to 20 years; if the offender causes or attempts to cause death, the statutory maximum is increased to any term of years (or to life).

The amendment amends § 2B5.3 (Criminal Infringement of Copyright or Trademark) at subsection (b)(5) to clarify that the enhancement in that subsection, which applies when the offense involved the risk of serious bodily injury, also applies when the offense involved the risk of death. This brings the language of that enhancement back into parallel with the corresponding enhancement in subsection (b)(13) of § 2B1.1 (Larceny, Embezzlement, and Other Forms of Theft; Offenses Involving Stolen Property; Property Damage or Destruction; Fraud and Deceit; Forgery; Offenses Involving Altered or Counterfeit Instruments Other than Counterfeit Bearer Obligations of the United States). The Commission envisioned, when it added the enhancement to § 2B5.3, that paralleling the fraud guideline would promote proportionality. See Appendix C to the Guidelines Manual, Amendment 590 ("The Commission determined that this kind of aggravating conduct in connection with infringement cases should be treated under the guidelines in the same way it is treated in connection with fraud cases; therefore, this enhancement is consistent with an identical provision in the fraud guideline."). Accordingly, the amendment also increases the minimum offense level in § 2B5.3(b)(5) from level 13 to level 14, bringing it back into parallel with the minimum offense level in § 2B1.1(b)(13).

Effective Date: The effective date of this amendment is November 1, 2009.

736. **Amendment:** The Commentary to § 1B1.8 captioned "Application Notes" is amended in Note 3 by striking "(e)(6) (Inadmissibility of Pleas," and inserting "(f) (Admissibility or Inadmissibility of a Plea,".

The Commentary to § 2G2.1 captioned "Statutory Provisions" is amended by inserting "(a)-(c), 2251(d)(1)(B)" after "2251".

The Commentary to § 2G2.2 captioned "Statutory Provisions" is amended by inserting "(a)-(b)" after "2252A".

The Commentary to § 2G2.2 captioned "Application Notes" is amended in Note 1 in the paragraph that begins "'Sexual abuse" by inserting "(a)-(c), § 2251(d)(1)(B)" after "2251".

The Commentary to § 2G2.3 captioned "Background" is amended by striking "twenty" and inserting "thirty".

Section 2G3.1(c)(1) is amended by inserting "Soliciting," after "Shipping,"; and by striking "Traffic) or § 2G2.4 (Possession of Materials Depicting a Minor Engaged in Sexually Explicit Conduct), as appropriate." and inserting "Traffic; Possessing Material Involving the Sexual Exploitation of a Minor).".

The Commentary to § 2J1.1 captioned "Application Notes" is amended in Note 3 by striking "(7)" and inserting "(8)".

The Commentary to § 4B1.2 captioned "Application Notes" is amended in Note 1 in the paragraph that begins "Unlawfully possessing a listed" by striking "(d)" and inserting "(c)".

The Commentary to § 5C1.2 captioned "Application Notes" is amended in Note 8 by striking "(c)(1), (3)" and inserting "(f), (i)".

The Commentary to § 5D1.2 captioned "Background" is amended by striking "(b)" and inserting "(c)".

Appendix A (Statutory Index) is amended by inserting after the line referenced to 18 U.S.C. § 2251(a),(b) the following:

Amendment 736 APPENDIX C - VOLUME III November 1, 2013

"18 U.S.C. § 2251(c)   2G2.1";

in the line referenced to 18 U.S.C. § 2251(c)(1)(A) by striking "(c)" and inserting "(d)";

in the line referenced to 18 U.S.C. § 2251(c)(1)(B) by striking "(c)" and inserting "(d)";

in the line referenced to 18 U.S.C. § 2252A by inserting "(a), (b)" after "2252A";

by inserting before the line referenced to 18 U.S.C. § 2252B the following:

"18 U.S.C. § 2252A(g)   2G2.6";

and in the line referenced to 42 U.S.C. § 3611(f) by striking "(f)" and inserting "(c)".

Reason for Amendment: This multi-part amendment makes various technical and conforming changes to the guidelines.

The amendment addresses several cases in which the Guidelines Manual refers to a guideline, or to a statute or rule, but the reference has become incorrect or obsolete. First, it makes technical changes in § 1B1.8 (Use of Certain Information) to address the fact that provisions that had been contained in subsection (e)(6) of Rule 11 of the Federal Rules of Criminal Procedure are now contained in subsection (f) of that rule. Second, it makes a technical change in § 2J1.1 (Contempt), Application Note 3, to address the fact that the provision that had been contained in subsection (b)(7)(C) of § 2B1.1 (Larceny, Embezzlement, and Other Forms of Theft; Offenses Involving Stolen Property; Property Damage or Destruction; Fraud and Deceit; Forgery; Offenses Involving Altered or Counterfeit Instruments Other than Counterfeit Bearer Obligations of the United States)) is now contained in subsection (b)(8)(C) of that guideline. Third, it makes a technical change in § 4B1.2 (Definitions of Terms Used in Section 4B1.1), Application Note 1, to address the fact that the offense that had been contained in subsection (d)(1) of 21 U.S.C. § 841 is now contained in subsection (c)(1) of that section. Fourth, it makes technical changes in § 5C1.2 (Limitation on Applicability of Statutory Minimum Sentences in Certain Cases), Application Note 8, to address the fact that subsections (c)(1) and (c)(3) of Rule 32 of the Federal Rules of Criminal Procedure are now contained in subsections (f) and (i) of that rule. Fifth, it makes a technical change to the Commentary in § 5D1.2 (Term of Supervised Release) to address the fact that the provision that had been contained in subsection (b) of § 5D1.2 is now contained in subsection (c) of that guideline. Sixth, it makes a technical change in Appendix A (Statutory Index) to address the fact that the offense that had been contained in subsection (f) of 42 U.S.C. § 3611 is now contained in subsection (c) of that section.

The amendment also resolves certain technical issues that have arisen in the Guidelines Manual with respect to child pornography offenses. First, it makes technical changes to the Commentary in § 2G2.1 (Sexually Exploiting a Minor by Production of Sexually Explicit Visual or Printed Material; Custodian Permitting Minor to Engage in Sexually Explicit Conduct; Advertisement for Minors to Engage in Production) to more accurately indicate which offenses under 18 U.S.C. § 2251 are referenced to § 2G2.1. Second, it makes technical changes to the Commentary in § 2G2.2 (Trafficking in Material Involving the Sexual Exploitation of a Minor; Receiving, Transporting, Shipping, Soliciting, or Advertising Material Involving the Sexual Exploitation of a Minor; Possessing Material Involving the Sexual Exploitation of a Minor with Intent to Traffic; Possessing Material Involving the Sexual Exploitation of a Minor) to address the fact that offenses under 18 U.S.C. § 2252A(g) are now covered by § 2G2.6 (Child Exploitation Enterprises)(see Appendix C

November 1, 2013 APPENDIX C - VOLUME III **Amendment 737**

to the Guidelines Manual, Amendment 701), while offenses under section 2252A(a) and (b) continue to be covered by § 2G2.2. Third, it makes a technical change to the Commentary in § 2G2.3 (Selling or Buying of Children for Use in the Production of Pornography) to address the fact that the statutory minimum sentence for a defendant convicted under 18 U.S.C. § 2251A is now 30 years imprisonment. Fourth, it makes technical changes in subsection (c)(1) of § 2G3.1 (Importing, Mailing, or Transporting Obscene Matter; Transferring Obscene Matter to a Minor; Misleading Domain Names) to address the fact that § 2G2.4 no longer exists, having been consolidated into § 2G2.2 effective November 1, 2004 (see Appendix C to the Guidelines Manual, Amendment 664). Fifth, it makes a technical change in Appendix A (Statutory Index) to address the fact that the offenses that had been contained in subsections (c)(1)(A) and (c)(1)(B) of 18 U.S.C. § 2251 are now contained in subsections (d)(1)(A) and (d)(1)(B) of that section. In doing so, it also provides the appropriate reference for the offense that is now contained in subsection (c) of that section. Sixth, it makes a technical change in Appendix A (Statutory Index) to address the fact that offenses under section 2252A(g) are now covered by § 2G2.6, while offenses under section 2252A(a) and (b) continue to be covered by § 2G2.2.

Effective Date: The effective date of this amendment is November 1, 2009.

737. **Amendment:** The Commentary to § 2A6.2 captioned "Application Notes" is amended in Note 4 in the second paragraph by striking "2" after "Note" and inserting "3".

The Commentary to § 2B1.1 captioned "Application Notes", as amended by Amendment 726, is further amended in Note 1, in the paragraph that begins "'Personal information' means", by striking "(i)" and inserting "(A)"; by striking "(ii)" and inserting "(B)"; by striking "(iii)" and inserting "(C)"; by striking "(iv)" and inserting "(D)"; by striking "(v)" and inserting "(E)"; by striking "(vi)" and inserting "(F)"; and by striking "(vii)" and inserting "(G)".

The Commentary to § 2B1.1 captioned "Application Notes" is amended in Note 3(F)(iii) by striking "276a" and inserting "3142".

The Commentary to § 2B1.1 captioned "Application Notes" is amended in Note 4(C)(iii) by striking "his" and inserting "the addressee's".

The Commentary to § 2B1.1 captioned "Application Notes" is amended in Note 7(E) by striking "Enhancements" and inserting "Chapter Three Adjustments".

The Commentary to § 2B1.1 captioned "Application Notes" is amended in Note 8(C) by striking "Enhancement" and inserting "Chapter Three Adjustment".

The Commentary to § 2B1.1 captioned "Application Notes" is amended in Note 9 by striking the paragraph that begins "'Telecommunications service' has the meaning" as follows:

"'Telecommunications service' has the meaning given that term in 18 U.S.C. § 1029(e)(9).";

and by inserting after the paragraph that begins "'Produce' includes manufacture" the following:

"'Telecommunications service' has the meaning given that term in 18 U.S.C. § 1029(e)(9).".

The Commentary to § 2B1.1 captioned "Application Notes", as amended by Amendment

726 is further amended in Note 14(A) by striking "this subsection" and inserting "subsection (b)(17)";

in the paragraph that begins "'Commodities law'" by striking "Commodities" before "Exchange" and inserting "Commodity"; by striking "Commodities" before "Futures" and inserting "Commodity";

in the paragraph that begins "'Commodity pool operator'" by striking "(4)" and inserting "(5)" each place it appears; by striking "Commodities" and inserting "Commodity";

in the paragraph that begins "'Commodity trading advisor'" by striking "(5)" and inserting "(6)" each place it appears; by striking "Commodities" and inserting "Commodity";

in the paragraph that begins "'Futures commission merchant'" by striking "Commodities" and inserting "Commodity";

in the paragraph that begins "'Introducing broker'" by striking "Commodities" and inserting "Commodity";

in the paragraph that begins "'Investment adviser'" by inserting "(a)(11)" after "202";

in the paragraph that begins "'Person associated with a broker or dealer'" by striking "(48)" and inserting "(18)";

and in the paragraph that begins "'Person associated with an investment adviser'" by inserting "(a)(17)" after "202".

The Commentary to § 2D1.6 captioned "Application Notes" is amended in Note 1 by inserting "a minimum offense level of 8 where the offense involves flunitrazepam (§ 2D1.1(c)(16));" after "(§ 2D1.1(c)(14));".

The Commentary to § 2G1.1 captioned "Application Notes" is amended in Note 1 in the paragraph that begins "'Commercial sex act'" by striking "(c)(1)" and inserting "(e)(3)".

The Commentary to § 2G1.3 captioned "Application Notes" is amended in Note 1 in the paragraph that begins "'Commercial sex act'" by striking "(c)(1)" and inserting "(e)(3)".

The Commentary to § 2G2.1 captioned "Statutory Provisions", as amended by Amendment 736, is further amended by striking "(b)" and inserting "(a)".

The Commentary to § 2H3.1 captioned "Application Notes", as amended by Amendment 726, is further amended in Note 4, in the paragraph that begins "'Personal information' means", by striking "(i)" and inserting "(A)"; by striking "(ii)" and inserting "(B)"; by striking "(iii)" and inserting "(C)"; by striking "(iv)" and inserting "(D)"; by striking "(v)" and inserting "(E)"; by striking "(vi)" and inserting "(F)"; and by striking "(vii)" and inserting "(G)".

The Commentary to § 2H3.1 captioned "Application Notes" is amended in Note 5 by striking "(i)" and inserting "(A)"; and by striking "(ii)" and inserting "(B)".

The Commentary to § 2J1.5 captioned "Statutory Provisions" is amended by striking "Provision" and inserting "Provisions"; and by striking "(2)" and inserting "(1)(B)".

The Commentary to § 2J1.5 captioned "Application Notes" is amended in Note 2 by striking "this offense" and inserting "an offense under 18 U.S.C. § 3146(b)(1)(B)".

The Commentary to § 2J1.5 captioned "Background" is amended by striking "This offense covered by this section" and inserting "The offense under 18 U.S.C. § 3146(b)(1)(B)".

The Commentary to § 3B1.2 captioned "Application Notes" is amended in Note 6 by striking "(3)" and inserting "(5)".

The Commentary following § 3D1.5 captioned "Illustrations of the Operation of the Multiple-Count Rules" is amended in example 3 by striking "he" and inserting "the defendant"; and by striking "(8)" and inserting "(9)".

Appendix A (Statutory Index), as amended by Amendment 733, is further amended by striking the line that begins "50 U.S.C. App. § 527(e)";

and by inserting after the line that begins "50 U.S.C. App. § 462" the following:

"50 U.S.C. App. § 527(e)   2X5.2".

Reason for Amendment: This amendment makes certain technical and conforming changes to commentary.

First, it updates obsolete statutory and guideline references in §§ 2A6.2 (Stalking or Domestic Violence), Application Note 4; 2B1.1 (Theft, Property Destruction, and Fraud), Application Notes 3(F)(iii) and 14(A); 2G1.1 (Promoting a Commercial Sex Act or Prohibited Sexual Conduct with an Individual Other than a Minor), Application Note 1; 2G1.3 (Promoting a Commercial Sex Act or Prohibited Sexual Conduct with a Minor; Transportation of Minors to Engage in a Commercial Sex Act or Prohibited Sexual Conduct; Travel to Engage in Commercial Sex Act or Prohibited Sexual Conduct with a Minor; Sex Trafficking of Children; Use of Interstate Facilities to Transport Information about a Minor), Application Note 1; 2G2.1 (Sexually Exploiting a Minor by Production of Sexually Explicit Visual or Printed Material; Custodian Permitting Minor to Engage in Sexually Explicit Conduct; Advertisement for Minors to Engage in Production), Statutory Provisions; 2J1.5 (Failure to Appear by Material Witness), Statutory Provisions; 3B1.2 (Mitigating Role), Application Note 6; and the Illustrations following 3D1.5 (Determining the Total Punishment).

Second, it makes clerical and stylistic changes to the Commentary to § 2B1.1; the Commentary to § 2H3.1 (Interception of Communications; Eavesdropping; Disclosure of Certain Private or Protected Information); and the Illustrations following § 3D1.5.

Third, it amends § 2D1.6 (Use of Communication Facility in Committing Drug Offense; Attempt or Conspiracy), Application Note 1, to ensure that its description of the various minimum offense levels that apply to controlled substances under § 2D1.1 (Unlawful Manufacturing, Importing, Exporting, or Trafficking (Including Possession with Intent to Commit These Offenses); Attempt or Conspiracy) is more comprehensive (i.e., by including in that description the minimum offense level that applies to flunitrazepam).

Finally, it amends Appendix A (Statutory Index) to ensure that the line reference to 50 U.S.C. App. § 527(e) is placed in the appropriate order.

Effective Date: The effective date of this amendment is November 1, 2009.

738. **Amendment:** Chapter Five, Part A, is amended in the Sentencing Table by redesignating Zones A, B, C, and D (as designated by Amendment 462, see USSG Appendix C, Amendment 462 (effective November 1, 1992)) as follows: Zone A (containing all guideline ranges having a minimum of zero months); Zone B (containing all guideline ranges having a minimum of at least one but not more than nine months); Zone C (containing all

Amendment 738

guideline ranges having a minimum of at least ten but not more than twelve months); and Zone D (containing all guideline ranges having a minimum of fifteen months or more).

The Commentary to § 5B1.1 captioned "Application Notes" is amended in Note 1(b) by striking "six" and inserting "nine"; and in Note 2 by striking "eight" and inserting "ten".

The Commentary to § 5C1.1 captioned "Application Notes" is amended in Note 3 in the first paragraph by striking "six" and inserting "nine";

in Note 4 by striking "eight, nine, or ten months" and inserting "ten or twelve months"; by striking "8-14" and inserting "10-16" both places it appears; by striking "sentence of four" and inserting "sentence of five" both places it appears; by striking "four" before "months community" and inserting "five"; by striking "five" after "and a sentence of" and inserting "ten";

by striking Note 6 as follows:

> "6. There may be cases in which a departure from the guidelines by substitution of a longer period of community confinement than otherwise authorized for an equivalent number of months of imprisonment is warranted to accomplish a specific treatment purpose (e.g., substitution of twelve months in an approved residential drug treatment program for twelve months of imprisonment). Such a substitution should be considered only in cases where the defendant's criminality is related to the treatment problem to be addressed and there is a reasonable likelihood that successful completion of the treatment program will eliminate that problem.",

and inserting the following:

> "6. There may be cases in which a departure from the sentencing options authorized for Zone C of the Sentencing Table (under which at least half the minimum term must be satisfied by imprisonment) to the sentencing options authorized for Zone B of the Sentencing Table (under which all or most of the minimum term may be satisfied by intermittent confinement, community confinement, or home detention instead of imprisonment) is appropriate to accomplish a specific treatment purpose. Such a departure should be considered only in cases where the court finds that (A) the defendant is an abuser of narcotics, other controlled substances, or alcohol, or suffers from a significant mental illness, and (B) the defendant's criminality is related to the treatment problem to be addressed.
>
> In determining whether such a departure is appropriate, the court should consider, among other things, (1) the likelihood that completion of the treatment program will successfully address the treatment problem, thereby reducing the risk to the public from further crimes of the defendant, and (2) whether imposition of less imprisonment than required by Zone C will increase the risk to the public from further crimes of the defendant.
>
> Examples: The following examples both assume the applicable guideline range is 12-18 months and the court departs in accordance with this application note. Under Zone C rules, the defendant must be sentenced to at least six months imprisonment. (1) The defendant is a nonviolent drug offender in Criminal History Category I and probation is not prohibited by statute. The court departs downward to impose a sentence of probation, with twelve

months of intermittent confinement, community confinement, or home detention and participation in a substance abuse treatment program as conditions of probation. (2) The defendant is convicted of a Class A or B felony, so probation is prohibited by statute (see § 5B1.1(b)). The court departs downward to impose a sentence of one month imprisonment, with eleven months in community confinement or home detention and participation in a substance abuse treatment program as conditions of supervised release.";

in Note 7 by striking the last sentence as follows:

"Generally, such defendants have failed to reform despite the use of such alternatives.";

in Note 8 by striking "twelve" and inserting "15"; and by redesignating Note 8 as Note 9 and inserting after Note 7 the following:

"8. In a case in which community confinement in a residential treatment program is imposed to accomplish a specific treatment purpose, the court should consider the effectiveness of the residential treatment program.".

Reason for Amendment: This amendment is a two-part amendment expanding the availability of alternatives to incarceration. The amendment provides a greater range of sentencing options to courts with respect to certain offenders by expanding Zones B and C of the Sentencing Table by one level each and addresses cases in which a departure from imprisonment to an alternative to incarceration (such as intermittent confinement, community confinement, or home confinement) may be appropriate to accomplish a specific treatment purpose.

The amendment is a result of the Commission's continued multi-year study of alternatives to incarceration. The Commission initiated this study in recognition of increased interest in alternatives to incarceration by all three branches of government and renewed public debate about the size of the federal prison population and the need for greater availability of alternatives to incarceration for certain nonviolent first offenders. See generally 28 U.S.C. §§ 994(g), (j).

As part of the study, the Commission held a two-day national symposium at which the Commission heard from experts on alternatives to incarceration, including federal and state judges, congressional staff, professors of law and the social sciences, corrections and alternative sentencing practitioners and specialists, federal and state prosecutors and defense attorneys, prison officials, and others involved in criminal justice. See United States Sentencing Commission, Symposium on Alternatives to Incarceration (July 2008). In considering the amendment, the Commission also reviewed federal sentencing data, public comment and testimony, recent scholarly literature, current federal and state practices, and feedback in various forms from federal judges.

First, the amendment expands Zones B and C of the Sentencing Table in Chapter Five. Specifically, it expands Zone B by one level for each Criminal History Category (taking this area from Zone C), and expands Zone C by one level for each Criminal History Category (taking this area from Zone D). Accordingly, under the amendment, defendants in Zone C with an applicable guideline range of 8-14 months or 9-15 months are moved to Zone B, and defendants in Zone D with an applicable guideline range of 12-18 months are moved to Zone C. Conforming changes also are made to §§ 5B1.1 (Imposition of a Term of Probation) and 5C1.1. In considering this one-level expansion, the Commission observed that approximately 42 percent of the Zone C offenders covered by the amendment and approximately 52 percent of the Zone D offenders covered by the amendment already receive sentences below the applicable guideline range.

The Commission estimates that of the 71,054 offenders sentenced in fiscal year 2009 for which complete sentencing guideline application information is available, 1,565 offenders in Zone C, or 2.2 percent, would have been in Zone B of the Sentencing Table under the amendment, and 2,734 offenders in Zone D, or 3.8 percent, would have been in Zone C. Not all of these offenders would have been eligible for an alternative to incarceration, however, because many were non-citizens who may have been subject to an immigration detainer and some were statutorily prohibited from being sentenced to a term of probation, see, e.g., 18 U.S.C. § 3561(a)(1) (prohibiting a defendant convicted of a Class A or Class B felony from being sentenced to a term of probation).

As a further reason for the zone expansion, Commission data indicate that courts often sentence offenders in Zone D with an applicable guideline range of 12-18 months to a term of imprisonment of 12 months and one day for the specific purpose of making such offenders eligible for credit for satisfactory behavior while in prison. See 18 U.S.C. § 3624(b). For such an offender, assuming the maximum "good time credit" is earned, the sentence effectively becomes approximately ten and one-half months. Given that prior to the amendment the highest guideline range in Zone C was 10-16 months, the Commission determined that offenders in Zone D with an applicable guideline range of 12-18 months, many of whom effectively serve a sentence at the lower end of the highest Zone C sentencing range, should be included in Zone C.

Second, the amendment clarifies and illustrates certain cases in which a departure may be appropriate to accomplish a specific treatment purpose. Specifically, it amends an existing departure provision at § 5C1.1 (Imposition of a Term of Imprisonment), Application Note 6. As amended, the application note states that a departure from the sentencing options authorized for Zone C of the Sentencing Table to accomplish a specific treatment purpose should be considered only in cases where the court finds that (A) the defendant is an abuser of narcotics, other controlled substances, or alcohol, or suffers from a significant mental illness, and (B) the defendant's criminality is related to the treatment problem to be addressed.

Under the application note as amended, the court may depart from the sentencing options authorized for Zone C (under which at least half the minimum term must be satisfied by imprisonment) to the sentencing options authorized for Zone B (under which all or most of the minimum term may be satisfied by intermittent confinement, community confinement, or home detention instead of imprisonment) to accomplish a specific treatment purpose. The application note also provides that, in determining whether such a departure is appropriate, the court should consider, among other things, two factors relating to public safety: (1) the likelihood that completion of the treatment program will successfully address the treatment problem, thereby reducing the risk to the public from further crimes of the defendant, and (2) whether imposition of less imprisonment than required by Zone C will increase the risk to the public from further crimes of the defendant. Some public comment, testimony, and research suggested that successful completion of treatment programs may reduce recidivism rates and that, for some defendants, confinement at home or in the community instead of imprisonment may better address both the defendant's need for treatment and the need to protect the public. Accordingly, the Commission amended the application note to clarify the criteria and to provide examples of such cases.

The amendment also makes two other changes to the Commentary to § 5C1.1 regarding the factors to be considered in determining whether to impose an alternative to incarceration. The amendment adds an application note providing that, in a case in which community confinement in a residential treatment program is imposed to accomplish a specific treatment purpose, the court should consider the effectiveness of the treatment program. The amendment also deletes as unnecessary the second sentence of Application Note 7.

Effective Date: The effective date of this amendment is November 1, 2010.

739. **Amendment:** Chapter Five, Part H, is amended in the Introductory Commentary by striking the first paragraph as follows:

" The following policy statements address the relevance of certain offender characteristics to the determination of whether a sentence should be outside the applicable guideline range and, in certain cases, to the determination of a sentence within the applicable guideline range. Under 28 U.S.C. § 994(d), the Commission is directed to consider whether certain specific offender characteristics 'have any relevance to the nature, extent, place of service, or other incidents of an appropriate sentence' and to take them into account only to the extent they are determined to be relevant by the Commission.",

and inserting the following:

" This Part addresses the relevance of certain specific offender characteristics in sentencing. The Sentencing Reform Act (the 'Act') contains several provisions regarding specific offender characteristics:

First, the Act directs the Commission to ensure that the guidelines and policy statements 'are entirely neutral' as to five characteristics – race, sex, national origin, creed, and socioeconomic status. See 28 U.S.C. § 994(d).

Second, the Act directs the Commission to consider whether eleven specific offender characteristics, 'among others', have any relevance to the nature, extent, place of service, or other aspects of an appropriate sentence, and to take them into account in the guidelines and policy statements only to the extent that they do have relevance. See 28 U.S.C. § 994(d).

Third, the Act directs the Commission to ensure that the guidelines and policy statements, in recommending a term of imprisonment or length of a term of imprisonment, reflect the 'general inappropriateness' of considering five of those characteristics – education; vocational skills; employment record; family ties and responsibilities; and community ties. See 28 U.S.C. § 994(e).

Fourth, the Act also directs the sentencing court, in determining the particular sentence to be imposed, to consider, among other factors, 'the history and characteristics of the defendant'. See 18 U.S.C. § 3553(a)(1).

Specific offender characteristics are taken into account in the guidelines in several ways. One important specific offender characteristic is the defendant's criminal history, see 28 U.S.C. § 994(d)(10), which is taken into account in the guidelines in Chapter Four (Criminal History and Criminal Livelihood). See § 5H1.8 (Criminal History). Another specific offender characteristic in the guidelines is the degree of dependence upon criminal history for a livelihood, see 28 U.S.C. § 994(d)(11), which is taken into account in Chapter Four, Part B (Career Offenders and Criminal Livelihood). See § 5H1.9 (Dependence upon Criminal Activity for a Livelihood). Other specific offender characteristics are accounted for elsewhere in this manual. See, e.g., §§ 2C1.1(a)(1) and 2C1.2(a)(1) (providing alternative base offense levels if the defendant was a public official); 3B1.3 (Abuse of Position of Trust or Use of Special Skill); and 3E1.1 (Acceptance of Responsibility).

Amendment 739 APPENDIX C - VOLUME III November 1, 2013

The Supreme Court has emphasized that the advisory guideline system should 'continue to move sentencing in Congress' preferred direction, helping to avoid excessive sentencing disparities while maintaining flexibility sufficient to individualize sentences where necessary.' See United States v. Booker, 543 U.S. 220, 264-65 (2005). Although the court must consider 'the history and characteristics of the defendant' among other factors, see 18 U.S.C. § 3553(a), in order to avoid unwarranted sentencing disparities the court should not give them excessive weight. Generally, the most appropriate use of specific offender characteristics is to consider them not as a reason for a sentence outside the applicable guideline range but for other reasons, such as in determining the sentence within the applicable guideline range, the type of sentence (e.g., probation or imprisonment) within the sentencing options available for the applicable Zone on the Sentencing Table, and various other aspects of an appropriate sentence. To avoid unwarranted sentencing disparities among defendants with similar records who have been found guilty of similar conduct, see 18 U.S.C. § 3553(a)(6), 28 U.S.C. § 991(b)(1)(B), the guideline range, which reflects the defendant's criminal conduct and the defendant's criminal history, should continue to be 'the starting point and the initial benchmark.' Gall v. United States, 552 U.S. 38, 49 (2007).

Accordingly, the purpose of this Part is to provide sentencing courts with a framework for addressing specific offender characteristics in a reasonably consistent manner. Using such a framework in a uniform manner will help 'secure nationwide consistency,' see Gall v. United States, 552 U.S. 38, 49 (2007), 'avoid unwarranted sentencing disparities,' see 28 U.S.C. § 991(b)(1)(B), 18 U.S.C. § 3553(a)(6), 'provide certainty and fairness,' see 28 U.S.C. § 991(b)(1)(B), and 'promote respect for the law,' see 18 U.S.C. § 3553(a)(2)(A).

This Part allocates specific offender characteristics into three general categories.

In the first category are specific offender characteristics the consideration of which Congress has prohibited (e.g., § 5H1.10 (Race, Sex, National Origin, Creed, Religion, and Socio-Economic Status)) or that the Commission has determined should be prohibited.

In the second category are specific offender characteristics that Congress directed the Commission to take into account in the guidelines only to the extent that they have relevance to sentencing. See 28 U.S.C. § 994(d). For some of these, the policy statements indicate that these characteristics may be relevant in determining whether a sentence outside the applicable guideline range is warranted (e.g., age; mental and emotional condition; physical condition). These characteristics may warrant a sentence outside the applicable guideline range if the characteristic, individually or in combination with other such characteristics, is present to an unusual degree and distinguishes the case from the typical cases covered by the guidelines. These specific offender characteristics also may be considered for other reasons, such as in determining the sentence within the applicable guideline range, the type of sentence (e.g., probation or imprisonment) within the sentencing options available for the applicable Zone on the Sentencing Table, and various other aspects of an appropriate sentence.";

in the second paragraph by striking "The Commission has determined that certain circumstances" and inserting the following:

"In the third category are specific offender characteristics that Congress directed the Commission to ensure are reflected in the guidelines and policy statements as generally inappropriate in recommending a term of imprisonment or length of a term of imprisonment. See 28 U.S.C. § 994(e). The policy statements indicate that these characteristics";

by striking "or to the determination of" and inserting ", the type of sentence (e.g., probation or imprisonment) within the sentencing options available for the applicable Zone on the Sentencing Table, or"; by striking "incidents" and inserting "aspects";

and by striking the last paragraph as follows:

"   In addition, 28 U.S.C. § 994(e) requires the Commission to assure that its guidelines and policy statements reflect the general inappropriateness of considering the defendant's education, vocational skills, employment record, and family ties and responsibilities in determining whether a term of imprisonment should be imposed or the length of a term of imprisonment.",

and inserting the following:

"   As with the other provisions in this manual, these policy statements 'are evolutionary in nature'. See Chapter One, Part A, Subpart 2 (Continuing Evolution and Role of the Guidelines); 28 U.S.C. § 994(o). The Commission expects, and the Sentencing Reform Act contemplates, that continuing research, experience, and analysis will result in modifications and revisions.

   The nature, extent, and significance of specific offender characteristics can involve a range of considerations. The Commission will continue to provide information to the courts on the relevance of specific offender characteristics in sentencing, as the Sentencing Reform Act contemplates. See, e.g., 28 U.S.C. § 995(a)(12)(A) (the Commission serves as a 'clearinghouse and information center' on federal sentencing). Among other things, this may include information on the use of specific offender characteristics, individually and in combination, in determining the sentence to be imposed (including, where available, information on rates of use, criteria for use, and reasons for use); the relationship, if any, between specific offender characteristics and (A) the 'forbidden factors' specified in 28 U.S.C. § 994(d) and (B) the 'discouraged factors' specified in 28 U.S.C. § 994(e); and the relationship, if any, between specific offender characteristics and the statutory purposes of sentencing.".

Section 5H1.1 is amended by striking the first sentence as follows:

"Age (including youth) is not ordinarily relevant in determining whether a departure is warranted.",

and inserting the following:

"Age (including youth) may be relevant in determining whether a departure is warranted, if considerations based on age, individually or in combination with other offender characteristics, are present to an unusual degree and distinguish the case from the typical cases covered by the guidelines.".

Section 5H1.3 is amended by striking the first paragraph as follows:

"Mental and emotional conditions are not ordinarily relevant in determining whether a departure is warranted, except as provided in Chapter Five, Part K, Subpart 2 (Other Grounds for Departure).",

and inserting the following:

"Mental and emotional conditions may be relevant in determining whether a departure is warranted, if such conditions, individually or in combination with other offender characteristics, are present to an unusual degree and distinguish the case from the typical cases covered by the guidelines. See also Chapter Five, Part K, Subpart 2 (Other Grounds for Departure).

In certain cases a downward departure may be appropriate to accomplish a specific treatment purpose. See § 5C1.1, Application Note 6.".

Section 5H1.4 is amended in the first paragraph by striking the first sentence as follows:

"Physical condition or appearance, including physique, is not ordinarily relevant in determining whether a departure may be warranted.",

and inserting the following:

"Physical condition or appearance, including physique, may be relevant in determining whether a departure is warranted, if the condition or appearance, individually or in combination with other offender characteristics, is present to an unusual degree and distinguishes the case from the typical cases covered by the guidelines.";

in the second sentence by striking "However, an" and inserting "An"; in the second paragraph by inserting "ordinarily" after "or abuse"; in the last sentence by striking "supervisory body" and inserting "probation office"; by inserting as the third paragraph the following:

"In certain cases a downward departure may be appropriate to accomplish a specific treatment purpose. See § 5C1.1, Application Note 6."; and

in the fourth paragraph, as amended by this amendment, by striking "Similarly, where" and inserting "In a case in which".

Section 5H1.11 is amended by inserting as the first paragraph the following:

"Military service may be relevant in determining whether a departure is warranted, if the military service, individually or in combination with other offender characteristics, is present to an unusual degree and distinguishes the case from the typical cases covered by the guidelines."; and

in the second paragraph, as amended by this amendment, by striking "Military, civic" and inserting "Civic".

Section 5K2.0(d)(1) is amended by striking "third and last sentences" and inserting "last sentence".

Reason for Amendment: This multi-part amendment revises the introductory commentary to Chapter Five, Part H (Specific Offender Characteristics), amends the policy statements relating to age, mental and emotional conditions, physical condition, and military service, and makes conforming changes to § 5K2.0 (Grounds for Departure). The amendment is a result of a review of the departure provisions in the Guidelines Manual begun by the Commission this year. See 74 Fed. Reg. 46478, 46479 (September 9, 2009). The Commission undertook this review, in part, in response to an observed decrease in reliance on departure provisions in the Guidelines Manual in favor of an increased use of variances.

First, the amendment revises the introductory commentary to Chapter Five, Part H. As amended, the introductory commentary explains that the purpose of Part H is to provide sentencing courts with a framework for addressing specific offender characteristics in a reasonably consistent manner. Using such a framework in a uniform manner will help "secure nationwide consistency," Gall v. United States, 552 U.S. 38, 49 (2007), "avoid unwarranted sentencing disparities," 28 U.S.C. § 991(b)(1)(B), and "promote respect for the law," 18 U.S.C. § 3553(a)(2)(A).

Accordingly, the amended introductory commentary outlines three categories of specific offender characteristics described in the Sentencing Reform Act and the statutory and guideline standards that apply to consideration of each category. Courts must consider "the history and characteristics of the defendant" among other factors. See 18 U.S.C. § 3553(a). However, in order to avoid unwarranted sentencing disparities, see 18 U.S.C. § 3553(a)(6), 28 U.S.C. § 991(b)(1)(B), courts should not give specific offender characteristics excessive weight. The guideline range, which reflects the defendant's criminal conduct and the defendant's criminal history, should continue to be "the starting point and the initial benchmark." Gall, supra, at 49.

The amended introductory commentary also states that the Commission will continue to provide information to the courts on the relevance of specific offender characteristics in sentencing, as contemplated by the Sentencing Reform Act. See, e.g., 28 U.S.C. § 995(a)(12)(A). The Commission expects that providing such information on an ongoing basis will promote nationwide consistency in the consideration of specific offender characteristics by courts and help avoid unwarranted sentencing disparities.

Second, the amendment amends several policy statements that cover specific offender characteristics addressed in 28 U.S.C. § 994(d): §§ 5H1.1 (Age), 5H1.3 (Mental and Emotional Conditions), and 5H1.4 (Physical Condition, Including Drug or Alcohol Dependence or Abuse; Gambling Addiction). As amended, these policy statements generally provide that age; mental and emotional conditions; and physical condition or appearance, including physique, "may be relevant in determining whether a departure is warranted, if [the offender characteristic], individually or in combination with other offender characteristics, is present to an unusual degree and distinguishes the case from the typical cases covered by the guidelines." The Commission adopted this departure standard after reviewing recent federal sentencing data, trial and appellate court case law, scholarly literature, public comment and testimony, and feedback in various forms from federal judges.

The amendment also amends §§ 5H1.3 and 5H1.4 to provide that in certain cases described in Application Note 6 to § 5C1.1 (Imposition of a Term of Imprisonment) a departure may be appropriate.

Third, the amendment amends § 5H1.11 (Military, Civic, Charitable, or Public Service; Employment-Related Contributions; Record of Prior Good Works) to draw a distinction between military service and the other circumstances covered by that policy statement. As amended, the policy statement provides that military service "may be relevant in determining whether a departure is warranted, if the military service, individually or in combination with other offender characteristics, is present to an unusual degree and distinguishes the case from the typical cases covered by the guidelines". The Commission determined that applying this departure standard to consideration of military service is appropriate because such service has been recognized as a traditional mitigating factor at sentencing. See, e.g., Porter v. McCollum, 130 S. Ct. 447, 455 (2009) ("Our Nation has a long tradition of according leniency to veterans in recognition of their service, especially for those who fought on the front lines . . . .").

Finally, the amendment makes conforming changes to § 5K2.0 (Grounds for Departure).

Effective Date: The effective date of this amendment is November 1, 2010.

Amendment 740 APPENDIX C - VOLUME III November 1, 2013

740. Amendment: The Commentary to § 2L1.2 captioned "Application Notes" is amended in Note 7 by striking "Consideration" and inserting "Based on Seriousness of a Prior Conviction".

The Commentary to § 2L1.2 captioned "Application Notes" is amended by adding at the end the following:

"8. Departure Based on Cultural Assimilation.—There may be cases in which a downward departure may be appropriate on the basis of cultural assimilation. Such a departure should be considered only in cases where (A) the defendant formed cultural ties primarily with the United States from having resided continuously in the United States from childhood, (B) those cultural ties provided the primary motivation for the defendant's illegal reentry or continued presence in the United States, and (C) such a departure is not likely to increase the risk to the public from further crimes of the defendant.

In determining whether such a departure is appropriate, the court should consider, among other things, (1) the age in childhood at which the defendant began residing continuously in the United States, (2) whether and for how long the defendant attended school in the United States, (3) the duration of the defendant's continued residence in the United States, (4) the duration of the defendant's presence outside the United States, (5) the nature and extent of the defendant's familial and cultural ties inside the United States, and the nature and extent of such ties outside the United States, (6) the seriousness of the defendant's criminal history, and (7) whether the defendant engaged in additional criminal activity after illegally reentering the United States.".

Reason for Amendment: This amendment addresses when a downward departure may be appropriate in an illegal reentry case sentenced under § 2L1.2 (Unlawfully Entering or Remaining in the United States) on the basis of the defendant's cultural assimilation to the United States.

Several circuits have upheld departures based on cultural assimilation. See, e.g., United States v. Rodriguez-Montelongo, 263 F.3d 429, 433 (5th Cir. 2001); United States v. Sanchez-Valencia, 148 F.3d 1273, 1274 (11th Cir. 1998); United States v. Lipman, 133 F.3d 726, 730 (9th Cir. 1998). Other circuits have declined to rule on whether such a departure may be warranted. See, e.g., United States v. Galarza-Payan, 441 F.3d 885, 889 (10th Cir. 2006) ("We need not address that debate in the altered post-Booker landscape."); United States v. Melendez-Torres, 420 F.3d 45, 51 n.3 (1st Cir. 2005); see also United States v. Ticas, 219 F. App'x 44, 45 (2d Cir. 2007) (acknowledging that the Second Circuit has never recognized cultural assimilation as a basis for a downward departure). Some circuits, though not foreclosing the possibility of cultural assimilation departures, have stated that district courts are within their discretion to deny such departures in light of a defendant's criminal past and society's increased interest in "keeping aliens who have committed crimes out of the United States following their deportation." United States v. Roche-Martinez, 467 F.3d 591, 595 (7th Cir. 2006); see also Galarza-Payan, supra, at 889-90 (stating that "in assessing the reasonableness of a sentence [] a particular defendant's cultural ties must be weighed against other factors such as (1) sentencing disparities among defendants with similar backgrounds and characteristics, and (2) the need for the sentence to reflect the seriousness of the crime and promote respect for the law").

In order to promote uniform consideration of cultural assimilation by courts, the amendment adds an application note to § 2L1.2 providing that a downward departure may be appropriate on the basis of cultural assimilation. The application note provides that such a departure may be appropriate if (A) the defendant formed cultural ties primarily with the United States from having resided continuously in the United States from childhood, (B) those cultural ties provided the primary motivation for the defendant's illegal reentry or continued presence in the United States, and (C) such a departure is not likely to increase the risk to the public from further crimes of the defendant. The application note also provides a non-exhaustive list of factors the court should consider in determining whether such a departure is appropriate.

Effective Date: The effective date of this amendment is November 1, 2010.

741. **Amendment:** Section 1B1.1 is amended by redesignating subdivisions (a) through (h) as (1) through (8), respectively; in subdivision (4) (as so redesignated) by striking "(a)" and inserting "(1)", and by striking "(c)" and inserting "(3)";

by striking the first paragraph as follows:

> "Except as specifically directed, the provisions of this manual are to be applied in the following order:",

and inserting the following:

> "(a) The court shall determine the kinds of sentence and the guideline range as set forth in the guidelines (see 18 U.S.C. § 3553(a)(4)) by applying the provisions of this manual in the following order, except as specifically directed:";

by redesignating subdivision (i) as subsection (b) and, in that subsection, by striking "Refer to" and inserting "The court shall then consider"; by striking "to" before "any"; and by adding at the end "See 18 U.S.C. § 3553(a)(5)."; and

by adding at the end the following:

> "(c) The court shall then consider the applicable factors in 18 U.S.C. § 3553(a) taken as a whole. See 18 U.S.C. § 3553(a).".

The Commentary to § 1B1.1 is amended by adding at the end the following:

> "Background: The court must impose a sentence 'sufficient, but not greater than necessary,' to comply with the purposes of sentencing set forth in 18 U.S.C. § 3553(a)(2). See 18 U.S.C. § 3553(a). Subsections (a), (b), and (c) are structured to reflect the three-step process used in determining the particular sentence to be imposed. If, after step (c), the court imposes a sentence that is outside the guidelines framework, such a sentence is considered a 'variance'. See Irizarry v. United States, 128 S. Ct. 2198, 2200-03 (2008) (describing within-range sentences and departures as 'sentences imposed under the framework set out in the Guidelines').".

Reason for Amendment: This amendment amends § 1B1.1 (Application Instructions) in light of United States v. Booker, 543 U.S. 220 (2005), and subsequent case law.

As explained more fully in Chapter One, Part A, Subpart 2 (Continuing Evolution and Role of the Guidelines) of the Guidelines Manual, a district court is required to properly calculate and consider the guidelines when sentencing. See 18 U.S.C. § 3553(a)(4); Booker, 543 U.S. at 264 ("The district courts, while not bound to apply the Guidelines, must . . . take them into account when sentencing."); Rita v. United States, 551 U.S. 338, 347-48 (2007) (stating that a district court should begin all sentencing proceedings by cor-

Amendment 741

rectly calculating the applicable Guidelines range); Gall v. United States, 552 U.S. 38, 49 (2007) ("As a matter of administration and to secure nationwide consistency, the Guidelines should be the starting point and the initial benchmark.").

After determining the guideline range, the district court should refer to the Guidelines Manual and consider whether the case warrants a departure. See 18 U.S.C. § 3553(a)(5). "'Departure' is a term of art under the Guidelines and refers only to non-Guidelines sentences imposed under the framework set out in the Guidelines." Irizarry v. United States, 128 S.Ct. 2198, 2202 (2008). A "variance" – i.e., a sentence outside the guideline range other than as provided for in the Guidelines Manual – is considered by the court only after departures have been considered.

Most circuits agree on a three-step approach, including the consideration of departure provisions in the Guidelines Manual, in determining the sentence to be imposed. See United States v. Dixon, 449 F.3d 194, 203-04 (1st Cir. 2006) (court must consider "any applicable departures"); United States v. Selioutsky, 409 F.3d 114, 118 (2d Cir. 2005) (court must consider "available departure authority"); United States v. Jackson, 467 F.3d 834, 838 (3d Cir. 2006) (same); United States v. Moreland, 437 F.3d 424, 433 (4th Cir. 2006) (departures "remain an important part of sentencing even after Booker"); United States v. Tzep-Mejia, 461 F.3d 522, 525 (5th Cir. 2006) ("Post-Booker case law recognizes three types of sentences under the new advisory sentencing regime: (1) a sentence within a properly calculated Guideline range; (2) a sentence that includes an upward or downward departure as allowed by the Guidelines, which sentence is also a Guideline sentence; or (3) a non-Guideline sentence which is either higher or lower than the relevant Guideline sentence." (internal footnote and citation omitted)); United States v. McBride, 434 F.3d 470, 476 (6th Cir. 2006) (district court "still required to consider . . . whether a Chapter 5 departure is appropriate"); United States v. Hawk Wing, 433 F.3d 622, 631 (8th Cir. 2006) ("the district court must decide if a traditional departure is appropriate", and after that must consider a variance (internal quotation omitted)); United States v. Robertson, 568 F.3d 1203, 1210 (10th Cir. 2009) (district courts must continue to apply departures); United States v. Jordi, 418 F.3d 1212, 1215 (11th Cir. 2005) (stating that "the application of the guidelines is not complete until the departures, if any, that are warranted are appropriately considered"). But see United States v. Johnson, 427 F.3d 423, 426 (7th Cir. 2006) (stating that departures are "obsolete").

The amendment resolves the circuit conflict and adopts the three-step approach followed by a majority of circuits in determining the sentence to be imposed. The amendment restructures § 1B1.1 into three subsections to reflect the three-step process. As amended, subsection (a) addresses how to apply the provisions in the Guidelines Manual to properly determine the kinds of sentence and the guideline range. Subsection (b) addresses the need to consider the policy statements and commentary to determine whether a departure is warranted. Subsection (c) addresses the need to consider the applicable factors under 18 U.S.C. § 3553(a) taken as a whole in determining the appropriate sentence. The amendment also adds background commentary referring to the statutory requirements of 18 U.S.C. § 3553(a) and defining the term "variance" as "a sentence that is outside the guidelines framework".

Effective Date: The effective date of this amendment is November 1, 2010.

742. **Amendment:** Section 4A1.1 is amended by striking "items (a) through (f)" and inserting "subsections (a) through (e)"; in subsection (c) by striking "item" and inserting "subsection"; by striking subsection (e) as follows:

"(e) Add 2 points if the defendant committed the instant offense less than two years after release from imprisonment on a sentence counted under (a) or (b) or while in imprisonment or escape status on such a sentence. If 2 points are added for item (d), add only 1 point for this item.";

and redesignating subsection (f) as (e); and in subsection (e) (as so redesignated) by striking "item" and inserting "subsection".

The Commentary to § 4A1.1 captioned "Application Notes" is amended by striking "item" and inserting "subsection" each place it appears; by striking Note 5 as follows:

"5. § 4A1.1(e). Two points are added if the defendant committed any part of the instant offense (i.e., any relevant conduct) less than two years following release from confinement on a sentence counted under § 4A1.1(a) or (b). This also applies if the defendant committed the instant offense while in imprisonment or escape status on such a sentence. Failure to report for service of a sentence of imprisonment is to be treated as an escape from such sentence. See § 4A1.2(n). However, if two points are added under § 4A1.1(d), only one point is added under § 4A1.1(e).";

and redesignating Note 6 as Note 5; and in Note 5 (as so redesignated) by striking "(f)" and inserting "(e)" each place it appears.

The Commentary to § 4A1.1 captioned "Background" is amended by striking "Subdivisions" and inserting "Subsections"; by striking "implements one measure of recency by adding" and inserting "adds"; and

by striking the paragraph that begins "Section 4A1.1(e)" as follows:

"   Section 4A1.1(e) implements another measure of recency by adding two points if the defendant committed any part of the instant offense less than two years immediately following his release from confinement on a sentence counted under § 4A1.1(a) or (b). Because of the potential overlap of (d) and (e), their combined impact is limited to three points. However, a defendant who falls within both (d) and (e) is more likely to commit additional crimes; thus, (d) and (e) are not completely combined.".

Section 4A1.2 is amended in subsection (a)(2) by striking "(f)" and inserting "(e)"; in subsection (k)(2) by striking subparagraph (A) as follows:

"(A)   Revocation of probation, parole, supervised release, special parole, or mandatory release may affect the points for § 4A1.1(e) in respect to the recency of last release from confinement.";

and by striking "(B)"; in subsection (l) by striking "(f)" and inserting "(e)", and by striking "; § 4A1.1(e) shall not apply"; in subsection (n) by striking "and (e)"; and in subsection (p) by striking "(f)" and inserting "(e)".

The Commentary to § 4A1.2 captioned "Application Notes" is amended in Note 12(A) by striking "subdivision" and inserting "subsection".

Reason for Amendment: This amendment addresses a factor included in the calculation of the criminal history score in Chapter Four of the Guidelines Manual. Specifically, this amendment eliminates the "recency" points provided in subsection (e) of § 4A1.1 (Criminal History Category). Under § 4A1.1(e), one or two points are added to the criminal history score if the defendant committed the instant offense less than two years after release from imprisonment on a sentence counted under subsection (a) or (b) or while in imprisonment or escape status on such a sentence. In addition to recency, subsections (a), (b), (c), (d), and (f) add points to the criminal history score to account for the seriousness of the prior offense and the status of the defendant. These other factors remain included in the criminal history score after the amendment.

The amendment is a result of the Commission's continued review of criminal history issues. This multi-year review was prompted in part because criminal history issues are often cited by sentencing courts as reasons for imposing non-government sponsored below range sentences, particularly in cases in which recency points were added to the criminal history score under § 4A1.1(e).

As part of its review, the Commission undertook analyses to determine the extent to which recency points contribute to the ability of the criminal history score to predict the defendant's risk of recidivism. See generally USSG Ch. 4, Pt. A, intro. comment ("To protect the public from further crimes of the particular defendant, the likelihood of recidivism and future criminal behavior must be considered."). Recent research isolating the effect of § 4A1.1(e) on the predictive ability of the criminal history score indicated that consideration of recency only minimally improves the predictive ability.

In addition, the Commission received public comment and testimony suggesting that the recency of the instant offense to the defendant's release from imprisonment does not necessarily reflect increased culpability. Public comment and testimony indicated that defendants who recidivate tend to do so relatively soon after being released from prison but suggested that, for many defendants, this may reflect the challenges to successful reentry after imprisonment rather than increased culpability.

Finally, Commission data indicated that many of the cases in which recency points apply are sentenced under Chapter Two guidelines that have provisions based on criminal history. The amendment responds to suggestions that recency points are not necessary to adequately account for criminal history in such cases.

Effective Date: The effective date of this amendment is November 1, 2010.

743. **Amendment:** The Commentary to § 2H1.1 captioned "Statutory Provisions" is amended by inserting "249," after "248,".

The Commentary to § 2H1.1 captioned "Application Notes" is amended in Note 4 by inserting "gender identity," after "gender,".

Section 3A1.1(a) is amended by inserting "gender identity," after "gender,".

The Commentary to § 3A1.1 captioned "Application Notes" is amended in Note 3 by inserting "gender identity," after "gender,"; and by adding after Note 4 the following:

> "5. For purposes of this guideline, 'gender identity' means actual or perceived gender-related characteristics. See 18 U.S.C. § 249(c)(4).".

The Commentary to § 3A1.1 captioned "Background" is amended in the first paragraph by striking the following:

> "(i.e., a primary motivation for the offense was the race, color, religion, national origin, ethnicity, gender, disability, or sexual orientation of the victim)";

and by adding at the end of that paragraph the following:

"In section 4703(a) of Public Law 111-84, Congress broadened the scope of that directive to include gender identity; to reflect that congressional action, the Commission has broadened the scope of this enhancement to include gender identity.".

Appendix A (Statutory Index) is amended by inserting after the line referenced to 18 U.S.C. § 247 the following:

"18 U.S.C. § 249   2H1.1";

and by inserting after the line referenced to 18 U.S.C. § 1369 the following:

"18 U.S.C. § 1389   2A2.2, 2A2.3, 2B1.1".

Reason for Amendment: This amendment responds to the Matthew Shepard and James Byrd, Jr. Hate Crimes Prevention Act (division E of Pub. L. 111-84) (the "Act"). The Act created two new offenses and amended a 1994 directive to the Commission regarding crimes motivated by hate.

The first new offense, 18 U.S.C. § 249 (Hate crime acts), makes it unlawful, whether or not acting under color of law, to willfully cause bodily injury to any person or, through the use of fire, a firearm, a dangerous weapon, or an explosive or incendiary device, to attempt to cause bodily injury to any person because of the actual or perceived race, color, religion, national origin, gender, sexual orientation, gender identity, or disability of any person. A person who violates 18 U.S.C. § 249 is subject to a term of imprisonment of up to 10 years or, if the offense includes kidnapping, aggravated sexual abuse, or an attempt to kill, or if death results from the offense, to imprisonment for any term of years or life. The amendment amends Appendix A (Statutory Index) to refer offenses under 18 U.S.C. § 249 to § 2H1.1 (Offenses Involving Individual Rights) because that guideline covers similar offenses, e.g., 18 U.S.C. §§ 241 (Conspiracy against rights) and 242 (Deprivation of rights under color of law), and contains appropriate enhancements to account for aggravating circumstances that may be involved in a section 249 offense, e.g., subsection (b)(1), which provides a 6-level increase if the offense was committed under color of law.

The Act also amended section 280003 of the Violent Crime Control and Law Enforcement Act of 1994 (Pub. L. 103-322; 28 U.S.C. § 994 note), which contains a directive to the Commission regarding hate crimes. The Commission implemented that directive by promulgating subsection (a) of § 3A1.1 (Hate Crime Motivation or Vulnerable Victim). See USSG App. C, Amendment 521 (effective November 1, 1995). The Act broadened the definition of "hate crime" in section 280003(a) to include crimes motivated by actual or perceived "gender identity", which has the effect of expanding the scope of the directive in section 280003(b) so that it now requires the Commission to provide an enhancement for crimes motivated by actual or perceived "gender identity". To reflect the broadened definition, the amendment amends § 3A1.1 so that the enhancement in subsection (a) covers crimes motivated by actual or perceived "gender identity" and makes conforming changes to §§ 2H1.1. The amendment also deletes as unnecessary the parenthetical in the Background to § 3A1.1, which provided an example of "hate crime motivation".

The second new offense, 18 U.S.C. § 1389 (Prohibition on attacks on United States servicemen on account of service), makes it unlawful to knowingly assault or batter a United States serviceman or an immediate family member of a United States serviceman, or to knowingly destroy or injure the property of such serviceman or immediate family member, on the account of the military service of that serviceman or the status of that individual as a United States serviceman. A person who violates 18 U.S.C. § 1389 is subject to a term of imprisonment of not more than 2 years in the case of a simple assault, or damage of not more than $500, of not more than 5 years in the case of damage of more than $500, or of not less than 6 months nor more than 10 years in the case of a battery, or an assault resulting in bodily injury. The Commission determined that offenses under 18 U.S.C. § 1389 are similar to offenses involving assault or property damage that are already referenced to §§ 2A2.2 (Aggravated Assault), 2A2.3 (Minor Assault), and 2B1.1 (Theft, Property Destruction, and Fraud) and therefore amended Appendix A (Statutory Index) to refer the new offense to those guidelines.

Effective Date: The effective date of this amendment is November 1, 2010.

744. Amendment: Section 8B2.1(b)(4) is amended by striking "subdivision" and inserting "subparagraph" each place it appears.

The Commentary to § 8B2.1 captioned "Application Notes" is amended in Note 2(D) by striking "subdivision" and inserting "subparagraph".

The Commentary to § 8B2.1 captioned "Application Notes" is amended by redesignating Note 6 as Note 7, and by inserting after Note 5 the following:

"6. Application of Subsection (b)(7).—Subsection (b)(7) has two aspects.

First, the organization should respond appropriately to the criminal conduct. The organization should take reasonable steps, as warranted under the circumstances, to remedy the harm resulting from the criminal conduct. These steps may include, where appropriate, providing restitution to identifiable victims, as well as other forms of remediation. Other reasonable steps to respond appropriately to the criminal conduct may include self-reporting and cooperation with authorities.

Second, the organization should act appropriately to prevent further similar criminal conduct, including assessing the compliance and ethics program and making modifications necessary to ensure the program is effective. The steps taken should be consistent with subsections (b)(5) and (c) and may include the use of an outside professional advisor to ensure adequate assessment and implementation of any modifications.";

and in Note 7, as redesignated by this amendment, by striking "subdivision" and inserting "subparagraph" each place it appears.

Section 8C2.5(f)(3) is amended in subparagraph (A) by striking "subdivision (B)" and inserting "subparagraphs (B) and (C)"; and by adding at the end the following:

"(C) Subparagraphs (A) and (B) shall not apply if—

(i) the individual or individuals with operational responsibility for the compliance and ethics program (see § 8B2.1(b)(2)(C)) have direct reporting obligations to the governing authority or an appropriate subgroup thereof (e.g., an audit committee of the board of directors);

(ii) the compliance and ethics program detected the offense before discovery outside the organization or before such discovery was reasonably likely;

(iii) the organization promptly reported the offense to appropriate governmental authorities; and

(iv) no individual with operational responsibility for the compliance and ethics program participated in, condoned, or was willfully ignorant of the offense.".

The Commentary to § 8C2.5 captioned "Application Notes" is amended in Note 10 in the second sentence by inserting "or (f)(3)(C)(iii)" after "subsection (f)(2)"; by redesignating Notes 11 through 14 as Notes 12 through 15, respectively; and by inserting after Note 10 the following:

"11. For purposes of subsection (f)(3)(C)(i), an individual has 'direct reporting obligations' to the governing authority or an appropriate subgroup thereof if the individual has express authority to communicate personally to the governing authority or appropriate subgroup thereof (A) promptly on any matter involving criminal conduct or potential criminal conduct, and (B) no less than annually on the implementation and effectiveness of the compliance and ethics program.".

Section 8D1.4 is amended by striking subsections (b) and (c) as follows:

"(b) If probation is imposed under § 8D1.1(a)(2), the following conditions may be appropriate to the extent they appear necessary to safeguard the organization's ability to pay any deferred portion of an order of restitution, fine, or assessment:

(1) The organization shall make periodic submissions to the court or probation officer, at intervals specified by the court, reporting on the organization's financial condition and results of business operations, and accounting for the disposition of all funds received.

(2) The organization shall submit to: (A) a reasonable number of regular or unannounced examinations of its books and records at appropriate business premises by the probation officer or experts engaged by the court; and (B) interrogation of knowledgeable individuals within the organization. Compensation to and costs of any experts engaged by the court shall be paid by the organization.

(3) The organization shall be required to notify the court or probation officer immediately upon learning of (A) any material adverse change in its business or financial condition or prospects, or (B) the commencement of any bankruptcy proceeding, major civil litigation, criminal prosecution, or administrative proceeding against the organization, or any investigation or formal inquiry by governmental authorities regarding the organization.

(4) The organization shall be required to make periodic payments, as specified by the court, in the following priority: (A) restitution; (B) fine; and (C) any other monetary sanction.

(c) If probation is ordered under § 8D1.1(a)(3), (4), (5), or (6), the following conditions may be appropriate:

(1) The organization shall develop and submit to the court an effective compliance and ethics program consistent with § 8B2.1 (Effective Compliance and Ethics Program). The organization shall include in

its submission a schedule for implementation of the compliance and ethics program.

(2) Upon approval by the court of a program referred to in subdivision (1), the organization shall notify its employees and shareholders of its criminal behavior and its program referred to in subdivision (1). Such notice shall be in a form prescribed by the court.

(3) The organization shall make periodic reports to the court or probation officer, at intervals and in a form specified by the court, regarding the organization's progress in implementing the program referred to in subdivision (1). Among other things, such reports shall disclose any criminal prosecution, civil litigation, or administrative proceeding commenced against the organization, or any investigation or formal inquiry by governmental authorities of which the organization learned since its last report.

(4) In order to monitor whether the organization is following the program referred to in subdivision (1), the organization shall submit to: (A) a reasonable number of regular or unannounced examinations of its books and records at appropriate business premises by the probation officer or experts engaged by the court; and (B) interrogation of knowledgeable individuals within the organization. Compensation to and costs of any experts engaged by the court shall be paid by the organization.",

and inserting the following:

"(b) If probation is imposed under § 8D1.1, the following conditions may be appropriate:

(1) The organization shall develop and submit to the court an effective compliance and ethics program consistent with § 8B2.1 (Effective Compliance and Ethics Program). The organization shall include in its submission a schedule for implementation of the compliance and ethics program.

(2) Upon approval by the court of a program referred to in paragraph (1), the organization shall notify its employees and shareholders of its criminal behavior and its program referred to in paragraph (1). Such notice shall be in a form prescribed by the court.

(3) The organization shall make periodic submissions to the court or probation officer, at intervals specified by the court, (A) reporting on the organization's financial condition and results of business operations, and accounting for the disposition of all funds received, and (B) reporting on the organization's progress in implementing the program referred to in paragraph (1). Among other things, reports under subparagraph (B) shall disclose any criminal prosecution, civil litigation, or administrative proceeding commenced against the organization, or any investigation or formal inquiry by governmental authorities of which the organization learned since its last report.

(4) The organization shall notify the court or probation officer im-

mediately upon learning of (A) any material adverse change in its business or financial condition or prospects, or (B) the commencement of any bankruptcy proceeding, major civil litigation, criminal prosecution, or administrative proceeding against the organization, or any investigation or formal inquiry by governmental authorities regarding the organization.

(5) The organization shall submit to: (A) a reasonable number of regular or unannounced examinations of its books and records at appropriate business premises by the probation officer or experts engaged by the court; and (B) interrogation of knowledgeable individuals within the organization. Compensation to and costs of any experts engaged by the court shall be paid by the organization.

(6) The organization shall make periodic payments, as specified by the court, in the following priority: (A) restitution; (B) fine; and (C) any other monetary sanction.".

The Commentary to § 8D1.4 captioned "Application Note" is amended in Note 1 by striking "(a)(3) through (6)"; and by striking "(c)(3)" and inserting "(b)(3)".

Reason for Amendment: This amendment makes several changes to Chapter Eight of the Guidelines Manual regarding the sentencing of organizations.

First, the amendment amends the Commentary to § 8B2.1 (Effective Compliance and Ethics Program) by adding an application note that clarifies the remediation efforts required to satisfy the seventh minimal requirement for an effective compliance and ethics program under subsection (b)(7). Subsection (b)(7) requires an organization, after criminal conduct has been detected, to take reasonable steps (1) to respond appropriately to the criminal conduct and (2) to prevent further similar criminal conduct.

The new application note describes the two aspects of subsection (b)(7). With respect to the first aspect, the application note provides that the organization should take reasonable steps, as warranted under the circumstances, to remedy the harm resulting from the criminal conduct. The application note further provides that such steps may include, where appropriate, providing restitution to identifiable victims, other forms of remediation, and self-reporting and cooperation with authorities. With respect to the second aspect, the application note provides that an organization should assess the compliance and ethics program and make modifications necessary to ensure the program is effective. The application note further provides that such steps should be consistent with § 8B2.1(b)(5) and (c), which also require assessment and modification of the program, and may include the use of an outside professional advisor to ensure adequate assessment and implementation of any modifications.

This application note was added in response to public comment and testimony suggesting that further guidance regarding subsection (b)(7) may encourage organizations to take reasonable steps upon discovery of criminal conduct. The steps outlined by the application note are consistent with factors considered by enforcement agencies in evaluating organizational compliance and ethics practices.

Second, the amendment amends subsection (f) of § 8C2.5 (Culpability Score) to create a limited exception to the general prohibition against applying the 3-level decrease for having an effective compliance and ethics program when an organization's high-level or substantial authority personnel are involved in the offense. Specifically, the amendment

Amendment 744 APPENDIX C - VOLUME III November 1, 2013

adds subsection (f)(3)(C), which allows an organization to receive the decrease if the organization meets four criteria: (1) the individual or individuals with operational responsibility for the compliance and ethics program have direct reporting obligations to the organization's governing authority or appropriate subgroup thereof; (2) the compliance and ethics program detected the offense before discovery outside the organization or before such discovery was reasonably likely; (3) the organization promptly reported the offense to the appropriate governmental authorities; and (4) no individual with operational responsibility for the compliance and ethics program participated in, condoned, or was willfully ignorant of the offense.

The new subsection (f)(3)(C) responds to concerns expressed in public comment and testimony that the general prohibition in § 8C2.5(f)(3) operates too broadly and that internal and external reporting of criminal conduct could be better encouraged by providing an exception to that general prohibition in appropriate cases.

The amendment also adds an application note that describes the "direct reporting obligations" necessary to meet the first criterion under § 8C2.5(f)(3)(C). The application note provides that an individual has "direct reporting obligations" if the individual has express authority to communicate personally to the governing authority "promptly on any matter involving criminal conduct or potential criminal conduct" and "no less than annually on the implementation and effectiveness of the compliance and ethics program". The application note responds to public comment and testimony regarding the challenges operational compliance personnel may face when seeking to report criminal conduct to the governing authority of an organization and encourages compliance and ethics policies that provide operational compliance personnel with access to the governing authority when necessary.

Third, the amendment amends § 8D1.4 (Recommended Conditions of Probation – Organizations (Policy Statement)) to augment and simplify the recommended conditions of probation for organizations. The amendment removes the distinction between conditions of probation imposed solely to enforce a monetary penalty and conditions of probation imposed for any other reason so that all conditional probation terms are available for consideration by the court in determining an appropriate sentence.

Finally, the amendment makes technical and conforming changes to various provisions in Chapter Eight.

Effective Date: The effective date of this amendment is November 1, 2010.

745. Amendment: Section 2B1.1(c)(4) is amended by inserting "or a paleontological resource" after "resource"; and by inserting "or Paleontological Resources" after "Heritage Resources" each place it appears.

The Commentary to § 2B1.1 captioned "Application Notes" is amended in Note 1 by inserting after the paragraph that begins "'National cemetery' means" the following:

> "'Paleontological resource' has the meaning given that term in Application Note 1 of the Commentary to § 2B1.5 (Theft of, Damage to, or Destruction of, Cultural Heritage Resources or Paleontological Resources; Unlawful Sale, Purchase, Exchange, Transportation, or Receipt of Cultural Heritage Resources or Paleontological Resources).".

The Commentary to § 2B1.1 captioned "Application Notes" is amended in Note 14(A) by inserting "and 18 U.S.C. § 1348" after "7 U.S.C. § 1 et seq.)".

Section 2B1.5 is amended in the heading by inserting "or Paleontological Resources" after

"Heritage Resources" each place it appears.

Section 2B1.5(b) is amended in each of paragraphs (1) and (2) by inserting "or paleontological resource" after "heritage resource"; and in paragraph (5) by inserting "or paleontological resources" after "heritage resources".

The Commentary to § 2B1.5 captioned "Statutory Provisions" is amended by inserting "470aaa–5," after "16 U.S.C. §§ ".

The Commentary to § 2B1.5 captioned "Application Notes" is amended in Note 1 by redesignating subparagraphs (A) through (G) as (i) through (vii), respectively; by striking "'Cultural Heritage Resource' Defined.—For purposes of this guideline, 'cultural heritage resource' means any of the following:" and inserting:

"Definitions.—For purposes of this guideline:

(A) 'Cultural heritage resource' means any of the following:";

by striking "(A)" before "has the meaning" and inserting "(I)"; by striking "(B)" before "includes" and inserting "(II)"; and by adding at the end the following:

"(B) 'Paleontological resource' has the meaning given such term in 16 U.S.C. § 470aaa.".

The Commentary to § 2B1.5 captioned "Application Notes" is amended in Note 2 by striking "Cultural Heritage" both places it appears; by striking "cultural heritage" each place it appears; and by inserting ", e.g.," after "See" each place it appears.

The Commentary to § 2B1.5 captioned "Application Notes" is amended in Note 5(B) by striking "cultural heritage"; in Note 6(A) by inserting "or paleontological resources" after "resources", and by striking "cultural heritage" after "involving a" each place it appears; in Note 8 by striking "cultural heritage" each place it appears; and in Note 9 by inserting "or paleontological resources" after "resources" the first place it appears; and by inserting "or paleontological resources" after "resources)".

Section 2D1.11(e) is amended in subdivisions (1)-(10) by inserting the following list I chemicals in the appropriate place in alphabetical order by subdivision as follows:

(1)   "1.3 KG or more of Iodine;",

(2)   "At least 376.2 G but less than 1.3 KG of Iodine;",

(3)   "At least 125.4 G but less than 376.2 G of Iodine;",

(4)   "At least 87.8 G but less than 125.4 G of Iodine;",

(5)   "At least 50.2 G but less than 87.8 G of Iodine;",

(6)   "At least 12.5 G but less than 50.2 G of Iodine;",

(7)   "At least 10 G but less than 12.5 G of Iodine;",

(8)   "At least 7.5 G but less than 10 G of Iodine;",

(9)   "At least 5 G but less than 7.5 G of Iodine;",

(10)   "Less than 5 G of Iodine;"; and

Amendment 745 APPENDIX C - VOLUME III November 1, 2013

in subdivisions (2)-(10), in list II chemicals, by striking the lines referenced to "Iodine", including the period, and in the lines referenced to "Toluene" by striking the semicolon and inserting a period.

Appendix A (Statutory Index) is amended by inserting after the line referenced to 16 U.S.C. § 413 the following:

"16 U.S.C. § 470aaa–5   2B1.1, 2B1.5"; and

by inserting after the line referenced to 42 U.S.C. § 1396h(b)(2) the following:

"42 U.S.C. § 1396w–2   2H3.1".

Reason for Amendment: This multi-part amendment responds to miscellaneous issues arising from legislation recently enacted and other miscellaneous guideline application issues.

First, the amendment responds to the Fraud Enforcement and Recovery Act of 2009, Pub. L. 111–21, which broadened 18 U.S.C. § 1348, a securities fraud statute, to cover commodities fraud. Offenses under 18 U.S.C. § 1348 are referenced in Appendix A (Statutory Index) to § 2B1.1 (Larceny, Embezzlement, and Other Forms of Theft; Offenses Involving Stolen Property; Property Damage or Destruction; Fraud and Deceit; Forgery; Offenses Involving Altered or Counterfeit Instruments Other than Counterfeit Bearer Obligations of the United States). Section 2B1.1 includes an enhancement at subsection (b)(17)(B) that applies when specified persons who have fiduciary duties violate commodities law. "Commodities law" is defined in Application Note 14 to mean the Commodities Exchange Act (7 U.S.C. § 1 et seq.), including the rules, regulations, and orders issued by the Commodity Futures Trading Commission. The amendment adds 18 U.S.C. § 1348 to the definition of "commodities law" for purposes of subsection (b)(17)(B). The Commission determined that including 18 U.S.C. § 1348 within the scope of subsection (b)(17)(B) is appropriate to reflect the expanded scope of the statute.

Second, the amendment responds to the Omnibus Public Land Management Act of 2009, Pub. L. 111–11, which created a new offense at 16 U.S.C. § 470aaa-5 making it unlawful to remove, damage, alter, traffic in, or make a false record relating to a paleontological resource on federal land. The amendment amends Appendix A (Statutory Index) to refer offenses under 16 U.S.C. § 470aaa-5 to §§ 2B1.1 and 2B1.5 (Theft of, Damage to, or Destruction of, Cultural Heritage Resources; Unlawful Sale, Purchase, Exchange, Transportation, or Receipt of Cultural Heritage Resources) because such offenses are similar either to offenses involving cultural heritage resources or, to the extent they involve false records, to fraud offenses. The amendment also makes technical and conforming changes to §§ 2B1.1 and 2B1.5.

Third, the amendment responds to the Children's Health Insurance Program Reauthorization Act of 2009, Pub. L. 111–3, which created a new Class A misdemeanor offense at 42 U.S.C. § 1396w-2 regarding the unlawful disclosure of certain protected information related to social security eligibility. The amendment amends Appendix A (Statutory Index) to refer offenses under 42 U.S.C. § 1396w-2 to § 2H3.1 (Interception of Communications; Eavesdropping; Disclosure of Certain Private or Protected Information) because such offenses involve invasions of privacy.

Fourth, the amendment responds to a regulatory change in which iodine was upgraded from a List II chemical to a List I chemical. Offenses involving listed chemicals are sentenced under § 2D1.11 (Unlawfully Distributing, Importing, Exporting or Possessing a

Listed Chemical; Attempt or Conspiracy). Because the maximum base offense level for List I chemicals (level 30) is higher than that for List II chemicals (level 28), the amendment increases the maximum base offense level for offenses involving iodine to level 30 and specifies the amount of iodine needed (1.3 kilograms) for base offense level 30 to apply.

Effective Date: The effective date of this amendment is November 1, 2010.

746. **Amendment:** The Commentary to § 1B1.3 captioned "Application Notes" is amended in Note 2 in the second paragraph by striking "(i)" and inserting "(A)"; and by striking "(ii)" and inserting "(B)"; in Note 6, in the first paragraph by striking "'is" and inserting "'was"; and by striking "was committed by the means set forth in" and inserting "involved conduct described in".

The Commentary to § 1B1.8 captioned "Application Notes" is amended in Note 2 by striking "Probation Service" and inserting "probation office".

The Commentary to § 1B1.9 captioned "Application Notes" is amended in Note 1 by inserting "or for which no imprisonment is authorized. See 18 U.S.C. § 3559" after "not more than five days".

The Commentary to § 1B1.11 captioned "Application Notes" is amended in Note 2 by striking "Guideline" and inserting "Guidelines".

The Commentary to § 1B1.13 captioned "Application Notes" is amended in Note 1 by striking "Subsection" and inserting "Subdivision".

The Commentary to § 2A1.1 captioned "Application Notes" is amended in Note 1 by inserting ", see § 2A4.1(c)(1)" after "occurs"; and by inserting ", see § 2E1.3(a)(2)" after "racketeering".

The Commentary to § 2A3.2 captioned "Application Notes" is amended in Note 5 by striking "kidnaping" and inserting "kidnapping" each place it appears.

The Commentary to § 2A3.3 captioned "Application Notes" is amended in Note 1 by inserting "years" before "; (B)".

The Commentary to § 2A3.5 captioned "Application Notes" is amended in Note 1 by striking "those terms in 42 U.S.C. § 16911(2), (3) and (4), respectively" and inserting "the terms 'tier I sex offender', 'tier II sex offender', and 'tier III sex offender', respectively, in 42 U.S.C. § 16911".

The Commentary to § 2B1.4 captioned "Application Notes" is amended in Note 1 by striking "Subsection of".

The Commentary to § 2B1.5 captioned "Application Notes" is amended in Note 1 by striking "299" and inserting "229"; and by striking "section 2(c) of Public Law 99–652 (40 U.S.C. § 1002(c))" and inserting "40 U.S.C. § 8902(a)(1)".

The Commentary to § 2B3.1 captioned "Application Notes" is amended in Note 2 by striking "(d)" and inserting "(D)".

The Commentary to § 2B4.1 captioned "Background" is amended in the fourth paragraph by striking "was recently increased from two to" and inserting "is"; and by striking "Violations" and all that follows through "to the Medicaid program." as follows:

Amendment 746 APPENDIX C - VOLUME III November 1, 2013

> "Violations of 42 U.S.C. §§ 1395nn(b)(1) and (b)(2), involve the offer or acceptance of a payment to refer an individual for services or items paid forunder the Medicare program. Similar provisions in 42 U.S.C. §§ 1396h(b)(1) and (b)(2) cover the offer or acceptance of a payment for referral to the Medicaid program.",

and inserting the following:

> "Violations of 42 U.S.C. § 1320a-7b involve the offer or acceptance of a payment to refer an individual for services or items paid for under a federal health care program (e.g., the Medicare and Medicaid programs).".

The Commentary to § 2B6.1 captioned "Background" is amended by striking "§§ 511 and 553(a)(2)" and inserting "§ 511"; and by inserting "§ 553(a)(2) and" before "2321".

The Commentary to § 2C1.1 captioned "Application Notes" is amended in Note 3 by striking "(A)" after "(b)(2)".

The Commentary to § 2C1.2 captioned "Application Notes" is amended in Note 4 by striking "or" before "Trust" and inserting "of".

Section 2D1.1(c) is amended in each of Notes (H) and (I) to the Drug Quantity Table by striking "(25)" and inserting "(30)".

The Commentary to § 2D1.11 captioned "Application Notes" is amended in Note 6 by striking "or" after "1319(c),"; by striking § 5124,"; and by inserting after "9603(b)" the following: ", and 49 U.S.C. § 5124 (relating to violations of laws and regulations enforced by the Department of Transportation with respect to the transportation of hazardous material)".

The Commentary to § 2D1.12 captioned "Application Notes" is amended in Note 3 by striking "or" after "1319(c),"; by striking § 5124,"; and by inserting after "9603(b)" the following: ", and 49 U.S.C. § 5124 (relating to violations of laws and regulations enforced by the Department of Transportation with respect to the transportation of hazardous material)".

Section 2D1.14(a)(1) is amended by striking "(3)" and inserting "(5)" both places it appears.

The Commentary to § 2D2.1 captioned "Background" is amended in the last paragraph by striking "Section 6371 of the Anti-Drug Abuse Act of 1988" and inserting "21 U.S.C. § 844(a)" both places it appears.

The Commentary to § 2G3.1 captioned "Application Notes" is amended in Note 1 in the paragraph that begins "'Distribution' means" by inserting "transmission," after "production,".

Section 2H4.2(b)(1) is amended by striking "(i)" and inserting "(A)"; and by striking "(ii)" and inserting "(B)".

The Commentary to § 2K1.3 captioned "Application Notes" is amended in Note 10 by striking "(1)" and inserting "(A)"; by striking "(2)" and inserting "(B)"; by striking "(3)" and inserting "(C)"; and by striking "(4)" and inserting "(D)".

The Commentary to § 2K2.1 captioned "Application Notes" is amended in Note 2 by inserting "That Is" after "Firearm"; and by inserting "that is" after "'semiautomatic firearm".

The Commentary to § 2K2.1 captioned "Application Notes" is amended in Note 10 in the first paragraph by striking "; § 4A1.2, comment. (n.3)"; in Note 11 by striking "(1)" and inserting "(A)"; by striking "(2)" and inserting "(B)"; by striking "(3)" and inserting "(C)"; and by striking "(4)" and inserting "(D)".

The Commentary to § 2K2.5 captioned "Application Notes" is amended in Note 2 by striking "(f)" and inserting "(g)"; and in Note 3 by inserting "See 18 U.S.C. § 924(a)(4)." after "other offense.".

The Commentary to § 2L2.1 captioned "Statutory Provisions" is amended by striking "(b)," after "1325"; and by inserting ", (d)" after "(c)".

The Commentary to § 2L2.2 captioned "Statutory Provisions" is amended by striking "(b)," after "1325"; and by inserting ", (d)" after "(c)".

The Commentary to § 2M3.1 captioned "Application Notes" is amended in Note 1 by striking "12356" and inserting "12958 (50 U.S.C. § 435 note)".

The Commentary to § 2M3.3 captioned "Statutory Provisions" is amended by striking "(b), (c)".

The Commentary to § 2M3.9 captioned "Application Notes" is amended in Note 3 by inserting "See 50 U.S.C. § 421(d)." after "imprisonment.".

The Commentary to § 2M6.1 captioned "Application Notes" is amended in Note 1 in the paragraph that begins "'Foreign terrorist" by striking "1219" and inserting "1189"; and in the paragraph that begins "'Restricted person" by striking "(b)" and inserting "(d)".

The Commentary to § 2Q1.2 captioned "Background" is amended by striking "last two" and inserting "fifth and sixth".

Section 2Q1.6(a)(1) is amended by striking "Substance" and inserting "Substances".

The Commentary to § 2Q2.1 captioned "Application Notes" is amended in Note 3 by inserting ", Subtitle B," after "7 C.F.R.".

Chapter Two, Part T, Subpart 2, is amended in the Introductory Commentary by striking "section" and inserting "subpart"; and by inserting "of Chapter 51 of Subtitle E" after "Subchapter J".

The Commentary to § 2X5.2 captioned "Statutory Provisions" is amended by striking "§ 1129(a),".

The Commentary to § 3C1.1 captioned "Application Notes" is amended in Note 4 by redesignating subdivisions (a) through (k) as (A) through (K); and in Note 5 by redesignating subdivisions (a) through (e) as (A) through (E).

The Commentary to § 3E1.1 captioned "Application Notes" is amended in Note 1 by redesignating subdivisions (a) through (h) as (A) through (H).

Section 5K2.17 is amended by striking "(A)" and inserting "(1)"; and by striking "(B)" and inserting "(2)".

Appendix A (Statutory Index) is amended in the line referenced to 7 U.S.C. § 13(f) by striking "(f)" and inserting "(e)";

in the line referenced to 8 U.S.C. § 1325(b) by striking "(b)" and inserting "(c)";

Amendment 746

in the line referenced to 8 U.S.C. § 1325(c) by striking "(c)" and inserting "(d)";

by inserting after the line referenced to 18 U.S.C. § 247 the following:

"18 U.S.C. § 248   2H1.1";

by striking the line referenced to 18 U.S.C. § 1129(a);

by inserting after the line referenced to 42 U.S.C. § 1320a-7b the following:

"42 U.S.C. § 1320a-8b   2X5.1, 2X5.2";

in the line referenced to 50 U.S.C. § 783(b) by striking "(b)"; and

by striking the line referenced to 50 U.S.C. § 783(c).

Reason for Amendment: This two-part amendment makes various technical and conforming changes to the guidelines.

First, the amendment makes changes to the Guidelines Manual to promote accuracy and completeness. For example, it corrects typographical errors, and it addresses cases in which the Guidelines Manual provides information (such as a reference to a guideline, statute, or regulation) that has become incorrect or obsolete. Specifically, it amends:

(1) § 1B1.3 (Relevant Conduct), Application Note 6, to ensure that two quotations contained in that note are accurate;

(2) § 1B1.8 (Use of Certain Information), Application Note 2, to revise a reference to the "Probation Service";

(3) § 1B1.9 (Class B or C Misdemeanors and Infractions), Application Note 1, to reflect that some infractions do not have any authorized term of imprisonment;

(4) § 1B1.11 (Use of Guidelines Manual in Effect on Date of Sentencing), Application Note 2, to correct a typographical error;

(5) § 2A1.1 (First Degree Murder), Application Note 1, to provide specific citations for the examples given;

(6) § 2A3.2 (Criminal Sexual Abuse of a Minor Under the Age of Sixteen Years (Statutory Rape) or Attempt to Commit Such Acts), Application Note 5, to correct typographical errors;

(7) § 2A3.3 (Criminal Sexual Abuse of a Ward or Attempt to Commit Such Acts), Application Note 1, to correct a typographical error;

(8) § 2A3.5 (Failure to Register as a Sex Offender), Application Note 1, to ensure that the statutory definitions referred to in that note are accurately cited;

(9) § 2B1.4 (Insider Trading), Application Note 1, to correct a typographical error;

(10) § 2B1.5 (Theft of, Damage to, or Destruction of, Cultural Heritage Re-

sources), Application Note 1, to provide updated citations to statutes and regulations;

(11) § 2B3.1 (Robbery), Application Note 2, to correct a typographical error;

(12) § 2B4.1 (Bribery in Procurement of Bank Loan and Other Commercial Bribery), Background, to provide an updated description and reference to the statute criminalizing bribery in connection with Medicare and Medicaid referrals;

(13) § 2B6.1 (Altering or Removing Motor Vehicle Identification Numbers), Background, to update the statutory maximum term of imprisonment for violations of 18 U.S.C. § 553(a)(2);

(14) § 2C1.1 (Offering, Giving, Soliciting, or Receiving a Bribe), Application Note 3, to ensure that the subsection relating to "loss" is accurately cited;

(15) § 2C1.2 (Offering, Giving, Soliciting, or Receiving a Gratuity), Application Note 4, to correct a typographical error;

(16) § 2D1.1 (Unlawful Manufacturing, Importing, Exporting, or Trafficking), in the Notes to the Drug Quantity Table, to provide updated citations to regulations;

(17) both § 2D1.11 (Unlawfully Distributing, Importing, Exporting or Possessing a Listed Chemical), Application Note 6, and § 2D1.12 (Unlawful Possession, Manufacture, Distribution, Transportation, Exportation, or Importation of Prohibited Flask, Equipment, Chemical, Product, or Material), Application Note 3, to provide a more accurate statutory citation and description;

(18) § 2D1.14 (Narco-Terrorism), subsection (a)(1), to provide an updated guideline reference;

(19) § 2D2.1 (Unlawful Possession), Commentary, to provide updated statutory references;

(20) § 2G3.1 (Importing, Mailing, or Transporting Obscene Matter), Application Note 1, to make the definition of "distribution" in that guideline consistent with the definition of "distribution" in the child pornography guidelines;

(21) § 2K2.1 (Unlawful Receipt, Possession, or Transportation of Firearms or Ammunition), Application Notes 2 and 10, to ensure that a quotation contained in Note 2 is accurate and that a citation in Note 10 is accurate;

(22) § 2K2.5 (Possession of Firearm or Dangerous Weapon in Federal Facility; Possession or Discharge of Firearm in School Zone), Application Notes 2 and 3, to provide updated statutory references;

(23) both § 2L2.1 (Trafficking in a Document Relating to Naturalization, Citizenship, or Legal Resident Status, or a United States Passport), Statutory Provisions, and § 2L2.2 (Fraudulently Acquiring Documents Relating to Naturalization, Citizenship, or Legal Resident Status for Own Use), Statutory Provisions, to provide updated statutory references;

(24) § 2M3.1 (Gathering or Transmitting National Defense Information to Aid a Foreign Government), Application Note 1, to provide an updated reference to an executive order;

(25) § 2M3.3 (Transmitting National Defense Information), to provide an updated statutory reference;

(26) § 2M3.9 (Disclosure of Information Identifying a Covert Agent), Application Note 3, to provide an updated statutory reference;

(27) § 2M6.1 (Unlawful Activity Involving Nuclear Material, Weapons, or Facilities, Biological Agents, Toxins, or Delivery Systems, Chemical Weapons, or Other Weapons of Mass Destruction), Application Note 1, to provide updated statutory references;

(28) § 2Q1.2 (Mishandling of Hazardous or Toxic Substances or Pesticides), Background, to provide updated guideline references;

(29) § 2Q1.6 (Hazardous or Injurious Devices on Federal Lands), subsection (a)(1), to correct a typographical error;

(30) § 2Q2.1 (Offenses Involving Fish, Wildlife, and Plants), Application Note 3, to provide a more complete reference to regulations;

(31) Chapter Two, Part T, Subpart 2 (Alcohol and Tobacco Taxes), Introductory Commentary, to provide a more complete statutory reference;

(32) § 2X5.2 (Class A Misdemeanors (Not Covered by Another Specific Offense Guideline)), to strike an erroneous statutory reference;

(33) Appendix A (Statutory Index), to provide updated statutory references and strike an erroneous statutory reference.

Second, the amendment makes a series of changes to the Guidelines Manual to promote stylistic consistency in how subdivisions are designated. When dividing guideline sections into subdivisions, the guidelines generally follow the structure used by Congress to divide statutory sections into subdivisions. Thus, a section is broken into subsections (starting with "(a)"), which are broken into paragraphs (starting with "(1)"), which are broken into subparagraphs (starting with "(A)"), which are broken into clauses (starting with "(i)"), which are broken into subclauses (starting with "(I)"). For a generic term, "subdivision" is also used. When dividing application notes into subdivisions, the guidelines generally follow the same structure, except that subsections and paragraphs are not used; the first subdivisions used are subparagraphs (starting with "(A)"). The amendment identifies places in the Guidelines Manual where these principles are not followed and brings them into conformity.

Effective Date: The effective date of this amendment is November 1, 2010.

747. **Amendment:** The Commentary to § 2B1.1 captioned "Application Notes" is amended in Note 1 by inserting "or Paleontological Resources" after "Resources" both places it appears.

The Commentary to § 2B1.1 captioned "Application Notes" is amended in Note 3 in the last paragraph by inserting "or Paleontological Resources" after "Resources"; by inserting "or paleontological resource" before ", loss"; by striking "cultural heritage" after "to that" and by striking "cultural heritage" after "of the".

The Commentary to § 2K1.3 captioned "Application Notes" is amended in Note 9 by striking "; § 4A1.2, comment. (n.3)".

The Commentary to § 2P1.1 captioned "Application Notes" is amended in Note 5 by striking the comma after "escape)" and inserting "and"; and by striking ", and § 4A1.1(e) (recency)".

The Commentary to § 3A1.2 captioned "Application Notes" is amended in Note 3 by striking "§ 2B3.1(a)" and inserting "§ 2B3.1(b)(1)".

The Commentary to § 3C1.1 captioned "Application Notes", as amended by Amendment 746, is amended in Note 4(F) by inserting "judge" after "magistrate"; and in Note 5(B) by striking "4(g)" and inserting "4(G)".

The Commentary to § 3C1.1 captioned "Application Notes" is amended in Note 9 by striking "his" and inserting "the defendant's"; and by striking "he" and inserting "the defendant".

The Commentary to § 3C1.2 captioned "Application Notes" is amended in Note 5 by striking "his" and inserting "the defendant's" and by striking "he" and inserting "the defendant".

The Commentary to § 3E1.1 captioned "Application Notes" is amended in Note 3 by striking "1(a)" and inserting "1(A)".

The Commentary to § 4B1.3 captioned "Application Notes" is amended in Note 2 by striking "(1)" and inserting "(A)"; by striking "(2)" and inserting "(B)"; and by striking "his" and inserting "the defendant's".

The Commentary to § 4B1.3 captioned "Background" is amended by striking "he" and inserting "the defendant"; and by striking "his" and inserting "the defendant's".

The Commentary to § 5B1.1 captioned "Application Notes", as amended by Amendment 738, is amended in Note 1 by redesignating subdivisions (a) and (b) as (A) and (B).

The Commentary to § 5D1.1 captioned "Application Notes" is amended in Note 1 by redesignating subdivisions (1) through (5) as (A) through (E).

The Commentary to § 5E1.5 captioned "Background" is amended by striking "1302c-9" and inserting "1320c-9".

The Commentary to § 5G1.2 captioned "Application Notes" is amended in Note 1 in the second paragraph by striking "(1)" and inserting "(A)" and by striking "(2)" and inserting "(B)".

The Commentary to § 5G1.3 captioned "Application Notes" is amended in Note 2(C) by striking "Judgement" and inserting "Judgment".

The Commentary to § 7B1.4 captioned "Application Notes" is amended in Note 2 by striking "Adequacy" and inserting "Departures Based on Inadequacy"; and in Note 3 by striking "he" and inserting "the defendant".

The Commentary to § 8A1.2 captioned "Application Notes" is amended in Note 2 by striking "and" after "Procedures" and inserting a comma; by inserting ", and Crime

Victims' Rights" after "Agreements"; and in Note 3 by redesignating subdivisions (a) through (j) as subdivisions (A) through (J).

Reason for Amendment: This amendment makes certain technical and conforming changes to commentary in the Guidelines Manual.

First, the amendment makes certain technical and conforming changes in connection with the amendments that the Commission submitted to Congress on April 29, 2010. Those conforming changes are as follows:

(1) Amendment 745 expanded the scope of § 2B1.5 (Theft of, Damage to, or Destruction of, Cultural Heritage Resources; Unlawful Sale, Purchase, Exchange, Transportation, or Receipt of Cultural Heritage Resources) to cover not only cultural heritage resources, but also paleontological resources. To reflect this expanded scope, conforming changes are made to § 2B1.1 (Theft, Property Destruction, and Fraud), Application Notes 1 and 3.

(2) Amendment 746 made a technical change to § 2K2.1 (Unlawful Receipt, Possession, or Transportation of Firearms or Ammunition), Application Note 10, to correct an inaccurate citation. To address a parallel inaccurate citation in § 2K1.3 (Unlawful Receipt, Possession, or Transportation of Explosive Materials; Prohibited Transactions Involving Explosive Materials), Application Note 9, a parallel technical change is made there.

(3) Amendment 742 eliminated the use of "recency" points in calculating the criminal history score. A conforming change is made in § 2P1.1 (Escape, Instigating or Assisting Escape), Application Note 5, to delete an obsolete reference to "recency."

Second, the amendment makes certain other stylistic and clerical changes to commentary in the Guidelines Manual. It amends § 3A1.2 (Official Victim), Application Note 3, to provide an accurate reference to an enhancement in the robbery guideline. It amends § 3C1.1 (Obstructing or Impeding the Administration of Justice), Application Note 4, to replace the obsolete term "magistrate" with the term "magistrate judge." It amends § 5E1.5 (Costs of Prosecution), Background, to correct a typographical error in a statutory citation. It amends § 7B1.4 (Term of Imprisonment), Application Note 2, and § 8A1.2 (Application Instructions - Organizations), Application Note 2, to provide accurate references to guideline titles. Finally, it makes certain other stylistic changes to promote stylistic consistency and gender neutrality.

Effective Date: The effective date of this amendment is November 1, 2010.

748. Amendment: Section 2D1.1(a)(5) is amended by adding at the end the following:

"If the resulting offense level is greater than level 32 and the defendant receives the 4-level ('minimal participant') reduction in § 3B1.2(a), decrease to level 32.".

Section 2D1.1(b) is amended by redesignating subdivisions (10) and (11) as subdivisions (13) and (16); by redesignating subdivisions (2) through (9) as subdivisions (3) through (10); by inserting after subdivision (1) the following:

"(2) If the defendant used violence, made a credible threat to use violence, or directed the use of violence, increase by 2 levels.";

by inserting after subdivision (10), as redesignated by this amendment, the following:

"(11) If the defendant bribed, or attempted to bribe, a law enforcement officer to facilitate the commission of the offense, increase by 2 levels.

(12) If the defendant maintained a premises for the purpose of manufacturing or distributing a controlled substance, increase by 2 levels.";

by inserting after subdivision (13), as redesignated by this amendment, the following:

"(14) If the defendant receives an adjustment under § 3B1.1 (Aggravating Role) and the offense involved 1 or more of the following factors:

(A) (i) the defendant used fear, impulse, friendship, affection, or some combination thereof to involve another individual in the illegal purchase, sale, transport, or storage of controlled substances, (ii) the individual received little or no compensation from the illegal purchase, sale, transport, or storage of controlled substances, and (iii) the individual had minimal knowledge of the scope and structure of the enterprise;

(B) the defendant, knowing that an individual was (i) less than 18 years of age, (ii) 65 or more years of age, (iii) pregnant, or (iv) unusually vulnerable due to physical or mental condition or otherwise particularly susceptible to the criminal conduct, distributed a controlled substance to that individual or involved that individual in the offense;

(C) the defendant was directly involved in the importation of a controlled substance;

(D) the defendant engaged in witness intimidation, tampered with or destroyed evidence, or otherwise obstructed justice in connection with the investigation or prosecution of the offense;

(E) the defendant committed the offense as part of a pattern of criminal conduct engaged in as a livelihood,

increase by 2 levels.

(15) If the defendant receives the 4-level ('minimal participant') reduction in § 3B1.2(a) and the offense involved all of the following factors:

(A) the defendant was motivated by an intimate or familial relationship or by threats or fear to commit the offense and was otherwise unlikely to commit such an offense;

(B) the defendant received no monetary compensation from the illegal purchase, sale, transport, or storage of controlled substances; and

(C) the defendant had minimal knowledge of the scope and structure of the enterprise,

decrease by 2 levels.".

Section 2D1.1(c) is amended in subdivision (1) in the third entry by striking "4.5" and

Amendment 748 APPENDIX C - VOLUME III November 1, 2013

inserting "8.4"; in subdivision (2) in the third entry by striking "1.5" and inserting "2.8"; by striking "4.5" and inserting "8.4"; in subdivision (3) in the third entry by striking "500" and inserting "840"; by striking "1.5" and inserting "2.8"; in subdivision (4) in the third entry by striking "150" and inserting "280"; by striking "500" and inserting "840"; in subdivision (5) in the third entry by striking "50" and inserting "196"; by striking "150" and inserting "280"; in subdivision (6) in the third entry by striking "35" and inserting "112"; by striking "50" and inserting "196"; in subdivision (7) in the third entry by striking "20" and inserting "28"; by striking "35" and inserting "112"; in subdivision (8) in the third entry by striking "5" and inserting "22.4"; by striking "20" and inserting "28"; in subdivision (9) in the third entry by striking "4" and inserting "16.8"; by striking "5" and inserting "22.4"; in subdivision (10) in the third entry by striking "3" and inserting "11.2"; by striking "4" and inserting "16.8"; in subdivision (11) in the third entry by striking "2" and inserting "5.6"; by striking "3" and inserting "11.2"; in subdivision (12) in the third entry by striking "1" and inserting "2.8"; by striking "2" and inserting "5.6"; in subdivision (13) in the third entry by striking "500 MG" and inserting "1.4 G"; by striking "1" and inserting "2.8"; and in subdivision (14) in the third entry by striking "500 MG" and inserting "1.4 G".

The Commentary to § 2D1.1 captioned "Application Notes" is amended in Note 3 by inserting:

"Application of Subsections (b)(1) and (b)(2).—

(A)   Application of Subsection (b)(1).—" before "Definitions";

by inserting "in subsection (b)(1)" after "weapon possession"; by striking "adjustment" and inserting "enhancement"; by striking "his" and inserting "the defendant's"; and by adding at the end the following:

"(B)   Interaction of Subsections (b)(1) and (b)(2).—The enhancements in subsections (b)(1) and (b)(2) may be applied cumulatively (added together), as is generally the case when two or more specific offense characteristics each apply. See § 1B1.1 (Application Instructions), Application Note 4(A). However, in a case in which the defendant merely possessed a dangerous weapon but did not use violence, make a credible threat to use violence, or direct the use of violence, subsection (b)(2) would not apply.".

The Commentary to § 2D1.1 captioned "Application Notes" is amended in Note 8 in the last paragraph by striking "(2)" and inserting "(3)".

The Commentary to § 2D1.1 captioned "Application Notes" is amended in Note 10(B) in the first paragraph by striking "(Except Cocaine Base)" after "Differing Controlled Substances"; and by striking the sentence beginning "To determine".

The Commentary to § 2D1.1 captioned "Application Notes" is amended in Note 10(C) by striking "(Except Cocaine Base)" after "Differing Controlled Substances"; and in subdivision (C)(iii) by striking "five kilograms of marihuana" and inserting "2 grams of cocaine base"; by inserting ", and the cocaine base is equivalent to 7.142 kilograms of marihuana" after "16 kilograms of marihuana"; and by striking "21" and inserting "23.142".

The Commentary to § 2D1.1 captioned "Application Notes" is amended in Note 10 by striking subdivision (D) as follows:

"(D)   Determining Base Offense Level in Offenses Involving Cocaine Base and Other Controlled Substances.—

(i) In General.—Except as provided in subdivision (ii), if the offense involves cocaine base ("crack") and one or more other controlled substance, determine the combined offense level as provided by subdivision (B) of this note, and reduce the combined offense level by 2 levels.

(ii) Exceptions to 2-level Reduction.—The 2-level reduction provided in subdivision (i) shall not apply in a case in which:

(I) the offense involved 4.5 kg or more, or less than 250 mg, of cocaine base; or

(II) the 2-level reduction results in a combined offense level that is less than the combined offense level that would apply under subdivision (B) of this note if the offense involved only the other controlled substance(s) (i.e., the controlled substance(s) other than cocaine base).

(iii) Examples.—

(I) The case involves 20 gm of cocaine base, 1.5 kg of cocaine, and 10 kg of marihuana. Under the Drug Equivalency Tables in subdivision (E) of this note, 20 gm of cocaine base converts to 400 kg of marihuana (20 gm x 20 kg = 400 kg), and 1.5 kg of cocaine converts to 300 kg of marihuana (1.5 kg x 200 gm = 300 kg), which, when added to the 10 kg of marihuana results in a combined equivalent quantity of 710 kg of marihuana. Under the Drug Quantity Table, 710 kg of marihuana corresponds to a combined offense level of 30, which is reduced by two levels to level 28. For the cocaine and marihuana, their combined equivalent quantity of 310 kg of marihuana corresponds to a combined offense level of 26 under the Drug Quantity Table. Because the combined offense level for all three drug types after the 2-level reduction is not less than the combined base offense level for the cocaine and marihuana, the combined offense level for all three drug types remains level 28.

(II) The case involves 5 gm of cocaine base and 6 kg of heroin. Under the Drug Equivalency Tables in subdivision (E) of this note, 5 gm of cocaine base converts to 100 kg of marihuana (5 gm x 20 kg = 100 kg), and 6 kg of heroin converts to 6,000 kg of marihuana (6,000 gm x 1 kg = 6,000 kg), which, when added together results in a combined equivalent quantity of 6,100 kg of marihuana. Under the Drug Quantity Table, 6,100 kg of marihuana corresponds to a combined offense level of 34, which is reduced by two levels to 32. For the heroin, the 6,000 kg of marihuana corresponds to an offense level 34 under the Drug Quantity Table. Because the combined offense level for the two drug types after the 2-level reduction is less than the offense level for the heroin, the reduction does not apply and the combined offense level for the two drugs remains level 34.";

and by redesignating subdivision (E) as subdivision (D).

The Commentary to § 2D1.1 captioned "Application Notes" is amended in Note 10(D), as redesignated by this amendment, in the table captioned "Cocaine and Other Schedule I and II Stimulants (and their immediate precursors)*" in the line referenced to Cocaine Base by striking "20 kg" and inserting "3,571 gm".

The Commentary to § 2D1.1 captioned "Application Notes" is amended in Note 18 by striking "(2)" and inserting "(3)", and by striking "(4)" and inserting "(5)";

in Note 19 by striking "(10)" and inserting "(13)" in both places;

in Note 20 by striking "(10)" and inserting "(13)" in both places;

in Note 21 by striking "(11)" and inserting "(16)" each place it appears;

in Note 23 by striking "(6)" and inserting "(7)" each place it appears;

in Note 25 by striking "(7)" and inserting "(8)" in both places;

and in Note 26 by striking "(8)" and inserting "(9)" in both places.

The Commentary to § 2D1.1 captioned "Application Notes" is amended by adding at the end the following:

> "27. Application of Subsection (b)(11).—Subsection (b)(11) does not apply if the purpose of the bribery was to obstruct or impede the investigation, prosecution, or sentencing of the defendant. Such conduct is covered by § 3C1.1 (Obstructing or Impeding the Administration of Justice) and, if applicable, § 2D1.1(b)(14)(D).
>
> 28. Application of Subsection (b)(12).—Subsection (b)(12) applies to a defendant who knowingly maintains a premises (i.e., a 'building, room, or enclosure,' see § 2D1.8, comment. (backg'd.)) for the purpose of manufacturing or distributing a controlled substance.
>
> Among the factors the court should consider in determining whether the defendant 'maintained' the premises are (A) whether the defendant held a possessory interest in (e.g., owned or rented) the premises and (B) the extent to which the defendant controlled access to, or activities at, the premises.
>
> Manufacturing or distributing a controlled substance need not be the sole purpose for which the premises was maintained, but must be one of the defendant's primary or principal uses for the premises, rather than one of the defendant's incidental or collateral uses for the premises. In making this determination, the court should consider how frequently the premises was used by the defendant for manufacturing or distributing a controlled substance and how frequently the premises was used by the defendant for lawful purposes.
>
> 29. Application of Subsection (b)(14).—
>
> > (A) Distributing to a Specified Individual or Involving Such an Individual in the Offense (Subsection (b)(14)(B)).—If the defendant distributes a controlled substance to an individual or involves an individual in the offense, as specified in subsection (b)(14)(B), the individual is not a 'vulnerable victim' for purposes of § 3A1.1(b).

(B) Directly Involved in the Importation of a Controlled Substance (Subsection (b)(14)(C)).—Subsection (b)(14)(C) applies if the defendant is accountable for the importation of a controlled substance under subsection (a)(1)(A) of § 1B1.3 (Relevant Conduct (Factors that Determine the Guideline Range)), i.e., the defendant committed, aided, abetted, counseled, commanded, induced, procured, or willfully caused the importation of a controlled substance.

If subsection (b)(3) or (b)(5) applies, do not apply subsection (b)(14)(C).

(C) Pattern of Criminal Conduct Engaged in as a Livelihood (Subsection (b)(14)(E)).—For purposes of subsection (b)(14)(E), 'pattern of criminal conduct' and 'engaged in as a livelihood' have the meaning given such terms in § 4B1.3 (Criminal Livelihood).".

The Commentary to § 2D1.1 captioned "Background" is amended by inserting after the paragraph that begins "For marihuana plants" the following:

" The last sentence of subsection (a)(5) implements the directive to the Commission in section 7(1) of Public Law 111–220.

Subsection (b)(2) implements the directive to the Commission in section 5 of Public Law 111–220.";

in the paragraph that begins "Specific Offense Characteristic" by striking "Specific Offense Characteristic (b)(2)" and inserting "Subsection (b)(3)";

by inserting after the paragraph that begins "The dosage weight" the following:

" Subsection (b)(11) implements the directive to the Commission in section 6(1) of Public Law 111–220.

Subsection (b)(12) implements the directive to the Commission in section 6(2) of Public Law 111–220.";

in the paragraph that begins "Subsection (b)(10)(A)" by striking "(10)" and inserting "(13)";

in the paragraph that begins "Subsections (b)(10)(C)(ii)" by striking "(10)" and inserting "(13)";

and by adding at the end the following:

" Subsection (b)(14) implements the directive to the Commission in section 6(3) of Public Law 111–220.

Subsection (b)(15) implements the directive to the Commission in section 7(2) of Public Law 111–220.".

Section 2D1.14(a)(1) is amended by striking "(11)" and inserting "(16)".

Section 2D2.1(b) is amended by striking "References" and inserting "Reference"; by striking subdivision (1) as follows:

"(1) If the defendant is convicted of possession of more than 5 grams of a mixture

Amendment 748

or substance containing cocaine base, apply § 2D1.1 (Unlawful Manufacturing, Importing, Exporting, or Trafficking) as if the defendant had been convicted of possession of that mixture or substance with intent to distribute.";

and by redesignating subdivision (2) as subdivision (1).

The Commentary to § 2D2.1 captioned "Background" is amended by striking "five" and inserting "three"; and by striking the last paragraph as follows:

" Section 2D2.1(b)(1) provides a cross reference to § 2D1.1 for possession of more than five grams of a mixture or substance containing cocaine base, an offense subject to an enhanced penalty under 21 U.S.C. § 844(a). Other cases for which enhanced penalties are provided under 21 U.S.C. § 844(a)(e.g., for a person with one prior conviction, possession of more than three grams of a mixture or substance containing cocaine base; for a person with two or more prior convictions, possession of more than one gram of a mixture or substance containing cocaine base) are to be sentenced in accordance with § 5G1.1(b).".

Section 2K2.4 captioned "Application Notes" is amended in Note 4 by inserting after the first paragraph the following:

"A sentence under this guideline also accounts for conduct that would subject the defendant to an enhancement under § 2D1.1(b)(2) (pertaining to use of violence, credible threat to use violence, or directing the use of violence). Do not apply that enhancement when determining the sentence for the underlying offense.".

The Commentary to § 3B1.4 captioned "Application Notes" is amended in Note 2 by adding at the end as the last sentence the following: "For example, if the defendant receives an enhancement under § 2D1.1(b)(14)(B) for involving an individual less than 18 years of age in the offense, do not apply this adjustment.".

The Commentary to § 3C1.1 captioned "Application Notes" is amended in Note 7 by adding at the end the following new paragraph:

"Similarly, if the defendant receives an enhancement under § 2D1.1(b)(14)(D), do not apply this adjustment.".

Reason for Amendment: This amendment implements the emergency directive in section 8 of the Fair Sentencing Act of 2010, Pub. L. 111–220 (the "Act"). The Act reduced the statutory penalties for cocaine base ("crack cocaine") offenses, eliminated the statutory mandatory minimum sentence for simple possession of crack cocaine, and contained directives requiring the Commission to review and amend the guidelines to account for specified aggravating and mitigating circumstances in certain drug cases. The emergency amendment authority provided in section 8 of the Act required the Commission to promulgate the guidelines, policy statements, or amendments provided for in the Act, and to make such conforming changes to the guidelines as the Commission determines necessary to achieve consistency with other guideline provisions and applicable law, not later than 90 days after the date of enactment of the Act.

First, the amendment amends the Drug Quantity Table in § 2D1.1 (Unlawful Manufacturing, Importing, Exporting, or Trafficking (Including Possession with Intent to Commit These Offenses); Attempt or Conspiracy) to account for the changes in the statutory penalties made in section 2 of the Act. Section 2 of the Act reduced the statutory penalties for offenses involving manufacturing or trafficking in crack cocaine by increasing the quantity thresholds required to trigger a mandatory minimum term of imprisonment. The quantity threshold required to trigger the 5-year mandatory minimum term of imprisonment was increased from 5 grams to 28 grams, and the quantity threshold required to trigger the 10-year mandatory minimum term of imprisonment was increased from 50 grams to 280 grams. See 21 U.S.C. §§ 841(b)(1)(A), (B), (C), 960(b)(1), (2), (3).

To account for these statutory changes, the amendment conforms the guideline penalty structure for crack cocaine offenses to the approach followed for other drugs, i.e., the base offense levels for crack cocaine are set in the Drug Quantity Table so that the statutory minimum penalties correspond to levels 26 and 32. See generally § 2D1.1, comment. (backg'd.). Accordingly, using the new drug quantities established by the Act, offenses involving 28 grams or more of crack cocaine are assigned a base offense level of 26, offenses involving 280 grams or more of crack cocaine are assigned a base offense level of 32, and other offense levels are established by extrapolating upward and downward. Conforming to this approach ensures that the relationship between the statutory penalties for crack cocaine offenses and the statutory penalties for offenses involving other drugs is consistently and proportionally reflected throughout the Drug Quantity Table.

To provide a means of obtaining a single offense level in cases involving crack cocaine and one or more other controlled substances, the amendment also establishes a marihuana equivalency for crack cocaine under which 1 gram of crack cocaine is equivalent to 3,571 grams of marihuana. (The marihuana equivalency for any controlled substance is a constant that can be calculated using any threshold in the Drug Quantity Table by dividing the amount of marihuana corresponding to that threshold by the amount of the other controlled substance corresponding to that threshold. For example, the threshold quantities at base offense level 26 are 100,000 grams of marihuana and 28 grams of crack cocaine; 100,000 grams divided by 28 is 3,571 grams.) In the commentary to § 2D1.1, the amendment makes a conforming change to the rules for cases involving both crack cocaine and one or more other controlled substances. The amendment deletes the special rules in Note 10(D) for cases involving crack cocaine and one or more other controlled substances, and revises Note 10(C) so that it provides an example of such a case.

Second, the amendment amends § 2D1.1 to add a sentence at the end of subsection (a)(5) (often referred to as the "mitigating role cap"). The new provision provides that if the offense level otherwise resulting from subsection (a)(5) is greater than level 32, and the defendant receives the 4-level ("minimal participant") reduction in subsection (a) of § 3B1.2 (Mitigating Role), the base offense level shall be decreased to level 32. This provision responds to section 7(1) of the Act, which directed the Commission to ensure that "if the defendant is subject to a minimal role adjustment under the guidelines, the base offense level for the defendant based solely on drug quantity shall not exceed level 32".

Third, the amendment amends § 2D1.1 to create a new specific offense characteristic at subsection (b)(2) providing an enhancement of 2 levels if the defendant used violence, made a credible threat to use violence, or directed the use of violence. The new specific offense characteristic responds to section 5 of the Act, which directed the Commission to "ensure that the guidelines provide an additional penalty increase of at least 2 offense levels if the defendant used violence, made a credible threat to use violence, or directed the use of violence during a drug trafficking offense."

The amendment also revises the commentary to § 2D1.1 to clarify how this new specific offense characteristic interacts with subsection (b)(1). Specifically, Application Note 3 is amended to provide that the enhancements in subsections (b)(1) (regarding possession of a dangerous weapon) and (b)(2) may be applied cumulatively. However, in a case in which the defendant merely possessed a dangerous weapon but did not use violence, make a credible threat to use violence, or direct the use of violence, subsection (b)(2) would not

Amendment 748   APPENDIX C - VOLUME III   November 1, 2013

apply.

In addition, the amendment makes a conforming change to the commentary to § 2K2.4 (Use of Firearm, Armor-Piercing Ammunition, or Explosive During or in Relation to Certain Crimes) to address cases in which the defendant is sentenced under both § 2D1.1 (for a drug trafficking offense) and § 2K2.4 (for an offense under 18 U.S.C. § 924(c)). In such a case, the sentence under § 2K2.4 accounts for any weapon enhancement; therefore, in determining the sentence under § 2D1.1, the weapon enhancement in § 2D1.1(b)(1) does not apply. See § 2K2.4, comment. (n. 4). The amendment amends this commentary to similarly provide that, in a case in which the defendant is sentenced under both §§ 2D1.1 and 2K2.4, the new enhancement at § 2D1.1(b)(2) also is accounted for by § 2K2.4 and, therefore, does not apply.

Fourth, the amendment amends § 2D1.1 to create a new specific offense characteristic at subsection (b)(11) providing an enhancement of 2 levels if the defendant bribed, or attempted to bribe, a law enforcement officer to facilitate the commission of the offense. The new specific offense characteristic responds to section 6(1) of the Act, which directed the Commission "to ensure an additional increase of at least 2 offense levels if . . . the defendant bribed, or attempted to bribe, a Federal, State, or local law enforcement official in connection with a drug trafficking offense".

The amendment also revises the commentary to § 2D1.1 to clarify how this new specific offense characteristic interacts with the adjustment at § 3C1.1 (Obstructing or Impeding the Administration of Justice). Specifically, new Application Note 27 provides that subsection (b)(11) does not apply if the purpose of the bribery was to obstruct or impede the investigation, prosecution, or sentencing of the defendant because such conduct is covered by § 3C1.1.

Fifth, the amendment amends § 2D1.1 to create a new specific offense characteristic at subsection (b)(12) providing an enhancement of 2 levels if the defendant maintained a premises for the purpose of manufacturing or distributing a controlled substance. The new specific offense characteristic responds to section 6(2) of the Act, which directed the Commission to "ensure an additional increase of at least 2 offense levels if . . . the defendant maintained an establishment for the manufacture or distribution of a controlled substance, as generally described in section 416 of the Controlled Substances Act (21 U.S.C. 856)".

The amendment also adds commentary in § 2D1.1 at Application Note 28 providing that among the factors the court should consider in determining whether the defendant "maintained" the premises are (A) whether the defendant held a possessory interest (e.g., owned or rented) the premises and (B) the extent to which the defendant controlled access to, or activities at, the premises. Application Note 28 also provides that manufacturing or distributing a controlled substance need not be the sole purpose for which the premises was maintained, but must be one of the defendant's primary or principal uses for the premises, rather than one of the defendant's incidental or collateral uses of the premises. In making this determination, the court should consider how frequently the premises was used by the defendant for manufacturing or distributing a controlled substance and how frequently the premises was used by the defendant for lawful purposes.

Sixth, the amendment amends § 2D1.1 to create a new specific offense characteristic at subsection (b)(14) that provides an enhancement of 2 levels if the defendant receives an adjustment under § 3B1.1 (Aggravating Role) and the offense involved one or more of five specified factors. The new specific offense characteristic responds to section 6(3) of the Act, which directed the Commission "to ensure an additional increase of at least 2 offense levels if . . . (A) the defendant is an organizer, leader, manager, or supervisor of drug

– 1212 –

trafficking activity subject to an aggravating role enhancement under the guidelines; and (B) the offense involved 1 or more of the following super-aggravating factors:

    (i)   The defendant--

        (I)   used another person to purchase, sell, transport, or store controlled substances;

        (II)   used impulse, fear, friendship, affection, or some combination thereof to involve such person in the offense; and

        (III)   such person had a minimum knowledge of the illegal enterprise and was to receive little or no compensation from the illegal transaction.

    (ii)   The defendant--

        (I)   knowingly distributed a controlled substance to a person under the age of 18 years, a person over the age of 64 years, or a pregnant individual;

        (II)   knowingly involved a person under the age of 18 years, a person over the age of 64 years, or a pregnant individual in drug trafficking;

        (III)   knowingly distributed a controlled substance to an individual who was unusually vulnerable due to physical or mental condition, or who was particularly susceptible to criminal conduct; or

        (IV)   knowingly involved an individual who was unusually vulnerable due to physical or mental condition, or who was particularly susceptible to criminal conduct, in the offense.

    (iii)   The defendant was involved in the importation into the United States of a controlled substance.

    (iv)   The defendant engaged in witness intimidation, tampered with or destroyed evidence, or otherwise obstructed justice in connection with the investigation or prosecution of the offense.

    (v)   The defendant committed the drug trafficking offense as part of a pattern of criminal conduct engaged in as a livelihood."

The amendment also revises the commentary to § 2D1.1 to provide guidance in applying the new specific offense characteristic at § 2D1.1(b)(14). Specifically, new Application Note 29 provides that if the defendant distributes a controlled substance to an individual or involves an individual in the offense, as specified in subsection (b)(14)(B), the individual is not a "vulnerable victim" for purposes of subsection (b) of § 3A1.1 (Hate Crime Motivation or Vulnerable Victim). Application Note 29 also provides that subsection (b)(14)(C) applies if the defendant committed, aided, abetted, counseled, commanded, induced, procured, or willfully caused the importation of a controlled substance. Subsection (b)(14)(C), however, does not apply if subsection (b)(3) or (b)(5) (as redesignated by the amendment) applies because the defendant's involvement in importation is adequately accounted for by those subsections. In addition, Application Note 29 defines "pattern of criminal conduct" and "engaged in as a livelihood" for purposes of subsection (b)(14)(E) as those terms are defined in § 4B1.3 (Criminal Livelihood).

The amendment also revises the commentary in § 3B1.4 (Using a Minor To Commit a Crime) and § 3C1.1 (Obstructing or Impeding the Administration of Justice) to specify how those adjustments interact with § 2D1.1(b)(14)(B) and (D), respectively. Specifically, Application Note 2 to § 3B1.4 is amended to clarify that the increase of two levels under this section would not apply if the defendant receives an enhancement under § 2D1.1(b)(14)(B).

Similarly, Application Note 7 to § 3C1.1 is amended to clarify that the increase of two levels under this section would not apply if the defendant receives an enhancement under § 2D1.1(b)(14)(D).

Seventh, the amendment amends § 2D1.1 to create a new specific offense characteristic providing a 2-level downward adjustment if the defendant receives the 4-level ("minimal participant") reduction in subsection (a) of § 3B1.2 (Mitigating Role) and the offense involved each of three additional specified factors: namely, the defendant was motivated by an intimate or familial relationship or by threats or fear to commit the offense when the defendant was otherwise unlikely to commit such an offense; was to receive no monetary compensation from the illegal purchase, sale, transport, or storage of controlled substances; and had minimal knowledge of the scope and structure of the enterprise. The specific offense characteristic responds to section 7(2) of the Act, which directed the Commission to ensure that "there is an additional reduction of 2 offense levels if the defendant—

(A)   otherwise qualifies for a minimal role adjustment under the guidelines and had a minimum knowledge of the illegal enterprise;

(B)   was to receive no monetary compensation from the illegal transaction; and

(C)   was motivated by an intimate or familial relationship or by threats or fear when the defendant was otherwise unlikely to commit such an offense."

Eighth, to reflect the renumbering of specific offense characteristics in § 2D1.1(b) by the amendment, technical and conforming changes are made to the commentary to § 2D1.1 and to § 2D1.14 (Narco-Terrorism).

Ninth, the amendment amends § 2D2.1 (Unlawful Possession; Attempt or Conspiracy) to account for the changes in the statutory penalties for simple possession of crack cocaine made in section 3 of the Act. Section 3 of the Act amended 21 U.S.C. § 844(a) to eliminate the 5-year mandatory minimum term of imprisonment (and 20-year statutory maximum) for simple possession of more than 5 grams of crack cocaine (or, for certain repeat offenders, more than 1 gram of crack cocaine). Accordingly, the statutory penalty for simple possession of crack cocaine is now the same as for simple possession of most other controlled substances: for a first offender, a maximum term of imprisonment of one year; for repeat offenders, maximum terms of 2 years or 3 years, and minimum terms of 15 days or 90 days, depending on the prior convictions. See 21 U.S.C. § 844(a). To account for this statutory change, the amendment deletes the cross reference at § 2D2.1(b)(1) under which an offender who possessed more than 5 grams of crack cocaine was sentenced under the drug trafficking guideline, § 2D1.1.

Effective Date: The effective date of this amendment is November 1, 2010.

749. Amendment: Section 2B1.1(b) is amended by redesignating subdivisions (8) through (17) as subdivisions (9) through (18); and by inserting after subdivision (7) the following:

"(8) If (A) the defendant was convicted of a Federal health care offense involving a Government health care program; and (B) the loss under subsection (b)(1) to the Government health care program was (i) more than $1,000,000, increase by 2 levels; (ii) more than $7,000,000, increase by 3 levels; or (iii) more than $20,000,000, increase by 4 levels.".

Section 2B1.1(b) is amended in subdivision (15), as redesignated by this amendment, by striking "(14)" and inserting "(15)".

The Commentary to § 2B1.1 captioned "Application Notes" is amended in Note 1 by inserting after the paragraph that begins "'Equity securities'" the following:

"'Federal health care offense' has the meaning given that term in 18 U.S.C. § 24.";

and by inserting after the paragraph that begins "'Foreign instrumentality'" the following:

"'Government health care program' means any plan or program that provides health benefits, whether directly, through insurance, or otherwise, which is funded directly, in whole or in part, by federal or state government. Examples of such programs are the Medicare program, the Medicaid program, and the CHIP program.".

The Commentary to § 2B1.1 captioned "Application Notes" is amended in Note 3(F) by adding at the end the following:

"(viii) Federal Health Care Offenses Involving Government Health Care Programs.—In a case in which the defendant is convicted of a Federal health care offense involving a Government health care program, the aggregate dollar amount of fraudulent bills submitted to the Government health care program shall constitute prima facie evidence of the amount of the intended loss, i.e., is evidence sufficient to establish the amount of the intended loss, if not rebutted.".

The Commentary to § 2B1.1 captioned "Application Notes" is amended in Note 7 by striking "(8)" and inserting "(9)" each place it appears;

in Note 8 by striking "(9)" and inserting "(10)" each place it appears;

in Note 9 by striking "(10)" and inserting "(11)" each place it appears;

in Note 10 by striking "(12)" and inserting "(13)" in both places;

in Note 11 and Note 12 by striking "(14)" and inserting "(15)" each place it appears;

in Note 13 by striking "(16)" and inserting "(17)" each place it appears and by striking "(14)" and inserting "(15)" in both places;

in Note 14 by striking "(b)(17)" and inserting "(b)(18)" each place it appears;

in Note 19 by striking "(16)" and inserting "(17)" and by striking "(11)" and inserting "(12)".

The Commentary to § 2B1.1 captioned "Background" is amended by inserting after the paragraph that begins "Subsection (b)(6)" the following:

"Subsection (b)(8) implements the directive to the Commission in section 10606 of Public Law 111–148.".

Amendment 749 APPENDIX C - VOLUME III November 1, 2013

The Commentary to § 2B1.1 captioned "Background" is amended in the paragraph that begins "Subsection (b)(8)(D)" by striking "(8)" and inserting "(9)";

in the paragraph that begins "Subsection (b)(9)" by striking "(9)" and inserting "(10)";

in the paragraph that begins "Subsections (b)(10)(A)(i)" by striking "(10)" and inserting "(11)";

in the paragraph that begins "Subsection (b)(10)(C)" by striking "(10)" and inserting "(11)";

in the paragraph that begins "Subsection (b)(11)" by striking "(11)" and inserting "(12)";

in the paragraph that begins "Subsection (b)(13)(B)" by striking "(13)" and inserting "(14)";

in the paragraph that begins "Subsection (b)(14)(A)" by striking "(14)" and inserting "(15)";

in the paragraph that begins "Subsection (b)(14)(B)(i)" by striking "(14)" and inserting "(15)";

in the paragraph that begins "Subsection (b)(15)" by striking "(15)" and inserting "(16)"; and

in the paragraph that begins "Subsection (b)(16)" by striking "(16)" and inserting "(17)" in both places.

The Commentary to § 3B1.2 captioned "Application Notes" is amended in Note 3(A) by adding at the end the following:

"Likewise, a defendant who is accountable under § 1B1.3 for a loss amount under § 2B1.1 (Theft, Property Destruction, and Fraud) that greatly exceeds the defendant's personal gain from a fraud offense and who had limited knowledge of the scope of the scheme is not precluded from consideration for an adjustment under this guideline. For example, a defendant in a health care fraud scheme, whose role in the scheme was limited to serving as a nominee owner and who received little personal gain relative to the loss amount, is not precluded from consideration for an adjustment under this guideline.".

Appendix A (Statutory Index) is amended by inserting after the line referenced to 12 U.S.C. § 4641 the following:

"12 U.S.C. § 5382   2H3.1";

by inserting after the in the line referenced to 15 U.S.C. § 78u(c) the following:

"15 U.S.C. § 78jjj(c)(1),(2)   2B1.1
15 U.S.C. § 78jjj(d)   2B1.1";

in the line referenced to 29 U.S.C. § 1131 by inserting "(a)" after "1131"; and

by inserting after the line referenced to 29 U.S.C. § 1141 the following:

"29 U.S.C. § 1149   2B1.1".

– 1216 –

Reason for Amendment: This amendment responds to the directive in section 10606(a)(2) of the Patient Protection and Affordable Care Act of 2010, Pub. L. 111–148 (the "Patient Protection Act"), and addresses certain new offenses created by the Patient Protection Act and by the Dodd-Frank Wall Street and Consumer Protection Act, Pub. L. 111–203 (the "Dodd-Frank Act").

Response to Directive

Section 10606(a)(2)(B) of the Patient Protection Act directed the Commission to—

> amend the Federal Sentencing Guidelines and policy statements applicable to persons convicted of Federal health care offenses involving Government health care programs to provide that the aggregate dollar amount of fraudulent bills submitted to the Government health care program shall constitute prima facie evidence of the amount of the intended loss by the defendant[.]

Section 10606(a)(2)(C) directed the Commission to amend the guidelines to provide—

(i) a 2-level increase in the offense level for any defendant convicted of a Federal health care offense relating to a Government health care program which involves a loss of not less than $1,000,000 and less than $7,000,000;

(ii) a 3-level increase in the offense level for any defendant convicted of a Federal health care offense relating to a Government health care program which involves a loss of not less than $7,000,000 and less than $20,000,000;

(iii) a 4-level increase in the offense level for any defendant convicted of a Federal health care offense relating to a Government health care program which involves a loss of not less than $20,000,000; and

(iv) if appropriate, otherwise amend the Federal Sentencing Guidelines and policy statements applicable to persons convicted of Federal health care offenses involving Government health care programs.

Section 10606(a)(3) required the Commission, in carrying out the directive, to "ensure reasonable consistency with other relevant directives and with other guidelines" and to "account for any aggravating or mitigating circumstances that might justify exceptions," among other requirements.

The amendment implements the directive by adding two provisions to § 2B1.1 (Theft, Property Destruction, and Fraud), both of which apply to cases in which "the defendant was convicted of a Federal health care offense involving a Government health care program".

The first provision is a new tiered enhancement at subsection (b)(8) that applies in such cases (i.e., Federal health care offenses involving a Government health care program) if the loss is more than $1,000,000. The enhancement is 2 levels if the loss is more than $1,000,000, 3 levels if the loss is more than $7,000,000, and 4 levels if the loss is more than $20,000,000. The tiers of the enhancement apply to loss amounts "more than" the specified dollar amounts rather than to loss amounts "not less than" the specified dollar amounts to "ensure reasonable consistency" as required by the directive. The consistent practice in the Guidelines Manual is to apply enhancements to loss amounts "more than" specified dollar amounts.

Amendment 749 APPENDIX C - VOLUME III November 1, 2013

The second provision is a new special rule in Application Note 3(F) for determining intended loss in a case in which the defendant is convicted of a Federal health care offense involving a Government health care program. The special rule provides that, in such a case, "the aggregate dollar amount of fraudulent bills submitted to the Government health care program shall constitute prima facie evidence of the amount of the intended loss, i.e., is evidence sufficient to establish the amount of the intended loss, if not rebutted". The special rule includes language making clear that the government's proof of intended loss may be rebutted by the defendant.

The amendment also adds definitions to the commentary in § 2B1.1 for the terms "Federal health care offense" and "Government health care program". "Federal health care offense" is defined to have the meaning given that term in 18 U.S.C. § 24, as required by section 10606(a)(1) of the Patient Protection Act. "Government health care program" is defined to mean "any plan or program that provides health benefits, whether directly, through insurance, or otherwise, which is funded directly, in whole or in part, by federal or state government." The amendment lists the Medicare program, the Medicaid program, and the CHIP program as examples of such programs. The Commission adopted this definition because health care fraud involving federally funded programs and health care fraud involving state-funded programs are similar offenses, committed in similar ways and posing similar harms to the taxpaying public. In addition, defining "Government health care program" in this manner avoids application difficulties likely to arise from a narrower definition that would require the disaggregation of losses program by program in cases in which the defendant defrauded both federal and state health care programs. Finally, the statutory language in the directive indicates congressional concern with health care fraud that adversely affects the public fisc beyond health care programs funded solely with federal funds.

Finally, the amendment amends Application Note 3(A) to § 3B1.2 (Mitigating Role) to make clear that a defendant who is accountable under § 1B1.3 (Relevant Conduct) for a loss amount under § 2B1.1 that greatly exceeds the defendant's personal gain from a fraud offense, and who had limited knowledge of the scope of the scheme, is not precluded from consideration for a mitigating role adjustment. The amended commentary provides as an example "a defendant in a health care fraud scheme, whose role in the scheme was limited to serving as a nominee owner and who received little personal gain relative to the loss amount". This part of the amendment is consistent with the directive in section 10606(a)(3)(D) of the Patient Protection Act that the Commission should "account for any aggravating or mitigating circumstances that might justify exceptions" to the new tiered enhancement.

New Offenses

In addition to responding to the directives, the amendment amends Appendix A (Statutory Index) to include offenses created by both the Patient Protection Act and the Dodd-Frank Act.

The Patient Protection Act created a new offense at 29 U.S.C. § 1149 that prohibits making a false statement in connection with the marketing or sale of a multiple employer welfare arrangement under the Employee Retirement Income Security Act. Pursuant to 29 U.S.C. § 1131(b), a person who commits this new offense is subject to a term of imprisonment of not more than 10 years. The amendment references the new offense at 29 U.S.C. § 1149 to § 2B1.1 because the offense has fraud or misrepresentation as a element of the offense. As a clerical change, the amendment also amends Appendix A (Statutory Index) to make clear that 29 U.S.C. § 1131(a), not the new § 1131(b), is referenced to § 2E5.3 (False Statements and Concealment of Facts in Relation to Documents Required by the

Employee Retirement Income Security Act; Failure to Maintain and Falsification of Records Required by the Labor Management Reporting and Disclosure Act; Destruction and Failure to Maintain Corporate Audit Records).

The Dodd-Frank Act created two new offenses, 12 U.S.C. § 5382 and 15 U.S.C. § 78jjj(d). With regard to 12 U.S.C. § 5382, under authority granted by sections 202-203 of the Dodd-Frank Act, the Secretary of the Treasury may make a "systemic risk determination" concerning a financial company and, if the company fails the determination, may commence the orderly liquidation of the company by appointing the Federal Deposit Insurance Corporation as receiver. Before making the appointment, the Secretary must either obtain the consent of the company or petition under seal for approval by a federal district court. The Dodd-Frank Act makes it a crime, codified at 12 U.S.C. § 5382, to recklessly disclose a systemic risk determination or the pendency of court proceedings on such a petition. A person who violates 12 U.S.C. § 5382 is subject to imprisonment for not more than five years. The amendment references 12 U.S.C. § 5382 to § 2H3.1 (Interception of Communications; Eavesdropping; Disclosure of Certain Private or Protected Information). Section 2H3.1 covers several criminal statutes with similar elements and the same maximum term of imprisonment.

The second new offense, 15 U.S.C. § 78jjj(d), makes it a crime for a person to falsely represent that he or she is a member of the Security Investor Protection Corporation or that any person or account is protected or eligible for protection under the Security Investor Protection Act. See Dodd-Frank Act, Pub. L. 111–203, § 929V. Section 78jjj also contains two other offenses, at subsections (c)(1) and (c)(2), that are not referenced in Appendix A (Statutory Index). All three subsections are subject to the same maximum term of imprisonment of five years. In addition, all three concern fraud and deceit: the newly created 15 U.S.C. § 78jjj(d) involves false representation; 15 U.S.C. § 78jjj(c)(1) involves fraud in connection with or in contemplation of a liquidation proceeding; and 15 U.S.C. § 78jjj(c)(2) involves fraudulent conversion of assets of the Security Investor Protection Corporation. The amendment references these offenses to § 2B1.1 because the elements of the offenses involve fraud and deceit.

Effective Date: The effective date of this amendment is November 1, 2011.

750. **Amendment:** Sections 2D1.1, 2D1.14, 2D2.1, 2K2.4, 3B1.4, and 3C1.1, effective November 1, 2010 (see Appendix C, Amendment 748), as set forth in Supplement to the 2010 Guidelines Manual (effective November 1, 2010); see also 75 FR 66188 (October 27, 2010), are repromulgated as follows:

PART A

The Drug Quantity Table in § 2D1.1(c) and Note 10 of the Commentary to § 2D1.1 captioned "Application Notes" are repromulgated without change.

PART B

All provisions of § 2D1.1 not repromulgated by Part A of this amendment are repromulgated without change, except as follows:

The Commentary to § 2D1.1 captioned "Application Notes" is amended by striking Note 28 as follows:

"28. Application of Subsection (b)(12).—Subsection (b)(12) applies to a defendant who knowingly maintains a premises (i.e., a 'building, room, or enclosure,' see § 2D1.8, comment. (backg'd.)) for the purpose of manufacturing or distributing a controlled substance.

Among the factors the court should consider in determining whether the defendant 'maintained' the premises are (A) whether the defendant held a possessory interest in (e.g., owned or rented) the premises and (B) the extent to which the defendant controlled access to, or activities at, the premises.

Manufacturing or distributing a controlled substance need not be the sole purpose for which the premises was maintained, but must be one of the defendant's primary or principal uses for the premises, rather than one of the defendant's incidental or collateral uses for the premises. In making this determination, the court should consider how frequently the premises was used by the defendant for manufacturing or distributing a controlled substance and how frequently the premises was used by the defendant for lawful purposes.",

and inserting a new Note 28 as follows:

"28. Application of Subsection (b)(12).—Subsection (b)(12) applies to a defendant who knowingly maintains a premises (i.e., a building, room, or enclosure) for the purpose of manufacturing or distributing a controlled substance, including storage of a controlled substance for the purpose of distribution.

Among the factors the court should consider in determining whether the defendant 'maintained' the premises are (A) whether the defendant held a possessory interest in (e.g., owned or rented) the premises and (B) the extent to which the defendant controlled access to, or activities at, the premises.

Manufacturing or distributing a controlled substance need not be the sole purpose for which the premises was maintained, but must be one of the defendant's primary or principal uses for the premises, rather than one of the defendant's incidental or collateral uses for the premises. In making this determination, the court should consider how frequently the premises was used by the defendant for manufacturing or distributing a controlled substance and how frequently the premises was used by the defendant for lawful purposes.".

Sections 2D1.14, 2K2.4, 3B1.4, and 3C1.1 are repromulgated without change.

PART C

Section 2D2.1 is repromulgated without change.

Reason for Amendment: This multi-part amendment re-promulgates as permanent the temporary, emergency amendment (effective Nov. 1, 2010) that implemented the emergency directive in section 8 of the Fair Sentencing Act of 2010, Pub. L. 111–220 (the "Act"). The Act reduced the statutory penalties for cocaine base ("crack cocaine") offenses, eliminated the statutory mandatory minimum sentence for simple possession of crack cocaine, and contained directives to the Commission to review and amend the guidelines to account for specified aggravating and mitigating circumstances in certain drug cases.

The emergency amendment authority provided in section 8 of the Act required the Commission to promulgate the guidelines, policy statements, or amendments provided for in the Act, and to make such conforming changes to the guidelines as the Commission determines necessary to achieve consistency with other guideline provisions and applicable law, not later than 90 days after the date of enactment of the Act. Pursuant to this emergency directive, the Commission promulgated an amendment effective November 1, 2010, that made temporary, emergency revisions to § 2D1.1 (Unlawful Manufacturing, Importing, Exporting, or Trafficking (Including Possession with Intent to Commit These Offenses); Attempt or Conspiracy) and § 2D2.1 (Unlawful Possession; Attempt or Conspiracy). Conforming changes to certain other guidelines were also promulgated on a temporary, emergency basis. See USSG App. C, Amendment 748 (effective November 1, 2010).

This amendment re-promulgates the temporary, emergency amendment. Part A re-promulgates the revisions to the crack cocaine quantity levels in the Drug Quantity Table in § 2D1.1 without change. Part B re-promulgates the various aggravating and mitigating provisions in § 2D1.1 without change, except for a revision to the new Application Note 28 (relating to the new enhancement for maintaining premises). Part C re-promulgates the revision to § 2D2.1 accounting for the reduction in the statutory penalties for simple possession of crack cocaine without change.

Part A. Changes to the Drug Quantity Table for Offenses Involving Crack Cocaine

Part A re-promulgates without change the emergency, temporary revisions to the Drug Quantity Table in § 2D1.1 and related revisions to Application Note 10 to account for the changes in the statutory penalties made in section 2 of the Act. Section 2 of the Act reduced the statutory penalties for offenses involving manufacturing or trafficking in crack cocaine by increasing the quantity thresholds required to trigger a mandatory minimum term of imprisonment. The quantity threshold required to trigger the 5-year mandatory minimum term of imprisonment was increased from 5 grams to 28 grams, and the quantity threshold required to trigger the 10-year mandatory minimum term of imprisonment was increased from 50 grams to 280 grams. See 21 U.S.C. §§ 841(b)(1)(A), (B), (C), 960(b)(1), (2), (3). The new mandatory minimum quantity threshold levels for crack cocaine offenses are consistent with the Commission's 2007 report to Congress, Cocaine and Federal Sentencing Policy, in which the Commission, based on available information, defined crack cocaine offenders who deal in quantities of one ounce (approximately 28 grams) or more in a single transaction as wholesalers.

To account for these statutory changes, the amendment conforms the guideline penalty structure for crack cocaine offenses to the approach followed for other drugs, i.e., the base offense levels for crack cocaine are set in the Drug Quantity Table so that the statutory minimum penalties correspond to levels 26 and 32, which was the approach used for crack cocaine offenses prior to November 1, 2007. See § 2D1.1, comment. (backg'd.); USSG App. C, Amendment 706 (effective November 1, 2007). Accordingly, using the new drug quantities established by the Act, offenses involving 28 grams or more of crack cocaine are assigned a base offense level of 26, offenses involving 280 grams or more of crack cocaine are assigned a base offense level of 32, and other offense levels are established by extrapolating proportionally upward and downward on the Drug Quantity Table. Conforming the guideline penalty structure for crack cocaine offenses to the approach followed for all other drugs ensures that the quantity-based relationship established by statute between crack cocaine offenses and offenses involving all other drugs is consistently and proportionally reflected throughout the Drug Quantity Table at all drug quantities.

Estimating the likely future sentencing impact of the amendment to the Drug Quantity Table is difficult because the reductions in the statutory penalties for crack cocaine offenses may result in changes in prosecutorial and other practices. With that important caveat, the Commission estimates that approximately 63 percent of crack cocaine offenders sentenced after November 1, 2011, will receive a lower sentence as a result of the change to the Drug Quantity Table, with an average sentence decrease of approximately 26 percent. For example, under the Drug Quantity Table in effect from November 1, 2007 through October 31, 2010, an offense involving 5 grams of crack cocaine was assigned a base offense level of 24, which corresponds to a guideline sentencing range of 51 to 63 months. Under the Drug Quantity Table as amended, 5 grams of crack cocaine is assigned a base offense level of 16, which corresponds to a guideline sentencing range of 21 to 27 months. Similarly, under the Drug Quantity Table in effect from November 1, 2007 through October 31, 2010, an offense involving 50 grams of crack cocaine was assigned a base offense level of 30, which corresponds to a guideline sentencing range of 97 to 121 months. Under the Drug Quantity Table as amended, 50 grams of crack cocaine is assigned a base offense level of 26, which corresponds to a guideline sentencing range of 63 to 78 months.

It is important to note that no crack cocaine offender will receive an increased sentence as a result of the amendment to the Drug Quantity Table. As indicated above, not all crack cocaine offenders sentenced after November 1, 2011, will receive a lower sentence as a result of the change to the Drug Quantity Table. This is the case for a variety of reasons. Among the reasons, compared to the Drug Quantity Table in effect from November 1, 2007 through October 31, 2010, the amendment does not lower the base offense levels, and therefore does not lower the sentences, for offenses involving the following quantities of crack cocaine: less than 500 milligrams; at least 28 grams but less than 35 grams; at least 280 grams but less than 500 grams; at least 840 grams but less than 1.5 kilograms; at least 2.8 kilograms but less than 4.5 kilograms; and 8.5 kilograms or more. In addition, some offenders are sentenced at the statutory mandatory minimum and therefore cannot have their sentences lowered by an amendment to the guidelines. See § 5G1.1(b) (Sentencing on a Single Count of Conviction). Other offenders are sentenced pursuant to §§ 4B1.1 (Career Offender) and 4B1.4 (Armed Career Criminal), which result in sentencing guideline ranges that are unaffected by a reduction in the Drug Quantity Table.

To provide a means of obtaining a single offense level in cases involving crack cocaine and one or more other controlled substances, the amendment also establishes a marihuana equivalency for crack cocaine under which 1 gram of crack cocaine is equivalent to 3,571 grams of marihuana. (The marihuana equivalency for any controlled substance is a constant that can be calculated using any threshold in the Drug Quantity Table by dividing the amount of marihuana corresponding to that threshold by the amount of the other controlled substance corresponding to that threshold. For example, the threshold quantities at base offense level 26 are 100,000 grams of marihuana and 28 grams of crack cocaine; 100,000 grams divided by 28 is 3,571 grams.) In the commentary to § 2D1.1, the amendment makes a conforming change to the rules for cases involving both crack cocaine and one or more other controlled substances. The amendment deletes the special rules in Note 10(D) for cases involving crack cocaine and one or more other controlled substances, and revises Note 10(C) so that it provides an example of such a case.

Part B. Aggravating and Mitigating Factors in Drug Trafficking Cases

Part B re-promulgates the temporary, emergency revisions to § 2D1.1 and accompanying commentary that account for certain aggravating and mitigating factors in drug trafficking cases. These changes implement directives to the Commission in sections 5, 6, and 7 of the Act. The emergency revisions are re-promulgated without change, except for the new Application Note 28 (relating to the new enhancement for maintaining a premises), as explained below.

First, Part B amends § 2D1.1 to add a sentence at the end of subsection (a)(5) (often referred to as the "mitigating role cap"). The new provision provides that if the offense level otherwise resulting from subsection (a)(5) is greater than level 32, and the defendant receives the 4-level ("minimal participant") reduction in subsection (a) of § 3B1.2 (Mitigating Role), the base offense level shall be decreased to level 32. This provision responds to section 7(1) of the Act, which directed the Commission to ensure that "if the defendant is subject to a minimal role adjustment under the guidelines, the base offense level for the defendant based solely on drug quantity shall not exceed level 32".

Second, Part B amends § 2D1.1 to create a new specific offense characteristic at subsection (b)(2) providing an enhancement of 2 levels if the defendant used violence, made a credible threat to use violence, or directed the use of violence. The new specific offense characteristic responds to section 5 of the Act, which directed the Commission to "ensure that the guidelines provide an additional penalty increase of at least 2 offense levels if the defendant used violence, made a credible threat to use violence, or directed the use of violence during a drug trafficking offense."

The amendment also revises the commentary to § 2D1.1 to clarify how this new specific offense characteristic interacts with subsection (b)(1), which provides an enhancement of 2 levels if a dangerous weapon (including a firearm) was possessed. Specifically, Application Note 3 is amended to provide that the enhancements in subsections (b)(1) and (b)(2) may be applied cumulatively. However, in a case in which the defendant merely possessed a dangerous weapon but did not use violence, make a credible threat to use violence, or direct the use of violence, subsection (b)(2) would not apply.

In addition, the amendment makes a conforming change to the commentary to § 2K2.4 (Use of Firearm, Armor-Piercing Ammunition, or Explosive During or in Relation to Certain Crimes) to address cases in which the defendant is sentenced under both § 2D1.1 (for a drug trafficking offense) and § 2K2.4 (for an offense under 18 U.S.C. § 924(c)). In such a case, the sentence under § 2K2.4 accounts for any weapon enhancement; therefore, in determining the sentence under § 2D1.1, the weapon enhancement in § 2D1.1(b)(1) does not apply. See § 2K2.4, comment. (n. 4). The amendment amends this commentary to similarly provide that, in a case in which the defendant is sentenced under both §§ 2D1.1 and 2K2.4, the new enhancement at § 2D1.1(b)(2) also is accounted for by § 2K2.4 and, therefore, does not apply.

Third, Part B amends § 2D1.1 to create a new specific offense characteristic at subsection (b)(11) providing an enhancement of 2 levels if the defendant bribed, or attempted to bribe, a law enforcement officer to facilitate the commission of the offense. The new specific offense characteristic responds to section 6(1) of the Act, which directed the Commission "to ensure an additional increase of at least 2 offense levels if . . . the defendant bribed, or attempted to bribe, a Federal, State, or local law enforcement official in connection with a drug trafficking offense".

The amendment also revises the commentary to § 2D1.1 to clarify how this new specific offense characteristic interacts with the adjustment at § 3C1.1 (Obstructing or Impeding the Administration of Justice). Specifically, new Application Note 27 provides that subsection (b)(11) does not apply if the purpose of the bribery was to obstruct or impede the investigation, prosecution, or sentencing of the defendant because such conduct is covered by § 3C1.1.

Fourth, Part B amends § 2D1.1 to create a new specific offense characteristic at subsection (b)(12) providing an enhancement of 2 levels if the defendant maintained premises for the purpose of manufacturing or distributing a controlled substance. The new specific offense characteristic responds to section 6(2) of the Act, which directed the Commission to "ensure an additional increase of at least 2 offense levels if . . . the defendant maintained an establishment for the manufacture or distribution of a controlled substance, as generally

Amendment 750

described in section 416 of the Controlled Substances Act (21 U.S.C. 856)".

The amendment also adds commentary in § 2D1.1 at Application Note 28 providing that the enhancement applies to a defendant who knowingly maintains premises (i.e., a building, room, or enclosure) for the purpose of maintaining or distributing a controlled substance. The new amendment differs from the temporary, emergency revisions in clarifying that distribution includes storage of a controlled substance for the purpose of distribution.

Application Note 28 also provides that among the factors the court should consider in determining whether the defendant "maintained" the premises are (A) whether the defendant held a possessory interest in (e.g., owned or rented) the premises and (B) the extent to which the defendant controlled access to, or activities at, the premises. Application Note 28 also provides that manufacturing or distributing a controlled substance need not be the sole purpose for which the premises was maintained, but must be one of the defendant's primary or principal uses for the premises, rather than one of the defendant's incidental or collateral uses of the premises. In making this determination, the court should consider how frequently the premises was used by the defendant for manufacturing or distributing a controlled substance and how frequently the premises was used by the defendant for lawful purposes.

Fifth, Part B amends § 2D1.1 to create a new specific offense characteristic at subsection (b)(14) providing an enhancement of 2 levels if the defendant receives an adjustment under § 3B1.1 (Aggravating Role) and the offense involved one or more of five specified factors. The new specific offense characteristic responds to section 6(3) of the Act, which directed the Commission "to ensure an additional increase of at least 2 offense levels if . . . (A) the defendant is an organizer, leader, manager, or supervisor of drug trafficking activity subject to an aggravating role enhancement under the guidelines; and (B) the offense involved 1 or more of the following super-aggravating factors:

    (i)   The defendant—

        (I)   used another person to purchase, sell, transport, or store controlled substances;

        (II)   used impulse, fear, friendship, affection, or some combination thereof to involve such person in the offense; and

        (III)   such person had a minimum knowledge of the illegal enterprise and was to receive little or no compensation from the illegal transaction.

    (ii)   The defendant—

        (I)   knowingly distributed a controlled substance to a person under the age of 18 years, a person over the age of 64 years, or a pregnant individual;

        (II)   knowingly involved a person under the age of 18 years, a person over the age of 64 years, or a pregnant individual in drug trafficking;

        (III)   knowingly distributed a controlled substance to an individual who was unusually vulnerable due to physical or mental condition, or who was particularly susceptible to criminal conduct; or

(IV) knowingly involved an individual who was unusually vulnerable due to physical or mental condition, or who was particularly susceptible to criminal conduct, in the offense.

(iii) The defendant was involved in the importation into the United States of a controlled substance.

(iv) The defendant engaged in witness intimidation, tampered with or destroyed evidence, or otherwise obstructed justice in connection with the investigation or prosecution of the offense.

(v) The defendant committed the drug trafficking offense as part of a pattern of criminal conduct engaged in as a livelihood."

The amendment also revises the commentary to § 2D1.1 to provide guidance in applying the new specific offense characteristic at § 2D1.1(b)(14). Specifically, new Application Note 29 provides that if the defendant distributes a controlled substance to an individual or involves an individual in the offense, as specified in subsection (b)(14)(B), the individual is not a "vulnerable victim" for purposes of subsection (b) of § 3A1.1 (Hate Crime Motivation or Vulnerable Victim). Application Note 29 also provides that subsection (b)(14)(C) applies if the defendant committed, aided, abetted, counseled, commanded, induced, procured, or willfully caused the importation of a controlled substance. Subsection (b)(14)(C), however, does not apply if subsection (b)(3) or (b)(5) (as redesignated by the amendment) applies because the defendant's involvement in importation is adequately accounted for by those subsections. In addition, Application Note 29 defines "pattern of criminal conduct" and "engaged in as a livelihood" for purposes of subsection (b)(14)(E) as those terms are defined in § 4B1.3 (Criminal Livelihood).

The amendment also revises the commentary in § 3B1.4 (Using a Minor To Commit a Crime) and § 3C1.1 (Obstructing or Impeding the Administration of Justice) to specify how those adjustments interact with § 2D1.1(b)(14)(B) and (D), respectively. Specifically, Application Note 2 to § 3B1.4 is amended to clarify that the increase of two levels under this section would not apply if the defendant receives an enhancement under § 2D1.1(b)(14)(B). Similarly, Application Note 7 to § 3C1.1 is amended to clarify that the increase of two levels under this section would not apply if the defendant receives an enhancement under § 2D1.1(b)(14)(D).

Sixth, Part B amends § 2D1.1 to create a new specific offense characteristic at subsection (b)(15) providing a 2-level downward adjustment if the defendant receives the 4-level ("minimal participant") reduction in subsection (a) of § 3B1.2 (Mitigating Role) and the offense involved each of three additional specified factors: namely, the defendant was motivated by an intimate or familial relationship or by threats or fear to commit the offense when the defendant was otherwise unlikely to commit such an offense; was to receive no monetary compensation from the illegal purchase, sale, transport, or storage of controlled substances; and had minimal knowledge of the scope and structure of the enterprise. The specific offense characteristic responds to section 7(2) of the Act, which directed the Commission to ensure that "there is an additional reduction of 2 offense levels if the defendant—

(A) otherwise qualifies for a minimal role adjustment under the guidelines and had a minimum knowledge of the illegal enterprise;

(B) was to receive no monetary compensation from the illegal transaction; and

(C) was motivated by an intimate or familial relationship or by threats or fear when the defendant was otherwise unlikely to commit such an offense."

Amendment 750

Seventh, to reflect the renumbering of specific offense characteristics in § 2D1.1(b) by the amendment, technical and conforming changes are made to the commentary to § 2D1.1 and to § 2D1.14 (Narco-Terrorism).

Part C. Simple Possession of Crack Cocaine

Part C re-promulgates without change the temporary, emergency revisions to § 2D2.1 to account for the changes in the statutory penalties for simple possession of crack cocaine made in section 3 of the Act. Section 3 of the Act amended 21 U.S.C. § 844(a) to eliminate the 5-year mandatory minimum term of imprisonment (and 20-year statutory maximum) for simple possession of more than 5 grams of crack cocaine (or, for certain repeat offenders, more than 1 gram of crack cocaine). Accordingly, the statutory penalty for simple possession of crack cocaine is now the same as for simple possession of most other controlled substances: for a first offender, a maximum term of imprisonment of one year; for repeat offenders, maximum terms of 2 years or 3 years, and minimum terms of 15 days or 90 days, depending on the prior convictions. See 21 U.S.C. § 844(a). To account for this statutory change, the amendment deletes the cross reference at § 2D2.1(b)(1) under which an offender who possessed more than 5 grams of crack cocaine was sentenced under the drug trafficking guideline, § 2D1.1.

Effective Date: The effective date of this amendment is November 1, 2011.

751. **Amendment:** The Commentary to § 2D1.1 captioned "Application Notes" is amended in Note 8, in the first paragraph by adding at the end as the last sentence the following:

> "Likewise, an adjustment under § 3B1.3 ordinarily would apply in a case in which the defendant is convicted of a drug offense resulting from the authorization of the defendant to receive scheduled substances from an ultimate user or long-term care facility. See 21 U.S.C. § 822(g).".

Reason for Amendment: This amendment makes changes to the Commentary to § 2D1.1 (Unlawful Manufacturing, Importing, Exporting, or Trafficking (Including Possession with Intent to Commit These Offenses); Attempt or Conspiracy) in response to the Secure and Responsible Drug Disposal Act of 2010, Pub. L. 111–273 (the "Act"). Section 3 of the Act amended 21 U.S.C. § 822 (Persons required to register) to authorize certain persons in possession of controlled substances (i.e., ultimate users and long-term care facilities) to deliver the controlled substances for the purpose of disposal. Section 4 of the Act contained a directive to the Commission to "review and, if appropriate, amend" the guidelines to ensure that the guidelines provide "an appropriate penalty increase of up to 2 offense levels above the sentence otherwise applicable in Part D of the Guidelines Manual if a person is convicted of a drug offense resulting from the authorization of that person to receive scheduled substances from an ultimate user or long-term care facility as set forth in the amendments made by section 3."

The amendment implements the directive by amending Application Note 8 to § 2D1.1 to provide that an adjustment under § 3B1.3 (Abuse of Position of Trust or Use of Special Skill) ordinarily would apply in a case in which the defendant is convicted of a drug offense resulting from the authorization of the defendant to receive scheduled substances from an ultimate user or long-term care facility. The amendment reflects the likelihood that in such a case the offender abused a position of trust (i.e., the authority provided by 21 U.S.C. § 822 to receive controlled substances for the purpose of disposal) to facilitate the commission or concealment of the offense.

Effective Date: The effective date of this amendment is November 1, 2011.

752. **Amendment:** The Commentary to § 2J1.1 captioned "Application Notes" is amended in

Note 2 by inserting "In such a case, do not apply § 2B1.1(b)(8)(C) (pertaining to a violation of a prior, specific judicial order)." after "failed to pay.".

Reason for Amendment: This amendment addresses a circuit conflict on whether the specific offense characteristic at subsection (b)(8)(C) of § 2B1.1 (Theft, Property Destruction, and Fraud) applies to a defendant convicted of an offense involving the willful failure to pay court-ordered child support (i.e., a violation of 18 U.S.C. § 228). The specific offense characteristic in § 2B1.1(b)(8)(C) applies if the offense involved "a violation of any prior, specific judicial or administrative order, injunction, decree, or process not addressed elsewhere in the guidelines".

It provides an enhancement of 2 levels and a minimum offense level of level 10.

Offenses under section 228 are referenced in Appendix A (Statutory Index) to § 2J1.1 (Contempt), which directs the court to apply § 2X5.1 (Other Offenses), which in turn directs the court to apply the most analogous offense guideline. The commentary to § 2J1.1 provides that, in a case involving a violation of section 228, the most analogous offense guideline is § 2B1.1. See § 2J1.1, comment. (n.2).

Some circuits have disagreed over whether to apply § 2B1.1(b)(8)(C) in a case involving a violation of section 228. The Second and Eleventh Circuits have held that applying § 2B1.1(b)(8)(C) in a section 228 case is permissible because the failure to pay the child support and the violation of the order are distinct harms. See United States v. Maloney, 406 F.3d 149, 153-54 (2d Cir. 2005); United States v. Phillips, 363 F.3d 1167, 1169 (11th Cir. 2004). However, the Seventh Circuit has held that applying § 2B1.1(b)(8)(C) in a section 228 case is impermissible double counting. See United States v. Bell, 598 F.3d 366 (7th Cir. 2010) ("apply[ing] both the cross-reference for § 228 and the enhancement for violation of a court or administrative order is impermissible double counting").

The amendment resolves the conflict by amending the commentary to § 2J1.1 to specify that, in a case involving a violation of section 228, § 2B1.1(b)(8)(C) does not apply. The Commission determined that in a section 228 case the fact that the offense involved a violation of a court order is adequately accounted for by the base offense level.

Effective Date: The effective date of this amendment is November 1, 2011.

753. **Amendment:** Section 2K2.1(a) is amended in subdivision (4)(B) by striking "or" before "(II) is"; and by adding at the end the following:

> "or (III) is convicted under 18 U.S.C. § 922(a)(6) or § 924(a)(1)(A) and committed the offense with knowledge, intent, or reason to believe that the offense would result in the transfer of a firearm or ammunition to a prohibited person;";

and in subdivision (6) by striking "or" before "(B)"; and by adding at the end the following:

> "or (C) is convicted under 18 U.S.C. § 922(a)(6) or § 924(a)(1)(A) and committed the offense with knowledge, intent, or reason to believe that the offense would result in the transfer of a firearm or ammunition to a prohibited person;".

Section 2K2.1(b) is amended by striking subdivision (6) as follows:

> "(6) If the defendant used or possessed any firearm or ammunition in connection with another felony offense; or possessed or transferred any firearm or ammunition with knowledge, intent, or reason to believe that it would be used or possessed in connection with another felony offense, increase by 4 levels. If the resulting offense level is less than level 18, increase to level 18.",

and inserting a new subdivision (6) as follows:

"(6) If the defendant—

(A) possessed any firearm or ammunition while leaving or attempting to leave the United States, or possessed or transferred any firearm or ammunition with knowledge, intent, or reason to believe that it would be transported out of the United States; or

(B) used or possessed any firearm or ammunition in connection with another felony offense; or possessed or transferred any firearm or ammunition with knowledge, intent, or reason to believe that it would be used or possessed in connection with another felony offense,

increase by 4 levels. If the resulting offense level is less than level 18, increase to level 18.".

The Commentary to § 2K2.1 captioned "Application Notes" is amended in Note 13(D) by inserting "(B)" after "(b)(6)".

The Commentary to § 2K2.1 captioned "Application Notes" is amended in Note 14 by inserting "(B)" after "(b)(6)" each place it appears.

The Commentary to § 2K2.1 captioned "Application Notes" is amended by adding at the end the following:

"15. Certain Convictions Under 18 U.S.C. §§ 922(a)(6), 922(d), and 924(a)(1)(A).—In a case in which the defendant is convicted under 18 U.S.C. §§ 922(a)(6), 922(d), or 924(a)(1)(A), a downward departure may be warranted if (A) none of the enhancements in subsection (b) apply, (B) the defendant was motivated by an intimate or familial relationship or by threats or fear to commit the offense and was otherwise unlikely to commit such an offense, and (C) the defendant received no monetary compensation from the offense.".

The Commentary to § 2M5.1 captioned "Statutory Provisions" is amended by inserting "22 U.S.C. § 8512; 50 U.S.C. § 1705;" after "2332d;".

Section 2M5.2(a)(2) is amended by inserting "(A)" before "non-fully"; and by striking "ten" and inserting "two, (B) ammunition for non-fully automatic small arms, and the number of rounds did not exceed 500, or (C) both".

The Commentary to § 2M5.2 captioned "Statutory Provisions" is amended by inserting ", 8512; 50 U.S.C. § 1705" after "2780".

The Commentary to § 2M5.3 captioned "Statutory Provisions" is amended by inserting "22 U.S.C. § 8512;" before "50 U.S.C. "; and by striking "§ 1701,".

Appendix A (Statutory Index) is amended by inserting after the line referenced to 22 U.S.C. § 4221 the following:

"22 U.S.C. § 8512   2M5.1, 2M5.2, 2M5.3";

by striking the line referenced to 50 U.S.C. § 1701;

and in the line referenced to 50 U.S.C. § 1705 by inserting "2M5.1, 2M5.2," before "2M5.3".

Reason for Amendment: This multi-part amendment is a result of the Commission's review of offenses involving firearms crossing the border. The Commission undertook this review in response to concerns that the illegal flow of firearms across the southwestern border of the United States is contributing to violence along the border and ultimately harming the national security of the United States. The Commission has considered sentencing data, heard testimony, and received comment on the general concern of firearms crossing the border illegally and a specific concern that "straw purchasers" (i.e., individuals who buy firearms on behalf of others, typically "prohibited persons" who are not allowed to buy or possess firearms themselves) are contributing to this illegal flow of firearms to a significant degree.

The amendment amends the primary firearms guideline, § 2K2.1 (Unlawful Receipt, Possession, or Transportation of Firearms or Ammunition; Prohibited Transactions Involving Firearms or Ammunition), to address the general concern of firearms crossing the border and the specific concern about straw purchasers. The amendment also amends the guideline for arms export violations, § 2M5.2 (Exportation of Arms, Munitions, or Military Equipment or Services Without Required Validated Export License), to provide greater penalties for export offenses involving small arms and more guidance on export offenses involving ammunition. Finally, the amendment revises the references in Appendix A (Statutory Index) for certain offenses, including providing a reference for a new offense created by the Comprehensive Iran Sanctions, Accountability, and Divestment Act of 2010, Pub. L. 111–195.

Firearms Leaving the United States

Subsection (b)(6) provides a 4-level enhancement, and a minimum offense level of 18, if the defendant used or possessed any firearm or ammunition in connection with another felony offense, or possessed or transferred any firearm or ammunition with knowledge, intent, or reason to believe that it would be used or possessed in connection with another felony offense. The amendment establishes a new prong (A) in subsection (b)(6) that applies "if the defendant possessed any firearm or ammunition while leaving or attempting to leave the United States; or possessed or transferred any firearm or ammunition with knowledge, intent, or reason to believe that it would be transferred out of the United States", and redesignates the existing provision as prong (B). Under the amendment, a defendant receives the 4-level enhancement and minimum offense level 18 if either prong applies. The Commission determined that possessing a firearm while leaving or attempting to leave the United States is conduct sufficiently similar in seriousness to possessing a firearm in connection with another felony offense to warrant similar punishment. Likewise, possessing or transferring a firearm with knowledge, intent, or reason to believe that it would be transported out of the United States is conduct sufficiently similar in seriousness to possessing or transferring a firearm with knowledge, intent, or reason to believe that it would be used or possessed in connection with another felony offense to warrant similar punishment.

Prior to the amendment, some courts have applied subsection (b)(6) to cases in which the defendant has transported or attempted to transport firearms across the border. These courts have concluded that because transporting a firearm outside the United States is generally a felony under federal law, such conduct may qualify as "another felony offense" for purposes of subsection (b)(6). See, e.g., United States v. Juarez, 626 F.3d 246 (5th Cir. 2010) (holding that, under the guideline as amended by the Commission in 2008, the district court did not plainly err in applying § 2K2.1(b)(6) to a defendant who transferred firearms with reason to believe they would be taken across the border in a manner that would violate 22 U.S.C. § 2778(b) and (c), which prohibits, among other things, the unlicensed export of defense articles and punishes such violations by up to 20 years' imprisonment). However, for clarity and to promote consistency of application, the Commission created a separate, distinct prong (A) in subsection (b)(6) to cover this conduct.

Straw Purchasers

Second, the amendment amends § 2K2.1 to address the concerns about straw purchasers. The amendment increases penalties for certain defendants convicted under 18 U.S.C. §§ 922(a)(6) or 924(a)(1)(A) for making a false statement in connection with a firearms transaction. Specifically, the amendment increases penalties for a defendant who is convicted under 18 U.S.C. §§ 922(a)(6) or 924(a)(1)(A) and committed the offense with knowledge, intent, or reason to believe that the offense would result in the transfer of a firearm or ammunition to a prohibited person. The base offense level for a defendant convicted under either of these statutes has been level 12, or level 18 if the offense involved a firearm described in 26 U.S.C. § 5845(a). See § 2K2.1(a)(5), (7). The amendment amends subsections (a)(4)(B) and (a)(6) to increase the base offense level for these defendants to level 14, or 20 if the offense involved either a semiautomatic firearm that is capable of accepting a large capacity magazine or a firearm described in 26 U.S.C. § 5845(a).

The amendment ensures that defendants convicted under 18 U.S.C. §§ 922(a)(6) or 924(a)(1)(A) receive the same punishment as defendants convicted under a third statute used to prosecute straw purchasers, 18 U.S.C. § 922(d), when the conduct is similar. Section 922(d) differs from 18 U.S.C. §§ 922(a)(6) and 924(a)(1)(A) in that it requires as an element of the offense that the defendant sell or otherwise dispose of a firearm or ammunition to a prohibited person knowing or having reasonable cause to believe that such person is a prohibited person. Section 2K2.1 has accounted for the increased offense seriousness and offender culpability in violations of 18 U.S.C. § 922(d) by providing base offense levels for convictions under section 922(d) that are generally 2 levels higher than for convictions under 18 U.S.C. §§ 922(a)(6) and 924(a)(1)(A). See § 2K2.1(a)(4)(B), (a)(6)(B). The Commission determined that defendants who are convicted under 18 U.S.C. §§ 922(a)(6) or 924(a)(1)(A) for making a false statement in connection with a firearms transaction and committed the offense with knowledge, intent, or reason to believe that the offense would result in the transfer of a firearm or ammunition to a prohibited person have engaged in conduct similar to the elements of 18 U.S.C. § 922(d), are similarly culpable, and therefore warrant a similar sentence under § 2K2.1.

In addition, the amendment provides a new Application Note 15 stating that, in a case in which the defendant is convicted under any of the three statutes, a downward departure may be warranted if (A) none of the enhancements in subsection (b) of § 2K2.1 apply, (B) the defendant was motivated by an intimate or familial relationship or by threats or fear to commit the offense and was otherwise unlikely to commit such an offense, and (C) the defendant received no monetary compensation from the offense. The Commission determined that a defendant meeting these criteria may be less culpable than the typical straw purchaser.

Export Offenses Involving Small Arms or Ammunition

Third, the amendment amends § 2M5.2 to narrow the application of the alternative base offense level of 14 at subsection (a)(2). The alternative base offense level of 14 has applied "if the offense involved only non-fully automatic small arms (rifles, handguns, or shotguns) and the number of weapons did not exceed ten." See § 2M5.2(a)(2). The amendment reduces the threshold number of small arms in subsection (a)(2) from ten to two. The Commission determined that export offenses involving more than two firearms are more serious and more likely to involve trafficking. Narrowing the application of subsection (a)(2) also brings § 2M5.2 into greater conformity with § 2K2.1 in how it accounts for the number of firearms involved in the offense. See § 2K2.1(b)(1) (providing a tiered enhancement of 2 to 10 levels if the offense involved three or more firearms); § 2K2.1, comment. (n.13) (specifying that the trafficking enhancement in § 2K2.1(b)(5) applies if the offense involved two or more firearms and other requirements are also met).

The amendment also amends § 2M5.2 to address cases in which the defendant possessed ammunition, either in a case involving ammunition only or in a case involving ammunition and small arms. There appears to be differences in how § 2M5.2 is being applied by the courts in such cases. Under the amendment, a defendant with ammunition will receive the alternative base offense level of 14 if the ammunition consisted of not more than 500 rounds of ammunition for small arms. Such ammunition typically is sold in quantities of not more than 500 rounds, depending on the manufacturer and the type of ammunition. The Commission determined that, as with export offenses involving more than two firearms, export offenses involving more than 500 rounds of ammunition are more serious and more likely to involve trafficking.

References in Appendix A (Statutory Index)

Fourth, the amendment amends Appendix A (Statutory Index) to expand the number of guidelines to which offenses under 50 U.S.C. § 1705 are referenced. Section 1705 makes it unlawful to violate, attempt to violate, conspire to violate, or cause a violation of any license, order, regulation, or prohibition issued under the International Emergency Economic Powers Act (50 U.S.C. § 1701 et seq.). Any person who willfully commits, willfully attempts or conspires to commit, or aids or abets in the commission of such an unlawful act may be imprisoned for not more than 20 years. See 50 U.S.C. § 1705(c). Appendix A (Statutory Index) previously contained two separate entries: the criminal offense, 50 U.S.C. § 1705, was referenced to § 2M5.3 (Providing Material Support or Resources to Designated Foreign Terrorist Organizations or Specially Designated Global Terrorists, or For a Terrorist Purpose), while another statute that contains no criminal offense, 50 U.S.C. § 1701, was referenced to § 2M5.3 as well as to §§ 2M5.1 (Evasion of Export Controls; Financial Transactions with Countries Supporting International Terrorism) and 2M5.2 (Exportation of Arms, Munitions, or Military Equipment or Services Without Required Validated Export License). The amendment revises the entry for 50 U.S.C. § 1705 to include all three guidelines, §§ 2M5.1, 2M5.2, and 2M5.3, and deletes as unnecessary the entry for 50 U.S.C. § 1701.

Finally, the amendment addresses a new offense created by the Comprehensive Iran Sanctions, Accountability, and Divestment Act of 2010, Pub. L. 111–195. Section 103 of that Act (22 U.S.C. § 8512) makes it unlawful to import into the United States certain goods or services of Iranian origin, or export to Iran certain goods, services, or technology, and provides that the penalties under 50 U.S.C. § 1705 apply to a violation. The amendment amends Appendix A (Statutory Index) to reference the new offense at 22 U.S.C. § 8512 to §§ 2M5.1, 2M5.2, and 2M5.3.

Effective Date: The effective date of this amendment is November 1, 2011.

754. **Amendment:** Section 2L1.2(b)(1)(A) is amended by inserting "if the conviction receives criminal history points under Chapter Four or by 12 levels if the conviction does not receive criminal history points" after "16 levels".

Section 2L1.2(b)(1)(B) is amended by inserting "if the conviction receives criminal history points under Chapter Four or by 8 levels if the conviction does not receive criminal

Amendment 754

history points" after "12 levels".

The Commentary to 2L1.2 captioned "Application Notes" is amended in Note 1 by adding at the end the following:

> "(C) Prior Convictions.—In determining the amount of an enhancement under subsection (b)(1), note that the levels in subsections (b)(1)(A) and (B) depend on whether the conviction receives criminal history points under Chapter Four (Criminal History and Criminal Livelihood), while subsections (b)(1)(C), (D), and (E) apply without regard to whether the conviction receives criminal history points.".

The Commentary to 2L1.2 captioned "Application Notes" is amended in Note 7 by inserting after "warranted. (B)" the following: "In a case in which the 12-level enhancement under subsection (b)(1)(A) or the 8-level enhancement in subsection (b)(1)(B) applies but that enhancement does not adequately reflect the extent or seriousness of the conduct underlying the prior conviction, an upward departure may be warranted. (C)".

Reason for Amendment: This amendment amends § 2L1.2 (Unlawfully Entering or Remaining in the United States) to limit the extent of the enhancement at subsection (b)(1) provided for certain offenders. Subsection (b)(1) provides an enhancement if the defendant previously was deported, or unlawfully remained in the United States, after a predicate conviction. The amount of the enhancement ranges from 16 levels to 4 levels, depending on the nature of the prior conviction. Specifically, prior to the amendment, subsection (b)(1)(A) has provided a 16-level increase for a prior conviction for a felony that is (i) a drug trafficking offense for which the sentence imposed exceeded 13 months, (ii) a crime of violence, (iii) a firearms offense, (iv) a child pornography offense, (v) a national security or terrorism offense, (vi) a human trafficking offense, or (vii) an alien smuggling offense; and subsection (b)(1)(B) has provided a 12-level increase for a felony drug trafficking offense for which the sentence imposed was 13 months or less. Both of these enhancements have applied regardless of whether the prior conviction received criminal history points under Chapter Four (Criminal History and Criminal Livelihood).

The amendment reduces the enhancements at subsections (b)(1)(A) and (B) to 12 or 8 levels, respectively, if the prior conviction does not receive criminal history points under Chapter Four. Subsections (b)(1)(A) and (B) as amended continue to provide a 16- or 12-level enhancement, as applicable, if the prior conviction receives criminal history points under Chapter Four. Thus, for reasons of proportionality, the amendment maintains the 4-level distinction between defendants who receive an enhancement under subsection (b)(1)(A) and those who receive an enhancement under subsection (b)(1)(B), regardless of whether the prior conviction receives criminal history points.

The amendment responds to case law and public comment regarding the magnitude of the enhancement when a defendant's predicate conviction does not receive criminal history points. Compare United States v. Amezcua-Vasquez, 567 F.3d 1050, 1055 (9th Cir. 2009) (defendant had two convictions that were 25 years old; court stated that the 16-level enhancement in § 2L1.2(b)(1)(A) "addresses the seriousness of the offense" but "does not . . . justify increasing a defendant's sentence by the same magnitude irrespective of the age of the prior conviction at the time of reentry" [emphasis in original]); with United States v. Chavez-Suarez, 597 F.3d 1137, 1139 (10th Cir. 2010) (defendant had a conviction that was 11 years old; court discussed Amezcua-Vasquez but was "not convinced that this conviction was so stale" as to require the sentencing court to vary downward from the 16-level enhancement).

Under the amendment, defendants with predicate offenses that qualify for an enhancement under subsections (b)(1)(A) and (B) continue to receive an enhancement, regardless of whether the prior convictions receive criminal history points under Chapter Four. Other provisions in the guidelines exclude consideration of a predicate conviction because of the age of the predicate conviction. See, e.g., § 2K1.3 (Unlawful Receipt, Possession, or Transportation of Explosive Materials; Prohibited Transactions Involving Explosive Materials), comment. (n.9); § 2K2.1 (Unlawful Receipt, Possession, or Transportation of Firearms or Ammunition; Prohibited Transactions Involving Firearms or Ammunition), comment. (n.10); § 4B1.2 (Definitions of Terms Used in Section 4B1.1), comment. (n.3). The amendment conforms § 2L1.2(b)(1)(A) and (B) more closely to those provisions, but because of the seriousness of the predicate offenses covered by subsection (b)(1)(A) and (B) reduces, rather than eliminates, the 16- and 12-level enhancements. See, e.g., Amezcua-Vasquez, 567 F.3d at 1055 (acknowledging that it is "reasonable to take some account of an aggravated felony, no matter how stale, in assessing the seriousness of an unlawful reentry into the country"). See also id. at 1055 (in certain cases in which the prior conviction is "stale", an enhancement may be appropriate to address the "seriousness" of the prior conviction but need not be of the "same magnitude"); Chavez-Suarez, 597 F.3d at 1139 (same). For similar reasons, the amendment also adds an upward departure provision at Application Note 7 for cases in which the lower 12- or 8-level enhancement does not adequately reflect the extent or seriousness of the conduct underlying the prior conviction. Conforming changes to the Commentary are also made.

Effective Date: The effective date of this amendment is November 1, 2011.

755. **Amendment:** The Commentary to § 3B1.2 captioned "Application Notes" is amended in Note 3(C) by inserting "is based on the totality of the circumstances and" after "adjustment,"; and by striking the last sentence as follows:

> "As with any other factual issue, the court, in weighing the totality of the circumstances, is not required to find, based solely on the defendant's bare assertion, that such a role adjustment is warranted.".

The Commentary to § 3B1.2 captioned "Application Notes" is amended in Note 4 by striking the last sentence as follows:

> "It is intended that the downward adjustment for a minimal participant will be used infrequently".

Reason for Amendment: This amendment deletes two sentences from the commentary to § 3B1.2 (Mitigating Role). Specifically, in Application Note 3(C), the amendment deletes the statement that "[a]s with any other factual issue, the court, in weighing the totality of the circumstances, is not required to find, based solely on the defendant's bare assertion, that such a role adjustment is warranted," while retaining the "totality of the circumstances" approach. In Application Note 4, the amendment deletes the sentence, "It is intended that the downward adjustment for a minimal participant will be used infrequently". The Commission determined that these two sentences are unnecessary and may have the unintended effect of discouraging courts from applying the mitigating role adjustment in otherwise appropriate circumstances.

Effective Date: The effective date of this amendment is November 1, 2011.

756. **Amendment:** Section 5D1.1 is amended by striking subsection (a) as follows:

> "(a) The court shall order a term of supervised release to follow imprisonment when a sentence of imprisonment of more than one year is imposed, or when required by statute.",

and inserting the following:

"(a) The court shall order a term of supervised release to follow imprisonment—

(1) when required by statute (see 18 U.S.C. § 3583(a)); or

(2) except as provided in subsection (c), when a sentence of imprisonment of more than one year is imposed.";

and in subsection (b) by adding at the end the following: "See 18 U.S.C. § 3583(a).".

Section 5D1.1 is amended by adding at the end the following:

"(c) The court ordinarily should not impose a term of supervised release in a case in which supervised release is not required by statute and the defendant is a deportable alien who likely will be deported after imprisonment.".

The Commentary to § 5D1.1 captioned "Application Notes" is amended by striking Notes 1 and 2 as follows:

"1. Under subsection (a), the court is required to impose a term of supervised release to follow imprisonment if a sentence of imprisonment of more than one year is imposed or if a term of supervised release is required by a specific statute. The court may depart from this guideline and not impose a term of supervised release if it determines that supervised release is neither required by statute nor required for any of the following reasons: (A) to protect the public welfare; (B) to enforce a financial condition; (C) to provide drug or alcohol treatment or testing; (D) to assist the reintegration of the defendant into the community; or (E) to accomplish any other sentencing purpose authorized by statute.

2. Under subsection (b), the court may impose a term of supervised release to follow a term of imprisonment of one year or less for any of the reasons set forth in Application Note 1.",

and inserting the following:

"1. Application of Subsection (a).—Under subsection (a), the court is required to impose a term of supervised release to follow imprisonment when supervised release is required by statute or, except as provided in subsection (c), when a sentence of imprisonment of more than one year is imposed. The court may depart from this guideline and not impose a term of supervised release if supervised release is not required by statute and the court determines, after considering the factors set forth in Note 3, that supervised release is not necessary.

2. Application of Subsection (b).—Under subsection (b), the court may impose a term of supervised release to follow a term of imprisonment in any other case, after considering the factors set forth in Note 3.

3. Factors to Be Considered.—

(A) Statutory Factors.—In determining whether to impose a term of supervised release, the court is required by statute to consider, among other factors:

		(i)	the nature and circumstances of the offense and the history and characteristics of the defendant;
		(ii)	the need to afford adequate deterrence to criminal conduct, to protect the public from further crimes of the defendant, and to provide the defendant with needed educational or vocational training, medical care, or other correctional treatment in the most effective manner;
		(iii)	the need to avoid unwarranted sentence disparities among defendants with similar records who have been found guilty of similar conduct; and
		(iv)	the need to provide restitution to any victims of the offense.
			See 18 U.S.C. § 3583(c).
	(B)		Criminal History.—The court should give particular consideration to the defendant's criminal history (which is one aspect of the 'history and characteristics of the defendant' in subparagraph (A)(i), above). In general, the more serious the defendant's criminal history, the greater the need for supervised release.
	(C)		Substance Abuse.—In a case in which a defendant sentenced to imprisonment is an abuser of controlled substances or alcohol, it is highly recommended that a term of supervised release also be imposed. See § 5H1.4 (Physical Condition, Including Drug or Alcohol Dependence or Abuse; Gambling Addiction).
4.			Community Confinement or Home Detention Following Imprisonment.—A term of supervised release must be imposed if the court wishes to impose a 'split sentence' under which the defendant serves a term of imprisonment followed by a period of community confinement or home detention pursuant to subsection (c)(2) or (d)(2) of § 5C1.1 (Imposition of a Term of Imprisonment). In such a case, the period of community confinement or home detention is imposed as a condition of supervised release.
5.			Application of Subsection (c).—In a case in which the defendant is a deportable alien specified in subsection (c) and supervised release is not required by statute, the court ordinarily should not impose a term of supervised release. Unless such a defendant legally returns to the United States, supervised release is unnecessary. If such a defendant illegally returns to the United States, the need to afford adequate deterrence and protect the public ordinarily is adequately served by a new prosecution. The court should, however, consider imposing a term of supervised release on such a defendant if the court determines it would provide an added measure of deterrence and protection based on the facts and circumstances of a particular case.".

Section 5D1.2(a) is amended in subdivision (1) by striking "three" and inserting "two"; and by adding at the end the following: "See 18 U.S.C. § 3583(b)(1).".

Section 5D1.2(a) is amended in subdivision (2) by striking "two years" and inserting "one year"; and by adding at the end the following: "See 18 U.S.C. § 3583(b)(2).".

Section 5D1.2(a) is amended in subdivision (3) by adding at the end the following: "See

Amendment 756

18 U.S.C. § 3583(b)(3).".

The Commentary to § 5D1.2 captioned "Application Notes" is amended by adding at the end the following:

> "4. <u>Factors Considered</u>.—The factors to be considered in determining the length of a term of supervised release are the same as the factors considered in determining whether to impose such a term. <u>See</u> 18 U.S.C. § 3583(c); Application Note 3 to § 5D1.1 (Imposition of a Term of Supervised Release). The court should ensure that the term imposed on the defendant is long enough to address the purposes of imposing supervised release on the defendant.
>
> 5. <u>Early Termination and Extension</u>.—The court has authority to terminate or extend a term of supervised release. <u>See</u> 18 U.S.C. § 3583(e)(1), (2). The court is encouraged to exercise this authority in appropriate cases. The prospect of exercising this authority is a factor the court may wish to consider in determining the length of a term of supervised release. For example, the court may wish to consider early termination of supervised release if the defendant is an abuser of narcotics, other controlled substances, or alcohol who, while on supervised release, successfully completes a treatment program, thereby reducing the risk to the public from further crimes of the defendant.".

Reason for Amendment: This amendment makes revisions to the supervised release guidelines, § 5D1.1 (Imposition of a Term of Supervised Release) and § 5D1.2 (Term of Supervised Release), in response to both the findings in the Commission's July 2010 report, <u>Federal Offenders Sentenced to Supervised Release</u>, and changes in federal immigration law and the federal offender population in recent years.

First, the amendment creates an exception to the general rule in § 5D1.1(a) that a term of supervised release be imposed when a sentence of imprisonment of more than one year is imposed or when required by statute. The exception, which appears in a new subsection (c) in § 5D1.1, states that supervised release ordinarily should not be imposed in a case in which supervised release is not required by statute and the defendant is a deportable alien who likely will be deported after imprisonment. A corresponding application note explains that imposing supervised release in such a case is generally unnecessary, although there may be particular cases in which it is appropriate. Non-citizens now are approximately half of the overall population of federal offenders, <u>see</u> 2010 Sourcebook of Federal Sentencing Statistics, Table 9 (showing that 47.5% of federal offenders in fiscal year 2010 were non-citizens), and supervised release is imposed in more than 91 percent of cases in which the defendant is a non-citizen, <u>see</u> <u>Federal Offenders Sentenced to Supervised Release</u> at 60. The Commission determined that such a high rate of imposition of supervised release for non-citizen offenders is unnecessary because "recent changes in our immigration law have made removal nearly an automatic result for a broad class of noncitizen offenders." <u>Padilla v. Kentucky</u>, 130 S. Ct. 1473, 1481 (2010); <u>see also id.</u> at 1478 ("[D]eportation or removal . . . is now virtually inevitable for a vast number of noncitizens convicted of crimes."). Furthermore, such offenders likely would face prosecution for a new offense under the federal immigration laws if they were to return illegally to the United States.

Second, the amendment lowers the minimum term of supervised release required by the guidelines for certain defendants (regardless of their citizenship status) when a statute does not require a higher minimum term. Section 5D1.2 requires the court to impose a term of supervised release of at least three years when the defendant is convicted of a Class A or B felony and at least two years when the defendant is convicted of a Class C or D felony. The amendment lowers these minimum terms to two years for a defendant convicted of a Class A and B felony and one year for a defendant convicted of a Class C or D felony. Thus, for reasons of proportionality, the amendment maintains a 1-year distinction in the minimum term of supervised release between a defendant convicted of a Class A or B felony and a defendant convicted of a Class C or D felony. The Commission determined that these lesser minimum terms should be sufficient in most cases because research indicates that the majority of defendants who violate a condition of supervised release do so during the first year of the term of supervised release. See Federal Offenders Sentenced to Supervised Release at 63 & n. 265. Furthermore, if an offender shows non-compliance during such a minimum term, the court may extend the term of supervision up to the statutory maximum. See 18 U.S.C. § 3583(e)(2). The amendment also adds commentary at new Application Note 5 encouraging courts to exercise their authority to terminate supervised release at any time after the expiration of one year of supervised release in appropriate cases. See 18 U.S.C. § 3583(e)(1).

Finally, the amendment adds commentary in §§ 5D1.1 and 5D1.2 that provides guidance on the factors a court should consider in deciding whether to order a term of supervised release (when not required by statute) and, if so, how long such a term should be. Such factors include the extent of an offender's criminal record, which research shows to be predictive of an offender's likelihood of complying with the conditions of supervision. See Federal Offenders Sentenced to Supervised Release at 66-67 (Figure 4) (noting that the rates of revocation for offenders increased steadily across the six Criminal History Categories (CHC), from 18.7% for offenders in CHC I to 59.8% in CHC VI).

Effective Date: The effective date of this amendment is November 1, 2011.

757. **Amendment:** Section 5K2.0(e) is amended by striking "written judgment and commitment order" and inserting "statement of reasons form".

The Commentary to § 5K2.0 captioned "Application Notes" is amended in Note 3(C) in the second paragraph by striking "written judgment and commitment order" and inserting "statement of reasons form"; and in Note 5 by striking "written judgment and commitment order" and inserting "statement of reasons form".

Section 6B1.2(b)(2) is amended by striking "departs from" and inserting "is outside"; by striking "specifically set forth in writing", and inserting "set forth with specificity"; and by striking "or judgment and commitment order" and inserting "form".

Section 6B1.2(c)(2) is amended by striking "departs from" and inserting "is outside"; by striking "specifically set forth in writing" and inserting "set forth with specificity"; and by striking "or judgment and commitment order" and inserting "form".

The Commentary to § 6B1.2 is amended in the second paragraph by striking "departs from" and inserting "is outside"; by striking "(i.e., that such departure is authorized by 18 U.S.C. § 3553(b)) and those reasons are specifically set forth in writing in the statement of reasons or the judgment and commitment order", and inserting" and those reasons are set forth with specificity in the statement of reasons form. See 18 U.S.C. § 3553(c)".

Appendix A (Statutory Index) is amended by inserting after the line referenced to 18 U.S.C. § 2237(a)(2)(B) the following:

"18 U.S.C. § 2237(b)(2)(B)(i)   2A1.3, 2A1.4

18 U.S.C. § 2237(b)(2)(B)(ii)(I)	2A2.1, 2A2.2
18 U.S.C. § 2237(b)(2)(B)(ii)(II)	2A4.1
18 U.S.C. § 2237(b)(2)(B)(ii)(III)	2A3.1
18 U.S.C. § 2237(b)(3)	2A2.2
18 U.S.C. § 2237(b)(4)	2A2.1, 2A2.2, 2G1.1, 2G1.3, 2G2.1, 2H4.1, 2L1.1";

and by inserting after the line referenced to 33 U.S.C. § 1908 the following:

"33 U.S.C. § 3851   2Q1.2".

Reason for Amendment: This two-part amendment addresses miscellaneous issues arising from recently enacted legislation and other guideline application issues.

Plea Agreements

First, the amendment updates the policy statement at § 6B1.2 (Standards for Acceptance of Plea Agreements) in light of United States v. Booker, 543 U.S. 220 (2005). Specifically, it amends § 6B1.2 to provide standards for acceptance of plea agreements when the sentence is outside the applicable guideline range, including when the sentence is a "variance" (i.e., a sentence that is outside the guidelines framework). These changes to § 6B1.2 are consistent with the changes to § 1B1.1 (Application Instructions) that the Commission promulgated last year, see USSG App. C, Amendment 741 (effective November 1, 2010), and reflect Booker and subsequent case law.

The amendment also responds to the Federal Judiciary Administrative Improvements Act of 2010, Pub. L. 111–174 (enacted May 27, 2010), which amended 18 U.S.C. § 3553(c)(2) to require that the reasons for a sentence be set forth in the statement of reasons form (rather than in the judgment and commitment order). The amendment makes appropriate clerical changes to § 6B1.2 and subsection (e) of § 5K2.0 (Grounds for Departure) to reflect this statutory change.

Coast Guard Authorization Act of 2010

Second, the amendment responds to the Coast Guard Authorization Act of 2010, Pub. L. 111–281 (enacted October 15, 2010), which provided statutory sentencing enhancements for certain offenses under 18 U.S.C. § 2237 (Criminal sanctions for failure to heave to, obstruction of boarding, or providing false information) and created a new criminal offense at 33 U.S.C. § 3851.

The amendment addresses the section 2237 offenses by expanding the range of guidelines to which certain section 2237 offenses are referenced. Section 2237 makes it unlawful for—

> the operator of a vessel to knowingly fail to obey a law enforcement order to heave to, see 18 U.S.C. § 2237(a)(1);
>
> a person on board a vessel to forcibly interfere with a law enforcement boarding or other law enforcement action, or to resist arrest, see 18 U.S.C. § 2237(a)(2)(A); or
>
> a person on board a vessel to provide materially false information to a law enforcement officer during a boarding regarding the vessel's destination, origin, ownership, registration, nationality, cargo, or crew, see 18 U.S.C. § 2237(a)(2)(B).

All three of these offenses are punishable by not more than 5 years of imprisonment. The first two are referenced in Appendix A (Statutory Index) to § 2A2.4 (Obstructing or Impeding Officers); the third is referenced to § 2B1.1 (Theft, Property Destruction, and Fraud). However, the Coast Guard Authorization Act of 2010 provided statutory sentencing enhancements that apply to persons convicted under either of the first two offenses under section 2237 (i.e., the failure-to-heave-to and forcible-interference offenses referenced to § 2A2.4; the statutory sentencing enhancements do not apply to the false-information offense referenced to § 2B1.1). The amendment addresses these new statutory sentencing enhancements by referencing them in Appendix A (Statutory Index) to Chapter Two offense guidelines most analogous to the conduct forming the basis for the statutory sentencing enhancements, as follows.

If the section 2237 offense results in death, the statutory maximum term of imprisonment is raised to any term of years or life. See 18 U.S.C. § 2237(b)(2)(B)(i). The Commission referenced this statutory sentencing enhancement to §§ 2A1.3 (Voluntary Manslaughter) and 2A1.4 (Involuntary Manslaughter) because the statutory sentencing enhancement involves death without proof of malice aforethought.

If the section 2237 offense involves an attempt to kill, kidnapping or an attempt to kidnap, or an offense under 18 U.S.C. § 2241 (aggravated sexual abuse), the statutory maximum term of imprisonment likewise is raised to any term of years or life. See 18 U.S.C. § 2237(b)(2)(B)(ii). The Commission referenced this statutory sentencing enhancement to §§ 2A2.1 (Assault with Intent to Commit Murder; Attempted Murder) and 2A2.2 (Aggravated Assault) to account for when the section 2237 offense involves an attempt to kill, because those guidelines apply to attempted murder and attempted manslaughter, respectively; to § 2A3.1 (Criminal Sexual Abuse; Attempt to Commit Criminal Sexual Abuse) to account for when the section 2237 offense involves an offense under 18 U.S.C. § 2241, because offenses under section 2241 are referenced to that guideline; and to § 2A4.1 (Kidnapping, Abduction, Unlawful Restraint) to account for when the section 2237 offense involves kidnapping or attempted kidnapping, because that guideline applies to kidnapping.

If the section 2237 offense results in serious bodily injury, the statutory maximum term of imprisonment is raised to 15 years. See 18 U.S.C. § 2237(b)(3). The Commission referenced this statutory sentencing enhancement to § 2A2.2 because a section 2237 offense involving this statutory sentencing enhancement is similar to an assault that results in bodily injury, and that guideline applies to such an assault. See USSG § 2A2.2, comment. (n.1) (defining aggravated assault to include any assault that involved serious bodily injury).

If the section 2237 offense involves knowing transportation under inhumane conditions, and is committed in the course of a violation of 8 U.S.C. § 1324; chapter 77 of title 18, United States Code; or section 113 or 117 of such title, the statutory maximum term of imprisonment is raised to 15 years. See 18 U.S.C. § 2237(b)(4). The Commission referenced this statutory sentencing enhancement to the following guidelines:

> to §§ 2A2.1 (Assault with Intent to Commit Murder; Attempted Murder) and 2A2.2 to account for when the section 2237 offense involves a violation of section 113, because section 113 offenses are referenced to those guidelines;

> to §§ 2G1.1 (Promoting a Commercial Sex Act or Prohibited Sexual Conduct with an Individual Other than a Minor), 2G1.3 (Promoting a Commercial Sex Act or Prohibited Sexual Conduct with a Minor; Transportation of Minors to Engage in a Commercial Sex Act or Prohibited Sexual Conduct; Travel to Engage in Com-

mercial Sex Act or Prohibited Sexual Conduct with a Minor; Sex Trafficking of Children; Use of Interstate Facilities to Transport Information about a Minor), and 2G2.1 (Sexually Exploiting a Minor by Production of Sexually Explicit Visual or Printed Material; Custodian Permitting Minor to Engage in Sexually Explicit Conduct; Advertisement for Minors to Engage in Production) to account for when the section 2237 offense involve a violation of 18 U.S.C. § 1591 (which is within chapter 77), because offenses under section 1591 are referenced to those guidelines;

to § 2H4.1 (Peonage, Involuntary Servitude, Slave Trade, and Child Soldiers) to account for when the section 2237 offense involves a violation of any provision of chapter 77 other than 18 U.S.C. § 1591, because such violations generally are referenced to that guideline; and

to § 2L1.1 (Smuggling, Transporting, or Harboring an Unlawful Alien) to account for when the section 2237 offense involves a violation of 8 U.S.C. § 1324, because section 1324 offenses are referenced to that guideline.

Finally, the amendment addresses the new criminal offense at 33 U.S.C. § 3851, which makes it a felony, punishable by imprisonment for not more than six years, to sell or distribute an organotin or to sell, distribute, make, use, or apply an anti-fouling system (e.g., paint) containing an organotin. The Commission referenced this offense to § 2Q1.2 (Mishandling of Hazardous or Toxic Substances or Pesticides; Recordkeeping, Tampering, and Falsification; Unlawfully Transporting Hazardous Materials in Commerce) because the offense involves pesticides known to be toxic.

Effective Date: The effective date of this amendment is November 1, 2011.

758. **Amendment:** Chapter Two is amended in the introductory commentary by inserting "and Related Adjustments" after "(Obstruction".

The Commentary to § 2J1.2 captioned "Application Notes" is amended in Note 2(A) by inserting "and Related Adjustments" after "(Obstruction"; and in Note 3 by inserting "and Related Adjustments" after "(Obstruction".

The Commentary to § 2J1.3 captioned "Application Notes" is amended in Note 2 by inserting "and Related Adjustments" after "(Obstruction"; and in Note 3 by inserting "and Related Adjustments" after "(Obstruction".

The Commentary to § 2J1.6 captioned "Application Notes" is amended in Note 2 by inserting "and Related Adjustments" after "(Obstruction"; and in Note 4 by striking "Obstruction of Justice" and inserting "Obstructing or Impeding the Administration of Justice".

The Commentary to § 2J1.9 captioned "Application Notes" is amended in Note 1 by inserting "and Related Adjustments" after "(Obstruction"; and in Note 2 by inserting "and Related Adjustments" after "(Obstruction".

Section 2Q2.1(c)(1) is amended by inserting "or paleontological resource" after "heritage resource"; and by inserting "or Paleontological Resources" after "Heritage Resources" in both places.

Section 3C1.1 is amended by striking "(A)" and inserting "(1)"; by striking "(B)" and inserting "(2)"; by striking "(i)" and inserting "(A)"; and by striking "(ii)" and inserting "(B)".

Section 4A1.2(k)(2) is amended by striking "(i)" and inserting "(A)"; by striking "(ii)" and inserting "(B)"; and by striking "(iii)" and inserting "(C)".

Section 4B1.1(b) is amended by redesignating (A) through (G) as (1) through (7).

The Commentary to § 5E1.2 captioned "Application Notes" is amended in Note 6 by inserting "and Related Adjustments" after "(Obstruction".

The Commentary to § 8A1.2 captioned "Application Notes" is amended in Note 2 by inserting "and Related Adjustments" after "(Obstruction".

Section 8B2.1(a) is amended by striking "(c)" and inserting "(b)".

The Commentary to § 8C2.3 captioned "Application Notes" is amended in Note 2 by inserting "and Related Adjustments" after "(Obstruction".

Reason for Amendment: This amendment makes various technical and conforming changes to the guidelines.

First, the amendment makes certain technical and conforming changes in connection with the amendments that the Commission submitted to Congress on April 29, 2010. See 75 Fed. Reg. 27388 (May 14, 2010); USSG App. C, Amendments 738–746. Those changes are as follows:

(1) Amendment 744 made changes to the organizational guidelines in Chapter Eight, including a change that consolidated subsections (b) and (c) of § 8D1.4 (Recommended Conditions of Probation — Organizations) into a single subsection (b). To reflect this consolidation, subsection (a) of § 8B2.1 (Effective Compliance and Ethics Program) is changed so that it refers to the correct subsection of § 8D1.4.

(2) Amendment 745 expanded the scope of § 2B1.5 (Theft of, Damage to, or Destruction of, Cultural Heritage Resources; Unlawful Sale, Purchase, Exchange, Transportation, or Receipt of Cultural Heritage Resources) to cover not only cultural heritage resources but also paleontological resources. To reflect this expanded scope, a conforming change is made to subsection (c)(1) of § 2Q2.1 (Offenses Involving Fish, Wildlife, and Plants).

Second, the amendment makes technical changes to § 3C1.1 (Obstructing or Impeding the Administration of Justice), subsection (k)(2) of § 4A1.2 (Definitions and Instructions for Computing Criminal History), and subsection (b) of § 4B1.1 (Career Offender) to promote stylistic consistency in how subdivisions are designated throughout the Guidelines Manual.

Finally, the amendment makes a series of changes throughout the Guidelines Manual to provide full and accurate references to the titles of Chapter Three, Part C (Obstruction and Related Adjustments) and § 3C1.1.

Effective Date: The effective date of this amendment is November 1, 2011.

759. Amendment: Section 1B1.10(b) is amended in subdivision (2) by striking "Limitations" and inserting "Limitation"; in subdivision (2)(A) by striking "In General" and inserting "Limitation"; in subdivision (2)(B) by inserting "for Substantial Assistance" after "Exception"; by striking "original"; by inserting "pursuant to a government motion to reflect the defendant's substantial assistance to authorities" after "of sentencing"; and by striking the last sentence as follows:

"However, if the original term of imprisonment constituted a non-guideline sentence determined pursuant to 18 U.S.C. § 3553(a) and United States v. Booker, 543 U.S. 220 (2005), a further reduction generally would not be appropriate.".

Amendment 759   APPENDIX C - VOLUME III   November 1, 2013

Section 1B1.10(c) is amended by striking "and"; and by inserting ", and 750 (parts A and C only)" before the period at the end.

The Commentary to § 1B1.10 captioned "Application Notes" is amended in Note 1(A) in the first sentence by inserting "(i.e., the guideline range that corresponds to the offense level and criminal history category determined pursuant to § 1B1.1(a), which is determined before consideration of any departure provision in the Guidelines Manual or any variance)" before the period; and in Note 1(B)(iii) by striking "original".

The Commentary to § 1B1.10 captioned "Application Notes" is amended in Note 3 in the first paragraph by striking "original" in both places; by striking "shall not" and inserting "may" in both places; by inserting "as provided in subsection (b)(2)(A)," after "Specifically,"; by inserting "no" before "less than the minimum"; by striking "41 to 51" and inserting "70 to 87"; by striking "41" and inserting "70"; by striking "30 to 37" and inserting "51 to 63"; by striking "to a term less than 30 months" and inserting ", but shall not reduce it to a term less than 51 months"; and by striking the second paragraph as follows:

> "If the original term of imprisonment imposed was less than the term of imprisonment provided by the guideline range applicable to the defendant at the time of sentencing, a reduction comparably less than the amended guideline range determined under subsection (b)(1) may be appropriate. For example, in a case in which: (A) the guideline range applicable to the defendant at the time of sentencing was 70 to 87 months; (B) the defendant's original term of imprisonment imposed was 56 months (representing a downward departure of 20 percent below the minimum term of imprisonment provided by the guideline range applicable to the defendant at the time of sentencing); and (C) the amended guideline range determined under subsection (b)(1) is 57 to 71 months, a reduction to a term of imprisonment of 46 months (representing a reduction of approximately 20 percent below the minimum term of imprisonment provided by the amended guideline range determined under subsection (b)(1)) would amount to a comparable reduction and may be appropriate.",

and inserting the following new paragraphs:

> "If the term of imprisonment imposed was outside the guideline range applicable to the defendant at the time of sentencing, the limitation in subsection (b)(2)(A) also applies. Thus, if the term of imprisonment imposed in the example provided above was not a sentence of 70 months (within the guidelines range) but instead was a sentence of 56 months (constituting a downward departure or variance), the court likewise may reduce the defendant's term of imprisonment, but shall not reduce it to a term less than 51 months.
>
> Subsection (b)(2)(B) provides an exception to this limitation, which applies if the term of imprisonment imposed was less than the term of imprisonment provided by the guideline range applicable to the defendant at the time of sentencing pursuant to a government motion to reflect the defendant's substantial assistance to authorities. In such a case, the court may reduce the defendant's term, but the reduction is not limited by subsection (b)(2)(A) to the minimum of the amended guideline range. Instead, as provided in subsection (b)(2)(B), the court may, if appropriate, provide a reduction comparably less than the amended guideline range. Thus, if the term of imprisonment imposed in the example provided above was 56 months pursuant to a government motion to reflect the defendant's substantial assistance to authorities (representing a downward departure of 20 percent below the minimum term of imprisonment provided by the guideline range applicable to the defendant at the time of sentencing), a reduction to a term of imprisonment of 41 months (representing a reduction of approximately 20 percent below the minimum term of imprison-

ment provided by the amended guideline range) would amount to a comparable reduction and may be appropriate.

The provisions authorizing such a government motion are § 5K1.1 (Substantial Assistance to Authorities) (authorizing, upon government motion, a downward departure based on the defendant's substantial assistance); 18 U.S.C. § 3553(e) (authorizing the court, upon government motion, to impose a sentence below a statutory minimum to reflect the defendant's substantial assistance); and Fed. R. Crim. P. 35(b) (authorizing the court, upon government motion, to reduce a sentence to reflect the defendant's substantial assistance).";

and in the fifth paragraph, as redesignated by this amendment, by inserting "See subsection (b)(2)(C)." after "time served.".

The Commentary to § 1B1.10 captioned "Application Notes" is amended by redesignating Note 4 as Note 5 and inserting after Note 3 the following:

> "4. Application to Amendment 750 (Parts A and C Only).—As specified in subsection (c), the parts of Amendment 750 that are covered by this policy statement are Parts A and C only. Part A amended the Drug Quantity Table in § 2D1.1 for crack cocaine and made related revisions to Application Note 10 to § 2D1.1. Part C deleted the cross reference in § 2D2.1(b) under which an offender who possessed more than 5 grams of crack cocaine was sentenced under § 2D1.1.".

The Commentary to § 1B1.10 captioned "Application Notes" is amended by adding at the end the following:

> "6. Use of Policy Statement in Effect on Date of Reduction.—Consistent with subsection (a) of § 1B1.11 (Use of Guidelines Manual in Effect on Date of Sentencing), the court shall use the version of this policy statement that is in effect on the date on which the court reduces the defendant's term of imprisonment as provided by 18 U.S.C. § 3582(c)(2).".

The Commentary to § 1B1.10 captioned "Background" is amended in the second paragraph by adding at the end as the last sentence the following:

> "The Supreme Court has concluded that proceedings under section 3582(c)(2) are not governed by United States v. Booker, 543 U.S. 220 (2005), and this policy statement remains binding on courts in such proceedings. See Dillon v. United States, 130 S. Ct. 2683 (2010).".

Reason for Amendment: This amendment amends § 1B1.10 (Reduction in Term of Imprisonment as a Result of Amended Guideline Range) (Policy Statement) in four ways. First, it expands the listing in § 1B1.10(c) to implement the directive in 28 U.S.C. § 994(u) with respect to guideline amendments that may be considered for retroactive application. Second, it amends § 1B1.10 to change the limitations that apply in cases in which the term of imprisonment was less than the minimum of the applicable guideline range at the time of sentencing. Third, it amends the commentary to § 1B1.10 to address an application issue about what constitutes the "applicable guideline range" for purposes of § 1B1.10. Fourth, it adds an application note to § 1B1.10 to specify that the court shall use the version of § 1B1.10 that is in effect on the date on which the court reduces the defendant's term of imprisonment as provided by 18 U.S.C. § 3582(c)(2).

First, the Commission has determined, under the applicable standards set forth in the

Amendment 759 APPENDIX C - VOLUME III   November 1, 2013

background commentary to § 1B1.10, that Amendment 750 (Parts A and C only) should be included in § 1B1.10(c) as an amendment that may be considered for retroactive application. Part A amended the Drug Quantity Table in § 2D1.1 (Unlawful Manufacturing, Importing, Exporting, or Trafficking (Including Possession with Intent to Commit These Offenses); Attempt or Conspiracy) for crack cocaine and made related revisions to Application Note 10 to § 2D1.1. Part C deleted the cross reference in § 2D2.1(b) under which an offender who possessed more than 5 grams of crack cocaine was sentenced under § 2D1.1.

Under the applicable standards set forth in the background commentary to § 1B1.10, the Commission considers, among other factors, (1) the purpose of the amendment, (2) the magnitude of the change in the guideline range made by the amendment, and (3) the difficulty of applying the amendment retroactively. See § 1B1.10, comment. (backg'd.). Applying those standards to Parts A and C of Amendment 750, the Commission determined that, among other factors:

(1) The purpose of Parts A and C of Amendment 750 was to account for the changes in the statutory penalties made by the Fair Sentencing Act of 2010, Pub. L. 111–220, 124 Stat. 2372, for offenses involving cocaine base ("crack cocaine"). See USSG App. C, Amend. 750 (Reason for Amendment). The Fair Sentencing Act of 2010 did not contain a provision making the statutory changes retroactive. The Act directed the Commission to promulgate guideline amendments implementing the Act. The guideline amendments implementing the Act have the effect of reducing the term of imprisonment recommended in the guidelines for certain defendants, and the Commission has a statutory duty to consider whether the resulting guideline amendments should be made available for retroactive application. See 28 U.S.C. § 994(u) ("If the Commission reduces the term of imprisonment recommended in the guidelines . . . it shall specify in what circumstances and by what amount sentences of prisoners . . . may be reduced."). In carrying out its statutory duty to consider whether to give Amendment 750 retroactive effect, the Commission also considered the purpose of the underlying statutory changes made by the Act. Those statutory changes reflect congressional action consistent with the Commission's long-held position that the then-existing statutory penalty structure for crack cocaine "significantly undermines the various congressional objectives set forth in the Sentencing Reform Act and elsewhere" (see USSG App. C, Amend. 706 (Reason for Amendment)). The Fair Sentencing Act of 2010 specified in its statutory text that its purpose was to "restore fairness to Federal cocaine sentencing" and provide "cocaine sentencing disparity reduction". See 124 Stat. at 2372.

It is important to note that the inclusion of Amendment 750 (Parts A and C) in § 1B1.10(c) only allows the guideline changes to be considered for retroactive application; it does not make any of the statutory changes in the Fair Sentencing Act of 2010 retroactive.

(2) The number of cases potentially involved is substantial, and the magnitude of the change in the guideline range is significant. As indicated in the Commission's analysis of cases potentially eligible for retroactive application of Parts A and C of Amendment 750, approximately 12,000 offenders would be eligible to seek a reduced sentence and the average sentence reduction would be approximately 23 percent.

(3) The administrative burdens of applying Parts A and C of Amendment 750

retroactively are manageable. This determination was informed by testimony at the Commission's June 1, 2011, public hearing on retroactivity and by other public comment received by the Commission on retroactivity. The Commission also considered the administrative burdens that were involved when its 2007 crack cocaine amendments were applied retroactively. See USSG App. C, Amendments 706 and 711 (amending the guidelines applicable to crack cocaine, effective November 1, 2007) and Amendment 713 (expanding the listing in § 1B1.10(c) to include Amendments 706 and 711 as amendments that may be considered for retroactive application, effective March 3, 2008). The Commission received comment and testimony indicating that those burdens were manageable and that motions routinely were decided based on the filings, without the need for a hearing or the presence of the defendant, and did not constitute full resentencings. The Commission determined that applying Parts A and C of Amendment 750 would likewise be manageable, given that, among other things, significantly fewer cases would be involved. As indicated in the Commission's Preliminary Crack Cocaine Retroactivity Report (April 2011 Data) regarding retroactive application of the 2007 crack cocaine amendments, approximately 25,500 offenders have requested a sentence reduction pursuant to retroactive application of the 2007 crack cocaine amendments and approximately 16,500 of those requests have been granted.

In addition, public safety will be considered in every case because § 1B1.10 requires the court, in determining whether and to what extent a reduction in the defendant's term of imprisonment is warranted, to consider the nature and seriousness of the danger to any person or the community that may be posed by such a reduction. See § 1B1.10, comment. (n.1(B)(ii)).

Second, in light of public comment and testimony and recent case law, the amendment amends § 1B1.10 to change the limitations that apply in cases in which the term of imprisonment was less than the minimum of the applicable guideline range at the time of sentencing. Under the amendment, the general limitation in subsection (b)(2)(A) continues to be that the court shall not reduce the defendant's term of imprisonment to a term that is less than the minimum of the amended guideline range. The amendment restricts the exception in subsection (b)(2)(B) to cases involving a government motion to reflect the defendant's substantial assistance to authorities (i.e., under § 5K1.1 (Substantial Assistance to Authorities), 18 U.S.C. § 3553(e), or Fed. R. Crim. P. 35(b)). For those cases, a reduction comparably less than the amended guideline range may be appropriate.

The version of § 1B1.10 currently in effect draws a different distinction for cases in which the term of imprisonment was less than the minimum of the applicable guideline range, one rule for downward departures (stating that "a reduction comparably less than the amended guideline range . . . may be appropriate") and another rule for variances (stating that "a further reduction generally would not be appropriate"). See § 1B1.10(b)(2)(B). The Commission has received public comment and testimony indicating that this distinction has been difficult to apply and has prompted litigation. The Commission has determined that, in the specific context of § 1B1.10, a single limitation applicable to both departures and variances furthers the need to avoid unwarranted sentencing disparities and avoids litigation in individual cases. The limitation that prohibits a reduction below the amended guideline range in such cases promotes conformity with the amended guideline range and avoids undue complexity and litigation.

Nonetheless, the Commission has determined that, in a case in which the term of imprisonment was below the guideline range pursuant to a government motion to reflect the defendant's substantial assistance to authorities (e.g., under § 5K1.1), a reduction comparably less than the amended guideline range may be appropriate. Section 5K1.1 implements the directive to the Commission in its organic statute to "assure that the guidelines reflect the general appropriateness of imposing a lower sentence than would otherwise be imposed . . . to take into account a defendant's substantial assistance in the investigation or prosecution of another person who has committed an offense." See 28 U.S.C. § 994(n). For other provisions authorizing such a government motion, see 18 U.S.C. § 3553(e) (authorizing the court, upon government motion, to impose a sentence below a statutory minimum to reflect a defendant's substantial assistance); Fed. R. Crim. P. 35(b) (authorizing the court, upon government motion, to reduce a sentence to reflect a defendant's substantial assistance). The guidelines and the relevant statutes have long recognized that defendants who provide substantial assistance are differently situated than other defendants and should be considered for a sentence below a guideline or statutory minimum even when defendants who are otherwise similar (but did not provide substantial assistance) are subject to a guideline or statutory minimum. Applying this principle when the guideline range has been reduced and made available for retroactive application under section 3582(c)(2) appropriately maintains this distinction and furthers the purposes of sentencing.

Third, the amendment amends the commentary to § 1B1.10 to address an application issue. Circuits have conflicting interpretations about when, if at all, the court applies a departure provision before determining the "applicable guideline range" for purposes of § 1B1.10. The First, Second, and Fourth Circuits have held that, for § 1B1.10 purposes, at least some departures (e.g., departures under § 4A1.3 (Departures Based on Inadequacy of Criminal History Category) (Policy Statement)) are considered before determining the applicable guideline range, while the Sixth, Eighth, and Tenth Circuits have held that "the only applicable guideline range is the one established before any departures". See United States v. Guyton, 636 F.3d 316, 320 (7th Cir. 2011) (collecting and discussing cases; holding that departures under § 5K1.1 are considered after determining the applicable guideline range but declining to address whether departures under § 4A1.3 are considered before or after). Effective November 1, 2010, the Commission amended § 1B1.1 (Application Instructions) to provide a three-step approach in determining the sentence to be imposed. See USSG App. C, Amend. 741 (Reason for Amendment). Under § 1B1.1 as so amended, the court first determines the guideline range and then considers departures. Id. ("As amended, subsection (a) addresses how to apply the provisions in the Guidelines Manual to properly determine the kinds of sentence and the guideline range. Subsection (b) addresses the need to consider the policy statements and commentary to determine whether a departure is warranted."). Consistent with the three-step approach adopted by Amendment 741 and reflected in § 1B1.1, the amendment adopts the approach of the Sixth, Eighth, and Tenth Circuits and amends Application Note 1 to clarify that the applicable guideline range referred to in § 1B1.10 is the guideline range determined pursuant to § 1B1.1(a), which is determined before consideration of any departure provision in the Guidelines Manual or any variance.

Fourth, the amendment adds an application note to § 1B1.10 to specify that, consistent with subsection (a) of § 1B1.11 (Use of Guidelines Manual in Effect on Date of Sentencing), the court shall use the version of § 1B1.10 that is in effect on the date on which the court reduces the defendant's term of imprisonment as provided by 18 U.S.C. § 3582(c)(2).

Finally, the amendment amends the commentary to § 1B1.10 to refer to Dillon v. United States, 130 S. Ct. 2683 (2010). In Dillon, the Supreme Court concluded that proceedings under section 3582(c)(2) are not governed by United States v. Booker, 543 U.S. 220 (2005), and that § 1B1.10 remains binding on courts in such proceedings.

Effective Date: The effective date of this amendment is November 1, 2011.

760. Amendment: The Commentary to § 2D1.1 captioned "Application Notes" is amended in Note 3(A) by striking ", and 2D2.1(b)(1)"; and inserting "and" before "2D1.12(c)(1)".

The Commentary to § 2J1.1 captioned "Application Notes" is amended in each of Note 2 and Note 3 by striking "§ 2B1.1(b)(8)(C)" and inserting "§ 2B1.1(b)(9)(C)".

The Commentary to § 2K2.4 captioned "Application Notes" is amended in Note 4 in the third paragraph by striking "§ 2K2.1(b)(6)" and inserting "§ 2K2.1(b)(6)(B)" in both places.

The Commentary following § 3D1.5 captioned "Illustrations of the Operation of the Multiple-Count Rules" is amended in Note 3 by striking "§ 2B1.1(b)(9)" and inserting "§ 2B1.1(b)(10)".

Reason for Amendment: This amendment makes certain technical and conforming changes in connection with certain recently promulgated amendments. See 76 Fed. Reg. 24960 (May 3, 2011). The technical and conforming changes are as follows:

(1) Amendment 749 renumbered specific offense characteristics in § 2B1.1 (Theft, Property Destruction, and Fraud), including the specific offense characteristic for violation of a prior, specific order (from (b)(8)(C) to (b)(9)(C)) and the specific offense characteristic for sophisticated means (from (b)(9) to (b)(10)). To reflect these renumberings, conforming changes are made to Application Notes 2 and 3 to § 2J1.1 (Contempt) and to the Commentary following § 3D1.5 (Determining the Total Punishment).

(2) Amendment 750 amended § 2D2.1 (Unlawful Possession; Attempt or Conspiracy) to delete a cross-reference at subsection (b)(1). To reflect this deletion, a conforming change is made to Application Note 3(A) to § 2D1.1 (Unlawful Manufacturing, Importing, Exporting, or Trafficking (Including Possession with Intent to Commit These Offenses); Attempt or Conspiracy).

(3) Amendment 753 renumbered the specific offense characteristic in § 2K2.1 (Unlawful Receipt, Possession, or Transportation of Firearms or Ammunition; Prohibited Transactions Involving Firearms or Ammunition) for using or possessing a firearm in connection with another felony offense from (b)(6) to (b)(6)(B). To reflect this renumbering, conforming changes are made to Application Note 4 to § 2K2.4 (Use of Firearm, Armor-Piercing Ammunition, or Explosive During or in Relation to Certain Crimes).

Effective Date: The effective date of this amendment is November 1, 2011.

UNITED STATES SENTENCING COMMISSION
GUIDELINES MANUAL
Supplement to Appendix C

PATTI B. SARIS
Chair

KETANJI B. JACKSON
Vice Chair

RICARDO H. HINOJOSA
Commissioner

DABNEY L. FRIEDRICH
Commissioner

JONATHAN J. WROBLEWSKI
Commissioner, Ex-officio

ISAAC FULWOOD, JR.
Commissioner, Ex-officio

This document contains amendments to the *Guidelines Manual* effective November 1, 2012, and November 1, 2013. For amendments effective November 1, 2004; October 24, 2005; November 1, 2005; March 27, 2006; September 12, 2006; November 1, 2006; May 1, 2007; November 1, 2007; February 6, 2008; March 3, 2008; May 1, 2008; November 1, 2008; November 1, 2009; November 1, 2010; and November 1, 2011, *see* Appendix C, Volume III. For amendments effective November 1, 1998; May 1, 2000; November 1, 2000; December 16, 2000; May 1, 2001; November 1, 2001; November 1, 2002; January 25, 2003; April 30, 2003; October 27, 2003; November 1, 2003; and November 5, 2003, *see* Appendix C, Volume II. For amendments effective November 1,1997, and earlier, *see* Appendix C, Volume I.

November 1, 2013   SUPPLEMENT TO APPENDIX C   **Amendment 761**

SUPPLEMENT TO APPENDIX C - AMENDMENTS TO THE GUIDELINES MANUAL

This supplement to Appendix C presents amendments to the guidelines, policy statements, and official commentary effective November 1, 2012, and November 1, 2013.

For amendments to the guidelines, policy statements, and official commentary effective November 1, 2004; October 24, 2005; November 1, 2005; March 27, 2006; September 12, 2006; November 1, 2006; May 1, 2007; November 1, 2007; February 6, 2008; March 3, 2008; May 1, 2008; November 1, 2008; November 1, 2009; November 1, 2010; and November 1, 2011, see Appendix C, Volume III. For amendments effective November 1, 1998; May 1, 2000; November 1, 2000; December 16, 2000; May 1, 2001; November 1, 2001; November 1, 2002; January 25, 2003; April 30, 2003; October 27, 2003; November 1, 2003; and November 5, 2003, see Appendix C, Volume II. For amendments effective November 1, 1997, and earlier, see Appendix C, Volume I.

The format under which the amendments are presented in Appendix C, including this supplement, is designed to facilitate a comparison between previously existing and amended provisions, in the event it becomes necessary to reference the former guideline, policy statement, or commentary language.

AMENDMENTS

761. Amendment: The Commentary to § 2B1.1 captioned "Application Notes" is amended in Note 3(E) by adding at the end the following:

"(iii) Notwithstanding clause (ii), in the case of a fraud involving a mortgage loan, if the collateral has not been disposed of by the time of sentencing, use the fair market value of the collateral as of the date on which the guilt of the defendant has been established, whether by guilty plea, trial, or plea of nolo contendere.

In such a case, there shall be a rebuttable presumption that the most recent tax assessment value of the collateral is a reasonable estimate of the fair market value. In determining whether the most recent tax assessment value is a reasonable estimate of the fair market value, the court may consider, among other factors, the recency of the tax assessment and the extent to which the jurisdiction's tax assessment practices reflect factors not relevant to fair market value.";

in Note 3(F) by adding at the end the following:

"(ix) Fraudulent Inflation or Deflation in Value of Securities or Commodities.—In a case involving the fraudulent inflation or deflation in the value of a publicly traded security or commodity, there shall be a rebuttable presumption that the actual loss attributable to the change in value of the security or commodity is the amount determined by—

(I) calculating the difference between the average price of the security or commodity during the period that the fraud occurred and the average price of the security or commodity during the 90-day period after the fraud was disclosed to the market, and

(II) multiplying the difference in average price by the number of shares outstanding.

Amendment 761   SUPPLEMENT TO APPENDIX C   November 1, 2013

> In determining whether the amount so determined is a reasonable estimate of the actual loss attributable to the change in value of the security or commodity, the court may consider, among other factors, the extent to which the amount so determined includes significant changes in value not resulting from the offense (e.g., changes caused by external market forces, such as changed economic circumstances, changed investor expectations, and new industry-specific or firm-specific facts, conditions, or events).";

in Note 12(A) by adding at the end the following:

> "(v) One or more of the criteria in clauses (i) through (iv) was likely to result from the offense but did not result from the offense because of federal government intervention, such as a 'bailout'.";

in Note 12(B)(ii) by adding at the end the following:

> "(VII) One or more of the criteria in subclauses (I) through (VI) was likely to result from the offense but did not result from the offense because of federal government intervention, such as a 'bailout'.";

in Note 19(A)(iv) by inserting before the period at the end the following: ", such as a risk of a significant disruption of a national financial market";

and in Note 19(C) by adding after the first paragraph the following new paragraph:

> "For example, a securities fraud involving a fraudulent statement made publicly to the market may produce an aggregate loss amount that is substantial but diffuse, with relatively small loss amounts suffered by a relatively large number of victims. In such a case, the loss table in subsection (b)(1) and the victims table in subsection (b)(2) may combine to produce an offense level that substantially overstates the seriousness of the offense. If so, a downward departure may be warranted.".

Section 2B1.4(b) is amended by striking "Characteristic" and inserting "Characteristics"; and by adding at the end the following:

> "(2) If the offense involved an organized scheme to engage in insider trading and the offense level determined above is less than level 14, increase to level 14.".

The Commentary to § 2B1.4 captioned "Application Note" is amended in the caption by striking "Note" and inserting "Notes"; by redesignating Note 1 as Note 2 and inserting before Note 2 (as so redesignated) the following:

> "1. Application of Subsection (b)(2).—For purposes of subsection (b)(2), an 'organized scheme to engage in insider trading' means a scheme to engage in insider trading that involves considered, calculated, systematic, or repeated efforts to obtain and trade on inside information, as distinguished from fortuitous or opportunistic instances of insider trading.
>
> The following is a non-exhaustive list of factors that the court may consider in determining whether the offense involved an organized scheme to engage in insider trading:
>
> (A) the number of transactions;
>
> (B) the dollar value of the transactions;

(C) the number of securities involved;

(D) the duration of the offense;

(E) the number of participants in the scheme (although such a scheme may exist even in the absence of more than one participant);

(F) the efforts undertaken to obtain material, nonpublic information;

(G) the number of instances in which material, nonpublic information was obtained; and

(H) the efforts undertaken to conceal the offense.";

in Note 2 (as so redesignated) by striking "only"; and by adding at the end the following new paragraph:

"Furthermore, § 3B1.3 should be applied if the defendant's employment in a position that involved regular participation or professional assistance in creating, issuing, buying, selling, or trading securities or commodities was used to facilitate significantly the commission or concealment of the offense. It would apply, for example, to a hedge fund professional who regularly participates in securities transactions or to a lawyer who regularly provides professional assistance in securities transactions, if the defendant's employment in such a position was used to facilitate significantly the commission or concealment of the offense. It ordinarily would not apply to a position such as a clerical worker in an investment firm, because such a position ordinarily does not involve special skill. See § 3B1.3, comment. (n. 4).".

The Commentary to § 2B1.4 captioned "Background" is amended by adding at the end the following new paragraph:

" Subsection (b)(2) implements the directive to the Commission in section 1079A(a)(1)(A) of Public Law 111–203.".

Reason for Amendment: This amendment responds to the two directives to the Commission in the Dodd-Frank Wall Street Reform and Consumer Protection Act, Pub. L. 111–203 (the "Act"). The first directive relates to securities fraud and similar offenses, and the second directive relates to mortgage fraud and financial institution fraud.

Securities Fraud and Similar Offenses

Section 1079A(a)(1)(A) of the Act directs the Commission to "review and, if appropriate, amend" the guidelines and policy statements applicable to "persons convicted of offenses relating to securities fraud or any other similar provision of law, in order to reflect the intent of Congress that penalties for the offenses under the guidelines and policy statements appropriately account for the potential and actual harm to the public and the financial markets from the offenses." Section 1079A(a)(1)(B) provides that in promulgating any such amendment the Commission shall—

(i) ensure that the guidelines and policy statements, particularly section 2B1.1(b)(14) and section 2B1.1(b)(17) (and any successors thereto), reflect—

(I) the serious nature of the offenses described in subparagraph (A);

(II) the need for an effective deterrent and appropriate punishment to prevent the offenses; and

		(III)	the effectiveness of incarceration in furthering the objectives described in subclauses (I) and (II);
	(ii)		consider the extent to which the guidelines appropriately account for the potential and actual harm to the public and the financial markets resulting from the offenses;
	(iii)		ensure reasonable consistency with other relevant directives and guidelines and Federal statutes;
	(iv)		make any necessary conforming changes to guidelines; and
	(v)		ensure that the guidelines adequately meet the purposes of sentencing, as set forth in section 3553(a)(2) of title 18, United States Code.

The amendment responds to this directive in two ways. First, the amendment amends the fraud guideline, § 2B1.1 (Theft, Property Destruction, and Fraud), to provide a special rule for determining actual loss in cases involving the fraudulent inflation or deflation in the value of a publicly traded security or commodity. Case law and comments received by the Commission indicate that determinations of loss in cases involving securities fraud and similar offenses are complex and that a variety of different methods are in use, possibly resulting in unwarranted sentencing disparities.

The amendment amends § 2B1.1 to provide a special rule regarding how to calculate actual loss in these types of cases. Specifically, the amendment creates a new Application Note 3(F)(ix) which establishes a rebuttable presumption that "the actual loss attributable to the change in value of the security or commodity is the amount determined by (I) calculating the difference between the average price of the security or commodity during the period that the fraud occurred and the average price of the security or commodity during the 90-day period after the fraud was disclosed to the market, and (II) multiplying the difference in average price by the number of shares outstanding." The special rule further provides that, "[i]n determining whether the amount so determined is a reasonable estimate of the actual loss attributable to the change in value of the security or commodity, the court may consider, among other factors, the extent to which the amount so determined includes significant changes in value not resulting from the offense (e.g., changes caused by external market forces, such as changed economic circumstances, changed investor expectations, and new industry-specific or firm-specific facts, conditions, or events)."

The special rule is based upon what is sometimes referred to as the "modified rescissory method" and should ordinarily provide a "reasonable estimate of the loss" as required by Application Note 3(C). This special rule is intended to provide courts a workable and consistent formula for calculating loss that "resulted from the offense." See § 2B1.1, comment. (n.3(A)(i)). By averaging the stock price during the period in which the fraud occurred and a set 90-day period after the fraud was discovered, the special rule reduces the impact on the loss calculation of factors other than the fraud, such as overall growth or decline in the price of the stock. See, e.g., United States v. Bakhit, 218 F. Supp. 2d 1232 (C.D. Cal. 2002); United States v. Snyder, 291 F.3d 1291 (11th Cir. 2002); United States v. Brown, 595 F.3d 498 (3d Cir. 2010); see also 15 U.S.C. § 78u-4(e) (statutorily setting forth a similar method for loss calculation in the context of private securities litigation). Furthermore, applying this special rule could "eliminate[ ], or at least reduce[ ], the complexity, uncertainty, and expense inherent in attempting to determine out-of-pocket losses on a case-by-case basis." See United States v. Grabske, 260 F. Supp. 2d. 866, 873-74 (N.D. Cal. 2002).

By applying a rebuttable presumption, however, the amendment also provides sufficient flexibility for a court to consider the extent to which the amount determined under the special rule includes significant changes in value not resulting from the offense (e.g., changes caused by external market forces, such as changed economic circumstances, changed investor expectations, and new industry-specific or firm-specific facts, conditions, or events).

The amendment also responds to the first directive by amending the insider trading guideline, § 2B1.4 (Insider Trading). First, it provides a new specific offense characteristic if the offense involved an "organized scheme to engage in insider trading." In such a case, the new specific offense characteristic provides a minimum offense level of 14. The commentary is also amended to provide factors the court may consider in determining whether the new minimum offense level applies.

The amendment reflects the Commission's view that a defendant who engages in considered, calculated, systematic, or repeated efforts to obtain and trade on inside information (as opposed to fortuitous or opportunistic instances of insider trading) warrants, at minimum, a short but definite period of incarceration. Sentencing data indicate that when a defendant engages in an organized insider trading scheme, the gain from the offense ordinarily triggers an enhancement under § 2B1.4(b)(1) of sufficient magnitude to result in a guideline range that requires a period of imprisonment. The amendment, however, ensures that the guidelines require a period of incarceration even in such a case involving relatively little gain.

The amendment also amends the commentary to § 2B1.4 to provide more guidance on the applicability of § 3B1.3 (Abuse of Position of Trust or Use of Special Skill) in insider trading cases. In particular, the new commentary in Application Note 2 provides that § 3B1.3 should be applied if the defendant's employment in a position that involved regular participation or professional assistance in creating, issuing, buying, selling, or trading securities or commodities was used to facilitate significantly the commission or concealment of the offense. The commentary further provides examples of positions that may qualify for the adjustment, including a hedge fund professional who regularly participates in securities transactions or a lawyer who regularly provides professional assistance in securities transactions. Individuals who occupy such positions possess special knowledge regarding the financial markets and the rules prohibiting insider trading, and generally are viewed as more culpable. See § 3B1.3, comment. (backg'd). The commentary also provides as an example of a position that would not qualify for the adjustment in § 3B1.4 a clerical worker in an investment firm. Such a position ordinarily does not involve special skill and is not generally viewed as more culpable.

<u>Mortgage Fraud and Financial Institution Fraud</u>

Section 1079A(a)(2)(A) of the Act directs the Commission to "review and, if appropriate, amend" the guidelines and policy statements applicable to "persons convicted of fraud offenses relating to financial institutions or federally related mortgage loans and any other similar provisions of law, to reflect the intent of Congress that the penalties for the offenses under the guidelines and policy statements ensure appropriate terms of imprisonment for offenders involved in substantial bank frauds or other frauds relating to financial institutions." Section 1079A(a)(2)(B) of the Act provides that, in promulgating any such amendment, the Commission shall—

  (i) ensure that the guidelines and policy statements reflect—

    (I) the serious nature of the offenses described in subparagraph (A);

Amendment 761 SUPPLEMENT TO APPENDIX C November 1, 2013

(II) the need for an effective deterrent and appropriate punishment to prevent the offenses; and

(III) the effectiveness of incarceration in furthering the objectives described in subclauses (I) and (II);

(ii) consider the extent to which the guidelines appropriately account for the potential and actual harm to the public and the financial markets resulting from the offenses;

(iii) ensure reasonable consistency with other relevant directives and guidelines and Federal statutes;

(iv) make any necessary conforming changes to guidelines; and

(v) ensure that the guidelines adequately meet the purposes of sentencing, as set forth in section 3553(a)(2) of title 18, United States Code.

The amendment responds to this directive in two ways.

First, the amendment adds language to the credits against loss rule, found in Application Note 3(E) of the commentary to § 2B1.1. Application Note 3(E)(i) generally provides that the determination of loss under subsection (b)(1) shall be reduced by the money returned and the fair market value of the property returned and services rendered to the victim before the offense was detected. In the context of a case involving collateral pledged or otherwise provided by the defendant, Application Note 3(E)(ii) provides that the loss to the victim shall be reduced by either "the amount the victim has recovered at the time of sentencing from disposition of the collateral, or if the collateral has not been disposed of by that time, the fair market value of the collateral at the time of sentencing."

The Commission received comment that, in cases involving mortgage fraud where the collateral has not been disposed of by the time of sentencing, the fair market value of the collateral may be difficult to determine and may require frequent updating, especially in cases involving multiple properties. The comments further indicate that the lack of a uniform process may result in unwarranted sentencing disparities.

The amendment responds to these concerns by establishing a new Application Note 3(E)(iii) applicable to fraud cases involving a mortgage loan where the underlying collateral has not been disposed of by the time of sentencing. In such a case, new Application Note 3(E)(iii) makes two changes to the calculation of credits against loss. First, the note changes the date on which the fair market value of the collateral is determined, from the time of sentencing to the date on which the guilt of the defendant has been established. This change is intended to avoid the need to reassess the fair market value of such collateral on multiple occasions up to the date of sentencing. Second, it establishes a rebuttable presumption that the most recent tax assessment value of the collateral is a reasonable estimate of the fair market value. In determining whether the tax assessment is a reasonable estimate of fair market value, the note further provides that the court may consider the recency of the tax assessment and the extent to which the jurisdiction's tax assessment practices reflect factors not relevant to fair market value, among other factors.

By structuring the special rule in this manner, the amendment addresses the need to provide a uniform practicable method for determining fair market value of undisposed collateral while providing sufficient flexibility for courts to address differences among jurisdictions regarding how closely the most recent tax assessment correlates to fair market value. The Commission heard concerns, for example, that, in some jurisdictions, the most recent tax assessment may be outdated or based upon factors, such as the age or status of the homeowner, that have no correlation to fair market value.

The amendment also responds to the second directive by amending the commentary regarding the application of § 2B1.1(b)(15)(B), which provides an enhancement of 4 levels if the offense involved specific types of financial harms (e.g., jeopardizing a financial institution or organization). This commentary, contained in Application Note 12 to § 2B1.1, provides a non-exhaustive list of factors the court shall consider in determining whether, as a result of the offense, the safety and soundness of a financial institution or an organization that was a publicly traded company or that had more than 1,000 employees was substantially jeopardized. For example, in the context of financial institutions, the court shall consider whether the financial institution became insolvent, was forced to reduce benefits to pensioners or insureds, was unable on demand to refund fully any deposit, payment, or investment, or was so depleted of its assets as to be forced to merge with another institution. Similarly, in the context of a covered organization, the court shall consider whether the organization became insolvent or suffered a substantial reduction in the value of its assets, filed for bankruptcy, suffered a substantial reduction in the value of its equity securities or its employee retirement accounts, or substantially reduced its workforce or employee pension benefits.

The amendment amends Application Note 12 to add as a new consideration whether one of the listed harms was likely to result from the offense, but did not result from the offense because of federal government intervention, such as a "bailout." This amendment reflects the Commission's intent that § 2B1.1(b)(15)(B) account for the risk of harm from the defendant's conduct and its view that a defendant should not avoid the application of the enhancement because the harm that was otherwise likely to result from the offense conduct did not occur because of fortuitous federal government intervention.

Departure Provisions

Finally, the amendment also responds to the Act's directives by amending the departure provisions in § 2B1.1 to provide two examples of cases in which a departure may be warranted.

First, the amendment amends Application Note 19(A)(iv), which provides that an upward departure may be warranted if the offense created a risk of substantial loss beyond the loss determined for purposes of subsection (b)(1). The amendment adds "risk of a significant disruption of a national financial market" as an example of such a risk. This part of the amendment responds to the requirement in the Act to consider whether the guidelines applicable to the offenses covered by the directives appropriately "account for the potential and actual harm to the public and the financial markets[.]"

The amendment also amends Application Note 19(C), which provides that a downward departure may be warranted if the offense level substantially overstates the seriousness of the offense, by adding an example of a case in which such a departure may be appropriate. The example provides that "a securities fraud involving a fraudulent statement made publicly to the market may produce an aggregate loss amount that is substantial but diffuse, with relatively small loss amounts suffered by a relatively large number of victims," and that, "in such a case, the loss table in subsection (b)(1) and the victims table in subsection (b)(2) may combine to produce an offense level that substantially overstates the seriousness of the offense." This part of the amendment responds to concerns raised in comment and case law that the cumulative impact of the loss table and the victims table may overstate the seriousness of the offense in certain cases.

Effective Date: The effective date of this amendment is November 1, 2012.

Amendment 762   SUPPLEMENT TO APPENDIX C   November 1, 2013

762. Amendment: The Commentary to § 2D1.1 captioned "Application Notes" is amended in Note 10(D) in the subdivision captioned "Cocaine and Other Schedule I and II Stimulants (and their immediate precursors)" by inserting after the entry relating to N-N-Dimethylamphetamine the following new entry:

    "1 gm of N-Benzylpiperazine =   100 gm of marihuana".

Reason for Amendment: This amendment responds to concerns raised by the Second Circuit Court of Appeals and others regarding the sentencing of offenders convicted of offenses involving BZP (N-Benzylpiperazine), which is a Schedule I stimulant. See United States v. Figueroa, 647 F.3d 466 (2d Cir. 2011). The amendment establishes a marijuana equivalency for BZP offenses in the Drug Equivalency Table provided in Application Note 10(D) in § 2D1.1 (Unlawful Manufacturing, Importing, Exporting, or Trafficking (Including Possession with Intent to Commit These Offenses); Attempt or Conspiracy). The marijuana equivalency established by the amendment provides that 1 gram of BZP equals 100 grams of marijuana.

Prior to the amendment, the Drug Equivalency Table did not include a marijuana equivalency for BZP. As a result, in offenses involving BZP, the court determined the base offense level using the marijuana equivalency of "the most closely related controlled substance" referenced in § 2D1.1. See § 2D1.1, comment. (n. 5). In determining the most closely related controlled substance, the commentary directs the court to consider (1) whether the controlled substance not referenced in § 2D1.1 has a chemical structure that is substantially similar to a controlled substance that is referenced in § 2D1.1, (2) whether the controlled substance not referenced in § 2D1.1 has a stimulant, depressant, or hallucinogenic effect similar to a controlled substance referenced in the guideline, and (3) whether a lesser or greater quantity of the controlled substance not referenced in § 2D1.1 is needed to produce a substantially similar effect as a controlled substance that is referenced in § 2D1.1.

In applying these factors, courts have reached different conclusions regarding which controlled substance referenced in § 2D1.1 is most closely related to BZP and have therefore used different marijuana equivalencies in sentencing BZP offenders. The Commission's review of case law and sentencing data indicate that some district courts have found that the controlled substance most closely related to BZP is amphetamine and used the marijuana equivalency for amphetamine, see United States v. Major, 801 F. Supp. 2d 511, 514 (E.D. Va. 2011) (using the marijuana equivalency for amphetamine at full potency), while other district courts have found that the controlled substance most related to BZP is MDMA, but at varying potencies. See United States v. Bennett, 659 F.3d 711, 715-16 (8th Cir. 2011) (affirming a district court's use of the marijuana equivalency for MDMA at full potency); United States v. Rose, 722 F. Supp. 2d 1286, 1289 (M.D. Ala. 2010) (concluding that BZP is most closely related to MDMA, but imposing a variance to reflect BZP's reduced potency compared to MDMA). The different findings of which controlled substance is the most closely related to BZP, and the application of different potencies of those controlled substances, have resulted in courts imposing vastly different sentence lengths for the same conduct.

The Commission reviewed scientific literature and received expert testimony and comment relating to BZP and concluded that BZP is a stimulant with pharmacologic properties similar to that of amphetamine, but is only one-tenth to one-twentieth as potent as amphetamine, depending on the particular user's history of drug abuse. Accordingly, in order to promote uniformity in sentencing BZP offenders and to reflect the best available scientific evidence, the amendment establishes a marijuana equivalency of 1 gram of BZP equals 100 grams of marijuana. This corresponds to one-twentieth of the marijuana

November 1, 2013 SUPPLEMENT TO APPENDIX C **Amendment 763**

equivalency for amphetamine, which is 1 gram of amphetamine equals 2 kilograms (or 2,000 grams) of marijuana.

Effective Date: The effective date of this amendment is November 1, 2012.

763. **Amendment:** Section 2D1.11 is amended in subsection (b) by adding at the end the following:

> "(6) If the defendant meets the criteria set forth in subdivisions (1)-(5) of subsection (a) of § 5C1.2 (Limitation on Applicability of Statutory Minimum Sentences in Certain Cases), decrease by 2 levels.".

The Commentary to 2D1.11 captioned "Application Notes" is amended by adding at the end the following:

> "9. Applicability of Subsection (b)(6).—The applicability of subsection (b)(6) shall be determined without regard to the offense of conviction. If subsection (b)(6) applies, § 5C1.2(b) does not apply. See § 5C1.2(b)(2) (requiring a minimum offense level of level 17 if the 'statutorily required minimum sentence is at least five years').".

Reason for Amendment: This amendment adds a new specific offense characteristic at subsection (b)(6) of § 2D1.11 (Unlawfully Distributing, Importing, Exporting or Possessing a Listed Chemical; Attempt or Conspiracy) that provides a 2-level decrease if the defendant meets the criteria set forth in subdivisions (1)–(5) of subsection (a) of § 5C1.2 (Limitation on Applicability of Statutory Minimum Sentences in Certain Cases) (commonly referred to as the "safety valve" criteria). The new specific offense characteristic in § 2D1.11 parallels the existing 2-level decrease at subsection (b)(16) of § 2D1.1 (Unlawful Manufacturing, Importing, Exporting, or Trafficking (Including Possession with Intent to Commit These Offenses); Attempt or Conspiracy).

The Commission in 1995 created the 2-level reduction in § 2D1.1 for offenders who meet the safety valve criteria in response to a directive in section 80001 of the Violent Crime Control and Law Enforcement Act of 1994, Pub. L. No. 103–322. Section 80001 provided an exception to otherwise applicable statutory minimum sentences for defendants convicted of specified drug offenses and who meet the criteria specified in 18 U.S.C. § 3553(f)(1)–(5), and directed the Commission to promulgate guidelines to carry out these purposes. The reduction in § 2D1.1 initially was limited to defendants whose offense level was level 26 or greater, see USSG App. C, Amendment 515 (effective November 1, 1995), but was subsequently expanded to apply to offenders with an offense level lower than level 26 to address proportionality concerns. See USSG App. C, Amendment 624 (effective November 1, 2001). Specifically, the Commission determined that limiting the applicability of the reduction to defendants with an offense level of level 26 or greater "is inconsistent with the general principles underlying the two-level reduction . . . to provide lesser punishment for first time, nonviolent offenders." Id.

For similar reasons of proportionality, this amendment expands application of the 2-level reduction to offenses involving list I and list II chemicals sentenced under § 2D1.11. List I chemicals are important to the manufacture of a controlled substance and usually become part of the final product, while list II chemicals are generally used as solvents, catalysts, and reagents. See USSG § 2D1.11, comment. (backg'd.). Section 2D1.11 is generally structured to provide base offense levels that are tied to, but less severe than, the base offense levels in § 2D1.1 for offenses involving the final product. The Commission determined that adding the 2-level reduction for meeting the safety valve criteria in § 2D1.11

Amendment 763 SUPPLEMENT TO APPENDIX C November 1, 2013

would promote the proportionality the Commission has intended to achieve between §§ 2D1.1 and 2D1.11.

The amendment also adds new commentary relating to the "safety valve" reduction in § 2D1.11 that is consistent with the commentary relating to the "safety valve" reduction in § 2D1.1. See USSG § 2D1.1, comment. (n. 21). The commentary makes clear that the new 2-level reduction in § 2D1.11 applies regardless of the offense of conviction, and that the minimum offense level of 17 in subsection (b) of § 5C1.2 (Limitation on Applicability of Statutory Minimum Sentences in Certain Cases) does not apply. Section 5C1.2(b) provides for an offense level not less than level 17 for defendants who meet the criteria of subdivisions (1)–(5) of section (a) in § 5C1.2 and for whom the statutorily required minimum sentence is at least 5 years. See USSG App. C, Amendment 624 (effective November 1, 2001). Since none of the offenses referenced to § 2D1.11 carries a statutory mandatory minimum, the minimum offense level of 17 at § 5C1.2(b) does not affect application of the new 2-level reduction in § 2D1.11.

Effective Date: The effective date of this amendment is November 1, 2012.

764. **Amendment:** The Commentary to § 2L1.2 captioned "Application Notes" is amended in Note 1(B)(vii) by inserting before the period at the end the following: ", but only if the revocation occurred before the defendant was deported or unlawfully remained in the United States".

Reason for Amendment: This amendment responds to a circuit conflict over the application of the enhancements found at § 2L1.2(b)(1)(A) and (B) to a defendant who was sentenced on two or more occasions for the same drug trafficking conviction (e.g., because of a revocation of probation, parole, or supervised release), such that there was a sentence imposed before the defendant's deportation, then an additional sentence imposed after the deportation. The amendment resolves the conflict by amending the definition of "sentence imposed" in Application Note 1(B)(vii) to § 2L1.2 (Unlawfully Entering or Remaining in the United States) to state that the length of the sentence imposed includes terms of imprisonment given upon revocation of probation, parole, or supervised release, but "only if the revocation occurred before the defendant was deported or unlawfully remained in the United States."

Section 2L1.2(b)(1) generally reflects the Commission's determination that both the seriousness and the timing of the prior offense for which the defendant was deported are relevant to assessing the defendant's culpability for the illegal reentry offense. A defendant who was deported after a conviction for a felony drug trafficking offense receives an enhancement under either prong (A) or (B) of subsection (b)(1), depending on the length of the sentence imposed. If the sentence imposed was more than 13 months, the defendant receives a 16-level enhancement to the base offense level under prong (A). If the sentence imposed was 13 months or less, the defendant receives a 12-level enhancement under prong (B). However, for defendants whose prior convictions are remote in time and thus do not receive criminal history points, these enhancements are reduced to 12 levels and 8 levels, respectively.

The majority of circuits that have considered the meaning of "sentence imposed" in this context have held that the later, additional sentence imposed after deportation does not lengthen the sentence imposed for purposes of the subsection (b)(1) enhancement. See United States v. Bustillos-Pena, 612 F.3d 863 (5th Cir. 2010); United States v. Lopez, 634 F.3d 948 (7th Cir. 2011); United States v. Rosales-Garcia, 667 F.3d 1348 (10th Cir. 2012); United States v. Guzman-Bera, 216 F.3d 1019 (11th Cir. 2000). Under the majority approach, if the sentence imposed was 13 months or less before the defendant was deported, and was only increased to more than 13 months after the deportation, the defendant is not subject to the enhancement in prong (A) because the "sentence imposed" includes only the sentence imposed before the deportation. Under this approach, such a defendant receives the enhancement in prong (B) instead.

The Second Circuit has reached the contrary conclusion, holding that defendants who had their sentences increased to more than 13 months upon revocation after deportation are subject to the enhancement in prong (A) because the "sentence imposed" includes the additional revocation sentence imposed after deportation. See United States v. Compres-Paulino, 393 F.3d 116 (2d Cir. 2004).

The amendment adopts the approach taken by the majority of circuits, with the result that the term of imprisonment imposed upon revocation counts toward the calculation of the offense level in § 2L1.2 only if it was imposed before the defendant was deported or unlawfully remained in the United States. According to public comment and testimony received by the Commission, and as courts have observed, the circumstances under which persons are found present in this country and have their probation, parole, or supervised release revoked for a prior offense vary widely. See Bustillos-Pena, 612 F.3d at 867-68 (describing differences among revocation proceedings). In some jurisdictions, the revocation is typically based on the offender's illegal return, while in others, the revocation is typically based on the offender's committing an additional crime. Furthermore, in some cases revocation proceedings commonly occur before the offender is sentenced on the illegal reentry offense, while in other cases the revocation occurs after the federal sentencing. See Rosales-Garcia, 667 F.3d at 1354 (observing that considering post-deportation revocation sentences could result in disparities based on the "happenstance" of whether that revocation occurred before or after the prosecution for the illegal reentry offense). Therefore, assessing the seriousness of the prior crime based on the sentence imposed before deportation should result in more consistent application of the enhancements in § 2L1.2(b)(1)(A) and (B) and promote uniformity in sentencing.

Effective Date: The effective date of this amendment is November 1, 2012.

765. **Amendment:** Section 2L2.2 is amended in subsection (b) by adding at the end the following:

>"(4) (Apply the Greater):
>
>>(A) If the defendant committed any part of the instant offense to conceal the defendant's membership in, or authority over, a military, paramilitary, or police organization that was involved in a serious human rights offense during the period in which the defendant was such a member or had such authority, increase by 2 levels. If the resulting offense level is less than level 13, increase to level 13.
>
>>(B) If the defendant committed any part of the instant offense to conceal the defendant's participation in (i) the offense of incitement to genocide, increase by 6 levels; or (ii) any other serious human rights offense, increase by 10 levels. If clause (ii) applies and the resulting offense level is less than level 25, increase to level 25.".

The Commentary to 2L2.2 captioned "Application Notes" is amended by redesignating Notes 4 and 5 as Notes 5 and 6, respectively; and by inserting after Note 3 the following:

>"4. <u>Application of Subsection (b)(4)</u>.—For purposes of subsection (b)(4):

'Serious human rights offense' means (A) violations of federal criminal laws relating to genocide, torture, war crimes, and the use or recruitment of child soldiers under sections 1091, 2340, 2340A, 2441, and 2442 of title 18, United States Code, see 28 U.S.C. § 509B(e); and (B) conduct that would have been a violation of any such law if the offense had occurred within the jurisdiction of the United States or if the defendant or the victim had been a national of the United States.

'The offense of incitement to genocide' means (A) violations of 18 U.S.C. § 1091(c); and (B) conduct that would have been a violation of such section if the offense had occurred within the jurisdiction of the United States or if the defendant or the victim had been a national of the United States.".

Chapter Three, Part A is amended by adding at the end the following new guideline and accompanying commentary:

"§ 3A1.5.   Serious Human Rights Offense

If the defendant was convicted of a serious human rights offense, increase the offense level as follows:

(a) If the defendant was convicted of an offense under 18 U.S.C. § 1091(c), increase by 2 levels.

(b) If the defendant was convicted of any other serious human rights offense, increase by 4 levels. If (1) death resulted, and (2) the resulting offense level is less than level 37, increase to level 37.

Commentary

Application Notes:

1. Definition.—For purposes of this guideline, 'serious human rights offense' means violations of federal criminal laws relating to genocide, torture, war crimes, and the use or recruitment of child soldiers under sections 1091, 2340, 2340A, 2441, and 2442 of title 18, United States Code. See 28 U.S.C. § 509B(e).

2. Application of Minimum Offense Level in Subsection (b).—The minimum offense level in subsection (b) is cumulative with any other provision in the guidelines. For example, if death resulted and this factor was specifically incorporated into the Chapter Two offense guideline, the minimum offense level in subsection (b) may also apply.

Background: This guideline covers a range of conduct considered to be serious human rights offenses, including genocide, war crimes, torture, and the recruitment or use of child soldiers. See generally 28 U.S.C. § 509B(e).

Serious human rights offenses generally have a statutory maximum term of imprisonment of 20 years, but if death resulted, a higher statutory maximum term of imprisonment of any term of years or life applies. See 18 U.S.C. §§ 1091(b), 2340A(a), 2442(b). For the offense of war crimes, a statutory maximum term of imprisonment of any term of years or life always applies. See 18 U.S.C. § 2441(a). For the offense of incitement to genocide, the statutory maximum term of imprisonment is five years. See 18 U.S.C. § 1091(c).".

Appendix A (Statutory Index) is amended by inserting after the line referenced to 18 U.S.C. § 2425 the following:

"18 U.S.C. § 2441   2X5.1".

Reason for Amendment: This amendment results from the Commission's multi-year review to ensure that the guidelines provide appropriate guidelines penalties for cases involving human rights violations. This amendment addresses human rights violators in two areas: defendants who are convicted of a human rights offense, and defendants who are convicted of immigration or naturalization fraud to conceal the defendant's involvement, or possible involvement, in a human rights offense.

Serious Human Rights Offenses

First, the amendment addresses defendants whose instant offense of conviction is a "serious human rights offense." In the Human Rights Enforcement Act of 2009, Pub. L. 111-122 (Dec. 22, 2009), Congress defined "serious human rights offenses" as "violations of Federal criminal laws relating to genocide, torture, war crimes, and the use or recruitment of child soldiers under sections 1091, 2340, 2340A, 2441, and 2442 of title 18, United States Code." In that legislation, Congress authorized a new section within the Department of Justice "with responsibility for the enforcement of laws against suspected participants in [such] offenses." That section was established the following year, when the Human Rights and Special Prosecutions Section was created in the Justice Department's Criminal Division. Serious human rights offenses generally have a statutory maximum term of imprisonment of 20 years, but if death resulted, a higher statutory maximum term of imprisonment of any term of years or life applies. See 18 U.S.C. §§ 1091(b), 2340A(a), 2442(b). For the offense of war crimes, a statutory maximum term of imprisonment of any term of years or life always applies. See 18 U.S.C. § 2441(a). For the offense of incitement to genocide, the statutory maximum term of imprisonment is five years. See 18 U.S.C. § 1091(c).

Serious human rights offenses can be committed in a variety of ways, including, for example, assault, kidnapping, and murder. As a result, the guidelines generally have addressed these offenses by referencing them to a number of different Chapter Two offense guidelines, such as §§ 2A1.1 (First Degree Murder), 2A1.2 (Second Degree Murder), 2A2.1 (Assault with Intent to Commit Murder; Attempted Murder), 2A2.2 (Aggravated Assault) and 2A4.1 (Kidnapping, Abduction, Unlawful Restraint). In addition, certain of these Chapter Two offense guidelines use as a base offense level the offense level from another guideline applicable to the underlying conduct (e.g., § 2H1.1 (Offenses Involving Individual Rights), which is the guideline to which genocide offenses are referenced). The offense of committing a war crime in violation of 18 U.S.C. § 2441, however, has not been referenced to any guideline prior to this amendment. The amendment amends Appendix A (Statutory Index) to reference these offenses to § 2X5.1 (Other Felony Offenses). Section 2X5.1 addresses the variety of ways in which a war crimes offense may be committed by generally directing the court to apply the most analogous offense guideline.

The amendment also establishes a new Chapter Three adjustment at § 3A1.5 (Serious Human Rights Offense) if the defendant was convicted of a serious human rights offense. The new guideline provides two tiers of adjustments, corresponding to the differing statutory penalties that apply to such offenses. The adjustment generally provides a 4-level increase if the defendant was convicted of a serious human rights offense, and a minimum offense level of 37 if death resulted. If the defendant was convicted of an offense under 18 U.S.C. § 1091(c) for inciting genocide, however, the adjustment provides a 2-level increase in light of the lesser statutory maximum penalty such offenses carry compared to the other

Amendment 765 SUPPLEMENT TO APPENDIX C November 1, 2013

offenses covered by this adjustment.

The new Chapter Three adjustment accounts for the particularly egregious nature of serious human rights offenses while generally maintaining the proportionality provided by the various Chapter Two guidelines that cover such offenses.

Immigration Fraud

Second, the amendment addresses cases in which the offense of conviction is for immigration or naturalization fraud and the defendant committed any part of the instant offense to conceal the defendant's involvement, or possible involvement, in a serious human rights offense. These offenders are sentenced under § 2L2.2 (Fraudulently Acquiring Documents Relating to Naturalization, Citizenship, or Legal Resident Status for Own Use; False Personation or Fraudulent Marriage by Alien to Evade Immigration Law; Fraudulently Acquiring or Improperly Using a United States Passport). The offenders covered by this amendment fall into two categories. In the first category are defendants who concealed their connection to a military, paramilitary, or police organization that was involved in a serious human rights offense. In the second category are defendants who concealed having participated in a serious human rights offense.

The amendment adds a new specific offense characteristic to § 2L2.2 at subsection (b)(4) that contains two subparagraphs. Subparagraph (A) applies if the defendant committed any part of the instant offense to conceal the defendant's membership in, or authority over, a military, paramilitary, or police organization that was involved in a serious human rights offense during the period in which the defendant was such a member or had such authority, and provides a 2-level increase and a minimum offense level of 13. Subparagraph (B) applies if the defendant committed any part of the instant offense to conceal the defendant's participation in a serious human rights offense, and provides a 6-level increase if the offense was incitement to genocide, or a 10-level increase and minimum offense level of 25 if the offense was any other serious human rights offense. The amendment also adds an application note defining the terms "serious human rights offense" and "the offense of incitement to genocide."

The new enhancement reflects the impact that such immigration fraud offenses can have on the ability of immigration and naturalization authorities to make fully informed decisions regarding the defendant's immigration petition, application or other request and is intended to ensure that the United States is not a safe haven for those who have committed serious human rights offenses.

Effective Date: The effective date of this amendment is November 1, 2012.

766. **Amendment:** The Commentary to § 4A1.2 captioned "Application Notes" is amended in Note 5 by striking "counted. Such offenses are not minor traffic infractions within the meaning of § 4A1.2(c)." and inserting "always counted, without regard to how the offense is classified. Paragraphs (1) and (2) of § 4A1.2(c) do not apply.".

Reason for Amendment: This amendment resolves differences among circuits regarding when prior sentences for the misdemeanor offenses of driving while intoxicated and driving under the influence (and any similar offenses by whatever name they are known) are counted toward the defendant's criminal history score.

Convictions for driving while intoxicated and similar offenses encompass a range of offense conduct. For example, convictions for driving while intoxicated and similar offenses can be classified as anything from traffic infractions to misdemeanors and felonies, and they are subject to a broad spectrum of penalties (ranging from a fine to years in custody for habitual offenders). When the prior offense is a felony, the sentence clearly counts toward the defendant's criminal history score because "[s]entences for all felony offenses are counted." See subsection (c) of § 4A1.2 (Definitions and Instructions for Computing Criminal History). However, when the prior sentence is for a misdemeanor or petty offense, circuits have taken different approaches, in part because of language added to § 4A1.2(c)(1). See USSG App. C, Amendment 352 (effective November 1, 1990) (adding "careless or reckless driving" to the offenses listed in § 4A1.2(c)(1)).

When the prior sentence is a misdemeanor or petty offense, § 4A1.2(c) specifies that the offense is counted, but with two exceptions, limited to cases in which the prior offense is on (or similar to an offense that is on) either of two lists. On the first list are offenses from "careless or reckless driving" to "trespassing." In such a case, the sentence is counted only if (A) the sentence was a term of probation of more than one year or a term of imprisonment of at least 30 days, or (B) the prior offense was similar to the instant offense. See § 4A1.2(c)(1). On the second list are offenses from "fish and game violations" to "vagrancy." In such a case, the sentence is never counted. See § 4A1.2(c)(2).

Most circuits have held that driving while intoxicated convictions, including misdemeanors and petty offenses, always count toward the criminal history score, without exception, even if the offense met the criteria for either of the two lists. These circuits have relied on Application Note 5 to § 4A1.2, which has provided:

> Sentences for Driving While Intoxicated or Under the Influence.—Convictions for driving while intoxicated or under the influence (and similar offenses by whatever name they are known) are counted. Such offenses are not minor traffic infractions within the meaning of § 4A1.2(c).

See United States v. Pando, 545 F.3d 682, 683-85 (8th Cir. 2008) (holding that a conviction for driving while ability impaired was properly included in defendant's criminal history, and rejecting defendant's argument that his offense was similar to careless or reckless driving); United States v. Thornton, 444 F.3d 1163, 1165-67 (9th Cir. 2006) (holding that driving with high blood alcohol level was properly included in defendant's criminal history, and rejecting defendant's argument that his conviction was "similar" to minor traffic infraction or public intoxication). See also United States v. LeBlanc, 45 F.3d 192, 195 (7th Cir. 1995) ("[A]pplication note [5] reflects the Sentencing Commission's conclusion 'that driving while intoxicated offenses are of sufficient gravity to merit inclusion in the defendant's criminal history, however they might be classified under state law.'"); United States v. Deigert, 916 F.2d 916, 918 (4th Cir. 1990) (holding that defendant's alcohol-related traffic offenses are counted under Application Note 5).

The Second Circuit took a different approach in United States v. Potes-Castillo, 638 F.3d 106 (2d Cir. 2011), holding that Application Note 5 could be read either (1) to "mean that, like felonies, driving while ability impaired sentences are always counted, without possibility of exception" or (2) "as setting forth the direction that driving while ability impaired sentences must not be treated as minor traffic infractions or local ordinance violations and excluded under section 4A1.2(c)(2)." Id. at 110-11. The Second Circuit adopted the second reading and, accordingly, held that a prior sentence for driving while ability impaired "should be treated like any other misdemeanor or petty offense, except that they cannot be exempted under section 4A1.2(c)(2)." Id. at 113. According to the Second Circuit, such a sentence can qualify for an exception, and therefore not be counted, under the first list (e.g., if it was similar to "careless or reckless driving" and the other criteria for a first-list exception were met).

The amendment resolves the issue by amending Application Note 5 to clarify that convic-

Amendment 766

tions for driving while intoxicated and similar offenses are always counted, without regard to how the offenses are classified. Further, the amendment states plainly that paragraphs (1) and (2) of § 4A1.2(c) do not apply.

This amendment reflects the Commission's view that convictions for driving while intoxicated and other similar offenses are sufficiently serious to always count toward a defendant's criminal history score. The amendment clarifies the Commission's intent and should result in more consistent calculation of criminal history scores among the circuits.

Effective Date: The effective date of this amendment is November 1, 2012.

767. **Amendment:** Section 5G1.2 is amended in subsection (b) by striking "Except as otherwise required by law (see § 5G1.1(a), (b)), the sentence imposed on each other count shall be the total punishment as determined in accordance with Part D of Chapter Three, and Part C of this Chapter." and inserting "For all counts not covered by subsection (a), the court shall determine the total punishment and shall impose that total punishment on each such count, except to the extent otherwise required by law.".

The Commentary to § 5G1.2 captioned "Application Notes" is amended in Note 1, in the first paragraph, by inserting before the period at the end of the first sentence the following: "and determining the defendant's guideline range on the Sentencing Table in Chapter Five, Part A (Sentencing Table)"; and

after the first paragraph, by inserting the following new paragraph:

"Note that the defendant's guideline range on the Sentencing Table may be affected or restricted by a statutorily authorized maximum sentence or a statutorily required minimum sentence not only in a single-count case, see § 5G1.1 (Sentencing on a Single Count of Conviction), but also in a multiple-count case. See Note 3, below."; and

by redesignating Note 3 as Note 4 and inserting after Note 2 the following:

"3. Application of Subsection (b).—

(A) In General.—Subsection (b) provides that, for all counts not covered by subsection (a), the court shall determine the total punishment (i.e., the combined length of the sentences to be imposed) and shall impose that total punishment on each such count, except to the extent otherwise required by law (such as where a statutorily required minimum sentence or a statutorily authorized maximum sentence otherwise requires).

(B) Effect on Guidelines Range of Mandatory Minimum or Statutory Maximum.—The defendant's guideline range on the Sentencing Table may be affected or restricted by a statutorily authorized maximum sentence or a statutorily required minimum sentence not only in a single-count case, see § 5G1.1, but also in a multiple-count case.

In particular, where a statutorily required minimum sentence on any count is greater than the maximum of the applicable guideline range, the statutorily required minimum sentence on that count shall be the guideline sentence on all counts. See § 5G1.1(b). Similarly, where a statutorily required minimum sentence on any count is greater than the minimum of the applicable guideline range, the guideline range for all counts is restricted by that statutorily required minimum sentence. See § 5G1.1(c)(2) and accompanying Commentary.

However, where a statutorily authorized maximum sentence on a particular count is less than the minimum of the applicable guideline range, the

sentence imposed on that count shall not be greater than the statutorily authorized maximum sentence on that count. See § 5G1.1(a).

(C) Examples.—The following examples illustrate how subsection (b) applies, and how the restrictions in subparagraph (B) operate, when a statutorily required minimum sentence is involved.

Defendant A and Defendant B are each convicted of the same four counts. Counts 1, 3, and 4 have statutory maximums of 10 years, 20 years, and 2 years, respectively. Count 2 has a statutory maximum of 30 years and a mandatory minimum of 10 years.

For Defendant A, the court determines that the final offense level is 19 and the defendant is in Criminal History Category I, which yields a guideline range on the Sentencing Table of 30 to 37 months. Because of the 10-year mandatory minimum on Count 2, however, Defendant A's guideline sentence is 120 months. See subparagraph (B), above. After considering that guideline sentence, the court determines that the appropriate 'total punishment' to be imposed on Defendant A is 120 months. Therefore, subsection (b) requires that the total punishment of 120 months be imposed on each of Counts 1, 2, and 3. The sentence imposed on Count 4 is limited to 24 months, because a statutory maximum of 2 years applies to that particular count.

For Defendant B, in contrast, the court determines that the final offense level is 30 and the defendant is in Criminal History Category II, which yields a guideline range on the Sentencing Table of 108 to 135 months. Because of the 10-year mandatory minimum on Count 2, however, Defendant B's guideline range is restricted to 120 to 135 months. See subparagraph (B), above. After considering that restricted guideline range, the court determines that the appropriate 'total punishment' to be imposed on Defendant B is 130 months. Therefore, subsection (b) requires that the total punishment of 130 months be imposed on each of Counts 2 and 3. The sentences imposed on Counts 1 and 4 are limited to 120 months (10 years) and 24 months (2 years), respectively, because of the applicable statutory maximums.

(D) Special Rule on Resentencing.—In a case in which (i) the defendant's guideline range on the Sentencing Table was affected or restricted by a statutorily required minimum sentence (as described in subparagraph (B)), (ii) the court is resentencing the defendant, and (iii) the statutorily required minimum sentence no longer applies, the defendant's guideline range for purposes of the remaining counts shall be redetermined without regard to the previous effect or restriction of the statutorily required minimum sentence.".

Reason for Amendment: This amendment responds to an application issue regarding the applicable guideline range in a case in which the defendant is sentenced on multiple counts of conviction, at least one of which involves a mandatory minimum sentence that is greater than the minimum of the otherwise applicable guideline range. The issue arises under § 5G1.2 (Sentencing on Multiple Counts of Conviction) when at least one count in a multiple-count case involves a mandatory minimum sentence that affects the otherwise applicable guideline range. In such cases, circuits differ over whether the guideline range is affected only for the count involving the mandatory minimum or for all counts in the case.

The Fifth Circuit has held that, in such a case, the effect on the guideline range applies to all counts in the case. See United States v. Salter, 241 F.3d 392, 395-96 (5th Cir. 2001). In that case, the guideline range on the Sentencing Table was 87 to 108 months, but one of the three counts carried a mandatory minimum sentence of 10 years (120 months), which resulted in a guideline sentence of 120 months. The Fifth Circuit instructed the district court that the appropriate guideline sentence was 120 months on each of the three counts.

The Ninth Circuit took a different approach in United States v. Evans-Martinez, 611 F.3d 635 (9th Cir. 2010), holding that, in such a case, "a mandatory minimum sentence becomes the starting point for any count that carries a mandatory minimum sentence higher than what would otherwise be the Guidelines sentencing range," but "[a]ll other counts . . . are sentenced based on the Guidelines sentencing range, regardless [of] the mandatory minimum sentences that apply to other counts." See id. at 637. The Ninth Circuit stated that it would be more "logical" to follow the Fifth Circuit's approach but "such logic is overcome by the precise language of the Sentencing Guidelines". See id.

The District of Columbia Circuit appears to follow an approach similar to the Ninth Circuit. See United States v. Kennedy, 133 F.3d 53, 60-61 (D.C. Cir. 1998) (one of two counts carried a mandatory sentence of life imprisonment; district court treated life imprisonment as the guidelines sentence for both counts; Court of Appeals reversed, holding that the appropriate guidelines range for the other count was 262 to 327 months).

The amendment adopts the approach followed by the Fifth Circuit and makes three changes to § 5G1.2. First, it amends § 5G1.2(b) to clarify that the court is to determine the total punishment and impose that total punishment on each count, except to the extent otherwise required by law.

Second, it amends the Commentary to clarify that the defendant's guideline range in a multiple-count case may be restricted by a mandatory minimum penalty or statutory maximum penalty (i.e., a mandatory minimum may increase the bottom of the otherwise applicable guideline range and a statutory maximum may decrease the top of the otherwise applicable guideline range) in a manner similar to how the guideline range in a single-count case may be restricted by a minimum or maximum penalty under § 5G1.1 (Sentencing on a Single Count of Conviction). Specifically, it clarifies that when any count involves a mandatory minimum that restricts the defendant's guideline range, the guideline range is restricted as to all counts. It also provides examples of how these restrictions operate.

Third, it amends the commentary to clarify that in a case in which (1) a defendant's guideline range was affected or restricted by a mandatory minimum penalty, (2) the court is resentencing the defendant, and (3) the mandatory minimum sentence no longer applies, the court shall redetermine the defendant's guideline range for purposes of the remaining counts without regard to the mandatory minimum penalty.

These changes resolve the application issue by clarifying the manner in which the Commission intended this guideline to operate, and by providing examples similar to those used in training probation officers and judges. When there is only one count, the guidelines provide a single guideline range, and that range may be restricted if a mandatory minimum is involved, as described in § 5G1.1 (Sentencing on a Single Count of Conviction). When there is more than one count, the guidelines also provide a single guideline range, and that range also may be restricted if a mandatory minimum is involved. These changes provide clarity and consistency for cases in which a mandatory minimum is present and are intended to ensure that sentencing courts resolve multiple-count cases in a straightforward, logical manner, with a single guideline range, a single set of findings and reasons, and a single set of departure and variance considerations.

Effective Date: The effective date of this amendment is November 1, 2012.

768. **Amendment:** Chapter Five, Part K, Subpart 2 is amended by striking § 5K2.19 and its accompanying commentary as follows:

> "§ 5K2.19. Post-Sentencing Rehabilitative Efforts (Policy Statement)
>
> > Post-sentencing rehabilitative efforts, even if exceptional, undertaken by a defendant after imposition of a term of imprisonment for the instant offense are not an appropriate basis for a downward departure when resentencing the defendant for that offense. (Such efforts may provide a basis for early termination of supervised release under 18 U.S.C. § 3583(e)(1).)
>
> > Commentary
>
> > Background: The Commission has determined that post-sentencing rehabilitative measures should not provide a basis for downward departure when resentencing a defendant initially sentenced to a term of imprisonment because such a departure would (1) be inconsistent with the policies established by Congress under 18 U.S.C. § 3624(b) and other statutory provisions for reducing the time to be served by an imprisoned person; and (2) inequitably benefit only those who gain the opportunity to be resentenced de novo.".

Reason for Amendment: The Commission's policy statement at § 5K2.19 (Post-Sentencing Rehabilitative Efforts) (Policy Statement) prohibits the consideration of post-sentencing rehabilitative efforts as a basis for downward departure when resentencing a defendant. Section 5K2.19 was promulgated in 2000 in response to a circuit conflict regarding whether sentencing courts may consider such rehabilitative efforts while in prison or on probation as a basis for downward departure at resentencing following an appeal. See USSG App. C, Amendment 602 (effective November 1, 2000). This amendment repeals § 5K2.19. The amendment responds to the Supreme Court's decision in Pepper v. United States, 131 S. Ct. 1229 (2011), which, in part relying on 18 U.S.C. § 3661, held among other things that "when a defendant's sentence has been set aside on appeal, a district court at resentencing may consider evidence of the defendant's postsentencing rehabilitation." The amendment repeals the policy statement in light of the Pepper decision.

Effective Date: The effective date of this amendment is November 1, 2012.

769. **Amendment:** Section 2P1.2 is amended in subsection (a)(3) by inserting after "currency," the following: "a mobile phone or similar device,".

Amendment 769 SUPPLEMENT TO APPENDIX C November 1, 2013

The Commentary to § 2P1.2 captioned "Application Notes" is amended by redesignating Notes 1 and 2 as Notes 2 and 3, respectively, and by inserting at the beginning the following:

"1. In this guideline, the term 'mobile phone or similar device' means a phone or other device as described in 18 U.S.C. § 1791(d)(1)(F).".

The Commentary to § 2T2.1 captioned "Statutory Provisions" is amended by inserting "15 U.S.C. § 377," before "26 U.S.C.".

The Commentary to § 2T2.2 captioned "Statutory Provisions" is amended by inserting "15 U.S.C. § 377," before "26 U.S.C.".

Appendix A (Statutory Index) is amended by inserting after the line referenced to 15 U.S.C. § 158 the following:

"15 U.S.C. § 377   2T2.1, 2T2.2";

by inserting after the line referenced to 18 U.S.C. § 43 the following:

"18 U.S.C. § 48   2G3.1";

by inserting after the line referenced to 18 U.S.C. § 1153 the following:

"18 U.S.C. § 1158   2B1.1, 2B5.3
18 U.S.C. § 1159   2B1.1";

by inserting after the line referenced to 18 U.S.C. § 1716D the following:

"18 U.S.C. § 1716E   2T2.2"; and

by striking the lines referenced to 41 U.S.C. § 53, 54, and 423(e) as follows:

"41 U.S.C. § 53   2B4.1
41 U.S.C. § 54   2B4.1
41 U.S.C. § 423(e)   2B1.1, 2C1.1"; and by inserting the following:

"41 U.S.C. § 2102   2B1.1, 2C1.1
41 U.S.C. § 2105   2B1.1, 2C1.1
41 U.S.C. § 8702   2B4.1
41 U.S.C. § 8707   2B4.1".

Reason for Amendment: This amendment responds to miscellaneous issues arising from recently enacted legislation.

Cell Phone Contraband Act of 2010

First, the amendment responds to the Cell Phone Contraband Act of 2010, Pub. L. 111–225 (enacted August 10, 2010), which amended 18 U.S.C. § 1791 (Providing or possessing contraband in prison) to make it a class A misdemeanor to provide a mobile phone or similar device to an inmate, or for an inmate to possess a mobile phone or similar device. Offenses under section 1791 are referenced in Appendix A (Statutory Index) to § 2P1.2 (Providing or Possessing Contraband in Prison). The penalty structure of section 1791 is

November 1, 2013   SUPPLEMENT TO APPENDIX C   **Amendment 769**

based on the type of contraband involved, and the other class A misdemeanors in section 1791 receive a base offense level of 6 in § 2P1.2. Under the amendment, the class A misdemeanor in section 1791 that applies when the contraband is a cell phone will also receive a base offense level of 6 in § 2P1.2. This change maintains the relationship between the penalty structures of the statute and the guideline.

Prevent All Cigarette Trafficking Act of 2009

Second, the amendment responds to the Prevent All Cigarette Trafficking Act of 2009 (PACT Act), Pub. L. 111–154 (enacted March 31, 2010). The PACT Act made a series of revisions to the Jenkins Act, 15 U.S.C. § 375 et seq., which is one of several laws governing the sale, shipment and taxation of cigarettes and smokeless tobacco.

The PACT Act raised the criminal penalty at 15 U.S.C. § 377 for a knowing violation of the Jenkins Act from a misdemeanor to a felony with a statutory maximum term of imprisonment of 3 years. The amendment amends Appendix A (Statutory Index) to reference section 377 offenses to § 2T2.1 (Non-Payment of Taxes) and § 2T2.2 (Regulatory Offenses). These two guidelines are the most analogous guidelines for a section 377 offense because the offense may involve either non-payment of taxes or regulatory offenses. Accordingly, the amendment also amends the Commentary to §§ 2T2.1 and 2T2.2 to add section 377 to their lists of statutory provisions. These lists indicate that § 2T2.1 applies if the conduct constitutes non-payment, evasion, or attempted evasion of taxes, and § 2T2.2 applies if the conduct is tantamount to a record-keeping violation rather than an effort to evade payment of taxes.

The PACT Act also created a new class A misdemeanor at 18 U.S.C. § 1716E, prohibiting the knowing shipment of cigarettes and smokeless tobacco through the United States mail. The amendment amends Appendix A (Statutory Index) to reference section 1716E offenses to § 2T2.2. Section 2T2.2 is the most analogous guideline because offenses under section 1716E are regulatory offenses.

Animal Crush Video Prohibition Act of 2010

Third, the amendment responds to the Animal Crush Video Prohibition Act of 2010, Pub. L. 111–294 (enacted December 9, 2010), which substantially revised the criminal offense at 18 U.S.C. § 48 (Animal crush videos). Section 48 makes it a crime to create or distribute an "animal crush video," which is defined by the statute in a manner that requires, among other things, that the depiction be obscene. The maximum term of imprisonment for a section 48 offense is 7 years. The amendment amends Appendix A (Statutory Index) to reference section 48 offenses to § 2G3.1 (Importing, Mailing, or Transporting Obscene Matter; Transferring Obscene Matter to a Minor; Misleading Domain Names). Section 2G3.1 is the most analogous guideline because obscenity is an element of section 48 offenses.

Indian Arts and Crafts Amendments Act of 2010

Fourth, the amendment responds to the Indian Arts and Crafts Amendments Act of 2010, Pub. L. 111–211 (enacted July 29, 2010), which amended the criminal offense at 18 U.S.C. § 1159 (Misrepresentation of Indian produced goods and services) to reduce penalties for first offenders when the value of the goods involved is less than $1,000. The maximum term of imprisonment under section 1159 had been 5 years for a first offender and 15 years for a repeat offender. The Act retained this penalty structure, except that the statutory maximum term of imprisonment for a first offender was reduced to 1 year in a case in which the value of the goods involved is less than $1,000. The amendment amends Appendix A (Statutory Index) to reference section 1159 offenses to § 2B1.1 (Theft, Property

Amendment 769 SUPPLEMENT TO APPENDIX C November 1, 2013

Destruction, and Fraud). Section 2B1.1 is the most analogous guideline because an offense under section 1159 has elements of fraud and deceit.

The amendment also addresses an existing offense, 18 U.S.C. § 1158 (Counterfeiting Indian Arts and Crafts Board trade mark), which makes it a crime to counterfeit or unlawfully affix a Government trademark used or devised by the Indian Arts and Crafts Board or to make any false statement for the purpose of obtaining the use of any such mark. The maximum term of imprisonment under section 1158 is 5 years for a first offender and 15 years for a repeat offender. The amendment amends Appendix A (Statutory Index) to reference section 1158 offenses to both §§ 2B1.1 and 2B5.3 (Criminal Infringement of Copyright or Trademark).

These two guidelines are the most analogous guidelines because an offense under section 1158 contains alternative sets of elements, one of which involves trademark infringement and one of which involves false statements.

Public Contracting Offenses

Finally, the amendment responds to Public Law 111–350 (enacted January 4, 2011), which enacted certain laws relating to public contracts as a new positive-law title of the Code — title 41, "Public Contracts". As part of this codification, two criminal offenses, 41 U.S.C. §§ 53 and 423(a)–(b), and their respective penalty provisions, 41 U.S.C. §§ 54 and 423(e), were given new title 41 section numbers: sections 8702 and 8707 for sections 53 and 54, respectively, and sections 2102 and 2105 for sections 423(a)–(b) and 423(e), respectively. The substantive offenses and their related penalties did not change. The amendment makes changes to Appendix A (Statutory Index) to reflect the renumbering and includes a reference for the new section 2102, whose predecessor section 423(a)–(b) was not referenced in Appendix A. The changes are technical.

Effective Date: The effective date of this amendment is November 1, 2012.

770. **Amendment:** The Commentary to § 1B1.10 captioned "Application Notes" is amended in Note 4 by striking "Application Note 10 to § 2D1.1" and inserting "the Drug Equivalency Tables in the Commentary to § 2D1.1 (see § 2D1.1, comment. (n.8))".

The Commentary to § 2D1.1 captioned "Application Notes" is amended by renumbering Notes 1 through 29 according to the following table:

Before Amendment	After Amendment
1	1
17	2
13	3
2	4
12	5
5	6
6	7
10	8
11	9

15	10
3	11
18	12
23	13
25	14
26	15
27	16
28	17
19	18(A)
20	18(B)
29	19
21	20
24	21
8	22
7	23
22	24
4	25
14	26(A)
16	26(B)
9	26(C);

and by rearranging those Notes, as so renumbered, to place them in proper numerical order.

The Commentary to § 2D1.1 captioned "Application Notes", as so renumbered and rearranged, is further amended by inserting headings at the beginning of certain notes, as follows (with Notes referred to by their new numbers):

Note	Heading to Be Inserted at the Beginning
1	"Mixture or Substance".—
2	"Plant".—
3	Classification of Controlled Substances.—
4	Applicability to "Counterfeit" Substances.—
5	Determining Drug Types and Drug Quantities.—

Amendment 770 SUPPLEMENT TO APPENDIX C November 1, 2013

7 Multiple Transactions or Multiple Drug Types.—

9 Determining Quantity Based on Doses, Pills, or Capsules.—

10 Determining Quantity of LSD.—

12 Application of Subsection (b)(5).—

18 Application of Subsection (b)(13).—

23 Cases Involving Mandatory Minimum Penalties.—

25 Cases Involving "Small Amount of Marihuana for No Remuneration".—

26 Departure Considerations.—

26(A) Downward Departure Based on Drug Quantity in Certain Reverse Sting Operations.—

26(B) Upward Departure Based on Drug Quantity.—

26(C) Upward Departure Based on Unusually High Purity.—

The Commentary to § 2D1.1 captioned "Application Notes", as so renumbered and rearranged and amended, is further amended as follows (with Notes referred to by their new numbers):

in Note 8(A) by striking "Note 5" and inserting "Note 6";

in Note 15 by redesignating (i), (ii), and (iii) as (A), (B), and (C), respectively;

in Note 18(A) by inserting before the period at the end of the heading the following: "(Subsection (b)(13)(A))"; and

in Note 18(B) by inserting before the period at the end of the heading the following: "(Subsection (b)(13)(C)B(D))", by redesignating its component subdivision (A) (beginning "Factors to Consider") as (i), and that subdivision's component subdivisions (i) through (iv) as (I) through (IV), respectively, and by redesignating its component subdivision (B) (beginning "Definitions") as (ii).

The Commentary to § 2D1.1 captioned "Background" is amended by striking the fifth through eighth undesignated paragraphs as follows:

" The last sentence of subsection (a)(5) implements the directive to the Commission in section 7(1) of Public Law 111–220.

Subsection (b)(2) implements the directive to the Commission in section 5 of Public Law 111–220.

Subsection (b)(3) is derived from Section 6453 of the Anti-Drug Abuse Act of 1988.

Frequently, a term of supervised release to follow imprisonment is required by statute for offenses covered by this guideline. Guidelines for the imposition, duration, and conditions of supervised release are set forth in Chapter Five, Part D (Supervised Release).";

in the paragraph beginning "The dosage weight" by striking "111 S.Ct. 1919" and inserting "500 U.S. 453"; and

by inserting before the paragraph beginning "Subsection (b)(11)" the following:

" Frequently, a term of supervised release to follow imprisonment is required by statute for offenses covered by this guideline. Guidelines for the imposition, duration, and conditions of supervised release are set forth in Chapter Five, Part D (Supervised Release).

The last sentence of subsection (a)(5) implements the directive to the Commission in section 7(1) of Public Law 111–220.

Subsection (b)(2) implements the directive to the Commission in section 5 of Public Law 111–220.

Subsection (b)(3) is derived from Section 6453 of the Anti-Drug Abuse Act of 1988.".

The Commentary to § 2D1.6 captioned "Application Note" is amended in Note 1 by striking "Note 12" and inserting "Note 5".

The Commentary to § 2D1.11 captioned "Application Notes", as amended by Amendment 763, is further amended by renumbering Notes 1 through 9 according to the following table:

Before Amendment	After Amendment
4	1
1	2
5	3
6	4
7	5
8	6
9	7
2	8
3	9;

and by rearranging those Notes, as so renumbered, to place them in proper numerical order.

The Commentary to § 2D1.11 captioned "Application Notes", as so renumbered and rearranged, is further amended by inserting headings at the beginning of certain notes, as follows (with Notes referred to by their new numbers):

Note	Heading to Be Inserted at the Beginning
2	Application of Subsection (b)(1).—
3	Application of Subsection (b)(2).—
4	Application of Subsection (b)(3).—

– 1273 –

Amendment 770   SUPPLEMENT TO APPENDIX C   November 1, 2013

    8   Application of Subsection (c)(1).—

    9   Offenses Involving Immediate Precursors or Other Controlled Substances Covered Under § 2D1.1.—

The Commentary to § 2D1.11 captioned "Application Notes", as so renumbered and rearranged and amended, is further amended in Note 9 (as so renumbered) by striking "Note 12" and inserting "Note 5".

The Commentary to § 5G1.2 captioned "Application Notes", as amended by Note 767, is further amended by amending Note 1 to read as follows:

    "1.   In General.—This section specifies the procedure for determining the specific sentence to be formally imposed on each count in a multiple-count case. The combined length of the sentences ('total punishment') is determined by the court after determining the adjusted combined offense level and the Criminal History Category and determining the defendant's guideline range on the Sentencing Table in Chapter Five, Part A (Sentencing Table).

          Note that the defendant's guideline range on the Sentencing Table may be affected or restricted by a statutorily authorized maximum sentence or a statutorily required minimum sentence not only in a single-count case, see § 5G1.1 (Sentencing on a Single Count of Conviction), but also in a multiple-count case. See Note 3, below.

          Except as otherwise required by subsection (e) or any other law, the total punishment is to be imposed on each count and the sentences on all counts are to be imposed to run concurrently to the extent allowed by the statutory maximum sentence of imprisonment for each count of conviction.

          This section applies to multiple counts of conviction (A) contained in the same indictment or information, or (B) contained in different indictments or informations for which sentences are to be imposed at the same time or in a consolidated proceeding.

          Usually, at least one of the counts will have a statutory maximum adequate to permit imposition of the total punishment as the sentence on that count. The sentence on each of the other counts will then be set at the lesser of the total punishment and the applicable statutory maximum, and be made to run concurrently with all or part of the longest sentence. If no count carries an adequate statutory maximum, consecutive sentences are to be imposed to the extent necessary to achieve the total punishment.".

Section 5K2.0 is amended in subsection (d)(1) by striking "the last sentence of 5K2.12 (Coercion and Duress), and 5K2.19 (Post-Sentencing Rehabilitative Efforts)" and inserting "and the last sentence of 5K2.12 (Coercion and Duress)".

Reason for Amendment: This proposed amendment makes certain technical and conforming changes to commentary in the Guidelines Manual.

First, it reorganizes the commentary to the drug trafficking guideline, § 2D1.1 (Unlawful Manufacturing, Importing, Exporting, or Trafficking (Including Possession with Intent to Commit These Offenses); Attempt or Conspiracy), so that the order of the application notes better reflects the order of the guidelines provisions to which they relate. The

November 1, 2013 SUPPLEMENT TO APPENDIX C **Amendment 771**

proposed amendment also makes stylistic changes to the Commentary to § 2D1.1, such as by adding headings to certain application notes. To reflect the renumbering of application notes in § 2D1.1, conforming changes are also made to the Commentary to § 1B1.10 and § 2D1.6.

Second, it makes certain clerical and stylistic changes in connection with certain recently promulgated amendments. See 77 Fed. Reg. 28226 (May 11, 2012). The clerical and stylistic changes are as follows:

(1) Amendment 763 made revisions to § 2D1.11 (Unlawfully Distributing, Importing, Exporting or Possessing a Listed Chemical; Attempt or Conspiracy). This proposed amendment reorganizes the commentary to § 2D1.11 so that the order of the application notes better reflects the order of the guidelines provisions to which they relate. The proposed amendment also makes stylistic changes to the Commentary to § 2D1.11 by adding headings to certain application notes.

(2) Amendment 767 made revisions to § 5G1.2 (Sentencing on Multiple Counts of Conviction), including a revision to Application Note 1. However, the amendatory instructions published in the Federal Register to implement those revisions included an erroneous instruction. This proposed amendment restates Application Note 1 in its entirety to ensure that it conforms with the version of Application Note 1 that appears in the unofficial, "reader-friendly" version of Amendment 7 that the Commission made available in May 2012.

(3) Amendment 768 repealed the policy statement at § 5K2.19 (Post-Sentencing Rehabilitative Efforts). However, a reference to that policy statement is contained in § 5K2.0 (Grounds for Departure). This proposed amendment revises § 5K2.0 to reflect the repeal of § 5K2.19.

Effective Date: The effective date of this amendment is November 1, 2012.

771. Amendment: Section 2B1.1(b) is amended by striking paragraph (5) as follows:

"(5) If the offense involved misappropriation of a trade secret and the defendant knew or intended that the offense would benefit a foreign government, foreign instrumentality, or foreign agent, increase by 2 levels.";

by renumbering paragraphs (6) through (8) as (5) through (7); by renumbering paragraphs (13) through (18) as (14) through (19); by inserting after paragraph (12) the following:

"(13) (Apply the greater) If the offense involved misappropriation of a trade secret and the defendant knew or intended—

(A) that the trade secret would be transported or transmitted out of the United States, increase by 2 levels; or

(B) that the offense would benefit a foreign government, foreign instrumentality, or foreign agent, increase by 4 levels.

If subparagraph (B) applies and the resulting offense level is less than level 14, increase to level 14."; and

in paragraph (16) (as so renumbered) by striking "(b)(15)(B)" and inserting "(b)(16)(B)".

Amendment 771 SUPPLEMENT TO APPENDIX C November 1, 2013

The Commentary to § 2B1.1 captioned "Application Notes" is amended in Note 6 by striking "(b)(7)" both places it appears and inserting "(b)(6)"; in Note 10 by striking "(b)(13)" both places it appears and inserting "(b)(14)"; in Note 11 by striking "(b)(15)(A)" both places it appears and inserting "(b)(16)(A)"; in Note 12 by striking "(b)(15)(B)" and inserting "(b)(16)(B)"; in Note 12(A) by striking "(b)(15)(B)(i)" and inserting "(b)(16)(B)(i)"; in Note 12(B) by striking "(b)(15)(B)(ii)" and inserting "(b)(16)(B)(ii)"; in Note 13 by striking "(b)(17)" both places it appears and inserting "(b)(18)"; in Note 13(B) by striking "(b)(17)(A)(iii)" both places it appears and inserting "(b)(18)(A)(iii)", and by striking "(b)(15)(B)" both places it appears and inserting "(b)(16)(B)"; in Note 14 by striking "(b)(18)" each place it appears and inserting "(b)(19)"; and in Note 19(B) by striking "(b)(17)(A)(iii)" and inserting "(b)(18)(A)(iii)".

The Commentary to § 2B1.1 captioned "Background" is amended by striking "(b)(6)", "(b)(8)", "(b)(14)(B)", "(b)(15)(A)", "(b)(15)(B)(i)", "(b)(16)", "(b)(17)", and "(b)(17)(B)" and inserting "(b)(5)", "(b)(7)", "(b)(15)(B)", "(b)(16)(A)", "(b)(16)(B)(i)", "(b)(17)", "(b)(18)", and "(b)(18)(B)", respectively; and by inserting before the paragraph that begins "Subsection (b)(15)(B)" (as so amended) the following:

"   Subsection (b)(13) implements the directive in section 3 of Public Law 112–269.".

Reason for Amendment: This amendment responds to section 3 of the Foreign and Economic Espionage Penalty Enhancement Act of 2012, Pub. L. 112–269 (enacted January 14, 2013), which contains a directive to the Commission regarding offenses involving stolen trade secrets or economic espionage.

Section 3(a) of the Act directs the Commission to "review and, if appropriate, amend" the guidelines "applicable to persons convicted of offenses relating to the transmission or attempted transmission of a stolen trade secret outside of the United States or economic espionage, in order to reflect the intent of Congress that penalties for such offenses under the Federal sentencing guidelines and policy statements appropriately reflect the seriousness of these offenses, account for the potential and actual harm caused by these offenses, and provide adequate deterrence against such offenses." Section 3(b) of the Act states that, in carrying out the directive, the Commission shall consider, among other things, whether the guidelines adequately address the simple misappropriation of a trade secret; the transmission or attempted transmission of a stolen trade secret outside of the United States; and the transmission or attempted transmission of a stolen trade secret outside of the United States that is committed or attempted to be committed for the benefit of a foreign government, foreign instrumentality, or foreign agent.

The offenses described in the directive may be prosecuted under 18 U.S.C. § 1831 (Economic espionage), which requires that the defendant specifically intend or know that the offense "will benefit any foreign government, foreign instrumentality, or foreign agent," and 18 U.S.C. § 1832 (Theft of trade secrets), which does not require such specific intent or knowledge. The statutory maximum terms of imprisonment are 15 years for a section 1831 offense and 10 years for a section 1832 offense. Both offenses are referenced in Appendix A (Statutory Index) to § 2B1.1 (Theft, Property Destruction, and Fraud).

In response to the directive, the amendment revises the existing specific offense characteristic at § 2B1.1(b)(5), which provides an enhancement of two levels "[i]f the offense involved misappropriation of a trade secret and the defendant knew or intended that the offense would benefit a foreign government, foreign instrumentality, or foreign agent," in two ways. First, it broadens the scope of the enhancement to provide a 2-level increase for trade secret offenses in which the defendant knew or intended that the trade secret would be transported or transmitted out of the United States. Second, it increases the severity of the enhancement to provide a 4-level enhancement and a minimum offense level of 14 for trade secret offenses in which the defendant knew or intended that the offense would benefit a foreign government, foreign instrumentality, or foreign agent. The enhancement also is redesignated as subsection (b)(13).

In responding to the directive, the Commission consulted with individuals or groups representing law enforcement, owners of trade secrets, victims of economic espionage offenses, the United States Department of Justice, the United States Department of Homeland Security, the United States Department of State, the Office of the United States Trade Representative, the Federal Public and Community Defenders, and standing advisory groups, among others. The Commission also considered relevant data and literature.

The Commission received public comment and testimony that the transmission of stolen trade secrets outside of the United States creates significant obstacles to effective investigation and prosecution and causes both increased harm to victims and more general harms to the nation. With respect to the victim, civil remedies may not be readily available or effective, and the transmission of a stolen trade secret outside of the United States substantially increases the risk that the trade secret will be exploited by a foreign competitor. In contrast, the simple movement of a stolen trade secret within a domestic multinational company (e. g., from a United States office to an overseas office of the same company) may not pose the same risks or harms. More generally, the Commission heard that foreign actors increasingly target United States companies for trade secret theft and that such offenses pose a growing threat to the nation's global competitiveness, economic growth, and national security. Accordingly, the Commission determined that a 2-level enhancement is warranted for cases in which the defendant knew or intended that a stolen trade secret would be transported or transmitted outside of the United States.

The Commission also received public comment and testimony that cases involving economic espionage (i.e., trade secret offenses that benefit foreign governments or entities under the substantial control of foreign governments) are particularly serious. In such cases, the United States is unlikely to obtain a foreign government's cooperation when seeking relief for the victim, and offenders backed by a foreign government likely will have significant financial resources to combat civil remedies. In addition, a foreign government's involvement increases the threat to the nation's economic and national security. Accordingly, the Commission determined that the existing enhancement for economic espionage should be increased from 2 to 4 levels and that such offenses should be subject to a minimum offense level of 14. This heightened enhancement is consistent with the higher statutory maximum penalties and fines applicable to such offenses and the Commission's established treatment of economic espionage as a more serious form of trade secret theft.

Consistent with the directive, the Commission also considered whether the guidelines appropriately account for the simple misappropriation of a trade secret. The Commission determined that such offenses are adequately accounted for by existing provisions in the Guidelines Manual, such as the loss table in § 2B1.1(b)(1), the sophisticated means enhancement at § 2B1.1(b)(10), and the adjustment for abuse of position of trust or use of special skill at § 3B1.3.

Effective Date: The effective date of this amendment is November 1, 2013.

772. **Amendment:** Section 2B1.1 is amended by inserting before paragraph (9) the following new paragraph:

"(8) (Apply the greater) If—

Amendment 772 SUPPLEMENT TO APPENDIX C November 1, 2013

    (A)   the offense involved conduct described in 18 U.S.C. § 670, increase by 2 levels; or

    (B)   the offense involved conduct described in 18 U.S.C. § 670, and the defendant was employed by, or was an agent of, an organization in the supply chain for the pre-retail medical product, increase by 4 levels.";

The Commentary to § 2B1.1 captioned "Application Notes" is amended in Note 1 by inserting after the paragraph that begins "'Personal information' means" the following:

"'Pre-retail medical product' has the meaning given that term in 18 U.S.C. § 670(e)."; and by inserting after the paragraph that begins "'Publicly traded company' means" the following:

"'Supply chain' has the meaning given that term in 18 U.S.C. § 670(e).";

in Note 3(F)(i) by striking "Note 9(A)" and inserting "Note 10(A)"; and

by renumbering Notes 7 through 19 as 8 through 20; by inserting after Note 6 the following:

    "7.   Application of Subsection (b)(8)(B).—If subsection (b)(8)(B) applies, do not apply an adjustment under § 3B1.3 (Abuse of Position of Trust or Use of Special Skill)."; and

in Note 20 (as so renumbered) by adding at the end of subparagraph (A)(ii) as the last sentence the following: "Similarly, an upward departure would be warranted in a case involving conduct described in 18 U.S.C. § 670 if the offense resulted in serious bodily injury or death, including serious bodily injury or death resulting from the use of the pre-retail medical product.".

The Commentary to § 2B1.1 captioned "Background" is amended by inserting before the paragraph that begins "Subsection (b)(9)(D)" the following:

    "   Subsection (b)(8) implements the directive to the Commission in section 7 of Public Law 112–186.".

However, if § 2B1.1(b) already contains a paragraph (8) because the renumbering of paragraphs by Amendment 771 has not taken effect, renumber the new paragraph inserted into § 2B1.1(b) as paragraph (8A) rather than paragraph (8), and revise the Commentary so that the new Note 7 inserted into the Application Notes and the new paragraph inserted into the Background refer to subsection (b)(8A) rather than subsection (b)(8).

Appendix A (Statutory Index) is amended by inserting after the line referenced to 18 U.S.C. § 669 the following:

    "18 U.S.C. § 670   2B1.1".

Reason for Amendment: This amendment responds to the Strengthening and Focusing Enforcement to Deter Organized Stealing and Enhance Safety Act of 2012, Pub. L. 112–186 (enacted October 5, 2012) (the "Act"), which addressed various offenses involving "pre-retail medical products," defined as "a medical product that has not yet been made available for retail purchase by a consumer." The Act created a new criminal offense at 18 U.S.C. § 670 for theft of pre-retail medical products, increased statutory penalties for certain related offenses when a pre-retail medical product is involved, and contained a directive to the Commission.

New Offense at 18 U.S.C. § 670

The new offense at section 670 makes it unlawful for any person in (or using any means or facility of) interstate or foreign commerce to—

(1) embezzle, steal, or by fraud or deception obtain, or knowingly and unlawfully take, carry away, or conceal a pre-retail medical product;

(2) knowingly and falsely make, alter, forge, or counterfeit the labeling or documentation (including documentation relating to origination or shipping) of a pre-retail medical product;

(3) knowingly possess, transport, or traffic in a pre-retail medical product that was involved in a violation of paragraph (1) or (2);

(4) with intent to defraud, buy, or otherwise obtain, a pre-retail medical product that has expired or been stolen;

(5) with intent to defraud, sell, or distribute, a pre-retail medical product that is expired or stolen; or

(6) attempt or conspire to violate any of paragraphs (1) through (5).

The offense generally carries a statutory maximum term of imprisonment of three years. If the offense is an "aggravated offense," however, higher statutory maximum terms of imprisonment are provided. The offense is an "aggravated offense" if—

(1) the defendant is employed by, or is an agent of, an organization in the supply chain for the pre-retail medical product; or

(2) the violation—

(A) involves the use of violence, force, or a threat of violence or force;

(B) involves the use of a deadly weapon;

(C) results in serious bodily injury or death, including serious bodily injury or death resulting from the use of the medical product involved; or

(D) is subsequent to a prior conviction for an offense under section 670.

Specifically, the higher statutory maximum terms of imprisonment are:

(1) Five years, if—

(A) the defendant is employed by, or is an agent of, an organization in the supply chain for the pre-retail medical product; or

(B) the violation (i) involves the use of violence, force, or a threat of violence or force, (ii) involves the use of a deadly weapon, or (iii) is subsequent to a prior conviction for an offense under section 670.

Amendment 772   SUPPLEMENT TO APPENDIX C   November 1, 2013

(2) 15 years, if the value of the medical products involved in the offense is $5,000 or greater.

(3) 20 years, if both (1) and (2) apply.

(4) 30 years, if the offense results in serious bodily injury or death, including serious bodily injury or death resulting from the use of the medical product involved.

The amendment amends Appendix A (Statutory Index) to reference the new offense at 18 U.S.C. § 670 to § 2B1.1 (Theft, Property Destruction, and Fraud). The Commission concluded that § 2B1.1 is the appropriate guideline because the elements of the new offense include theft or fraud.

Response to Directive

Section 7 of the Act directs the Commission to "review and, if appropriate, amend" the federal sentencing guidelines and policy statements applicable to the new offense and the related offenses "to reflect the intent of Congress that penalties for such offenses be sufficient to deter and punish such offenses, and appropriately account for the actual harm to the public from these offenses." The amendment amends § 2B1.1 to address offenses involving pre-retail medical products in two ways.

First, the amendment adds a new specific offense characteristic at § 2B1.1(b)(8) that provides a two-pronged enhancement with an instruction to apply the greater. Prong (A) provides a 2-level enhancement if the offense involved conduct described in 18 U.S.C. § 670. Prong (B) provides a 4-level enhancement if the offense involved conduct described in 18 U.S.C. § 670 and the defendant was employed by, or an agent of, an organization in the supply chain for the pre-retail product. Accompanying this new specific offense characteristic is new Commentary providing that, if prong (B) applies, "do not apply an adjustment under § 3B1.3 (Abuse of Position of Trust or Use of Special Skill)."

Based on public comment, testimony and sentencing data, the Commission concluded that an enhancement differentiating fraud and theft offenses involving medical products from those involving other products is warranted by the additional risk such offenses pose to public health and safety. In addition, such offenses undermine the public's confidence in the medical regulatory and distribution system. The Commission also concluded that the risks and harms it identified would be present in any theft or fraud offense involving a pre-retail medical product, regardless of the offense of conviction. Therefore application of the new specific offense characteristic is not limited to offenses charged under 18 U.S.C. § 670.

The amendment provides a 4-level enhancement for defendants who commit such offenses while employed in the supply chain for the pre-retail medical product. Such defendants are subject to an increased statutory maximum and the Commission determined that a heightened enhancement should apply to reflect the likelihood that the defendant's position in the supply chain facilitated the commission or concealment of the offense. Defendants who receive the 4-level enhancement are not subject to the adjustment at § 3B1.3 because the new enhancement adequately accounts for the concerns covered by § 3B1.3. The Commission determined that existing specific offense characteristics generally account for other aggravating factors included in the Act, such as loss, use or threat of force, risk of death or serious bodily injury, and weapon involvement, and therefore additional new specific offense characteristics are not necessary. See, e.g., §§ 2B1.1(b)(1), (b)(3), and (b)(15) (as redesignated by the amendment).

Second, it amends the upward departure provisions in the Commentary to § 2B1.1 at Application Note 19(A) to provide — as an example of a case in which an upward departure would be warranted — a case "involving conduct described in 18 U.S.C. § 670 if the offense resulted in serious bodily injury or death, including serious bodily injury or death resulting from the use of the pre-retail medical product." Public comment and testimony indicated that § 2B1.1 may not adequately account for the harm created by theft or fraud offenses involving pre-retail medical products when such serious bodily injury or death actually occurs as a result of the offense. For example, some pre-retail medical products are stolen as part of a scheme to re-sell them into the supply chain, but if the products have not been properly stored in the interim, their subsequent use can seriously injure the individual consumers who buy and use them. Thus, the amendment expands the scope of the existing upward departure provision to address such harms and to clarify that an upward departure is appropriate in such cases not only if serious bodily injury or death occurred during the theft or fraud, but also if such serious bodily injury or death resulted from the victim's use of a pre-retail medical product that had previously been obtained by theft or fraud.

Finally, the proposed amendment amends the Commentary to § 2B1.1 to provide relevant definitions and make other conforming changes.

Effective Date: The effective date of this amendment is November 1, 2013.

773. **Amendment:** Section 2B5.3(b) is amended by renumbering paragraph (5) as (6); by inserting after paragraph (4) the following:

"(5) If the offense involved a counterfeit drug, increase by 2 levels."; and

by inserting after paragraph (6) (as so renumbered) the following:

"(7) If the offense involved a counterfeit military good or service the use, malfunction, or failure of which is likely to cause (A) the disclosure of classified information; (B) impairment of combat operations; or (C) other significant harm to (i) a combat operation, (ii) a member of the Armed Forces, or (iii) national security, increase by 2 levels. If the resulting offense level is less than level 14, increase to level 14.".

The Commentary to § 2B5.3 captioned "Application Notes" is amended in Note 1 by inserting after the paragraph that begins "'Commercial advantage" the following:

"'Counterfeit drug' has the meaning given that term in 18 U.S.C. § 2320(f)(6).

"'Counterfeit military good or service' has the meaning given that term in 18 U.S.C. § 2320(f)(4).";

by renumbering Notes 3 and 4 as 4 and 5; by inserting after Note 2 the following:

"3. Application of Subsection (b)(7).—In subsection (b)(7), 'other significant harm to a member of the Armed Forces' means significant harm other than serious bodily injury or death. In a case in which the offense involved a counterfeit military good or service the use, malfunction, or failure of which is likely to cause serious bodily injury or death, subsection (b)(6)(A) (conscious or reckless risk of serious bodily injury or death) would apply."; and

in Note 5 (as so renumbered) by adding at the end the following:

"(D) The offense resulted in death or serious bodily injury.".

Amendment 773   SUPPLEMENT TO APPENDIX C   November 1, 2013

The Commentary to § 2B5.3 captioned "Background" is amended by inserting after the paragraph that begins "Subsection (b)(1)" the following:

"   Subsection (b)(5) implements the directive to the Commission in section 717 of Public Law 112–144.".

Appendix A (Statutory Index) is amended by striking the line referenced to 21 U.S.C. § 333(b) as follows:

"21 U.S.C. § 333(b)   2N2.1";

and inserting the following:

"21 U.S.C. § 333(b)(1)–(6)   2N2.1

21 U.S.C. § 333(b)(7)   2N1.1".

Reason for Amendment: This amendment responds to two recent Acts that made changes to 18 U.S.C. § 2320 (Trafficking in counterfeit goods or services). One Act increased penalties for offenses involving counterfeit military goods and services; the other increased penalties for offenses involving counterfeit drugs and included a directive to the Commission. The amendment also responds to recent statutory changes to 21 U.S.C. § 333 (Penalties for violations of the Federal Food, Drug, and Cosmetics Act) that increase penalties for offenses involving intentionally adulterated drugs.

<u>Section 2320 and Counterfeit Military Goods and Services</u>

First, the amendment responds to changes to section 2320 made by the National Defense Authorization Act for Fiscal Year 2012, Pub. L. 112–81 (enacted December 31, 2011) (the "NDAA"). In general, section 2320 prohibits trafficking in goods or services using a counterfeit mark, and provides a statutory maximum term of imprisonment of 10 years, or 20 years for a second or subsequent offense. If the offender knowingly or recklessly causes or attempts to cause serious bodily injury or death, the statutory maximum is increased to 20 years or any term of years or life, respectively. Offenses under section 2320 are referenced in Appendix A (Statutory Index) to § 2B5.3 (Criminal Infringement of Copyright or Trademark).

Section 818 of the NDAA amended section 2320 to add a new subsection (a)(3) that prohibits trafficking in counterfeit military goods and services, the use, malfunction, or failure of which is likely to cause serious bodily injury or death, the disclosure of classified information, impairment of combat operations, or other significant harm to a combat operation, a member of the Armed Forces, or national security. A "counterfeit military good or service" is defined as a good or service that uses a counterfeit mark and that (A) is falsely identified or labeled as meeting military specifications, or (B) is intended for use in a military or national security application. <u>See</u> 18 U.S.C. § 2320(f)(4). An individual who commits an offense under subsection (a)(3) is subject to a statutory maximum term of imprisonment of 20 years, or 30 years for a second or subsequent offense. <u>See</u> 18 U.S.C. § 2320(b)(3).

The legislative history of the NDAA indicates that Congress amended section 2320 because of concerns about national security and the protection of United States servicemen and women. After reviewing the legislative history, public comment, testimony, and data, the Commission determined that an offense involving counterfeit military goods and services that jeopardizes the safety of United States troops and compromises mission effectiveness warrants increased punishment.

Specifically, the amendment addresses offenses involving counterfeit military goods and services by amending § 2B5.3 to create a new specific offense characteristic at subsection (b)(7). Subsection (b)(7) provides a 2-level enhancement and a minimum offense level of 14 if the offense involves a counterfeit military good or service the use, malfunction, or failure of which is likely to cause the disclosure of classified information, impairment of combat operations, or other significant harm to a combat operation, a member of the Armed Forces, or to national security. The Commission set the minimum offense level at 14 so that it would be proportionate to the minimum offense level in the enhancement for "conscious or reckless risk of death or serious bodily injury" at subsection (b)(5)(A). That enhancement is moved from (b)(5)(A) to (b)(6)(A) by the amendment.

Although section 2320(a)(3) includes offenses that are likely to cause "serious bodily injury or death," the new specific offense characteristic does not because the Commission determined that such risk of harm is adequately addressed by the existing enhancement for offenses involving the "conscious or reckless risk of death or serious bodily injury." Consistent with that approach, the amendment includes commentary providing that the "other significant harm" specified in subsection (b)(7) does not include death or serious bodily injury and that § 2B5.3(b)(6)(A) would apply if the offense involved a counterfeit military good or service the use, malfunction, or failure of which is likely to cause serious bodily injury or death.

Section 2320 and Counterfeit Drugs

Second, the amendment responds to changes made by section 717 of the Food and Drug Administration Safety and Innovation Act, Pub. L. 112–144 (enacted July 9, 2012) (the "FDASIA"), which amended section 2320 to add a new subsection (a)(4) that prohibits trafficking in a counterfeit drug. A "counterfeit drug" is a drug, as defined by section 201 of the Federal Food, Drug, and Cosmetic Act (21 U.S.C. § 321), that uses a counterfeit mark. See 18 U.S.C. § 2320(f)(6). An individual who commits an offense under subsection (a)(4) is subject to the same statutory maximum term of imprisonment as for an offense involving a counterfeit military good or service — 20 years, or 30 years for a second or subsequent offense. See 18 U.S.C. § 2320(b)(3).

Section 717 of the FDASIA also contained a directive to the Commission to "review and amend, if appropriate" the guidelines and policy statements applicable to persons convicted of an offense described in section 2320(a)(4) — i.e., offenses involving counterfeit drugs — "in order to reflect the intent of Congress that such penalties be increased in comparison to those currently provided by the guidelines and policy statements." See Pub. L. 112–144, § 717(b)(1). In addition, section 717(b)(2) provides that, in responding to the directive, the Commission shall, among other things, ensure that the guidelines reflect the serious nature of section 2320(a)(4) offenses and consider the extent to which the guidelines account for the potential and actual harm to the public resulting from such offenses.

After reviewing the legislative history of the FDASIA, public comment, testimony, and data, the Commission determined that offenses involving counterfeit drugs involve a threat to public safety and undermine the public's confidence in the drug supply chain. Furthermore, unlike many other goods covered by the infringement guideline, offenses involving counterfeit drugs circumvent a regulatory scheme established to protect the health and safety of the public. Accordingly, the amendment responds to the directive by adding a new specific offense characteristic at § 2B5.3(b)(5) that provides a 2-level enhancement if the offense involves a counterfeit drug.

Amendment 773 SUPPLEMENT TO APPENDIX C November 1, 2013

Offenses Resulting in Death or Serious Bodily Injury

Third, the amendment amends the Commentary to § 2B5.3 to add a new upward departure consideration if the offense resulted in death or serious bodily injury. The addition of this departure consideration recognizes the distinction between an offense involving the risk of death or serious bodily injury and one in which death or serious bodily injury actually results. Departures for these reasons are already authorized in the guidelines, see §§ 5K2.1 (Death) (Policy Statement), 5K2.2 (Physical Injury) (Policy Statement), but the amendment is intended to heighten awareness of the availability of a departure in such cases.

Section 333 and Offenses Involving Intentionally Adulterated Drugs

Finally, the amendment provides a statutory reference for the new offense at 21 U.S.C. § 333(b)(7) created by section 716 of the FDASIA. Section 333(b)(7) applies to any person who knowingly and intentionally adulterates a drug such that the drug is adulterated under certain provisions of 21 U.S.C. § 351 and has a reasonable probability of causing serious adverse health consequences or death to humans or animals. It provides a statutory maximum term of imprisonment of 20 years.

The amendment amends Appendix A (Statutory Index) to reference offenses under section 333(b)(7) to § 2N1.1 (Tampering or Attempting to Tamper Involving Risk of Death or Bodily Injury). The Commission concluded that offenses under section 333(b)(7) are similar to tampering offenses under 18 U.S.C. § 1365 (Tampering with consumer products), which are referenced to § 2N1.1. In addition, the public health harms that Congress intended to target in adulteration cases are similar to those targeted by violations of section 1365(a) and are best addressed under § 2N1.1.

Effective Date: The effective date of this amendment is November 1, 2013.

774. **Amendment:** The Commentary to § 2T1.1 captioned "Application Notes" is amended in Note 1 by inserting "Tax Loss.—" at the beginning;

in Note 2 by inserting "Total Tax Loss Attributable to the Offense.—" at the beginning, and by redesignating subdivisions (a) through (e) as (A) through (E);

by inserting after Note 2 the following:

> "3. Unclaimed Credits, Deductions, and Exemptions.—In determining the tax loss, the court should account for the standard deduction and personal and dependent exemptions to which the defendant was entitled. In addition, the court should account for any unclaimed credit, deduction, or exemption that is needed to ensure a reasonable estimate of the tax loss, but only to the extent that (A) the credit, deduction, or exemption was related to the tax offense and could have been claimed at the time the tax offense was committed; (B) the credit, deduction, or exemption is reasonably and practicably ascertainable; and (C) the defendant presents information to support the credit, deduction, or exemption sufficiently in advance of sentencing to provide an adequate opportunity to evaluate whether it has sufficient indicia of reliability to support its probable accuracy (see § 6A1.3 (Resolution of Disputed Factors) (Policy Statement)).
>
> However, the court shall not account for payments to third parties made in a manner that encouraged or facilitated a separate violation of law (e.g., 'under the table' payments to employees or expenses incurred to obstruct justice).

The burden is on the defendant to establish any such credit, deduction, or exemption by a preponderance of the evidence. See § 6A1.3, comment.";

by striking "3. 'Criminal activity' means" and inserting the following:

"4. Application of Subsection (b)(1) (Criminal Activity).—'Criminal activity' means";

by striking "4. Sophisticated Means Enhancement.—" and inserting the following:

"5. Application of Subsection (b)(2) (Sophisticated Means).—";

by striking Notes 5 and 6 as follows:

"5. A 'credit claimed against tax' is an item that reduces the amount of tax directly. In contrast, a 'deduction' is an item that reduces the amount of taxable income.

6. 'Gross income,' for the purposes of this section, has the same meaning as it has in 26 U.S.C. § 61 and 26 C.F.R. § 1.61.";

and inserting the following:

"6. Other Definitions.—For purposes of this section:

A 'credit claimed against tax' is an item that reduces the amount of tax directly. In contrast, a 'deduction' is an item that reduces the amount of taxable income.

'Gross income' has the same meaning as it has in 26 U.S.C. § 61 and 26 C.F.R. § 1.61."; and

in Note 7 by inserting "Aggregation of Individual and Corporate Tax Loss.—" at the beginning.

Reason for Amendment: This amendment responds to a circuit conflict regarding whether a sentencing court, in calculating tax loss as defined in § 2T1.1 (Tax Evasion; Willful Failure to File Return, Supply Information, or Pay Tax; Fraudulent or False Returns, Statements, or Other Documents), may consider previously unclaimed credits, deductions, and exemptions that the defendant legitimately could have claimed if he or she had filed an accurate tax return.

The Tenth and Second Circuits have held that a sentencing court may give the defendant credit for a legitimate but unclaimed deduction. These circuit courts generally reason that, while a district court need not speculate about unclaimed deductions if the defendant offers weak support, nothing in the guidelines prohibits a sentencing court from considering evidence of unclaimed deductions where a defendant offers convincing proof. See United States v. Hoskins, 654 F.3d 1086, 1094 (10th Cir. 2011) ("[W]here defendant offers convincing proof — where the court's exercise is neither nebulous nor complex — nothing in the Guidelines prohibits a sentencing court from considering evidence of unclaimed deductions in analyzing a defendant's estimate of the tax loss suffered by the government."); United States v. Martinez-Rios, 143 F.3d 662, 671 (2d Cir. 1998) (holding that "the sentencing court need not base its tax loss calculation on gross unreported income if it can make a 'more accurate determination' of the intended loss and that determination of the tax loss involves giving the defendant the benefit of legitimate but unclaimed deductions"); United States v. Gordon, 291 F.3d 181, 187 (2d Cir. 2002) (applying Martinez-Rios, the court held that the district court erred when it refused to consider potential unclaimed deductions in its sentencing analysis).

Six other circuit courts — the Fourth, Fifth, Seventh, Eighth, Ninth, and Eleventh — have reached the opposite conclusion, directly or indirectly holding that a court may not consider unclaimed deductions to reduce the tax loss. These circuit courts generally reason that the "object of the [defendant's] offense" is established by the amount stated on the fraudulent return, and that courts should not be required to reconstruct the defendant's return based on speculation regarding the many hypothetical ways the defendant could have completed the return. See United States v. Delfino, 510 F.3d 468, 473 (4th Cir. 2007) ("The law simply does not require the district court to engage in [speculation as to what deductions would have been allowed], nor does it entitle the Delfinos to the benefit of deductions they might have claimed now that they stand convicted of tax evasion."); United States v. Phelps, 478 F.3d 680, 682 (5th Cir. 2007) (holding that the defendant could not reduce tax loss by taking a social security tax deduction that he did not claim on the false return); United States v. Chavin, 316 F.3d 666, 677 (7th Cir. 2002) ("Here, the object of [the defendant]'s offense was the amount by which he underreported and fraudulently stated his tax liability on his return; reference to other unrelated mistakes on the return such as unclaimed deductions tells us nothing about the amount of loss to the government that his scheme intended to create."); United States v. Psihos, 683 F.3d 777, 781-82 (7th Cir. 2012) (following Chavin in disallowing consideration of unclaimed deductions); United States v. Sherman, 372 F.App'x 668, 676–77 (8th Cir. 2010); United States v. Blevins, 542 F.3d 1200, 1203 (8th Cir. 2008) (declining to decide "whether an unclaimed tax benefit may ever offset tax loss," but finding the district court properly declined to reduce tax loss based on taxpayers' unclaimed deductions); United States v. Yip, 592 F.3d 1035, 1041 (9th Cir. 2010) ("We hold that § 2T1.1 does not entitle a defendant to reduce the tax loss charged to him by the amount of potentially legitimate, but unclaimed, deductions even if those deductions are related to the offense."); United States v. Clarke, 562 F.3d 1158, 1165 (11th Cir. 2009) (holding that the defendant was not entitled to a tax loss calculation based on a filing status other than the one he actually used; "[t]he district court did not err in computing the tax loss based on the fraudulent return Clarke actually filed, and not on the tax return Clarke could have filed but did not.").

The amendment resolves the conflict by amending the Commentary to § 2T1.1 to establish a new application note regarding the consideration of unclaimed credits, deductions, or exemptions in calculating a defendant's tax loss. This amendment reflects the Commission's view that consideration of legitimate unclaimed credits, deductions, or exemptions, subject to certain limitations and exclusions, is most consistent with existing provisions regarding the calculation of tax loss in § 2T1.1. See, e.g., USSG § 2T1.1, comment. (n.1) ("the guidelines contemplate that the court will simply make a reasonable estimate based on the available facts"); USSG § 2T1.1, comment. (backg'd.) ("a greater tax loss is obviously more harmful to the treasury and more serious than a smaller one with otherwise similar characteristics"); USSG § 2T1.1, comment. (n.1) (allowing a sentencing court to go beyond the presumptions set forth in the guideline if "the government or defense provides sufficient information for a more accurate assessment of the tax loss," and providing "the court should use any method of determining the tax loss that appears appropriate to reasonably calculate the loss that would have resulted had the offense been successfully completed").

The new application note first provides that courts should always account for the standard deduction and personal and dependent exemptions to which the defendant was entitled. The Commission received public comment and testimony that such deductions and exemptions are commonly considered and accepted by the government during the course of its investigation and during the course of plea negotiations. Consistent with this standard practice, the Commission determined that accounting for these generally undisputed and readily verifiable deductions and exemptions where they are not previously claimed (most commonly where the offense involves a failure to file a tax return) is appropriate.

The new application note further provides that courts should also account for any other previously unclaimed credit, deduction, or exemption that is needed to ensure a reasonable estimate of the tax loss, but only to the extent certain conditions are met. First, the credit, deduction, or exemption must be one that was related to the tax offense and could have been claimed at the time the tax offense was committed. This condition reflects the Commission's determination that a defendant should not be permitted to invoke unforeseen or after-the-fact changes or characterizations — such as offsetting losses that occur before or after the relevant tax year or substituting a more advantageous depreciation method or filing status — to lower the tax loss. To permit a defendant to optimize his return in this manner would unjustly reward defendants, and could require unjustifiable speculation and complexity at the sentencing hearing.

Second, the otherwise unclaimed credit, deduction, or exemption must be reasonably and practicably ascertainable. Consistent with the instruction in Application Note 1, this condition reaffirms the Commission's position that sentencing courts need only make a reasonable estimate of tax loss. In this regard, the Commission recognized that consideration of some unclaimed credits, deductions, or exemptions could require sentencing courts to make unnecessarily complex tax determinations, and therefore concluded that limiting consideration of unclaimed credits, deductions, or exemptions to those that are reasonably and practicably ascertainable is appropriate.

Third, the defendant must present information to support the credit, deduction, or exemption sufficiently in advance of sentencing to provide an adequate opportunity to evaluate whether it has sufficient indicia of reliability to support its probable accuracy. Consistent with the principles set forth in § 6A1.3 (Resolution of Disputed Factors) (Policy Statement), this condition ensures that the parties have an adequate opportunity to present information relevant to the court's consideration of any unclaimed credits, deductions, or exemptions raised at sentencing.

In addition, the new application note provides that certain categories of credits, deductions, or exemptions shall not be considered by the court in any case. In particular, "the court shall not account for payments to third parties made in a manner that encouraged or facilitated a separate violation of law (e.g., 'under the table' payments to employees or expenses incurred to obstruct justice)." The Commission determined that payments made in this manner result in additional harm to the tax system and the legal system as a whole. Therefore, to use them to reduce the tax loss would unjustifiably benefit the defendant and would result in a tax loss figure that understates the seriousness of the offense and the culpability of the defendant.

Finally, the application note makes clear that the burden is on the defendant to establish any credit, deduction, or exemption permitted under this new application note by a preponderance of the evidence, which is also consistent with the commentary in § 6A1.3.

Effective Date: The effective date of this amendment is November 1, 2013.

775. **Amendment:** The Commentary to § 3E1.1 captioned "Application Notes" is amended in Note 6 by adding at the end of the paragraph that begins "Because the Government" the following as the last sentence: "The government should not withhold such a motion based on interests not identified in § 3E1.1, such as whether the defendant agrees to waive his or

her right to appeal."; and

by adding after the paragraph that begins "Because the Government" the following new paragraph:

"If the government files such a motion, and the court in deciding whether to grant the motion also determines that the defendant has assisted authorities in the investigation or prosecution of his own misconduct by timely notifying authorities of his intention to enter a plea of guilty, thereby permitting the government to avoid preparing for trial and permitting the government and the court to allocate their resources efficiently, the court should grant the motion.".

The Commentary to § 3E1.1 captioned "Background" is amended in the paragraph that begins "Section 401(g)" by striking "the last paragraph" and inserting "the first sentence of the second paragraph".

Reason for Amendment: This amendment addresses two circuit conflicts involving the guideline for acceptance of responsibility, § 3E1.1 (Acceptance of Responsibility). A defendant who clearly demonstrates acceptance of responsibility for his offense receives a 2-level reduction under subsection (a) of § 3E1.1. The two circuit conflicts both involve the circumstances under which the defendant is eligible for a third level of reduction under subsection (b) of § 3E1.1. Subsection (b) provides:

(b) If the defendant qualifies for a decrease under subsection (a), the offense level determined prior to the operation of subsection (a) is level 16 or greater, and upon motion of the government stating that the defendant has assisted authorities in the investigation or prosecution of his own misconduct by timely notifying authorities of his intention to enter a plea of guilty, thereby permitting the government to avoid preparing for trial and permitting the government and the court to allocate their resources efficiently, decrease the offense level by 1 additional level.

The first circuit conflict involves the government's discretion under subsection (b) and, in particular, whether the government may withhold a motion based on an interest not identified in § 3E1.1, such as the defendant's refusal to waive his right to appeal. The second conflict involves the court's discretion under subsection (b) and, in particular, whether the court may decline to apply the third level of reduction when the government has moved for it.

These circuit conflicts are unusual in that they involve guideline and commentary provisions that Congress directly amended. See section 401(g) of the Prosecutorial Remedies and Other Tools to end the Exploitation of Children Today Act of 2003, Pub. L. 108–21 (the "PROTECT Act"); see also USSG App. C, Amendment 649 (effective April 30, 2003) (implementing amendments to the guidelines made directly by the PROTECT Act). They also implicate a congressional directive to the Commission not to "alter or repeal" the congressional amendments. See section 401(j)(4) of the PROTECT Act. Accordingly, in considering these conflicts, the Commission has not only reviewed public comment, sentencing data, case law, and the other types of information it ordinarily considers, but has also studied the operation of § 3E1.1 before the PROTECT Act, the congressional action to amend § 3E1.1, and the legislative history of that congressional action.

The Government's Discretion to Withhold the Motion

The first circuit conflict involves the government's discretion under subsection (b) and, in particular, whether the government may withhold a motion based on an interest not identified in § 3E1.1, such as the defendant's refusal to waive his right to appeal.

Several circuits have held that a defendant's refusal to sign an appellate waiver is a legitimate reason for the government to withhold a § 3E1.1(b) motion. See, e.g., United States v. Johnson, 581 F.3d 994, 1002 (9th Cir. 2009) (holding that "allocation and expenditure of prosecutorial resources for the purposes of defending an appeal is a rational basis" for such refusal); United States v. Deberry, 576 F.3d 708, 711 (7th Cir. 2009) (holding that requiring the defendant to sign an appeal waiver would avoid "expense and uncertainty" on appeal); United States v. Newson, 515 F.3d 374, 378 (5th Cir. 2008) (holding that the government's interests under § 3E1.1 encompass not only the government's time and effort at prejudgment stage but also at post-judgment proceedings).

In contrast, the Fourth Circuit has held that a defendant's refusal to sign an appellate waiver is not a legitimate reason for the government to withhold a § 3E1.1(b) motion. See United States v. Divens, 650 F.3d 343, 348 (4th Cir. 2011) (stating that "the text of § 3E1.1(b) reveals a concern for the efficient allocation of trial resources, not appellate resources" [emphasis in original]); see also United States v. Davis, No. 12-3552, slip op. at 5, __ F.3d __ (7th Cir., April 9, 2013) (Rovner, J., concurring) ("insisting that [the defendant] waive his right to appeal before he may receive the maximum credit under the Guidelines for accepting responsibility serves none of the interests identified in section 3E1.1"). The majority in Davis called for the conflict to be resolved, stating: "Resolution of this conflict is the province of the Supreme Court or the Sentencing Commission." Davis, slip op. at 3, __ F.3d at __ (per curiam). The Second Circuit, stating that the Fourth Circuit's reasoning in Divens applies "with equal force" to the defendant's request for an evidentiary hearing on sentencing issues, held that the government may not withhold a § 3E1.1 motion based upon such a request. See United States v. Lee, 653 F.3d 170, 175 (2d Cir. 2011).

The PROTECT Act added Commentary to § 3E1.1 stating that "[b]ecause the Government is in the best position to determine whether the defendant has assisted authorities in a manner that avoids preparing for trial, an adjustment under subsection (b) may only be granted upon a formal motion by the Government at the time of sentencing." See § 3E1.1, comment. (n.6). The PROTECT Act also amended § 3E1.1(b) to provide that the government motion state, among other things, that the defendant's notification of his intention to enter a plea of guilty permitted "the government to avoid preparing for trial and . . . the government and the court to allocate their resources efficiently . . .".

In its study of the PROTECT Act, the Commission could discern no congressional intent to allow decisions under § 3E1.1 to be based on interests not identified in § 3E1.1. Furthermore, consistent with Divens and the concurrence in Davis, the Commission determined that the defendant's waiver of his or her right to appeal is an example of an interest not identified in § 3E1.1. Accordingly, this amendment adds an additional sentence to the Commentary stating that "[t]he government should not withhold such a motion based on interests not identified in § 3E1.1, such as whether the defendant agrees to waive his or her right to appeal."

The Court's Discretion to Deny the Motion

The second conflict involves the court's discretion under subsection (b) and, in particular, whether the court may decline to apply the third level of reduction when the government has moved for it.

The Seventh Circuit has held that if the government makes the motion (and the other two requirements of subsection (b) are met, i.e., the defendant qualifies for the 2-level decrease and the offense level is level 16 or greater), the third level of reduction must be awarded. See United States v. Mount, 675 F.3d 1052 (7th Cir. 2012).

In contrast, the Fifth Circuit has held that the district court retains discretion to deny the motion. See United States v. Williamson, 598 F.3d 227, 230 (5th Cir. 2010). In Williamson, the defendant was convicted after jury trial but successfully appealed. After remand, he pled guilty to a lesser offense. The government moved for the third level of reduction, but the court declined to grant it because "regardless of however much additional trial preparation the government avoided through Williamson's guilty plea following remand, the preparation for the initial trial and the use of the court's resources for that trial meant that the § 3E1.1(b) benefits to the government and the court were not obtained". Id. at 231. The Fifth Circuit affirmed, holding that the decision whether to grant the third level of reduction "is the district court's — not the government's — even though the court may only do so on the government's motion". Id. at 230.

This amendment amends the Commentary to § 3E1.1 by adding the following statement: "If the government files such a motion, and the court in deciding whether to grant the motion also determines that the defendant has assisted authorities in the investigation or prosecution of his own misconduct by timely notifying authorities of his intention to enter a plea of guilty, thereby permitting the government to avoid preparing for trial and permitting the government and the court to allocate their resources efficiently, the court should grant the motion."

In its study of the PROTECT Act, the Commission could discern no congressional intent to take away from the court its responsibility under § 3E1.1 to make its own determination of whether the conditions were met. In particular, both the language added to the Commentary by the PROTECT Act and the legislative history of the PROTECT Act speak in terms of allowing the court discretion to "grant" the third level of reduction. See USSG § 3E1.1, comment. (n.6) (stating that the third level of reduction "may only be granted upon a formal motion by the Government"); H.R. Rep. No. 108-66, at 59 (2003) (Conf. Rep.) (stating that the PROTECT Act amendment would "only allow courts to grant an additional third point reduction for 'acceptance of responsibility' upon motion of the government."). In addition, the Commission observes that one of the considerations in § 3E1.1(b) is whether the defendant's actions permitted the court to allocate its resources efficiently, and the court is in the best position to make that determination. Accordingly, consistent with congressional intent, this amendment recognizes that the court continues to have discretion to decide whether to grant the third level of reduction.

Finally, and as mentioned above, the Commission in its study of the PROTECT Act could discern no congressional intent to allow decisions under § 3E1.1 to be based on interests not identified in § 3E1.1. For that reason, this amendment indicates that, if the government has filed the motion and the court also determines that the circumstances identified in § 3E1.1 are present, the court should grant the motion.

Effective Date: The effective date of this amendment is November 1, 2013.

776. **Amendment:** The Commentary to § 5G1.3 captioned "Background" is amended by striking the following: "In a case in which a defendant is subject to an undischarged sentence of imprisonment, the court generally has authority to impose an imprisonment sentence on the current offense to run concurrently with or consecutively to the prior undischarged term. 18 U.S.C. § 3584(a). Exercise of that authority,";

and inserting the following: "Federal courts generally 'have discretion to select whether the sentences they impose will run concurrently or consecutively with respect to other sentences that they impose, or that have been imposed in other proceedings, including state proceedings.' See Setser v. United States, 132 S. Ct. 1463, 1468 (2012); 18 U.S.C. § 3584(a). Federal courts also generally have discretion to order that the sentences they impose will run concurrently with or consecutively to other state sentences that are anticipated but not yet imposed. See Setser, 132 S. Ct. at 1468. Exercise of that discretion,".

Reason for Amendment: This amendment responds to a recent Supreme Court decision that federal courts have discretion to order that the sentence run consecutively to (or concurrently with) an anticipated, but not yet imposed, state sentence. See Setser v. United States, 132 S. Ct. 1463, 1468 (2012).

The discretion recognized in Setser for anticipated state sentences is similar to the discretion that federal courts have under 18 U.S.C. § 3584 for previously imposed sentences. Under section 3584, a federal court imposing a sentence generally has discretion to order that the sentence run consecutively to (or, in the alternative, concurrently with) a term of imprisonment previously imposed but not yet discharged. See 18 U.S.C. § 3584(a). Section 5G1.3 (Imposition of a Sentence on a Defendant Subject to an Undischarged Term of Imprisonment) provides guidance to the court in determining whether, and how, to use the discretion under section 3584, i.e., whether the sentence should run consecutively to (or, in the alternative, concurrently with) the prior undischarged term of imprisonment.

The amendment amends the background commentary to § 5G1.3 to include a statement that, in addition to the discretion provided by section 3584, federal courts also generally have discretion under Setser to order that the sentences they impose will run consecutively to or concurrently with other state sentences that are anticipated but not yet imposed. Determining whether, and how, to use this discretion will depend on the adequacy of the information available. See Setser, 132 S.Ct. at 1471 n.6 ("Of course, a district court should exercise the power to impose anticipatory consecutive (or concurrent) sentences intelligently. In some situations, a district court may have inadequate information and may forbear, but in other situations, that will not be the case."). Adding this statement to the guideline that applies to the court's discretion under section 3584 is intended to provide heightened awareness of the court's similar discretion under Setser.

Effective Date: The effective date of this amendment is November 1, 2013.

777. **Amendment:** The Commentary to § 2B1.1 captioned "Application Notes" is amended in Note 15 (as renumbered by Amendment 772) by striking "1a(5)" both places it appears and inserting "1a(11)"; by striking "1a(6)" both places it appears and inserting "1a(12)"; by striking "1a(20)" both places it appears and inserting "1a(28)"; and by striking "1a(23)" both places it appears and inserting "1a(31)".

Section 2B2.3(b) is amended by striking paragraph (1) as follows:

"(1) If the trespass occurred (A) at a secure government facility; (B) at a nuclear energy facility; (C) on a vessel or aircraft of the United States; (D) in a secure area of an airport or a seaport; (E) at a residence; (F) at Arlington National Cemetery or a cemetery under the control of the National Cemetery Administration; or (G) on a computer system used (i) to maintain or operate a critical infrastructure; or (ii) by or for a government entity in furtherance of the administration of justice, national defense, or national security, increase by 2 levels.";

and inserting the following:

"(1) (Apply the greater) If—

(A) the trespass occurred (i) at a secure government facility; (ii) at a nuclear energy facility; (iii) on a vessel or aircraft of the United States; (iv) in a secure area of an airport or a seaport; (v) at a residence; (vi) at Arlington National Cemetery or a cemetery under the control of the National Cemetery Administration; (vii) at any restricted building or grounds; or (viii) on a computer system used (I) to maintain or operate a critical infrastructure; or (II) by or for a government entity in furtherance of the administration of justice, national defense, or national security, increase by 2 levels; or

(B) the trespass occurred at the White House or its grounds, or the Vice President's official residence or its grounds, increase by 4 levels.".

The Commentary to § 2B2.3 captioned "Application Notes" is amended in Note 1 by inserting after the paragraph that begins "'Protected computer' means" the following:

"'Restricted building or grounds' has the meaning given that term in 18 U.S.C. § 1752."; and

in Note 2 by inserting "Application of Subsection (b)(3).—" at the beginning.

The Notes to the Drug Quantity Table in § 2D1.1(c) are amended in each of Notes (H) and (I) by striking "1308.11(d)(30)" and inserting "1308.11(d)(31)".

The Commentary to § 2J1.2 captioned "Application Notes" is amended in Note 2(A) by striking "Chapter Three, Part C" in the heading and inserting "§ 3C1.1"; and by striking "Chapter Three, Part C (Obstruction and Related Adjustments)" and inserting "§ 3C1.1 (Obstructing or Impeding the Administration of Justice)".

The Commentary to § 2J1.3 captioned "Application Notes" is amended in Note 2 by striking "Chapter Three, Part C (Obstruction and Related Adjustments)" and inserting "§ 3C1.1 (Obstructing or Impeding the Administration of Justice)"; and in Note 3 by striking "Chapter Three, Part C (Obstruction and Related Adjustments)" and inserting "§ 3C1.1".

The Commentary to § 2J1.6 captioned "Application Notes" is amended in Note 2 by striking "Chapter Three, Part C (Obstruction and Related Adjustments)" and inserting "§ 3C1.1 (Obstructing or Impeding the Administration of Justice)".

The Commentary to § 2J1.9 captioned "Application Notes" is amended in Note 1 by striking "Chapter Three, Part C (Obstruction and Related Adjustments)" and inserting "§ 3C1.1 (Obstructing or Impeding the Administration of Justice)"; and in Note 2 by striking "Chapter Three, Part C (Obstruction and Related Adjustments)" and inserting "§ 3C1.1".

The Commentary to § 4A1.1 captioned "Application Notes" is amended in each of Notes 2 and 3 by striking "court martial" and inserting "court-martial".

Section 4A1.2(g) is amended by striking "court martial" both places it appears and inserting "court-martial".

Appendix A (Statutory Index) is amended by inserting after the line referenced to 18 U.S.C. § 38 the following:

"18 U.S.C. § 39A   2A5.2";

in the line referenced to 18 U.S.C. § 554 by inserting "2M5.1," after "2B1.5,";

by inserting after the line referenced to 18 U.S.C. § 1513 the following:

"18 U.S.C. § 1514(c)   2J1.2";

by inserting after the line referenced to 18 U.S.C. § 1751(e) the following:

"18 U.S.C. § 1752   2A2.4, 2B2.3"; and

by inserting after the line referenced to 19 U.S.C. § 1586(e) the following:

"19 U.S.C. § 1590(d)(1)   2T3.1

19 U.S.C. § 1590(d)(2)   2D1.1".

Reason for Amendment: This amendment responds to recently enacted legislation and miscellaneous and technical guideline issues.

Aiming a Laser Pointer at an Aircraft

First, the amendment responds to Section 311 of the FAA Modernization and Reform Act of 2012, Pub. L. 112–95 (enacted February 14, 2012), which established a new criminal offense at 18 U.S.C. § 39A (Aiming a laser pointer at an aircraft). The offense applies to whoever knowingly aims the beam of a laser pointer at an aircraft in the special aircraft jurisdiction of the United States or at the flight path of such an aircraft. The statutory maximum term of imprisonment is five years.

The amendment amends Appendix A (Statutory Index) to reference section 39A offenses to § 2A5.2 (Interference with Flight Crew Member or Flight Attendant; Interference with Dispatch, Navigation, Operation, or Maintenance of Mass Transportation Vehicle). Section 2A5.2 is the most analogous guideline because the offense involves interference with an aircraft in flight.

Restraining the Harassment of a Victim or Witness

Second, the amendment responds to section 3(a) of the Child Protection Act of 2012, Pub. L. 112–206 (enacted December 7, 2012), which established a new offense at 18 U.S.C. § 1514(c) that makes it a criminal offense to knowingly and intentionally violate or attempt to violate an order issued under section 1514 (Civil action to restrain harassment of a victim or witness). The new offense has a statutory maximum term of imprisonment of five years.

The amendment amends Appendix A (Statutory Index) to reference section 1514(c) offenses to § 2J1.2 (Obstruction of Justice). Section 2J1.2 is the most analogous guideline because the offense involves interference with judicial proceedings.

Restricted Buildings and Grounds

Third, the amendment responds to the Federal Restricted Buildings and Grounds Improvement Act of 2011, Pub. L. 112–98 (enacted March 8, 2012), which amended the criminal offense at 18 U.S.C. § 1752 (Restricted building or grounds). As so amended, the statute defines "restricted buildings or grounds" to mean any restricted area (A) of the White House or its grounds, or the Vice President's official residence or its grounds; (B) of a building or grounds where the President or other person protected by the United States Secret Service is or will be temporarily visiting; or (C) of a building or grounds restricted in conjunction with an event designated as a special event of national significance. The statute makes it a crime to enter or remain; to impede or disrupt the orderly conduct of business or official functions; to obstruct or impede ingress or egress; or to engage in any physical violence against any person or property. The Act did not change the statutory maximum term of imprisonment, which is ten years if the person used or carried a deadly or dangerous weapon or firearm or if the offense results in significant bodily injury, and one year in any other case.

The amendment amends Appendix A (Statutory Index) to reference section 1752 offenses to § 2A2.4 (Obstructing or Impeding Officers) and § 2B2.3 (Trespass). These guidelines are most analogous because the elements of offenses under section 1752 involve either trespass at certain locations (i.e., locations permanently or temporarily protected by the Secret Service) or interference with official business at such locations, or both.

The amendment also amends § 2B2.3(b)(1) to ensure that a trespass under section 1752 provides a 4-level enhancement if the trespass occurred at the White House or the Vice President's official residence, or a 2-level enhancement if the trespass occurred at any other location permanently or temporarily protected by the Secret Service. Section 2B2.3(b)(1) provides a 2-level enhancement if the trespass occurred at locations that involve a significant federal interest, such as nuclear facilities, airports, and seaports. A trespass at a location protected by the Secret Service is no less serious than a trespass at other locations that involve a significant federal interest and warrants an equivalent enhancement of 2 levels. Section 2B2.3(b)(1) also provides a 2-level enhancement if the trespass occurred at a residence. A trespass at the residence of the President or the Vice President is more serious and poses a greater risk of harm than a trespass at an ordinary residence and warrants an enhancement of 4 levels.

Aviation Smuggling

Fourth, the amendment responds to the Ultralight Aircraft Smuggling Prevention Act of 2012, Pub. L. 112–93 (enacted February 10, 2012), which amended the criminal offense at 19 U.S.C. § 1590 (Aviation smuggling) to clarify that the term "aircraft" includes ultralight aircraft and to cover attempts and conspiracies. Section 1590 makes it unlawful for the pilot of an aircraft to transport merchandise, or for any individual on board any aircraft to possess merchandise, knowing that the merchandise will be introduced into the United States contrary to law. It is also unlawful for a person to transfer merchandise between an aircraft and a vessel on the high seas or in the customs waters of the United States unlawfully. The Act did not change the statutory maximum terms of imprisonment, which are 20 years if any of the merchandise involved was a controlled substance, see § 1590(d)(2), and five years otherwise, see § 1590(d)(1).

The amendment amends Appendix A (Statutory Index) to reference offenses under section 1590(d)(1) to § 2T3.1 (Evading Import Duties or Restrictions (Smuggling); Receiving or Trafficking in Smuggled Property). In such cases, § 2T3.1 is the most analogous guideline because the offense involves smuggling. The amendment also amends Appendix A (Statutory Index) to reference offenses under section 1590(d)(2) to § 2D1.1 (Unlawful Manufacturing, Importing, Exporting, or Trafficking (Including Possession with Intent to Commit These Offenses); Attempt or Conspiracy). In such cases, § 2D1.1 is the most analogous guideline because controlled substances are involved in these offenses.

Interaction Between Offense Guidelines in Chapter Two, Part J, and Certain Adjustments in Chapter Three, Part C

Fifth, the amendment responds to an application issue that may arise in cases in which the defendant is sentenced under an offense guideline in Chapter Two, Part J (Offenses Involving the Administration of Justice) and the defendant may also be subject to an adjustment under Chapter Three, Part C (Obstruction and Related Adjustments). Specifically, there are application notes in four Chapter Two, Part J guidelines that, it has been argued, preclude the court from applying adjustments in Chapter Three, Part C. See, e.g., United States v. Duong, 665 F.3d 364 (1st Cir. 2012) (observing that, "according to the literal terms" of the application notes, an adjustment under Chapter Three, Part C "'does not apply'", but "reject[ing] that premise").

The amendment amends the relevant application notes in Chapter Two, Part J (see §§ 2J1.2, comment. (n.2(A)); 2J1.3, comment. (n.2); 2J1.6, comment. (n.2); 2J1.9, comment. (n.1)) to clarify the Commission's intent that they restrict the court from applying § 3C1.1 (Obstructing or Impeding the Administration of Justice) but do not restrict the court from applying §§ 3C1.2, 3C1.3, and 3C1.4. These changes resolve the application issue consistent with Duong and promote clarity and consistency in the application of these adjustments.

Export Offenses Under 18 U.S.C. § 554

Sixth, the amendment broadens the range of guidelines to which export offenses under 18 U.S.C. § 554 (Smuggling goods from the United States) are referenced. Section 554 makes it unlawful to export or send from the United States (or attempt to do so) any merchandise, article, or object contrary to any law or regulation of the United States. It also makes it unlawful to receive, conceal, buy, sell, or in any manner facilitate the transportation, concealment, or sale of such merchandise, article, or object, prior to exportation, knowing the same to be intended for exportation contrary to any law or regulation of the United States. Offenses under section 554 have a statutory maximum term of imprisonment of ten years, and they are referenced in Appendix A (Statutory Index) to three guidelines: §§ 2B1.5 (Theft of, Damage to, or Destruction of, Cultural Heritage Resources or Paleontological Resources; Unlawful Sale, Purchase, Exchange, Transportation, or Receipt of Cultural Heritage Resources or Paleontological Resources), 2M5.2 (Exportation of Arms, Munitions, or Military Equipment or Services Without Required Validated Export License), and 2Q2.1 (Offenses Involving Fish, Wildlife, and Plants).

The amendment amends Appendix A (Statutory Index) to add § 2M5.1 (Evasion of Export Controls; Financial Transactions with Countries Supporting International Terrorism) to the list of guidelines to which offenses under section 554 are referenced. Not all offenses under section 554 involve munitions, cultural resources, or wildlife, so a reference to an additional guideline is warranted. For example, a section 554 offense may be based on the export of ordinary commercial goods in violation of economic sanctions or on the export of "dual-use" goods (i.e., goods that have both commercial and military applications). For such cases, the additional reference to § 2M5.1 promotes clarity and consistency in guideline application, and the penalty structure of § 2M5.1 provides appropriate distinctions between offenses that violate national security controls and offenses that do not.

Technical and Stylistic Changes

Finally, the amendment makes certain technical and stylistic changes to the Guidelines Manual. First, it amends the Commentary to § 2B1.1 (Theft, Property Destruction, and Fraud) to provide updated references to the definitions contained in 7 U.S.C. § 1a, which were renumbered by Public Law 111–203 (enacted July 21, 2010). Second, it amends the Notes to the Drug Quantity Table in § 2D1.1 (Unlawful Manufacturing, Importing, Exporting, or Trafficking (Including Possession with Intent to Commit These Offenses); Attempt or Conspiracy) to provide updated references to the definition of tetrahydrocannabinols contained in 21 C.F.R. § 1308.11(d), which were renumbered by 75 Fed. Reg. 79296 (December 20, 2010). Third, it makes several stylistic revisions in the Guidelines Manual to change "court martial" to "court-martial". The changes are not substantive.

Effective Date: The effective date of this amendment is November 1, 2013.

Amendment 778 SUPPLEMENT TO APPENDIX C November 1, 2013

778. Amendment: The Commentary to § 1B1.8 captioned "Application Notes" is amended in Note 3 by striking "(Inadmissibility of Pleas" and inserting "Pleas".

The Commentary to § 2M3.1 captioned "Application Notes" is amended in Note 1 by striking "12958" and inserting "13526".

The Commentary to § 8B2.1 captioned "Background" is amended by striking "805(a)(2)(5)" and inserting "805(a)(5)".

The Commentary to § 8D1.2 captioned "Application Note" is amended in Note 1 by striking "3561(b)" and inserting "3561(c)".

Reason for Amendment: This amendment makes certain technical changes to Commentary in the Guidelines Manual. The changes amend—

(1) Application Note 3 to § 1B1.8 (Use of Certain Information) to reflect a change to the heading of Rule 410 of the Federal Rules of Evidence;

(2) Application Note 1 to § 2M3.1 (Gathering or Transmitting National Defense Information to Aid a Foreign Government) to ensure that the Executive Order to which it refers is the most recent Executive Order; and

(3) the Background Commentary to § 8B2.1 (Effective Compliance and Ethics Program) and Application Note 1 to § 8D1.2 (Term of Probation - Organizations) to correct typographical errors in citations to certain statutes.

Effective Date: The effective date of this amendment is November 1, 2013.

779. Amendment: The Commentary to § 1B1.11 captioned "Background" is amended in the first paragraph by striking the following:

"Although aware of possible ex post facto clause challenges to application of the guidelines in effect at the time of sentencing, Congress did not believe that the ex post facto clause would apply to amended sentencing guidelines. S. Rep. No. 225, 98th Cong., 1st Sess. 77-78 (1983). While the Commission concurs in the policy expressed by Congress, courts to date have generally held that the ex post facto clause does apply to sentencing guideline amendments that subject the defendant to increased punishment.";

and inserting the following:

"However, the Supreme Court has held that the ex post facto clause applies to sentencing guideline amendments that subject the defendant to increased punishment. See Peugh v. United States, 133 S. Ct. 2072, 2078 (2013) (holding that 'there is an ex post facto violation when a defendant is sentenced under Guidelines promulgated after he committed his criminal acts and the new version provides a higher applicable Guidelines sentencing range than the version in place at the time of the offense')."; and

in the paragraph that begins "Subsection (b)(3)" by striking ", cert. denied, 493 U.S. 1062 (1990)".

Reason for Amendment: The Commission's policy statement at § 1B1.11 (Use of Guidelines in Effect on Date of Sentencing) provides that the court should apply the Guidelines Manual in effect on the date the defendant is sentenced unless the court determines that doing so would violate the ex post facto clause, in which case the court

–1296–

shall apply the Guidelines Manual in effect on the date the offense of conviction was committed. See § 1B1.11(a), (b)(1).

This amendment updates the Background Commentary to 1B1.11 to reflect the Supreme Court's decision in Peugh v. United States, 133 S. Ct. 2072 (2013), which held that "there is an ex post facto violation when a defendant is sentenced under Guidelines promulgated after he committed his criminal acts and the new version provides a higher applicable Guidelines sentencing range than the version in place at the time of the offense." Id. at 2078. The amendment inserts new language to refer to the Supreme Court's decision in Peugh and deletes obsolete language.

Effective Date: The effective date of this amendment is November 1, 2013.

APPENDIX D - SENTENCING WORKSHEETS

All the following Sentencing Worksheets were prepared by the United States Sentencing Commission and can be found on the Commission's website, www.ussc.gov.

PART A - WORKSHEETS FOR INDIVIDUALS

APPENDIX D   November 1, 2013

Worksheet A (Offense Level)

Defendant _____ District/Office _____

Docket Number (Year-Sequence-Defendant No.) ____ ____-____ ____ ____ ____-____

Count Number(s) _____ U.S. Code Title & Section _____ : _____
                                                        _____ : _____

Guidelines Manual Edition Used: 20___ (NOTE: worksheets keyed to the Manual effective November 1, 2010)

Instructions:

For each count of conviction (or stipulated offense), complete a separate Worksheet A. Exception: Use only a single Worksheet A where the offense level for a group of closely related counts is based primarily on aggregate value or quantity (see §3D1.2(d)) or where a count of conspiracy, solicitation, or attempt is grouped with a substantive count that was the sole object of the conspiracy, solicitation, or attempt (see §3D1.2(a) and (b)).

1. **Offense Level** (See Chapter Two)
   Enter the applicable base offense level and any specific offense characteristics from Chapter Two and explain the bases for these determinations. Enter the sum in the box provided.

Guideline	Description	Level
_____	_____	_____
_____	_____	_____
_____	_____	_____
_____	_____	_____
_____	_____	_____
_____	_____	_____

   Sum ☐

2. **Victim-Related Adjustments** (See Chapter Three, Part A)
   Enter the applicable section and adjustment. If more than one section is applicable, list each section and enter the combined adjustment. If no adjustment is applicable enter "0."   § _____   ☐

3. **Role in the Offense Adjustments** (See Chapter Three, Part B)
   Enter the applicable section and adjustment. If more than one section is applicable, list each section and enter the combined adjustment. If the adjustment reduces the offense level, enter a minus (-) sign in front of the adjustment. If no adjustment is applicable, enter "0."   § _____   ☐

4. **Obstruction Adjustments** (See Chapter Three, Part C)
   Enter the applicable section and adjustment. If more than one section is applicable, list each section and enter the combined adjustment. If no adjustment is applicable, enter "0."   § _____   ☐

5. **Adjusted Offense Level**
   Enter the sum of Items 1-4. If this worksheet does not cover all counts of conviction or stipulated offenses, complete Worksheet B. Otherwise, enter this result on Worksheet D, Item 1.   ☐

☐ *Check if the defendant is convicted of a single count. In such case, Worksheet B need not be completed.*

☐ *If the defendant has no criminal history, enter criminal history "I" here and on Item 4, Worksheet D. In such case, Worksheet C need not be completed.*

U.S. Sentencing Commission
November 22, 2010
H:\oesp\TRAINING\Worksheets\Worksheets-November2010.wpd

November 1, 2013   APPENDIX D

Worksheet B
(Multiple Counts or Stipulation to Additional Offenses)

Defendant _____   Docket Number _____

Instructions

Step 1: Determine if any of the counts group. (Note: All, some, or none of the counts may group. Some of the counts may have already been grouped in the application under Worksheet A, specifically, (1) counts grouped under §3D1.2(d), or (2) a count charging conspiracy, solicitation, or attempt that is grouped with the substantive count of conviction (see §3D1.2(a)). Explain the reasons for grouping:

_____

_____

Step 2: Using the box(es) provided below, for each group of closely related counts, enter the highest adjusted offense level from the various "A" Worksheets (Item 5) that comprise the group (see §3D1.3). (Note: A "group" may consist of a single count that has not grouped with any other count. In those instances, the offense level for the group will be the adjusted offense level for the single count.)

Step 3: Enter the number of units to be assigned to each group (see §3D1.4) as follows:

- One unit (1) for the group of closely related counts with the highest offense level
- An additional unit (1) for each group that is equally serious or 1 to 4 levels less serious
- An additional half unit (1/2) for each group that is 5 to 8 levels less serious
- No increase in units for groups that are 9 or more levels less serious

1. **Adjusted Offense Level for the First Group of Closely Related Counts**
   Count number(s):_____   ☐   _____ (unit)

2. **Adjusted Offense Level for the Second Group of Closely Related Counts**
   Count number(s):_____   ☐   _____ (unit)

3. **Adjusted Offense Level for the Third Group of Closely Related Counts**
   Count number(s):_____   ☐   _____ (unit)

4. **Adjusted Offense Level for the Fourth Group of Closely Related Counts**
   Count number(s):_____   ☐   _____ (unit)

5. **Adjusted Offense Level for the Fifth Group of Closely Related Counts**
   Count number(s):_____   ☐   _____ (unit)

6. **Total Units**   _____ (total units)

7. **Increase in Offense Level Based on Total Units (See §3D1.4)**

1 unit:	no increase	2 1/2 - 3 units:	add 3 levels
1 1/2 units:	add 1 level	3 1/2 - 5 units:	add 4 levels
2 units:	add 2 levels	More than 5 units:	add 5 levels

   ☐

8. **Highest of the Adjusted Offense Levels from Items 1-5 Above**   ☐

9. **Combined Adjusted Offense Level (See §3D1.4)**
   Enter the sum of Items 7 and 8 here and on Worksheet D, Item 1.   ☐

U.S. Sentencing Commission
November 22, 2010
H:\ocsp\TRAINING\Worksheets\Worksheets-November2010.wpd

APPENDIX D November 1, 2013

Worksheet C (Criminal History)

Defendant _____ Docket Number _____

Enter the Date Defendant Commenced Participation in Instant Offense (Earliest Date of Relevant Conduct) _____

1. <u>3 Points</u> for each prior ADULT sentence of imprisonment EXCEEDING ONE YEAR AND ONE MONTH <u>imposed within</u> 15 YEARS of the defendant's commencement of the instant offense OR resulting in <u>incarceration during</u> any part of that 15-YEAR period. (<u>See</u> §§4A1.1(a) and 4A1.2.)

2. <u>2 Points</u> for each prior sentence of imprisonment of AT LEAST 60 DAYS resulting from an offense committed ON OR AFTER the defendant's 18th birthday not counted under §4A1.1(a) <u>imposed within</u> 10 YEARS of the instant offense; and

   <u>2 Points</u> for each prior sentence of imprisonment of AT LEAST 60 DAYS resulting from an offense committed BEFORE the defendant's 18th birthday not counted under §4A1.1(a) from which the defendant was <u>released from confinement within</u> 5 YEARS of the instant offense. (<u>See</u> §§4A1.1(b) and 4A1.2.)

3. <u>1 Point</u> for each prior sentence resulting from an offense committed ON OR AFTER the defendant's 18th birthday not counted under §4A1.1(a) or §4A1.1(b) <u>imposed within</u> 10 YEARS of the instant offense; and

   <u>1 Point</u> for each prior sentence resulting from an offense committed BEFORE the defendant's 18th birthday not counted under §4A1.1(a) or §4A1.1(b) <u>imposed within</u> 5 YEARS of the instant offense. (<u>See</u> §§4A1.1(c) and 4A1.2.)

   NOTE: A maximum sum of <u>4 Points</u> may be given for the prior sentences in Item 3.

Date of Imposition	Offense	Sentence	Release Date**	Guideline Section	Criminal History Pts.

*   Indicate with an asterisk those offenses where defendant was sentenced as a juvenile.

** A release date is required in only two instances:

   a. When a sentence covered under §4A1.1(a) was imposed more than 15 years prior to the commencement of the instant offense but release from incarceration occurred within such 15-year period;

   b. When a sentence counted under §4A1.1(b) was imposed for an offense committed prior to age 18 and more than 5 years prior to the commencement of the instant offense, but release from incarceration occurred within such 5-year period; and

4. Sum of Criminal History Points for prior sentences under §§4A1.1(a), 4A1.1(b), and 4A1.1(c) (Items 1,2,3). ☐

November 1, 2013   APPENDIX D

Worksheet C   Page 2

Defendant _____   Docket Number _____

5. <u>2 Points</u> if the defendant committed the instant offense while <u>under any criminal justice sentence</u> (e.g., probation, parole, supervised release, imprisonment, work release, escape status). (See §§4A1.1(d) and 4A1.2.) List the type of control and identify the sentence from which control resulted. Otherwise, enter <u>0 Points</u>.

6. <u>1 Point</u> for each prior sentence resulting from a conviction of a crime of violence that did not receive any points under §4A1.1(a), (b), or (c) because such sentence was counted as a single sentence which also included another sentence resulting from a conviction for a crime of violence. (See §§4A1.1(e) and 4A1.2.) Identify the crimes of violence and briefly explain why the cases are considered a single sentence. Otherwise, enter <u>0 Points</u>.

_____
_____
_____
_____
_____
_____
_____
_____

7. **Total Criminal History Points** (Sum of Items 4-6)

8. **Criminal History Category** (Enter here and on Worksheet D, Item 4)

Total Points	Criminal History Category
0-1	I
2-3	II
4-6	III
7-9	IV
10-12	V
13 or more	VI

U.S. Sentencing Commission
November 22, 2010
H:\oesp\TRAINING\Worksheets\Worksheets-November2010.wpd

– 1303 –

APPENDIX D   November 1, 2013

Worksheet D (Guideline Worksheet)

Defendant _____   District _____

Docket Number _____

1. **Adjusted Offense Level** (From Worksheet A or B)
   If Worksheet B is required, enter the result from Worksheet B, Item 9.
   Otherwise, enter the result from Worksheet A, Item 5.

2. **Acceptance of Responsibility** (See Chapter Three, Part E)
   Enter the applicable reduction of 2 or 3 levels. If no adjustment is applicable, enter "0".

3. **Offense Level Total** (Item 1 less Item 2)

4. **Criminal History Category** (From Worksheet C)
   Enter the result from Worksheet C, Item 8.

5. **Terrorism/Career Offender/Criminal Livelihood/Armed Career Criminal/Repeat and Dangerous Sex Offender**
   (see Chapter Three, Part A, and Chapter Four, Part B)

   a. Offense Level Total

   If the provision for Career Offender (§4B1.1), Criminal Livelihood (§4B1.3), Armed Career Criminal (§4B1.4), or Repeat and Dangerous Sex Offender (§4B1.5) results in an offense level total higher than Item 3, enter the offense level total. Otherwise, enter "N/A."

   b. Criminal History Category

   If the provision for Terrorism (§3A1.4), Career Offender (§4B1.1), Armed Career Criminal (§4B1.4), or Repeat and Dangerous Sex Offender (§4B1.5) results in a criminal history category higher than Item 4, enter the applicable criminal history category. Otherwise, enter "N/A."

6. **Guideline Range from Sentencing Table**
   Enter the applicable guideline range from Chapter Five, Part A.   _____ Months

7. **Restricted Guideline Range** (See Chapter Five, Part G)
   If the statutorily authorized maximum sentence or the statutorily required minimum sentence restricts the guideline range (Item 6) (see §§5G1.1 and 5G1.2), enter either the restricted guideline range or any statutory maximum or minimum penalty that would modify the guideline range. Otherwise, enter "N/A."   _____ Months

   ☐ Check this box if §5C1.2 (Limitation on Applicability of Statutory Minimum Penalties in Certain Cases) is applicable.

8. **Undischarged Term of Imprisonment** (See §5G1.3)

   ☐ If the defendant is subject to an undischarged term of imprisonment, check this box and list the undischarged term(s) below.

   _____

   _____

U.S. Sentencing Commission
November 22, 2010
H:\oesp\TRAINING\Worksheets\Worksheets-November2010.wpd

November 1, 2013   APPENDIX D

Worksheet D   Page 2

Defendant _____ Docket Number _____

9. **Sentencing Options** (Check the applicable box that corresponds to the Guideline Range entered in Item 6 or Item 7, if applicable.)
(See Chapter Five, Sentencing Table)

    ☐ Zone A If checked, the following options are available (see §5B1.1):

- Fine (See §5E1.2(a))
- "Straight" Probation
- Imprisonment

    ☐ Zone B If checked, the <u>minimum term may be satisfied</u> by:

- Imprisonment
- Imprisonment of at least <u>one month</u> plus supervised release with a condition that substitutes community confinement or home detention for imprisonment (see §5C1.1(c)(2))
- Probation with a condition that substitutes intermittent confinement, community confinement, or home detention for imprisonment (see §5B1.1(a)(2) and §5C1.1(c)(3))

    ☐ Zone C If checked, the <u>minimum term may be satisfied</u> by:

- Imprisonment
- Imprisonment of at least <u>one-half of the minimum term</u> plus supervised release with a condition that substitutes community confinement or home detention for imprisonment (see §5C1.1(d)(2))

    ☐ Zone D If checked, the <u>minimum term shall be satisfied</u> by a sentence of imprisonment (see §5C1.1(f))

10. **Length of Term of Probation** (See §5B1.2)

If probation is imposed, the guideline for the length of such term of probation is: (Check applicable box)

    ☐ At least one year, but not more than five years if the offense level total is 6 or more

    ☐ No more than three years if the offense level total is 5 or less

11. **Conditions of Probation** (See §5B1.3)

List any mandatory conditions ((a)(1)-(10)), standard conditions ((c)(1)-(14)), and any other special conditions that may be applicable:

_____
_____
_____
_____
_____
_____
_____

U.S. Sentencing Commission
November 22, 2010
H:\oesp\TRAINING\Worksheets\Worksheets-November2010.wpd

APPENDIX D   November 1, 2013

Worksheet D   Page 3

Defendant _____   Docket Number _____

12. **Supervised Release** (See §§5D1.1 and 5D1.2)

    a. A term of supervised release is: (Check applicable box)

    ☐ Required because a term of imprisonment of more than one year is to be imposed or if required by statute

    ☐ Authorized but not required because a term of imprisonment of one year or less is to be imposed

    b. Length of Term (Guideline Range of Supervised Release): (Check applicable box)

    ☐ Class A or B Felony: Three to Five Year Term

    ☐ Class C or D Felony: Two to Three Year Term

    ☐ Class E Felony or Class A Misdemeanor: One Year Term

    c. Restricted Guideline Range of Supervision Release

    ☐ If a statutorily required term of supervised release impacts the guideline range, check this box and enter the required term. _____

13. **Conditions of Supervised Release** (See §5D1.3)
    List any mandatory conditions ((a)(1)-(8)), standard conditions ((c)(1)-(15)), and any other special conditions that may be applicable: _____
    _____

14. **Restitution** (See §5E1.1)

    a. If restitution is applicable, enter the amount. Otherwise enter "N/A" and the reason:_____
    _____

    b. Enter whether restitution is statutorily mandatory or discretionary: _____
    _____

    c. Enter whether restitution is by an order of restitution or <u>solely</u> as a condition of supervision. Enter the authorizing statute:
    _____

15. **Fines** (Guideline Range of Fines for Individual Defendants) (See §5E1.2)

    a. Special fine provisions   Minimum   Maximum
       ☐ Check box if any of the counts of conviction is
         for a statute with a special fine provision. (This
         does not include the general fine provisions of
         18 USC § 3571(b)(2), (d))

         Enter the sum of statutory maximum fines for all such counts $_____

    b. Fine Table (§5E1.2(c)(3))
       Enter the minimum and maximum fines $_____ $_____

    c. Guideline Range of Fines $_____ $_____
       (determined by the minimum of the fine table (Item 15(b))
       and the greater maximum above (Item 15(a) or 15(b)))

    d. Ability to Pay

       ☐ Check this box if the defendant does not have an ability to pay.

U.S. Sentencing Commission
November 22, 2010
H:\oesp\TRAINING\Worksheets\Worksheets-November2010.wpd

November 1, 2013 APPENDIX D

Worksheet D Page 4

Defendant _____ Docket Number _____

16. **Special Assessments** (See §5E1.3)

   Enter the total amount of special assessments required for all counts of conviction:

   - $25 for each misdemeanor count of conviction
   - Not less than $100 for each felony count of conviction

   $ _____

17. **Additional Factors**

   List any additional applicable guidelines, policy statements, and statutory provisions. Also list any applicable aggravating and mitigating factors that may warrant a sentence at a particular point either within or outside the applicable guideline range. Attach additional sheets as necessary.

   _____
   _____
   _____
   _____
   _____
   _____
   _____
   _____
   _____
   _____
   _____
   _____
   _____
   _____
   _____
   _____
   _____
   _____
   _____
   _____
   _____
   _____

Completed by _____ Date _____

U.S. Sentencing Commission
November 22, 2010
H:\oesp\TRAINING\Worksheets\Worksheets-November2010.wpd

APPENDIX DNovember 1, 2013

PART B - WORKSHEETS FOR ORGANIZATIONS

November 1, 2013   APPENDIX D

Organizational Worksheet A
(Offense Level)

Defendant _____   Docket Number _____

Docket Number (Year-Sequence-Defendant No.) _____ - _____ - _____

Count Number(s) _____ U.S. Code Title & Section _____ : _____

_____ : _____

Guidelines Manual Edition Used: 20 ___ (NOTE: worksheets keyed to the Manual effective November 1, 2001)

Instructions:
For each count of conviction (or stipulated offense listed at §8C2.1, complete a separate Worksheet A. Exceptions: Use only a single Worsheet A where the offense level for a group of closely related counts is based primarily on aggrregate value or quantity (See §3D1.2(d)) or where a count of conspiracy, solicitation, or attempt is grouped with a substantive count that was the sole object of the conspiracy, solicitation, or attempt (See §3D1.2(a) and (b)).

For counts of conviction (or stipulated offenses) not listed at §8C2.1, skip to Worksheet D, Item 1.

1. **Offense Level** (See §8C2.3).

    Enter the applicable base offense level and any specific offense characteristics from Chapter Two and explain the bases for these determinations. Enter the sum, the adjusted offense level, in the box provided below.

Guideline	**Description**	**Level**
_____	_____	_____
_____	_____	_____
_____	_____	_____

    If this worksheet does not cover all counts of conviction or stipulated offenses listed at §8C2.1, complete Worksheet B. Otherwise, enter this sum on Worksheet C, Item 1.

    Sum ☐

    (Adjusted Offense Level)

    Notes: _____

    _____

    Note: Chapter Three Parts A, B, C and E, **do not** apply to organizational defendants.

☐   Check if the defendant is convicted of a single count. In such case, Worksheet B need not be completed.

U.S. Sentencing Commission
December 17, 2001

APPENDIX D   November 1, 2013

Organizational Worksheet B
(Multiple Counts or Stipulation to Additional Offenses)

Defendant _____   Docket Number _____

Instructions

Step 1: Determine if any of the counts group. (Note: All, some, or none of the counts may group. Some of the counts may have already been grouped in the application under Worksheet A, specifically, (1) counts grouped under §3D1.2(d), or (2) a count charging conspiracy, solicitation, or attempt that is grouped with the substantive count of conviction (see §3D1.2(a)). Explain the reasons for grouping:

_____
_____

Step 2: Using the box(es) provided below, for each group of closely related counts, enter the highest adjusted offense level from the various "A" Worksheets (Worksheet A, Item 1) that comprise the group (see §3D1.3). (Note: A "group" may consist of a single count that has not grouped with any other count. In those instances, the offense level for the group will be the adjusted offense level for the single count.)

Step 3: Enter the number of units to be assigned to each group (see §3D1.4) as follows:

- One unit (1) for the group of closely related counts with the highest offense level
- An additional unit (1) for each group that is equally serious or 1 to 4 levels less serious
- An additional half unit (1/2) for each group that is 5 to 8 levels less serious
- No increase in units for groups that are 9 or more levels less serious

1. **Adjusted Offense Level for the First Group of Closely Related Counts**
   Count number(s): _____   ☐ _____(unit)

2. **Adjusted Offense Level for the Second Group of Closely Related Counts**
   Count number(s): _____   ☐ _____(unit)

3. **Adjusted Offense Level for the Third Group of Closely Related Counts**
   Count number(s): _____   ☐ _____(unit)

4. **Adjusted Offense Level for the Fourth Group of Closely Related Counts**
   Count number(s): _____   ☐ _____(unit)

5. **Adjusted Offense Level for the Fifth Group of Closely Related Counts**
   Count number(s): _____   ☐ _____(unit)

6. **Total Units**   _____
                                                                        (Total units)

7. **Increase in Offense Level Based on Total Units** (See §3D1.4)
   1 unit: no increase   2 1/2 - 3 units: add 3 levels
   1 1/2 units: add 1 level   3 1/2 - 5 units: add 4 levels   ☐
   2 units: add 2 levels   More than 5 units: add 5 levels

8. **Highest of the Adjusted Offense Levels from Items 1-5 Above**   ☐

9. **Combined Adjusted Offense Level** (See §3D1.4)
   Enter the sum of Items 7 and 8 here and on Worksheet C, Item 1.   ☐

U.S. Sentencing Commission
December 17, 2001

November 1, 2013   APPENDIX D

Organizational Worksheet C
(Base Fine, Culpability Score and Fine Range)

Defendant _____   Docket Number _____

1. **Offense Level Total**

    If Worksheet B is required, enter the combined adjusted offense level from Worksheet B, Item 9. Otherwise, enter the sum (the adjusted offense level) from Worksheet A, Item 1.

2. **Base Fine** (See §8C2.4(d))

    (a) Enter the amount from the Offense Level Fine Table (See §8C2.4(d)) corresponding to the offense level total in Item 1 above. $_____

    (b) Enter the pecuniary gain to the organization (See §8C2.4(a)(2)). $_____

    (c) Enter the pecuniary loss caused by the organization to the extent the loss was caused intentionally, knowingly, or recklessly (See §8C2.4(a)(3)). Note: the following Chapter Two guidelines have special instructions regarding the determination of pecuniary loss: §§2B4.1, 2C1.1, 2C1.2, 2E5.1, 2E5.6, and 2R1.1. $_____

    (d) Enter the amount from Item (a), (b), or (c) above, whichever is greatest. $_____

3. **Culpability Score** (See §8C2.5)

    (a) Start with five points and apply (b) through (g) below.   5

    (See §8C2.5(a))

    (b) Involvement/Tolerance (See §8C2.5(b))

    Enter the specific subdivision and points applicable. If more than one subdivision is applicable, use the greatest. If no adjustment is applicable, enter "0".   §_____

    (c) Prior History (See §8C2.5(c))

    Enter the specific subdivision and points applicable. If both subdivision are applicable, use the greater. If no adjustment is applicable, enter "0".   §_____

    Enter the earliest date of relevant conduct for the instant offense: _____

U.S. Sentencing Commission
December 17, 2001

APPENDIX D November 1, 2013

Organizational Worksheet C, Page Two

Defendant _____ Docket Number _____

    (d)   Violation of an Order (See §8C2.5(d))

           Enter the specific subdivision and points applicable. If both subdivisions are applicable, use the greater. If no adjustment is applicable, enter "0".   §_____   [____]

    (e)   Obstruction of Justice (See §8C2.5(e))

           If no adjustment is applicable, enter "0".   §_____   [____]

    (f)   Effective Program to Prevent and Detect Violations of Law (See §8C2.5(f))
           If no adjustment is applicable, enter "0".   §_____   [____]

    (g)   Self-Reporting, Cooperation, and Acceptance of Responsibility (See §8C2.5(g))

           Enter the specific subdivision and points applicable. If more than one subdivision is applicable, use the greatest. If no adjustment is applicable, enter "0".   §_____   [____]

4. **Total Culpability Score**

    Enter the total of Items 3(a) through 3(g).   _____

5. **Minimum and Maximum Multipliers** (See §8C2.6)

    Enter the minimum and the maximum multipliers from the table at §8C2.6 corresponding to the total culpability score in Item 4 above.
    Note: If the applicable Chapter Two guideline is §2R1.1, neither the minimum nor the maximum multiplier shall be less than 0.75. (See §2R1.1(d)(2)).

    (a)   Minimum Multiplier   _____

    (b)   Maximum Multiplier   _____

U.S. Sentencing Commission
December 17, 2001

Organizational Worksheet C, Page Three

Defendant _____ Docket Number _____

6. **Fine Range** (See §8C2.7)

    (a) Multiply the base fine (Item 2(d) above) by the minimum multiplier (Item 5(a) above) to establish the minimum of the fine range. Enter the result here and at Worksheet D, Item 4(a).

    Minimum of fine range $_____

    (b) Multiply the base fine (Item 2(d) above) by the maximum multiplier (Item 5(b) above) to establish the maximum of the fine range. Enter the result here and at Worksheet D, Item 4(a).

    Maximum of fine range $_____

7. **Disgorgement** (See §8C2.9)

    Skip this item if any pending or anticipated civil or administrative proceeding is expected to deprive the defendant of its gain from the offense.

    (a) Enter the amount of pecuniary gain to the defendant from Item 2(b) above $_____

    (b) Enter the amount of restitution already made and remedial costs already incurred. $_____

    (c) Enter the amount of restitution and other remedial costs to be ordered by the court. (See §§8B1.1 and 8B1.2.) $_____

    (d) Add Items (b) and (c) and enter the sum.

    (e) Subtract the sum of restitution and remedial costs (Item (d)) from the amount of pecuniary gain to the defendant (Item (a)) to determine undisgorged gain. Enter the result here and at Worksheet D, Item 4(b). Note: If the amount of undisgorged gain is less than zero, enter zero. $_____

U.S. Sentencing Commission
December 17, 2001

APPENDIX D   November 1, 2013

Organizational Worksheet D
(Guideline Worksheet)

Defendant _____   Docket Number _____

Note: Unless otherwise specified, all items on Worksheet D are applicable to **all** counts of conviction.

1. **Restitution** (See §8B1.1)

    a. If restitution is applicable, enter the amount. Otherwise enter "N/A" and the reason:
    _____

    b. Enter whether restitution is statutorily mandatory or discretionary:
    _____

    c. Enter whether restitution is by an order of restitution or solely as a condition of supervision. Enter the authorizing statute:
    _____

2. **Remedial Orders** (See §8B1.2), **Community Service** (See §8B1.3), **Order of Notice to Victims** (See §8B1.4)

    List if applicable. Otherwise enter "N/A".
    _____
    _____

3. **Criminal Purpose Organization** (See §8C1.1)

    If a preliminary determination indicates that the organization operated primarily for a criminal purpose or primarily by criminal means, enter the amount of the organization's net assets. This amount shall be the fine (subject to the statutory maximum) for all counts of conviction. $_____

4. **Guideline Range** (Only for counts listed under §8C2.1)

    (a) Enter the fine range from Worksheet C, Item 6 $_____ to $_____

    (b) Disgorgement (See §8C2.9)

    Enter the result from the Worksheet C, Item 7(e). The court shall add to the fine determined under §8C2.1 (Determining the Fine Within the Range) any undisgorged gain to the organization from the offense. $_____

5. **Counts Not Listed Under §8C2.1** (See §8C2.10)

    Enter the counts not listed under §8C2.1 and the statutory maximum fine for each count. The court may impose an additional fine for these counts.
    _____
    _____

U.S. Sentencing Commission
December 17, 2001

November 1, 2013   APPENDIX D

Organizational Worksheet D, Page Two
(Guideline Worksheet)

Defendant _____   Docket Number _____

6. **Fine Offset** (See §8C3.4)

   Multiply the total fines imposed upon individuals who each own at least
   five percent (5%) interest in the organization by those individuals' total percentage
   interest in the organization, and enter the result. The court **may** reduce the
   fine imposed on a closely held organization by an amount not to exceed the fine
   offset. $ _____

7. **Imposition of a Sentence of Probation** (See §8D1.1.)

   (a) Probation is required if any of the following apply. Check the applicable boxes(es).

   ☐ (1) Probation is necessary as a mechanism to secure payment of restitution (§8B1.1), enforce a remedial order (§8B1.2), or ensure completion of community service (§8B1.3).

   ☐ (2) Any monetary penalty imposed (i.e., restitution, fine, or special assessment) is not paid in full at the time of sentencing and restrictions appear necessary to safeguard the defendant's ability to make payments.

   ☐ (3) At the time of sentencing the organization has 50 or more employees and does not have an effective program to prevent and detect violations of law.

   ☐ (4) Within the last five years prior to sentencing, the organization has engaged in similar misconduct, as determined by a prior criminal adjudication, and any part of the misconduct underlying the instant offense occurred after that adjudication.

   ☐ (5) An individual within high-level personnel of the organization or the unit of the organization within which the instant offense was committed participated in the misconduct underlying the instant offense; and that individual within five years prior to sentencing engaged in similar misconduct, as determined by a prior criminal adjudication; and any part of the misconduct underlying the instant offense occurred after that adjudication.

   ☐ (6) Probation is necessary to ensure that changes are made within the organization to reduce the likelihood of future criminal conduct.

   ☐ (7) The sentence imposed upon the organization does not include a fine.

   ☐ (8) Probation is necessary to accomplish one or more of the purposes of sentencing set forth in 18 U.S.C. § 3553(a)(2). State purpose(s): _____

   _____

   _____

U.S. Sentencing Commission
December 17, 2001

Organizational Worksheet D, Page Three
(Guideline Worksheet)

Defendant _____ Docket Number _____

    (b) Length of Term of Probation (See §8D1.2)
          If probation is imposed, the guideline for the length of such term of probation is:
          (Check the applicable box)

        ☐ (1) At least one year, but not more than five years if the offense is a felony

        ☐ (2) No more than five years if the offense is a Class A misdemeanor

    (c) Conditions of Probation (See §§8D1.3 and 8D1.4)
          List any mandatory conditions (§8D1.3), recommended conditions (§8D1.4), and any other special conditions that may be applicable. _____
          _____
          _____

8. **Special Assessments** (See §8E1.1)

    Enter the total amount of special assessments required for all counts of conviction. $_____

9. **Additional Factors**

    List any additional applicable guidelines, policy statements, and statutory provisions. Also list any applicable aggravating and mitigating factors that may warrant a sentence at a particular point either within or outside the applicable guideline range. Attach additional sheets as necessary.

_____
_____
_____
_____
_____
_____
_____
_____
_____
_____
_____
_____

Completed by _____ Date _____

U.S. Sentencing Commission
December 17, 2001

APPENDIX E - FEDERAL RULES OF CRIMINAL PROCEDURE RELATING TO SENTENCING*

United States Code Annotated

Federal Rules of Criminal Procedure for the United States District Courts

VII. Post-Conviction Procedures

Rule 32. Sentencing and Judgment

(a) [Reserved.]

(b) **Time of Sentencing.**

(1) **In General.** The court must impose sentence without unnecessary delay.

(2) **Changing Time Limits.** The court may, for good cause, change any time limits prescribed in this rule.

(c) **Presentence Investigation.**

(1) **Required Investigation.**

(A) **In General.** The probation officer must conduct a presentence investigation and submit a report to the court before it imposes sentence unless:

(i) 18 U.S.C. § 3593(c) or another statute requires otherwise; or

(ii) the court finds that the information in the record enables it to meaningfully exercise its sentencing authority under 18 U.S.C. § 3553, and the court explains its finding on the record.

(B) **Restitution.** If the law permits restitution, the probation officer must conduct an investigation and submit a report that contains sufficient information for the court to order restitution.

(2) **Interviewing the Defendant.** The probation officer who interviews a defendant as part of a presentence investigation must, on request, give the defendant's attorney notice and a reasonable opportunity to attend the interview.

[Text of subdivision (d) effective until December 1, 2011, absent contrary Congressional action.]

(d) **Presentence Report.**

(1) **Applying the Advisory Sentencing Guidelines.** The presentence report must:

(A) identify all applicable guidelines and policy statements of the Sentencing Commission;

(B) calculate the defendant's offense level and criminal history category;

---

*Publisher's Note: This Appendix has been added by the Publisher. It is not included in the Commission's *Guidelines Manual*.

(C) state the resulting sentencing range and kinds of sentences available;

(D) identify any factor relevant to:

(i) the appropriate kind of sentence, or

(ii) the appropriate sentence within the applicable sentencing range; and

(E) identify any basis for departing from the applicable sentencing range.

(2) Additional Information. The presentence report must also contain the following:

(A) the defendant's history and characteristics, including:

(i) any prior criminal record;

(ii) the defendant's financial condition; and

(iii) any circumstances affecting the defendant's behavior that may be helpful in imposing sentence or in correctional treatment;

(B) information that assesses any financial, social, psychological, and medical impact on any victim;

(C) when appropriate, the nature and extent of nonprison programs and resources available to the defendant;

(D) when the law provides for restitution, information sufficient for a restitution order;

(E) if the court orders a study under 18 U.S.C. § 3552(b), any resulting report and recommendation;

(F) a statement of whether the government seeks forfeiture under Rule 32.2 and any other law; and

(G) any other information that the court requires, including information relevant to the factors under 18 U.S.C. § 3553(a).

(3) Exclusions. The presentence report must exclude the following:

(A) any diagnoses that, if disclosed, might seriously disrupt a rehabilitation program;

(B) any sources of information obtained upon a promise of confidentiality; and

(C) any other information that, if disclosed, might result in physical or other harm to the defendant or others.

[Text of subdivision (d) effective December 1, 2011, absent contrary Congressional action.]

(e) Disclosing the Report and Recommendation.

(1) Time to Disclose. Unless the defendant has consented in writing, the probation officer must not submit a presentence report to the court or disclose its contents to anyone until the defendant has pleaded guilty or nolo contendere, or has been found guilty.

(2) Minimum Required Notice. The probation officer must give the presentence report to the defendant, the defendant's attorney, and an attorney for the government at least 35 days before sentencing unless the defendant waives this minimum period.

(3) Sentence Recommendation. By local rule or by order in a case, the court may direct the probation officer not to disclose to anyone other than the court the officer's recommendation on the sentence.

(f) Objecting to the Report.

(1) Time to Object. Within 14 days after receiving the presentence report, the parties must state in writing any objections, including objections to material information, sentencing guideline ranges, and policy statements contained in or omitted from the report.

(2) Serving Objections. An objecting party must provide a copy of its objections to the opposing party and to the probation officer.

(3) Action on Objections. After receiving objections, the probation officer may meet with the parties to discuss the objections. The probation officer may then investigate further and revise the presentence report as appropriate.

(g) Submitting the Report. At least 7 days before sentencing, the probation officer must submit to the court and to the parties the presentence report and an addendum containing any unresolved objections, the grounds for those objections, and the probation officer's comments on them.

(h) Notice of Possible Departure from Sentencing Guidelines. Before the court may depart from the applicable sentencing range on a ground not identified for departure either in the presentence report or in a party's prehearing submission, the court must give the parties reasonable notice that it is contemplating such a departure. The notice must specify any ground on which the court is contemplating a departure.

(i) Sentencing.

(1) In General. At sentencing, the court:

(A) must verify that the defendant and the defendant's attorney have read and discussed the presentence report and any addendum to the report;

(B) must give to the defendant and an attorney for the government a written summary of--or summarize in camera--any information excluded from the presentence report under Rule 32(d)(3) on which the court will rely in sentencing, and give them a reasonable opportunity to comment on that information;

(C) must allow the parties' attorneys to comment on the probation officer's determinations and other matters relating to an appropriate sentence; and

(D) may, for good cause, allow a party to make a new objection at any time before sentence is imposed.

(2) Introducing Evidence; Producing a Statement. The court may permit the parties to introduce evidence on the objections. If a witness testifies at sentencing, Rule 26.2(a)-(d) and (f) applies. If a party fails to comply with a Rule 26.2 order to produce a witness's statement, the court must not consider that witness's testimony.

(3) Court Determinations. At sentencing, the court:

(A) may accept any undisputed portion of the presentence report as a finding of fact;

(B) must--for any disputed portion of the presentence report or other controverted matter--rule on the dispute or determine that a ruling is unnecessary either because the matter will not affect sentencing, or because the court will not consider the matter in sentencing; and

(C) must append a copy of the court's determinations under this rule to any copy of the presentence report made available to the Bureau of Prisons.

(4) Opportunity to Speak.

(A) By a Party. Before imposing sentence, the court must:

(i) provide the defendant's attorney an opportunity to speak on the defendant's behalf;

(ii) address the defendant personally in order to permit the defendant to speak or present any information to mitigate the sentence; and

(iii) provide an attorney for the government an opportunity to speak equivalent to that of the defendant's attorney.

(B) By a Victim. Before imposing sentence, the court must address any victim of the crime who is present at sentencing and must permit the victim to be reasonably heard.

(C) In Camera Proceedings. Upon a party's motion and for good cause, the court may hear in camera any statement made under Rule 32(i)(4).

(j) Defendant's Right to Appeal.

(1) Advice of a Right to Appeal.

(A) Appealing a Conviction. If the defendant pleaded not guilty and was convicted, after sentencing the court must advise the defendant of the right to appeal the conviction.

(B) Appealing a Sentence. After sentencing--regardless of the defendant's plea--the court must advise the defendant of any right to appeal the sentence.

(C) Appeal Costs. The court must advise a defendant who is unable to pay appeal costs of the right to ask for permission to appeal in forma pauperis.

(2) Clerk's Filing of Notice. If the defendant so requests, the clerk must immediately prepare and file a notice of appeal on the defendant's behalf.

(k) Judgment.

(1) In General. In the judgment of conviction, the court must set forth the plea, the jury verdict or the court's findings, the adjudication, and the sentence. If the defendant is found not guilty or is otherwise entitled to be discharged, the court must so order. The judge must sign the judgment, and the clerk must enter it.

(2) Criminal Forfeiture. Forfeiture procedures are governed by Rule 32.2.

CREDIT(S)

(As amended Feb. 28, 1966, eff. July 1, 1966; Apr. 24, 1972, eff. Oct. 1, 1972; Apr. 22, 1974, eff. Dec. 1, 1975; July 31, 1975, Pub.L. 94-64, § 3(31)-(34), 89 Stat. 376; Apr. 30, 1979, eff. Aug. 1, 1979, Dec. 1, 1980; Oct. 12, 1982, Pub.L. 97-291, § 3, 96 Stat. 1249; Apr. 28, 1983, eff. Aug. 1, 1983; Oct. 12, 1984, Pub.L. 98-473, Title II, § 215(a), 98 Stat. 2014; Nov. 10, 1986, Pub.L. 99-646, § 25(a), 100 State. 3597; Mar. 9, 1987, eff. Aug. 1, 1987; Apr. 25, 1989, eff. Dec. 1, 1989; Apr. 30, 1991, eff. Dec. 1, 1991; Apr. 22, 1993, eff. Dec. 1, 1993; Apr. 29, 1994, eff. Dec. 1, 1994; Sept. 13, 1994, Pub.L.

103-322, Title XXIII, § 230101(b), 108 Stat. 2078; Apr. 23, 1996, eff. Dec. 1, 1996; Apr. 24, 1996, Pub.L. 104-132, Title II, § 207(a), 110 Stat. 1236; Apr. 17, 2000, eff. Dec. 1, 2000; Apr. 29, 2002, eff. Dec. 1, 2002; Apr. 30, 2007, eff. Dec. 1, 2007; Apr. 23, 2008, eff. Dec. 1, 2008; Mar. 26, 2009, eff. Dec. 1, 2009; Apr. 26, 2011, eff. Dec. 1, 2011, absent contrary Congressional action.)

Rule 32.1. Revoking or Modifying Probation or Supervised Release

(a) Initial Appearance.

(1) Person In Custody. A person held in custody for violating probation or supervised release must be taken without unnecessary delay before a magistrate judge.

(A) If the person is held in custody in the district where an alleged violation occurred, the initial appearance must be in that district.

(B) If the person is held in custody in a district other than where an alleged violation occurred, the initial appearance must be in that district, or in an adjacent district if the appearance can occur more promptly there.

(2) Upon a Summons. When a person appears in response to a summons for violating probation or supervised release, a magistrate judge must proceed under this rule.

(3) Advice. The judge must inform the person of the following:

(A) the alleged violation of probation or supervised release;

(B) the person's right to retain counsel or to request that counsel be appointed if the person cannot obtain counsel; and

(C) the person's right, if held in custody, to a preliminary hearing under Rule 32.1(b)(1).

(4) Appearance in the District With Jurisdiction. If the person is arrested or appears in the district that has jurisdiction to conduct a revocation hearing-- either originally or by transfer of jurisdiction--the court must proceed under Rule 32.1(b)-(e).

(5) Appearance in a District Lacking Jurisdiction. If the person is arrested or appears in a district that does not have jurisdiction to conduct a revocation hearing, the magistrate judge must:

(A) if the alleged violation occurred in the district of arrest, conduct a preliminary hearing under Rule 32.1(b) and either:

(i) transfer the person to the district that has jurisdiction, if the judge finds probable cause to believe that a violation occurred; or

(ii) dismiss the proceedings and so notify the court that has jurisdiction, if the judge finds no probable cause to believe that a violation occurred; or

(B) if the alleged violation did not occur in the district of arrest, transfer the person to the district that has jurisdiction if:

(i) the government produces certified copies of the judgment, warrant, and warrant application, or produces copies of those certified documents by reliable electronic means; and

(ii) the judge finds that the person is the same person named in the warrant.

(6) Release or Detention. The magistrate judge may release or detain the person under 18

U.S.C. § 3143(a)(1) pending further proceedings. The burden of establishing by clear and convincing evidence that the person will not flee or pose a danger to any other person or to the community rests with the person.

(b) Revocation.

(1) Preliminary Hearing.

(A) In General. If a person is in custody for violating a condition of probation or supervised release, a magistrate judge must promptly conduct a hearing to determine whether there is probable cause to believe that a violation occurred. The person may waive the hearing.

(B) Requirements. The hearing must be recorded by a court reporter or by a suitable recording device. The judge must give the person:

(i) notice of the hearing and its purpose, the alleged violation, and the person's right to retain counsel or to request that counsel be appointed if the person cannot obtain counsel;

(ii) an opportunity to appear at the hearing and present evidence; and

(iii) upon request, an opportunity to question any adverse witness, unless the judge determines that the interest of justice does not require the witness to appear.

(C) Referral. If the judge finds probable cause, the judge must conduct a revocation hearing. If the judge does not find probable cause, the judge must dismiss the proceeding.

(2) Revocation Hearing. Unless waived by the person, the court must hold the revocation hearing within a reasonable time in the district having jurisdiction. The person is entitled to:

(A) written notice of the alleged violation;

(B) disclosure of the evidence against the person;

(C) an opportunity to appear, present evidence, and question any adverse witness unless the court determines that the interest of justice does not require the witness to appear;

(D) notice of the person's right to retain counsel or to request that counsel be appointed if the person cannot obtain counsel; and

(E) an opportunity to make a statement and present any information in mitigation.

(c) Modification.

(1) In General. Before modifying the conditions of probation or supervised release, the court must hold a hearing, at which the person has the right to counsel and an opportunity to make a statement and present any information in mitigation.

(2) Exceptions. A hearing is not required if:

(A) the person waives the hearing; or

(B) the relief sought is favorable to the person and does not extend the term of probation or of supervised release; and

(C) an attorney for the government has received notice of the relief sought, has had a reasonable opportunity to object, and has not done so.

(d) Disposition of the Case. The court's disposition of the case is governed by 18 U.S.C. § 3563 and § 3565 (probation) and § 3583 (supervised release).

(e) Producing a Statement. Rule 26.2(a)-(d) and (f) applies at a hearing under this rule. If a party fails to comply with a Rule 26.2 order to produce a witness's statement, the court must not consider that witness's testimony.

CREDIT(S)

(Added Apr. 30, 1979, eff. Dec. 1, 1980, and amended Nov. 10, 1986, Pub.L. 99-646, § 12(b), 100 Stat. 3594; Mar. 9, 1987, eff. Aug. 1, 1987; Apr. 25, 1989, eff. Dec. 1, 1989; Apr. 30, 1991, eff. Dec. 1, 1991; Apr. 22, 1993, eff. Dec. 1, 1993; Apr. 29, 2002, eff. Dec. 1, 2002; Apr. 25, 2005, eff. Dec. 1, 2005; Apr. 12, 2006, eff. Dec. 1, 2006; Apr. 28, 2010, eff. Dec. 1, 2010, absent contrary Congressional action.)

Rule 32.2. Criminal Forfeiture

(a) Notice to the Defendant. A court must not enter a judgment of forfeiture in a criminal proceeding unless the indictment or information contains notice to the defendant that the government will seek the forfeiture of property as part of any sentence in accordance with the applicable statute. The notice should not be designated as a count of the indictment or information. The indictment or information need not identify the property subject to forfeiture or specify the amount of any forfeiture money judgment that the government seeks.

(b) Entering a Preliminary Order of Forfeiture.

(1) Forfeiture Phase of the Trial.

(A) Forfeiture Determinations. As soon as practical after a verdict or finding of guilty, or after a plea of guilty or nolo contendere is accepted, on any count in an indictment or information regarding which criminal forfeiture is sought, the court must determine what property is subject to forfeiture under the applicable statute. If the government seeks forfeiture of specific property, the court must determine whether the government has established the requisite nexus between the property and the offense. If the government seeks a personal money judgment, the court must determine the amount of money that the defendant will be ordered to pay.

(B) Evidence and Hearing. The court's determination may be based on evidence already in the record, including any written plea agreement, and on any additional evidence or information submitted by the parties and accepted by the court as relevant and reliable. If the forfeiture is contested, on either party's request the court must conduct a hearing after the verdict or finding of guilty.

(2) Preliminary Order.

(A) Contents of a Specific Order. If the court finds that property is subject to forfeiture, it must promptly enter a preliminary order of forfeiture setting forth the amount of any money judgment, directing the forfeiture of specific property, and directing the forfeiture of any substitute property if the government has met the statutory criteria. The court must enter the order without regard to any third party's interest in the property. Determining whether a third party has such an interest must be deferred until any third party files a claim in an ancillary proceeding under Rule 32.2(c).

(B) Timing. Unless doing so is impractical, the court must enter the preliminary order sufficiently in advance of sentencing to allow the parties to suggest revisions or modifications before the order becomes final as to the defendant under Rule 32.2(b)(4).

(C) General Order. If, before sentencing, the court cannot identify all the specific property subject to forfeiture or calculate the total amount of the money judgment, the court may enter a forfeiture order that:

(i) lists any identified property;

(ii) describes other property in general terms; and

(iii) states that the order will be amended under Rule 32.2(e)(1) when additional specific property is identified or the amount of the money judgment has been calculated.

(3) Seizing Property. The entry of a preliminary order of forfeiture authorizes the Attorney General (or a designee) to seize the specific property subject to forfeiture; to conduct any discovery the court considers proper in identifying, locating, or disposing of the property; and to commence proceedings that comply with any statutes governing third-party rights. The court may include in the order of forfeiture conditions reasonably necessary to preserve the property's value pending any appeal.

(4) Sentence and Judgment.

(A) When Final. At sentencing--or at any time before sentencing if the defendant consents--the preliminary forfeiture order becomes final as to the defendant. If the order directs the defendant to forfeit specific property, it remains preliminary as to third parties until the ancillary proceeding is concluded under Rule 32.2(c).

(B) Notice and Inclusion in the Judgment. The court must include the forfeiture when orally announcing the sentence or must otherwise ensure that the defendant knows of the forfeiture at sentencing. The court must also include the forfeiture order, directly or by reference, in the judgment, but the court's failure to do so may be corrected at any time under Rule 36.

(C) Time to Appeal. The time for the defendant or the government to file an appeal from the forfeiture order, or from the court's failure to enter an order, begins to run when judgment is entered. If the court later amends or declines to amend a forfeiture order to include additional property under Rule 32.2(e), the defendant or the government may file an appeal regarding that property under Federal Rule of Appellate Procedure 4(b). The time for that appeal runs from the date when the order granting or denying the amendment becomes final.

(5) Jury Determination.

(A) Retaining the Jury. In any case tried before a jury, if the indictment or information states that the government is seeking forfeiture, the court must determine before the jury begins deliberating whether either party requests that the jury be retained to determine the forfeitability of specific property if it returns a guilty verdict.

(B) Special Verdict Form. If a party timely requests to have the jury determine forfeiture, the government must submit a proposed Special Verdict Form listing each property subject to forfeiture and asking the jury to determine whether the government has established the requisite nexus between the property and the offense committed by the defendant.

(6) Notice of the Forfeiture Order.

(A) Publishing and Sending Notice. If the court orders the forfeiture of specific property, the government must publish notice of the order and send notice to any person who reasonably appears to be a potential claimant with standing to contest the forfeiture in the ancillary proceeding.

(B) Content of the Notice. The notice must describe the forfeited property, state the times under the applicable statute when a petition contesting the forfeiture must be filed, and state the name and contact information for the government attorney to be served with the petition.

(C) Means of Publication; Exceptions to Publication Requirement. Publication must take place as described in Supplemental Rule G(4)(a)(iii) of the Federal Rules of Civil Procedure, and may be by any means described in Supplemental Rule G(4)(a)(iv). Publication is unnecessary if any exception in Supplemental Rule G(4)(a)(i) applies.

(D) Means of Sending the Notice. The notice may be sent in accordance with Supplemental Rules G(4)(b)(iii)-(v) of the Federal Rules of Civil Procedure.

(7) Interlocutory Sale. At any time before entry of a final forfeiture order, the court, in accordance with Supplemental Rule G(7) of the Federal Rules of Civil Procedure, may order the interlocutory sale of property alleged to be forfeitable.

(c) Ancillary Proceeding; Entering a Final Order of Forfeiture.

(1) In General. If, as prescribed by statute, a third party files a petition asserting an interest in the property to be forfeited, the court must conduct an ancillary proceeding, but no ancillary proceeding is required to the extent that the forfeiture consists of a money judgment.

(A) In the ancillary proceeding, the court may, on motion, dismiss the petition for lack of standing, for failure to state a claim, or for any other lawful reason. For purposes of the motion, the facts set forth in the petition are assumed to be true.

(B) After disposing of any motion filed under Rule 32.2(c)(1)(A) and before conducting a hearing on the petition, the court may permit the parties to conduct discovery in accordance with the Federal Rules of Civil Procedure if the court determines that discovery is necessary or desirable to resolve factual issues. When discovery ends, a party may move for summary judgment under Federal Rule of Civil Procedure 56.

(2) Entering a Final Order. When the ancillary proceeding ends, the court must enter a final order of forfeiture by amending the preliminary order as necessary to account for any third-party rights. If no third party files a timely petition, the preliminary order becomes the final order of forfeiture if the court finds that the defendant (or any combination of defendants convicted in the case) had an interest in the property that is forfeitable under the applicable statute. The defendant may not object to the entry of the final order on the ground that the property belongs, in whole or in part, to a codefendant or third party; nor may a third party object to the final order on the ground that the third party had an interest in the property.

(3) Multiple Petitions. If multiple third-party petitions are filed in the same case, an order dismissing or granting one petition is not appealable until rulings are made on all the petitions, unless the court determines that there is no just reason for delay.

(4) Ancillary Proceeding Not Part of Sentencing. An ancillary proceeding is not part of sentencing.

(d) Stay Pending Appeal. If a defendant appeals from a conviction or an order of forfeiture, the court may stay the order of forfeiture on terms appropriate to ensure that the property remains available pending appellate review. A stay does not delay the ancillary proceeding or the determination of a third party's rights or interests. If the court rules in favor of any third party while an appeal is pending, the court may amend the order of forfeiture but must not transfer any property interest to a third party until the decision on appeal becomes final, unless the defendant consents in writing or on the record.

(e) Subsequently Located Property; Substitute Property.

(1) In General. On the government's motion, the court may at any time enter an order of forfeiture or amend an existing order of forfeiture to include property that:

(A) is subject to forfeiture under an existing order of forfeiture but was located and identified after that order was entered; or

(B) is substitute property that qualifies for forfeiture under an applicable statute.

(2) Procedure. If the government shows that the property is subject to forfeiture under Rule 32.2(e)(1), the court must:

(A) enter an order forfeiting that property, or amend an existing preliminary or final order to include it; and

(B) if a third party files a petition claiming an interest in the property, conduct an ancillary proceeding under Rule 32.2(c).

(3) Jury Trial Limited. There is no right to a jury trial under Rule 32.2(e).

CREDIT(S)

(Added Apr. 17, 2000, eff. Dec. 1, 2000, and amended Apr. 29, 2002, eff. Dec. 1, 2002; Mar. 26, 2009, eff. Dec. 1, 2009.)

Rule 38. Staying a Sentence or a Disability

(a) Death Sentence. The court must stay a death sentence if the defendant appeals the conviction or sentence.

(b) Imprisonment.

(1) Stay Granted. If the defendant is released pending appeal, the court must stay a sentence of imprisonment.

(2) Stay Denied; Place of Confinement. If the defendant is not released pending appeal, the court may recommend to the Attorney General that the defendant be confined near the place of the trial or appeal for a period reasonably necessary to permit the defendant to assist in preparing the appeal.

(c) Fine. If the defendant appeals, the district court, or the court of appeals under Federal Rule of Appellate Procedure 8, may stay a sentence to pay a fine or a fine and costs. The court may stay the sentence on any terms considered appropriate and may require the defendant to:

(1) deposit all or part of the fine and costs into the district court's registry pending appeal;

(2) post a bond to pay the fine and costs; or

(3) submit to an examination concerning the defendant's assets and, if appropriate, order the defendant to refrain from dissipating assets.

(d) Probation. If the defendant appeals, the court may stay a sentence of probation. The court must set the terms of any stay.

(e) Restitution and Notice to Victims.

(1) In General. If the defendant appeals, the district court, or the court of appeals under Federal Rule of Appellate Procedure 8, may stay--on any terms considered appropriate--any sentence providing for restitution under 18 U.S.C. § 3556 or notice under 18 U.S.C. § 3555.

(2) Ensuring Compliance. The court may issue any order reasonably necessary to ensure compliance with a restitution order or a notice order after disposition of an appeal, including:

(A) a restraining order;

(B) an injunction;

(C) an order requiring the defendant to deposit all or part of any monetary restitution into the district court's registry; or

(D) an order requiring the defendant to post a bond.

(f) Forfeiture. A stay of a forfeiture order is governed by Rule 32.2(d).

(g) Disability. If the defendant's conviction or sentence creates a civil or employment disability under federal law, the district court, or the court of appeals under Federal Rule of Appellate Procedure 8, may stay the disability pending appeal on any terms considered appropriate. The court may issue any order reasonably necessary to protect the interest represented by the disability pending appeal, including a restraining order or an injunction.

CREDIT(S)

(As amended Dec. 27, 1948, eff. Jan. 1, 1949; Feb. 28, 1966, eff. July 1, 1966; Dec. 4, 1967, eff. July 1, 1968; Apr. 24, 1972, eff. Oct. 1, 1972; Oct. 12, 1984, Pub.L. 98-473, Title II, § 215(c), 98 Stat. 2016; Mar. 9, 1987, eff. Aug. 1, 1987; Apr. 17, 2000, eff. Dec. 1, 2000; Apr. 29, 2002, eff. Dec. 1, 2002.)

IX. General Provisions

Rule 58. Petty Offenses and Other Misdemeanors

(a) Scope.

(1) In General. These rules apply in petty offense and other misdemeanor cases and on appeal to a district judge in a case tried by a magistrate judge, unless this rule provides otherwise.

(2) Petty Offense Case Without Imprisonment. In a case involving a petty offense for which no sentence of imprisonment will be imposed, the court may follow any provision of these rules that is not inconsistent with this rule and that the court considers appropriate.

(3) Definition. As used in this rule, the term "petty offense for which no sentence of imprisonment will be imposed" means a petty offense for which the court determines that, in the event of conviction, no sentence of imprisonment will be imposed.

(b) Pretrial Procedure.

(1) Charging Document. The trial of a misdemeanor may proceed on an indictment, information, or complaint. The trial of a petty offense may also proceed on a citation or violation notice.

(2) Initial Appearance. At the defendant's initial appearance on a petty offense or other misdemeanor charge, the magistrate judge must inform the defendant of the following:

(A) the charge, and the minimum and maximum penalties, including imprisonment, fines, any special assessment under 18 U.S.C. § 3013, and restitution under 18 U.S.C. § 3556;

(B) the right to retain counsel;

(C) the right to request the appointment of counsel if the defendant is unable to retain counsel--unless the charge is a petty offense for which the appointment of counsel is not required;

(D) the defendant's right not to make a statement, and that any statement made may be used against the defendant;

(E) the right to trial, judgment, and sentencing before a district judge-- unless:

(i) the charge is a petty offense; or

(ii) the defendant consents to trial, judgment, and sentencing before a magistrate judge;

(F) the right to a jury trial before either a magistrate judge or a district judge--unless the charge is a petty offense; and

(G) any right to a preliminary hearing under Rule 5.1, and the general circumstances, if any, under which the defendant may secure pretrial release.

(3) Arraignment.

(A) Plea Before a Magistrate Judge. A magistrate judge may take the defendant's plea in a petty offense case. In every other misdemeanor case, a magistrate judge may take the plea only if the defendant consents either in writing or on the record to be tried before a magistrate judge and specifically waives trial before a district judge. The defendant may plead not guilty, guilty, or (with the consent of the magistrate judge) nolo contendere.

(B) Failure to Consent. Except in a petty offense case, the magistrate judge must order a defendant who does not consent to trial before a magistrate judge to appear before a district judge for further proceedings.

(c) Additional Procedures in Certain Petty Offense Cases. The following procedures also apply in a case involving a petty offense for which no sentence of imprisonment will be imposed:

(1) Guilty or Nolo Contendere Plea. The court must not accept a guilty or nolo contendere plea unless satisfied that the defendant understands the nature of the charge and the maximum possible penalty.

(2) Waiving Venue.

(A) Conditions of Waiving Venue. If a defendant is arrested, held, or present in a district different from the one where the indictment, information, complaint, citation, or violation notice is pending, the defendant may state in writing a desire to plead guilty or nolo contendere; to waive venue and trial in the district where the proceeding is pending; and to consent to the court's disposing of the case in the district where the defendant was arrested, is held, or is present.

(B) Effect of Waiving Venue. Unless the defendant later pleads not guilty, the prosecution will proceed in the district where the defendant was arrested, is held, or is present. The district clerk must notify the clerk in the original district of the defendant's waiver of venue. The defendant's statement of a desire to plead guilty or nolo contendere is not admissible against the defendant.

(3) Sentencing. The court must give the defendant an opportunity to be heard in mitigation and then proceed immediately to sentencing. The court may, however, postpone sentencing to allow the probation service to investigate or to permit either party to submit additional information.

(4) Notice of a Right to Appeal. After imposing sentence in a case tried on a not-guilty plea, the court must advise the defendant of a right to appeal the conviction and of any right to appeal the sentence. If the defendant was convicted on a plea of guilty or nolo contendere, the court must advise the defendant of any right to appeal the sentence.

(d) Paying a Fixed Sum in Lieu of Appearance.

(1) In General. If the court has a local rule governing forfeiture of collateral, the court may accept a fixed-sum payment in lieu of the defendant's appearance and end the case, but the fixed sum may not exceed the maximum fine allowed by law.

(2) Notice to Appear. If the defendant fails to pay a fixed sum, request a hearing, or appear in response to a citation or violation notice, the district clerk or a magistrate judge may issue a notice for the defendant to appear before the court on a date certain. The notice may give the defendant an additional opportunity to pay a fixed sum in lieu of appearance. The district clerk must serve the notice on the defendant by mailing a copy to the defendant's last known address.

(3) Summons or Warrant. Upon an indictment, or upon a showing by one of the other charging documents specified in Rule 58(b)(1) of probable cause to believe that an offense has been committed and that the defendant has committed it, the court may issue an arrest warrant or, if no warrant is requested by an attorney for the government, a summons. The showing of probable cause must be made under oath or under penalty of perjury, but the affiant need not appear before the court. If the defendant fails to appear before the court in response to a summons, the court may summarily issue a warrant for the defendant's arrest.

(e) Recording the Proceedings. The court must record any proceedings under this rule by using a court reporter or a suitable recording device.

(f) New Trial. Rule 33 applies to a motion for a new trial.

(g) Appeal.

(1) From a District Judge's Order or Judgment. The Federal Rules of Appellate Procedure govern an appeal from a district judge's order or a judgment of conviction or sentence.

(2) From a Magistrate Judge's Order or Judgment.

(A) Interlocutory Appeal. Either party may appeal an order of a magistrate judge to a district judge within 14 days of its entry if a district judge's order could similarly be appealed. The party appealing must file a notice with the clerk specifying the order being appealed and must serve a copy on the adverse party.

(B) Appeal from a Conviction or Sentence. A defendant may appeal a magistrate judge's judgment of conviction or sentence to a district judge within 14 days of its entry. To appeal, the defendant must file a notice with the clerk specifying the judgment being appealed and must serve a copy on an attorney for the government.

(C) Record. The record consists of the original papers and exhibits in the case; any transcript, tape, or other recording of the proceedings; and a certified copy of the docket entries. For purposes of the appeal, a copy of the record of the proceedings must be made available to a defendant who establishes by affidavit an inability to pay or give security for the record. The Director of the Administrative Office of the United States Courts must pay for those copies.

(D) Scope of Appeal. The defendant is not entitled to a trial de novo by a district judge. The scope of the appeal is the same as in an appeal to the court of appeals from a judgment entered by a district judge.

(3) Stay of Execution and Release Pending Appeal. Rule 38 applies to a stay of a judgment of conviction or sentence. The court may release the defendant pending appeal under the law relating to release pending appeal from a district court to a court of appeals.

CREDIT(S)

(Added May 1, 1990, eff. Dec. 1, 1990, and amended Apr. 30, 1991, eff. Dec. 1, 1991; Apr. 22, 1993, eff. Dec. 1, 1993; Apr. 29, 2002, eff. Dec. 1, 2002; Apr. 12, 2006, eff. Dec. 1, 2006; Mar. 26, 2009, eff. Dec. 1, 2009, absent contrary Congressional action.)

APPENDIX F - CASES APPLYING SPECIFIC SENTENCING GUIDELINES*

To retrieve the most recent published cases that apply any federal sentencing guideline, run the following query in a case law database on Westlaw: **he(u.s.s.g.) & da(aft 10/1/2005) % ci(fed.appx.).**

To retrieve only published cases that apply a specific federal sentencing guideline, such as 2K1.4, include the guideline number in the query. For example, use **he(u.s.s.g. +2 2K1.4) & da(aft 10/1/2005) % ci(fed.appx.)** To retrieve published cases applying § 2K1.4.

To retrieve both published and unpublished cases discussing the federal sentencing guidelines, use the following query: **u.s.s.g. "sentencing guideline"**.

---

*Publisher's Note: This Appendix has been added by the Publisher. It is not included in the Commission's *Guidelines Manual*.

APPENDIX G - TABLES

The following Tables were prepared by the United States Sentencing Commission.

November 1, 2013　　　　　APPENDIX G

The telephone number for the **USSC HelpLine** is (202) 502-4545. The hours of operation are from 8:30 a.m. to 5 p.m., Eastern time, Monday through Friday. The *Guidelines Manual* and other Commission publications and information are available on the Commission's web site at *www.ussc.gov*.

Fine Table (from §5E1.2 (Fines for Individual Defendants))

Offense Level	A Minimum	B Maximum
3 and below	$100	$5,000
4-5	$250	$5,000
6-7	$500	$5,000
8-9	$1,000	$10,000
10-11	$2,000	$20,000
12-13	$3,000	$30,000
14-15	$4,000	$40,000
16-17	$5,000	$50,000
18-19	$6,000	$60,000
20-22	$7,500	$75,000
23-25	$10,000	$100,000
26-28	$12,500	$125,000
29-31	$15,000	$150,000
32-34	$17,500	$175,000
35-37	$20,000	$200,000
38 and above	$25,000	$250,000

Revocation Table (from §7B1.4 (Term of Imprisonment (Policy Statement)))
(in months of imprisonment)

Criminal History Category*

Grade of Violation	I	II	III	IV	V	VI
Grade C	3-9	4-10	5-11	6-12	7-13	8-14
Grade B	4-10	6-12	8-14	12-18	18-24	21-27

Grade A　(1)　Except as provided in subdivision (2) below:

	I	II	III	IV	V	VI
	12-18	15-21	18-24	24-30	30-37	33-41

　　　　　(2)　Where the defendant was on probation or supervised release as a result of a sentence for a Class A felony:

	I	II	III	IV	V	VI
	24-30	27-33	30-37	37-46	46-57	51-63

*The criminal history category is the category applicable at the time the defendant originally was sentenced to a term of supervision.

APPENDIX G — November 1, 2013

SENTENCING TABLE
(in months of imprisonment)

Criminal History Category (Criminal History Points)

Zone	Offense Level	I (0 or 1)	II (2 or 3)	III (4, 5, 6)	IV (7, 8, 9)	V (10, 11, 12)	VI (13 or more)
Zone A	1	0-6	0-6	0-6	0-6	0-6	0-6
	2	0-6	0-6	0-6	0-6	0-6	1-7
	3	0-6	0-6	0-6	0-6	2-8	3-9
	4	0-6	0-6	0-6	2-8	4-10	6-12
	5	0-6	0-6	1-7	4-10	6-12	9-15
	6	0-6	1-7	2-8	6-12	9-15	12-18
Zone B	7	0-6	2-8	4-10	8-14	12-18	15-21
	8	0-6	4-10	6-12	10-16	15-21	18-24
	9	4-10	6-12	8-14	12-18	18-24	21-27
	10	6-12	8-14	10-16	15-21	21-27	24-30
	11	8-14	10-16	12-18	18-24	24-30	27-33
Zone C	12	10-16	12-18	15-21	21-27	27-33	30-37
Zone D	13	12-18	15-21	18-24	24-30	30-37	33-41
	14	15-21	18-24	21-27	27-33	33-41	37-46
	15	18-24	21-27	24-30	30-37	37-46	41-51
	16	21-27	24-30	27-33	33-41	41-51	46-57
	17	24-30	27-33	30-37	37-46	46-57	51-63
	18	27-33	30-37	33-41	41-51	51-63	57-71
	19	30-37	33-41	37-46	46-57	57-71	63-78
	20	33-41	37-46	41-51	51-63	63-78	70-87
	21	37-46	41-51	46-57	57-71	70-87	77-96
	22	41-51	46-57	51-63	63-78	77-96	84-105
	23	46-57	51-63	57-71	70-87	84-105	92-115
	24	51-63	57-71	63-78	77-96	92-115	100-125
	25	57-71	63-78	70-87	84-105	100-125	110-137
	26	63-78	70-87	78-97	92-115	110-137	120-150
	27	70-87	78-97	87-108	100-125	120-150	130-162
	28	78-97	87-108	97-121	110-137	130-162	140-175
	29	87-108	97-121	108-135	121-151	140-175	151-188
	30	97-121	108-135	121-151	135-168	151-188	168-210
	31	108-135	121-151	135-168	151-188	168-210	188-235
	32	121-151	135-168	151-188	168-210	188-235	210-262
	33	135-168	151-188	168-210	188-235	210-262	235-293
	34	151-188	168-210	188-235	210-262	235-293	262-327
	35	168-210	188-235	210-262	235-293	262-327	292-365
	36	188-235	210-262	235-293	262-327	292-365	324-405
	37	210-262	235-293	262-327	292-365	324-405	360-life
	38	235-293	262-327	292-365	324-405	360-life	360-life
	39	262-327	292-365	324-405	360-life	360-life	360-life
	40	292-365	324-405	360-life	360-life	360-life	360-life
	41	324-405	360-life	360-life	360-life	360-life	360-life
	42	360-life	360-life	360-life	360-life	360-life	360-life
	43	life	life	life	life	life	life

November 1, 2013